EBOOK

An eBook is available at **bookshelf.vitalsource.com**.

The code below provides access for one user.

FH4GHU78CQQ75TWT8GCM

To access the eBook, go to **bookshelf.vitalsource.com**, download the Bookshelf® that is right for your computer and enter your unique registration code.

Already have Bookshelf® installed? Simply redeem your code in Bookshelf® on your desktop or online.

For help, visit **wileydigitalsolutions.com.au/support**.

Financial Reporting Handbook

2019

Chartered Accountants Program

AUSTRALIA

Financial Reporting Handbook

Incorporating all the Standards as at 1 December 2018

2019

CHARTERED ACCOUNTANTS
AUSTRALIA + NEW ZEALAND

Global Accounting Alliance

Chartered
Accountants
Worldwide

Contents

Contents

eChapters

Statements of Accounting Concepts

Interpretations

Introduction

Accounting standards are the 'rules of the road' that govern the way that financial statements are prepared, with the objective of providing useful information that is relevant and faithfully represents what it purports to represent.

The role of the Accounting Professional and Ethical Standards Board (APESB)

The Accounting Professional and Ethical Standards Board (APESB) was established by Chartered Accountants ANZ (then the Institute of Chartered Accountants Australia) and CPA Australia in February 2006 in order to create an independent and more transparent body with responsibility for setting professional and ethical standards applicable to the accounting profession.

The APESB is responsible for the profession's ethical rulings on matters such as independence, changes in professional appointment, fees, advertising, etc. which are contained in APES 110 *Code of Ethics for Professional Accountants*. APES 110 incorporates the Code of Ethics for Professional Accountants (IESBA Code), which was issued by the International Ethics Standards Board for Accountants (IESBA) in July 2009, and some Australian-specific amendments and content. APES 110 is mandatory for members of Chartered Accountants ANZ, CPA Australia and the IPA.

Standard-setting process

Accounting standards in Australia are made by the AASB and referred to as AASB standards (AASBs). With the globalisation of business being a driving factor, the AASB prepares standards by adopting the content and wording of the International Financial Reporting Standards (IFRS) as set by the International Accounting Standards Board (IASB). Before being issued as AASBs, IFRS are amended only to comply with any Australian legislative requirements, for specific requirements related to not-for-profit accounting issues, and to reflect the reduced disclosure requirements (RDR) for entities that do not have public accountability.

Recent developments

In the past two years, a number of key standards have undergone significant changes that are either being applied for the first time in relation to the 30 June 2019 year end, or that become applicable during 2019.

Changes applicable to all entities

Wholesale revision to accounting for financial instruments has been introduced through IFRS/AASB 9 *Financial Instruments*. These changes were foreshadowed over several years by a number of versions of AASB 9 that introduced revised requirements for the classification and measurement of financial assets and liabilities. The complete version of AASB 9 is now operative for all entities, following its application date of annual reporting periods beginning on or after 1 January 2018. AASB 9 simplifies the complex requirements of its predecessor, IAS 39/AASB 139 *Financial Instruments: Recognition and Measurement* with changes in three key areas: classification and measurement of financial assets, impairment and hedge accounting.

Accounting for revenue has been clarified by the release of IFRS 15 *Revenue from Contracts with Customers*, issued by the IASB and the Financial Accounting Standards Board (FASB) internationally and as AASB 15 *Revenue from Contracts with Customers* in Australia. The core principle of AASB 15 requires entities to recognise revenue to depict the transfer of goods or services to customers in amounts that reflect the consideration (i. e. payment) to which entities expect to be entitled in exchange for those goods or services. AASB 15 was applicable for annual reporting periods beginning on or after 1 January 2018 for for-profit entities, and replaced the previous pronouncements on revenue:

- AASB 111 *Construction Contracts.*
- AASB 118 *Revenue.*
- Interpretation 13 *Customer Loyalty Programmes.*
- Interpretation 15 *Agreements for the Construction of Real Estate.*
- Interpretation 18 *Transfers of Assets from Customers.*
- Interpretation 131 *Revenue – Barter Transactions Involving Advertising Services.*
- Interpretation 1041 *Subscriber Acquisition Costs in the Telecommunications Industry.*

The long-awaited new lease accounting requirements are issued through IFRS/AASB 16 *Leases*. Although there are minimal changes in the standard for lessors, lessees may experience substantial changes with more leases being recognised and the resulting assets and liabilities included on the balance sheet. The key changes for lessees are that leases will no longer be classified as either operating leases or finance leases, so right-of-use (ROU) assets and lease liabilities will be recognised on the balance sheet, initially measured at present value of unavoidable future lease payments. There is an exception for lessees with short-term leases (12 months or less) and leases of low-value assets (US$5,000 or less), as these do not need to be recognised as assets and liabilities. This means for some entities with material off-balance-sheet leases, financial metrics derived from assets and liabilities (e. g. leverage ratios) will change so some entities may need to take care they continue to comply with their debt covenants. AASB 16 takes effect for annual reporting periods beginning on or after 1 January 2019, replacing AASB 117 *Leases*. Early adoption is permitted.

Insurers are likely to be significantly impacted by the new insurance Standard AASB 17 *Insurance Contracts*. This introduces a new measurement model for insurance liabilities, and will result in financial statements of insurers being more comparable across jurisdictions. AASB 4 *Insurance Contracts* currently permits entities in different jurisdictions to apply a wide variety of accounting practices to insurance contracts. AASB 17, based on IFRS 17, is the culmination of a long project which began in 1997 to develop a comprehensive set of accounting requirements for insurance contracts. The new standard applies to annual reporting periods beginning on or after 1 January 2021. Once AASB 17 becomes effective, AASB 1023 *General Insurance Contracts* and AASB 1038 *Life Insurance Contracts* will no longer apply. It should be noted however that AASB 17 does not apply to superannuation entities regulated by APRA and applying AASB 1056 *Superannuation Entities*. It also does not apply to not-for-profit public sector entities, which will continue to apply AASB 4, AASB 1023 and AASB 1038 after 1 January 2021.

A new interpretation – Interpretation 22 *Foreign Currency Transactions and Advance Consideration,* clarifies which exchange rate to use in reporting foreign currency transactions when a payment is made or received in advance. It is effective for reporting periods beginning on or after 1 January 2018.

The position on uncertain tax positions has been clarified through Interpretation 23 *Uncertainty over Income Tax Treatments,* applicable to annual reporting periods beginning on or after 1 January 2019. This Interpretation requires the effects of uncertain tax treatments to be taken into account when measuring tax amounts under AASB 112 *Income Taxes* if it not probable that the tax authority will accept the uncertain tax treatment. This Interpretation is based on the IASB version, and similar to Financial Accounting Standards Board (FASB) Interpretation FIN 48 dealing with uncertain tax positions. Interpretation 23 is likely to have a significant impact on the calculation of income tax liabilities for entities subject to issues such as transfer pricing.

Amendments for not-for-profit entities (NFPs)

As well as being impacted by the changes in AASB 9, AASB 15 and AASB 16, NFPs also have their own standard, AASB 1058 *Income of Not-for-Profit Entities*, addressing revenue recognition. Together, the new requirements are expected to result in better matching of income and related expenses as income recognition will now be deferred when there is a performance obligation or any other liability.

NFPs will need to apply AASB 15 if a transaction results from an enforceable agreement with another party and that agreement includes sufficiently specific performance obligations, so income is recognised as and when performance obligations are satisfied. To assist NFPs, a new Appendix F has been inserted in to AASB 15 containing guidance on how to identify an enforceable agreement, and whether sufficiently specific performance obligations exist within the agreement.

For all other revenue transactions for NFPs, AASB 1058 applies. This includes when an asset is acquired under beneficial circumstances for the purpose of furthering its objectives; as well as volunteer services.

AASB 1058 is effective for annual reporting periods beginning on or after 1 January 2019, and NFPs are permitted a one-year extension applying AASB 15 so the effective date aligns with AASB 1058.

One of the biggest impacts of the new requirements on NFPs arises from the interaction of AASB 16 and AASB 1058. NFP lessees holding a peppercorn lease (i. e. with significantly below-market payments) are required to capitalise the ROU asset on their balance sheet at fair value. In November 2018 the AASB announced it will issue an Exposure Draft proposing a temporary option to defer the peppercorn lease requirements, both because of the difficulties being experienced by some NFPs determining the fair value of their ROU assets, and because potentially the concurrent ACNC legislative review may result in fewer NFPs being required to apply AASB 16. Refer to the AASB website at aasb.gov.au for the latest on peppercorn leases.

Also new is AASB 1059 *Service Concession Arrangements: Grantors,* which introduces recognition and measurement requirements for assets and liabilities of public sector grantors in a service concession arrangement. It applies from 1 January 2020 and is expected to result in more infrastructure projects conducted via public-private partnerships being recognised on balance sheet.

Revised APES 110 *Code of Ethics for Professional Accountants*

In November 2018 the APESB issued a revised Code of Ethics for Professional Accountants (including independence standards). The Code has been restructured to facilitate usability and understanding of its requirements and brings the Australian Code into line with the IESBA's restructured International Code of Ethics for Professional Accountants. The restructured Australian Code incorporates the changes in relation to NOCLAR, Non Assurance Services to Audit or Assurance Clients (NAS) and audit partner rotation and is effective from 1 January 2020. All accountants need to be aware that their obligations have changed under the revised Code.

- APES 110 now explicitly addresses situations of non-compliance with laws and regulations (NOCLAR) which came into effect on 1 January 2018. This amendment allows accountants to set aside their duty of confidentiality when they come across non-compliance, providing a clear pathway to reporting to an appropriate authority. This means accountants can voice concerns about non-compliance, when legally permissible, without fear of breaching professional and ethical standards. Also included in this amended APES 110 are changes relating to the provision of non-assurance services to an audit clients.

- Applicable 1 January 2019 are further amendments on long association with audit clients. The most significant changes are to the rotation requirements through increasing the cooling-off period for engagement partners and review partners of public interest entities (PIEs).

- Further amendments in November 2018 saw the issue of a completely restructured Code, with a redefined structure and clearer guidelines designed to facilitate greater usability and understanding of its requirements, and enforcement by regulatory bodies. These changes are of particular relevance to accountants in business, as there are new and revised sections dealing with preparing and presenting information, and dealing with situations that create pressure to breach the fundamental principles. Restructured APES 110 is effective from 1 January 2020 with early adoption permitted.

Reduced disclosure requirements for Tier 2 entities

The AASB's Reduced Disclosure Regime (the RDR) reduces the disclosures required to be included in the financial statements for certain entities. AASB 1053 *Application of Tiers of Australian Accounting Standards* sets the framework for RDR by implementing a two-tier arrangement. Tier 1 (entities that have public accountability) apply full IFRS as included in the AASs. All other preparers of GPFS fall into Tier 2 and are able to apply the IFRS recognition and measurement requirements with substantially reduced disclosures. The disclosures that Tier 2 preparers can exclude from their financial statements are included by shading in the Standard.

The use of the RDR contained in AASB 1053 is an option for Tier 2 entities producing GPFS, and it must be applied in its entirety. Tier 2 entities are all those reporting entities that do not have public accountability. 'Public accountability' refers to entities that trade securities in a public market or hold assets in a fiduciary capacity. Typical entities that do not have public accountability and are likely to benefit from RDR include:

- unlisted public companies
- NFP private sector entities
- public sector entities other than the Federal Government and state, territory and local governments.

Tier 2 entities that take advantage of the RDR are required to follow the same recognition and measurement requirements as under the full suite of AASs, for these entities the major saving is potentially halving the number of disclosures they need to make. This reduction in disclosures means that Tier 2 entities are not be able to claim compliance with IFRS, but instead make a statement of compliance with the RDR.

Another important consideration for entities adopting the RDR is that the requirement to present true and fair financial statements remains. Entities need to consider whether they need to present additional disclosures above and beyond those required by the RDR.

As a result of its post implementation review of the Tier 2 requirements, the AASB issued ED 277 *Reduced Disclosure Requirements for Tier 2 Entities* to address concerns about the length and relevance of financial statements prepared using the RDR. This project is linked to the framework reform project mentioned above.

Future developments

Reforms to the Australian financial reporting framework, likely to impact on the 'reporting entity' concept, are being proposed by the AASB through ITC 39 *Applying the IASB's Revised Conceptual Framework and Solving the Reporting Entity and Special Purpose Financial Statement Problems,* removing the reporting entity concept contained in SAC 1 *Definition of the Reporting Entity.* The changes are in part driven by the recent release by the IASB of a revised Conceptual Framework that contains a much broader definition of reporting entity. The AASB's proposed changes incorporate removing the option that entities can lodge a special purpose financial statements (SPFS) with a regulator and the AASB is consulting on different options for Tier 2 reporting.

A number of other less significant changes to the standards and interpretations, for example through the annual improvements process, have also been implemented and other changes are proposed. To keep up to date with reporting changes refer to charteredaccountantsanz.com or aasb.gov.au.

Important information on versions of standards

This Handbook reflects the standards and interpretations issued by the AASB to 1 December 2018 as well as APES 110 issued in November 2018 and applicable 2020. As these pronouncements have various application dates, and the AASB updates standards and interpretations through the use of amending Standards rather than immediately amending the pronouncements, users will need to take care to check the version of the standard in this Handbook is the relevant version for their reporting period.

To access the compiled version of a standard or interpretation refer to the AASB website at aasb.gov.au. The AASB has a search tool to assist you to identify the correct version of a standard or an interpretation for a particular reporting period.

pronouncements have various application dates, and the AASB updates standards and interpretations through the use of amending Standards rather than immediately amending the pronouncements, users will need to take care to check the version of the standard in this Handbook is the relevant version for their reporting period.

To access the compiled version of a standard or interpretation refer to the AASB website at aasb.gov.au. The AASB has a search tool to assist you to identify the correct version of a standard or an interpretation for a particular reporting period.

FRAMEWORK
Framework for the Preparation and Presentation of Financial Statements

(Compiled June 2014)

This compiled Framework applies to annual reporting periods beginning on or after 1 July 2014. Early application is permitted. It incorporates relevant amendments made up to and including 4 June 2014.

Prepared on 15 March 2016 by the staff of the Australian Accounting Standards Board.

CONTENTS

COMPILATION DETAILS

COMPARISON WITH IASB FRAMEWORK

FRAMEWORK FOR THE PREPARATION AND PRESENTATION OF FINANCIAL STATEMENTS

FRAMEWORK

BASIS FOR CONCLUSIONS ON AASB CF 2013-1

COMPILATION DETAILS

Framework for the Preparation and Presentation of Financial Statements as amended

This compiled Framework applies to annual reporting periods beginning on or after 1 July 2014. It takes into account amendments up to and including 4 June 2014 and was prepared on 15 March 2016 by the staff of the Australian Accounting Standards Board (AASB).

This compilation is not a separate Framework issued by the AASB. Instead, it is a representation of the Framework (July 2004) as amended by other pronouncements, which are listed in the Table below.

Table of pronouncements

Pronouncement	Date made	Application date *(annual reporting periods ... on or after ...)*	Application, saving or transitional provisions
Framework	15 Jul 2004	*(beginning)* 1 Jan 2005	
AASB 2007-8	24 Sep 2007	*(beginning)* 1 Jan 2009	see (a) below
AASB 2007-10	13 Dec 2007	*(beginning)* 1 Jan 2009	see (a) below
AASB CF 2013-1	20 Dec 2013	*(ending)* 20 Dec 2013	see (b) below
AASB 2014-1	4 Jun 2014	Pt A *(beginning)* 1 Jul 2014	see (c) below

(a) Entities may elect to apply this Standard to annual reporting periods beginning on or after 1 January 2005 but before 1 January 2009, provided that AASB 101 *Presentation of Financial Statements* (September 2007) is also applied to such periods.

(b) Entities may elect to apply this pronouncement to periods beginning on or after 1 January 2005 that end before 20 December 2013.

(c) Entities may elect to apply Part A of this Standard to annual reporting periods beginning on or after 1 January 2005 but before 1 July 2014.

Table of amendments

Paragraph affected	How affected	By ... [paragraph]
Aus1.1	amended amended	AASB 2007-8 [7] AASB CF 2013-1 [5]
Aus1.4	amended	AASB CF 2013-1 [6]
Aus1.5	amended	AASB CF 2013-1 [7]
Aus1.6	deleted	AASB 2007-10 [10]
6-7	amended deleted	AASB 2007-10 [11] AASB CF 2013-1 [8]
8-20	deleted	AASB CF 2013-1 [8]
6-7	amended deleted	AASB 2007-10 [11] AASB CF 2013-1 [8]

Paragraph affected	How affected	By ... [paragraph]
21	amended deleted	AASB 2007-10 [12] AASB CF 2013-1 [8]
22	deleted	AASB CF 2013-1 [8]
23	amended	AASB 2007-10 [12]
24-46	deleted	AASB CF 2013-1 [9]
72	amended	AASB CF 2013-1 [10]
83	amended	AASB CF 2013-1 [11]
84	amended	AASB CF 2013-1 [12]
86	amended	AASB 2014-1A [31]
88	amended	AASB 2007-10 [13]
Appendix	added	AASB CF 2013-1 [13]

General terminology amendments

References to 'financial report(s)' that were amended to 'financial statements' by AASB 2007-10, paragraph 14, are not shown in the above Table of Amendments.

COMPARISON WITH IASB FRAMEWORK

The AASB *Framework* and the IASB *Framework*

This *Framework for the Preparation and Presentation of Financial Statements* as amended incorporates the *Conceptual Framework for Financial Reporting* as issued by the International Accounting Standards Board (IASB). Paragraphs that have been added to this *Framework* (and do not appear in the text of the IASB *Framework*) are identified with the prefix "Aus", followed by decimal numbering.

FRAMEWORK

The Australian Accounting Standards Board issued the *Framework for the Preparation and Presentation of Financial Statements* on 15 July 2004.

This compiled version of the *Framework* applies to annual reporting periods beginning on or after 1 July 2014. It incorporates relevant amendments contained in other AASB pronouncements up to and including 4 June 2014 (see Compilation Details).

FRAMEWORK FOR THE PREPARATION AND PRESENTATION OF FINANCIAL STATEMENTS

Application

Aus1.1   The concepts in this *Framework* are not set out as requirements for the purpose of preparing general purpose financial statements. This is consistent with the:

      (a)   [deleted]

      (b)   [deleted]

      (c)   *Australian Securities and Investments Commission Act 2001*, section 227(1).

Aus1.2   This *Framework* applies to periods beginning on or after 1 January 2005. [Note: For application dates of paragraphs changed or added by an amending pronouncement, see Compilation Details.]

Aus1.3   This *Framework* shall not be applied to annual reporting periods beginning before 1 January 2005.

Aus1.4   When applicable, this *Framework* supersedes:

(a)   Statement of Accounting Concepts SAC 2 *Objective of General Purpose Financial Reporting* as issued in August 1990;

(b)   Statement of Accounting Concepts SAC 3 *Qualitative Characteristics of Financial Information* as issued in August 1990; and

(c)   Statement of Accounting Concepts SAC 4 *Definition and Recognition of the Elements of Financial Statements* as issued in March 1995.

Aus1.5   SAC 2, SAC 3 and SAC 4 remain applicable until superseded by this *Framework*.

Introduction

Purpose and status

1   This *Framework* sets out the concepts that underlie the preparation and presentation of financial statements for external users. The purpose of the *Framework* is to:

(a)   assist the AASB in the development of future Australian Accounting Standards and in its review of existing Australian Accounting Standards, including evaluating proposed International Accounting Standards Board pronouncements;

(b)   assist the AASB in promoting harmonisation of regulations, accounting standards and procedures relating to the presentation of financial statements by providing a basis for reducing the number of alternative accounting treatments permitted by Australian Accounting Standards;

(c)   [deleted by the AASB];

(d)   assist preparers of financial statements in applying Australian Accounting Standards and in dealing with topics that have yet to form the subject of an Australian Accounting Standard;

(e)   assist auditors in forming an opinion as to whether financial statements conform with Australian Accounting Standards;

(f)   assist users of financial statements in interpreting the information contained in financial statements prepared in conformity with Australian Accounting Standards; and

(g)   provide those who are interested in the work of the AASB with information about its approach to the formulation of Australian Accounting Standards.

2   This *Framework* is not an Australian Accounting Standard and hence does not define standards for any particular measurement or disclosure issue. Nothing in this *Framework* overrides any specific Australian Accounting Standard.

3   The AASB recognises that in a limited number of cases there may be a conflict between the *Framework* and an Australian Accounting Standard. In those cases where there is a conflict, the requirements of the Australian Accounting Standard prevail over those of the *Framework*. As, however, the AASB will be guided by the *Framework* in the development of future Standards and in its review of existing Standards, the number of cases of conflict between the *Framework* and Australian Accounting Standards will diminish through time.

4   The *Framework* will be revised from time to time on the basis of the Board's experience of working with it.

Scope

5   The *Framework* deals with:

   (a)   the objective of financial statements;

   (b)   the qualitative characteristics that determine the usefulness of information in financial statements;

   (c)   the definition, recognition and measurement of the elements from which financial statements are constructed; and

   (d)   concepts of capital and capital maintenance.

6-8   [Deleted – replaced by concepts in the Appendix, Chapter 1]

Users and their information needs

9-11   [Deleted – replaced by concepts in the Appendix, Chapter 1]

The objective of financial statements

12-21 [Deleted – replaced by concepts in the Appendix, Chapter 1]

Underlying assumptions

Accrual basis

22   [Deleted]

Going concern

23   The financial statements are normally prepared on the assumption that an entity is a going concern and will continue in operation for the foreseeable future. Hence, it is assumed that the entity has neither the intention nor the need to liquidate or curtail materially the scale of its operations; if such an intention or need exists, the financial statements may have to be prepared on a different basis and, if so, the basis used is disclosed.

Qualitative characteristics of financial statements

24-46 [Deleted – replaced by concepts in the Appendix, Chapter 3]

The elements of financial statements

47   Financial statements portray the financial effects of transactions and other events by grouping them into broad classes according to their economic characteristics. These broad classes are termed the elements of financial statements. The elements directly related to the measurement of financial position in the balance sheet are assets, liabilities and equity. The elements directly related to the measurement of performance in the income statement are income and expenses. The cash flow statement usually reflects income statement elements and changes in balance sheet elements; accordingly, this *Framework* identifies no elements that are unique to this statement.

48   The presentation of these elements in the balance sheet and the income statement involves a process of sub-classification. For example, assets and liabilities may be classified by their nature or function in the business of the entity in order to display information in the manner most useful to users for purposes of making economic decisions.

Financial position

49   The elements directly related to the measurement of financial position are assets, liabilities and equity. These are defined as follows:

(a)   An asset is a resource controlled by the entity as a result of past events and from which future economic benefits are expected to flow to the entity.

(b)   A liability is a present obligation of the entity arising from past events, the settlement of which is expected to result in an outflow from the entity of resources embodying economic benefits.

(c)   Equity is the residual interest in the assets of the entity after deducting all its liabilities.

Aus49.1   In respect of not-for-profit entities in the public or private sector, in pursuing their objectives, goods and services are provided that have the capacity to satisfy human wants and needs. Assets provide a means for entities to achieve their objectives. Future economic benefits or service potential is the essence of assets. Future economic benefits is synonymous with the notion of service potential, and is used in this *Framework* as a reference also to service potential. Future economic benefits can be described as the scarce capacity to provide benefits to the entities that use them, and is common to all assets irrespective of their physical or other form.

50   The definitions of an asset and a liability identify their essential features but do not attempt to specify the criteria that need to be met before they are recognised in the balance sheet. Thus, the definitions embrace items that are not recognised as assets or liabilities in the balance sheet because they do not satisfy the criteria for recognition discussed in paragraphs 82 to 98. In particular, the expectation that future economic benefits will flow to or from an entity must be sufficiently certain to meet the probability criterion in paragraph 83 before an asset or liability is recognised.

51   In assessing whether an item meets the definition of an asset, liability or equity, attention needs to be given to its underlying substance and economic reality and not merely its legal form. Thus, for example, in the case of finance leases, the substance and economic reality are that the lessee acquires the economic benefits of the use of the leased asset for the major part of its useful life in return for entering into an obligation to pay for that right an amount approximating to the fair value of the asset and the related finance charge. Hence, the finance lease gives rise to items that satisfy the definition of an asset and a liability and are recognised as such in the lessee's balance sheet.

52   Balance sheets drawn up in accordance with current Australian Accounting Standards may include items that do not satisfy the definitions of an asset or liability and are not shown as part of equity. The definitions set out in paragraph 49 will, however, underlie future reviews of existing Australian Accounting Standards and the formulation of further Standards.

Assets

53   The future economic benefit embodied in an asset is the potential to contribute, directly or indirectly, to the flow of cash and cash equivalents to the entity. The potential may be a productive one that is part of the operating activities of the entity. It may also take the form of convertibility into cash or cash equivalents or a capability to reduce cash outflows, such as when an alternative manufacturing process lowers the costs of production.

54   An entity usually employs its assets to produce goods or services capable of satisfying the wants or needs of customers; because these goods or services can satisfy these wants or needs, customers are prepared to pay for them and hence contribute to the cash flow of the entity. Cash itself renders a service to the entity because of its command over other resources.

Aus54.1   In respect of not-for-profit entities, whether in the public or private sector, the future economic benefits are also used to provide goods and services in accordance with the entities' objectives. However, since the entities do not have the generation of profit as a principal objective, the provision of goods and services may not result in net cash inflows to the entities as the recipients of the goods and services may not transfer cash or other benefits to the entities in exchange.

Aus54.2   In respect of not-for-profit entities, the fact that they do not charge, or do not charge fully, their beneficiaries or customers for the goods and services they provide does not deprive those outputs of utility or value; nor does it preclude the entities from benefiting from the assets used to provide the goods and services. For example, assets such as monuments, museums, cathedrals and historical treasures provide needed or desired services to beneficiaries, typically at little or no direct cost to the beneficiaries. These assets benefit the entities by enabling them to meet their objectives of providing needed services to beneficiaries.

55   The future economic benefits embodied in an asset may flow to the entity in a number of ways. For example, an asset may be:

(a)   used singly or in combination with other assets in the production of goods or services to be sold by the entity;

(b)   exchanged for other assets;

(c)   used to settle a liability; or

(d)   distributed to the owners of the entity.

56   Many assets, for example, property, plant and equipment, have a physical form. However, physical form is not essential to the existence of an asset; hence patents and copyrights, for example, are assets if future economic benefits are expected to flow from them to the entity and if they are controlled by the entity.

57   Many assets, for example, receivables and property, are associated with legal rights, including the right of ownership. In determining the existence of an asset, the right of ownership is not essential; thus, for example, property held on a lease is an asset if the entity controls the benefits which are expected to flow from the property. Although the capacity of an entity to control benefits is usually the result of legal rights, an item may nonetheless satisfy the definition of an asset even when there is no legal control. For example, know-how obtained from a development activity may meet the definition of an asset when, by keeping that know-how secret, an entity controls the benefits that are expected to flow from it.

58   The assets of an entity result from past transactions or other past events. Entities normally obtain assets by purchasing or producing them, but other transactions or events may generate assets. Examples include property received by an entity from government as part of a program to encourage economic growth in an area, and the discovery of mineral deposits. Transactions or events expected to occur in the future do not, in themselves, give rise to assets. Hence, for example, an intention to purchase inventory does not, of itself, meet the definition of an asset.

59   There is a close association between incurring expenditure and generating assets but the two do not necessarily coincide. Hence, when an entity incurs expenditure, this may provide evidence that future economic benefits were sought but is not conclusive proof that an item satisfying the definition of an asset has been obtained. Similarly the absence of a related expenditure does not preclude an item from satisfying the definition of an asset and thus becoming a candidate for recognition in the balance sheet. For example, items that have been donated to the entity may satisfy the definition of an asset.

Liabilities

60   An essential characteristic of a liability is that the entity has a present obligation. An obligation is a duty or responsibility to act or perform in a certain way. Obligations may

be legally enforceable as a consequence of a binding contract or statutory requirement. This is normally the case, for example, with amounts payable for goods and services received. Obligations also arise, however, from normal business practice, custom and a desire to maintain good business relations or act in an equitable manner. If, for example, an entity decides as a matter of policy to rectify faults in its products even when these become apparent after the warranty period has expired, the amounts that are expected to be expended in respect of goods already sold are liabilities.

61   A distinction needs to be drawn between a present obligation and a future commitment. A decision by the management of an entity to acquire assets in the future does not, of itself, give rise to a present obligation. An obligation normally arises only when the asset is delivered or the entity enters into an irrevocable agreement to acquire the asset. In the latter case, the irrevocable nature of the agreement means that the economic consequences of failing to honour the obligation, for example, because of the existence of a substantial penalty, leave the entity with little, if any, discretion to avoid the outflow of resources to another party.

62   The settlement of a present obligation usually involves the entity giving up resources embodying economic benefits in order to satisfy the claim of the other party. Settlement of a present obligation may occur in a number of ways, for example, by:

(a)   payment of cash;

(b)   transfer of other assets;

(c)   provision of services;

(d)   replacement of that obligation with another obligation; or

(e)   conversion of the obligation to equity.

An obligation may also be extinguished by other means, such as a creditor waiving or forfeiting its rights.

63   Liabilities result from past transactions or other past events. Thus, for example, the acquisition of goods and the use of services give rise to trade payables (unless paid for in advance or on delivery), and the receipt of a bank loan results in an obligation to repay the loan. An entity may also recognise future rebates based on annual purchases by customers as liabilities; in this case, the sale of the goods in the past is the transaction that gives rise to the liability.

64   Some liabilities can be measured only by using a substantial degree of estimation. Some entities describe these liabilities as provisions. In some countries, such provisions are not regarded as liabilities because the concept of a liability is defined narrowly so as to include only amounts that can be established without the need to make estimates. The definition of a liability in paragraph 49 follows a broader approach. Thus, when a provision involves a present obligation and satisfies the rest of the definition, it is a liability even if the amount has to be estimated. Examples include provisions for payments to be made under existing warranties and provisions to cover pension obligations.

Equity

65   Although equity is defined in paragraph 49 as a residual, it may be sub-classified in the balance sheet. For example, in a corporate entity, funds contributed by shareholders, retained earnings, reserves representing appropriations of retained earnings and reserves representing capital maintenance adjustments may be shown separately. Such classifications can be relevant to the decision-making needs of the users of financial statements when they indicate legal or other restrictions on the ability of the entity to distribute or otherwise apply its equity. They may also reflect the fact that parties with ownership interests in an entity have differing rights in relation to the receipt of dividends or the repayment of contributed equity.

66   The creation of reserves is sometimes required by statute or other law in order to give the entity and its creditors an added measure of protection from the effects of

losses. Other reserves may be established if national tax law grants exemptions from, or reductions in, taxation liabilities when transfers to such reserves are made. The existence and size of these legal, statutory and tax reserves is information that can be relevant to the decision-making needs of users. Transfers to such reserves are appropriations of retained earnings rather than expenses.

67   The amount at which equity is shown in the balance sheet is dependent on the measurement of assets and liabilities. Normally, the aggregate amount of equity only by coincidence corresponds with the aggregate market value of the shares of the entity or the sum that could be raised by disposing of either the net assets on a piecemeal basis or the entity as a whole on a going concern basis.

68   Commercial, industrial and business activities are often undertaken by means of entities such as sole proprietorships, partnerships, trusts and various types of government business undertakings. The legal and regulatory framework for such entities is often different from that applying to corporate entities. For example, there may be few, if any, restrictions on the distribution to owners or other beneficiaries of amounts included in equity. Nevertheless, the definition of equity and the other aspects of this *Framework* that deal with equity are appropriate for such entities.

Performance

69   Profit is frequently used as a measure of performance or as the basis for other measures, such as return on investment or earnings per share. The elements directly related to the measurement of profit are income and expenses. The recognition and measurement of income and expenses, and hence profit, depends in part on the concepts of capital and capital maintenance used by the entity in preparing its financial statements. These concepts are discussed in paragraphs 102 to 110.

70   The elements of income and expenses are defined as follows.

   (a)   Income is increases in economic benefits during the accounting period in the form of inflows or enhancements of assets or decreases of liabilities that result in increases in equity, other than those relating to contributions from equity participants.

   (b)   Expenses are decreases in economic benefits during the accounting period in the form of outflows or depletions of assets or incurrences of liabilities that result in decreases in equity, other than those relating to distributions to equity participants.

71   The definitions of income and expenses identify their essential features but do not attempt to specify the criteria that would need to be met before they are recognised in the income statement. Criteria for the recognition of income and expenses are discussed in paragraphs 82 to 98.

72   Income and expenses may be presented in the income statement in different ways so as to provide information that is relevant for economic decision-making. For example, it is common practice to distinguish between those items of income and expenses that arise in the course of the ordinary activities of the entity and those that do not. This distinction is made on the basis that the source of an item is relevant in evaluating the ability of the entity to generate cash and cash equivalents in the future[1]. For example, incidental activities such as the disposal of a long-term investment are unlikely to recur on a regular basis. When distinguishing between items in this way, consideration needs to be given to the nature of the entity and its operations. Items that arise from the ordinary activities of one entity may be unusual in respect of another.

73   Distinguishing between items of income and expense and combining them in different ways also permits several measures of entity performance to be displayed. These have differing degrees of inclusiveness. For example, the income statement could display gross margin, profit or loss before taxation, and profit or loss.

---

1   For not-for-profit users, also see paragraph AusOB3.1.

Income

74   The definition of income encompasses both revenue and gains. Revenue arises in the course of the ordinary activities of an entity and is referred to by a variety of different names including sales, fees, interest, dividends, royalties and rent.

75   Gains represent other items that meet the definition of income and may, or may not, arise in the course of the ordinary activities of an entity. Gains represent increases in economic benefits and as such are no different in nature from revenue. Hence, they are not regarded as constituting a separate element in this *Framework*.

76   Gains include, for example, those arising on the disposal of non-current assets. The definition of income also includes unrealised gains; for example, those arising on the revaluation of marketable securities and those resulting from increases in the carrying amount of long-term assets. When gains are recognised in the income statement, they are usually displayed separately because knowledge of them is useful for the purpose of making economic decisions. Gains are often reported net of related expenses.

77   Various kinds of assets may be received or enhanced by income. Examples include cash, receivables and goods and services received in exchange for goods and services supplied. Income may also result from the settlement of liabilities. For example, an entity may provide goods and services to a lender in settlement of an obligation to repay an outstanding loan.

Expenses

78   The definition of expenses encompasses losses as well as those expenses that arise in the course of the ordinary activities of the entity. Expenses that arise in the course of the ordinary activities of the entity include, for example, cost of sales, wages and depreciation. They usually take the form of an outflow or depletion of assets such as cash and cash equivalents, inventory, property, plant and equipment.

79   Losses represent other items that meet the definition of expenses and may, or may not, arise in the course of the ordinary activities of the entity. Losses represent decreases in economic benefits and as such they are no different in nature from other expenses. Hence, they are not regarded as a separate element in this *Framework*.

80   Losses include, for example, those resulting from disasters such as fire and flood, as well as those arising on the disposal of non-current assets. The definition of expenses also includes unrealised losses, for example, those arising from the effects of increases in the rate of exchange for a foreign currency in respect of the borrowings of an entity in that currency. When losses are recognised in the income statement, they are usually displayed separately because knowledge of them is useful for the purpose of making economic decisions. Losses are often reported net of related income.

Capital maintenance adjustments

81   The revaluation or restatement of assets and liabilities gives rise to increases or decreases in equity. While these increases or decreases meet the definition of income and expenses, they are not included in the income statement under certain concepts of capital maintenance. Instead these items are included in equity as capital maintenance adjustments or revaluation reserves. These concepts of capital maintenance are discussed in paragraphs 102 to 110 of this *Framework*.

Recognition of the elements of financial statements

82   Recognition is the process of incorporating in the balance sheet or income statement an item that meets the definition of an element and satisfies the criteria for recognition set out in paragraph 83. It involves the depiction of the item in words and by a monetary amount and the inclusion of that amount in the balance sheet or income statement totals. Items that satisfy the recognition criteria should be recognised in the balance sheet or income statement. The failure to recognise such items is not rectified by disclosure of the accounting policies used nor by notes or explanatory material.

83   An item that meets the definition of an element should be recognised if:

    (a)   it is probable that any future economic benefit associated with the item will flow to or from the entity; and

    (b)   the item has a cost or value that can be measured with reliability.[2]

84   In assessing whether an item meets these criteria, and therefore qualifies for recognition in the financial statements, regard needs to be given to the materiality considerations discussed in Chapter 3 *Qualitative characteristics of useful financial information*. The interrelationship between the elements means that an item that meets the definition and recognition criteria for a particular element, for example, an asset, automatically requires the recognition of another element, for example, income or a liability.

The probability of future economic benefit

85   The concept of probability is used in the recognition criteria to refer to the degree of uncertainty that the future economic benefits associated with the item will flow to or from the entity. The concept is in keeping with the uncertainty that characterises the environment in which an entity operates. Assessments of the degree of uncertainty attaching to the flow of future economic benefits are made on the basis of the evidence available when the financial statements are prepared. For example, when it is probable that a receivable owed by an entity will be paid, it is then justifiable, in the absence of any evidence to the contrary, to recognise the receivable as an asset. For a large population of receivables, however, some degree of non-payment is normally considered probable; hence an expense representing the expected reduction in economic benefits is recognised.

Reliability of measurement

86   The second criterion for the recognition of an item is that it possesses a cost or value that can be measured with reliability. In many cases, cost or value must be estimated. The use of reasonable estimates is an essential part of the preparation of financial statements and does not undermine their reliability. When, however, a reasonable estimate cannot be made the item is not recognised in the balance sheet or income statement. For example, the expected proceeds from a lawsuit may meet the definitions of both an asset and income as well as the probability criterion for recognition. However, if it is not possible for the claim to be measured reliably, it should not be recognised as an asset or as income. The existence of the claim, however, would be disclosed in the notes, explanatory material or supplementary schedules.

87   An item that, at a particular point in time, fails to meet the recognition criteria in paragraph 83, may qualify for recognition at a later date as a result of subsequent circumstances or events.

88   An item that possesses the essential characteristics of an element but fails to meet the criteria for recognition may nonetheless warrant disclosure in the notes, explanatory material or in supplementary schedules. This is appropriate when knowledge of the item is considered to be relevant to the evaluation of the financial position, financial performance and cash flows of an entity by the users of financial statements.

Recognition of assets

89   An asset is recognised in the balance sheet when it is probable that the future economic benefits will flow to the entity and the asset has a cost or value that can be measured reliably.

90   An asset is not recognised in the balance sheet when expenditure has been incurred for which it is considered improbable that economic benefits will flow to the entity beyond the current accounting period. Instead, such a transaction results in the recognition

---

2   Information is reliable when it is complete, neutral and free from error.

of an expense in the income statement. This treatment does not imply either that the intention of management in incurring expenditure was other than to generate future economic benefits for the entity or that management was misguided. The only implication is that the degree of certainty that economic benefits will flow to the entity beyond the current accounting period is insufficient to warrant the recognition of an asset.

Recognition of liabilities

91   A liability is recognised in the balance sheet when it is probable that an outflow of resources embodying economic benefits will result from the settlement of a present obligation and the amount at which the settlement will take place can be measured reliably. In practice, obligations under contracts that are equally proportionately unperformed (for example, liabilities for inventory ordered but not yet received) are generally not recognised as liabilities in the financial statements. However, such obligations may meet the definition of liabilities and, provided the recognition criteria are met in the particular circumstances, may qualify for recognition. In such circumstances, recognition of liabilities entails recognition of related assets or expenses.

Recognition of income

92   Income is recognised in the income statement when an increase in future economic benefits related to an increase in an asset or a decrease of a liability has arisen that can be measured reliably. This means, in effect, that recognition of income occurs simultaneously with the recognition of increases in assets or decreases in liabilities (for example, the net increase in assets arising on a sale of goods or services or the decrease in liabilities arising from the waiver of a debt payable).

93   The procedures normally adopted in practice for recognising income, for example, the requirement that revenue should be earned, are applications of the recognition criteria in this *Framework*. Such procedures are generally directed at restricting the recognition as income to those items that can be measured reliably and have a sufficient degree of certainty.

Recognition of expenses

94   Expenses are recognised in the income statement when a decrease in future economic benefits related to a decrease in an asset or an increase of a liability has arisen that can be measured reliably. This means, in effect, that recognition of expenses occurs simultaneously with the recognition of an increase in liabilities or a decrease in assets (for example, the accrual of employee entitlements or the depreciation of equipment).

95   Expenses are recognised in the income statement on the basis of a direct association between the costs incurred and the earning of specific items of income. This process, commonly referred to as the matching of costs with revenues, involves the simultaneous or combined recognition of revenues and expenses that result directly and jointly from the same transactions or other events. For example, the various components of expense making up the cost of goods sold are recognised at the same time as the income derived from the sale of the goods. However, the application of the matching concept under this *Framework* does not allow the recognition of items in the balance sheet which do not meet the definition of assets or liabilities.

96   When economic benefits are expected to arise over several accounting periods and the association with income can only be broadly or indirectly determined, expenses are recognised in the income statement on the basis of systematic and rational allocation procedures. This is often necessary in recognising the expenses associated with the using up of assets such as property, plant, equipment, goodwill, patents and trademarks. In such cases, the expense is referred to as depreciation or amortisation. These allocation procedures are intended to recognise expenses in the accounting periods in which the economic benefits associated with these items are consumed or expire.

97   An expense is recognised immediately in the income statement when an expenditure produces no future economic benefits or when, and to the extent that, future economic benefits do not qualify, or cease to qualify, for recognition in the balance sheet as an asset.

98   An expense is also recognised in the income statement in those cases when a liability is incurred without the recognition of an asset, as when a liability under a product warranty arises.

Measurement of the elements of financial statements

99   Measurement is the process of determining the monetary amounts at which the elements of the financial statements are to be recognised and carried in the balance sheet and income statement. This involves the selection of the particular basis of measurement.

100   A number of different measurement bases are employed to different degrees and in varying combinations in financial statements, including the following.

(a)   *Historical cost* Assets are recorded at the amount of cash or cash equivalents paid or the fair value of the consideration given to acquire them at the time of their acquisition. Liabilities are recorded at the amount of proceeds received in exchange for the obligation, or in some circumstances (for example, income taxes), at the amounts of cash or cash equivalents expected to be paid to satisfy the liability in the normal course of business.

(b)   *Current cost* Assets are carried at the amount of cash or cash equivalents that would have to be paid if the same or an equivalent asset was acquired currently. Liabilities are carried at the undiscounted amount of cash or cash equivalents that would be required to settle the obligation currently.

(c)   *Realisable (settlement) value* Assets are carried at the amount of cash or cash equivalents that could currently be obtained by selling the asset in an orderly disposal. Liabilities are carried at their settlement values; that is, the undiscounted amounts of cash or cash equivalents expected to be paid to satisfy the liabilities in the normal course of business.

(d)   *Present value* Assets are carried at the present discounted value of the future net cash inflows that the item is expected to generate in the normal course of business. Liabilities are carried at the present discounted value of the future net cash outflows that are expected to be required to settle the liabilities in the normal course of business.

101   The measurement basis most commonly adopted by entities in preparing their financial statements is historical cost. This is usually combined with other measurement bases. For example, inventories are usually carried at the lower of cost and net realisable value, marketable securities may be carried at market value and pension liabilities are carried at their present value. Furthermore, some entities use the current cost basis as a response to the inability of the historical cost accounting model to deal with the effects of changing prices of non-monetary assets.

Concepts of capital and capital maintenance

Concepts of capital

102   A financial concept of capital is adopted by most entities in preparing their financial statements. Under a financial concept of capital, such as invested money or invested purchasing power, capital is synonymous with the net assets or equity of the entity. Under a physical concept of capital, such as operating capability, capital is regarded as the productive capacity of the entity based on, for example, units of output per day.

103   The selection of the appropriate concept of capital by an entity should be based on the needs of the users of its financial statements. Thus, a financial concept of capital

should be adopted if the users of financial statements are primarily concerned with the maintenance of nominal invested capital or the purchasing power of invested capital. If, however, the main concern of users is with the operating capability of the entity, a physical concept of capital should be used. The concept chosen indicates the goal to be attained in determining profit, even though there may be some measurement difficulties in making the concept operational.

Concepts of capital maintenance and the determination of profit

104   The concepts of capital in paragraph 102 give rise to the following concepts of capital maintenance.

(a)   *Financial capital maintenance* Under this concept, a profit is earned only if the financial (or money) amount of the net assets at the end of the period exceeds the financial (or money) amount of net assets at the beginning of the period, after excluding any distributions to, and contributions from, owners during the period. Financial capital maintenance can be measured in either nominal monetary units or units of constant purchasing power.

(b)   *Physical capital maintenance* Under this concept, a profit is earned only if the physical productive capacity (or operating capability) of the entity (or the resources or funds needed to achieve that capacity) at the end of the period exceeds the physical productive capacity at the beginning of the period, after excluding any distributions to, and contributions from, owners during the period.

105   The concept of capital maintenance is concerned with how an entity defines the capital that it seeks to maintain. It provides the linkage between the concepts of capital and the concepts of profit because it provides the point of reference by which profit is measured. It is a prerequisite for distinguishing between an entity's return on capital and its return of capital. Only inflows of assets in excess of amounts needed to maintain capital may be regarded as profit and therefore as a return on capital. Hence, profit is the residual amount that remains after expenses (including capital maintenance adjustments, where appropriate) have been deducted from income. If expenses exceed income, the residual amount is a net loss.

106   The physical capital maintenance concept requires the adoption of the current cost basis of measurement. The financial capital maintenance concept, however, does not require the use of a particular basis of measurement. Selection of the basis under this concept is dependent on the type of financial capital that the entity is seeking to maintain.

107   The principal difference between the two concepts of capital maintenance is the treatment of the effects of changes in the prices of assets and liabilities of the entity. In general terms, an entity has maintained its capital if it has as much capital at the end of the period as it had at the beginning of the period. Any amount over and above that required to maintain the capital at the beginning of the period is profit.

108   Under the concept of financial capital maintenance where capital is defined in terms of nominal monetary units, profit represents the increase in nominal money capital over the period. Thus, increases in the prices of assets held over the period, conventionally referred to as holding gains, are, conceptually, profits. They may not be recognised as such, however, until the assets are disposed of in an exchange transaction. When the concept of financial capital maintenance is defined in terms of constant purchasing power units, profit represents the increase in invested purchasing power over the period. Thus, only that part of the increase in the prices of assets that exceeds the increase in the general level of prices is regarded as profit. The rest of the increase is treated as a capital maintenance adjustment and, hence, as part of equity.

109   Under the concept of physical capital maintenance when capital is defined in terms of the physical productive capacity, profit represents the increase in that capital over the period. All price changes affecting the assets and liabilities of the entity are viewed as changes in the measurement of the physical productive capacity of the entity. Hence,

they are treated as capital maintenance adjustments that are part of equity and not as profit.

110   The selection of the measurement bases and concept of capital maintenance will determine the accounting model used in the preparation of the financial statements. Different accounting models exhibit different degrees of relevance and reliability and, as in other areas, management must seek a balance between relevance and reliability. This *Framework* is applicable to a range of accounting models and provides guidance on preparing and presenting the financial statements constructed under the chosen model. At the present time, it is not the intention of the AASB to prescribe a particular model other than in exceptional circumstances, such as for those entities reporting in the currency of a hyperinflationary economy. This intention will, however, be reviewed in the light of world developments.

APPENDIX
OBJECTIVE AND QUALITATIVE CHARACTERISTICS

This appendix is an integral part of the Framework for the Preparation and Presentation of Financial Statements (Framework) *and has the same status as other parts of the* Framework. *The appendix comprises two chapters – Chapter 1: The objective of general purpose financial reporting and Chapter 3: Qualitative characteristics of useful financial information.*

CHAPTER 1: THE OBJECTIVE OF GENERAL PURPOSE FINANCIAL REPORTING

CONTENTS

CHAPTER 1: THE OBJECTIVE OF GENERAL PURPOSE FINANCIAL REPORTING

Introduction

OB1   The objective of general purpose financial reporting forms the foundation of the *Framework*. Other aspects of the *Framework*—a reporting entity concept, the qualitative characteristics of, and the constraint on, useful financial information, elements of financial statements, recognition, measurement, presentation and disclosure—flow logically from the objective.

Objective, usefulness and limitations of general purpose financial reporting

OB2   The objective of general purpose financial reporting[1] is to provide financial information about the reporting entity that is useful to existing and potential investors, lenders and other creditors in making decisions about providing resources to the entity. Those decisions involve buying, selling or holding equity and debt instruments, and providing or settling loans and other forms of credit.

AusOB2.1   Among the users of financial information about a not-for-profit reporting entity are existing and potential resource providers (such as investors, lenders and other creditors, donors and taxpayers), recipients of goods and services (such as beneficiaries, for example, members of the community) and parties performing a review or oversight function on behalf of other users (such as advisers and members of parliament). Such users may make resource allocation decisions in relation to not-for-profit entities that differ from those identified in paragraph OB2. For example, parliaments decide, on behalf of constituents, whether to fund particular programmes for delivery by an entity, taxpayers decide who should represent them in government, donors decide whether to donate resources to an entity, and recipients decide whether they can continue to rely on the provision of goods and services from the entity or whether to seek alternative suppliers. In relation to not-for-profit entities, where pertinent, all references in this *Framework* to 'existing and potential investors, lenders and other creditors' (and related terms) should be read as a reference to this broader range of users.

OB3   Decisions by existing and potential investors about buying, selling or holding equity and debt instruments depend on the returns that they expect from an investment in those instruments, for example dividends, principal and interest payments or market price increases. Similarly, decisions by existing and potential lenders and other creditors about providing or settling loans and other forms of credit depend on the principal and interest payments or other returns that they expect. Investors', lenders' and other creditors' expectations about returns depend on their assessment of the amount, timing and uncertainty of (the prospects for) future net cash inflows to the entity. Consequently, existing and potential investors, lenders and other creditors need information to help them assess the prospects for future net cash inflows to an entity.

AusOB3.1   In respect of not-for-profit entities, users (such as certain existing and potential resource providers) are generally not concerned with obtaining a financial return on an investment in the entity. Rather, they are concerned with the ability of the entity to achieve its objectives (whether financial or non-financial), which in turn may depend, at least in part, on the entity's prospects for future net cash inflows. Users will, for example, be interested in the capability of the entity's resources to provide goods and services in the future. Accordingly, in relation to not-for-profit entities, where pertinent, references in this *Framework* to 'assessing prospects for future net cash inflows' (and related terms) should be read in the context of the common information needs of users of general purpose financial reports of not-for-profit entities described in this paragraph.

OB4   To assess an entity's prospects for future net cash inflows, existing and potential investors, lenders and other creditors need information about the resources of the entity, claims against the entity, and how efficiently and effectively the entity's management and governing board[2] have discharged their responsibilities to use the entity's resources. Examples of such responsibilities include protecting the entity's resources from unfavourable effects of economic factors such as price and technological changes and ensuring that the entity complies with applicable laws, regulations and contractual provisions.

---

1   Throughout this *Framework*, the terms *financial reports* and *financial reporting* refer to *general purpose financial reports* and *general purpose financial reporting* unless specifically indicated otherwise.

2   Throughout this *Framework*, the term *management* refers to *management and the governing board of an entity* unless specifically indicated otherwise.

Information about management's discharge of its responsibilities is also useful for decisions by existing investors, lenders and other creditors who have the right to vote on or otherwise influence management's actions.

OB5 Many existing and potential investors, lenders and other creditors cannot require reporting entities to provide information directly to them and must rely on general purpose financial reports for much of the financial information they need. Consequently, they are the primary users to whom general purpose financial reports are directed.

OB6 However, general purpose financial reports do not and cannot provide all of the information that existing and potential investors, lenders and other creditors need. Those users need to consider pertinent information from other sources, for example, general economic conditions and expectations, political events and political climate, and industry and company outlooks.

OB7 General purpose financial reports are not designed to show the value of a reporting entity; but they provide information to help existing and potential investors, lenders and other creditors to estimate the value of the reporting entity.

OB8 Individual primary users have different, and possibly conflicting, information needs and desires. The Board, in developing financial reporting standards, will seek to provide the information set that will meet the needs of the maximum number of primary users. However, focusing on common information needs does not prevent the reporting entity from including additional information that is most useful to a particular subset of primary users.

OB9 The management of a reporting entity is also interested in financial information about the entity. However, management need not rely on general purpose financial reports because it is able to obtain the financial information it needs internally.

OB10 Other parties, such as regulators and members of the public other than investors, lenders and other creditors, may also find general purpose financial reports useful. However, those reports are not primarily directed to these other groups.[3]

OB11 To a large extent, financial reports are based on estimates, judgements and models rather than exact depictions. The *Framework* establishes the concepts that underlie those estimates, judgements and models. The concepts are the goal towards which the Board and preparers of financial reports strive. As with most goals, the *Framework*'s vision of ideal financial reporting is unlikely to be achieved in full, at least not in the short term, because it takes time to understand, accept and implement new ways of analysing transactions and other events. Nevertheless, establishing a goal towards which to strive is essential if financial reporting is to evolve so as to improve its usefulness.

Information about a reporting entity's economic resources, claims against the entity and changes in resources and claims

OB12 General purpose financial reports provide information about the financial position of a reporting entity, which is information about the entity's economic resources and the claims against the reporting entity. Financial reports also provide information about the effects of transactions and other events that change a reporting entity's economic resources and claims. Both types of information provide useful input for decisions about providing resources to an entity.

Economic resources and claims

OB13 Information about the nature and amounts of a reporting entity's economic resources and claims can help users to identify the reporting entity's financial strengths and weaknesses. That information can help users to assess the reporting entity's liquidity and solvency, its needs for additional financing and how successful it is likely to be

---

3   For not-for-profit entities, see paragraph AusOB2.1.

in obtaining that financing. Information about priorities and payment requirements of existing claims helps users to predict how future cash flows will be distributed among those with a claim against the reporting entity.

OB14 Different types of economic resources affect a user's assessment of the reporting entity's prospects for future cash flows differently. Some future cash flows result directly from existing economic resources, such as accounts receivable. Other cash flows result from using several resources in combination to produce and market goods or services to customers. Although those cash flows cannot be identified with individual economic resources (or claims), users of financial reports need to know the nature and amount of the resources available for use in a reporting entity's operations.

Changes in economic resources and claims

OB15 Changes in a reporting entity's economic resources and claims result from that entity's financial performance (see paragraphs OB17–OB20) and from other events or transactions such as issuing debt or equity instruments (see paragraph OB21). To properly assess the prospects for future cash flows from the reporting entity, users need to be able to distinguish between both of these changes.

OB16 Information about a reporting entity's financial performance helps users to understand the return that the entity has produced on its economic resources. Information about the return the entity has produced provides an indication of how well management has discharged its responsibilities to make efficient and effective use of the reporting entity's resources. Information about the variability and components of that return is also important, especially in assessing the uncertainty of future cash flows. Information about a reporting entity's past financial performance and how its management discharged its responsibilities is usually helpful in predicting the entity's future returns on its economic resources.

Financial performance reflected by accrual accounting

OB17 Accrual accounting depicts the effects of transactions and other events and circumstances on a reporting entity's economic resources and claims in the periods in which those effects occur, even if the resulting cash receipts and payments occur in a different period. This is important because information about a reporting entity's economic resources and claims and changes in its economic resources and claims during a period provides a better basis for assessing the entity's past and future performance than information solely about cash receipts and payments during that period.

OB18 Information about a reporting entity's financial performance during a period, reflected by changes in its economic resources and claims other than by obtaining additional resources directly from investors and creditors (see paragraph OB21), is useful in assessing the entity's past and future ability to generate net cash inflows. That information indicates the extent to which the reporting entity has increased its available economic resources, and thus its capacity for generating net cash inflows through its operations rather than by obtaining additional resources directly from investors and creditors.

AusOB18.1 In respect of not-for-profit entities, information useful for assessing an entity's past and future ability to generate net cash inflows through its operations is, in turn, useful for assessing whether income from taxpayers, donors and other sources was sufficient, and is likely to remain sufficient, to meet the cost of a given volume and quality of goods and services the entity provides.

OB19 Information about a reporting entity's financial performance during a period may also indicate the extent to which events such as changes in market prices or interest rates have increased or decreased the entity's economic resources and claims, thereby affecting the entity's ability to generate net cash inflows.

Financial performance reflected by past cash flows

OB20 Information about a reporting entity's cash flows during a period also helps users to assess the entity's ability to generate future net cash inflows. It indicates how the reporting entity obtains and spends cash, including information about its borrowing and repayment of debt, cash dividends or other cash distributions to investors, and other factors that may affect the entity's liquidity or solvency. Information about cash flows helps users understand a reporting entity's operations, evaluate its financing and investing activities, assess its liquidity or solvency and interpret other information about financial performance.

Changes in economic resources and claims not resulting from financial performance

OB21 A reporting entity's economic resources and claims may also change for reasons other than financial performance, such as issuing additional ownership shares. Information about this type of change is necessary to give users a complete understanding of why the reporting entity's economic resources and claims changed and the implications of those changes for its future financial performance.

CHAPTER 3: QUALITATIVE CHARACTERISTICS OF USEFUL FINANCIAL INFORMATION

CONTENTS

CHAPTER 3: QUALITATIVE CHARACTERISTICS OF USEFUL FINANCIAL INFORMATION

Introduction

QC1 The qualitative characteristics of useful financial information discussed in this chapter identify the types of information that are likely to be most useful to the existing and potential investors, lenders and other creditors for making decisions about the reporting entity on the basis of information in its financial report (financial information).

QC2 Financial reports provide information about the reporting entity's economic resources, claims against the reporting entity and the effects of transactions and other events and

FRAMEWORK

conditions that change those resources and claims. (This information is referred to in the *Framework* as information about the economic phenomena.) Some financial reports also include explanatory material about management's expectations and strategies for the reporting entity, and other types of forward-looking information.

QC3   The qualitative characteristics of useful financial information[4] apply to financial information provided in financial statements, as well as to financial information provided in other ways. Cost, which is a pervasive constraint on the reporting entity's ability to provide useful financial information, applies similarly. However, the considerations in applying the qualitative characteristics and the cost constraint may be different for different types of information. For example, applying them to forward-looking information may be different from applying them to information about existing economic resources and claims and to changes in those resources and claims.

Qualitative characteristics of useful financial information

QC4   If financial information is to be useful, it must be relevant and faithfully represent what it purports to represent. The usefulness of financial information is enhanced if it is comparable, verifiable, timely and understandable.

Fundamental qualitative characteristics

QC5   The fundamental qualitative characteristics are *relevance* and *faithful representation*.

Relevance

QC6   Relevant financial information is capable of making a difference in the decisions made by users. Information may be capable of making a difference in a decision even if some users choose not to take advantage of it or are already aware of it from other sources.

QC7   Financial information is capable of making a difference in decisions if it has predictive value, confirmatory value or both.

QC8   Financial information has predictive value if it can be used as an input to processes employed by users to predict future outcomes. Financial information need not be a prediction or forecast to have predictive value. Financial information with predictive value is employed by users in making their own predictions.

QC9   Financial information has confirmatory value if it provides feedback about (confirms or changes) previous evaluations.

QC10   The predictive value and confirmatory value of financial information are interrelated. Information that has predictive value often also has confirmatory value. For example, revenue information for the current year, which can be used as the basis for predicting revenues in future years, can also be compared with revenue predictions for the current year that were made in past years. The results of those comparisons can help a user to correct and improve the processes that were used to make those previous predictions.

Materiality

QC11   Information is material if omitting it or misstating it could influence decisions that users make on the basis of financial information about a specific reporting entity. In other words, materiality is an entity-specific aspect of relevance based on the nature or magnitude, or both, of the items to which the information relates in the context of an individual entity's financial report. Consequently, the Board cannot specify a uniform quantitative threshold for materiality or predetermine what could be material in a particular situation.

---

4   Throughout this *Framework*, the terms *qualitative characteristics* and *constraint* refer to the qualitative characteristics of, and the constraint on, useful financial information.

Faithful representation

QC12 Financial reports represent economic phenomena in words and numbers. To be useful, financial information must not only represent relevant phenomena, but it must also faithfully represent the phenomena that it purports to represent. To be a perfectly faithful representation, a depiction would have three characteristics. It would be *complete, neutral* and *free from error*. Of course, perfection is seldom, if ever, achievable. The Board's objective is to maximise those qualities to the extent possible.

QC13 A complete depiction includes all information necessary for a user to understand the phenomenon being depicted, including all necessary descriptions and explanations. For example, a complete depiction of a group of assets would include, at a minimum, a description of the nature of the assets in the group, a numerical depiction of all of the assets in the group, and a description of what the numerical depiction represents (for example, original cost, adjusted cost or fair value). For some items, a complete depiction may also entail explanations of significant facts about the quality and nature of the items, factors and circumstances that might affect their quality and nature, and the process used to determine the numerical depiction.

QC14 A neutral depiction is without bias in the selection or presentation of financial information. A neutral depiction is not slanted, weighted, emphasised, de-emphasised or otherwise manipulated to increase the probability that financial information will be received favourably or unfavourably by users. Neutral information does not mean information with no purpose or no influence on behaviour. On the contrary, relevant financial information is, by definition, capable of making a difference in users' decisions.

QC15 Faithful representation does not mean accurate in all respects. Free from error means there are no errors or omissions in the description of the phenomenon, and the process used to produce the reported information has been selected and applied with no errors in the process. In this context, free from error does not mean perfectly accurate in all respects. For example, an estimate of an unobservable price or value cannot be determined to be accurate or inaccurate. However, a representation of that estimate can be faithful if the amount is described clearly and accurately as being an estimate, the nature and limitations of the estimating process are explained, and no errors have been made in selecting and applying an appropriate process for developing the estimate.

QC16 A faithful representation, by itself, does not necessarily result in useful information. For example, a reporting entity may receive property, plant and equipment through a government grant. Obviously, reporting that an entity acquired an asset at no cost would faithfully represent its cost, but that information would probably not be very useful. A slightly more subtle example is an estimate of the amount by which an asset's carrying amount should be adjusted to reflect an impairment in the asset's value. That estimate can be a faithful representation if the reporting entity has properly applied an appropriate process, properly described the estimate and explained any uncertainties that significantly affect the estimate. However, if the level of uncertainty in such an estimate is sufficiently large, that estimate will not be particularly useful. In other words, the relevance of the asset being faithfully represented is questionable. If there is no alternative representation that is more faithful, that estimate may provide the best available information.

Applying the fundamental qualitative characteristics

QC17 Information must be both relevant and faithfully represented if it is to be useful. Neither a faithful representation of an irrelevant phenomenon nor an unfaithful representation of a relevant phenomenon helps users make good decisions.

QC18 The most efficient and effective process for applying the fundamental qualitative characteristics would usually be as follows (subject to the effects of enhancing characteristics and the cost constraint, which are not considered in this example). First, identify an economic phenomenon that has the potential to be useful to users of the reporting entity's financial information. Second, identify the type of information about that phenomenon that would be most relevant if it is available and can be faithfully represented. Third, determine whether that information is available and can be faithfully represented. If so, the process of satisfying the fundamental qualitative characteristics ends at that point. If not, the process is repeated with the next most relevant type of information.

Enhancing qualitative characteristics

QC19 *Comparability, verifiability, timeliness* and *understandability* are qualitative characteristics that enhance the usefulness of information that is relevant and faithfully represented. The enhancing qualitative characteristics may also help determine which of two ways should be used to depict a phenomenon if both are considered equally relevant and faithfully represented.

Comparability

QC20 Users' decisions involve choosing between alternatives, for example, selling or holding an investment, or investing in one reporting entity or another. Consequently, information about a reporting entity is more useful if it can be compared with similar information about other entities and with similar information about the same entity for another period or another date.

QC21 Comparability is the qualitative characteristic that enables users to identify and understand similarities in, and differences among, items. Unlike the other qualitative characteristics, comparability does not relate to a single item. A comparison requires at least two items.

QC22 Consistency, although related to comparability, is not the same. Consistency refers to the use of the same methods for the same items, either from period to period within a reporting entity or in a single period across entities. Comparability is the goal; consistency helps to achieve that goal.

QC23 Comparability is not uniformity. For information to be comparable, like things must look alike and different things must look different. Comparability of financial information is not enhanced by making unlike things look alike any more than it is enhanced by making like things look different.

QC24 Some degree of comparability is likely to be attained by satisfying the fundamental qualitative characteristics. A faithful representation of a relevant economic phenomenon should naturally possess some degree of comparability with a faithful representation of a similar relevant economic phenomenon by another reporting entity.

QC25 Although a single economic phenomenon can be faithfully represented in multiple ways, permitting alternative accounting methods for the same economic phenomenon diminishes comparability.

Verifiability

QC26 Verifiability helps assure users that information faithfully represents the economic phenomena it purports to represent.

Verifiability means that different knowledgeable and independent observers could reach consensus, although not necessarily complete agreement, that a particular depiction is a faithful representation. Quantified information need not be a single point estimate to be verifiable. A range of possible amounts and the related probabilities can also be verified.

QC27 Verification can be direct or indirect. Direct verification means verifying an amount or other representation through direct observation, for example, by counting cash. Indirect verification means checking the inputs to a model, formula or other technique and recalculating the outputs using the same methodology. An example is verifying the carrying amount of inventory by checking the inputs (quantities and costs) and recalculating the ending inventory using the same cost flow assumption (for example, using the first-in, first-out method).

QC28   It may not be possible to verify some explanations and forward-looking financial information until a future period, if at all. To help users decide whether they want to use that information, it would normally be necessary to disclose the underlying assumptions, the methods of compiling the information and other factors and circumstances that support the information.

Timeliness

QC29   Timeliness means having information available to decision-makers in time to be capable of influencing their decisions. Generally, the older the information is the less useful it is. However, some information may continue to be timely long after the end of a reporting period because, for example, some users may need to identify and assess trends.

Understandability

QC30   Classifying, characterising and presenting information clearly and concisely makes it *understandable*.

QC31   Some phenomena are inherently complex and cannot be made easy to understand. Excluding information about those phenomena from financial reports might make the information in those financial reports easier to understand. However, those reports would be incomplete and therefore potentially misleading.

QC32   Financial reports are prepared for users who have a reasonable knowledge of business and economic activities and who review and analyse the information diligently. At times, even well-informed and diligent users may need to seek the aid of an adviser to understand information about complex economic phenomena.

Applying the enhancing qualitative characteristics

QC33   Enhancing qualitative characteristics should be maximised to the extent possible. However, the enhancing qualitative characteristics, either individually or as a group, cannot make information useful if that information is irrelevant or not faithfully represented.

QC34   Applying the enhancing qualitative characteristics is an iterative process that does not follow a prescribed order. Sometimes, one enhancing qualitative characteristic may have to be diminished to maximise another qualitative characteristic. For example, a temporary reduction in comparability as a result of prospectively applying a new financial reporting standard may be worthwhile to improve relevance or faithful representation in the longer term. Appropriate disclosures may partially compensate for non-comparability.

The cost constraint on useful financial reporting

QC35   Cost is a pervasive constraint on the information that can be provided by financial reporting. Reporting financial information imposes costs, and it is important that those costs are justified by the benefits of reporting that information. There are several types of costs and benefits to consider.

QC36   Providers of financial information expend most of the effort involved in collecting, processing, verifying and disseminating financial information, but users ultimately bear those costs in the form of reduced returns. Users of financial information also incur costs of analysing and interpreting the information provided. If needed information is not provided, users incur additional costs to obtain that information elsewhere or to estimate it.

QC37   Reporting financial information that is relevant and faithfully represents what it purports to represent helps users to make decisions with more confidence. This results in more efficient functioning of capital markets and a lower cost of capital for the economy as a whole. An individual investor, lender or other creditor also receives benefits by making more informed decisions. However, it is not possible for general purpose financial reports to provide all the information that every user finds relevant.

QC38 In applying the cost constraint, the Board assesses whether the benefits of reporting particular information are likely to justify the costs incurred to provide and use that information. When applying the cost constraint in developing a proposed financial reporting standard, the Board seeks information from providers of financial information, users, auditors, academics and others about the expected nature and quantity of the benefits and costs of that standard. In most situations, assessments are based on a combination of quantitative and qualitative information.

QC39 Because of the inherent subjectivity, different individuals' assessments of the costs and benefits of reporting particular items of financial information will vary. Therefore, the Board seeks to consider costs and benefits in relation to financial reporting generally, and not just in relation to individual reporting entities. That does not mean that assessments of costs and benefits always justify the same reporting requirements for all entities. Differences may be appropriate because of different sizes of entities, different ways of raising capital (publicly or privately), different users' needs or other factors.

BASIS FOR CONCLUSIONS ON AASB CF 2013-1

This Basis for Conclusions accompanies, but is not part of, the Framework. *The Basis for Conclusions was originally published with Accounting Framework AASB CF 2013-1* Amendments to the Australian Conceptual Framework *(December 2013).*

Background to the amendments introduced through AASB CF 2013-1

BC1 This Basis for Conclusions summarises the Australian Accounting Standards Board's (AASB) considerations in developing AASB CF 2013-1. Individual Board members gave greater weight to some factors than to others.

BC2 The amendments to the *Framework for the Preparation and Presentation of Financial Statements (Framework)* result from proposals that were included in AASB Exposure Draft ED 164 *An improved Conceptual Framework for Financial Reporting: The Objective of Financial Reporting and Qualitative Characteristics and Constraints of Decision-useful Financial Reporting Information* (AASB ED 164) published in June 2008. AASB ED 164 incorporated the International Accounting Standards Board's (IASB) May 2008 Exposure Draft of the same name.

BC3 The IASB has been undertaking a review of its conceptual framework for several years. Consistent with the AASB's policy of IFRS adoption, the AASB has been closely monitoring the work of the IASB. In September 2010, the IASB issued a revised IASB *Conceptual Framework for Financial Reporting* (IASB *Conceptual Framework*) containing two new chapters – Chapter 1: *The objective of general purpose financial reporting* and Chapter 3: *Qualitative characteristics of useful financial information*. The revised IASB *Conceptual Framework* includes a 'placeholder' for Chapter 2: *The reporting entity* and Chapter 4, which carries over the text of the IASB's *Framework for the Preparation and Presentation of Financial Statements*[1] (IASB *Framework* 2001) that was not superseded by Chapters 1 and 3 and therefore deals with concepts not yet reconsidered by the IASB. Further revised chapters are planned – see paragraph BC4 below.

---

1   The IASC's *Framework for the Preparation and Presentation of Financial Statements* (1989) was adopted by the IASB in April 2001.

BC4   As part of its review, the IASB has also issued:

     (a)   in March 2010, IASB Exposure Draft ED/2010/2 *Conceptual Framework for Financial Reporting: The Reporting Entity* (incorporated into AASB Exposure Draft ED 193 of the same name, also issued in March 2010); and

     (b)   in July 2013, IASB Discussion Paper DP/2013/1 *A Review of the Conceptual Framework for Financial Reporting* (incorporated into AASB Invitation to Comment ITC 29 *A Review of the IASB's Conceptual Framework for Financial Reporting*, also issued in July 2013). The Discussion Paper sets out the IASB's preliminary views on concepts relating to the elements of financial statements, recognition and derecognition, measurement, presentation and disclosure, and the IASB's plan to progress its reporting entity proposals.

BC5   In addition to the aspects of a conceptual framework noted in paragraph BC4(b) above, the IASB Discussion Paper DP/2013/1 also notes that while the IASB does not intend to fundamentally reconsider Chapter 1 and Chapter 3 as issued in September 2010, changes to these chapters may be necessary if work on the other aspects highlights areas in these chapters that require clarification or amendment. The IASB has also invited comment where respondents believe that changes are necessary to the existing chapters.

Application of the amendments to for-profit entities

BC6   The Board decided to make Chapters 1 and 3 of the September 2010 IASB *Conceptual Framework* applicable to for-profit entities, consistent with its IFRS-adoption policy. The Board decided to do this pragmatically by amending the *Framework* for the revised guidance rather than issuing a new framework document, pending completion of the IASB project.

BC7   The Board considered whether to introduce additional guidance in respect of for-profit entities in the public sector and decided that additional guidance is not necessary at this time.

Application of the amendments to not-for-profit entities

BC8   As part of its due process, through AASB ED 164, the AASB invited constituents to comment on the issues that would need to be considered if the proposed concepts relating to the objective of financial reporting and the qualitative characteristics of useful financial information were also to be applied to not-for-profit entities. Consistent with comments made in the joint report *A Report on the application to not-for-profit entities in the private and public sectors* (July 2008)[2] on the not-for-profit implications of the IASB Exposure Draft on these concepts, some respondents to AASB ED 164 commented that more emphasis would need to be given to accountability or stewardship, and less to reporting information for assessing cash flows, for the concepts to be suitable for such entities. Respondents were also concerned that a user group focussed on capital providers was too narrow to be a proxy for the common information needs of users of general purpose financial reports of not-for-profit entities.

BC9   The Board noted that the current focus of the IASB is on business entities in the private sector and that the IASB appears to no longer intend to consider, in the manner it initially proposed, the applicability of its revised concepts to not-for-profit entities in the private sector. In light of this, the Board decided to make Chapters 1 and 3 of the September 2010 IASB *Conceptual Framework* applicable to not-for-profit entities at the same time as for-profit entities, to be consistent with its IFRS-adoption and transaction-neutral policies. However, having regard to the feedback received on AASB ED 164 (see paragraph BC8), the Board decided to include additional

---

2   The Report was prepared by the Chairs and senior staff of the Australian Accounting Standards Board, Canadian Accounting Standards Board, New Zealand Financial Reporting Standards Board and the United Kingdom Accounting Standards Board.

guidance in respect of not-for-profit entities to the extent that matters are not adequately addressed by the IASB in Chapters 1 and 3 (see paragraphs BC11–BC15 below).

BC10 After the IASB has completed its review of its conceptual framework, the AASB intends reviewing the not-for-profit guidance included in its conceptual framework. As part of this process, the AASB will have further regard to the International Public Sector Accounting Standards Board's (IPSASB) decisions about its conceptual framework, particularly where the IPSASB's decisions are complementary to the IASB's decisions.[3]

Additional guidance for not-for-profit entities

BC11 The Board noted comments about the importance of accountability of management in respect of not-for-profit entities, and considered whether to make specific reference to the accountability (or stewardship) of management for the resources entrusted to it, similar to statements made in superseded paragraph 14 of the *Framework* and in Statement of Accounting Concepts SAC 2 *Objective of General Purpose Financial Reporting* (e. g. paragraphs 14, 27 and 44). The Board noted the IASB's acknowledgement of the role of stewardship and its rationale for not using the term 'stewardship' within Chapter 1. Paragraphs BC1.27 and BC1.28 of the IASB's Basis for Conclusions on Chapter 1 of the IASB *Conceptual Framework* (September 2010) state:

BC1.27 ... The Board did not intend to imply that assessing prospects for future cash flow or assessing the quality of management's stewardship is more important than the other. Both are important for making decisions about providing resources to an entity, and information about stewardship is also important for resource providers who have the ability to vote on, or otherwise influence, management's actions.

BC1.28 The Board decided not to use the term *stewardship* in the chapter because there would be difficulties in translating it into other languages. Instead, the Board described what stewardship encapsulates. Accordingly, the objective of financial reporting acknowledges that users make resource allocation decisions as well as decisions as to whether management has made efficient and effective use of the resources provided.

BC12 The Board noted that while the provision of information for accountability purposes is an important function of general purpose financial reporting, including in relation to not-for-profit entities, the rendering of accountability by reporting entities through general purpose financial reporting can be regarded as encompassed by the broader objective of providing information useful for making decisions about the allocation of resources. This is on the basis that users ultimately require accountability-related information for resource allocation decisions. Accordingly, in response to constituent feedback on AASB ED 164 in relation to accountability (see paragraph BC8), the Board concluded that the additional guidance it has included in respect of not-for-profit entities is consistent with the view that management accountability is encompassed within the objective of general purpose financial reporting of not-for-profit entities as described in the *Framework*.

BC13 In particular, the Board decided to develop additional guidance for not-for-profit entities that would:

(a)   identify the broad range of users of general purpose financial reports of not-for-profit entities (see paragraph AusOB2.1); and

---

3   In January 2013, the IPSASB issued *The Conceptual Framework for General Purpose Financial Reporting by Public Sector Entities* addressing some aspects of its conceptual framework: the role and authority of the conceptual framework, the objective and users of general purpose financial reports, qualitative characteristics, and the reporting entity. Chapters addressing other concepts, including the definition and recognition of elements of financial statements, measurement, and presentation, are being developed by the IPSASB.

(b)   adequately acknowledge that such users of general purpose financial reports of not-for-profit entities have common information needs relating to:

   (i)   how well the entity is meeting its objectives that are not primarily related to cash generation (see paragraphs AusOB3.1 and AusOB18.1); and

   (ii)   the ability of the entity's available resources to deliver future goods and services (see paragraph AusOB3.1).

In developing this not-for-profit specific guidance, the Board gave consideration to guidance included in the IPSASB conceptual framework chapters published in January 2013.

BC14   With regard to paragraph BC13(a), consistent with the IPSASB's *The Conceptual Framework for General Purpose Financial Reporting by Public Sector Entities* (and superseded paragraph 17 of SAC 2), the Board decided to particularly identify taxpayers as one of the users of general purpose financial reports of not-for-profit entities in paragraph AusOB2.1. As noted by the IPSASB, taxpayers usually provide resources to governments and other public sector entities involuntarily. In addition, as recipients of goods or services from public sector entities, taxpayers often do not have the discretion to choose an alternative supplier of those goods and services. Consequently, they have little direct or immediate capacity to make decisions about whether to provide resources to the government, the resources to be allocated for the provision of goods or services by a public sector entity or whether to purchase or consume the goods or services provided. However, they can make decisions about their voting preferences and representations they make to elected officials or other representative bodies based on information contained in general purpose financial reports – these decisions may have resource allocation consequences for certain not-for-profit entities.

BC15   With regard to paragraph BC13(b), the Board concluded that the common information needs of users of general purpose financial reports of not-for-profit entities include the entity's ability to achieve both its financial and non-financial objectives. For example, taxpayers may be interested in whether a not-for-profit entity in the public sector is delivering the services expected of it, that is, whether it is achieving its objectives and doing so economically and efficiently. Other resource providers, such as creditors, may principally be interested in the entity's ability to generate future cash inflows for timely payment of the entity's obligations to them; however, they may be indirectly concerned about the extent to which the entity is achieving its non-financial objectives, since the ability of the entity to generate future cash inflows will depend on its performance in this regard. The Board decided that it was important for such common user needs to be explicitly acknowledged in the amended chapters.

Other significant issues

Status of the *Framework*

BC16   The Board decided to take this opportunity to amend paragraph Aus1.1 of the *Framework* to remove the references to superseded or withdrawn pronouncements. Policy Statement 5 *The Nature and Purpose of Statements of Accounting Concepts* was withdrawn with effect for reporting periods beginning on or after 1 January 2005. Professional Statement APS 1 *Conformity with Accounting Standards and UIG Consensus Views* (which superseded APS 1 *Conformity of Accounting Standards*) has been superseded by Professional Standard APES 205 *Conformity with Accounting Standards* (December 2007), which does not make explicit reference to the non-mandatory status of the *Framework* or the Statements of Accounting Concepts.

Consequences for SAC 2

BC17   Superseded paragraph Aus14.1 of the *Framework* noted that a more detailed discussion of the objective of financial statements is provided in SAC 2. The Board decided that SAC 2 should be superseded as it is no longer necessary in light of the extensive discussion of the objective of general purpose financial reporting in paragraphs OB1 to OB21.

Status of SAC 1

BC18 The Board decided that the reporting entity concept expressed in Statement of Accounting Concepts SAC 1 *Definition of the Reporting Entity* still has its place in Australia. The concept is currently used to help identify those entities that must apply Australian Accounting Standards. Accordingly, the status of SAC 1 is retained (at least for now) in the Australian conceptual framework. The AASB intends to consider the manner in which to incorporate the IASB's forthcoming chapter on Reporting Entity (see paragraph BC4(a)) into the Australian conceptual framework in due course. This consideration would have regard to the interaction with other aspects of the IASB's Conceptual Framework project, other AASB projects (including reconsideration of the application of the reporting entity concept in Australia), and the AASB's approach to adopting IASB content for application by not-for-profit entities.

Effective date of the amendments

BC19 The Board decided that the amendments introduced by AASB CF 2013-1 should be applicable to general purpose financial statements of periods ending on or after the date of approval of the pronouncement, with allowance for earlier application.

BC20 The Board would not expect the incorporation of Chapters 1 and 3 of the IASB *Conceptual Framework* into the *Framework* to cause entities to change their accounting policies adopted under the existing *Framework*. Therefore, the application date provisions of these amendments would not be expected to have any practical significance. Nevertheless, the Board decided to identify an application date for these amendments and allow for earlier application, to avoid doubt about these aspects and for consistency with the application provisions of Accounting Standards.

AASB 1
First-time Adoption of Australian Accounting Standards
(Compiled December 2017)

For-profit (FP) entities

This compiled Standard applies to annual periods beginning on or after 1 January 2018 but before 1 January 2019. Earlier application is permitted for annual periods beginning after 24 July 2014 but before 1 January 2018. It incorporates relevant amendments made up to and including 12 December 2017.

Not-for-profit (NFP) entities – early application only

This compiled Standard does not apply mandatorily to NFP entities. However, early application is permitted for annual reporting periods beginning after 24 July 2014 but before 1 January 2019.

Prepared on 20 March 2018 by the staff of the Australian Accounting Standards Board.

Compilation no. 1

Compilation date: 31 December 2017

This note is not part of Accounting Standard AASB 1.

The following unincorporated amendments are not included in this compiled Standard.

- AASB 2017-4 *Amendments to Australian Accounting Standards — Uncertainty over income tax treatments.* This standard makes amendments to AASB 1 *First-time Adoption of Australian Accounting Standards* arising from AASB Interpretation 23 *Uncertainty over Income Tax Treatments*. This Standard applies to annual periods beginning on or after 1 January 2019, but earlier application is permitted.

- AASB 17 *Insurance Contracts* — Appendix D sets out the amendments to other Standards that are a consequence of the AASB issuing AASB 17 *Insurance Contracts*. This Standard is applicable from 1 January 2021. Earlier application is permitted, but entities must apply AASB 9 *Financial Instruments* and AASB 15 *Revenue from Contracts with Customers* first.

- AASB 1058 *Income of Not-for-Profit Entities* — Appendix D sets out the amendments to other Australian Accounting Standards that are a consequence of the AASB issuing this Standard. It is applicable from 1 January 2019. Earlier application is permitted, but amendments to AASB 117 apply before 1 January 2019 only if AASB 1058 is also applied to an earlier period. In addition, AASB 1 and AASB 16 amendments are applied to an earlier period only if AASB 16 is also applied to that period.

- AASB 16 *Leases* — Appendix D sets out the amendments to other Standards that are a consequence of the AASB issuing this Standard. It is applicable from 1 January 2019. Earlier application is permitted, but entities must apply AASB 15 *Revenue from Contracts with Customers* before applying this Standard.

- AASB 2016-7 *Amendments to Australian Accounting Standards — Deferral of AASB 15 for Not-for-Profit Entities.* This Standard defers the consequential amendments that were originally set out in AASB 2014-5 *Amendments to Australian Accounting Standards arising from AASB 15,* by restating the effective date of the amendments set out in AASB 2015-8 *Amendments to Australian Accounting*

Standards for not-for-profit entities. This Standard defers the application of AASB 15 to 1 January 2019. Earlier application is permitted provided AASB 1058 is also applied to the same period.

Entities early-adopting any amendments with later application dates will need to refer to the amending Standards that have not yet been incorporated into compilations. The abovementioned unincorporated amendments may be located on the AASB website at www.aasb.gov.au or on the Federal Register of Legislation website at www.legislation.gov.au.

CONTENTS

COMPARISON WITH IFRS 1
ACCOUNTING STANDARD
AASB 1 *FIRST-TIME ADOPTION OF AUSTRALIAN ACCOUNTING STANDARDS*

COMPILATION DETAILS

DELETED IFRS 1 TEXT

IMPLEMENTATION GUIDANCE ON IFRS 1 (available on the AASB website)

BASIS FOR CONCLUSIONS ON IFRS 1 (available on the AASB website)

Australian Accounting Standard AASB 1 *First-time Adoption of Australian Accounting Standards* (as amended) is set out in paragraphs 1 – Aus40.2 and Appendices A – F. All the paragraphs have equal authority. Paragraphs in **bold type** state the main principles. Terms defined in Appendix A are in *italics* the first time they appear in the Standard. AASB 1 is to be read in the context of other Australian Accounting Standards, including AASB 1048 *Interpretation of Standards*, which identifies the Australian Accounting Interpretations, and AASB 1057 *Application of Australian Accounting Standards*. In the absence of explicit guidance, AASB 108 *Accounting Policies, Changes in Accounting Estimates and Errors* provides a basis for selecting and applying accounting policies.

COMPARISON WITH IFRS 1

AASB 1 *First-time Adoption of Australian Accounting Standards* as amended incorporates IFRS 1 *First-time Adoption of International Financial Reporting Standards* issued and amended by the International Accounting Standards Board (IASB). Australian-specific paragraphs (which are not included in IFRS 1) are identified with the prefix "Aus" or "RDR". Paragraphs that apply only to not-for-profit entities begin by identifying their limited applicability.

Tier 1

For-profit entities complying with AASB 1 also comply with IFRS 1.

Not-for-profit entities' compliance with IFRS 1 will depend on whether any "Aus" paragraphs that specifically apply to not-for-profit entities provide additional guidance or contain applicable requirements that are inconsistent with IFRS 1.

Tier 2

Entities preparing general purpose financial statements under Australian Accounting Standards – Reduced Disclosure Requirements (Tier 2) will not be in compliance with IFRSs.

AASB 1053 *Application of Tiers of Australian Accounting Standards* explains the two tiers of reporting requirements.

ACCOUNTING STANDARD AASB 1

The Australian Accounting Standards Board made Accounting Standard AASB 1 *First-time Adoption of Australian Accounting Standards* under section 334 of the *Corporations Act 2001* on 24 July 2015.

This compiled version of AASB 1 applies to annual periods beginning on or after 1 January 2018 but before 1 January 2019 for for-profit entities. It incorporates relevant amendments contained in other AASB Standards made by the AASB up to and including 12 December 2017 (see Compilation Details).

ACCOUNTING STANDARD AASB 1
FIRST-TIME ADOPTION OF AUSTRALIAN ACCOUNTING STANDARDS

Objective

1   The objective of this Standard is to ensure that an entity's *first Australian-Accounting-Standards financial statements*, and its interim financial reports for part of the period covered by those financial statements, contain high quality information that:

    (a)   is transparent for users and comparable over all periods presented;

    (b)   provides a suitable starting point for accounting in accordance with Australian Accounting Standards[1]; and

    (c)   can be generated at a cost that does not exceed the benefits.

Scope

2   An entity shall apply this Standard in:

    (a)   its first Australian-Accounting-Standards financial statements; and

    (b)   each interim financial report, if any, that it presents in accordance with AASB 134 *Interim Financial Reporting* for part of the period covered by its first Australian-Accounting-Standards financial statements.

3   An entity's first Australian-Accounting-Standards financial statements are the first annual financial statements in which the entity adopts Australian Accounting Standards, by an explicit and unreserved statement in those financial statements of compliance with Australian Accounting Standards. Financial statements in accordance with Australian Accounting Standards are an entity's first Australian-Accounting-Standards financial statements if, for example, the entity:

    (a)   presented its most recent previous financial statements:

        (i)   in accordance with national requirements that are not consistent with Australian Accounting Standards or *International Financial Reporting Standards (IFRSs)* in all respects;

        (ii)   in conformity with Australian Accounting Standards or IFRSs in all respects, except that the financial statements did not contain an explicit and unreserved statement that they complied with Australian Accounting Standards or IFRSs;

        (iii)   containing an explicit statement of compliance with some, but not all, Australian Accounting Standards or IFRSs;

        (iv)   in accordance with national requirements inconsistent with Australian Accounting Standards or IFRSs, using some individual Australian Accounting Standards or IFRSs to account for items for which national requirements did not exist; or

        (v)   in accordance with national requirements, with a reconciliation of some amounts to the amounts determined in accordance with Australian Accounting Standards or IFRSs;

---

1   [Aus] The term 'Australian Accounting Standards' refers to Standards (including Interpretations) made by the AASB that apply to any reporting period beginning on or after 1 January 2005. In this context, the term encompasses Australian Accounting Standards – Reduced Disclosure Requirements, which some entities are permitted to apply in accordance with AASB 1053 *Application of Tiers of Australian Accounting Standards* in preparing general purpose financial statements.

(b)   prepared financial statements in accordance with Australian Accounting Standards or IFRSs for internal use only, without making them available to the entity's owners or any other external users;

(c)   prepared a reporting package in accordance with Australian Accounting Standards or IFRSs for consolidation purposes without preparing a complete set of financial statements as defined in AASB 101 *Presentation of Financial Statements* (as revised in 2007); or

(d)   did not present financial statements for previous periods.

Aus3.1   [Deleted by the AASB]

Aus3.2   In rare circumstances, a not-for-profit public sector entity may experience extreme difficulties in complying with the requirements of certain Australian Accounting Standards due to information deficiencies that have caused the entity to state non-compliance with *previous GAAP*. In these cases, the conditions specified in paragraph 3 for the application of this Standard are taken to be satisfied provided the entity:

     (a)   discloses in its first Australian-Accounting-Standards financial statements:

         (i)   an explanation of information deficiencies and its strategy for rectifying those deficiencies; and

         (ii)   the Australian Accounting Standards that have not been complied with; and

     (b)   makes an explicit and unreserved statement of compliance with other Australian Accounting Standards for which there are no information deficiencies.

4   This Standard applies when an entity first adopts Australian Accounting Standards. It does not apply when, for example, an entity:

     (a)   stops presenting financial statements in accordance with national requirements, having previously presented them as well as another set of financial statements that contained an explicit and unreserved statement of compliance with Australian Accounting Standards or IFRSs;

     (b)   presented financial statements in the previous year in accordance with national requirements and those financial statements contained an explicit and unreserved statement of compliance with Australian Accounting Standards or IFRSs; or

     (c)   presented financial statements in the previous year that contained an explicit and unreserved statement of compliance with Australian Accounting Standards or IFRSs, even if the auditors qualified their audit report on those financial statements.

4A   Notwithstanding the requirements in paragraphs 2 and 3, an entity that has applied Australian Accounting Standards or IFRSs in a previous reporting period, but whose most recent previous annual financial statements did not contain an explicit and unreserved statement of compliance with Australian Accounting Standards or IFRSs, must either apply this Standard or else apply Australian Accounting Standards retrospectively in accordance with AASB 108 *Accounting Policies, Changes in Accounting Estimates and Errors* as if the entity had never stopped applying Australian Accounting Standards or IFRSs.

4B   When an entity does not elect to apply this Standard in accordance with paragraph 4A, the entity shall nevertheless apply the disclosure requirements in paragraphs 23A–23B of AASB 1, in addition to the disclosure requirements in AASB 108.

5   This Standard does not apply to changes in accounting policies made by an entity that already applies Australian Accounting Standards. Such changes are the subject of:

AASB

(a)   requirements on changes in accounting policies in AASB 108 *Accounting Policies, Changes in Accounting Estimates and Errors*; and

(b)   specific transitional requirements in other Australian Accounting Standards.

Recognition and measurement

Opening Australian-Accounting-Standards statement of financial position

6   An entity shall prepare and present an *opening Australian-Accounting-Standards statement of financial position* at the *date of transition to Australian Accounting Standards*. This is the starting point for its accounting in accordance with Australian Accounting Standards.

Accounting policies

7   **An entity shall use the same accounting policies in its opening Australian-Accounting-Standards statement of financial position and throughout all periods presented in its first Australian-Accounting-Standards financial statements. Those accounting policies shall comply with each Australian Accounting Standard effective at the end of its *first Australian-Accounting-Standards reporting period*, except as specified in paragraphs 13–19 and Appendices B–E.**

8   An entity shall not apply different versions of Australian Accounting Standards that were effective at earlier dates. An entity may apply a new Standard that is not yet mandatory if that Standard permits early application.

Example: Consistent application of latest version of Australian Accounting Standards

Background

The end of entity A's first Australian-Accounting-Standards reporting period is 31 December 20X5. Entity A decides to present comparative information in those financial statements for one year only (see paragraph 21). Therefore, its date of transition to Australian Accounting Standards is the beginning of business on 1 January 20X4 (or, equivalently, close of business on 31 December 20X3). Entity A presented financial statements in accordance with its *previous GAAP* annually to 31 December each year up to, and including, 31 December 20X4.

Application of requirements

Entity A is required to apply the Australian Accounting Standards effective for periods ending on 31 December 20X5 in:

(a)   preparing and presenting its opening Australian-Accounting-Standards statement of financial position at 1 January 20X4; and

(b)   preparing and presenting its statement of financial position for 31 December 20X5 (including comparative amounts for 20X4), statement of comprehensive income, statement of changes in equity and statement of cash flows for the year to 31 December 20X5 (including comparative amounts for 20X4) and disclosures (including comparative information for 20X4).

If a new Standard is not yet mandatory but permits early application, entity A is permitted, but not required, to apply that Standard in its first Australian-Accounting-Standards financial statements.

---

9   The transitional provisions in other Australian Accounting Standards apply to changes in accounting policies made by an entity that already uses Australian Accounting Standards; they do not apply to a *first-time adopter*'s transition to Australian Accounting Standards, except as specified in Appendices B–E.

10 Except as described in paragraphs 13–19 and Appendices B–E, an entity shall, in its opening Australian-Accounting-Standards statement of financial position:

(a) recognise all assets and liabilities whose recognition is required by Australian Accounting Standards;

(b) not recognise items as assets or liabilities if Australian Accounting Standards do not permit such recognition;

(c) reclassify items that it recognised in accordance with previous GAAP as one type of asset, liability or component of equity, but are a different type of asset, liability or component of equity in accordance with Australian Accounting Standards; and

(d) apply Australian Accounting Standards in measuring all recognised assets and liabilities.

11 The accounting policies that an entity uses in its opening Australian-Accounting-Standards statement of financial position may differ from those that it used for the same date using its previous GAAP. The resulting adjustments arise from events and transactions before the date of transition to Australian Accounting Standards. Therefore, an entity shall recognise those adjustments directly in retained earnings (or, if appropriate, another category of equity) at the date of transition to Australian Accounting Standards.

12 This Standard establishes two categories of exceptions to the principle that an entity's opening Australian-Accounting-Standards statement of financial position shall comply with each Australian Accounting Standard:

(a) paragraphs 14–17 and Appendix B prohibit retrospective application of some aspects of other Australian Accounting Standards.

(b) Appendices C–E grant exemptions from some requirements of other Australian Accounting Standards.

Exceptions to the retrospective application of other Australian Accounting Standards

13 This Standard prohibits retrospective application of some aspects of other Australian Accounting Standards. These exceptions are set out in paragraphs 14–17 and Appendix B.

Estimates

14 **An entity's estimates in accordance with Australian Accounting Standards at the date of transition to Australian Accounting Standards shall be consistent with estimates made for the same date in accordance with previous GAAP (after adjustments to reflect any difference in accounting policies), unless there is objective evidence that those estimates were in error.**

15 An entity may receive information after the date of transition to Australian Accounting Standards about estimates that it had made under previous GAAP. In accordance with paragraph 14, an entity shall treat the receipt of that information in the same way as non-adjusting events after the reporting period in accordance with AASB 110 *Events after the Reporting Period*. For example, assume that an entity's date of transition to Australian Accounting Standards is 1 January 20X4 and new information on 15 July 20X4 requires the revision of an estimate made in accordance with previous GAAP at 31 December 20X3. The entity shall not reflect that new information in its opening Australian-Accounting-Standards statement of financial position (unless the estimates need adjustment for any differences in accounting policies or there is objective evidence that the estimates were in error). Instead, the entity shall reflect that new information in profit or loss (or, if appropriate, other comprehensive income) for the year ended 31 December 20X4.

AASB

16 An entity may need to make estimates in accordance with Australian Accounting Standards at the date of transition to Australian Accounting Standards that were not required at that date under previous GAAP. To achieve consistency with AASB 110, those estimates in accordance with Australian Accounting Standards shall reflect conditions that existed at the date of transition to Australian Accounting Standards. In particular, estimates at the date of transition to Australian Accounting Standards of market prices, interest rates or foreign exchange rates shall reflect market conditions at that date.

17 Paragraphs 14–16 apply to the opening Australian-Accounting-Standards statement of financial position. They also apply to a comparative period presented in an entity's first Australian-Accounting-Standards financial statements, in which case the references to the date of transition to Australian Accounting Standards are replaced by references to the end of that comparative period.

Exemptions from other Australian Accounting Standards

18 An entity may elect to use one or more of the exemptions contained in Appendices C–E. An entity shall not apply these exemptions by analogy to other items.

19 [Deleted]

Presentation and disclosure

20 This Standard does not provide exemptions from the presentation and disclosure requirements in other Australian Accounting Standards.

Comparative information

21 An entity's first Australian-Accounting-Standards financial statements shall include at least three statements of financial position, two statements of profit or loss and other comprehensive income, two separate statements of profit or loss (if presented), two statements of cash flows and two statements of changes in equity and related notes, including comparative information for all statements presented.

Non-Australian-Accounting-Standards comparative information and historical summaries

22 Some entities present historical summaries of selected data for periods before the first period for which they present full comparative information in accordance with Australian Accounting Standards. This Standard does not require such summaries to comply with the recognition and measurement requirements of Australian Accounting Standards. Furthermore, some entities present comparative information in accordance with previous GAAP as well as the comparative information required by AASB 101. In any financial statements containing historical summaries or comparative information in accordance with previous GAAP, an entity shall:

(a) label the previous GAAP information prominently as not being prepared in accordance with Australian Accounting Standards; and

(b) disclose the nature of the main adjustments that would make it comply with Australian Accounting Standards. An entity need not quantify those adjustments.

Explanation of transition to Australian Accounting Standards

23 **An entity shall explain how the transition from previous GAAP to Australian Accounting Standards affected its reported financial position, financial performance and cash flows.**

23A An entity that has applied Australian Accounting Standards or IFRSs in a previous period, as described in paragraph 4A, shall disclose:

(a) the reason it stopped applying Australian Accounting Standards or IFRSs; and

(b) the reason it is resuming or commencing the application of Australian Accounting Standards.

23B When an entity, in accordance with paragraph 4A, does not elect to apply AASB 1, the entity shall explain the reasons for electing to apply Australian Accounting Standards as if it had never stopped applying Australian Accounting Standards or IFRSs.

Reconciliations

24 To comply with paragraph 23, an entity's first Australian-Accounting-Standards financial statements shall include:

(a) reconciliations of its equity reported in accordance with previous GAAP to its equity in accordance with Australian Accounting Standards for both of the following dates:

(i) the date of transition to Australian Accounting Standards; and

(ii) the end of the latest period presented in the entity's most recent annual financial statements in accordance with previous GAAP.

(b) a reconciliation to its total comprehensive income in accordance with Australian Accounting Standards for the latest period in the entity's most recent annual financial statements. The starting point for that reconciliation shall be total comprehensive income in accordance with previous GAAP for the same period or, if an entity did not report such a total, profit or loss under previous GAAP.

(c) if the entity recognised or reversed any impairment losses for the first time in preparing its opening Australian-Accounting-Standards statement of financial position, the disclosures that AASB 136 *Impairment of Assets* would have required if the entity had recognised those impairment losses or reversals in the period beginning with the date of transition to Australian Accounting Standards.

25 The reconciliations required by paragraph 24(a) and (b) shall give sufficient detail to enable users to understand the material adjustments to the statement of financial position and statement of comprehensive income. If an entity presented a statement of cash flows under its previous GAAP, it shall also explain the material adjustments to the statement of cash flows.

26 If an entity becomes aware of errors made under previous GAAP, the reconciliations required by paragraph 24(a) and (b) shall distinguish the correction of those errors from changes in accounting policies.

27 AASB 108 does not apply to the changes in accounting policies an entity makes when it adopts Australian Accounting Standards or to changes in those policies until after it presents its first Australian-Accounting-Standards financial statements. Therefore, AASB 108's requirements about changes in accounting policies do not apply in an entity's first Australian-Accounting-Standards financial statements.

27A If during the period covered by its first Australian-Accounting-Standards financial statements an entity changes its accounting policies or its use of the exemptions contained in this Standard, it shall explain the changes between its first Australian-Accounting-Standards interim financial report and its first Australian-Accounting-Standards financial statements, in accordance with paragraph 23, and it shall update the reconciliations required by paragraph 24(a) and (b).

28 If an entity did not present financial statements for previous periods, its first Australian-Accounting-Standards financial statements shall disclose that fact.

Designation of financial assets or financial liabilities

29 An entity is permitted to designate a previously recognised financial asset as a financial asset measured at fair value through profit or loss in accordance with paragraph D19A.

The entity shall disclose the fair value of financial assets so designated at the date of designation and their classification and carrying amount in the previous financial statements.

29A An entity is permitted to designate a previously recognised financial liability as a financial liability at fair value through profit or loss in accordance with paragraph D19. The entity shall disclose the fair value of financial liabilities so designated at the date of designation and their classification and carrying amount in the previous financial statements.

Use of fair value as deemed cost

30   If an entity uses fair value in its opening Australian-Accounting-Standards statement of financial position as *deemed cost* for an item of property, plant and equipment, an investment property or an intangible asset (see paragraphs D5 and D7), the entity's first Australian-Accounting-Standards financial statements shall disclose, for each line item in the opening Australian-Accounting-Standards statement of financial position:

      (a)   the aggregate of those fair values; and

      (b)   the aggregate adjustment to the carrying amounts reported under previous GAAP.

Use of deemed cost for investments in subsidiaries, joint ventures and associates

31   Similarly, if an entity uses a deemed cost in its opening Australian-Accounting-Standards statement of financial position for an investment in a subsidiary, joint venture or associate in its separate financial statements (see paragraph D15), the entity's first Australian-Accounting-Standards separate financial statements shall disclose:

      (a)   the aggregate deemed cost of those investments for which deemed cost is their previous GAAP carrying amount;

      (b)   the aggregate deemed cost of those investments for which deemed cost is fair value; and

      (c)   the aggregate adjustment to the carrying amounts reported under previous GAAP.

Use of deemed cost for oil and gas assets

31A   If an entity uses the exemption in paragraph D8A(b) for oil and gas assets, it shall disclose that fact and the basis on which carrying amounts determined under previous GAAP were allocated.

Use of deemed cost for operations subject to rate regulation

31B   If an entity uses the exemption in paragraph D8B for operations subject to rate regulation, it shall disclose that fact and the basis on which carrying amounts were determined under previous GAAP.

Use of deemed cost after severe hyperinflation

31C   If an entity elects to measure assets and liabilities at fair value and to use that fair value as the deemed cost in its opening Australian-Accounting-Standards statement of financial position because of severe hyperinflation (see paragraphs D26–D30), the entity's first Australian-Accounting-Standards financial statements shall disclose an explanation of how, and why, the entity had, and then ceased to have, a functional currency that has both of the following characteristics:

      (a)   a reliable general price index is not available to all entities with transactions and balances in the currency.

      (b)   exchangeability between the currency and a relatively stable foreign currency does not exist.

Interim financial reports

32   To comply with paragraph 23, if an entity presents an interim financial report in accordance with AASB 134 for part of the period covered by its first Australian-Accounting-Standards financial statements, the entity shall satisfy the following requirements in addition to the requirements of AASB 134:

(a)   Each such interim financial report shall, if the entity presented an interim financial report for the comparable interim period of the immediately preceding financial year, include:

(i)   a reconciliation of its equity in accordance with previous GAAP at the end of that comparable interim period to its equity under Australian Accounting Standards at that date; and

(ii)   a reconciliation to its total comprehensive income in accordance with Australian Accounting Standards for that comparable interim period (current and year to date). The starting point for that reconciliation shall be total comprehensive income in accordance with previous GAAP for that period or, if an entity did not report such a total, profit or loss in accordance with previous GAAP.

(b)   In addition to the reconciliations required by (a), an entity's first interim financial report in accordance with AASB 134 for part of the period covered by its first Australian-Accounting-Standards financial statements shall include the reconciliations described in paragraph 24(a) and (b) (supplemented by the details required by paragraphs 25 and 26) or a cross-reference to another published document that includes these reconciliations.

(c)   If an entity changes its accounting policies or its use of the exemptions contained in this Standard, it shall explain the changes in each such interim financial report in accordance with paragraph 23 and update the reconciliations required by (a) and (b).

33   AASB 134 requires minimum disclosures, which are based on the assumption that users of the interim financial report also have access to the most recent annual financial statements. However, AASB 134 also requires an entity to disclose 'any events or transactions that are material to an understanding of the current interim period'. Therefore, if a first-time adopter did not, in its most recent annual financial statements in accordance with previous GAAP, disclose information material to an understanding of the current interim period, its interim financial report shall disclose that information or include a cross-reference to another published document that includes it.

Effective date

34   An entity shall apply this Standard if its first Australian-Accounting-Standards financial statements are for a period beginning on or after 1 January 2018. Earlier application is permitted for periods beginning after 24 July 2014 but before 1 January 2018.

35–39A   [Deleted by the AASB]

39AA   [Deleted]

39AC   AASB 2017-1 *Amendments to Australian Accounting Standards – Transfers of Investment Property, Annual Improvements 2014–2016 Cycle and Other Amendments* added paragraph D36 and amended paragraph D1. An entity shall apply that amendment when it applies AASB Interpretation 22 *Foreign Currency Transactions and Advance Consideration*, as identified in AASB 1048 *Interpretation of Standards*.

39AD   AASB 2017-1 *Amendments to Australian Accounting Standards – Transfers of Investment Property, Annual Improvements 2014–2016 Cycle and Other Amendments*, issued in February 2017, deleted paragraph 39AA. A for-profit entity shall apply those amendments for annual periods beginning on or after 1 January 2018. A not-for-profit entity shall apply those amendments for annual periods beginning on or after 1 January 2019.

39B [Deleted]

39C–39F [Deleted by the AASB]

39G [Deleted]

39H–39N [Deleted by the AASB]

39O Paragraphs B10 and B11 refer to AASB 9. If an entity applies this Standard but does not yet apply AASB 9, the references in paragraphs B10 and B11 to AASB 9 shall be read as references to AASB 139 *Financial Instruments: Recognition and Measurement*.

39P–39T [Deleted by the AASB]

39U [Deleted]

39V AASB 2014-1 *Amendments to Australian Accounting Standards*, issued in June 2014, amended paragraph D8B in the previous version of this Standard. An entity shall apply that amendment for annual periods beginning on or after 1 January 2016. Earlier application is permitted. If an entity applies AASB 14 for an earlier period, the amendment shall be applied for that earlier period.

39W AASB 2014-3 *Amendments to Australian Accounting Standards – Accounting for Acquisitions of Interests in Joint Operations*, issued in August 2014, amended paragraph C5 in the previous version of this Standard. An entity shall apply that amendment in annual periods beginning on or after 1 January 2016. If an entity applies related amendments to AASB 11 from AASB 2014-3 in an earlier period, the amendment to paragraph C5 shall be applied in that earlier period.

39X AASB 2014-5 *Amendments to Australian Accounting Standards arising from AASB 15*, issued in December 2014, amended the previous version of this Standard as follows: deleted paragraph D24 and its related heading and added paragraphs D34–D35 and their related heading. An entity shall apply those amendments when it applies AASB 15.

39Y AASB 2010-7 *Amendments to Australian Accounting Standards arising from AASB 9 (December 2010)* (as amended), AASB 2014-1 *Amendments to Australian Accounting Standards* and AASB 2014-7 *Amendments to Australian Accounting Standards arising from AASB 9 (December 2014)* amended the previous version of this Standard as follows: amended paragraphs 29, B1–B6, D1, D14, D19 and D20, deleted paragraph 39B and added paragraphs 29A, B8–B8G, B9, D19A–D19C, D33, E1 and E2. Paragraph 39G, added by AASB 2010-7, was deleted by AASB 2014-1. Paragraph 39U, added by AASB 2014-1, was deleted by AASB 2014-7. An entity shall apply those amendments when it applies AASB 9.

39Z AASB 2014-9 *Amendments to Australian Accounting Standards – Equity Method in Separate Financial Statements*, issued in December 2014, amended the previous version of this Standard as follows: amended paragraph D14 and added paragraph D15A. An entity shall apply those amendments for annual periods beginning on or after 1 January 2016. Earlier application is permitted. If an entity applies those amendments for an earlier period, it shall disclose that fact.

39AA AASB 2015-1 *Amendments to Australian Accounting Standards – Annual Improvements to Australian Accounting Standards 2012–2014 Cycle*, issued in January 2015, added paragraph E4A in the previous version of this Standard. An entity shall apply that amendment for annual periods beginning on or after 1 January 2016. Earlier application is permitted. If an entity applies that amendment for an earlier period it shall disclose that fact.

Withdrawal of IFRS 1 (issued 2003)

40 [Deleted by the AASB]

Commencement of the legislative instrument

Aus40.1   For legal purposes, this legislative instrument commences on 31 December 2017.

Withdrawal of AASB pronouncements

Aus40.2   This Standard repeals AASB 1 *First-time Adoption of Australian Accounting Standards* issued in May 2009. Despite the repeal, after the time this Standard starts to apply under section 334 of the Corporations Act (either generally or in relation to an individual entity), the repealed Standard continues to apply in relation to any period ending before that time as if the repeal had not occurred.

[Note: When this Standard applies under section 334 of the Corporations Act (either generally or in relation to an individual entity), it supersedes the application of the repealed Standard.]

APPENDIX A
DEFINED TERMS

This appendix is an integral part of the Standard.

date of transition to Australian Accounting Standards	The beginning of the earliest period for which an entity presents full comparative information under Australian Accounting Standards in its **first Australian-Accounting-Standards financial statements**.
deemed cost	An amount used as a surrogate for cost or depreciated cost at a given date. Subsequent depreciation or amortisation assumes that the entity had initially recognised the asset or liability at the given date and that its cost was equal to the deemed cost.
fair value	*Fair value* is the price that would be received to sell an asset or paid to transfer a liability in an orderly transaction between market participants at the measurement date. (See AASB 13.)
first Australian-Accounting-Standards financial statements	The first annual financial statements in which an entity adopts Australian Accounting Standards, by an explicit and unreserved statement of compliance with Australian Accounting Standards.
first Australian-Accounting-Standards reporting period	The latest reporting period covered by an entity's **first Australian-Accounting-Standards financial statements**.
first-time adopter	An entity that presents its **first Australian-Accounting-Standards financial statements**.
International Financial Reporting Standards (IFRSs)	Standards and Interpretations issued by the International Accounting Standards Board (IASB). They comprise: (a) International Financial Reporting Standards; (b) International Accounting Standards; (c) IFRIC Interpretations; and (d) SIC Interpretations.[(a)]
opening Australian-Accounting-Standards statement of financial position	An entity's statement of financial position at the **date of transition to Australian Accounting Standards**.
previous GAAP	The basis of accounting that a **first-time adopter** used immediately before adopting Australian Accounting Standards.

(a) Definition of IFRSs amended after the name changes introduced by the revised Constitution of the IFRS Foundation in 2010.

APPENDIX B
EXCEPTIONS TO THE RETROSPECTIVE APPLICATION OF OTHER AUSTRALIAN ACCOUNTING STANDARDS

This appendix is an integral part of the Standard.

B1   An entity shall apply the following exceptions:

   (a)   derecognition of financial assets and financial liabilities (paragraphs B2 and B3);

   (b)   hedge accounting (paragraphs B4–B6);

   (c)   non-controlling interests (paragraph B7);

   (d)   classification and measurement of financial assets (paragraph B8–B8C);

   (e)   impairment of financial assets (paragraphs B8D–B8G);

   (f)   embedded derivatives (paragraph B9); and

   (g)   government loans (paragraphs B10–B12).

Derecognition of financial assets and financial liabilities

B2   Except as permitted by paragraph B3, a first-time adopter shall apply the derecognition requirements in AASB 9 prospectively for transactions occurring on or after the date of transition to Australian Accounting Standards. For example, if a first-time adopter derecognised non-derivative financial assets or non-derivative financial liabilities in accordance with its previous GAAP as a result of a transaction that occurred before the date of transition to Australian Accounting Standards, it shall not recognise those assets and liabilities in accordance with Australian Accounting Standards (unless they qualify for recognition as a result of a later transaction or event).

B3   Despite paragraph B2, an entity may apply the derecognition requirements in AASB 9 retrospectively from a date of the entity's choosing, provided that the information needed to apply AASB 9 to financial assets and financial liabilities derecognised as a result of past transactions was obtained at the time of initially accounting for those transactions.

Hedge accounting

B4   As required by AASB 9, at the date of transition to Australian Accounting Standards an entity shall:

   (a)   measure all derivatives at fair value; and

   (b)   eliminate all deferred losses and gains arising on derivatives that were reported in accordance with previous GAAP as if they were assets or liabilities.

B5   An entity shall not reflect in its opening Australian-Accounting-Standards statement of financial position a hedging relationship of a type that does not qualify for hedge accounting in accordance with AASB 9 (for example, many hedging relationships where the hedging instrument is a stand-alone written option or a net written option; or where the hedged item is a net position in a cash flow hedge for another risk than foreign currency risk). However, if an entity designated a net position as a hedged item in accordance with previous GAAP, it may designate as a hedged item in accordance with Australian Accounting Standards an individual item within that net position, or a net position if that meets the requirements in paragraph 6.6.1 of AASB 9, provided that it does so no later than the date of transition to Australian Accounting Standards.

B6   If, before the date of transition to Australian Accounting Standards, an entity had designated a transaction as a hedge but the hedge does not meet the conditions for hedge accounting in AASB 9, the entity shall apply paragraphs 6.5.6 and 6.5.7 of AASB 9 to discontinue hedge accounting. Transactions entered into before the date of transition to Australian Accounting Standards shall not be retrospectively designated as hedges.

Non-controlling interests

B7   A first-time adopter shall apply the following requirements of AASB 10 prospectively from the date of transition to Australian Accounting Standards:

(a)   the requirement in paragraph B94 that total comprehensive income is attributed to the owners of the parent and to the non-controlling interests even if this results in the non-controlling interests having a deficit balance;

(b)   the requirements in paragraphs 23 and B96 for accounting for changes in the parent's ownership interest in a subsidiary that do not result in a loss of control; and

(c)   the requirements in paragraphs B97–B99 for accounting for a loss of control over a subsidiary, and the related requirements of paragraph 8A of AASB 5 *Non-current Assets Held for Sale and Discontinued Operations*.

However, if a first-time adopter elects to apply AASB 3 retrospectively to past business combinations, it shall also apply AASB 10 in accordance with paragraph C1 of this Standard.

Classification and measurement of financial instruments

B8   An entity shall assess whether a financial asset meets the conditions in paragraph 4.1.2 of AASB 9 or the conditions in paragraph 4.1.2A of AASB 9 on the basis of the facts and circumstances that exist at the date of transition to Australian Accounting Standards.

B8A   If it is impracticable to assess a modified time value of money element in accordance with paragraphs B4.1.9B–B4.1.9D of AASB 9 on the basis of the facts and circumstances that exist at the date of transition to Australian Accounting Standards, an entity shall assess the contractual cash flow characteristics of that financial asset on the basis of the facts and circumstances that existed at the date of transition to Australian Accounting Standards without taking into account the requirements related to the modification of the time value of money element in paragraphs B4.1.9B–B4.1.9D of AASB 9. (In this case, the entity shall also apply paragraph 42R of AASB 7 but references to 'paragraph 7.2.4 of AASB 9' shall be read to mean this paragraph and references to 'initial recognition of the financial asset' shall be read to mean 'at the date of transition to Australian Accounting Standards'.)

B8B   If it is impracticable to assess whether the fair value of a prepayment feature is insignificant in accordance with paragraph B4.1.12(c) of AASB 9 on the basis of the facts and circumstances that exist at the date of transition to Australian Accounting Standards, an entity shall assess the contractual cash flow characteristics of that financial asset on the basis of the facts and circumstances that existed at the date of transition to Australian Accounting Standards without taking into account the exception for prepayment features in paragraph B4.1.12 of AASB 9. (In this case, the entity shall also apply paragraph 42S of AASB 7 but references to 'paragraph 7.2.5 of AASB 9' shall be read to mean this paragraph and references to 'initial recognition of the financial asset' shall be read to mean 'at the date of transition to Australian Accounting Standards'.)

B8C   If it is impracticable (as defined in AASB 108) for an entity to apply retrospectively the effective interest method in AASB 9, the fair value of the financial asset or the financial liability at the date of transition to Australian Accounting Standards shall be

AASB

the new gross carrying amount of that financial asset or the new amortised cost of that financial liability at the date of transition to Australian Accounting Standards.

Impairment of financial assets

B8D   An entity shall apply the impairment requirements in Section 5.5 of AASB 9 retrospectively subject to paragraphs B8E–B8G and E1–E2 of that Standard.

B8E   At the date of transition to Australian Accounting Standards, an entity shall use reasonable and supportable information that is available without undue cost or effort to determine the credit risk at the date that financial instruments were initially recognised (or for loan commitments and financial guarantee contracts the date that the entity became a party to the irrevocable commitment in accordance with paragraph 5.5.6 of AASB 9) and compare that to the credit risk at the date of transition to Australian Accounting Standards (also see paragraphs B7.2.2–B7.2.3 of AASB 9).

B8F   When determining whether there has been a significant increase in credit risk since initial recognition, an entity may apply:

   (a)   the requirements in paragraph 5.5.10 and B5.5.22–B5.5.24 of AASB 9; and

   (b)   the rebuttable presumption in paragraph 5.5.11 of AASB 9 for contractual payments that are more than 30 days past due if an entity will apply the impairment requirements by identifying significant increases in credit risk since initial recognition for those financial instruments on the basis of past due information.

B8G   If, at the date of transition to Australian Accounting Standards, determining whether there has been a significant increase in credit risk since the initial recognition of a financial instrument would require undue cost or effort, an entity shall recognise a loss allowance at an amount equal to lifetime expected credit losses at each reporting date until that financial instrument is derecognised (unless that financial instrument is low credit risk at a reporting date, in which case paragraph B8F(a) applies).

Embedded derivatives

B9   A first-time adopter shall assess whether an embedded derivative is required to be separated from the host contract and accounted for as a derivative on the basis of the conditions that existed at the later of the date it first became a party to the contract and the date a reassessment is required by paragraph B4.3.11 of AASB 9.

Government loans

B10   A first-time adopter shall classify all government loans received as a financial liability or an equity instrument in accordance with AASB 132 *Financial Instruments: Presentation*. Except as permitted by paragraph B11, a first-time adopter shall apply the requirements in AASB 9 *Financial Instruments* and AASB 120 *Accounting for Government Grants and Disclosure of Government Assistance* prospectively to government loans existing at the date of transition to Australian Accounting Standards and shall not recognise the corresponding benefit of the government loan at a below-market rate of interest as a government grant. Consequently, if a first-time adopter did not, under its previous GAAP, recognise and measure a government loan at a below-market rate of interest on a basis consistent with Australian-Accounting-Standards requirements, it shall use its previous GAAP carrying amount of the loan at the date of transition to Australian Accounting Standards as the carrying amount of the loan in the opening Australian-Accounting-Standards statement of financial position. An entity shall apply AASB 9 to the measurement of such loans after the date of transition to Australian Accounting Standards.

B11   Despite paragraph B10, an entity may apply the requirements in AASB 9 and AASB 120 retrospectively to any government loan originated before the date of transition to

Australian Accounting Standards, provided that the information needed to do so had been obtained at the time of initially accounting for that loan.

B12 The requirements and guidance in paragraphs B10 and B11 do not preclude an entity from being able to use the exemptions described in paragraphs D19–D19C relating to the designation of previously recognised financial instruments at fair value through profit or loss.

APPENDIX C
EXEMPTIONS FOR BUSINESS COMBINATIONS

This appendix is an integral part of the Standard. An entity shall apply the following requirements to business combinations that the entity recognised before the date of transition to Australian Accounting Standards. This Appendix should only be applied to business combinations within the scope of AASB 3 Business Combinations.

C1 A first-time adopter may elect not to apply AASB 3 retrospectively to past business combinations (business combinations that occurred before the date of transition to Australian Accounting Standards). However, if a first-time adopter restates any business combination to comply with AASB 3, it shall restate all later business combinations and shall also apply AASB 10 from that same date. For example, if a first-time adopter elects to restate a business combination that occurred on 30 June 20X6, it shall restate all business combinations that occurred between 30 June 20X6 and the date of transition to Australian Accounting Standards, and it shall also apply AASB 10 from 30 June 20X6.

C2 An entity need not apply AASB 121 *The Effects of Changes in Foreign Exchange Rates* retrospectively to fair value adjustments and goodwill arising in business combinations that occurred before the date of transition to Australian Accounting Standards. If the entity does not apply AASB 121 retrospectively to those fair value adjustments and goodwill, it shall treat them as assets and liabilities of the entity rather than as assets and liabilities of the acquiree. Therefore, those goodwill and fair value adjustments either are already expressed in the entity's functional currency or are non-monetary foreign currency items, which are reported using the exchange rate applied in accordance with previous GAAP.

C3 An entity may apply AASB 121 retrospectively to fair value adjustments and goodwill arising in either:

    (a) all business combinations that occurred before the date of transition to Australian Accounting Standards; or

    (b) all business combinations that the entity elects to restate to comply with AASB 3, as permitted by paragraph C1 above.

C4 If a first-time adopter does not apply AASB 3 retrospectively to a past business combination, this has the following consequences for that business combination:

    (a) The first-time adopter shall keep the same classification (as an acquisition by the legal acquirer, a reverse acquisition by the legal acquiree, or a uniting of interests) as in its previous GAAP financial statements.

    (b) The first-time adopter shall recognise all its assets and liabilities at the date of transition to Australian Accounting Standards that were acquired or assumed in a past business combination, other than:

        (i) some financial assets and financial liabilities derecognised in accordance with previous GAAP (see paragraph B2); and

        (ii) assets, including goodwill, and liabilities that were not recognised in the acquirer's consolidated statement of financial position in accordance with previous GAAP and also would not qualify for recognition in accordance with Australian Accounting Standards in the separate statement of financial position of the acquiree (see (f)–(i) below).

The first-time adopter shall recognise any resulting change by adjusting retained earnings (or, if appropriate, another category of equity), unless the change results from the recognition of an intangible asset that was previously subsumed within goodwill (see (g)(i) below).

(c) The first-time adopter shall exclude from its opening Australian-Accounting-Standards statement of financial position any item recognised in accordance with previous GAAP that does not qualify for recognition as an asset or liability under Australian Accounting Standards. The first-time adopter shall account for the resulting change as follows:

    (i) the first-time adopter may have classified a past business combination as an acquisition and recognised as an intangible asset an item that does not qualify for recognition as an asset in accordance with AASB 138 *Intangible Assets*. It shall reclassify that item (and, if any, the related deferred tax and non-controlling interests) as part of goodwill (unless it deducted goodwill directly from equity in accordance with previous GAAP, see (g)(i) and (i) below).

    (ii) the first-time adopter shall recognise all other resulting changes in retained earnings.[2]

(d) Australian Accounting Standards require subsequent measurement of some assets and liabilities on a basis that is not based on original cost, such as fair value. The first-time adopter shall measure these assets and liabilities on that basis in its opening Australian-Accounting-Standards statement of financial position, even if they were acquired or assumed in a past business combination. It shall recognise any resulting change in the carrying amount by adjusting retained earnings (or, if appropriate, another category of equity), rather than goodwill.

(e) Immediately after the business combination, the carrying amount in accordance with previous GAAP of assets acquired and liabilities assumed in that business combination shall be their deemed cost in accordance with Australian Accounting Standards at that date. If Australian Accounting Standards require a cost-based measurement of those assets and liabilities at a later date, that deemed cost shall be the basis for cost-based depreciation or amortisation from the date of the business combination.

(f) If an asset acquired, or liability assumed, in a past business combination was not recognised in accordance with previous GAAP, it does not have a deemed cost of zero in the opening Australian-Accounting-Standards statement of financial position. Instead, the acquirer shall recognise and measure it in its consolidated statement of financial position on the basis that Australian Accounting Standards would require in the statement of financial position of the acquiree. To illustrate: if the acquirer had not, in accordance with its previous GAAP, capitalised finance leases acquired in a past business combination, it shall capitalise those leases in its consolidated financial statements, as AASB 117 *Leases* would require the acquiree to do in its Australian-Accounting-Standards statement of financial position. Similarly, if the acquirer had not, in accordance with its previous GAAP, recognised a contingent liability that still exists at the date of transition to Australian Accounting Standards, the acquirer shall recognise that contingent liability at that date unless AASB 137 *Provisions, Contingent Liabilities and Contingent Assets* would prohibit its recognition in the financial statements of the acquiree. Conversely, if an asset or liability was subsumed in goodwill in accordance with previous GAAP but would have been recognised separately under AASB 3, that asset or liability remains in goodwill unless Australian Accounting Standards would require its recognition in the financial statements of the acquiree.

---

2   Such changes include reclassifications from or to intangible assets if goodwill was not recognised in accordance with previous GAAP as an asset. This arises if, in accordance with previous GAAP, the entity (a) deducted goodwill directly from equity or (b) did not treat the business combination as an acquisition.

(g) The carrying amount of goodwill in the opening Australian-Accounting-Standards statement of financial position shall be its carrying amount in accordance with previous GAAP at the date of transition to Australian Accounting Standards, after the following two adjustments:

   (i) If required by (c)(i) above, the first-time adopter shall increase the carrying amount of goodwill when it reclassifies an item that it recognised as an intangible asset in accordance with previous GAAP. Similarly, if (f) above requires the first-time adopter to recognise an intangible asset that was subsumed in recognised goodwill in accordance with previous GAAP, the first-time adopter shall decrease the carrying amount of goodwill accordingly (and, if applicable, adjust deferred tax and non-controlling interests).

   (ii) Regardless of whether there is any indication that the goodwill may be impaired, the first-time adopter shall apply AASB 136 in testing the goodwill for impairment at the date of transition to Australian Accounting Standards and in recognising any resulting impairment loss in retained earnings (or, if so required by AASB 136, in revaluation surplus). The impairment test shall be based on conditions at the date of transition to Australian Accounting Standards.

(h) No other adjustments shall be made to the carrying amount of goodwill at the date of transition to Australian Accounting Standards. For example, the first-time adopter shall not restate the carrying amount of goodwill:

   (i) to exclude in-process research and development acquired in that business combination (unless the related intangible asset would qualify for recognition in accordance with AASB 138 in the statement of financial position of the acquiree);

   (ii) to adjust previous amortisation of goodwill;

   (iii) to reverse adjustments to goodwill that AASB 3 would not permit, but were made in accordance with previous GAAP because of adjustments to assets and liabilities between the date of the business combination and the date of transition to Australian Accounting Standards.

(i) If the first-time adopter recognised goodwill in accordance with previous GAAP as a deduction from equity:

   (i) it shall not recognise that goodwill in its opening Australian-Accounting-Standards statement of financial position. Furthermore, it shall not reclassify that goodwill to profit or loss if it disposes of the subsidiary or if the investment in the subsidiary becomes impaired.

   (ii) adjustments resulting from the subsequent resolution of a contingency affecting the purchase consideration shall be recognised in retained earnings.

(j) In accordance with its previous GAAP, the first-time adopter may not have consolidated a subsidiary acquired in a past business combination (for example, because the parent did not regard it as a subsidiary in accordance with previous GAAP or did not prepare consolidated financial statements). The first-time adopter shall adjust the carrying amounts of the subsidiary's assets and liabilities to the amounts that Australian Accounting Standards would require in the subsidiary's statement of financial position. The deemed cost of goodwill equals the difference at the date of transition to Australian Accounting Standards between:

   (i) the parent's interest in those adjusted carrying amounts; and

   (ii) the cost in the parent's separate financial statements of its investment in the subsidiary.

(k)　　The measurement of non-controlling interests and deferred tax follows from the measurement of other assets and liabilities. Therefore, the above adjustments to recognised assets and liabilities affect non-controlling interests and deferred tax.

C5　　The exemption for past business combinations also applies to past acquisitions of investments in associates, interests in joint ventures and interests in joint operations in which the activity of the joint operation constitutes a business, as defined in AASB 3. Furthermore, the date selected for paragraph C1 applies equally for all such acquisitions.

APPENDIX D
EXEMPTIONS FROM OTHER AUSTRALIAN ACCOUNTING STANDARDS

This appendix is an integral part of the Standard.

D1　　An entity may elect to use one or more of the following exemptions:

(a)　　share-based payment transactions (paragraphs D2 and D3);

(b)　　insurance contracts (paragraph D4);

(c)　　deemed cost (paragraphs D5–D8B);

(d)　　leases (paragraphs D9 and D9A);

(e)　　[deleted]

(f)　　cumulative translation differences (paragraphs D12 and D13);

(g)　　investments in subsidiaries, joint ventures and associates (paragraphs D14–D15A);

(h)　　assets and liabilities of subsidiaries, associates and joint ventures (paragraphs D16 and D17);

(i)　　compound financial instruments (paragraph D18);

(j)　　designation of previously recognised financial instruments (paragraphs D19–D19C);

(k)　　fair value measurement of financial assets or financial liabilities at initial recognition (paragraph D20);

(l)　　decommissioning liabilities included in the cost of property, plant and equipment (paragraphs D21 and D21A);

(m)　　financial assets or intangible assets accounted for in accordance with Interpretation 12 *Service Concession Arrangements* as identified in AASB 1048 *Interpretation of Standards* (paragraph D22);

(n)　　borrowing costs (paragraph D23);

(o)　　transfers of assets from customers (paragraph D24);

(p)　　extinguishing financial liabilities with equity instruments (paragraph D25);

(q)　　severe hyperinflation (paragraphs D26–D30);

(r)　　joint arrangements (paragraph D31);

(s)　　stripping costs in the production phase of a surface mine (paragraph D32);

(t)　　designation of contracts to buy or sell a non-financial item (paragraph D33);

(u)　　revenue (paragraphs D34 and D35); and

(v)　　foreign currency transactions and advance consideration (paragraph D36).

An entity shall not apply these exemptions by analogy to other items.

Share-based payment transactions

D2   A first-time adopter is encouraged, but not required, to apply AASB 2 *Share-based Payment* to equity instruments that were granted on or before 7 November 2002. A first-time adopter is also encouraged, but not required, to apply AASB 2 to equity instruments that were granted after 7 November 2002 and vested before the later of (a) the date of transition to Australian Accounting Standards and (b) 1 January 2005. However, if a first-time adopter elects to apply AASB 2 to such equity instruments, it may do so only if the entity has disclosed publicly the fair value of those equity instruments, determined at the measurement date, as defined in AASB 2. For all grants of equity instruments to which AASB 2 has not been applied (eg equity instruments granted on or before 7 November 2002), a first-time adopter shall nevertheless disclose the information required by paragraphs 44 and 45 of AASB 2. If a first-time adopter modifies the terms or conditions of a grant of equity instruments to which AASB 2 has not been applied, the entity is not required to apply paragraphs 26–29 of AASB 2 if the modification occurred before the date of transition to Australian Accounting Standards.

D3   A first-time adopter is encouraged, but not required, to apply AASB 2 to liabilities arising from share-based payment transactions that were settled before the date of transition to Australian Accounting Standards. A first-time adopter is also encouraged, but not required, to apply AASB 2 to liabilities that were settled before 1 January 2005. For liabilities to which AASB 2 is applied, a first-time adopter is not required to restate comparative information to the extent that the information relates to a period or date that is earlier than 7 November 2002.

Insurance contracts

D4   A first-time adopter may apply the transitional provisions in AASB 4 *Insurance Contracts*, AASB 1023 *General Insurance Contracts* and AASB 1038 *Life Insurance Contracts*. AASB 4 restricts changes in accounting policies for insurance contracts, including changes made by a first-time adopter.

Deemed cost

D5   An entity may elect to measure an item of property, plant and equipment at the date of transition to Australian Accounting Standards at its fair value and use that fair value as its deemed cost at that date.

D6   A first-time adopter may elect to use a previous GAAP revaluation of an item of property, plant and equipment at, or before, the date of transition to Australian Accounting Standards as deemed cost at the date of the revaluation, if the revaluation was, at the date of the revaluation, broadly comparable to:

(a)   fair value; or

(b)   cost or depreciated cost in accordance with Australian Accounting Standards, adjusted to reflect, for example, changes in a general or specific price index.

D7   The elections in paragraphs D5 and D6 are also available for:

(a)   investment property, if an entity elects to use the cost model in AASB 140 *Investment Property*; and

(b)   intangible assets that meet:

(i)   the recognition criteria in AASB 138 (including reliable measurement of original cost); and

(ii)   the criteria in AASB 138 for revaluation (including the existence of an active market).

An entity shall not use these elections for other assets or for liabilities.

D8   A first-time adopter may have established a deemed cost in accordance with previous GAAP for some or all of its assets and liabilities by measuring them at their fair value at one particular date because of an event such as a privatisation or initial public offering.

   (a)   If the measurement date is *at or before* the date of transition to Australian Accounting Standards, the entity may use such event-driven fair value measurements as deemed cost for Australian Accounting Standards at the date of that measurement.

   (b)   If the measurement date is *after* the date of transition to Australian Accounting Standards, but during the period covered by the first Australian-Accounting-Standards financial statements, the event-driven fair value measurements may be used as deemed cost when the event occurs. An entity shall recognise the resulting adjustments directly in retained earnings (or if appropriate, another category of equity) at the measurement date. At the date of transition to Australian Accounting Standards, the entity shall either establish the deemed cost by applying the criteria in paragraphs D5–D7 or measure assets and liabilities in accordance with the other requirements in this Standard.

D8A   Under some national accounting requirements exploration and development costs for oil and gas properties in the development or production phases are accounted for in cost centres that include all properties in a large geographical area. A first-time adopter using such accounting under previous GAAP may elect to measure oil and gas assets at the date of transition to Australian Accounting Standards on the following basis:

   (a)   exploration and evaluation assets at the amount determined under the entity's previous GAAP; and

   (b)   assets in the development or production phases at the amount determined for the cost centre under the entity's previous GAAP. The entity shall allocate this amount to the cost centre's underlying assets pro rata using reserve volumes or reserve values as of that date.

   The entity shall test exploration and evaluation assets and assets in the development and production phases for impairment at the date of transition to Australian Accounting Standards in accordance with AASB 6 *Exploration for and Evaluation of Mineral Resources* or AASB 136 respectively and, if necessary, reduce the amount determined in accordance with (a) or (b) above. For the purposes of this paragraph, oil and gas assets comprise only those assets used in the exploration, evaluation, development or production of oil and gas.

D8B   Some entities hold items of property, plant and equipment or intangible assets that are used, or were previously used, in operations subject to rate regulation. The carrying amount of such items might include amounts that were determined under previous GAAP but do not qualify for capitalisation in accordance with Australian Accounting Standards. If this is the case, a first-time adopter may elect to use the previous GAAP carrying amount of such an item at the date of transition to Australian Accounting Standards as deemed cost. If an entity applies this exemption to an item, it need not apply it to all items. At the date of transition to Australian Accounting Standards, an entity shall test for impairment in accordance with AASB 136 each item for which this exemption is used. For the purposes of this paragraph, operations are subject to rate regulation if they are governed by a framework for establishing the prices that can be charged to customers for goods or services and that framework is subject to oversight and/or approval by a rate regulator (as defined in AASB 14 *Regulatory Deferral Accounts*).

Leases

D9   A first-time adopter may apply the transitional provisions in Interpretation 4 *Determining whether an Arrangement contains a Lease* as identified in AASB 1048. Therefore, a first-time adopter may determine whether an arrangement existing at the date of transition to Australian Accounting Standards contains a lease on the basis of facts and circumstances existing at that date.

D9A If a first-time adopter made the same determination of whether an arrangement contained a lease in accordance with previous GAAP as that required by Interpretation 4 (as identified in AASB 1048) but at a date other than that required by Interpretation 4, the first-time adopter need not reassess that determination when it adopts Australian Accounting Standards. For an entity to have made the same determination of whether the arrangement contained a lease in accordance with previous GAAP, that determination would have to have given the same outcome as that resulting from applying AASB 117 *Leases* and Interpretation 4.

D10–D11 [Deleted]

Cumulative translation differences

D12 AASB 121 requires an entity:

(a) to recognise some translation differences in other comprehensive income and accumulate these in a separate component of equity; and

(b) on disposal of a foreign operation, to reclassify the cumulative translation difference for that foreign operation (including, if applicable, gains and losses on related hedges) from equity to profit or loss as part of the gain or loss on disposal.

D13 However, a first-time adopter need not comply with these requirements for cumulative translation differences that existed at the date of transition to Australian Accounting Standards. If a first-time adopter uses this exemption:

(a) the cumulative translation differences for all foreign operations are deemed to be zero at the date of transition to Australian Accounting Standards; and

(b) the gain or loss on a subsequent disposal of any foreign operation shall exclude translation differences that arose before the date of transition to Australian Accounting Standards and shall include later translation differences.

Investments in subsidiaries, joint ventures and associates

D14 When an entity prepares separate financial statements, AASB 127 requires it to account for its investments in subsidiaries, joint ventures and associates either:

(a) at cost;

(b) in accordance with AASB 9; or

(c) using the equity method as described in AASB 128.

D15 If a first-time adopter measures such an investment at cost in accordance with AASB 127, it shall measure that investment at one of the following amounts in its separate opening Australian-Accounting-Standards statement of financial position:

(a) cost determined in accordance with AASB 127; or

(b) deemed cost. The deemed cost of such an investment shall be its:

(i) fair value at the entity's date of transition to Australian Accounting Standards in its separate financial statements; or

(ii) previous GAAP carrying amount at that date.

A first-time adopter may choose either (i) or (ii) above to measure its investment in each subsidiary, joint venture or associate that it elects to measure using a deemed cost.

D15A If a first-time adopter accounts for such an investment using the equity method procedures as described in AASB 128:

(a)   the first-time adopter applies the exemption for past business combinations (Appendix C) to the acquisition of the investment.

(b)   if the entity becomes a first-time adopter for its separate financial statements earlier than for its consolidated financial statements, and

(i)   later than its parent, the entity shall apply paragraph D16 in its separate financial statements.

(ii)   later than its subsidiary, the entity shall apply paragraph D17 in its separate financial statements.

Assets and liabilities of subsidiaries, associates and joint ventures

D16   If a subsidiary becomes a first-time adopter later than its parent, the subsidiary shall, in its financial statements, measure its assets and liabilities at either:

(a)   the carrying amounts that would be included in the parent's consolidated financial statements, based on the parent's date of transition to Australian Accounting Standards, if no adjustments were made for consolidation procedures and for the effects of the business combination in which the parent acquired the subsidiary (this election is not available to a subsidiary of an investment entity, as defined in AASB 10, that is required to be measured at fair value through profit or loss); or

(b)   the carrying amounts required by the rest of this Standard, based on the subsidiary's date of transition to Australian Accounting Standards. These carrying amounts could differ from those described in (a):

(i)   when the exemptions in this Standard result in measurements that depend on the date of transition to Australian Accounting Standards.

(ii)   when the accounting policies used in the subsidiary's financial statements differ from those in the consolidated financial statements. For example, the subsidiary may use as its accounting policy the cost model in AASB 116 *Property, Plant and Equipment*, whereas the group may use the revaluation model.

A similar election is available to an associate or joint venture that becomes a first-time adopter later than an entity that has significant influence or joint control over it.

D17   However, if an entity becomes a first-time adopter later than its subsidiary (or associate or joint venture) the entity shall, in its consolidated financial statements, measure the assets and liabilities of the subsidiary (or associate or joint venture) at the same carrying amounts as in the financial statements of the subsidiary (or associate or joint venture), after adjusting for consolidation and equity accounting adjustments and for the effects of the business combination in which the entity acquired the subsidiary. Notwithstanding this requirement, a non-investment entity parent shall not apply the exception to consolidation that is used by any investment entity subsidiaries. Similarly, if a parent becomes a first-time adopter for its separate financial statements earlier or later than for its consolidated financial statements, it shall measure its assets and liabilities at the same amounts in both financial statements, except for consolidation adjustments.

Compound financial instruments

D18   AASB 132 *Financial Instruments: Presentation* requires an entity to split a compound financial instrument at inception into separate liability and equity components. If the liability component is no longer outstanding, retrospective application of AASB 132 involves separating two portions of equity. The first portion is in retained earnings and represents the cumulative interest accreted on the liability component. The other portion represents the original equity component. However, in accordance with this Standard, a first-time adopter need not separate these two portions if the liability component is no longer outstanding at the date of transition to Australian Accounting Standards.

Designation of previously recognised financial instruments

D19 AASB 9 permits a financial liability (provided it meets certain criteria) to be designated as a financial liability at fair value through profit or loss. Despite this requirement an entity is permitted to designate, at the date of transition to Australian Accounting Standards, any financial liability as at fair value through profit or loss provided the liability meets the criteria in paragraph 4.2.2 of AASB 9 at that date.

D19A An entity may designate a financial asset as measured at fair value through profit or loss in accordance with paragraph 4.1.5 of AASB 9 on the basis of the facts and circumstances that exist at the date of transition to Australian Accounting Standards.

D19B An entity may designate an investment in an equity instrument as at fair value through other comprehensive income in accordance with paragraph 5.7.5 of AASB 9 on the basis of the facts and circumstances that exist at the date of transition to Australian Accounting Standards.

D19C For a financial liability that is designated as a financial liability at fair value through profit or loss, an entity shall determine whether the treatment in paragraph 5.7.7 of AASB 9 would create an accounting mismatch in profit or loss on the basis of the facts and circumstances that exist at the date of transition to Australian Accounting Standards.

Fair value measurement of financial assets or financial liabilities at initial recognition

D20 Despite the requirements of paragraphs 7 and 9, an entity may apply the requirements in paragraph B5.1.2A(b) of AASB 9 prospectively to transactions entered into on or after the date of transition to Australian Accounting Standards.

Decommissioning liabilities included in the cost of property, plant and equipment

D21 Interpretation 1 *Changes in Existing Decommissioning, Restoration and Similar Liabilities* as identified in AASB 1048 requires specified changes in a decommissioning, restoration or similar liability to be added to or deducted from the cost of the asset to which it relates; the adjusted depreciable amount of the asset is then depreciated prospectively over its remaining useful life. A first-time adopter need not comply with these requirements for changes in such liabilities that occurred before the date of transition to Australian Accounting Standards. If a first-time adopter uses this exemption, it shall:

(a) measure the liability as at the date of transition to Australian Accounting Standards in accordance with AASB 137;

(b) to the extent that the liability is within the scope of Interpretation 1, estimate the amount that would have been included in the cost of the related asset when the liability first arose, by discounting the liability to that date using its best estimate of the historical risk-adjusted discount rate(s) that would have applied for that liability over the intervening period; and

(c) calculate the accumulated depreciation on that amount, as at the date of transition to Australian Accounting Standards, on the basis of the current estimate of the useful life of the asset, using the depreciation policy adopted by the entity in accordance with Australian Accounting Standards.

D21A An entity that uses the exemption in paragraph D8A(b) (for oil and gas assets in the development or production phases accounted for in cost centres that include all properties in a large geographical area under previous GAAP) shall, instead of applying paragraph D21 or Interpretation 1 (as identified in AASB 1048):

(a)   measure decommissioning, restoration and similar liabilities as at the date of transition to Australian Accounting Standards in accordance with AASB 137; and

(b)   recognise directly in retained earnings any difference between that amount and the carrying amount of those liabilities at the date of transition to Australian Accounting Standards determined under the entity's previous GAAP.

Financial assets or intangible assets accounted for in accordance with Interpretation 12

D22   A first-time adopter may apply the transitional provisions in Interpretation 12 as identified in AASB 1048.

Borrowing costs

D23   A first-time adopter can elect to apply the requirements of AASB 123 from the date of transition or from an earlier date as permitted by paragraph 28 of AASB 123. From the date on which an entity that applies this exemption begins to apply AASB 123, the entity:

(a)   shall not restate the borrowing cost component that was capitalised under previous GAAP and that was included in the carrying amount of assets at that date; and

(b)   shall account for borrowing costs incurred on or after that date in accordance with AASB 123, including those borrowing costs incurred on or after that date on qualifying assets already under construction.

D24   [Deleted]

Extinguishing financial liabilities with equity instruments

D25   A first-time adopter may apply the transitional provisions in Interpretation 19 *Extinguishing Financial Liabilities with Equity Instruments* as identified in AASB 1048.

Severe hyperinflation

D26   If an entity has a functional currency that was, or is, the currency of a hyperinflationary economy, it shall determine whether it was subject to severe hyperinflation before the date of transition to Australian Accounting Standards. This applies to entities that are adopting Australian Accounting Standards for the first time, as well as entities that have previously applied Australian Accounting Standards.

D27   The currency of a hyperinflationary economy is subject to severe hyperinflation if it has both of the following characteristics:

(a)   a reliable general price index is not available to all entities with transactions and balances in the currency.

(b)   exchangeability between the currency and a relatively stable foreign currency does not exist.

D28 The functional currency of an entity ceases to be subject to severe hyperinflation on the functional currency normalisation date. That is the date when the functional currency no longer has either, or both, of the characteristics in paragraph D27, or when there is a change in the entity's functional currency to a currency that is not subject to severe hyperinflation.

D29 When an entity's date of transition to Australian Accounting Standards is on, or after, the functional currency normalisation date, the entity may elect to measure all assets and liabilities held before the functional currency normalisation date at fair value on the date of transition to Australian Accounting Standards. The entity may use that fair value as the deemed cost of those assets and liabilities in the opening Australian-Accounting-Standards statement of financial position.

D30 When the functional currency normalisation date falls within a 12-month comparative period, the comparative period may be less than 12 months, provided that a complete set of financial statements (as required by paragraph 10 of AASB 101) is provided for that shorter period.

Joint arrangements

D31 A first-time adopter may apply the transition provisions in AASB 11 with the following exceptions:

(a) When applying the transition provisions in AASB 11, a first-time adopter shall apply these provisions at the date of transition to Australian Accounting Standards.

(b) When changing from proportionate consolidation to the equity method, a first-time adopter shall test for impairment the investment in accordance with AASB 136 as at the date of transition to Australian Accounting Standards, regardless of whether there is any indication that the investment may be impaired. Any resulting impairment shall be recognised as an adjustment to retained earnings at the date of transition to Australian Accounting Standards.

Stripping costs in the production phase of a surface mine

D32 A first-time adopter may apply the transitional provisions set out in paragraphs A1 to A4 of Interpretation 20 *Stripping Costs in the Production Phase of a Surface Mine* as identified in AASB 1048. In that paragraph, reference to the effective date shall be interpreted as 1 January 2016 or the beginning of the first Australian-Accounting-Standards reporting period, whichever is later.

Designation of contracts to buy or sell a non-financial item

D33 AASB 9 permits some contracts to buy or sell a non-financial item to be designated at inception as measured at fair value through profit or loss (see paragraph 2.5 of AASB 9). Despite this requirement an entity is permitted to designate, at the date of transition to Australian Accounting Standards, contracts that already exist on that date as measured at fair value through profit or loss but only if they meet the requirements of paragraph 2.5 of AASB 9 at that date and the entity designates all similar contracts.

Revenue

D34 A first-time adopter may apply the transition provisions in paragraph C5 of AASB 15. In those paragraphs references to the 'date of initial application' shall be interpreted as the beginning of the first Australian-Accounting-Standards reporting period. If a first-time adopter decides to apply those transition provisions, it shall also apply paragraph C6 of AASB 15.

D35 A first-time adopter is not required to restate contracts that were completed before the earliest period presented. A completed contract is a contract for which the entity has transferred all of the goods or services identified in accordance with previous GAAP.

Foreign currency transactions and advance consideration

D36 A first-time adopter need not apply AASB Interpretation 22 *Foreign Currency Transactions and Advance Consideration*, as identified in AASB 1048 *Interpretation of Standards*, to assets, expenses and income in the scope of that Interpretation initially recognised before the date of transition to Australian Accounting Standards.

APPENDIX E
SHORT-TERM EXEMPTIONS FROM AUSTRALIAN ACCOUNTING STANDARDS

This appendix is an integral part of the Standard.

Exemption from the requirement to restate comparative information for AASB 9

E1 If an entity's first Australian-Accounting-Standards reporting period begins before 1 January 2019 and the entity applies the completed version of AASB 9 (issued in 2014), the comparative information in the entity's first Australian-Accounting-Standards financial statements need not comply with AASB 7 *Financial Instruments: Disclosure* or the completed version of AASB 9 (issued in 2014), to the extent that the disclosures required by AASB 7 relate to items within the scope of AASB 9. For such entities, references to the 'date of transition to Australian Accounting Standards' shall mean, in the case of AASB 7 and AASB 9 (2014) only, the beginning of the first Australian-Accounting-Standards reporting period.

E2 An entity that chooses to present comparative information that does not comply with AASB 7 and the completed version of AASB 9 (issued in 2014) in its first year of transition shall:

(a) apply the requirements of its previous GAAP in place of the requirements of AASB 9 to comparative information about items within the scope of AASB 9.

(b) disclose this fact together with the basis used to prepare this information.

(c) treat any adjustment between the statement of financial position at the comparative period's reporting date (ie the statement of financial position that includes comparative information under previous GAAP) and the statement of financial position at the start of the *first Australian-Accounting-Standards reporting period* (ie the first period that includes information that complies with AASB 7 and the completed version of AASB 9 (issued in 2014)) as arising from a change in accounting policy and give the disclosures required by paragraph 28(a)–(e) and (f)(i) of AASB 108. Paragraph 28(f)(i) applies only to amounts presented in the statement of financial position at the comparative period's reporting date.

(d) apply paragraph 17(c) of AASB 101 to provide additional disclosures when compliance with the specific requirements in Australian Accounting Standards is insufficient to enable users to understand the impact of particular transactions, other events and conditions on the entity's financial position and financial performance.

E3–E7 [Deleted]

APPENDIX F
AUSTRALIAN REDUCED DISCLOSURE REQUIREMENTS

This appendix is an integral part of the Standard.

AusF1 **The following do not apply to entities preparing general purpose financial statements under Australian Accounting Standards – Reduced Disclosure Requirements:**

(a) **paragraphs 21, 22, 23, 24(b), 24(c), 25-31B, 32 and 33;**

(b) **in paragraph 6, the text "and present"; and**

(c) **in paragraph 24, the text "To comply with paragraph 23,".**

Entities applying Australian Accounting Standards – Reduced Disclosure Requirements may elect to comply with some or all of these excluded requirements.

AusF2 The requirements that do not apply to entities preparing general purpose financial statements under Australian Accounting Standards – Reduced Disclosure Requirements are also identified in this Standard by shading of the relevant text.

AusF3 **The RDR paragraph in this Standard applies only to entities preparing general purpose financial statements under Australian Accounting Standards – Reduced Disclosure Requirements.**

RDR21.1 In respect of entities applying Australian Accounting Standards – Reduced Disclosure Requirements, to comply with AASB 101, an entity's first Australian-Accounting-Standards-Reduced-Disclosure-Requirements financial statements shall include at least two statements of financial position, two statements of profit or loss and other comprehensive income, two separate statements of profit or loss (if presented), two statements of cash flows and two statements of changes in equity and related notes, including comparative information.

COMPILATION DETAILS

Accounting Standard AASB 1 *First-time Adoption of Australian Accounting Standards*

Compilation details are not part of AASB 1.

This compiled Standard applies to annual periods beginning on or after 1 January 2018 but before 1 January 2019 for for-profit entities. It takes into account amendments up to and including 12 December 2017 and was prepared on 20 March 2018 by the staff of the Australian Accounting Standards Board (AASB).

This compilation is not a separate Accounting Standard made by the AASB. Instead, it is a representation of AASB 1 (July 2015) as amended by other Accounting Standards, which are listed in the Table below.

Table of Standards

Standard	Date made	FRL identifier	Commencement date	Effective date (annual periods ... on or after ...)	Application, saving or transitional provisions
AASB 1	24 Jul 2015	F2015L01628	31 Dec 2017	(beginning) 1 Jan 2018	see (a) below
AASB 16	23 Feb 2016	F2016L00233	31 Dec 2018	(beginning) 1 Jan 2019	not compiled*
AASB 1058	9 Dec 2016	F2017L00042	31 Dec 2018	(beginning) 1 Jan 2019	not compiled*
AASB 2016-7	9 Dec 2016	F2017L00043	31 Dec 2016	(beginning) 1 Jan 2017	see (b) below
AASB 2017-1	13 Feb 2017	F2017L00193	31 Dec 2017	FP (beginning) 1 Jan 2018 NFP (beginning) 1 Jan 2019	see (c) below
AASB 17	19 Jul 2017	F2017L01184	31 Dec 2020	(beginning) 1 Jan 2021	not compiled*
AASB 2017-4	31 Jul 2017	F2017L01187	31 Dec 2018	(beginning) 1 Jan 2019	not compiled*
AASB 2017-5	12 Dec 2017	F2018L00067	31 Dec 2017	(beginning) 1 Jan 2018	see (d) below

* The amendments made by this Standard are not included in this compilation, which presents the principal Standard as applicable to annual periods beginning on or after 1 January 2018 but before 1 January 2019 for for-profit entities.

(a) Entities may elect to apply this Standard to annual periods beginning after 24 July 2014 but before 1 January 2018.

(b) As a result of AASB 2016-7 deferring the effective date of AASB 15 Revenue from Contracts with Customers (and its consequential amendments in AASB 2014-5) for not-for-profit entities from 1 January 2018 to 1 January 2019, AASB 1 (2015) applies to not-for-profit entities only to annual reporting periods beginning on or after 1 January 2019, instead of 1 January 2018. However, earlier application is permitted, provided that AASB 15 is also applied.

(c) For-profit (FP) entities and not-for-profit (NFP) entities may elect to apply the amendments made to AASB 1 by this Standard early, in advance of their particular mandatory effective dates.

(d) Entities may elect to apply this Standard to annual periods beginning before 1 January 2018.

Table of amendments

Paragraph affected	How affected	By ... [paragraph/page]
39AA	deleted	AASB 2017-1 [page 6]
39AC	added	AASB 2017-1 [page 5]
39AD	added	AASB 2017-1 [page 6]
B8	amended	AASB 2017-5 [12]
B8D	amended	AASB 2017-5 [13]
B12	amended	AASB 2017-5 [14]

Paragraph affected	How affected	By ... [paragraph/page]
D1	amended amended	AASB 2017-1 [page 6] AASB 2017-5 [15]
D36 (and heading)	added	AASB 2017-1 [page 6]
E3-E7 (and headings)	deleted	AASB 2017-1 [page 6]

DELETED IFRS 1 TEXT

Deleted IFRS 1 text is not part of AASB 1.

35 An entity shall apply the amendments in paragraphs D1(n) and D23 for annual periods beginning on or after 1 July 2009. If an entity applies IAS 23 *Borrowing Costs* (as revised in 2007) for an earlier period, those amendments shall be applied for that earlier period.

36 IFRS 3 *Business Combinations* (as revised in 2008) amended paragraphs 19, C1 and C4(f) and (g). If an entity applies IFRS 3 (revised 2008) for an earlier period, the amendments shall also be applied for that earlier period.

37 IAS 27 *Consolidated and Separate Financial Statements* (as amended in 2008) amended paragraphs B1 and B7. If an entity applies IAS 27 (amended 2008) for an earlier period, the amendments shall be applied for that earlier period.

38 *Cost of an Investment in a Subsidiary, Jointly Controlled Entity or Associate* (Amendments to IFRS 1 and IAS 27), issued in May 2008, added paragraphs 31, D1(g), D14 and D15. An entity shall apply those paragraphs for annual periods beginning on or after 1 July 2009. Earlier application is permitted. If an entity applies the paragraphs for an earlier period, it shall disclose that fact.

39 Paragraph B7 was amended by *Improvements to IFRSs* issued in May 2008. An entity shall apply those amendments for annual periods beginning on or after 1 July 2009. If an entity applies IAS 27 (amended 2008) for an earlier period, the amendments shall be applied for that earlier period.

39A *Additional Exemptions for First-time Adopters* (Amendments to IFRS 1), issued in July 2009, added paragraphs 31A, D8A, D9A and D21A and amended paragraph D1(c), (d) and (l). An entity shall apply those amendments for annual periods beginning on or after 1 January 2010. Earlier application is permitted. If an entity applies the amendments for an earlier period it shall disclose that fact.

39C IFRIC 19 *Extinguishing Financial Liabilities with Equity Instruments* added paragraph D25. An entity shall apply that amendment when it applies IFRIC 19.

39D *Limited Exemption from Comparative IFRS 7 Disclosures for First-time Adopters* (Amendment to IFRS 1), issued in January 2010, added paragraph E3. An entity shall apply that amendment for annual periods beginning on or after 1 July 2010. Earlier application is permitted. If an entity applies the amendment for an earlier period, it shall disclose that fact.

39E *Improvements to IFRSs* issued in May 2010 added paragraphs 27A, 31B and D8B and amended paragraphs 27, 32, D1(c) and D8. An entity shall apply those amendments for annual periods beginning on or after 1 January 2011. Earlier application is permitted. If an entity applies the amendments for an earlier period it shall disclose that fact. Entities that adopted IFRSs in periods before the effective date of IFRS 1 or applied IFRS 1 in a previous period are permitted to apply the amendment to paragraph D8 retrospectively in the first annual period after the amendment is effective. An entity applying paragraph D8 retrospectively shall disclose that fact.

39F *Disclosures—Transfers of Financial Assets* (Amendments to IFRS 7), issued in October 2010, added paragraph E4. An entity shall apply that amendment for annual periods beginning on or after 1 July 2011. Earlier application is permitted. If an entity applies the amendment for an earlier period, it shall disclose that fact.

39H *Severe Hyperinflation and Removal of Fixed Dates for First-time Adopters* (Amendments to IFRS 1), issued in December 2010, amended paragraphs B2, D1 and D20 and added paragraphs 31C and D26–D30. An entity shall apply those amendments for annual periods beginning on or after 1 July 2011. Earlier application is permitted.

39I IFRS 10 *Consolidated Financial Statements* and IFRS 11 *Joint Arrangements*, issued in May 2011, amended paragraphs 31, B7, C1, D1, D14 and D15 and added paragraph D31. An entity shall apply those amendments when it applies IFRS 10 and IFRS 11.

39J IFRS 13 *Fair Value Measurement,* issued in May 2011, deleted paragraph 19, amended the definition of fair value in Appendix A and amended paragraphs D15 and D20. An entity shall apply those amendments when it applies IFRS 13.

39K *Presentation of Items of Other Comprehensive Income* (Amendments to IAS 1), issued in June 2011, amended paragraph 21. An entity shall apply that amendment when it applies IAS 1 as amended in June 2011.

39L IAS 19 *Employee Benefits* (as amended in June 2011) amended paragraph D1, deleted paragraphs D10 and D11 and added paragraph E5. An entity shall apply those amendments when it applies IAS 19 (as amended in June 2011).

39M IFRIC 20 *Stripping Costs in the Production Phase of a Surface Mine* added paragraph D32 and amended paragraph D1. An entity shall apply that amendment when it applies IFRIC 20.

39N *Government Loans* (Amendments to IFRS 1), issued in March 2012, added paragraphs B1(f) and B10–B12. An entity shall apply those paragraphs for annual periods beginning on or after 1 January 2013. Earlier application is permitted.

39P *Annual Improvements 2009–2011 Cycle,* issued in May 2012, added paragraphs 4A–4B and 23A–23B. An entity shall apply that amendment retrospectively in accordance with IAS 8 *Accounting Policies, Changes in Accounting Estimates and Errors* for annual periods beginning on or after 1 January 2013. Earlier application is permitted. If an entity applies that amendment for an earlier period it shall disclose that fact.

39Q *Annual Improvements 2009–2011 Cycle,* issued in May 2012, amended paragraph D23. An entity shall apply that amendment retrospectively in accordance with IAS 8 *Accounting Policies, Changes in Accounting Estimates and Errors* for annual periods beginning on or after 1 January 2013. Earlier application is permitted. If an entity applies that amendment for an earlier period it shall disclose that fact.

39R *Annual Improvements 2009–2011 Cycle,* issued in May 2012, amended paragraph 21. An entity shall apply that amendment retrospectively in accordance with IAS 8 *Accounting Policies, Changes in Accounting Estimates and Errors* for annual periods beginning on or after 1 January 2013. Earlier application is permitted. If an entity applies that amendment for an earlier period it shall disclose that fact.

39S *Consolidated Financial Statements, Joint Arrangements and Disclosure of Interests in Other Entities: Transition Guidance* (Amendments to IFRS 10, IFRS 11 and IFRS 12), issued in June 2012, amended paragraph D31. An entity shall apply that amendment when it applies IFRS 11 (as amended in June 2012).

39T *Investment Entities* (Amendments to IFRS 10, IFRS 12 and IAS 27), issued in October 2012, amended paragraphs D16, D17 and Appendix C and added a heading and paragraphs E6–E7. An entity shall apply those amendments for annual periods beginning on or after 1 January 2014. Earlier application of *Investment Entities* is permitted. If an entity applies those amendments earlier it shall also apply all amendments included in *Investment Entities* at the same time.

40   This IFRS supersedes IFRS 1 (issued in 2003 and amended at May 2008).

AASB 2
Share-based Payment

(Compiled December 2017)

This compiled Standard applies to annual periods beginning on or after 1 January 2018. Earlier application is permitted for annual periods beginning after 24 July 2014 but before 1 January 2018. It incorporates relevant amendments made up to and including 12 December 2017.

Prepared on 20 April 2018 by the staff of the Australian Accounting Standards Board.

Compilation no. 1

Compilation date: 31 December 2017

CONTENTS

COMPARISON WITH IFRS 2
ACCOUNTING STANDARD
AASB 2 *SHARE-BASED PAYMENT*

APPENDICES

A. DEFINED TERMS

B. APPLICATION GUIDANCE

C. AUSTRALIAN REDUCED DISCLOSURE REQUIREMENTS

IMPLEMENTATION GUIDANCE

COMPILATION DETAILS

DELETED IFRS 2 TEXT

BASIS FOR CONCLUSIONS ON IFRS 2 (available on the AASB website)

Australian Accounting Standard AASB 2 *Share-based Payment* (as amended) is set out in paragraphs 1 – Aus64.2 and Appendices A – C. All the paragraphs have equal authority. Paragraphs in **bold type** state the main principles. Terms defined in Appendix A are in *italics* the first time they appear in the Standard. AASB 2 is to be read in the context of other Australian Accounting Standards, including AASB 1048 *Interpretation of Standards*, which identifies the Australian Accounting Interpretations, and AASB 1057 *Application of Australian Accounting Standards*. In the absence of explicit guidance, AASB 108 *Accounting Policies, Changes in Accounting Estimates and Errors* provides a basis for selecting and applying accounting policies.

COMPARISON WITH IFRS 2

AASB 2 *Share-based Payment* as amended incorporates IFRS 2 *Share-based Payment* as issued and as amended by the International Accounting Standards Board (IASB). Australian-specific paragraphs (which are not included in IFRS 2) are identified with the prefix "Aus" or "RDR". Paragraphs that apply only to not-for-profit entities begin by identifying their limited applicability.

Tier 1

For-profit entities complying with AASB 2 also comply with IFRS 2.

Not-for-profit entities' compliance with IFRS 2 will depend on whether any "Aus" paragraphs that specifically apply to not-for-profit entities provide additional guidance or contain applicable requirements that are inconsistent with IFRS 2.

Tier 2

Entities preparing general purpose financial statements under Australian Accounting Standards – Reduced Disclosure Requirements (Tier 2) will not be in compliance with IFRSs.

AASB 1053 *Application of Tiers of Australian Accounting Standards* explains the two tiers of reporting requirements.

ACCOUNTING STANDARD AASB 2

The Australian Accounting Standards Board made Accounting Standard AASB 2 *Share-based Payment* under section 334 of the *Corporations Act 2001* on 24 July 2015.

This compiled version of AASB 2 applies to annual periods beginning on or after 1 January 2018. It incorporates relevant amendments contained in other AASB Standards made by the AASB up to and including 12 December 2017 (see Compilation Details).

ACCOUNTING STANDARD AASB 2
SHARE-BASED PAYMENT

Objective

1 The objective of this Standard is to specify the financial reporting by an entity when it undertakes a *share-based payment transaction*. In particular, it requires an entity to reflect in its profit or loss and financial position the effects of share-based payment transactions, including expenses associated with transactions in which *share options* are granted to employees.

Scope

2 An entity shall apply this Standard in accounting for all share-based payment transactions, whether or not the entity can identify specifically some or all of the goods or services received, including:

(a) *equity-settled share-based payment transactions*,

(b) *cash-settled share-based payment transactions*, and

(c) transactions in which the entity receives or acquires goods or services and the terms of the arrangement provide either the entity or the supplier of those goods or services with a choice of whether the entity settles the transaction in cash (or other assets) or by issuing equity instruments,

except as noted in paragraphs 3A–6. In the absence of specifically identifiable goods or services, other circumstances may indicate that goods or services have been (or will be) received, in which case this Standard applies.

3 [Deleted]

3A A share-based payment transaction may be settled by another group entity (or a shareholder of any group entity) on behalf of the entity receiving or acquiring the goods or services. Paragraph 2 also applies to an entity that

(a) receives goods or services when another entity in the same group (or a shareholder of any group entity) has the obligation to settle the share-based payment transaction, or

(b) has an obligation to settle a share-based payment transaction when another entity in the same group receives the goods or services

unless the transaction is clearly for a purpose other than payment for goods or services supplied to the entity receiving them.

4 For the purposes of this Standard, a transaction with an employee (or other party) in his/her capacity as a holder of equity instruments of the entity is not a share-based payment transaction. For example, if an entity grants all holders of a particular class of its equity instruments the right to acquire additional equity instruments of the entity at a price that is less than the fair value of those equity instruments, and an employee receives such a right because he/she is a holder of equity instruments of that particular class, the granting or exercise of that right is not subject to the requirements of this Standard.

5 As noted in paragraph 2, this Standard applies to share-based payment transactions in which an entity acquires or receives goods or services. Goods includes inventories, consumables, property, plant and equipment, intangible assets and other non-financial assets. However, an entity shall not apply this Standard to transactions in which the

entity acquires goods as part of the net assets acquired in a business combination as defined by AASB 3 *Business Combinations*, in a combination of entities or businesses under common control as described in paragraphs B1–B4 of AASB 3, or the contribution of a business on the formation of a joint venture as defined by AASB 11 *Joint Arrangements*. Hence, equity instruments issued in a business combination in exchange for control of the acquiree are not within the scope of this Standard. However, equity instruments granted to employees of the acquiree in their capacity as employees (eg in return for continued service) are within the scope of this Standard. Similarly, the cancellation, replacement or other modification of *share-based payment arrangements* because of a business combination or other equity restructuring shall be accounted for in accordance with this Standard. AASB 3 provides guidance on determining whether equity instruments issued in a business combination are part of the consideration transferred in exchange for control of the acquiree (and therefore within the scope of AASB 3) or are in return for continued service to be recognised in the post-combination period (and therefore within the scope of this Standard).

6   This Standard does not apply to share-based payment transactions in which the entity receives or acquires goods or services under a contract within the scope of paragraphs 8–10 of AASB 132 *Financial Instruments: Presentation*[1] or paragraphs 2.4–2.7 of AASB 9 *Financial Instruments*.

6A   This Standard uses the term 'fair value' in a way that differs in some respects from the definition of fair value in AASB 13 *Fair Value Measurement*. Therefore, when applying AASB 2 an entity measures fair value in accordance with this Standard, not AASB 13.

Recognition

7   **An entity shall recognise the goods or services received or acquired in a share-based payment transaction when it obtains the goods or as the services are received. The entity shall recognise a corresponding increase in equity if the goods or services were received in an equity-settled share-based payment transaction, or a liability if the goods or services were acquired in a cash-settled share-based payment transaction.**

8   **When the goods or services received or acquired in a share-based payment transaction do not qualify for recognition as assets, they shall be recognised as expenses.**

9   Typically, an expense arises from the consumption of goods or services. For example, services are typically consumed immediately, in which case an expense is recognised as the counterparty renders service. Goods might be consumed over a period of time or, in the case of inventories, sold at a later date, in which case an expense is recognised when the goods are consumed or sold. However, sometimes it is necessary to recognise an expense before the goods or services are consumed or sold, because they do not qualify for recognition as assets. For example, an entity might acquire goods as part of the research phase of a project to develop a new product. Although those goods have not been consumed, they might not qualify for recognition as assets under the applicable Standard.

Equity-settled share-based payment transactions

Overview

10   **For equity-settled share-based payment transactions, the entity shall measure the goods or services received, and the corresponding increase in equity, directly, at the fair value of the goods or services received, unless that fair value cannot be estimated reliably. If the entity cannot estimate reliably the fair value of the goods or services received, the entity shall measure their value, and the**

---

1   The title of AASB 132 was amended in 2005.

corresponding increase in equity, indirectly, by reference to[2] the fair value of the equity instruments granted.

11 To apply the requirements of paragraph 10 to transactions with *employees and others providing similar services*,[3] the entity shall measure the fair value of the services received by reference to the fair value of the equity instruments granted, because typically it is not possible to estimate reliably the fair value of the services received, as explained in paragraph 12. The fair value of those equity instruments shall be measured at *grant date*.

12 Typically, shares, share options or other equity instruments are granted to employees as part of their remuneration package, in addition to a cash salary and other employment benefits. Usually, it is not possible to measure directly the services received for particular components of the employee's remuneration package. It might also not be possible to measure the fair value of the total remuneration package independently, without measuring directly the fair value of the equity instruments granted. Furthermore, shares or share options are sometimes granted as part of a bonus arrangement, rather than as a part of basic remuneration, eg as an incentive to the employees to remain in the entity's employ or to reward them for their efforts in improving the entity's performance. By granting shares or share options, in addition to other remuneration, the entity is paying additional remuneration to obtain additional benefits. Estimating the fair value of those additional benefits is likely to be difficult. Because of the difficulty of measuring directly the fair value of the services received, the entity shall measure the fair value of the employee services received by reference to the fair value of the equity instruments granted.

13 To apply the requirements of paragraph 10 to transactions with parties other than employees, there shall be a rebuttable presumption that the fair value of the goods or services received can be estimated reliably. That fair value shall be measured at the date the entity obtains the goods or the counterparty renders service. In rare cases, if the entity rebuts this presumption because it cannot estimate reliably the fair value of the goods or services received, the entity shall measure the goods or services received, and the corresponding increase in equity, indirectly, by reference to the fair value of the equity instruments granted, measured at the date the entity obtains the goods or the counterparty renders service.

13A In particular, if the identifiable consideration received (if any) by the entity appears to be less than the fair value of the equity instruments granted or liability incurred, typically this situation indicates that other consideration (ie unidentifiable goods or services) has been (or will be) received by the entity. The entity shall measure the identifiable goods or services received in accordance with this Standard. The entity shall measure the unidentifiable goods or services received (or to be received) as the difference between the fair value of the share-based payment and the fair value of any identifiable goods or services received (or to be received). The entity shall measure the unidentifiable goods or services received at the grant date. However, for cash-settled transactions, the liability shall be remeasured at the end of each reporting period until it is settled in accordance with paragraphs 30–33.

Transactions in which services are received

14 If the equity instruments granted *vest* immediately, the counterparty is not required to complete a specified period of service before becoming unconditionally entitled to those equity instruments. In the absence of evidence to the contrary, the entity shall presume that services rendered by the counterparty as consideration for the equity

---

2 This Standard uses the phrase 'by reference to' rather than 'at', because the transaction is ultimately measured by multiplying the fair value of the equity instruments granted, measured at the date specified in paragraph 11 or 13 (whichever is applicable), by the number of equity instruments that vest, as explained in paragraph 19.

3 In the remainder of this Standard, all references to employees also include others providing similar services.

instruments have been received. In this case, on grant date the entity shall recognise the services received in full, with a corresponding increase in equity.

15   If the equity instruments granted do not vest until the counterparty completes a specified period of service, the entity shall presume that the services to be rendered by the counterparty as consideration for those equity instruments will be received in the future, during the *vesting period*. The entity shall account for those services as they are rendered by the counterparty during the vesting period, with a corresponding increase in equity. For example:

(a)   if an employee is granted share options conditional upon completing three years' service, then the entity shall presume that the services to be rendered by the employee as consideration for the share options will be received in the future, over that three-year vesting period.

(b)   if an employee is granted share options conditional upon the achievement of a *performance condition* and remaining in the entity's employ until that performance condition is satisfied, and the length of the vesting period varies depending on when that performance condition is satisfied, the entity shall presume that the services to be rendered by the employee as consideration for the share options will be received in the future, over the expected vesting period. The entity shall estimate the length of the expected vesting period at grant date, based on the most likely outcome of the performance condition. If the performance condition is a *market condition*, the estimate of the length of the expected vesting period shall be consistent with the assumptions used in estimating the fair value of the options granted, and shall not be subsequently revised. If the performance condition is not a market condition, the entity shall revise its estimate of the length of the vesting period, if necessary, if subsequent information indicates that the length of the vesting period differs from previous estimates.

Transactions measured by reference to the fair value of the equity instruments granted

Determining the fair value of equity instruments granted

16   For transactions measured by reference to the fair value of the equity instruments granted, an entity shall measure the fair value of equity instruments granted at the *measurement date*, based on market prices if available, taking into account the terms and conditions upon which those equity instruments were granted (subject to the requirements of paragraphs 19–22).

17   If market prices are not available, the entity shall estimate the fair value of the equity instruments granted using a valuation technique to estimate what the price of those equity instruments would have been on the measurement date in an arm's length transaction between knowledgeable, willing parties. The valuation technique shall be consistent with generally accepted valuation methodologies for pricing financial instruments, and shall incorporate all factors and assumptions that knowledgeable, willing market participants would consider in setting the price (subject to the requirements of paragraphs 19–22).

18   Appendix B contains further guidance on the measurement of the fair value of shares and share options, focusing on the specific terms and conditions that are common features of a grant of shares or share options to employees.

Treatment of vesting conditions

19   A grant of equity instruments might be conditional upon satisfying specified vesting conditions. For example, a grant of shares or share options to an employee is typically conditional on the employee remaining in the entity's employ for a specified period of time. There might be performance conditions that must be satisfied, such as the entity achieving a specified growth in profit or a specified increase in the entity's share price. Vesting conditions, other than market conditions, shall not be taken into account

when estimating the fair value of the shares or share options at the measurement date. Instead, vesting conditions, other than market conditions, shall be taken into account by adjusting the number of equity instruments included in the measurement of the transaction amount so that, ultimately, the amount recognised for goods or services received as consideration for the equity instruments granted shall be based on the number of equity instruments that eventually vest. Hence, on a cumulative basis, no amount is recognised for goods or services received if the equity instruments granted do not vest because of failure to satisfy a *vesting condition*, other than a market condition, for example, the counterparty fails to complete a specified service period, or a performance condition is not satisfied, subject to the requirements of paragraph 21.

20   To apply the requirements of paragraph 19, the entity shall recognise an amount for the goods or services received during the vesting period based on the best available estimate of the number of equity instruments expected to vest and shall revise that estimate, if necessary, if subsequent information indicates that the number of equity instruments expected to vest differs from previous estimates. On vesting date, the entity shall revise the estimate to equal the number of equity instruments that ultimately vested, subject to the requirements of paragraph 21.

21   Market conditions, such as a target share price upon which vesting (or exercisability) is conditioned, shall be taken into account when estimating the fair value of the equity instruments granted. Therefore, for grants of equity instruments with market conditions, the entity shall recognise the goods or services received from a counterparty who satisfies all other vesting conditions (eg services received from an employee who remains in service for the specified period of service), irrespective of whether that market condition is satisfied.

Treatment of non-vesting conditions

21A   Similarly, an entity shall take into account all non-vesting conditions when estimating the fair value of the equity instruments granted. Therefore, for grants of equity instruments with non-vesting conditions, the entity shall recognise the goods or services received from a counterparty that satisfies all vesting conditions that are not market conditions (eg services received from an employee who remains in service for the specified period of service), irrespective of whether those non-vesting conditions are satisfied.

Treatment of a reload feature

22   For options with a *reload feature*, the reload feature shall not be taken into account when estimating the fair value of options granted at the measurement date. Instead, a *reload option* shall be accounted for as a new option grant, if and when a reload option is subsequently granted.

After vesting date

23   Having recognised the goods or services received in accordance with paragraphs 10–22, and a corresponding increase in equity, the entity shall make no subsequent adjustment to total equity after vesting date. For example, the entity shall not subsequently reverse the amount recognised for services received from an employee if the vested equity instruments are later forfeited or, in the case of share options, the options are not exercised. However, this requirement does not preclude the entity from recognising a transfer within equity, ie a transfer from one component of equity to another.

If the fair value of the equity instruments cannot be estimated reliably

24   The requirements in paragraphs 16–23 apply when the entity is required to measure a share-based payment transaction by reference to the fair value of the equity instruments granted. In rare cases, the entity may be unable to estimate reliably the fair value

of the equity instruments granted at the measurement date, in accordance with the requirements in paragraphs 16–22. In these rare cases only, the entity shall instead:

(a)   measure the equity instruments at their *intrinsic value*, initially at the date the entity obtains the goods or the counterparty renders service and subsequently at the end of each reporting period and at the date of final settlement, with any change in intrinsic value recognised in profit or loss. For a grant of share options, the share-based payment arrangement is finally settled when the options are exercised, are forfeited (eg upon cessation of employment) or lapse (eg at the end of the option's life).

(b)   recognise the goods or services received based on the number of equity instruments that ultimately vest or (where applicable) are ultimately exercised. To apply this requirement to share options, for example, the entity shall recognise the goods or services received during the vesting period, if any, in accordance with paragraphs 14 and 15, except that the requirements in paragraph 15(b) concerning a market condition do not apply. The amount recognised for goods or services received during the vesting period shall be based on the number of share options expected to vest. The entity shall revise that estimate, if necessary, if subsequent information indicates that the number of share options expected to vest differs from previous estimates. On vesting date, the entity shall revise the estimate to equal the number of equity instruments that ultimately vested. After vesting date, the entity shall reverse the amount recognised for goods or services received if the share options are later forfeited, or lapse at the end of the share option's life.

25   If an entity applies paragraph 24, it is not necessary to apply paragraphs 26–29, because any modifications to the terms and conditions on which the equity instruments were granted will be taken into account when applying the intrinsic value method set out in paragraph 24. However, if an entity settles a grant of equity instruments to which paragraph 24 has been applied:

(a)   if the settlement occurs during the vesting period, the entity shall account for the settlement as an acceleration of vesting, and shall therefore recognise immediately the amount that would otherwise have been recognised for services received over the remainder of the vesting period.

(b)   any payment made on settlement shall be accounted for as the repurchase of equity instruments, ie as a deduction from equity, except to the extent that the payment exceeds the intrinsic value of the equity instruments, measured at the repurchase date. Any such excess shall be recognised as an expense.

Modifications to the terms and conditions on which equity instruments were granted, including cancellations and settlements

26   An entity might modify the terms and conditions on which the equity instruments were granted. For example, it might reduce the exercise price of options granted to employees (ie reprice the options), which increases the fair value of those options. The requirements in paragraphs 27–29 to account for the effects of modifications are expressed in the context of share-based payment transactions with employees. However, the requirements shall also be applied to share-based payment transactions with parties other than employees that are measured by reference to the fair value of the equity instruments granted. In the latter case, any references in paragraphs 27–29 to grant date shall instead refer to the date the entity obtains the goods or the counterparty renders service.

27   The entity shall recognise, as a minimum, the services received measured at the grant date fair value of the equity instruments granted, unless those equity instruments do not vest because of failure to satisfy a vesting condition (other than a market condition) that was specified at grant date. This applies irrespective of any modifications to the terms and conditions on which the equity instruments were granted, or a cancellation or settlement of that grant of equity instruments. In addition, the entity shall recognise

the effects of modifications that increase the total fair value of the share-based payment arrangement or are otherwise beneficial to the employee. Guidance on applying this requirement is given in Appendix B.

28 If a grant of equity instruments is cancelled or settled during the vesting period (other than a grant cancelled by forfeiture when the vesting conditions are not satisfied):

    (a) the entity shall account for the cancellation or settlement as an acceleration of vesting, and shall therefore recognise immediately the amount that otherwise would have been recognised for services received over the remainder of the vesting period.

    (b) any payment made to the employee on the cancellation or settlement of the grant shall be accounted for as the repurchase of an equity interest, ie as a deduction from equity, except to the extent that the payment exceeds the fair value of the equity instruments granted, measured at the repurchase date. Any such excess shall be recognised as an expense. However, if the share-based payment arrangement included liability components, the entity shall remeasure the fair value of the liability at the date of cancellation or settlement. Any payment made to settle the liability component shall be accounted for as an extinguishment of the liability.

    (c) if new equity instruments are granted to the employee and, on the date when those new equity instruments are granted, the entity identifies the new equity instruments granted as replacement equity instruments for the cancelled equity instruments, the entity shall account for the granting of replacement equity instruments in the same way as a modification of the original grant of equity instruments, in accordance with paragraph 27 and the guidance in Appendix B. The incremental fair value granted is the difference between the fair value of the replacement equity instruments and the net fair value of the cancelled equity instruments, at the date the replacement equity instruments are granted. The net fair value of the cancelled equity instruments is their fair value, immediately before the cancellation, less the amount of any payment made to the employee on cancellation of the equity instruments that is accounted for as a deduction from equity in accordance with (b) above. If the entity does not identify new equity instruments granted as replacement equity instruments for the cancelled equity instruments, the entity shall account for those new equity instruments as a new grant of equity instruments.

28A If an entity or counterparty can choose whether to meet a non-vesting condition, the entity shall treat the entity's or counterparty's failure to meet that non-vesting condition during the vesting period as a cancellation.

29 If an entity repurchases vested equity instruments, the payment made to the employee shall be accounted for as a deduction from equity, except to the extent that the payment exceeds the fair value of the equity instruments repurchased, measured at the repurchase date. Any such excess shall be recognised as an expense.

Cash-settled share-based payment transactions

30 **For cash-settled share-based payment transactions, the entity shall measure the goods or services acquired and the liability incurred at the fair value of the liability, subject to the requirements of paragraphs 31–33D. Until the liability is settled, the entity shall remeasure the fair value of the liability at the end of each reporting period and at the date of settlement, with any changes in fair value recognised in profit or loss for the period.**

31 For example, an entity might grant share appreciation rights to employees as part of their remuneration package, whereby the employees will become entitled to a future cash payment (rather than an equity instrument), based on the increase in the entity's share price from a specified level over a specified period of time. Alternatively, an entity might grant to its employees a right to receive a future cash payment by granting to them a right to shares (including shares to be issued upon the exercise of

share options) that are redeemable, either mandatorily (for example, upon cessation of employment) or at the employee's option. These arrangements are examples of cash-settled share-based payment transactions. Share appreciation rights are used to illustrate some of the requirements in paragraphs 32–33D, however, the requirements in those paragraphs apply to all cash-settled share-based payment transactions.

32   The entity shall recognise the services received, and a liability to pay for those services, as the employees render service. For example, some share appreciation rights vest immediately, and the employees are therefore not required to complete a specified period of service to become entitled to the cash payment. In the absence of evidence to the contrary, the entity shall presume that the services rendered by the employees in exchange for the share appreciation rights have been received. Thus, the entity shall recognise immediately the services received and a liability to pay for them. If the share appreciation rights do not vest until the employees have completed a specified period of service, the entity shall recognise the services received, and a liability to pay for them, as the employees render service during that period.

33   The liability shall be measured, initially and at the end of each reporting period until settled, at the fair value of the share appreciation rights, by applying an option pricing model, taking into account the terms and conditions on which the share appreciation rights were granted, and the extent to which the employees have rendered service to date—subject to the requirements of paragraphs 33A–33D. An entity might modify the terms and conditions on which a cash-settled share-based payment is granted. Guidance for a modification of a share-based payment transaction that changes its classification from cash-settled to equity-settled is given in paragraphs B44A–B44C in Appendix B.

Treatment of vesting and non-vesting conditions

33A   A cash-settled share-based payment transaction might be conditional upon satisfying specified vesting conditions. There might be performance conditions that must be satisfied, such as the entity achieving a specified growth in profit or a specified increase in the entity's share price. Vesting conditions, other than market conditions, shall not be taken into account when estimating the fair value of the cash-settled share-based payment at the measurement date. Instead, vesting conditions, other than market conditions, shall be taken into account by adjusting the number of awards included in the measurement of the liability arising from the transaction.

33B   To apply the requirements in paragraph 33A, the entity shall recognise an amount for the goods or services received during the vesting period. That amount shall be based on the best available estimate of the number of awards that are expected to vest. The entity shall revise that estimate, if necessary, if subsequent information indicates that the number of awards that are expected to vest differs from previous estimates. On the vesting date, the entity shall revise the estimate to equal the number of awards that ultimately vested.

33C   Market conditions, such as a target share price upon which vesting (or exercisability) is conditioned, as well as non-vesting conditions, shall be taken into account when estimating the fair value of the cash-settled share-based payment granted and when remeasuring the fair value at the end of each reporting period and at the date of settlement.

33D   As a result of applying paragraphs 30–33C, the cumulative amount ultimately recognised for goods or services received as consideration for the cash-settled share-based payment is equal to the cash that is paid.

Share-based payment transactions with a net settlement feature for withholding tax obligations

33E   Tax laws or regulations may oblige an entity to withhold an amount for an employee's tax obligation associated with a share-based payment and transfer that amount, normally in cash, to the tax authority on the employee's behalf. To fulfil this obligation, the terms of the share-based payment arrangement may permit or require the entity to withhold the number of equity instruments equal to the monetary value of the employee's tax obligation from the total number of equity instruments that otherwise would have been issued to the employee upon exercise (or vesting) of the share-based payment (ie the share-based payment arrangement has a 'net settlement feature').

33F　As an exception to the requirements in paragraph 34, the transaction described in paragraph 33E shall be classified in its entirety as an equity-settled share-based payment transaction if it would have been so classified in the absence of the net settlement feature.

33G　The entity applies paragraph 29 of this Standard to account for the withholding of shares to fund the payment to the tax authority in respect of the employee's tax obligation associated with the share-based payment. Therefore, the payment made shall be accounted for as a deduction from equity for the shares withheld, except to the extent that the payment exceeds the fair value at the net settlement date of the equity instruments withheld.

33H　The exception in paragraph 33F does not apply to:

(a)　a share-based payment arrangement with a net settlement feature for which there is no obligation on the entity under tax laws or regulations to withhold an amount for an employee's tax obligation associated with that share-based payment; or

(b)　any equity instruments that the entity withholds in excess of the employee's tax obligation associated with the share-based payment (ie the entity withheld an amount of shares that exceeds the monetary value of the employee's tax obligation). Such excess shares withheld shall be accounted for as a cash-settled share-based payment when this amount is paid in cash (or other assets) to the employee.

Share-based payment transactions with cash alternatives

34　For share-based payment transactions in which the terms of the arrangement provide either the entity or the counterparty with the choice of whether the entity settles the transaction in cash (or other assets) or by issuing equity instruments, the entity shall account for that transaction, or the components of that transaction, as a cash-settled share-based payment transaction if, and to the extent that, the entity has incurred a liability to settle in cash or other assets, or as an equity-settled share-based payment transaction if, and to the extent that, no such liability has been incurred.

Share-based payment transactions in which the terms of the arrangement provide the counterparty with a choice of settlement

35　If an entity has granted the counterparty the right to choose whether a share-based payment transaction is settled in cash[4] or by issuing equity instruments, the entity has granted a compound financial instrument, which includes a debt component (ie the counterparty's right to demand payment in cash) and an equity component (ie the counterparty's right to demand settlement in equity instruments rather than in cash). For transactions with parties other than employees, in which the fair value of the goods or services received is measured directly, the entity shall measure the equity component of the compound financial instrument as the difference between the fair value of the goods or services received and the fair value of the debt component, at the date when the goods or services are received.

36　For other transactions, including transactions with employees, the entity shall measure the fair value of the compound financial instrument at the measurement date, taking into account the terms and conditions on which the rights to cash or equity instruments were granted.

4　In paragraphs 35–43, all references to cash also include other assets of the entity.

37   To apply paragraph 36, the entity shall first measure the fair value of the debt
      component, and then measure the fair value of the equity component—taking into
      account that the counterparty must forfeit the right to receive cash in order to receive
      the equity instrument. The fair value of the compound financial instrument is the sum
      of the fair values of the two components. However, share-based payment transactions
      in which the counterparty has the choice of settlement are often structured so that
      the fair value of one settlement alternative is the same as the other. For example, the
      counterparty might have the choice of receiving share options or cash-settled share
      appreciation rights. In such cases, the fair value of the equity component is zero, and
      hence the fair value of the compound financial instrument is the same as the fair value of
      the debt component. Conversely, if the fair values of the settlement alternatives differ,
      the fair value of the equity component usually will be greater than zero, in which case
      the fair value of the compound financial instrument will be greater than the fair value
      of the debt component.

38   The entity shall account separately for the goods or services received or acquired
      in respect of each component of the compound financial instrument. For the debt
      component, the entity shall recognise the goods or services acquired, and a liability to
      pay for those goods or services, as the counterparty supplies goods or renders service,
      in accordance with the requirements applying to cash-settled share-based payment
      transactions (paragraphs 30–33). For the equity component (if any), the entity shall
      recognise the goods or services received, and an increase in equity, as the counterparty
      supplies goods or renders service, in accordance with the requirements applying to
      equity-settled share-based payment transactions (paragraphs 10–29).

39   At the date of settlement, the entity shall remeasure the liability to its fair value. If
      the entity issues equity instruments on settlement rather than paying cash, the liability
      shall be transferred direct to equity, as the consideration for the equity instruments
      issued.

40   If the entity pays in cash on settlement rather than issuing equity instruments, that
      payment shall be applied to settle the liability in full. Any equity component previously
      recognised shall remain within equity. By electing to receive cash on settlement,
      the counterparty forfeited the right to receive equity instruments. However, this
      requirement does not preclude the entity from recognising a transfer within equity,
      ie a transfer from one component of equity to another.

Share-based payment transactions in which the terms of the arrangement provide the entity with a choice of settlement

41   For a share-based payment transaction in which the terms of the arrangement provide
      an entity with the choice of whether to settle in cash or by issuing equity instruments,
      the entity shall determine whether it has a present obligation to settle in cash and
      account for the share-based payment transaction accordingly. The entity has a present
      obligation to settle in cash if the choice of settlement in equity instruments has no
      commercial substance (eg because the entity is legally prohibited from issuing shares),
      or the entity has a past practice or a stated policy of settling in cash, or generally settles
      in cash whenever the counterparty asks for cash settlement.

42   If the entity has a present obligation to settle in cash, it shall account for the transaction
      in accordance with the requirements applying to cash-settled share-based payment
      transactions, in paragraphs 30–33.

43   If no such obligation exists, the entity shall account for the transaction in accordance
      with the requirements applying to equity-settled share-based payment transactions, in
      paragraphs 10–29. Upon settlement:

      (a)   if the entity elects to settle in cash, the cash payment shall be accounted for as
             the repurchase of an equity interest, ie as a deduction from equity, except as
             noted in (c) below.

      (b)   if the entity elects to settle by issuing equity instruments, no further accounting
             is required (other than a transfer from one component of equity to another, if
             necessary), except as noted in (c) below.

(c)   if the entity elects the settlement alternative with the higher fair value, as at the date of settlement, the entity shall recognise an additional expense for the excess value given, ie the difference between the cash paid and the fair value of the equity instruments that would otherwise have been issued, or the difference between the fair value of the equity instruments issued and the amount of cash that would otherwise have been paid, whichever is applicable.

Share-based payment transactions among group entities (2009 amendments)

43A   For share-based payment transactions among group entities, in its separate or individual financial statements, the entity receiving the goods or services shall measure the goods or services received as either an equity-settled or a cash-settled share-based payment transaction by assessing:

(a)   the nature of the awards granted, and

(b)   its own rights and obligations.

The amount recognised by the entity receiving the goods or services may differ from the amount recognised by the consolidated group or by another group entity settling the share-based payment transaction.

43B   The entity receiving the goods or services shall measure the goods or services received as an equity-settled share-based payment transaction when:

(a)   the awards granted are its own equity instruments, or

(b)   the entity has no obligation to settle the share-based payment transaction.

The entity shall subsequently remeasure such an equity-settled share-based payment transaction only for changes in non-market vesting conditions in accordance with paragraphs 19–21. In all other circumstances, the entity receiving the goods or services shall measure the goods or services received as a cash-settled share-based payment transaction.

43C   The entity settling a share-based payment transaction when another entity in the group receives the goods or services shall recognise the transaction as an equity-settled share-based payment transaction only if it is settled in the entity's own equity instruments. Otherwise, the transaction shall be recognised as a cash-settled share-based payment transaction.

43D   Some group transactions involve repayment arrangements that require one group entity to pay another group entity for the provision of the share-based payments to the suppliers of goods or services. In such cases, the entity that receives the goods or services shall account for the share-based payment transaction in accordance with paragraph 43B regardless of intragroup repayment arrangements.

Disclosures

44   An entity shall disclose information that enables users of the financial statements to understand the nature and extent of share-based payment arrangements that existed during the period.

45   To give effect to the principle in paragraph 44, the entity shall disclose at least the following:

(a)   a description of each type of share-based payment arrangement that existed at any time during the period, including the general terms and conditions of each arrangement, such as vesting requirements, the maximum term of options granted, and the method of settlement (eg whether in cash or equity). An entity with substantially similar types of share-based payment arrangements may aggregate this information, unless separate disclosure of each arrangement is necessary to satisfy the principle in paragraph 44.

(b)   the number and weighted average exercise prices of share options for each of the following groups of options:

    (i)   outstanding at the beginning of the period;

    (ii)   granted during the period;

    (iii)   forfeited during the period;

    (iv)   exercised during the period;

    (v)   expired during the period;

    (vi)   outstanding at the end of the period; and

    (vii)   exercisable at the end of the period.

(c)   for share options exercised during the period, the weighted average share price at the date of exercise. If options were exercised on a regular basis throughout the period, the entity may instead disclose the weighted average share price during the period.

(d)   for share options outstanding at the end of the period, the range of exercise prices and weighted average remaining contractual life. If the range of exercise prices is wide, the outstanding options shall be divided into ranges that are meaningful for assessing the number and timing of additional shares that may be issued and the cash that may be received upon exercise of those options.

46   An entity shall disclose information that enables users of the financial statements to understand how the fair value of the goods or services received, or the fair value of the equity instruments granted, during the period was determined.

47   If the entity has measured the fair value of goods or services received as consideration for equity instruments of the entity indirectly, by reference to the fair value of the equity instruments granted, to give effect to the principle in paragraph 46, the entity shall disclose at least the following:

(a)   for share options granted during the period, the weighted average fair value of those options at the measurement date and information on how that fair value was measured, including:

    (i)   the option pricing model used and the inputs to that model, including the weighted average share price, exercise price, expected volatility, option life, expected dividends, the risk-free interest rate and any other inputs to the model, including the method used and the assumptions made to incorporate the effects of expected early exercise;

    (ii)   how expected volatility was determined, including an explanation of the extent to which expected volatility was based on historical volatility; and

    (iii)   whether and how any other features of the option grant were incorporated into the measurement of fair value, such as a market condition.

(b)   for other equity instruments granted during the period (ie other than share options), the number and weighted average fair value of those equity instruments at the measurement date, and information on how that fair value was measured, including:

    (i)   if fair value was not measured on the basis of an observable market price, how it was determined;

    (ii)   whether and how expected dividends were incorporated into the measurement of fair value; and

    (iii)   whether and how any other features of the equity instruments granted were incorporated into the measurement of fair value.

(c)   for share-based payment arrangements that were modified during the period:

    (i)   an explanation of those modifications;

    (ii)   the incremental fair value granted (as a result of those modifications); and

       (iii)   information on how the incremental fair value granted was measured, consistently with the requirements set out in (a) and (b) above, where applicable.

48   If the entity has measured directly the fair value of goods or services received during the period, the entity shall disclose how that fair value was determined, eg whether fair value was measured at a market price for those goods or services.

49   If the entity has rebutted the presumption in paragraph 13, it shall disclose that fact, and give an explanation of why the presumption was rebutted.

50   An entity shall disclose information that enables users of the financial statements to understand the effect of share-based payment transactions on the entity's profit or loss for the period and on its financial position.

51   To give effect to the principle in paragraph 50, the entity shall disclose at least the following:

    (a)   the total expense recognised for the period arising from share-based payment transactions in which the goods or services received did not qualify for recognition as assets and hence were recognised immediately as an expense, including separate disclosure of that portion of the total expense that arises from transactions accounted for as equity-settled share-based payment transactions;

    (b)   for liabilities arising from share-based payment transactions:

        (i)   the total carrying amount at the end of the period; and

        (ii)   the total intrinsic value at the end of the period of liabilities for which the counterparty's right to cash or other assets had vested by the end of the period (eg vested share appreciation rights).

52   If the information required to be disclosed by this Standard does not satisfy the principles in paragraphs 44, 46 and 50, the entity shall disclose such additional information as is necessary to satisfy them. For example, if an entity has classified any share-based payment transactions as equity-settled in accordance with paragraph 33F, the entity shall disclose an estimate of the amount that it expects to transfer to the tax authority to settle the employee's tax obligation when it is necessary to inform users about the future cash flow effects associated with the share-based payment arrangement.

Transitional provisions

Aus52.1   Paragraphs 53–59 shall not be applied by entities that have previously applied AASB 2 (July 2004), unless required to do so by this or another Australian Accounting Standard.

53   For equity-settled share-based payment transactions, the entity shall apply this Standard to grants of shares, share options or other equity instruments that were granted after 7 November 2002 and had not yet vested at the effective date of this Standard.

54   The entity is encouraged, but not required, to apply this Standard to other grants of equity instruments if the entity has disclosed publicly the fair value of those equity instruments, determined at the measurement date.

55   For all grants of equity instruments to which this Standard is applied, the entity shall restate comparative information and, where applicable, adjust the opening balance of retained earnings for the earliest period presented.

56   For all grants of equity instruments to which this Standard has not been applied (eg equity instruments granted on or before 7 November 2002), the entity shall nevertheless disclose the information required by paragraphs 44 and 45.

57   If, after the Standard becomes effective, an entity modifies the terms or conditions of a grant of equity instruments to which this Standard has not been applied, the entity shall nevertheless apply paragraphs 26–29 to account for any such modifications.

58   For liabilities arising from share-based payment transactions existing at the effective
        date of this Standard, the entity shall apply the Standard retrospectively. For these
        liabilities, the entity shall restate comparative information, including adjusting the
        opening balance of retained earnings in the earliest period presented for which
        comparative information has been restated, except that the entity is not required to
        restate comparative information to the extent that the information relates to a period
        or date that is earlier than 7 November 2002.

59   The entity is encouraged, but not required, to apply retrospectively the Standard
        to other liabilities arising from share-based payment transactions, for example, to
        liabilities that were settled during a period for which comparative information is
        presented.

59A   An entity shall apply the amendments in paragraphs 30–31, 33–33H and B44A–B44C
        as set out below. Prior periods shall not be restated.

        (a)   The amendments in paragraphs B44A–B44C apply only to modifications that
                occur on or after the date that an entity first applies the amendments.

        (b)   The amendments in paragraphs 30–31 and 33–33D apply to share-based
                payment transactions that are unvested at the date that an entity first applies
                the amendments and to share-based payment transactions with a grant date
                on or after the date that an entity first applies the amendments. For unvested
                share-based payment transactions granted prior to the date that an entity first
                applies the amendments, an entity shall remeasure the liability at that date
                and recognise the effect of the remeasurement in opening retained earnings (or
                other component of equity, as appropriate) of the reporting period in which the
                amendments are first applied.

        (c)   The amendments in paragraphs 33E–33H and the amendment to paragraph
                52 apply to share-based payment transactions that are unvested (or vested but
                unexercised), at the date that an entity first applies the amendments and to
                share-based payment transactions with a grant date on or after the date that an
                entity first applies the amendments. For unvested (or vested but unexercised)
                share-based payment transactions (or components thereof) that were previously
                classified as cash-settled share-based payments but now are classified as equity-
                settled in accordance with the amendments, an entity shall reclassify the
                carrying value of the share-based payment liability to equity at the date that
                it first applies the amendments.

59B   Notwithstanding the requirements in paragraph 59A, an entity may apply the
        amendments in paragraph 63D retrospectively, subject to the transitional provisions
        in paragraphs 53–59 of this Standard, in accordance with AASB 108 *Accounting
        Policies, Changes in Accounting Estimates and Errors* if and only if it is possible
        without hindsight. If an entity elects retrospective application, it must do so for all
        of the amendments made by AASB 2016-5 *Amendments to Australian Accounting
        Standards – Classification and Measurement of Share-based Payment Transactions.*

Effective date

60   An entity shall apply this Standard for annual periods beginning on or after 1 January
        2018. Earlier application is encouraged for periods beginning after 24 July 2014 but
        before 1 January 2018. If an entity applies the Standard for a period beginning before
        1 January 2018, it shall disclose that fact.

61–63B [Deleted by the AASB]

63C   AASB 2014-7 *Amendments to Australian Accounting Standards arising from AASB 9
        (December 2014)*, issued in December 2014, amended paragraph 6 in the previous
        version of this Standard. An entity shall apply that amendment when it applies
        AASB 9.

63D   AASB 2016-5 *Amendments to Australian Accounting Standards – Classification and Measurement of Share-based Payment Transactions*, issued in July 2016, amended paragraphs 19, 30–31, 33, 52 and Aus52.1 and added paragraphs 33A–33H, 59A–59B, 63D and B44A–B44C and their related headings. An entity shall apply those amendments for annual periods beginning on or after 1 January 2018. Earlier application is permitted. If an entity applies the amendments for an earlier period, it shall disclose that fact.

Withdrawal of Interpretations

64   [Deleted by the AASB]

Commencement of the legislative instrument

Aus 64.1   For legal purposes, this legislative instrument commences on 31 December 2017.

Withdrawal of AASB pronouncements

Aus 64.2   This Standard repeals AASB 2 *Share-based Payment* issued in July 2004. Despite the repeal, after the time this Standard starts to apply under section 334 of the Corporations Act (either generally or in relation to an individual entity), the repealed Standard continues to apply in relation to any period ending before that time as if the repeal had not occurred.

[Note: When this Standard applies under section 334 of the Corporations Act (either generally or in relation to an individual entity), it supersedes the application of the repealed Standard.]

APPENDIX A
DEFINED TERMS

This appendix is an integral part of the Standard.

cash-settled share-based payment transaction	A **share-based payment transaction** in which the entity acquires goods or services by incurring a liability to transfer cash or other assets to the supplier of those goods or services for amounts that are based on the price (or value) of **equity instruments** (including shares or **share options**) of the entity or another group entity.
employees and others providing similar services	Individuals who render personal services to the entity and either
	(a) the individuals are regarded as employees for legal or tax purposes,
	(b) the individuals work for the entity under its direction in the same way as individuals who are regarded as employees for legal or tax purposes, or
	(c) the services rendered are similar to those rendered by employees.
	For example, the term encompasses all management personnel, ie those persons having authority and responsibility for planning, directing and controlling the activities of the entity, including non-executive directors.
equity instrument	A contract that evidences a residual interest in the assets of an entity after deducting all of its liabilities.[5]

---

5   The *Framework for the Preparation and Presentation of Financial Statements* defines a liability as a present obligation of the entity arising from past events, the settlement of which is expected to result in an outflow from the entity of resources embodying economic benefits (ie an outflow of cash or other assets of the entity).

equity instrument granted	The right (conditional or unconditional) to an **equity instrument** of the entity conferred by the entity on another party, under a **share-based payment arrangement**.
equity-settled share-based payment transaction	A **share-based payment transaction** in which the entity (a) receives goods or services as consideration for its own **equity instruments** (including shares or **share options**), or (b) receives goods or services but has no obligation to settle the transaction with the supplier.
fair value	The amount for which an asset could be exchanged, a liability settled, or an **equity instrument granted** could be exchanged, between knowledgeable, willing parties in an arm's length transaction.
grant date	The date at which the entity and another party (including an employee) agree to a **share-based payment arrangement**, being when the entity and the counterparty have a shared understanding of the terms and conditions of the arrangement. At grant date the entity confers on the counterparty the right to cash, other assets, or **equity instruments** of the entity, provided the specified **vesting conditions**, if any, are met. If that agreement is subject to an approval process (for example, by shareholders), grant date is the date when that approval is obtained.
intrinsic value	The difference between the **fair value** of the shares to which the counterparty has the (conditional or unconditional) right to subscribe or which it has the right to receive, and the price (if any) the counterparty is (or will be) required to pay for those shares. For example, a **share option** with an exercise price of CU15,[6] on a share with a fair value of CU20, has an intrinsic value of CU5.
market condition	A **performance condition** upon which the exercise price, vesting or exercisability of an **equity instrument** depends that is related to the market price (or value) of the entity's **equity instruments** (or the equity instruments of another entity in the same group), such as: (a) attaining a specified share price or a specified amount of **intrinsic value** of a **share option**; or (b) achieving a specified target that is based on the market price (or value) of the entity's **equity instruments** (or the equity instruments of another entity in the same group) relative to an index of market prices of **equity instruments** of other entities. A market condition requires the counterparty to complete a specified period of service (ie a **service condition**); the service requirement can be explicit or implicit.
measurement date	The date at which the **fair value** of the **equity instruments granted** is measured for the purposes of this Standard. For transactions with **employees and others providing similar services**, the measurement date is **grant date**. For transactions with parties other than employees (and those providing similar services), the measurement date is the date the entity obtains the goods or the counterparty renders service.

---

6   In this appendix, monetary amounts are denominated in 'currency units (CU)'.

performance condition	A **vesting condition** that requires: (a) the counterparty to complete a specified period of service (ie a **service condition**); the service requirement can be explicit or implicit; and (b) specified performance target(s) to be met while the counterparty is rendering the service required in (a). The period of achieving the performance target(s): (a) shall not extend beyond the end of the service period; and (b) may start before the service period on the condition that the commencement date of the performance target is not substantially before the commencement of the service period. A performance target is defined by reference to: (a) the entity's own operations (or activities) or the operations or activities of another entity in the same group (ie a non-market condition); or (b) the price (or value) of the entity's **equity instruments** or the equity instruments of another entity in the same group (including shares and **share options**) (ie a **market condition).** A performance target might relate either to the performance of the entity as a whole or to some part of the entity (or part of the group), such as a division or an individual employee.
reload feature	A feature that provides for an automatic grant of additional **share options** whenever the option holder exercises previously granted options using the entity's shares, rather than cash, to satisfy the exercise price.
reload option	A new **share option** granted when a share is used to satisfy the exercise price of a previous share option.
service condition	A **vesting condition** that requires the counterparty to complete a specified period of service during which services are provided to the entity. If the counterparty, regardless of the reason, ceases to provide service during the **vesting period**, it has failed to satisfy the condition. A service condition does not require a performance target to be met.
share-based payment arrangement	An agreement between the entity (or another group[7] entity or any shareholder of any group entity) and another party (including an employee) that entitles the other party to receive (a) cash or other assets of the entity for amounts that are based on the price (or value) of **equity instruments share options** (including shares or **share options**) of the entity or another group entity, or (b) **equity instruments** (including shares or **share options**) of the entity or another group entity, provided the specified **vesting conditions**, if any, are met.
share-based payment transaction	A transaction in which the entity (a) receives goods or services from the supplier of those goods or services (including an employee) in a **share-based payment arrangement**, or (b) incurs an obligation to settle the transaction with the supplier in a **share-based payment arrangement** when another group entity receives those goods or services.
share option	A contract that gives the holder the right, but not the obligation, to subscribe to the entity's shares at a fixed or determinable price for a specified period of time.
vest	To become an entitlement. Under a **share-based payment arrangement**, a counterparty's right to receive cash, other assets or **equity instruments** of the entity vests when the counterparty's entitlement is no longer conditional on the satisfaction of any **vesting conditions**.

7   A 'group' is defined in Appendix A of AASB 10 Consolidated Financial Statements as 'a parent and its subsidiaries' from the perspective of the reporting entity's ultimate parent.

| vesting condition | A condition that determines whether the entity receives the services that entitle the counterparty to receive cash, other assets or **equity instruments** of the entity, under a **share-based payment arrangement**. A vesting condition is either a **service condition** or a **performance condition**. |
| vesting period | The period during which all the specified **vesting conditions** of a **share-based payment arrangement** are to be satisfied. |

APPENDIX B
APPLICATION GUIDANCE

This appendix is an integral part of the Standard.

Estimating the fair value of equity instruments granted

B1   Paragraphs B2–B41 of this appendix discuss measurement of the fair value of shares and share options granted, focusing on the specific terms and conditions that are common features of a grant of shares or share options to employees. Therefore, it is not exhaustive. Furthermore, because the valuation issues discussed below focus on shares and share options granted to employees, it is assumed that the fair value of the shares or share options is measured at grant date. However, many of the valuation issues discussed below (eg determining expected volatility) also apply in the context of estimating the fair value of shares or share options granted to parties other than employees at the date the entity obtains the goods or the counterparty renders service.

Shares

B2   For shares granted to employees, the fair value of the shares shall be measured at the market price of the entity's shares (or an estimated market price, if the entity's shares are not publicly traded), adjusted to take into account the terms and conditions upon which the shares were granted (except for vesting conditions that are excluded from the measurement of fair value in accordance with paragraphs 19–21).

B3   For example, if the employee is not entitled to receive dividends during the vesting period, this factor shall be taken into account when estimating the fair value of the shares granted. Similarly, if the shares are subject to restrictions on transfer after vesting date, that factor shall be taken into account, but only to the extent that the post-vesting restrictions affect the price that a knowledgeable, willing market participant would pay for that share. For example, if the shares are actively traded in a deep and liquid market, post-vesting transfer restrictions may have little, if any, effect on the price that a knowledgeable, willing market participant would pay for those shares. Restrictions on transfer or other restrictions that exist during the vesting period shall not be taken into account when estimating the grant date fair value of the shares granted, because those restrictions stem from the existence of vesting conditions, which are accounted for in accordance with paragraphs 19–21.

Share options

B4   For share options granted to employees, in many cases market prices are not available, because the options granted are subject to terms and conditions that do not apply to traded options. If traded options with similar terms and conditions do not exist, the fair value of the options granted shall be estimated by applying an option pricing model.

B5 The entity shall consider factors that knowledgeable, willing market participants would consider in selecting the option pricing model to apply. For example, many employee options have long lives, are usually exercisable during the period between vesting date and the end of the options' life, and are often exercised early. These factors should be considered when estimating the grant date fair value of the options. For many entities, this might preclude the use of the Black-Scholes-Merton formula, which does not allow for the possibility of exercise before the end of the option's life and may not adequately reflect the effects of expected early exercise. It also does not allow for the possibility that expected volatility and other model inputs might vary over the option's life. However, for share options with relatively short contractual lives, or that must be exercised within a short period of time after vesting date, the factors identified above may not apply. In these instances, the Black-Scholes-Merton formula may produce a value that is substantially the same as a more flexible option pricing model.

B6 All option pricing models take into account, as a minimum, the following factors:

(a) the exercise price of the option;

(b) the life of the option;

(c) the current price of the underlying shares;

(d) the expected volatility of the share price;

(e) the dividends expected on the shares (if appropriate); and

(f) the risk-free interest rate for the life of the option.

B7 Other factors that knowledgeable, willing market participants would consider in setting the price shall also be taken into account (except for vesting conditions and reload features that are excluded from the measurement of fair value in accordance with paragraphs 19–22).

B8 For example, a share option granted to an employee typically cannot be exercised during specified periods (eg during the vesting period or during periods specified by securities regulators). This factor shall be taken into account if the option pricing model applied would otherwise assume that the option could be exercised at any time during its life. However, if an entity uses an option pricing model that values options that can be exercised only at the end of the options' life, no adjustment is required for the inability to exercise them during the vesting period (or other periods during the options' life), because the model assumes that the options cannot be exercised during those periods.

B9 Similarly, another factor common to employee share options is the possibility of early exercise of the option, for example, because the option is not freely transferable, or because the employee must exercise all vested options upon cessation of employment. The effects of expected early exercise shall be taken into account, as discussed in paragraphs B16–B21.

B10 Factors that a knowledgeable, willing market participant would not consider in setting the price of a share option (or other equity instrument) shall not be taken into account when estimating the fair value of share options (or other equity instruments) granted. For example, for share options granted to employees, factors that affect the value of the option from the individual employee's perspective only are not relevant to estimating the price that would be set by a knowledgeable, willing market participant.

Inputs to option pricing models

B11 In estimating the expected volatility of and dividends on the underlying shares, the objective is to approximate the expectations that would be reflected in a current market or negotiated exchange price for the option. Similarly, when estimating the effects of early exercise of employee share options, the objective is to approximate the expectations that an outside party with access to detailed information about employees' exercise behaviour would develop based on information available at the grant date.

B12   Often, there is likely to be a range of reasonable expectations about future volatility, dividends and exercise behaviour. If so, an expected value should be calculated, by weighting each amount within the range by its associated probability of occurrence.

B13   Expectations about the future are generally based on experience, modified if the future is reasonably expected to differ from the past. In some circumstances, identifiable factors may indicate that unadjusted historical experience is a relatively poor predictor of future experience. For example, if an entity with two distinctly different lines of business disposes of the one that was significantly less risky than the other, historical volatility may not be the best information on which to base reasonable expectations for the future.

B14   In other circumstances, historical information may not be available. For example, a newly listed entity will have little, if any, historical data on the volatility of its share price. Unlisted and newly listed entities are discussed further below.

B15   In summary, an entity should not simply base estimates of volatility, exercise behaviour and dividends on historical information without considering the extent to which the past experience is expected to be reasonably predictive of future experience.

Expected early exercise

B16   Employees often exercise share options early, for a variety of reasons. For example, employee share options are typically non-transferable. This often causes employees to exercise their share options early, because that is the only way for the employees to liquidate their position. Also, employees who cease employment are usually required to exercise any vested options within a short period of time, otherwise the share options are forfeited. This factor also causes the early exercise of employee share options. Other factors causing early exercise are risk aversion and lack of wealth diversification.

B17   The means by which the effects of expected early exercise are taken into account depends upon the type of option pricing model applied. For example, expected early exercise could be taken into account by using an estimate of the option's expected life (which, for an employee share option, is the period of time from grant date to the date on which the option is expected to be exercised) as an input into an option pricing model (eg the Black-Scholes-Merton formula). Alternatively, expected early exercise could be modelled in a binomial or similar option pricing model that uses contractual life as an input.

B18   Factors to consider in estimating early exercise include:

   (a)   the length of the vesting period, because the share option typically cannot be exercised until the end of the vesting period. Hence, determining the valuation implications of expected early exercise is based on the assumption that the options will vest. The implications of vesting conditions are discussed in paragraphs 19–21.

   (b)   the average length of time similar options have remained outstanding in the past.

   (c)   the price of the underlying shares. Experience may indicate that the employees tend to exercise options when the share price reaches a specified level above the exercise price.

   (d)   the employee's level within the organisation. For example, experience might indicate that higher-level employees tend to exercise options later than lower-level employees (discussed further in paragraph B21).

   (e)   expected volatility of the underlying shares. On average, employees might tend to exercise options on highly volatile shares earlier than on shares with low volatility.

B19   As noted in paragraph B17, the effects of early exercise could be taken into account by using an estimate of the option's expected life as an input into an option pricing model. When estimating the expected life of share options granted to a group of employees, the entity could base that estimate on an appropriately weighted average expected life for the entire employee group or on appropriately weighted average lives for subgroups of employees within the group, based on more detailed data about employees' exercise behaviour (discussed further below).

B20 Separating an option grant into groups for employees with relatively homogeneous exercise behaviour is likely to be important. Option value is not a linear function of option term; value increases at a decreasing rate as the term lengthens. For example, if all other assumptions are equal, although a two-year option is worth more than a one-year option, it is not worth twice as much. That means that calculating estimated option value on the basis of a single weighted average life that includes widely differing individual lives would overstate the total fair value of the share options granted. Separating options granted into several groups, each of which has a relatively narrow range of lives included in its weighted average life, reduces that overstatement.

B21 Similar considerations apply when using a binomial or similar model. For example, the experience of an entity that grants options broadly to all levels of employees might indicate that top-level executives tend to hold their options longer than middle-management employees hold theirs and that lower-level employees tend to exercise their options earlier than any other group. In addition, employees who are encouraged or required to hold a minimum amount of their employer's equity instruments, including options, might on average exercise options later than employees not subject to that provision. In those situations, separating options by groups of recipients with relatively homogeneous exercise behaviour will result in a more accurate estimate of the total fair value of the share options granted.

Expected volatility

B22 Expected volatility is a measure of the amount by which a price is expected to fluctuate during a period. The measure of volatility used in option pricing models is the annualised standard deviation of the continuously compounded rates of return on the share over a period of time. Volatility is typically expressed in annualised terms that are comparable regardless of the time period used in the calculation, for example, daily, weekly or monthly price observations.

B23 The rate of return (which may be positive or negative) on a share for a period measures how much a shareholder has benefited from dividends and appreciation (or depreciation) of the share price.

B24 The expected annualised volatility of a share is the range within which the continuously compounded annual rate of return is expected to fall approximately two-thirds of the time. For example, to say that a share with an expected continuously compounded rate of return of 12 per cent has a volatility of 30 per cent means that the probability that the rate of return on the share for one year will be between –18 per cent (12% – 30%) and 42 per cent (12% + 30%) is approximately two-thirds. If the share price is CU100 at the beginning of the year and no dividends are paid, the year-end share price would be expected to be between CU83.53 (CU100 $\times$ e$^{-0.18}$) and CU152.20 (CU100 $\times$ e$^{0.42}$) approximately two-thirds of the time.

B25 Factors to consider in estimating expected volatility include:

(a) implied volatility from traded share options on the entity's shares, or other traded instruments of the entity that include option features (such as convertible debt), if any.

(b) the historical volatility of the share price over the most recent period that is generally commensurate with the expected term of the option (taking into account the remaining contractual life of the option and the effects of expected early exercise).

(c) the length of time an entity's shares have been publicly traded. A newly listed entity might have a high historical volatility, compared with similar entities that have been listed longer. Further guidance for newly listed entities is given below.

(d)   the tendency of volatility to revert to its mean, ie its long-term average level, and other factors indicating that expected future volatility might differ from past volatility. For example, if an entity's share price was extraordinarily volatile for some identifiable period of time because of a failed takeover bid or a major restructuring, that period could be disregarded in computing historical average annual volatility.

(e)   appropriate and regular intervals for price observations. The price observations should be consistent from period to period. For example, an entity might use the closing price for each week or the highest price for the week, but it should not use the closing price for some weeks and the highest price for other weeks. Also, the price observations should be expressed in the same currency as the exercise price.

Newly listed entities

B26   As noted in paragraph B25, an entity should consider historical volatility of the share price over the most recent period that is generally commensurate with the expected option term. If a newly listed entity does not have sufficient information on historical volatility, it should nevertheless compute historical volatility for the longest period for which trading activity is available. It could also consider the historical volatility of similar entities following a comparable period in their lives. For example, an entity that has been listed for only one year and grants options with an average expected life of five years might consider the pattern and level of historical volatility of entities in the same industry for the first six years in which the shares of those entities were publicly traded.

Unlisted entities

B27   An unlisted entity will not have historical information to consider when estimating expected volatility. Some factors to consider instead are set out below.

B28   In some cases, an unlisted entity that regularly issues options or shares to employees (or other parties) might have set up an internal market for its shares. The volatility of those share prices could be considered when estimating expected volatility.

B29   Alternatively, the entity could consider the historical or implied volatility of similar listed entities, for which share price or option price information is available, to use when estimating expected volatility. This would be appropriate if the entity has based the value of its shares on the share prices of similar listed entities.

B30   If the entity has not based its estimate of the value of its shares on the share prices of similar listed entities, and has instead used another valuation methodology to value its shares, the entity could derive an estimate of expected volatility consistent with that valuation methodology. For example, the entity might value its shares on a net asset or earnings basis. It could consider the expected volatility of those net asset values or earnings.

Expected dividends

B31   Whether expected dividends should be taken into account when measuring the fair value of shares or options granted depends on whether the counterparty is entitled to dividends or dividend equivalents.

B32   For example, if employees were granted options and are entitled to dividends on the underlying shares or dividend equivalents (which might be paid in cash or applied to reduce the exercise price) between grant date and exercise date, the options granted should be valued as if no dividends will be paid on the underlying shares, ie the input for expected dividends should be zero.

B33   Similarly, when the grant date fair value of shares granted to employees is estimated, no adjustment is required for expected dividends if the employee is entitled to receive dividends paid during the vesting period.

B34 Conversely, if the employees are not entitled to dividends or dividend equivalents during the vesting period (or before exercise, in the case of an option), the grant date valuation of the rights to shares or options should take expected dividends into account. That is to say, when the fair value of an option grant is estimated, expected dividends should be included in the application of an option pricing model. When the fair value of a share grant is estimated, that valuation should be reduced by the present value of dividends expected to be paid during the vesting period.

B35 Option pricing models generally call for expected dividend yield. However, the models may be modified to use an expected dividend amount rather than a yield. An entity may use either its expected yield or its expected payments. If the entity uses the latter, it should consider its historical pattern of increases in dividends. For example, if an entity's policy has generally been to increase dividends by approximately 3 per cent per year, its estimated option value should not assume a fixed dividend amount throughout the option's life unless there is evidence that supports that assumption.

B36 Generally, the assumption about expected dividends should be based on publicly available information. An entity that does not pay dividends and has no plans to do so should assume an expected dividend yield of zero. However, an emerging entity with no history of paying dividends might expect to begin paying dividends during the expected lives of its employee share options. Those entities could use an average of their past dividend yield (zero) and the mean dividend yield of an appropriately comparable peer group.

Risk-free interest rate

B37 Typically, the risk-free interest rate is the implied yield currently available on zero-coupon government issues of the country in whose currency the exercise price is expressed, with a remaining term equal to the expected term of the option being valued (based on the option's remaining contractual life and taking into account the effects of expected early exercise). It may be necessary to use an appropriate substitute, if no such government issues exist or circumstances indicate that the implied yield on zero-coupon government issues is not representative of the risk-free interest rate (for example, in high inflation economies). Also, an appropriate substitute should be used if market participants would typically determine the risk-free interest rate by using that substitute, rather than the implied yield of zero-coupon government issues, when estimating the fair value of an option with a life equal to the expected term of the option being valued.

Capital structure effects

B38 Typically, third parties, not the entity, write traded share options. When these share options are exercised, the writer delivers shares to the option holder. Those shares are acquired from existing shareholders. Hence the exercise of traded share options has no dilutive effect.

B39 In contrast, if share options are written by the entity, new shares are issued when those share options are exercised (either actually issued or issued in substance, if shares previously repurchased and held in treasury are used). Given that the shares will be issued at the exercise price rather than the current market price at the date of exercise, this actual or potential dilution might reduce the share price, so that the option holder does not make as large a gain on exercise as on exercising an otherwise similar traded option that does not dilute the share price.

B40 Whether this has a significant effect on the value of the share options granted depends on various factors, such as the number of new shares that will be issued on exercise of the options compared with the number of shares already issued. Also, if the market already expects that the option grant will take place, the market may have already factored the potential dilution into the share price at the date of grant.

B41   However, the entity should consider whether the possible dilutive effect of the future exercise of the share options granted might have an impact on their estimated fair value at grant date. Option pricing models can be adapted to take into account this potential dilutive effect.

Modifications to equity-settled share-based payment arrangements

B42   Paragraph 27 requires that, irrespective of any modifications to the terms and conditions on which the equity instruments were granted, or a cancellation or settlement of that grant of equity instruments, the entity should recognise, as a minimum, the services received measured at the grant date fair value of the equity instruments granted, unless those equity instruments do not vest because of failure to satisfy a vesting condition (other than a market condition) that was specified at grant date. In addition, the entity should recognise the effects of modifications that increase the total fair value of the share-based payment arrangement or are otherwise beneficial to the employee.

B43   To apply the requirements of paragraph 27:

   (a)   if the modification increases the fair value of the equity instruments granted (eg by reducing the exercise price), measured immediately before and after the modification, the entity shall include the incremental fair value granted in the measurement of the amount recognised for services received as consideration for the equity instruments granted. The incremental fair value granted is the difference between the fair value of the modified equity instrument and that of the original equity instrument, both estimated as at the date of the modification. If the modification occurs during the vesting period, the incremental fair value granted is included in the measurement of the amount recognised for services received over the period from the modification date until the date when the modified equity instruments vest, in addition to the amount based on the grant date fair value of the original equity instruments, which is recognised over the remainder of the original vesting period. If the modification occurs after vesting date, the incremental fair value granted is recognised immediately, or over the vesting period if the employee is required to complete an additional period of service before becoming unconditionally entitled to those modified equity instruments.

   (b)   similarly, if the modification increases the number of equity instruments granted, the entity shall include the fair value of the additional equity instruments granted, measured at the date of the modification, in the measurement of the amount recognised for services received as consideration for the equity instruments granted, consistently with the requirements in (a) above. For example, if the modification occurs during the vesting period, the fair value of the additional equity instruments granted is included in the measurement of the amount recognised for services received over the period from the modification date until the date when the additional equity instruments vest, in addition to the amount based on the grant date fair value of the equity instruments originally granted, which is recognised over the remainder of the original vesting period.

   (c)   if the entity modifies the vesting conditions in a manner that is beneficial to the employee, for example, by reducing the vesting period or by modifying or eliminating a performance condition (other than a market condition, changes to which are accounted for in accordance with (a) above), the entity shall take the modified vesting conditions into account when applying the requirements of paragraphs 19–21.

B44 Furthermore, if the entity modifies the terms or conditions of the equity instruments granted in a manner that reduces the total fair value of the share-based payment arrangement, or is not otherwise beneficial to the employee, the entity shall nevertheless continue to account for the services received as consideration for the equity instruments granted as if that modification had not occurred (other than a cancellation of some or all the equity instruments granted, which shall be accounted for in accordance with paragraph 28). For example:

(a) if the modification reduces the fair value of the equity instruments granted, measured immediately before and after the modification, the entity shall not take into account that decrease in fair value and shall continue to measure the amount recognised for services received as consideration for the equity instruments based on the grant date fair value of the equity instruments granted.

(b) if the modification reduces the number of equity instruments granted to an employee, that reduction shall be accounted for as a cancellation of that portion of the grant, in accordance with the requirements of paragraph 28.

(c) if the entity modifies the vesting conditions in a manner that is not beneficial to the employee, for example, by increasing the vesting period or by modifying or adding a performance condition (other than a market condition, changes to which are accounted for in accordance with (a) above), the entity shall not take the modified vesting conditions into account when applying the requirements of paragraphs 19–21.

Accounting for a modification of a share-based payment transaction that changes its classification from cash-settled to equity-settled

B44A If the terms and conditions of a cash-settled share-based payment transaction are modified with the result that it becomes an equity-settled share-based payment transaction, the transaction is accounted for as such from the date of the modification. Specifically:

(a) The equity-settled share-based payment transaction is measured by reference to the fair value of the equity instruments granted at the modification date. The equity-settled share-based payment transaction is recognised in equity on the modification date to the extent to which goods or services have been received.

(b) The liability for the cash-settled share-based payment transaction as at the modification date is derecognised on that date.

(c) Any difference between the carrying amount of the liability derecognised and the amount of equity recognised on the modification date is recognised immediately in profit or loss.

B44B If, as a result of the modification, the vesting period is extended or shortened, the application of the requirements in paragraph B44A reflect the modified vesting period. The requirements in paragraph B44A apply even if the modification occurs after the vesting period.

B44C A cash-settled share-based payment transaction may be cancelled or settled (other than a transaction cancelled by forfeiture when the vesting conditions are not satisfied). If equity instruments are granted and, on that grant date, the entity identifies them as a replacement for the cancelled cash-settled share-based payment, the entity shall apply paragraphs B44A and B44B.

Share-based payment transactions among group entities (2009 amendments)

B45 Paragraphs 43A–43C address the accounting for share-based payment transactions among group entities in each entity's separate or individual financial statements.

Paragraphs B46–B61 discuss how to apply the requirements in paragraphs 43A–43C. As noted in paragraph 43D, share-based payment transactions among group entities may take place for a variety of reasons depending on facts and circumstances. Therefore, this discussion is not exhaustive and assumes that when the entity receiving the goods or services has no obligation to settle the transaction, the transaction is a parent's equity contribution to the subsidiary, regardless of any intragroup repayment arrangements.

B46   Although the discussion below focuses on transactions with employees, it also applies to similar share-based payment transactions with suppliers of goods or services other than employees. An arrangement between a parent and its subsidiary may require the subsidiary to pay the parent for the provision of the equity instruments to the employees. The discussion below does not address how to account for such an intragroup payment arrangement.

B47   Four issues are commonly encountered in share-based payment transactions among group entities. For convenience, the examples below discuss the issues in terms of a parent and its subsidiary.

Share-based payment arrangements involving an entity's own equity instruments

B48   The first issue is whether the following transactions involving an entity's own equity instruments should be accounted for as equity-settled or as cash-settled in accordance with the requirements of this Standard:

(a)   an entity grants to its employees rights to equity instruments of the entity (eg share options), and either chooses or is required to buy equity instruments (ie treasury shares) from another party, to satisfy its obligations to its employees; and

(b)   an entity's employees are granted rights to equity instruments of the entity (eg share options), either by the entity itself or by its shareholders, and the shareholders of the entity provide the equity instruments needed.

B49   The entity shall account for share-based payment transactions in which it receives services as consideration for its own equity instruments as equity-settled. This applies regardless of whether the entity chooses or is required to buy those equity instruments from another party to satisfy its obligations to its employees under the share-based payment arrangement. It also applies regardless of whether:

(a)   the employee's rights to the entity's equity instruments were granted by the entity itself or by its shareholder(s); or

(b)   the share-based payment arrangement was settled by the entity itself or by its shareholder(s).

B50   If the shareholder has an obligation to settle the transaction with its investee's employees, it provides equity instruments of its investee rather than its own. Therefore, if its investee is in the same group as the shareholder, in accordance with paragraph 43C, the shareholder shall measure its obligation in accordance with the requirements applicable to cash-settled share-based payment transactions in the shareholder's separate financial statements and those applicable to equity-settled share-based payment transactions in the shareholder's consolidated financial statements.

Share-based payment arrangements involving equity instruments of the parent

B51   The second issue concerns share-based payment transactions between two or more entities within the same group involving an equity instrument of another group entity. For example, employees of a subsidiary are granted rights to equity instruments of its parent as consideration for the services provided to the subsidiary.

B52 Therefore, the second issue concerns the following share-based payment arrangements:

(a) a parent grants rights to its equity instruments directly to the employees of its subsidiary: the parent (not the subsidiary) has the obligation to provide the employees of the subsidiary with the equity instruments; and

(b) a subsidiary grants rights to equity instruments of its parent to its employees: the subsidiary has the obligation to provide its employees with the equity instruments.

A parent grants rights to its equity instruments to the employees of its subsidiary (paragraph B52(a))

B53 The subsidiary does not have an obligation to provide its parent's equity instruments to the subsidiary's employees. Therefore, in accordance with paragraph 43B, the subsidiary shall measure the services received from its employees in accordance with the requirements applicable to equity-settled share-based payment transactions, and recognise a corresponding increase in equity as a contribution from the parent.

B54 The parent has an obligation to settle the transaction with the subsidiary's employees by providing the parent's own equity instruments. Therefore, in accordance with paragraph 43C, the parent shall measure its obligation in accordance with the requirements applicable to equity-settled share-based payment transactions.

A subsidiary grants rights to equity instruments of its parent to its employees (paragraph B52(b))

B55 Because the subsidiary does not meet either of the conditions in paragraph 43B, it shall account for the transaction with its employees as cash-settled. This requirement applies irrespective of how the subsidiary obtains the equity instruments to satisfy its obligations to its employees.

Share-based payment arrangements involving cash-settled payments to employees

B56 The third issue is how an entity that receives goods or services from its suppliers (including employees) should account for share-based arrangements that are cash-settled when the entity itself does not have any obligation to make the required payments to its suppliers. For example, consider the following arrangements in which the parent (not the entity itself) has an obligation to make the required cash payments to the employees of the entity:

(a) the employees of the entity will receive cash payments that are linked to the price of its equity instruments.

(b) the employees of the entity will receive cash payments that are linked to the price of its parent's equity instruments.

B57 The subsidiary does not have an obligation to settle the transaction with its employees. Therefore, the subsidiary shall account for the transaction with its employees as equity-settled, and recognise a corresponding increase in equity as a contribution from its parent. The subsidiary shall remeasure the cost of the transaction subsequently for any changes resulting from non-market vesting conditions not being met in accordance with paragraphs 19–21. This differs from the measurement of the transaction as cash-settled in the consolidated financial statements of the group.

B58 Because the parent has an obligation to settle the transaction with the employees, and the consideration is cash, the parent (and the consolidated group) shall measure its obligation in accordance with the requirements applicable to cash-settled share-based payment transactions in paragraph 43C.

AASB

Transfer of employees between group entities

B59   The fourth issue relates to group share-based payment arrangements that involve employees of more than one group entity. For example, a parent might grant rights to its equity instruments to the employees of its subsidiaries, conditional upon the completion of continuing service with the group for a specified period. An employee of one subsidiary might transfer employment to another subsidiary during the specified vesting period without the employee's rights to equity instruments of the parent under the original share-based payment arrangement being affected. If the subsidiaries have no obligation to settle the share-based payment transaction with their employees, they account for it as an equity-settled transaction. Each subsidiary shall measure the services received from the employee by reference to the fair value of the equity instruments at the date the rights to those equity instruments were originally granted by the parent as defined in Appendix A, and the proportion of the vesting period the employee served with each subsidiary.

B60   If the subsidiary has an obligation to settle the transaction with its employees in its parent's equity instruments, it accounts for the transaction as cash-settled. Each subsidiary shall measure the services received on the basis of grant date fair value of the equity instruments for the proportion of the vesting period the employee served with each subsidiary. In addition, each subsidiary shall recognise any change in the fair value of the equity instruments during the employee's service period with each subsidiary.

B61   Such an employee, after transferring between group entities, may fail to satisfy a vesting condition other than a market condition as defined in Appendix A, eg the employee leaves the group before completing the service period. In this case, because the vesting condition is service to the group, each subsidiary shall adjust the amount previously recognised in respect of the services received from the employee in accordance with the principles in paragraph 19. Hence, if the rights to the equity instruments granted by the parent do not vest because of an employee's failure to meet a vesting condition other than a market condition, no amount is recognised on a cumulative basis for the services received from that employee in the financial statements of any group entity.

APPENDIX C
AUSTRALIAN REDUCED DISCLOSURE
REQUIREMENTS

This appendix is an integral part of AASB 2.

AusC1   **The following do not apply to entities preparing general purpose financial statements under Australian Accounting Standards – Reduced Disclosure Requirements:**

   (a)   **paragraphs 45(c), 45(d), 46, 47(a), 47(b), 47(c)(ii), 47(c)(iii), 48-50, 51 and 52; and**

   (b)   **in paragraph 47, the text "to give effect to the principle in paragraph 46,".**

   Entities applying Australian Accounting Standards – Reduced Disclosure Requirements may elect to comply with some or all of these excluded requirements.

AusC2   The requirements that do not apply to entities preparing general purpose financial statements under Australian Accounting Standards – Reduced Disclosure Requirements are also identified in this Standard by shading of the relevant text.

AusC3　　RDR paragraphs in this Standard apply only to entities preparing general purpose financial statements under Australian Accounting Standards – Reduced Disclosure Requirements.

RDR46.1　For equity-settled share-based payment arrangements, an entity applying Australian Accounting Standards – Reduced Disclosure Requirements shall disclose information about how it measured the fair value of goods or services received or the fair value of the equity instruments granted. If a valuation methodology was used, the entity shall disclose the method and its reason for choosing it.

RDR46.2　For cash-settled share-based payment arrangements, an entity applying Australian Accounting Standards – Reduced Disclosure Requirements shall disclose information about how the liability was measured.

RDR50.1　An entity applying Australian Accounting Standards – Reduced Disclosure Requirements shall disclose the following information about the effect of share-based payment transactions on the entity's profit or loss for the period and on its financial position:

(a)　　the total expense recognised in profit or loss for the period; and

(b)　　the total carrying amount at the end of the period of liabilities arising from share-based payment transactions.

CONTENTS

GUIDANCE ON IMPLEMENTING
AASB 2 *SHARE-BASED PAYMENT*

AASB

GUIDANCE ON IMPLEMENTING
AASB 2 *SHARE-BASED PAYMENT*

This guidance accompanies, but is not part of, AASB 2.

Definition of grant date

IG1   AASB 2 defines grant date as the date at which the entity and the employee (or other party providing similar services) agree to a share-based payment arrangement, being when the entity and the counterparty have a shared understanding of the terms and conditions of the arrangement. At grant date the entity confers on the counterparty the right to cash, other assets, or equity instruments of the entity, provided the specified vesting conditions, if any, are met. If that agreement is subject to an approval process (for example, by shareholders), grant date is the date when that approval is obtained.

IG2   As noted above, grant date is when both parties agree to a share-based payment arrangement. The word 'agree' is used in its usual sense, which means that there must be both an offer and acceptance of that offer. Hence, the date at which one party makes an offer to another party is not grant date. The date of grant is when that other party accepts the offer. In some instances, the counterparty explicitly agrees to the arrangement, eg by signing a contract. In other instances, agreement might be implicit, eg for many share-based payment arrangements with employees, the employees' agreement is evidenced by their commencing to render services.

IG3   Furthermore, for both parties to have agreed to the share-based payment arrangement, both parties must have a shared understanding of the terms and conditions of the arrangement. Therefore, if some of the terms and conditions of the arrangement are agreed on one date, with the remainder of the terms and conditions agreed on a later date, then grant date is on that later date, when all of the terms and conditions have been agreed. For example, if an entity agrees to issue share options to an employee, but the exercise price of the options will be set by a compensation committee that meets in three months' time, grant date is when the exercise price is set by the compensation committee.

IG4   In some cases, grant date might occur after the employees to whom the equity instruments were granted have begun rendering services. For example, if a grant of equity instruments is subject to shareholder approval, grant date might occur some months after the employees have begun rendering services in respect of that grant. The Standard requires the entity to recognise the services when received. In this situation, the entity should estimate the grant date fair value of the equity instruments (eg by estimating the fair value of the equity instruments at the end of the reporting period), for the purposes of recognising the services received during the period between service commencement date and grant date. Once the date of grant has been established, the entity should revise the earlier estimate so that the amounts recognised for services received in respect of the grant are ultimately based on the grant date fair value of the equity instruments.

Definition of vesting conditions

IG4A   AASB 2 defines vesting conditions as the conditions that determine whether the entity receives the services that entitle the counterparty to receive cash, other assets or equity instruments of the entity under a share-based payment arrangement. The following flowchart illustrates the evaluation of whether a condition is a service or performance condition or a non-vesting condition.

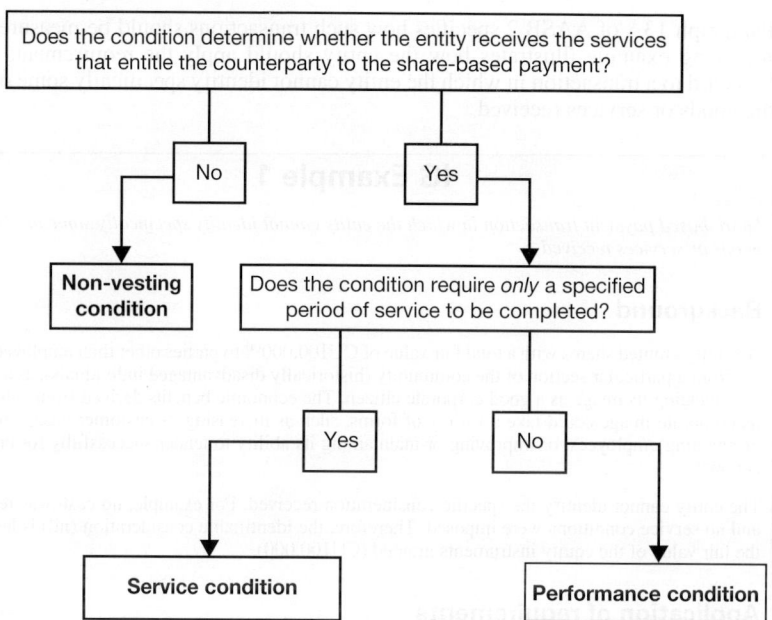

Transactions with parties other than employees

IG5 For transactions with parties other than employees (and others providing similar services) that are measured by reference to the fair value of the equity instruments granted, paragraph 13 of AASB 2 includes a rebuttable presumption that the fair value of the goods or services received can be estimated reliably. In these situations, paragraph 13 of AASB 2 requires the entity to measure that fair value at the date the entity obtains the goods or the counterparty renders service.

Transaction in which the entity cannot identify specifically some or all of the goods or services received

IG5A In some cases, however, it might be difficult to demonstrate that goods or services have been (or will be) received. For example, an entity may grant shares to a charitable organisation for nil consideration. It is usually not possible to identify the specific goods or services received in return for such a transaction. A similar situation might arise in transactions with other parties.

IG5B Paragraph 11 of AASB 2 requires transactions in which share-based payments are made to employees to be measured by reference to the fair value of the share-based payments at grant date.[8] Hence, the entity is not required to measure directly the fair value of the employee services received.

IG5C It should be noted that the phrase 'the fair value of the share-based payment' refers to the fair value of the particular share-based payment concerned. For example, an entity might be required by government legislation to issue some portion of its shares to nationals of a particular country that may be transferred only to other nationals of that country. Such a transfer restriction may affect the fair value of the shares concerned, and therefore those shares may have a fair value that is less than the fair value of otherwise identical shares that do not carry such restrictions. In this situation, the phrase 'the fair value of the share-based payment' would refer to the fair value of the restricted shares, not the fair value of other, unrestricted shares.

---

8 In AASB 2, all references to employees include others providing similar services.

IG5D Paragraph 13A of AASB 2 specifies how such transactions should be measured. The following example illustrates how the entity should apply the requirements of the Standard to a transaction in which the entity cannot identify specifically some or all of the goods or services received.

IG Example 1

Share-based payment transaction in which the entity cannot identify specifically some or all of the goods or services received

Background

An entity granted shares with a total fair value of CU100,000[a] to parties other than employees who are from a particular section of the community (historically disadvantaged individuals), as a means of enhancing its image as a good corporate citizen. The economic benefits derived from enhancing its corporate image could take a variety of forms, such as increasing its customer base, attracting or retaining employees, or improving or maintaining its ability to tender successfully for business contracts.

The entity cannot identify the specific consideration received. For example, no cash was received and no service conditions were imposed. Therefore, the identifiable consideration (nil) is less than the fair value of the equity instruments granted (CU100,000).

Application of requirements

Although the entity cannot identify the specific goods or services received, the circumstances indicate that goods or services have been (or will be) received, and therefore AASB 2 applies.

In this situation, because the entity cannot identify the specific goods or services received, the rebuttable presumption in paragraph 13 of AASB 2, that the fair value of the goods or services received can be estimated reliably, does not apply. The entity should instead measure the goods or services received by reference to the fair value of the equity instruments granted.

(a) In this example, and in all other examples in this guidance, monetary amounts are denominated in 'currency units (CU)'.

Measurement date for transactions with parties other than employees

IG6 If the goods or services are received on more than one date, the entity should measure the fair value of the equity instruments granted on each date when goods or services are received. The entity should apply that fair value when measuring the goods or services received on that date.

IG7 However, an approximation could be used in some cases. For example, if an entity received services continuously during a three-month period, and its share price did not change significantly during that period, the entity could use the average share price during the three-month period when estimating the fair value of the equity instruments granted.

Transitional arrangements

IG8 In paragraph 54 of AASB 2, the entity is encouraged, but not required, to apply the requirements of the Standard to other grants of equity instruments (ie grants other than those specified in paragraph 53 of the Standard), if the entity has disclosed publicly the fair value of those equity instruments, measured at the measurement date. For example, such equity instruments include equity instruments for which the entity has disclosed in the notes to its financial statements the information required in the US by SFAS 123 *Accounting for Stock-based Compensation*.

Equity-settled share-based payment transactions

IG9 For equity-settled transactions measured by reference to the fair value of the equity instruments granted, paragraph 19 of AASB 2 states that vesting conditions, other than market conditions,[9] are not taken into account when estimating the fair value of the shares or share options at the measurement date (ie grant date, for transactions with employees and others providing similar services). Instead, vesting conditions are taken into account by adjusting the number of equity instruments included in the measurement of the transaction amount so that, ultimately, the amount recognised for goods or services received as consideration for the equity instruments granted is based on the number of equity instruments that eventually vest. Hence, on a cumulative basis, no amount is recognised for goods or services received if the equity instruments granted do not vest because of failure to satisfy a vesting condition, eg the counterparty fails to complete a specified service period, or a performance condition is not satisfied. This accounting method is known as the modified grant date method, because the number of equity instruments included in the determination of the transaction amount is adjusted to reflect the outcome of the vesting conditions, but no adjustment is made to the fair value of those equity instruments. That fair value is estimated at grant date (for transactions with employees and others providing similar services) and not subsequently revised. Hence, neither increases nor decreases in the fair value of the equity instruments after grant date are taken into account when determining the transaction amount (other than in the context of measuring the incremental fair value transferred if a grant of equity instruments is subsequently modified).

IG10 To apply these requirements, paragraph 20 of AASB 2 requires the entity to recognise the goods or services received during the vesting period based on the best available estimate of the number of equity instruments expected to vest and to revise that estimate, if necessary, if subsequent information indicates that the number of equity instruments expected to vest differs from previous estimates. On vesting date, the entity revises the estimate to equal the number of equity instruments that ultimately vested (subject to the requirements of paragraph 21 concerning market conditions).

IG11 In the examples below, the share options granted all vest at the same time, at the end of a specified period. In some situations, share options or other equity instruments granted might vest in instalments over the vesting period. For example, suppose an employee is granted 100 share options, which will vest in instalments of 25 share options at the end of each year over the next four years. To apply the requirements of the Standard, the entity should treat each instalment as a separate share option grant, because each instalment has a different vesting period, and hence the fair value of each instalment will differ (because the length of the vesting period affects, for example, the likely timing of cash flows arising from the exercise of the options).

IG Example 1A

Background

An entity grants 100 share options to each of its 500 employees. Each grant is conditional upon the employee working for the entity over the next three years. The entity estimates that the fair value of each share option is CU15.

On the basis of a weighted average probability, the entity estimates that 20 per cent of employees will leave during the three-year period and therefore forfeit their rights to the share options.

---

9 In the remainder of this paragraph, the discussion of vesting conditions excludes market conditions, which are subject to the requirements of paragraph 21 of AASB 2.

Application of requirements

Scenario 1

If everything turns out exactly as expected, the entity recognises the following amounts during the vesting period, for services received as consideration for the share options.

Year	Calculation	Remuneration expense for period	Cumulative remuneration expense
		CU	CU
1	50,000 options × 80% × CU15 × $^1/_3$ years	200,000	200,000
2	(50,000 options × 80% × CU15 × $^2/_3$ years) – CU200,000	200,000	400,000
3	(50,000 options × 80% × CU15 × $^3/_3$ years) – CU400,000	200,000	600,000

Scenario 2

During year 1, 20 employees leave. The entity revises its estimate of total employee departures over the three-year period from 20 per cent (100 employees) to 15 per cent (75 employees). During year 2, a further 22 employees leave. The entity revises its estimate of total employee departures over the three-year period from 15 per cent to 12 per cent (60 employees). During year 3, a further 15 employees leave. Hence, a total of 57 employees forfeited their rights to the share options during the three-year period, and a total of 44,300 share options (443 employees × 100 options per employee) vested at the end of year 3.

Year	Calculation	Remuneration expense for period	Cumulative remuneration expense
		CU	CU
1	50,000 options × 85% × CU15 × $^1/_3$ years	212,500	212,500
2	(50,000 options × 88% × CU15 × $^2/_3$ years) – CU212,500	227,500	440,000
3	(44,300 options × CU15) – CU440,000	224,500	664,500

IG12   In Example 1A, the share options were granted conditionally upon the employees' completing a specified service period. In some cases, a share option or share grant might also be conditional upon the achievement of a specified performance target. Examples 2, 3 and 4 illustrate the application of the Standard to share option or share grants with performance conditions (other than market conditions, which are discussed in paragraph IG13 and illustrated in Examples 5 and 6). In Example 2, the length of the vesting period varies, depending on when the performance condition is satisfied. Paragraph 15 of the Standard requires the entity to estimate the length of the expected vesting period, based on the most likely outcome of the performance condition, and to revise that estimate, if necessary, if subsequent information indicates that the length of the vesting period is likely to differ from previous estimates.

IG Example 2

Grant with a performance condition, in which the length of the vesting period varies

Background

At the beginning of year 1, the entity grants 100 shares each to 500 employees, conditional upon the employees' remaining in the entity's employ during the vesting period. The shares will vest at the end of year 1 if the entity's earnings increase by more than 18 per cent; at the end of year 2 if the entity's earnings increase by more than an average of 13 per cent per year over the two-year period; and at the end of year 3 if the entity's earnings increase by more than an average of 10 per cent per year over the three-year period. The shares have a fair value of CU30 per share at the start of year 1, which equals the share price at grant date. No dividends are expected to be paid over the three-year period.

By the end of year 1, the entity's earnings have increased by 14 per cent, and 30 employees have left. The entity expects that earnings will continue to increase at a similar rate in year 2, and therefore expects that the shares will vest at the end of year 2. The entity expects, on the basis of a weighted average probability, that a further 30 employees will leave during year 2, and therefore expects that 440 employees will vest in 100 shares each at the end of year 2.

By the end of year 2, the entity's earnings have increased by only 10 per cent and therefore the shares do not vest at the end of year 2. 28 employees have left during the year. The entity expects that a further 25 employees will leave during year 3, and that the entity's earnings will increase by at least 6 per cent, thereby achieving the average of 10 per cent per year.

By the end of year 3, 23 employees have left and the entity's earnings had increased by 8 per cent, resulting in an average increase of 10.67 per cent per year. Therefore, 419 employees received 100 shares at the end of year 3.

Application of requirements

Year	Calculation	Remuneration expense for period	Cumulative remuneration expense
		CU	CU
1	440 employees × 100 shares × CU30 × $^{1}/_{2}$	660,000	660,000
2	(417 employees × 100 shares × CU30 × $^{2}/_{3}$) − CU660,000	174,000	834,000
3	(419 employees × 100 shares × CU30 × $^{3}/_{3}$) − CU834,000	423,000	1,257,000

IG Example 3

Grant with a performance condition, in which the number of equity instruments varies

Background

At the beginning of year 1, Entity A grants share options to each of its 100 employees working in the sales department. The share options will vest at the end of year 3, provided that the employees remain in the entity's employ, and provided that the volume of sales of a particular product increases by at least an average of 5 per cent per year. If the volume of sales of the product increases by an average of between 5 per cent and 10 per cent per year, each employee will receive 100 share options. If the volume of sales increases by an average of between 10 per cent and 15 per cent each year, each employee will receive 200 share options. If the volume of sales increases by an average of 15 per cent or more, each employee will receive 300 share options.

On grant date, Entity A estimates that the share options have a fair value of CU20 per option. Entity A also estimates that the volume of sales of the product will increase by an average of between 10 per cent and 15 per cent per year, and therefore expects that, for each employee who remains in service until the end of year 3, 200 share options will vest. The entity also estimates, on the basis of a weighted average probability, that 20 per cent of employees will leave before the end of year 3.

By the end of year 1, seven employees have left and the entity still expects that a total of 20 employees will leave by the end of year 3. Hence, the entity expects that 80 employees will remain in service for the three-year period. Product sales have increased by 12 per cent and the entity expects this rate of increase to continue over the next 2 years.

By the end of year 2, a further five employees have left, bringing the total to 12 to date. The entity now expects only three more employees will leave during year 3, and therefore expects a total of 15 employees will have left during the three-year period, and hence 85 employees are expected to remain. Product sales have increased by 18 per cent, resulting in an average of 15 per cent over the two years to date. The entity now expects that sales will average 15 per cent or more over the three-year period, and hence expects each sales employee to receive 300 share options at the end of year 3.

By the end of year 3, a further two employees have left. Hence, 14 employees have left during the three-year period, and 86 employees remain. The entity's sales have increased by an average of 16 per cent over the three years. Therefore, each of the 86 employees receives 300 share options.

Application of requirements

Year	Calculation	Remuneration expense for period CU	Cumulative remuneration expense CU
1	80 employees × 200 options × CU20 × $^1/_3$	106,667	106,667
2	(85 employees × 300 options × CU20 × $^2/_3$) – CU106,667	233,333	340,000
3	(86 employees × 300 options × CU20 × $^3/_3$) – CU340,000	176,000	516,000

IG Example 4

Grant with a performance condition, in which the exercise price varies

Background

At the beginning of year 1, an entity grants to a senior executive 10,000 share options, conditional upon the executive remaining in the entity's employ until the end of year 3. The exercise price is CU40. However, the exercise price drops to CU30 if the entity's earnings increase by at least an average of 10 per cent per year over the three-year period.

On grant date, the entity estimates that the fair value of the share options, with an exercise price of CU30, is CU16 per option. If the exercise price is CU40, the entity estimates that the share options have a fair value of CU12 per option.

During year 1, the entity's earnings increased by 12 per cent, and the entity expects that earnings will continue to increase at this rate over the next two years. The entity therefore expects that the earnings target will be achieved, and hence the share options will have an exercise price of CU30.

During year 2, the entity's earnings increased by 13 per cent, and the entity continues to expect that the earnings target will be achieved.

During year 3, the entity's earnings increased by only 3 per cent, and therefore the earnings target was not achieved. The executive completes three years' service, and therefore satisfies the service condition. Because the earnings target was not achieved, the 10,000 vested share options have an exercise price of CU40.

Application of requirements

Because the exercise price varies depending on the outcome of a performance condition that is not a market condition, the effect of that performance condition (ie the possibility that the exercise price might be CU40 and the possibility that the exercise price might be CU30) is not taken into account when estimating the fair value of the share options at grant date. Instead, the entity estimates the fair value of the share options at grant date under each scenario (ie exercise price of CU40 and exercise price of CU30) and ultimately revises the transaction amount to reflect the outcome of that performance condition, as illustrated below.

Year	Calculation	Remuneration expense for period	Cumulative remuneration expense
		CU	CU
1	10,000 options × CU16 × $^{1}/_{3}$	53,333	53,333
2	(10,000 options × CU16 × $^{2}/_{3}$) – CU53,333	53,334	106,667
3	(10,000 options × CU12 × $^{3}/_{3}$) – CU106,667	13,333	120,000

IG13 Paragraph 21 of the Standard requires market conditions, such as a target share price upon which vesting (or exercisability) is conditional, to be taken into account when estimating the fair value of the equity instruments granted. Therefore, for grants of equity instruments with market conditions, the entity recognises the goods or services received from a counterparty who satisfies all other vesting conditions (eg services received from an employee who remains in service for the specified period of service), irrespective of whether that market condition is satisfied. Example 5 illustrates these requirements.

IG Example 5

Grant with a market condition

Background

At the beginning of year 1, an entity grants to a senior executive 10,000 share options, conditional upon the executive remaining in the entity's employ until the end of year 3. However, the share options cannot be exercised unless the share price has increased from CU50 at the beginning of year 1 to above CU65 at the end of year 3. If the share price is above CU65 at the end of year 3, the share options can be exercised at any time during the next seven years, ie by the end of year 10.

The entity applies a binomial option pricing model, which takes into account the possibility that the share price will exceed CU65 at the end of year 3 (and hence the share options become exercisable) and the possibility that the share price will not exceed CU65 at the end of year 3 (and hence the options will be forfeited). It estimates the fair value of the share options with this market condition to be CU24 per option.

Application of requirements

Because paragraph 21 of the Standard requires the entity to recognise the services received from a counterparty who satisfies all other vesting conditions (eg services received from an employee who remains in service for the specified service period), irrespective of whether that market condition is satisfied, it makes no difference whether the share price target is achieved. The possibility that the share price target might not be achieved has already been taken into account when estimating the fair value of the share options at grant date. Therefore, if the entity expects the executive to complete the three-year service period, and the executive does so, the entity recognises the following amounts in years 1, 2 and 3:

Year	Calculation	Remuneration expense for period	Cumulative remuneration expense
		CU	CU
1	10,000 options × CU24 × $^1/_3$	80,000	80,000
2	(10,000 options × CU24 × $^2/_3$) – CU80,000	80,000	160,000
3	(10,000 options × CU24) – CU160,000	80,000	240,000

As noted above, these amounts are recognised irrespective of the outcome of the market condition. However, if the executive left during year 2 (or year 3), the amount recognised during year 1 (and year 2) would be reversed in year 2 (or year 3). This is because the service condition, in contrast to the market condition, was not taken into account when estimating the fair value of the share options at grant date. Instead, the service condition is taken into account by adjusting the transaction amount to be based on the number of equity instruments that ultimately vest, in accordance with paragraphs 19 and 20 of the Standard.

IG14   In Example 5, the outcome of the market condition did not change the length of the vesting period. However, if the length of the vesting period varies depending on when a performance condition is satisfied, paragraph 15 of the Standard requires the entity to presume that the services to be rendered by the employees as consideration for the equity instruments granted will be received in the future, over the expected vesting period. The entity is required to estimate the length of the expected vesting period at grant date, based on the most likely outcome of the performance condition. If the performance condition is a market condition, the estimate of the length of the expected vesting period must be consistent with the assumptions used in estimating the fair value of the share options granted, and is not subsequently revised. Example 6 illustrates these requirements.

IG Example 6

Grant with a market condition, in which the length of the vesting period varies

Background

At the beginning of year 1, an entity grants 10,000 share options with a ten-year life to each of ten senior executives. The share options will vest and become exercisable immediately if and when the entity's share price increases from CU50 to CU70, provided that the executive remains in service until the share price target is achieved.

The entity applies a binomial option pricing model, which takes into account the possibility that the share price target will be achieved during the ten-year life of the options, and the possibility that the target will not be achieved. The entity estimates that the fair value of the share options at grant date is CU25 per option. From the option pricing model, the entity determines that the mode of the distribution of possible vesting dates is five years. In other words, of all the possible outcomes, the most likely outcome of the market condition is that the share price target will be achieved at the end of year 5. Therefore, the entity estimates that the expected vesting period is five years. The entity also estimates that two executives will have left by the end of year 5, and therefore expects that 80,000 share options (10,000 share options × 8 executives) will vest at the end of year 5.

Throughout years 1–4, the entity continues to estimate that a total of two executives will leave by the end of year 5. However, in total three executives leave, one in each of years 3, 4 and 5. The share price target is achieved at the end of year 6. Another executive leaves during year 6, before the share price target is achieved.

Application of requirements

Paragraph 15 of the Standard requires the entity to recognise the services received over the expected vesting period, as estimated at grant date, and also requires the entity not to revise that estimate. Therefore, the entity recognises the services received from the executives over years 1–5. Hence, the transaction amount is ultimately based on 70,000 share options (10,000 share options × 7 executives who remain in service at the end of year 5).

Although another executive left during year 6, no adjustment is made, because the executive had already completed the expected vesting period of five years. Therefore, the entity recognises the following amounts in years 1–5:

Year	Calculation	Remuneration expense for period	Cumulative remuneration expense
		CU	CU
1	80,000 options × CU25 × $^1/_5$	400,000	400,000
2	(80,000 options × CU25 × $^2/_5$) – CU400,000	400,000	800,000
3	(80,000 options × CU25 × $^3/_5$) – CU800,000	400,000	1,200,000
4	(80,000 options × CU25 × $^4/_5$) – CU1,200,000	400,000	1,600,000
5	(70,000 options × CU25) – CU1,600,000	150,000	1,750,000

IG15 Paragraphs 26–29 and B42–B44 of the Standard set out requirements that apply if a share option is repriced (or the entity otherwise modifies the terms or conditions of a share-based payment arrangement). Examples 7–9 illustrate some of these requirements.

IG Example 7

Grant of share options that are subsequently repriced

Background

At the beginning of year 1, an entity grants 100 share options to each of its 500 employees. Each grant is conditional upon the employee remaining in service over the next three years. The entity estimates that the fair value of each option is CU15. On the basis of a weighted average probability, the entity estimates that 100 employees will leave during the three-year period and therefore forfeit their rights to the share options.

Suppose that 40 employees leave during year 1. Also suppose that by the end of year 1, the entity's share price has dropped, and the entity reprices its share options, and that the repriced share options vest at the end of year 3. The entity estimates that a further 70 employees will leave during years 2 and 3, and hence the total expected employee departures over the three-year vesting period is 110 employees. During year 2, a further 35 employees leave, and the entity estimates that a further 30 employees will leave during year 3, to bring the total expected employee departures over the three-year vesting period to 105 employees. During year 3, a total of 28 employees leave, and hence a total of 103 employees ceased employment during the vesting period. For the remaining 397 employees, the share options vested at the end of year 3.

The entity estimates that, at the date of repricing, the fair value of each of the original share options granted (ie before taking into account the repricing) is CU5 and that the fair value of each repriced share option is CU8.

Application of requirements

Paragraph 27 of the Standard requires the entity to recognise the effects of modifications that increase the total fair value of the share-based payment arrangement or are otherwise beneficial to the employee. If the modification increases the fair value of the equity instruments granted (eg by reducing the exercise price), measured immediately before and after the modification, paragraph B43(a) of Appendix B requires the entity to include the incremental fair value granted (ie the difference between the fair value of the modified equity instrument and that of the original equity instrument, both estimated as at the date of the modification) in the measurement of the amount recognised for services received as consideration for the equity instruments granted. If the modification occurs during the vesting period, the incremental fair value granted is included in the

AASB

measurement of the amount recognised for services received over the period from the modification date until the date when the modified equity instruments vest, in addition to the amount based on the grant date fair value of the original equity instruments, which is recognised over the remainder of the original vesting period.

The incremental value is CU3 per share option (CU8 – CU5). This amount is recognised over the remaining two years of the vesting period, along with remuneration expense based on the original option value of CU15.

The amounts recognised in years 1–3 are as follows:

Year	Calculation	Remuneration expense for period CU	Cumulative remuneration expense CU
1	(500 – 110) employees × 100 options × CU15 × $^1/_3$	195,000	195,000
2	(500 – 105) employees × 100 options × (CU15 × $^2/_3$ + CU3 × $^1/_2$) – CU195,000	259,250	454,250
3	(500 – 103) employees × 100 options × (CU15 + CU3) – CU454,250	260,350	714,600

IG Example 8

Grant of share options with a vesting condition that is subsequently modified

Background

At the beginning of year 1, the entity grants 1,000 share options to each member of its sales team, conditional upon the employee remaining in the entity's employ for three years, and the team selling more than 50,000 units of a particular product over the three-year period. The fair value of the share options is CU15 per option at the date of grant.

During year 2, the entity increases the sales target to 100,000 units. By the end of year 3, the entity has sold 55,000 units, and the share options are forfeited. Twelve members of the sales team have remained in service for the three-year period.

Application of requirements

Paragraph 20 of the Standard requires, for a performance condition that is not a market condition, the entity to recognise the services received during the vesting period based on the best available estimate of the number of equity instruments expected to vest and to revise that estimate, if necessary, if subsequent information indicates that the number of equity instruments expected to vest differs from previous estimates. On vesting date, the entity revises the estimate to equal the number of equity instruments that ultimately vested. However, paragraph 27 of the Standard requires, irrespective of any modifications to the terms and conditions on which the equity instruments were granted, or a cancellation or settlement of that grant of equity instruments, the entity to recognise, as a minimum, the services received, measured at the grant date fair value of the equity instruments granted, unless those equity instruments do not vest because of failure to satisfy a vesting condition (other than a market condition) that was specified at grant date. Furthermore, paragraph B44(c) of Appendix B specifies that, if the entity modifies the vesting conditions in a manner that is not beneficial to the employee, the entity does not take the modified vesting conditions into account when applying the requirements of paragraphs 19–21 of the Standard.

Therefore, because the modification to the performance condition made it less likely that the share options will vest, which was not beneficial to the employee, the entity takes no account of the modified performance condition when recognising the services received. Instead, it continues to recognise the services received over the three-year period based on the original vesting conditions. Hence, the entity ultimately recognises cumulative remuneration expense of CU180,000 over the three-year period (12 employees × 1,000 options × CU15).

The same result would have occurred if, instead of modifying the performance target, the entity had increased the number of years of service required for the share options to vest from three years to ten years. Because such a modification would make it less likely that the options will vest, which would not be beneficial to the employees, the entity would take no account of the modified service condition when recognising the services received. Instead, it would recognise the services received from the twelve employees who remained in service over the original three-year vesting period.

IG Example 9

Grant of shares, with a cash alternative subsequently added

Background

At the beginning of year 1, the entity grants 10,000 shares with a fair value of CU33 per share to a senior executive, conditional upon the completion of three years' service. By the end of year 2, the share price has dropped to CU25 per share. At that date, the entity adds a cash alternative to the grant, whereby the executive can choose whether to receive 10,000 shares or cash equal to the value of 10,000 shares on vesting date. The share price is CU22 on vesting date.

Application of requirements

Paragraph 27 of the Standard requires, irrespective of any modifications to the terms and conditions on which the equity instruments were granted, or a cancellation or settlement of that grant of equity instruments, the entity to recognise, as a minimum, the services received measured at the grant date fair value of the equity instruments granted, unless those equity instruments do not vest because of failure to satisfy a vesting condition (other than a market condition) that was specified at grant date. Therefore, the entity recognises the services received over the three-year period, based on the grant date fair value of the shares.

Furthermore, the addition of the cash alternative at the end of year 2 creates an obligation to settle in cash. In accordance with the requirements for cash-settled share-based payment transactions (paragraphs 30–33 of the Standard), the entity recognises the liability to settle in cash at the modification date, based on the fair value of the shares at the modification date and the extent to which the specified services have been received. Furthermore, the entity remeasures the fair value of the liability at the end of each reporting period and at the date of settlement, with any changes in fair value recognised in profit or loss for the period. Therefore, the entity recognises the following amounts:

Year	Calculation	Expense CU	Equity CU	Liability CU
1	Remuneration expense for year: 10,000 shares × CU33 × $^1/_3$	110,000	110,000	
2	Remuneration expense for year: (10,000 shares × CU33 × $^2/_3$) – CU110,000	110,000	110,000	
	Reclassify equity to liabilities: 10,000 shares × CU25 × $^2/_3$		(166,667)	166,667
3	Remuneration expense for year: (10,000 shares × CU33 × $^3/_3$) – CU220,000	110,000[a]	26,667	83,333
	Adjust liability to closing fair value: (CU166,667 + CU83,333) – (CU22 × 10,000 shares)	(30,000)		(30,000)
	Total	300,000	80,000	220,000

[a] Allocated between liabilities and equity, to bring in the final third of the liability based on the fair value of the shares as at the date of the modification.

AASB

IG15A If a share-based payment has a non-vesting condition that the counterparty can choose not to meet and the counterparty does not meet that non-vesting condition during the vesting period, paragraph 28A of the Standard requires that event to be treated as a cancellation. Example 9A illustrates the accounting for this type of event.

IG Example 9A

Share-based payment with vesting and non-vesting conditions when the counterparty can choose whether the non-vesting condition is met

Background

An entity grants an employee the opportunity to participate in a plan in which the employee obtains share options if he agrees to save 25 per cent of his monthly salary of CU400 for a three-year period. The monthly payments are made by deduction from the employee's salary. The employee may use the accumulated savings to exercise his options at the end of three years, or take a refund of his contributions at any point during the three-year period. The estimated annual expense for the share-based payment arrangement is CU120.

After 18 months, the employee stops paying contributions to the plan and takes a refund of contributions paid to date of CU1,800.

Application of requirements

There are three components to this plan: paid salary, salary deduction paid to the savings plan and share-based payment. The entity recognises an expense in respect of each component and a corresponding increase in liability or equity as appropriate. The requirement to pay contributions to the plan is a non-vesting condition, which the employee chooses not to meet in the second year. Therefore, in accordance with paragraphs 28(b) and 28A of the Standard, the repayment of contributions is treated as an extinguishment of the liability and the cessation of contributions in year 2 is treated as a cancellation.

YEAR 1	Expense	Cash	Liability	Equity
	CU	CU	CU	CU
Paid salary	3,600			
	(75% × 400 × 12)	(3,600)		
Salary deduction paid to the savings plan	1,200			
	(25% × 400 × 12)		(1,200)	
Share-based payment	120			(120)
Total	4,920	(3,600)	(1,200)	(120)

YEAR 2	Expense	Cash	Liability	Equity
Paid salary	4,200			
	(75% × 400 × 6 + 100% × 400 × 6)	(4,200)		
Salary deduction paid to the savings plan	600			
	(25% × 400 × 6)		(600)	
Refund of contributions to the employee		(1,800)	1800	
Share-based payment (acceleration of remaining expense)	240			(240)
	(120 × 3 − 120)			
Total	5,040	(6,000)	1,200	(240)

IG16 Paragraph 24 of the Standard requires that, in rare cases only, in which the Standard requires the entity to measure an equity-settled share-based payment transaction by reference to the fair value of the equity instruments granted, but the entity is unable to estimate reliably that fair value at the specified measurement date (eg grant date, for transactions with employees), the entity shall instead measure the transaction using an intrinsic value measurement method. Paragraph 24 also contains requirements on how to apply this method. The following example illustrates these requirements.

IG Example 10

Grant of share options that is accounted for by applying the intrinsic value method

Background

At the beginning of year 1, an entity grants 1,000 share options to 50 employees. The share options will vest at the end of year 3, provided the employees remain in service until then. The share options have a life of 10 years. The exercise price is CU60 and the entity's share price is also CU60 at the date of grant.

At the date of grant, the entity concludes that it cannot estimate reliably the fair value of the share options granted.

At the end of year 1, three employees have ceased employment and the entity estimates that a further seven employees will leave during years 2 and 3. Hence, the entity estimates that 80 per cent of the share options will vest.

Two employees leave during year 2, and the entity revises its estimate of the number of share options that it expects will vest to 86 per cent.

Two employees leave during year 3. Hence, 43,000 share options vested at the end of year 3.

The entity's share price during years 1–10, and the number of share options exercised during years 4–10, are set out below. Share options that were exercised during a particular year were all exercised at the end of that year.

Year	Share price at year-end	Number of share options exercised at year-end
1	63	0
2	65	0
3	75	0
4	88	6,000
5	100	8,000
6	90	5,000
7	96	9,000
8	105	8,000
9	108	5,000
10	115	2,000

Application of requirements

In accordance with paragraph 24 of the Standard, the entity recognises the following amounts in years 1–10.

AASB

Year	Calculation	Expense for period CU	Cumulative expense CU
1	50,000 options × 80% × (CU63 – CU60) × $^1/_3$ years	40,000	40,000
2	50,000 options × 86% × (CU65 – CU60) × $^2/_3$ years – CU40,000	103,333	143,333
3	43,000 options × (CU75 – CU60) – CU143,333	501,667	645,000
4	37,000 outstanding options × (CU88 – CU75) + 6,000 exercised options × (CU88 – CU75)	559,000	1,204,000
5	29,000 outstanding options × (CU100 – CU88) + 8,000 exercised options × (CU100 – CU88)	444,000	1,648,000
6	24,000 outstanding options × (CU90 – CU100) + 5,000 exercised options × (CU90 – CU100)	(290,000)	1,358,000
7	15,000 outstanding options × (CU96 – CU90) + 9,000 exercised options × (CU96 – CU90)	144,000	1,502,000
8	7,000 outstanding options × (CU105 – CU96) + 8,000 exercised options × (CU105 – CU96)	135,000	1,637,000
9	2,000 outstanding options × (CU108 – CU105) + 5,000 exercised options × (CU108 – CU105)	21,000	1,658,000
10	2,000 exercised options × (CU115 – CU108)	14,000	1,672,000

IG17   There are many different types of employee share and share option plans. The following example illustrates the application of AASB 2 to one particular type of plan—an employee share purchase plan. Typically, an employee share purchase plan provides employees with the opportunity to purchase the entity's shares at a discounted price. The terms and conditions under which employee share purchase plans operate differ from country to country. That is to say, not only are there many different types of employee share and share options plans, there are also many different types of employee share purchase plans. Therefore, the following example illustrates the application of AASB 2 to one specific employee share purchase plan.

IG Example 11

Employee share purchase plan

Background

An entity offers all its 1,000 employees the opportunity to participate in an employee share purchase plan. The employees have two weeks to decide whether to accept the offer. Under the terms of the plan, the employees are entitled to purchase a maximum of 100 shares each. The purchase price will be 20 per cent less than the market price of the entity's shares at the date the offer is accepted, and the purchase price must be paid immediately upon acceptance of the offer. All shares purchased must be held in trust for the employees, and cannot be sold for five years. The employee is not permitted to withdraw from the plan during that period. For example, if the employee ceases employment during the five-year period, the shares must nevertheless remain in the plan until the end of the five-year period. Any dividends paid during the five-year period will be held in trust for the employees until the end of the five-year period.

In total, 800 employees accept the offer and each employee purchases, on average, 80 shares, ie the employees purchase a total of 64,000 shares. The weighted-average market price of the shares at the purchase date is CU30 per share, and the weighted-average purchase price is CU24 per share.

Application of requirements

For transactions with employees, AASB 2 requires the transaction amount to be measured by reference to the fair value of the equity instruments granted (AASB 2, paragraph 11). To apply this requirement, it is necessary first to determine the type of equity instrument granted to the employees. Although the plan is described as an employee share purchase plan (ESPP), some ESPPs include option features and are therefore, in effect, share option plans. For example, an ESPP might include a 'look-back feature', whereby the employee is able to purchase shares at a discount, and choose whether the discount is applied to the entity's share price at the date of grant or its share price at the date of purchase. Or an ESPP might specify the purchase price, and then allow the employees a significant period of time to decide whether to participate in the plan. Another example of an option feature is an ESPP that permits the participating employees to cancel their participation before or at the end of a specified period and obtain a refund of amounts previously paid into the plan.

However, in this example, the plan includes no option features. The discount is applied to the share price at the purchase date, and the employees are not permitted to withdraw from the plan.

Another factor to consider is the effect of post-vesting transfer restrictions, if any. Paragraph B3 of AASB 2 states that, if shares are subject to restrictions on transfer after vesting date, that factor should be taken into account when estimating the fair value of those shares, but only to the extent that the post-vesting restrictions affect the price that a knowledgeable, willing market participant would pay for that share. For example, if the shares are actively traded in a deep and liquid market, post-vesting transfer restrictions may have little, if any, effect on the price that a knowledgeable, willing market participant would pay for those shares.

In this example, the shares are vested when purchased, but cannot be sold for five years after the date of purchase. Therefore, the entity should consider the valuation effect of the five-year post-vesting transfer restriction. This entails using a valuation technique to estimate what the price of the restricted share would have been on the purchase date in an arm's length transaction between knowledgeable, willing parties. Suppose that, in this example, the entity estimates that the fair value of each restricted share is CU28. In this case, the fair value of the equity instruments granted is CU4 per share (being the fair value of the restricted share of CU28 less the purchase price of CU24). Because 64,000 shares were purchased, the total fair value of the equity instruments granted is CU256,000.

In this example, there is no vesting period. Therefore, in accordance with paragraph 14 of AASB 2, the entity should recognise an expense of CU256,000 immediately.

However, in some cases, the expense relating to an ESPP might not be material. AASB 108 *Accounting Policies, Changes in Accounting Policies and Errors* states that the accounting policies in Australian Accounting Standards need not be applied when the effect of applying them is immaterial (AASB 108, paragraph 8). AASB 108 also states that an omission or misstatement of an item is material if it could, individually or collectively, influence the economic decisions that users make on the basis of the financial statements. Materiality depends on the size and nature of the omission or misstatement judged in the surrounding circumstances. The size or nature of the item, or a combination of both, could be the determining factor (AASB 108, paragraph 5). Therefore, in this example, the entity should consider whether the expense of CU256,000 is material.

AASB

Cash-settled share-based payment transactions

IG18 Paragraphs 30–33 of the Standard set out requirements for transactions in which an entity acquires goods or services by incurring liabilities to the supplier of those goods or services in amounts based on the price of the entity's shares or other equity instruments. The entity is required to recognise initially the goods or services acquired, and a liability to pay for those goods or services, when the entity obtains the goods or as the services are rendered, measured at the fair value of the liability. Thereafter, until the liability is settled, the entity is required to recognise changes in the fair value of the liability.

IG19 For example, an entity might grant share appreciation rights to employees as part of their remuneration package, whereby the employees will become entitled to a future cash payment (rather than an equity instrument), based on the increase in the entity's share price from a specified level over a specified period of time. If the share appreciation rights do not vest until the employees have completed a specified period of service, the entity recognises the services received, and a liability to pay for them, as the employees render service during that period. The liability is measured, initially and at the end of each reporting period until settled, at the fair value of the share appreciation rights in accordance with paragraphs 30–33D of AASB 2. Changes in fair value are recognised in profit or loss. Therefore, if the amount recognised for the services received was included in the carrying amount of an asset recognised in the entity's statement of financial position (for example, inventory), the carrying amount of that asset is not adjusted for the effects of the liability remeasurement. Example 12 illustrates these requirements for a cash-settled share-based payment transaction that is subject to a service condition. Example 12A illustrates these requirements for a cash-settled share-based payment transaction that is subject to a performance condition.

IG Example 12

Background

An entity grants 100 cash share appreciation rights (SARs) to each of its 500 employees, on condition that the employees remain in its employ for the next three years.

During year 1, 35 employees leave. The entity estimates that a further 60 will leave during years 2 and 3. During year 2, 40 employees leave and the entity estimates that a further 25 will leave during year 3. During year 3, 22 employees leave. At the end of year 3, 150 employees exercise their SARs, another 140 employees exercise their SARs at the end of year 4 and the remaining 113 employees exercise their SARs at the end of year 5.

The entity estimates the fair value of the SARs at the end of each year in which a liability exists as shown below. At the end of year 3, all SARs held by the remaining employees vest. The intrinsic values of the SARs at the date of exercise (which equal the cash paid out) at the end of years 3, 4 and 5 are also shown below.

Year	Fair value	Intrinsic value
1	CU14.40	
2	CU15.50	
3	CU18.20	CU15.00
4	CU21.40	CU20.00
5		CU25.00

Application of requirements

Year	Calculation	Expense CU	Liability CU
1	(500 – 95) employees × 100 SARs × CU14.40 × $^1/_3$	194,400	194,400
2	(500 – 100) employees × 100 SARs × CU15.50 × $^2/_3$ – CU194,400	218,933	413,333
3	(500 – 97 – 150) employees × 100 SARs × CU18.20 – CU413,333	47,127	460,460
	+ 150 employees × 100 SARs × CU15.00	225,000	
	Total	272,127	
4	(253 – 140) employees × 100 SARs × CU21.40 – CU460,460	(218,640)	241,820
	+ 140 employees × 100 SARs × CU20.00	280,000	
	Total	61,360	
5	CU0 – CU241,820	(241,820)	0
	+ 113 employees × 100 SARs × CU25.00	282,500	
	Total	40,680	
	Total	787,500	

IG Example 12A

Background

An entity grants 100 cash-settled share appreciation rights (SARs) to each of its 500 employees on the condition that the employees remain in its employ for the next three years and the entity reaches a revenue target (CU1 billion in sales) by the end of Year 3. The entity expects all employees to remain in its employ.

For simplicity, this example assumes that none of the employees' compensation qualifies for capitalisation as part of the cost of an asset.

At the end of Year 1, the entity expects that the revenue target will not be achieved by the end of Year 3. During Year 2, the entity's revenue increased significantly and it expects that it will continue to grow. Consequently, at the end of Year 2, the entity expects that the revenue target will be achieved by the end of Year 3.

At the end of Year 3, the revenue target is achieved and 150 employees exercise their SARs. Another 150 employees exercise their SARs at the end of Year 4 and the remaining 200 employees exercise their SARs at the end of Year 5.

Using an option pricing model, the entity estimates the fair value of the SARs, ignoring the revenue target performance condition and the employment-service condition, at the end of each year until all of the cash-settled share-based payments are settled. At the end of Year 3, all of the SARs vest. The following table shows the estimated fair value of the SARs at the end of each year and the intrinsic values of the SARs at the date of exercise (which equals the cash paid out).

Year	Fair value of one SAR	Intrinsic value of one SAR
1	CU14.40	–
2	CU15.50	–
3	CU18.20	CU15.00
4	CU21.40	CU20.00
5	CU25.00	CU25.00

Application of requirements

	Number of employees expected to satisfy the service condition	Best estimate of whether the revenue target will be met
Year 1	500	No
Year 2	500	Yes
Year 3	500	Yes

Year	Calculation	Expense	Liability
		CU	CU
1	SARs are not expected to vest: no expense is recognised	–	–
2	SARs are expected to vest: 500 employees × 100 SARs × CU15.50 × $^2/_3$	516,667	516,667
3	(500–150) employees × 100 SARs × CU18.20 × $^3/_3$ – CU516,667 120,333		637,000
	+ 150 employees × 100 SARs × CU15.00 225,000		
	Total	345,333	

AASB

4	(350–150) employees × 100 SARs × CU21.40 – CU637,000	209,000		428,000
	+ 150 employees × 100 SARs × CU20.00	300,000		
	Total		91,000	
5	(200–200) employees × 100 SARs × CU25.00 – CU428,000	(428,000)		–
	+ 200 employees × 100 SARs × CU25.00	500,000		
	Total		72,000	
	Total		1,025,000	

Share-based payment transactions with a net settlement feature for withholding tax obligations

IG19A Paragraphs 33E and 33F require an entity to classify an arrangement in its entirety as an equity-settled share-based payment transaction if it would have been so classified in the absence of a net settlement feature that obliges the entity to withhold an amount for an employee's tax obligation associated with a share-based payment. The entity transfers that amount, normally in cash, to the tax authority on the employee's behalf. Example 12B illustrates these requirements.

IG Example 12B

Background

The tax law in jurisdiction X requires entities to withhold an amount for an employee's tax obligation associated with a share-based payment and transfer that amount in cash to the tax authority on the employee's behalf.

On 1 January 20X1 an entity in jurisdiction X grants an award of 100 shares to an employee; that award is conditional upon the completion of four years' service. The entity expects that the employee will complete the service period. For simplicity, this example assumes that none of the employee's compensation qualifies for capitalisation as part of the cost of an asset.

The terms and conditions of the share-based payment arrangement require the entity to withhold shares from the settlement of the award to its employee in order to settle the employee's tax obligation (that is, the share-based payment arrangement has a 'net settlement feature'). Accordingly, the entity settles the transaction on a net basis by withholding the number of shares with a fair value equal to the monetary value of the employee's tax obligation and issuing the remaining shares to the employee on completion of the vesting period.

The employee's tax obligation associated with the award is calculated based on the fair value of the shares on the vesting date. The employee's applicable tax rate is 40 per cent.

At grant date, the fair value of each share is CU2. The fair value of each share at 31 December 20X4 is CU10.

The fair value of the shares on the vesting date is CU1,000 (100 shares × CU10 per share) and therefore the employee's tax obligation is CU400 (100 shares × CU10 × 40%). Accordingly, on the vesting date, the entity issues 60 shares to the employee and withholds 40 shares (CU400 = 40 shares × CU10 per share). The entity pays the fair value of the withheld shares in cash to the tax authority on the employee's behalf. In other words, it is as if the entity had issued all 100 vested shares to the employee, and at the same time, repurchased 40 shares at their fair value.

Application of requirements

		Dr.	Cr.	Cr.
		Expense	Equity	Liability
Year	Calculation	CU	CU	CU
1	100 shares × CU2 × $^1/_4$	50	(50)	–
2	100 shares × CU2 × $^2/_4$ – CU50	50	(50)	–
3	100 shares × CU2 × $^3/_4$ – (CU50 + CU50)	50	(50)	–
4	100 shares × CU2 × $^4/_4$ – (CU50 + CU50 + CU50)	50	(50)	–
	Total	200	(200)	–

The journal entries recorded by the entity are as follows:

During the vesting period

Accumulated compensation expense recognised over the vesting period

Dr Expense 200

Cr Equity   200

Recognition of the tax liability[a]

Dr Equity   400

Cr Liability   400

Settlement of tax obligation

Cash paid to the tax authority on the employee's behalf at the date of settlement

Dr Liability 400

Cr Cash   400

(a)   The entity considers disclosing an estimate of the amount that it expects to transfer to the tax authority at the end of each reporting period. The entity makes such disclosure when it determines that this information is necessary to inform users about the future cash flow effects associated with the share-based payment.

Accounting for a modification of a share-based payment transaction that changes its classification from cash-settled to equity-settled

IG19B   The following example illustrates the application of the requirements in paragraphs B44A of AASB 2 to a modification of the terms and conditions of a cash-settled share-based payment transaction that becomes an equity-settled share-based payment transaction.

IG Example 12C

Background

On 1 January 20X1 an entity grants 100 share appreciation rights (SARs) that will be settled in cash to each of 100 employees on the condition that employees will remain employed for the next four years.

On 31 December 20X1 the entity estimates that the fair value of each SAR is CU10 and consequently, the total fair value of the cash-settled award is CU100,000. On 31 December 20X2 the estimated fair value of each SAR is CU12 and consequently, the total fair value of the cash-settled award is CU120,000.

On 31 December 20X2 the entity cancels the SARs and, in their place, grants 100 share options to each employee on the condition that each employee remains in its employ for the next two years. Therefore the original vesting period is not changed. On this date the fair value of each share option is CU13.20 and consequently, the total fair value of the new grant is CU132,000. All of the employees are expected to and ultimately do provide the required service.

For simplicity, this example assumes that none of the employees' compensation qualifies for capitalisation as part of the cost of an asset.

Application of requirements

At the modification date (31 December 20X2), the entity applies paragraph B44A. Accordingly:

(a) from the date of the modification, the share options are measured by reference to their modification-date fair value and, at the modification date, the share options are recognised in equity to the extent to which the employees have rendered services;

(b) the liability for the SARs is derecognised at the modification date; and

(c) the difference between the carrying amount of the liability derecognised and the equity amount recognised at the modification date is recognised immediately in profit or loss.

At the modification date (31 December 20X2), the entity compares the fair value of the equity-settled replacement award for services provided through to the modification date (CU132,000 × 2/4 = CU66,000) with the fair value of the cash-settled original award for those services (CU120,000 × 2/4 = CU60,000). The difference (CU6,000) is recognised immediately in profit or loss at the date of the modification.

The remainder of the equity-settled share-based payment (measured at its modification-date fair value) is recognised in profit or loss over the remaining two-year vesting period from the date of the modification.

Year	Calculation	Dr. Expense CU	Cumulative expense CU	Cr. Equity CU	Cr. Liability CU
1	100 employees ×100 SARs × CU10 × $^1/_4$	25,000	–	–	25,000
2	*Remeasurement before the modification* 100 employees × 100 SARs × CU12.00 × $^2/_4$ −25,000	35,000	60,000	–	35,000
	Derecognition of the liability, recognition of the modification-date fair value amount in equity and recognition of the effect of settlement for CU6,000 (100 employees x 100 share options × CU13.20 × $^2/_4$) – (100 employees × 100 SARs × CU12.00 × $^2/_4$)	6,000	66,000	66,000	(60,000)
3	100 employees × 100 share options × CU13.20 × $^3/_4$ – CU66,000	33,000	99,000	33,000	–
4	100 employees x 100 share options × CU13.20 × $^4/_4$ – CU99,000	33,000	132,000	33,000	–
	Total			132,000	–

Share-based payment arrangements with cash alternatives

IG20 Some employee share-based payment arrangements permit the employee to choose whether to receive cash or equity instruments. In this situation, a compound financial instrument has been granted, ie a financial instrument with debt and equity components. Paragraph 37 of the Standard requires the entity to estimate the fair value of the compound financial instrument at grant date, by first measuring the fair value of the debt component, and then measuring the fair value of the equity component—taking into account that the employee must forfeit the right to receive cash to receive the equity instrument.

IG21 Typically, share-based payment arrangements with cash alternatives are structured so that the fair value of one settlement alternative is the same as the other. For example, the employee might have the choice of receiving share options or cash share appreciation rights. In such cases, the fair value of the equity component will be zero, and hence the fair value of the compound financial instrument will be the same as the fair value of the debt component. However, if the fair values of the settlement alternatives differ, usually the fair value of the equity component will be greater than zero, in which case the fair value of the compound financial instrument will be greater than the fair value of the debt component.

IG22 Paragraph 38 of the Standard requires the entity to account separately for the services received in respect of each component of the compound financial instrument. For the debt component, the entity recognises the services received, and a liability to pay for those services, as the counterparty renders service, in accordance with the requirements applying to cash-settled share-based payment transactions. For the equity component (if any), the entity recognises the services received, and an increase in equity, as the counterparty renders service, in accordance with the requirements applying to equity-settled share-based payment transactions. Example 13 illustrates these requirements.

AASB

IG Example 13

Background

An entity grants to an employee the right to choose either 1,000 phantom shares, ie a right to a cash payment equal to the value of 1,000 shares, or 1,200 shares. The grant is conditional upon the completion of three years' service. If the employee chooses the share alternative, the shares must be held for three years after vesting date.

At grant date, the entity's share price is CU50 per share. At the end of years 1, 2 and 3, the share price is CU52, CU55 and CU60 respectively. The entity does not expect to pay dividends in the next three years. After taking into account the effects of the post-vesting transfer restrictions, the entity estimates that the grant date fair value of the share alternative is CU48 per share.

At the end of year 3, the employee chooses:

Scenario 1: The cash alternative

Scenario 2: The equity alternative

Application of requirements

The fair value of the equity alternative is CU57,600 (1,200 shares × CU48). The fair value of the cash alternative is CU50,000 (1,000 phantom shares × CU50). Therefore, the fair value of the equity component of the compound instrument is CU7,600 (CU57,600 – CU50,000).

The entity recognises the following amounts:

Year		Expense CU	Equity CU	Liability CU
1	Liability component: $(1,000 \times CU52 \times {}^1/_3)$	17,333		17,333
	Equity component: $(CU7,600 \times {}^1/_3)$	2,533	2,533	
2	Liability component: $(1,000 \times CU55 \times {}^2/_3) - CU17,333$	19,333		19,333
	Equity component: $(CU7,600 \times {}^1/_3)$	2,533	2,533	
3	Liability component: $(1,000 \times CU60) - CU36,666$	23,334		23,334
	Equity component: $(CU7,600 \times {}^1/_3)$	2,534	2,534	
End Year 3	Scenario 1: cash of CU60,000 paid			
	Scenario 1 totals	67,600	7,600	0
	Scenario 2: 1,200 shares issued		60,000	(60,000)
	Scenario 2 totals	67,600	67,600	0

Share-based payment transactions among group entities

IG22A   Paragraphs 43A and 43B of AASB 2 specify the accounting requirements for share-based payment transactions among group entities in the separate or individual financial statements of the entity receiving the goods or services. Example 14 illustrates the journal entries in the separate or individual financial statements for a group transaction in which a parent grants rights to its equity instruments to the employees of its subsidiary.

IG Example 14

Share-based payment transactions in which a parent grants rights to its equity instruments to the employees of its subsidiary

Background

A parent grants 200 share options to each of 100 employees of its subsidiary, conditional upon the completion of two years' service with the subsidiary. The fair value of the share options on grant date is CU30 each. At grant date, the subsidiary estimates that 80 per cent of the employees will complete the two-year service period. This estimate does not change during the vesting period. At the end of the vesting period, 81 employees complete the required two years of service. The parent does not require the subsidiary to pay for the shares needed to settle the grant of share options.

Application of requirements

As required by paragraph B53 of the Standard, over the two-year vesting period, the subsidiary measures the services received from the employees in accordance with the requirements applicable to equity-settled share-based payment transactions. Thus, the subsidiary measures the services received from the employees on the basis of the fair value of the share options at grant date. An increase in equity is recognised as a contribution from the parent in the separate or individual financial statements of the subsidiary.

The journal entries recorded by the subsidiary for each of the two years are as follows:

Year 1

Dr Remuneration expense (200 × 100 × CU30 × 0.8/2)	CU240,000	
Cr Equity (Contribution from the parent)		
Year 2		CU240,000
Dr Remuneration expense (200 × 100 × CU30 × 0.81 – 240,000)	CU246,000	
Cr Equity (Contribution from the parent)		CU246,000

Illustrative disclosures

IG23 The following example illustrates the disclosure requirements in paragraphs 44–52 of the Standard.[10]

Extract from the Notes to the Financial Statements of Company Z for the year ended 31 December 20X5.

Share-based Payment

During the period ended 31 December 20X5, the Company had four share-based payment arrangements, which are described below.

Type of arrangement	Senior management share option plan	General employee share option plan	Executive share plan	Senior management share appreciation cash plan
Date of grant	1 January 20X4	1 January 20X5	1 January 20X5	1 July 20X5
Number granted	50,000	75,000	50,000	25,000
Contractual life	10 years	10 years	N/A	10 years
Vesting conditions	1.5 years' service and achievement of a share price target, which was achieved.	Three years' service.	Three years' service and achievement of a target growth in earnings per share.	Three years' service and achievement of a target increase in market share.

The estimated fair value of each share option granted in the general employee share option plan is CU23.60. This was calculated by applying a binomial option pricing model. The model inputs were the share price at grant date of CU50, exercise price of CU50, expected volatility of 30 per cent, no expected dividends, contractual life of ten years, and a risk-free interest rate of 5 per cent. To allow for the effects of early exercise, it was assumed that the employees would exercise the options after vesting date when the share price was twice the exercise price. Historical volatility was 40 per cent, which includes the early years of the Company's life; the Company expects the volatility of its share price to reduce as it matures.

The estimated fair value of each share granted in the executive share plan is CU50.00, which is equal to the share price at the date of grant.

---

10 Note that the illustrative example is not intended to be a template or model and is therefore not exhaustive. For example, it does not illustrate the disclosure requirements in paragraphs 47(c), 48 and 49 of the Standard.

Further details of the two share option plans are as follows:

	20X4		20X5	
	Number of options	Weighted average exercise price	Number of options	Weighted average exercise price
Outstanding at start of year	0	–	45,000	CU40
Granted	50,000	CU40	75,000	CU50
Forfeited	(5,000)	CU40	(8,000)	CU46
Exercised	0	–	(4,000)	CU40
Outstanding at end of year	45,000	CU40	108,000	CU46
Exercisable at end of year	0	CU40	38,000	CU40

The weighted average share price at the date of exercise for share options exercised during the period was CU52. The options outstanding at 31 December 20X5 had an exercise price of CU40 or CU50, and a weighted average remaining contractual life of 8.64 years.

	20X4	20X5
	CU	CU
Expense arising from share-based payment transactions	495,000	1,105,867
Expense arising from share and share option plans	495,000	1,007,000
Closing balance of liability for cash share appreciation plan	–	98,867
Expense arising from increase in fair value of liability for cash share appreciation plan	–	9,200

Summary of conditions for a counterparty to receive an equity instrument granted and of accounting treatments

IG24 The table below categorises, with examples, the various conditions that determine whether a counterparty receives an equity instrument granted and the accounting treatment of share-based payments with those conditions.

Summary of conditions that determine whether a counterparty receives an equity instrument granted

	VESTING CONDITIONS			NON-VESTING CONDITIONS		
		Performance conditions				
	Service conditions	Performance conditions that are market conditions	Other performance conditions	Neither the entity nor the counterparty can choose whether the condition is met	Counterparty can choose whether to meet the condition	Entity can choose whether to meet the condition
Example conditions	Requirement to remain in service for three years	Target based on the market price of the entity's equity instruments	Target based on a successful initial public offering with a specified service requirement	Target based on a commodity index	Paying contributions towards the exercise price of a share-based payment	Continuation of the plan by the entity
Include in grant-date fair value?	No	Yes	No	Yes	Yes	Yes[a]
	(paragraph 19)	(paragraph 21)	(paragraph 19)	(paragraph 21A)	(paragraph 28A)	(paragraph 28A)
Accounting treatment if the condition is not met after the grant date and during the vesting period	Forfeiture. The entity revises the expense to reflect the best available estimate of the number of equity instruments expected to vest.	No change to accounting. The entity continues to recognise the expense over the remainder of the vesting period.	Forfeiture. The entity revises the expense to reflect the best available estimate of the number of equity instruments expected to vest.	No change to accounting. The entity continues to recognise the expense over the remainder of the vesting period.	Cancellation. The entity recognises immediately the amount of the expense that would otherwise have been recognised over the remainder of the vesting period.	Cancellation. The entity recognises immediately the amount of the expense that would otherwise have been recognised over the remainder of the vesting period.
	(paragraph 19)	(paragraph 21)	(paragraph 19)	(paragraph 21A)	(paragraph 28A)	(paragraph 28A)

(a) In the calculation of the fair value of the share-based payment, the probability of continuation of the plan by the entity is assumed to be 100 per cent.

AASB

COMPILATION DETAILS

Accounting Standard AASB 2 *Share-based Payment*

Compilation details are not part of AASB 2.

This compiled Standard applies to annual periods beginning on or after 1 January 2018. It takes into account amendments up to and including 12 December 2017 and was prepared on 20 April 2018 by the staff of the Australian Accounting Standards Board (AASB).

This compilation is not a separate Accounting Standard made by the AASB. Instead, it is a representation of AASB 2 (July 2015) as amended by other Accounting Standards, which are listed in the Table below.

Table of Standards

Standard	Date made	FRL identifier	Commencement date	Effective date *(annual periods ... on or after ...)*	Application, saving or transitional provisions
AASB 2	24 Jul 2015	F2015L01603	31 Dec 2017	*(beginning)* 1 Jan 2018	see (a) below
AASB 2016-5	21 Jul 2016	F2016L01237	31 Dec 2017	*(beginning)* 1 Jan 2018	see (b) below
AASB 2017-5	12 Dec 2017	F2018L00067	31 Dec 2017	*(beginning)* 1 Jan 2018	see (b) below

(a)   Entities may elect to apply this Standard to annual periods beginning after 24 July 2014 but before 1 January 2018.

(b)   Entities may elect to apply this Standard to annual periods beginning before 1 January 2018.

Table of amendments

Paragraph affected	How affected	By ... [paragraph/page]
19	amended	AASB 2016-5 [page 5]
30-31	amended	AASB 2016-5 [page 6]
33	amended	AASB 2016-5 [page 6]
33A-33H (and headings)	added	AASB 2016-5 [page 6]
52	amended	AASB 2016-5 [page 7]
Aus52.1	amended	AASB 2016-5 [page 7]
59A-59B	added	AASB 2016-5 [page 7]
63D	added	AASB 2016-5 [page 8]
B44A-B44C (and heading)	added	AASB 2016-5 [page 8]
IG19	amended amended amended (Example 12A)	AASB 2016-5 [page 9] AASB 2017-5 [16] AASB 2017-5 [17]
IG19A (preceding heading)	amended	AASB 2017-5 [18]
IG19A-IG19B (and headings)	added	AASB 2016-5 [page 10]
IG19A	amended (Example 12B)	AASB 2017-5 [19]
IG19B	amended (Example 12C)	AASB 2017-5 [20]

DELETED IFRS 2 TEXT

Deleted IFRS 2 text is not part of AASB 2.

61 IFRS 3 (as revised in 2008) and *Improvements to IFRSs* issued in April 2009 amended paragraph 5. An entity shall apply those amendments for annual periods beginning on or after 1 July 2009. Earlier application is permitted. If an entity applies IFRS 3 (revised 2008) for an earlier period, the amendments shall also be applied for that earlier period.

62 An entity shall apply the following amendments retrospectively in annual periods beginning on or after 1 January 2009:

    (a) the requirements in paragraph 21A in respect of the treatment of non-vesting conditions;

    (b) the revised definitions of 'vest' and 'vesting conditions' in Appendix A;

    (c) the amendments in paragraphs 28 and 28A in respect of cancellations.

Earlier application is permitted. If an entity applies these amendments for a period beginning before 1 January 2009, it shall disclose that fact.

63 An entity shall apply the following amendments made by *Group Cash-settled Share-based Payment Transactions* issued in June 2009 retrospectively, subject to the transitional provisions in paragraphs 53–59, in accordance with IAS 8 *Accounting Policies, Changes in Accounting Estimates and Errors* for annual periods beginning on or after 1 January 2010:

    (a) the amendment of paragraph 2, the deletion of paragraph 3 and the addition of paragraphs 3A and 43A–43D and of paragraphs B45, B47, B50, B54, B56–B58 and B60 in Appendix B in respect of the accounting for transactions among group entities.

    (b) the revised definitions in Appendix A of the following terms:

        • cash-settled share-based payment transaction,

        • equity-settled share-based payment transaction,

        • share-based payment arrangement, and

        • share-based payment transaction.

If the information necessary for retrospective application is not available, an entity shall reflect in its separate or individual financial statements the amounts previously recognised in the group's consolidated financial statements. Earlier application is permitted. If an entity applies the amendments for a period beginning before 1 January 2010, it shall disclose that fact.

63A IFRS 10 *Consolidated Financial Statements* and IFRS 11, issued in May 2011, amended paragraph 5 and Appendix A. An entity shall apply those amendments when it applies IFRS 10 and IFRS 11.

63B *Annual Improvements to IFRSs 2010–2012 Cycle*, issued in December 2013, amended paragraphs 15 and 19. In Appendix A, the definitions of 'vesting conditions' and 'market condition' were amended and the definitions of 'performance condition' and '*service condition*' were added. An entity shall prospectively apply that amendment to share-based payment transactions for which the grant date is on or after 1 July 2014. Earlier application is permitted. If an entity applies that amendment for an earlier period it shall disclose that fact.

64 *Group Cash-settled Share-based Payment Transactions* issued in June 2009 supersedes IFRIC 8 *Scope of IFRS 2* and IFRIC 11 *IFRS 2—Group and Treasury Share Transactions*. The amendments made by that document incorporated the previous requirements set out in IFRIC 8 and IFRIC 11 as follows:

    (a) amended paragraph 2 and added paragraph 13A in respect of the accounting for transactions in which the entity cannot identify specifically some or all of

AASB

the goods or services received. Those requirements were effective for annual periods beginning on or after 1 May 2006.

(b)   added paragraphs B46, B48, B49, B51–B53, B55, B59 and B61 in Appendix B in respect of the accounting for transactions among group entities. Those requirements were effective for annual periods beginning on or after 1 March 2007.

Those requirements were applied retrospectively in accordance with the requirements of IAS 8, subject to the transitional provisions of IFRS 2.

AASB 3
Business Combinations
(Reissued August 2015)

This note is not part of Accounting Standard AASB 3.

The following unincorporated amendments are not included in this Standard.

- AASB 2018-1 *Amendments to Australian Accounting Standards — Annual Improvements 2015–2017 Cycle*. This Standard makes amendments to AASB 3 *Business Combinations*, AASB 11 *Joint Arrangements*, AASB 112 *Income Taxes* and AASB 123 *Borrowing Costs*. These amendments arise from the issuance of IFRS *Annual Improvements to IFRS Standards 2015–2017 Cycle* by the IASB in December 2017. This Standard applies to annual periods beginning on or after 1 January 2019, but earlier application is permitted.

- AASB 16 *Leases* — Appendix D sets out the amendments to other Standards that are a consequence of the AASB issuing this Standard. It is applicable from 1 January 2019. Earlier application is permitted, but entities must apply AASB 15 *Revenue from Contracts with Customers* before applying this Standard.

- AASB 17 *Insurance Contracts* — Appendix D sets out the amendments to other Standards that are a consequence of the AASB issuing AASB 17 *Insurance Contracts*. This Standard is applicable from 1 January 2021. Earlier application is permitted, but entities must apply AASB 9 *Financial Instruments* and AASB 15 *Revenue from Contracts with Customers* first.

- AASB 2016-7 *Amendments to Australian Accounting Standards — Deferral of AASB 15 for Not-for-Profit Entities*. This Standard defers the consequential amendments that were originally set out in AASB 2014-5 *Amendments to Australian Accounting Standards arising from AASB 15,* by restating the effective date of the amendments set out in AASB 2015-8 *Amendments to Australian Accounting Standards* for not-for-profit entities. This Standard defers the application of AASB 15 to 1 January 2019. Earlier application is permitted provided AASB 1058 is also applied to the same period.

Entities early-adopting any amendments with later application dates will need to refer to the amending Standards that have not yet been incorporated into compilations. The abovementioned unincorporated amendments may be located on the AASB website at www.aasb.gov.au or on the Federal Register of Legislation website at www.legislation.gov.au.

AASB

CONTENTS

COMPARISON WITH IFRS 3
ACCOUNTING STANDARD
AASB 3 *BUSINESS COMBINATIONS*

APPENDICES
A. DEFINED TERMS
B. APPLICATION GUIDANCE
C. AUSTRALIAN REDUCED DISCLOSURE REQUIREMENTS

DELETED IFRS 3 TEXT
BASIS FOR CONCLUSIONS ON AASB 2008-11

ILLUSTRATIVE EXAMPLES (available on the AASB website)
BASIS FOR CONCLUSIONS ON IFRS 3 (available on the AASB website)

Australian Accounting Standard AASB 3 *Business Combinations* is set out in paragraphs 1 – Aus68.2 and Appendices A – C. All the paragraphs have equal authority. Paragraphs in **bold type** state the main principles. Terms defined in Appendix A are in *italics* the first time they appear in the Standard. AASB 3 is to be read in the context of other Australian Accounting Standards, including AASB 1048 *Interpretation of Standards*, which identifies the Australian Accounting Interpretations, and AASB 1057 *Application of Australian Accounting Standards*. In the absence of explicit guidance, AASB 108 *Accounting Policies, Changes in Accounting Estimates and Errors* provides a basis for selecting and applying accounting policies.

COMPARISON WITH IFRS 3

AASB 3 *Business Combinations* incorporates IFRS 3 *Business Combinations* issued by the International Accounting Standards Board (IASB). Australian-specific paragraphs (which are not included in IFRS 3) are identified with the prefix "Aus" or "RDR". Paragraphs that apply only to not-for-profit entities begin by identifying their limited applicability.

Tier 1

For-profit entities complying with AASB 3 also comply with IFRS 3.

Not-for-profit entities' compliance with IFRS 3 will depend on whether any "Aus" paragraphs that specifically apply to not-for-profit entities provide additional guidance or contain applicable requirements that are inconsistent with IFRS 3.

Tier 2

Entities preparing general purpose financial statements under Australian Accounting Standards – Reduced Disclosure Requirements (Tier 2) will not be in compliance with IFRSs.

AASB 1053 *Application of Tiers of Australian Accounting Standards* explains the two tiers of reporting requirements.

ACCOUNTING STANDARD AASB 3

The Australian Accounting Standards Board makes Accounting Standard AASB 3 *Business Combinations* under section 334 of the *Corporations Act 2001*.

Kris Peach
Dated 7 August 2015   Chair – AASB

ACCOUNTING STANDARD AASB 3
BUSINESS COMBINATIONS

Objective

1   The objective of this Standard is to improve the relevance, reliability and comparability of the information that a reporting entity provides in its financial statements about a *business combination* and its effects. To accomplish that, this Standard establishes principles and requirements for how the *acquirer*:

   (a)   recognises and measures in its financial statements the *identifiable* assets acquired, the liabilities assumed and any *non-controlling interest* in the *acquiree*;

   (b)   recognises and measures the *goodwill* acquired in the business combination or a gain from a bargain purchase; and

   (c)   determines what information to disclose to enable users of the financial statements to evaluate the nature and financial effects of the business combination.

Aus1.1   Where assets and liabilities are transferred to a local government from
                another local government at no cost, or for nominal consideration, pursuant
                to legislation, ministerial directive or other externally imposed requirement,
                paragraphs Aus63.1–Aus63.9 shall be applied.

Scope

2   This Standard applies to a transaction or other event that meets the definition of a
                business combination. This Standard does not apply to:

(a)   the accounting for the formation of a joint arrangement in the financial
                statements of the joint arrangement itself.

(b)   the acquisition of an asset or a group of assets that does not constitute a
                business. In such cases the acquirer shall identify and recognise the individual
                identifiable assets acquired (including those assets that meet the definition of,
                and recognition criteria for, *intangible assets* in AASB 138 *Intangible Assets*)
                and liabilities assumed. The cost of the group shall be allocated to the individual
                identifiable assets and liabilities on the basis of their relative *fair values* at the
                date of purchase. Such a transaction or event does not give rise to goodwill.

(c)   a combination of entities or businesses under common control (paragraphs B1–
                B4 provide related application guidance).

Aus2.1   A restructure of administrative arrangements, as defined in Appendix A of
                AASB 1004 *Contributions*, is outside the scope of this Standard. AASB 1004
                specifies requirements for restructures of administrative arrangements.

2A   The requirements of this Standard do not apply to the acquisition by an investment
                entity, as defined in AASB 10 *Consolidated Financial Statements*, of an investment in
                a subsidiary that is required to be measured at fair value through profit or loss.

Identifying a business combination

3   **An entity shall determine whether a transaction or other event is a business
                combination by applying the definition in this Standard, which requires that the
                assets acquired and liabilities assumed constitute a business. If the assets acquired
                are not a business, the reporting entity shall account for the transaction or other
                event as an asset acquisition. Paragraphs B5–B12 provide guidance on identifying
                a business combination and the definition of a business.**

The acquisition method

4   **An entity shall account for each business combination by applying the acquisition
                method.**

5   Applying the acquisition method requires:

(a)   identifying the acquirer;

(b)   determining the *acquisition date*;

(c)   recognising and measuring the identifiable assets acquired, the liabilities
                assumed and any non-controlling interest in the acquiree; and

(d)   recognising and measuring goodwill or a gain from a bargain purchase.

Identifying the acquirer

6   **For each business combination, one of the combining entities shall be identified
                as the acquirer.**

7   The guidance in AASB 10 shall be used to identify the acquirer—the entity that obtains
                control of another entity, ie the acquiree. If a business combination has occurred but
                applying the guidance in AASB 10 does not clearly indicate which of the combining

entities is the acquirer, the factors in paragraphs B14–B18 shall be considered in making that determination.

Determining the acquisition date

8 **The acquirer shall identify the acquisition date, which is the date on which it obtains control of the acquiree.**

9 The date on which the acquirer obtains control of the acquiree is generally the date on which the acquirer legally transfers the consideration, acquires the assets and assumes the liabilities of the acquiree—the closing date. However, the acquirer might obtain control on a date that is either earlier or later than the closing date. For example, the acquisition date precedes the closing date if a written agreement provides that the acquirer obtains control of the acquiree on a date before the closing date. An acquirer shall consider all pertinent facts and circumstances in identifying the acquisition date.

Recognising and measuring the identifiable assets acquired, the liabilities assumed and any non-controlling interest in the acquiree

Recognition principle

10 **As of the acquisition date, the acquirer shall recognise, separately from goodwill, the identifiable assets acquired, the liabilities assumed and any non-controlling interest in the acquiree. Recognition of identifiable assets acquired and liabilities assumed is subject to the conditions specified in paragraphs 11 and 12.**

Recognition conditions

11 To qualify for recognition as part of applying the acquisition method, the identifiable assets acquired and liabilities assumed must meet the definitions of assets and liabilities in the *Framework for the Preparation and Presentation of Financial Statements* (as identified in AASB 1048 *Interpretation of Standards*)[1] at the acquisition date. For example, costs the acquirer expects but is not obliged to incur in the future to effect its plan to exit an activity of an acquiree or to terminate the employment of or relocate an acquiree's employees are not liabilities at the acquisition date. Therefore, the acquirer does not recognise those costs as part of applying the acquisition method. Instead, the acquirer recognises those costs in its post-combination financial statements in accordance with other Australian Accounting Standards.

12 In addition, to qualify for recognition as part of applying the acquisition method, the identifiable assets acquired and liabilities assumed must be part of what the acquirer and the acquiree (or its former *owners*) exchanged in the business combination transaction rather than the result of separate transactions. The acquirer shall apply the guidance in paragraphs 51–53 to determine which assets acquired or liabilities assumed are part of the exchange for the acquiree and which, if any, are the result of separate transactions to be accounted for in accordance with their nature and the applicable Australian Accounting Standards.

13 The acquirer's application of the recognition principle and conditions may result in recognising some assets and liabilities that the acquiree had not previously recognised as assets and liabilities in its financial statements. For example, the acquirer recognises the acquired identifiable intangible assets, such as a brand name, a patent or a customer relationship, that the acquiree did not recognise as assets in its financial statements because it developed them internally and charged the related costs to expense.

14 Paragraphs B28–B40 provide guidance on recognising operating leases and intangible assets. Paragraphs 22–28 specify the types of identifiable assets and liabilities that include items for which this Standard provides limited exceptions to the recognition principle and conditions.

AASB

---

1 In December 2013 the AASB amended the *Framework for the Preparation and Presentation of Financial Statements*.

Classifying or designating identifiable assets acquired and liabilities assumed in a business combination

15   At the acquisition date, the acquirer shall classify or designate the identifiable assets acquired and liabilities assumed as necessary to apply other Australian Accounting Standards subsequently. The acquirer shall make those classifications or designations on the basis of the contractual terms, economic conditions, its operating or accounting policies and other pertinent conditions as they exist at the acquisition date.

16   In some situations, Australian Accounting Standards provide for different accounting depending on how an entity classifies or designates a particular asset or liability. Examples of classifications or designations that the acquirer shall make on the basis of the pertinent conditions as they exist at the acquisition date include but are not limited to:

(a)   classification of particular financial assets and liabilities as measured at fair value through profit or loss or at amortised cost, or as a financial asset measured at fair value through other comprehensive income in accordance with AASB 9 *Financial Instruments*;

(b)   designation of a derivative instrument as a hedging instrument in accordance with AASB 9; and

(c)   assessment of whether an embedded derivative should be separated from a host contract in accordance with AASB 9 (which is a matter of 'classification' as this Standard uses that term).

17   This Standard provides two exceptions to the principle in paragraph 15:

(a)   classification of a lease contract as either an operating lease or a finance lease in accordance with AASB 117 *Leases*; and

(b)   classification of a contract as an insurance contract in accordance with AASB 4 *Insurance Contracts*.

The acquirer shall classify those contracts on the basis of the contractual terms and other factors at the inception of the contract (or, if the terms of the contract have been modified in a manner that would change its classification, at the date of that modification, which might be the acquisition date).

Measurement principle

18   The acquirer shall measure the identifiable assets acquired and the liabilities assumed at their acquisition-date fair values.

19   For each business combination, the acquirer shall measure at the acquisition date components of non-controlling interests in the acquiree that are present ownership interests and entitle their holders to a proportionate share of the entity's net assets in the event of liquidation at either:

(a)   fair value; or

(b)   the present ownership instruments' proportionate share in the recognised amounts of the acquiree's identifiable net assets.

All other components of non-controlling interests shall be measured at their acquisition-date fair values, unless another measurement basis is required by Australian Accounting Standards.

20   Paragraphs 24–31 specify the types of identifiable assets and liabilities that include items for which this Standard provides limited exceptions to the measurement principle.

Exceptions to the recognition or measurement principles

21   This Standard provides limited exceptions to its recognition and measurement principles. Paragraphs 22–31 specify both the particular items for which exceptions

are provided and the nature of those exceptions. The acquirer shall account for those items by applying the requirements in paragraphs 22–31, which will result in some items being:

(a)   recognised either by applying recognition conditions in addition to those in paragraphs 11 and 12 or by applying the requirements of other Australian Accounting Standards, with results that differ from applying the recognition principle and conditions.

(b)   measured at an amount other than their acquisition-date fair values.

Exception to the recognition principle
Contingent liabilities

22   AASB 137 *Provisions, Contingent Liabilities and Contingent Assets* defines a contingent liability as:

(a)   a possible obligation that arises from past events and whose existence will be confirmed only by the occurrence or non-occurrence of one or more uncertain future events not wholly within the control of the entity; or

(b)   a present obligation that arises from past events but is not recognised because:

(i)   it is not probable that an outflow of resources embodying economic benefits will be required to settle the obligation; or

(ii)   the amount of the obligation cannot be measured with sufficient reliability.

23   The requirements in AASB 137 do not apply in determining which contingent liabilities to recognise as of the acquisition date. Instead, the acquirer shall recognise as of the acquisition date a contingent liability assumed in a business combination if it is a present obligation that arises from past events and its fair value can be measured reliably. Therefore, contrary to AASB 137, the acquirer recognises a contingent liability assumed in a business combination at the acquisition date even if it is not probable that an outflow of resources embodying economic benefits will be required to settle the obligation. Paragraph 56 provides guidance on the subsequent accounting for contingent liabilities.

Exceptions to both the recognition and measurement principles
Income taxes

24   The acquirer shall recognise and measure a deferred tax asset or liability arising from the assets acquired and liabilities assumed in a business combination in accordance with AASB 112 *Income Taxes*.

25   The acquirer shall account for the potential tax effects of temporary differences and carryforwards of an acquiree that exist at the acquisition date or arise as a result of the acquisition in accordance with AASB 112.

Employee benefits

26   The acquirer shall recognise and measure a liability (or asset, if any) related to the acquiree's employee benefit arrangements in accordance with AASB 119 *Employee Benefits*.

Indemnification assets

27   The seller in a business combination may contractually indemnify the acquirer for the outcome of a contingency or uncertainty related to all or part of a specific asset or liability. For example, the seller may indemnify the acquirer against losses above a specified amount on a liability arising from a particular contingency; in other words, the seller will guarantee that the acquirer's liability will not exceed a specified amount. As a result, the acquirer obtains an indemnification asset. The acquirer shall recognise an indemnification asset at the same time that it recognises the indemnified item

AASB

measured on the same basis as the indemnified item, subject to the need for a valuation allowance for uncollectible amounts. Therefore, if the indemnification relates to an asset or a liability that is recognised at the acquisition date and measured at its acquisition-date fair value, the acquirer shall recognise the indemnification asset at the acquisition date measured at its acquisition-date fair value. For an indemnification asset measured at fair value, the effects of uncertainty about future cash flows because of collectibility considerations are included in the fair value measure and a separate valuation allowance is not necessary (paragraph B41 provides related application guidance).

28   In some circumstances, the indemnification may relate to an asset or a liability that is an exception to the recognition or measurement principles. For example, an indemnification may relate to a contingent liability that is not recognised at the acquisition date because its fair value is not reliably measurable at that date. Alternatively, an indemnification may relate to an asset or a liability, for example, one that results from an employee benefit, that is measured on a basis other than acquisition-date fair value. In those circumstances, the indemnification asset shall be recognised and measured using assumptions consistent with those used to measure the indemnified item, subject to management's assessment of the collectibility of the indemnification asset and any contractual limitations on the indemnified amount. Paragraph 57 provides guidance on the subsequent accounting for an indemnification asset.

Exceptions to the measurement principle
Reacquired rights

29   The acquirer shall measure the value of a reacquired right recognised as an intangible asset on the basis of the remaining contractual term of the related contract regardless of whether market participants would consider potential contractual renewals when measuring its fair value. Paragraphs B35 and B36 provide related application guidance.

Share-based payment transactions

30   The acquirer shall measure a liability or an equity instrument related to share-based payment transactions of the acquiree or the replacement of an acquiree's share-based payment transactions with share-based payment transactions of the acquirer in accordance with the method in AASB 2 *Share-based Payment* at the acquisition date. (This Standard refers to the result of that method as the 'market-based measure' of the share-based payment transaction.)

Assets held for sale

31   The acquirer shall measure an acquired non-current asset (or disposal group) that is classified as held for sale at the acquisition date in accordance with AASB 5 *Non-current Assets Held for Sale and Discontinued Operations* at fair value less costs to sell in accordance with paragraphs 15–18 of that Standard.

Recognising and measuring goodwill or a gain from a bargain purchase

32   The acquirer shall recognise goodwill as of the acquisition date measured as the excess of (a) over (b) below:

(a)   the aggregate of:

(i)   the consideration transferred measured in accordance with this Standard, which generally requires acquisition-date fair value (see paragraph 37);

(ii)   the amount of any non-controlling interest in the acquiree measured in accordance with this Standard; and

(iii) in a business combination achieved in stages (see paragraphs 41 and 42), the acquisition-date fair value of the acquirer's previously held equity interest in the acquiree.

(b) the net of the acquisition-date amounts of the identifiable assets acquired and the liabilities assumed measured in accordance with this Standard.

33 In a business combination in which the acquirer and the acquiree (or its former owners) exchange only equity interests, the acquisition-date fair value of the acquiree's equity interests may be more reliably measurable than the acquisition-date fair value of the acquirer's equity interests. If so, the acquirer shall determine the amount of goodwill by using the acquisition-date fair value of the acquiree's equity interests instead of the acquisition-date fair value of the equity interests transferred. To determine the amount of goodwill in a business combination in which no consideration is transferred, the acquirer shall use the acquisition-date fair value of the acquirer's interest in the acquiree in place of the acquisition-date fair value of the consideration transferred (paragraph 32(a)(i)). Paragraphs B46–B49 provide related application guidance.

Bargain purchases

34 Occasionally, an acquirer will make a bargain purchase, which is a business combination in which the amount in paragraph 32(b) exceeds the aggregate of the amounts specified in paragraph 32(a). If that excess remains after applying the requirements in paragraph 36, the acquirer shall recognise the resulting gain in profit or loss on the acquisition date. The gain shall be attributed to the acquirer.

35 A bargain purchase might happen, for example, in a business combination that is a forced sale in which the seller is acting under compulsion. However, the recognition or measurement exceptions for particular items discussed in paragraphs 22–31 may also result in recognising a gain (or change the amount of a recognised gain) on a bargain purchase.

36 Before recognising a gain on a bargain purchase, the acquirer shall reassess whether it has correctly identified all of the assets acquired and all of the liabilities assumed and shall recognise any additional assets or liabilities that are identified in that review. The acquirer shall then review the procedures used to measure the amounts this Standard requires to be recognised at the acquisition date for all of the following:

(a) the identifiable assets acquired and liabilities assumed;

(b) the non-controlling interest in the acquiree, if any;

(c) for a business combination achieved in stages, the acquirer's previously held equity interest in the acquiree; and

(d) the consideration transferred.

The objective of the review is to ensure that the measurements appropriately reflect consideration of all available information as of the acquisition date.

Consideration transferred

37 The consideration transferred in a business combination shall be measured at fair value, which shall be calculated as the sum of the acquisition-date fair values of the assets transferred by the acquirer, the liabilities incurred by the acquirer to former owners of the acquiree and the equity interests issued by the acquirer. (However, any portion of the acquirer's share-based payment awards exchanged for awards held by the acquiree's employees that is included in consideration transferred in the business combination shall be measured in accordance with paragraph 30 rather than at fair value.) Examples of potential forms of consideration include cash, other assets, a business or a subsidiary of the acquirer, *contingent consideration*, ordinary or preference equity instruments, options, warrants and member interests of *mutual entities*.

38 The consideration transferred may include assets or liabilities of the acquirer that have carrying amounts that differ from their fair values at the acquisition date (for example,

non-monetary assets or a business of the acquirer). If so, the acquirer shall remeasure the transferred assets or liabilities to their fair values as of the acquisition date and recognise the resulting gains or losses, if any, in profit or loss. However, sometimes the transferred assets or liabilities remain within the combined entity after the business combination (for example, because the assets or liabilities were transferred to the acquiree rather than to its former owners), and the acquirer therefore retains control of them. In that situation, the acquirer shall measure those assets and liabilities at their carrying amounts immediately before the acquisition date and shall not recognise a gain or loss in profit or loss on assets or liabilities it controls both before and after the business combination.

Contingent consideration

39   The consideration the acquirer transfers in exchange for the acquiree includes any asset or liability resulting from a contingent consideration arrangement (see paragraph 37). The acquirer shall recognise the acquisition-date fair value of contingent consideration as part of the consideration transferred in exchange for the acquiree.

40   The acquirer shall classify an obligation to pay contingent consideration that meets the definition of a financial instrument as a financial liability or as equity on the basis of the definitions of an equity instrument and a financial liability in paragraph 11 of AASB 132 *Financial Instruments: Presentation*. The acquirer shall classify as an asset a right to the return of previously transferred consideration if specified conditions are met. Paragraph 58 provides guidance on the subsequent accounting for contingent consideration.

Additional guidance for applying the acquisition method to particular types of business combinations

A business combination achieved in stages

41   An acquirer sometimes obtains control of an acquiree in which it held an equity interest immediately before the acquisition date. For example, on 31 December 20X1, Entity A holds a 35 per cent non-controlling equity interest in Entity B. On that date, Entity A purchases an additional 40 per cent interest in Entity B, which gives it control of Entity B. This Standard refers to such a transaction as a business combination achieved in stages, sometimes also referred to as a step acquisition.

42   In a business combination achieved in stages, the acquirer shall remeasure its previously held equity interest in the acquiree at its acquisition-date fair value and recognise the resulting gain or loss, if any, in profit or loss or other comprehensive income, as appropriate. In prior reporting periods, the acquirer may have recognised changes in the value of its equity interest in the acquiree in other comprehensive income. If so, the amount that was recognised in other comprehensive income shall be recognised on the same basis as would be required if the acquirer had disposed directly of the previously held equity interest.

A business combination achieved without the transfer of consideration

43   An acquirer sometimes obtains control of an acquiree without transferring consideration. The acquisition method of accounting for a business combination applies to those combinations. Such circumstances include:

(a)   The acquiree repurchases a sufficient number of its own shares for an existing investor (the acquirer) to obtain control.

(b)   Minority veto rights lapse that previously kept the acquirer from controlling an acquiree in which the acquirer held the majority voting rights.

(c)   The acquirer and acquiree agree to combine their businesses by contract alone. The acquirer transfers no consideration in exchange for control of an acquiree and holds no equity interests in the acquiree, either on the acquisition date or previously. Examples of business combinations achieved by contract alone include bringing two businesses together in a stapling arrangement or forming a dual listed corporation.

44   In a business combination achieved by contract alone, the acquirer shall attribute to the
        owners of the acquiree the amount of the acquiree's net assets recognised in accordance
        with this Standard. In other words, the equity interests in the acquiree held by parties
        other than the acquirer are a non-controlling interest in the acquirer's post-combination
        financial statements even if the result is that all of the equity interests in the acquiree
        are attributed to the non-controlling interest.

Measurement period

45   **If the initial accounting for a business combination is incomplete by the end
        of the reporting period in which the combination occurs, the acquirer shall
        report in its financial statements provisional amounts for the items for which
        the accounting is incomplete. During the measurement period, the acquirer shall
        retrospectively adjust the provisional amounts recognised at the acquisition date
        to reflect new information obtained about facts and circumstances that existed
        as of the acquisition date and, if known, would have affected the measurement
        of the amounts recognised as of that date. During the measurement period, the
        acquirer shall also recognise additional assets or liabilities if new information is
        obtained about facts and circumstances that existed as of the acquisition date and,
        if known, would have resulted in the recognition of those assets and liabilities as
        of that date. The measurement period ends as soon as the acquirer receives the
        information it was seeking about facts and circumstances that existed as of the
        acquisition date or learns that more information is not obtainable. However, the
        measurement period shall not exceed one year from the acquisition date.**

46   The measurement period is the period after the acquisition date during which the
        acquirer may adjust the provisional amounts recognised for a business combination.
        The measurement period provides the acquirer with a reasonable time to obtain the
        information necessary to identify and measure the following as of the acquisition date
        in accordance with the requirements of this Standard:

        (a)   the identifiable assets acquired, liabilities assumed and any non-controlling
                interest in the acquiree;

        (b)   the consideration transferred for the acquiree (or the other amount used in
                measuring goodwill);

        (c)   in a business combination achieved in stages, the equity interest in the acquiree
                previously held by the acquirer; and

        (d)   the resulting goodwill or gain on a bargain purchase.

47   The acquirer shall consider all pertinent factors in determining whether information
        obtained after the acquisition date should result in an adjustment to the provisional
        amounts recognised or whether that information results from events that occurred after
        the acquisition date. Pertinent factors include the date when additional information is
        obtained and whether the acquirer can identify a reason for a change to provisional
        amounts. Information that is obtained shortly after the acquisition date is more likely
        to reflect circumstances that existed at the acquisition date than is information obtained
        several months later. For example, unless an intervening event that changed its fair
        value can be identified, the sale of an asset to a third party shortly after the acquisition
        date for an amount that differs significantly from its provisional fair value measured at
        that date is likely to indicate an error in the provisional amount.

48   The acquirer recognises an increase (decrease) in the provisional amount recognised
        for an identifiable asset (liability) by means of a decrease (increase) in goodwill.
        However, new information obtained during the measurement period may sometimes
        result in an adjustment to the provisional amount of more than one asset or liability.
        For example, the acquirer might have assumed a liability to pay damages related
        to an accident in one of the acquiree's facilities, part or all of which are covered
        by the acquiree's liability insurance policy. If the acquirer obtains new information
        during the measurement period about the acquisition-date fair value of that liability, the
        adjustment to goodwill resulting from a change to the provisional amount recognised
        for the liability would be offset (in whole or in part) by a corresponding adjustment to

goodwill resulting from a change to the provisional amount recognised for the claim receivable from the insurer.

49   During the measurement period, the acquirer shall recognise adjustments to the provisional amounts as if the accounting for the business combination had been completed at the acquisition date. Thus, the acquirer shall revise comparative information for prior periods presented in financial statements as needed, including making any change in depreciation, amortisation or other income effects recognised in completing the initial accounting.

50   After the measurement period ends, the acquirer shall revise the accounting for a business combination only to correct an error in accordance with AASB 108 *Accounting Policies, Changes in Accounting Estimates and Errors*.

Determining what is part of the business combination transaction

51   **The acquirer and the acquiree may have a pre-existing relationship or other arrangement before negotiations for the business combination began, or they may enter into an arrangement during the negotiations that is separate from the business combination. In either situation, the acquirer shall identify any amounts that are not part of what the acquirer and the acquiree (or its former owners) exchanged in the business combination, ie amounts that are not part of the exchange for the acquiree. The acquirer shall recognise as part of applying the acquisition method only the consideration transferred for the acquiree and the assets acquired and liabilities assumed in the exchange for the acquiree. Separate transactions shall be accounted for in accordance with the relevant Australian Accounting Standards.**

52   A transaction entered into by or on behalf of the acquirer or primarily for the benefit of the acquirer or the combined entity, rather than primarily for the benefit of the acquiree (or its former owners) before the combination, is likely to be a separate transaction. The following are examples of separate transactions that are not to be included in applying the acquisition method:

(a)   a transaction that in effect settles pre-existing relationships between the acquirer and acquiree;

(b)   a transaction that remunerates employees or former owners of the acquiree for future services; and

(c)   a transaction that reimburses the acquiree or its former owners for paying the acquirer's acquisition-related costs.

Paragraphs B50–B62 provide related application guidance.

Acquisition-related costs

53   Acquisition-related costs are costs the acquirer incurs to effect a business combination. Those costs include finder's fees; advisory, legal, accounting, valuation and other professional or consulting fees; general administrative costs, including the costs of maintaining an internal acquisitions department; and costs of registering and issuing debt and equity securities. The acquirer shall account for acquisition-related costs as expenses in the periods in which the costs are incurred and the services are received, with one exception. The costs to issue debt or equity securities shall be recognised in accordance with AASB 132 and AASB 9.

Subsequent measurement and accounting

54   **In general, an acquirer shall subsequently measure and account for assets acquired, liabilities assumed or incurred and equity instruments issued in a business combination in accordance with other applicable Australian Accounting Standards for those items, depending on their nature. However, this Standard provides guidance on subsequently measuring and accounting for the following**

assets acquired, liabilities assumed or incurred and equity instruments issued in a business combination:

(a)   reacquired rights;

(b)   contingent liabilities recognised as of the acquisition date;

(c)   indemnification assets; and

(d)   contingent consideration.

Paragraph B63 provides related application guidance.

Reacquired rights

55   A reacquired right recognised as an intangible asset shall be amortised over the remaining contractual period of the contract in which the right was granted. An acquirer that subsequently sells a reacquired right to a third party shall include the carrying amount of the intangible asset in determining the gain or loss on the sale.

Contingent liabilities

56   After initial recognition and until the liability is settled, cancelled or expires, the acquirer shall measure a contingent liability recognised in a business combination at the higher of:

(a)   the amount that would be recognised in accordance with AASB 137; and

(b)   the amount initially recognised less, if appropriate, the cumulative amount of income recognised in accordance with the principles of AASB 15 *Revenue from Contracts with Customers*.

This requirement does not apply to contracts accounted for in accordance with AASB 9.

Indemnification assets

57   At the end of each subsequent reporting period, the acquirer shall measure an indemnification asset that was recognised at the acquisition date on the same basis as the indemnified liability or asset, subject to any contractual limitations on its amount and, for an indemnification asset that is not subsequently measured at its fair value, management's assessment of the collectibility of the indemnification asset. The acquirer shall derecognise the indemnification asset only when it collects the asset, sells it or otherwise loses the right to it.

Contingent consideration

58   Some changes in the fair value of contingent consideration that the acquirer recognises after the acquisition date may be the result of additional information that the acquirer obtained after that date about facts and circumstances that existed at the acquisition date. Such changes are measurement period adjustments in accordance with paragraphs 45–49. However, changes resulting from events after the acquisition date, such as meeting an earnings target, reaching a specified share price or reaching a milestone on a research and development project, are not measurement period adjustments. The acquirer shall account for changes in the fair value of contingent consideration that are not measurement period adjustments as follows:

(a)   Contingent consideration classified as equity shall not be remeasured and its subsequent settlement shall be accounted for within equity.

(b)   Other contingent consideration that:

(i)   is within the scope of AASB 9 shall be measured at fair value at each reporting date and changes in fair value shall be recognised in profit or loss in accordance with AASB 9.

(ii)   is not within the scope of AASB 9 shall be measured at fair value at each reporting date and changes in fair value shall be recognised in profit or loss.

Disclosures

59   The acquirer shall disclose information that enables users of its financial statements to evaluate the nature and financial effect of a business combination that occurs either:

(a)   during the current reporting period; or

(b)   after the end of the reporting period but before the financial statements are authorised for issue.

60   To meet the objective in paragraph 59, the acquirer shall disclose the information specified in paragraphs B64—B66.

61   The acquirer shall disclose information that enables users of its financial statements to evaluate the financial effects of adjustments recognised in the current reporting period that relate to business combinations that occurred in the period or previous reporting periods.

62   To meet the objective in paragraph 61, the acquirer shall disclose the information specified in paragraph B67.

63   If the specific disclosures required by this and other Australian Accounting Standards do not meet the objectives set out in paragraphs 59 and 61, the acquirer shall disclose whatever additional information is necessary to meet those objectives.

Restructures of local governments

Aus63.1   Where assets and liabilities are transferred to a local government from another local government at no cost, or for nominal consideration, pursuant to legislation, ministerial directive or other externally imposed requirement, the transferee local government shall recognise assets and liabilities and any gain or loss.

Aus63.2   Assets transferred to a local government from another local government at no cost, or for nominal consideration, by virtue of legislation, ministerial directive or other externally imposed requirement shall be recognised initially either at the amounts at which the assets were recognised by the transferor local government as at the date of the transfer, or at their fair values.

Aus63.3   A restructure of local governments involves the transfer of assets and liabilities of a local government to another local government, at no cost or for nominal consideration, by virtue of legislation, ministerial directive or other externally imposed requirement. This gives rise to assets and liabilities and a gain or loss of the transferee local government. A restructure of local governments may take the form of a new local government being constituted and other local governments being abolished as a result of a State government's policy to effectively amalgamate a number of local governments.

Aus63.4   A restructure of local governments involves a change in the resources controlled by the local governments involved in the restructure. The transferor local government will decrease its assets by the carrying amount of the assets transferred. The transferred assets will usually be recognised by the transferee at their carrying amounts in the books of the transferor at the time of the transfer. Such amounts provide a practical basis for recognising the transfer of assets, particularly when many assets are involved, as is usually the case in a restructure of local governments. However, the recognition of transferred assets at fair value is permitted by this Standard.

Aus63.5   The restructures of local governments referred to in paragraphs Aus63.3 and Aus63.4 do not involve transfers between the local government and its ownership group but give rise to a gain or loss that is recognised in the statement of comprehensive income.

Aus63.6   Assets and liabilities transferred during the reporting period and recognised in accordance with paragraph Aus63.1 shall be disclosed separately, by class, by way of note or otherwise, and the transferor local government shall be identified.

Aus63.7   Any gain or loss recognised in accordance with paragraph Aus63.1 shall be separately disclosed in the statement of comprehensive income.

Aus63.8   The disclosures required by paragraph Aus63.6 will assist users to identify the assets and liabilities recognised as a result of a restructure separately from other assets and liabilities and to identify the transferor local government. In addition, the disclosures required by paragraph Aus63.7 will assist users to identify separately the gain or loss which results from a restructure of local governments.

Aus63.9   Local governments are not required to apply paragraphs 59 to 63 and the related Appendix B Application Guidance paragraphs of this Standard when disclosing information about restructures of local governments.

Effective date and transition

Effective date

64   [Deleted by the AASB]

Aus64.1   This Standard applies to annual periods beginning on or after 1 January 2018. Earlier application is permitted for periods beginning after 24 July 2014 but before 1 January 2018.

64A   [Deleted]

64B–64C   [Deleted by the AASB]

64D   [Deleted]

64E–64G   [Deleted by the AASB]

64H   [Deleted]

64I   AASB 2014-1 *Amendments to Australian Accounting Standards*, issued in June 2014, amended the previous version of this Standard as follows: amended paragraphs 40 and 58 and added paragraph 67A and its related heading. An entity shall apply that amendment prospectively to business combinations for which the acquisition date is on or after 1 July 2014. Earlier application is permitted. An entity may apply the amendment earlier provided that AASB 9 and AASB 137 (both as amended by Part A of AASB 2014-1) have also been applied. If an entity applies that amendment earlier it shall disclose that fact

64J   AASB 2014-1, issued in June 2014, amended paragraph 2(a) in the previous version of this Standard. An entity shall apply that amendment prospectively for annual periods beginning on or after 1 July 2014. Earlier application is permitted. If an entity applies that amendment for an earlier period it shall disclose that fact.

64K   AASB 2014-5 *Amendments to Australian Accounting Standards arising from AASB 15*, issued in December 2014, amended paragraph 56 in the previous version of this Standard. An entity shall apply that amendment when it applies AASB 15.

64L   AASB 2010-7 *Amendments to Australian Accounting Standards arising from AASB 9 (December 2010)* (as amended), AASB 2014-1 *Amendments to Australian Accounting Standards* and AASB 2014-7 *Amendments to Australian Accounting Standards arising from AASB 9 (December 2014)* amended the previous version of this Standard as follows: amended paragraphs 16, 42, 53, 56, 58 and B41 and deleted paragraph 64A. Paragraph 64D, added by AASB 2010-7, was deleted by AASB 2014-1. Paragraph

AASB

64H, added by AASB 2014-1, was deleted by AASB 2014-7. An entity shall apply those amendments when it applies AASB 9.

Transition

65   [Deleted by the AASB]

Aus65.1   Assets and liabilities that arose from business combinations whose acquisition dates preceded the application of the previous version of this Standard shall not be adjusted upon application of this Standard. The previous version of the Standard applied prospectively to business combinations for which the acquisition date is on or after the beginning of the first annual reporting period beginning on or after 1 July 2009 and could be applied at the beginning of an annual reporting period that begins on or after 30 June 2007.

65A   Contingent consideration balances arising from business combinations whose acquisition dates preceded the date when an entity first applied this Standard as issued in 2008 shall not be adjusted upon first application of this Standard. Paragraphs 65B–65E shall be applied in the subsequent accounting for those balances. Paragraphs 65B–65E shall not apply to the accounting for contingent consideration balances arising from business combinations with acquisition dates on or after the date when the entity first applied this Standard as issued in 2008. In paragraphs 65B–65E business combination refers exclusively to business combinations whose acquisition date preceded the application of this Standard as issued in 2008.

65B   If a business combination agreement provides for an adjustment to the cost of the combination contingent on future events, the acquirer shall include the amount of that adjustment in the cost of the combination at the acquisition date if the adjustment is probable and can be measured reliably.

65C   A business combination agreement may allow for adjustments to the cost of the combination that are contingent on one or more future events. The adjustment might, for example, be contingent on a specified level of profit being maintained or achieved in future periods, or on the market price of the instruments issued being maintained. It is usually possible to estimate the amount of any such adjustment at the time of initially accounting for the combination without impairing the reliability of the information, even though some uncertainty exists. If the future events do not occur or the estimate needs to be revised, the cost of the business combination shall be adjusted accordingly.

65D   However, when a business combination agreement provides for such an adjustment, that adjustment is not included in the cost of the combination at the time of initially accounting for the combination if it either is not probable or cannot be measured reliably. If that adjustment subsequently becomes probable and can be measured reliably, the additional consideration shall be treated as an adjustment to the cost of the combination.

65E   In some circumstances, the acquirer may be required to make a subsequent payment to the seller as compensation for a reduction in the value of the assets given, equity instruments issued or liabilities incurred or assumed by the acquirer in exchange for control of the acquiree. This is the case, for example, when the acquirer guarantees the market price of equity or debt instruments issued as part of the cost of the business combination and is required to issue additional equity or debt instruments to restore the originally determined cost. In such cases, no increase in the cost of the business combination is recognised. In the case of equity instruments, the fair value of the additional payment is offset by an equal reduction in the value attributed to the instruments initially issued. In the case of debt instruments, the additional payment is regarded as a reduction in the premium or an increase in the discount on the initial issue.

66   An entity, such as a mutual entity, that has not yet applied AASB 3 and had one or more business combinations that were accounted for using the purchase method shall apply the transition provisions in paragraphs B68 and B69.

Income taxes

67 For business combinations in which the acquisition date was before the previous version of this Standard is applied, the acquirer shall apply the requirements of paragraph 68 of AASB 112, as amended by AASB 2008-3 *Amendments to Australian Accounting Standards arising from AASB 3 and AASB 127*, prospectively. That is to say, the acquirer shall not adjust the accounting for prior business combinations for previously recognised changes in recognised deferred tax assets. However, from the date when the previous version of this Standard is applied, the acquirer shall recognise, as an adjustment to profit or loss (or, if AASB 112 requires, outside profit or loss), changes in recognised deferred tax assets.

Reference to AASB 9

67A If an entity applies this Standard but does not yet apply AASB 9, any reference to AASB 9 should be read as a reference to AASB 139.

Withdrawal of IFRS 3 (2004)

68 [Deleted by the AASB]

Commencement of the legislative instrument

Aus68.1 For legal purposes, this legislative instrument commences on 31 December 2017.

Withdrawal of AASB pronouncements

Aus68.2 This Standard repeals AASB 3 *Business Combinations* issued in March 2008. Despite the repeal, after the time this Standard starts to apply under section 334 of the Corporations Act (either generally or in relation to an individual entity), the repealed Standard continues to apply in relation to any period ending before that time as if the repeal had not occurred.

[Note: When this Standard applies under section 334 of the Corporations Act (either generally or in relation to an individual entity), it supersedes the application of the repealed Standard.]

APPENDIX A
DEFINED TERMS

This appendix is an integral part of the Standard.

acquiree	The business or businesses that the **acquirer** obtains control of in a **business combination**.
acquirer	The entity that obtains control of the **acquiree**.
acquisition date	The date on which the **acquirer** obtains control of the **acquiree**.
business	An integrated set of activities and assets that is capable of being conducted and managed for the purpose of providing a return in the form of dividends, lower costs or other economic benefits directly to investors or other owners, members or participants.

business combination	A transaction or other event in which an **acquirer** obtains control of one or more **businesses**. Transactions sometimes referred to as 'true mergers' or 'mergers of equals' are also **business combinations** as that term is used in this Standard.
contingent consideration	Usually, an obligation of the **acquirer** to transfer additional assets or **equity interests** to the former owners of an **acquiree** as part of the exchange for control of the acquiree if specified future events occur or conditions are met. However, *contingent consideration* also may give the acquirer the right to the return of previously transferred consideration if specified conditions are met.
equity interests	For the purposes of this Standard, *equity interests* is used broadly to mean ownership interests of investor-owned entities and owner, member or participant interests of **mutual entities**.
fair value	*Fair value* is the price that would be received to sell an asset or paid to transfer a liability in an orderly transaction between market participants at the measurement date. (See AASB 13.)
goodwill	An asset representing the future economic benefits arising from other assets acquired in a **business combination** that are not individually identified and separately recognised.
identifiable	An asset is *identifiable* if it either: (a) is separable, ie capable of being separated or divided from the entity and sold, transferred, licensed, rented or exchanged, either individually or together with a related contract, identifiable asset or liability, regardless of whether the entity intends to do so; or (b) arises from contractual or other legal rights, regardless of whether those rights are transferable or separable from the entity or from other rights and obligations.
intangible asset	An **identifiable** non-monetary asset without physical substance.
mutual entity	An entity, other than an investor-owned entity, that provides dividends, lower costs or other economic benefits directly to its **owners**, members or participants. For example, a mutual insurance company, a credit union and a co-operative entity are all mutual entities.
non-controlling interest	The equity in a subsidiary not attributable, directly or indirectly, to a parent.
owners	For the purposes of this Standard, *owners* is used broadly to include holders of **equity interests** of investor-owned entities and owners or members of, or participants in, **mutual entities**.

APPENDIX B
APPLICATION GUIDANCE

This appendix is an integral part of the Standard.

Business combinations of entities under common control (application of paragraph 2(c))

B1   This Standard does not apply to a business combination of entities or businesses under common control. A business combination involving entities or businesses under common control is a business combination in which all of the combining entities or businesses are ultimately controlled by the same party or parties both before and after the business combination, and that control is not transitory.

B2 A group of individuals shall be regarded as controlling an entity when, as a result of contractual arrangements, they collectively have the power to govern its financial and operating policies so as to obtain benefits from its activities. Therefore, a business combination is outside the scope of this Standard when the same group of individuals has, as a result of contractual arrangements, ultimate collective power to govern the financial and operating policies of each of the combining entities so as to obtain benefits from their activities, and that ultimate collective power is not transitory.

B3 An entity may be controlled by an individual or by a group of individuals acting together under a contractual arrangement, and that individual or group of individuals may not be subject to the financial reporting requirements of Australian Accounting Standards. Therefore, it is not necessary for combining entities to be included as part of the same consolidated financial statements for a business combination to be regarded as one involving entities under common control.

B4 The extent of non-controlling interests in each of the combining entities before and after the business combination is not relevant to determining whether the combination involves entities under common control. Similarly, the fact that one of the combining entities is a subsidiary that has been excluded from the consolidated financial statements is not relevant to determining whether a combination involves entities under common control.

Identifying a business combination (application of paragraph 3)

B5 This Standard defines a business combination as a transaction or other event in which an acquirer obtains control of one or more businesses. An acquirer might obtain control of an acquiree in a variety of ways, for example:

(a) by transferring cash, cash equivalents or other assets (including net assets that constitute a business);

(b) by incurring liabilities;

(c) by issuing equity interests;

(d) by providing more than one type of consideration; or

(e) without transferring consideration, including by contract alone (see paragraph 43).

B6 A business combination may be structured in a variety of ways for legal, taxation or other reasons, which include but are not limited to:

(a) one or more businesses become subsidiaries of an acquirer or the net assets of one or more businesses are legally merged into the acquirer;

(b) one combining entity transfers its net assets, or its owners transfer their equity interests, to another combining entity or its owners;

(c) all of the combining entities transfer their net assets, or the owners of those entities transfer their equity interests, to a newly formed entity (sometimes referred to as a roll-up or put-together transaction); or

(d) a group of former owners of one of the combining entities obtains control of the combined entity.

Definition of a business (application of paragraph 3)

B7 A business consists of inputs and processes applied to those inputs that have the ability to create outputs. Although businesses usually have outputs, outputs are not required for an integrated set to qualify as a business. The three elements of a business are defined as follows:

(a) **Input:** Any economic resource that creates, or has the ability to create, outputs when one or more processes are applied to it. Examples include non-current assets (including intangible assets or rights to use non-current assets), intellectual property, the ability to obtain access to necessary materials or rights and employees.

(b)   **Process:** Any system, standard, protocol, convention or rule that when applied to an input or inputs, creates or has the ability to create outputs. Examples include strategic management processes, operational processes and resource management processes. These processes typically are documented, but an organised workforce having the necessary skills and experience following rules and conventions may provide the necessary processes that are capable of being applied to inputs to create outputs. (Accounting, billing, payroll and other administrative systems typically are not processes used to create outputs.)

(c)   **Output:** The result of inputs and processes applied to those inputs that provide or have the ability to provide a return in the form of dividends, lower costs or other economic benefits directly to investors or other owners, members or participants.

B8   To be capable of being conducted and managed for the purposes defined, an integrated set of activities and assets requires two essential elements—inputs and processes applied to those inputs, which together are or will be used to create outputs. However, a business need not include all of the inputs or processes that the seller used in operating that business if market participants are capable of acquiring the business and continuing to produce outputs, for example, by integrating the business with their own inputs and processes.

B9   The nature of the elements of a business varies by industry and by the structure of an entity's operations (activities), including the entity's stage of development. Established businesses often have many different types of inputs, processes and outputs, whereas new businesses often have few inputs and processes and sometimes only a single output (product). Nearly all businesses also have liabilities, but a business need not have liabilities.

B10   An integrated set of activities and assets in the development stage might not have outputs. If not, the acquirer should consider other factors to determine whether the set is a business. Those factors include, but are not limited to, whether the set:

(a)   has begun planned principal activities;

(b)   has employees, intellectual property and other inputs and processes that could be applied to those inputs;

(c)   is pursuing a plan to produce outputs; and

(d)   will be able to obtain access to customers that will purchase the outputs.

Not all of those factors need to be present for a particular integrated set of activities and assets in the development stage to qualify as a business.

B11   Determining whether a particular set of assets and activities is a business should be based on whether the integrated set is capable of being conducted and managed as a business by a market participant. Thus, in evaluating whether a particular set is a business, it is not relevant whether a seller operated the set as a business or whether the acquirer intends to operate the set as a business.

B12   In the absence of evidence to the contrary, a particular set of assets and activities in which goodwill is present shall be presumed to be a business. However, a business need not have goodwill.

Identifying the acquirer (application of paragraphs 6 and 7)

B13   The guidance in AASB 10 *Consolidated Financial Statements* shall be used to identify the acquirer—the entity that obtains control of the acquiree. If a business combination has occurred but applying the guidance in AASB 10 does not clearly indicate which of the combining entities is the acquirer, the factors in paragraphs B14–B18 shall be considered in making that determination.

B14   In a business combination effected primarily by transferring cash or other assets or by incurring liabilities, the acquirer is usually the entity that transfers the cash or other assets or incurs the liabilities.

B15   In a business combination effected primarily by exchanging equity interests, the acquirer is usually the entity that issues its equity interests. However, in some business combinations, commonly called 'reverse acquisitions', the issuing entity is the acquiree. Paragraphs B19–B27 provide guidance on accounting for reverse acquisitions. Other pertinent facts and circumstances shall also be considered in identifying the acquirer in a business combination effected by exchanging equity interests, including:

(a)   *the relative voting rights in the combined entity after the business combination*—The acquirer is usually the combining entity whose owners as a group retain or receive the largest portion of the voting rights in the combined entity. In determining which group of owners retains or receives the largest portion of the voting rights, an entity shall consider the existence of any unusual or special voting arrangements and options, warrants or convertible securities.

(b)   *the existence of a large minority voting interest in the combined entity if no other owner or organised group of owners has a significant voting interest*— The acquirer is usually the combining entity whose single owner or organised group of owners holds the largest minority voting interest in the combined entity.

(c)   *the composition of the governing body of the combined entity*—The acquirer is usually the combining entity whose owners have the ability to elect or appoint or to remove a majority of the members of the governing body of the combined entity.

(d)   *the composition of the senior management of the combined entity*—The acquirer is usually the combining entity whose (former) management dominates the management of the combined entity.

(e)   *the terms of the exchange of equity interests*—The acquirer is usually the combining entity that pays a premium over the pre-combination fair value of the equity interests of the other combining entity or entities.

B16   The acquirer is usually the combining entity whose relative size (measured in, for example, assets, revenues or profit) is significantly greater than that of the other combining entity or entities.

B17   In a business combination involving more than two entities, determining the acquirer shall include a consideration of, among other things, which of the combining entities initiated the combination, as well as the relative size of the combining entities.

B18   A new entity formed to effect a business combination is not necessarily the acquirer. If a new entity is formed to issue equity interests to effect a business combination, one of the combining entities that existed before the business combination shall be identified as the acquirer by applying the guidance in paragraphs B13–B17. In contrast, a new entity that transfers cash or other assets or incurs liabilities as consideration may be the acquirer.

Reverse acquisitions

B19   A reverse acquisition occurs when the entity that issues securities (the legal acquirer) is identified as the acquiree for accounting purposes on the basis of the guidance in paragraphs B13–B18. The entity whose equity interests are acquired (the legal acquiree) must be the acquirer for accounting purposes for the transaction to be considered a reverse acquisition. For example, reverse acquisitions sometimes occur when a private operating entity wants to become a public entity but does not want to register its equity shares. To accomplish that, the private entity will arrange for a public entity to acquire its equity interests in exchange for the equity interests of the public entity. In this example, the public entity is the **legal acquirer** because it issued its equity interests, and the private entity is the **legal acquiree** because its equity interests were acquired. However, application of the guidance in paragraphs B13–B18 results in identifying:

(a)   the public entity as the **acquiree** for accounting purposes (the accounting acquiree); and

(b)   the private entity as the **acquirer** for accounting purposes (the accounting acquirer).

The accounting acquiree must meet the definition of a business for the transaction to be accounted for as a reverse acquisition, and all of the recognition and measurement principles in this Standard, including the requirement to recognise goodwill, apply.

Measuring the consideration transferred

B20   In a reverse acquisition, the accounting acquirer usually issues no consideration for the acquiree. Instead, the accounting acquiree usually issues its equity shares to the owners of the accounting acquirer. Accordingly, the acquisition-date fair value of the consideration transferred by the accounting acquirer for its interest in the accounting acquiree is based on the number of equity interests the legal subsidiary would have had to issue to give the owners of the legal parent the same percentage equity interest in the combined entity that results from the reverse acquisition. The fair value of the number of equity interests calculated in that way can be used as the fair value of consideration transferred in exchange for the acquiree.

Preparation and presentation of consolidated financial statements

B21   Consolidated financial statements prepared following a reverse acquisition are issued under the name of the legal parent (accounting acquiree) but described in the notes as a continuation of the financial statements of the legal subsidiary (accounting acquirer), with one adjustment, which is to adjust retroactively the accounting acquirer's legal capital to reflect the legal capital of the accounting acquiree. That adjustment is required to reflect the capital of the legal parent (the accounting acquiree). Comparative information presented in those consolidated financial statements also is retroactively adjusted to reflect the legal capital of the legal parent (accounting acquiree).

B22   Because the consolidated financial statements represent the continuation of the financial statements of the legal subsidiary except for its capital structure, the consolidated financial statements reflect:

(a)   the assets and liabilities of the legal subsidiary (the accounting acquirer) recognised and measured at their pre-combination carrying amounts.

(b)   the assets and liabilities of the legal parent (the accounting acquiree) recognised and measured in accordance with this Standard.

(c)   the retained earnings and other equity balances of the legal subsidiary (accounting acquirer) **before** the business combination.

(d)   the amount recognised as issued equity interests in the consolidated financial statements determined by adding the issued equity interest of the legal subsidiary (the accounting acquirer) outstanding immediately before the business combination to the fair value of the legal parent (accounting acquiree). However, the equity structure (ie the number and type of equity interests issued) reflects the equity structure of the legal parent (the accounting acquiree), including the equity interests the legal parent issued to effect the combination. Accordingly, the equity structure of the legal subsidiary (the accounting acquirer) is restated using the exchange ratio established in the acquisition agreement to reflect the number of shares of the legal parent (the accounting acquiree) issued in the reverse acquisition.

(e)   the non-controlling interest's proportionate share of the legal subsidiary's (accounting acquirer's) pre-combination carrying amounts of retained earnings and other equity interests as discussed in paragraphs B23 and B24.

Non-controlling interest

B23 In a reverse acquisition, some of the owners of the legal acquiree (the accounting acquirer) might not exchange their equity interests for equity interests of the legal parent (the accounting acquiree). Those owners are treated as a non-controlling interest in the consolidated financial statements after the reverse acquisition. That is because the owners of the legal acquiree that do not exchange their equity interests for equity interests of the legal acquirer have an interest in only the results and net assets of the legal acquiree—not in the results and net assets of the combined entity. Conversely, even though the legal acquirer is the acquiree for accounting purposes, the owners of the legal acquirer have an interest in the results and net assets of the combined entity.

B24 The assets and liabilities of the legal acquiree are measured and recognised in the consolidated financial statements at their pre-combination carrying amounts (see paragraph B22(a)). Therefore, in a reverse acquisition the non-controlling interest reflects the non-controlling shareholders' proportionate interest in the pre-combination carrying amounts of the legal acquiree's net assets even if the non-controlling interests in other acquisitions are measured at their fair value at the acquisition date.

Earnings per share

B25 As noted in paragraph B22(d), the equity structure in the consolidated financial statements following a reverse acquisition reflects the equity structure of the legal acquirer (the accounting acquiree), including the equity interests issued by the legal acquirer to effect the business combination.

B26 In calculating the weighted average number of ordinary shares outstanding (the denominator of the earnings per share calculation) during the period in which the reverse acquisition occurs:

(a) the number of ordinary shares outstanding from the beginning of that period to the acquisition date shall be computed on the basis of the weighted average number of ordinary shares of the legal acquiree (accounting acquirer) outstanding during the period multiplied by the exchange ratio established in the merger agreement; and

(b) the number of ordinary shares outstanding from the acquisition date to the end of that period shall be the actual number of ordinary shares of the legal acquirer (the accounting acquiree) outstanding during that period.

B27 The basic earnings per share for each comparative period before the acquisition date presented in the consolidated financial statements following a reverse acquisition shall be calculated by dividing:

(a) the profit or loss of the legal acquiree attributable to ordinary shareholders in each of those periods by

(b) the legal acquiree's historical weighted average number of ordinary shares outstanding multiplied by the exchange ratio established in the acquisition agreement.

Recognising particular assets acquired and liabilities assumed (application of paragraphs 10–13)

Operating leases

B28 The acquirer shall recognise no assets or liabilities related to an operating lease in which the acquiree is the lessee except as required by paragraphs B29 and B30.

B29 The acquirer shall determine whether the terms of each operating lease in which the acquiree is the lessee are favourable or unfavourable. The acquirer shall recognise an intangible asset if the terms of an operating lease are favourable relative to market terms and a liability if the terms are unfavourable relative to market terms. Paragraph B42 provides guidance on measuring the acquisition-date fair value of assets subject to operating leases in which the acquiree is the lessor.

B30   An identifiable intangible asset may be associated with an operating lease, which may be evidenced by market participants' willingness to pay a price for the lease even if it is at market terms. For example, a lease of gates at an airport or of retail space in a prime shopping area might provide entry into a market or other future economic benefits that qualify as identifiable intangible assets, for example, as a customer relationship. In that situation, the acquirer shall recognise the associated identifiable intangible asset(s) in accordance with paragraph B31.

Intangible assets

B31   The acquirer shall recognise, separately from goodwill, the identifiable intangible assets acquired in a business combination. An intangible asset is identifiable if it meets either the separability criterion or the contractual-legal criterion.

B32   An intangible asset that meets the contractual-legal criterion is identifiable even if the asset is not transferable or separable from the acquiree or from other rights and obligations. For example:

    (a)   an acquiree leases a manufacturing facility under an operating lease that has terms that are favourable relative to market terms. The lease terms explicitly prohibit transfer of the lease (through either sale or sublease). The amount by which the lease terms are favourable compared with the terms of current market transactions for the same or similar items is an intangible asset that meets the contractual-legal criterion for recognition separately from goodwill, even though the acquirer cannot sell or otherwise transfer the lease contract.

    (b)   an acquiree owns and operates a nuclear power plant. The licence to operate that power plant is an intangible asset that meets the contractual-legal criterion for recognition separately from goodwill, even if the acquirer cannot sell or transfer it separately from the acquired power plant. An acquirer may recognise the fair value of the operating licence and the fair value of the power plant as a single asset for financial reporting purposes if the useful lives of those assets are similar.

    (c)   an acquiree owns a technology patent. It has licensed that patent to others for their exclusive use outside the domestic market, receiving a specified percentage of future foreign revenue in exchange. Both the technology patent and the related licence agreement meet the contractual-legal criterion for recognition separately from goodwill even if selling or exchanging the patent and the related licence agreement separately from one another would not be practical.

B33   The separability criterion means that an acquired intangible asset is capable of being separated or divided from the acquiree and sold, transferred, licensed, rented or exchanged, either individually or together with a related contract, identifiable asset or liability. An intangible asset that the acquirer would be able to sell, license or otherwise exchange for something else of value meets the separability criterion even if the acquirer does not intend to sell, license or otherwise exchange it. An acquired intangible asset meets the separability criterion if there is evidence of exchange transactions for that type of asset or an asset of a similar type, even if those transactions are infrequent and regardless of whether the acquirer is involved in them. For example, customer and subscriber lists are frequently licensed and thus meet the separability criterion. Even if an acquiree believes its customer lists have characteristics different from other customer lists, the fact that customer lists are frequently licensed generally means that the acquired customer list meets the separability criterion. However, a customer list acquired in a business combination would not meet the separability criterion if the terms of confidentiality or other agreements prohibit an entity from selling, leasing or otherwise exchanging information about its customers.

B34   An intangible asset that is not individually separable from the acquiree or combined entity meets the separability criterion if it is separable in combination with a related contract, identifiable asset or liability. For example:

    (a)   market participants exchange deposit liabilities and related depositor relationship intangible assets in observable exchange transactions. Therefore, the acquirer should recognise the depositor relationship intangible asset separately from goodwill.

(b)   an acquiree owns a registered trademark and documented but unpatented technical expertise used to manufacture the trademarked product. To transfer ownership of a trademark, the owner is also required to transfer everything else necessary for the new owner to produce a product or service indistinguishable from that produced by the former owner. Because the unpatented technical expertise must be separated from the acquiree or combined entity and sold if the related trademark is sold, it meets the separability criterion.

Reacquired rights

B35   As part of a business combination, an acquirer may reacquire a right that it had previously granted to the acquiree to use one or more of the acquirer's recognised or unrecognised assets. Examples of such rights include a right to use the acquirer's trade name under a franchise agreement or a right to use the acquirer's technology under a technology licensing agreement. A reacquired right is an identifiable intangible asset that the acquirer recognises separately from goodwill. Paragraph 29 provides guidance on measuring a reacquired right and paragraph 55 provides guidance on the subsequent accounting for a reacquired right.

B36   If the terms of the contract giving rise to a reacquired right are favourable or unfavourable relative to the terms of current market transactions for the same or similar items, the acquirer shall recognise a settlement gain or loss. Paragraph B52 provides guidance for measuring that settlement gain or loss.

Assembled workforce and other items that are not identifiable

B37   The acquirer subsumes into goodwill the value of an acquired intangible asset that is not identifiable as of the acquisition date. For example, an acquirer may attribute value to the existence of an assembled workforce, which is an existing collection of employees that permits the acquirer to continue to operate an acquired business from the acquisition date. An assembled workforce does not represent the intellectual capital of the skilled workforce—the (often specialised) knowledge and experience that employees of an acquiree bring to their jobs. Because the assembled workforce is not an identifiable asset to be recognised separately from goodwill, any value attributed to it is subsumed into goodwill.

B38   The acquirer also subsumes into goodwill any value attributed to items that do not qualify as assets at the acquisition date. For example, the acquirer might attribute value to potential contracts the acquiree is negotiating with prospective new customers at the acquisition date. Because those potential contracts are not themselves assets at the acquisition date, the acquirer does not recognise them separately from goodwill. The acquirer should not subsequently reclassify the value of those contracts from goodwill for events that occur after the acquisition date. However, the acquirer should assess the facts and circumstances surrounding events occurring shortly after the acquisition to determine whether a separately recognisable intangible asset existed at the acquisition date.

B39   After initial recognition, an acquirer accounts for intangible assets acquired in a business combination in accordance with the provisions of AASB 138 *Intangible Assets*. However, as described in paragraph 3 of AASB 138, the accounting for some acquired intangible assets after initial recognition is prescribed by other Australian Accounting Standards.

B40   The identifiability criteria determine whether an intangible asset is recognised separately from goodwill. However, the criteria neither provide guidance for measuring the fair value of an intangible asset nor restrict the assumptions used in measuring the fair value of an intangible asset. For example, the acquirer would take into account the assumptions that market participants would use when pricing the intangible asset, such as expectations of future contract renewals, in measuring fair value. It is not necessary for the renewals themselves to meet the identifiability criteria. (However, see paragraph 29, which establishes an exception to the fair value measurement principle for reacquired rights recognised in a business combination.) Paragraphs 36 and 37 of AASB 138 provide guidance for determining whether intangible assets should be combined into a single unit of account with other intangible or tangible assets.

Measuring the fair value of particular identifiable assets and a non-controlling interest in an acquiree (application of paragraphs 18 and 19)

Assets with uncertain cash flows (valuation allowances)

B41 The acquirer shall not recognise a separate valuation allowance as of the acquisition date for assets acquired in a business combination that are measured at their acquisition-date fair values because the effects of uncertainty about future cash flows are included in the fair value measure. For example, because this Standard requires the acquirer to measure acquired receivables, including loans, at their acquisition-date fair values in accounting for a business combination, the acquirer does not recognise a separate valuation allowance for the contractual cash flows that are deemed to be uncollectible at that date or a loss allowance for expected credit losses.

Assets subject to operating leases in which the acquiree is the lessor

B42 In measuring the acquisition-date fair value of an asset such as a building or a patent that is subject to an operating lease in which the acquiree is the lessor, the acquirer shall take into account the terms of the lease. In other words, the acquirer does not recognise a separate asset or liability if the terms of an operating lease are either favourable or unfavourable when compared with market terms as paragraph B29 requires for leases in which the acquiree is the lessee.

Assets that the acquirer intends not to use or to use in a way that is different from the way other market participants would use them

B43 To protect its competitive position, or for other reasons, the acquirer may intend not to use an acquired non-financial asset actively, or it may not intend to use the asset according to its highest and best use. For example, that might be the case for an acquired research and development intangible asset that the acquirer plans to use defensively by preventing others from using it. Nevertheless, the acquirer shall measure the fair value of the non-financial asset assuming its highest and best use by market participants in accordance with the appropriate valuation premise, both initially and when measuring fair value less costs of disposal for subsequent impairment testing.

Non-controlling interest in an acquiree

B44 This Standard allows the acquirer to measure a non-controlling interest in the acquiree at its fair value at the acquisition date. Sometimes an acquirer will be able to measure the acquisition-date fair value of a non-controlling interest on the basis of a quoted price in an active market for the equity shares (ie those not held by the acquirer). In other situations, however, a quoted price in an active market for the equity shares will not be available. In those situations, the acquirer would measure the fair value of the non-controlling interest using other valuation techniques.

B45 The fair values of the acquirer's interest in the acquiree and the non-controlling interest on a per-share basis might differ. The main difference is likely to be the inclusion of a control premium in the per-share fair value of the acquirer's interest in the acquiree or, conversely, the inclusion of a discount for lack of control (also referred to as a non-controlling interest discount) in the per-share fair value of the non-controlling interest if market participants would take into account such a premium or discount when pricing the non-controlling interest.

Measuring goodwill or a gain from a bargain purchase

Measuring the acquisition-date fair value of the acquirer's interest in the acquiree using valuation techniques (application of paragraph 33)

B46   In a business combination achieved without the transfer of consideration, the acquirer must substitute the acquisition-date fair value of its interest in the acquiree for the acquisition-date fair value of the consideration transferred to measure goodwill or a gain on a bargain purchase (see paragraphs 32–34).

Special considerations in applying the acquisition method to combinations of mutual entities (application of paragraph 33)

B47   When two mutual entities combine, the fair value of the equity or member interests in the acquiree (or the fair value of the acquiree) may be more reliably measurable than the fair value of the member interests transferred by the acquirer. In that situation, paragraph 33 requires the acquirer to determine the amount of goodwill by using the acquisition-date fair value of the acquiree's equity interests instead of the acquisition-date fair value of the acquirer's equity interests transferred as consideration. In addition, the acquirer in a combination of mutual entities shall recognise the acquiree's net assets as a direct addition to capital or equity in its statement of financial position, not as an addition to retained earnings, which is consistent with the way in which other types of entities apply the acquisition method.

B48   Although they are similar in many ways to other businesses, mutual entities have distinct characteristics that arise primarily because their members are both customers and owners. Members of mutual entities generally expect to receive benefits for their membership, often in the form of reduced fees charged for goods and services or patronage dividends. The portion of patronage dividends allocated to each member is often based on the amount of business the member did with the mutual entity during the year.

B49   A fair value measurement of a mutual entity should include the assumptions that market participants would make about future member benefits as well as any other relevant assumptions market participants would make about the mutual entity. For example, a present value technique may be used to measure the fair value of a mutual entity. The cash flows used as inputs to the model should be based on the expected cash flows of the mutual entity, which are likely to reflect reductions for member benefits, such as reduced fees charged for goods and services.

Determining what is part of the business combination transaction (application of paragraphs 51 and 52)

B50   The acquirer should consider the following factors, which are neither mutually exclusive nor individually conclusive, to determine whether a transaction is part of the exchange for the acquiree or whether the transaction is separate from the business combination:

(a)   **the reasons for the transaction**—Understanding the reasons why the parties to the combination (the acquirer and the acquiree and their owners, directors and managers—and their agents) entered into a particular transaction or arrangement may provide insight into whether it is part of the consideration transferred and the assets acquired or liabilities assumed. For example, if a transaction is arranged primarily for the benefit of the acquirer or the combined entity rather than primarily for the benefit of the acquiree or its former owners before the combination, that portion of the transaction price paid (and any related assets or liabilities) is less likely to be part of the exchange for the acquiree. Accordingly, the acquirer would account for that portion separately from the business combination.

(b)   **who initiated the transaction**—Understanding who initiated the transaction may also provide insight into whether it is part of the exchange for the acquiree.

For example, a transaction or other event that is initiated by the acquirer may be entered into for the purpose of providing future economic benefits to the acquirer or combined entity with little or no benefit received by the acquiree or its former owners before the combination. On the other hand, a transaction or arrangement initiated by the acquiree or its former owners is less likely to be for the benefit of the acquirer or the combined entity and more likely to be part of the business combination transaction.

(c)   **the timing of the transaction**—The timing of the transaction may also provide insight into whether it is part of the exchange for the acquiree. For example, a transaction between the acquirer and the acquiree that takes place during the negotiations of the terms of a business combination may have been entered into in contemplation of the business combination to provide future economic benefits to the acquirer or the combined entity. If so, the acquiree or its former owners before the business combination are likely to receive little or no benefit from the transaction except for benefits they receive as part of the combined entity.

Effective settlement of a pre-existing relationship between the acquirer and acquiree in a business combination (application of paragraph 52(a))

B51   The acquirer and acquiree may have a relationship that existed before they contemplated the business combination, referred to here as a 'pre-existing relationship'. A pre-existing relationship between the acquirer and acquiree may be contractual (for example, vendor and customer or licensor and licensee) or non-contractual (for example, plaintiff and defendant).

B52   If the business combination in effect settles a pre-existing relationship, the acquirer recognises a gain or loss, measured as follows:

(a)   for a pre-existing non-contractual relationship (such as a lawsuit), fair value.

(b)   for a pre-existing contractual relationship, the lesser of (i) and (ii):

(i)   the amount by which the contract is favourable or unfavourable from the perspective of the acquirer when compared with terms for current market transactions for the same or similar items. (An unfavourable contract is a contract that is unfavourable in terms of current market terms. It is not necessarily an onerous contract in which the unavoidable costs of meeting the obligations under the contract exceed the economic benefits expected to be received under it.)

(ii)   the amount of any stated settlement provisions in the contract available to the counterparty to whom the contract is unfavourable.

If (ii) is less than (i), the difference is included as part of the business combination accounting.

The amount of gain or loss recognised may depend in part on whether the acquirer had previously recognised a related asset or liability, and the reported gain or loss therefore may differ from the amount calculated by applying the above requirements.

B53   A pre-existing relationship may be a contract that the acquirer recognises as a reacquired right. If the contract includes terms that are favourable or unfavourable when compared with pricing for current market transactions for the same or similar items, the acquirer recognises, separately from the business combination, a gain or loss for the effective settlement of the contract, measured in accordance with paragraph B52.

Arrangements for contingent payments to employees or selling shareholders (application of paragraph 52(b))

B54   Whether arrangements for contingent payments to employees or selling shareholders are contingent consideration in the business combination or are separate transactions depends on the nature of the arrangements. Understanding the reasons why the acquisition agreement includes a provision for contingent payments, who initiated the arrangement and when the parties entered into the arrangement may be helpful in assessing the nature of the arrangement.

B55 If it is not clear whether an arrangement for payments to employees or selling shareholders is part of the exchange for the acquiree or is a transaction separate from the business combination, the acquirer should consider the following indicators:

(a) *Continuing employment*—The terms of continuing employment by the selling shareholders who become key employees may be an indicator of the substance of a contingent consideration arrangement. The relevant terms of continuing employment may be included in an employment agreement, acquisition agreement or some other document. A contingent consideration arrangement in which the payments are automatically forfeited if employment terminates is remuneration for post-combination services. Arrangements in which the contingent payments are not affected by employment termination may indicate that the contingent payments are additional consideration rather than remuneration.

(b) *Duration of continuing employment*—If the period of required employment coincides with or is longer than the contingent payment period, that fact may indicate that the contingent payments are, in substance, remuneration.

(c) *Level of remuneration*—Situations in which employee remuneration other than the contingent payments is at a reasonable level in comparison with that of other key employees in the combined entity may indicate that the contingent payments are additional consideration rather than remuneration.

(d) *Incremental payments to employees*—If selling shareholders who do not become employees receive lower contingent payments on a per-share basis than the selling shareholders who become employees of the combined entity, that fact may indicate that the incremental amount of contingent payments to the selling shareholders who become employees is remuneration.

(e) *Number of shares owned*—The relative number of shares owned by the selling shareholders who remain as key employees may be an indicator of the substance of the contingent consideration arrangement. For example, if the selling shareholders who owned substantially all of the shares in the acquiree continue as key employees, that fact may indicate that the arrangement is, in substance, a profit-sharing arrangement intended to provide remuneration for post-combination services. Alternatively, if selling shareholders who continue as key employees owned only a small number of shares of the acquiree and all selling shareholders receive the same amount of contingent consideration on a per-share basis, that fact may indicate that the contingent payments are additional consideration. The pre-acquisition ownership interests held by parties related to selling shareholders who continue as key employees, such as family members, should also be considered.

(f) *Linkage to the valuation*—If the initial consideration transferred at the acquisition date is based on the low end of a range established in the valuation of the acquiree and the contingent formula relates to that valuation approach, that fact may suggest that the contingent payments are additional consideration. Alternatively, if the contingent payment formula is consistent with prior profit-sharing arrangements, that fact may suggest that the substance of the arrangement is to provide remuneration.

(g) *Formula for determining consideration*—The formula used to determine the contingent payment may be helpful in assessing the substance of the arrangement. For example, if a contingent payment is determined on the basis of a multiple of earnings, that might suggest that the obligation is contingent consideration in the business combination and that the formula is intended to establish or verify the fair value of the acquiree. In contrast, a contingent payment that is a specified percentage of earnings might suggest that the obligation to employees is a profit-sharing arrangement to remunerate employees for services rendered.

(h)   *Other agreements and issues*—The terms of other arrangements with selling shareholders (such as agreements not to compete, executory contracts, consulting contracts and property lease agreements) and the income tax treatment of contingent payments may indicate that contingent payments are attributable to something other than consideration for the acquiree. For example, in connection with the acquisition, the acquirer might enter into a property lease arrangement with a significant selling shareholder. If the lease payments specified in the lease contract are significantly below market, some or all of the contingent payments to the lessor (the selling shareholder) required by a separate arrangement for contingent payments might be, in substance, payments for the use of the leased property that the acquirer should recognise separately in its post-combination financial statements. In contrast, if the lease contract specifies lease payments that are consistent with market terms for the leased property, the arrangement for contingent payments to the selling shareholder may be contingent consideration in the business combination.

Acquirer share-based payment awards exchanged for awards held by the acquiree's employees (application of paragraph 52(b))

B56   An acquirer may exchange its share-based payment awards[2] (replacement awards) for awards held by employees of the acquiree. Exchanges of share options or other share-based payment awards in conjunction with a business combination are accounted for as modifications of share-based payment awards in accordance with AASB 2 *Share-based Payment*. If the acquirer replaces the acquiree awards, either all or a portion of the market-based measure of the acquirer's replacement awards shall be included in measuring the consideration transferred in the business combination. Paragraphs B57–B62 provide guidance on how to allocate the market-based measure. However, in situations in which acquiree awards would expire as a consequence of a business combination and if the acquirer replaces those awards when it is not obliged to do so, all of the market-based measure of the replacement awards shall be recognised as remuneration cost in the post-combination financial statements in accordance with AASB 2. That is to say, none of the market-based measure of those awards shall be included in measuring the consideration transferred in the business combination. The acquirer is obliged to replace the acquiree awards if the acquiree or its employees have the ability to enforce replacement. For example, for the purposes of applying this guidance, the acquirer is obliged to replace the acquiree's awards if replacement is required by:

(a)   the terms of the acquisition agreement;

(b)   the terms of the acquiree's awards; or

(c)   applicable laws or regulations.

B57   To determine the portion of a replacement award that is part of the consideration transferred for the acquiree and the portion that is remuneration for post-combination service, the acquirer shall measure both the replacement awards granted by the acquirer and the acquiree awards as of the acquisition date in accordance with AASB 2. The portion of the market-based measure of the replacement award that is part of the consideration transferred in exchange for the acquiree equals the portion of the acquiree award that is attributable to pre-combination service.

B58   The portion of the replacement award attributable to pre-combination service is the market-based measure of the acquiree award multiplied by the ratio of the portion of the vesting period completed to the greater of the total vesting period or the original vesting period of the acquiree award. The vesting period is the period during which all the specified vesting conditions are to be satisfied. Vesting conditions are defined in AASB 2.

---

2   In paragraphs B56–B62 the term 'share-based payment awards' refers to vested or unvested share-based payment transactions.

B59 The portion of a non-vested replacement award attributable to post-combination service, and therefore recognised as remuneration cost in the post-combination financial statements, equals the total market-based measure of the replacement award less the amount attributed to pre-combination service. Therefore, the acquirer attributes any excess of the market-based measure of the replacement award over the market-based measure of the acquiree award to post-combination service and recognises that excess as remuneration cost in the post-combination financial statements. The acquirer shall attribute a portion of a replacement award to post-combination service if it requires post-combination service, regardless of whether employees had rendered all of the service required for their acquiree awards to vest before the acquisition date.

B60 The portion of a non-vested replacement award attributable to pre-combination service, as well as the portion attributable to post-combination service, shall reflect the best available estimate of the number of replacement awards expected to vest. For example, if the market-based measure of the portion of a replacement award attributed to pre-combination service is CU100 and the acquirer expects that only 95 per cent of the award will vest, the amount included in consideration transferred in the business combination is CU95. Changes in the estimated number of replacement awards expected to vest are reflected in remuneration cost for the periods in which the changes or forfeitures occur not as adjustments to the consideration transferred in the business combination. Similarly, the effects of other events, such as modifications or the ultimate outcome of awards with performance conditions, that occur after the acquisition date are accounted for in accordance with AASB 2 in determining remuneration cost for the period in which an event occurs.

B61 The same requirements for determining the portions of a replacement award attributable to pre-combination and post-combination service apply regardless of whether a replacement award is classified as a liability or as an equity instrument in accordance with the provisions of AASB 2. All changes in the market-based measure of awards classified as liabilities after the acquisition date and the related income tax effects are recognised in the acquirer's post-combination financial statements in the period(s) in which the changes occur.

B62 The income tax effects of replacement awards of share-based payments shall be recognised in accordance with the provisions of AASB 112 *Income Taxes*.

Equity-settled share-based payment transactions of the acquiree

B62A The acquiree may have outstanding share-based payment transactions that the acquirer does not exchange for its share-based payment transactions. If vested, those acquiree share-based payment transactions are part of the non-controlling interest in the acquiree and are measured at their market-based measure. If unvested, they are measured at their market-based measure as if the acquisition date were the grant date in accordance with paragraphs 19 and 30.

B62B The market-based measure of unvested share-based payment transactions is allocated to the non-controlling interest on the basis of the ratio of the portion of the vesting period completed to the greater of the total vesting period and the original vesting period of the share-based payment transaction. The balance is allocated to post-combination service.

Other Australian Accounting Standards that provide guidance on subsequent measurement and accounting (application of paragraph 54)

B63 Examples of other Australian Accounting Standards that provide guidance on subsequently measuring and accounting for assets acquired and liabilities assumed or incurred in a business combination include:

(a) AASB 138 prescribes the accounting for identifiable intangible assets acquired in a business combination. The acquirer measures goodwill at the amount recognised at the acquisition date less any accumulated impairment losses.

AASB 136 *Impairment of Assets* prescribes the accounting for impairment losses.

(b)   AASB 4 *Insurance Contracts* provides guidance on the subsequent accounting for an insurance contract acquired in a business combination.

(c)   AASB 112 prescribes the subsequent accounting for deferred tax assets (including unrecognised deferred tax assets) and liabilities acquired in a business combination.

(d)   AASB 2 provides guidance on subsequent measurement and accounting for the portion of replacement share-based payment awards issued by an acquirer that is attributable to employees' future services.

(e)   AASB 10 provides guidance on accounting for changes in a parent's ownership interest in a subsidiary after control is obtained.

Disclosures (application of paragraphs 59 and 61)

B64   To meet the objective in paragraph 59, the acquirer shall disclose the following information for each business combination that occurs during the reporting period:

(a)   the name and a description of the acquiree.

(b)   the acquisition date.

(c)   the percentage of voting equity interests acquired.

(d)   the primary reasons for the business combination and a description of how the acquirer obtained control of the acquiree.

(e)   a qualitative description of the factors that make up the goodwill recognised, such as expected synergies from combining operations of the acquiree and the acquirer, intangible assets that do not qualify for separate recognition or other factors.

(f)   the acquisition-date fair value of the total consideration transferred and the acquisition-date fair value of each major class of consideration, such as:

    (i)   cash;

    (ii)   other tangible or intangible assets, including a business or subsidiary of the acquirer;

    (iii)   liabilities incurred, for example, a liability for contingent consideration; and

    (iv)   equity interests of the acquirer, including the number of instruments or interests issued or issuable and the method of measuring the fair value of those instruments or interests.

(g)   for contingent consideration arrangements and indemnification assets:

    (i)   the amount recognised as of the acquisition date;

    (ii)   a description of the arrangement and the basis for determining the amount of the payment; and

    (iii)   an estimate of the range of outcomes (undiscounted) or, if a range cannot be estimated, that fact and the reasons why a range cannot be estimated. If the maximum amount of the payment is unlimited, the acquirer shall disclose that fact.

(h)   for acquired receivables:

    (i)   the fair value of the receivables;

    (ii)   the gross contractual amounts receivable; and

    (iii)   the best estimate at the acquisition date of the contractual cash flows not expected to be collected.

The disclosures shall be provided by major class of receivable, such as loans, direct finance leases and any other class of receivables.

(i) the amounts recognised as of the acquisition date for each major class of assets acquired and liabilities assumed.

(j) for each contingent liability recognised in accordance with paragraph 23, the information required in paragraph 85 of AASB 137 *Provisions, Contingent Liabilities and Contingent Assets*. If a contingent liability is not recognised because its fair value cannot be measured reliably, the acquirer shall disclose:

(i) the information required by paragraph 86 of AASB 137; and
(ii) the reasons why the liability cannot be measured reliably.

(k) the total amount of goodwill that is expected to be deductible for tax purposes.

(l) for transactions that are recognised separately from the acquisition of assets and assumption of liabilities in the business combination in accordance with paragraph 51:

(i) a description of each transaction;
(ii) how the acquirer accounted for each transaction;
(iii) the amounts recognised for each transaction and the line item in the financial statements in which each amount is recognised; and
(iv) if the transaction is the effective settlement of a pre-existing relationship, the method used to determine the settlement amount.

(m) the disclosure of separately recognised transactions required by (l) shall include the amount of acquisition-related costs and, separately, the amount of those costs recognised as an expense and the line item or items in the statement of comprehensive income in which those expenses are recognised. The amount of any issue costs not recognised as an expense and how they were recognised shall also be disclosed.

(n) in a bargain purchase (see paragraphs 34–36):

(i) the amount of any gain recognised in accordance with paragraph 34 and the line item in the statement of comprehensive income in which the gain is recognised; and
(ii) a description of the reasons why the transaction resulted in a gain.

(o) for each business combination in which the acquirer holds less than 100 per cent of the equity interests in the acquiree at the acquisition date:

(i) the amount of the non-controlling interest in the acquiree recognised at the acquisition date and the measurement basis for that amount; and
(ii) for each non-controlling interest in an acquiree measured at fair value, the valuation technique(s) and significant inputs used to measure that value.

(p) in a business combination achieved in stages:

(i) the acquisition-date fair value of the equity interest in the acquiree held by the acquirer immediately before the acquisition date; and
(ii) the amount of any gain or loss recognised as a result of remeasuring to fair value the equity interest in the acquiree held by the acquirer before the business combination (see paragraph 42) and the line item in the statement of comprehensive income in which that gain or loss is recognised.

(q) the following information:

(i) the amounts of revenue and profit or loss of the acquiree since the acquisition date included in the consolidated statement of comprehensive income for the reporting period; and
(ii) the revenue and profit or loss of the combined entity for the current reporting period as though the acquisition date for all business

combinations that occurred during the year had been as of the beginning of the annual reporting period.

If disclosure of any of the information required by this subparagraph is impracticable, the acquirer shall disclose that fact and explain why the disclosure is impracticable. This Standard uses the term 'impracticable' with the same meaning as in AASB 108 *Accounting Policies, Changes in Accounting Estimates and Errors*.

B65   For individually immaterial business combinations occurring during the reporting period that are material collectively, the acquirer shall disclose in aggregate the information required by paragraph B64(e)–(q).

B66   If the acquisition date of a business combination is after the end of the reporting period but before the financial statements are authorised for issue, the acquirer shall disclose the information required by paragraph B64 unless the initial accounting for the business combination is incomplete at the time the financial statements are authorised for issue. In that situation, the acquirer shall describe which disclosures could not be made and the reasons why they cannot be made.

B67   To meet the objective in paragraph 61, the acquirer shall disclose the following information for each material business combination or in the aggregate for individually immaterial business combinations that are material collectively:

(a)   if the initial accounting for a business combination is incomplete (see paragraph 45) for particular assets, liabilities, non-controlling interests or items of consideration and the amounts recognised in the financial statements for the business combination thus have been determined only provisionally:

   (i)   the reasons why the initial accounting for the business combination is incomplete;

   (ii)   the assets, liabilities, equity interests or items of consideration for which the initial accounting is incomplete; and

   (iii)   the nature and amount of any measurement period adjustments recognised during the reporting period in accordance with paragraph 49.

(b)   for each reporting period after the acquisition date until the entity collects, sells or otherwise loses the right to a contingent consideration asset, or until the entity settles a contingent consideration liability or the liability is cancelled or expires:

   (i)   any changes in the recognised amounts, including any differences arising upon settlement;

   (ii)   any changes in the range of outcomes (undiscounted) and the reasons for those changes; and

   (iii)   the valuation techniques and key model inputs used to measure contingent consideration.

(c)   for contingent liabilities recognised in a business combination, the acquirer shall disclose the information required by paragraphs 84 and 85 of AASB 137 for each class of provision.

(d)   a reconciliation of the carrying amount of goodwill at the beginning and end of the reporting period showing separately:

   (i)   the gross amount and accumulated impairment losses at the beginning of the reporting period.

   (ii)   additional goodwill recognised during the reporting period, except goodwill included in a disposal group that, on acquisition, meets the criteria to be classified as held for sale in accordance with AASB 5 *Non-current Assets Held for Sale and Discontinued Operations*.

   (iii)   adjustments resulting from the subsequent recognition of deferred tax assets during the reporting period in accordance with paragraph 67.

(iv) goodwill included in a disposal group classified as held for sale in accordance with AASB 5 and goodwill derecognised during the reporting period without having previously been included in a disposal group classified as held for sale.

(v) impairment losses recognised during the reporting period in accordance with AASB 136. (AASB 136 requires disclosure of information about the recoverable amount and impairment of goodwill in addition to this requirement.)

(vi) net exchange rate differences arising during the reporting period in accordance with AASB 121 *The Effects of Changes in Foreign Exchange Rates*.

(vii) any other changes in the carrying amount during the reporting period.

(viii) the gross amount and accumulated impairment losses at the end of the reporting period.

(e) the amount and an explanation of any gain or loss recognised in the current reporting period that both:

(i) relates to the identifiable assets acquired or liabilities assumed in a business combination that was effected in the current or previous reporting period; and

(ii) is of such a size, nature or incidence that disclosure is relevant to understanding the combined entity's financial statements.

Transitional provisions for business combinations involving only mutual entities or by contract alone (application of paragraph 66)

B68 [Deleted by the AASB]

AusB68.1 Paragraph Aus65.1 provides that this Standard applies prospectively to business combinations for which the acquisition date is on or after the beginning of the first annual reporting period beginning on or after 1 July 2009. Earlier application is permitted.

B69 The requirement to apply this Standard prospectively has the following effect for a business combination involving only mutual entities or by contract alone if the acquisition date for that business combination is before the application of the previous version of this Standard:

(a) *Classification*—An entity shall continue to classify the prior business combination in accordance with the entity's previous accounting policies for such combinations.

(b) *Previously recognised goodwill*—At the beginning of the first annual period in which the previous version of this Standard is applied, the carrying amount of goodwill arising from the prior business combination shall be its carrying amount at that date in accordance with the entity's previous accounting policies. In determining that amount, the entity shall eliminate the carrying amount of any accumulated amortisation of that goodwill and the corresponding decrease in goodwill. No other adjustments shall be made to the carrying amount of goodwill.

(c) *Goodwill previously recognised as a deduction from equity*—The entity's previous accounting policies may have resulted in goodwill arising from the prior business combination being recognised as a deduction from equity. In that situation the entity shall not recognise that goodwill as an asset at the beginning of the first annual period in which the previous version of this Standard is applied. Furthermore, the entity shall not recognise in profit or loss any part of that goodwill when it disposes of all or part of the business to which that goodwill relates or when a cash-generating unit to which the goodwill relates becomes impaired.

(d) *Subsequent accounting for goodwill*—From the beginning of the first annual period in which the previous version of this Standard is applied, an entity shall discontinue amortising goodwill arising from the prior business combination and shall test goodwill for impairment in accordance with AASB 136.

(e) *Previously recognised negative goodwill*—An entity that accounted for the prior business combination by applying the purchase method may have recognised a deferred credit for an excess of its interest in the net fair value of the acquiree's identifiable assets and liabilities over the cost of that interest (sometimes called negative goodwill). If so, the entity shall derecognise the carrying amount of that deferred credit at the beginning of the first annual period in which the previous version of this Standard is applied with a corresponding adjustment to the opening balance of retained earnings at that date.

APPENDIX C
AUSTRALIAN REDUCED DISCLOSURE REQUIREMENTS

This appendix is an integral part of the Standard.

AusC1   **The following do not apply to entities preparing general purpose financial statements under Australian Accounting Standards – Reduced Disclosure Requirements:**

      (a)   **paragraphs 59-63, Aus63.6–Aus63.9, B64(d), B64(e), B64(h), B64(k), B64(l), B64(m), B64(n)(ii), B64(q), B65, B66, B67(a)-(c) and B67(e);**

      (b)   **in the heading before paragraph B64, the text "(application of paragraphs 59 and 61)";**

      (c)   **in paragraph B64, the text "To meet the objective in paragraph 59,";**

      (d)   **in paragraph B64(j), the sentence "If a contingent liability ... liability cannot be measured reliably."; and**

      (e)   **in paragraph B67, the text "To meet the objective in paragraph 61,".**

      Entities applying Australian Accounting Standards – Reduced Disclosure Requirements may elect to comply with some or all of these excluded requirements.

AusC2   The requirements that do not apply to entities preparing general purpose financial statements under Australian Accounting Standards – Reduced Disclosure Requirements are also identified in this Standard by shading of the relevant text, except for comparative disclosures subject to RDR paragraphs.

AusC3   **RDR paragraphs in this Standard apply only to entities preparing general purpose financial statements under Australian Accounting Standards – Reduced Disclosure Requirements.**

RDRB65.1 For individually immaterial business combinations occurring during the reporting period that are material collectively, an acquirer applying Australian Accounting Standards – Reduced Disclosure Requirements shall disclose in aggregate the information required by paragraphs B64(f), B64(g), B64(i), B64(n)(i), B64(o)(i) and B64(p) and the first sentence of paragraph B64(j).

RDRB67.1 An entity applying Australian Accounting Standards – Reduced Disclosure Requirements is not required to disclose the reconciliation specified in paragraph B67(d) for prior periods.

DELETED IFRS 3 TEXT

Deleted IFRS 3 text is not part of AASB 3.

64   This IFRS shall be applied prospectively to business combinations for which the acquisition date is on or after the beginning of the first annual reporting period beginning on or after 1 July 2009. Earlier application is permitted. However, this IFRS shall be applied only at the beginning of an annual reporting period that begins on or after 30 June 2007. If an entity applies this IFRS before 1 July 2009, it shall disclose that fact and apply IAS 27 (as amended in 2008) at the same time.

64B   *Improvements to IFRSs* issued in May 2010 amended paragraphs 19, 30 and B56 and added paragraphs B62A and B62B. An entity shall apply those amendments for annual periods beginning on or after 1 July 2010. Earlier application is permitted. If an entity applies the amendments for an earlier period it shall disclose that fact. Application should be prospective from the date when the entity first applied this IFRS.

64C   Paragraphs 65A–65E were added by *Improvements to IFRSs* issued in May 2010. An entity shall apply those amendments for annual periods beginning on or after 1 July 2010. Earlier application is permitted. If an entity applies the amendments for an earlier period it shall disclose that fact. The amendments shall be applied to contingent consideration balances arising from business combinations with an acquisition date prior to the application of this IFRS, as issued in 2008.

64E   IFRS 10, issued in May 2011, amended paragraphs 7, B13, B63(e) and Appendix A. An entity shall apply those amendments when it applies IFRS 10.

64F   IFRS 13 *Fair Value Measurement*, issued in May 2011, amended paragraphs 20, 29, 33, 47, amended the definition of fair value in Appendix A and amended paragraphs B22, B40, B43–B46, B49 and B64. An entity shall apply those amendments when it applies IFRS 13.

64G   *Investment Entities* (Amendments to IFRS 10, IFRS 12 and IAS 27), issued in October 2012, amended paragraph 7 and added paragraph 2A. An entity shall apply those amendments for annual periods beginning on or after 1 January 2014. Earlier application of *Investment Entities* is permitted. If an entity applies these amendments earlier it shall also apply all amendments included in *Investment Entities* at the same time.

65   Assets and liabilities that arose from business combinations whose acquisition dates preceded the application of this Standard shall not be adjusted upon application of this Standard.

68   This IFRS supersedes IFRS 3 *Business Combinations* (as issued in 2004).

B68   Paragraph 64 provides that this IFRS applies prospectively to business combinations for which the acquisition date is on or after the beginning of the first annual reporting period beginning on or after 1 July 2009. Earlier application is permitted. However, an entity shall apply this IFRS only at the beginning of an annual reporting period that begins on or after 30 June 2007. If an entity applies this IFRS before its effective date, the entity shall disclose that fact and shall apply IAS 27 (as amended in 2008) at the same time.

BASIS FOR CONCLUSIONS ON AASB 2008-11

This Basis for Conclusions accompanies, but is not part of, AASB 3. The Basis for Conclusions was originally published with AASB 2008-11 Amendments to Australian Accounting Standard – Business Combinations Among Not-for-Profit Entities.

Background

BC1   This Basis for Conclusions summarises the Australian Accounting Standards Board's (AASB) decisions in reaching the conclusions in this Standard. Individual Board members gave greater weight to some factors than to others.

Significant issues

BC2   The AASB issued a revised AASB 3 *Business Combinations* in March 2008. At that time, the Board decided that the requirements of AASB 3 (March 2008) should only be available for early adoption by for-profit entities, until further work was undertaken on the implications of applying the requirements of AASB 3 (March 2008) to not-for-profit entities. Accordingly, the Board included in the Preface to AASB 3 (March 2008) the following statement:

> Prior to the mandatory application date of this Standard, being 1 July 2009, the AASB will consider its suitability for combinations among not-for-profit entities. In doing so, the AASB will have regard to the criteria being developed for judging when IFRSs should be modified for application by not-for-profit entities. Those criteria will assist in clarifying whether this Standard should be amended to include an additional scope exclusion or other amendments and, if so, the extent of that exclusion or other amendments in an Australian not-for-profit context. In light of this, not-for-profit entities cannot adopt this Standard prior to the mandatory application date.

BC3   As part of its subsequent deliberations, the Board noted the view of some that the difficulties in applying the acquisition method when a business combination does not involve consideration (including the difficulties of identifying an acquirer), which is often the case in business combinations among not-for-profit entities, means that the principles in AASB 3 (March 2008) are inappropriate for such combinations. However, the Board decided that, in principle, there is no conceptual basis for accounting for business combinations among not-for-profit entities differently from other analogous types of business combinations.

BC4   In particular, the Board noted that the types of difficulties noted in paragraph BC3 are also issues that may be encountered in business combinations of for-profit entities (such as combinations by contract alone). Therefore, consistent with transaction-neutral principles, the Board did not consider that there was sufficient reason to justify a different accounting treatment for business combinations among not-for-profit entities.

BC5   The Board observed that the motivations for business combinations among not-for-profit entities, such as to provide their beneficiaries with a broader range of, or access to, services and cost savings through economies of scale, are similar to those for business combinations among other entities. The Board noted a possible alternative to the acquisition method in AASB 3 for business combinations among not-for-profit entities might be the 'fresh start' method, especially where it is difficult to identify the acquirer. The fresh start method assumes that none of the combining entities survives the business combination as an independent reporting entity. Rather, the business combination is viewed as a transfer of the net assets of the combining entities to a new entity that assumes control over them. The Board noted the potential significant costs and practical difficulties that a fresh start alternative would impose, and therefore concluded that the potential advantages of using the fresh start method for some business combinations among not-for-profit entities would be outweighed by the disadvantages.

BC6   However, the Board noted that the accounting for business combinations may differ depending on whether entities, such as local governments or universities, are commonly controlled. In that regard, the Board confirmed that further work should be undertaken on its longer-term 'control in the public sector' project, which should include consideration of whether local governments or universities within a jurisdiction are subject to common control.

BC7   In the interim, the Board decided to maintain the status quo in respect of accounting for restructures of local governments by substantially incorporating the requirements originally transferred from AAS 27 *Financial Reporting by Local Governments* to superseded AASB 3 (as amended in December 2007 by AASB 2007-9 *Amendments to Australian Accounting Standards arising from the Review of AASs 27, 29 and 31*) into revised AASB 3 (March 2008, as amended). The Board noted that the relief carried forward from AAS 27 might be impacted by the progress it makes on its 'control in the public sector' project.

BC8 The Board noted that this approach to restructures of local governments, consistent with its general approach to the short-term review of AASs 27, 29 and 31, is pragmatic and a consequence of the past requirements in AAS 27.

BC9 The Board also considered the amendments made by the New Zealand Financial Reporting Standards Board to revised NZ IFRS 3 *Business Combinations* (March 2008) in the context of business combinations among not-for-profit entities, including definitions of public benefit entities, business and equity interests. In making its decision, the Board considered the work undertaken to date on Invitation to Comment ITC 14 *Not-for-Profit Entity Definition and Guidance*, which sought input on using the definition and guidance from NZ IAS 1 *Presentation of Financial Statements* in Australia. The Board suspended further work on ITC 14 until the development of guidelines that can be used for modifying IFRSs for application by not-for-profit entities. In light of this, the Board decided that no further changes should be made to AASB 3 (March 2008, as amended) in respect of not-for-profit entities.

AASB 4

Insurance Contracts

(Compiled July 2017)

For-profit (FP) entities

This compiled Standard applies to annual periods beginning on or after 1 January 2018 but before 1 January 2019. Earlier application is not permitted. It incorporates relevant amendments made up to and including 19 July 2017.

Not-for-profit (NFP) entities – early application only

This compiled Standard does not apply mandatorily to NFP entities. However, earlier application is permitted for annual reporting periods beginning on or after 1 January 2018 but before 1 January 2019.

Prepared on 20 March 2018 by the staff of the Australian Accounting Standards Board.

Compilation no. 2

Compilation date: 31 December 2017

This note is not part of Accounting Standard AASB 4.

The following unincorporated amendments are not included in this compiled Standard.

- AASB 16 *Leases* — Appendix D sets out the amendments to other Standards that are a consequence of the AASB issuing this Standard. It is applicable from 1 January 2019. Earlier application is permitted, but entities must apply AASB 15 *Revenue from Contracts with Customers* before applying this Standard.

- *AASB 2016-7 Amendments to Australian Accounting Standards — Deferral of AASB 15 for Not-for-Profit Entities.* This Standard defers the consequential amendments that were originally set out in AASB 2014-5 *Amendments to Australian Accounting Standards arising from AASB 15*, by restating the effective date of the amendments set out in AASB 2015-8 *Amendments to Australian Accounting Standards* for not-for-profit entities. This Standard defers the application of AASB 15 to 1 January 2019. Earlier application is permitted provided AASB 1058 is also applied to the same period.

Entities early-adopting any amendments with later application dates will need to refer to the amending Standards that have not yet been incorporated into compilations. The abovementioned unincorporated amendments may be located on the AASB website at www.aasb.gov.au or on the Federal Register of Legislation website at www.legislation.gov.au.

CONTENTS

COMPARISON WITH IFRS 4
ACCOUNTING STANDARD
AASB 4 *INSURANCE CONTRACTS*

AASB

Australian Accounting Standard AASB 4 *Insurance Contracts* (as amended) is set out in paragraphs 1 – 49 and Appendices A – C. All the paragraphs have equal authority. Paragraphs in **bold type** state the main principles. Terms defined in this Standard are in *italics* the first time they appear in the Standard. AASB 4 is to be read in the context of other Australian Accounting Standards, including AASB 1048 *Interpretation of Standards*, which identifies the Australian Accounting Interpretations, and AASB 1057 *Application of Australian Accounting Standards*. In the absence of explicit guidance, AASB 108 *Accounting Policies, Changes in Accounting Estimates and Errors* provides a basis for selecting and applying accounting policies.

COMPARISON WITH IFRS 4

AASB 4 *Insurance Contracts* as amended incorporates IFRS 4 *Insurance Contracts* as issued and amended by the International Accounting Standards Board (IASB). Australian-specific paragraphs (which are not included in IFRS 4) are identified with the prefix "Aus". Paragraphs that apply only to not-for-profit entities begin by identifying their limited applicability.

Tier 1

For-profit entities complying with AASB 4 also comply with IFRS 4.

Not-for-profit entities' compliance with IFRS 4 will depend on whether any "Aus" paragraphs that specifically apply to not-for-profit entities provide additional guidance or contain applicable requirements that are inconsistent with IFRS 4.

AASB 1053 *Application of Tiers of Australian Accounting Standards* explains the two tiers of reporting requirements.

ACCOUNTING STANDARD AASB 4

The Australian Accounting Standards Board made Accounting Standard AASB 4 *Insurance Contracts* under section 334 of the *Corporations Act 2001* on 7 August 2015.

This compiled version of AASB 4 applies to annual periods beginning on or after 1 January 2018 but before 1 January 2019 for for-profit entities. It incorporates relevant amendments contained in other AASB Standards made by the AASB up to and including 19 July 2017 (see Compilation Details).

ACCOUNTING STANDARD AASB 4
INSURANCE CONTRACTS

Objective

1   The objective of this Standard, in conjunction with AASB 1023 *General Insurance Contracts* and AASB 1038 *Life Insurance Contracts*, is to specify the financial reporting for *insurance contracts* by any entity that issues such contracts (described in this Standard as an *insurer*) until the AASB and the IASB complete the second phase of the project on insurance contracts. In particular, this Standard requires:

      (a)   limited improvements to accounting by insurers for insurance contracts.

      (b)   disclosure that identifies and explains the amounts in an insurer's financial statements arising from insurance contracts and helps users of those financial statements understand the amount, timing and uncertainty of future cash flows from insurance contracts.

Scope

2 An entity shall apply this Standard to:

    (a) insurance contracts (including *reinsurance contracts*) that it issues and reinsurance contracts that it holds.

    (b) financial instruments that it issues with a *discretionary participation feature* (see paragraph 35). AASB 7 *Financial Instruments: Disclosures* requires disclosure about financial instruments, including financial instruments that contain such features.

3 This Standard does not address other aspects of accounting by insurers, such as accounting for financial assets held by insurers and financial liabilities issued by insurers (see AASB 132 *Financial Instruments: Presentation*, AASB 7 and AASB 9 *Financial Instruments*), except:

    (a) paragraph 20A permits insurers that meet specified criteria to apply a temporary exemption from AASB 9;

    (b) paragraph 35B permits insurers to apply the overlay approach to designated financial assets; and

    (c) paragraph 45 permits insurers to reclassify in specified circumstances some or all of their financial assets so that the assets are measured at fair value through profit or loss.

Aus3.1 Notwithstanding paragraph 2, to comply with the requirements of this Standard, an entity shall apply:

    (a) AASB 1023 *General Insurance Contracts* to *general insurance contracts*, except for fixed-fee service contracts that meet the definition of an insurance contract under this Standard; and

    (b) AASB 1038 *Life Insurance Contracts* to *life insurance contracts*.

    Where this Standard provides an accounting policy choice, an entity shall apply that choice in the context of the requirements specified in AASB 1023 and AASB 1038, when applicable.

Aus3.2 This Standard includes only limited guidance in accounting for insurance contracts and disclosure requirements. AASB 1023 and AASB 1038 address all aspects of recognition, measurement and disclosure of general insurance contracts and life insurance contracts. The requirements of those Standards address a wider range of accounting requirements than this Standard, but enable simultaneous compliance with this Standard.

4 An entity shall not apply this Standard to:

    (a) product warranties issued directly by a manufacturer, dealer or retailer (see AASB 15 *Revenue from Contracts with Customers* and AASB 137 *Provisions, Contingent Liabilities and Contingent Assets*).

    (b) employers' assets and liabilities under employee benefit plans (see AASB 119 *Employee Benefits* and AASB 2 *Share-based Payment*) and retirement benefit obligations reported by defined benefit retirement plans (see AASB 1056 *Superannuation Entities*).

    (c) contractual rights or contractual obligations that are contingent on the future use of, or right to use, a non-financial item (for example, some licence fees, royalties, contingent lease payments and similar items), as well as a lessee's residual value guarantee embedded in a finance lease (see AASB 117 *Leases*, AASB 15 *Revenue from Contracts with Customers* and AASB 138 *Intangible Assets*).

    (d) financial guarantee contracts unless the issuer has previously asserted explicitly that it regards such contracts as insurance contracts and has used accounting applicable to insurance contracts, in which case the issuer may elect to apply either AASB 132, AASB 7 and AASB 9 or AASB 1023 to such financial

AASB

guarantee contracts. The issuer may make that election contract by contract, but the election for each contract is irrevocable.

(e) contingent consideration payable or receivable in a business combination (see AASB 3 *Business Combinations*).

(f) *direct insurance contracts* that the entity holds (ie direct insurance contracts in which the entity is the *policyholder*). However, a *cedant* shall apply this Standard to reinsurance contracts that it holds.

5 For ease of reference, this Standard describes any entity that issues an insurance contract as an insurer, whether or not the issuer is regarded as an insurer for legal or supervisory purposes. All references in paragraphs 3(a)–3(b), 20A–20Q, 35B–35N, 39B–39M and 46–49 to an insurer shall be read as also referring to an issuer of a financial instrument that contains a discretionary participation feature.

6 A reinsurance contract is a type of insurance contract. Accordingly, all references in this Standard to insurance contracts also apply to reinsurance contracts.

Aus6.1 This Standard applies to fixed-fee service contracts, described in paragraphs B6 and B7, which meet the definition of an insurance contract under this Standard.

Embedded derivatives

7 AASB 9 requires an entity to separate some embedded derivatives from their host contract, measure them at *fair value* and include changes in their fair value in profit or loss. AASB 9 applies to derivatives embedded in an insurance contract unless the embedded derivative is itself an insurance contract.

8 As an exception to the requirements in AASB 9, an insurer need not separate, and measure at fair value, a policyholder's option to surrender an insurance contract for a fixed amount (or for an amount based on a fixed amount and an interest rate), even if the exercise price differs from the carrying amount of the host *insurance liability*. However, the requirements in AASB 9 do apply to a put option or cash surrender option embedded in an insurance contract if the surrender value varies in response to the change in a financial variable (such as an equity or commodity price or index), or a non-financial variable that is not specific to a party to the contract. Furthermore, those requirements also apply if the holder's ability to exercise a put option or cash surrender option is triggered by a change in such a variable (for example, a put option that can be exercised if a stock market index reaches a specified level).

9 Paragraph 8 applies equally to options to surrender a financial instrument containing a discretionary participation feature.

Unbundling of deposit components

10 Some insurance contracts contain both an insurance component and a *deposit component*. In some cases, an insurer is required or permitted to *unbundle* those components:

(a) unbundling is required if both the following conditions are met:

(i) the insurer can measure the deposit component (including any embedded surrender options) separately (ie without considering the insurance component).

(ii) the insurer's accounting policies do not otherwise require it to recognise all obligations and rights arising from the deposit component.

(b) unbundling is permitted, but not required, if the insurer can measure the deposit component separately as in (a)(i) but its accounting policies require it to recognise all obligations and rights arising from the deposit component, regardless of the basis used to measure those rights and obligations.

(c)   unbundling is prohibited if an insurer cannot measure the deposit component separately as in (a)(i).

11   The following is an example of a case when an insurer's accounting policies do not require it to recognise all obligations arising from a deposit component. A cedant receives compensation for losses from a *reinsurer*, but the contract obliges the cedant to repay the compensation in future years. That obligation arises from a deposit component. If the cedant's accounting policies would otherwise permit it to recognise the compensation as income without recognising the resulting obligation, unbundling is required.

12   To unbundle a contract, an insurer shall:

(a)   apply this Standard to the insurance component.

(b)   apply AASB 9 to the deposit component.

Recognition and measurement

Temporary exemption from some other Australian Accounting Standards

13   Paragraphs 10–12 of AASB 108 *Accounting Policies, Changes in Accounting Estimates and Errors* specify criteria for an entity to use in developing an accounting policy if no Standard applies specifically to an item. However, this Standard exempts an insurer from applying those criteria to its accounting policies for:

(a)   insurance contracts that it issues (including related acquisition costs and related intangible assets, such as those described in paragraphs 31 and 32); and

(b)   reinsurance contracts that it holds.

14   Nevertheless, this Standard does not exempt an insurer from some implications of the criteria in paragraphs 10–12 of AASB 108. Specifically, an insurer:

(a)   shall not recognise as a liability any provisions for possible future claims, if those claims arise under insurance contracts that are not in existence at the end of the reporting period (such as catastrophe provisions and equalisation provisions).

(b)   shall carry out the *liability adequacy test* described in paragraphs 15–19.

(c)   shall remove an insurance liability (or a part of an insurance liability) from its statement of financial position when, and only when, it is extinguished— ie when the obligation specified in the contract is discharged or cancelled or expires.

(d)   shall not offset:

(i)   *reinsurance assets* against the related insurance liabilities; or

(ii)   income or expense from reinsurance contracts against the expense or income from the related insurance contracts.

(e)   shall consider whether its reinsurance assets are impaired (see paragraph 20).

Liability adequacy test

15   An insurer shall assess at the end of each reporting period whether its recognised insurance liabilities are adequate, using current estimates of future cash flows under its insurance contracts. If that assessment shows that the carrying amount of its insurance liabilities (less related deferred acquisition costs and related intangible assets, such as those discussed in paragraphs 31 and 32) is inadequate in the light of the estimated future cash flows, the entire deficiency shall be recognised in profit or loss.

16   If an insurer applies a liability adequacy test that meets specified minimum requirements, this Standard imposes no further requirements. The minimum requirements are the following:

(a)   The test considers current estimates of all contractual cash flows, and of related cash flows such as claims handling costs, as well as cash flows resulting from embedded options and guarantees.

(b)   If the test shows that the liability is inadequate, the entire deficiency is recognised in profit or loss.

17   If an insurer's accounting policies do not require a liability adequacy test that meets the minimum requirements of paragraph 16, the insurer shall:

    (a)   determine the carrying amount of the relevant insurance liabilities[1] less the carrying amount of:

        (i)   any related deferred acquisition costs; and

        (ii)   any related intangible assets, such as those acquired in a business combination or portfolio transfer (see paragraphs 31 and 32). However, related reinsurance assets are not considered because an insurer accounts for them separately (see paragraph 20).

    (b)   determine whether the amount described in (a) is less than the carrying amount that would be required if the relevant insurance liabilities were within the scope of AASB 137. If it is less, the insurer shall recognise the entire difference in profit or loss and decrease the carrying amount of the related deferred acquisition costs or related intangible assets or increase the carrying amount of the relevant insurance liabilities.

18   If an insurer's liability adequacy test meets the minimum requirements of paragraph 16, the test is applied at the level of aggregation specified in that test. If its liability adequacy test does not meet those minimum requirements, the comparison described in paragraph 17 shall be made at the level of a portfolio of contracts that are subject to broadly similar risks and managed together as a single portfolio.

19   The amount described in paragraph 17(b) (ie the result of applying AASB 137) shall reflect future investment margins (see paragraphs 27–29) if, and only if, the amount described in paragraph 17(a) also reflects those margins.

Impairment of reinsurance assets

20   If a cedant's reinsurance asset is impaired, the cedant shall reduce its carrying amount accordingly and recognise that impairment loss in profit or loss. A reinsurance asset is impaired if, and only if:

    (a)   there is objective evidence, as a result of an event that occurred after initial recognition of the reinsurance asset, that the cedant may not receive all amounts due to it under the terms of the contract; and

    (b)   that event has a reliably measurable impact on the amounts that the cedant will receive from the reinsurer.

Temporary exemption from AASB 9

20A   **AASB 9 addresses the accounting for financial instruments and is effective for annual periods beginning on or after 1 January 2018. However, for an insurer that meets the criteria in paragraph 20B, this Standard provides a temporary exemption that permits, but does not require, the insurer to apply AASB 139 *Financial Instruments: Recognition and Measurement* rather than AASB 9 for annual periods beginning before 1 January 2021. An insurer that applies the temporary exemption from AASB 9 shall:**

    (a)   **use the requirements in AASB 9 that are necessary to provide the disclosures required in paragraphs 39B–39J of this Standard; and**

---

1   The relevant insurance liabilities are those insurance liabilities (and related deferred acquisition costs and related intangible assets) for which the insurer's accounting policies do not require a liability adequacy test that meets the minimum requirements of paragraph 16.

(b)   **apply all other applicable Standards to its financial instruments, except as described in paragraphs 20A–20Q, 39B–39J and 46–47 of this Standard.**

20B   **An insurer may apply the temporary exemption from AASB 9 if, and only if:**

(a)   **it has not previously applied any version of AASB 9[2], other than only the requirements for the presentation of gains and losses on financial liabilities designated as at fair value through profit or loss in paragraphs 5.7.1(c), 5.7.7–5.7.9, 7.2.14 and B5.7.5–B5.7.20 of AASB 9; and**

(b)   **its activities are predominantly connected with insurance, as described in paragraph 20D, at its annual reporting date that immediately precedes 1 April 2016, or at a subsequent annual reporting date as specified in paragraph 20G.**

20C   An insurer applying the temporary exemption from AASB 9 is permitted to elect to apply only the requirements for the presentation of gains and losses on financial liabilities designated as at fair value through profit or loss in paragraphs 5.7.1(c), 5.7.7–5.7.9, 7.2.14 and B5.7.5–B5.7.20 of AASB 9. If an insurer elects to apply those requirements, it shall apply the relevant transition provisions in AASB 9, disclose the fact that it has applied those requirements and provide on an ongoing basis the related disclosures set out in paragraphs 10–11 of AASB 7 (as amended by AASB 9 (2010)).

20D   An insurer's activities are predominantly connected with insurance if, and only if:

(a)   the carrying amount of its liabilities arising from contracts within the scope of this Standard, AASB 1023 and AASB 1038, which includes any deposit components or embedded derivatives unbundled from insurance contracts applying paragraphs 7–12 of this Standard, is significant compared to the total carrying amount of all its liabilities; and

(b)   the percentage of the total carrying amount of its liabilities connected with insurance (see paragraph 20E) relative to the total carrying amount of all its liabilities is:

(i)   greater than 90 per cent; or

(ii)   less than or equal to 90 per cent but greater than 80 per cent, and the insurer does not engage in a significant activity unconnected with insurance (see paragraph 20F).

20E   For the purposes of applying paragraph 20D(b), liabilities connected with insurance comprise:

(a)   liabilities arising from contracts within the scope of this Standard, AASB 1023 and AASB 1038, as described in paragraph 20D(a);

(b)   non-derivative investment contract liabilities measured at fair value through profit or loss applying AASB 139 (including those designated as at fair value through profit or loss to which the insurer has applied the requirements in AASB 9 for the presentation of gains and losses (see paragraphs 20B(a) and 20C)); and

(c)   liabilities that arise because the insurer issues, or fulfils obligations arising from, the contracts in (a) and (b). Examples of such liabilities include derivatives used to mitigate risks arising from those contracts and from the assets backing those contracts, relevant tax liabilities such as the deferred tax liabilities for taxable temporary differences on liabilities arising from those contracts, and debt instruments issued that are included in the insurer's regulatory capital.

20F   In assessing whether it engages in a significant activity unconnected with insurance for the purposes of applying paragraph 20D(b)(ii), an insurer shall consider:

(a)   only those activities from which it may earn income and incur expenses; and

(b)   quantitative or qualitative factors (or both), including publicly available information such as the industry classification that users of financial statements apply to the insurer.

---

2   The Board issued successive principal versions of AASB 9 in 2009, 2010 and 2014.

20G Paragraph 20B(b) requires an entity to assess whether it qualifies for the temporary exemption from AASB 9 at its annual reporting date that immediately precedes 1 April 2016. After that date:

(a)   an entity that previously qualified for the temporary exemption from AASB 9 shall reassess whether its activities are predominantly connected with insurance at a subsequent annual reporting date if, and only if, there was a change in the entity's activities, as described in paragraphs 20H–20I, during the annual period that ended on that date.

(b)   an entity that previously did not qualify for the temporary exemption from AASB 9 is permitted to reassess whether its activities are predominantly connected with insurance at a subsequent annual reporting date before 31 December 2018 if, and only if, there was a change in the entity's activities, as described in paragraphs 20H–20I, during the annual period that ended on that date.

20H For the purposes of applying paragraph 20G, a change in an entity's activities is a change that:

(a)   is determined by the entity's senior management as a result of external or internal changes;

(b)   is significant to the entity's operations; and

(c)   is demonstrable to external parties.

Accordingly, such a change occurs only when the entity begins or ceases to perform an activity that is significant to its operations or significantly changes the magnitude of one of its activities; for example, when the entity has acquired, disposed of or terminated a business line.

20I   A change in an entity's activities, as described in paragraph 20H, is expected to be very infrequent. The following are not changes in an entity's activities for the purposes of applying paragraph 20G:

(a)   a change in the entity's funding structure that in itself does not affect the activities from which the entity earns income and incurs expenses.

(b)   the entity's plan to sell a business line, even if the assets and liabilities are classified as held for sale applying AASB 5 *Non-current Assets Held for Sale and Discontinued Operations*. A plan to sell a business line could change the entity's activities and give rise to a reassessment in the future but has yet to affect the liabilities recognised on its statement of financial position.

20J   If an entity no longer qualifies for the temporary exemption from AASB 9 as a result of a reassessment (see paragraph 20G(a)), then the entity is permitted to continue to apply the temporary exemption from AASB 9 only until the end of the annual period that began immediately after that reassessment. Nevertheless, the entity must apply AASB 9 for annual periods beginning on or after 1 January 2021. For example, if an entity determines that it no longer qualifies for the temporary exemption from AASB 9 applying paragraph 20G(a) on 31 December 2018 (the end of its annual period), then the entity is permitted to continue to apply the temporary exemption from AASB 9 only until 31 December 2019.

20K An insurer that previously elected to apply the temporary exemption from AASB 9 may at the beginning of any subsequent annual period irrevocably elect to apply AASB 9.

First-time adopter

20L   A first-time adopter, as defined in AASB 1 *First-time Adoption of Australian Accounting Standards*, may apply the temporary exemption from AASB 9 described in paragraph 20A if, and only if, it meets the criteria described in paragraph 20B. In applying paragraph 20B(b), the first-time adopter shall use the carrying amounts determined applying Standards at the date specified in that paragraph.

20M AASB 1 contains requirements and exemptions applicable to a first-time adopter. Those requirements and exemptions (for example, paragraphs D16–D17 of

AASB 1) do not override the requirements in paragraphs 20A–20Q and 39B–39J of this Standard. For example, the requirements and exemptions in AASB 1 do not override the requirement that a first-time adopter must meet the criteria specified in paragraph 20L to apply the temporary exemption from AASB 9.

20N A first-time adopter that discloses the information required by paragraphs 39B–39J shall use the requirements and exemptions in AASB 1 that are relevant to making the assessments required for those disclosures.

Temporary exemption from specific requirements in AASB 128

20O Paragraphs 35–36 of AASB 128 *Investments in Associates and Joint Ventures* require an entity to apply uniform accounting policies when using the equity method. Nevertheless, for annual periods beginning before 1 January 2021, an entity is permitted, but not required, to retain the relevant accounting policies applied by the associate or joint venture as follows:

(a) the entity applies AASB 9 but the associate or joint venture applies the temporary exemption from AASB 9; or

(b) the entity applies the temporary exemption from AASB 9 but the associate or joint venture applies AASB 9.

20P When an entity uses the equity method to account for its investment in an associate or joint venture:

(a) if AASB 9 was previously applied in the financial statements used to apply the equity method to that associate or joint venture (after reflecting any adjustments made by the entity), then AASB 9 shall continue to be applied.

(b) if the temporary exemption from AASB 9 was previously applied in the financial statements used to apply the equity method to that associate or joint venture (after reflecting any adjustments made by the entity), then AASB 9 may be subsequently applied.

20Q An entity may apply paragraphs 20O and 20P(b) separately for each associate or joint venture.

Changes in accounting policies

21 Paragraphs 22–30 apply both to changes made by an insurer that already applies IFRSs and to changes made by an insurer adopting Australian Accounting Standards for the first time.

22 An insurer may change its accounting policies for insurance contracts if, and only if, the change makes the financial statements more relevant to the economic decision-making needs of users and no less reliable, or more reliable and no less relevant to those needs. An insurer shall judge relevance and reliability by the criteria in AASB 108.

23 To justify changing its accounting policies for insurance contracts, an insurer shall show that the change brings its financial statements closer to meeting the criteria in AASB 108, but the change need not achieve full compliance with those criteria. The following specific issues are discussed below:

(a) current interest rates (paragraph 24);

(b) continuation of existing practices (paragraph 25);

(c) prudence (paragraph 26);

(d) future investment margins (paragraphs 27–29); and

(e) shadow accounting (paragraph 30).

Current market interest rates

24   An insurer is permitted, but not required, to change its accounting policies so that it remeasures designated insurance liabilities[3] to reflect current market interest rates and recognises changes in those liabilities in profit or loss. At that time, it may also introduce accounting policies that require other current estimates and assumptions for the designated liabilities. The election in this paragraph permits an insurer to change its accounting policies for designated liabilities, without applying those policies consistently to all similar liabilities as AASB 108 would otherwise require. If an insurer designates liabilities for this election, it shall continue to apply current market interest rates (and, if applicable, the other current estimates and assumptions) consistently in all periods to all these liabilities until they are extinguished.

Continuation of existing practices

25   An insurer may continue the following practices, but the introduction of any of them does not satisfy paragraph 22:

   (a)   measuring insurance liabilities on an undiscounted basis.

   (b)   measuring contractual rights to future investment management fees at an amount that exceeds their fair value as implied by a comparison with current fees charged by other market participants for similar services. It is likely that the fair value at inception of those contractual rights equals the origination costs paid, unless future investment management fees and related costs are out of line with market comparables.

   (c)   using non-uniform accounting policies for the insurance contracts (and related deferred acquisition costs and related intangible assets, if any) of subsidiaries, except as permitted by paragraph 24. If those accounting policies are not uniform, an insurer may change them if the change does not make the accounting policies more diverse and also satisfies the other requirements in this Standard.

Prudence

26   An insurer need not change its accounting policies for insurance contracts to eliminate excessive prudence. However, if an insurer already measures its insurance contracts with sufficient prudence, it shall not introduce additional prudence.

Future investment margins

27   An insurer need not change its accounting policies for insurance contracts to eliminate future investment margins. However, there is a rebuttable presumption that an insurer's financial statements will become less relevant and reliable if it introduces an accounting policy that reflects future investment margins in the measurement of insurance contracts, unless those margins affect the contractual payments. Two examples of accounting policies that reflect those margins are:

   (a)   using a discount rate that reflects the estimated return on the insurer's assets; or

   (b)   projecting the returns on those assets at an estimated rate of return, discounting those projected returns at a different rate and including the result in the measurement of the liability.

28   An insurer may overcome the rebuttable presumption described in paragraph 27 if, and only if, the other components of a change in accounting policies increase the relevance and reliability of its financial statements sufficiently to outweigh the decrease in relevance and reliability caused by the inclusion of future investment margins. For example, suppose that an insurer's existing accounting policies for insurance contracts involve excessively prudent assumptions set at inception and a discount rate prescribed by a regulator without direct reference to market conditions, and ignore some embedded options and guarantees. The insurer might make its

---

3   In this paragraph, insurance liabilities include related deferred acquisition costs and related intangible assets, such as those discussed in paragraphs 31 and 32.

financial statements more relevant and no less reliable by switching to a comprehensive investor-oriented basis of accounting that is widely used and involves:

(a) current estimates and assumptions;

(b) a reasonable (but not excessively prudent) adjustment to reflect risk and uncertainty;

(c) measurements that reflect both the intrinsic value and time value of embedded options and guarantees; and

(d) a current market discount rate, even if that discount rate reflects the estimated return on the insurer's assets.

29   In some measurement approaches, the discount rate is used to determine the present value of a future profit margin. That profit margin is then attributed to different periods using a formula. In those approaches, the discount rate affects the measurement of the liability only indirectly. In particular, the use of a less appropriate discount rate has a limited or no effect on the measurement of the liability at inception. However, in other approaches, the discount rate determines the measurement of the liability directly. In the latter case, because the introduction of an asset-based discount rate has a more significant effect, it is highly unlikely that an insurer could overcome the rebuttable presumption described in paragraph 27.

Shadow accounting

30   In some accounting models, realised gains or losses on an insurer's assets have a direct effect on the measurement of some or all of (a) its insurance liabilities, (b) related deferred acquisition costs and (c) related intangible assets, such as those described in paragraphs 31 and 32. An insurer is permitted, but not required, to change its accounting policies so that a recognised but unrealised gain or loss on an asset affects those measurements in the same way that a realised gain or loss does. The related adjustment to the insurance liability (or deferred acquisition costs or intangible assets) shall be recognised in other comprehensive income if, and only if, the unrealised gains or losses are recognised in other comprehensive income. This practice is sometimes described as 'shadow accounting'.

Insurance contracts acquired in a business combination or portfolio transfer

31   To comply with AASB 3, an insurer shall, at the acquisition date, measure at fair value the insurance liabilities assumed and *insurance assets* acquired in a business combination. However, an insurer is permitted, but not required, to use an expanded presentation that splits the fair value of acquired insurance contracts into two components:

(a) a liability measured in accordance with the insurer's accounting policies for insurance contracts that it issues; and

(b) an intangible asset, representing the difference between (i) the fair value of the contractual insurance rights acquired and insurance obligations assumed and (ii) the amount described in (a). The subsequent measurement of this asset shall be consistent with the measurement of the related insurance liability.

32   An insurer acquiring a portfolio of insurance contracts may use the expanded presentation described in paragraph 31.

33   The intangible assets described in paragraphs 31 and 32 are excluded from the scope of AASB 136 *Impairment of Assets* and AASB 138. However, AASB 136 and AASB 138 apply to customer lists and customer relationships reflecting the expectation of future contracts that are not part of the contractual insurance rights and contractual insurance obligations that existed at the date of a business combination or portfolio transfer.

Discretionary participation features

Discretionary participation features in insurance contracts

34   Some insurance contracts contain a discretionary participation feature as well as a *guaranteed element*. The issuer of such a contract:

    (a)   may, but need not, recognise the guaranteed element separately from the discretionary participation feature. If the issuer does not recognise them separately, it shall classify the whole contract as a liability. If the issuer classifies them separately, it shall classify the guaranteed element as a liability.

    (b)   shall, if it recognises the discretionary participation feature separately from the guaranteed element, classify that feature as either a liability or a separate component of equity. This Standard does not specify how the issuer determines whether that feature is a liability or equity. The issuer may split that feature into liability and equity components and shall use a consistent accounting policy for that split. The issuer shall not classify that feature as an intermediate category that is neither liability nor equity.

    (c)   may recognise all premiums received as revenue without separating any portion that relates to the equity component. The resulting changes in the guaranteed element and in the portion of the discretionary participation feature classified as a liability shall be recognised in profit or loss. If part or all of the discretionary participation feature is classified in equity, a portion of profit or loss may be attributable to that feature (in the same way that a portion may be attributable to non-controlling interests). The issuer shall recognise the portion of profit or loss attributable to any equity component of a discretionary participation feature as an allocation of profit or loss, not as expense or income (see AASB 101 *Presentation of Financial Statements*).

    (d)   shall, if the contract contains an embedded derivative within the scope of AASB 9, apply AASB 9 to that embedded derivative.

    (e)   shall, in all respects not described in paragraphs 14–20 and 34(a)–(d), continue its existing accounting policies for such contracts, unless it changes those accounting policies in a way that complies with paragraphs 21–30.

Discretionary participation features in financial instruments

35   The requirements in paragraph 34 also apply to a financial instrument that contains a discretionary participation feature. In addition:

    (a)   if the issuer classifies the entire discretionary participation feature as a liability, it shall apply the liability adequacy test in paragraphs 15–19 to the whole contract (ie both the guaranteed element and the discretionary participation feature). The issuer need not determine the amount that would result from applying AASB 9 to the guaranteed element.

    (b)   if the issuer classifies part or all of that feature as a separate component of equity, the liability recognised for the whole contract shall not be less than the amount that would result from applying AASB 9 to the guaranteed element. That amount shall include the intrinsic value of an option to surrender the contract, but need not include its time value if paragraph 9 exempts that option from measurement at fair value. The issuer need not disclose the amount that would result from applying AASB 9 to the guaranteed element, nor need it present that amount separately. Furthermore, the issuer need not determine that amount if the total liability recognised is clearly higher.

    (c)   although these contracts are financial instruments, the issuer may continue to recognise the premiums for those contracts as revenue and recognise as an expense the resulting increase in the carrying amount of the liability.

    (d)   although these contracts are financial instruments, an issuer applying paragraph 20(b) of AASB 7 to contracts with a discretionary participation feature shall disclose the total interest expense recognised in profit or loss, but need not calculate such interest expense using the effective interest method.

35A The temporary exemptions in paragraphs 20A, 20L and 20O and the overlay approach in paragraph 35B are also available to an issuer of a financial instrument that contains a discretionary participation feature. Accordingly, all references in paragraphs 3(a)–3(b), 20A–20Q, 35B–35N, 39B–39M and 46–49 to an insurer shall be read as also referring to an issuer of a financial instrument that contains a discretionary participation feature.

Presentation

The overlay approach

35B **An insurer is permitted, but not required, to apply the overlay approach to designated financial assets. An insurer that applies the overlay approach shall:**

    (a) **reclassify between profit or loss and other comprehensive income an amount that results in the profit or loss at the end of the reporting period for the designated financial assets being the same as if the insurer had applied AASB 139 to the designated financial assets. Accordingly, the amount reclassified is equal to the difference between:**

        (i) **the amount reported in profit or loss for the designated financial assets applying AASB 9; and**

        (ii) **the amount that would have been reported in profit or loss for the designated financial assets if the insurer had applied AASB 139.**

    (b) **apply all other applicable Standards to its financial instruments, except as described in paragraphs 35B–35N, 39K–39M and 48–49 of this Standard.**

35C **An insurer may elect to apply the overlay approach described in paragraph 35B only when it first applies AASB 9, including when it first applies AASB 9 after previously applying:**

    (a) **the temporary exemption from AASB 9 described in paragraph 20A; or**

    (b) **only the requirements for the presentation of gains and losses on financial liabilities designated as at fair value through profit or loss in paragraphs 5.7.1(c), 5.7.7–5.7.9, 7.2.14 and B5.7.5–B5.7.20 of AASB 9.**

35D An insurer shall present the amount reclassified between profit or loss and other comprehensive income applying the overlay approach:

    (a) in profit or loss as a separate line item; and

    (b) in other comprehensive income as a separate component of other comprehensive income.

35E A financial asset is eligible for designation for the overlay approach if, and only if, the following criteria are met:

    (a) it is measured at fair value through profit or loss applying AASB 9 but would not have been measured at fair value through profit or loss in its entirety applying AASB 139; and

    (b) it is not held in respect of an activity that is unconnected with contracts within the scope of this Standard, AASB 1023 or AASB 1038. Examples of financial assets that would not be eligible for the overlay approach are those assets held in respect of banking activities or financial assets held in funds relating to investment contracts that are outside the scope of this Standard, AASB 1023 or AASB 1038.

35F An insurer may designate an eligible financial asset for the overlay approach when it elects to apply the overlay approach (see paragraph 35C). Subsequently, it may designate an eligible financial asset for the overlay approach when, and only when:

    (a) that asset is initially recognised; or

    (b) that asset newly meets the criterion in paragraph 35E(b) having previously not met that criterion.

AASB

35G An insurer is permitted to designate eligible financial assets for the overlay approach applying paragraph 35F on an instrument-by-instrument basis.

35H When relevant, for the purposes of applying the overlay approach to a newly designated financial asset applying paragraph 35F(b):

(a) its fair value at the date of designation shall be its new amortised cost carrying amount; and

(b) the effective interest rate shall be determined based on its fair value at the date of designation.

35I An entity shall continue to apply the overlay approach to a designated financial asset until that financial asset is derecognised. However, an entity:

(a) shall de-designate a financial asset when the financial asset no longer meets the criterion in paragraph 35E(b). For example, a financial asset will no longer meet that criterion when an entity transfers that asset so that it is held in respect of its banking activities or when an entity ceases to be an insurer.

(b) may, at the beginning of any annual period, stop applying the overlay approach to all designated financial assets. An entity that elects to stop applying the overlay approach shall apply AASB 108 to account for the change in accounting policy.

35J When an entity de-designates a financial asset applying paragraph 35I(a), it shall reclassify from accumulated other comprehensive income to profit or loss as a reclassification adjustment (see AASB 101) any balance relating to that financial asset.

35K If an entity stops using the overlay approach applying the election in paragraph 35I(b) or because it is no longer an insurer, it shall not subsequently apply the overlay approach. An insurer that has elected to apply the overlay approach (see paragraph 35C) but has no eligible financial assets (see paragraph 35E) may subsequently apply the overlay approach when it has eligible financial assets.

Interaction with other requirements

35L Paragraph 30 of this Standard permits a practice that is sometimes described as 'shadow accounting'. If an insurer applies the overlay approach, shadow accounting may be applicable.

35M Reclassifying an amount between profit or loss and other comprehensive income applying paragraph 35B may have consequential effects for including other amounts in other comprehensive income, such as income taxes. An insurer shall apply the relevant Standard, such as AASB 112 *Income Taxes*, to determine any such consequential effects.

First-time adopter

35N If a first-time adopter elects to apply the overlay approach, it shall restate comparative information to reflect the overlay approach if, and only if, it restates comparative information to comply with AASB 9 (see paragraphs E1–E2 of AASB 1).

Disclosure

Explanation of recognised amounts

36 **An insurer shall disclose information that identifies and explains the amounts in its financial statements arising from insurance contracts.**

37 To comply with paragraph 36, an insurer shall disclose:

(a) its accounting policies for insurance contracts and related assets, liabilities, income and expense.

(b) the recognised assets, liabilities, income and expense (and, if it presents its statement of cash flows using the direct method, cash flows) arising from insurance contracts. Furthermore, if the insurer is a cedant, it shall disclose:

(i)   gains and losses recognised in profit or loss on buying reinsurance; and

(ii)   if the cedant defers and amortises gains and losses arising on buying reinsurance, the amortisation for the period and the amounts remaining unamortised at the beginning and end of the period.

(c)   the process used to determine the assumptions that have the greatest effect on the measurement of the recognised amounts described in (b). When practicable, an insurer shall also give quantified disclosure of those assumptions.

(d)   the effect of changes in assumptions used to measure insurance assets and insurance liabilities, showing separately the effect of each change that has a material effect on the financial statements.

(e)   reconciliations of changes in insurance liabilities, reinsurance assets and, if any, related deferred acquisition costs.

Nature and extent of risks arising from insurance contracts

38   **An insurer shall disclose information that enables users of its financial statements to evaluate the nature and extent of risks arising from insurance contracts.**

39   To comply with paragraph 38, an insurer shall disclose:

(a)   its objectives, policies and processes for managing risks arising from insurance contracts and the methods used to manage those risks.

(b)   [deleted]

(c)   information about *insurance risk* (both before and after risk mitigation by reinsurance), including information about:

    (i)   sensitivity to insurance risk (see paragraph 39A).

    (ii)   concentrations of insurance risk, including a description of how management determines concentrations and a description of the shared characteristic that identifies each concentration (eg type of insured event, geographical area, or currency).

    (iii)   actual claims compared with previous estimates (ie claims development). The disclosure about claims development shall go back to the period when the earliest material claim arose for which there is still uncertainty about the amount and timing of the claims payments, but need not go back more than ten years. An insurer need not disclose this information for claims for which uncertainty about the amount and timing of claims payments is typically resolved within one year.

(d)   information about credit risk, liquidity risk and market risk that paragraphs 31–42 of AASB 7 would require if the insurance contracts were within the scope of AASB 7. However:

    (i)   an insurer need not provide the maturity analyses required by paragraph 39(a) and (b) of AASB 7 if it discloses information about the estimated timing of the net cash outflows resulting from recognised insurance liabilities instead. This may take the form of an analysis, by estimated timing, of the amounts recognised in the statement of financial position.

    (ii)   if an insurer uses an alternative method to manage sensitivity to market conditions, such as an embedded value analysis, it may use that sensitivity analysis to meet the requirement in paragraph 40(a) of AASB 7. Such an insurer shall also provide the disclosures required by paragraph 41 of AASB 7.

(e)   information about exposures to market risk arising from embedded derivatives contained in a host insurance contract if the insurer is not required to, and does not, measure the embedded derivatives at fair value.

39A   To comply with paragraph 39(c)(i), an insurer shall disclose either (a) or (b) as follows:

    (a)   a sensitivity analysis that shows how profit or loss and equity would have been affected if changes in the relevant risk variable that were reasonably possible at the end of the reporting period had occurred; the methods and assumptions used in preparing the sensitivity analysis; and any changes from the previous period in the methods and assumptions used. However, if an insurer uses an alternative method to manage sensitivity to market conditions, such as an embedded value analysis, it may meet this requirement by disclosing that alternative sensitivity analysis and the disclosures required by paragraph 41 of AASB 7.

    (b)   qualitative information about sensitivity, and information about those terms and conditions of insurance contracts that have a material effect on the amount, timing and uncertainty of the insurer's future cash flows.

Disclosures about the temporary exemption from AASB 9

39B   An insurer that elects to apply the temporary exemption from AASB 9 shall disclose information to enable users of financial statements:

    (a)   to understand how the insurer qualified for the temporary exemption; and

    (b)   to compare insurers applying the temporary exemption with entities applying AASB 9.

39C   To comply with paragraph 39B(a), an insurer shall disclose the fact that it is applying the temporary exemption from AASB 9 and how the insurer concluded on the date specified in paragraph 20B(b) that it qualifies for the temporary exemption from AASB 9, including:

    (a)   if the carrying amount of its liabilities arising from contracts within the scope of this Standard (ie those liabilities described in paragraph 20E(a)) was less than or equal to 90 per cent of the total carrying amount of all its liabilities, the nature and carrying amounts of the liabilities connected with insurance that are not liabilities arising from contracts within the scope of this Standard (ie those liabilities described in paragraphs 20E(b) and 20E(c));

    (b)   if the percentage of the total carrying amount of its liabilities connected with insurance relative to the total carrying amount of all its liabilities was less than or equal to 90 per cent but greater than 80 per cent, how the insurer determined that it did not engage in a significant activity unconnected with insurance, including what information it considered; and

    (c)   if the insurer qualified for the temporary exemption from AASB 9 on the basis of a reassessment applying paragraph 20G(b):

        (i)   the reason for the reassessment;

        (ii)   the date on which the relevant change in its activities occurred; and

        (iii)   a detailed explanation of the change in its activities and a qualitative description of the effect of that change on the insurer's financial statements.

39D   If, applying paragraph 20G(a), an entity concludes that its activities are no longer predominantly connected with insurance, it shall disclose the following information in each reporting period before it begins to apply AASB 9:

    (a)   the fact that it no longer qualifies for the temporary exemption from AASB 9;

    (b)   the date on which the relevant change in its activities occurred; and

    (c)   a detailed explanation of the change in its activities and a qualitative description of the effect of that change on the entity's financial statements.

39E   To comply with paragraph 39B(b), an insurer shall disclose the fair value at the end of the reporting period and the amount of change in the fair value during that period for the following two groups of financial assets separately:

    (a)   financial assets with contractual terms that give rise on specified dates to cash flows that are solely payments of principal and interest on the principal amount outstanding (ie financial assets that meet the condition in paragraphs 4.1.2(b) and 4.1.2A(b) of AASB 9), excluding any financial asset that meets the definition of held for trading in AASB 9, or that is managed and whose performance is evaluated on a fair value basis (see paragraph B4.1.6 of AASB 9).

(b)   all financial assets other than those specified in paragraph 39E(a); that is, any financial asset:

    (i)   with contractual terms that do not give rise on specified dates to cash flows that are solely payments of principal and interest on the principal amount outstanding;

    (ii)   that meets the definition of held for trading in AASB 9; or

    (iii)   that is managed and whose performance is evaluated on a fair value basis.

39F   When disclosing the information in paragraph 39E, the insurer:

(a)   may deem the carrying amount of the financial asset measured applying AASB 139 to be a reasonable approximation of its fair value if the insurer is not required to disclose its fair value applying paragraph 29(a) of AASB 7 (eg short-term trade receivables); and

(b)   shall consider the level of detail necessary to enable users of financial statements to understand the characteristics of the financial assets.

39G   To comply with paragraph 39B(b), an insurer shall disclose information about the credit risk exposure, including significant credit risk concentrations, inherent in the financial assets described in paragraph 39E(a). At a minimum, an insurer shall disclose the following information for those financial assets at the end of the reporting period:

(a)   by credit risk rating grades as defined in AASB 7, the carrying amounts applying AASB 139 (in the case of financial assets measured at amortised cost, before adjusting for any impairment allowances).

(b)   for the financial assets described in paragraph 39E(a) that do not have low credit risk at the end of the reporting period, the fair value and the carrying amount applying AASB 139 (in the case of financial assets measured at amortised cost, before adjusting for any impairment allowances). For the purposes of this disclosure, paragraph B5.5.22 of AASB 9 provides the relevant requirements for assessing whether the credit risk on a financial instrument is considered low.

39H   To comply with paragraph 39B(b), an insurer shall disclose information about where a user of financial statements can obtain any publicly available AASB 9 information that relates to an entity within the group that is not provided in the group's consolidated financial statements for the relevant reporting period. For example, such AASB 9 information could be obtained from the publicly available individual or separate financial statements of an entity within the group that has applied AASB 9.

39I   If an entity elected to apply the exemption in paragraph 20O from particular requirements in AASB 128, it shall disclose that fact.

39J   If an entity applied the temporary exemption from AASB 9 when accounting for its investment in an associate or joint venture using the equity method (for example, see paragraph 20O(a)), the entity shall disclose the following, in addition to the information required by AASB 12 *Disclosure of Interests in Other Entities*:

(a)   the information described by paragraphs 39B–39H for each associate or joint venture that is material to the entity. The amounts disclosed shall be those included in the Australian-Accounting-Standards financial statements of the associate or joint venture after reflecting any adjustments made by the entity when using the equity method (see paragraph B14(a) of AASB 12), rather than the entity's share of those amounts.

(b)   the quantitative information described by paragraphs 39B–39H in aggregate for all individually immaterial associates or joint ventures. The aggregate amounts:

(i)   disclosed shall be the entity's share of those amounts; and

(ii)   for associates shall be disclosed separately from the aggregate amounts disclosed for joint ventures.

Disclosures about the overlay approach

39K   An insurer that applies the overlay approach shall disclose information to enable users of financial statements to understand:

(a)   how the total amount reclassified between profit or loss and other comprehensive income in the reporting period is calculated; and

(b)   the effect of that reclassification on the financial statements.

39L   To comply with paragraph 39K, an insurer shall disclose:

(a)   the fact that it is applying the overlay approach;

(b)   the carrying amount at the end of the reporting period of financial assets to which the insurer applies the overlay approach by class of financial asset;

(c)   the basis for designating financial assets for the overlay approach, including an explanation of any designated financial assets that are held outside the legal entity that issues contracts within the scope of this Standard;

(d)   an explanation of the total amount reclassified between profit or loss and other comprehensive income in the reporting period in a way that enables users of financial statements to understand how that amount is derived, including:

(i)   the amount reported in profit or loss for the designated financial assets applying AASB 9; and

(ii)   the amount that would have been reported in profit or loss for the designated financial assets if the insurer had applied AASB 139.

(e)   the effect of the reclassification described in paragraphs 35B and 35M on each affected line item in profit or loss; and

(f)   if during the reporting period the insurer has changed the designation of financial assets:

(i)   the amount reclassified between profit or loss and other comprehensive income in the reporting period relating to newly designated financial assets applying the overlay approach (see paragraph 35F(b));

(ii)   the amount that would have been reclassified between profit or loss and other comprehensive income in the reporting period if the financial assets had not been de-designated (see paragraph 35I(a)); and

(iii) the amount reclassified in the reporting period to profit or loss from accumulated other comprehensive income for financial assets that have been de-designated (see paragraph 35J).

39M   If an entity applied the overlay approach when accounting for its investment in an associate or joint venture using the equity method, the entity shall disclose the following, in addition to the information required by AASB 12:

(a)   the information described by paragraphs 39K–39L for each associate or joint venture that is material to the entity. The amounts disclosed shall be those included in the Australian-Accounting-Standards financial statements of the associate or joint venture after reflecting any adjustments made by the entity when using the equity method (see paragraph B14(a) of AASB 12), rather than the entity's share of those amounts.

(b)   the quantitative information described by paragraphs 39K–39L(d) and 39L(f), and the effect of the reclassification described in paragraph 35B on profit or loss and other comprehensive income in aggregate for all individually immaterial associates or joint ventures. The aggregate amounts:

(i)   disclosed shall be the entity's share of those amounts; and

(ii) for associates shall be disclosed separately from the aggregate amounts disclosed for joint ventures.

Effective date and transition

40   The transitional provisions in paragraphs 41–45 apply both to an entity that is already applying IFRSs when it first applies this Standard and to an entity that applies Australian Accounting Standards for the first time (a first-time adopter).

41   An entity shall apply this Standard for annual periods beginning on or after 1 January 2018. Earlier application is encouraged for periods beginning after 24 July 2014 but before 1 January 2018. If an entity applies this Standard for an earlier period, it shall disclose that fact.

41A–41B   [Deleted by the AASB]

41C   [Deleted]

41D   [Deleted]

41E   [Deleted by the AASB]

41F   [Deleted]

41G   AASB 2014-5 *Amendments to Australian Accounting Standards arising from AASB 15*, issued in December 2014, amended the previous version of this Standard as follows: amended paragraphs 4(a) and (c), B7, B18(h) and B21. An entity shall apply those amendments when it applies AASB 15.

41H   AASB 2010-7 *Amendments to Australian Accounting Standards arising from AASB 9 (December 2010)* (as amended), AASB 2014-1 *Amendments to Australian Accounting Standards* and AASB 2014-7 *Amendments to Australian Accounting Standards arising from AASB 9 (December 2014)* amended the previous version of this Standard as follows: amended paragraphs 3, 4, 7, 8, 12, 34, 35, 45, Appendix A and paragraphs B18–B20 and deleted paragraph 41C. Paragraph 41D, added by AASB 2010-7, was deleted by AASB 2014-1. Paragraph 41F, added by AASB 2014-1, was deleted by AASB 2014-7. An entity shall apply those amendments when it applies AASB 9.

Disclosure

42   An entity need not apply the disclosure requirements in this Standard to comparative information that relates to annual periods beginning before 1 January 2005, except for the disclosures required by paragraph 37(a) and (b) about accounting policies, and recognised assets, liabilities, income and expense (and cash flows if the direct method is used).

43   If it is impracticable to apply a particular requirement of paragraphs 10–35 to comparative information that relates to annual periods beginning before 1 January 2005, an entity shall disclose that fact. Applying the liability adequacy test (paragraphs 15–19) to such comparative information might sometimes be impracticable, but it is highly unlikely to be impracticable to apply other requirements of paragraphs 10–35 to such comparative information. AASB 108 explains the term 'impracticable'.

44   In applying paragraph 39(c)(iii), an entity need not disclose information about claims development that occurred earlier than five years before the end of the first financial year in which it applies this Standard. Furthermore, if it is impracticable, when an entity first applies this Standard, to prepare information about claims development that occurred before the beginning of the earliest period for which an entity presents full comparative information that complies with this Standard, the entity shall disclose that fact.

Redesignation of financial assets

45   Notwithstanding paragraph 4.4.1 of AASB 9, when an insurer changes its accounting policies for insurance liabilities, it is permitted, but not required, to reclassify some or all of its financial assets so that they are measured at fair value through profit or loss. This reclassification is permitted if an insurer changes accounting policies when it first applies this Standard and if it makes a subsequent policy change permitted by paragraph 22. The reclassification is a change in accounting policy and AASB 108 applies.

Applying AASB 4 with AASB 9

Temporary exemption from AASB 9

46   *Amendments to Australian Accounting Standards – Applying AASB 9* Financial Instruments *with AASB 4* Insurance Contracts, issued in October 2016, amended paragraphs 3 and 5, and added paragraphs 20A–20Q, 35A and 39B–39J and headings after paragraphs 20, 20K, 20N and 39A. An entity shall apply those amendments, which permit insurers that meet specified criteria to apply a temporary exemption from AASB 9, for annual periods beginning on or after 1 January 2018.

47   An entity that discloses the information required by paragraphs 39B–39J shall use the transitional provisions in AASB 9 that are relevant to making the assessments required for those disclosures. The date of initial application for that purpose shall be deemed to be the beginning of the first annual period beginning on or after 1 January 2018.

The overlay approach

48   *Amendments to Australian Accounting Standards – Applying AASB 9* Financial Instruments *with AASB 4* Insurance Contracts, issued in October 2016, amended paragraphs 3 and 5, and added paragraphs 35A–35N and 39K–39M and headings after paragraphs 35A, 35K, 35M and 39J. An entity shall apply those amendments, which permit insurers to apply the overlay approach to designated financial assets, when it first applies AASB 9 (see paragraph 35C).

49   An entity that elects to apply the overlay approach shall:

(a)   apply that approach retrospectively to designated financial assets on transition to AASB 9. Accordingly, for example, the entity shall recognise as an adjustment to the opening balance of accumulated other comprehensive income an amount equal to the difference between the fair value of the designated financial assets determined applying AASB 9 and their carrying amount determined applying AASB 139.

(b)   restate comparative information to reflect the overlay approach if, and only if, the entity restates comparative information applying AASB 9.

Commencement of the legislative instrument

Aus45.1   For legal purposes, this legislative instrument commences on 31 December 2017.

Withdrawal of AASB pronouncements

Aus45.2   This Standard repeals AASB 4 *Insurance Contracts* issued in July 2004. Despite the repeal, after the time this Standard starts to apply under section 334 of the Corporations Act (either generally or in relation to an individual entity), the repealed Standard continues to apply in relation to any period ending before that time as if the repeal had not occurred.

[Note: When this Standard applies under section 334 of the Corporations Act (either generally or in relation to an individual entity), it supersedes the application of the repealed Standard.]

APPENDIX A
DEFINED TERMS

This appendix is an integral part of the Standard.

cedant	The **policyholder** under a **reinsurance contract**.
deposit component	A contractual component that is not accounted for as a derivative under AASB 9 and would be within the scope of AASB 9 if it were a separate instrument.
direct insurance contract	An **insurance contract** that is not a **reinsurance contract**.

discretionary participation feature	A contractual right to receive, as a supplement to **guaranteed benefits**, additional benefits:
	
	(a) that are likely to be a significant portion of the total contractual benefits;
	(b) whose amount or timing is contractually at the discretion of the issuer; and
	(c) that are contractually based on:
	
	    (i) the performance of a specified pool of contracts or a specified type of contract;
	    (ii) realised and/or unrealised investment returns on a specified pool of assets held by the issuer; or
	    (iii) the profit or loss of the company, fund or other entity that issues the contract.

fair value	*Fair value* is the price that would be received to sell an asset or paid to transfer a liability in an orderly transaction between market participants at the measurement date. (See AASB 13.)
financial guarantee contract	A contract that requires the issuer to make specified payments to reimburse the holder for a loss it incurs because a specified debtor fails to make payment when due in accordance with the original or modified terms of a debt instrument.
financial risk	The risk of a possible future change in one or more of a specified interest rate, financial instrument price, commodity price, foreign exchange rate, index of prices or rates, credit rating or credit index or other variable, provided in the case of a non-financial variable that the variable is not specific to a party to the contract.
guaranteed benefits	Payments or other benefits to which a particular **policyholder** or investor has an unconditional right that is not subject to the contractual discretion of the issuer.
guaranteed element	An obligation to pay **guaranteed benefits**, included in a contract that contains a **discretionary participation feature**.
insurance asset	An **insurer's** net contractual rights under an **insurance contract**.
insurance contract	A contract under which one party (the **insurer**) accepts significant **insurance risk** from another party (the **policyholder**) by agreeing to compensate the policyholder if a specified uncertain future event (the **insured event**) adversely affects the policyholder. (See Appendix B for guidance on this definition.)

AASB

insurance liability	An **insurer's** net contractual obligations under an **insurance contract**.
insurance risk	Risk, other than **financial risk**, transferred from the holder of a contract to the issuer.
insured event	An uncertain future event that is covered by an **insurance contract** and creates **insurance risk**.
insurer	The party that has an obligation under an **insurance contract** to compensate a **policyholder** if an **insured event** occurs.
liability adequacy test	An assessment of whether the carrying amount of an **insurance liability** needs to be increased (or the carrying amount of related deferred acquisition costs or related intangible assets decreased), based on a review of future cash flows.
policyholder	A party that has a right to compensation under an **insurance contract** if an **insured event** occurs.
reinsurance assets	A **cedant's** net contractual rights under a **reinsurance contract**.
reinsurance contract	An **insurance contract** issued by one insurer (the **reinsurer**) to compensate another insurer (the **cedant**) for losses on one or more contracts issued by the cedant.
reinsurer	The party that has an obligation under a **reinsurance contract** to compensate a **cedant** if an **insured event** occurs.
unbundle	Account for the components of a contract as if they were separate contracts.

Additional Australian defined terms – see Appendix C.

APPENDIX B
DEFINITION OF AN INSURANCE CONTRACT

This appendix is an integral part of the Standard.

B1   This appendix gives guidance on the definition of an insurance contract in Appendix A. It addresses the following issues:

  (a)   the term 'uncertain future event' (paragraphs B2–B4);

  (b)   payments in kind (paragraphs B5–B7);

  (c)   insurance risk and other risks (paragraphs B8–B17);

  (d)   examples of insurance contracts (paragraphs B18–B21);

  (e)   significant insurance risk (paragraphs B22–B28); and

  (f)   changes in the level of insurance risk (paragraphs B29 and B30).

Uncertain future event

B2   Uncertainty (or risk) is the essence of an insurance contract. Accordingly, at least one of the following is uncertain at the inception of an insurance contract:

(a)   whether an *insured event* will occur;

(b)   when it will occur; or

(c)   how much the insurer will need to pay if it occurs.

B3   In some insurance contracts, the insured event is the discovery of a loss during the term of the contract, even if the loss arises from an event that occurred before the inception of the contract. In other insurance contracts, the insured event is an event that occurs during the term of the contract, even if the resulting loss is discovered after the end of the contract term.

B4   Some insurance contracts cover events that have already occurred, but whose financial effect is still uncertain. An example is a reinsurance contract that covers the direct insurer against adverse development of claims already reported by policyholders. In such contracts, the insured event is the discovery of the ultimate cost of those claims.

Payments in kind

B5   Some insurance contracts require or permit payments to be made in kind. An example is when the insurer replaces a stolen article directly, instead of reimbursing the policyholder. Another example is when an insurer uses its own hospitals and medical staff to provide medical services covered by the contracts.

B6   Some fixed-fee service contracts in which the level of service depends on an uncertain event meet the definition of an insurance contract in this Standard but are not regulated as insurance contracts in some countries. One example is a maintenance contract in which the service provider agrees to repair specified equipment after a malfunction. The fixed service fee is based on the expected number of malfunctions, but it is uncertain whether a particular machine will break down. The malfunction of the equipment adversely affects its owner and the contract compensates the owner (in kind, rather than cash). Another example is a contract for car breakdown services in which the provider agrees, for a fixed annual fee, to provide roadside assistance or tow the car to a nearby garage. The latter contract could meet the definition of an insurance contract even if the provider does not agree to carry out repairs or replace parts.

B7   Applying the Standard to the contracts described in paragraph B6 is likely to be no more burdensome than applying the Australian Accounting Standards that would be applicable if such contracts were outside the scope of this Standard:

(a)   There are unlikely to be material liabilities for malfunctions and breakdowns that have already occurred.

(b)   If AASB 15 applied, the service provider would recognise revenue when (or as) it transfers services to the customer (subject to other specified criteria). That approach is also acceptable under this Standard, which permits the service provider (i) to continue its existing accounting policies for these contracts unless they involve practices prohibited by paragraph 14 and (ii) to improve its accounting policies if so permitted by paragraphs 22–30.

(c)   The service provider considers whether the cost of meeting its contractual obligation to provide services exceeds the revenue received in advance. To do this, it applies the liability adequacy test described in paragraphs 15–19 of this Standard. If this Standard did not apply to these contracts, the service provider would apply AASB 137 to determine whether the contracts are onerous.

(d)   For these contracts, the disclosure requirements in this Standard are unlikely to add significantly to disclosures required by other Australian Accounting Standards.

Distinction between insurance risk and other risks

B8   The definition of an insurance contract refers to insurance risk, which this Standard
        defines as risk, other than *financial risk*, transferred from the holder of a contract to the
        issuer. A contract that exposes the issuer to financial risk without significant insurance
        risk is not an insurance contract.

B9   The definition of financial risk in Appendix A includes a list of financial and non-
        financial variables. That list includes non-financial variables that are not specific to a
        party to the contract, such as an index of earthquake losses in a particular region or
        an index of temperatures in a particular city. It excludes non-financial variables that
        are specific to a party to the contract, such as the occurrence or non-occurrence of a
        fire that damages or destroys an asset of that party. Furthermore, the risk of changes
        in the fair value of a non-financial asset is not a financial risk if the fair value reflects
        not only changes in market prices for such assets (a financial variable) but also the
        condition of a specific non-financial asset held by a party to a contract (a non-financial
        variable). For example, if a guarantee of the residual value of a specific car exposes the
        guarantor to the risk of changes in the car's physical condition, that risk is insurance
        risk, not financial risk.

B10   Some contracts expose the issuer to financial risk, in addition to significant insurance
        risk. For example, many life insurance contracts both guarantee a minimum rate of
        return to policyholders (creating financial risk) and promise death benefits that at some
        times significantly exceed the policyholder's account balance (creating insurance risk
        in the form of mortality risk). Such contracts are insurance contracts.

B11   Under some contracts, an insured event triggers the payment of an amount linked
        to a price index. Such contracts are insurance contracts, provided the payment that
        is contingent on the insured event can be significant. For example, a life-contingent
        annuity linked to a cost-of-living index transfers insurance risk because payment is
        triggered by an uncertain event—the survival of the annuitant. The link to the price
        index is an embedded derivative, but it also transfers insurance risk. If the resulting
        transfer of insurance risk is significant, the embedded derivative meets the definition
        of an insurance contract, in which case it need not be separated and measured at fair
        value (see paragraph 7 of this Standard).

B12   The definition of insurance risk refers to risk that the insurer accepts from the
        policyholder. In other words, insurance risk is a pre-existing risk transferred from the
        policyholder to the insurer. Thus, a new risk created by the contract is not insurance
        risk.

B13   The definition of an insurance contract refers to an adverse effect on the policyholder.
        The definition does not limit the payment by the insurer to an amount equal to the
        financial impact of the adverse event. For example, the definition does not exclude
        'new-for-old' coverage that pays the policyholder sufficient to permit replacement of
        a damaged old asset by a new asset. Similarly, the definition does not limit payment
        under a term life insurance contract to the financial loss suffered by the deceased's
        dependants, nor does it preclude the payment of predetermined amounts to quantify
        the loss caused by death or an accident.

B14   Some contracts require a payment if a specified uncertain event occurs, but do not
        require an adverse effect on the policyholder as a precondition for payment. Such a
        contract is not an insurance contract even if the holder uses the contract to mitigate
        an underlying risk exposure. For example, if the holder uses a derivative to hedge an
        underlying non-financial variable that is correlated with cash flows from an asset of the
        entity, the derivative is not an insurance contract because payment is not conditional
        on whether the holder is adversely affected by a reduction in the cash flows from the
        asset. Conversely, the definition of an insurance contract refers to an uncertain event for
        which an adverse effect on the policyholder is a contractual precondition for payment.
        This contractual precondition does not require the insurer to investigate whether the
        event actually caused an adverse effect, but permits the insurer to deny payment if it is
        not satisfied that the event caused an adverse effect.

B15   Lapse or persistency risk (ie the risk that the counterparty will cancel the contract earlier or later than the issuer had expected in pricing the contract) is not insurance risk because the payment to the counterparty is not contingent on an uncertain future event that adversely affects the counterparty. Similarly, expense risk (ie the risk of unexpected increases in the administrative costs associated with the servicing of a contract, rather than in costs associated with insured events) is not insurance risk because an unexpected increase in expenses does not adversely affect the counterparty.

B16   Therefore, a contract that exposes the issuer to lapse risk, persistency risk or expense risk is not an insurance contract unless it also exposes the issuer to insurance risk. However, if the issuer of that contract mitigates that risk by using a second contract to transfer part of that risk to another party, the second contract exposes that other party to insurance risk.

B17   An insurer can accept significant insurance risk from the policyholder only if the insurer is an entity separate from the policyholder. In the case of a mutual insurer, the mutual accepts risk from each policyholder and pools that risk. Although policyholders bear that pooled risk collectively in their capacity as owners, the mutual has still accepted the risk that is the essence of an insurance contract.

Examples of insurance contracts

B18   The following are examples of contracts that are insurance contracts, if the transfer of insurance risk is significant:

(a)   insurance against theft or damage to property.

(b)   insurance against product liability, professional liability, civil liability or legal expenses.

(c)   life insurance and prepaid funeral plans (although death is certain, it is uncertain when death will occur or, for some types of life insurance, whether death will occur within the period covered by the insurance).

(d)   life-contingent annuities and pensions (ie contracts that provide compensation for the uncertain future event—the survival of the annuitant or pensioner—to assist the annuitant or pensioner in maintaining a given standard of living, which would otherwise be adversely affected by his or her survival).

(e)   disability and medical cover.

(f)   surety bonds, fidelity bonds, performance bonds and bid bonds (ie contracts that provide compensation if another party fails to perform a contractual obligation, for example an obligation to construct a building).

(g)   credit insurance that provides for specified payments to be made to reimburse the holder for a loss it incurs because a specified debtor fails to make payment when due under the original or modified terms of a debt instrument. These contracts could have various legal forms, such as that of a guarantee, some types of letter of credit, a credit derivative default contract or an insurance contract. However, although these contracts meet the definition of an insurance contract, they also meet the definition of a financial guarantee contract in AASB 9 and are within the scope of AASB 132[4] and AASB 9, not this Standard (see paragraph 4(d)). Nevertheless, if an issuer of financial guarantee contracts has previously asserted explicitly that it regards such contracts as insurance contracts and has used accounting applicable to insurance contracts, the issuer may elect to apply either AASB 132[5] and AASB 9 or AASB 1023 to such financial guarantee contracts.

AASB

---

4   When an entity applies AASB 7, the reference to AASB 132 is replaced by a reference to AASB 7.

5   When an entity applies AASB 7, the reference to AASB 132 is replaced by a reference to AASB 7.

(h)   product warranties. Product warranties issued by another party for goods sold by a manufacturer, dealer or retailer are within the scope of this Standard. However, product warranties issued directly by a manufacturer, dealer or retailer are outside its scope, because they are within the scope of AASB 15 and AASB 137.

(i)   title insurance (ie insurance against the discovery of defects in title to land that were not apparent when the insurance contract was written). In this case, the insured event is the discovery of a defect in the title, not the defect itself.

(j)   travel assistance (ie compensation in cash or in kind to policyholders for losses suffered while they are travelling). Paragraphs B6 and B7 discuss some contracts of this kind.

(k)   catastrophe bonds that provide for reduced payments of principal, interest or both if a specified event adversely affects the issuer of the bond (unless the specified event does not create significant insurance risk, for example if the event is a change in an interest rate or foreign exchange rate).

(l)   insurance swaps and other contracts that require a payment based on changes in climatic, geological or other physical variables that are specific to a party to the contract.

(m)   reinsurance contracts.

B19   The following are examples of items that are not insurance contracts:

(a)   investment contracts that have the legal form of an insurance contract but do not expose the insurer to significant insurance risk, for example life insurance contracts in which the insurer bears no significant mortality risk (such contracts are non-insurance financial instruments or service contracts, see paragraphs B20 and B21).

(b)   contracts that have the legal form of insurance, but pass all significant insurance risk back to the policyholder through non-cancellable and enforceable mechanisms that adjust future payments by the policyholder as a direct result of insured losses, for example some financial reinsurance contracts or some group contracts (such contracts are normally non-insurance financial instruments or service contracts, see paragraphs B20 and B21).

(c)   self-insurance, in other words retaining a risk that could have been covered by insurance (there is no insurance contract because there is no agreement with another party).

(d)   contracts (such as gambling contracts) that require a payment if a specified uncertain future event occurs, but do not require, as a contractual precondition for payment, that the event adversely affects the policyholder. However, this does not preclude the specification of a predetermined payout to quantify the loss caused by a specified event such as death or an accident (see also paragraph B13).

(e)   derivatives that expose one party to financial risk but not insurance risk, because they require that party to make payment based solely on changes in one or more of a specified interest rate, financial instrument price, commodity price, foreign exchange rate, index of prices or rates, credit rating or credit index or other variable, provided in the case of a non-financial variable that the variable is not specific to a party to the contract (see AASB 9).

(f)   a credit-related guarantee (or letter of credit, credit derivative default contract or credit insurance contract) that requires payments even if the holder has not incurred a loss on the failure of the debtor to make payments when due (see AASB 9).

(g)   contracts that require a payment based on a climatic, geological or other physical variable that is not specific to a party to the contract (commonly described as weather derivatives).

(h) catastrophe bonds that provide for reduced payments of principal, interest or both, based on a climatic, geological or other physical variable that is not specific to a party to the contract.

B20 If the contracts described in paragraph B19 create financial assets or financial liabilities, they are within the scope of AASB 9. Among other things, this means that the parties to the contract use what is sometimes called deposit accounting, which involves the following:

(a) one party recognises the consideration received as a financial liability, rather than as revenue.

(b) the other party recognises the consideration paid as a financial asset, rather than as an expense.

B21 If the contracts described in paragraph B19 do not create financial assets or financial liabilities, AASB 15 applies. Under AASB 15, revenue is recognised when (or as) an entity satisfies a performance obligation by transferring a promised good or service to a customer in an amount that reflects the consideration to which the entity expects to be entitled.

Significant insurance risk

B22 A contract is an insurance contract only if it transfers significant insurance risk. Paragraphs B8–B21 discuss insurance risk. The following paragraphs discuss the assessment of whether insurance risk is significant.

B23 Insurance risk is significant if, and only if, an insured event could cause an insurer to pay significant additional benefits in any scenario, excluding scenarios that lack commercial substance (ie have no discernible effect on the economics of the transaction). If significant additional benefits would be payable in scenarios that have commercial substance, the condition in the previous sentence may be met even if the insured event is extremely unlikely or even if the expected (ie probability-weighted) present value of contingent cash flows is a small proportion of the expected present value of all the remaining contractual cash flows.

B24 The additional benefits described in paragraph B23 refer to amounts that exceed those that would be payable if no insured event occurred (excluding scenarios that lack commercial substance). Those additional amounts include claims handling and claims assessment costs, but exclude:

(a) the loss of the ability to charge the policyholder for future services. For example, in an investment-linked life insurance contract, the death of the policyholder means that the insurer can no longer perform investment management services and collect a fee for doing so. However, this economic loss for the insurer does not reflect insurance risk, just as a mutual fund manager does not take on insurance risk in relation to the possible death of the client. Therefore, the potential loss of future investment management fees is not relevant in assessing how much insurance risk is transferred by a contract.

(b) waiver on death of charges that would be made on cancellation or surrender. Because the contract brought those charges into existence, the waiver of these charges does not compensate the policyholder for a pre-existing risk. Hence, they are not relevant in assessing how much insurance risk is transferred by a contract.

(c) a payment conditional on an event that does not cause a significant loss to the holder of the contract. For example, consider a contract that requires the issuer to pay one million currency units if an asset suffers physical damage causing an insignificant economic loss of one currency unit to the holder. In this contract, the holder transfers to the insurer the insignificant risk of losing one currency unit. At the same time, the contract creates non-insurance risk that the issuer will need to pay 999,999 currency units if the specified event occurs. Because the issuer does not accept significant insurance risk from the holder, this contract is not an insurance contract.

(d)   possible reinsurance recoveries. The insurer accounts for these separately.

B25   An insurer shall assess the significance of insurance risk contract by contract, rather than by reference to materiality to the financial statements.[6] Thus, insurance risk may be significant even if there is a minimal probability of material losses for a whole book of contracts. This contract-by-contract assessment makes it easier to classify a contract as an insurance contract. However, if a relatively homogeneous book of small contracts is known to consist of contracts that all transfer insurance risk, an insurer need not examine each contract within that book to identify a few non-derivative contracts that transfer insignificant insurance risk.

B26   It follows from paragraphs B23–B25 that if a contract pays a death benefit exceeding the amount payable on survival, the contract is an insurance contract unless the additional death benefit is insignificant (judged by reference to the contract rather than to an entire book of contracts). As noted in paragraph B24(b), the waiver on death of cancellation or surrender charges is not included in this assessment if this waiver does not compensate the policyholder for a pre-existing risk. Similarly, an annuity contract that pays out regular sums for the rest of a policyholder's life is an insurance contract, unless the aggregate life-contingent payments are insignificant.

B27   Paragraph B23 refers to additional benefits. These additional benefits could include a requirement to pay benefits earlier if the insured event occurs earlier and the payment is not adjusted for the time value of money. An example is whole life insurance for a fixed amount (in other words, insurance that provides a fixed death benefit whenever the policyholder dies, with no expiry date for the cover). It is certain that the policyholder will die, but the date of death is uncertain. The insurer will suffer a loss on those individual contracts for which policyholders die early, even if there is no overall loss on the whole book of contracts.

B28   If an insurance contract is unbundled into a deposit component and an insurance component, the significance of insurance risk transfer is assessed by reference to the insurance component. The significance of insurance risk transferred by an embedded derivative is assessed by reference to the embedded derivative.

Changes in the level of insurance risk

B29   Some contracts do not transfer any insurance risk to the issuer at inception, although they do transfer insurance risk at a later time. For example, consider a contract that provides a specified investment return and includes an option for the policyholder to use the proceeds of the investment on maturity to buy a life-contingent annuity at the current annuity rates charged by the insurer to other new annuitants when the policyholder exercises the option. The contract transfers no insurance risk to the issuer until the option is exercised, because the insurer remains free to price the annuity on a basis that reflects the insurance risk transferred to the insurer at that time. However, if the contract specifies the annuity rates (or a basis for setting the annuity rates), the contract transfers insurance risk to the issuer at inception.

B30   A contract that qualifies as an insurance contract remains an insurance contract until all rights and obligations are extinguished or expire.

---

6   For this purpose, contracts entered into simultaneously with a single counterparty (or contracts that are otherwise interdependent) form a single contract.

APPENDIX C
AUSTRALIAN DEFINED TERMS

This appendix is an integral part of the Standard.

general insurance contract	An **insurance contract** that is not a **life insurance contract**.
life insurance contract	An **insurance contract**, or a financial instrument with a **discretionary participation feature**, regulated under the *Life Insurance Act 1995*, and similar contracts issued by entities operating outside Australia.

COMPILATION DETAILS

Accounting Standard AASB 4 *Insurance Contracts* as amended

Compilation details are not part of AASB 4.

This compiled Standard applies to annual periods beginning on or after 1 January 2018 but before 1 January 2019 for for-profit entities. It takes into account amendments up to and including 19 July 2017 and was prepared on 20 March 2018 by the staff of the Australian Accounting Standards Board (AASB).

This compilation is not a separate Accounting Standard made by the AASB. Instead, it is a representation of AASB 4 (August 2015) as amended by other Accounting Standards, which are listed in the Table below.

Table of Standards

Standard	Date made	FRL identifier	Commence-ment date	Effective date *(annual periods ... on or after ...)*	Application, saving or transitional provisions
AASB 4	7 Aug 2015	F2015L01623	31 Dec 2017	*(beginning)* 1 Jan 2018	see (a) below
AASB 16	23 Feb 2016	F2016L00233	31 Dec 2018	*(beginning)* 1 Jan 2019	not compiled*
AASB 2016-6	5 Oct 2016	F2016L01637	22 Oct 2016	*(beginning)* 1 Jan 2018	see (b) below
AASB 2016-7	9 Dec 2016	F2017L00043	31 Dec 2016	*(beginning)* 1 Jan 2017	see (c) below
AASB 2017-3	19 Jul 2017	F2017L01181	31 Dec 2017	*(beginning)* 1 Jan 2018	see (d) below

* The amendments made by this Standard are not included in this compilation, which presents the principal Standard as applicable to annual periods beginning on or after 1 January 2018 but before 1 January 2019 for for-profit entities.

(a) Entities may elect to apply this Standard to annual periods beginning after 24 July 2014 but before 1 January 2018.

(b) Earlier application of this Standard is not permitted.

(c) As a result of AASB 2016-7 deferring the effective date of AASB 15 *Revenue from Contracts with Customers* (and its consequential amendments in AASB 2014-5) for not-for-profit entities from 1 January 2018 to 1 January 2019, AASB 4 (2015) applies to not-for-profit entities only to annual reporting periods beginning on or after 1 January 2019, instead of 1 January 2018. However, earlier application is permitted, provided that AASB 15 is also applied.

(d) Earlier application of this Standard is not permitted.

Table of amendments

Paragraph affected	How affected	By ... [paragraph/page]
3	amended	AASB 2016-6 [page 5]
Aus 3.1	amended	AASB 2017-3 [page 5]
Aus 3.2	added	AASB 2017-3 [page 5]
5	amended	AASB 2016-6 [page 6]
20A-20Q (and headings)	added	AASB 2016-6 [page 6]
20D-20E	amended	AASB 2017-3 [page 6]
35A-35N (and headings)	added	AASB 2016-6 [page 8]
35E	amended	AASB 2017-3 [page 6]
39B-39M (and headings)	added	AASB 2016-6 [page 10]
46-49 (and headings)	added	AASB 2016-6 [page 13]

DELETED IFRS 4 TEXT

Deleted IFRS 4 text is not part of AASB 4.

41A   *Financial Guarantee Contracts* (Amendments to IAS 39 and IFRS 4), issued in August 2005, amended paragraphs 4(d), B18(g) and B19(f). An entity shall apply those amendments for annual periods beginning on or after 1 January 2006. Earlier application is encouraged. If an entity applies those amendments for an earlier period, it shall disclose that fact and apply the related amendments to IAS 39 and IAS 32[7] at the same time.

41B   IAS 1 (revised in 2007) amended the terminology used throughout IFRSs. In addition it amended paragraph 30. An entity shall apply those amendments for annual periods beginning on or after 1 January 2009. If an entity applies IAS 1 (revised 2007) for an earlier period, the amendments shall be applied for that earlier period.

41E   IFRS 13 *Fair Value Measurement*, issued in May 2011, amended the definition of fair value in Appendix A. An entity shall apply that amendment when it applies IFRS 13.

---

7   When an entity applies IFRS 7, the reference to IAS 32 is replaced by a reference to IFRS 7.

AASB 5

Non-current Assets Held for Sale and Discontinued Operations

(Reissued August 2015)

This note is not part of Accounting Standard AASB 5.

The following unincorporated amendments are not included in this Standard.

- AASB 17 *Insurance Contracts* — Appendix D sets out the amendments to other Standards that are a consequence of the AASB issuing AASB 17 *Insurance Contracts*. This Standard is applicable from 1 January 2021. Earlier application is permitted, but entities must apply AASB 9 *Financial Instruments* and AASB 15 *Revenue from Contracts with Customers* first.

Entities early-adopting any amendments with later application dates will need to refer to the amending Standards that have not yet been incorporated into compilations. The abovementioned unincorporated amendments may be located on the AASB website at www.aasb.gov.au or on the Federal Register of Legislation website at www.legislation.gov.au.

CONTENTS

COMPARISON WITH IFRS 5

ACCOUNTING STANDARD

AASB 5 *NON-CURRENT ASSETS HELD FOR SALE AND DISCONTINUED OPERATIONS*

AASB

APPENDICES
A. DEFINED TERMS
B. APPLICATION SUPPLEMENT
D. AUSTRALIAN REDUCED DISCLOSURE REQUIREMENTS

DELETED IFRS 5 TEXT

IMPLEMENTATION GUIDANCE ON IFRS 5 (available on the AASB website)
BASIS FOR CONCLUSIONS ON IFRS 5 (available on the AASB website)

Australian Accounting Standard AASB 5 *Non-current Assets Held for Sale and Discontinued Operations* is set out in paragraphs 1 – Aus45.2 and Appendices A, B and D. All the paragraphs have equal authority. Paragraphs in **bold type** state the main principles. Terms defined in Appendix A are in *italics* the first time they appear in the Standard. AASB 5 is to be read in the context of other Australian Accounting Standards, including AASB 1048 *Interpretation of Standards*, which identifies the Australian Accounting Interpretations, and AASB 1057 *Application of Australian Accounting Standards*. In the absence of explicit guidance, AASB 108 *Accounting Policies, Changes in Accounting Estimates and Errors* provides a basis for selecting and applying accounting policies.

COMPARISON WITH IFRS 5

AASB 5 *Non-current Assets Held for Sale and Discontinued Operations* incorporates IFRS 5 *Non-current Assets Held for Sale and Discontinued Operations* issued by the International Accounting Standards Board (IASB). Australian-specific paragraphs (which are not included in IFRS 5) are identified with the prefix "Aus". Paragraphs that apply only to not-for-profit entities begin by identifying their limited applicability.

Tier 1

For-profit entities complying with AASB 5 also comply with IFRS 5.

Not-for-profit entities' compliance with IFRS 5 will depend on whether any "Aus" paragraphs that specifically apply to not-for-profit entities provide additional guidance or contain applicable requirements that are inconsistent with IFRS 5.

Tier 2

Entities preparing general purpose financial statements under Australian Accounting Standards – Reduced Disclosure Requirements (Tier 2) will not be in compliance with IFRSs.

AASB 1053 *Application of Tiers of Australian Accounting Standards* explains the two tiers of reporting requirements.

ACCOUNTING STANDARD AASB 5

The Australian Accounting Standards Board makes Accounting Standard AASB 5 *Non-current Assets Held for Sale and Discontinued Operations* under section 334 of the *Corporations Act 2001*.

Kris Peach

Dated 7 August 2015   Chair – AASB

ACCOUNTING STANDARD AASB 5
NON-CURRENT ASSETS HELD FOR SALE AND DISCONTINUED OPERATIONS

Objective

1   The objective of this Standard is to specify the accounting for assets held for sale, and the presentation and disclosure of *discontinued operations*. In particular, the Standard requires:

    (a)   assets that meet the criteria to be classified as held for sale to be measured at the lower of carrying amount and *fair value* less *costs to sell*, and depreciation on such assets to cease; and

    (b)   assets that meet the criteria to be classified as held for sale to be presented separately in the statement of financial position and the results of discontinued operations to be presented separately in the statement of comprehensive income.

Scope

2   The classification and presentation requirements of this Standard apply to all recognised *non-current assets*[1] and to all *disposal groups* of an entity. The measurement requirements of this Standard apply to all recognised non-current assets and disposal groups (as set out in paragraph 4), except for those assets listed in paragraph 5 which shall continue to be measured in accordance with the Standard noted.

Aus2.1   **The requirements in this Standard do not apply to:**

    (a)   the restructuring of administrative arrangements; and

    (b)   the restructuring of administered activities of government departments.

Aus2.2   AASB 1004 *Contributions* includes requirements for the disclosure of assets, liabilities and items of equity resulting from the restructuring of administrative arrangements.

Aus2.3   An administered activity of a government department does not give rise to income and expenses of the department reporting the administered activity (see AASB 1050 *Administered Items*) and therefore, from the point of view of the department, the discontinuance of an administered activity does not give rise to a discontinued operation. However, if a government were to discontinue an activity that one of its departments had disclosed as an administered activity, from the point of view of that government the discontinuance may constitute a discontinued operation.

Aus2.4   Although AASB 3 *Business Combinations* contains requirements relating to the restructuring of local governments, these requirements only apply to the local government receiving assets or liabilities as a result of the restructuring. This Standard applies to the local government transferring assets and liabilities where the restructuring results in a discontinued operation of the transferor local government.

3   Assets classified as non-current in accordance with AASB 101 *Presentation of Financial Statements* shall not be reclassified as *current assets* until they meet the criteria to be classified as held for sale in accordance with this Standard. Assets of a class that an entity would normally regard as non-current that are acquired exclusively

---

1   For assets classified according to a liquidity presentation, non-current assets are assets that include amounts expected to be recovered more than twelve months after the reporting period. Paragraph 3 applies to the classification of such assets.

with a view to resale shall not be classified as current unless they meet the criteria to be classified as held for sale in accordance with this Standard.

4   Sometimes an entity disposes of a group of assets, possibly with some directly associated liabilities, together in a single transaction. Such a disposal group may be a group of *cash-generating units*, a single cash-generating unit, or part of a cash-generating unit.[2] The group may include any assets and any liabilities of the entity, including current assets, current liabilities and assets excluded by paragraph 5 from the measurement requirements of this Standard. If a non-current asset within the scope of the measurement requirements of this Standard is part of a disposal group, the measurement requirements of this Standard apply to the group as a whole, so that the group is measured at the lower of its carrying amount and fair value less costs to sell. The requirements for measuring the individual assets and liabilities within the disposal group are set out in paragraphs 18, 19 and 23.

5   The measurement provisions of this Standard[3] do not apply to the following assets, which are covered by the Australian Accounting Standards listed, either as individual assets or as part of a disposal group:

(a)   deferred tax assets (AASB 112 *Income Taxes*).

(b)   assets arising from employee benefits (AASB 119 *Employee Benefits*).

(c)   financial assets within the scope of AASB 9 *Financial Instruments*.

(d)   non-current assets that are accounted for in accordance with the fair value model in AASB 140 *Investment Property*.

(e)   non-current assets that are measured at fair value less costs to sell in accordance with AASB 141 *Agriculture*.

(f)   contractual rights under insurance contracts as defined in AASB 4 *Insurance Contracts*.

5A   The classification, presentation and measurement requirements in this Standard applicable to a non-current asset (or disposal group) that is classified as held for sale apply also to a non-current asset (or disposal group) that is classified as held for distribution to owners acting in their capacity as owners (held for distribution to owners).

5B   This Standard specifies the disclosures required in respect of non-current assets (or disposal groups) classified as held for sale or discontinued operations. Disclosures in other Standards do not apply to such assets (or disposal groups) unless those Standards require:

(a)   specific disclosures in respect of non-current assets (or disposal groups) classified as held for sale or discontinued operations; or

(b)   disclosures about measurement of assets and liabilities within a disposal group that are not within the scope of the measurement requirement of AASB 5 and such disclosures are not already provided in the other notes to the financial statements.

Additional disclosures about non-current assets (or disposal groups) classified as held for sale or discontinued operations may be necessary to comply with the general requirements of AASB 101, in particular paragraphs 15 and 125 of that Standard.

---

2   However, once the cash flows from an asset or group of assets are expected to arise principally from sale rather than continuing use, they become less dependent on cash flows arising from other assets, and a disposal group that was part of a cash-generating unit becomes a separate cash-generating unit.

3   Other than paragraphs 18 and 19, which require the assets in question to be measured in accordance with other applicable Australian Accounting Standards.

Classification of non-current assets (or disposal groups) as held for sale or as held for distribution to owners

6 **An entity shall classify a non-current asset (or disposal group) as held for sale if its carrying amount will be recovered principally through a sale transaction rather than through continuing use.**

7 For this to be the case, the asset (or disposal group) must be available for immediate sale in its present condition subject only to terms that are usual and customary for sales of such assets (or disposal groups) and its sale must be *highly probable*.

8 For the sale to be highly probable, the appropriate level of management must be committed to a plan to sell the asset (or disposal group), and an active programme to locate a buyer and complete the plan must have been initiated. Further, the asset (or disposal group) must be actively marketed for sale at a price that is reasonable in relation to its current fair value. In addition, the sale should be expected to qualify for recognition as a completed sale within one year from the date of classification, except as permitted by paragraph 9, and actions required to complete the plan should indicate that it is unlikely that significant changes to the plan will be made or that the plan will be withdrawn. The probability of shareholders' approval (if required in the jurisdiction) should be considered as part of the assessment of whether the sale is highly probable.

8A An entity that is committed to a sale plan involving loss of control of a subsidiary shall classify all the assets and liabilities of that subsidiary as held for sale when the criteria set out in paragraphs 6–8 are met, regardless of whether the entity will retain a non-controlling interest in its former subsidiary after the sale.

9 Events or circumstances may extend the period to complete the sale beyond one year. An extension of the period required to complete a sale does not preclude an asset (or disposal group) from being classified as held for sale if the delay is caused by events or circumstances beyond the entity's control and there is sufficient evidence that the entity remains committed to its plan to sell the asset (or disposal group). This will be the case when the criteria in Appendix B are met.

10 Sale transactions include exchanges of non-current assets for other non-current assets when the exchange has commercial substance in accordance with AASB 116 *Property, Plant and Equipment.*

11 When an entity acquires a non-current asset (or disposal group) exclusively with a view to its subsequent disposal, it shall classify the non-current asset (or disposal group) as held for sale at the acquisition date only if the one-year requirement in paragraph 8 is met (except as permitted by paragraph 9) and it is highly probable that any other criteria in paragraphs 7 and 8 that are not met at that date will be met within a short period following the acquisition (usually within three months).

12 If the criteria in paragraphs 7 and 8 are met after the reporting period, an entity shall not classify a non-current asset (or disposal group) as held for sale in those financial statements when issued. However, when those criteria are met after the reporting period but before the authorisation of the financial statements for issue, the entity shall disclose the information specified in paragraph 41(a), (b) and (d) in the notes.

12A A non-current asset (or disposal group) is classified as held for distribution to owners when the entity is committed to distribute the asset (or disposal group) to the owners. For this to be the case, the assets must be available for immediate distribution in their present condition and the distribution must be highly probable. For the distribution to be highly probable, actions to complete the distribution must have been initiated and should be expected to be completed within one year from the date of classification. Actions required to complete the distribution should indicate that it is unlikely that significant changes to the distribution will be made or that the distribution will be withdrawn. The probability of shareholders' approval (if required in the jurisdiction) should be considered as part of the assessment of whether the distribution is highly probable.

Non-current assets that are to be abandoned

13   An entity shall not classify as held for sale a non-current asset (or disposal group) that is to be abandoned. This is because its carrying amount will be recovered principally through continuing use. However, if the disposal group to be abandoned meets the criteria in paragraph 32(a)–(c), the entity shall present the results and cash flows of the disposal group as discontinued operations in accordance with paragraphs 33 and 34 at the date on which it ceases to be used. Non-current assets (or disposal groups) to be abandoned include non-current assets (or disposal groups) that are to be used to the end of their economic life and non-current assets (or disposal groups) that are to be closed rather than sold.

14   An entity shall not account for a non-current asset that has been temporarily taken out of use as if it had been abandoned.

Measurement of non-current assets (or disposal groups) classified as held for sale

Measurement of a non-current asset (or disposal group)

15   **An entity shall measure a non-current asset (or disposal group) classified as held for sale at the lower of its carrying amount and fair value less costs to sell.**

15A   **An entity shall measure a non-current asset (or disposal group) classified as held for distribution to owners at the lower of its carrying amount and fair value less costs to distribute.[4]**

16   If a newly acquired asset (or disposal group) meets the criteria to be classified as held for sale (see paragraph 11), applying paragraph 15 will result in the asset (or disposal group) being measured on initial recognition at the lower of its carrying amount had it not been so classified (for example, cost) and fair value less costs to sell. Hence, if the asset (or disposal group) is acquired as part of a business combination, it shall be measured at fair value less costs to sell.

17   When the sale is expected to occur beyond one year, the entity shall measure the costs to sell at their present value. Any increase in the present value of the costs to sell that arises from the passage of time shall be presented in profit or loss as a financing cost.

18   Immediately before the initial classification of the asset (or disposal group) as held for sale, the carrying amounts of the asset (or all the assets and liabilities in the group) shall be measured in accordance with applicable Australian Accounting Standards.

19   On subsequent remeasurement of a disposal group, the carrying amounts of any assets and liabilities that are not within the scope of the measurement requirements of this Standard, but are included in a disposal group classified as held for sale, shall be remeasured in accordance with applicable Australian Accounting Standards before the fair value less costs to sell of the disposal group is remeasured.

Recognition of impairment losses and reversals

20   An entity shall recognise an impairment loss for any initial or subsequent write-down of the asset (or disposal group) to fair value less costs to sell, to the extent that it has not been recognised in accordance with paragraph 19.

21   An entity shall recognise a gain for any subsequent increase in fair value less costs to sell of an asset, but not in excess of the cumulative impairment loss that has been recognised either in accordance with this Standard or previously in accordance with AASB 136 *Impairment of Assets*.

22   An entity shall recognise a gain for any subsequent increase in fair value less costs to sell of a disposal group:

---

4   Costs to distribute are the incremental costs directly attributable to the distribution, excluding finance costs and income tax expense.

(a)   to the extent that it has not been recognised in accordance with paragraph 19; but

(b)   not in excess of the cumulative impairment loss that has been recognised, either in accordance with this Standard or previously in accordance with AASB 136, on the non-current assets that are within the scope of the measurement requirements of this Standard.

23   The impairment loss (or any subsequent gain) recognised for a disposal group shall reduce (or increase) the carrying amount of the non-current assets in the group that are within the scope of the measurement requirements of this Standard, in the order of allocation set out in paragraphs 104(a) and (b) and 122 of AASB 136.

24   A gain or loss not previously recognised by the date of the sale of a non-current asset (or disposal group) shall be recognised at the date of derecognition. Requirements relating to derecognition are set out in:

(a)   paragraphs 67–72 of AASB 116 for property, plant and equipment, and

(b)   paragraphs 112–117 of AASB 138 *Intangible Assets* for intangible assets.

25   An entity shall not depreciate (or amortise) a non-current asset while it is classified as held for sale or while it is part of a disposal group classified as held for sale. Interest and other expenses attributable to the liabilities of a disposal group classified as held for sale shall continue to be recognised.

Changes to a plan of sale or to a plan of distribution to owners

26   If an entity has classified an asset (or disposal group) as held for sale or as held for distribution to owners, but the criteria in paragraphs 7–9 (for held for sale) or in paragraph 12A (for held for distribution to owners) are no longer met, the entity shall cease to classify the asset (or disposal group) as held for sale or held for distribution to owners (respectively). In such cases an entity shall follow the guidance in paragraphs 27–29 to account for this change except when paragraph 26A applies.

26A   If an entity reclassifies an asset (or disposal group) directly from being held for sale to being held for distribution to owners, or directly from being held for distribution to owners to being held for sale, then the change in classification is considered a continuation of the original plan of disposal. The entity:

(a)   shall not follow the guidance in paragraphs 27–29 to account for this change. The entity shall apply the classification, presentation and measurement requirements in this Standard that are applicable to the new method of disposal.

(b)   shall measure the non-current asset (or disposal group) by following the requirements in paragraph 15 (if reclassified as held for sale) or 15A (if reclassified as held for distribution to owners) and recognise any reduction or increase in the fair value less costs to sell/costs to distribute of the non-current asset (or disposal group) by following the requirements in paragraphs 20–25.

(c)   shall not change the date of classification in accordance with paragraphs 8 and 12A. This does not preclude an extension of the period required to complete a sale or a distribution to owners if the conditions in paragraph 9 are met.

27   The entity shall measure a non-current asset (or disposal group) that ceases to be classified as held for sale or as held for distribution to owners (or ceases to be included in a disposal group classified as held for sale or as held for distribution to owners) at the lower of:

(a)   its carrying amount before the asset (or disposal group) was classified as held for sale or as held for distribution to owners, adjusted for any depreciation, amortisation or revaluations that would have been recognised had the asset (or disposal group) not been classified as held for sale or as held for distribution to owners, and

(b)   its *recoverable amount* at the date of the subsequent decision not to sell or distribute.[5]

28   The entity shall include any required adjustment to the carrying amount of a non-current asset that ceases to be classified as held for sale or as held for distribution to owners in profit or loss[6] from continuing operations in the period in which the criteria in paragraphs 7–9 or 12A, respectively, are no longer met. Financial statements for the periods since classification as held for sale or as held for distribution to owners shall be amended accordingly if the disposal group or non-current asset that ceases to be classified as held for sale or as held for distribution to owners is a subsidiary, joint operation, joint venture, associate, or a portion of an interest in a joint venture or an associate. The entity shall present that adjustment in the same caption in the statement of comprehensive income used to present a gain or loss, if any, recognised in accordance with paragraph 37.

29   If an entity removes an individual asset or liability from a disposal group classified as held for sale, the remaining assets and liabilities of the disposal group to be sold shall continue to be measured as a group only if the group meets the criteria in paragraphs 7–9. If an entity removes an individual asset or liability from a disposal group classified as held for distribution to owners, the remaining assets and liabilities of the disposal group to be distributed shall continue to be measured as a group only if the group meets the criteria in paragraph 12A. Otherwise, the remaining non-current assets of the group that individually meet the criteria to be classified as held for sale (or as held for distribution to owners) shall be measured individually at the lower of their carrying amounts and fair values less costs to sell (or costs to distribute) at that date. Any non-current assets that do not meet the criteria for held for sale shall cease to be classified as held for sale in accordance with paragraph 26. Any non-current assets that do not meet the criteria for held for distribution to owners shall cease to be classified as held for distribution to owners in accordance with paragraph 26.

Presentation and disclosure

30   An entity shall present and disclose information that enables users of the financial statements to evaluate the financial effects of discontinued operations and disposals of non-current assets (or disposal groups).

Presenting discontinued operations

31   A *component of an entity* comprises operations and cash flows that can be clearly distinguished, operationally and for financial reporting purposes, from the rest of the entity. In other words, a component of an entity will have been a cash-generating unit or a group of cash-generating units while being held for use.

32   A discontinued operation is a component of an entity that either has been disposed of, or is classified as held for sale, and

(a)   represents a separate major line of business or geographical area of operations,

(b)   is part of a single co-ordinated plan to dispose of a separate major line of business or geographical area of operations or

(c)   is a subsidiary acquired exclusively with a view to resale.

---

5   If the non-current asset is part of a cash-generating unit, its recoverable amount is the carrying amount that would have been recognised after the allocation of any impairment loss arising on that cash-generating unit in accordance with AASB 136.

6   Unless the asset is property, plant and equipment or an intangible asset that had been revalued in accordance with AASB 116 or AASB 138 before classification as held for sale, in which case the adjustment shall be treated as a revaluation increase or decrease.

33   An entity shall disclose:

    (a)   a single amount in the statement of comprehensive income comprising the total of:

        (i)   the post-tax profit or loss of discontinued operations and

        (ii)   the post-tax gain or loss recognised on the measurement to fair value less costs to sell or on the disposal of the assets or disposal group(s) constituting the discontinued operation.

    (b)   an analysis of the single amount in (a) into:

        (i)   the revenue, expenses and pre-tax profit or loss of discontinued operations;

        (ii)   the related income tax expense as required by paragraph 81(h) of AASB 112.

        (iii)   the gain or loss recognised on the measurement to fair value less costs to sell or on the disposal of the assets or disposal group(s) constituting the discontinued operation; and

        (iv)   the related income tax expense as required by paragraph 81(h) of AASB 112.

    The analysis may be presented in the notes or in the statement of comprehensive income. If it is presented in the statement of comprehensive income it shall be presented in a section identified as relating to discontinued operations, ie separately from continuing operations. The analysis is not required for disposal groups that are newly acquired subsidiaries that meet the criteria to be classified as held for sale on acquisition (see paragraph 11).

    (c)   the net cash flows attributable to the operating, investing and financing activities of discontinued operations. These disclosures may be presented either in the notes or in the financial statements. These disclosures are not required for disposal groups that are newly acquired subsidiaries that meet the criteria to be classified as held for sale on acquisition (see paragraph 11).

    (d)   the amount of income from continuing operations and from discontinued operations attributable to owners of the parent. These disclosures may be presented either in the notes or in the statement of comprehensive income.

33A   If an entity presents the items of profit or loss in a separate statement as described in paragraph 10A of AASB 101, a section identified as relating to discontinued operations is presented in that statement.

34   An entity shall re-present the disclosures in paragraph 33 for prior periods presented in the financial statements so that the disclosures relate to all operations that have been discontinued by the end of the reporting period for the latest period presented.

35   Adjustments in the current period to amounts previously presented in discontinued operations that are directly related to the disposal of a discontinued operation in a prior period shall be classified separately in discontinued operations. The nature and amount of such adjustments shall be disclosed. Examples of circumstances in which these adjustments may arise include the following:

    (a)   the resolution of uncertainties that arise from the terms of the disposal transaction, such as the resolution of purchase price adjustments and indemnification issues with the purchaser.

    (b)   the resolution of uncertainties that arise from and are directly related to the operations of the component before its disposal, such as environmental and product warranty obligations retained by the seller.

    (c)   the settlement of employee benefit plan obligations, provided that the settlement is directly related to the disposal transaction.

AASB

36   If an entity ceases to classify a component of an entity as held for sale, the results of operations of the component previously presented in discontinued operations in accordance with paragraphs 33–35 shall be reclassified and included in income from continuing operations for all periods presented. The amounts for prior periods shall be described as having been re-presented.

36A   An entity that is committed to a sale plan involving loss of control of a subsidiary shall disclose the information required in paragraphs 33–36 when the subsidiary is a disposal group that meets the definition of a discontinued operation in accordance with paragraph 32.

Gains or losses relating to continuing operations

37   Any gain or loss on the remeasurement of a non-current asset (or disposal group) classified as held for sale that does not meet the definition of a discontinued operation shall be included in profit or loss from continuing operations.

Presentation of a non-current asset or disposal group classified as held for sale

38   An entity shall present a non-current asset classified as held for sale and the assets of a disposal group classified as held for sale separately from other assets in the statement of financial position. The liabilities of a disposal group classified as held for sale shall be presented separately from other liabilities in the statement of financial position. Those assets and liabilities shall not be offset and presented as a single amount. The major classes of assets and liabilities classified as held for sale shall be separately disclosed either in the statement of financial position or in the notes, except as permitted by paragraph 39. An entity shall present separately any cumulative income or expense recognised in other comprehensive income relating to a non-current asset (or disposal group) classified as held for sale.

39   If the disposal group is a newly acquired subsidiary that meets the criteria to be classified as held for sale on acquisition (see paragraph 11), disclosure of the major classes of assets and liabilities is not required.

40   An entity shall not reclassify or re-present amounts presented for non-current assets or for the assets and liabilities of disposal groups classified as held for sale in the statements of financial position for prior periods to reflect the classification in the statement of financial position for the latest period presented.

Additional disclosures

41   An entity shall disclose the following information in the notes in the period in which a non-current asset (or disposal group) has been either classified as held for sale or sold:

   (a)   a description of the non-current asset (or disposal group);

   (b)   a description of the facts and circumstances of the sale, or leading to the expected disposal, and the expected manner and timing of that disposal;

   (c)   the gain or loss recognised in accordance with paragraphs 20–22 and, if not separately presented in the statement of comprehensive income, the caption in the statement of comprehensive income that includes that gain or loss;

   (d)   if applicable, the reportable segment in which the non-current asset (or disposal group) is presented in accordance with AASB 8 Operating Segments.

42   If either paragraph 26 or paragraph 29 applies, an entity shall disclose, in the period of the decision to change the plan to sell the non-current asset (or disposal group), a description of the facts and circumstances leading to the decision and the effect of the decision on the results of operations for the period and any prior periods presented.

Transitional provisions

Aus42.1　The following transitional paragraph shall not be applied by entities that have previously applied this Standard, unless required to do so by another Australian Accounting Standard.

43　The Standard shall be applied prospectively to non-current assets (or disposal groups) that meet the criteria to be classified as held for sale and operations that meet the criteria to be classified as discontinued after the effective date of the Standard. An entity may apply the requirements of the Standard to all non-current assets (or disposal groups) that meet the criteria to be classified as held for sale and operations that meet the criteria to be classified as discontinued after any date before the effective date of the Standard, provided the valuations and other information needed to apply the Standard were obtained at the time those criteria were originally met.

Effective date

44　An entity shall apply this Standard for annual periods beginning on or after 1 January 2018. Earlier application is encouraged for periods beginning after 24 July 2014 but before 1 January 2018. If an entity applies the Standard for a period beginning before 1 January 2018, it shall disclose that fact.

44A–44E　[Deleted by the AASB]

44F　[Deleted]

44G–44I　[Deleted by the AASB]

44J　[Deleted]

44K　AASB 2010-7 *Amendments to Australian Accounting Standards arising from AASB 9 (December 2010)* (as amended) amended paragraph 5 in the previous version of this Standard. Paragraph 44F, added by AASB 2010-7, was deleted by AASB 2014-1 *Amendments to Australian Accounting Standards.* Paragraph 44J, added by AASB 2014-1, was deleted by AASB 2014-7 *Amendments to Australian Accounting Standards arising from AASB 9 (December 2014).* An entity shall apply those amendments when it applies AASB 9.

44L　AASB 2015-1 *Amendments to Australian Accounting Standards – Annual Improvements to Australian Accounting Standards 2012–2014 Cycle,* issued in January 2015, amended the previous version of this Standard as follows: amended paragraphs 26–29 and added paragraph 26A. An entity shall apply those amendments prospectively in accordance with AASB 108 *Accounting Policies, Changes in Accounting Estimates and Errors* to changes in a method of disposal that occur in annual periods beginning on or after 1 January 2016. Earlier application is permitted. If an entity applies those amendments for an earlier period it shall disclose that fact.

Withdrawal of IAS 35

45　[Deleted by the AASB]

Commencement of the legislative instrument

Aus45.1　For legal purposes, this legislative instrument commences on 31 December 2017.

Withdrawal of AASB pronouncements

Aus45.2　This Standard repeals AASB 5 *Non-current Assets Held for Sale and Discontinued Operations* issued in July 2004. Despite the repeal, after the time this Standard starts to apply under section 334 of the Corporations Act (either generally or in relation to an individual entity), the repealed Standard continues to apply in relation to any period ending before that time as if the repeal had not occurred.

[Note: When this Standard applies under section 334 of the Corporations Act (either generally or in relation to an individual entity), it supersedes the application of the repealed Standard.]

APPENDIX A
DEFINED TERMS

This appendix is an integral part of the Standard.

cash-generating unit	The smallest identifiable group of assets that generates cash inflows that are largely independent of the cash inflows from other assets or groups of assets.
component of an entity	Operations and cash flows that can be clearly distinguished, operationally and for financial reporting purposes, from the rest of the entity.
costs to sell	The incremental costs directly attributable to the disposal of an asset (or **disposal group**), excluding finance costs and income tax expense.
current asset	An entity shall classify an asset as current when: (a) it expects to realise the asset, or intends to sell or consume it, in its normal operating cycle; (b) it holds the asset primarily for the purpose of trading; (c) it expects to realise the asset within twelve months after the reporting period; or (d) the asset is cash or a cash equivalent (as defined in AASB 107) unless the asset is restricted from being exchanged or used to settle a liability for at least twelve months after the reporting period.
discontinued operation	A **component of an entity** that either has been disposed of or is classified as held for sale and: (a) represents a separate major line of business or geographical area of operations, (b) is part of a single co-ordinated plan to dispose of a separate major line of business or geographical area of operations or (c) is a subsidiary acquired exclusively with a view to resale.
disposal group	A group of assets to be disposed of, by sale or otherwise, together as a group in a single transaction, and liabilities directly associated with those assets that will be transferred in the transaction. The group includes goodwill acquired in a business combination if the group is a **cash-generating unit** to which goodwill has been allocated in accordance with the requirements of paragraphs 80–87 of AASB 136 *Impairment of Assets* or if it is an operation within such a cash-generating unit.
fair value	*Fair value* is the price that would be received to sell an asset or paid to transfer a liability in an orderly transaction between market participants at the measurement date. (See AASB 13.)
firm purchase commitment	An agreement with an unrelated party, binding on both parties and usually legally enforceable, that (a) specifies all significant terms, including the price and timing of the transactions, and (b) includes a disincentive for non-performance that is sufficiently large to make performance **highly probable.**
highly probable	Significantly more likely than **probable**.

non-current asset	An asset that does not meet the definition of a **current asset**.
probable	More likely than not.
recoverable amount	The higher of an asset's **fair value** less **costs to sell** and its **value in use**.
value in use[7]	The present value of estimated future cash flows expected to arise from the continuing use of an asset and from its disposal at the end of its useful life.

APPENDIX B
APPLICATION SUPPLEMENT

This appendix is an integral part of the Standard.

Extension of the period required to complete a sale

B1   As noted in paragraph 9, an extension of the period required to complete a sale does not preclude an asset (or disposal group) from being classified as held for sale if the delay is caused by events or circumstances beyond the entity's control and there is sufficient evidence that the entity remains committed to its plan to sell the asset (or disposal group). An exception to the one-year requirement in paragraph 8 shall therefore apply in the following situations in which such events or circumstances arise:

(a)   at the date an entity commits itself to a plan to sell a non-current asset (or disposal group) it reasonably expects that others (not a buyer) will impose conditions on the transfer of the asset (or disposal group) that will extend the period required to complete the sale, and:

(i)   actions necessary to respond to those conditions cannot be initiated until after a *firm purchase commitment* is obtained, and

(ii)   a firm purchase commitment is highly probable within one year.

(b)   an entity obtains a firm purchase commitment and, as a result, a buyer or others unexpectedly impose conditions on the transfer of a non-current asset (or disposal group) previously classified as held for sale that will extend the period required to complete the sale, and:

(i)   timely actions necessary to respond to the conditions have been taken, and

(ii)   a favourable resolution of the delaying factors is expected.

(c)   during the initial one-year period, circumstances arise that were previously considered unlikely and, as a result, a non-current asset (or disposal group) previously classified as held for sale is not sold by the end of that period, and:

(i)   during the initial one-year period the entity took action necessary to respond to the change in circumstances,

(ii)   the non-current asset (or disposal group) is being actively marketed at a price that is reasonable, given the change in circumstances, and

(iii)   the criteria in paragraphs 7 and 8 are met.

---

7   [Aus] Not-for-profit entities should refer to AASB 136 *Impairment of Assets* when the future economic benefits of an asset are not primarily dependent on the asset's ability to generate net cash inflows.

APPENDIX D
AUSTRALIAN REDUCED DISCLOSURE
REQUIREMENTS

This appendix is an integral part of the Standard.

AusD1   The following do not apply to entities preparing general purpose financial statements under Australian Accounting Standards – Reduced Disclosure Requirements:

         (a)   paragraphs 33(b), 33(d), 41(d) and 42; and

         (b)   the second and third sentences in paragraph 35, including paragraphs 35(a)–(c).

              Entities applying Australian Accounting Standards – Reduced Disclosure Requirements may elect to comply with some or all of these excluded requirements.

AusD2   The requirements that do not apply to entities preparing general purpose financial statements under Australian Accounting Standards – Reduced Disclosure Requirements are also identified in this Standard by shading of the relevant text.

DELETED IFRS 5 TEXT

Deleted IFRS 5 text is not part of AASB 5.

44A   IAS 1 (as revised in 2007) amended the terminology used throughout IFRSs. In addition it amended paragraphs 3 and 38, and added paragraph 33A. An entity shall apply those amendments for annual periods beginning on or after 1 January 2009. If an entity applies IAS 1 (revised 2007) for an earlier period, the amendments shall be applied for that earlier period.

44B   IAS 27 *Consolidated and Separate Financial Statements* (as amended in 2008) added paragraph 33(d). An entity shall apply that amendment for annual periods beginning on or after 1 July 2009. If an entity applies IAS 27 (amended 2008) for an earlier period, the amendment shall be applied for that earlier period. The amendment shall be applied retrospectively.

44C   Paragraphs 8A and 36A were added by *Improvements to IFRSs* issued in May 2008. An entity shall apply those amendments for annual periods beginning on or after 1 July 2009. Earlier application is permitted. However, an entity shall not apply the amendments for annual periods beginning before 1 July 2009 unless it also applies IAS 27 (as amended in January 2008). If an entity applies the amendments before 1 July 2009 it shall disclose that fact. An entity shall apply the amendments prospectively from the date at which it first applied IFRS 5, subject to the transitional provisions in paragraph 45 of IAS 27 (amended January 2008).

44D   Paragraphs 5A, 12A and 15A were added and paragraph 8 was amended by IFRIC 17 *Distributions of Non-cash Assets to Owners* in November 2008. Those amendments shall be applied prospectively to non-current assets (or disposal groups) that are classified as held for distribution to owners in annual periods beginning on or after 1 July 2009. Retrospective application is not permitted. Earlier application is permitted. If an entity applies the amendments for a period beginning before 1 July 2009 it shall disclose that fact and also apply IFRS 3 *Business Combinations* (as revised in 2008), IAS 27 (as amended in January 2008) and IFRIC 17.

44E   Paragraph 5B was added by *Improvements to IFRSs* issued in April 2009. An entity shall apply that amendment prospectively for annual periods beginning on or after 1 January 2010. Earlier application is permitted. If an entity applies the amendment for an earlier period it shall disclose that fact.

44G IFRS 11 *Joint Arrangements*, issued in May 2011, amended paragraph 28. An entity shall apply that amendment when it applies IFRS 11.

44H IFRS 13 *Fair Value Measurement*, issued in May 2011, amended the definition of fair value in Appendix A. An entity shall apply that amendment when it applies IFRS 13.

44I *Presentation of Items of Other Comprehensive Income* (Amendments to IAS 1), issued in June 2011, amended paragraph 33A. An entity shall apply that amendment when it applies IAS 1 as amended in June 2011.

45 This IFRS supersedes IAS 35 *Discontinuing Operations*.

AASB 6
Exploration for and Evaluation of Mineral Resources
(Reissued August 2015)

CONTENTS

COMPARISON WITH IFRS 6
ACCOUNTING STANDARD
AASB 6 *EXPLORATION FOR AND EVALUATION OF MINERAL RESOURCES*

from paragraph

APPENDICES
A. DEFINED TERMS
B. AUSTRALIAN DEFINED TERMS

BASIS FOR CONCLUSIONS ON IFRS 6 (available on the AASB website)

Australian Accounting Standard AASB 6 *Exploration for and Evaluation of Mineral Resources* is set out in paragraphs 1 – Aus27.2 and Appendices A – B. All the paragraphs have equal authority. Paragraphs in **bold type** state the main principles. Terms defined in this Standard are in *italics* the first time they appear in the Standard. AASB 6 is to be read in the context of other Australian Accounting Standards, including AASB 1048 *Interpretation of Standards*, which identifies the Australian Accounting Interpretations, and AASB 1057 *Application of Australian Accounting Standards*. In the absence of explicit guidance, AASB 108 *Accounting Policies, Changes in Accounting Estimates and Errors* provides a basis for selecting and applying accounting policies.

COMPARISON WITH IFRS 6

AASB 6 *Exploration for and Evaluation of Mineral Resources* incorporates IFRS 6 *Exploration for and Evaluation of Mineral Resources* issued by the International Accounting Standards Board (IASB). Australian-specific paragraphs (which are not included in IFRS 6) are identified with the prefix "Aus". Paragraphs that apply only to not-for-profit entities begin by identifying their limited applicability.

Tier 1

For-profit entities complying with AASB 6 also comply with IFRS 6.

Not-for-profit entities' compliance with IFRS 6 will depend on whether any "Aus" paragraphs that specifically apply to not-for-profit entities provide additional guidance or contain applicable requirements that are inconsistent with IFRS 6.

AASB 1053 *Application of Tiers of Australian Accounting Standards* explains the two tiers of reporting requirements.

ACCOUNTING STANDARD AASB 6

The Australian Accounting Standards Board makes Accounting Standard AASB 6 *Exploration for and Evaluation of Mineral Resources* under section 334 of the *Corporations Act 2001*.

Kris Peach

Dated 7 August 2015   Chair – AASB

ACCOUNTING STANDARD AASB 6
EXPLORATION FOR AND EVALUATION OF MINERAL RESOURCES

Objective

1   The objective of this Standard is to specify the financial reporting for the *exploration for and evaluation of mineral resources*.

2   In particular, the Standard requires:

    (a)   limited improvements to existing accounting practices for *exploration and evaluation expenditures*.

    (b)   entities that recognise *exploration and evaluation assets* to assess such assets for impairment in accordance with this Standard and measure any impairment in accordance with AASB 136 *Impairment of Assets*.

    (c)   disclosures that identify and explain the amounts in the entity's financial statements arising from the exploration for and evaluation of mineral resources and help users of those financial statements understand the amount, timing and certainty of future cash flows from any exploration and evaluation assets recognised.

Scope

3   An entity shall apply the Standard to exploration and evaluation expenditures that it incurs.

4   The Standard does not address other aspects of accounting by entities engaged in the exploration for and evaluation of mineral resources.

5   An entity shall not apply the Standard to expenditures incurred:

(a)   before the exploration for and evaluation of mineral resources, such as expenditures incurred before the entity has obtained the legal rights to explore a specific area.

(b)   after the technical feasibility and commercial viability of extracting a mineral resource are demonstrable.

Recognition of exploration and evaluation assets

Temporary exemption from AASB 108 paragraphs 11 and 12

6   When developing its accounting policies, an entity recognising exploration and evaluation assets shall apply paragraph 10 of AASB 108 *Accounting Policies, Changes in Accounting Estimates and Errors* and paragraphs Aus7.1 and Aus7.2 below.

7   Paragraphs 11 and 12 of AASB 108 specify sources of authoritative requirements and guidance that management is required to consider in developing an accounting policy for an item if no Standard applies specifically to that item. Subject to paragraphs 9 and 10 below, this Standard exempts an entity from applying those paragraphs to its accounting policies for the recognition and measurement of exploration and evaluation assets.

Treatment of exploration and evaluation expenditures

Aus7.1   An entity's accounting policy for the treatment of its exploration and evaluation expenditures shall be in accordance with the following requirements. For each *area of interest*, expenditures incurred in the exploration for and evaluation of mineral resources shall be:

(a)   expensed as incurred; or

(b)   partially or fully capitalised, and recognised as an exploration and evaluation asset if the requirements of paragraph Aus7.2 are satisfied.

An entity shall make this decision separately for each area of interest.

Aus7.2   An exploration and evaluation asset shall only be recognised in relation to an area of interest if the following conditions are satisfied:

(a)   the rights to tenure of the area of interest are current; and

(b)   at least one of the following conditions is also met:

(i)   the exploration and evaluation expenditures are expected to be recouped through successful development and exploitation of the area of interest, or alternatively, by its sale; and

(ii)   exploration and evaluation activities in the area of interest have not at the end of the reporting period reached a stage which permits a reasonable assessment of the existence or otherwise of *economically recoverable reserves*, and active and significant operations in, or in relation to, the area of interest are continuing.

Aus7.3 An area of interest refers to an individual geological area whereby the presence of a mineral deposit or an oil or natural gas field is considered favourable or has been proved to exist. It is common for an area of interest to contract in size progressively, as exploration and evaluation lead towards the identification of a mineral deposit or an oil or natural gas field, which may prove to contain economically recoverable reserves. When this happens during the exploration for and evaluation of mineral resources, exploration and evaluation expenditures are still included in the cost of the exploration and evaluation asset notwithstanding that the size of the area of interest may contract as the exploration and evaluation operations progress. In most cases, an area of interest will comprise a single mine or deposit or a separate oil or gas field.

Measurement of exploration and evaluation assets

Measurement at recognition

8 Exploration and evaluation assets shall be measured at cost.

Elements of cost of exploration and evaluation assets

9 An entity shall determine an accounting policy specifying which expenditures are recognised as exploration and evaluation assets and apply the policy consistently. In making this determination, an entity considers the degree to which the expenditure can be associated with finding specific mineral resources. The following are examples of expenditures that might be included in the initial measurement of exploration and evaluation assets (the list is not exhaustive):

(a) acquisition of rights to explore;

(b) topographical, geological, geochemical and geophysical studies;

(c) exploratory drilling;

(d) trenching;

(e) sampling; and

(f) activities in relation to evaluating the technical feasibility and commercial viability of extracting a mineral resource.

Aus9.1 In accordance with paragraph 9, where an entity recognises exploration and evaluation assets, direct and indirect costs associated with the exploration for and evaluation of mineral resources and which specifically relate to an area of interest are allocated to that area of interest. In making this allocation, no distinction is drawn between costs incurred within the entity and the cost of services performed by outside contractors or consultants on behalf of the entity.

Aus9.2 The costs of acquiring leases or other rights of tenure in the area of interest are included in the cost of the exploration and evaluation asset if they are acquired as part of the exploration for and evaluation of mineral resources.

Aus9.3 Indirect costs that are included in the cost of an exploration and evaluation asset include, among other things, charges for depreciation of equipment used in exploration and evaluation activities.

Aus9.4 General and administrative costs are allocated to, and included in, the cost of an exploration and evaluation asset, but only to the extent that those costs can be related directly to operational activities in the area of interest to which the exploration and evaluation asset relates. In all other cases, these costs are expensed as incurred. For example, general and administrative costs such as directors' fees, secretarial and share registry expenses, and salaries and other expenses of general management are recognised as expenses when incurred since they are only indirectly related to operational activities.

AASB

10   Expenditures related to the development of mineral resources shall not be recognised as exploration and evaluation assets. The *Framework for the Preparation and Presentation of Financial Statements* (as identified in AASB 1048 *Interpretation of Standards*) and AASB 138 *Intangible Assets* provide guidance on the recognition of assets arising from development.

11   In accordance with AASB 137 *Provisions, Contingent Liabilities and Contingent Assets* an entity recognises any obligations for removal and restoration that are incurred during a particular period as a consequence of having undertaken the exploration for and evaluation of mineral resources.

Measurement after recognition

12   After recognition, an entity shall apply either the cost model or the revaluation model to the exploration and evaluation assets. If the revaluation model is applied (either the model in AASB 116 *Property, Plant and Equipment* or the model in AASB 138) it shall be consistent with the classification of the assets (see paragraph 15).

Changes in accounting policies

13   **An entity may change its accounting policies for exploration and evaluation expenditures if the change makes the financial statements more relevant to the economic decision-making needs of users and no less reliable, or more reliable and no less relevant to those needs. An entity shall judge relevance and reliability using the criteria in AASB 108.**

Aus13.1   Notwithstanding paragraph 13, any change in an entity's accounting policy for exploration and evaluation expenditures shall also remain in accordance with paragraphs Aus7.1 and Aus7.2.

14   To justify changing its accounting policies for exploration and evaluation expenditures, an entity shall demonstrate that the change brings its financial statements closer to meeting the criteria in AASB 108, but the change need not achieve full compliance with those criteria.

Presentation

Classification of exploration and evaluation assets

15   An entity shall classify exploration and evaluation assets as tangible or intangible according to the nature of the assets acquired and apply the classification consistently.

16   Some exploration and evaluation assets are treated as intangible (eg drilling rights), whereas others are tangible (eg vehicles and drilling rigs). To the extent that a tangible asset is consumed in developing an intangible asset, the amount reflecting that consumption is part of the cost of the intangible asset. However, using a tangible asset to develop an intangible asset does not change a tangible asset into an intangible asset.

Reclassification of exploration and evaluation assets

17   An exploration and evaluation asset shall no longer be classified as such when the technical feasibility and commercial viability of extracting a mineral resource are demonstrable. Exploration and evaluation assets shall be assessed for impairment, and any impairment loss recognised, before reclassification.

Impairment

Recognition and measurement

18   **Exploration and evaluation assets shall be assessed for impairment when facts and circumstances suggest that the carrying amount of an exploration and evaluation asset may exceed its recoverable amount. When facts and circumstances suggest that the carrying amount exceeds the recoverable amount, an entity shall measure, present and disclose any resulting impairment loss in accordance with AASB 136, except as provided by paragraph 21 below.**

19   For the purposes of exploration and evaluation assets only, paragraph 20 of this Standard shall be applied rather than paragraphs 8–17 of AASB 136 when identifying an exploration and evaluation asset that may be impaired. Paragraph 20 uses the term 'assets' but applies equally to separate exploration and evaluation assets or a cash-generating unit.

20   One or more of the following facts and circumstances indicate that an entity should test exploration and evaluation assets for impairment (the list is not exhaustive):

(a)   the period for which the entity has the right to explore in the specific area has expired during the period or will expire in the near future, and is not expected to be renewed.

(b)   substantive expenditure on further exploration for and evaluation of mineral resources in the specific area is neither budgeted nor planned.

(c)   exploration for and evaluation of mineral resources in the specific area have not led to the discovery of commercially viable quantities of mineral resources and the entity has decided to discontinue such activities in the specific area.

(d)   sufficient data exist to indicate that, although a development in the specific area is likely to proceed, the carrying amount of the exploration and evaluation asset is unlikely to be recovered in full from successful development or by sale.

In any such case, or similar cases, the entity shall perform an impairment test in accordance with AASB 136. Any impairment loss is recognised as an expense in accordance with AASB 136.

Specifying the level at which exploration and evaluation assets are assessed for impairment

21   **An entity shall determine an accounting policy for allocating exploration and evaluation assets to cash-generating units or groups of cash-generating units for the purpose of assessing such assets for impairment. Each cash-generating unit or group of units to which an exploration and evaluation asset is allocated shall not be larger than an operating segment determined in accordance with AASB 8 *Operating Segments*.**

22   The level identified by the entity for the purposes of testing exploration and evaluation assets for impairment may comprise one or more cash-generating units.

Aus22.1   Notwithstanding paragraphs 21 and 22, the level identified by the entity for the purposes of testing exploration and evaluation assets for impairment shall be no larger than the area of interest to which the exploration and evaluation asset relates.

Disclosure

23   **An entity shall disclose information that identifies and explains the amounts recognised in its financial statements arising from the exploration for and evaluation of mineral resources.**

24   To comply with paragraph 23, an entity shall disclose:

   (a)   its accounting policies for exploration and evaluation expenditures including the recognition of exploration and evaluation assets.

   (b)   the amounts of assets, liabilities, income and expense and operating and investing cash flows arising from the exploration for and evaluation of mineral resources.

Aus24.1   In addition to the disclosure required by paragraph 24(b), an entity that recognises exploration and evaluation assets for any of its areas of interest shall, in disclosing the amounts of those assets, provide an explanation that recoverability of the carrying amount of the exploration and evaluation assets is dependent on successful development and commercial exploitation, or alternatively, sale of the respective areas of interest.

25   An entity shall treat exploration and evaluation assets as a separate class of assets and make the disclosures required by either AASB 116 or AASB 138 consistent with how the assets are classified.

Effective date

26   An entity shall apply this Standard for annual periods beginning on or after 1 January 2016. Earlier application is encouraged for periods beginning on or after 1 January 2014 but before 1 January 2016. If an entity applies the Standard for a period beginning before 1 January 2016, it shall disclose that fact.

Transitional provisions

27   If it is impracticable to apply a particular requirement of paragraph 18 to comparative information that relates to annual periods beginning before 1 January 2005, an entity shall disclose that fact. AASB 108 explains the term 'impracticable'.

Commencement of the legislative instrument

Aus27.1   For legal purposes, this legislative instrument commences on 31 December 2015.

Withdrawal of AASB pronouncements

Aus27.2   This Standard repeals AASB 6 *Exploration for and Evaluation of Mineral Resources* issued in December 2004. Despite the repeal, after the time this Standard starts to apply under section 334 of the Corporations Act (either generally or in relation to an individual entity), the repealed Standard continues to apply in relation to any period ending before that time as if the repeal had not occurred.

[Note: When this Standard applies under section 334 of the Corporations Act (either generally or in relation to an individual entity), it supersedes the application of the repealed Standard.]

APPENDIX A
DEFINED TERMS

This appendix is an integral part of the Standard.

exploration and evaluation assets	**Exploration and evaluation expenditures** recognised as assets in accordance with the entity's accounting policy.
exploration and evaluation expenditures	Expenditures incurred by an entity in connection with the **exploration for and evaluation of mineral resources** before the technical feasibility and commercial viability of extracting a mineral resource are demonstrable.
exploration for and evaluation of mineral resources	The search for mineral resources, including minerals, oil, natural gas and similar non-regenerative resources after the entity has obtained legal rights to explore in a specific area, as well as the determination of the technical feasibility and commercial viability of extracting the mineral resource.

APPENDIX B
AUSTRALIAN DEFINED TERMS

This appendix is an integral part of the Standard.

area of interest	An individual geological area which is considered to constitute a favourable environment for the presence of a mineral deposit or an oil or natural gas field, or has been proved to contain such a deposit or field.
economically recoverable reserves	The estimated quantity of product in an **area of interest** that can be expected to be profitably extracted, processed and sold under current and foreseeable economic conditions

AASB

AASB 7
Financial Instruments: Disclosures

(Compiled December 2017)

This compiled Standard applies to annual periods beginning on or after 1 January 2018 but before 1 January 2019. Earlier application is permitted for annual periods beginning after 24 July 2014 but before 1 January 2018. It incorporates relevant amendments made up to and including 12 December 2017.

Prepared on 20 May 2018 by the staff of the Australian Accounting Standards Board.

Compilation no. 1

Compilation date: 31 December 2017

This note is not part of Accounting Standard AASB 7.

The following unincorporated amendments are not included in this compiled Standard.

- AASB 16 *Leases* — Appendix D sets out the amendments to other Standards that are a consequence of the AASB issuing this Standard. It is applicable from 1 January 2019. Earlier application is permitted, but entities must apply AASB 15 *Revenue from Contracts with Customers* before applying this Standard.

- AASB 17 *Insurance Contracts* — Appendix D sets out the amendments to other Standards that are a consequence of the AASB issuing AASB 17 *Insurance Contracts*. This Standard is applicable from 1 January 2021. Earlier application is permitted, but entities must apply AASB 9 *Financial Instruments* and AASB 15 *Revenue from Contracts with Customers* first.

Entities early-adopting any amendments with later application dates will need to refer to the amending Standards that have not yet been incorporated into compilations. The abovementioned unincorporated amendments may be located on the AASB website at www.aasb.gov.au or on the Federal Register of Legislation website at www.legislation.gov.au.

CONTENTS

COMPARISON WITH IFRS 7
ACCOUNTING STANDARD
AASB 7 *FINANCIAL INSTRUMENTS: DISCLOSURES*

APPENDICES

A. DEFINED TERMS

B. APPLICATION GUIDANCE

D. AUSTRALIAN REDUCED DISCLOSURE REQUIREMENTS

COMPILATION DETAILS

DELETED IFRS 7 TEXT

IMPLEMENTATION GUIDANCE ON IFRS 7 (available on the AASB website)

BASIS FOR CONCLUSIONS ON IFRS 7 (available on the AASB website)

Australian Accounting Standard AASB 7 *Financial Instruments: Disclosures* (as amended) is set out in paragraphs 1 – Aus45.2 and Appendices A – B and D. All the paragraphs have equal authority. Paragraphs in **bold type** state the main principles. Terms defined in Appendix A are in *italics* the first time they appear in the Standard. AASB 7 is to be read in the context of other Australian Accounting Standards, including AASB 1048 *Interpretation of Standards*, which identifies the Australian Accounting Interpretations, and AASB 1057 *Application of Australian Accounting Standards*. In the absence of explicit guidance, AASB 108 *Accounting Policies, Changes in Accounting Estimates and Errors* provides a basis for selecting and applying accounting policies.

COMPARISON WITH IFRS 7

AASB 7 *Financial Instruments: Disclosures* (as amended) incorporates IFRS 7 *Financial Instruments: Disclosures* as issued and as amended by the International Accounting Standards Board (IASB). Australian-specific paragraphs (which are not included in IFRS 7) are identified with the prefix "Aus" or "RDR". Paragraphs that apply only to not-for-profit entities begin by identifying their limited applicability.

Tier 1

For-profit entities complying with AASB 7 also comply with IFRS 7.

Not-for-profit entities' compliance with IFRS 7 will depend on whether any "Aus" paragraphs that specifically apply to not-for-profit entities provide additional guidance or contain applicable requirements that are inconsistent with IFRS 7.

Tier 2

Entities preparing general purpose financial statements under Australian Accounting Standards – Reduced Disclosure Requirements (Tier 2) will not be in compliance with IFRSs.

AASB 1053 *Application of Tiers of Australian Accounting Standards* explains the two tiers of reporting requirements.

ACCOUNTING STANDARD AASB 7

The Australian Accounting Standards Board made Accounting Standard AASB 7 *Financial Instruments: Disclosures* under section 334 of the *Corporations Act 2001* on 7 August 2015.

This compiled version of AASB 7 applies to annual periods beginning on or after 1 January 2018 but before 1 January 2019. It incorporates relevant amendments contained in other AASB Standards made by the AASB up to and including 12 December 2017 (see Compilation Details).

ACCOUNTING STANDARD AASB 7
FINANCIAL INSTRUMENTS: DISCLOSURES

Objective

1   The objective of this Standard is to require entities to provide disclosures in their financial statements that enable users to evaluate:

(a)   the significance of financial instruments for the entity's financial position and performance; and

(b)   the nature and extent of risks arising from financial instruments to which the entity is exposed during the period and at the end of the reporting period, and how the entity manages those risks.

2   The principles in this Standard complement the principles for recognising, measuring and presenting financial assets and financial liabilities in AASB 132 *Financial Instruments: Presentation* and AASB 9 *Financial Instruments*.

Scope

3   This Standard shall be applied by all entities to all types of financial instruments, except:

    (a)   those interests in subsidiaries, associates or joint ventures that are accounted for in accordance with AASB 10 *Consolidated Financial Statements*, AASB 127 *Separate Financial Statements* or AASB 128 *Investments in Associates and Joint Ventures*. However, in some cases, AASB 10, AASB 127 or AASB 128 require or permit an entity to account for an interest in a subsidiary, associate or joint venture using AASB 9; in those cases, entities shall apply the requirements of this Standard and, for those measured at fair value, the requirements of AASB 13 *Fair Value Measurement*. Entities shall also apply this Standard to all derivatives linked to interests in subsidiaries, associates or joint ventures unless the derivative meets the definition of an equity instrument in AASB 132.

    (b)   employers' rights and obligations arising from employee benefit plans, to which AASB 119 *Employee Benefits* applies.

    (c)   [deleted]

    (d)   insurance contracts as defined in AASB 4 *Insurance Contracts*. However, this Standard applies to derivatives that are embedded in insurance contracts if AASB 9 requires the entity to account for them separately. Moreover, an issuer shall apply this Standard to *financial guarantee contracts* if the issuer applies AASB 9 in recognising and measuring the contracts, but shall apply AASB 4 if the issuer elects, in accordance with paragraph 4(d) of AASB 4, to apply AASB 4 in recognising and measuring them.

    (e)   financial instruments, contracts and obligations under share-based payment transactions to which AASB 2 *Share-based Payment* applies, except that this Standard applies to contracts within the scope of AASB 9.

    (f)   instruments that are required to be classified as equity instruments in accordance with paragraphs 16A and 16B or paragraphs 16C and 16D of AASB 132.

4   This Standard applies to recognised and unrecognised financial instruments. Recognised financial instruments include financial assets and financial liabilities that are within the scope of AASB 9. Unrecognised financial instruments include some financial instruments that, although outside the scope of AASB 9, are within the scope of this Standard.

5   This Standard applies to contracts to buy or sell a non-financial item that are within the scope of AASB 9.

5A   The credit risk disclosure requirements in paragraphs 35A–35N apply to those rights that AASB 15 *Revenue from Contracts with Customers* specifies are accounted for in accordance with AASB 9 for the purposes of recognising impairment gains or losses. Any reference to financial assets or financial instruments in these paragraphs shall include those rights unless otherwise specified.

Classes of financial instruments and level of disclosure

6   When this Standard requires disclosures by class of financial instrument, an entity shall group financial instruments into classes that are appropriate to the nature of the information disclosed and that take into account the characteristics of those financial instruments. An entity shall provide sufficient information to permit reconciliation to the line items presented in the statement of financial position.

Significance of financial instruments for financial position and performance

7   An entity shall disclose information that enables users of its financial statements
       to evaluate the significance of financial instruments for its financial position and
       performance.

Statement of financial position

Categories of financial assets and financial liabilities

8   The carrying amounts of each of the following categories, as specified in AASB 9,
       shall be disclosed either in the statement of financial position or in the notes:

       (a)   financial assets measured at fair value through profit or loss, showing
              separately (i) those designated as such upon initial recognition or subsequently
              in accordance with paragraph 6.7.1 of AASB 9 and (ii) those mandatorily
              measured at fair value through profit or loss in accordance with AASB 9.

       (b)–(d) [deleted]

       (e)   financial liabilities at fair value through profit or loss, showing separately
              (i) those designated as such upon initial recognition or subsequently in
              accordance with paragraph 6.7.1 of AASB 9 and (ii) those that meet the
              definition of held for trading in AASB 9.

       (f)   financial assets measured at amortised cost.

       (g)   financial liabilities measured at amortised cost.

       (h)   financial assets measured at fair value through other comprehensive income,
              showing separately (i) financial assets that are measured at fair value through
              other comprehensive income in accordance with paragraph 4.1.2A of AASB
              9; and (ii) investments in equity instruments designated as such upon initial
              recognition in accordance with paragraph 5.7.5 of AASB 9.

Financial assets or financial liabilities at fair value through profit or loss

9   If the entity has designated as measured at fair value through profit or loss a financial
       asset (or group of financial assets) that would otherwise be measured at fair value
       through other comprehensive income or amortised cost, it shall disclose:

       (a)   the maximum exposure to *credit risk* (see paragraph 36(a)) of the financial asset
              (or group of financial assets) at the end of the reporting period.

       (b)   the amount by which any related credit derivatives or similar instruments
              mitigate that maximum exposure to credit risk (see paragraph 36(b)).

       (c)   the amount of change, during the period and cumulatively, in the fair value
              of the financial asset (or group of financial assets) that is attributable to changes
              in the credit risk of the financial asset determined either:

              (i)   as the amount of change in its fair value that is not attributable to changes
                      in market conditions that give rise to *market risk*; or

              (ii)   using an alternative method the entity believes more faithfully represents
                      the amount of change in its fair value that is attributable to changes in the
                      credit risk of the asset.

              Changes in market conditions that give rise to market risk include changes in
              an observed (benchmark) interest rate, commodity price, foreign exchange rate
              or index of prices or rates.

      (d)   the amount of the change in the fair value of any related credit derivatives or similar instruments that has occurred during the period and cumulatively since the financial asset was designated.

10   If the entity has designated a financial liability as at fair value through profit or loss in accordance with paragraph 4.2.2 of AASB 9 and is required to present the effects of changes in that liability's credit risk in other comprehensive income (see paragraph 5.7.7 of AASB 9), it shall disclose:

    (a)   the amount of change, cumulatively, in the fair value of the financial liability that is attributable to changes in the credit risk of that liability (see paragraphs B5.7.13–B5.7.20 of AASB 9 for guidance on determining the effects of changes in a liability's credit risk).

    (b)   the difference between the financial liability's carrying amount and the amount the entity would be contractually required to pay at maturity to the holder of the obligation.

    (c)   any transfers of the cumulative gain or loss within equity during the period including the reason for such transfers.

    (d)   if a liability is derecognised during the period, the amount (if any) presented in other comprehensive income that was realised at derecognition.

10A   If an entity has designated a financial liability as at fair value through profit or loss in accordance with paragraph 4.2.2 of AASB 9 and is required to present all changes in the fair value of that liability (including the effects of changes in the credit risk of the liability) in profit or loss (see paragraphs 5.7.7 and 5.7.8 of AASB 9), it shall disclose:

    (a)   the amount of change, during the period and cumulatively, in the fair value of the financial liability that is attributable to changes in the credit risk of that liability (see paragraphs B5.7.13–B5.7.20 of AASB 9 for guidance on determining the effects of changes in a liability's credit risk); and

    (b)   the difference between the financial liability's carrying amount and the amount the entity would be contractually required to pay at maturity to the holder of the obligation.

11   The entity shall also disclose:

    (a)   a detailed description of the methods used to comply with the requirements in paragraphs 9(c), 10(a) and 10A(a) and paragraph 5.7.7(a) of AASB 9, including an explanation of why the method is appropriate.

    (b)   if the entity believes that the disclosure it has given, either in the statement of financial position or in the notes, to comply with the requirements in paragraph 9(c), 10(a) or 10A(a) or paragraph 5.7.7(a) of AASB 9 does not faithfully represent the change in the fair value of the financial asset or financial liability attributable to changes in its credit risk, the reasons for reaching this conclusion and the factors it believes are relevant.

    (c)   a detailed description of the methodology or methodologies used to determine whether presenting the effects of changes in a liability's credit risk in other comprehensive income would create or enlarge an accounting mismatch in profit or loss (see paragraphs 5.7.7 and 5.7.8 of AASB 9). If an entity is required to present the effects of changes in a liability's credit risk in profit or loss (see paragraph 5.7.8 of AASB 9), the disclosure must include a detailed description of the economic relationship described in paragraph B5.7.6 of AASB 9.

Investments in equity instruments designated at fair value through other comprehensive income

11A   If an entity has designated investments in equity instruments to be measured at fair value through other comprehensive income, as permitted by paragraph 5.7.5 of AASB 9, it shall disclose:

    (a)   which investments in equity instruments have been designated to be measured at fair value through other comprehensive income.

AASB

    (b)   the reasons for using this presentation alternative.

    (c)   the fair value of each such investment at the end of the reporting period.

    (d)   dividends recognised during the period, showing separately those related to investments derecognised during the reporting period and those related to investments held at the end of the reporting period.

    (e)   any transfers of the cumulative gain or loss within equity during the period including the reason for such transfers.

11B   If an entity derecognised investments in equity instruments measured at fair value through other comprehensive income during the reporting period, it shall disclose:

    (a)   the reasons for disposing of the investments.

    (b)   the fair value of the investments at the date of derecognition.

    (c)   the cumulative gain or loss on disposal.

Reclassification

12–12A [Deleted]

12B   An entity shall disclose if, in the current or previous reporting periods, it has reclassified any financial assets in accordance with paragraph 4.4.1 of AASB 9. For each such event, an entity shall disclose:

    (a)   the date of reclassification.

    (b)   a detailed explanation of the change in business model and a qualitative description of its effect on the entity's financial statements.

    (c)   the amount reclassified into and out of each category.

12C   For each reporting period following reclassification until derecognition, an entity shall disclose for assets reclassified out of the fair value through profit or loss category so that they are measured at amortised cost or fair value through other comprehensive income in accordance with paragraph 4.4.1 of AASB 9:

    (a)   the effective interest rate determined on the date of reclassification; and

    (b)   the interest revenue recognised.

12D   If, since its last annual reporting date, an entity has reclassified financial assets out of the fair value through other comprehensive income category so that they are measured at amortised cost or out of the fair value through profit or loss category so that they are measured at amortised cost or fair value through other comprehensive income it shall disclose:

    (a)   the fair value of the financial assets at the end of the reporting period; and

    (b)   the fair value gain or loss that would have been recognised in profit or loss or other comprehensive income during the reporting period if the financial assets had not been reclassified.

13   [Deleted]

Offsetting financial assets and financial liabilities

13A   The disclosures in paragraphs 13B–13E supplement the other disclosure requirements of this Standard and are required for all recognised financial instruments that are set off in accordance with paragraph 42 of AASB 132. These disclosures also apply to recognised financial instruments that are subject to an enforceable master netting arrangement or similar agreement, irrespective of whether they are set off in accordance with paragraph 42 of AASB 132.

13B   An entity shall disclose information to enable users of its financial statements to evaluate the effect or potential effect of netting arrangements on the entity's financial position. This includes the effect or potential effect of rights of set-off associated with the entity's recognised financial assets and recognised financial liabilities that are within the scope of paragraph 13A.

13C   To meet the objective in paragraph 13B, an entity shall disclose, at the end of the reporting period, the following quantitative information separately for recognised financial assets and recognised financial liabilities that are within the scope of paragraph 13A:

(a)   the gross amounts of those recognised financial assets and recognised financial liabilities;

(b)   the amounts that are set off in accordance with the criteria in paragraph 42 of AASB 132 when determining the net amounts presented in the statement of financial position;

(c)   the net amounts presented in the statement of financial position;

(d)   the amounts subject to an enforceable master netting arrangement or similar agreement that are not otherwise included in paragraph 13C(b), including:

(i)   amounts related to recognised financial instruments that do not meet some or all of the offsetting criteria in paragraph 42 of AASB 132; and

(ii)   amounts related to financial collateral (including cash collateral); and

(e)   the net amount after deducting the amounts in (d) from the amounts in (c) above.

The information required by this paragraph shall be presented in a tabular format, separately for financial assets and financial liabilities, unless another format is more appropriate.

13D   The total amount disclosed in accordance with paragraph 13C(d) for an instrument shall be limited to the amount in paragraph 13C(c) for that instrument.

13E   An entity shall include a description in the disclosures of the rights of set-off associated with the entity's recognised financial assets and recognised financial liabilities subject to enforceable master netting arrangements and similar agreements that are disclosed in accordance with paragraph 13C(d), including the nature of those rights.

13F   If the information required by paragraphs 13B–13E is disclosed in more than one note to the financial statements, an entity shall cross-refer between those notes.

Collateral

14   An entity shall disclose:

(a)   the carrying amount of financial assets it has pledged as collateral for liabilities or contingent liabilities, including amounts that have been reclassified in accordance with paragraph 3.2.23(a) of AASB 9; and

(b)   the terms and conditions relating to its pledge.

15   When an entity holds collateral (of financial or non-financial assets) and is permitted to sell or repledge the collateral in the absence of default by the owner of the collateral, it shall disclose:

(a)   the fair value of the collateral held;

(b)   the fair value of any such collateral sold or repledged, and whether the entity has an obligation to return it; and

(c)   the terms and conditions associated with its use of the collateral.

Allowance account for credit losses

16   [Deleted]

16A   The carrying amount of financial assets measured at fair value through other comprehensive income in accordance with paragraph 4.1.2A of AASB 9 is not reduced by a loss allowance and an entity shall not present the loss allowance separately in the statement of financial position as a reduction of the carrying amount of the financial asset. However, an entity shall disclose the loss allowance in the notes to the financial statements.

Compound financial instruments with multiple embedded derivatives

17   If an entity has issued an instrument that contains both a liability and an equity component (see paragraph 28 of AASB 132) and the instrument has multiple embedded derivatives whose values are interdependent (such as a callable convertible debt instrument), it shall disclose the existence of those features.

Defaults and breaches

18   For *loans payable* recognised at the end of the reporting period, an entity shall disclose:

(a)   details of any defaults during the period of principal, interest, sinking fund, or redemption terms of those loans payable;

(b)   the carrying amount of the loans payable in default at the end of the reporting period; and

(c)   whether the default was remedied, or the terms of the loans payable were renegotiated, before the financial statements were authorised for issue.

19   If, during the period, there were breaches of loan agreement terms other than those described in paragraph 18, an entity shall disclose the same information as required by paragraph 18 if those breaches permitted the lender to demand accelerated repayment (unless the breaches were remedied, or the terms of the loan were renegotiated, on or before the end of the reporting period).

Statement of comprehensive income

Items of income, expense, gains or losses

20   An entity shall disclose the following items of income, expense, gains or losses either in the statement of comprehensive income or in the notes:

(a)   net gains or net losses on:

(i)   financial assets or financial liabilities measured at fair value through profit or loss, showing separately those on financial assets or financial liabilities designated as such upon initial recognition or subsequently in accordance with paragraph 6.7.1 of AASB 9, and those on financial assets or financial liabilities that are mandatorily measured at fair value through profit or loss in accordance with AASB 9 (eg financial liabilities that meet the definition of held for trading in AASB 9). For financial liabilities designated as at fair value through profit or loss, an entity shall show separately the amount of gain or loss recognised in other comprehensive income and the amount recognised in profit or loss.

(ii)–(iv)   [deleted]

(v)   financial liabilities measured at amortised cost.

(vi)   financial assets measured at amortised cost.

(vii)   investments in equity instruments designated at fair value through other comprehensive income in accordance with paragraph 5.7.5 of AASB 9.

(viii)   financial assets measured at fair value through other comprehensive income in accordance with paragraph 4.1.2A of AASB 9, showing separately the amount of gain or loss recognised in other comprehensive income during the period and the amount reclassified upon derecognition from accumulated other comprehensive income to profit or loss for the period.

(b)   total interest revenue and total interest expense (calculated using the effective interest method) for financial assets that are measured at amortised cost or that are measured at fair value through other comprehensive income in accordance with paragraph 4.1.2A of AASB 9 (showing these amounts separately); or financial liabilities that are not measured at fair value through profit or loss.

(c) fee income and expense (other than amounts included in determining the effective interest rate) arising from:

    (i) financial assets and financial liabilities that are not at fair value through profit or loss; and

    (ii) trust and other fiduciary activities that result in the holding or investing of assets on behalf of individuals, trusts, retirement benefit plans, and other institutions.

(d) [deleted]

(e) [deleted]

20A An entity shall disclose an analysis of the gain or loss recognised in the statement of comprehensive income arising from the derecognition of financial assets measured at amortised cost, showing separately gains and losses arising from derecognition of those financial assets. This disclosure shall include the reasons for derecognising those financial assets.

Other disclosures

Accounting policies

21 In accordance with paragraph 117 of AASB 101 *Presentation of Financial Statements*, an entity discloses its significant accounting policies comprising the measurement basis (or bases) used in preparing the financial statements and the other accounting policies used that are relevant to an understanding of the financial statements.

Hedge accounting

21A An entity shall apply the disclosure requirements in paragraphs 21B–24F for those risk exposures that an entity hedges and for which it elects to apply hedge accounting. Hedge accounting disclosures shall provide information about:

(a) an entity's risk management strategy and how it is applied to manage risk;

(b) how the entity's hedging activities may affect the amount, timing and uncertainty of its future cash flows; and

(c) the effect that hedge accounting has had on the entity's statement of financial position, statement of comprehensive income and statement of changes in equity.

21B An entity shall present the required disclosures in a single note or separate section in its financial statements. However, an entity need not duplicate information that is already presented elsewhere, provided that the information is incorporated by cross-reference from the financial statements to some other statement, such as a management commentary or risk report, that is available to users of the financial statements on the same terms as the financial statements and at the same time. Without the information incorporated by cross-reference, the financial statements are incomplete.

21C When paragraphs 22A–24F require the entity to separate by risk category the information disclosed, the entity shall determine each risk category on the basis of the risk exposures an entity decides to hedge and for which hedge accounting is applied. An entity shall determine risk categories consistently for all hedge accounting disclosures.

21D To meet the objectives in paragraph 21A, an entity shall (except as otherwise specified below) determine how much detail to disclose, how much emphasis to place on different aspects of the disclosure requirements, the appropriate level of aggregation or disaggregation, and whether users of financial statements need additional explanations to evaluate the quantitative information disclosed. However, an entity shall use the same level of aggregation or disaggregation it uses for disclosure requirements of related information in this Standard and AASB 13 *Fair Value Measurement*.

The risk management strategy

22   [Deleted]

22A   An entity shall explain its risk management strategy for each risk category of risk exposures that it decides to hedge and for which hedge accounting is applied. This explanation should enable users of financial statements to evaluate (for example):

   (a)   how each risk arises.

   (b)   how the entity manages each risk; this includes whether the entity hedges an item in its entirety for all risks or hedges a risk component (or components) of an item and why.

   (c)   the extent of risk exposures that the entity manages.

22B   To meet the requirements in paragraph 22A, the information should include (but is not limited to) a description of:

   (a)   the hedging instruments that are used (and how they are used) to hedge risk exposures;

   (b)   how the entity determines the economic relationship between the hedged item and the hedging instrument for the purpose of assessing hedge effectiveness; and

   (c)   how the entity establishes the hedge ratio and what the sources of hedge ineffectiveness are.

22C   When an entity designates a specific risk component as a hedged item (see paragraph 6.3.7 of AASB 9) it shall provide, in addition to the disclosures required by paragraphs 22A and 22B, qualitative or quantitative information about:

   (a)   how the entity determined the risk component that is designated as the hedged item (including a description of the nature of the relationship between the risk component and the item as a whole); and

   (b)   how the risk component relates to the item in its entirety (for example, the designated risk component historically covered on average 80 per cent of the changes in fair value of the item as a whole).

The amount, timing and uncertainty of future cash flows

23   [Deleted]

23A   Unless exempted by paragraph 23C, an entity shall disclose by risk category quantitative information to allow users of its financial statements to evaluate the terms and conditions of hedging instruments and how they affect the amount, timing and uncertainty of future cash flows of the entity.

23B   To meet the requirement in paragraph 23A, an entity shall provide a breakdown that discloses:

   (a)   a profile of the timing of the nominal amount of the hedging instrument; and

   (b)   if applicable, the average price or rate (for example strike or forward prices etc) of the hedging instrument.

23C   In situations in which an entity frequently resets (ie discontinues and restarts) hedging relationships because both the hedging instrument and the hedged item frequently change (ie the entity uses a dynamic process in which both the exposure and the hedging instruments used to manage that exposure do not remain the same for long—such as in the example in paragraph B6.5.24(b) of AASB 9) the entity:

   (a)   is exempt from providing the disclosures required by paragraphs 23A and 23B.

   (b)   shall disclose:

      (i)   information about what the ultimate risk management strategy is in relation to those hedging relationships;

    (ii)   a description of how it reflects its risk management strategy by using hedge accounting and designating those particular hedging relationships; and

    (iii)   an indication of how frequently the hedging relationships are discontinued and restarted as part of the entity's process in relation to those hedging relationships.

23D   An entity shall disclose by risk category a description of the sources of hedge ineffectiveness that are expected to affect the hedging relationship during its term.

23E   If other sources of hedge ineffectiveness emerge in a hedging relationship, an entity shall disclose those sources by risk category and explain the resulting hedge ineffectiveness.

23F   For cash flow hedges, an entity shall disclose a description of any forecast transaction for which hedge accounting had been used in the previous period, but which is no longer expected to occur.

The effects of hedge accounting on financial position and performance

24   [Deleted]

24A   An entity shall disclose, in a tabular format, the following amounts related to items designated as hedging instruments separately by risk category for each type of hedge (fair value hedge, cash flow hedge or hedge of a net investment in a foreign operation):

    (a)   the carrying amount of the hedging instruments (financial assets separately from financial liabilities);

    (b)   the line item in the statement of financial position that includes the hedging instrument;

    (c)   the change in fair value of the hedging instrument used as the basis for recognising hedge ineffectiveness for the period; and

    (d)   the nominal amounts (including quantities such as tonnes or cubic metres) of the hedging instruments.

24B   An entity shall disclose, in a tabular format, the following amounts related to hedged items separately by risk category for the types of hedges as follows:

    (a)   for fair value hedges:

        (i)   the carrying amount of the hedged item recognised in the statement of financial position (presenting assets separately from liabilities);

        (ii)   the accumulated amount of fair value hedge adjustments on the hedged item included in the carrying amount of the hedged item recognised in the statement of financial position (presenting assets separately from liabilities);

        (iii)   the line item in the statement of financial position that includes the hedged item;

        (iv)   the change in value of the hedged item used as the basis for recognising hedge ineffectiveness for the period; and

        (v)   the accumulated amount of fair value hedge adjustments remaining in the statement of financial position for any hedged items that have ceased to be adjusted for hedging gains and losses in accordance with paragraph 6.5.10 of AASB 9.

    (b)   for cash flow hedges and hedges of a net investment in a foreign operation:

        (i)   the change in value of the hedged item used as the basis for recognising hedge ineffectiveness for the period (ie for cash flow hedges the change in value used to determine the recognised hedge ineffectiveness in accordance with paragraph 6.5.11(c) of AASB 9);

    (ii)   the balances in the cash flow hedge reserve and the foreign currency translation reserve for continuing hedges that are accounted for in accordance with paragraphs 6.5.11 and 6.5.13(a) of AASB 9; and

    (iii)   the balances remaining in the cash flow hedge reserve and the foreign currency translation reserve from any hedging relationships for which hedge accounting is no longer applied.

24C   An entity shall disclose, in a tabular format, the following amounts separately by risk category for the types of hedges as follows:

    (a)   for fair value hedges:

        (i)   hedge ineffectiveness—ie the difference between the hedging gains or losses of the hedging instrument and the hedged item—recognised in profit or loss (or other comprehensive income for hedges of an equity instrument for which an entity has elected to present changes in fair value in other comprehensive income in accordance with paragraph 5.7.5 of AASB 9); and

        (ii)   the line item in the statement of comprehensive income that includes the recognised hedge ineffectiveness.

    (b)   for cash flow hedges and hedges of a net investment in a foreign operation:

        (i)   hedging gains or losses of the reporting period that were recognised in other comprehensive income;

        (ii)   hedge ineffectiveness recognised in profit or loss;

        (iii)   the line item in the statement of comprehensive income that includes the recognised hedge ineffectiveness;

        (iv)   the amount reclassified from the cash flow hedge reserve or the foreign currency translation reserve into profit or loss as a reclassification adjustment (see AASB 101) (differentiating between amounts for which hedge accounting had previously been used, but for which the hedged future cash flows are no longer expected to occur, and amounts that have been transferred because the hedged item has affected profit or loss);

        (v)   the line item in the statement of comprehensive income that includes the reclassification adjustment (see AASB 101); and

        (vi)   for hedges of net positions, the hedging gains or losses recognised in a separate line item in the statement of comprehensive income (see paragraph 6.6.4 of AASB 9).

24D   When the volume of hedging relationships to which the exemption in paragraph 23C applies is unrepresentative of normal volumes during the period (ie the volume at the reporting date does not reflect the volumes during the period) an entity shall disclose that fact and the reason it believes the volumes are unrepresentative.

24E   An entity shall provide a reconciliation of each component of equity and an analysis of other comprehensive income in accordance with AASB 101 that, taken together:

    (a)   differentiates, at a minimum, between the amounts that relate to the disclosures in paragraph 24C(b)(i) and (b)(iv) as well as the amounts accounted for in accordance with paragraph 6.5.11(d)(i) and (d)(iii) of AASB 9;

    (b)   differentiates between the amounts associated with the time value of options that hedge transaction related hedged items and the amounts associated with the time value of options that hedge time-period related hedged items when an entity accounts for the time value of an option in accordance with paragraph 6.5.15 of AASB 9; and

    (c)   differentiates between the amounts associated with forward elements of forward contracts and the foreign currency basis spreads of financial instruments that hedge transaction related hedged items, and the amounts associated with forward elements of forward contracts and the foreign currency basis spreads of financial instruments that hedge time-period related hedged items when an entity accounts for those amounts in accordance with paragraph 6.5.16 of AASB 9.

24F An entity shall disclose the information required in paragraph 24E separately by risk category. This disaggregation by risk may be provided in the notes to the financial statements.

Option to designate a credit exposure as measured at fair value through profit or loss

24G If an entity designated a financial instrument, or a proportion of it, as measured at fair value through profit or loss because it uses a credit derivative to manage the credit risk of that financial instrument it shall disclose:

(a) for credit derivatives that have been used to manage the credit risk of financial instruments designated as measured at fair value through profit or loss in accordance with paragraph 6.7.1 of AASB 9, a reconciliation of each of the nominal amount and the fair value at the beginning and at the end of the period;

(b) the gain or loss recognised in profit or loss on designation of a financial instrument, or a proportion of it, as measured at fair value through profit or loss in accordance with paragraph 6.7.1 of AASB 9; and

(c) on discontinuation of measuring a financial instrument, or a proportion of it, at fair value through profit or loss, that financial instrument's fair value that has become the new carrying amount in accordance with paragraph 6.7.4 of AASB 9 and the related nominal or principal amount (except for providing comparative information in accordance with AASB 101, an entity does not need to continue this disclosure in subsequent periods).

Fair value

25 Except as set out in paragraph 29, for each class of financial assets and financial liabilities (see paragraph 6), an entity shall disclose the fair value of that class of assets and liabilities in a way that permits it to be compared with its carrying amount.

26 In disclosing fair values, an entity shall group financial assets and financial liabilities into classes, but shall offset them only to the extent that their carrying amounts are offset in the statement of financial position.

27–27B [Deleted]

28 In some cases, an entity does not recognise a gain or loss on initial recognition of a financial asset or financial liability because the fair value is neither evidenced by a quoted price in an active market for an identical asset or liability (ie a Level 1 input) nor based on a valuation technique that uses only data from observable markets (see paragraph B5.1.2A of AASB 9). In such cases, the entity shall disclose by class of financial asset or financial liability:

(a) its accounting policy for recognising in profit or loss the difference between the fair value at initial recognition and the transaction price to reflect a change in factors (including time) that market participants would take into account when pricing the asset or liability (see paragraph B5.1.2A(b) of AASB 9).

(b) the aggregate difference yet to be recognised in profit or loss at the beginning and end of the period and a reconciliation of changes in the balance of this difference.

(c) why the entity concluded that the transaction price was not the best evidence of fair value, including a description of the evidence that supports the fair value.

29 Disclosures of fair value are not required:

(a) when the carrying amount is a reasonable approximation of fair value, for example, for financial instruments such as short-term trade receivables and payables;

(b)   [deleted]

(c)   for a contract containing a discretionary participation feature (as described in AASB 4) if the fair value of that feature cannot be measured reliably.

30   In the case described in paragraph 29(c), an entity shall disclose information to help users of the financial statements make their own judgements about the extent of possible differences between the carrying amount of those contracts and their fair value, including:

(a)   the fact that fair value information has not been disclosed for these instruments because their fair value cannot be measured reliably;

(b)   a description of the financial instruments, their carrying amount, and an explanation of why fair value cannot be measured reliably;

(c)   information about the market for the instruments;

(d)   information about whether and how the entity intends to dispose of the financial instruments; and

(e)   if financial instruments whose fair value previously could not be reliably measured are derecognised, that fact, their carrying amount at the time of derecognition, and the amount of gain or loss recognised.

Nature and extent of risks arising from financial instruments

31   **An entity shall disclose information that enables users of its financial statements to evaluate the nature and extent of risks arising from financial instruments to which the entity is exposed at the end of the reporting period.**

32   The disclosures required by paragraphs 33–42 focus on the risks that arise from financial instruments and how they have been managed. These risks typically include, but are not limited to, credit risk, *liquidity risk* and market risk.

32A   Providing qualitative disclosures in the context of quantitative disclosures enables users to link related disclosures and hence form an overall picture of the nature and extent of risks arising from financial instruments. The interaction between qualitative and quantitative disclosures contributes to disclosure of information in a way that better enables users to evaluate an entity's exposure to risks.

Qualitative disclosures

33   For each type of risk arising from financial instruments, an entity shall disclose:

(a)   the exposures to risk and how they arise;

(b)   its objectives, policies and processes for managing the risk and the methods used to measure the risk; and

(c)   any changes in (a) or (b) from the previous period.

Quantitative disclosures

34   For each type of risk arising from financial instruments, an entity shall disclose:

(a)   summary quantitative data about its exposure to that risk at the end of the reporting period. This disclosure shall be based on the information provided internally to key management personnel of the entity (as defined in AASB 124 *Related Party Disclosures*), for example the entity's board of directors or chief executive officer.

(b)   the disclosures required by paragraphs 35A–42, to the extent not provided in accordance with (a).

(c)   concentrations of risk if not apparent from the disclosures made in accordance with (a) and (b).

35   If the quantitative data disclosed as at the end of the reporting period are unrepresentative of an entity's exposure to risk during the period, an entity shall provide further information that is representative.

Credit risk
Scope and objectives

35A   An entity shall apply the disclosure requirements in paragraphs 35F–35N to financial instruments to which the impairment requirements in AASB 9 are applied. However:

(a)   for trade receivables, contract assets and lease receivables, paragraph 35J(a) applies to those trade receivables, contract assets or lease receivables on which lifetime expected credit losses are recognised in accordance with paragraph 5.5.15 of AASB 9, if those financial assets are modified while more than 30 days past due; and

(b)   paragraph 35K(b) does not apply to lease receivables.

35B   The credit risk disclosures made in accordance with paragraphs 35F–35N shall enable users of financial statements to understand the effect of credit risk on the amount, timing and uncertainty of future cash flows. To achieve this objective, credit risk disclosures shall provide:

(a)   information about an entity's credit risk management practices and how they relate to the recognition and measurement of expected credit losses, including the methods, assumptions and information used to measure expected credit losses;

(b)   quantitative and qualitative information that allows users of financial statements to evaluate the amounts in the financial statements arising from expected credit losses, including changes in the amount of expected credit losses and the reasons for those changes; and

(c)   information about an entity's credit risk exposure (ie the credit risk inherent in an entity's financial assets and commitments to extend credit) including significant credit risk concentrations.

35C   An entity need not duplicate information that is already presented elsewhere, provided that the information is incorporated by cross-reference from the financial statements to other statements, such as a management commentary or risk report that is available to users of the financial statements on the same terms as the financial statements and at the same time. Without the information incorporated by cross-reference, the financial statements are incomplete.

35D   To meet the objectives in paragraph 35B, an entity shall (except as otherwise specified) consider how much detail to disclose, how much emphasis to place on different aspects of the disclosure requirements, the appropriate level of aggregation or disaggregation, and whether users of financial statements need additional explanations to evaluate the quantitative information disclosed.

35E   If the disclosures provided in accordance with paragraphs 35F–35N are insufficient to meet the objectives in paragraph 35B, an entity shall disclose additional information that is necessary to meet those objectives.

The credit risk management practices

35F   An entity shall explain its credit risk management practices and how they relate to the recognition and measurement of expected credit losses. To meet this objective an entity shall disclose information that enables users of financial statements to understand and evaluate:

(a)   how an entity determined whether the credit risk of financial instruments has increased significantly since initial recognition, including, if and how:

(i)   financial instruments are considered to have low credit risk in accordance with paragraph 5.5.10 of AASB 9, including the classes of financial instruments to which it applies; and

        (ii)   the presumption in paragraph 5.5.11 of AASB 9, that there have been significant increases in credit risk since initial recognition when financial assets are more than 30 days past due, has been rebutted;

(b)   an entity's definitions of default, including the reasons for selecting those definitions;

(c)   how the instruments were grouped if expected credit losses were measured on a collective basis;

(d)   how an entity determined that financial assets are credit-impaired financial assets;

(e)   an entity's write-off policy, including the indicators that there is no reasonable expectation of recovery and information about the policy for financial assets that are written-off but are still subject to enforcement activity; and

(f)   how the requirements in paragraph 5.5.12 of AASB 9 for the modification of contractual cash flows of financial assets have been applied, including how an entity:

        (i)   determines whether the credit risk on a financial asset that has been modified while the loss allowance was measured at an amount equal to lifetime expected credit losses, has improved to the extent that the loss allowance reverts to being measured at an amount equal to 12-month expected credit losses in accordance with paragraph 5.5.5 of AASB 9; and

        (ii)   monitors the extent to which the loss allowance on financial assets meeting the criteria in (i) is subsequently remeasured at an amount equal to lifetime expected credit losses in accordance with paragraph 5.5.3 of AASB 9.

35G   An entity shall explain the inputs, assumptions and estimation techniques used to apply the requirements in Section 5.5 of AASB 9. For this purpose an entity shall disclose:

(a)   the basis of inputs and assumptions and the estimation techniques used to:

        (i)   measure the 12-month and lifetime expected credit losses;

        (ii)   determine whether the credit risk of financial instruments has increased significantly since initial recognition; and

        (iii)   determine whether a financial asset is a credit-impaired financial asset.

(b)   how forward-looking information has been incorporated into the determination of expected credit losses, including the use of macroeconomic information; and

(c)   changes in the estimation techniques or significant assumptions made during the reporting period and the reasons for those changes.

Quantitative and qualitative information about amounts arising from expected credit losses

35H   To explain the changes in the loss allowance and the reasons for those changes, an entity shall provide, by class of financial instrument, a reconciliation from the opening balance to the closing balance of the loss allowance, in a table, showing separately the changes during the period for:

(a)   the loss allowance measured at an amount equal to 12-month expected credit losses;

(b)   the loss allowance measured at an amount equal to lifetime expected credit losses for:

        (i)   financial instruments for which credit risk has increased significantly since initial recognition but that are not credit-impaired financial assets;

        (ii)   financial assets that are credit-impaired at the reporting date (but that are not purchased or originated credit-impaired); and

         (iii)   trade receivables, contract assets or lease receivables for which the loss allowances are measured in accordance with paragraph 5.5.15 of AASB 9

    (c)   financial assets that are purchased or originated credit-impaired. In addition to the reconciliation, an entity shall disclose the total amount of undiscounted expected credit losses at initial recognition on financial assets initially recognised during the reporting period.

35I   To enable users of financial statements to understand the changes in the loss allowance disclosed in accordance with paragraph 35H, an entity shall provide an explanation of how significant changes in the gross carrying amount of financial instruments during the period contributed to changes in the loss allowance. The information shall be provided separately for financial instruments that represent the loss allowance as listed in paragraph 35H(a)–(c) and shall include relevant qualitative and quantitative information. Examples of changes in the gross carrying amount of financial instruments that contributed to the changes in the loss allowance may include:

    (a)   changes because of financial instruments originated or acquired during the reporting period;

    (b)   the modification of contractual cash flows on financial assets that do not result in a derecognition of those financial assets in accordance with AASB 9;

    (c)   changes because of financial instruments that were derecognised (including those that were written-off) during the reporting period; and

    (d)   changes arising from whether the loss allowance is measured at an amount equal to 12-month or lifetime expected credit losses.

35J   To enable users of financial statements to understand the nature and effect of modifications of contractual cash flows on financial assets that have not resulted in derecognition and the effect of such modifications on the measurement of expected credit losses, an entity shall disclose:

    (a)   the amortised cost before the modification and the net modification gain or loss recognised for financial assets for which the contractual cash flows have been modified during the reporting period while they had a loss allowance measured at an amount equal to lifetime expected credit losses; and

    (b)   the gross carrying amount at the end of the reporting period of financial assets that have been modified since initial recognition at a time when the loss allowance was measured at an amount equal to lifetime expected credit losses and for which the loss allowance has changed during the reporting period to an amount equal to 12-month expected credit losses.

35K   To enable users of financial statements to understand the effect of collateral and other credit enhancements on the amounts arising from expected credit losses, an entity shall disclose by class of financial instrument:

    (a)   the amount that best represents its maximum exposure to credit risk at the end of the reporting period without taking account of any collateral held or other credit enhancements (eg netting agreements that do not qualify for offset in accordance with AASB 132).

    (b)   a narrative description of collateral held as security and other credit enhancements, including:

         (i)   a description of the nature and quality of the collateral held;

         (ii)   an explanation of any significant changes in the quality of that collateral or credit enhancements as a result of deterioration or changes in the collateral policies of the entity during the reporting period; and

         (iii)   information about financial instruments for which an entity has not recognised a loss allowance because of the collateral.

    (c)   quantitative information about the collateral held as security and other credit enhancements (for example, quantification of the extent to which collateral and other credit enhancements mitigate credit risk) for financial assets that are credit-impaired at the reporting date.

35L An entity shall disclose the contractual amount outstanding on financial assets that were written off during the reporting period and are still subject to enforcement activity.

Credit risk exposure

35M To enable users of financial statements to assess an entity's credit risk exposure and understand its significant credit risk concentrations, an entity shall disclose, by *credit risk rating grades*, the gross carrying amount of financial assets and the exposure to credit risk on loan commitments and financial guarantee contracts. This information shall be provided separately for financial instruments:

    (a) for which the loss allowance is measured at an amount equal to 12-month expected credit losses;

    (b) for which the loss allowance is measured at an amount equal to lifetime expected credit losses and that are:

        (i) financial instruments for which credit risk has increased significantly

        (ii) financial assets that are credit-impaired at the reporting date (but that are not purchased or originated credit-impaired); and

        (iii) trade receivables, contract assets or lease receivables for which the loss allowances are measured in accordance with paragraph 5.5.15 of AASB 9.

    (c) that are purchased or originated credit-impaired financial assets.

35N For trade receivables, contract assets and lease receivables to which an entity applies paragraph 5.5.15 of AASB 9, the information provided in accordance with paragraph 35M may be based on a provision matrix (see paragraph B5.5.35 of AASB 9).

36 For all financial instruments within the scope of this Standard, but to which the impairment requirements in AASB 9 are not applied, an entity shall disclose by class of financial instrument:

    (a) the amount that best represents its maximum exposure to credit risk at the end of the reporting period without taking account of any collateral held or other credit enhancements (eg netting agreements that do not quality for offset in accordance with AASB 132); this disclosure is not required for financial instruments whose carrying amount best represents the maximum exposure to credit risk.

    (b) a description of collateral held as security and other credit enhancements, and their financial effect (eg quantification of the extent to which collateral and other credit enhancements mitigate credit risk) in respect of the amount that best represents the maximum exposure to credit risk (whether disclosed in accordance with (a) or represented by the carrying amount of a financial instrument).

    (c) [deleted]

    (d) [deleted]

37 [Deleted]

Collateral and other credit enhancements obtained

38 When an entity obtains financial or non-financial assets during the period by taking possession of collateral it holds as security or calling on other credit enhancements (eg guarantees), and such assets meet the recognition criteria in other Australian Accounting Standards, an entity shall disclose for such assets held at the reporting date:

    (a) the nature and carrying amount of the assets; and

    (b) when the assets are not readily convertible into cash, its policies for disposing of such assets or for using them in its operations.

Liquidity risk

39 An entity shall disclose:

(a) a maturity analysis for non-derivative financial liabilities (including issued financial guarantee contracts) that shows the remaining contractual maturities.

(b) a maturity analysis for derivative financial liabilities. The maturity analysis shall include the remaining contractual maturities for those derivative financial liabilities for which contractual maturities are essential for an understanding of the timing of the cash flows (see paragraph B11B).

(c) a description of how it manages the liquidity risk inherent in (a) and (b).

Market risk
Sensitivity analysis

40 Unless an entity complies with paragraph 41, it shall disclose:

(a) a sensitivity analysis for each type of market risk to which the entity is exposed at the end of the reporting period, showing how profit or loss and equity would have been affected by changes in the relevant risk variable that were reasonably possible at that date;

(b) the methods and assumptions used in preparing the sensitivity analysis; and

(c) changes from the previous period in the methods and assumptions used, and the reasons for such changes.

41 If an entity prepares a sensitivity analysis, such as value-at-risk, that reflects interdependencies between risk variables (eg interest rates and exchange rates) and uses it to manage financial risks, it may use that sensitivity analysis in place of the analysis specified in paragraph 40. The entity shall also disclose:

(a) an explanation of the method used in preparing such a sensitivity analysis, and of the main parameters and assumptions underlying the data provided; and

(b) an explanation of the objective of the method used and of limitations that may result in the information not fully reflecting the fair value of the assets and liabilities involved.

Other market risk disclosures

42 When the sensitivity analyses disclosed in accordance with paragraph 40 or 41 are unrepresentative of a risk inherent in a financial instrument (for example because the year-end exposure does not reflect the exposure during the year), the entity shall disclose that fact and the reason it believes the sensitivity analyses are unrepresentative.

Transfers of financial assets

42A The disclosure requirements in paragraphs 42B–42H relating to transfers of financial assets supplement the other disclosure requirements of this Standard. An entity shall present the disclosures required by paragraphs 42B–42H in a single note in its financial statements. An entity shall provide the required disclosures for all transferred financial assets that are not derecognised and for any continuing involvement in a transferred asset, existing at the reporting date, irrespective of when the related transfer transaction occurred. For the purposes of applying the disclosure requirements in those paragraphs, an entity transfers all or a part of a financial asset (the transferred financial asset) if, and only if, it either:

(a) transfers the contractual rights to receive the cash flows of that financial asset; or

(b) retains the contractual rights to receive the cash flows of that financial asset, but assumes a contractual obligation to pay the cash flows to one or more recipients in an arrangement.

42B An entity shall disclose information that enables users of its financial statements:

(a) to understand the relationship between transferred financial assets that are not derecognised in their entirety and the associated liabilities; and

(c)   the amount of any financial assets and financial liabilities in the statement of financial position that were previously designated as measured at fair value through profit or loss but are no longer so designated, distinguishing between those that AASB 9 requires an entity to reclassify and those that an entity elects to reclassify at the date of initial application.

In accordance with paragraph 7.2.2 of AASB 9, depending on the entity's chosen approach to applying AASB 9, the transition can involve more than one date of initial application. Therefore this paragraph may result in disclosure on more than one date of initial application. An entity shall present these quantitative disclosures in a table unless another format is more appropriate.

42J   In the reporting period that includes the date of initial application of AASB 9, an entity shall disclose qualitative information to enable users to understand:

(a)   how it applied the classification requirements in AASB 9 to those financial assets whose classification has changed as a result of applying AASB 9.

(b)   the reasons for any designation or de-designation of financial assets or financial liabilities as measured at fair value through profit or loss at the date of initial application.

In accordance with paragraph 7.2.2 of AASB 9, depending on the entity's chosen approach to applying AASB 9, the transition can involve more than one date of initial application. Therefore this paragraph may result in disclosure on more than one date of initial application.

42K   In the reporting period that an entity first applies the classification and measurement requirements for financial assets in AASB 9 (ie when the entity transitions from AASB 139 to AASB 9 for financial assets), it shall present the disclosures set out in paragraphs 42L–42O of this Standard as required by paragraph 7.2.15 of AASB 9.

42L   When required by paragraph 42K, an entity shall disclose the changes in the classifications of financial assets and financial liabilities as at the date of initial application of AASB 9, showing separately:

(a)   the changes in the carrying amounts on the basis of their measurement categories in accordance with AASB 139 (ie not resulting from a change in measurement attribute on transition to AASB 9); and

(b)   the changes in the carrying amounts arising from a change in measurement attribute on transition to AASB 9.

The disclosures in this paragraph need not be made after the annual reporting period in which the entity initially applies the classification and measurement requirements for financial assets in AASB 9.

42M   When required by paragraph 42K, an entity shall disclose the following for financial assets and financial liabilities that have been reclassified so that they are measured at amortised cost and, in the case of financial assets, that have been reclassified out of fair value through profit or loss so that they are measured at fair value through other comprehensive income, as a result of the transition to AASB 9:

(a)   the fair value of the financial assets or financial liabilities at the end of the reporting period; and

(b)   the fair value gain or loss that would have been recognised in profit or loss or other comprehensive income during the reporting period if the financial assets or financial liabilities had not been reclassified.

The disclosures in this paragraph need not be made after the annual reporting period in which the entity initially applies the classification and measurement requirements for financial assets in AASB 9.

42N   When required by paragraph 42K, an entity shall disclose the following for financial assets and financial liabilities that have been reclassified out of the fair value through profit or loss category as a result of the transition to AASB 9:

(a)   the effective interest rate determined on the date of initial application; and

(b)   the interest revenue or expense recognised.

If an entity treats the fair value of a financial asset or a financial liability as the new gross carrying amount at the date of initial application (see paragraph 7.2.11 of AASB 9), the disclosures in this paragraph shall be made for each reporting period until derecognition. Otherwise, the disclosures in this paragraph need not be made after the annual reporting period in which the entity initially applies the classification and measurement requirements for financial assets in AASB 9.

42O   When an entity presents the disclosures set out in paragraphs 42K–42N, those disclosures, and the disclosures in paragraph 25 of this Standard, must permit reconciliation between:

(a)   the measurement categories presented in accordance with AASB 139 and AASB 9; and

(b)   the class of financial instrument

as at the date of initial application.

42P   On the date of initial application of Section 5.5 of AASB 9, an entity is required to disclose information that would permit the reconciliation of the ending impairment allowances in accordance with AASB 139 and the provisions in accordance with AASB 137 to the opening loss allowances determined in accordance with AASB 9. For financial assets, this disclosure shall be provided by the related financial assets' measurement categories in accordance with AASB 139 and AASB 9, and shall show separately the effect of the changes in the measurement category on the loss allowance at that date.

42Q   In the reporting period that includes the date of initial application of AASB 9, an entity is not required to disclose the line item amounts that would have been reported in accordance with the classification and measurement requirements (which includes the requirements related to amortised cost measurement of financial assets and impairment in Sections 5.4 and 5.5 of AASB 9) of:

(a)   AASB 9 for prior periods; and

(b)   AASB 139 for the current period.

42R   In accordance with paragraph 7.2.4 of AASB 9, if it is impracticable (as defined in AASB 108) at the date of initial application of AASB 9 for an entity to assess a modified time value of money element in accordance with paragraphs B4.1.9B–B4.1.9D of AASB 9 based on the facts and circumstances that existed at the initial recognition of the financial asset, an entity shall assess the contractual cash flow characteristics of that financial asset based on the facts and circumstances that existed at the initial recognition of the financial asset without taking into account the requirements related to the modification of the time value of money element in paragraphs B4.1.9B–B4.1.9D of AASB 9. An entity shall disclose the carrying amount at the reporting date of the financial assets whose contractual cash flow characteristics have been assessed based on the facts and circumstances that existed at the initial recognition of the financial asset without taking into account the requirements related to the modification of the time value of money element in paragraphs B4.1.9B–B4.1.9D of AASB 9 until those financial assets are derecognised.

42S   In accordance with paragraph 7.2.5 of AASB 9, if it is impracticable (as defined in AASB 108) at the date of initial application for an entity to assess whether the fair value of a prepayment feature was insignificant in accordance with paragraphs B4.1.12(c) of AASB 9 based on the facts and circumstances that existed at the initial recognition of the financial asset, an entity shall assess the contractual cash flow characteristics of that financial asset based on the facts and circumstances that existed at the initial recognition of the financial asset without taking into account the exception for prepayment features in paragraph B4.1.12 of AASB 9. An entity shall disclose the carrying amount at the reporting date of the financial assets whose contractual cash flow characteristics have been assessed based on the facts and circumstances

AASB

that existed at the initial recognition of the financial asset without taking into account the exception for prepayment features in paragraph B4.1.12 of AASB 9 until those financial assets are derecognised.

Effective date and transition

43   An entity shall apply this Standard for annual periods beginning on or after 1 January 2018. Earlier application is encouraged for periods beginning after 24 July 2014 but before 1 January 2018. If an entity applies this Standard for an earlier period, it shall disclose that fact.

44–44D	[Deleted by the AASB]
44E	[Deleted]
44F	[Deleted]
44G	[Deleted by the AASB]
44H–44J	[Deleted]
44K–44M	[Deleted by the AASB]
44N	[Deleted]
44O–44R	[Deleted by the AASB]
44S–44W	[Deleted]
44X	[Deleted by the AASB]
44Y	[Deleted]

44Z   AASB 2010-7 *Amendments to Australian Accounting Standards arising from AASB 9 (December 2010)* (as amended), AASB 2014-1 *Amendments to Australian Accounting Standards* and AASB 2014-7 *Amendments to Australian Accounting Standards arising from AASB 9 (December 2014)* amended the previous version of this Standard as follows: amended paragraphs 3, 4, 8–11, 14, 20, 28–30, 36, 42C–42E, Appendix A and paragraphs B1, B5, B9, B10, B22 and B27, deleted paragraphs 12, 12A, 16, 22, 23, 24, 37, 44E, 44F, 44H–44J, 44S–44W, B4 and Appendix D and added paragraphs 5A, 10A, 11A, 11B, 12B–12D, 16A, 20A, 21A–21D, 22A–22C, 23A–23F, 24A–24G, 35A–35N, 42I–42S, 44ZA and B8A–B8J. Paragraph 44N, added by AASB 2010-7, was deleted by AASB 2014-1. Paragraph 44Y, added by AASB 2014-1, was deleted by AASB 2014-7. An entity shall apply those amendments when it applies AASB 9. Those amendments need not be applied to comparative information provided for periods before the date of initial application of AASB 9.

44ZA   In accordance with paragraph 7.1.2 of AASB 9, for annual reporting periods prior to 1 January 2018, an entity may elect to early apply only the requirements for the presentation of gains and losses on financial liabilities designated as at fair value through profit or loss in paragraphs 5.7.1(c), 5.7.7–5.7.9, 7.2.14 and B5.7.5–B5.7.20 of AASB 9 without applying the other requirements in AASB 9. If an entity elects to apply only those paragraphs of AASB 9, it shall disclose that fact and provide on an ongoing basis the related disclosures set out in paragraphs 10–11 of this Standard (as amended in the previous version of this Standard by AASB 2010-7 *Amendments to Australian Accounting Standards arising from AASB 9 (December 2010)*).

44AA   AASB 2015-1 *Amendments to Australian Accounting Standards – Annual Improvements to Australian Accounting Standards 2012–2014 Cycle*, issued in January 2015, amended the previous version of this Standard as follows: amended paragraphs 44R and B30 and added paragraph B30A. An entity shall apply those amendments retrospectively in accordance with AASB 108 *Accounting Policies, Changes in Accounting Estimates and Errors* for annual periods beginning on or after 1 January 2016, except that an entity need not apply the amendments to paragraphs B30 and B30A for any period presented that begins before the annual period for which the entity first applies those amendments. Earlier application of the amendments to paragraphs 44R, B30 and B30A is permitted. If an entity applies those amendments for an earlier period it shall disclose that fact.

44BB AASB 2015-2 *Amendments to Australian Accounting Standards – Disclosure Initiative: Amendments to AASB 101*, issued in January 2015, amended the previous version of this Standard as follows: amended paragraphs 21 and B5. An entity shall apply those amendments for annual periods beginning on or after 1 January 2016. Earlier application of those amendments is permitted.

Withdrawal of IAS 30

45 [Deleted by the AASB]

Commencement of the legislative instrument

Aus45.1 For legal purposes, this legislative instrument commences on 31 December 2017.

Withdrawal of AASB pronouncements

Aus45.2 This Standard repeals AASB 7 *Financial Instruments: Disclosures* issued in August 2005. Despite the repeal, after the time this Standard starts to apply under section 334 of the Corporations Act (either generally or in relation to an individual entity), the repealed Standard continues to apply in relation to any period ending before that time as if the repeal had not occurred.

[Note: When this Standard applies under section 334 of the Corporations Act (either generally or in relation to an individual entity), it supersedes the application of the repealed Standard.]

APPENDIX A
DEFINED TERMS

This appendix is an integral part of the Standard.

credit risk	The risk that one party to a financial instrument will cause a financial loss for the other party by failing to discharge an obligation.
credit risk rating grades	Rating of credit risk based on the risk of a default occurring on the financial instrument.
currency risk	The risk that the fair value or future cash flows of a financial instrument will fluctuate because of changes in foreign exchange rates.
interest rate risk	The risk that the fair value or future cash flows of a financial instrument will fluctuate because of changes in market interest rates.
liquidity risk	The risk that an entity will encounter difficulty in meeting obligations associated with financial liabilities that are settled by delivering cash or another financial asset.
loans payable	Loans payable are financial liabilities, other than short-term trade payables on normal credit terms.
market risk	The risk that the fair value or future cash flows of a financial instrument will fluctuate because of changes in market prices. Market risk comprises three types of risk: **currency risk**, **interest rate risk** and **other price risk**.
other price risk	The risk that the fair value or future cash flows of a financial instrument will fluctuate because of changes in market prices (other than those arising from **interest rate risk** or **currency risk**), whether those changes are caused by factors specific to the individual financial instrument or its issuer or by factors affecting all similar financial instruments traded in the market.

The following terms are defined in paragraph 11 of AASB 132, paragraph 9 of AASB 139, Appendix A of AASB 9 or Appendix A of AASB 13 and are used in this Standard with the meaning specified in AASB 132, AASB 139, AASB 9 and AASB 13.

- amortised cost of a financial asset or financial liability
- contract asset
- credit-impaired financial assets
- derecognition
- derivative
- dividends
- effective interest method
- equity instrument
- expected credit losses
- fair value
- financial asset
- financial guarantee contract
- financial instrument
- financial liability
- financial liability at fair value through profit or loss
- forecast transaction
- gross carrying amount of a financial asset
- hedging instrument
- held for trading
- impairment gains or losses
- loss allowance
- past due
- purchased or originated credit-impaired financial assets
- reclassification date
- regular way purchase or sale.

APPENDIX B
APPLICATION GUIDANCE

This appendix is an integral part of the Standard.

Classes of financial instruments and level of disclosure (paragraph 6)

B1   Paragraph 6 requires an entity to group financial instruments into classes that are appropriate to the nature of the information disclosed and that take into account the characteristics of those financial instruments. The classes described in paragraph 6 are determined by the entity and are, thus, distinct from the categories of financial instruments specified in AASB 9 (which determine how financial instruments are measured and where changes in fair value are recognised).

B2   In determining classes of financial instrument, an entity shall, at a minimum:

  (a)   distinguish instruments measured at amortised cost from those measured at fair value.

      (b)   treat as a separate class or classes those financial instruments outside the scope of this Standard.

B3   An entity decides, in the light of its circumstances, how much detail it provides to satisfy the requirements of this Standard, how much emphasis it places on different aspects of the requirements and how it aggregates information to display the overall picture without combining information with different characteristics. It is necessary to strike a balance between overburdening financial statements with excessive detail that may not assist users of financial statements and obscuring important information as a result of too much aggregation. For example, an entity shall not obscure important information by including it among a large amount of insignificant detail. Similarly, an entity shall not disclose information that is so aggregated that it obscures important differences between individual transactions or associated risks.

B4   [Deleted]

Other disclosure – accounting policies (paragraph 21)

B5   Paragraph 21 requires disclosure of the measurement basis (or bases) used in preparing the financial statements and the other accounting policies used that are relevant to an understanding of the financial statements. For financial instruments, such disclosure may include:

      (a)   for financial liabilities designated as at fair value through profit or loss:

           (i)   the nature of the financial liabilities the entity has designated as at fair value through profit or loss;

           (ii)   the criteria for so designating such financial liabilities on initial recognition; and

          (iii)   how the entity has satisfied the conditions in paragraph 4.2.2 of AASB 9 for such designation.

     (aa)   for financial assets designated as measured at fair value through profit or loss:

           (i)   the nature of the financial assets the entity has designated as measured at fair value through profit or loss; and

           (ii)   how the entity has satisfied the criteria in paragraph 4.1.5 of AASB 9 for such designation.

      (b)   [deleted]

      (c)   whether regular way purchases and sales of financial assets are accounted for at trade date or at settlement date (see paragraph 3.1.2 of AASB 9).

      (d)   [deleted]

      (e)   how net gains or net losses on each category of financial instrument are determined (see paragraph 20(a)), for example, whether the net gains or net losses on items at fair value through profit or loss include interest or dividend income.

      (f)   [deleted]

      (g)   [deleted]

     Paragraph 122 of AASB 101 also requires entities to disclose, along with its significant accounting policies or other notes, the judgements, apart from those involving estimations, that management has made in the process of applying the entity's accounting policies and that have the most significant effect on the amounts recognised in the financial statements.

Nature and extent of risks arising from financial instruments (paragraphs 31–42)

B6   The disclosures required by paragraphs 31–42 shall be either given in the financial statements or incorporated by cross-reference from the financial statements to some other statement, such as a management commentary or risk report, that is available to users of the financial statements on the same terms as the financial statements and at the same time. Without the information incorporated by cross-reference, the financial statements are incomplete.

Quantitative disclosures (paragraph 34)

B7   Paragraph 34(a) requires disclosures of summary quantitative data about an entity's exposure to risks based on the information provided internally to key management personnel of the entity. When an entity uses several methods to manage a risk exposure, the entity shall disclose information using the method or methods that provide the most relevant and reliable information. AASB 108 *Accounting Policies, Changes in Accounting Estimates and Errors* discusses relevance and reliability.

B8   Paragraph 34(c) requires disclosures about concentrations of risk. Concentrations of risk arise from financial instruments that have similar characteristics and are affected similarly by changes in economic or other conditions. The identification of concentrations of risk requires judgement taking into account the circumstances of the entity. Disclosure of concentrations of risk shall include:

    (a)   a description of how management determines concentrations;

    (b)   a description of the shared characteristic that identifies each concentration (eg counterparty, geographical area, currency or market); and

    (c)   the amount of the risk exposure associated with all financial instruments sharing that characteristic.

Credit risk management practices (paragraphs 35F–35G)

B8A   Paragraph 35F(b) requires the disclosure of information about how an entity has defined default for different financial instruments and the reasons for selecting those definitions. In accordance with paragraph 5.5.9 of AASB 9, the determination of whether lifetime expected credit losses should be recognised is based on the increase in the risk of a default occurring since initial recognition. Information about an entity's definitions of default that will assist users of financial statements in understanding how an entity has applied the expected credit loss requirements in AASB 9 may include:

    (a)   the qualitative and quantitative factors considered in defining default;

    (b)   whether different definitions have been applied to different types of financial instruments; and

    (c)   assumptions about the cure rate (ie the number of financial assets that return to a performing status) after a default occurred on the financial asset.

B8B   To assist users of financial statements in evaluating an entity's restructuring and modification policies, paragraph 35F(f)(ii) requires the disclosure of information about how an entity monitors the extent to which the loss allowance on financial assets previously disclosed in accordance with paragraph 35F(f)(i) are subsequently measured at an amount equal to lifetime expected credit losses in accordance with paragraph 5.5.3 of AASB 9. Quantitative information that will assist users in understanding the subsequent increase in credit risk of modified financial assets may include information about modified financial assets meeting the criteria in paragraph 35F(f)(i) for which the loss allowance has reverted to being measured at an amount equal to lifetime expected credit losses (ie a deterioration rate).

B8C   Paragraph 35G(a) requires the disclosure of information about the basis of inputs and assumptions and the estimation techniques used to apply the impairment requirements in AASB 9. An entity's assumptions and inputs used to measure expected credit losses or determine the extent of increases in credit risk since initial recognition may include information obtained from internal historical information or rating reports and assumptions about the expected life of financial instruments and the timing of the sale of collateral.

Changes in the loss allowance (paragraph 35H)

B8D   In accordance with paragraph 35H, an entity is required to explain the reasons for the changes in the loss allowance during the period. In addition to the reconciliation from the opening balance to the closing balance of the loss allowance, it may be necessary to provide a narrative explanation of the changes. This narrative explanation may include an analysis of the reasons for changes in the loss allowance during the period, including:

    (a)   the portfolio composition;

    (b)   the volume of financial instruments purchased or originated; and

    (c)   the severity of the expected credit losses.

B8E   For loan commitments and financial guarantee contracts the loss allowance is recognised as a provision. An entity should disclose information about the changes in the loss allowance for financial assets separately from those for loan commitments and financial guarantee contracts. However, if a financial instrument includes both a loan (ie financial asset) and an undrawn commitment (ie loan commitment) component and the entity cannot separately identify the expected credit losses on the loan commitment component from those on the financial asset component, the expected credit losses on the loan commitment should be recognised together with the loss allowance for the financial asset. To the extent that the combined expected credit losses exceed the gross carrying amount of the financial asset, the expected credit losses should be recognised as a provision.

Collateral (paragraph 35K)

B8F   Paragraph 35K requires the disclosure of information that will enable users of financial statements to understand the effect of collateral and other credit enhancements on the amount of expected credit losses. An entity is neither required to disclose information about the fair value of collateral and other credit enhancements nor is it required to quantify the exact value of the collateral that was included in the calculation of expected credit losses (ie the loss given default).

B8G   A narrative description of collateral and its effect on amounts of expected credit losses might include information about:

    (a)   the main types of collateral held as security and other credit enhancements (examples of the latter being guarantees, credit derivatives and netting agreements that do not qualify for offset in accordance with AASB 132);

    (b)   the volume of collateral held and other credit enhancements and its significance in terms of the loss allowance;

    (c)   the policies and processes for valuing and managing collateral and other credit enhancements;

    (d)   the main types of counterparties to collateral and other credit enhancements and their creditworthiness; and

    (e)   information about risk concentrations within the collateral and other credit enhancements.

Credit risk exposure (paragraphs 35M–35N)

B8H   Paragraph 35M requires the disclosure of information about an entity's credit risk exposure and significant concentrations of credit risk at the reporting date. A concentration of credit risk exists when a number of counterparties are located in a geographical region or are engaged in similar activities and have similar economic characteristics that would cause their ability to meet contractual obligations to be similarly affected by changes in economic or other conditions. An entity should provide information that enables users of financial statements to understand whether there are groups or portfolios of financial instruments with particular features that could affect a large portion of that group of financial instruments such as concentration to particular risks. This could include, for example, loan-to-value groupings, geographical, industry or issuer-type concentrations.

B8I   The number of credit risk rating grades used to disclose the information in accordance with paragraph 35M shall be consistent with the number that the entity reports to key management personnel for credit risk management purposes. If past due information is the only borrower-specific information available and an entity uses past due information to assess whether credit risk has increased significantly since initial recognition in accordance with paragraph 5.5.11 of AASB 9, an entity shall provide an analysis by past due status for those financial assets.

B8J   When an entity has measured expected credit losses on a collective basis, the entity may not be able to allocate the gross carrying amount of individual financial assets or the exposure to credit risk on loan commitments and financial guarantee contracts to the credit risk rating grades for which lifetime expected credit losses are recognised. In that case, an entity should apply the requirement in paragraph 35M to those financial instruments that can be directly allocated to a credit risk rating grade and disclose separately the gross carrying amount of financial instruments for which lifetime expected credit losses have been measured on a collective basis.

Maximum credit risk exposure (paragraph 36(a))

B9   Paragraphs 35K(a) and 36(a) require disclosure of the amount that best represents the entity's maximum exposure to credit risk. For a financial asset, this is typically the gross carrying amount, net of:

(a)   any amounts offset in accordance with AASB 132; and

(b)   any loss allowance recognised in accordance with AASB 9.

B10   Activities that give rise to credit risk and the associated maximum exposure to credit risk include, but are not limited to:

(a)   granting loans to customers and placing deposits with other entities. In these cases, the maximum exposure to credit risk is the carrying amount of the related financial assets.

(b)   entering into derivative contracts, eg foreign exchange contracts, interest rate swaps and credit derivatives. When the resulting asset is measured at fair value, the maximum exposure to credit risk at the end of the reporting period will equal the carrying amount.

(c)   granting financial guarantees. In this case, the maximum exposure to credit risk is the maximum amount the entity could have to pay if the guarantee is called on, which may be significantly greater than the amount recognised as a liability.

(d)   making a loan commitment that is irrevocable over the life of the facility or is revocable only in response to a material adverse change. If the issuer cannot settle the loan commitment net in cash or another financial instrument, the maximum credit exposure is the full amount of the commitment. This is because it is uncertain whether the amount of any undrawn portion may be drawn upon in the future. This may be significantly greater than the amount recognised as a liability.

Quantitative liquidity risk disclosures (paragraphs 34(a) and 39(a) and (b))

B10A   In accordance with paragraph 34(a) an entity discloses summary quantitative data about its exposure to liquidity risk on the basis of the information provided internally to key management personnel. An entity shall explain how those data are determined. If the outflows of cash (or another financial asset) included in those data could either:

    (a)   occur significantly earlier than indicated in the data, or

    (b)   be for significantly different amounts from those indicated in the data (eg for a derivative that is included in the data on a net settlement basis but for which the counterparty has the option to require gross settlement),

the entity shall state that fact and provide quantitative information that enables users of its financial statements to evaluate the extent of this risk unless that information is included in the contractual maturity analyses required by paragraph 39(a) or (b).

B11   In preparing the maturity analyses required by paragraph 39(a) and (b), an entity uses its judgement to determine an appropriate number of time bands. For example, an entity might determine that the following time bands are appropriate:

    (a)   not later than one month;

    (b)   later than one month and not later than three months;

    (c)   later than three months and not later than one year; and

    (d)   later than one year and not later than five years.

B11A   In complying with paragraph 39(a) and (b), an entity shall not separate an embedded derivative from a hybrid (combined) financial instrument. For such an instrument, an entity shall apply paragraph 39(a).

B11B   Paragraph 39(b) requires an entity to disclose a quantitative maturity analysis for derivative financial liabilities that shows remaining contractual maturities if the contractual maturities are essential for an understanding of the timing of the cash flows. For example, this would be the case for:

    (a)   an interest rate swap with a remaining maturity of five years in a cash flow hedge of a variable rate financial asset or liability.

    (b)   all loan commitments.

B11C   Paragraph 39(a) and (b) requires an entity to disclose maturity analyses for financial liabilities that show the remaining contractual maturities for some financial liabilities. In this disclosure:

    (a)   when a counterparty has a choice of when an amount is paid, the liability is allocated to the earliest period in which the entity can be required to pay. For example, financial liabilities that an entity can be required to repay on demand (eg demand deposits) are included in the earliest time band.

    (b)   when an entity is committed to make amounts available in instalments, each instalment is allocated to the earliest period in which the entity can be required to pay. For example, an undrawn loan commitment is included in the time band containing the earliest date it can be drawn down.

    (c)   for issued financial guarantee contracts the maximum amount of the guarantee is allocated to the earliest period in which the guarantee could be called.

B11D   The contractual amounts disclosed in the maturity analyses as required by paragraph 39(a) and (b) are the contractual undiscounted cash flows, for example:

    (a)   gross finance lease obligations (before deducting finance charges);

    (b)   prices specified in forward agreements to purchase financial assets for cash;

    (c)   net amounts for pay-floating/receive-fixed interest rate swaps for which net cash flows are exchanged;

    (d)   contractual amounts to be exchanged in a derivative financial instrument (eg a currency swap) for which gross cash flows are exchanged; and

    (e)   gross loan commitments.

Such undiscounted cash flows differ from the amount included in the statement of financial position because the amount in that statement is based on discounted

AASB

cash flows. When the amount payable is not fixed, the amount disclosed is determined by reference to the conditions existing at the end of the reporting period. For example, when the amount payable varies with changes in an index, the amount disclosed may be based on the level of the index at the end of the period.

B11E   Paragraph 39(c) requires an entity to describe how it manages the liquidity risk inherent in the items disclosed in the quantitative disclosures required in paragraph 39(a) and (b). An entity shall disclose a maturity analysis of financial assets it holds for managing liquidity risk (eg financial assets that are readily saleable or expected to generate cash inflows to meet cash outflows on financial liabilities), if that information is necessary to enable users of its financial statements to evaluate the nature and extent of liquidity risk.

B11F   Other factors that an entity might consider in providing the disclosure required in paragraph 39(c) include, but are not limited to, whether the entity:

   (a)   has committed borrowing facilities (eg commercial paper facilities) or other lines of credit (eg stand-by credit facilities) that it can access to meet liquidity needs;

   (b)   holds deposits at central banks to meet liquidity needs;

   (c)   has very diverse funding sources;

   (d)   has significant concentrations of liquidity risk in either its assets or its funding sources;

   (e)   has internal control processes and contingency plans for managing liquidity risk;

   (f)   has instruments that include accelerated repayment terms (eg on the downgrade of the entity's credit rating);

   (g)   has instruments that could require the posting of collateral (eg margin calls for derivatives);

   (h)   has instruments that allow the entity to choose whether it settles its financial liabilities by delivering cash (or another financial asset) or by delivering its own shares; or

   (i)   has instruments that are subject to master netting agreements.

B12–B16 [Deleted]

Market risk – sensitivity analysis (paragraphs 40 and 41)

B17   Paragraph 40(a) requires a sensitivity analysis for each type of market risk to which the entity is exposed. In accordance with paragraph B3, an entity decides how it aggregates information to display the overall picture without combining information with different characteristics about exposures to risks from significantly different economic environments. For example:

   (a)   an entity that trades financial instruments might disclose this information separately for financial instruments held for trading and those not held for trading.

   (b)   an entity would not aggregate its exposure to market risks from areas of hyperinflation with its exposure to the same market risks from areas of very low inflation.

   If an entity has exposure to only one type of market risk in only one economic environment, it would not show disaggregated information.

B18   Paragraph 40(a) requires the sensitivity analysis to show the effect on profit or loss and equity of reasonably possible changes in the relevant risk variable (eg prevailing market interest rates, currency rates, equity prices or commodity prices). For this purpose:

   (a)   entities are not required to determine what the profit or loss for the period would have been if relevant risk variables had been different. Instead, entities disclose the effect on profit or loss and equity at the end of the reporting period assuming that a reasonably possible change in the relevant risk variable had occurred at the end of the reporting period and had been applied to the risk exposures in existence at that date. For example, if an entity has a floating rate liability at the end of the year, the entity would disclose the effect on profit or loss (ie interest expense) for the current year if interest rates had varied by reasonably possible amounts.

(b)   entities are not required to disclose the effect on profit or loss and equity for each change within a range of reasonably possible changes of the relevant risk variable. Disclosure of the effects of the changes at the limits of the reasonably possible range would be sufficient.

B19   In determining what a reasonably possible change in the relevant risk variable is, an entity should consider:

(a)   the economic environments in which it operates. A reasonably possible change should not include remote or 'worst case' scenarios or 'stress tests'. Moreover, if the rate of change in the underlying risk variable is stable, the entity need not alter the chosen reasonably possible change in the risk variable. For example, assume that interest rates are 5 per cent and an entity determines that a fluctuation in interest rates of ±50 basis points is reasonably possible. It would disclose the effect on profit or loss and equity if interest rates were to change to 4.5 per cent or 5.5 per cent. In the next period, interest rates have increased to 5.5 per cent. The entity continues to believe that interest rates may fluctuate by ±50 basis points (ie that the rate of change in interest rates is stable). The entity would disclose the effect on profit or loss and equity if interest rates were to change to 5 per cent or 6 per cent. The entity would not be required to revise its assessment that interest rates might reasonably fluctuate by ±50 basis points, unless there is evidence that interest rates have become significantly more volatile.

(b)   the time frame over which it is making the assessment. The sensitivity analysis shall show the effects of changes that are considered to be reasonably possible over the period until the entity will next present these disclosures, which is usually its next annual reporting period.

B20   Paragraph 41 permits an entity to use a sensitivity analysis that reflects interdependencies between risk variables, such as a value-at-risk methodology, if it uses this analysis to manage its exposure to financial risks. This applies even if such a methodology measures only the potential for loss and does not measure the potential for gain. Such an entity might comply with paragraph 41(a) by disclosing the type of value-at-risk model used (eg whether the model relies on Monte Carlo simulations), an explanation about how the model works and the main assumptions (eg the holding period and confidence level). Entities might also disclose the historical observation period and weightings applied to observations within that period, an explanation of how options are dealt with in the calculations, and which volatilities and correlations (or, alternatively, Monte Carlo probability distribution simulations) are used.

B21   An entity shall provide sensitivity analyses for the whole of its business, but may provide different types of sensitivity analysis for different classes of financial instruments.

Interest rate risk

B22   *Interest rate risk* arises on interest-bearing financial instruments recognised in the statement of financial position (eg debt instruments acquired or issued) and on some financial instruments not recognised in the statement of financial position (eg some loan commitments).

Currency risk

B23   *Currency risk* (or foreign exchange risk) arises on financial instruments that are denominated in a foreign currency, ie in a currency other than the functional currency in which they are measured. For the purpose of this Standard, currency risk does not arise from financial instruments that are non-monetary items or from financial instruments denominated in the functional currency.

B24 A sensitivity analysis is disclosed for each currency to which an entity has significant exposure.

Other price risk

B25 *Other price risk* arises on financial instruments because of changes in, for example, commodity prices or equity prices. To comply with paragraph 40, an entity might disclose the effect of a decrease in a specified stock market index, commodity price, or other risk variable. For example, if an entity gives residual value guarantees that are financial instruments, the entity discloses an increase or decrease in the value of the assets to which the guarantee applies.

B26 Two examples of financial instruments that give rise to equity price risk are (a) a holding of equities in another entity and (b) an investment in a trust that in turn holds investments in equity instruments. Other examples include forward contracts and options to buy or sell specified quantities of an equity instrument and swaps that are indexed to equity prices. The fair values of such financial instruments are affected by changes in the market price of the underlying equity instruments.

B27 In accordance with paragraph 40(a), the sensitivity of profit or loss (that arises, for example, from instruments measured at fair value through profit or loss) is disclosed separately from the sensitivity of other comprehensive income (that arises, for example, from investments in equity instruments whose changes in fair value are presented in other comprehensive income).

B28 Financial instruments that an entity classifies as equity instruments are not remeasured. Neither profit or loss nor equity will be affected by the equity price risk of those instruments. Accordingly, no sensitivity analysis is required.

Derecognition (paragraphs 42C–42H)

Continuing involvement (paragraph 42C)

B29 The assessment of continuing involvement in a transferred financial asset for the purposes of the disclosure requirements in paragraphs 42E–42H is made at the level of the reporting entity. For example, if a subsidiary transfers to an unrelated third party a financial asset in which the parent of the subsidiary has continuing involvement, the subsidiary does not include the parent's involvement in the assessment of whether it has continuing involvement in the transferred asset in its separate or individual financial statements (ie when the subsidiary is the reporting entity). However, a parent would include its continuing involvement (or that of another member of the group) in a financial asset transferred by its subsidiary in determining whether it has continuing involvement in the transferred asset in its consolidated financial statements (ie when the reporting entity is the group).

B30 An entity does not have a continuing involvement in a transferred financial asset if, as part of the transfer, it neither retains any of the contractual rights or obligations inherent in the transferred financial asset nor acquires any new contractual rights or obligations relating to the transferred financial asset. An entity does not have continuing involvement in a transferred financial asset if it has neither an interest in the future performance of the transferred financial asset nor a responsibility under any circumstances to make payments in respect of the transferred financial asset in the future. The term 'payment' in this context does not include cash flows of the transferred financial asset that an entity collects and is required to remit to the transferee.

B30A When an entity transfers a financial asset, the entity may retain the right to service that financial asset for a fee that is included in, for example, a servicing contract. The entity assesses the servicing contract in accordance with the guidance in paragraphs 42C and B30 to decide whether the entity has continuing involvement as a result of the servicing contract for the purposes of the disclosure requirements. For example, a servicer will have continuing involvement in the transferred financial asset for the purposes of the disclosure requirements if the servicing fee is dependent on the amount or timing of the cash flows collected from the transferred financial asset. Similarly, a servicer has continuing involvement for the purposes of the disclosure requirements if a fixed fee would not be paid in full because of non-performance of the transferred financial asset. In these examples, the servicer has an interest in the future performance of the transferred financial asset. This assessment is independent of whether the fee to be received is expected to compensate the entity adequately for performing the servicing.

B31 Continuing involvement in a transferred financial asset may result from contractual provisions in the transfer agreement or in a separate agreement with the transferee or a third party entered into in connection with the transfer.

Transferred financial assets that are not derecognised in their entirety (paragraph 42D)

B32 Paragraph 42D requires disclosures when part or all of the transferred financial assets do not qualify for derecognition[1]. Those disclosures are required at each reporting date at which the entity continues to recognise the transferred financial assets, regardless of when the transfers occurred.

Types of continuing involvement (paragraphs 42E–42H)

B33 Paragraphs 42E–42H require qualitative and quantitative disclosures for each type of continuing involvement in derecognised financial assets. An entity shall aggregate its continuing involvement into types that are representative of the entity's exposure to risks. For example, an entity may aggregate its continuing involvement by type of financial instrument (eg guarantees or call options) or by type of transfer (eg factoring of receivables, securitisations and securities lending).

Maturity analysis for undiscounted cash outflows to repurchase transferred assets (paragraph 42E(e))

B34 Paragraph 42E(e) requires an entity to disclose a maturity analysis of the undiscounted cash outflows to repurchase derecognised financial assets or other amounts payable to the transferee in respect of the derecognised financial assets, showing the remaining contractual maturities of the entity's continuing involvement. This analysis distinguishes cash flows that are required to be paid (eg forward contracts), cash flows that the entity may be required to pay (eg written put options) and cash flows that the entity might choose to pay (eg purchased call options).

B35 An entity shall use its judgement to determine an appropriate number of time bands in preparing the maturity analysis required by paragraph 42E(e). For example, an entity might determine that the following maturity time bands are appropriate:

(a) not later than one month;

(b) later than one month and not later than three months;

(c) later than three months and not later than six months;

(d) later than six months and not later than one year;

(e) later than one year and not later than three years;

(f) later than three years and not later than five years; and

(g) more than five years.

B36 If there is a range of possible maturities, the cash flows are included on the basis of the earliest date on which the entity can be required or is permitted to pay.

---

1 [Aus] A cross-reference to a paragraph that contains disclosure requirements that do not apply to entities preparing general purpose financial statements under Australian Accounting Standards – Reduced Disclosure Requirements does not amend the requirements for such entities.

Qualitative information (paragraph 42E(f))

B37   The qualitative information required by paragraph 42E(f) includes a description of the derecognised financial assets and the nature and purpose of the continuing involvement retained after transferring those assets. It also includes a description of the risks to which an entity is exposed, including:

(a)   a description of how the entity manages the risk inherent in its continuing involvement in the derecognised financial assets.

(b)   whether the entity is required to bear losses before other parties, and the ranking and amounts of losses borne by parties whose interests rank lower than the entity's interest in the asset (ie its continuing involvement in the asset).

(c)   a description of any triggers associated with obligations to provide financial support or to repurchase a transferred financial asset.

Gain or loss on derecognition (paragraph 42G(a))

B38   Paragraph 42G(a) requires an entity to disclose the gain or loss on derecognition relating to financial assets in which the entity has continuing involvement. The entity shall disclose if a gain or loss on derecognition arose because the fair values of the components of the previously recognised asset (ie the interest in the asset derecognised and the interest retained by the entity) were different from the fair value of the previously recognised asset as a whole. In that situation, the entity shall also disclose whether the fair value measurements included significant inputs that were not based on observable market data, as described in paragraph 27A.

Supplementary information (paragraph 42H)

B39   The disclosures required in paragraphs 42D–42G may not be sufficient to meet the disclosure objectives in paragraph 42B. If this is the case, the entity shall disclose whatever additional information is necessary to meet the disclosure objectives. The entity shall decide, in the light of its circumstances, how much additional information it needs to provide to satisfy the information needs of users and how much emphasis it places on different aspects of the additional information. It is necessary to strike a balance between burdening financial statements with excessive detail that may not assist users of financial statements and obscuring information as a result of too much aggregation.

Offsetting financial assets and financial liabilities (paragraphs 13A–13F)

Scope (paragraph 13A)

B40   The disclosures in paragraphs 13B–13E are required for all recognised financial instruments that are set off in accordance with paragraph 42 of AASB 132. In addition, financial instruments are within the scope of the disclosure requirements in paragraphs 13B–13E if they are subject to an enforceable master netting arrangement or similar agreement that covers similar financial instruments and transactions, irrespective of whether the financial instruments are set off in accordance with paragraph 42 of AASB 132.

B41   The similar agreements referred to in paragraphs 13A and B40 include derivative clearing agreements, global master repurchase agreements, global master securities lending agreements, and any related rights to financial collateral. The similar financial instruments and transactions referred to in paragraph B40 include derivatives, sale and repurchase agreements, reverse sale and repurchase agreements, securities borrowing, and securities lending agreements. Examples of financial instruments that are not within the scope of paragraph 13A are loans and customer deposits at the same institution (unless they are set off in the statement of financial position), and financial instruments that are subject only to a collateral agreement.

Disclosure of quantitative information for recognised financial assets and recognised financial liabilities within the scope of paragraph 13A (paragraph 13C)

B42 Financial instruments disclosed in accordance with paragraph 13C may be subject to different measurement requirements (for example, a payable related to a repurchase agreement may be measured at amortised cost, while a derivative will be measured at fair value). An entity shall include instruments at their recognised amounts and describe any resulting measurement differences in the related disclosures.

Disclosure of the gross amounts of recognised financial assets and recognised financial liabilities within the scope of paragraph 13A (paragraph 13C(a))

B43 The amounts required by paragraph 13C(a) relate to recognised financial instruments that are set off in accordance with paragraph 42 of AASB 132. The amounts required by paragraph 13C(a) also relate to recognised financial instruments that are subject to an enforceable master netting arrangement or similar agreement irrespective of whether they meet the offsetting criteria. However, the disclosures required by paragraph 13C(a) do not relate to any amounts recognised as a result of collateral agreements that do not meet the offsetting criteria in paragraph 42 of AASB 132. Instead, such amounts are required to be disclosed in accordance with paragraph 13C(d).

Disclosure of the amounts that are set off in accordance with the criteria in paragraph 42 of AASB 132 (paragraph 13C(b))

B44 Paragraph 13C(b) requires that entities disclose the amounts set off in accordance with paragraph 42 of AASB 132 when determining the net amounts presented in the statement of financial position. The amounts of both the recognised financial assets and the recognised financial liabilities that are subject to set-off under the same arrangement will be disclosed in both the financial asset and financial liability disclosures. However, the amounts disclosed (in, for example, a table) are limited to the amounts that are subject to set-off. For example, an entity may have a recognised derivative asset and a recognised derivative liability that meet the offsetting criteria in paragraph 42 of AASB 132. If the gross amount of the derivative asset is larger than the gross amount of the derivative liability, the financial asset disclosure table will include the entire amount of the derivative asset (in accordance with paragraph 13C(a)) and the entire amount of the derivative liability (in accordance with paragraph 13C(b)). However, while the financial liability disclosure table will include the entire amount of the derivative liability (in accordance with paragraph 13C(a)), it will only include the amount of the derivative asset (in accordance with paragraph 13C(b)) that is equal to the amount of the derivative liability.

Disclosure of the net amounts presented in the statement of financial position (paragraph 13C(c))

B45 If an entity has instruments that meet the scope of these disclosures (as specified in paragraph 13A), but that do not meet the offsetting criteria in paragraph 42 of AASB 132, the amounts required to be disclosed by paragraph 13C(c) would equal the amounts required to be disclosed by paragraph 13C(a).

B46 The amounts required to be disclosed by paragraph 13C(c) must be reconciled to the individual line item amounts presented in the statement of financial position. For example, if an entity determines that the aggregation or disaggregation of individual financial statement line item amounts provides more relevant information, it must reconcile the aggregated or disaggregated amounts disclosed in paragraph 13C(c) back to the individual line item amounts presented in the statement of financial position.

Disclosure of the amounts subject to an enforceable master netting arrangement or similar agreement that are not otherwise included in paragraph 13C(b) (paragraph 13C(d))

B47   Paragraph 13C(d) requires that entities disclose amounts that are subject to an enforceable master netting arrangement or similar agreement that are not otherwise included in paragraph 13C(b). Paragraph 13C(d)(i) refers to amounts related to recognised financial instruments that do not meet some or all of the offsetting criteria in paragraph 42 of AASB 132 (for example, current rights of set-off that do not meet the criterion in paragraph 42(b) of AASB 132, or conditional rights of set-off that are enforceable and exercisable only in the event of default, or only in the event of insolvency or bankruptcy of any of the counterparties).

B48   Paragraph 13C(d)(ii) refers to amounts related to financial collateral, including cash collateral, both received and pledged. An entity shall disclose the fair value of those financial instruments that have been pledged or received as collateral. The amounts disclosed in accordance with paragraph 13C(d)(ii) should relate to the actual collateral received or pledged and not to any resulting payables or receivables recognised to return or receive back such collateral.

Limits on the amounts disclosed in paragraph 13C(d) (paragraph 13D)

B49   When disclosing amounts in accordance with paragraph 13C(d), an entity must take into account the effects of over-collateralisation by financial instrument. To do so, the entity must first deduct the amounts disclosed in accordance with paragraph 13C(d)(i) from the amount disclosed in accordance with paragraph 13C(c). The entity shall then limit the amounts disclosed in accordance with paragraph 13C(d)(ii) to the remaining amount in paragraph 13C(c) for the related financial instrument. However, if rights to collateral can be enforced across financial instruments, such rights can be included in the disclosure provided in accordance with paragraph 13D.

Description of the rights of set-off subject to enforceable master netting arrangements and similar agreements (paragraph 13E)

B50   An entity shall describe the types of rights of set-off and similar arrangements disclosed in accordance with paragraph 13C(d), including the nature of those rights. For example, an entity shall describe its conditional rights. For instruments subject to rights of set-off that are not contingent on a future event but that do not meet the remaining criteria in paragraph 42 of AASB 132, the entity shall describe the reason(s) why the criteria are not met. For any financial collateral received or pledged, the entity shall describe the terms of the collateral agreement (for example, when the collateral is restricted).

Disclosure by type of financial instrument or by counterparty

B51   The quantitative disclosures required by paragraph 13C(a)–(e) may be grouped by type of financial instrument or transaction (for example, derivatives, repurchase and reverse repurchase agreements or securities borrowing and securities lending agreements).

B52   Alternatively, an entity may group the quantitative disclosures required by paragraph 13C(a)–(c) by type of financial instrument, and the quantitative disclosures required by paragraph 13C(c)–(e) by counterparty. If an entity provides the required information by counterparty, the entity is not required to identify the counterparties by name. However, designation of counterparties (Counterparty A, Counterparty B, Counterparty C, etc) shall remain consistent from year to year for the years presented to maintain comparability. Qualitative disclosures shall be considered so that further information can be given about the types of counterparties. When disclosure of the amounts in paragraph 13C(c)–(e) is provided by counterparty, amounts that are individually significant in terms of total counterparty amounts shall be separately disclosed and the remaining individually insignificant counterparty amounts shall be aggregated into one line item.

Other

B53 The specific disclosures required by paragraphs 13C–13E are minimum requirements. To meet the objective in paragraph 13B an entity may need to supplement them with additional (qualitative) disclosures, depending on the terms of the enforceable master netting arrangements and related agreements, including the nature of the rights of set-off, and their effect or potential effect on the entity's financial position.

APPENDIX D
AUSTRALIAN REDUCED DISCLOSURE
REQUIREMENTS

This appendix is an integral part of the Standard.

AusD1 The following do not apply to entities preparing general purpose financial statements under Australian Accounting Standards – Reduced Disclosure Requirements:

(a) paragraphs 6, 9, 10(a)–(c), 10A, 11–11B, 12C, 13A–13F, 15, 18, 19, 20(c), 20A, 21B, 21C, 23A, 23B, 23C(a), 23D, 23E, 24A(b), 24A(d), 24B(a)(ii), 24B(a)(iii), 24B(a)(v), 24B(b)(ii), 24B(b)(iii), 24C(a)(ii), 24C(b)(iii), 24C(b)(v), 24D–24F, 24G(a), 24G(b), 25–42, 42C, 42D(d), 42D(e), 42E(a), 42E(b), 42E(d)–(f), 42F–42H, B1–B4, B6–B29 and B33–B53;

(b) in paragraph 8(a), the text ", showing separately ... in accordance with AASB 9";

(c) in paragraph 8(e), the text ", showing separately ... held for trading in AASB 9";

(d) in paragraph 20(a)(i), the text ", showing separately ... held for trading in AASB 9)";

(e) in paragraph 24C(b)(iv), the words following the text "... reclassification adjustment";

(f) in paragraphs 24A-24C, the text ", in a tabular format,"; and

(g) in paragraph 42D(f), the text "the total carrying amount of the original assets before the transfer,".

AusD2 The requirements that do not apply to entities preparing general purpose financial statements under Australian Accounting Standards – Reduced Disclosure Requirements are also identified in this Standard by shading of the relevant text.

AusD3 RDR paragraphs in this Standard apply only to entities preparing general purpose financial statements under Australian Accounting Standards – Reduced Disclosure Requirements.

RDR18.1 For *loans payable* recognised at the end of the reporting period for which there is a breach of terms or default of principal, interest, sinking fund, or redemption terms that has not been remedied by the end of the reporting period, an entity applying Australian Accounting Standards – Reduced Disclosure Requirements shall disclose the following:

(a) details of that breach or default;

(b) the carrying amount of the related loans payable at the end of the reporting period; and

(c) whether the breach or default was remedied, or the terms of the loans payable were renegotiated, before the financial statements were authorised for issue.

COMPILATION DETAILS

Accounting Standard AASB 7 *Financial Instruments: Disclosures*

Compilation details are not part of AASB 7.

This compiled Standard applies to annual periods beginning on or after 1 January 2018 but before 1 January 2019. It takes into account amendments up to and including 12 December 2017 and was prepared on 20 May 2018 by the staff of the Australian Accounting Standards Board (AASB).

This compilation is not a separate Accounting Standard made by the AASB. Instead, it is a representation of AASB 7 (August 2015) as amended by other Accounting Standards, which are listed in the Table below.

Table of Standards

Standard	Date made	FRL identifier	Commence-ment date	Effective date *(annual periods ... on or after ...)*	Application, saving or transitional provisions
AASB 7	7 Aug 2015	F2015L01610	31 Dec 2017	*(beginning)* 1 Jan 2018	see (a) below
AASB 16	23 Feb 2016	F2016L00233	31 Dec 2018	*(beginning)* 1 Jan 2019	not compiled*
AASB 17	19 Jul 2017	F2017L01184	31 Dec 2020	*(beginning)* 1 Jan 2021	not compiled*
AASB 2017-5	12 Dec 2017	F2018L00067	31 Dec 2017	*(beginning)* 1 Jan 2018	see (b) below

*   The amendments made by this Standard are not included in this compilation, which presents the principal Standard as applicable to annual periods beginning on or after 1 January 2018 but before 1 January 2019.

(a) Entities may elect to apply this Standard to annual periods beginning after 24 July 2014 but before 1 January 2018.

(b) Entities may elect to apply this Standard to annual periods beginning before 1 January 2018.

Table of amendments

Paragraph affected	How affected	By ... [paragraph/page]
B8B	amended	AASB 2017-5 [21]

DELETED IFRS 7 TEXT

Deleted IFRS 7 text is not part of AASB 7.

44   If an entity applies this IFRS for annual periods beginning before 1 January 2006, it need not present comparative information for the disclosures required by paragraphs 31–42 about the nature and extent of risks arising from financial instruments.

44A   IAS 1 (as revised in 2007) amended the terminology used throughout IFRSs. In addition it amended paragraphs 20, 21, 23(c) and (d), 27(c) and B5 of Appendix B. An entity shall apply those amendments for annual periods beginning on or after 1 January 2009. If an entity applies IAS 1 (revised 2007) for an earlier period, the amendments shall be applied for that earlier period.

44B   IFRS 3 (as revised in 2008) deleted paragraph 3(c). An entity shall apply that amendment for annual periods beginning on or after 1 July 2009. If an entity applies

IFRS 3 (revised 2008) for an earlier period, the amendment shall also be applied for that earlier period. However, the amendment does not apply to contingent consideration that arose from a business combination for which the acquisition date preceded the application of IFRS 3 (revised 2008). Instead, an entity shall account for such consideration in accordance with paragraphs 65A–65E of IFRS 3 (as amended in 2010).

44C   An entity shall apply the amendment in paragraph 3 for annual periods beginning on or after 1 January 2009. If an entity applies *Puttable Financial Instruments and Obligations Arising on Liquidation* (Amendments to IAS 32 and IAS 1), issued in February 2008, for an earlier period, the amendment in paragraph 3 shall be applied for that earlier period.

44D   Paragraph 3(a) was amended by *Improvements to IFRSs* issued in May 2008. An entity shall apply that amendment for annual periods beginning on or after 1 January 2009. Earlier application is permitted. If an entity applies the amendment for an earlier period it shall disclose that fact and apply for that earlier period the amendments to paragraph 1 of IAS 28, paragraph 1 of IAS 31 and paragraph 4 of IAS 32 issued in May 2008. An entity is permitted to apply the amendment prospectively.

44G   *Improving Disclosures about Financial Instruments* (Amendments to IFRS 7), issued in March 2009, amended paragraphs 27, 39 and B11 and added paragraphs 27A, 27B, B10A and B11A–B11F. An entity shall apply those amendments for annual periods beginning on or after 1 January 2009. An entity need not provide the disclosures required by the amendments for:

(a)   any annual or interim period, including any statement of financial position, presented within an annual comparative period ending before 31 December 2009, or

(b)   any statement of financial position as at the beginning of the earliest comparative period as at a date before 31 December 2009.

Earlier application is permitted. If an entity applies the amendments for an earlier period, it shall disclose that fact.[2]

44K   Paragraph 44B was amended by *Improvements to IFRSs* issued in May 2010. An entity shall apply that amendment for annual periods beginning on or after 1 July 2010. Earlier application is permitted.

44L   *Improvements to IFRSs* issued in May 2010 added paragraph 32A and amended paragraphs 34 and 36–38. An entity shall apply those amendments for annual periods beginning on or after 1 January 2011. Earlier application is permitted. If an entity applies the amendments for an earlier period it shall disclose that fact.

44M   *Disclosures—Transfers of Financial Assets* (Amendments to IFRS 7), issued in October 2010, deleted paragraph 13 and added paragraphs 42A–42H and B29–B39. An entity shall apply those amendments for annual periods beginning on or after 1 July 2011. Earlier application is permitted. If an entity applies the amendments from an earlier date, it shall disclose that fact. An entity need not provide the disclosures required by those amendments for any period presented that begins before the date of initial application of the amendments.

44O   IFRS 10 and IFRS 11 *Joint Arrangements*, issued in May 2011, amended paragraph 3. An entity shall apply that amendment when it applies IFRS 10 and IFRS 11.

44P   IFRS 13, issued in May 2011, amended paragraphs 3, 28 and 29 and Appendix A and deleted paragraphs 27–27B. An entity shall apply those amendments when it applies IFRS 13.

44Q   *Presentation of Items of Other Comprehensive Income* (Amendments to IAS 1), issued in June 2011, amended paragraph 27B. An entity shall apply that amendment when it applies IAS 1 as amended in June 2011.

---

2   Paragraph 44G was amended as a consequence of *Limited Exemption from Comparative IFRS 7 Disclosures for First-time Adopters* (Amendment to IFRS 1) issued in January 2010. The Board amended paragraph 44G to clarify its conclusions and intended transition for *Improving Disclosures about Financial Instruments* (Amendments to IFRS 7).

44R   *Disclosures—Offsetting Financial Assets and Financial Liabilities* (Amendments to IFRS 7), issued in December 2011, added paragraphs 13A–13F and B40–B53. An entity shall apply those amendments for annual periods beginning on or after 1 January 2013. An entity shall provide the disclosures required by those amendments retrospectively.

44X   *Investment Entities* (Amendments to IFRS 10, IFRS 12 and IAS 27), issued in October 2012, amended paragraph 3. An entity shall apply that amendment for annual periods beginning on or after 1 January 2014. Earlier application of *Investment Entities* is permitted. If an entity applies that amendment earlier it shall also apply all amendments included in *Investment Entities* at the same time.

45   This IFRS supersedes IAS 30 *Disclosures in the Financial Statements of Banks and Similar Financial Institutions*.

AASB 8
Operating Segments

(Compiled November 2015)

This compiled Standard applies to annual periods beginning on or after 1 January 2016. Earlier application is permitted for annual periods beginning on or after 1 January 2014 but before 1 January 2016. It incorporates relevant amendments made up to and including 11 November 2015.

Prepared on 7 December 2015 by the staff of the Australian Accounting Standards Board.

CONTENTS

AASB

DELETED IFRS 8 TEXT

IMPLEMENTATION GUIDANCE ON IFRS 8 (available on the AASB website)

BASIS FOR CONCLUSIONS ON IFRS 8 (available on the AASB website)

Australian Accounting Standard AASB 8 *Operating Segments* (as amended) is set out in paragraphs 1 – Aus37.2 and Appendices A and C. All the paragraphs have equal authority. Paragraphs in **bold type** state the main principles. AASB 8 is to be read in the context of other Australian Accounting Standards, including AASB 1048 *Interpretation of Standards*, which identifies the Australian Accounting Interpretations, and AASB 1057 *Application of Australian Accounting Standards*. In the absence of explicit guidance, AASB 108 *Accounting Policies, Changes in Accounting Estimates and Errors* provides a basis for selecting and applying accounting policies.

COMPARISON WITH IFRS 8

AASB 8 *Operating Segments* as amended incorporates IFRS 8 *Operating Segments* as issued and amended by the International Accounting Standards Board (IASB). Australian-specific paragraphs (which are not included in IFRS 8) are identified with the prefix "Aus". Paragraphs that apply only to not-for-profit entities begin by identifying their limited applicability.

Tier 1

For-profit entities complying with AASB 8 also comply with IFRS 8.

Not-for-profit entities' compliance with IFRS 8 will depend on whether any "Aus" paragraphs that specifically apply to not-for-profit entities provide additional guidance or contain applicable requirements that are inconsistent with IFRS 8.

Tier 2

Entities preparing general purpose financial statements under Australian Accounting Standards – Reduced Disclosure Requirements (Tier 2) will not be in compliance with IFRSs.

AASB 1053 *Application of Tiers of Australian Accounting Standards* explains the two tiers of reporting requirements.

ACCOUNTING STANDARD AASB 8

The Australian Accounting Standards Board made Accounting Standard AASB 8 *Operating Segments* under section 334 of the *Corporations Act 2001* on 7 August 2015.

This compiled version of AASB 8 applies to annual periods beginning on or after 1 January 2016. It incorporates relevant amendments contained in other AASB Standards made by the AASB up to and including 11 November 2015 (see Compilation Details).

ACCOUNTING STANDARD AASB 8
OPERATING SEGMENTS

Core principle

1   **An entity shall disclose information to enable users of its financial statements to evaluate the nature and financial effects of the business activities in which it engages and the economic environments in which it operates.**

Scope

2   This Standard shall apply to:

   (a)   the separate or individual financial statements of an entity:

   (i)   whose debt or equity instruments are traded in a public market (a domestic or foreign stock exchange or an over-the-counter market, including local and regional markets), or

   (ii)   that files, or is in the process of filing, its financial statements with a securities commission or other regulatory organisation for the purpose of issuing any class of instruments in a public market; and

   (b)   the consolidated financial statements of a group with a parent:

   (i)   whose debt or equity instruments are traded in a public market (a domestic or foreign stock exchange or an over-the-counter market, including local and regional markets), or

   (ii)   that files, or is in the process of filing, the consolidated financial statements with a securities commission or other regulatory organisation for the purpose of issuing any class of instruments in a public market.

3   If an entity that is not required to apply this Standard chooses to disclose information about segments that does not comply with this Standard, it shall not describe the information as segment information.

4   If a financial report contains both the consolidated financial statements of a parent that is within the scope of this Standard as well as the parent's separate financial statements, segment information is required only in the consolidated financial statements.

Operating segments

5   An operating segment is a component of an entity:

   (a)   that engages in business activities from which it may earn revenues and incur expenses (including revenues and expenses relating to transactions with other components of the same entity),

   (b)   whose operating results are regularly reviewed by the entity's chief operating decision maker to make decisions about resources to be allocated to the segment and assess its performance, and

   (c)   for which discrete financial information is available.

   An operating segment may engage in business activities for which it has yet to earn revenues, for example, start-up operations may be operating segments before earning revenues.

6   Not every part of an entity is necessarily an operating segment or part of an operating segment. For example, a corporate headquarters or some functional departments may not earn revenues or may earn revenues that are only incidental to the activities of the entity and would not be operating segments. For the purposes of this Standard, an entity's post-employment benefit plans are not operating segments.

7   The term 'chief operating decision maker' identifies a function, not necessarily a manager with a specific title. That function is to allocate resources to and assess the performance of the operating segments of an entity. Often the chief operating decision maker of an entity is its chief executive officer or chief operating officer but, for example, it may be a group of executive directors or others.

8   For many entities, the three characteristics of operating segments described in paragraph 5 clearly identify its operating segments. However, an entity may produce reports in which its business activities are presented in a variety of ways. If the chief operating decision maker uses more than one set of segment information, other factors may identify a single set of components as constituting an entity's operating segments,

including the nature of the business activities of each component, the existence of managers responsible for them, and information presented to the board of directors.

9   Generally, an operating segment has a segment manager who is directly accountable to and maintains regular contact with the chief operating decision maker to discuss operating activities, financial results, forecasts, or plans for the segment. The term 'segment manager' identifies a function, not necessarily a manager with a specific title. The chief operating decision maker also may be the segment manager for some operating segments. A single manager may be the segment manager for more than one operating segment. If the characteristics in paragraph 5 apply to more than one set of components of an organisation but there is only one set for which segment managers are held responsible, that set of components constitutes the operating segments.

10   The characteristics in paragraph 5 may apply to two or more overlapping sets of components for which managers are held responsible. That structure is sometimes referred to as a matrix form of organisation. For example, in some entities, some managers are responsible for different product and service lines worldwide, whereas other managers are responsible for specific geographical areas. The chief operating decision maker regularly reviews the operating results of both sets of components, and financial information is available for both. In that situation, the entity shall determine which set of components constitutes the operating segments by reference to the core principle.

Reportable segments

11   An entity shall report separately information about each operating segment that:

     (a)   has been identified in accordance with paragraphs 5–10 or results from aggregating two or more of those segments in accordance with paragraph 12, and

     (b)   exceeds the quantitative thresholds in paragraph 13.

     Paragraphs 14–19 specify other situations in which separate information about an operating segment shall be reported.

Aggregation criteria

12   Operating segments often exhibit similar long-term financial performance if they have similar economic characteristics. For example, similar long-term average gross margins for two operating segments would be expected if their economic characteristics were similar. Two or more operating segments may be aggregated into a single operating segment if aggregation is consistent with the core principle of this Standard, the segments have similar economic characteristics, and the segments are similar in each of the following respects:

     (a)   the nature of the products and services;

     (b)   the nature of the production processes;

     (c)   the type or class of customer for their products and services;

     (d)   the methods used to distribute their products or provide their services; and

     (e)   if applicable, the nature of the regulatory environment, for example, banking, insurance or public utilities.

Quantitative thresholds

13   An entity shall report separately information about an operating segment that meets any of the following quantitative thresholds:

     (a)   Its reported revenue, including both sales to external customers and intersegment sales or transfers, is 10 per cent or more of the combined revenue, internal and external, of all operating segments.

    (b)   The absolute amount of its reported profit or loss is 10 per cent or more of the greater, in absolute amount, of (i) the combined reported profit of all operating segments that did not report a loss and (ii) the combined reported loss of all operating segments that reported a loss.

    (c)   Its assets are 10 per cent or more of the combined assets of all operating segments.

    Operating segments that do not meet any of the quantitative thresholds may be considered reportable, and separately disclosed, if management believes that information about the segment would be useful to users of the financial statements.

14   An entity may combine information about operating segments that do not meet the quantitative thresholds with information about other operating segments that do not meet the quantitative thresholds to produce a reportable segment only if the operating segments have similar economic characteristics and share a majority of the aggregation criteria listed in paragraph 12.

15   If the total external revenue reported by operating segments constitutes less than 75 per cent of the entity's revenue, additional operating segments shall be identified as reportable segments (even if they do not meet the criteria in paragraph 13) until at least 75 per cent of the entity's revenue is included in reportable segments.

16   Information about other business activities and operating segments that are not reportable shall be combined and disclosed in an 'all other segments' category separately from other reconciling items in the reconciliations required by paragraph 28. The sources of the revenue included in the 'all other segments' category shall be described.

17   If management judges that an operating segment identified as a reportable segment in the immediately preceding period is of continuing significance, information about that segment shall continue to be reported separately in the current period even if it no longer meets the criteria for reportability in paragraph 13.

18   If an operating segment is identified as a reportable segment in the current period in accordance with the quantitative thresholds, segment data for a prior period presented for comparative purposes shall be restated to reflect the newly reportable segment as a separate segment, even if that segment did not satisfy the criteria for reportability in paragraph 13 in the prior period, unless the necessary information is not available and the cost to develop it would be excessive.

19   There may be a practical limit to the number of reportable segments that an entity separately discloses beyond which segment information may become too detailed. Although no precise limit has been determined, as the number of segments that are reportable in accordance with paragraphs 13–18 increases above ten, the entity should consider whether a practical limit has been reached.

Disclosure

20   An entity shall disclose information to enable users of its financial statements to evaluate the nature and financial effects of the business activities in which it engages and the economic environments in which it operates.

21   To give effect to the principle in paragraph 20, an entity shall disclose the following for each period for which a statement of comprehensive income is presented:

    (a)   general information as described in paragraph 22;

    (b)   information about reported segment profit or loss, including specified revenues and expenses included in reported segment profit or loss, segment assets, segment liabilities and the basis of measurement, as described in paragraphs 23–27; and

    (c)   reconciliations of the totals of segment revenues, reported segment profit or loss, segment assets, segment liabilities and other material segment items to corresponding entity amounts as described in paragraph 28.

Reconciliations of the amounts in the statement of financial position for reportable segments to the amounts in the entity's statement of financial position are required for each date at which a statement of financial position is presented. Information for prior periods shall be restated as described in paragraphs 29 and 30.

General information

22   An entity shall disclose the following general information:

(a)   factors used to identify the entity's reportable segments, including the basis of organisation (for example, whether management has chosen to organise the entity around differences in products and services, geographical areas, regulatory environments, or a combination of factors and whether operating segments have been aggregated);

(b)   the judgements made by management in applying the aggregation criteria in paragraph 12. This includes a brief description of the operating segments that have been aggregated in this way and the economic indicators that have been assessed in determining that the aggregated operating segments share similar economic characteristics; and

(c)   types of products and services from which each reportable segment derives its revenues.

Information about profit or loss, assets and liabilities

23   An entity shall report a measure of profit or loss for each reportable segment. An entity shall report a measure of total assets and liabilities for each reportable segment if such amounts are regularly provided to the chief operating decision maker. An entity shall also disclose the following about each reportable segment if the specified amounts are included in the measure of segment profit or loss reviewed by the chief operating decision maker, or are otherwise regularly provided to the chief operating decision maker, even if not included in that measure of segment profit or loss:

(a)   revenues from external customers;

(b)   revenues from transactions with other operating segments of the same entity;

(c)   interest revenue;

(d)   interest expense;

(e)   depreciation and amortisation;

(f)   material items of income and expense disclosed in accordance with paragraph 97 of AASB 101 *Presentation of Financial Statements;*

(g)   the entity's interest in the profit or loss of associates and joint ventures accounted for by the equity method;

(h)   income tax expense or income; and

(i)   material non-cash items other than depreciation and amortisation.

An entity shall report interest revenue separately from interest expense for each reportable segment unless a majority of the segment's revenues are from interest and the chief operating decision maker relies primarily on net interest revenue to assess the performance of the segment and make decisions about resources to be allocated to the segment. In that situation, an entity may report that segment's interest revenue net of its interest expense and disclose that it has done so.

24   An entity shall disclose the following about each reportable segment if the specified amounts are included in the measure of segment assets reviewed by the chief operating decision maker or are otherwise regularly provided to the chief operating decision maker, even if not included in the measure of segment assets:

(a)   the amount of investment in associates and joint ventures accounted for by the equity method, and

(b)   the amounts of additions to non-current assets[1] other than financial instruments, deferred tax assets, net defined benefit assets (see AASB 119 Employee Benefits) and rights arising under insurance contracts.

Measurement

25   The amount of each segment item reported shall be the measure reported to the chief operating decision maker for the purposes of making decisions about allocating resources to the segment and assessing its performance. Adjustments and eliminations made in preparing an entity's financial statements and allocations of revenues, expenses, and gains or losses shall be included in determining reported segment profit or loss only if they are included in the measure of the segment's profit or loss that is used by the chief operating decision maker. Similarly, only those assets and liabilities that are included in the measures of the segment's assets and segment's liabilities that are used by the chief operating decision maker shall be reported for that segment. If amounts are allocated to reported segment profit or loss, assets or liabilities, those amounts shall be allocated on a reasonable basis.

26   If the chief operating decision maker uses only one measure of an operating segment's profit or loss, the segment's assets or the segment's liabilities in assessing segment performance and deciding how to allocate resources, segment profit or loss, assets and liabilities shall be reported at those measures. If the chief operating decision maker uses more than one measure of an operating segment's profit or loss, the segment's assets or the segment's liabilities, the reported measures shall be those that management believes are determined in accordance with the measurement principles most consistent with those used in measuring the corresponding amounts in the entity's financial statements.

27   An entity shall provide an explanation of the measurements of segment profit or loss, segment assets and segment liabilities for each reportable segment. At a minimum, an entity shall disclose the following:

(a)   the basis of accounting for any transactions between reportable segments.

(b)   the nature of any differences between the measurements of the reportable segments' profits or losses and the entity's profit or loss before income tax expense or income and discontinued operations (if not apparent from the reconciliations described in paragraph 28). Those differences could include accounting policies and policies for allocation of centrally incurred costs that are necessary for an understanding of the reported segment information.

(c)   the nature of any differences between the measurements of the reportable segments' assets and the entity's assets (if not apparent from the reconciliations described in paragraph 28). Those differences could include accounting policies and policies for allocation of jointly used assets that are necessary for an understanding of the reported segment information.

(d)   the nature of any differences between the measurements of the reportable segments' liabilities and the entity's liabilities (if not apparent from the reconciliations described in paragraph 28). Those differences could include accounting policies and policies for allocation of jointly utilised liabilities that are necessary for an understanding of the reported segment information.

(e)   the nature of any changes from prior periods in the measurement methods used to determine reported segment profit or loss and the effect, if any, of those changes on the measure of segment profit or loss.

(f)   the nature and effect of any asymmetrical allocations to reportable segments. For example, an entity might allocate depreciation expense to a segment without allocating the related depreciable assets to that segment.

---

1   For assets classified according to a liquidity presentation, non-current assets are assets that include amounts expected to be recovered more than twelve months after the reporting period.

Reconciliations

28   An entity shall provide reconciliations of all of the following:

(a)   the total of the reportable segments' revenues to the entity's revenue.

(b)   the total of the reportable segments' measures of profit or loss to the entity's profit or loss before tax expense (tax income) and discontinued operations. However, if an entity allocates to reportable segments items such as tax expense (tax income), the entity may reconcile the total of the segments' measures of profit or loss to the entity's profit or loss after those items.

(c)   the total of the reportable segments' assets to the entity's assets if the segment assets are reported in accordance with paragraph 23.

(d)   the total of the reportable segments' liabilities to the entity's liabilities if segment liabilities are reported in accordance with paragraph 23.

(e)   the total of the reportable segments' amounts for every other material item of information disclosed to the corresponding amount for the entity.

All material reconciling items shall be separately identified and described. For example, the amount of each material adjustment needed to reconcile reportable segment profit or loss to the entity's profit or loss arising from different accounting policies shall be separately identified and described.

Restatement of previously reported information

29   If an entity changes the structure of its internal organisation in a manner that causes the composition of its reportable segments to change, the corresponding information for earlier periods, including interim periods, shall be restated unless the information is not available and the cost to develop it would be excessive. The determination of whether the information is not available and the cost to develop it would be excessive shall be made for each individual item of disclosure. Following a change in the composition of its reportable segments, an entity shall disclose whether it has restated the corresponding items of segment information for earlier periods.

30   If an entity has changed the structure of its internal organisation in a manner that causes the composition of its reportable segments to change and if segment information for earlier periods, including interim periods, is not restated to reflect the change, the entity shall disclose in the year in which the change occurs segment information for the current period on both the old basis and the new basis of segmentation, unless the necessary information is not available and the cost to develop it would be excessive.

Entity-wide disclosures

31   Paragraphs 32–34 apply to all entities subject to this Standard including those entities that have a single reportable segment. Some entities' business activities are not organised on the basis of differences in related products and services or differences in geographical areas of operations. Such an entity's reportable segments may report revenues from a broad range of essentially different products and services, or more than one of its reportable segments may provide essentially the same products and services. Similarly, an entity's reportable segments may hold assets in different geographical areas and report revenues from customers in different geographical areas, or more than one of its reportable segments may operate in the same geographical area. Information required by paragraphs 32–34 shall be provided only if it is not provided as part of the reportable segment information required by this Standard.

Information about products and services

32 An entity shall report the revenues from external customers for each product and service, or each group of similar products and services, unless the necessary information is not available and the cost to develop it would be excessive, in which case that fact shall be disclosed. The amounts of revenues reported shall be based on the financial information used to produce the entity's financial statements.

Information about geographical areas

33 An entity shall report the following geographical information, unless the necessary information is not available and the cost to develop it would be excessive:

(a) revenues from external customers (i) attributed to the entity's country of domicile and (ii) attributed to all foreign countries in total from which the entity derives revenues. If revenues from external customers attributed to an individual foreign country are material, those revenues shall be disclosed separately. An entity shall disclose the basis for attributing revenues from external customers to individual countries.

(b) non-current assets[2] other than financial instruments, deferred tax assets, post-employment benefit assets, and rights arising under insurance contracts (i) located in the entity's country of domicile and (ii) located in all foreign countries in total in which the entity holds assets. If assets in an individual foreign country are material, those assets shall be disclosed separately.

The amounts reported shall be based on the financial information that is used to produce the entity's financial statements. If the necessary information is not available and the cost to develop it would be excessive, that fact shall be disclosed. An entity may provide, in addition to the information required by this paragraph, subtotals of geographical information about groups of countries.

Information about major customers

34 An entity shall provide information about the extent of its reliance on its major customers. If revenues from transactions with a single external customer amount to 10 per cent or more of an entity's revenues, the entity shall disclose that fact, the total amount of revenues from each such customer, and the identity of the segment or segments reporting the revenues. The entity need not disclose the identity of a major customer or the amount of revenues that each segment reports from that customer. For the purposes of this Standard, a group of entities known to a reporting entity to be under common control shall be considered a single customer. However, judgement is required to assess whether a government (including government agencies and similar bodies whether local, national or international) and entities known to the reporting entity to be under the control of that government are considered a single customer. In assessing this, the reporting entity shall consider the extent of economic integration between those entities.

Transition and effective date

35 An entity shall apply this Standard in its annual financial statements for periods beginning on or after 1 January 2016. Earlier application is permitted for periods beginning on or after 1 January 2014 but before 1 January 2016. If an entity applies this Standard in its financial statements for a period before 1 January 2016, it shall disclose that fact.

---

2 For assets classified according to a liquidity presentation, non-current assets are assets that include amounts expected to be recovered more than twelve months after the reporting period.

35A   [Deleted by the AASB]

36   Segment information for prior years that is reported as comparative information
           for the initial year of application (including application of the amendment to
           paragraph 23 made in May 2009 in the previous version of this Standard) shall
           be restated to conform to the requirements of this Standard, unless the necessary
           information is not available and the cost to develop it would be excessive.

36A–36B   [Deleted by the AASB]

36C   AASB 2014-1 *Amendments to Australian Accounting Standards*, issued in June
           2014, amended paragraphs 22 and 28 in the previous version of this Standard.
           An entity shall apply those amendments for annual periods beginning on or
           after 1 July 2014. Earlier application is permitted. If an entity applies those
           amendments for an earlier period it shall disclose that fact.

Withdrawal of IAS 14

37   [Deleted by the AASB]

Commencement of the legislative instrument

Aus37.1   For legal purposes, this legislative instrument commences on 31 December
           2015.

Withdrawal of AASB pronouncements

Aus37.2   This Standard repeals AASB 8 *Operating Segments* issued in February 2007.
           Despite the repeal, after the time this Standard starts to apply under section 334
           of the Corporations Act (either generally or in relation to an individual entity),
           the repealed Standard continues to apply in relation to any period ending before
           that time as if the repeal had not occurred.

           [Note: When this Standard applies under section 334 of the Corporations
           Act (either generally or in relation to an individual entity), it supersedes the
           application of the repealed Standard.]

APPENDIX A
DEFINED TERM

This appendix is an integral part of the Standard.

operating segment	An operating segment is a component of an entity:
	(a) that engages in business activities from which it may earn revenues and incur expenses (including revenues and expenses relating to transactions with other components of the same entity),
	(b) whose operating results are regularly reviewed by the entity's chief operating decision maker to make decisions about resources to be allocated to the segment and assess its performance, and
	(c) for which discrete financial information is available.

APPENDIX C
AUSTRALIAN REDUCED DISCLOSURE
REQUREMENTS

This appendix is an integral part of the Standard.

AusC1 Paragraphs 5–34 do not apply to entities preparing general purpose financial statements under Australian Accounting Standards – Reduced Disclosure Requirements and are identified in this Standard by shading of the relevant text. This Standard applies to Tier 1 entities preparing general purpose financial statements in accordance with Australian Accounting Standards. Entities applying Australian Accounting Standards – Reduced Disclosure Requirements may elect to comply with some or all of the excluded requirements.

COMPILATION DETAILS

Accounting Standard AASB 8 *Operating Segments* as amended

Compilation details are not part of AASB 8.

This compiled Standard applies to annual periods beginning on or after 1 January 2016. It takes into account amendments up to and including 11 November 2015 and was prepared on 7 December 2015 by the staff of the Australian Accounting Standards Board (AASB).

This compilation is not a separate Accounting Standard made by the AASB. Instead, it is a representation of AASB 8 (August 2015) as amended by other Accounting Standards, which are listed in the Table below.

Table of Standards

Standard	Date made	FRLI identifier	Commencement date	Effective date *(annual periods ... on or after ...)*	Application, saving or transitional provisions
AASB 8	7 Aug 2015	F2015L01606	31 Dec 2015	*(beginning)* 1 Jan 2016	see (a) below
AASB 2015-9	11 Nov 2015	F2015L01832	31 Dec 2015	*(beginning)* 1 Jan 2016	see (b) below

(a) Entities may elect to apply this Standard to annual periods beginning on or after 1 January 2014 but before 1 January 2016.

(b) Entities may elect to apply this Standard to annual periods beginning before 1 January 2016.

Table of amendments

Paragraph affected	How affected	By ... [paragraph]
2	added	AASB 2015-9 [7]

DELETED IFRS 8 TEXT

Deleted IFRS 8 text is not part of AASB 8.

35A Paragraph 23 was amended by *Improvements to IFRSs* issued in April 2009. An entity shall apply that amendment for annual periods beginning on or after 1 January 2010.

Earlier application is permitted. If an entity applies the amendment for an earlier period it shall disclose that fact.

36A   IAS 1 (as revised in 2007) amended the terminology used throughout IFRSs. In addition it amended paragraph 23(f). An entity shall apply those amendments for annual periods beginning on or after 1 January 2009. If an entity applies IAS 1 (revised 2007) for an earlier period, the amendments shall be applied for that earlier period.

36B   IAS 24 *Related Party Disclosures* (as revised in 2009) amended paragraph 34 for annual periods beginning on or after 1 January 2011. If an entity applies IAS 24 (revised 2009) for an earlier period, it shall apply the amendment to paragraph 34 for that earlier period.

37   This IFRS supersedes IAS 14 *Segment Reporting*.

AASB 9
Financial Instruments
(Issued December 2014)

This note is not part of Accounting Standard AASB 9.

The following unincorporated amendments are not included in this Standard.

- AASB 2017-6 *Amendments to Australian Accounting Standards — Prepayment Features with Negative Compensation.* This Standard makes amendments to AASB 9 *Financial Instruments* arising from the issuance of IFRS *Prepayment Features with Negative Compensation* (Amendments to IFRS 9) by the IASB in October 2017. This Standard applies to annual periods beginning on or after 1 January 2019, but earlier application is permitted.

- AASB 17 *Insurance Contracts* — Appendix D sets out the amendments to other Standards that are a consequence of the AASB issuing AASB 17 *Insurance Contracts.* This Standard is applicable from 1 January 2021. Earlier application is permitted, but entities must apply AASB 9 *Financial Instruments* and AASB 15 *Revenue from Contracts with Customers* first.

- AASB 2016-8 *Amendments to Australian Accounting Standards — Australian Implementation Guidance for Not-for-Profit Entities.* This standard makes amendments to AASB 9 *Financial Instruments* and AASB 15 *Revenue from Contracts with Customers.* This Standard is applicable from 1 January 2019, but earlier application is permitted provided AASB 1058 is also applied to the same period. The amendments arise from the issuance of AASB 1058 *Income of Not-for-Profit Entities.*

- AASB 16 *Leases* — Appendix D sets out the amendments to other Standards that are a consequence of the AASB issuing this Standard. It is applicable from 1 January 2019. Earlier application is permitted, but entities must apply AASB 15 *Revenue from Contracts with Customers* before applying this Standard.

Entities early-adopting any amendments with later application dates will need to refer to the amending Standards that have not yet been incorporated into compilations. The abovementioned unincorporated amendments may be located on the AASB website at www.aasb.gov.au or on the Federal Register of Legislation website at www.legislation.gov.au.

CONTENTS

Australian Accounting Standard AASB 9 *Financial Instruments* is set out in paragraphs 1.1 – 7.2.28 and Appendices A and B. All the paragraphs have equal authority. Paragraphs in **bold type** state the main principles. Terms defined in Appendix A are in *italics* the first time they appear in the Standard. AASB 9 is to be read in the context of other Australian Accounting Standards, including AASB 1048 *Interpretation of Standards*, which identifies the Australian Accounting Interpretations. In the absence of explicit guidance, AASB 108 *Accounting Policies, Changes in Accounting Estimates and Errors* provides a basis for selecting and applying accounting policies.

PREFACE

Introduction

The Australian Accounting Standards Board (AASB) makes Australian Accounting Standards, including Interpretations, to be applied by:

(a) entities required by the *Corporations Act 2001* to prepare financial reports;

(b) governments in preparing financial statements for the whole of government and the General Government Sector (GGS); and

(c) entities in the private or public for-profit or not-for-profit sectors that are reporting entities or that prepare general purpose financial statements.

AASB 1053 *Application of Tiers of Australian Accounting Standards* establishes a differential reporting framework consisting of two tiers of reporting requirements for preparing general purpose financial statements:

(a)   Tier 1: Australian Accounting Standards; and

(b)   Tier 2: Australian Accounting Standards – Reduced Disclosure Requirements.

Tier 1 requirements incorporate International Financial Reporting Standards (IFRSs), including Interpretations, issued by the International Accounting Standards Board (IASB), with the addition of paragraphs on the applicability of each Standard in the Australian environment.

Publicly accountable for-profit private sector entities are required to adopt Tier 1 requirements, and therefore are required to comply with IFRSs. Furthermore, other for-profit private sector entities complying with Tier 1 requirements will simultaneously comply with IFRSs. Some other entities complying with Tier 1 requirements will also simultaneously comply with IFRSs.

Tier 2 requirements comprise the recognition and measurement requirements of Tier 1 but substantially reduced disclosure requirements in comparison with Tier 1.

Australian Accounting Standards also include requirements that are specific to Australian entities. These requirements may be located in Australian Accounting Standards that incorporate IFRSs or in other Australian Accounting Standards. In most instances, these requirements are either restricted to the not-for-profit or public sectors or include additional disclosures that address domestic, regulatory or other issues. These requirements do not prevent publicly accountable for-profit private sector entities from complying with IFRSs. In developing requirements for public sector entities, the AASB considers the requirements of International Public Sector Accounting Standards (IPSASs), as issued by the International Public Sector Accounting Standards Board (IPSASB) of the International Federation of Accountants.

COMPARISON WITH IFRS 9

AASB 9 *Financial Instruments* incorporates IFRS 9 *Financial Instruments* issued by the International Accounting Standards Board (IASB). Paragraphs that have been added to this Standard (and do not appear in the text of IFRS 9) are identified with the prefix "Aus", followed by the number of the preceding IASB paragraph and decimal numbering.

Entities that comply with AASB 9 will simultaneously be in compliance with IFRS 9.

ACCOUNTING STANDARD AASB 9

The Australian Accounting Standards Board makes Accounting Standard AASB 9 *Financial Instruments* under section 334 of the *Corporations Act 2001*.

Kris Peach

Dated 17 December 2014   Chair – AASB

ACCOUNTING STANDARD AASB 9

FINANCIAL INSTRUMENTS

Chapter 1 Objective and application

1.1   The objective of this Standard is to establish principles for the financial reporting of *financial assets* and *financial liabilities* that will present relevant and useful information to users of financial statements for their assessment of the amounts, timing and uncertainty of an entity's future cash flows.

Aus1.1   This Standard applies to:

    (a)   each entity that is required to prepare financial reports in accordance with Part 2M.3 of the Corporations Act and that is a reporting entity;

    (b)   general purpose financial statements of each other reporting entity; and

    (c)   financial statements that are, or are held out to be, general purpose financial statements.

Aus1.2   This Standard applies to annual reporting periods beginning on or after 1 January 2018.

Aus1.3   This Standard may be applied to reporting periods beginning after 24 July 2014 but before 1 January 2018. However, except as specified by paragraph 7.1.2, if an entity elects to apply this Standard early, it must disclose that fact and apply all of the requirements in this Standard at the same time (but see also paragraphs Aus1.4 and 7.2.21 of this Standard). It shall also, at the same time, apply the amendments in AASB 2010-7 *Amendments to Australian Accounting Standards arising from AASB 9 (December 2010) (as amended)*, Part E of AASB 2014-1 *Amendments to Australian Accounting Standards* and AASB 2014-7 *Amendments to Australian Accounting Standards arising from AASB 9 (December 2014)*.

Aus1.4   When applied or operative, this Standard supersedes AASB 9 *Financial Instruments* (December 2009, as amended) and AASB 9 *Financial Instruments* (December 2010, as amended). However, for annual reporting periods ending on or after 31 December 2009 that begin before 1 January 2018, an entity may elect to apply AASB 9 (December 2009) or AASB 9 (December 2010) instead of applying this Standard if, and only if, the entity's relevant date of initial application is before 1 February 2015, and except that AASB 9 (December 2010) may be applied early only as set out in that Standard.

Aus1.5   When applied or operative, this Standard supersedes Interpretation 9 *Reassessment of Embedded Derivatives*, as identified in AASB 1048 *Interpretation of Standards*. The requirements added to AASB 9 in December 2010 incorporate the requirements previously set out in paragraphs 5 and 7 of Interpretation 9. As a consequential amendment, AASB 1 *First-time Adoption of Australian Accounting Standards* incorporates the requirements previously set out in paragraph 8 of Interpretation 9.

Commencement

Aus1.6   This Standard commences on the day this Standard is made by the Australian Accounting Standards Board.

Chapter 2 Scope

2.1   This Standard shall be applied by all entities to all types of financial instruments except:

    (a)   those interests in subsidiaries, associates and joint ventures that are accounted for in accordance with AASB 10 *Consolidated Financial Statements*, AASB 127 *Separate Financial Statements* or AASB 128 *Investments in Associates and Joint Ventures*. However, in some cases, AASB 10, AASB 127 or AASB 128 require or permit an entity to account for an interest in a subsidiary, associate or joint venture in accordance with some or all of the requirements of this Standard. Entities shall also apply this Standard to derivatives on an interest in a subsidiary, associate or joint venture unless the derivative meets the definition of an equity instrument of the entity in AASB 132 *Financial Instruments: Presentation*.

    (b)   rights and obligations under leases to which AASB 117 *Leases* applies. However:

AASB

      (i)   lease receivables recognised by a lessor are subject to the derecognition and impairment requirements of this Standard;

      (ii)   finance lease payables recognised by a lessee are subject to the derecognition requirements of this Standard; and

      (iii) derivatives that are embedded in leases are subject to the embedded derivatives requirements of this Standard.

(c)   employers' rights and obligations under employee benefit plans, to which AASB 119 *Employee Benefits* applies.

(d)   financial instruments issued by the entity that meet the definition of an equity instrument in AASB 132 (including options and warrants) or that are required to be classified as an equity instrument in accordance with paragraphs 16A and 16B or paragraphs 16C and 16D of AASB 132. However, the holder of such equity instruments shall apply this Standard to those instruments, unless they meet the exception in (a).

(e)   rights and obligations arising under (i) an insurance contract as defined in AASB 4 *Insurance Contracts*, other than an issuer's rights and obligations arising under an insurance contract that meets the definition of a financial guarantee contract, or (ii) a contract that is within the scope of AASB 4 because it contains a discretionary participation feature. However, this Standard applies to a derivative that is embedded in a contract within the scope of AASB 4 if the derivative is not itself a contract within the scope of AASB 4. Moreover, if an issuer of financial guarantee contracts has previously asserted explicitly that it regards such contracts as insurance contracts and has used accounting that is applicable to insurance contracts, the issuer may elect to apply either this Standard or AASB 1023 *General Insurance Contracts* to such financial guarantee contracts (see paragraphs B2.5–B2.6). The issuer may make that election contract by contract, but the election for each contract is irrevocable.

(f)   any forward contract between an acquirer and a selling shareholder to buy or sell an acquiree that will result in a business combination within the scope of AASB 3 *Business Combinations* at a future acquisition date. The term of the forward contract should not exceed a reasonable period normally necessary to obtain any required approvals and to complete the transaction.

(g)   loan commitments other than those loan commitments described in paragraph 2.3. However, an issuer of loan commitments shall apply the impairment requirements of this Standard to loan commitments that are not otherwise within the scope of this Standard. Also, all loan commitments are subject to the derecognition requirements of this Standard.

(h)   financial instruments, contracts and obligations under share-based payment transactions to which AASB 2 *Share-based Payment* applies, except for contracts within the scope of paragraphs 2.4–2.7 of this Standard to which this Standard applies.

(i)   rights to payments to reimburse the entity for expenditure that it is required to make to settle a liability that it recognises as a provision in accordance with AASB 137 *Provisions, Contingent Liabilities and Contingent Assets*, or for which, in an earlier period, it recognised a provision in accordance with AASB 137.

(j)   rights and obligations within the scope of AASB 15 *Revenue from Contracts with Customers* that are financial instruments, except for those that AASB 15 specifies are accounted for in accordance with this Standard.

2.2   The impairment requirements of this Standard shall be applied to those rights that AASB 15 specifies are accounted for in accordance with this Standard for the purposes of recognising impairment gains or losses.

2.3 The following loan commitments are within the scope of this Standard:

(a) loan commitments that the entity designates as financial liabilities at fair value through profit or loss (see paragraph 4.2.2). An entity that has a past practice of selling the assets resulting from its loan commitments shortly after origination shall apply this Standard to all its loan commitments in the same class.

(b) loan commitments that can be settled net in cash or by delivering or issuing another financial instrument. These loan commitments are derivatives. A loan commitment is not regarded as settled net merely because the loan is paid out in instalments (for example, a mortgage construction loan that is paid out in instalments in line with the progress of construction).

(c) commitments to provide a loan at a below-market interest rate (see paragraph 4.2.1(d)).

2.4 This Standard shall be applied to those contracts to buy or sell a non-financial item that can be settled net in cash or another financial instrument, or by exchanging financial instruments, as if the contracts were financial instruments, with the exception of contracts that were entered into and continue to be held for the purpose of the receipt or delivery of a non-financial item in accordance with the entity's expected purchase, sale or usage requirements. However, this Standard shall be applied to those contracts that an entity designates as measured at fair value through profit or loss in accordance with paragraph 2.5.

2.5 A contract to buy or sell a non-financial item that can be settled net in cash or another financial instrument, or by exchanging financial instruments, as if the contract was a financial instrument, may be irrevocably designated as measured at fair value through profit or loss even if it was entered into for the purpose of the receipt or delivery of a non-financial item in accordance with the entity's expected purchase, sale or usage requirements. This designation is available only at inception of the contract and only if it eliminates or significantly reduces a recognition inconsistency (sometimes referred to as an 'accounting mismatch') that would otherwise arise from not recognising that contract because it is excluded from the scope of this Standard (see paragraph 2.4).

2.6 There are various ways in which a contract to buy or sell a non-financial item can be settled net in cash or another financial instrument or by exchanging financial instruments. These include:

(a) when the terms of the contract permit either party to settle it net in cash or another financial instrument or by exchanging financial instruments;

(b) when the ability to settle net in cash or another financial instrument, or by exchanging financial instruments, is not explicit in the terms of the contract, but the entity has a practice of settling similar contracts net in cash or another financial instrument or by exchanging financial instruments (whether with the counterparty, by entering into offsetting contracts or by selling the contract before its exercise or lapse);

(c) when, for similar contracts, the entity has a practice of taking delivery of the underlying and selling it within a short period after delivery for the purpose of generating a profit from short-term fluctuations in price or dealer's margin; and

(d) when the non-financial item that is the subject of the contract is readily convertible to cash.

A contract to which (b) or (c) applies is not entered into for the purpose of the receipt or delivery of the non-financial item in accordance with the entity's expected purchase, sale or usage requirements and, accordingly, is within the scope of this Standard. Other contracts to which paragraph 2.4 applies are evaluated to determine whether they were entered into and continue to be held for the purpose of the receipt or delivery of the non-financial item in accordance with the entity's expected purchase, sale or usage requirements and, accordingly, whether they are within the scope of this Standard.

2.7   A written option to buy or sell a non-financial item that can be settled net in cash or another financial instrument, or by exchanging financial instruments, in accordance with paragraph 2.6(a) or 2.6(d) is within the scope of this Standard. Such a contract cannot be entered into for the purpose of the receipt or delivery of the non-financial item in accordance with the entity's expected purchase, sale or usage requirements.

Chapter 3 Recognition and derecognition

3.1 Initial recognition

3.1.1 **An entity shall recognise a financial asset or a financial liability in its statement of financial position when, and only when, the entity becomes party to the contractual provisions of the instrument (see paragraphs B3.1.1 and B3.1.2). When an entity first recognises a financial asset, it shall classify it in accordance with paragraphs 4.1.1–4.1.5 and measure it in accordance with paragraphs 5.1.1–5.1.3. When an entity first recognises a financial liability, it shall classify it in accordance with paragraphs 4.2.1 and 4.2.2 and measure it in accordance with paragraph 5.1.1.**

Regular way purchase or sale of financial assets

3.1.2 **A** *regular way purchase or sale* **of financial assets shall be recognised and derecognised, as applicable, using trade date accounting or settlement date accounting (see paragraphs B3.1.3–B3.1.6).**

3.2 Derecognition of financial assets

3.2.1 In consolidated financial statements, paragraphs 3.2.2–3.2.9, B3.1.1, B3.1.2 and B3.2.1–B3.2.17 are applied at a consolidated level. Hence, an entity first consolidates all subsidiaries in accordance with AASB 10 and then applies those paragraphs to the resulting group.

3.2.2 **Before evaluating whether, and to what extent,** *derecognition* **is appropriate under paragraphs 3.2.3–3.2.9, an entity determines whether those paragraphs should be applied to a part of a financial asset (or a part of a group of similar financial assets) or a financial asset (or a group of similar financial assets) in its entirety, as follows.**

(a)   **Paragraphs 3.2.3–3.2.9 are applied to a part of a financial asset (or a part of a group of similar financial assets) if, and only if, the part being considered for derecognition meets one of the following three conditions.**

(i)   **The part comprises only specifically identified cash flows from a financial asset (or a group of similar financial assets). For example, when an entity enters into an interest rate strip whereby the counterparty obtains the right to the interest cash flows, but not the principal cash flows from a debt instrument, paragraphs 3.2.3–3.2.9 are applied to the interest cash flows.**

(ii)   **The part comprises only a fully proportionate (pro rata) share of the cash flows from a financial asset (or a group of similar financial assets). For example, when an entity enters into an arrangement whereby the counterparty obtains the rights to a 90 per cent share of all cash flows of a debt instrument, paragraphs 3.2.3–3.2.9 are applied to 90 per cent of those cash flows. If there is more than one counterparty, each counterparty is not required to have a proportionate share of the cash flows provided that the transferring entity has a fully proportionate share.**

(iii)   **The part comprises only a fully proportionate (pro rata) share of specifically identified cash flows from a financial asset (or a group of similar financial assets). For example, when an entity enters into an arrangement whereby the counterparty obtains the rights to a 90 per cent share of interest cash flows from a financial asset,** paragraphs 3.2.3–3.2.9 are applied to 90 per cent of those interest cash flows. If there is more than one counterparty, each counterparty is not required to have a proportionate share of the specifically identified cash flows provided that the transferring entity has a fully proportionate share.

(b)   In all other cases, paragraphs 3.2.3–3.2.9 are applied to the financial asset in its entirety (or to the group of similar financial assets in their entirety). For example, when an entity transfers (i) the rights to the first or the last 90 per cent of cash collections from a financial asset (or a group of financial assets), or (ii) the rights to 90 per cent of the cash flows from a group of receivables, but provides a guarantee to compensate the buyer for any credit losses up to 8 per cent of the principal amount of the receivables, paragraphs 3.2.3–3.2.9 are applied to the financial asset (or a group of similar financial assets) in its entirety.

In paragraphs 3.2.3–3.2.12, the term 'financial asset' refers to either a part of a financial asset (or a part of a group of similar financial assets) as identified in (a) above or, otherwise, a financial asset (or a group of similar financial assets) in its entirety.

3.2.3 An entity shall derecognise a financial asset when, and only when:

(a)   the contractual rights to the cash flows from the financial asset expire, or

(b)   it transfers the financial asset as set out in paragraphs 3.2.4 and 3.2.5 and the transfer qualifies for derecognition in accordance with paragraph 3.2.6.

(See paragraph 3.1.2 for regular way sales of financial assets.)

3.2.4 An entity transfers a financial asset if, and only if, it either:

(a)   transfers the contractual rights to receive the cash flows of the financial asset, or

(b)   retains the contractual rights to receive the cash flows of the financial asset, but assumes a contractual obligation to pay the cash flows to one or more recipients in an arrangement that meets the conditions in paragraph 3.2.5.

3.2.5 When an entity retains the contractual rights to receive the cash flows of a financial asset (the 'original asset'), but assumes a contractual obligation to pay those cash flows to one or more entities (the 'eventual recipients'), the entity treats the transaction as a transfer of a financial asset if, and only if, all of the following three conditions are met.

(a)   The entity has no obligation to pay amounts to the eventual recipients unless it collects equivalent amounts from the original asset. Short-term advances by the entity with the right of full recovery of the amount lent plus accrued interest at market rates do not violate this condition.

(b)   The entity is prohibited by the terms of the transfer contract from selling or pledging the original asset other than as security to the eventual recipients for the obligation to pay them cash flows.

(c)   The entity has an obligation to remit any cash flows it collects on behalf of the eventual recipients without material delay. In addition, the entity is not entitled to reinvest such cash flows, except for investments in cash or cash equivalents (as defined in AASB 107 *Statement of Cash Flows*) during the short settlement period from the collection date to the date of required remittance to the eventual recipients, and interest earned on such investments is passed to the eventual recipients.

3.2.6 When an entity transfers a financial asset (see paragraph 3.2.4), it shall evaluate the extent to which it retains the risks and rewards of ownership of the financial asset. In this case:

(a)   if the entity transfers substantially all the risks and rewards of ownership of the financial asset, the entity shall derecognise the financial asset and

AASB

recognise separately as assets or liabilities any rights and obligations created or retained in the transfer.

(b)   if the entity retains substantially all the risks and rewards of ownership of the financial asset, the entity shall continue to recognise the financial asset.

(c)   if the entity neither transfers nor retains substantially all the risks and rewards of ownership of the financial asset, the entity shall determine whether it has retained control of the financial asset. In this case:

   (i)   if the entity has not retained control, it shall derecognise the financial asset and recognise separately as assets or liabilities any rights and obligations created or retained in the transfer.

   (ii)   if the entity has retained control, it shall continue to recognise the financial asset to the extent of its continuing involvement in the financial asset (see paragraph 3.2.16).

3.2.7   The transfer of risks and rewards (see paragraph 3.2.6) is evaluated by comparing the entity's exposure, before and after the transfer, with the variability in the amounts and timing of the net cash flows of the transferred asset. An entity has retained substantially all the risks and rewards of ownership of a financial asset if its exposure to the variability in the present value of the future net cash flows from the financial asset does not change significantly as a result of the transfer (eg because the entity has sold a financial asset subject to an agreement to buy it back at a fixed price or the sale price plus a lender's return). An entity has transferred substantially all the risks and rewards of ownership of a financial asset if its exposure to such variability is no longer significant in relation to the total variability in the present value of the future net cash flows associated with the financial asset (eg because the entity has sold a financial asset subject only to an option to buy it back at its *fair value* at the time of repurchase or has transferred a fully proportionate share of the cash flows from a larger financial asset in an arrangement, such as a loan sub-participation, that meets the conditions in paragraph 3.2.5).

3.2.8   Often it will be obvious whether the entity has transferred or retained substantially all risks and rewards of ownership and there will be no need to perform any computations. In other cases, it will be necessary to compute and compare the entity's exposure to the variability in the present value of the future net cash flows before and after the transfer. The computation and comparison are made using as the discount rate an appropriate current market interest rate. All reasonably possible variability in net cash flows is considered, with greater weight being given to those outcomes that are more likely to occur.

3.2.9   Whether the entity has retained control (see paragraph 3.2.6(c)) of the transferred asset depends on the transferee's ability to sell the asset. If the transferee has the practical ability to sell the asset in its entirety to an unrelated third party and is able to exercise that ability unilaterally and without needing to impose additional restrictions on the transfer, the entity has not retained control. In all other cases, the entity has retained control.

Transfers that qualify for derecognition

3.2.10 If an entity transfers a financial asset in a transfer that qualifies for derecognition in its entirety and retains the right to service the financial asset for a fee, it shall recognise either a servicing asset or a servicing liability for that servicing contract. If the fee to be received is not expected to compensate the entity adequately for performing the servicing, a servicing liability for the servicing obligation shall be recognised at its fair value. If the fee to be received is expected to be more than adequate compensation for the servicing, a servicing asset shall be recognised for the servicing right at an amount determined on the basis of an allocation of the carrying amount of the larger financial asset in accordance with paragraph 3.2.13.

3.2.11 If, as a result of a transfer, a financial asset is derecognised in its entirety but the transfer results in the entity obtaining a new financial asset or assuming a new financial liability, or a servicing liability, the entity shall recognise the new financial asset, financial liability or servicing liability at fair value.

3.2.12 On derecognition of a financial asset in its entirety, the difference between:

(a) the carrying amount (measured at the date of derecognition) and

(b) the consideration received (including any new asset obtained less any new liability assumed)

shall be recognised in profit or loss.

3.2.13 If the transferred asset is part of a larger financial asset (eg when an entity transfers interest cash flows that are part of a debt instrument, see paragraph 3.2.2(a)) and the part transferred qualifies for derecognition in its entirety, the previous carrying amount of the larger financial asset shall be allocated between the part that continues to be recognised and the part that is derecognised, on the basis of the relative fair values of those parts on the date of the transfer. For this purpose, a retained servicing asset shall be treated as a part that continues to be recognised. The difference between:

(a) the carrying amount (measured at the date of derecognition) allocated to the part derecognised and

(b) the consideration received for the part derecognised (including any new asset obtained less any new liability assumed)

shall be recognised in profit or loss.

3.2.14 When an entity allocates the previous carrying amount of a larger financial asset between the part that continues to be recognised and the part that is derecognised, the fair value of the part that continues to be recognised needs to be measured. When the entity has a history of selling parts similar to the part that continues to be recognised or other market transactions exist for such parts, recent prices of actual transactions provide the best estimate of its fair value. When there are no price quotes or recent market transactions to support the fair value of the part that continues to be recognised, the best estimate of the fair value is the difference between the fair value of the larger financial asset as a whole and the consideration received from the transferee for the part that is derecognised.

Transfers that do not qualify for derecognition

3.2.15 If a transfer does not result in derecognition because the entity has retained substantially all the risks and rewards of ownership of the transferred asset, the entity shall continue to recognise the transferred asset in its entirety and shall recognise a financial liability for the consideration received. In subsequent periods, the entity shall recognise any income on the transferred asset and any expense incurred on the financial liability.

Continuing involvement in transferred assets

3.2.16 If an entity neither transfers nor retains substantially all the risks and rewards of ownership of a transferred asset, and retains control of the transferred asset, the entity continues to recognise the transferred asset to the extent of its continuing involvement. The extent of the entity's continuing involvement in the transferred asset is the extent to which it is exposed to changes in the value of the transferred asset. For example:

(a) When the entity's continuing involvement takes the form of guaranteeing the transferred asset, the extent of the entity's continuing involvement is the lower of (i) the amount of the asset and (ii) the maximum amount of the consideration received that the entity could be required to repay ('the guarantee amount').

(b) When the entity's continuing involvement takes the form of a written or purchased option (or both) on the transferred asset, the extent of the entity's continuing involvement is the amount of the transferred asset that the entity may repurchase. However, in the case of a written put option on an asset that is measured at fair value, the extent of the entity's continuing involvement is limited to the lower of the fair value of the transferred asset and the option exercise price (see paragraph B3.2.13).

(c) When the entity's continuing involvement takes the form of a cash-settled option or similar provision on the transferred asset, the extent of the entity's continuing involvement is measured in the same way as that which results from non-cash settled options as set out in (b) above.

3.2.17 When an entity continues to recognise an asset to the extent of its continuing involvement, the entity also recognises an associated liability. Despite the other measurement requirements in this Standard, the transferred asset and the associated liability are measured on a basis that reflects the rights and obligations that the entity has retained. The associated liability is measured in such a way that the net carrying amount of the transferred asset and the associated liability is:

(a) the amortised cost of the rights and obligations retained by the entity, if the transferred asset is measured at amortised cost, or

(b) equal to the fair value of the rights and obligations retained by the entity when measured on a stand-alone basis, if the transferred asset is measured at fair value.

3.2.18 The entity shall continue to recognise any income arising on the transferred asset to the extent of its continuing involvement and shall recognise any expense incurred on the associated liability.

3.2.19 For the purpose of subsequent measurement, recognised changes in the fair value of the transferred asset and the associated liability are accounted for consistently with each other in accordance with paragraph 5.7.1, and shall not be offset.

3.2.20 If an entity's continuing involvement is in only a part of a financial asset (eg when an entity retains an option to repurchase part of a transferred asset, or retains a residual interest that does not result in the retention of substantially all the risks and rewards of ownership and the entity retains control), the entity allocates the previous carrying amount of the financial asset between the part it continues to recognise under continuing involvement, and the part it no longer recognises on the basis of the relative fair values of those parts on the date of the transfer. For this purpose, the requirements of paragraph 3.2.14 apply. The difference between:

(a) the carrying amount (measured at the date of derecognition) allocated to the part that is no longer recognised and

(b) the consideration received for the part no longer recognised

shall be recognised in profit or loss.

3.2.21 If the transferred asset is measured at amortised cost, the option in this Standard to designate a financial liability as at fair value through profit or loss is not applicable to the associated liability.

All transfers

3.2.22 If a transferred asset continues to be recognised, the asset and the associated liability shall not be offset. Similarly, the entity shall not offset any income arising from the transferred asset with any expense incurred on the associated liability (see paragraph 42 of AASB 132).

3.2.23 If a transferor provides non-cash collateral (such as debt or equity instruments) to the transferee, the accounting for the collateral by the transferor and the transferee depends on whether the transferee has the right to sell or repledge the collateral and on whether the transferor has defaulted. The transferor and transferee shall account for the collateral as follows:

(a) If the transferee has the right by contract or custom to sell or repledge the collateral, then the transferor shall reclassify that asset in its statement of financial position (eg as a loaned asset, pledged equity instruments or repurchase receivable) separately from other assets.

(b) If the transferee sells collateral pledged to it, it shall recognise the proceeds from the sale and a liability measured at fair value for its obligation to return the collateral.

(c) If the transferor defaults under the terms of the contract and is no longer entitled to redeem the collateral, it shall derecognise the collateral, and the transferee shall recognise the collateral as its asset initially measured at fair value or, if it has already sold the collateral, derecognise its obligation to return the collateral.

(d) Except as provided in (c), the transferor shall continue to carry the collateral as its asset, and the transferee shall not recognise the collateral as an asset.

3.3 Derecognition of financial liabilities

3.3.1 An entity shall remove a financial liability (or a part of a financial liability) from its statement of financial position when, and only when, it is extinguished – ie when the obligation specified in the contract is discharged or cancelled or expires.

3.3.2 An exchange between an existing borrower and lender of debt instruments with substantially different terms shall be accounted for as an extinguishment of the original financial liability and the recognition of a new financial liability. Similarly, a substantial modification of the terms of an existing financial liability or a part of it (whether or not attributable to the financial difficulty of the debtor) shall be accounted for as an extinguishment of the original financial liability and the recognition of a new financial liability.

3.3.3 The difference between the carrying amount of a financial liability (or part of a financial liability) extinguished or transferred to another party and the consideration paid, including any non-cash assets transferred or liabilities assumed, shall be recognised in profit or loss.

3.3.4 If an entity repurchases a part of a financial liability, the entity shall allocate the previous carrying amount of the financial liability between the part that continues to be recognised and the part that is derecognised based on the relative fair values of those parts on the date of the repurchase. The difference between (a) the carrying amount allocated to the part derecognised and (b) the consideration paid, including any non-cash assets transferred or liabilities assumed, for the part derecognised shall be recognised in profit or loss.

Chapter 4 Classification

4.1 Classification of financial assets

4.1.1 Unless paragraph 4.1.5 applies, an entity shall classify financial assets as subsequently measured at amortised cost, fair value through other comprehensive income or fair value through profit or loss on the basis of both:

(a) the entity's business model for managing the financial assets and

(b) the contractual cash flow characteristics of the financial asset.

4.1.2 A financial asset shall be measured at amortised cost if both of the following conditions are met:

(a) the financial asset is held within a business model whose objective is to hold financial assets in order to collect contractual cash flows and

(b)   the contractual terms of the financial asset give rise on specified dates to cash flows that are solely payments of principal and interest on the principal amount outstanding.

Paragraphs B4.1.1–B4.1.26 provide guidance on how to apply these conditions.

4.1.2A   A financial asset shall be measured at fair value through other comprehensive income if both of the following conditions are met:

(a)   the financial asset is held within a business model whose objective is achieved by both collecting contractual cash flows and selling financial assets and

(b)   the contractual terms of the financial asset give rise on specified dates to cash flows that are solely payments of principal and interest on the principal amount outstanding.

Paragraphs B4.1.1–B4.1.26 provide guidance on how to apply these conditions.

4.1.3   For the purpose of applying paragraphs 4.1.2(b) and 4.1.2A(b):

(a)   principal is the fair value of the financial asset at initial recognition. Paragraph B4.1.7B provides additional guidance on the meaning of principal.

(b)   interest consists of consideration for the time value of money, for the credit risk associated with the principal amount outstanding during a particular period of time and for other basic lending risks and costs, as well as a profit margin. Paragraphs B4.1.7A and B4.1.9A–B4.1.9E provide additional guidance on the meaning of interest, including the meaning of the time value of money.

4.1.4   A financial asset shall be measured at fair value through profit or loss unless it is measured at amortised cost in accordance with paragraph 4.1.2 or at fair value through other comprehensive income in accordance with paragraph 4.1.2A. However an entity may make an irrevocable election at initial recognition for particular investments in *equity instruments* that would otherwise be measured at fair value through profit or loss to present subsequent changes in fair value in other comprehensive income (see paragraphs 5.7.5–5.7.6).

Option to designate a financial asset at fair value through profit or loss

4.1.5   Despite paragraphs 4.1.1–4.1.4, an entity may, at initial recognition, irrevocably designate a financial asset as measured at fair value through profit or loss if doing so eliminates or significantly reduces a measurement or recognition inconsistency (sometimes referred to as an 'accounting mismatch') that would otherwise arise from measuring assets or liabilities or recognising the gains and losses on them on different bases (see paragraphs B4.1.29–B4.1.32).

4.2 Classification of financial liabilities

4.2.1   An entity shall classify all financial liabilities as subsequently measured at amortised cost, except for:

(a)   *financial liabilities at fair value through profit or loss*. Such liabilities, including *derivatives* that are liabilities, shall be subsequently measured at fair value.

(b)   financial liabilities that arise when a transfer of a financial asset does not qualify for derecognition or when the continuing involvement approach applies. Paragraphs 3.2.15 and 3.2.17 apply to the measurement of such financial liabilities.

(c)   *financial guarantee contracts*. After initial recognition, an issuer of such a contract shall (unless paragraph 4.2.1(a) or (b) applies) subsequently measure it at the higher of:

(i) the amount of the *loss allowance* determined in accordance with Section 5.5 and

(ii) the amount initially recognised (see paragraph 5.1.1) less, when appropriate, the cumulative amount of income recognised in accordance with the principles of AASB 15.

(d) commitments to provide a loan at a below-market interest rate. An issuer of such a commitment shall (unless paragraph 4.2.1(a) applies) subsequently measure it at the higher of:

(i) the amount of the loss allowance determined in accordance with Section 5.5 and

(ii) the amount initially recognised (see paragraph 5.1.1) less, when appropriate, the cumulative amount of income recognised in accordance with the principles of AASB 15.

(e) contingent consideration recognised by an acquirer in a business combination to which AASB 3 applies. Such contingent consideration shall subsequently be measured at fair value with changes recognised in profit or loss.

Option to designate a financial liability at fair value through profit or loss

4.2.2 An entity may, at initial recognition, irrevocably designate a financial liability as measured at fair value through profit or loss when permitted by paragraph 4.3.5, or when doing so results in more relevant information, because either:

(a) it eliminates or significantly reduces a measurement or recognition inconsistency (sometimes referred to as 'an accounting mismatch') that would otherwise arise from measuring assets or liabilities or recognising the gains and losses on them on different bases (see paragraphs B4.1.29–B4.1.32); or

(b) a group of financial liabilities or financial assets and financial liabilities is managed and its performance is evaluated on a fair value basis, in accordance with a documented risk management or investment strategy, and information about the group is provided internally on that basis to the entity's key management personnel (as defined in AASB 124 *Related Party Disclosures*), for example, the entity's board of directors and chief executive officer (see paragraphs B4.1.33–B4.1.36).

4.3 Embedded derivatives

4.3.1 An embedded derivative is a component of a hybrid contract that also includes a non-derivative host – with the effect that some of the cash flows of the combined instrument vary in a way similar to a stand-alone derivative. An embedded derivative causes some or all of the cash flows that otherwise would be required by the contract to be modified according to a specified interest rate, financial instrument price, commodity price, foreign exchange rate, index of prices or rates, credit rating or credit index, or other variable, provided in the case of a non-financial variable that the variable is not specific to a party to the contract. A derivative that is attached to a *financial instrument* but is contractually transferable independently of that instrument, or has a different counterparty, is not an embedded derivative, but a separate financial instrument.

Hybrid contracts with financial asset hosts

4.3.2 If a hybrid contract contains a host that is an asset within the scope of this Standard, an entity shall apply the requirements in paragraphs 4.1.1–4.1.5 to the entire hybrid contract.

Other hybrid contracts

4.3.3 If a hybrid contract contains a host that is not an asset within the scope of this Standard, an embedded derivative shall be separated from the host and accounted for as a derivative under this Standard if, and only if:

(a) the economic characteristics and risks of the embedded derivative are not closely related to the economic characteristics and risks of the host (see paragraphs B4.3.5 and B4.3.8);

(b) a separate instrument with the same terms as the embedded derivative would meet the definition of a derivative; and

(c) the hybrid contract is not measured at fair value with changes in fair value recognised in profit or loss (ie a derivative that is embedded in a financial liability at fair value through profit or loss is not separated).

4.3.4 If an embedded derivative is separated, the host contract shall be accounted for in accordance with the appropriate Standards. This Standard does not address whether an embedded derivative shall be presented separately in the statement of financial position.

4.3.5 Despite paragraphs 4.3.3 and 4.3.4, if a contract contains one or more embedded derivatives and the host is not an asset within the scope of this Standard, an entity may designate the entire hybrid contract as at fair value through profit or loss unless:

(a) the embedded derivative(s) do(es) not significantly modify the cash flows that otherwise would be required by the contract; or

(b) it is clear with little or no analysis when a similar hybrid instrument is first considered that separation of the embedded derivative(s) is prohibited, such as a prepayment option embedded in a loan that permits the holder to prepay the loan for approximately its amortised cost.

4.3.6 If an entity is required by this Standard to separate an embedded derivative from its host, but is unable to measure the embedded derivative separately either at acquisition or at the end of a subsequent financial reporting period, it shall designate the entire hybrid contract as at fair value through profit or loss.

4.3.7 If an entity is unable to measure reliably the fair value of an embedded derivative on the basis of its terms and conditions, the fair value of the embedded derivative is the difference between the fair value of the hybrid contract and the fair value of the host. If the entity is unable to measure the fair value of the embedded derivative using this method, paragraph 4.3.6 applies and the hybrid contract is designated as at fair value through profit or loss.

4.4 Reclassification

4.4.1 When, and only when, an entity changes its business model for managing financial assets it shall reclassify all affected financial assets in accordance with paragraphs 4.1.1–4.1.4. See paragraphs 5.6.1–5.6.7, B4.4.1–B4.4.3 and B5.6.1–B5.6.2 for additional guidance on reclassifying financial assets.

4.4.2 An entity shall not reclassify any financial liability.

4.4.3 The following changes in circumstances are not reclassifications for the purposes of paragraphs 4.4.1–4.4.2:

(a) an item that was previously a designated and effective hedging instrument in a cash flow hedge or net investment hedge no longer qualifies as such;

(b) an item becomes a designated and effective hedging instrument in a cash flow hedge or net investment hedge; and

(c) changes in measurement in accordance with Section 6.7.

Chapter 5 Measurement

5.1 Initial measurement

5.1.1   Except for trade receivables within the scope of paragraph 5.1.3, at initial recognition, an entity shall measure a financial asset or financial liability at its fair value plus or minus, in the case of a financial asset or financial liability not at fair value through profit or loss, *transaction costs* that are directly attributable to the acquisition or issue of the financial asset or financial liability.

5.1.1A   However, if the fair value of the financial asset or financial liability at initial recognition differs from the transaction price, an entity shall apply paragraph B5.1.2A.

5.1.2   When an entity uses settlement date accounting for an asset that is subsequently measured at amortised cost, the asset is recognised initially at its fair value on the trade date (see paragraphs B3.1.3–B3.1.6).

5.1.3   Despite the requirement in paragraph 5.1.1, at initial recognition, an entity shall measure trade receivables at their transaction price (as defined in AASB 15) if the trade receivables do not contain a significant financing component in accordance with AASB 15 (or when the entity applies the practical expedient in accordance with paragraph 63 of AASB 15).

5.2 Subsequent measurement of financial assets

5.2.1   After initial recognition, an entity shall measure a financial asset in accordance with paragraphs 4.1.1–4.1.5 at:

     (a)   amortised cost;

     (b)   fair value through other comprehensive income; or

     (c)   fair value through profit or loss.

5.2.2   An entity shall apply the impairment requirements in Section 5.5 to financial assets that are measured at amortised cost in accordance with paragraph 4.1.2 and to financial assets that are measured at fair value through other comprehensive income in accordance with paragraph 4.1.2A.

5.2.3   An entity shall apply the hedge accounting requirements in paragraphs 6.5.8–6.5.14 (and, if applicable, paragraphs 89–94 of AASB 139 *Financial Instruments: Recognition and Measurement* for the fair value hedge accounting for a portfolio hedge of interest rate risk) to a financial asset that is designated as a hedged item.[1]

5.3 Subsequent measurement of financial liabilities

5.3.1   After initial recognition, an entity shall measure a financial liability in accordance with paragraphs 4.2.1–4.2.2.

5.3.2   An entity shall apply the hedge accounting requirements in paragraphs 6.5.8–6.5.14 (and, if applicable, paragraphs 89–94 of AASB 139 for the fair value hedge accounting for a portfolio hedge of interest rate risk) to a financial liability that is designated as a hedged item.

5.4 Amortised cost measurement

Financial assets

Effective interest method

5.4.1   Interest revenue shall be calculated by using the *effective interest method* (see Appendix A and paragraphs B5.4.1–B5.4.7). This shall be calculated by applying

---

1   In accordance with paragraph 7.2.21, an entity may choose as its accounting policy to continue to apply the hedge accounting requirements in AASB 139 instead of the requirements in Chapter 6 of this Standard. If an entity has made this election, the references in this Standard to particular hedge accounting requirements in Chapter 6 are not relevant. Instead the entity applies the relevant hedge accounting requirements in AASB 139.

AASB

the *effective interest rate* to the *gross carrying amount of a financial asset* except for:

    (a)   *purchased or originated credit-impaired financial assets*. For those financial assets, the entity shall apply the *credit-adjusted effective interest rate* to the *amortised cost of the financial asset* from initial recognition.

    (b)   financial assets that are not purchased or originated credit-impaired financial assets but subsequently have become *credit-impaired financial assets*. For those financial assets, the entity shall apply the effective interest rate to the amortised cost of the financial asset in subsequent reporting periods.

5.4.2   An entity that, in a reporting period, calculates interest revenue by applying the effective interest method to the amortised cost of a financial asset in accordance with paragraph 5.4.1(b), shall, in subsequent reporting periods, calculate the interest revenue by applying the effective interest rate to the gross carrying amount if the credit risk on the financial instrument improves so that the financial asset is no longer credit-impaired and the improvement can be related objectively to an event occurring after the requirements in paragraph 5.4.1(b) were applied (such as an improvement in the borrower's credit rating).

Modification of contractual cash flows

5.4.3   When the contractual cash flows of a financial asset are renegotiated or otherwise modified and the renegotiation or modification does not result in the derecognition of that financial asset in accordance with this Standard, an entity shall recalculate the gross carrying amount of the financial asset and shall recognise a *modification gain or loss* in profit or loss. The gross carrying amount of the financial asset shall be recalculated as the present value of the renegotiated or modified contractual cash flows that are discounted at the financial asset's original effective interest rate (or credit-adjusted effective interest rate for purchased or originated credit-impaired financial assets) or, when applicable, the revised effective interest rate calculated in accordance with paragraph 6.5.10. Any costs or fees incurred adjust the carrying amount of the modified financial asset and are amortised over the remaining term of the modified financial asset.

Write-off

5.4.4   An entity shall directly reduce the gross carrying amount of a financial asset when the entity has no reasonable expectations of recovering a financial asset in its entirety or a portion thereof. A write-off constitutes a derecognition event (see paragraph B3.2.16(r)).

5.5 Impairment

Recognition of expected credit losses

General approach

5.5.1   An entity shall recognise a loss allowance for *expected credit losses* on a financial asset that is measured in accordance with paragraphs 4.1.2 or 4.1.2A, a lease receivable, a *contract asset* or a loan commitment and a financial guarantee contract to which the impairment requirements apply in accordance with paragraphs 2.1(g), 4.2.1(c) or 4.2.1(d).

5.5.2   An entity shall apply the impairment requirements for the recognition and measurement of a loss allowance for financial assets that are measured at fair value through other comprehensive income in accordance with paragraph 4.1.2A. However, the loss allowance shall be recognised in other comprehensive income and shall not reduce the carrying amount of the financial asset in the statement of financial position.

5.5.3   Subject to paragraphs 5.5.13–5.5.16, at each reporting date, an entity shall measure the loss allowance for a financial instrument at an amount equal to the

lifetime expected credit losses if the credit risk on that financial instrument has increased significantly since initial recognition.

5.5.4 The objective of the impairment requirements is to recognise lifetime expected credit losses for all financial instruments for which there have been significant increases in credit risk since initial recognition – whether assessed on an individual or collective basis – considering all reasonable and supportable information, including that which is forward-looking.

5.5.5 Subject to paragraphs 5.5.13–5.5.16, if, at the reporting date, the credit risk on a financial instrument has not increased significantly since initial recognition, an entity shall measure the loss allowance for that financial instrument at an amount equal to *12-month expected credit losses*.

5.5.6 For loan commitments and financial guarantee contracts, the date that the entity becomes a party to the irrevocable commitment shall be considered to be the date of initial recognition for the purposes of applying the impairment requirements.

5.5.7 If an entity has measured the loss allowance for a financial instrument at an amount equal to lifetime expected credit losses in the previous reporting period, but determines at the current reporting date that paragraph 5.5.3 is no longer met, the entity shall measure the loss allowance at an amount equal to 12-month expected credit losses at the current reporting date.

5.5.8 An entity shall recognise in profit or loss, as an *impairment gain or loss*, the amount of expected credit losses (or reversal) that is required to adjust the loss allowance at the reporting date to the amount that is required to be recognised in accordance with this Standard.

Determining significant increases in credit risk

5.5.9 At each reporting date, an entity shall assess whether the credit risk on a financial instrument has increased significantly since initial recognition. When making the assessment, an entity shall use the change in the risk of a default occurring over the expected life of the financial instrument instead of the change in the amount of expected credit losses. To make that assessment, an entity shall compare the risk of a default occurring on the financial instrument as at the reporting date with the risk of a default occurring on the financial instrument as at the date of initial recognition and consider reasonable and supportable information, that is available without undue cost or effort, that is indicative of significant increases in credit risk since initial recognition.

5.5.10 An entity may assume that the credit risk on a financial instrument has not increased significantly since initial recognition if the financial instrument is determined to have low credit risk at the reporting date (see paragraphs B5.5.22–B5.5.24).

5.5.11 If reasonable and supportable forward-looking information is available without undue cost or effort, an entity cannot rely solely on *past due* information when determining whether credit risk has increased significantly since initial recognition. However, when information that is more forward-looking than past due status (either on an individual or a collective basis) is not available without undue cost or effort, an entity may use past due information to determine whether there have been significant increases in credit risk since initial recognition. Regardless of the way in which an entity assesses significant increases in credit risk, there is a rebuttable presumption that the credit risk on a financial asset has increased significantly since initial recognition when contractual payments are more than 30 days past due. An entity can rebut this presumption if the entity has reasonable and supportable information that is available without undue cost or effort, that demonstrates that the credit risk has not increased significantly since initial recognition even though the contractual payments are more than 30 days past due. When an entity determines that there have been significant increases in credit risk before contractual payments are more than 30 days past due, the rebuttable presumption does not apply.

Modified financial assets

5.5.12 If the contractual cash flows on a financial asset have been renegotiated or modified and the financial asset was not derecognised, an entity shall assess whether there has been a significant increase in the credit risk of the financial instrument in accordance with paragraph 5.5.3 by comparing:

(a) the risk of a default occurring at the reporting date (based on the modified contractual terms); and

(b) the risk of a default occurring at initial recognition (based on the original, unmodified contractual terms).

Purchased or originated credit-impaired financial assets

5.5.13 **Despite paragraphs 5.5.3 and 5.5.5, at the reporting date, an entity shall only recognise the cumulative changes in lifetime expected credit losses since initial recognition as a loss allowance for purchased or originated credit-impaired financial assets.**

5.5.14 At each reporting date, an entity shall recognise in profit or loss the amount of the change in lifetime expected credit losses as an impairment gain or loss. An entity shall recognise favourable changes in lifetime expected credit losses as an impairment gain, even if the lifetime expected credit losses are less than the amount of expected credit losses that were included in the estimated cash flows on initial recognition.

Simplified approach for trade receivables, contract assets and lease receivables

5.5.15 **Despite paragraphs 5.5.3 and 5.5.5, an entity shall always measure the loss allowance at an amount equal to lifetime expected credit losses for:**

(a) **trade receivables or contract assets that result from transactions that are within the scope of AASB 15, and that:**

(i) **do not contain a significant financing component in accordance with AASB 15 (or when the entity applies the practical expedient in accordance with paragraph 63 of AASB 15); or**

(ii) **contain a significant financing component in accordance with AASB 15, if the entity chooses as its accounting policy to measure the loss allowance at an amount equal to lifetime expected credit losses. That accounting policy shall be applied to all such trade receivables or contract assets but may be applied separately to trade receivables and contract assets.**

(b) **lease receivables that result from transactions that are within the scope of AASB 117, if the entity chooses as its accounting policy to measure the loss allowance at an amount equal to lifetime expected credit losses. That accounting policy shall be applied to all lease receivables but may be applied separately to finance and operating lease receivables.**

5.5.16 An entity may select its accounting policy for trade receivables, lease receivables and contract assets independently of each other.

Measurement of expected credit losses

5.5.17 **An entity shall measure expected credit losses of a financial instrument in a way that reflects:**

(a) **an unbiased and probability-weighted amount that is determined by evaluating a range of possible outcomes;**

(b) **the time value of money; and**

(c) **reasonable and supportable information that is available without undue cost or effort at the reporting date about past events, current conditions and forecasts of future economic conditions.**

5.5.18 When measuring expected credit losses, an entity need not necessarily identify every possible scenario. However, it shall consider the risk or probability that a credit loss occurs by reflecting the possibility that a credit loss occurs and the possibility that no credit loss occurs, even if the possibility of a credit loss occurring is very low.

5.5.19 The maximum period to consider when measuring expected credit losses is the maximum contractual period (including extension options) over which the entity is exposed to credit risk and not a longer period, even if that longer period is consistent with business practice.

5.5.20 However, some financial instruments include both a loan and an undrawn commitment component and the entity's contractual ability to demand repayment and cancel the undrawn commitment does not limit the entity's exposure to credit losses to the contractual notice period. For such financial instruments, and only those financial instruments, the entity shall measure expected credit losses over the period that the entity is exposed to credit risk and expected credit losses would not be mitigated by credit risk management actions, even if that period extends beyond the maximum contractual period.

5.6 Reclassification of financial assets

5.6.1 **If an entity reclassifies financial assets in accordance with paragraph 4.4.1, it shall apply the reclassification prospectively from the *reclassification date*. The entity shall not restate any previously recognised gains, losses (including impairment gains or losses) or interest. Paragraphs 5.6.2–5.6.7 set out the requirements for reclassifications.**

5.6.2 **If an entity reclassifies a financial asset out of the amortised cost measurement category and into the fair value through profit or loss measurement category, its fair value is measured at the reclassification date. Any gain or loss arising from a difference between the previous amortised cost of the financial asset and fair value is recognised in profit or loss.**

5.6.3 **If an entity reclassifies a financial asset out of the fair value through profit or loss measurement category and into the amortised cost measurement category, its fair value at the reclassification date becomes its new gross carrying amount. (See paragraph B5.6.2 for guidance on determining an effective interest rate and a loss allowance at the reclassification date.)**

5.6.4 **If an entity reclassifies a financial asset out of the amortised cost measurement category and into the fair value through other comprehensive income measurement category, its fair value is measured at the reclassification date. Any gain or loss arising from a difference between the previous amortised cost of the financial asset and fair value is recognised in other comprehensive income. The effective interest rate and the measurement of expected credit losses are not adjusted as a result of the reclassification. (See paragraph B5.6.1.)**

5.6.5 **If an entity reclassifies a financial asset out of the fair value through other comprehensive income measurement category and into the amortised cost measurement category, the financial asset is reclassified at its fair value at the reclassification date. However, the cumulative gain or loss previously recognised in other comprehensive income is removed from equity and adjusted against the fair value of the financial asset at the reclassification date. As a result, the financial asset is measured at the reclassification date as if it had always been measured at amortised cost. This adjustment affects other comprehensive income but does not affect profit or loss and therefore is not a reclassification adjustment (see AASB 101 *Presentation of Financial Statements*). The effective interest rate and the measurement of expected credit losses are not adjusted as a result of the reclassification. (See paragraph B5.6.1.)**

5.6.6 **If an entity reclassifies a financial asset out of the fair value through profit or loss measurement category and into the fair value through other comprehensive income measurement category, the financial asset continues to be measured at fair**

value. (See paragraph B5.6.2 for guidance on determining an effective interest rate and a loss allowance at the reclassification date.)

5.6.7   If an entity reclassifies a financial asset out of the fair value through other comprehensive income measurement category and into the fair value through profit or loss measurement category, the financial asset continues to be measured at fair value. The cumulative gain or loss previously recognised in other comprehensive income is reclassified from equity to profit or loss as a reclassification adjustment (see AASB 101) at the reclassification date.

5.7 Gains and losses

5.7.1   A gain or loss on a financial asset or financial liability that is measured at fair value shall be recognised in profit or loss unless:

(a)   it is part of a hedging relationship (see paragraphs 6.5.8–6.5.14 and, if applicable, paragraphs 89–94 of AASB 139 for the fair value hedge accounting for a portfolio hedge of interest rate risk);

(b)   it is an investment in an equity instrument and the entity has elected to present gains and losses on that investment in other comprehensive income in accordance with paragraph 5.7.5;

(c)   it is a financial liability designated as at fair value through profit or loss and the entity is required to present the effects of changes in the liability's *credit risk* in other comprehensive income in accordance with paragraph 5.7.7; or

(d)   it is a financial asset measured at fair value through other comprehensive income in accordance with paragraph 4.1.2A and the entity is required to recognise some changes in fair value in other comprehensive income in accordance with paragraph 5.7.10.

5.7.1A   *Dividends* are recognised in profit or loss only when:

(a)   the entity's right to receive payment of the dividend is established;

(b)   it is probable that the economic benefits associated with the dividend will flow to the entity; and

(c)   the amount of the dividend can be measured reliably.

5.7.2   A gain or loss on a financial asset that is measured at amortised cost and is not part of a hedging relationship (see paragraphs 6.5.8–6.5.14 and, if applicable, paragraphs 89–94 of AASB 139 for the fair value hedge accounting for a portfolio hedge of interest rate risk) shall be recognised in profit or loss when the financial asset is derecognised, reclassified in accordance with paragraph 5.6.2, through the amortisation process or in order to recognise impairment gains or losses. An entity shall apply paragraphs 5.6.2 and 5.6.4 if it reclassifies financial assets out of the amortised cost measurement category. A gain or loss on a financial liability that is measured at amortised cost and is not part of a hedging relationship (see paragraphs 6.5.8–6.5.14 and, if applicable, paragraphs 89–94 of AASB 139 for the fair value hedge accounting for a portfolio hedge of interest rate risk) shall be recognised in profit or loss when the financial liability is derecognised and through the amortisation process. (See paragraph B5.7.2 for guidance on foreign exchange gains or losses.)

5.7.3   A gain or loss on financial assets or financial liabilities that are hedged items in a hedging relationship shall be recognised in accordance with paragraphs 6.5.8–6.5.14 and, if applicable, paragraphs 89–94 of AASB 139 for the fair value hedge accounting for a portfolio hedge of interest rate risk.

5.7.4   If an entity recognises financial assets using settlement date accounting (see paragraphs 3.1.2, B3.1.3 and B3.1.6), any change in the fair value of the asset to be received during the period between the trade date and the settlement date is not recognised for assets measured at amortised cost. For assets measured at fair value, however, the change in fair value shall be recognised in profit or loss or in other comprehensive income, as appropriate in accordance with paragraph 5.7.1. The trade date shall be considered the date of initial recognition for the purposes of applying the impairment requirements.

Investments in equity instruments

5.7.5 At initial recognition, an entity may make an irrevocable election to present in other comprehensive income subsequent changes in the fair value of an investment in an equity instrument within the scope of this Standard that is neither *held for trading* nor contingent consideration recognised by an acquirer in a business combination to which AASB 3 applies. (See paragraph B5.7.3 for guidance on foreign exchange gains or losses.)

5.7.6 If an entity makes the election in paragraph 5.7.5, it shall recognise in profit or loss dividends from that investment in accordance with paragraph 5.7.1A.

Liabilities designated as at fair value through profit or loss

5.7.7 An entity shall present a gain or loss on a financial liability that is designated as at fair value through profit or loss in accordance with paragraph 4.2.2 or paragraph 4.3.5 as follows:

(a) The amount of change in the fair value of the financial liability that is attributable to changes in the credit risk of that liability shall be presented in other comprehensive income (see paragraphs B5.7.13–B5.7.20), and

(b) the remaining amount of change in the fair value of the liability shall be presented in profit or loss

unless the treatment of the effects of changes in the liability's credit risk described in (a) would create or enlarge an accounting mismatch in profit or loss (in which case paragraph 5.7.8 applies). Paragraphs B5.7.5–B5.7.7 and B5.7.10–B5.7.12 provide guidance on determining whether an accounting mismatch would be created or enlarged.

5.7.8 If the requirements in paragraph 5.7.7 would create or enlarge an accounting mismatch in profit or loss, an entity shall present all gains or losses on that liability (including the effects of changes in the credit risk of that liability) in profit or loss.

5.7.9 Despite the requirements in paragraphs 5.7.7 and 5.7.8, an entity shall present in profit or loss all gains and losses on loan commitments and financial guarantee contracts that are designated as at fair value through profit or loss.

Assets measured at fair value through other comprehensive income

5.7.10 A gain or loss on a financial asset measured at fair value through other comprehensive income in accordance with paragraph 4.1.2A shall be recognised in other comprehensive income, except for impairment gains or losses (see Section 5.5) and foreign exchange gains and losses (see paragraphs B5.7.2–B5.7.2A), until the financial asset is derecognised or reclassified. When the financial asset is derecognised the cumulative gain or loss previously recognised in other comprehensive income is reclassified from equity to profit or loss as a reclassification adjustment (see AASB 101). If the financial asset is reclassified out of the fair value through other comprehensive income measurement category, the entity shall account for the cumulative gain or loss that was previously recognised in other comprehensive income in accordance with paragraphs 5.6.5 and 5.6.7. Interest calculated using the effective interest method is recognised in profit or loss.

5.7.11 As described in paragraph 5.7.10, if a financial asset is measured at fair value through other comprehensive income in accordance with paragraph 4.1.2A, the amounts that are recognised in profit or loss are the same as the amounts that would have been recognised in profit or loss if the financial asset had been measured at amortised cost.

Chapter 6 Hedge accounting

6.1 Objective and scope of hedge accounting

6.1.1   The objective of hedge accounting is to represent, in the financial statements, the effect of an entity's risk management activities that use financial instruments to manage exposures arising from particular risks that could affect profit or loss (or other comprehensive income, in the case of investments in equity instruments for which an entity has elected to present changes in fair value in other comprehensive income in accordance with paragraph 5.7.5). This approach aims to convey the context of hedging instruments for which hedge accounting is applied in order to allow insight into their purpose and effect.

6.1.2   An entity may choose to designate a hedging relationship between a hedging instrument and a hedged item in accordance with paragraphs 6.2.1–6.3.7 and B6.2.1–B6.3.25. For hedging relationships that meet the qualifying criteria, an entity shall account for the gain or loss on the hedging instrument and the hedged item in accordance with paragraphs 6.5.1–6.5.14 and B6.5.1–B6.5.28. When the hedged item is a group of items, an entity shall comply with the additional requirements in paragraphs 6.6.1–6.6.6 and B6.6.1–B6.6.16.

6.1.3   For a fair value hedge of the interest rate exposure of a portfolio of financial assets or financial liabilities (and only for such a hedge), an entity may apply the hedge accounting requirements in AASB 139 instead of those in this Standard. In that case, the entity must also apply the specific requirements for the fair value hedge accounting for a portfolio hedge of interest rate risk and designate as the hedged item a portion that is a currency amount (see paragraphs 81A, 89A and AG114–AG132 of AASB 139).

6.2 Hedging instruments

Qualifying instruments

6.2.1   **A derivative measured at fair value through profit or loss may be designated as a hedging instrument, except for some written options (see paragraph B6.2.4).**

6.2.2   **A non-derivative financial asset or a non-derivative financial liability measured at fair value through profit or loss may be designated as a hedging instrument unless it is a financial liability designated as at fair value through profit or loss for which the amount of its change in fair value that is attributable to changes in the credit risk of that liability is presented in other comprehensive income in accordance with paragraph 5.7.7. For a hedge of foreign currency risk, the foreign currency risk component of a non-derivative financial asset or a non-derivative financial liability may be designated as a hedging instrument provided that it is not an investment in an equity instrument for which an entity has elected to present changes in fair value in other comprehensive income in accordance with paragraph 5.7.5.**

6.2.3   **For hedge accounting purposes, only contracts with a party external to the reporting entity (ie external to the group or individual entity that is being reported on) can be designated as hedging instruments.**

Designation of hedging instruments

6.2.4   A qualifying instrument must be designated in its entirety as a hedging instrument. The only exceptions permitted are:

   (a)   separating the intrinsic value and time value of an option contract and designating as the hedging instrument only the change in intrinsic value of an option and not the change in its time value (see paragraphs 6.5.15 and B6.5.29–B6.5.33);

   (b)   separating the forward element and the spot element of a forward contract and designating as the hedging instrument only the change in the value of the spot element of a forward contract and not the forward element; similarly, the foreign currency basis spread may be separated and excluded from the designation of a financial instrument as the hedging instrument (see paragraphs 6.5.16 and B6.5.34–B6.5.39); and

(c)   a proportion of the entire hedging instrument, such as 50 per cent of the nominal amount, may be designated as the hedging instrument in a hedging relationship. However, a hedging instrument may not be designated for a part of its change in fair value that results from only a portion of the time period during which the hedging instrument remains outstanding.

6.2.5   An entity may view in combination, and jointly designate as the hedging instrument, any combination of the following (including those circumstances in which the risk or risks arising from some hedging instruments offset those arising from others):

(a)   derivatives or a proportion of them; and

(b)   non-derivatives or a proportion of them.

6.2.6   However, a derivative instrument that combines a written option and a purchased option (for example, an interest rate collar) does not qualify as a hedging instrument if it is, in effect, a net written option at the date of designation (unless it qualifies in accordance with paragraph B6.2.4). Similarly, two or more instruments (or proportions of them) may be jointly designated as the hedging instrument only if, in combination, they are not, in effect, a net written option at the date of designation (unless it qualifies in accordance with paragraph B6.2.4).

6.3 Hedged items

Qualifying items

6.3.1   A hedged item can be a recognised asset or liability, an unrecognised *firm commitment*, a *forecast transaction* or a net investment in a foreign operation. The hedged item can be:

(a)   a single item; or

(b)   a group of items (subject to paragraphs 6.6.1–6.6.6 and B6.6.1–B6.6.16).

A hedged item can also be a component of such an item or group of items (see paragraphs 6.3.7 and B6.3.7–B6.3.25).

6.3.2   The hedged item must be reliably measurable.

6.3.3   If a hedged item is a forecast transaction (or a component thereof), that transaction must be highly probable.

6.3.4   An aggregated exposure that is a combination of an exposure that could qualify as a hedged item in accordance with paragraph 6.3.1 and a derivative may be designated as a hedged item (see paragraphs B6.3.3–B6.3.4). This includes a forecast transaction of an aggregated exposure (ie uncommitted but anticipated future transactions that would give rise to an exposure and a derivative) if that aggregated exposure is highly probable and, once it has occurred and is therefore no longer forecast, is eligible as a hedged item.

6.3.5   For hedge accounting purposes, only assets, liabilities, firm commitments or highly probable forecast transactions with a party external to the reporting entity can be designated as hedged items. Hedge accounting can be applied to transactions between entities in the same group only in the individual or separate financial statements of those entities and not in the consolidated financial statements of the group, except for the consolidated financial statements of an investment entity, as defined in AASB 10, where transactions between an investment entity and its subsidiaries measured at fair value through profit or loss will not be eliminated in the consolidated financial statements.

6.3.6   However, as an exception to paragraph 6.3.5, the foreign currency risk of an intragroup monetary item (for example, a payable/receivable between two subsidiaries) may qualify as a hedged item in the consolidated financial statements if it results in an exposure to foreign exchange rate gains or losses that are not fully eliminated on consolidation in accordance with AASB 121 *The Effects of Changes in Foreign*

Exchange Rates. In accordance with AASB 121, foreign exchange rate gains and losses on intragroup monetary items are not fully eliminated on consolidation when the intragroup monetary item is transacted between two group entities that have different functional currencies. In addition, the foreign currency risk of a highly probable forecast intragroup transaction may qualify as a hedged item in consolidated financial statements provided that the transaction is denominated in a currency other than the functional currency of the entity entering into that transaction and the foreign currency risk will affect consolidated profit or loss.

Designation of hedged items

6.3.7   An entity may designate an item in its entirety or a component of an item as the hedged item in a hedging relationship. An entire item comprises all changes in the cash flows or fair value of an item. A component comprises less than the entire fair value change or cash flow variability of an item. In that case, an entity may designate only the following types of components (including combinations) as hedged items:

(a)   only changes in the cash flows or fair value of an item attributable to a specific risk or risks (risk component), provided that, based on an assessment within the context of the particular market structure, the risk component is separately identifiable and reliably measurable (see paragraphs B6.3.8–B6.3.15). Risk components include a designation of only changes in the cash flows or the fair value of a hedged item above or below a specified price or other variable (a one-sided risk).

(b)   one or more selected contractual cash flows.

(c)   components of a nominal amount, ie a specified part of the amount of an item (see paragraphs B6.3.16–B6.3.20).

6.4 Qualifying criteria for hedge accounting

6.4.1   **A hedging relationship qualifies for hedge accounting only if all of the following criteria are met:**

(a)   **the hedging relationship consists only of eligible hedging instruments and eligible hedged items.**

(b)   **at the inception of the hedging relationship there is formal designation and documentation of the hedging relationship and the entity's risk management objective and strategy for undertaking the hedge. That documentation shall include identification of the hedging instrument, the hedged item, the nature of the risk being hedged and how the entity will assess whether the hedging relationship meets the hedge effectiveness requirements (including its analysis of the sources of hedge ineffectiveness and how it determines the *hedge ratio*).**

(c)   **the hedging relationship meets all of the following hedge effectiveness requirements:**

(i)   **there is an economic relationship between the hedged item and the hedging instrument (see paragraphs B6.4.4–B6.4.6);**

(ii)   **the effect of credit risk does not dominate the value changes that result from that economic relationship (see paragraphs B6.4.7–B6.4.8); and**

(iii) **the hedge ratio of the hedging relationship is the same as that resulting from the quantity of the hedged item that the entity actually hedges and the quantity of the hedging instrument that the entity actually uses to hedge that quantity of hedged item. However, that designation shall not reflect an imbalance between the weightings of the hedged item and the hedging instrument that would create hedge ineffectiveness (irrespective of whether recognised or not) that could** result in an accounting outcome that would be inconsistent with the purpose of hedge accounting (see paragraphs B6.4.9–B6.4.11).

6.5 Accounting for qualifying hedging relationships

6.5.1 An entity applies hedge accounting to hedging relationships that meet the qualifying criteria in paragraph 6.4.1 (which include the entity's decision to designate the hedging relationship).

6.5.2 There are three types of hedging relationships:

(a) fair value hedge: a hedge of the exposure to changes in fair value of a recognised asset or liability or an unrecognised firm commitment, or a component of any such item, that is attributable to a particular risk and could affect profit or loss.

(b) cash flow hedge: a hedge of the exposure to variability in cash flows that is attributable to a particular risk associated with all, or a component of, a recognised asset or liability (such as all or some future interest payments on variable-rate debt) or a highly probable forecast transaction, and could affect profit or loss.

(c) hedge of a net investment in a foreign operation as defined in AASB 121.

6.5.3 If the hedged item is an equity instrument for which an entity has elected to present changes in fair value in other comprehensive income in accordance with paragraph 5.7.5, the hedged exposure referred to in paragraph 6.5.2(a) must be one that could affect other comprehensive income. In that case, and only in that case, the recognised hedge ineffectiveness is presented in other comprehensive income.

6.5.4 A hedge of the foreign currency risk of a firm commitment may be accounted for as a fair value hedge or a cash flow hedge.

6.5.5 If a hedging relationship ceases to meet the hedge effectiveness requirement relating to the hedge ratio (see paragraph 6.4.1(c)(iii)) but the risk management objective for that designated hedging relationship remains the same, an entity shall adjust the hedge ratio of the hedging relationship so that it meets the qualifying criteria again (this is referred to in this Standard as 'rebalancing' – see paragraphs B6.5.7–B6.5.21).

6.5.6 An entity shall discontinue hedge accounting prospectively only when the hedging relationship (or a part of a hedging relationship) ceases to meet the qualifying criteria (after taking into account any rebalancing of the hedging relationship, if applicable). This includes instances when the hedging instrument expires or is sold, terminated or exercised. For this purpose, the replacement or rollover of a hedging instrument into another hedging instrument is not an expiration or termination if such a replacement or rollover is part of, and consistent with, the entity's documented risk management objective. Additionally, for this purpose there is not an expiration or termination of the hedging instrument if:

(a) as a consequence of laws or regulations or the introduction of laws or regulations, the parties to the hedging instrument agree that one or more clearing counterparties replace their original counterparty to become the new counterparty to each of the parties. For this purpose, a clearing counterparty is a central counterparty (sometimes called a 'clearing organisation' or 'clearing agency') or an entity or entities, for example, a clearing member of a clearing organisation or a client of a clearing member of a clearing organisation, that are acting as a counterparty in order to effect clearing by a central counterparty. However, when the parties to the hedging instrument replace their original counterparties with different counterparties the requirement in this subparagraph is met only if each of those parties effects clearing with the same central counterparty.

(b)   other changes, if any, to the hedging instrument are limited to those that are necessary to effect such a replacement of the counterparty. Such changes are limited to those that are consistent with the terms that would be expected if the hedging instrument were originally cleared with the clearing counterparty. These changes include changes in the collateral requirements, rights to offset receivables and payables balances, and charges levied.

Discontinuing hedge accounting can either affect a hedging relationship in its entirety or only a part of it (in which case hedge accounting continues for the remainder of the hedging relationship).

6.5.7   An entity shall apply:

(a)   paragraph 6.5.10 when it discontinues hedge accounting for a fair value hedge for which the hedged item is (or is a component of) a financial instrument measured at amortised cost; and

(b)   paragraph 6.5.12 when it discontinues hedge accounting for cash flow hedges.

Fair value hedges

6.5.8   As long as a fair value hedge meets the qualifying criteria in paragraph 6.4.1, the hedging relationship shall be accounted for as follows:

(a)   **the gain or loss on the hedging instrument shall be recognised in profit or loss (or other comprehensive income, if the hedging instrument hedges an equity instrument for which an entity has elected to present changes in fair value in other comprehensive income in accordance with paragraph 5.7.5).**

(b)   **the hedging gain or loss on the hedged item shall adjust the carrying amount of the hedged item (if applicable) and be recognised in profit or loss. If the hedged item is a financial asset (or a component thereof) that is measured at fair value through other comprehensive income in accordance with paragraph 4.1.2A, the hedging gain or loss on the hedged item shall be recognised in profit or loss. However, if the hedged item is an equity instrument for which an entity has elected to present changes in fair value in other comprehensive income in accordance with paragraph 5.7.5, those amounts shall remain in other comprehensive income. When a hedged item is an unrecognised firm commitment (or a component thereof), the cumulative change in the fair value of the hedged item subsequent to its designation is recognised as an asset or a liability with a corresponding gain or loss recognised in profit or loss.**

6.5.9   When a hedged item in a fair value hedge is a firm commitment (or a component thereof) to acquire an asset or assume a liability, the initial carrying amount of the asset or the liability that results from the entity meeting the firm commitment is adjusted to include the cumulative change in the fair value of the hedged item that was recognised in the statement of financial position.

6.5.10   Any adjustment arising from paragraph 6.5.8(b) shall be amortised to profit or loss if the hedged item is a financial instrument (or a component thereof) measured at amortised cost. Amortisation may begin as soon as an adjustment exists and shall begin no later than when the hedged item ceases to be adjusted for hedging gains and losses. The amortisation is based on a recalculated effective interest rate at the date that amortisation begins. In the case of a financial asset (or a component thereof) that is a hedged item and that is measured at fair value through other comprehensive income in accordance with paragraph 4.1.2A, amortisation applies in the same manner but to the amount that represents the cumulative gain or loss previously recognised in accordance with paragraph 6.5.8(b) instead of by adjusting the carrying amount.

Cash flow hedges

6.5.11   As long as a cash flow hedge meets the qualifying criteria in paragraph 6.4.1, the hedging relationship shall be accounted for as follows:

(a) the separate component of equity associated with the hedged item (cash flow hedge reserve) is adjusted to the lower of the following (in absolute amounts):

    (i) the cumulative gain or loss on the hedging instrument from inception of the hedge; and

    (ii) the cumulative change in fair value (present value) of the hedged item (ie the present value of the cumulative change in the hedged expected future cash flows) from inception of the hedge.

(b) the portion of the gain or loss on the hedging instrument that is determined to be an effective hedge (ie the portion that is offset by the change in the cash flow hedge reserve calculated in accordance with (a)) shall be recognised in other comprehensive income.

(c) any remaining gain or loss on the hedging instrument (or any gain or loss required to balance the change in the cash flow hedge reserve calculated in accordance with (a)) is hedge ineffectiveness that shall be recognised in profit or loss.

(d) the amount that has been accumulated in the cash flow hedge reserve in accordance with (a) shall be accounted for as follows:

    (i) if a hedged forecast transaction subsequently results in the recognition of a non-financial asset or non-financial liability, or a hedged forecast transaction for a non-financial asset or a non-financial liability becomes a firm commitment for which fair value hedge accounting is applied, the entity shall remove that amount from the cash flow hedge reserve and include it directly in the initial cost or other carrying amount of the asset or the liability. This is not a reclassification adjustment (see AASB 101) and hence it does not affect other comprehensive income.

    (ii) for cash flow hedges other than those covered by (i), that amount shall be reclassified from the cash flow hedge reserve to profit or loss as a reclassification adjustment (see AASB 101) in the same period or periods during which the hedged expected future cash flows affect profit or loss (for example, in the periods that interest income or interest expense is recognised or when a forecast sale occurs).

    (iii) however, if that amount is a loss and an entity expects that all or a portion of that loss will not be recovered in one or more future periods, it shall immediately reclassify the amount that is not expected to be recovered into profit or loss as a reclassification adjustment (see AASB 101).

6.5.12 When an entity discontinues hedge accounting for a cash flow hedge (see paragraphs 6.5.6 and 6.5.7(b)) it shall account for the amount that has been accumulated in the cash flow hedge reserve in accordance with paragraph 6.5.11(a) as follows:

(a) if the hedged future cash flows are still expected to occur, that amount shall remain in the cash flow hedge reserve until the future cash flows occur or until paragraph 6.5.11(d)(iii) applies. When the future cash flows occur, paragraph 6.5.11(d) applies.

(b) if the hedged future cash flows are no longer expected to occur, that amount shall be immediately reclassified from the cash flow hedge reserve to profit or loss as a reclassification adjustment (see AASB 101). A hedged future cash flow that is no longer highly probable to occur may still be expected to occur.

Hedges of a net investment in a foreign operation

6.5.13 Hedges of a net investment in a foreign operation, including a hedge of a monetary item that is accounted for as part of the net investment (see AASB 121), shall be accounted for similarly to cash flow hedges:

(a)   the portion of the gain or loss on the hedging instrument that is determined to be an effective hedge shall be recognised in other comprehensive income (see paragraph 6.5.11); and

(b)   the ineffective portion shall be recognised in profit or loss.

6.5.14 The cumulative gain or loss on the hedging instrument relating to the effective portion of the hedge that has been accumulated in the foreign currency translation reserve shall be reclassified from equity to profit or loss as a reclassification adjustment (see AASB 101) in accordance with paragraphs 48–49 of AASB 121 on the disposal or partial disposal of the foreign operation.

Accounting for the time value of options

6.5.15   When an entity separates the intrinsic value and time value of an option contract and designates as the hedging instrument only the change in intrinsic value of the option (see paragraph 6.2.4(a)), it shall account for the time value of the option as follows (see paragraphs B6.5.29–B6.5.33):

(a)   an entity shall distinguish the time value of options by the type of hedged item that the option hedges (see paragraph B6.5.29):

(i)   a transaction related hedged item; or

(ii)   a time-period related hedged item.

(b)   the change in fair value of the time value of an option that hedges a transaction related hedged item shall be recognised in other comprehensive income to the extent that it relates to the hedged item and shall be accumulated in a separate component of equity. The cumulative change in fair value arising from the time value of the option that has been accumulated in a separate component of equity (the 'amount') shall be accounted for as follows:

(i)   if the hedged item subsequently results in the recognition of a non-financial asset or a non-financial liability, or a firm commitment for a non-financial asset or a non-financial liability for which fair value hedge accounting is applied, the entity shall remove the amount from the separate component of equity and include it directly in the initial cost or other carrying amount of the asset or the liability. This is not a reclassification adjustment (see AASB 101) and hence does not affect other comprehensive income.

(ii)   for hedging relationships other than those covered by (i), the amount shall be reclassified from the separate component of equity to profit or loss as a reclassification adjustment (see AASB 101) in the same period or periods during which the hedged expected future cash flows affect profit or loss (for example, when a forecast sale occurs).

(iii) however, if all or a portion of that amount is not expected to be recovered in one or more future periods, the amount that is not expected to be recovered shall be immediately reclassified into profit or loss as a reclassification adjustment (see AASB 101).

(c)   the change in fair value of the time value of an option that hedges a time-period related hedged item shall be recognised in other comprehensive income to the extent that it relates to the hedged item and shall be accumulated in a separate component of equity. The time value at the date of designation of the option as a hedging instrument, to the extent that it relates to the hedged item, shall be amortised on a systematic and rational basis over the period during which the hedge adjustment for the option's intrinsic value could affect profit or loss (or other comprehensive income, if the hedged item is an equity instrument for which an entity has elected to present changes in fair value in other comprehensive income in accordance with paragraph 5.7.5). Hence, in each reporting period, the amortisation amount shall be reclassified from the separate component of equity to profit or loss as a reclassification adjustment (see AASB 101). However, if hedge accounting is discontinued for the hedging relationship that includes the change in intrinsic value of the option as the hedging instrument, the net amount (ie including cumulative amortisation) that has been accumulated in the separate component of equity shall be immediately reclassified into profit or loss as a reclassification adjustment (see AASB 101).

Accounting for the forward element of forward contracts and foreign currency basis spreads of financial instruments

6.5.16   When an entity separates the forward element and the spot element of a forward contract and designates as the hedging instrument only the change in the value of the spot element of the forward contract, or when an entity separates the foreign currency basis spread from a financial instrument and excludes it from the designation of that financial instrument as the hedging instrument (see paragraph 6.2.4(b)), the entity may apply paragraph 6.5.15 to the forward element of the forward contract or to the foreign currency basis spread in the same manner as it is applied to the time value of an option. In that case, the entity shall apply the application guidance in paragraphs B6.5.34–B6.5.39.

6.6 Hedges of a group of items

Eligibility of a group of items as the hedged item

6.6.1   **A group of items (including a group of items that constitute a net position; see paragraphs B6.6.1–B6.6.8) is an eligible hedged item only if:**

(a)   **it consists of items (including components of items) that are, individually, eligible hedged items;**

(b)   **the items in the group are managed together on a group basis for risk management purposes; and**

(c)   **in the case of a cash flow hedge of a group of items whose variabilities in cash flows are not expected to be approximately proportional to the overall variability in cash flows of the group so that offsetting risk positions arise:**

     (i)   **it is a hedge of foreign currency risk; and**

     (ii)   **the designation of that net position specifies the reporting period in which the forecast transactions are expected to affect profit or loss, as well as their nature and volume (see paragraphs B6.6.7–B6.6.8).**

Designation of a component of a nominal amount

6.6.2   A component that is a proportion of an eligible group of items is an eligible hedged item provided that designation is consistent with the entity's risk management objective.

6.6.3   A layer component of an overall group of items (for example, a bottom layer) is eligible for hedge accounting only if:

(a)   it is separately identifiable and reliably measurable;

(b)   the risk management objective is to hedge a layer component;

(c)   the items in the overall group from which the layer is identified are exposed to the same hedged risk (so that the measurement of the hedged layer is not significantly affected by which particular items from the overall group form part of the hedged layer);

(d)   for a hedge of existing items (for example, an unrecognised firm commitment or a recognised asset) an entity can identify and track the overall group of items from which the hedged layer is defined (so that the entity is able to comply with the requirements for the accounting for qualifying hedging relationships); and

(e)   any items in the group that contain prepayment options meet the requirements for components of a nominal amount (see paragraph B6.3.20).

Presentation

6.6.4   For a hedge of a group of items with offsetting risk positions (ie in a hedge of a net position) whose hedged risk affects different line items in the statement of profit or loss and other comprehensive income, any hedging gains or losses in that statement shall be presented in a separate line from those affected by the hedged items. Hence, in that statement the amount in the line item that relates to the hedged item itself (for example, revenue or cost of sales) remains unaffected.

6.6.5   For assets and liabilities that are hedged together as a group in a fair value hedge, the gain or loss in the statement of financial position on the individual assets and liabilities shall be recognised as an adjustment of the carrying amount of the respective individual items comprising the group in accordance with paragraph 6.5.8(b).

Nil net positions

6.6.6   When the hedged item is a group that is a nil net position (ie the hedged items among themselves fully offset the risk that is managed on a group basis), an entity is permitted to designate it in a hedging relationship that does not include a hedging instrument, provided that:

(a)   the hedge is part of a rolling net risk hedging strategy, whereby the entity routinely hedges new positions of the same type as time moves on (for example, when transactions move into the time horizon for which the entity hedges);

(b)   the hedged net position changes in size over the life of the rolling net risk hedging strategy and the entity uses eligible hedging instruments to hedge the net risk (ie when the net position is not nil);

(c)   hedge accounting is normally applied to such net positions when the net position is not nil and it is hedged with eligible hedging instruments; and

(d)   not applying hedge accounting to the nil net position would give rise to inconsistent accounting outcomes, because the accounting would not recognise the offsetting risk positions that would otherwise be recognised in a hedge of a net position.

6.7 Option to designate a credit exposure as measured at fair value through profit or loss

Eligibility of credit exposures for designation at fair value through profit or loss

6.7.1   If an entity uses a credit derivative that is measured at fair value through profit or loss to manage the credit risk of all, or a part of, a financial instrument (credit exposure) it may designate that financial instrument to the extent that it is so managed (ie all or a proportion of it) as measured at fair value through profit or loss if:

(a)   the name of the credit exposure (for example, the borrower, or the holder of a loan commitment) matches the reference entity of the credit derivative ('name matching'); and

(b)   the seniority of the financial instrument matches that of the instruments that can be delivered in accordance with the credit derivative.

An entity may make this designation irrespective of whether the financial instrument that is managed for credit risk is within the scope of this Standard (for example, an entity may designate loan commitments that are outside the scope of this Standard). The entity may designate that financial instrument at, or subsequent to, initial recognition, or while it is unrecognised. The entity shall document the designation concurrently.

Accounting for credit exposures designated at fair value through profit or loss

6.7.2   If a financial instrument is designated in accordance with paragraph 6.7.1 as measured at fair value through profit or loss after its initial recognition, or was previously not recognised, the difference at the time of designation between the carrying amount, if any, and the fair value shall immediately be recognised in profit or loss. For financial assets measured at fair value through other comprehensive income in accordance with paragraph 4.1.2A, the cumulative gain or loss previously recognised in other comprehensive income shall immediately be reclassified from equity to profit or loss as a reclassification adjustment (see AASB 101).

6.7.3 An entity shall discontinue measuring the financial instrument that gave rise to the credit risk, or a proportion of that financial instrument, at fair value through profit or loss if:

(a) the qualifying criteria in paragraph 6.7.1 are no longer met, for example:

(i) the credit derivative or the related financial instrument that gives rise to the credit risk expires or is sold, terminated or settled; or

(ii) the credit risk of the financial instrument is no longer managed using credit derivatives. For example, this could occur because of improvements in the credit quality of the borrower or the loan commitment holder or changes to capital requirements imposed on an entity; and

(b) the financial instrument that gives rise to the credit risk is not otherwise required to be measured at fair value through profit or loss (ie the entity's business model has not changed in the meantime so that a reclassification in accordance with paragraph 4.4.1 was required).

6.7.4 When an entity discontinues measuring the financial instrument that gives rise to the credit risk, or a proportion of that financial instrument, at fair value through profit or loss, that financial instrument's fair value at the date of discontinuation becomes its new carrying amount. Subsequently, the same measurement that was used before designating the financial instrument at fair value through profit or loss shall be applied (including amortisation that results from the new carrying amount). For example, a financial asset that had originally been classified as measured at amortised cost would revert to that measurement and its effective interest rate would be recalculated based on its new gross carrying amount on the date of discontinuing measurement at fair value through profit or loss.

Chapter 7 Effective date and transition

7.1 Effective date

7.1.1 [Deleted by the AASB – see paragraphs Aus1.2 and Aus1.3]

7.1.2 Despite the requirements in paragraph Aus1.3, for annual reporting periods beginning before 1 January 2018, an entity may elect to early apply only the requirements for the presentation of gains and losses on financial liabilities designated as at fair value through profit or loss in paragraphs 5.7.1(c), 5.7.7–5.7.9, 7.2.14 and B5.7.5–B5.7.20 without applying the other requirements in this Standard. If an entity elects to apply only those paragraphs, it shall disclose that fact and provide on an ongoing basis the related disclosures set out in paragraphs 10–11 of AASB 7 *Financial Instruments: Disclosures* (as amended by AASB 2010-7 *Amendments to Australian Accounting Standards arising from AASB 9 (December 2010)*). (See also paragraphs 7.2.2 and 7.2.15.)

7.1.3 [Deleted by the AASB]

7.1.4 [Deleted by the AASB]

7.2 Transition

7.2.1 An entity shall apply this Standard retrospectively, in accordance with AASB 108 *Accounting Policies, Changes in Accounting Estimates and Errors*, except as specified in paragraphs 7.2.4–7.2.26 and 7.2.28. This Standard shall not be applied to items that have already been derecognised at the date of initial application.

7.2.2   For the purposes of the transition provisions in paragraphs 7.2.1, 7.2.3–7.2.28 and Aus1.4, the date of initial application is the date when an entity first applies those requirements of this Standard and must be the beginning of a reporting period after 24 July 2014[2] . Depending on the entity's chosen approach to applying AASB 9, the transition can involve one or more than one date of initial application for different requirements.

Transition for classification and measurement (Chapters 4 and 5)

7.2.3   At the date of initial application, an entity shall assess whether a financial asset meets the condition in paragraphs 4.1.2(a) or 4.1.2A(a) on the basis of the facts and circumstances that exist at that date. The resulting classification shall be applied retrospectively irrespective of the entity's business model in prior reporting periods.

7.2.4   If, at the date of initial application, it is impracticable (as defined in AASB 108) for an entity to assess a modified time value of money element in accordance with paragraphs B4.1.9B–B4.1.9D on the basis of the facts and circumstances that existed at the initial recognition of the financial asset, an entity shall assess the contractual cash flow characteristics of that financial asset on the basis of the facts and circumstances that existed at the initial recognition of the financial asset without taking into account the requirements related to the modification of the time value of money element in paragraphs B4.1.9B–B4.1.9D. (See also paragraph 42R of AASB 7.)

7.2.5   If, at the date of initial application, it is impracticable (as defined in AASB 108) for an entity to assess whether the fair value of a prepayment feature was insignificant in accordance with paragraph B4.1.12(c) on the basis of the facts and circumstances that existed at the initial recognition of the financial asset, an entity shall assess the contractual cash flow characteristics of that financial asset on the basis of the facts and circumstances that existed at the initial recognition of the financial asset without taking into account the exception for prepayment features in paragraph B4.1.12. (See also paragraph 42S of AASB 7.)

7.2.6   If an entity measures a hybrid contract at fair value in accordance with paragraphs 4.1.2A, 4.1.4 or 4.1.5 but the fair value of the hybrid contract had not been measured in comparative reporting periods, the fair value of the hybrid contract in the comparative reporting periods shall be the sum of the fair values of the components (ie the non-derivative host and the embedded derivative) at the end of each comparative reporting period if the entity restates prior periods (see paragraph 7.2.15).

7.2.7   If an entity has applied paragraph 7.2.6 then at the date of initial application the entity shall recognise any difference between the fair value of the entire hybrid contract at the date of initial application and the sum of the fair values of the components of the hybrid contract at the date of initial application in the opening retained earnings (or other component of equity, as appropriate) of the reporting period that includes the date of initial application.

7.2.8   At the date of initial application an entity may designate:

(a)   a financial asset as measured at fair value through profit or loss in accordance with paragraph 4.1.5; or

(b)   an investment in an equity instrument as at fair value through other comprehensive income in accordance with paragraph 5.7.5.

Such a designation shall be made on the basis of the facts and circumstances that exist at the date of initial application. That classification shall be applied retrospectively.

7.2.9   At the date of initial application an entity:

---

2   The International Accounting Standards Board issued International Financial Reporting Standard IFRS 9 *Financial Instruments* on 24 July 2014.

(a) shall revoke its previous designation of a financial asset as measured at fair value through profit or loss if that financial asset does not meet the condition in paragraph 4.1.5.

(b) may revoke its previous designation of a financial asset as measured at fair value through profit or loss if that financial asset meets the condition in paragraph 4.1.5.

Such a revocation shall be made on the basis of the facts and circumstances that exist at the date of initial application. That classification shall be applied retrospectively.

7.2.10 At the date of initial application, an entity:

(a) may designate a financial liability as measured at fair value through profit or loss in accordance with paragraph 4.2.2(a).

(b) shall revoke its previous designation of a financial liability as measured at fair value through profit or loss if such designation was made at initial recognition in accordance with the condition now in paragraph 4.2.2(a) and such designation does not satisfy that condition at the date of initial application.

(c) may revoke its previous designation of a financial liability as measured at fair value through profit or loss if such designation was made at initial recognition in accordance with the condition now in paragraph 4.2.2(a) and such designation satisfies that condition at the date of initial application.

Such a designation and revocation shall be made on the basis of the facts and circumstances that exist at the date of initial application. That classification shall be applied retrospectively.

7.2.11 If it is impracticable (as defined in AASB 108) for an entity to apply retrospectively the effective interest method, the entity shall treat:

(a) the fair value of the financial asset or the financial liability at the end of each comparative period presented as the gross carrying amount of that financial asset or the amortised cost of that financial liability if the entity restates prior periods; and

(b) the fair value of the financial asset or the financial liability at the date of initial application as the new gross carrying amount of that financial asset or the new amortised cost of that financial liability at the date of initial application of this Standard.

7.2.12 If an entity previously accounted at cost (in accordance with AASB 139), for an investment in an equity instrument that does not have a quoted price in an active market for an identical instrument (ie a Level 1 input) (or for a derivative asset that is linked to and must be settled by delivery of such an equity instrument) it shall measure that instrument at fair value at the date of initial application. Any difference between the previous carrying amount and the fair value shall be recognised in the opening retained earnings (or other component of equity, as appropriate) of the reporting period that includes the date of initial application.

7.2.13 If an entity previously accounted for a derivative liability that is linked to, and must be settled by, delivery of an equity instrument that does not have a quoted price in an active market for an identical instrument (ie a Level 1 input) at cost in accordance with AASB 139, it shall measure that derivative liability at fair value at the date of initial application. Any difference between the previous carrying amount and the fair value shall be recognised in the opening retained earnings of the reporting period that includes the date of initial application.

7.2.14 At the date of initial application, an entity shall determine whether the treatment in paragraph 5.7.7 would create or enlarge an accounting mismatch in profit or loss on the basis of the facts and circumstances that exist at the date of initial application. This Standard shall be applied retrospectively on the basis of that determination.

7.2.14A At the date of initial application, an entity is permitted to make the designation in paragraph 2.5 for contracts that already exist on the date but only if it designates all similar contracts. The change in the net assets resulting from such designations shall be recognised in retained earnings at the date of initial application.

7.2.15 Despite the requirement in paragraph 7.2.1, an entity that adopts the classification and measurement requirements of this Standard (which include the requirements related to amortised cost measurement for financial assets and impairment in Sections 5.4 and 5.5) shall provide the disclosures set out in paragraphs 42L–42O of AASB 7 but need not restate prior periods. The entity may restate prior periods if, and only if, it is possible without the use of hindsight. If an entity does not restate prior periods, the entity shall recognise any difference between the previous carrying amount and the carrying amount at the beginning of the annual reporting period that includes the date of initial application in the opening retained earnings (or other component of equity, as appropriate) of the annual reporting period that includes the date of initial application. However, if an entity restates prior periods, the restated financial statements must reflect all of the requirements in this Standard. If an entity's chosen approach to applying AASB 9 results in more than one date of initial application for different requirements, this paragraph applies at each date of initial application (see paragraph 7.2.2). This would be the case, for example, if an entity elects to early apply only the requirements for the presentation of gains and losses on financial liabilities designated as at fair value through profit or loss in accordance with paragraph 7.1.2 before applying the other requirements in this Standard.

7.2.16 If an entity prepares interim financial reports in accordance with AASB 134 *Interim Financial Reporting* the entity need not apply the requirements in this Standard to interim periods prior to the date of initial application if it is impracticable (as defined in AASB 108).

Impairment (Section 5.5)

7.2.17 An entity shall apply the impairment requirements in Section 5.5 retrospectively in accordance with AASB 108 subject to paragraphs 7.2.15 and 7.2.18–7.2.20.

7.2.18 At the date of initial application, an entity shall use reasonable and supportable information that is available without undue cost or effort to determine the credit risk at the date that a financial instrument was initially recognised (or for loan commitments and financial guarantee contracts at the date that the entity became a party to the irrevocable commitment in accordance with paragraph 5.5.6) and compare that to the credit risk at the date of initial application of this Standard.

7.2.19 When determining whether there has been a significant increase in credit risk since initial recognition, an entity may apply:

    (a)   the requirements in paragraphs 5.5.10 and B5.5.22–B5.5.24; and

    (b)   the rebuttable presumption in paragraph 5.5.11 for contractual payments that are more than 30 days past due if an entity will apply the impairment requirements by identifying significant increases in credit risk since initial recognition for those financial instruments on the basis of past due information.

7.2.20 If, at the date of initial application, determining whether there has been a significant increase in credit risk since initial recognition would require undue cost or effort, an entity shall recognise a loss allowance at an amount equal to lifetime expected credit losses at each reporting date until that financial instrument is derecognised (unless that financial instrument is low credit risk at a reporting date, in which case paragraph 7.2.19(a) applies).

Transition for hedge accounting (Chapter 6)

7.2.21 When an entity first applies this Standard, it may choose as its accounting policy to continue to apply the hedge accounting requirements of AASB 139 instead of the requirements in Chapter 6 of this Standard. An entity shall apply that policy to all of its hedging relationships. An entity that chooses that policy shall also apply Interpretation 16 *Hedges of a Net Investment in a Foreign Operation* without the amendments that conform that Interpretation to the requirements in Chapter 6 of this Standard.

Aus7.2.21.1 AASB 2014-1 *Amendments to Australian Accounting Standards* and AASB 2014-7 *Amendments to Australian Accounting Standards arising from AASB 9 (December 2014)* amend paragraphs 3, 5–7, 14, 16, AG1, AG8 and IE5 of Interpretation 16 and add paragraphs 18A-18B to conform Interpretation 16 to the requirements in Chapter 6 of this Standard.

7.2.22 Except as provided in paragraph 7.2.26, an entity shall apply the hedge accounting requirements of this Standard prospectively.

7.2.23 To apply hedge accounting from the date of initial application of the hedge accounting requirements of this Standard, all qualifying criteria must be met as at that date.

7.2.24 Hedging relationships that qualified for hedge accounting in accordance with AASB 139 that also qualify for hedge accounting in accordance with the criteria of this Standard (see paragraph 6.4.1), after taking into account any rebalancing of the hedging relationship on transition (see paragraph 7.2.25(b)), shall be regarded as continuing hedging relationships.

7.2.25 On initial application of the hedge accounting requirements of this Standard, an entity:

(a) may start to apply those requirements from the same point in time as it ceases to apply the hedge accounting requirements of AASB 139; and

(b) shall consider the hedge ratio in accordance with AASB 139 as the starting point for rebalancing the hedge ratio of a continuing hedging relationship, if applicable. Any gain or loss from such a rebalancing shall be recognised in profit or loss.

7.2.26 As an exception to prospective application of the hedge accounting requirements of this Standard, an entity:

(a) shall apply the accounting for the time value of options in accordance with paragraph 6.5.15 retrospectively if, in accordance with AASB 139, only the change in an option's intrinsic value was designated as a hedging instrument in a hedging relationship. This retrospective application applies only to those hedging relationships that existed at the beginning of the earliest comparative period or were designated thereafter.

(b) may apply the accounting for the forward element of forward contracts in accordance with paragraph 6.5.16 retrospectively if, in accordance with AASB 139, only the change in the spot element of a forward contract was designated as a hedging instrument in a hedging relationship. This retrospective application applies only to those hedging relationships that existed at the beginning of the earliest comparative period or were designated thereafter. In addition, if an entity elects retrospective application of this accounting, it shall be applied to all hedging relationships that qualify for this election (ie on transition this election is not available on a hedging-relationship-by-hedging-relationship basis). The accounting for foreign currency basis spreads (see paragraph 6.5.16) may be applied retrospectively for those hedging relationships that existed at the beginning of the earliest comparative period or were designated thereafter.

(c) shall apply retrospectively the requirement of paragraph 6.5.6 that there is not an expiration or termination of the hedging instrument if:

(i) as a consequence of laws or regulations, or the introduction of laws or regulations, the parties to the hedging instrument agree that one or more clearing counterparties replace their original counterparty to become the new counterparty to each of the parties; and

(ii) other changes, if any, to the hedging instrument are limited to those that are necessary to effect such a replacement of the counterparty.

Entities that have applied AASB 9 (December 2009) or AASB 9 (December 2010) early

7.2.27 An entity shall apply the transition requirements in paragraphs 7.2.1–7.2.26 at the relevant date of initial application. An entity shall apply each of the transition provisions in paragraphs 7.2.3–7.2.14A and 7.2.17–7.2.26 only once (ie if an entity chooses an approach of applying AASB 9 that involves more than one date of initial application, it cannot apply any of those provisions again if they were already applied at an earlier date). (See paragraphs 7.2.2 and Aus1.4).

Aus7.2.27.1 An entity's chosen approach to applying AASB 9 may include applying AASB 9 (December 2009) or AASB 9 (December 2010) in advance of the Standard's mandatory application date. In these instances, an entity will have more than one date of initial application, and will have previously applied some or all of the transition provisions specified by AASB 9 (December 2009) or AASB 9 (December 2010). An entity cannot apply again a transition provision specified by paragraphs 7.2.3–7.2.14A and 7.2.17–7.2.26 of this Standard to the extent a similar provision has already been applied at an earlier date on early adoption of AASB 9 (December 2009) or AASB 9 (December 2010).

7.2.28 An entity that applied AASB 9 (December 2009) or AASB 9 (December 2010) and subsequently applies this Standard:

(a) shall revoke its previous designation of a financial asset as measured at fair value through profit or loss if that designation was previously made in accordance with the condition in paragraph 4.1.5 but that condition is no longer satisfied as a result of the application of this Standard;

(b) may designate a financial asset as measured at fair value through profit or loss if that designation would not have previously satisfied the condition in paragraph 4.1.5 but that condition is now satisfied as a result of the application of this Standard;

(c) shall revoke its previous designation of a financial liability as measured at fair value through profit or loss if that designation was previously made in accordance with the condition in paragraph 4.2.2(a) but that condition is no longer satisfied as a result of the application of this Standard; and

(d) may designate a financial liability as measured at fair value through profit or loss if that designation would not have previously satisfied the condition in paragraph 4.2.2(a) but that condition is now satisfied as a result of the application of this Standard.

Such a designation and revocation shall be made on the basis of the facts and circumstances that exist at the date of initial application of this Standard. That classification shall be applied retrospectively.

7.3 Withdrawal of IFRIC 9, IFRS 9 (2009), IFRS 9 (2010) and IFRS 9 (2013)

7.3.1 [Deleted by the AASB – see paragraph Aus1.5]

7.3.2 [Deleted by the AASB – see paragraph Aus1.4]

APPENDIX A
DEFINED TERMS

This appendix is an integral part of AASB 9.

12-month expected credit losses	The portion of **lifetime expected credit losses** that represent the **expected credit losses** that result from default events on a financial instrument that are possible within the 12 months after the reporting date.

amortised cost of a financial asset or financial liability	The amount at which the financial asset or financial liability is measured at initial recognition minus the principal repayments, plus or minus the cumulative amortisation using the **effective interest method** of any difference between that initial amount and the maturity amount and, for financial assets, adjusted for any **loss allowance**.
contract assets	Those rights that AASB 15 *Revenue from Contracts with Customers* specifies are accounted for in accordance with this Standard for the purposes of recognising and measuring impairment gains or losses.
credit-impaired financial asset	A financial asset is credit-impaired when one or more events that have a detrimental impact on the estimated future cash flows of that financial asset have occurred. Evidence that a financial asset is credit-impaired include observable data about the following events: (a) significant financial difficulty of the issuer or the borrower; (b) a breach of contract, such as a default or **past due** event; (c) the lender(s) of the borrower, for economic or contractual reasons relating to the borrower's financial difficulty, having granted to the borrower a concession(s) that the lender(s) would not otherwise consider; (d) it is becoming probable that the borrower will enter bankruptcy or other financial reorganisation; (e) the disappearance of an active market for that financial asset because of financial difficulties; or (f) the purchase or origination of a financial asset at a deep discount that reflects the incurred **credit losses**. It may not be possible to identify a single discrete event – instead, the combined effect of several events may have caused financial assets to become credit-impaired.
credit loss	The difference between all contractual cash flows that are due to an entity in accordance with the contract and all the cash flows that the entity expects to receive (ie all cash shortfalls), discounted at the original **effective interest rate** (or **credit-adjusted effective interest rate** for **purchased or originated credit-impaired financial assets**). An entity shall estimate cash flows by considering all contractual terms of the financial instrument (for example, prepayment, extension, call and similar options) through the expected life of that financial instrument. The cash flows that are considered shall include cash flows from the sale of collateral held or other credit enhancements that are integral to the contractual terms. There is a presumption that the expected life of a financial instrument can be estimated reliably. However, in those rare cases when it is not possible to reliably estimate the expected life of a financial instrument, the entity shall use the remaining contractual term of the financial instrument.
credit-adjusted effective interest rate	The rate that exactly discounts the estimated future cash payments or receipts through the expected life of the financial asset to the **amortised cost of a financial asset** that is a **purchased or originated credit-impaired financial asset**. When calculating the credit-adjusted effective interest rate, an entity shall estimate the expected cash flows by considering all contractual terms of the financial asset (for example, prepayment, extension, call and similar options) and **expected credit losses**. The calculation includes all fees and points paid or received between parties to the contract that are an integral part of the effective interest rate (see paragraphs B5.4.1–B5.4.3), **transaction costs**, and all other premiums or discounts. There is a presumption that the cash flows and the expected life of a group of similar financial instruments can be estimated reliably. However, in those rare cases when it is not possible to reliably estimate the cash flows or the remaining life of a financial instrument (or group of financial instruments), the entity shall use the contractual cash flows over the full contractual term of the financial instrument (or group of financial instruments).
derecognition	The removal of a previously recognised financial asset or financial liability from an entity's statement of financial position.

(Continued)

derivative	A financial instrument or other contract within the scope of this Standard with all three of the following characteristics.
	(a) its value changes in response to the change in a specified interest rate, financial instrument price, commodity price, foreign exchange rate, index of prices or rates, credit rating or credit index, or other variable, provided in the case of a non-financial variable that the variable is not specific to a party to the contract (sometimes called the 'underlying').
	(b) it requires no initial net investment or an initial net investment that is smaller than would be required for other types of contracts that would be expected to have a similar response to changes in market factors.
	(c) it is settled at a future date.
dividends	Distributions of profits to holders of equity instruments in proportion to their holdings of a particular class of capital.
effective interest method	The method that is used in the calculation of the **amortised cost of a financial asset or a financial liability** and in the allocation and recognition of the interest revenue or interest expense in profit or loss over the relevant period.
effective interest rate	The rate that exactly discounts estimated future cash payments or receipts through the expected life of the financial asset or financial liability to the **gross carrying amount of a financial asset** or to the **amortised cost of a financial liability**. When calculating the effective interest rate, an entity shall estimate the expected cash flows by considering all the contractual terms of the financial instrument (for example, prepayment, extension, call and similar options) but shall not consider the **expected credit losses**. The calculation includes all fees and points paid or received between parties to the contract that are an integral part of the effective interest rate (see paragraphs B5.4.1–B5.4.3), **transaction costs**, and all other premiums or discounts. There is a presumption that the cash flows and the expected life of a group of similar financial instruments can be estimated reliably. However, in those rare cases when it is not possible to reliably estimate the cash flows or the expected life of a financial instrument (or group of financial instruments), the entity shall use the contractual cash flows over the full contractual term of the financial instrument (or group of financial instruments).
expected credit losses	The weighted average of **credit losses** with the respective risks of a default occurring as the weights.
financial guarantee contract	A contract that requires the issuer to make specified payments to reimburse the holder for a loss it incurs because a specified debtor fails to make payment when due in accordance with the original or modified terms of a debt instrument.
financial liability at fair value through profit or loss	A financial liability that meets one of the following conditions.
	(a) it meets the definition of **held for trading.**
	(b) upon initial recognition it is designated by the entity as at fair value through profit or loss in accordance with paragraph 4.2.2 or 4.3.5.
	(c) it is designated either upon initial recognition or subsequently as at fair value through profit or loss in accordance with paragraph 6.7.1.
firm commitment	A binding agreement for the exchange of a specified quantity of resources at a specified price on a specified future date or dates.
forecast transaction	An uncommitted but anticipated future transaction.
gross carrying amount of a financial asset	The **amortised cost of a financial asset**, before adjusting for any **loss allowance**.
hedge ratio	The relationship between the quantity of the hedging instrument and the quantity of the hedged item in terms of their relative weighting.
held for trading	A financial asset or financial liability that:
	(a) is acquired or incurred principally for the purpose of selling or repurchasing it in the near term;
	(b) on initial recognition is part of a portfolio of identified financial instruments that are managed together and for which there is evidence of a recent actual pattern of short-term profit-taking; or
	(c) is a **derivative** (except for a derivative that is a financial guarantee contract or a designated and effective hedging instrument).

impairment gain or loss	Gains or losses that are recognised in profit or loss in accordance with paragraph 5.5.8 and that arise from applying the impairment requirements in Section 5.5.
lifetime expected credit losses	The **expected credit losses** that result from all possible default events over the expected life of a financial instrument.
loss allowance	The allowance for **expected credit losses** on financial assets measured in accordance with paragraph 4.1.2, lease receivables and **contract assets**, the accumulated impairment amount for financial assets measured in accordance with paragraph 4.1.2A and the provision for expected credit losses on loan commitments and **financial guarantee contracts**.
modification gain or loss	The amount arising from adjusting the **gross carrying amount of a financial asset** to reflect the renegotiated or modified contractual cash flows. The entity recalculates the gross carrying amount of a financial asset as the present value of the estimated future cash payments or receipts through the expected life of the renegotiated or modified financial asset that are discounted at the financial asset's original **effective interest rate** (or the original **credit-adjusted effective interest rate** for **purchased or originated credit-impaired financial assets**) or, when applicable, the revised **effective interest rate** calculated in accordance with paragraph 6.5.10.
	When estimating the expected cash flows of a financial asset, an entity shall consider all contractual terms of the financial asset (for example, prepayment, call and similar options) but shall not consider the **expected credit losses**, unless the financial asset is a **purchased or originated credit-impaired financial asset**, in which case an entity shall also consider the initial expected credit losses that were considered when calculating the original **credit-adjusted effective interest rate**.
past due	A financial asset is past due when a counterparty has failed to make a payment when that payment was contractually due.
purchased or originated credit-impaired financial asset	Purchased or originated financial asset(s) that are **credit-impaired** on initial recognition.
reclassification date	The first day of the first reporting period following the change in business model that results in an entity reclassifying financial assets.
regular way purchase or sale	A purchase or sale of a financial asset under a contract whose terms require delivery of the asset within the time frame established generally by regulation or convention in the marketplace concerned.
transaction costs	Incremental costs that are directly attributable to the acquisition, issue or disposal of a financial asset or financial liability (see paragraph B5.4.8). An incremental cost is one that would not have been incurred if the entity had not acquired, issued or disposed of the financial instrument.

The following terms are defined in paragraph 11 of AASB 132, Appendix A of AASB 7, Appendix A of AASB 13 or Appendix A of AASB 15 and are used in this Standard with the meanings specified in AASB 132, AASB 7, AASB 13 or AASB 15:

(a) credit risk;[3]

(b) equity instrument;

(c) fair value;

(d) financial asset;

(e) financial instrument;

(f) financial liability;

(g) transaction price.

---

3   This term (as defined in AASB 7) is used in the requirements for presenting the effects of changes in credit risk on liabilities designated as at fair value through profit or loss (see paragraph 5.7.7).

APPENDIX B
APPLICATION GUIDANCE

This appendix is an integral part of AASB 9.

Scope (Chapter 2)

B2.1   Some contracts require a payment based on climatic, geological or other physical variables. (Those based on climatic variables are sometimes referred to as 'weather derivatives'.) If those contracts are not within the scope of AASB 4 *Insurance Contracts* or AASB 1023 *General Insurance Contracts*, they are within the scope of this Standard.

B2.2   This Standard does not change the requirements relating to employee benefit plans that comply with AASB 1056 *Superannuation Entities* and royalty agreements based on the volume of sales or service revenues that are accounted for under AASB 15 *Revenue from Contracts with Customers*.

B2.3   Sometimes, an entity makes what it views as a 'strategic investment' in equity instruments issued by another entity, with the intention of establishing or maintaining a long-term operating relationship with the entity in which the investment is made. The investor or joint venturer entity uses AASB 128 *Investments in Associates and Joint Ventures* to determine whether the equity method of accounting shall be applied to such an investment.

B2.4   This Standard applies to the financial assets and financial liabilities of insurers, other than rights and obligations that paragraph 2.1(e) excludes because they arise under contracts within the scope of AASB 4.

B2.5   Financial guarantee contracts may have various legal forms, such as a guarantee, some types of letter of credit, a credit default contract or an insurance contract. Their accounting treatment does not depend on their legal form. The following are examples of the appropriate treatment (see paragraph 2.1(e)):

   (a)   Although a financial guarantee contract meets the definition of an insurance contract in AASB 4 if the risk transferred is significant, the issuer applies this Standard. Nevertheless, if the issuer has previously asserted explicitly that it regards such contracts as insurance contracts and has used accounting that is applicable to insurance contracts, the issuer may elect to apply either this Standard or AASB 1023 to such financial guarantee contracts. If this Standard applies, paragraph 5.1.1 requires the issuer to recognise a financial guarantee contract initially at fair value. If the financial guarantee contract was issued to an unrelated party in a stand-alone arm's length transaction, its fair value at inception is likely to equal the premium received, unless there is evidence to the contrary. Subsequently, unless the financial guarantee contract was designated at inception as at fair value through profit or loss or unless paragraphs 3.2.15–3.2.23 and B3.2.12–B3.2.17 apply (when a transfer of a financial asset does not qualify for derecognition or the continuing involvement approach applies), the issuer measures it at the higher of:

   (i)   the amount determined in accordance with Section 5.5; and

   (ii) the amount initially recognised less, when appropriate, the cumulative amount of income recognised in accordance with the principles of AASB 15 (see paragraph 4.2.1(c)).

   (b)   Some credit-related guarantees do not, as a precondition for payment, require that the holder is exposed to, and has incurred a loss on, the failure of the debtor to make payments on the guaranteed asset when due. An example of such a guarantee is one that requires payments in response to changes in a specified credit rating or credit index. Such guarantees are not financial guarantee contracts as defined in this Standard, and are not insurance contracts as defined in AASB 4. Such guarantees are derivatives and the issuer applies this Standard to them.

(c) If a financial guarantee contract was issued in connection with the sale of goods, the issuer applies AASB 15 in determining when it recognises the revenue from the guarantee and from the sale of goods.

B2.6 Assertions that an issuer regards contracts as insurance contracts are typically found throughout the issuer's communications with customers and regulators, contracts, business documentation and financial statements. Furthermore, insurance contracts are often subject to accounting requirements that are distinct from the requirements for other types of transaction, such as contracts issued by banks or commercial companies. In such cases, an issuer's financial statements typically include a statement that the issuer has used those accounting requirements.

Recognition and derecognition (Chapter 3)

Initial recognition (Section 3.1)

B3.1.1 As a consequence of the principle in paragraph 3.1.1, an entity recognises all of its contractual rights and obligations under derivatives in its statement of financial position as assets and liabilities, respectively, except for derivatives that prevent a transfer of financial assets from being accounted for as a sale (see paragraph B3.2.14). If a transfer of a financial asset does not qualify for derecognition, the transferee does not recognise the transferred asset as its asset (see paragraph B3.2.15).

B3.1.2 The following are examples of applying the principle in paragraph 3.1.1:

(a) Unconditional receivables and payables are recognised as assets or liabilities when the entity becomes a party to the contract and, as a consequence, has a legal right to receive or a legal obligation to pay cash.

(b) Assets to be acquired and liabilities to be incurred as a result of a firm commitment to purchase or sell goods or services are generally not recognised until at least one of the parties has performed under the agreement. For example, an entity that receives a firm order does not generally recognise an asset (and the entity that places the order does not recognise a liability) at the time of the commitment but, instead, delays recognition until the ordered goods or services have been shipped, delivered or rendered. If a firm commitment to buy or sell non-financial items is within the scope of this Standard in accordance with paragraphs 2.4–2.7, its net fair value is recognised as an asset or a liability on the commitment date (see paragraph B4.1.30(c)). In addition, if a previously unrecognised firm commitment is designated as a hedged item in a fair value hedge, any change in the net fair value attributable to the hedged risk is recognised as an asset or a liability after the inception of the hedge (see paragraphs 6.5.8(b) and 6.5.9).

(c) A forward contract that is within the scope of this Standard (see paragraph 2.1) is recognised as an asset or a liability on the commitment date, instead of on the date on which settlement takes place. When an entity becomes a party to a forward contract, the fair values of the right and obligation are often equal, so that the net fair value of the forward is zero. If the net fair value of the right and obligation is not zero, the contract is recognised as an asset or liability.

(d) Option contracts that are within the scope of this Standard (see paragraph 2.1) are recognised as assets or liabilities when the holder or writer becomes a party to the contract.

(e) Planned future transactions, no matter how likely, are not assets and liabilities because the entity has not become a party to a contract.

Regular way purchase or sale of financial assets

B3.1.3 A regular way purchase or sale of financial assets is recognised using either trade date accounting or settlement date accounting as described in paragraphs B3.1.5 and B3.1.6. An entity shall apply the same method consistently for all purchases and sales of financial assets that are classified in the same way in accordance with this Standard. For this purpose assets that are mandatorily measured at fair value through profit or loss form a separate classification from assets designated as measured at fair value through profit or loss. In addition, investments in equity instruments accounted for using the option provided in paragraph 5.7.5 form a separate classification.

B3.1.4 A contract that requires or permits net settlement of the change in the value of the contract is not a regular way contract. Instead, such a contract is accounted for as a derivative in the period between the trade date and the settlement date.

B3.1.5 The trade date is the date that an entity commits itself to purchase or sell an asset. Trade date accounting refers to (a) the recognition of an asset to be received and the liability to pay for it on the trade date, and (b) derecognition of an asset that is sold, recognition of any gain or loss on disposal and the recognition of a receivable from the buyer for payment on the trade date. Generally, interest does not start to accrue on the asset and corresponding liability until the settlement date when title passes.

B3.1.6 The settlement date is the date that an asset is delivered to or by an entity. Settlement date accounting refers to (a) the recognition of an asset on the day it is received by the entity, and (b) the derecognition of an asset and recognition of any gain or loss on disposal on the day that it is delivered by the entity. When settlement date accounting is applied an entity accounts for any change in the fair value of the asset to be received during the period between the trade date and the settlement date in the same way as it accounts for the acquired asset. In other words, the change in value is not recognised for assets measured at amortised cost; it is recognised in profit or loss for assets classified as financial assets measured at fair value through profit or loss; and it is recognised in other comprehensive income for financial assets measured at fair value through other comprehensive income in accordance with paragraph 4.1.2A and for investments in equity instruments accounted for in accordance with paragraph 5.7.5.

Derecognition of financial assets (Section 3.2)

B3.2.1 The following flow chart illustrates the evaluation of whether and to what extent a financial asset is derecognised.

[Flow chart has been positioned after paragraph B3.2.3 due to page constraints.]

Arrangements under which an entity retains the contractual rights to receive the cash flows of a financial asset, but assumes a contractual obligation to pay the cash flows to one or more recipients (paragraph 3.2.4(b))

B3.2.2 The situation described in paragraph 3.2.4(b) (when an entity retains the contractual rights to receive the cash flows of the financial asset, but assumes a contractual obligation to pay the cash flows to one or more recipients) occurs, for example, if the entity is a trust, and issues to investors beneficial interests in the underlying financial assets that it owns and provides servicing of those financial assets. In that case, the financial assets qualify for derecognition if the conditions in paragraphs 3.2.5 and 3.2.6 are met.

B3.2.3 In applying paragraph 3.2.5, the entity could be, for example, the originator of the financial asset, or it could be a group that includes a subsidiary that has acquired the financial asset and passes on cash flows to unrelated third party investors.

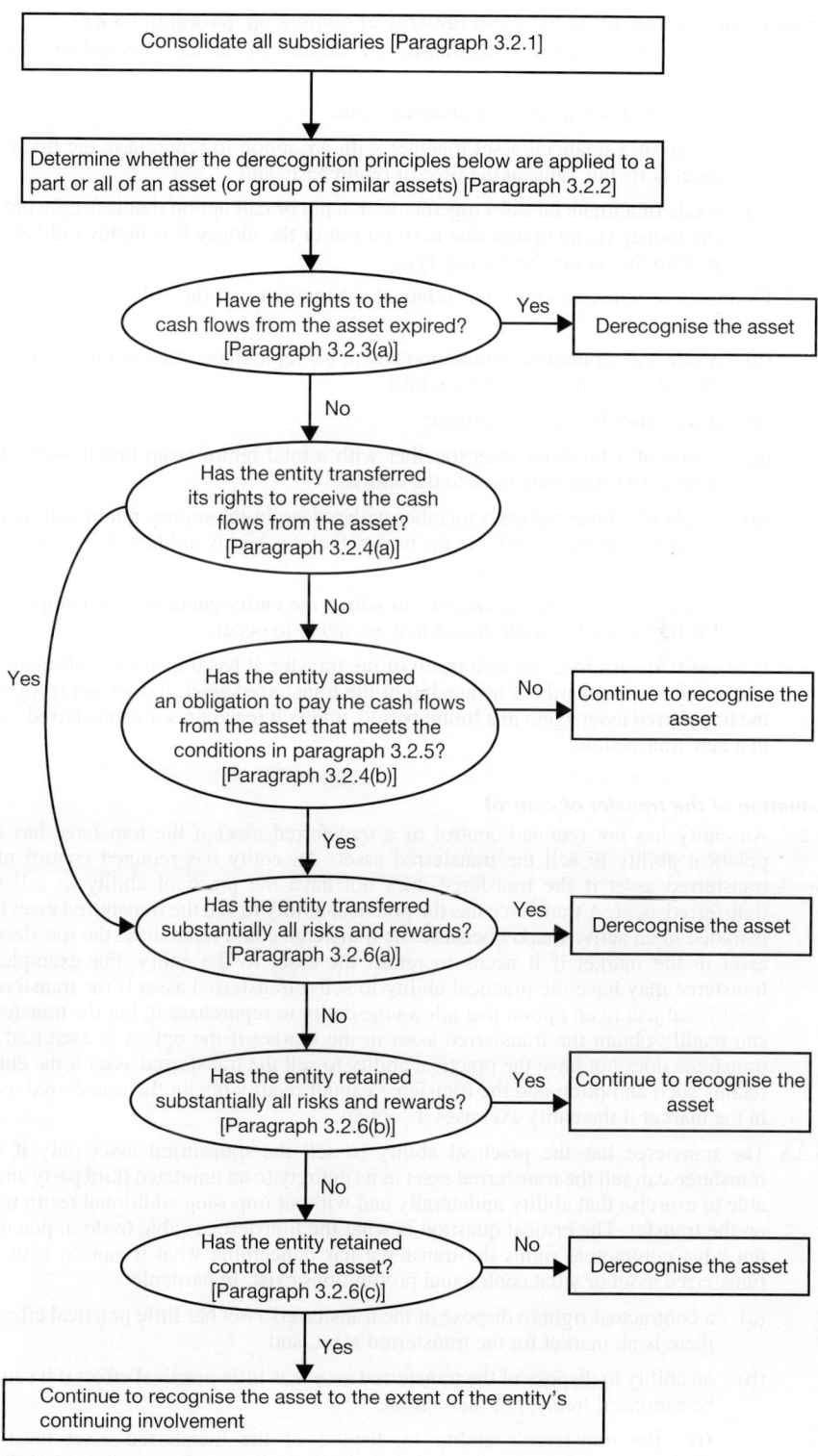

Evaluation of the transfer of risks and rewards of ownership (paragraph 3.2.6)

B3.2.4 Examples of when an entity has transferred substantially all the risks and rewards of ownership are:

    (a)   an unconditional sale of a financial asset;

    (b)   a sale of a financial asset together with an option to repurchase the financial asset at its fair value at the time of repurchase; and

    (c)   a sale of a financial asset together with a put or call option that is deeply out of the money (ie an option that is so far out of the money it is highly unlikely to go into the money before expiry).

B3.2.5 Examples of when an entity has retained substantially all the risks and rewards of ownership are:

    (a)   a sale and repurchase transaction where the repurchase price is a fixed price or the sale price plus a lender's return;

    (b)   a securities lending agreement;

    (c)   a sale of a financial asset together with a total return swap that transfers the market risk exposure back to the entity;

    (d)   a sale of a financial asset together with a deep in-the-money put or call option (ie an option that is so far in the money that it is highly unlikely to go out of the money before expiry); and

    (e)   a sale of short-term receivables in which the entity guarantees to compensate the transferee for credit losses that are likely to occur.

B3.2.6 If an entity determines that as a result of the transfer, it has transferred substantially all the risks and rewards of ownership of the transferred asset, it does not recognise the transferred asset again in a future period, unless it reacquires the transferred asset in a new transaction.

Evaluation of the transfer of control

B3.2.7 An entity has not retained control of a transferred asset if the transferee has the practical ability to sell the transferred asset. An entity has retained control of a transferred asset if the transferee does not have the practical ability to sell the transferred asset. A transferee has the practical ability to sell the transferred asset if it is traded in an active market because the transferee could repurchase the transferred asset in the market if it needs to return the asset to the entity. For example, a transferee may have the practical ability to sell a transferred asset if the transferred asset is subject to an option that allows the entity to repurchase it, but the transferee can readily obtain the transferred asset in the market if the option is exercised. A transferee does not have the practical ability to sell the transferred asset if the entity retains such an option and the transferee cannot readily obtain the transferred asset in the market if the entity exercises its option.

B3.2.8 The transferee has the practical ability to sell the transferred asset only if the transferee can sell the transferred asset in its entirety to an unrelated third party and is able to exercise that ability unilaterally and without imposing additional restrictions on the transfer. The critical question is what the transferee is able to do in practice, not what contractual rights the transferee has concerning what it can do with the transferred asset or what contractual prohibitions exist. In particular:

    (a)   a contractual right to dispose of the transferred asset has little practical effect if there is no market for the transferred asset, and

    (b)   an ability to dispose of the transferred asset has little practical effect if it cannot be exercised freely. For that reason:

        (i)   the transferee's ability to dispose of the transferred asset must be independent of the actions of others (ie it must be a unilateral ability), and

(ii)   the transferee must be able to dispose of the transferred asset without needing to attach restrictive conditions or 'strings' to the transfer (eg conditions about how a loan asset is serviced or an option giving the transferee the right to repurchase the asset).

B3.2.9 That the transferee is unlikely to sell the transferred asset does not, of itself, mean that the transferor has retained control of the transferred asset. However, if a put option or guarantee constrains the transferee from selling the transferred asset, then the transferor has retained control of the transferred asset. For example, if a put option or guarantee is sufficiently valuable it constrains the transferee from selling the transferred asset because the transferee would, in practice, not sell the transferred asset to a third party without attaching a similar option or other restrictive conditions. Instead, the transferee would hold the transferred asset so as to obtain payments under the guarantee or put option. Under these circumstances the transferor has retained control of the transferred asset.

Transfers that qualify for derecognition

B3.2.10 An entity may retain the right to a part of the interest payments on transferred assets as compensation for servicing those assets. The part of the interest payments that the entity would give up upon termination or transfer of the servicing contract is allocated to the servicing asset or servicing liability. The part of the interest payments that the entity would not give up is an interest-only strip receivable. For example, if the entity would not give up any interest upon termination or transfer of the servicing contract, the entire interest spread is an interest-only strip receivable. For the purposes of applying paragraph 3.2.13, the fair values of the servicing asset and interest-only strip receivable are used to allocate the carrying amount of the receivable between the part of the asset that is derecognised and the part that continues to be recognised. If there is no servicing fee specified or the fee to be received is not expected to compensate the entity adequately for performing the servicing, a liability for the servicing obligation is recognised at fair value.

B3.2.11 When measuring the fair values of the part that continues to be recognised and the part that is derecognised for the purposes of applying paragraph 3.2.13, an entity applies the fair value measurement requirements in AASB 13 *Fair Value Measurement* in addition to paragraph 3.2.14.

Transfers that do not qualify for derecognition

B3.2.12 The following is an application of the principle outlined in paragraph 3.2.15. If a guarantee provided by the entity for default losses on the transferred asset prevents a transferred asset from being derecognised because the entity has retained substantially all the risks and rewards of ownership of the transferred asset, the transferred asset continues to be recognised in its entirety and the consideration received is recognised as a liability.

Continuing involvement in transferred assets

B3.2.13 The following are examples of how an entity measures a transferred asset and the associated liability under paragraph 3.2.16.

All assets

(a)   If a guarantee provided by an entity to pay for default losses on a transferred asset prevents the transferred asset from being derecognised to the extent of the continuing involvement, the transferred asset at the date of the transfer is measured at the lower of (i) the carrying amount of the asset and (ii) the maximum amount of the consideration received in the transfer that the entity could be required to repay ('the guarantee amount'). The associated liability is initially measured at the guarantee amount plus the fair value of the guarantee (which is normally the consideration received for the guarantee). Subsequently, the initial fair value of the guarantee is recognised in profit or loss when (or as) the obligation is satisfied (in accordance with the principles of AASB 15) and the carrying value of the asset is reduced by any loss allowance.

Assets measured at amortised cost

(b)   If a put option obligation written by an entity or call option right held by an entity prevents a transferred asset from being derecognised and the entity measures the transferred asset at amortised cost, the associated liability is measured at its cost (ie the consideration received) adjusted for the amortisation of any difference between that cost and the gross carrying amount of the transferred asset at the expiration date of the option. For example, assume that the gross carrying amount of the asset on the date of the transfer is CU98 and that the consideration received is CU95. The gross carrying amount of the asset on the option exercise date will be CU100. The initial carrying amount of the associated liability is CU95 and the difference between CU95 and CU100 is recognised in profit or loss using the effective interest method. If the option is exercised, any difference between the carrying amount of the associated liability and the exercise price is recognised in profit or loss.

Assets measured at fair value

(c)   If a call option right retained by an entity prevents a transferred asset from being derecognised and the entity measures the transferred asset at fair value, the asset continues to be measured at its fair value. The associated liability is measured at (i) the option exercise price less the time value of the option if the option is in or at the money, or (ii) the fair value of the transferred asset less the time value of the option if the option is out of the money. The adjustment to the measurement of the associated liability ensures that the net carrying amount of the asset and the associated liability is the fair value of the call option right. For example, if the fair value of the underlying asset is CU80, the option exercise price is CU95 and the time value of the option is CU5, the carrying amount of the associated liability is CU75 (CU80 – CU5) and the carrying amount of the transferred asset is CU80 (ie its fair value).

(d)   If a put option written by an entity prevents a transferred asset from being derecognised and the entity measures the transferred asset at fair value, the associated liability is measured at the option exercise price plus the time value of the option. The measurement of the asset at fair value is limited to the lower of the fair value and the option exercise price because the entity has no right to increases in the fair value of the transferred asset above the exercise price of the option. This ensures that the net carrying amount of the asset and the associated liability is the fair value of the put option obligation. For example, if the fair value of the underlying asset is CU120, the option exercise price is CU100 and the time value of the option is CU5, the carrying amount of the associated liability is CU105 (CU100 + CU5) and the carrying amount of the asset is CU100 (in this case the option exercise price).

(e)   If a collar, in the form of a purchased call and written put, prevents a transferred asset from being derecognised and the entity measures the asset at fair value, it continues to measure the asset at fair value. The associated liability is measured at (i) the sum of the call exercise price and fair value of the put option less the time value of the call option, if the call option is in or at the money, or (ii) the sum of the fair value of the asset and the fair value of the put option less the time value of the call option if the call option is out of the money. The adjustment to the associated liability ensures that the net carrying amount of the asset and the associated liability is the fair value of the options held and written by the entity. For example, assume an entity transfers a financial asset that is measured at fair value while simultaneously purchasing a call with an exercise price of CU120 and writing a put with an exercise price of CU80. Assume also that the fair value of the asset is CU100 at the date of the transfer. The time value of the put and call are CU1 and CU5 respectively. In this case, the entity recognises an asset of CU100 (the fair value of the asset) and a liability of CU96 [(CU100 + CU1) – CU5]. This gives a net asset value of CU4, which is the fair value of the options held and written by the entity.

All transfers

B3.2.14 To the extent that a transfer of a financial asset does not qualify for derecognition, the transferor's contractual rights or obligations related to the transfer are not accounted for separately as derivatives if recognising both the derivative and either the transferred asset or the liability arising from the transfer would result in recognising the same rights or obligations twice. For example, a call option retained by the transferor may prevent a transfer of financial assets from being accounted for as a sale. In that case, the call option is not separately recognised as a derivative asset.

B3.2.15 To the extent that a transfer of a financial asset does not qualify for derecognition, the transferee does not recognise the transferred asset as its asset. The transferee derecognises the cash or other consideration paid and recognises a receivable from the transferor. If the transferor has both a right and an obligation to reacquire control of the entire transferred asset for a fixed amount (such as under a repurchase agreement), the transferee may measure its receivable at amortised cost if it meets the criteria in paragraph 4.1.2.

Examples

B3.2.16 The following examples illustrate the application of the derecognition principles of this Standard.

    (a) *Repurchase agreements and securities lending.* If a financial asset is sold under an agreement to repurchase it at a fixed price or at the sale price plus a lender's return or if it is loaned under an agreement to return it to the transferor, it is not derecognised because the transferor retains substantially all the risks and rewards of ownership. If the transferee obtains the right to sell or pledge the asset, the transferor reclassifies the asset in its statement of financial position, for example, as a loaned asset or repurchase receivable.

    (b) *Repurchase agreements and securities lending – assets that are substantially the same.* If a financial asset is sold under an agreement to repurchase the same or substantially the same asset at a fixed price or at the sale price plus a lender's return or if a financial asset is borrowed or loaned under an agreement to return the same or substantially the same asset to the transferor, it is not derecognised because the transferor retains substantially all the risks and rewards of ownership.

    (c) *Repurchase agreements and securities lending – right of substitution.* If a repurchase agreement at a fixed repurchase price or a price equal to the sale price plus a lender's return, or a similar securities lending transaction, provides the transferee with a right to substitute assets that are similar and of equal fair value to the transferred asset at the repurchase date, the asset sold or lent under a repurchase or securities lending transaction is not derecognised because the transferor retains substantially all the risks and rewards of ownership.

    (d) *Repurchase right of first refusal at fair value.* If an entity sells a financial asset and retains only a right of first refusal to repurchase the transferred asset at fair value if the transferee subsequently sells it, the entity derecognises the asset because it has transferred substantially all the risks and rewards of ownership.

    (e) *Wash sale transaction.* The repurchase of a financial asset shortly after it has been sold is sometimes referred to as a wash sale. Such a repurchase does not preclude derecognition provided that the original transaction met the derecognition requirements. However, if an agreement to sell a financial asset is entered into concurrently with an agreement to repurchase the same asset at a fixed price or the sale price plus a lender's return, then the asset is not derecognised.

    (f) *Put options and call options that are deeply in the money.* If a transferred financial asset can be called back by the transferor and the call option is

AASB

deeply in the money, the transfer does not qualify for derecognition because the transferor has retained substantially all the risks and rewards of ownership. Similarly, if the financial asset can be put back by the transferee and the put option is deeply in the money, the transfer does not qualify for derecognition because the transferor has retained substantially all the risks and rewards of ownership.

(g) *Put options and call options that are deeply out of the money.* A financial asset that is transferred subject only to a deep out-of-the-money put option held by the transferee or a deep out-of-the-money call option held by the transferor is derecognised. This is because the transferor has transferred substantially all the risks and rewards of ownership.

(h) *Readily obtainable assets subject to a call option that is neither deeply in the money nor deeply out of the money.* If an entity holds a call option on an asset that is readily obtainable in the market and the option is neither deeply in the money nor deeply out of the money, the asset is derecognised. This is because the entity (i) has neither retained nor transferred substantially all the risks and rewards of ownership, and (ii) has not retained control. However, if the asset is not readily obtainable in the market, derecognition is precluded to the extent of the amount of the asset that is subject to the call option because the entity has retained control of the asset.

(i) *A not readily obtainable asset subject to a put option written by an entity that is neither deeply in the money nor deeply out of the money.* If an entity transfers a financial asset that is not readily obtainable in the market, and writes a put option that is not deeply out of the money, the entity neither retains nor transfers substantially all the risks and rewards of ownership because of the written put option. The entity retains control of the asset if the put option is sufficiently valuable to prevent the transferee from selling the asset, in which case the asset continues to be recognised to the extent of the transferor's continuing involvement (see paragraph B3.2.9). The entity transfers control of the asset if the put option is not sufficiently valuable to prevent the transferee from selling the asset, in which case the asset is derecognised.

(j) *Assets subject to a fair value put or call option or a forward repurchase agreement.* A transfer of a financial asset that is subject only to a put or call option or a forward repurchase agreement that has an exercise or repurchase price equal to the fair value of the financial asset at the time of repurchase results in derecognition because of the transfer of substantially all the risks and rewards of ownership.

(k) *Cash-settled call or put options.* An entity evaluates the transfer of a financial asset that is subject to a put or call option or a forward repurchase agreement that will be settled net in cash to determine whether it has retained or transferred substantially all the risks and rewards of ownership. If the entity has not retained substantially all the risks and rewards of ownership of the transferred asset, it determines whether it has retained control of the transferred asset. That the put or the call or the forward repurchase agreement is settled net in cash does not automatically mean that the entity has transferred control (see paragraphs B3.2.9 and (g), (h) and (i) above).

(l) *Removal of accounts provision.* A removal of accounts provision is an unconditional repurchase (call) option that gives an entity the right to reclaim assets transferred subject to some restrictions. Provided that such an option results in the entity neither retaining nor transferring substantially all the risks and rewards of ownership, it precludes derecognition only to the extent of the amount subject to repurchase (assuming that the transferee cannot sell the assets). For example, if the carrying amount and proceeds from the transfer of loan assets are CU100,000 and any individual loan could be called back but the aggregate amount of loans that could be repurchased could not exceed CU10,000, CU90,000 of the loans would qualify for derecognition.

(m) *Clean-up calls.* An entity, which may be a transferor, that services transferred assets may hold a clean-up call to purchase remaining transferred assets when the amount of outstanding assets falls to a specified level at which the cost of servicing those assets becomes burdensome in relation to the benefits of servicing. Provided that such a clean-up call results in the entity neither retaining nor transferring substantially all the risks and rewards of ownership and the transferee cannot sell the assets, it precludes derecognition only to the extent of the amount of the assets that is subject to the call option.

(n) *Subordinated retained interests and credit guarantees.* An entity may provide the transferee with credit enhancement by subordinating some or all of its interest retained in the transferred asset. Alternatively, an entity may provide the transferee with credit enhancement in the form of a credit guarantee that could be unlimited or limited to a specified amount. If the entity retains substantially all the risks and rewards of ownership of the transferred asset, the asset continues to be recognised in its entirety. If the entity retains some, but not substantially all, of the risks and rewards of ownership and has retained control, derecognition is precluded to the extent of the amount of cash or other assets that the entity could be required to pay.

(o) *Total return swaps.* An entity may sell a financial asset to a transferee and enter into a total return swap with the transferee, whereby all of the interest payment cash flows from the underlying asset are remitted to the entity in exchange for a fixed payment or variable rate payment and any increases or declines in the fair value of the underlying asset are absorbed by the entity. In such a case, derecognition of all of the asset is prohibited.

(p) *Interest rate swaps.* An entity may transfer to a transferee a fixed rate financial asset and enter into an interest rate swap with the transferee to receive a fixed interest rate and pay a variable interest rate based on a notional amount that is equal to the principal amount of the transferred financial asset. The interest rate swap does not preclude derecognition of the transferred asset provided the payments on the swap are not conditional on payments being made on the transferred asset.

(q) *Amortising interest rate swaps.* An entity may transfer to a transferee a fixed rate financial asset that is paid off over time, and enter into an amortising interest rate swap with the transferee to receive a fixed interest rate and pay a variable interest rate based on a notional amount. If the notional amount of the swap amortises so that it equals the principal amount of the transferred financial asset outstanding at any point in time, the swap would generally result in the entity retaining substantial prepayment risk, in which case the entity either continues to recognise all of the transferred asset or continues to recognise the transferred asset to the extent of its continuing involvement. Conversely, if the amortisation of the notional amount of the swap is not linked to the principal amount outstanding of the transferred asset, such a swap would not result in the entity retaining prepayment risk on the asset. Hence, it would not preclude derecognition of the transferred asset provided the payments on the swap are not conditional on interest payments being made on the transferred asset and the swap does not result in the entity retaining any other significant risks and rewards of ownership on the transferred asset.

(r) *Write-off.* An entity has no reasonable expectations of recovering the contractual cash flows on a financial asset in its entirety or a portion thereof.

B3.2.17 This paragraph illustrates the application of the continuing involvement approach when the entity's continuing involvement is in a part of a financial asset.

Assume an entity has a portfolio of prepayable loans whose coupon and effective interest rate is 10 per cent and whose principal amount and amortised cost is CU10,000. It enters into a transaction in which, in return for a payment of CU9,115, the transferee obtains the right to CU9,000 of any collections of principal plus interest thereon at 9.5 per cent. The entity retains rights to CU1,000 of any collections of principal plus interest thereon at 10 per cent, plus the excess spread of 0.5 per cent on the remaining CU9,000 of principal. Collections from prepayments are allocated between the entity and the transferee proportionately in the ratio of 1:9, but any defaults are deducted from the entity's interest of CU1,000 until that interest is exhausted. The fair value of the loans at the date of the transaction is CU10,100 and the fair value of the excess spread of 0.5 per cent is CU40.

The entity determines that it has transferred some significant risks and rewards of ownership (for example, significant prepayment risk) but has also retained some significant risks and rewards of ownership (because of its subordinated retained interest) and has retained control. It therefore applies the continuing involvement approach.

To apply this Standard, the entity analyses the transaction as (a) a retention of a fully proportionate retained interest of CU1,000, plus (b) the subordination of that retained interest to provide credit enhancement to the transferee for credit losses.

The entity calculates that CU9,090 (90 per cent × CU10,100) of the consideration received of CU9,115 represents the consideration for a fully proportionate 90 per cent share. The remainder of the consideration received (CU25) represents consideration received for subordinating its retained interest to provide credit enhancement to the transferee for credit losses. In addition, the excess spread of 0.5 per cent represents consideration received for the credit enhancement. Accordingly, the total consideration received for the credit enhancement is CU65 (CU25 + CU40).

The entity calculates the gain or loss on the sale of the 90 per cent share of cash flows. Assuming that separate fair values of the 90 per cent part transferred and the 10 per cent part retained are not available at the date of the transfer, the entity allocates the carrying amount of the asset in accordance with paragraph 3.2.14 of AASB 9 as follows:

	Fair value	Percentage	Allocated carrying amount
Portion transferred	9,090	90%	9,000
Portion retained	1,010	10%	1,000
Total	**10,100**		**10,000**

The entity computes its gain or loss on the sale of the 90 per cent share of the cash flows by deducting the allocated carrying amount of the portion transferred from the consideration received, ie CU90 (CU9,090 – CU9,000). The carrying amount of the portion retained by the entity is CU1,000.

In addition, the entity recognises the continuing involvement that results from the subordination of its retained interest for credit losses. Accordingly, it recognises an asset of CU1,000 (the maximum amount of the cash flows it would not receive under the subordination), and an associated liability of CU1,065 (which is the maximum amount of the cash flows it would not receive under the subordination, ie CU1,000 plus the fair value of the subordination of CU65).

The entity uses all of the above information to account for the transaction as follows:

	Debit	Credit
Original asset	–	9,000
Asset recognised for subordination or the residual interest	1,000	–
Asset for the consideration received in the form of excess spread	40	–
Profit or loss (gain on transfer)	–	90
Liability	–	1,065
Cash received	9,115	–
Total	**10,155**	**10,155**

Immediately following the transaction, the carrying amount of the asset is CU2,040 comprising CU1,000, representing the allocated cost of the portion retained, and CU1,040, representing the entity's additional continuing involvement from the subordination of its retained interest for credit losses (which includes the excess spread of CU40).

In subsequent periods, the entity recognises the consideration received for the credit enhancement (CU65) on a time proportion basis, accrues interest on the recognised asset using the effective interest method and recognises any impairment losses on the recognised assets. As an example of the latter, assume that in the following year there is an impairment loss on the underlying loans of CU300. The entity reduces its recognised asset by CU600 (CU300 relating to its retained interest and CU300 relating to the additional continuing involvement that arises from the subordination of its retained interest for impairment losses), and reduces its recognised liability by CU300. The net result is a charge to profit or loss for impairment losses of CU300.

Derecognition of financial liabilities (Section 3.3)

B3.3.1 A financial liability (or part of it) is extinguished when the debtor either:

    (a) discharges the liability (or part of it) by paying the creditor, normally with cash, other financial assets, goods or services; or

    (b) is legally released from primary responsibility for the liability (or part of it) either by process of law or by the creditor. (If the debtor has given a guarantee this condition may still be met.)

B3.3.2 If an issuer of a debt instrument repurchases that instrument, the debt is extinguished even if the issuer is a market maker in that instrument or intends to resell it in the near term.

B3.3.3 Payment to a third party, including a trust (sometimes called 'in-substance defeasance'), does not, by itself, relieve the debtor of its primary obligation to the creditor, in the absence of legal release.

B3.3.4 If a debtor pays a third party to assume an obligation and notifies its creditor that the third party has assumed its debt obligation, the debtor does not derecognise the debt obligation unless the condition in paragraph B3.3.1(b) is met. If the debtor pays a third party to assume an obligation and obtains a legal release from its creditor, the debtor has extinguished the debt. However, if the debtor agrees to make payments on the debt to the third party or direct to its original creditor, the debtor recognises a new debt obligation to the third party.

B3.3.5 Although legal release, whether judicially or by the creditor, results in derecognition of a liability, the entity may recognise a new liability if the derecognition criteria in paragraphs 3.2.1–3.2.23 are not met for the financial assets transferred. If those criteria are not met, the transferred assets are not derecognised, and the entity recognises a new liability relating to the transferred assets.

B3.3.6 For the purpose of paragraph 3.3.2, the terms are substantially different if the discounted present value of the cash flows under the new terms, including any fees paid net of any fees received and discounted using the original effective interest rate, is at least 10 per cent different from the discounted present value of the remaining cash flows of the original financial liability. If an exchange of debt instruments or modification of terms is accounted for as an extinguishment, any costs or fees incurred are recognised as part of the gain or loss on the extinguishment. If the exchange or modification is not accounted for as an extinguishment, any costs or fees incurred adjust the carrying amount of the liability and are amortised over the remaining term of the modified liability.

B3.3.7 In some cases, a creditor releases a debtor from its present obligation to make payments, but the debtor assumes a guarantee obligation to pay if the party assuming primary responsibility defaults. In these circumstances the debtor:

    (a) recognises a new financial liability based on the fair value of its obligation for the guarantee, and

AASB

(b)   recognises a gain or loss based on the difference between (i) any proceeds paid
and (ii) the carrying amount of the original financial liability less the fair value
of the new financial liability.

Classification (Chapter 4)

Classification of financial assets (Section 4.1)

The entity's business model for managing financial assets

B4.1.1   Paragraph 4.1.1(a) requires an entity to classify financial assets on the basis of
the entity's business model for managing the financial assets, unless paragraph
4.1.5 applies. An entity assesses whether its financial assets meet the condition
in paragraph 4.1.2(a) or the condition in paragraph 4.1.2A(a) on the basis of the
business model as determined by the entity's key management personnel (as defined
in AASB 124 *Related Party Disclosures*).

B4.1.2   An entity's business model is determined at a level that reflects how groups of
financial assets are managed together to achieve a particular business objective.
The entity's business model does not depend on management's intentions for
an individual instrument. Accordingly, this condition is not an instrument-by-
instrument approach to classification and should be determined on a higher level
of aggregation. However, a single entity may have more than one business model
for managing its financial instruments. Consequently, classification need not be
determined at the reporting entity level. For example, an entity may hold a portfolio
of investments that it manages in order to collect contractual cash flows and another
portfolio of investments that it manages in order to trade to realise fair value
changes. Similarly, in some circumstances, it may be appropriate to separate a
portfolio of financial assets into subportfolios in order to reflect the level at which
an entity manages those financial assets. For example, that may be the case if an
entity originates or purchases a portfolio of mortgage loans and manages some of
the loans with an objective of collecting contractual cash flows and manages the
other loans with an objective of selling them.

B4.1.2A An entity's business model refers to how an entity manages its financial assets in
order to generate cash flows. That is, the entity's business model determines whether
cash flows will result from collecting contractual cash flows, selling financial assets
or both. Consequently, this assessment is not performed on the basis of scenarios
that the entity does not reasonably expect to occur, such as so-called 'worst case' or
'stress case' scenarios. For example, if an entity expects that it will sell a particular
portfolio of financial assets only in a stress case scenario, that scenario would not
affect the entity's assessment of the business model for those assets if the entity
reasonably expects that such a scenario will not occur. If cash flows are realised
in a way that is different from the entity's expectations at the date that the entity
assessed the business model (for example, if the entity sells more or fewer financial
assets than it expected when it classified the assets), that does not give rise to a prior
period error in the entity's financial statements (see AASB 108 *Accounting Policies,
Changes in Accounting Estimates and Errors*) nor does it change the classification
of the remaining financial assets held in that business model (ie those assets that the
entity recognised in prior periods and still holds) as long as the entity considered
all relevant information that was available at the time that it made the business
model assessment. However, when an entity assesses the business model for newly
originated or newly purchased financial assets, it must consider information about
how cash flows were realised in the past, along with all other relevant information.

B4.1.2B An entity's business model for managing financial assets is a matter of fact and not
merely an assertion. It is typically observable through the activities that the entity
undertakes to achieve the objective of the business model. An entity will need to
use judgement when it assesses its business model for managing financial assets and
that assessment is not determined by a single factor or activity. Instead, the entity

must consider all relevant evidence that is available at the date of the assessment. Such relevant evidence includes, but is not limited to:

(a) how the performance of the business model and the financial assets held within that business model are evaluated and reported to the entity's key management personnel;

(b) the risks that affect the performance of the business model (and the financial assets held within that business model) and, in particular, the way in which those risks are managed; and

(c) how managers of the business are compensated (for example, whether the compensation is based on the fair value of the assets managed or on the contractual cash flows collected).

A business model whose objective is to hold assets in order to collect contractual cash flows

B4.1.2C Financial assets that are held within a business model whose objective is to hold assets in order to collect contractual cash flows are managed to realise cash flows by collecting contractual payments over the life of the instrument. That is, the entity manages the assets held within the portfolio to collect those particular contractual cash flows (instead of managing the overall return on the portfolio by both holding and selling assets). In determining whether cash flows are going to be realised by collecting the financial assets' contractual cash flows, it is necessary to consider the frequency, value and timing of sales in prior periods, the reasons for those sales and expectations about future sales activity. However sales in themselves do not determine the business model and therefore cannot be considered in isolation. Instead, information about past sales and expectations about future sales provide evidence related to how the entity's stated objective for managing the financial assets is achieved and, specifically, how cash flows are realised. An entity must consider information about past sales within the context of the reasons for those sales and the conditions that existed at that time as compared to current conditions.

B4.1.3 Although the objective of an entity's business model may be to hold financial assets in order to collect contractual cash flows, the entity need not hold all of those instruments until maturity. Thus an entity's business model can be to hold financial assets to collect contractual cash flows even when sales of financial assets occur or are expected to occur in the future.

B4.1.3A The business model may be to hold assets to collect contractual cash flows even if the entity sells financial assets when there is an increase in the assets' credit risk. To determine whether there has been an increase in the assets' credit risk, the entity considers reasonable and supportable information, including forward looking information. Irrespective of their frequency and value, sales due to an increase in the assets' credit risk are not inconsistent with a business model whose objective is to hold financial assets to collect contractual cash flows because the credit quality of financial assets is relevant to the entity's ability to collect contractual cash flows. Credit risk management activities that are aimed at minimising potential credit losses due to credit deterioration are integral to such a business model. Selling a financial asset because it no longer meets the credit criteria specified in the entity's documented investment policy is an example of a sale that has occurred due to an increase in credit risk. However, in the absence of such a policy, the entity may demonstrate in other ways that the sale occurred due to an increase in credit risk.

B4.1.3B Sales that occur for other reasons, such as sales made to manage credit concentration risk (without an increase in the assets' credit risk), may also be consistent with a business model whose objective is to hold financial assets in order to collect contractual cash flows. In particular, such sales may be consistent with a business model whose objective is to hold financial assets in order to collect contractual cash flows if those sales are infrequent (even if significant in value) or insignificant in value both individually and in aggregate (even if frequent). If more than an infrequent number of such sales are made out of a portfolio and those sales are more than insignificant in value (either individually or in aggregate), the entity needs to assess whether and how such sales are consistent with an objective of collecting contractual cash flows. Whether a third party imposes the requirement to sell the financial assets, or that activity is at the entity's discretion, is not relevant to this assessment. An increase in the frequency or value of sales in a particular period is not necessarily inconsistent with an objective to hold financial assets in order to collect contractual cash flows, if an entity can explain the reasons for those sales and demonstrate why those sales do not reflect a change in the entity's business model. In addition, sales may be consistent with the objective of holding financial assets in order to collect contractual cash flows if the sales are made close to the maturity of the financial assets and the proceeds from the sales approximate the collection of the remaining contractual cash flows.

B4.1.4   The following are examples of when the objective of an entity's business model may be to hold financial assets to collect the contractual cash flows. This list of examples is not exhaustive. Furthermore, the examples are not intended to discuss all factors that may be relevant to the assessment of the entity's business model nor specify the relative importance of the factors.

Example	Analysis
Example 1 An entity holds investments to collect their contractual cash flows. The funding needs of the entity are predictable and the maturity of its financial assets is matched to the entity's estimated funding needs. The entity performs credit risk management activities with the objective of minimising credit losses. In the past, sales have typically occurred when the financial assets' credit risk has increased such that the assets no longer meet the credit criteria specified in the entity's documented investment policy. In addition, infrequent sales have occurred as a result of unanticipated funding needs. Reports to key management personnel focus on the credit quality of the financial assets and the contractual return. The entity also monitors fair values of the financial assets, among other information.	Although the entity considers, among other information, the financial assets' fair values from a liquidity perspective (ie the cash amount that would be realised if the entity needs to sell assets), the entity's objective is to hold the financial assets in order to collect the contractual cash flows. Sales would not contradict that objective if they were in response to an increase in the assets' credit risk, for example if the assets no longer meet the credit criteria specified in the entity's documented investment policy. Infrequent sales resulting from unanticipated funding needs (eg in a stress case scenario) also would not contradict that objective, even if such sales are significant in value.
Example 2 An entity's business model is to purchase portfolios of financial assets, such as loans. Those portfolios may or may not include financial assets that are credit impaired. If payment on the loans is not made on a timely basis, the entity attempts to realise the contractual cash flows through various means – for example, by contacting the debtor by mail, telephone or other methods. The entity's objective is to collect the contractual cash flows and the entity does not manage any of the loans in this portfolio with an objective of realising cash flows by selling them. In some cases, the entity enters into interest rate swaps to change the interest rate on particular financial assets in a portfolio from a floating interest rate to a fixed interest rate.	The objective of the entity's business model is to hold the financial assets in order to collect the contractual cash flows. The same analysis would apply even if the entity does not expect to receive all of the contractual cash flows (eg some of the financial assets are credit impaired at initial recognition). Moreover, the fact that the entity enters into derivatives to modify the cash flows of the portfolio does not in itself change the entity's business model.

Example	Analysis
Example 3 An entity has a business model with the objective of originating loans to customers and subsequently selling those loans to a securitisation vehicle. The securitisation vehicle issues instruments to investors. The originating entity controls the securitisation vehicle and thus consolidates it. The securitisation vehicle collects the contractual cash flows from the loans and passes them on to its investors. It is assumed for the purposes of this example that the loans continue to be recognised in the consolidated statement of financial position because they are not derecognised by the securitisation vehicle.	The consolidated group originated the loans with the objective of holding them to collect the contractual cash flows. However, the originating entity has an objective of realising cash flows on the loan portfolio by selling the loans to the securitisation vehicle, so for the purposes of its separate financial statements it would not be considered to be managing this portfolio in order to collect the contractual cash flows.
Example 4 A financial institution holds financial assets to meet liquidity needs in a 'stress case' scenario (eg, a run on the bank's deposits). The entity does not anticipate selling these assets except in such scenarios. The entity monitors the credit quality of the financial assets and its objective in managing the financial assets is to collect the contractual cash flows. The entity evaluates the performance of the assets on the basis of interest revenue earned and credit losses realised. However, the entity also monitors the fair value of the financial assets from a liquidity perspective to ensure that the cash amount that would be realised if the entity needed to sell the assets in a stress case scenario would be sufficient to meet the entity's liquidity needs. Periodically, the entity makes sales that are insignificant in value to demonstrate liquidity.	The objective of the entity's business model is to hold the financial assets to collect contractual cash flows. The analysis would not change even if during a previous stress case scenario the entity had sales that were significant in value in order to meet its liquidity needs. Similarly, recurring sales activity that is insignificant in value is not inconsistent with holding financial assets to collect contractual cash flows. In contrast, if an entity holds financial assets to meet its everyday liquidity needs and meeting that objective involves frequent sales that are significant in value, the objective of the entity's business model is not to hold the financial assets to collect contractual cash flows. Similarly, if the entity is required by its regulator to routinely sell financial assets to demonstrate that the assets are liquid, and the value of the assets sold is significant, the entity's business model is not to hold financial assets to collect contractual cash flows. Whether a third party imposes the requirement to sell the financial assets, or that activity is at the entity's discretion, is not relevant to the analysis.

A business model whose objective is achieved by both collecting contractual cash flows and selling financial assets

B4.1.4A   An entity may hold financial assets in a business model whose objective is achieved by both collecting contractual cash flows and selling financial assets. In this type of business model, the entity's key management personnel have made a decision that both collecting contractual cash flows and selling financial assets are integral to achieving the objective of the business model. There are various objectives that may be consistent with this type of business model. For example, the objective of the business model may be to manage everyday liquidity needs, to maintain a particular interest yield profile or to match the duration of the financial assets to the duration of the liabilities that those assets are funding. To achieve such an objective, the entity will both collect contractual cash flows and sell financial assets.

B4.1.4B   Compared to a business model whose objective is to hold financial assets to collect contractual cash flows, this business model will typically involve greater frequency and value of sales. This is because selling financial assets is integral to achieving the business model's objective instead of being only incidental to it. However, there is no threshold for the frequency or value of sales that must occur in this business model because both collecting contractual cash flows and selling financial assets are integral to achieving its objective.

B4.1.4C The following are examples of when the objective of the entity's business model may be achieved by both collecting contractual cash flows and selling financial assets. This list of examples is not exhaustive. Furthermore, the examples are not intended to describe all the factors that may be relevant to the assessment of the entity's business model nor specify the relative importance of the factors.

Example	Analysis
Example 5 An entity anticipates capital expenditure in a few years. The entity invests its excess cash in short and long-term financial assets so that it can fund the expenditure when the need arises. Many of the financial assets have contractual lives that exceed the entity's anticipated investment period. The entity will hold financial assets to collect the contractual cash flows and, when an opportunity arises, it will sell financial assets to re-invest the cash in financial assets with a higher return. The managers responsible for the portfolio are remunerated based on the overall return generated by the portfolio.	The objective of the business model is achieved by both collecting contractual cash flows and selling financial assets. The entity will make decisions on an ongoing basis about whether collecting contractual cash flows or selling financial assets will maximise the return on the portfolio until the need arises for the invested cash. In contrast, consider an entity that anticipates a cash outflow in five years to fund capital expenditure and invests excess cash in short-term financial assets. When the investments mature, the entity reinvests the cash in new short-term financial assets. The entity maintains this strategy until the funds are needed, at which time the entity uses the proceeds from the maturing financial assets to fund the capital expenditure. Only sales that are insignificant in value occur before maturity (unless there is an increase in credit risk). The objective of this contrasting business model is to hold financial assets to collect contractual cash flows.
Example 6 A financial institution holds financial assets to meet its everyday liquidity needs. The entity seeks to minimise the costs of managing those liquidity needs and therefore actively manages the return on the portfolio. That return consists of collecting contractual payments as well as gains and losses from the sale of financial assets. As a result, the entity holds financial assets to collect contractual cash flows and sells financial assets to reinvest in higher yielding financial assets or to better match the duration of its liabilities. In the past, this strategy has resulted in frequent sales activity and such sales have been significant in value. This activity is expected to continue in the future.	The objective of the business model is to maximise the return on the portfolio to meet everyday liquidity needs and the entity achieves that objective by both collecting contractual cash flows and selling financial assets. In other words, both collecting contractual cash flows and selling financial assets are integral to achieving the business model's objective.
Example 7 An insurer holds financial assets in order to fund insurance contract liabilities. The insurer uses the proceeds from the contractual cash flows on the financial assets to settle insurance contract liabilities as they come due. To ensure that the contractual cash flows from the financial assets are sufficient to settle those liabilities, the insurer undertakes significant buying and selling activity on a regular basis to rebalance its portfolio of assets and to meet cash flow needs as they arise.	The objective of the business model is to fund the insurance contract liabilities. To achieve this objective, the entity collects contractual cash flows as they come due and sells financial assets to maintain the desired profile of the asset portfolio. Thus both collecting contractual cash flows and selling financial assets are integral to achieving the business model's objective.

Other business models

B4.1.5 Financial assets are measured at fair value through profit or loss if they are not held within a business model whose objective is to hold assets to collect contractual cash flows or within a business model whose objective is achieved by both collecting contractual cash flows and selling financial assets (but see also paragraph 5.7.5). One business model that results in measurement at fair value through profit or loss is one in which an entity manages the financial assets with the objective of realising cash flows through the sale of the assets. The entity makes decisions based on the assets' fair values and manages the assets to realise those fair values. In this case, the entity's objective will typically result in active buying and selling. Even though the entity will collect contractual cash flows while it holds the financial assets, the objective of such a business model is not achieved by both collecting contractual cash flows and selling financial assets. This is because the collection of contractual cash flows is not integral to achieving the business model's objective; instead, it is incidental to it.

B4.1.6   A portfolio of financial assets that is managed and whose performance is evaluated on a fair value basis (as described in paragraph 4.2.2(b)) is neither held to collect contractual cash flows nor held both to collect contractual cash flows and to sell financial assets. The entity is primarily focused on fair value information and uses that information to assess the assets' performance and to make decisions. In addition, a portfolio of financial assets that meets the definition of held for trading is not held to collect contractual cash flows or held both to collect contractual cash flows and to sell financial assets. For such portfolios, the collection of contractual cash flows is only incidental to achieving the business model's objective. Consequently, such portfolios of financial assets must be measured at fair value through profit or loss.

Contractual cash flows that are solely payments of principal and interest on the principal amount outstanding

B4.1.7   Paragraph 4.1.1(b) requires an entity to classify a financial asset on the basis of its contractual cash flow characteristics if the financial asset is held within a business model whose objective is to hold assets to collect contractual cash flows or within a business model whose objective is achieved by both collecting contractual cash flows and selling financial assets, unless paragraph 4.1.5 applies. To do so, the condition in paragraphs 4.1.2(b) and 4.1.2A(b) requires an entity to determine whether the asset's contractual cash flows are solely payments of principal and interest on the principal amount outstanding.

B4.1.7A   Contractual cash flows that are solely payments of principal and interest on the principal amount outstanding are consistent with a basic lending arrangement. In a basic lending arrangement, consideration for the time value of money (see paragraphs B4.1.9A–B4.1.9E) and credit risk are typically the most significant elements of interest. However, in such an arrangement, interest can also include consideration for other basic lending risks (for example, liquidity risk) and costs (for example, administrative costs) associated with holding the financial asset for a particular period of time. In addition, interest can include a profit margin that is consistent with a basic lending arrangement. In extreme economic circumstances, interest can be negative if, for example, the holder of a financial asset either explicitly or implicitly pays for the deposit of its money for a particular period of time (and that fee exceeds the consideration that the holder receives for the time value of money, credit risk and other basic lending risks and costs). However, contractual terms that introduce exposure to risks or volatility in the contractual cash flows that is unrelated to a basic lending arrangement, such as exposure to changes in equity prices or commodity prices, do not give rise to contractual cash flows that are solely payments of principal and interest on the principal amount outstanding. An originated or a purchased financial asset can be a basic lending arrangement irrespective of whether it is a loan in its legal form.

B4.1.7B   In accordance with paragraph 4.1.3(a), principal is the fair value of the financial asset at initial recognition. However that principal amount may change over the life of the financial asset (for example, if there are repayments of principal).

B4.1.8   An entity shall assess whether contractual cash flows are solely payments of principal and interest on the principal amount outstanding for the currency in which the financial asset is denominated.

AASB

B4.1.9   Leverage is a contractual cash flow characteristic of some financial assets. Leverage increases the variability of the contractual cash flows with the result that they do not have the economic characteristics of interest. Stand-alone option, forward and swap contracts are examples of financial assets that include such leverage. Thus, such contracts do not meet the condition in paragraphs 4.1.2(b) and 4.1.2A(b) and cannot be subsequently measured at amortised cost or fair value through other comprehensive income.

Consideration for the time value of money

B4.1.9A   Time value of money is the element of interest that provides consideration for only the passage of time. That is, the time value of money element does not provide consideration for other risks or costs associated with holding the financial asset. In order to assess whether the element provides consideration for only the passage of time, an entity applies judgement and considers relevant factors such as the currency in which the financial asset is denominated and the period for which the interest rate is set.

B4.1.9B   However, in some cases, the time value of money element may be modified (ie imperfect). That would be the case, for example, if a financial asset's interest rate is periodically reset but the frequency of that reset does not match the tenor of the interest rate (for example, the interest rate resets every month to a one-year rate) or if a financial asset's interest rate is periodically reset to an average of particular short- and long-term interest rates. In such cases, an entity must assess the modification to determine whether the contractual cash flows represent solely payments of principal and interest on the principal amount outstanding. In some circumstances, the entity may be able to make that determination by performing a qualitative assessment of the time value of money element whereas, in other circumstances, it may be necessary to perform a quantitative assessment.

B4.1.9C   When assessing a modified time value of money element, the objective is to determine how different the contractual (undiscounted) cash flows could be from the (undiscounted) cash flows that would arise if the time value of money element was not modified (the benchmark cash flows). For example, if the financial asset under assessment contains a variable interest rate that is reset every month to a one-year interest rate, the entity would compare that financial asset to a financial instrument with identical contractual terms and the identical credit risk except the variable interest rate is reset monthly to a one-month interest rate. If the modified time value of money element could result in contractual (undiscounted) cash flows that are significantly different from the (undiscounted) benchmark cash flows, the financial asset does not meet the condition in paragraphs 4.1.2(b) and 4.1.2A(b). To make this determination, the entity must consider the effect of the modified time value of money element in each reporting period and cumulatively over the life of the financial instrument. The reason for the interest rate being set in this way is not relevant to the analysis. If it is clear, with little or no analysis, whether the contractual (undiscounted) cash flows on the financial asset under the assessment could (or could not) be significantly different from the (undiscounted) benchmark cash flows, an entity need not perform a detailed assessment.

B4.1.9D   When assessing a modified time value of money element, an entity must consider factors that could affect future contractual cash flows. For example, if an entity is assessing a bond with a five-year term and the variable interest rate is reset every six months to a five-year rate, the entity cannot conclude that the contractual cash flows are solely payments of principal and interest on the principal amount outstanding simply because the interest rate curve at the time of the assessment is such that the difference between a five-year interest rate and a six-month interest rate is not significant. Instead, the entity must also consider whether the relationship between the five-year interest rate and the six-month interest rate could change over the life of the instrument such that the contractual (undiscounted) cash flows over the life of the instrument could be significantly different from the (undiscounted) benchmark cash flows. However, an entity must consider only reasonably possible scenarios instead of every possible scenario. If an entity concludes that the contractual (undiscounted) cash flows could be significantly different from the (undiscounted) benchmark cash flows, the financial asset does not meet the condition in paragraphs 4.1.2(b) and 4.1.2A(b) and therefore cannot be measured at amortised cost or fair value through other comprehensive income.

B4.1.9E In some jurisdictions, the government or a regulatory authority sets interest rates. For example, such government regulation of interest rates may be part of a broad macroeconomic policy or it may be introduced to encourage entities to invest in a particular sector of the economy. In some of these cases, the objective of the time value of money element is not to provide consideration for only the passage of time. However, despite paragraphs B4.1.9A–B4.1.9D, a regulated interest rate shall be considered a proxy for the time value of money element for the purpose of applying the condition in paragraphs 4.1.2(b) and 4.1.2A(b) if that regulated interest rate provides consideration that is broadly consistent with the passage of time and does not provide exposure to risks or volatility in the contractual cash flows that are inconsistent with a basic lending arrangement.

Contractual terms that change the timing or amount of contractual cash flows

B4.1.10 If a financial asset contains a contractual term that could change the timing or amount of contractual cash flows (for example, if the asset can be prepaid before maturity or its term can be extended), the entity must determine whether the contractual cash flows that could arise over the life of the instrument due to that contractual term are solely payments of principal and interest on the principal amount outstanding. To make this determination, the entity must assess the contractual cash flows that could arise both before, and after, the change in contractual cash flows. The entity may also need to assess the nature of any contingent event (ie the trigger) that would change the timing or amount of the contractual cash flows. While the nature of the contingent event in itself is not a determinative factor in assessing whether the contractual cash flows are solely payments of principal and interest, it may be an indicator. For example, compare a financial instrument with an interest rate that is reset to a higher rate if the debtor misses a particular number of payments to a financial instrument with an interest rate that is reset to a higher rate if a specified equity index reaches a particular level. It is more likely in the former case that the contractual cash flows over the life of the instrument will be solely payments of principal and interest on the principal amount outstanding because of the relationship between missed payments and an increase in credit risk. (See also paragraph B4.1.18.)

B4.1.11 The following are examples of contractual terms that result in contractual cash flows that are solely payments of principal and interest on the principal amount outstanding:

(a) a variable interest rate that consists of consideration for the time value of money, the credit risk associated with the principal amount outstanding during a particular period of time (the consideration for credit risk may be determined at initial recognition only, and so may be fixed) and other basic lending risks and costs, as well as a profit margin;

(b) a contractual term that permits the issuer (ie the debtor) to prepay a debt instrument or permits the holder (ie the creditor) to put a debt instrument back to the issuer before maturity and the prepayment amount substantially represents unpaid amounts of principal and interest on the principal amount outstanding, which may include reasonable additional compensation for the early termination of the contract; and

AASB

(c)   a contractual term that permits the issuer or the holder to extend the contractual term of a debt instrument (ie an extension option) and the terms of the extension option result in contractual cash flows during the extension period that are solely payments of principal and interest on the principal amount outstanding, which may include reasonable additional compensation for the extension of the contract.

B4.1.12 Despite paragraph B4.1.10, a financial asset that would otherwise meet the condition in paragraphs 4.1.2(b) and 4.1.2A(b) but does not do so only as a result of a contractual term that permits (or requires) the issuer to prepay a debt instrument or permits (or requires) the holder to put a debt instrument back to the issuer before maturity is eligible to be measured at amortised cost or fair value through other comprehensive income (subject to meeting the condition in paragraph 4.1.2(a) or the condition in paragraph 4.1.2A(a)) if:

(a)   the entity acquires or originates the financial asset at a premium or discount to the contractual par amount;

(b)   the prepayment amount substantially represents the contractual par amount and accrued (but unpaid) contractual interest, which may include reasonable additional compensation for the early termination of the contract; and

(c)   when the entity initially recognises the financial asset, the fair value of the prepayment feature is insignificant.

B4.1.13 The following examples illustrate contractual cash flows that are solely payments of principal and interest on the principal amount outstanding. This list of examples is not exhaustive.

Instrument	Analysis
Instrument A Instrument A is a bond with a stated maturity date. Payments of principal and interest on the principal amount outstanding are linked to an inflation index of the currency in which the instrument is issued. The inflation link is not leveraged and the principal is protected.	The contractual cash flows are solely payments of principal and interest on the principal amount outstanding. Linking payments of principal and interest on the principal amount outstanding to an unleveraged inflation index resets the time value of money to a current level. In other words, the interest rate on the instrument reflects 'real' interest. Thus, the interest amounts are consideration for the time value of money on the principal amount outstanding. However, if the interest payments were indexed to another variable such as the debtor's performance (eg the debtor's net income) or an equity index, the contractual cash flows are not payments of principal and interest on the principal amount outstanding (unless the indexing to the debtor's performance results in an adjustment that only compensates the holder for changes in the credit risk of the instrument, such that contractual cash flows are solely payments of principal and interest). That is because the contractual cash flows reflect a return that is inconsistent with a basic lending arrangement (see paragraph B4.1.7A).
Instrument B Instrument B is a variable interest rate instrument with a stated maturity date that permits the borrower to choose the market interest rate on an ongoing basis. For example, at each interest rate reset date, the borrower can choose to pay three-month LIBOR for a three-month term or one-month LIBOR for a one-month term.	The contractual cash flows are solely payments of principal and interest on the principal amount outstanding as long as the interest paid over the life of the instrument reflects consideration for the time value of money, for the credit risk associated with the instrument and for other basic lending risks and costs, as well as a profit margin (see paragraph B4.1.7A). The fact that the LIBOR interest rate is reset during the life of the instrument does not in itself disqualify the instrument.

Instrument	Analysis
	However, if the borrower is able to choose to pay a one-month interest rate that is reset every three months, the interest rate is reset with a frequency that does not match the tenor of the interest rate. Consequently, the time value of money element is modified. Similarly, if an instrument has a contractual interest rate that is based on a term that can exceed the instrument's remaining life (for example, if an instrument with a five-year maturity pays a variable rate that is reset periodically but always reflects a five-year maturity), the time value of money element is modified. That is because the interest payable in each period is disconnected from the interest period.
	In such cases, the entity must qualitatively or quantitatively assess the contractual cash flows against those on an instrument that is identical in all respects except the tenor of the interest rate matches the interest period to determine if the cash flows are solely payments of principal and interest on the principal amount outstanding. (But see paragraph B4.1.9E for guidance on regulated interest rates.)
	For example, in assessing a bond with a five-year term that pays a variable rate that is reset every six months but always reflects a five-year maturity, an entity considers the contractual cash flows on an instrument that resets every six months to a six-month interest rate but is otherwise identical.
	The same analysis would apply if the borrower is able to choose between the lender's various published interest rates (eg the borrower can choose between the lender's published one-month variable interest rate and the lender's published three-month variable interest rate).
Instrument C Instrument C is a bond with a stated maturity date and pays a variable market interest rate. That variable interest rate is capped.	The contractual cash flows of both: (a) an instrument that has a fixed interest rate and (b) an instrument that has a variable interest rate are payments of principal and interest on the principal amount outstanding as long as the interest reflects consideration for the time value of money, for the credit risk associated with the instrument during the term of the instrument and for other basic lending risks and costs, as well as a profit margin. (See paragraph B4.1.7A)
	Consequently, an instrument that is a combination of (a) and (b) (eg a bond with an interest rate cap) can have cash flows that are solely payments of principal and interest on the principal amount outstanding. Such a contractual term may reduce cash flow variability by setting a limit on a variable interest rate (eg an interest rate cap or floor) or increase the cash flow variability because a fixed rate becomes variable.
Instrument D Instrument D is a full recourse loan and is secured by collateral.	The fact that a full recourse loan is collateralised does not in itself affect the analysis of whether the contractual cash flows are solely payments of principal and interest on the principal amount outstanding.
Instrument E Instrument E is issued by a regulated bank and has a stated maturity date. The instrument pays a fixed interest rate and all contractual cash flows are non-discretionary.	The holder would analyse the **contractual terms** of the financial instrument to determine whether they give rise to cash flows that are solely payments of principal and interest on the principal amount outstanding and thus are consistent with a basic lending arrangement.

(Continued)

AASB

(Continued)

Instrument	Analysis
However, the issuer is subject to legislation that permits or requires a national resolving authority to impose losses on holders of particular instruments, including Instrument E, in particular circumstances. For example, the national resolving authority has the power to write down the par amount of Instrument E or to convert it into a fixed number of the issuer's ordinary shares if the national resolving authority determines that the issuer is having severe financial difficulties, needs additional regulatory capital or is 'failing'.	That analysis would not consider the payments that arise only as a result of the national resolving authority's power to impose losses on the holders of Instrument E. That is because that power, and the resulting payments, are not **contractual terms** of the financial instrument. In contrast, the contractual cash flows would not be solely payments of principal and interest on the principal amount outstanding if the **contractual terms** of the financial instrument permit or require the issuer or another entity to impose losses on the holder (eg by writing down the par amount or by converting the instrument into a fixed number of the issuer's ordinary shares) as long as those contractual terms are genuine, even if the probability is remote that such a loss will be imposed.

B4.1.14 The following examples illustrate contractual cash flows that are not solely payments of principal and interest on the principal amount outstanding. This list of examples is not exhaustive.

Instrument	Analysis
Instrument F Instrument F is a bond that is convertible into a fixed number of equity instruments of the issuer.	The holder would analyse the convertible bond in its entirety. The contractual cash flows are not payments of principal and interest on the principal amount outstanding because they reflect a return that is inconsistent with a basic lending arrangement (see paragraph B4.1.7A); ie the return is linked to the value of the equity of the issuer.
Instrument G Instrument G is a loan that pays an inverse floating interest rate (ie the interest rate has an inverse relationship to market interest rates).	The contractual cash flows are not solely payments of principal and interest on the principal amount outstanding. The interest amounts are not consideration for the time value of money on the principal amount outstanding.
Instrument H Instrument H is a perpetual instrument but the issuer may call the instrument at any point and pay the holder the par amount plus accrued interest due. Instrument H pays a market interest rate but payment of interest cannot be made unless the issuer is able to remain solvent immediately afterwards. Deferred interest does not accrue additional interest.	The contractual cash flows are not payments of principal and interest on the principal amount outstanding. That is because the issuer may be required to defer interest payments and additional interest does not accrue on those deferred interest amounts. As a result, interest amounts are not consideration for the time value of money on the principal amount outstanding. If interest accrued on the deferred amounts, the contractual cash flows could be payments of principal and interest on the principal amount outstanding. The fact that Instrument H is perpetual does not in itself mean that the contractual cash flows are not payments of principal and interest on the principal amount outstanding. In effect, a perpetual instrument has continuous (multiple) extension options. Such options may result in contractual cash flows that are payments of principal and interest on the principal amount outstanding if interest payments are mandatory and must be paid in perpetuity.

Instrument	Analysis
	Also, the fact that Instrument H is callable does not mean that the contractual cash flows are not payments of principal and interest on the principal amount outstanding unless it is callable at an amount that does not substantially reflect payment of outstanding principal and interest on that principal amount outstanding. Even if the callable amount includes an amount that reasonably compensates the holder for the early termination of the instrument, the contractual cash flows could be payments of principal and interest on the principal amount outstanding. (See also paragraph B4.1.12.)

B4.1.15 In some cases a financial asset may have contractual cash flows that are described as principal and interest but those cash flows do not represent the payment of principal and interest on the principal amount outstanding as described in paragraphs 4.1.2(b), 4.1.2A(b) and 4.1.3 of this Standard.

B4.1.16 This may be the case if the financial asset represents an investment in particular assets or cash flows and hence the contractual cash flows are not solely payments of principal and interest on the principal amount outstanding. For example, if the contractual terms stipulate that the financial asset's cash flows increase as more automobiles use a particular toll road, those contractual cash flows are inconsistent with a basic lending arrangement. As a result, the instrument would not satisfy the condition in paragraphs 4.1.2(b) and 4.1.2A(b). This could be the case when a creditor's claim is limited to specified assets of the debtor or the cash flows from specified assets (for example, a 'non-recourse' financial asset).

B4.1.17 However, the fact that a financial asset is non-recourse does not in itself necessarily preclude the financial asset from meeting the condition in paragraphs 4.1.2(b) and 4.1.2A(b). In such situations, the creditor is required to assess ('look through to') the particular underlying assets or cash flows to determine whether the contractual cash flows of the financial asset being classified are payments of principal and interest on the principal amount outstanding. If the terms of the financial asset give rise to any other cash flows or limit the cash flows in a manner inconsistent with payments representing principal and interest, the financial asset does not meet the condition in paragraphs 4.1.2(b) and 4.1.2A(b). Whether the underlying assets are financial assets or non-financial assets does not in itself affect this assessment.

B4.1.18 A contractual cash flow characteristic does not affect the classification of the financial asset if it could have only a de minimis effect on the contractual cash flows of the financial asset. To make this determination, an entity must consider the possible effect of the contractual cash flow characteristic in each reporting period and cumulatively over the life of the financial instrument. In addition, if a contractual cash flow characteristic could have an effect on the contractual cash flows that is more than de minimis (either in a single reporting period or cumulatively) but that cash flow characteristic is not genuine, it does not affect the classification of a financial asset. A cash flow characteristic is not genuine if it affects the instrument's contractual cash flows only on the occurrence of an event that is extremely rare, highly abnormal and very unlikely to occur.

B4.1.19 In almost every lending transaction the creditor's instrument is ranked relative to the instruments of the debtor's other creditors. An instrument that is subordinated to other instruments may have contractual cash flows that are payments of principal and interest on the principal amount outstanding if the debtor's non-payment is a breach of contract and the holder has a contractual right to unpaid amounts of principal and interest on the principal amount outstanding even in the event of the debtor's bankruptcy. For example, a trade receivable that ranks its creditor as a general creditor would qualify as having payments of principal and interest on the principal amount outstanding. This is the case even if the debtor issued loans that are collateralised, which in the event of bankruptcy would give that loan holder priority over the claims of the general creditor in respect of the collateral but does not affect the contractual right of the general creditor to unpaid principal and other amounts due.

Contractually linked instruments

B4.1.20   In some types of transactions, an issuer may prioritise payments to the holders of financial assets using multiple contractually linked instruments that create concentrations of credit risk (tranches). Each tranche has a subordination ranking that specifies the order in which any cash flows generated by the issuer are allocated to the tranche. In such situations, the holders of a tranche have the right to payments of principal and interest on the principal amount outstanding only if the issuer generates sufficient cash flows to satisfy higher-ranking tranches.

B4.1.21   In such transactions, a tranche has cash flow characteristics that are payments of principal and interest on the principal amount outstanding only if:

(a)   the contractual terms of the tranche being assessed for classification (without looking through to the underlying pool of financial instruments) give rise to cash flows that are solely payments of principal and interest on the principal amount outstanding (eg the interest rate on the tranche is not linked to a commodity index);

(b)   the underlying pool of financial instruments has the cash flow characteristics set out in paragraphs B4.1.23 and B4.1.24; and

(c)   the exposure to credit risk in the underlying pool of financial instruments inherent in the tranche is equal to or lower than the exposure to credit risk of the underlying pool of financial instruments (for example, the credit rating of the tranche being assessed for classification is equal to or higher than the credit rating that would apply to a single tranche that funded the underlying pool of financial instruments).

B4.1.22   An entity must look through until it can identify the underlying pool of instruments that are creating (instead of passing through) the cash flows. This is the underlying pool of financial instruments.

B4.1.23   The underlying pool must contain one or more instruments that have contractual cash flows that are solely payments of principal and interest on the principal amount outstanding.

B4.1.24   The underlying pool of instruments may also include instruments that:

(a)   reduce the cash flow variability of the instruments in paragraph B4.1.23 and, when combined with the instruments in paragraph B4.1.23, result in cash flows that are solely payments of principal and interest on the principal amount outstanding (eg an interest rate cap or floor or a contract that reduces the credit risk on some or all of the instruments in paragraph B4.1.23); or

(b)   align the cash flows of the tranches with the cash flows of the pool of underlying instruments in paragraph B4.1.23 to address differences in and only in:

(i)   whether the interest rate is fixed or floating;

(ii)   the currency in which the cash flows are denominated, including inflation in that currency; or

(iii)   the timing of the cash flows.

B4.1.25   If any instrument in the pool does not meet the conditions in either paragraph B4.1.23 or paragraph B4.1.24, the condition in paragraph B4.1.21(b) is not met. In performing this assessment, a detailed instrument-by-instrument analysis of the pool may not be necessary. However, an entity must use judgement and perform sufficient analysis to determine whether the instruments in the pool meet the conditions in paragraphs B4.1.23–B4.1.24. (See also paragraph B4.1.18 for guidance on contractual cash flow characteristics that have only a de minimis effect.)

B4.1.26 If the holder cannot assess the conditions in paragraph B4.1.21 at initial recognition, the tranche must be measured at fair value through profit or loss. If the underlying pool of instruments can change after initial recognition in such a way that the pool may not meet the conditions in paragraphs B4.1.23–B4.1.24, the tranche does not meet the conditions in paragraph B4.1.21 and must be measured at fair value through profit or loss. However, if the underlying pool includes instruments that are collateralised by assets that do not meet the conditions in paragraphs B4.1.23–B4.1.24, the ability to take possession of such assets shall be disregarded for the purposes of applying this paragraph unless the entity acquired the tranche with the intention of controlling the collateral.

Option to designate a financial asset or financial liability as at fair value through profit or loss (Sections 4.1 and 4.2)

B4.1.27 Subject to the conditions in paragraphs 4.1.5 and 4.2.2, this Standard allows an entity to designate a financial asset, a financial liability, or a group of financial instruments (financial assets, financial liabilities or both) as at fair value through profit or loss provided that doing so results in more relevant information.

B4.1.28 The decision of an entity to designate a financial asset or financial liability as at fair value through profit or loss is similar to an accounting policy choice (although, unlike an accounting policy choice, it is not required to be applied consistently to all similar transactions). When an entity has such a choice, paragraph 14(b) of AASB 108 requires the chosen policy to result in the financial statements providing reliable and more relevant information about the effects of transactions, other events and conditions on the entity's financial position, financial performance or cash flows. For example, in the case of designation of a financial liability as at fair value through profit or loss, paragraph 4.2.2 sets out the two circumstances when the requirement for more relevant information will be met. Accordingly, to choose such designation in accordance with paragraph 4.2.2, the entity needs to demonstrate that it falls within one (or both) of these two circumstances.

Designation eliminates or significantly reduces an accounting mismatch

B4.1.29 Measurement of a financial asset or financial liability and classification of recognised changes in its value are determined by the item's classification and whether the item is part of a designated hedging relationship. Those requirements can create a measurement or recognition inconsistency (sometimes referred to as an 'accounting mismatch') when, for example, in the absence of designation as at fair value through profit or loss, a financial asset would be classified as subsequently measured at fair value through profit or loss and a liability the entity considers related would be subsequently measured at amortised cost (with changes in fair value not recognised). In such circumstances, an entity may conclude that its financial statements would provide more relevant information if both the asset and the liability were measured as at fair value through profit or loss.

B4.1.30 The following examples show when this condition could be met. In all cases, an entity may use this condition to designate financial assets or financial liabilities as at fair value through profit or loss only if it meets the principle in paragraph 4.1.5 or 4.2.2(a):

(a) an entity has liabilities under insurance contracts whose measurement incorporates current information (as permitted by paragraph 24 of AASB 4) and financial assets that it considers to be related and that would otherwise be measured at either fair value through other comprehensive income or amortised cost.

(b) an entity has financial assets, financial liabilities or both that share a risk, such as interest rate risk, and that gives rise to opposite changes in fair value that tend to offset each other. However, only some of the instruments would be measured at fair value through profit or loss (for example, those that are derivatives, or are classified as held for trading). It may also be the case that

AASB

the requirements for hedge accounting are not met because, for example, the requirements for hedge effectiveness in paragraph 6.4.1 are not met.

(c)   an entity has financial assets, financial liabilities or both that share a risk, such as interest rate risk, that gives rise to opposite changes in fair value that tend to offset each other and none of the financial assets or financial liabilities qualifies for designation as a hedging instrument because they are not measured at fair value through profit or loss. Furthermore, in the absence of hedge accounting there is a significant inconsistency in the recognition of gains and losses. For example, the entity has financed a specified group of loans by issuing traded bonds whose changes in fair value tend to offset each other. If, in addition, the entity regularly buys and sells the bonds but rarely, if ever, buys and sells the loans, reporting both the loans and the bonds at fair value through profit or loss eliminates the inconsistency in the timing of the recognition of the gains and losses that would otherwise result from measuring them both at amortised cost and recognising a gain or loss each time a bond is repurchased.

B4.1.31   In cases such as those described in the preceding paragraph, to designate, at initial recognition, the financial assets and financial liabilities not otherwise so measured as at fair value through profit or loss may eliminate or significantly reduce the measurement or recognition inconsistency and produce more relevant information. For practical purposes, the entity need not enter into all of the assets and liabilities giving rise to the measurement or recognition inconsistency at exactly the same time. A reasonable delay is permitted provided that each transaction is designated as at fair value through profit or loss at its initial recognition and, at that time, any remaining transactions are expected to occur.

B4.1.32   It would not be acceptable to designate only some of the financial assets and financial liabilities giving rise to the inconsistency as at fair value through profit or loss if to do so would not eliminate or significantly reduce the inconsistency and would therefore not result in more relevant information. However, it would be acceptable to designate only some of a number of similar financial assets or similar financial liabilities if doing so achieves a significant reduction (and possibly a greater reduction than other allowable designations) in the inconsistency. For example, assume an entity has a number of similar financial liabilities that sum to CU100 and a number of similar financial assets that sum to CU50 but are measured on a different basis. The entity may significantly reduce the measurement inconsistency by designating at initial recognition all of the assets but only some of the liabilities (for example, individual liabilities with a combined total of CU45) as at fair value through profit or loss. However, because designation as at fair value through profit or loss can be applied only to the whole of a financial instrument, the entity in this example must designate one or more liabilities in their entirety. It could not designate either a component of a liability (eg changes in value attributable to only one risk, such as changes in a benchmark interest rate) or a proportion (ie percentage) of a liability.

A group of financial liabilities or financial assets and financial liabilities is managed and its performance is evaluated on a fair value basis

B4.1.33   An entity may manage and evaluate the performance of a group of financial liabilities or financial assets and financial liabilities in such a way that measuring that group at fair value through profit or loss results in more relevant information. The focus in this instance is on the way the entity manages and evaluates performance, instead of on the nature of its financial instruments.

B4.1.34   For example, an entity may use this condition to designate financial liabilities as at fair value through profit or loss if it meets the principle in paragraph 4.2.2(b) and the entity has financial assets and financial liabilities that share one or more risks and those risks are managed and evaluated on a fair value basis in accordance with a documented policy of asset and liability management. An example could be an entity that has issued 'structured products' containing multiple embedded derivatives and manages the resulting risks on a fair value basis using a mix of derivative and non-derivative financial instruments.

B4.1.35 As noted above, this condition relies on the way the entity manages and evaluates performance of the group of financial instruments under consideration. Accordingly, (subject to the requirement of designation at initial recognition) an entity that designates financial liabilities as at fair value through profit or loss on the basis of this condition shall so designate all eligible financial liabilities that are managed and evaluated together.

B4.1.36 Documentation of the entity's strategy need not be extensive but should be sufficient to demonstrate compliance with paragraph 4.2.2(b). Such documentation is not required for each individual item, but may be on a portfolio basis. For example, if the performance management system for a department – as approved by the entity's key management personnel – clearly demonstrates that its performance is evaluated on this basis, no further documentation is required to demonstrate compliance with paragraph 4.2.2(b).

Embedded derivatives (Section 4.3)

B4.3.1 When an entity becomes a party to a hybrid contract with a host that is not an asset within the scope of this Standard, paragraph 4.3.3 requires the entity to identify any embedded derivative, assess whether it is required to be separated from the host contract and, for those that are required to be separated, measure the derivatives at fair value at initial recognition and subsequently at fair value through profit or loss.

B4.3.2 If a host contract has no stated or predetermined maturity and represents a residual interest in the net assets of an entity, then its economic characteristics and risks are those of an equity instrument, and an embedded derivative would need to possess equity characteristics related to the same entity to be regarded as closely related. If the host contract is not an equity instrument and meets the definition of a financial instrument, then its economic characteristics and risks are those of a debt instrument.

B4.3.3 An embedded non-option derivative (such as an embedded forward or swap) is separated from its host contract on the basis of its stated or implied substantive terms, so as to result in it having a fair value of zero at initial recognition. An embedded option-based derivative (such as an embedded put, call, cap, floor or swaption) is separated from its host contract on the basis of the stated terms of the option feature. The initial carrying amount of the host instrument is the residual amount after separating the embedded derivative.

B4.3.4 Generally, multiple embedded derivatives in a single hybrid contract are treated as a single compound embedded derivative. However, embedded derivatives that are classified as equity (see AASB 132 *Financial Instruments: Presentation*) are accounted for separately from those classified as assets or liabilities. In addition, if a hybrid contract has more than one embedded derivative and those derivatives relate to different risk exposures and are readily separable and independent of each other, they are accounted for separately from each other.

B4.3.5 The economic characteristics and risks of an embedded derivative are not closely related to the host contract (paragraph 4.3.3(a)) in the following examples. In these examples, assuming the conditions in paragraph 4.3.3(b) and (c) are met, an entity accounts for the embedded derivative separately from the host contract.

(a) A put option embedded in an instrument that enables the holder to require the issuer to reacquire the instrument for an amount of cash or other assets that varies on the basis of the change in an equity or commodity price or index is not closely related to a host debt instrument.

(b) An option or automatic provision to extend the remaining term to maturity of a debt instrument is not closely related to the host debt instrument unless there is a concurrent adjustment to the approximate current market rate of interest at the time of the extension. If an entity issues a debt instrument and the holder of that debt instrument writes a call option on the debt instrument to a third party, the issuer regards the call option as extending the term to maturity of the debt

AASB

instrument provided the issuer can be required to participate in or facilitate the remarketing of the debt instrument as a result of the call option being exercised.

(c)   Equity-indexed interest or principal payments embedded in a host debt instrument or insurance contract – by which the amount of interest or principal is indexed to the value of equity instruments – are not closely related to the host instrument because the risks inherent in the host and the embedded derivative are dissimilar.

(d)   Commodity-indexed interest or principal payments embedded in a host debt instrument or insurance contract – by which the amount of interest or principal is indexed to the price of a commodity (such as gold) – are not closely related to the host instrument because the risks inherent in the host and the embedded derivative are dissimilar.

(e)   A call, put, or prepayment option embedded in a host debt contract or host insurance contract is not closely related to the host contract unless:

   (i)   the option's exercise price is approximately equal on each exercise date to the amortised cost of the host debt instrument or the carrying amount of the host insurance contract; or

   (ii)   the exercise price of a prepayment option reimburses the lender for an amount up to the approximate present value of lost interest for the remaining term of the host contract. Lost interest is the product of the principal amount prepaid multiplied by the interest rate differential. The interest rate differential is the excess of the effective interest rate of the host contract over the effective interest rate the entity would receive at the prepayment date if it reinvested the principal amount prepaid in a similar contract for the remaining term of the host contract.

   The assessment of whether the call or put option is closely related to the host debt contract is made before separating the equity element of a convertible debt instrument in accordance with AASB 132.

(f)   Credit derivatives that are embedded in a host debt instrument and allow one party (the 'beneficiary') to transfer the credit risk of a particular reference asset, which it may not own, to another party (the 'guarantor') are not closely related to the host debt instrument. Such credit derivatives allow the guarantor to assume the credit risk associated with the reference asset without directly owning it.

B4.3.6   An example of a hybrid contract is a financial instrument that gives the holder a right to put the financial instrument back to the issuer in exchange for an amount of cash or other financial assets that varies on the basis of the change in an equity or commodity index that may increase or decrease (a 'puttable instrument'). Unless the issuer on initial recognition designates the puttable instrument as a financial liability at fair value through profit or loss, it is required to separate an embedded derivative (ie the indexed principal payment) under paragraph 4.3.3 because the host contract is a debt instrument under paragraph B4.3.2 and the indexed principal payment is not closely related to a host debt instrument under paragraph B4.3.5(a). Because the principal payment can increase and decrease, the embedded derivative is a non-option derivative whose value is indexed to the underlying variable.

B4.3.7   In the case of a puttable instrument that can be put back at any time for cash equal to a proportionate share of the net asset value of an entity (such as units of an open-ended mutual fund or some unit-linked investment products), the effect of separating an embedded derivative and accounting for each component is to measure the hybrid contract at the redemption amount that is payable at the end of the reporting period if the holder exercised its right to put the instrument back to the issuer.

B4.3.8 The economic characteristics and risks of an embedded derivative are closely related to the economic characteristics and risks of the host contract in the following examples. In these examples, an entity does not account for the embedded derivative separately from the host contract.

(a) An embedded derivative in which the underlying is an interest rate or interest rate index that can change the amount of interest that would otherwise be paid or received on an interest-bearing host debt contract or insurance contract is closely related to the host contract unless the hybrid contract can be settled in such a way that the holder would not recover substantially all of its recognised investment or the embedded derivative could at least double the holder's initial rate of return on the host contract and could result in a rate of return that is at least twice what the market return would be for a contract with the same terms as the host contract.

(b) An embedded floor or cap on the interest rate on a debt contract or insurance contract is closely related to the host contract, provided the cap is at or above the market rate of interest and the floor is at or below the market rate of interest when the contract is issued, and the cap or floor is not leveraged in relation to the host contract. Similarly, provisions included in a contract to purchase or sell an asset (eg a commodity) that establish a cap and a floor on the price to be paid or received for the asset are closely related to the host contract if both the cap and floor were out of the money at inception and are not leveraged.

(c) An embedded foreign currency derivative that provides a stream of principal or interest payments that are denominated in a foreign currency and is embedded in a host debt instrument (for example, a dual currency bond) is closely related to the host debt instrument. Such a derivative is not separated from the host instrument because AASB 121 *The Effects of Changes in Foreign Exchange Rates* requires foreign currency gains and losses on monetary items to be recognised in profit or loss.

(d) An embedded foreign currency derivative in a host contract that is an insurance contract or not a financial instrument (such as a contract for the purchase or sale of a non-financial item where the price is denominated in a foreign currency) is closely related to the host contract provided it is not leveraged, does not contain an option feature, and requires payments denominated in one of the following currencies:

  (i) the functional currency of any substantial party to that contract;

  (ii) the currency in which the price of the related good or service that is acquired or delivered is routinely denominated in commercial transactions around the world (such as the US dollar for crude oil transactions); or

  (iii) a currency that is commonly used in contracts to purchase or sell non-financial items in the economic environment in which the transaction takes place (eg a relatively stable and liquid currency that is commonly used in local business transactions or external trade).

(e) An embedded prepayment option in an interest-only or principal-only strip is closely related to the host contract provided the host contract (i) initially resulted from separating the right to receive contractual cash flows of a financial instrument that, in and of itself, did not contain an embedded derivative, and (ii) does not contain any terms not present in the original host debt contract.

(f) An embedded derivative in a host lease contract is closely related to the host contract if the embedded derivative is (i) an inflation-related index such as an index of lease payments to a consumer price index (provided that the lease is not leveraged and the index relates to inflation in the entity's own economic environment), (ii) contingent rentals based on related sales or (iii) contingent rentals based on variable interest rates.

AASB

(g) A unit-linking feature embedded in a host financial instrument or host insurance contract is closely related to the host instrument or host contract if the unit-denominated payments are measured at current unit values that reflect the fair values of the assets of the fund. A unit-linking feature is a contractual term that requires payments denominated in units of an internal or external investment fund.

(h) A derivative embedded in an insurance contract is closely related to the host insurance contract if the embedded derivative and host insurance contract are so interdependent that an entity cannot measure the embedded derivative separately (ie without considering the host contract).

Instruments containing embedded derivatives

B4.3.9 As noted in paragraph B4.3.1, when an entity becomes a party to a hybrid contract with a host that is not an asset within the scope of this Standard and with one or more embedded derivatives, paragraph 4.3.3 requires the entity to identify any such embedded derivative, assess whether it is required to be separated from the host contract and, for those that are required to be separated, measure the derivatives at fair value at initial recognition and subsequently. These requirements can be more complex, or result in less reliable measures, than measuring the entire instrument at fair value through profit or loss. For that reason this Standard permits the entire hybrid contract to be designated as at fair value through profit or loss.

B4.3.10 Such designation may be used whether paragraph 4.3.3 requires the embedded derivatives to be separated from the host contract or prohibits such separation. However, paragraph 4.3.5 would not justify designating the hybrid contract as at fair value through profit or loss in the cases set out in paragraph 4.3.5(a) and (b) because doing so would not reduce complexity or increase reliability.

Reassessment of embedded derivatives

B4.3.11 In accordance with paragraph 4.3.3, an entity shall assess whether an embedded derivative is required to be separated from the host contract and accounted for as a derivative when the entity first becomes a party to the contract. Subsequent reassessment is prohibited unless there is a change in the terms of the contract that significantly modifies the cash flows that otherwise would be required under the contract, in which case reassessment is required. An entity determines whether a modification to cash flows is significant by considering the extent to which the expected future cash flows associated with the embedded derivative, the host contract or both have changed and whether the change is significant relative to the previously expected cash flows on the contract.

B4.3.12 Paragraph B4.3.11 does not apply to embedded derivatives in contracts acquired in:

(a) a business combination (as defined in AASB 3 *Business Combinations*);

(b) a combination of entities or businesses under common control as described in paragraphs B1–B4 of AASB 3; or

(c) the formation of a joint venture as defined in AASB 11 *Joint Arrangements*

or their possible reassessment at the date of acquisition.[4]

Reclassification of financial assets (Section 4.4)

Reclassification of financial assets

B4.4.1 Paragraph 4.4.1 requires an entity to reclassify financial assets if the entity changes its business model for managing those financial assets. Such changes are expected to be very infrequent. Such changes are determined by the entity's senior management as a result of external or internal changes and must be significant to the entity's operations and demonstrable to external parties. Accordingly, a change in an entity's

---

4   AASB 3 addresses the acquisition of contracts with embedded derivatives in a business combination.

business model will occur only when an entity either begins or ceases to perform an activity that is significant to its operations; for example, when the entity has acquired, disposed of or terminated a business line. Examples of a change in business model include the following:

(a) An entity has a portfolio of commercial loans that it holds to sell in the short term. The entity acquires a company that manages commercial loans and has a business model that holds the loans in order to collect the contractual cash flows. The portfolio of commercial loans is no longer for sale, and the portfolio is now managed together with the acquired commercial loans and all are held to collect the contractual cash flows.

(b) A financial services firm decides to shut down its retail mortgage business. That business no longer accepts new business and the financial services firm is actively marketing its mortgage loan portfolio for sale.

B4.4.2 A change in the objective of the entity's business model must be effected before the reclassification date. For example, if a financial services firm decides on 15 February to shut down its retail mortgage business and hence must reclassify all affected financial assets on 1 April (ie the first day of the entity's next reporting period), the entity must not accept new retail mortgage business or otherwise engage in activities consistent with its former business model after 15 February.

B4.4.3 The following are not changes in business model:

(a) a change in intention related to particular financial assets (even in circumstances of significant changes in market conditions).

(b) the temporary disappearance of a particular market for financial assets.

(c) a transfer of financial assets between parts of the entity with different business models.

Measurement (Chapter 5)

Initial measurement (Section 5.1)

B5.1.1 The fair value of a financial instrument at initial recognition is normally the transaction price (ie the fair value of the consideration given or received, see also paragraph B5.1.2A and AASB 13). However, if part of the consideration given or received is for something other than the financial instrument, an entity shall measure the fair value of the financial instrument. For example, the fair value of a long-term loan or receivable that carries no interest can be measured as the present value of all future cash receipts discounted using the prevailing market rate(s) of interest for a similar instrument (similar as to currency, term, type of interest rate and other factors) with a similar credit rating. Any additional amount lent is an expense or a reduction of income unless it qualifies for recognition as some other type of asset.

B5.1.2 If an entity originates a loan that bears an off-market interest rate (eg 5 per cent when the market rate for similar loans is 8 per cent), and receives an upfront fee as compensation, the entity recognises the loan at its fair value, ie net of the fee it receives.

B5.1.2A The best evidence of the fair value of a financial instrument at initial recognition is normally the transaction price (ie the fair value of the consideration given or received, see also AASB 13). If an entity determines that the fair value at initial recognition differs from the transaction price as mentioned in paragraph 5.1.1A, the entity shall account for that instrument at that date as follows:

(a) at the measurement required by paragraph 5.1.1 if that fair value is evidenced by a quoted price in an active market for an identical asset or liability (ie a Level 1 input) or based on a valuation technique that uses only data from observable markets. An entity shall recognise the difference between the fair value at initial recognition and the transaction price as a gain or loss.

(b)   in all other cases, at the measurement required by paragraph 5.1.1, adjusted to defer the difference between the fair value at initial recognition and the transaction price. After initial recognition, the entity shall recognise that deferred difference as a gain or loss only to the extent that it arises from a change in a factor (including time) that market participants would take into account when pricing the asset or liability.

Subsequent measurement (Sections 5.2 and 5.3)

B5.2.1   If a financial instrument that was previously recognised as a financial asset is measured at fair value through profit or loss and its fair value decreases below zero, it is a financial liability measured in accordance with paragraph 4.2.1. However, hybrid contracts with hosts that are assets within the scope of this Standard are always measured in accordance with paragraph 4.3.2.

B5.2.2   The following example illustrates the accounting for transaction costs on the initial and subsequent measurement of a financial asset measured at fair value with changes through other comprehensive income in accordance with either paragraph 5.7.5 or 4.1.2A. An entity acquires a financial asset for CU100 plus a purchase commission of CU2. Initially, the entity recognises the asset at CU102. The reporting period ends one day later, when the quoted market price of the asset is CU100. If the asset were sold, a commission of CU3 would be paid. On that date, the entity measures the asset at CU100 (without regard to the possible commission on sale) and recognises a loss of CU2 in other comprehensive income. If the financial asset is measured at fair value through other comprehensive income in accordance with paragraph 4.1.2A, the transaction costs are amortised to profit or loss using the effective interest method.

B5.2.2A The subsequent measurement of a financial asset or financial liability and the subsequent recognition of gains and losses described in paragraph B5.1.2A shall be consistent with the requirements of this Standard.

Investments in equity instruments and contracts on those investments

B5.2.3   All investments in equity instruments and contracts on those instruments must be measured at fair value. However, in limited circumstances, cost may be an appropriate estimate of fair value. That may be the case if insufficient more recent information is available to measure fair value, or if there is a wide range of possible fair value measurements and cost represents the best estimate of fair value within that range.

B5.2.4   Indicators that cost might not be representative of fair value include:

(a)   a significant change in the performance of the investee compared with budgets, plans or milestones.

(b)   changes in expectation that the investee's technical product milestones will be achieved.

(c)   a significant change in the market for the investee's equity or its products or potential products.

(d)   a significant change in the global economy or the economic environment in which the investee operates.

(e)   a significant change in the performance of comparable entities, or in the valuations implied by the overall market.

(f)   internal matters of the investee such as fraud, commercial disputes, litigation, changes in management or strategy.

(g)   evidence from external transactions in the investee's equity, either by the investee (such as a fresh issue of equity), or by transfers of equity instruments between third parties.

B5.2.5 The list in paragraph B5.2.4 is not exhaustive. An entity shall use all information about the performance and operations of the investee that becomes available after the date of initial recognition. To the extent that any such relevant factors exist, they may indicate that cost might not be representative of fair value. In such cases, the entity must measure fair value.

B5.2.6 Cost is never the best estimate of fair value for investments in quoted equity instruments (or contracts on quoted equity instruments).

Amortised cost measurement (Section 5.4)

Effective interest method

B5.4.1 In applying the effective interest method, an entity identifies fees that are an integral part of the effective interest rate of a financial instrument. The description of fees for financial services may not be indicative of the nature and substance of the services provided. Fees that are an integral part of the effective interest rate of a financial instrument are treated as an adjustment to the effective interest rate, unless the financial instrument is measured at fair value, with the change in fair value being recognised in profit or loss. In those cases, the fees are recognised as revenue or expense when the instrument is initially recognised.

B5.4.2 Fees that are an integral part of the effective interest rate of a financial instrument include:

    (a) origination fees received by the entity relating to the creation or acquisition of a financial asset. Such fees may include compensation for activities such as evaluating the borrower's financial condition, evaluating and recording guarantees, collateral and other security arrangements, negotiating the terms of the instrument, preparing and processing documents and closing the transaction. These fees are an integral part of generating an involvement with the resulting financial instrument.

    (b) commitment fees received by the entity to originate a loan when the loan commitment is not measured in accordance with paragraph 4.2.1(a) and it is probable that the entity will enter into a specific lending arrangement. These fees are regarded as compensation for an ongoing involvement with the acquisition of a financial instrument. If the commitment expires without the entity making the loan, the fee is recognised as revenue on expiry.

    (c) origination fees paid on issuing financial liabilities measured at amortised cost. These fees are an integral part of generating an involvement with a financial liability. An entity distinguishes fees and costs that are an integral part of the effective interest rate for the financial liability from origination fees and transaction costs relating to the right to provide services, such as investment management services.

B5.4.3 Fees that are not an integral part of the effective interest rate of a financial instrument and are accounted for in accordance with AASB 15 include:

    (a) fees charged for servicing a loan;

    (b) commitment fees to originate a loan when the loan commitment is not measured in accordance with paragraph 4.2.1(a) and it is unlikely that a specific lending arrangement will be entered into; and

    (c) loan syndication fees received by an entity that arranges a loan and retains no part of the loan package for itself (or retains a part at the same effective interest rate for comparable risk as other participants).

B5.4.4 When applying the effective interest method, an entity generally amortises any fees, points paid or received, transaction costs and other premiums or discounts that are included in the calculation of the effective interest rate over the expected life of the financial instrument. However, a shorter period is used if this is the period to which the fees, points paid or received, transaction costs, premiums or discounts relate. This will be the case when the variable to which the fees, points paid or received, transaction costs, premiums or discounts relate is repriced to market rates before the expected maturity of the financial instrument. In such a case, the appropriate amortisation period is the period to the next such repricing date. For example, if a premium or discount on a floating-rate financial instrument reflects the interest that has accrued on that financial instrument since the interest was last paid, or changes in the market rates since the floating interest rate was reset to the market rates, it will be amortised to the next date when the floating interest is reset to market rates. This is because the premium or discount relates to the period to the next interest reset date because, at that date, the variable to which the premium or discount relates (ie interest rates) is reset to the market rates. If, however, the premium or discount results from a change in the credit spread over the floating rate specified in the financial instrument, or other variables that are not reset to the market rates, it is amortised over the expected life of the financial instrument.

B5.4.5 For floating-rate financial assets and floating-rate financial liabilities, periodic re-estimation of cash flows to reflect the movements in the market rates of interest alters the effective interest rate. If a floating-rate financial asset or a floating-rate financial liability is recognised initially at an amount equal to the principal receivable or payable on maturity, re-estimating the future interest payments normally has no significant effect on the carrying amount of the asset or the liability.

B5.4.6 If an entity revises its estimates of payments or receipts (excluding modifications in accordance with paragraph 5.4.3 and changes in estimates of expected credit losses), it shall adjust the gross carrying amount of the financial asset or amortised cost of a financial liability (or group of financial instruments) to reflect actual and revised estimated contractual cash flows. The entity recalculates the gross carrying amount of the financial asset or amortised cost of the financial liability as the present value of the estimated future contractual cash flows that are discounted at the financial instrument's original effective interest rate (or credit-adjusted effective interest rate for purchased or originated credit-impaired financial assets) or, when applicable, the revised effective interest rate calculated in accordance with paragraph 6.5.10. The adjustment is recognised in profit or loss as income or expense.

B5.4.7 In some cases a financial asset is considered credit-impaired at initial recognition because the credit risk is very high, and in the case of a purchase it is acquired at a deep discount. An entity is required to include the initial expected credit losses in the estimated cash flows when calculating the credit-adjusted effective interest rate for financial assets that are considered to be purchased or originated credit-impaired at initial recognition. However, this does not mean that a credit-adjusted effective interest rate should be applied solely because the financial asset has high credit risk at initial recognition.

Transaction costs

B5.4.8 Transaction costs include fees and commission paid to agents (including employees acting as selling agents), advisers, brokers and dealers, levies by regulatory agencies and security exchanges, and transfer taxes and duties. Transaction costs do not include debt premiums or discounts, financing costs or internal administrative or holding costs.

Write-off

B5.4.9 Write-offs can relate to a financial asset in its entirety or to a portion of it. For example, an entity plans to enforce the collateral on a financial asset and expects to recover no more than 30 per cent of the financial asset from the collateral. If the entity has no reasonable prospects of recovering any further cash flows from the financial asset, it should write off the remaining 70 per cent of the financial asset.

Impairment (Section 5.5)

Collective and individual assessment basis

B5.5.1   In order to meet the objective of recognising lifetime expected credit losses for significant increases in credit risk since initial recognition, it may be necessary to perform the assessment of significant increases in credit risk on a collective basis by considering information that is indicative of significant increases in credit risk on, for example, a group or sub-group of financial instruments. This is to ensure that an entity meets the objective of recognising lifetime expected credit losses when there are significant increases in credit risk, even if evidence of such significant increases in credit risk at the individual instrument level is not yet available.

B5.5.2   Lifetime expected credit losses are generally expected to be recognised before a financial instrument becomes past due. Typically, credit risk increases significantly before a financial instrument becomes past due or other lagging borrower-specific factors (for example, a modification or restructuring) are observed. Consequently when reasonable and supportable information that is more forward-looking than past due information is available without undue cost or effort, it must be used to assess changes in credit risk.

B5.5.3   However, depending on the nature of the financial instruments and the credit risk information available for particular groups of financial instruments, an entity may not be able to identify significant changes in credit risk for individual financial instruments before the financial instrument becomes past due. This may be the case for financial instruments such as retail loans for which there is little or no updated credit risk information that is routinely obtained and monitored on an individual instrument until a customer breaches the contractual terms. If changes in the credit risk for individual financial instruments are not captured before they become past due, a loss allowance based only on credit information at an individual financial instrument level would not faithfully represent the changes in credit risk since initial recognition.

B5.5.4   In some circumstances an entity does not have reasonable and supportable information that is available without undue cost or effort to measure lifetime expected credit losses on an individual instrument basis. In that case, lifetime expected credit losses shall be recognised on a collective basis that considers comprehensive credit risk information. This comprehensive credit risk information must incorporate not only past due information but also all relevant credit information, including forward-looking macroeconomic information, in order to approximate the result of recognising lifetime expected credit losses when there has been a significant increase in credit risk since initial recognition on an individual instrument level.

B5.5.5   For the purpose of determining significant increases in credit risk and recognising a loss allowance on a collective basis, an entity can group financial instruments on the basis of shared credit risk characteristics with the objective of facilitating an analysis that is designed to enable significant increases in credit risk to be identified on a timely basis. The entity should not obscure this information by grouping financial instruments with different risk characteristics. Examples of shared credit risk characteristics may include, but are not limited to, the:

    (a)   instrument type;

    (b)   credit risk ratings;

    (c)   collateral type;

    (d)   date of initial recognition;

    (e)   remaining term to maturity;

    (f)   industry;

    (g)   geographical location of the borrower; and

    (h)   the value of collateral relative to the financial asset if it has an impact on the probability of a default occurring (for example, non-recourse loans in some jurisdictions or loan-to-value ratios).

B5.5.6 Paragraph 5.5.4 requires that lifetime expected credit losses are recognised on all financial instruments for which there has been significant increases in credit risk since initial recognition. In order to meet this objective, if an entity is not able to group financial instruments for which the credit risk is considered to have increased significantly since initial recognition based on shared credit risk characteristics, the entity should recognise lifetime expected credit losses on a portion of the financial assets for which credit risk is deemed to have increased significantly. The aggregation of financial instruments to assess whether there are changes in credit risk on a collective basis may change over time as new information becomes available on groups of, or individual, financial instruments.

Timing of recognising lifetime expected credit losses

B5.5.7 The assessment of whether lifetime expected credit losses should be recognised is based on significant increases in the likelihood or risk of a default occurring since initial recognition (irrespective of whether a financial instrument has been repriced to reflect an increase in credit risk) instead of on evidence of a financial asset being credit-impaired at the reporting date or an actual default occurring. Generally, there will be a significant increase in credit risk before a financial asset becomes credit-impaired or an actual default occurs.

B5.5.8 For loan commitments, an entity considers changes in the risk of a default occurring on the loan to which a loan commitment relates. For financial guarantee contracts, an entity considers the changes in the risk that the specified debtor will default on the contract.

B5.5.9 The significance of a change in the credit risk since initial recognition depends on the risk of a default occurring as at initial recognition. Thus, a given change, in absolute terms, in the risk of a default occurring will be more significant for a financial instrument with a lower initial risk of a default occurring compared to a financial instrument with a higher initial risk of a default occurring.

B5.5.10 The risk of a default occurring on financial instruments that have comparable credit risk is higher the longer the expected life of the instrument; for example, the risk of a default occurring on an AAA-rated bond with an expected life of 10 years is higher than that on an AAA-rated bond with an expected life of five years.

B5.5.11 Because of the relationship between the expected life and the risk of a default occurring, the change in credit risk cannot be assessed simply by comparing the change in the absolute risk of a default occurring over time. For example, if the risk of a default occurring for a financial instrument with an expected life of 10 years at initial recognition is identical to the risk of a default occurring on that financial instrument when its expected life in a subsequent period is only five years, that may indicate an increase in credit risk. This is because the risk of a default occurring over the expected life usually decreases as time passes if the credit risk is unchanged and the financial instrument is closer to maturity. However, for financial instruments that only have significant payment obligations close to the maturity of the financial instrument the risk of a default occurring may not necessarily decrease as time passes. In such a case, an entity should also consider other qualitative factors that would demonstrate whether credit risk has increased significantly since initial recognition.

B5.5.12 An entity may apply various approaches when assessing whether the credit risk on a financial instrument has increased significantly since initial recognition or when measuring expected credit losses. An entity may apply different approaches for different financial instruments. An approach that does not include an explicit probability of default as an input per se, such as a credit loss rate approach, can be consistent with the requirements in this Standard, provided that an entity is able to separate the changes in the risk of a default occurring from changes in other drivers of expected credit losses, such as collateral, and considers the following when making the assessment:

  (a) the change in the risk of a default occurring since initial recognition;

    (b)   the expected life of the financial instrument; and

    (c)   reasonable and supportable information that is available without undue cost or effort that may affect credit risk.

B5.5.13 The methods used to determine whether credit risk has increased significantly on a financial instrument since initial recognition should consider the characteristics of the financial instrument (or group of financial instruments) and the default patterns in the past for comparable financial instruments. Despite the requirement in paragraph 5.5.9, for financial instruments for which default patterns are not concentrated at a specific point during the expected life of the financial instrument, changes in the risk of a default occurring over the next 12 months may be a reasonable approximation of the changes in the lifetime risk of a default occurring. In such cases, an entity may use changes in the risk of a default occurring over the next 12 months to determine whether credit risk has increased significantly since initial recognition, unless circumstances indicate that a lifetime assessment is necessary.

B5.5.14 However, for some financial instruments, or in some circumstances, it may not be appropriate to use changes in the risk of a default occurring over the next 12 months to determine whether lifetime expected credit losses should be recognised. For example, the change in the risk of a default occurring in the next 12 months may not be a suitable basis for determining whether credit risk has increased on a financial instrument with a maturity of more than 12 months when:

    (a)   the financial instrument only has significant payment obligations beyond the next 12 months;

    (b)   changes in relevant macroeconomic or other credit-related factors occur that are not adequately reflected in the risk of a default occurring in the next 12 months; or

    (c)   changes in credit-related factors only have an impact on the credit risk of the financial instrument (or have a more pronounced effect) beyond 12 months.

Determining whether credit risk has increased significantly since initial recognition

B5.5.15 When determining whether the recognition of lifetime expected credit losses is required, an entity shall consider reasonable and supportable information that is available without undue cost or effort and that may affect the credit risk on a financial instrument in accordance with paragraph 5.5.17(c). An entity need not undertake an exhaustive search for information when determining whether credit risk has increased significantly since initial recognition.

B5.5.16 Credit risk analysis is a multifactor and holistic analysis; whether a specific factor is relevant, and its weight compared to other factors, will depend on the type of product, characteristics of the financial instruments and the borrower as well as the geographical region. An entity shall consider reasonable and supportable information that is available without undue cost or effort and that is relevant for the particular financial instrument being assessed. However, some factors or indicators may not be identifiable on an individual financial instrument level. In such a case, the factors or indicators should be assessed for appropriate portfolios, groups of portfolios or portions of a portfolio of financial instruments to determine whether the requirement in paragraph 5.5.3 for the recognition of lifetime expected credit losses has been met.

B5.5.17 The following non-exhaustive list of information may be relevant in assessing changes in credit risk:

    (a)   significant changes in internal price indicators of credit risk as a result of a change in credit risk since inception, including, but not limited to, the credit spread that would result if a particular financial instrument or similar financial instrument with the same terms and the same counterparty were newly originated or issued at the reporting date.

(b)   other changes in the rates or terms of an existing financial instrument that would be significantly different if the instrument was newly originated or issued at the reporting date (such as more stringent covenants, increased amounts of collateral or guarantees, or higher income coverage) because of changes in the credit risk of the financial instrument since initial recognition.

(c)   significant changes in external market indicators of credit risk for a particular financial instrument or similar financial instruments with the same expected life. Changes in market indicators of credit risk include, but are not limited to:

   (i)   the credit spread;

   (ii)   the credit default swap prices for the borrower;

   (iii) the length of time or the extent to which the fair value of a financial asset has been less than its amortised cost; and

   (iv)   other market information related to the borrower, such as changes in the price of a borrower's debt and equity instruments.

(d)   an actual or expected significant change in the financial instrument's external credit rating.

(e)   an actual or expected internal credit rating downgrade for the borrower or decrease in behavioural scoring used to assess credit risk internally. Internal credit ratings and internal behavioural scoring are more reliable when they are mapped to external ratings or supported by default studies.

(f)   existing or forecast adverse changes in business, financial or economic conditions that are expected to cause a significant change in the borrower's ability to meet its debt obligations, such as an actual or expected increase in interest rates or an actual or expected significant increase in unemployment rates.

(g)   an actual or expected significant change in the operating results of the borrower. Examples include actual or expected declining revenues or margins, increasing operating risks, working capital deficiencies, decreasing asset quality, increased balance sheet leverage, liquidity, management problems or changes in the scope of business or organisational structure (such as the discontinuance of a segment of the business) that results in a significant change in the borrower's ability to meet its debt obligations.

(h)   significant increases in credit risk on other financial instruments of the same borrower.

(i)   an actual or expected significant adverse change in the regulatory, economic, or technological environment of the borrower that results in a significant change in the borrower's ability to meet its debt obligations, such as a decline in the demand for the borrower's sales product because of a shift in technology.

(j)   significant changes in the value of the collateral supporting the obligation or in the quality of third-party guarantees or credit enhancements, which are expected to reduce the borrower's economic incentive to make scheduled contractual payments or to otherwise have an effect on the probability of a default occurring. For example, if the value of collateral declines because house prices decline, borrowers in some jurisdictions have a greater incentive to default on their mortgages.

(k)   a significant change in the quality of the guarantee provided by a shareholder (or an individual's parents) if the shareholder (or parents) have an incentive and financial ability to prevent default by capital or cash infusion.

(l)   significant changes, such as reductions in financial support from a parent entity or other affiliate or an actual or expected significant change in the quality of credit enhancement, that are expected to reduce the borrower's economic incentive to make scheduled contractual payments. Credit quality enhancements or support include the consideration of the financial condition of the guarantor and/or, for interests issued in securitisations, whether subordinated interests are expected to be capable of absorbing expected credit losses (for example, on the loans underlying the security).

(m) expected changes in the loan documentation including an expected breach of contract that may lead to covenant waivers or amendments, interest payment holidays, interest rate step-ups, requiring additional collateral or guarantees, or other changes to the contractual framework of the instrument.

(n) significant changes in the expected performance and behaviour of the borrower, including changes in the payment status of borrowers in the group (for example, an increase in the expected number or extent of delayed contractual payments or significant increases in the expected number of credit card borrowers who are expected to approach or exceed their credit limit or who are expected to be paying the minimum monthly amount).

(o) changes in the entity's credit management approach in relation to the financial instrument; ie based on emerging indicators of changes in the credit risk of the financial instrument, the entity's credit risk management practice is expected to become more active or to be focused on managing the instrument, including the instrument becoming more closely monitored or controlled, or the entity specifically intervening with the borrower.

(p) past due information, including the rebuttable presumption as set out in paragraph 5.5.11.

B5.5.18 In some cases, the qualitative and non-statistical quantitative information available may be sufficient to determine that a financial instrument has met the criterion for the recognition of a loss allowance at an amount equal to lifetime expected credit losses. That is, the information does not need to flow through a statistical model or credit ratings process in order to determine whether there has been a significant increase in the credit risk of the financial instrument. In other cases, an entity may need to consider other information, including information from its statistical models or credit ratings processes. Alternatively, the entity may base the assessment on both types of information, ie qualitative factors that are not captured through the internal ratings process and a specific internal rating category at the reporting date, taking into consideration the credit risk characteristics at initial recognition, if both types of information are relevant.

More than 30 days past due rebuttable presumption

B5.5.19 The rebuttable presumption in paragraph 5.5.11 is not an absolute indicator that lifetime expected credit losses should be recognised, but is presumed to be the latest point at which lifetime expected credit losses should be recognised even when using forward-looking information (including macroeconomic factors on a portfolio level).

B5.5.20 An entity can rebut this presumption. However, it can do so only when it has reasonable and supportable information available that demonstrates that even if contractual payments become more than 30 days past due, this does not represent a significant increase in the credit risk of a financial instrument. For example when non-payment was an administrative oversight, instead of resulting from financial difficulty of the borrower, or the entity has access to historical evidence that demonstrates that there is no correlation between significant increases in the risk of a default occurring and financial assets on which payments are more than 30 days past due, but that evidence does identify such a correlation when payments are more than 60 days past due.

B5.5.21 An entity cannot align the timing of significant increases in credit risk and the recognition of lifetime expected credit losses to when a financial asset is regarded as credit-impaired or an entity's internal definition of default.

Financial instruments that have low credit risk at the reporting date

B5.5.22 The credit risk on a financial instrument is considered low for the purposes of paragraph 5.5.10, if the financial instrument has a low risk of default, the borrower has a strong capacity to meet its contractual cash flow obligations in the near term and adverse changes in economic and business conditions in the longer term may, but will not necessarily, reduce the ability of the borrower to fulfil its contractual cash flow obligations. Financial instruments are not considered to have low credit risk when they are regarded as having a low risk of loss simply because of the value of collateral and the financial instrument without that collateral would not be considered low credit risk. Financial instruments are also not considered to have low credit risk simply because they have a lower risk of default than the entity's other financial instruments or relative to the credit risk of the jurisdiction within which an entity operates.

B5.5.23 To determine whether a financial instrument has low credit risk, an entity may use its internal credit risk ratings or other methodologies that are consistent with a globally understood definition of low credit risk and that consider the risks and the type of financial instruments that are being assessed. An external rating of 'investment grade' is an example of a financial instrument that may be considered as having low credit risk. However, financial instruments are not required to be externally rated to be considered to have low credit risk. They should, however, be considered to have low credit risk from a market participant perspective taking into account all of the terms and conditions of the financial instrument.

B5.5.24 Lifetime expected credit losses are not recognised on a financial instrument simply because it was considered to have low credit risk in the previous reporting period and is not considered to have low credit risk at the reporting date. In such a case, an entity shall determine whether there has been a significant increase in credit risk since initial recognition and thus whether lifetime expected credit losses are required to be recognised in accordance with paragraph 5.5.3.

Modifications

B5.5.25 In some circumstances, the renegotiation or modification of the contractual cash flows of a financial asset can lead to the derecognition of the existing financial asset in accordance with this Standard. When the modification of a financial asset results in the derecognition of the existing financial asset and the subsequent recognition of the modified financial asset, the modified asset is considered a 'new' financial asset for the purposes of this Standard.

B5.5.26 Accordingly the date of the modification shall be treated as the date of initial recognition of that financial asset when applying the impairment requirements to the modified financial asset. This typically means measuring the loss allowance at an amount equal to 12-month expected credit losses until the requirements for the recognition of lifetime expected credit losses in paragraph 5.5.3 are met. However, in some unusual circumstances following a modification that results in derecognition of the original financial asset, there may be evidence that the modified financial asset is credit-impaired at initial recognition, and thus, the financial asset should be recognised as an originated credit-impaired financial asset. This might occur, for example, in a situation in which there was a substantial modification of a distressed asset that resulted in the derecognition of the original financial asset. In such a case, it may be possible for the modification to result in a new financial asset which is credit-impaired at initial recognition.

B5.5.27 If the contractual cash flows on a financial asset have been renegotiated or otherwise modified, but the financial asset is not derecognised, that financial asset is not automatically considered to have lower credit risk. An entity shall assess whether there has been a significant increase in credit risk since initial recognition on the basis of all reasonable and supportable information that is available without undue cost or effort. This includes historical and forward-looking information and an assessment of the credit risk over the expected life of the financial asset, which includes information about the circumstances that led to the modification. Evidence that the criteria for the recognition of lifetime expected credit losses are no longer met may include a history of up-to-date and timely payment performance against the modified contractual terms. Typically a customer would need to demonstrate consistently good payment behaviour over a period of time before the credit risk is considered to have decreased. For example, a history of missed or incomplete payments would not typically be erased by simply making one payment on time following a modification of the contractual terms.

Measurement of expected credit losses

Expected credit losses

B5.5.28 Expected credit losses are a probability-weighted estimate of credit losses (ie the present value of all cash shortfalls) over the expected life of the financial instrument. A cash shortfall is the difference between the cash flows that are due to an entity in accordance with the contract and the cash flows that the entity expects to receive. Because expected credit losses consider the amount and timing of payments, a credit loss arises even if the entity expects to be paid in full but later than when contractually due.

B5.5.29 For financial assets, a credit loss is the present value of the difference between:

(a) the contractual cash flows that are due to an entity under the contract; and

(b) the cash flows that the entity expects to receive.

B5.5.30 For undrawn loan commitments, a credit loss is the present value of the difference between:

(a) the contractual cash flows that are due to the entity if the holder of the loan commitment draws down the loan; and

(b) the cash flows that the entity expects to receive if the loan is drawn down.

B5.5.31 An entity's estimate of expected credit losses on loan commitments shall be consistent with its expectations of drawdowns on that loan commitment, ie it shall consider the expected portion of the loan commitment that will be drawn down within 12 months of the reporting date when estimating 12-month expected credit losses, and the expected portion of the loan commitment that will be drawn down over the expected life of the loan commitment when estimating lifetime expected credit losses.

B5.5.32 For a financial guarantee contract, the entity is required to make payments only in the event of a default by the debtor in accordance with the terms of the instrument that is guaranteed. Accordingly, cash shortfalls are the expected payments to reimburse the holder for a credit loss that it incurs less any amounts that the entity expects to receive from the holder, the debtor or any other party. If the asset is fully guaranteed, the estimation of cash shortfalls for a financial guarantee contract would be consistent with the estimations of cash shortfalls for the asset subject to the guarantee.

B5.5.33 For a financial asset that is credit-impaired at the reporting date, but that is not a purchased or originated credit-impaired financial asset, an entity shall measure the expected credit losses as the difference between the asset's gross carrying amount and the present value of estimated future cash flows discounted at the financial asset's original effective interest rate. Any adjustment is recognised in profit or loss as an impairment gain or loss.

B5.5.34 When measuring a loss allowance for a lease receivable, the cash flows used for determining the expected credit losses should be consistent with the cash flows used in measuring the lease receivable in accordance with AASB 117 *Leases*.

B5.5.35 An entity may use practical expedients when measuring expected credit losses if they are consistent with the principles in paragraph 5.5.17. An example of a practical expedient is the calculation of the expected credit losses on trade receivables using a provision matrix. The entity would use its historical credit loss experience (adjusted as appropriate in accordance with paragraphs B5.5.51–B5.5.52) for trade receivables to estimate the 12-month expected credit losses or the lifetime expected credit losses on the financial assets as relevant. A provision matrix might, for example, specify fixed provision rates depending on the number of days that a trade receivable is past due (for example, 1 per cent if not past due, 2 per cent if less than 30 days past due, 3 per cent if more than 30 days but less than 90 days past due, 20 per cent if 90–180 days past due etc). Depending on the diversity of its customer base, the entity would use appropriate groupings if its historical credit loss experience shows significantly different loss patterns for different customer segments. Examples of criteria that might be used to group assets include geographical region, product type, customer rating, collateral or trade credit insurance and type of customer (such as wholesale or retail).

Definition of default

B5.5.36 Paragraph 5.5.9 requires that when determining whether the credit risk on a financial instrument has increased significantly, an entity shall consider the change in the risk of a default occurring since initial recognition.

B5.5.37 When defining default for the purposes of determining the risk of a default occurring, an entity shall apply a default definition that is consistent with the definition used for internal credit risk management purposes for the relevant financial instrument and consider qualitative indicators (for example, financial covenants) when appropriate. However, there is a rebuttable presumption that default does not occur later than when a financial asset is 90 days past due unless an entity has reasonable and supportable information to demonstrate that a more lagging default criterion is more appropriate. The definition of default used for these purposes shall be applied consistently to all financial instruments unless information becomes available that demonstrates that another default definition is more appropriate for a particular financial instrument.

Period over which to estimate expected credit losses

B5.5.38 In accordance with paragraph 5.5.19, the maximum period over which expected credit losses shall be measured is the maximum contractual period over which the entity is exposed to credit risk. For loan commitments and financial guarantee contracts, this is the maximum contractual period over which an entity has a present contractual obligation to extend credit.

B5.5.39 However, in accordance with paragraph 5.5.20, some financial instruments include both a loan and an undrawn commitment component and the entity's contractual ability to demand repayment and cancel the undrawn commitment does not limit the entity's exposure to credit losses to the contractual notice period. For example, revolving credit facilities, such as credit cards and overdraft facilities, can be contractually withdrawn by the lender with as little as one day's notice. However, in practice lenders continue to extend credit for a longer period and may only withdraw the facility after the credit risk of the borrower increases, which could be too late to prevent some or all of the expected credit losses. These financial instruments generally have the following characteristics as a result of the nature of the financial instrument, the way in which the financial instruments are managed, and the nature of the available information about significant increases in credit risk:

(a) the financial instruments do not have a fixed term or repayment structure and usually have a short contractual cancellation period (for example, one day);

(b) the contractual ability to cancel the contract is not enforced in the normal day-to-day management of the financial instrument and the contract may only be cancelled when the entity becomes aware of an increase in credit risk at the facility level; and

(c) the financial instruments are managed on a collective basis.

B5.5.40 When determining the period over which the entity is expected to be exposed to credit risk, but for which expected credit losses would not be mitigated by the entity's normal credit risk management actions, an entity should consider factors such as historical information and experience about:

(a) the period over which the entity was exposed to credit risk on similar financial instruments;

(b) the length of time for related defaults to occur on similar financial instruments following a significant increase in credit risk; and

(c) the credit risk management actions that an entity expects to take once the credit risk on the financial instrument has increased, such as the reduction or removal of undrawn limits.

Probability-weighted outcome

B5.5.41 The purpose of estimating expected credit losses is neither to estimate a worst-case scenario nor to estimate the best-case scenario. Instead, an estimate of expected credit losses shall always reflect the possibility that a credit loss occurs and the possibility that no credit loss occurs even if the most likely outcome is no credit loss.

B5.5.42 Paragraph 5.5.17(a) requires the estimate of expected credit losses to reflect an unbiased and probability-weighted amount that is determined by evaluating a range of possible outcomes. In practice, this may not need to be a complex analysis. In some cases, relatively simple modelling may be sufficient, without the need for a large number of detailed simulations of scenarios. For example, the average credit losses of a large group of financial instruments with shared risk characteristics may be a reasonable estimate of the probability-weighted amount. In other situations, the identification of scenarios that specify the amount and timing of the cash flows for particular outcomes and the estimated probability of those outcomes will probably be needed. In those situations, the expected credit losses shall reflect at least two outcomes in accordance with paragraph 5.5.18.

B5.5.43 For lifetime expected credit losses, an entity shall estimate the risk of a default occurring on the financial instrument during its expected life. 12-month expected credit losses are a portion of the lifetime expected credit losses and represent the lifetime cash shortfalls that will result if a default occurs in the 12 months after the reporting date (or a shorter period if the expected life of a financial instrument is less than 12 months), weighted by the probability of that default occurring. Thus, 12-month expected credit losses are neither the lifetime expected credit losses that an entity will incur on financial instruments that it predicts will default in the next 12 months nor the cash shortfalls that are predicted over the next 12 months.

Time value of money

B5.5.44 Expected credit losses shall be discounted to the reporting date, not to the expected default or some other date, using the effective interest rate determined at initial recognition or an approximation thereof. If a financial instrument has a variable interest rate, expected credit losses shall be discounted using the current effective interest rate determined in accordance with paragraph B5.4.5.

B5.5.45 For purchased or originated credit-impaired financial assets, expected credit losses shall be discounted using the credit-adjusted effective interest rate determined at initial recognition.

B5.5.46 Expected credit losses on lease receivables shall be discounted using the same discount rate used in the measurement of the lease receivable in accordance with AASB 117.

B5.5.47 The expected credit losses on a loan commitment shall be discounted using the effective interest rate, or an approximation thereof, that will be applied when recognising the financial asset resulting from the loan commitment. This is because for the purpose of applying the impairment requirements, a financial asset that is recognised following a draw down on a loan commitment shall be treated as a continuation of that commitment instead of as a new financial instrument. The

AASB

expected credit losses on the financial asset shall therefore be measured considering the initial credit risk of the loan commitment from the date that the entity became a party to the irrevocable commitment.

B5.5.48   Expected credit losses on financial guarantee contracts or on loan commitments for which the effective interest rate cannot be determined shall be discounted by applying a discount rate that reflects the current market assessment of the time value of money and the risks that are specific to the cash flows but only if, and to the extent that, the risks are taken into account by adjusting the discount rate instead of adjusting the cash shortfalls being discounted.

Reasonable and supportable information

B5.5.49   For the purpose of this Standard, reasonable and supportable information is that which is reasonably available at the reporting date without undue cost or effort, including information about past events, current conditions and forecasts of future economic conditions. Information that is available for financial reporting purposes is considered to be available without undue cost or effort.

B5.5.50   An entity is not required to incorporate forecasts of future conditions over the entire expected life of a financial instrument. The degree of judgement that is required to estimate expected credit losses depends on the availability of detailed information. As the forecast horizon increases, the availability of detailed information decreases and the degree of judgement required to estimate expected credit losses increases. The estimate of expected credit losses does not require a detailed estimate for periods that are far in the future – for such periods, an entity may extrapolate projections from available, detailed information.

B5.5.51   An entity need not undertake an exhaustive search for information but shall consider all reasonable and supportable information that is available without undue cost or effort and that is relevant to the estimate of expected credit losses, including the effect of expected prepayments. The information used shall include factors that are specific to the borrower, general economic conditions and an assessment of both the current as well as the forecast direction of conditions at the reporting date. An entity may use various sources of data, that may be both internal (entity-specific) and external. Possible data sources include internal historical credit loss experience, internal ratings, credit loss experience of other entities and external ratings, reports and statistics. Entities that have no, or insufficient, sources of entity-specific data may use peer group experience for the comparable financial instrument (or groups of financial instruments).

B5.5.52   Historical information is an important anchor or base from which to measure expected credit losses. However, an entity shall adjust historical data, such as credit loss experience, on the basis of current observable data to reflect the effects of the current conditions and its forecasts of future conditions that did not affect the period on which the historical data is based, and to remove the effects of the conditions in the historical period that are not relevant to the future contractual cash flows. In some cases, the best reasonable and supportable information could be the unadjusted historical information, depending on the nature of the historical information and when it was calculated, compared to circumstances at the reporting date and the characteristics of the financial instrument being considered. Estimates of changes in expected credit losses should reflect, and be directionally consistent with, changes in related observable data from period to period (such as changes in unemployment rates, property prices, commodity prices, payment status or other factors that are indicative of credit losses on the financial instrument or in the group of financial instruments and in the magnitude of those changes). An entity shall regularly review the methodology and assumptions used for estimating expected credit losses to reduce any differences between estimates and actual credit loss experience.

B5.5.53   When using historical credit loss experience in estimating expected credit losses, it is important that information about historical credit loss rates is applied to groups that are defined in a manner that is consistent with the groups for which the historical credit loss rates were observed. Consequently, the method used shall enable each group of financial assets to be associated with information about past credit loss experience in groups of financial assets with similar risk characteristics and with relevant observable data that reflects current conditions.

B5.5.54 Expected credit losses reflect an entity's own expectations of credit losses. However, when considering all reasonable and supportable information that is available without undue cost or effort in estimating expected credit losses, an entity should also consider observable market information about the credit risk of the particular financial instrument or similar financial instruments.

Collateral

B5.5.55 For the purposes of measuring expected credit losses, the estimate of expected cash shortfalls shall reflect the cash flows expected from collateral and other credit enhancements that are part of the contractual terms and are not recognised separately by the entity. The estimate of expected cash shortfalls on a collateralised financial instrument reflects the amount and timing of cash flows that are expected from foreclosure on the collateral less the costs of obtaining and selling the collateral, irrespective of whether foreclosure is probable (ie the estimate of expected cash flows considers the probability of a foreclosure and the cash flows that would result from it). Consequently, any cash flows that are expected from the realisation of the collateral beyond the contractual maturity of the contract should be included in this analysis. Any collateral obtained as a result of foreclosure is not recognised as an asset that is separate from the collateralised financial instrument unless it meets the relevant recognition criteria for an asset in this or other Standards.

Reclassification of financial assets (Section 5.6)

B5.6.1 If an entity reclassifies financial assets in accordance with paragraph 4.4.1, paragraph 5.6.1 requires that the reclassification is applied prospectively from the reclassification date. Both the amortised cost measurement category and the fair value through other comprehensive income measurement category require that the effective interest rate is determined at initial recognition. Both of those measurement categories also require that the impairment requirements are applied in the same way. Consequently, when an entity reclassifies a financial asset between the amortised cost measurement category and the fair value through other comprehensive income measurement category:

    (a) the recognition of interest revenue will not change and therefore the entity continues to use the same effective interest rate.

    (b) the measurement of expected credit losses will not change because both measurement categories apply the same impairment approach. However if a financial asset is reclassified out of the fair value through other comprehensive income measurement category and into the amortised cost measurement category, a loss allowance would be recognised as an adjustment to the gross carrying amount of the financial asset from the reclassification date. If a financial asset is reclassified out of the amortised cost measurement category and into the fair value through other comprehensive income measurement category, the loss allowance would be derecognised (and thus would no longer be recognised as an adjustment to the gross carrying amount) but instead would be recognised as an accumulated impairment amount (of an equal amount) in other comprehensive income and would be disclosed from the reclassification date.

B5.6.2 However, an entity is not required to separately recognise interest revenue or impairment gains or losses for a financial asset measured at fair value through profit or loss. Consequently, when an entity reclassifies a financial asset out of the fair value through profit or loss measurement category, the effective interest rate is determined on the basis of the fair value of the asset at the reclassification date. In addition, for the purposes of applying Section 5.5 to the financial asset from the reclassification date, the date of the reclassification is treated as the date of initial recognition.

Gains and losses (Section 5.7)

B5.7.1 Paragraph 5.7.5 permits an entity to make an irrevocable election to present in other comprehensive income changes in the fair value of an investment in an equity instrument that is not held for trading. This election is made on an instrument-by-instrument (ie share-by-share) basis. Amounts presented in other comprehensive income shall not be subsequently transferred to profit or loss. However, the entity may transfer the cumulative gain or loss within equity. Dividends on such investments are recognised in profit or loss in accordance with paragraph 5.7.6 unless the dividend clearly represents a recovery of part of the cost of the investment.

B5.7.1A Unless paragraph 4.1.5 applies, paragraph 4.1.2A requires that a financial asset is measured at fair value through other comprehensive income if the contractual terms of the financial asset give rise to cash flows that are solely payments of principal and interest on the principal amount outstanding and the asset is held in a business model whose objective is achieved by both collecting contractual cash flows and selling financial assets. This measurement category recognises information in profit or loss as if the financial asset is measured at amortised cost, while the financial asset is measured in the statement of financial position at fair value. Gains or losses, other than those that are recognised in profit or loss in accordance with paragraphs 5.7.10–5.7.11, are recognised in other comprehensive income. When these financial assets are derecognised, cumulative gains or losses previously recognised in other comprehensive income are reclassified to profit or loss. This reflects the gain or loss that would have been recognised in profit or loss upon derecognition if the financial asset had been measured at amortised cost.

B5.7.2 An entity applies AASB 121 to financial assets and financial liabilities that are monetary items in accordance with AASB 121 and denominated in a foreign currency. AASB 121 requires any foreign exchange gains and losses on monetary assets and monetary liabilities to be recognised in profit or loss. An exception is a monetary item that is designated as a hedging instrument in a cash flow hedge (see paragraph 6.5.11), a hedge of a net investment (see paragraph 6.5.13) or a fair value hedge of an equity instrument for which an entity has elected to present changes in fair value in other comprehensive income in accordance with paragraph 5.7.5 (see paragraph 6.5.8).

B5.7.2A For the purpose of recognising foreign exchange gains and losses under AASB 121, a financial asset measured at fair value through other comprehensive income in accordance with paragraph 4.1.2A is treated as a monetary item. Accordingly, such a financial asset is treated as an asset measured at amortised cost in the foreign currency. Exchange differences on the amortised cost are recognised in profit or loss and other changes in the carrying amount are recognised in accordance with paragraph 5.7.10.

B5.7.3 Paragraph 5.7.5 permits an entity to make an irrevocable election to present in other comprehensive income subsequent changes in the fair value of particular investments in equity instruments. Such an investment is not a monetary item. Accordingly, the gain or loss that is presented in other comprehensive income in accordance with paragraph 5.7.5 includes any related foreign exchange component.

B5.7.4 If there is a hedging relationship between a non-derivative monetary asset and a non-derivative monetary liability, changes in the foreign currency component of those financial instruments are presented in profit or loss.

Liabilities designated as at fair value through profit or loss

B5.7.5 When an entity designates a financial liability as at fair value through profit or loss, it must determine whether presenting in other comprehensive income the effects of changes in the liability's credit risk would create or enlarge an accounting mismatch in profit or loss. An accounting mismatch would be created or enlarged if presenting the effects of changes in the liability's credit risk in other comprehensive income would result in a greater mismatch in profit or loss than if those amounts were presented in profit or loss.

B5.7.6   To make that determination, an entity must assess whether it expects that the effects of changes in the liability's credit risk will be offset in profit or loss by a change in the fair value of another financial instrument measured at fair value through profit or loss. Such an expectation must be based on an economic relationship between the characteristics of the liability and the characteristics of the other financial instrument.

B5.7.7   That determination is made at initial recognition and is not reassessed. For practical purposes the entity need not enter into all of the assets and liabilities giving rise to an accounting mismatch at exactly the same time. A reasonable delay is permitted provided that any remaining transactions are expected to occur. An entity must apply consistently its methodology for determining whether presenting in other comprehensive income the effects of changes in the liability's credit risk would create or enlarge an accounting mismatch in profit or loss. However, an entity may use different methodologies when there are different economic relationships between the characteristics of the liabilities designated as at fair value through profit or loss and the characteristics of the other financial instruments. AASB 7 requires an entity to provide qualitative disclosures in the notes to the financial statements about its methodology for making that determination.

B5.7.8   If such a mismatch would be created or enlarged, the entity is required to present all changes in fair value (including the effects of changes in the credit risk of the liability) in profit or loss. If such a mismatch would not be created or enlarged, the entity is required to present the effects of changes in the liability's credit risk in other comprehensive income.

B5.7.9   Amounts presented in other comprehensive income shall not be subsequently transferred to profit or loss. However, the entity may transfer the cumulative gain or loss within equity.

B5.7.10   The following example describes a situation in which an accounting mismatch would be created in profit or loss if the effects of changes in the credit risk of the liability were presented in other comprehensive income. A mortgage bank provides loans to customers and funds those loans by selling bonds with matching characteristics (eg amount outstanding, repayment profile, term and currency) in the market. The contractual terms of the loan permit the mortgage customer to prepay its loan (ie satisfy its obligation to the bank) by buying the corresponding bond at fair value in the market and delivering that bond to the mortgage bank. As a result of that contractual prepayment right, if the credit quality of the bond worsens (and, thus, the fair value of the mortgage bank's liability decreases), the fair value of the mortgage bank's loan asset also decreases. The change in the fair value of the asset reflects the mortgage customer's contractual right to prepay the mortgage loan by buying the underlying bond at fair value (which, in this example, has decreased) and delivering the bond to the mortgage bank. Consequently, the effects of changes in the credit risk of the liability (the bond) will be offset in profit or loss by a corresponding change in the fair value of a financial asset (the loan). If the effects of changes in the liability's credit risk were presented in other comprehensive income there would be an accounting mismatch in profit or loss. Consequently, the mortgage bank is required to present all changes in fair value of the liability (including the effects of changes in the liability's credit risk) in profit or loss.

B5.7.11   In the example in paragraph B5.7.10, there is a contractual linkage between the effects of changes in the credit risk of the liability and changes in the fair value of the financial asset (ie as a result of the mortgage customer's contractual right to prepay the loan by buying the bond at fair value and delivering the bond to the mortgage bank). However, an accounting mismatch may also occur in the absence of a contractual linkage.

B5.7.12   For the purposes of applying the requirements in paragraphs 5.7.7 and 5.7.8, an accounting mismatch is not caused solely by the measurement method that an entity uses to determine the effects of changes in a liability's credit risk. An accounting mismatch in profit or loss would arise only when the effects of changes in the liability's credit risk (as defined in AASB 7) are expected to be offset by changes in the fair value of another financial instrument. A mismatch that arises solely as a result of the measurement method (ie because an entity does not isolate changes in a liability's credit risk from some other changes in its fair value) does not affect the determination required by paragraphs 5.7.7 and 5.7.8. For example, an entity may not isolate changes in a liability's credit risk from changes in liquidity risk. If the entity presents the combined effect of both factors in other comprehensive income, a mismatch may occur because changes in liquidity risk may be included in the fair value measurement of the entity's financial assets and the entire fair value change of those assets is presented in profit or loss. However, such a mismatch is caused by measurement imprecision, not the offsetting relationship described in paragraph B5.7.6 and, therefore, does not affect the determination required by paragraphs 5.7.7 and 5.7.8.

The meaning of 'credit risk' (paragraphs 5.7.7 and 5.7.8)

B5.7.13 AASB 7 defines credit risk as 'the risk that one party to a financial instrument will cause a financial loss for the other party by failing to discharge an obligation'. The requirement in paragraph 5.7.7(a) relates to the risk that the issuer will fail to perform on that particular liability. It does not necessarily relate to the creditworthiness of the issuer. For example, if an entity issues a collateralised liability and a non-collateralised liability that are otherwise identical, the credit risk of those two liabilities will be different, even though they are issued by the same entity. The credit risk on the collateralised liability will be less than the credit risk of the non-collateralised liability. The credit risk for a collateralised liability may be close to zero.

B5.7.14 For the purposes of applying the requirement in paragraph 5.7.7(a), credit risk is different from asset-specific performance risk. Asset-specific performance risk is not related to the risk that an entity will fail to discharge a particular obligation but instead it is related to the risk that a single asset or a group of assets will perform poorly (or not at all).

B5.7.15 The following are examples of asset-specific performance risk:

(a)   a liability with a unit-linking feature whereby the amount due to investors is contractually determined on the basis of the performance of specified assets. The effect of that unit-linking feature on the fair value of the liability is asset-specific performance risk, not credit risk.

(b)   a liability issued by a structured entity with the following characteristics. The entity is legally isolated so the assets in the entity are ring-fenced solely for the benefit of its investors, even in the event of bankruptcy. The entity enters into no other transactions and the assets in the entity cannot be hypothecated. Amounts are due to the entity's investors only if the ring-fenced assets generate cash flows. Thus, changes in the fair value of the liability primarily reflect changes in the fair value of the assets. The effect of the performance of the assets on the fair value of the liability is asset-specific performance risk, not credit risk.

Determining the effects of changes in credit risk

B5.7.16 For the purposes of applying the requirement in paragraph 5.7.7(a), an entity shall determine the amount of change in the fair value of the financial liability that is attributable to changes in the credit risk of that liability either:

(a)   as the amount of change in its fair value that is not attributable to changes in market conditions that give rise to market risk (see paragraphs B5.7.17 and B5.7.18); or

(b) using an alternative method the entity believes more faithfully represents the amount of change in the liability's fair value that is attributable to changes in its credit risk.

B5.7.17 Changes in market conditions that give rise to market risk include changes in a benchmark interest rate, the price of another entity's financial instrument, a commodity price, a foreign exchange rate or an index of prices or rates.

B5.7.18 If the only significant relevant changes in market conditions for a liability are changes in an observed (benchmark) interest rate, the amount in paragraph B5.7.16(a) can be estimated as follows:

(a) First, the entity computes the liability's internal rate of return at the start of the period using the fair value of the liability and the liability's contractual cash flows at the start of the period. It deducts from this rate of return the observed (benchmark) interest rate at the start of the period, to arrive at an instrument-specific component of the internal rate of return.

(b) Next, the entity calculates the present value of the cash flows associated with the liability using the liability's contractual cash flows at the end of the period and a discount rate equal to the sum of (i) the observed (benchmark) interest rate at the end of the period and (ii) the instrument-specific component of the internal rate of return as determined in (a).

(c) The difference between the fair value of the liability at the end of the period and the amount determined in (b) is the change in fair value that is not attributable to changes in the observed (benchmark) interest rate. This is the amount to be presented in other comprehensive income in accordance with paragraph 5.7.7(a).

B5.7.19 The example in paragraph B5.7.18 assumes that changes in fair value arising from factors other than changes in the instrument's credit risk or changes in observed (benchmark) interest rates are not significant. This method would not be appropriate if changes in fair value arising from other factors are significant. In those cases, an entity is required to use an alternative method that more faithfully measures the effects of changes in the liability's credit risk (see paragraph B5.7.16(b)). For example, if the instrument in the example contains an embedded derivative, the change in fair value of the embedded derivative is excluded in determining the amount to be presented in other comprehensive income in accordance with paragraph 5.7.7(a).

B5.7.20 As with all fair value measurements, an entity's measurement method for determining the portion of the change in the liability's fair value that is attributable to changes in its credit risk must make maximum use of relevant observable inputs and minimum use of unobservable inputs.

Hedge accounting (Chapter 6)

Hedging instruments (Section 6.2)

Qualifying instruments

B6.2.1 Derivatives that are embedded in hybrid contracts, but that are not separately accounted for, cannot be designated as separate hedging instruments.

B6.2.2 An entity's own equity instruments are not financial assets or financial liabilities of the entity and therefore cannot be designated as hedging instruments.

B6.2.3 For hedges of foreign currency risk, the foreign currency risk component of a non-derivative financial instrument is determined in accordance with AASB 121.

Written options

B6.2.4 This Standard does not restrict the circumstances in which a derivative that is measured at fair value through profit or loss may be designated as a hedging instrument, except for some written options. A written option does not qualify as a hedging instrument unless it is designated as an offset to a purchased option, including one that is embedded in another financial instrument (for example, a written call option used to hedge a callable liability).

Designation of hedging instruments

B6.2.5 For hedges other than hedges of foreign currency risk, when an entity designates a non-derivative financial asset or a non-derivative financial liability measured at fair value through profit or loss as a hedging instrument, it may only designate the non-derivative financial instrument in its entirety or a proportion of it.

B6.2.6 A single hedging instrument may be designated as a hedging instrument of more than one type of risk, provided that there is a specific designation of the hedging instrument and of the different risk positions as hedged items. Those hedged items can be in different hedging relationships.

Hedged items (Section 6.3)

Qualifying items

B6.3.1 A firm commitment to acquire a business in a business combination cannot be a hedged item, except for foreign currency risk, because the other risks being hedged cannot be specifically identified and measured. Those other risks are general business risks.

B6.3.2 An equity method investment cannot be a hedged item in a fair value hedge. This is because the equity method recognises in profit or loss the investor's share of the investee's profit or loss, instead of changes in the investment's fair value. For a similar reason, an investment in a consolidated subsidiary cannot be a hedged item in a fair value hedge. This is because consolidation recognises in profit or loss the subsidiary's profit or loss, instead of changes in the investment's fair value. A hedge of a net investment in a foreign operation is different because it is a hedge of the foreign currency exposure, not a fair value hedge of the change in the value of the investment.

B6.3.3 Paragraph 6.3.4 permits an entity to designate as hedged items aggregated exposures that are a combination of an exposure and a derivative. When designating such a hedged item, an entity assesses whether the aggregated exposure combines an exposure with a derivative so that it creates a different aggregated exposure that is managed as one exposure for a particular risk (or risks). In that case, the entity may designate the hedged item on the basis of the aggregated exposure. For example:

(a) an entity may hedge a given quantity of highly probable coffee purchases in 15 months' time against price risk (based on US dollars) using a 15-month futures contract for coffee. The highly probable coffee purchases and the futures contract for coffee in combination can be viewed as a 15-month fixed-amount US dollar foreign currency risk exposure for risk management purposes (ie like any fixed-amount US dollar cash outflow in 15 months' time).

(b) an entity may hedge the foreign currency risk for the entire term of a 10-year fixed-rate debt denominated in a foreign currency. However, the entity requires fixed-rate exposure in its functional currency only for a short to medium term (say two years) and floating rate exposure in its functional currency for the remaining term to maturity. At the end of each of the two-year intervals (ie on a two-year rolling basis) the entity fixes the next two years' interest rate exposure (if the interest level is such that the entity wants to fix interest rates). In such a situation an entity may enter into a 10-year fixed-to-floating cross-currency interest rate swap that swaps the fixed-rate foreign currency debt into a variable-rate functional currency exposure. This is overlaid with a two-year interest rate swap that – on the basis of the functional currency – swaps variable-rate debt into fixed-rate debt. In effect, the fixed-rate foreign currency debt and the 10-year fixed-to-floating cross-currency interest rate swap in combination are viewed as a 10-year variable-rate debt functional currency exposure for risk management purposes.

B6.3.4 When designating the hedged item on the basis of the aggregated exposure, an entity considers the combined effect of the items that constitute the aggregated exposure for the purpose of assessing hedge effectiveness and measuring hedge ineffectiveness. However, the items that constitute the aggregated exposure remain accounted for separately. This means that, for example:

(a) derivatives that are part of an aggregated exposure are recognised as separate assets or liabilities measured at fair value; and

(b) if a hedging relationship is designated between the items that constitute the aggregated exposure, the way in which a derivative is included as part of an aggregated exposure must be consistent with the designation of that derivative as the hedging instrument at the level of the aggregated exposure. For example, if an entity excludes the forward element of a derivative from its designation as the hedging instrument for the hedging relationship between the items that constitute the aggregated exposure, it must also exclude the forward element when including that derivative as a hedged item as part of the aggregated exposure. Otherwise, the aggregated exposure shall include a derivative, either in its entirety or a proportion of it.

B6.3.5 Paragraph 6.3.6 states that in consolidated financial statements the foreign currency risk of a highly probable forecast intragroup transaction may qualify as a hedged item in a cash flow hedge, provided that the transaction is denominated in a currency other than the functional currency of the entity entering into that transaction and that the foreign currency risk will affect consolidated profit or loss. For this purpose an entity can be a parent, subsidiary, associate, joint arrangement or branch. If the foreign currency risk of a forecast intragroup transaction does not affect consolidated profit or loss, the intragroup transaction cannot qualify as a hedged item. This is usually the case for royalty payments, interest payments or management charges between members of the same group, unless there is a related external transaction. However, when the foreign currency risk of a forecast intragroup transaction will affect consolidated profit or loss, the intragroup transaction can qualify as a hedged item. An example is forecast sales or purchases of inventories between members of the same group if there is an onward sale of the inventory to a party external to the group. Similarly, a forecast intragroup sale of plant and equipment from the group entity that manufactured it to a group entity that will use the plant and equipment in its operations may affect consolidated profit or loss. This could occur, for example, because the plant and equipment will be depreciated by the purchasing entity and the amount initially recognised for the plant and equipment may change if the forecast intragroup transaction is denominated in a currency other than the functional currency of the purchasing entity.

B6.3.6 If a hedge of a forecast intragroup transaction qualifies for hedge accounting, any gain or loss is recognised in, and taken out of, other comprehensive income in accordance with paragraph 6.5.11. The relevant period or periods during which the foreign currency risk of the hedged transaction affects profit or loss is when it affects consolidated profit or loss.

Designation of hedged items

B6.3.7 A component is a hedged item that is less than the entire item. Consequently, a component reflects only some of the risks of the item of which it is a part or reflects the risks only to some extent (for example, when designating a proportion of an item).

Risk components

B6.3.8 To be eligible for designation as a hedged item, a risk component must be a separately identifiable component of the financial or the non-financial item, and the changes in the cash flows or the fair value of the item attributable to changes in that risk component must be reliably measurable.

B6.3.9 When identifying what risk components qualify for designation as a hedged item, an entity assesses such risk components within the context of the particular market structure to which the risk or risks relate and in which the hedging activity takes place. Such a determination requires an evaluation of the relevant facts and circumstances, which differ by risk and market.

B6.3.10   When designating risk components as hedged items, an entity considers whether the risk components are explicitly specified in a contract (contractually specified risk components) or whether they are implicit in the fair value or the cash flows of an item of which they are a part (non-contractually specified risk components). Non-contractually specified risk components can relate to items that are not a contract (for example, forecast transactions) or contracts that do not explicitly specify the component (for example, a firm commitment that includes only one single price instead of a pricing formula that references different underlyings). For example:

(a)   Entity A has a long-term supply contract for natural gas that is priced using a contractually specified formula that references commodities and other factors (for example, gas oil, fuel oil and other components such as transport charges). Entity A hedges the gas oil component in that supply contract using a gas oil forward contract. Because the gas oil component is specified by the terms and conditions of the supply contract it is a contractually specified risk component. Hence, because of the pricing formula, Entity A concludes that the gas oil price exposure is separately identifiable. At the same time, there is a market for gas oil forward contracts. Hence, Entity A concludes that the gas oil price exposure is reliably measurable. Consequently, the gas oil price exposure in the supply contract is a risk component that is eligible for designation as a hedged item.

(b)   Entity B hedges its future coffee purchases based on its production forecast. Hedging starts up to 15 months before delivery for part of the forecast purchase volume. Entity B increases the hedged volume over time (as the delivery date approaches). Entity B uses two different types of contracts to manage its coffee price risk:

(i)   exchange-traded coffee futures contracts; and

(ii) coffee supply contracts for Arabica coffee from Colombia delivered to a specific manufacturing site. These contracts price a tonne of coffee based on the exchange-traded coffee futures contract price plus a fixed price differential plus a variable logistics services charge using a pricing formula. The coffee supply contract is an executory contract in accordance with which Entity B takes actual delivery of coffee.

For deliveries that relate to the current harvest, entering into the coffee supply contracts allows Entity B to fix the price differential between the actual coffee quality purchased (Arabica coffee from Colombia) and the benchmark quality that is the underlying of the exchange-traded futures contract. However, for deliveries that relate to the next harvest, the coffee supply contracts are not yet available, so the price differential cannot be fixed. Entity B uses exchange-traded coffee futures contracts to hedge the benchmark quality component of its coffee price risk for deliveries that relate to the current harvest as well as the next harvest. Entity B determines that it is exposed to three different risks: coffee price risk reflecting the benchmark quality, coffee price risk reflecting the difference (spread) between the price for the benchmark quality coffee and the particular Arabica coffee from Colombia that it actually receives, and the variable logistics costs. For deliveries related to the current harvest, after Entity B enters into a coffee supply contract, the coffee price risk reflecting the benchmark quality is a contractually specified risk component because the pricing formula includes an indexation to the exchange-traded coffee futures contract price. Entity B concludes that this risk component is separately identifiable and reliably measurable. For deliveries related to the next harvest, Entity B has not yet entered into any coffee supply contracts (ie those deliveries are forecast transactions). Hence, the coffee price risk reflecting the benchmark quality is a non-contractually specified risk component. Entity B's analysis of the market structure takes into account how eventual deliveries of the particular coffee that it receives are priced. Hence, on the basis of this analysis of the market structure, Entity B concludes that the forecast transactions also involve the coffee price risk that reflects the benchmark quality as a risk component that is separately identifiable and reliably measurable even though it is not contractually specified. Consequently, Entity B may designate hedging relationships on a risk components basis (for the coffee price risk that reflects the benchmark quality) for coffee supply contracts as well as forecast transactions.

(c) Entity C hedges part of its future jet fuel purchases on the basis of its consumption forecast up to 24 months before delivery and increases the volume that it hedges over time. Entity C hedges this exposure using different types of contracts depending on the time horizon of the hedge, which affects the market liquidity of the derivatives. For the longer time horizons (12–24 months) Entity C uses crude oil contracts because only these have sufficient market liquidity. For time horizons of 6–12 months Entity C uses gas oil derivatives because they are sufficiently liquid. For time horizons up to six months Entity C uses jet fuel contracts. Entity C's analysis of the market structure for oil and oil products and its evaluation of the relevant facts and circumstances is as follows:

   (i) Entity C operates in a geographical area in which Brent is the crude oil benchmark. Crude oil is a raw material benchmark that affects the price of various refined oil products as their most basic input. Gas oil is a benchmark for refined oil products, which is used as a pricing reference for oil distillates more generally. This is also reflected in the types of derivative financial instruments for the crude oil and refined oil products markets of the environment in which Entity C operates, such as:

      • the benchmark crude oil futures contract, which is for Brent crude oil;

      • the benchmark gas oil futures contract, which is used as the pricing reference for distillates – for example, jet fuel spread derivatives cover the price differential between jet fuel and that benchmark gas oil; and

      • the benchmark gas oil crack spread derivative (ie the derivative for the price differential between crude oil and gas oil – a refining margin), which is indexed to Brent crude oil.

   (ii) the pricing of refined oil products does not depend on which particular crude oil is processed by a particular refinery because those refined oil products (such as gas oil or jet fuel) are standardised products.

Hence, Entity C concludes that the price risk of its jet fuel purchases includes a crude oil price risk component based on Brent crude oil and a gas oil price risk component, even though crude oil and gas oil are not specified in any contractual arrangement. Entity C concludes that these two risk components are separately identifiable and reliably measurable even though they are not contractually specified. Consequently, Entity C may designate hedging relationships for forecast jet fuel purchases on a risk components basis (for crude oil or gas oil). This analysis also means that if, for example, Entity C used crude oil derivatives based on West Texas Intermediate (WTI) crude oil, changes in the price differential between Brent crude oil and WTI crude oil would cause hedge ineffectiveness.

(d) Entity D holds a fixed-rate debt instrument. This instrument is issued in an environment with a market in which a large variety of similar debt instruments are compared by their spreads to a benchmark rate (for example, LIBOR) and variable-rate instruments in that environment are typically indexed to that benchmark rate. Interest rate swaps are frequently used to manage interest rate risk on the basis of that benchmark rate, irrespective of the spread of debt instruments to that benchmark rate. The price of fixed-rate debt instruments varies directly in response to changes in the benchmark rate as they happen.

Entity D concludes that the benchmark rate is a component that can be separately identified and reliably measured. Consequently, Entity D may designate hedging relationships for the fixed-rate debt instrument on a risk component basis for the benchmark interest rate risk.

B6.3.11 When designating a risk component as a hedged item, the hedge accounting requirements apply to that risk component in the same way as they apply to other hedged items that are not risk components. For example, the qualifying criteria apply, including that the hedging relationship must meet the hedge effectiveness requirements, and any hedge ineffectiveness must be measured and recognised.

B6.3.12 An entity can also designate only changes in the cash flows or fair value of a hedged item above or below a specified price or other variable (a 'one-sided risk'). The intrinsic value of a purchased option hedging instrument (assuming that it has the same principal terms as the designated risk), but not its time value, reflects a one-sided risk in a hedged item. For example, an entity can designate the variability of future cash flow outcomes resulting from a price increase of a forecast commodity purchase. In such a situation, the entity designates only cash flow losses that result from an increase in the price above the specified level. The hedged risk does not include the time value of a purchased option, because the time value is not a component of the forecast transaction that affects profit or loss.

B6.3.13 There is a rebuttable presumption that unless inflation risk is contractually specified, it is not separately identifiable and reliably measurable and hence cannot be designated as a risk component of a financial instrument. However, in limited cases, it is possible to identify a risk component for inflation risk that is separately identifiable and reliably measurable because of the particular circumstances of the inflation environment and the relevant debt market.

B6.3.14 For example, an entity issues debt in an environment in which inflation-linked bonds have a volume and term structure that results in a sufficiently liquid market that allows constructing a term structure of zero-coupon real interest rates. This means that for the respective currency, inflation is a relevant factor that is separately considered by the debt markets. In those circumstances the inflation risk component could be determined by discounting the cash flows of the hedged debt instrument using the term structure of zero-coupon real interest rates (ie in a manner similar to how a risk-free (nominal) interest rate component can be determined). Conversely, in many cases an inflation risk component is not separately identifiable and reliably measurable. For example, an entity issues only nominal interest rate debt in an environment with a market for inflation-linked bonds that is not sufficiently liquid to allow a term structure of zero-coupon real interest rates to be constructed. In this case the analysis of the market structure and of the facts and circumstances does not support the entity concluding that inflation is a relevant factor that is separately considered by the debt markets. Hence, the entity cannot overcome the rebuttable presumption that inflation risk that is not contractually specified is not separately identifiable and reliably measurable. Consequently, an inflation risk component would not be eligible for designation as the hedged item. This applies irrespective of any inflation hedging instrument that the entity has actually entered into. In particular, the entity cannot simply impute the terms and conditions of the actual inflation hedging instrument by projecting its terms and conditions onto the nominal interest rate debt.

B6.3.15 A contractually specified inflation risk component of the cash flows of a recognised inflation-linked bond (assuming that there is no requirement to account for an embedded derivative separately) is separately identifiable and reliably measurable, as long as other cash flows of the instrument are not affected by the inflation risk component.

Components of a nominal amount

B6.3.16 There are two types of components of nominal amounts that can be designated as the hedged item in a hedging relationship: a component that is a proportion of an entire item or a layer component. The type of component changes the accounting outcome. An entity shall designate the component for accounting purposes consistently with its risk management objective.

B6.3.17 An example of a component that is a proportion is 50 per cent of the contractual cash flows of a loan.

B6.3.18 A layer component may be specified from a defined, but open, population, or from a defined nominal amount. Examples include:

    (a) part of a monetary transaction volume, for example, the next FC10 cash flows from sales denominated in a foreign currency after the first FC20 in March 201X;[5]

    (b) a part of a physical volume, for example, the bottom layer, measuring 5 million cubic metres, of the natural gas stored in location XYZ;

    (c) a part of a physical or other transaction volume, for example, the first 100 barrels of the oil purchases in June 201X or the first 100 MWh of electricity sales in June 201X; or

    (d) a layer from the nominal amount of the hedged item, for example, the last CU80 million of a CU100 million firm commitment, the bottom layer of CU20 million of a CU100 million fixed-rate bond or the top layer of CU30 million from a total amount of CU100 million of fixed-rate debt that can be prepaid at fair value (the defined nominal amount is CU100 million).

B6.3.19 If a layer component is designated in a fair value hedge, an entity shall specify it from a defined nominal amount. To comply with the requirements for qualifying fair value hedges, an entity shall remeasure the hedged item for fair value changes (ie remeasure the item for fair value changes attributable to the hedged risk). The fair value hedge adjustment must be recognised in profit or loss no later than when the item is derecognised. Consequently, it is necessary to track the item to which the fair value hedge adjustment relates. For a layer component in a fair value hedge, this requires an entity to track the nominal amount from which it is defined. For example, in paragraph B6.3.18(d), the total defined nominal amount of CU100 million must be tracked in order to track the bottom layer of CU20 million or the top layer of CU30 million.

B6.3.20 A layer component that includes a prepayment option is not eligible to be designated as a hedged item in a fair value hedge if the prepayment option's fair value is affected by changes in the hedged risk, unless the designated layer includes the effect of the related prepayment option when determining the change in the fair value of the hedged item.

Relationship between components and the total cash flows of an item

B6.3.21 If a component of the cash flows of a financial or a non-financial item is designated as the hedged item, that component must be less than or equal to the total cash flows of the entire item. However, all of the cash flows of the entire item may be designated as the hedged item and hedged for only one particular risk (for example, only for those changes that are attributable to changes in LIBOR or a benchmark commodity price).

B6.3.22 For example, in the case of a financial liability whose effective interest rate is below LIBOR, an entity cannot designate:

    (a) a component of the liability equal to interest at LIBOR (plus the principal amount in case of a fair value hedge); and

    (b) a negative residual component.

B6.3.23 However, in the case of a fixed-rate financial liability whose effective interest rate is (for example) 100 basis points below LIBOR, an entity can designate as the hedged

_____

5   In this Standard monetary amounts are denominated in 'currency units' (CU) and 'foreign currency units' (FC).

item the change in the value of that entire liability (ie principal plus interest at LIBOR minus 100 basis points) that is attributable to changes in LIBOR. If a fixed-rate financial instrument is hedged some time after its origination and interest rates have changed in the meantime, the entity can designate a risk component equal to a benchmark rate that is higher than the contractual rate paid on the item. The entity can do so provided that the benchmark rate is less than the effective interest rate calculated on the assumption that the entity had purchased the instrument on the day when it first designates the hedged item. For example, assume that an entity originates a fixed-rate financial asset of CU100 that has an effective interest rate of 6 per cent at a time when LIBOR is 4 per cent. It begins to hedge that asset some time later when LIBOR has increased to 8 per cent and the fair value of the asset has decreased to CU90. The entity calculates that if it had purchased the asset on the date it first designates the related LIBOR interest rate risk as the hedged item, the effective yield of the asset based on its then fair value of CU90 would have been 9.5 per cent. Because LIBOR is less than this effective yield, the entity can designate a LIBOR component of 8 per cent that consists partly of the contractual interest cash flows and partly of the difference between the current fair value (ie CU90) and the amount repayable on maturity (ie CU100).

B6.3.24   If a variable-rate financial liability bears interest of (for example) three-month LIBOR minus 20 basis points (with a floor at zero basis points), an entity can designate as the hedged item the change in the cash flows of that entire liability (ie three-month LIBOR minus 20 basis points – including the floor) that is attributable to changes in LIBOR. Hence, as long as the three-month LIBOR forward curve for the remaining life of that liability does not fall below 20 basis points, the hedged item has the same cash flow variability as a liability that bears interest at three-month LIBOR with a zero or positive spread. However, if the three-month LIBOR forward curve for the remaining life of that liability (or a part of it) falls below 20 basis points, the hedged item has a lower cash flow variability than a liability that bears interest at three-month LIBOR with a zero or positive spread.

B6.3.25   A similar example of a non-financial item is a specific type of crude oil from a particular oil field that is priced off the relevant benchmark crude oil. If an entity sells that crude oil under a contract using a contractual pricing formula that sets the price per barrel at the benchmark crude oil price minus CU10 with a floor of CU15, the entity can designate as the hedged item the entire cash flow variability under the sales contract that is attributable to the change in the benchmark crude oil price. However, the entity cannot designate a component that is equal to the full change in the benchmark crude oil price. Hence, as long as the forward price (for each delivery) does not fall below CU25, the hedged item has the same cash flow variability as a crude oil sale at the benchmark crude oil price (or with a positive spread). However, if the forward price for any delivery falls below CU25, the hedged item has a lower cash flow variability than a crude oil sale at the benchmark crude oil price (or with a positive spread).

Qualifying criteria for hedge accounting (Section 6.4)

Hedge effectiveness

B6.4.1   Hedge effectiveness is the extent to which changes in the fair value or the cash flows of the hedging instrument offset changes in the fair value or the cash flows of the hedged item (for example, when the hedged item is a risk component, the relevant change in fair value or cash flows of an item is the one that is attributable to the hedged risk). Hedge ineffectiveness is the extent to which the changes in the fair value or the cash flows of the hedging instrument are greater or less than those on the hedged item.

B6.4.2   When designating a hedging relationship and on an ongoing basis, an entity shall analyse the sources of hedge ineffectiveness that are expected to affect the hedging relationship during its term. This analysis (including any updates in accordance with paragraph B6.5.21 arising from rebalancing a hedging relationship) is the basis for the entity's assessment of meeting the hedge effectiveness requirements.

B6.4.3 For the avoidance of doubt, the effects of replacing the original counterparty with a clearing counterparty and making the associated changes as described in paragraph 6.5.6 shall be reflected in the measurement of the hedging instrument and therefore in the assessment of hedge effectiveness and the measurement of hedge effectiveness.

Economic relationship between the hedged item and the hedging instrument

B6.4.4 The requirement that an economic relationship exists means that the hedging instrument and the hedged item have values that generally move in the opposite direction because of the same risk, which is the hedged risk. Hence, there must be an expectation that the value of the hedging instrument and the value of the hedged item will systematically change in response to movements in either the same underlying or underlyings that are economically related in such a way that they respond in a similar way to the risk that is being hedged (for example, Brent and WTI crude oil).

B6.4.5 If the underlyings are not the same but are economically related, there can be situations in which the values of the hedging instrument and the hedged item move in the same direction, for example, because the price differential between the two related underlyings changes while the underlyings themselves do not move significantly. That is still consistent with an economic relationship between the hedging instrument and the hedged item if the values of the hedging instrument and the hedged item are still expected to typically move in the opposite direction when the underlyings move.

B6.4.6 The assessment of whether an economic relationship exists includes an analysis of the possible behaviour of the hedging relationship during its term to ascertain whether it can be expected to meet the risk management objective. The mere existence of a statistical correlation between two variables does not, by itself, support a valid conclusion that an economic relationship exists.

The effect of credit risk

B6.4.7 Because the hedge accounting model is based on a general notion of offset between gains and losses on the hedging instrument and the hedged item, hedge effectiveness is determined not only by the economic relationship between those items (ie the changes in their underlyings) but also by the effect of credit risk on the value of both the hedging instrument and the hedged item. The effect of credit risk means that even if there is an economic relationship between the hedging instrument and the hedged item, the level of offset might become erratic. This can result from a change in the credit risk of either the hedging instrument or the hedged item that is of such a magnitude that the credit risk dominates the value changes that result from the economic relationship (ie the effect of the changes in the underlyings). A level of magnitude that gives rise to dominance is one that would result in the loss (or gain) from credit risk frustrating the effect of changes in the underlyings on the value of the hedging instrument or the hedged item, even if those changes were significant. Conversely, if during a particular period there is little change in the underlyings, the fact that even small credit risk-related changes in the value of the hedging instrument or the hedged item might affect the value more than the underlyings does not create dominance.

B6.4.8 An example of credit risk dominating a hedging relationship is when an entity hedges an exposure to commodity price risk using an uncollateralised derivative. If the counterparty to that derivative experiences a severe deterioration in its credit standing, the effect of the changes in the counterparty's credit standing might outweigh the effect of changes in the commodity price on the fair value of the hedging instrument, whereas changes in the value of the hedged item depend largely on the commodity price changes.

Hedge ratio

B6.4.9 In accordance with the hedge effectiveness requirements, the hedge ratio of the hedging relationship must be the same as that resulting from the quantity of the hedged item that the entity actually hedges and the quantity of the hedging instrument that the entity actually uses to hedge that quantity of hedged item. Hence, if an entity hedges less than 100 per cent of the exposure on an item, such as 85 per cent, it shall designate the hedging relationship using a hedge ratio that is the same as that resulting from 85 per cent of the exposure and the quantity of the hedging instrument that the entity actually uses to hedge those 85 per cent. Similarly, if, for example, an entity hedges an exposure using a nominal amount of 40 units of a financial instrument, it shall designate the hedging relationship using a hedge ratio that is the same as that resulting from that quantity of 40 units (ie the entity must not use a hedge ratio based on a higher quantity of units that it might hold in total or a lower quantity of units) and the quantity of the hedged item that it actually hedges with those 40 units.

B6.4.10 However, the designation of the hedging relationship using the same hedge ratio as that resulting from the quantities of the hedged item and the hedging instrument that the entity actually uses shall not reflect an imbalance between the weightings of the hedged item and the hedging instrument that would in turn create hedge ineffectiveness (irrespective of whether recognised or not) that could result in an accounting outcome that would be inconsistent with the purpose of hedge accounting. Hence, for the purpose of designating a hedging relationship, an entity must adjust the hedge ratio that results from the quantities of the hedged item and the hedging instrument that the entity actually uses if that is needed to avoid such an imbalance.

B6.4.11 Examples of relevant considerations in assessing whether an accounting outcome is inconsistent with the purpose of hedge accounting are:

(a) whether the intended hedge ratio is established to avoid recognising hedge ineffectiveness for cash flow hedges, or to achieve fair value hedge adjustments for more hedged items with the aim of increasing the use of fair value accounting, but without offsetting fair value changes of the hedging instrument; and

(b) whether there is a commercial reason for the particular weightings of the hedged item and the hedging instrument, even though that creates hedge ineffectiveness. For example, an entity enters into and designates a quantity of the hedging instrument that is not the quantity that it determined as the best hedge of the hedged item because the standard volume of the hedging instruments does not allow it to enter into that exact quantity of hedging instrument (a 'lot size issue'). An example is an entity that hedges 100 tonnes of coffee purchases with standard coffee futures contracts that have a contract size of 37,500 lbs (pounds). The entity could only use either five or six contracts (equivalent to 85.0 and 102.1 tonnes respectively) to hedge the purchase volume of 100 tonnes. In that case, the entity designates the hedging relationship using the hedge ratio that results from the number of coffee futures contracts that it actually uses, because the hedge ineffectiveness resulting from the mismatch in the weightings of the hedged item and the hedging instrument would not result in an accounting outcome that is inconsistent with the purpose of hedge accounting.

Frequency of assessing whether the hedge effectiveness requirements are met

B6.4.12 An entity shall assess at the inception of the hedging relationship, and on an ongoing basis, whether a hedging relationship meets the hedge effectiveness requirements. At a minimum, an entity shall perform the ongoing assessment at each reporting date or upon a significant change in the circumstances affecting the hedge effectiveness requirements, whichever comes first. The assessment relates to expectations about hedge effectiveness and is therefore only forward-looking.

Methods for assessing whether the hedge effectiveness requirements are met

B6.4.13 This Standard does not specify a method for assessing whether a hedging relationship meets the hedge effectiveness requirements. However, an entity shall use a method that captures the relevant characteristics of the hedging relationship including the sources of hedge ineffectiveness. Depending on those factors, the method can be a qualitative or a quantitative assessment.

B6.4.14 For example, when the critical terms (such as the nominal amount, maturity and underlying) of the hedging instrument and the hedged item match or are closely aligned, it might be possible for an entity to conclude on the basis of a qualitative assessment of those critical terms that the hedging instrument and the hedged item have values that will generally move in the opposite direction because of the same risk and hence that an economic relationship exists between the hedged item and the hedging instrument (see paragraphs B6.4.4–B6.4.6).

B6.4.15 The fact that a derivative is in or out of the money when it is designated as a hedging instrument does not in itself mean that a qualitative assessment is inappropriate. It depends on the circumstances whether hedge ineffectiveness arising from that fact could have a magnitude that a qualitative assessment would not adequately capture.

B6.4.16 Conversely, if the critical terms of the hedging instrument and the hedged item are not closely aligned, there is an increased level of uncertainty about the extent of offset. Consequently, the hedge effectiveness during the term of the hedging relationship is more difficult to predict. In such a situation it might only be possible for an entity to conclude on the basis of a quantitative assessment that an economic relationship exists between the hedged item and the hedging instrument (see paragraphs B6.4.4–B6.4.6). In some situations a quantitative assessment might also be needed to assess whether the hedge ratio used for designating the hedging relationship meets the hedge effectiveness requirements (see paragraphs B6.4.9–B6.4.11). An entity can use the same or different methods for those two different purposes.

B6.4.17 If there are changes in circumstances that affect hedge effectiveness, an entity may have to change the method for assessing whether a hedging relationship meets the hedge effectiveness requirements in order to ensure that the relevant characteristics of the hedging relationship, including the sources of hedge ineffectiveness, are still captured.

B6.4.18 An entity's risk management is the main source of information to perform the assessment of whether a hedging relationship meets the hedge effectiveness requirements. This means that the management information (or analysis) used for decision-making purposes can be used as a basis for assessing whether a hedging relationship meets the hedge effectiveness requirements.

B6.4.19 An entity's documentation of the hedging relationship includes how it will assess the hedge effectiveness requirements, including the method or methods used. The documentation of the hedging relationship shall be updated for any changes to the methods (see paragraph B6.4.17).

Accounting for qualifying hedging relationships (Section 6.5)

B6.5.1 An example of a fair value hedge is a hedge of exposure to changes in the fair value of a fixed-rate debt instrument arising from changes in interest rates. Such a hedge could be entered into by the issuer or by the holder.

B6.5.2 The purpose of a cash flow hedge is to defer the gain or loss on the hedging instrument to a period or periods in which the hedged expected future cash flows affect profit or loss. An example of a cash flow hedge is the use of a swap to change floating rate debt (whether measured at amortised cost or fair value) to fixed-rate debt (ie a hedge of a future transaction in which the future cash flows being hedged are the future interest payments). Conversely, a forecast purchase of an equity instrument that, once acquired, will be accounted for at fair value through profit or loss, is an example of an item that cannot be the hedged item in a cash flow hedge, because any gain or loss on the hedging instrument that would be deferred could not be appropriately reclassified to profit or loss during a period in which it would achieve offset. For the same reason, a forecast purchase of an equity instrument that, once acquired, will be accounted for at fair value with changes in fair value presented in other comprehensive income also cannot be the hedged item in a cash flow hedge.

B6.5.3 A hedge of a firm commitment (for example, a hedge of the change in fuel price relating to an unrecognised contractual commitment by an electric utility to purchase fuel at a fixed price) is a hedge of an exposure to a change in fair value. Accordingly, such a hedge is a fair value hedge. However, in accordance with paragraph 6.5.4, a hedge of the foreign currency risk of a firm commitment could alternatively be accounted for as a cash flow hedge.

Measurement of hedge ineffectiveness

B6.5.4 When measuring hedge ineffectiveness, an entity shall consider the time value of money. Consequently, the entity determines the value of the hedged item on a present value basis and therefore the change in the value of the hedged item also includes the effect of the time value of money.

B6.5.5 To calculate the change in the value of the hedged item for the purpose of measuring hedge ineffectiveness, an entity may use a derivative that would have terms that match the critical terms of the hedged item (this is commonly referred to as a 'hypothetical derivative'), and, for example for a hedge of a forecast transaction, would be calibrated using the hedged price (or rate) level. For example, if the hedge was for a two-sided risk at the current market level, the hypothetical derivative would represent a hypothetical forward contract that is calibrated to a value of nil at the time of designation of the hedging relationship. If the hedge was for example for a one-sided risk, the hypothetical derivative would represent the intrinsic value of a hypothetical option that at the time of designation of the hedging relationship is at the money if the hedged price level is the current market level, or out of the money if the hedged price level is above (or, for a hedge of a long position, below) the current market level. Using a hypothetical derivative is one possible way of calculating the change in the value of the hedged item. The hypothetical derivative replicates the hedged item and hence results in the same outcome as if that change in value was determined by a different approach. Hence, using a 'hypothetical derivative' is not a method in its own right but a mathematical expedient that can only be used to calculate the value of the hedged item. Consequently, a 'hypothetical derivative' cannot be used to include features in the value of the hedged item that only exist in the hedging instrument (but not in the hedged item). An example is debt denominated in a foreign currency (irrespective of whether it is fixed-rate or variable-rate debt). When using a hypothetical derivative to calculate the change in the value of such debt or the present value of the cumulative change in its cash flows, the hypothetical derivative cannot simply impute a charge for exchanging different currencies even though actual derivatives under which different currencies are exchanged might include such a charge (for example, cross-currency interest rate swaps).

B6.5.6 The change in the value of the hedged item determined using a hypothetical derivative may also be used for the purpose of assessing whether a hedging relationship meets the hedge effectiveness requirements.

Rebalancing the hedging relationship and changes to the hedge ratio

B6.5.7 Rebalancing refers to the adjustments made to the designated quantities of the hedged item or the hedging instrument of an already existing hedging relationship for the purpose of maintaining a hedge ratio that complies with the hedge effectiveness requirements. Changes to designated quantities of a hedged item or of a hedging instrument for a different purpose do not constitute rebalancing for the purpose of this Standard.

B6.5.8 Rebalancing is accounted for as a continuation of the hedging relationship in accordance with paragraphs B6.5.9–B6.5.21. On rebalancing, the hedge ineffectiveness of the hedging relationship is determined and recognised immediately before adjusting the hedging relationship.

B6.5.9 Adjusting the hedge ratio allows an entity to respond to changes in the relationship between the hedging instrument and the hedged item that arise from their underlyings or risk variables. For example, a hedging relationship in which the hedging instrument and the hedged item have different but related underlyings changes in response to a change in the relationship between those two underlyings (for example, different but related reference indices, rates or prices). Hence, rebalancing allows the continuation of a hedging relationship in situations in which the relationship between the hedging instrument and the hedged item changes in a way that can be compensated for by adjusting the hedge ratio.

B6.5.10 For example, an entity hedges an exposure to Foreign Currency A using a currency derivative that references Foreign Currency B and Foreign Currencies A and B are pegged (ie their exchange rate is maintained within a band or at an exchange rate set by a central bank or other authority). If the exchange rate between Foreign Currency A and Foreign Currency B were changed (ie a new band or rate was set), rebalancing the hedging relationship to reflect the new exchange rate would ensure that the hedging relationship would continue to meet the hedge effectiveness requirement for the hedge ratio in the new circumstances. In contrast, if there was a default on the currency derivative, changing the hedge ratio could not ensure that the hedging relationship would continue to meet that hedge effectiveness requirement. Hence, rebalancing does not facilitate the continuation of a hedging relationship in situations in which the relationship between the hedging instrument and the hedged item changes in a way that cannot be compensated for by adjusting the hedge ratio.

B6.5.11 Not every change in the extent of offset between the changes in the fair value of the hedging instrument and the hedged item's fair value or cash flows constitutes a change in the relationship between the hedging instrument and the hedged item. An entity analyses the sources of hedge ineffectiveness that it expected to affect the hedging relationship during its term and evaluates whether changes in the extent of offset are:

(a) fluctuations around the hedge ratio, which remains valid (ie continues to appropriately reflect the relationship between the hedging instrument and the hedged item); or

(b) an indication that the hedge ratio no longer appropriately reflects the relationship between the hedging instrument and the hedged item.

An entity performs this evaluation against the hedge effectiveness requirement for the hedge ratio, ie to ensure that the hedging relationship does not reflect an imbalance between the weightings of the hedged item and the hedging instrument that would create hedge ineffectiveness (irrespective of whether recognised or not) that could result in an accounting outcome that would be inconsistent with the purpose of hedge accounting. Hence, this evaluation requires judgement.

B6.5.12 Fluctuation around a constant hedge ratio (and hence the related hedge ineffectiveness) cannot be reduced by adjusting the hedge ratio in response to each particular outcome. Hence, in such circumstances, the change in the extent of offset is a matter of measuring and recognising hedge ineffectiveness but does not require rebalancing.

B6.5.13 Conversely, if changes in the extent of offset indicate that the fluctuation is around a hedge ratio that is different from the hedge ratio that is currently used for that hedging relationship, or that there is a trend leading away from that hedge ratio, hedge ineffectiveness can be reduced by adjusting the hedge ratio, whereas retaining the hedge ratio would increasingly produce hedge ineffectiveness. Hence, in such circumstances, an entity must evaluate whether the hedging relationship reflects an imbalance between the weightings of the hedged item and the hedging instrument that would create hedge ineffectiveness (irrespective of whether recognised or not) that could result in an accounting outcome that would be inconsistent with the purpose of hedge accounting. If the hedge ratio is adjusted, it also affects the measurement and recognition of hedge ineffectiveness because, on rebalancing, the hedge ineffectiveness of the hedging relationship must be determined and recognised immediately before adjusting the hedging relationship in accordance with paragraph B6.5.8.

B6.5.14 Rebalancing means that, for hedge accounting purposes, after the start of a hedging relationship an entity adjusts the quantities of the hedging instrument or the hedged item in response to changes in circumstances that affect the hedge ratio of that hedging relationship. Typically, that adjustment should reflect adjustments in the quantities of the hedging instrument and the hedged item that it actually uses. However, an entity must adjust the hedge ratio that results from the quantities of the hedged item or the hedging instrument that it actually uses if:

(a) the hedge ratio that results from changes to the quantities of the hedging instrument or the hedged item that the entity actually uses would reflect an imbalance that would create hedge ineffectiveness that could result in an accounting outcome that would be inconsistent with the purpose of hedge accounting; or

(b) an entity would retain quantities of the hedging instrument and the hedged item that it actually uses, resulting in a hedge ratio that, in new circumstances, would reflect an imbalance that would create hedge ineffectiveness that could result in an accounting outcome that would be inconsistent with the purpose of hedge accounting (ie an entity must not create an imbalance by omitting to adjust the hedge ratio).

B6.5.15 Rebalancing does not apply if the risk management objective for a hedging relationship has changed. Instead, hedge accounting for that hedging relationship shall be discontinued (despite that an entity might designate a new hedging relationship that involves the hedging instrument or hedged item of the previous hedging relationship as described in paragraph B6.5.28).

B6.5.16 If a hedging relationship is rebalanced, the adjustment to the hedge ratio can be effected in different ways:

(a) the weighting of the hedged item can be increased (which at the same time reduces the weighting of the hedging instrument) by:

(i) increasing the volume of the hedged item; or

(ii) decreasing the volume of the hedging instrument.

(b) the weighting of the hedging instrument can be increased (which at the same time reduces the weighting of the hedged item) by:

(i) increasing the volume of the hedging instrument; or

(ii) decreasing the volume of the hedged item.

Changes in volume refer to the quantities that are part of the hedging relationship. Hence, decreases in volumes do not necessarily mean that the items or transactions no longer exist, or are no longer expected to occur, but that they are not part of the hedging relationship. For example, decreasing the volume of the hedging instrument can result in the entity retaining a derivative, but only part of it might remain a hedging instrument of the hedging relationship. This could occur if the rebalancing could be effected only by reducing the volume of the hedging instrument in the hedging relationship, but with the entity retaining the volume that is no longer needed. In that case, the undesignated part of the derivative would be accounted for at fair value through profit or loss (unless it was designated as a hedging instrument in a different hedging relationship).

B6.5.17 Adjusting the hedge ratio by increasing the volume of the hedged item does not affect how the changes in the fair value of the hedging instrument are measured. The measurement of the changes in the value of the hedged item related to the previously designated volume also remains unaffected. However, from the date of rebalancing, the changes in the value of the hedged item also include the change in the value of the additional volume of the hedged item. These changes are measured starting from, and by reference to, the date of rebalancing instead of the date on which the hedging relationship was designated. For example, if an entity originally hedged a volume of 100 tonnes of a commodity at a forward price of CU80 (the forward price at inception of the hedging relationship) and added a volume of 10 tonnes on rebalancing when the forward price was CU90, the hedged item after rebalancing would comprise two layers: 100 tonnes hedged at CU80 and 10 tonnes hedged at CU90.

B6.5.18 Adjusting the hedge ratio by decreasing the volume of the hedging instrument does not affect how the changes in the value of the hedged item are measured. The measurement of the changes in the fair value of the hedging instrument related to the volume that continues to be designated also remains unaffected. However, from the date of rebalancing, the volume by which the hedging instrument was decreased is no longer part of the hedging relationship. For example, if an entity originally hedged the price risk of a commodity using a derivative volume of 100 tonnes as the hedging instrument and reduces that volume by 10 tonnes on rebalancing, a nominal amount of 90 tonnes of the hedging instrument volume would remain (see paragraph B6.5.16 for the consequences for the derivative volume (ie the 10 tonnes) that is no longer a part of the hedging relationship).

B6.5.19 Adjusting the hedge ratio by increasing the volume of the hedging instrument does not affect how the changes in the value of the hedged item are measured. The measurement of the changes in the fair value of the hedging instrument related to the previously designated volume also remains unaffected. However, from the date of rebalancing, the changes in the fair value of the hedging instrument also include the changes in the value of the additional volume of the hedging instrument. The changes are measured starting from, and by reference to, the date of rebalancing instead of the date on which the hedging relationship was designated. For example, if an entity originally hedged the price risk of a commodity using a derivative volume of 100 tonnes as the hedging instrument and added a volume of 10 tonnes on rebalancing, the hedging instrument after rebalancing would comprise a total derivative volume of 110 tonnes. The change in the fair value of the hedging instrument is the total change in the fair value of the derivatives that make up the total volume of 110 tonnes. These derivatives could (and probably would) have different critical terms, such as their forward rates, because they were entered into at different points in time (including the possibility of designating derivatives into hedging relationships after their initial recognition).

B6.5.20 Adjusting the hedge ratio by decreasing the volume of the hedged item does not affect how the changes in the fair value of the hedging instrument are measured. The measurement of the changes in the value of the hedged item related to the volume that continues to be designated also remains unaffected. However, from the date of rebalancing, the volume by which the hedged item was decreased is no longer part of the hedging relationship. For example, if an entity originally hedged a volume of 100 tonnes of a commodity at a forward price of CU80 and reduces that volume by 10 tonnes on rebalancing, the hedged item after rebalancing would be 90 tonnes hedged at CU80. The 10 tonnes of the hedged item that are no longer part of the hedging relationship would be accounted for in accordance with the requirements for the discontinuation of hedge accounting (see paragraphs 6.5.6–6.5.7 and B6.5.22–B6.5.28).

B6.5.21 When rebalancing a hedging relationship, an entity shall update its analysis of the sources of hedge ineffectiveness that are expected to affect the hedging relationship during its (remaining) term (see paragraph B6.4.2). The documentation of the hedging relationship shall be updated accordingly.

Discontinuation of hedge accounting

B6.5.22 Discontinuation of hedge accounting applies prospectively from the date on which the qualifying criteria are no longer met.

B6.5.23 An entity shall not de-designate and thereby discontinue a hedging relationship that:

(a)　still meets the risk management objective on the basis of which it qualified for hedge accounting (ie the entity still pursues that risk management objective); and

(b)　continues to meet all other qualifying criteria (after taking into account any rebalancing of the hedging relationship, if applicable).

B6.5.24　For the purposes of this Standard, an entity's risk management strategy is distinguished from its risk management objectives. The risk management strategy is established at the highest level at which an entity determines how it manages its risk. Risk management strategies typically identify the risks to which the entity is exposed and set out how the entity responds to them. A risk management strategy is typically in place for a longer period and may include some flexibility to react to changes in circumstances that occur while that strategy is in place (for example, different interest rate or commodity price levels that result in a different extent of hedging). This is normally set out in a general document that is cascaded down through an entity through policies containing more specific guidelines. In contrast, the risk management objective for a hedging relationship applies at the level of a particular hedging relationship. It relates to how the particular hedging instrument that has been designated is used to hedge the particular exposure that has been designated as the hedged item. Hence, a risk management strategy can involve many different hedging relationships whose risk management objectives relate to executing that overall risk management strategy. For example:

(a)　an entity has a strategy of managing its interest rate exposure on debt funding that sets ranges for the overall entity for the mix between variable-rate and fixed-rate funding. The strategy is to maintain between 20 per cent and 40 per cent of the debt at fixed rates. The entity decides from time to time how to execute this strategy (ie where it positions itself within the 20 per cent to 40 per cent range for fixed-rate interest exposure) depending on the level of interest rates. If interest rates are low the entity fixes the interest for more debt than when interest rates are high. The entity's debt is CU100 of variable-rate debt of which CU30 is swapped into a fixed-rate exposure. The entity takes advantage of low interest rates to issue an additional CU50 of debt to finance a major investment, which the entity does by issuing a fixed-rate bond. In the light of the low interest rates, the entity decides to set its fixed interest-rate exposure to 40 per cent of the total debt by reducing by CU20 the extent to which it previously hedged its variable-rate exposure, resulting in CU60 of fixed-rate exposure. In this situation the risk management strategy itself remains unchanged. However, in contrast the entity's execution of that strategy has changed and this means that, for CU20 of variable-rate exposure that was previously hedged, the risk management objective has changed (ie at the hedging relationship level). Consequently, in this situation hedge accounting must be discontinued for CU20 of the previously hedged variable-rate exposure. This could involve reducing the swap position by a CU20 nominal amount but, depending on the circumstances, an entity might retain that swap volume and, for example, use it for hedging a different exposure or it might become part of a trading book. Conversely, if an entity instead swapped a part of its new fixed-rate debt into a variable-rate exposure, hedge accounting would have to be continued for its previously hedged variable-rate exposure.

(b)　some exposures result from positions that frequently change, for example, the interest rate risk of an open portfolio of debt instruments. The addition of new debt instruments and the derecognition of debt instruments continuously change that exposure (ie it is different from simply running off a position that matures). This is a dynamic process in which both the exposure and the hedging instruments used to manage it do not remain the same for long. Consequently, an entity with such an exposure frequently adjusts the hedging instruments used to manage the interest rate risk as the exposure changes. For example, debt instruments with 24 months' remaining maturity are designated as the hedged item for interest rate risk for 24 months. The same procedure is applied to other time buckets or maturity periods. After a short period of time, the entity discontinues all, some or a part of the previously designated hedging relationships for maturity periods and designates new hedging relationships for maturity periods on the basis of their size and the hedging instruments that exist at that time. The discontinuation of hedge accounting in this situation reflects that those hedging relationships are established in such a way that the entity looks at a new hedging instrument and a new hedged item instead of the hedging instrument and the hedged item that were designated previously. The risk management strategy remains the same, but there is no risk management objective that continues for those previously designated hedging relationships, which as such no longer exist. In such a situation, the discontinuation of hedge accounting applies to the extent to which the risk management objective has changed. This depends on the situation of an entity and could, for example, affect all or only some hedging relationships of a maturity period, or only part of a hedging relationship.

(c) an entity has a risk management strategy whereby it manages the foreign currency risk of forecast sales and the resulting receivables. Within that strategy the entity manages the foreign currency risk as a particular hedging relationship only up to the point of the recognition of the receivable. Thereafter, the entity no longer manages the foreign currency risk on the basis of that particular hedging relationship. Instead, it manages together the foreign currency risk from receivables, payables and derivatives (that do not relate to forecast transactions that are still pending) denominated in the same foreign currency. For accounting purposes, this works as a 'natural' hedge because the gains and losses from the foreign currency risk on all of those items are immediately recognised in profit or loss. Consequently, for accounting purposes, if the hedging relationship is designated for the period up to the payment date, it must be discontinued when the receivable is recognised, because the risk management objective of the original hedging relationship no longer applies. The foreign currency risk is now managed within the same strategy but on a different basis. Conversely, if an entity had a different risk management objective and managed the foreign currency risk as one continuous hedging relationship specifically for that forecast sales amount and the resulting receivable until the settlement date, hedge accounting would continue until that date.

B6.5.25 The discontinuation of hedge accounting can affect:

(a) a hedging relationship in its entirety; or

(b) a part of a hedging relationship (which means that hedge accounting continues for the remainder of the hedging relationship).

B6.5.26 A hedging relationship is discontinued in its entirety when, as a whole, it ceases to meet the qualifying criteria. For example:

(a) the hedging relationship no longer meets the risk management objective on the basis of which it qualified for hedge accounting (ie the entity no longer pursues that risk management objective);

(b) the hedging instrument or instruments have been sold or terminated (in relation to the entire volume that was part of the hedging relationship); or

(c) there is no longer an economic relationship between the hedged item and the hedging instrument or the effect of credit risk starts to dominate the value changes that result from that economic relationship.

B6.5.27 A part of a hedging relationship is discontinued (and hedge accounting continues for its remainder) when only a part of the hedging relationship ceases to meet the qualifying criteria. For example:

(a) on rebalancing of the hedging relationship, the hedge ratio might be adjusted in such a way that some of the volume of the hedged item is no longer part of the hedging relationship (see paragraph B6.5.20); hence, hedge accounting is discontinued only for the volume of the hedged item that is no longer part of the hedging relationship; or

(b)   when the occurrence of some of the volume of the hedged item that is (or is a component of) a forecast transaction is no longer highly probable, hedge accounting is discontinued only for the volume of the hedged item whose occurrence is no longer highly probable. However, if an entity has a history of having designated hedges of forecast transactions and having subsequently determined that the forecast transactions are no longer expected to occur, the entity's ability to predict forecast transactions accurately is called into question when predicting similar forecast transactions. This affects the assessment of whether similar forecast transactions are highly probable (see paragraph 6.3.3) and hence whether they are eligible as hedged items.

B6.5.28   An entity can designate a new hedging relationship that involves the hedging instrument or hedged item of a previous hedging relationship for which hedge accounting was (in part or in its entirety) discontinued. This does not constitute a continuation of a hedging relationship but is a restart. For example:

(a)   a hedging instrument experiences such a severe credit deterioration that the entity replaces it with a new hedging instrument. This means that the original hedging relationship failed to achieve the risk management objective and is hence discontinued in its entirety. The new hedging instrument is designated as the hedge of the same exposure that was hedged previously and forms a new hedging relationship. Hence, the changes in the fair value or the cash flows of the hedged item are measured starting from, and by reference to, the date of designation of the new hedging relationship instead of the date on which the original hedging relationship was designated.

(b)   a hedging relationship is discontinued before the end of its term. The hedging instrument in that hedging relationship can be designated as the hedging instrument in another hedging relationship (for example, when adjusting the hedge ratio on rebalancing by increasing the volume of the hedging instrument or when designating a whole new hedging relationship).

Accounting for the time value of options

B6.5.29   An option can be considered as being related to a time period because its time value represents a charge for providing protection for the option holder over a period of time. However, the relevant aspect for the purpose of assessing whether an option hedges a transaction or time-period related hedged item are the characteristics of that hedged item, including how and when it affects profit or loss. Hence, an entity shall assess the type of hedged item (see paragraph 6.5.15(a)) on the basis of the nature of the hedged item (regardless of whether the hedging relationship is a cash flow hedge or a fair value hedge):

(a)   the time value of an option relates to a transaction related hedged item if the nature of the hedged item is a transaction for which the time value has the character of costs of that transaction. An example is when the time value of an option relates to a hedged item that results in the recognition of an item whose initial measurement includes transaction costs (for example, an entity hedges a commodity purchase, whether it is a forecast transaction or a firm commitment, against the commodity price risk and includes the transaction costs in the initial measurement of the inventory). As a consequence of including the time value of the option in the initial measurement of the particular hedged item, the time value affects profit or loss at the same time as that hedged item. Similarly, an entity that hedges a sale of a commodity, whether it is a forecast transaction or a firm commitment, would include the time value of the option as part of the cost related to that sale (hence, the time value would be recognised in profit or loss in the same period as the revenue from the hedged sale).

(b)   the time value of an option relates to a time-period related hedged item if the nature of the hedged item is such that the time value has the character of a cost for obtaining protection against a risk over a particular period of time (but the hedged item does not result in a transaction that involves the notion of a transaction cost in accordance with (a)). For example, if commodity inventory is hedged against a fair value decrease for six months using a commodity option with a corresponding life, the time value of the option would be allocated to profit or loss (ie amortised on a systematic and rational basis) over that six-month period. Another example is a hedge of a net investment in a foreign operation that is hedged for 18 months using a foreign-exchange option, which would result in allocating the time value of the option over that 18-month period.

B6.5.30 The characteristics of the hedged item, including how and when the hedged item affects profit or loss, also affect the period over which the time value of an option that hedges a time-period related hedged item is amortised, which is consistent with the period over which the option's intrinsic value can affect profit or loss in accordance with hedge accounting. For example, if an interest rate option (a cap) is used to provide protection against increases in the interest expense on a floating rate bond, the time value of that cap is amortised to profit or loss over the same period over which any intrinsic value of the cap would affect profit or loss:

(a) if the cap hedges increases in interest rates for the first three years out of a total life of the floating rate bond of five years, the time value of that cap is amortised over the first three years; or

(b) if the cap is a forward start option that hedges increases in interest rates for years two and three out of a total life of the floating rate bond of five years, the time value of that cap is amortised during years two and three.

B6.5.31 The accounting for the time value of options in accordance with paragraph 6.5.15 also applies to a combination of a purchased and a written option (one being a put option and one being a call option) that at the date of designation as a hedging instrument has a net nil time value (commonly referred to as a 'zero-cost collar'). In that case, an entity shall recognise any changes in time value in other comprehensive income, even though the cumulative change in time value over the total period of the hedging relationship is nil. Hence, if the time value of the option relates to:

(a) a transaction related hedged item, the amount of time value at the end of the hedging relationship that adjusts the hedged item or that is reclassified to profit or loss (see paragraph 6.5.15(b)) would be nil.

(b) a time-period related hedged item, the amortisation expense related to the time value is nil.

B6.5.32 The accounting for the time value of options in accordance with paragraph 6.5.15 applies only to the extent that the time value relates to the hedged item (aligned time value). The time value of an option relates to the hedged item if the critical terms of the option (such as the nominal amount, life and underlying) are aligned with the hedged item. Hence, if the critical terms of the option and the hedged item are not fully aligned, an entity shall determine the aligned time value, ie how much of the time value included in the premium (actual time value) relates to the hedged item (and therefore should be treated in accordance with paragraph 6.5.15). An entity determines the aligned time value using the valuation of the option that would have critical terms that perfectly match the hedged item.

B6.5.33 If the actual time value and the aligned time value differ, an entity shall determine the amount that is accumulated in a separate component of equity in accordance with paragraph 6.5.15 as follows:

(a) if, at inception of the hedging relationship, the actual time value is higher than the aligned time value, the entity shall:

(i) determine the amount that is accumulated in a separate component of equity on the basis of the aligned time value; and

(ii) account for the differences in the fair value changes between the two time values in profit or loss.

(b)   if, at inception of the hedging relationship, the actual time value is lower than the aligned time value, the entity shall determine the amount that is accumulated in a separate component of equity by reference to the lower of the cumulative change in fair value of:

    (i)   the actual time value; and

    (ii)   the aligned time value.

Any remainder of the change in fair value of the actual time value shall be recognised in profit or loss.

Accounting for the forward element of forward contracts and foreign currency basis spreads of financial instruments

B6.5.34   A forward contract can be considered as being related to a time period because its forward element represents charges for a period of time (which is the tenor for which it is determined). However, the relevant aspect for the purpose of assessing whether a hedging instrument hedges a transaction or time-period related hedged item are the characteristics of that hedged item, including how and when it affects profit or loss. Hence, an entity shall assess the type of hedged item (see paragraphs 6.5.16 and 6.5.15(a)) on the basis of the nature of the hedged item (regardless of whether the hedging relationship is a cash flow hedge or a fair value hedge):

(a)   the forward element of a forward contract relates to a transaction related hedged item if the nature of the hedged item is a transaction for which the forward element has the character of costs of that transaction. An example is when the forward element relates to a hedged item that results in the recognition of an item whose initial measurement includes transaction costs (for example, an entity hedges an inventory purchase denominated in a foreign currency, whether it is a forecast transaction or a firm commitment, against foreign currency risk and includes the transaction costs in the initial measurement of the inventory). As a consequence of including the forward element in the initial measurement of the particular hedged item, the forward element affects profit or loss at the same time as that hedged item. Similarly, an entity that hedges a sale of a commodity denominated in a foreign currency against foreign currency risk, whether it is a forecast transaction or a firm commitment, would include the forward element as part of the cost that is related to that sale (hence, the forward element would be recognised in profit or loss in the same period as the revenue from the hedged sale).

(b)   the forward element of a forward contract relates to a time-period related hedged item if the nature of the hedged item is such that the forward element has the character of a cost for obtaining protection against a risk over a particular period of time (but the hedged item does not result in a transaction that involves the notion of a transaction cost in accordance with (a)). For example, if commodity inventory is hedged against changes in fair value for six months using a commodity forward contract with a corresponding life, the forward element of the forward contract would be allocated to profit or loss (ie amortised on a systematic and rational basis) over that six-month period. Another example is a hedge of a net investment in a foreign operation that is hedged for 18 months using a foreign-exchange forward contract, which would result in allocating the forward element of the forward contract over that 18-month period.

B6.5.35   The characteristics of the hedged item, including how and when the hedged item affects profit or loss, also affect the period over which the forward element of a forward contract that hedges a time-period related hedged item is amortised, which is over the period to which the forward element relates. For example, if a forward contract hedges the exposure to variability in three-month interest rates for a three-month period that starts in six months' time, the forward element is amortised during the period that spans months seven to nine.

B6.5.36 The accounting for the forward element of a forward contract in accordance with paragraph 6.5.16 also applies if, at the date on which the forward contract is designated as a hedging instrument, the forward element is nil. In that case, an entity shall recognise any fair value changes attributable to the forward element in other comprehensive income, even though the cumulative fair value change attributable to the forward element over the total period of the hedging relationship is nil. Hence, if the forward element of a forward contract relates to:

(a) a transaction related hedged item, the amount in respect of the forward element at the end of the hedging relationship that adjusts the hedged item or that is reclassified to profit or loss (see paragraphs 6.5.15(b) and 6.5.16) would be nil.

(b) a time-period related hedged item, the amortisation amount related to the forward element is nil.

B6.5.37 The accounting for the forward element of forward contracts in accordance with paragraph 6.5.16 applies only to the extent that the forward element relates to the hedged item (aligned forward element). The forward element of a forward contract relates to the hedged item if the critical terms of the forward contract (such as the nominal amount, life and underlying) are aligned with the hedged item. Hence, if the critical terms of the forward contract and the hedged item are not fully aligned, an entity shall determine the aligned forward element, ie how much of the forward element included in the forward contract (actual forward element) relates to the hedged item (and therefore should be treated in accordance with paragraph 6.5.16). An entity determines the aligned forward element using the valuation of the forward contract that would have critical terms that perfectly match the hedged item.

B6.5.38 If the actual forward element and the aligned forward element differ, an entity shall determine the amount that is accumulated in a separate component of equity in accordance with paragraph 6.5.16 as follows:

(a) if, at inception of the hedging relationship, the absolute amount of the actual forward element is higher than that of the aligned forward element the entity shall:

(i) determine the amount that is accumulated in a separate component of equity on the basis of the aligned forward element; and

(ii) account for the differences in the fair value changes between the two forward elements in profit or loss.

(b) if, at inception of the hedging relationship, the absolute amount of the actual forward element is lower than that of the aligned forward element, the entity shall determine the amount that is accumulated in a separate component of equity by reference to the lower of the cumulative change in fair value of:

(i) the absolute amount of the actual forward element; and

(ii) the absolute amount of the aligned forward element.

Any remainder of the change in fair value of the actual forward element shall be recognised in profit or loss.

B6.5.39 When an entity separates the foreign currency basis spread from a financial instrument and excludes it from the designation of that financial instrument as the hedging instrument (see paragraph 6.2.4(b)), the application guidance in paragraphs B6.5.34–B6.5.38 applies to the foreign currency basis spread in the same manner as it is applied to the forward element of a forward contract.

Hedge of a group of items (Section 6.6)

Hedge of a net position

Eligibility for hedge accounting and designation of a net position

B6.6.1 A net position is eligible for hedge accounting only if an entity hedges on a net basis for risk management purposes. Whether an entity hedges in this way is a matter of fact (not merely of assertion or documentation). Hence, an entity cannot apply hedge accounting on a net basis solely to achieve a particular accounting outcome if that would not reflect its risk management approach. Net position hedging must form part of an established risk management strategy. Normally this would be approved by key management personnel as defined in AASB 124.

B6.6.2 For example, Entity A, whose functional currency is its local currency, has a firm commitment to pay FC150,000 for advertising expenses in nine months' time and a firm commitment to sell finished goods for FC150,000 in 15 months' time. Entity A enters into a foreign currency derivative that settles in nine months' time under which it receives FC100 and pays CU70. Entity A has no other exposures to FC. Entity A does not manage foreign currency risk on a net basis. Hence, Entity A cannot apply hedge accounting for a hedging relationship between the foreign currency derivative and a net position of FC100 (consisting of FC150,000 of the firm purchase commitment – ie advertising services – and FC149,900 (of the FC150,000) of the firm sale commitment) for a nine-month period.

B6.6.3 If Entity A did manage foreign currency risk on a net basis and did not enter into the foreign currency derivative (because it increases its foreign currency risk exposure instead of reducing it), then the entity would be in a natural hedged position for nine months. Normally, this hedged position would not be reflected in the financial statements because the transactions are recognised in different reporting periods in the future. The nil net position would be eligible for hedge accounting only if the conditions in paragraph 6.6.6 are met.

B6.6.4 When a group of items that constitute a net position is designated as a hedged item, an entity shall designate the overall group of items that includes the items that can make up the net position. An entity is not permitted to designate a non-specific abstract amount of a net position. For example, an entity has a group of firm sale commitments in nine months' time for FC100 and a group of firm purchase commitments in 18 months' time for FC120. The entity cannot designate an abstract amount of a net position up to FC20. Instead, it must designate a gross amount of purchases and a gross amount of sales that together give rise to the hedged net position. An entity shall designate gross positions that give rise to the net position so that the entity is able to comply with the requirements for the accounting for qualifying hedging relationships.

Application of the hedge effectiveness requirements to a hedge of a net position

B6.6.5 When an entity determines whether the hedge effectiveness requirements of paragraph 6.4.1(c) are met when it hedges a net position, it shall consider the changes in the value of the items in the net position that have a similar effect as the hedging instrument in conjunction with the fair value change on the hedging instrument. For example, an entity has a group of firm sale commitments in nine months' time for FC100 and a group of firm purchase commitments in 18 months' time for FC120. It hedges the foreign currency risk of the net position of FC20 using a forward exchange contract for FC20. When determining whether the hedge effectiveness requirements of paragraph 6.4.1(c) are met, the entity shall consider the relationship between:

(a) the fair value change on the forward exchange contract together with the foreign currency risk related changes in the value of the firm sale commitments; and

(b) the foreign currency risk related changes in the value of the firm purchase commitments.

B6.6.6 Similarly, if in the example in paragraph B6.6.5 the entity had a nil net position it would consider the relationship between the foreign currency risk related changes in the value of the firm sale commitments and the foreign currency risk related changes in the value of the firm purchase commitments when determining whether the hedge effectiveness requirements of paragraph 6.4.1(c) are met.

Cash flow hedges that constitute a net position

B6.6.7 When an entity hedges a group of items with offsetting risk positions (ie a net position), the eligibility for hedge accounting depends on the type of hedge. If the hedge is a fair value hedge, then the net position may be eligible as a hedged item. If, however, the hedge is a cash flow hedge, then the net position can only be eligible as a hedged item if it is a hedge of foreign currency risk and the designation of that net position specifies the reporting period in which the forecast transactions are expected to affect profit or loss and also specifies their nature and volume.

B6.6.8 For example, an entity has a net position that consists of a bottom layer of FC100 of sales and a bottom layer of FC150 of purchases. Both sales and purchases are denominated in the same foreign currency. In order to sufficiently specify the designation of the hedged net position, the entity specifies in the original documentation of the hedging relationship that sales can be of Product A or Product B and purchases can be of Machinery Type A, Machinery Type B and Raw Material A. The entity also specifies the volumes of the transactions by each nature. The entity documents that the bottom layer of sales (FC100) is made up of a forecast sales volume of the first FC70 of Product A and the first FC30 of Product B. If those sales volumes are expected to affect profit or loss in different reporting periods, the entity would include that in the documentation, for example, the first FC70 from sales of Product A that are expected to affect profit or loss in the first reporting period and the first FC30 from sales of Product B that are expected to affect profit or loss in the second reporting period. The entity also documents that the bottom layer of the purchases (FC150) is made up of purchases of the first FC60 of Machinery Type A, the first FC40 of Machinery Type B and the first FC50 of Raw Material A. If those purchase volumes are expected to affect profit or loss in different reporting periods, the entity would include in the documentation a disaggregation of the purchase volumes by the reporting periods in which they are expected to affect profit or loss (similarly to how it documents the sales volumes). For example, the forecast transaction would be specified as:

(a) the first FC60 of purchases of Machinery Type A that are expected to affect profit or loss from the third reporting period over the next ten reporting periods;

(b) the first FC40 of purchases of Machinery Type B that are expected to affect profit or loss from the fourth reporting period over the next 20 reporting periods; and

(c) the first FC50 of purchases of Raw Material A that are expected to be received in the third reporting period and sold, ie affect profit or loss, in that and the next reporting period.

Specifying the nature of the forecast transaction volumes would include aspects such as the depreciation pattern for items of property, plant and equipment of the same kind, if the nature of those items is such that the depreciation pattern could vary depending on how the entity uses those items. For example, if the entity uses items of Machinery Type A in two different production processes that result in straight-line depreciation over ten reporting periods and the units of production method respectively, its documentation of the forecast purchase volume for Machinery Type A would disaggregate that volume by which of those depreciation patterns will apply.

B6.6.9 For a cash flow hedge of a net position, the amounts determined in accordance with paragraph 6.5.11 shall include the changes in the value of the items in the net position that have a similar effect as the hedging instrument in conjunction with the fair value change on the hedging instrument. However, the changes in the value of the items in the net position that have a similar effect as the hedging instrument are recognised only once the transactions that they relate to are recognised, such as when a forecast sale is recognised as revenue. For example, an entity has a group of highly probable forecast sales in nine months' time for FC100 and a group of highly probable forecast purchases in 18 months' time for FC120. It hedges the foreign currency risk of the net position of FC20 using a forward exchange contract for FC20. When determining the amounts that are recognised in the cash flow hedge reserve in accordance with paragraph 6.5.11(a)–6.5.11(b), the entity compares:

(a)   the fair value change on the forward exchange contract together with the foreign currency risk related changes in the value of the highly probable forecast sales; with

(b)   the foreign currency risk related changes in the value of the highly probable forecast purchases.

However, the entity recognises only amounts related to the forward exchange contract until the highly probable forecast sales transactions are recognised in the financial statements, at which time the gains or losses on those forecast transactions are recognised (ie the change in the value attributable to the change in the foreign exchange rate between the designation of the hedging relationship and the recognition of revenue).

B6.6.10   Similarly, if in the example the entity had a nil net position it would compare the foreign currency risk related changes in the value of the highly probable forecast sales with the foreign currency risk related changes in the value of the highly probable forecast purchases. However, those amounts are recognised only once the related forecast transactions are recognised in the financial statements.

Layers of groups of items designated as the hedged item

B6.6.11   For the same reasons noted in paragraph B6.3.19, designating layer components of groups of existing items requires the specific identification of the nominal amount of the group of items from which the hedged layer component is defined.

B6.6.12   A hedging relationship can include layers from several different groups of items. For example, in a hedge of a net position of a group of assets and a group of liabilities, the hedging relationship can comprise, in combination, a layer component of the group of assets and a layer component of the group of liabilities.

Presentation of hedging instrument gains or losses

B6.6.13   If items are hedged together as a group in a cash flow hedge, they might affect different line items in the statement of profit or loss and other comprehensive income. The presentation of hedging gains or losses in that statement depends on the group of items.

B6.6.14   If the group of items does not have any offsetting risk positions (for example, a group of foreign currency expenses that affect different line items in the statement of profit or loss and other comprehensive income that are hedged for foreign currency risk) then the reclassified hedging instrument gains or losses shall be apportioned to the line items affected by the hedged items. This apportionment shall be done on a systematic and rational basis and shall not result in the grossing up of the net gains or losses arising from a single hedging instrument.

B6.6.15   If the group of items does have offsetting risk positions (for example, a group of sales and expenses denominated in a foreign currency hedged together for foreign currency risk) then an entity shall present the hedging gains or losses in a separate line item in the statement of profit or loss and other comprehensive income. Consider, for example, a hedge of the foreign currency risk of a net position of foreign currency sales of FC100 and foreign currency expenses of FC80 using a forward exchange contract for FC20. The gain or loss on the forward exchange contract that is reclassified from the cash flow hedge reserve to profit or loss (when the net position affects profit or loss) shall be presented in a separate line item from the hedged sales and expenses. Moreover, if the sales occur in an earlier period than the expenses, the sales revenue is still measured at the spot exchange rate in accordance with AASB 121. The related hedging gain or loss is presented in a separate line item, so that profit or loss reflects the effect of hedging the net position, with a corresponding adjustment to the cash flow hedge reserve. When the hedged expenses affect profit or loss in a later period, the hedging gain or loss previously recognised in the cash flow hedge reserve on the sales is reclassified to profit or loss and presented as a separate line item from those that include the hedged expenses, which are measured at the spot exchange rate in accordance with AASB 121.

B6.6.16 For some types of fair value hedges, the objective of the hedge is not primarily to offset the fair value change of the hedged item but instead to transform the cash flows of the hedged item. For example, an entity hedges the fair value interest rate risk of a fixed-rate debt instrument using an interest rate swap. The entity's hedge objective is to transform the fixed-interest cash flows into floating interest cash flows. This objective is reflected in the accounting for the hedging relationship by accruing the net interest accrual on the interest rate swap in profit or loss. In the case of a hedge of a net position (for example, a net position of a fixed-rate asset and a fixed-rate liability), this net interest accrual must be presented in a separate line item in the statement of profit or loss and other comprehensive income. This is to avoid the grossing up of a single instrument's net gains or losses into offsetting gross amounts and recognising them in different line items (for example, this avoids grossing up a net interest receipt on a single interest rate swap into gross interest revenue and gross interest expense).

Effective date and transition (Chapter 7)

Transition (Section 7.2)

Financial assets held for trading

B7.2.1 At the date of initial application of this Standard, an entity must determine whether the objective of the entity's business model for managing any of its financial assets meets the condition in paragraph 4.1.2(a) or the condition in paragraph 4.1.2A(a) or if a financial asset is eligible for the election in paragraph 5.7.5. For that purpose, an entity shall determine whether financial assets meet the definition of held for trading as if the entity had purchased the assets at the date of initial application.

Impairment

B7.2.2 On transition, an entity should seek to approximate the credit risk on initial recognition by considering all reasonable and supportable information that is available without undue cost or effort. An entity is not required to undertake an exhaustive search for information when determining, at the date of transition, whether there have been significant increases in credit risk since initial recognition. If an entity is unable to make this determination without undue cost or effort paragraph 7.2.20 applies.

B7.2.3 In order to determine the loss allowance on financial instruments initially recognised (or loan commitments or financial guarantee contracts to which the entity became a party to the contract) prior to the date of initial application, both on transition and until the derecognition of those items an entity shall consider information that is relevant in determining or approximating the credit risk at initial recognition. In order to determine or approximate the initial credit risk, an entity may consider internal and external information, including portfolio information, in accordance with paragraphs B5.5.1–B5.5.6.

B7.2.4 An entity with little historical information may use information from internal reports and statistics (that may have been generated when deciding whether to launch a new product), information about similar products or peer group experience for comparable financial instruments, if relevant.

DEFINITIONS (APPENDIX A)

Derivatives

BA.1 Typical examples of derivatives are futures and forward, swap and option contracts. A derivative usually has a notional amount, which is an amount of currency, a number of

AASB

shares, a number of units of weight or volume or other units specified in the contract. However, a derivative instrument does not require the holder or writer to invest or receive the notional amount at the inception of the contract. Alternatively, a derivative could require a fixed payment or payment of an amount that can change (but not proportionally with a change in the underlying) as a result of some future event that is unrelated to a notional amount. For example, a contract may require a fixed payment of CU1,000 if six-month LIBOR increases by 100 basis points. Such a contract is a derivative even though a notional amount is not specified.

BA.2 The definition of a derivative in this Standard includes contracts that are settled gross by delivery of the underlying item (eg a forward contract to purchase a fixed rate debt instrument). An entity may have a contract to buy or sell a non-financial item that can be settled net in cash or another financial instrument or by exchanging financial instruments (eg a contract to buy or sell a commodity at a fixed price at a future date). Such a contract is within the scope of this Standard unless it was entered into and continues to be held for the purpose of delivery of a non-financial item in accordance with the entity's expected purchase, sale or usage requirements. However, this Standard applies to such contracts for an entity's expected purchase, sale or usage requirements if the entity makes a designation in accordance with paragraph 2.5 (see paragraphs 2.4–2.7).

BA.3 One of the defining characteristics of a derivative is that it has an initial net investment that is smaller than would be required for other types of contracts that would be expected to have a similar response to changes in market factors. An option contract meets that definition because the premium is less than the investment that would be required to obtain the underlying financial instrument to which the option is linked. A currency swap that requires an initial exchange of different currencies of equal fair values meets the definition because it has a zero initial net investment.

BA.4 A regular way purchase or sale gives rise to a fixed price commitment between trade date and settlement date that meets the definition of a derivative. However, because of the short duration of the commitment it is not recognised as a derivative financial instrument. Instead, this Standard provides for special accounting for such regular way contracts (see paragraphs 3.1.2 and B3.1.3–B3.1.6).

BA.5 The definition of a derivative refers to non-financial variables that are not specific to a party to the contract. These include an index of earthquake losses in a particular region and an index of temperatures in a particular city. Non-financial variables specific to a party to the contract include the occurrence or non-occurrence of a fire that damages or destroys an asset of a party to the contract. A change in the fair value of a non-financial asset is specific to the owner if the fair value reflects not only changes in market prices for such assets (a financial variable) but also the condition of the specific non-financial asset held (a non-financial variable). For example, if a guarantee of the residual value of a specific car exposes the guarantor to the risk of changes in the car's physical condition, the change in that residual value is specific to the owner of the car.

Financial assets and liabilities held for trading

BA.6 Trading generally reflects active and frequent buying and selling, and financial instruments held for trading generally are used with the objective of generating a profit from short-term fluctuations in price or dealer's margin.

BA.7 Financial liabilities held for trading include:

   (a)   derivative liabilities that are not accounted for as hedging instruments;

   (b)   obligations to deliver financial assets borrowed by a short seller (ie an entity that sells financial assets it has borrowed and does not yet own);

   (c)   financial liabilities that are incurred with an intention to repurchase them in the near term (eg a quoted debt instrument that the issuer may buy back in the near term depending on changes in its fair value); and

(d)   financial liabilities that are part of a portfolio of identified financial instruments that are managed together and for which there is evidence of a recent pattern of short-term profit-taking.

BA.8 The fact that a liability is used to fund trading activities does not in itself make that liability one that is held for trading.

DELETED IFRS 9 TEXT

Deleted IFRS 9 text is not part of AASB 9.

Paragraph 7.1.1

An entity shall apply this Standard for annual periods beginning on or after 1 January 2018. Earlier application is permitted. If an entity elects to apply this Standard early, it must disclose that fact and apply all of the requirements in this Standard at the same time (but see also paragraphs 7.1.2, 7.2.21 and 7.3.2). It shall also, at the same time, apply the amendments in Appendix C.

Paragraph 7.1.3

Annual Improvements to IFRSs 2010–2012 Cycle, issued in December 2013, amended paragraphs 4.2.1 and 5.7.5 as a consequential amendment derived from the amendment to IFRS 3. An entity shall apply that amendment prospectively to business combinations to which the amendment to IFRS 3 applies.

Paragraph 7.1.4

IFRS 15, issued in May 2014, amended paragraphs 3.1.1, 4.2.1, 5.1.1, 5.2.1, 5.7.6, B3.2.13, B5.7.1, C5 and C42 and deleted paragraph C16 and its related heading. Paragraphs 5.1.3 and 5.7.1A, and a definition to Appendix A, were added. An entity shall apply those amendments when it applies IFRS 15.

Paragraph 7.3.1

This Standard supersedes IFRIC 9 *Reassessment of Embedded Derivatives*. The requirements added to IFRS 9 in October 2010 incorporated the requirements previously set out in paragraphs 5 and 7 of IFRIC 9. As a consequential amendment, IFRS 1 *First-time Adoption of International Financial Reporting Standards* incorporated the requirements previously set out in paragraph 8 of IFRIC 9.

Paragraph 7.3.2

This Standard supersedes IFRS 9 (2009), IFRS 9 (2010) and IFRS 9 (2013). However, for annual periods beginning before 1 January 2018, an entity may elect to apply those earlier versions of IFRS 9 instead of applying this Standard if, and only if, the entity's relevant date of initial application is before 1 February 2015.

AASB

AASB 10
Consolidated Financial Statements
(Compiled December 2017)

This compiled Standard applies to annual periods beginning on or after 1 January 2022. Earlier application is permitted for annual periods beginning on or after 1 January 2014 but before 1 January 2022. It incorporates relevant amendments made up to and including 12 December 2017.

Prepared on 20 April 2018 by the staff of the Australian Accounting Standards Board.

Compilation no. 2

Compilation date: 31 December 2017

CONTENTS

COMPARISON WITH IFRS 10
ACCOUNTING STANDARD
AASB 10 *CONSOLIDATED FINANCIAL STATEMENTS*

Australian Accounting Standard AASB 10 *Consolidated Financial Statements* (as amended) is set out in paragraphs 1 – Aus33.2 and Appendices A – C and E. All the paragraphs have equal authority. Paragraphs in **bold type** state the main principles. Terms defined in Appendix A are in *italics* the first time they appear in the Standard. AASB 10 is to be read in the context of other Australian Accounting Standards, including AASB 1048 *Interpretation of Standards*, which identifies the Australian Accounting Interpretations, and AASB 1057 *Application of Australian Accounting Standards*. In the absence of explicit guidance, AASB 108 *Accounting Policies, Changes in Accounting Estimates and Errors* provides a basis for selecting and applying accounting policies.

COMPARISON WITH IFRS 10

AASB 10 *Consolidated Financial Statements* as amended incorporates IFRS 10 *Consolidated Financial Statements* as issued and amended by the International Accounting Standards Board (IASB). Australian-specific paragraphs (which are not included in IFRS 10) are identified with the prefix "Aus". Paragraphs that apply only to not-for-profit entities begin by identifying their limited applicability.

Tier 1

For-profit entities complying with AASB 10 also comply with IFRS 10.

Not-for-profit entities' compliance with IFRS 10 will depend on whether any "Aus" paragraphs that specifically apply to not-for-profit entities provide additional guidance or contain applicable requirements that are inconsistent with IFRS 10.

AASB 1053 *Application of Tiers of Australian Accounting Standards* explains the two tiers of reporting requirements.

ACCOUNTING STANDARD AASB 10

The Australian Accounting Standards Board made Accounting Standard AASB 10 *Consolidated Financial Statements* under section 334 of the *Corporations Act 2001* on 24 July 2015.

This compiled version of AASB 10 applies to annual periods beginning on or after 1 January 2022. It incorporates relevant amendments contained in other AASB Standards made by the AASB up to and including 12 December 2017 (see Compilation Details).

ACCOUNTING STANDARD AASB 10
CONSOLIDATED FINANCIAL STATEMENTS

Objective

1   The objective of this Standard is to establish principles for the presentation and preparation of consolidated financial statements when an entity controls one or more other entities.

Meeting the objective

2   To meet the objective in paragraph 1, this Standard:

   (a)   requires an entity (the *parent*) that controls one or more other entities (*subsidiaries*) to present consolidated financial statements;

   (b)   defines the principle of *control*, and establishes control as the basis for consolidation;

   (c)   sets out how to apply the principle of control to identify whether an investor controls an investee and therefore must consolidate the investee;

(d)   sets out the accounting requirements for the preparation of consolidated financial statements; and

(e)   defines an investment entity and sets out an exception to consolidating particular subsidiaries of an investment entity.

3   This Standard does not deal with the accounting requirements for business combinations and their effect on consolidation, including goodwill arising on a business combination (see AASB 3 *Business Combinations*).

Scope

4   An entity that is a parent shall present consolidated financial statements. This Standard applies to all entities, except as follows:

(a)   a parent need not present consolidated financial statements if it meets all the following conditions:

  (i)   it is a wholly-owned subsidiary or is a partially-owned subsidiary of another entity and all its other owners, including those not otherwise entitled to vote, have been informed about, and do not object to, the parent not presenting consolidated financial statements;

  (ii)   its debt or equity instruments are not traded in a public market (a domestic or foreign stock exchange or an over-the-counter market, including local and regional markets);

  (iii) it did not file, nor is it in the process of filing, its financial statements with a securities commission or other regulatory organisation for the purpose of issuing any class of instruments in a public market; and

  (iv)   its ultimate or any intermediate parent produces financial statements that are available for public use and comply with IFRSs, in which subsidiaries are consolidated or are measured at fair value through profit or loss in accordance with this Standard.

(b)   [deleted]

(c)   [deleted]

Aus4.1   Notwithstanding paragraph 4(a)(iv), a parent that meets the criteria in paragraphs 4(a)(i), 4(a)(ii) and 4(a)(iii) need not present consolidated financial statements if its ultimate or any intermediate parent produces financial statements that are available for public use in which subsidiaries are consolidated or are measured at fair value through profit or loss in accordance with this Standard and:

(a)   the parent and its ultimate or intermediate parent are:

  (i)   both not-for-profit entities complying with Australian Accounting Standards; or

  (ii)   both entities complying with Australian Accounting Standards – Reduced Disclosure Requirements; or

(b)   the parent is an entity complying with Australian Accounting Standards – Reduced Disclosure Requirements and its ultimate or intermediate parent is a not-for-profit entity complying with Australian Accounting Standards.

Aus4.2   Notwithstanding paragraphs 4(a) and Aus4.1, the ultimate Australian parent shall present consolidated financial statements that consolidate its investments in subsidiaries in accordance with this Standard when either the parent or the group is a reporting entity or both the parent and the group are reporting entities, except if the ultimate Australian parent is required, in accordance with paragraph 31 of this Standard, to measure all of its subsidiaries at fair value through profit or loss.

4A This Standard does not apply to post-employment benefit plans or other long-term employee benefit plans to which AASB 119 *Employee Benefits* applies.

4B A parent that is an investment entity shall not present consolidated financial statements if it is required, in accordance with paragraph 31 of this Standard, to measure all of its subsidiaries at fair value through profit or loss.

Control

5 **An investor, regardless of the nature of its involvement with an entity (the investee), shall determine whether it is a parent by assessing whether it controls the investee.**

6 **An investor controls an investee when it is exposed, or has rights, to variable returns from its involvement with the investee and has the ability to affect those returns through its power over the investee.**

7 **Thus, an investor controls an investee if and only if the investor has all the following:**

(a) **power over the investee (see paragraphs 10–14);**

(b) **exposure, or rights, to variable returns from its involvement with the investee (see paragraphs 15 and 16); and**

(c) **the ability to use its power over the investee to affect the amount of the investor's returns (see paragraphs 17 and 18).**

8 An investor shall consider all facts and circumstances when assessing whether it controls an investee. The investor shall reassess whether it controls an investee if facts and circumstances indicate that there are changes to one or more of the three elements of control listed in paragraph 7 (see paragraphs B80–B85).

9 Two or more investors collectively control an investee when they must act together to direct the relevant activities. In such cases, because no investor can direct the activities without the co-operation of the others, no investor individually controls the investee. Each investor would account for its interest in the investee in accordance with the relevant Australian Accounting Standards, such as AASB 11 *Joint Arrangements*, AASB 128 *Investments in Associates and Joint Ventures* or AASB 9 *Financial Instruments*.

Power

10 An investor has power over an investee when the investor has existing rights that give it the current ability to direct the *relevant activities*, ie the activities that significantly affect the investee's returns.

11 Power arises from rights. Sometimes assessing power is straightforward, such as when power over an investee is obtained directly and solely from the voting rights granted by equity instruments such as shares, and can be assessed by considering the voting rights from those shareholdings. In other cases, the assessment will be more complex and require more than one factor to be considered, for example when power results from one or more contractual arrangements.

12 An investor with the current ability to direct the relevant activities has power even if its rights to direct have yet to be exercised. Evidence that the investor has been directing relevant activities can help determine whether the investor has power, but such evidence is not, in itself, conclusive in determining whether the investor has power over an investee.

13 If two or more investors each have existing rights that give them the unilateral ability to direct different relevant activities, the investor that has the current ability to direct the activities that most significantly affect the returns of the investee has power over the investee.

14   An investor can have power over an investee even if other entities have existing rights that give them the current ability to participate in the direction of the relevant activities, for example when another entity has *significant influence*. However, an investor that holds only protective rights does not have power over an investee (see paragraphs B26–B28), and consequently does not control the investee.

Returns

15   An investor is exposed, or has rights, to variable returns from its involvement with the investee when the investor's returns from its involvement have the potential to vary as a result of the investee's performance. The investor's returns can be only positive, only negative or both positive and negative.

16   Although only one investor can control an investee, more than one party can share in the returns of an investee. For example, holders of non-controlling interests can share in the profits or distributions of an investee.

Link between power and returns

17   An investor controls an investee if the investor not only has power over the investee and exposure or rights to variable returns from its involvement with the investee, but also has the ability to use its power to affect the investor's returns from its involvement with the investee.

18   Thus, an investor with decision-making rights shall determine whether it is a principal or an agent. An investor that is an agent in accordance with paragraphs B58–B72 does not control an investee when it exercises decision-making rights delegated to it.

Accounting requirements

19   **A parent shall prepare consolidated financial statements using uniform accounting policies for like transactions and other events in similar circumstances.**

20   Consolidation of an investee shall begin from the date the investor obtains control of the investee and cease when the investor loses control of the investee.

21   Paragraphs B86–B93 set out guidance for the preparation of consolidated financial statements.

Non-controlling interests

22   A parent shall present non-controlling interests in the consolidated statement of financial position within equity, separately from the equity of the owners of the parent.

23   Changes in a parent's ownership interest in a subsidiary that do not result in the parent losing control of the subsidiary are equity transactions (ie transactions with owners in their capacity as owners).

24   Paragraphs B94–B96 set out guidance for the accounting for non-controlling interests in consolidated financial statements.

Loss of control

25   If a parent loses control of a subsidiary, the parent:

  (a)   derecognises the assets and liabilities of the former subsidiary from the consolidated statement of financial position.

  (b)   recognises any investment retained in the former subsidiary and subsequently accounts for it and for any amounts owed by or to the former subsidiary in accordance with relevant Standards. That retained interest is remeasured, as described in paragraphs B98(b)(iii) and B99A. The remeasured value at the date that control is lost shall be regarded as the fair value on initial recognition of a financial asset in accordance with AASB 9 or the cost on initial recognition of an investment in an associate or joint venture, if applicable.

(c) recognises the gain or loss associated with the loss of control attributable to the former controlling interest, as specified in paragraphs B98–B99A.

26 Paragraphs B97–B99A set out guidance for the accounting for the loss of control of a subsidiary.

Determining whether an entity is an investment entity

27 **A parent shall determine whether it is an investment entity. An investment entity is an entity that:**

(a) **obtains funds from one or more investors for the purpose of providing those investor(s) with investment management services;**

(b) **commits to its investor(s) that its business purpose is to invest funds solely for returns from capital appreciation, investment income, or both; and**

(c) **measures and evaluates the performance of substantially all of its investments on a fair value basis.**

Paragraphs B85A–B85M provide related application guidance.

28 In assessing whether it meets the definition described in paragraph 27, an entity shall consider whether it has the following typical characteristics of an investment entity:

(a) it has more than one investment (see paragraphs B85O–B85P);

(b) it has more than one investor (see paragraphs B85Q–B85S);

(c) it has investors that are not related parties of the entity (see paragraphs B85T–B85U); and

(d) it has ownership interests in the form of equity or similar interests (see paragraphs B85V–B85W).

The absence of any of these typical characteristics does not necessarily disqualify an entity from being classified as an investment entity. An investment entity that does not have all of these typical characteristics provides additional disclosure required by paragraph 9A of AASB 12 *Disclosure of Interests in Other Entities*.

29 If facts and circumstances indicate that there are changes to one or more of the three elements that make up the definition of an investment entity, as described in paragraph 27, or the typical characteristics of an investment entity, as described in paragraph 28, a parent shall reassess whether it is an investment entity.

30 A parent that either ceases to be an investment entity or becomes an investment entity shall account for the change in its status prospectively from the date at which the change in status occurred (see paragraphs B100–B101).

Investment entities: Exception to consolidation

31 **Except as described in paragraph 32, an investment entity shall not consolidate its subsidiaries or apply AASB 3 when it obtains control of another entity. Instead, an investment entity shall measure an investment in a subsidiary at fair value through profit or loss in accordance with AASB 9.[1]**

32 Notwithstanding the requirement in paragraph 31, if an investment entity has a subsidiary that is not itself an investment entity and whose main purpose and activities are providing services that relate to the investment entity's investment activities (see paragraphs B85C–B85E), it shall consolidate that subsidiary in accordance with

---

1 Paragraph C7 of AASB 10 *Consolidated Financial Statements* states "If an entity applies this Standard but does not yet apply AASB 9, any reference in this Standard to AASB 9 shall be read as a reference to AASB 139 *Financial Instruments: Recognition and Measurement*."

paragraphs 19–26 of this Standard and apply the requirements of AASB 3 to the acquisition of any such subsidiary.

33   A parent of an investment entity shall consolidate all entities that it controls, including those controlled through an investment entity subsidiary, unless the parent itself is an investment entity.

Commencement of the legislative instrument

Aus33.1   For legal purposes, this legislative instrument commences on 30 June 2016.

Withdrawal of AASB pronouncements

Aus33.2   This Standard repeals AASB 10 *Consolidated Financial Statements* issued in August 2011. Despite the repeal, after the time this Standard starts to apply under section 334 of the Corporations Act (either generally or in relation to an individual entity), the repealed Standard continues to apply in relation to any period ending before that time as if the repeal had not occurred.

[Note: When this Standard applies under section 334 of the Corporations Act (either generally or in relation to an individual entity), it supersedes the application of the repealed Standard.]

APPENDIX A
DEFINED TERMS

This appendix is an integral part of the Standard.

consolidated financial statements	The financial statements of a **group** in which the assets, liabilities, equity, income, expenses and cash flows of the **parent** and its **subsidiaries** are presented as those of a single economic entity.
control of an investee	An investor controls an investee when the investor is exposed, or has rights, to variable returns from its involvement with the investee and has the ability to affect those returns through its power over the investee.
decision maker	An entity with decision-making rights that is either a principal or an agent for other parties.
group	A **parent** and its **subsidiaries**.
investment entity	An entity that: (a) obtains funds from one or more investors for the purpose of providing those investor(s) with investment management services; (b) commits to its investor(s) that its business purpose is to invest funds solely for returns from capital appreciation, investment income, or both; and (c) measures and evaluates the performance of substantially all of its investments on a fair value basis.
non-controlling interest	Equity in a **subsidiary** not attributable, directly or indirectly, to a **parent**.
parent	An entity that **controls** one or more entities.
power	Existing rights that give the current ability to direct the **relevant activities**.
protective rights	Rights designed to protect the interest of the party holding those rights without giving that party power over the entity to which those rights relate.
relevant activities	For the purpose of this Standard, relevant activities are activities of the investee that significantly affect the investee's returns.
removal rights	Rights to deprive the decision maker of its decision-making authority.
subsidiary	An entity that is controlled by another entity.

The following terms are defined in AASB 11, AASB 12 *Disclosure of Interests in Other Entities*, AASB 128 or AASB 124 *Related Party Disclosures* and are used in this Standard with the meanings specified in those Standards:

- associate
- interest in another entity
- joint venture
- key management personnel
- related party
- significant influence.

APPENDIX B
APPLICATION GUIDANCE

This appendix is an integral part of the Standard. It describes the application of paragraphs 1–33 and has the same authority as the other parts of the Standard.

B1   The examples in this appendix portray hypothetical situations. Although some aspects of the examples may be present in actual fact patterns, all facts and circumstances of a particular fact pattern would need to be evaluated when applying AASB 10.

Assessing control

B2   To determine whether it controls an investee an investor shall assess whether it has all the following:

(a)   power over the investee;

(b)   exposure, or rights, to variable returns from its involvement with the investee; and

(c)   the ability to use its power over the investee to affect the amount of the investor's returns.

B3   Consideration of the following factors may assist in making that determination:

(a)   the purpose and design of the investee (see paragraphs B5–B8);

(b)   what the relevant activities are and how decisions about those activities are made (see paragraphs B11–B13);

(c)   whether the rights of the investor give it the current ability to direct the relevant activities (see paragraphs B14–B54);

(d)   whether the investor is exposed, or has rights, to variable returns from its involvement with the investee (see paragraphs B55–B57); and

(e)   whether the investor has the ability to use its power over the investee to affect the amount of the investor's returns (see paragraphs B58–B72).

B4   When assessing control of an investee, an investor shall consider the nature of its relationship with other parties (see paragraphs B73–B75).

Purpose and design of an investee

B5   When assessing control of an investee, an investor shall consider the purpose and design of the investee in order to identify the relevant activities, how decisions about the relevant activities are made, who has the current ability to direct those activities and who receives returns from those activities.

B6   When an investee's purpose and design are considered, it may be clear that an investee is controlled by means of equity instruments that give the holder proportionate voting rights, such as ordinary shares in the investee. In this case, in the absence of any additional arrangements that alter decision-making, the assessment of control focuses on which party, if any, is able to exercise voting rights sufficient to determine the investee's operating and financing policies (see paragraphs B34–B50). In the most straightforward case, the investor that holds a majority of those voting rights, in the absence of any other factors, controls the investee.

B7   To determine whether an investor controls an investee in more complex cases, it may be necessary to consider some or all of the other factors in paragraph B3.

B8   An investee may be designed so that voting rights are not the dominant factor in deciding who controls the investee, such as when any voting rights relate to administrative tasks only and the relevant activities are directed by means of contractual arrangements. In such cases, an investor's consideration of the purpose and design of the investee shall also include consideration of the risks to which the investee was designed to be exposed, the risks it was designed to pass on to the parties involved with the investee and whether the investor is exposed to some or all of those risks. Consideration of the risks includes not only the downside risk, but also the potential for upside.

Power

B9   To have power over an investee, an investor must have existing rights that give it the current ability to direct the relevant activities. For the purpose of assessing power, only substantive rights and rights that are not protective shall be considered (see paragraphs B22–B28).

B10   The determination about whether an investor has power depends on the relevant activities, the way decisions about the relevant activities are made and the rights the investor and other parties have in relation to the investee.

Relevant activities and direction of relevant activities

B11   For many investees, a range of operating and financing activities significantly affect their returns. Examples of activities that, depending on the circumstances, can be relevant activities include, but are not limited to:

(a)   selling and purchasing of goods or services;

(b)   managing financial assets during their life (including upon default);

(c)   selecting, acquiring or disposing of assets;

(d)   researching and developing new products or processes; and

(e)   determining a funding structure or obtaining funding.

B12   Examples of decisions about relevant activities include but are not limited to:

(a)   establishing operating and capital decisions of the investee, including budgets; and

(b)   appointing and remunerating an investee's key management personnel or service providers and terminating their services or employment.

B13   In some situations, activities both before and after a particular set of circumstances arises or event occurs may be relevant activities. When two or more investors have the current ability to direct relevant activities and those activities occur at different times, the investors shall determine which investor is able to direct the activities that most significantly affect those returns consistently with the treatment of concurrent decision-making rights (see paragraph 13). The investors shall reconsider this assessment over time if relevant facts or circumstances change.

Application examples

Example 1

Two investors form an investee to develop and market a medical product. One investor is responsible for developing and obtaining regulatory approval of the medical product—that responsibility includes having the unilateral ability to make all decisions relating to the development of the product and to obtaining regulatory approval. Once the regulator has approved the product, the other investor will manufacture and market it—this investor has the unilateral ability to make all decisions about the manufacture and marketing of the product. If all the activities—developing and obtaining regulatory approval as well as manufacturing and marketing of the medical product— are relevant activities, each investor needs to determine whether it is able to direct the activities that *most* significantly affect the investee's returns. Accordingly, each investor needs to consider whether developing and obtaining regulatory approval or the manufacturing and marketing of the medical product is the activity that most significantly affects the investee's returns and whether it is able to direct that activity. In determining which investor has power, the investors would consider:

(a) the purpose and design of the investee;

(b) the factors that determine the profit margin, revenue and value of the investee as well as the value of the medical product;

(c) the effect on the investee's returns resulting from each investor's decision-making authority with respect to the factors in (b); and

(d) the investors' exposure to variability of returns.

In this particular example, the investors would also consider:

(e) the uncertainty of, and effort required in, obtaining regulatory approval (considering the investor's record of successfully developing and obtaining regulatory approval of medical products); and

(f) which investor controls the medical product once the development phase is successful.

Example 2

An investment vehicle (the investee) is created and financed with a debt instrument held by an investor (the debt investor) and equity instruments held by a number of other investors. The equity tranche is designed to absorb the first losses and to receive any residual return from the investee. One of the equity investors who holds 30 per cent of the equity is also the asset manager. The investee uses its proceeds to purchase a portfolio of financial assets, exposing the investee to the credit risk associated with the possible default of principal and interest payments of the assets. The transaction is marketed to the debt investor as an investment with minimal exposure to the credit risk associated with the possible default of the assets in the portfolio because of the nature of these assets and because the equity tranche is designed to absorb the first losses of the investee. The returns of the investee are significantly affected by the management of the investee's asset portfolio, which includes decisions about the selection, acquisition and disposal of the assets within portfolio guidelines and the management upon default of any portfolio assets. All those activities are managed by the asset manager until defaults reach a specified proportion of the portfolio value (ie when the value of the portfolio is such that the equity tranche of the investee has been consumed). From that time, a third-party trustee manages the assets according to the instructions of the debt investor. Managing the investee's asset portfolio is the relevant activity of the investee. The asset manager has the ability to direct the relevant activities until defaulted assets reach the specified proportion of the portfolio value; the debt investor has the ability to direct the relevant activities when the value of defaulted assets surpasses that specified proportion of the portfolio value. The asset manager and the debt investor each need to determine whether they are able to direct the activities that *most* significantly affect the investee's returns, including considering the purpose and design of the investee as well as each party's exposure to variability of returns.

Rights that give an investor power over an investee

B14 Power arises from rights. To have power over an investee, an investor must have existing rights that give the investor the current ability to direct the relevant activities. The rights that may give an investor power can differ between investees.

B15   Examples of rights that, either individually or in combination, can give an investor power include but are not limited to:

       (a)   rights in the form of voting rights (or potential voting rights) of an investee (see paragraphs B34–B50);

       (b)   rights to appoint, reassign or remove members of an investee's key management personnel who have the ability to direct the relevant activities;

       (c)   rights to appoint or remove another entity that directs the relevant activities;

       (d)   rights to direct the investee to enter into, or veto any changes to, transactions for the benefit of the investor; and

       (e)   other rights (such as decision-making rights specified in a management contract) that give the holder the ability to direct the relevant activities.

B16   Generally, when an investee has a range of operating and financing activities that significantly affect the investee's returns and when substantive decision-making with respect to these activities is required continuously, it will be voting or similar rights that give an investor power, either individually or in combination with other arrangements.

B17   When voting rights cannot have a significant effect on an investee's returns, such as when voting rights relate to administrative tasks only and contractual arrangements determine the direction of the relevant activities, the investor needs to assess those contractual arrangements in order to determine whether it has rights sufficient to give it power over the investee. To determine whether an investor has rights sufficient to give it power, the investor shall consider the purpose and design of the investee (see paragraphs B5–B8) and the requirements in paragraphs B51–B54 together with paragraphs B18–B20.

B18   In some circumstances it may be difficult to determine whether an investor's rights are sufficient to give it power over an investee. In such cases, to enable the assessment of power to be made, the investor shall consider evidence of whether it has the practical ability to direct the relevant activities unilaterally. Consideration is given, but is not limited, to the following, which, when considered together with its rights and the indicators in paragraphs B19 and B20, may provide evidence that the investor's rights are sufficient to give it power over the investee:

       (a)   The investor can, without having the contractual right to do so, appoint or approve the investee's key management personnel who have the ability to direct the relevant activities.

       (b)   The investor can, without having the contractual right to do so, direct the investee to enter into, or can veto any changes to, significant transactions for the benefit of the investor.

       (c)   The investor can dominate either the nominations process for electing members of the investee's governing body or the obtaining of proxies from other holders of voting rights.

       (d)   The investee's key management personnel are related parties of the investor (for example, the chief executive officer of the investee and the chief executive officer of the investor are the same person).

       (e)   The majority of the members of the investee's governing body are related parties of the investor.

B19   Sometimes there will be indications that the investor has a special relationship with the investee, which suggests that the investor has more than a passive interest in the investee. The existence of any individual indicator, or a particular combination of indicators, does not necessarily mean that the power criterion is met. However, having more than a passive interest in the investee may indicate that the investor has other related rights sufficient to give it power or provide evidence of existing power over an investee. For example, the following suggests that the investor has more than a passive interest in the investee and, in combination with other rights, may indicate power:

(a) The investee's key management personnel who have the ability to direct the relevant activities are current or previous employees of the investor.

(b) The investee's operations are dependent on the investor, such as in the following situations:

    (i) The investee depends on the investor to fund a significant portion of its operations.

    (ii) The investor guarantees a significant portion of the investee's obligations.

    (iii) The investee depends on the investor for critical services, technology, supplies or raw materials.

    (iv) The investor controls assets such as licences or trademarks that are critical to the investee's operations.

    (v) The investee depends on the investor for key management personnel, such as when the investor's personnel have specialised knowledge of the investee's operations.

(c) A significant portion of the investee's activities either involve or are conducted on behalf of the investor.

(d) The investor's exposure, or rights, to returns from its involvement with the investee is disproportionately greater than its voting or other similar rights. For example, there may be a situation in which an investor is entitled, or exposed, to more than half of the returns of the investee but holds less than half of the voting rights of the investee.

B20 The greater an investor's exposure, or rights, to variability of returns from its involvement with an investee, the greater is the incentive for the investor to obtain rights sufficient to give it power. Therefore, having a large exposure to variability of returns is an indicator that the investor may have power. However, the extent of the investor's exposure does not, in itself, determine whether an investor has power over the investee.

B21 When the factors set out in paragraph B18 and the indicators set out in paragraphs B19 and B20 are considered together with an investor's rights, greater weight shall be given to the evidence of power described in paragraph B18.

Substantive rights

B22 An investor, in assessing whether it has power, considers only substantive rights relating to an investee (held by the investor and others). For a right to be substantive, the holder must have the practical ability to exercise that right.

B23 Determining whether rights are substantive requires judgement, taking into account all facts and circumstances. Factors to consider in making that determination include but are not limited to:

(a) Whether there are any barriers (economic or otherwise) that prevent the holder (or holders) from exercising the rights. Examples of such barriers include but are not limited to:

    (i) financial penalties and incentives that would prevent (or deter) the holder from exercising its rights.

    (ii) an exercise or conversion price that creates a financial barrier that would prevent (or deter) the holder from exercising its rights.

    (iii) terms and conditions that make it unlikely that the rights would be exercised, for example, conditions that narrowly limit the timing of their exercise.

(iv)   the absence of an explicit, reasonable mechanism in the founding documents of an investee or in applicable laws or regulations that would allow the holder to exercise its rights.

(v)   the inability of the holder of the rights to obtain the information necessary to exercise its rights.

(vi)   operational barriers or incentives that would prevent (or deter) the holder from exercising its rights (eg the absence of other managers willing or able to provide specialised services or provide the services and take on other interests held by the incumbent manager).

(vii)   legal or regulatory requirements that prevent the holder from exercising its rights (eg where a foreign investor is prohibited from exercising its rights).

(b)   When the exercise of rights requires the agreement of more than one party, or when the rights are held by more than one party, whether a mechanism is in place that provides those parties with the practical ability to exercise their rights collectively if they choose to do so. The lack of such a mechanism is an indicator that the rights may not be substantive. The more parties that are required to agree to exercise the rights, the less likely it is that those rights are substantive. However, a board of directors whose members are independent of the decision maker may serve as a mechanism for numerous investors to act collectively in exercising their rights. Therefore, removal rights exercisable by an independent board of directors are more likely to be substantive than if the same rights were exercisable individually by a large number of investors.

(c)   Whether the party or parties that hold the rights would benefit from the exercise of those rights. For example, the holder of potential voting rights in an investee (see paragraphs B47–B50) shall consider the exercise or conversion price of the instrument. The terms and conditions of potential voting rights are more likely to be substantive when the instrument is in the money or the investor would benefit for other reasons (eg by realising synergies between the investor and the investee) from the exercise or conversion of the instrument.

B24   To be substantive, rights also need to be exercisable when decisions about the direction of the relevant activities need to be made. Usually, to be substantive, the rights need to be currently exercisable. However, sometimes rights can be substantive, even though the rights are not currently exercisable.

Application examples

Example 3

The investee has annual shareholder meetings at which decisions to direct the relevant activities are made. The next scheduled shareholders' meeting is in eight months. However, shareholders that individually or collectively hold at least 5 per cent of the voting rights can call a special meeting to change the existing policies over the relevant activities, but a requirement to give notice to the other shareholders means that such a meeting cannot be held for at least 30 days. Policies over the relevant activities can be changed only at special or scheduled shareholders' meetings. This includes the approval of material sales of assets as well as the making or disposing of significant investments.

The above fact pattern applies to examples 3A–3D described below. Each example is considered in isolation.

Example 3A

An investor holds a majority of the voting rights in the investee. The investor's voting rights are substantive because the investor is able to make decisions about the direction of the relevant activities when they need to be made. The fact that it takes 30 days before the investor can exercise its voting rights does not stop the investor from having the current ability to direct the relevant activities from the moment the investor acquires the shareholding.

Example 3B

An investor is party to a forward contract to acquire the majority of shares in the investee. The forward contract's settlement date is in 25 days. The existing shareholders are unable to change the existing policies over the relevant activities because a special meeting cannot be held for at least 30 days, at which point the forward contract will have been settled. Thus, the investor has rights that are essentially equivalent to the majority shareholder in example 3A above (ie the investor holding the forward contract can make decisions about the direction of the relevant activities when they need to be made). The investor's forward contract is a substantive right that gives the investor the current ability to direct the relevant activities even before the forward contract is settled.

Example 3C

An investor holds a substantive option to acquire the majority of shares in the investee that is exercisable in 25 days and is deeply in the money. The same conclusion would be reached as in example 3B.

Example 3D

An investor is party to a forward contract to acquire the majority of shares in the investee, with no other related rights over the investee. The forward contract's settlement date is in six months. In contrast to the examples above, the investor does not have the current ability to direct the relevant activities. The existing shareholders have the current ability to direct the relevant activities because they can change the existing policies over the relevant activities before the forward contract is settled.

B25 Substantive rights exercisable by other parties can prevent an investor from controlling the investee to which those rights relate. Such substantive rights do not require the holders to have the ability to initiate decisions. As long as the rights are not merely protective (see paragraphs B26–B28), substantive rights held by other parties may prevent the investor from controlling the investee even if the rights give the holders only the current ability to approve or block decisions that relate to the relevant activities.

Protective rights

B26 In evaluating whether rights give an investor power over an investee, the investor shall assess whether its rights, and rights held by others, are protective rights. Protective rights relate to fundamental changes to the activities of an investee or apply in exceptional circumstances. However, not all rights that apply in exceptional circumstances or are contingent on events are protective (see paragraphs B13 and B53).

B27 Because protective rights are designed to protect the interests of their holder without giving that party power over the investee to which those rights relate, an investor that holds only protective rights cannot have power or prevent another party from having power over an investee (see paragraph 14).

B28 Examples of protective rights include but are not limited to:

(a) a lender's right to restrict a borrower from undertaking activities that could significantly change the credit risk of the borrower to the detriment of the lender.

(b) the right of a party holding a non-controlling interest in an investee to approve capital expenditure greater than that required in the ordinary course of business, or to approve the issue of equity or debt instruments.

(c) the right of a lender to seize the assets of a borrower if the borrower fails to meet specified loan repayment conditions.

Franchises

B29 A franchise agreement for which the investee is the franchisee often gives the franchisor rights that are designed to protect the franchise brand. Franchise agreements typically give franchisors some decision-making rights with respect to the operations of the franchisee.

B30 Generally, franchisors' rights do not restrict the ability of parties other than the franchisor to make decisions that have a significant effect on the franchisee's returns. Nor do the rights of the franchisor in franchise agreements necessarily give the franchisor the current ability to direct the activities that significantly affect the franchisee's returns.

B31 It is necessary to distinguish between having the current ability to make decisions that significantly affect the franchisee's returns and having the ability to make decisions that protect the franchise brand. The franchisor does not have power over the franchisee if other parties have existing rights that give them the current ability to direct the relevant activities of the franchisee.

B32 By entering into the franchise agreement the franchisee has made a unilateral decision to operate its business in accordance with the terms of the franchise agreement, but for its own account.

B33 Control over such fundamental decisions as the legal form of the franchisee and its funding structure may be determined by parties other than the franchisor and may significantly affect the returns of the franchisee. The lower the level of financial support provided by the franchisor and the lower the franchisor's exposure to variability of returns from the franchisee the more likely it is that the franchisor has only protective rights.

Voting rights

B34 Often an investor has the current ability, through voting or similar rights, to direct the relevant activities. An investor considers the requirements in this section (paragraphs B35–B50) if the relevant activities of an investee are directed through voting rights.

Power with a majority of the voting rights

B35 An investor that holds more than half of the voting rights of an investee has power in the following situations, unless paragraph B36 or paragraph B37 applies:

(a) the relevant activities are directed by a vote of the holder of the majority of the voting rights, or

(b) a majority of the members of the governing body that directs the relevant activities are appointed by a vote of the holder of the majority of the voting rights.

Majority of the voting rights but no power

B36 For an investor that holds more than half of the voting rights of an investee, to have power over an investee, the investor's voting rights must be substantive, in accordance with paragraphs B22–B25, and must provide the investor with the current ability to direct the relevant activities, which often will be through determining operating and financing policies. If another entity has existing rights that provide that entity with the right to direct the relevant activities and that entity is not an agent of the investor, the investor does not have power over the investee.

B37 An investor does not have power over an investee, even though the investor holds the majority of the voting rights in the investee, when those voting rights are not substantive. For example, an investor that has more than half of the voting rights in an investee cannot have power if the relevant activities are subject to direction by a government, court, administrator, receiver, liquidator or regulator.

Power without a majority of the voting rights

B38 An investor can have power even if it holds less than a majority of the voting rights of an investee. An investor can have power with less than a majority of the voting rights of an investee, for example, through:

(a) a contractual arrangement between the investor and other vote holders (see paragraph B39);

(b)   rights arising from other contractual arrangements (see paragraph B40);

(c)   the investor's voting rights (see paragraphs B41–B45);

(d)   potential voting rights (see paragraphs B47–B50); or

(e)   a combination of (a)–(d).

Contractual arrangement with other vote holders

B39   A contractual arrangement between an investor and other vote holders can give the investor the right to exercise voting rights sufficient to give the investor power, even if the investor does not have voting rights sufficient to give it power without the contractual arrangement. However, a contractual arrangement might ensure that the investor can direct enough other vote holders on how to vote to enable the investor to make decisions about the relevant activities.

Rights from other contractual arrangements

B40   Other decision-making rights, in combination with voting rights, can give an investor the current ability to direct the relevant activities. For example, the rights specified in a contractual arrangement in combination with voting rights may be sufficient to give an investor the current ability to direct the manufacturing processes of an investee or to direct other operating or financing activities of an investee that significantly affect the investee's returns. However, in the absence of any other rights, economic dependence of an investee on the investor (such as relations of a supplier with its main customer) does not lead to the investor having power over the investee.

The investor's voting rights

B41   An investor with less than a majority of the voting rights has rights that are sufficient to give it power when the investor has the practical ability to direct the relevant activities unilaterally.

B42   When assessing whether an investor's voting rights are sufficient to give it power, an investor considers all facts and circumstances, including:

(a)   the size of the investor's holding of voting rights relative to the size and dispersion of holdings of the other vote holders, noting that:

   (i)   the more voting rights an investor holds, the more likely the investor is to have existing rights that give it the current ability to direct the relevant activities;

   (ii)   the more voting rights an investor holds relative to other vote holders, the more likely the investor is to have existing rights that give it the current ability to direct the relevant activities;

   (iii)   the more parties that would need to act together to outvote the investor, the more likely the investor is to have existing rights that give it the current ability to direct the relevant activities;

(b)   potential voting rights held by the investor, other vote holders or other parties (see paragraphs B47–B50);

(c)   rights arising from other contractual arrangements (see paragraph B40); and

(d)   any additional facts and circumstances that indicate the investor has, or does not have, the current ability to direct the relevant activities at the time that decisions need to be made, including voting patterns at previous shareholders' meetings.

B43   When the direction of relevant activities is determined by majority vote and an investor holds significantly more voting rights than any other vote holder or organised group of vote holders, and the other shareholdings are widely dispersed, it may be clear, after considering the factors listed in paragraph B42(a)–(c) alone, that the investor has power over the investee.

AASB

Application examples

Example 4

An investor acquires 48 per cent of the voting rights of an investee. The remaining voting rights are held by thousands of shareholders, none individually holding more than 1 per cent of the voting rights. None of the shareholders has any arrangements to consult any of the others or make collective decisions. When assessing the proportion of voting rights to acquire, on the basis of the relative size of the other shareholdings, the investor determined that a 48 per cent interest would be sufficient to give it control. In this case, on the basis of the absolute size of its holding and the relative size of the other shareholdings, the investor concludes that it has a sufficiently dominant voting interest to meet the power criterion without the need to consider any other evidence of power.

Example 5

Investor A holds 40 per cent of the voting rights of an investee and twelve other investors each hold 5 per cent of the voting rights of the investee. A shareholder agreement grants investor A the right to appoint, remove and set the remuneration of management responsible for directing the relevant activities. To change the agreement, a two-thirds majority vote of the shareholders is required. In this case, investor A concludes that the absolute size of the investor's holding and the relative size of the other shareholdings alone are not conclusive in determining whether the investor has rights sufficient to give it power. However, investor A determines that its contractual right to appoint, remove and set the remuneration of management is sufficient to conclude that it has power over the investee. The fact that investor A might not have exercised this right or the likelihood of investor A exercising its right to select, appoint or remove management shall not be considered when assessing whether investor A has power.

B44   In other situations, it may be clear after considering the factors listed in paragraph B42(a)–(c) alone that an investor does not have power.

Application example

Example 6

Investor A holds 45 per cent of the voting rights of an investee. Two other investors each hold 26 per cent of the voting rights of the investee. The remaining voting rights are held by three other shareholders, each holding 1 per cent. There are no other arrangements that affect decision-making. In this case, the size of investor A's voting interest and its size relative to the other shareholdings are sufficient to conclude that investor A does not have power. Only two other investors would need to co-operate to be able to prevent investor A from directing the relevant activities of the investee.

B45   However, the factors listed in paragraph B42(a)–(c) alone may not be conclusive. If an investor, having considered those factors, is unclear whether it has power, it shall consider additional facts and circumstances, such as whether other shareholders are passive in nature as demonstrated by voting patterns at previous shareholders' meetings. This includes the assessment of the factors set out in paragraph B18 and the indicators in paragraphs B19 and B20. The fewer voting rights the investor holds, and the fewer parties that would need to act together to outvote the investor, the more reliance would be placed on the additional facts and circumstances to assess whether the investor's rights are sufficient to give it power. When the facts and circumstances in paragraphs B18–B20 are considered together with the investor's rights, greater weight shall be given to the evidence of power in paragraph B18 than to the indicators of power in paragraphs B19 and B20.

Application examples

Example 7

An investor holds 45 per cent of the voting rights of an investee. Eleven other shareholders each hold 5 per cent of the voting rights of the investee. None of the shareholders has contractual arrangements to consult any of the others or make collective decisions. In this case, the absolute size of the investor's holding and the relative size of the other shareholdings alone are not conclusive in determining whether the investor has rights sufficient to give it power over the investee. Additional facts and circumstances that may provide evidence that the investor has, or does not have, power shall be considered.

Example 8

An investor holds 35 per cent of the voting rights of an investee. Three other shareholders each hold 5 per cent of the voting rights of the investee. The remaining voting rights are held by numerous other shareholders, none individually holding more than 1 per cent of the voting rights. None of the shareholders has arrangements to consult any of the others or make collective decisions. Decisions about the relevant activities of the investee require the approval of a majority of votes cast at relevant shareholders' meetings—75 per cent of the voting rights of the investee have been cast at recent relevant shareholders' meetings. In this case, the active participation of the other shareholders at recent shareholders' meetings indicates that the investor would not have the practical ability to direct the relevant activities unilaterally, regardless of whether the investor has directed the relevant activities because a sufficient number of other shareholders voted in the same way as the investor.

B46   If it is not clear, having considered the factors listed in paragraph B42(a)–(d), that the investor has power, the investor does not control the investee.

Potential voting rights

B47   When assessing control, an investor considers its potential voting rights as well as potential voting rights held by other parties, to determine whether it has power. Potential voting rights are rights to obtain voting rights of an investee, such as those arising from convertible instruments or options, including forward contracts. Those potential voting rights are considered only if the rights are substantive (see paragraphs B22–B25).

B48   When considering potential voting rights, an investor shall consider the purpose and design of the instrument, as well as the purpose and design of any other involvement the investor has with the investee. This includes an assessment of the various terms and conditions of the instrument as well as the investor's apparent expectations, motives and reasons for agreeing to those terms and conditions.

B49   If the investor also has voting or other decision-making rights relating to the investee's activities, the investor assesses whether those rights, in combination with potential voting rights, give the investor power.

B50   Substantive potential voting rights alone, or in combination with other rights, can give an investor the current ability to direct the relevant activities. For example, this is likely to be the case when an investor holds 40 per cent of the voting rights of an investee and, in accordance with paragraph B23, holds substantive rights arising from options to acquire a further 20 per cent of the voting rights.

Application examples

Example 9

Investor A holds 70 per cent of the voting rights of an investee. Investor B has 30 per cent of the voting rights of the investee as well as an option to acquire half of investor A's voting rights. The option is exercisable for the next two years at a fixed price that is deeply out of the money (and is expected to remain so for that two-year period). Investor A has been exercising its votes and is

---

actively directing the relevant activities of the investee. In such a case, investor A is likely to meet the power criterion because it appears to have the current ability to direct the relevant activities. Although investor B has currently exercisable options to purchase additional voting rights (that, if exercised, would give it a majority of the voting rights in the investee), the terms and conditions associated with those options are such that the options are not considered substantive.

Example 10

Investor A and two other investors each hold a third of the voting rights of an investee. The investee's business activity is closely related to investor A. In addition to its equity instruments, investor A also holds debt instruments that are convertible into ordinary shares of the investee at any time for a fixed price that is out of the money (but not deeply out of the money). If the debt were converted, investor A would hold 60 per cent of the voting rights of the investee. Investor A would benefit from realising synergies if the debt instruments were converted into ordinary shares. Investor A has power over the investee because it holds voting rights of the investee together with substantive potential voting rights that give it the current ability to direct the relevant activities.

Power when voting or similar rights do not have a significant effect on the investee's returns

B51 In assessing the purpose and design of an investee (see paragraphs B5–B8), an investor shall consider the involvement and decisions made at the investee's inception as part of its design and evaluate whether the transaction terms and features of the involvement provide the investor with rights that are sufficient to give it power. Being involved in the design of an investee alone is not sufficient to give an investor control. However, involvement in the design may indicate that the investor had the opportunity to obtain rights that are sufficient to give it power over the investee.

B52 In addition, an investor shall consider contractual arrangements such as call rights, put rights and liquidation rights established at the investee's inception. When these contractual arrangements involve activities that are closely related to the investee, then these activities are, in substance, an integral part of the investee's overall activities, even though they may occur outside the legal boundaries of the investee. Therefore, explicit or implicit decision-making rights embedded in contractual arrangements that are closely related to the investee need to be considered as relevant activities when determining power over the investee.

B53 For some investees, relevant activities occur only when particular circumstances arise or events occur. The investee may be designed so that the direction of its activities and its returns are predetermined unless and until those particular circumstances arise or events occur. In this case, only the decisions about the investee's activities when those circumstances or events occur can significantly affect its returns and thus be relevant activities. The circumstances or events need not have occurred for an investor with the ability to make those decisions to have power. The fact that the right to make decisions is contingent on circumstances arising or an event occurring does not, in itself, make those rights protective.

Application examples

Example 11

An investee's only business activity, as specified in its founding documents, is to purchase receivables and service them on a day-to-day basis for its investors. The servicing on a day-to-day basis includes the collection and passing on of principal and interest payments as they fall due. Upon default of a receivable the investee automatically puts the receivable to an investor as agreed separately in a put agreement between the investor and the investee. The only relevant activity is managing the receivables upon default because it is the only activity that can significantly affect the investee's returns. Managing the receivables before default is not a relevant activity because it does not require substantive decisions to be made that could significantly affect the investee's returns— the activities before default are predetermined and amount only to collecting cash flows as they fall due and passing them on to investors. Therefore, only the investor's right to manage the assets upon default should be considered when assessing the overall activities of the investee that significantly affect the investee's returns.

In this example, the design of the investee ensures that the investor has decision-making authority over the activities that significantly affect the returns at the only time that such decision-making authority is required. The terms of the put agreement are integral to the overall transaction and the establishment of the investee. Therefore, the terms of the put agreement together with the founding documents of the investee lead to the conclusion that the investor has power over the investee even though the investor takes ownership of the receivables only upon default and manages the defaulted receivables outside the legal boundaries of the investee.

Example 12

The only assets of an investee are receivables. When the purpose and design of the investee are considered, it is determined that the only relevant activity is managing the receivables upon default. The party that has the ability to manage the defaulting receivables has power over the investee, irrespective of whether any of the borrowers have defaulted.

B54 An investor may have an explicit or implicit commitment to ensure that an investee continues to operate as designed. Such a commitment may increase the investor's exposure to variability of returns and thus increase the incentive for the investor to obtain rights sufficient to give it power. Therefore a commitment to ensure that an investee operates as designed may be an indicator that the investor has power, but does not, by itself, give an investor power, nor does it prevent another party from having power.

Exposure, or rights, to variable returns from an investee

B55 When assessing whether an investor has control of an investee, the investor determines whether it is exposed, or has rights, to variable returns from its involvement with the investee.

B56 Variable returns are returns that are not fixed and have the potential to vary as a result of the performance of an investee. Variable returns can be only positive, only negative or both positive and negative (see paragraph 15). An investor assesses whether returns from an investee are variable and how variable those returns are on the basis of the substance of the arrangement and regardless of the legal form of the returns. For example, an investor can hold a bond with fixed interest payments. The fixed interest payments are variable returns for the purpose of this Standard because they are subject to default risk and they expose the investor to the credit risk of the issuer of the bond. The amount of variability (ie how variable those returns are) depends on the credit risk of the bond. Similarly, fixed performance fees for managing an investee's assets are variable returns because they expose the investor to the performance risk of the investee. The amount of variability depends on the investee's ability to generate sufficient income to pay the fee.

B57 Examples of returns include:

(a) dividends, other distributions of economic benefits from an investee (eg interest from debt securities issued by the investee) and changes in the value of the investor's investment in that investee.

(b) remuneration for servicing an investee's assets or liabilities, fees and exposure to loss from providing credit or liquidity support, residual interests in the investee's assets and liabilities on liquidation of that investee, tax benefits, and access to future liquidity that an investor has from its involvement with an investee.

(c) returns that are not available to other interest holders. For example, an investor might use its assets in combination with the assets of the investee, such as combining operating functions to achieve economies of scale, cost savings, sourcing scarce products, gaining access to proprietary knowledge or limiting some operations or assets, to enhance the value of the investor's other assets.

AASB

Link between power and returns

Delegated power

B58 When an investor with decision-making rights (a decision maker) assesses whether it controls an investee, it shall determine whether it is a principal or an agent. An investor shall also determine whether another entity with decision-making rights is acting as an agent for the investor. An agent is a party primarily engaged to act on behalf and for the benefit of another party or parties (the principal(s)) and therefore does not control the investee when it exercises its decision-making authority (see paragraphs 17 and 18). Thus, sometimes a principal's power may be held and exercisable by an agent, but on behalf of the principal. A decision maker is not an agent simply because other parties can benefit from the decisions that it makes.

B59 An investor may delegate its decision-making authority to an agent on some specific issues or on all relevant activities. When assessing whether it controls an investee, the investor shall treat the decision-making rights delegated to its agent as held by the investor directly. In situations where there is more than one principal, each of the principals shall assess whether it has power over the investee by considering the requirements in paragraphs B5–B54. Paragraphs B60–B72 provide guidance on determining whether a decision maker is an agent or a principal.

B60 A decision maker shall consider the overall relationship between itself, the investee being managed and other parties involved with the investee, in particular all the factors below, in determining whether it is an agent:

(a) the scope of its decision-making authority over the investee (paragraphs B62 and B63).

(b) the rights held by other parties (paragraphs B64–B67).

(c) the remuneration to which it is entitled in accordance with the remuneration agreement(s) (paragraphs B68–B70).

(d) the decision maker's exposure to variability of returns from other interests that it holds in the investee (paragraphs B71 and B72).

Different weightings shall be applied to each of the factors on the basis of particular facts and circumstances.

B61 Determining whether a decision maker is an agent requires an evaluation of all the factors listed in paragraph B60 unless a single party holds substantive rights to remove the decision maker (removal rights) and can remove the decision maker without cause (see paragraph B65).

The scope of the decision-making authority

B62 The scope of a decision maker's decision-making authority is evaluated by considering:

(a) the activities that are permitted according to the decision-making agreement(s) and specified by law, and

(b) the discretion that the decision maker has when making decisions about those activities.

B63 A decision maker shall consider the purpose and design of the investee, the risks to which the investee was designed to be exposed, the risks it was designed to pass on to the parties involved and the level of involvement the decision maker had in the design of an investee. For example, if a decision maker is significantly involved in the design of the investee (including in determining the scope of decision-making authority), that involvement may indicate that the decision maker had the opportunity and incentive to obtain rights that result in the decision maker having the ability to direct the relevant activities.

Rights held by other parties

B64   Substantive rights held by other parties may affect the decision maker's ability to direct the relevant activities of an investee. Substantive removal or other rights may indicate that the decision maker is an agent.

B65   When a single party holds substantive removal rights and can remove the decision maker without cause, this, in isolation, is sufficient to conclude that the decision maker is an agent. If more than one party holds such rights (and no individual party can remove the decision maker without the agreement of other parties) those rights are not, in isolation, conclusive in determining that a decision maker acts primarily on behalf and for the benefit of others. In addition, the greater the number of parties required to act together to exercise rights to remove a decision maker and the greater the magnitude of, and variability associated with, the decision maker's other economic interests (ie remuneration and other interests), the less the weighting that shall be placed on this factor.

B66   Substantive rights held by other parties that restrict a decision maker's discretion shall be considered in a similar manner to removal rights when evaluating whether the decision maker is an agent. For example, a decision maker that is required to obtain approval from a small number of other parties for its actions is generally an agent. (See paragraphs B22–B25 for additional guidance on rights and whether they are substantive.)

B67   Consideration of the rights held by other parties shall include an assessment of any rights exercisable by an investee's board of directors (or other governing body) and their effect on the decision-making authority (see paragraph B23(b)).

Remuneration

B68   The greater the magnitude of, and variability associated with, the decision maker's remuneration relative to the returns expected from the activities of the investee, the more likely the decision maker is a principal.

B69   In determining whether it is a principal or an agent the decision maker shall also consider whether the following conditions exist:

    (a)   The remuneration of the decision maker is commensurate with the services provided.

    (b)   The remuneration agreement includes only terms, conditions or amounts that are customarily present in arrangements for similar services and level of skills negotiated on an arm's length basis.

B70   A decision maker cannot be an agent unless the conditions set out in paragraph B69(a) and (b) are present. However, meeting those conditions in isolation is not sufficient to conclude that a decision maker is an agent.

Exposure to variability of returns from other interests

B71   A decision maker that holds other interests in an investee (eg investments in the investee or provides guarantees with respect to the performance of the investee), shall consider its exposure to variability of returns from those interests in assessing whether it is an agent. Holding other interests in an investee indicates that the decision maker may be a principal.

B72   In evaluating its exposure to variability of returns from other interests in the investee a decision maker shall consider the following:

    (a)   the greater the magnitude of, and variability associated with, its economic interests, considering its remuneration and other interests in aggregate, the more likely the decision maker is a principal.

    (b)   whether its exposure to variability of returns is different from that of the other investors and, if so, whether this might influence its actions. For example, this might be the case when a decision maker holds subordinated interests in, or provides other forms of credit enhancement to, an investee.

The decision maker shall evaluate its exposure relative to the total variability of returns of the investee. This evaluation is made primarily on the basis of returns expected from the activities of the investee but shall not ignore the decision maker's maximum exposure to variability of returns of the investee through other interests that the decision maker holds.

Application examples

Example 13

A decision maker (fund manager) establishes, markets and manages a publicly traded, regulated fund according to narrowly defined parameters set out in the investment mandate as required by its local laws and regulations. The fund was marketed to investors as an investment in a diversified portfolio of equity securities of publicly traded entities. Within the defined parameters, the fund manager has discretion about the assets in which to invest. The fund manager has made a 10 per cent pro rata investment in the fund and receives a market-based fee for its services equal to 1 per cent of the net asset value of the fund. The fees are commensurate with the services provided. The fund manager does not have any obligation to fund losses beyond its 10 per cent investment. The fund is not required to establish, and has not established, an independent board of directors. The investors do not hold any substantive rights that would affect the decision-making authority of the fund manager, but can redeem their interests within particular limits set by the fund.

Although operating within the parameters set out in the investment mandate and in accordance with the regulatory requirements, the fund manager has decision-making rights that give it the current ability to direct the relevant activities of the fund—the investors do not hold substantive rights that could affect the fund manager's decision-making authority. The fund manager receives a market-based fee for its services that is commensurate with the services provided and has also made a pro rata investment in the fund. The remuneration and its investment expose the fund manager to variability of returns from the activities of the fund without creating exposure that is of such significance that it indicates that the fund manager is a principal.

In this example, consideration of the fund manager's exposure to variability of returns from the fund together with its decision-making authority within restricted parameters indicates that the fund manager is an agent. Thus, the fund manager concludes that it does not control the fund.

Example 14

A decision maker establishes, markets and manages a fund that provides investment opportunities to a number of investors. The decision maker (fund manager) must make decisions in the best interests of all investors and in accordance with the fund's governing agreements. Nonetheless, the fund manager has wide decision-making discretion. The fund manager receives a market-based fee for its services equal to 1 per cent of assets under management and 20 per cent of all the fund's profits if a specified profit level is achieved. The fees are commensurate with the services provided.

Although it must make decisions in the best interests of all investors, the fund manager has extensive decision-making authority to direct the relevant activities of the fund. The fund manager is paid fixed and performance-related fees that are commensurate with the services provided. In addition, the remuneration aligns the interests of the fund manager with those of the other investors to increase the value of the fund, without creating exposure to variability of returns from the activities of the fund that is of such significance that the remuneration, when considered in isolation, indicates that the fund manager is a principal.

The above fact pattern and analysis applies to examples 14A–14C described below. Each example is considered in isolation.

Example 14A

The fund manager also has a 2 per cent investment in the fund that aligns its interests with those of the other investors. The fund manager does not have any obligation to fund losses beyond its 2 per cent investment. The investors can remove the fund manager by a simple majority vote, but only for breach of contract.

The fund manager's 2 per cent investment increases its exposure to variability of returns from the activities of the fund without creating exposure that is of such significance that it indicates that the fund manager is a principal. The other investors' rights to remove the fund manager are considered to be protective rights because they are exercisable only for breach of contract. In this example, although the fund manager has extensive decision-making authority and is exposed to variability of returns from its interest and remuneration, the fund manager's exposure indicates that the fund manager is an agent. Thus, the fund manager concludes that it does not control the fund.

Example 14B

The fund manager has a more substantial pro rata investment in the fund, but does not have any obligation to fund losses beyond that investment. The investors can remove the fund manager by a simple majority vote, but only for breach of contract.

In this example, the other investors' rights to remove the fund manager are considered to be protective rights because they are exercisable only for breach of contract. Although the fund manager is paid fixed and performance-related fees that are commensurate with the services provided, the combination of the fund manager's investment together with its remuneration could create exposure to variability of returns from the activities of the fund that is of such significance that it indicates that the fund manager is a principal. The greater the magnitude of, and variability associated with, the fund manager's economic interests (considering its remuneration and other interests in aggregate), the more emphasis the fund manager would place on those economic interests in the analysis, and the more likely the fund manager is a principal.

For example, having considered its remuneration and the other factors, the fund manager might consider a 20 per cent investment to be sufficient to conclude that it controls the fund. However, in different circumstances (ie if the remuneration or other factors are different), control may arise when the level of investment is different.

Example 14C

The fund manager has a 20 per cent pro rata investment in the fund, but does not have any obligation to fund losses beyond its 20 per cent investment. The fund has a board of directors, all of whose members are independent of the fund manager and are appointed by the other investors. The board appoints the fund manager annually. If the board decided not to renew the fund manager's contract, the services performed by the fund manager could be performed by other managers in the industry.

Although the fund manager is paid fixed and performance-related fees that are commensurate with the services provided, the combination of the fund manager's 20 per cent investment together with its remuneration creates exposure to variability of returns from the activities of the fund that is of such significance that it indicates that the fund manager is a principal. However, the investors have substantive rights to remove the fund manager—the board of directors provides a mechanism to ensure that the investors can remove the fund manager if they decide to do so.

In this example, the fund manager places greater emphasis on the substantive removal rights in the analysis. Thus, although the fund manager has extensive decision-making authority and is exposed to variability of returns of the fund from its remuneration and investment, the substantive rights held by the other investors indicate that the fund manager is an agent. Thus, the fund manager concludes that it does not control the fund.

Example 15

An investee is created to purchase a portfolio of fixed rate asset-backed securities, funded by fixed rate debt instruments and equity instruments. The equity instruments are designed to provide first loss protection to the debt investors and receive any residual returns of the investee. The transaction was marketed to potential debt investors as an investment in a portfolio of asset-backed securities with exposure to the credit risk associated with the possible default of the issuers of the asset-backed securities in the portfolio and to the interest rate risk associated with the management of the portfolio. On formation, the equity instruments represent 10 per cent of the value of the assets purchased. A decision maker (the asset manager) manages the active asset portfolio by making investment decisions within the parameters set out in the investee's prospectus. For those services, the asset manager receives a market-based fixed fee (ie 1 per cent of assets under management) and performance-related fees (ie 10 per cent of profits) if the investee's profits exceed a specified level. The fees are commensurate with the services provided. The asset manager holds 35 per cent of the equity in the investee. The remaining 65 per cent of the equity, and all the debt instruments, are held by a large number of widely dispersed unrelated third party investors. The asset manager can be removed, without cause, by a simple majority decision of the other investors.

The asset manager is paid fixed and performance-related fees that are commensurate with the services provided. The remuneration aligns the interests of the fund manager with those of the other investors to increase the value of the fund. The asset manager has exposure to variability of returns from the activities of the fund because it holds 35 per cent of the equity and from its remuneration.

Although operating within the parameters set out in the investee's prospectus, the asset manager has the current ability to make investment decisions that significantly affect the investee's returns—the removal rights held by the other investors receive little weighting in the analysis because those rights are held by a large number of widely dispersed investors. In this example, the asset manager places greater emphasis on its exposure to variability of returns of the fund from its equity interest, which is subordinate to the debt instruments. Holding 35 per cent of the equity creates subordinated exposure to losses and rights to returns of the investee, which are of such significance that it indicates that the asset manager is a principal. Thus, the asset manager concludes that it controls the investee.

Example 16

A decision maker (the sponsor) sponsors a multi-seller conduit, which issues short-term debt instruments to unrelated third party investors. The transaction was marketed to potential investors as an investment in a portfolio of highly rated medium-term assets with minimal exposure to the credit risk associated with the possible default by the issuers of the assets in the portfolio. Various transferors sell high quality medium-term asset portfolios to the conduit. Each transferor services the portfolio of assets that it sells to the conduit and manages receivables on default for a market-based servicing fee. Each transferor also provides first loss protection against credit losses from its asset portfolio through over-collateralisation of the assets transferred to the conduit. The sponsor establishes the terms of the conduit and manages the operations of the conduit for a market-based fee. The fee is commensurate with the services provided. The sponsor approves the sellers permitted to sell to the conduit, approves the assets to be purchased by the conduit and makes decisions about the funding of the conduit. The sponsor must act in the best interests of all investors.

The sponsor is entitled to any residual return of the conduit and also provides credit enhancement and liquidity facilities to the conduit. The credit enhancement provided by the sponsor absorbs losses of up to 5 per cent of all of the conduit's assets, after losses are absorbed by the transferors. The liquidity facilities are not advanced against defaulted assets. The investors do not hold substantive rights that could affect the decision-making authority of the sponsor.

Even though the sponsor is paid a market-based fee for its services that is commensurate with the services provided, the sponsor has exposure to variability of returns from the activities of the conduit because of its rights to any residual returns of the conduit and the provision of credit enhancement and liquidity facilities (ie the conduit is exposed to liquidity risk by using short-term debt instruments to fund medium-term assets). Even though each of the transferors has decision-making rights that affect the value of the assets of the conduit, the sponsor has extensive decision-making authority that gives it the current ability to direct the activities that most significantly affect the conduit's returns (ie the sponsor established the terms of the conduit, has the right to make decisions about the assets (approving the assets purchased and the transferors of those assets) and the funding of the conduit (for which new investment must be found on a regular basis)). The right to residual returns of the conduit and the provision of credit enhancement and liquidity facilities expose the sponsor to variability of returns from the activities of the conduit that is different from that of the other investors. Accordingly, that exposure indicates that the sponsor is a principal and thus the sponsor concludes that it controls the conduit. The sponsor's obligation to act in the best interest of all investors does not prevent the sponsor from being a principal.

Relationship with other parties

B73   When assessing control, an investor shall consider the nature of its relationship with other parties and whether those other parties are acting on the investor's behalf (ie they are 'de facto agents'). The determination of whether other parties are acting as de facto agents requires judgement, considering not only the nature of the relationship but also how those parties interact with each other and the investor.

B74   Such a relationship need not involve a contractual arrangement. A party is a de facto agent when the investor has, or those that direct the activities of the investor have, the ability to direct that party to act on the investor's behalf. In these circumstances, the investor shall consider its de facto agent's decision-making rights and its indirect exposure, or rights, to variable returns through the de facto agent together with its own when assessing control of an investee.

B75   The following are examples of such other parties that, by the nature of their relationship, might act as de facto agents for the investor:

(a)   the investor's related parties.

(b)   a party that received its interest in the investee as a contribution or loan from the investor.

(c)   a party that has agreed not to sell, transfer or encumber its interests in the investee without the investor's prior approval (except for situations in which the investor and the other party have the right of prior approval and the rights are based on mutually agreed terms by willing independent parties).

(d)   a party that cannot finance its operations without subordinated financial support from the investor.

(e)   an investee for which the majority of the members of its governing body or for which its key management personnel are the same as those of the investor.

(f)   a party that has a close business relationship with the investor, such as the relationship between a professional service provider and one of its significant clients.

Control of specified assets

B76   An investor shall consider whether it treats a portion of an investee as a deemed separate entity and, if so, whether it controls the deemed separate entity.

B77   An investor shall treat a portion of an investee as a deemed separate entity if and only if the following condition is satisfied:

> Specified assets of the investee (and related credit enhancements, if any) are the only source of payment for specified liabilities of, or specified other interests in, the investee. Parties other than those with the specified liability do not have rights or obligations related to the specified assets or to residual cash flows from those assets. In substance, none of the returns from the specified assets can be used by the remaining investee and none of the liabilities of the deemed separate entity are payable from the assets of the remaining investee. Thus, in substance, all the assets, liabilities and equity of that deemed separate entity are ring-fenced from the overall investee. Such a deemed separate entity is often called a 'silo'.

B78   When the condition in paragraph B77 is satisfied, an investor shall identify the activities that significantly affect the returns of the deemed separate entity and how those activities are directed in order to assess whether it has power over that portion of the investee. When assessing control of the deemed separate entity, the investor shall also consider whether it has exposure or rights to variable returns from its involvement with that deemed separate entity and the ability to use its power over that portion of the investee to affect the amount of the investor's returns.

B79   If the investor controls the deemed separate entity, the investor shall consolidate that portion of the investee. In that case, other parties exclude that portion of the investee when assessing control of, and in consolidating, the investee.

Continuous assessment

B80   An investor shall reassess whether it controls an investee if facts and circumstances indicate that there are changes to one or more of the three elements of control listed in paragraph 7.

B81   If there is a change in how power over an investee can be exercised, that change must be reflected in how an investor assesses its power over an investee. For example, changes to decision-making rights can mean that the relevant activities are no longer directed through voting rights, but instead other agreements, such as contracts, give another party or parties the current ability to direct the relevant activities.

B82   An event can cause an investor to gain or lose power over an investee without the investor being involved in that event. For example, an investor can gain power over an investee because decision-making rights held by another party or parties that previously prevented the investor from controlling an investee have lapsed.

B83 An investor also considers changes affecting its exposure, or rights, to variable returns from its involvement with an investee. For example, an investor that has power over an investee can lose control of an investee if the investor ceases to be entitled to receive returns or to be exposed to obligations, because the investor would fail to satisfy paragraph 7(b) (eg if a contract to receive performance-related fees is terminated).

B84 An investor shall consider whether its assessment that it acts as an agent or a principal has changed. Changes in the overall relationship between the investor and other parties can mean that an investor no longer acts as an agent, even though it has previously acted as an agent, and vice versa. For example, if changes to the rights of the investor, or of other parties, occur, the investor shall reconsider its status as a principal or an agent.

B85 An investor's initial assessment of control or its status as a principal or an agent would not change simply because of a change in market conditions (eg a change in the investee's returns driven by market conditions), unless the change in market conditions changes one or more of the three elements of control listed in paragraph 7 or changes the overall relationship between a principal and an agent.

Determining whether an entity is an investment entity

B85A An entity shall consider all facts and circumstances when assessing whether it is an investment entity, including its purpose and design. An entity that possesses the three elements of the definition of an investment entity set out in paragraph 27 is an investment entity. Paragraphs B85B–B85M describe the elements of the definition in more detail.

Business purpose

B85B The definition of an investment entity requires that the purpose of the entity is to invest solely for capital appreciation, investment income (such as dividends, interest or rental income), or both. Documents that indicate what the entity's investment objectives are, such as the entity's offering memorandum, publications distributed by the entity and other corporate or partnership documents, will typically provide evidence of an investment entity's business purpose. Further evidence may include the manner in which the entity presents itself to other parties (such as potential investors or potential investees); for example, an entity may present its business as providing medium-term investment for capital appreciation. In contrast, an entity that presents itself as an investor whose objective is to jointly develop, produce or market products with its investees has a business purpose that is inconsistent with the business purpose of an investment entity, because the entity will earn returns from the development, production or marketing activity as well as from its investments (see paragraph B85I).

B85C An investment entity may provide investment-related services (eg investment advisory services, investment management, investment support and administrative services), either directly or through a subsidiary, to third parties as well as to its investors, even if those activities are substantial to the entity, subject to the entity continuing to meet the definition of an investment entity.

B85D An investment entity may also participate in the following investment-related activities, either directly or through a subsidiary, if these activities are undertaken to maximise the investment return (capital appreciation or investment income) from its investees and do not represent a separate substantial business activity or a separate substantial source of income to the investment entity:

    (a)   providing management services and strategic advice to an investee; and

    (b)   providing financial support to an investee, such as a loan, capital commitment or guarantee.

B85E If an investment entity has a subsidiary that is not itself an investment entity and whose main purpose and activities are providing investment-related services or activities that relate to the investment entity's investment activities, such as those described in paragraphs B85C–B85D, to the entity or other parties, it shall consolidate that subsidiary in accordance with paragraph 32. If the subsidiary that provides the investment-related services or activities is itself an investment entity, the investment entity parent shall measure that subsidiary at fair value through profit or loss in accordance with paragraph 31.

Exit strategies

B85F An entity's investment plans also provide evidence of its business purpose. One feature that differentiates an investment entity from other entities is that an investment entity does not plan to hold its investments indefinitely; it holds them for a limited period. Because equity investments and non-financial asset investments have the potential to be held indefinitely, an investment entity shall have an exit strategy documenting how the entity plans to realise capital appreciation from substantially all of its equity investments and non-financial asset investments. An investment entity shall also have an exit strategy for any debt instruments that have the potential to be held indefinitely, for example perpetual debt investments. The entity need not document specific exit strategies for each individual investment but shall identify different potential strategies for different types or portfolios of investments, including a substantive time frame for exiting the investments. Exit mechanisms that are only put in place for default events, such as a breach of contract or non-performance, are not considered exit strategies for the purpose of this assessment.

B85G Exit strategies can vary by type of investment. For investments in private equity securities, examples of exit strategies include an initial public offering, a private placement, a trade sale of a business, distributions (to investors) of ownership interests in investees and sales of assets (including the sale of an investee's assets followed by a liquidation of the investee). For equity investments that are traded in a public market, examples of exit strategies include selling the investment in a private placement or in a public market. For real estate investments, an example of an exit strategy includes the sale of the real estate through specialised property dealers or the open market.

B85H An investment entity may have an investment in another investment entity that is formed in connection with the entity for legal, regulatory, tax or similar business reasons. In this case, the investment entity investor need not have an exit strategy for that investment, provided that the investment entity investee has appropriate exit strategies for its investments.

Earnings from investments

B85I An entity is not investing solely for capital appreciation, investment income, or both, if the entity or another member of the group containing the entity (ie the group that is controlled by the investment entity's ultimate parent) obtains, or has the objective of obtaining, other benefits from the entity's investments that are not available to other parties that are not related to the investee. Such benefits include:

(a) the acquisition, use, exchange or exploitation of the processes, assets or technology of an investee. This would include the entity or another group member having disproportionate, or exclusive, rights to acquire assets, technology, products or services of any investee; for example, by holding an option to purchase an asset from an investee if the asset's development is deemed successful;

(b) joint arrangements (as defined in AASB 11) or other agreements between the entity or another group member and an investee to develop, produce, market or provide products or services;

(c) financial guarantees or assets provided by an investee to serve as collateral for borrowing arrangements of the entity or another group member (however, an investment entity would still be able to use an investment in an investee as collateral for any of its borrowings);

(d) an option held by a related party of the entity to purchase, from that entity or another group member, an ownership interest in an investee of the entity;

(e)   except as described in paragraph B85J, transactions between the entity or another group member and an investee that:

   (i)   are on terms that are unavailable to entities that are not related parties of either the entity, another group member or the investee;

   (ii)   are not at fair value; or

   (iii)   represent a substantial portion of the investee's or the entity's business activity, including business activities of other group entities.

B85J   An investment entity may have a strategy to invest in more than one investee in the same industry, market or geographical area in order to benefit from synergies that increase the capital appreciation and investment income from those investees. Notwithstanding paragraph B85I(e), an entity is not disqualified from being classified as an investment entity merely because such investees trade with each other.

Fair value measurement

B85K   An essential element of the definition of an investment entity is that it measures and evaluates the performance of substantially all of its investments on a fair value basis, because using fair value results in more relevant information than, for example, consolidating its subsidiaries or using the equity method for its interests in associates or joint ventures. In order to demonstrate that it meets this element of the definition, an investment entity:

(a)   provides investors with fair value information and measures substantially all of its investments at fair value in its financial statements whenever fair value is required or permitted in accordance with Australian Accounting Standards; and

(b)   reports fair value information internally to the entity's key management personnel (as defined in AASB 124), who use fair value as the primary measurement attribute to evaluate the performance of substantially all of its investments and to make investment decisions.

B85L   In order to meet the requirement in B85K(a), an investment entity would:

(a)   elect to account for any investment property using the fair value model in AASB 140 *Investment Property*;

(b)   elect the exemption from applying the equity method in AASB 128 for its investments in associates and joint ventures; and

(c)   measure its financial assets at fair value using the requirements in AASB 9.

B85M   An investment entity may have some non-investment assets, such as a head office property and related equipment, and may also have financial liabilities. The fair value measurement element of the definition of an investment entity in paragraph 27(c) applies to an investment entity's investments. Accordingly, an investment entity need not measure its non-investment assets or its liabilities at fair value.

Typical characteristics of an investment entity

B85N   In determining whether it meets the definition of an investment entity, an entity shall consider whether it displays the typical characteristics of one (see paragraph 28). The absence of one or more of these typical characteristics does not necessarily disqualify an entity from being classified as an investment entity but indicates that additional judgement is required in determining whether the entity is an investment entity.

More than one investment

B85O   An investment entity typically holds several investments to diversify its risk and maximise its returns. An entity may hold a portfolio of investments directly or indirectly, for example by holding a single investment in another investment entity that itself holds several investments.

B85P There may be times when the entity holds a single investment. However, holding a single investment does not necessarily prevent an entity from meeting the definition of an investment entity. For example, an investment entity may hold only a single investment when the entity:

(a) is in its start-up period and has not yet identified suitable investments and, therefore, has not yet executed its investment plan to acquire several investments;

(b) has not yet made other investments to replace those it has disposed of;

(c) is established to pool investors' funds to invest in a single investment when that investment is unobtainable by individual investors (eg when the required minimum investment is too high for an individual investor); or

(d) is in the process of liquidation.

More than one investor

B85Q Typically, an investment entity would have several investors who pool their funds to gain access to investment management services and investment opportunities that they might not have had access to individually. Having several investors would make it less likely that the entity, or other members of the group containing the entity, would obtain benefits other than capital appreciation or investment income (see paragraph B85I).

B85R Alternatively, an investment entity may be formed by, or for, a single investor that represents or supports the interests of a wider group of investors (eg a pension fund, government investment fund or family trust).

B85S There may also be times when the entity temporarily has a single investor. For example, an investment entity may have only a single investor when the entity:

(a) is within its initial offering period, which has not expired and the entity is actively identifying suitable investors;

(b) has not yet identified suitable investors to replace ownership interests that have been redeemed; or

(c) is in the process of liquidation.

Unrelated investors

B85T Typically, an investment entity has several investors that are not related parties (as defined in AASB 124) of the entity or other members of the group containing the entity. Having unrelated investors would make it less likely that the entity, or other members of the group containing the entity, would obtain benefits other than capital appreciation or investment income (see paragraph B85I).

B85U However, an entity may still qualify as an investment entity even though its investors are related to the entity. For example, an investment entity may set up a separate 'parallel' fund for a group of its employees (such as key management personnel) or other related party investor(s), which mirrors the investments of the entity's main investment fund. This 'parallel' fund may qualify as an investment entity even though all of its investors are related parties.

Ownership interests

B85V An investment entity is typically, but is not required to be, a separate legal entity. Ownership interests in an investment entity are typically in the form of equity or similar interests (eg partnership interests), to which proportionate shares of the net assets of the investment entity are attributed. However, having different classes of investors, some of which have rights only to a specific investment or groups of investments or which have different proportionate shares of the net assets, does not preclude an entity from being an investment entity.

B85W In addition, an entity that has significant ownership interests in the form of debt that, in accordance with other applicable Australian Accounting Standards, does not meet the definition of equity, may still qualify as an investment entity, provided that the debt holders are exposed to variable returns from changes in the fair value of the entity's net assets.

Accounting requirements

Consolidation procedures

B86   Consolidated financial statements:

(a)   combine like items of assets, liabilities, equity, income, expenses and cash flows of the parent with those of its subsidiaries.

(b)   offset (eliminate) the carrying amount of the parent's investment in each subsidiary and the parent's portion of equity of each subsidiary (AASB 3 explains how to account for any related goodwill).

(c)   eliminate in full intragroup assets and liabilities, equity, income, expenses and cash flows relating to transactions between entities of the group (profits or losses resulting from intragroup transactions that are recognised in assets, such as inventory and fixed assets, are eliminated in full). Intragroup losses may indicate an impairment that requires recognition in the consolidated financial statements. AASB 112 *Income Taxes* applies to temporary differences that arise from the elimination of profits and losses resulting from intragroup transactions.

Uniform accounting policies

B87   If a member of the group uses accounting policies other than those adopted in the consolidated financial statements for like transactions and events in similar circumstances, appropriate adjustments are made to that group member's financial statements in preparing the consolidated financial statements to ensure conformity with the group's accounting policies.

Measurement

B88   An entity includes the income and expenses of a subsidiary in the consolidated financial statements from the date it gains control until the date when the entity ceases to control the subsidiary. Income and expenses of the subsidiary are based on the amounts of the assets and liabilities recognised in the consolidated financial statements at the acquisition date. For example, depreciation expense recognised in the consolidated statement of comprehensive income after the acquisition date is based on the fair values of the related depreciable assets recognised in the consolidated financial statements at the acquisition date.

Potential voting rights

B89   When potential voting rights, or other derivatives containing potential voting rights, exist, the proportion of profit or loss and changes in equity allocated to the parent and non-controlling interests in preparing consolidated financial statements is determined solely on the basis of existing ownership interests and does not reflect the possible exercise or conversion of potential voting rights and other derivatives, unless paragraph B90 applies.

B90   In some circumstances an entity has, in substance, an existing ownership interest as a result of a transaction that currently gives the entity access to the returns associated with an ownership interest. In such circumstances, the proportion allocated to the parent and non-controlling interests in preparing consolidated financial statements is determined by taking into account the eventual exercise of those potential voting rights and other derivatives that currently give the entity access to the returns.

B91   AASB 9 does not apply to interests in subsidiaries that are consolidated. When instruments containing potential voting rights in substance currently give access to the returns associated with an ownership interest in a subsidiary, the instruments are not subject to the requirements of AASB 9. In all other cases, instruments containing potential voting rights in a subsidiary are accounted for in accordance with AASB 9.

Reporting date

B92   The financial statements of the parent and its subsidiaries used in the preparation of the consolidated financial statements shall have the same reporting date. When the end of the reporting period of the parent is different from that of a subsidiary, the subsidiary prepares, for consolidation purposes, additional financial information as of the same date as the financial statements of the parent to enable the parent to consolidate the financial information of the subsidiary, unless it is impracticable to do so.

B93   If it is impracticable to do so, the parent shall consolidate the financial information of the subsidiary using the most recent financial statements of the subsidiary adjusted for the effects of significant transactions or events that occur between the date of those financial statements and the date of the consolidated financial statements. In any case, the difference between the date of the subsidiary's financial statements and that of the consolidated financial statements shall be no more than three months, and the length of the reporting periods and any difference between the dates of the financial statements shall be the same from period to period.

Non-controlling interests

B94   An entity shall attribute the profit or loss and each component of other comprehensive income to the owners of the parent and to the non-controlling interests. The entity shall also attribute total comprehensive income to the owners of the parent and to the non-controlling interests even if this results in the non-controlling interests having a deficit balance.

B95   If a subsidiary has outstanding cumulative preference shares that are classified as equity and are held by non-controlling interests, the entity shall compute its share of profit or loss after adjusting for the dividends on such shares, whether or not such dividends have been declared.

Changes in the proportion held by non-controlling interests

B96   When the proportion of the equity held by non-controlling interests changes, an entity shall adjust the carrying amounts of the controlling and non-controlling interests to reflect the changes in their relative interests in the subsidiary. The entity shall recognise directly in equity any difference between the amount by which the non-controlling interests are adjusted and the fair value of the consideration paid or received, and attribute it to the owners of the parent.

Loss of control

B97   A parent might lose control of a subsidiary in two or more arrangements (transactions). However, sometimes circumstances indicate that the multiple arrangements should be accounted for as a single transaction. In determining whether to account for the arrangements as a single transaction, a parent shall consider all the terms and conditions of the arrangements and their economic effects. One or more of the following indicate that the parent should account for the multiple arrangements as a single transaction:

(a)   They are entered into at the same time or in contemplation of each other.

(b)   They form a single transaction designed to achieve an overall commercial effect.

(c)   The occurrence of one arrangement is dependent on the occurrence of at least one other arrangement.

(d) One arrangement considered on its own is not economically justified, but it is economically justified when considered together with other arrangements. An example is when a disposal of shares is priced below market and is compensated for by a subsequent disposal priced above market.

B98 If a parent loses control of a subsidiary, it shall:

(a) derecognise:

(i) the assets (including any goodwill) and liabilities of the subsidiary at their carrying amounts at the date when control is lost; and

(ii) the carrying amount of any non-controlling interests in the former subsidiary at the date when control is lost (including any components of other comprehensive income attributable to them).

(b) recognise:

(i) the fair value of the consideration received, if any, from the transaction, event or circumstances that resulted in the loss of control;

(ii) if the transaction, event or circumstances that resulted in the loss of control involves a distribution of shares of the subsidiary to owners in their capacity as owners, that distribution; and

(iii) any investment retained in the former subsidiary at its fair value at the date when control is lost.

(c) reclassify to profit or loss, or transfer directly to retained earnings if required by other Standards, the amounts recognised in other comprehensive income in relation to the subsidiary on the basis described in paragraph B99.

(d) recognise any resulting difference as a gain or loss in profit or loss attributable to the parent.

B99 If a parent loses control of a subsidiary, the parent shall account for all amounts previously recognised in other comprehensive income in relation to that subsidiary on the same basis as would be required if the parent had directly disposed of the related assets or liabilities. Therefore, if a gain or loss previously recognised in other comprehensive income would be reclassified to profit or loss on the disposal of the related assets or liabilities, the parent shall reclassify the gain or loss from equity to profit or loss (as a reclassification adjustment) when it loses control of the subsidiary. If a revaluation surplus previously recognised in other comprehensive income would be transferred directly to retained earnings on the disposal of the asset, the parent shall transfer the revaluation surplus directly to retained earnings when it loses control of the subsidiary.

B99A If a parent loses control of a subsidiary that does not contain a business, as defined in AASB 3, as a result of a transaction involving an associate or a joint venture that is accounted for using the equity method, the parent determines the gain or loss in accordance with paragraphs B98–B99. The gain or loss resulting from the transaction (including the amounts previously recognised in other comprehensive income that would be reclassified to profit or loss in accordance with paragraph B99) is recognised in the parent's profit or loss only to the extent of the unrelated investors' interests in that associate or joint venture. The remaining part of the gain is eliminated against the carrying amount of the investment in that associate or joint venture. In addition, if the parent retains an investment in the former subsidiary and the former subsidiary is now an associate or a joint venture that is accounted for using the equity method, the parent recognises the part of the gain or loss resulting from the remeasurement at fair value of the investment retained in that former subsidiary in its profit or loss only to the extent of the unrelated investors' interests in the new associate or joint venture. The remaining part of that gain is eliminated against the carrying amount of the investment retained in the former subsidiary. If the parent retains an investment in the former subsidiary that is now accounted for in accordance with AASB 9, the part of the gain or loss resulting from the remeasurement at fair value of the investment retained in the former subsidiary is recognised in full in the parent's profit or loss.

Application examples

Example 17

A parent has a 100 per cent interest in a subsidiary that does not contain a business. The parent sells 70 per cent of its interest in the subsidiary to an associate in which it has a 20 per cent interest. As a consequence of this transaction the parent loses control of the subsidiary. The carrying amount of the net assets of the subsidiary is CU100 and the carrying amount of the interest sold is CU70 (CU70 = CU100 × 70%). The fair value of the consideration received is CU210, which is also the fair value of the interest sold. The investment retained in the former subsidiary is an associate accounted for using the equity method and its fair value is CU90. The gain determined in accordance with paragraphs B98–B99, before the elimination required by paragraph B99A, is CU200 (CU200 = CU210 + CU90 – CU100). This gain comprises two parts:

(a) the gain (CU140) resulting from the sale of the 70 per cent interest in the subsidiary to the associate. This gain is the difference between the fair value of the consideration received (CU210) and the carrying amount of the interest sold (CU70). According to paragraph B99A, the parent recognises in its profit or loss the amount of the gain attributable to the unrelated investors' interests in the existing associate. This is 80 per cent of this gain, that is CU112 (CU112 = CU140 × 80%). The remaining 20 per cent of the gain (CU28 = CU140 × 20%) is eliminated against the carrying amount of the investment in the existing associate.

(b) the gain (CU60) resulting from the remeasurement at fair value of the investment directly retained in the former subsidiary. This gain is the difference between the fair value of the investment retained in the former subsidiary (CU90) and 30 per cent of the carrying amount of the net assets of the subsidiary (CU30 = CU100 × 30%). According to paragraph B99A, the parent recognises in its profit or loss the amount of the gain attributable to the unrelated investors' interests in the new associate. This is 56 per cent (70% × 80%) of the gain, that is CU34 (CU34 = CU60 × 56%). The remaining 44 per cent of the gain CU26 (CU26 = CU60 × 44%) is eliminated against the carrying amount of the investment retained in the former subsidiary.

Accounting for a change in investment entity status

B100 When an entity ceases to be an investment entity, it shall apply AASB 3 to any subsidiary that was previously measured at fair value through profit or loss in accordance with paragraph 31. The date of the change of status shall be the deemed acquisition date. The fair value of the subsidiary at the deemed acquisition date shall represent the transferred deemed consideration when measuring any goodwill or gain from a bargain purchase that arises from the deemed acquisition. All subsidiaries shall be consolidated in accordance with paragraphs 19–24 of this Standard from the date of change of status.

B101 When an entity becomes an investment entity, it shall cease to consolidate its subsidiaries at the date of the change in status, except for any subsidiary that shall continue to be consolidated in accordance with paragraph 32. The investment entity shall apply the requirements of paragraphs 25 and 26 to those subsidiaries that it ceases to consolidate as though the investment entity had lost control of those subsidiaries at that date.

APPENDIX C
EFFECTIVE DATE AND TRANSITION

This appendix is an integral part of the Standard and has the same authority as the other parts of the Standard.

Effective date

C1 An entity shall apply this Standard for annual periods beginning on or after 1 July 2016. Earlier application is permitted for annual periods beginning on or after 1 January 2014 but before 1 July 2016. If an entity applies this Standard earlier, it shall disclose that fact and apply AASB 11, AASB 12, AASB 127 *Separate Financial Statements* and AASB 128 at the same time.

AusC1.1　　AASB 2015-6 *Amendments to Australian Accounting Standards – Extending Related Party Disclosures to Not-for-Profit Public Sector Entities* amended Example IG5 in Appendix E in the previous version of this Standard. An entity shall apply those amendments for annual periods beginning on or after 1 July 2016. Earlier application is permitted. Those amendments shall be applied prospectively as at the beginning of the annual period in which this Standard is initially applied.

C1A–C1B　　[Deleted by the AASB]

C1C　　AASB 2014-10 *Amendments to Australian Accounting Standards – Sale or Contribution of Assets between an Investor and its Associate or Joint Venture*, issued in December 2014, in conjunction with AASB 2015-10 *Amendments to Australian Accounting Standards – Effective Date of Amendments to AASB 10 and AASB 128* and AASB 2017-5 *Amendments to Australian Accounting Standards – Effective Date of Amendments to AASB 10 and AASB 128 and Editorial Corrections*, amended paragraphs 25–26 and added paragraph B99A. An entity shall apply those amendments prospectively to transactions occurring in annual periods beginning on or after 1 January 2022. Earlier application is permitted. If an entity applies those amendments earlier, it shall disclose that fact.

C1D　　AASB 2015-5 *Amendments to Australian Accounting Standards – Investment Entities: Applying the Consolidation Exception*, issued in January 2015, amended the previous version of the Standard as follows: amended paragraphs 4, Aus4.1, Aus4.2, 32, B85C, B85E and C2A and added paragraphs 4A–4B. An entity shall apply those amendments for annual periods beginning on or after 1 January 2016. Earlier application is permitted. If an entity applies those amendments for an earlier period it shall disclose that fact.

Transition

C2　　An entity shall apply this Standard retrospectively, in accordance with AASB 108 *Accounting Policies, Changes in Accounting Estimates and Errors*, except as specified in paragraphs C2A–C6.

C2A　　Notwithstanding the requirements of paragraph 28 of AASB 108, when this Standard is first applied, and, if later, when AASB 2013-5 *Amendments to Australian Accounting Standards – Investment Entities* and AASB 2015-5 are first applied, an entity need only present the quantitative information required by paragraph 28(f) of AASB 108 for the annual period immediately preceding the date of initial application of this Standard (the 'immediately preceding period'). An entity may also present this information for the current period or for earlier comparative periods, but is not required to do so.

C2B　　For the purposes of this Standard, the date of initial application is the beginning of the annual reporting period for which this Standard is applied for the first time.

C3　　At the date of initial application, an entity is not required to make adjustments to the previous accounting for its involvement with either:

(a)　　entities that would be consolidated at that date in accordance with AASB 127 *Consolidated and Separate Financial Statements* and Interpretation 112 *Consolidation—Special Purpose Entities* and are still consolidated in accordance with this Standard; or

(b)　　entities that would not be consolidated at that date in accordance with AASB 127 and Interpretation 112 and are not consolidated in accordance with this Standard.

C3A　　At the date of initial application, an entity shall assess whether it is an investment entity on the basis of the facts and circumstances that exist at that date. If, at the date of initial application, an entity concludes that it is an investment entity, it shall apply the requirements of paragraphs C3B–C3F instead of paragraphs C5–C5A.

C3B Except for any subsidiary that is consolidated in accordance with paragraph 32 (to which paragraphs C3 and C6 or paragraphs C4–C4C, whichever is relevant, apply), an investment entity shall measure its investment in each subsidiary at fair value through profit or loss as if the requirements of this Standard had always been effective. The investment entity shall retrospectively adjust both the annual period that immediately precedes the date of initial application and equity at the beginning of the immediately preceding period for any difference between:

(a)   the previous carrying amount of the subsidiary; and

(b)   the fair value of the investment entity's investment in the subsidiary.

The cumulative amount of any fair value adjustments previously recognised in other comprehensive income shall be transferred to retained earnings at the beginning of the annual period immediately preceding the date of initial application.

C3C Before the date that AASB 13 *Fair Value Measurement* is adopted, an investment entity shall use the fair value amounts that were previously reported to investors or to management, if those amounts represent the amount for which the investment could have been exchanged between knowledgeable, willing parties in an arm's length transaction at the date of the valuation.

C3D If measuring an investment in a subsidiary in accordance with paragraphs C3B–C3C is impracticable (as defined in AASB 108), an investment entity shall apply the requirements of this Standard at the beginning of the earliest period for which application of paragraphs C3B–C3C is practicable, which may be the current period. The investor shall retrospectively adjust the annual period that immediately precedes the date of initial application, unless the beginning of the earliest period for which application of this paragraph is practicable is the current period. If this is the case, the adjustment to equity shall be recognised at the beginning of the current period.

C3E If an investment entity has disposed of, or has lost control of, an investment in a subsidiary before the date of initial application of this Standard, the investment entity is not required to make adjustments to the previous accounting for that subsidiary.

C3F If an entity applies AASB 2013-5 for a period later than when it applies AASB 10 for the first time, references to 'the date of initial application' in paragraphs C3A–C3E shall be read as 'the beginning of the annual reporting period for which AASB 2013-5 is applied for the first time.'

C4 If, at the date of initial application, an investor concludes that it shall consolidate an investee that was not consolidated in accordance with AASB 127 and Interpretation 112, the investor shall:

(a)   if the investee is a business (as defined in AASB 3 *Business Combinations*), measure the assets, liabilities and non-controlling interests in that previously unconsolidated investee as if that investee had been consolidated (and thus had applied acquisition accounting in accordance with AASB 3) from the date when the investor obtained control of that investee on the basis of the requirements of this Standard. The investor shall adjust retrospectively the annual period immediately preceding the date of initial application. When the date that control was obtained is earlier than the beginning of the immediately preceding period, the investor shall recognise, as an adjustment to equity at the beginning of the immediately preceding period, any difference between:

(i)   the amount of assets, liabilities and non-controlling interests recognised; and

(ii)   the previous carrying amount of the investor's involvement with the investee.

(b)   if the investee is not a business (as defined in AASB 3), measure the assets, liabilities and non-controlling interests in that previously unconsolidated investee as if that investee had been consolidated (applying the acquisition method as described in AASB 3 but without recognising any goodwill for the investee) from the date when the investor obtained control of that investee on the basis of the requirements of this Standard. The investor shall adjust retrospectively the annual period immediately preceding the date of initial application. When the date that control was obtained is earlier than the beginning of the immediately preceding period, the investor shall recognise, as an adjustment to equity at the beginning of the immediately preceding period, any difference between:

(i)   the amount of assets, liabilities and non-controlling interests recognised; and

(ii)   the previous carrying amount of the investor's involvement with the investee.

C4A If measuring an investee's assets, liabilities and non-controlling interests in accordance with paragraph C4(a) or (b) is impracticable (as defined in AASB 108), an investor shall:

(a)   if the investee is a business, apply the requirements of AASB 3 as of the deemed acquisition date. The deemed acquisition date shall be the beginning of the earliest period for which application of paragraph C4(a) is practicable, which may be the current period.

(b)   if the investee is not a business, apply the acquisition method as described in AASB 3 but without recognising any goodwill for the investee as of the deemed acquisition date. The deemed acquisition date shall be the beginning of the earliest period for which the application of paragraph C4(b) is practicable, which may be the current period.

The investor shall adjust retrospectively the annual period immediately preceding the date of initial application, unless the beginning of the earliest period for which application of this paragraph is practicable is the current period. When the deemed acquisition date is earlier than the beginning of the immediately preceding period, the investor shall recognise, as an adjustment to equity at the beginning of the immediately preceding period, any difference between:

(c)   the amount of assets, liabilities and non-controlling interests recognised; and

(d)   the previous carrying amount of the investor's involvement with the investee.

If the earliest period for which application of this paragraph is practicable is the current period, the adjustment to equity shall be recognised at the beginning of the current period.

C4B When an investor applies paragraphs C4–C4A and the date that control was obtained in accordance with this Standard is later than the effective date of AASB 3 as revised in 2008 (AASB 3 (2008)), the reference to AASB 3 in paragraphs C4 and C4A shall be to AASB 3 (2008). If control was obtained before the effective date of AASB 3 (2008), an investor shall apply either AASB 3 (2008) or AASB 3 (issued in 2004).

C4C When an investor applies paragraphs C4–C4A and the date that control was obtained in accordance with this Standard is later than the effective date of AASB 127 as revised in 2008 (AASB 127 (2008)), an investor shall apply the requirements of this Standard for all periods that the investee is retrospectively consolidated in accordance with paragraphs C4–C4A. If control was obtained before the effective date of AASB 127 (2008), an investor shall apply either:

(a)   the requirements of this Standard for all periods that the investee is retrospectively consolidated in accordance with paragraphs C4–C4A; or

(b)   the requirements of the version of AASB 127 issued in 2004 (AASB 127 (2004)) for those periods prior to the effective date of AASB 127 (2008) and thereafter the requirements of this Standard for subsequent periods.

C5   If, at the date of initial application, an investor concludes that it will no longer consolidate an investee that was consolidated in accordance with AASB 127 and Interpretation 112, the investor shall measure its interest in the investee at the amount at which it would have been measured if the requirements of this Standard had been effective when the investor became involved with (but did not obtain control in accordance with this Standard), or lost control of, the investee. The investor shall adjust retrospectively the annual period immediately preceding the date of initial application. When the date that the investor became involved with (but did not obtain control in accordance with this Standard), or lost control of, the investee is earlier than the beginning of the immediately preceding period, the investor shall recognise, as an adjustment to equity at the beginning of the immediately preceding period, any difference between:

(a)   the previous carrying amount of the assets, liabilities and non-controlling interests; and

(b)   the recognised amount of the investor's interest in the investee.

C5A   If measuring the interest in the investee in accordance with paragraph C5 is impracticable (as defined in AASB 108), an investor shall apply the requirements of this Standard at the beginning of the earliest period for which application of paragraph C5 is practicable, which may be the current period. The investor shall adjust retrospectively the annual period immediately preceding the date of initial application, unless the beginning of the earliest period for which application of this paragraph is practicable is the current period. When the date that the investor became involved with (but did not obtain control in accordance with this Standard), or lost control of, the investee is earlier than the beginning of the immediately preceding period, the investor shall recognise, as an adjustment to equity at the beginning of the immediately preceding period, any difference between:

(a)   the previous carrying amount of the assets, liabilities and non-controlling interests; and

(b)   the recognised amount of the investor's interest in the investee.

If the earliest period for which application of this paragraph is practicable is the current period, the adjustment to equity shall be recognised at the beginning of the current period.

C6   Paragraphs 23, 25, B94 and B96–B99 were amendments to AASB 127 made in 2008 that were carried forward into AASB 10. Except when an entity applies paragraph C3, or is required to apply paragraphs C4–C5A, the entity shall apply the requirements in those paragraphs as follows:

(a)   An entity shall not restate any profit or loss attribution for reporting periods before it applied the amendment in paragraph B94 for the first time.

(b)   The requirements in paragraphs 23 and B96 for accounting for changes in ownership interests in a subsidiary after control is obtained do not apply to changes that occurred before an entity applied these amendments for the first time.

(c)   An entity shall not restate the carrying amount of an investment in a former subsidiary if control was lost before it applied the amendments in paragraphs 25 and B97–B99 for the first time. In addition, an entity shall not recalculate any gain or loss on the loss of control of a subsidiary that occurred before the amendments in paragraphs 25 and B97–B99 were applied for the first time.

References to the 'immediately preceding period'

C6A   Notwithstanding the references to the annual period immediately preceding the date of initial application (the 'immediately preceding period') in paragraphs C3B–C5A, an entity may also present adjusted comparative information for any earlier periods presented, but is not required to do so. If an entity does present adjusted comparative information for any earlier periods, all references to the 'immediately preceding period' in paragraphs C3B–C5A shall be read as the 'earliest adjusted comparative period presented'.

C6B   If an entity presents unadjusted comparative information for any earlier periods, it shall clearly identify the information that has not been adjusted, state that it has been prepared on a different basis, and explain that basis.

References to AASB 9

C7   If an entity applies this Standard but does not yet apply AASB 9, any reference in this Standard to AASB 9 shall be read as a reference to AASB 139 *Financial Instruments: Recognition and Measurement*.

Withdrawal of other IFRSs

C8–C9   [Deleted by the AASB]

APPENDIX E
AUSTRALIAN IMPLEMENTATION GUIDANCE FOR NOT-FOR-PROFIT ENTITIES

This appendix is an integral part of AASB 10 and has the same authority as the other parts of the Standard. The appendix applies only to not-for-profit entities. The appendix does not apply to for-profit entities or affect their application of AASB 10.

IG1   AASB 10 incorporates International Financial Reporting Standard IFRS 10 *Consolidated Financial Statements*, issued by the International Accounting Standards Board. Consequently, much of the text of the body of this Standard and Appendices A–C is expressed from the perspective of for-profit entities. The AASB has prepared this appendix to explain and illustrate the principles in the Standard for not-for-profit entities in the private and public sectors, particularly to address circumstances where a for-profit perspective does not readily translate to a not-for-profit perspective.

IG2   This appendix addresses a range of matters affecting not-for-profit entities broadly in the order in which the related paragraphs appear in the body of the Standard and in Appendix B. The appendix paragraphs are arranged under the same headings as in the body of the Standard or Appendix B. Cross-references to the paragraphs in the body of the Standard and to the other appendices are included to assist in relating the paragraphs in this appendix to the requirements of the Standard.

IG3   Illustrative examples are provided in the implementation guidance both within implementation guidance paragraphs and as discrete examples. The examples apply by analogy to types of not-for-profit entities other than those identified in the examples and similar circumstances. It is the facts and circumstances in any case, not simply the type of not-for-profit entity, that need to be assessed in determining whether one entity controls another entity.

Control

IG4   Paragraph 5 of AASB 10 sets out the fundamental requirement that an investor shall determine whether it controls an investee. As indicated by the reference in paragraph 11 to assessing power arising from contractual arrangements, the investor need not have a financial investment in the investee. In general terms, an investor and an investee are merely entities that have a relationship in which control of one entity (the investee) by the other (the investor) might arise.

Power

IG5   One of the criteria set out in paragraph 7 for control of an investee is that the investor has power over the investee. Paragraph 10 states that an investor has power over an investee when the investor has existing rights that give it the current ability to direct the relevant activities, that is, the activities that significantly affect the investee's returns. As an example, a not-for-profit investor would have power over an investee when the investor can require the investee to deploy its assets or incur liabilities in a way that affects the investee's returns (for example, in providing goods or services to the investor or other parties that assist in achieving or furthering the investee's objectives).

IG6   Paragraph 11 states that power arises from rights, and refers to voting rights granted by equity instruments and rights arising from contractual arrangements. While these rights will often be the source of power for for-profit entities, power will frequently arise through different sources for not-for-profit entities. For many not-for-profit entities, rights arising from administrative arrangements or statutory provisions will often be the source of power. Assessing the purpose and design of an investee will assist an investor to identify who has power over the investee, ie the current ability to direct the relevant activities (paragraph B5).

IG7   As an example of contractual or statutory arrangements, a not-for-profit investor often will have power over an investee that it has established when the constituting document or enabling legislation for the investee specifies the investor's rights to direct the operating and financing activities that may be carried out by the investee. However, the impact of the constituting document or legislation is evaluated in the context of the prevailing circumstances, as all facts and circumstances need to be considered in assessing whether an investor has power over an investee. For example, the purpose and design of an investee may point to the relevant activities of the investee and how decisions about the relevant activities are made. To illustrate, a government may not have power over a research and development corporation that operates under a mandate created, and limited, by that government's legislation if that or other legislation means that the power to direct the relevant activities is held by other entities that are not controlled by the government, such as participants in the research and development activities.

IG8   The research and development corporation example in the previous paragraph illustrates that an investor might not have power over an investee due to the rights of other parties in relation to the investee, as indicated in paragraph B10. As another example, subject to consideration of all the facts and circumstances, a State or Territory government normally would not have power to direct the relevant activities (ie the activities that significantly affect the returns) of a local government that determines through the council elected periodically by the local community how to deploy the local government's resources in the interests of the local community (even though those interests might coincide with or overlap the interests of the State or Territory government).

Rights that give an investor power over an investee

IG9   Paragraph B15 provides examples of rights that, either individually or in combination, can give an investor power in respect of an investee. In relation to not-for-profit investors, additional examples of such rights include:

(a)   rights to give policy directions to the governing body of the investee that give the holder the ability to direct the relevant activities of the investee; and

(b)   rights to approve or veto operating and capital budgets relating to the relevant activities of the investee.

IG10   A not-for-profit investor can have power over an investee even if it does not have responsibility for the day-to-day operation of the investee or the specific manner in which prescribed functions are performed by the investee. For example, legislation governing the establishment and operation of an independent statutory office (such as an auditor-general or the judiciary) sets out the broad parameters within which the office holder is required to operate, and results in the office holder operating in a manner consistent with the objectives set by the legislation. Whilst the holders of an independent statutory office are to act independently in discharging their responsibilities, the government typically provides the organisations that assist the statutory office holders in fulfilling their responsibilities. In such cases, the resources of those organisations remain government resources albeit that they are placed at the disposal of the office holders, subject to the office holders acting in accordance with their enabling legislation. Furthermore, the relevant activities of the organisations, including providing technical services to the statutory office holders, are generally subject to the same financial management, employment and administrative frameworks and policies as would apply to government-controlled entities such as government departments. Therefore, subject to other facts and circumstances, assuming the other control criteria are also satisfied, the organisations assisting the independent statutory office holders would be controlled by the government and would be consolidated into the whole of government general purpose financial statements.

IG11   Paragraph B19 lists a range of indicators that suggest that an investor has more than a passive interest in an investee, but notes that the existence of such indicators does not necessarily mean that the power criterion is met. The indicators listed include the investee's operations being dependent on the investor, such as dependence on the investor to fund a significant portion of its operations, guarantee a significant portion of its obligations or provide critical goods or services. Paragraph B40 also states that, in the absence of other rights, the economic dependence of an investee on the investor does not lead to the investor having power over the investee.

IG12   An example of the circumstances contemplated in paragraphs B19 and B40 is that a government may not have the current ability to direct the relevant activities of entities (such as private schools, private hospitals, private aged-care providers and universities) that are financially dependent on government funding, where the governing bodies of those entities have discretion with respect to whether they will accept resources from the government, or the manner in which their resources are to be deployed. This may be so even if government grants provided to such entities require them to comply with specified conditions. Although these entities might receive government grants for capital construction and operating costs subject to specified service standards or restrictions on user fees, their independent governing body may have ultimate discretion about how assets are deployed.

Substantive rights

IG13   Barriers that prevent a holder of rights from exercising them are considered in determining whether the rights are substantive, that is, whether the holder has the practical ability to exercise the rights (paragraph B22). Paragraph B23 provides examples of such barriers. For some not-for-profit investors, political, cultural, social or similar types of barriers might make it difficult for the investor to exercise rights held in relation to an investee. However, the investor's rights would be substantive, despite such barriers, if the investor can still choose to exercise those rights. For example, a government may have the power to appoint and remove the majority of members of the governing body of a railway authority without cause but may be reluctant to remove members because of sensitivity in the electorate regarding the previous government's involvement in the operation of the rail network. In this case, the government has substantive rights, irrespective of whether it chooses to exercise them.

IG14   Paragraph B24 states that to be substantive, rights need to be exercisable when decisions about the direction of the relevant activities need to be made. Usually this means that the rights need to be currently exercisable. However, paragraph B24 also notes that sometimes rights can be substantive even though they are not currently exercisable. For many not-for-profit investors, power over an investee may be obtained from existing statutory arrangements. Rights specified in substantively enacted legislation would be substantive rights that need to be considered by the investor in assessing control of an investee if it is assessed that the rights will be exercisable when decisions about the direction of the relevant activities need to be made. However, the power to enact or change legislation does not give the investor the current ability to direct relevant activities of the investee. Depending on circumstances, statutory arrangements may be in the nature of protective rights rather than substantive rights – see paragraphs IG15–IG17.

Protective rights

IG15 Protective rights are defined in Appendix A as rights designed to protect the interest of the party holding those rights without giving that party power over the entity to which those rights relate. Applying this principle to not-for-profit entities, protective rights include rights held by a government or other entity in order to protect, as distinct from enhance, the interests of the government, the beneficiaries of an entity or the public at large. In accordance with paragraph B27, such rights do not result in the investor (the government or other entity) having power over an investee or restricting another entity from having power over the investee.

IG16 Not-for-profit entities might hold regulatory powers that restrict the way in which regulated entities operate. The regulatory powers may be exercisable through an established framework within which entities are required to operate, including the ability to impose conditions or sanctions on their operations. Regulatory powers may represent protective rights, which do not give power (as defined in the Standard) over an investee, or substantive rights that need to be considered in determining control. For example, regulatory powers may represent substantive rights when they would have the effect of giving the regulator the ability to direct the relevant activities of an investee in particular circumstances. Not-for-profit investors are required by paragraph B26 to assess whether their rights (and rights held by others) are protective or substantive rights.

IG17 In addition to the examples in paragraph B28, examples of protective rights in relation to not-for-profit entities include:

(a) the right of a regulator to curtail or close the operations of entities that are not complying with regulations or other requirements. For example, a pollution control authority may be able to close down an entity's activities that breach environmental regulations.

(b) the right to remove members of the governing body of another entity under certain restricted circumstances. For example, for reasons relating to a lack of probity, a State government may be able to remove or suspend the councillors of a local government and appoint an administrator who is not directed by the State government in carrying out the functions of the local government.

(c) the right to appoint additional members to the governing body of another entity under certain restricted circumstances. For example, when the entity has failed to comply with performance standards, a regulator may be able to appoint appropriately qualified members who are in the same position as other members – they do not report to and are not directed by the regulator.

(d) the right of the government to remove tax deductibility for contributions to a not-for-profit entity if the entity significantly changes its objectives or activities.

(e) a philanthropic trust providing resources to a charity on condition that the net assets of the charity would be distributed to a similar organisation undertaking similar activities if the charity is liquidated.

Returns

Exposure, or rights, to variable returns from an investee

IG18 One of the criteria set out in paragraph 7 for control of an investee is that the investor has exposure, or rights, to variable returns from its involvement with the investee. The examples of returns in paragraph B57, particularly those in paragraph B57(c), indicate that the scope of the nature of returns is broad. In application to not-for-profit entities, the broad scope of the nature of returns encompasses financial, non-financial, direct and indirect benefits, whether positive or negative, including the achievement or furtherance of the investor's objectives.

IG19 An investor's exposure, or rights, to variable returns from its involvement with an investee may give rise to indirect, non-financial returns, such as when achieving or furthering the objectives of the investee contributes to the objectives of the investor. For example, the provision of goods and services by the investee to its beneficiaries may affect the extent to which the investor's social policy objectives are furthered. These returns to the investor would reflect factors such as the efficiency and effectiveness of delivery of the goods and services and changes in the outcomes for the beneficiaries.

Link between power and returns

IG20 The third criterion set out in paragraph 7 for control of an investee is that the investor has the ability to use its power over the investee to affect the amount of the investor's returns. As an example, the investor would have the ability to use its power over the investee when it can direct the investee to work with the investor to further the investor's objectives. However, the existence of congruent objectives alone is insufficient for a not-for-profit investor to conclude that it controls an investee.

Delegated power

IG21 An investor with decision-making rights (a decision maker) is required by paragraph B58 to determine whether it is a principal or an agent. Paragraphs B60 and B61 summarise factors to be taken into account in making that determination, such as the scope of the decision-making authority and the rights of other parties. The following examples illustrate these paragraphs in relation to not-for-profit entities.

IG22 A charity establishes a trust to fund and construct village dams, bores and other water infrastructure in several provinces of a developing country. The trustee is appointed by the charity to oversee the work of the trust. The trustee receives remuneration from the trust commensurate with the services provided and the skills applied, plus a performance bonus upon the successful completion of individual projects. The charity can replace the trustee at its discretion. The trustee therefore is an agent of the charity and cannot control the trust in its own right. In this case, the charity then needs to assess whether it controls the trust through the trustee. For example:

    (a)   the trustee may have power over the trust in having the current ability to direct its relevant activities, whether through a broad decision-making authority or as determined by the charity in respect of major aspects, such as project selection. Even if the trustee does not have exposure or rights to variable returns from the trust, the charity does so in terms of the extent to which its overseas aid objectives are achieved or furthered through the activities of the trust. Since the trustee (as an agent of the charity) can use its powers to affect the trust's non-financial returns, the three control criteria are satisfied in respect of the charity and the charity would control the trust; or

    (b)   the trustee may be permitted by development regulations of the provincial governments to provide only oversight of the trust's activities, which are carried out in general by management committees appointed by the relevant provincial government. In this case, the trustee does not have the power to direct the relevant activities of the trust, and accordingly the charity would not control the trust.

IG23 A government department acts in relation to an investee only as an agent of the responsible Minister when the department or an official of the department is merely authorised by the Minister to act on the Minister's behalf (in which case the department's activities in relation to the investee would be reflected in its reporting under AASB 1050 Administered Items).

IG24 Alternatively, a department acts as a principal under a delegation of powers from the Minister as the department or an official of the department exercises their own discretion, not subject to specific direction by the Minister. In this case, the department would report its activities in relation to the investee as its own transactions. The department would need to assess whether the delegated powers give it the current ability to direct the relevant activities of the investee and whether the other control criteria are satisfied in deciding whether the department controls the investee and should consolidate it.

Implementation examples

IG25 Examples IG1–IG5 illustrate the application of the three criteria for control (power over an investee, variable returns from involvement with the investee, and link between power and the investor's returns) in a range of circumstances. Example IG5 also illustrates the effect of delegated powers in the public sector.

IG26 Each example provides detailed information about the purpose and design of the investee, as a basis for assessing control of the investee. The sub-examples address the initial circumstances, and then vary the design of the investee, with the control assessment then reconsidered in each case. Examples IG3 and IG4 particularly distinguish substantive and protective rights held by an investor in relation to the investee. In any specific case, distinguishing substantive and protective rights requires analysis of the circumstances, including considering the reasons for different investors holding various rights in relation to the investee.

Implementation examples

Example IG1

A religious organisation ABC established a community housing program that provides low-cost housing. The program is operated by an incorporated association. The association's constitution states that its objective is to manage the community housing facility to meet the need for low-cost housing. The association has not issued any equity instruments.

The relevant activities of the association comprise:

- reviewing and selecting applicants for housing;
- the day-to-day operation of the housing program;
- maintaining the houses and common facilities; and
- improving and extending the housing facilities.

The board of governors of the association has 16 members, with eight appointed by (and subject to removal by) the religious organisation. The chair is appointed by the board from amongst the appointees of the religious organisation, and has a casting vote that is rarely exercised. The board meets regularly and reviews reports received from the association's management. Based on these reports, the board may confirm or override management decisions. In addition, the board makes decisions on major issues such as significant maintenance and investing further capital to build additional housing, after reviewing vacancy levels and the demand for housing.

The religious organisation owns the land on which the housing facilities stand and has contributed capital and operating funds to the association since it was established. The association owns the housing facilities.

The association retains any surplus resulting from the operation of the facilities and under its constitution is unable to provide a direct financial return to the religious organisation.

Example IG1A

Based on the facts and circumstances outlined above, the religious organisation controls the association.

The religious organisation appoints eight members of the board of governors, one of whom will become the chair, who has a casting vote. As a result, the religious organisation has power over the association through substantive rights that give it the current ability to direct the relevant activities of the association, regardless of whether the religious organisation chooses to exercise those substantive rights.

The religious organisation also has exposure or rights to variable returns from its involvement with the association. The religious organisation obtains non-financial returns through the association furthering its social objective of meeting the need for low-cost community housing. Although not

AASB

able to receive direct financial returns, the religious organisation obtains indirect returns through its ability to direct how the financial returns are to be employed in the community housing program.

The religious organisation also satisfies the final control criterion. Through its appointees on the board, the religious organisation has the ability to use its power to affect the nature and amount of its returns from the association.

The religious organisation satisfies all three criteria for control and therefore the religious organisation controls the association.

Example IG1B

In this example, the facts of Example IG1A apply, except that:

* the association's board of governors is elected through a public nomination and voting process that does not give rights to the religious organisation to appoint board members; and

* decisions made by the association's board are reviewed by the religious organisation, which may offer advice to the association.

Based on the revised facts and circumstances outlined above, the religious organisation does not have substantive rights relating to the association and therefore does not have power over the association.

The religious organisation's social objectives in relation to low-cost community housing are still being achieved and therefore it will still obtain indirect non-financial returns. However, congruence of objectives alone is insufficient to conclude that one entity controls another (see paragraph IG20).

The religious organisation does not have power and consequently does not have the ability to use power to affect the amount of the organisation's returns. The religious organisation is unable to satisfy two of the three control criteria and therefore the religious organisation does not control the association.

Example IG1C

In this example, the facts of Example IG1B apply, except that the association's constitution allows the religious organisation to change the manner in which the board of governors is determined, as it sees fit.

For example, the religious organisation has the unilateral ability to amend the constitution of the association to enable the religious organisation to appoint a majority of the board of governors, thus giving the religious organisation substantive rights that give it the current ability to direct the relevant activities of the association. Therefore, the religious organisation has power over the association through those substantive rights, regardless of whether the religious organisation chooses to exercise those rights.

Since the religious organisation has the ability to determine the composition of the board of governors and thus direct the relevant activities of the association, the religious organisation has exposure or rights to the same variable returns from its involvement with the association as set out for Example IG1A.

The religious organisation also satisfies the final control criterion. Through its ability to determine the composition of the board of governors, the religious organisation can use its power to affect the amount of its returns from the activities of the association.

The religious organisation satisfies all three of the control criteria and therefore the religious organisation controls the association. In this example, the design of the association as set out in its constitution indicates that the religious organisation has the ability to direct the relevant activities of the association even though a publicly elected board of governors has been established. This design reflects the special relationship between the religious organisation and the association.

Implementation examples

Example IG2

FGH Charity is a private sector not-for-profit organisation. Its objectives are to protect and serve the community by providing emergency first aid and increasing the first aid skills of the community. The charity provides first aid at sporting events and when natural disasters occur. The charity is funded via donations and the sale of first aid supplies (bandages, first aid kits, etc.). The board of the charity has 10 members.

The charity established TUV First Aid Training Ltd (TUV or the company) some years ago. The purpose of TUV is to provide first aid training courses to the general public for a fee. TUV has an eight-member board, with all members appointed by the board of FGH Charity.

The charity has the right to receive distributions of profits made by TUV.

The management of TUV is responsible for the day-to-day operations of the company. TUV's management is also responsible for developing the company's policies, including:

- the scope of the training courses, such as the type of courses and the maximum number of participants for each course;
- marketing plans for the courses, including the fee structure;
- the frequency and location of courses; and
- the use of in-house or off-the-shelf training materials.

These policies address the relevant activities of TUV, ie the activities that significantly affect the company's returns.

The board of TUV meets regularly to review reports from TUV management in order to assess the performance of the company. The board makes decisions about the company's activities and policies so as to optimise its outcomes. For example, the board might modify the scope or frequency of courses or revise the fee structure.

The TUV board also considers whether any profits should be distributed to the charity (FGH) as a financial return or used to improve or expand the company's activities.

Example IG2A

Based on the facts and circumstances outlined above, the charity controls TUV. The charity has power over TUV because its board appoints the board members of TUV, thus giving the charity the current ability to direct the relevant activities of the company. The charity is exposed to variable returns from its involvement with TUV, both financial returns (the right to receive distributions of profits from TUV) and non-financial returns (the furtherance of its objective of improving community first aid skills). Finally, the charity can use its power over TUV (via the board) to affect the nature and amount of returns it obtains through TUV.

Example IG2B

In this example, the facts of Example IG2A apply, except that:

- the charity does not have the right to receive distributions of profits from TUV since the constitution of the company prohibits distributions to its members; and
- all profits of TUV are to be reinvested into first aid training programs.

Based on the revised facts and circumstances, the charity controls TUV. The charity has power over TUV because it appoints the board of the company. Although it does not receive any financial returns, the charity obtains non-financial returns because TUV is fulfilling one of its objectives by increasing the first aid skills of the community. The charity is able to use its power over TUV to affect the nature and amount of its returns. Therefore, the three control criteria are satisfied.

Example IG2C

This example has the same facts as Example IG2B, except that:

- the charity cannot appoint the board members of TUV, except for the Chair, who must be a board member of the charity; and
- the charity has the right to veto appointments to the board of TUV, but only in exceptional circumstances – that is, when a potential board member is deemed unsuitable. This right has only been enforced once, when a proposed board member was found to have a history of fraudulent activities.

Based on these facts and circumstances, the charity does not control TUV. This is because the charity does not have the requisite power to direct the relevant activities of TUV – it appoints only one of the eight members of the board of TUV. Even though the charity has the right of veto over TUV

AASB

board appointments, this is only a protective right because it is a safeguard against having board members who could potentially interfere with the operations of the company and adversely affect its outcomes.

The charity had the opportunity and incentive when establishing TUV to obtain rights that would give it the ability to direct the relevant activities of TUV, but it did not do so. Being involved in the design of an investee is not sufficient to give an investor control (see paragraph B51 of the Standard).

Example IG2D

In this example, the facts of Example IG2C apply, except that:

- TUV's constitution permits its board to make financial distributions to other parties as decided by the board; and

- although the charity does not have any right to distributions of profits from TUV, to date TUV has always distributed its profits to the charity.

Based on these facts and circumstances, the charity does not control TUV because, as in Example IG2C, the charity does not have power over TUV to direct the relevant activities.

Even though TUV was established by the charity in order to further its objective regarding community first aid skills, and despite the charity historically receiving financial returns from TUV, the design of TUV does not give the charity power over TUV. The board of TUV is independent of the charity, there is no requirement for TUV to make distributions to the charity (or to any other party), and the charity has no right to demand financial returns.

Implementation example

Example IG3

The LMN local government (the Council) is created under a State's Local Government Act to operate for the peace, order and good government of its municipal district. The Council is administered by the councillors, who are elected directly by the local community in periodic elections. General requirements for the elections are set out in the Act.

Objectives of the Council

The Act specifies that the Council's primary objective is to achieve the best outcomes for the local community over the long term. In working to achieve this objective, the Council must have regard to:

- promoting the social, economic and environmental viability and sustainability of the municipal district;

- ensuring that resources are used efficiently and effectively and that services provided are accessible and equitable;

- the equitable imposition of rates and charges; and

- transparency and accountability in Council decision making.

Powers and Functions of the Council

The Council is empowered by the Act to do all things necessary and convenient for the achievement of its objectives and the performance of its functions, subject to any limitations under the Act or any other legislation (see the sections on the State Government's protective and substantive rights later in this example).

The Council's functions include:

- raising revenue to fund its functions and activities;

- planning for and providing services and facilities (including infrastructure) for the local community;

- strategic and land-use planning;

- making and enforcing local laws; and

- advocating proposals that are in the best interests of the district.

Activities of the Council

In carrying out its functions, the Council undertakes a wide range of activities, including the employment of staff, the imposition of rates and charges upon constituents, the establishment and implementation of policies and procedures, the purchase or sale of goods or services from or to constituents or other parties, the provision without charge of services such as parks and roads, transactions under financial contracts and prosecuting legal actions.

State Government Involvement with the Council

The State Government's objectives for the government of the municipal district are consistent with the objectives of the Council, since the State Government set out the Council's objectives in the State's Local Government Act.

Consequently, the Council is subject to a wide range of State Government regulatory powers, even though its day-to-day operations are carried out by the Council's staff under the direction of its elected councillors. The State Government's rights in respect of the Council are held primarily by the Minister for Local Government, but other Ministers also hold some additional powers, such as land-use planning powers held by the Minister for Planning.

The interest of the State Government in the activities of the Council is to ensure that the general objectives set out in the Act are being achieved or furthered. To that end, the State Government has an extensive range of rights (through its Ministers) to advise or guide the Council in its activities or, under particular circumstances, to intervene in the activities of the Council. The principal rights of the State Government are described in the following sections.

Protective rights of the State Government

Some of the State Government's rights are protective rights, as described in paragraph B26: rights that relate to fundamental changes to the activities of the Council (the investee) or that apply in exceptional circumstances. For example, the Minister has the following rights that are regarded as protective rights for the purpose of this example:

- restructure the municipal district through boundary changes;

- abolish the existing Council and constitute a new Council or Councils, with the Minister able to direct the transfer of property, income, assets, rights, liabilities, expenses and staff among Councils as part of the process;

- suspend all the councillors of the Council if the Minister is satisfied that there has been a serious failure to provide good government or serious unlawful acts by the Council – in which case an administrator is appointed to act as the Council and to perform its functions, powers and duties;

- appoint inspectors of municipal administration to examine any particular Council matter and make recommendations to the Council, and enforce those recommendations if the Council does not adopt them;

- revoke local laws passed by the Council where, in the Minister's opinion, the laws substantially restrict competition without appropriate justification;

- approve (or veto) Council entering into an entrepreneurial endeavour that exceeds 5% of the Council's revenue from rates and charges;

- approve (or veto) investment by the Council in types of financial instruments not already approved under the Act; and

- make guidelines concerning the Council's procurement policy or the provision of services by the Council so as to best meet the needs of the local community.

Substantive rights of the State Government

The State Government also has a range of rights that do not fall into the category of protective rights. For example, Ministers have the following rights that, for the purpose of this example, are classified as substantive rights:

- give directions concerning rates and charges to limit the rate of change in the Council's general income for a financial year;

- review the allowance category annually for the Council, including the limits and ranges of councillor allowances; and

- prepare a planning scheme for the district or authorise an amendment subject to any conditions that the Minister wishes to impose.

Control of the Council

Based on the facts and circumstances outlined above, does the State Government control the Council in accordance with the definition of control in the Standard? If not, who controls the Council?

Relevant activities

The State Government has numerous rights in relation to the Council. Whereas the State Government's protective rights cannot give power over the Council, the substantive rights do give the State Government the current ability to direct some activities of the Council.

However, paragraph 10 of the Standard states that an investor has power over an investee when the investor has the current ability to direct the *relevant activities*, ie the activities that *significantly affect* the investee's returns. Therefore, it is necessary to identify the relevant activities of the Council, and then assess the State Government's substantive rights in respect of those activities relative to the rights of other parties.

Judgement is required in identifying the relevant activities, as this requires identifying both the Council's returns and the activities of the Council that significantly affect those returns. As a not-for-profit entity, the Council's non-financial returns for the community are considered to be of primary importance, even though its objectives also include financial aspects, such as the efficient use of resources and equitable rates and charges. The objectives do not include the raising of revenue per se.

All of the Council's activities and functions contribute (whether positively or negatively) to the Council achieving or furthering its objectives. Thus they are activities that affect the financial and non-financial returns of the Council. But which activities *significantly affect* the Council's returns? Given the significance of non-financial returns for the Council, it is considered that the provision of services and facilities for the community and regulating other parties' activities in the community (eg property development, health services and shopping centres) are the activities that most significantly affect the Council's returns. Consequently, these are likely to be the *relevant activities* of the Council.

Power

Paragraph B10 states that whether an investor has power over an investee depends on, for example, the rights the investor and other parties have in relation to the investee. When two or more parties each have existing rights that give them the unilateral ability to direct different relevant activities, the party that has the current ability to direct the activities that most significantly affect the investee's returns has power over the investee (paragraph 13 of the Standard). Does the State Government have the power, the current ability, to direct the relevant activities of the Council?

The substantive rights of the State Government do give it the current ability to direct *some* of the activities of the Council, such as amending or replacing planning schemes. However, the State Government is unable to direct the major part of the activities that *significantly affect* the Council's returns. Therefore, the State Government does not hold power over the Council as described in the Standard.

The power to direct the relevant activities is held by the councillors of the Council, who direct, within the framework established by the State Government, the vast majority of the Council's activities that affect the returns from its operations.

The State Government's right to give directions to limit the rate of change in the Council's general income (rates and charges) is in the nature of price regulation rather than directing relevant activities. The raising of revenue itself is not a relevant activity, as identified above, because revenue by itself is not one of the Council's returns or objectives.

Returns

The State Government is exposed, or has rights, to variable returns from its involvement with the Council since the activities of the Council contribute to the achievement or furtherance of the State Government's objectives for the good government and appropriate development of the municipal district.

Ability to use power to affect returns

Since it was concluded above that in the circumstances presented the State Government does not have power (as described in the Standard) over the Council, then the third control criterion linking power and returns is also not satisfied. The State Government is able to affect the Council's returns, and thus its own indirect returns, through exercising its substantive rights. However, the State Government is unable to direct the activities that most significantly affect the Council's returns.

Control conclusion

The conclusion from the above assessment is that the State Government does not have power over the Council and therefore does not control the Council.

In this case, the Council would not be consolidated by any other entity. The councillors of the Council as a group are not investors as contemplated by the Standard. They are akin to the board of directors of a company, that is, the councillors are a part of the Council itself.

Alternative Outcome

The distinction between protective and substantive rights and the significance of the substantive rights to the Council's returns are matters for judgement in view of all the facts and circumstances in any particular situation. A different list or classification of relevant activities, protective rights and substantive rights from that presented in this example might change the conclusion on control of the Council.

Implementation examples

Example IG4

XYZ University was established under an Act of the State Government. The University receives approximately 40% of its total revenue in the form of grants for various purposes, comprising 30% from the Australian Government and 10% from the State Government. The University is required by the Act to submit an annual report to the State Minister for Education.

Objectives of the University

The Act specifies that the University's objects include:

- to provide higher education at an international standard;

- to undertake scholarship and research for the advancement of knowledge and the benefit of the well-being of the State, Australian and international communities;

- to equip graduates to excel in their careers and contribute to the life of the community; and

- to serve the State, Australian and international communities and the public interest by enriching cultural and community life and promoting critical and free inquiry and public debate.

Management of the University

The governing body of the University is the University Council. The Council consists of 17 members, five of whom were appointed directly or indirectly by the State Minister. Four members were elected by the staff and students of the University. The remaining eight members were appointed by the Council itself, comprising the three official members (the Chancellor, the Vice-Chancellor and the President of the Academic Board) and five other (non-official) members.

The Act specifies that the number of Minister-appointed members (five members in this case) must be equal to or greater than the number of non-official Council-appointed members (also five).

The Act specifies that the University Council's responsibilities, powers and functions include:

- approving the mission, strategic direction and annual budget and business plan of the University;

- establishing policies ('university statutes and regulations') relating to the governance and operation of the University, including trusts and endowments, and research, development, consultancy, commercial activities and other services undertaken for commercial organisations or public bodies;

- developing guidelines (if any) concerning the carrying out of commercial activities, finance and property matters, or any other related matter;

- overseeing the management of the property, finances and business affairs of the University, such as risk management across the University, including its commercial activities;

- any other powers and functions conferred on it by or under legislation or any university statute or regulation; and

- the power to do anything else necessary or convenient to be done for or in connection with its powers and functions.

Activities of the University

In carrying out its functions, the University undertakes a wide range of activities, including employing academic, teaching and administrative staff, determining fees and charges for courses provided to students and for commercial activities, entering into contracts, and forming or becoming a member of other entities.

State Government Involvement with the University

The State Government's objectives for the University are consistent with, but not limited to, those specified in the Act for the University. For example, the State Government anticipates State economic development as a result of the University's activities, such as the provision of housing and tourism services to international students.

The State Minister has the following powers and functions, which are classified in this example as substantive rights under the Standard:

- fix the remuneration and fees to be paid to Council members who are not full-time staff of the University or holders of statutory office;

- approve (or veto) University statutes and guidelines made by the Council;

- declare an activity to be a university commercial activity;

- make interim guidelines concerning university commercial activities and finance and property matters – these apply unless replaced by University-submitted guidelines approved by the Minister;

- certain rights specified in State Government grants provided to the University – some of the grants detail the education or research activities to be carried out under the grant;

- in conjunction with the State Treasurer, approve the limits and conditions (eg security) for University borrowings; and

- approve (or veto) the disposal of land that was previously Crown land granted to the University.

The Minister also has the following powers, which are classified as protective rights for the purpose of this example:

- request commercial and financial reports from the University;

- refer a university commercial activity or any aspect thereof to the auditor-general for investigation and report to the Minister; and

- certain rights specified in State Government grants provided to the University – some of the grants are required to be repaid if not applied as specified.

Australian Government Involvement with the University

The Australian Government's objectives for the University are consistent with, but not limited to, those specified in the State Act for the University. For example, the Australian Government anticipates national economic development as a result of the University's activities and may seek to advance foreign policy objectives through universities attracting international students.

The Australian Minister for Education also has the rights specified in Australian Government grants provided to the University. Some of these grants specify how they are to be applied to education or research activities (which are substantive rights for the purpose of this example) and some require their repayment if not applied as specified (protective rights for the purpose of this example).

The Minister can also request reports from the University.

University Council-directed Activities

As indicated above, the University's commercial activities and finance and property matters are subject to various State Government Ministerial powers, and government grants may be conditional. However, the University Council also has a range of powers and functions that it can exercise directly, such as the following:

- appoint the Vice-Chancellor, who is the chief executive officer of the University and responsible for the conduct of the University's affairs in all matters;

- determine the composition of borrowings within the parameters set by the State Government;

- approve the University's budget for a financial year, incorporating total revenue and the planned revenue sources, including planning the mix between teaching, research and commercial activities, the fees and charges to apply to those activities, and the type and value of government grants desired;

- determine the course mix and target student mix, such as vocational, undergraduate, graduate and executive courses, on-campus or distance learning, and local and international students;

- appoint staff and determine their terms and conditions;

- decide whether to operate through multiple campuses and how to utilise the University's infrastructure; and

- make university regulations with respect to any matter relating to the University.

Example IG4A

Control of the University

Based on the facts and circumstances outlined above, does the State Government or the Australian Government control the University in accordance with the definition of control in the Standard? If not, who controls the University?

Economic dependence

The State and Australian Governments each has a range of rights in relation to the University. The University may be economically dependent on the grants from those Governments in order to carry out its activities at their present scope and scale, but paragraphs B19 and B40 of the Standard make clear that economic dependence alone does not lead to the investor having power (as that term is used in AASB 10) over the investee. The State Government and Australian Government rights under some of their grants to the University to recover misapplied funds amount to protective rights. The repayment of such grants, potentially coupled with a reduction of Government grants in the future given the lack of compliance with grant conditions, may require the University to curtail its activities due to the reduction in funding. However, such a curtailment does not involve either Government in directing activities of the University, since it is the University that would determine which activities would be curtailed.

Relevant activities

Judgement is required to identify the University's *relevant activities*, that is, the activities that *significantly affect* the University's returns. All of the University's activities and functions contribute in some way (positive or negative) to the University achieving or furthering its objectives. Thus they are activities that affect the financial and non-financial returns of the University. However, as the University has fairly limited commercial activities in this example, the activities that most significantly affect the University's returns are the education and research activities.

Power

Protective rights held by the State and Australian Governments cannot give them power over the University. Instead, their substantive rights concerning the University's education and research activities (the relevant activities) need to be weighed against the rights of the University Council itself, in order to assess which party has the current ability to direct the activities that most significantly affect the University's returns (or outcomes).

It is the University Council that generally directs the education and research activities. For example, the Council decides the mix between education, research and commercial activities, the courses to be offered, the target student mix, the fee structure and how to use the University's infrastructure for the activities. Some grants from the State and Australian Governments direct how they are to be applied, but these affect only a relatively small proportion of the education and research activities overall. On balance, the University Council itself appears to have the current ability to direct the relevant activities of the University.

Since the State Minister is able to appoint members of the University Council, it is necessary to consider whether the State Minister has power over the University through substantive rights to appoint a majority of the members of the University Council. In this example, the State Minister can appoint only five of the 17 members of the University Council. Therefore, the State Government is unable to direct the relevant activities of the University through appointments to the University Council.

The State Government's substantive rights in relation to the University's commercial activities or business operations are not considered in this assessment of control, since they do not relate to the relevant activities.

Neither the State Government nor the Australian Government would have power (as described in the Standard) over the University.

Returns

The State and Australian Governments are exposed, or have rights, to variable returns from their involvement with the University since the activities of the University contribute to the achievement or furtherance of the State Government's and the Australian Government's objectives for higher education. The Governments have additional objectives regarding the activities of the University, but there is no need for a direct alignment between the Governments' objectives and the University's objectives.

Ability to use power to affect returns

Since it was concluded above that in the circumstances presented neither the State Government nor the Australian Government has power (as described in the Standard) over the University, then the third control criterion linking power and returns is also not satisfied. The Governments are able to affect the returns of the University, and thus their own indirect returns, through exercising their substantive rights. However, the Governments are unable to direct the activities that most significantly affect the University's returns.

Control conclusion

The conclusion from the above assessment is that neither the State Government nor the Australian Government has power over the University and therefore neither Government controls the University.

In this case, the University would not be consolidated by any other entity. The University Council as a group is not an investor as contemplated by the Standard. It is akin to the board of directors of a company, that is, the Council is a part of the University itself.

Example IG4B

In this example, the facts are the same as in Example IG4A except that:

*   XYZ University is a research university with extensive commercial activities, and teaching activities that are limited to a small range of graduate and executive courses;

*   the University receives approximately 30% of its total revenue in the form of grants for various purposes, comprising 10% from the Australian Government and 20% from the State Government;

*   50% of the total revenue is derived from commercial activities, and the balance of 20% from industry funding and course fees; and

*   the State Government requires all significant commercial activities and finance and property decisions of the University to be approved by the Minister.

Based on these revised facts and circumstances, the State Government's substantive rights in respect of the University's commercial activities and its finance and property matters have a much more significant role in the operations of the University than in Example IG4A. The substantive rights may now be of such effect that the State Government has the current ability to direct the activities that significantly affect the University's returns. In that case, the State Government would have power over the University as described in the Standard, satisfying the first control criterion.

As explained in Example IG4A, the State Government is exposed or has rights to variable returns from its involvement with the University, thus satisfying the second control criterion.

Finally, the State Government is able to use its power over the University's commercial activities to affect its returns from the University, thus meeting the third control criterion.

Control Conclusion

The conclusion from the above assessment is that in this case the State Government controls the University, assuming that the State Government's substantive rights give it the ability to direct the relevant activities of the University.

Implementation examples

Example IG5

A statutory authority SHS is established under State health services legislation to deliver services to the community. The statutory authority has a governing council that oversees the authority's operations and is responsible for its day-to-day operations. The State Health Minister, as part of their role in the State Government, appoints the authority's governing council and, subject to the Minister's approval, the authority's governing council appoints the chief executive of the authority.

The State Health Department acts as the 'system manager' for the State public health system. This role includes:

*   strategic leadership, such as the development of State-wide health service plans;

*   directions for the delivery of health services, such as entering into service agreements, capital works approval and management of State-wide industrial relations, including employment terms and conditions for the authority's employees; and

*   monitoring of performance (eg quality of health services and financial data) of the authority and taking remedial action when performance does not meet specified performance measures.

The Minister's approval, given on behalf of the State Government, is specifically required for the following major decisions:

*   entering into service agreements with the authority;

*   issuing binding health service directives;

*   finalisation of State-wide health service plans and capital works planning; and

*   employment and remuneration of the authority's executive staff.

Example IG5A

Based on the facts and circumstances outlined above, the Department generally acts as an agent of the State Government in relation to the statutory authority. This is evident from the restricted decision-making authority held by the Department. The Department does not control the statutory authority.

As the State Government appoints the statutory authority's governing council and approves the major decisions affecting the authority's activities, the State Government has the power to direct the relevant activities of the authority. Assuming that the other control criteria (variable returns and link between power and returns) are satisfied, as would be expected, then the State Government would control the statutory authority. As a result, the statutory authority would not be consolidated by the Department, but would be consolidated directly into the whole of government general purpose financial statements.

Example IG5B

The facts are the same as in Example IG5A except that:

*   the State Government has delegated the power to appoint members of the statutory authority's governing council to the Department head;

*   the appointment of the authority's chief executive by the governing council does not require Ministerial approval;

*   the State Government has delegated the power to approve the major decisions to the Department head; and

*   assessments of the Department's performance encompass the performance of the statutory authority.

In this example, the scope of the decision-making authority held by the Department has increased significantly as a result of the delegations by the State Government to the Department head. As the Department acts as a principal under the delegations, the Department has the current ability to direct the relevant activities of the authority so as to achieve the health service objectives of the Department. As the Department also has the ability to use its power over the authority to affect the nature and amount of the Department's returns, the Department controls the statutory authority.

> The Department would consolidate the statutory authority into its consolidated financial statements. The Department's consolidated financial statements would then be consolidated into the whole of government financial statements.

AUSTRALIAN APPLICATION GUIDANCE

This Australian application guidance accompanies, but is not part of AASB 10.

Exemption from presenting consolidated financial statements

AG1   The following table summarises the circumstances in which the exemption from presenting consolidated financial statements set out in paragraphs 4-Aus4.2 of this Standard may be available to a parent entity. The exemption is available only if the requirements of those paragraphs are satisfied. For example, the exemption is not available to a parent entity if it is a disclosing entity.

Same type of entity – same tier				
Ultimate or Intermediate Parent	FP – Tier 1	FP – Tier 2	NFP – Tier 1	NFP – Tier 2
Parent	FP – Tier 1	FP – Tier 2	NFP – Tier 1	NFP – Tier 2
Exemption	Available*	Available	Available	Available

Same type of entity – different tier				
Ultimate or Intermediate Parent	FP – Tier 1	FP – Tier 2	NFP – Tier 1	NFP – Tier 2
Parent	FP – Tier 2	FP – Tier 1	NFP – Tier 2	NFP – Tier 1
Exemption	Available*	Not available	Available	Not available

Different type of entity – same tier				
Ultimate or Intermediate Parent	FP – Tier 1	FP – Tier 2	NFP – Tier 1	NFP – Tier 2
Parent	NFP – Tier 1	NFP – Tier 2	FP – Tier 1	FP – Tier 2
Exemption	Available*	Available	Not available^	Available

Different type of entity – different tier				
Ultimate or Intermediate Parent	FP – Tier 1	FP – Tier 2	NFP – Tier 1	NFP – Tier 2
Parent	NFP – Tier 2	NFP – Tier 1	FP – Tier 2	FP – Tier 1
Exemption	Available*	Not available	Available	Not available

FP = For-profit entity
NFP = Not-for-profit entity
*   The exemption would not be available by reference to the intermediate parent when it is a for-profit public sector entity unable to claim compliance with IFRSs – see paragraph Aus16.2 of AASB 101 *Presentation of Financial Statements*.

^   When the parent entity's NFP ultimate or intermediate parent is able to claim compliance with IFRSs, the exemption is available.

Australian Accounting Standards consist of two tiers of reporting requirements for preparing general purpose financial statements:
(a)   Tier 1: Australian Accounting Standards; and

(b)   Tier 2: Australian Accounting Standards – Reduced Disclosure Requirements.

COMPILATION DETAILS

Accounting Standard AASB 10 *Consolidated Financial Statements* as amended

Compilation details are not part of AASB 10.

This compiled Standard applies to annual periods beginning on or after 1 January 2022. It takes into account amendments up to and including 12 December 2017 and was prepared on 20 April 2018 by the staff of the Australian Accounting Standards Board (AASB).

This compilation is not a separate Accounting Standard made by the AASB. Instead, it is a representation of AASB 10 (July 2015) as amended by other Accounting Standards, which are listed in the Table below.

Table of Standards

Standard	Date made	FRLI identifier	Commencement date	Effective date (*annual periods ... on or after ...*)	Application, saving or transitional provisions
AASB 10	24 July 2015	F2015L01617	30 Jun 2016	(*beginning*) 1 Jul 2016	see (a) below
AASB 2015-10	22 Dec 2015	F2016L00035	31 Dec 2015	(*beginning*) 1 Jan 2016	see (b) below
AASB 2017-5	12 Dec 2017	F2018L00067	31 Dec 2017	(*beginning*) 1 Jan 2018	see (c) below

(a) Entities may elect to apply this Standard to annual periods beginning on or after 1 January 2014 but before 1 July 2016, provided that AASB 11 *Joint Arrangements*, AASB 12 *Disclosure of Interests in Other Entities*, AASB 127 *Separate Financial Statements* and AASB 128 *Investments in Associates and Joint Ventures* are also applied to such periods.

(b) AASB 2015-10 defers the effective date of certain requirements included in AASB 10 to annual periods beginning on or after 1 January 2018 instead of 1 July 2016. Entities may elect to apply this Standard to annual periods beginning before 1 January 2016. Entities may elect to apply the deferred requirements to annual periods beginning on or after 1 January 2014 but before 1 January 2018.

(c) AASB 2017-5 defers the effective date of certain requirements included in AASB 10 to annual periods beginning on or after 1 January 2022 instead of 1 January 2018. Entities may elect to apply this Standard to annual periods beginning before 1 January 2018. Entities may elect to apply the deferred requirements to annual periods beginning on or after 1 January 2014 but before 1 January 2022.

Table of amendments

Paragraph affected	How affected	By ... [paragraph]
25-26	amended (for certain periods)	AASB 2015-10 [8]
	amended (for certain periods)	AASB 2017-5 [6]
B99A	deleted (for certain periods)	AASB 2015-10 [8]
	deleted (for certain periods)	AASB 2017-5 [6]
C1C	deleted (for certain periods)	AASB 2015-10 [8]
	amended	AASB 2015-10 [9, 10]
	deleted (for certain periods)	AASB 2017-5 [6]
	amended	AASB 2017-5 [7, 8]

DELETED IFRS 10 TEXT

Deleted IFRS 10 text is not part of AASB 10.

C1A *Consolidated Financial Statements, Joint Arrangements and Disclosure of Interests in Other Entities: Transition Guidance* (Amendments to IFRS 10, IFRS 11 and IFRS

12), issued in June 2012, amended paragraphs C2–C6 and added paragraphs C2A–C2B, C4A–C4C, C5A and C6A–C6B. An entity shall apply those amendments for annual periods beginning on or after 1 January 2013. If an entity applies IFRS 10 for an earlier period, it shall apply those amendments for that earlier period.

C1B   *Investment Entities* (Amendments to IFRS 10, IFRS 12 and IAS 27), issued in October 2012, amended paragraphs 2, 4, C2A, C6A and Appendix A and added paragraphs 27–33, B85A–B85W, B100–B101 and C3A–C3F. An entity shall apply those amendments for annual periods beginning on or after 1 January 2014. Early application is permitted. If an entity applies those amendments earlier, it shall disclose that fact and apply all amendments included in *Investment Entities* at the same time.

C8   This IFRS supersedes the requirements relating to consolidated financial statements in IAS 27 (as amended in 2008).

C9   This IFRS also supersedes SIC-12 *Consolidation—Special Purpose Entities*.

BASIS FOR CONCLUSIONS ON AASB 2011-5 AND AASB 2011-6

This Basis for Conclusions accompanies, but is not part of, AASB 10. The Basis for Conclusions was originally published with AASB 2011-6 Amendments to Australian Accounting Standards – Extending Relief from Consolidation, the Equity Method and Proportionate Consolidation – Reduced Disclosure Requirements.

Introduction

BC1   This Basis for Conclusions summarises the Australian Accounting Standards Board's considerations in reaching the conclusions in AASB 2011-5 *Amendments to Australian Accounting Standards – Extending Relief from Consolidation, the Equity Method and Proportionate Consolidation* and AASB 2011-6 *Amendments to Australian Accounting Standards – Extending Relief from Consolidation, the Equity Method and Proportionate Consolidation – Reduced Disclosure Requirements*. Individual Board members gave greater weight to some factors than to others.

Background

BC2   Paragraph 10 of AASB 127 *Consolidated and Separate Financial Statements* (in common with IAS 27 *Consolidated and Separate Financial Statements*) provides relief from preparing consolidated financial statements for parents that meet four criteria, including having an ultimate parent or an intermediate parent that prepares IFRS-compliant consolidated financial statements (paragraph 10(d)).

BC3   Due to the addition of Aus paragraphs in IFRSs as adopted in Australia, the financial statements of some entities applying Australian Accounting Standards are not IFRS compliant. This means that a parent that has an ultimate parent or other intermediate parent that prepares non-IFRS-compliant consolidated financial statements does not have access to the exemption from consolidation provided in paragraph 10 of AASB 127, even if the criteria in paragraphs 10(a) to 10(c) are met.

BC4   Similarly, investors need not apply the equity method when they meet the four criteria in paragraph 13(c) of AASB 128 *Investments in Associates* and venturers need not apply proportionate consolidation or the equity method when they meet the four criteria in paragraph 2(c) of AASB 131 *Interests in Joint Ventures*. The criteria in paragraph 10 of AASB 127, paragraph 13(c) of AASB 128 and paragraph 2(c) of AASB 131 are similar.

BC5   Consequently, the exemptions from the equity method and proportionate consolidation are also not available under those paragraphs to an investor or a venturer when its ultimate parent or intermediate parent prepares non-IFRS-compliant consolidated financial statements.

BC6 The AASB issued Exposure Draft ED 205 *Extending Relief from Consolidation, the Equity Method and Proportionate Consolidation* in September 2010. The AASB considered the submissions received from constituents and confirmed the principal approach proposed in the Exposure Draft.

New Zealand approach

BC7 During its development of ED 205, the AASB noted that a related issue was considered by the Financial Reporting Standards Board (FRSB) of the New Zealand Institute of Chartered Accountants in December 2008. This concerned the requirement in paragraph 10(d) of NZ IAS 27 *Consolidated and Separate Financial Statements* that the parent's financial statements must be 'available for public use'. Due to the reporting requirements in New Zealand, not all entities are required to file their financial statements with the Companies Office. Hence, when a parent of a group is not required to submit its financial statements, any intermediate subsidiaries were unable to use the paragraph 10 exemption. As a result, the FRSB inserted paragraph NZ 3.1 into NZ IAS 27 so that entities that qualify for differential reporting concessions were not required to comply with paragraph 10(d). In order to qualify for the exemption not to present consolidated financial statements, qualifying entities were still required to comply with all the other conditions in paragraph 10.

BC8 In addition, the AASB noted that the FRSB had inserted a similar exemption into NZ IAS 28 *Investments in Associates* (paragraph NZ 1.2) and NZ IAS 31 *Interests in Joint Ventures* (paragraph NZ 1.1), extending the relief from application of the equity method by investors and proportionate consolidation or the equity method by venturers.

BC9 The AASB did not follow the FRSB's specific approach for qualifying entities, given the different issues faced by the two Boards and the different financial reporting framework in New Zealand, including its differential reporting framework that involves modifications to the recognition and measurement requirements of IFRSs.

Extending the exemptions

BC10 The AASB considered the limitations on the exemptions and developed a view that relief from consolidation, the equity method and proportionate consolidation should be extended to a not-for-profit or Tier 2 parent, investor or venturer if it:

(a) has a parent higher up in the group that prepares consolidated financial statements (whether or not IFRS-compliant) that are available for public use and:

    (i) those consolidated financial statements incorporate the information that would otherwise have been presented in the parent's consolidated financial statements or the investor's or venturer's financial statements; or

    (ii) the parent, investor or venturer is an entity complying with Australian Accounting Standards – Reduced Disclosure Requirements ('Tier 2'); and

(b) meets the criteria in paragraphs 10(a) to 10(c) of AASB 127, paragraphs 13(c)(i) to 13(c)(iii) of AASB 128 or paragraphs 2(c)(i) to 2(c)(iii) of AASB 131, as relevant.

BC11 This view is based on the principle that financial statement users would be able to satisfy their information needs through the consolidated financial statements prepared by the parent higher up in the group. However, the AASB decided that such relief should not be available in relation to the General Government Sector (GGS) of each Federal, State and Territory Government due to the unique circumstances related to the GGS, its relationship to the whole of government and its macro-economic significance. The AASB also decided that the partial consolidation basis for GGS financial statements required by AASB 1049 *Whole of Government and General Government Sector Financial Reporting* would not be amended.

BC12 Consistent with IAS 27, IAS 28 *Investments in Associates* and IAS 31 *Interests in Joint Ventures*, the AASB decided that the existing relief provided under paragraph 10 of AASB 127, paragraph 13(c) of AASB 128 and paragraph 2(c) of AASB 131 should be retained. The extension of relief on the basis set out in paragraph BC10 does not change the present requirements for relief when the ultimate or intermediate parent is a for-profit Tier 1 entity – that entity is still required to prepare IFRS-compliant consolidated financial statements.

Not-for-profit ultimate or intermediate parent

BC13 When the ultimate or intermediate parent is a not-for-profit Tier 1 entity, and the parent, investor or venturer is a for-profit Tier 1 entity, the relief is not available where there are differences in the basis of accounting between the not-for-profit and for-profit entities as a result of the not-for-profit entity applying Standards or Aus paragraphs that contain requirements that are inconsistent with IFRS requirements. Extending relief to the for-profit Tier 1 parent, investor or venturer in this case would be beyond the scope of the relief available under IFRSs. However, the relief is available when the not-for-profit entity is not required to apply such inconsistent requirements. This is indicated by footnote to the table in paragraph AG1 of the Australian application guidance added to AASB 127. In this case, the for-profit Tier 1 entity would be able to claim compliance with IFRSs in that the relief is within the scope of the relief available under IFRSs.

BC14 The AASB considered the extension of relief to a for-profit Tier 2 parent, investor or venturer that has a not-for-profit ultimate or intermediate parent. The table in the Basis for Conclusions in ED 205 proposed that relief should be available to a parent, investor or venturer in these circumstances, which appears to be inconsistent with the circumstances addressed in paragraph BC13. The AASB considered three approaches to addressing the apparent inconsistency:

(a)   amend the table proposed in ED 205 to indicate that the relief would not be available;

(b)   retain the approach proposed in ED 205, that the relief would be available, and extend the justification in the Basis for Conclusions for this position; or

(c)   retain the approach proposed in ED 205 with no amendment to the justification.

BC15 The AASB adopted the approach in paragraph BC14(b), extending the relief, based on its judgement that the relief would be reasonable for Tier 2 parents, investors or venturers despite any differences in the basis of accounting in the consolidated financial statements of the ultimate or intermediate parent that are publicly available. Typically, the not-for-profit ultimate or intermediate parent would not be able to claim compliance with IFRSs, and the Tier 2 parent, investor or venturer could not do so.

For-profit public sector entities

BC16 The AASB decided that relief would not be available to a parent entity merely because the intermediate parent preparing consolidated financial statements is a for-profit Tier 1 public sector entity unable to claim compliance with IFRSs. This decision was made on the basis that a for-profit public sector entity may apply requirements in particular Standards, such as AASB 1004 Contributions, and Aus paragraphs in other Australian Accounting Standards that are inconsistent with an IFRS requirement. However, relief may be available to the parent entity on another basis permitted by the Standard.

BC17 Relief is (or is not) available to a for-profit public sector entity as the parent, investor or venturer on the same basis as for any other for-profit parent, investor or venturer.

Other changes

BC18 The AASB also decided that, consistent with paragraph 10(d) of AASB 127, the references to 'Australian equivalents to IFRSs' in paragraph 13(c)(iv) of AASB 128 and paragraph 2(c)(iv) of AASB 131 should be amended to 'International Financial Reporting Standards'.

BC19 The AASB decided to include the summary table set out in the Basis for Conclusions in the Exposure Draft as Australian application guidance accompanying, but not part of, the amended AASB 127. Whereas the table in the Exposure Draft addressed relief in relation to both not-for-profit entities and entities applying reduced disclosure requirements under AASB 1053 *Application of Tiers of Australian Accounting Standards*, the table added to the AASB 127 guidance by AASB 2011-5 addresses not-for-profit entities but not reduced disclosure requirements.

Reduced disclosure requirements

BC20 Exposure Draft ED 205, in addition to addressing relief for not-for-profit entities, also proposed the extension of relief to entities applying Australian Accounting Standards – Reduced Disclosure Requirements under AASB 1053. The AASB decided that relief should be extended to Tier 2 entities, either on the same basis as for not-for-profit entities or as addressed in paragraphs BC14 and BC15. Accounting Standard AASB 2011-6 provides this relief. That Standard also expands the table in the Australian application guidance accompanying AASB 127 to address entities applying reduced disclosure requirements.

BC21 Whereas AASB 2011-5 applies to annual reporting periods beginning on or after 1 July 2011, AASB 2011-6 applies to annual reporting periods beginning on or after 1 July 2013, being the application date of the reduced disclosure requirements under AASB 1053. Accordingly, two amending Standards were prepared to reflect the different application dates. Early application of each Standard is permitted. Early application of AASB 2011-6 requires early application of AASB 1053.

BASIS FOR CONCLUSIONS ON AASB 2013-5 AND DISSENTING VIEWS

This Basis for Conclusions accompanies, but is not part of, AASB 10. The Basis for Conclusions was originally published with AASB 2013-5 Amendments to Australian Accounting Standards – Investment Entities.

BC1 This Basis for Conclusions summarises the Australian Accounting Standards Board's (AASB) considerations in issuing AASB 2013-5 *Amendments to Australian Accounting Standard – Investment Entities*. Individual Board members gave greater weight to some factors than to others.

Background

BC2 AASB 2013-5 is the result of the AASB's due process, which began when the AASB issued Exposure Draft ED 220 *Investment Entities* (AASB ED 220) in September 2011 (incorporating International Accounting Standards Board [IASB] ED/2011/4 *Investment Entities*). That Exposure Draft proposed that an investment entity be required to account for investees that it controls at fair value through profit or loss, rather than consolidate them.

BC3 In the material accompanying ED 220, AASB members expressed concerns with the ED/2011/4 proposals, including:

(a) the exception to consolidation goes against the application of the well-established accounting concept of control, which is designed to result in the presentation of all the assets, liabilities, income and expenses of the group, and the amendments would result in a loss of relevant information for users of financial statements;

(b)   the basis of the exception to consolidation is the type of entity, rather than the underlying relationship between investors and investees; and

(c)   there are no clear principles underpinning the classification of entities as investment entities and the criteria for identifying investment entities are rule-based and open to opportunistic behaviour.

BC4   As evident from the responses to ED 220, views were divided among Australian constituents. Some expressed concerns similar to those of the AASB members. However, others expressed broad support for requiring some types of entities to account for controlled investees at fair value through profit or loss, rather than having them consolidate such entities.

BC5   The AASB expressed its concerns in its submission to the IASB on IASB ED/2011/4.

BC6   In October 2012, the IASB amended IFRS 10 *Consolidated Financial Statements*, IFRS 12 *Disclosures of Interest in Other Entities* and IAS 27 *Separate Financial Statements* for investment entities to provide an exception to consolidating particular subsidiaries for investment entities, requiring them instead to measure their investments in unconsolidated subsidiaries at fair value through profit or loss.

BC7   The AASB noted that its concerns with the ED/2011/4 proposals were not adequately addressed in the IASB amendments. The AASB also considered the disclosures required by the IASB amendments and noted that they require an investment entity to provide information about the exception to consolidation rather than addressing the loss of consolidation information that preparing a complete set of consolidated general purpose financial statements would provide.

BC8   Because of its concerns with the IASB amendments, the AASB decided to undertake further due process. After considering a number of different possible approaches to the recognition and measurement of controlled investees of investment entities, including (i) consolidation and (ii) fair value measurement with compensating disclosures, the AASB issued ED 233 *Australian Additional Disclosures – Investment Entities* in December 2012. It proposed to introduce the exception to consolidation for investment entities (as per the IASB amendments) and to require Australian additional disclosures for Australian entities that meet the IASB's investment entity criteria. The Australian additional disclosures proposed in ED 233 were in the form of:

•   consolidated financial statements prepared in a manner consistent with the definition of consolidated financial statements in Appendix A of AASB 10 *Consolidated Financial Statements*; and

•   a summary of the significant accounting policies used in preparing those consolidated financial statements that are not otherwise disclosed in accordance with AASB 101 *Presentation of Financial Statements*.

BC9   ED 233 also specifically asked respondents whether they have any alternative approaches/disclosure strategies that can be employed to minimise the adverse impact on the decision-making of the loss of consolidation information.

BC10 The AASB received 29 submissions on ED 233. The vast majority of respondents did not support the proposed Australian additional disclosures. These respondents expressed support for introducing the IASB amendments without Australian additional disclosures.

BC11 The AASB staff also conducted targeted outreach with users of financial statements and the limited feedback received indicated that if there were to be Australian additional disclosures required, an example of the information that would be relevant is information about the earnings and liabilities of subsidiaries of investment entities.

AASB deliberations on adopting the IASB amendments in Australia without Australian additional disclosures

BC12 The AASB considered three main approaches to introducing the IASB amendments for investment entities in Australia:

A.   issue the IASB amendments without Australian additional disclosures;

B.   issue the IASB amendments with Australian additional disclosures as proposed in AASB ED 233; and

C.   issue the IASB amendments with Australian additional disclosures that are reduced compared with the ED 233 proposals, in particular, disclosures about an unconsolidated subsidiary's total assets, total liabilities and total comprehensive income.

BC13 The AASB considered and rejected the approach of not adopting the IASB's amendments for Australian investment entities as this would result in Australian investment entities not being able to assert IFRS compliance, an outcome that would be contrary to the AASB's policy of having "... Tier 1 for-profit entities being IFRS compliant"[2].

BC14 The majority of AASB members expressed a preference for, or could at least accept, Approach A, consistent with the AASB's policy of IFRS adoption. Some members consider that the fair value of controlled entities can arguably be regarded as more relevant for users of financial statements of investment entities than consolidation information. Some other members consider that the IASB's criteria for determining investment entities lack rigour and could lead to inconsistent application. However, on balance, the majority of members are willing to accept, in the absence of evidence to the contrary, that the IASB amendments, including the disclosures required of investment entities in accordance with IFRS 12, would be sufficient to meet the needs of users of financial statements of investment entities, consistent with the feedback received from the vast majority of the respondents to ED 233.

BC15 This majority of AASB members could not accept Approach C as there was insufficient feedback from users to suggest that the reduced disclosures proposed in Approach C would be useful. Those AASB members did not think it appropriate to delay adoption while further input from users is sought.

BC16 The AASB noted the wide range of arguments put forward by respondents to ED 233 for favouring Approach A including the view that fair value information is most relevant for investors of investment entities in many circumstances; and the cost to Australian preparers of financial statements compared with other jurisdictions of providing Australian additional disclosures. However, despite accepting Approach A, the AASB did not accept all of those arguments. In particular, the AASB did not accept the arguments that requiring Australian additional disclosures would reduce comparability (as distinct from uniformity) between Australian investment entities and their international counterparts or would lead to the perception that Australian investment entities are not IFRS compliant.

BC17 On balance, the AASB decided to adopt Approach A. This was on the basis that the AASB would monitor the implementation of the IASB amendments for Australian investment entities. This would include monitoring the disclosures made in accordance with AASB 12 *Disclosure of Interests in Other Entities* and AASB 101 *Presentation of Financial Statements* paragraph 17(c)[3]. Such monitoring, which may be via a post-implementation review, would be undertaken with a view to potentially adding Australian additional disclosure requirements at a later stage, if it were to become evident that additional disclosures are warranted, noting that such disclosures might be different from those proposed in ED 233 or Approach C. Monitoring might also lead

---

2   AASB Policy Statement *Policies and Processes* March 2011, paragraph 7

3   AASB 101 paragraph 17(c) requires an entity to provide additional disclosures when compliance with the specific requirements in Australian Accounting Standards is insufficient to enable users to understand the impact of particular transactions, other events and conditions on the entity's financial position and financial performance.

to the AASB deciding to write to the IASB, informing it of the findings and concerns arising from the Australian experience.

GAAP/GFS harmonisation

BC18   In adopting Approach A, the AASB considered whether there would be any GAAP/GFS harmonisation implications that it would need to address in the context of AASB 1049 *Whole of Government and General Government Sector Financial Reporting*. The AASB noted that no such implications are expected to arise because, although the whole of government or general government sector might be a parent of an investment entity, the whole of government and general government sector would not themselves be investment entities.

Application to Tier 2

BC19   The AASB noted that the way in which the IASB has defined an investment entity (including that such an entity need not have more than one investor) could result in there being investment entities that do not have public accountability as defined in Appendix A of AASB 1053 *Application of Tiers of Australian Accounting Standards* and are therefore eligible to present Tier 2 general purpose financial statements.

BC20   In addition, the AASB considered the entities listed in Appendix B of AASB 1053 that are deemed to have public accountability. Whilst many investment entities would fall within the list of deemed entities, there could be a number of investment entities that would not be captured – for example, managed investment schemes that are investment entities but are not registered and therefore, again potentially eligible to present Tier 2 general purpose financial statements.

BC21   The AASB conducted due process on whether Tier 2 investment entities should be provided with any relief from the disclosures required by the IASB amendments through ED 220.

BC22   After considering constituent feedback, the AASB decided the disclosures in the IASB amendments for investment entities should be applied to both Tier 1 and Tier 2 investment entities as it considers those disclosures to be fundamental to the needs of users in decision-making. Accordingly, the AASB decided that it would not be appropriate to exempt those investment entities from any of the disclosures in the IASB amendments.

Dissenting views

Dissent of Peter Gibson, Jayne Godfrey, John O'Grady and Kevin M. Stevenson

DO1   In our opinion the exception to consolidation for investment entities that requires controlled investees to be measured at fair value through profit or loss rather than being consolidated is a violation of the basic principle that an entity should account for all of its assets, liabilities, income and expenses.

DO2   At the most fundamental level we do not see the provision of fair value information for investments as a substitute for, or an alternative to, consolidated information. Without the detailed consideration of that part of the financial position and financial performance of an entity represented by its controlled entities, fair value movements would not be sufficient for decision-making and offset too much information into a single line item.

DO3   We regard the exception as fundamentally based on a view that an entity's business model should determine accounting treatments. However, we do not believe that an entity's business model should drive how it accounts for its controlled investees. In our opinion, the business model approach and the IASB's criteria for determining investment entities, which we believe lack rigour, will lead to uncertainty in application and inconsistency of reporting between similar entities. This approach also has the potential to promote structuring opportunities to avoid consolidation. In turn, this would be to the detriment of providing useful, comparable information to users of financial statements.

DO4 We believe that providing exceptions to principles further complicates accounting, introduces unjustified complexity to financial statements and reduces comparability of entities' financial reports across sectors. It also creates a precedent for further, less rigorous standard-setting.

DO5 For Australia, the exception to consolidation would require de-consolidation of controlled entities when Australia has been well-served by the control principle and has been relatively free of criticism of off-balance-sheet accounting.

DO6 Additionally, we have not heard from users of financial statements of investment entities in Australia that consolidation information is not useful or relevant for decision-making.

DO7 Furthermore, if the fair values of controlled investments held by investment entities are relevant, we are of the view that they could be provided as supplementary disclosures in financial statements, consistent with the disclosure requirements in AASB 7 Financial Instruments: Disclosures for financial instruments with carrying amounts that differ from their fair value.

BASIS FOR CONCLUSIONS ON AASB 2013-8

This Basis for Conclusions accompanies, but is not part of, AASB 10. The Basis for Conclusions was originally published with AASB 2013-8 Amendments to Australian Accounting Standards – Australian Implementation Guidance for Not-for-Profit Entities – Control and Structured Entities.

Background

BC1 This Basis for Conclusions summarises the Australian Accounting Standards Board's considerations in reaching the conclusions in this Standard. Individual Board members gave greater weight to some factors than to others.

BC2 Before finalising the implementation guidance set out in this Standard, the Board issued Exposure Draft ED 238 *Consolidated Financial Statements – Australian Implementation Guidance for Not-for-Profit Entities* in March 2013. ED 238 proposed for public comment implementation guidance for not-for-profit entities in respect of both AASB 10 *Consolidated Financial Statements* and AASB 12 *Disclosure of Interests in Other Entities*. The Board considered the submissions received in response to ED 238 in deciding the implementation guidance to be added to those Standards.

BC3 In the process of developing the proposals in ED 238, the Board commissioned research into the implementation issues that had been encountered by not-for-profit entities in applying the notion of control (and related public sector guidance) in the superseded Accounting Standard AASB 127 *Consolidated and Separate Financial Statements*. Discussions were also held with constituents experienced in not-for-profit public sector and private sector financial reporting, to ascertain implementation issues that might be encountered in applying AASB 10 (which replaces AASB 127, in part) in a not-for-profit context. Based on the research findings and the nature of many of the issues identified, the Board concluded that the principles in AASB 10 could be applied in a not-for-profit context, albeit using professional judgement, and that certain aspects of those principles and the terminology adopted warranted specific implementation guidance for not-for-profit entities.

BC4 In addition, the Board noted that some of the issues identified through the research are fundamental to the notion of control and therefore beyond the scope of AASB 10. These issues include:

(a)   the nature of government departments as reporting entities;

(b)   the role that disclosure of disaggregated information in whole of government financial reports might play in providing relevant information to users; and

(c)   control of assets.

BC5   The Board concluded that, because they are beyond the scope of AASB 10 and would not impede the application of AASB 10 by not-for-profit entities, these issues do not need to be addressed prior to clarifying for not-for-profit entities the application of the notion of control in AASB 10. The Board noted that this approach is consistent with its policy of transaction neutrality. Accordingly, the Board decided to progress its Control in the Not-for-Profit Public and Private Sectors project in stages. The first stage, completed by the issue of this Standard, is intended to clarify the application of AASB 10 (and AASB 12) in a not-for-profit context. It is expected that later stages will address the associated fundamental issues noted above.

BC6   The Board also noted the current project of the International Public Sector Accounting Standards Board (IPSASB) to update its consolidation, joint ventures and associates Standards for the issuance of IFRS 10 *Consolidated Financial Statements* and its related IFRSs. The IPSASB published its Exposure Drafts in October 2013, but the AASB decided to finalise the implementation guidance for AASB 10 and AASB 12, having considered the decisions of the IPSASB as it developed its Exposure Drafts.

BC7   Since the implementation guidance does not change or depart from the principles in AASB 10, the types of harmonisation differences between AASB 10 and the ABS GFS Manual are not affected by the guidance. Accordingly, pre-existing GAAP/GFS differences were not addressed in ED 238.

BC8   The remainder of this Basis for Conclusions outlines the basis for the Board's decisions relating to the first stage of the project.

Significant issues

Nature and location of guidance relating to AASB 10

BC9   The Board considered whether the implementation guidance to be added to AASB 10 should be integrated into the body of that Standard as Aus paragraphs. The Board decided that, in general, consistent with a principles-based approach to drafting Standards, Aus paragraphs in the body of the Standard should be limited to those that either amend the requirements in AASB 10 or add new requirements. As the implementation guidance neither amends the requirements nor adds new requirements for not-for-profit entities, the Board decided that the guidance should not be presented as Aus paragraphs within the body of AASB 10. However, the Board decided to include one Aus paragraph in the body of the Standard as a signpost to the implementation guidance.

BC10   The Board then considered whether the guidance should be presented as Aus paragraphs located throughout the existing Application Guidance (Appendix B to AASB 10) or as a separate attachment to AASB 10. As Appendix B is integral to AASB 10 and therefore has the same authority as the other parts of the Standard, Aus paragraphs in Appendix B should also be limited to those that either amend the requirements in AASB 10 or add new requirements. Accordingly, the Board applied the same approach as stated in paragraph BC9 and decided to add the not-for-profit entity implementation guidance to AASB 10 as an attachment rather than as Aus paragraphs within Appendix B.

BC11   The implementation guidance is attached to AASB 10 as Appendix E. The Appendix is integral to the Standard and thus has the same authority as the body and other appendices of the Standard. The Board considered whether the guidance should merely accompany, and not be part of, AASB 10. To facilitate the guidance being applied consistently by not-for-profit entities, the Board decided to make the guidance integral to AASB 10.

BC12 The Appendix added to AASB 10 is labelled as Appendix E, to be consistent with the labelling of the appendices to IFRS 10 *Consolidated Financial Statements*. In IFRS 10, Appendix D consists of the consequential amendments to other Standards and Interpretations arising from the issuance of IFRS 10. AASB 10 does not have any Appendix D since those consequential amendments were made in AASB 2011-7 *Amendments to Australian Accounting Standards arising from the Consolidation and Joint Arrangements Standards* (August 2011), following the Board's practice of making amendments via separate Standards rather than through appendices to Standards.

Terminology in AASB 10

BC13 As AASB 10 incorporates IFRS 10, issued by the International Accounting Standards Board (IASB), the text of the body of AASB 10 and Appendices A–C is expressed from the perspective of for-profit entities in the private sector. The Board considered that some of the terminology in the Standard does not readily translate to a not-for-profit perspective and decided that it would be useful to explain that terminology for application in a not-for-profit context, rather than revise the terminology in some way for not-for-profit entities. The terms 'investor' and 'investee', for example, figure prominently in AASB 10, including in the definition of control, and are described in general terms in paragraph IG3 of Appendix E for AASB 10. The nature of 'returns', as another example, is also addressed in the implementation guidance. The Board believes the explanations provided will assist a not-for-profit entity to better relate to and apply the requirements of AASB 10.

Implementation guidance on control

BC14 In developing the implementation guidance, including some comprehensive examples, the Board sought to address the implementation issues that were identified in the research referred to in paragraph BC3 on the application of the notion of control by not-for-profit entities in the private and public sectors. For example, the guidance addresses rights arising from statutory arrangements (paragraphs IG6–IG7), economic dependence (paragraphs IG11–IG12), regulatory powers (paragraphs IG16–IG17), indirect returns (or benefits) to not-for-profit entities and congruent objectives (paragraphs IG18–IG20), and delegated power (paragraphs IG21–IG24).

BC15 The Board did not include implementation guidance in respect of some topics covered by AASB 10 due to the Board's assessment that the issues arise similarly for both for-profit entities and not-for-profit entities. For example, the requirements regarding de facto agents and control of specified assets raise issues in practice for any entity, not just not-for-profit entities.

Examples

BC16 To illustrate the requirements of AASB 10, the implementation guidance includes examples within guidance paragraphs as well as five discrete, comprehensive examples. The examples refer to particular types of not-for-profit entities, some in the private sector and others in the public sector. However, the Board intended that the examples apply by analogy to other types of not-for-profit entities and similar circumstances as relevant, rather than being limited to the specific cases presented.

BC17 The comprehensive examples emphasise a principles-based approach, which requires an analysis of the relevant activities of the investee and of the substantive rights of various investors in considering whether the investor has power (as that term is used in AASB 10) over the investee. The Board noted that it could be difficult to distinguish substantive rights from protective rights held by an investor in relation to an investee. Therefore, the Board decided to note in the introduction to the comprehensive examples that distinguishing substantive and protective rights requires analysis of the circumstances, including considering the reasons for different investors holding various rights in relation to the investee. The Board also decided to include a range of scenarios in most of the comprehensive examples to illustrate that alternative outcomes for the assessment of control by the investor reflect the facts and circumstances in any particular case.

BC18 The Board included specific comprehensive examples in respect of a local government (Example IG3) and a university (Example IG4), given the anticipated uncertainty in respect of how AASB 10 might apply in determining whether such entities are controlled by another entity. Two scenarios under which different control conclusions might be drawn are presented in the university example, whereas the local government example includes only one case, in which it is concluded that the local government is not controlled by another government. The Board took the view that this would be the normal outcome in relation to local governments under current arrangements in Australia, but noted in paragraph IG8 and at the end of Example IG3 that the assessment of whether a local government is controlled by another government would depend on the particular facts and circumstances.

BC19 Given the types of arrangements often found in the public sector, the Board also decided that an example concerning delegated powers and agency relationships affecting public sector entities would be useful guidance. Example IG5 presents two scenarios regarding whether a government department controls a statutory authority. The example might be relevant in some jurisdictions but not in others.

Former guidance in superseded AASB 127

BC20 The Board reviewed the specific public sector guidance in the superseded AASB 127 *Consolidated and Separate Financial Statements* (paragraphs Aus17.1–Aus17.10) in the context of the three criteria for control set out in AASB 10: power, returns, and a link between power and returns. Some of the guidance in the superseded AASB 127 was not incorporated into Appendix E, on the grounds that the Board considered that it was either inconsistent with or beyond the scope of the requirements of AASB 10 or no longer necessary. The following paragraphs address the major aspects of the guidance in the superseded AASB 127.

BC21 Paragraph Aus17.1 stated that AASB 127 did not attempt to identify all groups and reporting entities in the public sector. Nevertheless, paragraph Aus17.5 described the nature of some reporting entities in the public sector. Paragraph Aus17.7 also discussed identifying economic entities in relation to Ministerial portfolios and functions with separate objectives. The Board decided that it was not appropriate to include these general statements in the implementation guidance since the nature of reporting entities in the public sector is a fundamental issue beyond the scope of AASB 10 (see paragraph BC4).

BC22 The statement in paragraph Aus17.2 that control of an entity by the government may be indicated by the accountability of the entity to the Parliament (or the Executive or a Minister) and by the government holding the residual financial interest in the net assets of the entity has not been incorporated into the implementation guidance. Accountability to the Parliament, the Executive or a Minister might or might not indicate that the government has substantive rights in relation to the entity, so the power criterion might not be satisfied. Holding the residual financial interest in the entity shows that the government has exposure or rights to variable returns from the entity, but does not indicate whether the government has the ability to use power over the entity to affect the government's returns. Consequently, these two factors are insufficient to conclude whether an entity is controlled by the government.

BC23 Paragraph Aus17.3 listed circumstances that, individually or in combination, indicate that an entity is accountable to Parliament, the Executive or a Minister. The circumstances listed in paragraphs Aus17.3(a)–(d) are addressed in paragraphs B15 and IG9 in terms of rights that can give an investor power in relation to an investee. However, paragraph Aus17.3(e) has not been included in the implementation guidance because a requirement to submit reports to Parliament might reflect either protective or substantive rights, and hence is not useful as an indicator of power. Paragraph

Aus17.3(f) regarding an entity established through legislation has been updated and included in paragraph IG7.

BC24 Paragraph Aus17.4 listed circumstances that indicate whether a government has a residual financial interest in the net assets of another entity. These circumstances (exposure to residual liabilities and the right to receive residual net assets on dissolution of the entity) indicate that the government would be exposed to variable returns from the entity. These returns are covered by the investment returns noted in paragraph B57(a).

BC25 Paragraph Aus17.6 stated that a government will usually control statutory authorities that it has established through legislation. This circumstance has been addressed through paragraph IG7 in respect of whether the government has power over an entity established through legislation. Power is just one of the control criteria.

BC26 Restrictions on the allocation of funds between activities and the existence of separate administrations are listed in paragraph Aus17.7 as factors that may affect the ability of an entity to deploy resources and should be considered in determining the existence of a group in the public sector. The ability to deploy resources is relevant to assessing whether an investor has power over an investee (see paragraph IG5). Restrictions on the ability to deploy resources may reflect barriers that prevent the holder of rights from exercising them. Examples of barriers are listed in paragraph B23, including operational barriers and legal or regulatory requirements.

BC27 Paragraph Aus17.8 noted that for a government to control an entity, it must have the power to require the entity's assets to be deployed towards achieving the government's objectives, and listed various actions that the government might be able to direct in respect of the controlled entity's assets. Whether these circumstances result in the government controlling the entity under AASB 10 would depend on whether the government has power to direct the relevant activities of the entity. The actions listed are broadly consistent with the activities listed in paragraph B11 that can be relevant activities of an investee, depending on the circumstances of the investee.

BC28 Paragraph Aus17.9 outlined a range of circumstances in which a government does not control another entity, such as an entity dependent on government funding but able to decide whether to accept resources from the government and how to use the resources (paragraphs Aus17.9(a) and (c)). These examples are no longer needed as paragraphs IG11 and IG12 concerning economic dependence and paragraph IG20 in respect of congruent objectives adequately address the issues.

BC29 Paragraph Aus17.9(b) stated that a government acting as the trustee of a trust would not control the trust as it would not be able to deploy the resources of the trust for its own benefit. In contrast, the implementation guidance includes an example of a trust that is controlled through the trustee (paragraph IG22). Under AASB 10, the investor's returns from a trust may be indirect non-financial returns, which the former guidance did not acknowledge.

BC30 Regulatory powers were addressed in paragraph Aus17.9(d) as not giving rise to control of regulated entities. Paragraph IG16 states that regulatory powers may represent either substantive rights (which could result in control of regulated entities) or protective rights (which would not result in control). Examples of protective rights are included in paragraph IG17.

BC31 Paragraph Aus17.9(e) stated that under existing legislative arrangements, State and Territory governments do not control local governments. The Board reconsidered the question of control of local governments but did not reach a categoric view. As noted in paragraph BC18, the Board concluded that although a local government normally would not be controlled by another government under current arrangements, the assessment of whether a local government is controlled by another government would depend on the particular facts and circumstances (paragraph IG8). Example IG3 illustrates how a decision as to whether a local government is controlled by another government could be addressed.

BC32 The final paragraph in the former public sector guidance, paragraph Aus17.10, addressed government control of independent statutory offices such as auditors-general and the judiciary. The same examples have been incorporated into the implementation guidance in paragraph IG10, which addresses more particularly the organisations assisting the independent statutory office holders.

AASB 12 and structured entities

BC33 While considering issues regarding AASB 10, the Board noted that the definition of 'structured entity' in AASB 12 *Disclosure of Interests in Other Entities* does not readily translate to a not-for-profit perspective as it focusses on voting or similar rights, which have less significance in general for many not-for-profit entities. The Board decided to propose implementation guidance to assist not-for-profit entities in applying this definition. As AASB 12 applies to not-for-profit entities in conjunction with AASB 10, the Board included the proposals in the same Exposure Draft (ED 238).

BC34 After considering the submissions received on the ED, the Board decided to add implementation guidance as Appendix E to AASB 12, integral to the Standard and thus with the same authority as the body and other appendices of the Standard. These decisions reflect the decisions on the nature and location of guidance as set out in paragraphs BC9–BC12 in respect of the AASB 10 guidance.

BC35 The Board decided that the implementation guidance for AASB 12 should be based on the principle underlying the definition of structured entity, and identified that principle as limiting the scope of structured entities to entities that are controlled through less conventional means. This is based on the definition emphasising that voting or similar rights are not the dominant factor in deciding who controls a structured entity – and for for-profit entities, voting rights are a common or conventional means of determining control.

BC36 The Board identified administrative arrangements and statutory provisions (legislation) as common means by which control may be determined for many not-for-profit entities, particularly those in the public sector. Accordingly, the Board took the view that the reference to 'similar rights' in the definition of structured entity encompasses, for not-for-profit entities, administrative arrangements and statutory provisions. Thus, not-for-profit entities for which administrative arrangements or statutory provisions are dominant factors in determining control of the entity are not regarded as structured entities. Appendix E for AASB 12 includes a range of examples to illustrate this approach.

AASB 1049 amendments

BC37 AASB 1049 *Whole of Government and General Government Sector Financial Reporting* was not addressed in the consequential amendments arising from AASB 10 (and related Standards) that were included in AASB 2011-7 *Amendments to Australian Accounting Standards arising from the Consolidation and Joint Arrangements Standards* (August 2011), given that the Board intended to address the application of AASB 10 to not-for-profit entities through its Control in the Not-for-Profit Public and Private Sectors project. This Standard (AASB 2013-8) sets out the consequential amendments to AASB 1049 arising from AASB 10 and the related Standards. Most of these amendments are editorial.

BC38 The Board noted that paragraph 45 of AASB 1049 does not require the General Government Sector (GGS) financial statements to comply with any of the disclosure requirements of the superseded AASB 127 *Consolidated and Separate Financial Statements*. The Board reconsidered this position in respect of the disclosure requirements set out in AASB 12, and concluded that the GGS financial statements should not be required to comply with those requirements. This is effected through the amendments in this Standard to paragraph 45 of AASB 1049.

BC39 The Board took the view that the GGS financial statements need not be required to comply with the disclosure requirements of AASB 12 on the grounds that such disclosures would essentially duplicate AASB 12 disclosures in the whole of government financial statements. As entities included in the GGS financial statements are also included in the whole of government financial statements, the entities' association with structured entities could be addressed in either set of financial statements. The nature of the risks associated with interests in structured entities is unlikely to change between the GGS level and the whole of government level.

Main changes from the Exposure Draft

BC40 The main changes made by the Board to the implementation guidance proposed in ED 238 following consideration of respondents' comments are noted in the following paragraphs.

BC41 Some respondents considered that the major examples emphasised substantive and protective rights of various investors without adequately identifying the relevant activities of the investee and in some cases did not clearly apply the three criteria for control in coming to their conclusions. The Board agreed that the relevant activities of the investee should be addressed clearly, since an investor can have power over an investee only when it has substantive rights that give it the current ability to direct the relevant activities of the investee. The examples were amended accordingly, including addressing the control criteria more directly. Nevertheless, the Board retained the substantive and protective rights details in the examples, albeit with some reclassification, as part of the background information for the examples.

BC42 Of the four major examples proposed in the ED, three related specifically to public sector entities (local governments, universities, and government departments and authorities) and one to not-for-profit private sector entities (a religious organisation and an association). Some respondents requested additional not-for-profit private sector examples. The Board added a further major example (Example IG2) based on not-for-profit private sector entities (a charity and a company) and illustrating four scenarios. As stated in paragraph BC16, the Board also decided to note in the implementation guidance that the illustrative examples apply by analogy to types of not-for-profit entities other than those specifically identified in the examples and similar circumstances, as relevant (see paragraph IG3).

BC43 The ED proposed that rights specified in substantively enacted legislation could not give an investor the current ability to direct the relevant activities of an investee. This was questioned by some respondents, who compared substantive enactment of substantive rights with substantive rights that were exercisable only in the future. The Board reconsidered the issue and decided to change the guidance to acknowledge that in limited circumstances rights under substantively enacted legislation could become exercisable in time for making decisions about an investee's relevant activities. For example, the progression from substantively enacted legislation to enacted legislation may be merely a matter of the formal approval of the legislation by the Governor in Council within a limited timeframe.

BC44 Several respondents questioned whether the notion of delegation in the not-for-profit public sector was adequately reflected in the proposed example illustrating whether a government department controlled a statutory authority. The Board revised the example and paragraph IG24 to clarify that a delegate in the not-for-profit public sector is not an agent of the delegator. The Board also deleted references to 'delegated control' as it was not necessary to introduce a new term. The Board noted that the term 'delegation' has a narrower meaning in the not-for-profit public sector than its general usage in the Standard to denote an agent/principal relationship.

Issues raised but guidance not revised

BC45 The Board discussed a range of issues raised by respondents to ED 238 that did not lead to changes to the implementation guidance that had been proposed in the ED. The more significant such issues included requests for guidance concerning assessing the relative significance of the rights of different parties, a controlled local government scenario, collective control in the public sector, and the effect of removal rights in the public sector, and comments on the power to enact or change legislation.

BC46 Respondents noted the difficulty in many cases of identifying which investor has power over an investee when more than one investor is able to direct different relevant activities of the investee. The Board was asked to provide further guidance on how to identify which investor was able to direct the activities that most significantly affected the investee's returns. The Board concluded that it was not feasible to provide guidance for weighing the relative significance of different relevant activities since this would be subject to judgement in the context of the facts and circumstances in any particular case.

BC47 Some respondents to ED 238 noted that, unlike the other comprehensive examples, the local government example did not include an alternative scenario. The only scenario illustrated concluded that in the circumstances presented the local government was not controlled by the State government. Some respondents suggested that if it was not possible for a local government to be controlled by another government, then the guidance should state that. Other respondents suggested the addition of an alternative scenario so that the alternative control outcome would not be overlooked when the guidance was being applied. The Board decided that an alternative scenario was not required, since the proposed example already referred to the possibility of an alternative outcome (ie the local government being controlled by another government) in different circumstances or based on different judgements. The proposed implementation guidance also indicated that the assessment of whether a local government is controlled by another government would depend on the particular facts and circumstances. As noted in paragraph BC18, this approach has been retained in the implementation guidance.

BC48 The Board considered whether to extend the proposed example concerning whether a department controlled a statutory authority to address so-called collective rights at a whole of government level, under which a particular entity would be consolidated in the whole of government financial statements despite no individual entity or Minister in the jurisdiction being considered to control the particular entity. The Board decided not to extend the example on the basis that judgement would be required to determine in the circumstances whether the collective rights amounted to control at the whole of government level, with or without joint control by entities in the jurisdiction, or some other outcome.

BC49 The Board was asked to provide guidance regarding the implications of removal rights since, in the public sector, a government or a Minister will often have the right to dismiss key executives of public sector entities, such as the head of a department. The Board noted that the AASB 10 requirements relating to agency relationships and removal rights might be interpreted to imply that the key executives or their organisations act only as an agent of the government or Minister and therefore would be unable to control other entities. However, the Board considers that the requirements do not prevent intermediate parent entities from controlling other entities or preparing consolidated financial statements. For example, a department head is a part of the department, and a Minister's ability to remove the department head does not prevent the department from being able to control other entities. The Board concluded that specific implementation guidance was not required.

BC50 Some respondents questioned the position proposed in the ED that the power to enact or change legislation could not give an investor the current ability to direct the relevant activities of an investee. The Board affirmed this view for the implementation guidance (paragraph IG14). If the power to legislate were relevant to determining whether a government controlled other entities, then, subject to the constitutional reach of its powers, the government might be considered to control all of the entities in its jurisdiction (including private sector entities) since it could conceivably cause Parliament to pass legislation to enable it to direct the activities of any or all of those entities so as to achieve its economic and social objectives. However, the political and social barriers (see paragraph IG13) to passing such legislation mean that the government realistically would not have the ability to exercise such power, and thus the power would not represent substantive rights.

ACNC requirements

BC51 Some respondents to ED 238 commented that, in determining the application of AASB 10 to not-for-profit entities, the Board should have regard to the financial reporting requirements of the Australian Charities and Not-for-profits Commission (ACNC).

BC52 The Board considered the requirements for annual financial reports under the *Australian Charities and Not-for-profits Commission Act 2012* (ACNC Act) and the *Australian Charities and Not-for-profits Commission Regulation 2013* (ACNC Regulation), in particular Subdivisions 60-C 'Annual financial reports' and 60-G 'Collective and joint reporting' of the ACNC Act and Subdivisions 60-B 'Requirements for annual financial reports (core rules)' and 60-C 'Requirements for annual financial reports (special rules)' of the ACNC Regulation. For example, under joint reporting, two or more registered entities may be permitted to prepare and lodge a single financial report, which might or might not be consistent with the AASB 10 requirements for consolidated financial statements. Collective reporting would not be consistent with AASB 10.

BC53 The Board also noted that section 60.30 of the ACNC Regulation requires a registered entity to prepare a special purpose financial statement, if it is not required to and does not propose to prepare a general purpose financial statement. The Board's focus in setting accounting standards is on general purpose financial statements rather than special purpose financial statements.

BC54 The Board acknowledges that regulators might impose financial reporting requirements that differ from AASB Standards for their own regulatory purposes. The Board noted that the ACNC requirements would be expected to coincide with AASB Accounting Standards in most cases. However, the ACNC may permit registered entities to depart from AASB 10 in limited circumstances. The Board decided that it would not be appropriate for its requirements for general purpose financial statements to reflect those limited circumstances.

AASB 11
Joint Arrangements
(Reissued July 2015)

This note is not part of Accounting Standard AASB 11.

The following unincorporated amendments are not included in this Standard.

- AASB 2018-1 *Amendments to Australian Accounting Standards — Annual Improvements 2015–2017 Cycle*. This Standard makes amendments to AASB 3 *Business Combinations*, AASB 11 *Joint Arrangements*, AASB 112 *Income Taxes* and AASB 123 *Borrowing Costs*. These amendments arise from the issuance of IFRS *Annual Improvements to IFRS Standards 2015–2017 Cycle* by the IASB in December 2017. This Standard applies to annual periods beginning on or after 1 January 2019, but earlier application is permitted.

Entities early-adopting any amendments with later application dates will need to refer to the amending Standards that have not yet been incorporated into compilations. The abovementioned unincorporated amendments may be located on the AASB website at www.aasb.gov.au or on the Federal Register of Legislation website at www.legislation.gov.au.

CONTENTS

COMPARISON WITH IFRS 11
ACCOUNTING STANDARD
AASB 11 *JOINT ARRANGEMENTS*

APPENDICES
A. DEFINED TERMS
B. APPLICATION GUIDANCE
C. EFFECTIVE DATE, TRANSITION AND WITHDRAWAL OF OTHER IFRSs

                                    Chartered Accountants Australia and New Zealand

ILLUSTRATIVE EXAMPLES

DELETED IFRS 11 TEXT

INTRODUCTION TO IFRS 11 (available on the AASB website)

BASIS FOR CONCLUSIONS ON IFRS 11 (available on the AASB website)

Australian Accounting Standard AASB 11 *Joint Arrangements* is set out in paragraphs 1 – Aus27.2 and Appendices A – C. All the paragraphs have equal authority. Paragraphs in **bold type** state the main principles. Terms defined in Appendix A are in *italics* the first time they appear in the Standard. AASB 11 is to be read in the context of other Australian Accounting Standards, including AASB 1048 *Interpretation of Standards*, which identifies the Australian Accounting Interpretations, and AASB 1057 *Application of Australian Accounting Standards*. In the absence of explicit guidance, AASB 108 *Accounting Policies, Changes in Accounting Estimates and Errors* provides a basis for selecting and applying accounting policies.

COMPARISON WITH IFRS 11

AASB 11 *Joint Arrangements* incorporates IFRS 11 *Joint Arrangements* issued by the International Accounting Standards Board (IASB). Australian-specific paragraphs (which are not included in IFRS 11) are identified with the prefix "Aus". Paragraphs that apply only to not-for-profit entities begin by identifying their limited applicability.

Tier 1

For-profit entities complying with AASB 11 also comply with IFRS 11.

Not-for-profit entities' compliance with IFRS 11 will depend on whether any "Aus" paragraphs that specifically apply to not-for-profit entities provide additional guidance or contain applicable requirements that are inconsistent with IFRS 11.

AASB 1053 *Application of Tiers of Australian Accounting Standards* explains the two tiers of reporting requirements.

ACCOUNTING STANDARD AASB 11

The Australian Accounting Standards Board makes Accounting Standard AASB 11 *Joint Arrangements* under section 334 of the *Corporations Act 2001*.

Kris Peach

Dated 24 July 2015   Chair – AASB

ACCOUNTING STANDARD AASB 11
JOINT ARRANGEMENTS

Objective

1   **The objective of this Standard is to establish principles for financial reporting by entities that have an interest in arrangements that are controlled jointly (ie *joint arrangements*).**

Meeting the objective

2   To meet the objective in paragraph 1, this Standard defines *joint control* and requires an entity that is a *party to a joint arrangement* to determine the type of joint arrangement in which it is involved by assessing its rights and obligations and to account for those rights and obligations in accordance with that type of joint arrangement.

Scope

3   This Standard shall be applied by all entities that are a party to a joint arrangement.

Joint arrangements

4   A joint arrangement is an arrangement of which two or more parties have joint control.

5   A joint arrangement has the following characteristics:

(a)   The parties are bound by a contractual arrangement (see paragraphs B2–B4).

(b)   The contractual arrangement gives two or more of those parties joint control of the arrangement (see paragraphs 7–13).

6   A joint arrangement is either a *joint operation* or a *joint venture*.

Joint control

7   Joint control is the contractually agreed sharing of control of an arrangement, which exists only when decisions about the relevant activities require the unanimous consent of the parties sharing control.

8   An entity that is a party to an arrangement shall assess whether the contractual arrangement gives all the parties, or a group of the parties, control of the arrangement collectively. All the parties, or a group of the parties, control the arrangement collectively when they must act together to direct the activities that significantly affect the returns of the arrangement (ie the relevant activities).

9   Once it has been determined that all the parties, or a group of the parties, control the arrangement collectively, joint control exists only when decisions about the relevant activities require the unanimous consent of the parties that control the arrangement collectively.

10   In a joint arrangement, no single party controls the arrangement on its own. A party with joint control of an arrangement can prevent any of the other parties, or a group of the parties, from controlling the arrangement.

11   An arrangement can be a joint arrangement even though not all of its parties have joint control of the arrangement. This Standard distinguishes between parties that have joint control of a joint arrangement (*joint operators* or *joint venturers*) and parties that participate in, but do not have joint control of, a joint arrangement.

12   An entity will need to apply judgement when assessing whether all the parties, or a group of the parties, have joint control of an arrangement. An entity shall make this assessment by considering all facts and circumstances (see paragraphs B5–B11).

13   If facts and circumstances change, an entity shall reassess whether it still has joint control of the arrangement.

Types of joint arrangement

14   An entity shall determine the type of joint arrangement in which it is involved. The classification of a joint arrangement as a joint operation or a joint venture depends upon the rights and obligations of the parties to the arrangement.

15   A joint operation is a joint arrangement whereby the parties that have joint control of the arrangement have rights to the assets, and obligations for the liabilities, relating to the arrangement. Those parties are called joint operators.

16   A joint venture is a joint arrangement whereby the parties that have joint control of the arrangement have rights to the net assets of the arrangement. Those parties are called joint venturers.

17   An entity applies judgement when assessing whether a joint arrangement is a joint operation or a joint venture. An entity shall determine the type of joint arrangement in which it is involved by considering its rights and obligations arising from the arrangement. An entity assesses its rights and obligations by considering the structure and legal form of the arrangement, the terms agreed by the parties in the contractual arrangement and, when relevant, other facts and circumstances (see paragraphs B12–B33).

18   Sometimes the parties are bound by a framework agreement that sets up the general contractual terms for undertaking one or more activities. The framework agreement might set out that the parties establish different joint arrangements to deal with specific activities that form part of the agreement. Even though those joint arrangements are related to the same framework agreement, their type might be different if the parties' rights and obligations differ when undertaking the different activities dealt with in the framework agreement. Consequently, joint operations and joint ventures can coexist when the parties undertake different activities that form part of the same framework agreement.

19   If facts and circumstances change, an entity shall reassess whether the type of joint arrangement in which it is involved has changed.

Financial statements of parties to a joint arrangement

Joint operations

20   **A joint operator shall recognise in relation to its interest in a joint operation:**

    (a)   **its assets, including its share of any assets held jointly;**

    (b)   **its liabilities, including its share of any liabilities incurred jointly;**

    (c)   **its revenue from the sale of its share of the output arising from the joint operation;**

    (d)   **its share of the revenue from the sale of the output by the joint operation; and**

    (e)   **its expenses, including its share of any expenses incurred jointly.**

21   A joint operator shall account for the assets, liabilities, revenues and expenses relating to its interest in a joint operation in accordance with the Standards applicable to the particular assets, liabilities, revenues and expenses.

21A   When an entity acquires an interest in a joint operation in which the activity of the joint operation constitutes a business, as defined in AASB 3 *Business Combinations*, it shall apply, to the extent of its share in accordance with paragraph 20, all of the principles on business combinations accounting in AASB 3, and other Australian Accounting Standards, that do not conflict with the guidance in this Standard and disclose the information that is required in those Australian Accounting Standards in relation to business combinations. This applies to the acquisition of both the initial interest and additional interests in a joint operation in which the activity of the joint operation constitutes a business. The accounting for the acquisition of an interest in such a joint operation is specified in paragraphs B33A–B33D.

22   The accounting for transactions such as the sale, contribution or purchase of assets between an entity and a joint operation in which it is a joint operator is specified in paragraphs B34–B37.

23   A party that participates in, but does not have joint control of, a joint operation shall also account for its interest in the arrangement in accordance with paragraphs 20–22 if that party has rights to the assets, and obligations for the liabilities, relating to the joint operation. If a party that participates in, but does not have joint control of, a joint operation does not have rights to the assets, and obligations for the liabilities, relating to that joint operation, it shall account for its interest in the joint operation in accordance with the Standards applicable to that interest.

Joint ventures

24   A joint venturer shall recognise its interest in a joint venture as an investment
      and shall account for that investment using the equity method in accordance
      with AASB 128 *Investments in Associates and Joint Ventures* unless the entity is
      exempted from applying the equity method as specified in that standard.

25   A party that participates in, but does not have joint control of, a joint venture shall
      account for its interest in the arrangement in accordance with AASB 9 *Financial
      Instruments*, unless it has significant influence over the joint venture, in which case
      it shall account for it in accordance with AASB 128.

Separate financial statements

26   In its separate financial statements, a joint operator or joint venturer shall
      account for its interest in:

      (a)   a joint operation in accordance with paragraphs 20–22;

      (b)   a joint venture in accordance with paragraph 10 of AASB 127 *Separate
            Financial Statements*.

27   In its separate financial statements, a party that participates in, but does not have
      joint control of, a joint arrangement shall account for its interest in:

      (a)   a joint operation in accordance with paragraph 23;

      (b)   a joint venture in accordance with AASB 9, unless the entity has significant
            influence over the joint venture, in which case it shall apply paragraph 10
            of AASB 127.

Commencement of the legislative instrument

Aus27.1   For legal purposes, this legislative instrument commences on 31 December
           2015.

Withdrawal of AASB pronouncements

Aus27.2   This Standard repeals AASB 11 *Joint Arrangements* issued in August 2011.
           Despite the repeal, after the time this Standard starts to apply under section 334
           of the Corporations Act (either generally or in relation to an individual entity),
           the repealed Standard continues to apply in relation to any period ending before
           that time as if the repeal had not occurred.

           [Note: When this Standard applies under section 334 of the Corporations
           Act (either generally or in relation to an individual entity), it supersedes the
           application of the repealed Standard.]

APPENDIX A
DEFINED TERMS

This appendix is an integral part of the Standard.

joint arrangement	An arrangement of which two or more parties have **joint control**.
joint control	The contractually agreed sharing of control of an arrangement, which exists only when decisions about the relevant activities require the unanimous consent of the parties sharing control.
joint operation	A **joint arrangement** whereby the parties that have **joint control** of the arrangement have rights to the assets, and obligations for the liabilities, relating to the arrangement.

joint operator	A party to a **joint operation** that has **joint control** of that joint operation.
joint venture	A **joint arrangement** whereby the parties that have **joint control** of the arrangement have rights to the net assets of the arrangement.
joint venturer	A party to a **joint venture** that has **joint control** of that joint venture.
party to a joint arrangement	An entity that participates in a **joint arrangement**, regardless of whether that entity has **joint control** of the arrangement.
separate vehicle	A separately identifiable financial structure, including separate legal entities or entities recognised by statute, regardless of whether those entities have a legal personality.

The following terms are defined in AASB 127, AASB 128 or AASB 10 *Consolidated Financial Statements* and are used in this Standard with the meanings specified in those Standards:

- control of an investee
- equity method
- power
- protective rights
- relevant activities
- separate financial statements
- significant influence.

APPENDIX B
APPLICATION GUIDANCE

This appendix is an integral part of the Standard. It describes the application of paragraphs 1–27 and has the same authority as the other parts of the Standard.

B1   The examples in this appendix portray hypothetical situations. Although some aspects of the examples may be present in actual fact patterns, all relevant facts and circumstances of a particular fact pattern would need to be evaluated when applying AASB 11.

Joint arrangements

Contractual arrangement (paragraph 5)

B2   Contractual arrangements can be evidenced in several ways. An enforceable contractual arrangement is often, but not always, in writing, usually in the form of a contract or documented discussions between the parties. Statutory mechanisms can also create enforceable arrangements, either on their own or in conjunction with contracts between the parties.

B3   When joint arrangements are structured through a *separate vehicle* (see paragraphs B19–B33), the contractual arrangement, or some aspects of the contractual arrangement, will in some cases be incorporated in the articles, charter or by-laws of the separate vehicle.

B4   The contractual arrangement sets out the terms upon which the parties participate in the activity that is the subject of the arrangement. The contractual arrangement generally deals with such matters as:

(a)   the purpose, activity and duration of the joint arrangement.

(b)   how the members of the board of directors, or equivalent governing body, of the joint arrangement, are appointed.

(c)   the decision-making process: the matters requiring decisions from the parties, the voting rights of the parties and the required level of support for those matters. The decision-making process reflected in the contractual arrangement establishes joint control of the arrangement (see paragraphs B5–B11).

(d)   the capital or other contributions required of the parties.

(e)   how the parties share assets, liabilities, revenues, expenses or profit or loss relating to the joint arrangement.

Joint control (paragraphs 7–13)

B5   In assessing whether an entity has joint control of an arrangement, an entity shall assess first whether all the parties, or a group of the parties, control the arrangement. AASB 10 defines control and shall be used to determine whether all the parties, or a group of the parties, are exposed, or have rights, to variable returns from their involvement with the arrangement and have the ability to affect those returns through their power over the arrangement. When all the parties, or a group of the parties, considered collectively, are able to direct the activities that significantly affect the returns of the arrangement (ie the relevant activities), the parties control the arrangement collectively.

B6   After concluding that all the parties, or a group of the parties, control the arrangement collectively, an entity shall assess whether it has joint control of the arrangement. Joint control exists only when decisions about the relevant activities require the unanimous consent of the parties that collectively control the arrangement. Assessing whether the arrangement is jointly controlled by all of its parties or by a group of the parties, or controlled by one of its parties alone, can require judgement.

B7   Sometimes the decision-making process that is agreed upon by the parties in their contractual arrangement implicitly leads to joint control. For example, assume two parties establish an arrangement in which each has 50 per cent of the voting rights and the contractual arrangement between them specifies that at least 51 per cent of the voting rights are required to make decisions about the relevant activities. In this case, the parties have implicitly agreed that they have joint control of the arrangement because decisions about the relevant activities cannot be made without both parties agreeing.

B8   In other circumstances, the contractual arrangement requires a minimum proportion of the voting rights to make decisions about the relevant activities. When that minimum required proportion of the voting rights can be achieved by more than one combination of the parties agreeing together, that arrangement is not a joint arrangement unless the contractual arrangement specifies which parties (or combination of parties) are required to agree unanimously to decisions about the relevant activities of the arrangement.

Application examples

Example 1

Assume that three parties establish an arrangement: A has 50 per cent of the voting rights in the arrangement, B has 30 per cent and C has 20 per cent. The contractual arrangement between A, B and C specifies that at least 75 per cent of the voting rights are required to make decisions about the relevant activities of the arrangement. Even though A can block any decision, it does not control the arrangement because it needs the agreement of B. The terms of their contractual arrangement requiring at least 75 per cent of the voting rights to make decisions about the relevant activities imply that A and B have joint control of the arrangement because decisions about the relevant activities of the arrangement cannot be made without both A and B agreeing.

Example 2

Assume an arrangement has three parties: A has 50 per cent of the voting rights in the arrangement and B and C each have 25 per cent. The contractual arrangement between A, B and C specifies that at least 75 per cent of the voting rights are required to make decisions about the relevant activities

---

of the arrangement. Even though A can block any decision, it does not control the arrangement because it needs the agreement of either B or C. In this example, A, B and C collectively control the arrangement. However, there is more than one combination of parties that can agree to reach 75 per cent of the voting rights (ie either A and B or A and C). In such a situation, to be a joint arrangement the contractual arrangement between the parties would need to specify which combination of the parties is required to agree unanimously to decisions about the relevant activities of the arrangement.

Example 3

Assume an arrangement in which A and B each have 35 per cent of the voting rights in the arrangement with the remaining 30 per cent being widely dispersed. Decisions about the relevant activities require approval by a majority of the voting rights. A and B have joint control of the arrangement only if the contractual arrangement specifies that decisions about the relevant activities of the arrangement require both A and B agreeing.

B9   The requirement for unanimous consent means that any party with joint control of the arrangement can prevent any of the other parties, or a group of the parties, from making unilateral decisions (about the relevant activities) without its consent. If the requirement for unanimous consent relates only to decisions that give a party protective rights and not to decisions about the relevant activities of an arrangement, that party is not a party with joint control of the arrangement.

B10   A contractual arrangement might include clauses on the resolution of disputes, such as arbitration. These provisions may allow for decisions to be made in the absence of unanimous consent among the parties that have joint control. The existence of such provisions does not prevent the arrangement from being jointly controlled and, consequently, from being a joint arrangement.

Assessing joint control

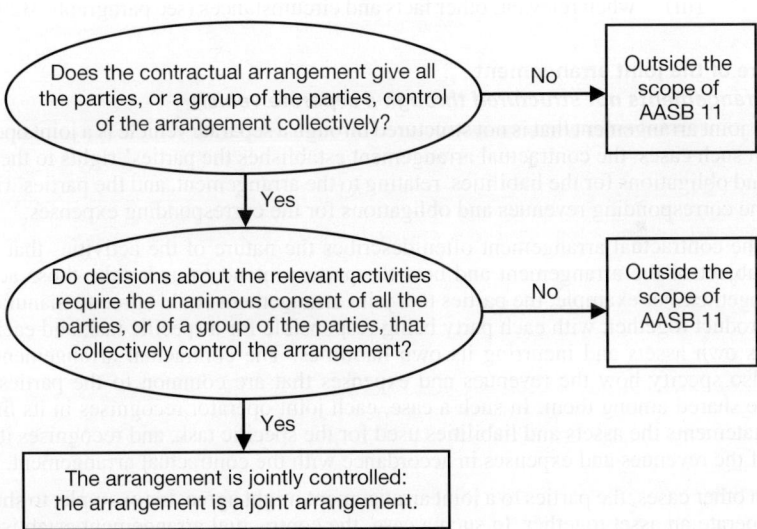

B11   When an arrangement is outside the scope of AASB 11, an entity accounts for its interest in the arrangement in accordance with relevant Australian Accounting Standards, such as AASB 10, AASB 128 or AASB 9.

Types of joint arrangement (paragraphs 14–19)

B12   Joint arrangements are established for a variety of purposes (eg as a way for parties to share costs and risks, or as a way to provide the parties with access to new technology or new markets), and can be established using different structures and legal forms.

B13   Some arrangements do not require the activity that is the subject of the arrangement to be undertaken in a separate vehicle. However, other arrangements involve the establishment of a separate vehicle.

B14   The classification of joint arrangements required by this Standard depends upon the parties' rights and obligations arising from the arrangement in the normal course of business. This Standard classifies joint arrangements as either joint operations or joint ventures. When an entity has rights to the assets, and obligations for the liabilities, relating to the arrangement, the arrangement is a joint operation. When an entity has rights to the net assets of the arrangement, the arrangement is a joint venture. Paragraphs B16–B33 set out the assessment an entity carries out to determine whether it has an interest in a joint operation or an interest in a joint venture.

Classification of a joint arrangement

B15   As stated in paragraph B14, the classification of joint arrangements requires the parties to assess their rights and obligations arising from the arrangement. When making that assessment, an entity shall consider the following:

    (a)   the structure of the joint arrangement (see paragraphs B16–B21).

    (b)   when the joint arrangement is structured through a separate vehicle:

        (i)   the legal form of the separate vehicle (see paragraphs B22–B24);

        (ii)   the terms of the contractual arrangement (see paragraphs B25–B28); and

        (iii)   when relevant, other facts and circumstances (see paragraphs B29–B33).

Structure of the joint arrangement
Joint arrangements not structured through a separate vehicle

B16   A joint arrangement that is not structured through a separate vehicle is a joint operation. In such cases, the contractual arrangement establishes the parties' rights to the assets, and obligations for the liabilities, relating to the arrangement, and the parties' rights to the corresponding revenues and obligations for the corresponding expenses.

B17   The contractual arrangement often describes the nature of the activities that are the subject of the arrangement and how the parties intend to undertake those activities together. For example, the parties to a joint arrangement could agree to manufacture a product together, with each party being responsible for a specific task and each using its own assets and incurring its own liabilities. The contractual arrangement could also specify how the revenues and expenses that are common to the parties are to be shared among them. In such a case, each joint operator recognises in its financial statements the assets and liabilities used for the specific task, and recognises its share of the revenues and expenses in accordance with the contractual arrangement.

B18   In other cases, the parties to a joint arrangement might agree, for example, to share and operate an asset together. In such a case, the contractual arrangement establishes the parties' rights to the asset that is operated jointly, and how output or revenue from the asset and operating costs are shared among the parties. Each joint operator accounts for its share of the joint asset and its agreed share of any liabilities, and recognises its share of the output, revenues and expenses in accordance with the contractual arrangement.

Joint arrangements structured through a separate vehicle

B19   A joint arrangement in which the assets and liabilities relating to the arrangement are held in a separate vehicle can be either a joint venture or a joint operation.

B20   Whether a party is a joint operator or a joint venturer depends on the party's rights to the assets, and obligations for the liabilities, relating to the arrangement that are held in the separate vehicle.

B21   As stated in paragraph B15, when the parties have structured a joint arrangement in a separate vehicle, the parties need to assess whether the legal form of the separate vehicle, the terms of the contractual arrangement and, when relevant, any other facts and circumstances give them:

(a)   rights to the assets, and obligations for the liabilities, relating to the arrangement (ie the arrangement is a joint operation); or

(b)   rights to the net assets of the arrangement (ie the arrangement is a joint venture).

Classification of a joint arrangement: assessment of the parties' rights and obligations arising from the arrangement

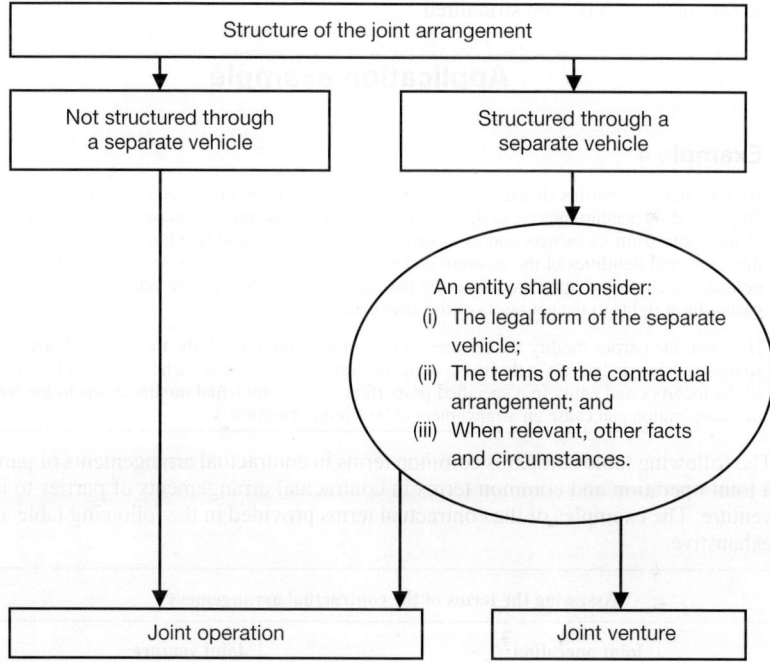

The legal form of the separate vehicle

B22   The legal form of the separate vehicle is relevant when assessing the type of joint arrangement. The legal form assists in the initial assessment of the parties' rights to the assets and obligations for the liabilities held in the separate vehicle, such as whether the parties have interests in the assets held in the separate vehicle and whether they are liable for the liabilities held in the separate vehicle.

B23   For example, the parties might conduct the joint arrangement through a separate vehicle, whose legal form causes the separate vehicle to be considered in its own right (ie the assets and liabilities held in the separate vehicle are the assets and liabilities of the separate vehicle and not the assets and liabilities of the parties). In such a case, the assessment of the rights and obligations conferred upon the parties by the legal form of the separate vehicle indicates that the arrangement is a joint venture. However, the terms agreed by the parties in their contractual arrangement (see paragraphs B25–B28) and, when relevant, other facts and circumstances (see paragraphs B29–B33) can override the assessment of the rights and obligations conferred upon the parties by the legal form of the separate vehicle.

B24   The assessment of the rights and obligations conferred upon the parties by the legal form of the separate vehicle is sufficient to conclude that the arrangement is a joint operation only if the parties conduct the joint arrangement in a separate vehicle whose legal form does not confer separation between the parties and the separate vehicle (ie the assets and liabilities held in the separate vehicle are the parties' assets and liabilities).

Assessing the terms of the contractual arrangement

B25   In many cases, the rights and obligations agreed to by the parties in their contractual arrangements are consistent, or do not conflict, with the rights and obligations conferred on the parties by the legal form of the separate vehicle in which the arrangement has been structured.

B26   In other cases, the parties use the contractual arrangement to reverse or modify the rights and obligations conferred by the legal form of the separate vehicle in which the arrangement has been structured.

Application example

Example 4

Assume that two parties structure a joint arrangement in an incorporated entity. Each party has a 50 per cent ownership interest in the incorporated entity. The incorporation enables the separation of the entity from its owners and as a consequence the assets and liabilities held in the entity are the assets and liabilities of the incorporated entity. In such a case, the assessment of the rights and obligations conferred upon the parties by the legal form of the separate vehicle indicates that the parties have rights to the net assets of the arrangement.

However, the parties modify the features of the corporation through their contractual arrangement so that each has an interest in the assets of the incorporated entity and each is liable for the liabilities of the incorporated entity in a specified proportion. Such contractual modifications to the features of a corporation can cause an arrangement to be a joint operation.

B27   The following table compares common terms in contractual arrangements of parties to a joint operation and common terms in contractual arrangements of parties to a joint venture. The examples of the contractual terms provided in the following table are not exhaustive.

Assessing the terms of the contractual arrangement		
	Joint operation	**Joint venture**
The terms of the contractual arrangement	The contractual arrangement provides the parties to the joint arrangement with rights to the assets, and obligations for the liabilities, relating to the arrangement.	The contractual arrangement provides the parties to the joint arrangement with rights to the net assets of the arrangement (ie it is the separate vehicle, not the parties, that has rights to the assets, and obligations for the liabilities, relating to the arrangement).
Rights to assets	The contractual arrangement establishes that the parties to the joint arrangement share all interests (eg rights, title or ownership) in the assets relating to the arrangement in a specified proportion (eg in proportion to the parties' ownership interest in the arrangement or in proportion to the activity carried out through the arrangement that is directly attributed to them).	The contractual arrangement establishes that the assets brought into the arrangement or subsequently acquired by the joint arrangement are the arrangement's assets. The parties have no interests (ie no rights, title or ownership) in the assets of the arrangement.

	Joint operation	Joint venture
Obligations for liabilities	The contractual arrangement establishes that the parties to the joint arrangement share all liabilities, obligations, costs and expenses in a specified proportion (eg in proportion to the parties' ownership interest in the arrangement or in proportion to the activity carried out through the arrangement that is directly attributed to them).	The contractual arrangement establishes that the joint arrangement is liable for the debts and obligations of the arrangement.
		The contractual arrangement establishes that the parties to the joint arrangement are liable to the arrangement only to the extent of their respective investments in the arrangement or to their respective obligations to contribute any unpaid or additional capital to the arrangement, or both.
	The contractual arrangement establishes that the parties to the joint arrangement are liable for claims raised by third parties.	The contractual arrangement states that creditors of the joint arrangement do not have rights of recourse against any party with respect to debts or obligations of the arrangement.
Revenues, expenses, profit or loss	The contractual arrangement establishes the allocation of revenues and expenses on the basis of the relative performance of each party to the joint arrangement. For example, the contractual arrangement might establish that revenues and expenses are allocated on the basis of the capacity that each party uses in a plant operated jointly, which could differ from their ownership interest in the joint arrangement. In other instances, the parties might have agreed to share the profit or loss relating to the arrangement on the basis of a specified proportion such as the parties' ownership interest in the arrangement. This would not prevent the arrangement from being a joint operation if the parties have rights to the assets, and obligations for the liabilities, relating to the arrangement.	The contractual arrangement establishes each party's share in the profit or loss relating to the activities of the arrangement.
Guarantees	The parties to joint arrangements are often required to provide guarantees to third parties that, for example, receive a service from, or provide financing to, the joint arrangement. The provision of such guarantees, or the commitment by the parties to provide them, does not, by itself, determine that the joint arrangement is a joint operation. The feature that determines whether the joint arrangement is a joint operation or a joint venture is whether the parties have obligations for the liabilities relating to the arrangement (for some of which the parties might or might not have provided a guarantee).	

B28   When the contractual arrangement specifies that the parties have rights to the assets, and obligations for the liabilities, relating to the arrangement, they are parties to a joint operation and do not need to consider other facts and circumstances (paragraphs B29–B33) for the purposes of classifying the joint arrangement.

Assessing other facts and circumstances

B29   When the terms of the contractual arrangement do not specify that the parties have rights to the assets, and obligations for the liabilities, relating to the arrangement, the parties shall consider other facts and circumstances to assess whether the arrangement is a joint operation or a joint venture.

B30   A joint arrangement might be structured in a separate vehicle whose legal form confers separation between the parties and the separate vehicle. The contractual terms agreed among the parties might not specify the parties' rights to the assets and obligations for the liabilities, yet consideration of other facts and circumstances can lead to such an arrangement being classified as a joint operation. This will be the case when other facts and circumstances give the parties rights to the assets, and obligations for the liabilities, relating to the arrangement.

B31   When the activities of an arrangement are primarily designed for the provision of output to the parties, this indicates that the parties have rights to substantially all the economic benefits of the assets of the arrangement. The parties to such arrangements often ensure their access to the outputs provided by the arrangement by preventing the arrangement from selling output to third parties.

B32   The effect of an arrangement with such a design and purpose is that the liabilities incurred by the arrangement are, in substance, satisfied by the cash flows received from the parties through their purchases of the output. When the parties are substantially the only source of cash flows contributing to the continuity of the operations of the arrangement, this indicates that the parties have an obligation for the liabilities relating to the arrangement.

Application example

Example 5

Assume that two parties structure a joint arrangement in an incorporated entity (entity C) in which each party has a 50 per cent ownership interest. The purpose of the arrangement is to manufacture materials required by the parties for their own, individual manufacturing processes. The arrangement ensures that the parties operate the facility that produces the materials to the quantity and quality specifications of the parties.

The legal form of entity C (an incorporated entity) through which the activities are conducted initially indicates that the assets and liabilities held in entity C are the assets and liabilities of entity C. The contractual arrangement between the parties does not specify that the parties have rights to the assets or obligations for the liabilities of entity C. Accordingly, the legal form of entity C and the terms of the contractual arrangement indicate that the arrangement is a joint venture.

However, the parties also consider the following aspects of the arrangement:

-     The parties agreed to purchase all the output produced by entity C in a ratio of 50:50. Entity C cannot sell any of the output to third parties, unless this is approved by the two parties to the arrangement. Because the purpose of the arrangement is to provide the parties with output they require, such sales to third parties are expected to be uncommon and not material.

-     The price of the output sold to the parties is set by both parties at a level that is designed to cover the costs of production and administrative expenses incurred by entity C. On the basis of this operating model, the arrangement is intended to operate at a break-even level.

From the fact pattern above, the following facts and circumstances are relevant:

-     The obligation of the parties to purchase all the output produced by entity C reflects the exclusive dependence of entity C upon the parties for the generation of cash flows and, thus, the parties have an obligation to fund the settlement of the liabilities of entity C.

-     The fact that the parties have rights to all the output produced by entity C means that the parties are consuming, and therefore have rights to, all the economic benefits of the assets of entity C.

These facts and circumstances indicate that the arrangement is a joint operation. The conclusion about the classification of the joint arrangement in these circumstances would not change if, instead of the parties using their share of the output themselves in a subsequent manufacturing process, the parties sold their share of the output to third parties.

If the parties changed the terms of the contractual arrangement so that the arrangement was able to sell output to third parties, this would result in entity C assuming demand, inventory and credit risks. In that scenario, such a change in the facts and circumstances would require reassessment of the classification of the joint arrangement. Such facts and circumstances would indicate that the arrangement is a joint venture.

B33 The following flow chart reflects the assessment an entity follows to classify an arrangement when the joint arrangement is structured through a separate vehicle:

Classification of a joint arrangement structured through a separate vehicle

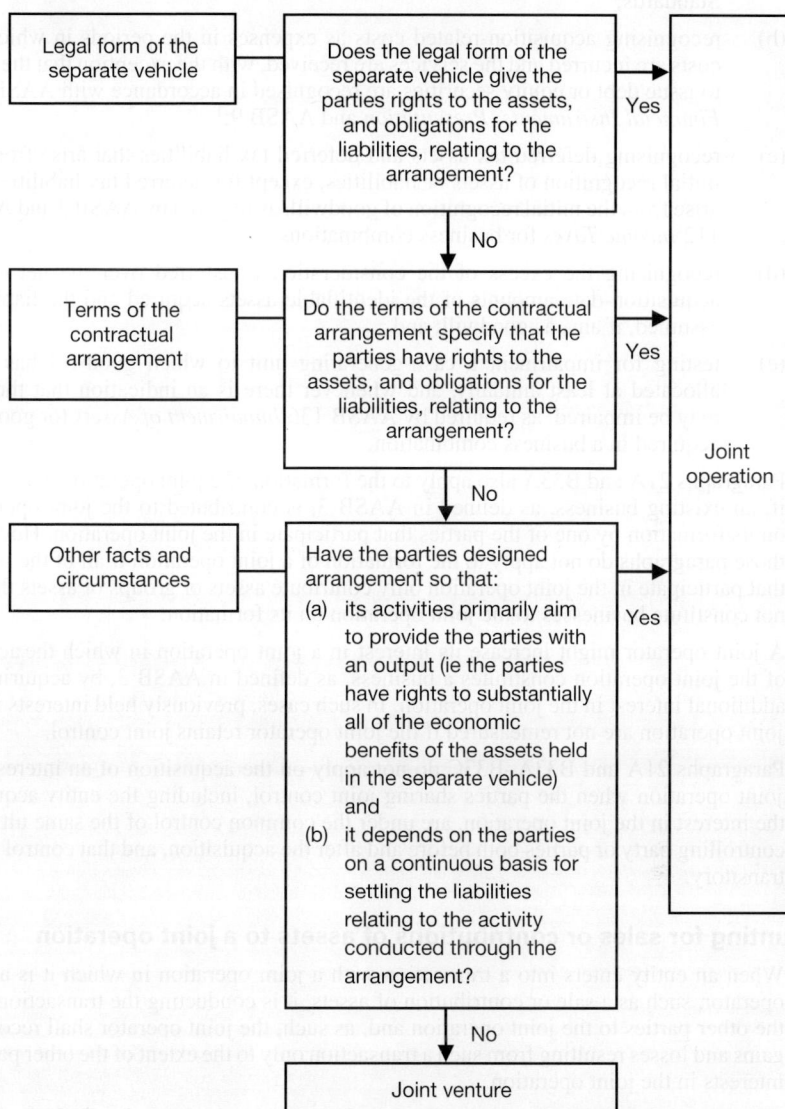

Financial statements of parties to a joint arrangement (paragraphs 21A–22)

Accounting for acquisitions of interests in joint operations

B33A When an entity acquires an interest in a joint operation in which the activity of the joint operation constitutes a business, as defined in AASB 3, it shall apply, to the extent of its share in accordance with paragraph 20, all of the principles on business combinations accounting in AASB 3, and other Australian Accounting Standards, that do not conflict with the guidance in this Standard and disclose the information required by those Australian Accounting Standards in relation to business combinations. The principles on business combinations accounting that do not conflict with the guidance in this Standard include but are not limited to:

(a)   measuring identifiable assets and liabilities at fair value, other than items for which exceptions are given in AASB 3 and other Australian Accounting Standards;

(b)   recognising acquisition-related costs as expenses in the periods in which the costs are incurred and the services are received, with the exception that the costs to issue debt or equity securities are recognised in accordance with AASB 132 *Financial Instruments: Presentation* and AASB 9;[1]

(c)   recognising deferred tax assets and deferred tax liabilities that arise from the initial recognition of assets or liabilities, except for deferred tax liabilities that arise from the initial recognition of goodwill, as required by AASB 3 and AASB 112 *Income Taxes* for business combinations;

(d)   recognising the excess of the consideration transferred over the net of the acquisition-date amounts of the identifiable assets acquired and the liabilities assumed, if any, as goodwill; and

(e)   testing for impairment a cash-generating unit to which goodwill has been allocated at least annually, and whenever there is an indication that the unit may be impaired, as required by AASB 136 *Impairment of Assets* for goodwill acquired in a business combination.

B33B   Paragraphs 21A and B33A also apply to the formation of a joint operation if, and only if, an existing business, as defined in AASB 3, is contributed to the joint operation on its formation by one of the parties that participate in the joint operation. However, those paragraphs do not apply to the formation of a joint operation if all of the parties that participate in the joint operation only contribute assets or groups of assets that do not constitute businesses to the joint operation on its formation.

B33C   A joint operator might increase its interest in a joint operation in which the activity of the joint operation constitutes a business, as defined in AASB 3, by acquiring an additional interest in the joint operation. In such cases, previously held interests in the joint operation are not remeasured if the joint operator retains joint control.

B33D   Paragraphs 21A and B33A–B33C do not apply on the acquisition of an interest in a joint operation when the parties sharing joint control, including the entity acquiring the interest in the joint operation, are under the common control of the same ultimate controlling party or parties both before and after the acquisition, and that control is not transitory.

Accounting for sales or contributions of assets to a joint operation

B34   When an entity enters into a transaction with a joint operation in which it is a joint operator, such as a sale or contribution of assets, it is conducting the transaction with the other parties to the joint operation and, as such, the joint operator shall recognise gains and losses resulting from such a transaction only to the extent of the other parties' interests in the joint operation.

B35   When such transactions provide evidence of a reduction in the net realisable value of the assets to be sold or contributed to the joint operation, or of an impairment loss of those assets, those losses shall be recognised fully by the joint operator.

Accounting for purchases of assets from a joint operation

B36   When an entity enters into a transaction with a joint operation in which it is a joint operator, such as a purchase of assets, it shall not recognise its share of the gains and losses until it resells those assets to a third party.

---

1   If an entity applies these amendments but does not yet apply AASB 9, the reference in these amendments to AASB 9 shall be read as a reference to AASB 139 *Financial Instruments: Recognition and Measurement*.

B37 When such transactions provide evidence of a reduction in the net realisable value of the assets to be purchased or of an impairment loss of those assets, a joint operator shall recognise its share of those losses.

APPENDIX C
EFFECTIVE DATE, TRANSITION AND WITHDRAWAL OF OTHER IFRSs

This appendix is an integral part of the Standard and has the same authority as the other parts of the Standard.

Effective date

C1 An entity shall apply this Standard for annual periods beginning on or after 1 January 2016. Earlier application is permitted for periods beginning on or after 1 January 2014 but before 1 January 2016. If an entity applies this Standard earlier, it shall disclose that fact and apply AASB 10, AASB 12 *Disclosure of Interests in Other Entities*, AASB 127 and AASB 128 at the same time.

C1A [Deleted by the AASB]

C1AA AASB 2014-3 *Amendments to Australian Accounting Standards – Accounting for Acquisitions of Interests in Joint Operations*, issued in August 2014, amended the previous version of this Standard as follows: amended the heading after paragraph B33 and added paragraphs 21A, B33A–B33D and C14A and their related headings. An entity shall apply those amendments prospectively in annual periods beginning on or after 1 January 2016. Earlier application is permitted. If an entity applies those amendments in an earlier period it shall disclose that fact.

Transition

C1B Notwithstanding the requirements of paragraph 28 of AASB 108 *Accounting Policies, Changes in Accounting Estimates and Errors*, when this Standard is first applied, an entity need only present the quantitative information required by paragraph 28(f) of AASB 108 for the annual period immediately preceding the first annual period for which AASB 11 is applied (the 'immediately preceding period'). An entity may also present this information for the current period or for earlier comparative periods, but is not required to do so.

Joint ventures—transition from proportionate consolidation to the equity method

C2 When changing from proportionate consolidation to the equity method, an entity shall recognise its investment in the joint venture as at the beginning of the immediately preceding period. That initial investment shall be measured as the aggregate of the carrying amounts of the assets and liabilities that the entity had previously proportionately consolidated, including any goodwill arising from acquisition. If the goodwill previously belonged to a larger cash-generating unit, or to a group of cash-generating units, the entity shall allocate goodwill to the joint venture on the basis of the relative carrying amounts of the joint venture and the cash-generating unit or group of cash-generating units to which it belonged.

C3 The opening balance of the investment determined in accordance with paragraph C2 is regarded as the deemed cost of the investment at initial recognition. An entity shall apply paragraphs 40–43 of AASB 128 to the opening balance of the investment to assess whether the investment is impaired and shall recognise any impairment loss as an adjustment to retained earnings at the beginning of the immediately preceding period. The initial recognition exception in paragraphs 15 and 24 of AASB 112

Income Taxes does not apply when the entity recognises an investment in a joint venture resulting from applying the transition requirements for joint ventures that had previously been proportionately consolidated.

C4   If aggregating all previously proportionately consolidated assets and liabilities results in negative net assets, an entity shall assess whether it has legal or constructive obligations in relation to the negative net assets and, if so, the entity shall recognise the corresponding liability. If the entity concludes that it does not have legal or constructive obligations in relation to the negative net assets, it shall not recognise the corresponding liability but it shall adjust retained earnings at the beginning of the immediately preceding period. The entity shall disclose this fact, along with its cumulative unrecognised share of losses of its joint ventures as at the beginning of the immediately preceding period and at the date at which this Standard is first applied.

C5   An entity shall disclose a breakdown of the assets and liabilities that have been aggregated into the single line investment balance as at the beginning of the immediately preceding period. That disclosure shall be prepared in an aggregated manner for all joint ventures for which an entity applies the transition requirements referred to in paragraphs C2–C6.

C6   After initial recognition, an entity shall account for its investment in the joint venture using the equity method in accordance with AASB 128.

Joint operations—transition from the equity method to accounting for assets and liabilities

C7   When changing from the equity method to accounting for assets and liabilities in respect of its interest in a joint operation, an entity shall, at the beginning of the immediately preceding period, derecognise the investment that was previously accounted for using the equity method and any other items that formed part of the entity's net investment in the arrangement in accordance with paragraph 38 of AASB 128 and recognise its share of each of the assets and the liabilities in respect of its interest in the joint operation, including any goodwill that might have formed part of the carrying amount of the investment.

C8   An entity shall determine its interest in the assets and liabilities relating to the joint operation on the basis of its rights and obligations in a specified proportion in accordance with the contractual arrangement. An entity measures the initial carrying amounts of the assets and liabilities by disaggregating them from the carrying amount of the investment at the beginning of the immediately preceding period on the basis of the information used by the entity in applying the equity method.

C9   Any difference arising from the investment previously accounted for using the equity method together with any other items that formed part of the entity's net investment in the arrangement in accordance with paragraph 38 of AASB 128, and the net amount of the assets and liabilities, including any goodwill, recognised shall be:

(a)   offset against any goodwill relating to the investment with any remaining difference adjusted against retained earnings at the beginning of the immediately preceding period, if the net amount of the assets and liabilities, including any goodwill, recognised is higher than the investment (and any other items that formed part of the entity's net investment) derecognised.

(b)   adjusted against retained earnings at the beginning of the immediately preceding period, if the net amount of the assets and liabilities, including any goodwill, recognised is lower than the investment (and any other items that formed part of the entity's net investment) derecognised.

C10   An entity changing from the equity method to accounting for assets and liabilities shall provide a reconciliation between the investment derecognised, and the assets and liabilities recognised, together with any remaining difference adjusted against retained earnings, at the beginning of the immediately preceding period.

C11 The initial recognition exception in paragraphs 15 and 24 of AASB 112 does not apply when the entity recognises assets and liabilities relating to its interest in a joint operation.

Transition provisions in an entity's separate financial statements

C12 An entity that, in accordance with paragraph 10 of AASB 127, was previously accounting in its separate financial statements for its interest in a joint operation as an investment at cost or in accordance with AASB 9 shall:

  (a) derecognise the investment and recognise the assets and the liabilities in respect of its interest in the joint operation at the amounts determined in accordance with paragraphs C7–C9.

  (b) provide a reconciliation between the investment derecognised, and the assets and liabilities recognised, together with any remaining difference adjusted in retained earnings, at the beginning of the immediately preceding period.

C13 The initial recognition exception in paragraphs 15 and 24 of AASB 112 does not apply when the entity recognises assets and liabilities relating to its interest in a joint operation in its separate financial statements resulting from applying the transition requirements for joint operations referred to in paragraph C12.

References to the 'immediately preceding period'

C13A Notwithstanding the references to the 'immediately preceding period' in paragraphs C2–C12, an entity may also present adjusted comparative information for any earlier periods presented, but is not required to do so. If an entity does present adjusted comparative information for any earlier periods, all references to the 'immediately preceding period' in paragraphs C2–C12 shall be read as the 'earliest adjusted comparative period presented'.

C13B If an entity presents unadjusted comparative information for any earlier periods, it shall clearly identify the information that has not been adjusted, state that it has been prepared on a different basis, and explain that basis.

References to AASB 9

C14 If an entity applies this Standard but does not yet apply AASB 9, any reference to AASB 9 shall be read as a reference to AASB 139 *Financial Instruments: Recognition and Measurement*.

Accounting for acquisitions of interests in joint operations

C14A AASB 2014-3, issued in August 2014, amended the previous version of this Standard as follows: amended the heading after paragraph B33 and added paragraphs 21A, B33A–B33D, C1AA and their related headings. An entity shall apply those amendments prospectively for acquisitions of interests in joint operations in which the activities of the joint operations constitute businesses, as defined in AASB 3, for those acquisitions occurring from the beginning of the first period in which it applies those amendments. Consequently, amounts recognised for acquisitions of interests in joint operations occurring in prior periods shall not be adjusted.

Withdrawal of other IFRSs

C15 [Deleted by the AASB]

ILLUSTRATIVE EXAMPLES
AASB 11 *JOINT ARRANGEMENTS*

These examples accompany, but are not part of, AASB 11. They illustrate aspects of AASB 11 but are not intended to provide interpretative guidance.

IE1   These examples portray hypothetical situations illustrating the judgements that might be used when applying AASB 11 in different situations. Although some aspects of the examples may be present in actual fact patterns, all relevant facts and circumstances of a particular fact pattern would need to be evaluated when applying AASB 11.

Example 1 – Construction services

IE2   A and B (the parties) are two companies whose businesses are the provision of many types of public and private construction services. They set up a contractual arrangement to work together for the purpose of fulfilling a contract with a government for the design and construction of a road between two cities. The contractual arrangement determines the participation shares of A and B and establishes joint control of the arrangement, the subject matter of which is the delivery of the road.

IE3   The parties set up a separate vehicle (entity Z) through which to conduct the arrangement. Entity Z, on behalf of A and B, enters into the contract with the government. In addition, the assets and liabilities relating to the arrangement are held in entity Z. The main feature of entity Z's legal form is that the parties, not entity Z, have rights to the assets, and obligations for the liabilities, of the entity.

IE4   The contractual arrangement between A and B additionally establishes that:

(a)   the rights to all the assets needed to undertake the activities of the arrangement are shared by the parties on the basis of their participation shares in the arrangement;

(b)   the parties have several and joint responsibility for all operating and financial obligations relating to the activities of the arrangement on the basis of their participation shares in the arrangement; and

(c)   the profit or loss resulting from the activities of the arrangement is shared by A and B on the basis of their participation shares in the arrangement.

IE5   For the purposes of co-ordinating and overseeing the activities, A and B appoint an operator, who will be an employee of one of the parties. After a specified time, the role of the operator will rotate to an employee of the other party. A and B agree that the activities will be executed by the operator's employees on a 'no gain or loss' basis.

IE6   In accordance with the terms specified in the contract with the government, entity Z invoices the construction services to the government on behalf of the parties.

Analysis

IE7   The joint arrangement is carried out through a separate vehicle whose legal form does not confer separation between the parties and the separate vehicle (ie the assets and liabilities held in entity Z are the parties' assets and liabilities). This is reinforced by the terms agreed by the parties in their contractual arrangement, which state that A and B have rights to the assets, and obligations for the liabilities, relating to the arrangement that is conducted through entity Z. The joint arrangement is a joint operation.

IE8   A and B each recognise in their financial statements their share of the assets (eg property, plant and equipment, accounts receivable) and their share of any liabilities resulting from the arrangement (eg accounts payable to third parties) on the basis of their agreed participation share. Each also recognises its share of the revenue and expenses resulting from the construction services provided to the government through entity Z.

Example 2 – Shopping centre operated jointly

IE9 Two real estate companies (the parties) set up a separate vehicle (entity X) for the purpose of acquiring and operating a shopping centre. The contractual arrangement between the parties establishes joint control of the activities that are conducted in entity X. The main feature of entity X's legal form is that the entity, not the parties, has rights to the assets, and obligations for the liabilities, relating to the arrangement. These activities include the rental of the retail units, managing the car park, maintaining the centre and its equipment, such as lifts, and building the reputation and customer base for the centre as a whole.

IE10 The terms of the contractual arrangement are such that:

    (a)   entity X owns the shopping centre. The contractual arrangement does not specify that the parties have rights to the shopping centre.

    (b)   the parties are not liable in respect of the debts, liabilities or obligations of entity X. If entity X is unable to pay any of its debts or other liabilities or to discharge its obligations to third parties, the liability of each party to any third party will be limited to the unpaid amount of that party's capital contribution.

    (c)   the parties have the right to sell or pledge their interests in entity X.

    (d)   each party receives a share of the income from operating the shopping centre (which is the rental income net of the operating costs) in accordance with its interest in entity X.

Analysis

IE11 The joint arrangement is carried out through a separate vehicle whose legal form causes the separate vehicle to be considered in its own right (ie the assets and liabilities held in the separate vehicle are the assets and liabilities of the separate vehicle and not the assets and liabilities of the parties). In addition, the terms of the contractual arrangement do not specify that the parties have rights to the assets, or obligations for the liabilities, relating to the arrangement. Instead, the terms of the contractual arrangement establish that the parties have rights to the net assets of entity X.

IE12 On the basis of the description above, there are no other facts and circumstances that indicate that the parties have rights to substantially all the economic benefits of the assets relating to the arrangement, and that the parties have an obligation for the liabilities relating to the arrangement. The joint arrangement is a joint venture.

IE13 The parties recognise their rights to the net assets of entity X as investments and account for them using the equity method.

Example 3 – Joint manufacturing and distribution of a product

IE14 Companies A and B (the parties) have set up a strategic and operating agreement (the framework agreement) in which they have agreed the terms according to which they will conduct the manufacturing and distribution of a product (product P) in different markets.

IE15 The parties have agreed to conduct manufacturing and distribution activities by establishing joint arrangements, as described below:

    (a)   Manufacturing activity: the parties have agreed to undertake the manufacturing activity through a joint arrangement (the manufacturing arrangement). The manufacturing arrangement is structured in a separate vehicle (entity M) whose legal form causes it to be considered in its own right (ie the assets and liabilities held in entity M are the assets and liabilities of entity M and not the assets and liabilities of the parties). In accordance with the framework agreement, the parties have committed themselves to purchasing the whole production of product P manufactured by the manufacturing arrangement in accordance with their ownership interests in entity M. The parties subsequently sell product P to another arrangement, jointly controlled by the two parties themselves, that has been established exclusively for the distribution of product P as described below. Neither the framework agreement nor the contractual arrangement between A and B dealing with the manufacturing activity specifies that the parties have rights to the assets, and obligations for the liabilities, relating to the manufacturing activity.

(b)   Distribution activity: the parties have agreed to undertake the distribution activity through a joint arrangement (the distribution arrangement). The parties have structured the distribution arrangement in a separate vehicle (entity D) whose legal form causes it to be considered in its own right (ie the assets and liabilities held in entity D are the assets and liabilities of entity D and not the assets and liabilities of the parties). In accordance with the framework agreement, the distribution arrangement orders its requirements for product P from the parties according to the needs of the different markets where the distribution arrangement sells the product. Neither the framework agreement nor the contractual arrangement between A and B dealing with the distribution activity specifies that the parties have rights to the assets, and obligations for the liabilities, relating to the distribution activity.

IE16   In addition, the framework agreement establishes:

(a)   that the manufacturing arrangement will produce product P to meet the requirements for product P that the distribution arrangement places on the parties;

(b)   the commercial terms relating to the sale of product P by the manufacturing arrangement to the parties. The manufacturing arrangement will sell product P to the parties at a price agreed by A and B that covers all production costs incurred. Subsequently, the parties sell the product to the distribution arrangement at a price agreed by A and B.

(c)   that any cash shortages that the manufacturing arrangement may incur will be financed by the parties in accordance with their ownership interests in entity M.

Analysis

IE17   The framework agreement sets up the terms under which parties A and B conduct the manufacturing and distribution of product P. These activities are undertaken through joint arrangements whose purpose is either the manufacturing or the distribution of product P.

IE18   The parties carry out the manufacturing arrangement through entity M whose legal form confers separation between the parties and the entity. In addition, neither the framework agreement nor the contractual arrangement dealing with the manufacturing activity specifies that the parties have rights to the assets, and obligations for the liabilities, relating to the manufacturing activity. However, when considering the following facts and circumstances the parties have concluded that the manufacturing arrangement is a joint operation:

(a)   The parties have committed themselves to purchasing the whole production of product P manufactured by the manufacturing arrangement. Consequently, A and B have rights to substantially all the economic benefits of the assets of the manufacturing arrangement.

(b)   The manufacturing arrangement manufactures product P to meet the quantity and quality needs of the parties so that they can fulfil the demand for product P of the distribution arrangement. The exclusive dependence of the manufacturing arrangement upon the parties for the generation of cash flows and the parties' commitments to provide funds when the manufacturing arrangement incurs any cash shortages indicate that the parties have an obligation for the liabilities of the manufacturing arrangement, because those liabilities will be settled through the parties' purchases of product P or by the parties' direct provision of funds.

IE19 The parties carry out the distribution activities through entity D, whose legal form confers separation between the parties and the entity. In addition, neither the framework agreement nor the contractual arrangement dealing with the distribution activity specifies that the parties have rights to the assets, and obligations for the liabilities, relating to the distribution activity.

IE20 There are no other facts and circumstances that indicate that the parties have rights to substantially all the economic benefits of the assets relating to the distribution arrangement or that the parties have an obligation for the liabilities relating to that arrangement. The distribution arrangement is a joint venture.

IE21 A and B each recognise in their financial statements their share of the assets (eg property, plant and equipment, cash) and their share of any liabilities resulting from the manufacturing arrangement (eg accounts payable to third parties) on the basis of their ownership interest in entity M. Each party also recognises its share of the expenses resulting from the manufacture of product P incurred by the manufacturing arrangement and its share of the revenues relating to the sales of product P to the distribution arrangement.

IE22 The parties recognise their rights to the net assets of the distribution arrangement as investments and account for them using the equity method.

Variation

IE23 Assume that the parties agree that the manufacturing arrangement described above is responsible not only for manufacturing product P, but also for its distribution to third-party customers.

IE24 The parties also agree to set up a distribution arrangement like the one described above to distribute product P exclusively to assist in widening the distribution of product P in additional specific markets.

IE25 The manufacturing arrangement also sells product P directly to the distribution arrangement. No fixed proportion of the production of the manufacturing arrangement is committed to be purchased by, or to be reserved to, the distribution arrangement.

Analysis

IE26 The variation has affected neither the legal form of the separate vehicle in which the manufacturing activity is conducted nor the contractual terms relating to the parties' rights to the assets, and obligations for the liabilities, relating to the manufacturing activity. However, it causes the manufacturing arrangement to be a self-financed arrangement because it is able to undertake trade on its own behalf, distributing product P to third-party customers and, consequently, assuming demand, inventory and credit risks. Even though the manufacturing arrangement might also sell product P to the distribution arrangement, in this scenario the manufacturing arrangement is not dependent on the parties to be able to carry out its activities on a continuous basis. In this case, the manufacturing arrangement is a joint venture.

IE27 The variation has no effect on the classification of the distribution arrangement as a joint venture.

IE28 The parties recognise their rights to the net assets of the manufacturing arrangement and their rights to the net assets of the distribution arrangement as investments and account for them using the equity method.

Example 4 – Bank operated jointly

IE29 Banks A and B (the parties) agreed to combine their corporate, investment banking, asset management and services activities by establishing a separate vehicle (bank C). Both parties expect the arrangement to benefit them in different ways. Bank A believes that the arrangement could enable it to achieve its strategic plans to increase its size, offering an opportunity to exploit its full potential for organic growth through

AASB

an enlarged offering of products and services. Bank B expects the arrangement to reinforce its offering in financial savings and market products.

IE30   The main feature of bank C's legal form is that it causes the separate vehicle to be considered in its own right (ie the assets and liabilities held in the separate vehicle are the assets and liabilities of the separate vehicle and not the assets and liabilities of the parties). Banks A and B each have a 40 per cent ownership interest in bank C, with the remaining 20 per cent being listed and widely held. The shareholders' agreement between bank A and bank B establishes joint control of the activities of bank C.

IE31   In addition, bank A and bank B entered into an irrevocable agreement under which, even in the event of a dispute, both banks agree to provide the necessary funds in equal amount and, if required, jointly and severally, to ensure that bank C complies with the applicable legislation and banking regulations, and honours any commitments made to the banking authorities. This commitment represents the assumption by each party of 50 per cent of any funds needed to ensure that bank C complies with legislation and banking regulations.

Analysis

IE32   The joint arrangement is carried out through a separate vehicle whose legal form confers separation between the parties and the separate vehicle. The terms of the contractual arrangement do not specify that the parties have rights to the assets, or obligations for the liabilities, of bank C, but it establishes that the parties have rights to the net assets of bank C. The commitment by the parties to provide support if bank C is not able to comply with the applicable legislation and banking regulations is not by itself a determinant that the parties have an obligation for the liabilities of bank C. There are no other facts and circumstances that indicate that the parties have rights to substantially all the economic benefits of the assets of bank C and that the parties have an obligation for the liabilities of bank C. The joint arrangement is a joint venture.

IE33   Both banks A and B recognise their rights to the net assets of bank C as investments and account for them using the equity method.

Example 5 – Oil and gas exploration, development and production activities

IE34   Companies A and B (the parties) set up a separate vehicle (entity H) and a Joint Operating Agreement (JOA) to undertake oil and gas exploration, development and production activities in country O. The main feature of entity H's legal form is that it causes the separate vehicle to be considered in its own right (ie the assets and liabilities held in the separate vehicle are the assets and liabilities of the separate vehicle and not the assets and liabilities of the parties).

IE35   Country O has granted entity H permits for the oil and gas exploration, development and production activities to be undertaken in a specific assigned block of land (fields).

IE36   The shareholders' agreement and JOA agreed by the parties establish their rights and obligations relating to those activities. The main terms of those agreements are summarised below.

Shareholders' agreement

IE37   The board of entity H consists of a director from each party. Each party has a 50 per cent shareholding in entity H. The unanimous consent of the directors is required for any resolution to be passed.

Joint Operating Agreement (JOA)

IE38   The JOA establishes an Operating Committee. This Committee consists of one representative from each party. Each party has a 50 per cent participating interest in the Operating Committee.

IE39 The Operating Committee approves the budgets and work programmes relating to the activities, which also require the unanimous consent of the representatives of each party. One of the parties is appointed as operator and is responsible for managing and conducting the approved work programmes.

IE40 The JOA specifies that the rights and obligations arising from the exploration, development and production activities shall be shared among the parties in proportion to each party's shareholding in entity H. In particular, the JOA establishes that the parties share:

(a) the rights and the obligations arising from the exploration and development permits granted to entity H (eg the permits, rehabilitation liabilities, any royalties and taxes payable);

(b) the production obtained; and

(c) all costs associated with all work programmes.

IE41 The costs incurred in relation to all the work programmes are covered by cash calls on the parties. If either party fails to satisfy its monetary obligations, the other is required to contribute to entity H the amount in default. The amount in default is regarded as a debt owed by the defaulting party to the other party.

Analysis

IE42 The parties carry out the joint arrangement through a separate vehicle whose legal form confers separation between the parties and the separate vehicle. The parties have been able to reverse the initial assessment of their rights and obligations arising from the legal form of the separate vehicle in which the arrangement is conducted. They have done this by agreeing terms in the JOA that entitle them to rights to the assets (eg exploration and development permits, production, and any other assets arising from the activities) and obligations for the liabilities (eg all costs and obligations arising from the work programmes) that are held in entity H. The joint arrangement is a joint operation.

IE43 Both company A and company B recognise in their financial statements their own share of the assets and of any liabilities resulting from the arrangement on the basis of their agreed participating interest. On that basis, each party also recognises its share of the revenue (from the sale of their share of the production) and its share of the expenses.

Example 6 – Liquefied natural gas arrangement

IE44 Company A owns an undeveloped gas field that contains substantial gas resources. Company A determines that the gas field will be economically viable only if the gas is sold to customers in overseas markets. To do so, a liquefied natural gas (LNG) facility must be built to liquefy the gas so that it can be transported by ship to the overseas markets.

IE45 Company A enters into a joint arrangement with company B in order to develop and operate the gas field and the LNG facility. Under that arrangement, companies A and B (the parties) agree to contribute the gas field and cash, respectively, to a new separate vehicle, entity C. In exchange for those contributions, the parties each take a 50 per cent ownership interest in entity C. The main feature of entity C's legal form is that it causes the separate vehicle to be considered in its own right (ie the assets and liabilities held in the separate vehicle are the assets and liabilities of the separate vehicle and not the assets and liabilities of the parties).

IE46 The contractual arrangement between the parties specifies that:

(a) companies A and B must each appoint two members to the board of entity C. The board of directors must unanimously agree the strategy and investments made by entity C.

(b) day-to-day management of the gas field and LNG facility, including development and construction activities, will be undertaken by the staff of company B in accordance with the directions jointly agreed by the parties. Entity C will reimburse B for the costs it incurs in managing the gas field and LNG facility.

(c)   entity C is liable for taxes and royalties on the production and sale of LNG as well as for other liabilities incurred in the ordinary course of business, such as accounts payable, site restoration and decommissioning liabilities.

(d)   companies A and B have equal shares in the profit from the activities carried out in the arrangement and, as such, are entitled to equal shares of any dividends distributed by entity C.

IE47   The contractual arrangement does not specify that either party has rights to the assets, or obligations for the liabilities, of entity C.

IE48   The board of entity C decides to enter into a financing arrangement with a syndicate of lenders to help fund the development of the gas field and construction of the LNG facility. The estimated total cost of the development and construction is CU1,000 million.[2]

IE49   The lending syndicate provides entity C with a CU700 million loan. The arrangement specifies that the syndicate has recourse to companies A and B only if entity C defaults on the loan arrangement during the development of the field and construction of the LNG facility. The lending syndicate agrees that it will not have recourse to companies A and B once the LNG facility is in production because it has assessed that the cash inflows that entity C should generate from LNG sales will be sufficient to meet the loan repayments. Although at this time the lenders have no recourse to companies A and B, the syndicate maintains protection against default by entity C by taking a lien on the LNG facility.

Analysis

IE50   The joint arrangement is carried out through a separate vehicle whose legal form confers separation between the parties and the separate vehicle. The terms of the contractual arrangement do not specify that the parties have rights to the assets, or obligations for the liabilities, of entity C, but they establish that the parties have rights to the net assets of entity C. The recourse nature of the financing arrangement during the development of the gas field and construction of the LNG facility (ie companies A and B providing separate guarantees during this phase) does not, by itself, impose on the parties an obligation for the liabilities of entity C (ie the loan is a liability of entity C). Companies A and B have separate liabilities, which are their guarantees to repay that loan if entity C defaults during the development and construction phase.

IE51   There are no other facts and circumstances that indicate that the parties have rights to substantially all the economic benefits of the assets of entity C and that the parties have an obligation for the liabilities of entity C. The joint arrangement is a joint venture.

IE52   The parties recognise their rights to the net assets of entity C as investments and account for them using the equity method.

Example 7—Accounting for acquisitions of interests in joint operations in which the activity constitutes a business

IE53   Companies A, B and C have joint control of Joint Operation D whose activity constitutes a business, as defined in AASB 3 *Business Combinations*.

IE54   Company E acquires company A's 40 per cent ownership interest in Joint Operation D at a cost of CU300 and incurs acquisition-related costs of CU50.

IE55   The contractual arrangement between the parties that Company E joined as part of the acquisition establishes that Company E's shares in several assets and liabilities differ from its ownership interest in Joint Operation D. The following table sets out Company

---

2   In these examples monetary amounts are denominated in 'currency units (CU)'.

E's share in the assets and liabilities related to Joint Operation D as established in the contractual arrangement between the parties:

	Company E's share in the assets and liabilities related to Joint Operation D
Property, plant and equipment	48%
Intangible assets (excluding goodwill)	90%
Accounts receivable	40%
Inventory	40%
Retirement benefit obligations	15%
Accounts payable	40%
Contingent liabilities	56%

Analysis

IE56 Company E recognises in its financial statements its share of the assets and liabilities resulting from the contractual arrangement (see paragraph 20).

IE57 It applies the principles on business combinations accounting in AASB 3 and other Australian Accounting Standards for identifying, recognising, measuring and classifying the assets acquired, and the liabilities assumed, on the acquisition of the interest in Joint Operation D. This is because Company E acquired an interest in a joint operation in which the activity constitutes a business (see paragraph 21A).

IE58 However, Company E does not apply the principles on business combinations accounting in AASB 3 and other Australian Accounting Standards that conflict with the guidance in this Standard. Consequently, in accordance with paragraph 20, Company E recognises, and therefore measures, in relation to its interest in Joint Operation D, only its share in each of the assets that are jointly held and in each of the liabilities that are incurred jointly, as stated in the contractual arrangement. Company E does not include in its assets and liabilities the shares of the other parties in Joint Operation D.

IE59 AASB 3 requires the acquirer to measure the identifiable assets acquired and the liabilities assumed at their acquisition-date fair values with limited exceptions; for example, deferred tax assets and deferred tax liabilities are not measured at fair value but are measured in accordance with AASB 112 *Income Taxes*. Such measurement does not conflict with this Standard and thus those requirements apply.

IE60 Consequently, Company E determines the fair value, or other measure specified in AASB 3, of its share in the identifiable assets and liabilities related to Joint Operation D. The following table sets out the fair value or other measure specified by AASB 3 of Company E's shares in the identifiable assets and liabilities related to Joint Operation D:

	Fair value or other measure specified by AASB 3 for Company E's shares in the identifiable assets and liabilities of Joint Operation D
	CU
Property, plant and equipment	138
Intangible assets (excluding goodwill)	72
Accounts receivable	84
Inventory	70
Retirement benefit obligations	(12)

AASB

	Fair value or other measure specified by AASB 3 for Company E's shares in the identifiable assets and liabilities of Joint Operation D
	CU
Accounts payable	(48)
Contingent liabilities	(52)
Deferred tax liability	(24)
Net assets	**228**

IE61   In accordance with AASB 3, the excess of the consideration transferred over the amount allocated to Company E's shares in the net identifiable assets is recognised as goodwill:

Consideration transferred	CU300
Company E's shares in the identifiable assets and liabilities relating to its interest in the joint operation	CU228
Goodwill	**CU72**

IE62   Acquisition-related costs of CU50 are not considered to be part of the consideration transferred for the interest in the joint operation. They are recognised as expenses in profit or loss in the period that the costs are incurred and the services are received (see paragraph 53 of AASB 3).

Example 8—Contributing the right to use know-how to a joint operation in which the activity constitutes a business

IE63   Companies A and B are two companies whose business is the construction of high performance batteries for diverse applications.

IE64   In order to develop batteries for electric vehicles they set up a contractual arrangement (Joint Operation Z) to work together. Companies A and B share joint control of Joint Operation Z. This arrangement is a joint operation in which the activity constitutes a business, as defined in AASB 3.

IE65   After several years, the joint operators (Companies A and B) concluded that it is feasible to develop a battery for electric vehicles using Material M. However, processing Material M requires specialist know-how and thus far, Material M has only been used in the production of cosmetics.

IE66   In order to get access to existing know-how in processing Material M, Companies A and B arrange for Company C to join as another joint operator by acquiring an interest in Joint Operation Z from Companies A and B and becoming a party to the contractual arrangements.

IE67   Company C's business so far has been solely the development and production of cosmetics. It has long-standing and extensive knowledge in processing Material M.

IE68   In exchange for its share in Joint Operation Z, Company C pays cash to Companies A and B and grants the right to use its know-how in processing Material M for the purposes of Joint Operation Z. In addition, Company C seconds some of its employees who are experienced in processing Material M to Joint Operation Z. However, Company C does not transfer control of the know-how to Companies A and B or Joint Operation Z because it retains all the rights to it. In particular, Company C is entitled to withdraw the right to use its know-how in processing Material M and to withdraw its seconded employees without any restrictions or compensation to Companies A and B or Joint Operation Z if it ceases its participation in Joint Operation Z.

IE69 The fair value of Company C's know-how on the date of the acquisition of the interest in the joint operation is CU1,000. Immediately before the acquisition, the carrying amount of the know-how in the financial statements of Company C was CU300.

Analysis

IE70 Company C has acquired an interest in Joint Operation Z in which the activity of the joint operation constitutes a business, as defined in AASB 3.

IE71 In accounting for the acquisition of its interest in the joint operation, Company C applies all the principles on business combinations accounting in AASB 3 and other Australian Accounting Standards that do not conflict with the guidance in this Standard (see paragraph 21A). Company C therefore recognises in its financial statements its share of the assets and liabilities resulting from the contractual arrangement (see paragraph 20).

IE72 Company C granted the right to use its know-how in processing Material M to Joint Operation Z as part of joining Joint Operation Z as a joint operator. However, Company C retains control of this right because it is entitled to withdraw the right to use its know-how in processing Material M and to withdraw its seconded employees without any restrictions or any compensation to Companies A and B or Joint Operation Z if it ceases its participation in Joint Operation Z.

IE73 Consequently, Company C continues to recognise the know-how in processing Material M after the acquisition of the interest in Joint Operation Z because it retains all the rights to it. This means that Company C will continue to recognise the know-how based on its carrying amount of CU300. As a consequence of retaining control of the right to use the know-how that it granted to the joint operation, Company C has granted the right to use the know-how to itself. Consequently, Company C does not remeasure the know-how, and it does not recognise a gain or loss on the grant of the right to use it.

DELETED IFRS 11 TEXT

Deleted IFRS 11 text is not part of AASB 11.

C1A *Consolidated Financial Statements, Joint Arrangements and Disclosure of Interests in Other Entities: Transition Guidance* (Amendments to IFRS 10, IFRS 11 and IFRS 12), issued in June 2012, amended paragraphs C2–C5, C7–C10 and C12 and added paragraphs C1B and C12A–C12B. An entity shall apply those amendments for annual periods beginning on or after 1 January 2013. If an entity applies IFRS 11 for an earlier period, it shall apply those amendments for that earlier period.

C15 This IFRS supersedes the following IFRSs:

    (a)   IAS 31 *Interests in Joint Ventures*; and

    (b)   SIC-13 *Jointly Controlled Entities—Non-Monetary Contributions by Venturers*.

AASB 12
Disclosure of Interests in Other Entities

(Compiled February 2017)

This compiled Standard applies to annual periods beginning on or after 1 January 2017. Earlier application is not permitted. It incorporates relevant amendments made up to and including 13 February 2017.

Prepared on 20 April 2017 by the staff of the Australian Accounting Standards Board.

Compilation no. 1

Compilation date: 13 February 2017

CONTENTS

B. APPLICATION GUIDANCE

C. EFFECTIVE DATE AND TRANSITION

E. AUSTRALIAN IMPLEMENTATION GUIDANCE FOR NOT-FOR-PROFIT ENTITIES

F. AUSTRALIAN REDUCED DISCLOSURE REQUIREMENTS

COMPILATION DETAILS

DELETED IFRS 12 TEXT

BASIS FOR CONCLUSIONS ON IFRS 12 (available on the AASB website)

Accounting Standard AASB 12 *Disclosure of Interests in Other Entities* as amended is set out in paragraphs 1 – Aus31.2 and Appendices A – C and E – F. All the paragraphs have equal authority. Paragraphs in **bold type** state the main principles. Terms defined in Appendix A are in *italics* the first time they appear in the Standard. AASB 12 is to be read in the context of other Australian Accounting Standards, including AASB 1048 *Interpretation of Standards*, which identifies the Australian Accounting Interpretations, and AASB 1057 *Application of Australian Accounting Standards*. In the absence of explicit guidance, AASB 108 *Accounting Policies, Changes in Accounting Estimates and Errors* provides a basis for selecting and applying accounting policies.

COMPARISON WITH IFRS 12

AASB 12 *Disclosure of Interests in Other Entities* incorporates IFRS 12 *Disclosure of Interests in Other Entities* issued by the International Accounting Standards Board (IASB). Australian-specific paragraphs (which are not included in IFRS 12) are identified with the prefix "Aus". Paragraphs that apply only to not-for-profit entities begin by identifying their limited applicability.

Tier 1

For-profit entities complying with AASB 12 also comply with IFRS 12.

Not-for-profit entities' compliance with IFRS 12 will depend on whether any "Aus" paragraphs that specifically apply to not-for-profit entities provide additional guidance or contain applicable requirements that are inconsistent with IFRS 12.

Tier 2

Entities preparing general purpose financial statements under Australian Accounting Standards – Reduced Disclosure Requirements (Tier 2) will not be in compliance with IFRSs.

AASB 1053 *Application of Tiers of Australian Accounting Standards* explains the two tiers of reporting requirements.

ACCOUNTING STANDARD AASB 12

The Australian Accounting Standards Board made Accounting Standard AASB 12 *Disclosure of Interests in Other Entities* under section 334 of the *Corporations Act 2001* on 7 August 2015.

This compiled version of AASB 12 applies to annual reporting periods beginning on or after 1 January 2017. It incorporates relevant amendments contained in other AASB Standards made by the AASB up to and including 13 February 2017 (see Compilation Details).

ACCOUNTING STANDARD AASB 12
DISCLOSURE OF INTERESTS IN OTHER ENTITIES

Objective

1   The objective of this Standard is to require an entity to disclose information that enables users of its financial statements to evaluate:

   (a)   the nature of, and risks associated with, its *interests in other entities*; and

   (b)   the effects of those interests on its financial position, financial performance and cash flows.

Meeting the objective

2   To meet the objective in paragraph 1, an entity shall disclose:

   (a)   the significant judgements and assumptions it has made in determining:

      (i)   the nature of its interest in another entity or arrangement;

      (ii)   the type of joint arrangement in which it has an interest (paragraphs 7–9);

      (iii)   that it meets the definition of an investment entity, if applicable (paragraph 9A); and

   (b)   information about its interests in:

      (i)   subsidiaries (paragraphs 10–19);

      (ii)   joint arrangements and associates (paragraphs 20–23); and

      (iii)   *structured entities* that are not controlled by the entity (unconsolidated structured entities) (paragraphs 24–31).

3   If the disclosures required by this Standard, together with disclosures required by other Standards, do not meet the objective in paragraph 1, an entity shall disclose whatever additional information is necessary to meet that objective.

4   An entity shall consider the level of detail necessary to satisfy the disclosure objective and how much emphasis to place on each of the requirements in this Standard. It shall aggregate or disaggregate disclosures so that useful information is not obscured by either the inclusion of a large amount of insignificant detail or the aggregation of items that have different characteristics (see paragraphs B2–B6).

Scope

5   This Standard shall be applied by an entity that has an interest in any of the following:

   (a)   subsidiaries

   (b)   joint arrangements (ie joint operations or joint ventures)

   (c)   associates

   (d)   unconsolidated structured entities.

5A   Except as described in paragraph B17, the requirements in this Standard apply to an entity's interests listed in paragraph 5 that are classified (or included in a disposal group that is classified) as held for sale or discontinued operations in accordance with AASB 5 *Non-current Assets Held for Sale and Discontinued Operations*.

6   This Standard does not apply to:

   (a)   post-employment benefit plans or other long-term employee benefit plans to which AASB 119 *Employee Benefits* applies.

   (b)   an entity's separate financial statements to which AASB 127 *Separate Financial Statements* applies. However:

(i) if an entity has interests in unconsolidated structured entities and prepares separate financial statements as its only financial statements, it shall apply the requirements in paragraphs 24–31 when preparing those separate financial statements.

(ii) an investment entity that prepares financial statements in which all of its subsidiaries are measured at fair value through profit or loss in accordance with paragraph 31 of AASB 10 shall present the disclosures relating to investment entities required by this Standard.

(c) an interest held by an entity that participates in, but does not have joint control of, a joint arrangement unless that interest results in significant influence over the arrangement or is an interest in a structured entity.

(d) an interest in another entity that is accounted for in accordance with AASB 9 *Financial Instruments*. However, an entity shall apply this Standard:

(i) when that interest is an interest in an associate or a joint venture that, in accordance with AASB 128 *Investments in Associates and Joint Ventures*, is measured at fair value through profit or loss; or

(ii) when that interest is an interest in an unconsolidated structured entity.

Significant judgements and assumptions

7 An entity shall disclose information about significant judgements and assumptions it has made (and changes to those judgements and assumptions) in determining:

(a) that it has control of another entity, ie an investee as described in paragraphs 5 and 6 of AASB 10 *Consolidated Financial Statements*;

(b) that it has joint control of an arrangement or significant influence over another entity; and

(c) the type of joint arrangement (ie joint operation or joint venture) when the arrangement has been structured through a separate vehicle.

8 The significant judgements and assumptions disclosed in accordance with paragraph 7 include those made by the entity when changes in facts and circumstances are such that the conclusion about whether it has control, joint control or significant influence changes during the reporting period.

9 To comply with paragraph 7, an entity shall disclose, for example, significant judgements and assumptions made in determining that:

(a) it does not control another entity even though it holds more than half of the voting rights of the other entity.

(b) it controls another entity even though it holds less than half of the voting rights of the other entity.

(c) it is an agent or a principal (see paragraphs B58–B72 of AASB 10).

(d) it does not have significant influence even though it holds 20 per cent or more of the voting rights of another entity.

(e) it has significant influence even though it holds less than 20 per cent of the voting rights of another entity.

Investment entity status

9A When a parent determines that it is an investment entity in accordance with paragraph 27 of AASB 10, the investment entity shall disclose information about significant judgements and assumptions it has made in determining that it is an investment entity. If the investment entity does not have one or more of the typical characteristics of an investment entity (see paragraph 28 of AASB 10), it shall disclose its reasons for concluding that it is nevertheless an investment entity.

9B   When an entity becomes, or ceases to be, an investment entity, it shall disclose the change of investment entity status and the reasons for the change. In addition, an entity that becomes an investment entity shall disclose the effect of the change of status on the financial statements for the period presented, including:

(a)   the total fair value, as of the date of change of status, of the subsidiaries that cease to be consolidated;

(b)   the total gain or loss, if any, calculated in accordance with paragraph B101 of AASB 10; and

(c)   the line item(s) in profit or loss in which the gain or loss is recognised (if not presented separately).

Interests in subsidiaries

10   **An entity shall disclose information that enables users of its consolidated financial statements**

(a)   **to understand:**

(i)   **the composition of the group; and**

(ii)   **the interest that non-controlling interests have in the group's activities and cash flows (paragraph 12); and**

(b)   **to evaluate:**

(i)   **the nature and extent of significant restrictions on its ability to access or use assets, and settle liabilities, of the group (paragraph 13);**

(ii)   **the nature of, and changes in, the risks associated with its interests in consolidated structured entities (paragraphs 14–17);**

(iii) **the consequences of changes in its ownership interest in a subsidiary that do not result in a loss of control (paragraph 18); and**

(iv)   **the consequences of losing control of a subsidiary during the reporting period (paragraph 19).**

11   When the financial statements of a subsidiary used in the preparation of consolidated financial statements are as of a date or for a period that is different from that of the consolidated financial statements (see paragraphs B92 and B93 of AASB 10), an entity shall disclose:

(a)   the date of the end of the reporting period of the financial statements of that subsidiary; and

(b)   the reason for using a different date or period.

The interest that non-controlling interests have in the group's activities and cash flows

12   An entity shall disclose for each of its subsidiaries that have non-controlling interests that are material to the reporting entity:

(a)   the name of the subsidiary.

(b)   the principal place of business (and country of incorporation if different from the principal place of business) of the subsidiary.

(c)   the proportion of ownership interests held by non-controlling interests.

(d)   the proportion of voting rights held by non-controlling interests, if different from the proportion of ownership interests held.

(e)   the profit or loss allocated to non-controlling interests of the subsidiary during the reporting period.

(f)   accumulated non-controlling interests of the subsidiary at the end of the reporting period.

(g)   summarised financial information about the subsidiary (see paragraph B10).

The nature and extent of significant restrictions

13   An entity shall disclose:

    (a)   significant restrictions (eg statutory, contractual and regulatory restrictions) on its ability to access or use the assets and settle the liabilities of the group, such as:

        (i)   those that restrict the ability of a parent or its subsidiaries to transfer cash or other assets to (or from) other entities within the group.

        (ii)   guarantees or other requirements that may restrict dividends and other capital distributions being paid, or loans and advances being made or repaid, to (or from) other entities within the group.

    (b)   the nature and extent to which protective rights of non-controlling interests can significantly restrict the entity's ability to access or use the assets and settle the liabilities of the group (such as when a parent is obliged to settle liabilities of a subsidiary before settling its own liabilities, or approval of non-controlling interests is required either to access the assets or to settle the liabilities of a subsidiary).

    (c)   the carrying amounts in the consolidated financial statements of the assets and liabilities to which those restrictions apply.

Nature of the risks associated with an entity's interests in consolidated structured entities

14   An entity shall disclose the terms of any contractual arrangements that could require the parent or its subsidiaries to provide financial support to a consolidated structured entity, including events or circumstances that could expose the reporting entity to a loss (eg liquidity arrangements or credit rating triggers associated with obligations to purchase assets of the structured entity or provide financial support).

15   If during the reporting period a parent or any of its subsidiaries has, without having a contractual obligation to do so, provided financial or other support to a consolidated structured entity (eg purchasing assets of or instruments issued by the structured entity), the entity shall disclose:

    (a)   the type and amount of support provided, including situations in which the parent or its subsidiaries assisted the structured entity in obtaining financial support; and

    (b)   the reasons for providing the support.

16   If during the reporting period a parent or any of its subsidiaries has, without having a contractual obligation to do so, provided financial or other support to a previously unconsolidated structured entity and that provision of support resulted in the entity controlling the structured entity, the entity shall disclose an explanation of the relevant factors in reaching that decision.

17   An entity shall disclose any current intentions to provide financial or other support to a consolidated structured entity, including intentions to assist the structured entity in obtaining financial support.

Consequences of changes in a parent's ownership interest in a subsidiary that do not result in a loss of control

18   An entity shall present a schedule that shows the effects on the equity attributable to owners of the parent of any changes in its ownership interest in a subsidiary that do not result in a loss of control.

Consequences of losing control of a subsidiary during the reporting period

19　An entity shall disclose the gain or loss, if any, calculated in accordance with paragraph 25 of AASB 10, and:

　(a)　the portion of that gain or loss attributable to measuring any investment retained in the former subsidiary at its fair value at the date when control is lost; and

　(b)　the line item(s) in profit or loss in which the gain or loss is recognised (if not presented separately).

Interests in unconsolidated subsidiaries (investment entities)

19A　An investment entity that, in accordance with AASB 10, is required to apply the exception to consolidation and instead account for its investment in a subsidiary at fair value through profit or loss shall disclose that fact.

19B　For each unconsolidated subsidiary, an investment entity shall disclose:

　(a)　the subsidiary's name;

　(b)　the principal place of business (and country of incorporation if different from the principal place of business) of the subsidiary; and

　(c)　the proportion of ownership interest held by the investment entity and, if different, the proportion of voting rights held.

19C　If an investment entity is the parent of another investment entity, the parent shall also provide the disclosures in 19B(a)–(c) for investments that are controlled by its investment entity subsidiary. The disclosure may be provided by including, in the financial statements of the parent, the financial statements of the subsidiary (or subsidiaries) that contain the above information.

19D　An investment entity shall disclose:

　(a)　the nature and extent of any significant restrictions (eg resulting from borrowing arrangements, regulatory requirements or contractual arrangements) on the ability of an unconsolidated subsidiary to transfer funds to the investment entity in the form of cash dividends or to repay loans or advances made to the unconsolidated subsidiary by the investment entity; and

　(b)　any current commitments or intentions to provide financial or other support to an unconsolidated subsidiary, including commitments or intentions to assist the subsidiary in obtaining financial support.

19E　If, during the reporting period, an investment entity or any of its subsidiaries has, without having a contractual obligation to do so, provided financial or other support to an unconsolidated subsidiary (eg purchasing assets of, or instruments issued by, the subsidiary or assisting the subsidiary in obtaining financial support), the entity shall disclose:

　(a)　the type and amount of support provided to each unconsolidated subsidiary; and

　(b)　the reasons for providing the support.

19F　An investment entity shall disclose the terms of any contractual arrangements that could require the entity or its unconsolidated subsidiaries to provide financial support to an unconsolidated, controlled, structured entity, including events or circumstances that could expose the reporting entity to a loss (eg liquidity arrangements or credit rating triggers associated with obligations to purchase assets of the structured entity or to provide financial support).

19G　If during the reporting period an investment entity or any of its unconsolidated subsidiaries has, without having a contractual obligation to do so, provided financial or other support to an unconsolidated, structured entity that the investment entity did not control, and if that provision of support resulted in the investment entity controlling the structured entity, the investment entity shall disclose an explanation of the relevant factors in reaching the decision to provide that support.

Interests in joint arrangements and associates

20 An entity shall disclose information that enables users of its financial statements to evaluate:

    (a) **the nature, extent and financial effects of its interests in joint arrangements and associates, including the nature and effects of its contractual relationship with the other investors with joint control of, or significant influence over, joint arrangements and associates (paragraphs 21 and 22); and**

    (b) **the nature of, and changes in, the risks associated with its interests in joint ventures and associates (paragraph 23).**

Nature, extent and financial effects of an entity's interests in joint arrangements and associates

21 An entity shall disclose:

    (a) for each joint arrangement and associate that is material to the reporting entity:

        (i) the name of the joint arrangement or associate.

        (ii) the nature of the entity's relationship with the joint arrangement or associate (by, for example, describing the nature of the activities of the joint arrangement or associate and whether they are strategic to the entity's activities).

        (iii) the principal place of business (and country of incorporation, if applicable and different from the principal place of business) of the joint arrangement or associate.

        (iv) the proportion of ownership interest or participating share held by the entity and, if different, the proportion of voting rights held (if applicable).

    (b) for each joint venture and associate that is material to the reporting entity:

        (i) whether the investment in the joint venture or associate is measured using the equity method or at fair value.

        (ii) summarised financial information about the joint venture or associate as specified in paragraphs B12 and B13.

        (iii) if the joint venture or associate is accounted for using the equity method, the fair value of its investment in the joint venture or associate, if there is a quoted market price for the investment.

    (c) financial information as specified in paragraph B16 about the entity's investments in joint ventures and associates that are not individually material:

        (i) in aggregate for all individually immaterial joint ventures and, separately,

        (ii) in aggregate for all individually immaterial associates.

21A An investment entity need not provide the disclosures required by paragraphs 21(b)–21(c).

22 An entity shall also disclose:

    (a) the nature and extent of any significant restrictions (eg resulting from borrowing arrangements, regulatory requirements or contractual arrangements between investors with joint control of or significant influence over a joint venture or an associate) on the ability of joint ventures or associates to transfer funds to the entity in the form of cash dividends, or to repay loans or advances made by the entity.

    (b) when the financial statements of a joint venture or associate used in applying the equity method are as of a date or for a period that is different from that of the entity:

        (i) the date of the end of the reporting period of the financial statements of that joint venture or associate; and

(ii)   the reason for using a different date or period.

(c)   the unrecognised share of losses of a joint venture or associate, both for the reporting period and cumulatively, if the entity has stopped recognising its share of losses of the joint venture or associate when applying the equity method.

Risks associated with an entity's interests in joint ventures and associates

23   An entity shall disclose:

(a)   commitments that it has relating to its joint ventures separately from the amount of other commitments as specified in paragraphs B18–B20.

(b)   in accordance with AASB 137 *Provisions, Contingent Liabilities and Contingent Assets*, unless the probability of loss is remote, contingent liabilities incurred relating to its interests in joint ventures or associates (including its share of contingent liabilities incurred jointly with other investors with joint control of, or significant influence over, the joint ventures or associates), separately from the amount of other contingent liabilities.

Interests in unconsolidated structured entities

24   **An entity shall disclose information that enables users of its financial statements:**

(a)   **to understand the nature and extent of its interests in unconsolidated structured entities (paragraphs 26–28); and**

(b)   **to evaluate the nature of, and changes in, the risks associated with its interests in unconsolidated structured entities (paragraphs 29–31).**

25   The information required by paragraph 24(b) includes information about an entity's exposure to risk from involvement that it had with unconsolidated structured entities in previous periods (eg sponsoring the structured entity), even if the entity no longer has any contractual involvement with the structured entity at the reporting date.

25A   An investment entity need not provide the disclosures required by paragraph 24 for an unconsolidated structured entity that it controls and for which it presents the disclosures required by paragraphs 19A–19G.

Nature of interests

26   An entity shall disclose qualitative and quantitative information about its interests in unconsolidated structured entities, including, but not limited to, the nature, purpose, size and activities of the structured entity and how the structured entity is financed.

27   If an entity has sponsored an unconsolidated structured entity for which it does not provide information required by paragraph 29 (eg because it does not have an interest in the entity at the reporting date), the entity shall disclose:

(a)   how it has determined which structured entities it has sponsored;

(b)   *income from those structured entities* during the reporting period, including a description of the types of income presented; and

(c)   the carrying amount (at the time of transfer) of all assets transferred to those structured entities during the reporting period.

28   An entity shall present the information in paragraph 27(b) and (c) in tabular format, unless another format is more appropriate, and classify its sponsoring activities into relevant categories (see paragraphs B2–B6).

Nature of risks

29   An entity shall disclose in tabular format, unless another format is more appropriate, a summary of:

(a)   the carrying amounts of the assets and liabilities recognised in its financial statements relating to its interests in unconsolidated structured entities.

    (b)   the line items in the statement of financial position in which those assets and liabilities are recognised.

    (c)   the amount that best represents the entity's maximum exposure to loss from its interests in unconsolidated structured entities, including how the maximum exposure to loss is determined. If an entity cannot quantify its maximum exposure to loss from its interests in unconsolidated structured entities it shall disclose that fact and the reasons.

    (d)   a comparison of the carrying amounts of the assets and liabilities of the entity that relate to its interests in unconsolidated structured entities and the entity's maximum exposure to loss from those entities.

30   If during the reporting period an entity has, without having a contractual obligation to do so, provided financial or other support to an unconsolidated structured entity in which it previously had or currently has an interest (for example, purchasing assets of or instruments issued by the structured entity), the entity shall disclose:

    (a)   the type and amount of support provided, including situations in which the entity assisted the structured entity in obtaining financial support; and

    (b)   the reasons for providing the support.

31   An entity shall disclose any current intentions to provide financial or other support to an unconsolidated structured entity, including intentions to assist the structured entity in obtaining financial support.

Commencement of the legislative instrument

Aus31.1   For legal purposes, this legislative instrument commences on 31 December 2015.

Withdrawal of AASB pronouncements

Aus31.2   This Standard repeals AASB 12 *Disclosure of Interests in Other Entities* issued in August 2011. Despite the repeal, after the time this Standard starts to apply under section 334 of the Corporations Act (either generally or in relation to an individual entity), the repealed Standard continues to apply in relation to any period ending before that time as if the repeal had not occurred.

    [Note: When this Standard applies under section 334 of the Corporations Act (either generally or in relation to an individual entity), it supersedes the application of the repealed Standard.]

APPENDIX A
DEFINED TERMS

This appendix is an integral part of the Standard.

income from a structured entity	For the purpose of this Standard, income from a **structured entity** includes, but is not limited to, recurring and non-recurring fees, interest, dividends, gains or losses on the remeasurement or derecognition of interests in structured entities and gains or losses from the transfer of assets and liabilities to the structured entity.

(Continued)

funding by issuing to those investors notes that are linked to entity Z's credit risk (credit-linked notes) and uses the proceeds to invest in a portfolio of risk-free financial assets. The structured entity obtains exposure to entity Z's credit risk by entering into a credit default swap (CDS) with a swap counterparty. The CDS passes entity Z's credit risk to the structured entity in return for a fee paid by the swap counterparty. The investors in the structured entity receive a higher return that reflects both the structured entity's return from its asset portfolio and the CDS fee. The swap counterparty does not have involvement with the structured entity that exposes it to variability of returns from the performance of the structured entity because the CDS transfers variability to the structured entity, rather than absorbing variability of returns of the structured entity.

Summarised financial information for subsidiaries, joint ventures and associates (paragraphs 12 and 21)

B10   For each subsidiary that has non-controlling interests that are material to the reporting entity, an entity shall disclose:

    (a)   dividends paid to non-controlling interests.

    (b)   summarised financial information about the assets, liabilities, profit or loss and cash flows of the subsidiary that enables users to understand the interest that non-controlling interests have in the group's activities and cash flows. That information might include but is not limited to, for example, current assets, non-current assets, current liabilities, non-current liabilities, revenue, profit or loss and total comprehensive income.

B11   The summarised financial information required by paragraph B10(b) shall be the amounts before inter-company eliminations.

B12   For each joint venture and associate that is material to the reporting entity, an entity shall disclose:

    (a)   dividends received from the joint venture or associate.

    (b)   summarised financial information for the joint venture or associate (see paragraphs B14 and B15) including, but not necessarily limited to:

        (i)   current assets.

        (ii)   non-current assets.

        (iii)   current liabilities.

        (iv)   non-current liabilities.

        (v)   revenue.

        (vi)   profit or loss from continuing operations.

        (vii)   post-tax profit or loss from discontinued operations.

        (viii) other comprehensive income.

        (ix)   total comprehensive income.

B13   In addition to the summarised financial information required by paragraph B12, an entity shall disclose for each joint venture that is material to the reporting entity the amount of:

    (a)   cash and cash equivalents included in paragraph B12(b)(i).

    (b)   current financial liabilities (excluding trade and other payables and provisions) included in paragraph B12(b)(iii).

    (c)   non-current financial liabilities (excluding trade and other payables and provisions) included in paragraph B12(b)(iv).

    (d)   depreciation and amortisation.

    (e)   interest income.

    (f)   interest expense.

    (g)   income tax expense or income.

B14 The summarised financial information presented in accordance with paragraphs B12 and B13 shall be the amounts included in the Australian-Accounting-Standards financial statements of the joint venture or associate (and not the entity's share of those amounts). If the entity accounts for its interest in the joint venture or associate using the equity method:

(a) the amounts included in the Australian-Accounting-Standards financial statements of the joint venture or associate shall be adjusted to reflect adjustments made by the entity when using the equity method, such as fair value adjustments made at the time of acquisition and adjustments for differences in accounting policies.

(b) the entity shall provide a reconciliation of the summarised financial information presented to the carrying amount of its interest in the joint venture or associate.

B15 An entity may present the summarised financial information required by paragraphs B12 and B13 on the basis of the joint venture's or associate's financial statements if:

(a) the entity measures its interest in the joint venture or associate at fair value in accordance with AASB 128; and

(b) the joint venture or associate does not prepare Australian-Accounting-Standards financial statements and preparation on that basis would be impracticable or cause undue cost.

In that case, the entity shall disclose the basis on which the summarised financial information has been prepared.

B16 An entity shall disclose, in aggregate, the carrying amount of its interests in all individually immaterial joint ventures or associates that are accounted for using the equity method. An entity shall also disclose separately the aggregate amount of its share of those joint ventures' or associates':

(a) profit or loss from continuing operations.

(b) post-tax profit or loss from discontinued operations.

(c) other comprehensive income.

(d) total comprehensive income.

An entity provides the disclosures separately for joint ventures and associates.

B17 When an entity's interest in a subsidiary, a joint venture or an associate (or a portion of its interest in a joint venture or an associate) is classified (or included in a disposal group that is classified) as held for sale in accordance with AASB 5, the entity is not required to disclose summarised financial information for that subsidiary, joint venture or associate in accordance with paragraphs B10–B16.

Commitments for joint ventures (paragraph 23(a))

B18 An entity shall disclose total commitments it has made but not recognised at the reporting date (including its share of commitments made jointly with other investors with joint control of a joint venture) relating to its interests in joint ventures. Commitments are those that may give rise to a future outflow of cash or other resources.

B19 Unrecognised commitments that may give rise to a future outflow of cash or other resources include:

(a) unrecognised commitments to contribute funding or resources as a result of, for example:

(i) the constitution or acquisition agreements of a joint venture (that, for example, require an entity to contribute funds over a specific period).

(ii) capital-intensive projects undertaken by a joint venture.

(iii) unconditional purchase obligations, comprising procurement of equipment, inventory or services that an entity is committed to purchasing from, or on behalf of, a joint venture.

        (iv)   unrecognised commitments to provide loans or other financial support to a joint venture.

        (v)   unrecognised commitments to contribute resources to a joint venture, such as assets or services.

        (vi)   other non-cancellable unrecognised commitments relating to a joint venture.

    (b)   unrecognised commitments to acquire another party's ownership interest (or a portion of that ownership interest) in a joint venture if a particular event occurs or does not occur in the future.

B20   The requirements and examples in paragraphs B18 and B19 illustrate some of the types of disclosure required by paragraph 18 of AASB 124 *Related Party Disclosures*.

Interests in unconsolidated structured entities (paragraphs 24–31)

Structured entities

B21   A structured entity is an entity that has been designed so that voting or similar rights are not the dominant factor in deciding who controls the entity, such as when any voting rights relate to administrative tasks only and the relevant activities are directed by means of contractual arrangements.

B22   A structured entity often has some or all of the following features or attributes:

    (a)   restricted activities.

    (b)   a narrow and well-defined objective, such as to effect a tax-efficient lease, carry out research and development activities, provide a source of capital or funding to an entity or provide investment opportunities for investors by passing on risks and rewards associated with the assets of the structured entity to investors.

    (c)   insufficient equity to permit the structured entity to finance its activities without subordinated financial support.

    (d)   financing in the form of multiple contractually linked instruments to investors that create concentrations of credit or other risks (tranches).

B23   Examples of entities that are regarded as structured entities include, but are not limited to:

    (a)   securitisation vehicles.

    (b)   asset-backed financings.

    (c)   some investment funds.

B24   An entity that is controlled by voting rights is not a structured entity simply because, for example, it receives funding from third parties following a restructuring.

Nature of risks from interests in unconsolidated structured entities (paragraphs 29–31)

B25   In addition to the information required by paragraphs 29–31, an entity shall disclose additional information that is necessary to meet the disclosure objective in paragraph 24(b).

B26   Examples of additional information that, depending on the circumstances, might be relevant to an assessment of the risks to which an entity is exposed when it has an interest in an unconsolidated structured entity are:

    (a)   the terms of an arrangement that could require the entity to provide financial support to an unconsolidated structured entity (eg liquidity arrangements or credit rating triggers associated with obligations to purchase assets of the structured entity or provide financial support), including:

(i)   a description of events or circumstances that could expose the reporting entity to a loss.

(ii)   whether there are any terms that would limit the obligation.

(iii)   whether there are any other parties that provide financial support and, if so, how the reporting entity's obligation ranks with those of other parties.

(b)   losses incurred by the entity during the reporting period relating to its interests in unconsolidated structured entities.

(c)   the types of income the entity received during the reporting period from its interests in unconsolidated structured entities.

(d)   whether the entity is required to absorb losses of an unconsolidated structured entity before other parties, the maximum limit of such losses for the entity, and (if relevant) the ranking and amounts of potential losses borne by parties whose interests rank lower than the entity's interest in the unconsolidated structured entity.

(e)   information about any liquidity arrangements, guarantees or other commitments with third parties that may affect the fair value or risk of the entity's interests in unconsolidated structured entities.

(f)   any difficulties an unconsolidated structured entity has experienced in financing its activities during the reporting period.

(g)   in relation to the funding of an unconsolidated structured entity, the forms of funding (eg commercial paper or medium-term notes) and their weighted-average life. That information might include maturity analyses of the assets and funding of an unconsolidated structured entity if the structured entity has longer-term assets funded by shorter-term funding.

APPENDIX C
EFFECTIVE DATE AND TRANSITION

This appendix is an integral part of the Standard and has the same authority as the other parts of the Standard.

Effective date and transition

C1   An entity shall apply this Standard for annual periods beginning on or after 1 January 2016. Earlier application is permitted for periods beginning on or after 1 January 2014 but before 1 January 2016.

C1A–C1B   [Deleted by the AASB]

C1C   AASB 2015-5 *Amendments to Australian Accounting Standards – Investment Entities: Applying the Consolidation Exception*, issued in January 2015, amended paragraph 6 in the previous version of the Standard. An entity shall apply that amendment for annual periods beginning on or after 1 January 2016. Earlier application is permitted. If an entity applies that amendment for an earlier period it shall disclose that fact.

C1D   AASB 2017-2 *Amendments to Australian Accounting Standards – Further Annual Improvements 2014–2016 Cycle*, issued in February 2017, added paragraph 5A and amended paragraph B17. An entity shall apply those amendments retrospectively in accordance with AASB 108 *Accounting Policies, Changes in Accounting Estimates and Errors* for annual periods beginning on or after 1 January 2017.

C2   [Deleted by the AASB]

C2A   The disclosure requirements of this Standard need not be applied for any period presented that begins before the annual period immediately preceding the first annual period for which AASB 12 is applied.

AASB

C2B   The disclosure requirements of paragraphs 24–31 and the corresponding guidance in paragraphs B21–B26 of this Standard need not be applied for any period presented that begins before the first annual period for which AASB 12 is applied.

References to AASB 9

C3   If an entity applies this Standard but does not yet apply AASB 9, any reference to AASB 9 shall be read as a reference to AASB 139 *Financial Instruments: Recognition and Measurement*.

APPENDIX E

AUSTRALIAN IMPLEMENTATION GUIDANCE FOR NOT-FOR-PROFIT ENTITIES

This appendix is an integral part of the Standard and has the same authority as the other parts of the Standard. The appendix applies only to not-for-profit entities. The appendix does not apply to for-profit entities or affect their application of AASB 12.

IG1   AASB 12 incorporates International Financial Reporting Standard IFRS 12 *Disclosure of Interests in Other Entities*, issued by the International Accounting Standards Board. Consequently, some of the text of this Standard particularly reflects the perspective of for-profit entities. The AASB has prepared this appendix to explain and illustrate the definition of 'structured entity' in the Standard for not-for-profit entities in the private and public sectors, to address circumstances where the for-profit perspective does not readily translate to a not-for-profit perspective.

IG2   AASB 12 includes specific disclosure requirements regarding both consolidated and unconsolidated structured entities. Some of those disclosures are not required of entities preparing general purpose financial statements under Australian Accounting Standards – Reduced Disclosure Requirements.

Structured entities

IG3   A structured entity is defined in Appendix A of AASB 12 as follows:

"An entity that has been designed so that voting or similar rights are not the dominant factor in deciding who controls the entity, such as when any voting rights relate to administrative tasks only and the relevant activities are directed by means of contractual arrangements."

Relevant activities are defined in AASB 10 as the activities of an entity that significantly affect the entity's returns. The current ability to direct the relevant activities is necessary in order for one entity to control another.

IG4   Paragraph B22 of AASB 12 states that structured entities often have some or all of the following features or attributes: restricted activities, a narrow and well-defined objective, insufficient equity to finance its activities without subordinated financial support, and financing tranches in the form of multiple contractually linked instruments. Paragraph B23 gives examples of structured entities: securitisation vehicles, asset-backed financings and some investment funds.

IG5   The definition of a structured entity depends on voting or similar rights not being the dominant factor in deciding who controls an entity. Voting rights are a common feature in many for-profit entities, having a dominant role in determining who controls an entity. Accordingly, the principle underlying the definition limits the scope of structured entities to entities that are controlled through less conventional means. The features listed in paragraph B22 and the examples in paragraph B23 also suggest that structured entities constitute a limited class of entity.

IG6 It is common for not-for-profit entities to be established by administrative arrangements or legislation, especially in the public sector. Therefore, if the administrative arrangements or legislation are dominant factors in determining control of such an entity, the entity is not a structured entity. The AASB 12 disclosures regarding structured entities, such as the provision of financial support without a contractual obligation, are not particularly relevant to such entities, given the expectation of ongoing government funding through appropriations to supplement any other revenue sources.

IG7 Applying the principle underlying the definition of a structured entity means that structured entities have been designed so that less conventional means – in the context of not-for-profit entities – are the dominant factor in determining who controls the entity. This approach limits, for not-for-profit entities, the scope of structured entities to entities that have been designed so that voting or similar rights, including administrative arrangements or statutory provisions, are not the dominant factor in determining control of the entity.

IG8 To illustrate the definition of a structured entity, an entity for which contractual arrangements are significant to determining control of the entity is a structured entity. This would include entities for which most of the activities are predetermined, with the relevant activities limited in scope but directed through contractual arrangements. Examples of such entities are included in paragraph B23. Another example would be a partnership between a government and a private sector entity, being a partnership established and directed by contractual arrangements. On that basis, the partnership is a structured entity, regardless of the rights (if any) that the government and the entity have in relation to the partnership. If the government guarantees a certain level of revenue for its private sector partner, for example, the AASB 12 disclosures concerning the provision of financial support would be particularly relevant, whether the partnership is a consolidated or an unconsolidated structured entity for the government. However, the mere fact that a government provides funding to another entity does not make that entity a structured entity.

IG9 Not-for-profit private sector entities will also need to identify any structured entities with which they are associated. For example, a not-for-profit private sector entity may have established or sponsored a community service organisation whose relevant activities are directed by means of contractual arrangements. Those arrangements might require the not-for-profit private sector entity to provide financial support in specified circumstances to the community service organisation, or alternatively the entity might choose to provide financial or other support to the organisation without the contractual obligation to do so (eg due to the economic dependency of the organisation upon the entity). The AASB 12 disclosure requirements would be relevant in both circumstances as the community service organisation is a structured entity. Paragraph 31, for example, would require the not-for-profit private sector entity to disclose any current intentions to provide support to an unconsolidated structured entity.

APPENDIX F
AUSTRALIAN REDUCED DISCLOSURE
REQUIREMENTS

This appendix is an integral part of the Standard and has the same authority as the other parts of the Standard.

AusF1 **The following do not apply to entities preparing general purpose financial statements under Australian Accounting Standards – Reduced Disclosure Requirements:**

(a) **paragraphs 9(a), 9(d), 9(e), 10(a)(ii), 10(b)(ii)–(iv), 11(b), 12, 13(a)(ii), 13(b), 14, 16, 18, 19, 20(b), 21(a)(ii), 21(b)(ii), 21(c), 22, 24(b), 25, 27–29, B10–B17, B25 and B26; and**

(b)   in paragraph 26, the text "qualitative and quantitative".

        Entities applying Australian Accounting Standards – Reduced Disclosure Requirements may elect to comply with some or all of these excluded requirements.

AusF2   The requirements that do not apply to entities preparing general purpose financial statements under Australian Accounting Standards – Reduced Disclosure Requirements are also identified in this Standard by shading of the relevant text.

COMPILATION DETAILS

Accounting Standard AASB 12 *Disclosure of Interests in Other Entities* as amended

Compilation details are not part of AASB 12.

This compiled Standard applies to annual periods beginning on or after 1 January 2017. It takes into account amendments up to and including 13 February 2017 and was prepared on 20 April 2017 by the staff of the Australian Accounting Standards Board (AASB).

This compilation is not a separate Accounting Standard made by the AASB. Instead, it is a representation of AASB 12 (August 2015) as amended by other Accounting Standards, which are listed in the Table below.

Table of Standards

Standard	Date made	FRL identifier	Commencement date	Effective date *(annual periods ... on or after ...)*	Application, saving or transitional provisions
AASB 12	7 Aug 2015	F2015L01536	31 Dec 2015	*(beginning)* 1 Jan 2016	see (a) below
AASB 2017-2	13 Feb 2017	F2017L00194	13 Feb 2017	*(beginning)* 1 Jan 2017	see (b) below

(a) Entities may elect to apply this Standard to annual periods beginning on or after 1 January 2014 but before 1 January 2016.

(b) Entities are not permitted to apply this Standard early.

Table of amendments

Paragraph affected	How affected	By ... [paragraph/page]
5A	added	AASB 2017-2 [page 5]
B17	amended	AASB 2017-2 [page 6]
C1D	added	AASB 2017-2 [page 6]

DELETED IFRS 12 TEXT

Deleted IFRS 12 text is not part of AASB 12.

C1A   *Consolidated Financial Statements, Joint Arrangements and Disclosure of Interests in Other Entities: Transition Guidance* (Amendments to IFRS 10, IFRS 11 and IFRS 12), issued in June 2012, added paragraphs C2A–C2B. An entity shall apply those amendments for annual periods beginning on or after 1 January 2013. If an entity applies IFRS 12 for an earlier period, it shall apply those amendments for that earlier period.

C1B   *Investment Entities* (Amendments to IFRS 10, IFRS 12 and IAS 27), issued in October 2012, amended paragraph 2 and Appendix A, and added paragraphs 9A–9B, 19A–19G, 21A and 25A. An entity shall apply those amendments for annual periods beginning on or after 1 January 2014. Early adoption is permitted. If an entity applies those amendments earlier, it shall disclose that fact and apply all amendments included in *Investment Entities* at the same time.

C2   An entity is encouraged to provide information required by this IFRS earlier than annual periods beginning on or after 1 January 2013. Providing some of the disclosures required by this IFRS does not compel the entity to comply with all the requirements of this IFRS or to apply IFRS 10, IFRS 11, IAS 27 (as amended in 2011) and IAS 28 (as amended in 2011) early.

AASB 13
Fair Value Measurement

(Issued August 2015)

This note is not part of Accounting Standard AASB 13.

The following unincorporated amendments are not included in this Standard.

*   AASB 16 *Leases* — Appendix D sets out the amendments to other Standards that are a consequence of the AASB issuing this Standard. It is applicable from 1 January 2019. Earlier application is permitted, but entities must apply AASB 15 *Revenue from Contracts with Customers* before applying this Standard.

Entities early-adopting any amendments with later application dates will need to refer to the amending Standards that have not yet been incorporated into compilations. The abovementioned unincorporated amendments may be located on the AASB website at www.aasb.gov.au or on the Federal Register of Legislation website at www.legislation.gov.au.

CONTENTS

COMPARISON WITH IFRS 13
ACCOUNTING STANDARD
AASB 13 *FAIR VALUE MEASUREMENT*

APPENDICES
A. DEFINED TERMS
B. APPLICATION GUIDANCE
C. EFFECTIVE DATE AND TRANSITION
E. AUSTRALIAN REDUCED DISCLOSURE REQUIREMENTS

DELETED IFRS 13 TEXT
BASIS FOR CONCLUSIONS ON AASB 2015-7

ILLUSTRATIVE EXAMPLES (available on the AASB website)
BASIS FOR CONCLUSIONS ON IFRS 13 (available on the AASB website)

AASB

> Australian Accounting Standard AASB 13 *Fair Value Measurement* is set out in paragraphs 1 – Aus99.2 and Appendices A – C and E. All the paragraphs have equal authority. Paragraphs in **bold type** state the main principles. Terms defined in Appendix A are in *italics* the first time they appear in the Standard. AASB 13 is to be read in the context of other Australian Accounting Standards, including AASB 1048 *Interpretation of Standards*, which identifies the Australian Accounting Interpretations, and AASB 1057 *Application of Australian Accounting Standards*. In the absence of explicit guidance, AASB 108 *Accounting Policies, Changes in Accounting Estimates and Errors* provides a basis for selecting and applying accounting policies.

COMPARISON WITH IFRS 13

AASB 13 *Fair Value Measurement* incorporates IFRS 13 *Fair Value Measurement* issued by the International Accounting Standards Board (IASB). Australian-specific paragraphs (which are not included in IFRS 13) are identified with the prefix "Aus". Paragraphs that apply only to not-for-profit entities begin by identifying their limited applicability.

Tier 1

For-profit entities complying with AASB 13 also comply with IFRS 13.

Not-for-profit entities' compliance with IFRS 13 will depend on whether any "Aus" paragraphs that specifically apply to not-for-profit entities provide additional guidance or contain applicable requirements that are inconsistent with IFRS 13.

Tier 2

Entities preparing general purpose financial statements under Australian Accounting Standards – Reduced Disclosure Requirements (Tier 2) will not be in compliance with IFRSs.

AASB 1053 *Application of Tiers of Australian Accounting Standards* explains the two tiers of reporting requirements.

ACCOUNTING STANDARD AASB 13

The Australian Accounting Standards Board makes Accounting Standard AASB 13 *Fair Value Measurement* under section 334 of the *Corporations Act 2001*.

Kris Peach

Dated 7 August 2015   Chair – AASB

ACCOUNTING STANDARD AASB 13
FAIR VALUE MEASUREMENT

Objective

1   **This Standard:**

    (a)   **defines** *fair value*;

    (b)   **sets out in a single Standard a framework for measuring fair value; and**

    (c)   **requires disclosures about fair value measurements.**

2   Fair value is a market-based measurement, not an entity-specific measurement. For some assets and liabilities, observable market transactions or market information might be available. For other assets and liabilities, observable market transactions and market information might not be available. However, the objective of a fair value measurement in both cases is the same—to estimate the price at which an *orderly transaction* to sell the asset or to transfer the liability would take place between *market participants* at the measurement date under current market conditions (ie an *exit price* at the measurement date from the perspective of a market participant that holds the asset or owes the liability).

3   When a price for an identical asset or liability is not observable, an entity measures fair value using another valuation technique that maximises the use of relevant *observable inputs* and minimises the use of *unobservable inputs*. Because fair value is a market-based measurement, it is measured using the assumptions that market participants would use when pricing the asset or liability, including assumptions about risk. As a result, an entity's intention to hold an asset or to settle or otherwise fulfil a liability is not relevant when measuring fair value.

4   The definition of fair value focuses on assets and liabilities because they are a primary subject of accounting measurement. In addition, this Standard shall be applied to an entity's own equity instruments measured at fair value.

Scope

5   **This Standard applies when another Standard requires or permits fair value measurements or disclosures about fair value measurements (and measurements, such as fair value less costs to sell, based on fair value or disclosures about those measurements), except as specified in paragraphs 6 and 7.**

6   The measurement and disclosure requirements of this Standard do not apply to the following:

    (a)   share-based payment transactions within the scope of AASB 2 *Share-based Payment*;

    (b)   leasing transactions within the scope of AASB 117 *Leases*; and

(c)   measurements that have some similarities to fair value but are not fair value, such as net realisable value in AASB 102 *Inventories* or value in use in AASB 136 *Impairment of Assets*.

7   The disclosures required by this Standard are not required for the following:

(a)   plan assets measured at fair value in accordance with AASB 119 *Employee Benefits*;

(b)   [deleted by the AASB]

(c)   assets for which recoverable amount is fair value less costs of disposal in accordance with AASB 136.

8   The fair value measurement framework described in this Standard applies to both initial and subsequent measurement if fair value is required or permitted by other Australian Accounting Standards.

Measurement

Definition of fair value

9   **This Standard defines fair value as the price that would be received to sell an asset or paid to transfer a liability in an orderly transaction between market participants at the measurement date.**

10   Paragraph B2 describes the overall fair value measurement approach.

The asset or liability

11   **A fair value measurement is for a particular asset or liability. Therefore, when measuring fair value an entity shall take into account the characteristics of the asset or liability if market participants would take those characteristics into account when pricing the asset or liability at the measurement date. Such characteristics include, for example, the following:**

(a)   **the condition and location of the asset; and**

(b)   **restrictions, if any, on the sale or use of the asset.**

12   The effect on the measurement arising from a particular characteristic will differ depending on how that characteristic would be taken into account by market participants.

13   The asset or liability measured at fair value might be either of the following:

(a)   a stand-alone asset or liability (eg a financial instrument or a non-financial asset); or

(b)   a group of assets, a group of liabilities or a group of assets and liabilities (eg a cash-generating unit or a business).

14   Whether the asset or liability is a stand-alone asset or liability, a group of assets, a group of liabilities or a group of assets and liabilities for recognition or disclosure purposes depends on its *unit of account*. The unit of account for the asset or liability shall be determined in accordance with the Standard that requires or permits the fair value measurement, except as provided in this Standard.

The transaction

15   **A fair value measurement assumes that the asset or liability is exchanged in an orderly transaction between market participants to sell the asset or transfer the liability at the measurement date under current market conditions.**

16   **A fair value measurement assumes that the transaction to sell the asset or transfer the liability takes place either:**

(a)   **in the *principal market* for the asset or liability; or**

        (b)   in the absence of a principal market, in the *most advantageous market* for the asset or liability.

17   An entity need not undertake an exhaustive search of all possible markets to identify the principal market or, in the absence of a principal market, the most advantageous market, but it shall take into account all information that is reasonably available. In the absence of evidence to the contrary, the market in which the entity would normally enter into a transaction to sell the asset or to transfer the liability is presumed to be the principal market or, in the absence of a principal market, the most advantageous market.

18   If there is a principal market for the asset or liability, the fair value measurement shall represent the price in that market (whether that price is directly observable or estimated using another valuation technique), even if the price in a different market is potentially more advantageous at the measurement date.

19   The entity must have access to the principal (or most advantageous) market at the measurement date. Because different entities (and businesses within those entities) with different activities may have access to different markets, the principal (or most advantageous) market for the same asset or liability might be different for different entities (and businesses within those entities). Therefore, the principal (or most advantageous) market (and thus, market participants) shall be considered from the perspective of the entity, thereby allowing for differences between and among entities with different activities.

20   Although an entity must be able to access the market, the entity does not need to be able to sell the particular asset or transfer the particular liability on the measurement date to be able to measure fair value on the basis of the price in that market.

21   Even when there is no observable market to provide pricing information about the sale of an asset or the transfer of a liability at the measurement date, a fair value measurement shall assume that a transaction takes place at that date, considered from the perspective of a market participant that holds the asset or owes the liability. That assumed transaction establishes a basis for estimating the price to sell the asset or to transfer the liability.

Market participants

22   **An entity shall measure the fair value of an asset or a liability using the assumptions that market participants would use when pricing the asset or liability, assuming that market participants act in their economic best interest.**

23   In developing those assumptions, an entity need not identify specific market participants. Rather, the entity shall identify characteristics that distinguish market participants generally, considering factors specific to all the following:

        (a)   the asset or liability;

        (b)   the principal (or most advantageous) market for the asset or liability; and

        (c)   market participants with whom the entity would enter into a transaction in that market.

The price

24   **Fair value is the price that would be received to sell an asset or paid to transfer a liability in an orderly transaction in the principal (or most advantageous) market at the measurement date under current market conditions (ie an exit price) regardless of whether that price is directly observable or estimated using another valuation technique.**

25   The price in the principal (or most advantageous) market used to measure the fair value of the asset or liability shall not be adjusted for *transaction costs*. Transaction costs shall be accounted for in accordance with other Australian Accounting Standards. Transaction costs are not a characteristic of an asset or a liability; rather, they are

specific to a transaction and will differ depending on how an entity enters into a transaction for the asset or liability.

26 Transaction costs do not include *transport costs*. If location is a characteristic of the asset (as might be the case, for example, for a commodity), the price in the principal (or most advantageous) market shall be adjusted for the costs, if any, that would be incurred to transport the asset from its current location to that market.

Application to non-financial assets

Highest and best use for non-financial assets

27 **A fair value measurement of a non-financial asset takes into account a market participant's ability to generate economic benefits by using the asset in its *highest and best use* or by selling it to another market participant that would use the asset in its highest and best use.**

28 The highest and best use of a non-financial asset takes into account the use of the asset that is physically possible, legally permissible and financially feasible, as follows:

(a) A use that is physically possible takes into account the physical characteristics of the asset that market participants would take into account when pricing the asset (eg the location or size of a property).

(b) A use that is legally permissible takes into account any legal restrictions on the use of the asset that market participants would take into account when pricing the asset (eg the zoning regulations applicable to a property).

(c) A use that is financially feasible takes into account whether a use of the asset that is physically possible and legally permissible generates adequate income or cash flows (taking into account the costs of converting the asset to that use) to produce an investment return that market participants would require from an investment in that asset put to that use.

29 Highest and best use is determined from the perspective of market participants, even if the entity intends a different use. However, an entity's current use of a non-financial asset is presumed to be its highest and best use unless market or other factors suggest that a different use by market participants would maximise the value of the asset.

30 To protect its competitive position, or for other reasons, an entity may intend not to use an acquired non-financial asset actively or it may intend not to use the asset according to its highest and best use. For example, that might be the case for an acquired intangible asset that the entity plans to use defensively by preventing others from using it. Nevertheless, the entity shall measure the fair value of a non-financial asset assuming its highest and best use by market participants.

Valuation premise for non-financial assets

31 The highest and best use of a non-financial asset establishes the valuation premise used to measure the fair value of the asset, as follows:

(a) The highest and best use of a non-financial asset might provide maximum value to market participants through its use in combination with other assets as a group (as installed or otherwise configured for use) or in combination with other assets and liabilities (eg a business).

(i) If the highest and best use of the asset is to use the asset in combination with other assets or with other assets and liabilities, the fair value of the asset is the price that would be received in a current transaction to sell the asset assuming that the asset would be used with other assets or with other assets and liabilities and that those assets and liabilities (ie its complementary assets and the associated liabilities) would be available to market participants.

(ii) Liabilities associated with the asset and with the complementary assets include liabilities that fund working capital, but do not include liabilities used to fund assets other than those within the group of assets.

(iii)   Assumptions about the highest and best use of a non-financial asset shall be consistent for all the assets (for which highest and best use is relevant) of the group of assets or the group of assets and liabilities within which the asset would be used.

(b)   The highest and best use of a non-financial asset might provide maximum value to market participants on a stand-alone basis. If the highest and best use of the asset is to use it on a stand-alone basis, the fair value of the asset is the price that would be received in a current transaction to sell the asset to market participants that would use the asset on a stand-alone basis.

32   The fair value measurement of a non-financial asset assumes that the asset is sold consistently with the unit of account specified in other Australian Accounting Standards (which may be an individual asset). That is the case even when that fair value measurement assumes that the highest and best use of the asset is to use it in combination with other assets or with other assets and liabilities because a fair value measurement assumes that the market participant already holds the complementary assets and the associated liabilities.

33   Paragraph B3 describes the application of the valuation premise concept for non-financial assets.

Application to liabilities and an entity's own equity instruments

General principles

34   **A fair value measurement assumes that a financial or non-financial liability or an entity's own equity instrument (eg equity interests issued as consideration in a business combination) is transferred to a market participant at the measurement date. The transfer of a liability or an entity's own equity instrument assumes the following:**

(a)   **A liability would remain outstanding and the market participant transferee would be required to fulfil the obligation. The liability would not be settled with the counterparty or otherwise extinguished on the measurement date.**

(b)   **An entity's own equity instrument would remain outstanding and the market participant transferee would take on the rights and responsibilities associated with the instrument. The instrument would not be cancelled or otherwise extinguished on the measurement date.**

35   Even when there is no observable market to provide pricing information about the transfer of a liability or an entity's own equity instrument (eg because contractual or other legal restrictions prevent the transfer of such items), there might be an observable market for such items if they are held by other parties as assets (eg a corporate bond or a call option on an entity's shares).

36   In all cases, an entity shall maximise the use of relevant observable inputs and minimise the use of unobservable inputs to meet the objective of a fair value measurement, which is to estimate the price at which an orderly transaction to transfer the liability or equity instrument would take place between market participants at the measurement date under current market conditions.

Liabilities and equity instruments held by other parties as assets

37   **When a quoted price for the transfer of an identical or a similar liability or entity's own equity instrument is not available and the identical item is held by another party as an asset, an entity shall measure the fair value of the liability or equity instrument from the perspective of a market participant that holds the identical item as an asset at the measurement date.**

38   In such cases, an entity shall measure the fair value of the liability or equity instrument as follows:

(a)   using the quoted price in an *active market* for the identical item held by another party as an asset, if that price is available.

(b)   if that price is not available, using other observable inputs, such as the quoted price in a market that is not active for the identical item held by another party as an asset.

(c)   if the observable prices in (a) and (b) are not available, using another valuation technique, such as:

(i)   an *income approach* (eg a present value technique that takes into account the future cash flows that a market participant would expect to receive from holding the liability or equity instrument as an asset; see paragraphs B10 and B11).

(ii) a *market approach* (eg using quoted prices for similar liabilities or equity instruments held by other parties as assets; see paragraphs B5–B7).

39   An entity shall adjust the quoted price of a liability or an entity's own equity instrument held by another party as an asset only if there are factors specific to the asset that are not applicable to the fair value measurement of the liability or equity instrument. An entity shall ensure that the price of the asset does not reflect the effect of a restriction preventing the sale of that asset. Some factors that may indicate that the quoted price of the asset should be adjusted include the following:

(a)   The quoted price for the asset relates to a similar (but not identical) liability or equity instrument held by another party as an asset. For example, the liability or equity instrument may have a particular characteristic (eg the credit quality of the issuer) that is different from that reflected in the fair value of the similar liability or equity instrument held as an asset.

(b)   The unit of account for the asset is not the same as for the liability or equity instrument. For example, for liabilities, in some cases the price for an asset reflects a combined price for a package comprising both the amounts due from the issuer and a third-party credit enhancement. If the unit of account for the liability is not for the combined package, the objective is to measure the fair value of the issuer's liability, not the fair value of the combined package. Thus, in such cases, the entity would adjust the observed price for the asset to exclude the effect of the third-party credit enhancement.

Liabilities and equity instruments not held by other parties as assets

40   When a quoted price for the transfer of an identical or a similar liability or entity's own equity instrument is not available and the identical item is not held by another party as an asset, an entity shall measure the fair value of the liability or equity instrument using a valuation technique from the perspective of a market participant that owes the liability or has issued the claim on equity.

41   For example, when applying a present value technique an entity might take into account either of the following:

(a)   the future cash outflows that a market participant would expect to incur in fulfilling the obligation, including the compensation that a market participant would require for taking on the obligation (see paragraphs B31–B33).

(b)   the amount that a market participant would receive to enter into or issue an identical liability or equity instrument, using the assumptions that market participants would use when pricing the identical item (eg having the same credit characteristics) in the principal (or most advantageous) market for issuing a liability or an equity instrument with the same contractual terms.

Non-performance risk

42   The fair value of a liability reflects the effect of *non-performance risk*. Non-performance risk includes, but may not be limited to, an entity's own credit risk (as defined in AASB 7 *Financial Instruments: Disclosures*). Non-performance risk is assumed to be the same before and after the transfer of the liability.

43   When measuring the fair value of a liability, an entity shall take into account the effect of its credit risk (credit standing) and any other factors that might influence the likelihood that the obligation will or will not be fulfilled. That effect may differ depending on the liability, for example:

    (a)   whether the liability is an obligation to deliver cash (a financial liability) or an obligation to deliver goods or services (a non-financial liability).

    (b)   the terms of credit enhancements related to the liability, if any.

44   The fair value of a liability reflects the effect of non-performance risk on the basis of its unit of account. The issuer of a liability issued with an inseparable third-party credit enhancement that is accounted for separately from the liability shall not include the effect of the credit enhancement (eg a third-party guarantee of debt) in the fair value measurement of the liability. If the credit enhancement is accounted for separately from the liability, the issuer would take into account its own credit standing and not that of the third party guarantor when measuring the fair value of the liability.

Restriction preventing the transfer of a liability or an entity's own equity instrument

45   When measuring the fair value of a liability or an entity's own equity instrument, an entity shall not include a separate input or an adjustment to other *inputs* relating to the existence of a restriction that prevents the transfer of the item. The effect of a restriction that prevents the transfer of a liability or an entity's own equity instrument is either implicitly or explicitly included in the other inputs to the fair value measurement.

46   For example, at the transaction date, both the creditor and the obligor accepted the transaction price for the liability with full knowledge that the obligation includes a restriction that prevents its transfer. As a result of the restriction being included in the transaction price, a separate input or an adjustment to an existing input is not required at the transaction date to reflect the effect of the restriction on transfer. Similarly, a separate input or an adjustment to an existing input is not required at subsequent measurement dates to reflect the effect of the restriction on transfer.

Financial liability with a demand feature

47   The fair value of a financial liability with a demand feature (eg a demand deposit) is not less than the amount payable on demand, discounted from the first date that the amount could be required to be paid.

Application to financial assets and financial liabilities with offsetting positions in market risks or counterparty credit risk

48   An entity that holds a group of financial assets and financial liabilities is exposed to market risks (as defined in AASB 7) and to the credit risk (as defined in AASB 7) of each of the counterparties. If the entity manages that group of financial assets and financial liabilities on the basis of its net exposure to either market risks or credit risk, the entity is permitted to apply an exception to this Standard for measuring fair value. That exception permits an entity to measure the fair value of a group of financial assets and financial liabilities on the basis of the price that would be received to sell a net long position (ie an asset) for a particular risk exposure or paid to transfer a net short position (ie a liability) for a particular risk exposure in an orderly transaction between market participants at the measurement date under current market conditions. Accordingly, an entity shall measure the fair value of the group of financial assets and financial liabilities consistently with how market participants would price the net risk exposure at the measurement date.

49   An entity is permitted to use the exception in paragraph 48 only if the entity does all the following:

    (a)   manages the group of financial assets and financial liabilities on the basis of the entity's net exposure to a particular market risk (or risks) or to the credit risk of a particular counterparty in accordance with the entity's documented risk management or investment strategy;

(b)   provides information on that basis about the group of financial assets and financial liabilities to the entity's key management personnel, as defined in AASB 124 *Related Party Disclosures*; and

(c)   is required or has elected to measure those financial assets and financial liabilities at fair value in the statement of financial position at the end of each reporting period.

50   The exception in paragraph 48 does not pertain to financial statement presentation. In some cases the basis for the presentation of financial instruments in the statement of financial position differs from the basis for the measurement of financial instruments, for example, if a Standard does not require or permit financial instruments to be presented on a net basis. In such cases an entity may need to allocate the portfolio-level adjustments (see paragraphs 53–56) to the individual assets or liabilities that make up the group of financial assets and financial liabilities managed on the basis of the entity's net risk exposure. An entity shall perform such allocations on a reasonable and consistent basis using a methodology appropriate in the circumstances.

51   An entity shall make an accounting policy decision in accordance with AASB 108 *Accounting Policies, Changes in Accounting Estimates and Errors* to use the exception in paragraph 48. An entity that uses the exception shall apply that accounting policy, including its policy for allocating bid-ask adjustments (see paragraphs 53–55) and credit adjustments (see paragraph 56), if applicable, consistently from period to period for a particular portfolio.

52   The exception in paragraph 48 applies only to financial assets, financial liabilities and other contracts within the scope of AASB 9 *Financial Instruments* (or AASB 139 *Financial Instruments: Recognition and Measurement*, if AASB 9 has not yet been adopted). The references to financial assets and financial liabilities in paragraphs 48–51 and 53–56 should be read as applying to all contracts within the scope of, and accounted for in accordance with, AASB 9 (or AASB 139, if AASB 9 has not yet been adopted), regardless of whether they meet the definitions of financial assets or financial liabilities in AASB 132 *Financial Instruments: Presentation*.

Exposure to market risks

53   When using the exception in paragraph 48 to measure the fair value of a group of financial assets and financial liabilities managed on the basis of the entity's net exposure to a particular market risk (or risks), the entity shall apply the price within the bid-ask spread that is most representative of fair value in the circumstances to the entity's net exposure to those market risks (see paragraphs 70 and 71).

54   When using the exception in paragraph 48, an entity shall ensure that the market risk (or risks) to which the entity is exposed within that group of financial assets and financial liabilities is substantially the same. For example, an entity would not combine the interest rate risk associated with a financial asset with the commodity price risk associated with a financial liability because doing so would not mitigate the entity's exposure to interest rate risk or commodity price risk. When using the exception in paragraph 48, any basis risk resulting from the market risk parameters not being identical shall be taken into account in the fair value measurement of the financial assets and financial liabilities within the group.

55   Similarly, the duration of the entity's exposure to a particular market risk (or risks) arising from the financial assets and financial liabilities shall be substantially the same. For example, an entity that uses a 12-month futures contract against the cash flows associated with 12 months' worth of interest rate risk exposure on a five-year financial instrument within a group made up of only those financial assets and financial liabilities measures the fair value of the exposure to 12-month interest rate risk on a net basis and the remaining interest rate risk exposure (ie years 2–5) on a gross basis.

AASB

Exposure to the credit risk of a particular counterparty

56   When using the exception in paragraph 48 to measure the fair value of a group of
      financial assets and financial liabilities entered into with a particular counterparty, the
      entity shall include the effect of the entity's net exposure to the credit risk of that
      counterparty or the counterparty's net exposure to the credit risk of the entity in the
      fair value measurement when market participants would take into account any existing
      arrangements that mitigate credit risk exposure in the event of default (eg a master
      netting agreement with the counterparty or an agreement that requires the exchange
      of collateral on the basis of each party's net exposure to the credit risk of the other
      party). The fair value measurement shall reflect market participants' expectations about
      the likelihood that such an arrangement would be legally enforceable in the event of
      default.

Fair value at initial recognition

57   When an asset is acquired or a liability is assumed in an exchange transaction for that
      asset or liability, the transaction price is the price paid to acquire the asset or received to
      assume the liability (an *entry price*). In contrast, the fair value of the asset or liability
      is the price that would be received to sell the asset or paid to transfer the liability
      (an exit price). Entities do not necessarily sell assets at the prices paid to acquire them.
      Similarly, entities do not necessarily transfer liabilities at the prices received to assume
      them.

58   In many cases the transaction price will equal the fair value (eg that might be the case
      when on the transaction date the transaction to buy an asset takes place in the market
      in which the asset would be sold).

59   When determining whether fair value at initial recognition equals the transaction price,
      an entity shall take into account factors specific to the transaction and to the asset or
      liability. Paragraph B4 describes situations in which the transaction price might not
      represent the fair value of an asset or a liability at initial recognition.

60   If another Standard requires or permits an entity to measure an asset or a liability
      initially at fair value and the transaction price differs from fair value, the entity shall
      recognise the resulting gain or loss in profit or loss unless that Standard specifies
      otherwise.

Valuation techniques

**61   An entity shall use valuation techniques that are appropriate in the circumstances
      and for which sufficient data are available to measure fair value, maximising the
      use of relevant observable inputs and minimising the use of unobservable inputs.**

62   The objective of using a valuation technique is to estimate the price at which an orderly
      transaction to sell the asset or to transfer the liability would take place between market
      participants at the measurement date under current market conditions. Three widely
      used valuation techniques are the market approach, the *cost approach* and the income
      approach. The main aspects of those approaches are summarised in paragraphs B5–
      B11. An entity shall use valuation techniques consistent with one or more of those
      approaches to measure fair value.

63   In some cases a single valuation technique will be appropriate (eg when valuing
      an asset or a liability using quoted prices in an active market for identical assets
      or liabilities). In other cases, multiple valuation techniques will be appropriate (eg
      that might be the case when valuing a cash-generating unit). If multiple valuation
      techniques are used to measure fair value, the results (ie respective indications of
      fair value) shall be evaluated considering the reasonableness of the range of values
      indicated by those results. A fair value measurement is the point within that range that
      is most representative of fair value in the circumstances.

64   If the transaction price is fair value at initial recognition and a valuation technique that
      uses unobservable inputs will be used to measure fair value in subsequent periods, the

valuation technique shall be calibrated so that at initial recognition the result of the valuation technique equals the transaction price. Calibration ensures that the valuation technique reflects current market conditions, and it helps an entity to determine whether an adjustment to the valuation technique is necessary (eg there might be a characteristic of the asset or liability that is not captured by the valuation technique). After initial recognition, when measuring fair value using a valuation technique or techniques that use unobservable inputs, an entity shall ensure that those valuation techniques reflect observable market data (eg the price for a similar asset or liability) at the measurement date.

65 Valuation techniques used to measure fair value shall be applied consistently. However, a change in a valuation technique or its application (eg a change in its weighting when multiple valuation techniques are used or a change in an adjustment applied to a valuation technique) is appropriate if the change results in a measurement that is equally or more representative of fair value in the circumstances. That might be the case if, for example, any of the following events take place:

(a) new markets develop;

(b) new information becomes available;

(c) information previously used is no longer available;

(d) valuation techniques improve; or

(e) market conditions change.

66 Revisions resulting from a change in the valuation technique or its application shall be accounted for as a change in accounting estimate in accordance with AASB 108. However, the disclosures in AASB 108 for a change in accounting estimate are not required for revisions resulting from a change in a valuation technique or its application.

Inputs to valuation techniques

General principles
67 **Valuation techniques used to measure fair value shall maximise the use of relevant observable inputs and minimise the use of unobservable inputs.**

68 Examples of markets in which inputs might be observable for some assets and liabilities (eg financial instruments) include exchange markets, dealer markets, brokered markets and principal-to-principal markets (see paragraph B34).

69 An entity shall select inputs that are consistent with the characteristics of the asset or liability that market participants would take into account in a transaction for the asset or liability (see paragraphs 11 and 12). In some cases those characteristics result in the application of an adjustment, such as a premium or discount (eg a control premium or non-controlling interest discount). However, a fair value measurement shall not incorporate a premium or discount that is inconsistent with the unit of account in the Standard that requires or permits the fair value measurement (see paragraphs 13 and 14). Premiums or discounts that reflect size as a characteristic of the entity's holding (specifically, a blockage factor that adjusts the quoted price of an asset or a liability because the market's normal daily trading volume is not sufficient to absorb the quantity held by the entity, as described in paragraph 80) rather than as a characteristic of the asset or liability (eg a control premium when measuring the fair value of a controlling interest) are not permitted in a fair value measurement. In all cases, if there is a quoted price in an active market (ie a *Level 1 input*) for an asset or a liability, an entity shall use that price without adjustment when measuring fair value, except as specified in paragraph 79.

Inputs based on bid and ask prices
70 If an asset or a liability measured at fair value has a bid price and an ask price (eg an input from a dealer market), the price within the bid-ask spread that is most representative of fair value in the circumstances shall be used to measure fair value

regardless of where the input is categorised within the fair value hierarchy (ie Level 1, 2 or 3; see paragraphs 72–90). The use of bid prices for asset positions and ask prices for liability positions is permitted, but is not required.

71   This Standard does not preclude the use of mid-market pricing or other pricing conventions that are used by market participants as a practical expedient for fair value measurements within a bid-ask spread.

Fair value hierarchy

72   To increase consistency and comparability in fair value measurements and related disclosures, this Standard establishes a fair value hierarchy that categorises into three levels (see paragraphs 76–90) the inputs to valuation techniques used to measure fair value. The fair value hierarchy gives the highest priority to quoted prices (unadjusted) in active markets for identical assets or liabilities (Level 1 inputs) and the lowest priority to unobservable inputs (*Level 3 inputs*).

73   In some cases, the inputs used to measure the fair value of an asset or a liability might be categorised within different levels of the fair value hierarchy. In those cases, the fair value measurement is categorised in its entirety in the same level of the fair value hierarchy as the lowest level input that is significant to the entire measurement. Assessing the significance of a particular input to the entire measurement requires judgement, taking into account factors specific to the asset or liability. Adjustments to arrive at measurements based on fair value, such as costs to sell when measuring fair value less costs to sell, shall not be taken into account when determining the level of the fair value hierarchy within which a fair value measurement is categorised.

74   The availability of relevant inputs and their relative subjectivity might affect the selection of appropriate valuation techniques (see paragraph 61). However, the fair value hierarchy prioritises the inputs to valuation techniques, not the valuation techniques used to measure fair value. For example, a fair value measurement developed using a present value technique might be categorised within Level 2 or Level 3, depending on the inputs that are significant to the entire measurement and the level of the fair value hierarchy within which those inputs are categorised.

75   If an observable input requires an adjustment using an unobservable input and that adjustment results in a significantly higher or lower fair value measurement, the resulting measurement would be categorised within Level 3 of the fair value hierarchy. For example, if a market participant would take into account the effect of a restriction on the sale of an asset when estimating the price for the asset, an entity would adjust the quoted price to reflect the effect of that restriction. If that quoted price is a *Level 2 input* and the adjustment is an unobservable input that is significant to the entire measurement, the measurement would be categorised within Level 3 of the fair value hierarchy.

Level 1 inputs

76   Level 1 inputs are quoted prices (unadjusted) in active markets for identical assets or liabilities that the entity can access at the measurement date.

77   A quoted price in an active market provides the most reliable evidence of fair value and shall be used without adjustment to measure fair value whenever available, except as specified in paragraph 79.

78   A Level 1 input will be available for many financial assets and financial liabilities, some of which might be exchanged in multiple active markets (eg on different exchanges). Therefore, the emphasis within Level 1 is on determining both of the following:

(a)   the principal market for the asset or liability or, in the absence of a principal market, the most advantageous market for the asset or liability; and

(b)   whether the entity can enter into a transaction for the asset or liability at the price in that market at the measurement date.

79   An entity shall not make an adjustment to a Level 1 input except in the following circumstances:

     (a)   when an entity holds a large number of similar (but not identical) assets or liabilities (eg debt securities) that are measured at fair value and a quoted price in an active market is available but not readily accessible for each of those assets or liabilities individually (ie given the large number of similar assets or liabilities held by the entity, it would be difficult to obtain pricing information for each individual asset or liability at the measurement date). In that case, as a practical expedient, an entity may measure fair value using an alternative pricing method that does not rely exclusively on quoted prices (eg matrix pricing). However, the use of an alternative pricing method results in a fair value measurement categorised within a lower level of the fair value hierarchy.

     (b)   when a quoted price in an active market does not represent fair value at the measurement date. That might be the case if, for example, significant events (such as transactions in a principal-to-principal market, trades in a brokered market or announcements) take place after the close of a market but before the measurement date. An entity shall establish and consistently apply a policy for identifying those events that might affect fair value measurements. However, if the quoted price is adjusted for new information, the adjustment results in a fair value measurement categorised within a lower level of the fair value hierarchy.

     (c)   when measuring the fair value of a liability or an entity's own equity instrument using the quoted price for the identical item traded as an asset in an active market and that price needs to be adjusted for factors specific to the item or the asset (see paragraph 39). If no adjustment to the quoted price of the asset is required, the result is a fair value measurement categorised within Level 1 of the fair value hierarchy. However, any adjustment to the quoted price of the asset results in a fair value measurement categorised within a lower level of the fair value hierarchy.

80   If an entity holds a position in a single asset or liability (including a position comprising a large number of identical assets or liabilities, such as a holding of financial instruments) and the asset or liability is traded in an active market, the fair value of the asset or liability shall be measured within Level 1 as the product of the quoted price for the individual asset or liability and the quantity held by the entity. That is the case even if a market's normal daily trading volume is not sufficient to absorb the quantity held and placing orders to sell the position in a single transaction might affect the quoted price.

Level 2 inputs

81   Level 2 inputs are inputs other than quoted prices included within Level 1 that are observable for the asset or liability, either directly or indirectly.

82   If the asset or liability has a specified (contractual) term, a Level 2 input must be observable for substantially the full term of the asset or liability. Level 2 inputs include the following:

     (a)   quoted prices for similar assets or liabilities in active markets.

     (b)   quoted prices for identical or similar assets or liabilities in markets that are not active.

     (c)   inputs other than quoted prices that are observable for the asset or liability, for example:

         (i)   interest rates and yield curves observable at commonly quoted intervals;

         (ii)   implied volatilities; and

         (iii)   credit spreads.

     (d)   *market-corroborated inputs.*

AASB

83   Adjustments to Level 2 inputs will vary depending on factors specific to the asset or
       liability. Those factors include the following:

   (a)   the condition or location of the asset;

   (b)   the extent to which inputs relate to items that are comparable to the asset or
           liability (including those factors described in paragraph 39); and

   (c)   the volume or level of activity in the markets within which the inputs are
           observed.

84   An adjustment to a Level 2 input that is significant to the entire measurement might
       result in a fair value measurement categorised within Level 3 of the fair value hierarchy
       if the adjustment uses significant unobservable inputs.

85   Paragraph B35 describes the use of Level 2 inputs for particular assets and liabilities.

Level 3 inputs

86   Level 3 inputs are unobservable inputs for the asset or liability.

87   Unobservable inputs shall be used to measure fair value to the extent that relevant
       observable inputs are not available, thereby allowing for situations in which there
       is little, if any, market activity for the asset or liability at the measurement date.
       However, the fair value measurement objective remains the same, ie an exit price
       at the measurement date from the perspective of a market participant that holds the
       asset or owes the liability. Therefore, unobservable inputs shall reflect the assumptions
       that market participants would use when pricing the asset or liability, including
       assumptions about risk.

88   Assumptions about risk include the risk inherent in a particular valuation technique
       used to measure fair value (such as a pricing model) and the risk inherent in the inputs
       to the valuation technique. A measurement that does not include an adjustment for risk
       would not represent a fair value measurement if market participants would include one
       when pricing the asset or liability. For example, it might be necessary to include a risk
       adjustment when there is significant measurement uncertainty (eg when there has been
       a significant decrease in the volume or level of activity when compared with normal
       market activity for the asset or liability, or similar assets or liabilities, and the entity
       has determined that the transaction price or quoted price does not represent fair value,
       as described in paragraphs B37–B47).

89   An entity shall develop unobservable inputs using the best information available in the
       circumstances, which might include the entity's own data. In developing unobservable
       inputs, an entity may begin with its own data, but it shall adjust those data if reasonably
       available information indicates that other market participants would use different data
       or there is something particular to the entity that is not available to other market
       participants (eg an entity-specific synergy). An entity need not undertake exhaustive
       efforts to obtain information about market participant assumptions. However, an entity
       shall take into account all information about market participant assumptions that is
       reasonably available. Unobservable inputs developed in the manner described above
       are considered market participant assumptions and meet the objective of a fair value
       measurement.

90   Paragraph B36 describes the use of Level 3 inputs for particular assets and liabilities.

Disclosure

**91   An entity shall disclose information that helps users of its financial statements
       assess both of the following:**

   **(a)   for assets and liabilities that are measured at fair value on a recurring
           or non-recurring basis in the statement of financial position after initial
           recognition, the valuation techniques and inputs used to develop those
           measurements.**

> (b)   **for recurring fair value measurements using significant unobservable inputs (Level 3), the effect of the measurements on profit or loss or other comprehensive income for the period.**

92   To meet the objectives in paragraph 91, an entity shall consider all the following:

(a)   the level of detail necessary to satisfy the disclosure requirements;

(b)   how much emphasis to place on each of the various requirements;

(c)   how much aggregation or disaggregation to undertake; and

(d)   whether users of financial statements need additional information to evaluate the quantitative information disclosed.

If the disclosures provided in accordance with this Standard and other Australian Accounting Standards are insufficient to meet the objectives in paragraph 91, an entity shall disclose additional information necessary to meet those objectives.

93   To meet the objectives in paragraph 91, an entity shall disclose, at a minimum, the following information for each class of assets and liabilities (see paragraph 94 for information on determining appropriate classes of assets and liabilities) measured at fair value (including measurements based on fair value within the scope of this Standard) in the statement of financial position after initial recognition:

(a)   for recurring and non-recurring fair value measurements, the fair value measurement at the end of the reporting period, and for non-recurring fair value measurements, the reasons for the measurement. Recurring fair value measurements of assets or liabilities are those that other Australian Accounting Standards require or permit in the statement of financial position at the end of each reporting period. Non-recurring fair value measurements of assets or liabilities are those that other Australian Accounting Standards require or permit in the statement of financial position in particular circumstances (eg when an entity measures an asset held for sale at fair value less costs to sell in accordance with AASB 5 *Non-current Assets Held for Sale and Discontinued Operations* because the asset's fair value less costs to sell is lower than its carrying amount).

(b)   for recurring and non-recurring fair value measurements, the level of the fair value hierarchy within which the fair value measurements are categorised in their entirety (Level 1, 2 or 3).

(c)   for assets and liabilities held at the end of the reporting period that are measured at fair value on a recurring basis, the amounts of any transfers between Level 1 and Level 2 of the fair value hierarchy, the reasons for those transfers and the entity's policy for determining when transfers between levels are deemed to have occurred (see paragraph 95). Transfers into each level shall be disclosed and discussed separately from transfers out of each level.

(d)   for recurring and non-recurring fair value measurements categorised within Level 2 and Level 3 of the fair value hierarchy, a description of the valuation technique(s) and the inputs used in the fair value measurement. If there has been a change in valuation technique (eg changing from a market approach to an income approach or the use of an additional valuation technique), the entity shall disclose that change and the reason(s) for making it. For fair value measurements categorised within Level 3 of the fair value hierarchy, an entity shall provide quantitative information about the significant unobservable inputs used in the fair value measurement. An entity is not required to create quantitative information to comply with this disclosure requirement if quantitative unobservable inputs are not developed by the entity when measuring fair value (eg when an entity uses prices from prior transactions or third-party pricing information without adjustment). However, when providing this disclosure an entity cannot ignore quantitative unobservable inputs that are significant to the fair value measurement and are reasonably available to the entity.

AASB

(e) for recurring fair value measurements categorised within Level 3 of the fair value hierarchy, a reconciliation from the opening balances to the closing balances, disclosing separately changes during the period attributable to the following:

    (i) total gains or losses for the period recognised in profit or loss, and the line item(s) in profit or loss in which those gains or losses are recognised.

    (ii) total gains or losses for the period recognised in other comprehensive income, and the line item(s) in other comprehensive income in which those gains or losses are recognised.

    (iii) purchases, sales, issues and settlements (each of those types of changes disclosed separately).

    (iv) the amounts of any transfers into or out of Level 3 of the fair value hierarchy, the reasons for those transfers and the entity's policy for determining when transfers between levels are deemed to have occurred (see paragraph 95). Transfers into Level 3 shall be disclosed and discussed separately from transfers out of Level 3.

(f) for recurring fair value measurements categorised within Level 3 of the fair value hierarchy, the amount of the total gains or losses for the period in (e)(i) included in profit or loss that is attributable to the change in unrealised gains or losses relating to those assets and liabilities held at the end of the reporting period, and the line item(s) in profit or loss in which those unrealised gains or losses are recognised.

(g) for recurring and non-recurring fair value measurements categorised within Level 3 of the fair value hierarchy, a description of the valuation processes used by the entity (including, for example, how an entity decides its valuation policies and procedures and analyses changes in fair value measurements from period to period).

(h) for recurring fair value measurements categorised within Level 3 of the fair value hierarchy:

    (i) for all such measurements, a narrative description of the sensitivity of the fair value measurement to changes in unobservable inputs if a change in those inputs to a different amount might result in a significantly higher or lower fair value measurement. If there are interrelationships between those inputs and other unobservable inputs used in the fair value measurement, an entity shall also provide a description of those interrelationships and of how they might magnify or mitigate the effect of changes in the unobservable inputs on the fair value measurement. To comply with that disclosure requirement, the narrative description of the sensitivity to changes in unobservable inputs shall include, at a minimum, the unobservable inputs disclosed when complying with (d).

    (ii) for financial assets and financial liabilities, if changing one or more of the unobservable inputs to reflect reasonably possible alternative assumptions would change fair value significantly, an entity shall state that fact and disclose the effect of those changes. The entity shall disclose how the effect of a change to reflect a reasonably possible alternative assumption was calculated. For that purpose, significance shall be judged with respect to profit or loss, and total assets or total liabilities, or, when changes in fair value are recognised in other comprehensive income, total equity.

(i) for recurring and non-recurring fair value measurements, if the highest and best use of a non-financial asset differs from its current use, an entity shall disclose that fact and why the non-financial asset is being used in a manner that differs from its highest and best use.

Aus93.1 Notwithstanding paragraph 93, in respect of not-for-profit public sector entities, for assets within the scope of AASB 116 *Property, Plant and Equipment* for which the future economic benefits are not primarily dependent on the asset's ability to generate net cash inflows, the following requirements do not apply:

(a) in paragraph 93(d), the text "For fair value measurements categorised within Level 3 of the fair value hierarchy, an entity shall provide quantitative information about the significant unobservable inputs used in the fair value measurement. An entity is not required to create quantitative information to comply with this disclosure requirement if quantitative unobservable inputs are not developed by the entity when measuring fair value (eg when an entity uses prices from prior transactions or third-party pricing information without adjustment). However, when providing this disclosure an entity cannot ignore quantitative unobservable inputs that are significant to the fair value measurement and are reasonably available to the entity.";

(b) paragraph 93(f); and

(c) paragraph 93(h)(i).

94 An entity shall determine appropriate classes of assets and liabilities on the basis of the following:

(a) the nature, characteristics and risks of the asset or liability; and

(b) the level of the fair value hierarchy within which the fair value measurement is categorised.

The number of classes may need to be greater for fair value measurements categorised within Level 3 of the fair value hierarchy because those measurements have a greater degree of uncertainty and subjectivity. Determining appropriate classes of assets and liabilities for which disclosures about fair value measurements should be provided requires judgement. A class of assets and liabilities will often require greater disaggregation than the line items presented in the statement of financial position. However, an entity shall provide information sufficient to permit reconciliation to the line items presented in the statement of financial position. If another Standard specifies the class for an asset or a liability, an entity may use that class in providing the disclosures required in this Standard if that class meets the requirements in this paragraph.

95 An entity shall disclose and consistently follow its policy for determining when transfers between levels of the fair value hierarchy are deemed to have occurred in accordance with paragraph 93(c) and (e)(iv). The policy about the timing of recognising transfers shall be the same for transfers into the levels as for transfers out of the levels. Examples of policies for determining the timing of transfers include the following:

(a) the date of the event or change in circumstances that caused the transfer.

(b) the beginning of the reporting period.

(c) the end of the reporting period.

96 If an entity makes an accounting policy decision to use the exception in paragraph 48, it shall disclose that fact.

97 For each class of assets and liabilities not measured at fair value in the statement of financial position but for which the fair value is disclosed, an entity shall disclose the information required by paragraph 93(b), (d) and (i). However, an entity is not required to provide the quantitative disclosures about significant unobservable inputs used in fair value measurements categorised within Level 3 of the fair value hierarchy required by paragraph 93(d). For such assets and liabilities, an entity does not need to provide the other disclosures required by this Standard.

98 For a liability measured at fair value and issued with an inseparable third-party credit enhancement, an issuer shall disclose the existence of that credit enhancement and whether it is reflected in the fair value measurement of the liability.

AASB

99   An entity shall present the quantitative disclosures required by this Standard in a tabular format unless another format is more appropriate.

Commencement of the legislative instrument

Aus99.1   For legal purposes, this legislative instrument commences on 31 December 2017.

Withdrawal of AASB pronouncements

Aus99.2   This Standard repeals AASB 13 *Fair Value Measurement* issued in September 2011. Despite the repeal, after the time this Standard starts to apply under section 334 of the Corporations Act (either generally or in relation to an individual entity), the repealed Standard continues to apply in relation to any period ending before that time as if the repeal had not occurred.

[Note: When this Standard applies under section 334 of the Corporations Act (either generally or in relation to an individual entity), it supersedes the application of the repealed Standard.]

APPENDIX A
DEFINED TERMS

This appendix is an integral part of the Standard.

active market	A market in which transactions for the asset or liability take place with sufficient frequency and volume to provide pricing information on an ongoing basis.
cost approach	A valuation technique that reflects the amount that would be required currently to replace the service capacity of an asset (often referred to as current replacement cost).
entry price	The price paid to acquire an asset or received to assume a liability in an exchange transaction.
exit price	The price that would be received to sell an asset or paid to transfer a liability.
expected cash flow	The probability-weighted average (ie mean of the distribution) of possible future cash flows.
fair value	The price that would be received to sell an asset or paid to transfer a liability in an orderly transaction between market participants at the measurement date.
highest and best use	The use of a non-financial asset by market participants that would maximise the value of the asset or the group of assets and liabilities (eg a business) within which the asset would be used.
income approach	Valuation techniques that convert future amounts (eg cash flows or income and expenses) to a single current (ie discounted) amount. The fair value measurement is determined on the basis of the value indicated by current market expectations about those future amounts.

inputs	The assumptions that market participants would use when pricing the asset or liability, including assumptions about risk, such as the following: (a) the risk inherent in a particular valuation technique used to measure fair value (such as a pricing model); and (b) the risk inherent in the inputs to the valuation technique. Inputs may be observable or unobservable.
Level 1 inputs	Quoted prices (unadjusted) in active markets for identical assets or liabilities that the entity can access at the measurement date.
Level 2 inputs	Inputs other than quoted prices included within Level 1 that are observable for the asset or liability, either directly or indirectly.
Level 3 inputs	Unobservable inputs for the asset or liability.
market approach	A valuation technique that uses prices and other relevant information generated by market transactions involving identical or comparable (ie similar) assets, liabilities or a group of assets and liabilities, such as a business.
market-corroborated inputs	Inputs that are derived principally from or corroborated by observable market data by correlation or other means.
market participant	Buyers and sellers in the principal (or most advantageous) market for the asset or liability that have all of the following characteristics: (a) They are independent of each other, ie they are not related parties as defined in AASB 124, although the price in a related party transaction may be used as an input to a fair value measurement if the entity has evidence that the transaction was entered into at market terms. (b) They are knowledgeable, having a reasonable understanding about the asset or liability and the transaction using all available information, including information that might be obtained through due diligence efforts that are usual and customary. (c) They are able to enter into a transaction for the asset or liability. (d) They are willing to enter into a transaction for the asset or liability, ie they are motivated but not forced or otherwise compelled to do so.
most advantageous market	The market that maximises the amount that would be received to sell the asset or minimises the amount that would be paid to transfer the liability, after taking into account transaction costs and transport costs.
non-performance risk	The risk that an entity will not fulfil an obligation. Non-performance risk includes, but may not be limited to, the entity's own credit risk.
observable inputs	Inputs that are developed using market data, such as publicly available information about actual events or transactions, and that reflect the assumptions that market participants would use when pricing the asset or liability.
orderly transaction	A transaction that assumes exposure to the market for a period before the measurement date to allow for marketing activities that are usual and customary for transactions involving such assets or liabilities; it is not a forced transaction (eg a forced liquidation or distress sale).
principal market	The market with the greatest volume and level of activity for the asset or liability.
risk premium	Compensation sought by risk-averse market participants for bearing the uncertainty inherent in the cash flows of an asset or a liability. Also referred to as a 'risk adjustment'.

AASB

transaction costs	The costs to sell an asset or transfer a liability in the principal (or most advantageous) market for the asset or liability that are directly attributable to the disposal of the asset or the transfer of the liability and meet both of the following criteria:
	(a) They result directly from and are essential to that transaction.
	(b) They would not have been incurred by the entity had the decision to sell the asset or transfer the liability not been made (similar to costs to sell, as defined in AASB 5).
transport costs	The costs that would be incurred to transport an asset from its current location to its principal (or most advantageous) market.
unit of account	The level at which an asset or a liability is aggregated or disaggregated in a Standard for recognition purposes.
unobservable inputs	Inputs for which market data are not available and that are developed using the best information available about the assumptions that market participants would use when pricing the asset or liability.

APPENDIX B

APPLICATION GUIDANCE

This appendix is an integral part of the Standard. It describes the application of paragraphs 1–99 and has the same authority as the other parts of the Standard.

B1   The judgements applied in different valuation situations may be different. This appendix describes the judgements that might apply when an entity measures fair value in different valuation situations.

The fair value measurement approach

B2   The objective of a fair value measurement is to estimate the price at which an orderly transaction to sell the asset or to transfer the liability would take place between market participants at the measurement date under current market conditions. A fair value measurement requires an entity to determine all the following:

(a)   the particular asset or liability that is the subject of the measurement (consistently with its unit of account).

(b)   for a non-financial asset, the valuation premise that is appropriate for the measurement (consistently with its highest and best use).

(c)   the principal (or most advantageous) market for the asset or liability.

(d)   the valuation technique(s) appropriate for the measurement, considering the availability of data with which to develop inputs that represent the assumptions that market participants would use when pricing the asset or liability and the level of the fair value hierarchy within which the inputs are categorised.

Valuation premise for non-financial assets (paragraphs 31–33)

B3   When measuring the fair value of a non-financial asset used in combination with other assets as a group (as installed or otherwise configured for use) or in combination with other assets and liabilities (eg a business), the effect of the valuation premise depends on the circumstances. For example:

(a)   the fair value of the asset might be the same whether the asset is used on a stand-alone basis or in combination with other assets or with other assets and liabilities. That might be the case if the asset is a business that market participants would continue to operate. In that case, the transaction would involve valuing the business in its entirety. The use of the assets as a group in an ongoing business would generate synergies that would be available to market participants (ie market participant synergies that, therefore, should affect the fair value of the asset on either a stand-alone basis or in combination with other assets or with other assets and liabilities).

(b)   an asset's use in combination with other assets or with other assets and liabilities might be incorporated into the fair value measurement through adjustments to the value of the asset used on a stand-alone basis That might be the case if the asset is a machine and the fair value measurement is determined using an observed price for a similar machine (not installed or otherwise configured for use), adjusted for transport and installation costs so that the fair value measurement reflects the current condition and location of the machine (installed and configured for use).

(c)   an asset's use in combination with other assets or with other assets and liabilities might be incorporated into the fair value measurement through the market participant assumptions used to measure the fair value of the asset. For example, if the asset is work in progress inventory that is unique and market participants would convert the inventory into finished goods, the fair value of the inventory would assume that market participants have acquired or would acquire any specialised machinery necessary to convert the inventory into finished goods.

(d)   an asset's use in combination with other assets or with other assets and liabilities might be incorporated into the valuation technique used to measure the fair value of the asset. That might be the case when using the multi-period excess earnings method to measure the fair value of an intangible asset because that valuation technique specifically takes into account the contribution of any complementary assets and the associated liabilities in the group in which such an intangible asset would be used.

(e)   in more limited situations, when an entity uses an asset within a group of assets, the entity might measure the asset at an amount that approximates its fair value when allocating the fair value of the asset group to the individual assets of the group. That might be the case if the valuation involves real property and the fair value of improved property (ie an asset group) is allocated to its component assets (such as land and improvements).

Fair value at initial recognition (paragraphs 57–60)

B4   When determining whether fair value at initial recognition equals the transaction price, an entity shall take into account factors specific to the transaction and to the asset or liability. For example, the transaction price might not represent the fair value of an asset or a liability at initial recognition if any of the following conditions exist:

(a)   The transaction is between related parties, although the price in a related party transaction may be used as an input into a fair value measurement if the entity has evidence that the transaction was entered into at market terms.

(b)   The transaction takes place under duress or the seller is forced to accept the price in the transaction. For example, that might be the case if the seller is experiencing financial difficulty.

(c)   The unit of account represented by the transaction price is different from the unit of account for the asset or liability measured at fair value. For example, that might be the case if the asset or liability measured at fair value is only one of the elements in the transaction (eg in a business combination), the transaction includes unstated rights and privileges that are measured separately in accordance with another Standard, or the transaction price includes transaction costs.

(d)   The market in which the transaction takes place is different from the principal market (or most advantageous market). For example, those markets might be different if the entity is a dealer that enters into transactions with customers in the retail market, but the principal (or most advantageous) market for the exit transaction is with other dealers in the dealer market.

Valuation techniques (paragraphs 61–66)

Market approach

B5   The market approach uses prices and other relevant information generated by market transactions involving identical or comparable (ie similar) assets, liabilities or a group of assets and liabilities, such as a business.

B6   For example, valuation techniques consistent with the market approach often use market multiples derived from a set of comparables. Multiples might be in ranges with a different multiple for each comparable. The selection of the appropriate multiple within the range requires judgement, considering qualitative and quantitative factors specific to the measurement.

B7   Valuation techniques consistent with the market approach include matrix pricing. Matrix pricing is a mathematical technique used principally to value some types of financial instruments, such as debt securities, without relying exclusively on quoted prices for the specific securities, but rather relying on the securities' relationship to other benchmark quoted securities.

Cost approach

B8   The cost approach reflects the amount that would be required currently to replace the service capacity of an asset (often referred to as current replacement cost).

B9   From the perspective of a market participant seller, the price that would be received for the asset is based on the cost to a market participant buyer to acquire or construct a substitute asset of comparable utility, adjusted for obsolescence. That is because a market participant buyer would not pay more for an asset than the amount for which it could replace the service capacity of that asset. Obsolescence encompasses physical deterioration, functional (technological) obsolescence and economic (external) obsolescence and is broader than depreciation for financial reporting purposes (an allocation of historical cost) or tax purposes (using specified service lives). In many cases the current replacement cost method is used to measure the fair value of tangible assets that are used in combination with other assets or with other assets and liabilities.

Income approach

B10   The income approach converts future amounts (eg cash flows or income and expenses) to a single current (ie discounted) amount. When the income approach is used, the fair value measurement reflects current market expectations about those future amounts.

B11   Those valuation techniques include, for example, the following:

    (a)   present value techniques (see paragraphs B12–B30);

    (b)   option pricing models, such as the Black-Scholes-Merton formula or a binomial model (ie a lattice model), that incorporate present value techniques and reflect both the time value and the intrinsic value of an option; and

    (c)   the multi-period excess earnings method, which is used to measure the fair value of some intangible assets.

Present value techniques

B12   Paragraphs B13–B30 describe the use of present value techniques to measure fair value. Those paragraphs focus on a discount rate adjustment technique and an *expected cash flow* (expected present value) technique. Those paragraphs neither prescribe the use of a single specific present value technique nor limit the use of present value techniques to measure fair value to the techniques discussed. The present value technique used to measure fair value will depend on facts and circumstances specific to the asset or liability being measured (eg whether prices for comparable assets or liabilities can be observed in the market) and the availability of sufficient data.

The components of a present value measurement

B13 Present value (ie an application of the income approach) is a tool used to link future amounts (eg cash flows or values) to a present amount using a discount rate. A fair value measurement of an asset or a liability using a present value technique captures all the following elements from the perspective of market participants at the measurement date:

(a) an estimate of future cash flows for the asset or liability being measured.

(b) expectations about possible variations in the amount and timing of the cash flows representing the uncertainty inherent in the cash flows.

(c) the time value of money, represented by the rate on risk-free monetary assets that have maturity dates or durations that coincide with the period covered by the cash flows and pose neither uncertainty in timing nor risk of default to the holder (ie a risk-free interest rate).

(d) the price for bearing the uncertainty inherent in the cash flows (ie a *risk premium*).

(e) other factors that market participants would take into account in the circumstances.

(f) for a liability, the non-performance risk relating to that liability, including the entity's (ie the obligor's) own credit risk.

General principles

B14 Present value techniques differ in how they capture the elements in paragraph B13. However, all the following general principles govern the application of any present value technique used to measure fair value:

(a) Cash flows and discount rates should reflect assumptions that market participants would use when pricing the asset or liability.

(b) Cash flows and discount rates should take into account only the factors attributable to the asset or liability being measured.

(c) To avoid double-counting or omitting the effects of risk factors, discount rates should reflect assumptions that are consistent with those inherent in the cash flows. For example, a discount rate that reflects the uncertainty in expectations about future defaults is appropriate if using contractual cash flows of a loan (ie a discount rate adjustment technique). That same rate should not be used if using expected (ie probability-weighted) cash flows (ie an expected present value technique) because the expected cash flows already reflect assumptions about the uncertainty in future defaults; instead, a discount rate that is commensurate with the risk inherent in the expected cash flows should be used.

(d) Assumptions about cash flows and discount rates should be internally consistent. For example, nominal cash flows, which include the effect of inflation, should be discounted at a rate that includes the effect of inflation. The nominal risk-free interest rate includes the effect of inflation. Real cash flows, which exclude the effect of inflation, should be discounted at a rate that excludes the effect of inflation. Similarly, after-tax cash flows should be discounted using an after-tax discount rate. Pre-tax cash flows should be discounted at a rate consistent with those cash flows.

(e) Discount rates should be consistent with the underlying economic factors of the currency in which the cash flows are denominated.

AASB

Risk and uncertainty

B15   A fair value measurement using present value techniques is made under conditions of uncertainty because the cash flows used are estimates rather than known amounts. In many cases both the amount and timing of the cash flows are uncertain. Even contractually fixed amounts, such as the payments on a loan, are uncertain if there is risk of default.

B16   Market participants generally seek compensation (ie a risk premium) for bearing the uncertainty inherent in the cash flows of an asset or a liability. A fair value measurement should include a risk premium reflecting the amount that market participants would demand as compensation for the uncertainty inherent in the cash flows. Otherwise, the measurement would not faithfully represent fair value. In some cases determining the appropriate risk premium might be difficult. However, the degree of difficulty alone is not a sufficient reason to exclude a risk premium.

B17   Present value techniques differ in how they adjust for risk and in the type of cash flows they use. For example:

     (a)   The discount rate adjustment technique (see paragraphs B18–B22) uses a risk-adjusted discount rate and contractual, promised or most likely cash flows.

     (b)   Method 1 of the expected present value technique (see paragraph B25) uses risk-adjusted expected cash flows and a risk-free rate.

     (c)   Method 2 of the expected present value technique (see paragraph B26) uses expected cash flows that are not risk-adjusted and a discount rate adjusted to include the risk premium that market participants require. That rate is different from the rate used in the discount rate adjustment technique.

Discount rate adjustment technique

B18   The discount rate adjustment technique uses a single set of cash flows from the range of possible estimated amounts, whether contractual or promised (as is the case for a bond) or most likely cash flows. In all cases, those cash flows are conditional upon the occurrence of specified events (eg contractual or promised cash flows for a bond are conditional on the event of no default by the debtor). The discount rate used in the discount rate adjustment technique is derived from observed rates of return for comparable assets or liabilities that are traded in the market. Accordingly, the contractual, promised or most likely cash flows are discounted at an observed or estimated market rate for such conditional cash flows (ie a market rate of return).

B19   The discount rate adjustment technique requires an analysis of market data for comparable assets or liabilities. Comparability is established by considering the nature of the cash flows (eg whether the cash flows are contractual or non-contractual and are likely to respond similarly to changes in economic conditions), as well as other factors (eg credit standing, collateral, duration, restrictive covenants and liquidity). Alternatively, if a single comparable asset or liability does not fairly reflect the risk inherent in the cash flows of the asset or liability being measured, it may be possible to derive a discount rate using data for several comparable assets or liabilities in conjunction with the risk-free yield curve (ie using a 'build-up' approach).

B20   To illustrate a build-up approach, assume that Asset A is a contractual right to receive CU800[1] in one year (ie there is no timing uncertainty). There is an established market for comparable assets, and information about those assets, including price information, is available. Of those comparable assets:

     (a)   Asset B is a contractual right to receive CU1,200 in one year and has a market price of CU1,083. Thus, the implied annual rate of return (ie a one-year market rate of return) is 10.8 per cent $[(CU1,200/CU1,083) - 1]$.

     (b)   Asset C is a contractual right to receive CU700 in two years and has a market price of CU566. Thus, the implied annual rate of return (ie a two-year market rate of return) is 11.2 per cent $[(CU700/CU566)^{0.5} - 1]$.

---

1   In this Standard monetary amounts are denominated in 'currency units (CU)'.

(c) All three assets are comparable with respect to risk (ie dispersion of possible pay-offs and credit).

B21 On the basis of the timing of the contractual payments to be received for Asset A relative to the timing for Asset B and Asset C (ie one year for Asset B versus two years for Asset C), Asset B is deemed more comparable to Asset A. Using the contractual payment to be received for Asset A (CU800) and the one-year market rate derived from Asset B (10.8 per cent), the fair value of Asset A is CU722 (CU800/1.108). Alternatively, in the absence of available market information for Asset B, the one-year market rate could be derived from Asset C using the build-up approach. In that case the two-year market rate indicated by Asset C (11.2 per cent) would be adjusted to a one-year market rate using the term structure of the risk-free yield curve. Additional information and analysis might be required to determine whether the risk premiums for one-year and two-year assets are the same. If it is determined that the risk premiums for one-year and two-year assets are not the same, the two-year market rate of return would be further adjusted for that effect.

B22 When the discount rate adjustment technique is applied to fixed receipts or payments, the adjustment for risk inherent in the cash flows of the asset or liability being measured is included in the discount rate. In some applications of the discount rate adjustment technique to cash flows that are not fixed receipts or payments, an adjustment to the cash flows may be necessary to achieve comparability with the observed asset or liability from which the discount rate is derived.

Expected present value technique

B23 The expected present value technique uses as a starting point a set of cash flows that represents the probability-weighted average of all possible future cash flows (ie the expected cash flows). The resulting estimate is identical to expected value, which, in statistical terms, is the weighted average of a discrete random variable's possible values with the respective probabilities as the weights. Because all possible cash flows are probability-weighted, the resulting expected cash flow is not conditional upon the occurrence of any specified event (unlike the cash flows used in the discount rate adjustment technique).

B24 In making an investment decision, risk-averse market participants would take into account the risk that the actual cash flows may differ from the expected cash flows. Portfolio theory distinguishes between two types of risk:

(a) unsystematic (diversifiable) risk, which is the risk specific to a particular asset or liability.

(b) systematic (non-diversifiable) risk, which is the common risk shared by an asset or a liability with the other items in a diversified portfolio.

Portfolio theory holds that in a market in equilibrium, market participants will be compensated only for bearing the systematic risk inherent in the cash flows. (In markets that are inefficient or out of equilibrium, other forms of return or compensation might be available.)

B25 Method 1 of the expected present value technique adjusts the expected cash flows of an asset for systematic (ie market) risk by subtracting a cash risk premium (ie risk-adjusted expected cash flows). Those risk-adjusted expected cash flows represent a certainty-equivalent cash flow, which is discounted at a risk-free interest rate. A certainty-equivalent cash flow refers to an expected cash flow (as defined), adjusted for risk so that a market participant is indifferent to trading a certain cash flow for an expected cash flow. For example, if a market participant was willing to trade an expected cash flow of CU1,200 for a certain cash flow of CU1,000, the CU1,000 is the certainty equivalent of the CU1,200 (ie the CU200 would represent the cash risk premium). In that case the market participant would be indifferent as to the asset held.

B26 In contrast, Method 2 of the expected present value technique adjusts for systematic (ie market) risk by applying a risk premium to the risk-free interest rate. Accordingly, the expected cash flows are discounted at a rate that corresponds to an expected rate associated with probability-weighted cash flows (ie an expected rate of return). Models used for pricing risky assets, such as the capital asset pricing model, can be used to estimate the expected rate of return. Because the discount rate used in the discount rate adjustment technique is a rate of return relating to conditional cash flows, it is likely to be higher than the discount rate used in Method 2 of the expected present value technique, which is an expected rate of return relating to expected or probability-weighted cash flows.

B27   To illustrate Methods 1 and 2, assume that an asset has expected cash flows of CU780 in one year determined on the basis of the possible cash flows and probabilities shown below. The applicable risk-free interest rate for cash flows with a one-year horizon is 5 per cent, and the systematic risk premium for an asset with the same risk profile is 3 per cent.

Possible cash flows	Probability	Probability-weighted cash flows
CU500	15%	CU75
CU800	60%	CU480
CU900	25%	CU225
Expected cash flows		CU780

B28   In this simple illustration, the expected cash flows (CU780) represent the probability-weighted average of the three possible outcomes. In more realistic situations, there could be many possible outcomes. However, to apply the expected present value technique, it is not always necessary to take into account distributions of all possible cash flows using complex models and techniques. Rather, it might be possible to develop a limited number of discrete scenarios and probabilities that capture the array of possible cash flows. For example, an entity might use realised cash flows for some relevant past period, adjusted for changes in circumstances occurring subsequently (eg changes in external factors, including economic or market conditions, industry trends and competition as well as changes in internal factors affecting the entity more specifically), taking into account the assumptions of market participants.

B29   In theory, the present value (ie the fair value) of the asset's cash flows is the same whether determined using Method 1 or Method 2, as follows:

(a)   Using Method 1, the expected cash flows are adjusted for systematic (ie market) risk. In the absence of market data directly indicating the amount of the risk adjustment, such adjustment could be derived from an asset pricing model using the concept of certainty equivalents. For example, the risk adjustment (ie the cash risk premium of CU22) could be determined using the systematic risk premium of 3 per cent (CU780 – [CU780 × (1.05/1.08)]), which results in risk-adjusted expected cash flows of CU758 (CU780 – CU22). The CU758 is the certainty equivalent of CU780 and is discounted at the risk-free interest rate (5 per cent). The present value (ie the fair value) of the asset is CU722 (CU758/1.05).

(b)   Using Method 2, the expected cash flows are not adjusted for systematic (ie market) risk. Rather, the adjustment for that risk is included in the discount rate. Thus, the expected cash flows are discounted at an expected rate of return of 8 per cent (ie the 5 per cent risk-free interest rate plus the 3 per cent systematic risk premium). The present value (ie the fair value) of the asset is CU722 (CU780/1.08).

B30   When using an expected present value technique to measure fair value, either Method 1 or Method 2 could be used. The selection of Method 1 or Method 2 will depend on facts and circumstances specific to the asset or liability being measured, the extent to which sufficient data are available and the judgements applied.

Applying present value techniques to liabilities and an entity's own equity instruments not held by other parties as assets (paragraphs 40 and 41)

B31   When using a present value technique to measure the fair value of a liability that is not held by another party as an asset (eg a decommissioning liability), an entity shall, among other things, estimate the future cash outflows that market participants would expect to incur in fulfilling the obligation. Those future cash outflows shall include market participants' expectations about the costs of fulfilling the obligation and the compensation that a market participant would require for taking on the obligation. Such compensation includes the return that a market participant would require for the following:

    (a)   undertaking the activity (ie the value of fulfilling the obligation; eg by using resources that could be used for other activities); and

    (b)   assuming the risk associated with the obligation (ie a risk premium that reflects the risk that the actual cash outflows might differ from the expected cash outflows; see paragraph B33).

B32   For example, a non-financial liability does not contain a contractual rate of return and there is no observable market yield for that liability. In some cases the components of the return that market participants would require will be indistinguishable from one another (eg when using the price a third party contractor would charge on a fixed fee basis). In other cases an entity needs to estimate those components separately (eg when using the price a third party contractor would charge on a cost plus basis because the contractor in that case would not bear the risk of future changes in costs).

B33   An entity can include a risk premium in the fair value measurement of a liability or an entity's own equity instrument that is not held by another party as an asset in one of the following ways:

    (a)   by adjusting the cash flows (ie as an increase in the amount of cash outflows); or

    (b)   by adjusting the rate used to discount the future cash flows to their present values (ie as a reduction in the discount rate).

    An entity shall ensure that it does not double-count or omit adjustments for risk. For example, if the estimated cash flows are increased to take into account the compensation for assuming the risk associated with the obligation, the discount rate should not be adjusted to reflect that risk.

Inputs to valuation techniques (paragraphs 67–71)

B34   Examples of markets in which inputs might be observable for some assets and liabilities (eg financial instruments) include the following:

    (a)   *Exchange markets.* In an exchange market, closing prices are both readily available and generally representative of fair value. An example of such a market is the London Stock Exchange.

    (b)   *Dealer markets.* In a dealer market, dealers stand ready to trade (either buy or sell for their own account), thereby providing liquidity by using their capital to hold an inventory of the items for which they make a market. Typically bid and ask prices (representing the price at which the dealer is willing to buy and the price at which the dealer is willing to sell, respectively) are more readily available than closing prices. Over-the-counter markets (for which prices are publicly reported) are dealer markets. Dealer markets also exist for some other assets and liabilities, including some financial instruments, commodities and physical assets (eg used equipment).

    (c)   *Brokered markets.* In a brokered market, brokers attempt to match buyers with sellers but do not stand ready to trade for their own account. In other words, brokers do not use their own capital to hold an inventory of the items for

AASB

which they make a market. The broker knows the prices bid and asked by the respective parties, but each party is typically unaware of another party's price requirements. Prices of completed transactions are sometimes available. Brokered markets include electronic communication networks, in which buy and sell orders are matched, and commercial and residential real estate markets.

(d)   *Principal-to-principal markets.* In a principal-to-principal market, transactions, both originations and resales, are negotiated independently with no intermediary. Little information about those transactions may be made available publicly.

Fair value hierarchy (paragraphs 72–90)

Level 2 inputs (paragraphs 81–85)

B35   Examples of Level 2 inputs for particular assets and liabilities include the following:

(a)   *Receive-fixed, pay-variable interest rate swap based on the London Interbank Offered Rate (LIBOR) swap rate.* A Level 2 input would be the LIBOR swap rate if that rate is observable at commonly quoted intervals for substantially the full term of the swap.

(b)   *Receive-fixed, pay-variable interest rate swap based on a yield curve denominated in a foreign currency.* A Level 2 input would be the swap rate based on a yield curve denominated in a foreign currency that is observable at commonly quoted intervals for substantially the full term of the swap. That would be the case if the term of the swap is 10 years and that rate is observable at commonly quoted intervals for 9 years, provided that any reasonable extrapolation of the yield curve for year 10 would not be significant to the fair value measurement of the swap in its entirety.

(c)   *Receive-fixed, pay-variable interest rate swap based on a specific bank's prime rate.* A Level 2 input would be the bank's prime rate derived through extrapolation if the extrapolated values are corroborated by observable market data, for example, by correlation with an interest rate that is observable over substantially the full term of the swap.

(d)   *Three-year option on exchange-traded shares.* A Level 2 input would be the implied volatility for the shares derived through extrapolation to year 3 if both of the following conditions exist:

(i)   Prices for one-year and two-year options on the shares are observable.

(ii)   The extrapolated implied volatility of a three-year option is corroborated by observable market data for substantially the full term of the option.

In that case the implied volatility could be derived by extrapolating from the implied volatility of the one-year and two-year options on the shares and corroborated by the implied volatility for three-year options on comparable entities' shares, provided that correlation with the one-year and two-year implied volatilities is established.

(e)   *Licensing arrangement.* For a licensing arrangement that is acquired in a business combination and was recently negotiated with an unrelated party by the acquired entity (the party to the licensing arrangement), a Level 2 input would be the royalty rate in the contract with the unrelated party at inception of the arrangement.

(f)   *Finished goods inventory at a retail outlet.* For finished goods inventory that is acquired in a business combination, a Level 2 input would be either a price to customers in a retail market or a price to retailers in a wholesale market, adjusted for differences between the condition and location of the inventory item and the comparable (ie similar) inventory items so that the fair value measurement reflects the price that would be received in a transaction to sell the inventory to another retailer that would complete the requisite selling efforts. Conceptually, the fair value measurement will be the same, whether adjustments are made to a retail price (downward) or to a wholesale price (upward). Generally, the price that requires the least amount of subjective adjustments should be used for the fair value measurement.

(g) *Building held and used.* A Level 2 input would be the price per square metre for the building (a valuation multiple) derived from observable market data, eg multiples derived from prices in observed transactions involving comparable (ie similar) buildings in similar locations.

(h) *Cash-generating unit.* A Level 2 input would be a valuation multiple (eg a multiple of earnings or revenue or a similar performance measure) derived from observable market data, eg multiples derived from prices in observed transactions involving comparable (ie similar) businesses, taking into account operational, market, financial and non-financial factors.

Level 3 inputs (paragraphs 86–90)

B36 Examples of Level 3 inputs for particular assets and liabilities include the following:

(a) *Long-dated currency swap.* A Level 3 input would be an interest rate in a specified currency that is not observable and cannot be corroborated by observable market data at commonly quoted intervals or otherwise for substantially the full term of the currency swap. The interest rates in a currency swap are the swap rates calculated from the respective countries' yield curves.

(b) *Three-year option on exchange-traded shares.* A Level 3 input would be historical volatility, ie the volatility for the shares derived from the shares' historical prices. Historical volatility typically does not represent current market participants' expectations about future volatility, even if it is the only information available to price an option.

(c) *Interest rate swap.* A Level 3 input would be an adjustment to a mid-market consensus (non-binding) price for the swap developed using data that are not directly observable and cannot otherwise be corroborated by observable market data.

(d) *Decommissioning liability assumed in a business combination.* A Level 3 input would be a current estimate using the entity's own data about the future cash outflows to be paid to fulfil the obligation (including market participants' expectations about the costs of fulfilling the obligation and the compensation that a market participant would require for taking on the obligation to dismantle the asset) if there is no reasonably available information that indicates that market participants would use different assumptions. That Level 3 input would be used in a present value technique together with other inputs, eg a current risk-free interest rate or a credit-adjusted risk-free rate if the effect of the entity's credit standing on the fair value of the liability is reflected in the discount rate rather than in the estimate of future cash outflows.

(e) *Cash-generating unit.* A Level 3 input would be a financial forecast (eg of cash flows or profit or loss) developed using the entity's own data if there is no reasonably available information that indicates that market participants would use different assumptions.

Measuring fair value when the volume or level of activity for an asset or a liability has significantly decreased

B37 The fair value of an asset or a liability might be affected when there has been a significant decrease in the volume or level of activity for that asset or liability in relation to normal market activity for the asset or liability (or similar assets or liabilities). To determine whether, on the basis of the evidence available, there has been a significant decrease in the volume or level of activity for the asset or liability, an entity shall evaluate the significance and relevance of factors such as the following:

(a)   There are few recent transactions.

(b)   Price quotations are not developed using current information.

(c)   Price quotations vary substantially either over time or among market-makers (eg some brokered markets).

(d)   Indices that previously were highly correlated with the fair values of the asset or liability are demonstrably uncorrelated with recent indications of fair value for that asset or liability.

(e)   There is a significant increase in implied liquidity risk premiums, yields or performance indicators (such as delinquency rates or loss severities) for observed transactions or quoted prices when compared with the entity's estimate of expected cash flows, taking into account all available market data about credit and other non-performance risk for the asset or liability.

(f)   There is a wide bid-ask spread or significant increase in the bid-ask spread.

(g)   There is a significant decline in the activity of, or there is an absence of, a market for new issues (ie a primary market) for the asset or liability or similar assets or liabilities.

(h)   Little information is publicly available (eg for transactions that take place in a principal-to-principal market).

B38   If an entity concludes that there has been a significant decrease in the volume or level of activity for the asset or liability in relation to normal market activity for the asset or liability (or similar assets or liabilities), further analysis of the transactions or quoted prices is needed. A decrease in the volume or level of activity on its own may not indicate that a transaction price or quoted price does not represent fair value or that a transaction in that market is not orderly. However, if an entity determines that a transaction or quoted price does not represent fair value (eg there may be transactions that are not orderly), an adjustment to the transactions or quoted prices will be necessary if the entity uses those prices as a basis for measuring fair value and that adjustment may be significant to the fair value measurement in its entirety. Adjustments also may be necessary in other circumstances (eg when a price for a similar asset requires significant adjustment to make it comparable to the asset being measured or when the price is stale).

B39   This Standard does not prescribe a methodology for making significant adjustments to transactions or quoted prices. See paragraphs 61–66 and B5–B11 for a discussion of the use of valuation techniques when measuring fair value. Regardless of the valuation technique used, an entity shall include appropriate risk adjustments, including a risk premium reflecting the amount that market participants would demand as compensation for the uncertainty inherent in the cash flows of an asset or a liability (see paragraph B17). Otherwise, the measurement does not faithfully represent fair value. In some cases determining the appropriate risk adjustment might be difficult. However, the degree of difficulty alone is not a sufficient basis on which to exclude a risk adjustment. The risk adjustment shall be reflective of an orderly transaction between market participants at the measurement date under current market conditions.

B40   If there has been a significant decrease in the volume or level of activity for the asset or liability, a change in valuation technique or the use of multiple valuation techniques may be appropriate (eg the use of a market approach and a present value technique). When weighting indications of fair value resulting from the use of multiple valuation techniques, an entity shall consider the reasonableness of the range of fair value measurements. The objective is to determine the point within the range that is most representative of fair value under current market conditions. A wide range of fair value measurements may be an indication that further analysis is needed.

B41   Even when there has been a significant decrease in the volume or level of activity for the asset or liability, the objective of a fair value measurement remains the same. Fair value is the price that would be received to sell an asset or paid to transfer a liability in an orderly transaction (ie not a forced liquidation or distress sale) between market participants at the measurement date under current market conditions.

B42 Estimating the price at which market participants would be willing to enter into a transaction at the measurement date under current market conditions if there has been a significant decrease in the volume or level of activity for the asset or liability depends on the facts and circumstances at the measurement date and requires judgement. An entity's intention to hold the asset or to settle or otherwise fulfil the liability is not relevant when measuring fair value because fair value is a market-based measurement, not an entity-specific measurement.

Identifying transactions that are not orderly

B43 The determination of whether a transaction is orderly (or is not orderly) is more difficult if there has been a significant decrease in the volume or level of activity for the asset or liability in relation to normal market activity for the asset or liability (or similar assets or liabilities). In such circumstances it is not appropriate to conclude that all transactions in that market are not orderly (ie forced liquidations or distress sales). Circumstances that may indicate that a transaction is not orderly include the following:

(a) There was not adequate exposure to the market for a period before the measurement date to allow for marketing activities that are usual and customary for transactions involving such assets or liabilities under current market conditions.

(b) There was a usual and customary marketing period, but the seller marketed the asset or liability to a single market participant.

(c) The seller is in or near bankruptcy or receivership (ie the seller is distressed).

(d) The seller was required to sell to meet regulatory or legal requirements (ie the seller was forced).

(e) The transaction price is an outlier when compared with other recent transactions for the same or a similar asset or liability.

An entity shall evaluate the circumstances to determine whether, on the weight of the evidence available, the transaction is orderly.

B44 An entity shall consider all the following when measuring fair value or estimating market risk premiums:

(a) If the evidence indicates that a transaction is not orderly, an entity shall place little, if any, weight (compared with other indications of fair value) on that transaction price.

(b) If the evidence indicates that a transaction is orderly, an entity shall take into account that transaction price. The amount of weight placed on that transaction price when compared with other indications of fair value will depend on the facts and circumstances, such as the following:

(i) the volume of the transaction.

(ii) the comparability of the transaction to the asset or liability being measured.

(iii) the proximity of the transaction to the measurement date.

(c) If an entity does not have sufficient information to conclude whether a transaction is orderly, it shall take into account the transaction price. However, that transaction price may not represent fair value (ie the transaction price is not necessarily the sole or primary basis for measuring fair value or estimating market risk premiums). When an entity does not have sufficient information to conclude whether particular transactions are orderly, the entity shall place less weight on those transactions when compared with other transactions that are known to be orderly.

An entity need not undertake exhaustive efforts to determine whether a transaction is orderly, but it shall not ignore information that is reasonably available. When an entity is a party to a transaction, it is presumed to have sufficient information to conclude whether the transaction is orderly.

Using quoted prices provided by third parties

B45 This Standard does not preclude the use of quoted prices provided by third parties, such as pricing services or brokers, if an entity has determined that the quoted prices provided by those parties are developed in accordance with this Standard.

B46 If there has been a significant decrease in the volume or level of activity for the asset or liability, an entity shall evaluate whether the quoted prices provided by third parties are developed using current information that reflects orderly transactions or a valuation technique that reflects market participant assumptions (including assumptions about risk). In weighting a quoted price as an input to a fair value measurement, an entity places less weight (when compared with other indications of fair value that reflect the results of transactions) on quotes that do not reflect the result of transactions.

B47 Furthermore, the nature of a quote (eg whether the quote is an indicative price or a binding offer) shall be taken into account when weighting the available evidence, with more weight given to quotes provided by third parties that represent binding offers.

APPENDIX C
EFFECTIVE DATE AND TRANSITION

This appendix is an integral part of the Standard and has the same authority as the other parts of the Standard.

C1 An entity shall apply this Standard for annual periods beginning on or after 1 January 2018. Earlier application is permitted for periods beginning after 24 July 2014 but before 1 January 2018. If an entity applies this Standard for an earlier period, it shall disclose that fact.

AusC1.1 Paragraphs C2 and C3 shall not be applied by an entity that has previously applied AASB 13, unless required to do so by another Standard.

C2 This Standard shall be applied prospectively as of the beginning of the annual period in which it is initially applied.

C3 The disclosure requirements of this Standard need not be applied in comparative information provided for periods before initial application of this Standard.

C4 [Deleted by the AASB]

C5 AASB 2014-7 *Amendments to Australian Accounting Standards arising from AASB 9 (December 2014)*, issued in December 2014, amended paragraph 52 in the previous version of this Standard. An entity shall apply that amendment when it applies AASB 9.

APPENDIX E
AUSTRALIAN REDUCED DISCLOSURE REQUIREMENTS

This appendix is an integral part of the Standard and has the same authority as the other parts of the Standard.

AusE1   The text "both of" in the lead in of paragraph 91 and paragraphs 91(b), 93(b)–(i), 95 and 97–99 of this Standard do not apply to entities preparing general purpose financial statements under Australian Accounting Standards – Reduced Disclosure Requirements. Entities applying Australian Accounting Standards – Reduced Disclosure Requirements may elect to comply with some or all of these excluded requirements.

AusE2   The requirements that do not apply to entities preparing general purpose financial statements under Australian Accounting Standards – Reduced Disclosure Requirements are also identified in this Standard by shading of the relevant text.

DELETED IFRS 13 TEXT

Deleted IFRS 13 text is not part of AASB 13.

7   The disclosures required by this IFRS are not required for the following:

(a)   ... ;

(b)   retirement benefit plan investments measured at fair value in accordance with IAS 26 *Accounting and Reporting by Retirement Benefit Plans*; and

(c)   ...

C4   *Annual Improvements Cycle 2011–2013* issued in December 2013 amended paragraph 52. An entity shall apply that amendment for annual periods beginning on or after 1 July 2014. An entity shall apply that amendment prospectively from the beginning of the annual period in which IFRS 13 was initially applied. Earlier application is permitted. If an entity applies that amendment for an earlier period it shall disclose that fact.

BASIS FOR CONCLUSIONS ON AASB 2015-7

This Basis for Conclusions accompanies, but is not part of, AASB 13. The Basis for Conclusions was originally published with AASB 2015-7 Amendments to Australian Accounting Standards – Fair Value Disclosures of Not-for-Profit Public Sector Entities.

Background

BC1   This Basis for Conclusions summarises the Australian Accounting Standards Board's considerations in reaching the conclusions in the Amending Standard. Individual Board members gave greater weight to some factors than to others.

BC2   AASB 13 *Fair Value Measurement* applies to annual reporting periods beginning on or after 1 January 2013. In 2014, the Board received feedback about AASB 13 from not-for-profit public sector entities following their implementation of the Standard, including feedback about some of the specified disclosures. These constituents were concerned that the costs of presenting the disclosures specified by the Standard, including potential disclosure overload for users of not-for-profit public sector general purpose financial statements, exceeded their benefits. The Board noted that it had considered similar issues in 2011 when making AASB 13, and had decided that no amendment to AASB 13 was necessary. However, following the feedback received, the Board decided, as a narrow scope project, to revisit whether some disclosure relief should be made available to not-for-profit public sector entities.

BC3   The Board undertook targeted outreach in late 2014 to further understand which disclosures were of concern to not-for-profit public sector entities, in particular, local governments, and the reasons for their concern. The Board's outreach activity included feedback from government entities, valuation experts and auditors. The Board received mixed feedback as to whether disclosure relief was necessary at this time.

BC4 In December 2014, the Board decided to limit its consideration of disclosure relief to:

(a) assets within the scope of AASB 116 *Property, Plant and Equipment* that are primarily held for their current service potential (for example, roads and water supply infrastructure) rather than to generate future net cash inflows; and

(b) disclosures in AASB 13 that apply solely to fair value measurements categorised within Level 3 in the fair value hierarchy. These disclosures help meet the objective noted in paragraph 91(b) of the Standard of providing users with information as to how fair value measurements using significant unobservable inputs affected profit or loss or other comprehensive income for the period, by requiring disclosure of information about the relative subjectivity of the fair value measurement.

BC5 The Board concluded that the feedback received did not suggest that a wider project scope was necessary to address matters raised about fair value disclosures (see also paragraphs BC7, BC18 and BC19). In April 2015, the Board evaluated these disclosures against its *Process for Modifying IFRSs for PBE/NFP ('Process')*. The *Process* allows for departures from the requirements of the equivalent International Financial Reporting Standard (IFRS) where not-for-profit specific reasons for the departure exist. The Board concluded that, for the interim, in relation to these assets, it is appropriate to depart from its policy of transaction neutrality for cost-benefit reasons in relation to certain disclosures specified by the Standard.

BC6 The Board issued Exposure Draft ED 262 *Fair Value Disclosures of Not-for-Profit Public Sector Entities* in May 2015. ED 262 exposed for public comment the Board's proposals to relieve not-for-profit public sector entities from certain disclosures specified by AASB 13, including the Board's rationale for its proposals. Following the consultation period, and after considering constituent comments received on the Exposure Draft, the Board decided to proceed with its proposals to make amendments to AASB 13 to relieve not-for-profit public sector entities from disclosing, for assets within the scope of AASB 116 that are primarily held for their current service potential rather than to generate future net cash inflows:

(a) for recurring and non-recurring fair value measurements categorised within Level 3 of the fair value hierarchy, quantitative information about the significant unobservable inputs used in the fair value measurement;

(b) for recurring fair value measurements categorised within Level 3 of the fair value hierarchy, the amount of the total gains and losses for the period included in profit or loss that is attributable to the change in unrealised gains or losses relating to the assets held at the end of the reporting period, and the line item(s) in profit or loss in which those unrealised gains or losses are recognised; and

(c) for recurring fair value measurements categorised within Level 3 of the fair value hierarchy, a narrative description of the sensitivity of the fair value measurement to changes in unobservable inputs if a change in those inputs to a different amount might result in a significantly higher or lower fair value measurement. Where there are interrelationships between those inputs and other unobservable inputs used in the fair value measurement, the disclosure of a description of those interrelationships and of how they might magnify or mitigate the effect of changes in the unobservable inputs on the fair value measurement will also not be required.

BC7 The Board intends to revisit the relief pending the outcome of related current Board projects, including its projects on the review of the Reduced Disclosure Regime (Tier 2), Australian Reporting Framework, and Conceptual Framework, to assess the extent to which outcomes from those projects address the factors that led to the Board's decisions noted above. The Board acknowledged that constituents also had other concerns with applying AASB 13, including various measurement concerns. The Board noted that these issues were beyond the scope of the current narrow-scope project, but would be considered as part of a broader future Board project.

Significant issues

Property, plant and equipment held by not-for-profit public sector entities

BC8 The Board discussed the prevailing practice in the Australian not-for-profit public sector, compared to other sectors, of revaluing property, plant and equipment subsequent to initial measurement and recognition. It noted that assets such as road infrastructure and national parks were typically only held by public sector entities, but did not consider the nature of such assets in itself to be a sufficient sector specific differentiator, as assets held by private sector entities may similarly vary significantly across entities operating in different industries.

BC9 The Board noted that property, plant and equipment is primarily held for the purposes of delivering the not-for-profit entity's public service objectives rather than being held to generate net cash inflows. The Board considered whether the relief should be extended to similar assets held by not-for-profit entities in the private sector. The Board observed that private sector entities, including not-for-profit private sector entities, may similarly hold assets other than for the purpose of generating net cash inflows. However, given the diversity of assets held by not-for-profit public sector entities, the information about assets held for their current service potential was likely to be different from such assets held by private sector entities.

BC10 The Board considered the extent and variety of long-lived assets measured on the fair value basis in the public sector and noted the resultant impact on the number of classes of assets determined for the purposes of satisfying the disclosure requirements of AASB 13. The Board observed that, in many instances, the valuation technique applied to these assets used unobservable inputs (Level 3 inputs) and that the assets were predominantly categorised within Level 3 in the fair value hierarchy for the purposes of making the disclosures specified by AASB 13. The Board discussed examples of fair value disclosures made in published financial statements of not-for-profit public sector entities. The Board observed that the reported range of many inputs, for example, the cost per square metre applied in the valuation of heritage buildings and the adjustment made to reflect the market-participant restricted use of an asset, varied widely within an asset class. The Board noted that this variation is likely to be a function of the number of assets grouped into each class, and that it may be impractical for entities to provide disclosures at a more disaggregated level.

Balance of costs and benefits

BC11 The Board concluded that it is appropriate to depart from its policy of transaction neutrality for assets within the scope of AASB 116 that are primarily held for their current service potential rather than to generate future net cash inflows for cost-benefit reasons. This conclusion takes into account the extent and variety of long-lived assets held by public sector entities measured on the fair value basis and categorised within Level 3 in the fair value hierarchy.

BC12 As part of its considerations, the Board had regard to the benefits of the disclosures recognised by the International Accounting Standards Board (IASB) in its Basis for Conclusions to IFRS 13 *Fair Value Measurement*. Having regard to its observations in paragraphs BC8-BC10, the Board considered that the relative costs of requiring not-for-profit public sector entities to disclose quantitative information about the significant unobservable inputs in fair value measurements of property, plant and equipment that are categorised within Level 3 in the fair value hierarchy, and the narrative description of the sensitivity of certain fair value measurements to changes in unobservable inputs, would generally be greater than they are for private sector entities. At the same time, the benefits would not be as great having regard to the number of assets leading to a wide range of inputs within each class of assets for which disclosure is made and the information needs of users for such assets, particularly in the context of the very specialised nature and limited alternative use of the assets. The Board similarly considered the costs of making the disclosure specified by paragraph 93(f) of AASB 13 to exceed the benefits to users of the disclosure, given the relative usefulness of the

AASB

additional information to users of not-for-profit public sector general purpose financial statements.

BC13   As part of its consideration of the costs versus the benefits of presenting the disclosures specified by paragraphs 93(d), 93(f) and 93(h)(i) of AASB 13, the Board observed that many not-for-profit public sector entities had only recently applied AASB 13. The Board discussed whether the concerns raised were reflective of underlying costs associated with implementing the Standard in a not-for-profit public sector environment, or whether the costs were largely transitional in nature. For example, the Board noted that the requirement to disclose a narrative description of the sensitivity of certain fair value measurements to unobservable inputs was likely to be transitional as it did not appear to be well understood in practice despite an example of the disclosure being included in the Illustrative Examples accompanying IFRS 13. The Board decided that the relative costs to not-for-profit public sector entities of presenting these disclosures were more than transitional in nature.

BC14   The Board also observed that IFRS 13 has not yet been incorporated into International Public Sector Accounting Standards (IPSASs) as issued by the International Public Sector Accounting Standards Board (IPSASB) of the International Federation of Accountants. Accordingly, for not-for-profit public sector entities, the extent of the disclosures specified by Australian Accounting Standards of the fair value measurements of property, plant and equipment held primarily for their current service potential presently exceeds those specified under IPSASs. The Board noted that future decisions of the IPSASB on public sector measurement and the accounting for heritage and infrastructure assets may prompt a need to revisit its present decisions on the costs versus benefits of the relief provided (see also paragraph BC7).

BC15   The Board decided that it was not necessary to provide relief to entities from disclosing the reconciliation of movements in each class of assets measured at fair value and categorised within Level 3 in the fair value hierarchy required by paragraph 93(e) of AASB 13 or the valuation processes used by the entity required by paragraph 93(g). The Board decided that these disclosures provided useful information without imposing significant additional ongoing costs. In particular, the Board considered that the information required to prepare the necessary reconciliations was likely in many cases to be available in the underlying accounting records.

BC16   The Board noted that entities would continue to be required to disclose a description of the valuation technique(s) and the inputs used in the fair value measurement in accordance with paragraph 93(d) of AASB 13. The Board expects, in most instances, that this disclosure together with other disclosures specified in AASB 13 and other Australian Accounting Standards (for example, AASB 101 *Presentation of Financial Statements* and AASB 116), would provide users of not-for-profit public sector general purpose financial statements with sufficient information about fair value measurements for decision-making purposes. The Board observed that the relief introduced into AASB 13 by this Standard does not override the general disclosure objective of AASB 13 as described in paragraph 91 of that Standard.

BC17   The Board observed that paragraph Aus93.1 of AASB 13 does not prevent a not-for-profit public sector entity from presenting some, or all, of the disclosures specified in paragraphs 93(d), 93(f) and 93(h)(i) in its general purpose financial statements.

Other issues

Extension of relief to other assets held by not-for-profit public sector entities

BC18   The Board discussed whether the relief from disclosure should be extended to include investment properties within the scope of AASB 140 *Investment Property* or financial assets held by not-for-profit public sector entities that are measured at fair value and categorised within Level 3 of the fair value hierarchy. The Board decided not to extend the relief to such assets as it did not regard there to be differences in the purposes these assets are held, whether held by a for-profit private sector entity or not-for-profit public sector entity. Further, the Board considered that, for such assets, the costs of providing the disclosures did not outweigh the benefits from making those disclosures in general purpose financial statements. The Board noted that, unlike property, plant and equipment, there was not necessarily a significant difference between the sectors with regard to the extent to which fair value measurement is applied to these assets.

BC19 The Board also discussed whether the relief from disclosure should be extended to include other assets (besides financial assets and investment properties) held by not-for-profit public sector entities that are measured at fair value and not held primarily for their current service potential. The Board noted that it had decided to keep the scope of its project narrow, and observed the role of materiality when considering whether specified disclosures should be included in general purpose financial statements.

Application date and transitional provisions

BC20 The Board considered the application date of the amendments to AASB 13. The Board decided that the amendments should apply to annual reporting periods beginning on or after 1 July 2016, and to permit early adoption of the amendments. The Board noted that early adoption would allow not-for-profit public sector entities to immediately access the disclosure relief.

BC21 The Board decided that no specific transitional provisions were necessary as the amendments relate to providing relief from disclosure. Accordingly, the requirements of AASB 108 *Accounting Policies, Changes in Accounting Estimates and Errors* apply to the amendments.

AASB 14

Regulatory Deferral Accounts

(Issued June 2014)

CONTENTS

PREFACE

COMPARISON WITH IFRS

ACCOUNTING STANDARD

AASB 14 *REGULATORY DEFERRAL ACCOUNTS*

ILLUSTRATIVE EXAMPLES (available on the AASB website)

BASIS FOR CONCLUSIONS ON IFRS 14 (available on the AASB website)

> Australian Accounting Standard AASB 14 *Regulatory Deferral Accounts* is set out in paragraphs 1 – 36 and Appendices A – C. All the paragraphs have equal authority. Paragraphs in **bold type** state the main principles. Terms defined in Appendix A are in *italics* the first time they appear in the Standard. AASB 14 is

to be read in the context of other Australian Accounting Standards, including AASB 1048 *Interpretation of Standards*, which identifies the Australian Accounting Interpretations. In the absence of explicit guidance, AASB 108 *Accounting Policies, Changes in Accounting Estimates and Errors* provides a basis for selecting and applying accounting policies.

PREFACE

Introduction

The Australian Accounting Standards Board (AASB) makes Australian Accounting Standards, including Interpretations, to be applied by:

(a)   entities required by the *Corporations Act 2001* to prepare financial reports;

(b)   governments in preparing financial statements for the whole of government and the General Government Sector (GGS); and

(c)   entities in the private or public for-profit or not-for-profit sectors that are reporting entities or that prepare general purpose financial statements.

AASB 1053 *Application of Tiers of Australian Accounting Standards* establishes a differential reporting framework consisting of two tiers of reporting requirements for preparing general purpose financial statements:

(a)   Tier 1: Australian Accounting Standards; and

(b)   Tier 2: Australian Accounting Standards – Reduced Disclosure Requirements.

Tier 1 requirements incorporate International Financial Reporting Standards (IFRSs), including Interpretations, issued by the International Accounting Standards Board (IASB), with the addition of paragraphs on the applicability of each Standard in the Australian environment.

Publicly accountable for-profit private sector entities are required to adopt Tier 1 requirements, and therefore are required to comply with IFRSs. Furthermore, other for-profit private sector entities complying with Tier 1 requirements will simultaneously comply with IFRSs. Some other entities complying with Tier 1 requirements will also simultaneously comply with IFRSs.

Tier 2 requirements comprise the recognition and measurement requirements of Tier 1 but substantially reduced disclosure requirements in comparison with Tier 1.

Australian Accounting Standards also include requirements that are specific to Australian entities. These requirements may be located in Australian Accounting Standards that incorporate IFRSs or in other Australian Accounting Standards. In most instances, these requirements are either restricted to the not-for-profit or public sectors or include additional disclosures that address domestic, regulatory or other issues. These requirements do not prevent publicly accountable for-profit private sector entities from complying with IFRSs. In developing requirements for public sector entities, the AASB considers the requirements of International Public Sector Accounting Standards (IPSASs), as issued by the International Public Sector Accounting Standards Board (IPSASB) of the International Federation of Accountants.

Reduced disclosure requirements

Disclosure requirements under Tier 2 are the same as those under Tier 1.

COMPARISON WITH IFRS

AASB 14 *Regulatory Deferral Accounts* incorporates IFRS 14 *Regulatory Deferral Accounts* issued by the International Accounting Standards Board (IASB). Paragraphs that have been added to this Standard (and do not appear in the text of IFRS) are identified with the prefix "Aus", followed by the number of the preceding IASB paragraph and decimal numbering. Paragraphs that apply only to not-for-profit entities begin by identifying their limited applicability.

Entities that comply with AASB 14 will simultaneously be in compliance with IFRS 14.

ACCOUNTING STANDARD AASB 14

The Australian Accounting Standards Board makes Accounting Standard AASB 14 *Regulatory Deferral Accounts* under section 334 of the *Corporations Act 2001*.

Kevin M. Stevenson

Dated 4 June 2014   Chair – AASB

ACCOUNTING STANDARD AASB 14
REGULATORY DEFERRAL ACCOUNTS

Objective

1   The objective of this Standard is to specify the financial reporting requirements for *regulatory deferral account balances* that arise when an entity provides goods or services to customers at a price or rate that is subject to *rate regulation*.

2   In meeting this objective, the Standard requires:

   (a)   limited changes to the accounting policies that were applied in accordance with previous generally accepted accounting principles (*previous GAAP*) for regulatory deferral account balances, which are primarily related to the presentation of these accounts; and

   (b)   disclosures that:

      (i)   identify and explain the amounts recognised in the entity's financial statements that arise from rate regulation; and

      (ii)   help users of the financial statements to understand the amount, timing and uncertainty of future cash flows from any regulatory deferral account balances that are recognised.

3   The requirements of this Standard permit an entity within its scope to continue to account for regulatory deferral account balances in its financial statements in accordance with its previous GAAP when it adopts Australian Accounting Standards, subject to the limited changes referred to in paragraph 2 above.

4   In addition, this Standard provides some exceptions to, or exemptions from, the requirements of other Standards. All specified requirements for reporting regulatory deferral account balances, and any exceptions to, or exemptions from, the requirements of other Standards that are related to those balances, are contained within this Standard instead of within those other Standards.

Application

Aus4.1   **This Standard applies to:**

   (a)   **each entity that is required to prepare financial reports in accordance with Part 2M.3 of the Corporations Act and that is a reporting entity;**

   (b)   **general purpose financial statements of each other reporting entity; and**

   (c)   **financial statements that are, or are held out to be, general purpose financial statements.**

Aus4.2	This Standard applies to annual reporting periods beginning on or after 1 January 2016.
Aus4.3	This Standard may be applied to annual reporting periods beginning on or after 1 January 2005 but before 1 January 2016. When an entity applies this Standard to such an annual reporting period, it shall disclose that fact.

Commencement

Aus4.4	This Standard commences on the day this Standard is made by the Australian Accounting Standards Board.

Scope

5 An entity is permitted to apply the requirements of this Standard in its *first Australian-Accounting-Standards financial statements* if and only if it:

    (a) conducts rate-regulated activities; and

    (b) recognised amounts that qualify as regulatory deferral account balances in its financial statements in accordance with its previous GAAP.

6 An entity shall apply the requirements of this Standard in its financial statements for subsequent periods if and only if, in its first Australian-Accounting-Standards financial statements, it recognised regulatory deferral account balances by electing to apply the requirements of this Standard.

7 This Standard does not address other aspects of accounting by entities that are engaged in rate-regulated activities. By applying the requirements in this Standard, any amounts that are permitted or required to be recognised as assets or liabilities in accordance with other Standards shall not be included within the amounts classified as regulatory deferral account balances.

8 An entity that is within the scope of, and that elects to apply, this Standard shall apply all of its requirements to all regulatory deferral account balances that arise from all of the entity's rate-regulated activities.

Recognition, measurement, impairment and derecognition

Temporary exemption from paragraph 11 of AASB 108 *Accounting Policies, Changes in Accounting Estimates and Errors*

9 An entity that has rate-regulated activities and that is within the scope of, and elects to apply, this Standard shall apply paragraphs 10 and 12 of AASB 108 when developing its accounting policies for the recognition, measurement, impairment and derecognition of regulatory deferral account balances.

10 Paragraphs 11–12 of AASB 108 specify sources of requirements and guidance that management is required or permitted to consider in developing an accounting policy for an item, if no relevant Standard applies specifically to that item. This Standard exempts an entity from applying paragraph 11 of AASB 108 to its accounting policies for the recognition, measurement, impairment and derecognition of regulatory deferral account balances. Consequently, entities that recognise regulatory deferral account balances, either as separate items or as part of the carrying value of other assets and liabilities, in accordance with their previous GAAP, are permitted to continue to recognise those balances in accordance with this Standard through the exemption from paragraph 11 of AASB 108, subject to any presentation changes required by paragraphs 18–19 of this Standard.

Continuation of existing accounting policies

11   On initial application of this Standard, an entity shall continue to apply
        its previous GAAP accounting policies for the recognition, measurement,
        impairment and derecognition of regulatory deferral account balances, except
        for any changes permitted by paragraphs 13–15. However, the presentation of
        such amounts shall comply with the presentation requirements of this Standard,
        which may require changes to the entity's previous GAAP presentation policies
        (see paragraphs 18–19).

12   An entity shall apply the policies established in accordance with paragraph 11
        consistently in subsequent periods, except for any changes permitted by paragraphs
        13–15.

Changes in accounting policies

13   An entity shall not change its accounting policies in order to start to recognise
        regulatory deferral account balances. An entity may only change its accounting
        policies for the recognition, measurement, impairment and derecognition of
        regulatory deferral account balances if the change makes the financial statements
        more relevant to the economic decision-making needs of users and no less
        reliable[1], or more reliable and no less relevant to those needs. An entity shall
        judge relevance and reliability using the criteria in paragraph 10 of AASB 108.

14   This Standard does not exempt entities from applying paragraphs 10 or 14–15 of AASB
        108 to changes in accounting policy. To justify changing its accounting policies for
        regulatory deferral account balances, an entity shall demonstrate that the change brings
        its financial statements closer to meeting the criteria in paragraph 10 of AASB 108.
        However, the change does not need to achieve full compliance with those criteria for
        the recognition, measurement, impairment and derecognition of regulatory deferral
        account balances.

15   Paragraphs 13–14 apply both to changes made on initial application of this Standard
        and to changes made in subsequent reporting periods.

Interaction with other Standards

16   Any specific exception, exemption or additional requirements related to the
        interaction of this Standard with other Standards are contained within this
        Standard (see paragraphs B7–B28). In the absence of any such exception,
        exemption or additional requirements, other Standards shall apply to regulatory
        deferral account balances in the same way as they apply to assets, liabilities,
        income and expenses that are recognised in accordance with other Standards.

17   In some situations, another Standard might need to be applied to a regulatory deferral
        account balance that has been measured in accordance with an entity's accounting
        policies that are established in accordance with paragraphs 11–12 in order to reflect that
        balance appropriately in the financial statements. For example, the entity might have
        rate-regulated activities in a foreign country for which the transactions and regulatory
        deferral account balances are denominated in a currency that is not the functional
        currency of the reporting entity. The regulatory deferral account balances and the
        movements in those balances are translated by applying AASB 121 *The Effects of
        Changes in Foreign Exchange Rates*.

---

1   In December 2013, the AASB amended the *Framework for the Preparation and Presentation of Financial
    Statements* (as identified in AASB 1048 *Interpretation of Standards*). The term "faithful representation"
    encompasses the main characteristics that the previous version of the Framework called "reliability". The
    requirement in paragraph 13 of this Standard is based on the requirements of AASB 108, which retains
    the term "reliable".

Presentation

Changes in presentation

18   This Standard introduces presentation requirements, outlined in paragraphs 20–26, for regulatory deferral account balances that are recognised in accordance with paragraphs 11–12. When this Standard is applied, the regulatory deferral account balances are recognised in the statement of financial position in addition to the assets and liabilities that are recognised in accordance with other Standards. These presentation requirements separate the impact of recognising regulatory deferral account balances from the financial reporting requirements of other Standards.

19   In addition to the items that are required to be presented in the statement of financial position and in the statement(s) of profit or loss and other comprehensive income in accordance with AASB 101 *Presentation of Financial Statements*, an entity applying this Standard shall present all regulatory deferral account balances and the movements in those balances in accordance with paragraphs 20–26.

Classification of regulatory deferral account balances

20   **An entity shall present separate line items in the statement of financial position for:**

    (a)   **the total of all regulatory deferral account debit balances; and**

    (b)   **the total of all regulatory deferral account credit balances.**

21   **When an entity presents current and non-current assets, and current and non-current liabilities, as separate classifications in its statement of financial position, it shall not classify the totals of regulatory deferral account balances as current or non-current. Instead, the separate line items required by paragraph 20 shall be distinguished from the assets and liabilities that are presented in accordance with other Standards by the use of sub-totals, which are drawn before the regulatory deferral account balances are presented.**

Classification of movements in regulatory deferral account balances

22   **An entity shall present, in the other comprehensive income section of the statement of profit or loss and other comprehensive income, the net movement in all regulatory deferral account balances for the reporting period that relate to items recognised in other comprehensive income. Separate line items shall be used for the net movement related to items that, in accordance with other Standards:**

    (a)   **will not be reclassified subsequently to profit or loss; and**

    (b)   **will be reclassified subsequently to profit or loss when specific conditions are met.**

23   **An entity shall present a separate line item in the profit or loss section of the statement of profit or loss and other comprehensive income, or in the separate statement of profit or loss, for the remaining net movement in all regulatory deferral account balances for the reporting period, excluding movements that are not reflected in profit or loss, such as amounts acquired. This separate line item shall be distinguished from the income and expenses that are presented in accordance with other Standards by the use of a sub-total, which is drawn before the net movement in regulatory deferral account balances.**

24   When an entity recognises a deferred tax asset or a deferred tax liability as a result of recognising regulatory deferral account balances, the entity shall present the resulting deferred tax asset (liability) and the related movement in that deferred tax asset (liability) with the related regulatory deferral account balances and movements in those balances, instead of within the total presented in accordance with AASB 112 *Income Taxes* for deferred tax assets (liabilities) and the tax expense (income) (see paragraphs B9–B12).

25   When an entity presents a discontinued operation or a disposal group in accordance with AASB 5 *Non-current Assets Held for Sale and Discontinued Operations*, the entity shall present any related regulatory deferral account balances and the net movement in those balances, as applicable, with the regulatory deferral account balances and movements in those balances, instead of within the disposal groups or discontinued operations (see paragraphs B19–B22).

26   When an entity presents earnings per share in accordance with AASB 133 *Earnings per Share*, the entity shall present additional basic and diluted earnings per share, which are calculated using the earnings amounts required by AASB 133 but excluding the movements in regulatory deferral account balances (see paragraphs B13–B14).

Disclosure

Objective

27   **An entity that elects to apply this Standard shall disclose information that enables users to assess:**

    (a)   **the nature of, and the risks associated with, the rate regulation that establishes the price(s) that the entity can charge customers for the goods or services it provides; and**

    (b)   **the effects of that rate regulation on its financial position, financial performance and cash flows.**

28   If any of the disclosures set out in paragraphs 30–36 are not considered relevant to meet the objective in paragraph 27, they may be omitted from the financial statements. If the disclosures provided in accordance with paragraphs 30–36 are insufficient to meet the objective in paragraph 27, an entity shall disclose additional information that is necessary to meet that objective.

29   To meet the disclosure objective in paragraph 27, an entity shall consider all of the following:

    (a)   the level of detail that is necessary to satisfy the disclosure requirements;

    (b)   how much emphasis to place on each of the various requirements;

    (c)   how much aggregation or disaggregation to undertake; and

    (d)   whether users of financial statements need additional information to evaluate the quantitative information disclosed.

Explanation of activities subject to rate regulation

30   To help a user of the financial statements assess the nature of, and the risks associated with, the entity's rate-regulated activities, an entity shall, for each type of rate-regulated activity, disclose:

    (a)   a brief description of the nature and extent of the rate-regulated activity and the nature of the regulatory rate-setting process;

    (b)   the identity of the rate regulator(s). If the rate regulator is a related party (as defined in AASB 124 *Related Party Disclosures*), the entity shall disclose that fact, together with an explanation of how it is related;

    (c)   how the future recovery of each class (ie each type of cost or income) of regulatory deferral account debit balance or reversal of each class of regulatory deferral account credit balance is affected by risks and uncertainty, for example:

       (i)   demand risk (for example, changes in consumer attitudes, the availability of alternative sources of supply or the level of competition);

> (ii) regulatory risk (for example, the submission or approval of a rate-setting application or the entity's assessment of the expected future regulatory actions); and
>
> (iii) other risks (for example, currency or other market risks).

31 [Deleted by the AASB]

Explanation of recognised amounts

32 An entity shall disclose the basis on which regulatory deferral account balances are recognised and derecognised, and how they are measured initially and subsequently, including how regulatory deferral account balances are assessed for recoverability and how any impairment loss is allocated.

33 For each type of rate-regulated activity, an entity shall disclose the following information for each class of regulatory deferral account balance:

(a) a reconciliation of the carrying amount at the beginning and the end of the period, in a table unless another format is more appropriate. The entity shall apply judgement in deciding the level of detail necessary (see paragraphs 28–29), but the following components would usually be relevant:

> (i) the amounts that have been recognised in the current period in the statement of financial position as regulatory deferral account balances;
>
> (ii) the amounts that have been recognised in the statement(s) of profit or loss and other comprehensive income relating to balances that have been recovered (sometimes described as amortised) or reversed in the current period; and
>
> (iii) other amounts, separately identified, that affected the regulatory deferral account balances, such as impairments, items acquired or assumed in a business combination, items disposed of, or the effects of changes in foreign exchange rates or discount rates;

(b) the rate of return or discount rate (including a zero rate or a range of rates, when applicable) used to reflect the time value of money that is applicable to each class of regulatory deferral account balance; and

(c) the remaining periods over which the entity expects to recover (or amortise) the carrying amount of each class of regulatory deferral account debit balance or to reverse each class of regulatory deferral account credit balance.

34 When rate regulation affects the amount and timing of an entity's income tax expense (income), the entity shall disclose the impact of the rate regulation on the amounts of current and deferred tax recognised. In addition, the entity shall separately disclose any regulatory deferral account balance that relates to taxation and the related movement in that balance.

35 When an entity provides disclosures in accordance with AASB 12 *Disclosure of Interests in Other Entities* for an interest in a subsidiary, associate or joint venture that has rate-regulated activities and for which regulatory deferral account balances are recognised in accordance with this Standard, the entity shall disclose the amounts that are included for the regulatory deferral account debit and credit balances and the net movement in those balances for the interests disclosed (see paragraphs B25–B28).

36 When an entity concludes that a regulatory deferral account balance is no longer fully recoverable or reversible, it shall disclose that fact, the reason why it is not recoverable or reversible and the amount by which the regulatory deferral account balance has been reduced.

APPENDIX A
DEFINED TERMS

This appendix is an integral part of AASB 14.

First Australian-Accounting-Standards financial statements	The first annual financial statements in which an entity adopts Australian Accounting Standards, by an explicit and unreserved statement of compliance with Australian Accounting Standards.
First-time adopter	An entity that presents its **first Australian-Accounting-Standards financial statements**.
Previous GAAP	The basis of accounting that a **first-time adopter** used immediately before adopting Australian Accounting Standards.
Rate-regulated activities	An entity's activities that are subject to **rate regulation**.
Rate regulation	A framework for establishing the prices that can be charged to customers for goods or services and that framework is subject to oversight and/or approval by a **rate regulator**.
Rate regulator	An authorised body that is empowered by statute or regulation to establish the rate or a range of rates that bind an entity. The **rate regulator** may be a third-party body or a related party of the entity, including the entity's own governing board, if that body is required by statute or regulation to set rates both in the interest of the customers and to ensure the overall financial viability of the entity.
Regulatory deferral account balance	The balance of any expense (or income) account that would not be recognised as an asset or a liability in accordance with other Standards, but that qualifies for deferral because it is included, or is expected to be included, by the **rate regulator** in establishing the rate(s) that can be charged to customers.

APPENDIX B
APPLICATION GUIDANCE

This appendix is an integral part of AASB 14.

Rate-regulated activities

B1 Historically, rate regulation applied to all activities of an entity. However, with acquisitions, diversification and deregulation, rate regulation may now apply to only a portion of an entity's activities, resulting in it having both regulated and non-regulated activities. This Standard applies only to the rate-regulated activities that are subject to statutory or regulatory restrictions through the actions of a rate regulator, regardless of the type of entity or the industry to which it belongs.

B2 An entity shall not apply this Standard to activities that are self-regulated, ie activities that are not subject to a pricing framework that is overseen and/or approved by a rate regulator. This does not prevent the entity from being eligible to apply this Standard when:

(a) the entity's own governing body or a related party establishes rates both in the interest of the customers and to ensure the overall financial viability of the entity within a specified pricing framework; and

(b)   the framework is subject to oversight and/or approval by an authorised body that is empowered by statute or regulation.

Continuation of existing accounting policies

B3   For the purposes of this Standard, a regulatory deferral account balance is defined as the balance of any expense (or income) account that would not be recognised as an asset or a liability in accordance with other Standards, but that qualifies for deferral because it is included, or is expected to be included, by the rate regulator in establishing the rate(s) that can be charged to customers. Some items of expense (income) may be outside the regulated rate(s) because, for example, the amounts are not expected to be accepted by the rate regulator or because they are not within the scope of the rate regulation. Consequently, such an item is recognised as income or expense as incurred, unless another Standard permits or requires it to be included in the carrying amount of an asset or liability.

B4   In some cases, other Standards explicitly prohibit an entity from recognising, in the statement of financial position, regulatory deferral account balances that might be recognised, either separately or included within other line items such as property, plant and equipment in accordance with previous GAAP accounting policies. However, in accordance with paragraph 11 of this Standard, an entity that elects to apply this Standard in its first Australian-Accounting-Standards financial statements applies the exemption from paragraph 11 of AASB 108 in order to continue to apply its previous GAAP accounting policies for the recognition, measurement, impairment, and derecognition of regulatory deferral account balances. Such accounting policies may include, for example, the following practices:

(a)   recognising a regulatory deferral account debit balance when the entity has the right, as a result of the actual or expected actions of the rate regulator, to increase rates in future periods in order to recover its allowable costs (ie the costs for which the regulated rate(s) is intended to provide recovery);

(b)   recognising, as a regulatory deferral account debit or credit balance, an amount that is equivalent to any loss or gain on the disposal or retirement of both items of property, plant and equipment and of intangible assets, which is expected to be recovered or reversed through future rates;

(c)   recognising a regulatory deferral account credit balance when the entity is required, as a result of the actual or expected actions of the rate regulator, to decrease rates in future periods in order to reverse over-recoveries of allowable costs (ie amounts in excess of the recoverable amount specified by the rate regulator); and

(d)   measuring regulatory deferral account balances on an undiscounted basis or on a discounted basis that uses an interest or discount rate specified by the rate regulator.

B5   The following are examples of the types of costs that rate regulators might allow in rate-setting decisions and that an entity might, therefore, recognise in regulatory deferral account balances:

(i)   volume or purchase price variances;

(ii)   costs of approved 'green energy' initiatives (in excess of amounts that are capitalised as part of the cost of property, plant and equipment in accordance with AASB 116 *Property, Plant and Equipment*);

(iii)   non-directly-attributable overhead costs that are treated as capital costs for rate regulation purposes (but are not permitted, in accordance with AASB 116, to be included in the cost of an item of property, plant and equipment);

(iv)   project cancellation costs;

(v)   storm damage costs; and

AASB

(vi)   deemed interest (including amounts allowed for funds that are used during construction that provide the entity with a return on the owner's equity capital as well as borrowings).

B6   Regulatory deferral account balances usually represent timing differences between the recognition of items of income or expenses for regulatory purposes and the recognition of those items for financial reporting purposes. When an entity changes an accounting policy on the first-time adoption of Australian Accounting Standards or on the initial application of a new or revised Standard, new or revised timing differences may arise that create new or revised regulatory deferral account balances. The prohibition in paragraph 13 that prevents an entity from changing its accounting policy in order to start to recognise regulatory deferral account balances does not prohibit the recognition of the new or revised regulatory deferral account balances that are created because of other changes in accounting policies required by Australian Accounting Standards. This is because the recognition of regulatory deferral account balances for such timing differences would be consistent with the existing recognition policy applied in accordance with paragraph 11 and would not represent the introduction of a new accounting policy. Similarly, paragraph 13 does not prohibit the recognition of regulatory deferral account balances arising from timing differences that did not exist immediately prior to the date of transition to Australian Accounting Standards but are consistent with the entity's accounting policies established in accordance with paragraph 11 (for example, storm damage costs).

Applicability of other Standards

B7   An entity that is within the scope of, and that elects to apply, the requirements of this Standard shall continue to apply its previous GAAP accounting policies for the recognition, measurement, impairment and derecognition of regulatory deferral account balances. However, paragraphs 16–17 state that, in some situations, other Standards might also need to be applied to regulatory deferral account balances in order to reflect them appropriately in the financial statements. The following paragraphs outline how some other Standards interact with the requirements of this Standard. In particular, the following paragraphs clarify specific exceptions to, and exemptions from, other Standards and additional presentation and disclosure requirements that are expected to be applicable.

Application of AASB 110 *Events after the Reporting Period*

B8   An entity may need to use estimates and assumptions in the recognition and measurement of its regulatory deferral account balances. For events that occur between the end of the reporting period and the date when the financial statements are authorised for issue, the entity shall apply AASB 110 to identify whether those estimates and assumptions should be adjusted to reflect those events.

Application of AASB 112 *Income Taxes*

B9   AASB 112 requires, with certain limited exceptions, an entity to recognise a deferred tax liability and (subject to certain conditions) a deferred tax asset for all temporary differences. A rate-regulated entity shall apply AASB 112 to all of its activities, including its rate-regulated activities, to identify the amount of income tax that is to be recognised.

B10   In some rate-regulatory schemes, the rate regulator permits or requires an entity to increase its future rates in order to recover some or all of the entity's income tax expense. In such circumstances, this might result in the entity recognising a regulatory deferral account balance in the statement of financial position related to income tax, in accordance with its accounting policies established in accordance with paragraphs 11–12. The recognition of this regulatory deferral account balance that relates to income tax might itself create an additional temporary difference for which a further deferred tax amount would be recognised.

B11 Notwithstanding the presentation and disclosure requirements of AASB 112, when an entity recognises a deferred tax asset or a deferred tax liability as a result of recognising regulatory deferral account balances, the entity shall not include that deferred tax amount within the total deferred tax asset (liability) balances. Instead, the entity shall present the deferred tax asset (liability) that arises as a result of recognising regulatory deferral account balances either:

(a) with the line items that are presented for the regulatory deferral account debit balances and credit balances; or

(b) as a separate line item alongside the related regulatory deferral account debit balances and credit balances.

B12 Similarly, when an entity recognises the movement in a deferred tax asset (liability) that arises as a result of recognising regulatory deferral account balances, the entity shall not include the movement in that deferred tax amount within the tax expense (income) line item that is presented in the statement(s) of profit or loss and other comprehensive income in accordance with AASB 112. Instead, the entity shall present the movement in the deferred tax asset (liability) that arises as a result of recognising regulatory deferral account balances either:

(a) with the line items that are presented in the statement(s) of profit or loss and other comprehensive income for the movements in regulatory deferral account balances; or

(b) as a separate line item alongside the related line items that are presented in the statement(s) of profit or loss and other comprehensive income for the movements in regulatory deferral account balances.

Application of AASB 133 *Earnings per Share*

B13 Paragraph 66 of AASB 133 requires some entities to present, in the statement of profit or loss and other comprehensive income, basic and diluted earnings per share both for profit or loss from continuing operations and profit or loss that is attributable to the ordinary equity holders of the parent entity. In addition, paragraph 68 of AASB 133 requires an entity that reports a discontinued operation to disclose the basic and diluted amounts per share for the discontinued operation, either in the statement of profit or loss and other comprehensive income or in the notes.

B14 For each earnings per share amount presented in accordance with AASB 133, an entity applying this Standard shall present additional basic and diluted earnings per share amounts that are calculated in the same way, except that those amounts shall exclude the net movement in the regulatory deferral account balances. Consistent with the requirement in paragraph 73 of AASB 133, an entity shall present the earnings per share required by paragraph 26 of this Standard with equal prominence to the earnings per share required by AASB 133 for all periods presented.

Application of AASB 136 *Impairment of Assets*

B15 Paragraphs 11–12 require an entity to continue to apply its previous GAAP accounting policies for the identification, recognition, measurement and reversal of any impairment of its recognised regulatory deferral account balances. Consequently, AASB 136 does not apply to the separate regulatory deferral account balances recognised.

B16 However, AASB 136 might require an entity to perform an impairment test on a cash-generating unit (CGU) that includes regulatory deferral account balances. This test might be required because the CGU contains goodwill, or because one or more of the impairment indicators described in AASB 136 have been identified relating to the CGU. In such situations, paragraphs 74–79 of AASB 136 contain requirements for identifying the recoverable amount and the carrying amount of a CGU. An entity shall apply those requirements to decide whether any of the regulatory deferral account balances recognised are included in the carrying amount of the CGU for the purpose of the impairment test. The remaining requirements of AASB 136 shall then be applied to any impairment loss that is recognised as a result of this test.

Application of AASB 3 *Business Combinations*

B17 The core principle of AASB 3 is that an acquirer of a business recognises the assets acquired and the liabilities assumed at their acquisition-date fair values. AASB 3 provides limited exceptions to its recognition and measurement principles. Paragraph B18 of this Standard provides an additional exception.

B18 Paragraphs 11–12 require an entity to continue to apply its previous GAAP accounting policies for the recognition, measurement, impairment and derecognition of regulatory deferral account balances. Consequently, if an entity acquires a business, it shall apply, in its consolidated financial statements, its accounting policies established in accordance with paragraphs 11–12 for the recognition and measurement of the acquiree's regulatory deferral account balances at the date of acquisition. The acquiree's regulatory deferral account balances shall be recognised in the consolidated financial statements of the acquirer in accordance with the acquirer's policies, irrespective of whether the acquiree recognises those balances in its own financial statements.

Application of AASB 5 *Non-current Assets Held for Sale and Discontinued Operations*

B19 Paragraphs 11–12 require an entity to continue to apply its previous accounting policies for the recognition, measurement, impairment and derecognition of regulatory deferral account balances. Consequently, the measurement requirements of AASB 5 shall not apply to the regulatory deferral account balances recognised.

B20 Paragraph 33 of AASB 5 requires a single amount to be presented for discontinued operations in the statement(s) of profit or loss and other comprehensive income. Notwithstanding the requirements of that paragraph, when an entity that elects to apply this Standard presents a discontinued operation, it shall not include the movement in regulatory deferral account balances that arose from the rate-regulated activities of the discontinued operation within the line items that are required by paragraph 33 of AASB 5. Instead, the entity shall present the movement in regulatory deferral account balances that arose from the rate-regulated activities of the discontinued operation either:

(a) within the line item that is presented for movements in the regulatory deferral account balances related to profit or loss; or

(b) as a separate line item alongside the related line item that is presented for movements in the regulatory deferral account balances related to profit or loss.

B21 Similarly, notwithstanding the requirements of paragraph 38 of AASB 5, when an entity presents a disposal group, the entity shall not include the total of the regulatory deferral account debit balances and credit balances that are part of the disposal group within the line items that are required by paragraph 38 of AASB 5. Instead, the entity shall present the total of the regulatory deferral account debit balances and credit balances that are part of the disposal group either:

(a) within the line items that are presented for the regulatory deferral account debit balances and credit balances; or

(b) as separate line items alongside the other regulatory deferral account debit balances and credit balances.

B22 If the entity chooses to include the regulatory deferral account balances and movements in those balances that are related to the disposal group or discontinued operation within the related regulated deferral account line items, it may be necessary to disclose them separately as part of the analysis of the regulatory deferral account line items described by paragraph 33 of this Standard.

Application of AASB 10 *Consolidated Financial Statements* and AASB 128 *Investments in Associates and Joint Ventures*

B23 Paragraph 19 of AASB 10 requires that a "parent shall prepare consolidated financial statements using uniform accounting policies for like transactions and other events in similar circumstances". Paragraph 8 of this Standard requires that an entity that is within the scope of, and elects to apply, this Standard shall apply all of its requirements to all regulatory deferral account balances arising from all of the entity's rate-regulated activities. Consequently, if a parent recognises regulatory deferral account balances in its consolidated financial statements in accordance with this Standard, it shall apply the same accounting policies to the regulatory deferral account balances arising in all of its subsidiaries. This shall apply irrespective of whether the subsidiaries recognise those balances in their own financial statements.

B24 Similarly, paragraphs 35–36 of AASB 128 require that, in applying the equity method, an "entity's financial statements shall be prepared using uniform accounting policies for like transactions and events in similar circumstances". Consequently, adjustments shall be made to make the associate's or joint venture's accounting policies for the recognition, measurement, impairment and derecognition of regulatory deferral account balances conform to those of the investing entity in applying the equity method.

Application of AASB 12 *Disclosure of Interests in Other Entities*

B25 Paragraph 12(e) of AASB 12 requires an entity to disclose, for each of its subsidiaries that have non-controlling interests that are material to the reporting entity, the profit or loss that was allocated to non-controlling interests of the subsidiary during the reporting period. An entity that recognises regulatory deferral account balances in accordance with this Standard shall disclose the net movement in regulatory deferral account balances that is included within the amounts that are required to be disclosed by paragraph 12(e) of AASB 12.

B26 Paragraph 12(g) of AASB 12 requires an entity to disclose, for each of its subsidiaries that have non-controlling interests that are material to the reporting entity, summarised financial information about the subsidiary, as specified in paragraph B10 of AASB 12. Similarly, paragraph 21(b)(ii) of AASB 12 requires an entity to disclose, for each joint venture and associate that is material to the reporting entity, summarised financial information as specified in paragraphs B12–B13 of AASB 12. Paragraph B16 of AASB 12 specifies the summary financial information that an entity is required to disclose for all other associates and joint ventures that are not individually material in accordance with paragraph 21(c) of AASB 12.

B27 In addition to the information specified in paragraphs 12, 21, B10, B12–B13 and B16 of AASB 12, an entity that recognises regulatory deferral account balances in accordance with this Standard shall also disclose the total regulatory deferral account debit balance, the total regulatory deferral account credit balance and the net movements in those balances, split between amounts recognised in profit or loss and amounts recognised in other comprehensive income, for each entity for which those AASB 12 disclosures are required.

B28 Paragraph 19 of AASB 12 specifies the information that an entity is required to disclose when the entity recognises a gain or loss on losing control of a subsidiary, calculated in accordance with paragraph 25 of AASB 10. In addition to the information required by paragraph 19 of AASB 12, an entity that elects to apply this Standard shall disclose the portion of that gain or loss that is attributable to derecognising regulatory deferral account balances in the former subsidiary at the date when control is lost.

AASB

APPENDIX C
EFFECTIVE DATE AND TRANSITION

This appendix is an integral part of AASB 14.

Effective date and transition

Effective date

C1   [Deleted by the AASB]

DELETED IFRS 14 TEXT

Deleted IFRS 14 text is not part of AASB 14.

Paragraph 31

The disclosures required by paragraph 30 shall be given in the financial statements either directly in the notes or incorporated by cross-reference from the financial statements to some other statement, such as a management commentary or risk report, that is available to users of the financial statements on the same terms as the financial statements and at the same time. If the information is not included in the financial statements directly or incorporated by cross-reference, the financial statements are incomplete.

Paragraph C1

An entity shall apply this Standard if its first annual IFRS financial statements are for a period beginning on or after 1 January 2016. Earlier application is permitted. If an entity applies this Standard in its first annual IFRS financial statements for an earlier period, it shall disclose that fact.

BASIS FOR CONCLUSIONS

This Basis for Conclusions accompanies, but is not part of, AASB 14.

Background

BC1   This Basis for Conclusions summarises the Australian Accounting Standards Board's (AASB) considerations in issuing AASB 14 *Regulatory Deferral Accounts*. Individual Board members gave greater weight to some factors than to others.

Background

BC2   AASB 14 is the result of the AASB's due process, which began when the AASB issued Exposure Draft ED 240 *Regulatory Deferral Accounts* (AASB ED 240) in May 2013 (incorporating International Accounting Standards Board [IASB] ED/2013/5 *Regulatory Deferral Accounts*). That Exposure Draft proposed an interim Standard to permit first-time adopters of Australian Accounting Standards [International Financial Reporting Standards (IFRS)] to continue to account for regulatory deferral account balances in their financial statements in accordance with their previous GAAP. The proposed interim standard was not intended, in any way, to anticipate the outcome of the IASB's longer term Rate-regulated Activities project.

BC3   In the Preface to ED 240, the AASB expressed the view that it did not expect the proposed interim standard, if it were to be incorporated into Australian Accounting Standards, would have a significant impact on entities in Australia as the Standard could conceivably only affect entities that adopt Australian Accounting Standards for the first time and have recognised regulatory deferral account balances under their previous GAAP.

BC4 The AASB received two comment letters on ED 240, which expressed broad support for issuing the interim standard, acknowledging that it would be an interim measure while the IASB develops a Discussion Paper under its comprehensive Rate-regulated Activities project. One respondent expressed the view that they were not aware of any entities in Australia whose financial statements would be directly impacted by the proposals in ED 240.

BC5 In its comment letter to the IASB on ED/2013/5, the AASB raised the following key concerns:

(a) the proposals could result in the IASB inappropriately setting a precedent of introducing additional interim standards for first-time adopters of IFRS to encourage transition to IFRS; and

(b) the proposals would reduce comparability between first-time adopters of IFRS that choose to apply the proposals and those that already apply IFRS or first-time adopters of IFRS that do not elect to apply the proposals.

BC6 In January 2014, the IASB issued IFRS 14 *Regulatory Deferral Accounts* (incorporating the proposals in ED/2013/5 without substantive changes) for annual reporting periods beginning on or after 1 January 2016, with early application permitted. The AASB noted that its concerns with the ED/2013/5 proposals, expressed in its submission to the IASB, were not addressed in IFRS 14.

BC7 After further considering the types of entities that might be affected by the requirements of AASB 14 (including a newly listed rate-regulated entity from a foreign jurisdiction and a foreign rate-regulated entity that 'back door' lists in Australia), the AASB expects that the practical impact of adopting AASB 14 in Australia would be minimal.

BC8 The AASB noted that its concerns (see paragraph BC5 above) are not so great as to cause it to make a decision that would be seen as not adopting IFRS more broadly. Accordingly, given the interim nature of IFRS 14 (and therefore AASB 14) and the expected practical impact of AASB 14, consistent with its policy of adopting IFRS in Australia, the AASB decided to issue AASB 14 on the basis that to do so would not be contrary to the best interests of the Australian economy.

BC9 The AASB also noted that, currently under AASB 1 *First-time Adoption of Australian Accounting Standards*, if a first-time adopter recognises property, plant and equipment or intangible assets used in rate-regulated activities and the carrying amounts of such items include amounts determined under the entity's previous GAAP that do not qualify for capitalisation in accordance with Australian Accounting Standards, the first-time adopter may elect to use its previous GAAP carrying amount of such items at the date of transition to Australian Accounting Standards as deemed cost (paragraph D8B of AASB 1). A similar exemption is also available to a first-time adopter with oil and gas properties, whereby the entity may elect to account for its exploration and evaluation assets at the amount determined under the entity's previous GAAP on transition to Australian Accounting Standards (paragraph D8A of AASB 1). The AASB considered that the exemption in AASB 14 that would permit first-time adopters to continue to account for amounts related to rate regulation in accordance with their previous GAAP when they first-time adopt Australian Accounting Standards is somewhat similar to these exemptions in AASB 1. Therefore, AASB 14 would be broadly consistent with the approach taken by the AASB to allowing first-time adopters to 'grandfather' previous GAAP when transitioning to Australian Accounting Standards.

DISSENTING OPINION

Dissent of Peter Gibson and Steve Mitsas

DO1 AASB 14 *Regulatory Deferral Accounts* is consistent with the AASB's policy of incorporating IFRSs into Australian Accounting Standards. While we generally support that policy, from a 'first principles' basis we do not agree with the key approach in AASB 14 that allows the continuation of accounting policies that are inconsistent with existing recognition and measurement requirements in other Australian Accounting Standards for late first-time adopters of Australian Accounting Standards.

DO2 Despite AASB 14 being described as an interim standard, it risks perpetuating differences in the recognition and measurement of assets and liabilities, and detracts from the comparability of financial statements, across similar entities. On this basis, we do not support adoption of AASB 14.

AASB 15

Revenue from Contracts with Customers

(Compiled December 2016)

For-profit (FP) entities

This compiled Standard applies to annual periods beginning on or after 1 January 2018 but before 1 January 2019. Earlier application is permitted. It incorporates relevant amendments made up to and including 9 December 2016.

Not-for-profit (NFP) entities – early application only

This compiled Standard does not apply mandatorily to NFP entities. However, earlier application is permitted for annual reporting periods beginning before 1 January 2019.

Prepared on 20 March 2018 by the staff of the Australian Accounting Standards Board.

Compilation no. 2

Compilation date: 31 December 2017

This note is not part of Accounting Standard AASB 15.

The following unincorporated amendments are not included in this compiled Standard.

- AASB 2018-4 *Amendments to Australian Accounting Standards — Australian Implementation Guidance for Not-for-Profit Public Sector Licensors.* This standard makes amendments to AASB 15 *Revenue from Contracts with Customers* and AASB 16 *Leases.* It applies to annual periods beginning on or after 1 January 2019, but earlier application is permitted.

- AASB 17 *Insurance Contracts* — Appendix D sets out the amendments to other Standards that are a consequence of the AASB issuing AASB 17 *Insurance Contracts.* This Standard is applicable from 1 January 2021. Earlier application is permitted, but entities must apply AASB 9 *Financial Instruments* and AASB 15 *Revenue from Contracts with Customers* first.

- AASB 1058 *Income of Not-for-Profit Entities* — Appendix D sets out the amendments to other Australian Accounting Standards that are a consequence of the AASB issuing this Standard. It is applicable from 1 January 2019. Earlier application is permitted, but amendments to AASB 117 apply before 1 January 2019 only if AASB 1058 is also applied to an earlier period. In addition, AASB 1 and AASB 16 amendments are applied to an earlier period only if AASB 16 is also applied to that period.

- AASB 2016-8 *Amendments to Australian Accounting Standards — Australian Implementation Guidance for Not-for-Profit Entities.* This standard makes amendments to AASB 9 *Financial Instruments* and AASB 15 *Revenue from Contracts with Customers.* The amendments arise from the issuance of AASB 1058 *Income of Not-for-Profit Entities.*

- AASB 16 *Leases* — Appendix D sets out the amendments to other Standards that are a consequence of the AASB issuing this Standard. It is applicable from 1 January 2019. Earlier application is permitted, but entities must apply AASB 15 *Revenue from Contracts with Customers* before applying this Standard.

- AASB 2016-7 *Amendments to Australian Accounting Standards — Deferral of AASB 15 for Not-for-Profit Entities.* This Standard defers the consequential amendments that were originally set out in AASB 2014-5 *Amendments to Australian Accounting Standards arising from AASB 15,* by restating the effective date of the amendments set out in AASB 2015-8 *Amendments to Australian Accounting Standards* for not-for-profit entities. This Standard defers the application of AASB

AASB

15 to 1 January 2019. Earlier application is permitted provided AASB 1058 is also applied to the same period.

Entities early-adopting any amendments with later application dates will need to refer to the amending Standards that have not yet been incorporated into compilations. The abovementioned unincorporated amendments may be located on the AASB website at www.aasb.gov.au or on the Federal Register of Legislation website at www.legislation.gov.au.

CONTENTS

COMPARISON WITH IFRS 15
ACCOUNTING STANDARD
AASB 15 *REVENUE FROM CONTRACTS WITH CUSTOMERS*

APPENDICES

A. DEFINED TERMS

B. APPLICATION GUIDANCE

C. EFFECTIVE DATE AND TRANSITION

E. AUSTRALIAN REDUCED DISCLOSURE REQUIREMENTS

COMPILATION DETAILS

DELETED IFRS 15 TEXT

INTRODUCTION TO IFRS 15 (available on the AASB website)

ILLUSTRATIVE EXAMPLES (available on the AASB website)

BASIS FOR CONCLUSIONS ON IFRS 15 (available on the AASB website)

Australian Accounting Standard AASB 15 *Revenue from Contracts with Customers* (as amended) is set out in paragraphs 1 – Aus129.1 and Appendices A – C and E. All the paragraphs have equal authority. Paragraphs in **bold type** state the main principles. Terms defined in Appendix A are in *italics* the first time they appear in the Standard. AASB 15 is to be read in the context of other Australian Accounting Standards, including AASB 1048 *Interpretation of Standards*, which identifies the Australian Accounting Interpretations, and AASB 1057 *Application of Australian Accounting Standards*. In the absence of explicit guidance, AASB 108 *Accounting Policies, Changes in Accounting Estimates and Errors* provides a basis for selecting and applying accounting policies.

COMPARISON WITH IFRS 15

AASB 15 *Revenue from Contracts with Customers* as amended incorporates IFRS 15 *Revenue from Contracts with Customers* as issued and amended by the International Accounting Standards Board (IASB). Australian-specific paragraphs (which are not included in IFRS 15) are identified with the prefix "Aus". Paragraphs that apply only to not-for-profit entities begin by identifying their limited applicability.

Tier 1

For-profit entities complying with AASB 15 also comply with IFRS 15.

Not-for-profit entities' compliance with IFRS 15 will depend on whether any "Aus" paragraphs that specifically apply to not-for-profit entities provide additional guidance or contain applicable requirements that are inconsistent with IFRS 15.

Tier 2

Entities preparing general purpose financial statements under Australian Accounting Standards – Reduced Disclosure Requirements (Tier 2) will not be in compliance with IFRSs.

AASB 1053 *Application of Tiers of Australian Accounting Standards* explains the two tiers of reporting requirements.

ACCOUNTING STANDARD AASB 15

The Australian Accounting Standards Board made Accounting Standard AASB 15 *Revenue from Contracts with Customers* under section 334 of the *Corporations Act 2001* on 12 December 2014.

This compiled version of AASB 15 applies to annual periods beginning on or after 1 January 2018 but before 1 January 2019 for for-profit entities. It incorporates relevant amendments contained in other AASB Standards made by the AASB up to and including 9 December 2016 (see Compilation Details).

ACCOUNTING STANDARD AASB 15
REVENUE FROM CONTRACTS WITH CUSTOMERS

Objective

1 **The objective of this Standard is to establish the principles that an entity shall apply to report useful information to users of financial statements about the nature, amount, timing and uncertainty of *revenue* and cash flows arising from a *contract* with a *customer*.**

Meeting the objective

2 To meet the objective in paragraph 1, the core principle of this Standard is that an entity shall recognise revenue to depict the transfer of promised goods or services to customers in an amount that reflects the consideration to which the entity expects to be entitled in exchange for those goods or services.

3 An entity shall consider the terms of the contract and all relevant facts and circumstances when applying this Standard. An entity shall apply this Standard, including the use of any practical expedients, consistently to contracts with similar characteristics and in similar circumstances.

4 This Standard specifies the accounting for an individual contract with a customer. However, as a practical expedient, an entity may apply this Standard to a portfolio of contracts (or *performance obligations*) with similar characteristics if the entity reasonably expects that the effects on the financial statements of applying this Standard to the portfolio would not differ materially from applying this Standard to the individual contracts (or performance obligations) within that portfolio. When accounting for a portfolio, an entity shall use estimates and assumptions that reflect the size and composition of the portfolio.

Scope

5 An entity shall apply this Standard to all contracts with customers, except the following:

  (a) lease contracts within the scope of AASB 117 *Leases*;

  (b) insurance contracts within the scope of AASB 4 *Insurance Contracts*;

  (c) financial instruments and other contractual rights or obligations within the scope of AASB 9 *Financial Instruments*, AASB 10 *Consolidated Financial Statements*, AASB 11 *Joint Arrangements*, AASB 127 *Separate Financial Statements* and AASB 128 *Investments in Associates and Joint Ventures*; and

  (d) non-monetary exchanges between entities in the same line of business to facilitate sales to customers or potential customers. For example, this Standard would not apply to a contract between two oil companies that agree to an exchange of oil to fulfil demand from their customers in different specified locations on a timely basis.

6   An entity shall apply this Standard to a contract (other than a contract listed in paragraph 5) only if the counterparty to the contract is a customer. A customer is a party that has contracted with an entity to obtain goods or services that are an output of the entity's ordinary activities in exchange for consideration. A counterparty to the contract would not be a customer if, for example, the counterparty has contracted with the entity to participate in an activity or process in which the parties to the contract share in the risks and benefits that result from the activity or process (such as developing an asset in a collaboration arrangement) rather than to obtain the output of the entity's ordinary activities.

7   A contract with a customer may be partially within the scope of this Standard and partially within the scope of other Standards listed in paragraph 5.

     (a)   If the other Standards specify how to separate and/or initially measure one or more parts of the contract, then an entity shall first apply the separation and/or measurement requirements in those Standards. An entity shall exclude from the *transaction price* the amount of the part (or parts) of the contract that are initially measured in accordance with other Standards and shall apply paragraphs 73–86 to allocate the amount of the transaction price that remains (if any) to each performance obligation within the scope of this Standard and to any other parts of the contract identified by paragraph 7(b).

     (b)   If the other Standards do not specify how to separate and/or initially measure one or more parts of the contract, then the entity shall apply this Standard to separate and/or initially measure the part (or parts) of the contract.

8   This Standard specifies the accounting for the incremental costs of obtaining a contract with a customer and for the costs incurred to fulfil a contract with a customer if those costs are not within the scope of another Standard (see paragraphs 91–104). An entity shall apply those paragraphs only to the costs incurred that relate to a contract with a customer (or part of that contract) that is within the scope of this Standard.

Recognition

Identifying the contract

9   **An entity shall account for a contract with a customer that is within the scope of this Standard only when all of the following criteria are met:**

     (a)   **the parties to the contract have approved the contract (in writing, orally or in accordance with other customary business practices) and are committed to perform their respective obligations;**

     (b)   **the entity can identify each party's rights regarding the goods or services to be transferred;**

     (c)   **the entity can identify the payment terms for the goods or services to be transferred;**

     (d)   **the contract has commercial substance (ie the risk, timing or amount of the entity's future cash flows is expected to change as a result of the contract); and**

     (e)   **it is probable that the entity will collect the consideration to which it will be entitled in exchange for the goods or services that will be transferred to the customer. In evaluating whether collectability of an amount of consideration is probable, an entity shall consider only the customer's ability and intention to pay that amount of consideration when it is due. The amount of consideration to which the entity will be entitled may be less than the price stated in the contract if the consideration is variable because the entity may offer the customer a price concession (see paragraph 52).**

10   A contract is an agreement between two or more parties that creates enforceable rights and obligations. Enforceability of the rights and obligations in a contract is a matter of law. Contracts can be written, oral or implied by an entity's customary business practices. The practices and processes for establishing contracts with customers vary

across legal jurisdictions, industries and entities. In addition, they may vary within an entity (for example, they may depend on the class of customer or the nature of the promised goods or services). An entity shall consider those practices and processes in determining whether and when an agreement with a customer creates enforceable rights and obligations.

11   Some contracts with customers may have no fixed duration and can be terminated or modified by either party at any time. Other contracts may automatically renew on a periodic basis that is specified in the contract. An entity shall apply this Standard to the duration of the contract (ie the contractual period) in which the parties to the contract have present enforceable rights and obligations.

12   For the purpose of applying this Standard, a contract does not exist if each party to the contract has the unilateral enforceable right to terminate a wholly unperformed contract without compensating the other party (or parties). A contract is wholly unperformed if both of the following criteria are met:

   (a)   the entity has not yet transferred any promised goods or services to the customer; and

   (b)   the entity has not yet received, and is not yet entitled to receive, any consideration in exchange for promised goods or services.

13   If a contract with a customer meets the criteria in paragraph 9 at contract inception, an entity shall not reassess those criteria unless there is an indication of a significant change in facts and circumstances. For example, if a customer's ability to pay the consideration deteriorates significantly, an entity would reassess whether it is probable that the entity will collect the consideration to which the entity will be entitled in exchange for the remaining goods or services that will be transferred to the customer.

14   If a contract with a customer does not meet the criteria in paragraph 9, an entity shall continue to assess the contract to determine whether the criteria in paragraph 9 are subsequently met.

15   When a contract with a customer does not meet the criteria in paragraph 9 and an entity receives consideration from the customer, the entity shall recognise the consideration received as revenue only when either of the following events has occurred:

   (a)   the entity has no remaining obligations to transfer goods or services to the customer and all, or substantially all, of the consideration promised by the customer has been received by the entity and is non-refundable; or

   (b)   the contract has been terminated and the consideration received from the customer is non-refundable.

16   An entity shall recognise the consideration received from a customer as a liability until one of the events in paragraph 15 occurs or until the criteria in paragraph 9 are subsequently met (see paragraph 14). Depending on the facts and circumstances relating to the contract, the liability recognised represents the entity's obligation to either transfer goods or services in the future or refund the consideration received. In either case, the liability shall be measured at the amount of consideration received from the customer.

Combination of contracts

17   An entity shall combine two or more contracts entered into at or near the same time with the same customer (or related parties of the customer) and account for the contracts as a single contract if one or more of the following criteria are met:

   (a)   the contracts are negotiated as a package with a single commercial objective;

   (b)   the amount of consideration to be paid in one contract depends on the price or performance of the other contract; or

   (c)   the goods or services promised in the contracts (or some goods or services promised in each of the contracts) are a single performance obligation in accordance with paragraphs 22–30.

Contract modifications

18   A contract modification is a change in the scope or price (or both) of a contract that is approved by the parties to the contract. In some industries and jurisdictions, a contract modification may be described as a change order, a variation or an amendment. A contract modification exists when the parties to a contract approve a modification that either creates new or changes existing enforceable rights and obligations of the parties to the contract. A contract modification could be approved in writing, by oral agreement or implied by customary business practices. If the parties to the contract have not approved a contract modification, an entity shall continue to apply this Standard to the existing contract until the contract modification is approved.

19   A contract modification may exist even though the parties to the contract have a dispute about the scope or price (or both) of the modification or the parties have approved a change in the scope of the contract but have not yet determined the corresponding change in price. In determining whether the rights and obligations that are created or changed by a modification are enforceable, an entity shall consider all relevant facts and circumstances including the terms of the contract and other evidence. If the parties to a contract have approved a change in the scope of the contract but have not yet determined the corresponding change in price, an entity shall estimate the change to the transaction price arising from the modification in accordance with paragraphs 50–54 on estimating variable consideration and paragraphs 56–58 on constraining estimates of variable consideration.

20   An entity shall account for a contract modification as a separate contract if both of the following conditions are present:

     (a)   the scope of the contract increases because of the addition of promised goods or services that are distinct (in accordance with paragraphs 26–30); and

     (b)   the price of the contract increases by an amount of consideration that reflects the entity's *stand-alone selling prices* of the additional promised goods or services and any appropriate adjustments to that price to reflect the circumstances of the particular contract. For example, an entity may adjust the stand-alone selling price of an additional good or service for a discount that the customer receives, because it is not necessary for the entity to incur the selling-related costs that it would incur when selling a similar good or service to a new customer.

21   If a contract modification is not accounted for as a separate contract in accordance with paragraph 20, an entity shall account for the promised goods or services not yet transferred at the date of the contract modification (ie the remaining promised goods or services) in whichever of the following ways is applicable:

     (a)   An entity shall account for the contract modification as if it were a termination of the existing contract and the creation of a new contract, if the remaining goods or services are distinct from the goods or services transferred on or before the date of the contract modification. The amount of consideration to be allocated to the remaining performance obligations (or to the remaining distinct goods or services in a single performance obligation identified in accordance with paragraph 22(b)) is the sum of:

         (i)   the consideration promised by the customer (including amounts already received from the customer) that was included in the estimate of the transaction price and that had not been recognised as revenue; and

         (ii)   the consideration promised as part of the contract modification.

     (b)   An entity shall account for the contract modification as if it were a part of the existing contract if the remaining goods or services are not distinct and, therefore, form part of a single performance obligation that is partially satisfied at the date of the contract modification. The effect that the contract modification has on the transaction price, and on the entity's measure of progress towards complete satisfaction of the performance obligation, is recognised as an adjustment to revenue (either as an increase in or a reduction of revenue) at the date of the contract modification (ie the adjustment to revenue is made on a cumulative catch-up basis).

(c)   If the remaining goods or services are a combination of items (a) and (b), then the entity shall account for the effects of the modification on the unsatisfied (including partially unsatisfied) performance obligations in the modified contract in a manner that is consistent with the objectives of this paragraph.

Identifying performance obligations

22   At contract inception, an entity shall assess the goods or services promised in a contract with a customer and shall identify as a performance obligation each promise to transfer to the customer either:

    (a)   a good or service (or a bundle of goods or services) that is distinct; or

    (b)   a series of distinct goods or services that are substantially the same and that have the same pattern of transfer to the customer (see paragraph 23).

23   A series of distinct goods or services has the same pattern of transfer to the customer if both of the following criteria are met:

    (a)   each distinct good or service in the series that the entity promises to transfer to the customer would meet the criteria in paragraph 35 to be a performance obligation satisfied over time; and

    (b)   in accordance with paragraphs 39–40, the same method would be used to measure the entity's progress towards complete satisfaction of the performance obligation to transfer each distinct good or service in the series to the customer.

Promises in contracts with customers

24   A contract with a customer generally explicitly states the goods or services that an entity promises to transfer to a customer. However, the performance obligations identified in a contract with a customer may not be limited to the goods or services that are explicitly stated in that contract. This is because a contract with a customer may also include promises that are implied by an entity's customary business practices, published policies or specific statements if, at the time of entering into the contract, those promises create a valid expectation of the customer that the entity will transfer a good or service to the customer.

25   Performance obligations do not include activities that an entity must undertake to fulfil a contract unless those activities transfer a good or service to a customer. For example, a services provider may need to perform various administrative tasks to set up a contract. The performance of those tasks does not transfer a service to the customer as the tasks are performed. Therefore, those setup activities are not a performance obligation.

Distinct goods or services

26   Depending on the contract, promised goods or services may include, but are not limited to, the following:

    (a)   sale of goods produced by an entity (for example, inventory of a manufacturer);

    (b)   resale of goods purchased by an entity (for example, merchandise of a retailer);

    (c)   resale of rights to goods or services purchased by an entity (for example, a ticket resold by an entity acting as a principal, as described in paragraphs B34–B38);

    (d)   performing a contractually agreed-upon task (or tasks) for a customer;

    (e)   providing a service of standing ready to provide goods or services (for example, unspecified updates to software that are provided on a when-and-if-available basis) or of making goods or services available for a customer to use as and when the customer decides;

(f) providing a service of arranging for another party to transfer goods or services to a customer (for example, acting as an agent of another party, as described in paragraphs B34–B38);

(g) granting rights to goods or services to be provided in the future that a customer can resell or provide to its customer (for example, an entity selling a product to a retailer promises to transfer an additional good or service to an individual who purchases the product from the retailer);

(h) constructing, manufacturing or developing an asset on behalf of a customer;

(i) granting licences (see paragraphs B52–B63B); and

(j) granting options to purchase additional goods or services (when those options provide a customer with a material right, as described in paragraphs B39–B43).

27 A good or service that is promised to a customer is distinct if both of the following criteria are met:

(a) the customer can benefit from the good or service either on its own or together with other resources that are readily available to the customer (ie the good or service is capable of being distinct); and

(b) the entity's promise to transfer the good or service to the customer is separately identifiable from other promises in the contract (ie the promise to transfer the good or service is distinct within the context of the contract).

28 A customer can benefit from a good or service in accordance with paragraph 27(a) if the good or service could be used, consumed, sold for an amount that is greater than scrap value or otherwise held in a way that generates economic benefits. For some goods or services, a customer may be able to benefit from a good or service on its own. For other goods or services, a customer may be able to benefit from the good or service only in conjunction with other readily available resources. A readily available resource is a good or service that is sold separately (by the entity or another entity) or a resource that the customer has already obtained from the entity (including goods or services that the entity will have already transferred to the customer under the contract) or from other transactions or events. Various factors may provide evidence that the customer can benefit from a good or service either on its own or in conjunction with other readily available resources. For example, the fact that the entity regularly sells a good or service separately would indicate that a customer can benefit from the good or service on its own or with other readily available resources.

29 In assessing whether an entity's promises to transfer goods or services to the customer are separately identifiable in accordance with paragraph 27(b), the objective is to determine whether the nature of the promise, within the context of the contract, is to transfer each of those goods or services individually or, instead, to transfer a combined item or items to which the promised goods or services are inputs. Factors that indicate that two or more promises to transfer goods or services to a customer are not separately identifiable include, but are not limited to, the following:

(a) the entity provides a significant service of integrating the goods or services with other goods or services promised in the contract into a bundle of goods or services that represent the combined output or outputs for which the customer has contracted. In other words, the entity is using the goods or services as inputs to produce or deliver the combined output or outputs specified by the customer. A combined output or outputs might include more than one phase, element or unit.

(b) one or more of the goods or services significantly modifies or customises, or are significantly modified or customised by, one or more of the other goods or services promised in the contract.

(c) the goods or services are highly interdependent or highly interrelated. In other words, each of the goods or services is significantly affected by one or more of the other goods or services in the contract. For example, in some cases, two or more goods or services are significantly affected by each other because the entity would not be able to fulfil its promise by transferring each of the goods or services independently.

30   If a promised good or service is not distinct, an entity shall combine that good or service with other promised goods or services until it identifies a bundle of goods or services that is distinct. In some cases, that would result in the entity accounting for all the goods or services promised in a contract as a single performance obligation.

Satisfaction of performance obligations

31   An entity shall recognise revenue when (or as) the entity satisfies a performance obligation by transferring a promised good or service (ie an asset) to a customer. An asset is transferred when (or as) the customer obtains control of that asset.

32   For each performance obligation identified in accordance with paragraphs 22–30, an entity shall determine at contract inception whether it satisfies the performance obligation over time (in accordance with paragraphs 35–37) or satisfies the performance obligation at a point in time (in accordance with paragraph 38). If an entity does not satisfy a performance obligation over time, the performance obligation is satisfied at a point in time.

33   Goods and services are assets, even if only momentarily, when they are received and used (as in the case of many services). Control of an asset refers to the ability to direct the use of, and obtain substantially all of the remaining benefits from, the asset. Control includes the ability to prevent other entities from directing the use of, and obtaining the benefits from, an asset. The benefits of an asset are the potential cash flows (inflows or savings in outflows) that can be obtained directly or indirectly in many ways, such as by:

(a)   using the asset to produce goods or provide services (including public services);

(b)   using the asset to enhance the value of other assets;

(c)   using the asset to settle liabilities or reduce expenses;

(d)   selling or exchanging the asset;

(e)   pledging the asset to secure a loan; and

(f)   holding the asset.

34   When evaluating whether a customer obtains control of an asset, an entity shall consider any agreement to repurchase the asset (see paragraphs B64–B76).

Performance obligations satisfied over time

35   An entity transfers control of a good or service over time and, therefore, satisfies a performance obligation and recognises revenue over time, if one of the following criteria is met:

(a)   the customer simultaneously receives and consumes the benefits provided by the entity's performance as the entity performs (see paragraphs B3–B4);

(b)   the entity's performance creates or enhances an asset (for example, work in progress) that the customer controls as the asset is created or enhanced (see paragraph B5); or

(c)   the entity's performance does not create an asset with an alternative use to the entity (see paragraph 36) and the entity has an enforceable right to payment for performance completed to date (see paragraph 37).

36   An asset created by an entity's performance does not have an alternative use to an entity if the entity is either restricted contractually from readily directing the asset for another use during the creation or enhancement of that asset or limited practically from readily directing the asset in its completed state for another use. The assessment of whether an asset has an alternative use to the entity is made at contract inception. After contract inception, an entity shall not update the assessment of the alternative use of an asset unless the parties to the contract approve a contract modification

that substantively changes the performance obligation. Paragraphs B6–B8 provide guidance for assessing whether an asset has an alternative use to an entity.

37 An entity shall consider the terms of the contract, as well as any laws that apply to the contract, when evaluating whether it has an enforceable right to payment for performance completed to date in accordance with paragraph 35(c). The right to payment for performance completed to date does not need to be for a fixed amount. However, at all times throughout the duration of the contract, the entity must be entitled to an amount that at least compensates the entity for performance completed to date if the contract is terminated by the customer or another party for reasons other than the entity's failure to perform as promised. Paragraphs B9–B13 provide guidance for assessing the existence and enforceability of a right to payment and whether an entity's right to payment would entitle the entity to be paid for its performance completed to date.

Performance obligations satisfied at a point in time

38 If a performance obligation is not satisfied over time in accordance with paragraphs 35–37, an entity satisfies the performance obligation at a point in time. To determine the point in time at which a customer obtains control of a promised asset and the entity satisfies a performance obligation, the entity shall consider the requirements for control in paragraphs 31–34. In addition, an entity shall consider indicators of the transfer of control, which include, but are not limited to, the following:

(a) The entity has a present right to payment for the asset—if a customer is presently obliged to pay for an asset, then that may indicate that the customer has obtained the ability to direct the use of, and obtain substantially all of the remaining benefits from, the asset in exchange.

(b) The customer has legal title to the asset—legal title may indicate which party to a contract has the ability to direct the use of, and obtain substantially all of the remaining benefits from, an asset or to restrict the access of other entities to those benefits. Therefore, the transfer of legal title of an asset may indicate that the customer has obtained control of the asset. If an entity retains legal title solely as protection against the customer's failure to pay, those rights of the entity would not preclude the customer from obtaining control of an asset.

(c) The entity has transferred physical possession of the asset—the customer's physical possession of an asset may indicate that the customer has the ability to direct the use of, and obtain substantially all of the remaining benefits from, the asset or to restrict the access of other entities to those benefits. However, physical possession may not coincide with control of an asset. For example, in some repurchase agreements and in some consignment arrangements, a customer or consignee may have physical possession of an asset that the entity controls. Conversely, in some bill-and-hold arrangements, the entity may have physical possession of an asset that the customer controls. Paragraphs B64–B76, B77–B78 and B79–B82 provide guidance on accounting for repurchase agreements, consignment arrangements and bill-and-hold arrangements, respectively.

(d) The customer has the significant risks and rewards of ownership of the asset—the transfer of the significant risks and rewards of ownership of an asset to the customer may indicate that the customer has obtained the ability to direct the use of, and obtain substantially all of the remaining benefits from, the asset. However, when evaluating the risks and rewards of ownership of a promised asset, an entity shall exclude any risks that give rise to a separate performance obligation in addition to the performance obligation to transfer the asset. For example, an entity may have transferred control of an asset to a customer but not yet satisfied an additional performance obligation to provide maintenance services related to the transferred asset.

(e) The customer has accepted the asset—the customer's acceptance of an asset may indicate that it has obtained the ability to direct the use of, and obtain substantially all of the remaining benefits from, the asset. To evaluate the effect of a contractual customer acceptance clause on when control of an asset is transferred, an entity shall consider the guidance in paragraphs B83–B86.

Measuring progress towards complete satisfaction of a performance obligation

39   For each performance obligation satisfied over time in accordance with paragraphs 35–37, an entity shall recognise revenue over time by measuring the progress towards complete satisfaction of that performance obligation. The objective when measuring progress is to depict an entity's performance in transferring control of goods or services promised to a customer (ie the satisfaction of an entity's performance obligation).

40   An entity shall apply a single method of measuring progress for each performance obligation satisfied over time and the entity shall apply that method consistently to similar performance obligations and in similar circumstances. At the end of each reporting period, an entity shall remeasure its progress towards complete satisfaction of a performance obligation satisfied over time.

Methods for measuring progress

41   Appropriate methods of measuring progress include output methods and input methods. Paragraphs B14–B19 provide guidance for using output methods and input methods to measure an entity's progress towards complete satisfaction of a performance obligation. In determining the appropriate method for measuring progress, an entity shall consider the nature of the good or service that the entity promised to transfer to the customer.

42   When applying a method for measuring progress, an entity shall exclude from the measure of progress any goods or services for which the entity does not transfer control to a customer. Conversely, an entity shall include in the measure of progress any goods or services for which the entity does transfer control to a customer when satisfying that performance obligation.

43   As circumstances change over time, an entity shall update its measure of progress to reflect any changes in the outcome of the performance obligation. Such changes to an entity's measure of progress shall be accounted for as a change in accounting estimate in accordance with AASB 108 *Accounting Policies, Changes in Accounting Estimates and Errors*.

Reasonable measures of progress

44   An entity shall recognise revenue for a performance obligation satisfied over time only if the entity can reasonably measure its progress towards complete satisfaction of the performance obligation. An entity would not be able to reasonably measure its progress towards complete satisfaction of a performance obligation if it lacks reliable information that would be required to apply an appropriate method of measuring progress.

45   In some circumstances (for example, in the early stages of a contract), an entity may not be able to reasonably measure the outcome of a performance obligation, but the entity expects to recover the costs incurred in satisfying the performance obligation. In those circumstances, the entity shall recognise revenue only to the extent of the costs incurred until such time that it can reasonably measure the outcome of the performance obligation.

Measurement

46   **When (or as) a performance obligation is satisfied, an entity shall recognise as revenue the amount of the transaction price (which excludes estimates of variable consideration that are constrained in accordance with paragraphs 56–58) that is allocated to that performance obligation.**

Determining the transaction price

47 An entity shall consider the terms of the contract and its customary business practices to determine the transaction price. The transaction price is the amount of consideration to which an entity expects to be entitled in exchange for transferring promised goods or services to a customer, excluding amounts collected on behalf of third parties (for example, some sales taxes). The consideration promised in a contract with a customer may include fixed amounts, variable amounts, or both.

48 The nature, timing and amount of consideration promised by a customer affect the estimate of the transaction price. When determining the transaction price, an entity shall consider the effects of all of the following:

(a) variable consideration (see paragraphs 50–55 and 59);

(b) constraining estimates of variable consideration (see paragraphs 56–58);

(c) the existence of a significant financing component in the contract (see paragraphs 60–65);

(d) non-cash consideration (see paragraphs 66–69); and

(e) consideration payable to a customer (see paragraphs 70–72).

49 For the purpose of determining the transaction price, an entity shall assume that the goods or services will be transferred to the customer as promised in accordance with the existing contract and that the contract will not be cancelled, renewed or modified.

Variable consideration

50 If the consideration promised in a contract includes a variable amount, an entity shall estimate the amount of consideration to which the entity will be entitled in exchange for transferring the promised goods or services to a customer.

51 An amount of consideration can vary because of discounts, rebates, refunds, credits, price concessions, incentives, performance bonuses, penalties or other similar items. The promised consideration can also vary if an entity's entitlement to the consideration is contingent on the occurrence or non-occurrence of a future event. For example, an amount of consideration would be variable if either a product was sold with a right of return or a fixed amount is promised as a performance bonus on achievement of a specified milestone.

52 The variability relating to the consideration promised by a customer may be explicitly stated in the contract. In addition to the terms of the contract, the promised consideration is variable if either of the following circumstances exists:

(a) the customer has a valid expectation arising from an entity's customary business practices, published policies or specific statements that the entity will accept an amount of consideration that is less than the price stated in the contract. That is, it is expected that the entity will offer a price concession. Depending on the jurisdiction, industry or customer this offer may be referred to as a discount, rebate, refund or credit.

(b) other facts and circumstances indicate that the entity's intention, when entering into the contract with the customer, is to offer a price concession to the customer.

53 An entity shall estimate an amount of variable consideration by using either of the following methods, depending on which method the entity expects to better predict the amount of consideration to which it will be entitled:

(a) The expected value—the expected value is the sum of probability-weighted amounts in a range of possible consideration amounts. An expected value may be an appropriate estimate of the amount of variable consideration if an entity has a large number of contracts with similar characteristics.

(b) The most likely amount—the most likely amount is the single most likely amount in a range of possible consideration amounts (ie the single most likely outcome of the contract). The most likely amount may be an appropriate estimate of the amount of variable consideration if the contract has only two possible outcomes (for example, an entity either achieves a performance bonus or does not).

54   An entity shall apply one method consistently throughout the contract when estimating the effect of an uncertainty on an amount of variable consideration to which the entity will be entitled. In addition, an entity shall consider all the information (historical, current and forecast) that is reasonably available to the entity and shall identify a reasonable number of possible consideration amounts. The information that an entity uses to estimate the amount of variable consideration would typically be similar to the information that the entity's management uses during the bid-and-proposal process and in establishing prices for promised goods or services.

Refund liabilities

55   An entity shall recognise a refund liability if the entity receives consideration from a customer and expects to refund some or all of that consideration to the customer. A refund liability is measured at the amount of consideration received (or receivable) for which the entity does not expect to be entitled (ie amounts not included in the transaction price). The refund liability (and corresponding change in the transaction price and, therefore, the *contract liability*) shall be updated at the end of each reporting period for changes in circumstances. To account for a refund liability relating to a sale with a right of return, an entity shall apply the guidance in paragraphs B20–B27.

Constraining estimates of variable consideration

56   An entity shall include in the transaction price some or all of an amount of variable consideration estimated in accordance with paragraph 53 only to the extent that it is highly probable that a significant reversal in the amount of cumulative revenue recognised will not occur when the uncertainty associated with the variable consideration is subsequently resolved.

57   In assessing whether it is highly probable that a significant reversal in the amount of cumulative revenue recognised will not occur once the uncertainty related to variable consideration is subsequently resolved, an entity shall consider both the likelihood and the magnitude of the revenue reversal. Factors that could increase the likelihood or the magnitude of a revenue reversal include, but are not limited to, any of the following:

(a)   the amount of consideration is highly susceptible to factors outside the entity's influence. Those factors may include volatility in a market, the judgement or actions of third parties, weather conditions and a high risk of obsolescence of the promised good or service.

(b)   the uncertainty about the amount of consideration is not expected to be resolved for a long period of time.

(c)   the entity's experience (or other evidence) with similar types of contracts is limited, or that experience (or other evidence) has limited predictive value.

(d)   the entity has a practice of either offering a broad range of price concessions or changing the payment terms and conditions of similar contracts in similar circumstances.

(e)   the contract has a large number and broad range of possible consideration amounts.

58   An entity shall apply paragraph B63 to account for consideration in the form of a sales-based or usage-based royalty that is promised in exchange for a licence of intellectual property.

Reassessment of variable consideration

59   At the end of each reporting period, an entity shall update the estimated transaction price (including updating its assessment of whether an estimate of variable consideration is constrained) to represent faithfully the circumstances present at the

end of the reporting period and the changes in circumstances during the reporting period. The entity shall account for changes in the transaction price in accordance with paragraphs 87–90.

The existence of a significant financing component in the contract

60 In determining the transaction price, an entity shall adjust the promised amount of consideration for the effects of the time value of money if the timing of payments agreed to by the parties to the contract (either explicitly or implicitly) provides the customer or the entity with a significant benefit of financing the transfer of goods or services to the customer. In those circumstances, the contract contains a significant financing component. A significant financing component may exist regardless of whether the promise of financing is explicitly stated in the contract or implied by the payment terms agreed to by the parties to the contract.

61 The objective when adjusting the promised amount of consideration for a significant financing component is for an entity to recognise revenue at an amount that reflects the price that a customer would have paid for the promised goods or services if the customer had paid cash for those goods or services when (or as) they transfer to the customer (ie the cash selling price). An entity shall consider all relevant facts and circumstances in assessing whether a contract contains a financing component and whether that financing component is significant to the contract, including both of the following:

    (a)   the difference, if any, between the amount of promised consideration and the cash selling price of the promised goods or services; and

    (b)   the combined effect of both of the following:

        (i)   the expected length of time between when the entity transfers the promised goods or services to the customer and when the customer pays for those goods or services; and

        (ii)   the prevailing interest rates in the relevant market.

62 Notwithstanding the assessment in paragraph 61, a contract with a customer would not have a significant financing component if any of the following factors exist:

    (a)   the customer paid for the goods or services in advance and the timing of the transfer of those goods or services is at the discretion of the customer.

    (b)   a substantial amount of the consideration promised by the customer is variable and the amount or timing of that consideration varies on the basis of the occurrence or non-occurrence of a future event that is not substantially within the control of the customer or the entity (for example, if the consideration is a sales-based royalty).

    (c)   the difference between the promised consideration and the cash selling price of the good or service (as described in paragraph 61) arises for reasons other than the provision of finance to either the customer or the entity, and the difference between those amounts is proportional to the reason for the difference. For example, the payment terms might provide the entity or the customer with protection from the other party failing to adequately complete some or all of its obligations under the contract.

63 As a practical expedient, an entity need not adjust the promised amount of consideration for the effects of a significant financing component if the entity expects, at contract inception, that the period between when the entity transfers a promised good or service to a customer and when the customer pays for that good or service will be one year or less.

64 To meet the objective in paragraph 61 when adjusting the promised amount of consideration for a significant financing component, an entity shall use the discount rate that would be reflected in a separate financing transaction between the entity and its customer at contract inception. That rate would reflect the credit characteristics of the party receiving financing in the contract, as well as any collateral or security

AASB

provided by the customer or the entity, including assets transferred in the contract. An entity may be able to determine that rate by identifying the rate that discounts the nominal amount of the promised consideration to the price that the customer would pay in cash for the goods or services when (or as) they transfer to the customer. After contract inception, an entity shall not update the discount rate for changes in interest rates or other circumstances (such as a change in the assessment of the customer's credit risk).

65   An entity shall present the effects of financing (interest revenue or interest expense) separately from revenue from contracts with customers in the statement of comprehensive income. Interest revenue or interest expense is recognised only to the extent that a *contract asset* (or receivable) or a contract liability is recognised in accounting for a contract with a customer.

Non-cash consideration

66   To determine the transaction price for contracts in which a customer promises consideration in a form other than cash, an entity shall measure the non-cash consideration (or promise of non-cash consideration) at fair value.

67   If an entity cannot reasonably estimate the fair value of the non-cash consideration, the entity shall measure the consideration indirectly by reference to the stand-alone selling price of the goods or services promised to the customer (or class of customer) in exchange for the consideration.

68   The fair value of the non-cash consideration may vary because of the form of the consideration (for example, a change in the price of a share to which an entity is entitled to receive from a customer). If the fair value of the non-cash consideration promised by a customer varies for reasons other than only the form of the consideration (for example, the fair value could vary because of the entity's performance), an entity shall apply the requirements in paragraphs 56–58.

69   If a customer contributes goods or services (for example, materials, equipment or labour) to facilitate an entity's fulfilment of the contract, the entity shall assess whether it obtains control of those contributed goods or services. If so, the entity shall account for the contributed goods or services as non-cash consideration received from the customer.

Consideration payable to a customer

70   Consideration payable to a customer includes cash amounts that an entity pays, or expects to pay, to the customer (or to other parties that purchase the entity's goods or services from the customer). Consideration payable to a customer also includes credit or other items (for example, a coupon or voucher) that can be applied against amounts owed to the entity (or to other parties that purchase the entity's goods or services from the customer). An entity shall account for consideration payable to a customer as a reduction of the transaction price and, therefore, of revenue unless the payment to the customer is in exchange for a distinct good or service (as described in paragraphs 26–30) that the customer transfers to the entity. If the consideration payable to a customer includes a variable amount, an entity shall estimate the transaction price (including assessing whether the estimate of variable consideration is constrained) in accordance with paragraphs 50–58.

71   If consideration payable to a customer is a payment for a distinct good or service from the customer, then an entity shall account for the purchase of the good or service in the same way that it accounts for other purchases from suppliers. If the amount of consideration payable to the customer exceeds the fair value of the distinct good or service that the entity receives from the customer, then the entity shall account for such an excess as a reduction of the transaction price. If the entity cannot reasonably estimate the fair value of the good or service received from the customer, it shall account for all of the consideration payable to the customer as a reduction of the transaction price.

72   Accordingly, if consideration payable to a customer is accounted for as a reduction of the transaction price, an entity shall recognise the reduction of revenue when (or as) the later of either of the following events occurs:

(a)   the entity recognises revenue for the transfer of the related goods or services to the customer; and

(b)   the entity pays or promises to pay the consideration (even if the payment is conditional on a future event). That promise might be implied by the entity's customary business practices.

Allocating the transaction price to performance obligations

73   **The objective when allocating the transaction price is for an entity to allocate the transaction price to each performance obligation (or distinct good or service) in an amount that depicts the amount of consideration to which the entity expects to be entitled in exchange for transferring the promised goods or services to the customer.**

74   To meet the allocation objective, an entity shall allocate the transaction price to each performance obligation identified in the contract on a relative stand-alone selling price basis in accordance with paragraphs 76–80, except as specified in paragraphs 81–83 (for allocating discounts) and paragraphs 84–86 (for allocating consideration that includes variable amounts).

75   Paragraphs 76–86 do not apply if a contract has only one performance obligation. However, paragraphs 84–86 may apply if an entity promises to transfer a series of distinct goods or services identified as a single performance obligation in accordance with paragraph 22(b) and the promised consideration includes variable amounts.

Allocation based on stand-alone selling prices

76   To allocate the transaction price to each performance obligation on a relative stand-alone selling price basis, an entity shall determine the stand-alone selling price at contract inception of the distinct good or service underlying each performance obligation in the contract and allocate the transaction price in proportion to those stand-alone selling prices.

77   The stand-alone selling price is the price at which an entity would sell a promised good or service separately to a customer. The best evidence of a stand-alone selling price is the observable price of a good or service when the entity sells that good or service separately in similar circumstances and to similar customers. A contractually stated price or a list price for a good or service may be (but shall not be presumed to be) the stand-alone selling price of that good or service.

78   If a stand-alone selling price is not directly observable, an entity shall estimate the stand-alone selling price at an amount that would result in the allocation of the transaction price meeting the allocation objective in paragraph 73. When estimating a stand-alone selling price, an entity shall consider all information (including market conditions, entity-specific factors and information about the customer or class of customer) that is reasonably available to the entity. In doing so, an entity shall maximise the use of observable inputs and apply estimation methods consistently in similar circumstances.

79   Suitable methods for estimating the stand-alone selling price of a good or service include, but are not limited to, the following:

(a)   Adjusted market assessment approach—an entity could evaluate the market in which it sells goods or services and estimate the price that a customer in that market would be willing to pay for those goods or services. That approach might also include referring to prices from the entity's competitors for similar goods or services and adjusting those prices as necessary to reflect the entity's costs and margins.

AASB

(b)   Expected cost plus a margin approach—an entity could forecast its expected costs of satisfying a performance obligation and then add an appropriate margin for that good or service.

(c)   Residual approach—an entity may estimate the stand-alone selling price by reference to the total transaction price less the sum of the observable stand-alone selling prices of other goods or services promised in the contract. However, an entity may use a residual approach to estimate, in accordance with paragraph 78, the stand-alone selling price of a good or service only if one of the following criteria is met:

(i)   the entity sells the same good or service to different customers (at or near the same time) for a broad range of amounts (ie the selling price is highly variable because a representative stand-alone selling price is not discernible from past transactions or other observable evidence); or

(ii)   the entity has not yet established a price for that good or service and the good or service has not previously been sold on a stand-alone basis (ie the selling price is uncertain).

80   A combination of methods may need to be used to estimate the stand-alone selling prices of the goods or services promised in the contract if two or more of those goods or services have highly variable or uncertain stand-alone selling prices. For example, an entity may use a residual approach to estimate the aggregate stand-alone selling price for those promised goods or services with highly variable or uncertain stand-alone selling prices and then use another method to estimate the stand-alone selling prices of the individual goods or services relative to that estimated aggregate stand-alone selling price determined by the residual approach. When an entity uses a combination of methods to estimate the stand-alone selling price of each promised good or service in the contract, the entity shall evaluate whether allocating the transaction price at those estimated stand-alone selling prices would be consistent with the allocation objective in paragraph 73 and the requirements for estimating stand-alone selling prices in paragraph 78.

Allocation of a discount

81   A customer receives a discount for purchasing a bundle of goods or services if the sum of the stand-alone selling prices of those promised goods or services in the contract exceeds the promised consideration in a contract. Except when an entity has observable evidence in accordance with paragraph 82 that the entire discount relates to only one or more, but not all, performance obligations in a contract, the entity shall allocate a discount proportionately to all performance obligations in the contract. The proportionate allocation of the discount in those circumstances is a consequence of the entity allocating the transaction price to each performance obligation on the basis of the relative stand-alone selling prices of the underlying distinct goods or services.

82   An entity shall allocate a discount entirely to one or more, but not all, performance obligations in the contract if all of the following criteria are met:

(a)   the entity regularly sells each distinct good or service (or each bundle of distinct goods or services) in the contract on a stand-alone basis;

(b)   the entity also regularly sells on a stand-alone basis a bundle (or bundles) of some of those distinct goods or services at a discount to the stand-alone selling prices of the goods or services in each bundle; and

(c)   the discount attributable to each bundle of goods or services described in paragraph 82(b) is substantially the same as the discount in the contract and an analysis of the goods or services in each bundle provides observable evidence of the performance obligation (or performance obligations) to which the entire discount in the contract belongs.

83   If a discount is allocated entirely to one or more performance obligations in the contract in accordance with paragraph 82, an entity shall allocate the discount before using

the residual approach to estimate the stand-alone selling price of a good or service in accordance with paragraph 79(c).

Allocation of variable consideration

84   Variable consideration that is promised in a contract may be attributable to the entire contract or to a specific part of the contract, such as either of the following:

    (a)   one or more, but not all, performance obligations in the contract (for example, a bonus may be contingent on an entity transferring a promised good or service within a specified period of time); or

    (b)   one or more, but not all, distinct goods or services promised in a series of distinct goods or services that forms part of a single performance obligation in accordance with paragraph 22(b) (for example, the consideration promised for the second year of a two-year cleaning service contract will increase on the basis of movements in a specified inflation index).

85   An entity shall allocate a variable amount (and subsequent changes to that amount) entirely to a performance obligation or to a distinct good or service that forms part of a single performance obligation in accordance with paragraph 22(b) if both of the following criteria are met:

    (a)   the terms of a variable payment relate specifically to the entity's efforts to satisfy the performance obligation or transfer the distinct good or service (or to a specific outcome from satisfying the performance obligation or transferring the distinct good or service); and

    (b)   allocating the variable amount of consideration entirely to the performance obligation or the distinct good or service is consistent with the allocation objective in paragraph 73 when considering all of the performance obligations and payment terms in the contract.

86   The allocation requirements in paragraphs 73–83 shall be applied to allocate the remaining amount of the transaction price that does not meet the criteria in paragraph 85.

Changes in the transaction price

87   After contract inception, the transaction price can change for various reasons, including the resolution of uncertain events or other changes in circumstances that change the amount of consideration to which an entity expects to be entitled in exchange for the promised goods or services.

88   An entity shall allocate to the performance obligations in the contract any subsequent changes in the transaction price on the same basis as at contract inception. Consequently, an entity shall not reallocate the transaction price to reflect changes in stand-alone selling prices after contract inception. Amounts allocated to a satisfied performance obligation shall be recognised as revenue, or as a reduction of revenue, in the period in which the transaction price changes.

89   An entity shall allocate a change in the transaction price entirely to one or more, but not all, performance obligations or distinct goods or services promised in a series that forms part of a single performance obligation in accordance with paragraph 22(b) only if the criteria in paragraph 85 on allocating variable consideration are met.

90   An entity shall account for a change in the transaction price that arises as a result of a contract modification in accordance with paragraphs 18–21. However, for a change in the transaction price that occurs after a contract modification, an entity shall apply paragraphs 87–89 to allocate the change in the transaction price in whichever of the following ways is applicable:

    (a)   An entity shall allocate the change in the transaction price to the performance obligations identified in the contract before the modification if, and to the extent that, the change in the transaction price is attributable to an amount of variable consideration promised before the modification and the modification is accounted for in accordance with paragraph 21(a).

(b) In all other cases in which the modification was not accounted for as a separate contract in accordance with paragraph 20, an entity shall allocate the change in the transaction price to the performance obligations in the modified contract (ie the performance obligations that were unsatisfied or partially unsatisfied immediately after the modification).

Contract costs

Incremental costs of obtaining a contract

91 **An entity shall recognise as an asset the incremental costs of obtaining a contract with a customer if the entity expects to recover those costs.**

92 The incremental costs of obtaining a contract are those costs that an entity incurs to obtain a contract with a customer that it would not have incurred if the contract had not been obtained (for example, a sales commission).

93 Costs to obtain a contract that would have been incurred regardless of whether the contract was obtained shall be recognised as an expense when incurred, unless those costs are explicitly chargeable to the customer regardless of whether the contract is obtained.

94 As a practical expedient, an entity may recognise the incremental costs of obtaining a contract as an expense when incurred if the amortisation period of the asset that the entity otherwise would have recognised is one year or less.

Costs to fulfil a contract

95 **If the costs incurred in fulfilling a contract with a customer are not within the scope of another Standard (for example, AASB 102 *Inventories*, AASB 116 *Property, Plant and Equipment* or AASB 138 *Intangible Assets*), an entity shall recognise an asset from the costs incurred to fulfil a contract only if those costs meet all of the following criteria:**

(a) **the costs relate directly to a contract or to an anticipated contract that the entity can specifically identify (for example, costs relating to services to be provided under renewal of an existing contract or costs of designing an asset to be transferred under a specific contract that has not yet been approved);**

(b) **the costs generate or enhance resources of the entity that will be used in satisfying (or in continuing to satisfy) performance obligations in the future; and**

(c) **the costs are expected to be recovered.**

96 For costs incurred in fulfilling a contract with a customer that are within the scope of another Standard, an entity shall account for those costs in accordance with those other Standards.

97 Costs that relate directly to a contract (or a specific anticipated contract) include any of the following:

(a) direct labour (for example, salaries and wages of employees who provide the promised services directly to the customer);

(b) direct materials (for example, supplies used in providing the promised services to a customer);

(c) allocations of costs that relate directly to the contract or to contract activities (for example, costs of contract management and supervision, insurance and depreciation of tools and equipment used in fulfilling the contract);

(d) costs that are explicitly chargeable to the customer under the contract; and

(e)   other costs that are incurred only because an entity entered into the contract (for example, payments to subcontractors).

98   An entity shall recognise the following costs as expenses when incurred:

(a)   general and administrative costs (unless those costs are explicitly chargeable to the customer under the contract, in which case an entity shall evaluate those costs in accordance with paragraph 97);

(b)   costs of wasted materials, labour or other resources to fulfil the contract that were not reflected in the price of the contract;

(c)   costs that relate to satisfied performance obligations (or partially satisfied performance obligations) in the contract (ie costs that relate to past performance); and

(d)   costs for which an entity cannot distinguish whether the costs relate to unsatisfied performance obligations or to satisfied performance obligations (or partially satisfied performance obligations).

Amortisation and impairment

99   An asset recognised in accordance with paragraph 91 or 95 shall be amortised on a systematic basis that is consistent with the transfer to the customer of the goods or services to which the asset relates. The asset may relate to goods or services to be transferred under a specific anticipated contract (as described in paragraph 95(a)).

100   An entity shall update the amortisation to reflect a significant change in the entity's expected timing of transfer to the customer of the goods or services to which the asset relates. Such a change shall be accounted for as a change in accounting estimate in accordance with AASB 108.

101   An entity shall recognise an impairment loss in profit or loss to the extent that the carrying amount of an asset recognised in accordance with paragraph 91 or 95 exceeds:

(a)   the remaining amount of consideration that the entity expects to receive in exchange for the goods or services to which the asset relates; less

(b)   the costs that relate directly to providing those goods or services and that have not been recognised as expenses (see paragraph 97).

102   For the purposes of applying paragraph 101 to determine the amount of consideration that an entity expects to receive, an entity shall use the principles for determining the transaction price (except for the requirements in paragraphs 56–58 on constraining estimates of variable consideration) and adjust that amount to reflect the effects of the customer's credit risk.

103   Before an entity recognises an impairment loss for an asset recognised in accordance with paragraph 91 or 95, the entity shall recognise any impairment loss for assets related to the contract that are recognised in accordance with another Standard (for example, AASB 102, AASB 116 and AASB 138). After applying the impairment test in paragraph 101, an entity shall include the resulting carrying amount of the asset recognised in accordance with paragraph 91 or 95 in the carrying amount of the cash-generating unit to which it belongs for the purpose of applying AASB 136 *Impairment of Assets* to that cash-generating unit.

104   An entity shall recognise in profit or loss a reversal of some or all of an impairment loss previously recognised in accordance with paragraph 101 when the impairment conditions no longer exist or have improved. The increased carrying amount of the asset shall not exceed the amount that would have been determined (net of amortisation) if no impairment loss had been recognised previously.

Presentation

105   **When either party to a contract has performed, an entity shall present the contract in the statement of financial position as a contract asset or a contract**

AASB

liability, depending on the relationship between the entity's performance and the customer's payment. An entity shall present any unconditional rights to consideration separately as a receivable.

106   If a customer pays consideration, or an entity has a right to an amount of consideration that is unconditional (ie a receivable), before the entity transfers a good or service to the customer, the entity shall present the contract as a contract liability when the payment is made or the payment is due (whichever is earlier). A contract liability is an entity's obligation to transfer goods or services to a customer for which the entity has received consideration (or an amount of consideration is due) from the customer.

107   If an entity performs by transferring goods or services to a customer before the customer pays consideration or before payment is due, the entity shall present the contract as a contract asset, excluding any amounts presented as a receivable. A contract asset is an entity's right to consideration in exchange for goods or services that the entity has transferred to a customer. An entity shall assess a contract asset for impairment in accordance with AASB 9. An impairment of a contract asset shall be measured, presented and disclosed on the same basis as a financial asset that is within the scope of AASB 9 (see also paragraph 113(b)).

108   A receivable is an entity's right to consideration that is unconditional. A right to consideration is unconditional if only the passage of time is required before payment of that consideration is due. For example, an entity would recognise a receivable if it has a present right to payment even though that amount may be subject to refund in the future. An entity shall account for a receivable in accordance with AASB 9. Upon initial recognition of a receivable from a contract with a customer, any difference between the measurement of the receivable in accordance with AASB 9 and the corresponding amount of revenue recognised shall be presented as an expense (for example, as an impairment loss).

109   This Standard uses the terms 'contract asset' and 'contract liability' but does not prohibit an entity from using alternative descriptions in the statement of financial position for those items. If an entity uses an alternative description for a contract asset, the entity shall provide sufficient information for a user of the financial statements to distinguish between receivables and contract assets.

Disclosure

110   **The objective of the disclosure requirements is for an entity to disclose sufficient information to enable users of financial statements to understand the nature, amount, timing and uncertainty of revenue and cash flows arising from contracts with customers. To achieve that objective, an entity shall disclose qualitative and quantitative information about all of the following:**

(a)   **its contracts with customers (see paragraphs 113–122);**

(b)   **the significant judgements, and changes in the judgements, made in applying this Standard to those contracts (see paragraphs 123–126); and**

(c)   **any assets recognised from the costs to obtain or fulfil a contract with a customer in accordance with paragraph 91 or 95 (see paragraphs 127–128).**

111   An entity shall consider the level of detail necessary to satisfy the disclosure objective and how much emphasis to place on each of the various requirements. An entity shall aggregate or disaggregate disclosures so that useful information is not obscured by either the inclusion of a large amount of insignificant detail or the aggregation of items that have substantially different characteristics.

112   An entity need not disclose information in accordance with this Standard if it has provided the information in accordance with another Standard.

Contracts with customers

113 An entity shall disclose all of the following amounts for the reporting period unless those amounts are presented separately in the statement of comprehensive income in accordance with other Standards:

(a) revenue recognised from contracts with customers, which the entity shall disclose separately from its other sources of revenue; and

(b) any impairment losses recognised (in accordance with AASB 9) on any receivables or contract assets arising from an entity's contracts with customers, which the entity shall disclose separately from impairment losses from other contracts.

Disaggregation of revenue

114 An entity shall disaggregate revenue recognised from contracts with customers into categories that depict how the nature, amount, timing and uncertainty of revenue and cash flows are affected by economic factors. An entity shall apply the guidance in paragraphs B87–B89 when selecting the categories to use to disaggregate revenue.

115 In addition, an entity shall disclose sufficient information to enable users of financial statements to understand the relationship between the disclosure of disaggregated revenue (in accordance with paragraph 114) and revenue information that is disclosed for each reportable segment, if the entity applies AASB 8 *Operating Segments*.

Contract balances

116 An entity shall disclose all of the following:

(a) the opening and closing balances of receivables, contract assets and contract liabilities from contracts with customers, if not otherwise separately presented or disclosed;

(b) revenue recognised in the reporting period that was included in the contract liability balance at the beginning of the period; and

(c) revenue recognised in the reporting period from performance obligations satisfied (or partially satisfied) in previous periods (for example, changes in transaction price).

117 An entity shall explain how the timing of satisfaction of its performance obligations (see paragraph 119(a)) relates to the typical timing of payment (see paragraph 119(b)) and the effect that those factors have on the contract asset and the contract liability balances. The explanation provided may use qualitative information.

118 An entity shall provide an explanation of the significant changes in the contract asset and the contract liability balances during the reporting period. The explanation shall include qualitative and quantitative information. Examples of changes in the entity's balances of contract assets and contract liabilities include any of the following:

(a) changes due to business combinations;

(b) cumulative catch-up adjustments to revenue that affect the corresponding contract asset or contract liability, including adjustments arising from a change in the measure of progress, a change in an estimate of the transaction price (including any changes in the assessment of whether an estimate of variable consideration is constrained) or a contract modification;

(c) impairment of a contract asset;

(d) a change in the time frame for a right to consideration to become unconditional (ie for a contract asset to be reclassified to a receivable); and

(e) a change in the time frame for a performance obligation to be satisfied (ie for the recognition of revenue arising from a contract liability).

AASB

Performance obligations

119   An entity shall disclose information about its performance obligations in contracts with customers, including a description of all of the following:

     (a)   when the entity typically satisfies its performance obligations (for example, upon shipment, upon delivery, as services are rendered or upon completion of service), including when performance obligations are satisfied in a bill-and-hold arrangement;

     (b)   the significant payment terms (for example, when payment is typically due, whether the contract has a significant financing component, whether the consideration amount is variable and whether the estimate of variable consideration is typically constrained in accordance with paragraphs 56–58);

     (c)   the nature of the goods or services that the entity has promised to transfer, highlighting any performance obligations to arrange for another party to transfer goods or services (ie if the entity is acting as an agent);

     (d)   obligations for returns, refunds and other similar obligations; and

     (e)   types of warranties and related obligations.

Transaction price allocated to the remaining performance obligations

120   An entity shall disclose the following information about its remaining performance obligations:

     (a)   the aggregate amount of the transaction price allocated to the performance obligations that are unsatisfied (or partially unsatisfied) as of the end of the reporting period; and

     (b)   an explanation of when the entity expects to recognise as revenue the amount disclosed in accordance with paragraph 120(a), which the entity shall disclose in either of the following ways:

         (i)   on a quantitative basis using the time bands that would be most appropriate for the duration of the remaining performance obligations; or

         (ii)   by using qualitative information.

121   As a practical expedient, an entity need not disclose the information in paragraph 120 for a performance obligation if either of the following conditions is met:

     (a)   the performance obligation is part of a contract that has an original expected duration of one year or less; or

     (b)   the entity recognises revenue from the satisfaction of the performance obligation in accordance with paragraph B16.

122   An entity shall explain qualitatively whether it is applying the practical expedient in paragraph 121 and whether any consideration from contracts with customers is not included in the transaction price and, therefore, not included in the information disclosed in accordance with paragraph 120. For example, an estimate of the transaction price would not include any estimated amounts of variable consideration that are constrained (see paragraphs 56–58).

Significant judgements in the application of this Standard

123   An entity shall disclose the judgements, and changes in the judgements, made in applying this Standard that significantly affect the determination of the amount and timing of revenue from contracts with customers. In particular, an entity shall explain the judgements, and changes in the judgements, used in determining both of the following:

     (a)   the timing of satisfaction of performance obligations (see paragraphs 124–125); and

(b) the transaction price and the amounts allocated to performance obligations (see paragraph 126).

Determining the timing of satisfaction of performance obligations

124 For performance obligations that an entity satisfies over time, an entity shall disclose both of the following:

(a) the methods used to recognise revenue (for example, a description of the output methods or input methods used and how those methods are applied); and

(b) an explanation of why the methods used provide a faithful depiction of the transfer of goods or services.

125 For performance obligations satisfied at a point in time, an entity shall disclose the significant judgements made in evaluating when a customer obtains control of promised goods or services.

Determining the transaction price and the amounts allocated to performance obligations

126 An entity shall disclose information about the methods, inputs and assumptions used for all of the following:

(a) determining the transaction price, which includes, but is not limited to, estimating variable consideration, adjusting the consideration for the effects of the time value of money and measuring non-cash consideration;

(b) assessing whether an estimate of variable consideration is constrained;

(c) allocating the transaction price, including estimating stand-alone selling prices of promised goods or services and allocating discounts and variable consideration to a specific part of the contract (if applicable); and

(d) measuring obligations for returns, refunds and other similar obligations.

Assets recognised from the costs to obtain or fulfil a contract with a customer

127 An entity shall describe both of the following:

(a) the judgements made in determining the amount of the costs incurred to obtain or fulfil a contract with a customer (in accordance with paragraph 91 or 95); and

(b) the method it uses to determine the amortisation for each reporting period.

128 An entity shall disclose all of the following:

(a) the closing balances of assets recognised from the costs incurred to obtain or fulfil a contract with a customer (in accordance with paragraph 91 or 95), by main category of asset (for example, costs to obtain contracts with customers, pre-contract costs and setup costs); and

(b) the amount of amortisation and any impairment losses recognised in the reporting period.

Practical expedients

129 If an entity elects to use the practical expedient in either paragraph 63 (about the existence of a significant financing component) or paragraph 94 (about the incremental costs of obtaining a contract), the entity shall disclose that fact.

Commencement of the legislative instrument

Aus129.1 **This Standard commences on the day this Standard is made by the Australian Accounting Standards Board.**

APPENDIX A
DEFINED TERMS

This appendix is an integral part of AASB 15.

contract	An agreement between two or more parties that creates enforceable rights and obligations.
contract asset	An entity's right to consideration in exchange for goods or services that the entity has transferred to a **customer** when that right is conditioned on something other than the passage of time (for example, the entity's future performance).
contract liability	An entity's obligation to transfer goods or services to a **customer** for which the entity has received consideration (or the amount is due) from the customer.
customer	A party that has contracted with an entity to obtain goods or services that are an output of the entity's ordinary activities in exchange for consideration.
income	Increases in economic benefits during the accounting period in the form of inflows or enhancements of assets or decreases of liabilities that result in an increase in equity, other than those relating to contributions from equity participants.
performance obligation	A promise in a **contract** with a **customer** to transfer to the customer either: (a) a good or service (or a bundle of goods or services) that is distinct; or (b) a series of distinct goods or services that are substantially the same and that have the same pattern of transfer to the customer.
revenue	**Income** arising in the course of an entity's ordinary activities.
stand-alone selling price (of a good or service)	The price at which an entity would sell a promised good or service separately to a **customer**.
transaction price (for a contract with a customer)	The amount of consideration to which an entity expects to be entitled in exchange for transferring promised goods or services to a **customer**, excluding amounts collected on behalf of third parties.

APPENDIX B
APPLICATION GUIDANCE

This appendix is an integral part of AASB 15. It describes the application of paragraphs 1–129 and has the same authority as the other parts of AASB 15.

B1   This application guidance is organised into the following categories:

      (a)   performance obligations satisfied over time (paragraphs B2–B13);

      (b)   methods for measuring progress towards complete satisfaction of a performance obligation (paragraphs B14–B19);

      (c)   sale with a right of return (paragraphs B20–B27);

      (d)   warranties (paragraphs B28–B33);

      (e)   principal versus agent considerations (paragraphs B34–B38);

      (f)   customer options for additional goods or services (paragraphs B39–B43);

(g)	customers' unexercised rights (paragraphs B44–B47);
(h)	non-refundable upfront fees (and some related costs) (paragraphs B48–B51);
(i)	licensing (paragraphs B52–B63B);
(j)	repurchase agreements (paragraphs B64–B76);
(k)	consignment arrangements (paragraphs B77–B78);
(l)	bill-and-hold arrangements (paragraphs B79–B82);
(m)	customer acceptance (paragraphs B83–B86); and
(n)	disclosure of disaggregated revenue (paragraphs B87–B89).

Performance obligations satisfied over time

B2   In accordance with paragraph 35, a performance obligation is satisfied over time if one of the following criteria is met:

(a)	the customer simultaneously receives and consumes the benefits provided by the entity's performance as the entity performs (see paragraphs B3–B4);
(b)	the entity's performance creates or enhances an asset (for example, work in progress) that the customer controls as the asset is created or enhanced (see paragraph B5); or
(c)	the entity's performance does not create an asset with an alternative use to the entity (see paragraphs B6–B8) and the entity has an enforceable right to payment for performance completed to date (see paragraphs B9–B13).

Simultaneous receipt and consumption of the benefits of the entity's performance (paragraph 35(a))

B3   For some types of performance obligations, the assessment of whether a customer receives the benefits of an entity's performance as the entity performs and simultaneously consumes those benefits as they are received will be straightforward. Examples include routine or recurring services (such as a cleaning service) in which the receipt and simultaneous consumption by the customer of the benefits of the entity's performance can be readily identified.

B4   For other types of performance obligations, an entity may not be able to readily identify whether a customer simultaneously receives and consumes the benefits from the entity's performance as the entity performs. In those circumstances, a performance obligation is satisfied over time if an entity determines that another entity would not need to substantially re-perform the work that the entity has completed to date if that other entity were to fulfil the remaining performance obligation to the customer. In determining whether another entity would not need to substantially re-perform the work the entity has completed to date, an entity shall make both of the following assumptions:

(a)	disregard potential contractual restrictions or practical limitations that otherwise would prevent the entity from transferring the remaining performance obligation to another entity; and
(b)	presume that another entity fulfilling the remainder of the performance obligation would not have the benefit of any asset that is presently controlled by the entity and that would remain controlled by the entity if the performance obligation were to transfer to another entity.

Customer controls the asset as it is created or enhanced (paragraph 35(b))

B5   In determining whether a customer controls an asset as it is created or enhanced in accordance with paragraph 35(b), an entity shall apply the requirements for control in paragraphs 31–34 and 38. The asset that is being created or enhanced (for example, a work-in-progress asset) could be either tangible or intangible.

Entity's performance does not create an asset with an alternative use (paragraph 35(c))

B6   In assessing whether an asset has an alternative use to an entity in accordance with paragraph 36, an entity shall consider the effects of contractual restrictions and practical limitations on the entity's ability to readily direct that asset for another use, such as selling it to a different customer. The possibility of the contract with the customer being terminated is not a relevant consideration in assessing whether the entity would be able to readily direct the asset for another use.

B7   A contractual restriction on an entity's ability to direct an asset for another use must be substantive for the asset not to have an alternative use to the entity. A contractual restriction is substantive if a customer could enforce its rights to the promised asset if the entity sought to direct the asset for another use. In contrast, a contractual restriction is not substantive if, for example, an asset is largely interchangeable with other assets that the entity could transfer to another customer without breaching the contract and without incurring significant costs that otherwise would not have been incurred in relation to that contract.

B8   A practical limitation on an entity's ability to direct an asset for another use exists if an entity would incur significant economic losses to direct the asset for another use. A significant economic loss could arise because the entity either would incur significant costs to rework the asset or would only be able to sell the asset at a significant loss. For example, an entity may be practically limited from redirecting assets that either have design specifications that are unique to a customer or are located in remote areas.

Right to payment for performance completed to date (paragraph 35(c))

B9   In accordance with paragraph 37, an entity has a right to payment for performance completed to date if the entity would be entitled to an amount that at least compensates the entity for its performance completed to date in the event that the customer or another party terminates the contract for reasons other than the entity's failure to perform as promised. An amount that would compensate an entity for performance completed to date would be an amount that approximates the selling price of the goods or services transferred to date (for example, recovery of the costs incurred by an entity in satisfying the performance obligation plus a reasonable profit margin) rather than compensation for only the entity's potential loss of profit if the contract were to be terminated. Compensation for a reasonable profit margin need not equal the profit margin expected if the contract was fulfilled as promised, but an entity should be entitled to compensation for either of the following amounts:

    (a)   a proportion of the expected profit margin in the contract that reasonably reflects the extent of the entity's performance under the contract before termination by the customer (or another party); or

    (b)   a reasonable return on the entity's cost of capital for similar contracts (or the entity's typical operating margin for similar contracts) if the contract-specific margin is higher than the return the entity usually generates from similar contracts.

B10   An entity's right to payment for performance completed to date need not be a present unconditional right to payment. In many cases, an entity will have an unconditional right to payment only at an agreed-upon milestone or upon complete satisfaction of the performance obligation. In assessing whether it has a right to payment for performance completed to date, an entity shall consider whether it would have an enforceable right to demand or retain payment for performance completed to date if the contract were to be terminated before completion for reasons other than the entity's failure to perform as promised.

B11   In some contracts, a customer may have a right to terminate the contract only at specified times during the life of the contract or the customer might not have any right to terminate the contract. If a customer acts to terminate a contract without having the right to terminate the contract at that time (including when a customer fails to perform its obligations as promised), the contract (or other laws) might entitle the entity to continue to transfer to the customer the goods or services promised in the contract and require the customer to pay the consideration promised in exchange for those goods or services. In those circumstances, an entity has a right to payment for performance completed to date because the entity has a right to continue to perform its obligations in accordance with the contract and to require the customer to perform its obligations (which include paying the promised consideration).

B12 In assessing the existence and enforceability of a right to payment for performance completed to date, an entity shall consider the contractual terms as well as any legislation or legal precedent that could supplement or override those contractual terms. This would include an assessment of whether:

(a) legislation, administrative practice or legal precedent confers upon the entity a right to payment for performance to date even though that right is not specified in the contract with the customer;

(b) relevant legal precedent indicates that similar rights to payment for performance completed to date in similar contracts have no binding legal effect; or

(c) an entity's customary business practices of choosing not to enforce a right to payment has resulted in the right being rendered unenforceable in that legal environment. However, notwithstanding that an entity may choose to waive its right to payment in similar contracts, an entity would continue to have a right to payment to date if, in the contract with the customer, its right to payment for performance to date remains enforceable.

B13 The payment schedule specified in a contract does not necessarily indicate whether an entity has an enforceable right to payment for performance completed to date. Although the payment schedule in a contract specifies the timing and amount of consideration that is payable by a customer, the payment schedule might not necessarily provide evidence of the entity's right to payment for performance completed to date. This is because, for example, the contract could specify that the consideration received from the customer is refundable for reasons other than the entity failing to perform as promised in the contract.

Methods for measuring progress towards complete satisfaction of a performance obligation

B14 Methods that can be used to measure an entity's progress towards complete satisfaction of a performance obligation satisfied over time in accordance with paragraphs 35–37 include the following:

(a) output methods (see paragraphs B15–B17); and

(b) input methods (see paragraphs B18–B19).

Output methods

B15 Output methods recognise revenue on the basis of direct measurements of the value to the customer of the goods or services transferred to date relative to the remaining goods or services promised under the contract. Output methods include methods such as surveys of performance completed to date, appraisals of results achieved, milestones reached, time elapsed and units produced or units delivered. When an entity evaluates whether to apply an output method to measure its progress, the entity shall consider whether the output selected would faithfully depict the entity's performance towards complete satisfaction of the performance obligation. An output method would not provide a faithful depiction of the entity's performance if the output selected would fail to measure some of the goods or services for which control has transferred to the customer. For example, output methods based on units produced or units delivered would not faithfully depict an entity's performance in satisfying a performance obligation if, at the end of the reporting period, the entity's performance has produced work in progress or finished goods controlled by the customer that are not included in the measurement of the output.

B16   As a practical expedient, if an entity has a right to consideration from a customer in an amount that corresponds directly with the value to the customer of the entity's performance completed to date (for example, a service contract in which an entity bills a fixed amount for each hour of service provided), the entity may recognise revenue in the amount to which the entity has a right to invoice.

B17   The disadvantages of output methods are that the outputs used to measure progress may not be directly observable and the information required to apply them may not be available to an entity without undue cost. Therefore, an input method may be necessary.

Input methods

B18   Input methods recognise revenue on the basis of the entity's efforts or inputs to the satisfaction of a performance obligation (for example, resources consumed, labour hours expended, costs incurred, time elapsed or machine hours used) relative to the total expected inputs to the satisfaction of that performance obligation. If the entity's efforts or inputs are expended evenly throughout the performance period, it may be appropriate for the entity to recognise revenue on a straight-line basis.

B19   A shortcoming of input methods is that there may not be a direct relationship between an entity's inputs and the transfer of control of goods or services to a customer. Therefore, an entity shall exclude from an input method the effects of any inputs that, in accordance with the objective of measuring progress in paragraph 39, do not depict the entity's performance in transferring control of goods or services to the customer. For instance, when using a cost-based input method, an adjustment to the measure of progress may be required in the following circumstances:

     (a)   When a cost incurred does not contribute to an entity's progress in satisfying the performance obligation. For example, an entity would not recognise revenue on the basis of costs incurred that are attributable to significant inefficiencies in the entity's performance that were not reflected in the price of the contract (for example, the costs of unexpected amounts of wasted materials, labour or other resources that were incurred to satisfy the performance obligation).

     (b)   When a cost incurred is not proportionate to the entity's progress in satisfying the performance obligation. In those circumstances, the best depiction of the entity's performance may be to adjust the input method to recognise revenue only to the extent of that cost incurred. For example, a faithful depiction of an entity's performance might be to recognise revenue at an amount equal to the cost of a good used to satisfy a performance obligation if the entity expects at contract inception that all of the following conditions would be met:

         (i)   the good is not distinct;

         (ii)   the customer is expected to obtain control of the good significantly before receiving services related to the good;

         (iii)   the cost of the transferred good is significant relative to the total expected costs to completely satisfy the performance obligation; and

         (iv)   the entity procures the good from a third party and is not significantly involved in designing and manufacturing the good (but the entity is acting as a principal in accordance with paragraphs B34–B38).

Sale with a right of return

B20   In some contracts, an entity transfers control of a product to a customer and also grants the customer the right to return the product for various reasons (such as dissatisfaction with the product) and receive any combination of the following:

     (a)   a full or partial refund of any consideration paid;

    (b)   a credit that can be applied against amounts owed, or that will be owed, to the entity; and

    (c)   another product in exchange.

B21   To account for the transfer of products with a right of return (and for some services that are provided subject to a refund), an entity shall recognise all of the following:

    (a)   revenue for the transferred products in the amount of consideration to which the entity expects to be entitled (therefore, revenue would not be recognised for the products expected to be returned);

    (b)   a refund liability; and

    (c)   an asset (and corresponding adjustment to cost of sales) for its right to recover products from customers on settling the refund liability.

B22   An entity's promise to stand ready to accept a returned product during the return period shall not be accounted for as a performance obligation in addition to the obligation to provide a refund.

B23   An entity shall apply the requirements in paragraphs 47–72 (including the requirements for constraining estimates of variable consideration in paragraphs 56–58) to determine the amount of consideration to which the entity expects to be entitled (ie excluding the products expected to be returned). For any amounts received (or receivable) for which an entity does not expect to be entitled, the entity shall not recognise revenue when it transfers products to customers but shall recognise those amounts received (or receivable) as a refund liability. Subsequently, at the end of each reporting period, the entity shall update its assessment of amounts for which it expects to be entitled in exchange for the transferred products and make a corresponding change to the transaction price and, therefore, in the amount of revenue recognised.

B24   An entity shall update the measurement of the refund liability at the end of each reporting period for changes in expectations about the amount of refunds. An entity shall recognise corresponding adjustments as revenue (or reductions of revenue).

B25   An asset recognised for an entity's right to recover products from a customer on settling a refund liability shall initially be measured by reference to the former carrying amount of the product (for example, inventory) less any expected costs to recover those products (including potential decreases in the value to the entity of returned products). At the end of each reporting period, an entity shall update the measurement of the asset arising from changes in expectations about products to be returned. An entity shall present the asset separately from the refund liability.

B26   Exchanges by customers of one product for another of the same type, quality, condition and price (for example, one colour or size for another) are not considered returns for the purposes of applying this Standard.

B27   Contracts in which a customer may return a defective product in exchange for a functioning product shall be evaluated in accordance with the guidance on warranties in paragraphs B28–B33.

Warranties

B28   It is common for an entity to provide (in accordance with the contract, the law or the entity's customary business practices) a warranty in connection with the sale of a product (whether a good or service). The nature of a warranty can vary significantly across industries and contracts. Some warranties provide a customer with assurance that the related product will function as the parties intended because it complies with agreed-upon specifications. Other warranties provide the customer with a service in addition to the assurance that the product complies with agreed-upon specifications.

B29   If a customer has the option to purchase a warranty separately (for example, because the warranty is priced or negotiated separately), the warranty is a distinct service because the entity promises to provide the service to the customer in addition to the product that has the functionality described in the contract. In those circumstances, an entity shall account for the promised warranty as a performance obligation in accordance with paragraphs 22–30 and allocate a portion of the transaction price to that performance obligation in accordance with paragraphs 73–86.

B30   If a customer does not have the option to purchase a warranty separately, an entity shall account for the warranty in accordance with AASB 137 *Provisions, Contingent Liabilities and Contingent Assets* unless the promised warranty, or a part of the promised warranty, provides the customer with a service in addition to the assurance that the product complies with agreed-upon specifications.

B31   In assessing whether a warranty provides a customer with a service in addition to the assurance that the product complies with agreed-upon specifications, an entity shall consider factors such as:

   (a)   Whether the warranty is required by law—if the entity is required by law to provide a warranty, the existence of that law indicates that the promised warranty is not a performance obligation because such requirements typically exist to protect customers from the risk of purchasing defective products.

   (b)   The length of the warranty coverage period—the longer the coverage period, the more likely it is that the promised warranty is a performance obligation because it is more likely to provide a service in addition to the assurance that the product complies with agreed-upon specifications.

   (c)   The nature of the tasks that the entity promises to perform—if it is necessary for an entity to perform specified tasks to provide the assurance that a product complies with agreed-upon specifications (for example, a return shipping service for a defective product), then those tasks likely do not give rise to a performance obligation.

B32   If a warranty, or a part of a warranty, provides a customer with a service in addition to the assurance that the product complies with agreed-upon specifications, the promised service is a performance obligation. Therefore, an entity shall allocate the transaction price to the product and the service. If an entity promises both an assurance-type warranty and a service-type warranty but cannot reasonably account for them separately, the entity shall account for both of the warranties together as a single performance obligation.

B33   A law that requires an entity to pay compensation if its products cause harm or damage does not give rise to a performance obligation. For example, a manufacturer might sell products in a jurisdiction in which the law holds the manufacturer liable for any damages (for example, to personal property) that might be caused by a consumer using a product for its intended purpose. Similarly, an entity's promise to indemnify the customer for liabilities and damages arising from claims of patent, copyright, trademark or other infringement by the entity's products does not give rise to a performance obligation. The entity shall account for such obligations in accordance with AASB 137.

Principal versus agent considerations

B34   When another party is involved in providing goods or services to a customer, the entity shall determine whether the nature of its promise is a performance obligation to provide the specified goods or services itself (ie the entity is a principal) or to arrange for those goods or services to be provided by the other party (ie the entity is an agent). An entity determines whether it is a principal or an agent for each specified good or service promised to the customer. A specified good or service is a distinct good or service (or a distinct bundle of goods or services) to be provided to the customer (see paragraphs 27–30). If a contract with a customer includes more than one specified good or service, an entity could be a principal for some specified goods or services and an agent for others.

B34A   To determine the nature of its promise (as described in paragraph B34), the entity shall:

> (a) identify the specified goods or services to be provided to the customer (which, for example, could be a right to a good or service to be provided by another party (see paragraph 26)); and
>
> (b) assess whether it controls (as described in paragraph 33) each specified good or service before that good or service is transferred to the customer.

B35 An entity is a principal if it controls the specified good or service before that good or service is transferred to a customer. However, an entity does not necessarily control a specified good if the entity obtains legal title to that good only momentarily before legal title is transferred to a customer. An entity that is a principal may satisfy its performance obligation to provide the specified good or service itself or it may engage another party (for example, a subcontractor) to satisfy some or all of the performance obligation on its behalf.

B35A When another party is involved in providing goods or services to a customer, an entity that is a principal obtains control of any one of the following:

> (a) a good or another asset from the other party that it then transfers to the customer.
>
> (b) a right to a service to be performed by the other party, which gives the entity the ability to direct that party to provide the service to the customer on the entity's behalf.
>
> (c) a good or service from the other party that it then combines with other goods or services in providing the specified good or service to the customer. For example, if an entity provides a significant service of integrating goods or services (see paragraph 29(a)) provided by another party into the specified good or service for which the customer has contracted, the entity controls the specified good or service before that good or service is transferred to the customer. This is because the entity first obtains control of the inputs to the specified good or service (which includes goods or services from other parties) and directs their use to create the combined output that is the specified good or service.

B35B When (or as) an entity that is a principal satisfies a performance obligation, the entity recognises revenue in the gross amount of consideration to which it expects to be entitled in exchange for the specified good or service transferred.

B36 An entity is an agent if the entity's performance obligation is to arrange for the provision of the specified good or service by another party. An entity that is an agent does not control the specified good or service provided by another party before that good or service is transferred to the customer. When (or as) an entity that is an agent satisfies a performance obligation, the entity recognises revenue in the amount of any fee or commission to which it expects to be entitled in exchange for arranging for the specified goods or services to be provided by the other party. An entity's fee or commission might be the net amount of consideration that the entity retains after paying the other party the consideration received in exchange for the goods or services to be provided by that party.

B37 Indicators that an entity controls the specified good or service before it is transferred to the customer (and is therefore a principal (see paragraph B35)) include, but are not limited to, the following:

> (a) the entity is primarily responsible for fulfilling the promise to provide the specified good or service. This typically includes responsibility for the acceptability of the specified good or service (for example, primary responsibility for the good or service meeting customer specifications). If the entity is primarily responsible for fulfilling the promise to provide the specified good or service, this may indicate that the other party involved in providing the specified good or service is acting on the entity's behalf.
>
> (b) the entity has inventory risk before the specified good or service has been transferred to a customer or after transfer of control to the customer (for example, if the customer has a right of return). For example, if the entity obtains, or commits itself to obtain, the specified good or service before obtaining a contract with a customer, that may indicate that the entity has the ability to

AASB

direct the use of, and obtain substantially all of the remaining benefits from, the good or service before it is transferred to the customer.

(c) the entity has discretion in establishing the price for the specified good or service. Establishing the price that the customer pays for the specified good or service may indicate that the entity has the ability to direct the use of that good or service and obtain substantially all of the remaining benefits. However, an agent can have discretion in establishing prices in some cases. For example, an agent may have some flexibility in setting prices in order to generate additional revenue from its service of arranging for goods or services to be provided by other parties to customers.

B37A The indicators in paragraph B37 may be more or less relevant to the assessment of control depending on the nature of the specified good or service and the terms and conditions of the contract. In addition, different indicators may provide more persuasive evidence in different contracts.

B38 If another entity assumes the entity's performance obligations and contractual rights in the contract so that the entity is no longer obliged to satisfy the performance obligation to transfer the specified good or service to the customer (ie the entity is no longer acting as the principal), the entity shall not recognise revenue for that performance obligation. Instead, the entity shall evaluate whether to recognise revenue for satisfying a performance obligation to obtain a contract for the other party (ie whether the entity is acting as an agent).

Customer options for additional goods and services

B39 Customer options to acquire additional goods or services for free or at a discount come in many forms, including sales incentives, customer award credits (or points), contract renewal options or other discounts on future goods or services.

B40 If, in a contract, an entity grants a customer the option to acquire additional goods or services, that option gives rise to a performance obligation in the contract only if the option provides a material right to the customer that it would not receive without entering into that contract (for example, a discount that is incremental to the range of discounts typically given for those goods or services to that class of customer in that geographical area or market). If the option provides a material right to the customer, the customer in effect pays the entity in advance for future goods or services and the entity recognises revenue when those future goods or services are transferred or when the option expires.

B41 If a customer has the option to acquire an additional good or service at a price that would reflect the stand-alone selling price for that good or service, that option does not provide the customer with a material right even if the option can be exercised only by entering into a previous contract. In those cases, the entity has made a marketing offer that it shall account for in accordance with this Standard only when the customer exercises the option to purchase the additional goods or services.

B42 Paragraph 74 requires an entity to allocate the transaction price to performance obligations on a relative stand-alone selling price basis. If the stand-alone selling price for a customer's option to acquire additional goods or services is not directly observable, an entity shall estimate it. That estimate shall reflect the discount that the customer would obtain when exercising the option, adjusted for both of the following:

(a) any discount that the customer could receive without exercising the option; and

(b) the likelihood that the option will be exercised.

B43 If a customer has a material right to acquire future goods or services and those goods or services are similar to the original goods or services in the contract and are provided in accordance with the terms of the original contract, then an entity may, as a practical alternative to estimating the stand-alone selling price of the option, allocate the transaction price to the optional goods or services by reference to the goods or services expected to be provided and the corresponding expected consideration. Typically, those types of options are for contract renewals.

Customers' unexercised rights

B44 In accordance with paragraph 106, upon receipt of a prepayment from a customer, an entity shall recognise a contract liability in the amount of the prepayment for its performance obligation to transfer, or to stand ready to transfer, goods or services in the future. An entity shall derecognise that contract liability (and recognise revenue) when it transfers those goods or services and, therefore, satisfies its performance obligation.

B45 A customer's non-refundable prepayment to an entity gives the customer a right to receive a good or service in the future (and obliges the entity to stand ready to transfer a good or service). However, customers may not exercise all of their contractual rights. Those unexercised rights are often referred to as breakage.

B46 If an entity expects to be entitled to a breakage amount in a contract liability, the entity shall recognise the expected breakage amount as revenue in proportion to the pattern of rights exercised by the customer. If an entity does not expect to be entitled to a breakage amount, the entity shall recognise the expected breakage amount as revenue when the likelihood of the customer exercising its remaining rights becomes remote. To determine whether an entity expects to be entitled to a breakage amount, the entity shall consider the requirements in paragraphs 56–58 on constraining estimates of variable consideration.

B47 An entity shall recognise a liability (and not revenue) for any consideration received that is attributable to a customer's unexercised rights for which the entity is required to remit to another party, for example, a government entity in accordance with applicable unclaimed property laws.

Non-refundable upfront fees (and some related costs)

B48 In some contracts, an entity charges a customer a non-refundable upfront fee at or near contract inception. Examples include joining fees in health club membership contracts, activation fees in telecommunication contracts, setup fees in some services contracts and initial fees in some supply contracts.

B49 To identify performance obligations in such contracts, an entity shall assess whether the fee relates to the transfer of a promised good or service. In many cases, even though a non-refundable upfront fee relates to an activity that the entity is required to undertake at or near contract inception to fulfil the contract, that activity does not result in the transfer of a promised good or service to the customer (see paragraph 25). Instead, the upfront fee is an advance payment for future goods or services and, therefore, would be recognised as revenue when those future goods or services are provided. The revenue recognition period would extend beyond the initial contractual period if the entity grants the customer the option to renew the contract and that option provides the customer with a material right as described in paragraph B40.

B50 If the non-refundable upfront fee relates to a good or service, the entity shall evaluate whether to account for the good or service as a separate performance obligation in accordance with paragraphs 22–30.

B51 An entity may charge a non-refundable fee in part as compensation for costs incurred in setting up a contract (or other administrative tasks as described in paragraph 25). If those setup activities do not satisfy a performance obligation, the entity shall disregard those activities (and related costs) when measuring progress in accordance with paragraph B19. That is because the costs of setup activities do not depict the transfer of services to the customer. The entity shall assess whether costs incurred in setting up a contract have resulted in an asset that shall be recognised in accordance with paragraph 95.

Licensing

B52   A licence establishes a customer's rights to the intellectual property of an entity. Licences of intellectual property may include, but are not limited to, licences of any of the following:

    (a)   software and technology;

    (b)   motion pictures, music and other forms of media and entertainment;

    (c)   franchises; and

    (d)   patents, trademarks and copyrights.

B53   In addition to a promise to grant a licence (or licences) to a customer, an entity may also promise to transfer other goods or services to the customer. Those promises may be explicitly stated in the contract or implied by an entity's customary business practices, published policies or specific statements (see paragraph 24). As with other types of contracts, when a contract with a customer includes a promise to grant a licence (or licences) in addition to other promised goods or services, an entity applies paragraphs 22–30 to identify each of the performance obligations in the contract.

B54   If the promise to grant a licence is not distinct from other promised goods or services in the contract in accordance with paragraphs 26–30, an entity shall account for the promise to grant a licence and those other promised goods or services together as a single performance obligation. Examples of licences that are not distinct from other goods or services promised in the contract include the following:

    (a)   a licence that forms a component of a tangible good and that is integral to the functionality of the good; and

    (b)   a licence that the customer can benefit from only in conjunction with a related service (such as an online service provided by the entity that enables, by granting a licence, the customer to access content).

B55   If the licence is not distinct, an entity shall apply paragraphs 31–38 to determine whether the performance obligation (which includes the promised licence) is a performance obligation that is satisfied over time or satisfied at a point in time.

B56   If the promise to grant the licence is distinct from the other promised goods or services in the contract and, therefore, the promise to grant the licence is a separate performance obligation, an entity shall determine whether the licence transfers to a customer either at a point in time or over time. In making this determination, an entity shall consider whether the nature of the entity's promise in granting the licence to a customer is to provide the customer with either:

    (a)   a right to access the entity's intellectual property as it exists throughout the licence period; or

    (b)   a right to use the entity's intellectual property as it exists at the point in time at which the licence is granted.

Determining the nature of the entity's promise

B57   [Deleted]

B58   The nature of an entity's promise in granting a licence is a promise to provide a right to access the entity's intellectual property if all of the following criteria are met:

    (a)   the contract requires, or the customer reasonably expects, that the entity will undertake activities that significantly affect the intellectual property to which the customer has rights (see paragraphs B59 and B59A);

    (b)   the rights granted by the licence directly expose the customer to any positive or negative effects of the entity's activities identified in paragraph B58(a); and

    (c)   those activities do not result in the transfer of a good or a service to the customer as those activities occur (see paragraph 25).

B59   Factors that may indicate that a customer could reasonably expect that an entity will undertake activities that significantly affect the intellectual property include the entity's customary business practices, published policies or specific statements. Although not determinative, the existence of a shared economic interest (for example, a sales-based royalty) between the entity and the customer related to the intellectual property to which the customer has rights may also indicate that the customer could reasonably expect that the entity will undertake such activities.

B59A   An entity's activities significantly affect the intellectual property to which the customer has rights when either:

   (a)   those activities are expected to significantly change the form (for example, the design or content) or the functionality (for example, the ability to perform a function or task) of the intellectual property; or

   (b)   the ability of the customer to obtain benefit from the intellectual property is substantially derived from, or dependent upon, those activities. For example, the benefit from a brand is often derived from, or dependent upon, the entity's ongoing activities that support or maintain the value of the intellectual property.

   Accordingly, if the intellectual property to which the customer has rights has significant stand-alone functionality, a substantial portion of the benefit of that intellectual property is derived from that functionality. Consequently, the ability of the customer to obtain benefit from that intellectual property would not be significantly affected by the entity's activities unless those activities significantly change its form or functionality. Types of intellectual property that often have significant stand-alone functionality include software, biological compounds or drug formulas, and completed media content (for example, films, television shows and music recordings).

B60   If the criteria in paragraph B58 are met, an entity shall account for the promise to grant a licence as a performance obligation satisfied over time because the customer will simultaneously receive and consume the benefit from the entity's performance of providing access to its intellectual property as the performance occurs (see paragraph 35(a)). An entity shall apply paragraphs 39–45 to select an appropriate method to measure its progress towards complete satisfaction of that performance obligation to provide access.

B61   If the criteria in paragraph B58 are not met, the nature of an entity's promise is to provide a right to use the entity's intellectual property as that intellectual property exists (in terms of form and functionality) at the point in time at which the licence is granted to the customer. This means that the customer can direct the use of, and obtain substantially all of the remaining benefits from, the licence at the point in time at which the licence transfers. An entity shall account for the promise to provide a right to use the entity's intellectual property as a performance obligation satisfied at a point in time. An entity shall apply paragraph 38 to determine the point in time at which the licence transfers to the customer. However, revenue cannot be recognised for a licence that provides a right to use the entity's intellectual property before the beginning of the period during which the customer is able to use and benefit from the licence. For example, if a software licence period begins before an entity provides (or otherwise makes available) to the customer a code that enables the customer to immediately use the software, the entity would not recognise revenue before that code has been provided (or otherwise made available).

B62   An entity shall disregard the following factors when determining whether a licence provides a right to access the entity's intellectual property or a right to use the entity's intellectual property:

   (a)   Restrictions of time, geographical region or use—those restrictions define the attributes of the promised licence, rather than define whether the entity satisfies its performance obligation at a point in time or over time.

   (b)   Guarantees provided by the entity that it has a valid patent to intellectual property and that it will defend that patent from unauthorised use—a promise to defend a patent right is not a performance obligation because the act of defending a patent protects the value of the entity's intellectual property assets and provides

Bill-and-hold arrangements

B79 A bill-and-hold arrangement is a contract under which an entity bills a customer for a product but the entity retains physical possession of the product until it is transferred to the customer at a point in time in the future. For example, a customer may request an entity to enter into such a contract because of the customer's lack of available space for the product or because of delays in the customer's production schedules.

B80 An entity shall determine when it has satisfied its performance obligation to transfer a product by evaluating when a customer obtains control of that product (see paragraph 38). For some contracts, control is transferred either when the product is delivered to the customer's site or when the product is shipped, depending on the terms of the contract (including delivery and shipping terms). However, for some contracts, a customer may obtain control of a product even though that product remains in an entity's physical possession. In that case, the customer has the ability to direct the use of, and obtain substantially all of the remaining benefits from, the product even though it has decided not to exercise its right to take physical possession of that product. Consequently, the entity does not control the product. Instead, the entity provides custodial services to the customer over the customer's asset.

B81 In addition to applying the requirements in paragraph 38, for a customer to have obtained control of a product in a bill-and-hold arrangement, all of the following criteria must be met:

(a) the reason for the bill-and-hold arrangement must be substantive (for example, the customer has requested the arrangement);

(b) the product must be identified separately as belonging to the customer;

(c) the product currently must be ready for physical transfer to the customer; and

(d) the entity cannot have the ability to use the product or to direct it to another customer.

B82 If an entity recognises revenue for the sale of a product on a bill-and-hold basis, the entity shall consider whether it has remaining performance obligations (for example, for custodial services) in accordance with paragraphs 22–30 to which the entity shall allocate a portion of the transaction price in accordance with paragraphs 73–86.

Customer acceptance

B83 In accordance with paragraph 38(e), a customer's acceptance of an asset may indicate that the customer has obtained control of the asset. Customer acceptance clauses allow a customer to cancel a contract or require an entity to take remedial action if a good or service does not meet agreed-upon specifications. An entity shall consider such clauses when evaluating when a customer obtains control of a good or service.

B84 If an entity can objectively determine that control of a good or service has been transferred to the customer in accordance with the agreed-upon specifications in the contract, then customer acceptance is a formality that would not affect the entity's determination of when the customer has obtained control of the good or service. For example, if the customer acceptance clause is based on meeting specified size and weight characteristics, an entity would be able to determine whether those criteria have been met before receiving confirmation of the customer's acceptance. The entity's experience with contracts for similar goods or services may provide evidence that a good or service provided to the customer is in accordance with the agreed-upon specifications in the contract. If revenue is recognised before customer acceptance, the entity still must consider whether there are any remaining performance obligations (for example, installation of equipment) and evaluate whether to account for them separately.

B85 However, if an entity cannot objectively determine that the good or service provided to the customer is in accordance with the agreed-upon specifications in the contract, then the entity would not be able to conclude that the customer has obtained control until the entity receives the customer's acceptance. That is because in that circumstance the entity cannot determine that the customer has the ability to direct the use of, and obtain substantially all of the remaining benefits from, the good or service.

B86 If an entity delivers products to a customer for trial or evaluation purposes and the customer is not committed to pay any consideration until the trial period lapses, control of the product is not transferred to the customer until either the customer accepts the product or the trial period lapses.

Disclosure of disaggregated revenue

B87 Paragraph 114 requires an entity to disaggregate revenue from contracts with customers into categories that depict how the nature, amount, timing and uncertainty of revenue and cash flows are affected by economic factors. Consequently, the extent to which an entity's revenue is disaggregated for the purposes of this disclosure depends on the facts and circumstances that pertain to the entity's contracts with customers. Some entities may need to use more than one type of category to meet the objective in paragraph 114 for disaggregating revenue. Other entities may meet the objective by using only one type of category to disaggregate revenue.

B88 When selecting the type of category (or categories) to use to disaggregate revenue, an entity shall consider how information about the entity's revenue has been presented for other purposes, including all of the following:

(a) disclosures presented outside the financial statements (for example, in earnings releases, annual reports or investor presentations);

(b) information regularly reviewed by the chief operating decision maker for evaluating the financial performance of operating segments; and

(c) other information that is similar to the types of information identified in paragraph B88(a) and (b) and that is used by the entity or users of the entity's financial statements to evaluate the entity's financial performance or make resource allocation decisions.

B89 Examples of categories that might be appropriate include, but are not limited to, all of the following:

(a) type of good or service (for example, major product lines);

(b) geographical region (for example, country or region);

(c) market or type of customer (for example, government and non-government customers);

(d) type of contract (for example, fixed-price and time-and-materials contracts);

(e) contract duration (for example, short-term and long-term contracts);

(f) timing of transfer of goods or services (for example, revenue from goods or services transferred to customers at a point in time and revenue from goods or services transferred over time); and

(g) sales channels (for example, goods sold directly to consumers and goods sold through intermediaries).

APPENDIX C
EFFECTIVE DATE AND TRANSITION

This appendix is an integral part of AASB 15 and has the same authority as the other parts of AASB 15.

Effective date

C1   An entity shall apply this Standard for annual reporting periods beginning on or after 1 January 2018. Earlier application is permitted. If an entity applies this Standard earlier, it shall disclose that fact.

AusC1.1   Notwithstanding paragraph C1, this Standard applies to not-for-profit entities for annual reporting periods beginning on or after 1 January 2019. Earlier application is permitted, provided that AASB 1058 *Income of Not-for-Profit Entities* is also applied to the same period. If a not-for-profit entity applies this Standard earlier, it shall disclose that fact.

C1B   AASB 2016-3 *Amendments to Australian Accounting Standards – Clarifications to AASB 15*, issued in May 2016, amended paragraphs 26, 27, 29, B1, B34–B38, B52–B53, B58, C2, C5 and C7, deleted paragraph B57 and added paragraphs B34A, B35A, B35B, B37A, B59A, B63A, B63B, C7A and C8A. An entity shall apply those amendments for annual reporting periods beginning on or after 1 January 2018. Earlier application is permitted. If an entity applies those amendments for an earlier period, it shall disclose that fact.

Transition

C2   For the purposes of the transition requirements in paragraphs C3–C8A:

    (a)   the date of initial application is the start of the reporting period in which an entity first applies this Standard; and

    (b)   a completed contract is a contract for which the entity has transferred all of the goods or services identified in accordance with AASB 111 *Construction Contracts*, AASB 118 *Revenue* and related Interpretations.

C3   An entity shall apply this Standard using one of the following two methods:

    (a)   retrospectively to each prior reporting period presented in accordance with AASB 108 *Accounting Policies, Changes in Accounting Estimates and Errors*, subject to the expedients in paragraph C5; or

    (b)   retrospectively with the cumulative effect of initially applying this Standard recognised at the date of initial application in accordance with paragraphs C7–C8.

C4   Notwithstanding the requirements of paragraph 28 of AASB 108, when this Standard is first applied, an entity need only present the quantitative information required by paragraph 28(f) of AASB 108 for the annual reporting period immediately preceding the first annual reporting period for which this Standard is applied (the 'immediately preceding period') and only if the entity applies this Standard retrospectively in accordance with paragraph C3(a). An entity may also present this information for the current period or for earlier comparative periods, but is not required to do so.

C5   An entity may use one or more of the following practical expedients when applying this Standard retrospectively in accordance with paragraph C3(a):

    (a)   for completed contracts, an entity need not restate contracts that:

        (i)   begin and end within the same annual reporting period; or

        (ii)   are completed contracts at the beginning of the earliest period presented.

    (b)   for completed contracts that have variable consideration, an entity may use the transaction price at the date the contract was completed rather than estimating variable consideration amounts in the comparative reporting periods.

    (c)   for contracts that were modified before the beginning of the earliest period presented, an entity need not retrospectively restate the contract for those contract modifications in accordance with paragraphs 20–21. Instead, an entity shall reflect the aggregate effect of all of the modifications that occur before the beginning of the earliest period presented when:

      (i)   identifying the satisfied and unsatisfied performance obligations;

      (ii)   determining the transaction price; and

      (iii) allocating the transaction price to the satisfied and unsatisfied performance obligations.

  (d)   for all reporting periods presented before the date of initial application, an entity need not disclose the amount of the transaction price allocated to the remaining performance obligations and an explanation of when the entity expects to recognise that amount as revenue (see paragraph 120).

C6   For any of the practical expedients in paragraph C5 that an entity uses, the entity shall apply that expedient consistently to all contracts within all reporting periods presented. In addition, the entity shall disclose all of the following information:

  (a)   the expedients that have been used; and

  (b)   to the extent reasonably possible, a qualitative assessment of the estimated effect of applying each of those expedients.

C7   If an entity elects to apply this Standard retrospectively in accordance with paragraph C3(b), the entity shall recognise the cumulative effect of initially applying this Standard as an adjustment to the opening balance of retained earnings (or other component of equity, as appropriate) of the annual reporting period that includes the date of initial application. Under this transition method, an entity may elect to apply this Standard retrospectively only to contracts that are not completed contracts at the date of initial application (for example, 1 January 2018 for an entity with a 31 December year-end).

C7A An entity applying this Standard retrospectively in accordance with paragraph C3(b) may also use the practical expedient described in paragraph C5(c), either:

  (a)   for all contract modifications that occur before the beginning of the earliest period presented; or

  (b)   for all contract modifications that occur before the date of initial application.

If an entity uses this practical expedient, the entity shall apply the expedient consistently to all contracts and disclose the information required by paragraph C6.

C8   For reporting periods that include the date of initial application, an entity shall provide both of the following additional disclosures if this Standard is applied retrospectively in accordance with paragraph C3(b):

  (a)   the amount by which each financial statement line item is affected in the current reporting period by the application of this Standard as compared to AASB 111, AASB 118 and related Interpretations that were in effect before the change; and

  (b)   an explanation of the reasons for significant changes identified in C8(a).

C8A An entity shall apply AASB 2016-3 *Amendments to Australian Accounting Standards – Clarifications to AASB 15* (see paragraph C1B) retrospectively in accordance with AASB 108. In applying the amendments retrospectively, an entity shall apply the amendments as if they had been included in AASB 15 at the date of initial application. Consequently, an entity does not apply the amendments to reporting periods or to contracts to which the requirements of AASB 15 are not applied in accordance with paragraphs C2–C8. For example, if an entity applies AASB 15 in accordance with paragraph C3(b) only to contracts that are not completed contracts at the date of initial application, the entity does not restate the completed contracts at the date of initial application of AASB 15 for the effects of these amendments.

References to AASB 9

C9   If an entity applies this Standard but does not yet apply AASB 9 *Financial Instruments*, any reference in this Standard to AASB 9 shall be read as a reference to AASB 139 *Financial Instruments: Recognition and Measurement*.

Withdrawal of other Standards

C10   [Deleted by the AASB]

AusC10.1   When applied or operative, this Standard supersedes:

     (a)   AASB 111 *Construction Contracts*;

     (b)   AASB 118 *Revenue*;

     (c)   Interpretation 13 *Customer Loyalty Programmes*;

     (d)   Interpretation 15 *Agreements for the Construction of Real Estate*;

     (e)   Interpretation 18 *Transfers of Assets from Customers*;

     (f)   Interpretation 131 *Revenue – Barter Transactions Involving Advertising Services*; and

     (g)   Interpretation 1042 *Subscriber Acquisition Costs in the Telecommunications Industry*.

APPENDIX E
AUSTRALIAN REDUCED DISCLOSURE REQUIREMENTS

This appendix is an integral part of AASB 15 and has the same authority as the other parts of AASB 15.

AusE1   **The following do not apply to entities preparing general purpose financial statements under Australian Accounting Standards – Reduced Disclosure Requirements:**

     (a)   **paragraphs 115, 116(b), 116(c), 117, 118, 120–122, 124(b), 126, 127(a); and**

     (b)   **in paragraph 128(a), the text ", by main category of asset (for example, costs to obtain contracts with customers, pre-contract costs and setup costs)".**

     Entities applying Australian Accounting Standards – Reduced Disclosure Requirements may elect to comply with some or all of these excluded requirements.

AusE2   The requirements that do not apply to entities preparing general purpose financial statements under Australian Accounting Standards – Reduced Disclosure Requirements are also identified in this Standard by shading of the relevant text.

COMPILATION DETAILS

Accounting Standard AASB 15 *Revenue from Contracts with Customers* as amended

Compilation details are not part of AASB 15.

This compiled Standard applies to annual periods beginning on or after 1 January 2018 but before 1 January 2019 for for-profit entities. It takes into account amendments up to and including 9 December 2016 and was prepared on 20 March 2018 by the staff of the Australian Accounting Standards Board (AASB).

This compilation is not a separate Accounting Standard made by the AASB. Instead, it is a representation of AASB 15 (December 2014) as amended by other Accounting Standards, which are listed in the Table below.

Table of Standards

Standard	Date made	FRL identifier	Commencement date	Effective date *(annual periods ... on or after ...)*	Application, saving or transitional provisions
AASB 15	12 Dec 2014	F2015L00115	12 Dec 2014	*(beginning)* 1 Jan 2018	see (a) below
AASB 2015-8	22 Oct 2015	F2015L01840	31 Dec 2016	*(beginning)* 1 Jan 2017	see (b) below
AASB 16	23 Feb 2016	F2016L00233	31 Dec 2018	*(beginning)* 1 Jan 2019	not compiled*
AASB 2016-3	11 May 2016	F2016L00825	31 Dec 2017	*(beginning)* 1 Jan 2018	see (c) below
AASB 1058	9 Dec 2016	F2017L00042	31 Dec 2018	*(beginning)* 1 Jan 2019	not compiled*
AASB 2016-7	9 Dec 2016	F2017L00043	31 Dec 2016	*(beginning)* 1 Jan 2017	see (d) below
AASB 2016-8	9 Dec 2016	F2017L00044	31 Dec 2018	*(beginning)* 1 Jan 2019	not compiled*
AASB 17	19 Jul 2017	F2017L01184	31 Dec 2020	*(beginning)* 1 Jan 2021	not compiled*

*   The amendments made by this Standard are not included in this compilation, which presents the principal Standard as applicable to annual reporting periods beginning on or after 1 January 2018 but before 1 January 2019 for for-profit entities.

(a)   AASB 15 applies to annual periods beginning on or after 1 January 2018 (instead of 1 January 2017) as a result of amendments made by AASB 2015-8 *Amendments to Australian Accounting Standards – Effective Date of AASB 15.*

(b)   Entities may elect to apply this Standard to annual periods beginning before 1 January 2017.

(c)   Entities may elect to apply this Standard to annual periods beginning before 1 January 2018.

(d)   AASB 2016-7 deferred the effective date of AASB 15 (and its consequential amendments in AASB 2014-5) for not-for-profit entities to annual reporting periods beginning on or after 1 January 2019, instead of 1 January 2018. However, earlier application is permitted, provided that AASB 1058 *Income of Not-for-Profit Entities* is also applied.

Table of amendments

Paragraph affected	How affected	By ... [paragraph/page]
Aus4.1 (and preceding heading)	deleted	AASB 2015-8 [9]
Aus4.2-Aus4.3	deleted	AASB 2015-8 [7]
Aus4.4	renumbered as AusC10.1	AASB 2015-8 [10]
Aus4.5-Aus4.6 (and preceding heading)	deleted	AASB 2015-8 [11]
Aus4.7 (preceding heading)	deleted	AASB 2015-8 [12]
Aus4.7	renumbered as Aus129.1	AASB 2015-8 [12]
26-27	amended	AASB 2016-3 [page 5]
29	amended	AASB 2016-3 [page 6]
Aus129.1 (preceding heading)	added	AASB 2015-8 [12]
B1	amended	AASB 2016-3 [page 7]
B34-B38	amended	AASB 2016-3 [page 7]
B34A	added	AASB 2016-3 [page 7]
B35A-B35B	added	AASB 2016-3 [page 7]

(Continued)

(Continued)

Paragraph affected	How affected	By ... [paragraph/page]
B37A	added	AASB 2016-3 [page 8]
B52-B53	amended	AASB 2016-3 [page 8]
B57	deleted	AASB 2016-3 [page 9]
B58	amended	AASB 2016-3 [page 9]
B59A	added	AASB 2016-3 [page 10]
B63A-B63B	added	AASB 2016-3 [page 10]
C1	added	AASB 2015-8 [7]
AusC1.1	added	AASB 2016-7 [4]
C1B	added	AASB 2016-3 [page 11]
C2	amended	AASB 2016-3 [page 11]
C5	amended	AASB 2016-3 [page 11]
C7	amended	AASB 2016-3 [page 12]
C7A	added	AASB 2016-3 [page 12]
C8A	added	AASB 2016-3 [page 12]
Appendix E	added	AASB 2015-8 [11]

DELETED IFRS 15 TEXT

Deleted IFRS 15 text is not part of AASB 15.

C10   This Standard supersedes the following Standards:

    (a)   IAS 11 *Construction Contracts*;

    (b)   IAS 18 *Revenue*;

    (c)   IFRIC 13 *Customer Loyalty Programmes*;

    (d)   IFRIC 15 *Agreements for the Construction of Real Estate*;

    (e)   IFRIC 18 *Transfers of Assets from Customers*; and

    (f)   SIC-31 *Revenue—Barter Transactions Involving Advertising Services.*

AASB 16
Leases

(Issued February 2016)

This note is not part of Accounting Standard AASB 16.

The following unincorporated amendments are not included in this Standard.

- AASB 2018-4 *Amendments to Australian Accounting Standards — Australian Implementation Guidance for Not-for-Profit Public Sector Licensors.* This standard makes amendments to AASB *15 Revenue from Contracts with Customers* and AASB 16 *Leases.* It applies to annual periods beginning on or after 1 January 2019, but earlier application is permitted.

- AASB 2018-3 *Amendments to Australian Accounting Standards — Reduced Disclosure Requirements.* This Standard makes amendments to AASB 16 *Leases* and AASB 1058 Income of *Not-for-Profit Entities.* These amendments establish Reduced Disclosure Requirements for entities preparing general purpose financial statements under *Australian Accounting Standards — Reduced Disclosure Requirements.* It applies to annual periods beginning on or after 1 January 2019, but earlier application is permitted.

- AASB 1058 *Income of Not-for-Profit Entities* — Appendix D sets out the amendments to other Australian Accounting Standards that are a consequence of the AASB issuing this Standard. It is applicable from 1 January 2019. Earlier application is permitted, but amendments to AASB 117 apply before 1 January 2019 only if AASB 1058 is also applied to an earlier period. In addition, AASB 1 and AASB 16 amendments are applied to an earlier period only if AASB 16 is also applied to that period.

- AASB 1059 *Service Concession Arrangements: Grantors* — Appendix D sets out the amendments to other AASBs that are a consequence of the AASB issuing this Standard. It is applicable from 1 January 2019, but earlier application is permitted.

Entities early-adopting any amendments with later application dates will need to refer to the amending Standards that have not yet been incorporated into compilations. The abovementioned unincorporated amendments may be located on the AASB website at www.aasb.gov.au or on the Federal Register of Legislation website at www.legislation.gov.au.

CONTENTS

PREFACE

COMPARISON WITH IFRS 16

ACCOUNTING STANDARD

AASB 16 *LEASES*

APPENDICES

A. DEFINED TERMS

B. APPLICATION GUIDANCE

C. EFFECTIVE DATE AND TRANSITION

D. AMENDMENTS TO OTHER STANDARDS

DELETED IFRS 16 TEXT

ILLUSTRATIVE EXAMPLES (available on the AASB website)

BASIS FOR CONCLUSIONS ON IFRS 16 (available on the AASB website)

Australian Accounting Standard AASB 16 *Leases* is set out in paragraphs 1 – Aus103.1 and Appendices A – D. All the paragraphs have equal authority. Paragraphs in **bold type** state the main principles. Terms defined in Appendix A are in *italics* the first time they appear in the Standard. AASB 16 is to be read in the context of other Australian Accounting Standards, including AASB 1048 *Interpretation of Standards*, which identifies the Australian Accounting Interpretations, and AASB 1057 *Application of Australian Accounting Standards*. In the absence of explicit guidance, AASB 108 *Accounting Policies, Changes in Accounting Estimates and Errors* provides a basis for selecting and applying accounting policies.

PREFACE

Introduction

The Australian Accounting Standards Board (AASB) develops, issues and maintains Australian Accounting Standards, including Interpretations. The AASB is an Australian Government agency under the *Australian Securities and Investments Commission Act 2001*.

AASB 1057 *Application of Australian Accounting Standards* identifies the application of Standards to entities and financial statements. AASB 1053 *Application of Tiers of Australian Accounting Standards* establishes a differential reporting framework consisting of two tiers of reporting requirements for preparing general purpose financial statements.

What this Standard requires

AASB 16 introduces a single lessee accounting model and requires a lessee to recognise assets and liabilities for all leases with a term of more than 12 months, unless the underlying asset is of low value. A lessee is required to recognise a right-of-use asset representing its right to use the underlying leased asset and a lease liability representing its obligations to make lease payments.

A lessee measures right-of-use assets similarly to other non-financial assets (such as property, plant and equipment) and lease liabilities similarly to other financial liabilities. As a consequence, a lessee recognises depreciation of the right-of-use asset and interest on the lease liability, and also classifies cash repayments of the lease liability into a principal portion and an interest portion and presents them in the statement of cash flows applying AASB 107 *Statement of Cash Flows*.

Assets and liabilities arising from a lease are initially measured on a present value basis. The measurement includes non-cancellable lease payments (including inflation-linked payments), and also includes payments to be made in optional periods if the lessee is reasonably certain to exercise an option to extend the lease, or not to exercise an option to terminate the lease.

AASB 16 contains disclosure requirements for lessees. Lessees will need to apply judgement in deciding upon the information to disclose to meet the objective of providing a basis for users of financial statements to assess the effect that leases have on the financial position, financial performance and cash flows of the lessee.

AASB 16 substantially carries forward the lessor accounting requirements in AASB 117 *Leases*. Accordingly, a lessor continues to classify its leases as operating leases or finance leases, and to account for those two types of leases differently.

AASB 16 also requires enhanced disclosures to be provided by lessors that will improve information disclosed about a lessor's risk exposure, particularly to residual value risk.

Application date

This Standard is applicable to annual reporting periods beginning on or after 1 January 2019 (see paragraph C1). Earlier application is permitted for entities that apply AASB 15 *Revenue from Contracts with Customers* at or before the date of initial application of this Standard.

Why we have issued this Standard

Leasing is an important activity for many entities. It is a means of gaining access to assets, of obtaining finance and of reducing an entity's exposure to the risks of asset ownership. The prevalence of leasing means that it is important that users of financial statements have a complete and understandable picture of an entity's leasing activities.

The previous accounting model for leases required lessees and lessors to classify their leases as either finances leases or operating leases and account for those two types of leases differently. That model was criticised for failing to meet the needs of users of financial statements because it did not always provide a faithful representation of leasing transactions. In particular, it did not require lessees to recognise assets and liabilities arising from operating leases.

Accordingly, the International Accounting Standards Board (IASB) and the US national standard-setter, the Financial Accounting Standards Board (FASB), initiated a joint project to develop a new approach to lease accounting that requires a lessee to recognise assets and liabilities for the rights and obligations created by leases. This approach will result in a more faithful representation of a lessee's assets and liabilities and, together with enhanced disclosures, will provide greater transparency of a lessee's financial leverage and capital employed.

Reduced disclosure requirements

Disclosure requirements under Tier 2 will be determined through a separate due process with amendments being made subsequently to this Standard as required.

COMPARISON WITH IFRS 16

AASB 16 *Leases* incorporates IFRS 16 *Leases* issued by the International Accounting Standards Board (IASB). Australian-specific paragraphs (which are not included in IFRS 16) are identified with the prefix "Aus". Paragraphs that apply only to not-for-profit entities begin by identifying their limited applicability.

Tier 1

For-profit entities complying with AASB 16 also comply with IFRS 16.

Not-for-profit entities' compliance with IFRS 16 will depend on whether any "Aus" paragraphs that specifically apply to not-for-profit entities provide additional guidance or contain applicable requirements that are inconsistent with IFRS 16.

AASB 1053 *Application of Tiers of Australian Accounting Standards* explains the two tiers of reporting requirements.

ACCOUNTING STANDARD AASB 16

The Australian Accounting Standards Board makes Accounting Standard AASB 16 *Leases* under section 334 of the *Corporations Act 2001*.

Dated 23 February 2016

Kris Peach
Chair – AASB

ACCOUNTING STANDARD AASB 16
LEASES

Objective

1   This Standard sets out the principles for the recognition, measurement, presentation and disclosure of *leases*. The objective is to ensure that *lessees* and

lessors provide relevant information in a manner that faithfully represents those transactions. This information gives a basis for users of financial statements to assess the effect that leases have on the financial position, financial performance and cash flows of an entity.

2   An entity shall consider the terms and conditions of *contracts* and all relevant facts and circumstances when applying this Standard. An entity shall apply this Standard consistently to contracts with similar characteristics and in similar circumstances.

Scope

3   An entity shall apply this Standard to all leases, including leases of *right-of-use assets* in a *sublease*, except for:

(a)   leases to explore for or use minerals, oil, natural gas and similar non-regenerative resources;

(b)   leases of biological assets within the scope of AASB 141 *Agriculture* held by a lessee;

(c)   service concession arrangements within the scope of Interpretation 12 *Service Concession Arrangements*;

(d)   licences of intellectual property granted by a lessor within the scope of AASB 15 *Revenue from Contracts with Customers*; and

(e)   rights held by a lessee under licensing agreements within the scope of AASB 138 *Intangible Assets* for such items as motion picture films, video recordings, plays, manuscripts, patents and copyrights.

4   A lessee may, but is not required to, apply this Standard to leases of intangible assets other than those described in paragraph 3(e).

Recognition exemptions (paragraphs B3–B8)

5   A lessee may elect not to apply the requirements in paragraphs 22–49 to:

(a)   *short-term leases*; and

(b)   leases for which the *underlying asset* is of low value (as described in paragraphs B3–B8).

6   If a lessee elects not to apply the requirements in paragraphs 22–49 to either short-term leases or leases for which the underlying asset is of low value, the lessee shall recognise the *lease payments* associated with those leases as an expense on either a straight-line basis over the *lease term* or another systematic basis. The lessee shall apply another systematic basis if that basis is more representative of the pattern of the lessee's benefit.

7   If a lessee accounts for short-term leases applying paragraph 6, the lessee shall consider the lease to be a new lease for the purposes of this Standard if:

(a)   there is a *lease modification*; or

(b)   there is any change in the lease term (for example, the lessee exercises an option not previously included in its determination of the lease term).

8   The election for short-term leases shall be made by class of underlying asset to which the right of use relates. A class of underlying asset is a grouping of underlying assets of a similar nature and use in an entity's operations. The election for leases for which the underlying asset is of low value can be made on a lease-by-lease basis.

Identifying a lease (paragraphs B9–B33)

9   At inception of a contract, an entity shall assess whether the contract is, or contains, a lease. A contract is, or contains, a lease if the contract conveys the right to control the use of an identified asset for a period of time in exchange for

consideration. **Paragraphs B9–B31 set out guidance on the assessment of whether a contract is, or contains, a lease.**

10   A period of time may be described in terms of the amount of use of an identified asset (for example, the number of production units that an item of equipment will be used to produce).

11   An entity shall reassess whether a contract is, or contains, a lease only if the terms and conditions of the contract are changed.

Separating components of a contract

12   For a contract that is, or contains, a lease, an entity shall account for each lease component within the contract as a lease separately from non-lease components of the contract, unless the entity applies the practical expedient in paragraph 15. Paragraphs B32–B33 set out guidance on separating components of a contract.

Lessee

13   For a contract that contains a lease component and one or more additional lease or non-lease components, a lessee shall allocate the consideration in the contract to each lease component on the basis of the relative stand-alone price of the lease component and the aggregate stand-alone price of the non-lease components.

14   The relative stand-alone price of lease and non-lease components shall be determined on the basis of the price the lessor, or a similar supplier, would charge an entity for that component, or a similar component, separately. If an observable stand-alone price is not readily available, the lessee shall estimate the stand-alone price, maximising the use of observable information.

15   As a practical expedient, a lessee may elect, by class of underlying asset, not to separate non-lease components from lease components, and instead account for each lease component and any associated non-lease components as a single lease component. A lessee shall not apply this practical expedient to embedded derivatives that meet the criteria in paragraph 4.3.3 of AASB 9 *Financial Instruments*.

16   Unless the practical expedient in paragraph 15 is applied, a lessee shall account for non-lease components applying other applicable Standards.

Lessor

17   For a contract that contains a lease component and one or more additional lease or non-lease components, a lessor shall allocate the consideration in the contract applying paragraphs 73–90 of AASB 15.

Lease term (paragraphs B34–B41)

18   An entity shall determine the lease term as the non-cancellable period of a lease, together with both:

(a)   periods covered by an option to extend the lease if the lessee is reasonably certain to exercise that option; and

(b)   periods covered by an option to terminate the lease if the lessee is reasonably certain not to exercise that option.

19   In assessing whether a lessee is reasonably certain to exercise an option to extend a lease, or not to exercise an option to terminate a lease, an entity shall consider all relevant facts and circumstances that create an economic incentive for the lessee to exercise the option to extend the lease, or not to exercise the option to terminate the lease, as described in paragraphs B37–B40.

20   A lessee shall reassess whether it is reasonably certain to exercise an extension option, or not to exercise a termination option, upon the occurrence of either a significant event or a significant change in circumstances that:

(a)   is within the control of the lessee; and

(b)   affects whether the lessee is reasonably certain to exercise an option not previously included in its determination of the lease term, or not to exercise an option previously included in its determination of the lease term (as described in paragraph B41).

21   An entity shall revise the lease term if there is a change in the non-cancellable period of a lease. For example, the non-cancellable period of a lease will change if:

(a)   the lessee exercises an option not previously included in the entity's determination of the lease term;

(b)   the lessee does not exercise an option previously included in the entity's determination of the lease term;

(c)   an event occurs that contractually obliges the lessee to exercise an option not previously included in the entity's determination of the lease term; or

(d)   an event occurs that contractually prohibits the lessee from exercising an option previously included in the entity's determination of the lease term.

Lessee

Recognition

22   At the *commencement date*, a lessee shall recognise a right-of-use asset and a lease liability.

Measurement

Initial measurement
Initial measurement of the right-of-use asset

23   At the commencement date, a lessee shall measure the right-of-use asset at cost.

24   The cost of the right-of-use asset shall comprise:

(a)   the amount of the initial measurement of the lease liability, as described in paragraph 26;

(b)   any lease payments made at or before the commencement date, less any *lease incentives* received;

(c)   any *initial direct costs* incurred by the lessee; and

(d)   an estimate of costs to be incurred by the lessee in dismantling and removing the underlying asset, restoring the site on which it is located or restoring the underlying asset to the condition required by the terms and conditions of the lease, unless those costs are incurred to produce inventories. The lessee incurs the obligation for those costs either at the commencement date or as a consequence of having used the underlying asset during a particular period.

25   A lessee shall recognise the costs described in paragraph 24(d) as part of the cost of the right-of-use asset when it incurs an obligation for those costs. A lessee applies AASB 102 *Inventories* to costs that are incurred during a particular period as a consequence of having used the right-of-use asset to produce inventories during that period. The obligations for such costs accounted for applying this Standard or AASB 102 are recognised and measured applying AASB 137 *Provisions, Contingent Liabilities and Contingent Assets*.

Initial measurement of the lease liability

26   At the commencement date, a lessee shall measure the lease liability at the present value of the lease payments that are not paid at that date. The lease payments shall be discounted using the *interest rate implicit in the lease*, if that rate can be readily determined. If that rate cannot be readily determined, the lessee shall use the *lessee's incremental borrowing rate*.

27   At the commencement date, the lease payments included in the measurement of the
      lease liability comprise the following payments for the right to use the underlying asset
      during the lease term that are not paid at the commencement date:

      (a)   *fixed payments* (including in-substance fixed payments as described in
             paragraph B42), less any lease incentives receivable;

      (b)   *variable lease payments* that depend on an index or a rate, initially measured
             using the index or rate as at the commencement date (as described in paragraph
             28);

      (c)   amounts expected to be payable by the lessee under *residual value guarantees*;

      (d)   the exercise price of a purchase option if the lessee is reasonably certain to
             exercise that option (assessed considering the factors described in paragraphs
             B37–B40); and

      (e)   payments of penalties for terminating the lease, if the lease term reflects the
             lessee exercising an option to terminate the lease.

28   Variable lease payments that depend on an index or a rate described in paragraph 27(b)
      include, for example, payments linked to a consumer price index, payments linked to
      a benchmark interest rate (such as LIBOR) or payments that vary to reflect changes in
      market rental rates.

Subsequent measurement
Subsequent measurement of the right-of-use asset

**29   After the commencement date, a lessee shall measure the right-of-use asset
      applying a cost model, unless it applies either of the measurement models
      described in paragraphs 34 and 35.**

Cost model

30   To apply a cost model, a lessee shall measure the right-of-use asset at cost:

      (a)   less any accumulated depreciation and any accumulated impairment losses; and

      (b)   adjusted for any remeasurement of the lease liability specified in paragraph
             36(c).

31   A lessee shall apply the depreciation requirements in AASB 116 *Property, Plant
      and Equipment* in depreciating the right-of-use asset, subject to the requirements in
      paragraph 32.

32   If the lease transfers ownership of the underlying asset to the lessee by the end of
      the lease term or if the cost of the right-of-use asset reflects that the lessee will
      exercise a purchase option, the lessee shall depreciate the right-of-use asset from the
      commencement date to the end of the *useful life* of the underlying asset. Otherwise,
      the lessee shall depreciate the right-of-use asset from the commencement date to the
      earlier of the end of the *useful life* of the right-of-use asset or the end of the lease term.

33   A lessee shall apply AASB 136 *Impairment of Assets* to determine whether the right-
      of-use asset is impaired and to account for any impairment loss identified.

Other measurement models

34   If a lessee applies the fair value model in AASB 140 *Investment Property* to its
      investment property, the lessee shall also apply that fair value model to right-of-use
      assets that meet the definition of investment property in AASB 140.

35   If right-of-use assets relate to a class of property, plant and equipment to which the
      lessee applies the revaluation model in AASB 116, a lessee may elect to apply that
      revaluation model to all of the right-of-use assets that relate to that class of property,
      plant and equipment.

Subsequent measurement of the lease liability

36   After the commencement date, a lessee shall measure the lease liability by:

    (a)   increasing the carrying amount to reflect interest on the lease liability;

    (b)   reducing the carrying amount to reflect the lease payments made; and

    (c)   remeasuring the carrying amount to reflect any reassessment or lease modifications specified in paragraphs 39–46, or to reflect revised in-substance fixed lease payments (see paragraph B42).

37   Interest on the lease liability in each period during the lease term shall be the amount that produces a constant periodic rate of interest on the remaining balance of the lease liability. The periodic rate of interest is the discount rate described in paragraph 26, or if applicable the revised discount rate described in paragraph 41, paragraph 43 or paragraph 45(c).

38   After the commencement date, a lessee shall recognise in profit or loss, unless the costs are included in the carrying amount of another asset applying other applicable Standards, both:

    (a)   interest on the lease liability; and

    (b)   variable lease payments not included in the measurement of the lease liability in the period in which the event or condition that triggers those payments occurs.

Reassessment of the lease liability

39   After the commencement date, a lessee shall apply paragraphs 40–43 to remeasure the lease liability to reflect changes to the lease payments. A lessee shall recognise the amount of the remeasurement of the lease liability as an adjustment to the right-of-use asset. However, if the carrying amount of the right-of-use asset is reduced to zero and there is a further reduction in the measurement of the lease liability, a lessee shall recognise any remaining amount of the remeasurement in profit or loss.

40   A lessee shall remeasure the lease liability by discounting the revised lease payments using a revised discount rate, if either:

    (a)   there is a change in the lease term, as described in paragraphs 20–21. A lessee shall determine the revised lease payments on the basis of the revised lease term; or

    (b)   there is a change in the assessment of an option to purchase the underlying asset, assessed considering the events and circumstances described in paragraphs 20–21 in the context of a purchase option. A lessee shall determine the revised lease payments to reflect the change in amounts payable under the purchase option.

41   In applying paragraph 40, a lessee shall determine the revised discount rate as the interest rate implicit in the lease for the remainder of the lease term, if that rate can be readily determined, or the lessee's incremental borrowing rate at the date of reassessment, if the interest rate implicit in the lease cannot be readily determined.

42   A lessee shall remeasure the lease liability by discounting the revised lease payments, if either:

    (a)   there is a change in the amounts expected to be payable under a residual value guarantee. A lessee shall determine the revised lease payments to reflect the change in amounts expected to be payable under the residual value guarantee.

    (b)   there is a change in future lease payments resulting from a change in an index or a rate used to determine those payments, including for example a change to reflect changes in market rental rates following a market rent review. The lessee shall remeasure the lease liability to reflect those revised lease payments only when there is a change in the cash flows (ie when the adjustment to the lease payments takes effect). A lessee shall determine the revised lease payments for the remainder of the lease term based on the revised contractual payments.

AASB

43 In applying paragraph 42, a lessee shall use an unchanged discount rate, unless the change in lease payments results from a change in floating interest rates. In that case, the lessee shall use a revised discount rate that reflects changes in the interest rate.

Lease modifications

44 A lessee shall account for a lease modification as a separate lease if both:

(a) the modification increases the scope of the lease by adding the right to use one or more underlying assets; and

(b) the consideration for the lease increases by an amount commensurate with the stand-alone price for the increase in scope and any appropriate adjustments to that stand-alone price to reflect the circumstances of the particular contract.

45 For a lease modification that is not accounted for as a separate lease, at the *effective date of the lease modification* a lessee shall:

(a) allocate the consideration in the modified contract applying paragraphs 13–16;

(b) determine the lease term of the modified lease applying paragraphs 18–19; and

(c) remeasure the lease liability by discounting the revised lease payments using a revised discount rate. The revised discount rate is determined as the interest rate implicit in the lease for the remainder of the lease term, if that rate can be readily determined, or the lessee's incremental borrowing rate at the effective date of the modification, if the interest rate implicit in the lease cannot be readily determined.

46 For a lease modification that is not accounted for as a separate lease, the lessee shall account for the remeasurement of the lease liability by:

(a) decreasing the carrying amount of the right-of-use asset to reflect the partial or full termination of the lease for lease modifications that decrease the scope of the lease. The lessee shall recognise in profit or loss any gain or loss relating to the partial or full termination of the lease.

(b) making a corresponding adjustment to the right-of-use asset for all other lease modifications.

Presentation

47 A lessee shall either present in the statement of financial position, or disclose in the notes:

(a) right-of-use assets separately from other assets. If a lessee does not present right-of-use assets separately in the statement of financial position, the lessee shall:

(i) include right-of-use assets within the same line item as that within which the corresponding underlying assets would be presented if they were owned; and

(ii) disclose which line items in the statement of financial position include those right-of-use assets.

(b) lease liabilities separately from other liabilities. If the lessee does not present lease liabilities separately in the statement of financial position, the lessee shall disclose which line items in the statement of financial position include those liabilities.

48 The requirement in paragraph 47(a) does not apply to right-of-use assets that meet the definition of investment property, which shall be presented in the statement of financial position as investment property.

49 In the statement of profit or loss and other comprehensive income, a lessee shall present interest expense on the lease liability separately from the depreciation charge for the right-of-use asset. Interest expense on the lease liability is a component of finance costs, which paragraph 82(b) of AASB 101 *Presentation of Financial*

Statements requires to be presented separately in the statement of profit or loss and other comprehensive income.

50   In the statement of cash flows, a lessee shall classify:

(a)   cash payments for the principal portion of the lease liability within financing activities;

(b)   cash payments for the interest portion of the lease liability applying the requirements in AASB 107 *Statement of Cash Flows* for interest paid; and

(c)   short-term lease payments, payments for leases of low-value assets and variable lease payments not included in the measurement of the lease liability within operating activities.

Disclosure

51   The objective of the disclosures is for lessees to disclose information in the notes that, together with the information provided in the statement of financial position, statement of profit or loss and statement of cash flows, gives a basis for users of financial statements to assess the effect that leases have on the financial position, financial performance and cash flows of the lessee. Paragraphs 52–60 specify requirements on how to meet this objective.

52   A lessee shall disclose information about its leases for which it is a lessee in a single note or separate section in its financial statements. However, a lessee need not duplicate information that is already presented elsewhere in the financial statements, provided that the information is incorporated by cross-reference in the single note or separate section about leases.

53   A lessee shall disclose the following amounts for the reporting period:

(a)   depreciation charge for right-of-use assets by class of underlying asset;

(b)   interest expense on lease liabilities;

(c)   the expense relating to short-term leases accounted for applying paragraph 6. This expense need not include the expense relating to leases with a lease term of one month or less;

(d)   the expense relating to leases of low-value assets accounted for applying paragraph 6. This expense shall not include the expense relating to short-term leases of low-value assets included in paragraph 53(c);

(e)   the expense relating to variable lease payments not included in the measurement of lease liabilities;

(f)   income from subleasing right-of-use assets;

(g)   total cash outflow for leases;

(h)   additions to right-of-use assets;

(i)   gains or losses arising from sale and leaseback transactions; and

(j)   the carrying amount of right-of-use assets at the end of the reporting period by class of underlying asset.

54   A lessee shall provide the disclosures specified in paragraph 53 in a tabular format, unless another format is more appropriate. The amounts disclosed shall include costs that a lessee has included in the carrying amount of another asset during the reporting period.

55   A lessee shall disclose the amount of its lease commitments for short-term leases accounted for applying paragraph 6 if the portfolio of short-term leases to which it is committed at the end of the reporting period is dissimilar to the portfolio of short-term leases to which the short-term lease expense disclosed applying paragraph 53(c) relates.

56   If right-of-use assets meet the definition of investment property, a lessee shall apply the disclosure requirements in AASB 140. In that case, a lessee is not required to provide the disclosures in paragraph 53(a), (f), (h) or (j) for those right-of-use assets.

57   If a lessee measures right-of-use assets at revalued amounts applying AASB 116, the lessee shall disclose the information required by paragraph 77 of AASB 116 for those right-of-use assets.

58   A lessee shall disclose a maturity analysis of lease liabilities applying paragraphs 39 and B11 of AASB 7 *Financial Instruments: Disclosures* separately from the maturity analyses of other financial liabilities.

59   In addition to the disclosures required in paragraphs 53–58, a lessee shall disclose additional qualitative and quantitative information about its leasing activities necessary to meet the disclosure objective in paragraph 51 (as described in paragraph B48). This additional information may include, but is not limited to, information that helps users of financial statements to assess:

(a)   the nature of the lessee's leasing activities;

(b)   future cash outflows to which the lessee is potentially exposed that are not reflected in the measurement of lease liabilities. This includes exposure arising from:

(i)   variable lease payments (as described in paragraph B49);

(ii)   extension options and termination options (as described in paragraph B50);

(iii)   residual value guarantees (as described in paragraph B51); and

(iv)   leases not yet commenced to which the lessee is committed.

(c)   restrictions or covenants imposed by leases; and

(d)   sale and leaseback transactions (as described in paragraph B52).

60   A lessee that accounts for short-term leases or leases of low-value assets applying paragraph 6 shall disclose that fact.

Lessor

Classification of leases (paragraphs B53–B58)

61   A lessor shall classify each of its leases as either an *operating lease* or a *finance lease*.

62   A lease is classified as a finance lease if it transfers substantially all the risks and rewards incidental to ownership of an underlying asset. A lease is classified as an operating lease if it does not transfer substantially all the risks and rewards incidental to ownership of an underlying asset.

63   Whether a lease is a finance lease or an operating lease depends on the substance of the transaction rather than the form of the contract. Examples of situations that individually or in combination would normally lead to a lease being classified as a finance lease are:

(a)   the lease transfers ownership of the underlying asset to the lessee by the end of the lease term;

(b)   the lessee has the option to purchase the underlying asset at a price that is expected to be sufficiently lower than the *fair value* at the date the option becomes exercisable for it to be reasonably certain, at the *inception date*, that the option will be exercised;

(c)   the lease term is for the major part of the *economic life* of the underlying asset even if title is not transferred;

(d)   at the inception date, the present value of the lease payments amounts to at least substantially all of the fair value of the underlying asset; and

(e)   the underlying asset is of such a specialised nature that only the lessee can use it without major modifications.

64   Indicators of situations that individually or in combination could also lead to a lease being classified as a finance lease are:

(a)   if the lessee can cancel the lease, the lessor's losses associated with the cancellation are borne by the lessee;

(b)   gains or losses from the fluctuation in the fair value of the residual accrue to the lessee (for example, in the form of a rent rebate equaling most of the sales proceeds at the end of the lease); and

(c)   the lessee has the ability to continue the lease for a secondary period at a rent that is substantially lower than market rent.

65   The examples and indicators in paragraphs 63–64 are not always conclusive. If it is clear from other features that the lease does not transfer substantially all the risks and rewards incidental to ownership of an underlying asset, the lease is classified as an operating lease. For example, this may be the case if ownership of the underlying asset transfers at the end of the lease for a variable payment equal to its then fair value, or if there are variable lease payments, as a result of which the lessor does not transfer substantially all such risks and rewards.

66   Lease classification is made at the inception date and is reassessed only if there is a lease modification. Changes in estimates (for example, changes in estimates of the economic life or of the residual value of the underlying asset), or changes in circumstances (for example, default by the lessee), do not give rise to a new classification of a lease for accounting purposes.

Finance leases

Recognition and measurement

67   **At the commencement date, a lessor shall recognise assets held under a finance lease in its statement of financial position and present them as a receivable at an amount equal to the *net investment in the lease*.**

Initial measurement

68   The lessor shall use the interest rate implicit in the lease to measure the net investment in the lease. In the case of a sublease, if the interest rate implicit in the sublease cannot be readily determined, an intermediate lessor may use the discount rate used for the head lease (adjusted for any initial direct costs associated with the sublease) to measure the net investment in the sublease.

69   Initial direct costs, other than those incurred by manufacturer or dealer lessors, are included in the initial measurement of the net investment in the lease and reduce the amount of income recognised over the lease term. The interest rate implicit in the lease is defined in such a way that the initial direct costs are included automatically in the net investment in the lease; there is no need to add them separately.

Initial measurement of the lease payments included in the net investment in the lease

70   At the commencement date, the lease payments included in the measurement of the net investment in the lease comprise the following payments for the right to use the underlying asset during the lease term that are not received at the commencement date:

(a)   fixed payments (including in-substance fixed payments as described in paragraph B42), less any lease incentives payable;

(b)   variable lease payments that depend on an index or a rate, initially measured using the index or rate as at the commencement date;

(c)   any residual value guarantees provided to the lessor by the lessee, a party related to the lessee or a third party unrelated to the lessor that is financially capable of discharging the obligations under the guarantee;

    (d)   the exercise price of a purchase option if the lessee is reasonably certain to exercise that option (assessed considering the factors described in paragraph B37); and

    (e)   payments of penalties for terminating the lease, if the lease term reflects the lessee exercising an option to terminate the lease.

Manufacturer or dealer lessors

71   At the commencement date, a manufacturer or dealer lessor shall recognise the following for each of its finance leases:

    (a)   revenue being the fair value of the underlying asset, or, if lower, the present value of the lease payments accruing to the lessor, discounted using a market rate of interest;

    (b)   the cost of sale being the cost, or carrying amount if different, of the underlying asset less the present value of the *unguaranteed residual value*; and

    (c)   selling profit or loss (being the difference between revenue and the cost of sale) in accordance with its policy for outright sales to which AASB 15 applies. A manufacturer or dealer lessor shall recognise selling profit or loss on a finance lease at the commencement date, regardless of whether the lessor transfers the underlying asset as described in AASB 15.

72   Manufacturers or dealers often offer to customers the choice of either buying or leasing an asset. A finance lease of an asset by a manufacturer or dealer lessor gives rise to profit or loss equivalent to the profit or loss resulting from an outright sale of the underlying asset, at normal selling prices, reflecting any applicable volume or trade discounts.

73   Manufacturer or dealer lessors sometimes quote artificially low rates of interest in order to attract customers. The use of such a rate would result in a lessor recognising an excessive portion of the total income from the transaction at the commencement date. If artificially low rates of interest are quoted, a manufacturer or dealer lessor shall restrict selling profit to that which would apply if a market rate of interest were charged.

74   A manufacturer or dealer lessor shall recognise as an expense costs incurred in connection with obtaining a finance lease at the commencement date because they are mainly related to earning the manufacturer or dealer's selling profit. Costs incurred by manufacturer or dealer lessors in connection with obtaining a finance lease are excluded from the definition of initial direct costs and, thus, are excluded from the net investment in the lease.

Subsequent measurement

75   A lessor shall recognise finance income over the lease term, based on a pattern reflecting a constant periodic rate of return on the lessor's net investment in the lease.

76   A lessor aims to allocate finance income over the lease term on a systematic and rational basis. A lessor shall apply the lease payments relating to the period against the *gross investment in the lease* to reduce both the principal and the *unearned finance income*.

77   A lessor shall apply the derecognition and impairment requirements in AASB 9 to the net investment in the lease. A lessor shall review regularly estimated unguaranteed residual values used in computing the gross investment in the lease. If there has been a reduction in the estimated unguaranteed residual value, the lessor shall revise the income allocation over the lease term and recognise immediately any reduction in respect of amounts accrued.

78   A lessor that classifies an asset under a finance lease as held for sale (or includes it in a disposal group that is classified as held for sale) applying AASB 5 *Non-current Assets*

Held for Sale and Discontinued Operations shall account for the asset in accordance with that Standard.

Lease modifications

79   A lessor shall account for a modification to a finance lease as a separate lease if both:

(a)   the modification increases the scope of the lease by adding the right to use one or more underlying assets; and

(b)   the consideration for the lease increases by an amount commensurate with the stand-alone price for the increase in scope and any appropriate adjustments to that stand-alone price to reflect the circumstances of the particular contract.

80   For a modification to a finance lease that is not accounted for as a separate lease, a lessor shall account for the modification as follows:

(a)   if the lease would have been classified as an operating lease had the modification been in effect at the inception date, the lessor shall:

(i)   account for the lease modification as a new lease from the effective date of the modification; and

(ii)   measure the carrying amount of the underlying asset as the net investment in the lease immediately before the effective date of the lease modification.

(b)   otherwise, the lessor shall apply the requirements of AASB 9.

Operating leases

Recognition and measurement

81   **A lessor shall recognise lease payments from operating leases as income on either a straight-line basis or another systematic basis. The lessor shall apply another systematic basis if that basis is more representative of the pattern in which benefit from the use of the underlying asset is diminished.**

82   A lessor shall recognise costs, including depreciation, incurred in earning the lease income as an expense.

83   A lessor shall add initial direct costs incurred in obtaining an operating lease to the carrying amount of the underlying asset and recognise those costs as an expense over the lease term on the same basis as the lease income.

84   The depreciation policy for depreciable underlying assets subject to operating leases shall be consistent with the lessor's normal depreciation policy for similar assets. A lessor shall calculate depreciation in accordance with AASB 116 and AASB 138.

85   A lessor shall apply AASB 136 to determine whether an underlying asset subject to an operating lease is impaired and to account for any impairment loss identified.

86   A manufacturer or dealer lessor does not recognise any selling profit on entering into an operating lease because it is not the equivalent of a sale.

Lease modifications

87   A lessor shall account for a modification to an operating lease as a new lease from the effective date of the modification, considering any prepaid or accrued lease payments relating to the original lease as part of the lease payments for the new lease.

Presentation

88   A lessor shall present underlying assets subject to operating leases in its statement of financial position according to the nature of the underlying asset.

AASB

Disclosure

89   The objective of the disclosures is for lessors to disclose information in the notes that, together with the information provided in the statement of financial position, statement of profit or loss and statement of cash flows, gives a basis for users of financial statements to assess the effect that leases have on the financial position, financial performance and cash flows of the lessor. Paragraphs 90–97 specify requirements on how to meet this objective.

90   A lessor shall disclose the following amounts for the reporting period:

    (a)   for finance leases:

        (i)   selling profit or loss;

        (ii)   finance income on the net investment in the lease; and

        (iii) income relating to variable lease payments not included in the measurement of the net investment in the lease.

    (b)   for operating leases, lease income, separately disclosing income relating to variable lease payments that do not depend on an index or a rate.

91   A lessor shall provide the disclosures specified in paragraph 90 in a tabular format, unless another format is more appropriate.

92   A lessor shall disclose additional qualitative and quantitative information about its leasing activities necessary to meet the disclosure objective in paragraph 89. This additional information includes, but is not limited to, information that helps users of financial statements to assess:

    (a)   the nature of the lessor's leasing activities; and

    (b)   how the lessor manages the risk associated with any rights it retains in underlying assets. In particular, a lessor shall disclose its risk management strategy for the rights it retains in underlying assets, including any means by which the lessor reduces that risk. Such means may include, for example, buy-back agreements, residual value guarantees or variable lease payments for use in excess of specified limits.

Finance leases

93   A lessor shall provide a qualitative and quantitative explanation of the significant changes in the carrying amount of the net investment in finance leases.

94   A lessor shall disclose a maturity analysis of the lease payments receivable, showing the undiscounted lease payments to be received on an annual basis for a minimum of each of the first five years and a total of the amounts for the remaining years. A lessor shall reconcile the undiscounted lease payments to the net investment in the lease. The reconciliation shall identify the unearned finance income relating to the lease payments receivable and any discounted unguaranteed residual value.

Operating leases

95   For items of property, plant and equipment subject to an operating lease, a lessor shall apply the disclosure requirements of AASB 116. In applying the disclosure requirements in AASB 116, a lessor shall disaggregate each class of property, plant and equipment into assets subject to operating leases and assets not subject to operating leases. Accordingly, a lessor shall provide the disclosures required by AASB 116 for assets subject to an operating lease (by class of underlying asset) separately from owned assets held and used by the lessor.

96   A lessor shall apply the disclosure requirements in AASB 136, AASB 138, AASB 140 and AASB 141 for assets subject to operating leases.

97   A lessor shall disclose a maturity analysis of lease payments, showing the undiscounted lease payments to be received on an annual basis for a minimum of each of the first five years and a total of the amounts for the remaining years.

Sale and leaseback transactions

98   If an entity (the seller-lessee) transfers an asset to another entity (the buyer-lessor) and leases that asset back from the buyer-lessor, both the seller-lessee and the buyer-lessor shall account for the transfer contract and the lease applying paragraphs 99–103.

Assessing whether the transfer of the asset is a sale

99   An entity shall apply the requirements for determining when a performance obligation is satisfied in AASB 15 to determine whether the transfer of an asset is accounted for as a sale of that asset.

Transfer of the asset is a sale

100   If the transfer of an asset by the seller-lessee satisfies the requirements of AASB 15 to be accounted for as a sale of the asset:

(a)   the seller-lessee shall measure the right-of-use asset arising from the leaseback at the proportion of the previous carrying amount of the asset that relates to the right of use retained by the seller-lessee. Accordingly, the seller-lessee shall recognise only the amount of any gain or loss that relates to the rights transferred to the buyer-lessor.

(b)   the buyer-lessor shall account for the purchase of the asset applying applicable Standards, and for the lease applying the lessor accounting requirements in this Standard.

101   If the fair value of the consideration for the sale of an asset does not equal the fair value of the asset, or if the payments for the lease are not at market rates, an entity shall make the following adjustments to measure the sale proceeds at fair value:

(a)   any below-market terms shall be accounted for as a prepayment of lease payments; and

(b)   any above-market terms shall be accounted for as additional financing provided by the buyer-lessor to the seller-lessee.

102   The entity shall measure any potential adjustment required by paragraph 101 on the basis of the more readily determinable of:

(a)   the difference between the fair value of the consideration for the sale and the fair value of the asset; and

(b)   the difference between the present value of the contractual payments for the lease and the present value of payments for the lease at market rates.

Transfer of the asset is not a sale

103   If the transfer of an asset by the seller-lessee does not satisfy the requirements of AASB 15 to be accounted for as a sale of the asset:

(a)   the seller-lessee shall continue to recognise the transferred asset and shall recognise a financial liability equal to the transfer proceeds. It shall account for the financial liability applying AASB 9.

(b)   the buyer-lessor shall not recognise the transferred asset and shall recognise a financial asset equal to the transfer proceeds. It shall account for the financial asset applying AASB 9.

Commencement of the legislative instrument

Aus103.1   For legal purposes, this legislative instrument commences on 31 December 2018.

APPENDIX A
DEFINED TERMS

This appendix is an integral part of the Standard.

commencement date of the lease (commencement date)	The date on which a **lessor** makes an **underlying asset** available for use by a **lessee**.
economic life	Either the period over which an asset is expected to be economically usable by one or more users or the number of production or similar units expected to be obtained from an asset by one or more users.
effective date of the modification	The date when both parties agree to a **lease modification**.
fair value	For the purpose of applying the **lessor** accounting requirements in this Standard, the amount for which an asset could be exchanged, or a liability settled, between knowledgeable, willing parties in an arm's length transaction.
finance lease	A **lease** that transfers substantially all the risks and rewards incidental to ownership of an **underlying asset**.
fixed payments	Payments made by a **lessee** to a **lessor** for the right to use an **underlying asset** during the **lease term**, excluding **variable lease payments**.
gross investment in the lease	The sum of: (a) the **lease payments** receivable by a **lessor** under a **finance lease**; and (b) any **unguaranteed residual value** accruing to the lessor.
inception date of the lease (inception date)	The earlier of the date of a **lease** agreement and the date of commitment by the parties to the principal terms and conditions of the lease.
initial direct costs	Incremental costs of obtaining a **lease** that would not have been incurred if the lease had not been obtained, except for such costs incurred by a manufacturer or dealer **lessor** in connection with a **finance lease**.
interest rate implicit in the lease	The rate of interest that causes the present value of (a) the **lease payments** and (b) the **unguaranteed residual value** to equal the sum of (i) the **fair value** of the **underlying asset** and (ii) any **initial direct costs** of the lessor.
lease	A contract, or part of a contract, that conveys the right to use an asset (the **underlying asset**) for a period of time in exchange for consideration.
lease incentives	Payments made by a **lessor** to a **lessee** associated with a **lease**, or the reimbursement or assumption by a lessor of costs of a lessee.
lease modification	A change in the scope of a **lease**, or the consideration for a lease, that was not part of the original terms and conditions of the lease (for example, adding or terminating the right to use one or more **underlying assets**, or extending or shortening the contractual **lease term**).

lease payments	Payments made by a **lessee** to a **lessor** relating to the right to use an **underlying asset** during the **lease term**, comprising the following: (a) **fixed payments** (including in-substance fixed payments), less any **lease incentives**; (b) **variable lease payments** that depend on an index or a rate; (c) the exercise price of a purchase option if the lessee is reasonably certain to exercise that option; and (d) payments of penalties for terminating the **lease**, if the lease term reflects the lessee exercising an option to terminate the lease. For the lessee, lease payments also include amounts expected to be payable by the lessee under **residual value guarantees**. Lease payments do not include payments allocated to non-lease components of a contract, unless the lessee elects to combine non-lease components with a lease component and to account for them as a single lease component. For the lessor, lease payments also include any residual value guarantees provided to the lessor by the lessee, a party related to the lessee or a third party unrelated to the lessor that is financially capable of discharging the obligations under the guarantee. Lease payments do not include payments allocated to non-lease components.
lease term	The non-cancellable period for which a **lessee** has the right to use an **underlying asset**, together with both: (a) periods covered by an option to extend the **lease** if the lessee is reasonably certain to exercise that option; and (b) periods covered by an option to terminate the lease if the lessee is reasonably certain not to exercise that option.
lessee	An entity that obtains the right to use an **underlying asset** for a period of time in exchange for consideration.
lessee's incremental borrowing rate	The rate of interest that a **lessee** would have to pay to borrow over a similar term, and with a similar security, the funds necessary to obtain an asset of a similar value to the **right-of-use asset** in a similar economic environment.
lessor	An entity that provides the right to use an **underlying asset** for a period of time in exchange for consideration.
net investment in the lease	The **gross investment in the lease** discounted at the **interest rate implicit in the lease**.
operating lease	A **lease** that does not transfer substantially all the risks and rewards incidental to ownership of an **underlying asset**.
optional lease payments	Payments to be made by a **lessee** to a **lessor** for the right to use an **underlying asset** during periods covered by an option to extend or terminate a **lease** that are not included in the **lease term**.
period of use	The total period of time that an asset is used to fulfil a contract with a customer (including any non-consecutive periods of time).
residual value guarantee	A guarantee made to a **lessor** by a party unrelated to the lessor that the value (or part of the value) of an **underlying asset** at the end of a **lease** will be at least a specified amount.
right-of-use asset	An asset that represents a **lessee's** right to use an **underlying asset** for the **lease term**.
short-term lease	A **lease** that, at the **commencement date**, has a **lease term** of 12 months or less. A lease that contains a purchase option is not a short-term lease.
sublease	A transaction for which an **underlying asset** is re-leased by a **lessee** ('intermediate lessor') to a third party, and the **lease** ('head lease') between the head lessor and lessee remains in effect.
underlying asset	An asset that is the subject of a **lease**, for which the right to use that asset has been provided by a **lessor** to a **lessee**.

AASB

unearned finance income	The difference between: (a) the **gross investment in the lease**; and (b) the **net investment in the lease**.
unguaranteed residual value	That portion of the residual value of the **underlying asset**, the realisation of which by a **lessor** is not assured or is guaranteed solely by a party related to the lessor.
variable lease payments	The portion of payments made by a **lessee** to a **lessor** for the right to use an **underlying asset** during the **lease term** that varies because of changes in facts or circumstances occurring after the **commencement date**, other than the passage of time.

Terms defined in other Standards and used in this Standard with the same meaning

contract	An agreement between two or more parties that creates enforceable rights and obligations.
useful life	The period over which an asset is expected to be available for use by an entity; or the number of production or similar units expected to be obtained from an asset by an entity.

APPENDIX B

APPLICATION GUIDANCE

This appendix is an integral part of the Standard. It describes the application of paragraphs 1–103 and has the same authority as the other parts of the Standard.

Portfolio application

B1   This Standard specifies the accounting for an individual lease. However, as a practical expedient, an entity may apply this Standard to a portfolio of leases with similar characteristics if the entity reasonably expects that the effects on the financial statements of applying this Standard to the portfolio would not differ materially from applying this Standard to the individual leases within that portfolio. If accounting for a portfolio, an entity shall use estimates and assumptions that reflect the size and composition of the portfolio.

Combination of contracts

B2   In applying this Standard, an entity shall combine two or more contracts entered into at or near the same time with the same counterparty (or related parties of the counterparty), and account for the contracts as a single contract if one or more of the following criteria are met:

(a)   the contracts are negotiated as a package with an overall commercial objective that cannot be understood without considering the contracts together;

(b)   the amount of consideration to be paid in one contract depends on the price or performance of the other contract; or

(c)   the rights to use underlying assets conveyed in the contracts (or some rights to use underlying assets conveyed in each of the contracts) form a single lease component as described in paragraph B32.

Recognition exemption: leases for which the underlying asset is of low value (paragraphs 5–8)

B3   Except as specified in paragraph B7, this Standard permits a lessee to apply paragraph 6 to account for leases for which the underlying asset is of low value. A lessee shall assess the value of an underlying asset based on the value of the asset when it is new, regardless of the age of the asset being leased.

B4   The assessment of whether an underlying asset is of low value is performed on an absolute basis. Leases of low-value assets qualify for the accounting treatment in paragraph 6 regardless of whether those leases are material to the lessee. The assessment is not affected by the size, nature or circumstances of the lessee. Accordingly, different lessees are expected to reach the same conclusions about whether a particular underlying asset is of low value.

B5   An underlying asset can be of low value only if:

    (a)   the lessee can benefit from use of the underlying asset on its own or together with other resources that are readily available to the lessee; and

    (b)   the underlying asset is not highly dependent on, or highly interrelated with, other assets.

B6   A lease of an underlying asset does not qualify as a lease of a low-value asset if the nature of the asset is such that, when new, the asset is typically not of low value. For example, leases of cars would not qualify as leases of low-value assets because a new car would typically not be of low value.

B7   If a lessee subleases an asset, or expects to sublease an asset, the head lease does not qualify as a lease of a low-value asset.

B8   Examples of low-value underlying assets can include tablet and personal computers, small items of office furniture and telephones.

Identifying a lease (paragraphs 9–11)

B9   To assess whether a contract conveys the right to control the use of an identified asset (see paragraphs B13–B20) for a period of time, an entity shall assess whether, throughout the *period of use*, the customer has both of the following:

    (a)   the right to obtain substantially all of the economic benefits from use of the identified asset (as described in paragraphs B21–B23); and

    (b)   the right to direct the use of the identified asset (as described in paragraphs B24–B30).

B10   If the customer has the right to control the use of an identified asset for only a portion of the term of the contract, the contract contains a lease for that portion of the term.

B11   A contract to receive goods or services may be entered into by a joint arrangement, or on behalf of a joint arrangement, as defined in AASB 11 *Joint Arrangements*. In this case, the joint arrangement is considered to be the customer in the contract. Accordingly, in assessing whether such a contract contains a lease, an entity shall assess whether the joint arrangement has the right to control the use of an identified asset throughout the period of use.

B12   An entity shall assess whether a contract contains a lease for each potential separate lease component. Refer to paragraph B32 for guidance on separate lease components.

Identified asset

B13   An asset is typically identified by being explicitly specified in a contract. However, an asset can also be identified by being implicitly specified at the time that the asset is made available for use by the customer.

Substantive substitution rights

B14   Even if an asset is specified, a customer does not have the right to use an identified asset if the supplier has the substantive right to substitute the asset throughout the period of use. A supplier's right to substitute an asset is substantive only if both of the following conditions exist:

    (a)   the supplier has the practical ability to substitute alternative assets throughout the period of use (for example, the customer cannot prevent the supplier from substituting the asset and alternative assets are readily available to the supplier or could be sourced by the supplier within a reasonable period of time); and

    (b)   the supplier would benefit economically from the exercise of its right to substitute the asset (ie the economic benefits associated with substituting the asset are expected to exceed the costs associated with substituting the asset).

B15   If the supplier has a right or an obligation to substitute the asset only on or after either a particular date or the occurrence of a specified event, the supplier's substitution right is not substantive because the supplier does not have the practical ability to substitute alternative assets throughout the period of use.

B16   An entity's evaluation of whether a supplier's substitution right is substantive is based on facts and circumstances at inception of the contract and shall exclude consideration of future events that, at inception of the contract, are not considered likely to occur. Examples of future events that, at inception of the contract, would not be considered likely to occur and, thus, should be excluded from the evaluation include:

    (a)   an agreement by a future customer to pay an above market rate for use of the asset;

    (b)   the introduction of new technology that is not substantially developed at inception of the contract;

    (c)   a substantial difference between the customer's use of the asset, or the performance of the asset, and the use or performance considered likely at inception of the contract; and

    (d)   a substantial difference between the market price of the asset during the period of use, and the market price considered likely at inception of the contract.

B17   If the asset is located at the customer's premises or elsewhere, the costs associated with substitution are generally higher than when located at the supplier's premises and, therefore, are more likely to exceed the benefits associated with substituting the asset.

B18   The supplier's right or obligation to substitute the asset for repairs and maintenance, if the asset is not operating properly or if a technical upgrade becomes available does not preclude the customer from having the right to use an identified asset.

B19   If the customer cannot readily determine whether the supplier has a substantive substitution right, the customer shall presume that any substitution right is not substantive.

Portions of assets

B20   A capacity portion of an asset is an identified asset if it is physically distinct (for example, a floor of a building). A capacity or other portion of an asset that is not physically distinct (for example, a capacity portion of a fibre optic cable) is not an identified asset, unless it represents substantially all of the capacity of the asset and thereby provides the customer with the right to obtain substantially all of the economic benefits from use of the asset.

Right to obtain economic benefits from use

B21   To control the use of an identified asset, a customer is required to have the right to obtain substantially all of the economic benefits from use of the asset throughout the period of use (for example, by having exclusive use of the asset throughout that period).

A customer can obtain economic benefits from use of an asset directly or indirectly in many ways, such as by using, holding or sub-leasing the asset. The economic benefits from use of an asset include its primary output and by-products (including potential cash flows derived from these items), and other economic benefits from using the asset that could be realised from a commercial transaction with a third party.

B22   When assessing the right to obtain substantially all of the economic benefits from use of an asset, an entity shall consider the economic benefits that result from use of the asset within the defined scope of a customer's right to use the asset (see paragraph B30). For example:

     (a)   if a contract limits the use of a motor vehicle to only one particular territory during the period of use, an entity shall consider only the economic benefits from use of the motor vehicle within that territory, and not beyond.

     (b)   if a contract specifies that a customer can drive a motor vehicle only up to a particular number of miles during the period of use, an entity shall consider only the economic benefits from use of the motor vehicle for the permitted mileage, and not beyond.

B23   If a contract requires a customer to pay the supplier or another party a portion of the cash flows derived from use of an asset as consideration, those cash flows paid as consideration shall be considered to be part of the economic benefits that the customer obtains from use of the asset. For example, if the customer is required to pay the supplier a percentage of sales from use of retail space as consideration for that use, that requirement does not prevent the customer from having the right to obtain substantially all of the economic benefits from use of the retail space. This is because the cash flows arising from those sales are considered to be economic benefits that the customer obtains from use of the retail space, a portion of which it then pays to the supplier as consideration for the right to use that space.

Right to direct the use

B24   A customer has the right to direct the use of an identified asset throughout the period of use only if either:

     (a)   the customer has the right to direct how and for what purpose the asset is used throughout the period of use (as described in paragraphs B25–B30); or

     (b)   the relevant decisions about how and for what purpose the asset is used are predetermined and:

         (i)   the customer has the right to operate the asset (or to direct others to operate the asset in a manner that it determines) throughout the period of use, without the supplier having the right to change those operating instructions; or

         (ii)   the customer designed the asset (or specific aspects of the asset) in a way that predetermines how and for what purpose the asset will be used throughout the period of use.

How and for what purpose the asset is used

B25   A customer has the right to direct how and for what purpose the asset is used if, within the scope of its right of use defined in the contract, it can change how and for what purpose the asset is used throughout the period of use. In making this assessment, an entity considers the decision-making rights that are most relevant to changing how and for what purpose the asset is used throughout the period of use. Decision-making rights are relevant when they affect the economic benefits to be derived from use. The decision-making rights that are most relevant are likely to be different for different contracts, depending on the nature of the asset and the terms and conditions of the contract.

B26   Examples of decision-making rights that, depending on the circumstances, grant the right to change how and for what purpose the asset is used, within the defined scope of the customer's right of use, include:

(a)   rights to change the type of output that is produced by the asset (for example, to decide whether to use a shipping container to transport goods or for storage, or to decide upon the mix of products sold from retail space);

(b)   rights to change when the output is produced (for example, to decide when an item of machinery or a power plant will be used);

(c)   rights to change where the output is produced (for example, to decide upon the destination of a truck or a ship, or to decide where an item of equipment is used); and

(d)   rights to change whether the output is produced, and the quantity of that output (for example, to decide whether to produce energy from a power plant and how much energy to produce from that power plant).

B27   Examples of decision-making rights that do not grant the right to change how and for what purpose the asset is used include rights that are limited to operating or maintaining the asset. Such rights can be held by the customer or the supplier. Although rights such as those to operate or maintain an asset are often essential to the efficient use of an asset, they are not rights to direct how and for what purpose the asset is used and are often dependent on the decisions about how and for what purpose the asset is used. However, rights to operate an asset may grant the customer the right to direct the use of the asset if the relevant decisions about how and for what purpose the asset is used are predetermined (see paragraph B24(b)(i)).

Decisions determined during and before the period of use

B28   The relevant decisions about how and for what purpose the asset is used can be predetermined in a number of ways. For example, the relevant decisions can be predetermined by the design of the asset or by contractual restrictions on the use of the asset.

B29   In assessing whether a customer has the right to direct the use of an asset, an entity shall consider only rights to make decisions about the use of the asset during the period of use, unless the customer designed the asset (or specific aspects of the asset) as described in paragraph B24(b)(ii). Consequently, unless the conditions in paragraph B24(b)(ii) exist, an entity shall not consider decisions that are predetermined before the period of use. For example, if a customer is able only to specify the output of an asset before the period of use, the customer does not have the right to direct the use of that asset. The ability to specify the output in a contract before the period of use, without any other decision-making rights relating to the use of the asset, gives a customer the same rights as any customer that purchases goods or services.

Protective rights

B30   A contract may include terms and conditions designed to protect the supplier's interest in the asset or other assets, to protect its personnel, or to ensure the supplier's compliance with laws or regulations. These are examples of protective rights. For example, a contract may (i) specify the maximum amount of use of an asset or limit where or when the customer can use the asset, (ii) require a customer to follow particular operating practices, or (iii) require a customer to inform the supplier of changes in how an asset will be used. Protective rights typically define the scope of the customer's right of use but do not, in isolation, prevent the customer from having the right to direct the use of an asset.

B31   The following flowchart may assist entities in making the assessment of whether a contract is, or contains, a lease.

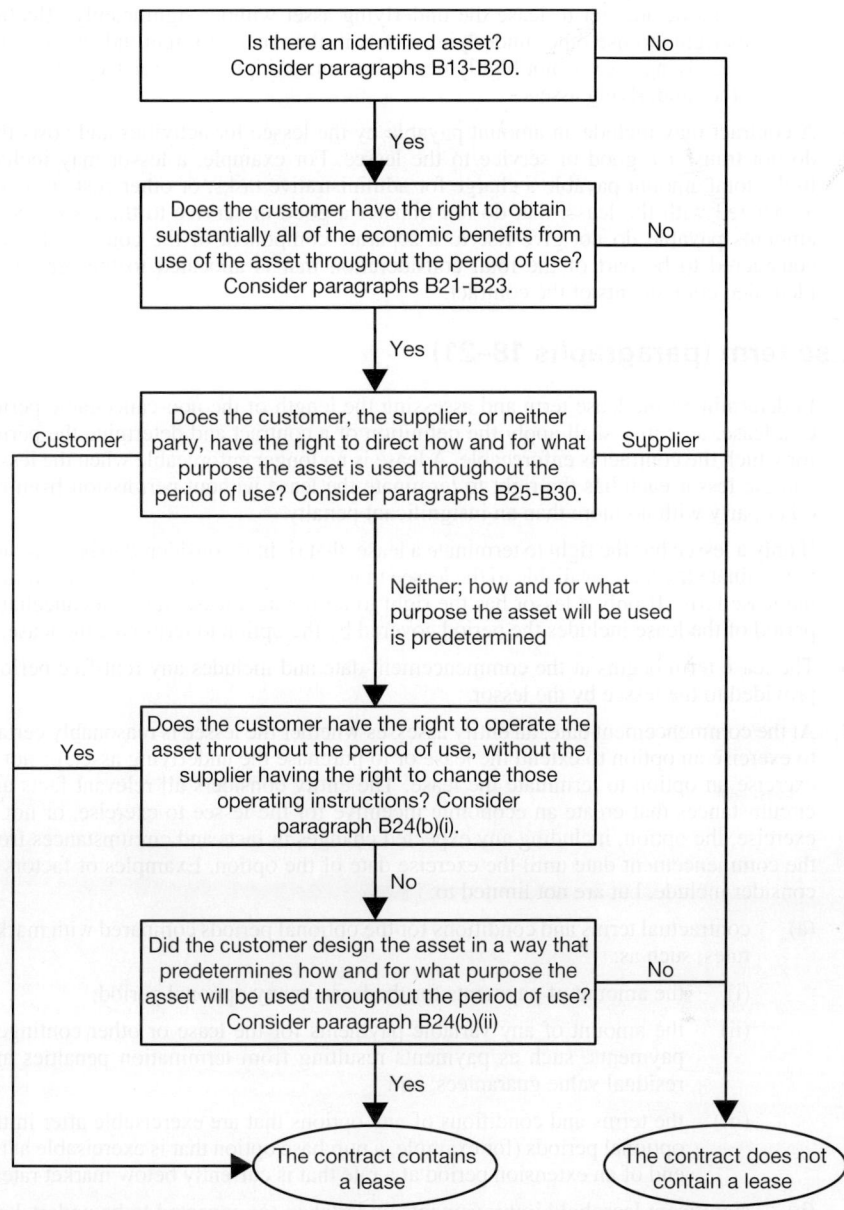

Separating components of a contract (paragraphs 12–17)

B32   The right to use an underlying asset is a separate lease component if both:

   (a)   the lessee can benefit from use of the underlying asset either on its own or together with other resources that are readily available to the lessee. Readily available resources are goods or services that are sold or leased separately (by the lessor or other suppliers) or resources that the lessee has already obtained (from the lessor or from other transactions or events); and

   (b)   the underlying asset is neither highly dependent on, nor highly interrelated with, the other underlying assets in the contract. For example, the fact that a lessee could decide not to lease the underlying asset without significantly affecting its rights to use other underlying assets in the contract might indicate that the underlying asset is not highly dependent on, or highly interrelated with, those other underlying assets.

B33   A contract may include an amount payable by the lessee for activities and costs that do not transfer a good or service to the lessee. For example, a lessor may include in the total amount payable a charge for administrative tasks, or other costs it incurs associated with the lease, that do not transfer a good or service to the lessee. Such amounts payable do not give rise to a separate component of the contract, but are considered to be part of the total consideration that is allocated to the separately identified components of the contract.

Lease term (paragraphs 18–21)

B34   In determining the lease term and assessing the length of the non-cancellable period of a lease, an entity shall apply the definition of a contract and determine the period for which the contract is enforceable. A lease is no longer enforceable when the lessee and the lessor each has the right to terminate the lease without permission from the other party with no more than an insignificant penalty.

B35   If only a lessee has the right to terminate a lease, that right is considered to be an option to terminate the lease available to the lessee that an entity considers when determining the lease term. If only a lessor has the right to terminate a lease, the non-cancellable period of the lease includes the period covered by the option to terminate the lease.

B36   The lease term begins at the commencement date and includes any rent-free periods provided to the lessee by the lessor.

B37   At the commencement date, an entity assesses whether the lessee is reasonably certain to exercise an option to extend the lease or to purchase the underlying asset, or not to exercise an option to terminate the lease. The entity considers all relevant facts and circumstances that create an economic incentive for the lessee to exercise, or not to exercise, the option, including any expected changes in facts and circumstances from the commencement date until the exercise date of the option. Examples of factors to consider include, but are not limited to:

(a)   contractual terms and conditions for the optional periods compared with market rates, such as:

(i)   the amount of payments for the lease in any optional period;

(ii)   the amount of any variable payments for the lease or other contingent payments, such as payments resulting from termination penalties and residual value guarantees; and

(iii) the terms and conditions of any options that are exercisable after initial optional periods (for example, a purchase option that is exercisable at the end of an extension period at a rate that is currently below market rates).

(b)   significant leasehold improvements undertaken (or expected to be undertaken) over the term of the contract that are expected to have significant economic benefit for the lessee when the option to extend or terminate the lease, or to purchase the underlying asset, becomes exercisable;

(c)   costs relating to the termination of the lease, such as negotiation costs, relocation costs, costs of identifying another underlying asset suitable for the lessee's needs, costs of integrating a new asset into the lessee's operations, or termination penalties and similar costs, including costs associated with returning the underlying asset in a contractually specified condition or to a contractually specified location;

(d)   the importance of that underlying asset to the lessee's operations, considering, for example, whether the underlying asset is a specialised asset, the location of the underlying asset and the availability of suitable alternatives; and

(e)   conditionality associated with exercising the option (ie when the option can be exercised only if one or more conditions are met), and the likelihood that those conditions will exist.

B38   An option to extend or terminate a lease may be combined with one or more other contractual features (for example, a residual value guarantee) such that the lessee guarantees the lessor a minimum or fixed cash return that is substantially the same regardless of whether the option is exercised. In such cases, and notwithstanding the guidance on in-substance fixed payments in paragraph B42, an entity shall assume that the lessee is reasonably certain to exercise the option to extend the lease, or not to exercise the option to terminate the lease.

B39   The shorter the non-cancellable period of a lease, the more likely a lessee is to exercise an option to extend the lease or not to exercise an option to terminate the lease. This is because the costs associated with obtaining a replacement asset are likely to be proportionately higher the shorter the non-cancellable period.

B40   A lessee's past practice regarding the period over which it has typically used particular types of assets (whether leased or owned), and its economic reasons for doing so, may provide information that is helpful in assessing whether the lessee is reasonably certain to exercise, or not to exercise, an option. For example, if a lessee has typically used particular types of assets for a particular period of time or if the lessee has a practice of frequently exercising options on leases of particular types of underlying assets, the lessee shall consider the economic reasons for that past practice in assessing whether it is reasonably certain to exercise an option on leases of those assets.

B41   Paragraph 20 specifies that, after the commencement date, a lessee reassesses the lease term upon the occurrence of a significant event or a significant change in circumstances that is within the control of the lessee and affects whether the lessee is reasonably certain to exercise an option not previously included in its determination of the lease term, or not to exercise an option previously included in its determination of the lease term. Examples of significant events or changes in circumstances include:

(a)   significant leasehold improvements not anticipated at the commencement date that are expected to have significant economic benefit for the lessee when the option to extend or terminate the lease, or to purchase the underlying asset, becomes exercisable;

(b)   a significant modification to, or customisation of, the underlying asset that was not anticipated at the commencement date;

(c)   the inception of a sublease of the underlying asset for a period beyond the end of the previously determined lease term; and

(d)   a business decision of the lessee that is directly relevant to exercising, or not exercising, an option (for example, a decision to extend the lease of a complementary asset, to dispose of an alternative asset or to dispose of a business unit within which the right-of-use asset is employed).

In-substance fixed lease payments (paragraphs 27(a), 36(c) and 70(a))

B42   Lease payments include any in-substance fixed lease payments. In-substance fixed lease payments are payments that may, in form, contain variability but that, in substance, are unavoidable. In-substance fixed lease payments exist, for example, if:

(a)   payments are structured as variable lease payments, but there is no genuine variability in those payments. Those payments contain variable clauses that do not have real economic substance. Examples of those types of payments include:

(i)   payments that must be made only if an asset is proven to be capable of operating during the lease, or only if an event occurs that has no genuine possibility of not occurring; or

(ii)   payments that are initially structured as variable lease payments linked to the use of the underlying asset but for which the variability will be resolved at some point after the commencement date so that the payments become fixed for the remainder of the lease term. Those payments become in-substance fixed payments when the variability is resolved.

(b)   there is more than one set of payments that a lessee could make, but only one of those sets of payments is realistic. In this case, an entity shall consider the realistic set of payments to be lease payments.

(c)   there is more than one realistic set of payments that a lessee could make, but it must make at least one of those sets of payments. In this case, an entity shall consider the set of payments that aggregates to the lowest amount (on a discounted basis) to be lease payments.

Lessee involvement with the underlying asset before the commencement date

Costs of the lessee relating to the construction or design of the underlying asset

B43   An entity may negotiate a lease before the underlying asset is available for use by the lessee. For some leases, the underlying asset may need to be constructed or redesigned for use by the lessee. Depending on the terms and conditions of the contract, a lessee may be required to make payments relating to the construction or design of the asset.

B44   If a lessee incurs costs relating to the construction or design of an underlying asset, the lessee shall account for those costs applying other applicable Standards, such as AASB 116. Costs relating to the construction or design of an underlying asset do not include payments made by the lessee for the right to use the underlying asset. Payments for the right to use an underlying asset are payments for a lease, regardless of the timing of those payments.

Legal title to the underlying asset

B45   A lessee may obtain legal title to an underlying asset before that legal title is transferred to the lessor and the asset is leased to the lessee. Obtaining legal title does not in itself determine how to account for the transaction.

B46   If the lessee controls (or obtains control of) the underlying asset before that asset is transferred to the lessor, the transaction is a sale and leaseback transaction that is accounted for applying paragraphs 98–103.

B47   However, if the lessee does not obtain control of the underlying asset before the asset is transferred to the lessor, the transaction is not a sale and leaseback transaction. For example, this may be the case if a manufacturer, a lessor and a lessee negotiate a transaction for the purchase of an asset from the manufacturer by the lessor, which is in turn leased to the lessee. The lessee may obtain legal title to the underlying asset before legal title transfers to the lessor. In this case, if the lessee obtains legal title to the underlying asset but does not obtain control of the asset before it is transferred to the lessor, the transaction is not accounted for as a sale and leaseback transaction, but as a lease.

Lessee disclosures (paragraph 59)

B48   In determining whether additional information about leasing activities is necessary to meet the disclosure objective in paragraph 51, a lessee shall consider:

(a)   whether that information is relevant to users of financial statements. A lessee shall provide additional information specified in paragraph 59 only if that information is expected to be relevant to users of financial statements. In this context, this is likely to be the case if it helps those users to understand:

(i)   the flexibility provided by leases. Leases may provide flexibility if, for example, a lessee can reduce its exposure by exercising termination options or renewing leases with favourable terms and conditions.

      (ii)   restrictions imposed by leases. Leases may impose restrictions, for example, by requiring the lessee to maintain particular financial ratios.

      (iii)   sensitivity of reported information to key variables. Reported information may be sensitive to, for example, future variable lease payments.

      (iv)   exposure to other risks arising from leases.

      (v)   deviations from industry practice. Such deviations may include, for example, unusual or unique lease terms and conditions that affect a lessee's lease portfolio.

  (b)   whether that information is apparent from information either presented in the primary financial statements or disclosed in the notes. A lessee need not duplicate information that is already presented elsewhere in the financial statements.

B49   Additional information relating to variable lease payments that, depending on the circumstances, may be needed to satisfy the disclosure objective in paragraph 51 could include information that helps users of financial statements to assess, for example:

  (a)   the lessee's reasons for using variable lease payments and the prevalence of those payments;

  (b)   the relative magnitude of variable lease payments to fixed payments;

  (c)   key variables upon which variable lease payments depend and how payments are expected to vary in response to changes in those key variables; and

  (d)   other operational and financial effects of variable lease payments.

B50   Additional information relating to extension options or termination options that, depending on the circumstances, may be needed to satisfy the disclosure objective in paragraph 51 could include information that helps users of financial statements to assess, for example:

  (a)   the lessee's reasons for using extension options or termination options and the prevalence of those options;

  (b)   the relative magnitude of *optional lease payments* to lease payments;

  (c)   the prevalence of the exercise of options that were not included in the measurement of lease liabilities; and

  (d)   other operational and financial effects of those options.

B51   Additional information relating to residual value guarantees that, depending on the circumstances, may be needed to satisfy the disclosure objective in paragraph 51 could include information that helps users of financial statements to assess, for example:

  (a)   the lessee's reasons for providing residual value guarantees and the prevalence of those guarantees;

  (b)   the magnitude of a lessee's exposure to residual value risk;

  (c)   the nature of underlying assets for which those guarantees are provided; and

  (d)   other operational and financial effects of those guarantees.

B52   Additional information relating to sale and leaseback transactions that, depending on the circumstances, may be needed to satisfy the disclosure objective in paragraph 51 could include information that helps users of financial statements to assess, for example:

  (a)   the lessee's reasons for sale and leaseback transactions and the prevalence of those transactions;

  (b)   key terms and conditions of individual sale and leaseback transactions;

  (c)   payments not included in the measurement of lease liabilities; and

  (d)   the cash flow effect of sale and leaseback transactions in the reporting period.

AASB

Lessor lease classification (paragraphs 61–66)

B53   The classification of leases for lessors in this Standard is based on the extent to which the lease transfers the risks and rewards incidental to ownership of an underlying asset. Risks include the possibilities of losses from idle capacity or technological obsolescence and of variations in return because of changing economic conditions. Rewards may be represented by the expectation of profitable operation over the underlying asset's economic life and of gain from appreciation in value or realisation of a residual value.

B54   A lease contract may include terms and conditions to adjust the lease payments for particular changes that occur between the inception date and the commencement date (such as a change in the lessor's cost of the underlying asset or a change in the lessor's cost of financing the lease). In that case, for the purposes of classifying the lease, the effect of any such changes shall be deemed to have taken place at the inception date.

B55   When a lease includes both land and buildings elements, a lessor shall assess the classification of each element as a finance lease or an operating lease separately applying paragraphs 62–66 and B53–B54. In determining whether the land element is an operating lease or a finance lease, an important consideration is that land normally has an indefinite economic life.

B56   Whenever necessary in order to classify and account for a lease of land and buildings, a lessor shall allocate lease payments (including any lump-sum upfront payments) between the land and the buildings elements in proportion to the relative fair values of the leasehold interests in the land element and buildings element of the lease at the inception date. If the lease payments cannot be allocated reliably between these two elements, the entire lease is classified as a finance lease, unless it is clear that both elements are operating leases, in which case the entire lease is classified as an operating lease.

B57   For a lease of land and buildings in which the amount for the land element is immaterial to the lease, a lessor may treat the land and buildings as a single unit for the purpose of lease classification and classify it as a finance lease or an operating lease applying paragraphs 62–66 and B53–B54. In such a case, a lessor shall regard the economic life of the buildings as the economic life of the entire underlying asset.

Sublease classification

B58   In classifying a sublease, an intermediate lessor shall classify the sublease as a finance lease or an operating lease as follows:

(a)   if the head lease is a short-term lease that the entity, as a lessee, has accounted for applying paragraph 6, the sublease shall be classified as an operating lease.

(b)   otherwise, the sublease shall be classified by reference to the right-of-use asset arising from the head lease, rather than by reference to the underlying asset (for example, the item of property, plant or equipment that is the subject of the lease).

APPENDIX C
EFFECTIVE DATE AND TRANSITION

This appendix is an integral part of the Standard and has the same authority as the other parts of the Standard.

Effective date

C1   An entity shall apply this Standard for annual reporting periods beginning on or after 1 January 2019. Earlier application is permitted for entities that apply AASB 15 *Revenue from Contracts with Customers* at or before the date of initial application of this Standard. If an entity applies this Standard earlier, it shall disclose that fact.

Transition

C2   For the purposes of the requirements in paragraphs C1–C19, the date of initial application is the beginning of the annual reporting period in which an entity first applies this Standard.

Definition of a lease

C3   As a practical expedient, an entity is not required to reassess whether a contract is, or contains, a lease at the date of initial application. Instead, the entity is permitted:

(a)   to apply this Standard to contracts that were previously identified as leases applying AASB 117 *Leases* and Interpretation 4 *Determining whether an Arrangement contains a Lease*. The entity shall apply the transition requirements in paragraphs C5–C18 to those leases.

(b)   not to apply this Standard to contracts that were not previously identified as containing a lease applying AASB 117 and Interpretation 4.

C4   If an entity chooses the practical expedient in paragraph C3, it shall disclose that fact and apply the practical expedient to all of its contracts. As a result, the entity shall apply the requirements in paragraphs 9–11 only to contracts entered into (or changed) on or after the date of initial application.

Lessees

C5   A lessee shall apply this Standard to its leases either:

(a)   retrospectively to each prior reporting period presented applying AASB 108 *Accounting Policies, Changes in Accounting Estimates and Errors*; or

(b)   retrospectively with the cumulative effect of initially applying the Standard recognised at the date of initial application in accordance with paragraphs C7–C13.

C6   A lessee shall apply the election described in paragraph C5 consistently to all of its leases in which it is a lessee.

C7   If a lessee elects to apply this Standard in accordance with paragraph C5(b), the lessee shall not restate comparative information. Instead, the lessee shall recognise the cumulative effect of initially applying this Standard as an adjustment to the opening balance of retained earnings (or other component of equity, as appropriate) at the date of initial application.

Leases previously classified as operating leases

C8   If a lessee elects to apply this Standard in accordance with paragraph C5(b), the lessee shall:

(a)   recognise a lease liability at the date of initial application for leases previously classified as an operating lease applying AASB 117. The lessee shall measure that lease liability at the present value of the remaining lease payments, discounted using the lessee's incremental borrowing rate at the date of initial application.

(b)   recognise a right-of-use asset at the date of initial application for leases previously classified as an operating lease applying AASB 117. The lessee shall choose, on a lease-by-lease basis, to measure that right-of-use asset at either:

(i)   its carrying amount as if the Standard had been applied since the commencement date, but discounted using the lessee's incremental borrowing rate at the date of initial application; or

(ii)   an amount equal to the lease liability, adjusted by the amount of any prepaid or accrued lease payments relating to that lease recognised in the statement of financial position immediately before the date of initial application.

(b)   adjust the leaseback right-of-use asset for any deferred gains or losses that relate to off-market terms recognised in the statement of financial position immediately before the date of initial application.

Amounts previously recognised in respect of business combinations

C19   If a lessee previously recognised an asset or a liability applying AASB 3 *Business Combinations* relating to favourable or unfavourable terms of an operating lease acquired as part of a business combination, the lessee shall derecognise that asset or liability and adjust the carrying amount of the right-of-use asset by a corresponding amount at the date of initial application.

References to AASB 9

C20   If an entity applies this Standard but does not yet apply AASB 9 *Financial Instruments*, any reference in this Standard to AASB 9 shall be read as a reference to AASB 139 *Financial Instruments: Recognition and Measurement*.

Withdrawal of other Standards

C21   [Deleted by the AASB]

Withdrawal of AASB pronouncements

AusC21.1   This Standard repeals AASB 117 *Leases* issued in August 2015. Despite the repeal, after the time this Standard starts to apply under section 334 of the Corporations Act (either generally or in relation to an individual entity), the repealed Standard continues to apply in relation to any period ending before that time as if the repeal had not occurred.

            [Note: When this Standard applies under section 334 of the Corporations Act (either generally or in relation to an individual entity), it supersedes the application of the repealed Standard.]

AusC21.2   When applied or operative, this Standard supersedes:

(a)   Interpretation 4 *Determining whether an Arrangement contains a Lease*;

(b)   Interpretation 115 *Operating Leases—Incentives*; and

(c)   Interpretation 127 *Evaluating the Substance of Transactions Involving the Legal Form of a Lease*.

APPENDIX D
AMENDMENTS TO OTHER STANDARDS

This appendix sets out the amendments to other Standards that are a consequence of the AASB issuing this Standard. An entity shall apply the amendments for annual periods beginning on or after 1 January 2019. If an entity applies this Standard for an earlier period, it shall also apply these amendments for that earlier period.

An entity is not permitted to apply AASB 16 before applying AASB 15 Revenue from Contracts with Customers *(see paragraph C1).*

> Amendments are made to the latest principal version of a Standard (or an Interpretation), unless otherwise indicated.
>
> The amendments set out in this appendix also apply, as far as possible, to earlier principal versions of the amended Standards and Interpretations when this Standard is applied for earlier periods, as necessary.

This Standard uses underlining, striking out and other typographical material to identify some of the amendments to a Standard or an Interpretation, in order to make the amendments more understandable. However, the amendments made by this Standard do not include that underlining, striking out or other typographical material. Amended paragraphs are shown with deleted text struck through and new text is underlined. Ellipses (...) are used to help provide the context within which amendments are made and also to indicate text that is not amended.

AASB 1 *First-time Adoption of Australian Accounting Standards* (July 2015)

Paragraph 30 is amended and paragraph 39AB is added.

Use of fair value as deemed cost

30 If an entity uses fair value in its opening Australian-Accounting-Standards statement of financial position as *deemed cost* for an item of property, plant and equipment, an investment property, or an intangible asset or a right-of-use asset (see paragraphs D5 and D7), the entity's first Australian-Accounting-Standards financial statements shall disclose, for each line item in the opening Australian-Accounting-Standards statement of financial position:

(a) ...

Effective date

...

39AB AASB 16 *Leases*, issued in February 2016, amended paragraphs 30, C4, D1, D7, D8B and D9, deleted paragraph D9A and added paragraphs D9B–D9E An entity shall apply those amendments when it applies AASB 16.

Paragraph C4 is amended.

Exemptions for business combinations

...

C4 If a first-time adopter does not apply AASB 3 retrospectively to a past business combination, this has the following consequences for that business combination:

(a) ...

(f) If an asset acquired, or liability assumed, in a past business combination was not recognised in accordance with previous GAAP, it does not have a deemed cost of zero in the opening Australian-Accounting-Standards statement of financial position. Instead, the acquirer shall recognise and measure it in its consolidated statement of financial position on the basis that Australian Accounting Standards would require in the statement of financial position of the acquiree. To illustrate: if the acquirer had not, in accordance with its previous GAAP, capitalised finance leases acquired in a past business combination in which the acquiree was a lessee, it shall capitalise those leases in its consolidated financial statements, as AASB 117 AASB 16 *Leases* would require the acquiree to do in its Australian-Accounting-Standards statement of financial position. Similarly, if the acquirer had not, in accordance with its previous GAAP, recognised a contingent liability that still exists at the date of transition to Australian Accounting Standards, the acquirer shall recognise that contingent liability at that date unless AASB 137 *Provisions, Contingent Liabilities and Contingent Assets* would prohibit its recognition in the financial statements of the acquiree. Conversely, if an asset or liability was subsumed in goodwill in accordance with previous GAAP but would have been recognised separately under AASB 3, that asset or liability remains in goodwill unless Australian Accounting Standards would require its recognition in the financial statements of the acquiree.

(g)   ...

In Appendix D, paragraphs D1, D7, D8B and D9 are amended. Paragraph D9A is deleted. Paragraphs D9B–D9E are added.

Exemptions from other Australian Accounting Standards

...

D1   An entity may elect to use one or more of the following exemptions:

(a)   ...

(d)   leases (paragraphs D9 and ~~D9A~~ D9B–D9E);

...

Deemed cost

...

D7   The elections in paragraphs D5 and D6 are also available for:

(a)   investment property, if an entity elects to use the cost model in AASB 140 *Investment Property*; ~~and~~

(aa)   right-of-use assets (AASB 16 *Leases*); and

(b)   ...

        ...

D8B   Some entities hold items of property, plant and equipment, <u>right-of-use assets</u> or intangible assets that are used, or were previously used, in operations subject to rate regulation. The carrying amount of such items might include amounts that were determined under previous GAAP but do not qualify for capitalisation in accordance with Australian Accounting Standards. If this is the case, a first-time adopter may elect to use the previous GAAP carrying amount of such an item at the date of transition to Australian Accounting Standards as deemed cost. If an entity applies this exemption to an item, it need not apply it to all items. At the date of transition to Australian Accounting Standards, an entity shall test for impairment in accordance with AASB 136 each item for which this exemption is used. For the purposes of this paragraph, operations are subject to rate regulation if they are governed by a framework for establishing the prices that can be charged to customers for goods or services and that framework is subject to oversight and/or approval by a rate regulator (as defined in AASB 14 *Regulatory Deferral Accounts*).

Leases

D9   ~~A first-time adopter may apply the transitional provisions in Interpretation 4 *Determining whether an Arrangement contains a Lease* as identified in AASB 1048. Therefore, a first-time adopter may determine whether an arrangement existing at the date of transition to Australian Accounting Standards contains a lease on the basis of facts and circumstances existing at that date.~~ <u>A first-time adopter may assess whether a contract existing at the date of transition to Australian Accounting Standards contains a lease by applying paragraphs 9–11 of AASB 16 to those contracts on the basis of facts and circumstances existing at that date.</u>

D9A   [Deleted] ~~If a first-time adopter made the same determination of whether an arrangement contained a lease in accordance with previous GAAP as that required~~

~~by Interpretation 4 (as identified in AASB 1048) but at a date other than that required by Interpretation 4, the first-time adopter need not reassess that determination when it adopts Australian Accounting Standards. For an entity to have made the same determination of whether the arrangement contained a lease in accordance with previous GAAP, that determination would have to have given the same outcome as that resulting from applying AASB 117 *Leases* and Interpretation 4.~~

D9B When a first-time adopter that is a lessee recognises lease liabilities and right-of-use assets, it may apply the following approach to all of its leases (subject to the practical expedients described in paragraph D9D):

    (a) measure a lease liability at the date of transition to Australian Accounting Standards. A lessee following this approach shall measure that lease liability at the present value of the remaining lease payments (see paragraph D9E), discounted using the lessee's incremental borrowing rate (see paragraph D9E) at the date of transition to Australian Accounting Standards.

    (b) measure a right-of-use asset at the date of transition to Australian Accounting Standards. The lessee shall choose, on a lease-by-lease basis, to measure that right-of-use asset at either:

        (i) its carrying amount as if AASB 16 had been applied since the commencement date of the lease (see paragraph D9E), but discounted using the lessee's incremental borrowing rate at the date of transition to Australian Accounting Standards; or

        (ii) an amount equal to the lease liability, adjusted by the amount of any prepaid or accrued lease payments relating to that lease recognised in the statement of financial position immediately before the date of transition to Australian Accounting Standards.

    (c) apply AASB 136 to right-of-use assets at the date of transition to Australian Accounting Standards.

D9C Notwithstanding the requirements in paragraph D9B, a first-time adopter that is a lessee shall measure the right-of-use asset at fair value at the date of transition to Australian Accounting Standards for leases that meet the definition of investment property in AASB 140 and are measured using the fair value model in AASB 140 from the date of transition to Australian Accounting Standards.

D9D A first-time adopter that is a lessee may do one or more of the following at the date of transition to Australian Accounting Standards, applied on a lease-by-lease basis:

    (a) apply a single discount rate to a portfolio of leases with reasonably similar characteristics (for example, a similar remaining lease term for a similar class of underlying asset in a similar economic environment).

    (b) elect not to apply the requirements in paragraph D9B to leases for which the lease term (see paragraph D9E) ends within 12 months of the date of transition to Australian Accounting Standards. Instead, the entity shall account for (including disclosure of information about) these leases as if they were short-term leases accounted for in accordance with paragraph 6 of AASB 16.

    (c) elect not to apply the requirements in paragraph D9B to leases for which the underlying asset is of low value (as described in paragraphs B3-B8 of AASB 16). Instead, the entity shall account for (including disclosure of information about) these leases in accordance with paragraph 6 of AASB 16.

    (d) exclude initial direct costs (see paragraph D9E) from the measurement of the right-of-use asset at the date of transition to Australian Accounting Standards.

    (e) use hindsight, such as in determining the lease term if the contract contains options to extend or terminate the lease.

D9E Lease payments, lessee, lessee's incremental borrowing rate, commencement date of the lease, initial direct costs and lease term are defined terms in AASB 16 and are used in this Standard with the same meaning.

AASB 3 *Business Combinations* (August 2015)

Paragraphs 14 and 17 are amended and paragraphs 28A and 28B and their related heading, and paragraph 64M, are added.

Recognition conditions

...

14   Paragraphs ~~B28 B40~~ B31–B40 provide guidance on recognising ~~operating leases and~~ intangible assets. Paragraphs 22–28B specify the types of identifiable assets and liabilities that include items for which this Standard provides limited exceptions to the recognition principle and conditions.

Classifying or designating identifiable assets acquired and liabilities assumed in a business combination

...

17   This Standard provides two exceptions to the principle in paragraph 15:

    (a)   classification of a lease contract in which the acquiree is the lessor as either an operating lease or a finance lease in accordance with ~~AASB 117~~ AASB 16 *Leases*; and

    (b)   ...

Leases in which the acquiree is the lessee

28A   The acquirer shall recognise right-of-use assets and lease liabilities for leases identified in accordance with AASB 16 in which the acquiree is the lessee. The acquirer is not required to recognise right-of-use assets and lease liabilities for:

    (a)   leases for which the lease term (as defined in AASB 16) ends within 12 months of the acquisition date; or

    (b)   leases for which the underlying asset is of low value (as described in paragraphs B3–B0 of AASB 16).

28B   The acquirer shall measure the lease liability at the present value of the remaining lease payments (as defined in AASB 16) as if the acquired lease were a new lease at the acquisition date. The acquirer shall measure the right-of-use asset at the same amount as the lease liability, adjusted to reflect favourable or unfavourable terms of the lease when compared with market terms.

Effective date

...

64M   AASB 16, issued in February 2016, amended paragraphs 14, 17, B32 and B42, deleted paragraphs B28–B30 and their related heading and added paragraphs 28A–28B and their related heading. An entity shall apply those amendments when it applies AASB 16.

In Appendix B, paragraphs B28–B30 and their related heading are deleted and paragraphs B32 and B42 are amended.

~~Operating leases~~

B28   [Deleted] ~~The acquirer shall recognise no assets or liabilities related to an operating lease in which the acquiree is the lessee except as required by paragraphs B29 and B30.~~

B29 [Deleted] ~~The acquirer shall determine whether the terms of each operating lease in which the acquiree is the lessee are favourable or unfavourable. The acquirer shall recognise an intangible asset if the terms of an operating lease are favourable relative to market terms and a liability if the terms are unfavourable relative to market terms. Paragraph B42 provides guidance on measuring the acquisition-date fair value of assets subject to operating leases in which the acquiree is the lessor.~~

B30 [Deleted] ~~An identifiable intangible asset may be associated with an operating lease, which may be evidenced by market participants' willingness to pay a price for the lease even if it is at market terms. For example, a lease of gates at an airport or of retail space in a prime shopping area might provide entry into a market or other future economic benefits that qualify as identifiable intangible assets, for example, as a customer relationship. In that situation, the acquirer shall recognise the associated identifiable intangible asset(s) in accordance with paragraph B31.~~

Intangible assets

...

B32 An intangible asset that meets the contractual-legal criterion is identifiable even if the asset is not transferable or separable from the acquiree or from other rights and obligations. For example:

   (a) [deleted] ~~an acquiree leases a manufacturing facility under an operating lease that has terms that are favourable relative to market terms. The lease terms explicitly prohibit transfer of the lease (through either sale or sublease). The amount by which the lease terms are favourable compared with the terms of current market transactions for the same or similar items is an intangible asset that meets the contractual-legal criterion for recognition separately from goodwill, even though the acquirer cannot sell or otherwise transfer the lease contract.~~

   (b) ...

Assets subject to operating leases in which the acquiree is the lessor

B42 In measuring the acquisition-date fair value of an asset such as a building or a patent that is subject to an operating lease in which the acquiree is the lessor, the acquirer shall take into account the terms of the lease. ~~In other words, t~~The acquirer does not recognise a separate asset or liability if the terms of an operating lease are either favourable or unfavourable when compared with market terms ~~as paragraph B29 requires for leases in which the acquiree is the lessee~~.

AASB 4 *Insurance Contracts* (August 2015)

> Paragraph 4 is amended and paragraph 41I is added.

Scope

...

4 An entity shall not apply this Standard to:

   (a) ...

   (c) contractual rights or contractual obligations that are contingent on the future use of, or right to use, a non-financial item (for example, some licence fees, royalties, ~~contingent~~ variable lease payments and similar items), as well as a lessee's residual value guarantee embedded in a ~~finance~~ lease (see ~~AASB 117~~ AASB 16 *Leases*, AASB 15 *Revenue from Contracts with Customers* and AASB 138 *Intangible Assets*).

   (d) ...

Effective date and transition

...

41I   AASB 16, issued in February 2016, amended paragraph 4. An entity shall apply that
       amendment when it applies AASB 16.

AASB 7 *Financial Instruments: Disclosures* (August 2015)

Paragraph 29 is amended and paragraph 44CC is added.

Fair value

...

29   Disclosures of fair value are not required:

      (a)   ...

      (b)   for an investment in equity instruments that do not have a quoted price in an
             active market for an identical instrument (ie a Level 1 input), or derivatives
             linked to such equity instruments, that is measured at cost in accordance with
             AASB 139 because its fair value cannot otherwise be measured reliably; ~~or~~

      (c)   for a contract containing a discretionary participation feature (as described in
             AASB 4) if the fair value of that feature cannot be measured reliably; or

      (d)   for lease liabilities.

Effective date and transition

...

44CC AASB 16 *Leases*, issued in February 2016, amended paragraphs 29 and B11D. An
      entity shall apply those amendments when it applies AASB 16.

In Appendix B, paragraph B11D is amended.

Quantitative liquidity risk disclosures (paragraphs 34(a) and 39(a) and (b))

...

B11D The contractual amounts disclosed in the maturity analyses as required by paragraph
      39(a) and (b) are the contractual undiscounted cash flows, for example:

      (a)   gross ~~finance~~ lease ~~obligations~~ liabilities (before deducting finance charges);

      (b)   ...

AASB 9 *Financial Instruments* (December 2014)

Paragraph 2.1 and paragraph 5.5.15 are amended and paragraph 7.1.5 is added.

Chapter 2 Scope

**2.1   This Standard shall be applied by all entities to all types of financial instruments
         except:**

      (a)   ...

      **(b)   rights and obligations under leases to which ~~AASB 117~~ AASB 16 *Leases*
               applies. However:**

(i)   finance lease receivables (ie <u>net investments in finance leases</u>) and <u>operating lease receivables</u> recognised by a lessor are subject to the derecognition and impairment requirements of this Standard;

(ii)   <s>finance</s> lease <s>payables</s> <u>liabilities</u> recognised by a lessee are subject to the derecognition requirements <u>in paragraph 3.3.1</u> of this Standard; and

(iii) derivatives that are embedded in leases are subject to the embedded derivatives requirements of this Standard.

(c)   ...

Simplified approach for trade receivables, contract assets and lease receivables

5.5.15 Despite paragraphs 5.5.3 and 5.5.5, an entity shall always measure the loss allowance at an amount equal to lifetime expected credit losses for:

(a)   ...

(b)   lease receivables that result from transactions that are within the scope of <s>AASB 117</s> <u>AASB 16</u>, if the entity chooses as its accounting policy to measure the loss allowance at an amount equal to lifetime expected credit losses. That accounting policy shall be applied to all lease receivables but may be applied separately to finance and operating lease receivables.

...

7.1 Effective date

...

7.1.5 <u>AASB 16, issued in February 2016, amended paragraphs 2.1, 5.5.15, B4.3.8, B5.5.34 and B5.5.46. An entity shall apply those amendments when it applies AASB 16.</u>

In Appendix B, paragraphs B4.3.8, B5.5.34 and B5.5.46 are amended.

Embedded derivatives (Section 4.3)

...

B4.3.8 The economic characteristics and risks of an embedded derivative are closely related to the economic characteristics and risks of the host contract in the following examples. In these examples, an entity does not account for the embedded derivative separately from the host contract.

(a)   ...

(f)   An embedded derivative in a host lease contract is closely related to the host contract if the embedded derivative is (i) an inflation-related index such as an index of lease payments to a consumer price index (provided that the lease is not leveraged and the index relates to inflation in the entity's own economic environment), (ii) <s>contingent rentals</s> <u>variable lease payments</u> based on related sales or (iii) <s>contingent rentals</s> <u>variable lease payments</u> based on variable interest rates.

(g)   ...

Expected credit losses

...

B5.5.34 When measuring a loss allowance for a lease receivable, the cash flows used for determining the expected credit losses should be consistent with the cash flows used in measuring the lease receivable in accordance with <s>AASB 117</s> <u>AASB 16</u> *Leases*.

...

Time value of money

...

B5.5.46 Expected credit losses on lease receivables shall be discounted using the same discount rate used in the measurement of the lease receivable in accordance with ~~AASB 117~~ AASB 16.

...

AASB 13 *Fair Value Measurement* (August 2015)

Paragraph 6 is amended.

Scope

...

6   The measurement and disclosure requirements of this Standard do not apply to the following:

(a)   ...

(b)   leasing transactions ~~within the scope of AASB 117~~ accounted for in accordance with AASB 16 *Leases*; and

(c)   ...

In Appendix C, paragraph C6 is added.

Effective date and transition

...

C6   AASB 16 *Leases*, issued in February 2016, amended paragraph 6. An entity shall apply that amendment when it applies AASB 16.

AASB 15 *Revenue from Contracts with Customers* (December 2014)

Paragraphs 5 and 97 are amended.

Scope

5   An entity shall apply this Standard to all contracts with customers, except the following:

(a)   lease contracts within the scope of ~~AASB 117~~ AASB 16 *Leases*;

(b)   ...

Costs to fulfil a contract

...

97   Costs that relate directly to a contract (or a specific anticipated contract) include any of the following:

(a)   ...

(c)   allocations of costs that relate directly to the contract or to contract activities (for example, costs of contract management and supervision, insurance and depreciation of tools, ~~and~~ equipment and right-of-use assets used in fulfilling the contract);

(d) ...

In Appendix B, paragraphs B66 and B70 are amended.

A forward or a call option

B66 If an entity has an obligation or a right to repurchase the asset (a forward or a call option), a customer does not obtain control of the asset because the customer is limited in its ability to direct the use of, and obtain substantially all of the remaining benefits from, the asset even though the customer may have physical possession of the asset. Consequently, the entity shall account for the contract as either of the following:

(a) a lease in accordance with ~~AASB 117~~ AASB 16 *Leases* if the entity can or must repurchase the asset for an amount that is less than the original selling price of the asset, unless the contract is part of a sale and leaseback transaction. If the contract is part of a sale and leaseback transaction, the entity shall continue to recognise the asset and shall recognise a financial liability for any consideration received from the customer. The entity shall account for the financial liability in accordance with AASB 9; or

(b) ...

A put option

B70 If an entity has an obligation to repurchase the asset at the customer's request (a put option) at a price that is lower than the original selling price of the asset, the entity shall consider at contract inception whether the customer has a significant economic incentive to exercise that right. The customer's exercising of that right results in the customer effectively paying the entity consideration for the right to use a specified asset for a period of time. Therefore, if the customer has a significant economic incentive to exercise that right, the entity shall account for the agreement as a lease in accordance with ~~AASB 117~~ AASB 16, unless the contract is part of a sale and leaseback transaction. If the contract is part of a sale and leaseback transaction, the entity shall continue to recognise the asset and shall recognise a financial liability for any consideration received from the customer. The entity shall account for the financial liability in accordance with AASB 9.

...

In Appendix C, paragraph C1A is added.

Effective date

...

C1A AASB 16 *Leases*, issued in February 2016, amended paragraphs 5, 97, B66 and B70. An entity shall apply those amendments when it applies AASB 16.

AASB 101 *Presentation of Financial Statements* (July 2015)

Paragraph 123 is amended and paragraph 139Q is added.

Disclosure of accounting policies

...

123   In the process of applying the entity's accounting policies, management makes various judgements, apart from those involving estimations, that can significantly affect the amounts it recognises in the financial statements. For example, management makes judgements in determining:

(a)   ...

(b)   when substantially all the significant risks and rewards of ownership of financial assets and, for lessors, ~~lease~~ assets subject to leases are transferred to other entities; and

(c)   ...

Transition and effective date

...

139Q   AASB 16 *Leases*, issued in February 2016, amended paragraph 123. An entity shall apply that amendment when it applies AASB 16.

AASB 102 *Inventories* (July 2015)

Paragraph 12 is amended and paragraph 40G is added.

Costs of conversion

12   The costs of conversion of inventories include costs directly related to the units of production, such as direct labour. They also include a systematic allocation of fixed and variable production overheads that are incurred in converting materials into finished goods. Fixed production overheads are those indirect costs of production that remain relatively constant regardless of the volume of production, such as depreciation and maintenance of factory buildings, ~~and~~ equipment and right-of-use assets used in the production process, and the cost of factory management and administration. Variable production overheads are those indirect costs of production that vary directly, or nearly directly, with the volume of production, such as indirect materials and indirect labour.

...

Effective date

...

40G   AASB 16 *Leases*, issued in February 2016, amended paragraph 12. An entity shall apply that amendment when it applies AASB 16.

AASB 107 *Statement of Cash Flows* (August 2015)

Paragraphs Aus58.1 and Aus58.2 are renumbered to Aus52.1 and Aus52.2 respectively and with their related headings "Commencement of the legislative instrument" and "Withdrawal of AASB pronouncements" are relocated to follow paragraph 52.

Paragraphs 17 and 44 are amended and paragraph 59 is added.

Financing activities

17 The separate disclosure of cash flows arising from financing activities is important because it is useful in predicting claims on future cash flows by providers of capital to the entity. Examples of cash flows arising from financing activities are:

(a) ...

(e) cash payments by a lessee for the reduction of the outstanding liability relating to a ~~finance~~ lease.

Non-cash transactions

...

44 Many investing and financing activities do not have a direct impact on current cash flows although they do affect the capital and asset structure of an entity. The exclusion of non-cash transactions from the statement of cash flows is consistent with the objective of a statement of cash flows as these items do not involve cash flows in the current period. Examples of non-cash transactions are:

(a) the acquisition of assets either by assuming directly related liabilities or by means of a ~~finance~~ lease;

(b) ...

Effective date

...

59 AASB 16 *Leases*, issued in February 2016, amended paragraphs 17 and 44. An entity shall apply those amendments when it applies AASB 16.

In the Illustrative examples accompanying AASB 107, Example A is amended.

A Statement of cash flows for an entity other than a financial institution

...

3 The following additional information is also relevant for the preparation of the statements of cash flows:

- ...

- during the period, the group acquired property, plant and equipment and right-of-use assets relating to property, plant and equipment with an aggregate cost of 1,250, of which 900 ~~was acquired by means of finance leases~~ related to right-of-use assets. Cash payments of 350 were made to purchase property, plant and equipment.

- ...

Direct method statement of cash flows (paragraph 18(a))

20X2

...

Cash flows from financing activities

...

Payment of ~~finance~~ lease liabilities (90)

...

Depreciation

...

44   An entity allocates the amount initially recognised in respect of an item of property, plant and equipment to its significant parts and depreciates separately each such part. For example, it may be appropriate to depreciate separately the airframe and engines of an aircraft, whether owned or subject to a finance lease. Similarly, if an entity acquires property, plant and equipment subject to an operating lease in which it is the lessor, it may be appropriate to depreciate separately amounts reflected in the cost of that item that are attributable to favourable or unfavourable lease terms relative to market terms.

...

Derecognition

...

68   The gain or loss arising from the derecognition of an item of property, plant and equipment shall be included in profit or loss when the item is derecognised (unless AASB 117 AASB 16 *Leases* requires otherwise on a sale and leaseback). Gains shall not be classified as revenue.

...

69   The disposal of an item of property, plant and equipment may occur in a variety of ways (eg by sale, by entering into a finance lease or by donation). The date of disposal of an item of property, plant and equipment is the date the recipient obtains control of that item in accordance with the requirements for determining when a performance obligation is satisfied in AASB 15. AASB 117 AASB 16 applies to disposal by a sale and leaseback.

...

Effective date

...

81L   AASB 16, issued in February 2016, deleted paragraphs 4 and 27 and amended paragraphs 5, 10, 44 and 68–69. An entity shall apply those amendments when it applies AASB 16.

AASB 121 *The Effects of Changes in Foreign Exchange Rates* (August 2015)

Paragraph 16 is amended and paragraph 60K is added.

Monetary items

16   The essential feature of a monetary item is a right to receive (or an obligation to deliver) a fixed or determinable number of units of currency. Examples include: pensions and other employee benefits to be paid in cash; provisions that are to be settled in cash; lease liabilities; and cash dividends that are recognised as a liability. Similarly, a contract to receive (or deliver) a variable number of the entity's own equity instruments or a variable amount of assets in which the fair value to be received (or delivered) equals a fixed or determinable number of units of currency is a monetary item. Conversely, the essential feature of a non-monetary item is the absence of a right to receive (or an obligation to deliver) a fixed or determinable number of units of currency. Examples include: amounts prepaid for goods and services (eg prepaid rent); goodwill; intangible assets; inventories; property, plant and equipment; right-of-use assets; and provisions that are to be settled by the delivery of a non-monetary asset.

Effective date and transition

...

60K AASB 16 *Leases*, issued in February 2016, amended paragraph 16. An entity shall apply that amendment when it applies AASB 16.

AASB 123 *Borrowing Costs* (August 2015)

Paragraph 6 is amended and paragraph 29C is added.

Definitions

...

6 Borrowing costs may include:

(a) ...

(d) ~~finance charges~~ interest in respect of ~~finance~~ leases liabilities recognised in accordance with ~~AASB 117~~ AASB 16 *Leases*; and

(e) ...

Effective date

...

29C AASB 16, issued in February 2016, amended paragraph 6. An entity shall apply that amendment when it applies AASB 16.

AASB 132 *Financial Instruments: Presentation* (August 2015)

Paragraph 97S is added and paragraphs AG9 and AG10 in the Application Guidance are amended.

Effective date and transition

...

97S AASB 16 *Leases*, issued in February 2016, amended paragraphs AG9 and AG10. An entity shall apply those amendments when it applies AASB 16.

Appendix

Definitions (paragraphs 11-14)
Financial assets and financial liabilities

...

AG9 ~~Under AASB 117 *Leases* a finance lease is regarded as primarily~~ A lease typically creates an entitlement of the lessor to receive, and an obligation of the lessee to pay, a stream of payments that are substantially the same as blended payments of principal and interest under a loan agreement. The lessor accounts for its investment in the amount receivable under a finance lease ~~the~~ ~~contract~~ rather than the ~~leased~~ underlying asset itself that is subject to the finance lease. Accordingly, a lessor regards a finance lease as a financial instrument. ~~An operating lease, on the other hand, is regarded as primarily an uncompleted contract committing the lessor to provide the use of an asset in future periods in exchange for consideration similar to a fee for a service.~~ Under AASB 16, a lessor does not recognise its entitlement to receive lease payments under an operating lease. The lessor continues to account for the ~~leased~~ underlying asset itself rather than any amount receivable in the future under the contract. Accordingly, ~~a finance lease is regarded as a financial instrument and an operating lease is not regarded~~

as a financial instrument (except as regards individual payments currently due and payable) a lessor does not regard an operating lease as a financial instrument, except as regards individual payments currently due and payable by the lessee.

AG10 Physical assets (such as inventories, property, plant and equipment), leased right-of-use assets and intangible assets (such as patents and trademarks) are not financial assets. Control of such physical assets, right-of-use assets and intangible assets creates an opportunity to generate an inflow of cash or another financial asset, but it does not give rise to a present right to receive cash or another financial asset.

...

AASB 134 *Interim Financial Reporting* (August 2015)

In the Illustrative examples accompanying AASB 134, paragraphs B7 and C7 are amended.

~~Contingent~~ Variable lease payments

B7 ~~Contingent~~ Variable lease payments based on sales can be an example of a legal or constructive obligation that is recognised as a liability. If a lease provides for ~~contingent~~ variable payments based on the lessee achieving a certain level of annual sales, an obligation can arise in the interim periods of the financial year before the required annual level of sales has been achieved, if that required level of sales is expected to be achieved and the entity, therefore, has no realistic alternative but to make the future lease payment.

C Examples of the use of estimates

...

C7 **Revaluations and fair value accounting:** AASB 116 *Property, Plant and Equipment* allows an entity to choose as its accounting policy the revaluation model whereby items of property, plant and equipment are revalued to fair value. AASB 16 *Leases* allows a lessee to measure right-of-use assets applying the revaluation model in AASB 116 if those right-of-use assets relate to a class of property, plant and equipment to which the lessee applies the revaluation model in AASB 116. Similarly, AASB 140 *Investment Property* requires an entity to measure the fair value of investment property. For those measurements, an entity may rely on professionally qualified valuers at annual reporting dates though not at interim reporting dates.

...

AASB 137 *Provisions, Contingent Liabilities and Contingent Assets* (August 2015)

Paragraph 5 is amended and paragraph 102 is added.

Scope

...

5 When another Standard deals with a specific type of provision, contingent liability or contingent asset, an entity applies that Standard instead of this Standard. For example, some types of provisions are addressed in Standards on:

(a) ...

(c) leases (see ~~AASB 117~~ AASB 16 *Leases*). However, ~~as AASB 117 contains no specific requirements to deal with operating leases that have become onerous,~~

this Standard applies to such cases this Standard applies to any lease that becomes onerous before the commencement date of the lease as defined in AASB 16. This Standard also applies to short-term leases and leases for which the underlying asset is of low value accounted for in accordance with paragraph 6 of AASB 16 and that have become onerous;

(d) ...

Effective date

...

102 AASB 16, issued in February 2016, amended paragraph 5. An entity shall apply that amendment when it applies AASB 16.

In the Guidance on implementing AASB 137, in Section C, Example 8 is deleted.

Example 8 An onerous contract

[Deleted] An entity operates profitably from a factory that it has leased under an operating lease. ...

Conclusion A provision is recognised for the best estimate of the unavoidable lease payments (see paragraphs 5(c), 14 and 66).

AASB 138 *Intangible Assets* (August 2015)

Paragraphs 3, 6, 113 and 114 are amended and paragraph 130L is added.

Scope

...

3 If another Standard prescribes the accounting for a specific type of intangible asset, an entity applies that Standard instead of this Standard. For example, this Standard does not apply to:

(a) ...

(c) leases that are within the scope of AASB 117 of intangible assets accounted for in accordance with AASB 16 *Leases*.

(d) ...

6 In the case of a finance lease, the underlying asset may be either tangible or intangible. After initial recognition, a lessee accounts for an intangible asset held under a finance lease in accordance with this Standard. Rights held by a lessee under licensing agreements for items such as motion picture films, video recordings, plays, manuscripts, patents and copyrights are excluded from the scope of AASB 117 and are within the scope of this Standard and are excluded from the scope of AASB 16.

...

Retirements and disposals

...

113 The gain or loss arising from the derecognition of an intangible asset shall be determined as the difference between the net disposal proceeds, if any, and the carrying amount of the asset. It shall be recognised in profit or loss when the asset is derecognised (unless AASB 117 AASB 16 requires otherwise on a sale and leaseback.) Gains shall not be classified as revenue.

114   The disposal of an intangible asset may occur in a variety of ways (eg by sale, by
        entering into a finance lease, or by donation). The date of disposal of an intangible
        asset is the date that the recipient obtains control of that asset in accordance with the
        requirements for determining when a performance obligation is satisfied in AASB 15
        Revenue from Contracts with Customers. ~~AASB 117~~ AASB 16 applies to disposal by
        a sale and leaseback.

Transitional provisions and effective date

...

130L   AASB 16, issued in February 2016, amended paragraphs 3, 6, 113 and 114. An entity
        shall apply those amendments when it applies AASB 16.

AASB 139 *Financial Instruments: Recognition and Measurement* (July 2004)

> The following amendments apply only when AASB 16 is applied early in conjunction with the July 2004
> version of AASB 139.
>
> Paragraph 2 is amended, paragraph 103V is added and in the Application Guidance paragraph AG33 is
> amended.

Scope

2   This Standard shall be applied by all entities to all types of financial instruments
        except:

        (a)   ...

        (b)   rights and obligations under leases to which ~~AASB 117~~ AASB 16 *Leases*
                applies. However:

                (i)   finance lease receivables (ie net investments in finance leases) and
                        operating lease receivables recognised by a lessor are subject to
                        the *derecognition* and impairment provisions of this Standard (see
                        paragraphs 15–37 and 58, 59, 63–65 and Appendix A paragraphs
                        AG36–AG52 and AG84–AG93);

                (ii)   ~~finance~~ lease ~~payables~~ liabilities recognised by a lessee are subject
                        to the derecognition provisions in paragraph 39 of this Standard ~~(see
                        paragraphs 39–42 and Appendix A paragraphs AG57–AG63)~~; and

                (iii)   ...

Effective date and transition

...

103V   AASB 16, issued in February 2016, amended paragraphs 2 and AG33. An entity shall
        apply those amendments when it applies AASB 16.

Appendix A
Embedded derivatives (paragraphs 10–13)

...

AG33   The economic characteristics and risks of an embedded derivative are closely related to
        the economic characteristics and risks of the host contract in the following examples.
        In these examples, an entity does not account for the embedded derivative separately
        from the host contract.

        (a)   ...

AASB 16

(f)   An embedded derivative in a host lease contract is closely related to the host
        contract if the embedded derivative is (i) an inflation-related index such as an
        index of lease payments to a consumer price index (provided that the lease is
        not leveraged and the index relates to inflation in the entity's own economic
        environment), (ii) ~~contingent rentals~~ variable lease payments based on related
        sales or (iii) ~~contingent rentals~~ variable lease payments based on variable
        interest rates.

(g)   ...

AASB 140 *Investment Property* (August 2015)

Paragraphs 3, 6, 25, 26 and 34 are deleted, paragraphs 5, 7-9, 16, 20, 30, 41, 50, 53, 53A, 54, 56, 60-62, 67,
69, 74, 75, 77 and 78 are amended and paragraphs 19A, 29A, 40A, 84B and 85F are added.

Scope

...

3   [Deleted] ~~Among other things, this Standard applies to the measurement in a lessee's~~
        ~~financial statements of investment property interests held under a lease accounted for as~~
        ~~a finance lease and to the measurement in a lessor's financial statements of investment~~
        ~~property provided to a lessee under an operating lease. This Standard does not deal~~
        ~~with matters covered in AASB 117 Leases, including:~~

        (a)   ~~classification of leases as finance leases or operating leases;~~

        (b)   ~~recognition of lease income from investment property (see also AASB 15~~
                ~~Revenue from Contracts with Customers);~~

        (c)   ~~measurement in a lessee's financial statements of property interests held under~~
                ~~a lease accounted for as an operating lease;~~

        (d)   ~~measurement in a lessor's financial statements of its net investment in a finance~~
                ~~lease;~~

        (e)   ~~accounting for sale and leaseback transactions; and~~

        (f)   ~~disclosure about finance leases and operating leases.~~

                ...

Definitions

5   The following terms are used in this Standard with the meanings specified:

        ...

        Investment property is property (land or a building—or part of a building—or
        both) held (by the owner or by the lessee as a right-of-use asset ~~under a finance~~
        ~~lease~~) to earn rentals or for capital appreciation or both, rather than for:

        (a)   use in the production or supply of goods or services or for administrative
                purposes; or

        (b)   sale in the ordinary course of business.

        Owner-occupied property is property held (by the owner or by the lessee as a right-
        of-use asset ~~under a finance lease~~) for use in the production or supply of goods
        or services or for administrative purposes.

Classification of property as investment property or owner-occupied property

6   [Deleted] ~~A property interest that is held by a lessee under an operating lease may~~
        ~~be classified and accounted for as investment property if, and only if, the property~~

~~would otherwise meet the definition of an investment property and the lessee uses the fair value model set out in paragraphs 33–55 for the asset recognised. This classification alternative is available on a property-by-property basis. However, once this classification alternative is selected for one such property interest held under an operating lease, all property classified as investment property shall be accounted for using the fair value model. When this classification alternative is selected, any interest so classified is included in the disclosures required by paragraphs 74–78.~~

7   Investment property is held to earn rentals or for capital appreciation or both. Therefore, an investment property generates cash flows largely independently of the other assets held by an entity. This distinguishes investment property from owner-occupied property. The production or supply of goods or services (or the use of property for administrative purposes) generates cash flows that are attributable not only to property, but also to other assets used in the production or supply process. AASB 116 applies to <u>owned</u> owner-occupied property <u>and AASB 16 applies to owner-occupied property held by a lessee as a right-of-use asset</u>.

8   The following are examples of investment property:

    (a)   ...

    (c)   a building owned by the entity (or <u>a right-of-use asset relating to a building</u> held by the entity ~~under a finance lease~~) and leased out under one or more operating leases.

    (d)   ...

9   The following are examples of items that are not investment property and are therefore outside the scope of this Standard:

    (a)   ...

    (c)   owner-occupied property (see AASB 116 <u>and AASB 16</u>), including (among other things) property held for future use as owner-occupied property, property held for future development and subsequent use as owner-occupied property, property occupied by employees (whether or not the employees pay rent at market rates) and owner-occupied property awaiting disposal.

    (d)   ...

Recognition

16   <u>An owned</u> ~~I~~investment property shall be recognised as an asset when, and only when:

    (a)   it is probable that the future economic benefits that are associated with the investment property will flow to the entity; and

    (b)   the cost of the investment property can be measured reliably.

    ...

19A   <u>An investment property held by a lessee as a right-of-use asset shall be recognised in accordance with AASB 16.</u>

Measurement at recognition

20   **An <u>owned</u> investment property shall be measured initially at its cost. Transaction costs shall be included in the initial measurement.**

    ...

25   [Deleted] ~~The initial cost of a property interest held under a lease and classified as an investment property shall be as prescribed for a finance lease by paragraph 20 of AASB 117, ie the asset shall be recognised at the lower of the fair value of the property and the present value of the minimum lease payments. An equivalent amount shall be recognised as a liability in accordance with that same paragraph.~~

26   [Deleted] ~~Any premium paid for a lease is treated as part of the minimum lease payments for this purpose, and is therefore included in the cost of the asset, but is excluded from the liability. If a property interest held under a lease is classified as investment property, the item accounted for at fair value is that interest and not the underlying property. Guidance on measuring the fair value of a property interest is set out for the fair value model in paragraphs 33–35, 40, 41, 48, 50 and 52 and in AASB 13. That guidance is also relevant to the measurement of fair value when that value is used as cost for initial recognition purposes.~~

        ...

29A   An investment property held by a lessee as a right-of-use asset shall be measured initially at its cost in accordance with AASB 16.

Measurement after recognition

Accounting policy

30   **With the exceptions noted in paragraphs 32A ~~and 34~~, an entity shall choose as its accounting policy either the fair value model in paragraphs 33–55 or the cost model in paragraph 56 and shall apply that policy to all of its investment property.**

        ...

Fair value model

...

34   [Deleted] ~~When a property interest held by a lessee under an operating lease is classified as an investment property under paragraph 6, paragraph 30 is not elective; the fair value model shall be applied.~~

        ...

40A   When a lessee uses the fair value model to measure an investment property that is held as a right-of-use asset, it shall measure the right-of-use asset, and not the underlying property, at fair value.

41   ~~Paragraph 25~~ AASB 16 specifies the basis for initial recognition of the cost of ~~an interest in a leased property~~ an investment property held by a lessee as a right-of-use asset. Paragraph 33 requires the ~~interest in the leased property~~ investment property held by a lessee as a right-of-use asset to be remeasured, if necessary, to fair value if the entity chooses the fair value model. ~~In a lease negotiated~~ When lease payments are at market rates, the fair value of ~~an interest in a leased property~~ an investment property held by a lessee as a right-of-use asset at acquisition, net of all expected lease payments (including those relating to recognised lease liabilities), should be zero. ~~This fair value does not change regardless of whether, for accounting purposes, a leased asset and liability are recognised at fair value or at the present value of minimum lease payments, in accordance with paragraph 20 of AASB 117.~~ Thus, remeasuring a ~~leased~~ right-of-use asset from cost in accordance with ~~paragraph 25~~ AASB 16 to fair value in accordance with paragraph 33 (taking into account the requirements in paragraph 50) should not give rise to any initial gain or loss, unless fair value is measured at different times. This could occur when an election to apply the fair value model is made after initial recognition.

        ...

50   In determining the carrying amount of investment property under the fair value model, an entity does not double-count assets or liabilities that are recognised as separate assets or liabilities. For example:

        (a)   ...

        (d)   the fair value of investment property held by a lessee as a right-of-use asset ~~under a lease~~ reflects expected cash flows (including ~~contingent rent that is~~ variable lease payments that are expected to become payable). Accordingly, if a valuation obtained for a property is net of all payments expected to be made,

AASB

it will be necessary to add back any recognised lease liability, to arrive at the carrying amount of the investment property using the fair value model.

...

Inability to measure fair value reliably

53   **There is a rebuttable presumption that an entity can reliably measure the fair value of an investment property on a continuing basis. However, in exceptional cases, there is clear evidence when an entity first acquires an investment property (or when an existing property first becomes investment property after a change in use) that the fair value of the investment property is not reliably measurable on a continuing basis. This arises when, and only when, the market for comparable properties is inactive (eg there are few recent transactions, price quotations are not current or observed transaction prices indicate that the seller was forced to sell) and alternative reliable measurements of fair value (for example, based on discounted cash flow projections) are not available. If an entity determines that the fair value of an investment property under construction is not reliably measurable but expects the fair value of the property to be reliably measurable when construction is complete, it shall measure that investment property under construction at cost until either its fair value becomes reliably measurable or construction is completed (whichever is earlier). If an entity determines that the fair value of an investment property (other than an investment property under construction) is not reliably measurable on a continuing basis, the entity shall measure that investment property using the cost model in AASB 116 for owned investment property or in accordance with AASB 16 for investment property held by a lessee as a right-of-use asset. The residual value of the investment property shall be assumed to be zero. The entity shall continue to apply AASB 116 or AASB 16 until disposal of the investment property.**

53A   Once an entity becomes able to measure reliably the fair value of an investment property under construction that has previously been measured at cost, it shall measure that property at its fair value. Once construction of that property is complete, it is presumed that fair value can be measured reliably. If this is not the case, in accordance with paragraph 53, the property shall be accounted for using the cost model in accordance with AASB 116 for owned assets or AASB 16 for investment property held by a lessee as a right-of-use asset.

...

54   In the exceptional cases when an entity is compelled, for the reason given in paragraph 53, to measure an investment property using the cost model in accordance with AASB 116 or AASB 16, it measures at fair value all its other investment property, including investment property under construction. In these cases, although an entity may use the cost model for one investment property, the entity shall continue to account for each of the remaining properties using the fair value model.

...

Cost model

56   ~~After initial recognition, an entity that chooses the cost model shall measure all of its investment properties in accordance with AASB 116's requirements for that model, other than those that meet the criteria to be classified as held for sale (or are included in a disposal group that is classified as held for sale) in accordance with AASB 5 Non-current Assets Held for Sale and Discontinued Operations. Investment properties that meet the criteria to be classified as held for sale (or are included in a disposal group that is classified as held for sale) shall be measured in accordance with AASB 5.~~

After initial recognition, an entity that chooses the cost model shall measure investment property:

(a) in accordance with AASB 5 *Non-current Assets Held for Sale and Discontinued Operations* if it meets the criteria to be classified as held for sale (or is included in a disposal group that is classified as held for sale);

(b) in accordance with AASB 16 if it is held by a lessee as a right-of-use asset and is not held for sale in accordance with AASB 5; and

(c) in accordance with the requirements in AASB 116 for the cost model in all other cases.

Transfers

...

60 For a transfer from investment property carried at fair value to owner-occupied property or inventories, the property's deemed cost for subsequent accounting in accordance with AASB 116, AASB 16 or AASB 102 shall be its fair value at the date of change in use.

61 If an owner-occupied property becomes an investment property that will be carried at fair value, an entity shall apply AASB 116 for owned property and AASB 16 for property held by a lessee as a right-of-use asset up to the date of change in use. The entity shall treat any difference at that date between the carrying amount of the property in accordance with AASB 116 or AASB 16 and its fair value in the same way as a revaluation in accordance with AASB 116.

62 Up to the date when an owner-occupied property becomes an investment property carried at fair value, an entity depreciates the property (or the right-of-use asset) and recognises any impairment losses that have occurred. The entity treats any difference at that date between the carrying amount of the property in accordance with AASB 116 or AASB 16 and its fair value in the same way as a revaluation in accordance with AASB 116. In other words:

(a) ...

Disposals

...

67 The disposal of an investment property may be achieved by sale or by entering into a finance lease. The date of disposal for investment property that is sold is the date the recipient obtains control of the investment property in accordance with the requirements for determining when a performance obligation is satisfied in AASB 15. AASB 117 AASB 16 applies to a disposal effected by entering into a finance lease and to a sale and leaseback.

...

69 Gains or losses arising from the retirement or disposal of investment property shall be determined as the difference between the net disposal proceeds and the carrying amount of the asset and shall be recognised in profit or loss (unless AASB 117 AASB 16 requires otherwise on a sale and leaseback) in the period of the retirement or disposal.

...

Disclosure

Fair value model and cost model

74 The disclosures below apply in addition to those in AASB 117 AASB 16. In accordance with AASB 117 AASB 16, the owner of an investment property provides lessors' disclosures about leases into which it has entered. An entity A lessee that holds an investment property as a right-of-use asset under a finance or operating lease provides lessees' disclosures as required by AASB 16 for finance leases and lessors' disclosures as required by AASB 16 for any operating leases into which it has entered.

AASB

75   An entity shall disclose:

      (a)   ...

      (b)   [deleted] ~~if it applies the fair value model, whether, and in what~~
             ~~circumstances, property interests held under operating leases are classified~~
             ~~and accounted for as investment property.~~

      (c)   ...

Fair value model

      ...

77   When a valuation obtained for investment property is adjusted significantly for
      the purpose of the financial statements, for example to avoid double-counting
      of assets or liabilities that are recognised as separate assets and liabilities as
      described in paragraph 50, the entity shall disclose a reconciliation between
      the valuation obtained and the adjusted valuation included in the financial
      statements, showing separately the aggregate amount of any recognised lease
      ~~obligations~~ liabilities that have been added back, and any other significant
      adjustments.

78   In the exceptional cases referred to in paragraph 53, when an entity measures
      investment property using the cost model in AASB 116 or in accordance with
      AASB 16, the reconciliation required by paragraph 76 shall disclose amounts
      relating to that investment property separately from amounts relating to other
      investment property. In addition, an entity shall disclose:

      (a)   ...

AASB 16

84B   An entity applying AASB 16, and its related amendments to this Standard, for
      the first time shall apply the transition requirements in Appendix C of AASB 16
      to its investment property held as a right-of-use asset.

Effective date

      ...

85F   AASB 16, issued in February 2016, amended the scope of AASB 140 by defining
      investment property to include both owned investment property and property held by
      a lessee as a right-of-use asset. AASB 16 amended paragraphs 5, 7, 8, 9, 16, 20, 30,
      41, 50, 53, 53A, 54, 56, 60, 61, 62, 67, 69, 74, 75, 77 and 78, added paragraphs 19A,
      29A, 40A and 84B and its related heading and deleted paragraphs 3, 6, 25, 26 and 34.
      An entity shall apply those amendments when it applies AASB 16.

AASB 141 *Agriculture* (August 2015)

Paragraph 2 is amended and paragraph 64 is added.

Scope

      ...

2   This Standard does not apply to:

      (a)   ...

      (e)   right-of-use assets arising from a lease of land related to agricultural activity
             (see AASB 16 *Leases*).

      ...

Effective date and transition

...

64 AASB 16, issued in February 2016, amended paragraph 2. An entity shall apply that amendment when it applies AASB 16.

AASB 1023 *General Insurance Contracts* (July 2004)

Paragraph 2.2(e) is amended.

2 Scope

Transactions outside the scope of this Standard

2.2 This Standard does not apply to:

(a) ...

(e) contractual rights or contractual obligations that are contingent on the future use of, or right to use, a non-financial item (for example, some license fees, royalties, ~~contingent~~ variable lease payments and similar items), as well as a lessee's residual value guarantee embedded in a ~~finance~~ lease (see AASB 15, ~~AASB 117~~ AASB 16 *Leases* and AASB 138 *Intangible Assets*);

(f) ...

Interpretation 1 *Changes in Existing Decommissioning, Restoration and Similar Liabilities*

The References paragraph is amended.

References

• AASB 16 *Leases*

• AASB 101 *Presentation of Financial Statements*

• ...

Paragraph 2 is amended and paragraph 9B is added.

Scope

2 This Interpretation applies to changes in the measurement of any existing decommissioning, restoration or similar liability that is both:

(a) recognised as part of the cost of an item of property, plant and equipment in accordance with AASB 116 or as part of the cost of a right-of-use asset in accordance with AASB 16; and

(b) ...

Effective date

...

9B AASB 16, issued in February 2016, amended paragraph 2. An entity shall apply that amendment when it applies AASB 16.

Interpretation 12 *Service Concession Arrangements*

> The References paragraph is amended.

References

- ...

- AASB 15 *Revenue from Contracts with Customers*

- AASB 16 *Leases*

- ...

- ~~AASB 117 *Leases*~~

- ...

- ~~AASB Interpretation 4 *Determining whether an Arrangement contains a Lease*~~

- ...

> Paragraph 28F is added.

Effective date

...

28F   AASB 16, issued in February 2016, amended paragraph AG8. An entity shall apply those amendments when it applies AASB 16.

> In Appendix A, paragraph AG8 is amended.

Appendix A
Scope (paragraph 5)

...

AG8   The operator may have a right to use the separable infrastructure described in paragraph AG7(a), or the facilities used to provide ancillary unregulated services described in paragraph AG7(b). In either case, there may in substance be a lease from the grantor to the operator; if so, it shall be accounted for in accordance with ~~AASB 117~~ AASB 16.

> Information note 1 and Information note 2 accompanying Interpretation 12 are amended.

Information note 1
Accounting framework for public-to-private service arrangements

...

The diagram below summarises the accounting for service arrangements established by Interpretation 12.

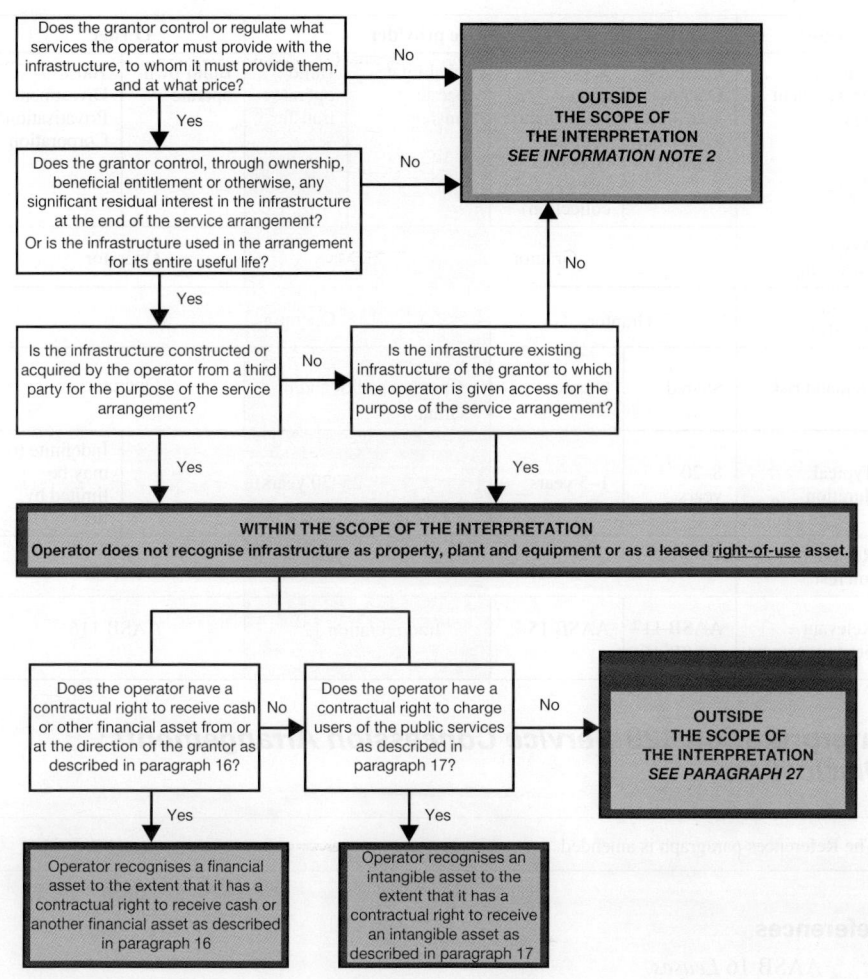

Information note 2

References to AASB pronouncements that apply to typical types of public-to-private arrangements

...

The table sets out the typical types of arrangements for private sector participation in the provision of public sector services and provides references to Australian Accounting Standards that apply to those arrangements. The list of arrangements types is not exhaustive. The purpose of the table is to highlight the continuum of arrangements. It is not the IFRIC's intention to convey the impression that bright lines exist between the accounting requirements for public-to-private arrangements.

Category	Lessee	Service provider				Owner	
Typical arrangement types	Lease (eg Operator leases asset from grantor)	Service and/or maintenance contract (specific tasks eg debt collection)	Rehabilitate-operate-transfer	Build-operate-transfer	Build-own-operate	100% Divestment/ Privatisation/ Corporation
Asset ownership	Grantor					Operator	
Capital investment	Grantor		Operator				
Demand risk	Shared	Grantor	Operator and/or and/or Grantor		Operator		
Typical duration	8–20 years	1–5 years	25–30 years			Indefinite (or may be limited by licence)	
Residual interest	Grantor				Operator		
Relevant pronouncement	~~AASB 117~~ AASB 16	AASB 15	Interpretation 12		AASB 116		

Interpretation 129 *Service Concession Arrangements: Disclosures*

> The References paragraph is amended.

References

- AASB 16 *Leases*
- ...
- ~~AASB 117 *Leases*~~
- ...

> Paragraph 5 is amended.

Issue

...

5   Certain aspects and disclosures relating to some service concession arrangements are already addressed by existing Australian Accounting Standards (eg AASB 116 applies to acquisitions of items of property, plant and equipment, ~~AASB 117~~ AASB 16 applies to leases of assets, and AASB 138 applies to acquisitions of intangible assets). However, a service concession arrangement may involve executory contracts that are not addressed in Australian Accounting Standards, unless the contracts are onerous, in which case AASB 137 applies. Therefore, this Interpretation addresses additional disclosures of service concession arrangements.

> Paragraph Aus7.3 is added.

Effective date

...

Aus7.3   AASB 16, issued in February 2016, amended paragraph 5. An entity shall apply that amendment when it applies AASB 16.

Interpretation 132 *Intangible Assets—Web Site Costs*

The References paragraph is amended.

References

- ...
- AASB 15 *Revenue from Contracts with Customers*
- AASB 16 *Leases*
- ...
- ~~AASB 117 *Leases*~~
- ...

Paragraph 6 is amended.

Issue

...

6   AASB 138 does not apply to intangible assets held by an entity for sale in the ordinary course of business (see AASB 102 and AASB 15) or leases ~~that fall within the scope of AASB 117~~ of intangible assets accounted for in accordance with AASB 16. Accordingly, this Interpretation does not apply to expenditure on the development or operation of a web site (or web site software) for sale to another entity or that is accounted for in accordance with AASB 16. ~~When a web site is leased under an operating lease, the lessor applies this Interpretation. When a web site is leased under a finance lease, the lessee applies this Interpretation after initial recognition of the leased asset.~~

Paragraph Aus10.3 is added.

Effective date

...

Aus10.3   AASB 16, issued in February 2016, amended paragraph 6. An entity shall apply that amendment when it applies AASB 16.

DELETED IFRS 16 TEXT

Deleted IFRS 16 text is not part of AASB 16.

C21   This Standard supersedes the following Standards and Interpretations:

    (a)   IAS 17 *Leases*;

    (b)   IFRIC 4 *Determining whether an Arrangement contains a Lease*;

    (c)   SIC-15 *Operating Leases—Incentives*; and

    (d)   SIC-27 *Evaluating the Substance of Transactions Involving the Legal Form of a Lease*.

with substantial variability over a long period. To provide useful information about these features, the approach adopted in AASB 17:

(a) combines current measurement of the future cash flows with the recognition of profit over the period services are provided under the contract;

(b) presents insurance service results (including presentation of insurance revenue) separately from insurance finance income or expenses; and

(c) requires an entity to make an accounting policy choice portfolio-by-portfolio of whether to recognise all insurance finance income or expenses for the reporting period in profit or loss or to recognise some of that income or expenses in other comprehensive income.

The key principles in AASB 17 are that an entity:

(a) identifies as insurance contracts those contracts under which the entity accepts significant insurance risk from another party (the policyholder) by agreeing to compensate the policyholder if a specified uncertain future event (the insured event) adversely affects the policyholder.

(b) separates specified embedded derivatives, distinct investment components and distinct performance obligations from the insurance contracts.

(c) divides the contracts into groups it will recognise and measure.

(d) recognises and measures groups of insurance contracts at:

    (i) a risk-adjusted present value of the future cash flows (the fulfilment cash flows) that incorporates all of the available information about the fulfilment cash flows in a way that is consistent with observable market information; plus (if this value is a liability) or minus (if this value is an asset)

    (ii) an amount representing the unearned profit in the group of contracts (the contractual service margin).

(e) recognises the profit from a group of insurance contracts over the period the entity provides insurance coverage, and as the entity is released from risk. If a group of contracts is or becomes loss-making, an entity recognises the loss immediately.

(f) presents separately insurance revenue, insurance service expenses and insurance finance income or expenses.

(g) discloses information to enable users of financial statements to assess the effect that contracts within the scope of AASB 17 have on the financial position, financial performance and cash flows of an entity. To do this, an entity discloses qualitative and quantitative information about:

    (i) the amounts recognised in its financial statements from insurance contracts;

    (ii) the significant judgements, and changes in those judgements, made when applying the Standard; and

    (iii) the nature and extent of the risks from contracts within the scope of this Standard.

Application date

This Standard is applicable to annual reporting periods beginning on or after 1 January 2021 (see paragraph C1). Earlier application is permitted for entities that apply AASB 9 *Financial Instruments* and AASB 15 *Revenue from Contracts with Customers* on or before the date of initial application of this Standard.

Who this Standard applies to

This Standard does not apply to:

(a) superannuation entities applying AASB 1056 *Superannuation Entities*; and

(b) not-for-profit public sector entities.

The AASB is undertaking further outreach to determine the applicability of this Standard to those entities. The AASB's views in that regard will be subject to its usual due process.

Why we have issued this Standard

When Australia adopted IFRS, the IASB had a project considering insurance accounting on its agenda with the intention to replace IFRS 4 *Insurance Contracts* (incorporated into AASB 4) with a more comprehensive set of requirements. Given that position, as permitted by AASB 4, the AASB decided to retain AASB 1023 and AASB 1038 pending the outcome of the IASB's project to replace IFRS 4. At the time, the AASB noted that compliance with AASB 1023 and AASB 1038 would result in simultaneous compliance with AASB 4.

At the international level, the IASB was aware that the approach in IFRS 4 *Insurance Contracts* allowed entities in other jurisdictions to use a wide variety of accounting practices for insurance contracts, reflecting national accounting requirements and variations of those requirements. The differences in accounting treatment across jurisdictions and products made it difficult for investors and analysts to understand and compare insurers' results across various jurisdictions. Most stakeholders, including insurers, agreed on the need for a common global insurance accounting standard even though opinions varied as to what it should be.

IFRS 17 *Insurance Contracts* is the conclusion of a project that began in 1997, which sought input from numerous stakeholders around the world to develop a set of comprehensive, global accounting requirements. The AASB considered the requirements and potential for increased comparability with international jurisdictions and also across industries that apply IFRS. This was weighed against the cost of superseding existing Australian requirements that insurers had already been applying. On balance, the AASB decided that the benefits outweighed the costs and therefore decided to incorporate IFRS 17 into AASB 17.

Reduced disclosure requirements

Disclosure requirements under Tier 2 will be determined through a separate due process with amendments being made subsequently to this Standard as required.

COMPARISON WITH IFRS 17

AASB 17 *Insurance Contracts* incorporates IFRS 17 *Insurance Contracts* issued by the International Accounting Standards Board (IASB). Australian-specific paragraphs (which are not included in IFRS 17) are identified with the prefix "Aus". Paragraphs that apply only to not-for-profit entities begin by identifying their limited applicability.

Tier 1

For-profit entities complying with AASB 17 also comply with IFRS 17.

Not-for-profit entities' compliance with IFRS 17 will depend on whether any "Aus" paragraphs that specifically apply to not-for-profit entities provide additional guidance or contain applicable requirements that are inconsistent with IFRS 17.

AASB 1053 *Application of Tiers of Australian Accounting Standards* explains the two tiers of reporting requirements.

ACCOUNTING STANDARD AASB 17

The Australian Accounting Standards Board makes Accounting Standard AASB 17 *Insurance Contracts* under section 334 of the *Corporations Act 2001*.

Kris Peach

Dated 19 July 2017

Chair – AASB

ACCOUNTING STANDARD AASB 17
INSURANCE CONTRACTS

Objective

1   **AASB 17** *Insurance Contracts* **establishes principles for the recognition, measurement, presentation and disclosure of** *insurance contracts* **within the scope of the Standard. The objective of AASB 17 is to ensure that an entity provides relevant information that faithfully represents those contracts. This information gives a basis for users of financial statements to assess the effect that insurance contracts have on the entity's financial position, financial performance and cash flows.**

2   An entity shall consider its substantive rights and obligations, whether they arise from a contract, law or regulation, when applying AASB 17. A contract is an agreement between two or more parties that creates enforceable rights and obligations. Enforceability of the rights and obligations in a contract is a matter of law. Contracts can be written, oral or implied by an entity's customary business practices. Contractual terms include all terms in a contract, explicit or implied, but an entity shall disregard terms that have no commercial substance (ie no discernible effect on the economics of the contract). Implied terms in a contract include those imposed by law or regulation. The practices and processes for establishing contracts with customers vary across legal jurisdictions, industries and entities. In addition, they may vary within an entity (for example, they may depend on the class of customer or the nature of the promised goods or services).

Scope

3   An entity shall apply AASB 17 to:

  (a)   insurance contracts, including *reinsurance contracts*, it issues;

  (b)   reinsurance contracts it holds; and

  (c)   *investment contracts with discretionary participation features* it issues, provided the entity also issues insurance contracts.

4   All references in AASB 17 to insurance contracts also apply to:

  (a)   reinsurance contracts held, except:

   (i)   for references to insurance contracts issued; and

   (ii)   as described in paragraphs 60–70.

  (b)   investment contracts with discretionary participation features as set out in paragraph 3(c), except for the reference to insurance contracts in paragraph 3(c) and as described in paragraph 71.

5   All references in AASB 17 to insurance contracts issued also apply to insurance contracts acquired by the entity in a transfer of insurance contracts or a business combination other than reinsurance contracts held.

6   Appendix A defines an insurance contract and paragraphs B2–B30 of Appendix B provide guidance on the definition of an insurance contract.

7   An entity shall not apply AASB 17 to:

  (a)   warranties provided by a manufacturer, dealer or retailer in connection with the sale of its goods or services to a customer (see AASB 15 *Revenue from Contracts with Customers*).

  (b)   employers' assets and liabilities from employee benefit plans (see AASB 119 *Employee Benefits* and AASB 2 *Share-based Payment*).

(c)   contractual rights or contractual obligations contingent on the future use of, or the right to use, a non-financial item (for example, some licence fees, royalties, variable and other contingent lease payments and similar items: see AASB 15, AASB 138 *Intangible Assets* and AASB 16 *Leases*).

(d)   residual value guarantees provided by a manufacturer, dealer or retailer and a lessee's residual value guarantees when they are embedded in a lease (see AASB 15 and AASB 16).

(e)   financial guarantee contracts, unless the issuer has previously asserted explicitly that it regards such contracts as insurance contracts and has used accounting applicable to insurance contracts. The issuer shall choose to apply either AASB 17 or AASB 132 *Financial Instruments: Presentation*, AASB 7 *Financial Instruments: Disclosures* and AASB 9 *Financial Instruments* to such financial guarantee contracts. The issuer may make that choice contract by contract, but the choice for each contract is irrevocable.

(f)   contingent consideration payable or receivable in a business combination (see AASB 3 *Business Combinations*).

(g)   insurance contracts in which the entity is the *policyholder*, unless those contracts are reinsurance contracts held (see paragraph 3(b)).

8   Some contracts meet the definition of an insurance contract but have as their primary purpose the provision of services for a fixed fee. An entity may choose to apply AASB 15 instead of AASB 17 to such contracts that it issues if, and only if, specified conditions are met. The entity may make that choice contract by contract, but the choice for each contract is irrevocable. The conditions are:

(a)   the entity does not reflect an assessment of the risk associated with an individual customer in setting the price of the contract with that customer;

(b)   the contract compensates the customer by providing services, rather than by making cash payments to the customer; and

(c)   the *insurance risk* transferred by the contract arises primarily from the customer's use of services rather than from uncertainty over the cost of those services.

Combination of insurance contracts

9   A set or series of insurance contracts with the same or a related counterparty may achieve, or be designed to achieve, an overall commercial effect. In order to report the substance of such contracts, it may be necessary to treat the set or series of contracts as a whole. For example, if the rights or obligations in one contract do nothing other than entirely negate the rights or obligations in another contract entered into at the same time with the same counterparty, the combined effect is that no rights or obligations exist.

Separating components from an insurance contract (paragraphs B31–B35)

10   An insurance contract may contain one or more components that would be within the scope of another Standard if they were separate contracts. For example, an insurance contract may include an *investment component* or a service component (or both). An entity shall apply paragraphs 11–13 to identify and account for the components of the contract.

11   An entity shall:

(a)   apply AASB 9 to determine whether there is an embedded derivative to be separated and, if there is, how to account for that derivative.

(b)   separate from a host insurance contract an investment component if, and only if, that investment component is distinct (see paragraphs B31–B32). The entity shall apply AASB 9 to account for the separated investment component.

AASB

12   After applying paragraph 11 to separate any cash flows related to embedded derivatives and distinct investment components, an entity shall separate from the host insurance contract any promise to transfer distinct goods or non-insurance services to a policyholder, applying paragraph 7 of AASB 15. The entity shall account for such promises applying AASB 15. In applying paragraph 7 of AASB 15 to separate the promise, the entity shall apply paragraphs B33–B35 of AASB 17 and, on initial recognition, shall:

(a)   apply AASB 15 to attribute the cash inflows between the insurance component and any promises to provide distinct goods or non-insurance services; and

(b)   attribute the cash outflows between the insurance component and any promised goods or non-insurance services accounted for applying AASB 15 so that:

(i)   cash outflows that relate directly to each component are attributed to that component; and

(ii)   any remaining cash outflows are attributed on a systematic and rational basis, reflecting the cash outflows the entity would expect to arise if that component were a separate contract.

13   After applying paragraphs 11–12, an entity shall apply AASB 17 to all remaining components of the host insurance contract. Hereafter, all references in AASB 17 to embedded derivatives refer to derivatives that have not been separated from the host insurance contract and all references to investment components refer to investment components that have not been separated from the host insurance contract (except those references in paragraphs B31–B32).

Level of aggregation of insurance contracts

14   **An entity shall identify *portfolios of insurance contracts*. A portfolio comprises contracts subject to similar risks and managed together. Contracts within a product line would be expected to have similar risks and hence would be expected to be in the same portfolio if they are managed together. Contracts in different product lines (for example single premium fixed annuities compared with regular term life assurance) would not be expected to have similar risks and hence would be expected to be in different portfolios.**

15   **Paragraphs 16–24 apply to insurance contracts issued. The requirements for the level of aggregation of reinsurance contracts held are set out in paragraph 61.**

16   **An entity shall divide a portfolio of insurance contracts issued into a minimum of:**

(a)   **a group of contracts that are onerous at initial recognition, if any;**

(b)   **a group of contracts that at initial recognition have no significant possibility of becoming onerous subsequently, if any; and**

(c)   **a group of the remaining contracts in the portfolio, if any.**

17   If an entity has reasonable and supportable information to conclude that a set of contracts will all be in the same group applying paragraph 16, it may measure the set of contracts to determine if the contracts are onerous (see paragraph 47) and assess the set of contracts to determine if the contracts have no significant possibility of becoming onerous subsequently (see paragraph 19). If the entity does not have reasonable and supportable information to conclude that a set of contracts will all be in the same group, it shall determine the group to which contracts belong by considering individual contracts.

18   For contracts issued to which an entity applies the premium allocation approach (see paragraphs 53–59), the entity shall assume no contracts in the portfolio are onerous at initial recognition, unless facts and circumstances indicate otherwise. An entity shall assess whether contracts that are not onerous at initial recognition have no significant possibility of becoming onerous subsequently by assessing the likelihood of changes in applicable facts and circumstances.

19   For contracts issued to which an entity does not apply the premium allocation approach (see paragraphs 53–59), an entity shall assess whether contracts that are not onerous at initial recognition have no significant possibility of becoming onerous:

   (a)   based on the likelihood of changes in assumptions which, if they occurred, would result in the contracts becoming onerous.

   (b)   using information about estimates provided by the entity's internal reporting. Hence, in assessing whether contracts that are not onerous at initial recognition have no significant possibility of becoming onerous:

      (i)   an entity shall not disregard information provided by its internal reporting about the effect of changes in assumptions on different contracts on the possibility of their becoming onerous; but

      (ii)   an entity is not required to gather additional information beyond that provided by the entity's internal reporting about the effect of changes in assumptions on different contracts.

20   If, applying paragraphs 14–19, contracts within a portfolio would fall into different groups only because law or regulation specifically constrains the entity's practical ability to set a different price or level of benefits for policyholders with different characteristics, the entity may include those contracts in the same group. The entity shall not apply this paragraph by analogy to other items.

21   An entity is permitted to subdivide the groups described in paragraph 16. For example, an entity may choose to divide the portfolios into:

   (a)   more groups that are not onerous at initial recognition—if the entity's internal reporting provides information that distinguishes:

      (i)   different levels of profitability; or

      (ii)   different possibilities of contracts becoming onerous after initial recognition; and

   (b)   more than one group of contracts that are onerous at initial recognition—if the entity's internal reporting provides information at a more detailed level about the extent to which the contracts are onerous.

22   An entity shall not include contracts issued more than one year apart in the same group. To achieve this the entity shall, if necessary, further divide the groups described in paragraphs 16–21.

23   A *group of insurance contracts* shall comprise a single contract if that is the result of applying paragraphs 14–22.

24   An entity shall apply the recognition and measurement requirements of AASB 17 to the groups of contracts issued determined by applying paragraphs 14–23. An entity shall establish the groups at initial recognition, and shall not reassess the composition of the groups subsequently. To measure a group of contracts, an entity may estimate the *fulfilment cash flows* at a higher level of aggregation than the group or portfolio, provided the entity is able to include the appropriate fulfilment cash flows in the measurement of the group, applying paragraphs 32(a), 40(a)(i) and 40(b), by allocating such estimates to groups of contracts.

Recognition

25   An entity shall recognise a group of insurance contracts it issues from the earliest of the following:

   (a)   the beginning of the *coverage period* of the group of contracts;

   (b)   the date when the first payment from a policyholder in the group becomes due; and

   (c)   for a group of onerous contracts, when the group becomes onerous.

26   If there is no contractual due date, the first payment from the policyholder is deemed to be due when it is received. An entity is required to determine whether any contracts form a group of onerous contracts applying paragraph 16 before the earlier of the dates set out in paragraphs 25(a) and 25(b) if facts and circumstances indicate there is such a group.

27   An entity shall recognise an asset or liability for any *insurance acquisition cash flows* relating to a group of issued insurance contracts that the entity pays or receives before the group is recognised, unless it chooses to recognise them as expenses or income applying paragraph 59(a). An entity shall derecognise the asset or liability resulting from such insurance acquisition cash flows when the group of insurance contracts to which the cash flows are allocated is recognised (see paragraph 38(b)).

28   In recognising a group of insurance contracts in a reporting period, an entity shall include only contracts issued by the end of the reporting period and shall make estimates for the discount rates at the date of initial recognition (see paragraph B73) and the coverage units provided in the reporting period (see paragraph B119). An entity may issue more contracts in the group after the end of a reporting period, subject to paragraph 22. An entity shall add the contracts to the group in the reporting period in which the contracts are issued. This may result in a change to the determination of the discount rates at the date of initial recognition applying paragraph B73. An entity shall apply the revised rates from the start of the reporting period in which the new contracts are added to the group.

Measurement (paragraphs B36–B119)

29   An entity shall apply paragraphs 30–52 to all groups of insurance contracts within the scope of AASB 17, with the following exceptions:

    (a)   for groups of insurance contracts meeting either of the criteria specified in paragraph 53, an entity may simplify the measurement of the group using the premium allocation approach in paragraphs 55–59.

    (b)   for groups of reinsurance contracts held, an entity shall apply paragraphs 32–46 as required by paragraphs 63–70. Paragraphs 45 (on *insurance contracts with direct participation features*) and 47–52 (on onerous contracts) do not apply to groups of reinsurance contracts held.

    (c)   for groups of investment contracts with discretionary participation features, an entity shall apply paragraphs 32–52 as modified by paragraph 71.

30   When applying AASB 121 *The Effects of Changes in Foreign Exchange Rates* to a group of insurance contracts that generate cash flows in a foreign currency, an entity shall treat the group of contracts, including the *contractual service margin*, as a monetary item.

31   In the financial statements of an entity that issues insurance contracts, the fulfilment cash flows shall not reflect the non-performance risk of that entity (non-performance risk is defined in AASB 13 *Fair Value Measurement*).

Measurement on initial recognition (paragraphs B36–B95)

32   **On initial recognition, an entity shall measure a group of insurance contracts at the total of:**

    (a)   **the fulfilment cash flows, which comprise:**

        (i)   **estimates of future cash flows (paragraphs 33–35);**

        (ii)   **an adjustment to reflect the time value of money and the *financial risks* related to the future cash flows, to the extent that the financial risks are not included in the estimates of the future cash flows (paragraph 36); and**

        (iii)   **a *risk adjustment for non-financial risk* (paragraph 37).**

    (b)   **the contractual service margin, measured applying paragraphs 38–39.**

Estimates of future cash flows (paragraphs B36–B71)

33 An entity shall include in the measurement of a group of insurance contracts all the future cash flows within the boundary of each contract in the group (see paragraph 34). Applying paragraph 24, an entity may estimate the future cash flows at a higher level of aggregation and then allocate the resulting fulfilment cash flows to individual groups of contracts. The estimates of future cash flows shall:

    (a) incorporate, in an unbiased way, all reasonable and supportable information available without undue cost or effort about the amount, timing and uncertainty of those future cash flows (see paragraphs B37–B41). To do this, an entity shall estimate the expected value (ie the probability-weighted mean) of the full range of possible outcomes.

    (b) reflect the perspective of the entity, provided that the estimates of any relevant market variables are consistent with observable market prices for those variables (see paragraphs B42–B53).

    (c) be current—the estimates shall reflect conditions existing at the measurement date, including assumptions at that date about the future (see paragraphs B54–B60).

    (d) be explicit—the entity shall estimate the adjustment for non-financial risk separately from the other estimates (see paragraph B90). The entity also shall estimate the cash flows separately from the adjustment for the time value of money and financial risk, unless the most appropriate measurement technique combines these estimates (see paragraph B46).

34 Cash flows are within the boundary of an insurance contract if they arise from substantive rights and obligations that exist during the reporting period in which the entity can compel the policyholder to pay the premiums or in which the entity has a substantive obligation to provide the policyholder with services (see paragraphs B61–B71). A substantive obligation to provide services ends when:

    (a) the entity has the practical ability to reassess the risks of the particular policyholder and, as a result, can set a price or level of benefits that fully reflects those risks; or

    (b) both of the following criteria are satisfied:

        (i) the entity has the practical ability to reassess the risks of the portfolio of insurance contracts that contains the contract and, as a result, can set a price or level of benefits that fully reflects the risk of that portfolio; and

        (ii) the pricing of the premiums for coverage up to the date when the risks are reassessed does not take into account the risks that relate to periods after the reassessment date.

35 An entity shall not recognise as a liability or as an asset any amounts relating to expected premiums or expected claims outside the boundary of the insurance contract. Such amounts relate to future insurance contracts.

Discount rates (paragraphs B72–B85)

36 An entity shall adjust the estimates of future cash flows to reflect the time value of money and the financial risks related to those cash flows, to the extent that the financial risks are not included in the estimates of cash flows. The discount rates applied to the estimates of the future cash flows described in paragraph 33 shall:

    (a) reflect the time value of money, the characteristics of the cash flows and the liquidity characteristics of the insurance contracts;

    (b) be consistent with observable current market prices (if any) for financial instruments with cash flows whose characteristics are consistent with those of the insurance contracts, in terms of, for example, timing, currency and liquidity; and

    (c)   exclude the effect of factors that influence such observable market prices but do not affect the future cash flows of the insurance contracts.

Risk adjustment for non-financial risk (paragraphs B86–B92)

37   An entity shall adjust the estimate of the present value of the future cash flows to reflect the compensation that the entity requires for bearing the uncertainty about the amount and timing of the cash flows that arises from non-financial risk.

Contractual service margin

38   The contractual service margin is a component of the asset or liability for the group of insurance contracts that represents the unearned profit the entity will recognise as it provides services in the future. An entity shall measure the contractual service margin on initial recognition of a group of insurance contracts at an amount that, unless paragraph 47 (on onerous contracts) applies, results in no income or expenses arising from:

    (a)   the initial recognition of an amount for the fulfilment cash flows, measured by applying paragraphs 32–37;

    (b)   the derecognition at the date of initial recognition of any asset or liability recognised for insurance acquisition cash flows applying paragraph 27; and

    (c)   any cash flows arising from the contracts in the group at that date.

39   For insurance contracts acquired in a transfer of insurance contracts or a business combination, an entity shall apply paragraph 38 in accordance with paragraphs B93–B95.

Subsequent measurement

40   The carrying amount of a group of insurance contracts at the end of each reporting period shall be the sum of:

    (a)   the *liability for remaining coverage* comprising:

        (i)   the fulfilment cash flows related to future service allocated to the group at that date, measured applying paragraphs 33–37 and B36–B92;

        (ii)   the contractual service margin of the group at that date, measured applying paragraphs 43–46; and

    (b)   the *liability for incurred claims*, comprising the fulfilment cash flows related to past service allocated to the group at that date, measured applying paragraphs 33–37 and B36–B92.

41   An entity shall recognise income and expenses for the following changes in the carrying amount of the liability for remaining coverage:

    (a)   insurance revenue—for the reduction in the liability for remaining coverage because of services provided in the period, measured applying paragraphs B120–B124;

    (b)   insurance service expenses—for losses on groups of onerous contracts, and reversals of such losses (see paragraphs 47–52); and

    (c)   insurance finance income or expenses—for the effect of the time value of money and the effect of financial risk as specified in paragraph 87.

42   An entity shall recognise income and expenses for the following changes in the carrying amount of the liability for incurred claims:

    (a)   insurance service expenses—for the increase in the liability because of claims and expenses incurred in the period, excluding any investment components;

    (b)   insurance service expenses—for any subsequent changes in fulfilment cash flows relating to incurred claims and incurred expenses; and

    (c)   insurance finance income or expenses—for the effect of the time value of money and the effect of financial risk as specified in paragraph 87.

Contractual service margin (paragraphs B96–B119)

43   The contractual service margin at the end of the reporting period represents the profit in the group of insurance contracts that has not yet been recognised in profit or loss because it relates to the future service to be provided under the contracts in the group.

44   For *insurance contracts without direct participation features*, the carrying amount of the contractual service margin of a group of contracts at the end of the reporting period equals the carrying amount at the start of the reporting period adjusted for:

    (a)   the effect of any new contracts added to the group (see paragraph 28);

    (b)   interest accreted on the carrying amount of the contractual service margin during the reporting period, measured at the discount rates specified in paragraph B72(b);

    (c)   the changes in fulfilment cash flows relating to future service as specified in paragraphs B96–B100, except to the extent that:

        (i)   such increases in the fulfilment cash flows exceed the carrying amount of the contractual service margin, giving rise to a loss (see paragraph 48(a)); or

        (ii)   such decreases in the fulfilment cash flows are allocated to the loss component of the liability for remaining coverage applying paragraph 50(b).

    (d)   the effect of any currency exchange differences on the contractual service margin; and

    (e)   the amount recognised as insurance revenue because of the transfer of services in the period, determined by the allocation of the contractual service margin remaining at the end of the reporting period (before any allocation) over the current and remaining coverage period applying paragraph B119.

45   For insurance contracts with direct participation features (see paragraphs B101–B118), the carrying amount of the contractual service margin of a group of contracts at the end of the reporting period equals the carrying amount at the start of the reporting period adjusted for the amounts specified in subparagraphs (a)–(e) below. An entity is not required to identify these adjustments separately. Instead, a combined amount may be determined for some, or all, of the adjustments. The adjustments are:

    (a)   the effect of any new contracts added to the group (see paragraph 28);

    (b)   the entity's share of the change in the fair value of the *underlying items* (see paragraph B104(b)(i)), except to the extent that:

        (i)   paragraph B115 (on risk mitigation) applies;

        (ii)   the entity's share of a decrease in the fair value of the underlying items exceeds the carrying amount of the contractual service margin, giving rise to a loss (see paragraph 48); or

        (iii)   the entity's share of an increase in the fair value of the underlying items reverses the amount in (ii).

    (c)   the changes in fulfilment cash flows relating to future service, as specified in paragraphs B101–B118, except to the extent that:

        (i)   paragraph B115 (on risk mitigation) applies;

        (ii)   such increases in the fulfilment cash flows exceed the carrying amount of the contractual service margin, giving rise to a loss (see paragraph 48); or

        (iii)   such decreases in the fulfilment cash flows are allocated to the loss component of the liability for remaining coverage applying paragraph 50(b).

AASB

(d)   the effect of any currency exchange differences arising on the contractual service margin; and

(e)   the amount recognised as insurance revenue because of the transfer of services in the period, determined by the allocation of the contractual service margin remaining at the end of the reporting period (before any allocation) over the current and remaining coverage period, applying paragraph B119.

46   Some changes in the contractual service margin offset changes in the fulfilment cash flows for the liability for remaining coverage, resulting in no change in the total carrying amount of the liability for remaining coverage. To the extent that changes in the contractual service margin do not offset changes in the fulfilment cash flows for the liability for remaining coverage, an entity shall recognise income and expenses for the changes, applying paragraph 41.

Onerous contracts

47   An insurance contract is onerous at the date of initial recognition if the fulfilment cash flows allocated to the contract, any previously recognised acquisition cash flows and any cash flows arising from the contract at the date of initial recognition in total are a net outflow. Applying paragraph 16(a), an entity shall group such contracts separately from contracts that are not onerous. To the extent that paragraph 17 applies, an entity may identify the group of onerous contracts by measuring a set of contracts rather than individual contracts. An entity shall recognise a loss in profit or loss for the net outflow for the group of onerous contracts, resulting in the carrying amount of the liability for the group being equal to the fulfilment cash flows and the contractual service margin of the group being zero.

48   A group of insurance contracts becomes onerous (or more onerous) on subsequent measurement if the following amounts exceed the carrying amount of the contractual service margin:

(a)   unfavourable changes in the fulfilment cash flows allocated to the group arising from changes in estimates of future cash flows relating to future service; and

(b)   for a group of insurance contracts with direct participation features, the entity's share of a decrease in the fair value of the underlying items.

Applying paragraphs 44(c)(i), 45(b)(ii) and 45(c)(ii), an entity shall recognise a loss in profit or loss to the extent of that excess.

49   An entity shall establish (or increase) a loss component of the liability for remaining coverage for an onerous group depicting the losses recognised applying paragraphs 47–48. The loss component determines the amounts that are presented in profit or loss as reversals of losses on onerous groups and are consequently excluded from the determination of insurance revenue.

50   After an entity has recognised a loss on an onerous group of insurance contracts, it shall allocate:

(a)   the subsequent changes in fulfilment cash flows of the liability for remaining coverage specified in paragraph 51 on a systematic basis between:

(i)   the loss component of the liability for remaining coverage; and

(ii)   the liability for remaining coverage, excluding the loss component.

(b)   any subsequent decrease in fulfilment cash flows allocated to the group arising from changes in estimates of future cash flows relating to future service and any subsequent increases in the entity's share in the fair value of the underlying items solely to the loss component until that component is reduced to zero. Applying paragraphs 44(c)(ii), 45(b)(iii) and 45(c)(iii), an entity shall adjust the contractual service margin only for the excess of the decrease over the amount allocated to the loss component.

51 The subsequent changes in the fulfilment cash flows of the liability for remaining coverage to be allocated applying paragraph 50(a) are:

(a) estimates of the present value of future cash flows for claims and expenses released from the liability for remaining coverage because of incurred insurance service expenses;

(b) changes in the risk adjustment for non-financial risk recognised in profit or loss because of the release from risk; and

(c) insurance finance income or expenses.

52 The systematic allocation required by paragraph 50(a) shall result in the total amounts allocated to the loss component in accordance with paragraphs 48–50 being equal to zero by the end of the coverage period of a group of contracts.

Premium allocation approach

53 An entity may simplify the measurement of a group of insurance contracts using the premium allocation approach set out in paragraphs 55–59 if, and only if, at the inception of the group:

(a) the entity reasonably expects that such simplification would produce a measurement of the liability for remaining coverage for the group that would not differ materially from the one that would be produced applying the requirements in paragraphs 32–52; or

(b) the coverage period of each contract in the group (including coverage arising from all premiums within the contract boundary determined at that date applying paragraph 34) is one year or less.

54 The criterion in paragraph 53(a) is not met if at the inception of the group an entity expects significant variability in the fulfilment cash flows that would affect the measurement of the liability for remaining coverage during the period before a claim is incurred. Variability in the fulfilment cash flows increases with, for example:

(a) the extent of future cash flows relating to any derivatives embedded in the contracts; and

(b) the length of the coverage period of the group of contracts.

55 Using the premium allocation approach, an entity shall measure the liability for remaining coverage as follows:

(a) on initial recognition, the carrying amount of the liability is:

(i) the premiums, if any, received at initial recognition;

(ii) minus any insurance acquisition cash flows at that date, unless the entity chooses to recognise the payments as an expense applying paragraph 59(a); and

(iii) plus or minus any amount arising from the derecognition at that date of the asset or liability recognised for insurance acquisition cash flows applying paragraph 27.

(b) at the end of each subsequent reporting period, the carrying amount of the liability is the carrying amount at the start of the reporting period:

(i) plus the premiums received in the period;

(ii) minus insurance acquisition cash flows; unless the entity chooses to recognise the payments as an expense applying paragraph 59(a);

(iii) plus any amounts relating to the amortisation of insurance acquisition cash flows recognised as an expense in the reporting period; unless the entity chooses to recognise insurance acquisition cash flows as an expense applying paragraph 59(a);

(iv) plus any adjustment to a financing component, applying paragraph 56;

AASB

(v)   minus the amount recognised as insurance revenue for coverage provided in that period (see paragraph B126); and

(vi)   minus any investment component paid or transferred to the liability for incurred claims.

56   If insurance contracts in the group have a significant financing component, an entity shall adjust the carrying amount of the liability for remaining coverage to reflect the time value of money and the effect of financial risk using the discount rates specified in paragraph 36, as determined on initial recognition. The entity is not required to adjust the carrying amount of the liability for remaining coverage to reflect the time value of money and the effect of financial risk if, at initial recognition, the entity expects that the time between providing each part of the coverage and the related premium due date is no more than a year.

57   If at any time during the coverage period, facts and circumstances indicate that a group of insurance contracts is onerous, an entity shall calculate the difference between:

(a)   the carrying amount of the liability for remaining coverage determined applying paragraph 55; and

(b)   the fulfilment cash flows that relate to remaining coverage of the group, applying paragraphs 33–37 and B36–B92. However, if, in applying paragraph 59(b), the entity does not adjust the liability for incurred claims for the time value of money and the effect of financial risk, it shall not include in the fulfilment cash flows any such adjustment.

58   To the extent that the fulfilment cash flows described in paragraph 57(b) exceed the carrying amount described in paragraph 57(a), the entity shall recognise a loss in profit or loss and increase the liability for remaining coverage.

59   In applying the premium allocation approach, an entity:

(a)   may choose to recognise any insurance acquisition cash flows as expenses when it incurs those costs, provided that the coverage period of each contract in the group at initial recognition is no more than one year.

(b)   shall measure the liability for incurred claims for the group of insurance contracts at the fulfilment cash flows relating to incurred claims, applying paragraphs 33–37 and B36–B92. However, the entity is not required to adjust future cash flows for the time value of money and the effect of financial risk if those cash flows are expected to be paid or received in one year or less from the date the claims are incurred.

Reinsurance contracts held

60   The requirements in AASB 17 are modified for reinsurance contracts held, as set out in paragraphs 61–70.

61   An entity shall divide portfolios of reinsurance contracts held applying paragraphs 14–24, except that the references to onerous contracts in those paragraphs shall be replaced with a reference to contracts on which there is a net gain on initial recognition. For some reinsurance contracts held, applying paragraphs 14–24 will result in a group that comprises a single contract.

Recognition

62   Instead of applying paragraph 25, an entity shall recognise a group of reinsurance contracts held:

(a)   if the reinsurance contracts held provide proportionate coverage—at the beginning of the coverage period of the group of reinsurance contracts held or at the initial recognition of any underlying contract, whichever is the later; and

(b)   in all other cases—from the beginning of the coverage period of the group of reinsurance contracts held.

Measurement

63 In applying the measurement requirements of paragraphs 32–36 to reinsurance contracts held, to the extent that the underlying contracts are also measured applying those paragraphs, the entity shall use consistent assumptions to measure the estimates of the present value of the future cash flows for the group of reinsurance contracts held and the estimates of the present value of the future cash flows for the group(s) of underlying insurance contracts. In addition, the entity shall include in the estimates of the present value of the future cash flows for the group of reinsurance contracts held the effect of any risk of non-performance by the issuer of the reinsurance contract, including the effects of collateral and losses from disputes.

64 Instead of applying paragraph 37, an entity shall determine the risk adjustment for non-financial risk so that it represents the amount of risk being transferred by the holder of the group of reinsurance contracts to the issuer of those contracts.

65 The requirements of paragraph 38 that relate to determining the contractual service margin on initial recognition are modified to reflect the fact that for a group of reinsurance contracts held there is no unearned profit but instead a net cost or net gain on purchasing the reinsurance. Hence, on initial recognition:

(a) the entity shall recognise any net cost or net gain on purchasing the group of reinsurance contracts held as a contractual service margin measured at an amount equal to the sum of the fulfilment cash flows, the amount derecognised at that date of any asset or liability previously recognised for cash flows related to the group of reinsurance contracts held, and any cash flows arising at that date; unless

(b) the net cost of purchasing reinsurance coverage relates to events that occurred before the purchase of the group of reinsurance contracts, in which case, notwithstanding the requirements of paragraph B5, the entity shall recognise such a cost immediately in profit or loss as an expense.

66 Instead of applying paragraph 44, an entity shall measure the contractual service margin at the end of the reporting period for a group of reinsurance contracts held as the carrying amount determined at the start of the reporting period, adjusted for:

(a) the effect of any new contracts added to the group (see paragraph 28);

(b) interest accreted on the carrying amount of the contractual service margin, measured at the discount rates specified in paragraph B72(b);

(c) changes in the fulfilment cash flows to the extent that the change:

(i) relates to future service; unless

(ii) the change results from a change in fulfilment cash flows allocated to a group of underlying insurance contracts that does not adjust the contractual service margin for the group of underlying insurance contracts.

(d) the effect of any currency exchange differences arising on the contractual service margin; and

(e) the amount recognised in profit or loss because of services received in the period, determined by the allocation of the contractual service margin remaining at the end of the reporting period (before any allocation) over the current and remaining coverage period of the group of reinsurance contracts held, applying paragraph B119.

67 Changes in the fulfilment cash flows that result from changes in the risk of non-performance by the issuer of a reinsurance contract held do not relate to future service and shall not adjust the contractual service margin.

68 Reinsurance contracts held cannot be onerous. Accordingly, the requirements of paragraphs 47–52 do not apply.

Premium allocation approach for reinsurance contracts held

69   An entity may use the premium allocation approach set out in paragraphs 55–56 and 59 (adapted to reflect the features of reinsurance contracts held that differ from insurance contracts issued, for example the generation of expenses or reduction in expenses rather than revenue) to simplify the measurement of a group of reinsurance contracts held, if at the inception of the group:

(a)   the entity reasonably expects the resulting measurement would not differ materially from the result of applying the requirements in paragraphs 63–68; or

(b)   the coverage period of each contract in the group of reinsurance contracts held (including coverage from all premiums within the contract boundary determined at that date applying paragraph 34) is one year or less.

70   An entity cannot meet the condition in paragraph 69(a) if, at the inception of the group, an entity expects significant variability in the fulfilment cash flows that would affect the measurement of the asset for remaining coverage during the period before a claim is incurred. Variability in the fulfilment cash flows increases with, for example:

(a)   the extent of future cash flows relating to any derivatives embedded in the contracts; and

(b)   the length of the coverage period of the group of reinsurance contracts held.

Investment contracts with discretionary participation features

71   An investment contract with discretionary participation features does not include a transfer of significant insurance risk. Consequently, the requirements in AASB 17 for insurance contracts are modified for investment contracts with discretionary participation features as follows:

(a)   the date of initial recognition (see paragraph 25) is the date the entity becomes party to the contract.

(b)   the contract boundary (see paragraph 34) is modified so that cash flows are within the contract boundary if they result from a substantive obligation of the entity to deliver cash at a present or future date. The entity has no substantive obligation to deliver cash if it has the practical ability to set a price for the promise to deliver the cash that fully reflects the amount of cash promised and related risks.

(c)   the allocation of the contractual service margin (see paragraphs 44(e) and 45(e)) is modified so that the entity shall recognise the contractual service margin over the duration of the group of contracts in a systematic way that reflects the transfer of investment services under the contract.

Modification and derecognition

Modification of an insurance contract

72   If the terms of an insurance contract are modified, for example by agreement between the parties to the contract or by a change in regulation, an entity shall derecognise the original contract and recognise the modified contract as a new contract, applying AASB 17 or other applicable Standards if, and only if, any of the conditions in (a)–(c) are satisfied. The exercise of a right included in the terms of a contract is not a modification. The conditions are that:

(a)   if the modified terms had been included at contract inception:

(i)   the modified contract would have been excluded from the scope of AASB 17, applying paragraphs 3–8;

(ii)   an entity would have separated different components from the host insurance contract applying paragraphs 10–13, resulting in a different insurance contract to which AASB 17 would have applied;

(iii)   the modified contract would have had a substantially different contract boundary applying paragraph 34; or

(iv)   the modified contract would have been included in a different group of contracts applying paragraphs 14–24.

(b)   the original contract met the definition of an *insurance contract with direct participation features*, but the modified contract no longer meets that definition, or vice versa; or

(c)   the entity applied the premium allocation approach in paragraphs 53–59 or paragraphs 69–70 to the original contract, but the modifications mean that the contract no longer meets the eligibility criteria for that approach in paragraph 53 or paragraph 69.

73   If a contract modification meets none of the conditions in paragraph 72, the entity shall treat changes in cash flows caused by the modification as changes in estimates of fulfilment cash flows by applying paragraphs 40–52.

Derecognition

74   An entity shall derecognise an insurance contract when, and only when:

(a)   it is extinguished, ie when the obligation specified in the insurance contract expires or is discharged or cancelled; or

(b)   any of the conditions in paragraph 72 are met.

75   When an insurance contract is extinguished, the entity is no longer at risk and is therefore no longer required to transfer any economic resources to satisfy the insurance contract. For example, when an entity buys reinsurance, it shall derecognise the underlying insurance contract(s) when, and only when, the underlying insurance contract(s) is or are extinguished.

76   An entity derecognises an insurance contract from within a group of contracts by applying the following requirements in AASB 17:

(a)   the fulfilment cash flows allocated to the group are adjusted to eliminate the present value of the future cash flows and risk adjustment for non-financial risk relating to the rights and obligations that have been derecognised from the group, applying paragraphs 40(a)(i) and 40(b);

(b)   the contractual service margin of the group is adjusted for the change in fulfilment cash flows described in (a), to the extent required by paragraphs 44(c) and 45(c), unless paragraph 77 applies; and

(c)   the number of coverage units for expected remaining coverage is adjusted to reflect the coverage units derecognised from the group, and the amount of the contractual service margin recognised in profit or loss in the period is based on that adjusted number, applying paragraph B119.

77   When an entity derecognises an insurance contract because it transfers the contract to a third party or derecognises an insurance contract and recognises a new contract applying paragraph 72, the entity shall instead of applying paragraph 76(b):

(a)   adjust the contractual service margin of the group from which the contract has been derecognised, to the extent required by paragraphs 44(c) and 45(c), for the difference between (i) and either (ii) for contracts transferred to a third party or (iii) for contracts derecognised applying paragraph 72:

(i)   the change in the carrying amount of the group of insurance contracts resulting from the derecognition of the contract, applying paragraph 76(a).

(ii)   the premium charged by the third party.

(iii)   the premium the entity would have charged had it entered into a contract with equivalent terms as the new contract at the date of the contract modification, less any additional premium charged for the modification.

AASB

(b)   measure the new contract recognised applying paragraph 72 assuming that the entity received the premium described in (a)(iii) at the date of the modification.

Presentation in the statement of financial position

78   **An entity shall present separately in the statement of financial position the carrying amount of groups of:**

(a)   **insurance contracts issued that are assets;**

(b)   **insurance contracts issued that are liabilities;**

(c)   **reinsurance contracts held that are assets; and**

(d)   **reinsurance contracts held that are liabilities.**

79   An entity shall include any assets or liabilities for insurance acquisition cash flows recognised applying paragraph 27 in the carrying amount of the related groups of insurance contracts issued, and any assets or liabilities for cash flows related to groups of reinsurance contracts held (see paragraph 65(a)) in the carrying amount of the groups of reinsurance contracts held.

Recognition and presentation in the statement(s) of financial performance (paragraphs B120–B136)

80   **Applying paragraphs 41 and 42, an entity shall disaggregate the amounts recognised in the statement(s) of profit or loss and other comprehensive income (hereafter referred to as the statement(s) of financial performance) into:**

(a)   **an insurance service result (paragraphs 83–86), comprising insurance revenue and insurance service expenses; and**

(b)   **insurance finance income or expenses (paragraphs 87–92).**

81   An entity is not required to disaggregate the change in the risk adjustment for non-financial risk between the insurance service result and insurance finance income or expenses. If an entity does not make such a disaggregation, it shall include the entire change in the risk adjustment for non-financial risk as part of the insurance service result.

82   **An entity shall present income or expenses from reinsurance contracts held separately from the expenses or income from insurance contracts issued.**

Insurance service result

83   **An entity shall present in profit or loss insurance revenue arising from the groups of insurance contracts issued. Insurance revenue shall depict the provision of coverage and other services arising from the group of insurance contracts at an amount that reflects the consideration to which the entity expects to be entitled in exchange for those services. Paragraphs B120–B127 specify how an entity measures insurance revenue.**

84   **An entity shall present in profit or loss insurance service expenses arising from a group of insurance contracts issued, comprising incurred claims (excluding repayments of investment components), other incurred insurance service expenses and other amounts as described in paragraph 103(b).**

85   **Insurance revenue and insurance service expenses presented in profit or loss shall exclude any investment components. An entity shall not present premium information in profit or loss if that information is inconsistent with paragraph 83.**

86   An entity may present the income or expenses from a group of reinsurance contracts held (see paragraphs 60–70), other than insurance finance income or expenses, as a single amount; or the entity may present separately the amounts recovered from the reinsurer and an allocation of the premiums paid that together give a net amount equal

to that single amount. If an entity presents separately the amounts recovered from the reinsurer and an allocation of the premiums paid, it shall:

(a) treat reinsurance cash flows that are contingent on claims on the underlying contracts as part of the claims that are expected to be reimbursed under the reinsurance contract held;

(b) treat amounts from the reinsurer that it expects to receive that are not contingent on claims of the underlying contracts (for example, some types of ceding commissions) as a reduction in the premiums to be paid to the reinsurer; and

(c) not present the allocation of premiums paid as a reduction in revenue.

Insurance finance income or expenses (see paragraphs B128–B136)

87 Insurance finance income or expenses comprises the change in the carrying amount of the group of insurance contracts arising from:

(a) **the effect of the time value of money and changes in the time value of money; and**

(b) **the effect of financial risk and changes in financial risk; but**

(c) **excluding any such changes for groups of insurance contracts with direct participation features that would adjust the contractual service margin but do not do so when applying paragraphs 45(b)(ii), 45(b)(iii), 45(c)(ii) or 45(c)(iii). These are included in insurance service expenses.**

88 Unless paragraph 89 applies, an entity shall make an accounting policy choice between:

(a) **including insurance finance income or expenses for the period in profit or loss; or**

(b) **disaggregating insurance finance income or expenses for the period to include in profit or loss an amount determined by a systematic allocation of the expected total insurance finance income or expenses over the duration of the group of contracts, applying paragraphs B130–B133.**

89 For insurance contracts with direct participation features, for which the entity holds the underlying items, an entity shall make an accounting policy choice between:

(a) **including insurance finance income or expenses for the period in profit or loss; or**

(b) **disaggregating insurance finance income or expenses for the period to include in profit or loss an amount that eliminates accounting mismatches with income or expenses included in profit or loss on the underlying items held, applying paragraphs B134–B136.**

90 If an entity chooses the accounting policy set out in paragraph 88(b) or in paragraph 89(b), it shall include in other comprehensive income the difference between the insurance finance income or expenses measured on the basis set out in those paragraphs and the total insurance finance income or expenses for the period.

91 If an entity transfers a group of insurance contracts or derecognises an insurance contract applying paragraph 77:

(a) **it shall reclassify to profit or loss as a reclassification adjustment (see AASB 101 *Presentation of Financial Statements*) any remaining amounts for the group (or contract) that were previously recognised in other comprehensive income because the entity chose the accounting policy set out in paragraph 88(b).**

(b) **it shall not reclassify to profit or loss as a reclassification adjustment (see AASB 101) any remaining amounts for the group (or contract) that were**

previously recognised in other comprehensive income because the entity chose the accounting policy set out in paragraph 89(b).

92   Paragraph 30 requires an entity to treat an insurance contract as a monetary item under AASB 121 for the purpose of translating foreign exchange items into the entity's functional currency. An entity includes exchange differences on changes in the carrying amount of groups of insurance contracts in the statement of profit or loss, unless they relate to changes in the carrying amount of groups of insurance contracts included in other comprehensive income applying paragraph 90, in which case they shall be included in other comprehensive income.

Disclosure

93   **The objective of the disclosure requirements is for an entity to disclose information in the notes that, together with the information provided in the statement of financial position, statement(s) of financial performance and statement of cash flows, gives a basis for users of financial statements to assess the effect that contracts within the scope of AASB 17 have on the entity's financial position, financial performance and cash flows. To achieve that objective, an entity shall disclose qualitative and quantitative information about:**

    (a)   **the amounts recognised in its financial statements for contracts within the scope of AASB 17 (see paragraphs 97–116);**

    (b)   **the significant judgements, and changes in those judgements, made when applying AASB 17 (see paragraphs 117–120); and**

    (c)   **the nature and extent of the risks from contracts within the scope of AASB 17 (see paragraphs 121–132).**

94   An entity shall consider the level of detail necessary to satisfy the disclosure objective and how much emphasis to place on each of the various requirements. If the disclosures provided, applying paragraphs 97–132, are not enough to meet the objective in paragraph 93, an entity shall disclose additional information necessary to meet that objective.

95   An entity shall aggregate or disaggregate information so that useful information is not obscured either by the inclusion of a large amount of insignificant detail or by the aggregation of items that have different characteristics.

96   Paragraphs 29–31 of AASB 101 set out requirements relating to materiality and aggregation of information. Examples of aggregation bases that might be appropriate for information disclosed about insurance contracts are:

    (a)   type of contract (for example, major product lines);

    (b)   geographical area (for example, country or region); or

    (c)   reportable segment, as defined in AASB 8 *Operating Segments*.

Explanation of recognised amounts

97   Of the disclosures required by paragraphs 98–109, only those in paragraphs 98–100 and 102–105 apply to contracts to which the premium allocation approach has been applied. If an entity uses the premium allocation approach, it shall also disclose:

    (a)   which of the criteria in paragraphs 53 and 69 it has satisfied;

    (b)   whether it makes an adjustment for the time value of money and the effect of financial risk applying paragraphs 56 and 57(b); and

    (c)   the method it has chosen to recognise insurance acquisition cash flows applying paragraph 59(a).

98   An entity shall disclose reconciliations that show how the net carrying amounts of contracts within the scope of AASB 17 changed during the period because of cash flows and income and expenses recognised in the statement(s) of financial performance. Separate reconciliations shall be disclosed for insurance contracts issued

and reinsurance contracts held. An entity shall adapt the requirements of paragraphs 100–109 to reflect the features of reinsurance contracts held that differ from insurance contracts issued; for example, the generation of expenses or reduction in expenses rather than revenue.

99 An entity shall provide enough information in the reconciliations to enable users of financial statements to identify changes from cash flows and amounts that are recognised in the statement(s) of financial performance. To comply with this requirement, an entity shall:

(a) disclose, in a table, the reconciliations set out in paragraphs 100–105; and

(b) for each reconciliation, present the net carrying amounts at the beginning and at the end of the period, disaggregated into a total for groups of contracts that are assets and a total for groups of contracts that are liabilities, that equal the amounts presented in the statement of financial position applying paragraph 78.

100 An entity shall disclose reconciliations from the opening to the closing balances separately for each of:

(a) the net liabilities (or assets) for the remaining coverage component, excluding any loss component.

(b) any loss component (see paragraphs 47–52 and 57–58).

(c) the liabilities for incurred claims. For insurance contracts to which the premium allocation approach described in paragraphs 53–59 or 69–70 has been applied, an entity shall disclose separate reconciliations for:

(i) the estimates of the present value of the future cash flows; and

(ii) the risk adjustment for non-financial risk.

101 For insurance contracts other than those to which the premium allocation approach described in paragraphs 53–59 or 69–70 has been applied, an entity shall also disclose reconciliations from the opening to the closing balances separately for each of:

(a) the estimates of the present value of the future cash flows;

(b) the risk adjustment for non-financial risk; and

(c) the contractual service margin.

102 The objective of the reconciliations in paragraphs 100–101 is to provide different types of information about the insurance service result.

103 An entity shall separately disclose in the reconciliations required in paragraph 100 each of the following amounts related to insurance services, if applicable:

(a) insurance revenue.

(b) insurance service expenses, showing separately:

(i) incurred claims (excluding investment components) and other incurred insurance service expenses;

(ii) amortisation of insurance acquisition cash flows;

(iii) changes that relate to past service, ie changes in fulfilment cash flows relating to the liability for incurred claims; and

(iv) changes that relate to future service, ie losses on onerous groups of contracts and reversals of such losses.

(c) investment components excluded from insurance revenue and insurance service expenses.

104 An entity shall separately disclose in the reconciliations required in paragraph 101 each of the following amounts related to insurance services, if applicable:

(a) changes that relate to future service, applying paragraphs B96–B118, showing separately:

(i)   changes in estimates that adjust the contractual service margin;

(ii)   changes in estimates that do not adjust the contractual service margin, ie losses on groups of onerous contracts and reversals of such losses; and

(iii)   the effects of contracts initially recognised in the period.

(b)   changes that relate to current service, ie:

(i)   the amount of the contractual service margin recognised in profit or loss to reflect the transfer of services;

(ii)   the change in the risk adjustment for non-financial risk that does not relate to future service or past service; and

(iii)   *experience adjustments* (see paragraphs B96(a), B97(c) and B113(a)).

(c)   changes that relate to past service, ie changes in fulfilment cash flows relating to incurred claims (see paragraphs B97(b) and B113(a)).

105   To complete the reconciliations in paragraphs 100–101, an entity shall also disclose separately each of the following amounts not related to insurance services provided in the period, if applicable:

(a)   cash flows in the period, including:

(i)   premiums received for insurance contracts issued (or paid for reinsurance contracts held);

(ii)   insurance acquisition cash flows; and

(iii)   incurred claims paid and other insurance service expenses paid for insurance contracts issued (or recovered under reinsurance contracts held), excluding insurance acquisition cash flows.

(b)   the effect of changes in the risk of non-performance by the issuer of reinsurance contracts held;

(c)   insurance finance income or expenses; and

(d)   any additional line items that may be necessary to understand the change in the net carrying amount of the insurance contracts.

106   For insurance contracts issued other than those to which the premium allocation approach described in paragraphs 53–59 has been applied, an entity shall disclose an analysis of the insurance revenue recognised in the period comprising:

(a)   the amounts relating to the changes in the liability for remaining coverage as specified in paragraph B124, separately disclosing:

(i)   the insurance service expenses incurred during the period as specified in paragraph B124(a);

(ii)   the change in the risk adjustment for non-financial risk, as specified in paragraph B124(b); and

(iii)   the amount of the contractual service margin recognised in profit or loss because of the transfer of services in the period, as specified in paragraph B124(c).

(b)   the allocation of the portion of the premiums that relate to the recovery of insurance acquisition cash flows.

107   For insurance contracts other than those to which the premium allocation approach described in paragraphs 53–59 or 69–70 has been applied, an entity shall disclose the effect on the statement of financial position separately for insurance contracts issued and reinsurance contracts held that are initially recognised in the period, showing their effect at initial recognition on:

(a)   the estimates of the present value of future cash outflows, showing separately the amount of the insurance acquisition cash flows;

(b)   the estimates of the present value of future cash inflows;

(c)   the risk adjustment for non-financial risk; and

(d)   the contractual service margin.

108   In the disclosures required by paragraph 107, an entity shall separately disclose amounts resulting from:

(a)   contracts acquired from other entities in transfers of insurance contracts or business combinations; and

(b)   groups of contracts that are onerous.

109   For insurance contracts other than those to which the premium allocation approach described in paragraphs 53–59 or 69–70 has been applied, an entity shall disclose an explanation of when it expects to recognise the contractual service margin remaining at the end of the reporting period in profit or loss, either quantitatively, in appropriate time bands, or by providing qualitative information. Such information shall be provided separately for insurance contracts issued and reinsurance contracts held.

Insurance finance income or expenses

110   An entity shall disclose and explain the total amount of insurance finance income or expenses in the reporting period. In particular, an entity shall explain the relationship between insurance finance income or expenses and the investment return on its assets, to enable users of its financial statements to evaluate the sources of finance income or expenses recognised in profit or loss and other comprehensive income.

111   For contracts with direct participation features, the entity shall describe the composition of the underlying items and disclose their fair value.

112   For contracts with direct participation features, if an entity chooses not to adjust the contractual service margin for some changes in the fulfilment cash flows, applying paragraph B115, it shall disclose the effect of that choice on the adjustment to the contractual service margin in the current period.

113   For contracts with direct participation features, if an entity changes the basis of disaggregation of insurance finance income or expenses between profit or loss and other comprehensive income, applying paragraph B135, it shall disclose, in the period when the change in approach occurred:

(a)   the reason why the entity was required to change the basis of disaggregation;

(b)   the amount of any adjustment for each financial statement line item affected; and

(c)   the carrying amount of the group of insurance contracts to which the change applied at the date of the change.

Transition amounts

114   An entity shall provide disclosures that enable users of financial statements to identify the effect of groups of insurance contracts measured at the transition date applying the modified retrospective approach (see paragraphs C6–C19) or the fair value approach (see paragraphs C20–C24) on the contractual service margin and insurance revenue in subsequent periods. Hence an entity shall disclose the reconciliation of the contractual service margin applying paragraph 101(c), and the amount of insurance revenue applying paragraph 103(a), separately for:

(a)   insurance contracts that existed at the transition date to which the entity has applied the modified retrospective approach;

(b)   insurance contracts that existed at the transition date to which the entity has applied the fair value approach; and

(c)   all other insurance contracts.

115   For all periods in which disclosures are made applying paragraphs 114(a) or 114(b), to enable users of financial statements to understand the nature and significance of the methods used and judgements applied in determining the transition amounts, an

entity shall explain how it determined the measurement of insurance contracts at the transition date.

116   An entity that chooses to disaggregate insurance finance income or expenses between profit or loss and other comprehensive income applies paragraphs C18(b), C19(b), C24(b) and C24(c) to determine the cumulative difference between the insurance finance income or expenses that would have been recognised in profit or loss and the total insurance finance income or expenses at the transition date for the groups of insurance contracts to which the disaggregation applies. For all periods in which amounts determined applying these paragraphs exist, the entity shall disclose a reconciliation from the opening to the closing balance of the cumulative amounts included in other comprehensive income for financial assets measured at fair value through other comprehensive income related to the groups of insurance contracts. The reconciliation shall include, for example, gains or losses recognised in other comprehensive income in the period and gains or losses previously recognised in other comprehensive income in previous periods reclassified in the period to profit or loss.

Significant judgements in applying AASB 17

117   An entity shall disclose the significant judgements and changes in judgements made in applying AASB 17. Specifically, an entity shall disclose the inputs, assumptions and estimation techniques used, including:

(a)   the methods used to measure insurance contracts within the scope of AASB 17 and the processes for estimating the inputs to those methods. Unless impracticable, an entity shall also provide quantitative information about those inputs.

(b)   any changes in the methods and processes for estimating inputs used to measure contracts, the reason for each change, and the type of contracts affected.

(c)   to the extent not covered in (a), the approach used:

(i)   to distinguish changes in estimates of future cash flows arising from the exercise of discretion from other changes in estimates of future cash flows for contracts without direct participation features (see paragraph B98);

(ii)   to determine the risk adjustment for non-financial risk, including whether changes in the risk adjustment for non-financial risk are disaggregated into an insurance service component and an insurance finance component or are presented in full in the insurance service result;

(iii)   to determine discount rates; and

(iv)   to determine investment components.

118   If, applying paragraph 88(b) or paragraph 89(b), an entity chooses to disaggregate insurance finance income or expenses into amounts presented in profit or loss and amounts presented in other comprehensive income, the entity shall disclose an explanation of the methods used to determine the insurance finance income or expenses recognised in profit or loss.

119   An entity shall disclose the confidence level used to determine the risk adjustment for non-financial risk. If the entity uses a technique other than the confidence level technique for determining the risk adjustment for non-financial risk, it shall disclose the technique used and the confidence level corresponding to the results of that technique.

120   An entity shall disclose the yield curve (or range of yield curves) used to discount cash flows that do not vary based on the returns on underlying items, applying paragraph 36. When an entity provides this disclosure in aggregate for a number of groups of insurance contracts, it shall provide such disclosures in the form of weighted averages, or relatively narrow ranges.

Nature and extent of risks that arise from contracts within the scope of AASB 17

121   An entity shall disclose information that enables users of its financial statements to evaluate the nature, amount, timing and uncertainty of future cash flows that arise from

contracts within the scope of AASB 17. Paragraphs 122–132 contain requirements for disclosures that would normally be necessary to meet this requirement.

122   These disclosures focus on the insurance and financial risks that arise from insurance contracts and how they have been managed. Financial risks typically include, but are not limited to, credit risk, liquidity risk and market risk.

123   If the information disclosed about an entity's exposure to risk at the end of the reporting period is not representative of its exposure to risk during the period, the entity shall disclose that fact, the reason why the period-end exposure is not representative, and further information that is representative of its risk exposure during the period.

124   For each type of risk arising from contracts within the scope of AASB 17, an entity shall disclose:

(a)   the exposures to risks and how they arise;

(b)   the entity's objectives, policies and processes for managing the risks and the methods used to measure the risks; and

(c)   any changes in (a) or (b) from the previous period.

125   For each type of risk arising from contracts within the scope of AASB 17, an entity shall disclose:

(a)   summary quantitative information about its exposure to that risk at the end of the reporting period. This disclosure shall be based on the information provided internally to the entity's key management personnel.

(b)   the disclosures required by paragraphs 127–132, to the extent not provided applying (a) of this paragraph.

126   An entity shall disclose information about the effect of the regulatory frameworks in which it operates; for example, minimum capital requirements or required interest-rate guarantees. If an entity applies paragraph 20 in determining the groups of insurance contracts to which it applies the recognition and measurement requirements of AASB 17, it shall disclose that fact.

All types of risk—concentrations of risk

127   An entity shall disclose information about concentrations of risk arising from contracts within the scope of AASB 17, including a description of how the entity determines the concentrations, and a description of the shared characteristic that identifies each concentration (for example, the type of *insured event*, industry, geographical area, or currency). Concentrations of financial risk might arise, for example, from interest-rate guarantees that come into effect at the same level for a large number of contracts. Concentrations of financial risk might also arise from concentrations of non-financial risk; for example, if an entity provides product liability protection to pharmaceutical companies and also holds investments in those companies.

Insurance and market risks—sensitivity analysis

128   An entity shall disclose information about sensitivities to changes in risk exposures arising from contracts within the scope of AASB 17. To comply with this requirement, an entity shall disclose:

(a)   a sensitivity analysis that shows how profit or loss and equity would have been affected by changes in risk exposures that were reasonably possible at the end of the reporting period:

(i)   for insurance risk—showing the effect for insurance contracts issued, before and after risk mitigation by reinsurance contracts held; and

(ii)   for each type of market risk—in a way that explains the relationship between the sensitivities to changes in risk exposures arising from insurance contracts and those arising from financial assets held by the entity.

(b)   the methods and assumptions used in preparing the sensitivity analysis; and

(c)   changes from the previous period in the methods and assumptions used in preparing the sensitivity analysis, and the reasons for such changes.

129   If an entity prepares a sensitivity analysis that shows how amounts different from those specified in paragraph 128(a) are affected by changes in risk exposures and uses that sensitivity analysis to manage risks arising from contracts within the scope of AASB 17, it may use that sensitivity analysis in place of the analysis specified in paragraph 128(a). The entity shall also disclose:

(a)   an explanation of the method used in preparing such a sensitivity analysis and of the main parameters and assumptions underlying the information provided; and

(b)   an explanation of the objective of the method used and of any limitations that may result in the information provided.

Insurance risk—claims development

130   An entity shall disclose actual claims compared with previous estimates of the undiscounted amount of the claims (ie claims development). The disclosure about claims development shall start with the period when the earliest material claim(s) arose and for which there is still uncertainty about the amount and timing of the claims payments at the end of the reporting period; but the disclosure is not required to start more than 10 years before the end of the reporting period. The entity is not required to disclose information about the development of claims for which uncertainty about the amount and timing of the claims payments is typically resolved within one year. An entity shall reconcile the disclosure about claims development with the aggregate carrying amount of the groups of insurance contracts, which the entity discloses applying paragraph 100(c).

Credit risk—other information

131   For credit risk that arises from contracts within the scope of AASB 17, an entity shall disclose:

(a)   the amount that best represents its maximum exposure to credit risk at the end of the reporting period, separately for insurance contracts issued and reinsurance contracts held; and

(b)   information about the credit quality of reinsurance contracts held that are assets.

Liquidity risk—other information

132   For liquidity risk arising from contracts within the scope of AASB 17, an entity shall disclose:

(a)   a description of how it manages the liquidity risk.

(b)   separate maturity analyses for groups of insurance contracts issued that are liabilities and groups of reinsurance contracts held that are liabilities that show, as a minimum, net cash flows of the groups for each of the first five years after the reporting date and in aggregate beyond the first five years. An entity is not required to include in these analyses liabilities for remaining coverage measured applying paragraphs 55–59. The analyses may take the form of:

(i)   an analysis, by estimated timing, of the remaining contractual undiscounted net cash flows; or

(ii)   an analysis, by estimated timing, of the estimates of the present value of the future cash flows.

(c)   the amounts that are payable on demand, explaining the relationship between such amounts and the carrying amount of the related groups of contracts, if not disclosed applying (b) of this paragraph.

Commencement of the legislative instrument

Aus132.1   For legal purposes, this legislative instrument commences on 31 December 2020.

APPENDIX A
DEFINED TERMS

This appendix is an integral part of AASB 17 Insurance Contracts.

contractual service margin	A component of the carrying amount of the asset or liability for a **group of insurance contracts** representing the unearned profit the entity will recognise as it provides services under the **insurance contracts** in the group.
coverage period	The period during which the entity provides coverage for **insured events**. This period includes the coverage that relates to all premiums within the boundary of the **insurance contract**.
experience adjustment	A difference between: (a) for premium receipts (and any related cash flows such as **insurance acquisition cash flows** and insurance premium taxes)—the estimate at the beginning of the period of the amounts expected in the period and the actual cash flows in the period; or (b) for insurance service expenses (excluding insurance acquisition expenses)—the estimate at the beginning of the period of the amounts expected to be incurred in the period and the actual amounts incurred in the period.
financial risk	The risk of a possible future change in one or more of a specified interest rate, financial instrument price, commodity price, currency exchange rate, index of prices or rates, credit rating or credit index or other variable, provided in the case of a non-financial variable that the variable is not specific to a party to the contract.
fulfilment cash flows	An explicit, unbiased and probability-weighted estimate (ie expected value) of the present value of the future cash outflows minus the present value of the future cash inflows that will arise as the entity fulfils **insurance contracts**, including a **risk adjustment for non-financial risk**.
group of insurance contracts	A set of **insurance contracts** resulting from the division of a **portfolio of insurance contracts** into, at a minimum, contracts written within a period of no longer than one year and that, at initial recognition: (a) are onerous, if any; (b) have no significant possibility of becoming onerous subsequently, if any; or (c) do not fall into either (a) or (b), if any.
insurance acquisition cash flows	Cash flows arising from the costs of selling, underwriting and starting a **group of insurance contracts** that are directly attributable to the **portfolio of insurance contracts** to which the group belongs. Such cash flows include cash flows that are not directly attributable to individual contracts or **groups of insurance contracts** within the portfolio.
insurance contract	A contract under which one party (the issuer) accepts significant **insurance risk** from another party (the **policyholder**) by agreeing to compensate the **policyholder** if a specified uncertain future event (the **insured event**) adversely affects the **policyholder**.

insurance contract with direct participation features	An **insurance contract** for which, at inception: (a) the contractual terms specify that the **policyholder** participates in a share of a clearly identified pool of **underlying items**; (b) the entity expects to pay to the **policyholder** an amount equal to a substantial share of the fair value returns on the **underlying items**; and (c) the entity expects a substantial proportion of any change in the amounts to be paid to the **policyholder** to vary with the change in fair value of the **underlying items**.
insurance contract without direct participation features	An **insurance contract** that is not an **insurance contract with direct participation features**.
insurance risk	Risk, other than **financial risk**, transferred from the holder of a contract to the issuer.
insured event	An uncertain future event covered by an **insurance contract** that creates **insurance risk**.
investment component	The amounts that an **insurance contract** requires the entity to repay to a **policyholder** even if an **insured event** does not occur.

investment contract with discretionary participation features	A financial instrument that provides a particular investor with the contractual right to receive, as a supplement to an amount not subject to the discretion of the issuer, additional amounts:
	(a) that are expected to be a significant portion of the total contractual benefits;
	(b) the timing or amount of which are contractually at the discretion of the issuer; and
	(c) that are contractually based on:
	    (i) the returns on a specified pool of contracts or a specified type of contract;
	    (ii) realised and/or unrealised investment returns on a specified pool of assets held by the issuer; or
	    (iii) the profit or loss of the entity or fund that issues the contract.

liability for incurred claims	An entity's obligation to investigate and pay valid claims for **insured events** that have already occurred, including events that have occurred but for which claims have not been reported, and other incurred insurance expenses.
liability for remaining coverage	An entity's obligation to investigate and pay valid claims under existing **insurance contracts** for **insured events** that have not yet occurred (ie the obligation that relates to the unexpired portion of the **coverage period**).
policyholder	A party that has a right to compensation under an **insurance contract** if an **insured event** occurs.
portfolio of insurance contracts	**Insurance contracts** subject to similar risks and managed together.
reinsurance contract	An **insurance contract** issued by one entity (the reinsurer) to compensate another entity for claims arising from one or more **insurance contracts** issued by that other entity (underlying contracts).
risk adjustment for non-financial risk	The compensation an entity requires for bearing the uncertainty about the amount and timing of the cash flows that arises from non-financial risk as the entity fulfils **insurance contracts**.
underlying items	Items that determine some of the amounts payable to a **policyholder**. **Underlying items** can comprise any items; for example, a reference portfolio of assets, the net assets of the entity, or a specified subset of the net assets of the entity.

APPENDIX B
APPLICATION GUIDANCE

This appendix is an integral part of AASB 17 Insurance Contracts.

B1   This appendix provides guidance on the following:

(a)   definition of an insurance contract (see paragraphs B2–B30);

(b)   separation of components from an insurance contract (see paragraphs B31–B35);

(c)   measurement (see paragraphs B36–B119);

(d)   insurance revenue (see paragraphs B120–B127);

(e)   insurance finance income or expenses (see paragraphs B128–B136); and

(f)   interim financial statements (see paragraph B137).

Definition of an insurance contract (Appendix A)

B2   This section provides guidance on the definition of an insurance contract as specified in Appendix A. It addresses the following:

(a)   uncertain future event (see paragraphs B3–B5);

(b)   payments in kind (see paragraph B6);

(c)   the distinction between insurance risk and other risks (see paragraphs B7–B16);

(d)   significant insurance risk (see paragraphs B17–B23);

(e)   changes in the level of insurance risk (see paragraphs B24–B25); and

(f)   examples of insurance contracts (see paragraphs B26–B30).

Uncertain future event

B3   Uncertainty (or risk) is the essence of an insurance contract. Accordingly, at least one of the following is uncertain at the inception of an insurance contract:

(a)   the probability of an insured event occurring;

(b)   when the insured event will occur; or

(c)   how much the entity will need to pay if the insured event occurs.

B4   In some insurance contracts, the insured event is the discovery of a loss during the term of the contract, even if that loss arises from an event that occurred before the inception of the contract. In other insurance contracts, the insured event is an event that occurs during the term of the contract, even if the resulting loss is discovered after the end of the contract term.

B5   Some insurance contracts cover events that have already occurred but the financial effect of which is still uncertain. An example is an insurance contract that provides coverage against an adverse development of an event that has already occurred. In such contracts, the insured event is the determination of the ultimate cost of those claims.

Payments in kind

B6   Some insurance contracts require or permit payments to be made in kind. In such cases, the entity provides goods or services to the policyholder to settle the entity's obligation to compensate the policyholder for insured events. An example is when the entity replaces a stolen article instead of reimbursing the policyholder for the amount of its loss. Another example is when an entity uses its own hospitals and medical staff to provide medical services covered by the insurance contract. Such contracts are insurance contracts, even though the claims are settled in kind. Fixed-fee service contracts that meet the conditions specified in paragraph 8 are also insurance contracts, but applying paragraph 8, an entity may choose to account for them applying either AASB 17 or AASB 15 *Revenue from Contracts with Customers*.

The distinction between insurance risk and other risks

B7   The definition of an insurance contract requires that one party accepts significant insurance risk from another party. AASB 17 defines insurance risk as 'risk, other than financial risk, transferred from the holder of a contract to the issuer'. A contract that exposes the issuer to financial risk without significant insurance risk is not an insurance contract.

B8   The definition of financial risk in Appendix A refers to financial and non-financial variables. Examples of non-financial variables not specific to a party to the contract include an index of earthquake losses in a particular region or temperatures in a particular city. Financial risk excludes risk from non-financial variables that are specific to a party to the contract, such as the occurrence or non-occurrence of a fire that damages or destroys an asset of that party. Furthermore, the risk of changes in the fair value of a non-financial asset is not a financial risk if the fair value reflects changes in the market prices for such assets (ie a financial variable) and the condition of a specific non-financial asset held by a party to a contract (ie a non-financial variable). For example, if a guarantee of the residual value of a specific car in which the policyholder has an insurable interest exposes the guarantor to the risk of changes in the car's physical condition, that risk is insurance risk, not financial risk.

B9   Some contracts expose the issuer to financial risk in addition to significant insurance risk. For example, many life insurance contracts guarantee a minimum rate of return to policyholders, creating financial risk, and at the same time promise death benefits that may significantly exceed the policyholder's account balance, creating insurance risk in the form of mortality risk. Such contracts are insurance contracts.

B10   Under some contracts, an insured event triggers the payment of an amount linked to a price index. Such contracts are insurance contracts, provided that the payment contingent on the insured event could be significant. For example, a life-contingent annuity linked to a cost-of-living index transfers insurance risk because the payment is triggered by an uncertain future event—the survival of the person who receives the annuity. The link to the price index is a derivative, but it also transfers insurance risk because the number of payments to which the index applies depends on the survival of the annuitant. If the resulting transfer of insurance risk is significant, the derivative meets the definition of an insurance contract, in which case it shall not be separated from the host contract (see paragraph 11(a)).

B11   Insurance risk is the risk the entity accepts from the policyholder. This means the entity must accept, from the policyholder, a risk to which the policyholder was already exposed. Any new risk created by the contract for the entity or the policyholder is not insurance risk.

B12   The definition of an insurance contract refers to an adverse effect on the policyholder. This definition does not limit the payment by the entity to an amount equal to the financial effect of the adverse event. For example, the definition includes 'new for old' coverage that pays the policyholder an amount that permits the replacement of a used and damaged asset with a new one. Similarly, the definition does not limit the payment under a life insurance contract to the financial loss suffered by the deceased's dependants, nor does it exclude contracts that specify the payment of predetermined amounts to quantify the loss caused by death or an accident.

B13   Some contracts require a payment if a specified uncertain future event occurs, but do not require an adverse effect on the policyholder as a precondition for the payment. This type of contract is not an insurance contract even if the holder uses it to mitigate an underlying risk exposure. For example, if the holder uses a derivative to hedge an underlying financial or non-financial variable correlated with the cash flows from an asset of the entity, the derivative is not an insurance contract because the payment is not conditional on whether the holder is adversely affected by a reduction in the cash flows from the asset. The definition of an insurance contract refers to an uncertain future event for which an adverse effect on the policyholder is a contractual precondition for payment. A contractual precondition does not require the entity to investigate whether the event actually caused an adverse effect, but it does permit the entity to deny the payment if it is not satisfied that the event did cause an adverse effect.

B14   Lapse or persistency risk (the risk that the policyholder will cancel the contract earlier or later than the issuer had expected when pricing the contract) is not insurance risk because the resulting variability in the payment to the policyholder is not contingent on an uncertain future event that adversely affects the policyholder. Similarly, expense risk (ie the risk of unexpected increases in the administrative costs associated with the servicing of a contract, rather than in the costs associated with insured events) is not insurance risk because an unexpected increase in such expenses does not adversely affect the policyholder.

B15   Consequently, a contract that exposes the entity to lapse risk, persistency risk or expense risk is not an insurance contract unless it also exposes the entity to significant insurance risk. However, if the entity mitigates its risk by using a second contract to transfer part of the non-insurance risk to another party, the second contract exposes the other party to insurance risk.

B16   An entity can accept significant insurance risk from the policyholder only if the entity is separate from the policyholder. In the case of a mutual entity, the mutual entity accepts risk from each policyholder and pools that risk. Although policyholders bear that pooled risk collectively because they hold the residual interest in the entity, the mutual entity is a separate entity that has accepted the risk.

Significant insurance risk

B17   A contract is an insurance contract only if it transfers significant insurance risk. Paragraphs B7–B16 discuss insurance risk. Paragraphs B18–B23 discuss the assessment of whether the insurance risk is significant.

B18   Insurance risk is significant if, and only if, an insured event could cause the issuer to pay additional amounts that are significant in any single scenario, excluding scenarios that have no commercial substance (ie no discernible effect on the economics of the transaction). If an insured event could mean significant additional amounts would be payable in any scenario that has commercial substance, the condition in the previous sentence can be met even if the insured event is extremely unlikely, or even if the expected (ie probability-weighted) present value of the contingent cash flows is a small proportion of the expected present value of the remaining cash flows from the insurance contract.

B19   In addition, a contract transfers significant insurance risk only if there is a scenario that has commercial substance in which the issuer has a possibility of a loss on a present value basis. However, even if a reinsurance contract does not expose the issuer to the possibility of a significant loss, that contract is deemed to transfer significant insurance risk if it transfers to the reinsurer substantially all the insurance risk relating to the reinsured portions of the underlying insurance contracts.

B20   The additional amounts described in paragraph B18 are determined on a present-value basis. If an insurance contract requires payment when an event with uncertain timing occurs and if the payment is not adjusted for the time value of money, there may be scenarios in which the present value of the payment increases, even if its nominal value is fixed. An example is insurance that provides a fixed death benefit when the policyholder dies, with no expiry date for the cover (often referred to as whole-life insurance for a fixed amount). It is certain that the policyholder will die, but the date of death is uncertain. Payments may be made when an individual policyholder dies earlier than expected. Because those payments are not adjusted for the time value of money, significant insurance risk could exist even if there is no overall loss on the portfolio of contracts. Similarly, contractual terms that delay timely reimbursement to the policyholder can eliminate significant insurance risk. An entity shall use the discount rates required in paragraph 36 to determine the present value of the additional amounts.

B21   The additional amounts described in paragraph B18 refer to the present value of amounts that exceed those that would be payable if no insured event had occurred (excluding scenarios that lack commercial substance). Those additional amounts include claims handling and assessment costs, but exclude:

(a)   the loss of the ability to charge the policyholder for future service. For example, in an investment-linked life insurance contract, the death of the policyholder means that the entity can no longer perform investment management services and collect a fee for doing so. However, this economic loss for the entity does not result from insurance risk, just as a mutual fund manager does not take on insurance risk in relation to the possible death of a client. Consequently, the potential loss of future investment management fees is not relevant when assessing how much insurance risk is transferred by a contract.

(b)   a waiver, on death, of charges that would be made on cancellation or surrender. Because the contract brought those charges into existence, their waiver does not compensate the policyholder for a pre-existing risk. Consequently, they are not relevant when assessing how much insurance risk is transferred by a contract.

(c)   a payment conditional on an event that does not cause a significant loss to the holder of the contract. For example, consider a contract that requires the issuer to pay CU1 million[1] if an asset suffers physical damage that causes an insignificant economic loss of CU1 to the holder. In this contract, the holder transfers the insignificant risk of losing CU1 to the issuer. At the same time, the contract creates a non-insurance risk that the issuer will need to pay CU999,999 if the specified event occurs. Because there is no scenario in which an insured event causes a significant loss to the holder of the contract, the issuer does not accept significant insurance risk from the holder and this contract is not an insurance contract.

(d)   possible reinsurance recoveries. The entity accounts for these separately.

B22   An entity shall assess the significance of insurance risk contract by contract. Consequently, the insurance risk can be significant even if there is minimal probability of significant losses for a portfolio or group of contracts.

B23   It follows from paragraphs B18–B22 that, if a contract pays a death benefit that exceeds the amount payable on survival, the contract is an insurance contract unless the additional death benefit is not significant (judged by reference to the contract itself rather than to an entire portfolio of contracts). As noted in paragraph B21(b), the waiver on death of cancellation or surrender charges is not included in this assessment if that waiver does not compensate the policyholder for a pre-existing risk. Similarly, an annuity contract that pays out regular sums for the rest of a policyholder's life is an insurance contract, unless the aggregate life-contingent payments are insignificant.

Changes in the level of insurance risk

B24   For some contracts, the transfer of insurance risk to the issuer occurs after a period of time. For example, consider a contract that provides a specified investment return and includes an option for the policyholder to use the proceeds of the investment on maturity to buy a life-contingent annuity at the same rates the entity charges other new annuitants at the time the policyholder exercises that option. Such a contract transfers insurance risk to the issuer only after the option is exercised, because the entity remains free to price the annuity on a basis that reflects the insurance risk that will be transferred to the entity at that time. Consequently, the cash flows that would occur on the exercise of the option fall outside the boundary of the contract, and before exercise there are no insurance cash flows within the boundary of the contract. However, if the contract

---

1   CU denotes currency unit.

specifies the annuity rates (or a basis other than market rates for setting the annuity rates), the contract transfers insurance risk to the issuer because the issuer is exposed to the risk that the annuity rates will be unfavourable to the issuer when the policyholder exercises the option. In that case, the cash flows that would occur when the option is exercised are within the boundary of the contract.

B25 A contract that meets the definition of an insurance contract remains an insurance contract until all rights and obligations are extinguished (ie discharged, cancelled or expired), unless the contract is derecognised applying paragraphs 74–77, because of a contract modification.

Examples of insurance contracts

B26 The following are examples of contracts that are insurance contracts if the transfer of insurance risk is significant:

(a) insurance against theft or damage.

(b) insurance against product liability, professional liability, civil liability or legal expenses.

(c) life insurance and prepaid funeral plans (although death is certain, it is uncertain when death will occur or, for some types of life insurance, whether death will occur within the period covered by the insurance).

(d) life-contingent annuities and pensions, ie contracts that provide compensation for the uncertain future event—the survival of the annuitant or pensioner—to provide the annuitant or pensioner with a level of income that would otherwise be adversely affected by his or her survival. (Employers' liabilities that arise from employee benefit plans and retirement benefit obligations reported by defined benefit retirement plans are outside the scope of AASB 17, applying paragraph 7(b)).

(e) insurance against disability and medical costs.

(f) surety bonds, fidelity bonds, performance bonds and bid bonds, ie contracts that compensate the holder if another party fails to perform a contractual obligation; for example, an obligation to construct a building.

(g) product warranties. Product warranties issued by another party for goods sold by a manufacturer, dealer or retailer are within the scope of AASB 17. However, product warranties issued directly by a manufacturer, dealer or retailer are outside the scope of AASB 17 applying paragraph 7(a), and are instead within the scope of AASB 15 or AASB 137 *Provisions, Contingent Liabilities and Contingent Assets*.

(h) title insurance (insurance against the discovery of defects in the title to land or buildings that were not apparent when the insurance contract was issued). In this case, the insured event is the discovery of a defect in the title, not the defect itself.

(i) travel insurance (compensation in cash or in kind to policyholders for losses suffered in advance of, or during, travel).

(j) catastrophe bonds that provide for reduced payments of principal, interest or both, if a specified event adversely affects the issuer of the bond (unless the specified event does not create significant insurance risk; for example, if the event is a change in an interest rate or a foreign exchange rate).

(k) insurance swaps and other contracts that require a payment depending on changes in climatic, geological or other physical variables that are specific to a party to the contract.

B27   The following are examples of items that are not insurance contracts:

(a)   investment contracts that have the legal form of an insurance contract but do not transfer significant insurance risk to the issuer. For example, life insurance contracts in which the entity bears no significant mortality or morbidity risk are not insurance contracts; such contracts are financial instruments or service contracts—see paragraph B28. Investment contracts with discretionary participation features do not meet the definition of an insurance contract; however, they are within the scope of AASB 17 provided they are issued by an entity that also issues insurance contracts, applying paragraph 3(c).

(b)   contracts that have the legal form of insurance, but return all significant insurance risk to the policyholder through non-cancellable and enforceable mechanisms that adjust future payments by the policyholder to the issuer as a direct result of insured losses. For example, some financial reinsurance contracts or some group contracts return all significant insurance risk to the policyholders; such contracts are normally financial instruments or service contracts (see paragraph B28).

(c)   self-insurance (ie retaining a risk that could have been covered by insurance). In such situations, there is no insurance contract because there is no agreement with another party. Thus, if an entity issues an insurance contract to its parent, subsidiary or fellow subsidiary, there is no insurance contract in the consolidated financial statements because there is no contract with another party. However, for the individual or separate financial statements of the issuer or holder, there is an insurance contract.

(d)   contracts (such as gambling contracts) that require a payment if a specified uncertain future event occurs, but do not require, as a contractual precondition for payment, the event to adversely affect the policyholder. However, this does not exclude from the definition of an insurance contract contracts that specify a predetermined payout to quantify the loss caused by a specified event such as a death or an accident (see paragraph B12).

(e)   derivatives that expose a party to financial risk but not insurance risk, because the derivatives require that party to make (or give them the right to receive) payment solely based on the changes in one or more of a specified interest rate, a financial instrument price, a commodity price, a foreign exchange rate, an index of prices or rates, a credit rating or a credit index or any other variable, provided that, in the case of a non-financial variable, the variable is not specific to a party to the contract.

(f)   credit-related guarantees that require payments even if the holder has not incurred a loss on the failure of the debtor to make payments when due; such contracts are accounted for applying AASB 9 *Financial Instruments* (see paragraph B29).

(g)   contracts that require a payment that depends on a climatic, geological or any other physical variable not specific to a party to the contract (commonly described as weather derivatives).

(h)   contracts that provide for reduced payments of principal, interest or both, that depend on a climatic, geological or any other physical variable, the effect of which is not specific to a party to the contract (commonly referred to as catastrophe bonds).

B28   An entity shall apply other applicable Standards, such as AASB 9 and AASB 15, to the contracts described in paragraph B27.

B29   The credit-related guarantees and credit insurance contracts discussed in paragraph B27(f) can have various legal forms, such as that of a guarantee, some types of letters of credit, a credit default contract or an insurance contract. Those contracts are insurance contracts if they require the issuer to make specified payments to reimburse the holder for a loss that the holder incurs because a specified debtor fails to make payment when due to the policyholder applying the original or modified terms of a debt instrument. However, such insurance contracts are excluded from the scope of AASB 17 unless

AASB 17

the issuer has previously asserted explicitly that it regards the contracts as insurance contracts and has used accounting applicable to insurance contracts (see paragraph 7(e)).

B30   Credit-related guarantees and credit insurance contracts that require payment, even if the policyholder has not incurred a loss on the failure of the debtor to make payments when due, are outside the scope of AASB 17 because they do not transfer significant insurance risk. Such contracts include those that require payment:

     (a)   regardless of whether the counterparty holds the underlying debt instrument; or

     (b)   on a change in the credit rating or the credit index, rather than on the failure of a specified debtor to make payments when due.

Separating components from an insurance contract (paragraphs 10–13)

Investment components (paragraph 11(b))

B31   Paragraph 11(b) requires an entity to separate a distinct investment component from the host insurance contract. An investment component is distinct if, and only if, both the following conditions are met:

     (a)   the investment component and the insurance component are not highly interrelated.

     (b)   a contract with equivalent terms is sold, or could be sold, separately in the same market or the same jurisdiction, either by entities that issue insurance contracts or by other parties. The entity shall take into account all information reasonably available in making this determination. The entity is not required to undertake an exhaustive search to identify whether an investment component is sold separately.

B32   An investment component and an insurance component are highly interrelated if, and only if:

     (a)   the entity is unable to measure one component without considering the other. Thus, if the value of one component varies according to the value of the other, an entity shall apply AASB 17 to account for the combined investment and insurance component; or

     (b)   the policyholder is unable to benefit from one component unless the other is also present. Thus, if the lapse or maturity of one component in a contract causes the lapse or maturity of the other, the entity shall apply AASB 17 to account for the combined investment component and insurance component.

Promises to transfer distinct goods or non-insurance services (paragraph 12)

B33   Paragraph 12 requires an entity to separate from an insurance contract a promise to transfer distinct goods or non-insurance services to a policyholder. For the purpose of separation, an entity shall not consider activities that an entity must undertake to fulfil a contract unless the entity transfers a good or service to the policyholder as those activities occur. For example, an entity may need to perform various administrative tasks to set up a contract. The performance of those tasks does not transfer a service to the policyholder as the tasks are performed.

B34   A good or non-insurance service promised to a policyholder is distinct if the policyholder can benefit from the good or service either on its own or together with other resources readily available to the policyholder. Readily available resources are goods or services that are sold separately (by the entity or by another entity), or resources that the policyholder has already got (from the entity or from other transactions or events).

B35   A good or non-insurance service that is promised to the policyholder is not distinct if:

(a)   the cash flows and risks associated with the good or service are highly interrelated with the cash flows and risks associated with the insurance components in the contract; and

(b)   the entity provides a significant service in integrating the good or non-insurance service with the insurance components.

Measurement (paragraphs 29–71)

Estimates of future cash flows (paragraphs 33–35)

B36   This section addresses:

(a)   unbiased use of all reasonable and supportable information available without undue cost or effort (see paragraphs B37–B41);

(b)   market variables and non-market variables (see paragraphs B42–B53);

(c)   using current estimates (see paragraphs B54–B60); and

(d)   cash flows within the contract boundary (see paragraphs B61–B71).

Unbiased use of all reasonable and supportable information available without undue cost or effort (paragraph 33(a))

B37   The objective of estimating future cash flows is to determine the expected value, or probability-weighted mean, of the full range of possible outcomes, considering all reasonable and supportable information available at the reporting date without undue cost or effort. Reasonable and supportable information available at the reporting date without undue cost or effort includes information about past events and current conditions, and forecasts of future conditions (see paragraph B41). Information available from an entity's own information systems is considered to be available without undue cost or effort.

B38   The starting point for an estimate of the cash flows is a range of scenarios that reflects the full range of possible outcomes. Each scenario specifies the amount and timing of the cash flows for a particular outcome, and the estimated probability of that outcome. The cash flows from each scenario are discounted and weighted by the estimated probability of that outcome to derive an expected present value. Consequently, the objective is not to develop a most likely outcome, or a more-likely-than-not outcome, for future cash flows.

B39   When considering the full range of possible outcomes, the objective is to incorporate all reasonable and supportable information available without undue cost or effort in an unbiased way, rather than to identify every possible scenario. In practice, developing explicit scenarios is unnecessary if the resulting estimate is consistent with the measurement objective of considering all reasonable and supportable information available without undue cost or effort when determining the mean. For example, if an entity estimates that the probability distribution of outcomes is broadly consistent with a probability distribution that can be described completely with a small number of parameters, it will be sufficient to estimate the smaller number of parameters. Similarly, in some cases, relatively simple modelling may give an answer within an acceptable range of precision, without the need for many detailed simulations. However, in some cases, the cash flows may be driven by complex underlying factors and may respond in a non-linear fashion to changes in economic conditions. This may happen if, for example, the cash flows reflect a series of interrelated options that are implicit or explicit. In such cases, more sophisticated stochastic modelling is likely to be necessary to satisfy the measurement objective.

B40   The scenarios developed shall include unbiased estimates of the probability of catastrophic losses under existing contracts. Those scenarios exclude possible claims under possible future contracts.

B41   An entity shall estimate the probabilities and amounts of future payments under existing contracts on the basis of information obtained including:

(a) information about claims already reported by policyholders.

(b) other information about the known or estimated characteristics of the insurance contracts.

(c) historical data about the entity's own experience, supplemented when necessary with historical data from other sources. Historical data is adjusted to reflect current conditions, for example, if:

    (i) the characteristics of the insured population differ (or will differ, for example, because of adverse selection) from those of the population that has been used as a basis for the historical data;

    (ii) there are indications that historical trends will not continue, that new trends will emerge or that economic, demographic and other changes may affect the cash flows that arise from the existing insurance contracts; or

    (iii) there have been changes in items such as underwriting procedures and claims management procedures that may affect the relevance of historical data to the insurance contracts.

(d) current price information, if available, for reinsurance contracts and other financial instruments (if any) covering similar risks, such as catastrophe bonds and weather derivatives, and recent market prices for transfers of insurance contracts. This information shall be adjusted to reflect the differences between the cash flows that arise from those reinsurance contracts or other financial instruments, and the cash flows that would arise as the entity fulfils the underlying contracts with the policyholder.

Market variables and non-market variables

B42 AASB 17 identifies two types of variables:

(a) market variables—variables that can be observed in, or derived directly from, markets (for example, prices of publicly traded securities and interest rates); and

(b) non-market variables—all other variables (for example, the frequency and severity of insurance claims and mortality).

B43 Market variables will generally give rise to financial risk (for example, observable interest rates) and non-market variables will generally give rise to non-financial risk (for example, mortality rates). However, this will not always be the case. For example, there may be assumptions that relate to financial risks for which variables cannot be observed in, or derived directly from, markets (for example, interest rates that cannot be observed in, or derived directly from, markets).

Market variables (paragraph 33(b))

B44 Estimates of market variables shall be consistent with observable market prices at the measurement date. An entity shall maximise the use of observable inputs and shall not substitute its own estimates for observable market data except as described in paragraph 79 of AASB 13 *Fair Value Measurement*. Consistent with AASB 13, if variables need to be derived (for example, because no observable market variables exist) they shall be as consistent as possible with observable market variables.

B45 Market prices blend a range of views about possible future outcomes and also reflect the risk preferences of market participants. Consequently, they are not a single-point forecast of the future outcome. If the actual outcome differs from the previous market price, this does not mean that the market price was 'wrong'.

B46 An important application of market variables is the notion of a replicating asset or a replicating portfolio of assets. A replicating asset is one whose cash flows *exactly* match, in all scenarios, the contractual cash flows of a group of insurance contracts in amount, timing and uncertainty. In some cases, a replicating asset may exist for some of the cash flows that arise from a group of insurance contracts. The fair value of that asset reflects both the expected present value of the cash flows from the asset and the risk associated with those cash flows. If a replicating portfolio of assets exists for some of the cash flows that arise from a group of insurance contracts, the entity can use the fair value of those assets to measure the relevant fulfilment cash flows instead of explicitly estimating the cash flows and discount rate.

B47   AASB 17 does not require an entity to use a replicating portfolio technique. However, if a replicating asset or portfolio does exist for some of the cash flows that arise from insurance contracts and an entity chooses to use a different technique, the entity shall satisfy itself that a replicating portfolio technique would be unlikely to lead to a materially different measurement of those cash flows.

B48   Techniques other than a replicating portfolio technique, such as stochastic modelling techniques, may be more robust or easier to implement if there are significant interdependencies between cash flows that vary based on returns on assets and other cash flows. Judgement is required to determine the technique that best meets the objective of consistency with observable market variables in specific circumstances. In particular, the technique used must result in the measurement of any options and guarantees included in the insurance contracts being consistent with observable market prices (if any) for such options and guarantees.

Non-market variables

B49   Estimates of non-market variables shall reflect all reasonable and supportable evidence available without undue cost or effort, both external and internal.

B50   Non-market external data (for example, national mortality statistics) may have more or less relevance than internal data (for example, internally developed mortality statistics), depending on the circumstances. For example, an entity that issues life insurance contracts shall not rely solely on national mortality statistics, but shall consider all other reasonable and supportable internal and external sources of information available without undue cost or effort when developing unbiased estimates of probabilities for mortality scenarios for its insurance contracts. In developing those probabilities, an entity shall give more weight to the more persuasive information. For example:

(a)   internal mortality statistics may be more persuasive than national mortality data if national data is derived from a large population that is not representative of the insured population. This might be because, for example, the demographic characteristics of the insured population could significantly differ from those of the national population, meaning that an entity would need to place more weight on the internal data and less weight on the national statistics.

(b)   conversely, if the internal statistics are derived from a small population with characteristics that are believed to be close to those of the national population, and the national statistics are current, an entity shall place more weight on the national statistics.

B51   Estimated probabilities for non-market variables shall not contradict observable market variables. For example, estimated probabilities for future inflation rate scenarios shall be as consistent as possible with probabilities implied by market interest rates.

B52   In some cases, an entity may conclude that market variables vary independently of non-market variables. If so, the entity shall consider scenarios that reflect the range of outcomes for the non-market variables, with each scenario using the same observed value of the market variable.

B53   In other cases, market variables and non-market variables may be correlated. For example, there may be evidence that lapse rates (a non-market variable) are correlated with interest rates (a market variable). Similarly, there may be evidence that claim levels for house or car insurance are correlated with economic cycles and therefore with interest rates and expense amounts. The entity shall ensure that the probabilities for the scenarios and the risk adjustments for the non-financial risk that relates to the market variables are consistent with the observed market prices that depend on those market variables.

Using current estimates (paragraph 33(c))

B54 In estimating each cash flow scenario and its probability, an entity shall use all reasonable and supportable information available without undue cost or effort. An entity shall review the estimates that it made at the end of the previous reporting period and update them. In doing so, an entity shall consider whether:

(a) the updated estimates faithfully represent the conditions at the end of the reporting period.

(b) the changes in estimates faithfully represent the changes in conditions during the period. For example, suppose that estimates were at one end of a reasonable range at the beginning of the period. If the conditions have not changed, shifting the estimates to the other end of the range at the end of the period would not faithfully represent what has happened during the period. If an entity's most recent estimates are different from its previous estimates, but conditions have not changed, it shall assess whether the new probabilities assigned to each scenario are justified. In updating its estimates of those probabilities, the entity shall consider both the evidence that supported its previous estimates and all newly available evidence, giving more weight to the more persuasive evidence.

B55 The probability assigned to each scenario shall reflect the conditions at the end of the reporting period. Consequently, applying AASB 110 *Events after the Reporting Period*, an event occurring after the end of the reporting period that resolves an uncertainty that existed at the end of the reporting period does not provide evidence of the conditions that existed at that date. For example, there may be a 20 per cent probability at the end of the reporting period that a major storm will strike during the remaining six months of an insurance contract. After the end of the reporting period but before the financial statements are authorised for issue, a major storm strikes. The fulfilment cash flows under that contract shall not reflect the storm that, with hindsight, is known to have occurred. Instead, the cash flows included in the measurement include the 20 per cent probability apparent at the end of the reporting period (with disclosure applying AASB 110 that a non-adjusting event occurred after the end of the reporting period).

B56 Current estimates of expected cash flows are not necessarily identical to the most recent actual experience. For example, suppose that mortality experience in the reporting period was 20 per cent worse than the previous mortality experience and previous expectations of mortality experience. Several factors could have caused the sudden change in experience, including:

(a) lasting changes in mortality;

(b) changes in the characteristics of the insured population (for example, changes in underwriting or distribution, or selective lapses by policyholders in unusually good health);

(c) random fluctuations; or

(d) identifiable non-recurring causes.

B57 An entity shall investigate the reasons for the change in experience and develop new estimates of cash flows and probabilities in the light of the most recent experience, the earlier experience and other information. The result for the example in paragraph B56 would typically be that the expected present value of death benefits changes, but not by as much as 20 per cent. In the example in paragraph B56, if mortality rates continue to be significantly higher than the previous estimates for reasons that are expected to continue, the estimated probability assigned to the high-mortality scenarios will increase.

B58 Estimates of non-market variables shall include information about the current level of insured events and information about trends. For example, mortality rates have

AASB

consistently declined over long periods in many countries. The determination of the fulfilment cash flows reflects the probabilities that would be assigned to each possible trend scenario, taking account of all reasonable and supportable information available without undue cost or effort.

B59   Similarly, if cash flows allocated to a group of insurance contracts are sensitive to inflation, the determination of the fulfilment cash flows shall reflect current estimates of possible future inflation rates. Because inflation rates are likely to be correlated with interest rates, the measurement of fulfilment cash flows shall reflect the probabilities for each inflation scenario in a way that is consistent with the probabilities implied by the market interest rates used in estimating the discount rate (see paragraph B51).

B60   When estimating the cash flows, an entity shall take into account current expectations of future events that might affect those cash flows. The entity shall develop cash flow scenarios that reflect those future events, as well as unbiased estimates of the probability of each scenario. However, an entity shall not take into account current expectations of future changes in legislation that would change or discharge the present obligation or create new obligations under the existing insurance contract until the change in legislation is substantively enacted.

Cash flows within the contract boundary (paragraph 34)

B61   Estimates of cash flows in a scenario shall include all cash flows within the boundary of an existing contract and no other cash flows. An entity shall apply paragraph 2 in determining the boundary of an existing contract.

B62   Many insurance contracts have features that enable policyholders to take actions that change the amount, timing, nature or uncertainty of the amounts they will receive. Such features include renewal options, surrender options, conversion options and options to stop paying premiums while still receiving benefits under the contracts. The measurement of a group of insurance contracts shall reflect, on an expected value basis, the entity's current estimates of how the policyholders in the group will exercise the options available, and the risk adjustment for non-financial risk shall reflect the entity's current estimates of how the actual behaviour of the policyholders may differ from the expected behaviour. This requirement to determine the expected value applies regardless of the number of contracts in a group; for example it applies even if the group comprises a single contract. Thus, the measurement of a group of insurance contracts shall not assume a 100 per cent probability that policyholders will:

(a)   surrender their contracts, if there is some probability that some of the policyholders will not; or

(b)   continue their contracts, if there is some probability that some of the policyholders will not.

B63   When an issuer of an insurance contract is required by the contract to renew or otherwise continue the contract, it shall apply paragraph 34 to assess whether premiums and related cash flows that arise from the renewed contract are within the boundary of the original contract.

B64   Paragraph 34 refers to an entity's practical ability to set a price at a future date (a renewal date) that fully reflects the risks in the contract from that date. An entity has that practical ability in the absence of constraints that prevent the entity from setting the same price it would for a new contract with the same characteristics as the existing contract issued on that date, or if it can amend the benefits to be consistent with the price it will charge. Similarly, an entity has that practical ability to set a price when it can reprice an existing contract so that the price reflects overall changes in the risks in a portfolio of insurance contracts, even if the price set for each individual policyholder does not reflect the change in risk for that specific policyholder. When assessing whether the entity has the practical ability to set a price that fully reflects the risks in the contract or portfolio, it shall consider all the risks that it would consider when underwriting equivalent contracts on the renewal date for the remaining coverage. In determining the estimates of future cash flows at the end of a reporting period, an entity shall reassess the boundary of an insurance contract to include the effect of changes in circumstances on the entity's substantive rights and obligations.

B65   Cash flows within the boundary of an insurance contract are those that relate directly to the fulfilment of the contract, including cash flows for which the entity has discretion over the amount or timing. The cash flows within the boundary include:

(a)   premiums (including premium adjustments and instalment premiums) from a policyholder and any additional cash flows that result from those premiums.

(b)   payments to (or on behalf of) a policyholder, including claims that have already been reported but have not yet been paid (ie reported claims), incurred claims for events that have occurred but for which claims have not been reported and all future claims for which the entity has a substantive obligation (see paragraph 34).

(c)   payments to (or on behalf of) a policyholder that vary depending on returns on underlying items.

(d)   payments to (or on behalf of) a policyholder resulting from derivatives, for example, options and guarantees embedded in the contract, to the extent that those options and guarantees are not separated from the insurance contract (see paragraph 11(a)).

(e)   an allocation of insurance acquisition cash flows attributable to the portfolio to which the contract belongs.

(f)   claim handling costs (ie the costs the entity will incur in investigating, processing and resolving claims under existing insurance contracts, including legal and loss-adjusters' fees and internal costs of investigating claims and processing claim payments).

(g)   costs the entity will incur in providing contractual benefits paid in kind.

(h)   policy administration and maintenance costs, such as costs of premium billing and handling policy changes (for example, conversions and reinstatements). Such costs also include recurring commissions that are expected to be paid to intermediaries if a particular policyholder continues to pay the premiums within the boundary of the insurance contract.

(i)   transaction-based taxes (such as premium taxes, value added taxes and goods and services taxes) and levies (such as fire service levies and guarantee fund assessments) that arise directly from existing insurance contracts, or that can be attributed to them on a reasonable and consistent basis.

(j)   payments by the insurer in a fiduciary capacity to meet tax obligations incurred by the policyholder, and related receipts.

(k)   potential cash inflows from recoveries (such as salvage and subrogation) on future claims covered by existing insurance contracts and, to the extent that they do not qualify for recognition as separate assets, potential cash inflows from recoveries on past claims.

(l)   an allocation of fixed and variable overheads (such as the costs of accounting, human resources, information technology and support, building depreciation, rent, and maintenance and utilities) directly attributable to fulfilling insurance contracts. Such overheads are allocated to groups of contracts using methods that are systematic and rational, and are consistently applied to all costs that have similar characteristics.

(m)   any other costs specifically chargeable to the policyholder under the terms of the contract.

B66   The following cash flows shall not be included when estimating the cash flows that will arise as the entity fulfils an existing insurance contract:

(a)   investment returns. Investments are recognised, measured and presented separately.

AASB

(b)   cash flows (payments or receipts) that arise under reinsurance contracts held. Reinsurance contracts held are recognised, measured and presented separately.

(c)   cash flows that may arise from future insurance contracts, ie cash flows outside the boundary of existing contracts (see paragraphs 34–35).

(d)   cash flows relating to costs that cannot be directly attributed to the portfolio of insurance contracts that contain the contract, such as some product development and training costs. Such costs are recognised in profit or loss when incurred.

(e)   cash flows that arise from abnormal amounts of wasted labour or other resources that are used to fulfil the contract. Such costs are recognised in profit or loss when incurred.

(f)   income tax payments and receipts the insurer does not pay or receive in a fiduciary capacity. Such payments and receipts are recognised, measured and presented separately applying AASB 112 *Income Taxes*.

(g)   cash flows between different components of the reporting entity, such as policyholder funds and shareholder funds, if those cash flows do not change the amount that will be paid to the policyholders.

(h)   cash flows arising from components separated from the insurance contract and accounted for using other applicable Standards (see paragraphs 10–13).

Contracts with cash flows that affect or are affected by cash flows to policyholders of other contracts

B67   Some insurance contracts affect the cash flows to policyholders of other contracts by requiring:

(a)   the policyholder to share with policyholders of other contracts the returns on the same specified pool of underlying items; and

(b)   either:

(i)   the policyholder to bear a reduction in their share of the returns on the underlying items because of payments to policyholders of other contracts that share in that pool, including payments arising under guarantees made to policyholders of those other contracts; or

(ii)   policyholders of other contracts to bear a reduction in their share of returns on the underlying items because of payments to the policyholder, including payments arising from guarantees made to the policyholder.

B68   Sometimes, such contracts will affect the cash flows to policyholders of contracts in other groups. The fulfilment cash flows of each group reflect the extent to which the contracts in the group cause the entity to be affected by expected cash flows, whether to policyholders in that group or to policyholders in another group. Hence the fulfilment cash flows for a group:

(a)   include payments arising from the terms of existing contracts to policyholders of contracts in other groups, regardless of whether those payments are expected to be made to current or future policyholders; and

(b)   exclude payments to policyholders in the group that, applying (a), have been included in the fulfilment cash flows of another group.

B69   For example, to the extent that payments to policyholders in one group are reduced from a share in the returns on underlying items of CU350 to CU250 because of payments of a guaranteed amount to policyholders in another group, the fulfilment cash flows of the first group would include the payments of CU100 (ie would be CU350) and the fulfilment cash flows of the second group would exclude CU100 of the guaranteed amount.

B70   Different practical approaches can be used to determine the fulfilment cash flows of groups of contracts that affect or are affected by cash flows to policyholders of contracts in other groups. In some cases, an entity might be able to identify the change in the underlying items and resulting change in the cash flows only at a higher level of aggregation than the groups. In such cases, the entity shall allocate the effect of the change in the underlying items to each group on a systematic and rational basis.

B71 After all the coverage has been provided to the contracts in a group, the fulfilment cash flows may still include payments expected to be made to current policyholders in other groups or future policyholders. An entity is not required to continue to allocate such fulfilment cash flows to specific groups but can instead recognise and measure a liability for such fulfilment cash flows arising from all groups.

Discount rates (paragraph 36)

B72 An entity shall use the following discount rates in applying AASB 17:

   (a) to measure the fulfilment cash flows—current discount rates applying paragraph 36;

   (b) to determine the interest to accrete on the contractual service margin applying paragraph 44(b) for insurance contracts without direct participation features— discount rates determined at the date of initial recognition of a group of contracts, applying paragraph 36 to nominal cash flows that do not vary based on the returns on any underlying items;

   (c) to measure the changes to the contractual service margin applying paragraph B96(a)–B96(c) for insurance contracts without direct participation features— discount rates applying paragraph 36 determined on initial recognition;

   (d) for groups of contracts applying the premium allocation approach that have a significant financing component, to adjust the carrying amount of the liability for remaining coverage applying paragraph 56—discount rates applying paragraph 36 determined on initial recognition;

   (e) if an entity chooses to disaggregate insurance finance income or expenses between profit or loss and other comprehensive income (see paragraph 88), to determine the amount of the insurance finance income or expenses included in profit or loss:

      (i) for groups of insurance contracts for which changes in assumptions that relate to financial risk do not have a substantial effect on the amounts paid to policyholders, applying paragraph B131—discount rates determined at the date of initial recognition of a group of contracts, applying paragraph 36 to nominal cash flows that do not vary based on the returns on any underlying items;

      (ii) for groups of insurance contracts for which changes in assumptions that relate to financial risk have a substantial effect on the amounts paid to policyholders, applying paragraph B132(a)(i)—discount rates that allocate the remaining revised expected finance income or expenses over the remaining duration of the group of contracts at a constant rate; and

      (iii) for groups of contracts applying the premium allocation approach applying paragraphs 59(b) and B133—discount rates determined at the date of the incurred claim, applying paragraph 36 to nominal cash flows that do not vary based on the returns on any underlying items.

B73 To determine the discount rates at the date of initial recognition of a group of contracts described in paragraphs B72(b)–B72(e), an entity may use weighted-average discount rates over the period that contracts in the group are issued, which applying paragraph 22 cannot exceed one year.

B74 Estimates of discount rates shall be consistent with other estimates used to measure insurance contracts to avoid double counting or omissions; for example:

   (a) cash flows that do not vary based on the returns on any underlying items shall be discounted at rates that do not reflect any such variability;

     (b)   cash flows that vary based on the returns on any financial underlying items shall be:

         (i)   discounted using rates that reflect that variability; or

         (ii)   adjusted for the effect of that variability and discounted at a rate that reflects the adjustment made.

     (c)   nominal cash flows (ie those that include the effect of inflation) shall be discounted at rates that include the effect of inflation; and

     (d)   real cash flows (ie those that exclude the effect of inflation) shall be discounted at rates that exclude the effect of inflation.

B75   Paragraph B74(b) requires cash flows that vary based on the returns on underlying items to be discounted using rates that reflect that variability, or to be adjusted for the effect of that variability and discounted at a rate that reflects the adjustment made. The variability is a relevant factor regardless of whether it arises because of contractual terms or because the entity exercises discretion, and regardless of whether the entity holds the underlying items.

B76   Cash flows that vary with returns on underlying items with variable returns, but that are subject to a guarantee of a minimum return, do not vary solely based on the returns on the underlying items, even when the guaranteed amount is lower than the expected return on the underlying items. Hence, an entity shall adjust the rate that reflects the variability of the returns on the underlying items for the effect of the guarantee, even when the guaranteed amount is lower than the expected return on the underlying items.

B77   AASB 17 does not require an entity to divide estimated cash flows into those that vary based on the returns on underlying items and those that do not. If an entity does not divide the estimated cash flows in this way, the entity shall apply discount rates appropriate for the estimated cash flows as a whole; for example, using stochastic modelling techniques or risk-neutral measurement techniques.

B78   Discount rates shall include only relevant factors, ie factors that arise from the time value of money, the characteristics of the cash flows and the liquidity characteristics of the insurance contracts. Such discount rates may not be directly observable in the market. Hence, when observable market rates for an instrument with the same characteristics are not available, or observable market rates for similar instruments are available but do not separately identify the factors that distinguish the instrument from the insurance contracts, an entity shall estimate the appropriate rates. AASB 17 does not require a particular estimation technique for determining discount rates. In applying an estimation technique, an entity shall:

     (a)   maximise the use of observable inputs (see paragraph B44) and reflect all reasonable and supportable information on non-market variables available without undue cost or effort, both external and internal (see paragraph B49). In particular, the discount rates used shall not contradict any available and relevant market data, and any non-market variables used shall not contradict observable market variables.

     (b)   reflect current market conditions from the perspective of a market participant.

     (c)   exercise judgement to assess the degree of similarity between the features of the insurance contracts being measured and the features of the instrument for which observable market prices are available and adjust those prices to reflect the differences between them.

B79   For cash flows of insurance contracts that do not vary based on the returns on underlying items, the discount rate reflects the yield curve in the appropriate currency for instruments that expose the holder to no or negligible credit risk, adjusted to reflect the liquidity characteristics of the group of insurance contracts. That adjustment shall reflect the difference between the liquidity characteristics of the group of insurance contracts and the liquidity characteristics of the assets used to determine the yield curve. Yield curves reflect assets traded in active markets that the holder can typically sell readily at any time without incurring significant costs. In contrast, under some insurance contracts the entity cannot be forced to make payments earlier than the occurrence of insured events, or dates specified in the contracts.

B80 Hence, for cash flows of insurance contracts that do not vary based on the returns on underlying items, an entity may determine discount rates by adjusting a liquid risk-free yield curve to reflect the differences between the liquidity characteristics of the financial instruments that underlie the rates observed in the market and the liquidity characteristics of the insurance contracts (a bottom-up approach).

B81 Alternatively, an entity may determine the appropriate discount rates for insurance contracts based on a yield curve that reflects the current market rates of return implicit in a fair value measurement of a reference portfolio of assets (a top-down approach). An entity shall adjust that yield curve to eliminate any factors that are not relevant to the insurance contracts, but is not required to adjust the yield curve for differences in liquidity characteristics of the insurance contracts and the reference portfolio.

B82 In estimating the yield curve described in paragraph B81:

    (a) if there are observable market prices in active markets for assets in the reference portfolio, an entity shall use those prices (consistent with paragraph 69 of AASB 13).

    (b) if a market is not active, an entity shall adjust observable market prices for similar assets to make them comparable to market prices for the assets being measured (consistent with paragraph 83 of AASB 13).

    (c) if there is no market for assets in the reference portfolio, an entity shall apply an estimation technique. For such assets (consistent with paragraph 89 of AASB 13) an entity shall:

        (i) develop unobservable inputs using the best information available in the circumstances. Such inputs might include the entity's own data and, in the context of AASB 17, the entity might place more weight on long-term estimates than on short-term fluctuations; and

        (ii) adjust those data to reflect all information about market participant assumptions that is reasonably available.

B83 In adjusting the yield curve, an entity shall adjust market rates observed in recent transactions in instruments with similar characteristics for movements in market factors since the transaction date, and shall adjust observed market rates to reflect the degree of dissimilarity between the instrument being measured and the instrument for which transaction prices are observable. For cash flows of insurance contracts that do not vary based on the returns on the assets in the reference portfolio, such adjustments include:

    (a) adjusting for differences between the amount, timing and uncertainty of the cash flows of the assets in the portfolio and the amount, timing and uncertainty of the cash flows of the insurance contracts; and

    (b) excluding market risk premiums for credit risk, which are relevant only to the assets included in the reference portfolio.

B84 In principle, for cash flows of insurance contracts that do not vary based on the returns of the assets in the reference portfolio, there should be a single illiquid risk-free yield curve that eliminates all uncertainty about the amount and timing of cash flows. However, in practice the top-down approach and the bottom-up approach may result in different yield curves, even in the same currency. This is because of the inherent limitations in estimating the adjustments made under each approach, and the possible lack of an adjustment for different liquidity characteristics in the top-down approach. An entity is not required to reconcile the discount rate determined under its chosen approach with the discount rate that would have been determined under the other approach.

B85 AASB 17 does not specify restrictions on the reference portfolio of assets used in applying paragraph B81. However, fewer adjustments would be required to eliminate factors that are not relevant to the insurance contracts when the reference portfolio of assets has similar characteristics. For example, if the cash flows from the insurance contracts do not vary based on the returns on underlying items, fewer adjustments would be required if an entity used debt instruments as a starting point rather than equity instruments. For debt instruments, the objective would be to eliminate from the total bond yield the effect of credit risk and other factors that are not relevant to the insurance contracts. One way to estimate the effect of credit risk is to use the market price of a credit derivative as a reference point.

Risk adjustment for non-financial risk (paragraph 37)

B86   The risk adjustment for non-financial risk relates to risk arising from insurance contracts other than financial risk. Financial risk is included in the estimates of the future cash flows or the discount rate used to adjust the cash flows. The risks covered by the risk adjustment for non-financial risk are insurance risk and other non-financial risks such as lapse risk and expense risk (see paragraph B14).

B87   The risk adjustment for non-financial risk for insurance contracts measures the compensation that the entity would require to make the entity indifferent between:

   (a)   fulfilling a liability that has a range of possible outcomes arising from non-financial risk; and

   (b)   fulfilling a liability that will generate fixed cash flows with the same expected present value as the insurance contracts.

   For example, the risk adjustment for non-financial risk would measure the compensation the entity would require to make it indifferent between fulfilling a liability that—because of non-financial risk—has a 50 per cent probability of being CU90 and a 50 per cent probability of being CU110, and fulfilling a liability that is fixed at CU100. As a result, the risk adjustment for non-financial risk conveys information to users of financial statements about the amount charged by the entity for the uncertainty arising from non-financial risk about the amount and timing of cash flows.

B88   Because the risk adjustment for non-financial risk reflects the compensation the entity would require for bearing the non-financial risk arising from the uncertain amount and timing of the cash flows, the risk adjustment for non-financial risk also reflects:

   (a)   the degree of diversification benefit the entity includes when determining the compensation it requires for bearing that risk; and

   (b)   both favourable and unfavourable outcomes, in a way that reflects the entity's degree of risk aversion.

B89   The purpose of the risk adjustment for non-financial risk is to measure the effect of uncertainty in the cash flows that arise from insurance contracts, other than uncertainty arising from financial risk. Consequently, the risk adjustment for non-financial risk shall reflect all non-financial risks associated with the insurance contracts. It shall not reflect the risks that do not arise from the insurance contracts, such as general operational risk.

B90   The risk adjustment for non-financial risk shall be included in the measurement in an explicit way. The risk adjustment for non-financial risk is conceptually separate from the estimates of future cash flows and the discount rates that adjust those cash flows. The entity shall not double-count the risk adjustment for non-financial risk by, for example, also including the risk adjustment for non-financial risk implicitly when determining the estimates of future cash flows or the discount rates. The discount rates that are disclosed to comply with paragraph 120 shall not include any implicit adjustments for non-financial risk.

B91   AASB 17 does not specify the estimation technique(s) used to determine the risk adjustment for non-financial risk. However, to reflect the compensation the entity would require for bearing the non-financial risk, the risk adjustment for non-financial risk shall have the following characteristics:

(a) risks with low frequency and high severity will result in higher risk adjustments for non-financial risk than risks with high frequency and low severity;

(b) for similar risks, contracts with a longer duration will result in higher risk adjustments for non-financial risk than contracts with a shorter duration;

(c) risks with a wider probability distribution will result in higher risk adjustments for non-financial risk than risks with a narrower distribution;

(d) the less that is known about the current estimate and its trend, the higher will be the risk adjustment for non-financial risk; and

(e) to the extent that emerging experience reduces uncertainty about the amount and timing of cash flows, risk adjustments for non-financial risk will decrease and vice versa.

B92 An entity shall apply judgement when determining an appropriate estimation technique for the risk adjustment for non-financial risk. When applying that judgement, an entity shall also consider whether the technique provides concise and informative disclosure so that users of financial statements can benchmark the entity's performance against the performance of other entities. Paragraph 119 requires an entity that uses a technique other than the confidence level technique for determining the risk adjustment for non-financial risk to disclose the technique used and the confidence level corresponding to the results of that technique.

Initial recognition of transfers of insurance contracts and business combinations (paragraph 39)

B93 When an entity acquires insurance contracts issued or reinsurance contracts held in a transfer of insurance contracts that do not form a business or in a business combination, the entity shall apply paragraphs 14–24 to identify the groups of contracts acquired, as if it had entered into the contracts on the date of the transaction.

B94 An entity shall use the consideration received or paid for the contracts as a proxy for the premiums received. The consideration received or paid for the contracts excludes the consideration received or paid for any other assets and liabilities acquired in the same transaction. In a business combination, the consideration received or paid is the fair value of the contracts at that date. In determining that fair value, an entity shall not apply paragraph 47 of AASB 13 (relating to demand features).

B95 Unless the premium allocation approach for the liability for remaining coverage in paragraphs 55–59 applies, on initial recognition the contractual service margin is calculated applying paragraph 38 for acquired insurance contracts issued and paragraph 65 for acquired reinsurance contracts held using the consideration received or paid for the contracts as a proxy for the premiums received or paid at the date of initial recognition. If acquired insurance contracts issued are onerous, applying paragraph 47, the entity shall recognise the excess of the fulfilment cash flows over the consideration paid or received as part of goodwill or gain on a bargain purchase for contracts acquired in a business combination or as a loss in profit or loss for contracts acquired in a transfer. The entity shall establish a loss component of the liability for remaining coverage for that excess, and apply paragraphs 49–52 to allocate subsequent changes in fulfilment cash flows to that loss component.

Changes in the carrying amount of the contractual service margin for insurance contracts without direct participation features (paragraph 44)

B96 For insurance contracts without direct participation features, paragraph 44(c) requires an adjustment to the contractual service margin of a group of insurance contracts for changes in fulfilment cash flows that relate to future service. These changes comprise:

(a) experience adjustments arising from premiums received in the period that relate to future service, and related cash flows such as insurance acquisition cash flows and premium-based taxes, measured at the discount rates specified in paragraph B72(c);

AASB

(b)   changes in estimates of the present value of the future cash flows in the liability for remaining coverage, except those described in paragraph B97(a), measured at the discount rates specified in paragraph B72(c);

(c)   differences between any investment component expected to become payable in the period and the actual investment component that becomes payable in the period, measured at the discount rates specified in paragraph B72(c); and

(d)   changes in the risk adjustment for non-financial risk that relate to future service.

B97   An entity shall not adjust the contractual service margin for a group of insurance contracts without direct participation features for the following changes in fulfilment cash flows because they do not relate to future service:

(a)   the effect of the time value of money and changes in the time value of money and the effect of financial risk and changes in financial risk (being the effect, if any, on estimated future cash flows and the effect of a change in discount rate);

(b)   changes in estimates of fulfilment cash flows in the liability for incurred claims; and

(c)   experience adjustments, except those described in paragraph B96(a).

B98   The terms of some insurance contracts without direct participation features give an entity discretion over the cash flows to be paid to policyholders. A change in the discretionary cash flows is regarded as relating to future service, and accordingly adjusts the contractual service margin. To determine how to identify a change in discretionary cash flows, an entity shall specify at inception of the contract the basis on which it expects to determine its commitment under the contract; for example, based on a fixed interest rate, or on returns that vary based on specified asset returns.

B99   An entity shall use that specification to distinguish between the effect of changes in assumptions that relate to financial risk on that commitment (which do not adjust the contractual service margin) and the effect of discretionary changes to that commitment (which adjust the contractual service margin).

B100   If an entity cannot specify at inception of the contract what it regards as its commitment under the contract and what it regards as discretionary, it shall regard its commitment to be the return implicit in the estimate of the fulfilment cash flows at inception of the contract, updated to reflect current assumptions that relate to financial risk.

Changes in the carrying amount of the contractual service margin for insurance contracts with direct participation features (paragraph 45)

B101   Insurance contracts with direct participation features are insurance contracts that are substantially investment-related service contracts under which an entity promises an investment return based on underlying items. Hence, they are defined as insurance contracts for which:

(a)   the contractual terms specify that the policyholder participates in a share of a clearly identified pool of underlying items (see paragraphs B105–B106);

(b)   the entity expects to pay to the policyholder an amount equal to a substantial share of the fair value returns on the underlying items (see paragraph B107); and

(c)   the entity expects a substantial proportion of any change in the amounts to be paid to the policyholder to vary with the change in fair value of the underlying items (see paragraph B107).

B102   An entity shall assess whether the conditions in paragraph B101 are met using its expectations at inception of the contract and shall not reassess the conditions afterwards, unless the contract is modified, applying paragraph 72.

B103   To the extent that insurance contracts in a group affect the cash flows to policyholders of contracts in other groups (see paragraphs B67–B71), an entity shall assess whether the conditions in paragraph B101 are met by considering the cash flows that the entity expects to pay the policyholders determined applying paragraphs B68–B70.

B104 The conditions in paragraph B101 ensure that insurance contracts with direct participation features are contracts under which the entity's obligation to the policyholder is the net of:

(a) the obligation to pay the policyholder an amount equal to the fair value of the underlying items; and

(b) a variable fee (see paragraphs B110–B118) that the entity will deduct from (a) in exchange for the future service provided by the insurance contract, comprising:

(i) the entity's share of the fair value of the underlying items; less

(ii) fulfilment cash flows that do not vary based on the returns on underlying items.

B105 A share referred to in paragraph B101(a) does not preclude the existence of the entity's discretion to vary the amounts paid to the policyholder. However, the link to the underlying items must be enforceable (see paragraph 2).

B106 The pool of underlying items referred to in paragraph B101(a) can comprise any items, for example a reference portfolio of assets, the net assets of the entity, or a specified subset of the net assets of the entity, as long as they are clearly identified by the contract. An entity need not hold the identified pool of underlying items. However, a clearly identified pool of underlying items does not exist when:

(a) an entity can change the underlying items that determine the amount of the entity's obligation with retrospective effect; or

(b) there are no underlying items identified, even if the policyholder could be provided with a return that generally reflects the entity's overall performance and expectations, or the performance and expectations of a subset of assets the entity holds. An example of such a return is a crediting rate or dividend payment set at the end of the period to which it relates. In this case, the obligation to the policyholder reflects the crediting rate or dividend amounts the entity has set, and does not reflect identified underlying items.

B107 Paragraph B101(b) requires that the entity expects a substantial share of the fair value returns on the underlying items will be paid to the policyholder and paragraph B101(c) requires that the entity expects a substantial proportion of any change in the amounts to be paid to the policyholder to vary with the change in fair value of the underlying items. An entity shall:

(a) interpret the term 'substantial' in both paragraphs in the context of the objective of insurance contracts with direct participation features being contracts under which the entity provides investment-related services and is compensated for the services by a fee that is determined by reference to the underlying items; and

(b) assess the variability in the amounts in paragraphs B101(b) and B101(c):

(i) over the duration of the group of insurance contracts; and

(ii) on a present value probability-weighted average basis, not a best or worst outcome basis (see paragraphs B37–B38).

B108 For example, if the entity expects to pay a substantial share of the fair value returns on underlying items, subject to a guarantee of a minimum return, there will be scenarios in which:

(a) the cash flows that the entity expects to pay to the policyholder vary with the changes in the fair value of the underlying items because the guaranteed return and other cash flows that do not vary based on the returns on underlying items do not exceed the fair value return on the underlying items; and

(b) the cash flows that the entity expects to pay to the policyholder do not vary with the changes in the fair value of the underlying items because the guaranteed return and other cash flows that do not vary based on the returns on underlying items exceed the fair value return on the underlying items.

The entity's assessment of the variability in paragraph B101(c) for this example will reflect a present value probability-weighted average of all these scenarios.

B109   Reinsurance contracts issued and reinsurance contracts held cannot be insurance contracts with direct participation features for the purposes of AASB 17.

B110   For insurance contracts with direct participation features, the contractual service margin is adjusted to reflect the variable nature of the fee. Hence, changes in the amounts set out in paragraph B104 are treated as set out in paragraphs B111–B114.

B111   Changes in the obligation to pay the policyholder an amount equal to the fair value of the underlying items (paragraph B104(a)) do not relate to future service and do not adjust the contractual service margin.

B112   Changes in the entity's share of the fair value of the underlying items (paragraph B104(b)(i)) relate to future service and adjust the contractual service margin, applying paragraph 45(b).

B113   Changes in the fulfilment cash flows that do not vary based on the returns on underlying items (paragraph B104(b)(ii)) comprise:

(a)   changes in estimates of the fulfilment cash flows other than those specified in (b). An entity shall apply paragraphs B96–B97, consistent with insurance contracts without direct participation features, to determine to what extent they relate to future service and, applying paragraph 45(c), adjust the contractual service margin. All the adjustments are measured using current discount rates.

(b)   the change in the effect of the time value of money and financial risks not arising from the underlying items; for example, the effect of financial guarantees. These relate to future service and, applying paragraph 45(c), adjust the contractual service margin, except to the extent that paragraph B115 applies.

B114   An entity is not required to identify the adjustments to the contractual service margin required by paragraphs B112 and B113 separately. Instead, a combined amount may be determined for some or all of the adjustments.

Risk mitigation

B115   To the extent that an entity meets the conditions in paragraph B116, it may choose not to recognise a change in the contractual service margin to reflect some or all of the changes in the effect of financial risk on the entity's share of the underlying items (see paragraph B112) or the fulfilment cash flows set out in paragraph B113(b).

B116   To apply paragraph B115, an entity must have a previously documented risk-management objective and strategy for using derivatives to mitigate financial risk arising from the insurance contracts and, in applying that objective and strategy:

(a)   the entity uses a derivative to mitigate the financial risk arising from the insurance contracts.

(b)   an economic offset exists between the insurance contracts and the derivative, ie the values of the insurance contracts and the derivative generally move in opposite directions because they respond in a similar way to the changes in the risk being mitigated. An entity shall not consider accounting measurement differences in assessing the economic offset.

(c)   credit risk does not dominate the economic offset.

B117   The entity shall determine the fulfilment cash flows in a group to which paragraph B115 applies in a consistent manner in each reporting period.

B118   If any of the conditions in paragraph B116 ceases to be met, an entity shall:

(a)   cease to apply paragraph B115 from that date; and

(b)   not make any adjustment for changes previously recognised in profit or loss.

Recognition of the contractual service margin in profit or loss

B119 An amount of the contractual service margin for a group of insurance contracts is recognised in profit or loss in each period to reflect the services provided under the group of insurance contracts in that period (see paragraphs 44(e), 45(e) and 66(e)). The amount is determined by:

(a) identifying the coverage units in the group. The number of coverage units in a group is the quantity of coverage provided by the contracts in the group, determined by considering for each contract the quantity of the benefits provided under a contract and its expected coverage duration.

(b) allocating the contractual service margin at the end of the period (before recognising any amounts in profit or loss to reflect the services provided in the period) equally to each coverage unit provided in the current period and expected to be provided in the future.

(c) recognising in profit or loss the amount allocated to coverage units provided in the period.

Insurance revenue (paragraphs 83 and 85)

B120 The total insurance revenue for a group of insurance contracts is the consideration for the contracts, ie the amount of premiums paid to the entity:

(a) adjusted for a financing effect; and

(b) excluding any investment components.

B121 Paragraph 83 requires the amount of insurance revenue recognised in a period to depict the transfer of promised services at an amount that reflects the consideration to which the entity expects to be entitled in exchange for those services. The total consideration for a group of contracts covers the following amounts:

(a) amounts related to the provision of services, comprising:

(i) insurance service expenses, excluding any amounts allocated to the loss component of the liability for remaining coverage;

(ii) the risk adjustment for non-financial risk, excluding any amounts allocated to the loss component of the liability for remaining coverage; and

(iii) the contractual service margin.

(b) amounts related to insurance acquisition cash flows.

B122 Insurance revenue for a period relating to the amounts described in paragraph B121(a) is determined as set out in paragraphs B123–B124. Insurance revenue for a period relating to the amounts described in paragraph B121(b) is determined as set out in paragraph B125.

B123 Applying AASB 15, when an entity provides services, it derecognises the performance obligation for those services and recognises revenue. Consistently, applying AASB 17, when an entity provides services in a period, it reduces the liability for remaining coverage for the services provided and recognises insurance revenue. The reduction in the liability for remaining coverage that gives rise to insurance revenue excludes changes in the liability that do not relate to services expected to be covered by the consideration received by the entity. Those changes are:

(a) changes that do not relate to services provided in the period, for example:

(i) changes resulting from cash inflows from premiums received;

(ii) changes that relate to investment components in the period;

(iii) changes that relate to transaction-based taxes collected on behalf of third parties (such as premium taxes, value added taxes and goods and services taxes) (see paragraph B65(i));

    (iv)   insurance finance income or expenses;

    (v)   insurance acquisition cash flows (see paragraph B125); and

    (vi)   derecognition of liabilities transferred to a third party.

  (b)   changes that relate to services, but for which the entity does not expect consideration, ie increases and decreases in the loss component of the liability for remaining coverage (see paragraphs 47–52).

B124 Consequently, insurance revenue for the period can also be analysed as the total of the changes in the liability for remaining coverage in the period that relates to services for which the entity expects to receive consideration. Those changes are:

  (a)   insurance service expenses incurred in the period (measured at the amounts expected at the beginning of the period), excluding:

    (i)   amounts allocated to the loss component of the liability for remaining coverage applying paragraph 51(a);

    (ii)   repayments of investment components;

    (iii)   amounts that relate to transaction-based taxes collected on behalf of third parties (such as premium taxes, value added taxes and goods and services taxes) (see paragraph B65(i)); and

    (iv)   insurance acquisition expenses (see paragraph B125).

  (b)   the change in the risk adjustment for non-financial risk, excluding:

    (i)   changes included in insurance finance income or expenses applying paragraph 87;

    (ii)   changes that adjust the contractual service margin because they relate to future service applying paragraphs 44(c) and 45(c); and

    (iii)   amounts allocated to the loss component of the liability for remaining coverage applying paragraph 51(b).

  (c)   the amount of the contractual service margin recognised in profit or loss in the period, applying paragraphs 44(e) and 45(e).

B125 An entity shall determine insurance revenue related to insurance acquisition cash flows by allocating the portion of the premiums that relate to recovering those cash flows to each reporting period in a systematic way on the basis of the passage of time. An entity shall recognise the same amount as insurance service expenses.

B126 When an entity applies the premium allocation approach in paragraphs 55–58, insurance revenue for the period is the amount of expected premium receipts (excluding any investment component and adjusted to reflect the time value of money and the effect of financial risk, if applicable, applying paragraph 56) allocated to the period. The entity shall allocate the expected premium receipts to each period of coverage:

  (a)   on the basis of the passage of time; but

  (b)   if the expected pattern of release of risk during the coverage period differs significantly from the passage of time, then on the basis of the expected timing of incurred insurance service expenses.

B127 An entity shall change the basis of allocation between paragraphs B126(a) and B126(b) as necessary if facts and circumstances change.

Insurance finance income or expenses (paragraphs 87–92)

B128 Paragraph 87 requires an entity to include in insurance finance income or expenses the effect of changes in assumptions that relate to financial risk. For the purposes of AASB 17:

(a)   assumptions about inflation based on an index of prices or rates or on prices of assets with inflation-linked returns are assumptions that relate to financial risk; and

(b)   assumptions about inflation based on an entity's expectation of specific price changes are not assumptions that relate to financial risk.

B129   Paragraphs 88–89 require an entity to make an accounting policy choice as to whether to disaggregate insurance finance income or expenses for the period between profit or loss and other comprehensive income. An entity shall apply its choice of accounting policy to portfolios of insurance contracts. In assessing the appropriate accounting policy for a portfolio of insurance contracts, applying paragraph 13 of AASB 108 *Accounting Policies, Changes in Accounting Estimates and Errors*, the entity shall consider for each portfolio the assets that the entity holds and how it accounts for those assets.

B130   If paragraph 88(b) applies, an entity shall include in profit or loss an amount determined by a systematic allocation of the expected total finance income or expenses over the duration of the group of insurance contracts. In this context, a systematic allocation is an allocation of the total expected finance income or expenses of a group of insurance contracts over the duration of the group that:

(a)   is based on characteristics of the contracts, without reference to factors that do not affect the cash flows expected to arise under the contracts. For example, the allocation of the finance income or expenses shall not be based on expected recognised returns on assets if those expected recognised returns do not affect the cash flows of the contracts in the group.

(b)   results in the amounts recognised in other comprehensive income over the duration of the group of contracts totalling zero. The cumulative amount recognised in other comprehensive income at any date is the difference between the carrying amount of the group of contracts and the amount that the group would be measured at when applying the systematic allocation.

B131   For groups of insurance contracts for which changes in assumptions that relate to financial risk do not have a substantial effect on the amounts paid to the policyholder, the systematic allocation is determined using the discount rates specified in paragraph B72(e)(i).

B132   For groups of insurance contracts for which changes in assumptions that relate to financial risk have a substantial effect on the amounts paid to the policyholders:

(a)   a systematic allocation for the finance income or expenses arising from the estimates of future cash flows can be determined in one of the following ways:

(i)   using a rate that allocates the remaining revised expected finance income or expenses over the remaining duration of the group of contracts at a constant rate; or

(ii)   for contracts that use a crediting rate to determine amounts due to the policyholders—using an allocation that is based on the amounts credited in the period and expected to be credited in future periods.

(b)   a systematic allocation for the finance income or expenses arising from the risk adjustment for non-financial risk, if separately disaggregated from other changes in the risk adjustment for non-financial risk applying paragraph 81, is determined using an allocation consistent with that used for the allocation for the finance income or expenses arising from the future cash flows.

(c)   a systematic allocation for the finance income or expenses arising from the contractual service margin is determined:

(i)   for insurance contracts that do not have direct participation features, using the discount rates specified in paragraph B72(b); and

AASB

(ii)   for insurance contracts with direct participation features, using an allocation consistent with that used for the allocation for the finance income or expenses arising from the future cash flows.

B133 In applying the premium allocation approach to insurance contracts described in paragraphs 53–59, an entity may be required, or may choose, to discount the liability for incurred claims. In such cases, it may choose to disaggregate the insurance finance income or expenses applying paragraph 88(b). If the entity makes this choice, it shall determine the insurance finance income or expenses in profit or loss using the discount rate specified in paragraph B72(e)(iii).

B134 Paragraph 89 applies if an entity, either by choice or because it is required to, holds the underlying items for insurance contracts with direct participation features. If an entity chooses to disaggregate insurance finance income or expenses applying paragraph 89(b), it shall include in profit or loss expenses or income that exactly match the income or expenses included in profit or loss for the underlying items, resulting in the net of the two separately presented items being nil.

B135 An entity may qualify for the accounting policy choice in paragraph 89 in some periods but not in others because of a change in whether it holds the underlying items. If such a change occurs, the accounting policy choice available to the entity changes from that set out in paragraph 88 to that set out in paragraph 89, or vice versa. Hence, an entity might change its accounting policy between that set out in paragraph 88(b) and that set out in paragraph 89(b). In making such a change an entity shall:

(a)   include the accumulated amount previously included in other comprehensive income by the date of the change as a reclassification adjustment in profit or loss in the period of change and in future periods, as follows:

(i)   if the entity had previously applied paragraph 88(b)—the entity shall include in profit or loss the accumulated amount included in other comprehensive income before the change as if the entity were continuing the approach in paragraph 88(b) based on the assumptions that applied immediately before the change; and

(ii)   if the entity had previously applied paragraph 89(b)—the entity shall include in profit or loss the accumulated amount included in other comprehensive income before the change as if the entity were continuing the approach in paragraph 89(b) based on the assumptions that applied immediately before the change.

(b)   not restate prior period comparative information.

B136 When applying paragraph B135(a), an entity shall not recalculate the accumulated amount previously included in other comprehensive income as if the new disaggregation had always applied; and the assumptions used for the reclassification in future periods shall not be updated after the date of the change.

Interim financial statements

B137 Notwithstanding the requirement in AASB 134 *Interim Financial Reporting* that the frequency of an entity's reporting shall not affect the measurement of its annual results, an entity shall not change the treatment of accounting estimates made in previous interim financial statements when applying AASB 17 in subsequent interim financial statements or in the annual reporting period.

APPENDIX C
EFFECTIVE DATE AND TRANSITION

This appendix is an integral part of AASB 17 Insurance Contracts.

Effective date

C1 An entity shall apply AASB 17 for annual reporting periods beginning on or after 1 January 2021. If an entity applies AASB 17 earlier, it shall disclose that fact. Early application is permitted for entities that apply AASB 9 *Financial Instruments* and AASB 15 *Revenue from Contracts with Customers* on or before the date of initial application of AASB 17.

C2 For the purposes of the transition requirements in paragraphs C1 and C3–C33:

    (a) the date of initial application is the beginning of the annual reporting period in which an entity first applies AASB 17; and

    (b) the transition date is the beginning of the annual reporting period immediately preceding the date of initial application.

Transition

C3 An entity shall apply AASB 17 retrospectively unless impracticable, except that:

    (a) an entity is not required to present the quantitative information required by paragraph 28(f) of AASB 108 *Accounting Policies, Changes in Accounting Estimates and Errors*; and

    (b) an entity shall not apply the option in paragraph B115 for periods before the date of initial application of AASB 17.

C4 To apply AASB 17 retrospectively, an entity shall at the transition date:

    (a) identify, recognise and measure each group of insurance contracts as if AASB 17 had always applied;

    (b) derecognise any existing balances that would not exist had AASB 17 always applied; and

    (c) recognise any resulting net difference in equity.

C5 If, and only if, it is impracticable for an entity to apply paragraph C3 for a group of insurance contracts, an entity shall apply the following approaches instead of applying paragraph C4(a):

    (a) the modified retrospective approach in paragraphs C6–C19, subject to paragraph C6(a); or

    (b) the fair value approach in paragraphs C20–C24.

Modified retrospective approach

C6 The objective of the modified retrospective approach is to achieve the closest outcome to retrospective application possible using reasonable and supportable information available without undue cost or effort. Accordingly, in applying this approach, an entity shall:

    (a) use reasonable and supportable information. If the entity cannot obtain reasonable and supportable information necessary to apply the modified retrospective approach, it shall apply the fair value approach.

    (b) maximise the use of information that would have been used to apply a fully retrospective approach, but need only use information available without undue cost or effort.

C7 Paragraphs C9–C19 set out permitted modifications to retrospective application in the following areas:

    (a) assessments of insurance contracts or groups of insurance contracts that would have been made at the date of inception or initial recognition;

    (b) amounts related to the contractual service margin or loss component for insurance contracts without direct participation features;

    (c)   amounts related to the contractual service margin or loss component for insurance contracts with direct participation features; and

    (d)   insurance finance income or expenses.

C8   To achieve the objective of the modified retrospective approach, an entity is permitted to use each modification in paragraphs C9–C19 only to the extent that an entity does not have reasonable and supportable information to apply a retrospective approach.

Assessments at inception or initial recognition

C9   To the extent permitted by paragraph C8, an entity shall determine the following matters using information available at the transition date:

    (a)   how to identify groups of insurance contracts, applying paragraphs 14–24;

    (b)   whether an insurance contract meets the definition of an insurance contract with direct participation features, applying paragraphs B101–B109; and

    (c)   how to identify discretionary cash flows for insurance contracts without direct participation features, applying paragraphs B98–B100.

C10   To the extent permitted by paragraph C8, an entity shall not apply paragraph 22 to divide groups into those that do not include contracts issued more than one year apart.

Determining the contractual service margin or loss component for groups of insurance contracts without direct participation features

C11   To the extent permitted by paragraph C8, for contracts without direct participation features, an entity shall determine the contractual service margin or loss component of the liability for remaining coverage (see paragraphs 49–52) at the transition date by applying paragraphs C12–C16.

C12   To the extent permitted by paragraph C8, an entity shall estimate the future cash flows at the date of initial recognition of a group of insurance contracts as the amount of the future cash flows at the transition date (or earlier date, if the future cash flows at that earlier date can be determined retrospectively, applying paragraph C4(a)), adjusted by the cash flows that are known to have occurred between the date of initial recognition of a group of insurance contracts and the transition date (or earlier date). The cash flows that are known to have occurred include cash flows resulting from contracts that ceased to exist before the transition date.

C13   To the extent permitted by paragraph C8, an entity shall determine the discount rates that applied at the date of initial recognition of a group of insurance contracts (or subsequently):

    (a)   using an observable yield curve that, for at least three years immediately before the transition date, approximates the yield curve estimated applying paragraphs 36 and B72–B85, if such an observable yield curve exists.

    (b)   if the observable yield curve in paragraph (a) does not exist, estimate the discount rates that applied at the date of initial recognition (or subsequently) by determining an average spread between an observable yield curve and the yield curve estimated applying paragraphs 36 and B72–B85, and applying that spread to that observable yield curve. That spread shall be an average over at least three years immediately before the transition date.

C14   To the extent permitted by paragraph C8, an entity shall determine the risk adjustment for non-financial risk at the date of initial recognition of a group of insurance contracts (or subsequently) by adjusting the risk adjustment for non-financial risk at the transition date by the expected release of risk before the transition date. The expected release of risk shall be determined by reference to the release of risk for similar insurance contracts that the entity issues at the transition date.

C15   If applying paragraphs C12–C14 results in a contractual service margin at the date of initial recognition, to determine the contractual service margin at the date of transition an entity shall:

(a) if the entity applies C13 to estimate the discount rates that apply on initial recognition, use those rates to accrete interest on the contractual service margin; and

(b) to the extent permitted by paragraph C8, determine the amount of the contractual service margin recognised in profit or loss because of the transfer of services before the transition date, by comparing the remaining coverage units at that date with the coverage units provided under the group of contracts before the transition date (see paragraph B119).

C16 If applying paragraphs C12–C14 results in a loss component of the liability for remaining coverage at the date of initial recognition, an entity shall determine any amounts allocated to the loss component before the transition date applying paragraphs C12–C14 and using a systematic basis of allocation.

Determining the contractual service margin or loss component for groups of insurance contracts with direct participation features

C17 To the extent permitted by paragraph C8, for contracts with direct participation features an entity shall determine the contractual service margin or loss component of the liability for remaining coverage at the transition date as:

(a) the total fair value of the underlying items at that date; minus

(b) the fulfilment cash flows at that date; plus or minus

(c) an adjustment for:

    (i) amounts charged by the entity to the policyholders (including amounts deducted from the underlying items) before that date.

    (ii) amounts paid before that date that would not have varied based on the underlying items.

    (iii) the change in the risk adjustment for non-financial risk caused by the release from risk before that date. The entity shall estimate this amount by reference to the release of risk for similar insurance contracts that the entity issues at the transition date.

(d) if (a)–(c) result in a contractual service margin—minus the amount of the contractual service margin that relates to services provided before that date. The total of (a)–(c) is a proxy for the total contractual service margin for all services to be provided under the group of contracts, ie before any amounts that would have been recognised in profit or loss for services provided. The entity shall estimate the amounts that would have been recognised in profit or loss for services provided by comparing the remaining coverage units at the transition date with the coverage units provided under the group of contracts before the transition date; or

(e) if (a)–(c) result in a loss component—adjust the loss component to nil and increase the liability for remaining coverage excluding the loss component by the same amount.

Insurance finance income or expenses

C18 For groups of insurance contracts that, applying paragraph C10, include contracts issued more than one year apart:

(a) an entity is permitted to determine the discount rates at the date of initial recognition of a group specified in paragraphs B72(b)–B72(e)(ii) and the discount rates at the date of the incurred claim specified in paragraph B72(e)(iii) at the transition date instead of at the date of initial recognition or incurred claim.

(b) if an entity chooses to disaggregate insurance finance income or expenses between amounts included in profit or loss and amounts included in other comprehensive income applying paragraphs 88(b) or 89(b), the entity needs to determine the cumulative amount of insurance finance income or expenses recognised in other comprehensive income at the transition date to apply paragraph 91(a) in future periods. The entity is permitted to determine that cumulative difference either by applying paragraph C19(b) or:

    (i)   as nil, unless (ii) applies; and

    (ii)   for insurance contracts with direct participation features to which paragraph B134 applies, as equal to the cumulative amount recognised in other comprehensive income on the underlying items.

C19   For groups of insurance contracts that do not include contracts issued more than one year apart:

    (a)   if an entity applies paragraph C13 to estimate the discount rates that applied at initial recognition (or subsequently), it shall also determine the discount rates specified in paragraphs B72(b)–B72(e) applying paragraph C13; and

    (b)   if an entity chooses to disaggregate insurance finance income or expenses between amounts included in profit or loss and amounts included in other comprehensive income, applying paragraphs 88(b) or 89(b), the entity needs to determine the cumulative amount of insurance finance income or expenses recognised in other comprehensive income at the transition date to apply paragraph 91(a) in future periods. The entity shall determine that cumulative difference:

        (i)   for insurance contracts for which an entity will apply the methods of systematic allocation set out in paragraph B131—if the entity applies paragraph C13 to estimate the discount rates at initial recognition—using the discount rates that applied at the date of initial recognition, also applying paragraph C13;

        (ii)   for insurance contracts for which an entity will apply the methods of systematic allocation set out in paragraph B132—on the basis that the assumptions that relate to financial risk that applied at the date of initial recognition are those that apply on the transition date, ie as nil;

        (iii) for insurance contracts for which an entity will apply the methods of systematic allocation set out in paragraph B133—if the entity applies paragraph C13 to estimate the discount rates at initial recognition (or subsequently)—using the discount rates that applied at the date of the incurred claim, also applying paragraph C13; and

        (iv) for insurance contracts with direct participation features to which paragraph B134 applies—as equal to the cumulative amount recognised in other comprehensive income on the underlying items.

Fair value approach

C20   To apply the fair value approach, an entity shall determine the contractual service margin or loss component of the liability for remaining coverage at the transition date as the difference between the fair value of a group of insurance contracts at that date and the fulfilment cash flows measured at that date. In determining that fair value, an entity shall not apply paragraph 47 of AASB 13 *Fair Value Measurement* (relating to demand features).

C21   In applying the fair value approach, an entity may apply paragraph C22 to determine:

    (a)   how to identify groups of insurance contracts, applying paragraphs 14–24;

    (b)   whether an insurance contract meets the definition of an insurance contract with direct participation features, applying paragraphs B101–B109; and

    (c)   how to identify discretionary cash flows for insurance contracts without direct participation features, applying paragraphs B98–B100.

C22   An entity may choose to determine the matters in paragraph C21 using:

    (a)   reasonable and supportable information for what the entity would have determined given the terms of the contract and the market conditions at the date of inception or initial recognition, as appropriate; or

    (b)   reasonable and supportable information available at the transition date.

C23   In applying the fair value approach, an entity is not required to apply paragraph 22, and may include in a group contracts issued more than one year apart. An entity shall only divide groups into those including only contracts issued within a year (or less) if it has reasonable and supportable information to make the division. Whether or not an entity applies paragraph 22, it is permitted to determine the discount rates at the date of initial recognition of a group specified in paragraphs B72(b)–B72(e)(ii) and the discount rates at the date of the incurred claim specified in paragraph B72(e)(iii) at the transition date instead of at the date of initial recognition or incurred claim.

C24   In applying the fair value approach, if an entity chooses to disaggregate insurance finance income or expenses between profit or loss and other comprehensive income, it is permitted to determine the cumulative amount of insurance finance income or expenses recognised in other comprehensive income at the transition date:

    (a)   retrospectively—but only if it has reasonable and supportable information to do so; or

    (b)   as nil—unless (c) applies; and

    (c)   for insurance contracts with direct participation features to which paragraph B134 applies—as equal to the cumulative amount recognised in other comprehensive income from the underlying items.

Comparative information

C25   Notwithstanding the reference to the annual reporting period immediately preceding the date of initial application in paragraph C2(b), an entity may also present adjusted comparative information applying AASB 17 for any earlier periods presented, but is not required to do so. If an entity does present adjusted comparative information for any earlier periods, the reference to 'the beginning of the annual reporting period immediately preceding the date of initial application' in paragraph C2(b) shall be read as 'the beginning of the earliest adjusted comparative period presented'.

C26   An entity is not required to provide the disclosures specified in paragraphs 93–132 for any period presented before the beginning of the annual reporting period immediately preceding the date of initial application.

C27   If an entity presents unadjusted comparative information and disclosures for any earlier periods, it shall clearly identify the information that has not been adjusted, disclose that it has been prepared on a different basis, and explain that basis.

C28   An entity need not disclose previously unpublished information about claims development that occurred earlier than five years before the end of the annual reporting period in which it first applies AASB 17. However, if an entity does not disclose that information, it shall disclose that fact.

Redesignation of financial assets

C29   At the date of initial application of AASB 17, an entity that had applied AASB 9 to annual reporting periods before the initial application of AASB 17:

    (a)   may reassess whether an eligible financial asset meets the condition in paragraph 4.1.2(a) or paragraph 4.1.2A(a) of AASB 9. A financial asset is eligible only if the financial asset is not held in respect of an activity that is unconnected with contracts within the scope of AASB 17. Examples of financial assets that would not be eligible for reassessment are financial assets held in respect of banking activities or financial assets held in funds relating to investment contracts that are outside the scope of AASB 17.

(b)   shall revoke its previous designation of a financial asset as measured at fair value through profit or loss if the condition in paragraph 4.1.5 of AASB 9 is no longer met because of the application of AASB 17.

(c)   may designate a financial asset as measured at fair value through profit or loss if the condition in paragraph 4.1.5 of AASB 9 is met.

(d)   may designate an investment in an equity instrument as at fair value through other comprehensive income applying paragraph 5.7.5 of AASB 9.

(e)   may revoke its previous designation of an investment in an equity instrument as at fair value through other comprehensive income applying paragraph 5.7.5 of AASB 9.

C30   An entity shall apply paragraph C29 on the basis of the facts and circumstances that exist at the date of initial application of AASB 17. An entity shall apply those designations and classifications retrospectively. In doing so, the entity shall apply the relevant transition requirements in AASB 9. The date of initial application for that purpose shall be deemed to be the date of initial application of AASB 17.

C31   An entity that applies paragraph C29 is not required to restate prior periods to reflect such changes in designations or classifications. The entity may restate prior periods only if it is possible without the use of hindsight. If an entity restates prior periods, the restated financial statements must reflect all the requirements of AASB 9 for those affected financial assets. If an entity does not restate prior periods, the entity shall recognise, in the opening retained earnings (or other component of equity, as appropriate) at the date of initial application, any difference between:

(a)   the previous carrying amount of those financial assets; and

(b)   the carrying amount of those financial assets at the date of initial application.

C32   When an entity applies paragraph C29, it shall disclose in that annual reporting period for those financial assets by class:

(a)   if paragraph C29(a) applies—its basis for determining eligible financial assets;

(b)   if any of paragraphs C29(a)–C29(e) apply:

        (i)   the measurement category and carrying amount of the affected financial assets determined immediately before the date of initial application of AASB 17; and

        (ii)   the new measurement category and carrying amount of the affected financial assets determined after applying paragraph C29.

(c)   if paragraph C29(b) applies—the carrying amount of financial assets in the statement of financial position that were previously designated as measured at fair value through profit or loss applying paragraph 4.1.5 of AASB 9 that are no longer so designated.

C33   When an entity applies paragraph C29, the entity shall disclose in that annual reporting period qualitative information that would enable users of financial statements to understand:

(a)   how it applied paragraph C29 to financial assets the classification of which has changed on initially applying AASB 17;

(b)   the reasons for any designation or de-designation of financial assets as measured at fair value through profit or loss applying paragraph 4.1.5 of AASB 9; and

(c)   why the entity came to any different conclusions in the new assessment applying paragraphs 4.1.2(a) or 4.1.2A(a) of AASB 9.

Withdrawal of other IFRS Standards

C34   [Deleted by the AASB]

APPENDIX D
AMENDMENTS TO OTHER AUSTRALIAN ACCOUNTING STANDARDS

This appendix sets out the amendments to other Standards that are a consequence of the Australian Accounting Standards Board issuing AASB 17 Insurance Contracts. *An entity shall apply these amendments when it applies AASB 17.*

An entity is not permitted to apply AASB 17 before applying AASB 9 Financial Instruments *and AASB 15* Revenue from Contracts with Customers *(see paragraph C1).*

Amendments are made to the latest principal version of a Standard (or an Interpretation) as subsequently amended, unless otherwise indicated.

The amendments set out in this appendix also apply, as far as possible and necessary, to earlier principal versions of the Standards and Interpretations that are identified in this appendix when this Standard is applied prior to 1 January 2021.

This appendix uses underlining, striking out and other typographical material to identify some of the amendments to a Standard or an Interpretation, in order to make the amendments more understandable. However, the amendments made by this appendix do not include that underlining, striking out or other typographical material. Amended paragraphs are shown with deleted text struck through and new text is underlined. Ellipses (...) are used to help provide the context within which amendments are made and also to indicate text that is not amended.

AASB 1 *First-time Adoption of Australian Accounting Standards* (July 2015, as amended)

Paragraph 39AE is added.

Effective date

...

39AE AASB 17 *Insurance Contracts*, issued in July 2017, amended paragraphs B1 and D1, deleted the heading before paragraph D4 and paragraph D4, and after paragraph B12 added a heading and paragraph B13. An entity shall apply those amendments when it applies AASB 17.

In Appendix B, paragraph B1 is amended. After paragraph B12, a heading and paragraph B13 are added.

Appendix B
Exceptions to the retrospective application of other Australian Accounting Standards

...

B1 An entity shall apply the following exceptions:

(a) ...

(f) embedded derivatives (paragraph B9); ~~and~~

(g) government loans (paragraphs B10–B12)~~.~~ ; and

(h) insurance contracts (paragraph B13).

...

Insurance contracts

B13 An entity shall apply the transition provisions in paragraphs C1–C24 and C28 in
     Appendix C of AASB 17 to contracts within the scope of AASB 17. The references in
     those paragraphs in AASB 17 to the transition date shall be read as the date of transition
     to Australian Accounting Standards.

In Appendix D, paragraph D1 is amended and paragraph D4 and its related heading are deleted.

Appendix D
Exemptions from other Australian Accounting Standards

...

D1   An entity may elect to use one or more of the following exemptions:

(a)   ...

(b)   [deleted] ~~insurance contracts (paragraph D4);~~

(c)   ...

~~Insurance contracts~~

D4   [Deleted] ~~A first time adopter may apply the transitional provisions in AASB 4
     Insurance Contracts, AASB 1023 General Insurance Contracts and AASB 1038 Life
     Insurance Contracts. AASB 4 restricts changes in accounting policies for insurance
     contracts, including changes made by a first time adopter.~~

AASB 3 *Business Combinations* (August 2015, as amended but excluding AASB 16)

The following amendments apply only when AASB 17 is not applied in conjunction with AASB 16 *Leases*.

Paragraphs 17, 20, 21 and 35 are amended. After paragraph 31, a heading and paragraph 31A are added. Paragraph 64N is added.

Classifying or designating identifiable assets acquired and liabilities assumed in a business combination

...

17   This Standard provides ~~two~~an exception~~s~~ to the principle in paragraph 15:

(a)   classification of a lease contract as either an operating lease or a finance lease
        in accordance with AASB 117 *Leases*. ~~; and~~

(b)   [deleted] ~~classification of a contract as an insurance contract in accordance with
        AASB 4 Insurance Contracts.~~

The acquirer shall classify those contracts on the basis of the contractual terms and
other factors at the inception of the contract (or, if the terms of the contract have
been modified in a manner that would change its classification, at the date of that
modification, which might be the acquisition date).

...

Measurement principle

...

20   Paragraphs 24 ~~31~~31A specify the types of identifiable assets and liabilities that
     include items for which this Standard provides limited exceptions to the measurement
     principle.

Exceptions to the recognition or measurement principles

21 This Standard provides limited exceptions to its recognition and measurement principles. Paragraphs 22–~~31~~31A specify both the particular items for which exceptions are provided and the nature of those exceptions. The acquirer shall account for those items by applying the requirements in paragraphs 22–~~31~~31A, which will result in some items being:

...

Insurance contracts

31A The acquirer shall measure a group of contracts within the scope of AASB 17 *Insurance Contracts* acquired in a business combination as a liability or asset in accordance with paragraphs 39 and B93–B95 of AASB 17, at the acquisition date.

...

Bargain purchases

...

35 A bargain purchase might happen, for example, in a business combination that is a forced sale in which the seller is acting under compulsion. However, the recognition or measurement exceptions for particular items discussed in paragraphs 22–~~31~~31A may also result in recognising a gain (or change the amount of a recognised gain) on a bargain purchase.

...

Effective date

...

64N AASB 17, issued in July 2017, amended paragraphs 17, 20, 21, 35 and B63, and after paragraph 31 added a heading and paragraph 31A. An entity shall apply those amendments when it applies AASB 17.

In Appendix B, paragraph B63 is amended.

Other Australian Accounting Standards that provide guidance on subsequent measurement and accounting (application of paragraph 54)

B63 Examples of other Australian Accounting Standards that provide guidance on subsequently measuring and accounting for assets acquired and liabilities assumed or incurred in a business combination include:

(a) ...

(b) [deleted] ~~AASB 4 *Insurance Contracts* provides guidance on the subsequent accounting for an insurance contract acquired in a business combination.~~

(c) ...

AASB 3 *Business Combinations* (August 2015, as amended, including by AASB 16)

The following amendments apply only when AASB 17 is applied in conjunction with AASB 16.

Paragraphs 17, 20, 21 and 35 are amended. After paragraph 31, a heading and paragraph 31A are added. Paragraph 64N is added.

Classifying or designating identifiable assets acquired and liabilities assumed in a business combination

...

17   This Standard provides ~~two~~an ~~exceptions~~exception to the principle in paragraph 15:

(a)   classification of a lease contract in which the acquiree is the lessor as either an operating lease or a finance lease in accordance with AASB 16 *Leases*. ~~; and~~

(b)   [deleted] ~~classification of a contract as an insurance contract in accordance with AASB 4 Insurance Contracts.~~

The acquirer shall classify those contracts on the basis of the contractual terms and other factors at the inception of the contract (or, if the terms of the contract have been modified in a manner that would change its classification, at the date of that modification, which might be the acquisition date).

...

Measurement principle

...

20   Paragraphs 24–~~31~~31A specify the types of identifiable assets and liabilities that include items for which this Standard provides limited exceptions to the measurement principle.

Exceptions to the recognition or measurement principles

21   This Standard provides limited exceptions to its recognition and measurement principles. Paragraphs 22–~~31~~31A specify both the particular items for which exceptions are provided and the nature of those exceptions. The acquirer shall account for those items by applying the requirements in paragraphs 22–~~31~~31A, which will result in some items being:

...

Insurance contracts

31A   The acquirer shall measure a group of contracts within the scope of AASB 17 *Insurance Contracts* acquired in a business combination as a liability or asset in accordance with paragraphs 39 and B93–B95 of AASB 17, at the acquisition date.

...

Bargain purchases

...

35   A bargain purchase might happen, for example, in a business combination that is a forced sale in which the seller is acting under compulsion. However, the recognition or measurement exceptions for particular items discussed in paragraphs 22–~~31~~31A may also result in recognising a gain (or change the amount of a recognised gain) on a bargain purchase.

...

Effective date

...

64N   AASB 17, issued in July 2017, amended paragraphs 17, 20, 21, 35 and B63, and after paragraph 31 added a heading and paragraph 31A. An entity shall apply those amendments when it applies AASB 17.

In Appendix B, paragraph B63 is amended.

AASB 17

Other Australian Accounting Standards that provide guidance on subsequent measurement and accounting (application of paragraph 54)

B63 Examples of other Australian Accounting Standards that provide guidance on subsequently measuring and accounting for assets acquired and liabilities assumed or incurred in a business combination include:

(a) ...

(b) [deleted] ~~AASB 4 *Insurance Contracts* provides guidance on the subsequent accounting for an insurance contract acquired in a business combination.~~

(c) ...

AASB 5 *Non-current Assets Held for Sale and Discontinued Operations* (August 2015, as amended)

> Paragraph 5 is amended. Paragraph 44M is added.

Scope

...

5 The measurement provisions of this Standard [footnote omitted] do not apply to the following assets, which are covered by the Standards listed, either as individual assets or as part of a disposal group:

(a) ...

(f) ~~contractual rights under insurance contracts as defined in AASB 4~~groups of contracts within the scope of AASB 17 *Insurance Contracts*.

...

Effective date

...

44M AASB 17, issued in July 2017, amended paragraph 5. An entity shall apply that amendment when it applies AASB 17.

AASB 7 *Financial Instruments: Disclosures* (August 2015, as amended but excluding AASB 16)

> The following amendments apply only when AASB 17 is not applied in conjunction with AASB 16.
>
> Paragraphs 3, 8 and 29 are amended. Paragraph 30 is deleted. Paragraph 44DD is added.

Scope

3 This Standard shall be applied by all entities to all types of financial instruments, except:

(a) ...

(d) ~~insurance~~ contracts ~~as defined in AASB 4~~within the scope of AASB 17 *Insurance Contracts*. However, this Standard applies to~~:~~

    (i) derivatives that are embedded in ~~insurance~~ contracts within the scope of AASB 17, if AASB 9 requires the entity to account for them separately~~.~~; and

    (ii) investment components that are separated from contracts within the scope of AASB 17, if AASB 17 requires such separation.

Moreover, an issuer shall apply this Standard to *financial guarantee contracts* if the issuer applies AASB 9 in recognising and measuring the contracts, but shall apply ~~AASB 4~~AASB 17 if the issuer elects, in accordance with paragraph 4~~(d)~~ ~~of AASB 4~~7(e) of AASB 17, to apply ~~AASB 4~~AASB 17 in recognising and measuring them.

(e)   ...

Categories of financial assets and financial liabilities

8   The carrying amounts of each of the following categories, as specified in AASB 9, shall be disclosed either in the statement of financial position or in the notes:

(a)   financial assets measured at fair value through profit or loss, showing separately (i) those designated as such upon initial recognition or subsequently in accordance with paragraph 6.7.1 of AASB 9; (ii) those measured as such in accordance with the election in paragraph 3.3.5 of AASB 9; (iii) those measured as such in accordance with the election in paragraph 33A of AASB 132 and (~~iii~~iv) those mandatorily measured at fair value through profit or loss in accordance with AASB 9.

(b)   ...

Fair value

...

29   Disclosures of fair value are not required:

(a)   ...

(c)   [deleted]~~for a contract containing a discretionary participation feature (as described in AASB 4) if the fair value of that feature cannot be measured reliably.~~

30   [Deleted]~~In the case described in paragraph 29(c), an entity shall disclose information to help users of the financial statements make their own judgements about the extent of possible differences between the carrying amount of those contracts and their fair value, including:~~

(a)   ~~the fact that fair value information has not been disclosed for these instruments because their fair value cannot be measured reliably;~~

(b)   ~~a description of the financial instruments, their carrying amount, and an explanation of why fair value cannot be measured reliably;~~

(c)   ~~information about the market for the instruments;~~

(d)   ~~information about whether and how the entity intends to dispose of the financial instruments; and~~

(e)   ~~if financial instruments whose fair value previously could not be reliably measured are derecognised, that fact, their carrying amount at the time of derecognition, and the amount of gain or loss recognised.~~

...

Effective date and transition

...

44DD   AASB 17, issued in July 2017, amended paragraphs 3, 8 and 29 and deleted paragraph 30. An entity shall apply those amendments when it applies AASB 17.

AASB 7 *Financial Instruments: Disclosures* (August 2015, as amended, including by AASB 16)

The following amendments apply only when AASB 17 is applied in conjunction with AASB 16.

Paragraphs 3, 8 and 29 are amended. Paragraph 30 is deleted. Paragraph 44DD is added.

Scope

3 This Standard shall be applied by all entities to all types of financial instruments, except:

(a) ...

(d) ~~insurance~~ contracts ~~as defined in AASB 4~~ within the scope of AASB 17 *Insurance Contracts*. However, this Standard applies to:

(i) derivatives that are embedded in ~~insurance~~ contracts within the scope of AASB 17, if AASB 9 requires the entity to account for them separately~~,~~; and

(ii) investment components that are separated from contracts within the scope of AASB 17, if AASB 17 requires such separation.

Moreover, an issuer shall apply this Standard to *financial guarantee contracts* if the issuer applies AASB 9 in recognising and measuring the contracts, but shall apply ~~AASB 4~~AASB 17 if the issuer elects, in accordance with paragraph ~~4(d) of AASB 4~~7(e) of AASB 17, to apply ~~AASB 4~~AASB 17 in recognising and measuring them.

(e) ...

Categories of financial assets and financial liabilities

8 The carrying amounts of each of the following categories, as specified in AASB 9, shall be disclosed either in the statement of financial position or in the notes:

(a) financial assets measured at fair value through profit or loss, showing separately (i) those designated as such upon initial recognition or subsequently in accordance with paragraph 6.7.1 of AASB 9; (ii) those measured as such in accordance with the election in paragraph 3.3.5 of AASB 9; (iii) those measured as such in accordance with the election in paragraph 33A of AASB 132 and (~~iii~~iv) those mandatorily measured at fair value through profit or loss in accordance with AASB 9.

(b) ...

Fair value

...

29 Disclosures of fair value are not required:

(a) when the carrying amount is a reasonable approximation of fair value, for example, for financial instruments such as short-term trade receivables and payables; or

(b) [deleted]

(c) [deleted]~~for a contract containing a discretionary participation feature (as described in AASB 4) if the fair value of that feature cannot be measured reliably; or~~

(d) for lease liabilities.

30   [Deleted]~~In the case described in paragraph 29(c), an entity shall disclose information~~
~~to help users of the financial statements make their own judgements about the extent~~
~~of possible differences between the carrying amount of those contracts and their fair~~
~~value, including:~~

   (a)   ~~the fact that fair value information has not been disclosed for these instruments~~
~~because their fair value cannot be measured reliably;~~

   (b)   ~~a description of the financial instruments, their carrying amount, and an~~
~~explanation of why fair value cannot be measured reliably;~~

   (e)   ~~information about the market for the instruments;~~

   (d)   ~~information about whether and how the entity intends to dispose of the financial~~
~~instruments; and~~

   (e)   ~~if financial instruments whose fair value previously could not be reliably~~
~~measured are derecognised, that fact, their carrying amount at the time of~~
~~derecognition, and the amount of gain or loss recognised.~~

         ...

Effective date and transition

   ...

44DD AASB 17, issued in July 2017, amended paragraphs 3, 8 and 29 and deleted paragraph
      30. An entity shall apply those amendments when it applies AASB 17.

AASB 9 *Financial Instruments* (December 2014, as amended)

> Paragraph 2.1 is amended. Paragraphs 3.3.5 and 7.1.6 are added.

Chapter 2 Scope

2.1   This Standard shall be applied by all entities to all types of financial instruments
      except:

   (a)   ...

   (e)   rights and obligations arising under ~~(i) an insurance~~ a contract ~~as defined~~
~~in AASB 4~~within the scope of AASB 17 *Insurance Contracts*, other than
         an issuer's rights and obligations arising under an insurance contract that
         meets the definition of a financial guarantee contract~~, or (ii) a contract~~
~~that is within the scope of AASB 4 because it contains a discretionary~~
~~participation feature~~. However, this Standard applies to (i) a derivative
         that is embedded in a contract within the scope of ~~AASB 4~~AASB 17, if
         the derivative is not itself a contract within the scope of ~~AASB 4~~AASB 17;
         and (ii) an investment component that is separated from a contract
         within the scope of AASB 17, if AASB 17 requires such separation.
         Moreover, if an issuer of financial guarantee contracts has previously
         asserted explicitly that it regards such contracts as insurance contracts
         and has used accounting that is applicable to insurance contracts, the
         issuer may elect to apply either this Standard or ~~AASB 1023 *General*~~
~~*Insurance Contracts*~~AASB 17 to such financial guarantee contracts (see
         paragraphs B2.5–B2.6). The issuer may make that election contract by
         contract, but the election for each contract is irrevocable.

   ...

3.3 Derecognition of financial liabilities

   ...

3.3.5 Some entities operate, either internally or externally, an investment fund that provides investors with benefits determined by units in the fund and recognise financial liabilities for the amounts to be paid to those investors. Similarly, some entities issue groups of insurance contracts with direct participation features and those entities hold the underlying items. Some such funds or underlying items include the entity's financial liability (for example, a corporate bond issued). Despite the other requirements in this Standard for the derecognition of financial liabilities, an entity may elect not to derecognise its financial liability that is included in such a fund or is an underlying item when, and only when, the entity repurchases its financial liability for such purposes. Instead, the entity may elect to continue to account for that instrument as a financial liability and to account for the repurchased instrument as if the instrument were a financial asset, and measure it at fair value through profit or loss in accordance with this Standard. That election is irrevocable and made on an instrument-by-instrument basis. For the purposes of this election, insurance contracts include investment contracts with discretionary participation features. (See AASB 17 for terms used in this paragraph that are defined in that Standard.)

...

7.1 Effective date

...

7.1.6 AASB 17, issued in July 2017, amended paragraphs 2.1, B2.1, B2.4, B2.5 and B4.1.30, and added paragraph 3.3.5. An entity shall apply those amendments when it applies AASB 17.

In Appendix B, paragraphs B2.1, B2.4, B2.5 and B4.1.30 are amended.

Scope (Chapter 2)

B2.1 Some contracts require a payment based on climatic, geological or other physical variables. (Those based on climatic variables are sometimes referred to as 'weather derivatives'.) If those contracts are not within the scope of ~~AASB 4~~AASB 17 *Insurance Contracts* ~~or AASB 1023 General Insurance Contracts~~, they are within the scope of this Standard.

...

B2.4 This Standard applies to the financial assets and financial liabilities of insurers, other than rights and obligations that paragraph 2.1(e) excludes because they arise under contracts within the scope of ~~AASB 4~~AASB 17.

B2.5 Financial guarantee contracts may have various legal forms, such as a guarantee, some types of letter of credit, a credit default contract or an insurance contract. Their accounting treatment does not depend on their legal form. The following are examples of the appropriate treatment (see paragraph 2.1(e)):

  (a) Although a financial guarantee contract meets the definition of an insurance contract in ~~AASB 4~~AASB 17 (see paragraph 7(e) of AASB 17) if the risk transferred is significant, the issuer applies this Standard. Nevertheless, if the issuer has previously asserted explicitly that it regards such contracts as insurance contracts and has used accounting that is applicable to insurance contracts, the issuer may elect to apply either this Standard or ~~AASB 1023~~AASB 17 to such financial guarantee contracts....

  (b) Some credit-related guarantees do not, as a precondition for payment, require that the holder is exposed to, and has incurred a loss on, the failure of the debtor to make payments on the guaranteed asset when due. An example of such a guarantee is one that requires payments in response to changes in a specified credit rating or credit index. Such guarantees are not financial guarantee contracts as defined in this Standard, and are not insurance contracts as defined in ~~AASB 4~~AASB 17. Such guarantees are derivatives and the issuer applies this Standard to them.

(c)   ...

Designation eliminates or significantly reduces an accounting mismatch

...

B4.1.30   The following examples show when this condition could be met. In all cases, an entity may use this condition to designate financial assets or financial liabilities as at fair value through profit or loss only if it meets the principle in paragraph 4.1.5 or 4.2.2(a):

(a)   an entity has ~~liabilities under insurance~~ contracts within the scope of AASB 17 (the measurement of which ~~whose measurement~~ incorporates current information ~~(as permitted by paragraph 24 of AASB 4)~~ and financial assets that it considers to be related and that would otherwise be measured at either fair value through other comprehensive income or amortised cost.

(b)   ...

AASB 15 *Revenue from Contracts with Customers* (December 2014, as amended)

> Paragraph 5 is amended.

Scope

5   An entity shall apply this Standard to all contracts with customers, except the following:

(a)   ...

(b)   ~~insurance~~ contracts within the scope of ~~AASB 4~~AASB 17 *Insurance Contracts*~~;~~ . However, an entity may choose to apply this Standard to insurance contracts that have as their primary purpose the provision of services for a fixed fee in accordance with paragraph 8 of AASB 17.

(c)   ...

> In Appendix C, paragraph C1C is added.

Effective date

...

C1C   AASB 17, issued in July 2017, amended paragraph 5. An entity shall apply that amendment when it applies AASB 17.

AASB 101 *Presentation of Financial Statements* (July 2015, as amended)

> Paragraphs 7, 54 and 82 are amended. Paragraph 139R is added.

Definitions

7   ...

Other comprehensive income **comprises items of income and expense (including reclassification adjustments) that are not recognised in profit or loss as required or permitted by other Australian Accounting Standards.**

The components of other comprehensive income include:

(a)　...

(g)　... ; ~~and~~

(h)　... <u>. - ;</u>

(i)　<u>insurance finance income and expenses from contracts issued within the scope of AASB 17 *Insurance Contracts* excluded from profit or loss when total insurance finance income or expenses is disaggregated to include in profit or loss an amount determined by a systematic allocation applying paragraph 88(b) of AASB 17, or by an amount that eliminates accounting mismatches with the finance income or expenses arising on the underlying items, applying paragraph 89(b) of AASB 17; and</u>

(j)　<u>finance income and expenses from reinsurance contracts held excluded from profit or loss when total reinsurance finance income or expenses is disaggregated to include in profit or loss an amount determined by a systematic allocation applying paragraph 88(b) of AASB 17.</u>

　　　...

Information to be presented in the statement of financial position

54　The statement of financial position shall include line items that present the following amounts:

(a)　...

(da)　<u>**groups of contracts within the scope of AASB 17 that are assets, disaggregated as required by paragraph 78 of AASB 17;**</u>

(e)　...

(ma)　<u>**groups of contracts within the scope of AASB 17 that are liabilities, disaggregated as required by paragraph 78 of AASB 17;**</u>

(n)　...

Information to be presented in the profit or loss section or the statement of profit or loss

82　In addition to items required by other Australian Accounting Standards, the profit or loss section or the statement of profit or loss shall include line items that present the following amounts for the period:

(a)　revenue, presenting separately<u>:</u>

　　　(i)　<u>interest revenue calculated using the effective interest method; and</u>

　　　(ii)　<u>insurance revenue (see AASB 17);</u>

(aa)　...

(ab)　<u>**insurance service expenses from contracts issued within the scope of AASB 17 (see AASB 17);**</u>

(ac)　<u>**income or expenses from reinsurance contracts held (see AASB 17);**</u>

(b)　...

(bb)　<u>**insurance finance income or expenses from contracts issued within the scope of AASB 17 (see AASB 17);**</u>

(bc)　<u>**finance income or expenses from reinsurance contracts held (see AASB 17);**</u>

(c)　...

Transition and effective date

　　　...

139R　<u>AASB 17, issued in July 2017, amended paragraphs 7, 54 and 82. An entity shall apply those amendments when it applies AASB 17.</u>

Exemptions from applying the equity method

...

18   When an investment in an associate or a joint venture is held by, or is held indirectly through, an entity that is a venture capital organisation, or a mutual fund, unit trust and similar entities including investment-linked insurance funds, the entity may elect to measure that investment at fair value through profit or loss in accordance with AASB 9. An example of an investment-linked insurance fund is a fund held by an entity as the underlying items for a group of insurance contracts with direct participation features. For the purposes of this election, insurance contracts include investment contracts with discretionary participation features. An entity shall make this election separately for each associate or joint venture, at initial recognition of the associate or joint venture. (See AASB 17 *Insurance Contracts* for terms used in this paragraph that are defined in that Standard.)

...

Effective date and transition

...

45F   AASB 17, issued in July 2017, amended paragraph 18. An entity shall apply that amendment when it applies AASB 17.

AASB 132 *Financial Instruments: Presentation* (August 2015, as amended)

> Paragraph 4 is amended. Paragraphs 33A and 97T are added.

Scope

4   This Standard shall be applied by all entities to all types of financial instruments except:

(a)   ...

(d)   ~~insurance~~ contracts ~~as defined in AASB 4~~within the scope of AASB 17 *Insurance Contracts*. However, this Standard applies to:

   (i)   derivatives that are embedded in ~~insurance~~ contracts within the scope of AASB 17, if AASB 9 requires the entity to account for them separately~~.~~; and

   (ii)   investment components that are separated from contracts within the scope of AASB 17, if AASB 17 requires such separation.

   Moreover, an issuer shall apply this Standard to financial guarantee contracts if the issuer applies AASB 9 in recognising and measuring the contracts, but shall apply ~~AASB 4~~AASB 17 if the issuer elects, in accordance with paragraph ~~4(d) of AASB 4~~7(e) of AASB 17, to apply ~~AASB 4~~AASB 17 in recognising and measuring them.

(e)   [deleted]~~financial instruments that are within the scope of AASB 4 because they contain a discretionary participation feature. The issuer of these instruments is exempt from applying to these features paragraphs 15–3 and AG25–AG3 of this Standard regarding the distinction between financial liabilities and equity instruments. However, these instruments are subject to all other requirements of this Standard. Furthermore, this Standard applies to derivatives that are embedded in these instruments (see AASB 9).~~

(f)   ...

Treasury shares (see also paragraph AG36)

...

33A   Some entities operate, either internally or externally, an investment fund that provides investors with benefits determined by units in the fund and recognise financial liabilities for the amounts to be paid to those investors. Similarly, some entities issue groups of insurance contracts with direct participation features and those entities hold the underlying items. Some such funds or underlying items include the entity's treasury shares. Despite paragraph 33, an entity may elect not to deduct from equity a treasury share that is included in such a fund or is an underlying item when, and only when, an entity reacquires its own equity instrument for such purposes. Instead, the entity may elect to continue to account for that treasury share as equity and to account for the reacquired instrument as if the instrument were a financial asset and measure it at fair value through profit or loss in accordance with AASB 9. That election is irrevocable and made on an instrument-by-instrument basis. For the purposes of this election, insurance contracts include investment contracts with discretionary participation features. (See AASB 17 for terms used in this paragraph that are defined in that Standard.)

...

Effective date and transition

...

97T   AASB 17, issued in July 2017, amended paragraphs 4 and AG8, and added paragraph 33A. An entity shall apply those amendments when it applies AASB 17.

In the Application Guidance, paragraph AG8 is amended.

Financial assets and financial liabilities

...

AG8   The ability to exercise a contractual right or the requirement to satisfy a contractual obligation may be absolute, or it may be contingent on the occurrence of a future event. For example, a financial guarantee is a contractual right of the lender to receive cash from the guarantor, and a corresponding contractual obligation of the guarantor to pay the lender, if the borrower defaults. The contractual right and obligation exist because of a past transaction or event (assumption of the guarantee), even though the lender's ability to exercise its right and the requirement for the guarantor to perform under its obligation are both contingent on a future act of default by the borrower. A contingent right and obligation meet the definition of a financial asset and a financial liability, even though such assets and liabilities are not always recognised in the financial statements. Some of these contingent rights and obligations may be ~~insurance~~ contracts within the scope of ~~AASB 4~~AASB 17.

AASB 136 *Impairment of Assets* (August 2015, as amended)

Paragraph 2 is amended. Paragraph 140N is added.

Scope

2   **This Standard shall be applied in accounting for the impairment of all assets, other than:**

   (a)   ...

   (h)   ~~deferred acquisition costs, and intangible assets, arising from an insurer's contractual rights under insurance~~ contracts within the scope of ~~AASB 4~~

AASB 17 *Insurance Contracts, AASB 1023 ~~General Insurance Contracts~~* ~~and AASB 1038~~ *~~Life Insurance Contracts~~* that are assets; and

(i) ...

Transition provisions and effective date

...

140N AASB 17, issued in July 2017, amended paragraph 2. An entity shall apply that amendment when it applies AASB

AASB 137 *Provisions, Contingent Liabilities and Contingent Assets* (August 2015, as amended)

> Paragraph 5 is amended. Paragraph 103 is added.

Scope

...

5   When another Standard deals with a specific type of provision, contingent liability or contingent asset, an entity applies that Standard instead of this Standard. For example, some types of provisions are addressed in Standards on:

(a)   ...

(e)   insurance contracts and other contracts within the scope of ~~(see AASB 4~~ AASB 17 *Insurance Contracts, AASB 1023 ~~General Insurance Contracts,~~* ~~and AASB 1038~~ *~~Life Insurance Contracts~~*). ~~However, this Standard applies to provisions, contingent liabilities and contingent assets of an insurer, other than those arising from its contractual obligations and rights under insurance contracts within the scope of AASB 4, AASB 1023 or AASB 1038;~~

(f)   ...

Effective date

...

103   AASB 17, issued in July 2017, amended paragraph 5. An entity shall apply that amendment when it applies AASB 17.

AASB 138 *Intangible Assets* (August 2015, as amended)

> Paragraph 3 is amended. Paragraph 130M is added.

Scope

...

3   If another Standard prescribes the accounting for a specific type of intangible asset, an entity applies that Standard instead of this Standard. For example, this Standard does not apply to:

(a)   ...

(g)   deferred acquisition costs, and intangible assets, arising from an insurer's contractual rights under insurance contracts within the scope of ~~AASB 4~~ AASB 17 *Insurance Contracts*. ~~AASB 4 sets out specific disclosure requirements for those deferred acquisition costs but not for those intangible assets. Therefore, the disclosure requirements in this Standard apply to those intangible assets.~~

(h) ...

Transitional provisions and effective date

...

130M AASB 17, issued in July 2017, amended paragraph 3. An entity shall apply that amendment when it applies AASB 17.

AASB 140 *Investment Property* (August 2015, as amended)

Paragraph 32B is amended. Paragraph 85H is added.

Accounting policy

...

32B Some ~~insurers and other~~ entities operate, either internally or externally, an investment~~an internal property~~ fund that provides investors with benefits determined by units in the fund. ~~issues notional units, with some units held by investors in linked contracts and others held by the entity~~Similarly, some entities issue insurance contracts with direct participation features, for which the underlying items include investment property. For the purposes of paragraphs 32A–32B only, insurance contracts include investment contracts with discretionary participation features. Paragraph 32A does not permit an entity to measure ~~the~~ property held by the fund (or property that is an underlying item) partly at cost and partly at fair value. (See AASB 17 *Insurance Contracts* for terms used in this paragraph that are defined in that Standard.)

...

Effective date

...

85H AASB 17, issued in July 2017, amended paragraph 32B. An entity shall apply that amendment when it applies AASB 17.

AASB 1023 *General Insurance Contracts* (July 2004, as amended)

Paragraph 1.1 is amended.

1 Application

1.1 This Standard applies to:

(a) ~~each entity that is required to prepare financial reports in accordance with Part 2M.3 of the Corporations Act and that is a reporting entity;~~

(~~a~~b) general purpose financial statements of each ~~other~~ not-for-profit public sector reporting entity; and

(~~b~~c) financial statements of each not-for-profit public sector entity that are, or are held out to be, general purpose financial statements.

AASB 1038 *Life Insurance Contracts* (July 2004, as amended)

Paragraph 1.1 is amended.

1 Application

1.1 This Standard applies to each entity that is:

 (a) a life insurer; or

 (b) the parent in a group that includes a life insurer;

 when the entity is a not-for-profit public sector entity that:

 (~~c~~) ~~is a reporting entity that is required to prepare financial reports in accordance with Part 2M.3 of the Corporations Act;~~

 (~~d~~c) is ~~an other~~ a reporting entity and prepares general purpose financial statements; or

 (~~e~~d) prepares financial statements that are, or are held out to be, general purpose financial statements.

AASB 1057 *Application of Australian Accounting Standards* (July 2015, as amended)

> Paragraphs 5, 12 and 26 are amended. Paragraphs 5A, 6A and 11A are added.

Application of Australian Accounting Standards

5 Unless otherwise specified in paragraphs 6<u>5</u>A–21, Australian Accounting Standards apply to:

 (a) ...

5A AASB 4 *Insurance Contracts* applies to:

 (a) general purpose financial statements of each not-for-profit public sector reporting entity; and

 (b) financial statements of each not-for-profit public sector entity that are, or are held out to be, general purpose financial statements.

  ...

6A AASB 17 *Insurance Contracts* applies to:

 (a) each entity that is required to prepare financial reports in accordance with Part 2M.3 of the Corporations Act and that is a reporting entity;

 (b) general purpose financial statements of each other reporting entity; and

 (c) financial statements that are, or are held out to be, general purpose financial statements;

 except when the entity is:

 (d) a superannuation entity applying AASB 1056; or

 (e) a not-for-profit public sector entity.

  ...

11A AASB 1023 *General Insurance Contracts* applies to:

 (a) general purpose financial statements of each not-for-profit public sector reporting entity; and

 (b) financial statements of each not-for-profit public sector entity that are, or are held out to be, general purpose financial statements.

12 AASB 1038 *Life Insurance Contracts* applies to:

 (a) a life insurer; or

 (b) the parent in a group that includes a life insurer;

 when the entity is a not-for-profit public sector entity that:

(c) is a reporting entity that is required to prepare financial reports in accordance with Part 2M.3 of the Corporations Act;

(d̶c̲) is an~~other~~ a reporting entity and prepares general purpose financial statements; or

(e̶d̲) prepares financial statements that are, or are held out to be, general purpose financial statements.

...

Application of Australian Interpretations

...

26 Interpretation 1047 *Professional Indemnity Claims Liabilities in Medical Defence Organisations* applies to entities that are or include medical defence organisations as follows:

(a) ~~each entity that is required to prepare financial reports in accordance with Part 2M.3 of the Corporations Act and that is a reporting entity;~~

(a̲b̶) general purpose financial statements of each ~~other~~ not-for-profit public sector reporting entity; and

(b̲c̶) financial statements of each not-for-profit public sector entity that are, or are held out to be, general purpose financial statements.

AASB 1058 *Income of Not-for-Profit Entities* (December 2016)

AASB

Paragraph 7 is amended.

Scope (paragraphs B2-B11)

7 An entity shall apply this Standard to transactions where the consideration to acquire an asset is significantly less than fair value principally to enable the entity to further its objectives, and the receipt of volunteer services, except for:

(a) ...

(b) ~~insurance~~ contracts within the scope of ~~AASB 4~~ AASB 17 *Insurance Contracts*, ~~AASB 1023 General Insurance Contracts or AASB 1038 Life Insurance Contracts~~;

(c) ...

In Appendix C, paragraph C1A is added.

Effective date

...

C1A AASB 17, issued in July 2017, amended paragraph 7. An entity shall apply that amendment when it applies AASB 17.

Interpretation 127 *Evaluating the Substance of Transactions Involving the Legal Form of a Lease*

The references paragraph is amended.

References

...

*   ~~AASB 4~~AASB 17 *Insurance Contracts*
*   ...
*   ~~AASB 1023 *General Insurance Contracts*~~

...

Paragraph 7 is amended.

Consensus

...

7   Other obligations of an arrangement, including any guarantees provided and obligations incurred upon early termination, shall be accounted for under AASB 137, ~~AASB 1023 or~~ AASB 9 or AASB 17, depending on the terms.

The effective date paragraph is amended.

Effective date

...

C1A   AASB 17, issued in July 2017, amended paragraph 7. An entity shall apply that amendment when it applies AASB 17.

Interpretation 1047 *Professional Indemnity Claims Liabilities in Medical Defence Organisations*

Paragraph 10 is amended.

Application

~~10~~   This Interpretation applies to entities that are or include medical defence organisations as follows:

(a)   ~~each entity that is required to prepare financial reports in accordance with Part 2M.3 of the Corporations Act and that is a reporting entity;~~

(a~~b~~)   general purpose financial statements of each ~~other~~ not-for-profit public sector reporting entity; and

(~~b~~c)   financial statements of each not-for-profit public sector entity that are, or are held out to be, general purpose financial statements.

DELETED IFRS 17 TEXT

Deleted IFRS 17 text is not part of AASB 17.

7(b)   ... and retirement benefit obligations reported by defined benefit retirement plans (see IAS 26 *Accounting and Reporting by Retirement Benefit Plans*).

C34   IFRS 17 supersedes IFRS 4 *Insurance Contracts*, as amended in 2016.

AASB BASIS FOR CONCLUSIONS

This AASB Basis for Conclusions accompanies, but is not part of, AASB 17.

Introduction

AusBC1 This Basis for Conclusions summarises the Australian Accounting Standards Board's (AASB) considerations in reaching the conclusions regarding the substantive Australian-specific issues pertinent to IFRS 17 *Insurance Contracts* as incorporated into AASB 17 *Insurance Contracts*. In making decisions, individual Board members gave greater weight to some factors than to others.

Australian-specific issues

AusBC2 In issuing IFRS 17 the International Accounting Standards Board (IASB) replaced its existing Standard on insurance, namely IFRS 4 *Insurance Contracts*. IFRS 4 allowed entities to use a wide variety of accounting practices for insurance contracts, reflecting national accounting requirements. In the Australian context, those national accounting requirements (including Reduced Disclosure Requirements (RDR) concessions) were contained in:

(a) AASB 4 *Insurance Contracts*;

(b) AASB 1023 *General Insurance Contracts*;

(c) AASB 1038 *Life Insurance Contracts*; and

(d) Interpretation 1047 *Professional Indemnity Claims Liabilities in Medical Defence Organisations*.

AusBC3 In addition, AASB 1056 *Superannuation Entities* includes requirements applicable to a superannuation entity acting in the capacity of an insurer.

AusBC4 IFRS 17 was developed by the IASB from a for-profit perspective. Accordingly, and consistent with the AASB's *Process for Modifying IFRSs for PBE/NFP*, the AASB considered whether it would be suitable for not-for-profit (NFP) entities.

AusBC5 Within the context of replacing existing Australian requirements and addressing NFP issues, Australian-specific issues that are the subject of this Basis for Conclusions relate to the implications for:

(a) AASB 4, AASB 1023 and AASB 1038 (including Australian-specific disclosure requirements) – see paragraphs AusBC6 – AusBC11;

(b) Interpretation 1047 – see paragraphs AusBC14 – AusBC17;

(c) AASB 1056 – see paragraphs AusBC18 – AusBC22;

(d) NFP and public sector entities (including for-profit public sector entities) – see paragraphs AusBC23 – AusBC30; and

(e) RDR – see paragraphs AusBC31 – AusBC32.

Some of these issues have been resolved through the issue of AASB 17, others will be the subject of further due process (including in a forthcoming ED on Australian-specific issues arising from AASB 17), as noted where relevant below.

Implications for AASB 4, AASB 1023 and AASB 1038

AusBC6 The AASB noted that adopting IFRS 17 would supersede AASB 4, AASB 1023 and AASB 1038 and therefore change current accounting requirements for insurance contracts. The AASB acknowledged that doing so would improve financial reporting in some respects but not in other respects.

AusBC7 Regarding the key aspects, the AASB noted that:

(a) the main improvements include:

(i) greater clarity around the accounting for acquisition costs, particularly for general insurance; and

      (ii)   greater alignment with other industries of the basis for revenue recognition for insurance contracts with coverage periods greater than one year; and

   (b)   the main areas not improved include:

      (i)   use of historical (inception-date) discount rates in accounting for the contractual service margin (CSM) under the 'general model';

      (ii)   use of 'coverage period' (rather than pattern of service provision) as the basis for recognising the CSM in profit over the contract life; and

      (iii) the level of aggregation of contracts for accounting purposes.

AusBC8   In weighing up these issues, the AASB also acknowledged the precedent it established when it decided not to adopt IAS 26 *Accounting and Reporting by Retirement Benefit Plans* in favour of retaining the Australian accounting requirements specified in AAS 25 *Financial Reporting by Superannuation Plans*. This decision was subsequently reconfirmed when the AASB issued AASB 1056 to supersede AAS 25.

AusBC9   In considering the facts and circumstances surrounding the AASB's decisions not to adopt IAS 26 (and thereby have an exception to its IFRS adoption policy), the AASB concluded that the legislative environment as well as tailored financial reporting requirements for superannuation entities (which were not adequately addressed in IAS 26) justified the need for a specific Australian pronouncement (see paragraphs BC7 – BC11 of AASB 1056). In contrast, overall, the AASB concluded that IFRS 17 represents a comprehensive, internationally consistent, set of financial reporting requirements for Australian insurers, despite the issues noted in paragraph AusBC7(b).

AusBC10   On balance, the AASB considered that the benefits arising from international harmonisation in relation to the accounting for insurance contracts, and the greater alignment of the basis for revenue recognition with other industries noted in paragraph AusBC7(a)(ii), outweighed the drawbacks noted in paragraph AusBC7(b). Accordingly, the AASB decided to supersede AASB 4, AASB 1023 and AASB 1038 (and Interpretation 1047 – see paragraphs AusBC14 – AusBC17) for for-profit private sector entities with the issue of AASB 17. NFP private sector entities and public sector entities are discussed in paragraphs AusBC23 – AusBC30.

AusBC11   The AASB noted that a consequence of its decision to supersede AASB 1023 and AASB 1038 is that Australian specific disclosures (eg paragraphs 17.8 and 17.10(c) of AASB 1038 relating to regulatory capital disclosures and conformance with the *Life Insurance Act 1995*) are no longer required. However, as a separate project the AASB intends to review the usefulness and necessity of those disclosures under AASB 17 at a future date prior to AASB 17 becoming mandatory.

AusBC12   The AASB further considered the interaction between AASB 4, AASB 1023 and AASB 1038, noting that compliance with either AASB 1023 or AASB 1038 simultaneously achieved compliance with AASB 4. However, the AASB observed that this fact was not explicitly stated in AASB 4 itself, which resulted in divergent interpretations of whether an insurer could apply either of the AASB 9 *Financial Instruments* deferral or overlay approaches introduced with AASB 2016-6 *Amendments to Australian Accounting Standards – Applying AASB 9* Financial Instruments *with AASB 4* Insurance Contracts.

AusBC13   The AASB decided to clarify paragraph Aus3.1 and insert paragraph Aus3.2 in AASB 4 to replicate similar wording already present in AASB 1023 and AASB 1038 to highlight the simultaneous compliance noted above. Furthermore, the AASB decided to clearly indicate that liabilities in scope of AASB 1023 and AASB 1038 are included in an insurer's consideration of whether it qualifies for either the deferral or overlay approaches. The AASB noted that these amendments are purely mechanical and for clarification only, expecting no change in practice arising from these amendments.

Implications for Interpretation 1047

AusBC14   Interpretation 1047 was originally issued in June 2002 to address divergent views as to whether a Medical Defence Organisation (MDO) should recognise a liability for future claims arising from the medical indemnity insurance it offered given the MDO had discretion on whether to pay claims made by members. The Interpretation required that a MDO recognise its obligations in a manner consistent with the principles in AASB 1023.

AusBC15   After 1 July 2003, the *Medical Indemnity Act 2002* came into effect and regulatory arrangements allowed only authorised general insurers to offer medical indemnity insurance. In August 2016 the AASB noted feedback from staff outreach to industry stakeholders indicating that all medical indemnity insurance had, as of then, been transferred to authorised general insurers (or subsidiaries thereof).

AusBC16   Also at its August 2016 meeting, the AASB noted that some business written by MDOs prior to 1 July 2003 could still be in existence, and therefore might still require the guidance of Interpretation 1047. However, on balance, based on the feedback from staff outreach to industry stakeholders, the AASB concluded that any such remaining business would be immaterial to the financial statements of the affected insurers.

AusBC17   Accordingly, the AASB decided to supersede Interpretation 1047 for for-profit private sector entities upon the adoption of IFRS 17 given it was no longer materially relevant, could result in a perceived 'difference' from IFRS if retained and no longer reflected predominant current practice. NFP private sector entities and public sector entities are discussed in paragraphs AusBC23 – AusBC30.

Implications for AASB 1056 *Superannuation Entities*

AusBC18   The AASB issued Exposure Draft ED 223 *Superannuation Entities* (December 2011) proposing new accounting requirements for superannuation entities as part of the AASB's comprehensive review of AAS 25. ED 223 proposed that superannuation entities must measure any liabilities arising from insurance arrangements provided to members in accordance with the approach in AASB 119 *Employee Benefits* for defined benefit plans.

AusBC19   The AASB issued AASB 1056 in June 2014 instead requiring that superannuation entities apply the defined benefit member liability measurement requirements of AASB 1056, as opposed to AASB 119, in response to feedback received on ED 223.

AusBC20   When issuing AASB 17 the AASB was aware that a superannuation entity acting in the capacity of an insurer would apply the insurance requirements of AASB 1056 and not those of AASB 17 because AASB 1056 effectively overrides AASB 17 for a superannuation entity acting in the capacity of an insurer. The AASB noted this would mean superannuation entities could not claim compliance with IFRS. However, the AASB noted that superannuation entities could not claim IFRS compliance anyway because AASB 1056 does not incorporate the corresponding IASB Standard. Accordingly, the AASB decided that no amendments were necessary to the insurance requirements of AASB 1056 as IFRS compliance is not an objective in this limited circumstance. For the avoidance of doubt, the AASB also decided to prevent superannuation entities from applying AASB 17 through an amendment to AASB 1057 *Application of Australian Accounting Standards*. Consequently, the AASB deleted a cross-reference to IAS 26 from paragraph 7(b) of AASB 17 instead of replacing it with a cross-reference to AASB 1056.

AusBC21   The AASB also considered groups where the consolidated financial statements of a superannuation entity include an insurance subsidiary that applies AASB 17. On this issue the AASB noted that no significant issues were brought to its attention during the development of either AASB 1056 or AASB 17, nor since.

AusBC22   Accordingly, the AASB decided to issue AASB 17 without any consequential amendments to the insurance requirements of AASB 1056 in relation to this matter. However, the AASB decided that it would add a specific matter for comment on this matter to its forthcoming ED on Australian-specific issues arising from AASB 17.

Implications for NFP and public sector entities

AusBC23   When issuing a new accounting Standard the AASB considers the applicability of that Standard to all sectors of the economy. In the case of AASB 17, the incorporation of IFRS 17 means that the for-profit private sector is largely considered through the IASB's due process – see paragraphs AusBC6 – AusBC11.

AusBC24   However, the IASB does not explicitly consider:

(a)   NFP entities in the public and private sectors; and

(b)   for-profit entities in the public sector.

AusBC25   The AASB decided that additional consideration is warranted for such entities. To that end, the AASB established a short-term project to consider the applicability and suitability of AASB 17 to them.

AusBC26   At the time of issuing AASB 17, that project was in the process of developing proposals for exposure in the AASB's forthcoming ED on Australian-specific issues arising from AASB 17.

AusBC27   Notwithstanding the above project, the AASB was aware of key concerns from the NFP public sector in particular that need further consideration before a decision is made about whether those entities should be subject to AASB 17 without amendment. Chiefly among those concerns was AASB 17 applicability to statutory obligations such as Medicare, the National Disability Insurance Scheme or worker's compensation insurance.

AusBC28   The AASB acknowledged those concerns and decided to temporarily exclude NFP public sector entities from the scope of AASB 17 pending the outcome of its separate project to address these issues. Until such time as the NFP public sector issues are addressed, those affected entities continue to be subject to AASB 4, AASB 1023 and AASB 1038 (and, potentially, Interpretation 1047).

AusBC29   The AASB noted that NFP private sector entities (eg. some health insurers) often enter into insurance contracts that are substantively similar to those entered into by for-profit entities. Accordingly, the AASB decided not to restrict NFP private sector entities from applying AASB 17, rather allowing those entities to decide to apply AASB 17 prior to 1 January 2021. However, the AASB may propose additional application guidance, where necessary, as part of the forthcoming ED on Australian-specific issues arising from AASB 17, the aim of which is to be operative before the mandatory application date of AASB 17.

AusBC30   The AASB also noted that for-profit public sector entities could enter into arrangements that exhibit characteristics of insurance contracts but are entered into through legislative means as opposed to contractual means. These types of arrangements will also be considered in the AASB's forthcoming ED on Australian-specific issues. However, for-profit public sector entities are not prohibited from applying AASB 17 as their not-for-profit counterparts are.

Implications for RDR

AusBC31   At the time of issuing AASB 17, the AASB was in the process of reviewing its Tier 2 decision-making framework and RDR for existing Standards through ED 277 *Reduced Disclosure Requirements for Tier 2 Entities* (issued in January 2017). Accordingly, the AASB decided not to consider any new pronouncements for RDR concessions until that review is finalised. Consistent with this decision, AASB 17 and its consequential amendments do not include any RDR concessions.

AusBC32   Once the AASB has finalised its Tier 2 decision-making framework it will make RDR proposals, where appropriate, for AASB 17 and its consequential amendments.

AASB 101
Presentation of Financial Statements
(Compiled December 2017)

For-profit (FP) entities

This compiled Standard applies to annual periods beginning on or after 1 January 2018 but before 1 January 2019. Earlier application is permitted for annual periods beginning after 24 July 2014 but before 1 January 2018. It incorporates relevant amendments made up to and including 12 December 2017.

Not-for-profit (NFP) entities – early application only

This compiled Standard does not apply mandatorily to NFP entities. However, early application is permitted for annual reporting periods beginning after 24 July 2014 but before 1 January 2019.

Prepared on 20 May 2018 by the staff of the Australian Accounting Standards Board.

Compilation no. 1

Compilation date: 31 December 2017

This note is not part of Accounting Standard AASB 101.

The following unincorporated amendments are not included in this compiled Standard.

- AASB 17 *Insurance Contracts* — Appendix D sets out the amendments to other Standards that are a consequence of the AASB issuing AASB 17 *Insurance Contracts*. This Standard is applicable from 1 January 2021. Earlier application is permitted, but entities must apply AASB 9 *Financial Instruments* and AASB 15 *Revenue from Contracts with Customers* first.

- AASB 1058 *Income of Not-for-Profit Entities* — Appendix D sets out the amendments to other Australian Accounting Standards that are a consequence of the AASB issuing this Standard. It is applicable from 1 January 2019. Earlier application is permitted, but amendments to AASB 117 apply before 1 January 2019 only if AASB 1058 is also applied to an earlier period. In addition, AASB 1 and AASB 16 amendments are applied to an earlier period only if AASB 16 is also applied to that period.

- AASB 16 *Leases* — Appendix D sets out the amendments to other Standards that are a consequence of the AASB issuing this Standard. It is applicable from 1 January 2019. Earlier application is permitted, but entities must apply AASB 15 *Revenue from Contracts with Customers* before applying this Standard.

- AASB 2016-7 *Amendments to Australian Accounting Standards — Deferral of AASB 15 for Not-for-Profit Entities*. This Standard defers the consequential amendments that were originally set out in AASB 2014-5 *Amendments to Australian Accounting Standards arising from AASB 15,* by restating the effective date of the amendments set out in AASB 2015-8 *Amendments to Australian Accounting Standards* for not-for-profit entities. This Standard defers the application of AASB 15 to 1 January 2019. Earlier application is permitted provided AASB 1058 is also applied to the same period.

Entities early-adopting any amendments with later application dates will need to refer to the amending Standards that have not yet been incorporated into compilations. The abovementioned unincorporated amendments may be located on the AASB website at www.aasb.gov.au or on the Federal Register of Legislation website at www.legislation.gov.au.

CONTENTS

APPENDICES
A. AUSTRALIAN DEFINED TERMS
B. AUSTRALIAN REDUCED DISCLOSURE REQUIREMENTS

COMPILATION DETAILS
DELETED IAS 1 TEXT

IMPLEMENTATION GUIDANCE ON IAS 1 (available on the AASB website)
BASIC FOR CONCLUSIONS ON IAS 1 (available on the AASB website)

Australian Accounting Standard AASB 101 *Presentation of Financial Statements* (as amended) is set out in paragraphs 1 – Aus140.2 and Appendices A – B. All the paragraphs have equal authority. Paragraphs in **bold type** state the main principles. AASB 101 is to be read in the context of other Australian Accounting Standards, including AASB 1048 *Interpretation of Standards*, which identifies the Australian Accounting Interpretations, and AASB 1057 *Application of Australian Accounting Standards*. In the absence of explicit guidance, AASB 108 *Accounting Policies, Changes in Accounting Estimates and Errors* provides a basis for selecting and applying accounting policies.

COMPARISON WITH IAS 1

AASB 101 *Presentation of Financial Statements* as amended incorporates IAS 1 *Presentation of Financial Statements* as issued and amended by the International Accounting Standards Board (IASB). Australian-specific paragraphs (which are not included in IAS 1) are identified with the prefix "Aus" or "RDR". Paragraphs that apply only to not-for-profit entities begin by identifying their limited applicability.

Tier 1

For-profit entities complying with AASB 101 also comply with IAS 1.

Not-for-profit entities' compliance with IAS 1 will depend on whether any "Aus" paragraphs that specifically apply to not-for-profit entities provide additional guidance or contain applicable requirements that are inconsistent with IAS 1.

Tier 2

Entities preparing general purpose financial statements under Australian Accounting Standards – Reduced Disclosure Requirements (Tier 2) will not be in compliance with IFRSs.

AASB 1053 *Application of Tiers of Australian Accounting Standards* explains the two tiers of reporting requirements.

ACCOUNTING STANDARD AASB 101

The Australian Accounting Standards Board made Accounting Standard AASB 101 *Presentation of Financial Statements* under section 334 of the *Corporations Act 2001* on 24 July 2015.

This compiled version of AASB 101 applies to annual periods beginning on or after 1 January 2018 but before 1 January 2019 for for-profit entities. It incorporates relevant amendments contained in other AASB Standards made by the AASB up to and including 12 December 2017 (see Compilation Details).

ACCOUNTING STANDARD AASB 101
PRESENTATION OF FINANCIAL STATEMENTS

Objective

1   This Standard prescribes the basis for presentation of general purpose financial statements to ensure comparability both with the entity's financial statements of previous periods and with the financial statements of other entities. It sets out overall requirements for the presentation of financial statements, guidelines for their structure and minimum requirements for their content.

Scope

2   [Deleted by the AASB]

3   Other Australian Accounting Standards set out the recognition, measurement and disclosure requirements for specific transactions and other events.

4   This Standard does not apply to the structure and content of condensed interim financial statements prepared in accordance with AASB 134 *Interim Financial Reporting*. However, paragraphs 15–35 apply to such financial statements. This Standard applies equally to all entities, including those that present consolidated financial statements in accordance with AASB 10 *Consolidated Financial Statements* and those that present separate financial statements in accordance with AASB 127 *Separate Financial Statements*.

5   This Standard uses terminology that is suitable for profit-oriented entities, including public sector business entities. If entities with not-for-profit activities in the private sector or the public sector apply this Standard, they may need to amend the descriptions used for particular line items in the financial statements and for the financial statements themselves.

6   Similarly, entities that do not have equity as defined in AASB 132 *Financial Instruments: Presentation* (eg some mutual funds) and entities whose share capital is not equity (eg some co-operative entities) may need to adapt the financial statement presentation of members' or unitholders' interests.

Definitions

7   **The following terms are used in this Standard with the meanings specified:**

   General purpose financial statements (referred to as 'financial statements') are those intended to meet the needs of users who are not in a position to require an entity to prepare reports tailored to their particular information needs.

   Impracticable Applying a requirement is impracticable when the entity cannot apply it after making every reasonable effort to do so.

   International Financial Reporting Standards (IFRSs) are Standards and Interpretations issued by the International Accounting Standards Board (IASB). They comprise:

(a)   International Financial Reporting Standards;

(b)   International Accounting Standards;

(c)   IFRIC Interpretations; and

(d)   SIC Interpretations.[1]

Material Omissions or misstatements of items are material if they could, individually or collectively, influence the economic decisions that users make on the basis of the financial statements. Materiality depends on the size and nature of the omission or misstatement judged in the surrounding circumstances. The size or nature of the item, or a combination of both, could be the determining factor.

Assessing whether an omission or misstatement could influence economic decisions of users, and so be material, requires consideration of the characteristics of those users. The *Framework for the Preparation and Presentation of Financial Statements* states in paragraph 25[2] that 'users are assumed to have a reasonable knowledge of business and economic activities and accounting and a willingness to study the information with reasonable diligence.' Therefore, the assessment needs to take into account how users with such attributes could reasonably be expected to be influenced in making economic decisions.

Notes contain information in addition to that presented in the statement of financial position, statement(s) of profit or loss and other comprehensive income, statement of changes in equity and statement of cash flows. Notes provide narrative descriptions or disaggregations of items presented in those statements and information about items that do not qualify for recognition in those statements.

Other comprehensive income comprises items of income and expense (including reclassification adjustments) that are not recognised in profit or loss as required or permitted by other Australian Accounting Standards.

The components of other comprehensive income include:

(a)   changes in revaluation surplus (see AASB 116 *Property, Plant and Equipment* and AASB 138 *Intangible Assets*);

(b)   remeasurements of defined benefit plans (see AASB 119 *Employee Benefits*);

(c)   gains and losses arising from translating the financial statements of a foreign operation (see AASB 121 *The Effects of Changes in Foreign Exchange Rates*);

(d)   gains and losses from investments in equity instruments designated at fair value through other comprehensive income in accordance with paragraph 5.7.5 of AASB 9 *Financial Instruments*;

(da)   gains and losses on financial assets measured at fair value through other comprehensive income in accordance with paragraph 4.1.2A of AASB 9.

(e)   the effective portion of gains and losses on hedging instruments in a cash flow hedge and the gains and losses on hedging instruments that hedge investments in equity instruments measured at fair value through other comprehensive income in accordance with paragraph 5.7.5 of AASB 9 (see Chapter 6 of AASB 9);

(f)   for particular liabilities designated as at fair value through profit or loss, the amount of the change in fair value that is attributable to changes in the liability's credit risk (see paragraph 5.7.7 of AASB 9);

(g)   changes in the value of the time value of options when separating the intrinsic value and time value of an option contract and designating as the hedging instrument only the changes in the intrinsic value (see Chapter 6 of AASB 9); and

---

1   Definition of IFRSs amended after the name changes introduced by the revised Constitution of the IFRS Foundation in 2010.

2   In December 2013 the AASB amended the *Framework for the Preparation and Presentation of Financial Statements*. The *Framework* is identified in AASB 1048 *Interpretation of Standards*. Paragraph 25 was superseded by Chapter 3 of the *Framework*.

(h) changes in the value of the forward elements of forward contracts when separating the forward element and spot element of a forward contract and designating as the hedging instrument only the changes in the spot element, and changes in the value of the foreign currency basis spread of a financial instrument when excluding it from the designation of that financial instrument as the hedging instrument (see Chapter 6 of AASB 9).

Owners **are holders of instruments classified as equity.**

Profit or loss **is the total of income less expenses, excluding the components of other comprehensive income.**

Reclassification adjustments **are amounts reclassified to profit or loss in the current period that were recognised in other comprehensive income in the current or previous periods.**

Total comprehensive income **is the change in equity during a period resulting from transactions and other events, other than those changes resulting from transactions with owners in their capacity as owners.**

Total comprehensive income comprises all components of 'profit or loss' and of 'other comprehensive income'.

8 Although this Standard uses the terms 'other comprehensive income', 'profit or loss' and 'total comprehensive income', an entity may use other terms to describe the totals as long as the meaning is clear. For example, an entity may use the term 'net income' to describe profit or loss.

8A The following terms are described in AASB 132 *Financial Instruments: Presentation* and are used in this Standard with the meaning specified in AASB 132:

(a) puttable financial instrument classified as an equity instrument (described in paragraphs 16A and 16B of AASB 132)

(b) an instrument that imposes on the entity an obligation to deliver to another party a pro rata share of the net assets of the entity only on liquidation and is classified as an equity instrument (described in paragraphs 16C and 16D of AASB 132).

Financial statements

Purpose of financial statements

9 Financial statements are a structured representation of the financial position and financial performance of an entity. The objective of financial statements is to provide information about the financial position, financial performance and cash flows of an entity that is useful to a wide range of users in making economic decisions. Financial statements also show the results of the management's stewardship of the resources entrusted to it. To meet this objective, financial statements provide information about an entity's:

(a) assets;

(b) liabilities;

(c) equity;

(d) income and expenses, including gains and losses;

(e) contributions by and distributions to owners in their capacity as owners; and

(f) cash flows.

This information, along with other information in the notes, assists users of financial statements in predicting the entity's future cash flows and, in particular, their timing and certainty.

Complete set of financial statements

10 **A complete set of financial statements comprises:**

(a) **a statement of financial position as at the end of the period;**

(b)   a statement of profit or loss and other comprehensive income for the period;

(c)   a statement of changes in equity for the period;

(d)   a statement of cash flows for the period;

(e)   notes, comprising significant accounting policies and other explanatory information;

(ea)   comparative information in respect of the preceding period as specified in paragraphs 38 and 38A; and

(f)   a statement of financial position as at the beginning of the preceding period when an entity applies an accounting policy retrospectively or makes a retrospective restatement of items in its financial statements, or when it reclassifies items in its financial statements in accordance with paragraphs 40A–40D.

An entity may use titles for the statements other than those used in this Standard. For example, an entity may use the title 'statement of comprehensive income' instead of 'statement of profit or loss and other comprehensive income'.

10A   An entity may present a single statement of profit or loss and other comprehensive income, with profit or loss and other comprehensive income presented in two sections. The sections shall be presented together, with the profit or loss section presented first followed directly by the other comprehensive income section. An entity may present the profit or loss section in a separate statement of profit or loss. If so, the separate statement of profit or loss shall immediately precede the statement presenting comprehensive income, which shall begin with profit or loss.

11   An entity shall present with equal prominence all of the financial statements in a complete set of financial statements.

12   [Deleted]

13   Many entities present, outside the financial statements, a financial review by management that describes and explains the main features of the entity's financial performance and financial position, and the principal uncertainties it faces. Such a report may include a review of:

(a)   the main factors and influences determining financial performance, including changes in the environment in which the entity operates, the entity's response to those changes and their effect, and the entity's policy for investment to maintain and enhance financial performance, including its dividend policy;

(b)   the entity's sources of funding and its targeted ratio of liabilities to equity; and

(c)   the entity's resources not recognised in the statement of financial position in accordance with Australian Accounting Standards.

14   Many entities also present, outside the financial statements, reports and statements such as environmental reports and value added statements, particularly in industries in which environmental factors are significant and when employees are regarded as an important user group. Reports and statements presented outside financial statements are outside the scope of Australian Accounting Standards.

General features

Fair presentation and compliance with Standards

15   Financial statements shall present fairly the financial position, financial performance and cash flows of an entity. Fair presentation requires the faithful representation of the effects of transactions, other events and conditions in accordance with the definitions and recognition criteria for assets, liabilities,

---

3   Paragraphs 15–24 contain references to the objective of financial statements set out in the *Framework for the Preparation and Presentation of Financial Statements* (as identified in AASB 1048). In December 2013 the AASB amended the *Framework*, and thereby replaced the objective of financial statements with the objective of general purpose financial reporting: see Chapter 1 of the *Framework*.

income and expenses set out in the *Framework*.[3] The application of Australian Accounting Standards, with additional disclosure when necessary, is presumed to result in financial statements that achieve a fair presentation.

16   An entity whose financial statements comply with IFRSs shall make an explicit and unreserved statement of such compliance in the notes. An entity shall not describe financial statements as complying with IFRSs unless they comply with all the requirements of IFRSs.

Aus16.1   [Deleted by the AASB]

Aus16.2   Compliance with Australian Accounting Standards by for-profit entities will not necessarily lead to compliance with IFRSs. This circumstance arises when the entity is a for-profit government department to which particular Standards apply, such as AASB 1004 *Contributions*, and to which Aus paragraphs in various other Australian Accounting Standards apply, and the entity applies a requirement that is inconsistent with an IFRS requirement.

Aus16.3   Not-for-profit entities need not comply with the paragraph 16 requirement to make an explicit and unreserved statement of compliance with IFRSs.

17   In virtually all circumstances, an entity achieves a fair presentation by compliance with applicable Australian Accounting Standards. A fair presentation also requires an entity:

    (a)   to select and apply accounting policies in accordance with AASB 108 *Accounting Policies, Changes in Accounting Estimates and Errors*. AASB 108 sets out a hierarchy of authoritative guidance that management considers in the absence of an Australian Accounting Standard that specifically applies to an item.

    (b)   to present information, including accounting policies, in a manner that provides relevant, reliable, comparable and understandable information.

    (c)   to provide additional disclosures when compliance with the specific requirements in Australian Accounting Standards is insufficient to enable users to understand the impact of particular transactions, other events and conditions on the entity's financial position and financial performance.

18   An entity cannot rectify inappropriate accounting policies either by disclosure of the accounting policies used or by notes or explanatory material.

19   In the extremely rare circumstances in which management concludes that compliance with a requirement in an Australian Accounting Standard would be so misleading that it would conflict with the objective of financial statements set out in the *Framework*, the entity shall depart from that requirement in the manner set out in paragraph 20 if the relevant regulatory framework requires, or otherwise does not prohibit, such a departure.

Aus19.1   In relation to paragraph 19, the following shall not depart from a requirement in an Australian Accounting Standard:

    (a)   entities required to prepare financial reports under Part 2M.3 of the Corporations Act;

    (b)   private and public sector not-for-profit entities; and

    (c)   entities applying Australian Accounting Standards – Reduced Disclosure Requirements.

20   When an entity departs from a requirement of an Australian Accounting Standard in accordance with paragraph 19, it shall disclose:

    (a)   that management has concluded that the financial statements present fairly the entity's financial position, financial performance and cash flows;

    (b)   that it has complied with applicable Australian Accounting Standards, except that it has departed from a particular requirement to achieve a fair presentation;

AASB

(c)   the title of the Australian Accounting Standard from which the entity
      has departed, the nature of the departure, including the treatment that
      the Australian Accounting Standard would require, the reason why that
      treatment would be so misleading in the circumstances that it would conflict
      with the objective of financial statements set out in the *Framework*, and the
      treatment adopted; and

(d)   for each period presented, the financial effect of the departure on each item
      in the financial statements that would have been reported in complying with
      the requirement.

21   When an entity has departed from a requirement of an Australian Accounting
     Standard in a prior period, and that departure affects the amounts recognised in
     the financial statements for the current period, it shall make the disclosures set
     out in paragraph 20(c) and (d).

22   Paragraph 21 applies, for example, when an entity departed in a prior period from a
     requirement in an Australian Accounting Standard for the measurement of assets or
     liabilities and that departure affects the measurement of changes in assets and liabilities
     recognised in the current period's financial statements.

23   In the extremely rare circumstances in which management concludes that
     compliance with a requirement in an Australian Accounting Standard would be
     so misleading that it would conflict with the objective of financial statements set
     out in the *Framework*, but the relevant regulatory framework prohibits departure
     from the requirement, the entity shall, to the maximum extent possible, reduce the
     perceived misleading aspects of compliance by disclosing:

(a)   the title of the Australian Accounting Standard in question, the nature
      of the requirement, and the reason why management has concluded that
      complying with that requirement is so misleading in the circumstances
      that it conflicts with the objective of financial statements set out in the
      Framework; and

(b)   for each period presented, the adjustments to each item in the financial
      statements that management has concluded would be necessary to achieve
      a fair presentation.

24   For the purpose of paragraphs 19–23, an item of information would conflict with the
     objective of financial statements when it does not represent faithfully the transactions,
     other events and conditions that it either purports to represent or could reasonably
     be expected to represent and, consequently, it would be likely to influence economic
     decisions made by users of financial statements. When assessing whether complying
     with a specific requirement in an Australian Accounting Standard would be so
     misleading that it would conflict with the objective of financial statements set out in
     the *Framework*, management considers:

(a)   why the objective of financial statements is not achieved in the particular
      circumstances; and

(b)   how the entity's circumstances differ from those of other entities that comply
      with the requirement. If other entities in similar circumstances comply with
      the requirement, there is a rebuttable presumption that the entity's compliance
      with the requirement would not be so misleading that it would conflict with the
      objective of financial statements set out in the *Framework*.

Going concern

25   When preparing financial statements, management shall make an assessment
     of an entity's ability to continue as a going concern. An entity shall prepare
     financial statements on a going concern basis unless management either intends to
     liquidate the entity or to cease trading, or has no realistic alternative but to do so.
     When management is aware, in making its assessment, of material uncertainties
     related to events or conditions that may cast significant doubt upon the entity's
     ability to continue as a going concern, the entity shall disclose those uncertainties.

> When an entity does not prepare financial statements on a going concern basis, it shall disclose that fact, together with the basis on which it prepared the financial statements and the reason why the entity is not regarded as a going concern.

26   In assessing whether the going concern assumption is appropriate, management takes into account all available information about the future, which is at least, but is not limited to, twelve months from the end of the reporting period. The degree of consideration depends on the facts in each case. When an entity has a history of profitable operations and ready access to financial resources, the entity may reach a conclusion that the going concern basis of accounting is appropriate without detailed analysis. In other cases, management may need to consider a wide range of factors relating to current and expected profitability, debt repayment schedules and potential sources of replacement financing before it can satisfy itself that the going concern basis is appropriate.

Accrual basis of accounting

27   **An entity shall prepare its financial statements, except for cash flow information, using the accrual basis of accounting.**

28   When the accrual basis of accounting is used, an entity recognises items as assets, liabilities, equity, income and expenses (the elements of financial statements) when they satisfy the definitions and recognition criteria for those elements in the *Framework*.[4]

Materiality and aggregation

29   **An entity shall present separately each material class of similar items. An entity shall present separately items of a dissimilar nature or function unless they are immaterial.**

30   Financial statements result from processing large numbers of transactions or other events that are aggregated into classes according to their nature or function. The final stage in the process of aggregation and classification is the presentation of condensed and classified data, which form line items in the financial statements. If a line item is not individually material, it is aggregated with other items either in those statements or in the notes. An item that is not sufficiently material to warrant separate presentation in those statements may warrant separate presentation in the notes.

30A   When applying this and other Australian Accounting Standards an entity shall decide, taking into consideration all relevant facts and circumstances, how it aggregates information in the financial statements, which include the notes. An entity shall not reduce the understandability of its financial statements by obscuring material information with immaterial information or by aggregating material items that have different natures or functions.

31   Some Australian Accounting Standards specify information that is required to be included in the financial statements, which include the notes. An entity need not provide a specific disclosure required by an Australian Accounting Standard if the information resulting from that disclosure is not material. This is the case even if the Australian Accounting Standard contains a list of specific requirements or describes them as minimum requirements. An entity shall also consider whether to provide additional disclosures when compliance with the specific requirements in Australian Accounting Standards is insufficient to enable users of financial statements to understand the impact of particular transactions, other events and conditions on the entity's financial position and financial performance.

Offsetting

32   **An entity shall not offset assets and liabilities or income and expenses, unless required or permitted by an Australian Accounting Standard.**

---

4   The *Framework for the Preparation and Presentation of Financial Statements* was amended by the AASB in December 2013.

33   An entity reports separately both assets and liabilities, and income and expenses. Offsetting in the statement(s) of profit or loss and other comprehensive income or financial position, except when offsetting reflects the substance of the transaction or other event, detracts from the ability of users both to understand the transactions, other events and conditions that have occurred and to assess the entity's future cash flows. Measuring assets net of valuation allowances—for example, obsolescence allowances on inventories and doubtful debts allowances on receivables—is not offsetting.

34   AASB 15 *Revenue from Contracts with Customers* requires an entity to measure revenue from contracts with customers at the amount of consideration to which the entity expects to be entitled in exchange for transferring promised goods or services. For example, the amount of revenue recognised reflects any trade discounts and volume rebates the entity allows. An entity undertakes, in the course of its ordinary activities, other transactions that do not generate revenue but are incidental to the main revenue-generating activities. An entity presents the results of such transactions, when this presentation reflects the substance of the transaction or other event, by netting any income with related expenses arising on the same transaction. For example:

    (a)   an entity presents gains and losses on the disposal of non-current assets, including investments and operating assets, by deducting from the amount of consideration on disposal the carrying amount of the asset and related selling expenses; and

    (b)   an entity may net expenditure related to a provision that is recognised in accordance with AASB 137 *Provisions, Contingent Liabilities and Contingent Assets* and reimbursed under a contractual arrangement with a third party (for example, a supplier's warranty agreement) against the related reimbursement.

35   In addition, an entity presents on a net basis gains and losses arising from a group of similar transactions, for example, foreign exchange gains and losses or gains and losses arising on financial instruments held for trading. However, an entity presents such gains and losses separately if they are material.

Frequency of reporting

36   An entity shall present a complete set of financial statements (including comparative information) at least annually. When an entity changes the end of its reporting period and presents financial statements for a period longer or shorter than one year, an entity shall disclose, in addition to the period covered by the financial statements:

    (a)   the reason for using a longer or shorter period, and

    (b)   the fact that amounts presented in the financial statements are not entirely comparable.

37   Normally, an entity consistently prepares financial statements for a one-year period. However, for practical reasons, some entities prefer to report, for example, for a 52-week period. This Standard does not preclude this practice.

Comparative information
Minimum comparative information

38   Except when Australian Accounting Standards permit or require otherwise, an entity shall present comparative information in respect of the preceding period for all amounts reported in the current period's financial statements. An entity shall include comparative information for narrative and descriptive information if it is relevant to understanding the current period's financial statements.

38A   An entity shall present, as a minimum, two statements of financial position, two statements of profit or loss and other comprehensive income, two separate statements of profit or loss (if presented), two statements of cash flows and two statements of changes in equity, and related notes.

38B   In some cases, narrative information provided in the financial statements for the preceding period(s) continues to be relevant in the current period. For example, an entity discloses in the current period details of a legal dispute, the outcome of which was uncertain at the end of the preceding period and is yet to be resolved. Users may benefit from the disclosure of information that the uncertainty existed at the end of the preceding period and from the disclosure of information about the steps that have been taken during the period to resolve the uncertainty.

Additional comparative information

38C   An entity may present comparative information in addition to the minimum comparative financial statements required by Australian Accounting Standards, as long as that information is prepared in accordance with Australian Accounting Standards. This comparative information may consist of one or more statements referred to in paragraph 10, but need not comprise a complete set of financial statements. When this is the case, the entity shall present related note information for those additional statements.

38D   For example, an entity may present a third statement of profit or loss and other comprehensive income (thereby presenting the current period, the preceding period and one additional comparative period). However, the entity is not required to present a third statement of financial position, a third statement of cash flows or a third statement of changes in equity (ie an additional financial statement comparative). The entity is required to present, in the notes to the financial statements, the comparative information related to that additional statement of profit or loss and other comprehensive income.

39–40 [Deleted]

Change in accounting policy, retrospective restatement or reclassification

40A   An entity shall present a third statement of financial position as at the beginning of the preceding period in addition to the minimum comparative financial statements required in paragraph 38A if:

(a)   it applies an accounting policy retrospectively, makes a retrospective restatement of items in its financial statements or reclassifies items in its financial statements; and

(b)   the retrospective application, retrospective restatement or the reclassification has a material effect on the information in the statement of financial position at the beginning of the preceding period.

40B   In the circumstances described in paragraph 40A, an entity shall present three statements of financial position as at:

(a)   the end of the current period;

(b)   the end of the preceding period; and

(c)   the beginning of the preceding period.

40C   When an entity is required to present an additional statement of financial position in accordance with paragraph 40A, it must disclose the information required by paragraphs 41–44 and AASB 108. However, it need not present the related notes to the opening statement of financial position as at the beginning of the preceding period.

40D   The date of that opening statement of financial position shall be as at the beginning of the preceding period regardless of whether an entity's financial statements present comparative information for earlier periods (as permitted in paragraph 38C).

41   If an entity changes the presentation or classification of items in its financial statements, it shall reclassify comparative amounts unless reclassification is impracticable. When an entity reclassifies comparative amounts, it shall disclose (including as at the beginning of the preceding period):

(a)   the nature of the reclassification;

(b)   the amount of each item or class of items that is reclassified; and

(c)   the reason for the reclassification.

42   **When it is impracticable to reclassify comparative amounts, an entity shall disclose:**

(a)   **the reason for not reclassifying the amounts, and**

(b)   **the nature of the adjustments that would have been made if the amounts had been reclassified.**

43   Enhancing the inter-period comparability of information assists users in making economic decisions, especially by allowing the assessment of trends in financial information for predictive purposes. In some circumstances, it is impracticable to reclassify comparative information for a particular prior period to achieve comparability with the current period. For example, an entity may not have collected data in the prior period(s) in a way that allows reclassification, and it may be impracticable to recreate the information.

44   AASB 108 sets out the adjustments to comparative information required when an entity changes an accounting policy or corrects an error.

Consistency of presentation

45   **An entity shall retain the presentation and classification of items in the financial statements from one period to the next unless:**

(a)   **it is apparent, following a significant change in the nature of the entity's operations or a review of its financial statements, that another presentation or classification would be more appropriate having regard to the criteria for the selection and application of accounting policies in AASB 108; or**

(b)   **an Australian Accounting Standard requires a change in presentation.**

46   For example, a significant acquisition or disposal, or a review of the presentation of the financial statements, might suggest that the financial statements need to be presented differently. An entity changes the presentation of its financial statements only if the changed presentation provides information that is reliable and more relevant to users of the financial statements and the revised structure is likely to continue, so that comparability is not impaired. When making such changes in presentation, an entity reclassifies its comparative information in accordance with paragraphs 41 and 42.

Structure and content

Introduction

47   This Standard requires particular disclosures in the statement of financial position or the statement(s) of profit or loss and other comprehensive income, or in the statement of changes in equity and requires disclosure of other line items either in those statements or in the notes. AASB 107 *Statement of Cash Flows* sets out requirements for the presentation of cash flow information.

48   This Standard sometimes uses the term 'disclosure' in a broad sense, encompassing items presented in the financial statements. Disclosures are also required by other Australian Accounting Standards. Unless specified to the contrary elsewhere in this Standard or in another Australian Accounting Standard, such disclosures may be made in the financial statements.

Identification of the financial statements

49   **An entity shall clearly identify the financial statements and distinguish them from other information in the same published document.**

50   Australian Accounting Standards apply only to financial statements, and not necessarily to other information presented in an annual report, a regulatory filing, or another document. Therefore, it is important that users can distinguish information that

is prepared using Australian Accounting Standards from other information that may be useful to users but is not the subject of those requirements.

51 **An entity shall clearly identify each financial statement and the notes. In addition, an entity shall display the following information prominently, and repeat it when necessary for the information presented to be understandable:**

    (a) **the name of the reporting entity or other means of identification, and any change in that information from the end of the preceding reporting period;**

    (b) **whether the financial statements are of an individual entity or a group of entities;**

    (c) **the date of the end of the reporting period or the period covered by the set of financial statements or notes;**

    (d) **the presentation currency, as defined in AASB 121; and**

    (e) **the level of rounding used in presenting amounts in the financial statements.**

52 An entity meets the requirements in paragraph 51 by presenting appropriate headings for pages, statements, notes, columns and the like. Judgement is required in determining the best way of presenting such information. For example, when an entity presents the financial statements electronically, separate pages are not always used; an entity then presents the above items to ensure that the information included in the financial statements can be understood.

53 An entity often makes financial statements more understandable by presenting information in thousands or millions of units of the presentation currency. This is acceptable as long as the entity discloses the level of rounding and does not omit material information.

Statement of financial position

Information to be presented in the statement of financial position

54 **The statement of financial position shall include line items that present the following amounts:**

    (a) **property, plant and equipment;**

    (b) **investment property;**

    (c) **intangible assets;**

    (d) **financial assets (excluding amounts shown under (e), (h) and (i));**

    (e) **investments accounted for using the equity method;**

    (f) **biological assets within the scope of AASB 141 *Agriculture*;**

    (g) **inventories;**

    (h) **trade and other receivables;**

    (i) **cash and cash equivalents;**

    (j) **the total of assets classified as held for sale and assets included in disposal groups classified as held for sale in accordance with AASB 5 *Non-current Assets Held for Sale and Discontinued Operations*;**

    (k) **trade and other payables;**

    (l) **provisions;**

    (m) **financial liabilities (excluding amounts shown under (k) and (l));**

    (n) **liabilities and assets for current tax, as defined in AASB 112 *Income Taxes*;**

    (o) **deferred tax liabilities and deferred tax assets, as defined in AASB 112;**

    (p) **liabilities included in disposal groups classified as held for sale in accordance with AASB 5;**

AASB

(q)   non-controlling interests, presented within equity; and

(r)   issued capital and reserves attributable to owners of the parent.

55   An entity shall present additional line items (including by disaggregating the line items listed in paragraph 54), headings and subtotals in the statement of financial position when such presentation is relevant to an understanding of the entity's financial position.

55A   When an entity presents subtotals in accordance with paragraph 55, those subtotals shall:

(a)   be comprised of line items made up of amounts recognised and measured in accordance with Australian Accounting Standards;

(b)   be presented and labelled in a manner that makes the line items that constitute the subtotal clear and understandable;

(c)   be consistent from period to period, in accordance with paragraph 45; and

(d)   not be displayed with more prominence than the subtotals and totals required in Australian Accounting Standards for the statement of financial position.

56   **When an entity presents current and non-current assets, and current and non-current liabilities, as separate classifications in its statement of financial position, it shall not classify deferred tax assets (liabilities) as current assets (liabilities).**

57   This Standard does not prescribe the order or format in which an entity presents items. Paragraph 54 simply lists items that are sufficiently different in nature or function to warrant separate presentation in the statement of financial position. In addition:

(a)   line items are included when the size, nature or function of an item or aggregation of similar items is such that separate presentation is relevant to an understanding of the entity's financial position; and

(b)   the descriptions used and the ordering of items or aggregation of similar items may be amended according to the nature of the entity and its transactions, to provide information that is relevant to an understanding of the entity's financial position. For example, a financial institution may amend the above descriptions to provide information that is relevant to the operations of a financial institution.

58   An entity makes the judgement about whether to present additional items separately on the basis of an assessment of:

(a)   the nature and liquidity of assets;

(b)   the function of assets within the entity; and

(c)   the amounts, nature and timing of liabilities.

59   The use of different measurement bases for different classes of assets suggests that their nature or function differs and, therefore, that an entity presents them as separate line items. For example, different classes of property, plant and equipment can be carried at cost or at revalued amounts in accordance with AASB 116.

Current/non-current distinction

60   **An entity shall present current and non-current assets, and current and non-current liabilities, as separate classifications in its statement of financial position in accordance with paragraphs 66–76 except when a presentation based on liquidity provides information that is reliable and more relevant. When that exception applies, an entity shall present all assets and liabilities in order of liquidity.**

61   **Whichever method of presentation is adopted, an entity shall disclose the amount expected to be recovered or settled after more than twelve months for each asset and liability line item that combines amounts expected to be recovered or settled:**

(a)   **no more than twelve months after the reporting period, and**

(b)   **more than twelve months after the reporting period.**

62   When an entity supplies goods or services within a clearly identifiable operating cycle, separate classification of current and non-current assets and liabilities in the statement of financial position provides useful information by distinguishing the net assets that are continuously circulating as working capital from those used in the entity's long-term operations. It also highlights assets that are expected to be realised within the current operating cycle, and liabilities that are due for settlement within the same period.

63   For some entities, such as financial institutions, a presentation of assets and liabilities in increasing or decreasing order of liquidity provides information that is reliable and more relevant than a current/non-current presentation because the entity does not supply goods or services within a clearly identifiable operating cycle.

64   In applying paragraph 60, an entity is permitted to present some of its assets and liabilities using a current/non-current classification and others in order of liquidity when this provides information that is reliable and more relevant. The need for a mixed basis of presentation might arise when an entity has diverse operations.

65   Information about expected dates of realisation of assets and liabilities is useful in assessing the liquidity and solvency of an entity. AASB 7 *Financial Instruments: Disclosures* requires disclosure of the maturity dates of financial assets and financial liabilities. Financial assets include trade and other receivables, and financial liabilities include trade and other payables. Information on the expected date of recovery of non-monetary assets such as inventories and expected date of settlement for liabilities such as provisions is also useful, whether assets and liabilities are classified as current or as non-current. For example, an entity discloses the amount of inventories that are expected to be recovered more than twelve months after the reporting period.

Current assets

66   **An entity shall classify an asset as current when:**

    (a)   **it expects to realise the asset, or intends to sell or consume it, in its normal operating cycle;**

    (b)   **it holds the asset primarily for the purpose of trading;**

    (c)   **it expects to realise the asset within twelve months after the reporting period; or**

    (d)   **the asset is cash or a cash equivalent (as defined in AASB 107) unless the asset is restricted from being exchanged or used to settle a liability for at least twelve months after the reporting period.**

    An entity shall classify all other assets as non-current.

67   This Standard uses the term 'non-current' to include tangible, intangible and financial assets of a long-term nature. It does not prohibit the use of alternative descriptions as long as the meaning is clear.

68   The operating cycle of an entity is the time between the acquisition of assets for processing and their realisation in cash or cash equivalents. When the entity's normal operating cycle is not clearly identifiable, it is assumed to be twelve months. Current assets include assets (such as inventories and trade receivables) that are sold, consumed or realised as part of the normal operating cycle even when they are not expected to be realised within twelve months after the reporting period. Current assets also include assets held primarily for the purpose of trading (examples include some financial assets that meet the definition of held for trading in AASB 9) and the current portion of non-current financial assets.

Current liabilities

69   **An entity shall classify a liability as current when:**

    (a)   **it expects to settle the liability in its normal operating cycle;**

    (b)   **it holds the liability primarily for the purpose of trading;**

AASB

(c)   the liability is due to be settled within twelve months after the reporting period; or

(d)   it does not have an unconditional right to defer settlement of the liability for at least twelve months after the reporting period (see paragraph 73). Terms of a liability that could, at the option of the counterparty, result in its settlement by the issue of equity instruments do not affect its classification.

An entity shall classify all other liabilities as non-current.

70   Some current liabilities, such as trade payables and some accruals for employee and other operating costs, are part of the working capital used in the entity's normal operating cycle. An entity classifies such operating items as current liabilities even if they are due to be settled more than twelve months after the reporting period. The same normal operating cycle applies to the classification of an entity's assets and liabilities. When the entity's normal operating cycle is not clearly identifiable, it is assumed to be twelve months.

71   Other current liabilities are not settled as part of the normal operating cycle, but are due for settlement within twelve months after the reporting period or held primarily for the purpose of trading. Examples are some financial liabilities that meet the definition of held for trading in AASB 9, bank overdrafts, and the current portion of non-current financial liabilities, dividends payable, income taxes and other non-trade payables. Financial liabilities that provide financing on a long-term basis (ie are not part of the working capital used in the entity's normal operating cycle) and are not due for settlement within twelve months after the reporting period are non-current liabilities, subject to paragraphs 74 and 75.

72   An entity classifies its financial liabilities as current when they are due to be settled within twelve months after the reporting period, even if:

(a)   the original term was for a period longer than twelve months, and

(b)   an agreement to refinance, or to reschedule payments, on a long-term basis is completed after the reporting period and before the financial statements are authorised for issue.

73   If an entity expects, and has the discretion, to refinance or roll over an obligation for at least twelve months after the reporting period under an existing loan facility, it classifies the obligation as non-current, even if it would otherwise be due within a shorter period. However, when refinancing or rolling over the obligation is not at the discretion of the entity (for example, there is no arrangement for refinancing), the entity does not consider the potential to refinance the obligation and classifies the obligation as current.

74   When an entity breaches a provision of a long-term loan arrangement on or before the end of the reporting period with the effect that the liability becomes payable on demand, it classifies the liability as current, even if the lender agreed, after the reporting period and before the authorisation of the financial statements for issue, not to demand payment as a consequence of the breach. An entity classifies the liability as current because, at the end of the reporting period, it does not have an unconditional right to defer its settlement for at least twelve months after that date.

75   However, an entity classifies the liability as non-current if the lender agreed by the end of the reporting period to provide a period of grace ending at least twelve months after the reporting period, within which the entity can rectify the breach and during which the lender cannot demand immediate repayment.

76   In respect of loans classified as current liabilities, if the following events occur between the end of the reporting period and the date the financial statements are authorised for issue, those events are disclosed as non-adjusting events in accordance with AASB 110 *Events after the Reporting Period*:

(a)   refinancing on a long-term basis;

(b)   rectification of a breach of a long-term loan arrangement; and

(c)   the granting by the lender of a period of grace to rectify a breach of a long-term loan arrangement ending at least twelve months after the reporting period.

Information to be presented either in the statement of financial position or in the notes

77   An entity shall disclose, either in the statement of financial position or in the notes, further subclassifications of the line items presented, classified in a manner appropriate to the entity's operations.

78   The detail provided in subclassifications depends on the requirements of Australian Accounting Standards and on the size, nature and function of the amounts involved. An entity also uses the factors set out in paragraph 58 to decide the basis of subclassification. The disclosures vary for each item, for example:

(a)   items of property, plant and equipment are disaggregated into classes in accordance with AASB 116;

(b)   receivables are disaggregated into amounts receivable from trade customers, receivables from related parties, prepayments and other amounts;

(c)   inventories are disaggregated, in accordance with AASB 102 *Inventories*, into classifications such as merchandise, production supplies, materials, work in progress and finished goods;

(d)   provisions are disaggregated into provisions for employee benefits and other items; and

(e)   equity capital and reserves are disaggregated into various classes, such as paid-in capital, share premium and reserves.

79   An entity shall disclose the following, either in the statement of financial position or the statement of changes in equity, or in the notes:

(a)   for each class of share capital:

(i)   the number of shares authorised;

(ii)   the number of shares issued and fully paid, and issued but not fully paid;

(iii)   par value per share, or that the shares have no par value;

(iv)   a reconciliation of the number of shares outstanding at the beginning and at the end of the period;

(v)   the rights, preferences and restrictions attaching to that class including restrictions on the distribution of dividends and the repayment of capital;

(vi)   shares in the entity held by the entity or by its subsidiaries or associates; and

(vii)   shares reserved for issue under options and contracts for the sale of shares, including terms and amounts; and

(b)   a description of the nature and purpose of each reserve within equity.

80   An entity without share capital, such as a partnership or trust, shall disclose information equivalent to that required by paragraph 79(a), showing changes during the period in each category of equity interest, and the rights, preferences and restrictions attaching to each category of equity interest.

80A   If an entity has reclassified

(a)   a puttable financial instrument classified as an equity instrument, or

(b)   an instrument that imposes on the entity an obligation to deliver to another party a pro rata share of the net assets of the entity only on liquidation and is classified as an equity instrument

between financial liabilities and equity, it shall disclose the amount reclassified into and out of each category (financial liabilities or equity), and the timing and reason for that reclassification.

Statement of profit or loss and other comprehensive income

81   [Deleted]

81A   The statement of profit or loss and other comprehensive income (statement of comprehensive income) shall present, in addition to the profit or loss and other comprehensive income sections:

(a)   profit or loss;

(b)   total other comprehensive income;

(c)   comprehensive income for the period, being the total of profit or loss and other comprehensive income.

If an entity presents a separate statement of profit or loss it does not present the profit or loss section in the statement presenting comprehensive income.

81B   An entity shall present the following items, in addition to the profit or loss and other comprehensive income sections, as allocation of profit or loss and other comprehensive income for the period:

(a)   profit or loss for the period attributable to:

(i)   non-controlling interests, and

(ii)   owners of the parent.

(b)   comprehensive income for the period attributable to:

(i)   non-controlling interests, and

(ii)   owners of the parent.

If an entity presents profit or loss in a separate statement it shall present (a) in that statement.

Information to be presented in the profit or loss section or the statement of profit or loss

82 In addition to items required by other Australian Accounting Standards, the profit or loss section or the statement of profit or loss shall include line items that present the following amounts for the period:

(a)   revenue, presenting separately interest revenue calculated using the effective interest method;

(aa)   gains and losses arising from the derecognition of financial assets measured at amortised cost;

(b)   finance costs;

(ba)   impairment losses (including reversals of impairment losses or impairment gains) determined in accordance with Section 5.5 of AASB 9;

(c)   share of the profit or loss of associates and joint ventures accounted for using the equity method;

(ca)   if a financial asset is reclassified out of the amortised cost measurement category so that it is measured at fair value through profit or loss, any gain or loss arising from a difference between the previous amortised cost of the financial asset and its fair value at the reclassification date (as defined in AASB 9);

(cb)   if a financial asset is reclassified out of the fair value through other comprehensive income measurement category so that it is measured at fair value through profit or loss, any cumulative gain or loss previously recognised in other comprehensive income that is reclassified to profit or loss;

(d)   tax expense;

(e)   [deleted]

(ea)   a single amount for the total of discontinued operations (see AASB 5).

(f)–(i) [deleted]

Information to be presented in the other comprehensive income section

82A   The other comprehensive income section shall present line items for the amounts for the period of:

(a)   items of other comprehensive income (excluding amounts in paragraph (b)), classified by nature and grouped into those that, in accordance with other Australian Accounting Standards:

(i)   will not be reclassified subsequently to profit or loss; and

(ii)   will be reclassified subsequently to profit or loss when specific conditions are met.

(b)   the share of the other comprehensive income of associates and joint ventures accounted for using the equity method, separated into the share of items that, in accordance with other Australian Accounting Standards:

(i)   will not be reclassified subsequently to profit or loss; and

(ii)   will be reclassified subsequently to profit or loss when specific conditions are met.

83–84 [Deleted]

85   **An entity shall present additional line items (including by disaggregating the line items listed in paragraph 82), headings and subtotals in the statement(s) presenting profit or loss and other comprehensive income when such presentation is relevant to an understanding of the entity's financial performance.**

85A   When an entity presents subtotals in accordance with paragraph 85, those subtotals shall:

(a)   be comprised of line items made up of amounts recognised and measured in accordance with Australian Accounting Standards;

(b)   be presented and labelled in a manner that makes the line items that constitute the subtotal clear and understandable;

(c)   be consistent from period to period, in accordance with paragraph 45; and

(d)   not be displayed with more prominence than the subtotals and totals required in Australian Accounting Standards for the statement(s) presenting profit or loss and other comprehensive income.

85B   An entity shall present the line items in the statement(s) presenting profit or loss and other comprehensive income that reconcile any subtotals presented in accordance with paragraph 85 with the subtotals or totals required in Australian Accounting Standards for such statement(s).

86   Because the effects of an entity's various activities, transactions and other events differ in frequency, potential for gain or loss and predictability, disclosing the components of financial performance assists users in understanding the financial performance achieved and in making projections of future financial performance. An entity includes additional line items in the statement(s) presenting profit or loss and other comprehensive income and it amends the descriptions used and the ordering of items when this is necessary to explain the elements of financial performance. An entity considers factors including materiality and the nature and function of the items of income and expense. For example, a financial institution may amend the descriptions to provide information that is relevant to the operations of a financial institution. An entity does not offset income and expense items unless the criteria in paragraph 32 are met.

87   **An entity shall not present any items of income or expense as extraordinary items, in the statement(s) presenting profit or loss and other comprehensive income or in the notes.**

Profit or loss for the period

88   An entity shall recognise all items of income and expense in a period in profit or loss unless an Australian Accounting Standard requires or permits otherwise.

89   Some Australian Accounting Standards specify circumstances when an entity recognises particular items outside profit or loss in the current period. AASB 108 specifies two such circumstances: the correction of errors and the effect of changes in accounting policies. Other Australian Accounting Standards require or permit components of other comprehensive income that meet the *Framework*'s[5] definition of income or expense to be excluded from profit or loss (see paragraph 7).

Other comprehensive income for the period

90   An entity shall disclose the amount of income tax relating to each item of other comprehensive income, including reclassification adjustments, either in the statement of profit or loss and other comprehensive income or in the notes.

91   An entity may present items of other comprehensive income either:

(a)   net of related tax effects, or

(b)   before related tax effects with one amount shown for the aggregate amount of income tax relating to those items.

If an entity elects alternative (b), it shall allocate the tax between the items that might be reclassified subsequently to the profit or loss section and those that will not be reclassified subsequently to the profit or loss section.

92   An entity shall disclose reclassification adjustments relating to components of other comprehensive income.

93   Other Australian Accounting Standards specify whether and when amounts previously recognised in other comprehensive income are reclassified to profit or loss. Such reclassifications are referred to in this Standard as reclassification adjustments. A reclassification adjustment is included with the related component of other comprehensive income in the period that the adjustment is reclassified to profit or loss. These amounts may have been recognised in other comprehensive income as unrealised gains in the current or previous periods. Those unrealised gains must be deducted from other comprehensive income in the period in which the realised gains are reclassified to profit or loss to avoid including them in total comprehensive income twice.

94   An entity may present reclassification adjustments in the statement(s) of profit or loss and other comprehensive income or in the notes. An entity presenting reclassification adjustments in the notes presents the items of other comprehensive income after any related reclassification adjustments.

95   Reclassification adjustments arise, for example, on disposal of a foreign operation (see AASB 121) and when some hedged forecast cash flows affect profit or loss (see paragraph 6.5.11(d) of AASB 9 in relation to cash flow hedges).

96   Reclassification adjustments do not arise on changes in revaluation surplus recognised in accordance with AASB 116 or AASB 138 or on remeasurements of defined benefit plans recognised in accordance with AASB 119. These components are recognised in other comprehensive income and are not reclassified to profit or loss in subsequent periods. Changes in revaluation surplus may be transferred to retained earnings in subsequent periods as the asset is used or when it is derecognised (see AASB 116 and AASB 138). In accordance with AASB 9, reclassification adjustments do not arise if a cash flow hedge or the accounting for the time value of an option (or the forward element of a forward contract or the foreign currency basis spread of a financial instrument) result in amounts that are removed from the cash flow hedge reserve or a separate component of equity, respectively, and included directly in the initial cost or

---

5   The *Framework for the Preparation and Presentation of Financial Statements* was amended by the AASB in December 2013.

other carrying amount of an asset or a liability. These amounts are directly transferred to assets or liabilities.

Information to be presented in the statement(s) of profit or loss and other comprehensive income or in the notes

97   **When items of income or expense are material, an entity shall disclose their nature and amount separately.**

98   Circumstances that would give rise to the separate disclosure of items of income and expense include:

(a)   write-downs of inventories to net realisable value or of property, plant and equipment to recoverable amount, as well as reversals of such write-downs;

(b)   restructurings of the activities of an entity and reversals of any provisions for the costs of restructuring;

(c)   disposals of items of property, plant and equipment;

(d)   disposals of investments;

(e)   discontinued operations;

(f)   litigation settlements; and

(g)   other reversals of provisions.

99   **An entity shall present an analysis of expenses recognised in profit or loss using a classification based on either their nature or their function within the entity, whichever provides information that is reliable and more relevant.**

100   Entities are encouraged to present the analysis in paragraph 99 in the statement(s) presenting profit or loss and other comprehensive income.

101   Expenses are subclassified to highlight components of financial performance that may differ in terms of frequency, potential for gain or loss and predictability. This analysis is provided in one of two forms.

102   The first form of analysis is the 'nature of expense' method. An entity aggregates expenses within profit or loss according to their nature (for example, depreciation, purchases of materials, transport costs, employee benefits and advertising costs), and does not reallocate them among functions within the entity. This method may be simple to apply because no allocations of expenses to functional classifications are necessary. An example of a classification using the nature of expense method is as follows:

Revenue	X
Other income	X
Changes in inventories of finished goods and work in progress	X
Raw materials and consumables used	X
Employee benefits expense	X
Depreciation and amortisation expense	X
Other expenses	X
Total expenses	(X)
Profit before tax	X

103   The second form of analysis is the 'function of expense' or 'cost of sales' method and classifies expenses according to their function as part of cost of sales or, for example,

the costs of distribution or administrative activities. At a minimum, an entity discloses its cost of sales under this method separately from other expenses. This method can provide more relevant information to users than the classification of expenses by nature, but allocating costs to functions may require arbitrary allocations and involve considerable judgement. An example of a classification using the function of expense method is as follows:

Revenue	X
Cost of sales	(X)
Gross profit	X
Other income	X
Distribution costs	(X)
Administrative expenses	(X)
Other expenses	(X)
Profit before tax	X

104   An entity classifying expenses by function shall disclose additional information on the nature of expenses, including depreciation and amortisation expense and employee benefits expense.

105   The choice between the function of expense method and the nature of expense method depends on historical and industry factors and the nature of the entity. Both methods provide an indication of those costs that might vary, directly or indirectly, with the level of sales or production of the entity. Because each method of presentation has merit for different types of entities, this Standard requires management to select the presentation that is reliable and more relevant. However, because information on the nature of expenses is useful in predicting future cash flows, additional disclosure is required when the function of expense classification is used. In paragraph 104, 'employee benefits' has the same meaning as in AASB 119.

Statement of changes in equity

Information to be presented in the statement of changes in equity

106   **An entity shall present a statement of changes in equity as required by paragraph 10. The statement of changes in equity includes the following information:**

(a)   **total comprehensive income for the period, showing separately the total amounts attributable to owners of the parent and to non-controlling interests;**

(b)   **for each component of equity, the effects of retrospective application or retrospective restatement recognised in accordance with AASB 108; and**

(c)   **[deleted]**

(d)   **for each component of equity, a reconciliation between the carrying amount at the beginning and the end of the period, separately (as a minimum) disclosing changes resulting from:**

(i)   **profit or loss;**

(ii)   **other comprehensive income; and**

(iii)   **transactions with owners in their capacity as owners, showing separately contributions by and distributions to owners and changes in ownership interests in subsidiaries that do not result in a loss of control.**

Information to be presented in the statement of changes in equity or in the notes

106A For each component of equity an entity shall present, either in the statement of changes in equity or in the notes, an analysis of other comprehensive income by item (see paragraph 106(d)(ii)).

107 An entity shall present, either in the statement of changes in equity or in the notes, the amount of dividends recognised as distributions to owners during the period, and the related amount of dividends per share.

108 In paragraph 106, the components of equity include, for example, each class of contributed equity, the accumulated balance of each class of other comprehensive income and retained earnings.

109 Changes in an entity's equity between the beginning and the end of the reporting period reflect the increase or decrease in its net assets during the period. Except for changes resulting from transactions with owners in their capacity as owners (such as equity contributions, reacquisitions of the entity's own equity instruments and dividends) and transaction costs directly related to such transactions, the overall change in equity during a period represents the total amount of income and expense, including gains and losses, generated by the entity's activities during that period.

110 AASB 108 requires retrospective adjustments to effect changes in accounting policies, to the extent practicable, except when the transition provisions in another Australian Accounting Standard require otherwise. AASB 108 also requires restatements to correct errors to be made retrospectively, to the extent practicable. Retrospective adjustments and retrospective restatements are not changes in equity but they are adjustments to the opening balance of retained earnings, except when an Australian Accounting Standard requires retrospective adjustment of another component of equity. Paragraph 106(b) requires disclosure in the statement of changes in equity of the total adjustment to each component of equity resulting from changes in accounting policies and, separately, from corrections of errors. These adjustments are disclosed for each prior period and the beginning of the period.

Statement of cash flows

111 Cash flow information provides users of financial statements with a basis to assess the ability of the entity to generate cash and cash equivalents and the needs of the entity to utilise those cash flows. AASB 107 sets out requirements for the presentation and disclosure of cash flow information.

Notes
Structure

112 The notes shall:

(a) present information about the basis of preparation of the financial statements and the specific accounting policies used in accordance with paragraphs 117–124;

(b) disclose the information required by Australian Accounting Standards that is not presented elsewhere in the financial statements; and

(c) provide information that is not presented elsewhere in the financial statements, but is relevant to an understanding of any of them.

113 An entity shall, as far as practicable, present notes in a systematic manner. In determining a systematic manner, the entity shall consider the effect on the understandability and comparability of its financial statements. An entity shall cross-reference each item in the statements of financial position and in the statement(s) of profit or loss and other comprehensive income, and in the statements of changes in equity and of cash flows to any related information in the notes.

114   Examples of systematic ordering or grouping of the notes include:

(a)   giving prominence to the areas of its activities that the entity considers to be most relevant to an understanding of its financial performance and financial position, such as grouping together information about particular operating activities;

(b)   grouping together information about items measured similarly such as assets measured at fair value; or

(c)   following the order of the line items in the statement(s) of profit or loss and other comprehensive income and the statement of financial position, such as:

(i)   statement of compliance with IFRSs (see paragraph 16);

(ii)   significant accounting policies applied (see paragraph 117);

(iii)   supporting information for items presented in the statements of financial position and in the statement(s) of profit or loss and other comprehensive income, and in the statements of changes in equity and of cash flows, in the order in which each statement and each line item is presented; and

(iv)   other disclosures, including:

(1)   contingent liabilities (see AASB 137) and unrecognised contractual commitments; and

(2)   non-financial disclosures, eg the entity's financial risk management objectives and policies (see AASB 7).

115   [Deleted]

116   An entity may present notes providing information about the basis of preparation of the financial statements and specific accounting policies as a separate section of the financial statements.

Disclosure of accounting policies

117   An entity shall disclose its significant accounting policies comprising:

(a)   the measurement basis (or bases) used in preparing the financial statements; and

(b)   the other accounting policies used that are relevant to an understanding of the financial statements.

118   It is important for an entity to inform users of the measurement basis or bases used in the financial statements (for example, historical cost, current cost, net realisable value, fair value or recoverable amount) because the basis on which an entity prepares the financial statements significantly affects users' analysis. When an entity uses more than one measurement basis in the financial statements, for example when particular classes of assets are revalued, it is sufficient to provide an indication of the categories of assets and liabilities to which each measurement basis is applied.

119   In deciding whether a particular accounting policy should be disclosed, management considers whether disclosure would assist users in understanding how transactions, other events and conditions are reflected in reported financial performance and financial position. Each entity considers the nature of its operations and the policies that the users of its financial statements would expect to be disclosed for that type of entity. Disclosure of particular accounting policies is especially useful to users when those policies are selected from alternatives allowed in Australian Accounting Standards. An example is disclosure of whether an entity applies the fair value or cost model to its investment property (see AASB 140 *Investment Property*). Some Australian Accounting Standards specifically require disclosure of particular accounting policies, including choices made by management between different policies they allow. For example, AASB 116 requires disclosure of the measurement bases used for classes of property, plant and equipment.

120   [Deleted]

121   An accounting policy may be significant because of the nature of the entity's operations even if amounts for current and prior periods are not material. It is also appropriate to disclose each significant accounting policy that is not specifically required by Australian Accounting Standards but the entity selects and applies in accordance with AASB 108.

122   An entity shall disclose, along with its significant accounting policies or other notes, the judgements, apart from those involving estimations (see paragraph 125), that management has made in the process of applying the entity's accounting policies and that have the most significant effect on the amounts recognised in the financial statements.

123   In the process of applying the entity's accounting policies, management makes various judgements, apart from those involving estimations, that can significantly affect the amounts it recognises in the financial statements. For example, management makes judgements in determining:

(a)   [deleted]

(b)   when substantially all the significant risks and rewards of ownership of financial assets and lease assets are transferred to other entities;

(c)   whether, in substance, particular sales of goods are financing arrangements and therefore do not give rise to revenue; and

(d)   whether the contractual terms of a financial asset give rise on specified dates to cash flows that are solely payments of principal and interest on the principal amount outstanding.

124   Some of the disclosures made in accordance with paragraph 122 are required by other Australian Accounting Standards. For example, AASB 12 *Disclosure of Interests in Other Entities* requires an entity to disclose the judgements it has made in determining whether it controls another entity. AASB 140 *Investment Property* requires disclosure of the criteria developed by the entity to distinguish investment property from owner-occupied property and from property held for sale in the ordinary course of business, when classification of the property is difficult.

Sources of estimation uncertainty

125   An entity shall disclose information about the assumptions it makes about the future, and other major sources of estimation uncertainty at the end of the reporting period, that have a significant risk of resulting in a material adjustment to the carrying amounts of assets and liabilities within the next financial year. In respect of those assets and liabilities, the notes shall include details of:

(a)   their nature, and

(b)   their carrying amount as at the end of the reporting period.

126   Determining the carrying amounts of some assets and liabilities requires estimation of the effects of uncertain future events on those assets and liabilities at the end of the reporting period. For example, in the absence of recently observed market prices, future-oriented estimates are necessary to measure the recoverable amount of classes of property, plant and equipment, the effect of technological obsolescence on inventories, provisions subject to the future outcome of litigation in progress, and long-term employee benefit liabilities such as pension obligations. These estimates involve assumptions about such items as the risk adjustment to cash flows or discount rates, future changes in salaries and future changes in prices affecting other costs.

127   The assumptions and other sources of estimation uncertainty disclosed in accordance with paragraph 125 relate to the estimates that require management's most difficult, subjective or complex judgements. As the number of variables and assumptions affecting the possible future resolution of the uncertainties increases, those judgements become more subjective and complex, and the potential for a consequential material adjustment to the carrying amounts of assets and liabilities normally increases accordingly.

128   The disclosures in paragraph 125 are not required for assets and liabilities with a significant risk that their carrying amounts might change materially within the next financial year if, at the end of the reporting period, they are measured at fair value based on a quoted price in an active market for an identical asset or liability. Such fair values might change materially within the next financial year but these changes would not arise from assumptions or other sources of estimation uncertainty at the end of the reporting period.

129   An entity presents the disclosures in paragraph 125 in a manner that helps users of financial statements to understand the judgements that management makes about the future and about other sources of estimation uncertainty. The nature and extent of the information provided vary according to the nature of the assumption and other circumstances. Examples of the types of disclosures an entity makes are:

    (a)   the nature of the assumption or other estimation uncertainty;

    (b)   the sensitivity of carrying amounts to the methods, assumptions and estimates underlying their calculation, including the reasons for the sensitivity;

    (c)   the expected resolution of an uncertainty and the range of reasonably possible outcomes within the next financial year in respect of the carrying amounts of the assets and liabilities affected; and

    (d)   an explanation of changes made to past assumptions concerning those assets and liabilities, if the uncertainty remains unresolved.

130   This Standard does not require an entity to disclose budget information or forecasts in making the disclosures in paragraph 125.

131   Sometimes it is impracticable to disclose the extent of the possible effects of an assumption or another source of estimation uncertainty at the end of the reporting period. In such cases, the entity discloses that it is reasonably possible, on the basis of existing knowledge, that outcomes within the next financial year that are different from the assumption could require a material adjustment to the carrying amount of the asset or liability affected. In all cases, the entity discloses the nature and carrying amount of the specific asset or liability (or class of assets or liabilities) affected by the assumption.

132   The disclosures in paragraph 122 of particular judgements that management made in the process of applying the entity's accounting policies do not relate to the disclosures of sources of estimation uncertainty in paragraph 125.

133   Other Australian Accounting Standards require the disclosure of some of the assumptions that would otherwise be required in accordance with paragraph 125. For example, AASB 137 requires disclosure, in specified circumstances, of major assumptions concerning future events affecting classes of provisions. AASB 13 *Fair Value Measurement* requires disclosure of significant assumptions (including the valuation technique(s) and inputs) the entity uses when measuring the fair values of assets and liabilities that are carried at fair value.

Capital

134   An entity shall disclose information that enables users of its financial statements to evaluate the entity's objectives, policies and processes for managing capital.

135   To comply with paragraph 134, the entity discloses the following:

    (a)   qualitative information about its objectives, policies and processes for managing capital, including:

        (i)   a description of what it manages as capital;

        (ii)   when an entity is subject to externally imposed capital requirements, the nature of those requirements and how those requirements are incorporated into the management of capital; and

        (iii)   how it is meeting its objectives for managing capital.

    (b)   summary quantitative data about what it manages as capital. Some entities regard some financial liabilities (eg some forms of subordinated debt) as part of capital. Other entities regard capital as excluding some components of equity (eg components arising from cash flow hedges).

    (c)   any changes in (a) and (b) from the previous period.

    (d)   whether during the period it complied with any externally imposed capital requirements to which it is subject.

    (e)   when the entity has not complied with such externally imposed capital requirements, the consequences of such non-compliance.

The entity bases these disclosures on the information provided internally to key management personnel.

136   An entity may manage capital in a number of ways and be subject to a number of different capital requirements. For example, a conglomerate may include entities that undertake insurance activities and banking activities and those entities may operate in several jurisdictions. When an aggregate disclosure of capital requirements and how capital is managed would not provide useful information or distorts a financial statement user' understanding of an entity's capital resources, the entity shall disclose separate information for each capital requirement to which the entity is subject.

Aus136.1   An entity that is required to prepare financial reports in accordance with Part 2M.3 of the Corporations Act and that is not a reporting entity need not present the disclosures required by paragraphs 134–136.

Aus136.2   Notwithstanding paragraph Aus136.1, a not-for-profit entity need not present the disclosures required by paragraphs 134–136.

Puttable financial instruments classified as equity

136A For puttable financial instruments classified as equity instruments, an entity shall disclose (to the extent not disclosed elsewhere):

    (a)   summary quantitative data about the amount classified as equity;

    (b)   its objectives, policies and processes for managing its obligation to repurchase or redeem the instruments when required to do so by the instrument holders, including any changes from the previous period;

    (c)   the expected cash outflow on redemption or repurchase of that class of financial instruments; and

    (d)   information about how the expected cash outflow on redemption or repurchase was determined.

Other disclosures

137 An entity shall disclose in the notes:

    (a)   the amount of dividends proposed or declared before the financial statements were authorised for issue but not recognised as a distribution to owners during the period, and the related amount per share; and

    (b)   the amount of any cumulative preference dividends not recognised.

138 An entity shall disclose the following, if not disclosed elsewhere in information published with the financial statements:

    (a)   the domicile and legal form of the entity, its country of incorporation and the address of its registered office (or principal place of business, if different from the registered office);

    (b)   a description of the nature of the entity's operations and its principal activities;

    (c)   the name of the parent and the ultimate parent of the group; and

    (d)   if it is a limited life entity, information regarding the length of its life.

Transition and effective date

139   An entity shall apply this Standard for annual periods beginning on or after 1 January 2018. Earlier application is permitted for periods beginning after 24 July 2014 but before 1 January 2018. If an entity adopts this Standard for an earlier period, it shall disclose that fact.

139A–139D [Deleted by the AASB]

139E   [Deleted]

139F   [Deleted by the AASB]

139G   [Deleted]

139H–139L [Deleted by the AASB]

139M   [Deleted]

139N   AASB 2014-5 *Amendments to Australian Accounting Standards arising from AASB 15*, issued in December 2014, amended paragraph 34 in the previous version of this Standard. An entity shall apply that amendment when it applies AASB 15.

139O   AASB 2010-7 *Amendments to Australian Accounting Standards arising from AASB 9 (December 2010)* (as amended), AASB 2014-1 *Amendments to Australian Accounting Standards* and AASB 2014-7 *Amendments to Australian Accounting Standards arising from AASB 9 (December 2014)*, amended the previous version of this Standard as follows: amended paragraphs Aus1.8, 7, 68, 71, 82, 93, 95, 96, 106 and 123 and deleted paragraph 139E. Paragraph 139G, added by AASB 2010-7, was deleted by AASB 2014-1. Paragraph 139M, added by AASB 2014-1, was deleted by AASB 2014-7. An entity shall apply those amendments when it applies AASB 9.

139P   AASB 2015-2 *Amendments to Australian Accounting Standards – Disclosure Initiative: Amendments to AASB 101*, issued in January 2015, amended the previous version of this Standard as follows: amended paragraphs Aus1.8, 10, 31, 54–55, 82A, 85, 113–114, 117, 119 and 122, added paragraphs 30A, 55A and 85A–85B and deleted paragraphs 115 and 120. An entity shall apply those amendments for annual periods beginning on or after 1 January 2016. Earlier application is permitted. Entities are not required to disclose the information required by paragraphs 28–30 of AASB 108 in relation to these amendments.

Withdrawal of IAS 1 (revised 2003)

140   [Deleted by the AASB]

Commencement of the legislative instrument

Aus140.1   For legal purposes, this legislative instrument commences on 31 December 2017.

Withdrawal of AASB pronouncements

Aus140.2   This Standard repeals AASB 101 *Presentation of Financial Statements* issued in September 2007. Despite the repeal, after the time this Standard starts to apply under section 334 of the Corporations Act (either generally or in relation to an individual entity), the repealed Standard continues to apply in relation to any period ending before that time as if the repeal had not occurred.

        [Note: When this Standard applies under section 334 of the Corporations Act (either generally or in relation to an individual entity), it supersedes the application of the repealed Standard.]

APPENDIX A

AUSTRALIAN DEFINED TERMS

This appendix is an integral part of AASB 101.

Aus7.1   [Deleted by the AASB]

Aus7.2   **In respect of public sector entities, *local governments, governments* and most, if not all, *government departments* are *reporting entities*:**

reporting entity means an entity in respect of which it is reasonable to expect the existence of users who rely on the entity's general purpose financial statement for information that will be useful to them for making and evaluating decisions about the allocation of resources. A reporting entity can be a single entity or a group comprising a parent and all of its subsidiaries.

government means the Australian Government, the Government of the Australian Capital Territory, New South Wales, the Northern Territory, Queensland, South Australia, Tasmania, Victoria or Western Australia.

government department means a government controlled entity, created pursuant to administrative arrangements or otherwise designated as a government department by the government which controls it.

local government means an entity comprising all entities controlled by a governing body elected or appointed pursuant to a Local Government Act or similar legislation.

APPENDIX B

AUSTRALIAN REDUCED DISCLOSURE REQUIREMENTS

This appendix is an integral part of AASB 101.

AusB1   **The following do not apply to entities preparing general purpose financial statements under Australian Accounting Standards – Reduced Disclosure Requirements:**

    (a)   **paragraphs 10(f), 15, 16, Aus16.3, 40A-40D, 42(b), 61, 65, 80A, 82(aa), 85B, 90, 92, 94, 104, 131, 134–136 and 136A–138; and**

    (b)   **in paragraph 107, the text ", and the related amount of dividends per share".**

Entities applying Australian Accounting Standards – Reduced Disclosure Requirements may elect to comply with some or all of these excluded requirements.

AusB2   The requirements that do not apply to entities preparing general purpose financial statements under Australian Accounting Standards – Reduced Disclosure Requirements are also identified in this Standard by shading of the relevant text.

AusB3   **RDR paragraphs in this Standard apply only to entities preparing general purpose financial statements under Australian Accounting Standards – Reduced Disclosure Requirements.**

RDR15.1   **Financial statements shall present fairly the financial position, financial performance and cash flows of an entity applying Australian Accounting Standards – Reduced Disclosure Requirements. Fair presentation requires the faithful representation of the effects of transactions, other events and conditions in accordance with the definitions and recognition criteria for** assets, liabilities, income and expenses set out in the *Framework*. The application of Australian Accounting Standards – Reduced Disclosure Requirements, with additional disclosure when necessary, is presumed to result in financial statements that achieve a fair presentation.

RDR16.1 Entities applying Australian Accounting Standards – Reduced Disclosure Requirements would not be able to state compliance with IFRSs.

COMPILATION DETAILS

Accounting Standard AASB 101 *Presentation of Financial Statements*

Compilation details are not part of AASB 101.

This compiled Standard applies to annual periods beginning on or after 1 January 2018 but before 1 January 2019 for for-profit entities. It takes into account amendments up to and including 12 December 2017 and was prepared on 20 May 2018 by the staff of the Australian Accounting Standards Board (AASB).

This compilation is not a separate Accounting Standard made by the AASB. Instead, it is a representation of AASB 101 (July 2015) as amended by other Accounting Standards, which are listed in the Table below.

Table of Standards

Standard	Date made	FRL identifier	Commencement date	Effective date (*annual periods ... on or after ...*)	Application, saving or transitional provisions
AASB 101	24 Jul 2015	F2015L01626	31 Dec 2017	(*beginning*) 1 Jan 2018	see (a) below
AASB 16	23 Feb 2016	F2016L00233	31 Dec 2018	(*beginning*) 1 Jan 2019	not compiled*
AASB 1058	9 Dec 2016	F2017L00042	31 Dec 2018	(*beginning*) 1 Jan 2019	not compiled*
AASB 2016-7	9 Dec 2016	F2017L00043	31 Dec 2016	(*beginning*) 1 Jan 2017	see (b) below
AASB 17	19 Jul 2017	F2017L01184	31 Dec 2020	(*beginning*) 1 Jan 2021	not compiled*
AASB 2017-5	12 Dec 2017	F2018L00067	31 Dec 2017	(*beginning*) 1 Jan 2018	see (c) below

* The amendments made by this Standard are not included in this compilation, which presents the principal Standard as applicable to annual periods beginning on or after 1 January 2018 but before 1 January 2019 for for-profit entities.

(a) Entities may elect to apply this Standard to annual periods beginning after 24 July 2014 but before 1 January 2018.

(b) As a result of AASB 2016-7 deferring the effective date of AASB 15 *Revenue from Contracts with Customers* (and its consequential amendments in AASB 2014-5) for not-for-profit entities from 1 January 2018 to 1 January 2019, AASB 101 (2015) applies to not-for-profit entities only to annual reporting periods beginning on or after 1 January 2019, instead of 1 January 2018. However, earlier application is permitted, provided that AASB 15 is also applied.

(c) Entities may elect to apply this Standard to annual periods beginning before 1 January 2018.

Table of amendments

Paragraph affected	How affected	By … [paragraph]
95	amended	AASB 2017-5 [22]
Aus136.1	amended	AASB 2017-5 [23]

DELETED IAS 1 TEXT

Deleted IAS 1 text is not part of AASB 101.

2   **An entity shall apply this Standard in preparing and presenting general purpose financial statements in accordance with International Financial Reporting Standards (IFRSs).**

139A IAS 27 (as amended in 2008) amended paragraph 106. An entity shall apply that amendment for annual periods beginning on or after 1 July 2009. If an entity applies IAS 27 (amended 2008) for an earlier period, the amendment shall be applied for that earlier period. The amendment shall be applied retrospectively.

139B *Puttable Financial Instruments and Obligations Arising on Liquidation* (Amendments to IAS 32 and IAS 1), issued in February 2008, amended paragraph 138 and inserted paragraphs 8A, 80A and 136A. An entity shall apply those amendments for annual periods beginning on or after 1 January 2009. Earlier application is permitted. If an entity applies the amendments for an earlier period, it shall disclose that fact and apply the related amendments to IAS 32, IAS 39, IFRS 7 and IFRIC 2 *Members' Shares in Co-operative Entities and Similar Instruments* at the same time.

139C Paragraphs 68 and 71 were amended by *Improvements to IFRSs* issued in May 2008. An entity shall apply those amendments for annual periods beginning on or after 1 January 2009. Earlier application is permitted. If an entity applies the amendments for an earlier period it shall disclose that fact.

139D Paragraph 69 was amended by *Improvements to IFRSs* issued in April 2009. An entity shall apply that amendment for annual periods beginning on or after 1 January 2010. Earlier application is permitted. If an entity applies the amendment for an earlier period it shall disclose that fact.

139F Paragraphs 106 and 107 were amended and paragraph 106A was added by *Improvements to IFRSs* issued in May 2010. An entity shall apply those amendments for annual periods beginning on or after 1 January 2011. Earlier application is permitted.

139H IFRS 10 and IFRS 12, issued in May 2011, amended paragraphs 4, 119, 123 and 124. An entity shall apply those amendments when it applies IFRS 10 and IFRS 12.

139I IFRS 13, issued in May 2011, amended paragraphs 128 and 133. An entity shall apply those amendments when it applies IFRS 13.

139J *Presentation of Items of Other Comprehensive Income* (Amendments to IAS 1), issued in June 2011, amended paragraphs 7, 10, 82, 85–87, 90, 91, 94, 100 and 115, added paragraphs 10A, 81A, 81B and 82A, and deleted paragraphs 12, 81, 83 and 84. An entity shall apply those amendments for annual periods beginning on or after 1 July 2012. Earlier application is permitted. If an entity applies the amendments for an earlier period it shall disclose that fact.

139K IAS 19 *Employee Benefits* (as amended in June 2011) amended the definition of 'other comprehensive income' in paragraph 7 and paragraph 96. An entity shall apply those amendments when it applies IAS 19 (as amended in June 2011).

AASB

139L *Annual Improvements 2009–2011 Cycle*, issued in May 2012, amended paragraphs 10, 38 and 41, deleted paragraphs 39–40 and added paragraphs 38A–38D and 40A–40D. An entity shall apply that amendment retrospectively in accordance with IAS 8 *Accounting Policies, Changes in Accounting Estimates and Errors* for annual periods beginning on or after 1 January 2013. Earlier application is permitted. If an entity applies that amendment for an earlier period it shall disclose that fact.

140 This Standard supersedes IAS 1 *Presentation of Financial Statements* revised in 2003, as amended in 2005.

AASB 102
Inventories

(Reissued July 2015)

This note is not part of Accounting Standard AASB 102.

The following unincorporated amendments are not included in this Standard.

- AASB 1058 *Income of Not-for-Profit Entities* — Appendix D sets out the amendments to other Australian Accounting Standards that are a consequence of the AASB issuing this Standard. It is applicable from 1 January 2019. Earlier application is permitted, but amendments to AASB 117 apply before 1 January 2019 only if AASB 1058 is also applied to an earlier period. In addition, AASB 1 and AASB 16 amendments are applied to an earlier period only if AASB 16 is also applied to that period.

- AASB 16 *Leases* — Appendix D sets out the amendments to other Standards that are a consequence of the AASB issuing this Standard. It is applicable from 1 January 2019. Earlier application is permitted, but entities must apply AASB 15 *Revenue from Contracts with Customers* before applying this Standard.

- AASB 2016-7 *Amendments to Australian Accounting Standards — Deferral of AASB 15 for Not-for-Profit Entities.* This Standard defers the consequential amendments that were originally set out in AASB 2014-5 *Amendments to Australian Accounting Standards arising from AASB 15,* by restating the effective date of the amendments set out in AASB 2015-8 *Amendments to Australian Accounting Standards* for not-for-profit entities. This Standard defers the application of AASB 15 to 1 January 2019. Earlier application is permitted provided AASB 1058 is also applied to the same period.

Entities early-adopting any amendments with later application dates will need to refer to the amending Standards that have not yet been incorporated into compilations. The abovementioned unincorporated amendments may be located on the AASB website at www.aasb.gov.au or on the Federal Register of Legislation website at www.legislation.gov.au.

AASB

CONTENTS

Australian Accounting Standard AASB 102 *Inventories* is set out in paragraphs 1 – Aus42.4 and Appendices A – B. All the paragraphs have equal authority. Paragraphs in **bold type** state the main principles. AASB 102 is to be read in the context of other Australian Accounting Standards, including AASB 1048 *Interpretation of Standards*, which identifies the Australian Accounting Interpretations, and AASB 1057 *Application of Australian Accounting Standards*. In the absence of explicit guidance, AASB 108 *Accounting Policies, Changes in Accounting Estimates and Errors* provides a basis for selecting and applying accounting policies.

COMPARISON WITH IAS 2

AASB 102 *Inventories* incorporates IAS 2 *Inventories* issued by the International Accounting Standards Board (IASB). Australian-specific paragraphs (which are not included in IAS 2) are identified with the prefix "Aus" or "RDR". Paragraphs that apply only to not-for-profit entities begin by identifying their limited applicability.

Tier 1

For-profit entities complying with AASB 102 also comply with IAS 2.

Not-for-profit entities' compliance with IAS 2 will depend on whether any "Aus" paragraphs that specifically apply to not-for-profit entities provide additional guidance or contain applicable requirements that are inconsistent with IAS 2.

Tier 2

Entities preparing general purpose financial statements under Australian Accounting Standards – Reduced Disclosure Requirements (Tier 2) will not be in compliance with IFRSs.

AASB 1053 *Application of Tiers of Australian Accounting Standards* explains the two tiers of reporting requirements.

ACCOUNTING STANDARD AASB 102

The Australian Accounting Standards Board makes Accounting Standard AASB 102 *Inventories* under section 334 of the Corporations Act 2001.

Kris Peach

Dated 24 July 2015   Chair – AASB

ACCOUNTING STANDARD AASB 102
INVENTORIES

Objective

1   The objective of this Standard is to prescribe the accounting treatment for inventories. A primary issue in accounting for inventories is the amount of cost to be recognised as an asset and carried forward until the related revenues are recognised. This Standard provides guidance on the determination of cost and its subsequent recognition as an expense, including any write-down to net realisable value. It also provides guidance on the cost formulas that are used to assign costs to inventories.

Scope

2   This Standard applies to all inventories, except:

    (a)   [deleted]

    (b)   **financial instruments (see AASB 132 *Financial Instruments: Presentation* and AASB 9 *Financial Instruments*); and**

    (c)   **biological assets related to agricultural activity and agricultural produce at the point of harvest (see AASB 141 *Agriculture*).**

Aus2.1   **Notwithstanding paragraph 2, in respect of not-for-profit entities, this Standard does not apply to work in progress of services to be provided for no or nominal consideration directly in return from the recipients.**

3   This Standard does not apply to the measurement of inventories held by:

    (a)   **producers of agricultural and forest products, agricultural produce after harvest, and minerals and mineral products, to the extent that they are measured at net realisable value in accordance with well-established practices in those industries. When such inventories are measured at net realisable value, changes in that value are recognised in profit or loss in the period of the change.**

    (b)   **commodity broker-traders who measure their inventories at fair value less costs to sell. When such inventories are measured at fair value less costs to sell, changes in fair value less costs to sell are recognised in profit or loss in the period of the change.**

4   The inventories referred to in paragraph 3(a) are measured at net realisable value at certain stages of production. This occurs, for example, when agricultural crops have been harvested or minerals have been extracted and sale is assured under a forward contract or a government guarantee, or when an active market exists and there is a negligible risk of failure to sell. These inventories are excluded from only the measurement requirements of this Standard.

5   Broker-traders are those who buy or sell commodities for others or on their own account. The inventories referred to in paragraph 3(b) are principally acquired with the purpose of selling in the near future and generating a profit from fluctuations in price or broker-traders' margin. When these inventories are measured at fair value less costs to sell, they are excluded from only the measurement requirements of this Standard.

Definitions

6   The following terms are used in this Standard with the meanings specified:

        Inventories are assets:

        (a)   held for sale in the ordinary course of business;

        (b)   in the process of production for such sale; or

        (c)   in the form of materials or supplies to be consumed in the production process or in the rendering of services.

        Net realisable value is the estimated selling price in the ordinary course of business less the estimated costs of completion and the estimated costs necessary to make the sale.

        Fair value is the price that would be received to sell an asset or paid to transfer a liability in an orderly transaction between market participants at the measurement date. (See AASB 13 *Fair Value Measurement*.)

7   Net realisable value refers to the net amount that an entity expects to realise from the sale of inventory in the ordinary course of business. Fair value reflects the price at which an orderly transaction to sell the same inventory in the principal (or most advantageous) market for that inventory would take place between market participants at the measurement date. The former is an entity-specific value; the latter is not. Net realisable value for inventories may not equal fair value less costs to sell.

8   Inventories encompass goods purchased and held for resale including, for example, merchandise purchased by a retailer and held for resale, or land and other property held for resale. Inventories also encompass finished goods produced, or work in progress being produced, by the entity and include materials and supplies awaiting use in the production process. Costs incurred to fulfil a contract with a customer that do not give rise to inventories (or assets within the scope of another Standard) are accounted for in accordance with AASB 15 *Revenue from Contracts with Customers*.

Measurement of inventories

9   Inventories shall be measured at the lower of cost and net realisable value.

Aus9.1   Notwithstanding paragraph 9, each not-for-profit entity shall measure inventories held for distribution at cost, adjusted when applicable for any loss of service potential.

Aus9.2   Not-for-profit entities would need to use judgment in determining the factors relevant to the circumstances in assessing whether there is a loss of service potential for inventories held for distribution. For many inventories held for distribution, a loss of service potential would be identified and measured based on the existence of a current replacement cost that is lower than the original acquisition cost or other subsequent carrying amount. For other inventories held for distribution, a loss of service potential might be identified and measured based on a loss of operating capacity due to obsolescence. Different bases for determining whether there has been a loss of service potential and the measurement of that loss may apply to different inventories held for distribution within the same entity.

Cost of inventories

10   The cost of inventories shall comprise all costs of purchase, costs of conversion and other costs incurred in bringing the inventories to their present location and condition.

Aus10.1   Notwithstanding paragraph 10, in respect of not-for-profit entities, where inventories are acquired at no cost, or for nominal consideration, the cost shall be the current replacement cost as at the date of acquisition.

Costs of purchase

11 The costs of purchase of inventories comprise the purchase price, import duties and other taxes (other than those subsequently recoverable by the entity from the taxing authorities), and transport, handling and other costs directly attributable to the acquisition of finished goods, materials and services. Trade discounts, rebates and other similar items are deducted in determining the costs of purchase.

Costs of conversion

12 The costs of conversion of inventories include costs directly related to the units of production, such as direct labour. They also include a systematic allocation of fixed and variable production overheads that are incurred in converting materials into finished goods. Fixed production overheads are those indirect costs of production that remain relatively constant regardless of the volume of production, such as depreciation and maintenance of factory buildings and equipment, and the cost of factory management and administration. Variable production overheads are those indirect costs of production that vary directly, or nearly directly, with the volume of production, such as indirect materials and indirect labour.

13 The allocation of fixed production overheads to the costs of conversion is based on the normal capacity of the production facilities. Normal capacity is the production expected to be achieved on average over a number of periods or seasons under normal circumstances, taking into account the loss of capacity resulting from planned maintenance. The actual level of production may be used if it approximates normal capacity. The amount of fixed overhead allocated to each unit of production is not increased as a consequence of low production or idle plant. Unallocated overheads are recognised as an expense in the period in which they are incurred. In periods of abnormally high production, the amount of fixed overhead allocated to each unit of production is decreased so that inventories are not measured above cost. Variable production overheads are allocated to each unit of production on the basis of the actual use of the production facilities.

14 A production process may result in more than one product being produced simultaneously. This is the case, for example, when joint products are produced or when there is a main product and a by-product. When the costs of conversion of each product are not separately identifiable, they are allocated between the products on a rational and consistent basis. The allocation may be based, for example, on the relative sales value of each product either at the stage in the production process when the products become separately identifiable, or at the completion of production. Most by-products, by their nature, are immaterial. When this is the case, they are often measured at net realisable value and this value is deducted from the cost of the main product. As a result, the carrying amount of the main product is not materially different from its cost.

Other costs

15 Other costs are included in the cost of inventories only to the extent that they are incurred in bringing the inventories to their present location and condition. For example, it may be appropriate to include non-production overheads or the costs of designing products for specific customers in the cost of inventories.

16 Examples of costs excluded from the cost of inventories and recognised as expenses in the period in which they are incurred are:

(a) abnormal amounts of wasted materials, labour or other production costs;

(b) storage costs, unless those costs are necessary in the production process before a further production stage;

(c) administrative overheads that do not contribute to bringing inventories to their present location and condition; and

(d) selling costs.

17   AASB 123 *Borrowing Costs* identifies limited circumstances where borrowing costs are included in the cost of inventories.

18   An entity may purchase inventories on deferred settlement terms. When the arrangement effectively contains a financing element, that element, for example a difference between the purchase price for normal credit terms and the amount paid, is recognised as interest expense over the period of the financing.

Cost of inventories of a service provider

19   [Deleted]

Cost of agricultural produce harvested from biological assets

20   In accordance with AASB 141 *Agriculture* inventories comprising agricultural produce that an entity has harvested from its biological assets are measured on initial recognition at their fair value less costs to sell at the point of harvest. This is the cost of the inventories at that date for application of this Standard.

Techniques for the measurement of cost

21   Techniques for the measurement of the cost of inventories, such as the standard cost method or the retail method, may be used for convenience if the results approximate cost. Standard costs take into account normal levels of materials and supplies, labour, efficiency and capacity utilisation. They are regularly reviewed and, if necessary, revised in the light of current conditions.

22   The retail method is often used in the retail industry for measuring inventories of large numbers of rapidly changing items with similar margins for which it is impracticable to use other costing methods. The cost of the inventory is determined by reducing the sales value of the inventory by the appropriate percentage gross margin. The percentage used takes into consideration inventory that has been marked down to below its original selling price. An average percentage for each retail department is often used.

Cost formulas

23   **The cost of inventories of items that are not ordinarily interchangeable and goods or services produced and segregated for specific projects shall be assigned by using specific identification of their individual costs.**

24   Specific identification of cost means that specific costs are attributed to identified items of inventory. This is the appropriate treatment for items that are segregated for a specific project, regardless of whether they have been bought or produced. However, specific identification of costs is inappropriate when there are large numbers of items of inventory that are ordinarily interchangeable. In such circumstances, the method of selecting those items that remain in inventories could be used to obtain predetermined effects on profit or loss.

25   **The cost of inventories, other than those dealt with in paragraph 23, shall be assigned by using the first-in, first-out (FIFO) or weighted average cost formula. An entity shall use the same cost formula for all inventories having a similar nature and use to the entity. For inventories with a different nature or use, different cost formulas may be justified.**

26   For example, inventories used in one operating segment may have a use to the entity different from the same type of inventories used in another operating segment. However, a difference in geographical location of inventories (or in the respective tax rules), by itself, is not sufficient to justify the use of different cost formulas.

27   The FIFO formula assumes that the items of inventory that were purchased or produced first are sold first, and consequently the items remaining in inventory at the end of the period are those most recently purchased or produced. Under the weighted average cost formula, the cost of each item is determined from the weighted average of the cost of similar items at the beginning of a period and the cost of similar items purchased or

produced during the period. The average may be calculated on a periodic basis, or as each additional shipment is received, depending upon the circumstances of the entity.

Net realisable value

28   The cost of inventories may not be recoverable if those inventories are damaged, if they have become wholly or partially obsolete, or if their selling prices have declined. The cost of inventories may also not be recoverable if the estimated costs of completion or the estimated costs to be incurred to make the sale have increased. The practice of writing inventories down below cost to net realisable value is consistent with the view that assets should not be carried in excess of amounts expected to be realised from their sale or use.

29   Inventories are usually written down to net realisable value item by item. In some circumstances, however, it may be appropriate to group similar or related items. This may be the case with items of inventory relating to the same product line that have similar purposes or end uses, are produced and marketed in the same geographical area, and cannot be practicably evaluated separately from other items in that product line. It is not appropriate to write inventories down on the basis of a classification of inventory, for example, finished goods, or all the inventories in a particular operating segment.

30   Estimates of net realisable value are based on the most reliable evidence available at the time the estimates are made, of the amount the inventories are expected to realise. These estimates take into consideration fluctuations of price or cost directly relating to events occurring after the end of the period to the extent that such events confirm conditions existing at the end of the period.

31   Estimates of net realisable value also take into consideration the purpose for which the inventory is held. For example, the net realisable value of the quantity of inventory held to satisfy firm sales or service contracts is based on the contract price. If the sales contracts are for less than the inventory quantities held, the net realisable value of the excess is based on general selling prices. Provisions may arise from firm sales contracts in excess of inventory quantities held or from firm purchase contracts. Such provisions are dealt with under AASB 137 *Provisions, Contingent Liabilities and Contingent Assets*.

32   Materials and other supplies held for use in the production of inventories are not written down below cost if the finished products in which they will be incorporated are expected to be sold at or above cost. However, when a decline in the price of materials indicates that the cost of the finished products exceeds net realisable value, the materials are written down to net realisable value. In such circumstances, the replacement cost of the materials may be the best available measure of their net realisable value.

33   A new assessment is made of net realisable value in each subsequent period. When the circumstances that previously caused inventories to be written down below cost no longer exist or when there is clear evidence of an increase in net realisable value because of changed economic circumstances, the amount of the write-down is reversed (ie the reversal is limited to the amount of the original write-down) so that the new carrying amount is the lower of the cost and the revised net realisable value. This occurs, for example, when an item of inventory that is carried at net realisable value, because its selling price has declined, is still on hand in a subsequent period and its selling price has increased.

Recognition as an expense

34   **When inventories are sold, the carrying amount of those inventories shall be recognised as an expense in the period in which the related revenue is recognised. The amount of any write-down of inventories to net realisable value and all losses of inventories shall be recognised as an expense in the period the write-down or loss occurs. The amount of any reversal of any write-down of inventories, arising**

from an increase in net realisable value, shall be recognised as a reduction in the amount of inventories recognised as an expense in the period in which the reversal occurs.

Aus34.1   When inventories held for distribution by a not-for-profit entity are distributed, the carrying amount of those inventories shall be recognised as an expense. The amount of any write-down of inventories for loss of service potential and all losses of inventories shall be recognised as an expense in the period in which the write-down or loss occurs. The amount of any reversal of any write-down of inventories arising from a reversal of the circumstances that gave rise to the loss of service potential shall be recognised as a reduction in the amount of inventories recognised as an expense in the period in which the reversal occurs.

35   Some inventories may be allocated to other asset accounts, for example, inventory used as a component of self-constructed property, plant or equipment. Inventories allocated to another asset in this way are recognised as an expense during the useful life of that asset.

Disclosure

36   The financial statements shall disclose:

    (a)   the accounting policies adopted in measuring inventories, including the cost formula used;

    (b)   the total carrying amount of inventories and the carrying amount in classifications appropriate to the entity;

    (c)   the carrying amount of inventories carried at fair value less costs to sell;

    (d)   the amount of inventories recognised as an expense during the period;

    (e)   the amount of any write-down of inventories recognised as an expense in the period in accordance with paragraph 34;

    (f)   the amount of any reversal of any write-down that is recognised as a reduction in the amount of inventories recognised as expense in the period in accordance with paragraph 34;

    (g)   the circumstances or events that led to the reversal of a write-down of inventories in accordance with paragraph 34; and

    (h)   the carrying amount of inventories pledged as security for liabilities.

Aus36.1   Notwithstanding paragraph 36, in respect of not-for-profit entities, the financial statements shall disclose:

    (a)   the accounting policies adopted in measuring inventories held for distribution, including the cost formula used;

    (b)   the total carrying amount of inventories held for distribution and the carrying amount in classifications appropriate to the entity;

    (c)   the amount of inventories held for distribution recognised as an expense during the period in accordance with paragraph Aus34.1;

    (d)   the amount of any write-down of inventories held for distribution recognised as an expense in the period in accordance with paragraph Aus34.1;

    (e)   the amount of any reversal of any write-down that is recognised as a reduction in the amount of inventories held for distribution recognised as expense in the period in accordance with paragraph Aus34.1;

    (f)   the circumstances or events that led to the reversal of a write-down of inventories held for distribution in accordance with paragraph Aus34.1;

(g)   the carrying amount of inventories held for distribution pledged as
        security for liabilities; and

(h)   the basis on which any loss of service potential of inventories held
        for distribution is assessed, or the bases when more than one basis is
        used.

37   Information about the carrying amounts held in different classifications of inventories
      and the extent of the changes in these assets is useful to financial statement
      users. Common classifications of inventories are merchandise, production supplies,
      materials, work in progress and finished goods.

38   The amount of inventories recognised as an expense during the period, which
      is often referred to as cost of sales, consists of those costs previously included
      in the measurement of inventory that has now been sold and unallocated
      production overheads and abnormal amounts of production costs of inventories. The
      circumstances of the entity may also warrant the inclusion of other amounts, such as
      distribution costs.

39   Some entities adopt a format for profit or loss that results in amounts being disclosed
      other than the cost of inventories recognised as an expense during the period. Under
      this format, an entity presents an analysis of expenses using a classification based on
      the nature of expenses. In this case, the entity discloses the costs recognised as an
      expense for raw materials and consumables, labour costs and other costs together with
      the amount of the net change in inventories for the period.

Effective date

40   An entity shall apply this Standard for annual periods beginning on or after 1 January
      2018. Earlier application is encouraged for periods beginning after 24 July 2014 but
      before 1 January 2018. If an entity applies this Standard for a period beginning before
      1 January 2018, it shall disclose that fact.

40A   [Deleted]

40B   [Deleted]

40C   [Deleted by the AASB]

40D   [Deleted]

40E   AASB 2014-5 *Amendments to Australian Accounting Standards arising from AASB 15*,
      issued in December 2014, amended the previous version of this Standard as follows:
      amended paragraphs 2, 8, 29 and 37 and deleted paragraph 19. An entity shall apply
      those amendments when it applies AASB 15.

40F   AASB 2010-7 *Amendments to Australian Accounting Standards arising from AASB
      9 (December 2010)* (as amended) amended the previous version of this Standard as
      follows: amended paragraph 2(b) and deleted paragraph 40A. Paragraph 40B, added by
      AASB 2010-7, was deleted by AASB 2014-1 *Amendments to Australian Accounting
      Standards*. Paragraph 40D, added by AASB 2014-1 was deleted by AASB 2014-7
      *Amendments to Australian Accounting Standards arising from AASB 9 (December
      2014)*. An entity shall apply those amendments when it applies AASB 9.

Withdrawal of other pronouncements

41–42 [Deleted by the AASB]

Transition

Aus42.1   **Not-for-profit entities shall apply paragraph Aus9.1 and measure
          inventories held for distribution at cost, adjusted when applicable for any
          loss of service potential, on a prospective basis from the beginning of the
          annual period to which this Standard is first applied.**

Aus42.2   Under paragraph Aus42.1, not-for-profit entities shall make any necessary adjustment to the opening balance of inventories held for distribution, previously carried at the lower of cost and current replacement cost, against opening retained earnings for the current annual period. Accordingly, comparative information is not adjusted.

Commencement of the legislative instrument

Aus42.3   For legal purposes, this legislative instrument commences on 31 December 2017.

Withdrawal of AASB pronouncements

Aus42.4   This Standard repeals AASB 102 *Inventories* issued in July 2004. Despite the repeal, after the time this Standard starts to apply under section 334 of the Corporations Act (either generally or in relation to an individual entity), the repealed Standard continues to apply in relation to any period ending before that time as if the repeal had not occurred.

[Note: When this Standard applies under section 334 of the Corporations Act (either generally or in relation to an individual entity), it supersedes the application of the repealed Standard.]

APPENDIX A
AUSTRALIAN DEFINED TERMS

This appendix is an integral part of AASB 102.

Aus6.1   **The following terms are also used in this Standard with the meanings specified.**

A *not-for-profit entity* is an entity whose principal objective is not the generation of profit. A not-for-profit entity can be a single entity or a group of entities comprising the parent entity and each of the entities that it controls.

In respect of not-for-profit entities, *current replacement cost* is the cost the entity would incur to acquire the asset at the end of the reporting period.

In respect of not-for-profit entities, *inventories held for distribution* are assets:

(a)   held for distribution at no or nominal consideration in the ordinary course of operations;

(b)   in the process of production for distribution at no or nominal consideration in the ordinary course of operations; or

(c)   in the form of materials or supplies to be consumed in the production process or in the rendering of services at no or nominal consideration.[1]

Aus8.1   A not-for-profit entity may hold inventories whose future economic benefits or service potential are not directly related to their ability to generate net cash inflows. These types of inventories may arise when an entity has determined to distribute certain goods at no charge or for a nominal amount. In these cases, the future economic benefits or service potential of the inventory for financial reporting purposes is reflected by the amount the entity would need to pay

---

1   Paragraphs 10–18 and 20–27 in this Standard apply to both inventories (as defined in paragraph 6) and inventories held for distribution (as defined in paragraph Aus6.1).

to acquire the economic benefits or service potential if this was necessary to achieve the objectives of the entity. Where the economic benefits or service potential cannot be acquired in the market, an estimate of replacement cost will need to be made. If the purpose for which the inventory is held changes, then the inventory is valued using the provisions of paragraph 9.

Aus8.2 The replacement cost that an entity would be prepared to incur in respect of an item of inventory would reflect any obsolescence or any other impairment.

APPENDIX B
AUSTRALIAN REDUCED DISCLOSURE REQUIREMENTS

This appendix is an integral part of AASB 102.

AusB1 **Paragraphs 36(c), 36(g) and Aus36.1(f) of this Standard do not apply to entities preparing general purpose financial statements under Australian Accounting Standards – Reduced Disclosure Requirements. Entities applying Australian Accounting Standards – Reduced Disclosure Requirements may elect to comply with some or all of these excluded requirements.**

AusB2 The requirements that do not apply to entities preparing general purpose financial statements under Australian Accounting Standards – Reduced Disclosure Requirements are also identified in this Standard by shading of the relevant text.

DELETED IAS 2 TEXT

Deleted IAS 2 text is not part of AASB 102.

40C IFRS 13, issued in May 2011, amended the definition of fair value in paragraph 6 and amended paragraph 7. An entity shall apply those amendments when it applies IFRS 13.

41 This Standard supersedes IAS 2 *Inventories* (revised in 1993).

42 This Standard supersedes SIC-1 *Consistency—Different Cost Formulas for Inventories.*

BASIS FOR CONCLUSIONS ON AASB 2007-5

This Basis for Conclusions accompanies, but is not part of, AASB 102. The Basis for Conclusions was originally published with AASB 2007-5 Amendments to Australian Accounting Standard – Inventories Held for Distribution by Not-for-Profit Entities.

Background relating to standards on inventories

BC1 For reporting periods beginning prior to 1 January 2005, under AASB 1019 *Inventories* (now superseded by AASB 102 *Inventories*), inventories were defined only in terms of items held for sale or in the process of sale. The treatment of items in the nature of inventories that were not held for sale needed to be determined by analogy because they were not explicitly covered by AASB 1019.

BC2 Inventories held for distribution by not-for-profit entities were scoped into AASB 102, issued in July 2004, and were required to be measured at the lower of cost and current replacement cost.

BC3 This is the same as the requirement in the International Public Sector Accounting Standards Board's IPSAS 12 *Inventories* issued in July 2001. (IPSAS 12 has since been revised in December 2006 for application from 1 January 2008.)

BC4 The Board notes that inventories held for distribution do not include major spare parts and stand-by equipment that qualify as property, plant and equipment, which are discussed in AASB 116 *Property, Plant and Equipment* at paragraphs 8 and 12.

Background relating to key issue

BC5 A number of constituents raised issues with the Board relating to the conceptual soundness of applying the lower of cost and current replacement cost treatment to inventories held for distribution as well as the practicality of its application to certain types of inventories held for distribution.

BC6 The Board considered the view that writing down inventory held for distribution when its current replacement cost falls below cost may result in the recognition of impairments when the service potential to the entity of those inventories remains unchanged. In addition, the Board noted that the service potential to the entity of inventories held for distribution may fall, but that current replacement cost to the entity may remain higher than the original cost. The Board concluded that this is in part because the lower of cost and current replacement cost requirement focuses on financial values, whereas the service potential of inventories held for distribution by many not-for-profit entities is considered in physical terms.

BC7 The Board also considered the practical problem that current replacement costs are sometimes not readily available for many of the inventories held for distribution that have long lives because they have not been replenished for long periods. In some cases, such inventories may have maintained their service potential, but may no longer be available in the form held by the entity.

BC8 The Board noted that a for-profit entity will readily know its costs and its net realisable values, because most businesses buy and sell inventories regularly. In a not-for-profit entity that holds inventories for distribution and buys and distributes them regularly, the lower of cost and current replacement cost requirement has been viewed as the nearest available equivalent requirement.

BC9 The Board noted that the practical problems emerge when the inventories held for distribution are retained over the long term and replacement costs are not readily available. A major part of the burden is the possible need to maintain records of three prices for each type of inventory: (1) the cost; (2) the up-to-date replacement cost in case there is a need for write down; and (3) in the event that the replacement cost has previously fallen below cost, that replacement cost [carrying amount]. The Board also noted that the records of the three prices might also need to be maintained to facilitate the reversal of write downs in the event that the circumstances that previously caused inventories to be written down below cost no longer exist or when there is clear evidence of an increase in current replacement cost because of changed economic circumstances.

Alternative solutions

BC10 The Board considered developing a proposed solution only in respect of long-lived inventories held for distribution by not-for-profit entities in order to address the practical problems raised by constituents. However, the Board concluded that it would be more appropriate to develop a solution for all types of inventories held for distribution by not-for-profit entities that addresses the issues at both the principle and practical levels. This is because the Board prefers a solution based on a high-level principle that can be applied consistently by all not-for-profit entities in a manner that best suits the character of their inventories held for distribution.

BC11 Among the possible solutions considered by the Board was applying an AASB 136 *Impairment of Assets*-style impairment test, however, it was noted that this would have many of the problems already associated with the existing requirements.

Cost adjusted when applicable for any loss of service potential

BC12 The Board noted that the lower of cost and net realisable value requirement in AASB 102 in respect of inventories other than those held for distribution can be viewed as being based on a notion of recognising a loss of service potential in a for-profit environment. That is, an entity that seeks to sell inventories for more than they cost generally considers the service potential of those inventories in financial terms. If net realisable value falls below cost, the entity can be viewed as suffering a loss of service potential.

BC13 The Board observed that the lower of cost and current replacement cost requirement for measuring inventories held for distribution by not-for-profit entities can be viewed as seeking to emulate the approach taken for other inventories and its focus is also on a loss of value in financial terms. However, the Board considered that this financial measure of the loss of service potential may not always be the most relevant measure in respect of inventories held for distribution by not-for-profit entities for the reasons outlined in paragraph BC6.

BC14 The Board considered that the measurement of inventories held for distribution by not-for-profit entities at cost, adjusted when applicable for any loss of service potential, is consistent with the *Framework for the Preparation and Presentation of Financial Statements*, which notes at paragraph Aus49.1: In respect of not-for-profit entities in the public or private sector, in pursuing their objectives, goods and services are provided that have the capacity to satisfy human wants and needs. Assets provide a means for entities to achieve their objectives. Future economic benefits or service potential is the essence of assets. Future economic benefits is synonymous with the notion of service potential, and is used in this Framework as a reference also to service potential. Future economic benefits can be described as the scarce capacity to provide benefits to the entities that use them, and is common to all assets irrespective of their physical or other form.

BC15 The Board noted that a fall in the current replacement cost of inventories held for distribution may at times indicate a loss of service potential, but that this is not necessarily always the case, and that a loss of service potential may at times be identified on other, more relevant, bases. For example, obsolescence, which may occur with or without there being a fall in current replacement cost, may be the main factor leading to a loss of service potential for many not-for-profit entities. The term 'obsolescence' covers both 'technical obsolescence' and 'functional obsolescence'. Technical obsolescence occurs when an item still functions for some or all of the tasks it was originally acquired to do, but no longer matches existing technologies. Functional obsolescence occurs when an item no longer functions the way it did when it was first acquired. In either case, a loss of service potential may need to be recognised.

BC16 The Board also considered that a problem with a purely physical service potential approach is identifying ways in which physical service potential would be measured. However, the Board concluded that many not-for-profit entities will often be more likely to monitor the service potential of their inventories held for distribution than they are to monitor the current replacement costs of those inventories. The Board considered that this is especially likely to be the case when those inventories are important to maintaining its functions or operating capability and, therefore, often in cases when it is most likely to be material to the financial statements.

BC17 The Board considers that there is a need for the circumstances of a not-for-profit entity to be the determining factor behind its manner of assessing any loss of service potential for inventories held for distribution. The measurement requirement for inventories held for distribution would require each not-for-profit entity to identify the basis (or bases) for determining any loss of service potential that best suits the circumstances relating to the entity. Different bases may apply to different inventories held for distribution within the same entity.

BC18 There was considerable support for the approach of requiring inventories held for distribution to be measured at cost, adjusted for any loss of service potential, in the submissions on Exposure Draft ED 154 *Proposed Amendments to AASB 102 – Inventories Held for Distribution by Not-for-Profit Entities*. However, some submissions expressed concerns that the lower of cost and current replacement cost requirement is being applied without difficulty by many entities and argued that it might be unnecessarily disruptive to introduce the change proposed in ED 154.

BC19 The Board noted that a current replacement cost that is lower than cost might be a common way of identifying and measuring a loss of service potential for inventories held for distribution. Accordingly, many entities are likely to continue their existing practices under a revised AASB 102, and the Board concluded few entities would be disrupted by the change.

BC20 The Board concluded that the requirement to measure inventories held for distribution at cost, adjusted when applicable for any loss of service potential, would give rise to more relevant information that better reflects the various accountabilities of not-for-profit entities. In addition, the Board concluded that the requirement is likely to be more appropriate in practical terms than the former requirement in some circumstances.

Transition

BC21 The Board considered that, in some cases, measuring at the lower of cost and current replacement cost versus measuring at cost, adjusted when applicable for any loss of service potential, would give rise to different carrying amounts for inventories held for distribution. The Board concluded that, on transition to the changed requirement, it is appropriate to require not-for-profit entities to adjust any difference prospectively against opening retained earnings and not amend comparative information on the basis that:

(a) there are likely to be practical problems associated with trying to retrospectively determine whether there have been further losses of service potential and precisely when they occurred, which may not be overcome by the impracticability override in AASB 108 *Accounting Policies, Changes in Accounting Estimates and Errors*;

(b) the relatively short period of development involved in amending AASB 102 and, therefore, the absence of a long period during which constituents would be made aware of the changes; and

(c) requiring rather than permitting the prospective transitional approach is desirable from a comparability viewpoint.

AASB 107
Statement of Cash Flows
(Compiled March 2016)

This compiled Standard applies to annual periods beginning on or after 1 January 2017 but before 1 January 2019. Earlier application is permitted for annual periods beginning on or after 1 January 2014 but before 1 January 2017. It incorporates relevant amendments made up to and including 23 March 2016.

Prepared on 20 March 2017 by the staff of the Australian Accounting Standards Board.

Compilation no. 1

Compilation date: 31 December 2016

This note is not part of Accounting Standard AASB 107.

The following unincorporated amendments are not included in this compiled Standard.

- AASB 17 *Insurance Contracts* — Appendix D sets out the amendments to other Standards that are a consequence of the AASB issuing AASB 17 *Insurance Contracts*. This Standard is applicable from 1 January 2021. Earlier application is permitted, but entities must apply AASB 9 *Financial Instruments* and AASB 15 *Revenue from Contracts with Customers* first.

- AASB 16 *Leases* — Appendix D sets out the amendments to other Standards that are a consequence of the AASB issuing this Standard. It is applicable from 1 January 2019. Earlier application is permitted, but entities must apply AASB 15 *Revenue from Contracts with Customers* before applying this Standard.

Entities early-adopting any amendments with later application dates will need to refer to the amending Standards that have not yet been incorporated into compilations. The abovementioned unincorporated amendments may be located on the AASB website at www.aasb.gov.au or on the Federal Register of Legislation website at www.legislation.gov.au.

AASB

CONTENTS

APPENDIX

A. AUSTRALIAN REDUCED DISCLOSURE REQUIREMENTS

ILLUSTRATIVE EXAMPLES

A. STATEMENT OF CASH FLOWS FOR AN ENTITY OTHER THAN A FINANCIAL INSTITUTION

B. STATEMENT OF CASH FLOWS FOR A FINANCIAL INSTITUTION

C. RECONCILIATION OF LIABILITIES ARISING FROM FINANCING ACTIVITIES

COMPILATION DETAILS

DELETED IAS 7 TEXT

BASIS FOR CONCLUSIONS ON IAS 7 (available on the AASB website)

Accounting Standard AASB 107 *Statement of Cash Flows* (as amended) is set out in paragraphs 1 – 60 and Appendix A. All the paragraphs have equal authority. Paragraphs in **bold type** state the main principles. AASB 107 is to be read in the context of other Australian Accounting Standards, including AASB 1048 *Interpretation of Standards*, which identifies the Australian Accounting Interpretations, and AASB 1057 *Application of Australian Accounting Standards*. In the absence of explicit guidance, AASB 108 *Accounting Policies, Changes in Accounting Estimates and Errors* provides a basis for selecting and applying accounting policies.

COMPARISON WITH IAS 7

AASB 107 *Statement of Cash Flows* as amended incorporates IAS 7 *Statement of Cash Flows* as issued and amended by the International Accounting Standards Board (IASB). Australian-specific paragraphs (which are not included in IAS 7) are identified with the prefix "Aus". Paragraphs that apply only to not-for-profit entities begin by identifying their limited applicability.

Tier 1

For-profit entities complying with AASB 107 also comply with IAS 7.

Not-for-profit entities' compliance with IAS 7 will depend on whether any "Aus" paragraphs that specifically apply to not-for-profit entities provide additional guidance or contain applicable requirements that are inconsistent with IAS 7.

Tier 2

Entities preparing general purpose financial statements under Australian Accounting Standards – Reduced Disclosure Requirements (Tier 2) will not be in compliance with IFRSs.

AASB 1053 *Application of Tiers of Australian Accounting Standards* explains the two tiers of reporting requirements.

ACCOUNTING STANDARD AASB 107

The Australian Accounting Standards Board made Accounting Standard AASB 107 *Statement of Cash Flows* under section 334 of the *Corporations Act 2001* on 7 August 2015.

This compiled version of AASB 107 applies to annual periods beginning on or after 1 January 2017 but before 1 January 2019. It incorporates relevant amendments contained in other AASB Standards made by the AASB up to and including 23 March 2016 (see Compilation Details).

ACCOUNTING STANDARD AASB 107
STATEMENT OF CASH FLOWS

Objective

Information about the cash flows of an entity is useful in providing users of financial statements with a basis to assess the ability of the entity to generate cash and cash equivalents and the needs of the entity to utilise those cash flows. The economic decisions that are taken by users require an evaluation of the ability of an entity to generate cash and cash equivalents and the timing and certainty of their generation.

The objective of this Standard is to require the provision of information about the historical changes in cash and cash equivalents of an entity by means of a statement of cash flows which classifies cash flows during the period from operating, investing and financing activities.

Scope

1   **An entity shall prepare a statement of cash flows in accordance with the requirements of this Standard and shall present it as an integral part of its financial statements for each period for which financial statements are presented.**

2   [Deleted by the AASB]

3   Users of an entity's financial statements are interested in how the entity generates and uses cash and cash equivalents. This is the case regardless of the nature of the entity's activities and irrespective of whether cash can be viewed as the product of the entity, as may be the case with a financial institution. Entities need cash for essentially the same reasons however different their principal revenue-producing activities might be. They need cash to conduct their operations, to pay their obligations, and to provide returns to their investors.

Benefits of cash flow information

4   A statement of cash flows, when used in conjunction with the rest of the financial statements, provides information that enables users to evaluate the changes in net assets of an entity, its financial structure (including its liquidity and solvency) and its ability to affect the amounts and timing of cash flows in order to adapt to changing circumstances and opportunities. Cash flow information is useful in assessing the ability of the entity to generate cash and cash equivalents and enables users to develop models to assess and compare the present value of the future cash flows of different entities. It also enhances the comparability of the reporting of operating performance by different entities because it eliminates the effects of using different accounting treatments for the same transactions and events.

5   Historical cash flow information is often used as an indicator of the amount, timing and certainty of future cash flows. It is also useful in checking the accuracy of past assessments of future cash flows and in examining the relationship between profitability and net cash flow and the impact of changing prices.

Definitions

6   **The following terms are used in this Standard with the meanings specified:**

Cash **comprises cash on hand and demand deposits.**

Cash equivalents **are short-term, highly liquid investments that are readily convertible to known amounts of cash and which are subject to an insignificant risk of changes in value.**

Cash flows **are inflows and outflows of cash and cash equivalents.**

Operating activities **are the principal revenue-producing activities of the entity and other activities that are not investing or financing activities.**

Investing activities **are the acquisition and disposal of long-term assets and other investments not included in cash equivalents.**

Financing activities **are activities that result in changes in the size and composition of the contributed equity and borrowings of the entity.**

Cash and cash equivalents

7   Cash equivalents are held for the purpose of meeting short-term cash commitments rather than for investment or other purposes. For an investment to qualify as a cash equivalent it must be readily convertible to a known amount of cash and be subject to an insignificant risk of changes in value. Therefore, an investment normally qualifies as a cash equivalent only when it has a short maturity of, say, three months or less from the date of acquisition. Equity investments are excluded from cash equivalents unless they are, in substance, cash equivalents, for example in the case of preferred shares acquired within a short period of their maturity and with a specified redemption date.

8   Bank borrowings are generally considered to be financing activities. However, in some countries, bank overdrafts which are repayable on demand form an integral part of an entity's cash management. In these circumstances, bank overdrafts are included as a component of cash and cash equivalents. A characteristic of such banking arrangements is that the bank balance often fluctuates from being positive to overdrawn.

9   Cash flows exclude movements between items that constitute cash or cash equivalents because these components are part of the cash management of an entity rather than part of its operating, investing and financing activities. Cash management includes the investment of excess cash in cash equivalents.

Presentation of a statement of cash flows

10   **The statement of cash flows shall report cash flows during the period classified by operating, investing and financing activities.**

11   An entity presents its cash flows from operating, investing and financing activities in a manner which is most appropriate to its business. Classification by activity provides information that allows users to assess the impact of those activities on the financial position of the entity and the amount of its cash and cash equivalents. This information may also be used to evaluate the relationships among those activities.

12   A single transaction may include cash flows that are classified differently. For example, when the cash repayment of a loan includes both interest and capital, the interest element may be classified as an operating activity and the capital element is classified as a financing activity.

Operating activities

13   The amount of cash flows arising from operating activities is a key indicator of the extent to which the operations of the entity have generated sufficient cash flows to repay loans, maintain the operating capability of the entity, pay dividends and make new investments without recourse to external sources of financing. Information about the specific components of historical operating cash flows is useful, in conjunction with other information, in forecasting future operating cash flows.

14   Cash flows from operating activities are primarily derived from the principal revenue-producing activities of the entity. Therefore, they generally result from the transactions and other events that enter into the determination of profit or loss. Examples of cash flows from operating activities are:

(a)   cash receipts from the sale of goods and the rendering of services;

(b)   cash receipts from royalties, fees, commissions and other revenue;

(c)   cash payments to suppliers for goods and services;

(d)   cash payments to and on behalf of employees;

(e)   cash receipts and cash payments of an insurance entity for premiums and claims, annuities and other policy benefits;

(f)   cash payments or refunds of income taxes unless they can be specifically identified with financing and investing activities; and

(g)   cash receipts and payments from contracts held for dealing or trading purposes.

Some transactions, such as the sale of an item of plant, may give rise to a gain or loss that is included in recognised profit or loss. The cash flows relating to such transactions are cash flows from investing activities. However, cash payments to manufacture or acquire assets held for rental to others and subsequently held for sale as described in paragraph 68A of AASB 116 *Property, Plant and Equipment* are cash flows from operating activities. The cash receipts from rents and subsequent sales of such assets are also cash flows from operating activities.

15   An entity may hold securities and loans for dealing or trading purposes, in which case they are similar to inventory acquired specifically for resale. Therefore, cash flows arising from the purchase and sale of dealing or trading securities are classified as operating activities. Similarly, cash advances and loans made by financial institutions are usually classified as operating activities since they relate to the main revenue-producing activity of that entity.

Investing activities

16   The separate disclosure of cash flows arising from investing activities is important because the cash flows represent the extent to which expenditures have been made for resources intended to generate future income and cash flows. Only expenditures that result in a recognised asset in the statement of financial position are eligible for classification as investing activities. Examples of cash flows arising from investing activities are:

(a)   cash payments to acquire property, plant and equipment, intangibles and other long-term assets. These payments include those relating to capitalised development costs and self-constructed property, plant and equipment;

(b)   cash receipts from sales of property, plant and equipment, intangibles and other long-term assets;

(c)   cash payments to acquire equity or debt instruments of other entities and interests in joint ventures (other than payments for those instruments considered to be cash equivalents or those held for dealing or trading purposes);

(d)   cash receipts from sales of equity or debt instruments of other entities and interests in joint ventures (other than receipts for those instruments considered to be cash equivalents and those held for dealing or trading purposes);

(e)   cash advances and loans made to other parties (other than advances and loans made by a financial institution);

(f)   cash receipts from the repayment of advances and loans made to other parties (other than advances and loans of a financial institution);

(g)   cash payments for futures contracts, forward contracts, option contracts and swap contracts except when the contracts are held for dealing or trading purposes, or the payments are classified as financing activities; and

(h)   cash receipts from futures contracts, forward contracts, option contracts and swap contracts except when the contracts are held for dealing or trading purposes, or the receipts are classified as financing activities.

When a contract is accounted for as a hedge of an identifiable position the cash flows of the contract are classified in the same manner as the cash flows of the position being hedged.

Financing activities

17   The separate disclosure of cash flows arising from financing activities is important because it is useful in predicting claims on future cash flows by providers of capital to the entity. Examples of cash flows arising from financing activities are:

(a)   cash proceeds from issuing shares or other equity instruments;

(b)   cash payments to owners to acquire or redeem the entity's shares;

(c)   cash proceeds from issuing debentures, loans, notes, bonds, mortgages and other short-term or long-term borrowings;

(d)   cash repayments of amounts borrowed; and

(e)   cash payments by a lessee for the reduction of the outstanding liability relating to a finance lease.

Reporting cash flows from operating activities

18   **An entity shall report cash flows from operating activities using either:**

(a)   **the direct method, whereby major classes of gross cash receipts and gross cash payments are disclosed; or**

(b)   **the indirect method, whereby profit or loss is adjusted for the effects of transactions of a non-cash nature, any deferrals or accruals of past or future operating cash receipts or payments, and items of income or expense associated with investing or financing cash flows.**

19   Entities are encouraged to report cash flows from operating activities using the direct method. The direct method provides information which may be useful in estimating future cash flows and which is not available under the indirect method. Under the direct method, information about major classes of gross cash receipts and gross cash payments may be obtained either:

(a)   from the accounting records of the entity; or

(b)   by adjusting sales, cost of sales (interest and similar income and interest expense and similar charges for a financial institution) and other items in the statement of comprehensive income for:

(i)   changes during the period in inventories and operating receivables and payables;

(ii)   other non-cash items; and

(iii)   other items for which the cash effects are investing or financing cash flows.

20   Under the indirect method, the net cash flow from operating activities is determined by adjusting profit or loss for the effects of:

(a) changes during the period in inventories and operating receivables and payables;

(b) non-cash items such as depreciation, provisions, deferred taxes, unrealised foreign currency gains and losses, and undistributed profits of associates; and

(c) all other items for which the cash effects are investing or financing cash flows.

Alternatively, the net cash flow from operating activities may be presented under the indirect method by showing the revenues and expenses disclosed in the statement of comprehensive income and the changes during the period in inventories and operating receivables and payables.

Aus20.1 [Deleted by the AASB]

Aus20.2 Not-for-profit entities that use the direct method and that highlight the net cost of services in their statement of comprehensive income for the reporting period shall disclose in the complete set of financial statements a reconciliation of cash flows arising from operating activities to net cost of services as reported in the statement of comprehensive income.

Reporting cash flows from investing and financing activities

21 **An entity shall report separately major classes of gross cash receipts and gross cash payments arising from investing and financing activities, except to the extent that cash flows described in paragraphs 22 and 24 are reported on a net basis.**

Reporting cash flows on a net basis

22 **Cash flows arising from the following operating, investing or financing activities may be reported on a net basis:**

(a) **cash receipts and payments on behalf of customers when the cash flows reflect the activities of the customer rather than those of the entity; and**

(b) **cash receipts and payments for items in which the turnover is quick, the amounts are large, and the maturities are short.**

23 Examples of cash receipts and payments referred to in paragraph 22(a) are:

(a) the acceptance and repayment of demand deposits of a bank;

(b) funds held for customers by an investment entity; and

(c) rents collected on behalf of, and paid over to, the owners of properties.

23A Examples of cash receipts and payments referred to in paragraph 22(b) are advances made for, and the repayment of:

(a) principal amounts relating to credit card customers;

(b) the purchase and sale of investments; and

(c) other short-term borrowings, for example, those which have a maturity period of three months or less.

24 **Cash flows arising from each of the following activities of a financial institution may be reported on a net basis:**

(a) **cash receipts and payments for the acceptance and repayment of deposits with a fixed maturity date;**

(b) **the placement of deposits with and withdrawal of deposits from other financial institutions; and**

(c) **cash advances and loans made to customers and the repayment of those advances and loans.**

AASB

Foreign currency cash flows

25   **Cash flows arising from transactions in a foreign currency shall be recorded in an entity's functional currency by applying to the foreign currency amount the exchange rate between the functional currency and the foreign currency at the date of the cash flow.**

26   **The cash flows of a foreign subsidiary shall be translated at the exchange rates between the functional currency and the foreign currency at the dates of the cash flows.**

27   Cash flows denominated in a foreign currency are reported in a manner consistent with AASB 121 *The Effects of Changes in Foreign Exchange Rates*. This permits the use of an exchange rate that approximates the actual rate. For example, a weighted average exchange rate for a period may be used for recording foreign currency transactions or the translation of the cash flows of a foreign subsidiary. However, AASB 121 does not permit use of the exchange rate at the end of the reporting period when translating the cash flows of a foreign subsidiary.

28   Unrealised gains and losses arising from changes in foreign currency exchange rates are not cash flows. However, the effect of exchange rate changes on cash and cash equivalents held or due in a foreign currency is reported in the statement of cash flows in order to reconcile cash and cash equivalents at the beginning and the end of the period. This amount is presented separately from cash flows from operating, investing and financing activities and includes the differences, if any, had those cash flows been reported at end of period exchange rates.

29   [Deleted]

30   [Deleted]

Interest and dividends

31   **Cash flows from interest and dividends received and paid shall each be disclosed separately. Each shall be classified in a consistent manner from period to period as either operating, investing or financing activities.**

32   The total amount of interest paid during a period is disclosed in the statement of cash flows whether it has been recognised as an expense in profit or loss or capitalised in accordance with AASB 123 *Borrowing Costs*.

33   Interest paid and interest and dividends received are usually classified as operating cash flows for a financial institution. However, there is no consensus on the classification of these cash flows for other entities. Interest paid and interest and dividends received may be classified as operating cash flows because they enter into the determination of profit or loss. Alternatively, interest paid and interest and dividends received may be classified as financing cash flows and investing cash flows respectively, because they are costs of obtaining financial resources or returns on investments.

34   Dividends paid may be classified as a financing cash flow because they are a cost of obtaining financial resources. Alternatively, dividends paid may be classified as a component of cash flows from operating activities in order to assist users to determine the ability of an entity to pay dividends out of operating cash flows.

Taxes on income

35   **Cash flows arising from taxes on income shall be separately disclosed and shall be classified as cash flows from operating activities unless they can be specifically identified with financing and investing activities.**

36   Taxes on income arise on transactions that give rise to cash flows that are classified as operating, investing or financing activities in a statement of cash flows. While tax expense may be readily identifiable with investing or financing activities, the related

tax cash flows are often impracticable to identify and may arise in a different period from the cash flows of the underlying transaction. Therefore, taxes paid are usually classified as cash flows from operating activities. However, when it is practicable to identify the tax cash flow with an individual transaction that gives rise to cash flows that are classified as investing or financing activities the tax cash flow is classified as an investing or financing activity as appropriate. When tax cash flows are allocated over more than one class of activity, the total amount of taxes paid is disclosed.

Investments in subsidiaries, associates and joint ventures

37   When accounting for an investment in an associate, a joint venture or a subsidiary accounted for by use of the equity or cost method, an investor restricts its reporting in the statement of cash flows to the cash flows between itself and the investee, for example, to dividends and advances.

38   An entity that reports its interest in an associate or a joint venture using the equity method includes in its statement of cash flows the cash flows in respect of its investments in the associate or joint venture, and distributions and other payments or receipts between it and the associate or joint venture.

Changes in ownership interests in subsidiaries and other businesses

39   **The aggregate cash flows arising from obtaining or losing control of subsidiaries or other businesses shall be presented separately and classified as investing activities.**

40   **An entity shall disclose, in aggregate, in respect of both obtaining and losing control of subsidiaries or other businesses during the period each of the following:**

   (a)   **the total consideration paid or received;**

   (b)   **the portion of the consideration consisting of cash and cash equivalents;**

   (c)   **the amount of cash and cash equivalents in the subsidiaries or other businesses over which control is obtained or lost; and**

   (d)   **the amount of the assets and liabilities other than cash or cash equivalents in the subsidiaries or other businesses over which control is obtained or lost, summarised by each major category.**

40A   An investment entity, as defined in AASB 10 *Consolidated Financial Statements*, need not apply paragraphs 40(c) or 40(d) to an investment in a subsidiary that is required to be measured at fair value through profit or loss.

41   The separate presentation of the cash flow effects of obtaining or losing control of subsidiaries or other businesses as single line items, together with the separate disclosure of the amounts of assets and liabilities acquired or disposed of, helps to distinguish those cash flows from the cash flows arising from the other operating, investing and financing activities. The cash flow effects of losing control are not deducted from those of obtaining control.

42   The aggregate amount of the cash paid or received as consideration for obtaining or losing control of subsidiaries or other businesses is reported in the statement of cash flows net of cash and cash equivalents acquired or disposed of as part of such transactions, events or changes in circumstances.

42A   Cash flows arising from changes in ownership interests in a subsidiary that do not result in a loss of control shall be classified as cash flows from financing activities, unless the subsidiary is held by an investment entity, as defined in AASB 10, and is required to be measured at fair value through profit or loss.

42B   Changes in ownership interests in a subsidiary that do not result in a loss of control, such as the subsequent purchase or sale by a parent of a subsidiary's equity instruments, are accounted for as equity transactions (see AASB 10), unless the subsidiary is held by an investment entity and is required to be measured at fair value through profit or loss. Accordingly, the resulting cash flows are classified in the same way as other transactions with owners described in paragraph 17.

Non-cash transactions

43 **Investing and financing transactions that do not require the use of cash or cash equivalents shall be excluded from a statement of cash flows. Such transactions shall be disclosed elsewhere in the financial statements in a way that provides all the relevant information about these investing and financing activities.**

44 Many investing and financing activities do not have a direct impact on current cash flows although they do affect the capital and asset structure of an entity. The exclusion of non-cash transactions from the statement of cash flows is consistent with the objective of a statement of cash flows as these items do not involve cash flows in the current period. Examples of non-cash transactions are:

(a) the acquisition of assets either by assuming directly related liabilities or by means of a finance lease;

(b) the acquisition of an entity by means of an equity issue; and

(c) the conversion of debt to equity.

Changes in liabilities arising from financing activities

44A An entity shall provide disclosures that enable users of financial statements to evaluate changes in liabilities arising from financing activities, including both changes arising from cash flows and non-cash changes.

44B To the extent necessary to satisfy the requirement in paragraph 44A, an entity shall disclose the following changes in liabilities arising from financing activities:

(a) changes from financing cash flows;

(b) changes arising from obtaining or losing control of subsidiaries or other businesses;

(c) the effect of changes in foreign exchange rates;

(d) changes in fair values; and

(e) other changes.

44C Liabilities arising from financing activities are liabilities for which cash flows were, or future cash flows will be, classified in the statement of cash flows as cash flows from financing activities. In addition, the disclosure requirement in paragraph 44A also applies to changes in financial assets (for example, assets that hedge liabilities arising from financing activities) if cash flows from those financial assets were, or future cash flows will be, included in cash flows from financing activities.

44D One way to fulfil the disclosure requirement in paragraph 44A is by providing a reconciliation between the opening and closing balances in the statement of financial position for liabilities arising from financing activities, including the changes identified in paragraph 44B. Where an entity discloses such a reconciliation, it shall provide sufficient information to enable users of the financial statements to link items included in the reconciliation to the statement of financial position and the statement of cash flows.

44E If an entity provides the disclosure required by paragraph 44A in combination with disclosures of changes in other assets and liabilities, it shall disclose the changes in liabilities arising from financing activities separately from changes in those other assets and liabilities.

Components of cash and cash equivalents

45 An entity shall disclose the components of cash and cash equivalents and shall present a reconciliation of the amounts in its statement of cash flows with the equivalent items reported in the statement of financial position.

46 In view of the variety of cash management practices and banking arrangements around the world and in order to comply with AASB 101 *Presentation of Financial Statements*, an entity discloses the policy which it adopts in determining the composition of cash and cash equivalents.

47 The effect of any change in the policy for determining components of cash and cash equivalents, for example, a change in the classification of financial instruments previously considered to be part of an entity's investment portfolio, is reported in accordance with AASB 108 *Accounting Policies, Changes in Accounting Estimates and Errors*.

Other disclosures

48 An entity shall disclose, together with a commentary by management, the amount of significant cash and cash equivalent balances held by the entity that are not available for use by the group.

49 There are various circumstances in which cash and cash equivalent balances held by an entity are not available for use by the group. Examples include cash and cash equivalent balances held by a subsidiary that operates in a country where exchange controls or other legal restrictions apply when the balances are not available for general use by the parent or other subsidiaries.

50 Additional information may be relevant to users in understanding the financial position and liquidity of an entity. Disclosure of this information, together with a commentary by management, is encouraged and may include:

    (a) the amount of undrawn borrowing facilities that may be available for future operating activities and to settle capital commitments, indicating any restrictions on the use of these facilities;

    (b) [deleted]

    (c) the aggregate amount of cash flows that represent increases in operating capacity separately from those cash flows that are required to maintain operating capacity; and

    (d) the amount of the cash flows arising from the operating, investing and financing activities of each reportable segment (see AASB 8 *Operating Segments*).

51 The separate disclosure of cash flows that represent increases in operating capacity and cash flows that are required to maintain operating capacity is useful in enabling the user to determine whether the entity is investing adequately in the maintenance of its operating capacity. An entity that does not invest adequately in the maintenance of its operating capacity may be prejudicing future profitability for the sake of current liquidity and distributions to owners.

52 The disclosure of segmental cash flows enables users to obtain a better understanding of the relationship between the cash flows of the business as a whole and those of its component parts and the availability and variability of segmental cash flows.

Effective date

53 This Standard becomes operative for financial statements covering periods beginning on or after 1 January 2016. Earlier application is permitted for periods beginning on or after 1 January 2014 but before 1 January 2016.

54–58 [Deleted by the AASB]

60   AASB 2016-2 *Amendments to Australian Accounting Standards – Disclosure Initiative: Amendments to AASB 107*, issued in March 2016, added paragraphs 44A–44E. An entity shall apply those amendments for annual periods beginning on or after 1 January 2017. Earlier application is permitted. When the entity first applies those amendments, it is not required to provide comparative information for preceding periods.

Commencement of the legislative instrument

Aus58.1   For legal purposes, this legislative instrument commences on 31 December 2015.

Withdrawal of AASB pronouncements

Aus58.2   This Standard repeals AASB 107 *Statement of Cash Flows* issued in July 2004. Despite the repeal, after the time this Standard starts to apply under section 334 of the Corporations Act (either generally or in relation to an individual entity), the repealed Standard continues to apply in relation to any period ending before that time as if the repeal had not occurred.

[Note: When this Standard applies under section 334 of the Corporations Act (either generally or in relation to an individual entity), it supersedes the application of the repealed Standard.]

APPENDIX A
AUSTRALIAN REDUCED DISCLOSURE REQUIREMENTS

This appendix is an integral part of the Standard and has the same authority as the other parts of the Standard.

AusA1   **Paragraphs Aus20.2, 40, 41, 44A-44E, 46, 50(d) and 52 of this Standard do not apply to entities preparing general purpose financial statements under Australian Accounting Standards – Reduced Disclosure Requirements. Entities applying Australian Accounting Standards – Reduced Disclosure Requirements may elect to comply with some or all of these excluded requirements.**

AusA2   The requirements that do not apply to entities preparing general purpose financial statements under Australian Accounting Standards – Reduced Disclosure Requirements are also identified in this Standard by shading of the relevant text.

ILLUSTRATIVE EXAMPLES

These illustrative examples accompany, but are not part of, AASB 107.

A. Statement of cash flows for an entity other than a financial institution

1   The examples show only current period amounts. Corresponding amounts for the preceding period are required to be presented in accordance with AASB 101 *Presentation of Financial Statements*.

2   Information from the statement of comprehensive income and statement of financial position is provided to show how the statements of cash flows under the direct method

and indirect method have been derived. Neither the statement of comprehensive income nor the statement of financial position is presented in conformity with the disclosure and presentation requirements of other Standards.

3   The following additional information is also relevant for the preparation of the statements of cash flows:

- all of the shares of a subsidiary were acquired for 590. The fair values of assets acquired and liabilities assumed were as follows:

Inventories	100
Accounts receivable	100
Cash	40
Property, plant and equipment	650
Trade payables	100
Long-term debt	200

- 250 was raised from the issue of share capital and a further 250 was raised from long-term borrowings.

- interest expense was 400, of which 170 was paid during the period. Also, 100 relating to interest expense of the prior period was paid during the period.

- dividends paid were 1,200.

- the liability for tax at the beginning and end of the period was 1,000 and 400 respectively. During the period, a further 200 tax was provided for. Withholding tax on dividends received amounted to 100.

- during the period, the group acquired property, plant and equipment with an aggregate cost of 1,250 of which 900 was acquired by means of finance leases. Cash payments of 350 were made to purchase property, plant and equipment.

- plant with original cost of 80 and accumulated depreciation of 60 was sold for 20.

- accounts receivable as at the end of 20X2 include 100 of interest receivable.

Consolidated statement of comprehensive income for the period ended 20X2[a]

Sales	30,650
Cost of sales	(26,000)
Gross profit	4,650
Depreciation	(450)
Administrative and selling expenses	(910)
Interest expense	(400)
Investment income	500
Foreign exchange loss	(40)
Profit before taxation	3,350
Taxes on income	(300)
Profit	3,050

(a) The entity did not recognise any components of other comprehensive income in the period ended 20X2

AASB

Consolidated statement of financial position as at end of 20X2

	20X2		20X1	
Assets				
Cash and cash equivalents		230		160
Accounts receivable		1,900		1,200
Inventory		1,000		1,950
Portfolio investments		2,500		2,500
Property, plant and equipment at cost	3,730		1,910	
Accumulated depreciation	(1,450)		(1,060)	
Property, plant and equipment net		2,280		850
Total assets		7,910		6,660
Liabilities				
Trade payables		250		1,890
Interest payable		230		100
Income taxes payable		400		1,000
Long-term debt		2,300		1,040
Total liabilities		3,180		4,030
Shareholders' equity				
Share capital		1,500		1,250
Retained earnings		3,230		1,380
Total shareholders' equity		4,730		2,630
Total liabilities and shareholders' equity		7,910		6,660

Direct method statement of cash flows (paragraph 18(a))

	20X2
Cash flows from operating activities	
Cash receipts from customers	30,150
Cash paid to suppliers and employees	(27,600)
Cash generated from operations	2,550
Interest paid	(270)
Income taxes paid	(900)
Net cash from operating activities	1,380

Cash flows from investing activities

Acquisition of subsidiary X, net of cash acquired (Note A)	(550)	
Purchase of property, plant and equipment (Note B)	(350)	
Proceeds from sale of equipment	20	
Interest received	200	
Dividends received	200	
Net cash used in investing activities		(480)

Cash flows from financing activities

Proceeds from issue of share capital	250	
Proceeds from long-term borrowings	250	
Payment of finance lease liabilities	(90)	
Dividends paid[a]	(1,200)	
Net cash used in financing activities		(790)

Net increase in cash and cash equivalents		110
Cash and cash equivalents at beginning of period (Note C)		120
Cash and cash equivalents at end of period (Note C)		230

(a) This could also be shown as an operating cash flow.

Indirect method statement of cash flows (paragraph 18(b))

	20X2	
Cash flows from operating activities		
Profit before taxation	3,350	
Adjustments for:		
Depreciation	450	
Foreign exchange loss	40	
Investment income	(500)	
Interest expense	400	
	3,740	
Increase in trade and other receivables	(500)	
Decrease in inventories	1,050	
Decrease in trade payables	(1,740)	
Cash generated from operations	2,550	
Interest paid	(270)	
Income taxes paid	(900)	
Net cash from operating activities		1,380

(Continued)

(Continued)

Indirect method statement of cash flows (paragraph 18(b))		
		20X2
Cash flows from investing activities		
Acquisition of subsidiary X net of cash acquired (Note A)	(550)	
Purchase of property, plant and equipment (Note B)	(350)	
Proceeds from sale of equipment	20	
Interest received	200	
Dividends received	200	
Net cash used in investing activities		(480)
Cash flows from financing activities		
Proceeds from issue of share capital	250	
Proceeds from long-term borrowings	250	
Payment of finance lease liabilities	(90)	
Dividends paid[(a)]	(1,200)	
Net cash used in financing activities		(790)
Net increase in cash and cash equivalents		110
Cash and cash equivalents at beginning of period (Note C)		120
Cash and cash equivalents at end of period (Note C)		230

(a) This could also be shown as an operating cash flow.

Notes to the statement of cash flows (direct method and indirect method)

A. Obtaining control of subsidiary

During the period the Group obtained control of subsidiary X. The fair values of assets acquired and liabilities assumed were as follows:

Cash	40
Inventories	100
Accounts receivable	100
Property, plant and equipment	650
Trade payables	(100)
Long-term debt	(200)
Total purchase price paid in cash	590
Less: Cash of subsidiary X acquired	(40)
Cash paid to obtain control net of cash acquired	550

B. Property, plant and equipment

During the period, the Group acquired property, plant and equipment with an aggregate cost of 1,250 of which 900 was acquired by means of finance leases. Cash payments of 350 were made to purchase property, plant and equipment.

C. Cash and cash equivalents

Cash and cash equivalents consist of cash on hand and balances with banks, and investments in money market instruments. Cash and cash equivalents included in the statement of cash flows comprise the following amounts in the statement of financial position:

	20X2	20X1
Cash on hand and balances with banks	40	25
Short-term investments	190	135
Cash and cash equivalents as previously reported	230	160
Effect of exchange rate changes	–	(40)
Cash and cash equivalents as restated	230	120

Cash and cash equivalents at the end of the period include deposits with banks of 100 held by a subsidiary which are not freely remissible to the holding company because of currency exchange restrictions.

The Group has undrawn borrowing facilities of 2,000 of which 700 may be used only for future expansion.

D. Segment information

	Segment A	Segment B	Total
Cash flows from:			
Operating activities	1,520	(140)	1,380
Investing activities	(640)	160	(480)
Financing activities	(570)	(220)	(790)
	310	(200)	110

E. Reconciliation of liabilities arising from financing activities

	20X1	Cash flows	Non-cash changes Acquisition	Non-cash changes New leases	20X2
Long-term borrowings	1,040	250	200	–	1,490
Lease liabilities		(90)		900	810
Long-term debt	1,040	160	200	900	2,300

Alternative presentation (indirect method)

As an alternative, in an indirect method statement of cash flows, operating profit before working capital changes is sometimes presented as follows:

Revenues excluding investment income	30,650	
Operating expense excluding depreciation	(26,910)	
Operating profit before working capital changes		3,740

B. Statement of cash flows for a financial institution

1 The example shows only current period amounts. Comparative amounts for the preceding period are required to be presented in accordance with AASB 101 *Presentation of Financial Statements*.

2 The example is presented using the direct method.

	20X2
Cash flows from operating activities	
Interest and commission receipts	28,447
Interest payments	(23,463)
Recoveries on loans previously written off	237
Cash payments to employees and suppliers	(997)
	4,224
(Increase) decrease in operating assets:	
Short-term funds	(650)
Deposits held for regulatory or monetary control purposes	234
Funds advanced to customers	(288)
Net increase in credit card receivables	(360)
Other short-term negotiable securities	(120)
Increase (decrease) in operating liabilities:	
Deposits from customers	600
Negotiable certificates of deposit	(200)
Net cash from operating activities before income tax	3,440
Income taxes paid	(100)
Net cash from operating activities	3,340
Cash flows from investing activities	
Disposal of subsidiary Y	50
Dividends received	200

Interest received	300
Proceeds from sales of non-dealing securities	1,200
Purchase of non-dealing securities	(600)
Purchase of property, plant and equipment	(500)
Net cash from investing activities	650

Cash flows from financing activities		
Issue of loan capital	1,000	
Issue of preference shares by subsidiary undertaking	800	
Repayment of long-term borrowings	(200)	
Net decrease in other borrowings	(1,000)	
Dividends paid	(400)	
Net cash from financing activities		200
Effects of exchange rate changes on cash and cash equivalents		600
Net increase in cash and cash equivalents		4,790
Cash and cash equivalents at beginning of period		4,050
Cash and cash equivalents at end of period		8,840

C. Reconciliation of liabilities arising from financing activities

1   This example illustrates one possible way of providing the disclosures required by paragraphs 44A–44E.

2   The example shows only current period amounts. Corresponding amounts for the preceding period are required to be presented in accordance with AASB 101 *Presentation of Financial Statements*.

	20X1	Cash flows	Non-cash changes			20X2
			Acquisition	**Foreign exchange movement**	**Fair value changes**	
Long-term borrowings	22,000	(1,000)	–	–	–	21,000
Short-term borrowings	10,000	(500)	–	200	–	9,700
Lease liabilities	4,000	(800)	300	–	–	3,500
Assets held to hedge long-term borrowings	(675)	150	–	–	(25)	(550)
Total liabilities from financing activities	35,325	(2,150)	300	200	(25)	33,650

COMPILATION DETAILS

Accounting Standard AASB 107 *Statement of Cash Flows* as amended

Compilation details are not part of AASB 107.

This compiled Standard applies to annual periods beginning on or after 1 January 2017 but before 1 January 2019. It takes into account amendments up to and including 23 March 2016 and was prepared on 20 March 2017 by the staff of the Australian Accounting Standards Board (AASB).

This compilation is not a separate Accounting Standard made by the AASB. Instead, it is a representation of AASB 107 (August 2015) as amended by other Accounting Standards, which are listed in the Table below.

Table of Standards

Standard	Date made	FRL identifier	Commencement date	Effective date *(annual periods ... on or after ...)*	Application, saving or transitional provisions
AASB 107	7 Aug 2015	F2015L01538	31 Dec 2015	*(beginning)* 1 Jan 2016	see (a) below
AASB 16	23 Feb 2016	F2016L00233	31 Dec 2018	*(beginning)* 1 Jan 2019	not compiled*
AASB 2016-2	23 Mar 2016	F2016L00395	31 Dec 2016	*(beginning)* 1 Jan 2017	see (b) below

*   The amendments made by this Standard are not included in this compilation, which presents the principal Standard as applicable to annual periods beginning on or after 1 January 2017 but before 1 January 2019.

(a) Entities may elect to apply this Standard to periods beginning on or after 1 January 2014 but before 1 January 2016.

(b) Entities may elect to apply this Standard to annual periods beginning before 1 January 2017.

Table of amendments

Paragraph affected	How affected	By ... [paragraph/page]
44A-44E (and preceding heading)	added	AASB 2016-2 [page 5]
60	added	AASB 2016-2 [page 6]
AusA1	amended	AASB 2016-2 [page 6]
Illustrative example A	amended	AASB 2016-2 [page 6]
Illustrative example C	added	AASB 2016-2 [page 7]

DELETED IAS 7 TEXT

Deleted IAS 7 text is not part of AASB 107.

2   This Standard supersedes IAS 7 *Statement of Changes in Financial Position*, approved in July 1977.

3   ... Accordingly, this Standard requires all entities to present a statement of cash flows. [the last sentence of the paragraph]

54 IAS 27 (as amended in 2008) amended paragraphs 39–42 and added paragraphs 42A and 42B. An entity shall apply those amendments for annual periods beginning on or after 1 July 2009. If an entity applies IAS 27 (amended 2008) for an earlier period, the amendments shall be applied for that earlier period. The amendments shall be applied retrospectively.

55 Paragraph 14 was amended by *Improvements to IFRSs* issued in May 2008. An entity shall apply that amendment for annual periods beginning on or after 1 January 2009. Earlier application is permitted. If an entity applies the amendment for an earlier period it shall disclose that fact and apply paragraph 68A of IAS 16.

56 Paragraph 16 was amended by *Improvements to IFRSs* issued in April 2009. An entity shall apply that amendment for annual periods beginning on or after 1 January 2010. Earlier application is permitted. If an entity applies the amendment for an earlier period it shall disclose that fact.

57 IFRS 10 and IFRS 11 *Joint Arrangements*, issued in May 2011, amended paragraphs 37, 38 and 42B and deleted paragraph 50(b). An entity shall apply those amendments when it applies IFRS 10 and IFRS 11.

58 *Investment Entities* (Amendments to IFRS 10, IFRS 12 and IAS 27), issued in October 2012, amended paragraphs 42A and 42B and added paragraph 40A. An entity shall apply those amendments for annual periods beginning on or after 1 January 2014. Earlier application of *Investment Entities* is permitted. If an entity applies those amendments earlier it shall also apply all amendments included in *Investment Entities* at the same time.

AASB 108
Accounting Policies, Changes in Accounting Estimates and Errors
(Reissued August 2015)

CONTENTS

COMPARISON WITH IAS 8

ACCOUNTING STANDARD

AASB 108 *ACCOUNTING POLICIES, CHANGES IN ACCOUNTING ESTIMATES AND ERRORS*

APPENDIX

A. AUSTRALIAN REDUCED DISCLOSURE REQUIREMENTS

DELETED IAS 8 TEXT

IMPLEMENTATION GUIDANCE ON IAS 8 (available on the AASB website)

BASIS FOR CONCLUSIONS ON IAS 8 (available on the AASB website)

         Chartered Accountants Australia and New Zealand

Australian Accounting Standard AASB 108 *Accounting Policies, Changes in Accounting Estimates and Errors* is set out in paragraphs 1 – Aus56.2 and Appendix A. All the paragraphs have equal authority. Paragraphs in **bold type** state the main principles. AASB 108 is to be read in the context of other Australian Accounting Standards, including AASB 1048 *Interpretation of Standards*, which identifies the Australian Accounting Interpretations, and AASB 1057 *Application of Australian Accounting Standards*.

COMPARISON WITH IAS 8

AASB 108 *Accounting Policies, Changes in Accounting Estimates and Errors* incorporates IAS 8 *Accounting Policies, Changes in Accounting Estimates and Errors* issued by the International Accounting Standards Board (IASB). Australian-specific paragraphs (which are not included in IAS 8) are identified with the prefix "Aus" or "RDR". Paragraphs that apply only to not-for-profit entities begin by identifying their limited applicability.

Tier 1

For-profit entities complying with AASB 108 also comply with IAS 8.

Not-for-profit entities' compliance with IAS 8 will depend on whether any "Aus" paragraphs that specifically apply to not-for-profit entities provide additional guidance or contain applicable requirements that are inconsistent with IAS 8.

Tier 2

Entities preparing general purpose financial statements under Australian Accounting Standards – Reduced Disclosure Requirements (Tier 2) will not be in compliance with IFRSs.

AASB 1053 *Application of Tiers of Australian Accounting Standards* explains the two tiers of reporting requirements.

ACCOUNTING STANDARD AASB 108

The Australian Accounting Standards Board makes Accounting Standard AASB 108 *Accounting Policies, Changes in Accounting Estimates and Errors* under section 334 of the Corporations Act 2001.

Kris Peach

Dated 7 August 2015   Chair – AASB

ACCOUNTING STANDARD AASB 108
ACCOUNTING POLICIES, CHANGES IN ACCOUNTING ESTIMATES AND ERRORS

Objective

1   The objective of this Standard is to prescribe the criteria for selecting and changing accounting policies, together with the accounting treatment and disclosure of changes in accounting policies, changes in accounting estimates and corrections of errors. The Standard is intended to enhance the relevance and reliability of an entity's financial statements, and the comparability of those financial statements over time and with the financial statements of other entities.

2   Disclosure requirements for accounting policies, except those for changes in accounting policies, are set out in AASB 101 *Presentation of Financial Statements*.

Scope

3 This Standard shall be applied in selecting and applying accounting policies, and accounting for changes in accounting policies, changes in accounting estimates and corrections of prior period errors.

4 The tax effects of corrections of prior period errors and of retrospective adjustments made to apply changes in accounting policies are accounted for and disclosed in accordance with AASB 112 *Income Taxes*.

Definitions

5 The following terms are used in this Standard with the meanings specified:

Accounting policies are the specific principles, bases, conventions, rules and practices applied by an entity in preparing and presenting financial statements.

A *change in accounting estimate* is an adjustment of the carrying amount of an asset or a liability, or the amount of the periodic consumption of an asset, that results from the assessment of the present status of, and expected future benefits and obligations associated with, assets and liabilities. Changes in accounting estimates result from new information or new developments and, accordingly, are not corrections of errors.

Material Omissions or misstatements of items are material if they could, individually or collectively, influence the economic decisions that users make on the basis of the financial statements. Materiality depends on the size and nature of the omission or misstatement judged in the surrounding circumstances. The size or nature of the item, or a combination of both, could be the determining factor.

Prior period errors are omissions from, and misstatements in, the entity's financial statements for one or more prior periods arising from a failure to use, or misuse of, reliable information that:

(a) was available when financial statements for those periods were authorised for issue; and

(b) could reasonably be expected to have been obtained and taken into account in the preparation and presentation of those financial statements.

Such errors include the effects of mathematical mistakes, mistakes in applying accounting policies, oversights or misinterpretations of facts, and fraud.

Retrospective application is applying a new accounting policy to transactions, other events and conditions as if that policy had always been applied.

Retrospective restatement is correcting the recognition, measurement and disclosure of amounts of elements of financial statements as if a prior period error had never occurred.

Impracticable Applying a requirement is impracticable when the entity cannot apply it after making every reasonable effort to do so. For a particular prior period, it is impracticable to apply a change in an accounting policy retrospectively or to make a retrospective restatement to correct an error if:

(a) the effects of the retrospective application or retrospective restatement are not determinable;

(b) the retrospective application or retrospective restatement requires assumptions about what management's intent would have been in that period; or

(c) the retrospective application or retrospective restatement requires significant estimates of amounts and it is impossible to distinguish objectively information about those estimates that:

       (i)   provides evidence of circumstances that existed on the date(s) as at which those amounts are to be recognised, measured or disclosed; and

       (ii)   would have been available when the financial statements for that prior period were authorised for issue from other information.

Prospective application of a change in accounting policy and of recognising the effect of a change in an accounting estimate, respectively, are:

(a)   applying the new accounting policy to transactions, other events and conditions occurring after the date as at which the policy is changed; and

(b)   recognising the effect of the change in the accounting estimate in the current and future periods affected by the change.

6   Assessing whether an omission or misstatement could influence economic decisions of users, and so be material, requires consideration of the characteristics of those users. The *Framework for the Preparation and Presentation of Financial Statements* states in paragraph 25[1] that 'users are assumed to have a reasonable knowledge of business and economic activities and accounting and a willingness to study the information with reasonable diligence.' Therefore, the assessment needs to take into account how users with such attributes could reasonably be expected to be influenced in making economic decisions.

Accounting policies

Selection and application of accounting policies

7   **When an Australian Accounting Standard[2] specifically applies to a transaction, other event or condition, the accounting policy or policies applied to that item shall be determined by applying the Standard.**

8   Australian Accounting Standards set out accounting policies that the AASB has concluded result in financial statements containing relevant and reliable information about the transactions, other events and conditions to which they apply. Those policies need not be applied when the effect of applying them is immaterial. However, it is inappropriate to make, or leave uncorrected, immaterial departures from Australian Accounting Standards to achieve a particular presentation of an entity's financial position, financial performance or cash flows.

9   Australian Accounting Standards are accompanied by guidance to assist entities in applying their requirements. All such guidance states whether it is an integral part of Australian Accounting Standards. Guidance that is an integral part of the Australian Accounting Standards is mandatory. Guidance that is not an integral part of the Australian Accounting Standards does not contain requirements for financial statements.

10   **In the absence of an Australian Accounting Standard that specifically applies to a transaction, other event or condition, management shall use its judgement in developing and applying an accounting policy that results in information that is:**

(a)   **relevant to the economic decision-making needs of users; and**

(b)   **reliable, in that the financial statements:**

       (i)   **represent faithfully the financial position, financial performance and cash flows of the entity;**

---

1   In December 2013 the AASB amended the Framework for the Preparation and Presentation of Financial Statements. The Framework is identified in AASB 1048 Interpretation of Standards. Paragraph 25 was superseded by Chapter 3 of the Framework.

2   [Aus] The term 'Australian Accounting Standards' refers to Standards (including Interpretations) made by the AASB that apply to any reporting period beginning on or after 1 January 2005. In this context, the term encompasses Australian Accounting Standards – Reduced Disclosure Requirements, which some entities are permitted to apply in accordance with AASB 1053 Application of Tiers of Australian Accounting Standards in preparing general purpose financial statements.

(ii) reflect the economic substance of transactions, other events and conditions, and not merely the legal form;

(iii) are neutral, ie free from bias;

(iv) are prudent; and

(v) are complete in all material respects.

11 In making the judgement described in paragraph 10, management shall refer to, and consider the applicability of, the following sources in descending order:

(a) the requirements in Australian Accounting Standards dealing with similar and related issues; and

(b) the definitions, recognition criteria and measurement concepts for assets, liabilities, income and expenses in the *Framework*.[3]

12 In making the judgement described in paragraph 10, management may also consider the most recent pronouncements of other standard-setting bodies that use a similar conceptual framework to develop accounting standards, other accounting literature and accepted industry practices, to the extent that these do not conflict with the sources in paragraph 11.

Consistency of accounting policies

13 An entity shall select and apply its accounting policies consistently for similar transactions, other events and conditions, unless an Australian Accounting Standard specifically requires or permits categorisation of items for which different policies may be appropriate. If an Australian Accounting Standard requires or permits such categorisation, an appropriate accounting policy shall be selected and applied consistently to each category.

Changes in accounting policies

14 An entity shall change an accounting policy only if the change:

(a) is required by an Australian Accounting Standard; or

(b) results in the financial statements providing reliable and more relevant information about the effects of transactions, other events or conditions on the entity's financial position, financial performance or cash flows.

15 Users of financial statements need to be able to compare the financial statements of an entity over time to identify trends in its financial position, financial performance and cash flows. Therefore, the same accounting policies are applied within each period and from one period to the next unless a change in accounting policy meets one of the criteria in paragraph 14.

16 The following are not changes in accounting policies:

(a) the application of an accounting policy for transactions, other events or conditions that differ in substance from those previously occurring; and

(b) the application of a new accounting policy for transactions, other events or conditions that did not occur previously or were immaterial.

17 The initial application of a policy to revalue assets in accordance with AASB 116 *Property, Plant and Equipment* or AASB 138 *Intangible Assets* is a change in an accounting policy to be dealt with as a revaluation in accordance with AASB 116 or AASB 138, rather than in accordance with this Standard.

18 Paragraphs 19–31 do not apply to the change in accounting policy described in paragraph 17.

---

3 In December 2013 the AASB amended the *Framework for the Preparation and Presentation of Financial Statements*.

Applying changes in accounting policies

19   Subject to paragraph 23:

(a)   an entity shall account for a change in accounting policy resulting from the initial application of an Australian Accounting Standard in accordance with the specific transitional provisions, if any, in that Australian Accounting Standard; and

(b)   when an entity changes an accounting policy upon initial application of an Australian Accounting Standard that does not include specific transitional provisions applying to that change, or changes an accounting policy voluntarily, it shall apply the change retrospectively.

20   For the purpose of this Standard, early application of an Australian Accounting Standard is not a voluntary change in accounting policy.

21   In the absence of an Australian Accounting Standard that specifically applies to a transaction, other event or condition, management may, in accordance with paragraph 12, apply an accounting policy from the most recent pronouncements of other standard-setting bodies that use a similar conceptual framework to develop accounting standards. If, following an amendment of such a pronouncement, the entity chooses to change an accounting policy, that change is accounted for and disclosed as a voluntary change in accounting policy.

Retrospective application

22   Subject to paragraph 23, when a change in accounting policy is applied retrospectively in accordance with paragraph 19(a) or (b), the entity shall adjust the opening balance of each affected component of equity for the earliest prior period presented and the other comparative amounts disclosed for each prior period presented as if the new accounting policy had always been applied.

Limitations on retrospective application

23   When retrospective application is required by paragraph 19(a) or (b), a change in accounting policy shall be applied retrospectively except to the extent that it is impracticable to determine either the period-specific effects or the cumulative effect of the change.

24   When it is impracticable to determine the period-specific effects of changing an accounting policy on comparative information for one or more prior periods presented, the entity shall apply the new accounting policy to the carrying amounts of assets and liabilities as at the beginning of the earliest period for which retrospective application is practicable, which may be the current period, and shall make a corresponding adjustment to the opening balance of each affected component of equity for that period.

25   When it is impracticable to determine the cumulative effect, at the beginning of the current period, of applying a new accounting policy to all prior periods, the entity shall adjust the comparative information to apply the new accounting policy prospectively from the earliest date practicable.

26   When an entity applies a new accounting policy retrospectively, it applies the new accounting policy to comparative information for prior periods as far back as is practicable. Retrospective application to a prior period is not practicable unless it is practicable to determine the cumulative effect on the amounts in both the opening and closing statements of financial position for that period. The amount of the resulting adjustment relating to periods before those presented in the financial statements is made to the opening balance of each affected component of equity of the earliest prior period presented. Usually the adjustment is made to retained earnings. However, the adjustment may be made to another component of equity (for example, to comply with an Australian Accounting Standard). Any other information about prior periods, such as historical summaries of financial data, is also adjusted as far back as is practicable.

27   When it is impracticable for an entity to apply a new accounting policy retrospectively, because it cannot determine the cumulative effect of applying the policy to all prior periods, the entity, in accordance with paragraph 25, applies the new policy prospectively from the start of the earliest period practicable. It therefore disregards the portion of the cumulative adjustment to assets, liabilities and equity arising before that date. Changing an accounting policy is permitted even if it is impracticable to apply the policy prospectively for any prior period. Paragraphs 50–53 provide guidance on when it is impracticable to apply a new accounting policy to one or more prior periods.

Disclosure

28   **When initial application of an Australian Accounting Standard has an effect on the current period or any prior period, would have such an effect except that it is impracticable to determine the amount of the adjustment, or might have an effect on future periods, an entity shall disclose:**

(a)   **the title of the Australian Accounting Standard;**

(b)   **when applicable, that the change in accounting policy is made in accordance with its transitional provisions;**

(c)   **the nature of the change in accounting policy;**

(d)   **when applicable, a description of the transitional provisions;**

(e)   **when applicable, the transitional provisions that might have an effect on future periods;**

(f)   **for the current period and each prior period presented, to the extent practicable, the amount of the adjustment:**

  (i)   **for each financial statement line item affected; and**

  (ii)   **if AASB 133 *Earnings per Share* applies to the entity, for basic and diluted earnings per share;**

(g)   **the amount of the adjustment relating to periods before those presented, to the extent practicable; and**

(h)   **if retrospective application required by paragraph 19(a) or (b) is impracticable for a particular prior period, or for periods before those presented, the circumstances that led to the existence of that condition and a description of how and from when the change in accounting policy has been applied.**

Financial statements of subsequent periods need not repeat these disclosures.

29   **When a voluntary change in accounting policy has an effect on the current period or any prior period, would have an effect on that period except that it is impracticable to determine the amount of the adjustment, or might have an effect on future periods, an entity shall disclose:**

(a)   **the nature of the change in accounting policy;**

(b)   **the reasons why applying the new accounting policy provides reliable and more relevant information;**

(c)   **for the current period and each prior period presented, to the extent practicable, the amount of the adjustment:**

  (i)   **for each financial statement line item affected; and**

  (ii)   **if AASB 133 applies to the entity, for basic and diluted earnings per share;**

(d)   **the amount of the adjustment relating to periods before those presented, to the extent practicable; and**

(e)   **if retrospective application is impracticable for a particular prior period, or for periods before those presented, the circumstances that led to the existence of that condition and a description of how and from when the change in accounting policy has been applied.**

Financial statements of subsequent periods need not repeat these disclosures.

30   When an entity has not applied a new Australian Accounting Standard that has been issued but is not yet effective, the entity shall disclose:

(a)   this fact; and

(b)   known or reasonably estimable information relevant to assessing the possible impact that application of the new Australian Accounting Standard will have on the entity's financial statements in the period of initial application.

31   In complying with paragraph 30, an entity considers disclosing:

(a)   the title of the new Australian Accounting Standard;

(b)   the nature of the impending change or changes in accounting policy;

(c)   the date by which application of the Australian Accounting Standard is required;

(d)   the date as at which it plans to apply the Australian Accounting Standard initially; and

(e)   either:

(i)   a discussion of the impact that initial application of the Australian Accounting Standard is expected to have on the entity's financial statements; or

(ii)   if that impact is not known or reasonably estimable, a statement to that effect.

Changes in accounting estimates

32   As a result of the uncertainties inherent in business activities, many items in financial statements cannot be measured with precision but can only be estimated. Estimation involves judgements based on the latest available, reliable information. For example, estimates may be required of:

(a)   bad debts;

(b)   inventory obsolescence;

(c)   the fair value of financial assets or financial liabilities;

(d)   the useful lives of, or expected pattern of consumption of the future economic benefits embodied in, depreciable assets; and

(e)   warranty obligations.

33   The use of reasonable estimates is an essential part of the preparation of financial statements and does not undermine their reliability.

34   An estimate may need revision if changes occur in the circumstances on which the estimate was based or as a result of new information or more experience. By its nature, the revision of an estimate does not relate to prior periods and is not the correction of an error.

35   A change in the measurement basis applied is a change in an accounting policy, and is not a change in an accounting estimate. When it is difficult to distinguish a change in an accounting policy from a change in an accounting estimate, the change is treated as a change in an accounting estimate.

36   The effect of a change in an accounting estimate, other than a change to which paragraph 37 applies, shall be recognised prospectively by including it in profit or loss in:

(a)   the period of the change, if the change affects that period only; or

(b)   the period of the change and future periods, if the change affects both.

37   To the extent that a change in an accounting estimate gives rise to changes in assets and liabilities, or relates to an item of equity, it shall be recognised by adjusting

the carrying amount of the related asset, liability or equity item in the period of the change.

38   Prospective recognition of the effect of a change in an accounting estimate means that the change is applied to transactions, other events and conditions from the date of the change in estimate. A change in an accounting estimate may affect only the current period's profit or loss, or the profit or loss of both the current period and future periods. For example, a change in the estimate of the amount of bad debts affects only the current period's profit or loss and therefore is recognised in the current period. However, a change in the estimated useful life of, or the expected pattern of consumption of the future economic benefits embodied in, a depreciable asset affects depreciation expense for the current period and for each future period during the asset's remaining useful life. In both cases, the effect of the change relating to the current period is recognised as income or expense in the current period. The effect, if any, on future periods is recognised as income or expense in those future periods.

Disclosure

39   **An entity shall disclose the nature and amount of a change in an accounting estimate that has an effect in the current period or is expected to have an effect in future periods, except for the disclosure of the effect on future periods when it is impracticable to estimate that effect.**

40   **If the amount of the effect in future periods is not disclosed because estimating it is impracticable, an entity shall disclose that fact.**

Errors

41   Errors can arise in respect of the recognition, measurement, presentation or disclosure of elements of financial statements. Financial statements do not comply with Australian Accounting Standards if they contain either material errors or immaterial errors made intentionally to achieve a particular presentation of an entity's financial position, financial performance or cash flows. Potential current period errors discovered in that period are corrected before the financial statements are authorised for issue. However, material errors are sometimes not discovered until a subsequent period, and these prior period errors are corrected in the comparative information presented in the financial statements for that subsequent period (see paragraphs 42–47).

42   **Subject to paragraph 43, an entity shall correct material prior period errors retrospectively in the first set of financial statements authorised for issue after their discovery by:**

(a)   **restating the comparative amounts for the prior period(s) presented in which the error occurred; or**

(b)   **if the error occurred before the earliest prior period presented, restating the opening balances of assets, liabilities and equity for the earliest prior period presented.**

Limitations on retrospective restatement

43   **A prior period error shall be corrected by retrospective restatement except to the extent that it is impracticable to determine either the period-specific effects or the cumulative effect of the error.**

44   **When it is impracticable to determine the period-specific effects of an error on comparative information for one or more prior periods presented, the entity shall restate the opening balances of assets, liabilities and equity for the earliest period for which retrospective restatement is practicable (which may be the current period).**

45   **When it is impracticable to determine the cumulative effect, at the beginning of the current period, of an error on all prior periods, the entity shall restate the**

comparative information to correct the error prospectively from the earliest date practicable.

46   The correction of a prior period error is excluded from profit or loss for the period in which the error is discovered. Any information presented about prior periods, including any historical summaries of financial data, is restated as far back as is practicable.

47   When it is impracticable to determine the amount of an error (eg a mistake in applying an accounting policy) for all prior periods, the entity, in accordance with paragraph 45, restates the comparative information prospectively from the earliest date practicable. It therefore disregards the portion of the cumulative restatement of assets, liabilities and equity arising before that date. Paragraphs 50–53 provide guidance on when it is impracticable to correct an error for one or more prior periods.

48   Corrections of errors are distinguished from changes in accounting estimates. Accounting estimates by their nature are approximations that may need revision as additional information becomes known. For example, the gain or loss recognised on the outcome of a contingency is not the correction of an error.

Disclosure of prior period errors

49   In applying paragraph 42, an entity shall disclose the following:

   (a)   the nature of the prior period error;

   (b)   for each prior period presented, to the extent practicable, the amount of the correction:

      (i)   for each financial statement line item affected; and

      (ii)   if AASB 133 applies to the entity, for basic and diluted earnings per share;

   (c)   the amount of the correction at the beginning of the earliest prior period presented; and

   (d)   if retrospective restatement is impracticable for a particular prior period, the circumstances that led to the existence of that condition and a description of how and from when the error has been corrected.

   Financial statements of subsequent periods need not repeat these disclosures.

Impracticability in respect of retrospective application and retrospective

50   In some circumstances, it is impracticable to adjust comparative information for one or more prior periods to achieve comparability with the current period. For example, data may not have been collected in the prior period(s) in a way that allows either retrospective application of a new accounting policy (including, for the purpose of paragraphs 51–53, its prospective application to prior periods) or retrospective restatement to correct a prior period error, and it may be impracticable to recreate the information.

51   It is frequently necessary to make estimates in applying an accounting policy to elements of financial statements recognised or disclosed in respect of transactions, other events or conditions. Estimation is inherently subjective, and estimates may be developed after the reporting period. Developing estimates is potentially more difficult when retrospectively applying an accounting policy or making a retrospective restatement to correct a prior period error, because of the longer period of time that might have passed since the affected transaction, other event or condition occurred. However, the objective of estimates related to prior periods remains the same as for estimates made in the current period, namely, for the estimate to reflect the circumstances that existed when the transaction, other event or condition occurred.

52   Therefore, retrospectively applying a new accounting policy or correcting a prior period error requires distinguishing information that

(a)   provides evidence of circumstances that existed on the date(s) as at which the transaction, other event or condition occurred, and

(b)   would have been available when the financial statements for that prior period were authorised for issue

from other information. For some types of estimates (eg a fair value measurement that uses significant unobservable inputs), it is impracticable to distinguish these types of information. When retrospective application or retrospective restatement would require making a significant estimate for which it is impossible to distinguish these two types of information, it is impracticable to apply the new accounting policy or correct the prior period error retrospectively.

53   Hindsight should not be used when applying a new accounting policy to, or correcting amounts for, a prior period, either in making assumptions about what management's intentions would have been in a prior period or estimating the amounts recognised, measured or disclosed in a prior period. For example, when an entity corrects a prior period error in calculating its liability for employees' accumulated sick leave in accordance with AASB 119 *Employee Benefits*, it disregards information about an unusually severe influenza season during the next period that became available after the financial statements for the prior period were authorised for issue. The fact that significant estimates are frequently required when amending comparative information presented for prior periods does not prevent reliable adjustment or correction of the comparative information.

Effective date

54   An entity shall apply this Standard for annual periods beginning on or after 1 January 2018. Earlier application is encouraged for periods beginning after 24 July 2014 but before 1 January 2018. If an entity applies this Standard for a period beginning before 1 January 2018, it shall disclose that fact.

54A   [Deleted]

54B   [Deleted]

54C   [Deleted by the AASB]

54D   [Deleted]

54E   AASB 2010-7 *Amendments to Australian Accounting Standards arising from AASB 9 (December 2010)* (as amended) amended the previous version of this Standard as follows: amended paragraph 53 and deleted paragraph 54A. Paragraph 54B, added by AASB 2010-7, was deleted by AASB 2014-1 *Amendments to Australian Accounting Standards*. Paragraph 54D, added by AASB 2014-1, was deleted by AASB 2014-7 *Amendments to Australian Accounting Standards arising from AASB 9 (December 2014)*. An entity shall apply those amendments when it applies AASB 9.

Withdrawal of other pronouncements

55–56 [Deleted by the AASB]

Commencement of the legislative instrument

Aus56.1   For legal purposes, this legislative instrument commences on 31 December 2017.

Withdrawal of AASB pronouncements

Aus56.2   This Standard repeals AASB 108 *Accounting Policies, Changes in Accounting Estimates and Errors* issued in July 2004. Despite the repeal, after the time this Standard starts to apply under section 334 of the Corporations Act (either generally or in relation to an individual entity), the repealed Standard continues to apply in relation to any period ending before that time as if the repeal had not occurred.

[Note: When this Standard applies under section 334 of the Corporations Act (either generally or in relation to an individual entity), it supersedes the application of the repealed Standard.]

APPENDIX A
AUSTRALIAN REDUCED DISCLOSURE REQUIREMENTS

This appendix is an integral part of the Standard.

AusA1 **Paragraphs 28(b), 28(d), 28(e), 28(h), 30, 31 and 40 of this Standard do not apply to entities preparing general purpose financial statements under Australian Accounting Standards – Reduced Disclosure Requirements. Entities applying Australian Accounting Standards – Reduced Disclosure Requirements may elect to comply with some or all of these excluded requirements.**

AusA2 The requirements that do not apply to entities preparing general purpose financial statements under Australian Accounting Standards – Reduced Disclosure Requirements are also identified in this Standard by shading of the relevant text.

AusA3 **The RDR paragraph in this Standard applies only to entities preparing general purpose financial statements under Australian Accounting Standards – Reduced Disclosure Requirements.**

RDR28.1 **An entity applying Australian Accounting Standards – Reduced Disclosure Requirements shall disclose an explanation if it is impracticable to determine the amounts required to be disclosed by paragraph 28(f)(i) or 28(g).**

DELETED IAS 8 TEXT

Deleted IAS 8 text is not part of AASB 108.

54C IFRS 13 *Fair Value Measurement*, issued in May 2011, amended paragraph 52. An entity shall apply that amendment when it applies IFRS 13.

55 This Standard supersedes IAS 8 *Net Profit or Loss for the Period, Fundamental Errors and Changes in Accounting Policies*, revised in 1993.

56 This Standard supersedes the following Interpretations:

(a) SIC-2 *Consistency—Capitalisation of Borrowing Costs*; and

(b) SIC-18 *Consistency—Alternative Methods*.

AASB 110

Events after the Reporting Period

(Compiled December 2017)

This compiled Standard applies to annual periods beginning on or after 1 January 2018. Earlier application is permitted for annual periods beginning after 24 July 2014 but before 1 January 2018. It incorporates relevant amendments made up to and including 12 December 2017.

Prepared on 20 May 2018 by the staff of the Australian Accounting Standards Board.

Compilation no. 1

Compilation date: 31 December 2017

CONTENTS

Australian Accounting Standard AASB 110 *Events after the Reporting Period* (as amended) is set out in paragraphs 1 – Aus24.2 and Appendix A. All the paragraphs have equal authority. Paragraphs in **bold type** state the main principles. AASB 110 is to be read in the context of other Australian Accounting Standards, including AASB 1048 *Interpretation of Standards*, which identifies the Australian Accounting Interpretations, and AASB 1057 *Application of Australian Accounting Standards*. In the absence of explicit guidance, AASB 108 *Accounting Policies, Changes in Accounting Estimates and Errors* provides a basis for selecting and applying accounting policies.

COMPARISON WITH IAS 10

AASB 110 *Events after the Reporting Period* as amended incorporates IAS 10 *Events after the Reporting Period* as issued and amended by the International Accounting Standards Board (IASB). Australian-specific paragraphs (which are not included in IAS 10) are identified with the prefix "Aus" or "RDR". Paragraphs that apply only to not-for-profit entities begin by identifying their limited applicability.

Tier 1

For-profit entities complying with AASB 110 also comply with IAS 10.

Not-for-profit entities' compliance with IAS 10 will depend on whether any "Aus" paragraphs that specifically apply to not-for-profit entities provide additional guidance or contain applicable requirements that are inconsistent with IAS 10.

Tier 2

Entities preparing general purpose financial statements under Australian Accounting Standards – Reduced Disclosure Requirements (Tier 2) will not be in compliance with IFRSs.

AASB 1053 *Application of Tiers of Australian Accounting Standards* explains the two tiers of reporting requirements.

ACCOUNTING STANDARD AASB 110

The Australian Accounting Standards Board made Accounting Standard AASB 110 *Events after the Reporting Period* under section 334 of the *Corporations Act 2001* on 24 July 2015.

This compiled version of AASB 110 applies to annual periods beginning on or after 1 January 2018. It incorporates relevant amendments contained in other AASB Standards made by the AASB up to and including 12 December 2017 (see Compilation Details).

ACCOUNTING STANDARD AASB 110
EVENTS AFTER THE REPORTING PERIOD

Objective

1   The objective of this Standard is to prescribe:

(a)   when an entity should adjust its financial statements for events after the reporting period; and

(b)   the disclosures that an entity should give about the date when the financial statements were authorised for issue and about events after the reporting period.

The Standard also requires that an entity should not prepare its financial statements on a going concern basis if events after the reporting period indicate that the going concern assumption is not appropriate.

Scope

2   **This Standard shall be applied in the accounting for, and disclosure of, events after the reporting period.**

Definitions

3   **The following terms are used in this Standard with the meanings specified:**

Events after the reporting period **are those events, favourable and unfavourable, that occur between the end of the reporting period and the date when the financial statements are authorised for issue. Two types of events can be identified:**

(a)   **those that provide evidence of conditions that existed at the end of the reporting period (***adjusting events after the reporting period***); and**

(b)   **those that are indicative of conditions that arose after the reporting period (***non-adjusting events after the reporting period***).**

4   The process involved in authorising the financial statements for issue will vary depending upon the management structure, statutory requirements and procedures followed in preparing and finalising the financial statements.

5   In some cases, an entity is required to submit its financial statements to its shareholders for approval after the financial statements have been issued. In such cases, the financial statements are authorised for issue on the date of issue, not the date when shareholders approve the financial statements.

Example

The management of an entity completes draft financial statements for the year to 31 December 20X1 on 28 February 20X2. On 18 March 20X2, the board of directors reviews the financial statements and authorises them for issue. The entity announces its profit and selected other financial information on 19 March 20X2. The financial statements are made available to shareholders and others on 1 April 20X2. The shareholders approve the financial statements at their annual meeting on 15 May 20X2 and the approved financial statements are then filed with a regulatory body on 17 May 20X2.

The financial statements are authorised for issue on 18 March 20X2 (date of board authorisation for issue).

---

6   In some cases, the management of an entity is required to issue its financial statements to a supervisory board (made up solely of non-executives) for approval. In such cases, the financial statements are authorised for issue when the management authorises them for issue to the supervisory board.

Example

On 18 March 20X2, the management of an entity authorises financial statements for issue to its supervisory board. The supervisory board is made up solely of non-executives and may include representatives of employees and other outside interests. The supervisory board approves the financial statements on 26 March 20X2. The financial statements are made available to shareholders and others on 1 April 20X2. The shareholders approve the financial statements at their annual meeting on 15 May 20X2 and the financial statements are then filed with a regulatory body on 17 May 20X2.

The financial statements are authorised for issue on 18 March 20X2 (date of management authorisation for issue to the supervisory board).

---

7   Events after the reporting period include all events up to the date when the financial statements are authorised for issue, even if those events occur after the public announcement of profit or of other selected financial information.

Recognition and measurement

Adjusting events after the reporting period

8   **An entity shall adjust the amounts recognised in its financial statements to reflect adjusting events after the reporting period.**

9   The following are examples of adjusting events after the reporting period that require an entity to adjust the amounts recognised in its financial statements, or to recognise items that were not previously recognised:

     (a)   the settlement after the reporting period of a court case that confirms that the entity had a present obligation at the end of the reporting period. The entity adjusts any previously recognised provision related to this court case in accordance with AASB 137 *Provisions, Contingent Liabilities and Contingent Assets* or recognises a new provision. The entity does not merely disclose a contingent liability because the settlement provides additional evidence that would be considered in accordance with paragraph 16 of AASB 137.

     (b)   the receipt of information after the reporting period indicating that an asset was impaired at the end of the reporting period, or that the amount of a previously recognised impairment loss for that asset needs to be adjusted. For example:

         (i)   the bankruptcy of a customer that occurs after the reporting period usually confirms that the customer was credit-impaired at the end of the reporting period; and

         (ii)   the sale of inventories after the reporting period may give evidence about their net realisable value at the end of the reporting period.

     (c)   the determination after the reporting period of the cost of assets purchased, or the proceeds from assets sold, before the end of the reporting period.

     (d)   the determination after the reporting period of the amount of profit-sharing or bonus payments, if the entity had a present legal or constructive obligation at the end of the reporting period to make such payments as a result of events before that date (see AASB 119 *Employee Benefits*).

     (e)   the discovery of fraud or errors that show that the financial statements are incorrect.

Non-adjusting events after the reporting period

10   **An entity shall not adjust the amounts recognised in its financial statements to reflect non-adjusting events after the reporting period.**

11   An example of a non-adjusting event after the reporting period is a decline in fair value of investments between the end of the reporting period and the date when the financial statements are authorised for issue. The decline in fair value does not normally relate to the condition of the investments at the end of the reporting period, but reflects circumstances that have arisen subsequently. Therefore, an entity does not adjust the amounts recognised in its financial statements for the investments. Similarly, the entity does not update the amounts disclosed for the investments as at the end of the reporting period, although it may need to give additional disclosure under paragraph 21.

Dividends

12   **If an entity declares dividends to holders of equity instruments (as defined in AASB 132 *Financial Instruments: Presentation*) after the reporting period, the entity shall not recognise those dividends as a liability at the end of the reporting period.**

13   If dividends are declared after the reporting period but before the financial statements are authorised for issue, the dividends are not recognised as a liability at the end of the reporting period because no obligation exists at that time. Such dividends are disclosed in the notes in accordance with AASB 101 *Presentation of Financial Statements*.

Going concern

14   **An entity shall not prepare its financial statements on a going concern basis if management determines after the reporting period either that it intends to liquidate the entity or to cease trading, or that it has no realistic alternative but to do so.**

15   Deterioration in operating results and financial position after the reporting period may indicate a need to consider whether the going concern assumption is still appropriate. If the going concern assumption is no longer appropriate, the effect is so pervasive that this Standard requires a fundamental change in the basis of accounting, rather than an adjustment to the amounts recognised within the original basis of accounting.

16   AASB 101 specifies required disclosures if:

    (a)   the financial statements are not prepared on a going concern basis; or

    (b)   management is aware of material uncertainties related to events or conditions that may cast significant doubt upon the entity's ability to continue as a going concern. The events or conditions requiring disclosure may arise after the reporting period.

Disclosure

Date of authorisation for issue

17   **An entity shall disclose the date when the financial statements were authorised for issue and who gave that authorisation. If the entity's owners or others have the power to amend the financial statements after issue, the entity shall disclose that fact.**

18   It is important for users to know when the financial statements were authorised for issue, because the financial statements do not reflect events after this date.

Updating disclosure about conditions at the end of the reporting period

19   **If an entity receives information after the reporting period about conditions that existed at the end of the reporting period, it shall update disclosures that relate to those conditions, in the light of the new information.**

20   In some cases, an entity needs to update the disclosures in its financial statements to reflect information received after the reporting period, even when the information does not affect the amounts that it recognises in its financial statements. One example of the need to update disclosures is when evidence becomes available after the reporting period about a contingent liability that existed at the end of the reporting period. In addition to considering whether it should recognise or change a provision under AASB 137, an entity updates its disclosures about the contingent liability in the light of that evidence.

Non-adjusting events after the reporting period

21   **If non-adjusting events after the reporting period are material, non-disclosure could influence the economic decisions that users make on the basis of the financial statements. Accordingly, an entity shall disclose the following for each material category of non-adjusting event after the reporting period:**

    (a)   **the nature of the event; and**

    (b)   **an estimate of its financial effect, or a statement that such an estimate cannot be made.**

22   The following are examples of non-adjusting events after the reporting period that would generally result in disclosure:

(a)   a major business combination after the reporting period (AASB 3 *Business Combinations* requires specific disclosures in such cases) or disposing of a major subsidiary;

(b)   announcing a plan to discontinue an operation;

(c)   major purchases of assets, classification of assets as held for sale in accordance with AASB 5 *Non-current Assets Held for Sale and Discontinued Operations*, other disposals of assets, or expropriation of major assets by government;

(d)   the destruction of a major production plant by a fire after the reporting period;

(e)   announcing, or commencing the implementation of, a major restructuring (see AASB 137);

(f)   major ordinary share transactions and potential ordinary share transactions after the reporting period (AASB 133 *Earnings per Share* requires an entity to disclose a description of such transactions, other than when such transactions involve capitalisation or bonus issues, share splits or reverse share splits all of which are required to be adjusted under AASB 133);

(g)   abnormally large changes after the reporting period in asset prices or foreign exchange rates;

(h)   changes in tax rates or tax laws enacted or announced after the reporting period that have a significant effect on current and deferred tax assets and liabilities (see AASB 112 *Income Taxes*);

(i)   entering into significant commitments or contingent liabilities, for example, by issuing significant guarantees; and

(j)   commencing major litigation arising solely out of events that occurred after the reporting period.

Effective date

23   An entity shall apply this Standard for annual periods beginning on or after 1 January 2018. Earlier application is encouraged for periods beginning after 24 July 2014 but before 1 January 2018. If an entity applies this Standard for a period beginning before 1 January 2018, it shall disclose that fact.

23A   [Deleted by the AASB]

23B   AASB 2014-7 *Amendments to Australian Accounting Standards arising from AASB 9 (December 2014)* issued in December 2014 amended paragraph 9 in the previous version of this Standard. An entity shall apply that amendment when it applies AASB 9.

Withdrawal of IAS 10 (revised 1999)

24   [Deleted by the AASB]

Commencement of the legislative instrument

Aus24.1   For legal purposes, this legislative instrument commences on 31 December 2017.

Withdrawal of AASB pronouncements

Aus24.2   This Standard repeals AASB 110 *Events after the Reporting Period* issued in July 2004. Despite the repeal, after the time this Standard starts to apply under section 334 of the Corporations Act (either generally or in relation to an individual entity), the repealed Standard continues to apply in relation to any period ending before that time as if the repeal had not occurred.

[Note: When this Standard applies under section 334 of the Corporations Act (either generally or in relation to an individual entity), it supersedes the application of the repealed Standard.]

APPENDIX A
AUSTRALIAN REDUCED DISCLOSURE REQUIREMENTS

This appendix is an integral part of the Standard.

AusA1   **The following do not apply to entities preparing general purpose financial statements under Australian Accounting Standards – Reduced Disclosure Requirements:**

(a)   **paragraphs 13, 19 and 20; and**

(b)   **in paragraph 22(a), the text "(AASB 3 ... in such cases)".**

Entities applying Australian Accounting Standards – Reduced Disclosure Requirements may elect to comply with some or all of these excluded requirements.

AusA2   The requirements that do not apply to entities preparing general purpose financial statements under Australian Accounting Standards – Reduced Disclosure Requirements are also identified in this Standard by shading of the relevant text.

COMPILATION DETAILS

Accounting Standard AASB 110 *Events after the Reporting Period*

Compilation details are not part of AASB 110.

This compiled Standard applies to annual periods beginning on or after 1 January 2018. It takes into account amendments up to and including 12 December 2017 and was prepared on 20 May 2018 by the staff of the Australian Accounting Standards Board (AASB).

This compilation is not a separate Accounting Standard made by the AASB. Instead, it is a representation of AASB 110 (August 2015) as amended by other Accounting Standards, which are listed in the Table below.

Table of Standards

Standard	Date made	FRL identifier	Commencement date	Effective date *(annual periods ... on or after ...)*	Application, saving or transitional provisions
AASB 110	7 Aug 2015	F2015L01553	31 Dec 2017	*(beginning)* 1 Jan 2018	see (a) below
AASB 2017-5	12 Dec 2017	F2018L00067	31 Dec 2017	*(beginning)* 1 Jan 2018	see (b) below

(a) Entities may elect to apply this Standard to annual periods beginning after 24 July 2014 but before 1 January 2018.

(b) Entities may elect to apply this Standard to annual periods beginning before 1 January 2018.

Table of amendments

Paragraph affected	How affected	By ... [paragraph/page]
9(b)(i)	amended	AASB 2017-5 [24]

DELETED IAS 10 TEXT

Deleted IAS 10 text is not part of AASB 110.

23A   IFRS 13, issued in May 2011, amended paragraph 11. An entity shall apply that amendment when it applies IFRS 13.

24   This Standard supersedes IAS 10 *Events After the Balance Sheet Date* (revised in 1999).

AASB 112

Income Taxes

(Compiled February 2016)

This compiled Standard applies to annual periods beginning on or after 1 January 2018 but before 1 January 2019. Earlier application is permitted for annual periods beginning after 24 July 2014 but before 1 January 2018. It incorporates relevant amendments made up to and including 24 February 2016.

Prepared on 20 March 2017 by the staff of the Australian Accounting Standards Board.

Compilation no. 1

Compilation date: 31 December 2016

This note is not part of Accounting Standard AASB 112.

The following unincorporated amendments are not included in this compiled Standard.

- AASB 2018-1 *Amendments to AAS — Annual Improvements 2015–2017 Cycle*. This Standard makes amendments to AASB 3 *Business Combinations*, AASB 11 *Joint Arrangements*, AASB 112 *Income Taxes* and AASB 123 *Borrowing Costs*. These amendments arise from the issuance of IFRS *Annual Improvements to IFRS Standards 2015–2017 Cycle* by the IASB in December 2017. This Standard applies to annual periods beginning on or after 1 January 2019, but earlier application is permitted.

- AASB 1058 *Income of Not-for-Profit Entities* — Appendix D sets out the amendments to other Australian Accounting Standards that are a consequence of the AASB issuing this Standard. It is applicable from 1 January 2019. Earlier application is permitted, but amendments to AASB 117 apply before 1 January 2019 only if AASB 1058 is also applied to an earlier period. In addition, AASB 1 and AASB 16 amendments are applied to an earlier period only if AASB 16 is also applied to that period.

- AASB 16 *Leases* — Appendix D sets out the amendments to other Standards that are a consequence of the AASB issuing this Standard. It is applicable from 1 January 2019. Earlier application is permitted, but entities must apply AASB 15 *Revenue from Contracts with Customers* before applying this Standard.

- AASB 2016-7 *Amendments to Australian Accounting Standards — Deferral of AASB 15 for Not-for-Profit Entities*. This Standard defers the consequential amendments that were originally set out in AASB 2014-5 *Amendments to Australian Accounting Standards arising from AASB 15,* by restating the effective date of the amendments set out in AASB 2015-8 *Amendments to Australian Accounting Standards* for not-for-profit entities. This Standard defers the application of AASB 15 to 1 January 2019. Earlier application is permitted provided AASB 1058 is also applied to the same period.

Entities early-adopting any amendments with later application dates will need to refer to the amending Standards that have not yet been incorporated into compilations. The abovementioned unincorporated amendments may be located on the AASB website at www.aasb.gov.au or on the Federal Register of Legislation website at www.legislation.gov.au.

CONTENTS

AASB

COMPILATION DETAILS

DELETED IAS 12 TEXT

BASIS FOR CONCLUSIONS ON IAS 12 (available on the AASB website)

Australian Accounting Standard AASB 112 *Income Taxes* (as amended) is set out in paragraphs 1 – Aus99.2 and Appendix A. All the paragraphs have equal authority. Paragraphs in **bold type** state the main principles. AASB 112 is to be read in the context of other Australian Accounting Standards, including AASB 1048 *Interpretation of Standards*, which identifies the Australian Accounting Interpretations, and AASB 1057 *Application of Australian Accounting Standards*. In the absence of explicit guidance, AASB 108 *Accounting Policies, Changes in Accounting Estimates and Errors* provides a basis for selecting and applying accounting policies.

COMPARISON WITH IAS 12

AASB 112 *Income Taxes* as amended incorporates IAS 12 *Income Taxes* as issued and amended by the International Accounting Standards Board (IASB). Australian-specific paragraphs (which are not included in IAS 12) are identified with the prefix "Aus" or "RDR". Paragraphs that apply only to not-for-profit entities begin by identifying their limited applicability.

Tier 1

For-profit entities complying with AASB 112 also comply with IAS 12.

Not-for-profit entities' compliance with IAS 12 will depend on whether any "Aus" paragraphs that specifically apply to not-for-profit entities provide additional guidance or contain applicable requirements that are inconsistent with IAS 12.

Tier 2

Entities preparing general purpose financial statements under Australian Accounting Standards – Reduced Disclosure Requirements (Tier 2) will not be in compliance with IFRSs.

AASB 1053 *Application of Tiers of Australian Accounting Standards* explains the two tiers of reporting requirements.

ACCOUNTING STANDARD AASB 112

The Australian Accounting Standards Board made Accounting Standard AASB 112 *Income Taxes* under section 334 of the *Corporations Act 2001* on 7 August 2015.

This compiled version of AASB 112 applies to annual periods beginning on or after 1 January 2018 but before 1 January 2019. It incorporates relevant amendments contained in other AASB Standards made by the AASB up to and including 24 February 2016 (see Compilation Details).

ACCOUNTING STANDARD AASB 112
INCOME TAXES

Objective

The objective of this Standard is to prescribe the accounting treatment for income taxes. The principal issue in accounting for income taxes is how to account for the current and future tax consequences of:

(a)   the future recovery (settlement) of the carrying amount of assets (liabilities) that are recognised in an entity's statement of financial position; and

(b)   transactions and other events of the current period that are recognised in an entity's financial statements.

It is inherent in the recognition of an asset or liability that the reporting entity expects to recover or settle the carrying amount of that asset or liability. If it is probable that recovery or settlement of that carrying amount will make future tax payments larger (smaller) than they would be if such recovery or settlement were to have no tax consequences, this Standard requires an entity to recognise a deferred tax liability (deferred tax asset), with certain limited exceptions.

This Standard requires an entity to account for the tax consequences of transactions and other events in the same way that it accounts for the transactions and other events themselves. Thus, for transactions and other events recognised in profit or loss, any related tax effects are also recognised in profit or loss. For transactions and other events recognised outside profit or loss (either in other comprehensive income or directly in equity), any related tax effects are also recognised outside profit or loss (either in other comprehensive income or directly in equity, respectively). Similarly, the recognition of deferred tax assets and liabilities in a business combination affects the amount of goodwill arising in that business combination or the amount of the bargain purchase gain recognised.

This Standard also deals with the recognition of deferred tax assets arising from unused tax losses or unused tax credits, the presentation of income taxes in the financial statements and the disclosure of information relating to income taxes.

Scope

1   This Standard shall be applied in accounting for income taxes.

2   For the purposes of this Standard, income taxes include all domestic and foreign taxes which are based on taxable profits. Income taxes also include taxes, such as withholding taxes, which are payable by a subsidiary, associate or joint arrangement on distributions to the reporting entity.

Aus2.1   For public sector entities and for the purposes of this Standard, income taxes also include forms of income tax that may be payable by a public sector entity under their own enabling legislation or other authority. These forms of income tax are often referred to as "income tax equivalents".

3   [Deleted]

4   This Standard does not deal with the methods of accounting for government grants (see AASB 120 *Accounting for Government Grants and Disclosure of Government Assistance* or, for not-for-profit entities, AASB 1004 *Contributions*) or investment tax credits. However, this Standard does deal with the accounting for temporary differences that may arise from such grants or investment tax credits.

Definitions

5   **The following terms are used in this Standard with the meanings specified:**

Accounting profit **is profit or loss for a period before deducting tax expense.**

Taxable profit **(***tax loss***) is the profit (loss) for a period, determined in accordance with the rules established by the taxation authorities, upon which income taxes are payable (recoverable).**

Tax expense **(***tax income***) is the aggregate amount included in the determination of profit or loss for the period in respect of current tax and deferred tax.**

Current tax **is the amount of income taxes payable (recoverable) in respect of the taxable profit (tax loss) for a period.**

Deferred tax liabilities **are the amounts of income taxes payable in future periods in respect of taxable temporary differences.**

Deferred tax assets are the amounts of income taxes recoverable in future periods in respect of:

(a)   deductible temporary differences;

(b)   the carryforward of unused tax losses; and

(c)   the carryforward of unused tax credits.

Temporary differences are differences between the carrying amount of an asset or liability in the statement of financial position and its tax base. Temporary differences may be either:

(a)   *taxable temporary differences*, which are temporary differences that will result in taxable amounts in determining taxable profit (tax loss) of future periods when the carrying amount of the asset or liability is recovered or settled; or

(b)   *deductible temporary differences*, which are temporary differences that will result in amounts that are deductible in determining taxable profit (tax loss) of future periods when the carrying amount of the asset or liability is recovered or settled.

The *tax base* of an asset or liability is the amount attributed to that asset or liability for tax purposes.

6   Tax expense (tax income) comprises current tax expense (current tax income) and deferred tax expense (deferred tax income).

Tax base

7   The tax base of an asset is the amount that will be deductible for tax purposes against any taxable economic benefits that will flow to an entity when it recovers the carrying amount of the asset. If those economic benefits will not be taxable, the tax base of the asset is equal to its carrying amount.

Examples

1	A machine cost 100. For tax purposes, depreciation of 30 has already been deducted in the current and prior periods and the remaining cost will be deductible in future periods, either as depreciation or through a deduction on disposal. Revenue generated by using the machine is taxable, any gain on disposal of the machine will be taxable and any loss on disposal will be deductible for tax purposes. *The tax base of the machine is 70.*
2	Interest receivable has a carrying amount of 100. The related interest revenue will be taxed on a cash basis. *The tax base of the interest receivable is nil.*
3	Trade receivables have a carrying amount of 100. The related revenue has already been included in taxable profit (tax loss). *The tax base of the trade receivables is 100.*
4	Dividends receivable from a subsidiary have a carrying amount of 100. The dividends are not taxable. *In substance, the entire carrying amount of the asset is deductible against the economic benefits. Consequently, the tax base of the dividends receivable is 100.*[a]
5	A loan receivable has a carrying amount of 100. The repayment of the loan will have no tax consequences. *The tax base of the loan is 100.*

(a)   Under this analysis, there is no taxable temporary difference. An alternative analysis is that the accrued dividends receivable have a tax base of nil and that a tax rate of nil is applied to the resulting taxable temporary difference of 100. Under both analyses, there is no deferred tax liability.

---

8   The tax base of a liability is its carrying amount, less any amount that will be deductible for tax purposes in respect of that liability in future periods. In the case of revenue which is received in advance, the tax base of the resulting liability is its carrying amount, less any amount of the revenue that will not be taxable in future periods.

Examples

1	Current liabilities include accrued expenses with a carrying amount of 100. The related expense will be deducted for tax purposes on a cash basis. *The tax base of the accrued expenses is nil.*
2	Current liabilities include interest revenue received in advance, with a carrying amount of 100. The related interest revenue was taxed on a cash basis. *The tax base of the interest received in advance is nil.*
3	Current liabilities include accrued expenses with a carrying amount of 100. The related expense has already been deducted for tax purposes. *The tax base of the accrued expenses is 100.*
4	Current liabilities include accrued fines and penalties with a carrying amount of 100. Fines and penalties are not deductible for tax purposes. *The tax base of the accrued fines and penalties is 100.*[a]
5	A loan payable has a carrying amount of 100. The repayment of the loan will have no tax consequences. *The tax base of the loan is 100.*

(a) Under this analysis, there is no deductible temporary difference. An alternative analysis is that the accrued fines and penalties payable have a tax base of nil and that a tax rate of nil is applied to the resulting deductible temporary difference of 100. Under both analyses, there is no deferred tax asset.

9   Some items have a tax base but are not recognised as assets and liabilities in the statement of financial position. For example, research costs are recognised as an expense in determining accounting profit in the period in which they are incurred but may not be permitted as a deduction in determining taxable profit (tax loss) until a later period. The difference between the tax base of the research costs, being the amount the taxation authorities will permit as a deduction in future periods, and the carrying amount of nil is a deductible temporary difference that results in a deferred tax asset.

10   Where the tax base of an asset or liability is not immediately apparent, it is helpful to consider the fundamental principle upon which this Standard is based: that an entity shall, with certain limited exceptions, recognise a deferred tax liability (asset) whenever recovery or settlement of the carrying amount of an asset or liability would make future tax payments larger (smaller) than they would be if such recovery or settlement were to have no tax consequences. Example C following paragraph 51A illustrates circumstances when it may be helpful to consider this fundamental principle, for example, when the tax base of an asset or liability depends on the expected manner of recovery or settlement.

11   In consolidated financial statements, temporary differences are determined by comparing the carrying amounts of assets and liabilities in the consolidated financial statements with the appropriate tax base. The tax base is determined by reference to a consolidated tax return in those jurisdictions in which such a return is filed. In other jurisdictions, the tax base is determined by reference to the tax returns of each entity in the group.

Recognition of current tax liabilities and current tax assets

12   **Current tax for current and prior periods shall, to the extent unpaid, be recognised as a liability. If the amount already paid in respect of current and prior periods exceeds the amount due for those periods, the excess shall be recognised as an asset.**

13   **The benefit relating to a tax loss that can be carried back to recover current tax of a previous period shall be recognised as an asset.**

14   When a tax loss is used to recover current tax of a previous period, an entity recognises the benefit as an asset in the period in which the tax loss occurs because it is probable that the benefit will flow to the entity and the benefit can be reliably measured.

Recognition of deferred tax liabilities and deferred tax assets

Taxable temporary differences

15   A deferred tax liability shall be recognised for all taxable temporary differences, except to the extent that the deferred tax liability arises from:

    (a)   the initial recognition of goodwill; or

    (b)   the initial recognition of an asset or liability in a transaction which:

        (i)   is not a business combination; and

        (ii)   at the time of the transaction, affects neither accounting profit nor taxable profit (tax loss).

However, for taxable temporary differences associated with investments in subsidiaries, branches and associates, and interests in joint arrangements, a deferred tax liability shall be recognised in accordance with paragraph 39.

16   It is inherent in the recognition of an asset that its carrying amount will be recovered in the form of economic benefits that flow to the entity in future periods. When the carrying amount of the asset exceeds its tax base, the amount of taxable economic benefits will exceed the amount that will be allowed as a deduction for tax purposes. This difference is a taxable temporary difference and the obligation to pay the resulting income taxes in future periods is a deferred tax liability. As the entity recovers the carrying amount of the asset, the taxable temporary difference will reverse and the entity will have taxable profit. This makes it probable that economic benefits will flow from the entity in the form of tax payments. Therefore, this Standard requires the recognition of all deferred tax liabilities, except in certain circumstances described in paragraphs 15 and 39.

Example

An asset which cost 150 has a carrying amount of 100. Cumulative depreciation for tax purposes is 90 and the tax rate is 25%.

The tax base of the asset is 60 (cost of 150 less cumulative tax depreciation of 90). To recover the carrying amount of 100, the entity must earn taxable income of 100, but will only be able to deduct tax depreciation of 60. Consequently, the entity will pay income taxes of 10 (40 at 25%) when it recovers the carrying amount of the asset. The difference between the carrying amount of 100 and the tax base of 60 is a taxable temporary difference of 40. Therefore, the entity recognises a deferred tax liability of 10 (40 at 25%) representing the income taxes that it will pay when it recovers the carrying amount of the asset.

---

17   Some temporary differences arise when income or expense is included in accounting profit in one period but is included in taxable profit in a different period. Such temporary differences are often described as timing differences. The following are examples of temporary differences of this kind which are taxable temporary differences and which therefore result in deferred tax liabilities:

    (a)   interest revenue is included in accounting profit on a time proportion basis but may, in some jurisdictions, be included in taxable profit when cash is collected. The tax base of any receivable recognised in the statement of financial position with respect to such revenues is nil because the revenues do not affect taxable profit until cash is collected;

    (b)   depreciation used in determining taxable profit (tax loss) may differ from that used in determining accounting profit. The temporary difference is the difference between the carrying amount of the asset and its tax base which is the original cost of the asset less all deductions in respect of that asset permitted by the taxation authorities in determining taxable profit of the current and prior periods. A taxable temporary difference arises, and results in a deferred tax liability, when tax depreciation is accelerated (if tax depreciation is less rapid than accounting depreciation, a deductible temporary difference arises, and results in a deferred tax asset); and

(c)   development costs may be capitalised and amortised over future periods in determining accounting profit but deducted in determining taxable profit in the period in which they are incurred. Such development costs have a tax base of nil as they have already been deducted from taxable profit. The temporary difference is the difference between the carrying amount of the development costs and their tax base of nil.

18   Temporary differences also arise when:

     (a)   the identifiable assets acquired and liabilities assumed in a business combination are recognised at their fair values in accordance with AASB 3 *Business Combinations*, but no equivalent adjustment is made for tax purposes (see paragraph 19);

     (b)   assets are revalued and no equivalent adjustment is made for tax purposes (see paragraph 20);

     (c)   goodwill arises in a business combination (see paragraph 21);

     (d)   the tax base of an asset or liability on initial recognition differs from its initial carrying amount, for example when an entity benefits from non-taxable government grants related to assets (see paragraphs 22, 33 and Aus33.1); or

     (e)   the carrying amount of investments in subsidiaries, branches and associates or interests in joint arrangements becomes different from the tax base of the investment or interest (see paragraphs 38–45).

Business combinations

19   With limited exceptions, the identifiable assets acquired and liabilities assumed in a business combination are recognised at their fair values at the acquisition date. Temporary differences arise when the tax bases of the identifiable assets acquired and liabilities assumed are not affected by the business combination or are affected differently. For example, when the carrying amount of an asset is increased to fair value but the tax base of the asset remains at cost to the previous owner, a taxable temporary difference arises which results in a deferred tax liability. The resulting deferred tax liability affects goodwill (see paragraph 66).

Assets carried at fair value

20   Australian Accounting Standards permit or require certain assets to be carried at fair value or to be revalued (see, for example, AASB 116 *Property, Plant and Equipment*, AASB 138 *Intangible Assets*, AASB 140 *Investment Property* and AASB 9 *Financial Instruments*). In some jurisdictions, the revaluation or other restatement of an asset to fair value affects taxable profit (tax loss) for the current period. As a result, the tax base of the asset is adjusted and no temporary difference arises. In other jurisdictions, the revaluation or restatement of an asset does not affect taxable profit in the period of the revaluation or restatement and, consequently, the tax base of the asset is not adjusted. Nevertheless, the future recovery of the carrying amount will result in a taxable flow of economic benefits to the entity and the amount that will be deductible for tax purposes will differ from the amount of those economic benefits. The difference between the carrying amount of a revalued asset and its tax base is a temporary difference and gives rise to a deferred tax liability or asset. This is true even if:

     (a)   the entity does not intend to dispose of the asset. In such cases, the revalued carrying amount of the asset will be recovered through use and this will generate taxable income which exceeds the depreciation that will be allowable for tax purposes in future periods; or

     (b)   tax on capital gains is deferred if the proceeds of the disposal of the asset are invested in similar assets. In such cases, the tax will ultimately become payable on sale or use of the similar assets.

a deferred tax asset in respect of the income taxes that will be recoverable in future periods.

Example

An entity recognises a liability of 100 for accrued product warranty costs. For tax purposes, the product warranty costs will not be deductible until the entity pays claims. The tax rate is 25%.

The tax base of the liability is nil (carrying amount of 100, less the amount that will be deductible for tax purposes in respect of that liability in future periods). In settling the liability for its carrying amount, the entity will reduce its future taxable profit by an amount of 100 and, consequently, reduce its future tax payments by 25 (100 at 25%). The difference between the carrying amount of 100 and the tax base of nil is a deductible temporary difference of 100. Therefore, the entity recognises a deferred tax asset of 25 (100 at 25%), provided that it is probable that the entity will earn sufficient taxable profit in future periods to benefit from a reduction in tax payments.

---

26   The following are examples of deductible temporary differences that result in deferred tax assets:

(a)   retirement benefit costs may be deducted in determining accounting profit as service is provided by the employee, but deducted in determining taxable profit either when contributions are paid to a fund by the entity or when retirement benefits are paid by the entity. A temporary difference exists between the carrying amount of the liability and its tax base; the tax base of the liability is usually nil. Such a deductible temporary difference results in a deferred tax asset as economic benefits will flow to the entity in the form of a deduction from taxable profits when contributions or retirement benefits are paid;

(b)   research costs are recognised as an expense in determining accounting profit in the period in which they are incurred but may not be permitted as a deduction in determining taxable profit (tax loss) until a later period. The difference between the tax base of the research costs, being the amount the taxation authorities will permit as a deduction in future periods, and the carrying amount of nil is a deductible temporary difference that results in a deferred tax asset;

(c)   with limited exceptions, an entity recognises the identifiable assets acquired and liabilities assumed in a business combination at their fair values at the acquisition date. When a liability assumed is recognised at the acquisition date but the related costs are not deducted in determining taxable profits until a later period, a deductible temporary difference arises which results in a deferred tax asset. A deferred tax asset also arises when the fair value of an identifiable asset acquired is less than its tax base. In both cases, the resulting deferred tax asset affects goodwill (see paragraph 66); and

(d)   certain assets may be carried at fair value, or may be revalued, without an equivalent adjustment being made for tax purposes (see paragraph 20). A deductible temporary difference arises if the tax base of the asset exceeds its carrying amount.

Example illustrating paragraph 26(d)

Identification of a deductible temporary difference at the end of Year 2:

Entity A purchases for CU1,000, at the beginning of Year 1, a debt instrument with a nominal value of CU1,000 payable on maturity in 5 years with an interest rate of 2% payable at the end of each year. The effective interest rate is 2%. The debt instrument is measured at fair value.

At the end of Year 2, the fair value of the debt instrument has decreased to CU918 as a result of an increase in market interest rates to 5%. It is probable that Entity A will collect all the contractual cash flows if it continues to hold the debt instrument.

Any gains (losses) on the debt instrument are taxable (deductible) only when realised. The gains (losses) arising on the sale or maturity of the debt instrument are calculated for tax purposes as the difference between the amount collected and the original cost of the debt instrument.

> Accordingly, the tax base of the debt instrument is its original cost.
>
> *The difference between the carrying amount of the debt instrument in Entity A's statement of financial position of CU918 and its tax base of CU1,000 gives rise to a deductible temporary difference of CU82 at the end of Year 2 (see paragraphs 20 and 26(d)), irrespective of whether Entity A expects to recover the carrying amount of the debt instrument by sale or by use, ie by holding it and collecting contractual cash flows, or a combination of both.*
>
> *This is because deductible temporary differences are differences between the carrying amount of an asset or liability in the statement of financial position and its tax base that will result in amounts that are deductible in determining taxable profit (tax loss) of future periods, when the carrying amount of the asset or liability is recovered or settled (see paragraph 5). Entity A obtains a deduction equivalent to the tax base of the asset of CU1,000 in determining taxable profit (tax loss) either on sale or on maturity.*

27   The reversal of deductible temporary differences results in deductions in determining taxable profits of future periods. However, economic benefits in the form of reductions in tax payments will flow to the entity only if it earns sufficient taxable profits against which the deductions can be offset. Therefore, an entity recognises deferred tax assets only when it is probable that taxable profits will be available against which the deductible temporary differences can be utilised.

27A   When an entity assesses whether taxable profits will be available against which it can utilise a deductible temporary difference, it considers whether tax law restricts the sources of taxable profits against which it may make deductions on the reversal of that deductible temporary difference. If tax law imposes no such restrictions, an entity assesses a deductible temporary difference in combination with all of its other deductible temporary differences. However, if tax law restricts the utilisation of losses to deduction against income of a specific type, a deductible temporary difference is assessed in combination only with other deductible temporary differences of the appropriate type.

28   It is probable that taxable profit will be available against which a deductible temporary difference can be utilised when there are sufficient taxable temporary differences relating to the same taxation authority and the same taxable entity which are expected to reverse:

   (a)   in the same period as the expected reversal of the deductible temporary difference; or

   (b)   in periods into which a tax loss arising from the deferred tax asset can be carried back or forward.

   In such circumstances, the deferred tax asset is recognised in the period in which the deductible temporary differences arise.

29   When there are insufficient taxable temporary differences relating to the same taxation authority and the same taxable entity, the deferred tax asset is recognised to the extent that:

   (a)   it is probable that the entity will have sufficient taxable profit relating to the same taxation authority and the same taxable entity in the same period as the reversal of the deductible temporary difference (or in the periods into which a tax loss arising from the deferred tax asset can be carried back or forward). In evaluating whether it will have sufficient taxable profit in future periods, an entity:

      (i)   compares the deductible temporary differences with future taxable profit that excludes tax deductions resulting from the reversal of those deductible temporary differences. This comparison shows the extent to which the future taxable profit is sufficient for the entity to deduct the amounts resulting from the reversal of those deductible temporary differences; and

      (ii)   ignores taxable amounts arising from deductible temporary differences that are expected to originate in future periods, because the deferred

AASB

tax asset arising from these deductible temporary differences will itself require future taxable profit in order to be utilised; or

(b)   tax planning opportunities are available to the entity that will create taxable profit in appropriate periods.

29A   The estimate of probable future taxable profit may include the recovery of some of an entity's assets for more than their carrying amount if there is sufficient evidence that it is probable that the entity will achieve this. For example, when an asset is measured at fair value, the entity shall consider whether there is sufficient evidence to conclude that it is probable that the entity will recover the asset for more than its carrying amount. This may be the case, for example, when an entity expects to hold a fixed-rate debt instrument and collect the contractual cash flows.

30   Tax planning opportunities are actions that the entity would take in order to create or increase taxable income in a particular period before the expiry of a tax loss or tax credit carryforward. For example, in some jurisdictions, taxable profit may be created or increased by:

(a)   electing to have interest income taxed on either a received or receivable basis;

(b)   deferring the claim for certain deductions from taxable profit;

(c)   selling, and perhaps leasing back, assets that have appreciated but for which the tax base has not been adjusted to reflect such appreciation; and

(d)   selling an asset that generates non-taxable income (such as, in some jurisdictions, a government bond) in order to purchase another investment that generates taxable income.

Where tax planning opportunities advance taxable profit from a later period to an earlier period, the utilisation of a tax loss or tax credit carryforward still depends on the existence of future taxable profit from sources other than future originating temporary differences.

31   When an entity has a history of recent losses, the entity considers the guidance in paragraphs 35 and 36.

32   [Deleted]

Goodwill

32A   If the carrying amount of goodwill arising in a business combination is less than its tax base, the difference gives rise to a deferred tax asset. The deferred tax asset arising from the initial recognition of goodwill shall be recognised as part of the accounting for a business combination to the extent that it is probable that taxable profit will be available against which the deductible temporary difference could be utilised.

Initial recognition of an asset or liability

33   One case when a deferred tax asset arises on initial recognition of an asset is when a non-taxable government grant related to an asset is deducted in arriving at the carrying amount of the asset but, for tax purposes, is not deducted from the asset's depreciable amount (in other words its tax base); the carrying amount of the asset is less than its tax base and this gives rise to a deductible temporary difference. Government grants may also be set up as deferred income in which case the difference between the deferred income and its tax base of nil is a deductible temporary difference. Whichever method of presentation an entity adopts, the entity does not recognise the resulting deferred tax asset, for the reason given in paragraph 22.

Aus33.1   In respect of not-for-profit entities, a deferred tax asset will not arise on a non-taxable government grant relating to an asset. Under AASB 1004 *Contributions*, a not-for-profit entity accounts for the receipt of non-taxable government grants as income rather than as deferred income when those grants are controlled by the entity. As such, a temporary difference does not arise.

Unused tax losses and unused tax credits

34 **A deferred tax asset shall be recognised for the carryforward of unused tax losses and unused tax credits to the extent that it is probable that future taxable profit will be available against which the unused tax losses and unused tax credits can be utilised.**

35 The criteria for recognising deferred tax assets arising from the carryforward of unused tax losses and tax credits are the same as the criteria for recognising deferred tax assets arising from deductible temporary differences. However, the existence of unused tax losses is strong evidence that future taxable profit may not be available. Therefore, when an entity has a history of recent losses, the entity recognises a deferred tax asset arising from unused tax losses or tax credits only to the extent that the entity has sufficient taxable temporary differences or there is convincing other evidence that sufficient taxable profit will be available against which the unused tax losses or unused tax credits can be utilised by the entity. In such circumstances, paragraph 82 requires disclosure of the amount of the deferred tax asset and the nature of the evidence supporting its recognition.

36 An entity considers the following criteria in assessing the probability that taxable profit will be available against which the unused tax losses or unused tax credits can be utilised:

(a) whether the entity has sufficient taxable temporary differences relating to the same taxation authority and the same taxable entity, which will result in taxable amounts against which the unused tax losses or unused tax credits can be utilised before they expire;

(b) whether it is probable that the entity will have taxable profits before the unused tax losses or unused tax credits expire;

(c) whether the unused tax losses result from identifiable causes which are unlikely to recur; and

(d) whether tax planning opportunities (see paragraph 30) are available to the entity that will create taxable profit in the period in which the unused tax losses or unused tax credits can be utilised.

To the extent that it is not probable that taxable profit will be available against which the unused tax losses or unused tax credits can be utilised, the deferred tax asset is not recognised.

Reassessment of unrecognised deferred tax assets

37 At the end of each reporting period, an entity reassesses unrecognised deferred tax assets. The entity recognises a previously unrecognised deferred tax asset to the extent that it has become probable that future taxable profit will allow the deferred tax asset to be recovered. For example, an improvement in trading conditions may make it more probable that the entity will be able to generate sufficient taxable profit in the future for the deferred tax asset to meet the recognition criteria set out in paragraph 24 or 34. Another example is when an entity reassesses deferred tax assets at the date of a business combination or subsequently (see paragraphs 67 and 68).

Investments in subsidiaries, branches and associates and interests in joint arrangements

38 Temporary differences arise when the carrying amount of investments in subsidiaries, branches and associates or interests in joint arrangements (namely the parent or investor's share of the net assets of the subsidiary, branch, associate or investee, including the carrying amount of goodwill) becomes different from the tax base (which is often cost) of the investment or interest. Such differences may arise in a number of different circumstances, for example:

(a) the existence of undistributed profits of subsidiaries, branches, associates and joint arrangements;

(b)   changes in foreign exchange rates when a parent and its subsidiary are based in different countries; and

(c)   a reduction in the carrying amount of an investment in an associate to its recoverable amount.

In consolidated financial statements, the temporary difference may be different from the temporary difference associated with that investment in the parent's separate financial statements if the parent carries the investment in its separate financial statements at cost or revalued amount.

39   An entity shall recognise a deferred tax liability for all taxable temporary differences associated with investments in subsidiaries, branches and associates, and interests in joint arrangements, except to the extent that both of the following conditions are satisfied:

    (a)   the parent, investor, joint venturer or joint operator is able to control the timing of the reversal of the temporary difference; and

    (b)   it is probable that the temporary difference will not reverse in the foreseeable future.

40   As a parent controls the dividend policy of its subsidiary, it is able to control the timing of the reversal of temporary differences associated with that investment (including the temporary differences arising not only from undistributed profits but also from any foreign exchange translation differences). Furthermore, it would often be impracticable to determine the amount of income taxes that would be payable when the temporary difference reverses. Therefore, when the parent has determined that those profits will not be distributed in the foreseeable future the parent does not recognise a deferred tax liability. The same considerations apply to investments in branches.

41   The non-monetary assets and liabilities of an entity are measured in its functional currency (see AASB 121 *The Effects of Changes in Foreign Exchange Rates*). If the entity's taxable profit or tax loss (and, hence, the tax base of its non-monetary assets and liabilities) is determined in a different currency, changes in the exchange rate give rise to temporary differences that result in a recognised deferred tax liability or (subject to paragraph 24) asset. The resulting deferred tax is charged or credited to profit or loss (see paragraph 58).

42   An investor in an associate does not control that entity and is usually not in a position to determine its dividend policy. Therefore, in the absence of an agreement requiring that the profits of the associate will not be distributed in the foreseeable future, an investor recognises a deferred tax liability arising from taxable temporary differences associated with its investment in the associate. In some cases, an investor may not be able to determine the amount of tax that would be payable if it recovers the cost of its investment in an associate, but can determine that it will equal or exceed a minimum amount. In such cases, the deferred tax liability is measured at this amount.

43   The arrangement between the parties to a joint arrangement usually deals with the distribution of the profits and identifies whether decisions on such matters require the consent of all the parties or a group of the parties. When the joint venturer or joint operator can control the timing of the distribution of its share of the profits of the joint arrangement and it is probable that its share of the profits will not be distributed in the foreseeable future, a deferred tax liability is not recognised.

44   An entity shall recognise a deferred tax asset for all deductible temporary differences arising from investments in subsidiaries, branches and associates, and interests in joint arrangements, to the extent that, and only to the extent that, it is probable that:

    (a)   the temporary difference will reverse in the foreseeable future; and

    (b)   taxable profit will be available against which the temporary difference can be utilised.

45   In deciding whether a deferred tax asset is recognised for deductible temporary differences associated with its investments in subsidiaries, branches and associates, and

its interests in joint arrangements, an entity considers the guidance set out in paragraphs 28 to 31.

Measurement

46   **Current tax liabilities (assets) for the current and prior periods shall be measured at the amount expected to be paid to (recovered from) the taxation authorities, using the tax rates (and tax laws) that have been enacted or substantively enacted by the end of the reporting period.**

47   **Deferred tax assets and liabilities shall be measured at the tax rates that are expected to apply to the period when the asset is realised or the liability is settled, based on tax rates (and tax laws) that have been enacted or substantively enacted by the end of the reporting period.**

48   Current and deferred tax assets and liabilities are usually measured using the tax rates (and tax laws) that have been enacted. However, in some jurisdictions, announcements of tax rates (and tax laws) by the government have the substantive effect of actual enactment, which may follow the announcement by a period of several months. In these circumstances, tax assets and liabilities are measured using the announced tax rate (and tax laws).

49   When different tax rates apply to different levels of taxable income, deferred tax assets and liabilities are measured using the average rates that are expected to apply to the taxable profit (tax loss) of the periods in which the temporary differences are expected to reverse.

50   [Deleted]

51   **The measurement of deferred tax liabilities and deferred tax assets shall reflect the tax consequences that would follow from the manner in which the entity expects, at the end of the reporting period, to recover or settle the carrying amount of its assets and liabilities.**

51A   In some jurisdictions, the manner in which an entity recovers (settles) the carrying amount of an asset (liability) may affect either or both of:

(a)   the tax rate applicable when the entity recovers (settles) the carrying amount of the asset (liability); and

(b)   the tax base of the asset (liability).

In such cases, an entity measures deferred tax liabilities and deferred tax assets using the tax rate and the tax base that are consistent with the expected manner of recovery or settlement.

Example A

An item of property, plant and equipment has a carrying amount of 100 and a tax base of 60. A tax rate of 20% would apply if the item were sold and a tax rate of 30% would apply to other income.

The entity recognises a deferred tax liability of 8 (40 at 20%) if it expects to sell the item without further use and a deferred tax liability of 12 (40 at 30%) if it expects to retain the item and recover its carrying amount through use.

Example B

An item or property, plant and equipment with a cost of 100 and a carrying amount of 80 is revalued to 150. No equivalent adjustment is made for tax purposes. Cumulative depreciation for tax purposes is 30 and the tax rate is 30%. If the item is sold for more than cost, the cumulative tax depreciation of 30 will be included in taxable income but sale proceeds in excess of cost will not be taxable.

The tax base of the item is 70 and there is a taxable temporary difference of 80. If the entity expects to recover the carrying amount by using the item, it must generate taxable income of 150, but will only be able to deduct depreciation of 70. On this basis, there is a deferred tax liability of 24 (80 at 30%). If the entity expects to recover the carrying amount by selling

---

the item immediately for proceeds of 150, the deferred tax liability is computed as follows:

	Taxable Temporary Difference	Tax Rate	Deferred Tax Liability
Cumulative tax depreciation	30	30%	9
Proceeds in excess of cost	50	nil	–
Total	80		9

(note: in accordance with paragraph 61A, the additional deferred tax that arises on the revaluation is recognised in other comprehensive income)

Example C

The facts are as in example B, except that if the item is sold for more than cost, the cumulative tax depreciation will be included in taxable income (taxed at 30%) and the sale proceeds will be taxed at 40%, after deducting an inflation-adjusted cost of 110.

If the entity expects to recover the carrying amount by using the item, it must generate taxable income of 150, but will only be able to deduct depreciation of 70. On this basis, the tax base is 70, there is a taxable temporary difference of 80 and there is a deferred tax liability of 24 (80 at 30%), as in example B.

If the entity expects to recover the carrying amount by selling the item immediately for proceeds of 150, the entity will be able to deduct the indexed cost of 110. The net proceeds of 40 will be taxed at 40%. In addition, the cumulative tax depreciation of 30 will be included in taxable income and taxed at 30%. On this basis, the tax base is 80 (110 less 30), there is a taxable temporary difference of 70 and there is a deferred tax liability of 25 (40 at 40% plus 30 at 30%). If the tax base is not immediately apparent in this example, it may be helpful to consider the fundamental principle set out in paragraph 10.

(note: in accordance with paragraph 61A, the additional deferred tax that arises on the revaluation is recognised in other comprehensive income)

51B   If a deferred tax liability or deferred tax asset arises from a non-depreciable asset measured using the revaluation model in AASB 116, the measurement of the deferred tax liability or deferred tax asset shall reflect the tax consequences of recovering the carrying amount of the non-depreciable asset through sale, regardless of the basis of measuring the carrying amount of that asset. Accordingly, if the tax law specifies a tax rate applicable to the taxable amount derived from the sale of an asset that differs from the tax rate applicable to the taxable amount derived from using an asset, the former rate is applied in measuring the deferred tax liability or asset related to a non-depreciable asset.

51C   If a deferred tax liability or asset arises from investment property that is measured using the fair value model in AASB 140, there is a rebuttable presumption that the carrying amount of the investment property will be recovered through sale. Accordingly, unless the presumption is rebutted, the measurement of the deferred tax liability or deferred tax asset shall reflect the tax consequences of recovering the carrying amount of the investment property entirely through sale. This presumption is rebutted if the investment property is depreciable and is held within a business model whose objective is to consume substantially all of the economic benefits embodied in the investment property over time, rather than through sale. If the presumption is rebutted, the requirements of paragraphs 51 and 51A shall be followed.

Example illustrating paragraph 51C

An investment property has a cost of 100 and fair value of 150. It is measured using the fair value model in AASB 140. It comprises land with a cost of 40 and fair value of 60 and a building with a cost of 60 and fair value of 90. The land has an unlimited useful life.

Cumulative depreciation of the building for tax purposes is 30. Unrealised changes in the fair value of the investment property do not affect taxable profit. If the investment property is sold for more than cost, the reversal of the cumulative tax depreciation of 30 will be included in taxable profit and taxed at an ordinary tax rate of 30%. For sales proceeds in excess of cost, tax law specifies tax rates of 25% for assets held for less than two years and 20% for assets held for two years or more.

Because the investment property is measured using the fair value model in AASB 140, there is a rebuttable presumption that the entity will recover the carrying amount of the investment property entirely through sale. If that presumption is not rebutted, the deferred tax reflects the tax consequences of recovering the carrying amount entirely through sale, even if the entity expects to earn rental income from the property before sale.

The tax base of the land if it is sold is 40 and there is a taxable temporary difference of 20 (60 – 40). The tax base of the building if it is sold is 30 (60 – 30) and there is a taxable temporary difference of 60 (90 – 30). As a result, the total taxable temporary difference relating to the investment property is 80 (20 + 60).

In accordance with paragraph 47, the tax rate is the rate expected to apply to the period when the investment property is realised. Thus, the resulting deferred tax liability is computed as follows, if the entity expects to sell the property after holding it for more than two years:

	Taxable Temporary Difference	Tax Rate	Deferred Tax Liability
Cumulative tax depreciation	30	30%	9
Proceeds in excess of cost	50	20%	10
Total	80		19

If the entity expects to sell the property after holding it for less than two years, the above computation would be amended to apply a tax rate of 25%, rather than 20%, to the proceeds in excess of cost.

If, instead, the entity holds the building within a business model whose objective is to consume substantially all of the economic benefits embodied in the building over time, rather than through sale, this presumption would be rebutted for the building. However, the land is not depreciable. Therefore the presumption of recovery through sale would not be rebutted for the land. It follows that the deferred tax liability would reflect the tax consequences of recovering the carrying amount of the building through use and the carrying amount of the land through sale.

The tax base of the building if it is used is 30 (60 – 30) and there is a taxable temporary difference of 60 (90 – 30), resulting in a deferred tax liability of 18 (60 at 30%).

The tax base of the land if it is sold is 40 and there is a taxable temporary difference of 20 (60 – 40), resulting in a deferred tax liability of 4 (20 at 20%).

As a result, if the presumption of recovery through sale is rebutted for the building, the deferred tax liability relating to the investment property is 22 (18 + 4).

51D   The rebuttable presumption in paragraph 51C also applies when a deferred tax liability or a deferred tax asset arises from measuring investment property in a business combination if the entity will use the fair value model when subsequently measuring that investment property.

51E   Paragraphs 51B–51D do not change the requirements to apply the principles in paragraphs 24–33 (deductible temporary differences) and paragraphs 34–36 (unused tax losses and unused tax credits) of this Standard when recognising and measuring deferred tax assets.

52   [moved and renumbered 51A]

52A   In some jurisdictions, income taxes are payable at a higher or lower rate if part or all of the net profit or retained earnings is paid out as a dividend to shareholders of the entity. In some other jurisdictions, income taxes may be refundable or payable if part or all of the net profit or retained earnings is paid out as a dividend to shareholders of the entity. In these circumstances, current and deferred tax assets and liabilities are measured at the tax rate applicable to undistributed profits.

52B   In the circumstances described in paragraph 52A, the income tax consequences of dividends are recognised when a liability to pay the dividend is recognised. The income

AASB

tax consequences of dividends are more directly linked to past transactions or events than to distributions to owners. Therefore, the income tax consequences of dividends are recognised in profit or loss for the period as required by paragraph 58 except to the extent that the income tax consequences of dividends arise from the circumstances described in paragraph 58(a) and (b).

Example illustrating paragraphs 52A and 52B

The following example deals with the measurement of current and deferred tax assets and liabilities for an entity in a jurisdiction where income taxes are payable at a higher rate on undistributed profits (50%) with an amount being refundable when profits are distributed. The tax rate on distributed profits is 35%.

At the end of the reporting period, 31 December 20X1, the entity does not recognise a liability for dividends proposed or declared after the reporting period. As a result, no dividends are recognised in the year 20X1. Taxable income for 20X1 is 100,000. The net taxable temporary difference for the year 20X1 is 40,000.

The entity recognises a current tax liability and a current income tax expense of 50,000. No asset is recognised for the amount potentially recoverable as a result of future dividends. The entity also recognises a deferred tax liability and deferred tax expense of 20,000 (40,000 at 50%) representing the income taxes that the entity will pay when it recovers or settles the carrying amounts of its assets and liabilities based on the tax rate applicable to undistributed profits.

Subsequently, on 15 March 20X2 the entity recognises dividends of 10,000 from previous operating profits as a liability.

On 15 March 20X2, the entity recognises the recovery of income taxes of 1,500 (15% of the dividends recognised as a liability) as a current tax asset and as a reduction of current income tax expense for 20X2.

---

53   **Deferred tax assets and liabilities shall not be discounted.**

54   The reliable determination of deferred tax assets and liabilities on a discounted basis requires detailed scheduling of the timing of the reversal of each temporary difference. In many cases such scheduling is impracticable or highly complex. Therefore, it is inappropriate to require discounting of deferred tax assets and liabilities. To permit, but not to require, discounting would result in deferred tax assets and liabilities which would not be comparable between entities. Therefore, this Standard does not require or permit the discounting of deferred tax assets and liabilities.

55   Temporary differences are determined by reference to the carrying amount of an asset or liability. This applies even where that carrying amount is itself determined on a discounted basis, for example in the case of retirement benefit obligations (see AASB 119 *Employee Benefits*).

56   **The carrying amount of a deferred tax asset shall be reviewed at the end of each reporting period. An entity shall reduce the carrying amount of a deferred tax asset to the extent that it is no longer probable that sufficient taxable profit will be available to allow the benefit of part or all of that deferred tax asset to be utilised. Any such reduction shall be reversed to the extent that it becomes probable that sufficient taxable profit will be available.**

Recognition of current and deferred tax

57   Accounting for the current and deferred tax effects of a transaction or other event is consistent with the accounting for the transaction or event itself. Paragraphs 58 to 68C implement this principle.

Items recognised in profit or loss

58   **Current and deferred tax shall be recognised as income or an expense and included in profit or loss for the period, except to the extent that the tax arises from:**

(a)   a transaction or event which is recognised, in the same or a different period, outside profit or loss, either in other comprehensive income or directly in equity (see paragraphs 61A–65); or

(b)   a business combination (other than the acquisition by an investment entity, as defined in AASB 10 *Consolidated Financial Statements*, of a subsidiary that is required to be measured at fair value through profit or loss) (see paragraphs 66–68).

59   Most deferred tax liabilities and deferred tax assets arise where income or expense is included in accounting profit in one period, but is included in taxable profit (tax loss) in a different period. The resulting deferred tax is recognised in profit or loss. Examples are when:

(a)   interest, royalty or dividend revenue is received in arrears and is included in accounting profit in accordance with AASB 15 *Revenue from Contracts with Customers*, AASB 139 *Financial Instruments: Recognition and Measurement* or AASB 9 *Financial Instruments*, as relevant, but is included in taxable profit (tax loss) on a cash basis; and

(b)   costs of intangible assets have been capitalised in accordance with AASB 138 and are being amortised in profit or loss, but were deducted for tax purposes when they were incurred.

60   The carrying amount of deferred tax assets and liabilities may change even though there is no change in the amount of the related temporary differences. This can result, for example, from:

(a)   a change in tax rates or tax laws;

(b)   a reassessment of the recoverability of deferred tax assets; or

(c)   a change in the expected manner of recovery of an asset.

The resulting deferred tax is recognised in profit or loss, except to the extent that it relates to items previously recognised outside profit or loss (see paragraph 63).

Items recognised outside profit or loss

61   [Deleted]

61A   **Current tax and deferred tax shall be recognised outside profit or loss if the tax relates to items that are recognised, in the same or a different period, outside profit or loss. Therefore, current tax and deferred tax that relates to items that are recognised, in the same or a different period:**

(a)   **in other comprehensive income, shall be recognised in other comprehensive income (see paragraph 62).**

(b)   **directly in equity, shall be recognised directly in equity (see paragraph 62A).**

62   Australian Accounting Standards require or permit particular items to be recognised in other comprehensive income. Examples of such items are:

(a)   a change in carrying amount arising from the revaluation of property, plant and equipment (see AASB 116); and

(b)   [deleted]

(c)   exchange differences arising on the translation of the financial statements of a foreign operation (see AASB 121).

(d)   [deleted]

62A   Australian Accounting Standards require or permit particular items to be credited or charged directly to equity. Examples of such items are:

(a)   an adjustment to the opening balance of retained earnings resulting from either a change in accounting policy that is applied retrospectively or the correction of an error (see AASB 108 *Accounting Policies, Changes in Accounting Estimates and Errors*); and

(b)   amounts arising on initial recognition of the equity component of a compound financial instrument (see paragraph 23).

63   In exceptional circumstances it may be difficult to determine the amount of current and deferred tax that relates to items recognised outside profit or loss (either in other comprehensive income or directly in equity). This may be the case, for example, when:

(a)   there are graduated rates of income tax and it is impossible to determine the rate at which a specific component of taxable profit (tax loss) has been taxed;

(b)   a change in the tax rate or other tax rules affects a deferred tax asset or liability relating (in whole or in part) to an item that was previously recognised outside profit or loss; or

(c)   an entity determines that a deferred tax asset should be recognised, or should no longer be recognised in full, and the deferred tax asset relates (in whole or in part) to an item that was previously recognised outside profit or loss.

In such cases, the current and deferred tax related to items that are recognised outside profit or loss are based on a reasonable pro rata allocation of the current and deferred tax of the entity in the tax jurisdiction concerned, or other method that achieves a more appropriate allocation in the circumstances.

64   AASB 116 does not specify whether an entity should transfer each year from revaluation surplus to retained earnings an amount equal to the difference between the depreciation or amortisation on a revalued asset and the depreciation or amortisation based on the cost of that asset. If an entity makes such a transfer, the amount transferred is net of any related deferred tax. Similar considerations apply to transfers made on disposal of an item of property, plant or equipment.

65   When an asset is revalued for tax purposes and that revaluation is related to an accounting revaluation of an earlier period, or to one that is expected to be carried out in a future period, the tax effects of both the asset revaluation and the adjustment of the tax base are recognised in other comprehensive income in the periods in which they occur. However, if the revaluation for tax purposes is not related to an accounting revaluation of an earlier period, or to one that is expected to be carried out in a future period, the tax effects of the adjustment of the tax base are recognised in profit or loss.

65A   When an entity pays dividends to its shareholders, it may be required to pay a portion of the dividends to taxation authorities on behalf of shareholders. In many jurisdictions, this amount is referred to as a withholding tax. Such an amount paid or payable to taxation authorities is charged to equity as a part of the dividends.

Deferred tax arising from a business combination

66   As explained in paragraphs 19 and 26(c), temporary differences may arise in a business combination. In accordance with AASB 3, an entity recognises any resulting deferred tax assets (to the extent that they meet the recognition criteria in paragraph 24) or deferred tax liabilities as identifiable assets and liabilities at the acquisition date. Consequently, those deferred tax assets and deferred tax liabilities affect the amount of goodwill or the bargain purchase gain the entity recognises. However, in accordance with paragraph 15(a), an entity does not recognise deferred tax liabilities arising from the initial recognition of goodwill.

67   As a result of a business combination, the probability of realising a pre-acquisition deferred tax asset of the acquirer could change. An acquirer may consider it probable that it will recover its own deferred tax asset that was not recognised before the business combination. For example, the acquirer may be able to utilise the benefit of its unused tax losses against the future taxable profit of the acquiree. Alternatively, as a result of the business combination it might no longer be probable that future taxable profit will allow the deferred tax asset to be recovered. In such cases, the acquirer recognises a change in the deferred tax asset in the period of the business combination, but does not include it as part of the accounting for the business combination. Therefore, the

acquirer does not take it into account in measuring the goodwill or bargain purchase gain it recognises in the business combination.

68 The potential benefit of the acquiree's income tax loss carryforwards or other deferred tax assets might not satisfy the criteria for separate recognition when a business combination is initially accounted for but might be realised subsequently. An entity shall recognise acquired deferred tax benefits that it realises after the business combination as follows:

(a) Acquired deferred tax benefits recognised within the measurement period that result from new information about facts and circumstances that existed at the acquisition date shall be applied to reduce the carrying amount of any goodwill related to that acquisition. If the carrying amount of that goodwill is zero, any remaining deferred tax benefits shall be recognised in profit or loss.

(b) All other acquired deferred tax benefits realised shall be recognised in profit or loss (or, if this Standard so requires, outside profit or loss).

Current and deferred tax arising from share-based payment transactions

68A In some tax jurisdictions, an entity receives a tax deduction (ie an amount that is deductible in determining taxable profit) that relates to remuneration paid in shares, share options or other equity instruments of the entity. The amount of that tax deduction may differ from the related cumulative remuneration expense, and may arise in a later accounting period. For example, in some jurisdictions, an entity may recognise an expense for the consumption of employee services received as consideration for share options granted, in accordance with AASB 2 *Share-based Payment*, and not receive a tax deduction until the share options are exercised, with the measurement of the tax deduction based on the entity's share price at the date of exercise.

68B As with the research costs discussed in paragraphs 9 and 26(b) of this Standard, the difference between the tax base of the employee services received to date (being the amount the taxation authorities will permit as a deduction in future periods), and the carrying amount of nil, is a deductible temporary difference that results in a deferred tax asset. If the amount the taxation authorities will permit as a deduction in future periods is not known at the end of the period, it shall be estimated, based on information available at the end of the period. For example, if the amount that the taxation authorities will permit as a deduction in future periods is dependent upon the entity's share price at a future date, the measurement of the deductible temporary difference should be based on the entity's share price at the end of the period.

68C As noted in paragraph 68A, the amount of the tax deduction (or estimated future tax deduction, measured in accordance with paragraph 68B) may differ from the related cumulative remuneration expense. Paragraph 58 of the Standard requires that current and deferred tax should be recognised as income or an expense and included in profit or loss for the period, except to the extent that the tax arises from (a) a transaction or event that is recognised, in the same or a different period, outside profit or loss, or (b) a business combination (other than the acquisition by an investment entity of a subsidiary that is required to be measured at fair value through profit or loss). If the amount of the tax deduction (or estimated future tax deduction) exceeds the amount of the related cumulative remuneration expense, this indicates that the tax deduction relates not only to remuneration expense but also to an equity item. In this situation, the excess of the associated current or deferred tax should be recognised directly in equity.

Presentation

Tax assets and tax liabilities

69–70 [Deleted]

Offset

71 **An entity shall offset current tax assets and current tax liabilities if, and only if, the entity:**

(a)   has a legally enforceable right to set off the recognised amounts; and

(b)   intends either to settle on a net basis, or to realise the asset and settle the liability simultaneously.

72   Although current tax assets and liabilities are separately recognised and measured they are offset in the statement of financial position subject to criteria similar to those established for financial instruments in AASB 132. An entity will normally have a legally enforceable right to set off a current tax asset against a current tax liability when they relate to income taxes levied by the same taxation authority and the taxation authority permits the entity to make or receive a single net payment.

73   In consolidated financial statements, a current tax asset of one entity in a group is offset against a current tax liability of another entity in the group if, and only if, the entities concerned have a legally enforceable right to make or receive a single net payment and the entities intend to make or receive such a net payment or to recover the asset and settle the liability simultaneously.

74   **An entity shall offset deferred tax assets and deferred tax liabilities if, and only if:**

(a)   **the entity has a legally enforceable right to set off current tax assets against current tax liabilities; and**

(b)   **the deferred tax assets and the deferred tax liabilities relate to income taxes levied by the same taxation authority on either:**

(i)   **the same taxable entity; or**

(ii)   **different taxable entities which intend either to settle current tax liabilities and assets on a net basis, or to realise the assets and settle the liabilities simultaneously, in each future period in which significant amounts of deferred tax liabilities or assets are expected to be settled or recovered.**

75   To avoid the need for detailed scheduling of the timing of the reversal of each temporary difference, this Standard requires an entity to set off a deferred tax asset against a deferred tax liability of the same taxable entity if, and only if, they relate to income taxes levied by the same taxation authority and the entity has a legally enforceable right to set off current tax assets against current tax liabilities.

76   In rare circumstances, an entity may have a legally enforceable right of set-off, and an intention to settle net, for some periods but not for others. In such rare circumstances, detailed scheduling may be required to establish reliably whether the deferred tax liability of one taxable entity will result in increased tax payments in the same period in which a deferred tax asset of another taxable entity will result in decreased payments by that second taxable entity.

Tax expense

Tax expense (income) related to profit or loss from ordinary activities

77   **The tax expense (income) related to profit or loss from ordinary activities shall be presented as part of profit or loss in the statement(s) of profit or loss and other comprehensive income.**

77A   [Deleted]

Exchange differences on deferred foreign tax liabilities or assets

78   AASB 121 requires certain exchange differences to be recognised as income or expense but does not specify where such differences should be presented in the statement of comprehensive income. Accordingly, where exchange differences on deferred foreign tax liabilities or assets are recognised in the statement of comprehensive income, such differences may be classified as deferred tax expense (income) if that presentation is considered to be the most useful to financial statement users.

Disclosure

79 **The major components of tax expense (income) shall be disclosed separately.**

80 Components of tax expense (income) may include:

(a) current tax expense (income);

(b) any adjustments recognised in the period for current tax of prior periods;

(c) the amount of deferred tax expense (income) relating to the origination and reversal of temporary differences;

(d) the amount of deferred tax expense (income) relating to changes in tax rates or the imposition of new taxes;

(e) the amount of the benefit arising from a previously unrecognised tax loss, tax credit or temporary difference of a prior period that is used to reduce current tax expense;

(f) the amount of the benefit from a previously unrecognised tax loss, tax credit or temporary difference of a prior period that is used to reduce deferred tax expense;

(g) deferred tax expense arising from the write-down, or reversal of a previous write-down, of a deferred tax asset in accordance with paragraph 56; and

(h) the amount of tax expense (income) relating to those changes in accounting policies and errors that are included in profit or loss in accordance with AASB 108, because they cannot be accounted for retrospectively.

81 **The following shall also be disclosed separately:**

(a) **the aggregate current and deferred tax relating to items that are charged or credited directly to equity (see paragraph 62A);**

(ab) **the amount of income tax relating to each component of other comprehensive income (see paragraph 62 and AASB 101);**

(b) **[deleted]**

(c) **an explanation of the relationship between tax expense (income) and accounting profit in either or both of the following forms:**

(i) **a numerical reconciliation between tax expense (income) and the product of accounting profit multiplied by the applicable tax rate(s), disclosing also the basis on which the applicable tax rate(s) is (are) computed; or**

(ii) **a numerical reconciliation between the average effective tax rate and the applicable tax rate, disclosing also the basis on which the applicable tax rate is computed;**

(d) **an explanation of changes in the applicable tax rate(s) compared to the previous accounting period;**

(e) **the amount (and expiry date, if any) of deductible temporary differences, unused tax losses, and unused tax credits for which no deferred tax asset is recognised in the statement of financial position;**

(f) **the aggregate amount of temporary differences associated with investments in subsidiaries, branches and associates and interests in joint arrangements, for which deferred tax liabilities have not been recognised (see paragraph 39);**

(g) **in respect of each type of temporary difference, and in respect of each type of unused tax losses and unused tax credits:**

(i) **the amount of the deferred tax assets and liabilities recognised in the statement of financial position for each period presented;**

> (ii)   the amount of the deferred tax income or expense recognised in profit or loss, if this is not apparent from the changes in the amounts recognised in the statement of financial position;

(h)   in respect of discontinued operations, the tax expense relating to:

>   (i)   the gain or loss on discontinuance; and

>   (ii)   the profit or loss from the ordinary activities of the discontinued operation for the period, together with the corresponding amounts for each prior period presented;

(i)   the amount of income tax consequences of dividends to shareholders of the entity that were proposed or declared before the financial statements were authorised for issue, but are not recognised as a liability in the financial statements;

(j)   if a business combination in which the entity is the acquirer causes a change in the amount recognised for its pre-acquisition deferred tax asset (see paragraph 67), the amount of that change; and

(k)   if the deferred tax benefits acquired in a business combination are not recognised at the acquisition date but are recognised after the acquisition date (see paragraph 68), a description of the event or change in circumstances that caused the deferred tax benefits to be recognised.

82   An entity shall disclose the amount of a deferred tax asset and the nature of the evidence supporting its recognition, when:

(a)   the utilisation of the deferred tax asset is dependent on future taxable profits in excess of the profits arising from the reversal of existing taxable temporary differences; and

(b)   the entity has suffered a loss in either the current or preceding period in the tax jurisdiction to which the deferred tax asset relates.

82A   In the circumstances described in paragraph 52A, an entity shall disclose the nature of the potential income tax consequences that would result from the payment of dividends to its shareholders. In addition, the entity shall disclose the amounts of the potential income tax consequences practically determinable and whether there are any potential income tax consequences not practically determinable.

83   [Deleted]

84   The disclosures required by paragraph 81(c) enable users of financial statements to understand whether the relationship between tax expense (income) and accounting profit is unusual and to understand the significant factors that could affect that relationship in the future. The relationship between tax expense (income) and accounting profit may be affected by such factors as revenue that is exempt from taxation, expenses that are not deductible in determining taxable profit (tax loss), the effect of tax losses and the effect of foreign tax rates.

85   In explaining the relationship between tax expense (income) and accounting profit, an entity uses an applicable tax rate that provides the most meaningful information to the users of its financial statements. Often, the most meaningful rate is the domestic rate of tax in the country in which the entity is domiciled, aggregating the tax rate applied for national taxes with the rates applied for any local taxes which are computed on a substantially similar level of taxable profit (tax loss). However, for an entity operating in several jurisdictions, it may be more meaningful to aggregate separate reconciliations prepared using the domestic rate in each individual jurisdiction. The following example illustrates how the selection of the applicable tax rate affects the presentation of the numerical reconciliation.

Example illustrating paragraph 85

In 19X2, an entity has accounting profit in its own jurisdiction (country A) of 1,500 (19X1: 2,000) and in country B of 1,500 (19X1: 500). The tax rate is 30% in country A and 20% in country B. In country A, expenses of 100 (19X1: 200) are not deductible for tax purposes.

The following is an example of a reconciliation to the domestic tax rate.

	19X1	19X2
Accounting profit	2,500	3,000
Tax at the domestic rate of 30%	750	900
Tax effect of expenses that are not deductible for tax purposes	60	30
Effect of lower tax rates in country B	(50)	(150)
Tax expense	760	780

The following is an example of a reconciliation prepared by aggregating separate reconciliations for each national jurisdiction. Under this method, the effect of differences between the reporting entity's own domestic tax rate and the domestic tax rate in other jurisdictions does not appear as a separate item in the reconciliation. An entity may need to discuss the effect of significant changes in either tax rates, or the mix of profits earned in different jurisdictions, in order to explain changes in the applicable tax rate(s), as required by paragraph 81(d).

	19X1	19X2
Accounting profit	2,500	3,000
Tax at the domestic rates applicable to profits in the country concerned	700	750
Tax effect of expenses that are not deductible for tax purposes	60	30
Tax expense	760	780

---

86 The average effective tax rate is the tax expense (income) divided by the accounting profit.

87 It would often be impracticable to compute the amount of unrecognised deferred tax liabilities arising from investments in subsidiaries, branches and associates and interests in joint arrangements (see paragraph 39). Therefore, this Standard requires an entity to disclose the aggregate amount of the underlying temporary differences but does not require disclosure of the deferred tax liabilities. Nevertheless, where practicable, entities are encouraged to disclose the amounts of the unrecognised deferred tax liabilities because financial statement users may find such information useful.

87A Paragraph 82A requires an entity to disclose the nature of the potential income tax consequences that would result from the payment of dividends to its shareholders. An entity discloses the important features of the income tax systems and the factors that will affect the amount of the potential income tax consequences of dividends.

87B It would sometimes not be practicable to compute the total amount of the potential income tax consequences that would result from the payment of dividends to shareholders. This may be the case, for example, where an entity has a large number of foreign subsidiaries. However, even in such circumstances, some portions of the total amount may be easily determinable. For example, in a consolidated group, a parent and some of its subsidiaries may have paid income taxes at a higher rate on undistributed profits and be aware of the amount that would be refunded on the payment of future dividends to shareholders from consolidated retained earnings. In this case,

AASB

that refundable amount is disclosed. If applicable, the entity also discloses that there are additional potential income tax consequences not practicably determinable. In the parent's separate financial statements, if any, the disclosure of the potential income tax consequences relates to the parent's retained earnings.

87C   An entity required to provide the disclosures in paragraph 82A may also be required to provide disclosures related to temporary differences associated with investments in subsidiaries, branches and associates or interests in joint arrangements. In such cases, an entity considers this in determining the information to be disclosed under paragraph 82A. For example, an entity may be required to disclose the aggregate amount of temporary differences associated with investments in subsidiaries for which no deferred tax liabilities have been recognised (see paragraph 81(f)). If it is impracticable to compute the amounts of unrecognised deferred tax liabilities (see paragraph 87) there may be amounts of potential income tax consequences of dividends not practicably determinable related to these subsidiaries.

88   An entity discloses any tax-related contingent liabilities and contingent assets in accordance with AASB 137 *Provisions, Contingent Liabilities and Contingent Assets*. Contingent liabilities and contingent assets may arise, for example, from unresolved disputes with the taxation authorities. Similarly, where changes in tax rates or tax laws are enacted or announced after the reporting period, an entity discloses any significant effect of those changes on its current and deferred tax assets and liabilities (see AASB 110 *Events after the Reporting Period*).

Effective date

89   This Standard becomes operative for financial statements covering periods beginning on or after 1 January 2018. Earlier application is permitted for periods beginning after 24 July 2014 but before 1 January 2018. If an entity applies this Standard for financial statements covering periods beginning before 1 January 2018, the entity shall disclose that fact.

90–92   [Deleted by the AASB]

93   Paragraph 68 shall be applied prospectively from the effective date of AASB 3 (as revised in 2008) to the recognition of deferred tax assets acquired in business combinations.

94   Therefore, entities shall not adjust the accounting for prior business combinations if tax benefits failed to satisfy the criteria for separate recognition as of the acquisition date and are recognised after the acquisition date, unless the benefits are recognised within the measurement period and result from new information about facts and circumstances that existed at the acquisition date. Other tax benefits recognised shall be recognised in profit or loss (or, if this Standard so requires, outside profit or loss).

95   [Deleted by the AASB]

96   [Deleted]

97   [Deleted]

98–98C [Deleted by the AASB]

98D   [Deleted]

98E   AASB 2014-5 *Amendments to Australian Accounting Standards arising from AASB 15*, issued in December 2014, amended paragraph 59 in the previous version of this Standard. An entity shall apply that amendment when it applies AASB 15.

98F   AASB 2010-7 *Amendments to Australian Accounting Standards arising from AASB 9 (December 2010)* (as amended) amended the previous version of this Standard as follows: amended paragraph 20 and deleted paragraph 96. Paragraph 97, added by AASB 2010-7, was deleted by AASB 2014-1 *Amendments to Australian Accounting Standards*. Paragraph 98D, added by AASB 2014-1, was deleted by AASB 2014-7 *Amendments to Australian Accounting Standards arising from AASB 9 (December 2014)*. An entity shall apply those amendments when it applies AASB 9.

98H   AASB 2016-1 *Amendments to Australian Accounting Standards – Recognition of Deferred Tax Assets for Unrealised Losses*, issued in February 2016, amended paragraph 29 and added paragraphs 27A, 29A and the example following paragraph 26. An entity shall apply those amendments for annual periods beginning on or after 1 January 2017. Earlier application is permitted. If an entity applies those amendments for an earlier period, it shall disclose that fact. An entity shall apply those amendments retrospectively in accordance with AASB 108 *Accounting Policies, Changes in Accounting Estimates and Errors*. However, on initial application of the amendment, the change in the opening equity of the earliest comparative period may be recognised in opening retained earnings (or in another component of equity, as appropriate), without allocating the change between opening retained earnings and other components of equity. If an entity applies this relief, it shall disclose that fact.

Withdrawal of SIC-21

99   [Deleted by the AASB]

Commencement of the legislative instrument

Aus99.1   For legal purposes, this legislative instrument commences on 31 December 2017.

Withdrawal of AASB pronouncements

Aus99.2   This Standard repeals AASB 112 *Income Taxes* issued in July 2004. Despite the repeal, after the time this Standard starts to apply under section 334 of the Corporations Act (either generally or in relation to an individual entity), the repealed Standard continues to apply in relation to any period ending before that time as if the repeal had not occurred.

[Note: When this Standard applies under section 334 of the Corporations Act (either generally or in relation to an individual entity), it supersedes the application of the repealed Standard.]

APPENDIX A
AUSTRALIAN REDUCED DISCLOSURE REQUIREMENTS

This appendix is an integral part of the Standard.

AusA1   **The following do not apply to entities preparing general purpose financial statements under Australian Accounting Standards – Reduced Disclosure Requirements:**

(a)   paragraphs 81(ab), 81(f), 81(i)-(k), 82 and 87-87C; and

(b)   the second sentence in paragraph 82A.

Entities applying Australian Accounting Standards – Reduced Disclosure Requirements may elect to comply with some or all of these excluded requirements.

AusA2   The requirements that do not apply to entities preparing general purpose financial statements under Australian Accounting Standards – Reduced Disclosure Requirements are also identified in this Standard by shading of the relevant text.

AusA3   The RDR paragraph in this Standard applies only to entities preparing general purpose financial statements under Australian Accounting Standards – Reduced Disclosure Requirements.

RDR81.1   An entity applying Australian Accounting Standards – Reduced Disclosure Requirements shall disclose the aggregate amount of current and deferred income tax relating to items recognised in other comprehensive income.

ILLUSTRATIVE EXAMPLES

These illustrative examples accompany, but are not part of, AASB 112.

Examples of temporary differences

A. Examples of circumstances that give rise to taxable temporary differences

All taxable temporary differences give rise to a deferred tax liability.

Transactions that affect profit or loss

1   Interest revenue is received in arrears and is included in accounting profit on a time apportionment basis but is included in taxable profit on a cash basis.

2   Revenue from the sale of goods is included in accounting profit when goods are delivered but is included in taxable profit when cash is collected. (*note: as explained in B3 below, there is also a **deductible** temporary difference associated with any related inventory*).

3   Depreciation of an asset is accelerated for tax purposes.

4   Development costs have been capitalised and will be amortised to the statement of comprehensive income but were deducted in determining taxable profit in the period in which they were incurred.

5   Prepaid expenses have already been deducted on a cash basis in determining the taxable profit of the current or previous periods.

Transactions that affect the statement of financial position

6   Depreciation of an asset is not deductible for tax purposes and no deduction will be available for tax purposes when the asset is sold or scrapped. (*note: paragraph 15(b) of the Standard prohibits recognition of the resulting deferred tax liability unless the asset was acquired in a business combination, see also paragraph 22 of the Standard.*)

7   A borrower records a loan at the proceeds received (which equal the amount due at maturity), less transaction costs. Subsequently, the carrying amount of the loan is increased by amortisation of the transaction costs to accounting profit. The transaction costs were deducted for tax purposes in the period when the loan was first recognised. (*notes: (1) the taxable temporary difference is the amount of transaction costs already deducted in determining the taxable profit of current or prior periods, less the cumulative amount amortised to accounting profit; and (2) as the initial recognition of the loan affects taxable profit, the exception in paragraph 15(b) of the Standard does not apply. Therefore, the borrower recognises the deferred tax liability.*)

8   A loan payable was measured on initial recognition at the amount of the net proceeds, net of transaction costs. The transaction costs are amortised to accounting profit over the life of the loan. Those transaction costs are not deductible in determining the taxable profit of future, current or prior periods. (*notes: (1) the taxable temporary difference is the amount of unamortised transaction costs; and (2) paragraph 15(b) of the Standard prohibits recognition of the resulting deferred tax liability.*)

9   The liability component of a compound financial instrument (for example a convertible bond) is measured at a discount to the amount repayable on maturity (see AASB 132

Financial Instruments: Presentation). The discount is not deductible in determining taxable profit (tax loss).

Fair value adjustments and revaluations

10   Financial assets or investment property are carried at fair value which exceeds cost but no equivalent adjustment is made for tax purposes.

11   An entity revalues property, plant and equipment (under the revaluation model treatment in AASB 116 *Property, Plant and Equipment*) but no equivalent adjustment is made for tax purposes. (*note: paragraph 61A of the Standard requires the related deferred tax to be recognised in other comprehensive income.*)

Business combinations and consolidation

12   The carrying amount of an asset is increased to fair value in a business combination and no equivalent adjustment is made for tax purposes. (*Note that on initial recognition, the resulting deferred tax liability increases goodwill or decreases the amount of any bargain purchase gain recognised. See paragraph 66 of the Standard.*)

13   Reductions in the carrying amount of goodwill are not deductible in determining taxable profit and the cost of the goodwill would not be deductible on disposal of the business. (*Note that paragraph 15(a) of the Standard prohibits recognition of the resulting deferred tax liability.*)

14   Unrealised losses resulting from intragroup transactions are eliminated by inclusion in the carrying amount of inventory or property, plant and equipment.

15   Retained earnings of subsidiaries, branches, associates and joint ventures are included in consolidated retained earnings, but income taxes will be payable if the profits are distributed to the reporting parent. (*note: paragraph 39 of the Standard prohibits recognition of the resulting deferred tax liability if the parent, investor or venturer is able to control the timing of the reversal of the temporary difference and it is probable that the temporary difference will not reverse in the foreseeable future.*)

16   Investments in foreign subsidiaries, branches or associates or interests in foreign joint ventures are affected by changes in foreign exchange rates. (*notes: (1) there may be either a taxable temporary difference or a deductible temporary difference; and (2) paragraph 39 of the Standard prohibits recognition of the resulting deferred tax liability if the parent, investor or venturer is able to control the timing of the reversal of the temporary difference and it is probable that the temporary difference will not reverse in the foreseeable future.*)

17   The non-monetary assets and liabilities of an entity are measured in its functional currency but the taxable profit or tax loss is determined in a different currency. (*notes: (1) there may be either a taxable temporary difference or a deductible temporary difference; (2) where there is a taxable temporary difference, the resulting deferred tax liability is recognised (paragraph 41 of the Standard); and (3) the deferred tax is recognised in profit or loss, see paragraph 58 of the Standard.*)

Hyperinflation

18   Non-monetary assets are restated in terms of the measuring unit current at the end of the reporting period (see AASB 129 *Financial Reporting in Hyperinflationary Economies*) and no equivalent adjustment is made for tax purposes. (*notes: (1) the deferred tax is recognised in profit or loss; and (2) if, in addition to the restatement, the non-monetary assets are also revalued, the deferred tax relating to the revaluation is recognised in other comprehensive income and the deferred tax relating to the restatement is recognised in profit or loss.*)

B. Examples of circumstances that give rise to deductible temporary differences

All deductible temporary differences give rise to a deferred tax asset. However, some deferred tax assets may not satisfy the recognition criteria in paragraph 24 of the Standard.

AASB

Transactions that affect profit or loss

1   Retirement benefit costs are deducted in determining accounting profit as service is provided by the employee, but are not deducted in determining taxable profit until the entity pays either retirement benefits or contributions to a fund. *(note: similar deductible temporary differences arise where other expenses, such as product warranty costs or interest, are deductible on a cash basis in determining taxable profit.)*

2   Accumulated depreciation of an asset in the financial statements is greater than the cumulative depreciation allowed up to the end of the reporting period for tax purposes.

3   The cost of inventories sold before the end of the reporting period is deducted in determining accounting profit when goods or services are delivered but is deducted in determining taxable profit when cash is collected. *(note: as explained in A2 above, there is also a **taxable** temporary difference associated with the related trade receivable.)*

4   The net realisable value of an item of inventory, or the recoverable amount of an item of property, plant or equipment, is less than the previous carrying amount and an entity therefore reduces the carrying amount of the asset, but that reduction is ignored for tax purposes until the asset is sold.

5   Research costs (or organisation or other start-up costs) are recognised as an expense in determining accounting profit but are not permitted as a deduction in determining taxable profit until a later period.

6   Income is deferred in the statement of financial position but has already been included in taxable profit in current or prior periods.

7   A government grant which is included in the statement of financial position as deferred income will not be taxable in future periods. *(note: paragraph 24 of the Standard prohibits the recognition of the resulting deferred tax asset, see also paragraph 33 of the Standard.)*

Fair value adjustments and revaluations

8   Financial assets or investment property are carried at fair value which is less than cost, but no equivalent adjustment is made for tax purposes.

Business combinations and consolidation

9   A liability is recognised at its fair value in a business combination, but none of the related expense is deducted in determining taxable profit until a later period. *(Note that the resulting deferred tax asset decreases goodwill or increases the amount of any bargain purchase gain recognised. See paragraph 66 of the Standard.)*

10   [Deleted]

11   Unrealised profits resulting from intragroup transactions are eliminated from the carrying amount of assets, such as inventory or property, plant or equipment, but no equivalent adjustment is made for tax purposes.

12   Investments in foreign subsidiaries, branches or associates or interests in foreign joint ventures are affected by changes in foreign exchange rates. *(notes: (1) there may be a taxable temporary difference or a deductible temporary difference; and (2) paragraph 44 of the Standard requires recognition of the resulting deferred tax asset to the extent, and only to the extent, that it is probable that: (a) the temporary difference will reverse in the foreseeable future; and (b) taxable profit will be available against which the temporary difference can be utilised).*

13   The non-monetary assets and liabilities of an entity are measured in its functional currency but the taxable profit or tax loss is determined in a different currency. *(notes: (1) there may be either a taxable temporary difference or a deductible temporary difference; (2) where there is a deductible temporary difference, the resulting deferred tax asset is recognised to the extent that it is probable that sufficient taxable profit will be available (paragraph 41 of the Standard); and (3) the deferred tax is recognised in profit or loss, see paragraph 58 of the Standard.)*

C. Examples of circumstances where the carrying amount of an asset or liability is equal to its tax base

1   Accrued expenses have already been deducted in determining an entity's current tax liability for the current or earlier periods.

2   A loan payable is measured at the amount originally received and this amount is the same as the amount repayable on final maturity of the loan.

3   Accrued expenses will never be deductible for tax purposes.

4   Accrued income will never be taxable.

Illustrative computations and presentation

Extracts from statements of financial position and statements of comprehensive income are provided to show the effects on these financial statements of the transactions described below. These extracts do not necessarily conform with all the disclosure and presentation requirements of other Standards.

All the examples below assume that the entities concerned have no transaction other than those described.

Example 1 – Depreciable assets

An entity buys equipment for 10,000 and depreciates it on a straight-line basis over its expected useful life of five years. For tax purposes, the equipment is depreciated at 25% a year on a straight-line basis. Tax losses may be carried back against taxable profit of the previous five years. In year 0, the entity's taxable profit was 5,000. The tax rate is 40%.

The entity will recover the carrying amount of the equipment by using it to manufacture goods for resale. Therefore, the entity's current tax computation is as follows:

	Year				
	1	**2**	**3**	**4**	**5**
Taxable income	2,000	2,000	2,000	2,000	2,000
Depreciation for tax purposes	2,500	2,500	2,500	2,500	0
Taxable profit (tax loss)	(500)	(500)	(500)	(500)	2,000
Current tax expense (income) at 40%	(200)	(200)	(200)	(200)	800

The entity recognises a current tax asset at the end of years 1 to 4 because it recovers the benefit of the tax loss against the taxable profit of year 0.

The temporary differences associated with the equipment and the resulting deferred tax asset and liability and deferred tax expense and income are as follows:

	Year				
	1	**2**	**3**	**4**	**5**
Carrying amount	8,000	6,000	4,000	2,000	0
Tax base	7,500	5,000	2,500	0	0
Taxable temporary difference	500	1,000	1,500	2,000	0
Opening deferred tax liability	0	200	400	600	800
Deferred tax expense (income)	200	200	200	200	(800)
Closing deferred tax liability	200	400	600	800	0

The entity recognises the deferred tax liability in years 1 to 4 because the reversal of the taxable temporary difference will create taxable income in subsequent years. The entity's statement of comprehensive income includes the following:

	Year				
	1	2	3	4	5
Income	2,000	2,000	2,000	2,000	2,000
Depreciation	2,000	2,000	2,000	2,000	2,000
Profit before tax	0	0	0	0	0
Current tax expense (income)	(200)	(200)	(200)	(200)	800
Deferred tax expense (income)	200	200	200	200	(800)
Total tax expense (income)	0	0	0	0	0
Profit for the period	0	0	0	0	0

Example 2 – Deferred tax assets and liabilities

The example deals with an entity over the two-year period, X5 and X6. In X5 the enacted income tax rate was 40% of taxable profit. In X6 the enacted income tax rate was 35% of taxable profit.

Charitable donations are recognised as an expense when they are paid and are not deductible for tax purposes.

In X5, the entity was notified by the relevant authorities that they intend to pursue an action against the entity with respect to sulphur emissions. Although as at December X6 the action had not yet come to court the entity recognised a liability of 700 in X5 being its best estimate of the fine arising from the action. Fines are not deductible for tax purposes.

In X2, the entity incurred 1,250 of costs in relation to the development of a new product. These costs were deducted for tax purposes in X2. For accounting purposes, the entity capitalised this expenditure and amortised it on the straight-line basis over five years. At 31/12/X4, the unamortised balance of these product development costs was 500.

In X5, the entity entered into an agreement with its existing employees to provide healthcare benefits to retirees. The entity recognises as an expense the cost of this plan as employees provide service. No payments to retirees were made for such benefits in X5 or X6. Healthcare costs are deductible for tax purposes when payments are made to retirees. The entity has determined that it is probable that taxable profit will be available against which any resulting deferred tax asset can be utilised.

Buildings are depreciated for accounting purposes at 5% a year on a straight-line basis and at 10% a year on a straight-line basis for tax purposes. Motor vehicles are depreciated for accounting purposes at 20% a year on a straight-line basis and at 25% a year on a straight-line basis for tax purposes. A full year's depreciation is charged for accounting purposes in the year that an asset is acquired.

At 1/1/X6, the building was revalued to 65,000 and the entity estimated that the remaining useful life of the building was 20 years from the date of the revaluation. The revaluation did not affect taxable profit in X6 and the taxation authorities did not adjust the tax base of the building to reflect the revaluation. In X6, the entity transferred 1,033 from revaluation surplus to retained earnings. This represents the difference of 1,590 between the actual depreciation on the building (3,250) and equivalent depreciation based on the cost of the building (1,660, which is the book value at 1/1/X6 of 33,200 divided by the remaining useful life of 20 years), less the related deferred tax of 557 (see paragraph 64 of the Standard).

Current tax expense

	X5	X6
Accounting profit	8,775	8,740
Add		
Depreciation for accounting purposes	4,800	8,250
Charitable donations	500	350
Fine for environmental pollution	700	–
Product development costs	250	250
Healthcare benefits	2,000	1,000
	17,025	18,590
Deduct		
Depreciation for tax purposes	(8,100)	(11,850)
Taxable profit	8,925	6,740
Current tax expense at 40%	3,570	
Current tax expense at 35%		2,359

AASB

Carrying amounts of property, plant and equipment

	Building	Motor vehicles	Total
Balance at 31/12/X4	50,000	10,000	60,000
Additions X5	6,000	–	6,000
Balance at 31/12/X5	56,000	10,000	66,000
Elimination of accumulated depreciation on revaluation at 1/1/X6	(22,800)	–	(22,800)
Revaluation at 1/1/X6	31,800	–	31,800
Balance at 1/1/X6	65,000	10,000	75,000
Additions X6	–	15,000	15,000
	65,000	25,000	90,000

(*Continued*)

(Continued)

	Building	Motor vehicles	Total
Accumulated depreciation	5%	20%	
Balance at 31/12/X4	20,000	4,000	24,000
Depreciation X5	2,800	2,000	4,800
Balance at 31/12/X5	22,800	6,000	28,800
Revaluation at 1/1/X6	(22,800)	–	(22,800)
Balance at 1/1/X6	–	6,000	6,000
Depreciation X6	3,250	5,000	8,250
Balance at 31/12/X6	3,250	11,000	14,250
Carrying amount			
31/12/X4	30,000	6,000	36,000
31/12/X5	33,200	4,000	37,200
31/12/X6	61,750	14,000	75,750

Tax base of property, plant and equipment

	Building	Motor vehicles	Total
Cost			
Balance at 31/12/X4	50,000	10,000	60,000
Additions X5	6,000	–	6,000
Balance at 31/12/X5	56,000	10,000	66,000
Additions X6	–	15,000	15,000
Balance at 31/12/X6	56,000	25,000	81,000
Accumulated depreciation	10%	25%	
Balance at 31/12/X4	40,000	5,000	45,000
Depreciation X5	5,600	2,500	8,100
Balance at 31/12/X5	45,600	7,500	53,100
Depreciation X6	5,600	6,250	11,850
Balance 31/12/X6	51,200	13,750	64,950

	Building	Motor vehicles	Total
Tax base			
31/12/X4	10,000	5,000	15,000
31/12/X5	10,400	2,500	12,900
31/12/X6	4,800	11,250	16,050

Deferred tax assets, liabilities and expense at 31/12/X4

	Carrying amount	Tax base	Temporary differences
Accounts receivable	500	500	–
Inventory	2,000	2,000	–
Product development costs	500	–	500
Investments	33,000	33,000	–
Property, plant & equipment	36,000	15,000	21,000
TOTAL ASSETS	72,000	50,500	21,500
Current income taxes payable	3,000	3,000	–
Accounts payable	500	500	–
Fines payable	–	–	–
Liability for healthcare benefits	–	–	–
Long-term debt	20,000	20,000	–
Deferred income taxes	8,600	8,600	–
TOTAL LIABILITIES	32,100	32,100	
Share capital	5,000	5,000	–
Revaluation surplus	–	–	–
Retained earnings	34,900	13,400	
TOTAL LIABILITIES/EQUITY	72,000	50,500	
TEMPORARY DIFFERENCES			21,500
Deferred tax liability	21,500 at 40%		8,600
Deferred tax asset	–		
Net deferred tax liability			8,600

Deferred tax assets, liabilities and expense at 31/12/X5

	Carrying amount	Tax base	Temporary differences
Accounts receivable	500	500	–
Inventory	2,000	2,000	–
Product development costs	250	–	250
Investments	33,000	33,000	–
Property, plant & equipment	37,200	12,900	24,300
TOTAL ASSETS	72,950	48,400	24,550
Current income taxes payable	3,570	3,570	–
Accounts payable	500	500	–
Fines payable	700	700	–
Liability for healthcare benefits	2,000	–	(2,000)
Long-term debt	12,475	12,475	–
Deferred income taxes	9,020	9,020	
TOTAL LIABILITIES	28,265	26,265	(2,000)
Share capital	5,000	5,000	
Revaluation surplus	–	–	
Retained earnings	30,685	17,135	
TOTAL LIABILITIES/EQUITY	72,950	48,400	

TEMPORARY DIFFERENCES			22,550
Deferred tax liability	24,550 at 40%		9,820
Deferred tax asset	2,000 at 40%		(800)
Net deferred tax liability			9,020
Less: Opening deferred tax liability			(8,600)
Deferred tax expense (income) related to the origination and reversal of temporary differences			420

Deferred tax assets, liabilities and expense at 31/12/X6

	Carrying amount	Tax base	Temporary differences
Accounts receivable	500	500	–
Inventory	2,000	2,000	–
Product development costs	–	–	–
Investments	33,000	33,000	–
Property, plant & equipment	75,750	16,050	59,700
TOTAL ASSETS	111,250	51,550	59,700
Current income taxes payable	2,359	2,359	–
Accounts payable	500	500	–
Fines payable	700	700	
Liability for healthcare benefits	3,000	–	(3,000)
Long-term debt	12,805	12,805	–
Deferred income taxes	19,845	19,845	
TOTAL LIABILITIES	39,209	36,209	(3,000)
Share capital	5,000	5,000	
Revaluation surplus	19,637		–
Retained earnings	47,404	10,341	
TOTAL LIABILITIES/EQUITY	111,250	51,550	

TEMPORARY DIFFERENCES		56,700
Deferred tax liability	59,700 at 35%	20,895
Deferred tax asset	3,000 at 35%	(1,050)
Net deferred tax liability		19,845
Less: Opening deferred tax liability		(9,020)
Adjustment to opening deferred tax liability resulting from reduction in tax rate	22,550 at 5%	1,127
Deferred tax attributable to revaluation surplus	31,800 at 35%	(11,130)
Deferred tax expense (income) related to the origination and reversal of temporary differences		822

AASB

Illustrative disclosure

The amounts to be disclosed in accordance with the Standard are as follows:

Major components of tax expense (income) (paragraph 79)

	X5	X6
Current tax expense	3,570	2,359
Deferred tax expense relating to the origination and reversal of temporary differences:	420	822
Deferred tax expense (income) resulting from reduction in tax rate	–	(1,127)
Tax expense	3,990	2,054

Income tax relating to the components of other comprehensive income (paragraph 81(ab))

Deferred tax relating to revaluation of building	–	(11,130)

In addition, deferred tax of 557 was transferred in X6 from retained earnings to revaluation surplus. This relates to the difference between the actual depreciation on the building and equivalent depreciation based on the cost of the building.

Explanation of the relationship between tax expense and accounting profit (paragraph 81(c))

The Standard permits two alternative methods of explaining the relationship between tax expense (income) and accounting profit. Both of these formats are illustrated below.

(i)   a numerical reconciliation between tax expense (income) and the product of accounting profit multiplied by the applicable tax rate(s), disclosing also the basis on which the applicable tax rate(s) is (are) computed

	X5	X6
Accounting profit	8,775	8,740
Tax at the applicable tax rate of 35% (X5: 40%)	3,510	3,059
Tax effect of expenses that are not deductible in determining taxable profit:		
Charitable donations	200	122
Fines for environmental pollution	280	–
Reduction in opening deferred taxes resulting from reduction in tax rate	–	(1,127)
Tax expense	3,990	2,054

The applicable tax rate is the aggregate of the national income tax rate of 30% (X5: 35%) and the local income tax rate of 5%.

(ii)   a numerical reconciliation between the average effective tax rate and the applicable tax rate, disclosing also the basis on which the applicable tax rate is computed

	X5 %	X6 %
Applicable tax rate	40.0	35.0
Tax effect of expenses that are not deductible for tax purposes:		
Charitable donations	2.3	1.4
Fines for environmental pollution	3.2	–
Effect on opening deferred taxes of reduction in tax rate	–	(12.9)
Average effective tax rate (tax expense divided by profit before tax)	45.5	23.5

The applicable tax rate is the aggregate of the national income tax rate of 30% (X5: 35%) and the local income tax rate of 5%.

An explanation of changes in the applicable tax rate(s) compared to the previous accounting period (paragraph 81(d))

In X6, the government enacted a change in the national income tax rate from 35% to 30%.

In respect of each type of temporary difference, and in respect of each type of unused tax losses and unused tax credits:

(i)   **the amount of the deferred tax assets and liabilities recognised in the statement of financial position for each period presented;**

(ii)   **the amount of the deferred tax income or expense recognised in profit or loss for each period presented, if this is not apparent from the changes in the amounts recognised in the statement of financial position (paragraph 81(g)).**

	X5	X6
Accelerated depreciation for tax purposes	9,720	10,322
Liabilities for healthcare benefits that are deducted for tax purposes only when paid	(800)	(1,050)
Product development costs deducted from taxable profit in earlier years	100	–
Revaluation, net of related depreciation	–	10,573
Deferred tax liability	9,020	19,845

(note: the amount of the deferred tax income or expense recognised in profit or loss for the current year is apparent from the changes in the amounts recognised in the statement of financial position)

Example 3 – Business combinations

On 1 January X5 entity A acquired 100 per cent of the shares of entity B at a cost of 600. At the acquisition date, the tax base in A's tax jurisdiction of A's investment in B is 600. Reductions in the carrying amount of goodwill are not deductible for tax purposes, and the cost of the goodwill would also not be deductible if B were to dispose of its underlying business. The tax rate in A's tax jurisdiction is 30 per cent and the tax rate in B's tax jurisdiction is 40 per cent.

The fair value of the identifiable assets acquired and liabilities assumed (excluding deferred tax assets and liabilities) by A is set out in the following table, together with their tax bases in B's tax jurisdiction and the resulting temporary differences.

	Amount recognised at acquisition	Tax base	Temporary differences
Property, plant and equipment	270	155	115
Accounts receivable	210	210	–
Inventory	174	124	50
Retirement benefit obligations	(30)	–	(30)
Accounts payable	(120)	(120)	–
Identifiable assets acquired and liabilities assumed, excluding deferred tax	504	369	135

The deferred tax asset arising from the retirement benefit obligations is offset against the deferred tax liabilities arising from the property, plant and equipment and inventory (see paragraph 74 of the Standard).

No deduction is available in B's tax jurisdiction for the cost of the goodwill. Therefore, the tax base of the goodwill in B's jurisdiction is nil. However, in accordance with paragraph 15(a) of the Standard, A recognises no deferred tax liability for the taxable temporary difference associated with the goodwill in B's tax jurisdiction.

The carrying amount, in A's consolidated financial statements, of its investment in B is made up as follows:

Fair value of identifiable assets acquired and liabilities assumed, excluding deferred tax	504
Deferred tax liability (135 at 40%)	(54)
Fair value of identifiable assets acquired and liabilities assumed	450
Goodwill	150
Carrying amount	600

Because, at the acquisition date, the tax base in A's tax jurisdiction, of A's investment in B is 600, no temporary difference is associated in A's tax jurisdiction with the investment.

During X5, B's equity (incorporating the fair value adjustments made as a result of the business combination) changed as follows:

At 1 January X5	450
Retained profit for X5 (net profit of 150, less dividend payable of 80)	70
At 31 December X5	520

A recognises a liability for any withholding tax or other taxes that it will incur on the accrued dividend receivable of 80.

At 31 December X5, the carrying amount of A's underlying investment in B, excluding the accrued dividend receivable, is as follows:

Net assets of B	520
Goodwill	150
Carrying amount	670

The temporary difference associated with A's underlying investment is 70. This amount is equal to the cumulative retained profit since the acquisition date.

If A has determined that it will not sell the investment in the foreseeable future and that B will not distribute its retained profits in the foreseeable future, no deferred tax liability is recognised in relation to A's investment in B (see paragraphs 39 and 40 of the Standard). Note that this exception would apply for an investment in an associate only if there is an agreement requiring that the profits of the associate will not be distributed in the foreseeable future (see paragraph 42 of the Standard). A discloses the amount of the temporary difference for which no deferred tax is recognised, ie 70 (see paragraph 81(f) of the Standard).

If A expects to sell the investment in B, or that B will distribute its retained profits in the foreseeable future, A recognises a deferred tax liability to the extent that the temporary difference is expected to reverse. The tax rate reflects the manner in which A expects to recover the carrying amount of its investment (see paragraph 51 of the Standard). A recognises the deferred tax in other comprehensive income to the extent that the deferred tax results from foreign exchange translation differences that have been recognised in other comprehensive income (paragraph 61A of the Standard). A discloses separately:

(a)   the amount of deferred tax that has been recognised in other comprehensive income (paragraph 81(ab) of the Standard); and

(b)   the amount of any remaining temporary difference which is not expected to reverse in the foreseeable future and for which, therefore, no deferred tax is recognised (see paragraph 81(f) of the Standard).

Example 4 – Compound financial instruments

An entity receives a non-interest-bearing convertible loan of 1,000 on 31 December X4 repayable at par on 1 January X8. In accordance with AASB 132 *Financial Instruments: Presentation* the entity classifies the instrument's liability component as a liability and the equity component as equity. The entity assigns an initial carrying amount of 751 to the liability component of the convertible loan and 249 to the equity component. Subsequently, the entity recognises imputed discount as interest expense at an annual rate of 10% on the carrying amount of the liability component at the beginning of the year. The tax authorities do not allow the entity to claim any deduction for the imputed discount on the liability component of the convertible loan. The tax rate is 40%.

The temporary differences associated with the liability component and the resulting deferred tax liability and deferred tax expense and income are as follows:

	Year			
	X4	**X5**	**X6**	**X7**
Carrying amount of liability component	751	826	909	1,000
Tax base	1,000	1,000	1,000	1,000
Taxable temporary difference	249	174	91	–

(Continued)

(Continued)

	Year			
	X4	**X5**	**X6**	**X7**
Opening deferred tax liability at 40%	0	100	70	37
Deferred tax charged to equity	100	–	–	–
Deferred tax expense (income)	–	(30)	(33)	(37)
Closing deferred tax liability at 40%	100	70	37	–

As explained in paragraph 23 of the Standard, at 31 December X4, the entity recognises the resulting deferred tax liability by adjusting the initial carrying amount of the equity component of the convertible liability. Therefore, the amounts recognised at that date are as follows:

Liability component	751
Deferred tax liability	100
Equity component (249 less 100)	149
	1,000

Subsequent changes in the deferred tax liability are recognised in profit or loss as tax income (see paragraph 23 of the Standard). Therefore, the entity's profit or loss includes the following:

	Year			
	X4	**X5**	**X6**	**X7**
Interest expense (imputed discount)	–	75	83	91
Deferred tax expense (income)	–	(30)	(33)	(37)
	–	45	50	54

Example 5 – Share-based payment transactions

In accordance with AASB 2 *Share-based Payment*, an entity has recognised an expense for the consumption of employee services received as consideration for share options granted. A tax deduction will not arise until the options are exercised, and the deduction is based on the options' intrinsic value at exercise date.

As explained in paragraph 68B of the Standard, the difference between the tax base of the employee services received to date (being the amount the taxation authorities will permit as a deduction in future periods in respect of those services), and the carrying amount of nil, is a deductible temporary difference that results in a deferred tax asset. Paragraph 68B requires that, if the amount the taxation authorities will permit as a deduction in future periods is not known at the end of the period, it should be estimated, based on information available at the end of the period. If the amount that the taxation authorities will permit as a deduction in future periods is dependent upon the entity's share price at a future date, the measurement of the deductible temporary difference should be based on the entity's share price at the end of the period. Therefore, in this example, the estimated future tax deduction (and hence the measurement of the deferred tax asset) should be based on the options' intrinsic value at the end of the period.

As explained in paragraph 68C of the Standard, if the tax deduction (or estimated future tax deduction) exceeds the amount of the related cumulative remuneration expense, this indicates that the tax deduction relates not only to remuneration expense but also to an equity item. In this situation, paragraph 68C requires that the excess of the associated current or deferred tax should be recognised directly in equity.

The entity's tax rate is 40 per cent. The options were granted at the start of year 1, vested at the end of year 3 and were exercised at the end of year 5. Details of the expense recognised for employee services received and consumed in each accounting period, the number of options outstanding at each year-end, and the intrinsic value of the options at each year-end, are as follows:

	Employee services expense	Number of options at year-end	Intrinsic value per option
Year 1	188,000	50,000	5
Year 2	185,000	45,000	8
Year 3	190,000	40,000	13
Year 4	0	40,000	17
Year 5	0	40,000	20

The entity recognises a deferred tax asset and deferred tax income in years 1–4 and current tax income in year 5 as follows. In years 4 and 5, some of the deferred and current tax income is recognised directly in equity, because the estimated (and actual) tax deduction exceeds the cumulative remuneration expense.

Year 1

Deferred tax asset and deferred tax income:

$$(50,000 \times 5 \times {}^1/_3{}^{(a)} \times 0.40) = \qquad 33,333$$

(a) The tax base of the employee services received is based on the intrinsic value of the options, and those options were granted for three years' services. Because only one year's services have been received to date, it is necessary to multiply the option's intrinsic value by one-third to arrive at the tax base of the employee services received in year 1.

The deferred tax income is all recognised in profit or loss, because the estimated future tax deduction of 83,333 (50,000 × 5 × $^1/_3$) is less than the cumulative remuneration expense of 188,000.

Year 2

Deferred tax asset at year-end:

$(45,000 \times 8 \times {}^2/_3 \times 0.40) =$	96,000	
Less deferred tax asset at start of year	(33,333)	
Deferred tax income for year		62,667*

* This amount consists of the following:

Deferred tax income for the temporary difference
between the tax base of the employee services
received during the year and their carrying amount
of nil:

$(45,000 \times 8 \times {}^1/_3 \times 0.40)$	48,000	

Tax income resulting from an adjustment to the tax
base of employee services received in previous
years:

(a) increase in intrinsic value: $(45,000 \times 3 \times {}^1/_3 \times 0.40)$	18,000	
(b) decrease in number of options: $(5,000 \times 5 \times {}^1/_3 \times 0.40)$	(3,333)	
Deferred tax income for year		62,667

The deferred tax income is all recognised in profit or loss, because the estimated future tax deduction of 240,000 ($45,000 \times 8 \times {}^2/_3$) is less than the cumulative remuneration expense of 373,000 (188,000 + 185,000).

Year 3

Deferred tax asset at year-end:

$(40,000 \times 13 \times 0.40) =$	208,000	
Less deferred tax asset at start of year	(96,000)	
Deferred tax income for year	112,000	

The deferred tax income is all recognised in profit or loss, because the estimated future tax deduction of 520,000 ($40,000 \times 13$) is less than the cumulative remuneration expense of 563,000 (188,000 + 185,000 + 190,000).

Year 4

Deferred tax asset at year-end:

$(40,000 \times 17 \times 0.40) =$	272,000	
Less deferred tax asset at start of year	(208,000)	
Deferred tax income for year		64,000

The deferred tax income is recognised partly in profit or loss and partly directly in equity as follows:

Estimated future tax deduction $(40,000 \times 17) =$	680,000	
Cumulative remuneration expense	563,000	
Excess tax deduction		117,000
Deferred tax income for year	64,000	
Excess recognised directly in equity $(117,000 \times 0.40) =$	46,800	
Recognised in profit or loss		17,200

Year 5

Deferred tax expense (reversal of deferred tax asset)	272,000	
Amount recognised directly in equity (reversal of cumulative deferred tax income recognised directly in equity)	46,800	
Amount recognised in profit or loss		225,200
Current tax income based on intrinsic value of options at exercise date $(40,000 \times 20 \times 0.40) =$	320,000	
Amount recognised in profit or loss $(563,000 \times 0.40) =$	225,200	
Amount recognised directly in equity		94,800

Summary

	Statement of comprehensive income				Statement of financial position	
	Employee services expense	Current tax expense (income)	Deferred tax expense (income)	Total tax expense (income)	Equity	Deferred tax asset
Year 1	188,000	0	(33,333)	(33,333)	0	33,333
Year 2	185,000	0	(62,667)	(62,667)	0	96,000
Year 3	190,000	0	(112,000)	(112,000)	0	208,000
Year 4	0	0	(17,200)	(17,200)	(46,800)	272,000
Year 5	0	(225,200)	225,200	0	46,800	0
					(94,800)	
Totals	563,000	(225,200)	0	(225,200)	(94,800)	0

Example 6 – Replacement awards in a business combination

On 1 January 20X1 Entity A acquired 100 per cent of Entity B. Entity A pays cash consideration of CU400 to the former owners of Entity B.

At the acquisition date Entity B had outstanding employee share options with a market-based measure of CU100. The share options were fully vested. As part of the business combination Entity B's outstanding share options are replaced by share options of Entity A (replacement awards) with a market-based measure of CU100 and an intrinsic value of CU80. The replacement awards are fully vested. In accordance with paragraphs B56–B62 of AASB 3 *Business Combinations*, the replacement awards are part of the consideration transferred for Entity B. A tax deduction for the replacement awards will not arise until the options are exercised. The tax deduction will be based on the share options' intrinsic value at that date. Entity A's tax rate is 40 per cent. Entity A recognises a deferred tax asset of CU32 (CU80 intrinsic value × 40%) on the replacement awards at the acquisition date.

Entity A measures the identifiable net assets obtained in the business combination (excluding deferred tax assets and liabilities) at CU450. The tax base of the identifiable net assets obtained is CU300. Entity A recognises a deferred tax liability of CU60 ((CU450 – CU300) × 40%) on the identifiable net assets at the acquisition date.

Goodwill is calculated as follows:

	CU
Cash consideration	400
Market-based measure of replacement awards	100
Total consideration transferred	500
Identifiable net assets, excluding deferred tax assets and liabilities	(450)
Deferred tax asset	32
Deferred tax liability	60
Goodwill	**78**

Reductions in the carrying amount of goodwill are not deductible for tax purposes. In accordance with paragraph 15(a) of the Standard, Entity A recognises no deferred tax liability for the taxable temporary difference associated with the goodwill recognised in the business combination.

The accounting entry for the business combination is as follows:

		CU	CU
Dr	Goodwill	78	
Dr	Identifiable net assets	450	
Dr	Deferred tax asset	32	
	Cr Cash		400
	Cr Equity (replacement awards)		100
	Cr Deferred tax liability		60

On 31 December 20X1 the intrinsic value of the replacement awards is CU120. Entity A recognises a deferred tax asset of CU48 (CU120 × 40%). Entity A recognises deferred tax income of CU16 (CU48 – CU32) from the increase in the intrinsic value of the replacement awards. The accounting entry is as follows:

		CU	CU
Dr	Deferred tax asset	16	
	Cr Deferred tax income		16

If the replacement awards had not been tax-deductible under current tax law, Entity A would not have recognised a deferred tax asset on the acquisition date. Entity A would have accounted for any subsequent events that result in a tax deduction related to the replacement award in the deferred tax income or expense of the period in which the subsequent event occurred.

Paragraphs B56–B62 of AASB 3 provide guidance on determining which portion of a replacement award is part of the consideration transferred in a business combination and which portion is attributable to future service and thus a post-combination remuneration expense. Deferred tax assets and liabilities on replacement awards that are post-combination expenses are accounted for in accordance with the general principles as illustrated in Example 5.

Example 7—Debt instruments measured at fair value

Debt instruments

At 31 December 20X1, Entity Z holds a portfolio of three debt instruments:

Debt Instrument	Cost (CU)	Fair value (CU)	Contractual interest rate
A	2,000,000	1,942,857	2.00%
B	750,000	778,571	9.00%
C	2,000,000	1,961,905	3.00%

Entity Z acquired all the debt instruments on issuance for their nominal value. The terms of the debt instruments require the issuer to pay the nominal value of the debt instruments on their maturity on 31 December 20X2.

Interest is paid at the end of each year at the contractually fixed rate, which equalled the market interest rate when the debt instruments were acquired. At the end of 20X1, the market interest rate is 5 per cent, which has caused the fair value of Debt Instruments A and C to fall below their cost and the fair value of Debt Instrument B to rise above its cost. It is probable that Entity Z will receive all the contractual cash flows if it continues to hold the debt instruments.

At the end of 20X1, Entity Z expects that it will recover the carrying amounts of Debt Instruments A and B through use, ie by continuing to hold them and collecting contractual cash flows, and Debt Instrument C by sale at the beginning of 20X2 for its fair value on 31 December 20X1. It is assumed that no other tax planning opportunity is available to Entity Z that would enable it to sell Debt Instrument B to generate a capital gain against which it could offset the capital loss arising from selling Debt Instrument C.

The debt instruments are measured at fair value through other comprehensive income in accordance with AASB 9 *Financial Instruments* (or AASB 139 *Financial Instruments: Recognition and Measurement*[1]).

Tax law
The tax base of the debt instruments is cost, which tax law allows to be offset either on maturity when principal is paid or against the sale proceeds when the debt instruments are sold. Tax law specifies that gains (losses) on the debt instruments are taxable (deductible) only when realised.

Tax law distinguishes ordinary gains and losses from capital gains and losses. Ordinary losses can be offset against both ordinary gains and capital gains. Capital losses can only be offset against capital gains. Capital losses can be carried forward for 5 years and ordinary losses can be carried forward for 20 years.

Ordinary gains are taxed at 30 per cent and capital gains are taxed at 10 per cent.

Tax law classifies interest income from the debt instruments as 'ordinary' and gains and losses arising on the sale of the debt instruments as 'capital'. Losses that arise if the issuer of the debt instrument fails to pay the principal on maturity are classified as ordinary by tax law.

General
On 31 December 20X1, Entity Z has, from other sources, taxable temporary differences of CU50,000 and deductible temporary differences of CU430,000, which will reverse in ordinary taxable profit (or ordinary tax loss) in 20X2.

At the end of 20X1, it is probable that Entity Z will report to the tax authorities an ordinary tax loss of CU200,000 for the year 20X2. This tax loss includes all taxable economic benefits and tax deductions for which temporary differences exist on 31 December 20X1 and that are classified as ordinary by tax law. These amounts contribute equally to the loss for the period according to tax law.

Entity Z has no capital gains against which it can utilise capital losses arising in the years 20X1–20X2.

Except for the information given in the previous paragraphs, there is no further information that is relevant to Entity Z's accounting for deferred taxes in the period 20X1–20X2.

---

1   AASB 9 replaced AASB 139. AASB 9 applies to all items that were previously within the scope of AASB139.

Temporary differences

At the end of 20X1, Entity Z identifies the following temporary differences:

	Carrying amount (CU)	Tax base (CU)	Taxable temporary differences (CU)	Deductible temporary differences (CU)
Debt Instrument A	1,942,857	2,000,000		
57,143				
Debt Instrument B	778,571	750,000	28,571	
Debt Instrument C	1,961,905	2,000,000		38,095
Other sources	Not specified		50,000	430,000

The difference between the carrying amount of an asset or liability and its tax base gives rise to a deductible (taxable) temporary difference (see paragraphs 20 and 26(d) of the Standard). This is because deductible (taxable) temporary differences are differences between the carrying amount of an asset or liability in the statement of financial position and its tax base, which will result in amounts that are deductible (taxable) in determining taxable profit (tax loss) of future periods when the carrying amount of the asset or liability is recovered or settled (see paragraph 5 of the Standard).

Utilisation of deductible temporary differences

With some exceptions, deferred tax assets arising from deductible temporary differences are recognised to the extent that sufficient future taxable profit will be available against which the deductible temporary differences are utilised (see paragraph 24 of the Standard).

Paragraphs 28–29 of AASB 112 identify the sources of taxable profits against which an entity can utilise deductible temporary differences. They include:

(a)   future reversal of existing taxable temporary differences;

(b)   taxable profit in future periods; and

(c)   tax planning opportunities.

The deductible temporary difference that arises from Debt Instrument C is assessed separately for utilisation. This is because tax law classifies the loss resulting from recovering the carrying amount of Debt Instrument C by sale as capital and allows capital losses to be offset only against capital gains (see paragraph 27A of the Standard).

The separate assessment results in not recognising a deferred tax asset for the deductible temporary difference that arises from Debt Instrument C because Entity Z has no source of taxable profit available that tax law classifies as capital.

In contrast, the deductible temporary difference that arises from Debt Instrument A and other sources are assessed for utilisation in combination with one another. This is because their related tax deductions would be classified as ordinary by tax law.

The tax deductions represented by the deductible temporary differences related to Debt Instrument A are classified as ordinary because the tax law classifies the effect on taxable profit (tax loss) from deducting the tax base on maturity as ordinary.

In assessing the utilisation of deductible temporary differences on 31 December 20X1, the following two steps are performed by Entity Z.

AASB

Step 1: Utilisation of deductible temporary differences because of the reversal of taxable temporary differences (see paragraph 28 of the Standard)

Entity Z first assesses the availability of taxable temporary differences as follows:

	(CU)
Expected reversal of deductible temporary differences in 20X2	
From Debt Instrument A	57,143
From other sources	430,000
Total reversal of deductible temporary differences	487,143
Expected reversal of taxable temporary differences in 20X2	
From Debt Instrument B	(28,571)
From other sources	(50,000)
Total reversal of taxable temporary differences	(78,571)
Utilisation because of the reversal of taxable temporary differences (Step 1)	78,571
Remaining deductible temporary differences to be assessed for utilisation in Step 2 (487,143 – 78,571)	408,572

In Step 1, Entity Z can recognise a deferred tax asset in relation to a deductible temporary difference of CU78,571.

Step 2: Utilisation of deductible temporary differences because of future taxable profit (see paragraph 29(a) of the Standard)

In this step, Entity Z assesses the availability of future taxable profit as follows:

	(CU)
Probable future tax profit (loss) in 20X2 (upon which income taxes are payable (recoverable))	(200,000)
Add back: reversal of deductible temporary differences expected to reverse in 20X2	487,143
Less: reversal of taxable temporary differences (utilised in Step 1)	(78,571)
Probable taxable profit excluding tax deductions for assessing utilisation of deductible temporary differences in 20X2	208,572
Remaining deductible temporary differences to be assessed for utilisation from Step 1	408,572
Utilisation because of future taxable profit (Step 2)	208,572
Utilisation because of the reversal of taxable temporary differences (Step 1)	78,571
Total utilisation of deductible temporary differences	287,143

The tax loss of CU200,000 includes the taxable economic benefit of CU2 million from the collection of the principal of Debt Instrument A and the equivalent tax deduction, because it is probable that Entity Z will recover the debt instrument for more than its carrying amount (see paragraph 29A of the Standard).

The utilisation of deductible temporary differences is not, however, assessed against probable future taxable profit for a period upon which income taxes are payable (see paragraph 5 of the Standard). Instead, the utilisation of deductible temporary differences is assessed against probable future taxable profit that excludes tax deductions resulting from the reversal of deductible temporary differences (see paragraph 29(a) of the Standard). Assessing the utilisation of deductible temporary differences against probable future taxable profits without excluding those deductions would lead to double counting the deductible temporary differences in that assessment.

In Step 2, Entity Z determines that it can recognise a deferred tax asset in relation to a future taxable profit, excluding tax deductions resulting from the reversal of deductible temporary differences, of CU208,572. Consequently, the total utilisation of deductible temporary differences amounts to CU287,143 (CU78,571 (Step 1) + CU208,572 (Step 2)).

Measurement of deferred tax assets and deferred tax liabilities

Entity Z presents the following deferred tax assets and deferred tax liabilities in its financial statements on 31 December 20X1:

	(CU)
Total taxable temporary differences	78,571
Total utilisation of deductible temporary differences	287,143
Deferred tax liabilities (78,571 at 30%)	23,571
Deferred tax assets (287,143 at 30%)	86,143

The deferred tax assets and the deferred tax liabilities are measured using the tax rate for ordinary gains of 30 per cent, in accordance with the expected manner of recovery (settlement) of the underlying assets (liabilities) (see paragraph 51 of the Standard).

Allocation of changes in deferred tax assets between profit or loss and other comprehensive income

Changes in deferred tax that arise from items that are recognised in profit or loss are recognised in profit or loss (see paragraph 58 of the Standard). Changes in deferred tax that arise from items that are recognised in other comprehensive income are recognised in other comprehensive income (see paragraph 61A of the Standard).

Entity Z did not recognise deferred tax assets for all of its deductible temporary differences at 31 December 20X1, and according to tax law all the tax deductions represented by the deductible temporary differences contribute equally to the tax loss for the period. Consequently, the assessment of the utilisation of deductible temporary differences does not specify whether the taxable profits are utilised for deferred tax items that are recognised in profit or loss (ie the deductible temporary differences from other sources) or whether instead the taxable profits are utilised for deferred tax items that are recognised in other comprehensive income (ie the deductible temporary differences related to debt instruments classified as fair value through other comprehensive income).

For such situations, paragraph 63 of the Standard requires the changes in deferred taxes to be allocated to profit or loss and other comprehensive income on a reasonable pro rata basis or by another method that achieves a more appropriate allocation in the circumstances.

COMPILATION DETAILS

Accounting Standard AASB 112 *Income Taxes* as amended

Compilation details are not part of AASB 112.

This compiled Standard applies to annual periods beginning on or after 1 January 2018 but before 1 January 2019. It takes into account amendments up to and including 24 February 2016 and was prepared on 20 March 2017 by the staff of the Australian Accounting Standards Board (AASB).

This compilation is not a separate Accounting Standard made by the AASB. Instead, it is a representation of AASB 112 (August 2015) as amended by other Accounting Standards, which are listed in the Table below.

Table of Standards

Standard	Date made	FRL identifier	Commence-ment date	Effective date *(annual periods ... on or after ...)*	Application, saving or transitional provisions
AASB 112	7 Aug 2015	F2015L01601	31 Dec 2017	*(beginning)* 1 Jan 2018	see (a) below
AASB 16	23 Feb 2016	F2016L00233	31 Dec 2018	*(beginning)* 1 Jan 2019	not compiled*
AASB 2016-1	24 Feb 2016	F2016L00231	31 Dec 2016	*(beginning)* 1 Jan 2017	see (b) below

*   The amendments made by this Standard are not included in this compilation, which presents the principal Standard as applicable to annual periods beginning on or after 1 January 2018 but before 1 January 2019.
(a) Entities may elect to apply this Standard to periods beginning after 24 July 2014 but before 1 January 2018.
(b) Entities may elect to apply this Standard to annual periods beginning before 1 January 2017.

Table of amendments to Standard

Paragraph affected	How affected	By ... [paragraph/page]
26 (example)	added	AASB 2016-1 [page 6]
27	added	AASB 2016-1 [page 6]
29	amended	AASB 2016-1 [page 7]
29A	added	AASB 2016-1 [page 7]
98H	added	AASB 2016-1 [page 7]

Table of amendments to illustrative examples

Paragraph affected	How affected	By ... [paragraph/page]
Illustrative computations and presentation		
Example 7	added	AASB 2016-1 [page 8]

DELETED IAS 12 TEXT

Deleted IAS 12 text is not part of AASB 112.

90   This Standard supersedes IAS 12 *Accounting for Taxes on Income*, approved in 1979.

91   Paragraphs 52A, 52B, 65A, 81(i), 82A, 87A, 87B, 87C and the deletion of paragraphs 3 and 50 become operative for annual financial statements[1] covering periods beginning on or after 1 January 2001. Earlier adoption is encouraged. If earlier adoption affects the financial statements, an entity shall disclose that fact.

> 1   Paragraph 91 refers to 'annual financial statements' in line with more explicit language for writing effective dates adopted in 1998. Paragraph 89 refers to 'financial statements'.

92   IAS 1 (as revised in 2007) amended the terminology used throughout IFRSs. In addition it amended paragraphs 23, 52, 58, 60, 62, 63, 65, 68C, 77 and 81, deleted paragraph 61 and added paragraphs 61A, 62A and 77A. An entity shall apply those amendments for annual periods beginning on or after 1 January 2009. If an entity applies IAS 1 (revised 2007) for an earlier period, the amendments shall be applied for that earlier period.

95   IFRS 3 (as revised in 2008) amended paragraphs 21 and 67 and added paragraphs 32A and 81(j) and (k). An entity shall apply those amendments for annual periods beginning on or after 1 July 2009. If an entity applies IFRS 3 (revised 2008) for an earlier period, the amendments shall also be applied for that earlier period.

98   Paragraph 52 was renumbered as 51A, paragraph 10 and the examples following paragraph 51A were amended, and paragraphs 51B and 51C and the following example and paragraphs 51D, 51E and 99 were added by *Deferred Tax: Recovery of Underlying Assets*, issued in December 2010. An entity shall apply those amendments for annual periods beginning on or after 1 January 2012. Earlier application is permitted. If an entity applies the amendments for an earlier period, it shall disclose that fact.

98A   IFRS 11 *Joint Arrangements*, issued in May 2011, amended paragraphs 2, 15, 18(e), 24, 38, 39, 43–45, 81(f), 87 and 87C. An entity shall apply those amendments when it applies IFRS 11.

98B   *Presentation of Items of Other Comprehensive Income* (Amendments to IAS 1), issued in June 2011, amended paragraph 77 and deleted paragraph 77A. An entity shall apply those amendments when it applies IAS 1 as amended in June 2011.

98C   *Investment Entities* (Amendments to IFRS 10, IFRS 12 and IAS 27), issued in October 2012, amended paragraphs 58 and 68C. An entity shall apply those amendments for annual periods beginning on or after 1 January 2014. Earlier application of *Investment Entities* is permitted. If an entity applies those amendments earlier it shall also apply all amendments included in *Investment Entities* at the same time.

99   The amendments made by *Deferred Tax: Recovery of Underlying Assets*, issued in December 2010, supersede SIC Interpretation 21 *Income Taxes—Recovery of Revalued Non-Depreciable Assets*.

AASB 116

Property, Plant and Equipment

(Compiled June 2016)

This compiled Standard applies to annual periods beginning on or after 1 January 2018 but before 1 January 2019. Earlier application is permitted. It incorporates relevant amendments made up to and including 27 June 2016.

Prepared on 20 March 2017 by the staff of the Australian Accounting Standards Board.

Compilation no. 1

Compilation date: 31 December 2016

This note is not part of Accounting Standard AASB 116.

The following unincorporated amendments are not included in this compiled Standard.

- AASB 17 *Insurance Contracts* — Appendix D sets out the amendments to other Standards that are a consequence of the AASB issuing AASB 17 *Insurance Contracts*. This Standard is applicable from 1 January 2021. Earlier application is permitted, but entities must apply AASB 9 *Financial Instruments* and AASB 15 *Revenue from Contracts with Customers* first.

- AASB 1058 *Income of Not-for-Profit Entities* — Appendix D sets out the amendments to other Australian Accounting Standards that are a consequence of the AASB issuing this Standard. It is applicable from 1 January 2019. Earlier application is permitted, but amendments to AASB 117 apply before 1 January 2019 only if AASB 1058 is also applied to an earlier period. In addition, AASB 1 and AASB 16 amendments are applied to an earlier period only if AASB 16 is also applied to that period.

- AASB 16 *Leases* — Appendix D sets out the amendments to other Standards that are a consequence of the AASB issuing this Standard. It is applicable from 1 January 2019. Earlier application is permitted, but entities must apply AASB 15 *Revenue from Contracts with Customers* before applying this Standard.

- AASB 2016-7 *Amendments to Australian Accounting Standards — Deferral of AASB 15 for Not-for-Profit Entities.* This Standard defers the consequential amendments that were originally set out in AASB 2014-5 *Amendments to Australian Accounting Standards arising from AASB 15,* by restating the effective date of the amendments set out in AASB 2015-8 *Amendments to Australian Accounting Standards* for not-for-profit entities. This Standard defers the application of AASB 15 to 1 January 2019. Earlier application is permitted provided AASB 1058 is also applied to the same period.

Entities early-adopting any amendments with later application dates will need to refer to the amending Standards that have not yet been incorporated into compilations. The abovementioned unincorporated amendments may be located on the AASB website at www.aasb.gov.au or on the Federal Register of Legislation website at www.legislation.gov.au.

CONTENTS

APPENDICES

A. AUSTRALIAN DEFINED TERMS

B. AUSTRALIAN REDUCED DISCLOSURE REQUIREMENTS

AUSTRALIAN IMPLEMENTATION GUIDANCE

COMPILATION DETAILS

DELETED IAS 16 TEXT

BASIS FOR CONCLUSIONS ON IAS 16 (available on the AASB website)

> Australian Accounting Standard AASB 116 *Property, Plant and Equipment* (as amended) is set out in paragraphs 1 – Aus83.2 and Appendices A – B. All the paragraphs have equal authority. Paragraphs in **bold type** state the main principles. AASB 116 is to be read in the context of other Australian Accounting Standards, including AASB 1048 *Interpretation of Standards*, which identifies the Australian Accounting Interpretations, and AASB 1057 *Application of Australian Accounting Standards*. In the absence of explicit guidance, AASB 108 *Accounting Policies, Changes in Accounting Estimates and Errors* provides a basis for selecting and applying accounting policies.

COMPARISON WITH IAS 16

AASB 116 *Property, Plant and Equipment* as amended incorporates IAS 16 *Presentation of Financial Statements* as issued and amended by the International Accounting Standards Board (IASB). Australian-specific paragraphs (which are not included in IAS 16) are identified with the prefix "Aus" or "RDR". Paragraphs that apply only to not-for-profit entities begin by identifying their limited applicability.

Tier 1

For-profit entities complying with AASB 116 also comply with IAS 16.

Not-for-profit entities' compliance with IAS 16 will depend on whether any "Aus" paragraphs that specifically apply to not-for-profit entities provide additional guidance or contain applicable requirements that are inconsistent with IAS 16.

Tier 2

Entities preparing general purpose financial statements under Australian Accounting Standards – Reduced Disclosure Requirements (Tier 2) will not be in compliance with IFRSs.

AASB 1053 *Application of Tiers of Australian Accounting Standards* explains the two tiers of reporting requirements.

ACCOUNTING STANDARD AASB 116

The Australian Accounting Standards Board made Accounting Standard AASB 116 *Property, Plant and Equipment* under section 334 of the *Corporations Act 2001* on 7 August 2015.

This compiled version of AASB 116 applies to annual periods beginning on or after 1 January 2018 but before 1 January 2019. It incorporates relevant amendments contained in other AASB Standards made by the AASB up to and including 27 June 2016 (see Compilation Details).

ACCOUNTING STANDARD AASB 116
PROPERTY, PLANT AND EQUIPMENT

Objective

1   The objective of this Standard is to prescribe the accounting treatment for property, plant and equipment so that users of the financial statements can discern information about an entity's investment in its property, plant and equipment and the changes in such investment. The principal issues in accounting for property, plant and equipment are the recognition of the assets, the determination of their carrying amounts and the depreciation charges and impairment losses to be recognised in relation to them.

Scope

2   **This Standard shall be applied in accounting for property, plant and equipment except when another Standard requires or permits a different accounting treatment.**

3   This Standard does not apply to:

     (a)   property, plant and equipment classified as held for sale in accordance with AASB 5 *Non-current Assets Held for Sale and Discontinued Operations*.

     (b)   biological assets related to agricultural activity other than bearer plants (see AASB 141 *Agriculture*). This Standard applies to bearer plants but it does not apply to the produce on bearer plants.

     (c)   the recognition and measurement of exploration and evaluation assets (see AASB 6 *Exploration for and Evaluation of Mineral Resources*).

     (d)   mineral rights and mineral reserves such as oil, natural gas and similar non-regenerative resources.

     However, this Standard applies to property, plant and equipment used to develop or maintain the assets described in (b)–(d).

4   Other Standards may require recognition of an item of property, plant and equipment based on an approach different from that in this Standard. For example, AASB 117

Leases requires an entity to evaluate its recognition of an item of leased property, plant and equipment on the basis of the transfer of risks and rewards. However, in such cases other aspects of the accounting treatment for these assets, including depreciation, are prescribed by this Standard.

5 An entity using the cost model for investment property in accordance with AASB 140 *Investment Property* shall use the cost model in this Standard.

Definitions

6 The following terms are used in this Standard with the meanings specified:

A *bearer plant* is a living plant that:

(a) is used in the production or supply of agricultural produce;

(b) is expected to bear produce for more than one period; and

(c) has a remote likelihood of being sold as agricultural produce, except for incidental scrap sales.

(Paragraphs 5A–5B of AASB 141 elaborate on this definition of a bearer plant.)

Carrying amount is the amount at which an asset is recognised after deducting any accumulated depreciation and accumulated impairment losses.

Cost is the amount of cash or cash equivalents paid or the fair value of the other consideration given to acquire an asset at the time of its acquisition or construction or, where applicable, the amount attributed to that asset when initially recognised in accordance with the specific requirements of other Australian Accounting Standards, eg AASB 2 *Share-based Payment*.

Depreciable amount is the cost of an asset, or other amount substituted for cost, less its residual value.

Depreciation is the systematic allocation of the depreciable amount of an asset over its useful life.

Entity-specific value is the present value of the cash flows an entity expects to arise from the continuing use of an asset and from its disposal at the end of its useful life or expects to incur when settling a liability.

Fair value is the price that would be received to sell an asset or paid to transfer a liability in an orderly transaction between market participants at the measurement date. (See AASB 13 *Fair Value Measurement*.)

An *impairment loss* is the amount by which the carrying amount of an asset exceeds its recoverable amount.

Property, plant and equipment are tangible items that:

(a) are held for use in the production or supply of goods or services, for rental to others, or for administrative purposes; and

(b) are expected to be used during more than one period.

Recoverable amount is the higher of an asset's fair value less costs to sell and its value in use.

The *residual value* of an asset is the estimated amount that an entity would currently obtain from disposal of the asset, after deducting the estimated costs of disposal, if the asset were already of the age and in the condition expected at the end of its useful life.

Useful life is:

(a) the period over which an asset is expected to be available for use by an entity; or

(b) the number of production or similar units expected to be obtained from the asset by an entity.

Recognition

7   **The cost of an item of property, plant and equipment shall be recognised as an asset if, and only if:**

        (a)   **it is probable that future economic benefits associated with the item will flow to the entity; and**

        (b)   **the cost of the item can be measured reliably.**

8   Items such as spare parts, stand-by equipment and servicing equipment are recognised in accordance with this Standard when they meet the definition of property, plant and equipment. Otherwise, such items are classified as inventory.

9   This Standard does not prescribe the unit of measure for recognition, ie what constitutes an item of property, plant and equipment. Thus, judgement is required in applying the recognition criteria to an entity's specific circumstances. It may be appropriate to aggregate individually insignificant items, such as moulds, tools and dies, and to apply the criteria to the aggregate value.

10   An entity evaluates under this recognition principle all its property, plant and equipment costs at the time they are incurred. These costs include costs incurred initially to acquire or construct an item of property, plant and equipment and costs incurred subsequently to add to, replace part of, or service it.

Initial costs

11   Items of property, plant and equipment may be acquired for safety or environmental reasons. The acquisition of such property, plant and equipment, although not directly increasing the future economic benefits of any particular existing item of property, plant and equipment, may be necessary for an entity to obtain the future economic benefits from its other assets. Such items of property, plant and equipment qualify for recognition as assets because they enable an entity to derive future economic benefits from related assets in excess of what could be derived had those items not been acquired. For example, a chemical manufacturer may install new chemical handling processes to comply with environmental requirements for the production and storage of dangerous chemicals; related plant enhancements are recognised as an asset because without them the entity is unable to manufacture and sell chemicals. However, the resulting carrying amount of such an asset and related assets is reviewed for impairment in accordance with AASB 136 *Impairment of Assets*.

Subsequent costs

12   Under the recognition principle in paragraph 7, an entity does not recognise in the carrying amount of an item of property, plant and equipment the costs of the day-to-day servicing of the item. Rather, these costs are recognised in profit or loss as incurred. Costs of day-to-day servicing are primarily the costs of labour and consumables, and may include the cost of small parts. The purpose of these expenditures is often described as for the 'repairs and maintenance' of the item of property, plant and equipment.

13   Parts of some items of property, plant and equipment may require replacement at regular intervals. For example, a furnace may require relining after a specified number of hours of use, or aircraft interiors such as seats and galleys may require replacement several times during the life of the airframe. Items of property, plant and equipment may also be acquired to make a less frequently recurring replacement, such as replacing the interior walls of a building, or to make a nonrecurring replacement. Under the recognition principle in paragraph 7, an entity recognises in the carrying amount of an item of property, plant and equipment the cost of replacing part of such an item when that cost is incurred if the recognition criteria are met. The carrying amount of those parts that are replaced is derecognised in accordance with the derecognition provisions of this Standard (see paragraphs 67–72).

14   A condition of continuing to operate an item of property, plant and equipment (for example, an aircraft) may be performing regular major inspections for faults regardless of whether parts of the item are replaced. When each major inspection is performed, its cost is recognised in the carrying amount of the item of property, plant and equipment as a replacement if the recognition criteria are satisfied. Any remaining carrying amount of the cost of the previous inspection (as distinct from physical parts) is derecognised. This occurs regardless of whether the cost of the previous inspection was identified in the transaction in which the item was acquired or constructed. If necessary, the estimated cost of a future similar inspection may be used as an indication of what the cost of the existing inspection component was when the item was acquired or constructed.

Measurement at recognition

15   **An item of property, plant and equipment that qualifies for recognition as an asset shall be measured at its cost.**

Aus15.1   **Notwithstanding paragraph 15, in respect of not-for-profit entities, where an asset is acquired at no cost, or for a nominal cost, the cost is its fair value as at the date of acquisition.**

Aus15.2   In respect of not-for-profit entities, an item of property, plant and equipment may be gifted or contributed to the entity. For example, land may be contributed to a local government by a developer at no or nominal consideration to enable the local government to develop parks, roads and paths in the development. An asset may also be acquired for no or nominal consideration through the exercise of powers of sequestration. Under these circumstances the cost of the item is its fair value as at the date it is acquired.

Aus15.3   In respect of not-for-profit entities, for the purposes of this Standard, the initial recognition at fair value of an item of property, plant and equipment, acquired at no or nominal cost, consistent with the requirements of paragraph Aus15.1, does not constitute a revaluation. Accordingly, the revaluation requirements in paragraph 31, and the supporting commentary in paragraphs 32 to 35, only apply where an entity elects to revalue an item of property, plant and equipment in subsequent reporting periods.

Elements of cost

16   The cost of an item of property, plant and equipment comprises:

    (a)   its purchase price, including import duties and non-refundable purchase taxes, after deducting trade discounts and rebates.

    (b)   any costs directly attributable to bringing the asset to the location and condition necessary for it to be capable of operating in the manner intended by management.

    (c)   the initial estimate of the costs of dismantling and removing the item and restoring the site on which it is located, the obligation for which an entity incurs either when the item is acquired or as a consequence of having used the item during a particular period for purposes other than to produce inventories during that period.

17   Examples of directly attributable costs are:

    (a)   costs of employee benefits (as defined in AASB 119 *Employee Benefits*) arising directly from the construction or acquisition of the item of property, plant and equipment;

    (b)   costs of site preparation;

    (c)   initial delivery and handling costs;

    (d)   installation and assembly costs;

    (e)   costs of testing whether the asset is functioning properly, after deducting the net proceeds from selling any items produced while bringing the asset to that location and condition (such as samples produced when testing equipment); and

    (f)   professional fees.

18   An entity applies AASB 102 *Inventories* to the costs of obligations for dismantling, removing and restoring the site on which an item is located that are incurred during a particular period as a consequence of having used the item to produce inventories during that period. The obligations for costs accounted for in accordance with AASB 102 or AASB 116 are recognised and measured in accordance with AASB 137 *Provisions, Contingent Liabilities and Contingent Assets*.

19   Examples of costs that are not costs of an item of property, plant and equipment are:

    (a)   costs of opening a new facility;

    (b)   costs of introducing a new product or service (including costs of advertising and promotional activities);

    (c)   costs of conducting business in a new location or with a new class of customer (including costs of staff training); and

    (d)   administration and other general overhead costs.

20   Recognition of costs in the carrying amount of an item of property, plant and equipment ceases when the item is in the location and condition necessary for it to be capable of operating in the manner intended by management. Therefore, costs incurred in using or redeploying an item are not included in the carrying amount of that item. For example, the following costs are not included in the carrying amount of an item of property, plant and equipment:

    (a)   costs incurred while an item capable of operating in the manner intended by management has yet to be brought into use or is operated at less than full capacity;

    (b)   initial operating losses, such as those incurred while demand for the item's output builds up; and

    (c)   costs of relocating or reorganising part or all of an entity's operations.

21   Some operations occur in connection with the construction or development of an item of property, plant and equipment, but are not necessary to bring the item to the location and condition necessary for it to be capable of operating in the manner intended by management. These incidental operations may occur before or during the construction or development activities. For example, income may be earned through using a building site as a car park until construction starts. Because incidental operations are not necessary to bring an item to the location and condition necessary for it to be capable of operating in the manner intended by management, the income and related expenses of incidental operations are recognised in profit or loss and included in their respective classifications of income and expense.

22   The cost of a self-constructed asset is determined using the same principles as for an acquired asset. If an entity makes similar assets for sale in the normal course of business, the cost of the asset is usually the same as the cost of constructing an asset for sale (see AASB 102). Therefore, any internal profits are eliminated in arriving at such costs. Similarly, the cost of abnormal amounts of wasted material, labour, or other resources incurred in self-constructing an asset is not included in the cost of the asset. AASB 123 *Borrowing Costs* establishes criteria for the recognition of interest as a component of the carrying amount of a self-constructed item of property, plant and equipment.

22A   Bearer plants are accounted for in the same way as self-constructed items of property, plant and equipment before they are in the location and condition necessary to be capable of operating in the manner intended by management. Consequently, references to 'construction' in this Standard should be read as covering activities that are necessary to cultivate the bearer plants before they are in the location and condition necessary to be capable of operating in the manner intended by management.

Measurement of cost

23   The cost of an item of property, plant and equipment is the cash price equivalent at the recognition date. If payment is deferred beyond normal credit terms, the difference between the cash price equivalent and the total payment is recognised as interest over the period of credit unless such interest is capitalised in accordance with AASB 123.

24   One or more items of property, plant and equipment may be acquired in exchange for a non-monetary asset or assets, or a combination of monetary and non-monetary assets. The following discussion refers simply to an exchange of one non-monetary asset for another, but it also applies to all exchanges described in the preceding sentence. The cost of such an item of property, plant and equipment is measured at fair value unless (a) the exchange transaction lacks commercial substance or (b) the fair value of neither the asset received nor the asset given up is reliably measurable. The acquired item is measured in this way even if an entity cannot immediately derecognise the asset given up. If the acquired item is not measured at fair value, its cost is measured at the carrying amount of the asset given up.

25   An entity determines whether an exchange transaction has commercial substance by considering the extent to which its future cash flows are expected to change as a result of the transaction. An exchange transaction has commercial substance if:

(a)   the configuration (risk, timing and amount) of the cash flows of the asset received differs from the configuration of the cash flows of the asset transferred; or

(b)   the entity-specific value of the portion of the entity's operations affected by the transaction changes as a result of the exchange; and

(c)   the difference in (a) or (b) is significant relative to the fair value of the assets exchanged.

For the purpose of determining whether an exchange transaction has commercial substance, the entity-specific value of the portion of the entity's operations affected by the transaction shall reflect post-tax cash flows. The result of these analyses may be clear without an entity having to perform detailed calculations.

26   The fair value of an asset is reliably measurable if (a) the variability in the range of reasonable fair value measurements is not significant for that asset or (b) the probabilities of the various estimates within the range can be reasonably assessed and used when measuring fair value. If an entity is able to measure reliably the fair value of either the asset received or the asset given up, then the fair value of the asset given up is used to measure the cost of the asset received unless the fair value of the asset received is more clearly evident.

27   The cost of an item of property, plant and equipment held by a lessee under a finance lease is determined in accordance with AASB 117.

28   The carrying amount of an item of property, plant and equipment may be reduced by government grants in accordance with AASB 120 *Accounting for Government Grants and Disclosure of Government Assistance*.

Measurement after recognition

29   **An entity shall choose either the cost model in paragraph 30 or the revaluation model in paragraph 31 as its accounting policy and shall apply that policy to an entire class of property, plant and equipment.**

Cost model

30   After recognition as an asset, an item of property, plant and equipment shall
        be carried at its cost less any accumulated depreciation and any accumulated
        impairment losses.

Revaluation model

31   After recognition as an asset, an item of property, plant and equipment whose fair
        value can be measured reliably shall be carried at a revalued amount, being its fair
        value at the date of the revaluation less any subsequent accumulated depreciation
        and subsequent accumulated impairment losses. Revaluations shall be made with
        sufficient regularity to ensure that the carrying amount does not differ materially
        from that which would be determined using fair value at the end of the reporting
        period.

32–33   [Deleted]

34   The frequency of revaluations depends upon the changes in fair values of the items of
        property, plant and equipment being revalued. When the fair value of a revalued asset
        differs materially from its carrying amount, a further revaluation is required. Some
        items of property, plant and equipment experience significant and volatile changes
        in fair value, thus necessitating annual revaluation. Such frequent revaluations are
        unnecessary for items of property, plant and equipment with only insignificant changes
        in fair value. Instead, it may be necessary to revalue the item only every three or five
        years.

35   When an item of property, plant and equipment is revalued, the carrying amount of
        that asset is adjusted to the revalued amount. At the date of the revaluation, the asset
        is treated in one of the following ways:

        (a)   the gross carrying amount is adjusted in a manner that is consistent with the
                revaluation of the carrying amount of the asset. For example, the gross carrying
                amount may be restated by reference to observable market data or it may be
                restated proportionately to the change in the carrying amount. The accumulated
                depreciation at the date of the revaluation is adjusted to equal the difference
                between the gross carrying amount and the carrying amount of the asset after
                taking into account accumulated impairment losses; or

        (b)   the accumulated depreciation is eliminated against the gross carrying amount
                of the asset.

        The amount of the adjustment of accumulated depreciation forms part of the increase
        or decrease in carrying amount that is accounted for in accordance with paragraphs 39,
        Aus39.1, 40, Aus40.1 and Aus40.2.

36   **If an item of property, plant and equipment is revalued, the entire class of
        property, plant and equipment to which that asset belongs shall be revalued.**

37   A class of property, plant and equipment is a grouping of assets of a similar nature and
        use in an entity's operations. The following are examples of separate classes:

        (a)   land;

        (b)   land and buildings;

        (c)   machinery;

        (d)   ships;

        (e)   aircraft;

        (f)   motor vehicles;

        (g)   furniture and fixtures;

        (h)   office equipment; and

        (i)   bearer plants.

38   The items within a class of property, plant and equipment are revalued simultaneously to avoid selective revaluation of assets and the reporting of amounts in the financial statements that are a mixture of costs and values as at different dates. However, a class of assets may be revalued on a rolling basis provided revaluation of the class of assets is completed within a short period and provided the revaluations are kept up to date.

39   **If an asset's carrying amount is increased as a result of a revaluation, the increase shall be recognised in other comprehensive income and accumulated in equity under the heading of revaluation surplus. However, the increase shall be recognised in profit or loss to the extent that it reverses a revaluation decrease of the same asset previously recognised in profit or loss.**

Aus39.1   **Notwithstanding paragraph 39, in respect of not-for-profit entities, if the carrying amount of a class of assets is increased as a result of a revaluation, the net revaluation increase shall be recognised in other comprehensive income and accumulated in equity under the heading of revaluation surplus. However, the net revaluation increase shall be recognised in profit or loss to the extent that it reverses a net revaluation decrease of the same class of assets previously recognised in profit or loss.**

40   **If an asset's carrying amount is decreased as a result of a revaluation, the decrease shall be recognised in profit or loss. However, the decrease shall be recognised in other comprehensive income to the extent of any credit balance existing in the revaluation surplus in respect of that asset. The decrease recognised in other comprehensive income reduces the amount accumulated in equity under the heading of revaluation surplus.**

Aus40.1   **Notwithstanding paragraph 40, in respect of not-for-profit entities, if the carrying amount of a class of assets decreased as a result of a revaluation, the net revaluation decrease shall be recognised in profit or loss. However, the net revaluation decrease shall be recognised in other comprehensive income to the extent of any credit balance existing in any revaluation surplus in respect of that same class of asset. The net revaluation decrease recognised in other comprehensive income reduces the amount accumulated in equity under the heading of revaluation surplus.**

Aus40.2   **Notwithstanding paragraph 40, in respect of not-for-profit entities, revaluation increases and revaluation decreases relating to individual assets within a class of property, plant and equipment shall be offset against one another within that class but shall not be offset in respect of assets in different classes.**

41   The revaluation surplus included in equity in respect of an item of property, plant and equipment may be transferred directly to retained earnings when the asset is derecognised. This may involve transferring the whole of the surplus when the asset is retired or disposed of. However, some of the surplus may be transferred as the asset is used by an entity. In such a case, the amount of the surplus transferred would be the difference between depreciation based on the revalued carrying amount of the asset and depreciation based on the asset's original cost. Transfers from revaluation surplus to retained earnings are not made through profit or loss.

42   The effects of taxes on income, if any, resulting from the revaluation of property, plant and equipment are recognised and disclosed in accordance with AASB 112 *Income Taxes*.

Depreciation

43   **Each part of an item of property, plant and equipment with a cost that is significant in relation to the total cost of the item shall be depreciated separately.**

44   An entity allocates the amount initially recognised in respect of an item of property, plant and equipment to its significant parts and depreciates separately each such part. For example, it may be appropriate to depreciate separately the airframe and engines of an aircraft, whether owned or subject to a finance lease. Similarly, if an entity acquires

property, plant and equipment subject to an operating lease in which it is the lessor, it may be appropriate to depreciate separately amounts reflected in the cost of that item that are attributable to favourable or unfavourable lease terms relative to market terms.

45 A significant part of an item of property, plant and equipment may have a useful life and a depreciation method that are the same as the useful life and the depreciation method of another significant part of that same item. Such parts may be grouped in determining the depreciation charge.

46 To the extent that an entity depreciates separately some parts of an item of property, plant and equipment, it also depreciates separately the remainder of the item. The remainder consists of the parts of the item that are individually not significant. If an entity has varying expectations for these parts, approximation techniques may be necessary to depreciate the remainder in a manner that faithfully represents the consumption pattern and/or useful life of its parts.

47 An entity may choose to depreciate separately the parts of an item that do not have a cost that is significant in relation to the total cost of the item.

48 The depreciation charge for each period shall be recognised in profit or loss unless it is included in the carrying amount of another asset.

49 The depreciation charge for a period is usually recognised in profit or loss. However, sometimes, the future economic benefits embodied in an asset are absorbed in producing other assets. In this case, the depreciation charge constitutes part of the cost of the other asset and is included in its carrying amount. For example, the depreciation of manufacturing plant and equipment is included in the costs of conversion of inventories (see AASB 102). Similarly, depreciation of property, plant and equipment used for development activities may be included in the cost of an intangible asset recognised in accordance with AASB 138 *Intangible Assets*.

Depreciable amount and depreciation period

50 The depreciable amount of an asset shall be allocated on a systematic basis over its useful life.

51 The residual value and the useful life of an asset shall be reviewed at least at each financial year-end and, if expectations differ from previous estimates, the change(s) shall be accounted for as a change in an accounting estimate in accordance with AASB 108 *Accounting Policies, Changes in Accounting Estimates and Errors*.

52 Depreciation is recognised even if the fair value of the asset exceeds its carrying amount, as long as the asset's residual value does not exceed its carrying amount. Repair and maintenance of an asset do not negate the need to depreciate it.

53 The depreciable amount of an asset is determined after deducting its residual value. In practice, the residual value of an asset is often insignificant and therefore immaterial in the calculation of the depreciable amount.

54 The residual value of an asset may increase to an amount equal to or greater than the asset's carrying amount. If it does, the asset's depreciation charge is zero unless and until its residual value subsequently decreases to an amount below the asset's carrying amount.

55 Depreciation of an asset begins when it is available for use, ie when it is in the location and condition necessary for it to be capable of operating in the manner intended by management. Depreciation of an asset ceases at the earlier of the date that the asset is classified as held for sale (or included in a disposal group that is classified as held for sale) in accordance with AASB 5 and the date that the asset is derecognised. Therefore, depreciation does not cease when the asset becomes idle or is retired from active use unless the asset is fully depreciated. However, under usage methods of depreciation the depreciation charge can be zero while there is no production.

56 The future economic benefits embodied in an asset are consumed by an entity principally through its use. However, other factors, such as technical or commercial

obsolescence and wear and tear while an asset remains idle, often result in the diminution of the economic benefits that might have been obtained from the asset. Consequently, all the following factors are considered in determining the useful life of an asset:

(a) expected usage of the asset. Usage is assessed by reference to the asset's expected capacity or physical output.

(b) expected physical wear and tear, which depends on operational factors such as the number of shifts for which the asset is to be used and the repair and maintenance programme, and the care and maintenance of the asset while idle.

(c) technical or commercial obsolescence arising from changes or improvements in production, or from a change in the market demand for the product or service output of the asset. Expected future reductions in the selling price of an item that was produced using an asset could indicate the expectation of technical or commercial obsolescence of the asset, which, in turn, might reflect a reduction of the future economic benefits embodied in the asset.

(d) legal or similar limits on the use of the asset, such as the expiry dates of related leases.

57 The useful life of an asset is defined in terms of the asset's expected utility to the entity. The asset management policy of the entity may involve the disposal of assets after a specified time or after consumption of a specified proportion of the future economic benefits embodied in the asset. Therefore, the useful life of an asset may be shorter than its economic life. The estimation of the useful life of the asset is a matter of judgement based on the experience of the entity with similar assets.

58 Land and buildings are separable assets and are accounted for separately, even when they are acquired together. With some exceptions, such as quarries and sites used for landfill, land has an unlimited useful life and therefore is not depreciated. Buildings have a limited useful life and therefore are depreciable assets. An increase in the value of the land on which a building stands does not affect the determination of the depreciable amount of the building.

59 If the cost of land includes the costs of site dismantlement, removal and restoration, that portion of the land asset is depreciated over the period of benefits obtained by incurring those costs. In some cases, the land itself may have a limited useful life, in which case it is depreciated in a manner that reflects the benefits to be derived from it.

Depreciation method

60 The depreciation method used shall reflect the pattern in which the asset's future economic benefits are expected to be consumed by the entity.

61 The depreciation method applied to an asset shall be reviewed at least at each financial year-end and, if there has been a significant change in the expected pattern of consumption of the future economic benefits embodied in the asset, the method shall be changed to reflect the changed pattern. Such a change shall be accounted for as a change in an accounting estimate in accordance with AASB 108.

62 A variety of depreciation methods can be used to allocate the depreciable amount of an asset on a systematic basis over its useful life. These methods include the straight-line method, the diminishing balance method and the units of production method. Straight-line depreciation results in a constant charge over the useful life if the asset's residual value does not change. The diminishing balance method results in a decreasing charge over the useful life. The units of production method results in a charge based on the expected use or output. The entity selects the method that most closely reflects the expected pattern of consumption of the future economic benefits embodied in the asset. That method is applied consistently from period to period unless there is a change in the expected pattern of consumption of those future economic benefits.

62A   A depreciation method that is based on revenue that is generated by an activity that includes the use of an asset is not appropriate. The revenue generated by an activity that includes the use of an asset generally reflects factors other than the consumption of the economic benefits of the asset. For example, revenue is affected by other inputs and processes, selling activities and changes in sales volumes and prices. The price component of revenue may be affected by inflation, which has no bearing upon the way in which an asset is consumed.

Impairment

63   To determine whether an item of property, plant and equipment is impaired, an entity applies AASB 136 *Impairment of Assets*. That Standard explains how an entity reviews the carrying amount of its assets, how it determines the recoverable amount of an asset, and when it recognises, or reverses the recognition of, an impairment loss.

64   [Deleted]

Compensation for impairment

65   **Compensation from third parties for items of property, plant and equipment that were impaired, lost or given up shall be included in profit or loss when the compensation becomes receivable.**

66   Impairments or losses of items of property, plant and equipment, related claims for or payments of compensation from third parties and any subsequent purchase or construction of replacement assets are separate economic events and are accounted for separately as follows:

     (a)   impairments of items of property, plant and equipment are recognised in accordance with AASB 136;

     (b)   derecognition of items of property, plant and equipment retired or disposed of is determined in accordance with this Standard;

     (c)   compensation from third parties for items of property, plant and equipment that were impaired, lost or given up is included in determining profit or loss when it becomes receivable; and

     (d)   the cost of items of property, plant and equipment restored, purchased or constructed as replacements is determined in accordance with this Standard.

Derecognition

67   **The carrying amount of an item of property, plant and equipment shall be derecognised:**

     (a)   **on disposal; or**

     (b)   **when no future economic benefits are expected from its use or disposal.**

68   **The gain or loss arising from the derecognition of an item of property, plant and equipment shall be included in profit or loss when the item is derecognised (unless AASB 117 requires otherwise on a sale and leaseback). Gains shall not be classified as revenue.**

68A   However, an entity that, in the course of its ordinary activities, routinely sells items of property, plant and equipment that it has held for rental to others shall transfer such assets to inventories at their carrying amount when they cease to be rented and become held for sale. The proceeds from the sale of such assets shall be recognised as revenue in accordance with AASB 15 *Revenue from Contracts with Customers*. AASB 5 does not apply when assets that are held for sale in the ordinary course of business are transferred to inventories.

69   The disposal of an item of property, plant and equipment may occur in a variety of ways (eg by sale, by entering into a finance lease or by donation). The date of disposal of an item of property, plant and equipment is the date the recipient obtains control of

that item in accordance with the requirements for determining when a performance obligation is satisfied in AASB 15. AASB 117 applies to disposal by a sale and leaseback.

70   If, under the recognition principle in paragraph 7, an entity recognises in the carrying amount of an item of property, plant and equipment the cost of a replacement for part of the item, then it derecognises the carrying amount of the replaced part regardless of whether the replaced part had been depreciated separately. If it is not practicable for an entity to determine the carrying amount of the replaced part, it may use the cost of the replacement as an indication of what the cost of the replaced part was at the time it was acquired or constructed.

71   **The gain or loss arising from the derecognition of an item of property, plant and equipment shall be determined as the difference between the net disposal proceeds, if any, and the carrying amount of the item.**

72   The amount of consideration to be included in the gain or loss arising from the derecognition of an item of property, plant and equipment is determined in accordance with the requirements for determining the transaction price in paragraphs 47–72 of AASB 15. Subsequent changes to the estimated amount of the consideration included in the gain or loss shall be accounted for in accordance with the requirements for changes in the transaction price in AASB 15.

Disclosure

73   **The financial statements shall disclose, for each class of property, plant and equipment:**

    (a)   **the measurement bases used for determining the gross carrying amount;**

    (b)   **the depreciation methods used;**

    (c)   **the useful lives or the depreciation rates used;**

    (d)   **the gross carrying amount and the accumulated depreciation (aggregated with accumulated impairment losses) at the beginning and end of the period; and**

    (e)   **a reconciliation of the carrying amount at the beginning and end of the period showing:**

        (i)   **additions;**

        (ii)   **assets classified as held for sale or included in a disposal group classified as held for sale in accordance with AASB 5 and other disposals;**

        (iii)   **acquisitions through business combinations;**

        (iv)   **increases or decreases resulting from revaluations under paragraphs 31, 39, Aus39.1, 40, Aus40.1 and Aus40.2 and from impairment losses recognised or reversed in other comprehensive income in accordance with AASB 136;**

        (v)   **impairment losses recognised in profit or loss in accordance with AASB 136;**

        (vi)   **impairment losses reversed in profit or loss in accordance with AASB 136;**

        (vii)   **depreciation;**

        (viii)   **the net exchange differences arising on the translation of the financial statements from the functional currency into a different presentation currency, including the translation of a foreign operation into the presentation currency of the reporting entity; and**

        (ix)   **other changes.**

74   **The financial statements shall also disclose:**

    (a)   **the existence and amounts of restrictions on title, and property, plant and equipment pledged as security for liabilities;**

    (b)   **the amount of expenditures recognised in the carrying amount of an item of property, plant and equipment in the course of its construction;**

    (c)   **the amount of contractual commitments for the acquisition of property, plant and equipment; and**

    (d)   **if it is not disclosed separately in the statement of comprehensive income, the amount of compensation from third parties for items of property, plant and equipment that were impaired, lost or given up that is included in profit or loss.**

75   Selection of the depreciation method and estimation of the useful life of assets are matters of judgement. Therefore, disclosure of the methods adopted and the estimated useful lives or depreciation rates provides users of financial statements with information that allows them to review the policies selected by management and enables comparisons to be made with other entities. For similar reasons, it is necessary to disclose:

    (a)   depreciation, whether recognised in profit or loss or as a part of the cost of other assets, during a period; and

    (b)   accumulated depreciation at the end of the period.

76   In accordance with AASB 108 an entity discloses the nature and effect of a change in an accounting estimate that has an effect in the current period or is expected to have an effect in subsequent periods. For property, plant and equipment, such disclosure may arise from changes in estimates with respect to:

    (a)   residual values;

    (b)   the estimated costs of dismantling, removing or restoring items of property, plant and equipment;

    (c)   useful lives; and

    (d)   depreciation methods.

77   **If items of property, plant and equipment are stated at revalued amounts, the following shall be disclosed in addition to the disclosures required by AASB 13:**

    (a)   **the effective date of the revaluation;**

    (b)   **whether an independent valuer was involved;**

    (c)–(d) [deleted]

    (e)   **for each revalued class of property, plant and equipment, the carrying amount that would have been recognised had the assets been carried under the cost model; and**

    (f)   **the revaluation surplus, indicating the change for the period and any restrictions on the distribution of the balance to shareholders.**

Aus77.1   **Notwithstanding paragraph 77(e), in respect of not-for-profit entities, for each revalued class of property, plant and equipment, the requirement to disclose the carrying amount that would have been recognised had the assets been carried under the cost model does not apply.**

78   In accordance with AASB 136 an entity discloses information on impaired property, plant and equipment in addition to the information required by paragraph 73(e) (iv)–(vi).

79   Users of financial statements may also find the following information relevant to their needs:

    (a)   the carrying amount of temporarily idle property, plant and equipment;

    (b)   the gross carrying amount of any fully depreciated property, plant and equipment that is still in use;

(c)   the carrying amount of property, plant and equipment retired from active use and not classified as held for sale in accordance with AASB 5; and

(d)   when the cost model is used, the fair value of property, plant and equipment when this is materially different from the carrying amount.

Therefore, entities are encouraged to disclose these amounts.

Transitional provisions

80   [Deleted by the AASB]

80A   Paragraph 35 in the previous version of this Standard was amended by AASB 2014-1 *Amendments to Australian Accounting Standards*. An entity shall apply that amendment to all revaluations recognised in annual periods beginning on or after the date of initial application of that amendment and in the immediately preceding annual period. An entity may also present adjusted comparative information for any earlier periods presented, but it is not required to do so. If an entity presents unadjusted comparative information for any earlier periods, it shall clearly identify the information that has not been adjusted, state that it has been presented on a different basis and explain that basis.

80B   In the reporting period when AASB 2014-6 *Amendments to Australian Accounting Standards – Agriculture: Bearer Plants* is first applied an entity need not disclose the quantitative information required by paragraph 28(f) of IAS 8 for the current period. However, an entity shall present the quantitative information required by paragraph 28(f) of IAS 8 for each prior period presented.

80C   An entity may elect to measure an item of bearer plants at its fair value at the beginning of the earliest period presented in the financial statements for the reporting period in which the entity first applies AASB 2014-6 and use that fair value as its deemed cost at that date. Any difference between the previous carrying amount and fair value shall be recognised in opening retained earnings at the beginning of the earliest period presented.

Effective date

81   An entity shall apply this Standard for annual periods beginning on or after 1 January 2018. Earlier application is encouraged for periods beginning on or after 1 January 2014 but before 1 January 2018. If an entity applies this Standard for a period beginning before 1 January 2018, it shall disclose that fact.

81A–81D   [Deleted by the AASB]

81E   Paragraph 5 in the previous version of this Standard was amended by AASB 2008-5 *Amendments to Australian Accounting Standards arising from the Annual Improvements Project* issued in July 2008. An entity shall apply that amendment prospectively for annual periods beginning on or after 1 January 2009. Earlier application is permitted if an entity also applies the amendments to paragraphs 8, 9, 22, 48, 53, 53A, 53B, 54, 57 and 85B of AASB 140 at the same time. If an entity applies the amendment for an earlier period it shall disclose that fact.

81F–81G   [Deleted by the AASB]

81H   AASB 2014-1 *Amendments to Australian Accounting Standards*, issued in June 2014 amended the previous version of this Standard as follows: amended paragraph 35 and added paragraph 80A. An entity shall apply that amendment for annual periods beginning on or after 1 July 2014. Earlier application is permitted. If an entity applies that amendment for an earlier period it shall disclose that fact.

81I   AASB 2014-4 *Amendments to Australian Accounting Standards – Clarification of Acceptable Methods of Depreciation and Amortisation*, issued in August 2014, amended the previous version of this Standard as follows: amended paragraph 56 and added paragraph 62A. An entity shall apply those amendments prospectively for annual periods beginning on or after 1 January 2016. Earlier application is permitted. If an entity applies those amendments for an earlier period it shall disclose that fact.

81J   AASB 2014-5 *Amendments to Australian Accounting Standards arising from AASB 15*, issued in December 2014, amended the previous version of this Standard as follows: amended paragraphs 68A, 69 and 72. An entity shall apply those amendments when it applies AASB 15.

81K   AASB 2014-6 *Amendments to Australian Accounting Standards – Agriculture: Bearer Plants*, issued in December 2014, amended the previous version of this Standard as follows: amended paragraphs 3, 6 and 37 and added paragraphs 22A and 80B–80C. An entity shall apply those amendments for annual periods beginning on or after 1 January 2016. Earlier application is permitted. If an entity applies those amendments for an earlier period, it shall disclose that fact. An entity shall apply those amendments retrospectively, in accordance with AASB 108, except as specified in paragraph 80C.

Withdrawal of other pronouncements

82–83 [Deleted by the AASB]

Commencement of the legislative instrument

Aus83.1   For legal purposes, this legislative instrument commences on 31 December 2016.

Withdrawal of AASB pronouncements

Aus83.2   When applied or operative, this Standard repeals AASB 116 *Property, Plant and Equipment* issued in July 2004. Despite the repeal, after the time this Standard starts to apply under section 334 of the Corporations Act (either generally or in relation to an individual entity), the repealed Standard continues to apply in relation to any period ending before that time as if the repeal had not occurred.

[Note: When this Standard applies under section 334 of the Corporations Act (either generally or in relation to an individual entity), it supersedes the application of the repealed Standard.]

APPENDIX A
AUSTRALIAN DEFINED TERMS

This appendix is an integral part of the Standard.

Aus6.1   **The following term is also used in this Standard with the meaning specified.**

A *not-for-profit entity* is an entity whose principal objective is not the generation of profit. A not-for-profit entity can be a single entity or a group of entities comprising the parent and each of the entities that it controls.

Aus6.2   Examples of property, plant and equipment held by not-for-profit public sector entities and for-profit government departments include, but are not limited to, infrastructure, cultural, community and heritage assets.

APPENDIX B
AUSTRALIAN REDUCED DISCLOSURE REQUIREMENTS

This appendix is an integral part of the Standard.

AusB1 **Paragraphs 73(e)(viii), 74(b), 74(d), 77(e), Aus77.1 and 79 of this Standard do not apply to entities preparing general purpose financial statements under Australian Accounting Standards – Reduced Disclosure Requirements. Entities applying Australian Accounting Standards – Reduced Disclosure Requirements may elect to comply with some or all of these excluded requirements.**

AusB2 The requirements that do not apply to entities preparing general purpose financial statements under Australian Accounting Standards – Reduced Disclosure Requirements are also identified in this Standard by shading of the relevant text, except for comparative disclosures subject to RDR paragraphs.

AusB3 **The RDR paragraph in this Standard applies only to entities preparing general purpose financial statements under Australian Accounting Standards – Reduced Disclosure Requirements.**

RDR73.1 **An entity applying Australian Accounting Standards – Reduced Disclosure Requirements is not required to disclose the reconciliation specified in paragraph 73(e) for prior periods.**

AUSTRALIAN IMPLEMENTATION GUIDANCE

This guidance accompanies, but is not part of, AASB 116. This guidance is pertinent to not-for-profit public sector entities and for-profit government departments that hold heritage or cultural assets.

G1 In accordance with paragraphs 7(b), 15 and Aus15.1 of AASB 116, only those heritage and cultural assets that can be reliably measured are recognised. It depends on the circumstances as to whether the reliable measurement recognition criterion can be satisfied in relation to a particular heritage or cultural asset. Heritage and cultural assets acquired at no cost, or for a nominal cost, are required to be initially recognised at fair value as at the date of acquisition. Depending on circumstances, it may not be possible to reliably measure the fair value as at the date of acquisition of a heritage or cultural asset.

G2 Of those heritage and cultural assets that satisfy the reliable measurement criterion for initial recognition purposes, paragraph 29 of AASB 116 permits, but does not require, revaluation. However, under AASB 1049 *Whole of Government and General Government Sector Financial Reporting*, GGSs and whole of governments are required to adopt those optional treatments in Australian Accounting Standards that are aligned with the principles or rules in the Australian Bureau of Statistics Government Finance Statistics (GFS) Manual. Consequently, those entities would be required to adopt a revaluation model for heritage and cultural assets recognised under AASB 116 where the reliable measurement recognition criterion is satisfied.

G3 Furthermore, given the nature of many heritage and cultural assets that meet the recognition criteria, those assets may not have limited useful lives (for example, when the entity adopts appropriate curatorial and preservation policies), and therefore may not be subject to depreciation. However, entities should consider whether the requirements of AASB 136 *Impairment of Assets* apply to such assets.

G4 The curatorial and preservation policies referred to in paragraph G3 above would typically be those developed and monitored by qualified personnel and include the following:

(a) a clearly stated objective about the holding and preservation of items;

(b)   a well-developed plan to achieve the objective, including demonstration of how the policy will be implemented, based on advice by appropriately qualified experts;

(c)   monitoring procedures; and

(d)   periodic reviews.

In addition, there would be evidence that the policies have been adopted by the governing body of the entity.

COMPILATION DETAILS

Accounting Standard AASB 116 *Property, Plant and Equipment* as amended

Compilation details are not part of AASB 116.

This compiled Standard applies to annual periods beginning on or after 1 January 2018 but before 1 January 2019. It takes into account amendments up to and including 27 June 2016 and was prepared on 20 March 2017 by the staff of the Australian Accounting Standards Board (AASB).

This compilation is not a separate Accounting Standard made by the AASB. Instead, it is a representation of AASB 116 (August 2015) as amended by other Accounting Standards, which are listed in the Table below.

Table of Standards

Standard	Date made	FRLI identifier	Commence-ment date	Effective date *(annual periods ... on or after ...)*	Application, saving or transitional provisions
AASB 116	7 Aug 2015	F2015L01572	31 Dec 2016	*(beginning)* 1 Jan 2018	see (a) below
AASB 2015-8	22 Oct 2015	F2015L01840	31 Dec 2016	*(beginning)* 1 Jan 2017	see (b) below
AASB 16	23 Feb 2016	F2016L00233	31 Dec 2018	*(beginning)* 1 Jan 2019	not compiled*
AASB 2016-4	27 Jun 2016	F2016L01173	31 Dec 2016	*(beginning)* 1 Jan 2017	see (c) below
AASB 1058	9 Dec 2016	F2017L00042	31 Dec 2018	*(beginning)* 1 Jan 2019	not compiled*

*   The amendments made by this Standard are not included in this compilation, which presents the principal Standard as applicable to annual reporting periods beginning on or after 1 January 2018 but before 1 January 2019.

(a) AASB 116 applies to annual periods beginning on or after 1 January 2018 (instead of 1 January 2017) as a result of amendments made by AASB 2015-8 *Amendments to Australian Accounting Standards – Effective Date of AASB 15*.

(b) Entities may elect to apply this Standard to annual periods beginning before 1 January 2017, provided that AASB 15 *Revenue from Contracts with Customers* is also applied.

(c) Entities may elect to apply this Standard to annual reporting periods beginning before 1 January 2017.

Table of amendments

Paragraph affected	How affected	By ... [paragraph]
81	amended	AASB 2015-8 [13]
G3	amended	AASB 2016-4 [8]

DELETED IAS 16 TEXT

Deleted IAS 16 text is not part of AASB 116.

80   The requirements of paragraphs 24–26 regarding the initial measurement of an item of property, plant and equipment acquired in an exchange of assets transaction shall be applied prospectively only to future transactions.

81A   An entity shall apply the amendments in paragraph 3 for annual periods beginning on or after 1 January 2006. If an entity applies IFRS 6 for an earlier period, those amendments shall be applied for that earlier period.

81B   IAS 1 *Presentation of Financial Statements* (as revised in 2007) amended the terminology used throughout IFRSs. In addition it amended paragraphs 39, 40 and 73(e)(iv). An entity shall apply those amendments for annual periods beginning on or after 1 January 2009. If an entity applies IAS 1 (revised 2007) for an earlier period, the amendments shall be applied for that earlier period.

81C   IFRS 3 *Business Combinations* (as revised in 2008) amended paragraph 44. An entity shall apply that amendment for annual periods beginning on or after 1 July 2009. If an entity applies IFRS 3 (revised 2008) for an earlier period, the amendment shall also be applied for that earlier period.

81D   Paragraphs 6 and 69 were amended and paragraph 68A was added by *Improvements to IFRSs* issued in May 2008. An entity shall apply those amendments for annual periods beginning on or after 1 January 2009. Earlier application is permitted. If an entity applies the amendments for an earlier period it shall disclose that fact and at the same time apply the related amendments to IAS 7 *Statement of Cash Flows*.

81F   IFRS 13, issued in May 2011, amended the definition of fair value in paragraph 6, amended paragraphs 26, 35 and 77 and deleted paragraphs 32 and 33. An entity shall apply those amendments when it applies IFRS 13.

81G   *Annual Improvements 2009–2011 Cycle*, issued in May 2012, amended paragraph 8. An entity shall apply that amendment retrospectively in accordance with IAS 8 *Accounting Policies, Changes in Accounting Estimates and Errors* for annual periods beginning on or after 1 January 2013. Earlier application is permitted. If an entity applies that amendment for an earlier period it shall disclose that fact.

82   This Standard supersedes IAS 16 *Property, Plant and Equipment* (revised in 1998).

83   This Standard supersedes the following Interpretations:

(a)   SIC-6 *Costs of Modifying Existing Software*;

(b)   SIC-14 *Property, Plant and Equipment—Compensation for the Impairment or Loss of Items*; and

(c)   SIC-23 *Property, Plant and Equipment—Major Inspection or Overhaul Costs*.

AASB 117
Leases
(Reissued August 2015)

This note is not part of Accounting Standard AASB 117.

The following unincorporated amendments are not included in this Standard.

- AASB 1058 *Income of Not-for-Profit Entities* — Appendix D sets out the amendments to other Australian Accounting Standards that are a consequence of the AASB issuing this Standard. It is applicable from 1 January 2019. Earlier application is permitted, but amendments to AASB 117 apply before 1 January 2019 only if AASB 1058 is also applied to an earlier period. In addition, AASB 1 and AASB 16 amendments are applied to an earlier period only if AASB 16 is also applied to that period.

Entities early-adopting any amendments with later application dates will need to refer to the amending Standards that have not yet been incorporated into compilations. The abovementioned unincorporated amendments may be located on the AASB website at www.aasb.gov.au or on the Federal Register of Legislation website at www.legislation.gov.au.

CONTENTS

APPENDIX

A. AUSTRALIAN REDUCED DISCLOSURE REQUIREMENTS

GUIDANCE ON IMPLEMENTING AASB 117 LEASES

DELETED IAS 17 TEXT

BASIS FOR CONCLUSIONS ON IAS 17 (available on the AASB website)

Australian Accounting Standard AASB 117 *Leases* is set out in paragraphs 1 – Aus70.2 and Appendix A. All the paragraphs have equal authority. Paragraphs in **bold type** state the main principles. AASB 117 is to be read in the context of other Australian Accounting Standards, including AASB 1048 *Interpretation of Standards*, which identifies the Australian Accounting Interpretations, and AASB 1057 *Application of Australian Accounting Standards*. In the absence of explicit guidance, AASB 108 *Accounting Policies, Changes in Accounting Estimates and Errors* provides a basis for selecting and applying accounting policies.

COMPARISON WITH IAS 17

AASB 117 *Leases* incorporates IAS 17 *Leases* issued by the International Accounting Standards Board (IASB). Australian-specific paragraphs (which are not included in IAS 17) are identified with the prefix "Aus". Paragraphs that apply only to not-for-profit entities begin by identifying their limited applicability.

Tier 1

For-profit entities complying with AASB 117 also comply with IAS 17.

Not-for-profit entities' compliance with IAS 17 will depend on whether any "Aus" paragraphs that specifically apply to not-for-profit entities provide additional guidance or contain applicable requirements that are inconsistent with IAS 17.

Tier 2

Entities preparing general purpose financial statements under Australian Accounting Standards – Reduced Disclosure Requirements (Tier 2) will not be in compliance with IFRSs.

AASB 1053 *Application of Tiers of Australian Accounting Standards* explains the two tiers of reporting requirements.

ACCOUNTING STANDARD AASB 117

The Australian Accounting Standards Board makes Accounting Standard AASB 117 *Leases* under section 334 of the *Corporations Act 2001*.

Kris Peach

Dated 7 August 2015

Chair – AASB

ACCOUNTING STANDARD AASB 117
LEASES

Objective

1   The objective of this Standard is to prescribe, for lessees and lessors, the appropriate accounting policies and disclosure to apply in relation to leases.

Scope

2   **This Standard shall be applied in accounting for all leases other than:**

   (a)   **leases to explore for or use minerals, oil, natural gas and similar non-regenerative resources; and**

   (b)   **licensing agreements for such items as motion picture films, video recordings, plays, manuscripts, patents and copyrights.**

   However, this Standard shall not be applied as the basis of measurement for:

   (a)   **property held by lessees that is accounted for as investment property (see AASB 140 *Investment Property*);**

   (b)   **investment property provided by lessors under operating leases (see AASB 140);**

   (c)   **biological assets within the scope of AASB 141 *Agriculture* held by lessees under finance leases; or**

   (d)   **biological assets within the scope of AASB 141 provided by lessors under operating leases.**

3   This Standard applies to agreements that transfer the right to use assets even though substantial services by the lessor may be called for in connection with the operation or maintenance of such assets. This Standard does not apply to agreements that are contracts for services that do not transfer the right to use assets from one contracting party to the other.

Definitions

4   **The following terms are used in this Standard with the meanings specified:**

   A *lease* is an agreement whereby the lessor conveys to the lessee in return for a payment or series of payments the right to use an asset for an agreed period of time.

   A *finance lease* is a lease that transfers substantially all the risks and rewards incidental to ownership of an asset. Title may or may not eventually be transferred.

   An *operating lease* is a lease other than a finance lease.

   A *non-cancellable lease* is a lease that is cancellable only:

   (a)   **upon the occurrence of some remote contingency;**

   (b)   **with the permission of the lessor;**

   (c)   **if the lessee enters into a new lease for the same or an equivalent asset with the same lessor; or**

   (d)   **upon payment by the lessee of such an additional amount that, at inception of the lease, continuation of the lease is reasonably certain.**

   The *inception of the lease* is the earlier of the date of the lease agreement and the date of commitment by the parties to the principal provisions of the lease. As at this date:

(a)   a lease is classified as either an operating or a finance lease; and

(b)   in the case of a finance lease, the amounts to be recognised at the commencement of the lease term are determined.

The *commencement of the lease term* is the date from which the lessee is entitled to exercise its right to use the leased asset. It is the date of initial recognition of the lease (ie the recognition of the assets, liabilities, income or expenses resulting from the lease, as appropriate).

The *lease term* is the non-cancellable period for which the lessee has contracted to lease the asset together with any further terms for which the lessee has the option to continue to lease the asset, with or without further payment, when at the inception of the lease it is reasonably certain that the lessee will exercise the option.

Minimum lease payments are the payments over the lease term that the lessee is or can be required to make, excluding contingent rent, costs for services and taxes to be paid by and reimbursed to the lessor, together with:

(a)   for a lessee, any amounts guaranteed by the lessee or by a party related to the lessee; or

(b)   for a lessor, any residual value guaranteed to the lessor by:

(i)   the lessee;

(ii)   a party related to the lessee; or

(iii) a third party unrelated to the lessor that is financially capable of discharging the obligations under the guarantee.

However, if the lessee has an option to purchase the asset at a price that is expected to be sufficiently lower than fair value at the date the option becomes exercisable for it to be reasonably certain, at the inception of the lease, that the option will be exercised, the minimum lease payments comprise the minimum payments payable over the lease term to the expected date of exercise of this purchase option and the payment required to exercise it.

Fair value is the amount for which an asset could be exchanged, or a liability settled, between knowledgeable, willing parties in an arm's length transaction.

Economic life is either:

(a)   the period over which an asset is expected to be economically usable by one or more users; or

(b)   the number of production or similar units expected to be obtained from the asset by one or more users.

Useful life is the estimated remaining period, from the commencement of the lease term, without limitation by the lease term, over which the economic benefits embodied in the asset are expected to be consumed by the entity.

Guaranteed residual value is:

(a)   for a lessee, that part of the residual value that is guaranteed by the lessee or by a party related to the lessee (the amount of the guarantee being the maximum amount that could, in any event, become payable); and

(b)   for a lessor, that part of the residual value that is guaranteed by the lessee or by a third party unrelated to the lessor that is financially capable of discharging the obligations under the guarantee.

Unguaranteed residual value is that portion of the residual value of the leased asset, the realisation of which by the lessor is not assured or is guaranteed solely by a party related to the lessor.

Initial direct costs are incremental costs that are directly attributable to negotiating and arranging a lease, except for such costs incurred by manufacturer or dealer lessors.

AASB

Gross investment in the lease is the aggregate of:

(a)   the minimum lease payments receivable by the lessor under a finance lease, and

(b)   any unguaranteed residual value accruing to the lessor.

Net investment in the lease is the gross investment in the lease discounted at the interest rate implicit in the lease.

Unearned finance income is the difference between:

(a)   the gross investment in the lease, and

(b)   the net investment in the lease.

The *interest rate implicit in the lease* is the discount rate that, at the inception of the lease, causes the aggregate present value of (a) the minimum lease payments and (b) the unguaranteed residual value to be equal to the sum of (i) the fair value of the leased asset and (ii) any initial direct costs of the lessor.

The *lessee's incremental borrowing rate of interest* is the rate of interest the lessee would have to pay on a similar lease or, if that is not determinable, the rate that, at the inception of the lease, the lessee would incur to borrow over a similar term, and with a similar security, the funds necessary to purchase the asset.

Contingent rent is that portion of the lease payments that is not fixed in amount but is based on the future amount of a factor that changes other than with the passage of time (eg percentage of future sales, amount of future use, future price indices, future market rates of interest).

5   A lease agreement or commitment may include a provision to adjust the lease payments for changes in the construction or acquisition cost of the leased property or for changes in some other measure of cost or value, such as general price levels, or in the lessor's costs of financing the lease, during the period between the inception of the lease and the commencement of the lease term. If so, the effect of any such changes shall be deemed to have taken place at the inception of the lease for the purposes of this Standard.

6   The definition of a lease includes contracts for the hire of an asset that contain a provision giving the hirer an option to acquire title to the asset upon the fulfilment of agreed conditions. These contracts are sometimes known as hire purchase contracts.

6A   AASB 117 uses the term 'fair value' in a way that differs in some respects from the definition of fair value in AASB 13 *Fair Value Measurement*. Therefore, when applying AASB 117 an entity measures fair value in accordance with AASB 117, not AASB 13.

Classification of leases

7   The classification of leases adopted in this Standard is based on the extent to which risks and rewards incidental to ownership of a leased asset lie with the lessor or the lessee. Risks include the possibilities of losses from idle capacity or technological obsolescence and of variations in return because of changing economic conditions. Rewards may be represented by the expectation of profitable operation over the asset's economic life and of gain from appreciation in value or realisation of a residual value.

8   **A lease is classified as a finance lease if it transfers substantially all the risks and rewards incidental to ownership. A lease is classified as an operating lease if it does not transfer substantially all the risks and rewards incidental to ownership.**

9   Because the transaction between a lessor and a lessee is based on a lease agreement between them, it is appropriate to use consistent definitions. The application of these definitions to the differing circumstances of the lessor and lessee may result in the same lease being classified differently by them. For example, this may be the case if the lessor benefits from a residual value guarantee provided by a party unrelated to the lessee.

10 Whether a lease is a finance lease or an operating lease depends on the substance of the transaction rather than the form of the contract.[1] Examples of situations that individually or in combination would normally lead to a lease being classified as a finance lease are:

(a) the lease transfers ownership of the asset to the lessee by the end of the lease term;

(b) the lessee has the option to purchase the asset at a price that is expected to be sufficiently lower than the fair value at the date the option becomes exercisable for it to be reasonably certain, at the inception of the lease, that the option will be exercised;

(c) the lease term is for the major part of the economic life of the asset even if title is not transferred;

(d) at the inception of the lease the present value of the minimum lease payments amounts to at least substantially all of the fair value of the leased asset; and

(e) the leased assets are of such a specialised nature that only the lessee can use them without major modifications.

11 Indicators of situations that individually or in combination could also lead to a lease being classified as a finance lease are:

(a) if the lessee can cancel the lease, the lessor's losses associated with the cancellation are borne by the lessee;

(b) gains or losses from the fluctuation in the fair value of the residual accrue to the lessee (for example, in the form of a rent rebate equalling most of the sales proceeds at the end of the lease); and

(c) the lessee has the ability to continue the lease for a secondary period at a rent that is substantially lower than market rent.

12 The examples and indicators in paragraphs 10 and 11 are not always conclusive. If it is clear from other features that the lease does not transfer substantially all risks and rewards incidental to ownership, the lease is classified as an operating lease. For example, this may be the case if ownership of the asset transfers at the end of the lease for a variable payment equal to its then fair value, or if there are contingent rents, as a result of which the lessee does not have substantially all such risks and rewards.

13 Lease classification is made at the inception of the lease. If at any time the lessee and the lessor agree to change the provisions of the lease, other than by renewing the lease, in a manner that would have resulted in a different classification of the lease under the criteria in paragraphs 7–12 if the changed terms had been in effect at the inception of the lease, the revised agreement is regarded as a new agreement over its term. However, changes in estimates (for example, changes in estimates of the economic life or of the residual value of the leased property), or changes in circumstances (for example, default by the lessee), do not give rise to a new classification of a lease for accounting purposes.

14–15 [Deleted]

15A When a lease includes both land and buildings elements, an entity assesses the classification of each element as a finance or an operating lease separately in accordance with paragraphs 7–13. In determining whether the land element is an operating or a finance lease, an important consideration is that land normally has an indefinite economic life.

16 Whenever necessary in order to classify and account for a lease of land and buildings, the minimum lease payments (including any lump-sum upfront payments) are allocated between the land and the buildings elements in proportion to the relative fair values of the leasehold interests in the land element and buildings element of the

---

1 See also Interpretation 127 *Evaluating the Substance of Transactions Involving the Legal Form of a Lease*, as identified in AASB 1048 *Interpretation of Standards*.

lease at the inception of the lease. If the lease payments cannot be allocated reliably between these two elements, the entire lease is classified as a finance lease, unless it is clear that both elements are operating leases, in which case the entire lease is classified as an operating lease.

17   For a lease of land and buildings in which the amount that would initially be recognised for the land element, in accordance with paragraph 20, is immaterial, the land and buildings may be treated as a single unit for the purpose of lease classification and classified as a finance or operating lease in accordance with paragraphs 7–13. In such a case, the economic life of the buildings is regarded as the economic life of the entire leased asset.

18   Separate measurement of the land and buildings elements is not required when the lessee's interest in both land and buildings is classified as an investment property in accordance with AASB 140 and the fair value model is adopted. Detailed calculations are required for this assessment only if the classification of one or both elements is otherwise uncertain.

19   In accordance with AASB 140, it is possible for a lessee to classify a property interest held under an operating lease as an investment property. If it does, the property interest is accounted for as if it were a finance lease and, in addition, the fair value model is used for the asset recognised. The lessee shall continue to account for the lease as a finance lease, even if a subsequent event changes the nature of the lessee's property interest so that it is no longer classified as investment property. This will be the case if, for example, the lessee:

(a)   occupies the property, which is then transferred to owner-occupied property at a deemed cost equal to its fair value at the date of change in use; or

(b)   grants a sublease that transfers substantially all of the risks and rewards incidental to ownership of the interest to an unrelated third party. Such a sublease is accounted for by the lessee as a finance lease to the third party, although it may be accounted for as an operating lease by the third party.

Leases in the financial statements of lessees

Finance leases

Initial recognition

20   **At the commencement of the lease term, lessees shall recognise finance leases as assets and liabilities in their statements of financial position at amounts equal to the fair value of the leased property or, if lower, the present value of the minimum lease payments, each determined at the inception of the lease. The discount rate to be used in calculating the present value of the minimum lease payments is the interest rate implicit in the lease, if this is practicable to determine; if not, the lessee's incremental borrowing rate shall be used. Any initial direct costs of the lessee are added to the amount recognised as an asset.**

21   Transactions and other events are accounted for and presented in accordance with their substance and financial reality and not merely with legal form. Although the legal form of a lease agreement is that the lessee may acquire no legal title to the leased asset, in the case of finance leases the substance and financial reality are that the lessee acquires the economic benefits of the use of the leased asset for the major part of its economic life in return for entering into an obligation to pay for that right an amount approximating, at the inception of the lease, the fair value of the asset and the related finance charge.

22   If such lease transactions are not reflected in the lessee's statement of financial position, the economic resources and the level of obligations of an entity are understated, thereby distorting financial ratios. Therefore, it is appropriate for a finance lease to be recognised in the lessee's statement of financial position both as an asset and as an obligation to pay future lease payments. At the commencement of the lease term, the asset and the liability for the future lease payments are recognised in the statement of financial position at the same amounts except for any initial direct costs of the lessee that are added to the amount recognised as an asset.

23   It is not appropriate for the liabilities for leased assets to be presented in the financial statements as a deduction from the leased assets. If for the presentation of liabilities in the statement of financial position a distinction is made between current and non-current liabilities, the same distinction is made for lease liabilities.

24   Initial direct costs are often incurred in connection with specific leasing activities, such as negotiating and securing leasing arrangements. The costs identified as directly attributable to activities performed by the lessee for a finance lease are added to the amount recognised as an asset.

Subsequent measurement

25   **Minimum lease payments shall be apportioned between the finance charge and the reduction of the outstanding liability. The finance charge shall be allocated to each period during the lease term so as to produce a constant periodic rate of interest on the remaining balance of the liability. Contingent rents shall be charged as expenses in the periods in which they are incurred.**

26   In practice, in allocating the finance charge to periods during the lease term, a lessee may use some form of approximation to simplify the calculation.

27   **A finance lease gives rise to depreciation expense for depreciable assets as well as finance expense for each accounting period. The depreciation policy for depreciable leased assets shall be consistent with that for depreciable assets that are owned, and the depreciation recognised shall be calculated in accordance with AASB 116** *Property, Plant and Equipment* **and AASB 138** *Intangible Assets*. **If there is no reasonable certainty that the lessee will obtain ownership by the end of the lease term, the asset shall be fully depreciated over the shorter of the lease term and its useful life.**

28   The depreciable amount of a leased asset is allocated to each accounting period during the period of expected use on a systematic basis consistent with the depreciation policy the lessee adopts for depreciable assets that are owned. If there is reasonable certainty that the lessee will obtain ownership by the end of the lease term, the period of expected use is the useful life of the asset; otherwise the asset is depreciated over the shorter of the lease term and its useful life.

29   The sum of the depreciation expense for the asset and the finance expense for the period is rarely the same as the lease payments payable for the period, and it is, therefore, inappropriate simply to recognise the lease payments payable as an expense. Accordingly, the asset and the related liability are unlikely to be equal in amount after the commencement of the lease term.

30   To determine whether a leased asset has become impaired, an entity applies AASB 136 *Impairment of Assets*.

Disclosures

31   **Lessees shall, in addition to meeting the requirements of AASB 7** *Financial Instruments: Disclosures*, **make the following disclosures for finance leases:**

(a)   **for each class of asset, the net carrying amount at the end of the reporting period.**

(b)   **a reconciliation between the total of future minimum lease payments at the end of the reporting period, and their present value. In addition, an entity shall disclose the total of future minimum lease payments at the end of the reporting period, and their present value, for each of the following periods:**

(i)   **not later than one year;**

(ii)   **later than one year and not later than five years;**

(iii)   **later than five years.**

(c)   contingent rents recognised as an expense in the period.

(d)   the total of future minimum sublease payments expected to be received under non-cancellable subleases at the end of the reporting period.

(e)   a general description of the lessee's material leasing arrangements including, but not limited to, the following:

    (i)   the basis on which contingent rent payable is determined;

    (ii)   the existence and terms of renewal or purchase options and escalation clauses; and

    (iii) restrictions imposed by lease arrangements, such as those concerning dividends, additional debt, and further leasing.

32   In addition, the requirements for disclosure in accordance with AASB 116, AASB 136, AASB 138, AASB 140 and AASB 141 apply to lessees for assets leased under finance leases.

Operating leases

33   **Lease payments under an operating lease shall be recognised as an expense on a straight-line basis over the lease term unless another systematic basis is more representative of the time pattern of the user's benefit.**[2]

34   For operating leases, lease payments (excluding costs for services such as insurance and maintenance) are recognised as an expense on a straight-line basis unless another systematic basis is representative of the time pattern of the user's benefit, even if the payments are not on that basis.

Disclosures

35   **Lessees shall, in addition to meeting the requirements of AASB 7, make the following disclosures for operating leases:**

(a)   the total of future minimum lease payments under non-cancellable operating leases for each of the following periods:

    (i)   not later than one year;

    (ii)   later than one year and not later than five years;

    (iii) later than five years.

(b)   the total of future minimum sublease payments expected to be received under non-cancellable subleases at the end of the reporting period.

(c)   lease and sublease payments recognised as an expense in the period, with separate amounts for minimum lease payments, contingent rents, and sublease payments.

(d)   a general description of the lessee's significant leasing arrangements including, but not limited to, the following:

    (i)   the basis on which contingent rent payable is determined;

    (ii)   the existence and terms of renewal or purchase options and escalation clauses; and

    (iii) restrictions imposed by lease arrangements, such as those concerning dividends, additional debt and further leasing.

---

2   See also Interpretation 115 *Operating Leases—Incentives*, as identified in AASB 1048 *Interpretation of Standards*.

Leases in the financial statements of lessors

Finance leases

Initial recognition

36   **Lessors shall recognise assets held under a finance lease in their statements of financial position and present them as a receivable at an amount equal to the net investment in the lease.**

37   Under a finance lease substantially all the risks and rewards incidental to legal ownership are transferred by the lessor, and thus the lease payment receivable is treated by the lessor as repayment of principal and finance income to reimburse and reward the lessor for its investment and services.

38   Initial direct costs are often incurred by lessors and include amounts such as commissions, legal fees and internal costs that are incremental and directly attributable to negotiating and arranging a lease. They exclude general overheads such as those incurred by a sales and marketing team. For finance leases other than those involving manufacturer or dealer lessors, initial direct costs are included in the initial measurement of the finance lease receivable and reduce the amount of income recognised over the lease term. The interest rate implicit in the lease is defined in such a way that the initial direct costs are included automatically in the finance lease receivable; there is no need to add them separately. Costs incurred by manufacturer or dealer lessors in connection with negotiating and arranging a lease are excluded from the definition of initial direct costs. As a result, they are excluded from the net investment in the lease and are recognised as an expense when the selling profit is recognised, which for a finance lease is normally at the commencement of the lease term.

Subsequent measurement

39   **The recognition of finance income shall be based on a pattern reflecting a constant periodic rate of return on the lessor's net investment in the finance lease.**

40   A lessor aims to allocate finance income over the lease term on a systematic and rational basis. This income allocation is based on a pattern reflecting a constant periodic return on the lessor's net investment in the finance lease. Lease payments relating to the period, excluding costs for services, are applied against the gross investment in the lease to reduce both the principal and the unearned finance income.

41   Estimated unguaranteed residual values used in computing the lessor's gross investment in the lease are reviewed regularly. If there has been a reduction in the estimated unguaranteed residual value, the income allocation over the lease term is revised and any reduction in respect of amounts accrued is recognised immediately.

41A   An asset under a finance lease that is classified as held for sale (or included in a disposal group that is classified as held for sale) in accordance with AASB 5 *Non-current Assets Held for Sale and Discontinued Operations* shall be accounted for in accordance with that Standard.

42   **Manufacturer or dealer lessors shall recognise selling profit or loss in the period, in accordance with the policy followed by the entity for outright sales. If artificially low rates of interest are quoted, selling profit shall be restricted to that which would apply if a market rate of interest were charged. Costs incurred by manufacturer or dealer lessors in connection with negotiating and arranging a lease shall be recognised as an expense when the selling profit is recognised.**

43   Manufacturers or dealers often offer to customers the choice of either buying or leasing an asset. A finance lease of an asset by a manufacturer or dealer lessor gives rise to two types of income:

   (a)   profit or loss equivalent to the profit or loss resulting from an outright sale of the asset being leased, at normal selling prices, reflecting any applicable volume or trade discounts; and

   (b)   finance income over the lease term.

44   The sales revenue recognised at the commencement of the lease term by a manufacturer or dealer lessor is the fair value of the asset, or, if lower, the present value of the minimum lease payments accruing to the lessor, computed at a market rate of interest. The cost of sale recognised at the commencement of the lease term is the cost, or carrying amount if different, of the leased property less the present value of the unguaranteed residual value. The difference between the sales revenue and the cost of sale is the selling profit, which is recognised in accordance with the entity's policy for outright sales.

45   Manufacturer or dealer lessors sometimes quote artificially low rates of interest in order to attract customers. The use of such a rate would result in an excessive portion of the total income from the transaction being recognised at the time of sale. If artificially low rates of interest are quoted, selling profit is restricted to that which would apply if a market rate of interest were charged.

46   Costs incurred by a manufacturer or dealer lessor in connection with negotiating and arranging a finance lease are recognised as an expense at the commencement of the lease term because they are mainly related to earning the manufacturer's or dealer's selling profit.

Disclosures

47   Lessors shall, in addition to meeting the requirements in AASB 7, disclose the following for finance leases:

   (a)   a reconciliation between the gross investment in the lease at the end of the reporting period, and the present value of minimum lease payments receivable at the end of the reporting period. In addition, an entity shall disclose the gross investment in the lease and the present value of minimum lease payments receivable at the end of the reporting period, for each of the following periods:

   (i)   not later than one year;

   (ii)   later than one year and not later than five years;

   (iii)   later than five years.

   (b)   unearned finance income.

   (c)   the unguaranteed residual values accruing to the benefit of the lessor.

   (d)   the accumulated allowance for uncollectible minimum lease payments receivable.

   (e)   contingent rents recognised as income in the period.

   (f)   a general description of the lessor's material leasing arrangements.

48   As an indicator of growth it is often useful also to disclose the gross investment less unearned income in new business added during the period, after deducting the relevant amounts for cancelled leases.

Operating leases

49   Lessors shall present assets subject to operating leases in their statements of financial position according to the nature of the asset.

50   Lease income from operating leases shall be recognised in income on a straight-line basis over the lease term, unless another systematic basis is more representative of the time pattern in which use benefit derived from the leased asset is diminished.[3]

51   Costs, including depreciation, incurred in earning the lease income are recognised as an expense. Lease income (excluding receipts for services provided such as insurance

---

3   See also Interpretation 115 *Operating Leases—Incentives*, as identified in AASB 1048 *Interpretation of Standards*.

and maintenance) is recognised on a straight-line basis over the lease term even if the receipts are not on such a basis, unless another systematic basis is more representative of the time pattern in which use benefit derived from the leased asset is diminished.

52 **Initial direct costs incurred by lessors in negotiating and arranging an operating lease shall be added to the carrying amount of the leased asset and recognised as an expense over the lease term on the same basis as the lease income.**

53 **The depreciation policy for depreciable leased assets shall be consistent with the lessor's normal depreciation policy for similar assets, and depreciation shall be calculated in accordance with AASB 116 and AASB 138.**

54 To determine whether a leased asset has become impaired, an entity applies AASB 136.

55 A manufacturer or dealer lessor does not recognise any selling profit on entering into an operating lease because it is not the equivalent of a sale.

Disclosures

56 **Lessors shall, in addition to meeting the requirements of AASB 7, disclose the following for operating leases:**

    (a) **the future minimum lease payments under non-cancellable operating leases in the aggregate and for each of the following periods:**

        (i) **not later than one year;**

        (ii) **later than one year and not later than five years;**

        (iii) **later than five years.**

    (b) **total contingent rents recognised as income in the period.**

    (c) **a general description of the lessor's leasing arrangements.**

57 In addition, the disclosure requirements in AASB 116, AASB 136, AASB 138, AASB 140 and AASB 141 apply to lessors for assets provided under operating leases.

Sale and leaseback transactions

58 A sale and leaseback transaction involves the sale of an asset and the leasing back of the same asset. The lease payment and the sale price are usually interdependent because they are negotiated as a package. The accounting treatment of a sale and leaseback transaction depends upon the type of lease involved.

59 **If a sale and leaseback transaction results in a finance lease, any excess of sales proceeds over the carrying amount shall not be immediately recognised as income by a seller-lessee. Instead, it shall be deferred and amortised over the lease term.**

60 If the leaseback is a finance lease, the transaction is a means whereby the lessor provides finance to the lessee, with the asset as security. For this reason it is not appropriate to regard an excess of sales proceeds over the carrying amount as income. Such excess is deferred and amortised over the lease term.

61 **If a sale and leaseback transaction results in an operating lease, and it is clear that the transaction is established at fair value, any profit or loss shall be recognised immediately. If the sale price is below fair value, any profit or loss shall be recognised immediately except that, if the loss is compensated for by future lease payments at below market price, it shall be deferred and amortised in proportion to the lease payments over the period for which the asset is expected to be used. If the sale price is above fair value, the excess over fair value shall be deferred and amortised over the period for which the asset is expected to be used.**

62 If the leaseback is an operating lease, and the lease payments and the sale price are at fair value, there has in effect been a normal sale transaction and any profit or loss is recognised immediately.

63   For operating leases, if the fair value at the time of a sale and leaseback transaction is less than the carrying amount of the asset, a loss equal to the amount of the difference between the carrying amount and fair value shall be recognised immediately.

64   For finance leases, no such adjustment is necessary unless there has been an impairment in value, in which case the carrying amount is reduced to recoverable amount in accordance with AASB 136.

65   Disclosure requirements for lessees and lessors apply equally to sale and leaseback transactions. The required description of material leasing arrangements leads to disclosure of unique or unusual provisions of the agreement or terms of the sale and leaseback transactions.

66   Sale and leaseback transactions may trigger the separate disclosure criteria in AASB 101 *Presentation of Financial Statements*.

Transitional provisions

67–68 [Deleted by the AASB]

68A   An entity shall reassess the classification of land elements of unexpired leases at the date it adopts the amendments referred to in paragraph 69A on the basis of information existing at the inception of those leases. It shall recognise a lease newly classified as a finance lease retrospectively in accordance with AASB 108 *Accounting Policies, Changes in Accounting Estimates and Errors*. However, if an entity does not have the information necessary to apply the amendments retrospectively, it shall:

(a)   apply the amendments to those leases on the basis of the facts and circumstances existing on the date it adopts the amendments; and

(b)   recognise the asset and liability related to a land lease newly classified as a finance lease at their fair values on that date; any difference between those fair values is recognised in retained earnings.

Effective date

69   An entity shall apply this Standard for annual periods beginning on or after 1 January 2016. Earlier application is encouraged for periods beginning on or after 1 January 2014 but before 1 January 2016. If an entity applies this Standard for a period beginning before 1 January 2016, it shall disclose that fact.

69A   In the previous version of this Standard, paragraphs 14 and 15 were deleted, and paragraphs 15A and 68A were added as part of AASB 2009-5 *Further Amendments to Australian Accounting Standards arising from the Annual Improvements Project* issued in May 2009. An entity shall apply those amendments for annual periods beginning on or after 1 January 2010. Earlier application is permitted. If an entity applies the amendments for an earlier period it shall disclose that fact.

Withdrawal of IAS 17 (revised 1997)

70   [Deleted by the AASB]

Commencement of the legislative instrument

Aus70.1   For legal purposes, this legislative instrument commences on 31 December 2015.

Withdrawal of AASB pronouncements

Aus70.2   This Standard repeals AASB 117 *Leases* issued in July 2004. Despite the repeal, after the time this Standard starts to apply under section 334 of the Corporations Act (either generally or in relation to an individual entity), the repealed Standard continues to apply in relation to any period ending before that time as if the repeal had not occurred.

[Note: When this Standard applies under section 334 of the Corporations Act (either generally or in relation to an individual entity), it supersedes the application of the repealed Standard.]

APPENDIX A
AUSTRALIAN REDUCED DISCLOSURE REQUIREMENTS

This appendix is an integral part of the Standard.

AusA1   **The following do not apply to entities preparing general purpose financial statements under Australian Accounting Standards – Reduced Disclosure Requirements:**

    (a)   paragraphs 31(c), 31(d), 35(b) and 48;

    (b)   in paragraph 31(b), the text "a reconciliation ... present value." and, in the second sentence, the text "In addition, an entity shall disclose" and "and their present value,";

    (c)   in paragraph 35(c), the text ", with separate amounts ... sublease payments"; and

    (d)   in paragraph 56(a), the words "in the aggregate and".

    Entities applying Australian Accounting Standards – Reduced Disclosure Requirements may elect to comply with some or all of these excluded requirements.

AusA2   The requirements that do not apply to entities preparing general purpose financial statements under Australian Accounting Standards – Reduced Disclosure Requirements are also identified in this Standard by shading of the relevant text.

GUIDANCE ON IMPLEMENTING AASB 117 *LEASES*

This guidance accompanies, but is not part of, AASB 117.

Illustrative examples of sale and leaseback transactions that result in operating leases

A sale and leaseback transaction that results in an operating lease may give rise to profit or a loss, the determination and treatment of which depends on the leased asset's carrying amount, fair value and selling price. The table below shows the requirements of the Standard in various circumstances.

Sale price at fair value (paragraph 61)	Carrying amount equal to fair value	Carrying amount less than fair value	Carrying amount above fair value
Profit	no profit	recognise profit immediately	not applicable
Loss	no loss	not applicable	recognise loss immediately

Sale price below fair value (paragraph 61)	Carrying amount equal to fair value	Carrying amount less than fair value	Carrying amount above fair value
Profit	no profit	recognise profit immediately	no profit (note 1)
Loss not compensated for by future lease payments at below market price	recognise loss immediately	recognise loss immediately	(note 1)
Loss compensated for by future lease payments at below market price	defer and amortise loss	defer and amortise loss	(note 1)

Sale price above fair value (paragraph 61)	Carrying amount equal to fair value	Carrying amount less than fair value	Carrying amount above fair value
Profit	defer and amortise profit	defer and amortise excess profit (note 3)	defer and amortise profit (note 2)
Loss	no loss	no loss	(note 1)

Note 1   These parts of the table represent circumstances dealt with in paragraph 63 of the Standard. Paragraph 63 requires the carrying amount of an asset to be written down to fair value where it is subject to a sale and leaseback.

Note 2   Profit is the difference between fair value and sale price because the carrying amount would have been written down to fair value in accordance with paragraph 63.

Note 3   The excess profit (the excess of sale price over fair value) is deferred and amortised over the period for which the asset is expected to be used. Any excess of fair value over carrying amount is recognised immediately.

DELETED IAS 17 TEXT

Deleted IAS 17 text is not part of AASB 117.

67   **Subject to paragraph 68, retrospective application of this Standard is encouraged but not required. If the Standard is not applied retrospectively, the balance of any pre-existing finance lease is deemed to have been properly determined by the lessor and shall be accounted for thereafter in accordance with the provisions of this Standard.**

68   **An entity that has previously applied IAS 17 (revised 1997) shall apply the amendments made by this Standard retrospectively for all leases or, if IAS 17 (revised 1997) was not applied retrospectively, for all leases entered into since it first applied that Standard.**

70   This Standard supersedes IAS 17 *Leases* (revised in 1997).

AASB 119
Employee Benefits

(Reissued August 2015)

This note is not part of Accounting Standard AASB 119.

The following unincorporated amendments are not included in this Standard.

- AASB 17 *Insurance Contracts* — Appendix D sets out the amendments to other Standards that are a consequence of the AASB issuing AASB 17 *Insurance Contracts*. This Standard is applicable from 1 January 2021. Earlier application is permitted, but entities must apply AASB 9 *Financial Instruments* and AASB 15 *Revenue from Contracts with Customers* first.

- AASB 2018-2 *Amendments to Australian Accounting Standards — Plan Amendment, Curtailment or Settlement*. This Standard makes amendments to AASB 119 *Employee Benefits* arising from the issuance of IFRS *Plan Amendment, Curtailment or Settlement* (Amendments to IAS 19) by the IASB in February 2018. It applies to annual reporting periods beginning on or after 1 January 2019, but earlier application is permitted.

Entities early-adopting any amendments with later application dates will need to refer to the amending Standards that have not yet been incorporated into compilations. The abovementioned unincorporated amendments may be located on the AASB website at www.aasb.gov.au or on the Federal Register of Legislation website at www.legislation.gov.au.

CONTENTS

COMPARISON WITH IAS 19
ACCOUNTING STANDARD
AASB 119 *EMPLOYEE BENEFITS*

APPENDICES

A. APPLICATION GUIDANCE

C. AUSTRALIAN REDUCED DISCLOSURE REQUIREMENTS

DELETED IAS 19 TEXT

BASIS FOR CONCLUSIONS ON IAS 19 (available on the AASB website)

> Australian Accounting Standard AASB 119 *Employee Benefits* is set out in paragraphs 1 – Aus177.2 and
> Appendices A and C. All the paragraphs have equal authority. Paragraphs in **bold type** state the main
> principles. AASB 119 is to be read in the context of other Australian Accounting Standards, including
> AASB 1048 *Interpretation of Standards*, which identifies the Australian Accounting Interpretations, and
> AASB 1057 *Application of Australian Accounting Standards*. In the absence of explicit guidance, AASB
> 108 *Accounting Policies, Changes in Accounting Estimates and Errors* provides a basis for selecting and
> applying accounting policies.

COMPARISON WITH IAS 19

AASB 119 *Employee Benefits* incorporates IAS 19 *Employee Benefits* issued by the
International Accounting Standards Board (IASB). Australian-specific paragraphs (which are
not included in IAS 19) are identified with the prefix "Aus" or "RDR". Paragraphs that apply
only to not-for-profit entities begin by identifying their limited applicability.

Tier 1

For-profit entities complying with AASB 119 also comply with IAS 19.

Not-for-profit entities' compliance with IAS 19 will depend on whether any "Aus" paragraphs
that specifically apply to not-for-profit entities provide additional guidance or contain
applicable requirements that are inconsistent with IAS 19.

Tier 2

Entities preparing general purpose financial statements under Australian Accounting
Standards – Reduced Disclosure Requirements (Tier 2) will not be in compliance with IFRSs.

AASB 1053 *Application of Tiers of Australian Accounting Standards* explains the two tiers
of reporting requirements.

ACCOUNTING STANDARD AASB 119

The Australian Accounting Standards Board makes Accounting Standard AASB 119
Employee Benefits under section 334 of the *Corporations Act 2001*.

Kris Peach

Dated 7 August 2015   Chair – AASB

ACCOUNTING STANDARD AASB 119
EMPLOYEE BENEFITS

Objective

1   The objective of this Standard is to prescribe the accounting and disclosure for
        employee benefits. The Standard requires an entity to recognise:

        (a)   a liability when an employee has provided service in exchange for employee
                benefits to be paid in the future; and

(b)   an expense when the entity consumes the economic benefit arising from service provided by an employee in exchange for employee benefits.

Scope

2   **This Standard shall be applied by an employer in accounting for all employee benefits, except those to which AASB 2 *Share-based Payment* applies.**

3   This Standard does not deal with reporting by employee benefit plans (see AAS 25 *Financial Reporting by Superannuation Plans* or AASB 1056 *Superannuation Entities*, as appropriate).

4   The employee benefits to which this Standard applies include those provided:

(a)   under formal plans or other formal agreements between an entity and individual employees, groups of employees or their representatives;

(b)   under legislative requirements, or through industry arrangements, whereby entities are required to contribute to national, state, industry or other multi-employer plans; or

(c)   by those informal practices that give rise to a constructive obligation. Informal practices give rise to a constructive obligation where the entity has no realistic alternative but to pay employee benefits. An example of a constructive obligation is where a change in the entity's informal practices would cause unacceptable damage to its relationship with employees.

5   Employee benefits include:

(a)   short-term employee benefits, such as the following, if expected to be settled wholly before twelve months after the end of the annual reporting period in which the employees render the related services:

(i)   wages, salaries and social security contributions;

(ii)   paid annual leave and paid sick leave;

(iii) profit-sharing and bonuses; and

(iv)   non-monetary benefits (such as medical care, housing, cars and free or subsidised goods or services) for current employees;

(b)   post-employment benefits, such as the following:

(i)   retirement benefits (eg pensions and lump sum payments on retirement); and

(ii)   other post-employment benefits, such as post-employment life insurance and post-employment medical care;

(c)   other long-term employee benefits, such as the following:

(i)   long-term paid absences such as long-service leave or sabbatical leave;

(ii)   jubilee or other long-service benefits; and

(iii) long-term disability benefits; and

(d)   termination benefits.

6   Employee benefits include benefits provided either to employees or to their dependants or beneficiaries and may be settled by payments (or the provision of goods or services) made either directly to the employees, to their spouses, children or other dependants or to others, such as insurance companies.

7   An employee may provide services to an entity on a full-time, part-time, permanent, casual or temporary basis. For the purpose of this Standard, employees include directors and other management personnel.

Definitions

8   The following terms are used in this Standard with the meanings specified:

Definitions of employee benefits

Employee benefits are all forms of consideration given by an entity in exchange for service rendered by employees or for the termination of employment.

Short-term employee benefits are employee benefits (other than termination benefits) that are expected to be settled wholly before twelve months after the end of the annual reporting period in which the employees render the related service.

Post-employment benefits are employee benefits (other than termination benefits and short-term employee benefits) that are payable after the completion of employment.

Other long-term employee benefits are all employee benefits other than short-term employee benefits, post-employment benefits and termination benefits.

Termination benefits are employee benefits provided in exchange for the termination of an employee's employment as a result of either:

(a)   an entity's decision to terminate an employee's employment before the normal retirement date; or

(b)   an employee's decision to accept an offer of benefits in exchange for the termination of employment.

Definitions relating to classification of plans

Post-employment benefit plans are formal or informal arrangements under which an entity provides post-employment benefits for one or more employees.

Defined contribution plans are post-employment benefit plans under which an entity pays fixed contributions into a separate entity (a fund) and will have no legal or constructive obligation to pay further contributions if the fund does not hold sufficient assets to pay all employee benefits relating to employee service in the current and prior periods.

Defined benefit plans are post-employment benefit plans other than defined contribution plans.

Multi-employer plans are defined contribution plans (other than state plans) or defined benefit plans (other than state plans) that:

(a)   pool the assets contributed by various entities that are not under common control; and

(b)   use those assets to provide benefits to employees of more than one entity, on the basis that contribution and benefit levels are determined without regard to the identity of the entity that employs the employees.

Definitions relating to the net defined benefit liability (asset)

The *net defined benefit liability* (asset) is the deficit or surplus, adjusted for any effect of limiting a net defined benefit asset to the asset ceiling.

The *deficit or surplus* is:

(a)   the present value of the defined benefit obligation less

(b)   the fair value of plan assets (if any).

The *asset ceiling* is the present value of any economic benefits available in the form of refunds from the plan or reductions in future contributions to the plan.

The *present value of a defined benefit obligation* is the present value, without deducting any plan assets, of expected future payments required to settle the obligation resulting from employee service in the current and prior periods.

Plan assets comprise:

(a)   assets held by a long-term employee benefit fund; and

(b)   qualifying insurance policies.

Assets held by a long-term employee benefit fund are assets (other than non-transferable financial instruments issued by the reporting entity) that:

(a)   are held by an entity (a fund) that is legally separate from the reporting entity and exists solely to pay or fund employee benefits; and

(b)   are available to be used only to pay or fund employee benefits, are not available to the reporting entity's own creditors (even in bankruptcy), and cannot be returned to the reporting entity, unless either:

    (i)   the remaining assets of the fund are sufficient to meet all the related employee benefit obligations of the plan or the reporting entity; or

    (ii)   the assets are returned to the reporting entity to reimburse it for employee benefits already paid.

A *qualifying insurance policy* is an insurance policy[1] issued by an insurer that is not a related party (as defined in AASB 124 *Related Party Disclosures*) of the reporting entity, if the proceeds of the policy:

(a)   can be used only to pay or fund employee benefits under a defined benefit plan; and

(b)   are not available to the reporting entity's own creditors (even in bankruptcy) and cannot be paid to the reporting entity, unless either:

    (i)   the proceeds represent surplus assets that are not needed for the policy to meet all the related employee benefit obligations; or

    (ii)   the proceeds are returned to the reporting entity to reimburse it for employee benefits already paid.

Fair value is the price that would be received to sell an asset or paid to transfer a liability in an orderly transaction between market participants at the measurement date. (See AASB 13 *Fair Value Measurement*.)

Definitions relating to defined benefit cost

Service cost comprises:

(a)   *current service cost*, which is the increase in the present value of the defined benefit obligation resulting from employee service in the current period;

(b)   *past service cost*, which is the change in the present value of the defined benefit obligation for employee service in prior periods, resulting from a plan amendment (the introduction or withdrawal of, or changes to, a defined benefit plan) or a curtailment (a significant reduction by the entity in the number of employees covered by a plan); and

(c)   any gain or loss on settlement.

Net interest on the net defined benefit liability (asset) is the change during the period in the net defined benefit liability (asset) that arises from the passage of time.

Remeasurements of the net defined benefit liability (asset) comprise:

(a)   actuarial gains and losses;

(b)   the return on plan assets, excluding amounts included in net interest on the net defined benefit liability (asset); and

(c)   any change in the effect of the asset ceiling, excluding amounts included in net interest on the net defined benefit liability (asset).

---

1   A qualifying insurance policy is not necessarily an insurance contract, as defined in AASB 4 *Insurance Contracts*.

Actuarial gains and losses are changes in the present value of the defined benefit obligation resulting from:

(a)   experience adjustments (the effects of differences between the previous actuarial assumptions and what has actually occurred); and

(b)   the effects of changes in actuarial assumptions.

The *return on plan assets* is interest, dividends and other income derived from the plan assets, together with realised and unrealised gains or losses on the plan assets, less:

(a)   any costs of managing plan assets; and

(b)   any tax payable by the plan itself, other than tax included in the actuarial assumptions used to measure the present value of the defined benefit obligation.

A *settlement* is a transaction that eliminates all further legal or constructive obligations for part or all of the benefits provided under a defined benefit plan, other than a payment of benefits to, or on behalf of, employees that is set out in the terms of the plan and included in the actuarial assumptions.

Short-term employee benefits

9   Short-term employee benefits include items such as the following, if expected to be settled wholly before twelve months after the end of the annual reporting period in which the employees render the related services:

(a)   wages, salaries and social security contributions;

(b)   paid annual leave and paid sick leave;

(c)   profit-sharing and bonuses; and

(d)   non-monetary benefits (such as medical care, housing, cars and free or subsidised goods or services) for current employees.

10   An entity need not reclassify a short-term employee benefit if the entity's expectations of the timing of settlement change temporarily. However, if the characteristics of the benefit change (such as a change from a non-accumulating benefit to an accumulating benefit) or if a change in expectations of the timing of settlement is not temporary, then the entity considers whether the benefit still meets the definition of short-term employee benefits.

Recognition and measurement

All short-term employee benefits

11   When an employee has rendered service to an entity during an accounting period, the entity shall recognise the undiscounted amount of short-term employee benefits expected to be paid in exchange for that service:

(a)   as a liability (accrued expense), after deducting any amount already paid. If the amount already paid exceeds the undiscounted amount of the benefits, an entity shall recognise that excess as an asset (prepaid expense) to the extent that the prepayment will lead to, for example, a reduction in future payments or a cash refund.

(b)   as an expense, unless another Australian Accounting Standard requires or permits the inclusion of the benefits in the cost of an asset (see, for example, AASB 102 *Inventories* and AASB 116 *Property, Plant and Equipment*).

12   Paragraphs 13, 16 and 19 explain how an entity shall apply paragraph 11 to short-term employee benefits in the form of paid absences and profit-sharing and bonus plans.

Short-term paid absences

13   An entity shall recognise the expected cost of short-term employee benefits in the form of paid absences under paragraph 11 as follows:

    (a)   **in the case of accumulating paid absences, when the employees render service that increases their entitlement to future paid absences.**

    (b)   **in the case of non-accumulating paid absences, when the absences occur.**

14   An entity may pay employees for absence for various reasons including holidays, sickness and short-term disability, maternity or paternity, jury service and military service. Entitlement to paid absences falls into two categories:

    (a)   accumulating; and

    (b)   non-accumulating.

15   Accumulating paid absences are those that are carried forward and can be used in future periods if the current period's entitlement is not used in full. Accumulating paid absences may be either vesting (in other words, employees are entitled to a cash payment for unused entitlement on leaving the entity) or non-vesting (when employees are not entitled to a cash payment for unused entitlement on leaving). An obligation arises as employees render service that increases their entitlement to future paid absences. The obligation exists, and is recognised, even if the paid absences are non-vesting, although the possibility that employees may leave before they use an accumulated non-vesting entitlement affects the measurement of that obligation.

16   **An entity shall measure the expected cost of accumulating paid absences as the additional amount that the entity expects to pay as a result of the unused entitlement that has accumulated at the end of the reporting period.**

17   The method specified in the previous paragraph measures the obligation at the amount of the additional payments that are expected to arise solely from the fact that the benefit accumulates. In many cases, an entity may not need to make detailed computations to estimate that there is no material obligation for unused paid absences. For example, a sick leave obligation is likely to be material only if there is a formal or informal understanding that unused paid sick leave may be taken as paid annual leave.

Example illustrating paragraphs 16 and 17

An entity has 100 employees, who are each entitled to five working days of paid sick leave for each year. Unused sick leave may be carried forward for one calendar year. Sick leave is taken first out of the current year's entitlement and then out of any balance brought forward from the previous year (a LIFO basis). At 31 December 20X1 the average unused entitlement is two days per employee. The entity expects, on the basis of experience that is expected to continue, that 92 employees will take no more than five days of paid sick leave in 20X2 and that the remaining eight employees will take an average of six and a half days each.

The entity expects that it will pay an additional twelve days of sick pay as a result of the unused entitlement that has accumulated at 31 December 20X1 (one and a half days each, for eight employees). Therefore, the entity recognises a liability equal to twelve days of sick pay.

---

18   Non-accumulating paid absences do not carry forward: they lapse if the current period's entitlement is not used in full and do not entitle employees to a cash payment for unused entitlement on leaving the entity. This is commonly the case for sick pay (to the extent that unused past entitlement does not increase future entitlement), maternity or paternity leave and paid absences for jury service or military service. An entity recognises no liability or expense until the time of the absence, because employee service does not increase the amount of the benefit.

Profit-sharing and bonus plans

19   An entity shall recognise the expected cost of profit-sharing and bonus payments under paragraph 11 when, and only when:

    (a)   the entity has a present legal or constructive obligation to make such payments as a result of past events; and

    (b)   a reliable estimate of the obligation can be made.

    A present obligation exists when, and only when, the entity has no realistic alternative but to make the payments.

20   Under some profit-sharing plans, employees receive a share of the profit only if they remain with the entity for a specified period. Such plans create a constructive obligation as employees render service that increases the amount to be paid if they remain in service until the end of the specified period. The measurement of such constructive obligations reflects the possibility that some employees may leave without receiving profit-sharing payments.

Example illustrating paragraph 20

A profit-sharing plan requires an entity to pay a specified proportion of its profit for the year to employees who serve throughout the year. If no employees leave during the year, the total profit-sharing payments for the year will be 3 per cent of profit. The entity estimates that staff turnover will reduce the payments to 2.5 per cent of profit.

The entity recognises a liability and an expense of 2.5 per cent of profit.

---

21   An entity may have no legal obligation to pay a bonus. Nevertheless, in some cases, an entity has a practice of paying bonuses. In such cases, the entity has a constructive obligation because the entity has no realistic alternative but to pay the bonus. The measurement of the constructive obligation reflects the possibility that some employees may leave without receiving a bonus.

22   An entity can make a reliable estimate of its legal or constructive obligation under a profit-sharing or bonus plan when, and only when:

    (a)   the formal terms of the plan contain a formula for determining the amount of the benefit;

    (b)   the entity determines the amounts to be paid before the financial statements are authorised for issue; or

    (c)   past practice gives clear evidence of the amount of the entity's constructive obligation.

23   An obligation under profit-sharing and bonus plans results from employee service and not from a transaction with the entity's owners. Therefore, an entity recognises the cost of profit-sharing and bonus plans not as a distribution of profit but as an expense.

24   If profit-sharing and bonus payments are not expected to be settled wholly before twelve months after the end of the annual reporting period in which the employees render the related service, those payments are other long-term employee benefits (see paragraphs 153–158).

Disclosure

25   Although this Standard does not require specific disclosures about short-term employee benefits, other Australian Accounting Standards may require disclosures. For example, AASB 124 requires disclosures about employee benefits for key management personnel. AASB 101 *Presentation of Financial Statements* requires disclosure of employee benefits expense.

Post-employment benefits: distinction between defined contribution plans and defined benefit plans

26   Post-employment benefits include items such as the following:

    (a)   retirement benefits (eg pensions and lump sum payments on retirement); and

    (b)   other post-employment benefits, such as post-employment life insurance and post-employment medical care.

Arrangements whereby an entity provides post-employment benefits are post-employment benefit plans. An entity applies this Standard to all such arrangements whether or not they involve the establishment of a separate entity to receive contributions and to pay benefits.

27   Post-employment benefit plans are classified as either defined contribution plans or defined benefit plans, depending on the economic substance of the plan as derived from its principal terms and conditions.

28   Under defined contribution plans the entity's legal or constructive obligation is limited to the amount that it agrees to contribute to the fund. Thus, the amount of the post-employment benefits received by the employee is determined by the amount of contributions paid by an entity (and perhaps also the employee) to a post-employment benefit plan or to an insurance company, together with investment returns arising from the contributions. In consequence, actuarial risk (that benefits will be less than expected) and investment risk (that assets invested will be insufficient to meet expected benefits) fall, in substance, on the employee.

29   Examples of cases where an entity's obligation is not limited to the amount that it agrees to contribute to the fund are when the entity has a legal or constructive obligation through:

    (a)   a plan benefit formula that is not linked solely to the amount of contributions and requires the entity to provide further contributions if assets are insufficient to meet the benefits in the plan benefit formula;

    (b)   a guarantee, either indirectly through a plan or directly, of a specified return on contributions; or

    (c)   those informal practices that give rise to a constructive obligation. For example, a constructive obligation may arise where an entity has a history of increasing benefits for former employees to keep pace with inflation even where there is no legal obligation to do so.

30   Under defined benefit plans:

    (a)   the entity's obligation is to provide the agreed benefits to current and former employees; and

    (b)   actuarial risk (that benefits will cost more than expected) and investment risk fall, in substance, on the entity. If actuarial or investment experience are worse than expected, the entity's obligation may be increased.

31   Paragraphs 32–49 explain the distinction between defined contribution plans and defined benefit plans in the context of multi-employer plans, defined benefit plans that share risks between entities under common control, state plans and insured benefits.

Multi-employer plans

32   **An entity shall classify a multi-employer plan as a defined contribution plan or a defined benefit plan under the terms of the plan (including any constructive obligation that goes beyond the formal terms).**

33   If an entity participates in a multi-employer defined benefit plan, unless paragraph 34 applies, it shall:

    (a)   account for its proportionate share of the defined benefit obligation, plan assets and cost associated with the plan in the same way as for any other defined benefit plan; and

    (b)   disclose the information required by paragraphs 135–148 (excluding paragraph 148(d)).

34   When sufficient information is not available to use defined benefit accounting for a multi-employer defined benefit plan, an entity shall:

    (a)   account for the plan in accordance with paragraphs 51 and 52 as if it were a defined contribution plan; and

    (b)   disclose the information required by paragraph 148.

35   One example of a multi-employer defined benefit plan is one where:

    (a)   the plan is financed on a pay-as-you-go basis: contributions are set at a level that is expected to be sufficient to pay the benefits falling due in the same period; and future benefits earned during the current period will be paid out of future contributions; and

    (b)   employees' benefits are determined by the length of their service and the participating entities have no realistic means of withdrawing from the plan without paying a contribution for the benefits earned by employees up to the date of withdrawal. Such a plan creates actuarial risk for the entity: if the ultimate cost of benefits already earned at the end of the reporting period is more than expected, the entity will have either to increase its contributions or to persuade employees to accept a reduction in benefits. Therefore, such a plan is a defined benefit plan.

36   Where sufficient information is available about a multi-employer defined benefit plan, an entity accounts for its proportionate share of the defined benefit obligation, plan assets and post-employment cost associated with the plan in the same way as for any other defined benefit plan. However, an entity may not be able to identify its share of the underlying financial position and performance of the plan with sufficient reliability for accounting purposes. This may occur if:

    (a)   the plan exposes the participating entities to actuarial risks associated with the current and former employees of other entities, with the result that there is no consistent and reliable basis for allocating the obligation, plan assets and cost to individual entities participating in the plan; or

    (b)   the entity does not have access to sufficient information about the plan to satisfy the requirements of this Standard.

In those cases, an entity accounts for the plan as if it were a defined contribution plan and discloses the information required by paragraph 148.

37   There may be a contractual agreement between the multi-employer plan and its participants that determines how the surplus in the plan will be distributed to the participants (or the deficit funded). A participant in a multi-employer plan with such an agreement that accounts for the plan as a defined contribution plan in accordance with paragraph 34 shall recognise the asset or liability that arises from the contractual agreement and the resulting income or expense in profit or loss.

Example illustrating paragraph 37

An entity participates in a multi-employer defined benefit plan that does not prepare plan valuations on an AASB 119 basis. It therefore accounts for the plan as if it were a defined contribution plan. A non-AASB 119 funding valuation shows a deficit of CU100 million[(a)] in the plan. The plan has agreed under contract a schedule of contributions with the participating employers in the plan that

> will eliminate the deficit over the next five years. The entity's total contributions under the contract are CU8 million.
>
> *The entity recognises a liability for the contributions adjusted for the time value of money and an equal expense in profit or loss.*
>
> ───────────
>
> (a)   In this Standard monetary amounts are denominated in 'currency units (CU)'.

38   Multi-employer plans are distinct from group administration plans. A group administration plan is merely an aggregation of single employer plans combined to allow participating employers to pool their assets for investment purposes and reduce investment management and administration costs, but the claims of different employers are segregated for the sole benefit of their own employees. Group administration plans pose no particular accounting problems because information is readily available to treat them in the same way as any other single employer plan and because such plans do not expose the participating entities to actuarial risks associated with the current and former employees of other entities. The definitions in this Standard require an entity to classify a group administration plan as a defined contribution plan or a defined benefit plan in accordance with the terms of the plan (including any constructive obligation that goes beyond the formal terms).

39   **In determining when to recognise, and how to measure, a liability relating to the wind-up of a multi-employer defined benefit plan, or the entity's withdrawal from a multi-employer defined benefit plan, an entity shall apply AASB 137 *Provisions, Contingent Liabilities and Contingent Assets*.**

Defined benefit plans that share risks between entities under common control

40   Defined benefit plans that share risks between entities under common control, for example, a parent and its subsidiaries, are not multi-employer plans.

41   An entity participating in such a plan shall obtain information about the plan as a whole measured in accordance with this Standard on the basis of assumptions that apply to the plan as a whole. If there is a contractual agreement or stated policy for charging to individual group entities the net defined benefit cost for the plan as a whole measured in accordance with this Standard, the entity shall, in its separate or individual financial statements, recognise the net defined benefit cost so charged. If there is no such agreement or policy, the net defined benefit cost shall be recognised in the separate or individual financial statements of the group entity that is legally the sponsoring employer for the plan. The other group entities shall, in their separate or individual financial statements, recognise a cost equal to their contribution payable for the period.

42   Participation in such a plan is a related party transaction for each individual group entity. An entity shall therefore, in its separate or individual financial statements, disclose the information required by paragraph 149.

State plans

43   **An entity shall account for a state plan in the same way as for a multi-employer plan (see paragraphs 32–39).**

44   State plans are established by legislation to cover all entities (or all entities in a particular category, for example, a specific industry) and are operated by national or local government or by another body (for example, an autonomous agency created specifically for this purpose) that is not subject to control or influence by the reporting entity. Some plans established by an entity provide both compulsory benefits, as a substitute for benefits that would otherwise be covered under a state plan, and additional voluntary benefits. Such plans are not state plans.

45   State plans are characterised as defined benefit or defined contribution, depending on the entity's obligation under the plan. Many state plans are funded on a pay-as-you-go

AASB 119

basis: contributions are set at a level that is expected to be sufficient to pay the required benefits falling due in the same period; future benefits earned during the current period will be paid out of future contributions. Nevertheless, in most state plans the entity has no legal or constructive obligation to pay those future benefits: its only obligation is to pay the contributions as they fall due and if the entity ceases to employ members of the state plan, it will have no obligation to pay the benefits earned by its own employees in previous years. For this reason, state plans are normally defined contribution plans. However, when a state plan is a defined benefit plan an entity applies paragraphs 32–39.

Insured benefits

46   **An entity may pay insurance premiums to fund a post-employment benefit plan. The entity shall treat such a plan as a defined contribution plan unless the entity will have (either directly, or indirectly through the plan) a legal or constructive obligation either:**

    (a)   to pay the employee benefits directly when they fall due; or

    (b)   to pay further amounts if the insurer does not pay all future employee benefits relating to employee service in the current and prior periods.

   If the entity retains such a legal or constructive obligation, the entity shall treat the plan as a defined benefit plan.

47   The benefits insured by an insurance policy need not have a direct or automatic relationship with the entity's obligation for employee benefits. Post-employment benefit plans involving insurance policies are subject to the same distinction between accounting and funding as other funded plans.

48   Where an entity funds a post-employment benefit obligation by contributing to an insurance policy under which the entity (either directly, indirectly through the plan, through the mechanism for setting future premiums or through a related party relationship with the insurer) retains a legal or constructive obligation, the payment of the premiums does not amount to a defined contribution arrangement. It follows that the entity:

    (a)   accounts for a qualifying insurance policy as a plan asset (see paragraph 8); and

    (b)   recognises other insurance policies as reimbursement rights (if the policies satisfy the criterion in paragraph 116).

49   Where an insurance policy is in the name of a specified plan participant or a group of plan participants and the entity does not have any legal or constructive obligation to cover any loss on the policy, the entity has no obligation to pay benefits to the employees and the insurer has sole responsibility for paying the benefits. The payment of fixed premiums under such contracts is, in substance, the settlement of the employee benefit obligation, rather than an investment to meet the obligation. Consequently, the entity no longer has an asset or a liability. Therefore, an entity treats such payments as contributions to a defined contribution plan.

Post-employment benefits: defined contribution plans

50   Accounting for defined contribution plans is straightforward because the reporting entity's obligation for each period is determined by the amounts to be contributed for that period. Consequently, no actuarial assumptions are required to measure the obligation or the expense and there is no possibility of any actuarial gain or loss. Moreover, the obligations are measured on an undiscounted basis, except where they are not expected to be settled wholly before twelve months after the end of the annual reporting period in which the employees render the related service.

Recognition and measurement

51   When an employee has rendered service to an entity during a period, the entity shall recognise the contribution payable to a defined contribution plan in exchange for that service:

(a)   as a liability (accrued expense), after deducting any contribution already paid. If the contribution already paid exceeds the contribution due for service before the end of the reporting period, an entity shall recognise that excess as an asset (prepaid expense) to the extent that the prepayment will lead to, for example, a reduction in future payments or a cash refund.

(b)   as an expense, unless another Australian Accounting Standard requires or permits the inclusion of the contribution in the cost of an asset (see, for example, AASB 102 and AASB 116).

52   When contributions to a defined contribution plan are not expected to be settled wholly before twelve months after the end of the annual reporting period in which the employees render the related service, they shall be discounted using the discount rate specified in paragraph 83.

Disclosure

53   An entity shall disclose the amount recognised as an expense for defined contribution plans.

54   Where required by AASB 124 an entity discloses information about contributions to defined contribution plans for key management personnel.

Post-employment benefits: defined benefit plans

55   Accounting for defined benefit plans is complex because actuarial assumptions are required to measure the obligation and the expense and there is a possibility of actuarial gains and losses. Moreover, the obligations are measured on a discounted basis because they may be settled many years after the employees render the related service.

Recognition and measurement

56   Defined benefit plans may be unfunded, or they may be wholly or partly funded by contributions by an entity, and sometimes its employees, into an entity, or fund, that is legally separate from the reporting entity and from which the employee benefits are paid. The payment of funded benefits when they fall due depends not only on the financial position and the investment performance of the fund but also on an entity's ability, and willingness, to make good any shortfall in the fund's assets. Therefore, the entity is, in substance, underwriting the actuarial and investment risks associated with the plan. Consequently, the expense recognised for a defined benefit plan is not necessarily the amount of the contribution due for the period.

57   Accounting by an entity for defined benefit plans involves the following steps:

(a)   determining the deficit or surplus. This involves:

(i)   using an actuarial technique, the projected unit credit method, to make a reliable estimate of the ultimate cost to the entity of the benefit that employees have earned in return for their service in the current and prior periods (see paragraphs 67–69). This requires an entity to determine how much benefit is attributable to the current and prior periods (see paragraphs 70–74) and to make estimates (actuarial assumptions) about demographic variables (such as employee turnover and mortality) and financial variables (such as future increases in salaries and medical costs) that will affect the cost of the benefit (see paragraphs 75–98).

(ii) discounting that benefit in order to determine the present value of the defined benefit obligation and the current service cost (see paragraphs 67–69 and 83–86).

(iii) deducting the fair value of any plan assets (see paragraphs 113–115) from the present value of the defined benefit obligation.

(b) determining the amount of the net defined benefit liability (asset) as the amount of the deficit or surplus determined in (a), adjusted for any effect of limiting a net defined benefit asset to the asset ceiling (see paragraph 64).

(c) determining amounts to be recognised in profit or loss:

(i) current service cost (see paragraphs 70–74).

(ii) any past service cost and gain or loss on settlement (see paragraphs 99–112).

(iii) net interest on the net defined benefit liability (asset) (see paragraphs 123–126).

(d) determining the remeasurements of the net defined benefit liability (asset), to be recognised in other comprehensive income, comprising:

(i) actuarial gains and losses (see paragraphs 128 and 129);

(ii) return on plan assets, excluding amounts included in net interest on the net defined benefit liability (asset) (see paragraph 130); and

(iii) any change in the effect of the asset ceiling (see paragraph 64), excluding amounts included in net interest on the net defined benefit liability (asset).

Where an entity has more than one defined benefit plan, the entity applies these procedures for each material plan separately.

58 **An entity shall determine the net defined benefit liability (asset) with sufficient regularity that the amounts recognised in the financial statements do not differ materially from the amounts that would be determined at the end of the reporting period.**

59 This Standard encourages, but does not require, an entity to involve a qualified actuary in the measurement of all material post-employment benefit obligations. For practical reasons, an entity may request a qualified actuary to carry out a detailed valuation of the obligation before the end of the reporting period. Nevertheless, the results of that valuation are updated for any material transactions and other material changes in circumstances (including changes in market prices and interest rates) up to the end of the reporting period.

60 In some cases, estimates, averages and computational short cuts may provide a reliable approximation of the detailed computations illustrated in this Standard.

Accounting for the constructive obligation

61 **An entity shall account not only for its legal obligation under the formal terms of a defined benefit plan, but also for any constructive obligation that arises from the entity's informal practices. Informal practices give rise to a constructive obligation where the entity has no realistic alternative but to pay employee benefits. An example of a constructive obligation is where a change in the entity's informal practices would cause unacceptable damage to its relationship with employees.**

62 The formal terms of a defined benefit plan may permit an entity to terminate its obligation under the plan. Nevertheless, it is usually difficult for an entity to terminate its obligation under a plan (without payment) if employees are to be retained. Therefore, in the absence of evidence to the contrary, accounting for post-employment benefits assumes that an entity that is currently promising such benefits will continue to do so over the remaining working lives of employees.

Examples illustrating paragraph 71

1   A defined benefit plan provides a lump sum benefit of CU100 payable on retirement for each year of service.

A benefit of CU100 is attributed to each year. The current service cost is the present value of CU100. The present value of the defined benefit obligation is the present value of CU100, multiplied by the number of years of service up to the end of the reporting period.

If the benefit is payable immediately when the employee leaves the entity, the current service cost and the present value of the defined benefit obligation reflect the date at which the employee is expected to leave. Thus, because of the effect of discounting, they are less than the amounts that would be determined if the employee left at the end of the reporting period.

2   A plan provides a monthly pension of 0.2 per cent of final salary for each year of service. The pension is payable from the age of 65.

Benefit equal to the present value, at the expected retirement date, of a monthly pension of 0.2 per cent of the estimated final salary payable from the expected retirement date until the expected date of death is attributed to each year of service. The current service cost is the present value of that benefit. The present value of the defined benefit obligation is the present value of monthly pension payments of 0.2 per cent of final salary, multiplied by the number of years of service up to the end of the reporting period. The current service cost and the present value of the defined benefit obligation are discounted because pension payments begin at the age of 65.

---

72   Employee service gives rise to an obligation under a defined benefit plan even if the benefits are conditional on future employment (in other words they are not vested). Employee service before the vesting date gives rise to a constructive obligation because, at the end of each successive reporting period, the amount of future service that an employee will have to render before becoming entitled to the benefit is reduced. In measuring its defined benefit obligation, an entity considers the probability that some employees may not satisfy any vesting requirements. Similarly, although some post-employment benefits, for example, post-employment medical benefits, become payable only if a specified event occurs when an employee is no longer employed, an obligation is created when the employee renders service that will provide entitlement to the benefit if the specified event occurs. The probability that the specified event will occur affects the measurement of the obligation, but does not determine whether the obligation exists.

Examples illustrating paragraph 72

1   A plan pays a benefit of CU100 for each year of service. The benefits vest after ten years of service.

A benefit of CU100 is attributed to each year. In each of the first ten years, the current service cost and the present value of the obligation reflect the probability that the employee may not complete ten years of service.

2   A plan pays a benefit of CU100 for each year of service, excluding service before the age of 25. The benefits vest immediately.

No benefit is attributed to service before the age of 25 because service before that date does not lead to benefits (conditional or unconditional). A benefit of CU100 is attributed to each subsequent year.

---

73   The obligation increases until the date when further service by the employee will lead to no material amount of further benefits. Therefore, all benefit is attributed to periods ending on or before that date. Benefit is attributed to individual accounting periods under the plan's benefit formula. However, if an employee's service in later years will lead to a materially higher level of benefit than in earlier years, an entity attributes benefit on a straight-line basis until the date when further service by the employee will lead to no material amount of further benefits. That is because the employee's service throughout the entire period will ultimately lead to benefit at that higher level.

Examples illustrating paragraph 73

1   A plan pays a lump sum benefit of CU1,000 that vests after ten years of service. The plan provides no further benefit for subsequent service.

A benefit of CU100 (CU1,000 divided by ten) is attributed to each of the first ten years.

The current service cost in each of the first ten years reflects the probability that the employee may not complete ten years of service. No benefit is attributed to subsequent years.

2   A plan pays a lump sum retirement benefit of CU2,000 to all employees who are still employed at the age of 55 after twenty years of service, or who are still employed at the age of 65, regardless of their length of service.

For employees who join before the age of 35, service first leads to benefits under the plan at the age of 35 (an employee could leave at the age of 30 and return at the age of 33, with no effect on the amount or timing of benefits). Those benefits are conditional on further service. Also, service beyond the age of 55 will lead to no material amount of further benefits. For these employees, the entity attributes benefit of CU100 (CU2,000 divided by twenty) to each year from the age of 35 to the age of 55.

For employees who join between the ages of 35 and 45, service beyond twenty years will lead to no material amount of further benefits. For these employees, the entity attributes benefit of 100 (2,000 divided by twenty) to each of the first twenty years.

For an employee who joins at the age of 55, service beyond ten years will lead to no material amount of further benefits. For this employee, the entity attributes benefit of CU200 (CU2,000 divided by ten) to each of the first ten years.

For all employees, the current service cost and the present value of the obligation reflect the probability that the employee may not complete the necessary period of service.

3   A post-employment medical plan reimburses 40 per cent of an employee's post-employment medical costs if the employee leaves after more than ten and less than twenty years of service and 50 per cent of those costs if the employee leaves after twenty or more years of service.

Under the plan's benefit formula, the entity attributes 4 per cent of the present value of the expected medical costs (40 per cent divided by ten) to each of the first ten years and 1 per cent (10 per cent divided by ten) to each of the second ten years. The current service cost in each year reflects the probability that the employee may not complete the necessary period of service to earn part or all of the benefits. For employees expected to leave within ten years, no benefit is attributed.

4   A post-employment medical plan reimburses 10 per cent of an employee's post-employment medical costs if the employee leaves after more than ten and less than twenty years of service and 50 per cent of those costs if the employee leaves after twenty or more years of service.

Service in later years will lead to a materially higher level of benefit than in earlier years. Therefore, for employees expected to leave after twenty or more years, the entity attributes benefit on a straight-line basis under paragraph 71. Service beyond twenty years will lead to no material amount of further benefits. Therefore, the benefit attributed to each of the first twenty years is 2.5 per cent of the present value of the expected medical costs (50 per cent divided by twenty).

For employees expected to leave between ten and twenty years, the benefit attributed to each of the first ten years is 1 per cent of the present value of the expected medical costs.

For these employees, no benefit is attributed to service between the end of the tenth year and the estimated date of leaving.

For employees expected to leave within ten years, no benefit is attributed.

74   Where the amount of a benefit is a constant proportion of final salary for each year of service, future salary increases will affect the amount required to settle the obligation that exists for service before the end of the reporting period, but do not create an additional obligation. Therefore:

(a)   for the purpose of paragraph 70(b), salary increases do not lead to further benefits, even though the amount of the benefits is dependent on final salary; and

(b)   the amount of benefit attributed to each period is a constant proportion of the salary to which the benefit is linked.

Example illustrating paragraph 74

Employees are entitled to a benefit of 3 per cent of final salary for each year of service before the age of 55.

Benefit of 3 per cent of estimated final salary is attributed to each year up to the age of 55. This is the date when further service by the employee will lead to no material amount of further benefits under the plan. No benefit is attributed to service after that age.

Actuarial assumptions

75   **Actuarial assumptions shall be unbiased and mutually compatible.**

76   Actuarial assumptions are an entity's best estimates of the variables that will determine the ultimate cost of providing post-employment benefits. Actuarial assumptions comprise:

   (a)   demographic assumptions about the future characteristics of current and former employees (and their dependants) who are eligible for benefits. Demographic assumptions deal with matters such as:

      (i)   mortality (see paragraphs 81 and 82);

      (ii)   rates of employee turnover, disability and early retirement;

      (iii) the proportion of plan members with dependants who will be eligible for benefits;

      (iv)   the proportion of plan members who will select each form of payment option available under the plan terms; and

      (v)   claim rates under medical plans.

   (b)   financial assumptions, dealing with items such as:

      (i)   the discount rate (see paragraphs 83–86);

      (ii)   benefit levels, excluding any cost of the benefits to be met by employees, and future salary (see paragraphs 87–95);

      (iii) in the case of medical benefits, future medical costs, including claim handling costs (ie the costs that will be incurred in processing and resolving claims, including legal and adjuster's fees) (see paragraphs 96–98); and

      (iv)   taxes payable by the plan on contributions relating to service before the reporting date or on benefits resulting from that service.

77   Actuarial assumptions are unbiased if they are neither imprudent nor excessively conservative.

78   Actuarial assumptions are mutually compatible if they reflect the economic relationships between factors such as inflation, rates of salary increase and discount rates. For example, all assumptions that depend on a particular inflation level (such as assumptions about interest rates and salary and benefit increases) in any given future period assume the same inflation level in that period.

79   An entity determines the discount rate and other financial assumptions in nominal (stated) terms, unless estimates in real (inflation-adjusted) terms are more reliable, for example, in a hyperinflationary economy (see AASB 129 *Financial Reporting in Hyperinflationary Economies*), or where the benefit is index-linked and there is a deep market in index-linked bonds of the same currency and term.

80   **Financial assumptions shall be based on market expectations, at the end of the reporting period, for the period over which the obligations are to be settled.**

Actuarial assumptions: mortality

81   **An entity shall determine its mortality assumptions by reference to its best estimate of the mortality of plan members both during and after employment.**

82 In order to estimate the ultimate cost of the benefit an entity takes into consideration expected changes in mortality, for example by modifying standard mortality tables with estimates of mortality improvements.

Actuarial assumptions: discount rate

83 **The rate used to discount post-employment benefit obligations (both funded and unfunded) shall be determined by reference to market yields at the end of the reporting period on high quality corporate bonds. For currencies for which there is no deep market in such high quality corporate bonds, the market yields (at the end of the reporting period) on government bonds denominated in that currency shall be used. The currency and term of the corporate bonds or government bonds shall be consistent with the currency and estimated term of the post-employment benefit obligations.**

Aus83.1 **Notwithstanding paragraph 83, in respect of not-for-profit public sector entities, post-employment benefit obligations denominated in Australian currency shall be discounted using market yields on government bonds.**

84 One actuarial assumption that has a material effect is the discount rate. The discount rate reflects the time value of money but not the actuarial or investment risk. Furthermore, the discount rate does not reflect the entity-specific credit risk borne by the entity's creditors, nor does it reflect the risk that future experience may differ from actuarial assumptions.

85 The discount rate reflects the estimated timing of benefit payments. In practice, an entity often achieves this by applying a single weighted average discount rate that reflects the estimated timing and amount of benefit payments and the currency in which the benefits are to be paid.

86 In some cases, there may be no deep market in bonds with a sufficiently long maturity to match the estimated maturity of all the benefit payments. In such cases, an entity uses current market rates of the appropriate term to discount shorter-term payments, and estimates the discount rate for longer maturities by extrapolating current market rates along the yield curve. The total present value of a defined benefit obligation is unlikely to be particularly sensitive to the discount rate applied to the portion of benefits that is payable beyond the final maturity of the available corporate or government bonds.

Actuarial assumptions: salaries, benefits and medical costs

87 **An entity shall measure its defined benefit obligations on a basis that reflects:**

(a) **the benefits set out in the terms of the plan (or resulting from any constructive obligation that goes beyond those terms) at the end of the reporting period;**

(b) **any estimated future salary increases that affect the benefits payable;**

(c) **the effect of any limit on the employer's share of the cost of the future benefits;**

(d) **contributions from employees or third parties that reduce the ultimate cost to the entity of those benefits; and**

(e) **estimated future changes in the level of any state benefits that affect the benefits payable under a defined benefit plan, if, and only if, either:**

(i) **those changes were enacted before the end of the reporting period; or**

(ii) **historical data, or other reliable evidence, indicate that those state benefits will change in some predictable manner, for example, in line with future changes in general price levels or general salary levels.**

88 Actuarial assumptions reflect future benefit changes that are set out in the formal terms of a plan (or a constructive obligation that goes beyond those terms) at the end of the reporting period. This is the case if, for example:

(a) the entity has a history of increasing benefits, for example, to mitigate the effects of inflation, and there is no indication that this practice will change in the future;

(b) the entity is obliged, by either the formal terms of a plan (or a constructive obligation that goes beyond those terms) or legislation, to use any surplus in the plan for the benefit of plan participants (see paragraph 108(c)); or

(c) benefits vary in response to a performance target or other criteria. For example, the terms of the plan may state that it will pay reduced benefits or require additional contributions from employees if the plan assets are insufficient. The measurement of the obligation reflects the best estimate of the effect of the performance target or other criteria.

89   Actuarial assumptions do not reflect future benefit changes that are not set out in the formal terms of the plan (or a constructive obligation) at the end of the reporting period. Such changes will result in:

(a) past service cost, to the extent that they change benefits for service before the change; and

(b) current service cost for periods after the change, to the extent that they change benefits for service after the change.

90   Estimates of future salary increases take account of inflation, seniority, promotion and other relevant factors, such as supply and demand in the employment market.

91   Some defined benefit plans limit the contributions that an entity is required to pay. The ultimate cost of the benefits takes account of the effect of a limit on contributions. The effect of a limit on contributions is determined over the shorter of:

(a) the estimated life of the entity; and

(b) the estimated life of the plan.

92   Some defined benefit plans require employees or third parties to contribute to the cost of the plan. Contributions by employees reduce the cost of the benefits to the entity. An entity considers whether third-party contributions reduce the cost of the benefits to the entity, or are a reimbursement right as described in paragraph 116. Contributions by employees or third parties are either set out in the formal terms of the plan (or arise from a constructive obligation that goes beyond those terms), or are discretionary. Discretionary contributions by employees or third parties reduce service cost upon payment of these contributions to the plan.

93   Contributions from employees or third parties set out in the formal terms of the plan either reduce service cost (if they are linked to service), or affect remeasurements of the net defined benefit liability (asset) (if they are not linked to service). An example of contributions that are not linked to service is when the contributions are required to reduce a deficit arising from losses on plan assets or from actuarial losses. If contributions from employees or third parties are linked to service, those contributions reduce the service cost as follows:

(a) if the amount of the contributions is dependent on the number of years of service, an entity shall attribute the contributions to periods of service using the same attribution method required by paragraph 70 for the gross benefit (ie either using the plan's contribution formula or on a straight-line basis); or

(b) if the amount of the contributions is independent of the number of years of service, the entity is permitted to recognise such contributions as a reduction of the service cost in the period in which the related service is rendered. Examples of contributions that are independent of the number of years of service include those that are a fixed percentage of the employee's salary, a fixed amount throughout the service period or dependent on the employee's age.

Paragraph A1 provides related application guidance.

94   For contributions from employees or third parties that are attributed to periods of service in accordance with paragraph 93(a), changes in the contributions result in:

(a) current and past service cost (if those changes are not set out in the formal terms of a plan and do not arise from a constructive obligation); or

(b) actuarial gains and losses (if those changes are set out in the formal terms of a plan, or arise from a constructive obligation).

95 Some post-employment benefits are linked to variables such as the level of state retirement benefits or state medical care. The measurement of such benefits reflects the best estimate of such variables, based on historical data and other reliable evidence.

96 Assumptions about medical costs shall take account of estimated future changes in the cost of medical services, resulting from both inflation and specific changes in medical costs.

97 Measurement of post-employment medical benefits requires assumptions about the level and frequency of future claims and the cost of meeting those claims. An entity estimates future medical costs on the basis of historical data about the entity's own experience, supplemented where necessary by historical data from other entities, insurance companies, medical providers or other sources. Estimates of future medical costs consider the effect of technological advances, changes in health care utilisation or delivery patterns and changes in the health status of plan participants.

98 The level and frequency of claims is particularly sensitive to the age, health status and sex of employees (and their dependants) and may be sensitive to other factors such as geographical location. Therefore, historical data are adjusted to the extent that the demographic mix of the population differs from that of the population used as a basis for the data. They are also adjusted where there is reliable evidence that historical trends will not continue.

Past service cost and gains and losses on settlement

99 Before determining past service cost, or a gain or loss on settlement, an entity shall remeasure the net defined benefit liability (asset) using the current fair value of plan assets and current actuarial assumptions (including current market interest rates and other current market prices) reflecting the benefits offered under the plan before the plan amendment, curtailment or settlement.

100 An entity need not distinguish between past service cost resulting from a plan amendment, past service cost resulting from a curtailment and a gain or loss on settlement if these transactions occur together. In some cases, a plan amendment occurs before a settlement, such as when an entity changes the benefits under the plan and settles the amended benefits later. In those cases an entity recognises past service cost before any gain or loss on settlement.

101 A settlement occurs together with a plan amendment and curtailment if a plan is terminated with the result that the obligation is settled and the plan ceases to exist. However, the termination of a plan is not a settlement if the plan is replaced by a new plan that offers benefits that are, in substance, the same.

Past service cost

102 Past service cost is the change in the present value of the defined benefit obligation resulting from a plan amendment or curtailment.

103 An entity shall recognise past service cost as an expense at the earlier of the following dates:

(a) when the plan amendment or curtailment occurs; and

(b) when the entity recognises related restructuring costs (see AASB 137) or termination benefits (see paragraph 165).

104 A plan amendment occurs when an entity introduces, or withdraws, a defined benefit plan or changes the benefits payable under an existing defined benefit plan.

AASB

105   A curtailment occurs when an entity significantly reduces the number of employees covered by a plan. A curtailment may arise from an isolated event, such as the closing of a plant, discontinuance of an operation or termination or suspension of a plan.

106   Past service cost may be either positive (when benefits are introduced or changed so that the present value of the defined benefit obligation increases) or negative (when benefits are withdrawn or changed so that the present value of the defined benefit obligation decreases).

107   Where an entity reduces benefits payable under an existing defined benefit plan and, at the same time, increases other benefits payable under the plan for the same employees, the entity treats the change as a single net change.

108   Past service cost excludes:

   (a)   the effect of differences between actual and previously assumed salary increases on the obligation to pay benefits for service in prior years (there is no past service cost because actuarial assumptions allow for projected salaries);

   (b)   underestimates and overestimates of discretionary pension increases when an entity has a constructive obligation to grant such increases (there is no past service cost because actuarial assumptions allow for such increases);

   (c)   estimates of benefit improvements that result from actuarial gains or from the return on plan assets that have been recognised in the financial statements if the entity is obliged, by either the formal terms of a plan (or a constructive obligation that goes beyond those terms) or legislation, to use any surplus in the plan for the benefit of plan participants, even if the benefit increase has not yet been formally awarded (there is no past service cost because the resulting increase in the obligation is an actuarial loss, see paragraph 88); and

   (d)   the increase in vested benefits (ie benefits that are not conditional on future employment, see paragraph 72) when, in the absence of new or improved benefits, employees complete vesting requirements (there is no past service cost because the entity recognised the estimated cost of benefits as current service cost as the service was rendered).

Gains and losses on settlement

109   The gain or loss on a settlement is the difference between:

   (a)   the present value of the defined benefit obligation being settled, as determined on the date of settlement; and

   (b)   the settlement price, including any plan assets transferred and any payments made directly by the entity in connection with the settlement.

110   An entity shall recognise a gain or loss on the settlement of a defined benefit plan when the settlement occurs.

111   A settlement occurs when an entity enters into a transaction that eliminates all further legal or constructive obligation for part or all of the benefits provided under a defined benefit plan (other than a payment of benefits to, or on behalf of, employees in accordance with the terms of the plan and included in the actuarial assumptions). For example, a one-off transfer of significant employer obligations under the plan to an insurance company through the purchase of an insurance policy is a settlement; a lump sum cash payment, under the terms of the plan, to plan participants in exchange for their rights to receive specified post-employment benefits is not.

112   In some cases, an entity acquires an insurance policy to fund some or all of the employee benefits relating to employee service in the current and prior periods. The acquisition of such a policy is not a settlement if the entity retains a legal or constructive obligation (see paragraph 46) to pay further amounts if the insurer does not pay the employee benefits specified in the insurance policy. Paragraphs 116–119 deal with the recognition and measurement of reimbursement rights under insurance policies that are not plan assets.

Recognition and measurement: plan assets

Fair value of plan assets

113 The fair value of any plan assets is deducted from the present value of the defined benefit obligation in determining the deficit or surplus.

114 Plan assets exclude unpaid contributions due from the reporting entity to the fund, as well as any non-transferable financial instruments issued by the entity and held by the fund. Plan assets are reduced by any liabilities of the fund that do not relate to employee benefits, for example, trade and other payables and liabilities resulting from derivative financial instruments.

115 Where plan assets include qualifying insurance policies that exactly match the amount and timing of some or all of the benefits payable under the plan, the fair value of those insurance policies is deemed to be the present value of the related obligations (subject to any reduction required if the amounts receivable under the insurance policies are not recoverable in full).

Reimbursements

116 **When, and only when, it is virtually certain that another party will reimburse some or all of the expenditure required to settle a defined benefit obligation, an entity shall:**

   (a) **recognise its right to reimbursement as a separate asset. The entity shall measure the asset at fair value.**

   (b) **disaggregate and recognise changes in the fair value of its right to reimbursement in the same way as for changes in the fair value of plan assets (see paragraphs 124 and 125). The components of defined benefit cost recognised in accordance with paragraph 120 may be recognised net of amounts relating to changes in the carrying amount of the right to reimbursement.**

117 Sometimes, an entity is able to look to another party, such as an insurer, to pay part or all of the expenditure required to settle a defined benefit obligation. Qualifying insurance policies, as defined in paragraph 8, are plan assets. An entity accounts for qualifying insurance policies in the same way as for all other plan assets and paragraph 116 is not relevant (see paragraphs 46–49 and 115).

118 When an insurance policy held by an entity is not a qualifying insurance policy, that insurance policy is not a plan asset. Paragraph 116 is relevant to such cases: the entity recognises its right to reimbursement under the insurance policy as a separate asset, rather than as a deduction in determining the defined benefit deficit or surplus. Paragraph 140(b) requires the entity to disclose a brief description of the link between the reimbursement right and the related obligation.

119 If the right to reimbursement arises under an insurance policy that exactly matches the amount and timing of some or all of the benefits payable under a defined benefit plan, the fair value of the reimbursement right is deemed to be the present value of the related obligation (subject to any reduction required if the reimbursement is not recoverable in full).

Components of defined benefit cost

120 **An entity shall recognise the components of defined benefit cost, except to the extent that another Australian Accounting Standard requires or permits their inclusion in the cost of an asset, as follows:**

   (a) **service cost (see paragraphs 66–112) in profit or loss;**

   (b) **net interest on the net defined benefit liability (asset) (see paragraphs 123–126) in profit or loss; and**

   (c) **remeasurements of the net defined benefit liability (asset) (see paragraphs 127–130) in other comprehensive income.**

121   Other Australian Accounting Standards require the inclusion of some employee benefit costs within the cost of assets, such as inventories and property, plant and equipment (see AASB 102 and AASB 116). Any post-employment benefit costs included in the cost of such assets include the appropriate proportion of the components listed in paragraph 120.

122   Remeasurements of the net defined benefit liability (asset) recognised in other comprehensive income shall not be reclassified to profit or loss in a subsequent period. However, the entity may transfer those amounts recognised in other comprehensive income within equity.

Net interest on the net defined benefit liability (asset)

123   Net interest on the net defined benefit liability (asset) shall be determined by multiplying the net defined benefit liability (asset) by the discount rate specified in paragraph 83, both as determined at the start of the annual reporting period, taking account of any changes in the net defined benefit liability (asset) during the period as a result of contribution and benefit payments.

124   Net interest on the net defined benefit liability (asset) can be viewed as comprising interest income on plan assets, interest cost on the defined benefit obligation and interest on the effect of the asset ceiling mentioned in paragraph 64.

125   Interest income on plan assets is a component of the return on plan assets, and is determined by multiplying the fair value of the plan assets by the discount rate specified in paragraph 83, both as determined at the start of the annual reporting period, taking account of any changes in the plan assets held during the period as a result of contributions and benefit payments. The difference between the interest income on plan assets and the return on plan assets is included in the remeasurement of the net defined benefit liability (asset).

126   Interest on the effect of the asset ceiling is part of the total change in the effect of the asset ceiling, and is determined by multiplying the effect of the asset ceiling by the discount rate specified in paragraph 83, both as determined at the start of the annual reporting period. The difference between that amount and the total change in the effect of the asset ceiling is included in the remeasurement of the net defined benefit liability (asset).

Remeasurements of the net defined benefit liability (asset)

127   Remeasurements of the net defined benefit liability (asset) comprise:

    (a)   actuarial gains and losses (see paragraphs 128 and 129);

    (b)   the return on plan assets (see paragraph 130), excluding amounts included in net interest on the net defined benefit liability (asset) (see paragraph 125); and

    (c)   any change in the effect of the asset ceiling, excluding amounts included in net interest on the net defined benefit liability (asset) (see paragraph 126).

128   Actuarial gains and losses result from increases or decreases in the present value of the defined benefit obligation because of changes in actuarial assumptions and experience adjustments. Causes of actuarial gains and losses include, for example:

    (a)   unexpectedly high or low rates of employee turnover, early retirement or mortality or of increases in salaries, benefits (if the formal or constructive terms of a plan provide for inflationary benefit increases) or medical costs;

    (b)   the effect of changes to assumptions concerning benefit payment options;

    (c)   the effect of changes in estimates of future employee turnover, early retirement or mortality or of increases in salaries, benefits (if the formal or constructive terms of a plan provide for inflationary benefit increases) or medical costs; and

    (d)   the effect of changes in the discount rate.

129 Actuarial gains and losses do not include changes in the present value of the defined benefit obligation because of the introduction, amendment, curtailment or settlement of the defined benefit plan, or changes to the benefits payable under the defined benefit plan. Such changes result in past service cost or gains or losses on settlement.

130 In determining the return on plan assets, an entity deducts the costs of managing the plan assets and any tax payable by the plan itself, other than tax included in the actuarial assumptions used to measure the defined benefit obligation (paragraph 76). Other administration costs are not deducted from the return on plan assets.

Presentation

Offset

131 An entity shall offset an asset relating to one plan against a liability relating to another plan when, and only when, the entity:

   (a) has a legally enforceable right to use a surplus in one plan to settle obligations under the other plan; and

   (b) intends either to settle the obligations on a net basis, or to realise the surplus in one plan and settle its obligation under the other plan simultaneously.

132 The offsetting criteria are similar to those established for financial instruments in AASB 132 *Financial Instruments: Presentation*.

Current/non-current distinction

133 Some entities distinguish current assets and liabilities from non-current assets and liabilities. This Standard does not specify whether an entity should distinguish current and non-current portions of assets and liabilities arising from post-employment benefits.

Components of defined benefit cost

134 Paragraph 120 requires an entity to recognise service cost and net interest on the net defined benefit liability (asset) in profit or loss. This Standard does not specify how an entity should present service cost and net interest on the net defined benefit liability (asset). An entity presents those components in accordance with AASB 101.

Disclosure

135 An entity shall disclose information that:

   (a) explains the characteristics of its defined benefit plans and risks associated with them (see paragraph 139);

   (b) identifies and explains the amounts in its financial statements arising from its defined benefit plans (see paragraphs 140–144); and

   (c) describes how its defined benefit plans may affect the amount, timing and uncertainty of the entity's future cash flows (see paragraphs 145–147).

136 To meet the objectives in paragraph 135, an entity shall consider all the following:

   (a) the level of detail necessary to satisfy the disclosure requirements;

   (b) how much emphasis to place on each of the various requirements;

   (c) how much aggregation or disaggregation to undertake; and

   (d) whether users of financial statements need additional information to evaluate the quantitative information disclosed.

137 If the disclosures provided in accordance with the requirements in this Standard and other Australian Accounting Standards are insufficient to meet the objectives in paragraph 135, an entity shall disclose additional information necessary to meet those objectives. For example, an entity may present an analysis of the present value of the

defined benefit obligation that distinguishes the nature, characteristics and risks of the obligation. Such a disclosure could distinguish:

(a)   between amounts owing to active members, deferred members, and pensioners.

(b)   between vested benefits and accrued but not vested benefits.

(c)   between conditional benefits, amounts attributable to future salary increases and other benefits.

138   An entity shall assess whether all or some disclosures should be disaggregated to distinguish plans or groups of plans with materially different risks. For example, an entity may disaggregate disclosure about plans showing one or more of the following features:

(a)   different geographical locations.

(b)   different characteristics such as flat salary pension plans, final salary pension plans or post-employment medical plans.

(c)   different regulatory environments.

(d)   different reporting segments.

(e)   different funding arrangements (eg wholly unfunded, wholly or partly funded).

Characteristics of defined benefit plans and risks associated with them

139   An entity shall disclose:

(a)   information about the characteristics of its defined benefit plans, including:

(i)   the nature of the benefits provided by the plan (eg final salary defined benefit plan or contribution-based plan with guarantee).

(ii)   a description of the regulatory framework in which the plan operates, for example the level of any minimum funding requirements, and any effect of the regulatory framework on the plan, such as the asset ceiling (see paragraph 64).

(iii)   a description of any other entity's responsibilities for the governance of the plan, for example responsibilities of trustees or of board members of the plan.

(b)   a description of the risks to which the plan exposes the entity, focused on any unusual, entity-specific or plan-specific risks, and of any significant concentrations of risk. For example, if plan assets are invested primarily in one class of investments, eg property, the plan may expose the entity to a concentration of property market risk.

(c)   a description of any plan amendments, curtailments and settlements.

Explanation of amounts in the financial statements

140   An entity shall provide a reconciliation from the opening balance to the closing balance for each of the following, if applicable:

(a)   the net defined benefit liability (asset), showing separate reconciliations for:

(i)   plan assets.

(ii)   the present value of the defined benefit obligation.

(iii)   the effect of the asset ceiling.

(b)   any reimbursement rights. An entity shall also describe the relationship between any reimbursement right and the related obligation.

141   Each reconciliation listed in paragraph 140 shall show each of the following, if applicable:

(a)   current service cost.

(b)   interest income or expense.

    (c)   remeasurements of the net defined benefit liability (asset), showing separately:

        (i)   the return on plan assets, excluding amounts included in interest in (b).

        (ii)   actuarial gains and losses arising from changes in demographic assumptions (see paragraph 76(a)).

        (iii)   actuarial gains and losses arising from changes in financial assumptions (see paragraph 76(b)).

        (iv)   changes in the effect of limiting a net defined benefit asset to the asset ceiling, excluding amounts included in interest in (b). An entity shall also disclose how it determined the maximum economic benefit available, ie whether those benefits would be in the form of refunds, reductions in future contributions or a combination of both.

    (d)   past service cost and gains and losses arising from settlements. As permitted by paragraph 100, past service cost and gains and losses arising from settlements need not be distinguished if they occur together.

    (e)   the effect of changes in foreign exchange rates.

    (f)   contributions to the plan, showing separately those by the employer and by plan participants.

    (g)   payments from the plan, showing separately the amount paid in respect of any settlements.

    (h)   the effects of business combinations and disposals.

142   An entity shall disaggregate the fair value of the plan assets into classes that distinguish the nature and risks of those assets, subdividing each class of plan asset into those that have a quoted market price in an active market (as defined in AASB 13 *Fair Value Measurement*) and those that do not. For example, and considering the level of disclosure discussed in paragraph 136, an entity could distinguish between:

    (a)   cash and cash equivalents;

    (b)   equity instruments (segregated by industry type, company size, geography etc);

    (c)   debt instruments (segregated by type of issuer, credit quality, geography etc);

    (d)   real estate (segregated by geography etc);

    (e)   derivatives (segregated by type of underlying risk in the contract, for example, interest rate contracts, foreign exchange contracts, equity contracts, credit contracts, longevity swaps etc);

    (f)   investment funds (segregated by type of fund);

    (g)   asset-backed securities; and

    (h)   structured debt.

143   An entity shall disclose the fair value of the entity's own transferable financial instruments held as plan assets, and the fair value of plan assets that are property occupied by, or other assets used by, the entity.

144   An entity shall disclose the significant actuarial assumptions used to determine the present value of the defined benefit obligation (see paragraph 76). Such disclosure shall be in absolute terms (eg as an absolute percentage, and not just as a margin between different percentages and other variables). When an entity provides disclosures in total for a grouping of plans, it shall provide such disclosures in the form of weighted averages or relatively narrow ranges.

Amount, timing and uncertainty of future cash flows

145   An entity shall disclose:

    (a)   a sensitivity analysis for each significant actuarial assumption (as disclosed under paragraph 144) as of the end of the reporting period, showing how the defined benefit obligation would have been affected by changes in the relevant actuarial assumption that were reasonably possible at that date.

(b)   the methods and assumptions used in preparing the sensitivity analyses required by (a) and the limitations of those methods.

(c)   changes from the previous period in the methods and assumptions used in preparing the sensitivity analyses, and the reasons for such changes.

146   An entity shall disclose a description of any asset-liability matching strategies used by the plan or the entity, including the use of annuities and other techniques, such as longevity swaps, to manage risk.

147   To provide an indication of the effect of the defined benefit plan on the entity's future cash flows, an entity shall disclose:

(a)   a description of any funding arrangements and funding policy that affect future contributions.

(b)   the expected contributions to the plan for the next annual reporting period.

(c)   information about the maturity profile of the defined benefit obligation. This will include the weighted average duration of the defined benefit obligation and may include other information about the distribution of the timing of benefit payments, such as a maturity analysis of the benefit payments.

Multi-employer plans

148   If an entity participates in a multi-employer defined benefit plan, it shall disclose:

(a)   a description of the funding arrangements, including the method used to determine the entity's rate of contributions and any minimum funding requirements.

(b)   a description of the extent to which the entity can be liable to the plan for other entities' obligations under the terms and conditions of the multi-employer plan.

(c)   a description of any agreed allocation of a deficit or surplus on:

(i)   wind-up of the plan; or

(ii)   the entity's withdrawal from the plan.

(d)   if the entity accounts for that plan as if it were a defined contribution plan in accordance with paragraph 34, it shall disclose the following, in addition to the information required by (a)–(c) and instead of the information required by paragraphs 139–147:

(i)   the fact that the plan is a defined benefit plan.

(ii)   the reason why sufficient information is not available to enable the entity to account for the plan as a defined benefit plan.

(iii)   the expected contributions to the plan for the next annual reporting period.

(iv)   information about any deficit or surplus in the plan that may affect the amount of future contributions, including the basis used to determine that deficit or surplus and the implications, if any, for the entity.

(v)   an indication of the level of participation of the entity in the plan compared with other participating entities. Examples of measures that might provide such an indication include the entity's proportion of the total contributions to the plan or the entity's proportion of the total number of active members, retired members, and former members entitled to benefits, if that information is available.

Defined benefit plans that share risks between entities under common control

149   If an entity participates in a defined benefit plan that shares risks between entities under common control, it shall disclose:

(a) the contractual agreement or stated policy for charging the net defined benefit cost or the fact that there is no such policy.

(b) the policy for determining the contribution to be paid by the entity.

(c) if the entity accounts for an allocation of the net defined benefit cost as noted in paragraph 41, all the information about the plan as a whole required by paragraphs 135–147.

(d) if the entity accounts for the contribution payable for the period as noted in paragraph 41, the information about the plan as a whole required by paragraphs 135–137, 139, 142–144 and 147(a) and (b).

150 The information required by paragraph 149(c) and (d) can be disclosed by cross-reference to disclosures in another group entity's financial statements if:

(a) that group entity's financial statements separately identify and disclose the information required about the plan; and

(b) that group entity's financial statements are available to users of the financial statements on the same terms as the financial statements of the entity and at the same time as, or earlier than, the financial statements of the entity.

Disclosure requirements in other Australian Accounting Standards

151 Where required by AASB 124 an entity discloses information about:

(a) related party transactions with post-employment benefit plans; and

(b) post-employment benefits for key management personnel.

152 Where required by AASB 137 an entity discloses information about contingent liabilities arising from post-employment benefit obligations.

Other long-term employee benefits

153 Other long-term employee benefits include items such as the following, if not expected to be settled wholly before twelve months after the end of the annual reporting period in which the employees render the related service:

(a) long-term paid absences such as long-service or sabbatical leave;

(b) jubilee or other long-service benefits;

(c) long-term disability benefits;

(d) profit-sharing and bonuses; and

(e) deferred remuneration.

154 The measurement of other long-term employee benefits is not usually subject to the same degree of uncertainty as the measurement of post-employment benefits. For this reason, this Standard requires a simplified method of accounting for other long-term employee benefits. Unlike the accounting required for post-employment benefits, this method does not recognise remeasurements in other comprehensive income.

Recognition and measurement

155 **In recognising and measuring the surplus or deficit in an other long-term employee benefit plan, an entity shall apply paragraphs 56–98 and 113–115. An entity shall apply paragraphs 116–119 in recognising and measuring any reimbursement right.**

156 **For other long-term employee benefits, an entity shall recognise the net total of the following amounts in profit or loss, except to the extent that another Australian Accounting Standard requires or permits their inclusion in the cost of an asset:**

(a) **service cost (see paragraphs 66–112);**

(b) **net interest on the net defined benefit liability (asset) (see paragraphs 123–126); and**

(c)   **remeasurements of the net defined benefit liability (asset) (see paragraphs 127–130).**

157   One form of other long-term employee benefit is long-term disability benefit. If the level of benefit depends on the length of service, an obligation arises when the service is rendered. Measurement of that obligation reflects the probability that payment will be required and the length of time for which payment is expected to be made. If the level of benefit is the same for any disabled employee regardless of years of service, the expected cost of those benefits is recognised when an event occurs that causes a long-term disability.

Disclosure

158   Although this Standard does not require specific disclosures about other long-term employee benefits, other Australian Accounting Standards may require disclosures. For example, AASB 124 requires disclosures about employee benefits for key management personnel. AASB 101 requires disclosure of employee benefits expense.

Termination benefits

159   This Standard deals with termination benefits separately from other employee benefits because the event that gives rise to an obligation is the termination of employment rather than employee service. Termination benefits result from either an entity's decision to terminate the employment or an employee's decision to accept an entity's offer of benefits in exchange for termination of employment.

160   Termination benefits do not include employee benefits resulting from termination of employment at the request of the employee without an entity's offer, or as a result of mandatory retirement requirements, because those benefits are post-employment benefits. Some entities provide a lower level of benefit for termination of employment at the request of the employee (in substance, a post-employment benefit) than for termination of employment at the request of the entity. The difference between the benefit provided for termination of employment at the request of the employee and a higher benefit provided at the request of the entity is a termination benefit.

161   The form of the employee benefit does not determine whether it is provided in exchange for service or in exchange for termination of the employee's employment. Termination benefits are typically lump sum payments, but sometimes also include:

(a)   enhancement of post-employment benefits, either indirectly through an employee benefit plan or directly.

(b)   salary until the end of a specified notice period if the employee renders no further service that provides economic benefits to the entity.

162   Indicators that an employee benefit is provided in exchange for services include the following:

(a)   the benefit is conditional on future service being provided (including benefits that increase if further service is provided).

(b)   the benefit is provided in accordance with the terms of an employee benefit plan.

163   Some termination benefits are provided in accordance with the terms of an existing employee benefit plan. For example, they may be specified by statute, employment contract or union agreement, or may be implied as a result of the employer's past practice of providing similar benefits. As another example, if an entity makes an offer of benefits available for more than a short period, or there is more than a short period between the offer and the expected date of actual termination, the entity considers whether it has established a new employee benefit plan and hence whether the benefits offered under that plan are termination benefits or post-employment benefits. Employee benefits provided in accordance with the terms of an employee benefit plan are termination benefits if they both result from an entity's decision to terminate an employee's employment and are not conditional on future service being provided.

164   Some employee benefits are provided regardless of the reason for the employee's departure. The payment of such benefits is certain (subject to any vesting or minimum service requirements) but the timing of their payment is uncertain. Although such benefits are described in some jurisdictions as termination indemnities or termination gratuities, they are post-employment benefits rather than termination benefits, and an entity accounts for them as post-employment benefits.

Recognition

165   An entity shall recognise a liability and expense for termination benefits at the earlier of the following dates:

(a)   when the entity can no longer withdraw the offer of those benefits; and

(b)   when the entity recognises costs for a restructuring that is within the scope of AASB 137 and involves the payment of termination benefits.

166   For termination benefits payable as a result of an employee's decision to accept an offer of benefits in exchange for the termination of employment, the time when an entity can no longer withdraw the offer of termination benefits is the earlier of:

(a)   when the employee accepts the offer; and

(b)   when a restriction (eg a legal, regulatory or contractual requirement or other restriction) on the entity's ability to withdraw the offer takes effect. This would be when the offer is made, if the restriction existed at the time of the offer.

167   For termination benefits payable as a result of an entity's decision to terminate an employee's employment, the entity can no longer withdraw the offer when the entity has communicated to the affected employees a plan of termination meeting all of the following criteria:

(a)   Actions required to complete the plan indicate that it is unlikely that significant changes to the plan will be made.

(b)   The plan identifies the number of employees whose employment is to be terminated, their job classifications or functions and their locations (but the plan need not identify each individual employee) and the expected completion date.

(c)   The plan establishes the termination benefits that employees will receive in sufficient detail that employees can determine the type and amount of benefits they will receive when their employment is terminated.

168   When an entity recognises termination benefits, the entity may also have to account for a plan amendment or a curtailment of other employee benefits (see paragraph 103).

Measurement

169   An entity shall measure termination benefits on initial recognition, and shall measure and recognise subsequent changes, in accordance with the nature of the employee benefit, provided that if the termination benefits are an enhancement to post-employment benefits, the entity shall apply the requirements for post-employment benefits. Otherwise:

(a)   if the termination benefits are expected to be settled wholly before twelve months after the end of the annual reporting period in which the termination benefit is recognised, the entity shall apply the requirements for short-term employee benefits.

(b)   if the termination benefits are not expected to be settled wholly before twelve months after the end of the annual reporting period, the entity shall apply the requirements for other long-term employee benefits.

170   Because termination benefits are not provided in exchange for service, paragraphs 70–74 relating to the attribution of the benefit to periods of service are not relevant.

Example illustrating paragraphs 159–170

Background

As a result of a recent acquisition, an entity plans to close a factory in ten months and, at that time, terminate the employment of all of the remaining employees at the factory. Because the entity needs the expertise of the employees at the factory to complete some contracts, it announces a plan of termination as follows.

Each employee who stays and renders service until the closure of the factory will receive on the termination date a cash payment of CU30,000. Employees leaving before closure of the factory will receive CU10,000.

There are 120 employees at the factory. At the time of announcing the plan, the entity expects 20 of them to leave before closure. Therefore, the total expected cash outflows under the plan are CU3,200,000 (ie 20 × CU10,000 + 100 × CU30,000). As required by paragraph 160, the entity accounts for benefits provided in exchange for termination of employment as termination benefits and accounts for benefits provided in exchange for services as short-term employee benefits.

Termination benefits

The benefit provided in exchange for termination of employment is CU10,000. This is the amount that an entity would have to pay for terminating the employment regardless of whether the employees stay and render service until closure of the factory or they leave before closure. Even though the employees can leave before closure, the termination of all employees' employment is a result of the entity's decision to close the factory and terminate their employment (ie all employees will leave employment when the factory closes). Therefore the entity recognises a liability of CU1,200,000 (ie 120 × CU10,000) for the termination benefits provided in accordance with the employee benefit plan at the earlier of when the plan of termination is announced and when the entity recognises the restructuring costs associated with the closure of the factory.

Benefits provided in exchange for service

The incremental benefits that employees will receive if they provide services for the full ten-month period are in exchange for services provided over that period. The entity accounts for them as short-term employee benefits because the entity expects to settle them before twelve months after the end of the annual reporting period. In this example, discounting is not required, so an expense of CU200,000 (ie CU2,000,000 ÷ 10) is recognised in each month during the service period of ten months, with a corresponding increase in the carrying amount of the liability.

Disclosure

171   Although this Standard does not require specific disclosures about termination benefits, other Australian Accounting Standards may require disclosures. For example, AASB 124 requires disclosures about employee benefits for key management personnel. AASB 101 requires disclosure of employee benefits expense.

Transition and effective date

172   An entity shall apply this Standard for annual periods beginning on or after 1 January 2016. Earlier application is permitted for periods beginning on or after 1 January 2014 but before 1 January 2016. If an entity applies this Standard for an earlier period, it shall disclose that fact.

Aus172.1   Paragraphs 173(a) and (b) shall not be applied by an entity that has previously applied AASB 119, unless required to do so by another Standard.

173   An entity shall apply this Standard retrospectively, in accordance with AASB 108 *Accounting Policies, Changes in Accounting Estimates and Errors*, except that:

(a)   an entity need not adjust the carrying amount of assets outside the scope of this Standard for changes in employee benefit costs that were included in the carrying amount before the date of initial application. The date of initial application is the beginning of the earliest prior period presented in the first financial statements in which the entity adopts this Standard.

(b)   in financial statements for periods beginning before 1 January 2014, an entity need not present comparative information for the disclosures required by paragraph 145 about the sensitivity of the defined benefit obligation.

174   [Deleted by the AASB]

175   AASB 2014-1 *Amendments to Australian Accounting Standards*, issued in June 2014, amended paragraphs 93–94 in the previous version of this Standard. An entity shall apply those amendments for annual periods beginning on or after 1 July 2014 retrospectively in accordance with AASB 108 *Accounting Policies, Changes in Accounting Estimates and Errors*. Earlier application is permitted. If an entity applies those amendments for an earlier period, it shall disclose that fact.

176   AASB 2015-1 *Amendments to Australian Accounting Standards – Annual Improvements to Australian Accounting Standards 2012–2014 Cycle*, issued in January 2015, amended the previous version of this Standard as follows: amended paragraph 83 and added paragraph 177. An entity shall apply that amendment for annual periods beginning on or after 1 January 2016. Earlier application is permitted. If an entity applies that amendment for an earlier period it shall disclose that fact.

177   An entity shall apply the amendment in paragraph 176 from the beginning of the earliest comparative period presented in the first financial statements in which the entity applies the amendment. Any initial adjustment arising from the application of the amendment shall be recognised in retained earnings at the beginning of that period.

Commencement of the legislative instrument

Aus177.1   For legal purposes, this legislative instrument commences on 31 December 2015.

Withdrawal of AASB pronouncements

Aus177.2   This Standard repeals AASB 119 *Employee Benefits* issued in September 2011. Despite the repeal, after the time this Standard starts to apply under section 334 of the Corporations Act (either generally or in relation to an individual entity), the repealed Standard continues to apply in relation to any period ending before that time as if the repeal had not occurred.

[Note: When this Standard applies under section 334 of the Corporations Act (either generally or in relation to an individual entity), it supersedes the application of the repealed Standard.]

APPENDIX A
APPLICATION GUIDANCE

This appendix is an integral part of the Standard. It describes the application of paragraphs 92–93 and has the same authority as the other parts of the Standard.

A1   The accounting requirements for contributions from employees or third parties are illustrated in the diagram below.

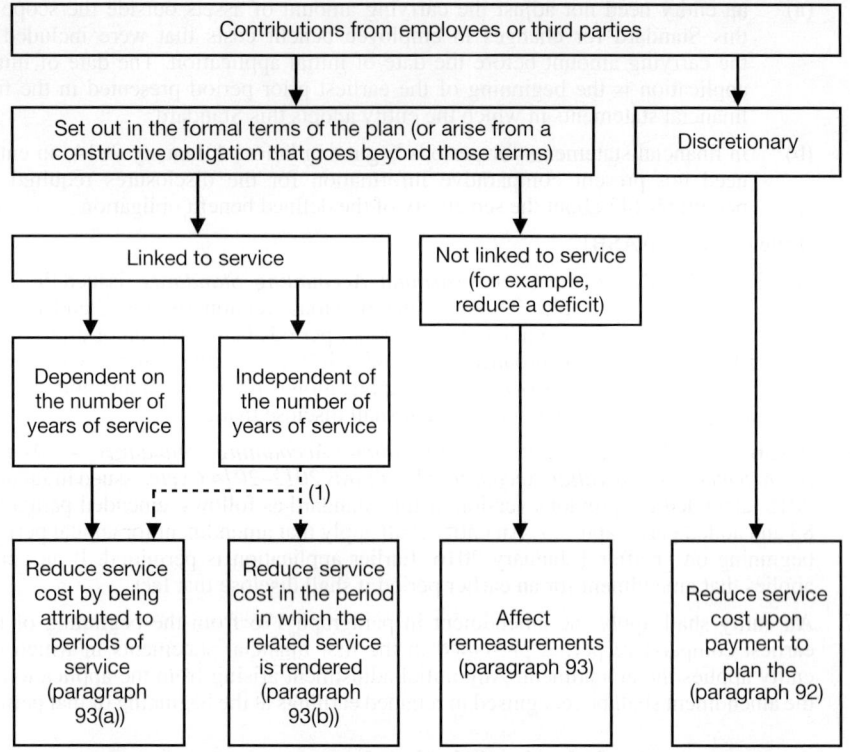

(1) This dotted arrow means that an entity is permitted to choose either accounting.

APPENDIX C
AUSTRALIAN REDUCED DISCLOSURE REQUIREMENT

This appendix is an integral part of the Standard.

AusC1   The following do not apply to entities preparing general purpose financial statements under Australian Accounting Standards – Reduced Disclosure Requirements:

(a)   in paragraph 25, the text "For example, AASB 124 requires disclosures about employee benefits for key management personnel. AASB 101 *Presentation of Financial Statements* requires disclosure of employee benefits expense.";

(b)   paragraphs 54, 135(c), 137, 139(c), 141(a)–(e), 141(h), 145–147, 148(d)(v) and 149–151;

(c)   in paragraph 139(a), the text ", including:" and associated paragraphs (i)–(iii);

(d)   in paragraph 140(b), the text "An entity shall also describe the relationship between any reimbursement right and the related obligation.";

(e) in paragraph 141(f), the text ", showing separately those by the employer and by plan participants";

(f) in paragraph 141(g), the text ", showing separately the amount paid in respect of any settlements";

(g) in paragraph 142, the text ", subdividing each class ... could distinguish between:" and associated paragraphs (a)–(h);

(h) in paragraph 144, the text "Such disclosure shall ... relatively narrow ranges.";

(i) in paragraph 148(d)(iv), the text ", including the basis used to determine that deficit or surplus";

(j) in paragraph 158, the text "AASB 124 requires disclosures about employee benefits for key management personnel."; and

(k) in paragraph 171, the text "AASB 124 requires disclosures about employee benefits for key management personnel."

Entities applying Australian Accounting Standards – Reduced Disclosure Requirements may elect to comply with some or all of these excluded requirements.

AusC2 The requirements that do not apply to entities preparing general purpose financial statements under Australian Accounting Standards – Reduced Disclosure Requirements are also identified in this Standard by shading of the relevant text.

AusC3 **The RDR paragraph in this Standard applies only to entities preparing general purpose financial statements under Australian Accounting Standards – Reduced Disclosure Requirements.**

RDR140.1 An entity applying Australian Accounting Standards – Reduced Disclosure Requirements is not required to disclose the reconciliations specified in paragraphs 140 and 141 for prior periods.

DELETED IAS 19 TEXT

Deleted IAS 19 text is not part of AASB 119.

174 IFRS 13, issued in May 2011, amended the definition of fair value in paragraph 8 and amended paragraph 113. An entity shall apply those amendments when it applies IFRS 13.

AASB 120

Accounting for Government Grants and Disclosure of Government Assistance

(Reissued August 2015)

CONTENTS

COMPARISON WITH IAS 20

ACCOUNTING STANDARD

AASB 120 *ACCOUNTING FOR GOVERNMENT GRANTS AND DISCLOSURE OF GOVERNMENT ASSISTANCE*

DELETED IAS 20 TEXT

BASIS FOR CONCLUSIONS ON IAS 20 (available on the AASB website)

Australian Accounting Standard AASB 120 *Accounting for Government Grants and Disclosure of Government Assistance* is set out in paragraphs 1 – Aus48.2. All the paragraphs have equal authority. Paragraphs in **bold type** state the main principles. AASB 120 is to be read in the context of other Australian Accounting Standards, including AASB 1048 *Interpretation of Standards*, which identifies the Australian Accounting Interpretations, and AASB 1057 *Application of Australian Accounting Standards*. In the absence of explicit guidance, AASB 108 *Accounting Policies, Changes in Accounting Estimates and Errors* provides a basis for selecting and applying accounting policies.

COMPARISON WITH IAS 20

AASB 120 *Accounting for Government Grants and Disclosure of Government Assistance* incorporates IAS 20 *Accounting for Government Grants and Disclosure of Government Assistance* issued by the International Accounting Standards Board (IASB). Australian-specific paragraphs (which are not included in IAS 20) are identified with the prefix "Aus". Paragraphs that apply only to not-for-profit entities begin by identifying their limited applicability.

Tier 1

For-profit entities complying with AASB 120 also comply with IAS 20.

Not-for-profit entities' compliance with IAS 20 will depend on whether any "Aus" paragraphs that specifically apply to not-for-profit entities provide additional guidance or contain applicable requirements that are inconsistent with IAS 20.

AASB 1053 *Application of Tiers of Australian Accounting Standards* explains the two tiers of reporting requirements.

ACCOUNTING STANDARD AASB 120

The Australian Accounting Standards Board makes Accounting Standard AASB 120 *Accounting for Government Grants and Disclosure of Government Assistance* under section 334 of the *Corporations Act 2001*.

Kris Peach

Dated 7 August 2015   Chair – AASB

ACCOUNTING STANDARD AASB 120
ACCOUNTING FOR GOVERNMENT GRANTS AND DISCLOSURE OF GOVERNMENT ASSISTANCE[1]

Scope

1   **This Standard shall be applied in accounting for, and in the disclosure of, government grants and in the disclosure of other forms of government assistance.**

2   This Standard does not deal with:

(a)   the special problems arising in accounting for government grants in financial statements reflecting the effects of changing prices or in supplementary information of a similar nature.

(b)   government assistance that is provided for an entity in the form of benefits that are available in determining taxable profit or tax loss, or are determined or limited on the basis of income tax liability. Examples of such benefits are income tax holidays, investment tax credits, accelerated depreciation allowances and reduced income tax rates.

(c)   government participation in the ownership of the entity.

(d)   government grants covered by AASB 141 *Agriculture*.

---

1   As part of AASB 2008-5 *Amendments to Australian Accounting Standards arising from the Annual Improvements Project* issued in July 2008 the Board amended terminology used in this Standard to be consistent with other Australian Accounting Standards as follows: (a) 'taxable income' was amended to 'taxable profit or tax loss', (b) 'recognised as income/expense' was amended to 'recognised in profit or loss', (c) 'credited directly to shareholders' interests/equity' was amended to 'recognised outside profit or loss', and (d) 'revision to an accounting estimate' was amended to 'change in accounting estimate'.

Definitions

3   The following terms are used in this Standard with the meanings specified:

Government refers to government, government agencies and similar bodies whether local, national or international.

Government assistance is action by government designed to provide an economic benefit specific to an entity or range of entities qualifying under certain criteria. Government assistance for the purpose of this Standard does not include benefits provided only indirectly through action affecting general trading conditions, such as the provision of infrastructure in development areas or the imposition of trading constraints on competitors.

Government grants are assistance by government in the form of transfers of resources to an entity in return for past or future compliance with certain conditions relating to the operating activities of the entity. They exclude those forms of government assistance which cannot reasonably have a value placed upon them and transactions with government which cannot be distinguished from the normal trading transactions of the entity.[2]

Grants related to assets are government grants whose primary condition is that an entity qualifying for them should purchase, construct or otherwise acquire long-term assets. Subsidiary conditions may also be attached restricting the type or location of the assets or the periods during which they are to be acquired or held.

Grants related to income are government grants other than those related to assets.

Forgivable loans are loans which the lender undertakes to waive repayment of under certain prescribed conditions.

Fair value is the price that would be received to sell an asset or paid to transfer a liability in an orderly transaction between market participants at the measurement date. (See AASB 13 *Fair Value Measurement*.)

4   Government assistance takes many forms varying both in the nature of the assistance given and in the conditions which are usually attached to it. The purpose of the assistance may be to encourage an entity to embark on a course of action which it would not normally have taken if the assistance was not provided.

5   The receipt of government assistance by an entity may be significant for the preparation of the financial statements for two reasons. Firstly, if resources have been transferred, an appropriate method of accounting for the transfer must be found. Secondly, it is desirable to give an indication of the extent to which the entity has benefited from such assistance during the reporting period. This facilitates comparison of an entity's financial statements with those of prior periods and with those of other entities.

6   Government grants are sometimes called by other names such as subsidies, subventions, or premiums.

Government grants

7   Government grants, including non-monetary grants at fair value, shall not be recognised until there is reasonable assurance that:

(a)   the entity will comply with the conditions attaching to them; and

(b)   the grants will be received.

8   A government grant is not recognised until there is reasonable assurance that the entity will comply with the conditions attaching to it, and that the grant will be received. Receipt of a grant does not of itself provide conclusive evidence that the conditions attaching to the grant have been or will be fulfilled.

---

2   See also Interpretation 110 *Government Assistance—No Specific Relation to Operating Activities*, as identified in AASB 1048 *Interpretation of Standards*.

9   The manner in which a grant is received does not affect the accounting method to be adopted in regard to the grant. Thus a grant is accounted for in the same manner whether it is received in cash or as a reduction of a liability to the government.

10   A forgivable loan from government is treated as a government grant when there is reasonable assurance that the entity will meet the terms for forgiveness of the loan.

10A   The benefit of a government loan at a below-market rate of interest is treated as a government grant. The loan shall be recognised and measured in accordance with AASB 9 *Financial Instruments*. The benefit of the below-market rate of interest shall be measured as the difference between the initial carrying value of the loan determined in accordance with AASB 9 and the proceeds received. The benefit is accounted for in accordance with this Standard. The entity shall consider the conditions and obligations that have been, or must be, met when identifying the costs for which the benefit of the loan is intended to compensate.

11   Once a government grant is recognised, any related contingent liability or contingent asset is treated in accordance with AASB 137 *Provisions, Contingent Liabilities and Contingent Assets*.

12   Government grants shall be recognised in profit or loss on a systematic basis over the periods in which the entity recognises as expenses the related costs for which the grants are intended to compensate.

13   There are two broad approaches to the accounting for government grants: the capital approach, under which a grant is recognised outside profit or loss, and the income approach, under which a grant is recognised in profit or loss over one or more periods.

14   Those in support of the capital approach argue as follows:

(a)   government grants are a financing device and should be dealt with as such in the statement of financial position rather than be recognised in profit or loss to offset the items of expense that they finance. Because no repayment is expected, such grants should be recognised outside profit or loss.

(b)   it is inappropriate to recognise government grants in profit or loss, because they are not earned but represent an incentive provided by government without related costs.

15   Arguments in support of the income approach are as follows:

(a)   because government grants are receipts from a source other than shareholders, they should not be recognised directly in equity but should be recognised in profit or loss in appropriate periods.

(b)   government grants are rarely gratuitous. The entity earns them through compliance with their conditions and meeting the envisaged obligations. They should therefore be recognised in profit or loss over the periods in which the entity recognises as expenses the related costs for which the grant is intended to compensate.

(c)   because income and other taxes are expenses, it is logical to deal also with government grants, which are an extension of fiscal policies, in profit or loss.

16   It is fundamental to the income approach that government grants should be recognised in profit or loss on a systematic basis over the periods in which the entity recognises as expenses the related costs for which the grant is intended to compensate. Recognition of government grants in profit or loss on a receipts basis is not in accordance with the accrual accounting assumption (see AASB 101 *Presentation of Financial Statements*) and would be acceptable only if no basis existed for allocating a grant to periods other than the one in which it was received.

17   In most cases the periods over which an entity recognises the costs or expenses related to a government grant are readily ascertainable. Thus grants in recognition of specific expenses are recognised in profit or loss in the same period as the relevant expenses. Similarly, grants related to depreciable assets are usually recognised in profit or loss over the periods and in the proportions in which depreciation expense on those assets is recognised.

18   Grants related to non-depreciable assets may also require the fulfilment of certain obligations and would then be recognised in profit or loss over the periods that bear the cost of meeting the obligations. As an example, a grant of land may be conditional upon the erection of a building on the site and it may be appropriate to recognise the grant in profit or loss over the life of the building.

19   Grants are sometimes received as part of a package of financial or fiscal aids to which a number of conditions are attached. In such cases, care is needed in identifying the conditions giving rise to costs and expenses which determine the periods over which the grant will be earned. It may be appropriate to allocate part of a grant on one basis and part on another.

20   A government grant that becomes receivable as compensation for expenses or losses already incurred or for the purpose of giving immediate financial support to the entity with no future related costs shall be recognised in profit or loss of the period in which it becomes receivable.

21   In some circumstances, a government grant may be awarded for the purpose of giving immediate financial support to an entity rather than as an incentive to undertake specific expenditures. Such grants may be confined to a particular entity and may not be available to a whole class of beneficiaries. These circumstances may warrant recognising a grant in profit or loss of the period in which the entity qualifies to receive it, with disclosure to ensure that its effect is clearly understood.

22   A government grant may become receivable by an entity as compensation for expenses or losses incurred in a previous period. Such a grant is recognised in profit or loss of the period in which it becomes receivable, with disclosure to ensure that its effect is clearly understood.

Non-monetary government grants

23   A government grant may take the form of a transfer of a non-monetary asset, such as land or other resources, for the use of the entity. In these circumstances it is usual to assess the fair value of the non-monetary asset and to account for both grant and asset at that fair value. An alternative course that is sometimes followed is to record both asset and grant at a nominal amount.

Presentation of grants related to assets

24   Government grants related to assets, including non-monetary grants at fair value, shall be presented in the statement of financial position either by setting up the grant as deferred income or by deducting the grant in arriving at the carrying amount of the asset.

25   Two methods of presentation in financial statements of grants (or the appropriate portions of grants) related to assets are regarded as acceptable alternatives.

26   One method recognises the grant as deferred income that is recognised in profit or loss on a systematic basis over the useful life of the asset.

27   The other method deducts the grant in calculating the carrying amount of the asset. The grant is recognised in profit or loss over the life of a depreciable asset as a reduced depreciation expense.

28   The purchase of assets and the receipt of related grants can cause major movements in the cash flow of an entity. For this reason and in order to show the gross investment in assets, such movements are often disclosed as separate items in the statement of cash flows regardless of whether or not the grant is deducted from the related asset for presentation purposes in the statement of financial position.

Presentation of grants related to income

29   Grants related to income are presented as part of profit or loss, either separately or under a general heading such as 'Other income'; alternatively, they are deducted in reporting the related expense.

29A [Deleted]

30 Supporters of the first method claim that it is inappropriate to net income and expense items and that separation of the grant from the expense facilitates comparison with other expenses not affected by a grant. For the second method it is argued that the expenses might well not have been incurred by the entity if the grant had not been available and presentation of the expense without offsetting the grant may therefore be misleading.

31 Both methods are regarded as acceptable for the presentation of grants related to income. Disclosure of the grant may be necessary for a proper understanding of the financial statements. Disclosure of the effect of the grants on any item of income or expense which is required to be separately disclosed is usually appropriate.

Repayment of government grants

32 A government grant that becomes repayable shall be accounted for as a change in accounting estimate (see AASB 108 *Accounting Policies, Changes in Accounting Estimates and Errors*). Repayment of a grant related to income shall be applied first against any unamortised deferred credit recognised in respect of the grant. To the extent that the repayment exceeds any such deferred credit, or when no deferred credit exists, the repayment shall be recognised immediately in profit or loss. Repayment of a grant related to an asset shall be recognised by increasing the carrying amount of the asset or reducing the deferred income balance by the amount repayable. The cumulative additional depreciation that would have been recognised in profit or loss to date in the absence of the grant shall be recognised immediately in profit or loss.

33 Circumstances giving rise to repayment of a grant related to an asset may require consideration to be given to the possible impairment of the new carrying amount of the asset.

Government assistance

34 Excluded from the definition of government grants in paragraph 3 are certain forms of government assistance which cannot reasonably have a value placed upon them and transactions with government which cannot be distinguished from the normal trading transactions of the entity.

35 Examples of assistance that cannot reasonably have a value placed upon them are free technical or marketing advice and the provision of guarantees. An example of assistance that cannot be distinguished from the normal trading transactions of the entity is a government procurement policy that is responsible for a portion of the entity's sales. The existence of the benefit might be unquestioned but any attempt to segregate the trading activities from government assistance could well be arbitrary.

36 The significance of the benefit in the above examples may be such that disclosure of the nature, extent and duration of the assistance is necessary in order that the financial statements may not be misleading.

37 [Deleted]

38 In this Standard, government assistance does not include the provision of infrastructure by improvement to the general transport and communication network and the supply of improved facilities such as irrigation or water reticulation which is available on an ongoing indeterminate basis for the benefit of an entire local community.

Disclosure

39 The following matters shall be disclosed:

   (a) the accounting policy adopted for government grants, including the methods of presentation adopted in the financial statements;

AASB

(b)   the nature and extent of government grants recognised in the financial statements and an indication of other forms of government assistance from which the entity has directly benefited; and

(c)   unfulfilled conditions and other contingencies attaching to government assistance that has been recognised.

Transitional provisions

40   [Deleted by the AASB]

Effective date

41   This Standard becomes operative for financial statements covering periods beginning on or after 1 January 2018. Earlier application is permitted for periods beginning after 24 July 2014 but before 1 January 2018. If an entity applies the amendments for an earlier period it shall disclose that fact.

42   [Deleted by the AASB]

43   In the previous version of this Standard, paragraph 37 was deleted and paragraph 10A added by AASB 2008-5 *Amendments to Australian Accounting Standards arising from the Annual Improvements Project* issued in July 2008. An entity shall apply those amendments prospectively to government loans received in periods beginning on or after 1 January 2009. Earlier application is permitted. If an entity applies the amendments for an earlier period it shall disclose that fact.

44   [Deleted]

45–46 [Deleted by the AASB]

47   [Deleted]

48   AASB 2010-7 *Amendments to Australian Accounting Standards arising from AASB 9 (December 2010)* (as amended) amended the previous version of this Standard as follows: amended paragraph 10A. Paragraph 44, added by AASB 2010-7, was deleted by AASB 2014-1 *Amendments to Australian Accounting Standards*. Paragraph 47, added by AASB 2014-1, was deleted by AASB 2014-7 *Amendments to Australian Accounting Standards arising from AASB 9 (December 2014)*. An entity shall apply those amendments when it applies AASB 9.

Commencement of the legislative instrument

Aus48.1   For legal purposes, this legislative instrument commences on 31 December 2017.

Withdrawal of AASB pronouncements

Aus48.2   This Standard repeals AASB 120 *Accounting for Government Grants and Disclosure of Government Assistance* issued in July 2004. Despite the repeal, after the time this Standard starts to apply under section 334 of the Corporations Act (either generally or in relation to an individual entity), the repealed Standard continues to apply in relation to any period ending before that time as if the repeal had not occurred.

[Note: When this Standard applies under section 334 of the Corporations Act (either generally or in relation to an individual entity), it supersedes the application of the repealed Standard.]

DELETED IAS 20 TEXT

Deleted IAS 20 text is not part of AASB 120.

40   **An entity adopting the Standard for the first time shall:**

    (a)   **comply with the disclosure requirements, where appropriate; and**

    (b)   **either:**

       (i)   **adjust its financial statements for the change in accounting policy in accordance with IAS 8; or**

       (ii)   **apply the accounting provisions of the Standard only to grants or portions of grants becoming receivable or repayable after the effective date of the Standard.**

42   IAS 1 (as revised in 2007) amended the terminology used throughout IFRSs. In addition it added paragraph 29A. An entity shall apply those amendments for annual periods beginning on or after 1 January 2009. If an entity applies IAS 1 (revised 2007) for an earlier period, the amendments shall be applied for that earlier period.

45   IFRS 13, issued in May 2011, amended the definition of fair value in paragraph 3. An entity shall apply that amendment when it applies IFRS 13.

46   *Presentation of Items of Other Comprehensive Income* (Amendments to IAS 1), issued in June 2011, amended paragraph 29 and deleted paragraph 29A. An entity shall apply those amendments when it applies IAS 1 as amended in June 2011.

AASB 121

The Effects of Changes in Foreign Exchange Rates

(Reissued August 2015)

This note is not part of Accounting Standard AASB 121.

The following unincorporated amendments are not included in this Standard.

- AASB 16 *Leases* — Appendix D sets out the amendments to other Standards that are a consequence of the AASB issuing this Standard. It is applicable from 1 January 2019. Earlier application is permitted, but entities must apply AASB 15 *Revenue from Contracts with Customers* before applying this Standard.

Entities early-adopting any amendments with later application dates will need to refer to the amending Standards that have not yet been incorporated into compilations. The abovementioned unincorporated amendments may be located on the AASB website at www.aasb.gov.au or on the Federal Register of Legislation website at www.legislation.gov.au.

CONTENTS

APPENDIX

A. AUSTRALIAN REDUCED DISCLOSURE REQUIREMENTS

DELETED IAS 21 TEXT

BASIS FOR CONCLUSIONS ON IAS 21 (available on the AASB website)

> Australian Accounting Standard AASB 121 *The Effects of Changes in Foreign Exchange Rates* is set out in paragraphs 1 – Aus62.2 and Appendix A. All the paragraphs have equal authority. Paragraphs in **bold type** state the main principles. AASB 121 is to be read in the context of other Australian Accounting Standards, including AASB 1048 *Interpretation of Standards*, which identifies the Australian Accounting Interpretations, and AASB 1057 *Application of Australian Accounting Standards*. In the absence of explicit guidance, AASB 108 *Accounting Policies, Changes in Accounting Estimates and Errors* provides a basis for selecting and applying accounting policies.

COMPARISON WITH IAS 21

AASB 121 *The Effects of Changes in Foreign Exchange Rates* incorporates IAS 21 *The Effects of Changes in Foreign Exchange Rates* issued by the International Accounting Standards Board (IASB). Australian-specific paragraphs (which are not included in IAS 21) are identified with the prefix "Aus". Paragraphs that apply only to not-for-profit entities begin by identifying their limited applicability.

Tier 1

For-profit entities complying with AASB 121 also comply with IAS 21.

Not-for-profit entities' compliance with IAS 21 will depend on whether any "Aus" paragraphs that specifically apply to not-for-profit entities provide additional guidance or contain applicable requirements that are inconsistent with IAS 21.

Tier 2

Entities preparing general purpose financial statements under Australian Accounting Standards – Reduced Disclosure Requirements (Tier 2) will not be in compliance with IFRSs.

AASB 1053 *Application of Tiers of Australian Accounting Standards* explains the two tiers of reporting requirements.

ACCOUNTING STANDARD AASB 121

The Australian Accounting Standards Board makes Accounting Standard AASB 121 *The Effects of Changes in Foreign Exchange Rates* under section 334 of the *Corporations Act 2001*.

Kris Peach

Dated 7 August 2015   Chair – AASB

ACCOUNTING STANDARD AASB 121
THE EFFECTS OF CHANGES IN FOREIGN EXCHANGE RATES

Objective

1   An entity may carry on foreign activities in two ways. It may have transactions in foreign currencies or it may have foreign operations. In addition, an entity may present its financial statements in a foreign currency. The objective of this Standard is to prescribe how to include foreign currency transactions and foreign operations in the financial statements of an entity and how to translate financial statements into a presentation currency.

2   The principal issues are which exchange rate(s) to use and how to report the effects of changes in exchange rates in the financial statements.

Scope

3   This Standard shall be applied:[1]

   (a)   in accounting for transactions and balances in foreign currencies, except for those derivative transactions and balances that are within the scope of AASB 9 *Financial Instruments*;

   (b)   in translating the results and financial position of foreign operations that are included in the financial statements of the entity by consolidation or the equity method; and

   (c)   in translating an entity's results and financial position into a presentation currency.

4   AASB 9 applies to many foreign currency derivatives and, accordingly, these are excluded from the scope of this Standard. However, those foreign currency derivatives that are not within the scope of AASB 9 (eg some foreign currency derivatives that are embedded in other contracts) are within the scope of this Standard. In addition, this Standard applies when an entity translates amounts relating to derivatives from its functional currency to its presentation currency.

5   This Standard does not apply to hedge accounting for foreign currency items, including the hedging of a net investment in a foreign operation. AASB 9 applies to hedge accounting.

6   This Standard applies to the presentation of an entity's financial statements in a foreign currency and sets out requirements for the resulting financial statements to be described as complying with Australian Accounting Standards. For translations of financial information into a foreign currency that do not meet these requirements, this Standard specifies information to be disclosed.

7   This Standard does not apply to the presentation in a statement of cash flows of the cash flows arising from transactions in a foreign currency, or to the translation of cash flows of a foreign operation (see AASB 107 *Statement of Cash Flows*).

Definitions

8   The following terms are used in this Standard with the meanings specified:

   Closing rate is the spot exchange rate at the end of the reporting period.

---

1   See also Interpretation 107 *Introduction of the Euro*, as identified in AASB 1048 *Interpretation of Standards*.

Exchange difference is the difference resulting from translating a given number of units of one currency into another currency at different exchange rates.

Exchange rate is the ratio of exchange for two currencies.

Fair value is the price that would be received to sell an asset or paid to transfer a liability in an orderly transaction between market participants at the measurement date. (See AASB 13 *Fair Value Measurement*.)

Foreign currency is a currency other than the functional currency of the entity.

Foreign operation is an entity that is a subsidiary, associate, joint arrangement or branch of a reporting entity, the activities of which are based or conducted in a country or currency other than those of the reporting entity.

Functional currency is the currency of the primary economic environment in which the entity operates.

A *group* is a parent and all its subsidiaries.

Monetary items are units of currency held and assets and liabilities to be received or paid in a fixed or determinable number of units of currency.

Net investment in a foreign operation is the amount of the reporting entity's interest in the net assets of that operation.

Presentation currency is the currency in which the financial statements are presented.

Spot exchange rate is the exchange rate for immediate delivery.

Elaboration on the definitions

Functional currency

9   The primary economic environment in which an entity operates is normally the one in which it primarily generates and expends cash. An entity considers the following factors in determining its functional currency:

   (a)   the currency:

      (i)   that mainly influences sales prices for goods and services (this will often be the currency in which sales prices for its goods and services are denominated and settled); and

      (ii)   of the country whose competitive forces and regulations mainly determine the sales prices of its goods and services.

   (b)   the currency that mainly influences labour, material and other costs of providing goods or services (this will often be the currency in which such costs are denominated and settled).

10   The following factors may also provide evidence of an entity's functional currency:

   (a)   the currency in which funds from financing activities (ie issuing debt and equity instruments) are generated.

   (b)   the currency in which receipts from operating activities are usually retained.

11   The following additional factors are considered in determining the functional currency of a foreign operation, and whether its functional currency is the same as that of the reporting entity (the reporting entity, in this context, being the entity that has the foreign operation as its subsidiary, branch, associate or joint arrangement):

   (a)   whether the activities of the foreign operation are carried out as an extension of the reporting entity, rather than being carried out with a significant degree of autonomy. An example of the former is when the foreign operation only sells goods imported from the reporting entity and remits the proceeds to it. An example of the latter is when the operation accumulates cash and other monetary items, incurs expenses, generates income and arranges borrowings, all substantially in its local currency.

(b)   whether transactions with the reporting entity are a high or a low proportion of the foreign operation's activities.

(c)   whether cash flows from the activities of the foreign operation directly affect the cash flows of the reporting entity and are readily available for remittance to it.

(d)   whether cash flows from the activities of the foreign operation are sufficient to service existing and normally expected debt obligations without funds being made available by the reporting entity.

12   When the above indicators are mixed and the functional currency is not obvious, management uses its judgement to determine the functional currency that most faithfully represents the economic effects of the underlying transactions, events and conditions. As part of this approach, management gives priority to the primary indicators in paragraph 9 before considering the indicators in paragraphs 10 and 11, which are designed to provide additional supporting evidence to determine an entity's functional currency.

13   An entity's functional currency reflects the underlying transactions, events and conditions that are relevant to it. Accordingly, once determined, the functional currency is not changed unless there is a change in those underlying transactions, events and conditions.

14   If the functional currency is the currency of a hyperinflationary economy, the entity's financial statements are restated in accordance with AASB 129 *Financial Reporting in Hyperinflationary Economies*. An entity cannot avoid restatement in accordance with AASB 129 by, for example, adopting as its functional currency a currency other than the functional currency determined in accordance with this Standard (such as the functional currency of its parent).

Net investment in a foreign operation

15   An entity may have a monetary item that is receivable from or payable to a foreign operation. An item for which settlement is neither planned nor likely to occur in the foreseeable future is, in substance, a part of the entity's net investment in that foreign operation, and is accounted for in accordance with paragraphs 32 and 33. Such monetary items may include long-term receivables or loans. They do not include trade receivables or trade payables.

15A   The entity that has a monetary item receivable from or payable to a foreign operation described in paragraph 15 may be any subsidiary of the group. For example, an entity has two subsidiaries, A and B. Subsidiary B is a foreign operation. Subsidiary A grants a loan to Subsidiary B. Subsidiary A's loan receivable from Subsidiary B would be part of the entity's net investment in Subsidiary B if settlement of the loan is neither planned nor likely to occur in the foreseeable future. This would also be true if Subsidiary A were itself a foreign operation.

Monetary items

16   The essential feature of a monetary item is a right to receive (or an obligation to deliver) a fixed or determinable number of units of currency. Examples include: pensions and other employee benefits to be paid in cash; provisions that are to be settled in cash; and cash dividends that are recognised as a liability. Similarly, a contract to receive (or deliver) a variable number of the entity's own equity instruments or a variable amount of assets in which the fair value to be received (or delivered) equals a fixed or determinable number of units of currency is a monetary item. Conversely, the essential feature of a non-monetary item is the absence of a right to receive (or an obligation to deliver) a fixed or determinable number of units of currency. Examples include: amounts prepaid for goods and services (eg prepaid rent); goodwill; intangible assets; inventories; property, plant and equipment; and provisions that are to be settled by the delivery of a non-monetary asset.

Summary of the approach required by this Standard

17   In preparing financial statements, each entity—whether a stand-alone entity, an entity with foreign operations (such as a parent) or a foreign operation (such as a subsidiary or branch)—determines its functional currency in accordance with paragraphs 9–14. The entity translates foreign currency items into its functional currency and reports the effects of such translation in accordance with paragraphs 20–37 and 50.

18   Many reporting entities comprise a number of individual entities (eg a group is made up of a parent and one or more subsidiaries). Various types of entities, whether members of a group or otherwise, may have investments in associates or joint arrangements. They may also have branches. It is necessary for the results and financial position of each individual entity included in the reporting entity to be translated into the currency in which the reporting entity presents its financial statements. This Standard permits the presentation currency of a reporting entity to be any currency (or currencies). The results and financial position of any individual entity within the reporting entity whose functional currency differs from the presentation currency are translated in accordance with paragraphs 38–50.

19   This Standard also permits a stand-alone entity preparing financial statements or an entity preparing separate financial statements in accordance with AASB 127 *Separate Financial Statements* to present its financial statements in any currency (or currencies). If the entity's presentation currency differs from its functional currency, its results and financial position are also translated into the presentation currency in accordance with paragraphs 38–50.

Reporting foreign currency transactions in the functional currency

Initial recognition

20   A foreign currency transaction is a transaction that is denominated or requires settlement in a foreign currency, including transactions arising when an entity:

   (a)   buys or sells goods or services whose price is denominated in a foreign currency;

   (b)   borrows or lends funds when the amounts payable or receivable are denominated in a foreign currency; or

   (c)   otherwise acquires or disposes of assets, or incurs or settles liabilities, denominated in a foreign currency.

21   **A foreign currency transaction shall be recorded, on initial recognition in the functional currency, by applying to the foreign currency amount the spot exchange rate between the functional currency and the foreign currency at the date of the transaction.**

22   The date of a transaction is the date on which the transaction first qualifies for recognition in accordance with Australian Accounting Standards. For practical reasons, a rate that approximates the actual rate at the date of the transaction is often used, for example, an average rate for a week or a month might be used for all transactions in each foreign currency occurring during that period. However, if exchange rates fluctuate significantly, the use of the average rate for a period is inappropriate.

Reporting at the ends of subsequent reporting periods

23   **At the end of each reporting period:**

   (a)   **foreign currency monetary items shall be translated using the closing rate;**

> (b)   **non-monetary items that are measured in terms of historical cost in a foreign currency shall be translated using the exchange rate at the date of the transaction; and**
>
> (c)   **non-monetary items that are measured at fair value in a foreign currency shall be translated using the exchange rates at the date when the fair value was measured.**

24   The carrying amount of an item is determined in conjunction with other relevant Standards. For example, property, plant and equipment may be measured in terms of fair value or historical cost in accordance with AASB 116 *Property, Plant and Equipment*. Whether the carrying amount is determined on the basis of historical cost or on the basis of fair value, if the amount is determined in a foreign currency it is then translated into the functional currency in accordance with this Standard.

25   The carrying amount of some items is determined by comparing two or more amounts. For example, the carrying amount of inventories is the lower of cost and net realisable value in accordance with AASB 102 *Inventories*. Similarly, in accordance with AASB 136 *Impairment of Assets*, the carrying amount of an asset for which there is an indication of impairment is the lower of its carrying amount before considering possible impairment losses and its recoverable amount. When such an asset is non-monetary and is measured in a foreign currency, the carrying amount is determined by comparing:

> (a)   the cost or carrying amount, as appropriate, translated at the exchange rate at the date when that amount was determined (ie the rate at the date of the transaction for an item measured in terms of historical cost); and
>
> (b)   the net realisable value or recoverable amount, as appropriate, translated at the exchange rate at the date when that value was determined (eg the closing rate at the end of the reporting period).

The effect of this comparison may be that an impairment loss is recognised in the functional currency but would not be recognised in the foreign currency, or vice versa.

26   When several exchange rates are available, the rate used is that at which the future cash flows represented by the transaction or balance could have been settled if those cash flows had occurred at the measurement date. If exchangeability between two currencies is temporarily lacking, the rate used is the first subsequent rate at which exchanges could be made.

Recognition of exchange differences

27   As noted in paragraphs 3(a) and 5, AASB 9 applies to hedge accounting for foreign currency items. The application of hedge accounting requires an entity to account for some exchange differences differently from the treatment of exchange differences required by this Standard. For example, AASB 9 requires that exchange differences on monetary items that qualify as hedging instruments in a cash flow hedge are recognised initially in other comprehensive income to the extent that the hedge is effective.

28   **Exchange differences arising on the settlement of monetary items or on translating monetary items at rates different from those at which they were translated on initial recognition during the period or in previous financial statements shall be recognised in profit or loss in the period in which they arise, except as described in paragraph 32.**

29   When monetary items arise from a foreign currency transaction and there is a change in the exchange rate between the transaction date and the date of settlement, an exchange difference results. When the transaction is settled within the same accounting period as that in which it occurred, all the exchange difference is recognised in that period. However, when the transaction is settled in a subsequent accounting period, the exchange difference recognised in each period up to the date of settlement is determined by the change in exchange rates during each period.

30 **When a gain or loss on a non-monetary item is recognised in other comprehensive income, any exchange component of that gain or loss shall be recognised in other comprehensive income. Conversely, when a gain or loss on a non-monetary item is recognised in profit or loss, any exchange component of that gain or loss shall be recognised in profit or loss.**

31 Other Australian Accounting Standards require some gains and losses to be recognised in other comprehensive income. For example, AASB 116 requires some gains and losses arising on a revaluation of property, plant and equipment to be recognised in other comprehensive income. When such an asset is measured in a foreign currency, paragraph 23(c) of this Standard requires the revalued amount to be translated using the rate at the date the value is determined, resulting in an exchange difference that is also recognised in other comprehensive income.

32 **Exchange differences arising on a monetary item that forms part of a reporting entity's net investment in a foreign operation (see paragraph 15) shall be recognised in profit or loss in the separate financial statements of the reporting entity or the individual financial statements of the foreign operation, as appropriate. In the financial statements that include the foreign operation and the reporting entity (eg consolidated financial statements when the foreign operation is a subsidiary), such exchange differences shall be recognised initially in other comprehensive income and reclassified from equity to profit or loss on disposal of the net investment in accordance with paragraph 48.**

33 When a monetary item forms part of a reporting entity's net investment in a foreign operation and is denominated in the functional currency of the reporting entity, an exchange difference arises in the foreign operation's individual financial statements in accordance with paragraph 28. If such an item is denominated in the functional currency of the foreign operation, an exchange difference arises in the reporting entity's separate financial statements in accordance with paragraph 28. If such an item is denominated in a currency other than the functional currency of either the reporting entity or the foreign operation, an exchange difference arises in the reporting entity's separate financial statements and in the foreign operation's individual financial statements in accordance with paragraph 28. Such exchange differences are recognised in other comprehensive income in the financial statements that include the foreign operation and the reporting entity (ie financial statements in which the foreign operation is consolidated or accounted for using the equity method).

34 When an entity keeps its books and records in a currency other than its functional currency, at the time the entity prepares its financial statements all amounts are translated into the functional currency in accordance with paragraphs 20–26. This produces the same amounts in the functional currency as would have occurred had the items been recorded initially in the functional currency. For example, monetary items are translated into the functional currency using the closing rate, and non-monetary items that are measured on a historical cost basis are translated using the exchange rate at the date of the transaction that resulted in their recognition.

Change in functional currency

35 **When there is a change in an entity's functional currency, the entity shall apply the translation procedures applicable to the new functional currency prospectively from the date of the change.**

36 As noted in paragraph 13, the functional currency of an entity reflects the underlying transactions, events and conditions that are relevant to the entity. Accordingly, once the functional currency is determined, it can be changed only if there is a change to those underlying transactions, events and conditions. For example, a change in the currency that mainly influences the sales prices of goods and services may lead to a change in an entity's functional currency.

37   The effect of a change in functional currency is accounted for prospectively. In other words, an entity translates all items into the new functional currency using the exchange rate at the date of the change. The resulting translated amounts for non-monetary items are treated as their historical cost. Exchange differences arising from the translation of a foreign operation previously recognised in other comprehensive income in accordance with paragraphs 32 and 39(c) are not reclassified from equity to profit or loss until the disposal of the operation.

Use of a presentation currency other than the functional currency

Translation to the presentation currency

38   An entity may present its financial statements in any currency (or currencies). If the presentation currency differs from the entity's functional currency, it translates its results and financial position into the presentation currency. For example, when a group contains individual entities with different functional currencies, the results and financial position of each entity are expressed in a common currency so that consolidated financial statements may be presented.

39   **The results and financial position of an entity whose functional currency is not the currency of a hyperinflationary economy shall be translated into a different presentation currency using the following procedures:**

     (a)   **assets and liabilities for each statement of financial position presented (ie including comparatives) shall be translated at the closing rate at the date of that statement of financial position;**

     (b)   **income and expenses for each statement presenting profit or loss and other comprehensive income (ie including comparatives) shall be translated at exchange rates at the dates of the transactions; and**

     (c)   **all resulting exchange differences shall be recognised in other comprehensive income.**

40   For practical reasons, a rate that approximates the exchange rates at the dates of the transactions, for example an average rate for the period, is often used to translate income and expense items. However, if exchange rates fluctuate significantly, the use of the average rate for a period is inappropriate.

41   The exchange differences referred to in paragraph 39(c) result from:

     (a)   translating income and expenses at the exchange rates at the dates of the transactions and assets and liabilities at the closing rate.

     (b)   translating the opening net assets at a closing rate that differs from the previous closing rate.

These exchange differences are not recognised in profit or loss because the changes in exchange rates have little or no direct effect on the present and future cash flows from operations. The cumulative amount of the exchange differences is presented in a separate component of equity until disposal of the foreign operation. When the exchange differences relate to a foreign operation that is consolidated but not wholly-owned, accumulated exchange differences arising from translation and attributable to non-controlling interests are allocated to, and recognised as part of, non-controlling interests in the consolidated statement of financial position.

42   **The results and financial position of an entity whose functional currency is the currency of a hyperinflationary economy shall be translated into a different presentation currency using the following procedures:**

     (a)   **all amounts (ie assets, liabilities, equity items, income and expenses, including comparatives) shall be translated at the closing rate at the date of the most recent statement of financial position, except that**

(b)   when amounts are translated into the currency of a non-hyperinflationary economy, comparative amounts shall be those that were presented as current year amounts in the relevant prior year financial statements (ie not adjusted for subsequent changes in the price level or subsequent changes in exchange rates).

43   When an entity's functional currency is the currency of a hyperinflationary economy, the entity shall restate its financial statements in accordance with AASB 129 before applying the translation method set out in paragraph 42, except for comparative amounts that are translated into a currency of a non-hyperinflationary economy (see paragraph 42(b)). When the economy ceases to be hyperinflationary and the entity no longer restates its financial statements in accordance with AASB 129, it shall use as the historical costs for translation into the presentation currency the amounts restated to the price level at the date the entity ceased restating its financial statements.

Translation of a foreign operation

44   Paragraphs 45–47, in addition to paragraphs 38–43, apply when the results and financial position of a foreign operation are translated into a presentation currency so that the foreign operation can be included in the financial statements of the reporting entity by consolidation or the equity method.

45   The incorporation of the results and financial position of a foreign operation with those of the reporting entity follows normal consolidation procedures, such as the elimination of intragroup balances and intragroup transactions of a subsidiary (see AASB 10 *Consolidated Financial Statements*). However, an intragroup monetary asset (or liability), whether short-term or long-term, cannot be eliminated against the corresponding intragroup liability (or asset) without showing the results of currency fluctuations in the consolidated financial statements. This is because the monetary item represents a commitment to convert one currency into another and exposes the reporting entity to a gain or loss through currency fluctuations. Accordingly, in the consolidated financial statements of the reporting entity, such an exchange difference is recognised in profit or loss or, if it arises from the circumstances described in paragraph 32, it is recognised in other comprehensive income and accumulated in a separate component of equity until the disposal of the foreign operation.

46   When the financial statements of a foreign operation are as of a date different from that of the reporting entity, the foreign operation often prepares additional statements as of the same date as the reporting entity's financial statements. When this is not done, AASB 10 allows the use of a different date provided that the difference is no greater than three months and adjustments are made for the effects of any significant transactions or other events that occur between the different dates. In such a case, the assets and liabilities of the foreign operation are translated at the exchange rate at the end of the reporting period of the foreign operation. Adjustments are made for significant changes in exchange rates up to the end of the reporting period of the reporting entity in accordance with AASB 10. The same approach is used in applying the equity method to associates and joint ventures in accordance with AASB 128.

47   **Any goodwill arising on the acquisition of a foreign operation and any fair value adjustments to the carrying amounts of assets and liabilities arising on the acquisition of that foreign operation shall be treated as assets and liabilities of the foreign operation. Thus they shall be expressed in the functional currency of the foreign operation and shall be translated at the closing rate in accordance with paragraphs 39 and 42.**

Disposal or partial disposal of a foreign operation

48   **On the disposal of a foreign operation, the cumulative amount of the exchange differences relating to that foreign operation, recognised in other comprehensive income and accumulated in the separate component of equity, shall be reclassified**

from equity to profit or loss (as a reclassification adjustment) when the gain or loss on disposal is recognised (see AASB 101 *Presentation of Financial Statements*).

48A   In addition to the disposal of an entity's entire interest in a foreign operation, the following partial disposals are accounted for as disposals:

    (a)   when the partial disposal involves the loss of control of a subsidiary that includes a foreign operation, regardless of whether the entity retains a non-controlling interest in its former subsidiary after the partial disposal; and

    (b)   when the retained interest after the partial disposal of an interest in a joint arrangement or a partial disposal of an interest in an associate that includes a foreign operation is a financial asset that includes a foreign operation.

48B   On disposal of a subsidiary that includes a foreign operation, the cumulative amount of the exchange differences relating to that foreign operation that have been attributed to the non-controlling interests shall be derecognised, but shall not be reclassified to profit or loss.

48C   **On the partial disposal of a subsidiary that includes a foreign operation, the entity shall re-attribute the proportionate share of the cumulative amount of the exchange differences recognised in other comprehensive income to the non-controlling interests in that foreign operation. In any other partial disposal of a foreign operation the entity shall reclassify to profit or loss only the proportionate share of the cumulative amount of the exchange differences recognised in other comprehensive income.**

48D   A partial disposal of an entity's interest in a foreign operation is any reduction in an entity's ownership interest in a foreign operation, except those reductions in paragraph 48A that are accounted for as disposals.

49   An entity may dispose or partially dispose of its interest in a foreign operation through sale, liquidation, repayment of share capital or abandonment of all, or part of, that entity. A write-down of the carrying amount of a foreign operation, either because of its own losses or because of an impairment recognised by the investor, does not constitute a partial disposal. Accordingly, no part of the foreign exchange gain or loss recognised in other comprehensive income is reclassified to profit or loss at the time of a write-down.

Tax effects of all exchange differences

50   Gains and losses on foreign currency transactions and exchange differences arising on translating the results and financial position of an entity (including a foreign operation) into a different currency may have tax effects. AASB 112 *Income Taxes* applies to these tax effects.

Disclosure

51   **In paragraphs 53 and 55–57 references to 'functional currency' apply, in the case of a group, to the functional currency of the parent.**

52   **An entity shall disclose:**

    (a)   **the amount of exchange differences recognised in profit or loss except for those arising on financial instruments measured at fair value through profit or loss in accordance with AASB 9; and**

    (b)   **net exchange differences recognised in other comprehensive income and accumulated in a separate component of equity, and a reconciliation of the amount of such exchange differences at the beginning and end of the period.**

53   **When the presentation currency is different from the functional currency, that fact shall be stated, together with disclosure of the functional currency and the reason for using a different presentation currency.**

54 **When there is a change in the functional currency of either the reporting entity or a significant foreign operation, that fact and the reason for the change in functional currency shall be disclosed.**

55 **When an entity presents its financial statements in a currency that is different from its functional currency, it shall describe the financial statements as complying with Australian Accounting Standards only if they comply with all the requirements of Australian Accounting Standards including the translation method set out in paragraphs 39 and 42.**

56 An entity sometimes presents its financial statements or other financial information in a currency that is not its functional currency without meeting the requirements of paragraph 55. For example, an entity may convert into another currency only selected items from its financial statements. Or, an entity whose functional currency is not the currency of a hyperinflationary economy may convert the financial statements into another currency by translating all items at the most recent closing rate. Such conversions are not in accordance with Australian Accounting Standards and the disclosures set out in paragraph 57 are required.

57 **When an entity displays its financial statements or other financial information in a currency that is different from either its functional currency or its presentation currency and the requirements of paragraph 55 are not met, it shall:**

    (a) **clearly identify the information as supplementary information to distinguish it from the information that complies with Australian Accounting Standards;**

    (b) **disclose the currency in which the supplementary information is displayed; and**

    (c) **disclose the entity's functional currency and the method of translation used to determine the supplementary information.**

Effective date and transition

58 An entity shall apply this Standard for annual periods beginning on or after 1 January 2018. Earlier application is encouraged for periods beginning after 24 July 2014 but before 1 January 2018. If an entity applies this Standard for a period beginning before 1 January 2018, it shall disclose that fact.

58A–60A [Deleted by the AASB]

60B AASB 2008-3 *Amendments to Australian Accounting Standards arising from AASB 3 and AASB 127* amended the previous version of this Standard as follows: added paragraphs 48A–48D and amended paragraph 49. An entity shall apply those amendments prospectively for annual periods beginning on or after 1 July 2009. If an entity applies AASB 127 (amended 2008) for an earlier period, the amendments shall be applied for that earlier period.

60C [Deleted]

60D [Deleted by the AASB]

60E [Deleted]

60F–60H [Deleted by the AASB]

Withdrawal of other pronouncements

61–62 [Deleted by the AASB]

Commencement of the legislative instrument

Aus62.1 For legal purposes, this legislative instrument commences on 31 December 2017.

Withdrawal of AASB pronouncements

Aus62.2   This Standard repeals AASB 121 *The Effects of Changes in Foreign Exchange Rates* issued in July 2004. Despite the repeal, after the time this Standard starts to apply under section 334 of the Corporations Act (either generally or in relation to an individual entity), the repealed Standard continues to apply in relation to any period ending before that time as if the repeal had not occurred.

[Note: When this Standard applies under section 334 of the Corporations Act (either generally or in relation to an individual entity), it supersedes the application of the repealed Standard.]

APPENDIX A

AUSTRALIAN REDUCED DISCLOSURE REQUIREMENTS

This appendix is an integral part of the Standard.

AusA1   **Paragraphs 55-57 of this Standard do not apply to entities preparing general purpose financial statements under Australian Accounting Standards – Reduced Disclosure Requirements. Entities applying Australian Accounting Standards – Reduced Disclosure Requirements may elect to comply with some or all of these excluded requirements.**

AusA1   The requirements that do not apply to entities preparing general purpose financial statements under Australian Accounting Standards – Reduced Disclosure Requirements are also identified in this Standard by shading of the relevant text.

DELETED IAS 21 TEXT

Deleted IAS 21 text is not part of AASB 121.

58A   *Net Investment in a Foreign Operation* (Amendment to IAS 21), issued in December 2005, added paragraph 15A and amended paragraph 33. An entity shall apply those amendments for annual periods beginning on or after 1 January 2006. Earlier application is encouraged.

59   An entity shall apply paragraph 47 prospectively to all acquisitions occurring after the beginning of the financial reporting period in which this Standard is first applied. Retrospective application of paragraph 47 to earlier acquisitions is permitted. For an acquisition of a foreign operation treated prospectively but which occurred before the date on which this Standard is first applied, the entity shall not restate prior years and accordingly may, when appropriate, treat goodwill and fair value adjustments arising on that acquisition as assets and liabilities of the entity rather than as assets and liabilities of the foreign operation. Therefore, those goodwill and fair value adjustments either are already expressed in the entity's functional currency or are non-monetary foreign currency items, which are reported using the exchange rate at the date of the acquisition.

60   All other changes resulting from the application of this Standard shall be accounted for in accordance with the requirements of IAS 8 *Accounting Policies, Changes in Accounting Estimates and Errors.*

60A   IAS 1 (as revised in 2007) amended the terminology used throughout IFRSs. In addition it amended paragraphs 27, 30–33, 37, 39, 41, 45, 48 and 52. An entity shall apply those amendments for annual periods beginning on or after 1 January 2009. If an entity applies IAS 1 (revised 2007) for an earlier period, the amendments shall be applied for that earlier period.

60D   Paragraph 60B was amended by *Improvements to IFRSs* issued in May 2010. An entity shall apply that amendment for annual periods beginning on or after 1 July 2010. Earlier application is permitted.

60F   IFRS 10 and IFRS 11 *Joint Arrangements*, issued in May 2011, amended paragraphs 3(b), 8, 11, 18, 19, 33, 44–46 and 48A. An entity shall apply those amendments when it applies IFRS 10 and IFRS 11.

60G   IFRS 13, issued in May 2011, amended the definition of fair value in paragraph 8 and amended paragraph 23. An entity shall apply those amendments when it applies IFRS 13.

60H   *Presentation of Items of Other Comprehensive Income* (Amendments to IAS 1), issued in June 2011, amended paragraph 39. An entity shall apply that amendment when it applies IAS 1 as amended in June 2011.

61   This Standard supersedes IAS 21 *The Effects of Changes in Foreign Exchange Rates* (revised in 1993).

62   This Standard supersedes the following Interpretations:

   (a)   SIC-11 *Foreign Exchange—Capitalisation of Losses Resulting from Severe Currency Devaluations*;

   (b)   SIC-19 *Reporting Currency—Measurement and Presentation of Financial Statements under IAS 21 and IAS 29*; and

   (c)   SIC-30 *Reporting Currency—Translation from Measurement Currency to Presentation Currency.*

AASB 123
Borrowing Costs
(Reissued August 2015)

This note is not part of Accounting Standard AASB 123.

The following unincorporated amendments are not included in this Standard.

- AASB 2018-1 *Amendments to Australian Accounting Standards — Annual Improvements 2015–2017 Cycle*. This Standard makes amendments to AASB 3 *Business Combinations*, AASB 11 *Joint Arrangements*, AASB 112 *Income Taxes* and AASB 123 *Borrowing Costs*. These amendments arise from the issuance of IFRS *Annual Improvements to IFRS Standards 2015–2017 Cycle* by the IASB in December 2017. This Standard applies to annual periods beginning on or after 1 January 2019, but earlier application is permitted.

- AASB 16 *Leases* — Appendix D sets out the amendments to other Standards that are a consequence of the AASB issuing this Standard. It is applicable from 1 January 2019. Earlier application is permitted, but entities must apply AASB 15 *Revenue from Contracts with Customers* before applying this Standard.

Entities early-adopting any amendments with later application dates will need to refer to the amending Standards that have not yet been incorporated into compilations. The abovementioned unincorporated amendments may be located on the AASB website at www.aasb.gov.au or on the Federal Register of Legislation website at www.legislation.gov.au.

CONTENTS

COMPARISON WITH IAS 23
ACCOUNTING STANDARD
AASB 123 *BORROWING COSTS*

     Chartered Accountants Australia and New Zealand

APPENDIX

A. AUSTRALIAN REDUCED DISCLOSURE REQUIREMENTS

DELETED IAS 23 TEXT

BASIS FOR CONCLUSIONS

BASIS FOR CONCLUSIONS ON IAS 23 (available on the AASB website)

> Australian Accounting Standard AASB 123 *Borrowing Costs* is set out in paragraphs 1 – Aus30.2 and Appendix A. All the paragraphs have equal authority. Paragraphs in **bold type** state the main principles. AASB 123 is to be read in the context of other Australian Accounting Standards, including AASB 1048 *Interpretation of Standards*, which identifies the Australian Accounting Interpretations, and AASB 1057 *Application of Australian Accounting Standards*. In the absence of explicit guidance, AASB 108 *Accounting Policies, Changes in Accounting Estimates and Errors* provides a basis for selecting and applying accounting policies.

COMPARISON WITH IAS 23

AASB 123 *Borrowing Costs* incorporates IAS 23 *Borrowing Costs* issued by the International Accounting Standards Board (IASB). Australian-specific paragraphs (which are not included in IAS 23) are identified with the prefix "Aus" or "RDR". Paragraphs that apply only to not-for-profit entities begin by identifying their limited applicability.

Tier 1

For-profit entities complying with AASB 123 also comply with IAS 23.

Not-for-profit entities' compliance with IAS 23 will depend on whether any "Aus" paragraphs that specifically apply to not-for-profit entities provide additional guidance or contain applicable requirements that are inconsistent with IAS 23.

Tier 2

Entities preparing general purpose financial statements under Australian Accounting Standards – Reduced Disclosure Requirements (Tier 2) will not be in compliance with IFRSs.

AASB 1053 *Application of Tiers of Australian Accounting Standards* explains the two tiers of reporting requirements.

ACCOUNTING STANDARD AASB 123

The Australian Accounting Standards Board makes Accounting Standard AASB 123 *Borrowing Costs* under section 334 of the *Corporations Act 2001*.

Dated 7 August 2015

Kris Peach
Chair – AASB

ACCOUNTING STANDARD AASB 123
BORROWING COSTS

Core principle

1   **Borrowing costs that are directly attributable to the acquisition, construction or production of a qualifying asset form part of the cost of that asset. Other borrowing costs are recognised as an expense.**

Aus1.1   In respect of not-for-profit public sector entities, borrowing costs may be expensed in accordance with paragraph Aus8.1.

Scope

2   An entity shall apply this Standard in accounting for borrowing costs.

3   The Standard does not deal with the actual or imputed cost of equity, including preferred capital not classified as a liability.

4   An entity is not required to apply the Standard to borrowing costs directly attributable to the acquisition, construction or production of:

    (a)   a qualifying asset measured at fair value, for example a biological asset within the scope of AASB 141 *Agriculture*; or

    (b)   inventories that are manufactured, or otherwise produced, in large quantities on a repetitive basis.

Definitions

5   This Standard uses the following terms with the meanings specified:

Borrowing costs are interest and other costs that an entity incurs in connection with the borrowing of funds.

A *qualifying asset* is an asset that necessarily takes a substantial period of time to get ready for its intended use or sale.

6   Borrowing costs may include:

    (a)   interest expense calculated using the effective interest method as described in AASB 9;

    (b)   [deleted]

    (c)   [deleted]

    (d)   finance charges in respect of finance leases recognised in accordance with AASB 117 *Leases*; and

    (e)   exchange differences arising from foreign currency borrowings to the extent that they are regarded as an adjustment to interest costs.

7   Depending on the circumstances, any of the following may be qualifying assets:

    (a)   inventories

    (b)   manufacturing plants

    (c)   power generation facilities

    (d)   intangible assets

    (e)   investment properties

    (f)   bearer plants.

Financial assets, and inventories that are manufactured, or otherwise produced, over a short period of time, are not qualifying assets. Assets that are ready for their intended use or sale when acquired are not qualifying assets.

Recognition

8   **An entity shall capitalise borrowing costs that are directly attributable to the acquisition, construction or production of a qualifying asset as part of the cost of that asset. An entity shall recognise other borrowing costs as an expense in the period in which it incurs them.**

Aus8.1   **A not-for-profit public sector entity may elect to recognise borrowing costs as an expense in the period in which they are incurred regardless of how the borrowings are applied.**

Aus8.2   In respect of not-for-profit public sector entities, paragraphs 9–26, 27 and 28 apply only when an entity elects to capitalise borrowing costs that are directly attributable to the acquisition, construction or production of a qualifying asset as part of the cost of that asset.

9   Borrowing costs that are directly attributable to the acquisition, construction or production of a qualifying asset are included in the cost of that asset. Such borrowing costs are capitalised as part of the cost of the asset when it is probable that they will result in future economic benefits to the entity and the costs can be measured reliably. When an entity applies AASB 129 *Financial Reporting in Hyperinflationary Economies*, it recognises as an expense the part of borrowing costs that compensates for inflation during the same period in accordance with paragraph 21 of that Standard.

Borrowing costs eligible for capitalisation

10   The borrowing costs that are directly attributable to the acquisition, construction or production of a qualifying asset are those borrowing costs that would have been avoided if the expenditure on the qualifying asset had not been made. When an entity borrows funds specifically for the purpose of obtaining a particular qualifying asset, the borrowing costs that directly relate to that qualifying asset can be readily identified.

11   It may be difficult to identify a direct relationship between particular borrowings and a qualifying asset and to determine the borrowings that could otherwise have been avoided. Such a difficulty occurs, for example, when the financing activity of an entity is co-ordinated centrally. Difficulties also arise when a group uses a range of debt instruments to borrow funds at varying rates of interest, and lends those funds on various bases to other entities in the group. Other complications arise through the use of loans denominated in or linked to foreign currencies, when the group operates in highly inflationary economies, and from fluctuations in exchange rates. As a result, the determination of the amount of borrowing costs that are directly attributable to the acquisition of a qualifying asset is difficult and the exercise of judgement is required.

12   **To the extent that an entity borrows funds specifically for the purpose of obtaining a qualifying asset, the entity shall determine the amount of borrowing costs eligible for capitalisation as the actual borrowing costs incurred on that borrowing during the period less any investment income on the temporary investment of those borrowings.**

13   The financing arrangements for a qualifying asset may result in an entity obtaining borrowed funds and incurring associated borrowing costs before some or all of the funds are used for expenditures on the qualifying asset. In such circumstances, the funds are often temporarily invested pending their expenditure on the qualifying asset. In determining the amount of borrowing costs eligible for capitalisation during a period, any investment income earned on such funds is deducted from the borrowing costs incurred.

14   **To the extent that an entity borrows funds generally and uses them for the purpose of obtaining a qualifying asset, the entity shall determine the amount of borrowing costs eligible for capitalisation by applying a capitalisation rate to the expenditures on that asset. The capitalisation rate shall be the weighted average of the borrowing costs applicable to the borrowings of the entity that are outstanding during the period, other than borrowings made specifically for the purpose of obtaining a qualifying asset. The amount of borrowing costs that an entity capitalises during a period shall not exceed the amount of borrowing costs it incurred during that period.**

15   In some circumstances, it is appropriate to include all borrowings of the parent and its subsidiaries when computing a weighted average of the borrowing costs; in other

circumstances, it is appropriate for each subsidiary to use a weighted average of the borrowing costs applicable to its own borrowings.

Excess of the carrying amount of the qualifying asset over recoverable amount

16   When the carrying amount or the expected ultimate cost of the qualifying asset exceeds its recoverable amount or net realisable value, the carrying amount is written down or written off in accordance with the requirements of other Standards. In certain circumstances, the amount of the write-down or write-off is written back in accordance with those other Standards.

Commencement of capitalisation

17   **An entity shall begin capitalising borrowing costs as part of the cost of a qualifying asset on the commencement date. The commencement date for capitalisation is the date when the entity first meets all of the following conditions:**

(a)   **it incurs expenditures for the asset;**

(b)   **it incurs borrowing costs; and**

(c)   **it undertakes activities that are necessary to prepare the asset for its intended use or sale.**

18   Expenditures on a qualifying asset include only those expenditures that have resulted in payments of cash, transfers of other assets or the assumption of interest-bearing liabilities. Expenditures are reduced by any progress payments received and grants received in connection with the asset (see AASB 120 *Accounting for Government Grants and Disclosure of Government Assistance*). The average carrying amount of the asset during a period, including borrowing costs previously capitalised, is normally a reasonable approximation of the expenditures to which the capitalisation rate is applied in that period.

19   The activities necessary to prepare the asset for its intended use or sale encompass more than the physical construction of the asset. They include technical and administrative work prior to the commencement of physical construction, such as the activities associated with obtaining permits prior to the commencement of the physical construction. However, such activities exclude the holding of an asset when no production or development that changes the asset's condition is taking place. For example, borrowing costs incurred while land is under development are capitalised during the period in which activities related to the development are being undertaken. However, borrowing costs incurred while land acquired for building purposes is held without any associated development activity do not qualify for capitalisation.

Suspension of capitalisation

20   **An entity shall suspend capitalisation of borrowing costs during extended periods in which it suspends active development of a qualifying asset.**

21   An entity may incur borrowing costs during an extended period in which it suspends the activities necessary to prepare an asset for its intended use or sale. Such costs are costs of holding partially completed assets and do not qualify for capitalisation. However, an entity does not normally suspend capitalising borrowing costs during a period when it carries out substantial technical and administrative work. An entity also does not suspend capitalising borrowing costs when a temporary delay is a necessary part of the process of getting an asset ready for its intended use or sale. For example, capitalisation continues during the extended period that high water levels delay construction of a bridge, if such high water levels are common during the construction period in the geographical region involved.

Cessation of capitalisation

22 **An entity shall cease capitalising borrowing costs when substantially all the activities necessary to prepare the qualifying asset for its intended use or sale are complete.**

23 An asset is normally ready for its intended use or sale when the physical construction of the asset is complete even though routine administrative work might still continue. If minor modifications, such as the decoration of a property to the purchaser's or user's specification, are all that are outstanding, this indicates that substantially all the activities are complete.

24 **When an entity completes the construction of a qualifying asset in parts and each part is capable of being used while construction continues on other parts, the entity shall cease capitalising borrowing costs when it completes substantially all the activities necessary to prepare that part for its intended use or sale.**

25 A business park comprising several buildings, each of which can be used individually, is an example of a qualifying asset for which each part is capable of being usable while construction continues on other parts. An example of a qualifying asset that needs to be complete before any part can be used is an industrial plant involving several processes which are carried out in sequence at different parts of the plant within the same site, such as a steel mill.

Disclosure

26 **An entity shall disclose:**

    (a) **the amount of borrowing costs capitalised during the period; and**

    (b) **the capitalisation rate used to determine the amount of borrowing costs eligible for capitalisation.**

Aus26.1 **A not-for-profit public sector entity shall disclose the accounting policy adopted for borrowing costs.**

Transitional provisions

Aus26.2 **Paragraphs 27 and 28 shall not be applied by an entity that has previously applied AASB 123, unless required to do so by another Standard.**

27 **When application of this Standard constitutes a change in accounting policy, an entity shall apply the Standard to borrowing costs relating to qualifying assets for which the commencement date for capitalisation is on or after the effective date.**

28 **However, an entity may designate any date before the effective date and apply the Standard to borrowing costs relating to all qualifying assets for which the commencement date for capitalisation is on or after that date.**

Effective date

29 An entity shall apply the Standard for annual periods beginning on or after 1 January 2018. Earlier application is permitted for periods beginning after 24 July 2014 but before 1 January 2018. If an entity applies the Standard from a date before 1 January 2018, it shall disclose that fact.

29A [Deleted by the AASB]

29B AASB 2014-7 *Amendments to Australian Accounting Standards arising from AASB 9 (December 2014)*, issued in December 2014, amended paragraph 6 in the previous version of this Standard. An entity shall apply that amendment when it applies AASB 9.

Withdrawal of IAS 23 (revised 1993)

30   [Deleted by the AASB]

Commencement of the legislative instrument

Aus30.1   For legal purposes, this legislative instrument commences on 31 December 2017.

Withdrawal of AASB pronouncements

Aus30.2   This Standard repeals AASB 123 *Borrowing Costs* issued in June 2007. Despite the repeal, after the time this Standard starts to apply under section 334 of the Corporations Act (either generally or in relation to an individual entity), the repealed Standard continues to apply in relation to any period ending before that time as if the repeal had not occurred.

[Note: When this Standard applies under section 334 of the Corporations Act (either generally or in relation to an individual entity), it supersedes the application of the repealed Standard.]

APPENDIX A
AUSTRALIAN REDUCED DISCLOSURE REQUIREMENTS

This appendix is an integral part of the Standard.

AusA1   **Paragraph 26(b) of this Standard does not apply to entities preparing general purpose financial statements under Australian Accounting Standards – Reduced Disclosure Requirements. Entities applying Australian Accounting Standards – Reduced Disclosure Requirements may elect to comply with this excluded requirement.**

AusA2   The requirement that does not apply to entities preparing general purpose financial statements under Australian Accounting Standards – Reduced Disclosure Requirements are also identified in this Standard by shading of the relevant text.

DELETED IAS 23 TEXT

Deleted IAS 23 text is not part of AASB 123.

29A   Paragraph 6 was amended by *Improvements to IFRSs* issued in May 2008. An entity shall apply that amendment for annual periods beginning on or after 1 January 2009. Earlier application is permitted. If an entity applies the amendment for an earlier period it shall disclose that fact.

30   This Standard supersedes IAS 23 *Borrowing Costs* revised in 1993.

BASIS FOR CONCLUSIONS

This Basis for Conclusions accompanies, but is not part of, AASB 123.

Background

BC1   This Basis for Conclusions summarises the Australian Accounting Standards Board's considerations in reaching the conclusions in this Standard. Individual Board members gave greater weight to some factors than to others.

BC2 Before the mandatory application date of revised AASB 123 *Borrowing Costs* in 2009, the Board conducted a review of the requirement in AASB 123 for not-for-profit entities to capitalise borrowing costs that are directly attributable to the acquisition, construction or production of a qualifying asset as part of the cost of that asset. As a result of that review, in April 2009 the Board issued AASB 2009-1 *Amendments to Australian Accounting Standards – Borrowing Costs of Not-for-Profit Public Sector Entities*. AASB 2009-1 amended AASB 123 to allow not-for-profit public sector entities to expense borrowing costs as incurred, regardless of how the borrowings are applied.

BC3 The Board intended for the relief granted under AASB 2009-1 to be of an interim nature pending the outcome of:

(a) the work of the New Zealand Financial Reporting Standards Board (FRSB)[1] on the relationship between depreciated replacement cost and borrowing costs, in which the AASB agreed to participate;

(b) the AASB and FRSB work on developing a Process for Modifying, or Introducing Additional Requirements to, IFRSs for PBE/NFP; and

(c) the International Public Sector Accounting Standards Board's (IPSASB's) Borrowing Costs project.

BC4 In March 2011, the AASB decided to reactivate its project on the application of AASB 123 by not-for-profit public sector entities, and evaluate the election for not-for-profit public sector entities to expense immediately all borrowing costs against its *Process for Modifying IFRSs for PBE/NFP ('Process')*.

BC5 In September 2014, the Board discussed the modification for not-for-profit public sector entities to expense borrowing costs that are directly attributable to the acquisition, construction or production of a qualifying asset against its *Process*. The Board noted that the International Valuation Standards Council issued Technical Information Paper 2 *The Cost Approach for Tangible Assets* in April 2012, which includes discussion of inputs included in a model based on the cost approach, and that the IPSASB's Borrowing Cost project was on hold pending completion of the IPSASB's Conceptual Framework project.

BC6 The Board noted that it would not be appropriate for the accounting for borrowing costs of not-for-profit public sector entities to differ from that of for-profit entities merely because the Board may favour a different treatment conceptually. The Board confirmed that departure from the requirements of IAS 23 *Borrowing Costs* should only be permitted where not-for-profit specific reasons for departure exist.

BC7 The Board decided, on evaluation of IAS 23 against its *Process*, that the modification for not-for-profit public sector entities should be retained in AASB 123. The Board decided to add a Basis for Conclusions to AASB 123 to reflect its conclusions in this regard.

Significant issues

GAAP/GFS convergence

BC8 The Board weighed its policy on GAAP/GFS harmonisation against its policy of transaction neutrality, noting that requiring not-for-profit public sector entities to capitalise borrowing costs that are directly attributable to the acquisition, construction or production of a qualifying asset as part of the cost of that asset would create a further difference between Generally Accepted Accounting Principles (GAAP) and Government Finance Statistics (GFS). The Board considered the costs of tracking reconciling differences over the useful life of the assets, and noted that public sector infrastructure assets may have a longer useful life than most assets held by private sector entities.

---

1 The FRSB has since been succeeded by the New Zealand Accounting Standards Board (NZASB).

reporting entity. If the reporting entity is itself such a plan, the sponsoring employers are also related to the reporting entity.

(vi)   The entity is controlled or jointly controlled by a person identified in (a).

(vii) A person identified in (a)(i) has significant influence over the entity or is a member of the key management personnel of the entity (or of a parent of the entity).

(viii) The entity, or any member of a group of which it is a part, provides key management personnel services to the reporting entity or to the parent of the reporting entity.

A *related party transaction* is a transfer of resources, services or obligations between a reporting entity and a related party, regardless of whether a price is charged.

Close members of the family of a person are those family members who may be expected to influence, or be influenced by, that person in their dealings with the entity and include:

(a)   that person's children and spouse or domestic partner;

(b)   children of that person's spouse or domestic partner; and

(c)   dependants of that person or that person's spouse or domestic partner.

Compensation includes all employee benefits (as defined in AASB 119 *Employee Benefits*) including employee benefits to which AASB 2 *Share-based Payment* applies. Employee benefits are all forms of consideration paid, payable or provided by the entity, or on behalf of the entity, in exchange for services rendered to the entity. It also includes such consideration paid on behalf of a parent of the entity in respect of the entity. Compensation includes:

(a)   short-term employee benefits, such as wages, salaries and social security contributions, paid annual leave and paid sick leave, profit-sharing and bonuses (if payable within twelve months of the end of the period) and non-monetary benefits (such as medical care, housing, cars and free or subsidised goods or services) for current employees;

(b)   post-employment benefits such as pensions, other retirement benefits, post-employment life insurance and post-employment medical care;

(c)   other long-term employee benefits, including long-service leave or sabbatical leave, jubilee or other long-service benefits, long-term disability benefits and, if they are not payable wholly within twelve months after the end of the period, profit-sharing, bonuses and deferred compensation;

(d)   termination benefits; and

(e)   share-based payment.

Key management personnel are those persons having authority and responsibility for planning, directing and controlling the activities of the entity, directly or indirectly, including any director (whether executive or otherwise) of that entity.

Government refers to government, government agencies and similar bodies whether local, national or international.

A *government-related entity* is an entity that is controlled, jointly controlled or significantly influenced by a government.

The terms 'control' and 'investment entity', 'joint control' and 'significant influence' are defined in AASB 10, AASB 11 *Joint Arrangements* and AASB 128 *Investments in Associates and Joint Ventures* respectively and are used in this Standard with the meanings specified in those Australian Accounting Standards.

10   In considering each possible related party relationship, attention is directed to the substance of the relationship and not merely the legal form.

11   In the context of this Standard, the following are not related parties:

    (a)   two entities simply because they have a director or other member of key management personnel in common or because a member of key management personnel of one entity has significant influence over the other entity.

    (b)   two joint venturers simply because they share joint control of a joint venture.

    (c)   (i)   providers of finance,

         (ii)   trade unions,

         (iii)   public utilities, and

         (iv)   departments and agencies of a government that does not control, jointly control or significant influence the reporting entity,

        simply by virtue of their normal dealings with an entity (even though they may affect the freedom of action of an entity or participate in its decision-making process).

    (d)   a customer, supplier, franchisor, distributor or general agent with whom an entity transacts a significant volume of business, simply by virtue of the resulting economic dependence.

12   In the definition of a related party, an associate includes subsidiaries of the associate and a joint venture includes subsidiaries of the joint venture. Therefore, for example, an associate's subsidiary and the investor that has significant influence over the associate are related to each other.

Disclosures

All entities

13   **Relationships between a parent and its subsidiaries shall be disclosed irrespective of whether there have been transactions between them. An entity shall disclose the name of its parent and, if different, the ultimate controlling party. If neither the entity's parent nor the ultimate controlling party produces consolidated financial statements available for public use, the name of the next most senior parent that does so shall also be disclosed.**

Aus13.1   When any of the parent entities and/or ultimate controlling parties named in accordance with paragraph 13 is incorporated or otherwise constituted outside Australia, an entity shall:

    (a)   identify which of those entities is incorporated overseas and where; and

    (b)   disclose the name of the ultimate controlling entity incorporated within Australia.

14   To enable users of financial statements to form a view about the effects of related party relationships on an entity, it is appropriate to disclose the related party relationship when control exists, irrespective of whether there have been transactions between the related parties.

15   The requirement to disclose related party relationships between a parent and its subsidiaries is in addition to the disclosure requirements in AASB 127 and AASB 12 *Disclosure of Interests in Other Entities*.

16   Paragraph 13 refers to the next most senior parent. This is the first parent in the group above the immediate parent that produces consolidated financial statements available for public use.

17   **An entity shall disclose key management personnel compensation in total and for each of the following categories:**

    (a)   short-term employee benefits;

    (b)   post-employment benefits;

    (c)   other long-term benefits;

(d)   termination benefits; and

(e)   share-based payment.

17A   If an entity obtains key management personnel services from another entity (the 'management entity'), the entity is not required to apply the requirements in paragraph 17 to the compensation paid or payable by the management entity to the management entity's employees or directors.

18   If an entity has had related party transactions during the periods covered by the financial statements, it shall disclose the nature of the related party relationship as well as information about those transactions and outstanding balances, including commitments, necessary for users to understand the potential effect of the relationship on the financial statements. These disclosure requirements are in addition to those in paragraph 17. At a minimum, disclosures shall include:

(a)   the amount of the transactions;

(b)   the amount of outstanding balances, including commitments, and:

(i)   their terms and conditions, including whether they are secured, and the nature of the consideration to be provided in settlement; and

(ii)   details of any guarantees given or received;

(c)   provisions for doubtful debts related to the amount of outstanding balances; and

(d)   the expense recognised during the period in respect of bad or doubtful debts due from related parties.

18A   Amounts incurred by the entity for the provision of key management personnel services that are provided by a separate management entity shall be disclosed.

19   The disclosures required by paragraph 18 shall be made separately for each of the following categories:

(a)   the parent;

(b)   entities with joint control of, or significant influence over, the entity;

(c)   subsidiaries;

(d)   associates;

(e)   joint ventures in which the entity is a joint venturer;

(f)   key management personnel of the entity or its parent; and

(g)   other related parties.

20   The classification of amounts payable to, and receivable from, related parties in the different categories as required in paragraph 19 is an extension of the disclosure requirement in AASB 101 *Presentation of Financial Statements* for information to be presented either in the statement of financial position or in the notes. The categories are extended to provide a more comprehensive analysis of related party balances and apply to related party transactions.

21   The following are examples of transactions that are disclosed if they are with a related party:

(a)   purchases or sales of goods (finished or unfinished);

(b)   purchases or sales of property and other assets;

(c)   rendering or receiving of services;

(d)   leases;

(e)   transfers of research and development;

(f)   transfers under licence agreements;

(g)   transfers under finance arrangements (including loans and equity contributions in cash or in kind);

(h)   provision of guarantees or collateral;

(i)   commitments to do something if a particular event occurs or does not occur in the future, including executory contracts[1] (recognised and unrecognised); and

(j)   settlement of liabilities on behalf of the entity or by the entity on behalf of that related party.

22   Participation by a parent or subsidiary in a defined benefit plan that shares risks between group entities is a transaction between related parties (see paragraph 42 of AASB 119).

23   Disclosures that related party transactions were made on terms equivalent to those that prevail in arm's length transactions are made only if such terms can be substantiated.

24   Items of a similar nature may be disclosed in aggregate except when separate disclosure is necessary for an understanding of the effects of related party transactions on the financial statements of the entity.

Government-related entities

25   A reporting entity is exempt from the disclosure requirements of paragraph 18 in relation to related party transactions and outstanding balances, including commitments, with:

(a)   a government that has control or joint control of, or significant influence over, the reporting entity; and

(b)   another entity that is a related party because the same government has control or joint control of, or significant influence over, both the reporting entity and the other entity.

26   If a reporting entity applies the exemption in paragraph 25, it shall disclose the following about the transactions and related outstanding balances referred to in paragraph 25:

(a)   the name of the government and the nature of its relationship with the reporting entity (ie control, joint control or significant influence);

(b)   the following information in sufficient detail to enable users of the entity's financial statements to understand the effect of related party transactions on its financial statements:

(i)   the nature and amount of each individually significant transaction; and

(ii)   for other transactions that are collectively, but not individually, significant, a qualitative or quantitative indication of their extent. Types of transactions include those listed in paragraph 21.

27   In using its judgement to determine the level of detail to be disclosed in accordance with the requirements in paragraph 26(b), the reporting entity shall consider the closeness of the related party relationship and other factors relevant in establishing the level of significance of the transaction such as whether it is:

(a)   significant in terms of size;

(b)   carried out on non-market terms;

(c)   outside normal day-to-day business operations, such as the purchase and sale of businesses;

(d)   disclosed to regulatory or supervisory authorities;

(e)   reported to senior management;

(f)   subject to shareholder approval.

---

1   AASB 137 *Provisions, Contingent Liabilities and Contingent Assets* defines executory contracts as contracts under which neither party has performed any of its obligations or both parties have partially performed their obligations to an equal extent.

Effective date and transition

28   [Deleted by the AASB]

Aus28.1   An entity shall apply this Standard for annual periods beginning on or after 1
           July 2016. Earlier application is permitted for periods beginning on or after 1
           January 2014 but before 1 July 2016. If an entity applies this Standard for a
           period beginning before 1 July 2016, it shall disclose that fact.

Aus28.2   AASB 2015-6 *Amendments to Australian Accounting Standards – Extending
           Related Party Disclosures to Not-for-Profit Public Sector Entities* amended
           the previous version of this Standard as follows: deleted paragraph Aus1.3,
           amended paragraph Aus9.1 and added the Australian Implementation Guidance
           for Not-for-Profit Public Sector Entities. An entity shall apply those
           amendments for annual periods beginning on or after 1 July 2016. Earlier
           application is permitted. Those amendments shall be applied prospectively as
           at the beginning of the annual period in which this Standard is initially applied.
           For example, a not-for-profit public sector entity shall apply this Standard
           prospectively as at the beginning of the annual period in which this Standard
           is initially applied.

28A–28B   [Deleted by the AASB]

28C   AASB 2014-1 *Amendments to Australian Accounting Standards*, issued in June 2014,
        amended the previous version of this Standard as follows: amended paragraph 9 and
        added paragraphs 17A and 18A. An entity shall apply that amendment for annual
        periods beginning on or after 1 July 2014. Earlier application is permitted. If an entity
        applies that amendment for an earlier period it shall disclose that fact.

Withdrawal of IAS 24 (2003)

29   [Deleted by the AASB]

Commencement of the legislative instrument

Aus29.1 For legal purposes, this legislative instrument commences on 30 June 2016.

Withdrawal of AASB pronouncements

Aus29.2   This Standard repeals AASB 124 *Related Party Disclosures* issued in December
           2009. Despite the repeal, after the time this Standard starts to apply under
           section 334 of the Corporations Act (either generally or in relation to an
           individual entity), the repealed Standard continues to apply in relation to any
           period ending before that time as if the repeal had not occurred.

           [Note: When this Standard applies under section 334 of the Corporations
           Act (either generally or in relation to an individual entity), it supersedes the
           application of the repealed Standard.]

APPENDIX A
AUSTRALIAN DEFINED TERMS

This appendix is an integral part of AASB 124.

Aus9.1   **The following terms are also used in this Standard with the meaning
           specified.**

           Director **means:**

           (a)   a person who is a director under the Corporations Act; and

(b) in the case of entities governed by bodies not called a board of directors, a person who, regardless of the name that is given to the position, is appointed to the position of member of the governing body, council, commission or authority.

Remuneration is *compensation* as defined in this Standard.

Aus9.1.1 Although the defined term 'compensation' is used in this Standard rather than the term '*remuneration*', both words refer to the same concept and all references in the Corporations Act to the remuneration of directors and executives is taken as referring to compensation as defined and explained in this Standard.

APPENDIX B
AUSTRALIAN REDUCED DISCLOSURE REQUIREMENTS

This appendix is an integral part of AASB 124.

AusB1 The following do not apply to entities preparing general purpose financial statements under Australian Accounting Standards – Reduced Disclosure Requirements:

(a) paragraphs Aus13.1, 26 and 27;

(b) in paragraph 17, the text "and for each of ... (e) share-based payment"; and

(c) in paragraph 22, the text "(see paragraph 42 of AASB 119)".

Entities applying Australian Accounting Standards – Reduced Disclosure Requirements may elect to comply with some or all of these excluded requirements.

AusB2 The requirements that do not apply to entities preparing general purpose financial statements under Australian Accounting Standards – Reduced Disclosure Requirements are also identified in this Standard by shading of the relevant text.

AUSTRALIAN IMPLEMENTATION GUIDANCE FOR NOT-FOR-PROFIT PUBLIC SECTOR ENTITIES

This guidance is an integral part of AASB 124 and has the same authority as the other parts of the Standard. The guidance applies only to public sector entities. The guidance does not apply to private sector entities or affect their application of AASB 124.

IG1 AASB 124 *Related Party Disclosures* incorporates International Financial Reporting Standard IAS 24 *Related Party Disclosures*, issued by the International Accounting Standards Board. Consequently, much of the text of the body of this Standard and the Illustrative Examples is expressed from the perspective of for-profit entities. The AASB has prepared this guidance to explain and illustrate the principles in the Standard to assist application of the Standard by not-for-profit public sector entities, particularly to address circumstances where a for-profit perspective does not readily translate to a not-for-profit public sector perspective. This guidance also assists not-for-profit public sector entities in determining the extent of the information necessary to meet the objective of the Standard. This guidance does not remove the need for judgement to be applied by an entity in complying with the requirements of the Standard.

IG2 This guidance addresses a range of matters affecting not-for-profit public sector entities broadly in the order in which the related paragraphs appear in the body of the Standard.

Illustrative examples are provided in the implementation guidance. The examples apply by analogy to types of not-for-profit public sector entities other than those identified in the examples and similar circumstances. It is the facts and circumstances in any case, not simply the type of not-for-profit public sector entity, that need to be assessed in determining the appropriate disclosures that apply.

Identification of key management personnel

IG3   Paragraph 9 of the Standard defines key management personnel as being those persons having the authority and responsibility for planning, directing and controlling the activities of the entity, directly or indirectly, including any director (whether executive or otherwise) of the entity. In a public sector context, entities should consider the facts and circumstances, including the terms of the relevant legislative instruments that give rise to the entity, in assessing whether a person is a member of the key management personnel, as defined, of the entity. For example, the facts and circumstances may reflect that not all persons described as 'senior executive staff' or 'Secretary' or 'Minister' may be a member of the key management personnel of the entity. Similarly, in relation to a not-for-profit public sector entity, the facts and circumstances may reflect that a person's powers do not give rise to a capacity to direct or control the activities of an entity, where the powers are only ceremonial or procedural in substance.

IG4   Normally, the determination of key management personnel is similar for entities in the public sector and the private sector. However, ministerial-type roles do not normally arise in a private sector context. A Minister would be a member of the key management personnel of an entity that is within the Minister's portfolio if the Minister has the "authority and responsibility for planning, directing and controlling the activities of the entity, directly or indirectly". In some entities or jurisdictions, the responsible Minister may not, in substance, have such authority and responsibility over the activities of the entity, and consequently would not meet the definition of key management personnel.

IG5   A Minister may be a member of the key management personnel of an entity where the Minister's role and responsibilities result in the Minister forming part of the group of persons tasked with determining the direction of the entity. It would be uncommon for a Minister to be a member of the key management personnel of an entity that is within their portfolio where the entity is not otherwise controlled by the government, as the government's powers and functions (executed by the Minister) in relation to that entity would have formed part of the government's assessment of whether it controls the entity. Whether a Minister is a member of the key management personnel of an entity controlled by the government will depend on the facts and circumstances that apply in each instance, as the determination of the key management personnel of an entity is made on an entity by entity basis. Accordingly, a member of the key management personnel of the government is not necessarily also a member of the key management personnel of each entity controlled by that government (see also paragraph IG10).

IG6   Examples 1–6 illustrate application of the definition of key management personnel by not-for-profit public sector entities. These examples do not limit the persons who may be key management personnel of a not-for-profit public sector entity to only those roles described.

Example 1

Minister A is the Australian Minister for Education and Training. Minister A administers their portfolio through the Department of Education and Training (the Department), a controlled entity of the Australian Government. Minister A is accountable to Parliament for the actions of the Department. As part of the portfolio, the Minister is responsible for:

- education policy and programs including schools, vocational, higher education and Indigenous education, but excluding migrant adult education;
- education and training transitions policy and programs;
- science awareness programs in schools;

- training, including apprenticeships and training services;
- policy, co-ordination and support for education exports and services; and
- income support policies and programs for students and apprentices.
- Minister B is the Assistant Minister for Education and Training. Assistant Ministers are appointed to assist Ministers in prioritising work, to provide a training experience for future Ministers, to facilitate public access to the Ministers and to enable the bureaucracy to have an ongoing point of contact so that parliamentary correspondence and other parliamentary administrative issues are neither overlooked nor downgraded. As an Assistant Minister, Minister B cannot:
- sit as a Minister in Cabinet;
- attend a meeting of the Executive Council or sign Executive Council Minutes on behalf of the Minister;
- perform any duties in Parliament on behalf of the Minister including answering questions without notice, presenting Ministerial Statements, tabling documents and introducing legislation; or
- appear before a Committee of Parliament on behalf of the Minister.

The Department is responsible for delivering national policies and programs that help Australians access quality early childhood education, school education, higher education, vocational education and training, international education and research. The Department is headed by the Secretary of the Department, who reports to the Australian Minister for Education and Training. At the same time, the Secretary also makes reports to the Assistant Minister for Education and Training. The Secretary of the Department, and two Associate Secretaries and a Deputy Secretary within the Department, operate as the executive management team responsible for the day-to-day delivery of the Department's services.

Based on the facts and circumstances above, Minister A, the Secretary of the Department, and the two Associate Secretaries and Deputy Secretary are members of the key management personnel of the Department as they have the authority and responsibility for planning, directing and controlling the activities of the entity. Minister A's role is akin to that of a director in a company, as the Minister discharges their role and responsibilities regarding the Department and is ultimately responsible for the performance of the Department. Minister B is not a member of the key management personnel of the Department as Minister B's role supports that of the Minister, rather than having any authority and responsibility for planning, directing and controlling the activities of the Department in Minister B's own right.

Example 2

The Cabinet is a group within the Australian Government (the Commonwealth of Australia) comprising the Prime Minister and a number of senior Ministers. All current Ministers are part of the Executive Council, but not all Ministers are also part of Cabinet. The Governor-General is the chair of the Executive Council.

Minister A, the Australian Minister for Education and Training, is part of Cabinet. Minister B, the Assistant Minister for Education and Training is not part of Cabinet but is part of the Executive Council. Minister D, the Minister for Justice, is also not part of Cabinet but is part of the Executive Council.

Cabinet's role is to direct the overall government policy and make decisions about national issues. In Cabinet meetings, Ministers also present bills from their government departments. Cabinet examines these bills, and recommends whether bills should proceed to Parliament or changes should be made. A Minister who is not part of Cabinet may be invited to a Cabinet meeting to speak about developments within their portfolio. The Cabinet is accountable to Parliament for the running of the government.

The Executive Council is a constitutional body charged with advising the Governor-General. Legally, members of the Executive Council are chosen by the Governor-General; however, in practice, all current Ministers are part of the Executive Council. The Executive Council acts as a formal ratification body for the decisions of Cabinet, and is required to undertake a range of functions including making proclamations, regulations and ordinances as delegated by various Acts of Parliament, issuing writs for elections, appointing public servants and recommending the appointment of judges.

Section 61 of the Australian Constitution provides that "The executive power of the Commonwealth is vested in the Queen and is exercisable by the Governor-General as the Queen's representative, and extends to the execution and maintenance of this Constitution, and of the laws of the

Commonwealth". However, the Governor-General is bound by convention to follow the advice of the Executive Council.

Based on the facts and circumstances above, Minister A is a member of the key management personnel of the Australian Government. As part of Cabinet and having regard to Cabinet's powers, Minister A has the authority and responsibility for planning, directing and controlling the activities of the Australian Government. In addition, as a member of the key management personnel of the Australian Government, Minister A is also a related party of any entities controlled by the Australian Government, consistent with paragraph 9 of the Standard.

Minister B and Minister D are unlikely to be members of the key management personnel of the Australian Government as, although they are part of the Executive Council, they are outside the group of persons responsible for making decisions about the overall running of the government. Further, in substance, neither the members of the Executive Council nor Governor-General have the authority and responsibility for directing and controlling the activities of the Australian Government, and accordingly, are not members of the key management personnel of the Australian Government reporting entity.

Example 3

University XYZ is a not-for-profit public sector entity established under an Act of the State Government. The State Government has determined that it does not control the University.

The governing body of the University is the University Council. The University Council consists of 17 members, five of whom are appointed directly or indirectly by the State Minister for Education. The Chair of the University Council is the Chancellor, who is the formal head of the University. The Chancellor is responsible for ensuring the efficient operation of the University Council in the performance of its governance role, presiding at ceremonial occasions of the University and acting as a signatory to official statutory reports of the University.

The Act specifies that the University Council's responsibilities, powers and functions include:

- approving the mission, strategic direction and annual budget and business plan of the University;
- establishing policies ('university statutes and regulations') relating to the governance and operation of the University, including trusts and endowments, and research, development, consultancy, commercial activities and other services undertaken for commercial organisations or public bodies;
- developing guidelines (if any) concerning the carrying out of commercial activities, finance and property matters, or any other related matter;
- overseeing the management of the property, finances and business affairs of the University, such as risk management across the University, including its commercial activities;
- any other powers and functions conferred on it by or under legislation or any university statute or regulation; and
- the power to do anything else necessary or convenient to be done for or in connection with its powers and functions.

The University Council has a range of powers and functions that it can exercise directly, including the following:

- appointing the Vice-Chancellor, who is the chief executive officer of the University and responsible for the conduct of the University's affairs in all matters;
- determining the composition of borrowings within the parameters set by the State Government;
- approving the University's budget for a financial year, incorporating total revenue and the planned revenue sources, including planning the mix between teaching, research and commercial activities, the fees and charges to apply to those activities, and the type and value of government grants desired;
- determining the course mix and target student mix, such as vocational, undergraduate, graduate and executive courses, on-campus or distance learning, and local and international students;
- appointing staff and determining their terms and conditions;
- deciding whether to operate through multiple campuses and how to utilise the University's infrastructure; and

- making university regulations with respect to any matter relating to the University.

The University Council has delegated the day-to-day management responsibilities and other functions to the University's executive and other senior staff in order to be able to focus on the broader policy and strategic issues.

The State Minister for Education has the following powers and functions as part of the Minister's role in the State Government:

- fixing the remuneration and fees to be paid to University Council members who are not full-time staff of the University or holders of statutory office;
- approving (or vetoing) University statutes and guidelines made by the University Council;
- declaring an activity to be a university commercial activity;
- making interim guidelines concerning university commercial activities and finance and property matters – these apply unless replaced by University-submitted guidelines approved by the Minister;
- in conjunction with the State Treasurer, approving the limits and conditions (eg security) for University borrowings;
- approving (or vetoing) the disposal of land that was previously Crown land granted to the University;
- requesting commercial and financial reports from the University;
- referring a university commercial activity or any aspect thereof to the auditor-general for investigation; and
- ensuring that the University complies with certain rights specified in State Government grants provided to the University – some of the grants are required to be repaid if not applied as specified.

Based on the facts and circumstances above, as the State Government has determined that it does not control the University, it is unlikely that the State Minister for Education, as the executor of the State Government's powers, is a member of the key management personnel of the University, as the evaluation of control includes an assessment of the State Government's ability to direct the activities that most significantly affect the University's outcomes. The State Minister's powers and functions (provided to the position) may restrict the way in which the University operates, but do not of themselves give the State Minister authority and responsibility for the activities of the University.

Rather, based on the facts and circumstances above, it is the University Council (who are akin to a board of directors, with the Chancellor akin to a non-executive chairman) and the University's executive and other senior staff who have the authority and responsibility for planning, directing and controlling the activities of the University.

The purpose of this Example is to assist entities with the identification of key management personnel of a not-for-profit public sector entity. However, an entity should also consider whether the State Minister for Education, or the State Government, will otherwise meet the definition of a related party of the University (see paragraph 9 of the Standard).

AASB

Example 4

The LMN local government (the Council) is a local government entity created under a State's Local Government Act (the Act) and is subject to a wide range of State Government regulatory powers. The interest of the State Government in the activities of the Council is primarily to ensure that the general objectives set out in the Act are being achieved or furthered. The State Government's rights in respect of the Council are held primarily by the State Minister for Local Government. These rights allow the State Government (via the State Minister for Local Government) to advise or guide the Council in its activities, or under particular circumstances, to intervene in the activities of the Council.

Minister X is the State Minister for Local Government. The Minister administers their portfolio through the Local Government branch of the State Department of Transport, Planning and Local Infrastructure (the Department). As part of the Minister's role and responsibilities, Minister X is responsible for:

- the scrutiny of councils, including municipal boundaries;
- making recommendations for allocation of project grants to local governments for projects;
- overseeing tendering processes for council services;

- ensuring the concerns of local governments are communicated to the State Cabinet; and
- the coordination of council community and infrastructure work at a State level.

The Council's primary objective is to achieve the best outcomes for the local community over the long term. The Council is empowered by the Act to do all things necessary and convenient for the achievement of its objectives and the performance of its functions, subject to any limitations under the Act or any other legislation.

The Council is administered by 10 councillors, who are elected directly by the local community in periodic elections. The Council's functions include raising revenue to fund its functions and activities, and planning for and providing services and facilities (including infrastructure) for the local community. In carrying out its functions, the Council undertakes a wide range of activities including the imposition of rates and charges upon constituents, and the provision without charge of services such as parks and roads. The day-to-day operations of the Council are carried out by council staff under the direction of its elected councillors.

The State Government has determined that it does not control the Council.

Based on the facts and circumstances above, Minister X is not a member of the key management personnel of the Council, as the Minister's role does not extend to having the authority and responsibility for planning, directing and controlling the activities of the Council itself. Having concluded that the State Government does not control the council, Minister X's role as executor of the State Government's powers and rights over the Council cannot of itself enable Minister X to meet the definition of key management personnel of the Council. Rather, in this example, it is the councillors and senior council staff who have the authority and responsibility for the activities of the Council (similar to a board of directors and senior management of a company).

The purpose of this Example is to assist entities with the identification of key management personnel of a not-for-profit public sector entity. However, an entity should also consider whether Minister X, or the State Government, will otherwise meet the definition of a related party of the Council (see paragraph 9 of the Standard).

Example 5

Minister E, the State Minister for Education, Minister F, the State Minister for Children and Early Childhood, and Minister G, the State Minister for Higher Education and Skills, administer their portfolios wholly through the State Department of Education (the Department), a controlled entity of the State Government.

The day-to-day operations of the Department are managed by an Executive Board comprising the Secretary of the Department and the head of each of the Department's divisions. The Executive Board is the governance and decision-making body for the Department accountable for the:

- strategic direction and leadership of the Department;
- management of the Department;
- decision-making and risk management;
- monitoring and evaluation of the Department's activities; and
- compliance and stakeholder management.

The Department reports to the three Ministers, separately or jointly as appropriate to the nature of the Ministers' portfolio. The Ministers are jointly accountable to Parliament for the actions of the Department.

Based on the facts and circumstances above, Minister E, Minister F and Minister G, and the members of the Executive Board are members of the key management personnel of the Department as they have the authority and responsibility for planning, directing and controlling the activities of the Department. The Ministers' roles are akin to that of directors in a company, even though each has responsibility only to the extent of their respective portfolios, as they discharge their roles and responsibilities regarding the Department and are ultimately responsible for the performance of the Department.

Example 6

Statutory authority SLA is a statutory authority of the State Government tasked with providing legal information, advice and representation to financially disadvantaged residents of the State. As a statutory authority, SLA was established under its own enabling legislation, which sets out its functions, powers and responsibilities. Its remit is such that it generally operates independently of any governmental direction or influence.

SLA is funded by the State Government to undertake state law matters. The State Government may specify areas to which certain of the funds granted should be allocated. SLA is a controlled entity of the State Government.

The execution and authority for the day-to-day operations of SLA are the responsibility of its executive management team, who report to the Board of SLA. The Board is the statutory authority's governing body and is responsible for managing SLA and ensuring that its objectives are achieved. The Board is responsible for deciding SLA's priorities and strategies, leading its policy direction and ensuring its sound and prudent financial management. Board members are appointed by the State Governor in Council, on advice of the State Minister for Justice.

SLA is accountable to the State Government for the delivery of legal assistance services. As a statutory authority, the Board of SLA reports to the State Minister for Justice, who is responsible to Parliament for the oversight of statutory authorities within the Minister's portfolio.

SLA's enabling legislation provides that the Board must:

• if asked by the State Minister for Justice, give the Minister a report on any issue relevant to its functions, other than about legal assistance for a particular person; and

• act upon a written direction given by the State Minister for Justice about the performance of SLA's functions or exercise of its powers, and its policies, priorities or guidelines, including priorities in legal assistance funding. The direction cannot be about giving legal assistance to a particular person.

While SLA generally operates independently of any governmental direction or influence, from time to time, the State Minister for Justice has requested various reports and required SLA to act as directed.

Based on the facts and circumstances above, the Board and executive management team of SLA are members of the key management personnel of the entity, as they ultimately have the authority and responsibility for planning, directing and controlling the activities of the entity. In this fact pattern, the State Minister for Justice is also a member of the key management personnel of SLA, as the powers vested in the Minister's role also give the Minister authority and responsibility for planning, directing and controlling the activities of the entity, as SLA is required to act in accordance with the Minister's written directions (which may relate to SLA's execution of its remit).

The purpose of this Example is to assist entities with the identification of key management personnel of a not-for-profit public sector entity. However, consideration should also be given to whether the State Government is a related party of SLA (see paragraph 9 of the Standard).

Key management personnel compensation

IG7 In the public sector, Ministers are normally compensated through one or more central government agencies or authorities. In relation to not-for-profit public sector entities, the central government agency typically operates as a management entity for the purposes of applying paragraph 17A of the Standard.

IG8 Paragraph 18A of the Standard requires disclosure of amounts incurred by the entity preparing general purpose financial statements for the key management personnel services that are provided by a separate management entity. No disclosure is required to comply with the requirement in paragraph 18A where an entity is not obligated to reimburse the management entity for key management personnel services it has obtained.

Related party transactions

IG9 Paragraph 18 of the Standard requires an entity to disclose information about transactions that have occurred between the entity and its related parties, including transactions between the entity and its key management personnel or key management personnel of the entity's parent, that is necessary for users to understand the potential effect of the relationship on the financial statements.

IG10 Ministers, councillors and other senior public servants may qualify as a related party of a public sector entity under one or more of the criteria set down in paragraph (a) in the definition of 'related party' in AASB 124. For example, a Minister who is a member of the key management personnel of the Commonwealth or State government is, under the definition of 'related party', a related party not only of the Commonwealth or State government consolidated entity but also of each controlled entity of that government (see Example 2 in paragraph IG6). In such instances, the Standard requires the controlled government entity to disclose related party transactions with that Minister which are necessary to meet the objective noted in paragraph 1 of the Standard, whether or not the Minister has responsibility for the entity.

IG11   A related party transaction is a transfer of resources, services or obligations between an entity and its related party, regardless of whether a price is charged. In the not-for-profit public sector, many entities are likely to engage frequently with persons who are a related party of that entity in the course of delivering the entity's public service objectives, including the raising of funds (for example, rates and taxes) to meet those objectives. These related party transactions often occur on terms and conditions no different to those applying to the general public (for example, the Medicare rebate or public school fees). A not-for-profit public sector entity may determine that information about related party transactions occurring during the course of delivering its public service objectives and which occur on no different terms to that of the general public is not material for disclosure in its general purpose financial statements and accordingly need not be disclosed. Guidance relevant to an entity's assessment of the materiality of a disclosure to its general purpose financial statements is included in AASB 101 *Presentation of Financial Statements* and AASB 108 *Accounting Policies, Changes in Accounting Estimates and Errors*. The factors described in paragraph 27 of the Standard may also assist an entity in making this determination.

IG12   Examples 7–8 describe different types of related party transactions that may occur between not-for-profit public sector entities and their related parties:

Example 7

Councillor P is a member of the key management personnel of the LMN local government (the Council). The Council's functions include raising revenue to fund its functions and activities, and planning for and providing services and facilities (including infrastructure) for the local community. In carrying out its functions, the Council undertakes a wide range of activities including the imposition of rates and charges upon constituents, and the provision without charge of services such as parks and roads.

Councillor P is a ratepayer residing within the Council's constituency. As such, Councillor P takes advantage of the availability of free public access to local parks and libraries. Councillor P also used the swimming pool at the Council's Recreation Centre twice during the financial year, paying the casual entry fee applicable to the general public each time. The recreation centre has approximately 20,000 visitors each financial year.

All of the transactions described above between the Council and Councillor P are related party transactions of the Council considered for disclosure in the Council's general purpose financial statements. Based on the facts and circumstances described, the Council may determine that these transactions are unlikely to influence the decisions that users of the Council's financial statements make having regard to both the extent of the transactions, and that the transactions have occurred between the Council and Councillor P within a public service provider/ taxpayer relationship.

Example 8

Minister Z, the State Minister for Planning, has responsibility for a range of functions and, in certain circumstances, has the power to intervene on matters associated with planning and heritage processes. Minister Z is a member of the key management personnel of State Government H.

Entity MED is a controlled entity of State Government H, and operates within the State Health sector. Entity MED is currently seeking State development approval for a potentially contentious new building.

Around this time, Entity MED enters into a contract with Entity STU, an entity wholly-owned and controlled by a close member of Minister Z's family for Entity STU to provide cleaning services at various current and future Entity MED locations, including the new building when completed. The cleaning contract was won by Entity STU in an open tender. Minister Z has declared information

---

about the contract to provide cleaning services to Cabinet and it is included as part of the Minister's Register of Members' Interests. During the reporting period, Entity STU rendered services of $50,000 to Entity MED. No amounts remain outstanding at Entity STU's reporting date. Entity MED assesses the cleaning services rendered to be a material component of its total operating expenses.

Entity STU is a related party of Entity MED in accordance with the definition of a related party in paragraph 9 of the Standard. The provision of $50,000 cleaning services by Entity STU to Entity MED described above is a related party transaction of Entity MED as there has been a transfer of services and resources between Entity MED and Entity STU. Based on the facts and circumstances described, management of Entity MED may determine that information about the transaction is material for disclosure in its general purpose financial statements as there has been a transfer of resources occurring other than as a result of a public service provider/ taxpayer relationship between related parties and the amount of the transaction is material to Entity MED.

The provision of $50,000 cleaning services by Entity STU to Entity MED described above is also a related party transaction of State Government H as Minister Z is a member of the key management personnel of State Government H and Entity MED is a controlled entity of State Government H. State Government H should separately assess whether the related party transaction is material for disclosure in the whole-of-government financial statements.

Government-related entities

IG13 Paragraph 25 of the Standard provides a limited exemption from the disclosure requirements of paragraph 18 for government-related entities, subject to the alternative disclosures in paragraph 26 of the Standard. An entity considers, on balance, the range of factors included in paragraph 27, as well as any additional relevant factors, in determining the extent of the disclosure required by paragraph 26(b). In some instances, the presence of a single factor identified in paragraph 27 will not be sufficient to inform the entity of the level of individual or collective significance of the transaction. For example, a requirement of legislation to report on various transactions to Parliament may not of itself inform a not-for-profit public sector entity of the significance of a transaction to itself where the entity's objective is to carry out such transactions, and consequently, the entity should also have regard to other factors in forming its assessment of the significance of the transaction. In other instances, a single factor may be adequate to establish the extent of the significance of the transaction to the entity.

IG14 Individually significant transactions would normally form a small subset, by number, of the total related party transactions of the entity. Paragraph IE3 in the Illustrative Examples accompanying the Standard provides examples of disclosure to comply with paragraph 26(b).

ILLUSTRATIVE EXAMPLES

The following examples accompany, but are not part of, AASB 124 Related Party Disclosures. They illustrate:

* *the partial exemption for government-related entities; and*

* *how the definition of a related party would apply in specified circumstances.*

In the examples, references to 'financial statements' relate to the individual, separate or consolidated financial statements.

Partial exemption for government-related entities

Example 1 – Exemption from disclosure (paragraph 25)

IE1 Government G directly or indirectly controls Entities 1 and 2 and Entities A, B, C and D. Person X is a member of the key management personnel of Entity 1.

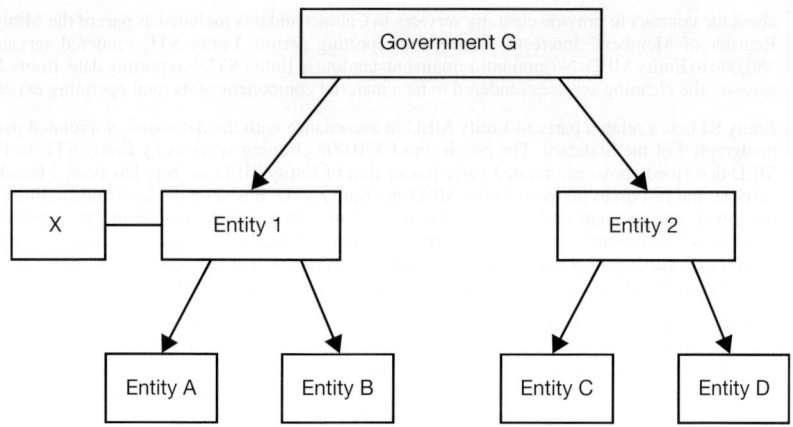

IE2   For Entity A's financial statements, the exemption in paragraph 25 applies to:

    (a)   transactions with Government G; and

    (b)   transactions with Entities 1 and 2 and Entities B, C and D.

However, that exemption does not apply to transactions with Person X.

Disclosure requirements when exemption applies (paragraph 26)

IE3   In Entity A's financial statements, an example of disclosure to comply with paragraph 26(b)(i) for **individually** significant transactions could be:

Example of disclosure for individually significant transaction carried out on non-market terms

On 15 January 20X1 Entity A, a utility company in which Government G indirectly owns 75 per cent of outstanding shares, sold a 10 hectare piece of land to another government-related utility company for CU5 million.[2] On 31 December 20X0 a plot of land in a similar location, of a similar size and with similar characteristics, was sold for CU3 million. There had not been any appreciation or depreciation of the land in the intervening period. See note X [of the financial statements] for disclosure of government assistance as required by AASB 120 *Accounting for Government Grants and Disclosure of Government Assistance* and notes Y and Z [of the financial statements] for compliance with other relevant Australian Accounting Standards.

Example of disclosure for individually significant transaction because of size of transaction

In the year ended December 20X1 Government G provided Entity A, a utility company in which Government G indirectly owns 75 per cent of outstanding shares, with a loan equivalent to 50 per cent of its funding requirement, repayable in quarterly instalments over the next five years. Interest is charged on the loan at a rate of 3 per cent, which is comparable to that charged on Entity A's bank loans.[3] See notes Y and Z [of the financial statements] for compliance with other relevant Australian Accounting Standards.

Example of disclosure of collectively significant transactions

In Entity A's financial statements, an example of disclosure to comply with paragraph 26(b)(ii) for **collectively** significant transactions could be:

---

2   In these examples monetary amounts are denominated in 'currency units (CU)'.

3   If the reporting entity had concluded that this transaction constituted government assistance it would have needed to consider the disclosure requirements in AASB 120.

Government G, indirectly, owns 75 per cent of Entity A's outstanding shares. Entity A's significant transactions with Government G and other entities controlled, jointly controlled or significantly influenced by Government G are [a large portion of its sales of goods and purchases of raw materials] or [about 50 per cent of its sales of goods and about 35 per cent of its purchases of raw materials].

The company also benefits from guarantees by Government G of the company's bank borrowing. See note X [of the financial statements] for disclosure of government assistance as required by AASB 120 *Accounting for Government Grants and Disclosure of Government Assistance* and notes Y and Z [of the financial statements] for compliance with other relevant Australian Accounting Standards.

Definition of a related party

*The references are to subparagraphs of the definition of a **related party** in paragraph 9 of AASB 124.*

Example 2 – Associates and subsidiaries

IE4   Parent entity has a controlling interest in Subsidiaries A, B and C and has significant influence over Associates 1 and 2. Subsidiary C has significant influence over Associate 3.

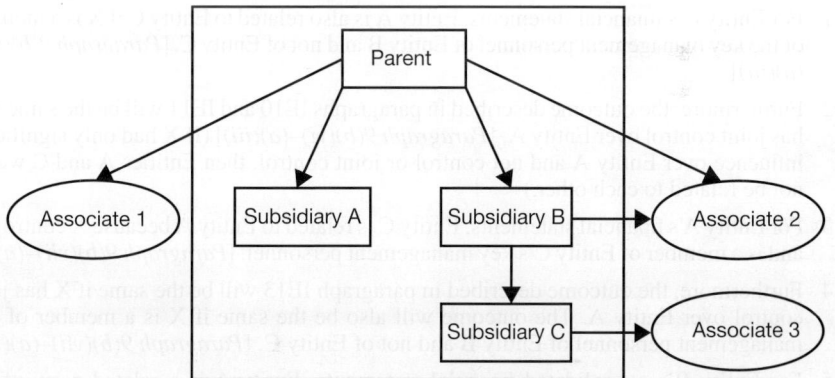

IE5   For Parent's separate financial statements, Subsidiaries A, B and C and Associates 1, 2 and 3 are related parties. [*Paragraph 9(b)(i) and (ii)*]

IE6   For Subsidiary A's financial statements, Parent, Subsidiaries B and C and Associates 1, 2 and 3 are related parties. For Subsidiary B's separate financial statements, Parent, Subsidiaries A and C and Associates 1, 2 and 3 are related parties. For Subsidiary C's financial statements, Parent, Subsidiaries A and B and Associates 1, 2 and 3 are related parties. [*Paragraph 9(b)(i) and (ii)*]

IE7   For the financial statements of Associates 1, 2 and 3, Parent and Subsidiaries A, B and C are related parties. Associates 1, 2 and 3 are not related to each other. [*Paragraph 9(b)(ii)*]

IE8   For Parent's consolidated financial statements, Associates 1, 2 and 3 are related to the Group. [*Paragraph 9(b)(ii)*]

Example 3 – Key management personnel

IE9   A person, X, has a 100 per cent investment in Entity A and is a member of the key management personnel of Entity C. Entity B has a 100 per cent investment in Entity C.

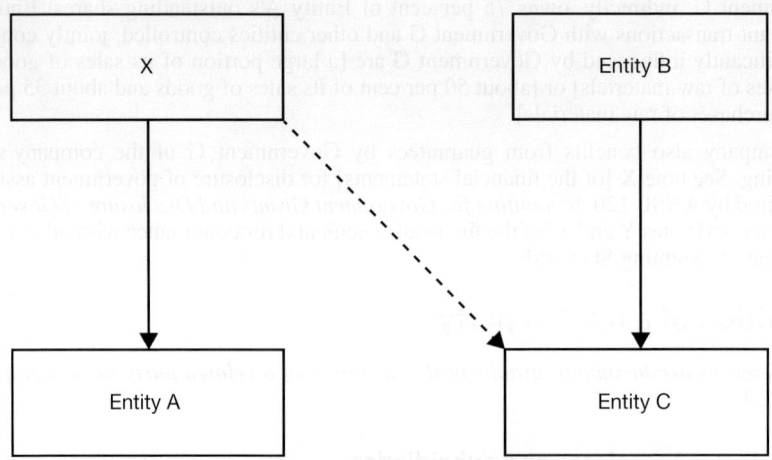

IE10   For Entity C's financial statements, Entity A is related to Entity C because X controls Entity A and is a member of the key management personnel of Entity C. [*Paragraph 9(b)(vi)–(a)(iii)*]

IE11   For Entity C's financial statements, Entity A is also related to Entity C if X is a member of the key management personnel of Entity B and not of Entity C. [*Paragraph 9(b)(vi)–(a)(iii)*]

IE12   Furthermore, the outcome described in paragraphs IE10 and IE11 will be the same if X has joint control over Entity A. [*Paragraph 9(b)(vi)–(a)(iii)*] (If X had only significant influence over Entity A and not control or joint control, then Entities A and C would not be related to each other.)

IE13   For Entity A's financial statements, Entity C is related to Entity A because X controls A and is a member of Entity C's key management personnel. [*Paragraph 9(b)(vii)–(a)(i)*]

IE14   Furthermore, the outcome described in paragraph IE13 will be the same if X has joint control over Entity A. The outcome will also be the same if X is a member of key management personnel of Entity B and not of Entity C. [*Paragraph 9(b)(vii)–(a)(i)*]

IE15   For Entity B's consolidated financial statements, Entity A is a related party of the Group if X is a member of key management personnel of the Group. [*Paragraph 9(b)(vi)–(a)(iii)*]

Example 4 – Person as investor

IE16   A person, X, has an investment in Entity A and Entity B.

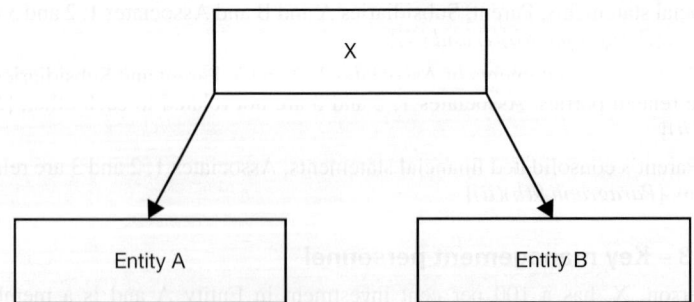

IE17   For Entity A's financial statements, if X controls or jointly controls Entity A, Entity B is related to Entity A when X has control, joint control or significant influence over Entity B. [*Paragraph 9(b)(vi)–(a)(i) and 9(b)(vii)–(a)(i)*]

IE18 For Entity B's financial statements, if X controls or jointly controls Entity A, Entity A is related to Entity B when X has control, joint control or significant influence over Entity B. [*Paragraph 9(b)(vi)–(a)(i) and 9(b)(vi)–(a)(ii)*]

IE19 If X has significant influence over both Entity A and Entity B, Entities A and B are not related to each other.

Example 5 – Close members of the family holding investments

IE20 A person, X, is the domestic partner of Y. X has an investment in Entity A and Y has an investment in Entity B.

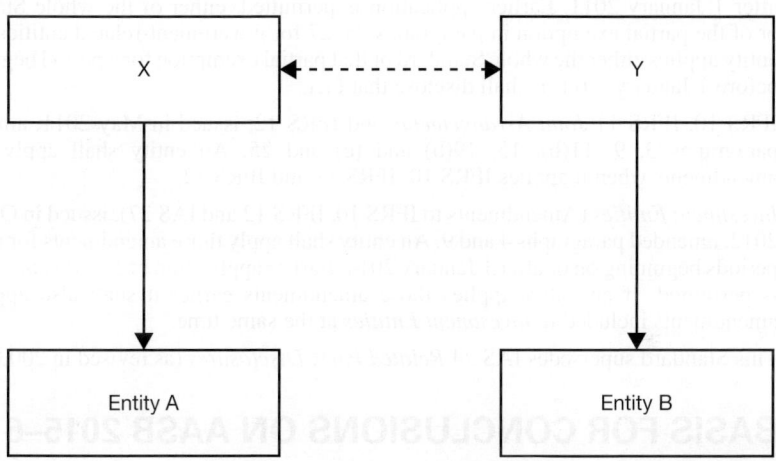

IE21 For Entity A's financial statements, if X controls or jointly controls Entity A, Entity B is related to Entity A when Y has control, joint control or significant influence over Entity B. [*Paragraph 9(b)(vi)–(a)(i) and 9(b)(vii)–(a)(i)*]

IE22 For Entity B's financial statements, if X controls or jointly controls Entity A, Entity A is related to Entity B when Y has control, joint control or significant influence over Entity B. [*Paragraph 9(b)(vi)–(a)(i) and 9(b)(vi)–(a)(ii)*]

IE23 If X has significant influence over Entity A and Y has significant influence over Entity B, Entities A and B are not related to each other.

Example 6 – Entity with joint control

IE24 Entity A has both (i) joint control over Entity B and (ii) joint control or significant influence over Entity C.

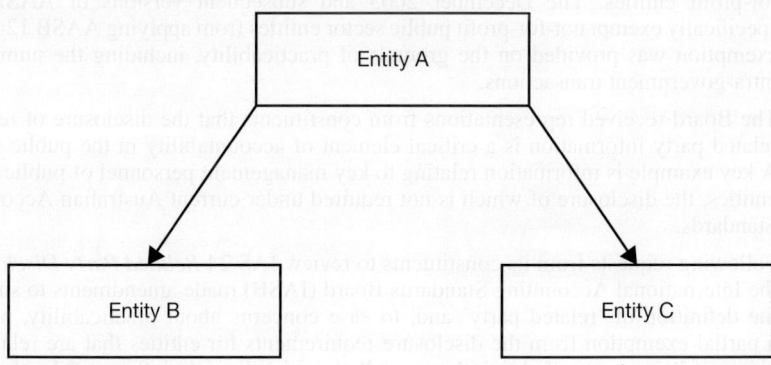

IE25 For Entity B's financial statements, Entity C is related to Entity B. [*Paragraph 9(b)(iii) and (iv)*]

IE26 Similarly, for Entity C's financial statements, Entity B is related to Entity C. [*Paragraph 9(b)(iii) and (iv)*]

DELETED IAS 24 TEXT

Deleted IAS 24 text is not part of AASB 124.

28 An entity shall apply this Standard retrospectively for annual periods beginning on or after 1 January 2011. Earlier application is permitted, either of the whole Standard or of the partial exemption in paragraphs 25–27 for government-related entities. If an entity applies either the whole Standard or that partial exemption for a period beginning before 1 January 2011, it shall disclose that fact.

28A IFRS 10, IFRS 11 *Joint Arrangements* and IFRS 12, issued in May 2011, amended paragraphs 3, 9, 11(b), 15, 19(b) and (e) and 25. An entity shall apply those amendments when it applies IFRS 10, IFRS 11 and IFRS 12.

28B *Investment Entities* (Amendments to IFRS 10, IFRS 12 and IAS 27), issued in October 2012, amended paragraphs 4 and 9. An entity shall apply those amendments for annual periods beginning on or after 1 January 2014. Earlier application of *Investment Entities* is permitted. If an entity applies those amendments earlier it shall also apply all amendments included in *Investment Entities* at the same time.

29 This Standard supersedes IAS 24 *Related Party Disclosures* (as revised in 2003).

BASIS FOR CONCLUSIONS ON AASB 2015–6

This Basis for Conclusions accompanies, but is not part of, AASB 124. The Basis for Conclusions was originally published with AASB 2015-6 Amendments to Australian Accounting Standards – Extending Related Party Disclosures to Not-for-Profit Public Sector Entities.

Background

BC1 This Basis for Conclusions summarises the Australian Accounting Standards Board's considerations in deciding to extend the scope of AASB 124 *Related Party Disclosures* (December 2009) to the not-for-profit public sector. Individual Board members gave greater weight to some factors than to others.

BC2 The first version of AASB 124, AASB 124 *Related Party Disclosures* (July 2004), applied explicitly to general purpose financial statements of companies and other for-profit entities. The December 2005 and subsequent versions of AASB 124 specifically exempt not-for-profit public sector entities from applying AASB 124. This exemption was provided on the grounds of practicability, including the number of intra-government transactions.

BC3 The Board received representations from constituents that the disclosure of relevant related party information is a critical element of accountability in the public sector. A key example is information relating to key management personnel of public sector entities, the disclosure of which is not required under current Australian Accounting Standards.

BC4 Following requests from its constituents to review IAS 24 *Related Party Disclosures*, the International Accounting Standards Board (IASB) made amendments to simplify the definition of 'related party' and, to ease concerns about practicability, provide a partial exemption from the disclosure requirements for entities that are related by virtue of being controlled, jointly controlled or significantly influenced by the same government. The Board incorporated the revised IAS 24 into AASB 124 (December 2009). The Board noted that this version of AASB 124 provides a more appropriate basis for application by not for profit public sector entities than the previous versions, as transactions between government-related entities of the same jurisdiction are exempted partially from disclosure.

BC5 Therefore, in furtherance of its policy of promulgating transaction-neutral Standards to the extent feasible, the Board initiated a project to consider issues relating to extending the scope of AASB 124 (December 2009) to not-for-profit public sector entities. The Board issued Exposure Draft ED 214 *Extending Related Party Disclosures to the Not-for-Profit Public Sector* in July 2011. ED 214 exposed for public comment the Board's proposal to extend the scope of AASB 124 to include not-for-profit public sector entities. The ED explained the Board's reasons for its proposals, including its considerations as to the applicability of AASB 124 to a not-for-profit public sector context. In addition, public roundtables were conducted with public sector constituents to identify concerns and implementation issues arising from the Board's proposals.

BC6 In finalising its proposals that not-for-profit public sector entities be required to apply AASB 124 unamended, the Board addressed a range of issues, including consideration of:

(a) amending the definition of 'key management personnel' for such entities;

(b) amending the requirements to provide such entities with some relief from disclosure of ministerial compensation;

(c) exempting such entities from disclosing certain related party transactions with Ministers;

(d) not requiring general government sector (GGS) financial statements to comply with AASB 124;

(e) adding a public sector perspective to AASB 124, for example by inserting an alternative definition for the term 'business' in paragraph 5 of AASB 124; and

(f) extending the disclosure requirements in AASB 124 for key management personnel.

Each of these issues and the outcome of the Board's considerations are noted below.

BC7 In finalising its proposals, the Board also considered constituent feedback for implementation guidance to be developed to assist not-for-profit public sector entities in applying AASB 124. The Board noted that while some information about Ministerial or senior executive compensation or related party transactions may be disclosed pursuant to other legislation or directives, the requirement to apply AASB 124 will be the first time that information about a not-for-profit public sector entity's related parties is specified by Australian Accounting Standards for inclusion in its general purpose financial statements. Consequently, such entities may not have previously considered challenges in implementing the Standard's requirements in a not-for-profit public sector environment. The Board considered that these entities may also have difficulty in identifying and determining the extent of the information necessary to meet the objective of AASB 124, as described in paragraph 1 of the Standard. Accordingly, the Board determined that the final amendments would include implementation guidance to assist not-for-profit public sector entities with their implementation of the Standard.

Significant issues

Definition of key management personnel

BC8 The Board considered whether an amendment of the definition of key management personnel for the not-for-profit public sector would be necessary to facilitate a decision to remove the not-for-profit public sector exemption from AASB 124, but decided that the present definition was suitable. The AASB noted that, in a public sector context, entities should consider the facts and circumstances in assessing whether a person is a member of the key management personnel, as defined, of the entity.

BC9 The Board considered that normally, the determination of key management personnel will be similar for entities in the public sector or the private sector. For example, a not-for-profit public sector entity will need to determine whether all, or only certain, of its senior executive service employees meet the definition of key management personnel. However, the Board acknowledged constituents' concerns that the determination of key management personnel may not be straightforward in the not-for-profit public sector given ministerial-type roles. The Board noted that it does not regard a Minister to always be a member of the key management personnel of a not-for-profit public sector entity; rather, this is dependent on the particular circumstances of the jurisdiction and of the entity. Accordingly, the Board decided to add guidance to the Standard, in the absence of a private sector analogy, to assist not-for-profit public sector entities in applying the definition of key management personnel to Ministers, as ministerial-type roles do not usually arise in a private sector context.

BC10 The Board also noted that an entity may determine that a relevant Minister may not meet the definition of key management personnel of an entity. However, the Board observed that this did not preclude that Minister from being otherwise identified as a related party of the entity, for example, where the Minister is a member of the key management personnel of the entity's parent.

Key management personnel compensation – Ministers

BC11 Respondents to ED 214 raised concerns that the requirements of AASB 124 pertaining to the disclosure of key management personnel compensation would be onerous if applicable to Ministers, noting also that any attribution of a Ministerial salary across entities coming under the responsibility of that Minister's portfolio would involve significant judgement.

BC12 The Board considered whether some relief was necessary with respect to the compensation of a Minister who is a member of the key management personnel of an entity. The Board observed that Ministers are typically remunerated through Parliament via a central agency, and that a Minister's compensation, while related to their responsibilities, may not be related to services performed for any specific entity or group of entities.

BC13 The Board noted the addition of paragraphs 17A and 18A into AASB 124 since the comment period on ED 214 closed. These paragraphs were inserted into AASB 124 by AASB 2014-1 *Amendments to Australian Accounting Standards* (June 2014) to address the disclosures that apply where members of the key management personnel are not employees of the reporting entity (see paragraphs BC51 and BC52 of IAS 24). The Board considered that these paragraphs will be of relevance to a not-for-profit public sector entity when considering the disclosure of the compensation of a Minister who has been identified as part of the key management personnel of the entity, and may alleviate the respondents' concerns noted in paragraph BC11. Accordingly, the Board decided that no amendment to AASB 124 to address the disclosure of ministerial compensation was necessary at this time. However, the Board decided to add implementation guidance to clarify the manner it considers paragraph 17A operates in relation to a Minister's compensation.

Related party transactions

BC14 The definition of 'related party' in AASB 124 separately addresses persons and entities related to the entity preparing general purpose financial statements. The partial exemption in AASB 124 from the disclosure requirements for government-related entities applies only in relation to those entities specified in paragraphs 25(a) and 25(b) of that Standard, and not also to persons who are related parties covered by paragraph 17 (key management personnel compensation) or paragraph 18 (transactions during the periods covered by the financial statements) of AASB 124.

BC15 Having regard to the partial exemption for government-related entities in AASB 124, the Board considered whether providing an exemption for the disclosure of related party transactions with Ministers or local government councillors was justified by any circumstances unique to the public sector and that may not have been considered by the IASB, whose mandate is limited to for-profit entities. The Board's consideration included the role of Ministers in a government and how onerous the disclosures required under AASB 124 might be. As part of its consideration, the Board had regard to the New Zealand Accounting Standards Board's decisions relating to disclosures of related party transactions with Ministers.

BC16 The Board observed that Ministers who are members of the key management personnel of their government would also be related parties not only of the government but also of each controlled entity of the government. Accordingly, a subsidiary government entity will be required to disclose related party transactions with Ministers who may have no responsibility for the entity to the extent the disclosures are considered material, from the entity's perspective, for disclosure. For example, the Board noted that in Example 1 of the Illustrative Examples accompanying AASB 124, Entities 1¬, 2, A, B, C and D will be required to disclose in their financial statements related party transactions between a Minister who is a member of the key management personnel of Government G and the entity, even where the Minister's portfolio does not include the entity.

BC17 The Board noted that, as is often the case with related party transactions, judgement would be required as to when transactions are material, especially when qualitative assessments are made about the nature of transactions. The Board considered situations in which key management personnel of a not-for-profit public sector entity, including Ministers or local government councillors where so identified, paid taxes, levies or other statutory charges or fees faced generally by citizens, or used public services such as state hospitals or schools. The Board does not expect, absent unusual circumstances, that the application of materiality would result in disclosure in many of these situations. In contrast, a commercial contract entered into by a Minister or local government councillor with a related public sector entity may be relevant for disclosure, similar to a commercial contract between a member of the key management personnel of a for-profit entity and the for-profit entity (for example, a contract to provide accountancy services between the entity and an entity controlled by a member of its key management personnel). Accordingly, the Board observed that a not-for-profit public sector entity would also need to apply judgement in determining the extent of information it needs to collect to meet the objective of AASB 124, as there is little value in an entity incurring significant costs to obtain data that is immaterial for disclosure. The Board noted that it would expect appropriate criteria to be identified so that information about transactions that are possibly material (for example, transactions that have occurred at a different price or volume to that applying to the general public) is captured for assessment.

BC18 Having regard to the role of materiality, the Board decided that no specific exemption from disclosure of the related party transactions with key management personnel of a not-for-profit public sector entity, including any Ministers or local government councillors where so identified, was necessary. However, to respond to constituents' requests for clarification on the extent of disclosures required of related party transactions that occur in the not-for-profit public sector, the Board decided to add implementation guidance to AASB 124 to assist not-for-profit public sector entities in this regard.

Transactions with Ministers acting in their collective government capacity

BC19 The Board considered whether transactions with Ministers who are related parties and who are acting in their collective government capacity would be assessed as being with the government and eligible for the partial exemption from disclosure in paragraphs 25 and 26 of AASB 124. The Board decided that such transactions were in substance transactions between the entity and the government-related entity, rather than being transactions with the Ministers in their own right, and that no clarification to the Standard was necessary in this regard (however, see also paragraphs BC20–BC22 below).

Government-related entities

BC20 The Board noted that not-for-profit public sector entities were previously excluded from applying the Standard on grounds of practicability, including having regard to the number of intra-government transactions. In extending the Standard to apply to not-for-profit public sector entities, the Board considered the extent of transactions for which disclosure may be necessary to comply with paragraph 26 of the Standard.

BC21 In its considerations, the Board had regard to the IASB's reasons for including the partial exemption, being to resolve concerns raised when the Standard was applied in environments where government control is pervasive. The Board noted that the IASB had indicated that it did not intend to require the entity to identify every government-related entity or to quantify in detail every transaction with such entities, as such a requirement would negate the exemption (see paragraph BC43 of IAS 24).

BC22 The Board noted that it shared the IASB's view communicated in paragraph BC45 of IAS 24. Paragraph BC45 of IAS 24 states:

BC45 The Board noted that this requirement should not be too onerous for the reporting entity because:

(a) individually significant transactions should be a small subset, by number, of total related party transactions;

(b) the reporting entity should know what those transactions are; and

(c) reporting such items on an exceptional basis takes into account cost-benefit considerations.

Nevertheless, the Board decided to add implementation guidance to the Standard to respond to constituent concerns about the extent of disclosure required by paragraph 26.

Other issues

Applicability to the general government sector

BC23 Respondents to the Exposure Draft sought clarification as to whether related party disclosures would be required in general purpose financial statements of entities in the general government sector (GGS). The Board noted the requirements in AASB 1049 *Whole of Government and General Government Sector Financial Reporting* for GGS and whole of government financial statements to be made available at the same time and, if presented separately, to be cross-referenced to each other. The Board also noted that there may be considerable overlap between the related party disclosures for the GGS and whole of government financial statements, and that exempting GGS entities from the scope of the Standard may reduce complexity and duplication of disclosures.

BC24 The Board noted that the issue of related party disclosures by subsidiary entities is also relevant to for-profit entities, and considered that related party disclosures for the GGS entity need not be the same as the disclosures for the whole-of-government or other public sector entities. Accordingly, the Board decided that GGS financial statements should not be exempt from complying with the Standard.

Public sector perspective

BC25 The Board considered whether amendment was necessary to AASB 124, for example, to paragraphs 5 and 27, to add a public sector perspective to the Standard. The Board decided that amendment was not necessary in this regard and that the addition of limited implementation guidance in respect of not-for-profit public sector entities would provide a sufficient public sector perspective to the Standard.

BC26 For example, the Board considered whether an alternative definition (to that in Appendix A of AASB 3 *Business Combinations*) for the term 'business' in paragraph 5 of AASB 124 was necessary. The Board decided that an alternative definition is not required, which is consistent with its decision when it reissued AASB 3 in March 2008. In the Board's view, the term 'business' can be read broadly. In particular, the phrase "lower costs or other economic benefits directly to investors or other owners, members or participants" in the definition of 'business' in AASB 3 is broad and can be applied by not-for-profit public sector entities.

Extending the disclosures of key management personnel of public sector entities

BC27 In finalising the amendments, the Board considered requests from some public sector constituents for additional disclosures (such as salary banding disclosures) for key management personnel in the public sector. Some constituents also queried whether additional disclosures similar to those required by section 300A of the *Corporations Act 2001* of key management personnel of listed companies should be required in respect of key management personnel of government business enterprises, based on the view that for-profit government business enterprises should be regarded as at least as publicly accountable as such entities.

BC28 The Board follows a policy of transaction neutrality in the requirements in Standards. Therefore, the Board decided not to require any compensation or other related party disclosures for key management personnel of public sector entities in addition to those specified of key management personnel of private sector entities, including in instances where a not for profit public sector entity has availed itself of the relief in paragraph 17A of AASB 124. The Board was not convinced that there was a not for profit sector specific reason to impose disclosures that exceed the requirements for for-profit entities.

Reduced disclosure requirements

BC29 The Board considered whether amendment was required to the reduced disclosure requirements specified in paragraph Aus1.11 for application by not-for-profit public sector entities, and decided that no amendment was necessary in this regard. Accordingly, the reduced disclosure requirements set out in AASB 124 that apply to Tier 2 not-for-profit public sector entities are the same as those applying to other Tier 2 entities.

Application date and transitional provisions

BC30 The Board considered the application date and transitional provisions of the amendments to extend the scope of AASB 124 to include not for profit public sector entities. The Board acknowledged constituent concerns about the ability of existing systems, processes and controls to capture the information required, and requests for a lengthy transition period prior to mandatory application of the amendments.

BC31 The Board was disinclined to unnecessarily further extend the period to which these amendments are on issue before mandatory application, having made its key decisions on the amendments in 2012, and as the finalised amendments are largely as were exposed. Further, the Board noted that Australian Implementation Guidance to AASB 10 *Consolidated Financial Statements* relating to the application of control by not-for-profit entities had been issued by the Board in October 2013. The Board also noted that the forthcoming issue of an amending standard extending the scope of AASB 124 to not-for-profit public sector entities has been signalled in its publicly available work program. Accordingly, the Board decided that the amendments should apply to annual reporting periods beginning on or after 1 July 2016.

BC32 However, having regard to constituent concerns, the Board decided not to require comparative related party disclosures to be presented in the period of initial application of the amendments.

AASB 127

Separate Financial Statements

(Reissued August 2015)

CONTENTS

COMPARISON WITH IAS 27
ACCOUNTING STANDARD
AASB 127 *SEPARATE FINANCIAL STATEMENTS*

from paragraph

APPENDIX
A. AUSTRALIAN REDUCED DISCLOSURE REQUIREMENTS

DELETED IAS 27 TEXT

BASIS FOR CONCLUSIONS ON IAS 27 (available on the AASB website)

> Australian Accounting Standard AASB 127 *Separate Financial Statements* is set out in paragraphs 1 –
> Aus20.2 and Appendix A. All the paragraphs have equal authority. Paragraphs in **bold type** state the main
> principles. AASB 127 is to be read in the context of other Australian Accounting Standards, including
> AASB 1048 *Interpretation of Standards*, which identifies the Australian Accounting Interpretations, and
> AASB 1057 *Application of Australian Accounting Standards*. In the absence of explicit guidance, AASB
> 108 *Accounting Policies, Changes in Accounting Estimates and Errors* provides a basis for selecting and
> applying accounting policies.

COMPARISON WITH IAS 27

AASB 127 *Separate Financial Statements* incorporates IAS 27 *Separate Financial
Statements* issued by the International Accounting Standards Board (IASB). Australian-
specific paragraphs (which are not included in IAS 27) are identified with the prefix "Aus" or
"RDR". Paragraphs that apply only to not-for-profit entities begin by identifying their limited
applicability.

Tier 1

For-profit entities complying with AASB 127 also comply with IAS 27.

Not-for-profit entities' compliance with IAS 27 will depend on whether any "Aus" paragraphs that specifically apply to not-for-profit entities provide additional guidance or contain applicable requirements that are inconsistent with IAS 27.

Tier 2

Entities preparing general purpose financial statements under Australian Accounting Standards – Reduced Disclosure Requirements (Tier 2) will not be in compliance with IFRSs.

AASB 1053 *Application of Tiers of Australian Accounting Standards* explains the two tiers of reporting requirements.

ACCOUNTING STANDARD AASB 127

The Australian Accounting Standards Board makes Accounting Standard AASB 127 *Separate Financial Statements* under section 334 of the *Corporations Act 2001*.

Kris Peach

Dated 7 August 2015 Chair – AASB

ACCOUNTING STANDARD AASB 127
SEPARATE FINANCIAL STATEMENTS

Objective

1   The objective of this Standard is to prescribe the accounting and disclosure requirements for investments in subsidiaries, joint ventures and associates when an entity prepares separate financial statements.

Scope

2   **This Standard shall be applied in accounting for investments in subsidiaries, joint ventures and associates when an entity elects, or is required by local regulations, to present separate financial statements.**

3   This Standard does not mandate which entities produce separate financial statements. It applies when an entity prepares separate financial statements that comply with Australian Accounting Standards.

Definitions

4   **The following terms are used in this Standard with the meanings specified:**

Consolidated financial statements **are the financial statements of a group in which the assets, liabilities, equity, income, expenses and cash flows of the parent and its subsidiaries are presented as those of a single economic entity.**

Separate financial statements **are those presented by an entity in which the entity could elect, subject to the requirements in this Standard, to account for its investments in subsidiaries, joint ventures and associates either at cost, in accordance with AASB 9** *Financial Instruments*, **or using the equity method as described in AASB 128** *Investments in Associates and Joint Ventures*.

5   The following terms are defined in Appendix A of AASB 10 *Consolidated Financial Statements*, Appendix A of AASB 11 *Joint Arrangements* and paragraph 3 of AASB 128:

- associate
- control of an investee
- equity method
- group
- investment entity
- joint control
- joint venture
- joint venturer
- parent
- significant influence
- subsidiary.

6   Separate financial statements are those presented in addition to consolidated financial statements or in addition to the financial statements of an investor that does not have investments in subsidiaries but has investments in associates or joint ventures in which the investments in associates or joint ventures are required by AASB 128 to be accounted for using the equity method, other than in the circumstances set out in paragraphs 8–8A.

7   The financial statements of an entity that does not have a subsidiary, associate or joint venturer's interest in a joint venture are not separate financial statements.

8   An entity that is exempted in accordance with paragraphs 4(a), Aus4.1 and Aus4.2 of AASB 10 from consolidation or paragraphs 17, Aus17.1 and Aus17.2 of AASB 128 from applying the equity method may present separate financial statements as its only financial statements.

8A   An investment entity that is required, throughout the current period and all comparative periods presented, to apply the exception to consolidation for all of its subsidiaries in accordance with paragraph 31 of AASB 10 presents separate financial statements as its only financial statements.

Preparation of separate financial statements

9   **Separate financial statements shall be prepared in accordance with all applicable Standards, except as provided in paragraph 10.**

10   **When an entity prepares separate financial statements, it shall account for investments in subsidiaries, joint ventures and associates either:**

   (a)   at cost;

   (b)   in accordance with AASB 9; or

   (c)   using the equity method as described in AASB 128.

   The entity shall apply the same accounting for each category of investments. Investments accounted for at cost or using the equity method shall be accounted for in accordance with AASB 5 *Non-current Assets Held for Sale and Discontinued Operations* when they are classified as held for sale or for distribution (or included in a disposal group that is classified as held for sale or for distribution). The measurement of investments accounted for in accordance with AASB 9 is not changed in such circumstances.

11   If an entity elects, in accordance with paragraph 18 of AASB 128, to measure its investments in associates or joint ventures at fair value through profit or loss in accordance with AASB 9, it shall also account for those investments in the same way in its separate financial statements.

11A If a parent is required, in accordance with paragraph 31 of AASB 10, to measure its investment in a subsidiary at fair value through profit or loss in accordance with

AASB 9, it shall also account for its investment in a subsidiary in the same way in its separate financial statements.

11B When a parent ceases to be an investment entity, or becomes an investment entity, it shall account for the change from the date when the change in status occurred, as follows:

    (a)   when an entity ceases to be an investment entity, the entity shall account for an investment in a subsidiary in accordance with paragraph 10. The date of the change of status shall be the deemed acquisition date. The fair value of the subsidiary at the deemed acquisition date shall represent the transferred deemed consideration when accounting for the investment in accordance with paragraph 10.

        (i)   [deleted]

        (ii)   [deleted]

    (b)   when an entity becomes an investment entity, it shall account for an investment in a subsidiary at fair value through profit or loss in accordance with AASB 9. The difference between the previous carrying amount of the subsidiary and its fair value at the date of the change of status of the investor shall be recognised as a gain or loss in profit or loss. The cumulative amount of any gain or loss previously recognised in other comprehensive income in respect of those subsidiaries shall be treated as if the investment entity had disposed of those subsidiaries at the date of change in status.

12   Dividends from a subsidiary, a joint venture or an associate are recognised in the separate financial statements of an entity when the entity's right to receive the dividend is established. The dividend is recognised in profit or loss unless the entity elects to use the equity method, in which case the dividend is recognised as a reduction from the carrying amount of the investment.

13 When a parent reorganises the structure of its group by establishing a new entity as its parent in a manner that satisfies the following criteria:

    (a)   the new parent obtains control of the original parent by issuing equity instruments in exchange for existing equity instruments of the original parent;

    (b)   the assets and liabilities of the new group and the original group are the same immediately before and after the reorganisation; and

    (c)   the owners of the original parent before the reorganisation have the same absolute and relative interests in the net assets of the original group and the new group immediately before and after the reorganisation,

and the new parent accounts for its investment in the original parent in accordance with paragraph 10(a) in its separate financial statements, the new parent shall measure cost at the carrying amount of its share of the equity items shown in the separate financial statements of the original parent at the date of the reorganisation.

14 Similarly, an entity that is not a parent might establish a new entity as its parent in a manner that satisfies the criteria in paragraph 13. The requirements in paragraph 13 apply equally to such reorganisations. In such cases, references to 'original parent' and 'original group' are to the 'original entity'.

Disclosure

15   An entity shall apply all applicable Standards when providing disclosures in its separate financial statements, including the requirements in paragraphs 16–17.

16   When a parent, in accordance with paragraphs 4(a), Aus4.1 and Aus4.2 of AASB 10, elects not to prepare consolidated financial statements and instead prepares separate financial statements, it shall disclose in those separate financial statements:

(a)   the fact that the financial statements are separate financial statements; that the exemption from consolidation has been used; the name and principal place of business (and country of incorporation, if different) of the entity whose consolidated financial statements that comply with International Financial Reporting Standards have been produced for public use; and the address where those consolidated financial statements are obtainable.

(b)   a list of significant investments in subsidiaries, joint ventures and associates, including:

    (i)   the name of those investees.

    (ii)   the principal place of business (and country of incorporation, if different) of those investees.

    (iii)   its proportion of the ownership interest (and its proportion of the voting rights, if different) held in those investees.

(c)   a description of the method used to account for the investments listed under (b).

Aus16.1   When a not-for-profit parent, in accordance with paragraphs 4(a), Aus4.1 and Aus4.2 of AASB 10, elects not to prepare consolidated financial statements and instead prepares separate financial statements, it shall disclose in those separate financial statements the disclosures specified in paragraph 16, with the exception that the reference in paragraph 16(a) to 'International Financial Reporting Standards' is replaced by a reference to 'Australian Accounting Standards'.

16A   When an investment entity that is a parent (other than a parent covered by paragraphs 16–Aus16.1) prepares, in accordance with paragraph 8A, separate financial statements as its only financial statements, it shall disclose that fact. The investment entity shall also present the disclosures relating to investment entities required by AASB 12 *Disclosure of Interests in Other Entities*.

17   When a parent (other than a parent covered by paragraphs 16–Aus16.1 or paragraph 16A) or an investor with joint control of, or significant influence over, an investee prepares separate financial statements, the parent or investor shall identify the financial statements prepared in accordance with AASB 10, AASB 11 or AASB 128 to which they relate. The parent or investor shall also disclose in its separate financial statements:

(a)   the fact that the statements are separate financial statements and the reasons why those statements are prepared if not required by law.

(b)   a list of significant investments in subsidiaries, joint ventures and associates, including:

    (i)   the name of those investees.

    (ii)   the principal place of business (and country of incorporation, if different) of those investees.

    (iii)   its proportion of the ownership interest (and its proportion of the voting rights, if different) held in those investees.

(c)   a description of the method used to account for the investments listed under (b).

Effective date and transition

18   An entity shall apply this Standard for annual periods beginning on or after 1 January 2016. Earlier application is permitted for periods beginning after 1 January 2014 but before 1 January 2016. If an entity applies this Standard earlier, it shall disclose that fact and apply AASB 10, AASB 11, AASB 12 and AASB 128 at the same time.

18A   AASB 2013-5 *Amendments to Australian Accounting Standards – Investment Entities*, issued in August 2013, amended the previous version of this Standard as follows: amended paragraphs 5, 6, 17 and 18, and added paragraphs 8A, 11A–11B, 16A and 18B–18I. An entity shall apply those amendments for annual periods beginning on or after 1 January 2014. Early adoption is permitted. If an entity applies those amendments earlier, it shall disclose that fact and apply all amendments included in *Investment Entities* at the same time.

18B If, at the date of initial application of AASB 2013-5 (which, for the purposes of this Standard, is the beginning of the annual reporting period for which those amendments are applied for the first time), a parent concludes that it is an investment entity, it shall apply paragraphs 18C–18I to its investment in a subsidiary.

18C At the date of initial application, an investment entity that previously measured its investment in a subsidiary at cost shall instead measure that investment at fair value through profit or loss as if the requirements of this Standard had always been effective. The investment entity shall adjust retrospectively the annual period immediately preceding the date of initial application and shall adjust retained earnings at the beginning of the immediately preceding period for any difference between:

(a) the previous carrying amount of the investment; and

(b) the fair value of the investor's investment in the subsidiary.

18D At the date of initial application, an investment entity that previously measured its investment in a subsidiary at fair value through other comprehensive income shall continue to measure that investment at fair value. The cumulative amount of any fair value adjustment previously recognised in other comprehensive income shall be transferred to retained earnings at the beginning of the annual period immediately preceding the date of initial application.

18E At the date of initial application, an investment entity shall not make adjustments to the previous accounting for an interest in a subsidiary that it had previously elected to measure at fair value through profit or loss in accordance with AASB 9, as permitted in paragraph 10.

18F Before the date that AASB 13 *Fair Value Measurement* is adopted, an investment entity shall use the fair value amounts previously reported to investors or to management, if those amounts represent the amount for which the investment could have been exchanged between knowledgeable, willing parties in an arm's length transaction at the date of the valuation.

18G If measuring the investment in the subsidiary in accordance with paragraphs 18C–18F is impracticable (as defined in AASB 108 *Accounting Policies, Changes in Accounting Estimates and Errors*), an investment entity shall apply the requirements of this Standard at the beginning of the earliest period for which application of paragraphs 18C–18F is practicable, which may be the current period. The investor shall adjust retrospectively the annual period immediately preceding the date of initial application, unless the beginning of the earliest period for which application of this paragraph is practicable is the current period. When the date that it is practicable for the investment entity to measure the fair value of the subsidiary is earlier than the beginning of the immediately preceding period, the investor shall adjust equity at the beginning of the immediately preceding period for any difference between:

(a) the previous carrying amount of the investment; and

(b) the fair value of the investor's investment in the subsidiary.

If the earliest period for which application of this paragraph is practicable is the current period, the adjustment to equity shall be recognised at the beginning of the current period.

18H If an investment entity has disposed of, or lost control of, an investment in a subsidiary before the date of initial application of AASB 2013-5, the investment entity is not required to make adjustments to the previous accounting for that investment.

18I Notwithstanding the references to the annual period immediately preceding the date of initial application (the 'immediately preceding period') in paragraphs 18C–18G, an entity may also present adjusted comparative information for any earlier periods presented, but is not required to do so. If an entity does present adjusted comparative information for any earlier periods, all references to the 'immediately preceding period' in paragraphs 18C–18G shall be read as the 'earliest adjusted comparative period presented'. If an entity presents unadjusted comparative information for any earlier periods, it shall clearly identify the information that has not been adjusted, state that it has been prepared on a different basis, and explain that basis.

18J AASB 2014-9 *Amendments to Australian Accounting Standards – Equity Method in Separate Financial Statements*, issued in December 2014, amended the previous version of this Standard as follows: amended paragraphs 4–7, 10, 11B and 12. An entity shall apply those amendments for annual periods beginning on or after 1 January 2016 retrospectively in accordance with AASB 108 *Accounting Policies, Changes in Accounting Estimates and Errors*. Earlier application is permitted. If an entity applies those amendments for an earlier period, it shall disclose that fact.

References to AASB 9

19 If an entity applies this Standard but does not yet apply AASB 9, any reference to AASB 9 shall be read as a reference to AASB 139 *Financial Instruments: Recognition and Measurement*.

Withdrawal of IAS 27 (2008)

20 [Deleted by the AASB]

Commencement of the legislative instrument

Aus20.1 For legal purposes, this legislative instrument commences on 31 December 2015.

Withdrawal of AASB pronouncements

Aus20.2 This Standard repeals AASB 127 *Separate Financial Statements* issued in August 2011. Despite the repeal, after the time this Standard starts to apply under section 334 of the Corporations Act (either generally or in relation to an individual entity), the repealed Standard continues to apply in relation to any period ending before that time as if the repeal had not occurred.

[Note: When this Standard applies under section 334 of the Corporations Act (either generally or in relation to an individual entity), it supersedes the application of the repealed Standard.]

APPENDIX A
AUSTRALIAN REDUCED DISCLOSURE
REQUIREMENTS

This appendix is an integral part of AASB 127.

AusA1 **The following do not apply to entities preparing general purpose financial statements under Australian Accounting Standards – Reduced Disclosure Requirements:**

(a) **paragraphs 16, Aus16.1, 17(b) and 17(c);**

(b) **in paragraph 17, the text "paragraphs 16–Aus16.1 or"; and**

(c) **in paragraph 17(a), the text "and the reasons why those statements are prepared if not required by law".**

Entities applying Australian Accounting Standards – Reduced Disclosure Requirements may elect to comply with some or all of these excluded requirements.

AusA2　The requirements that do not apply to entities preparing general purpose financial statements under Australian Accounting Standards – Reduced Disclosure Requirements are also identified in this Standard by shading of the relevant text.

AusA3　**The RDR paragraph in this Standard applies only to entities preparing general purpose financial statements under Australian Accounting Standards – Reduced Disclosure Requirements.**

RDR17.1　**A parent or an investor with joint control of, or significant influence over, an investee, that prepares separate financial statements applying Australian Accounting Standards – Reduced Disclosure Requirements, shall disclose the methods used to account for the investment when the investment is significant.**

DELETED IAS 27 TEXT

Deleted IAS 27 text is not part of AASB 127.

20　This Standard is issued concurrently with IFRS 10. Together, the two IFRSs supersede IAS 27 *Consolidated and Separate Financial Statements* (as amended in 2008).

AASB 128
Investments in Associates and Joint Ventures
(Compiled December 2017)

This compiled Standard applies to annual periods beginning on or after 1 January 2022. Earlier application is permitted for annual periods beginning after 24 July 2014 but before 1 January 2022. It incorporates relevant amendments made up to and including 12 December 2017.

Prepared on 20 April 2018 by the staff of the Australian Accounting Standards Board.

Compilation no. 2

Compilation date: 31 December 2017

This note is not part of Accounting Standard AASB 128.

The following unincorporated amendments are not included in this compiled Standard.

- AASB 2017-7 *Amendments to Australian Accounting Standards — Long-term Interests in Associates and Joint Ventures.* This Standard makes amendments to AASB 128 *Investments in Associates and Joint Ventures* arising from the issuance of IFRS *Long-term Interests in Associates and Joint Ventures* (Amendments to IAS 28) by the IASB in October 2017. This Standard applies to annual periods beginning on or after 1 January 2019, but earlier application is permitted.

- AASB 17 *Insurance Contracts* — Appendix D sets out the amendments to other Standards that are a consequence of the AASB issuing AASB 17 *Insurance Contracts.* This Standard is applicable from 1 January 2021. Earlier application is permitted, but entities must apply *AASB 9 Financial Instruments* and *AASB 15 Revenue from Contracts with Customers* first.

- AASB 1058 *Income of Not-for-Profit Entities* — Appendix D sets out the amendments to other Australian Accounting Standards that are a consequence of the AASB issuing this Standard. It is applicable from 1 January 2019. Earlier application is permitted, but amendments to AASB 117 apply before 1 January 2019 only if AASB 1058 is also applied to an earlier period. In addition, AASB 1 and AASB 16 amendments are applied to an earlier period only if AASB 16 is also applied to that period.

Entities early-adopting any amendments with later application dates will need to refer to the amending Standards that have not yet been incorporated into compilations. The abovementioned unincorporated amendments may be located on the AASB website at www.aasb.gov.au or on the Federal Register of Legislation website at www.legislation.gov.au.

CONTENTS

COMPILATION DETAILS

DELETED IAS 28 TEXT

BASIS FOR CONCLUSIONS ON AASB 2011-5 and AASB 2011-6

BASIS FOR CONCLUSIONS ON AASB 2015-4

BASIS FOR CONCLUSIONS ON IAS 28 (available on the AASB website)

AASB

Australian Accounting Standard AASB 128 *Investments in Associates and Joint Ventures* (as amended) is set out in paragraphs 1 – Aus47.2. All the paragraphs have equal authority. Paragraphs in **bold type** state the main principles. AASB 128 is to be read in the context of other Australian Accounting Standards, including AASB 1048 *Interpretation of Standards*, which identifies the Australian Accounting Interpretations, and AASB 1057 *Application of Australian Accounting Standards*. In the absence of explicit guidance, AASB 108 *Accounting Policies, Changes in Accounting Estimates and Errors* provides a basis for selecting and applying accounting policies.

COMPARISON WITH IAS 28

AASB 128 *Investments in Associates and Joint Ventures* as amended incorporates IAS 28 *Investments in Associates and Joint Ventures* as issued and amended by the International Accounting Standards Board (IASB). Australian-specific paragraphs (which are not included in IAS 28) are identified with the prefix "Aus". Paragraphs that apply only to not-for-profit entities begin by identifying their limited applicability.

Tier 1

For-profit entities complying with AASB 128 also comply with IAS 28.

Not-for-profit entities' compliance with IAS 28 will depend on whether any "Aus" paragraphs that specifically apply to not-for-profit entities provide additional guidance or contain applicable requirements that are inconsistent with IAS 28.

AASB 1053 *Application of Tiers of Australian Accounting Standards* explains the two tiers of reporting requirements.

ACCOUNTING STANDARD AASB 128

The Australian Accounting Standards Board made Accounting Standard AASB 128 *Investments in Associates and Joint Ventures* under section 334 of the *Corporations Act 2001* on 7 August 2015.

This compiled version of AASB 128 applies to annual periods beginning on or after 1 January 2022. It incorporates relevant amendments contained in other AASB Standards made by the AASB up to and including 12 December 2017 (see Compilation Details).

ACCOUNTING STANDARD AASB 128
INVESTMENTS IN ASSOCIATES AND JOINT VENTURES

Objective

1   The objective of this Standard is to prescribe the accounting for investments in associates and to set out the requirements for the application of the equity method when accounting for investments in associates and joint ventures.

Scope

2   This Standard shall be applied by all entities that are investors with joint control of, or significant influence over, an investee.

Definitions

3   The following terms are used in this Standard with the meanings specified:

An *associate* is an entity over which the investor has significant influence.

Consolidated financial statements are the financial statements of a group in which assets, liabilities, equity, income, expenses and cash flows of the parent and its subsidiaries are presented as those of a single economic entity.

The *equity method* is a method of accounting whereby the investment is initially recognised at cost and adjusted thereafter for the post-acquisition change in the investor's share of the investee's net assets. The investor's profit or loss includes its share of the investee's profit or loss and the investor's other comprehensive income includes its share of the investee's other comprehensive income.

A *joint arrangement* is an arrangement of which two or more parties have joint control.

Joint control is the contractually agreed sharing of control of an arrangement, which exists only when decisions about the relevant activities require the unanimous consent of the parties sharing control.

A *joint venture* is a joint arrangement whereby the parties that have joint control of the arrangement have rights to the net assets of the arrangement.

A *joint venturer* is a party to a joint venture that has joint control of that joint venture.

Significant influence is the power to participate in the financial and operating policy decisions of the investee but is not control or joint control of those policies.

4   The following terms are defined in paragraph 4 of AASB 127 *Separate Financial Statements* and in Appendix A of AASB 10 *Consolidated Financial Statements* and are used in this Standard with the meanings specified in the Standards in which they are defined:

- control of an investee
- group
- parent
- separate financial statements
- subsidiary.

Significant influence

5   If an entity holds, directly or indirectly (eg through subsidiaries), 20 per cent or more of the voting power of the investee, it is presumed that the entity has significant influence, unless it can be clearly demonstrated that this is not the case. Conversely, if the entity holds, directly or indirectly (eg through subsidiaries), less than 20 per cent of the voting power of the investee, it is presumed that the entity does not have significant influence, unless such influence can be clearly demonstrated. A substantial or majority ownership by another investor does not necessarily preclude an entity from having significant influence.

6   The existence of significant influence by an entity is usually evidenced in one or more of the following ways:

(a)   representation on the board of directors or equivalent governing body of the investee;

(b)   participation in policy-making processes, including participation in decisions about dividends or other distributions;

(c)   material transactions between the entity and its investee;

(d)   interchange of managerial personnel; or

(e)   provision of essential technical information.

7   An entity may own share warrants, share call options, debt or equity instruments that are convertible into ordinary shares, or other similar instruments that have the potential, if exercised or converted, to give the entity additional voting power or to reduce another party's voting power over the financial and operating policies of another entity (ie potential voting rights). The existence and effect of potential voting rights that are currently exercisable or convertible, including potential voting rights held by other entities, are considered when assessing whether an entity has significant influence. Potential voting rights are not currently exercisable or convertible when, for example, they cannot be exercised or converted until a future date or until the occurrence of a future event.

8   In assessing whether potential voting rights contribute to significant influence, the entity examines all facts and circumstances (including the terms of exercise of the potential voting rights and any other contractual arrangements whether considered individually or in combination) that affect potential rights, except the intentions of management and the financial ability to exercise or convert those potential rights.

9   An entity loses significant influence over an investee when it loses the power to participate in the financial and operating policy decisions of that investee. The loss of significant influence can occur with or without a change in absolute or relative ownership levels. It could occur, for example, when an associate becomes subject to the control of a government, court, administrator or regulator. It could also occur as a result of a contractual arrangement.

AASB

Equity method

10 Under the equity method, on initial recognition the investment in an associate or a joint venture is recognised at cost, and the carrying amount is increased or decreased to recognise the investor's share of the profit or loss of the investee after the date of acquisition. The investor's share of the investee's profit or loss is recognised in the investor's profit or loss. Distributions received from an investee reduce the carrying amount of the investment. Adjustments to the carrying amount may also be necessary for changes in the investor's proportionate interest in the investee arising from changes in the investee's other comprehensive income. Such changes include those arising from the revaluation of property, plant and equipment and from foreign exchange translation differences. The investor's share of those changes is recognised in the investor's other comprehensive income (see AASB 101 *Presentation of Financial Statements*).

11 The recognition of income on the basis of distributions received may not be an adequate measure of the income earned by an investor on an investment in an associate or a joint venture because the distributions received may bear little relation to the performance of the associate or joint venture. Because the investor has joint control of, or significant influence over, the investee, the investor has an interest in the associate's or joint venture's performance and, as a result, the return on its investment. The investor accounts for this interest by extending the scope of its financial statements to include its share of the profit or loss of such an investee. As a result, application of the equity method provides more informative reporting of the investor's net assets and profit or loss.

12 When potential voting rights or other derivatives containing potential voting rights exist, an entity's interest in an associate or a joint venture is determined solely on the basis of existing ownership interests and does not reflect the possible exercise or conversion of potential voting rights and other derivative instruments, unless paragraph 13 applies.

13 In some circumstances, an entity has, in substance, an existing ownership as a result of a transaction that currently gives it access to the returns associated with an ownership interest. In such circumstances, the proportion allocated to the entity is determined by taking into account the eventual exercise of those potential voting rights and other derivative instruments that currently give the entity access to the returns.

14 AASB 9 *Financial Instruments* does not apply to interests in associates and joint ventures that are accounted for using the equity method. When instruments containing potential voting rights in substance currently give access to the returns associated with an ownership interest in an associate or a joint venture, the instruments are not subject to AASB 9. In all other cases, instruments containing potential voting rights in an associate or a joint venture are accounted for in accordance with AASB 9.

15 Unless an investment, or a portion of an investment, in an associate or a joint venture is classified as held for sale in accordance with AASB 5 *Non-current Assets Held for Sale and Discontinued Operations*, the investment, or any retained interest in the investment not classified as held for sale, shall be classified as a non-current asset.

Application of the equity method

16 An entity with joint control of, or significant influence over, an investee shall account for its investment in an associate or a joint venture using the equity method except when that investment qualifies for exemption in accordance with paragraphs 17–19.

Exemptions from applying the equity method

17 An entity need not apply the equity method to its investment in an associate or a joint venture if the entity is a parent that is exempt from preparing consolidated financial statements by the scope exception in paragraphs 4(a), Aus4.1 and Aus4.2 of AASB 10 or if all the following apply:

(a) The entity is a wholly-owned subsidiary, or is a partially-owned subsidiary of another entity and its other owners, including those not otherwise entitled to vote, have been informed about, and do not object to, the entity not applying the equity method.

(b) The entity's debt or equity instruments are not traded in a public market (a domestic or foreign stock exchange or an over-the-counter market, including local and regional markets).

(c) The entity did not file, nor is it in the process of filing, its financial statements with a securities commission or other regulatory organisation, for the purpose of issuing any class of instruments in a public market.

(d) The ultimate or any intermediate parent of the entity produces financial statements available for public use that comply with International Financial Reporting Standards, in which subsidiaries are consolidated or are measured at fair value through profit or loss in accordance with AASB 10.

Aus17.1 Notwithstanding paragraph 17(d), an entity that meets the criteria in paragraphs 17(a), 17(b) and 17(c) need not apply the equity method in accounting for an interest in an associate or joint venture if its ultimate or any intermediate parent produces financial statements that are available for public use in which subsidiaries are consolidated or are measured at fair value through profit or loss in accordance with AASB 10 and:

    (a) the investor or the joint venturer and its ultimate or intermediate parent are:

        (i) both not-for-profit entities complying with Australian Accounting Standards; or

        (ii) both entities complying with Australian Accounting Standards – Reduced Disclosure Requirements; or

    (b) the investor or the joint venturer is an entity complying with Australian Accounting Standards – Reduced Disclosure Requirements and its ultimate or intermediate parent is a not-for-profit entity complying with Australian Accounting Standards.

Aus17.2 Notwithstanding paragraphs 17 and Aus17.1, the ultimate Australian entity shall apply the equity method in accounting for interests in associates and joint ventures in accordance with this Standard when either the entity or the group is a reporting entity, or both the entity and the group are reporting entities, except if the ultimate Australian parent is required, in accordance with paragraph 31 of AASB 10, to measure all of its subsidiaries at fair value through profit or loss.

18 When an investment in an associate or a joint venture is held by, or is held indirectly through, an entity that is a venture capital organisation, or a mutual fund, unit trust and similar entities including investment-linked insurance funds, the entity may elect to measure that investment at fair value through profit or loss in accordance with AASB 9. An entity shall make this election separately for each associate or joint venture, at initial recognition of the associate or joint venture.

19 When an entity has an investment in an associate, a portion of which is held indirectly through a venture capital organisation, or a mutual fund, unit trust and similar entities including investment-linked insurance funds, the entity may elect to measure that portion of the investment in the associate at fair value through profit or loss in accordance with AASB 9 regardless of whether the venture capital organisation, or the mutual fund, unit trust and similar entities including investment-linked insurance funds, has significant influence over that portion of the investment. If the entity makes that election, the entity shall apply the equity method to any remaining portion of its investment in an associate that is not held through a venture capital organisation, or a mutual fund, unit trust and similar entities including investment-linked insurance funds.

Classification as held for sale

20   An entity shall apply AASB 5 to an investment, or a portion of an investment, in an associate or a joint venture that meets the criteria to be classified as held for sale. Any retained portion of an investment in an associate or a joint venture that has not been classified as held for sale shall be accounted for using the equity method until disposal of the portion that is classified as held for sale takes place. After the disposal takes place, an entity shall account for any retained interest in the associate or joint venture in accordance with AASB 9 unless the retained interest continues to be an associate or a joint venture, in which case the entity uses the equity method.

21   When an investment, or a portion of an investment, in an associate or a joint venture previously classified as held for sale no longer meets the criteria to be so classified, it shall be accounted for using the equity method retrospectively as from the date of its classification as held for sale. Financial statements for the periods since classification as held for sale shall be amended accordingly.

Discontinuing the use of the equity method

22   **An entity shall discontinue the use of the equity method from the date when its investment ceases to be an associate or a joint venture as follows:**

(a)   **If the investment becomes a subsidiary, the entity shall account for its investment in accordance with AASB 3** *Business Combinations* **and AASB 10.**

(b)   **If the retained interest in the former associate or joint venture is a financial asset, the entity shall measure the retained interest at fair value. The fair value of the retained interest shall be regarded as its fair value on initial recognition as a financial asset in accordance with AASB 9. The entity shall recognise in profit or loss any difference between:**

(i)   **the fair value of any retained interest and any proceeds from disposing of a part interest in the associate or joint venture; and**

(ii)   **the carrying amount of the investment at the date the equity method was discontinued.**

(c)   **When an entity discontinues the use of the equity method, the entity shall account for all amounts previously recognised in other comprehensive income in relation to that investment on the same basis as would have been required if the investee had directly disposed of the related assets or liabilities.**

23   Therefore, if a gain or loss previously recognised in other comprehensive income by the investee would be reclassified to profit or loss on the disposal of the related assets or liabilities, the entity reclassifies the gain or loss from equity to profit or loss (as a reclassification adjustment) when the equity method is discontinued. For example, if an associate or a joint venture has cumulative exchange differences relating to a foreign operation and the entity discontinues the use of the equity method, the entity shall reclassify to profit or loss the gain or loss that had previously been recognised in other comprehensive income in relation to the foreign operation.

24   **If an investment in an associate becomes an investment in a joint venture or an investment in a joint venture becomes an investment in an associate, the entity continues to apply the equity method and does not remeasure the retained interest.**

Changes in ownership interest

25   If an entity's ownership interest in an associate or a joint venture is reduced, but the investment continues to be classified either as an associate or a joint venture respectively, the entity shall reclassify to profit or loss the proportion of the gain or loss that had previously been recognised in other comprehensive income relating to that

reduction in ownership interest if that gain or loss would be required to be reclassified to profit or loss on the disposal of the related assets or liabilities.

Equity method procedures

26 Many of the procedures that are appropriate for the application of the equity method are similar to the consolidation procedures described in AASB 10. Furthermore, the concepts underlying the procedures used in accounting for the acquisition of a subsidiary are also adopted in accounting for the acquisition of an investment in an associate or a joint venture.

27 A group's share in an associate or a joint venture is the aggregate of the holdings in that associate or joint venture by the parent and its subsidiaries. The holdings of the group's other associates or joint ventures are ignored for this purpose. When an associate or a joint venture has subsidiaries, associates or joint ventures, the profit or loss, other comprehensive income and net assets taken into account in applying the equity method are those recognised in the associate's or joint venture's financial statements (including the associate's or joint venture's share of the profit or loss, other comprehensive income and net assets of its associates and joint ventures), after any adjustments necessary to give effect to uniform accounting policies (see paragraphs 35–36A).

28 Gains and losses resulting from 'upstream' and 'downstream' transactions involving assets that do not constitute a business, as defined in AASB 3, between an entity (including its consolidated subsidiaries) and its associate or joint venture are recognised in the entity's financial statements only to the extent of unrelated investors' interests in the associate or joint venture. 'Upstream' transactions are, for example, sales of assets from an associate or a joint venture to the investor. The entity's share in the associate's or the joint venture's gains or losses resulting from these transactions is eliminated. 'Downstream' transactions are, for example, sales or contributions of assets from the investor to its associate or its joint venture.

29 When downstream transactions provide evidence of a reduction in the net realisable value of the assets to be sold or contributed, or of an impairment loss of those assets, those losses shall be recognised in full by the investor. When upstream transactions provide evidence of a reduction in the net realisable value of the assets to be purchased or of an impairment loss of those assets, the investor shall recognise its share in those losses.

30 The gain or loss resulting from the contribution of non-monetary assets that do not constitute a business, as defined in AASB 3, to an associate or a joint venture in exchange for an equity interest in that associate or joint venture shall be accounted for in accordance with paragraph 28, except when the contribution lacks commercial substance, as that term is described in AASB 116 *Property, Plant and Equipment*. If such a contribution lacks commercial substance, the gain or loss is regarded as unrealised and is not recognised unless paragraph 31 also applies. Such unrealised gains and losses shall be eliminated against the investment accounted for using the equity method and shall not be presented as deferred gains or losses in the entity's consolidated statement of financial position or in the entity's statement of financial position in which investments are accounted for using the equity method.

31 If, in addition to receiving an equity interest in an associate or a joint venture, an entity receives monetary or non-monetary assets, the entity recognises in full in profit or loss the portion of the gain or loss on the non-monetary contribution relating to the monetary or non-monetary assets received.

31A The gain or loss resulting from a downstream transaction involving assets that constitute a business, as defined in AASB 3, between an entity (including its consolidated subsidiaries) and its associate or joint venture is recognised in full in the investor's financial statements.

31B An entity might sell or contribute assets in two or more arrangements (transactions). When determining whether assets that are sold or contributed constitute a business, as defined in AASB 3, an entity shall consider whether the sale or contribution of those assets is part of multiple arrangements that should be accounted for as a single transaction in accordance with the requirements in paragraph B97 of AASB 10.

32   An investment is accounted for using the equity method from the date on which it becomes an associate or a joint venture. On acquisition of the investment, any difference between the cost of the investment and the entity's share of the net fair value of the investee's identifiable assets and liabilities is accounted for as follows:

(a)   Goodwill relating to an associate or a joint venture is included in the carrying amount of the investment. Amortisation of that goodwill is not permitted.

(b)   Any excess of the entity's share of the net fair value of the investee's identifiable assets and liabilities over the cost of the investment is included as income in the determination of the entity's share of the associate or joint venture's profit or loss in the period in which the investment is acquired.

Appropriate adjustments to the entity's share of the associate's or joint venture's profit or loss after acquisition are made in order to account, for example, for depreciation of the depreciable assets based on their fair values at the acquisition date. Similarly, appropriate adjustments to the entity's share of the associate's or joint venture's profit or loss after acquisition are made for impairment losses such as for goodwill or property, plant and equipment.

33   **The most recent available financial statements of the associate or joint venture are used by the entity in applying the equity method. When the end of the reporting period of the entity is different from that of the associate or joint venture, the associate or joint venture prepares, for the use of the entity, financial statements as of the same date as the financial statements of the entity unless it is impracticable to do so.**

34   **When, in accordance with paragraph 33, the financial statements of an associate or a joint venture used in applying the equity method are prepared as of a date different from that used by the entity, adjustments shall be made for the effects of significant transactions or events that occur between that date and the date of the entity's financial statements. In any case, the difference between the end of the reporting period of the associate or joint venture and that of the entity shall be no more than three months. The length of the reporting periods and any difference between the ends of the reporting periods shall be the same from period to period.**

35   **The entity's financial statements shall be prepared using uniform accounting policies for like transactions and events in similar circumstances.**

36   Except as described in paragraph 36A, if an associate or a joint venture uses accounting policies other than those of the entity for like transactions and events in similar circumstances, adjustments shall be made to make the associate's or joint venture's accounting policies conform to those of the entity when the associate's or joint venture's financial statements are used by the entity in applying the equity method.

36A   Notwithstanding the requirement in paragraph 36, if an entity that is not itself an investment entity has an interest in an associate or joint venture that is an investment entity, the entity may, when applying the equity method, elect to retain the fair value measurement applied by that investment entity associate or joint venture to the investment entity associate's or joint venture's interests in subsidiaries. This election is made separately for each investment entity associate or joint venture, at the later of the date on which (a) the investment entity associate or joint venture is initially recognised; (b) the associate or joint venture becomes an investment entity; and (c) the investment entity associate or joint venture first becomes a parent.

37   If an associate or a joint venture has outstanding cumulative preference shares that are held by parties other than the entity and are classified as equity, the entity computes its share of profit or loss after adjusting for the dividends on such shares, whether or not the dividends have been declared.

38   If an entity's share of losses of an associate or a joint venture equals or exceeds its interest in the associate or joint venture, the entity discontinues recognising its share of further losses. The interest in an associate or a joint venture is the carrying amount

of the investment in the associate or joint venture determined using the equity method together with any long-term interests that, in substance, form part of the entity's net investment in the associate or joint venture. For example, an item for which settlement is neither planned nor likely to occur in the foreseeable future is, in substance, an extension of the entity's investment in that associate or joint venture. Such items may include preference shares and long-term receivables or loans, but do not include trade receivables, trade payables or any long-term receivables for which adequate collateral exists, such as secured loans. Losses recognised using the equity method in excess of the entity's investment in ordinary shares are applied to the other components of the entity's interest in an associate or a joint venture in the reverse order of their seniority (ie priority in liquidation).

39　　After the entity's interest is reduced to zero, additional losses are provided for, and a liability is recognised, only to the extent that the entity has incurred legal or constructive obligations or made payments on behalf of the associate or joint venture. If the associate or joint venture subsequently reports profits, the entity resumes recognising its share of those profits only after its share of the profits equals the share of losses not recognised.

Impairment losses

40　　After application of the equity method, including recognising the associate's or joint venture's losses in accordance with paragraph 38, the entity applies paragraphs 41A–41C to determine whether there is any objective evidence that its net investment in the associate or joint venture is impaired.

41　　The entity applies the impairment requirements in AASB 9 to its other interests in the associate or joint venture that are in the scope of AASB 9 and that do not constitute part of the net investment.

41A　　The net investment in an associate or joint venture is impaired and impairment losses are incurred if, and only if, there is objective evidence of impairment as a result of one or more events that occurred after the initial recognition of the net investment (a 'loss event') and that loss event (or events) has an impact on the estimated future cash flows from the net investment that can be reliably estimated. It may not be possible to identify a single, discrete event that caused the impairment. Rather the combined effect of several events may have caused the impairment. Losses expected as a result of future events, no matter how likely, are not recognised. Objective evidence that the net investment is impaired includes observable data that comes to the attention of the entity about the following loss events:

(a)　　significant financial difficulty of the associate or joint venture;

(b)　　a breach of contract, such as a default or delinquency in payments by the associate or joint venture;

(c)　　the entity, for economic or legal reasons relating to its associate's or joint venture's financial difficulty, granting to the associate or joint venture a concession that the entity would not otherwise consider;

(d)　　it becoming probable that the associate or joint venture will enter bankruptcy or other financial reorganisation; or

(e)　　the disappearance of an active market for the net investment because of financial difficulties of the associate or joint venture.

41B　　The disappearance of an active market because the associate's or joint venture's equity or financial instruments are no longer publicly traded is not evidence of impairment. A downgrade of an associate's or joint venture's credit rating or a decline in the fair value of the associate or joint venture, is not of itself, evidence of impairment, although it may be evidence of impairment when considered with other available information.

41C　　In addition to the types of events in paragraph 41A, objective evidence of impairment for the net investment in the equity instruments of the associate or joint venture includes information about significant changes with an adverse effect that have taken

AASB

place in the technological, market, economic or legal environment in which the associate or joint venture operates, and indicates that the cost of the investment in the equity instrument may not be recovered. A significant or prolonged decline in the fair value of an investment in an equity instrument below its cost is also objective evidence of impairment.

42   Because goodwill that forms part of the carrying amount of the net investment in an associate or a joint venture is not separately recognised, it is not tested for impairment separately by applying the requirements for impairment testing goodwill in AASB 136 *Impairment of Assets*. Instead, the entire carrying amount of the investment is tested for impairment in accordance with AASB 136 as a single asset, by comparing its recoverable amount (higher of value in use and fair value less costs to sell) with its carrying amount whenever application of paragraphs 41A–41C indicates that the net investment may be impaired. An impairment loss recognised in those circumstances is not allocated to any asset, including goodwill, that forms part of the carrying amount of the net investment in the associate or joint venture. Accordingly, any reversal of that impairment loss is recognised in accordance with AASB 136 to the extent that the recoverable amount of the net investment subsequently increases. In determining the value in use of the net investment, an entity estimates:

(a)   its share of the present value of the estimated future cash flows expected to be generated by the associate or joint venture, including the cash flows from the operations of the associate or joint venture and the proceeds from the ultimate disposal of the investment; or

(b)   the present value of the estimated future cash flows expected to arise from dividends to be received from the investment and from its ultimate disposal.

Using appropriate assumptions, both methods give the same result.

43   The recoverable amount of an investment in an associate or a joint venture shall be assessed for each associate or joint venture, unless the associate or joint venture does not generate cash inflows from continuing use that are largely independent of those from other assets of the entity.

Separate financial statements

44   An investment in an associate or a joint venture shall be accounted for in the entity's separate financial statements in accordance with paragraph 10 of AASB 127.

Effective date and transition

45   An entity shall apply this Standard for annual periods beginning on or after 1 January 2018. Earlier application is permitted for periods beginning after 24 July 2014 but before 1 January 2018. If an entity applies this Standard earlier, it shall disclose that fact and apply AASB 10, AASB 11 *Joint Arrangements*, AASB 12 *Disclosure of Interests in Other Entities* and AASB 127 at the same time.

45A   AASB 2014-7 *Amendments to Australian Accounting Standards arising from AASB 9 (December 2014)*, issued in December 2014, amended the previous version of this Standard as follows: amended paragraphs 40–42 and added paragraphs 41A–41C. An entity shall apply those amendments when it applies AASB 9.

45B   AASB 2014-9 *Amendments to Australian Accounting Standards – Equity Method in Separate Financial Statements*, issued in December 2014, amended paragraph 25 in the previous version of this Standard. An entity shall apply that amendment for annual periods beginning on or after 1 January 2016 retrospectively in accordance with AASB 108 *Accounting Policies, Changes in Accounting Estimates and Errors*. Earlier application is permitted. If an entity applies that amendment for an earlier period, it shall disclose that fact.

45C   AASB 2014-10 *Amendments to Australian Accounting Standards – Sale or Contribution of Assets between an Investor and its Associate or Joint Venture*, issued in December 2014, in conjunction with AASB 2015-10 *Amendments to Australian*

Accounting Standards – Effective Date of Amendments to AASB 10 and AASB 128 and AASB 2017-5 Amendments to Australian Accounting Standards – Effective Date of Amendments to AASB 10 and AASB 128 and Editorial Corrections, amended paragraphs 28 and 30 and added paragraphs 31A–31B. An entity shall apply those amendments prospectively to the sale or contribution of assets occurring in annual periods beginning on or after 1 January 2022. Earlier application is permitted. If an entity applies those amendments earlier, it shall disclose that fact.

45D   AASB 2015-5 *Amendments to Australian Accounting Standards – Investment Entities: Applying the Consolidation Exception*, issued in January 2015, amended the previous version of this Standard as follows: amended paragraphs 17, Aus17.1, Aus17.2, 27 and 36 and added paragraph 36A. An entity shall apply those amendments for annual periods beginning on or after 1 January 2016. Earlier application is permitted. If an entity applies those amendments for an earlier period, it shall disclose that fact.

45E   AASB 2017-1 *Amendments to Australian Accounting Standards – Transfers of Investment Property, Annual Improvements 2014–2016 Cycle and Other Amendments*, issued in February 2017, amended paragraphs 18 and 36A. A for-profit entity shall apply those amendments retrospectively in accordance with AASB 108 for annual periods beginning on or after 1 January 2018. A not-for-profit entity shall apply those amendments retrospectively in accordance with AASB 108 for annual periods beginning on or after 1 January 2019. Earlier application is permitted. If an entity applies those amendments for an earlier period, it shall disclose that fact.

References to AASB 9

46   If an entity applies this Standard but does not yet apply AASB 9, any reference to AASB 9 shall be read as a reference to AASB 139.

Withdrawal of IAS 28 (2003)

47   [Deleted by the AASB]

Commencement of the legislative instrument

Aus47.1   For legal purposes, this legislative instrument commences on 31 December 2017.

Withdrawal of AASB pronouncements

Aus47.2   This Standard repeals AASB 128 *Investments in Associates and Joint Ventures* issued in August 2011. Despite the repeal, after the time this Standard starts to apply under section 334 of the Corporations Act (either generally or in relation to an individual entity), the repealed Standard continues to apply in relation to any period ending before that time as if the repeal had not occurred.

[Note: When this Standard applies under section 334 of the Corporations Act (either generally or in relation to an individual entity), it supersedes the application of the repealed Standard.]

COMPILATION DETAILS

Accounting Standard AASB 128 *Investments in Associates and Joint Ventures*

Compilation details are not part of AASB 128.

This compiled Standard applies to annual periods beginning on or after 1 January 2022. It takes into account amendments up to and including 12 December 2017 and was prepared on 20 April 2018 by the staff of the Australian Accounting Standards Board (AASB).

This compilation is not a separate Accounting Standard made by the AASB. Instead, it is a representation of AASB 128 (August 2015) as amended by other Accounting Standards, which are listed in the Table below.

Table of Standards

Standard	Date made	FRLI identifier	Commencement date	Effective date (*annual periods ... on or after ...*)	Application, saving or transitional provisions
AASB 128	7 Aug 2015	F2015L01543	31 Dec 2017	(*beginning*) 1 Jan 2018	see (a) below
AASB 2015-10	22 Dec 2015	F2016L00035	31 Dec 2015	(*beginning*) 1 Jan 2016	see (b) below
AASB 1058	9 Dec 2016	F2017L00042	31 Dec 2018	(*beginning*) 1 Jan 2019	not compiled*
AASB 2017-1	13 Feb 2017	F2017L00193	31 Dec 2017	FP (*beginning*) 1 Jan 2018 NFP (*beginning*) 1 Jan 2019	see (c) below
AASB 17	19 Jul 2017	F2017L01184	31 Dec 2020	(*beginning*) 1 Jan 2021	not compiled*
AASB 2017-5	12 Dec 2017	F2018L00067	31 Dec 2017	(*beginning*) 1 Jan 2018	see (d) below
AASB 2017-7	12 Dec 2017	F2018L00065	31 Dec 2018	(*beginning*) 1 Jan 2019	not compiled*

* The amendments made by this Standard are not included in this compilation, which presents the principal Standard as applicable to annual periods beginning on or after 1 January 2022 as at 31 December 2017.

(a) Entities may elect to apply this Standard to annual periods beginning after 24 July 2014 but before 1 January 2018, provided that AASB 10 *Consolidated Financial Statements*, AASB 11 *Joint Arrangements*, AASB 12 *Disclosure of Interests in Other Entities* and AASB 127 *Separate Financial Statements* are also applied to such periods.

(b) This Standard amended AASB 128 for annual periods beginning on or after 1 January 2018. Entities may elect to apply the amendments in this Standard to annual periods beginning before 1 January 2018.

(c) For-profit (FP) entities and not-for-profit (NFP) entities may elect to apply the amendments made to AASB 128 by this Standard early, in advance of their specific mandatory effective dates.

(d) AASB 2017-5 deferred the effective date of certain requirements included in AASB 128 to annual periods beginning on or after 1 January 2022 instead of 1 January 2018. Entities may elect to apply the deferred requirements to annual periods beginning before 1 January 2022.

Table of amendments

Paragraph affected	How affected	By ... [paragraph/page]
18	amended	AASB 2017-1 [page 7]
28	amended (for certain periods)	AASB 2017-5 [9]
30	amended (for certain periods)	AASB 2017-5 [9]
31A-31B	deleted (for certain periods)	AASB 2017-5 [9]
36A	amended	AASB 2017-1 [page 8]
37	amended	AASB 2017-5 [25]

Paragraph affected	How affected	By ... [paragraph/page]
45C	amended deleted (for certain periods) amended	AASB 2015-10 [11, 12] AASB 2017-5 [9] AASB 2017-5 [10, 11]
45E	added	AASB 2017-1 [page 8]

DELETED IAS 28 TEXT

Deleted IAS 28 text is not part of AASB 128.

47   This Standard supersedes IAS 28 *Investments in Associates* (as revised in 2003).

BASIS FOR CONCLUSIONS ON AASB 2011-5 AND AASB 2011-6

This Basis for Conclusions accompanies, but is not part of, AASB 128. The Basis for Conclusions was originally published with AASB 2011-6 Amendments to Australian Accounting Standards – Extending Relief from Consolidation, the Equity Method and Proportionate Consolidation – Reduced Disclosure Requirements.

Introduction

BC1   This Basis for Conclusions summarises the Australian Accounting Standards Board's considerations in reaching the conclusions in AASB 2011-5 *Amendments to Australian Accounting Standards – Extending Relief from Consolidation, the Equity Method and Proportionate Consolidation* and AASB 2011-6 *Amendments to Australian Accounting Standards – Extending Relief from Consolidation, the Equity Method and Proportionate Consolidation – Reduced Disclosure Requirements*. Individual Board members gave greater weight to some factors than to others.

Background

BC2   Paragraph 10 of AASB 127 *Consolidated and Separate Financial Statements* (in common with IAS 27 *Consolidated and Separate Financial Statements*) provides relief from preparing consolidated financial statements for parents that meet four criteria, including having an ultimate parent or an intermediate parent that prepares IFRS-compliant consolidated financial statements (paragraph 10(d)).

BC3   Due to the addition of Aus paragraphs in IFRSs as adopted in Australia, the financial statements of some entities applying Australian Accounting Standards are not IFRS compliant. This means that a parent that has an ultimate parent or other intermediate parent that prepares non-IFRS-compliant consolidated financial statements does not have access to the exemption from consolidation provided in paragraph 10 of AASB 127, even if the criteria in paragraphs 10(a) to 10(c) are met.

BC4   Similarly, investors need not apply the equity method when they meet the four criteria in paragraph 13(c) of AASB 128 *Investments in Associates* and venturers need not apply proportionate consolidation or the equity method when they meet the four criteria in paragraph 2(c) of AASB 131 *Interests in Joint Ventures*. The criteria in paragraph 10 of AASB 127, paragraph 13(c) of AASB 128 and paragraph 2(c) of AASB 131 are similar.

BC5   Consequently, the exemptions from the equity method and proportionate consolidation are also not available under those paragraphs to an investor or a venturer when its ultimate parent or intermediate parent prepares non-IFRS-compliant consolidated financial statements.

BC6 The AASB issued Exposure Draft ED 205 *Extending Relief from Consolidation, the Equity Method and Proportionate Consolidation* in September 2010. The AASB considered the submissions received from constituents and confirmed the principal approach proposed in the Exposure Draft.

New Zealand approach

BC7 During its development of ED 205, the AASB noted that a related issue was considered by the Financial Reporting Standards Board (FRSB) of the New Zealand Institute of Chartered Accountants in December 2008. This concerned the requirement in paragraph 10(d) of NZ IAS 27 *Consolidated and Separate Financial Statements* that the parent's financial statements must be 'available for public use'. Due to the reporting requirements in New Zealand, not all entities are required to file their financial statements with the Companies Office. Hence, when a parent of a group is not required to submit its financial statements, any intermediate subsidiaries were unable to use the paragraph 10 exemption. As a result, the FRSB inserted paragraph NZ 3.1 into NZ IAS 27 so that entities that qualify for differential reporting concessions were not required to comply with paragraph 10(d). In order to qualify for the exemption not to present consolidated financial statements, qualifying entities were still required to comply with all the other conditions in paragraph 10.

BC8 In addition, the AASB noted that the FRSB had inserted a similar exemption into NZ IAS 28 *Investments in Associates* (paragraph NZ 1.2) and NZ IAS 31 *Interests in Joint Ventures* (paragraph NZ 1.1), extending the relief from application of the equity method by investors and proportionate consolidation or the equity method by venturers.

BC9 The AASB did not follow the FRSB's specific approach for qualifying entities, given the different issues faced by the two Boards and the different financial reporting framework in New Zealand, including its differential reporting framework that involves modifications to the recognition and measurement requirements of IFRSs.

Extending the exemptions

BC10 The AASB considered the limitations on the exemptions and developed a view that relief from consolidation, the equity method and proportionate consolidation should be extended to a not-for-profit or Tier 2 parent, investor or venturer if it:

    (a)   has a parent higher up in the group that prepares consolidated financial statements (whether or not IFRS-compliant) that are available for public use and:

        (i)   those consolidated financial statements incorporate the information that would otherwise have been presented in the parent's consolidated financial statements or the investor's or venturer's financial statements; or

        (ii)   the parent, investor or venturer is an entity complying with Australian Accounting Standards – Reduced Disclosure Requirements ('Tier 2'); and

    (b)   meets the criteria in paragraphs 10(a) to 10(c) of AASB 127, paragraphs 13(c)(i) to 13(c)(iii) of AASB 128 or paragraphs 2(c)(i) to 2(c)(iii) of AASB 131, as relevant.

BC11 This view is based on the principle that financial statement users would be able to satisfy their information needs through the consolidated financial statements prepared by the parent higher up in the group. However, the AASB decided that such relief should not be available in relation to the General Government Sector (GGS) of each Federal, State and Territory Government due to the unique circumstances related to the GGS, its relationship to the whole of government and its macro-economic significance. The AASB also decided that the partial consolidation basis for GGS financial statements required by AASB 1049 *Whole of Government and General Government Sector Financial Reporting* would not be amended.

BC12 Consistent with IAS 27, IAS 28 *Investments in Associates* and IAS 31 *Interests in Joint Ventures*, the AASB decided that the existing relief provided under paragraph 10 of AASB 127, paragraph 13(c) of AASB 128 and paragraph 2(c) of AASB 131 should be retained. The extension of relief on the basis set out in paragraph BC10 does not change the present requirements for relief when the ultimate or intermediate parent is a for-profit Tier 1 entity – that entity is still required to prepare IFRS-compliant consolidated financial statements.

Not-for-profit ultimate or intermediate parent

BC13 When the ultimate or intermediate parent is a not-for-profit Tier 1 entity, and the parent, investor or venturer is a for-profit Tier 1 entity, the relief is not available where there are differences in the basis of accounting between the not-for-profit and for-profit entities as a result of the not-for-profit entity applying Standards or Aus paragraphs that contain requirements that are inconsistent with IFRS requirements. Extending relief to the for-profit Tier 1 parent, investor or venturer in this case would be beyond the scope of the relief available under IFRSs. However, the relief is available when the not-for-profit entity is not required to apply such inconsistent requirements. This is indicated by footnote to the table in paragraph AG1 of the Australian application guidance added to AASB 127. In this case, the for-profit Tier 1 entity would be able to claim compliance with IFRSs in that the relief is within the scope of the relief available under IFRSs.

BC14 The AASB considered the extension of relief to a for-profit Tier 2 parent, investor or venturer that has a not-for-profit ultimate or intermediate parent. The table in the Basis for Conclusions in ED 205 proposed that relief should be available to a parent, investor or venturer in these circumstances, which appears to be inconsistent with the circumstances addressed in paragraph BC13. The AASB considered three approaches to addressing the apparent inconsistency:

(a)   amend the table proposed in ED 205 to indicate that the relief would not be available;

(b)   retain the approach proposed in ED 205, that the relief would be available, and extend the justification in the Basis for Conclusions for this position; or

(c)   retain the approach proposed in ED 205 with no amendment to the justification.

BC15 The AASB adopted the approach in paragraph BC14(b), extending the relief, based on its judgement that the relief would be reasonable for Tier 2 parents, investors or venturers despite any differences in the basis of accounting in the consolidated financial statements of the ultimate or intermediate parent that are publicly available. Typically, the not-for-profit ultimate or intermediate parent would not be able to claim compliance with IFRSs, and the Tier 2 parent, investor or venturer could not do so.

For-profit public sector entities

BC16 The AASB decided that relief would not be available to a parent entity merely because the intermediate parent preparing consolidated financial statements is a for-profit Tier 1 public sector entity unable to claim compliance with IFRSs. This decision was made on the basis that a for-profit public sector entity may apply requirements in particular Standards, such as AASB 1004 Contributions, and Aus paragraphs in other Australian Accounting Standards that are inconsistent with an IFRS requirement. However, relief may be available to the parent entity on another basis permitted by the Standard.

BC17 Relief is (or is not) available to a for-profit public sector entity as the parent, investor or venturer on the same basis as for any other for-profit parent, investor or venturer.

Other changes

BC18 The AASB also decided that, consistent with paragraph 10(d) of AASB 127, the references to 'Australian equivalents to IFRSs' in paragraph 13(c)(iv) of AASB 128 and paragraph 2(c)(iv) of AASB 131 should be amended to 'International Financial Reporting Standards'.

BC19 The AASB decided to include the summary table set out in the Basis for Conclusions in the Exposure Draft as Australian application guidance accompanying, but not part of, the amended AASB 127. Whereas the table in the Exposure Draft addressed relief in relation to both not-for-profit entities and entities applying reduced disclosure requirements under AASB 1053 *Application of Tiers of Australian Accounting Standards*, the table added to the AASB 127 guidance by AASB 2011-5 addresses not-for-profit entities but not reduced disclosure requirements.

Reduced disclosure requirements

BC20 Exposure Draft ED 205, in addition to addressing relief for not-for-profit entities, also proposed the extension of relief to entities applying Australian Accounting Standards – Reduced Disclosure Requirements under AASB 1053. The AASB decided that relief should be extended to Tier 2 entities, either on the same basis as for not-for-profit entities or as addressed in paragraphs BC14 and BC15. Accounting Standard AASB 2011-6 provides this relief. That Standard also expands the table in the Australian application guidance accompanying AASB 127 to address entities applying reduced disclosure requirements.

BC21 Whereas AASB 2011-5 applies to annual reporting periods beginning on or after 1 July 2011, AASB 2011-6 applies to annual reporting periods beginning on or after 1 July 2013, being the application date of the reduced disclosure requirements under AASB 1053. Accordingly, two amending Standards were prepared to reflect the different application dates. Early application of each Standard is permitted. Early application of AASB 2011-6 requires early application of AASB 1053.

BASIS FOR CONCLUSIONS ON AASB 2015-4

This Basis for Conclusions accompanies, but is not part of, AASB 128. The Basis for Conclusions was originally published with AASB 2015-4 Amendments to Australian Accounting Standards – Financial Reporting Requirements for Australian Groups with a Foreign Parent.

Introduction

BC1 This Basis for Conclusions summarises the Australian Accounting Standards Board's considerations in reaching the conclusions in AASB 2015-4 *Amendments to Australian Accounting Standards – Financial Reporting Requirements for Australian Groups with a Foreign Parent*. Individual Board members gave greater weight to some factors than to others.

BC2 In September 2014, the Board identified that the requirements of AASB 10 *Consolidated Financial Statements* and AASB 128 *Investments in Associates and Joint Ventures* in relation to the requirement for an Australian parent entity to apply the requirements of AASB 10 and/or AASB 128 when either the parent or the group is a reporting entity, or both the parent and the group are reporting entities, were not aligned. Specifically, AASB 10 requires the ultimate Australian parent to prepare consolidated financial statements, even where the entity has a foreign parent that prepares consolidated financial statements that comply with IFRSs, when either the parent or the group is a reporting entity or both the parent and the group are reporting entities. AASB 128 did not include a similar requirement in relation to the application of the equity method by the ultimate Australian parent.

BC3 The Board noted that this difference arose when issuing AASB 128 in 2011 in which the Board adopted the IFRS wording in IAS 28 paragraph 17(d) without amendment. The superseded AASB 128 *Investments in Associates* (July 2004) included similar relief for parent entities from applying the equity method in accounting for an interest in an associate or joint venture, but limited that relief to parent entities other than the ultimate Australian parent.

BC4 In December 2014 the Board decided that the relief in AASB 128 should apply to the ultimate Australian entity, rather than the ultimate Australian parent, to better align the requirements in AASB 128 with the relief available in AASB 10.

BC5 The Board decided to conduct further research before deciding whether to undertake a project to reconsider whether to limit the exceptions in AASB 10 and AASB 128 from presenting consolidated financial statements or applying the equity method to entities other than the ultimate Australian entity. In the interim, the Board decided to amend AASB 128 to require that the ultimate Australian entity apply the equity method in accounting for an interest in an associate or joint venture, to be consistent with the requirement in AASB 10 for the ultimate Australian parent to present consolidated financial statements when either the parent or the group is a reporting entity or both the parent and the group are reporting entities. The amendment aligns the requirements of AASB 10 and AASB 128 in this regard and is substantively consistent with the limitation on the relief previously available to entities under the superseded AASB 128.

AASB 129
Financial Reporting in Hyperinflationary Economies
(Reissued August 2015)

CONTENTS

COMPARISON WITH IAS 29
ACCOUNTING STANDARD
AASB 129 *FINANCIAL REPORTING IN HYPERINFLATIONARY ECONOMIES*

BASIS FOR CONCLUSIONS ON IAS 29 (available on AASB website)

Australian Accounting Standard AASB 129 *Financial Reporting in Hyperinflationary Economies* is set out in paragraphs 1 – Aus41.2. All the paragraphs have equal authority. Paragraphs in **bold type** state the main principles. AASB 129 is to be read in the context of other Australian Accounting Standards, including AASB 1048 *Interpretation of Standards*, which identifies the Australian Accounting Interpretations, and AASB 1057 *Application of Australian Accounting Standards*. In the absence of explicit guidance, AASB 108 *Accounting Policies, Changes in Accounting Estimates and Errors* provides a basis for selecting and applying accounting policies.

COMPARISON WITH IAS 29

AASB 129 *Financial Reporting in Hyperinflationary Economies* incorporates IAS 29 *Financial Reporting in Hyperinflationary Economies* issued by the International Accounting Standards Board (IASB). Australian-specific paragraphs (which are not included in IAS 29) are identified with the prefix "Aus". Paragraphs that apply only to not-for-profit entities begin by identifying their limited applicability.

Tier 1

For-profit entities complying with AASB 129 also comply with IAS 29.

Not-for-profit entities' compliance with IAS 29 will depend on whether any "Aus" paragraphs that specifically apply to not-for-profit entities provide additional guidance or contain applicable requirements that are inconsistent with IAS 29.

AASB 1053 *Application of Tiers of Australian Accounting Standards* explains the two tiers of reporting requirements.

ACCOUNTING STANDARD AASB 129

The Australian Accounting Standards Board makes Accounting Standard AASB 129 *Financial Reporting in Hyperinflationary Economies* under section 334 of the *Corporations Act 2001*.

Kris Peach

Dated 7 August 2015

Chair – AASB

ACCOUNTING STANDARD AASB 129
FINANCIAL REPORTING IN HYPERINFLATIONARY ECONOMIES[1]

Scope

1   This Standard shall be applied to the financial statements, including the consolidated financial statements, of any entity whose functional currency is the currency of a hyperinflationary economy.

2   In a hyperinflationary economy, reporting of operating results and financial position in the local currency without restatement is not useful. Money loses purchasing power at such a rate that comparison of amounts from transactions and other events that have occurred at different times, even within the same accounting period, is misleading.

3   This Standard does not establish an absolute rate at which hyperinflation is deemed to arise. It is a matter of judgement when restatement of financial statements in accordance with this Standard becomes necessary. Hyperinflation is indicated by characteristics of the economic environment of a country which include, but are not limited to, the following:

(a)   the general population prefers to keep its wealth in non-monetary assets or in a relatively stable foreign currency. Amounts of local currency held are immediately invested to maintain purchasing power;

---

1   As part of AASB 2008-5 *Amendments to Australian Accounting Standards arising from the Annual Improvements Project* issued in July 2008, the Board changed terms used in AASB 129 to be consistent with other Australian Accounting Standards as follows: (a) 'market value' was amended to 'fair value', and (b) 'results of operations' and 'net income' were amended to 'profit or loss'.

(b)   the general population regards monetary amounts not in terms of the local currency but in terms of a relatively stable foreign currency. Prices may be quoted in that currency;

(c)   sales and purchases on credit take place at prices that compensate for the expected loss of purchasing power during the credit period, even if the period is short;

(d)   interest rates, wages and prices are linked to a price index; and

(e)   the cumulative inflation rate over three years is approaching, or exceeds, 100%.

4   It is preferable that all entities that report in the currency of the same hyperinflationary economy apply this Standard from the same date. Nevertheless, this Standard applies to the financial statements of any entity from the beginning of the reporting period in which it identifies the existence of hyperinflation in the country in whose currency it reports.

The restatement of financial statements

5   Prices change over time as the result of various specific or general political, economic and social forces. Specific forces such as changes in supply and demand and technological changes may cause individual prices to increase or decrease significantly and independently of each other. In addition, general forces may result in changes in the general level of prices and therefore in the general purchasing power of money.

6   Entities that prepare financial statements on the historical cost basis of accounting do so without regard either to changes in the general level of prices or to increases in specific prices of recognised assets or liabilities. The exceptions to this are those assets and liabilities that the entity is required, or chooses, to measure at fair value. For example, property, plant and equipment may be revalued to fair value and biological assets are generally required to be measured at fair value. Some entities, however, present financial statements that are based on a current cost approach that reflects the effects of changes in the specific prices of assets held.

7   In a hyperinflationary economy, financial statements, whether they are based on a historical cost approach or a current cost approach, are useful only if they are expressed in terms of the measuring unit current at the end of the reporting period. As a result, this Standard applies to the financial statements of entities reporting in the currency of a hyperinflationary economy. Presentation of the information required by this Standard as a supplement to unrestated financial statements is not permitted. Furthermore, separate presentation of the financial statements before restatement is discouraged.

8   **The financial statements of an entity whose functional currency is the currency of a hyperinflationary economy, whether they are based on a historical cost approach or a current cost approach, shall be stated in terms of the measuring unit current at the end of the reporting period. The corresponding figures for the previous period required by AASB 101** *Presentation of Financial Statements* **and any information in respect of earlier periods shall also be stated in terms of the measuring unit current at the end of the reporting period. For the purpose of presenting comparative amounts in a different presentation currency, paragraphs 42(b) and 43 of AASB 121** *The Effects of Changes in Foreign Exchange Rates* **apply.**

9   **The gain or loss on the net monetary position shall be included in profit or loss and separately disclosed.**

10   The restatement of financial statements in accordance with this Standard requires the application of certain procedures as well as judgement. The consistent application of these procedures and judgements from period to period is more important than the precise accuracy of the resulting amounts included in the restated financial statements.

Historical cost financial statements

Statement of financial position

11 Statement of financial position amounts not already expressed in terms of the measuring unit current at the end of the reporting period are restated by applying a general price index.

12 Monetary items are not restated because they are already expressed in terms of the monetary unit current at the end of the reporting period. Monetary items are money held and items to be received or paid in money.

13 Assets and liabilities linked by agreement to changes in prices, such as index linked bonds and loans, are adjusted in accordance with the agreement in order to ascertain the amount outstanding at the end of the reporting period. These items are carried at this adjusted amount in the restated statement of financial position.

14 All other assets and liabilities are non-monetary. Some non-monetary items are carried at amounts current at the end of the reporting period, such as net realisable value and fair value, so they are not restated. All other non-monetary assets and liabilities are restated.

15 Most non-monetary items are carried at cost or cost less depreciation; hence they are expressed at amounts current at their date of acquisition. The restated cost, or cost less depreciation, of each item is determined by applying to its historical cost and accumulated depreciation the change in a general price index from the date of acquisition to the end of the reporting period. For example, property, plant and equipment, inventories of raw materials and merchandise, goodwill, patents, trademarks and similar assets are restated from the dates of their purchase. Inventories of partly-finished and finished goods are restated from the dates on which the costs of purchase and of conversion were incurred.

16 Detailed records of the acquisition dates of items of property, plant and equipment may not be available or capable of estimation. In these rare circumstances, it may be necessary, in the first period of application of this Standard, to use an independent professional assessment of the value of the items as the basis for their restatement.

17 A general price index may not be available for the periods for which the restatement of property, plant and equipment is required by this Standard. In these circumstances, it may be necessary to use an estimate based, for example, on the movements in the exchange rate between the functional currency and a relatively stable foreign currency.

18 Some non-monetary items are carried at amounts current at dates other than that of acquisition or that of the statement of financial position, for example property, plant and equipment that has been revalued at some earlier date. In these cases, the carrying amounts are restated from the date of the revaluation.

19 The restated amount of a non-monetary item is reduced, in accordance with appropriate Australian Accounting Standards, when it exceeds its recoverable amount. For example, restated amounts of property, plant and equipment, goodwill, patents and trademarks are reduced to recoverable amount and restated amounts of inventories are reduced to net realisable value.

20 An investee that is accounted for under the equity method may report in the currency of a hyperinflationary economy. The statement of financial position and statement of comprehensive income of such an investee are restated in accordance with this Standard in order to calculate the investor's share of its net assets and profit or loss. When the restated financial statements of the investee are expressed in a foreign currency they are translated at closing rates.

21 The impact of inflation is usually recognised in borrowing costs. It is not appropriate both to restate the capital expenditure financed by borrowing and to capitalise that part of the borrowing costs that compensates for the inflation during the same period. This part of the borrowing costs is recognised as an expense in the period in which the costs are incurred.

22   An entity may acquire assets under an arrangement that permits it to defer payment without incurring an explicit interest charge. Where it is impracticable to impute the amount of interest, such assets are restated from the payment date and not the date of purchase.

23   [Deleted]

24   At the beginning of the first period of application of this Standard, the components of owners' equity, except retained earnings and any revaluation surplus, are restated by applying a general price index from the dates the components were contributed or otherwise arose. Any revaluation surplus that arose in previous periods is eliminated. Restated retained earnings are derived from all the other amounts in the restated statement of financial position.

25   At the end of the first period and in subsequent periods, all components of owners' equity are restated by applying a general price index from the beginning of the period or the date of contribution, if later. The movements for the period in owners' equity are disclosed in accordance with AASB 101.

Statement of comprehensive income

26   This Standard requires that all items in the statement of comprehensive income are expressed in terms of the measuring unit current at the end of the reporting period. Therefore all amounts need to be restated by applying the change in the general price index from the dates when the items of income and expenses were initially recorded in the financial statements.

Gain or loss on net monetary position

27   In a period of inflation, an entity holding an excess of monetary assets over monetary liabilities loses purchasing power and an entity with an excess of monetary liabilities over monetary assets gains purchasing power to the extent the assets and liabilities are not linked to a price level. This gain or loss on the net monetary position may be derived as the difference resulting from the restatement of non-monetary assets, owners' equity and items in the statement of comprehensive income and the adjustment of index linked assets and liabilities. The gain or loss may be estimated by applying the change in a general price index to the weighted average for the period of the difference between monetary assets and monetary liabilities.

28   The gain or loss on the net monetary position is included in profit or loss. The adjustment to those assets and liabilities linked by agreement to changes in prices made in accordance with paragraph 13 is offset against the gain or loss on net monetary position. Other income and expense items, such as interest income and expense, and foreign exchange differences related to invested or borrowed funds, are also associated with the net monetary position. Although such items are separately disclosed, it may be helpful if they are presented together with the gain or loss on net monetary position in the statement of comprehensive income.

Current cost financial statements

Statement of financial position

29   Items stated at current cost are not restated because they are already expressed in terms of the measuring unit current at the end of the reporting period. Other items in the statement of financial position are restated in accordance with paragraphs 11 to 25.

Statement of comprehensive income

30   The current cost statement of comprehensive income, before restatement, generally reports costs current at the time at which the underlying transactions or events occurred. Cost of sales and depreciation are recorded at current costs at the time of consumption; sales and other expenses are recorded at their money amounts when they occurred.

Therefore all amounts need to be restated into the measuring unit current at the end of the reporting period by applying a general price index.

Gain or loss on net monetary position

31   The gain or loss on the net monetary position is accounted for in accordance with paragraphs 27 and 28.

Taxes

32   The restatement of financial statements in accordance with this Standard may give rise to differences between the carrying amount of individual assets and liabilities in the statement of financial position and their tax bases. These differences are accounted for in accordance with AASB 112 *Income Taxes*.

Statement of cash flows

33   This Standard requires that all items in the statement of cash flows are expressed in terms of the measuring unit current at the end of the reporting period.

Corresponding figures

34   Corresponding figures for the previous reporting period, whether they were based on a historical cost approach or a current cost approach, are restated by applying a general price index so that the comparative financial statements are presented in terms of the measuring unit current at the end of the reporting period. Information that is disclosed in respect of earlier periods is also expressed in terms of the measuring unit current at the end of the reporting period. For the purpose of presenting comparative amounts in a different presentation currency, paragraphs 42(b) and 43 of AASB 121 apply.

Consolidated financial statements

35   A parent that reports in the currency of a hyperinflationary economy may have subsidiaries that also report in the currencies of hyperinflationary economies. The financial statements of any such subsidiary need to be restated by applying a general price index of the country in whose currency it reports before they are included in the consolidated financial statements issued by its parent. Where such a subsidiary is a foreign subsidiary, its restated financial statements are translated at closing rates. The financial statements of subsidiaries that do not report in the currencies of hyperinflationary economies are dealt with in accordance with AASB 121.

36   If financial statements with different ends of the reporting periods are consolidated, all items, whether non-monetary or monetary, need to be restated into the measuring unit current at the date of the consolidated financial statements.

Selection and use of the general price index

37   The restatement of financial statements in accordance with this Standard requires the use of a general price index that reflects changes in general purchasing power. It is preferable that all entities that report in the currency of the same economy use the same index.

Economies ceasing to be hyperinflationary

38   **When an economy ceases to be hyperinflationary and an entity discontinues the preparation and presentation of financial statements prepared in accordance with this Standard, it shall treat the amounts expressed in the measuring unit current**

at the end of the previous reporting period as the basis for the carrying amounts in its subsequent financial statements.

Disclosures

39   The following disclosures shall be made:

   (a)   the fact that the financial statements and the corresponding figures for previous periods have been restated for the changes in the general purchasing power of the functional currency and, as a result, are stated in terms of the measuring unit current at the end of the reporting period;

   (b)   whether the financial statements are based on a historical cost approach or a current cost approach; and

   (c)   the identity and level of the price index at the end of the reporting period and the movement in the index during the current and the previous reporting period.

40   The disclosures required by this Standard are needed to make clear the basis of dealing with the effects of inflation in the financial statements. They are also intended to provide other information necessary to understand that basis and the resulting amounts.

Effective date

41   This Standard becomes operative for financial statements covering periods beginning on or after 1 January 2016. Earlier application is permitted for periods beginning on or after 1 January 2014 but before 1 January 2016.

Commencement of the legislative instrument

Aus41.1   For legal purposes, this legislative instrument commences on 31 December 2015.

Withdrawal of AASB pronouncements

Aus41.2   This Standard repeals AASB 129 *Financial Reporting in Hyperinflationary Economies* issued in July 2004. Despite the repeal, after the time this Standard starts to apply under section 334 of the Corporations Act (either generally or in relation to an individual entity), the repealed Standard continues to apply in relation to any period ending before that time as if the repeal had not occurred.

[Note: When this Standard applies under section 334 of the Corporations Act (either generally or in relation to an individual entity), it supersedes the application of the repealed Standard.]

AASB 132
Financial Instruments: Presentation

(Reissued August 2015)

This note is not part of Accounting Standard AASB 132.

The following unincorporated amendments are not included in this Standard.

- AASB 17 *Insurance Contracts* — Appendix D sets out the amendments to other Standards that are a consequence of the AASB issuing AASB 17 *Insurance Contracts*. This Standard is applicable from 1 January 2021. Earlier application is permitted, but entities must apply AASB 9 *Financial Instruments* and AASB 15 *Revenue from Contracts with Customers* first.

- AASB 16 *Leases* — Appendix D sets out the amendments to other Standards that are a consequence of the AASB issuing this Standard. It is applicable from 1 January 2019. Earlier application is permitted, but entities must apply AASB 15 *Revenue from Contracts with Customers* before applying this Standard.

- AASB 2016-7 *Amendments to Australian Accounting Standards — Deferral of AASB 15 for Not-for-Profit Entities*. This Standard defers the consequential amendments that were originally set out in AASB 2014-5 *Amendments to Australian Accounting Standards arising from AASB 15,* by restating the effective date of the amendments set out in AASB 2015-8 *Amendments to Australian Accounting Standards* for not-for-profit entities. This Standard defers the application of AASB 15 to 1 January 2019. Earlier application is permitted provided AASB 1058 is also applied to the same period.

Entities early-adopting any amendments with later application dates will need to refer to the amending Standards that have not yet been incorporated into compilations. The abovementioned unincorporated amendments may be located on the AASB website at www.aasb.gov.au or on the Federal Register of Legislation website at www.legislation.gov.au.

CONTENTS

APPENDIX
A. APPLICATION GUIDANCE

ILLUSTRATIVE EXAMPLES
DELETED IAS 32 TEXT

BASIS FOR CONCLUSIONS ON IAS 32 (available on the AASB website)

Accounting Standard AASB 132 *Financial Instruments: Presentation* is set out in paragraphs 1 – Aus100.2 and the Appendix. All the paragraphs have equal authority. Paragraphs in **bold type** state the main principles. AASB 132 is to be read in the context of other Australian Accounting Standards, including AASB 1048 *Interpretation of Standards*, which identifies the Australian Accounting Interpretations, and AASB 1057 *Application of Australian Accounting Standards*. In the absence of explicit guidance, AASB 108 *Accounting Policies, Changes in Accounting Estimates and Errors* provides a basis for selecting and applying accounting policies.

COMPARISON WITH IAS 32

AASB 132 *Financial Instruments: Presentation* incorporates IAS 32 *Financial Instruments: Presentation* issued by the International Accounting Standards Board (IASB). Australian-specific paragraphs (which are not included in IAS 32) are identified with the prefix "Aus". Paragraphs that apply only to not-for-profit entities begin by identifying their limited applicability.

Tier 1

For-profit entities complying with AASB 132 also comply with IAS 32.

Not-for-profit entities' compliance with IAS 32 will depend on whether any "Aus" paragraphs that specifically apply to not-for-profit entities provide additional guidance or contain applicable requirements that are inconsistent with IAS 32.

AASB 1053 *Application of Tiers of Australian Accounting Standards* explains the two tiers of reporting requirements.

ACCOUNTING STANDARD AASB 132

The Australian Accounting Standards Board makes Accounting Standard AASB 132 *Financial Instruments: Presentation* under section 334 of the *Corporations Act 2001*.

Kris Peach

Dated 7 August 2015   Chair – AASB

ACCOUNTING STANDARD AASB 132
FINANCIAL INSTRUMENTS: PRESENTATION

Objective

1   [Deleted]

2   The objective of this Standard is to establish principles for presenting financial instruments as liabilities or equity and for offsetting financial assets and financial liabilities. It applies to the classification of financial instruments, from the perspective of the issuer, into financial assets, financial liabilities and equity instruments; the classification of related interest, dividends, losses and gains; and the circumstances in which financial assets and financial liabilities should be offset.

3   The principles in this Standard complement the principles for recognising and measuring financial assets and financial liabilities in AASB 9 *Financial Instruments*, and for disclosing information about them in AASB 7 *Financial Instruments: Disclosures*.

Scope

4   **This Standard shall be applied by all entities to all types of financial instruments except:**

     (a)   **those interests in subsidiaries, associates or joint ventures that are accounted for in accordance with AASB 10** *Consolidated Financial Statements*, **AASB 127** *Separate Financial Statements* **or AASB 128** *Investments in Associates and Joint Ventures*. **However, in some cases, AASB 10, AASB 127 or AASB 128 require or permit an entity to account for an interest in a subsidiary, associate or joint venture using AASB 9; in those cases, entities shall apply the requirements of this Standard. Entities shall also apply this Standard to all derivatives linked to interests in subsidiaries, associates or joint ventures.**

     (b)   **employers' rights and obligations under employee benefit plans, to which AASB 119** *Employee Benefits* **applies.**

     (c)   **[deleted]**

     (d)   **insurance contracts as defined in AASB 4** *Insurance Contracts*. **However, this Standard applies to derivatives that are embedded in insurance contracts if AASB 9 requires the entity to account for them separately. Moreover, an issuer shall apply this Standard to financial guarantee contracts if the issuer applies AASB 9 in recognising and measuring the contracts, but shall apply AASB 4 if the issuer elects, in accordance with paragraph 4(d) of AASB 4, to apply AASB 4 in recognising and measuring them.**

     (e)   **financial instruments that are within the scope of AASB 4 because they contain a discretionary participation feature. The issuer of these instruments is exempt from applying to these features paragraphs 15–32 and AG25–AG35 of this Standard regarding the distinction between financial liabilities and equity instruments. However, these instruments are subject to all other requirements of this Standard. Furthermore, this Standard applies to derivatives that are embedded in these instruments (see AASB 9).**

     (f)   **financial instruments, contracts and obligations under share-based payment transactions to which AASB 2** *Share-based Payment* **applies, except for**

         (i)   **contracts within the scope of paragraphs 8–10 of this Standard, to which this Standard applies,**

    (ii)   **paragraphs 33 and 34 of this Standard, which shall be applied to treasury shares purchased, sold, issued or cancelled in connection with employee share option plans, employee share purchase plans, and all other share-based payment arrangements.**

5–7   [Deleted]

8   **This Standard shall be applied to those contracts to buy or sell a non-financial item that can be settled net in cash or another financial instrument, or by exchanging financial instruments, as if the contracts were financial instruments, with the exception of contracts that were entered into and continue to be held for the purpose of the receipt or delivery of a non-financial item in accordance with the entity's expected purchase, sale or usage requirements. However, this Standard shall be applied to those contracts that an entity designates as measured at fair value through profit or loss in accordance with paragraph 2.5 of AASB 9** *Financial Instruments***.**

9   There are various ways in which a contract to buy or sell a non-financial item can be settled net in cash or another financial instrument or by exchanging financial instruments. These include:

    (a)   when the terms of the contract permit either party to settle it net in cash or another financial instrument or by exchanging financial instruments;

    (b)   when the ability to settle net in cash or another financial instrument, or by exchanging financial instruments, is not explicit in the terms of the contract, but the entity has a practice of settling similar contracts net in cash or another financial instrument, or by exchanging financial instruments (whether with the counterparty, by entering into offsetting contracts or by selling the contract before its exercise or lapse);

    (c)   when, for similar contracts, the entity has a practice of taking delivery of the underlying and selling it within a short period after delivery for the purpose of generating a profit from short-term fluctuations in price or dealer's margin; and

    (d)   when the non-financial item that is the subject of the contract is readily convertible to cash.

    A contract to which (b) or (c) applies is not entered into for the purpose of the receipt or delivery of the non-financial item in accordance with the entity's expected purchase, sale or usage requirements, and, accordingly, is within the scope of this Standard. Other contracts to which paragraph 8 applies are evaluated to determine whether they were entered into and continue to be held for the purpose of the receipt or delivery of the non-financial item in accordance with the entity's expected purchase, sale or usage requirement, and accordingly, whether they are within the scope of this Standard.

10   A written option to buy or sell a non-financial item that can be settled net in cash or another financial instrument, or by exchanging financial instruments, in accordance with paragraph 9(a) or (d) is within the scope of this Standard. Such a contract cannot be entered into for the purpose of the receipt or delivery of the non-financial item in accordance with the entity's expected purchase, sale or usage requirements.

Definitions (see also paragraphs AG3–AG23)

11   **The following terms are used in this Standard with the meanings specified:**

    A *financial instrument* **is any contract that gives rise to a financial asset of one entity and a financial liability or equity instrument of another entity.**

    A *financial asset* **is any asset that is:**

    (a)   **cash;**

    (b)   **an equity instrument of another entity;**

    (c)   **a contractual right:**

        (i)   **to receive cash or another financial asset from another entity; or**

(ii)   to exchange financial assets or financial liabilities with another entity under conditions that are potentially favourable to the entity; or

(d)   a contract that will or may be settled in the entity's own equity instruments and is:

(i)   a non-derivative for which the entity is or may be obliged to receive a variable number of the entity's own equity instruments; or

(ii)   a derivative that will or may be settled other than by the exchange of a fixed amount of cash or another financial asset for a fixed number of the entity's own equity instruments. For this purpose the entity's own equity instruments do not include puttable financial instruments classified as equity instruments in accordance with paragraphs 16A and 16B, instruments that impose on the entity an obligation to deliver to another party a pro rata share of the net assets of the entity only on liquidation and are classified as equity instruments in accordance with paragraphs 16C and 16D, or instruments that are contracts for the future receipt or delivery of the entity's own equity instruments.

A *financial liability* is any liability that is:

(a)   a contractual obligation:

(i)   to deliver cash or another financial asset to another entity; or

(ii)   to exchange financial assets or financial liabilities with another entity under conditions that are potentially unfavourable to the entity; or

(b)   a contract that will or may be settled in the entity's own equity instruments and is:

(i)   a non-derivative for which the entity is or may be obliged to deliver a variable number of the entity's own equity instruments; or

(ii)   a derivative that will or may be settled other than by the exchange of a fixed amount of cash or another financial asset for a fixed number of the entity's own equity instruments. For this purpose, rights, options or warrants to acquire a fixed number of the entity's own equity instruments for a fixed amount of any currency are equity instruments if the entity offers the rights, options or warrants pro rata to all of its existing owners of the same class of its own non-derivative equity instruments. Also, for these purposes the entity's own equity instruments do not include puttable financial instruments that are classified as equity instruments in accordance with paragraphs 16A and 16B, instruments that impose on the entity an obligation to deliver to another party a pro rata share of the net assets of the entity only on liquidation and are classified as equity instruments in accordance with paragraphs 16C and 16D, or instruments that are contracts for the future receipt or delivery of the entity's own equity instruments.

As an exception, an instrument that meets the definition of a financial liability is classified as an equity instrument if it has all the features and meets the conditions in paragraphs 16A and 16B or paragraphs 16C and 16D.

An *equity instrument* is any contract that evidences a residual interest in the assets of an entity after deducting all of its liabilities.

Fair value is the price that would be received to sell an asset or paid to transfer a liability in an orderly transaction between market participants at the measurement date. (See AASB 13 *Fair Value Measurement*.)

A *puttable instrument* is a financial instrument that gives the holder the right to put the instrument back to the issuer for cash or another financial asset or is

automatically put back to the issuer on the occurrence of an uncertain future event or the death or retirement of the instrument holder.

12   The following terms are defined in Appendix A of AASB 9 or paragraph 9 of AASB 139 *Financial Instruments: Recognition and Measurement* and are used in this Standard with the meaning specified in AASB 139 and AASB 9.

- amortised cost of a financial asset or financial liability
- derecognition
- derivative
- effective interest method
- financial guarantee contract
- financial liability at fair value through profit or loss
- firm commitment
- forecast transaction
- hedge effectiveness
- hedged item
- hedging instrument
- held for trading
- regular way purchase or sale
- transaction costs.

13   In this Standard, 'contract' and 'contractual' refer to an agreement between two or more parties that has clear economic consequences that the parties have little, if any, discretion to avoid, usually because the agreement is enforceable by law. Contracts, and thus financial instruments, may take a variety of forms and need not be in writing.

14   In this Standard, 'entity' includes individuals, partnerships, incorporated bodies, trusts and government agencies.

Presentation

Liabilities and equity (see also paragraphs AG13–AG14J and AG25–AG29A)

15   **The issuer of a financial instrument shall classify the instrument, or its component parts, on initial recognition as a financial liability, a financial asset or an equity instrument in accordance with the substance of the contractual arrangement and the definitions of a financial liability, a financial asset and an equity instrument.**

16   When an issuer applies the definitions in paragraph 11 to determine whether a financial instrument is an equity instrument rather than a financial liability, the instrument is an equity instrument if, and only if, both conditions (a) and (b) below are met.

(a)   The instrument includes no contractual obligation:

    (i)   to deliver cash or another financial asset to another entity; or

    (ii)   to exchange financial assets or financial liabilities with another entity under conditions that are potentially unfavourable to the issuer.

(b)   If the instrument will or may be settled in the issuer's own equity instruments, it is:

    (i)   a non-derivative that includes no contractual obligation for the issuer to deliver a variable number of its own equity instruments; or

    (ii)   a derivative that will be settled only by the issuer exchanging a fixed amount of cash or another financial asset for a fixed number of its own equity instruments. For this purpose, rights, options or warrants to acquire a fixed number of the entity's own equity instruments for a fixed amount of any currency are equity instruments if the entity offers the rights, options or warrants pro rata to all of its existing owners of the same class of its own non-derivative equity instruments. Also, for these purposes the issuer's own equity instruments do not include instruments that have all the features and meet the conditions described in paragraphs 16A and 16B or paragraphs 16C and 16D, or instruments that are contracts for the future receipt or delivery of the issuer's own equity instruments.

A contractual obligation, including one arising from a derivative financial instrument, that will or may result in the future receipt or delivery of the issuer's own equity instruments, but does not meet conditions (a) and (b) above, is not an equity instrument. As an exception, an instrument that meets the definition of a financial liability is classified as an equity instrument if it has all the features and meets the conditions in paragraphs 16A and 16B or paragraphs 16C and 16D.

Puttable instruments

16A   A puttable financial instrument includes a contractual obligation for the issuer to repurchase or redeem that instrument for cash or another financial asset on exercise of the put. As an exception to the definition of a financial liability, an instrument that includes such an obligation is classified as an equity instrument if it has all the following features:

(a)   It entitles the holder to a pro rata share of the entity's net assets in the event of the entity's liquidation. The entity's net assets are those assets that remain after deducting all other claims on its assets. A pro rata share is determined by:

    (i)   dividing the entity's net assets on liquidation into units of equal amount; and

    (ii)   multiplying that amount by the number of the units held by the financial instrument holder.

(b)   The instrument is in the class of instruments that is subordinate to all other classes of instruments. To be in such a class the instrument:

    (i)   has no priority over other claims to the assets of the entity on liquidation, and

    (ii)   does not need to be converted into another instrument before it is in the class of instruments that is subordinate to all other classes of instruments.

(c)   All financial instruments in the class of instruments that is subordinate to all other classes of instruments have identical features. For example, they must all be puttable, and the formula or other method used to calculate the repurchase or redemption price is the same for all instruments in that class.

(d)   Apart from the contractual obligation for the issuer to repurchase or redeem the instrument for cash or another financial asset, the instrument does not include any contractual obligation to deliver cash or another financial asset to another entity, or to exchange financial assets or financial liabilities with another entity under conditions that are potentially unfavourable to the entity, and it is not a contract that will or may be settled in the entity's own equity instruments as set out in subparagraph (b) of the definition of a financial liability.

(e)   The total expected cash flows attributable to the instrument over the life of the instrument are based substantially on the profit or loss, the change in the recognised net assets or the change in the fair value of the recognised and unrecognised net assets of the entity over the life of the instrument (excluding any effects of the instrument).

AASB

16B   For an instrument to be classified as an equity instrument, in addition to the instrument having all the above features, the issuer must have no other financial instrument or contract that has:

(a)   total cash flows based substantially on the profit or loss, the change in the recognised net assets or the change in the fair value of the recognised and unrecognised net assets of the entity (excluding any effects of such instrument or contract) and

(b)   the effect of substantially restricting or fixing the residual return to the puttable instrument holders.

For the purposes of applying this condition, the entity shall not consider non-financial contracts with a holder of an instrument described in paragraph 16A that have contractual terms and conditions that are similar to the contractual terms and conditions of an equivalent contract that might occur between a non-instrument holder and the issuing entity. If the entity cannot determine that this condition is met, it shall not classify the puttable instrument as an equity instrument.

Instruments, or components of instruments, that impose on the entity an obligation to deliver to another party a pro rata share of the net assets of the entity only on liquidation

16C   Some financial instruments include a contractual obligation for the issuing entity to deliver to another entity a pro rata share of its net assets only on liquidation. The obligation arises because liquidation either is certain to occur and outside the control of the entity (for example, a limited life entity) or is uncertain to occur but is at the option of the instrument holder. As an exception to the definition of a financial liability, an instrument that includes such an obligation is classified as an equity instrument if it has all the following features:

(a)   It entitles the holder to a pro rata share of the entity's net assets in the event of the entity's liquidation. The entity's net assets are those assets that remain after deducting all other claims on its assets. A pro rata share is determined by:

(i)   dividing the net assets of the entity on liquidation into units of equal amount; and

(ii)   multiplying that amount by the number of the units held by the financial instrument holder.

(b)   The instrument is in the class of instruments that is subordinate to all other classes of instruments. To be in such a class the instrument:

(i)   has no priority over other claims to the assets of the entity on liquidation, and

(ii)   does not need to be converted into another instrument before it is in the class of instruments that is subordinate to all other classes of instruments.

(c)   All financial instruments in the class of instruments that is subordinate to all other classes of instruments must have an identical contractual obligation for the issuing entity to deliver a pro rata share of its net assets on liquidation.

16D   For an instrument to be classified as an equity instrument, in addition to the instrument having all the above features, the issuer must have no other financial instrument or contract that has:

(a)   total cash flows based substantially on the profit or loss, the change in the recognised net assets or the change in the fair value of the recognised and unrecognised net assets of the entity (excluding any effects of such instrument or contract) and

(b)   the effect of substantially restricting or fixing the residual return to the instrument holders.

For the purposes of applying this condition, the entity shall not consider non-financial contracts with a holder of an instrument described in paragraph 16C that have contractual terms and conditions that are similar to the contractual terms and conditions of an equivalent contract that might occur between a non-instrument holder and the issuing entity. If the entity cannot determine that this condition is met, it shall not classify the instrument as an equity instrument.

Reclassification of puttable instruments and instruments that impose on the entity an obligation to deliver to another party a pro rata share of the net assets of the entity only on liquidation

16E An entity shall classify a financial instrument as an equity instrument in accordance with paragraphs 16A and 16B or paragraphs 16C and 16D from the date when the instrument has all the features and meets the conditions set out in those paragraphs. An entity shall reclassify a financial instrument from the date when the instrument ceases to have all the features or meet all the conditions set out in those paragraphs. For example, if an entity redeems all its issued non-puttable instruments and any puttable instrument that remain outstanding have all the features and meet all the conditions in paragraphs 16A and 16B, the entity shall reclassify the puttable instruments as equity instruments from the date when it redeems the non-puttable instruments.

16F An entity shall account as follows for the reclassification of an instrument in accordance with paragraph 16E:

(a) It shall reclassify an equity instrument as a financial liability from the date when the instrument ceases to have all the features or meet the conditions in paragraphs 16A and 16B or paragraphs 16C and 16D. The financial liability shall be measured at the instrument's fair value at the date of reclassification. The entity shall recognise in equity any difference between the carrying value of the equity instrument and the fair value of the financial liability at the date of reclassification.

(b) It shall reclassify a financial liability as equity from the date when the instrument has all the features and meets the conditions set out in paragraphs 16A and 16B or paragraphs 16C and 16D. An equity instrument shall be measured at the carrying value of the financial liability at the date of reclassification.

No contractual obligation to deliver cash or another financial asset (paragraph 16(a))

17 With the exception of the circumstances described in paragraphs 16A and 16B or paragraphs 16C and 16D, a critical feature in differentiating a financial liability from an equity instrument is the existence of a contractual obligation of one party to the financial instrument (the issuer) either to deliver cash or another financial asset to the other party (the holder) or to exchange financial assets or financial liabilities with the holder under conditions that are potentially unfavourable to the issuer. Although the holder of an equity instrument may be entitled to receive a pro rata share of any dividends or other distributions of equity, the issuer does not have a contractual obligation to make such distributions because it cannot be required to deliver cash or another financial asset to another party.

18 The substance of a financial instrument, rather than its legal form, governs its classification in the entity's statement of financial position. Substance and legal form are commonly consistent, but not always. Some financial instruments take the legal form of equity but are liabilities in substance and others may combine features associated with equity instruments and features associated with financial liabilities. For example:

(a) a preference share that provides for mandatory redemption by the issuer for a fixed or determinable amount at a fixed or determinable future date, or gives the holder the right to require the issuer to redeem the instrument at or after a particular date for a fixed or determinable amount, is a financial liability.

(b) a financial instrument that gives the holder the right to put it back to the issuer for cash or another financial asset (a 'puttable instrument') is a financial liability, except for those instruments classified as equity instruments in accordance with paragraphs 16A and 16B or paragraphs 16C and 16D. The financial instrument is a financial liability even when the amount of cash or other financial assets is determined on the basis of an index or other item that has the potential to increase or decrease. The existence of an option for the holder to put the instrument back to the issuer for cash or another financial asset means that the puttable instrument meets the definition of a financial liability, except for those instruments classified as equity instruments in accordance with paragraphs 16A and 16B or paragraphs 16C and 16D. For example, open-ended mutual funds, unit trusts, partnerships and some co-operative entities may provide their unitholders or members with a right to redeem their interests in the issuer at any time for cash, which results in the unitholders' or members' interests being classified as financial liabilities, except for those instruments classified as equity instruments in accordance with paragraphs 16A and 16B or paragraphs 16C and 16D. However, classification as a financial liability does not preclude the use of descriptors such as 'net asset value attributable to unitholders' and 'change in net asset value attributable to unitholders' in the financial statements of an entity that has no contributed equity (such as some mutual funds and unit trusts, see Illustrative Example 7) or the use of additional disclosure to show that total members' interests comprise items such as reserves that meet the definition of equity and puttable instruments that do not (see Illustrative Example 8).

19   If an entity does not have an unconditional right to avoid delivering cash or another financial asset to settle a contractual obligation, the obligation meets the definition of a financial liability, except for those instruments classified as equity instruments in accordance with paragraphs 16A and 16B or paragraphs 16C and 16D. For example:

(a)   a restriction on the ability of an entity to satisfy a contractual obligation, such as lack of access to foreign currency or the need to obtain approval for payment from a regulatory authority, does not negate the entity's contractual obligation or the holder's contractual right under the instrument.

(b)   a contractual obligation that is conditional on a counterparty exercising its right to redeem is a financial liability because the entity does not have the unconditional right to avoid delivering cash or another financial asset.

20   A financial instrument that does not explicitly establish a contractual obligation to deliver cash or another financial asset may establish an obligation indirectly through its terms and conditions. For example:

(a)   a financial instrument may contain a non-financial obligation that must be settled if, and only if, the entity fails to make distributions or to redeem the instrument. If the entity can avoid a transfer of cash or another financial asset only by settling the non-financial obligation, the financial instrument is a financial liability.

(b)   a financial instrument is a financial liability if it provides that on settlement the entity will deliver either:

(i)   cash or another financial asset; or

(ii)   its own shares whose value is determined to exceed substantially the value of the cash or other financial asset.

Although the entity does not have an explicit contractual obligation to deliver cash or another financial asset, the value of the share settlement alternative is such that the entity will settle in cash. In any event, the holder has in substance been guaranteed receipt of an amount that is at least equal to the cash settlement option (see paragraph 21).

Settlement in the entity's own equity instruments (paragraph 16(b))

21   A contract is not an equity instrument solely because it may result in the receipt or delivery of the entity's own equity instruments. An entity may have a contractual right or obligation to receive or deliver a number of its own shares or other equity instruments that varies so that the fair value of the entity's own equity instruments to

be received or delivered equals the amount of the contractual right or obligation. Such a contractual right or obligation may be for a fixed amount or an amount that fluctuates in part or in full in response to changes in a variable other than the market price of the entity's own equity instruments (eg an interest rate, a commodity price or a financial instrument price). Two examples are (a) a contract to deliver as many of the entity's own equity instruments as are equal in value to CU100,[1] and (b) a contract to deliver as many of the entity's own equity instruments as are equal in value to the value of 100 ounces of gold. Such a contract is a financial liability of the entity even though the entity must or can settle it by delivering its own equity instruments. It is not an equity instrument because the entity uses a variable number of its own equity instruments as a means to settle the contract. Accordingly, the contract does not evidence a residual interest in the entity's assets after deducting all of its liabilities.

22 Except as stated in paragraph 22A, a contract that will be settled by the entity (receiving or) delivering a fixed number of its own equity instruments in exchange for a fixed amount of cash or another financial asset is an equity instrument. For example, an issued share option that gives the counterparty a right to buy a fixed number of the entity's shares for a fixed price or for a fixed stated principal amount of a bond is an equity instrument. Changes in the fair value of a contract arising from variations in market interest rates that do not affect the amount of cash or other financial assets to be paid or received, or the number of equity instruments to be received or delivered, on settlement of the contract do not preclude the contract from being an equity instrument. Any consideration received (such as the premium received for a written option or warrant on the entity's own shares) is added directly to equity. Any consideration paid (such as the premium paid for a purchased option) is deducted directly from equity. Changes in the fair value of an equity instrument are not recognised in the financial statements.

22A If the entity's own equity instruments to be received, or delivered, by the entity upon settlement of a contract are puttable financial instruments with all the features and meeting the conditions described in paragraphs 16A and 16B, or instruments that impose on the entity an obligation to deliver to another party a pro rata share of the net assets of the entity only on liquidation with all the features and meeting the conditions described in paragraphs 16C and 16D, the contract is a financial asset or a financial liability. This includes a contract that will be settled by the entity receiving or delivering a fixed number of such instruments in exchange for a fixed amount of cash or another financial asset.

23 With the exception of the circumstances described in paragraphs 16A and 16B or paragraphs 16C and 16D, a contract that contains an obligation for an entity to purchase its own equity instruments for cash or another financial asset gives rise to a financial liability for the present value of the redemption amount (for example, for the present value of the forward repurchase price, option exercise price or other redemption amount). This is the case even if the contract itself is an equity instrument. One example is an entity's obligation under a forward contract to purchase its own equity instruments for cash. The financial liability is recognised initially at the present value of the redemption amount, and is reclassified from equity. Subsequently, the financial liability is measured in accordance with AASB 9. If the contract expires without delivery, the carrying amount of the financial liability is reclassified to equity. An entity's contractual obligation to purchase its own equity instruments gives rise to a financial liability for the present value of the redemption amount even if the obligation to purchase is conditional on the counterparty exercising a right to redeem (eg a written put option that gives the counterparty the right to sell an entity's own equity instruments to the entity for a fixed price).

24 A contract that will be settled by the entity delivering or receiving a fixed number of its own equity instruments in exchange for a variable amount of cash or another financial asset is a financial asset or financial liability. An example is a contract for the entity to deliver 100 of its own equity instruments in return for an amount of cash calculated to equal the value of 100 ounces of gold.

---

1   In this Standard, monetary amounts are denominated in 'currency units (CU)'.

Contingent settlement provisions

25   A financial instrument may require the entity to deliver cash or another financial asset, or otherwise to settle it in such a way that it would be a financial liability, in the event of the occurrence or non-occurrence of uncertain future events (or on the outcome of uncertain circumstances) that are beyond the control of both the issuer and the holder of the instrument, such as a change in a stock market index, consumer price index, interest rate or taxation requirements, or the issuer's future revenues, net income or debt-to-equity ratio. The issuer of such an instrument does not have the unconditional right to avoid delivering cash or another financial asset (or otherwise to settle it in such a way that it would be a financial liability). Therefore, it is a financial liability of the issuer unless:

(a)   the part of the contingent settlement provision that could require settlement in cash or another financial asset (or otherwise in such a way that it would be a financial liability) is not genuine;

(b)   the issuer can be required to settle the obligation in cash or another financial asset (or otherwise to settle it in such a way that it would be a financial liability) only in the event of liquidation of the issuer; or

(c)   the instrument has all the features and meets the conditions in paragraphs 16A and 16B.

Settlement options

26   When a derivative financial instrument gives one party a choice over how it is settled (eg the issuer or the holder can choose settlement net in cash or by exchanging shares for cash), it is a financial asset or a financial liability unless all of the settlement alternatives would result in it being an equity instrument.

27   An example of a derivative financial instrument with a settlement option that is a financial liability is a share option that the issuer can decide to settle net in cash or by exchanging its own shares for cash. Similarly, some contracts to buy or sell a non-financial item in exchange for the entity's own equity instruments are within the scope of this Standard because they can be settled either by delivery of the non-financial item or net in cash or another financial instrument (see paragraphs 8–10). Such contracts are financial assets or financial liabilities and not equity instruments.

Compound financial instruments (see also paragraphs AG30–AG35 and Illustrative Examples 9–12)

28   The issuer of a non-derivative financial instrument shall evaluate the terms of the financial instrument to determine whether it contains both a liability and an equity component. Such components shall be classified separately as financial liabilities, financial assets or equity instruments in accordance with paragraph 15.

29   An entity recognises separately the components of a financial instrument that (a) creates a financial liability of the entity and (b) grants an option to the holder of the instrument to convert it into an equity instrument of the entity. For example, a bond or similar instrument convertible by the holder into a fixed number of ordinary shares of the entity is a compound financial instrument. From the perspective of the entity, such an instrument comprises two components: a financial liability (a contractual arrangement to deliver cash or another financial asset) and an equity instrument (a call option granting the holder the right, for a specified period of time, to convert it into a fixed number of ordinary shares of the entity). The economic effect of issuing such an instrument is substantially the same as issuing simultaneously a debt instrument with an early settlement provision and warrants to purchase ordinary shares, or issuing a debt instrument with detachable share purchase warrants. Accordingly, in all cases, the entity presents the liability and equity components separately in its statement of financial position.

30 Classification of the liability and equity components of a convertible instrument is not revised as a result of a change in the likelihood that a conversion option will be exercised, even when exercise of the option may appear to have become economically advantageous to some holders. Holders may not always act in the way that might be expected because, for example, the tax consequences resulting from conversion may differ among holders. Furthermore, the likelihood of conversion will change from time to time. The entity's contractual obligation to make future payments remains outstanding until it is extinguished through conversion, maturity of the instrument or some other transaction.

31 AASB 9 deals with the measurement of financial assets and financial liabilities. Equity instruments are instruments that evidence a residual interest in the assets of an entity after deducting all of its liabilities. Therefore, when the initial carrying amount of a compound financial instrument is allocated to its equity and liability components, the equity component is assigned the residual amount after deducting from the fair value of the instrument as a whole the amount separately determined for the liability component. The value of any derivative features (such as a call option) embedded in the compound financial instrument other than the equity component (such as an equity conversion option) is included in the liability component. The sum of the carrying amounts assigned to the liability and equity components on initial recognition is always equal to the fair value that would be ascribed to the instrument as a whole. No gain or loss arises from initially recognising the components of the instrument separately.

32 Under the approach described in paragraph 31, the issuer of a bond convertible into ordinary shares first determines the carrying amount of the liability component by measuring the fair value of a similar liability (including any embedded non-equity derivative features) that does not have an associated equity component. The carrying amount of the equity instrument represented by the option to convert the instrument into ordinary shares is then determined by deducting the fair value of the financial liability from the fair value of the compound financial instrument as a whole.

Treasury shares (see also paragraph AG36)

33 **If an entity reacquires its own equity instruments, those instruments ('treasury shares') shall be deducted from equity. No gain or loss shall be recognised in profit or loss on the purchase, sale, issue or cancellation of an entity's own equity instruments. Such treasury shares may be acquired and held by the entity or by other members of the consolidated group. Consideration paid or received shall be recognised directly in equity.**

34 The amount of treasury shares held is disclosed separately either in the statement of financial position or in the notes, in accordance with AASB 101 *Presentation of Financial Statements*. An entity provides disclosure in accordance with AASB 124 *Related Party Disclosures* if the entity reacquires its own equity instruments from related parties.

Interest, dividends, losses and gains (see also paragraph AG37)

35 **Interest, dividends, losses and gains relating to a financial instrument or a component that is a financial liability shall be recognised as income or expense in profit or loss. Distributions to holders of an equity instrument shall be recognised by the entity directly in equity. Transaction costs of an equity transaction shall be accounted for as a deduction from equity.**

35A Income tax relating to distributions to holders of an equity instrument and to transaction costs of an equity transaction shall be accounted for in accordance with AASB 112 *Income Taxes*.

36 The classification of a financial instrument as a financial liability or an equity instrument determines whether interest, dividends, losses and gains relating to that instrument are recognised as income or expense in profit or loss. Thus, dividend

(d) financial assets are set aside in trust by a debtor for the purpose of discharging an obligation without those assets having been accepted by the creditor in settlement of the obligation (for example, a sinking fund arrangement); or

(e) obligations incurred as a result of events giving rise to losses are expected to be recovered from a third party by virtue of a claim made under an insurance contract.

50 An entity that undertakes a number of financial instrument transactions with a single counterparty may enter into a 'master netting arrangement' with that counterparty. Such an agreement provides for a single net settlement of all financial instruments covered by the agreement in the event of default on, or termination of, any one contract. These arrangements are commonly used by financial institutions to provide protection against loss in the event of bankruptcy or other circumstances that result in a counterparty being unable to meet its obligations. A master netting arrangement commonly creates a right of set-off that becomes enforceable and affects the realisation or settlement of individual financial assets and financial liabilities only following a specified event of default or in other circumstances not expected to arise in the normal course of business. A master netting arrangement does not provide a basis for offsetting unless both of the criteria in paragraph 42 are satisfied. When financial assets and financial liabilities subject to a master netting arrangement are not offset, the effect of the arrangement on an entity's exposure to credit risk is disclosed in accordance with paragraph 36 of AASB 7.

51-95 [Deleted]

Effective date and transition

96 An entity shall apply this Standard for annual periods beginning on or after 1 January 2018. Earlier application is permitted for periods beginning after 24 July 2014 but before 1 January 2018. If an entity applies this Standard for a period beginning before 1 January 2018, it shall disclose that fact.

96A AASB 2008-2 *Amendments to Australian Accounting Standards – Puttable Financial Instruments and Obligations arising on Liquidation*, issued in March 2008, required financial instruments that contain all the features and meet the conditions in paragraphs 16A and 16B or paragraphs 16C and 16D to be classified as an equity instrument, amended paragraphs 11, 16, 17–19, 22, 23, 25, AG13, AG14 and AG27, and inserted paragraphs 16A–16F, 22A, 96B, 96C, 97C, AG14A–AG14J and AG29A. An entity shall apply those amendments for annual periods beginning on or after 1 January 2009. Earlier application is permitted. If an entity applies the changes for an earlier period, it shall disclose that fact and apply the related amendments to AASB 101, AASB 139, AASB 7 and Interpretation 2 at the same time.

96B AASB 2008-2 *Amendments to Australian Accounting Standards – Puttable Financial Instruments and Obligations arising on Liquidation* introduced a limited scope exception in the previous version of this Standard; therefore, an entity shall not apply the exception by analogy.

96C The classification of instruments under this exception shall be restricted to the accounting for such an instrument under AASB 101, AASB 132, AASB 139, AASB 7 and AASB 9. The instrument shall not be considered an equity instrument under other guidance, for example AASB 2.

97 This Standard shall be applied retrospectively.

97A [Deleted by the AASB]

97B AASB 2008-3 *Amendments to Australian Accounting Standards arising from AASB 3 and AASB 127* deleted paragraph 4(c) in the previous version of this Standard. An entity shall apply that amendment for annual periods beginning on or after 1 July 2009. If an entity applies AASB 3 (revised 2008) for an earlier period, the amendment shall also be applied for that earlier period. However, the amendment does not apply to contingent consideration that arose from a business combination for which the acquisition date preceded the application of AASB 3 (revised 2008). Instead, an entity shall account for such consideration in accordance with paragraphs 65A–65E of AASB 3.

97C   When applying the amendments described in paragraph 96A, an entity is required to split a compound financial instrument with an obligation to deliver to another party a pro rata share of the net assets of the entity only on liquidation into separate liability and equity components. If the liability component is no longer outstanding, a retrospective application of those amendments to AASB 132 would involve separating two components of equity. The first component would be in retained earnings and represent the cumulative interest accreted on the liability component. The other component would represent the original equity component. Therefore, an entity need not separate these two components if the liability component is no longer outstanding at the date of application of the amendments.

97D–97E [Deleted by the AASB]

97F   [Deleted]

97G   Paragraph 97B was added in the previous version of this Standard by AASB 2010-3 *Amendments to Australian Accounting Standards arising from the Annual Improvements Project* issued in June 2010. An entity shall apply the last two sentences of paragraph 97B for annual periods beginning on or after 1 July 2010. Earlier application is permitted.

97H   [Deleted]

97I–97O [Deleted by the AASB]

97P   [Deleted]

97Q   AASB 2014-5 *Amendments to Australian Accounting Standards arising from AASB 15*, issued in December 2014, amended paragraph AG21 in the previous version of this Standard. An entity shall apply that amendment when it applies AASB 15.

97R   AASB 2010-7 *Amendments to Australian Accounting Standards arising from AASB 9 (December 2010)* (as amended), AASB 2014-1 *Amendments to Australian Accounting Standards* and AASB 2014-7 *Amendments to Australian Accounting Standards arising from AASB 9 (December 2014)* amended the previous version of this Standard as follows: amended paragraphs 3, 4, 8, 12, 23, 31, 42, 96C, AG2 and AG30 and deleted paragraph 97F. Paragraph 97H, added by AASB 2010-7, was deleted by AASB 2014-1. Paragraph 97P, added by AASB 2014-1, was deleted by AASB 2014-7. An entity shall apply those amendments when it applies AASB 9.

Withdrawal of other pronouncements

98–100 [Deleted by the AASB]

Commencement of the legislative instrument

Aus100.1   For legal purposes, this legislative instrument commences on 31 December 2017.

Withdrawal of AASB pronouncements

Aus100.2   This Standard repeals AASB 132 *Financial Instruments: Presentation* issued in July 2004. Despite the repeal, after the time this Standard starts to apply under section 334 of the Corporations Act (either generally or in relation to an individual entity), the repealed Standard continues to apply in relation to any period ending before that time as if the repeal had not occurred.

[Note: When this Standard applies under section 334 of the Corporations Act (either generally or in relation to an individual entity), it supersedes the application of the repealed Standard.]

APPENDIX
APPLICATION GUIDANCE

This appendix is an integral part of the Standard.

AG1   This Application Guidance explains the application of particular aspects of the Standard.

AG2   The Standard does not deal with the recognition or measurement of financial instruments. Requirements about the recognition and measurement of financial assets and financial liabilities are set out in AASB 9.

Definitions (paragraphs 11–14)

Financial assets and financial liabilities

AG3   Currency (cash) is a financial asset because it represents the medium of exchange and is therefore the basis on which all transactions are measured and recognised in financial statements. A deposit of cash with a bank or similar financial institution is a financial asset because it represents the contractual right of the depositor to obtain cash from the institution or to draw a cheque or similar instrument against the balance in favour of a creditor in payment of a financial liability.

AG4   Common examples of financial assets representing a contractual right to receive cash in the future and corresponding financial liabilities representing a contractual obligation to deliver cash in the future are:

(a)   trade accounts receivable and payable;

(b)   notes receivable and payable;

(c)   loans receivable and payable; and

(d)   bonds receivable and payable.

In each case, one party's contractual right to receive (or obligation to pay) cash is matched by the other party's corresponding obligation to pay (or right to receive).

AG5   Another type of financial instrument is one for which the economic benefit to be received or given up is a financial asset other than cash. For example, a note payable in government bonds gives the holder the contractual right to receive and the issuer the contractual obligation to deliver government bonds, not cash. The bonds are financial assets because they represent obligations of the issuing government to pay cash. The note is, therefore, a financial asset of the note holder and a financial liability of the note issuer.

AG6   'Perpetual' debt instruments (such as 'perpetual' bonds, debentures and capital notes) normally provide the holder with the contractual right to receive payments on account of interest at fixed dates extending into the indefinite future, either with no right to receive a return of principal or a right to a return of principal under terms that make it very unlikely or very far in the future. For example, an entity may issue a financial instrument requiring it to make annual payments in perpetuity equal to a stated interest rate of 8 per cent applied to a stated par or principal amount of CU1,000.[2] Assuming 8 per cent to be the market rate of interest for the instrument when issued, the issuer assumes a contractual obligation to make a stream of future interest payments having a fair value (present value) of CU1,000 on initial recognition. The holder and issuer of the instrument have a financial asset and a financial liability, respectively.

AG7   A contractual right or contractual obligation to receive, deliver or exchange financial instruments is itself a financial instrument. A chain of contractual rights or contractual obligations meets the definition of a financial instrument if it will ultimately lead to the receipt or payment of cash or to the acquisition or issue of an equity instrument.

---

2   In this guidance, monetary amounts are denominated in 'currency units (CU)'.

AG8 The ability to exercise a contractual right or the requirement to satisfy a contractual obligation may be absolute, or it may be contingent on the occurrence of a future event. For example, a financial guarantee is a contractual right of the lender to receive cash from the guarantor, and a corresponding contractual obligation of the guarantor to pay the lender, if the borrower defaults. The contractual right and obligation exist because of a past transaction or event (assumption of the guarantee), even though the lender's ability to exercise its right and the requirement for the guarantor to perform under its obligation are both contingent on a future act of default by the borrower. A contingent right and obligation meet the definition of a financial asset and a financial liability, even though such assets and liabilities are not always recognised in the financial statements. Some of these contingent rights and obligations may be insurance contracts within the scope of AASB 4.

AG9 Under AASB 117 *Leases* a finance lease is regarded as primarily an entitlement of the lessor to receive, and an obligation of the lessee to pay, a stream of payments that are substantially the same as blended payments of principal and interest under a loan agreement. The lessor accounts for its investment in the amount receivable under the lease contract rather than the leased asset itself. An operating lease, on the other hand, is regarded as primarily an uncompleted contract committing the lessor to provide the use of an asset in future periods in exchange for consideration similar to a fee for a service. The lessor continues to account for the leased asset itself rather than any amount receivable in the future under the contract. Accordingly, a finance lease is regarded as a financial instrument and an operating lease is not regarded as a financial instrument (except as regards individual payments currently due and payable).

AG10 Physical assets (such as inventories, property, plant and equipment), leased assets and intangible assets (such as patents and trademarks) are not financial assets. Control of such physical and intangible assets creates an opportunity to generate an inflow of cash or another financial asset, but it does not give rise to a present right to receive cash or another financial asset.

AG11 Assets (such as prepaid expenses) for which the future economic benefit is the receipt of goods or services, rather than the right to receive cash or another financial asset, are not financial assets. Similarly, items such as deferred revenue and most warranty obligations are not financial liabilities because the outflow of economic benefits associated with them is the delivery of goods and services rather than a contractual obligation to pay cash or another financial asset.

AG12 Liabilities or assets that are not contractual (such as income taxes that are created as a result of statutory requirements imposed by governments) are not financial liabilities or financial assets. Accounting for income taxes is dealt with in AASB 112. Similarly, constructive obligations, as defined in AASB 137 *Provisions, Contingent Liabilities and Contingent Assets*, do not arise from contracts and are not financial liabilities.

Equity instruments

AG13 Examples of equity instruments include non-puttable ordinary shares, some puttable instruments (see paragraphs 16A and 16B), some instruments that impose on the entity an obligation to deliver to another party a pro rata share of the net assets of the entity only on liquidation (see paragraphs 16C and 16D), some types of preference shares (see paragraphs AG25 and AG26), and warrants or written call options that allow the holder to subscribe for or purchase a fixed number of non-puttable ordinary shares in the issuing entity in exchange for a fixed amount of cash or another financial asset. An entity's obligation to issue or purchase a fixed number of its own equity instruments in exchange for a fixed amount of cash or another financial asset is an equity instrument of the entity (except as stated in paragraph 22A). However, if such a contract contains an obligation for the entity to pay cash or another financial asset (other than a contract classified as equity in accordance with paragraphs 16A and 16B or paragraphs 16C and 16D), it also gives rise to a liability for the present value of the redemption amount (see paragraph AG27(a)). An issuer of non-puttable ordinary shares assumes a liability when it formally acts to make a distribution and becomes legally obliged to the shareholders to do so. This may be the case following the declaration of a dividend or when the entity is being wound up and any assets remaining after the satisfaction of liabilities become distributable to shareholders.

AG14 A purchased call option or other similar contract acquired by an entity that gives it the right to reacquire a fixed number of its own equity instruments in exchange for delivering a fixed amount of cash or another financial asset is not a financial asset of the entity (except as stated in paragraph 22A). Instead, any consideration paid for such a contract is deducted from equity.

The class of instruments that is subordinate to all other classes (paragraphs 16A(b) and 16C(b))

AG14A One of the features of paragraphs 16A and 16C is that the financial instrument is in the class of instruments that is subordinate to all other classes.

AG14B When determining whether an instrument is in the subordinate class, an entity evaluates the instrument's claim on liquidation as if it were to liquidate on the date when it classifies the instrument. An entity shall reassess the classification if there is a change in relevant circumstances. For example, if the entity issues or redeems another financial instrument, this may affect whether the instrument in question is in the class of instruments that is subordinate to all other classes.

AG14C An instrument that has a preferential right on liquidation of the entity is not an instrument with an entitlement to a pro rata share of the net assets of the entity. For example, an instrument has a preferential right on liquidation if it entitles the holder to a fixed dividend on liquidation, in addition to a share of the entity's net assets, when other instruments in the subordinate class with a right to a pro rata share of the net assets of the entity do not have the same right on liquidation.

AG14D If an entity has only one class of financial instruments, that class shall be treated as if it were subordinate to all other classes.

Total expected cash flows attributable to the instrument over the life of the instrument (paragraph 16A(e))

AG14E The total expected cash flows of the instrument over the life of the instrument must be substantially based on the profit or loss, change in the recognised net assets or fair value of the recognised and unrecognised net assets of the entity over the life of the instrument. Profit or loss and the change in the recognised net assets shall be measured in accordance with relevant Australian Accounting Standards.

Transactions entered into by an instrument holder other than as owner of the entity (paragraphs 16A and 16C)

AG14F The holder of a puttable financial instrument or an instrument that imposes on the entity an obligation to deliver to another party a pro rata share of the net assets of the entity only on liquidation may enter into transactions with the entity in a role other than that of an owner. For example, an instrument holder may also be an employee of the entity. Only the cash flows and the contractual terms and conditions of the instrument that relate to the instrument holder as an owner of the entity shall be considered when assessing whether the instrument should be classified as equity under paragraph 16A or paragraph 16C.

AG14G An example is a limited partnership that has limited and general partners. Some general partners may provide a guarantee to the entity and may be remunerated for providing that guarantee. In such situations, the guarantee and the associated cash flows relate to the instrument holders in their role as guarantors and not in their roles as owners of the entity. Therefore, such a guarantee and the associated cash flows would not result in the general partners being considered subordinate to the limited partners, and would be disregarded when assessing whether the contractual terms of the limited partnership instruments and the general partnership instruments are identical.

AG14H Another example is a profit or loss sharing arrangement that allocates profit or loss to the instrument holders on the basis of services rendered or business generated during the current and previous years. Such arrangements are transactions with instrument holders in their role as non-owners and should not be considered when assessing the features listed in paragraph 16A or paragraph 16C. However, profit or loss sharing arrangements that allocate profit or loss to instrument holders based on the nominal amount of their instruments relative to others in the class represent transactions with the instrument holders in their roles as owners and should be considered when assessing the features listed in paragraph 16A or paragraph 16C.

AG14I The cash flows and contractual terms and conditions of a transaction between the instrument holder (in the role as a non-owner) and the issuing entity must be similar to an equivalent transaction that might occur between a non-instrument holder and the issuing entity.

No other financial instrument or contract with total cash flows that substantially fixes or restricts the residual return to the instrument holder (paragraphs 16B and 16D)

AG14J A condition for classifying as equity a financial instrument that otherwise meets the criteria in paragraph 16A or paragraph 16C is that the entity has no other financial instrument or contract that has (a) total cash flows based substantially on the profit or loss, the change in the recognised net assets or the change in the fair value of the recognised and unrecognised net assets of the entity and (b) the effect of substantially restricting or fixing the residual return. The following instruments, when entered into on normal commercial terms with unrelated parties, are unlikely to prevent instruments that otherwise meet the criteria in paragraph 16A or paragraph 16C from being classified as equity:

(a) instruments with total cash flows substantially based on specific assets of the entity.

(b) instruments with total cash flows based on a percentage of revenue.

(c) contracts designed to reward individual employees for services rendered to the entity.

(d) contracts requiring the payment of an insignificant percentage of profit for services rendered or goods provided.

Derivative financial instruments

AG15 Financial instruments include primary instruments (such as receivables, payables and equity instruments) and derivative financial instruments (such as financial options, futures and forwards, interest rate swaps and currency swaps). Derivative financial instruments meet the definition of a financial instrument and, accordingly, are within the scope of this Standard.

AG16 Derivative financial instruments create rights and obligations that have the effect of transferring between the parties to the instrument one or more of the financial risks inherent in an underlying primary financial instrument. On inception, derivative financial instruments give one party a contractual right to exchange financial assets or financial liabilities with another party under conditions that are potentially favourable, or a contractual obligation to exchange financial assets or financial liabilities with another party under conditions that are potentially unfavourable. However, they generally[3] do not result in a transfer of the underlying primary financial instrument on inception of the contract, nor does such a transfer necessarily take place on maturity of the contract. Some instruments embody both a right and an obligation to make an exchange. Because the terms of the exchange are determined on inception of the derivative instrument, as prices in financial markets change those terms may become either favourable or unfavourable.

AG17 A put or call option to exchange financial assets or financial liabilities (ie financial instruments other than an entity's own equity instruments) gives the holder a right to obtain potential future economic benefits associated with changes in the fair value of the financial instrument underlying the contract. Conversely, the writer of an option assumes an obligation to forgo potential future economic benefits or bear potential losses of economic benefits associated with changes in the fair value of the

---

3   This is true of most, but not all derivatives, eg in some cross-currency interest rate swaps principal is exchanged on inception (and re-exchanged on maturity).

underlying financial instrument. The contractual right of the holder and obligation of the writer meet the definition of a financial asset and a financial liability, respectively. The financial instrument underlying an option contract may be any financial asset, including shares in other entities and interest-bearing instruments. An option may require the writer to issue a debt instrument, rather than transfer a financial asset, but the instrument underlying the option would constitute a financial asset of the holder if the option were exercised. The option-holder's right to exchange the financial asset under potentially favourable conditions and the writer's obligation to exchange the financial asset under potentially unfavourable conditions are distinct from the underlying financial asset to be exchanged upon exercise of the option. The nature of the holder's right and of the writer's obligation are not affected by the likelihood that the option will be exercised.

AG18 Another example of a derivative financial instrument is a forward contract to be settled in six months' time in which one party (the purchaser) promises to deliver CU1,000,000 cash in exchange for CU1,000,000 face amount of fixed rate government bonds, and the other party (the seller) promises to deliver CU1,000,000 face amount of fixed rate government bonds in exchange for CU1,000,000 cash. During the six months, both parties have a contractual right and a contractual obligation to exchange financial instruments. If the market price of the government bonds rises above CU1,000,000, the conditions will be favourable to the purchaser and unfavourable to the seller; if the market price falls below CU1,000,000, the effect will be the opposite. The purchaser has a contractual right (a financial asset) similar to the right under a call option held and a contractual obligation (a financial liability) similar to the obligation under a put option written; the seller has a contractual right (a financial asset) similar to the right under a put option held and a contractual obligation (a financial liability) similar to the obligation under a call option written. As with options, these contractual rights and obligations constitute financial assets and financial liabilities separate and distinct from the underlying financial instruments (the bonds and cash to be exchanged). Both parties to a forward contract have an obligation to perform at the agreed time, whereas performance under an option contract occurs only if and when the holder of the option chooses to exercise it.

AG19 Many other types of derivative instruments embody a right or obligation to make a future exchange, including interest rate and currency swaps, interest rate caps, collars and floors, loan commitments, note issuance facilities and letters of credit. An interest rate swap contract may be viewed as a variation of a forward contract in which the parties agree to make a series of future exchanges of cash amounts, one amount calculated with reference to a floating interest rate and the other with reference to a fixed interest rate. Futures contracts are another variation of forward contracts, differing primarily in that the contracts are standardised and traded on an exchange.

Contracts to buy or sell non-financial items (paragraphs 8–10)

AG20 Contracts to buy or sell non-financial items do not meet the definition of a financial instrument because the contractual right of one party to receive a non-financial asset or service and the corresponding obligation of the other party do not establish a present right or obligation of either party to receive, deliver or exchange a financial asset. For example, contracts that provide for settlement only by the receipt or delivery of a non-financial item (eg an option, futures or forward contract on silver) are not financial instruments. Many commodity contracts are of this type. Some are standardised in form and traded on organised markets in much the same fashion as some derivative financial instruments. For example, a commodity futures contract may be bought and sold readily for cash because it is listed for trading on an exchange and may change hands many times. However, the parties buying and selling the contract are, in effect, trading the underlying commodity. The ability to buy or sell a commodity contract for cash, the ease with which it may be bought or sold and the possibility of negotiating a cash settlement of the obligation to receive or deliver the commodity do not alter the fundamental character of the contract in a way that creates a financial instrument. Nevertheless, some contracts to buy or sell non-financial items that can be settled net or by exchanging financial instruments, or in which the non-financial item is readily convertible to cash, are within the scope of the Standard as if they were financial instruments (see paragraph 8).

AG21 Except as required by AASB 15 *Revenue from Contracts with Customers*, a contract that involves the receipt or delivery of physical assets does not give rise to a financial asset of one party and a financial liability of the other party unless any corresponding payment is deferred past the date on which the physical assets are transferred. Such is the case with the purchase or sale of goods on trade credit.

AG22 Some contracts are commodity-linked, but do not involve settlement through the physical receipt or delivery of a commodity. They specify settlement through cash payments that are determined according to a formula in the contract, rather than through payment of fixed amounts. For example, the principal amount of a bond may be calculated by applying the market price of oil prevailing at the maturity of the bond to a fixed quantity of oil. The principal is indexed by reference to a commodity price, but is settled only in cash. Such a contract constitutes a financial instrument.

AG23 The definition of a financial instrument also encompasses a contract that gives rise to a non-financial asset or non-financial liability in addition to a financial asset or financial liability. Such financial instruments often give one party an option to exchange a financial asset for a non-financial asset. For example, an oil-linked bond may give the holder the right to receive a stream of fixed periodic interest payments and a fixed amount of cash on maturity, with the option to exchange the principal amount for a fixed quantity of oil. The desirability of exercising this option will vary from time to time depending on the fair value of oil relative to the exchange ratio of cash for oil (the exchange price) inherent in the bond. The intentions of the bondholder concerning the exercise of the option do not affect the substance of the component assets. The financial asset of the holder and the financial liability of the issuer make the bond a financial instrument, regardless of the other types of assets and liabilities also created.

AG24 [Deleted]

Presentation

Liabilities and equity (paragraphs 15–27)

No contractual obligation to deliver cash or another financial asset (paragraphs 17–20)

AG25 Preference shares may be issued with various rights. In determining whether a preference share is a financial liability or an equity instrument, an issuer assesses the particular rights attaching to the share to determine whether it exhibits the fundamental characteristic of a financial liability. For example, a preference share that provides for redemption on a specific date or at the option of the holder contains a financial liability because the issuer has an obligation to transfer financial assets to the holder of the share. The potential inability of an issuer to satisfy an obligation to redeem a preference share when contractually required to do so, whether because of a lack of funds, a statutory restriction or insufficient profits or reserves, does not negate the obligation. An option of the issuer to redeem the shares for cash does not satisfy the definition of a financial liability because the issuer does not have a present obligation to transfer financial assets to the shareholders. In this case, redemption of the shares is solely at the discretion of the issuer. An obligation may arise, however, when the issuer of the shares exercises its option, usually by formally notifying the shareholders of an intention to redeem the shares.

AG26 When preference shares are non-redeemable, the appropriate classification is determined by the other rights that attach to them. Classification is based on an assessment of the substance of the contractual arrangements and the definitions of a financial liability and an equity instrument. When distributions to holders of the preference shares, whether cumulative or non-cumulative, are at the discretion of the issuer, the shares are equity instruments. The classification of a preference share as an equity instrument or a financial liability is not affected by, for example:

(a)   a history of making distributions;

(b)   an intention to make distributions in the future;

(c) a possible negative impact on the price of ordinary shares of the issuer if distributions are not made (because of restrictions on paying dividends on the ordinary shares if dividends are not paid on the preference shares);

(d) the amount of the issuer's reserves;

(e) an issuer's expectation of a profit or loss for a period; or

(f) an ability or inability of the issuer to influence the amount of its profit or loss for the period.

Settlement in the entity's own equity instruments (paragraphs 21–24)

AG27 The following examples illustrate how to classify different types of contracts on an entity's own equity instruments:

(a) A contract that will be settled by the entity receiving or delivering a fixed number of its own shares for no future consideration, or exchanging a fixed number of its own shares for a fixed amount of cash or another financial asset, is an equity instrument (except as stated in paragraph 22A). Accordingly, any consideration received or paid for such a contract is added directly to or deducted directly from equity. One example is an issued share option that gives the counterparty a right to buy a fixed number of the entity's shares for a fixed amount of cash. However, if the contract requires the entity to purchase (redeem) its own shares for cash or another financial asset at a fixed or determinable date or on demand, the entity also recognises a financial liability for the present value of the redemption amount (with the exception of instruments that have all the features and meet the conditions in paragraphs 16A and 16B or paragraphs 16C and 16D). One example is an entity's obligation under a forward contract to repurchase a fixed number of its own shares for a fixed amount of cash.

(b) An entity's obligation to purchase its own shares for cash gives rise to a financial liability for the present value of the redemption amount even if the number of shares that the entity is obliged to repurchase is not fixed or if the obligation is conditional on the counterparty exercising a right to redeem (except as stated in paragraphs 16A and 16B or paragraphs 16C and 16D). One example of a conditional obligation is an issued option that requires the entity to repurchase its own shares for cash if the counterparty exercises the option.

(c) A contract that will be settled in cash or another financial asset is a financial asset or financial liability even if the amount of cash or another financial asset that will be received or delivered is based on changes in the market price of the entity's own equity (except as stated in paragraphs 16A and 16B or paragraphs 16C and 16D). One example is a net cash-settled share option.

(d) A contract that will be settled in a variable number of the entity's own shares whose value equals a fixed amount or an amount based on changes in an underlying variable (eg a commodity price) is a financial asset or a financial liability. An example is a written option to buy gold that, if exercised, is settled net in the entity's own instruments by the entity delivering as many of those instruments as are equal to the value of the option contract. Such a contract is a financial asset or financial liability even if the underlying variable is the entity's own share price rather than gold. Similarly, a contract that will be settled in a fixed number of the entity's own shares, but the rights attaching to those shares will be varied so that the settlement value equals a fixed amount or an amount based on changes in an underlying variable, is a financial asset or a financial liability.

Contingent settlement provisions (paragraph 25)

AG28 Paragraph 25 requires that if a part of a contingent settlement provision that could require settlement in cash or another financial asset (or in another way that would result in the instrument being a financial liability) is not genuine, the settlement provision does not affect the classification of a financial instrument. Thus, a contract that requires settlement in cash or a variable number of the entity's own shares only on the occurrence of an event that is extremely rare, highly abnormal and very unlikely to occur is an equity instrument. Similarly, settlement in a fixed number of an entity's own shares may be contractually precluded in circumstances that are outside the control of the entity, but if these circumstances have no genuine possibility of occurring, classification as an equity instrument is appropriate.

Treatment in consolidated financial statements

AG29 In consolidated financial statements, an entity presents non-controlling interests— ie the interests of other parties in the equity and income of its subsidiaries—in accordance with AASB 101 and AASB 10. When classifying a financial instrument (or a component of it) in consolidated financial statements, an entity considers all terms and conditions agreed between members of the group and the holders of the instrument in determining whether the group as a whole has an obligation to deliver cash or another financial asset in respect of the instrument or to settle it in a manner that results in liability classification. When a subsidiary in a group issues a financial instrument and a parent or other group entity agrees additional terms directly with the holders of the instrument (eg a guarantee), the group may not have discretion over distributions or redemption. Although the subsidiary may appropriately classify the instrument without regard to these additional terms in its individual financial statements, the effect of other agreements between members of the group and the holders of the instrument is considered in order to ensure that consolidated financial statements reflect the contracts and transactions entered into by the group as a whole. To the extent that there is such an obligation or settlement provision, the instrument (or the component of it that is subject to the obligation) is classified as a financial liability in consolidated financial statements.

AG29A Some types of instruments that impose a contractual obligation on the entity are classified as equity instruments in accordance with paragraphs 16A and 16B or paragraphs 16C and 16D. Classification in accordance with those paragraphs is an exception to the principles otherwise applied in this Standard to the classification of an instrument. This exception is not extended to the classification of non-controlling interests in the consolidated financial statements. Therefore, instruments classified as equity instruments in accordance with either paragraphs 16A and 16B or paragraphs 16C and 16D in the separate or individual financial statements that are non-controlling interests are classified as liabilities in the consolidated financial statements of the group.

Compound financial instruments (paragraphs 28–32)

AG30 Paragraph 28 applies only to issuers of non-derivative compound financial instruments. Paragraph 28 does not deal with compound financial instruments from the perspective of holders. AASB 9 deals with the classification and measurement of financial assets that are compound financial instruments from the holder's perspective.

AG31 A common form of compound financial instrument is a debt instrument with an embedded conversion option, such as a bond convertible into ordinary shares of the issuer, and without any other embedded derivative features. Paragraph 28 requires the issuer of such a financial instrument to present the liability component and the equity component separately in the statement of financial position, as follows:

(a) The issuer's obligation to make scheduled payments of interest and principal is a financial liability that exists as long as the instrument is not converted. On initial recognition, the fair value of the liability component is the present value of the contractually determined stream of future cash flows discounted at the rate of interest applied at that time by the market to instruments of comparable credit status and providing substantially the same cash flows, on the same terms, but without the conversion option.

(b) The equity instrument is an embedded option to convert the liability into equity of the issuer. This option has value on initial recognition even when it is out of the money.

AG32 On conversion of a convertible instrument at maturity, the entity derecognises the liability component and recognises it as equity. The original equity component remains as equity (although it may be transferred from one line item within equity to another). There is no gain or loss on conversion at maturity.

AG33 When an entity extinguishes a convertible instrument before maturity through an early redemption or repurchase in which the original conversion privileges are unchanged, the entity allocates the consideration paid and any transaction costs for the repurchase or redemption to the liability and equity components of the instrument at the date of the transaction. The method used in allocating the consideration paid and transaction costs to the separate components is consistent with that used in the original allocation to the separate components of the proceeds received by the entity when the convertible instrument was issued, in accordance with paragraphs 28–32.

AG34 Once the allocation of the consideration is made, any resulting gain or loss is treated in accordance with accounting principles applicable to the related component, as follows:

(a) the amount of gain or loss relating to the liability component is recognised in profit or loss; and

(b) the amount of consideration relating to the equity component is recognised in equity.

AG35 An entity may amend the terms of a convertible instrument to induce early conversion, for example by offering a more favourable conversion ratio or paying other additional consideration in the event of conversion before a specified date. The difference, at the date the terms are amended, between the fair value of the consideration the holder receives on conversion of the instrument under the revised terms and the fair value of the consideration the holder would have received under the original terms is recognised as a loss in profit or loss.

Treasury shares (paragraphs 33 and 34)

AG36 An entity's own equity instruments are not recognised as a financial asset regardless of the reason for which they are reacquired. Paragraph 33 requires an entity that reacquires its own equity instruments to deduct those equity instruments from equity. However, when an entity holds its own equity on behalf of others, eg a financial institution holding its own equity on behalf of a client, there is an agency relationship and as a result those holdings are not included in the entity's statement of financial position.

Interest, dividends, losses and gains (paragraphs 35–41)

AG37 The following example illustrates the application of paragraph 35 to a compound financial instrument. Assume that a non-cumulative preference share is mandatorily redeemable for cash in five years, but that dividends are payable at the discretion of the entity before the redemption date. Such an instrument is a compound financial instrument, with the liability component being the present value of the redemption amount. The unwinding of the discount on this component is recognised in profit or loss and classified as interest expense. Any dividends paid relate to the equity component and, accordingly, are recognised as a distribution of profit or loss. A similar treatment would apply if the redemption was not mandatory but at the option of the holder, or if the share was mandatorily convertible into a variable number of ordinary shares calculated to equal a fixed amount or an amount based on changes in an underlying variable (eg commodity). However, if any unpaid dividends are added to the redemption amount, the entire instrument is a liability. In such a case, any dividends are classified as interest expense.

Offsetting a financial asset and a financial liability (paragraphs 42–50)

AG38 [Deleted]

Criterion that an entity 'currently has a legally enforceable right to set off the recognised amounts' (paragraph 42(a))

AG38A A right of set off may be currently available or it may be contingent on a future event (for example, the right may be triggered or exercisable only on the occurrence of some future event, such as the default, insolvency or bankruptcy of one of the counterparties). Even if the right of set off is not contingent on a future event, it may only be legally enforceable in the normal course of business, or in the event of default, or in the event of insolvency or bankruptcy, of one or all of the counterparties.

AG38B To meet the criterion in paragraph 42(a), an entity must currently have a legally enforceable right of set-off. This means that the right of set-off:

(a) must not be contingent on a future event; and

(b) must be legally enforceable in all of the following circumstances:

(i) the normal course of business;

(ii) the event of default; and

(iii) the event of insolvency or bankruptcy

of the entity and all of the counterparties.

AG38C The nature and extent of the right of set-off, including any conditions attached to its exercise and whether it would remain in the event of default or insolvency or bankruptcy, may vary from one legal jurisdiction to another. Consequently, it cannot be assumed that the right of set-off is automatically available outside of the normal course of business. For example, the bankruptcy or insolvency laws of a jurisdiction may prohibit, or restrict, the right of set-off in the event of bankruptcy or insolvency in some circumstances.

AG38D The laws applicable to the relationships between the parties (for example, contractual provisions, the laws governing the contract, or the default, insolvency or bankruptcy laws applicable to the parties) need to be considered to ascertain whether the right of set-off is enforceable in the normal course of business, in an event of default, and in the event of insolvency or bankruptcy, of the entity and all of the counterparties (as specified in paragraph AG38B(b)).

Criterion that an entity 'intends either to settle on a net basis, or to realise the asset and settle the liability simultaneously' (paragraph 42(b))

AG38E To meet the criterion in paragraph 42(b) an entity must intend either to settle on a net basis or to realise the asset and settle the liability simultaneously. Although the entity may have a right to settle net, it may still realise the asset and settle the liability separately.

AG38F If an entity can settle amounts in a manner such that the outcome is, in effect, equivalent to net settlement, the entity will meet the net settlement criterion in paragraph 42(b). This will occur if, and only if, the gross settlement mechanism has features that eliminate or result in insignificant credit and liquidity risk, and that will process receivables and payables in a single settlement process or cycle. For example, a gross settlement system that has all of the following characteristics would meet the net settlement criterion in paragraph 42(b):

(a) financial assets and financial liabilities eligible for set-off are submitted at the same point in time for processing;

(b) once the financial assets and financial liabilities are submitted for processing, the parties are committed to fulfil the settlement obligation;

(c) there is no potential for the cash flows arising from the assets and liabilities to change once they have been submitted for processing (unless the processing fails—see (d) below);

(d) assets and liabilities that are collateralised with securities will be settled on a securities transfer or similar system (for example, delivery versus payment), so that if the transfer of securities fails, the processing of the related receivable or payable for which the securities are collateral will also fail (and vice versa);

(e) any transactions that fail, as outlined in (d), will be re-entered for processing until they are settled;

(f) settlement is carried out through the same settlement institution (for example, a settlement bank, a central bank or a central securities depository); and

(g) an intraday credit facility is in place that will provide sufficient overdraft amounts to enable the processing of payments at the settlement date for each of the parties, and it is virtually certain that the intraday credit facility will be honoured if called upon.

AG39 The Standard does not provide special treatment for so-called 'synthetic instruments', which are groups of separate financial instruments acquired and held to emulate the characteristics of another instrument. For example, a floating rate long-term debt combined with an interest rate swap that involves receiving floating payments and making fixed payments synthesises a fixed rate long-term debt. Each of the individual financial instruments that together constitute a 'synthetic instrument' represents a contractual right or obligation with its own terms and conditions and each may be transferred or settled separately. Each financial instrument is exposed to risks that may differ from the risks to which other financial instruments are exposed. Accordingly, when one financial instrument in a 'synthetic instrument' is an asset and another is a liability, they are not offset and presented in an entity's statement of financial position on a net basis unless they meet the criteria for offsetting in paragraph 42.

AG40 [Deleted]

ILLUSTRATIVE EXAMPLES

CONTENTS

from paragraph

ILLUSTRATIVE EXAMPLES

These examples accompany, but are not part of, AASB 132.

Accounting for contracts on equity instruments of an entity

IE1   The following examples[4] illustrate the application of paragraphs 15–27 and AASB 9 to the accounting for contracts on an entity's own equity instruments (other than the financial instruments specified in paragraphs 16A and 16B or paragraphs 16C and 16D).

Example 1: Forward to buy shares

IE2   This example illustrates the journal entries for forward purchase contracts on an entity's own shares that will be settled (a) net in cash, (b) net in shares or (c) by delivering cash in exchange for shares. It also discusses the effect of settlement options (see (d) below). To simplify the illustration, it is assumed that no dividends are paid on the underlying shares (ie the 'carry return' is zero) so that the present value of the forward price equals the spot price when the fair value of the forward contract is zero. The fair value of the forward has been computed as the difference between the market share price and the present value of the fixed forward price.

Assumptions:

Contract date	1 February 20X2
Maturity date	31 January 20X3
Market price per share on 1 February 20X2	CU100
Market price per share on 31 December 20X2	CU110
Market price per share on 31 January 20X3	CU106
Fixed forward price to be paid on 31 January 20X3	CU104
Present value of forward price on 1 February 20X2	CU100
Number of shares under forward contract	1,000
Fair value of forward on 1 February 20X2	CU0
Fair value of forward on 31 December 20X2	CU6,300
Fair value of forward on 31 January 20X3	CU2,000

(a) Cash for cash ('net cash settlement')

IE3   In this subsection, the forward purchase contract on the entity's own shares will be settled net in cash, ie there is no receipt or delivery of the entity's own shares upon settlement of the forward contract.

On 1 February 20X2, Entity A enters into a contract with Entity B to receive the fair value of 1,000 of Entity A's own outstanding ordinary shares as of 31 January 20X3 in exchange for a payment of CU104,000 in cash (ie CU104 per share) on 31 January 20X3. The contract will be settled net in cash. Entity A records the following journal entries.

1 February 20X2

The price per share when the contract is agreed on 1 February 20X2 is CU100. The initial fair value of the forward contract on 1 February 20X2 is zero.

No entry is required because the fair value of the derivative is zero and no cash is paid or received.

---

4   In these examples, monetary amounts are denominated in 'currency units (CU)'.

31 December 20X2

On 31 December 20X2, the market price per share has increased to CU110 and, as a result, the fair value of the forward contract has increased to CU6,300.

Dr	Forward asset	CU6,300
	Cr	Gain	CU6,300

To record the increase in the fair value of the forward contract.

31 January 20X3

On 31 January 20X3, the market price per share has decreased to CU106. The fair value of the forward contract is CU2,000 ([CU106 × 1,000] – CU104,000).

On the same day, the contract is settled net in cash. Entity A has an obligation to deliver CU104,000 to Entity B and Entity B has an obligation to deliver CU106,000 (CU106 × 1,000) to Entity A, so Entity B pays the net amount of CU2,000 to Entity A.

Dr	Loss	CU4,300
	Cr	Forward asset	CU4,300

To record the decrease in the fair value of the forward contract (ie CU4,300 = CU6,300 – CU2,000).

Dr	Cash	CU2,000
	Cr	Forward asset	CU2,000

To record the settlement of the forward contract.

(b) Shares for shares ('net share settlement')

IE4 Assume the same facts as in (a) except that settlement will be made net in shares instead of net in cash. Entity A's journal entries are the same as those shown in (a) above, except for recording the settlement of the forward contract, as follows:

31 January 20X3

The contract is settled net in shares. Entity A has an obligation to deliver CU104,000 (CU104 × 1,000) worth of its shares to Entity B and Entity B has an obligation to deliver CU106,000 (CU106 × 1,000) worth of shares to Entity A. Thus, Entity B delivers a net amount of CU2,000 (CU106,000 – CU104,000) worth of shares to Entity A, ie 18.9 shares (CU2,000/CU106).

Dr	Equity	CU2,000
	Cr	Forward asset	CU2,000

To record the settlement of the forward contract.

(c) Cash for shares ('gross physical settlement')

IE5 Assume the same facts as in (a) except that settlement will be made by delivering a fixed amount of cash and receiving a fixed number of Entity A's shares. Similarly to (a) and (b) above, the price per share that Entity A will pay in one year is fixed at CU104. Accordingly, Entity A has an obligation to pay CU104,000 in cash to Entity B (CU104 × 1,000) and Entity B has an obligation to deliver 1,000 of Entity A's outstanding shares to Entity A in one year. Entity A records the following journal entries.

1 February 20X2

Dr	Equity	CU100,000	
	Cr	Liability	CU100,000

To record the obligation to deliver CU104,000 in one year at its
present value of CU100,000 discounted using an appropriate interest
rate (see AASB 9, paragraph B5.1.1).

31 December 20X2

Dr	Interest expense	CU3,660	
	Cr	Liability	CU3,660

To accrue interest in accordance with the effective interest method on
the liability for the share redemption amount.

31 January 20X3

Dr	Interest expense	CU340	
	Cr	Liability	CU340

To accrue interest in accordance with the effective interest method on
the liability for the share redemption amount.

Entity A delivers CU104,000 in cash to Entity B and Entity B delivers 1,000 of Entity A's shares to Entity A.

Dr	Liability	CU104,000	
	Cr	Cash	CU104,000

To record the settlement of the obligation to redeem Entity A's own shares for cash.

(d) Settlement options

IE6   The existence of settlement options (such as net in cash, net in shares or by an exchange of cash and shares) has the result that the forward repurchase contract is a financial asset or a financial liability. If one of the settlement alternatives is to exchange cash for shares ((c) above), Entity A recognises a liability for the obligation to deliver cash, as illustrated in (c) above. Otherwise, Entity A accounts for the forward contract as a derivative.

Example 2: Forward to sell shares

IE7   This example illustrates the journal entries for forward sale contracts on an entity's own shares that will be settled (a) net in cash, (b) net in shares or (c) by receiving cash in exchange for shares. It also discusses the effect of settlement options (see (d) below). To simplify the illustration, it is assumed that no dividends are paid on the underlying shares (ie the 'carry return' is zero) so that the present value of the forward price equals the spot price when the fair value of the forward contract is zero. The fair value of the forward has been computed as the difference between the market share price and the present value of the fixed forward price.

Assumptions:

Contract date	1 February 20X2
Maturity date	31 January 20X3

Market price per share on 1 February 20X2	CU100
Market price per share on 31 December 20X2	CU110
Market price per share on 31 January 20X3	CU106
Fixed forward price to be paid on 31 January 20X3	CU104
Present value of forward price on 1 February 20X2	CU100
Number of shares under forward contract	1,000
Fair value of forward on 1 February 20X2	CU0
Fair value of forward on 31 December 20X2	(CU6,300)
Fair value of forward on 31 January 20X3	(CU2,000)

(a) Cash for cash ('net cash settlement')

IE8   On 1 February 20X2, Entity A enters into a contract with Entity B to pay the fair value of 1,000 of Entity A's own outstanding ordinary shares as of 31 January 20X3 in exchange for CU104,000 in cash (ie CU104 per share) on 31 January 20X3. The contract will be settled net in cash. Entity A records the following journal entries.

1 February 20X2

No entry is required because the fair value of the derivative is zero and no cash is paid or received.

31 December 20X2

| Dr | Loss | CU6,300 | |
| | Cr | Forward liability | | CU6,300 |

To record the decrease in the fair value of the forward contract.

31 January 20X3

| Dr | Forward liability | CU4,300 | |
| | Cr | Gain | | CU4,300 |

To record the increase in the fair value of the forward contract (ie CU4,300 = CU6,300 – CU2,000).

The contract is settled net in cash. Entity B has an obligation to deliver CU104,000 to Entity A, and Entity A has an obligation to deliver CU106,000 (CU106 × 1,000) to Entity B. Thus, Entity A pays the net amount of CU2,000 to Entity B.

| Dr | Forward liability | CU2,000 | |
| | Cr | Cash | | C2,000 |

To record the settlement of the forward contract.

(b) Shares for shares ('net share settlement')

IE9   Assume the same facts as in (a) except that settlement will be made net in shares instead of net in cash. Entity A's journal entries are the same as those shown in (a), except:

31 January 20X3

The contract is settled net in shares. Entity A has a right to receive CU104,000 (CU104 × 1,000) worth of its shares and an obligation to deliver CU106,000 (CU106 × 1,000) worth of its shares to Entity B. Thus, Entity A delivers a net amount of

CU2,000 (CU106,000 – CU104,000) worth of its shares to Entity B, ie 18.9 shares (CU2,000/CU106).

Dr	Forward liability	CU2,000	
	Cr Equity		CU2,000

To record the settlement of the forward contract. The issue of the entity's own shares is treated as an equity transaction.

(c) Shares for cash ('gross physical settlement')

IE10 Assume the same facts as in (a), except that settlement will be made by receiving a fixed amount of cash and delivering a fixed number of the entity's own shares. Similarly to (a) and (b) above, the price per share that Entity A will receive in one year is fixed at CU104. Accordingly, Entity A has a right to receive CU104,000 in cash (CU104 × 1,000) and an obligation to deliver 1,000 of its own shares in one year. Entity A records the following journal entries.

1 February 20X2

No entry is made on 1 February. No cash is paid or received because the forward has an initial fair value of zero. A forward contract to deliver a fixed number of Entity A's own shares in exchange for a fixed amount of cash or another financial asset meets the definition of an equity instrument because it cannot be settled otherwise than through the delivery of shares in exchange for cash.

31 December 20X2

No entry is made on 31 December because no cash is paid or received and a contract to deliver a fixed number of Entity A's own shares in exchange for a fixed amount of cash meets the definition of an equity instrument of the entity.

31 January 20X3

On 31 January 20X3, Entity A receives CU104,000 in cash and delivers 1,000 shares.

Dr	Cash	CU104,000	
	Cr Equity		CU104,000

To record the settlement of the forward contract.

(d) Settlement options

IE11 The existence of settlement options (such as net in cash, net in shares or by an exchange of cash and shares) has the result that the forward contract is a financial asset or a financial liability. It does not meet the definition of an equity instrument because it can be settled otherwise than by Entity A repurchasing a fixed number of its own shares in exchange for paying a fixed amount of cash or another financial asset. Entity A recognises a derivative asset or liability, as illustrated in (a) and (b) above. The accounting entry to be made on settlement depends on how the contract is actually settled.

Example 3: Purchased call option on shares

IE12 This example illustrates the journal entries for a purchased call option right on the entity's own shares that will be settled (a) net in cash, (b) net in shares or (c) by delivering cash in exchange for the entity's own shares. It also discusses the effect of settlement options (see (d) below):

Assumptions:	
Contract date	1 February 20X2
Exercise date	31 January 20X3
	(European terms, ie it can be exercised only at maturity)
Exercise right holder	Reporting entity (Entity A)
Market price per share on 1 February 20X2	CU100
Market price per share on 31 December 20X2	CU104
Market price per share on 31 January 20X3	CU104
Fixed exercise price to be paid on 31 January 20X3	CU102
Number of shares under option contract	1,000
Fair value of option on 1 February 20X2	CU5,000
Fair value of option on 31 December 20X2	CU3,000
Fair value of option on 31 January 20X3	CU2,000

(a) Cash for cash ('net cash settlement')

IE13   On 1 February 20X2, Entity A enters into a contract with Entity B that gives Entity B the obligation to deliver, and Entity A the right to receive the fair value of 1,000 of Entity A's own ordinary shares as of 31 January 20X3 in exchange for CU102,000 in cash (ie CU102 per share) on 31 January 20X3, if Entity A exercises that right. The contract will be settled net in cash. If Entity A does not exercise its right, no payment will be made. Entity A records the following journal entries.

1 February 20X2

The price per share when the contract is agreed on 1 February 20X2 is CU100. The initial fair value of the option contract on 1 February 20X2 is CU5,000, which Entity A pays to Entity B in cash on that date. On that date, the option has no intrinsic value, only time value, because the exercise price of CU102 exceeds the market price per share of CU100 and it would therefore not be economic for Entity A to exercise the option. In other words, the call option is out of the money.

Dr	Call option asset	CU5,000	
	Cr Cash		CU5,000

To recognise the purchased call option.

31 December 20X2

On 31 December 20X2, the market price per share has increased to CU104. The fair value of the call option has decreased to CU3,000, of which CU2,000 is intrinsic value ([CU104 – CU102] × 1,000), and CU1,000 is the remaining time value.

Dr	Loss	CU2,000	
	Cr Call option asset		CU2,000

To record the decrease in the fair value of the call option.

31 January 20X3

On 31 January 20X3, the market price per share is still CU104. The fair value of the call option has decreased to CU2,000, which is all intrinsic value ([CU104 – CU102] × 1,000) because no time value remains.

| Dr | Loss | CU1,000 | |
| | Cr | Call option asset | CU1,000 |

To record the decrease in the fair value of the call option.

On the same day, Entity A exercises the call option and the contract is settled net in cash. Entity B has an obligation to deliver CU104,000 (CU104 × 1,000) to Entity A in exchange for CU102,000 (CU102 × 1,000) from Entity A, so Entity A receives a net amount of CU2,000.

| Dr | Cash | CU2,000 | |
| | Cr | Call option asset | CU2,000 |

To record the settlement of the option contract.

(b) Shares for shares ('net share settlement')

IE14 Assume the same facts as in (a) except that settlement will be made net in shares instead of net in cash. Entity A's journal entries are the same as those shown in (a) except for recording the settlement of the option contract as follows:

31 January 20X3

Entity A exercises the call option and the contract is settled net in shares. Entity B has an obligation to deliver CU104,000 (CU104 × 1,000) worth of Entity A's shares to Entity A in exchange for CU102,000 (CU102 × 1,000) worth of Entity A's shares. Thus, Entity B delivers the net amount of CU2,000 worth of shares to Entity A, ie 19.2 shares (CU2,000/CU104).

| Dr | Equity | CU2,000 | |
| | Cr | Call option asset | CU2,000 |

To record the settlement of the option contract. The settlement is accounted for as a treasury share transaction (ie no gain or loss).

(c) Cash for shares ('gross physical settlement')

IE15 Assume the same facts as in (a) except that settlement will be made by receiving a fixed number of shares and paying a fixed amount of cash, if Entity A exercises the option. Similarly to (a) and (b) above, the exercise price per share is fixed at CU102. Accordingly, Entity A has a right to receive 1,000 of Entity A's own outstanding shares in exchange for CU102,000 (CU102 × 1,000) in cash, if Entity A exercises its option. Entity A records the following journal entries.

1 February 20X2

| Dr | Equity | CU5,000 | |
| | Cr | Cash | CU5,000 |

To record the cash paid in exchange for the right to receive Entity A's own shares in one year for a fixed price. The premium paid is recognised in equity.

31 December 20X2

No entry is made on 31 December because no cash is paid or received and a contract that gives a right to receive a fixed number of Entity A's own shares in exchange for a fixed amount of cash meets the definition of an equity instrument of the entity.

31 January 20X3

Entity A exercises the call option and the contract is settled gross. Entity B has an obligation to deliver 1,000 of Entity A's shares in exchange for CU102,000 in cash.

31 December 20X2

No entry is made on 31 December because no cash is paid or received and a contract to deliver a fixed number of Entity A's own shares in exchange for a fixed amount of cash meets the definition of an equity instrument of the entity.

31 January 20X3

Entity B exercises the call option and the contract is settled gross. Entity A has an obligation to deliver 1,000 shares in exchange for CU102,000 in cash.

Dr Cash	CU102,000	
Cr Equity		CU102,000

To record the settlement of the option contract.

(d) Settlement options

IE21 The existence of settlement options (such as net in cash, net in shares or by an exchange of cash and shares) has the result that the call option is a financial liability. It does not meet the definition of an equity instrument because it can be settled otherwise than by Entity A issuing a fixed number of its own shares in exchange for receiving a fixed amount of cash or another financial asset. Entity A recognises a derivative liability, as illustrated in (a) and (b) above. The accounting entry to be made on settlement depends on how the contract is actually settled.

Example 5: Purchased put option on shares

IE22 This example illustrates the journal entries for a purchased put option on the entity's own shares that will be settled (a) net in cash, (b) net in shares or (c) by delivering cash in exchange for shares. It also discusses the effect of settlement options (see (d) below).

Assumptions:	
Contract date	1 February 20X2
Exercise date	31 January 20X3
	(European terms, ie it can be exercised only at maturity)
Exercise right holder	Reporting entity (Entity A)
Market price per share on 1 February 20X2	CU100
Market price per share on 31 December 20X2	CU95
Market price per share on 31 January 20X3	CU95
Fixed exercise price to be paid on 31 January 20X3	CU98
Number of shares under option contract	1,000
Fair value of option on 1 February 20X2	CU5,000
Fair value of option on 31 December 20X2	CU4,000
Fair value of option on 31 January 20X3	CU3,000

(a) Cash for cash ('net cash settlement')

IE23 On 1 February 20X2, Entity A enters into a contract with Entity B that gives Entity A the right to sell, and Entity B the obligation to buy the fair value of 1,000 of Entity A's own outstanding ordinary shares as of 31 January 20X3 at a strike price of CU98,000 (ie CU98 per share) on 31 January 20X3, if Entity A exercises that right. The contract will be settled net in cash. If Entity A does not exercise its right, no payment will be made. Entity A records the following journal entries.

1 February 20X2

The price per share when the contract is agreed on 1 February 20X2 is CU100. The initial fair value of the option contract on 1 February 20X2 is CU5,000, which Entity A pays to Entity B in cash on that date. On that date, the option has no intrinsic value, only time value, because the exercise price of CU98 is less than the market price per share of CU100. Therefore it would not be economic for Entity A to exercise the option. In other words, the put option is out of the money.

Dr	Put option asset	CU5,000	
	Cr Cash		CU5,000

To recognise the purchased put option.

31 December 20X2

On 31 December 20X2 the market price per share has decreased to CU95. The fair value of the put option has decreased to CU4,000, of which CU3,000 is intrinsic value ([CU98 – CU95] × 1,000) and CU1,000 is the remaining time value.

Dr	Loss	CU1,000	
	Cr Put option asset		CU1,000

To record the decrease in the fair value of the put option.

31 January 20X3

On 31 January 20X3 the market price per share is still CU95. The fair value of the put option has decreased to CU3,000, which is all intrinsic value ([CU98 – CU95] × 1,000) because no time value remains.

Dr	Loss	CU1,000	
	Cr Put option asset		CU1,000

To record the decrease in the fair value of the option.

On the same day, Entity A exercises the put option and the contract is settled net in cash. Entity B has an obligation to deliver CU98,000 to Entity A and Entity A has an obligation to deliver CU95,000 (CU95 × 1,000) to Entity B, so Entity B pays the net amount of CU3,000 to Entity A.

Dr	Cash	CU3,000	
	Cr Put option asset		CU3,000

To record the settlement of the option contract.

(b) Shares for shares ('net share settlement')

IE24   Assume the same facts as in (a) except that settlement will be made net in shares instead of net in cash. Entity A's journal entries are the same as shown in (a), except:

31 January 20X3

Entity A exercises the put option and the contract is settled net in shares. In effect, Entity B has an obligation to deliver CU98,000 worth of Entity A's shares to Entity A, and Entity A has an obligation to deliver CU95,000 worth of Entity A's shares (CU95 × 1,000) to Entity B, so Entity B delivers the net amount of CU3,000 worth of shares to Entity A, ie 31.6 shares (CU3,000/CU95).

Dr	Equity	CU3,000	
	Cr Put option asset		CU3,000

To record the settlement of the option contract.

(c) Cash for shares ('gross physical settlement')

IE25 Assume the same facts as in (a) except that settlement will be made by receiving a fixed amount of cash and delivering a fixed number of Entity A's shares, if Entity A exercises the option. Similarly to (a) and (b) above, the exercise price per share is fixed at CU98. Accordingly, Entity B has an obligation to pay CU98,000 in cash to Entity A (CU98 × 1,000) in exchange for 1,000 of Entity A's outstanding shares, if Entity A exercises its option. Entity A records the following journal entries.

1 February 20X2

Dr	Equity	CU5,000	
	Cr Cash		CU5,000

To record the cash received in exchange for the right to deliver Entity A's own shares in one year for a fixed price. The premium paid is recognised directly in equity. Upon exercise, it results in the issue of a fixed number of shares in exchange for a fixed price.

31 December 20X2

No entry is made on 31 December because no cash is paid or received and a contract to deliver a fixed number of Entity A's own shares in exchange for a fixed amount of cash meets the definition of an equity instrument of Entity A.

31 January 20X3

Entity A exercises the put option and the contract is settled gross. Entity B has an obligation to deliver CU98,000 in cash to Entity A in exchange for 1,000 shares.

Dr	Cash	CU98,000	
	Cr Equity		CU98,000

To record the settlement of the option contract.

(d) Settlement options

IE26 The existence of settlement options (such as net in cash, net in shares or by an exchange of cash and shares) has the result that the put option is a financial asset. It does not meet the definition of an equity instrument because it can be settled otherwise than by Entity A issuing a fixed number of its own shares in exchange for receiving a fixed amount of cash or another financial asset. Entity A recognises a derivative asset, as illustrated in (a) and (b) above. The accounting entry to be made on settlement depends on how the contract is actually settled.

Example 6: Written put option on shares

IE27 This example illustrates the journal entries for a written put option on the entity's own shares that will be settled (a) net in cash, (b) net in shares or (c) by delivering cash in exchange for shares. It also discusses the effect of settlement options (see (d) below).

Assumptions:	
Contract date	1 February 20X2
Exercise date	31 January 20X3

	(European terms, ie it can be exercised only at maturity)
Exercise right holder	Counterparty (Entity B)
Market price per share on 1 February 20X2	CU100
Market price per share on 31 December 20X2	CU95
Market price per share on 31 January 20X3	CU95
Fixed exercise price to be paid on 31 January 20X3	CU98
Present value of exercise price on 1 February 20X2	CU95
Number of shares under option contract	1,000
Fair value of option on 1 February 20X2	CU5,000
Fair value of option on 31 December 20X2	CU4,000
Fair value of option on 31 January 20X3	CU3,000

(a) Cash for cash ('net cash settlement')

IE28   Assume the same facts as in Example 5(a) above, except that Entity A has written a put option on its own shares instead of having purchased a put option on its own shares. Accordingly, on 1 February 20X2, Entity A enters into a contract with Entity B that gives Entity B the right to receive and Entity A the obligation to pay the fair value of 1,000 of Entity A's outstanding ordinary shares as of 31 January 20X3 in exchange for CU98,000 in cash (ie CU98 per share) on 31 January 20X3, if Entity B exercises that right. The contract will be settled net in cash. If Entity B does not exercise its right, no payment will be made. Entity A records the following journal entries.

1 February 20X2

Dr	Cash	CU5,000	
	Cr Put option liability		CU5,000

To recognise the written put option.

31 December 20X2

Dr	Put option liability	CU1,000	
	Cr Gain		CU1,000

To record the decrease in the fair value of the put option.

31 January 20X3

Dr	Put option liability	CU1,000	
	Cr Gain		CU1,000

To record the decrease in the fair value of the put option.

On the same day, Entity B exercises the put option and the contract is settled net in cash. Entity A has an obligation to deliver CU98,000 to Entity B, and Entity B has an obligation to deliver CU95,000 (CU95 × 1,000) to Entity A. Thus, Entity A pays the net amount of CU3,000 to Entity B.

Dr	Put option liability	CU3,000	
	Cr Cash		CU3,000

To record the settlement of the option contract.

(b) Shares for shares ('net share settlement')

IE29   Assume the same facts as in (a) except that settlement will be made net in shares
instead of net in cash. Entity A's journal entries are the same as those in (a), except for
the following:

31 January 20X3

Entity B exercises the put option and the contract is settled net in shares. In effect,
Entity A has an obligation to deliver CU98,000 worth of shares to Entity B, and Entity
B has an obligation to deliver CU95,000 worth of Entity A's shares (CU95 × 1,000)
to Entity A. Thus, Entity A delivers the net amount of CU3,000 worth of Entity A's
shares to Entity B, ie 31.6 shares (3,000/95).

>   Dr   Put option liability   CU3,000
>   Cr   Equity   CU3,000
>   *To record the settlement of the option contract. The issue of Entity A's*
>   *own shares is accounted for as an equity transaction.*

(c) Cash for shares ('gross physical settlement')

IE30   Assume the same facts as in (a) except that settlement will be made by delivering a
fixed amount of cash and receiving a fixed number of shares, if Entity B exercises the
option. Similarly to (a) and (b) above, the exercise price per share is fixed at CU98.
Accordingly, Entity A has an obligation to pay CU98,000 in cash to Entity B (CU98
× 1,000) in exchange for 1,000 of Entity A's outstanding shares, if Entity B exercises
its option. Entity A records the following journal entries.

1 February 20X2

>   Dr   Cash   CU5,000
>   Cr Equity   CU5,000
>   *To recognise the option premium received of CU5,000 in equity.*

>   Dr   Equity   CU95,000
>   Cr Liability   CU95,000
>   *To recognise the present value of the obligation to deliver CU98,000*
>   *in one year, ie CU95,000, as a liability.*

31 December 20X2

>   Dr   Interest expense   CU2,750
>   Cr Liability   CU2,750
>   *To accrue interest in accordance with the effective interest method on*
>   *the liability for the share redemption amount.*

31 January 20X3

>   Dr   Interest expense   CU250
>   Cr Liability   CU250
>   *To accrue interest in accordance with the effective interest method on*
>   *the liability for the share redemption amount.*

On the same day, Entity B exercises the put option and the contract is settled gross. Entity A has an obligation to deliver CU98,000 in cash to Entity B in exchange for CU95,000 worth of shares (CU95 × 1,000).

Dr	Liability	CU98,000	
	Cr Cash		CU98,000

To record the settlement of the option contract.

(d) Settlement options

IE31 The existence of settlement options (such as net in cash, net in shares or by an exchange of cash and shares) has the result that the written put option is a financial liability. If one of the settlement alternatives is to exchange cash for shares ((c) above), Entity A recognises a liability for the obligation to deliver cash, as illustrated in (c) above. Otherwise, Entity A accounts for the put option as a derivative liability.

Entities such as mutual funds and co-operatives whose share capital is not equity as defined in AASB 132

Example 7: Entities with no equity

IE32 The following example illustrates a format of a statement of comprehensive income and statement of financial position that may be used by entities such as mutual funds that do not have equity as defined in AASB 132. Other formats are possible.

Statement of comprehensive income for the year ended 31 December 20X1

	20X1	20X0
	CU	CU
Revenue	2,956	1,718
Expenses (classified by nature or function)	(644)	(614)
Profit from operating activities	2,312	1,104
Finance costs		
– other finance costs	(47)	(47)
– distributions to unitholders	(50)	(50)
Change in net assets attributable to unitholders	2,215	1,007

Statement of financial position at 31 December 20X1

	20X1		20X0	
	CU	CU	CU	CU
ASSETS				
Non-current assets (classified in accordance with AASB 101)	91,374		78,484	
Total non-current assets		91,374		78,484
Current assets (classified in accordance with AASB 101)	1,422		1,769	
Total current assets		1,422		1,769
Total assets		92,796		80,253
LIABILITIES				
Current liabilities (classified in accordance with AASB 101)	647		66	
Total current liabilities		(647)		(66)
Non-current liabilities excluding net assets attributable to unitholders (classified in accordance with AASB 101)	280		136	
		(280)		(136)
Net assets attributable to unitholders		91,869		80,051

Example 8: Entities with some equity

IE33 The following example illustrates a format of a statement of comprehensive income and statement of financial position that may be used by entities whose share capital is not equity as defined in AASB 132 because the entity has an obligation to repay the share capital on demand but does not have all the features or meet the conditions in paragraphs 16A and 16B or paragraphs 16C and 16D. Other formats are possible.

Statement of comprehensive income for the year ended 31 December 20X1

	20X1	20X0
	CU	CU
Revenue	472	498
Expenses (classified by nature or function)	(367)	(396)
Profit from operating activities	105	102
Finance costs		
– other finance costs	(4)	(4)
– distributions to members	(50)	(50)
Change in net assets attributable to members	51	48

Statement of financial position at 31 December 20X1

	20X1	20X1	20X0	20X0
	CU	CU	CU	CU
ASSETS				
Non-current assets (classified in accordance with AASB 101)	908		830	
Total non-current assets		908		830
Current assets (classified in accordance with AASB 101)	383		350	
Total current assets		383		350
Total assets		1,291		1,180
LIABILITIES				
Current liabilities (classified in accordance with AASB 101)	372		338	
Share capital repayable on demand	202		161	
Total current liabilities		(574)		(499)
Total assets less current liabilities		717		681
Non-current liabilities (classified in accordance with AASB 101)	187		196	
		(187)		(196)
OTHER COMPONENTS OF EQUITY[(a)]				
Reserves eg revaluation surplus, retained earnings etc	530		485	
		530		485
		717		681
MEMORANDUM NOTE – Total members' interests				
Share capital repayable on demand		202		161
Reserves		530		485
		732		646

(a) In this example, the entity has no obligation to deliver a share of its reserves to its members.

Accounting for compound financial instruments

Example 9: Separation of a compound financial instrument on initial recognition

IE34 Paragraph 28 describes how the components of a compound financial instrument are separated by the entity on initial recognition. The following example illustrates how such a separation is made.

IE35 An entity issues 2,000 convertible bonds at the start of year 1. The bonds have a three-year term, and are issued at par with a face value of CU1,000 per bond, giving total proceeds of CU2,000,000. Interest is payable annually in arrears at a nominal annual interest rate of 6 per cent. Each bond is convertible at any time up to maturity into 250 ordinary shares. When the bonds are issued, the prevailing market interest rate for similar debt without conversion options is 9 per cent.

IE36 The liability component is measured first, and the difference between the proceeds of the bond issue and the fair value of the liability is assigned to the equity component. The present value of the liability component is calculated using a discount rate of 9 per cent, the market interest rate for similar bonds having no conversion rights, as shown below.

	CU
Present value of the principal – CU2,000,000 payable at the end of three years	1,544,367
Present value of the interest – CU120,000 payable annually in arrears for three years	303,755
Total liability component	1,848,122
Equity component (by deduction)	151,878
Proceeds of the bond issue	2,000,000

Example 10: Separation of a compound financial instrument with multiple embedded derivative features

IE37 The following example illustrates the application of paragraph 31 to the separation of the liability and equity components of a compound financial instrument with multiple embedded derivative features.

IE38 Assume that the proceeds received on the issue of a callable convertible bond are CU60. The value of a similar bond without a call or equity conversion option is CU57. Based on an option pricing model, it is determined that the value to the entity of the embedded call feature in a similar bond without an equity conversion option is CU2. In this case, the value allocated to the liability component under paragraph 31 is CU55 (CU57 – CU2) and the value allocated to the equity component is CU5 (CU60 – CU55).

Example 11: Repurchase of a convertible instrument

IE39 The following example illustrates how an entity accounts for a repurchase of a convertible instrument. For simplicity, at inception, the face amount of the instrument is assumed to be equal to the aggregate carrying amount of its liability and equity components in the financial statements, ie no original issue premium or discount exists. Also, for simplicity, tax considerations have been omitted from the example.

IE40 On 1 January 20X0, Entity A issued a 10 per cent convertible debenture with a face value of CU1,000 maturing on 31 December 20X9. The debenture is convertible into ordinary shares of Entity A at a conversion price of CU25 per share. Interest is payable half-yearly in cash. At the date of issue, Entity A could have issued non-convertible debt with a ten-year term bearing a coupon interest rate of 11 per cent.

IE41 In the financial statements of Entity A the carrying amount of the debenture was allocated on issue as follows:

	CU
Liability component	
Present value of 20 half-yearly interest payments of CU50, discounted at 11%	597
Present value of CU1,000 due in 10 years, discounted at 11%, compounded half-yearly	343
	940
Equity component	
(difference between CU1,000 total proceeds and CU940 allocated above)	60
Total proceeds	1,000

IE42   On 1 January 20X5, the convertible debenture has a fair value of CU1,700.

IE43   Entity A makes a tender offer to the holder of the debenture to repurchase the debenture for CU1,700, which the holder accepts. At the date of repurchase, Entity A could have issued non-convertible debt with a five-year term bearing a coupon interest rate of 8 per cent.

IE44   The repurchase price is allocated as follows:

	Carrying value	Fair value	Difference
Liability component:	CU	CU	CU
Present value of 10 remaining half-yearly interest payments of CU50, discounted at 11% and 8%, respectively	377	405	
Present value of CU1,000 due in 5 years, discounted at 11% and 8%, compounded half-yearly, respectively	585	676	
	962	1,081	(119)
Equity component	60	619[(a)]	(559)
Total	1,022	1,700	(678)

(a) This amount represents the difference between the fair value amount allocated to the liability component and the repurchase price of CU1,700.

IE45   Entity A recognises the repurchase of the debenture as follows:

Dr	Liability component	CU962	
Dr	Debt settlement expense (profit or loss)	CU119	
	Cr Cash		CU1,081

To recognise the repurchase of the liability component.

Dr	Equity	CU619	
	Cr Cash		CU619

To recognise the cash paid for the equity component.

IE46   The equity component remains as equity, but may be transferred from one line item within equity to another.

Example 12: Amendment of the terms of a convertible instrument to induce early conversion

IE47   The following example illustrates how an entity accounts for the additional consideration paid when the terms of a convertible instrument are amended to induce early conversion.

IE48   On 1 January 20X0, Entity A issued a 10 per cent convertible debenture with a face value of CU1,000 with the same terms as described in Example 11. On 1 January 20X1, to induce the holder to convert the convertible debenture promptly, Entity A reduces the conversion price to CU20 if the debenture is converted before 1 March 20X1 (ie within 60 days).

IE49   Assume the market price of Entity A's ordinary shares on the date the terms are amended is CU40 per share. The fair value of the incremental consideration paid by Entity A is calculated as follows:

*Number of ordinary shares to be issued to debenture holders under **amended** conversion terms:*

Face amount	CU1,000
New conversion price	/CU20 per share
Number of ordinary shares to be issued on conversion	50 shares

*Number of ordinary shares to be issued to debenture holders under **original** conversion terms:*

Face amount	CU1,000
Original conversion price	/CU25 per share
Number of ordinary shares to be issued on conversion	40 shares

Number of incremental ordinary shares issued upon conversion	10 shares

*Value of **incremental** ordinary shares issued upon conversion*	
CU40 per share x 10 incremental shares	CU400

IE50   The incremental consideration of CU400 is recognised as a loss in profit or loss.

DELETED IAS 32 TEXT

Deleted IAS 32 text is not part of AASB 132.

97A   IAS 1 (as revised in 2007) amended the terminology used throughout IFRSs. In addition it amended paragraph 40. An entity shall apply those amendments for annual periods beginning on or after 1 January 2009. If an entity applies IAS 1 (revised 2007) for an earlier period, the amendments shall be applied for that earlier period.

97D   Paragraph 4 was amended by *Improvements to IFRSs* issued in May 2008. An entity shall apply that amendment for annual periods beginning on or after 1 January 2009. Earlier application is permitted. If an entity applies the amendment for an earlier period it shall disclose that fact and apply for that earlier period the amendments to paragraph 3 of IFRS 7, paragraph 1 of IAS 28 and paragraph 1 of IAS 31 issued in May 2008. An entity is permitted to apply the amendment prospectively.

97E   Paragraphs 11 and 16 were amended by *Classification of Rights Issues* issued in October 2009. An entity shall apply that amendment for annual periods beginning on or after 1 February 2010. Earlier application is permitted. If an entity applies the amendment for an earlier period, it shall disclose that fact.

97I   IFRS 10 and IFRS 11 *Joint Arrangements*, issued in May 2011, amended paragraphs 4(a) and AG29. An entity shall apply those amendments when it applies IFRS 10 and IFRS 11.

97J   IFRS 13, issued in May 2011, amended the definition of fair value in paragraph 11 and amended paragraphs 23 and AG31. An entity shall apply those amendments when it applies IFRS 13.

97K   *Presentation of Items of Other Comprehensive Income* (Amendments to IAS 1), issued in June 2011, amended paragraph 40. An entity shall apply that amendment when it applies IAS 1 as amended in June 2011.

97L   *Offsetting Financial Assets and Financial Liabilities* (Amendments to IAS 32), issued in December 2011, deleted paragraph AG38 and added paragraphs AG38A–AG38F. An entity shall apply those amendments for annual periods beginning on or after 1 January 2014. An entity shall apply those amendments retrospectively. Earlier application is permitted. If an entity applies those amendments from an earlier date, it shall disclose that fact and shall also make the disclosures required by *Disclosures— Offsetting Financial Assets and Financial Liabilities* (Amendments to IFRS 7) issued in December 2011.

97M   *Disclosures—Offsetting Financial Assets and Financial Liabilities* (Amendments to IFRS 7), issued in December 2011, amended paragraph 43 by requiring an entity to disclose the information required in paragraphs 13B–13E of IFRS 7 for recognised financial assets that are within the scope of paragraph 13A of IFRS 7. An entity shall

AASB

apply that amendment for annual periods beginning on or after 1 January 2013 and interim periods within those annual periods. An entity shall provide the disclosures required by this amendment retrospectively.

97N *Annual Improvements 2009–2011 Cycle*, issued in May 2012, amended paragraphs 35, 37 and 39 and added paragraph 35A. An entity shall apply that amendment retrospectively in accordance with IAS 8 *Accounting Policies, Changes in Accounting Estimates and Errors* for annual periods beginning on or after 1 January 2013. Earlier application is permitted. If an entity applies that amendment for an earlier period it shall disclose that fact.

97O *Investment Entities* (Amendments to IFRS 10, IFRS 12 and IAS 27), issued in October 2012, amended paragraph 4. An entity shall apply that amendment for annual periods beginning on or after 1 January 2014. Earlier application of *Investment Entities* is permitted. If an entity applies that amendment earlier it shall also apply all amendments included in *Investment Entities* at the same time.

98   This Standard supersedes IAS 32 *Financial Instruments: Disclosure and Presentation* revised in 2000.[4]

> 4   In August 2005 the IASB relocated all disclosures relating to financial instruments to IFRS 7 Financial Instruments: Disclosures.

99   This Standard supersedes the following Interpretations:

(a)   SIC-5 *Classification of Financial Instruments—Contingent Settlement Provisions*;

(b)   SIC-16 *Share Capital—Reacquired Own Equity Instruments (Treasury Shares)*; and

(c)   SIC-17 *Equity—Costs of an Equity Transaction*.

100 This Standard withdraws draft SIC Interpretation D34 *Financial Instruments— Instruments or Rights Redeemable by the Holder*.

AASB 133
Earnings per Share

(Compiled November 2015)

This compiled Standard applies to annual periods beginning on or after 1 January 2018. Earlier application is permitted for annual periods beginning after 24 July 2014 but before 1 January 2018. It incorporates relevant amendments made up to and including 11 November 2015.

Prepared on 7 December 2015 by the staff of the Australian Accounting Standards Board.

CONTENTS

COMPARISON WITH IAS 33
ACCOUNTING STANDARD
AASB 133 *EARNINGS PER SHARE*

from paragraph

APPENDICES
A. APPLICATION GUIDANCE
B. AUSTRALIAN REDUCED DISCLOSURE REQUIREMENTS

ILLUSTRATIVE EXAMPLES

COMPILATION DETAILS

DELETED IAS 33 TEXT

BASIS FOR CONCLUSIONS ON IAS 33 (available on the AASB website)

Australian Accounting Standard AASB 133 *Earnings per Share* (as amended) is set out in paragraphs 1 – Aus76.2 and Appendices A and C. All the paragraphs have equal authority. Paragraphs in **bold type** state the main principles. AASB 133 is to be read in the context of other Australian Accounting Standards, including AASB 1048 *Interpretation of Standards*, which identifies the Australian Accounting Interpretations, and AASB 1057 *Application of Australian Accounting Standards*. In the absence of explicit guidance, AASB 108 *Accounting Policies, Changes in Accounting Estimates and Errors* provides a basis for selecting and applying accounting policies.

COMPARISON WITH IAS 33

AASB 133 *Earnings per Share* as amended incorporates IAS 33 *Earnings per Share* as issued and amended by the International Accounting Standards Board (IASB). Australian-specific paragraphs (which are not included in IAS 33) are identified with the prefix "Aus". Paragraphs that apply only to not-for-profit entities begin by identifying their limited applicability.

Tier 1

For-profit entities complying with AASB 133 also comply with IAS 33.

Not-for-profit entities' compliance with IAS 33 will depend on whether any "Aus" paragraphs that specifically apply to not-for-profit entities provide additional guidance or contain applicable requirements that are inconsistent with IAS 33.

Tier 2

Entities preparing general purpose financial statements under Australian Accounting Standards – Reduced Disclosure Requirements (Tier 2) will not be in compliance with IFRSs.

AASB 1053 *Application of Tiers of Australian Accounting Standards* explains the two tiers of reporting requirements.

ACCOUNTING STANDARD AASB 133

The Australian Accounting Standards Board made Accounting Standard AASB 133 *Earnings per Share* under section 334 of the *Corporations Act 2001* on 7 August 2015.

This compiled version of AASB 133 applies to annual periods beginning on or after 1 January 2018. It incorporates relevant amendments contained in other AASB Standards made by the AASB up to and including 11 November 2015 (see Compilation Details).

ACCOUNTING STANDARD AASB 133
EARNINGS PER SHARE

Objective

1   The objective of this Standard is to prescribe principles for the determination and presentation of earnings per share, so as to improve performance comparisons between different entities in the same reporting period and between different reporting periods for the same entity. Even though earnings per share data have limitations because of the different accounting policies that may be used for determining 'earnings', a

consistently determined denominator enhances financial reporting. The focus of this Standard is on the denominator of the earnings per share calculation.

Scope

2 **This Standard shall apply to:**

(a) **the separate or individual financial statements of an entity:**

(i) **whose ordinary shares or potential ordinary shares are traded in a public market (a domestic or foreign stock exchange or an over-the-counter market, including local and regional markets) or**

(ii) **that files, or is in the process of filing, its financial statements with a securities commission or other regulatory organisation for the purpose of issuing ordinary shares in a public market; and**

(b) **the consolidated financial statements of a group with a parent:**

(i) **whose ordinary shares or potential ordinary shares are traded in a public market (a domestic or foreign stock exchange or an over-the-counter market, including local and regional markets) or**

(ii) **that files, or is in the process of filing, its financial statements with a securities commission or other regulatory organisation for the purpose of issuing ordinary shares in a public market.**

3 **An entity that discloses earnings per share shall calculate and disclose earnings per share in accordance with this Standard.**

4 **When an entity presents both consolidated financial statements and separate financial statements prepared in accordance with AASB 10 *Consolidated Financial Statements* and AASB 127 *Separate Financial Statements* respectively, the disclosures required by this Standard need be presented only on the basis of the consolidated information. An entity that chooses to disclose earnings per share based on its separate financial statements shall present such earnings per share information only in its statement of comprehensive income. An entity shall not present such earnings per share information in the consolidated financial statements.**

4A **If an entity presents items of profit or loss in a separate statement as described in paragraph 10A of AASB 101 *Presentation of Financial Statements*, it presents earnings per share only in that separate statement.**

Definitions

5 **The following terms are used in this Standard with the meanings specified:**

Antidilution **is an increase in earnings per share or a reduction in loss per share resulting from the assumption that convertible instruments are converted, that options or warrants are exercised, or that ordinary shares are issued upon the satisfaction of specified conditions.**

A *contingent share agreement* is an agreement to issue shares that is dependent on the satisfaction of specified conditions.

Contingently issuable ordinary shares **are ordinary shares issuable for little or no cash or other consideration upon the satisfaction of specified conditions in a contingent share agreement.**

Dilution **is a reduction in earnings per share or an increase in loss per share resulting from the assumption that convertible instruments are converted, that options or warrants are exercised, or that ordinary shares are issued upon the satisfaction of specified conditions.**

Options, warrants and their equivalents **are financial instruments that give the holder the right to purchase ordinary shares.**

An *ordinary share* is an equity instrument that is subordinate to all other classes of equity instruments.

A *potential ordinary share* is a financial instrument or other contract that may entitle its holder to ordinary shares.

Put options on ordinary shares are contracts that give the holder the right to sell ordinary shares at a specified price for a given period.

6 Ordinary shares participate in profit for the period only after other types of shares such as preference shares have participated. An entity may have more than one class of ordinary shares. Ordinary shares of the same class have the same rights to receive dividends.

7 Examples of potential ordinary shares are:

(a) financial liabilities or equity instruments, including preference shares, that are convertible into ordinary shares;

(b) options and warrants;

(c) shares that would be issued upon the satisfaction of conditions resulting from contractual arrangements, such as the purchase of a business or other assets.

8 Terms defined in AASB 132 *Financial Instruments: Presentation* are used in this Standard with the meanings specified in paragraph 11 of AASB 132, unless otherwise noted. AASB 132 defines financial instrument, financial asset, financial liability and equity instrument, and provides guidance on applying those definitions. AASB 13 *Fair Value Measurement* defines fair value and sets out requirements for applying that definition.

Measurement

Basic earnings per share

9 **An entity shall calculate basic earnings per share amounts for profit or loss attributable to ordinary equity holders of the parent entity and, if presented, profit or loss from continuing operations attributable to those equity holders.**

10 **Basic earnings per share shall be calculated by dividing profit or loss attributable to ordinary equity holders of the parent entity (the numerator) by the weighted average number of ordinary shares outstanding (the denominator) during the period.**

11 The objective of basic earnings per share information is to provide a measure of the interests of each ordinary share of a parent entity in the performance of the entity over the reporting period.

Earnings

12 **For the purpose of calculating basic earnings per share, the amounts attributable to ordinary equity holders of the parent entity in respect of:**

(a) **profit or loss from continuing operations attributable to the parent entity; and**

(b) **profit or loss attributable to the parent entity**

shall be the amounts in (a) and (b) adjusted for the after-tax amounts of preference dividends, differences arising on the settlement of preference shares, and other similar effects of preference shares classified as equity.

13 All items of income and expense attributable to ordinary equity holders of the parent entity that are recognised in a period, including tax expense and dividends on preference shares classified as liabilities are included in the determination of profit or loss for the period attributable to ordinary equity holders of the parent entity (see AASB 101).

14   The after-tax amount of preference dividends that is deducted from profit or loss is:

      (a)   the after-tax amount of any preference dividends on non-cumulative preference shares declared in respect of the period; and

      (b)   the after-tax amount of the preference dividends for cumulative preference shares required for the period, whether or not the dividends have been declared. The amount of preference dividends for the period does not include the amount of any preference dividends for cumulative preference shares paid or declared during the current period in respect of previous periods.

15   Preference shares that provide for a low initial dividend to compensate an entity for selling the preference shares at a discount, or an above-market dividend in later periods to compensate investors for purchasing preference shares at a premium, are sometimes referred to as increasing rate preference shares. Any original issue discount or premium on increasing rate preference shares is amortised to retained earnings using the effective interest method and treated as a preference dividend for the purposes of calculating earnings per share.

16   Preference shares may be repurchased under an entity's tender offer to the holders. The excess of the fair value of the consideration paid to the preference shareholders over the carrying amount of the preference shares represents a return to the holders of the preference shares and a charge to retained earnings for the entity. This amount is deducted in calculating profit or loss attributable to ordinary equity holders of the parent entity.

17   Early conversion of convertible preference shares may be induced by an entity through favourable changes to the original conversion terms or the payment of additional consideration. The excess of the fair value of the ordinary shares or other consideration paid over the fair value of the ordinary shares issuable under the original conversion terms is a return to the preference shareholders, and is deducted in calculating profit or loss attributable to ordinary equity holders of the parent entity.

18   Any excess of the carrying amount of preference shares over the fair value of the consideration paid to settle them is added in calculating profit or loss attributable to ordinary equity holders of the parent entity.

Shares

19   **For the purpose of calculating basic earnings per share, the number of ordinary shares shall be the weighted average number of ordinary shares outstanding during the period.**

20   Using the weighted average number of ordinary shares outstanding during the period reflects the possibility that the amount of shareholders' capital varied during the period as a result of a larger or smaller number of shares being outstanding at any time. The weighted average number of ordinary shares outstanding during the period is the number of ordinary shares outstanding at the beginning of the period, adjusted by the number of ordinary shares bought back or issued during the period multiplied by a time-weighting factor. The time-weighting factor is the number of days that the shares are outstanding as a proportion of the total number of days in the period; a reasonable approximation of the weighted average is adequate in many circumstances.

21   Shares are usually included in the weighted average number of shares from the date consideration is receivable (which is generally the date of their issue), for example:

      (a)   ordinary shares issued in exchange for cash are included when cash is receivable;

      (b)   ordinary shares issued on the voluntary reinvestment of dividends on ordinary or preference shares are included when dividends are reinvested;

      (c)   ordinary shares issued as a result of the conversion of a debt instrument to ordinary shares are included from the date that interest ceases to accrue;

      (d)   ordinary shares issued in place of interest or principal on other financial instruments are included from the date that interest ceases to accrue;

AASB

deemed to have been converted into ordinary shares at the beginning of the period or, if later, the date of the issue of the potential ordinary shares.

37   Dilutive potential ordinary shares shall be determined independently for each period presented. The number of dilutive potential ordinary shares included in the year-to-date period is not a weighted average of the dilutive potential ordinary shares included in each interim computation.

38   Potential ordinary shares are weighted for the period they are outstanding. Potential ordinary shares that are cancelled or allowed to lapse during the period are included in the calculation of diluted earnings per share only for the portion of the period during which they are outstanding. Potential ordinary shares that are converted into ordinary shares during the period are included in the calculation of diluted earnings per share from the beginning of the period to the date of conversion; from the date of conversion, the resulting ordinary shares are included in both basic and diluted earnings per share.

39   The number of ordinary shares that would be issued on conversion of dilutive potential ordinary shares is determined from the terms of the potential ordinary shares. When more than one basis of conversion exists, the calculation assumes the most advantageous conversion rate or exercise price from the standpoint of the holder of the potential ordinary shares.

40   A subsidiary, joint venture or associate may issue to parties other than the parent or investors with joint control of, or significant influence over, the investee potential ordinary shares that are convertible into either ordinary shares of the subsidiary, joint venture or associate, or ordinary shares of the parent or investors with joint control of, or significant influence (the reporting entity) over, the investee. If these potential ordinary shares of the subsidiary, joint venture or associate have a dilutive effect on the basic earnings per share of the reporting entity, they are included in the calculation of diluted earnings per share.

Dilutive potential ordinary shares

41   **Potential ordinary shares shall be treated as dilutive when, and only when, their conversion to ordinary shares would decrease earnings per share or increase loss per share from continuing operations.**

42   An entity uses profit or loss from continuing operations attributable to the parent entity as the control number to establish whether potential ordinary shares are dilutive or antidilutive. Profit or loss from continuing operations attributable to the parent entity is adjusted in accordance with paragraph 12 and excludes items relating to discontinued operations.

43   Potential ordinary shares are antidilutive when their conversion to ordinary shares would increase earnings per share or decrease loss per share from continuing operations. The calculation of diluted earnings per share does not assume conversion, exercise, or other issue of potential ordinary shares that would have an antidilutive effect on earnings per share.

44   In determining whether potential ordinary shares are dilutive or antidilutive, each issue or series of potential ordinary shares is considered separately rather than in aggregate. The sequence in which potential ordinary shares are considered may affect whether they are dilutive. Therefore, to maximise the dilution of basic earnings per share, each issue or series of potential ordinary shares is considered in sequence from the most dilutive to the least dilutive, ie dilutive potential ordinary shares with the lowest 'earnings per incremental share' are included in the diluted earnings per share calculation before those with a higher earnings per incremental share. Options and warrants are generally included first because they do not affect the numerator of the calculation.

Options, warrants and their equivalents

45   **For the purpose of calculating diluted earnings per share, an entity shall assume the exercise of dilutive options and warrants of the entity. The assumed proceeds from these instruments shall be regarded as having been received from the issue of ordinary shares at the average market price of ordinary shares during the period. The difference between the number of ordinary shares issued and the number of ordinary shares that would have been issued at the average market price of ordinary shares during the period shall be treated as an issue of ordinary shares for no consideration.**

46   Options and warrants are dilutive when they would result in the issue of ordinary shares for less than the average market price of ordinary shares during the period. The amount of the dilution is the average market price of ordinary shares during the period minus the issue price. Therefore, to calculate diluted earnings per share, potential ordinary shares are treated as consisting of both the following:

      (a)   a contract to issue a certain number of the ordinary shares at their average market price during the period. Such ordinary shares are assumed to be fairly priced and to be neither dilutive nor antidilutive. They are ignored in the calculation of diluted earnings per share.

      (b)   a contract to issue the remaining ordinary shares for no consideration. Such ordinary shares generate no proceeds and have no effect on profit or loss attributable to ordinary shares outstanding. Therefore, such shares are dilutive and are added to the number of ordinary shares outstanding in the calculation of diluted earnings per share.

47   Options and warrants have a dilutive effect only when the average market price of ordinary shares during the period exceeds the exercise price of the options or warrants (ie they are 'in the money'). Previously reported earnings per share are not retroactively adjusted to reflect changes in prices of ordinary shares.

47A   For share options and other share-based payment arrangements to which AASB 2 *Share-based Payment* applies, the issue price referred to in paragraph 46 and the exercise price referred to in paragraph 47 shall include the fair value (measured in accordance with AASB 2) of any goods or services to be supplied to the entity in the future under the share option or other share-based payment arrangement.

48   Employee share options with fixed or determinable terms and non-vested ordinary shares are treated as options in the calculation of diluted earnings per share, even though they may be contingent on vesting. They are treated as outstanding on the grant date. Performance-based employee share options are treated as contingently issuable shares because their issue is contingent upon satisfying specified conditions in addition to the passage of time.

Convertible instruments

49   The dilutive effect of convertible instruments shall be reflected in diluted earnings per share in accordance with paragraphs 33 and 36.

50   Convertible preference shares are antidilutive whenever the amount of the dividend on such shares declared in or accumulated for the current period per ordinary share obtainable on conversion exceeds basic earnings per share. Similarly, convertible debt is antidilutive whenever its interest (net of tax and other changes in income or expense) per ordinary share obtainable on conversion exceeds basic earnings per share.

51   The redemption or induced conversion of convertible preference shares may affect only a portion of the previously outstanding convertible preference shares. In such cases, any excess consideration referred to in paragraph 17 is attributed to those shares that are redeemed or converted for the purpose of determining whether the remaining outstanding preference shares are dilutive. The shares redeemed or converted are considered separately from those shares that are not redeemed or converted.

Contingently issuable shares

52   As in the calculation of basic earnings per share, contingently issuable ordinary shares are treated as outstanding and included in the calculation of diluted earnings per share if the conditions are satisfied (ie the events have occurred). Contingently issuable shares are included from the beginning of the period (or from the date of the contingent share agreement, if later). If the conditions are not satisfied, the number of contingently issuable shares included in the diluted earnings per share calculation is based on the number of shares that would be issuable if the end of the period were the end of the contingency period. Restatement is not permitted if the conditions are not met when the contingency period expires.

53   If attainment or maintenance of a specified amount of earnings for a period is the condition for contingent issue and if that amount has been attained at the end of the reporting period but must be maintained beyond the end of the reporting period for an additional period, then the additional ordinary shares are treated as outstanding, if the effect is dilutive, when calculating diluted earnings per share. In that case, the calculation of diluted earnings per share is based on the number of ordinary shares that would be issued if the amount of earnings at the end of the reporting period were the amount of earnings at the end of the contingency period. Because earnings may change in a future period, the calculation of basic earnings per share does not include such contingently issuable ordinary shares until the end of the contingency period because not all necessary conditions have been satisfied.

54   The number of ordinary shares contingently issuable may depend on the future market price of the ordinary shares. In that case, if the effect is dilutive, the calculation of diluted earnings per share is based on the number of ordinary shares that would be issued if the market price at the end of the reporting period were the market price at the end of the contingency period. If the condition is based on an average of market prices over a period of time that extends beyond the end of the reporting period, the average for the period of time that has lapsed is used. Because the market price may change in a future period, the calculation of basic earnings per share does not include such contingently issuable ordinary shares until the end of the contingency period because not all necessary conditions have been satisfied.

55   The number of ordinary shares contingently issuable may depend on future earnings and future prices of the ordinary shares. In such cases, the number of ordinary shares included in the diluted earnings per share calculation is based on both conditions (ie earnings to date and the current market price at the end of the reporting period). Contingently issuable ordinary shares are not included in the diluted earnings per share calculation unless both conditions are met.

56   In other cases, the number of ordinary shares contingently issuable depends on a condition other than earnings or market price (for example, the opening of a specific number of retail stores). In such cases, assuming that the present status of the condition remains unchanged until the end of the contingency period, the contingently issuable ordinary shares are included in the calculation of diluted earnings per share according to the status at the end of the reporting period.

57   Contingently issuable potential ordinary shares (other than those covered by a contingent share agreement, such as contingently issuable convertible instruments) are included in the diluted earnings per share calculation as follows:

(a)   an entity determines whether the potential ordinary shares may be assumed to be issuable on the basis of the conditions specified for their issue in accordance with the contingent ordinary share provisions in paragraphs 52–56; and

(b)   if those potential ordinary shares should be reflected in diluted earnings per share, an entity determines their impact on the calculation of diluted earnings per share by following the provisions for options and warrants in paragraphs 45–48, the provisions for convertible instruments in paragraphs 49–51, the provisions for contracts that may be settled in ordinary shares or cash in paragraphs 58–61, or other provisions, as appropriate.

However, exercise or conversion is not assumed for the purpose of calculating diluted earnings per share unless exercise or conversion of similar outstanding potential ordinary shares that are not contingently issuable is assumed.

Contracts that may be settled in ordinary shares or cash

58   **When an entity has issued a contract that may be settled in ordinary shares or cash at the entity's option, the entity shall presume that the contract will be settled in ordinary shares, and the resulting potential ordinary shares shall be included in diluted earnings per share if the effect is dilutive.**

59   When such a contract is presented for accounting purposes as an asset or a liability, or has an equity component and a liability component, the entity shall adjust the numerator for any changes in profit or loss that would have resulted during the period if the contract had been classified wholly as an equity instrument. That adjustment is similar to the adjustments required in paragraph 33.

60   **For contracts that may be settled in ordinary shares or cash at the holder's option, the more dilutive of cash settlement and share settlement shall be used in calculating diluted earnings per share.**

61   An example of a contract that may be settled in ordinary shares or cash is a debt instrument that, on maturity, gives the entity the unrestricted right to settle the principal amount in cash or in its own ordinary shares. Another example is a written put option that gives the holder a choice of settling in ordinary shares or cash.

Purchased options

62   Contracts such as purchased put options and purchased call options (ie options held by the entity on its own ordinary shares) are not included in the calculation of diluted earnings per share because including them would be antidilutive. The put option would be exercised only if the exercise price were higher than the market price and the call option would be exercised only if the exercise price were lower than the market price.

Written put options

63   **Contracts that require the entity to repurchase its own shares, such as written put options and forward purchase contracts, are reflected in the calculation of diluted earnings per share if the effect is dilutive. If these contracts are 'in the money' during the period (ie the exercise or settlement price is above the average market price for that period), the potential dilutive effect on earnings per share shall be calculated as follows:**

    (a)   **it shall be assumed that at the beginning of the period sufficient ordinary shares will be issued (at the average market price during the period) to raise proceeds to satisfy the contract;**

    (b)   **it shall be assumed that the proceeds from the issue are used to satisfy the contract (ie to buy back ordinary shares); and**

    (c)   **the incremental ordinary shares (the difference between the number of ordinary shares assumed issued and the number of ordinary shares received from satisfying the contract) shall be included in the calculation of diluted earnings per share.**

Retrospective adjustments

64   **If the number of ordinary or potential ordinary shares outstanding increases as a result of a capitalisation, bonus issue or share split, or decreases as a result of a reverse share split, the calculation of basic and diluted earnings per share for all periods presented shall be adjusted retrospectively. If these changes occur after the reporting period but before the financial statements are authorised for issue, the per share calculations for those and any prior period financial statements presented shall be based on the new number of shares. The fact that per share calculations reflect such changes in the number of shares shall be disclosed. In addition, basic and diluted earnings per share of all periods presented shall be**

adjusted for the effects of errors and adjustments resulting from changes in accounting policies accounted for retrospectively.

65   An entity does not restate diluted earnings per share of any prior period presented for changes in the assumptions used in earnings per share calculations or for the conversion of potential ordinary shares into ordinary shares.

Presentation

66   **An entity shall present in the statement of comprehensive income basic and diluted earnings per share for profit or loss from continuing operations attributable to the ordinary equity holders of the parent entity and for profit or loss attributable to the ordinary equity holders of the parent entity for the period for each class of ordinary shares that has a different right to share in profit for the period. An entity shall present basic and diluted earnings per share with equal prominence for all periods presented.**

67   Earnings per share is presented for every period for which a statement of comprehensive income is presented. If diluted earnings per share is reported for at least one period, it shall be reported for all periods presented, even if it equals basic earnings per share. If basic and diluted earnings per share are equal, dual presentation can be accomplished in one line in the statement of comprehensive income.

67A   If an entity presents items of profit or loss in a separate statement as described in paragraph 10A of AASB 101, it presents basic and diluted earnings per share, as required in paragraphs 66 and 67, in that separate statement.

68   **An entity that reports a discontinued operation shall disclose the basic and diluted amounts per share for the discontinued operation either in the statement of comprehensive income or in the notes.**

68A   If an entity presents items of profit or loss in a separate statement as described in paragraph 10A of AASB 101, it presents basic and diluted earnings per share for the discontinued operation, as required in paragraph 68, in that separate statement or in the notes.

69   **An entity shall present basic and diluted earnings per share, even if the amounts are negative (ie a loss per share).**

Disclosure

70   **An entity shall disclose the following:**

    (a)   **the amounts used as the numerators in calculating basic and diluted earnings per share, and a reconciliation of those amounts to profit or loss attributable to the parent entity for the period. The reconciliation shall include the individual effect of each class of instruments that affects earnings per share.**

    (b)   **the weighted average number of ordinary shares used as the denominator in calculating basic and diluted earnings per share, and a reconciliation of these denominators to each other. The reconciliation shall include the individual effect of each class of instruments that affects earnings per share.**

    (c)   **instruments (including contingently issuable shares) that could potentially dilute basic earnings per share in the future, but were not included in the calculation of diluted earnings per share because they are antidilutive for the period(s) presented.**

    (d)   **a description of ordinary share transactions or potential ordinary share transactions, other than those accounted for in accordance with paragraph 64, that occur after the reporting period and that would have changed significantly the number of ordinary shares or potential ordinary shares** outstanding at the end of the period if those transactions had occurred before the end of the reporting period.

71 Examples of transactions in paragraph 70(d) include:

(a) an issue of shares for cash;

(b) an issue of shares when the proceeds are used to repay debt or preference shares outstanding at the end of the reporting period;

(c) the redemption of ordinary shares outstanding;

(d) the conversion or exercise of potential ordinary shares outstanding at the end of the reporting period into ordinary shares;

(e) an issue of options, warrants, or convertible instruments; and

(f) the achievement of conditions that would result in the issue of contingently issuable shares.

Earnings per share amounts are not adjusted for such transactions occurring after the reporting period because such transactions do not affect the amount of capital used to produce profit or loss for the period.

72 Financial instruments and other contracts generating potential ordinary shares may incorporate terms and conditions that affect the measurement of basic and diluted earnings per share. These terms and conditions may determine whether any potential ordinary shares are dilutive and, if so, the effect on the weighted average number of shares outstanding and any consequent adjustments to profit or loss attributable to ordinary equity holders. The disclosure of the terms and conditions of such financial instruments and other contracts is encouraged, if not otherwise required (see AASB 7 *Financial Instruments: Disclosures*).

73 If an entity discloses, in addition to basic and diluted earnings per share, amounts per share using a reported component of the statement of comprehensive income other than one required by this Standard, such amounts shall be calculated using the weighted average number of ordinary shares determined in accordance with this Standard. Basic and diluted amounts per share relating to such a component shall be disclosed with equal prominence and presented in the notes. An entity shall indicate the basis on which the numerator(s) is (are) determined, including whether amounts per share are before tax or after tax. If a component of the statement of comprehensive income is used that is not reported as a line item in the statement of comprehensive income, a reconciliation shall be provided between the component used and a line item that is reported in the statement of comprehensive income.

73A Paragraph 73 applies also to an entity that discloses, in addition to basic and diluted earnings per share, amounts per share using a reported item of profit or loss, other than one required by this Standard.

Effective date

74 An entity shall apply this Standard for annual periods beginning on or after 1 January 2018. Earlier application is encouraged for periods beginning after 24 July 2014 but before 1 January 2018. If an entity applies the Standard for a period beginning before 1 January 2018, it shall disclose that fact.

74A–74D [Deleted by the AASB]

74E AASB 2014-7 *Amendments to Australian Accounting Standards arising from AASB 9 (December 2014)*, issued in December 2014, amended paragraph 34 in the previous version of this Standard. An entity shall apply that amendment when it applies AASB 9.

Withdrawal of other pronouncements

75–76 [Deleted by the AASB]

Commencement of the legislative instrument

Aus76.1   For legal purposes, this legislative instrument commences on 31 December 2017.

Withdrawal of AASB pronouncements

Aus76.2   This Standard repeals AASB 133 *Earnings per Share* issued in July 2004. Despite the repeal, after the time this Standard starts to apply under section 334 of the Corporations Act (either generally or in relation to an individual entity), the repealed Standard continues to apply in relation to any period ending before that time as if the repeal had not occurred.

[Note: When this Standard applies under section 334 of the Corporations Act (either generally or in relation to an individual entity), it supersedes the application of the repealed Standard.]

APPENDIX A
APPLICATION GUIDANCE

This appendix is an integral part of the Standard.

Profit or loss attributable to the parent entity

A1   For the purpose of calculating earnings per share based on the consolidated financial statements, profit or loss attributable to the parent entity refers to profit or loss of the consolidated entity after adjusting for non-controlling interests.

Rights issues

A2   The issue of ordinary shares at the time of exercise or conversion of potential ordinary shares does not usually give rise to a bonus element. This is because the potential ordinary shares are usually issued for fair value, resulting in a proportionate change in the resources available to the entity. In a rights issue, however, the exercise price is often less than the fair value of the shares. Therefore, as noted in paragraph 27(b), such a rights issue includes a bonus element. If a rights issue is offered to all existing shareholders, the number of ordinary shares to be used in calculating basic and diluted earnings per share for all periods before the rights issue is the number of ordinary shares outstanding before the issue, multiplied by the following factor:

$$\frac{\text{Fair value per share immediately before the exercise of rights}}{\text{Theoretical ex-rights fair value per hare}}$$

The theoretical ex-rights fair value per share is calculated by adding the aggregate fair value of the shares immediately before the exercise of the rights to the proceeds from the exercise of the rights, and dividing by the number of shares outstanding after the exercise of the rights. Where the rights are to be publicly traded separately from the shares before the exercise date, fair value is measured at the close of the last day on which the shares are traded together with the rights.

Control number

A3   To illustrate the application of the control number notion described in paragraphs 42 and 43, assume that an entity has profit from continuing operations attributable to the parent entity of CU4,800,[1] a loss from discontinued operations attributable to the parent entity of (CU7,200), a loss attributable to the parent entity of (CU2,400), and 2,000 ordinary shares and 400 potential ordinary shares outstanding. The entity's basic earnings per share is CU2.40 for continuing operations, (CU3.60) for discontinued operations and (CU1.20) for the loss. The 400 potential ordinary shares are included in the diluted earnings per share calculation because the resulting CU2.00 earnings per share for continuing operations is dilutive, assuming no profit or loss impact of those 400 potential ordinary shares. Because profit from continuing operations attributable to the parent entity is the control number, the entity also includes those 400 potential ordinary shares in the calculation of the other earnings per share amounts, even though the resulting earnings per share amounts are antidilutive to their comparable basic earnings per share amounts, ie the loss per share is less [(CU3.00) per share for the loss from discontinued operations and (CU1.00) per share for the loss].

Average market price of ordinary shares

A4   For the purpose of calculating diluted earnings per share, the average market price of ordinary shares assumed to be issued is calculated on the basis of the average market price of the ordinary shares during the period. Theoretically, every market transaction for an entity's ordinary shares could be included in the determination of the average market price. As a practical matter, however, a simple average of weekly or monthly prices is usually adequate.

A5   Generally, closing market prices are adequate for calculating the average market price. When prices fluctuate widely, however, an average of the high and low prices usually produces a more representative price. The method used to calculate the average market price is used consistently unless it is no longer representative because of changed conditions. For example, an entity that uses closing market prices to calculate the average market price for several years of relatively stable prices might change to an average of high and low prices if prices start fluctuating greatly and the closing market prices no longer produce a representative average price.

Options, warrants and their equivalents

A6   Options or warrants to purchase convertible instruments are assumed to be exercised to purchase the convertible instrument whenever the average prices of both the convertible instrument and the ordinary shares obtainable upon conversion are above the exercise price of the options or warrants. However, exercise is not assumed unless conversion of similar outstanding convertible instruments, if any, is also assumed.

A7   Options or warrants may permit or require the tendering of debt or other instruments of the entity (or its parent or a subsidiary) in payment of all or a portion of the exercise price. In the calculation of diluted earnings per share, those options or warrants have a dilutive effect if (a) the average market price of the related ordinary shares for the period exceeds the exercise price or (b) the selling price of the instrument to be tendered is below that at which the instrument may be tendered under the option or warrant agreement and the resulting discount establishes an effective exercise price below the market price of the ordinary shares obtainable upon exercise. In the calculation of diluted earnings per share, those options or warrants are assumed to be exercised and the debt or other instruments are assumed to be tendered. If tendering cash is more advantageous to the option or warrant holder and the contract permits tendering cash, tendering of cash is assumed. Interest (net of tax) on any debt assumed to be tendered is added back as an adjustment to the numerator.

---

1   In this guidance, monetary amounts are denominated in 'currency units (CU)'.

A8   Similar treatment is given to preference shares that have similar provisions or to other instruments that have conversion options that permit the investor to pay cash for a more favourable conversion rate.

A9   The underlying terms of certain options or warrants may require the proceeds received from the exercise of those instruments to be applied to redeem debt or other instruments of the entity (or its parent or a subsidiary). In the calculation of diluted earnings per share, those options or warrants are assumed to be exercised and the proceeds applied to purchase the debt at its average market price rather than to purchase ordinary shares. However, the excess proceeds received from the assumed exercise over the amount used for the assumed purchase of debt are considered (ie assumed to be used to buy back ordinary shares) in the diluted earnings per share calculation. Interest (net of tax) on any debt assumed to be purchased is added back as an adjustment to the numerator.

Written put options

A10   To illustrate the application of paragraph 63, assume that an entity has outstanding 120 written put options on its ordinary shares with an exercise price of CU35. The average market price of its ordinary shares for the period is CU28. In calculating diluted earnings per share, the entity assumes that it issued 150 shares at CU28 per share at the beginning of the period to satisfy its put obligation of CU4,200. The difference between the 150 ordinary shares issued and the 120 ordinary shares received from satisfying the put option (30 incremental ordinary shares) is added to the denominator in calculating diluted earnings per share.

Instruments of subsidiaries, joint ventures or associates

A11   Potential ordinary shares of a subsidiary, joint venture or associate convertible into either ordinary shares of the subsidiary, joint venture or associate, or ordinary shares of the parent or investors with joint control of, or significant influence (the reporting entity) over, the investee are included in the calculation of diluted earnings per share as follows:

(a)   instruments issued by a subsidiary, joint venture or associate that enable their holders to obtain ordinary shares of the subsidiary, joint venture or associate are included in calculating the diluted earnings per share data of the subsidiary, joint venture or associate. Those earnings per share are then included in the reporting entity's earnings per share calculations based on the reporting entity's holding of the instruments of the subsidiary, joint venture or associate.

(b)   instruments of a subsidiary, joint venture or associate that are convertible into the reporting entity's ordinary shares are considered among the potential ordinary shares of the reporting entity for the purpose of calculating diluted earnings per share. Likewise, options or warrants issued by a subsidiary, joint venture or associate to purchase ordinary shares of the reporting entity are considered among the potential ordinary shares of the reporting entity in the calculation of consolidated diluted earnings per share.

A12   For the purpose of determining the earnings per share effect of instruments issued by a reporting entity that are convertible into ordinary shares of a subsidiary, joint venture or associate, the instruments are assumed to be converted and the numerator (profit or loss attributable to ordinary equity holders of the parent entity) adjusted as necessary in accordance with paragraph 33. In addition to those adjustments, the numerator is adjusted for any change in the profit or loss recorded by the reporting entity (such as dividend income or equity method income) that is attributable to the increase in the number of ordinary shares of the subsidiary, joint venture or associate outstanding as a result of the assumed conversion. The denominator of the diluted earnings per share calculation is not affected because the number of ordinary shares of the reporting entity outstanding would not change upon assumed conversion.

Participating equity instruments and two-class ordinary shares

A13 The equity of some entities includes:

(a) instruments that participate in dividends with ordinary shares according to a predetermined formula (for example, two for one) with, at times, an upper limit on the extent of participation (for example, up to, but not beyond, a specified amount per share).

(b) a class of ordinary shares with a different dividend rate from that of another class of ordinary shares but without prior or senior rights.

A14 For the purpose of calculating diluted earnings per share, conversion is assumed for those instruments described in paragraph A13 that are convertible into ordinary shares if the effect is dilutive. For those instruments that are not convertible into a class of ordinary shares, profit or loss for the period is allocated to the different classes of shares and participating equity instruments in accordance with their dividend rights or other rights to participate in undistributed earnings. To calculate basic and diluted earnings per share:

(a) profit or loss attributable to ordinary equity holders of the parent entity is adjusted (a profit reduced and a loss increased) by the amount of dividends declared in the period for each class of shares and by the contractual amount of dividends (or interest on participating bonds) that must be paid for the period (for example, unpaid cumulative dividends).

(b) the remaining profit or loss is allocated to ordinary shares and participating equity instruments to the extent that each instrument shares in earnings as if all of the profit or loss for the period had been distributed. The total profit or loss allocated to each class of equity instrument is determined by adding together the amount allocated for dividends and the amount allocated for a participation feature.

(c) the total amount of profit or loss allocated to each class of equity instrument is divided by the number of outstanding instruments to which the earnings are allocated to determine the earnings per share for the instrument.

For the calculation of diluted earnings per share, all potential ordinary shares assumed to have been issued are included in outstanding ordinary shares.

Partly paid shares

A15 Where ordinary shares are issued but not fully paid, they are treated in the calculation of basic earnings per share as a fraction of an ordinary share to the extent that they were entitled to participate in dividends during the period relative to a fully paid ordinary share.

A16 To the extent that partly paid shares are not entitled to participate in dividends during the period they are treated as the equivalent of warrants or options in the calculation of diluted earnings per share. The unpaid balance is assumed to represent proceeds used to purchase ordinary shares. The number of shares included in diluted earnings per share is the difference between the number of shares subscribed and the number of shares assumed to be purchased.

APPENDIX C
AUSTRALIAN REDUCED DISCLOSURE REQUIREMENTS

This appendix is an integral part of the Standard.

AusC1   Paragraphs 3–73A and the Application Guidance Appendix do not apply to entities preparing general purpose financial statements under Australian Accounting Standards – Reduced Disclosure Requirements and are identified in this Standard by shading of the relevant text. This Standard applies to relevant Tier 1 entities preparing general purpose financial statements in accordance with Australian Accounting Standards and to relevant Tier 2 entities that elect to comply with this Standard. Entities applying Australian Accounting Standards – Reduced Disclosure Requirements may elect to comply with some or all of the excluded requirements.

ILLUSTRATIVE EXAMPLES

CONTENTS

ILLUSTRATIVE EXAMPLES

These examples accompany, but are not part of, AASB 133.

Example 1 Increasing rate preference shares

Reference: AASB 133, paragraphs 12 and 15

Entity D issued non-convertible, non-redeemable class A cumulative preference shares of CU100 par value on 1 January 20X1. The class A preference shares are entitled to a cumulative annual dividend of CU7 per share starting in 20X4.

At the time of issue, the market rate dividend yield on the class A preference shares was 7 per cent a year. Thus, Entity D could have expected to receive proceeds of approximately CU100 per class A preference share if the dividend rate of CU7 per share had been in effect at the date of issue.

In consideration of the dividend payment terms, however, the class A preference shares were issued at CU81.63 per share, ie at a discount of CU18.37 per share. The issue price can be calculated by taking the present value of CU100, discounted at 7 per cent over a three-year period.

Because the shares are classified as equity, the original issue discount is amortised to retained earnings using the effective interest method and treated as a preference dividend for earnings per share purposes. To calculate basic earnings per share, the following imputed dividend per class A preference share is deducted to determine the profit or loss attributable to ordinary equity holders of the parent entity:

Year	Carrying amount of class A preference shares 1 January	Imputed[(a)] dividend	Carrying[(b)] amount of class A preference shares 31 December	Dividend paid
	CU	CU	CU	CU
20X1	81.63	5.71	87.34	–
20X2	87.34	6.12	93.46	–
20X3	93.46	6.54	100.00	–
Thereafter:	100.00	7.00	107.00	(7.00)

(a) at 7%

(b) This is before dividend payment.

Example 2 Weighted average number of ordinary shares

Reference: AASB 133, paragraphs 19–21

		Shares issued	Treasury[(a)] shares	Shares outstanding
1 January 20X1	Balance at beginning of year	2,000	300	1,700
31 May 20X1	Issue of new shares for cash	800	–	2,500
1 December 20X1	Purchase of treasury shares for cash	–	250	2,250
31 December 20X1	Balance at year-end	2,800	550	2,250

Calculation of weighted average:

$(1,700 \times {}^5/_{12}) + (2,500 \times {}^6/_{12}) + (2,250 \times {}^1/_{12}) = 2,146$ shares or

$(1,700 \times {}^{12}/_{12}) + (800 \times {}^7/_{12}) - (250 \times {}^1/_{12}) = 2,146$ shares

(a) Treasury shares are equity instruments reacquired and held by the issuing entity itself or by its subsidiaries.

Example 3 Bonus issue

Reference: AASB 133, paragraphs 26, 27(a) and 28

Profit attributable to ordinary equity holders of the parent entity 20X0	CU180
Profit attributable to ordinary equity holders of the parent entity 20X1	CU600
Ordinary shares outstanding until 30 September 20X1	200
Bonus issue 1 October 20X1	2 ordinary shares for each ordinary share outstanding at 30 September 20X1
	$200 \times 2 = 400$

Basic earnings per share 20X1 $\dfrac{\text{CU600}}{(200 + 400)} = \text{CU1.00}$

Basic earnings per share 20X0 $\dfrac{\text{CU180}}{(200 + 400)} = \text{CU0.30}$

Because the bonus issue was without consideration, it is treated as if it had occurred before the beginning of 20X0, the earliest period presented.

Example 4 Rights issue

Reference: AASB 133, paragraphs 26, 27(b) and A2

		20X0	20X1	20X2
Profit attributable to ordinary equity holders of the parent entity		CU1,100	CU1,500	CU1,800

Shares outstanding before rights issue	500 shares
Rights issue	One new share for each five outstanding shares
	(100 new shares total)
	Exercise price: CU5.00
	Date of rights issue: 1 January 20X1
	Last date to exercise rights: 1 March 20X1
Market price of one ordinary share immediately before exercise on 1 March 20X1:	CU11.00
Reporting date	31 December

Calculation of theoretical ex-rights value per share

$$\frac{\text{Fair value of all outstanding shares before the exercise of rights} + \text{total amount received from exercise of rights}}{\text{Number of shares outstanding before exercise} + \text{number of shares issued in the exercise}}$$

$$\frac{(\text{CU11.00} \times 500 \text{ shares}) + (\text{CU5.00} \times 100 \text{ shares})}{500 \text{ shares} + 100 \text{ shares}}$$

Theoretical ex-rights value per share = CU10.00

Calculation of adjustment factor

$$\frac{\text{Fair value per share before exercise of rights}}{\text{Theoretical ex-rights value per share}} \quad \frac{\text{CU11.00}}{\text{CU10.00}} = 1.10$$

Calculation of basic earnings per share

		20X0	20X1	20X2
20X0 basic EPS as originally reported:	CU1,100 ÷ 500 shares	CU2.20		
20X0 basic EPS restated for rights issue:	$\dfrac{\text{CU1,100}}{(500 \text{ shares} \times 1.1)}$	CU2.00		
20X1 basic EPS including effects of rights issue:	$\dfrac{\text{CU1,500}}{(500 \times 1.1 \times {}^2/_{12}) + (600 \times {}^{10}/_{12})}$		CU2.54	
20X2 basic EPS:	CU1,800 ÷ 600 shares			CU3.00

Example 5 Effects of share options on diluted earnings per share

Reference: AASB 133, paragraphs 45–47

Profit attributable to ordinary equity holders of the parent entity for year 20X1	CU1,200,000
Weighted average number of ordinary shares outstanding during year 20X1	500,000 shares
Average market price of one ordinary share during year 20X1	CU20.00
Weighted average number of shares under option during year 20X1	100,000 shares
Exercise price for shares under option during year 20X1	CU15.00

Calculation of earnings per share

	Earnings	Shares	Per share
Profit attributable to ordinary equity holders of the parent entity for year 20X1	CU1,200,000		
Weighted average shares outstanding during year 20X1		500,000	
Basic earnings per share			CU2.40
Weighted average number of shares under option		100,000	
Weighted average number of shares that would have been issued at average market price: $(100,000 \times CU15.00) \div CU20.00$	(a)	(75,000)	
Diluted earnings per share	CU1,200,000	525,000	CU2.29

(a) Earnings have not increased because the total number of shares has increased only by the number of shares (25,000) deemed to have been issued for no consideration (see paragraph 46(b) of the Standard).

Example 5A Determining the exercise price of employee share options

Weighted average number of unvested share options per employee	1,000
Weighted average amount per employee to be recognised over the remainder of the vesting period for employee services to be rendered as consideration for the share options, determined in accordance with AASB 2 *Share-based Payment*	CU1,200
Cash exercise price of unvested share options	CU15

Calculation of adjusted exercise price

Fair value of services yet to be rendered per employee:	CU1,200
Fair value of services yet to be rendered per option: $(CU1,200 \div 1,000)$	CU1.20
Total exercise price of share options: $(CU15.00 + CU1.20)$	CU16.20

Example 6 Convertible bonds[2]

Reference: AASB 133, paragraphs 33, 34, 36 and 49

Profit attributable to ordinary equity holders of the parent entity	CU1,004
Ordinary shares outstanding	1,000
Basic earnings per share	CU1.00
Convertible bonds	100
Each block of 10 bonds is convertible into three ordinary shares	
Interest expense for the current year relating to the liability component of the convertible bonds	CU10
Current and deferred tax relating to that interest expense	CU4

Note: the interest expense includes amortisation of the discount arising on initial recognition of the liability component (see AASB 132 Financial Instruments: Presentation*).*

Adjusted profit attributable to ordinary equity holders of the parent entity	CU1,004 + CU10 – CU4 = CU1,010
Number of ordinary shares resulting from conversion of bonds	30
Number of ordinary shares used to calculate diluted earnings per share	1,000 + 30 = 1,030
Diluted earnings per share	$\dfrac{CU1,010}{1,030}$ = CU0.98

Example 7 Contingently issuable shares

Reference: AASB 133, paragraphs 19, 24, 36, 37, 41–43 and 52

Ordinary shares outstanding during 20X1	1,000,000 (there were no options, warrants or convertible instruments outstanding during the period)

An agreement related to a recent business combination provides for the issue of additional ordinary shares based on the following conditions:

	5,000 additional ordinary shares for each new retail site opened during 20X1
	1,000 additional ordinary shares for each CU1,000 of consolidated profit in excess of CU2,000,000 for the year ended 31 December 20X1
Retail sites opened during the year:	one on 1 May 20X1
	one on 1 September 20X1
Consolidated year-to-date profit attributable to ordinary equity holders of the parent entity:	CU1,100,000 as of 31 March 20X1
	CU2,300,000 as of 30 June 20X1
	CU1,900,000 as of 30 September 20X1 (including a CU450,000 loss from a discontinued operation)
	CU2,900,000 as of 31 December 20X1

---

2   This example does not illustrate the classification of the components of convertible financial instruments as liabilities and equity or the classification of related interest and dividends as expenses and equity as required by AASB 132.

Basic earnings per share

	First quarter	Second quarter	Third quarter	Fourth quarter	Full year
Numerator (CU)	1,100,000	1,200,000	(400,000)	1,000,000	2,900,000
Denominator:					
Ordinary shares outstanding	1,000,000	1,000,000	1,000,000	1,000,000	1,000,000
Retail site contingency	–	3,333[a]	6,667[b]	10,000	5,000[c]
Earnings contingency[d]	–	–	–	–	–
Total shares	1,000,000	1,003,333	1,006,667	1,010,000	1,005,000
Basic earnings per share (CU)	1.10	1.20	(0.40)	0.99	2.89

(a) $5,000 \text{ shares} \times \frac{2}{3}$

(b) $5,000 \text{ shares} + (5,000 \text{ shares} \times \frac{1}{3})$

(c) $(5,000 \text{ shares} \times \frac{8}{12}) + (5,000 \text{ shares} \times \frac{4}{12})$

(d) The earnings contingency has no effect on basic earnings per share because it is not certain that the condition is satisfied until the end of the contingency period. The effect is negligible for the fourth-quarter and full-year calculations because it is not certain that the condition is met until the last day of the period.

Diluted earnings per share

	First quarter	Second quarter	Third quarter	Fourth quarter	Full year
Numerator (CU)	1,100,000	1,200,000	(400,000)	1,000,000	2,900,000
Denominator:					
Ordinary shares outstanding	1,000,000	1,000,000	1,000,000	1,000,000	1,000,000
Retail site contingency	–	5,000	10,000	10,000	10,000
Earnings contingency	–[a]	300,000[b]	–[c]	900,000[d]	900,000[d]
Total shares	1,000,000	1,305,000	1,010,000	1,910,000	1,910,000
Diluted earnings per share (CU)	1.10	0.92	(0.40)[e]	0.52	1.52

(a) Company A does not have year-to-date profit exceeding CU2,000,000 at 31 March 20X1. The Standard does not permit projecting future earnings levels and including the related contingent shares.

(b) [(CU2,300,000 – CU2,000,000) ÷ 1,000] × 1,000 shares = 300,000 shares.

(c) Year-to-date profit is less than CU2,000,000.

(d) [(CU2,900,000 – CU2,000,000) ÷ 1,000] × 1,000 shares = 900,000 shares.

(e) Because the loss during the third quarter is attributable to a loss from a discontinued operation, the antidilution rules do not apply. The control number (ie profit or loss from, continuing operations attributable to the equity holders of the parent entity) is positive. Accordingly, the effect of potential ordinary shares is included in the calculation of diluted earnings per share.

Example 8 Convertible bonds settled in shares or cash at the issuer's option

Reference: AASB 133, paragraphs 31–33, 36, 58 and 59

An entity issues 2,000 convertible bonds at the beginning of Year 1. The bonds have a three-year term, and are issued at par with a face value of CU1,000 per bond, giving total proceeds of CU2,000,000. Interest is payable annually in arrears at a nominal annual interest rate of

6 per cent. Each bond is convertible at any time up to maturity into 250 ordinary shares. The entity has an option to settle the principal amount of the convertible bonds in ordinary shares or in cash.

When the bonds are issued, the prevailing market interest rate for similar debt without a conversion option is 9 per cent. At the issue date, the market price of one ordinary share is CU3. Income tax is ignored.

Profit attributable to ordinary equity holders of the parent entity Year 1	CU1,000,000
Ordinary shares outstanding	1,200,000
Convertible bonds outstanding	2,000
Allocation of proceeds of the bond issue:	
Liability component	CU1,848,122[(a)]
Equity component	CU151,878
	CU2,000,000

(a) This represents the present value of the principal and interest discounted at 9% – CU2,000,000 payable at the end of three years; CU120,000 payable annually in arrears for three years.

The liability and equity components would be determined in accordance with AASB 132 *Financial Instruments: Presentation*. These amounts are recognised as the initial carrying amounts of the liability and equity components. The amount assigned to the issuer conversion option equity element is an addition to equity and is not adjusted.

Basic earnings per share Year 1:

$$\frac{CU1,000,000}{1,200,000} = CU0.83 \text{ per ordinary share}$$

Diluted earnings per share Year 1:

It is presumed that the issuer will settle the contract by the issue of ordinary shares. The dilutive effect is therefore calculated in accordance with paragraph 59 of the Standard.

$$\frac{CU1,000,000 + CU166,331^{(a)}}{1,200,000 + 500,000^{(b)}} = CU0.69 \text{ per ordinary share}$$

(a) Profit is adjusted for the accretion of CU166,331 (CU1,848,122 × 9%) of the liability because of the passage of time.
(b) 500,000 ordinary shares = 250 ordinary shares × 2,000 convertible bonds

Example 9 Calculation of weighted average number of shares: determining the order in which to include dilutive instruments[3]

Primary reference: AASB 133, paragraph 44

Secondary reference: AASB 133, paragraphs 10, 12, 19, 31–33, 36, 41–47, 49 and 50

---

3   This example does not illustrate the classification of the components of convertible financial instruments as liabilities and equity or the classification of related interest and dividends as expenses and equity as required by AASB 132.

Earnings	CU
Profit from continuing operations attributable to the parent entity	16,400,000
Less dividends on preference shares	(6,400,000)
Profit from continuing operations attributable to ordinary equity holders of the parent entity	10,000,000
Loss from discontinued operations attributable to the parent entity	(4,000,000)
Profit attributable to ordinary equity holders of the parent entity	6,000,000
Ordinary shares outstanding	2,000,000
Average market price of one ordinary share during year	CU75.00

Potential ordinary shares

Options	100,000 with exercise price of CU60
Convertible preference shares	800,000 shares with a par value of CU100 entitled to a cumulative dividend of CU8 per share. Each preference share is convertible to two ordinary shares.
5% convertible bonds	Nominal amount CU100,000,000. Each CU1,000 bond is convertible to 20 ordinary shares. There is no amortisation of premium or discount affecting the determination of interest expense.
Tax rate	40%

Increase in earnings attributable to ordinary equity holders on conversion of potential ordinary shares

		Increase in earnings	Increase in number of ordinary shares	Earnings per incremental share
		CU		CU
Options				
Increase in earnings		Nil		
Incremental shares issued for no consideration	100,000 × (CU75 – CU60) ÷ CU75		20,000	Nil
Convertible preference shares				
Increase in profit	CU800,000 × 100 × 0.08	6,400,000		
Incremental shares	2 × 800,000		1,600,000	4.00
5% convertible bonds				
Increase in profit	CU100,000,000 × 0.05 ×(1 – 0.40)	3,000,000		
Incremental shares	100,000 × 20		2,000,000	1.50

The order in which to include the dilutive instruments is therefore:

1   Options
2   5% convertible bonds
3   Convertible preference shares

Calculation of diluted earnings per share

	Profit from continuing operations attributable to ordinary equity holders of the parent entity (control number)	Ordinary shares	Per share	
	CU		CU	
As reported	10,000,000	2,000,000	5.00	
Options	–	20,000		
	10,000,000	2,020,000	4.95	Dilutive
5% convertible bonds	3,000,000	2,000,000		
	13,000,000	4,020,000	3.23	Dilutive
Convertible preference shares	6,400,000	1,600,000		
	19,400,000	5,620,000	3.45	Antidilutive

Because diluted earnings per share is increased when taking the convertible preference shares into account (from CU3.23 to CU3.45), the convertible preference shares are antidilutive and are ignored in the calculation of diluted earnings per share. Therefore, diluted earnings per share for profit from continuing operations is CU3.23:

	Basic EPS	Diluted EPS
	CU	CU
Profit from continuing operations attributable to ordinary equity holders of the parent entity	5.00	3.23
Loss from discontinued operations attributable to ordinary equity holders of the parent entity	(2.00)[a]	(0.99)[b]
Profit attributable to ordinary equity holders of the parent entity	3.00[c]	2.24[d]

(a) (CU4,000,000) ÷ 2,000,000 = (CU2.00)
(b) (CU4,000,000) ÷ 4,020,000 = (CU0.99)
(c) CU6,000,000 ÷ 2,000,000 = CU3.00
(d) (CU6,000,000 + CU3,000,000) ÷ 4,020,000 = CU2.24

Example 10 Instruments of a subsidiary: calculation of basic and diluted earnings per share[4]

Reference: AASB 133, paragraphs 40, A11 and A12

Parent:

Profit attributable to ordinary equity holders of the parent entity	CU12,000 (excluding any earnings of, or dividends paid by, the subsidiary)
Ordinary shares outstanding	10,000
Instruments of subsidiary owned by the parent	800 ordinary shares
	30 warrants exercisable to purchase ordinary shares of subsidiary
	300 convertible preference shares

---

4   This example does not illustrate the classification of the components of convertible financial instruments as liabilities and equity or the classification of related interest and dividends as expenses and equity as required by AASB 132.

Subsidiary:

Profit	CU5,400
Ordinary shares outstanding	1,000
Warrants	150, exercisable to purchase ordinary shares of the subsidiary
Exercise price	CU10
Average market price of one ordinary share	CU20
Convertible preference shares	400, each convertible into one ordinary share
Dividends on preference shares	CU1 per share

No inter-company eliminations or adjustments were necessary except for dividends.

For the purposes of this illustration, income taxes have been ignored.

Subsidiary's earnings per share

Basic EPS   CU5.00 calculated:

$$\frac{CU5,400^{(a)} + CU400^{(b)}}{1,000^{(c)}}$$

Diluted EPS   CU3.66 calculated:

$$\frac{CU5,400^{(d)}}{(1,000 + 75^{(e)} + 400^{(f)})}$$

(a) Subsidiary's profit attributable to ordinary equity holders.
(b) Dividends paid by subsidiary on convertible preference shares.
(c) Subsidiary's ordinary shares outstanding.
(d) Subsidiary's profit attributable to ordinary equity holders (CU5,000) increased by CU400 preference dividends for the purpose of calculating diluted earnings per share.
(e) Incremental shares from warrants, calculated: $[(CU20 - CU10) \div CU20] \times 150$.
(f) Subsidiary's ordinary shares assumed outstanding from conversion of convertible preference shares, calculated: 400 convertible preference shares × conversion factor of 1.

Consolidated earnings per share

Basic EPS   CU1.63 calculated:

$$\frac{CU12,000^{(a)} + CU4,300^{(b)}}{10,000^{(c)}}$$

Diluted EPS   CU1.61 calculated:

$$\frac{CU12,000 + CU2,928^{(d)} + CU55^{(e)} + CU1,098^{(f)}}{10,000}$$

(a) Parent's profit attributable to ordinary equity holders of the parent entity
(b) Portion of subsidiary's profit to be included in consolidated basic earnings per share, calculated: $(800 \times CU5.00) + (300 \times CU1.00)$.
(c) Parent's ordinary shares outstanding.
(d) Parent's proportionate interest in subsidiary's earnings attributable to ordinary shares, calculated: $(800 \div 1,000) \times (1,000 \text{ shares} \times CU3.66 \text{ per share})$.
(e) Parent's proportionate interest in subsidiary's earnings attributable to warrants, calculated: $(30 \div 150) \times (75 \text{ incremental shares} \times CU3.66 \text{ per share})$.
(f) Parent's proportionate interest in subsidiary's earnings attributable to convertible preference shares, calculated: $(300 \div 400) \times (400 \text{ shares from conversion} \times CU3.66 \text{ per share})$.

Example 11 Participating equity instruments and two-class ordinary shares[5]

Reference: AASB 133, paragraphs A13 and A14

Profit attributable to equity holders of the parent entity	CU100,000
Ordinary shares outstanding	10,000

5   This example does not illustrate the classification of the components of convertible financial instruments as liabilities and equity or the classification of related interest and dividends as expenses and equity as required by AASB 132.

AASB

Non-convertible preference shares	6,000
Non-cumulative annual dividend on preference shares (before any dividend is paid on ordinary shares)	CU5.50 per share

After ordinary shares have been paid a dividend of CU2.10 per share, the preference shares participate in any additional dividends on a 20:80 ratio with ordinary shares (ie after preference and ordinary shares have been paid dividends of CU5.50 and CU2.10 per share, respectively, preference shares participate in any additional dividends at a rate of one-fourth of the amount paid to ordinary shares on a per-share basis).

Dividends on preference shares paid	CU33,000	(CU5.50 per share)
Dividends on ordinary shares paid	CU21,000	(CU2.10 per share)

Basic earnings per share is calculated as follows:

	CU	CU
Profit attributable to equity holders of the parent entity		100,000
Less dividends paid:		
Preference	33,000	
Ordinary	21,000	
		(54,000)
Undistributed earnings		46,000

Allocation of undistributed earnings:

Allocation per ordinary share = A

Allocation per preference share = B; B = $^1/_4$ A

$$(A \times 10,000) + (^1/_4 \times A \times 6,000) = CU46,000$$
$$A = CU46,000 \div (10,000 + 1,500)$$
$$A = CU4.00$$
$$B = ^1/_4 \, A$$
$$B = CU1.00$$

Basic per share amounts:

	Preference shares	Ordinary shares
Distributed earnings	CU5.50	CU2.10
Undistributed earnings	CU1.00	CU4.00
Totals	CU6.50	CU6.10

Example 12 Calculation and presentation of basic and diluted earnings per share (comprehensive example)[6]

This example illustrates the quarterly and annual calculations of basic and diluted earnings per share in the year 20X1 for Company A, which has a complex capital structure. The control number is profit or loss from continuing operations attributable to the parent entity. Other facts assumed are as follows:

---

6   This example does not illustrate the classification of the components of convertible financial instruments as liabilities and equity or the classification of related interest and dividends as expenses and equity as required by AASB 132.

Average market price of ordinary shares: The average market prices of ordinary shares for the calendar year 20X1 were as follows:

First quarter	CU49
Second quarter	CU60
Third quarter	CU67
Fourth quarter	CU67

The average market price of ordinary shares from 1 July to 1 September 20X1 was CU65.

Ordinary shares: The number of ordinary shares outstanding at the beginning of 20X1 was 5,000,000. On 1 March 20X1, 200,000 ordinary shares were issued for cash.

Convertible bonds: In the last quarter of 20X0, 5 per cent convertible bonds with a principal amount of CU12,000,000 due in 20 years were sold for cash at CU1,000 (par). Interest is payable twice a year, on 1 November and 1 May. Each CU1,000 bond is convertible into 40 ordinary shares. No bonds were converted in 20X0. The entire issue was converted on 1 April 20X1 because the issue was called by Company A.

Convertible preference shares: In the second quarter of 20X0, 800,000 convertible preference shares were issued for assets in a purchase transaction. The quarterly dividend on each convertible preference share is CU0.05, payable at the end of the quarter for shares outstanding at that date. Each share is convertible into one ordinary share. Holders of 600,000 convertible preference shares converted their preference shares into ordinary shares on 1 June 20X1.

Warrants: Warrants to buy 600,000 ordinary shares at CU55 per share for a period of five years were issued on 1 January 20X1. All outstanding warrants were exercised on 1 September 20X1.

Options: Options to buy 1,500,000 ordinary shares at CU75 per share for a period of 10 years were issued on 1 July 20X1. No options were exercised during 20X1 because the exercise price of the options exceeded the market price of the ordinary shares.

Tax rate: The tax rate was 40 per cent for 20X1.

20X1	Profit (loss) from continuing operations attributable to the parent entity[a]	Profit (loss) attributable to the parent entity
	CU	CU
First quarter	5,000,000	5,000,000
Second quarter	6,500,000	6,500,000
Third quarter	1,000,000	(1,000,000)[b]
Fourth quarter	(700,000)	(700,000)
Full year	11,800,000	9,800,000

(a) This is the control number (before adjusting for preference dividends).
(b) Company A had a CU2,000,000 loss (net of tax) from discontinued operations in the third quarter.

First Quarter 20X1

Basic EPS calculation	CU
Profit from continuing operations attributable to the parent entity	5,000,000
Less: preference share dividends	(40,000)[a]
Profit attributable to ordinary equity holders of the parent entity	4,960,000

Dates	Shares outstanding	Fraction of period	Weighted-average shares
1 January–28 February	5,000,000	$^2/_3$	3,333,333
Issue of ordinary shares on 1 March			
1 March–31 March	200,000	$^1/_3$	1,733,333
Weighted-average shares	5,200,000		5,066,666
Basic EPS			**CU0.98**

Diluted EPS calculation

Profit attributable to ordinary equity holders of the parent entity			CU4,960,000
Plus: profit impact of assumed conversions			
Preference share dividends	CU40,000	(a)	
Interest on 5% convertible bonds	CU90,000	(b)	
Effect of assumed conversions			CU130,000
Profit attributable to ordinary equity holders of the parent entity including assumed conversions			CU5,090,000
Weighted-average shares			5,066,666
Plus: incremental shares from assumed conversions			
Warrants		0 (c)	
Convertible preference shares		800,000	
5% convertible bonds		480,000	
Dilutive potential ordinary shares			1,280,000
Adjusted weighted-average shares			6,346,666
Diluted EPS			**CU0.80**

(a) 800,000 shares × CU0.05
(b) (CU12,000,000 × 5%) ÷ 4; less taxes at 40%
(c) The warrants were not assumed to be exercised because they were antidilutive in the period
(CU55 [exercise price] > CU49 [average price]).

Second Quarter 20X1

Basic EPS calculation

	CU
Profit from continuing operations attributable to the parent entity	6,500,000
Less: preference share dividends	(10,000)(a)
Profit attributable to ordinary equity holders of the parent entity	6,490,000

Dates	Shares outstanding	Fraction of period	Weighted-average shares
1 April	5,200,000		
Conversion of 5% bonds on 1 April	480,000		
1 April–31 May	5,680,000	$^2/_3$	3,786,666
Conversion of preference shares 1 June	600,000		
1 June–30 June	6,280,000	$^1/_3$	2,093,333
Weighted-average shares			5,880,000
Basic EPS			**CU1.10**

Diluted EPS calculation

Profit attributable to ordinary equity holders of the parent entity		CU6,490,000
Plus: profit impact of assumed conversions		
Preference share dividends	CU10,000[a]	
Effect of assumed conversions		CU10,000
Profit attributable to ordinary equity holders of the parent entity including assumed conversions		CU6,500,000
Weighted-average shares		5,880,000
Plus: incremental shares from assumed conversions		
Warrants	50,000[b]	
Convertible preference shares	600,000[c]	
Dilutive potential ordinary shares		650,000
Adjusted weighted-average shares		6,530,000
Diluted EPS		***CU1.00***

(a) 200,000 shares × CU0.05
(b) CU55 × 600,000 = CU33,000,000; CU33,000,000 ÷ CU60 = 550,000; 600,000 – 550,000 = 50,000 shares OR [(CU60 – CU55) ÷ CU60] × 600,000 shares = 50,000 shares
(c) (800,000 shares × $\frac{2}{3}$) + (200,000 shares × $\frac{1}{3}$)

Third Quarter 20X1

Basic EPS calculation

	CU
Profit from continuing operations attributable to the parent entity	1,000,000
Less: preference share dividends	(10,000)
Profit from continuing operations attributable to ordinary equity holders of the parent entity	990,000
Loss from discontinued operations attributable to the parent entity	(2,000,000)
Loss attributable to ordinary equity holders of the parent entity	(1,010,000)

Dates	Shares outstanding	Fraction of period	Weighted-average shares
1 July–31 August	6,280,000	$^2/_3$	4,186,666
Exercise of warrants on 1 September	600,000		
1 September–30 September	6,880,000	$^1/_3$	2,293,333
Weighted-average shares			6,480,000

Basic EPS	
Profit from continuing operations	***CU0.15***
Loss from discontinued operations	***(CU0.31)***
Loss	***(CU0.16)***

Diluted EPS calculation

Profit from continuing operations attributable to ordinary equity holders of the parent entity	CU990,000
Plus: profit impact of assumed conversions	
Preference share dividends	CU10,000

Effect of assumed conversions	CU10,000
Profit from continuing operations attributable to ordinary equity holders of the parent entity including assumed conversions	CU1,000,000
Loss from discontinued operations attributable to the parent entity	(CU2,000,000)
Loss attributable to ordinary equity holders of the parent entity including assumed conversions	(CU1,000,000)

Weighted-average shares		6,480,000
Plus: incremental shares from assumed conversions		
Warrants	61,538[a]	
Convertible preference shares	200,000	
Dilutive potential ordinary shares		261,538
Adjusted weighted-average shares		6,741,538

Diluted EPS	
Profit from continuing operations	***CU0.15***
Loss from discontinued operations	***(CU0.30)***
Loss	***(CU0.15)***

(a) [(CU65 − CU55) ÷ CU65] × 600,000 = 92,308 shares; 92,308 × 2/3 = 61,538 shares

Note: The incremental shares from assumed conversions are included in calculating the diluted per-share amounts for the loss from discontinued operations and loss even though they are antidilutive. This is because the control number (profit from continuing operations attributable to ordinary equity holders of the parent entity, adjusted for preference dividends) was positive (ie profit, rather than loss).

Fourth Quarter 20X1

Basic EPS calculation	CU
Loss from continuing operations attributable to the parent entity	(700,000)
Add: preference share dividends	(10,000)
Loss attributable to ordinary equity holders of the parent entity	(710,000)

Dates	*Shares outstanding*	*Fraction of period*	*Weighted-average shares*
1 October–31 December	6,880,000	3/3	6,880,000
Weighted-average shares			6,880,000

Basic and diluted EPS	
Loss attributable to ordinary equity holders of the parent entity	***(CU0.10)***

Note: The incremental shares from assumed conversions are not included in calculating the diluted per-share amounts because the control number (loss from continuing operations attributable to ordinary equity holders of the parent entity adjusted for preference dividends) was negative (ie a loss, rather than profit).

Full Year 20X1

Basic EPS calculation	CU
Profit from continuing operations attributable to the parent entity	11,800,000
Less: preference share dividends	(70,000)
Profit from continuing operations attributable to ordinary equity holders of the parent entity	11,730,000
Loss from discontinued operations attributable to the parent entity	(2,000,000)
Profit attributable to ordinary equity holders of the parent entity	9,730,000

Dates	Shares outstanding	Fraction of period	Weighted-average shares
1 January–28 February	5,000,000	$^2/_{12}$	833,333
Issue of ordinary shares on 1 March	200,000		
1 March–31 March	5,200,000	$^1/_{12}$	433,333
Conversion of 5% bonds on 1 April	480,000		
1 April–31 May	5,680,000	$^2/_{12}$	946,667
Conversion of preference shares on 1 June	600,000		
1 June–31 August	6,280,000	$^3/_{12}$	1,570,000
Exercise of warrants on 1 September	600,000		
1 September–31 December	6,880,000	$^4/_{12}$	2,293,333
Weighted-average shares			6,076,667

Basic EPS

Profit from continuing operations	***CU1.93***
Loss from discontinued operations	***(CU0.33)***
Profit	***CU1.60***

Diluted EPS calculation

Profit from continuing operations attributable to ordinary equity holders of the parent entity		CU11,730,000
Plus: profit impact of assumed conversions		
Preference share dividends	CU70,000	
Interest on 5% convertible bonds	CU90,000[(a)]	
Effect of assumed conversions		CU160,000
Profit from continuing operations attributable to ordinary equity holders of the parent entity including assumed conversions		CU11,890,000
Loss from discontinued operations attributable to the parent entity		(CU2,000,000)
Profit attributable to ordinary equity holders of the parent entity including assumed conversions		CU9,890,000
Weighted-average shares		6,076,667
Plus: incremental shares from assumed conversions		
Warrants	14,880[(b)]	
Convertible preference shares	450,000[(c)]	
5% convertible bonds	120,000[(d)]	
Dilutive potential ordinary shares		584,880
Adjusted weighted-average shares		6,661,547

Diluted EPS

Profit from continuing operations	***CU1.78***
Loss from discontinued operations	***(CU0.30)***
Profit	***CU1.48***

(a) (CU12,000,000 × 5%) ÷ 4; less taxes at 40%.

(b) [(CU57.125* − CU55) ÷ CU57.125] × 600,000 = 22,320 shares; 22,320 × $\frac{8}{12}$ = 14,880 shares*.

   The average market price from 1 January 20X1 to 1 September 20X1.

(c) (800,000 shares × $\frac{5}{12}$) + (200,000 shares × $\frac{7}{12}$).

(d) 480,000 shares × $\frac{3}{12}$.

AASB

The following illustrates how Company A might present its earnings per share data in its statement of comprehensive income. Note that the amounts per share for the loss from discontinued operations are not required to be presented in the statement of comprehensive income.

For the year ended 20X1

	CU
Earnings per ordinary share	
Profit from continuing operations	1.93
Loss from discontinued operations	(0.33)
Profit	1.60
Diluted earnings per ordinary share	
Profit from continuing operations	1.78
Loss from discontinued operations	(0.30)
Profit	1.48

The following table includes the quarterly and annual earnings per share data for Company A. The purpose of this table is to illustrate that the sum of the four quarters' earnings per share data will not necessarily equal the annual earnings per share data. The Standard does not require disclosure of this information.

	First quarter	Second quarter	Third quarter	Fourth quarter	Full year
	CU	CU	CU	CU	CU
Basic EPS					
Profit (loss) from continuing operations	0.98	1.10	0.15	(0.10)	1.93
Loss from discontinued operations	–	–	(0.31)	–	(0.33)
Profit (loss)	0.98	1.10	(0.16)	(0.10)	1.60
Diluted EPS					
Profit (loss) from continuing operations	0.80	1.00	0.15	(0.10)	1.78
Loss from discontinued operations	–	–	(0.30)	–	(0.30)
Profit (loss)	0.80	1.00	(0.15)	(0.10)	1.48

COMPILATION DETAILS

Accounting Standard AASB 133 *Earnings per Share* as amended

Compilation details are not part of AASB 133.

This compiled Standard applies to annual periods beginning on or after 1 January 2018. It takes into account amendments up to and including 11 November 2015 and was prepared on 7 December 2015 by the staff of the Australian Accounting Standards Board (AASB).

This compilation is not a separate Accounting Standard made by the AASB. Instead, it is a representation of AASB 133 (August 2015) as amended by other Accounting Standards, which are listed in the Table below.

Table of Standards

Standard	Date made	FRLI identifier	Commence-ment date	Application date(*annual periods ... on or after ...*)	Application, saving or transitional provisions
AASB 133	7 Aug 2015	F2015L01616	31 Dec 2017	*(beginning)* 1 Jan 2018	see (a) below
AASB 2015-9	11 Nov 2015	F2015L01832	31 Dec 2015	*(beginning)* 1 Jan 2018	see (b) below

(a) Entities may elect to apply this Standard to annual periods beginning after 24 July 2014 but before 1 January 2018.

(b) This Standard applies to annual periods beginning on or after 1 January 2016 and may be applied to annual periods beginning before 1 January 2016. The amendments to AASB 133 (August 2015) apply to annual periods beginning on or after 1 January 2018.

Table of amendments

Paragraph affected	How affected	By ... [paragraph]
2	added	AASB 2015-9 [10]

DELETED IAS 33 TEXT

Deleted IAS 33 text is not part of AASB 133.

74A IAS 1 (as revised in 2007) amended the terminology used throughout IFRSs. In addition it added paragraphs 4A, 67A, 68A and 73A. An entity shall apply those amendments for annual periods beginning on or after 1 January 2009. If an entity applies IAS 1 (revised 2007) for an earlier period, the amendments shall be applied for that earlier period.

74B IFRS 10 and IFRS 11 *Joint Arrangements*, issued in May 2011, amended paragraphs 4, 40 and A11. An entity shall apply those amendments when it applies IFRS 10 and IFRS 11.

74C IFRS 13, issued in May 2011, amended paragraphs 8, 47A and A2. An entity shall apply those amendments when it applies IFRS 13.

74D *Presentation of Items of Other Comprehensive Income* (Amendments to IAS 1), issued in June 2011, amended paragraphs 4A, 67A, 68A and 73A. An entity shall apply those amendments when it applies IAS 1 as amended in June 2011.

75 This Standard supersedes IAS 33 *Earnings Per Share* (issued in 1997).

76 This Standard supersedes SIC-24 *Earnings Per Share—Financial Instruments and Other Contracts that May Be Settled in Shares*.

AASB 134

Interim Financial Reporting

(Compiled December 2017)

For-profit (FP) entities

This compiled Standard applies to annual periods beginning on or after 1 January 2018 but before 1 January 2019. Earlier application is permitted for annual periods beginning on or after 1 January 2014 but before 1 January 2018. It incorporates relevant amendments made up to and including 12 December 2017.

Not-for-profit (NPF) entities – early application only

This compiled Standard does not apply mandatorily to NFP entities. However, early application is permitted for annual reporting periods beginning on or after 1 January 2014 but before 1 January 2019.

Prepared on 20 May 2018 by the staff of the Australian Accounting Standards Board.

Compilation no. 2

Compilation date: 31 December 2017

This note is not part of Accounting Standard AASB 134.

The following unincorporated amendments are not included in this compiled Standard.

- AASB 16 *Leases* — Appendix D sets out the amendments to other Standards that are a consequence of the AASB issuing this Standard. It is applicable from 1 January 2019. Earlier application is permitted, but entities must apply AASB 15 *Revenue from Contracts with Customers* before applying this Standard.

- AASB 2016-7 *Amendments to Australian Accounting Standards — Deferral of AASB 15 for Not-for-Profit Entities*. This Standard defers the consequential amendments that were originally set out in AASB 2014-5 *Amendments to Australian Accounting Standards arising from AASB 15*, by restating the effective date of the amendments set out in AASB 2015-8 *Amendments to Australian Accounting Standards* for not-for-profit entities. This Standard defers the application of AASB 15 to 1 January 2019. Earlier application is permitted provided AASB 1058 is also applied to the same period.

Entities early-adopting any amendments with later application dates will need to refer to the amending Standards that have not yet been incorporated into compilations. The abovementioned unincorporated amendments may be located on the AASB website at www.aasb.gov.au or on the Federal Register of Legislation website at www.legislation.gov.au.

CONTENTS

COMPARISON WITH IAS 34

ACCOUNTING STANDARD

AASB 134 *INTERIM FINANCIAL REPORTING*

from paragraph

APPENDIX
A. AUSTRALIAN REDUCED DISCLOSURE REQUIREMENTS

ILLUSTRATIVE EXAMPLES
A. ILLUSTRATION OF PERIODS REQUIRED TO BE PRESENTED
B. EXAMPLES OF APPLYING THE RECOGNITION AND MEASUREMENT
   PRINCIPLES
C. EXAMPLES OF THE USE OF ESTIMATES

COMPILATION DETAILS
DELETED IAS 34 TEXT

BASIS FOR CONCLUSIONS ON IAS 34 (available on the AASB website)

Australian Accounting Standard AASB 134 *Interim Financial Reporting* (as amended) is set out in paragraphs 1 – Aus57.2 and Appendix A. All the paragraphs have equal authority. Paragraphs in **bold type** state the main principles. AASB 134 is to be read in the context of other Australian Accounting Standards, including AASB 1048 *Interpretation of Standards*, which identifies the Australian Accounting Interpretations, and AASB 1057 *Application of Australian Accounting Standards*. In the absence of explicit guidance, AASB 108 *Accounting Policies, Changes in Accounting Estimates and Errors* provides a basis for selecting and applying accounting policies.

COMPARISON WITH IAS 34

AASB 134 *Interim Financial Reporting* as amended incorporates IAS 34 *Interim Financial Reporting* as issued and amended by the International Accounting Standards Board (IASB). Australian-specific paragraphs (which are not included in IAS 34) are identified with the prefix "Aus" or "RDR". Paragraphs that apply only to not-for-profit entities begin by identifying their limited applicability.

AASB

Tier 1

For-profit entities complying with AASB 134 also comply with IAS 34.

Not-for-profit entities' compliance with IAS 34 will depend on whether any "Aus" paragraphs that specifically apply to not-for-profit entities provide additional guidance or contain applicable requirements that are inconsistent with IAS 34.

Tier 2

Entities preparing general purpose financial statements under Australian Accounting Standards – Reduced Disclosure Requirements (Tier 2) will not be in compliance with IFRSs.

AASB 1053 *Application of Tiers of Australian Accounting Standards* explains the two tiers of reporting requirements.

ACCOUNTING STANDARD AASB 134

The Australian Accounting Standards Board made Accounting Standard AASB 134 *Interim Financial Reporting* under section 334 of the *Corporations Act 2001* on 7 August 2015.

This compiled version of AASB 134 applies to annual periods beginning on or after 1 January 2018 but before 1 January 2019 for for-profit entities. It incorporates relevant amendments contained in other AASB Standards made by the AASB up to and including 12 December 2017 (see Compilation Details).

ACCOUNTING STANDARD AASB 134
INTERIM FINANCIAL REPORTING

Objective

The objective of this Standard is to prescribe the minimum content of an interim financial report and to prescribe the principles for recognition and measurement in complete or condensed financial statements for an interim period. Timely and reliable interim financial reporting improves the ability of investors, creditors, and others to understand an entity's capacity to generate earnings and cash flows and its financial condition and liquidity.

Scope

1   This Standard does not mandate which entities should be required to publish interim financial reports, how frequently, or how soon after the end of an interim period. However, governments, securities regulators, stock exchanges, and accountancy bodies often require entities whose debt or equity securities are publicly traded to publish interim financial reports. This Standard applies if an entity is required or elects to publish an interim financial report in accordance with Australian Accounting Standards. The International Accounting Standards Committee[1] encourages publicly traded entities to provide interim financial reports that conform to the recognition, measurement, and disclosure principles set out in this Standard. Specifically, publicly traded entities are encouraged:

   (a)   to provide interim financial reports at least as of the end of the first half of their financial year; and

   (b)   to make their interim financial reports available not later than 60 days after the end of the interim period.

---

1   The International Accounting Standards Committee was succeeded by the International Accounting Standards Board, which began operations in 2001.

Aus1.1 Under the Corporations Act, disclosing entities are required to prepare half-year financial reports. Disclosing entities may also voluntarily prepare other general purpose interim financial reports. This Standard prescribes the form and content of general purpose interim financial reports, including half-year financial reports prepared by disclosing entities.

Aus1.2 Interim financial reports that are intended to be special purpose financial reports do not fall within the scope of this Standard. However, interim financial reports that are purported to be special purpose financial reports but have the characteristics of general purpose financial statements fall within the scope of this Standard. Interim financial reports that are widely available but lack the characteristics of general purpose financial statements are not regarded as general purpose financial statements. An example is selected interim summary financial information, such as turnover and profit, voluntarily released by some entities. In some cases, professional judgement is needed to determine whether particular interim financial reports are general purpose financial statements.

2 Each financial report, annual or interim, is evaluated on its own for conformity to Australian Accounting Standards. The fact that an entity may not have provided interim financial reports during a particular financial year or may have provided interim financial reports that do not comply with this Standard does not prevent the entity's annual financial statements from conforming to Australian Accounting Standards if they otherwise do so.

Aus2.1 **This Standard does not apply to interim financial reports for the General Government Sector of each government.**

3 If an entity's interim financial report is described as complying with Australian Accounting Standards, it must comply with all of the requirements of this Standard. Paragraph 19 requires certain disclosures in that regard.

Definitions

4 **The following terms are used in this Standard with the meanings specified:**

Interim period **is a financial reporting period shorter than a full financial year.**

Interim financial report **means a financial report containing either a complete set of financial statements (as described in AASB 101** *Presentation of Financial Statements***) or a set of condensed financial statements (as described in this Standard) for an interim period.**

Content of an interim financial report

5 AASB 101 defines a complete set of financial statements as including the following components:

(a) a statement of financial position as at the end of the period;

(b) a statement of profit or loss and other comprehensive income for the period;

(c) a statement of changes in equity for the period;

(d) a statement of cash flows for the period;

(e) notes, comprising significant accounting policies and other explanatory information;

(ea) comparative information in respect of the preceding period as specified in paragraphs 38 and 38A of AASB 101; and

(f) a statement of financial position as at the beginning of the preceding period when an entity applies an accounting policy retrospectively or makes a retrospective restatement of items in its financial statements, or when it reclassifies items in its financial statements in accordance with paragraphs 40A–40D of AASB 101.

An entity may use titles for the statements other than those used in this Standard. For example, an entity may use the title 'statement of comprehensive income' instead of 'statement of profit or loss and other comprehensive income'.

6   In the interest of timeliness and cost considerations and to avoid repetition of information previously reported, an entity may be required to or may elect to provide less information at interim dates as compared with its annual financial statements. This Standard defines the minimum content of an interim financial report as including condensed financial statements and selected explanatory notes. The interim financial report is intended to provide an update on the latest complete set of annual financial statements. Accordingly, it focuses on new activities, events, and circumstances and does not duplicate information previously reported.

7   Nothing in this Standard is intended to prohibit or discourage an entity from publishing a complete set of financial statements (as described in AASB 101) in its interim financial report, rather than condensed financial statements and selected explanatory notes. Nor does this Standard prohibit or discourage an entity from including in condensed interim financial statements more than the minimum line items or selected explanatory notes as set out in this Standard. The recognition and measurement guidance in this Standard applies also to complete financial statements for an interim period, and such statements would include all of the disclosures required by this Standard (particularly the selected note disclosures in paragraph 16A) as well as those required by other Australian Accounting Standards.

Minimum components of an interim financial report

8   An interim financial report shall include, at a minimum, the following components:

   (a)   a condensed statement of financial position;

   (b)   a condensed statement or condensed statements of profit or loss and other comprehensive income;

   (c)   a condensed statement of changes in equity;

   (d)   a condensed statement of cash flows; and

   (e)   selected explanatory notes.

8A   If an entity presents items of profit or loss in a separate statement as described in paragraph 10A of AASB 101, it presents interim condensed information from that statement.

Form and content of interim financial statements

9   If an entity publishes a complete set of financial statements in its interim financial report, the form and content of those statements shall conform to the requirements of AASB 101 for a complete set of financial statements.

10   If an entity publishes a set of condensed financial statements in its interim financial report, those condensed statements shall include, at a minimum, each of the headings and subtotals that were included in its most recent annual financial statements and the selected explanatory notes as required by this Standard. Additional line items or notes shall be included if their omission would make the condensed interim financial statements misleading.

11   In the statement that presents the components of profit or loss for an interim period, an entity shall present basic and diluted earnings per share for that period when the entity is within the scope of AASB 133 *Earnings per Share*.[2]

11A   If an entity presents items of profit or loss in a separate statement as described in paragraph 10A of AASB 101, it presents basic and diluted earnings per share in that statement.

---

2   This paragraph was amended by AASB 2008-5 *Amendments to Australian Accounting Standards arising from the Annual Improvements Project* issued in July 2008 to clarify the scope of AASB 134.

12   AASB 101 provides guidance on the structure of financial statements. The Implementation Guidance for IAS 1 illustrates ways in which the statement of financial position, statement of comprehensive income and statement of changes in equity may be presented.

13   [Deleted]

14   An interim financial report is prepared on a consolidated basis if the entity's most recent annual financial statements were consolidated statements. The parent's separate financial statements are not consistent or comparable with the consolidated statements in the most recent annual financial report. If an entity's annual financial report included the parent's separate financial statements in addition to consolidated financial statements, this Standard neither requires nor prohibits the inclusion of the parent's separate statements in the entity's interim financial report.

Significant events and transactions

15   An entity shall include in its interim financial report an explanation of events and transactions that are significant to an understanding of the changes in financial position and performance of the entity since the end of the last annual reporting period. Information disclosed in relation to those events and transactions shall update the relevant information presented in the most recent annual financial report.

15A   A user of an entity's interim financial report will have access to the most recent annual financial report of that entity. Therefore, it is unnecessary for the notes to an interim financial report to provide relatively insignificant updates to the information that was reported in the notes in the most recent annual financial report.

15B   The following is a list of events and transactions for which disclosures would be required if they are significant: the list is not exhaustive.

     (a)   the write-down of inventories to net realisable value and the reversal of such a write-down;

     (b)   recognition of a loss from the impairment of financial assets, property, plant and equipment, intangible assets, assets arising from contracts with customers, or other assets, and the reversal of such an impairment loss;

     (c)   the reversal of any provisions for the costs of restructuring;

     (d)   acquisitions and disposals of items of property, plant and equipment;

     (e)   commitments for the purchase of property, plant and equipment;

     (f)   litigation settlements;

     (g)   corrections of prior period errors;

     (h)   changes in the business or economic circumstances that affect the fair value of the entity's financial assets and financial liabilities, whether those assets or liabilities are recognised at fair value or amortised cost;

     (i)   any loan default or breach of a loan agreement that has not been remedied on or before the end of the reporting period;

     (j)   related party transactions;

     (k)   transfers between levels of the fair value hierarchy used in measuring the fair value of financial instruments;

     (l)   changes in the classification of financial assets as a result of a change in the purpose or use of those assets; and

     (m)   changes in contingent liabilities or contingent assets.

15C   Individual Australian Accounting Standards provide guidance regarding disclosure requirements for many of the items listed in paragraph 15B. When an event or transaction is significant to an understanding of the changes in an entity's financial position or performance since the last annual reporting period, its interim financial

seasonal are encouraged to consider reporting such information in addition to the information called for in the preceding paragraph.

22   Part A of the illustrative examples accompanying this Standard illustrates the periods required to be presented by an entity that reports half-yearly and an entity that reports quarterly.

Materiality

23   **In deciding how to recognise, measure, classify, or disclose an item for interim financial reporting purposes, materiality shall be assessed in relation to the interim period financial data. In making assessments of materiality, it shall be recognised that interim measurements may rely on estimates to a greater extent than measurements of annual financial data.**

24   AASB 101 and AASB 108 *Accounting Policies, Changes in Accounting Estimates and Errors* define an item as material if its omission or misstatement could influence the economic decisions of users of the financial statements. AASB 101 requires separate disclosure of material items, including (for example) discontinued operations, and AASB 108 requires disclosure of changes in accounting estimates, errors, and changes in accounting policies. The two Standards do not contain quantified guidance as to materiality.

25   While judgement is always required in assessing materiality, this Standard bases the recognition and disclosure decision on data for the interim period by itself for reasons of understandability of the interim figures. Thus, for example, unusual items, changes in accounting policies or estimates, and errors are recognised and disclosed on the basis of materiality in relation to interim period data to avoid misleading inferences that might result from non-disclosure. The overriding goal is to ensure that an interim financial report includes all information that is relevant to understanding an entity's financial position and performance during the interim period.

Disclosure in annual financial statements

26   **If an estimate of an amount reported in an interim period is changed significantly during the final interim period of the financial year but a separate financial report is not published for that final interim period, the nature and amount of that change in estimate shall be disclosed in a note to the annual financial statements for that financial year.**

27   AASB 108 requires disclosure of the nature and (if practicable) the amount of a change in estimate that either has a material effect in the current period or is expected to have a material effect in subsequent periods. Paragraph 16A(d) of this Standard requires similar disclosure in an interim financial report. Examples include changes in estimate in the final interim period relating to inventory write-downs, restructurings, or impairment losses that were reported in an earlier interim period of the financial year. The disclosure required by the preceding paragraph is consistent with the AASB 108 requirement and is intended to be narrow in scope—relating only to the change in estimate. An entity is not required to include additional interim period financial information in its annual financial statements.

Recognition and measurement

Same accounting policies as annual

28   **An entity shall apply the same accounting policies in its interim financial statements as are applied in its annual financial statements, except for accounting policy changes made after the date of the most recent annual financial statements that are to be reflected in the next annual financial statements. However, the frequency of an entity's reporting (annual, half-yearly, or quarterly) shall**

not affect the measurement of its annual results. To achieve that objective, measurements for interim reporting purposes shall be made on a year-to-date basis.

29   Requiring that an entity apply the same accounting policies in its interim financial statements as in its annual statements may seem to suggest that interim period measurements are made as if each interim period stands alone as an independent reporting period. However, by providing that the frequency of an entity's reporting shall not affect the measurement of its annual results, paragraph 28 acknowledges that an interim period is a part of a larger financial year. Year-to-date measurements may involve changes in estimates of amounts reported in prior interim periods of the current financial year. But the principles for recognising assets, liabilities, income, and expenses for interim periods are the same as in annual financial statements.

30   To illustrate:

   (a)   the principles for recognising and measuring losses from inventory write-downs, restructurings, or impairments in an interim period are the same as those that an entity would follow if it prepared only annual financial statements. However, if such items are recognised and measured in one interim period and the estimate changes in a subsequent interim period of that financial year, the original estimate is changed in the subsequent interim period either by accrual of an additional amount of loss or by reversal of the previously recognised amount;

   (b)   a cost that does not meet the definition of an asset at the end of an interim period is not deferred in the statement of financial position either to await future information as to whether it has met the definition of an asset or to smooth earnings over interim periods within a financial year; and

   (c)   income tax expense is recognised in each interim period based on the best estimate of the weighted average annual income tax rate expected for the full financial year. Amounts accrued for income tax expense in one interim period may have to be adjusted in a subsequent interim period of that financial year if the estimate of the annual income tax rate changes.

31   Under the *Framework for the Preparation and Presentation of Financial Statements* (the *Framework*) (as identified in AASB 1048 *Interpretation of Standards*),[3] recognition is the 'process of incorporating in the balance sheet or income statement an item that meets the definition of an element and satisfies the criteria for recognition'. The definitions of assets, liabilities, income, and expenses are fundamental to recognition, at the end of both annual and interim financial reporting periods.

32   For assets, the same tests of future economic benefits apply at interim dates and at the end of an entity's financial year. Costs that, by their nature, would not qualify as assets at financial year-end would not qualify at interim dates either. Similarly, a liability at the end of an interim reporting period must represent an existing obligation at that date, just as it must at the end of an annual reporting period.

33   An essential characteristic of income (revenue) and expenses is that the related inflows and outflows of assets and liabilities have already taken place. If those inflows or outflows have taken place, the related revenue and expense are recognised; otherwise they are not recognised. The *Framework* says that 'expenses are recognised in the income statement when a decrease in future economic benefits related to a decrease in an asset or an increase of a liability has arisen that can be measured reliably... [The] *Framework* does not allow the recognition of items in the balance sheet which do not meet the definition of assets or liabilities.'

34   In measuring the assets, liabilities, income, expenses, and cash flows reported in its financial statements, an entity that reports only annually is able to take into account information that becomes available throughout the financial year. Its measurements are, in effect, on a year-to-date basis.

---

3   In December 2013 the AASB amended the *Framework for the Preparation and Presentation of Financial Statements*.

35   An entity that reports half-yearly uses information available by mid-year or shortly
        thereafter in making the measurements in its financial statements for the first six-
        month period and information available by year-end or shortly thereafter for the
        twelve-month period. The twelve-month measurements will reflect possible changes
        in estimates of amounts reported for the first six-month period. The amounts reported
        in the interim financial report for the first six-month period are not retrospectively
        adjusted. Paragraphs 16A(d) and 26 require, however, that the nature and amount of
        any significant changes in estimates be disclosed.

36   An entity that reports more frequently than half-yearly measures income and expenses
        on a year-to-date basis for each interim period using information available when each
        set of financial statements is being prepared. Amounts of income and expenses reported
        in the current interim period will reflect any changes in estimates of amounts reported
        in prior interim periods of the financial year. The amounts reported in prior interim
        periods are not retrospectively adjusted. Paragraphs 16A(d) and 26 require, however,
        that the nature and amount of any significant changes in estimates be disclosed.

Revenues received seasonally, cyclically, or occasionally

37   **Revenues that are received seasonally, cyclically, or occasionally within a financial
        year shall not be anticipated or deferred as of an interim date if anticipation or
        deferral would not be appropriate at the end of the entity's financial year.**

38   Examples include dividend revenue, royalties, and government grants. Additionally,
        some entities consistently earn more revenues in certain interim periods of a financial
        year than in other interim periods, for example, seasonal revenues of retailers. Such
        revenues are recognised when they occur.

Costs incurred unevenly during the financial year

39   **Costs that are incurred unevenly during an entity's financial year shall be
        anticipated or deferred for interim reporting purposes if, and only if, it is also
        appropriate to anticipate or defer that type of cost at the end of the financial year.**

Applying the recognition and measurement principles

40   Part B of the illustrative examples accompanying this Standard provides examples of
        applying the general recognition and measurement principles set out in paragraphs
        28–39.

Use of estimates

41   **The measurement procedures to be followed in an interim financial report shall be
        designed to ensure that the resulting information is reliable and that all material
        financial information that is relevant to an understanding of the financial position
        or performance of the entity is appropriately disclosed. While measurements in
        both annual and interim financial reports are often based on reasonable estimates,
        the preparation of interim financial reports generally will require a greater use
        of estimation methods than annual financial reports.**

42   Part C of the illustrative examples accompanying this Standard provides examples of
        the use of estimates in interim periods.

Restatement of previously reported interim periods

43   **A change in accounting policy, other than one for which the transition is specified
        by a new Australian Accounting Standard, shall be reflected by:**

        **(a)   restating the financial statements of prior interim periods of the current
                 financial year and the comparable interim periods of any prior financial
                 years that will be restated in the annual financial statements in accordance
                 with AASB 108; or**

(b)   when it is impracticable to determine the cumulative effect at the beginning of the financial year of applying a new accounting policy to all prior periods, adjusting the financial statements of prior interim periods of the current financial year, and comparable interim periods of prior financial years to apply the new accounting policy prospectively from the earliest date practicable.

44   One objective of the preceding principle is to ensure that a single accounting policy is applied to a particular class of transactions throughout an entire financial year. Under AASB 108, a change in accounting policy is reflected by retrospective application, with restatement of prior period financial data as far back as is practicable. However, if the cumulative amount of the adjustment relating to prior financial years is impracticable to determine, then under AASB 108 the new policy is applied prospectively from the earliest date practicable. The effect of the principle in paragraph 43 is to require that within the current financial year any change in accounting policy is applied either retrospectively or, if that is not practicable, prospectively, from no later than the beginning of the financial year.

45   To allow accounting changes to be reflected as of an interim date within the financial year would allow two differing accounting policies to be applied to a particular class of transactions within a single financial year. The result would be interim allocation difficulties, obscured operating results, and complicated analysis and understandability of interim period information.

Effective date

46   This Standard becomes operative for financial statements covering periods beginning on or after 1 January 2018. Earlier application is encouraged for periods beginning on or after 1 January 2014 but before 1 January 2018.

47–54   [Deleted by the AASB]

55   AASB 2014-5 *Amendments to Australian Accounting Standards arising from AASB 15*, issued in December 2014, amended paragraphs 15B and 16A in the previous version of this Standard. An entity shall apply those amendments when it applies AASB 15.

56   AASB 2015-1 *Amendments to Australian Accounting Standards – Annual Improvements to Australian Accounting Standards 2012–2014 Cycle*, issued in January 2015, amended paragraph 16A in the previous version of this Standard. An entity shall apply that amendment retrospectively in accordance with AASB 108 *Accounting Policies, Changes in Accounting Estimates and Errors* for annual periods beginning on or after 1 January 2016. Earlier application is permitted. If an entity applies the amendment for an earlier period it shall disclose that fact.

57   AASB 2015-2 *Amendments to Australian Accounting Standards – Disclosure Initiative: Amendments to AASB 101*, issued in January 2015, amended paragraph 5 in the previous version of this Standard. An entity shall apply that amendment for annual periods beginning on or after 1 January 2016. Earlier application of that amendment is permitted.

Commencement of the legislative instrument

Aus57.1   For legal purposes, this legislative instrument commences on 31 December 2016.

Withdrawal of AASB pronouncements

Aus57.2   This Standard repeals AASB 134 *Interim Financial Reporting* issued in July 2004. Despite the repeal, after the time this Standard starts to apply under section 334 of the Corporations Act (either generally or in relation to an individual entity), the repealed Standard continues to apply in relation to any period ending before that time as if the repeal had not occurred.

[Note: When this Standard applies under section 334 of the Corporations Act (either generally or in relation to an individual entity), it supersedes the application of the repealed Standard.]

APPENDIX A
AUSTRALIAN REDUCED DISCLOSURE REQUIREMENTS

This appendix is an integral part of the Standard.

AusA1   **The following do not apply to entities preparing general purpose financial statements under Australian Accounting Standards – Reduced Disclosure Requirements:**

    (a)   paragraphs 5(f), 16A(g), 19 and 21;

    (b)   in paragraph 16A(i), the sentence "In the case of ... required by AASB 3 *Business Combinations.*"; and

    (c)   in paragraph 16A(l), the text "115".

    Entities applying Australian Accounting Standards – Reduced Disclosure Requirements may elect to comply with some or all of these excluded requirements.

AusA2   The requirements that do not apply to entities preparing general purpose financial statements under Australian Accounting Standards – Reduced Disclosure Requirements are also identified in this Standard by shading of the relevant text.

AusA3   **The RDR paragraph in this Standard applies only to entities preparing general purpose financial statements under Australian Accounting Standards – Reduced Disclosure Requirements.**

RDR19.1   **If an entity's interim financial report is in compliance with this Standard as it applies to entities applying the Australian Accounting Standards – Reduced Disclosure Requirements, that fact shall be disclosed. An interim financial report shall not be described as complying with Australian Accounting Standards – Reduced Disclosure Requirements unless it complies with all of the requirements of Australian Accounting Standards – Reduced Disclosure Requirements.**

ILLUSTRATIVE EXAMPLES

These illustrative examples accompany, but are not part of, AASB 134.

A. Illustration of periods required to be presented

The following examples illustrate application of the principle in paragraph 20.

Entity publishes interim financial reports half-yearly

A1   The entity's financial year ends 31 December (calendar year). The entity will present the following financial statements (condensed or complete) in its half-yearly interim financial report as of 30 June 20X1:

Statement of financial position:		
At	30 June 20X1	31 December 20X0
Statement of comprehensive income:		
6 months ending	30 June 20X1	30 June 20X0
Statement of cash flows:		
6 months ending	30 June 20X1	30 June 20X0
Statement of changes in equity:		
6 months ending	30 June 20X1	30 June 20X0

Entity publishes interim financial reports quarterly

A2 The entity's financial year ends 31 December (calendar year). The entity will present the following financial statements (condensed or complete) in its quarterly interim financial report as of 30 June 20X1:

Statement of financial position:		
At	30 June 20X1	31 December 20X0
Statement of comprehensive income:		
6 months ending	30 June 20X1	30 June 20X0
3 months ending	30 June 20X1	30 June 20X0
Statement of cash flows:		
6 months ending	30 June 20X1	30 June 20X0
Statement of changes in equity:		
6 months ending	30 June 20X1	30 June 20X0

B. Examples of applying the recognition and measurement principles

The following are examples of applying the general recognition and measurement principles set out in paragraphs 28–39.

Employer payroll taxes and insurance contributions

B1 If employer payroll taxes or contributions to government-sponsored insurance funds are assessed on an annual basis, the employer's related expense is recognised in interim periods using an estimated average annual effective payroll tax or contribution rate, even though a large portion of the payments may be made early in the financial year. A common example is an employer payroll tax or insurance contribution that is imposed up to a certain maximum level of earnings per employee. For higher income employees, the maximum income is reached before the end of the financial year, and the employer makes no further payments through the end of the year.

Major planned periodic maintenance or overhaul

B2 The cost of a planned major periodic maintenance or overhaul or other seasonal expenditure that is expected to occur late in the year is not anticipated for interim reporting purposes unless an event has caused the entity to have a legal or constructive obligation. The mere intention or necessity to incur expenditure related to the future is not sufficient to give rise to an obligation.

Provisions

B3 A provision is recognised when an entity has no realistic alternative but to make a transfer of economic benefits as a result of an event that has created a legal or constructive obligation. The amount of the obligation is adjusted upward or downward, with a corresponding loss or gain recognised in profit or loss, if the entity's best estimate of the amount of the obligation changes.

AASB

B4   The Standard requires that an entity apply the same criteria for recognising and measuring a provision at an interim date as it would at the end of its financial year. The existence or non-existence of an obligation to transfer benefits is not a function of the length of the reporting period. It is a question of fact.

Year-end bonuses

B5   The nature of year-end bonuses varies widely. Some are earned simply by continued employment during a time period. Some bonuses are earned based on a monthly, quarterly, or annual measure of operating result. They may be purely discretionary, contractual, or based on years of historical precedent.

B6   A bonus is anticipated for interim reporting purposes if, and only if, (a) the bonus is a legal obligation or past practice would make the bonus a constructive obligation for which the entity has no realistic alternative but to make the payments, and (b) a reliable estimate of the obligation can be made. AASB 119 *Employee Benefits* provides guidance.

Contingent lease payments

B7   Contingent lease payments can be an example of a legal or constructive obligation that is recognised as a liability. If a lease provides for contingent payments based on the lessee achieving a certain level of annual sales, an obligation can arise in the interim periods of the financial year before the required annual level of sales has been achieved, if that required level of sales is expected to be achieved and the entity, therefore, has no realistic alternative but to make the future lease payment.

Intangible assets

B8   An entity will apply the definition and recognition criteria for an intangible asset in the same way in an interim period as in an annual period. Costs incurred before the recognition criteria for an intangible asset are met are recognised as an expense. Costs incurred after the specific point in time at which the criteria are met are recognised as part of the cost of an intangible asset. 'Deferring' costs as assets in an interim statement of financial position in the hope that the recognition criteria will be met later in the financial year is not justified.

Pensions

B9   Pension cost for an interim period is calculated on a year-to-date basis by using the actuarially determined pension cost rate at the end of the prior financial year, adjusted for significant market fluctuations since that time and for significant one-off events, such as plan amendments, curtailments and settlements.

Vacations, holidays, and other short-term compensated absences

B10   Accumulating paid absences are those that are carried forward and can be used in future periods if the current period's entitlement is not used in full. AASB 119 *Employee Benefits* requires that an entity measure the expected cost of and obligation for accumulating paid absences at the amount the entity expects to pay as a result of the unused entitlement that has accumulated at the end of the reporting period. That principle is also applied at the end of interim financial reporting periods. Conversely, an entity recognises no expense or liability for non-accumulating paid absences at the end of an interim reporting period, just as it recognises none at the end of an annual reporting period.

Other planned but irregularly occurring costs

B11   An entity's budget may include certain costs expected to be incurred irregularly during the financial year, such as charitable contributions and employee training costs. Those costs generally are discretionary even though they are planned and tend to recur from year to year. Recognising an obligation at the end of an interim financial reporting period for such costs that have not yet been incurred generally is not consistent with the definition of a liability.

Measuring interim income tax expense

B12   Interim period income tax expense is accrued using the tax rate that would be applicable to expected total annual earnings, that is, the estimated average annual effective income tax rate applied to the pre-tax income of the interim period.

B13   This is consistent with the basic concept set out in paragraph 28 that the same accounting recognition and measurement principles shall be applied in an interim financial report as are applied in annual financial statements. Income taxes are assessed on an annual basis. Interim period income tax expense is calculated by applying to an interim period's pre-tax income the tax rate that would be applicable to expected total annual earnings, that is, the estimated average annual effective income tax rate. That estimated average annual rate would reflect a blend of the progressive tax rate structure expected to be applicable to the full year's earnings including enacted or substantively enacted changes in the income tax rates scheduled to take effect later in the financial year. AASB 112 *Income Taxes* provides guidance on substantively enacted changes in tax rates. The estimated average annual income tax rate would be re-estimated on a year-to-date basis, consistent with paragraph 28 of the Standard. Paragraph 16A requires disclosure of a significant change in estimate.

B14   To the extent practicable, a separate estimated average annual effective income tax rate is determined for each taxing jurisdiction and applied individually to the interim period pre-tax income of each jurisdiction. Similarly, if different income tax rates apply to different categories of income (such as capital gains or income earned in particular industries), to the extent practicable a separate rate is applied to each individual category of interim period pre-tax income. While that degree of precision is desirable, it may not be achievable in all cases, and a weighted average of rates across jurisdictions or across categories of income is used if it is a reasonable approximation of the effect of using more specific rates.

B15   To illustrate the application of the foregoing principle, an entity reporting quarterly expects to earn 10,000 pre-tax each quarter and operates in a jurisdiction with a tax rate of 20 per cent on the first 20,000 of annual earnings and 30 per cent on all additional earnings. Actual earnings match expectations. The following table shows the amount of income tax expense that is reported in each quarter:

	1st Quarter	2nd Quarter	3rd Quarter	4th Quarter	Annual
Tax expense	2,500	2,500	2,500	2,500	10,000

10,000 of tax is expected to be payable for the full year on 40,000 of pre-tax income.

B16   As another illustration, an entity reports quarterly, earns 15,000 pre-tax profit in the first quarter but expects to incur losses of 5,000 in each of the three remaining quarters (thus having zero income for the year), and operates in a jurisdiction in which its estimated average annual income tax rate is expected to be 20 per cent. The following table shows the amount of income tax expense that is reported in each quarter:

	1st Quarter	2nd Quarter	3rd Quarter	4th Quarter	Annual
Tax expense	3,000	(1,000)	(1,000)	(1,000)	0

Difference in financial reporting year and tax year

B17   If the financial reporting year and the income tax year differ, income tax expense for the interim periods of that financial reporting year is measured using separate weighted average estimated effective tax rates for each of the income tax years applied to the portion of pre-tax income earned in each of those income tax years.

B18   To illustrate, an entity's financial reporting year ends 30 June and it reports quarterly. Its taxable year ends 31 December. For the financial year that begins 1 July, Year 1 and ends 30 June, Year 2, the entity earns 10,000 pre-tax each quarter. The estimated average annual income tax rate is 30 per cent in Year 1 and 40 per cent in Year 2.

	Quarter ending 30 Sept	Quarter ending 31 Dec	Quarter ending 31 Mar	Quarter ending 30 June	Year ending 30 June
	Year 1	Year 1	Year 2	Year 2	Year 2
Tax expense	3,000	3,000	4,000	4,000	14,000

Tax credits

B19 Some tax jurisdictions give taxpayers credits against the tax payable based on amounts of capital expenditures, exports, research and development expenditures, or other bases. Anticipated tax benefits of this type for the full year are generally reflected in computing the estimated annual effective income tax rate, because those credits are granted and calculated on an annual basis under most tax laws and regulations. On the other hand, tax benefits that relate to a one-off event are recognised in computing income tax expense in that interim period, in the same way that special tax rates applicable to particular categories of income are not blended into a single effective annual tax rate. Moreover, in some jurisdictions tax benefits or credits, including those related to capital expenditures and levels of exports, while reported on the income tax return, are more similar to a government grant and are recognised in the interim period in which they arise.

Tax loss and tax credit carrybacks and carryforwards

B20 The benefits of a tax loss carryback are reflected in the interim period in which the related tax loss occurs. AASB 112 provides that 'the benefit relating to a tax loss that can be carried back to recover current tax of a previous period shall be recognised as an asset'. A corresponding reduction of tax expense or increase of tax income is also recognised.

B21 AASB 112 provides that 'a deferred tax asset shall be recognised for the carryforward of unused tax losses and unused tax credits to the extent that it is probable that future taxable profit will be available against which the unused tax losses and unused tax credits can be utilised'. AASB 112 provides criteria for assessing the probability of taxable profit against which the unused tax losses and credits can be utilised. Those criteria are applied at the end of each interim period and, if they are met, the effect of the tax loss carryforward is reflected in the computation of the estimated average annual effective income tax rate.

B22 To illustrate, an entity that reports quarterly has an operating loss carryforward of 10,000 for income tax purposes at the start of the current financial year for which a deferred tax asset has not been recognised. The entity earns 10,000 in the first quarter of the current year and expects to earn 10,000 in each of the three remaining quarters. Excluding the carryforward, the estimated average annual income tax rate is expected to be 40 per cent. Tax expense is as follows:

	1st Quarter	2nd Quarter	3rd Quarter	4th Quarter	Annual
Tax expense	3,000	3,000	3,000	3,000	12,000

Contractual or anticipated purchase price changes

B23 Volume rebates or discounts and other contractual changes in the prices of raw materials, labour, or other purchased goods and services are anticipated in interim periods, by both the payer and the recipient, if it is probable that they have been earned or will take effect. Thus, contractual rebates and discounts are anticipated but discretionary rebates and discounts are not anticipated because the resulting asset or liability would not satisfy the conditions in the *Framework* that an asset must be a resource controlled by the entity as a result of a past event and that a liability must be a present obligation whose settlement is expected to result in an outflow of resources.

Depreciation and amortisation

B24 Depreciation and amortisation for an interim period is based only on assets owned during that interim period. It does not take into account asset acquisitions or dispositions planned for later in the financial year.

Inventories

B25 Inventories are measured for interim financial reporting by the same principles as at financial year-end. AASB 102 *Inventories* establishes standards for recognising and measuring inventories. Inventories pose particular problems at the end of any financial reporting period because of the need to determine inventory quantities, costs, and net realisable values. Nonetheless, the same measurement principles are applied for interim inventories. To save cost and time, entities often use estimates to measure inventories at interim dates to a greater extent than at the end of annual reporting periods. Following are examples of how to apply the net realisable value test at an interim date and how to treat manufacturing variances at interim dates.

Net realisable value of inventories

B26 The net realisable value of inventories is determined by reference to selling prices and related costs to complete and dispose at interim dates. An entity will reverse a write-down to net realisable value in a subsequent interim period only if it would be appropriate to do so at the end of the financial year.

B27 [Deleted]

Interim period manufacturing cost variances

B28 Price, efficiency, spending, and volume variances of a manufacturing entity are recognised in income at interim reporting dates to the same extent that those variances are recognised in income at financial year-end. Deferral of variances that are expected to be absorbed by year-end is not appropriate because it could result in reporting inventory at the interim date at more or less than its portion of the actual cost of manufacture.

Foreign currency translation gains and losses

B29 Foreign currency translation gains and losses are measured for interim financial reporting by the same principles as at financial year-end.

B30 AASB 121 *The Effects of Changes in Foreign Exchange Rates* specifies how to translate the financial statements for foreign operations into the presentation currency, including guidelines for using average or closing foreign exchange rates and guidelines for recognising the resulting adjustments in profit or loss, or in other comprehensive income. Consistently with AASB 121, the actual average and closing rates for the interim period are used. Entities do not anticipate some future changes in foreign exchange rates in the remainder of the current financial year in translating foreign operations at an interim date.

B31 If AASB 121 requires translation adjustments to be recognised as income or expense in the period in which they arise, that principle is applied during each interim period. Entities do not defer some foreign currency translation adjustments at an interim date if the adjustment is expected to reverse before the end of the financial year.

Interim financial reporting in hyperinflationary economies

B32 Interim financial reports in hyperinflationary economies are prepared by the same principles as at financial year-end.

B33   AASB 129 *Financial Reporting in Hyperinflationary Economies* requires that the financial statements of an entity that reports in the currency of a hyperinflationary economy be stated in terms of the measuring unit current at the end of the reporting period, and the gain or loss on the net monetary position is included in net income. Also, comparative financial data reported for prior periods are restated to the current measuring unit.

B34   Entities follow those same principles at interim dates, thereby presenting all interim data in the measuring unit as of the end of the interim period, with the resulting gain or loss on the net monetary position included in the interim period's net income. Entities do not annualise the recognition of the gain or loss. Nor do they use an estimated annual inflation rate in preparing an interim financial report in a hyperinflationary economy.

Impairment of assets

B35   AASB 136 *Impairment of Assets* requires that an impairment loss be recognised if the recoverable amount has declined below carrying amount.

B36   This Standard requires that an entity apply the same impairment testing, recognition, and reversal criteria at an interim date as it would at the end of its financial year. That does not mean, however, that an entity must necessarily make a detailed impairment calculation at the end of each interim period. Rather, an entity will review for indications of significant impairment since the end of the most recent financial year to determine whether such a calculation is needed.

C. Examples of the use of estimates

The following examples illustrate application of the principle in paragraph 41.

C1   **Inventories:** Full stock-taking and valuation procedures may not be required for inventories at interim dates, although it may be done at financial year-end. It may be sufficient to make estimates at interim dates based on sales margins.

C2   **Classifications of current and non-current assets and liabilities:** Entities may do a more thorough investigation for classifying assets and liabilities as current or non-current at annual reporting dates than at interim dates.

C3   **Provisions:** Determination of the appropriate amount of a provision (such as a provision for warranties, environmental costs, and site restoration costs) may be complex and often costly and time-consuming. Entities sometimes engage outside experts to assist in the annual calculations. Making similar estimates at interim dates often entails updating of the prior annual provision rather than the engaging of outside experts to do a new calculation.

C4   **Pensions:** AASB 119 *Employee Benefits* requires an entity to determine the present value of defined benefit obligations and the fair value of plan assets at the end of each reporting period and encourages an entity to involve a professionally qualified actuary in measurement of the obligations. For interim reporting purposes, reliable measurement is often obtainable by extrapolation of the latest actuarial valuation.

C5   **Income taxes:** Entities may calculate income tax expense and deferred income tax liability at annual dates by applying the tax rate for each individual jurisdiction to measures of income for each jurisdiction. Paragraph B14 acknowledges that while that degree of precision is desirable at interim reporting dates as well, it may not be achievable in all cases, and a weighted average of rates across jurisdictions or across categories of income is used if it is a reasonable approximation of the effect of using more specific rates.

C6   **Contingencies:** The measurement of contingencies may involve the opinions of legal experts or other advisers. Formal reports from independent experts are sometimes obtained with respect to contingencies. Such opinions about litigation, claims, assessments, and other contingencies and uncertainties may or may not also be needed at interim dates.

C7   **Revaluations and fair value accounting:** AASB 116 *Property, Plant and Equipment* allows an entity to choose as its accounting policy the revaluation model whereby items of property, plant and equipment are revalued to fair value. Similarly, AASB 140 *Investment Property* requires an entity to measure the fair value of investment property. For those measurements, an entity may rely on professionally qualified valuers at annual reporting dates though not at interim reporting dates.

C8   **Intercompany reconciliations:** Some intercompany balances that are reconciled on a detailed level in preparing consolidated financial statements at financial year-end might be reconciled at a less detailed level in preparing consolidated financial statements at an interim date.

C9   **Specialised industries:** Because of complexity, costliness, and time, interim period measurements in specialised industries might be less precise than at financial year-end. An example would be calculation of insurance reserves by insurance companies.

COMPILATION DETAILS

Accounting Standard AASB 134 *Interim Financial Reporting* as amended

Compilation details are not part of AASB 134.

This compiled Standard applies to annual periods beginning on or after 1 January 2018 but before 1 January 2019 for for-profit entities. It takes into account amendments up to and including 12 December 2017 and was prepared on 20 May 2018 by the staff of the Australian Accounting Standards Board (AASB).

This compilation is not a separate Accounting Standard made by the AASB. Instead, it is a representation of AASB 134 (August 2015) as amended by other Accounting Standards, which are listed in the Table below.

Table of Standards

Standard	Date made	FRL identifier	Commence-ment date	Effective date (annual periods ... on or after ...)	Application, saving or transitional provisions
AASB 134	7 Aug 2015	F2015L01557	31 Dec 2016	*(beginning)* 1 Jan 2018	see (a) below
AASB 2015-8	22 Oct 2015	F2015L01840	31 Dec 2016	*(beginning)* 1 Jan 2017	see (b) below
AASB 16	23 Feb 2016	F2016L00233	31 Dec 2018	*(beginning)* 1 Jan 2019	not compiled*
AASB 2016-7	9 Dec 2016	F2017L00043	31 Dec 2016	*(beginning)* 1 Jan 2017	see (c) below
AASB 2017-5	12 Dec 2017	F2018L00067	31 Dec 2017	*(beginning)* 1 Jan 2018	see (d) below

*   The amendments made by this Standard are not included in this compilation, which presents the principal Standard as applicable to annual reporting periods beginning on or after 1 January 2018 but before 1 January 2019 for for-profit entities.

(a) AASB 134 applies to annual periods beginning on or after 1 January 2018 (instead of 1 January 2017) as a result of amendments made by AASB 2015-8 *Amendments to Australian Accounting Standards – Effective Date of AASB 15*. Entities may elect to apply this Standard to annual periods beginning on or after 1 January 2014 but before 1 January 2018.

(b) Entities may elect to apply this Standard to annual periods beginning before 1 January 2017, provided that AASB 15 *Revenue from Contracts with Customers* is also applied.

(c) As a result of AASB 2016-7 deferring the effective date of AASB 15 *Revenue from Contracts with Customers* (and its consequential amendments in AASB 2014-5) for not-for-profit entities from 1 January 2018 to 1 January 2019, AASB 134 (2015) applies to not-for-profit entities only to annual reporting periods beginning on or after 1 January 2019, instead of 1 January 2018. However, earlier application is permitted, provided that AASB 15 is also applied.

(d) Entities may elect to apply this Standard to annual periods beginning before 1 January 2018.

Table of amendments

Paragraph affected	How affected	By ... [paragraph/page]
46	amended	AASB 2015-8 [13]
55	amended	AASB 2017-5 [26]

DELETED IAS 34 TEXT

Deleted IAS 34 text is not part of AASB 134.

47   IAS 1 (as revised in 2007) amended the terminology used throughout IFRSs. In addition it amended paragraphs 4, 5, 8, 11, 12 and 20, deleted paragraph 13 and added paragraphs 8A and 11A. An entity shall apply those amendments for annual periods beginning on or after 1 January 2009. If an entity applies IAS 1 (revised 2007) for an earlier period, the amendments shall be applied for that earlier period.

48   IFRS 3 (as revised in 2008) amended paragraph 16(i). An entity shall apply that amendment for annual periods beginning on or after 1 July 2009. If an entity applies IFRS 3 (revised 2008) for an earlier period, the amendment shall also be applied for that earlier period.

49   Paragraphs 15, 27, 35 and 36 were amended, paragraphs 15A–15C and 16A were added and paragraphs 16–18 were deleted by *Improvements to IFRSs* in May 2010. An entity shall apply those amendments for annual periods beginning on or after 1 January 2011. Earlier application is permitted. If an entity applies the amendments for an earlier period it shall disclose that fact.

50   IFRS 13, issued in May 2011, added paragraph 16A(j). An entity shall apply that amendment when it applies IFRS 13.

51   *Presentation of Items of Other Comprehensive Income* (Amendments to IAS 1), issued in June 2011, amended paragraphs 8, 8A, 11A and 20. An entity shall apply those amendments when it applies IAS 1 as amended in June 2011.

52   *Annual Improvements 2009–2011 Cycle*, issued in May 2012, amended paragraph 5 as a consequential amendment derived from the amendment to IAS 1 *Presentation of Financial Statements*. An entity shall apply that amendment retrospectively in accordance with IAS 8 *Accounting Policies, Changes in Accounting Estimates and Errors* for annual periods beginning on or after 1 January 2013. Earlier application is permitted. If an entity applies that amendment for an earlier period it shall disclose that fact.

53   *Annual Improvements 2009–2011 Cycle*, issued in May 2012, amended paragraph 16A. An entity shall apply that amendment retrospectively in accordance with IAS 8 *Accounting Policies, Changes in Accounting Estimates and Errors* for annual periods beginning on or after 1 January 2013. Earlier application is permitted. If an entity applies that amendment for an earlier period it shall disclose that fact.

54   *Investment Entities* (Amendments to IFRS 10, IFRS 12 and IAS 27), issued in October 2012, amended paragraph 16A. An entity shall apply that amendment for annual periods beginning on or after 1 January 2014. Earlier application of *Investment Entities* is permitted. If an entity applies that amendment earlier it shall also apply all amendments included in *Investment Entities* at the same time.

AASB 136
Impairment of Assets

(Compiled June 2016)

This compiled Standard applies to annual periods beginning on or after 1 January 2018. Earlier application is permitted. It incorporates relevant amendments made up to and including 27 June 2016.

Prepared on 20 March 2017 by the staff of the Australian Accounting Standards Board.

Compilation no. 1

Compilation date: 31 December 2016

This note is not part of Accounting Standard AASB 136.

The following unincorporated amendments are not included in this compiled Standard.

- AASB 17 *Insurance Contracts* — Appendix D sets out the amendments to other Standards that are a consequence of the AASB issuing AASB 17 *Insurance Contracts.* This Standard is applicable from 1 January 2021. Earlier application is permitted, but entities must apply AASB 9 *Financial Instruments* and AASB 15 *Revenue from Contracts with Customers* first.

- AASB 2016-7 *Amendments to Australian Accounting Standards — Deferral of AASB 15 for Not-for-Profit Entities.* This Standard defers the consequential amendments that were originally set out in AASB 2014-5 *Amendments to Australian Accounting Standards arising from AASB 15,* by restating the effective date of the amendments set out in AASB 2015-8 *Amendments to Australian Accounting Standards* for not-for-profit entities. This Standard defers the application of AASB 15 to 1 January 2019. Earlier application is permitted provided AASB 1058 is also applied to the same period.

Entities early-adopting any amendments with later application dates will need to refer to the amending Standards that have not yet been incorporated into compilations. The abovementioned unincorporated amendments may be located on the AASB website at www.aasb.gov.au or on the Federal Register of Legislation website at www.legislation.gov.au.

AASB

CONTENTS

APPENDICES

A. USING PRESENT VALUE TECHNIQUES TO MEASURE VALUE IN USE

C. IMPAIRMENT TESTING CASH-GENERATING UNITS WITH GOODWILL AND NON-CONTROLLING INTERESTS

D. AUSTRALIAN DEFINED TERMS

E. AUSTRALIAN REDUCED DISCLOSURE REQUIREMENTS

ILLUSTRATIVE EXAMPLES

COMPILATION DETAILS

DELETED IAS 36 TEXT

BASIS FOR CONCLUSIONS ON AASB 2016-4

BASIS FOR CONCLUSIONS ON IAS 36 (available on the AASB website)

Australian Accounting Standard AASB 136 *Impairment of Assets* (ass amended) is set out in paragraphs 1 – Aus141.2 and Appendices A and C – E. All the paragraphs have equal authority. Paragraphs in **bold type** state the main principles. AASB 136 is to be read in the context of other Australian Accounting Standards, including AASB 1048 *Interpretation of Standards*, which identifies the Australian Accounting Interpretations, and AASB 1057 *Application of Australian Accounting Standards*. In the absence of explicit guidance, AASB 108 *Accounting Policies, Changes in Accounting Estimates and Errors* provides a basis for selecting and applying accounting policies.

COMPARISON WITH IAS 36

AASB 136 *Impairment of Assets* as amended incorporates IAS 36 *Impairment of Assets* as issued and amended by the International Accounting Standards Board (IASB). Australian-specific paragraphs (which are not included in IAS 36) are identified with the prefix "Aus". Paragraphs that apply only to not-for-profit entities begin by identifying their limited applicability.

Tier 1

For-profit entities complying with AASB 136 also comply with IAS 36.

Not-for-profit entities' compliance with IAS 36 will depend on whether any "Aus" paragraphs that specifically apply to not-for-profit entities provide additional guidance or contain applicable requirements that are inconsistent with IAS 36.

Tier 2

Entities preparing general purpose financial statements under Australian Accounting Standards – Reduced Disclosure Requirements (Tier 2) will not be in compliance with IFRSs.

AASB 1053 *Application of Tiers of Australian Accounting Standards* explains the two tiers of reporting requirements.

ACCOUNTING STANDARD AASB 136

The Australian Accounting Standards Board made Accounting Standard AASB 136 *Impairment of Assets* under section 334 of the *Corporations Act 2001* on 14 August 2015.

This compiled version of AASB 136 applies to annual periods beginning on or after 1 January 2018. It incorporates relevant amendments contained in other AASB Standards made by the AASB up to and including 27 June 2016 (see Compilation Details).

ACCOUNTING STANDARD AASB 136
IMPAIRMENT OF ASSETS

Objective

1   The objective of this Standard is to prescribe the procedures that an entity applies to ensure that its assets are carried at no more than their recoverable amount. An asset is carried at more than its recoverable amount if its carrying amount exceeds the amount to be recovered through use or sale of the asset. If this is the case, the asset is described as impaired and the Standard requires the entity to recognise an impairment loss. The Standard also specifies when an entity should reverse an impairment loss and prescribes disclosures.

Scope

2   **This Standard shall be applied in accounting for the impairment of all assets, other than:**

   (a)   **inventories (see AASB 102 *Inventories*);**

   (b)   **contract assets and assets arising from costs to obtain or fulfil a contract that are recognised in accordance with AASB 15 *Revenue from Contracts with Customers*;**

   (c)   **deferred tax assets (see AASB 112 *Income Taxes*);**

    (d)   assets arising from employee benefits (see AASB 119 *Employee Benefits*);

    (e)   financial assets that are within the scope of AASB 9 *Financial Instruments*;

    (f)   investment property that is measured at fair value (see AASB 140 *Investment Property*);

    (g)   biological assets related to agricultural activity within the scope of AASB 141 *Agriculture* that are measured at fair value less costs to sell;

    (h)   deferred acquisition costs, and intangible assets, arising from an insurer's contractual rights under insurance contracts within the scopes of AASB 4 *Insurance Contracts*, AASB 1023 *General Insurance Contracts* and AASB 1038 *Life Insurance Contracts*; and

    (i)   non-current assets (or disposal groups) classified as held for sale in accordance with AASB 5 *Non-current Assets Held for Sale and Discontinued Operations*.

3   This Standard does not apply to inventories, assets arising from construction contracts, deferred tax assets, assets arising from employee benefits, or assets classified as held for sale (or included in a disposal group that is classified as held for sale) because existing Standards applicable to these assets contain requirements for recognising and measuring these assets.

4   This Standard applies to financial assets classified as:

    (a)   subsidiaries, as defined in AASB 10 *Consolidated Financial Statements*;

    (b)   associates, as defined in AASB 128 *Investments in Associates and Joint Ventures*; and

    (c)   joint ventures, as defined in AASB 11 *Joint Arrangements*.

For impairment of other financial assets, refer to AASB 9.

5   This Standard does not apply to financial assets within the scope of AASB 9, investment property measured at fair value within the scope of AASB 140, or biological assets related to agricultural activity measured at fair value less costs to sell within the scope of AASB 141. However, this Standard applies to assets that are carried at revalued amount (ie fair value at the date of the revaluation less any subsequent accumulated depreciation and subsequent accumulated impairment losses) in accordance with other Australian Accounting Standards, such as the revaluation model in AASB 116 *Property, Plant and Equipment* and AASB 138 *Intangible Assets*. The only difference between an asset's fair value and its fair value less costs of disposal is the direct incremental costs attributable to the disposal of the asset.

    (a)   If the disposal costs are negligible, the recoverable amount of the revalued asset is necessarily close to, or greater than, its revalued amount. In this case, after the revaluation requirements have been applied, it is unlikely that the revalued asset is impaired and recoverable amount need not be estimated.

    (b)   [deleted]

    (c)   If the disposal costs are not negligible, the fair value less costs of disposal of the revalued asset is necessarily less than its fair value. Therefore, the revalued asset will be impaired if its value in use is less than its revalued amount. In this case, after the revaluation requirements have been applied, an entity applies this Standard to determine whether the asset may be impaired.

Aus5.1   Many assets of not-for-profit entities that are not held primarily for their ability to generate net cash inflows are typically specialised assets held for continuing use of their service capacity. Given that these assets are rarely sold, their cost of disposal is typically negligible. The recoverable amount of such assets is expected to be materially the same as fair value, determined under AASB 13 *Fair Value Measurement*, with the consequence that this Standard:

    (a)   does not apply to such assets that are regularly revalued to fair value under the revaluation model in AASB 116 and AASB 138; and

(b) applies to such assets accounted for under the cost model in AASB 116 and AASB 138.

Definitions

6 The following terms are used in this Standard with the meanings specified:

Carrying amount is the amount at which an asset is recognised after deducting any accumulated depreciation (amortisation) and accumulated impairment losses thereon.

A *cash-generating unit* is the smallest identifiable group of assets that generates cash inflows that are largely independent of the cash inflows from other assets or groups of assets.

Corporate assets are assets other than goodwill that contribute to the future cash flows of both the cash-generating unit under review and other cash-generating units.

Costs of disposal are incremental costs directly attributable to the disposal of an asset or cash-generating unit, excluding finance costs and income tax expense.

Depreciable amount is the cost of an asset, or other amount substituted for cost in the financial statements, less its residual value.

Depreciation (Amortisation) is the systematic allocation of the depreciable amount of an asset over its useful life.[1]

Fair value is the price that would be received to sell an asset or paid to transfer a liability in an orderly transaction between market participants at the measurement date. (See AASB 13 *Fair Value Measurement*.)

An *impairment loss* is the amount by which the carrying amount of an asset or a cash-generating unit exceeds its recoverable amount.

The *recoverable amount* of an asset or a cash-generating unit is the higher of its fair value less costs of disposal and its value in use.

Useful life is either:

(a) the period of time over which an asset is expected to be used by the entity; or

(b) the number of production or similar units expected to be obtained from the asset by the entity.

Value in use is the present value of the future cash flows expected to be derived from an asset or cash-generating unit.

Identifying an asset that may be impaired

7 Paragraphs 8–17 specify when recoverable amount shall be determined. These requirements use the term 'an asset' but apply equally to an individual asset or a cash-generating unit. The remainder of this Standard is structured as follows:

(a) paragraphs 18–57 set out the requirements for measuring recoverable amount. These requirements also use the term 'an asset' but apply equally to an individual asset and a cash-generating unit.

(b) paragraphs 58–108 set out the requirements for recognising and measuring impairment losses. Recognition and measurement of impairment losses for individual assets other than goodwill are dealt with in paragraphs 58–64. Paragraphs 65–108 deal with the recognition and measurement of impairment losses for cash-generating units and goodwill.

---

1 In the case of an intangible asset, the term 'amortisation' is generally used instead of 'depreciation'. The two terms have the same meaning.

(c) paragraphs 109–116 set out the requirements for reversing an impairment loss recognised in prior periods for an asset or a cash-generating unit. Again, these requirements use the term 'an asset' but apply equally to an individual asset or a cash-generating unit. Additional requirements for an individual asset are set out in paragraphs 117–121, for a cash-generating unit in paragraphs 122 and 123, and for goodwill in paragraphs 124 and 125.

(d) paragraphs 126–133 specify the information to be disclosed about impairment losses and reversals of impairment losses for assets and cash-generating units. Paragraphs 134–137 specify additional disclosure requirements for cash-generating units to which goodwill or intangible assets with indefinite useful lives have been allocated for impairment testing purposes.

8 An asset is impaired when its carrying amount exceeds its recoverable amount. Paragraphs 12–14 describe some indications that an impairment loss may have occurred. If any of those indications is present, an entity is required to make a formal estimate of recoverable amount. Except as described in paragraph 10, this Standard does not require an entity to make a formal estimate of recoverable amount if no indication of an impairment loss is present.

9 **An entity shall assess at the end of each reporting period whether there is any indication that an asset may be impaired. If any such indication exists, the entity shall estimate the recoverable amount of the asset.**

10 **Irrespective of whether there is any indication of impairment, an entity shall also:**

(a) **test an intangible asset with an indefinite useful life or an intangible asset not yet available for use for impairment annually by comparing its carrying amount with its recoverable amount. This impairment test may be performed at any time during an annual period, provided it is performed at the same time every year. Different intangible assets may be tested for impairment at different times. However, if such an intangible asset was initially recognised during the current annual period, that intangible asset shall be tested for impairment before the end of the current annual period.**

(b) **test goodwill acquired in a business combination for impairment annually in accordance with paragraphs 80–99.**

11 The ability of an intangible asset to generate sufficient future economic benefits to recover its carrying amount is usually subject to greater uncertainty before the asset is available for use than after it is available for use. Therefore, this Standard requires an entity to test for impairment, at least annually, the carrying amount of an intangible asset that is not yet available for use.

12 **In assessing whether there is any indication that an asset may be impaired, an entity shall consider, as a minimum, the following indications:**

External sources of information

(a) **there are observable indications that the asset's value has declined during the period significantly more than would be expected as a result of the passage of time or normal use.**

(b) **significant changes with an adverse effect on the entity have taken place during the period, or will take place in the near future, in the technological, market, economic or legal environment in which the entity operates or in the market to which an asset is dedicated.**

(c) **market interest rates or other market rates of return on investments have increased during the period, and those increases are likely to affect the discount rate used in calculating an asset's value in use and decrease the asset's recoverable amount materially.**

(d) **the carrying amount of the net assets of the entity is more than its market capitalisation.**

Internal sources of information

(e) **evidence is available of obsolescence or physical damage of an asset.**

(f) **significant changes with an adverse effect on the entity have taken place during the period, or are expected to take place in the near future, in the extent to which, or manner in which, an asset is used or is expected to be used. These changes include the asset becoming idle, plans to discontinue or restructure the operation to which an asset belongs, plans to dispose of an asset before the previously expected date, and reassessing the useful life of an asset as finite rather than indefinite.[2]**

(g) **evidence is available from internal reporting that indicates that the economic performance of an asset is, or will be, worse than expected.**

Dividend from a subsidiary, joint venture or associate

(h) **for an investment in a subsidiary, joint venture or associate, the investor recognises a dividend from the investment and evidence is available that:**

    (i) **the carrying amount of the investment in the separate financial statements exceeds the carrying amounts in the consolidated financial statements of the investee's net assets, including associated goodwill; or**

    (ii) **the dividend exceeds the total comprehensive income of the subsidiary, joint venture or associate in the period the dividend is declared.**

13 The list in paragraph 12 is not exhaustive. An entity may identify other indications that an asset may be impaired and these would also require the entity to determine the asset's recoverable amount or, in the case of goodwill, perform an impairment test in accordance with paragraphs 80–99.

14 Evidence from internal reporting that indicates that an asset may be impaired includes the existence of:

(a) cash flows for acquiring the asset, or subsequent cash needs for operating or maintaining it, that are significantly higher than those originally budgeted;

(b) actual net cash flows or operating profit or loss flowing from the asset that are significantly worse than those budgeted;

(c) a significant decline in budgeted net cash flows or operating profit, or a significant increase in budgeted loss, flowing from the asset; or

(d) operating losses or net cash outflows for the asset, when current period amounts are aggregated with budgeted amounts for the future.

15 As indicated in paragraph 10, this Standard requires an intangible asset with an indefinite useful life or not yet available for use and goodwill to be tested for impairment, at least annually. Apart from when the requirements in paragraph 10 apply, the concept of materiality applies in identifying whether the recoverable amount of an asset needs to be estimated. For example, if previous calculations show that an asset's recoverable amount is significantly greater than its carrying amount, the entity need not re-estimate the asset's recoverable amount if no events have occurred that would eliminate that difference. Similarly, previous analysis may show that an asset's recoverable amount is not sensitive to one (or more) of the indications listed in paragraph 12.

16 As an illustration of paragraph 15, if market interest rates or other market rates of return on investments have increased during the period, an entity is not required to make a formal estimate of an asset's recoverable amount in the following cases:

---

2   Once an asset meets the criteria to be classified as held for sale (or is included in a disposal group that is classified as held for sale), it is excluded from the scope of this Standard and is accounted for in accordance with AASB 5 *Non-current Assets Held for Sale and Discontinued Operations.*

(a)   if the discount rate used in calculating the asset's value in use is unlikely to be affected by the increase in these market rates. For example, increases in short-term interest rates may not have a material effect on the discount rate used for an asset that has a long remaining useful life.

(b)   if the discount rate used in calculating the asset's value in use is likely to be affected by the increase in these market rates but previous sensitivity analysis of recoverable amount shows that:

    (i)   it is unlikely that there will be a material decrease in recoverable amount because future cash flows are also likely to increase (eg in some cases, an entity may be able to demonstrate that it adjusts its revenues to compensate for any increase in market rates); or

    (ii)   the decrease in recoverable amount is unlikely to result in a material impairment loss.

17   If there is an indication that an asset may be impaired, this may indicate that the remaining useful life, the depreciation (amortisation) method or the residual value for the asset needs to be reviewed and adjusted in accordance with the Standard applicable to the asset, even if no impairment loss is recognised for the asset.

Measuring recoverable amount

18   This Standard defines recoverable amount as the higher of an asset's or cash-generating unit's fair value less costs of disposal and its value in use. Paragraphs 19–57 set out the requirements for measuring recoverable amount. These requirements use the term 'an asset' but apply equally to an individual asset or a cash-generating unit.

19   It is not always necessary to determine both an asset's fair value less costs of disposal and its value in use. If either of these amounts exceeds the asset's carrying amount, the asset is not impaired and it is not necessary to estimate the other amount.

20   It may be possible to measure fair value less costs of disposal, even if there is not a quoted price in an active market for an identical asset. However, sometimes it will not be possible to measure fair value less costs of disposal because there is no basis for making a reliable estimate of the price at which an orderly transaction to sell the asset would take place between market participants at the measurement date under current market conditions. In this case, the entity may use the asset's value in use as its recoverable amount.

21   If there is no reason to believe that an asset's value in use materially exceeds its fair value less costs of disposal, the asset's fair value less costs of disposal may be used as its recoverable amount. This will often be the case for an asset that is held for disposal. This is because the value in use of an asset held for disposal will consist mainly of the net disposal proceeds, as the future cash flows from continuing use of the asset until its disposal are likely to be negligible.

22   Recoverable amount is determined for an individual asset, unless the asset does not generate cash inflows that are largely independent of those from other assets or groups of assets. If this is the case, recoverable amount is determined for the cash-generating unit to which the asset belongs (see paragraphs 65–103), unless either:

(a)   the asset's fair value less costs of disposal is higher than its carrying amount; or

(b)   the asset's value in use can be estimated to be close to its fair value less costs of disposal and fair value less costs of disposal can be measured.

23   In some cases, estimates, averages and computational short cuts may provide reasonable approximations of the detailed computations illustrated in this Standard for determining fair value less costs of disposal or value in use.

Measuring the recoverable amount of an intangible asset with an indefinite useful life

24 Paragraph 10 requires an intangible asset with an indefinite useful life to be tested for impairment annually by comparing its carrying amount with its recoverable amount, irrespective of whether there is any indication that it may be impaired. However, the most recent detailed calculation of such an asset's recoverable amount made in a preceding period may be used in the impairment test for that asset in the current period, provided all of the following criteria are met:

(a) if the intangible asset does not generate cash inflows from continuing use that are largely independent of those from other assets or groups of assets and is therefore tested for impairment as part of the cash-generating unit to which it belongs, the assets and liabilities making up that unit have not changed significantly since the most recent recoverable amount calculation;

(b) the most recent recoverable amount calculation resulted in an amount that exceeded the asset's carrying amount by a substantial margin; and

(c) based on an analysis of events that have occurred and circumstances that have changed since the most recent recoverable amount calculation, the likelihood that a current recoverable amount determination would be less than the asset's carrying amount is remote.

Fair value less costs of disposal

25–27 [Deleted]

28 Costs of disposal, other than those that have been recognised as liabilities, are deducted in measuring fair value less costs of disposal. Examples of such costs are legal costs, stamp duty and similar transaction taxes, costs of removing the asset, and direct incremental costs to bring an asset into condition for its sale. However, termination benefits (as defined in AASB 119) and costs associated with reducing or reorganising a business following the disposal of an asset are not direct incremental costs to dispose of the asset.

29 Sometimes, the disposal of an asset would require the buyer to assume a liability and only a single fair value less costs of disposal is available for both the asset and the liability. Paragraph 78 explains how to deal with such cases.

Value in use

30 **The following elements shall be reflected in the calculation of an asset's value in use:**

(a) **an estimate of the future cash flows the entity expects to derive from the asset;**

(b) **expectations about possible variations in the amount or timing of those future cash flows;**

(c) **the time value of money, represented by the current market risk-free rate of interest;**

(d) **the price for bearing the uncertainty inherent in the asset; and**

(e) **other factors, such as illiquidity, that market participants would reflect in pricing the future cash flows the entity expects to derive from the asset.**

31 Estimating the value in use of an asset involves the following steps:

(a) estimating the future cash inflows and outflows to be derived from continuing use of the asset and from its ultimate disposal; and

(b) applying the appropriate discount rate to those future cash flows.

32 The elements identified in paragraph 30(b), (d) and (e) can be reflected either as adjustments to the future cash flows or as adjustments to the discount rate. Whichever approach an entity adopts to reflect expectations about possible variations in the

AASB

amount or timing of future cash flows, the result shall be to reflect the expected present value of the future cash flows, ie the weighted average of all possible outcomes. Appendix A provides additional guidance on the use of present value techniques in measuring an asset's value in use.

Basis for estimates of future cash flows

33   In measuring value in use an entity shall:

    (a)   **base cash flow projections on reasonable and supportable assumptions that represent management's best estimate of the range of economic conditions that will exist over the remaining useful life of the asset. Greater weight shall be given to external evidence.**

    (b)   **base cash flow projections on the most recent financial budgets/forecasts approved by management, but shall exclude any estimated future cash inflows or outflows expected to arise from future restructurings or from improving or enhancing the asset's performance. Projections based on these budgets/forecasts shall cover a maximum period of five years, unless a longer period can be justified.**

    (c)   **estimate cash flow projections beyond the period covered by the most recent budgets/forecasts by extrapolating the projections based on the budgets/forecasts using a steady or declining growth rate for subsequent years, unless an increasing rate can be justified. This growth rate shall not exceed the long-term average growth rate for the products, industries, or country or countries in which the entity operates, or for the market in which the asset is used, unless a higher rate can be justified.**

34   Management assesses the reasonableness of the assumptions on which its current cash flow projections are based by examining the causes of differences between past cash flow projections and actual cash flows. Management shall ensure that the assumptions on which its current cash flow projections are based are consistent with past actual outcomes, provided the effects of subsequent events or circumstances that did not exist when those actual cash flows were generated make this appropriate.

35   Detailed, explicit and reliable financial budgets/forecasts of future cash flows for periods longer than five years are generally not available. For this reason, management's estimates of future cash flows are based on the most recent budgets/forecasts for a maximum of five years. Management may use cash flow projections based on financial budgets/forecasts over a period longer than five years if it is confident that these projections are reliable and it can demonstrate its ability, based on past experience, to forecast cash flows accurately over that longer period.

36   Cash flow projections until the end of an asset's useful life are estimated by extrapolating the cash flow projections based on the financial budgets/forecasts using a growth rate for subsequent years. This rate is steady or declining, unless an increase in the rate matches objective information about patterns over a product or industry lifecycle. If appropriate, the growth rate is zero or negative.

37   When conditions are favourable, competitors are likely to enter the market and restrict growth. Therefore, entities will have difficulty in exceeding the average historical growth rate over the long term (say, twenty years) for the products, industries, or country or countries in which the entity operates, or for the market in which the asset is used.

38   In using information from financial budgets/forecasts, an entity considers whether the information reflects reasonable and supportable assumptions and represents management's best estimate of the set of economic conditions that will exist over the remaining useful life of the asset.

Composition of estimates of future cash flows

39 **Estimates of future cash flows shall include:**

    (a) **projections of cash inflows from the continuing use of the asset;**

    (b) **projections of cash outflows that are necessarily incurred to generate the cash inflows from continuing use of the asset (including cash outflows to prepare the asset for use) and can be directly attributed, or allocated on a reasonable and consistent basis, to the asset; and**

    (c) **net cash flows, if any, to be received (or paid) for the disposal of the asset at the end of its useful life.**

40 Estimates of future cash flows and the discount rate reflect consistent assumptions about price increases attributable to general inflation. Therefore, if the discount rate includes the effect of price increases attributable to general inflation, future cash flows are estimated in nominal terms. If the discount rate excludes the effect of price increases attributable to general inflation, future cash flows are estimated in real terms (but include future specific price increases or decreases).

41 Projections of cash outflows include those for the day-to-day servicing of the asset as well as future overheads that can be attributed directly, or allocated on a reasonable and consistent basis, to the use of the asset.

42 When the carrying amount of an asset does not yet include all the cash outflows to be incurred before it is ready for use or sale, the estimate of future cash outflows includes an estimate of any further cash outflow that is expected to be incurred before the asset is ready for use or sale. For example, this is the case for a building under construction or for a development project that is not yet completed.

43 To avoid double-counting, estimates of future cash flows do not include:

    (a) cash inflows from assets that generate cash inflows that are largely independent of the cash inflows from the asset under review (for example, financial assets such as receivables); and

    (b) cash outflows that relate to obligations that have been recognised as liabilities (for example, payables, pensions or provisions).

44 **Future cash flows shall be estimated for the asset in its current condition. Estimates of future cash flows shall not include estimated future cash inflows or outflows that are expected to arise from:**

    (a) **a future restructuring to which an entity is not yet committed; or**

    (b) **improving or enhancing the asset's performance.**

45 Because future cash flows are estimated for the asset in its current condition, value in use does not reflect:

    (a) future cash outflows or related cost savings (for example reductions in staff costs) or benefits that are expected to arise from a future restructuring to which an entity is not yet committed; or

    (b) future cash outflows that will improve or enhance the asset's performance or the related cash inflows that are expected to arise from such outflows.

46 A restructuring is a programme that is planned and controlled by management and materially changes either the scope of the business undertaken by an entity or the manner in which the business is conducted. AASB 137 *Provisions, Contingent Liabilities and Contingent Assets* contains guidance clarifying when an entity is committed to a restructuring.

47 When an entity becomes committed to a restructuring, some assets are likely to be affected by this restructuring. Once the entity is committed to the restructuring:

    (a) its estimates of future cash inflows and cash outflows for the purpose of determining value in use reflect the cost savings and other benefits from the restructuring (based on the most recent financial budgets/forecasts approved by management); and

(b)   its estimates of future cash outflows for the restructuring are included in a restructuring provision in accordance with AASB 137.

Illustrative Example 5 illustrates the effect of a future restructuring on a value in use calculation.

48   Until an entity incurs cash outflows that improve or enhance the asset's performance, estimates of future cash flows do not include the estimated future cash inflows that are expected to arise from the increase in economic benefits associated with the cash outflow (see Illustrative Example 6).

49   Estimates of future cash flows include future cash outflows necessary to maintain the level of economic benefits expected to arise from the asset in its current condition. When a cash-generating unit consists of assets with different estimated useful lives, all of which are essential to the ongoing operation of the unit, the replacement of assets with shorter lives is considered to be part of the day-to-day servicing of the unit when estimating the future cash flows associated with the unit. Similarly, when a single asset consists of components with different estimated useful lives, the replacement of components with shorter lives is considered to be part of the day-to-day servicing of the asset when estimating the future cash flows generated by the asset.

50   Estimates of future cash flows shall not include:

(a)   cash inflows or outflows from financing activities; or

(b)   income tax receipts or payments.

51   Estimated future cash flows reflect assumptions that are consistent with the way the discount rate is determined. Otherwise, the effect of some assumptions will be counted twice or ignored. Because the time value of money is considered by discounting the estimated future cash flows, these cash flows exclude cash inflows or outflows from financing activities. Similarly, because the discount rate is determined on a pre-tax basis, future cash flows are also estimated on a pre-tax basis.

52   The estimate of net cash flows to be received (or paid) for the disposal of an asset at the end of its useful life shall be the amount that an entity expects to obtain from the disposal of the asset in an arm's length transaction between knowledgeable, willing parties, after deducting the estimated costs of disposal.

53   The estimate of net cash flows to be received (or paid) for the disposal of an asset at the end of its useful life is determined in a similar way to an asset's fair value less costs of disposal, except that, in estimating those net cash flows:

(a)   an entity uses prices prevailing at the date of the estimate for similar assets that have reached the end of their useful life and have operated under conditions similar to those in which the asset will be used.

(b)   the entity adjusts those prices for the effect of both future price increases due to general inflation and specific future price increases or decreases. However, if estimates of future cash flows from the asset's continuing use and the discount rate exclude the effect of general inflation, the entity also excludes this effect from the estimate of net cash flows on disposal.

53A   Fair value differs from value in use. Fair value reflects the assumptions market participants would use when pricing the asset. In contrast, value in use reflects the effects of factors that may be specific to the entity and not applicable to entities in general. For example, fair value does not reflect any of the following factors to the extent that they would not be generally available to market participants:

(a)   additional value derived from the grouping of assets (such as the creation of a portfolio of investment properties in different locations);

(b)   synergies between the asset being measured and other assets;

(c)   legal rights or legal restrictions that are specific only to the current owner of the asset; and

(d)   tax benefits or tax burdens that are specific to the current owner of the asset.

Foreign currency future cash flows

54 Future cash flows are estimated in the currency in which they will be generated and then discounted using a discount rate appropriate for that currency. An entity translates the present value using the spot exchange rate at the date of the value in use calculation.

Discount rate

55 The discount rate (rates) shall be a pre-tax rate (rates) that reflect(s) current market assessments of:

(a) the time value of money; and

(b) the risks specific to the asset for which the future cash flow estimates have not been adjusted.

56 A rate that reflects current market assessments of the time value of money and the risks specific to the asset is the return that investors would require if they were to choose an investment that would generate cash flows of amounts, timing and risk profile equivalent to those that the entity expects to derive from the asset. This rate is estimated from the rate implicit in current market transactions for similar assets or from the weighted average cost of capital of a listed entity that has a single asset (or a portfolio of assets) similar in terms of service potential and risks to the asset under review. However, the discount rate(s) used to measure an asset's value in use shall not reflect risks for which the future cash flow estimates have been adjusted. Otherwise, the effect of some assumptions will be double-counted.

57 When an asset-specific rate is not directly available from the market, an entity uses surrogates to estimate the discount rate. Appendix A provides additional guidance on estimating the discount rate in such circumstances.

Recognising and measuring an impairment loss

58 Paragraphs 59–64 set out the requirements for recognising and measuring impairment losses for an individual asset other than goodwill. Recognising and measuring impairment losses for cash-generating units and goodwill are dealt with in paragraphs 65–108.

59 If, and only if, the recoverable amount of an asset is less than its carrying amount, the carrying amount of the asset shall be reduced to its recoverable amount. That reduction is an impairment loss.

60 An impairment loss shall be recognised immediately in profit or loss, unless the asset is carried at revalued amount in accordance with another Standard (for example, in accordance with the revaluation model in AASB 116). Any impairment loss of a revalued asset shall be treated as a revaluation decrease in accordance with that other Standard.

61 An impairment loss on a non-revalued asset is recognised in profit or loss. However, an impairment loss on a revalued asset is recognised in other comprehensive income to the extent that the impairment loss does not exceed the amount in the revaluation surplus for that same asset. Such an impairment loss on a revalued asset reduces the revaluation surplus for that asset.

Aus61.1 Notwithstanding paragraph 61, in respect of not-for-profit entities, an impairment loss on a revalued asset is recognised in other comprehensive income to the extent that the impairment loss does not exceed the amount in the revaluation surplus for the class of asset. Such an impairment loss on a revalued asset reduces the revaluation surplus for the class of asset.

62 When the amount estimated for an impairment loss is greater than the carrying amount of the asset to which it relates, an entity shall recognise a liability if, and only if, that is required by another Standard.

63 After the recognition of an impairment loss, the depreciation (amortisation) charge for the asset shall be adjusted in future periods to allocate the asset's

revised carrying amount, less its residual value (if any), on a systematic basis over its remaining useful life.

64 If an impairment loss is recognised, any related deferred tax assets or liabilities are determined in accordance with AASB 112 by comparing the revised carrying amount of the asset with its tax base (see Illustrative Example 3).

Cash-generating units and goodwill

65 Paragraphs 66–108 and Appendix C set out the requirements for identifying the cash-generating unit to which an asset belongs and determining the carrying amount of, and recognising impairment losses for, cash-generating units and goodwill.

Identifying the cash-generating unit to which an asset belongs

66 **If there is any indication that an asset may be impaired, recoverable amount shall be estimated for the individual asset. If it is not possible to estimate the recoverable amount of the individual asset, an entity shall determine the recoverable amount of the cash-generating unit to which the asset belongs (the asset's cash-generating unit).**

67 The recoverable amount of an individual asset cannot be determined if:

(a) the asset's value in use cannot be estimated to be close to its fair value less costs of disposal (for example, when the future cash flows from continuing use of the asset cannot be estimated to be negligible); and

(b) the asset does not generate cash inflows that are largely independent of those from other assets.

In such cases, value in use and, therefore, recoverable amount, can be determined only for the asset's cash-generating unit.

Example

A mining entity owns a private railway to support its mining activities. The private railway could be sold only for scrap value and it does not generate cash inflows that are largely independent of the cash inflows from the other assets of the mine.

It is not possible to estimate the recoverable amount of the private railway because its value in use cannot be determined and is probably different from scrap value. Therefore, the entity estimates the recoverable amount of the cash-generating unit to which the private railway belongs, ie the mine as a whole.

---

68 As defined in paragraph 6, an asset's cash-generating unit is the smallest group of assets that includes the asset and generates cash inflows that are largely independent of the cash inflows from other assets or groups of assets. Identification of an asset's cash-generating unit involves judgement. If recoverable amount cannot be determined for an individual asset, an entity identifies the lowest aggregation of assets that generate largely independent cash inflows.

Example

A bus company provides services under contract with a municipality that requires minimum service on each of five separate routes. Assets devoted to each route and the cash flows from each route can be identified separately. One of the routes operates at a significant loss.

Because the entity does not have the option to curtail any one bus route, the lowest level of identifiable cash inflows that are largely independent of the cash inflows from other assets or groups of assets is the cash inflows generated by the five routes together. The cash-generating unit for each route is the bus company as a whole.

---

69 Cash inflows are inflows of cash and cash equivalents received from parties external to the entity. In identifying whether cash inflows from an asset (or group of assets) are

largely independent of the cash inflows from other assets (or groups of assets), an entity considers various factors including how management monitors the entity's operations (such as by product lines, businesses, individual locations, districts or regional areas) or how management makes decisions about continuing or disposing of the entity's assets and operations. Illustrative Example 1 gives examples of identification of a cash-generating unit.

70   **If an active market exists for the output produced by an asset or group of assets, that asset or group of assets shall be identified as a cash-generating unit, even if some or all of the output is used internally. If the cash inflows generated by any asset or cash-generating unit are affected by internal transfer pricing, an entity shall use management's best estimate of future price(s) that could be achieved in arm's length transactions in estimating:**

(a)   **the future cash inflows used to determine the asset's or cash-generating unit's value in use; and**

(b)   **the future cash outflows used to determine the value in use of any other assets or cash-generating units that are affected by the internal transfer pricing.**

71   Even if part or all of the output produced by an asset or a group of assets is used by other units of the entity (for example, products at an intermediate stage of a production process), this asset or group of assets forms a separate cash-generating unit if the entity could sell the output on an active market. This is because the asset or group of assets could generate cash inflows that would be largely independent of the cash inflows from other assets or groups of assets. In using information based on financial budgets/forecasts that relates to such a cash-generating unit, or to any other asset or cash-generating unit affected by internal transfer pricing, an entity adjusts this information if internal transfer prices do not reflect management's best estimate of future prices that could be achieved in arm's length transactions.

72   **Cash-generating units shall be identified consistently from period to period for the same asset or types of assets, unless a change is justified.**

73   If an entity determines that an asset belongs to a cash-generating unit different from that in previous periods, or that the types of assets aggregated for the asset's cash-generating unit have changed, paragraph 130 requires disclosures about the cash-generating unit, if an impairment loss is recognised or reversed for the cash-generating unit.

Recoverable amount and carrying amount of a cash-generating unit

74   The recoverable amount of a cash-generating unit is the higher of the cash-generating unit's fair value less costs of disposal and its value in use. For the purpose of determining the recoverable amount of a cash-generating unit, any reference in paragraphs 19–57 to 'an asset' is read as a reference to 'a cash-generating unit'.

75   **The carrying amount of a cash-generating unit shall be determined on a basis consistent with the way the recoverable amount of the cash-generating unit is determined.**

76   The carrying amount of a cash-generating unit:

(a)   includes the carrying amount of only those assets that can be attributed directly, or allocated on a reasonable and consistent basis, to the cash-generating unit and will generate the future cash inflows used in determining the cash-generating unit's value in use; and

(b)   does not include the carrying amount of any recognised liability, unless the recoverable amount of the cash-generating unit cannot be determined without consideration of this liability.

This is because fair value less costs of disposal and value in use of a cash-generating unit are determined excluding cash flows that relate to assets that are not part of the cash-generating unit and liabilities that have been recognised (see paragraphs 28 and 43).

77   When assets are grouped for recoverability assessments, it is important to include in the cash-generating unit all assets that generate or are used to generate the relevant stream of cash inflows. Otherwise, the cash-generating unit may appear to be fully recoverable when in fact an impairment loss has occurred. In some cases, although some assets contribute to the estimated future cash flows of a cash-generating unit, they cannot be allocated to the cash-generating unit on a reasonable and consistent basis. This might be the case for goodwill or corporate assets such as head office assets. Paragraphs 80–103 explain how to deal with these assets in testing a cash-generating unit for impairment.

78   It may be necessary to consider some recognised liabilities to determine the recoverable amount of a cash-generating unit. This may occur if the disposal of a cash-generating unit would require the buyer to assume the liability. In this case, the fair value less costs of disposal (or the estimated cash flow from ultimate disposal) of the cash-generating unit is the price to sell the assets of the cash-generating unit and the liability together, less the costs of disposal. To perform a meaningful comparison between the carrying amount of the cash-generating unit and its recoverable amount, the carrying amount of the liability is deducted in determining both the cash-generating unit's value in use and its carrying amount.

Example

A company operates a mine in a country where legislation requires that the owner must restore the site on completion of its mining operations. The cost of restoration includes the replacement of the overburden, which must be removed before mining operations commence. A provision for the costs to replace the overburden was recognised as soon as the overburden was removed. The amount provided was recognised as part of the cost of the mine and is being depreciated over the mine's useful life. The carrying amount of the provision for restoration costs is CU500,[(a)] which is equal to the present value of the restoration costs.

The entity is testing the mine for impairment. The cash-generating unit for the mine is the mine as a whole. The entity has received various offers to buy the mine at a price of around CU800. This price reflects the fact that the buyer will assume the obligation to restore the overburden. Disposal costs for the mine are negligible. The value in use of the mine is approximately CU1,200, excluding restoration costs. The carrying amount of the mine is CU1,000.

The cash-generating unit's fair value less costs of disposal is CU800. This amount considers restoration costs that have already been provided for. As a consequence, the value in use for the cash-generating unit is determined after consideration of the restoration costs and is estimated to be CU700 (CU1,200 less CU500). The carrying amount of the cash-generating unit is CU500, which is the carrying amount of the mine (CU1,000) less the carrying amount of the provision for restoration costs (CU500). Therefore, the recoverable amount of the cash-generating unit exceeds its carrying amount.

(a)   In this Standard, monetary amounts are denominated in 'currency units (CU)'.

---

79   For practical reasons, the recoverable amount of a cash-generating unit is sometimes determined after consideration of assets that are not part of the cash-generating unit (for example, receivables or other financial assets) or liabilities that have been recognised (for example, payables, pensions and other provisions). In such cases, the carrying amount of the cash-generating unit is increased by the carrying amount of those assets and decreased by the carrying amount of those liabilities.

Goodwill

Allocating goodwill to cash-generating units

80   **For the purpose of impairment testing, goodwill acquired in a business combination shall, from the acquisition date, be allocated to each of the acquirer's cash-generating units, or groups of cash-generating units, that is expected to benefit from the synergies of the combination, irrespective of whether other assets or liabilities of the acquiree are assigned to those units or groups of units. Each unit or group of units to which the goodwill is so allocated shall:**

(a)   represent the lowest level within the entity at which the goodwill is monitored for internal management purposes; and

(b)   not be larger than an operating segment as defined by paragraph 5 of AASB 8 *Operating Segments* before aggregation.

81   Goodwill recognised in a business combination is an asset representing the future economic benefits arising from other assets acquired in a business combination that are not individually identified and separately recognised. Goodwill does not generate cash flows independently of other assets or groups of assets, and often contributes to the cash flows of multiple cash-generating units. Goodwill sometimes cannot be allocated on a non-arbitrary basis to individual cash-generating units, but only to groups of cash-generating units. As a result, the lowest level within the entity at which the goodwill is monitored for internal management purposes sometimes comprises a number of cash-generating units to which the goodwill relates, but to which it cannot be allocated. References in paragraphs 83–99 and Appendix C to a cash-generating unit to which goodwill is allocated should be read as references also to a group of cash-generating units to which goodwill is allocated.

82   Applying the requirements in paragraph 80 results in goodwill being tested for impairment at a level that reflects the way an entity manages its operations and with which the goodwill would naturally be associated. Therefore, the development of additional reporting systems is typically not necessary.

83   A cash-generating unit to which goodwill is allocated for the purpose of impairment testing may not coincide with the level at which goodwill is allocated in accordance with AASB 121 *The Effects of Changes in Foreign Exchange Rates* for the purpose of measuring foreign currency gains and losses. For example, if an entity is required by AASB 121 to allocate goodwill to relatively low levels for the purpose of measuring foreign currency gains and losses, it is not required to test the goodwill for impairment at that same level unless it also monitors the goodwill at that level for internal management purposes.

84   If the initial allocation of goodwill acquired in a business combination cannot be completed before the end of the annual period in which the business combination is effected, that initial allocation shall be completed before the end of the first annual period beginning after the acquisition date.

85   In accordance with AASB 3 *Business Combinations*, if the initial accounting for a business combination can be determined only provisionally by the end of the period in which the combination is effected, the acquirer:

(a)   accounts for the combination using those provisional values; and

(b)   recognises any adjustments to those provisional values as a result of completing the initial accounting within the measurement period, which will not exceed twelve months from the acquisition date.

In such circumstances, it might also not be possible to complete the initial allocation of the goodwill recognised in the combination before the end of the annual period in which the combination is effected. When this is the case, the entity discloses the information required by paragraph 133.

86   If goodwill has been allocated to a cash-generating unit and the entity disposes of an operation within that unit, the goodwill associated with the operation disposed of shall be:

(a)   included in the carrying amount of the operation when determining the gain or loss on disposal; and

(b)   measured on the basis of the relative values of the operation disposed of and the portion of the cash-generating unit retained, unless the entity can demonstrate that some other method better reflects the goodwill associated with the operation disposed of.

Example

An entity sells for CU100 an operation that was part of a cash-generating unit to which goodwill has been allocated. The goodwill allocated to the unit cannot be identified or associated with an asset group at a level lower than that unit, except arbitrarily. The recoverable amount of the portion of the cash-generating unit retained is CU300.

Because the goodwill allocated to the cash-generating unit cannot be non-arbitrarily identified or associated with an asset group at a level lower than that unit, the goodwill associated with the operation disposed of is measured on the basis of the relative values of the operation disposed of and the portion of the unit retained. Therefore, 25 per cent of the goodwill allocated to the cash-generating unit is included in the carrying amount of the operation that is sold.

87   **If an entity reorganises its reporting structure in a way that changes the composition of one or more cash-generating units to which goodwill has been allocated, the goodwill shall be reallocated to the units affected. This reallocation shall be performed using a relative value approach similar to that used when an entity disposes of an operation within a cash-generating unit, unless the entity can demonstrate that some other method better reflects the goodwill associated with the reorganised units.**

Example

Goodwill had previously been allocated to cash-generating unit A. The goodwill allocated to A cannot be identified or associated with an asset group at a level lower than A, except arbitrarily. A is to be divided and integrated into three other cash-generating units, B, C and D.

Because the goodwill allocated to A cannot be non-arbitrarily identified or associated with an asset group at a level lower than A, it is reallocated to units B, C and D on the basis of the relative values of the three portions of A before those portions are integrated with B, C and D.

Testing cash-generating units with goodwill for impairment

88   **When, as described in paragraph 81, goodwill relates to a cash-generating unit but has not been allocated to that unit, the unit shall be tested for impairment, whenever there is an indication that the unit may be impaired, by comparing the unit's carrying amount, excluding any goodwill, with its recoverable amount. Any impairment loss shall be recognised in accordance with paragraph 104.**

89   If a cash-generating unit described in paragraph 88 includes in its carrying amount an intangible asset that has an indefinite useful life or is not yet available for use and that asset can be tested for impairment only as part of the cash-generating unit, paragraph 10 requires the unit also to be tested for impairment annually.

90   **A cash-generating unit to which goodwill has been allocated shall be tested for impairment annually, and whenever there is an indication that the unit may be impaired, by comparing the carrying amount of the unit, including the goodwill, with the recoverable amount of the unit. If the recoverable amount of the unit exceeds the carrying amount of the unit, the unit and the goodwill allocated to that unit shall be regarded as not impaired. If the carrying amount of the unit exceeds the recoverable amount of the unit, the entity shall recognise the impairment loss in accordance with paragraph 104.**

91–95 [Deleted]

Timing of impairment tests

96   **The annual impairment test for a cash-generating unit to which goodwill has been allocated may be performed at any time during an annual period, provided the test is performed at the same time every year. Different cash-generating units may be tested for impairment at different times. However, if some or all of the goodwill allocated to a cash-generating unit was acquired in a business combination during**

the current annual period, that unit shall be tested for impairment before the end of the current annual period.

97   If the assets constituting the cash-generating unit to which goodwill has been allocated are tested for impairment at the same time as the unit containing the goodwill, they shall be tested for impairment before the unit containing the goodwill. Similarly, if the cash-generating units constituting a group of cash-generating units to which goodwill has been allocated are tested for impairment at the same time as the group of units containing the goodwill, the individual units shall be tested for impairment before the group of units containing the goodwill.

98   At the time of impairment testing a cash-generating unit to which goodwill has been allocated, there may be an indication of an impairment of an asset within the unit containing the goodwill. In such circumstances, the entity tests the asset for impairment first, and recognises any impairment loss for that asset before testing for impairment the cash-generating unit containing the goodwill. Similarly, there may be an indication of an impairment of a cash-generating unit within a group of units containing the goodwill. In such circumstances, the entity tests the cash-generating unit for impairment first, and recognises any impairment loss for that unit, before testing for impairment the group of units to which the goodwill is allocated.

99   The most recent detailed calculation made in a preceding period of the recoverable amount of a cash-generating unit to which goodwill has been allocated may be used in the impairment test of that unit in the current period provided all of the following criteria are met:

    (a)   the assets and liabilities making up the unit have not changed significantly since the most recent recoverable amount calculation;

    (b)   the most recent recoverable amount calculation resulted in an amount that exceeded the carrying amount of the unit by a substantial margin; and

    (c)   based on an analysis of events that have occurred and circumstances that have changed since the most recent recoverable amount calculation, the likelihood that a current recoverable amount determination would be less than the current carrying amount of the unit is remote.

Corporate assets

100   Corporate assets include group or divisional assets such as the building of a headquarters or a division of the entity, EDP equipment or a research centre. The structure of an entity determines whether an asset meets this Standard's definition of corporate assets for a particular cash-generating unit. The distinctive characteristics of corporate assets are that they do not generate cash inflows independently of other assets or groups of assets and their carrying amount cannot be fully attributed to the cash-generating unit under review.

101   Because corporate assets do not generate separate cash inflows, the recoverable amount of an individual corporate asset cannot be determined unless management has decided to dispose of the asset. As a consequence, if there is an indication that a corporate asset may be impaired, recoverable amount is determined for the cash-generating unit or group of cash-generating units to which the corporate asset belongs, and is compared with the carrying amount of this cash-generating unit or group of cash-generating units. Any impairment loss is recognised in accordance with paragraph 104.

102   In testing a cash-generating unit for impairment, an entity shall identify all the corporate assets that relate to the cash-generating unit under review. If a portion of the carrying amount of a corporate asset:

    (a)   can be allocated on a reasonable and consistent basis to that unit, the entity shall compare the carrying amount of the unit, including the portion of the carrying amount of the corporate asset allocated to the unit, with its recoverable amount. Any impairment loss shall be recognised in accordance with paragraph 104.

(b)   cannot be allocated on a reasonable and consistent basis to that unit, the entity shall:

(i)   compare the carrying amount of the unit, excluding the corporate asset, with its recoverable amount and recognise any impairment loss in accordance with paragraph 104;

(ii)   identify the smallest group of cash-generating units that includes the cash-generating unit under review and to which a portion of the carrying amount of the corporate asset can be allocated on a reasonable and consistent basis; and

(iii) compare the carrying amount of that group of cash-generating units, including the portion of the carrying amount of the corporate asset allocated to that group of units, with the recoverable amount of the group of units. Any impairment loss shall be recognised in accordance with paragraph 104.

103   Illustrative Example 8 illustrates the application of these requirements to corporate assets.

Impairment loss for a cash-generating unit

104   An impairment loss shall be recognised for a cash-generating unit (the smallest group of cash-generating units to which goodwill or a corporate asset has been allocated) if, and only if, the recoverable amount of the unit (group of units) is less than the carrying amount of the unit (group of units). The impairment loss shall be allocated to reduce the carrying amount of the assets of the unit (group of units) in the following order:

(a)   first, to reduce the carrying amount of any goodwill allocated to the cash-generating unit (group of units); and

(b)   then, to the other assets of the unit (group of units) pro rata on the basis of the carrying amount of each asset in the unit (group of units).

These reductions in carrying amounts shall be treated as impairment losses on individual assets and recognised in accordance with paragraph 60.

105   In allocating an impairment loss in accordance with paragraph 104, an entity shall not reduce the carrying amount of an asset below the highest of:

(a)   its fair value less costs of disposal (if measurable);

(b)   its value in use (if determinable); and

(c)   zero.

The amount of the impairment loss that would otherwise have been allocated to the asset shall be allocated pro rata to the other assets of the unit (group of units).

106   If it is not practicable to estimate the recoverable amount of each individual asset of a cash-generating unit, this Standard requires an arbitrary allocation of an impairment loss between the assets of that unit, other than goodwill, because all assets of a cash-generating unit work together.

107   If the recoverable amount of an individual asset cannot be determined (see paragraph 67):

(a)   an impairment loss is recognised for the asset if its carrying amount is greater than the higher of its fair value less costs of disposal and the results of the allocation procedures described in paragraphs 104 and 105; and

(b)   no impairment loss is recognised for the asset if the related cash-generating unit is not impaired. This applies even if the asset's fair value less costs of disposal is less than its carrying amount.

Example

A machine has suffered physical damage but is still working, although not as well as before it was damaged. The machine's fair value less costs of disposal is less than its carrying amount. The machine does not generate independent cash inflows. The smallest identifiable group of assets that includes the machine and generates cash inflows that are largely independent of the cash inflows from other assets is the production line to which the machine belongs. The recoverable amount of the production line shows that the production line taken as a whole is not impaired.

Assumption 1: budgets/forecasts approved by management reflect no commitment of management to replace the machine.

The recoverable amount of the machine alone cannot be estimated because the machine's value in use:

(a)   *may differ from its fair value less costs of disposal; and*

(b)   *can be determined only for the cash-generating unit to which the machine belongs (the production line).*

The production line is not impaired. Therefore, no impairment loss is recognised for the machine. Nevertheless, the entity may need to reassess the depreciation period or the depreciation method for the machine. Perhaps a shorter depreciation period or a faster depreciation method is required to reflect the expected remaining useful life of the machine or the pattern in which economic benefits are expected to be consumed by the entity.

Assumption 2: budgets/forecasts approved by management reflect a commitment of management to replace the machine and sell it in the near future. Cash flows from continuing use of the machine until its disposal are estimated to be negligible.

The machine's value in use can be estimated to be close to its fair value less costs of disposal. Therefore, the recoverable amount of the machine can be determined and no consideration is given to the cash-generating unit to which the machine belongs (ie the production line). Because the machine's fair value less costs of disposal is less than its carrying amount, an impairment loss is recognised for the machine.

---

108 **After the requirements in paragraphs 104 and 105 have been applied, a liability shall be recognised for any remaining amount of an impairment loss for a cash-generating unit if, and only if, that is required by another Standard.**

Reversing an impairment loss

109   Paragraphs 110–116 set out the requirements for reversing an impairment loss recognised for an asset or a cash-generating unit in prior periods. These requirements use the term 'an asset' but apply equally to an individual asset or a cash-generating unit. Additional requirements for an individual asset are set out in paragraphs 117–121, for a cash-generating unit in paragraphs 122 and 123 and for goodwill in paragraphs 124 and 125.

110   **An entity shall assess at the end of each reporting period whether there is any indication that an impairment loss recognised in prior periods for an asset other than goodwill may no longer exist or may have decreased. If any such indication exists, the entity shall estimate the recoverable amount of that asset.**

111   **In assessing whether there is any indication that an impairment loss recognised in prior periods for an asset other than goodwill may no longer exist or may have decreased, an entity shall consider, as a minimum, the following indications:**

External sources of information

(a)   **there are observable indications that the asset's value has increased significantly during the period.**

(b)   **significant changes with a favourable effect on the entity have taken place during the period, or will take place in the near future, in the technological, market, economic or legal environment in which the entity operates or in the market to which the asset is dedicated.**

(c)   market interest rates or other market rates of return on investments have decreased during the period, and those decreases are likely to affect the discount rate used in calculating the asset's value in use and increase the asset's recoverable amount materially.

Internal sources of information

(d)   significant changes with a favourable effect on the entity have taken place during the period, or are expected to take place in the near future, in the extent to which, or manner in which, the asset is used or is expected to be used. These changes include costs incurred during the period to improve or enhance the asset's performance or restructure the operation to which the asset belongs.

(e)   evidence is available from internal reporting that indicates that the economic performance of the asset is, or will be, better than expected.

112   Indications of a potential decrease in an impairment loss in paragraph 111 mainly mirror the indications of a potential impairment loss in paragraph 12.

113   If there is an indication that an impairment loss recognised for an asset other than goodwill may no longer exist or may have decreased, this may indicate that the remaining useful life, the depreciation (amortisation) method or the residual value may need to be reviewed and adjusted in accordance with the Standard applicable to the asset, even if no impairment loss is reversed for the asset.

114   An impairment loss recognised in prior periods for an asset other than goodwill shall be reversed if, and only if, there has been a change in the estimates used to determine the asset's recoverable amount since the last impairment loss was recognised. If this is the case, the carrying amount of the asset shall, except as described in paragraph 117, be increased to its recoverable amount. That increase is a reversal of an impairment loss.

115   A reversal of an impairment loss reflects an increase in the estimated service potential of an asset, either from use or from sale, since the date when an entity last recognised an impairment loss for that asset. Paragraph 130 requires an entity to identify the change in estimates that causes the increase in estimated service potential. Examples of changes in estimates include:

(a)   a change in the basis for recoverable amount (ie whether recoverable amount is based on fair value less costs of disposal or value in use);

(b)   if recoverable amount was based on value in use, a change in the amount or timing of estimated future cash flows or in the discount rate; or

(c)   if recoverable amount was based on fair value less costs of disposal, a change in estimate of the components of fair value less costs of disposal.

116   An asset's value in use may become greater than the asset's carrying amount simply because the present value of future cash inflows increases as they become closer. However, the service potential of the asset has not increased. Therefore, an impairment loss is not reversed just because of the passage of time (sometimes called the 'unwinding' of the discount), even if the recoverable amount of the asset becomes higher than its carrying amount.

Reversing an impairment loss for an individual asset

117   The increased carrying amount of an asset other than goodwill attributable to a reversal of an impairment loss shall not exceed the carrying amount that would have been determined (net of amortisation or depreciation) had no impairment loss been recognised for the asset in prior years.

118   Any increase in the carrying amount of an asset other than goodwill above the carrying amount that would have been determined (net of amortisation or depreciation) had

no impairment loss been recognised for the asset in prior years is a revaluation. In accounting for such a revaluation, an entity applies the Standard applicable to the asset.

119 **A reversal of an impairment loss for an asset other than goodwill shall be recognised immediately in profit or loss, unless the asset is carried at revalued amount in accordance with another Standard (for example, the revaluation model in AASB 116). Any reversal of an impairment loss of a revalued asset shall be treated as a revaluation increase in accordance with that other Standard.**

120 A reversal of an impairment loss on a revalued asset is recognised in other comprehensive income and increases the revaluation surplus for that asset. However, to the extent that an impairment loss on the same revalued asset was previously recognised in profit or loss, a reversal of that impairment loss is also recognised in profit or loss.

Aus120.1 Notwithstanding paragraph 120, in respect of not-for-profit entities, a reversal of an impairment loss on a revalued asset is recognised in other comprehensive income and increases the revaluation surplus. However, to the extent that an impairment loss on the same class of asset was previously recognised in profit or loss, a reversal of that impairment loss is also recognised in profit or loss.

121 **After a reversal of an impairment loss is recognised, the depreciation (amortisation) charge for the asset shall be adjusted in future periods to allocate the asset's revised carrying amount, less its residual value (if any), on a systematic basis over its remaining useful life.**

Reversing an impairment loss for a cash-generating unit

122 **A reversal of an impairment loss for a cash-generating unit shall be allocated to the assets of the unit, except for goodwill, pro rata with the carrying amounts of those assets. These increases in carrying amounts shall be treated as reversals of impairment losses for individual assets and recognised in accordance with paragraph 119.**

123 **In allocating a reversal of an impairment loss for a cash-generating unit in accordance with paragraph 122, the carrying amount of an asset shall not be increased above the lower of:**

(a) **its recoverable amount (if determinable); and**

(b) **the carrying amount that would have been determined (net of amortisation or depreciation) had no impairment loss been recognised for the asset in prior periods.**

The amount of the reversal of the impairment loss that would otherwise have been allocated to the asset shall be allocated pro rata to the other assets of the unit, except for goodwill.

Reversing an impairment loss for goodwill

124 **An impairment loss recognised for goodwill shall not be reversed in a subsequent period.**

125 AASB 138 *Intangible Assets* prohibits the recognition of internally generated goodwill. Any increase in the recoverable amount of goodwill in the periods following the recognition of an impairment loss for that goodwill is likely to be an increase in internally generated goodwill, rather than a reversal of the impairment loss recognised for the acquired goodwill.

Disclosure

126 **An entity shall disclose the following for each class of assets:**

(a) **the amount of impairment losses recognised in profit or loss during the period and the line item(s) of the statement of comprehensive income in which those impairment losses are included.**

(b)   the amount of reversals of impairment losses recognised in profit or loss during the period and the line item(s) of the statement of comprehensive income in which those impairment losses are reversed.

(c)   the amount of impairment losses on revalued assets recognised in other comprehensive income during the period.

(d)   the amount of reversals of impairment losses on revalued assets recognised in other comprehensive income during the period.

127   A class of assets is a grouping of assets of similar nature and use in an entity's operations.

128   The information required in paragraph 126 may be presented with other information disclosed for the class of assets. For example, this information may be included in a reconciliation of the carrying amount of property, plant and equipment, at the beginning and end of the period, as required by AASB 116.

129   An entity that reports segment information in accordance with AASB 8 shall disclose the following for each reportable segment:

(a)   the amount of impairment losses recognised in profit or loss and in other comprehensive income during the period.

(b)   the amount of reversals of impairment losses recognised in profit or loss and in other comprehensive income during the period.

130   An entity shall disclose the following for an individual asset (including goodwill) or a cash-generating unit, for which an impairment loss has been recognised or reversed during the period:

(a)   the events and circumstances that led to the recognition or reversal of the impairment loss.

(b)   the amount of the impairment loss recognised or reversed.

(c)   for an individual asset:

    (i)   the nature of the asset; and

    (ii)   if the entity reports segment information in accordance with AASB 8, the reportable segment to which the asset belongs.

(d)   for a cash-generating unit:

    (i)   a description of the cash-generating unit (such as whether it is a product line, a plant, a business operation, a geographical area, or a reportable segment as defined in AASB 8);

    (ii)   the amount of the impairment loss recognised or reversed by class of assets and, if the entity reports segment information in accordance with AASB 8, by reportable segment; and

    (iii)   if the aggregation of assets for identifying the cash-generating unit has changed since the previous estimate of the cash-generating unit's recoverable amount (if any), a description of the current and former way of aggregating assets and the reasons for changing the way the cash-generating unit is identified.

(e)   the recoverable amount of the asset (cash-generating unit) and whether the recoverable amount of the asset (cash-generating unit) is its fair value less costs of disposal or its value in use.

(f)   if the recoverable amount is fair value less costs of disposal, the entity shall disclose the following information:

    (i)   the level of the fair value hierarchy (see AASB 13) within which the fair value measurement of the asset (cash-generating unit) is categorised in its entirety (without taking into account whether the 'costs of disposal' are observable);

(ii)   for fair value measurements categorised within Level 2 and Level 3 of the fair value hierarchy, a description of the valuation technique(s) used to measure fair value less costs of disposal. If there has been a change in valuation technique, the entity shall disclose that change and the reason(s) for making it; and

(iii)   for fair value measurements categorised within Level 2 and Level 3 of the fair value hierarchy, each key assumption on which management has based its determination of fair value less costs of disposal. Key assumptions are those to which the asset's (cash-generating unit's) recoverable amount is most sensitive. The entity shall also disclose the discount rate(s) used in the current measurement and previous measurement if fair value less costs of disposal is measured using a present value technique.

(g)   if recoverable amount is value in use, the discount rate(s) used in the current estimate and previous estimate (if any) of value in use.

131   An entity shall disclose the following information for the aggregate impairment losses and the aggregate reversals of impairment losses recognised during the period for which no information is disclosed in accordance with paragraph 130:

(a)   the main classes of assets affected by impairment losses and the main classes of assets affected by reversals of impairment losses.

(b)   the main events and circumstances that led to the recognition of these impairment losses and reversals of impairment losses.

132   An entity is encouraged to disclose assumptions used to determine the recoverable amount of assets (cash-generating units) during the period. However, paragraph 134 requires an entity to disclose information about the estimates used to measure the recoverable amount of a cash-generating unit when goodwill or an intangible asset with an indefinite useful life is included in the carrying amount of that unit.

133   If, in accordance with paragraph 84, any portion of the goodwill acquired in a business combination during the period has not been allocated to a cash-generating unit (group of units) at the end of the reporting period, the amount of the unallocated goodwill shall be disclosed together with the reasons why that amount remains unallocated.

Estimates used to measure recoverable amounts of cash-generating units containing goodwill or intangible assets with indefinite useful lives

134   An entity shall disclose the information required by (a)–(f) for each cash-generating unit (group of units) for which the carrying amount of goodwill or intangible assets with indefinite useful lives allocated to that unit (group of units) is significant in comparison with the entity's total carrying amount of goodwill or intangible assets with indefinite useful lives:

(a)   the carrying amount of goodwill allocated to the unit (group of units).

(b)   the carrying amount of intangible assets with indefinite useful lives allocated to the unit (group of units).

(c)   the basis on which the unit's (group of units') recoverable amount has been determined (ie value in use or fair value less costs of disposal).

(d)   if the unit's (group of units') recoverable amount is based on value in use:

(i)   each key assumption on which management has based its cash flow projections for the period covered by the most recent budgets/forecasts. Key assumptions are those to which the unit's (group of units') recoverable amount is most sensitive.

(ii) a description of management's approach to determining the value(s) assigned to each key assumption, whether those value(s) reflect past experience or, if appropriate, are consistent with external sources of information, and, if not, how and why they differ from past experience or external sources of information.

(iii) the period over which management has projected cash flows based on financial budgets/forecasts approved by management and, when a period greater than five years is used for a cash-generating unit (group of units), an explanation of why that longer period is justified.

(iv) the growth rate used to extrapolate cash flow projections beyond the period covered by the most recent budgets/forecasts, and the justification for using any growth rate that exceeds the long-term average growth rate for the products, industries, or country or countries in which the entity operates, or for the market to which the unit (group of units) is dedicated.

(v) the discount rate(s) applied to the cash flow projections.

(e) if the unit's (group of units') recoverable amount is based on fair value less costs of disposal, the valuation technique(s) used to measure fair value less costs of disposal. An entity is not required to provide the disclosures required by AASB 13. If fair value less costs of disposal is not measured using a quoted price for an identical unit (group of units), an entity shall disclose the following information:

(i) each key assumption on which management has based its determination of fair value less costs of disposal. Key assumptions are those to which the unit's (group of units') recoverable amount is most sensitive.

(ii) a description of management's approach to determining the value (or values) assigned to each key assumption, whether those values reflect past experience or, if appropriate, are consistent with external sources of information, and, if not, how and why they differ from past experience or external sources of information.

(iiA) the level of the fair value hierarchy (see AASB 13) within which the fair value measurement is categorised in its entirety (without giving regard to the observability of 'costs of disposal').

(iiB) if there has been a change in valuation technique, the change and the reason(s) for making it.

If fair value less costs of disposal is measured using discounted cash flow projections, an entity shall disclose the following information:

(iii) the period over which management has projected cash flows.

(iv) the growth rate used to extrapolate cash flow projections.

(v) the discount rate(s) applied to the cash flow projections.

(f) if a reasonably possible change in a key assumption on which management has based its determination of the unit's (group of units') recoverable amount would cause the unit's (group of units') carrying amount to exceed its recoverable amount:

(i) the amount by which the unit's (group of units') recoverable amount exceeds its carrying amount.

       (ii)   the value assigned to the key assumption.

       (iii)   the amount by which the value assigned to the key assumption must change, after incorporating any consequential effects of that change on the other variables used to measure recoverable amount, in order for the unit's (group of units') recoverable amount to be equal to its carrying amount.

135   If some or all of the carrying amount of goodwill or intangible assets with indefinite useful lives is allocated across multiple cash-generating units (groups of units), and the amount so allocated to each unit (group of units) is not significant in comparison with the entity's total carrying amount of goodwill or intangible assets with indefinite useful lives, that fact shall be disclosed, together with the aggregate carrying amount of goodwill or intangible assets with indefinite useful lives allocated to those units (groups of units). In addition, if the recoverable amounts of any of those units (groups of units) are based on the same key assumption(s) and the aggregate carrying amount of goodwill or intangible assets with indefinite useful lives allocated to them is significant in comparison with the entity's total carrying amount of goodwill or intangible assets with indefinite useful lives, an entity shall disclose that fact, together with:

(a)   the aggregate carrying amount of goodwill allocated to those units (groups of units).

(b)   the aggregate carrying amount of intangible assets with indefinite useful lives allocated to those units (groups of units).

(c)   a description of the key assumption(s).

(d)   a description of management's approach to determining the value(s) assigned to the key assumption(s), whether those value(s) reflect past experience or, if appropriate, are consistent with external sources of information, and, if not, how and why they differ from past experience or external sources of information.

(e)   if a reasonably possible change in the key assumption(s) would cause the aggregate of the units' (groups of units') carrying amounts to exceed the aggregate of their recoverable amounts:

       (i)   the amount by which the aggregate of the units' (groups of units') recoverable amounts exceeds the aggregate of their carrying amounts.

       (ii)   the value(s) assigned to the key assumption(s).

       (iii) the amount by which the value(s) assigned to the key assumption(s) must change, after incorporating any consequential effects of the change on the other variables used to measure recoverable amount, in order for the aggregate of the units' (groups of units') recoverable amounts to be equal to the aggregate of their carrying amounts.

136   The most recent detailed calculation made in a preceding period of the recoverable amount of a cash-generating unit (group of units) may, in accordance with paragraph 24 or 99, be carried forward and used in the impairment test for that unit (group of units) in the current period provided specified criteria are met. When this is the case, the information for that unit (group of units) that is incorporated into the disclosures required by paragraphs 134 and 135 relate to the carried forward calculation of recoverable amount.

137   Illustrative Example 9 illustrates the disclosures required by paragraphs 134 and 135.

AASB

Transition provisions and effective date

138   [Deleted]

139   [Deleted by the AASB]

Aus139.1   An entity shall apply this Standard for annual periods beginning on or after 1 January 2018. Earlier application is encouraged for periods beginning after 24 July 2014 but before 1 January 2018. If an entity applies the Standard for a period beginning before 1 January 2018, it shall disclose that fact.

140–140C   [Deleted by the AASB]

140D AASB 2008-7 *Amendments to Australian Accounting Standards – Cost of an Investment in a Subsidiary, Jointly Controlled Entity or Associate*, issued in July 2008, added paragraph 12(h) in the previous version of this Standard. An entity shall apply that amendment prospectively for annual periods beginning on or after 1 January 2009. Earlier application is permitted. If an entity applies the related amendments in paragraphs 4 and 38A of AASB 127 (July 2004, as amended) or paragraphs 4 and 38A of AASB 127 (March 2008, as amended) for an earlier period, it shall apply the amendment in paragraph 12(h) at the same time.

140E AASB 2009-5 *Further Amendments to Australian Accounting Standards arising from the Annual Improvements Project*, issued in May 2009, amended paragraph 80(b) in the previous version of this Standard. An entity shall apply that amendment prospectively for annual periods beginning on or after 1 January 2010. Earlier application is permitted. If an entity applies the amendment for an earlier period it shall disclose that fact.

140F   [Deleted]

140G   [Deleted]

140H–140J   [Deleted by the AASB]

140K   [Deleted]

140L AASB 2014-5 *Amendments to Australian Accounting Standards arising from AASB 15*, issued in December 2014, amended paragraph 2 in the previous version of this Standard. An entity shall apply that amendment when it applies IFRS 15.

140M AASB 2010-7 *Amendments to Australian Accounting Standards arising from AASB 9 (December 2010)* (as amended) and AASB 2014-7 *Amendments to Australian Accounting Standards arising from AASB 9 (December 2014)* amended the previous version of this Standard as follows: amended paragraphs 2(e), 4 and 5 and deleted paragraph 140F. Paragraph 140G, added by AASB 2010-7, was deleted by AASB 2014-1 *Amendments to Australian Accounting Standards*. Paragraph 140K, added by AASB 2014-1, was deleted by AASB 2014-7. An entity shall apply those amendments when it applies AASB 9.

Withdrawal of IAS 36 (issued 1998)

141   [Deleted by the AASB]

Commencement of the legislative instrument

Aus141.1   For legal purposes, this legislative instrument commences on 31 December 2017.

Withdrawal of AASB pronouncements

Aus141.2 This Standard repeals AASB 136 *Impairment of Assets* issued in July 2004. Despite the repeal, after the time this Standard starts to apply under section 334 of the Corporations Act (either generally or in relation to an individual entity), the repealed Standard continues to apply in relation to any period ending before that time as if the repeal had not occurred.

[Note: When this Standard applies under section 334 of the Corporations Act (either generally or in relation to an individual entity), it supersedes the application of the repealed Standard.]

APPENDIX A
USING PRESENT VALUE TECHNIQUES TO MEASURE VALUE IN USE

This appendix is an integral part of the Standard. It provides guidance on the use of present value techniques in measuring value in use. Although the guidance uses the term 'asset', it equally applies to a group of assets forming a cash-generating unit.

The components of a present value measurement

A1 The following elements together capture the economic differences between assets:

(a) an estimate of the future cash flow, or in more complex cases, series of future cash flows the entity expects to derive from the asset;

(b) expectations about possible variations in the amount or timing of those cash flows;

(c) the time value of money, represented by the current market risk-free rate of interest;

(d) the price for bearing the uncertainty inherent in the asset; and

(e) other, sometimes unidentifiable, factors (such as illiquidity) that market participants would reflect in pricing the future cash flows the entity expects to derive from the asset.

A2 This appendix contrasts two approaches to computing present value, either of which may be used to estimate the value in use of an asset, depending on the circumstances. Under the 'traditional' approach, adjustments for factors (b)–(e) described in paragraph A1 are embedded in the discount rate. Under the 'expected cash flow' approach, factors (b), (d) and (e) cause adjustments in arriving at risk-adjusted expected cash flows. Whichever approach an entity adopts to reflect expectations about possible variations in the amount or timing of future cash flows, the result should be to reflect the expected present value of the future cash flows, ie the weighted average of all possible outcomes.

General principles

A3 The techniques used to estimate future cash flows and interest rates will vary from one situation to another depending on the circumstances surrounding the asset in question. However, the following general principles govern any application of present value techniques in measuring assets:

(a) interest rates used to discount cash flows should reflect assumptions that are consistent with those inherent in the estimated cash flows. Otherwise, the effect of some assumptions will be double-counted or ignored. For example, a discount rate of 12 per cent might be applied to contractual cash flows of a loan receivable. That rate reflects expectations about future defaults from loans with particular characteristics. That same 12 per cent rate should not be used to discount expected cash flows because those cash flows already reflect assumptions about future defaults.

(b)   estimated cash flows and discount rates should be free from both bias and factors unrelated to the asset in question. For example, deliberately understating estimated net cash flows to enhance the apparent future profitability of an asset introduces a bias into the measurement.

(c)   estimated cash flows or discount rates should reflect the range of possible outcomes rather than a single most likely, minimum or maximum possible amount.

Traditional and expected cash flow approaches to present value

Traditional approach

A4   Accounting applications of present value have traditionally used a single set of estimated cash flows and a single discount rate, often described as 'the rate commensurate with the risk'. In effect, the traditional approach assumes that a single discount rate convention can incorporate all the expectations about the future cash flows and the appropriate risk premium. Therefore, the traditional approach places most of the emphasis on selection of the discount rate.

A5   In some circumstances, such as those in which comparable assets can be observed in the marketplace, a traditional approach is relatively easy to apply. For assets with contractual cash flows, it is consistent with the manner in which marketplace participants describe assets, as in 'a 12 per cent bond'.

A6   However, the traditional approach may not appropriately address some complex measurement problems, such as the measurement of non-financial assets for which no market for the item or a comparable item exists. A proper search for 'the rate commensurate with the risk' requires analysis of at least two items—an asset that exists in the marketplace and has an observed interest rate and the asset being measured. The appropriate discount rate for the cash flows being measured must be inferred from the observable rate of interest in that other asset. To draw that inference, the characteristics of the other asset's cash flows must be similar to those of the asset being measured. Therefore, the measurer must do the following:

(a)   identify the set of cash flows that will be discounted;

(b)   identify another asset in the marketplace that appears to have similar cash flow characteristics;

(c)   compare the cash flow sets from the two items to ensure that they are similar (for example, are both sets contractual cash flows, or is one contractual and the other an estimated cash flow?);

(d)   evaluate whether there is an element in one item that is not present in the other (for example, is one less liquid than the other?); and

(e)   evaluate whether both sets of cash flows are likely to behave (ie vary) in a similar fashion in changing economic conditions.

Expected cash flow approach

A7 The expected cash flow approach is, in some situations, a more effective measurement tool than the traditional approach. In developing a measurement, the expected cash flow approach uses all expectations about possible cash flows instead of the single most likely cash flow. For example, a cash flow might be CU100, CU200 or CU300 with probabilities of 10 per cent, 60 per cent and 30 per cent, respectively. The expected cash flow is CU220. The expected cash flow approach thus differs from the traditional approach by focusing on direct analysis of the cash flows in question and on more explicit statements of the assumptions used in the measurement.

A8 The expected cash flow approach also allows use of present value techniques when the timing of cash flows is uncertain. For example, a cash flow of CU1,000 may be received in one year, two years or three years with probabilities of 10 per cent, 60 per cent and 30 per cent, respectively. The example below shows the computation of expected present value in that situation.

Present value of CU1,000 in 1 year at 5%	CU952.38	
Probability	10.00%	CU95.24
Present value of CU1,000 in 2 years at 5.25%	CU902.73	
Probability	60.00%	CU541.64
Present value of CU1,000 in 3 years at 5.50%	CU851.61	
Probability	30.00%	CU255.48
Expected present value		CU892.36

A9 The expected present value of CU892.36 differs from the traditional notion of a best estimate of CU902.73 (the 60 per cent probability). A traditional present value computation applied to this example requires a decision about which of the possible timings of cash flows to use and, accordingly, would not reflect the probabilities of other timings. This is because the discount rate in a traditional present value computation cannot reflect uncertainties in timing.

A10 The use of probabilities is an essential element of the expected cash flow approach. Some question whether assigning probabilities to highly subjective estimates suggests greater precision than, in fact, exists. However, the proper application of the traditional approach (as described in paragraph A6) requires the same estimates and subjectivity without providing the computational transparency of the expected cash flow approach.

A11 Many estimates developed in current practice already incorporate the elements of expected cash flows informally. In addition, accountants often face the need to measure an asset using limited information about the probabilities of possible cash flows. For example, an accountant might be confronted with the following situations:

(a) the estimated amount falls somewhere between CU50 and CU250, but no amount in the range is more likely than any other amount. Based on that limited information, the estimated expected cash flow is CU150 [(50 + 250)/2].

(b) the estimated amount falls somewhere between CU50 and CU250, and the most likely amount is CU100. However, the probabilities attached to each amount are unknown. Based on that limited information, the estimated expected cash flow is CU133.33 [(50 + 100 + 250)/3].

(c) the estimated amount will be CU50 (10 per cent probability), CU250 (30 per cent probability), or CU100 (60 per cent probability). Based on that limited information, the estimated expected cash flow is CU140 [(50 × 0.10) + (250 × 0.30) + (100 × 0.60)].

In each case, the estimated expected cash flow is likely to provide a better estimate of value in use than the minimum, most likely or maximum amount taken alone.

A12   The application of an expected cash flow approach is subject to a cost-benefit constraint. In some cases, an entity may have access to extensive data and may be able to develop many cash flow scenarios. In other cases, an entity may not be able to develop more than general statements about the variability of cash flows without incurring substantial cost. The entity needs to balance the cost of obtaining additional information against the additional reliability that information will bring to the measurement.

A13   Some maintain that expected cash flow techniques are inappropriate for measuring a single item or an item with a limited number of possible outcomes. They offer an example of an asset with two possible outcomes: a 90 per cent probability that the cash flow will be CU10 and a 10 per cent probability that the cash flow will be CU1,000. They observe that the expected cash flow in that example is CU109 and criticise that result as not representing either of the amounts that may ultimately be paid.

A14   Assertions like the one just outlined reflect underlying disagreement with the measurement objective. If the objective is accumulation of costs to be incurred, expected cash flows may not produce a representationally faithful estimate of the expected cost. However, this Standard is concerned with measuring the recoverable amount of an asset. The recoverable amount of the asset in this example is not likely to be CU10, even though that is the most likely cash flow. This is because a measurement of CU10 does not incorporate the uncertainty of the cash flow in the measurement of the asset. Instead, the uncertain cash flow is presented as if it were a certain cash flow. No rational entity would sell an asset with these characteristics for CU10.

Discount rate

A15   Whichever approach an entity adopts for measuring the value in use of an asset, interest rates used to discount cash flows should not reflect risks for which the estimated cash flows have been adjusted. Otherwise, the effect of some assumptions will be double-counted.

A16   When an asset-specific rate is not directly available from the market, an entity uses surrogates to estimate the discount rate. The purpose is to estimate, as far as possible, a market assessment of:

   (a)   the time value of money for the periods until the end of the asset's useful life; and

   (b)   factors (b), (d) and (e) described in paragraph A1, to the extent those factors have not caused adjustments in arriving at estimated cash flows.

A17   As a starting point in making such an estimate, the entity might take into account the following rates:

   (a)   the entity's weighted average cost of capital determined using techniques such as the Capital Asset Pricing Model;

   (b)   the entity's incremental borrowing rate; and

   (c)   other market borrowing rates.

A18   However, these rates must be adjusted:

   (a)   to reflect the way that the market would assess the specific risks associated with the asset's estimated cash flows; and

   (b)   to exclude risks that are not relevant to the asset's estimated cash flows or for which the estimated cash flows have been adjusted.

   Consideration should be given to risks such as country risk, currency risk and price risk.

A19 The discount rate is independent of the entity's capital structure and the way the entity financed the purchase of the asset, because the future cash flows expected to arise from an asset do not depend on the way in which the entity financed the purchase of the asset.

A20 Paragraph 55 requires the discount rate used to be a pre-tax rate. Therefore, when the basis used to estimate the discount rate is post-tax, that basis is adjusted to reflect a pre-tax rate.

A21 An entity normally uses a single discount rate for the estimate of an asset's value in use. However, an entity uses separate discount rates for different future periods where value in use is sensitive to a difference in risks for different periods or to the term structure of interest rates.

APPENDIX C
IMPAIRMENT TESTING CASH-GENERATING UNITS WITH GOODWILL AND NON-CONTROLLING INTERESTS

This appendix is an integral part of the Standard.

C1 In accordance with AASB 3, the acquirer measures and recognises goodwill as of the acquisition date as the excess of (a) over (b) below:

    (a)   the aggregate of:

        (i)   the consideration transferred measured in accordance with AASB 3, which generally requires acquisition-date fair value;

        (ii)   the amount of any non-controlling interest in the acquiree measured in accordance with AASB 3; and

        (iii)   in a business combination achieved in stages, the acquisition-date fair value of the acquirer's previously held equity interest in the acquiree.

    (b)   the net of the acquisition-date amounts of the identifiable assets acquired and liabilities assumed measured in accordance with AASB 3.

Allocation of goodwill

C2 Paragraph 80 of this Standard requires goodwill acquired in a business combination to be allocated to each of the acquirer's cash-generating units, or groups of cash-generating units, expected to benefit from the synergies of the combination, irrespective of whether other assets or liabilities of the acquiree are assigned to those units, or groups of units. It is possible that some of the synergies resulting from a business combination will be allocated to a cash-generating unit in which the non-controlling interest does not have an interest.

Testing for impairment

C3 Testing for impairment involves comparing the recoverable amount of a cash-generating unit with the carrying amount of the cash-generating unit.

C4 If an entity measures non-controlling interests as its proportionate interest in the net identifiable assets of a subsidiary at the acquisition date, rather than at fair value, goodwill attributable to non-controlling interests is included in the recoverable amount of the related cash-generating unit but is not recognised in the parent's consolidated financial statements. As a consequence, an entity shall gross up the carrying amount of goodwill allocated to the unit to include the goodwill attributable to the non-controlling interest. This adjusted carrying amount is then compared with the recoverable amount of the unit to determine whether the cash-generating unit is impaired.

Allocating an impairment loss

C5   Paragraph 104 requires any identified impairment loss to be allocated first to reduce the carrying amount of goodwill allocated to the unit and then to the other assets of the unit pro rata on the basis of the carrying amount of each asset in the unit.

C6   If a subsidiary, or part of a subsidiary, with a non-controlling interest is itself a cash-generating unit, the impairment loss is allocated between the parent and the non-controlling interest on the same basis as that on which profit or loss is allocated.

C7   If a subsidiary, or part of a subsidiary, with a non-controlling interest is part of a larger cash-generating unit, goodwill impairment losses are allocated to the parts of the cash-generating unit that have a non-controlling interest and the parts that do not. The impairment losses should be allocated to the parts of the cash-generating unit on the basis of:

     (a)   to the extent that the impairment relates to goodwill in the cash-generating unit, the relative carrying values of the goodwill of the parts before the impairment; and

     (b)   to the extent that the impairment relates to identifiable assets in the cash-generating unit, the relative carrying values of the net identifiable assets of the parts before the impairment. Any such impairment is allocated to the assets of the parts of each unit pro rata on the basis of the carrying amount of each asset in the part.

In those parts that have a non-controlling interest, the impairment loss is allocated between the parent and the non-controlling interest on the same basis as that on which profit or loss is allocated.

C8   If an impairment loss attributable to a non-controlling interest relates to goodwill that is not recognised in the parent's consolidated financial statements (see paragraph C4), that impairment is not recognised as a goodwill impairment loss. In such cases, only the impairment loss relating to the goodwill that is allocated to the parent is recognised as a goodwill impairment loss.

C9   Illustrative Example 7 illustrates the impairment testing of a non-wholly-owned cash-generating unit with goodwill.

APPENDIX D
AUSTRALIAN DEFINED TERMS

This appendix is an integral part of the Standard.

Aus6.1   [Deleted by the AASB]

Aus6.2   **The following terms are also used in this Standard with the meaning specified.**

     A *not-for-profit entity* is an entity whose principal objective is not the generation of profit. A not-for-profit entity can be a single entity or a group of entities comprising the parent and each of the entities that it controls.

APPENDIX E
AUSTRALIAN REDUCED DISCLOSURE REQUIREMENTS

This appendix is an integral part of the Standard.

AusE1   **The following do not apply to entities preparing general purpose financial statements under Australian Accounting Standards – Reduced Disclosure Requirements:**

         (a)   **paragraphs 129, 130(a)–(d), 130(f)–(g) and 131–137; and**

         (b)   **in paragraph 130(e), the text "and whether ... value in use".**

     Entities applying Australian Accounting Standards – Reduced Disclosure Requirements may elect to comply with some or all of these excluded requirements.

AusE2   The requirements that do not apply to entities preparing general purpose financial statements under Australian Accounting Standards – Reduced Disclosure Requirements are also identified in this Standard by shading of the relevant text.

ILLUSTRATIVE EXAMPLES

CONTENTS

AASB

ILLUSTRATIVE EXAMPLES

These examples accompany, but are not part of, AASB 136. All the examples assume that the entities concerned have no transactions other than those described. In the examples monetary amounts are denominated in 'currency units (CU)'.

Example 1 Identification of cash-generating units

The purpose of this example is:

(a)   *to indicate how cash-generating units are identified in various situations; and*

(b)   *to highlight certain factors that an entity may consider in identifying the cash-generating unit to which an asset belongs.*

A Retail store chain

Background

IE1   Store X belongs to a retail store chain M. X makes all its retail purchases through M's purchasing centre. Pricing, marketing, advertising and human resources policies (except for hiring X's cashiers and sales staff) are decided by M. M also owns five other stores in the same city as X (although in different neighbourhoods) and 20 other stores in other cities. All stores are managed in the same way as X. X and four other stores were purchased five years ago and goodwill was recognised.

What is the cash-generating unit for X (X's cash-generating unit)?

Analysis

IE2   In identifying X's cash-generating unit, an entity considers whether, for example:

(a)   internal management reporting is organised to measure performance on a store-by-store basis; and

(b)   the business is run on a store-by-store profit basis or on a region/city basis.

IE3   All M's stores are in different neighbourhoods and probably have different customer bases. So, although X is managed at a corporate level, X generates cash inflows that are largely independent of those of M's other stores. Therefore, it is likely that X is a cash-generating unit.

IE4   If X's cash-generating unit represents the lowest level within M at which the goodwill is monitored for internal management purposes, M applies to that cash-generating unit the impairment test described in paragraph 90 of AASB 136. If information about the carrying amount of goodwill is not available and monitored for internal management purposes at the level of X's cash-generating unit, M applies to that cash-generating unit the impairment test described in paragraph 88 of AASB 136.

B Plant for an intermediate step in a production process

Background

IE5   A significant raw material used for plant Y's final production is an intermediate product bought from plant X of the same entity. X's products are sold to Y at a transfer price that passes all margins to X. Eighty per cent of Y's final production is sold to customers outside of the entity. Sixty per cent of X's final production is sold to Y and the remaining 40 per cent is sold to customers outside of the entity.

For each of the following cases, what are the cash-generating units for X and Y?

Case 1: X could sell the products it sells to Y in an active market. Internal transfer prices are higher than market prices.

Case 2: There is no active market for the products X sells to Y.

Analysis
Case 1

IE6   X could sell its products in an active market and, so, generate cash inflows that would be largely independent of the cash inflows from Y. Therefore, it is likely that X is a separate cash-generating unit, although part of its production is used by Y (see paragraph 70 of AASB 136).

IE7   It is likely that Y is also a separate cash-generating unit. Y sells 80 per cent of its products to customers outside of the entity. Therefore, its cash inflows can be regarded as largely independent.

IE8   Internal transfer prices do not reflect market prices for X's output. Therefore, in determining value in use of both X and Y, the entity adjusts financial budgets/forecasts to reflect management's best estimate of future prices that could be achieved in arm's length transactions for those of X's products that are used internally (see paragraph 70 of AASB 136).

Case 2

IE9   It is likely that the recoverable amount of each plant cannot be assessed independently of the recoverable amount of the other plant because:

    (a)   the majority of X's production is used internally and could not be sold in an active market. So, cash inflows of X depend on demand for Y's products. Therefore, X cannot be considered to generate cash inflows that are largely independent of those of Y.

    (b)   the two plants are managed together.

IE10 As a consequence, it is likely that X and Y together are the smallest group of assets that generates cash inflows that are largely independent.

C Single product entity
Background

IE11 Entity M produces a single product and owns plants A, B and C. Each plant is located in a different continent. A produces a component that is assembled in either B or C. The combined capacity of B and C is not fully utilised. M's products are sold worldwide from either B or C. For example, B's production can be sold in C's continent if the products can be delivered faster from B than from C. Utilisation levels of B and C depend on the allocation of sales between the two sites.

For each of the following cases, what are the cash-generating units for A, B and C?

Case 1: There is an active market for A's products.

Case 2: There is no active market for A's products.

Analysis
Case 1

IE12 It is likely that A is a separate cash-generating unit because there is an active market for its products (see Example B – Plant for an intermediate step in a production process, Case 1).

IE13 Although there is an active market for the products assembled by B and C, cash inflows for B and C depend on the allocation of production across the two sites. It is unlikely that the future cash inflows for B and C can be determined individually. Therefore, it is likely that B and C together are the smallest identifiable group of assets that generates cash inflows that are largely independent.

IE14 In determining the value in use of A and B plus C, M adjusts financial budgets/forecasts to reflect its best estimate of future prices that could be achieved in arm's length transactions for A's products (see paragraph 70 of AASB 136).

Case 2

IE15 It is likely that the recoverable amount of each plant cannot be assessed independently because:

    (a)   there is no active market for A's products. Therefore, A's cash inflows depend on sales of the final product by B and C.

    (b)   although there is an active market for the products assembled by B and C, cash inflows for B and C depend on the allocation of production across the two sites. It is unlikely that the future cash inflows for B and C can be determined individually.

IE16 As a consequence, it is likely that A, B and C together (ie M as a whole) are the smallest identifiable group of assets that generates cash inflows that are largely independent.

D Magazine titles

Background

IE17 A publisher owns 150 magazine titles of which 70 were purchased and 80 were self-created. The price paid for a purchased magazine title is recognised as an intangible asset. The costs of creating magazine titles and maintaining the existing titles are recognised as an expense when incurred. Cash inflows from direct sales and advertising are identifiable for each magazine title. Titles are managed by customer segments. The level of advertising income for a magazine title depends on the range of titles in the customer segment to which the magazine title relates. Management has a policy to abandon old titles before the end of their economic lives and replace them immediately with new titles for the same customer segment.

    What is the cash-generating unit for an individual magazine title?

Analysis

IE18 It is likely that the recoverable amount of an individual magazine title can be assessed. Even though the level of advertising income for a title is influenced, to a certain extent, by the other titles in the customer segment, cash inflows from direct sales and advertising are identifiable for each title. In addition, although titles are managed by customer segments, decisions to abandon titles are made on an individual title basis.

IE19 Therefore, it is likely that individual magazine titles generate cash inflows that are largely independent of each other and that each magazine title is a separate cash-generating unit.

E Building half-rented to others and half-occupied for own use

Background

IE20 M is a manufacturing company. It owns a headquarters building that used to be fully occupied for internal use. After down-sizing, half of the building is now used internally and half rented to third parties. The lease agreement with the tenant is for five years.

    What is the cash-generating unit of the building?

Analysis

IE21 The primary purpose of the building is to serve as a corporate asset, supporting M's manufacturing activities. Therefore, the building as a whole cannot be considered to generate cash inflows that are largely independent of the cash inflows from the entity as a whole. So, it is likely that the cash-generating unit for the building is M as a whole.

IE22 The building is not held as an investment. Therefore, it would not be appropriate to determine the value in use of the building based on projections of future market related rents.

Example 2 Calculation of value in use and recognition of an impairment loss

In this example, tax effects are ignored.

Background and calculation of value in use

IE23   At the end of 20X0, entity T acquires entity M for CU10,000. M has manufacturing plants in three countries.

Schedule 1. Data at the end of 20X0

End of 20X0	*Allocation of purchase price*	*Fair value of identifiable assets*	*Goodwill*[a]
	CU	CU	CU
Activities in Country A	3,000	2,000	1,000
Activities in Country B	2,000	1,500	500
Activities in Country C	5,000	3,500	1,500
Total	10,000	7,000	3,000

(a) Activities in each country represent the lowest level at which the goodwill is monitored for internal management purposes (determined as the difference between the purchase price of the activities in each country, as specified in the purchase agreement, and the fair value of the identifiable assets).

IE23A   Because goodwill has been allocated to the activities in each country, each of those activities must be tested for impairment annually or more frequently if there is any indication that it may be impaired (see paragraph 90 of AASB 136).

IE24   The recoverable amounts (ie higher of value in use and fair value less costs of disposal) of the cash-generating units are determined on the basis of value in use calculations. At the end of 20X0 and 20X1, the value in use of each cash-generating unit exceeds its carrying amount. Therefore the activities in each country and the goodwill allocated to those activities are regarded as not impaired.

IE25   At the beginning of 20X2, a new government is elected in Country A. It passes legislation significantly restricting exports of T's main product. As a result, and for the foreseeable future, T's production in Country A will be cut by 40 per cent.

IE26   The significant export restriction and the resulting production decrease require T also to estimate the recoverable amount of the Country A operations at the beginning of 20X2.

IE27   T uses straight-line depreciation over a 12-year life for the Country A identifiable assets and anticipates no residual value.

IE28   To determine the value in use for the Country A cash-generating unit (see Schedule 2), T:

   (a)   prepares cash flow forecasts derived from the most recent financial budgets/forecasts for the next five years (years 20X2–20X6) approved by management.

   (b)   estimates subsequent cash flows (years 20X7–20Y2) based on declining growth rates. The growth rate for 20X7 is estimated to be 3 per cent. This rate is lower than the average long-term growth rate for the market in Country A.

   (c)   selects a 15 per cent discount rate, which represents a pre-tax rate that reflects current market assessments of the time value of money and the risks specific to the Country A cash-generating unit.

Recognition and measurement of impairment loss

IE29 The recoverable amount of the Country A cash-generating unit is CU1,360.

IE30 T compares the recoverable amount of the Country A cash-generating unit with its carrying amount (see Schedule 3).

IE31 Because the carrying amount exceeds the recoverable amount by CU1,473, T recognises an impairment loss of CU1,473 immediately in profit or loss. The carrying amount of the goodwill that relates to the Country A operations is reduced to zero before reducing the carrying amount of other identifiable assets within the Country A cash-generating unit (see paragraph 104 of AASB 136).

IE32 Tax effects are accounted for separately in accordance with AASB 112 *Income Taxes* (see Illustrative Example 3A).

Schedule 2. Calculation of the value in use of the Country A cash-generating unit at the beginning of 20X2

Year	Long-term growth rates	Future cash flows	Present value factor at 15% discount rate[a]	Discounted future cash flows
		CU		CU
20X2 (n=1)		230[b]	0.86957	200
20X3		253[b]	0.75614	191
20X4		273[b]	0.65752	180
20X5		290[b]	0.57175	166
20X6		304[b]	0.49718	151
20X7	3%	313[c]	0.43233	135
20X8	(2%)	307[c]	0.37594	115
20X9	(6%)	289[c]	0.32690	94
20Y0	(15%)	245[c]	0.28426	70
20Y1	(25%)	184[c]	0.24719	45
20Y2	(67%)	61[c]	0.21494	13
Value in use				1,360

(a) The present value factor is calculated as $k = 1/(1+a)^n$, where a = discount rate and n = period of discount.
(b) Based on management's best estimate of net cash flow projections (after the 40% cut).
(c) Based on an extrapolation from preceding year cash flow using declining growth rates.

Schedule 3. Calculation and allocation of the impairment loss for the Country A cash-generating unit at the beginning of 20X2

Beginning of 20X2	Goodwill	Identifiable assets	Total
	CU	CU	CU
Historical cost	1,000	2,000	3,000
Accumulated depreciation (20X1)	–	(167)	(167)
Carrying amount	1,000	1,833	2,833
Impairment loss	(1,000)	(473)	(1,473)
Carrying amount after impairment loss	–	1,360	1,360

Example 3 Deferred tax effects

Use the data for entity T as presented in Example 2, with supplementary information as provided in this example.

A Deferred tax effects of the recognition of an impairment loss

IE33   At the beginning of 20X2, the tax base of the identifiable assets of the Country A cash-generating unit is CU900. Impairment losses are not deductible for tax purposes. The tax rate is 40 per cent.

IE34   The recognition of an impairment loss on the assets of the Country A cash-generating unit reduces the taxable temporary difference related to those assets. The deferred tax liability is reduced accordingly.

Beginning of 20X2	Identifiable assets before impairment loss	Impairment loss	Identifiable assets after impairment loss
	CU	CU	CU
Carrying amount (Example 2)	1,833	(473)	1,360
Tax base	900	–	900
Taxable temporary difference	933	(473)	460
Deferred tax liability at 40%	373	(189)	184

IE35   In accordance with AASB 112 *Income Taxes*, no deferred tax relating to the goodwill was recognised initially. Therefore, the impairment loss relating to the goodwill does not give rise to a deferred tax adjustment.

B Recognition of an impairment loss creates a deferred tax asset

IE36   An entity has an identifiable asset with a carrying amount of CU1,000. Its recoverable amount is CU650. The tax rate is 30 per cent and the tax base of the asset is CU800. Impairment losses are not deductible for tax purposes. The effect of the impairment loss is as follows:

	Before impairment	Effect of impairment	After impairment
	CU	CU	CU
Carrying amount	1,000	(350)	650
Tax base	800	–	800
Taxable (deductible) temporary difference	200	(350)	(150)
Deferred tax liability (asset) at 30%	60	(105)	(45)

IE37   In accordance with AASB 112, the entity recognises the deferred tax asset to the extent that it is probable that taxable profit will be available against which the deductible temporary difference can be utilised.

Example 4 Reversal of an impairment loss

Use the data for entity T as presented in Example 2, with supplementary information as provided in this example. In this example, tax effects are ignored.

Background

IE38   In 20X3, the government is still in office in Country A, but the business situation is improving. The effects of the export laws on T's production are proving to be less drastic than initially expected by management. As a result, management estimates that production will increase by 30 per cent. This favourable change requires T to re-estimate the recoverable amount of the net assets of the Country A operations (see paragraphs 110 and 111 of AASB 136). The cash-generating unit for the net assets of the Country A operations is still the Country A operations.

IE39   Calculations similar to those in Example 2 show that the recoverable amount of the Country A cash-generating unit is now CU1,910.

Reversal of impairment loss

IE40   T compares the recoverable amount and the net carrying amount of the Country A cash-generating unit.

Schedule 1. Calculation of the carrying amount of the Country A cash-generating unit at the end of 20X3

	Goodwill	Identifiable assets	Total
	CU	CU	CU
Beginning of 20X2 (Example 2)			
Historical cost	1,000	2,000	3,000
Accumulated depreciation	–	(167)	(167)
Impairment loss	(1,000)	(473)	(1,473)
Carrying amount after impairment loss	–	1,360	1,360
End of 20X3			
Additional depreciation (2 years)[a]	–	(247)	(247)
Carrying amount	–	1,113	1,113
Recoverable amount			1,910
Excess of recoverable amount over carrying amount			797

(a) After recognition of the impairment loss at the beginning of 20X2, T revised the depreciation charge for the Country A identifiable assets (from CU166.7 per year to CU123.6 per year), based on the revised carrying amount and remaining useful life (11 years).

IE41   There has been a favourable change in the estimates used to determine the recoverable amount of the Country A net assets since the last impairment loss was recognised. Therefore, in accordance with paragraph 114 of AASB 136, T recognises a reversal of the impairment loss recognised in 20X2.

IE42   In accordance with paragraphs 122 and 123 of AASB 136, T increases the carrying amount of the Country A identifiable assets by CU387 (see Schedule 3), ie up to the lower of recoverable amount (CU1,910) and the identifiable assets' depreciated historical cost (CU1,500) (see Schedule 2). This increase is recognised immediately in profit or loss.

IE43 In accordance with paragraph 124 of AASB 136, the impairment loss on goodwill is not reversed.

Schedule 2. Determination of the depreciated historical cost of the Country A identifiable assets at the end of 20X3

End of 20X3	Identifiable assets
	CU
Historical cost	2,000
Accumulated depreciation *(166.7 × 3 years)*	(500)
Depreciated historical cost	1,500
Carrying amount (Schedule 1)	1,113
Difference	387

Schedule 3. Carrying amount of the Country A assets at the end of 20X3

End of 20X3	Goodwill	Identifiable assets	Total
	CU	CU	CU
Gross carrying amount	1,000	2,000	3,000
Accumulated amortisation	–	(414)	(414)
Accumulated impairment loss	(1,000)	(473)	(1,473)
Carrying amount	–	1,113	1,113
Reversal of impairment loss	0	387	387
Carrying amount after reversal of impairment loss	–	1,500	1,500

Example 5 Treatment of a future restructuring

In this example, tax effects are ignored.

Background

IE44 At the end of 20X0, entity K tests a plant for impairment. The plant is a cash-generating unit. The plant's assets are carried at depreciated historical cost. The plant has a carrying amount of CU3,000 and a remaining useful life of 10 years.

IE45 The plant's recoverable amount (ie higher of value in use and fair value less costs of disposal) is determined on the basis of a value in use calculation. Value in use is calculated using a pre-tax discount rate of 14 per cent.

IE46 Management approved budgets reflect that:

(a) at the end of 20X3, the plant will be restructured at an estimated cost of CU100. Since K is not yet committed to the restructuring, a provision has not been recognised for the future restructuring costs.

(b) there will be future benefits from this restructuring in the form of reduced future cash outflows.

IE47 At the end of 20X2, K becomes committed to the restructuring. The costs are still estimated to be CU100 and a provision is recognised accordingly. The plant's estimated future cash flows reflected in the most recent management approved budgets are given in paragraph IE51 and a current discount rate is the same as at the end of 20X0.

IE48 At the end of 20X3, actual restructuring costs of CU100 are incurred and paid. Again, the plant's estimated future cash flows reflected in the most recent management approved budgets and a current discount rate are the same as those estimated at the end of 20X2.

At the end of 20X0

Schedule 1. Calculation of the plant's value in use at the end of 20X0

Year	Future cash flows	Discounted at 14%
	CU	CU
20X1	300[(a)]	263
20X2	280[(b)]	215
20X3	420[(b)]	283
20X4	520[(b)]	308
20X5	350[(b)]	182
20X6	420[(b)]	191
20X7	480[(b)]	192
20X8	480[(b)]	168
20X9	460[(b)]	141
20X10	400[(b)]	108
		2,051

(a) Excludes estimated restructuring costs reflected in management budgets.
(b) Excludes estimated benefits expected from the restructuring reflected in management budgets.

IE49 The plant's recoverable amount (ie value in use) is less than its carrying amount. Therefore, K recognises an impairment loss for the plant.

Schedule 2. Calculation of the impairment loss at the end of 20X0

	Plant
	CU
Carrying amount before impairment loss	3,000
Recoverable amount (Schedule 1)	2,051
Impairment loss	(949)
Carrying amount after impairment loss	2,051

At the end of 20X1

IE50 No event occurs that requires the plant's recoverable amount to be re-estimated. Therefore, no calculation of the recoverable amount is required to be performed.

At the end of 20X2

IE51 The entity is now committed to the restructuring. Therefore, in determining the plant's value in use, the benefits expected from the restructuring are considered in forecasting cash flows. This results in an increase in the estimated future cash flows used to determine value in use at the end of 20X0. In accordance with paragraphs 110 and 111 of AASB 136, the recoverable amount of the plant is re-determined at the end of 20X2.

Schedule 3. Calculation of the plant's value in use at the end of 20X2

Year	Future cash flows	Discounted at 14%
	CU	CU
20X3	420[(a)]	368
20X4	570[(b)]	439
20X5	380[(b)]	256
20X6	450[(b)]	266
20X7	510[(b)]	265
20X8	510[(b)]	232
20X9	480[(b)]	192
20X10	410[(b)]	144
		2,162

(a) Excludes estimated restructuring costs because a liability has already been recognised.
(b) Includes estimated benefits expected from the restructuring reflected in management budgets.

IE52 The plant's recoverable amount (value in use) is higher than its carrying amount (see Schedule 4). Therefore, K reverses the impairment loss recognised for the plant at the end of 20X0.

Schedule 4. Calculation of the reversal of the impairment loss at the end of 20X2

	Plant
	CU
Carrying amount at the end of 20X0 (Schedule 2)	2,051
End of 20X2	
Depreciation charge (for 20X1 and 20X2–Schedule 5)	(410)
Carrying amount before reversal	1,641
Recoverable amount (Schedule 3)	2,162
Reversal of the impairment loss	521
Carrying amount after reversal	2,162
Carrying amount: depreciated historical cost (Schedule 5)	2,400[(a)]

(a) The reversal does not result in the carrying amount of the plant exceeding what its carrying amount would have been at depreciated historical cost. Therefore, the full reversal of the impairment loss is recognised.

At the end of 20X3

IE53 There is a cash outflow of CU100 when the restructuring costs are paid. Even though a cash outflow has taken place, there is no change in the estimated future cash flows used to determine value in use at the end of 20X2. Therefore, the plant's recoverable amount is not calculated at the end of 20X3.

AASB

Schedule 5. Summary of the carrying amount of the plant

End of year	Depreciated historical cost	Recoverable amount	Adjusted depreciation charge	Impairment loss	Carrying amount after impairment
	CU	CU	CU	CU	CU
20X0	3,000	2,051	0	(949)	2,051
20X1	2,700	nc	(205)	0	1,846
20X2	2,400	2,162	(205)	521	2,162
20X3	2,100	nc	(270)	0	1,892

nc = not calculated as there is no indication that the impairment loss may have increased/decreased.

Example 6 Treatment of future costs

In this example, tax effects are ignored.

Background

IE54　At the end of 20X0, entity F tests a machine for impairment. The machine is a cash-generating unit. It is carried at depreciated historical cost and its carrying amount is CU150,000. It has an estimated remaining useful life of 10 years.

IE55　The machine's recoverable amount (ie higher of value in use and fair value less costs of disposal) is determined on the basis of a value in use calculation. Value in use is calculated using a pre-tax discount rate of 14 per cent.

IE56　Management approved budgets reflect:

(a)　estimated costs necessary to maintain the level of economic benefit expected to arise from the machine in its current condition; and

(b)　that in 20X4, costs of CU25,000 will be incurred to enhance the machine's performance by increasing its productive capacity.

IE57　At the end of 20X4, costs to enhance the machine's performance are incurred. The machine's estimated future cash flows reflected in the most recent management approved budgets are given in paragraph IE60 and a current discount rate is the same as at the end of 20X0.

At the end of 20X0

Schedule 1. Calculation of the machine's value in use at the end of 20X0

Year	Future cash flows	Discounted at 14%
	CU	CU
20X1	22,165[(a)]	19,443
20X2	21,450[(a)]	16,505
20X3	20,550[(a)]	13,871
20X4	24,725[(a),(b)]	14,639
20X5	25,325[(a),(c)]	13,153
20X6	24,825[(a),(c)]	11,310
20X7	24,123[(a),(c)]	9,640
20X8	25,533[(a),(c)]	8,951

(Continued)

(Continued)

Year	Future cash flows	Discounted at 14%
	CU	CU
20X9	24,234[(a),(c)]	7,452
20X10	22,850[(a),(c)]	6,164
Value in use		121,128

(a) Includes estimated costs necessary to maintain the level of economic benefit expected to arise from the machine in its current condition.

(b) Excludes estimated costs to enhance the machine's performance reflected in management budgets.

(c) Excludes estimated benefits expected from enhancing the machine's performance reflected in management budgets.

IE58 The machine's recoverable amount (value in use) is less than its carrying amount. Therefore, F recognises an impairment loss for the machine.

Schedule 2. Calculation of the impairment loss at the end of 20X0

	Machine
	CU
Carrying amount before impairment loss	150,000
Recoverable amount (Schedule 1)	121,128
Impairment loss	(28,872)
Carrying amount after impairment loss	121,128

Years 20X1–20X3

IE59 No event occurs that requires the machine's recoverable amount to be re-estimated. Therefore, no calculation of recoverable amount is required to be performed.

At the end of 20X4

IE60 The costs to enhance the machine's performance are incurred. Therefore, in determining the machine's value in use, the future benefits expected from enhancing the machine's performance are considered in forecasting cash flows. This results in an increase in the estimated future cash flows used to determine value in use at the end of 20X0. As a consequence, in accordance with paragraphs 110 and 111 of AASB 136, the recoverable amount of the machine is recalculated at the end of 20X4.

Schedule 3. Calculation of the machine's value in use at the end of 20X4

Year	Future cash flows[(a)]	Discounted at 14%
	CU	CU
20X5	30,321	26,597
20X6	32,750	25,200
20X7	31,721	21,411
20X8	31,950	18,917
20X9	33,100	17,191
20X10	27,999	12,756
Value in use		122,072

(a) Includes estimated benefits expected from enhancing the machine's performance reflected in management budgets.

IE61 The machine's recoverable amount (ie value in use) is higher than the machine's carrying amount and depreciated historical cost (see Schedule 4). Therefore, K reverses the impairment loss recognised for the machine at the end of 20X0 so that the machine is carried at depreciated historical cost.

Schedule 4. Calculation of the reversal of the impairment loss at the end of 20X4

	Machine
	CU
Carrying amount at the end of 20X0 (Schedule 2)	121,128
End of 20X4	
Depreciation charge (20X1 to 20X4 – Schedule 5)	(48,452)
Costs to enhance the asset's performance	25,000
Carrying amount before reversal	97,676
Recoverable amount (Schedule 3)	122,072
Reversal of the impairment loss	17,324
Carrying amount after reversal	115,000
Carrying amount: depreciated historical cost (Schedule 5)	115,000[a]

(a) The value in use of the machine exceeds what its carrying amount would have been at depreciated historical cost. Therefore, the reversal is limited to an amount that does not result in the carrying amount of the machine exceeding depreciated historical cost.

Schedule 5. Summary of the carrying amount of the machine

Year	*Depreciated historical cost*	*Recoverable amount*	*Adjusted depreciated charge*	*Impairment loss*	*Carrying amount after impairment*
	CU	*CU*	*CU*	*CU*	*CU*
20X0	150,000	121,128	0	(28,872)	121,128
20X1	135,000	nc	(12,113)	0	109,015
20X2	120,000	nc	(12,113)	0	96,902
20X3	105,000	nc	(12,113)	0	84,789
20X4	90,000		(12,113)		
enhancement	25,000		–		
	115,000	122,072	(12,113)	17,324	115,000
20X5	95,833	nc	(19,167)	0	95,833

nc = not calculated as there is no indication that the impairment loss may have increased/decreased.

Example 7 Impairment testing cash-generating units with goodwill and non-controlling interests

A Non-controlling interests measured initially as a proportionate share of the net identifiable assets

In this example, tax effects are ignored.

Background

IE62 Parent acquires an 80 per cent ownership interest in Subsidiary for CU2,100 on 1 January 20X3. At that date, Subsidiary's net identifiable assets have a fair value of CU1,500. Parent chooses to measure the non-controlling interests as the proportionate interest of Subsidiary's net identifiable assets of CU300 (20% of CU1,500). Goodwill of CU900 is the difference between the aggregate of the consideration transferred and the amount of the non-controlling interests (CU2,100 + CU300) and the net identifiable assets (CU1,500).

IE63   The assets of Subsidiary together are the smallest group of assets that generate cash inflows that are largely independent of the cash inflows from other assets or groups of assets. Therefore Subsidiary is a cash-generating unit. Because other cash-generating units of Parent are expected to benefit from the synergies of the combination, the goodwill of CU500 related to those synergies has been allocated to other cash-generating units within Parent. Because the cash-generating unit comprising Subsidiary includes goodwill within its carrying amount, it must be tested for impairment annually, or more frequently if there is an indication that it may be impaired (see paragraph 90 of AASB 136).

IE64   At the end of 20X3, Parent determines that the recoverable amount of cash-generating unit Subsidiary is CU1,000. The carrying amount of the net assets of Subsidiary, excluding goodwill, is CU1,350.

Testing Subsidiary (cash-generating unit) for impairment

IE65   Goodwill attributable to non-controlling interests is included in Subsidiary's recoverable amount of CU1,000 but has not been recognised in Parent's consolidated financial statements. Therefore, in accordance with paragraph C4 of Appendix C of AASB 136, the carrying amount of Subsidiary is grossed up to include goodwill attributable to the non-controlling interests, before being compared with the recoverable amount of CU1,000. Goodwill attributable to Parent's 80 per cent interest in Subsidiary at the acquisition date is CU400 after allocating CU500 to other cash-generating units within Parent. Therefore, goodwill attributable to the 20 per cent non-controlling interests in Subsidiary at the acquisition date is CU100.

Schedule 1. Testing Subsidiary for impairment at the end of 20X3

End of 20X3	Goodwill of Subsidiary	Net identifiable assets	Total
	CU	CU	CU
Carrying amount	400	1,350	1,750
Unrecognised non-controlling interests	100	–	100
Adjusted carrying amount	500	1,350	1,850
Recoverable amount			1,000
Impairment loss			850

Allocating the impairment loss

IE66   In accordance with paragraph 104 of AASB 136, the impairment loss of CU850 is allocated to the assets in the unit by first reducing the carrying amount of goodwill.

IE67   Therefore, CU500 of the CU850 impairment loss for the unit is allocated to the goodwill. In accordance with paragraph C6 of Appendix C of AASB 136, if the partially-owned subsidiary is itself a cash-generating unit, the goodwill impairment loss is allocated to the controlling and non-controlling interests on the same basis as that on which profit or loss is allocated. In this example, profit or loss is allocated on the basis of relative ownership interests. Because the goodwill is recognised only to the extent of Parent's 80 per cent ownership interest in Subsidiary, Parent recognises only 80 per cent of that goodwill impairment loss (ie CU400).

IE68 The remaining impairment loss of CU350 is recognised by reducing the carrying amounts of Subsidiary's identifiable assets (see Schedule 2).

Schedule 2. Allocation of the impairment loss for Subsidiary at the end of 20X3

End of 20X3	Goodwill	Net identifiable assets	Total
	CU	CU	CU
Carrying amount	400	1,350	1,750
Impairment loss	(400)	(350)	(750)
Carrying amount after impairment loss	–	1,000	1,000

B Non-controlling interests measured initially at fair value and the related subsidiary is a stand-alone cash-generating unit

In this example, tax effects are ignored.

Background

IE68A Parent acquires an 80 per cent ownership interest in Subsidiary for CU2,100 on 1 January 20X3. At that date, Subsidiary's net identifiable assets have a fair value of CU1,500. Parent chooses to measure the non-controlling interests at fair value, which is CU350. Goodwill of CU950 is the difference between the aggregate of the consideration transferred and the amount of the non-controlling interests (CU2,100 + CU350) and the net identifiable assets (CU1,500).

IE68B The assets of Subsidiary together are the smallest group of assets that generate cash inflows that are largely independent of the cash inflows from other assets or groups of assets. Therefore, Subsidiary is a cash-generating unit. Because other cash-generating units of Parent are expected to benefit from the synergies of the combination, the goodwill of CU500 related to those synergies has been allocated to other cash-generating units within Parent. Because Subsidiary includes goodwill within its carrying amount, it must be tested for impairment annually, or more frequently if there is an indication that it might be impaired (see paragraph 90 of AASB 136).

Testing Subsidiary for impairment

IE68C At the end of 20X3, Parent determines that the recoverable amount of cash-generating unit Subsidiary is CU1,650. The carrying amount of the net assets of Subsidiary, excluding goodwill, is CU1,350.

Schedule 1. Testing Subsidiary for impairment at the end of 20X3

End of 20X3	Goodwill	Net identifiable assets	Total
	CU	CU	CU
Carrying amount	450	1,350	1,800
Recoverable amount			1,650
Impairment loss			150

Allocating the impairment loss

IE68D In accordance with paragraph 104 of AASB 136, the impairment loss of CU150 is allocated to the assets in the unit by first reducing the carrying amount of goodwill.

IE68E Therefore, the full amount of impairment loss of CU150 for the unit is allocated to the goodwill. In accordance with paragraph C6 of Appendix C of AASB 136, if the partially-owned subsidiary is itself a cash-generating unit, the goodwill impairment loss is allocated to the controlling and non-controlling interests on the same basis as that on which profit or loss is allocated.

C Non-controlling interests measured initially at fair value and the related subsidiary is part of a larger cash-generating unit

In this example, tax effects are ignored.

Background

IE68F Suppose that, for the business combination described in paragraph IE68A of Example 7B, the assets of Subsidiary will generate cash inflows together with other assets or groups of assets of Parent. Therefore, rather than Subsidiary being the cash-generating unit for the purposes of impairment testing, Subsidiary becomes part of a larger cash-generating unit, Z. Other cash-generating units of Parent are also expected to benefit from the synergies of the combination. Therefore, goodwill related to those synergies, in the amount of CU500, has been allocated to those other cash-generating units. Z's goodwill related to previous business combinations is CU800.

IE68G Because Z includes goodwill within its carrying amount, both from Subsidiary and from previous business combinations, it must be tested for impairment annually, or more frequently if there is an indication that it might be impaired (see paragraph 90 of AASB 136).

Testing Subsidiary for impairment

IE68H At the end of 20X3, Parent determines that the recoverable amount of cash-generating unit Z is CU3,300. The carrying amount of the net assets of Z, excluding goodwill, is CU2,250.

Schedule 3. Testing Z for impairment at the end of 20X3

End of 20X3	Goodwill	Net identifiable assets	Total
	CU	CU	CU
Carrying amount	1,250	2,250	3,500
Recoverable amount			3,300
Impairment loss			200

Allocating the impairment loss

IE68I In accordance with paragraph 104 of AASB 136, the impairment loss of CU200 is allocated to the assets in the unit by first reducing the carrying amount of goodwill. Therefore, the full amount of impairment loss of CU200 for cash-generating unit Z is allocated to the goodwill. In accordance with paragraph C7 of Appendix C of AASB 136, if the partially-owned Subsidiary forms part of a larger cash-generating unit, the goodwill impairment loss would be allocated first to the parts of the cash-generating unit, Z, and then to the controlling and non-controlling interests of the partially-owned Subsidiary.

IE68J Parent allocates the impairment loss to the parts of the cash-generating unit on the basis of the relative carrying values of the goodwill of the parts before the impairment. In this example Subsidiary is allocated 36 per cent of the impairment (450/1,250). The impairment loss is then allocated to the controlling and non-controlling interests on the same basis as that on which profit or loss is allocated.

Example 8 Allocation of corporate assets

In this example, tax effects are ignored.

Background

IE69 Entity M has three cash-generating units: A, B and C. The carrying amounts of those units do not include goodwill. There are adverse changes in the technological environment in which M operates. Therefore, M conducts impairment tests of each of its cash-generating units. At the end of 20X0, the carrying amounts of A, B and C are CU100, CU150 and CU200 respectively.

IE70 The operations are conducted from a headquarters. The carrying amount of the headquarters is CU200: a headquarters building of CU150 and a research centre of CU50. The relative carrying amounts of the cash-generating units are a reasonable indication of the proportion of the headquarters building devoted to each cash-generating unit. The carrying amount of the research centre cannot be allocated on a reasonable basis to the individual cash-generating units.

IE71 The remaining estimated useful life of cash-generating unit A is 10 years. The remaining useful lives of B, C and the headquarters are 20 years. The headquarters is depreciated on a straight-line basis.

IE72 The recoverable amount (ie higher of value in use and fair value less costs of disposal) of each cash-generating unit is based on its value in use. Value in use is calculated using a pre-tax discount rate of 15 per cent.

Identification of corporate assets

IE73 In accordance with paragraph 102 of AASB 136, M first identifies all the corporate assets that relate to the individual cash-generating units under review. The corporate assets are the headquarters building and the research centre.

IE74 M then decides how to deal with each of the corporate assets:

(a) the carrying amount of the headquarters building can be allocated on a reasonable and consistent basis to the cash-generating units under review; and

(b) the carrying amount of the research centre cannot be allocated on a reasonable and consistent basis to the individual cash-generating units under review.

Allocation of corporate assets

IE75 The carrying amount of the headquarters building is allocated to the carrying amount of each individual cash-generating unit. A weighted allocation basis is used because the estimated remaining useful life of A's cash-generating unit is 10 years, whereas the estimated remaining useful lives of B and C's cash-generating units are 20 years.

Schedule 1. Calculation of a weighted allocation of the carrying amount of the headquarters building

End of 20X0	A	B	C	Total
	CU	CU	CU	CU
Carrying amount	100	150	200	450
Useful life	10 years	20 years	20 years	
Weighting based on useful life	1	2	2	
Carrying amount after weighting	100	300	400	800
Pro-rata allocation of the building	12%	38%	50%	100%
	(100/800)	*(300/800)*	*(400/800)*	

(Continued)

(Continued)

End of 20X0	A	B	C	Total
	CU	CU	CU	CU
Allocation of the carrying amount of the building (based on pro-rata above)	19	56	75	150
Carrying amount (after allocation of the building)	119	206	275	600

Determination of recoverable amount and calculation of impairment losses

IE76 Paragraph 102 of AASB 136 requires first that the recoverable amount of each individual cash-generating unit be compared with its carrying amount, including the portion of the carrying amount of the headquarters building allocated to the unit, and any resulting impairment loss recognised. Paragraph 102 of AASB 136 then requires the recoverable amount of M as a whole (ie the smallest group of cash-generating units that includes the research centre) to be compared with its carrying amount, including both the headquarters building and the research centre.

Schedule 2. Calculation of A, B, C and M's value in use at the end of 20X0

	A		B		C		M	
Year	Future cash flows	Discount at 15%	Future cash flows	Discount at 15%	Future cash flows	Discount at 15%	Future cash flows	Discount at 15%
	CU	CU	CU	CU	CU	CU	CU	CU
1	18	16	9	8	10	9	39	34
2	31	23	16	12	20	15	72	54
3	37	24	24	16	34	22	105	69
4	42	24	29	17	44	25	128	73
5	47	24	32	16	51	25	143	71
6	52	22	33	14	56	24	155	67
7	55	21	34	13	60	22	162	61
8	55	18	35	11	63	21	166	54
9	53	15	35	10	65	18	167	48
10	48	12	35	9	66	16	169	42
11			36	8	66	14	132	28
12			35	7	66	12	131	25
13			35	6	66	11	131	21
14			33	5	65	9	128	18
15			30	4	62	8	122	15
16			26	3	60	6	115	12

(Continued)

(Continued)

	A		B		C		M	
Year	Future cash flows	Discount at 15%	Future cash flows	Discount at 15%	Future cash flows	Discount at 15%	Future cash flows	Discount at 15%
	CU	CU	CU	CU	CU	CU	CU	CU
17			22	2	57	5	108	10
18			18	1	51	4	97	8
19			14	1	43	3	85	6
20			10	1	35	2	71	4
Value in use		199		164		271		720[(a)]

(a) It is assumed that the research centre generates additional future cash flows for the entity as a whole. Therefore, the sum of the value in use of each individual cash-generating unit is less than the value in use of the business as a whole. The additional cash flows are not attributable to the headquarters building.

Schedule 3. Impairment testing A, B and C

End of 20X0	A	B	C
	CU	CU	CU
Carrying amount (after allocation of the building) (Schedule 1)	119	206	275
Recoverable amount (Schedule 2)	199	164	271
Impairment loss	0	(42)	(4)

IE77 The next step is to allocate the impairment losses between the assets of the cash-generating units and the headquarters building.

Schedule 4. Allocation of the impairment losses for cash-generating units B and C

Cash-generating unit	**B**		**C**	
	CU		CU	
To headquarters building	(12)	$(42 \times {}^{56}/_{206})$	(1)	$(4 \times {}^{75}/_{275})$
To assets in cash-generating unit	(30)	$(42 \times {}^{150}/_{206})$	(3)	$(4 \times {}^{200}/_{275})$
	(42)		(4)	

IE78 Because the research centre could not be allocated on a reasonable and consistent basis to A, B and C's cash-generating units, M compares the carrying amount of the smallest group of cash-generating units to which the carrying amount of the research centre can be allocated (ie M as a whole) to its recoverable amount.

Schedule 5. Impairment testing the smallest group of cash-generating units to which the carrying amount of the research centre can be allocated (ie M as a whole)

End of 20X0	A	B	C	Building	Research centre	M
	CU	CU	CU	CU	CU	CU
Carrying amount	100	150	200	150	50	650

(Continued)

(Continued)

End of 20X0	A	B	C	Building	Research centre	M
	CU	CU	CU	CU	CU	CU
Impairment loss arising from the first step of the test	–	(30)	(3)	(13)	–	(46)
Carrying amount after the first step of the test	100	120	197	137	50	604
Recoverable amount (Schedule 2)						720
Impairment loss for the 'larger' cash-generating unit						0

IE79 Therefore, no additional impairment loss results from the application of the impairment test to M as a whole. Only an impairment loss of CU46 is recognised as a result of the application of the first step of the test to A, B and C.

Example 9 Disclosures about cash-generating units with goodwill or intangible assets with indefinite useful lives

The purpose of this example is to illustrate the disclosures required by paragraphs 134 and 135 of AASB 136.

Background

IE80 Entity M is a multinational manufacturing firm that uses geographical segments for reporting segment information. M's three reportable segments are Europe, North America and Asia. Goodwill has been allocated for impairment testing purposes to three individual cash-generating units—two in Europe (units A and B) and one in North America (unit C)—and to one group of cash-generating units (comprising operation XYZ) in Asia. Units A, B and C and operation XYZ each represent the lowest level within M at which the goodwill is monitored for internal management purposes.

IE81 M acquired unit C, a manufacturing operation in North America, in December 20X2. Unlike M's other North American operations, C operates in an industry with high margins and high growth rates, and with the benefit of a 10-year patent on its primary product. The patent was granted to C just before M's acquisition of C. As part of accounting for the acquisition of C, M recognised, in addition to the patent, goodwill of CU3,000 and a brand name of CU1,000. M's management has determined that the brand name has an indefinite useful life. M has no other intangible assets with indefinite useful lives.

IE82 The carrying amounts of goodwill and intangible assets with indefinite useful lives allocated to units A, B and C and to operation XYZ are as follows:

	Goodwill	Intangible assets with indefinite useful lives
	CU	CU
A	350	
B	450	
C	3,000	1,000
XYZ	1,200	
Total	5,000	1,000

IE83   During the year ending 31 December 20X3, M determines that there is no impairment of any of its cash-generating units or group of cash-generating units containing goodwill or intangible assets with indefinite useful lives. The recoverable amounts (ie higher of value in use and fair value less costs of disposal) of those units and group of units are determined on the basis of value in use calculations. M has determined that the recoverable amount calculations are most sensitive to changes in the following assumptions:

Units A and B	Unit C	Operation XYZ
Gross margin during the budget period (budget period is 4 years)	5-year US government bond rate during the budget period (budget period is 5 years)	Gross margin during the budget period (budget period is 5 years)
Raw materials price inflation during the budget period	Raw materials price inflation during the budget period	Japanese yen/US dollar exchange rate during the budget period
Market share during the budget period	Market share during the budget period	Market share during the budget period
Growth rate used to extrapolate cash flows beyond the budget period	Growth rate used to extrapolate cash flows beyond the budget period	Growth rate used to extrapolate cash flows beyond the budget period

IE84   Gross margins during the budget period for A, B and XYZ are estimated by M based on average gross margins achieved in the period immediately before the start of the budget period, increased by 5 per cent per year for anticipated efficiency improvements. A and B produce complementary products and are operated by M to achieve the same gross margins.

IE85   Market shares during the budget period are estimated by M based on average market shares achieved in the period immediately before the start of the budget period, adjusted each year for any anticipated growth or decline in market shares. M anticipates that:

   (a)   market shares for A and B will differ, but will each grow during the budget period by 3 per cent per year as a result of ongoing improvements in product quality.

   (b)   C's market share will grow during the budget period by 6 per cent per year as a result of increased advertising expenditure and the benefits from the protection of the 10-year patent on its primary product.

   (c)   XYZ's market share will remain unchanged during the budget period as a result of the combination of ongoing improvements in product quality and an anticipated increase in competition.

IE86   A and B purchase raw materials from the same European suppliers, whereas C's raw materials are purchased from various North American suppliers. Raw materials price inflation during the budget period is estimated by M to be consistent with forecast consumer price indices published by government agencies in the relevant European and North American countries.

IE87   The 5-year US government bond rate during the budget period is estimated by M to be consistent with the yield on such bonds at the beginning of the budget period. The Japanese yen/US dollar exchange rate is estimated by M to be consistent with the average market forward exchange rate over the budget period.

IE88   M uses steady growth rates to extrapolate beyond the budget period cash flows for A, B, C and XYX. The growth rates for A, B and XYZ are estimated by M to be consistent with publicly available information about the long-term average growth rates for the markets in which A, B and XYZ operate. However, the growth rate for C exceeds the long-term average growth rate for the market in which C operates. M's management is of the opinion that this is reasonable in the light of the protection of the 10-year patent on C's primary product.

IE89 M includes the following disclosure in the notes to its financial statements for the year ending 31 December 20X3.

Impairment tests for goodwill and intangible assets with indefinite lives

Goodwill has been allocated for impairment testing purposes to three individual cash-generating units—two in Europe (units A and B) and one in North America (unit C)—and to one group of cash-generating units (comprising operation XYZ) in Asia. The carrying amount of goodwill allocated to unit C and operation XYZ is significant in comparison with the total carrying amount of goodwill, but the carrying amount of goodwill allocated to each of units A and B is not. Nevertheless, the recoverable amounts of units A and B are based on some of the same key assumptions, and the aggregate carrying amount of goodwill allocated to those units is significant.

Operation XYZ

The recoverable amount of operation XYZ has been determined based on a value in use calculation. That calculation uses cash flow projections based on financial budgets approved by management covering a five-year period, and a discount rate of 8.4 per cent. Cash flows beyond that five-year period have been extrapolated using a steady 6.3 per cent growth rate. This growth rate does not exceed the long-term average growth rate for the market in which XYZ operates. Management believes that any reasonably possible change in the key assumptions on which XYZ's recoverable amount is based would *not* cause XYZ's carrying amount to exceed its recoverable amount.

Unit C

The recoverable amount of unit C has also been determined based on a value in use calculation. That calculation uses cash flow projections based on financial budgets approved by management covering a five-year period, and a discount rate of 9.2 per cent. C's cash flows beyond the five-year period are extrapolated using a steady 12 per cent growth rate. This growth rate exceeds by 4 percentage points the long-term average growth rate for the market in which C operates. However, C benefits from the protection of a 10-year patent on its primary product, granted in December 20X2. Management believes that a 12 per cent growth rate is reasonable in the light of that patent. Management also believes that any reasonably possible change in the key assumptions on which C's recoverable amount is based would *not* cause C's carrying amount to exceed its recoverable amount.

Units A and B

The recoverable amounts of units A and B have been determined on the basis of value in use calculations. Those units produce complementary products, and their recoverable amounts are based on some of the same key assumptions. Both value in use calculations use cash flow projections based on financial budgets approved by management covering a four-year period, and a discount rate of 7.9 per cent. Both sets of cash flows beyond the four-year period are extrapolated using a steady 5 per cent growth rate. This growth rate does not exceed the long-term average growth rate for the market in which A and B operate. Cash flow projections during the budget period for both A and B are also based on the same expected gross margins during the budget period and the same raw materials price inflation during the budget period. Management believes that any reasonably possible change in any of these key assumptions would *not* cause the aggregate carrying amount of A and B to exceed the aggregate recoverable amount of those units.

	Operation XYZ	*Unit C*	*Units A and B (in aggregate)*
Carrying amount of goodwill	CU1,200	CU3,000	CU800
Carrying amount of brand name with indefinite useful life	–	CU1,000	–
Key assumptions used in value in use calculations[(a)]			
Key assumption	Budgeted gross margins	5-year US government bond rate	Budgeted gross margins
Basis for determining value(s) assigned to key assumption	Average gross margins achieved in period immediately before the budget period, increased for expected efficiency improvements.	Yield on 5-year US government bonds at the beginning of the budget period.	Average gross margins achieved in period immediately before the budget period, increased for expected efficiency improvements.
	Values assigned to key assumption reflect past experience, except for efficiency improvements. Management believes improvements of 5% per year are reasonably achievable.	Value assigned to key assumption is consistent with external sources of information.	Values assigned to key assumption reflect past experience, except for efficiency improvements. Management believes improvements of 5% per year are reasonably achievable.
Key assumption	Japanese yen/US dollar exchange rate during the budget period	Raw materials price inflation	Raw materials price inflation
Basis for determining value(s) assigned to key assumption	Average market forward exchange rate over the budget period.	Forecast consumer price indices during the budget period for North American countries from which raw materials are purchased.	Forecast consumer price indices during the budget period for European countries from which raw materials are purchased.
	Value assigned to key assumption is consistent with external sources of information.	Value assigned to key assumption is consistent with external sources of information.	Value assigned to key assumption is consistent with external sources of information.
Key assumption	Budgeted market share	Budgeted market share	
Basis for determining value(s) assigned to key assumption	Average market share in period immediately before the budget period.	Average market share in period immediately before the budget period, increased each year for anticipated growth in market share.	

	Operation XYZ	Unit C	Units A and B (in aggregate)
	Value assigned to key assumption reflects past experience. No change in market share expected as a result of ongoing product quality improvements coupled with anticipated increase in competition.	Management believes market share growth of 6% per year is reasonably achievable due to increased advertising expenditure, the benefits from the protection of the 10-year patent on C's primary product, and the expected synergies to be achieved from operating C as part of M's North American segment.	

(a) The key assumptions shown in this table for units A and B are only those that are used in the recoverable amount calculations for both units.

COMPILATION DETAILS

Accounting Standard AASB 136 *Impairment of Assets* as amended

Compilation details are not part of AASB 136.

This compiled Standard applies to annual periods beginning on or after 1 January 2018. It takes into account amendments up to and including 27 June 2016 and was prepared on 20 March 2017 by the staff of the Australian Accounting Standards Board (AASB).

This compilation is not a separate Accounting Standard made by the AASB. Instead, it is a representation of AASB 136 (August 2015) as amended by other Accounting Standards, which are listed in the Table below.

Table of Standards

Standard	Date made	FRL identifier	Commence-ment date	Effective date (annual periods ... on or after ...)	Application, saving or transitional provisions
AASB 136	14 Aug 2015	F2015L01622	31 Dec 2017	*(beginning)* 1 Jan 2018	see (a) below
AASB 2016-4	27 Jun 2016	F2016L01173	31 Dec 2016	*(beginning)* 1 Jan 2017	see (b) below

(a) Entities may elect to apply this Standard to annual periods beginning after 24 July 2014 but before 1 January 2018.
(b) Entities may elect to apply this Standard to annual periods beginning before 1 January 2017.

Table of amendments

Paragraph affected	How affected	By ... [paragraph/page]
Aus5.1	added	AASB 2016-4 [7]
Aus6.1	deleted	AASB 2016-4 [4]
Aus6.2	amended	AASB 2016-4 [5]
Aus32.1–Aus32.2	deleted	AASB 2016-4 [6]

BASIS FOR CONCLUSIONS ON AASB 2016-4

The Basis for Conclusions accompanying AASB 2016-4 *Amendments to Australian Accounting Standards – Recoverable Amount of Non-Cash-Generating Specialised Assets of Not-for-Profit Entities* is attached to this compiled Standard.

DELETED IAS 36 TEXT

Deleted IAS 36 text is not part of AASB 136.

139 An entity shall apply this Standard:

    (a)   to goodwill and intangible assets acquired in business combinations for which the agreement date is on or after 31 March 2004; and

    (b)   to all other assets prospectively from the beginning of the first annual period beginning on or after 31 March 2004.

140 Entities to which paragraph 139 applies are encouraged to apply the requirements of this Standard before the effective dates specified in paragraph 139. However, if an entity applies this Standard before those effective dates, it also shall apply IFRS 3 and IAS 38 (as revised in 2004) at the same time.

140A IAS 1 *Presentation of Financial Statements* (as revised in 2007) amended the terminology used throughout IFRSs. In addition it amended paragraphs 61, 120, 126 and 129. An entity shall apply those amendments for annual periods beginning on or after 1 January 2009. If an entity applies IAS 1 (revised 2007) for an earlier period, the amendments shall be applied for that earlier period.

140B IFRS 3 (as revised in 2008) amended paragraphs 65, 81, 85 and 139, deleted paragraphs 91–95 and 138 and added Appendix C. An entity shall apply those amendments for annual periods beginning on or after 1 July 2009. If an entity applies IFRS 3 (revised 2008) for an earlier period, the amendments shall also be applied for that earlier period.

140C Paragraph 134(e) was amended by *Improvements to IFRSs* issued in May 2008. An entity shall apply that amendment for annual periods beginning on or after 1 January 2009. Earlier application is permitted. If an entity applies the amendment for an earlier period it shall disclose that fact.

140H IFRS 10 and IFRS 11, issued in May 2011, amended paragraph 4, the heading above paragraph 12(h) and paragraph 12(h). An entity shall apply those amendments when it applies IFRS 10 and IFRS 11.

140I IFRS 13, issued in May 2011, amended paragraphs 5, 6, 12, 20, 22, 28, 78, 105, 111, 130 and 134, deleted paragraphs 25–27 and added paragraph 53A. An entity shall apply those amendments when it applies IFRS 13.

140J In May 2013 paragraphs 130 and 134 and the heading above paragraph 138 were amended. An entity shall apply those amendments retrospectively for annual periods beginning on or after 1 January 2014. Earlier application is permitted. An entity shall not apply those amendments in periods (including comparative periods) in which it does not also apply IFRS 13.

141 This Standard supersedes IAS 36 *Impairment of Assets* (issued in 1998).

BASIS FOR CONCLUSIONS ON AASB 2016-4

This Basis for Conclusions accompanies, but is not part of, AASB 136. The Basis for Conclusions was originally published with AASB 2016-4 Amendments to Australian Accounting Standards – Recoverable Amount of Non-Cash-Generating Specialised Assets of Not-for-Profit Entities.

BC1   This Basis for Conclusions summarises the Australian Accounting Standards Board's considerations in reaching the conclusions in Accounting Standard AASB 2016-4 *Amendments to Australian Accounting Standards – Recoverable Amount of Non-Cash-Generating Specialised Assets of Not-for-Profit Entities*. Individual AASB members gave greater weight to some factors than to others.

Background

BC2   Under AASB 136 *Impairment of Assets* (July 2004 and August 2015), an impairment loss is the amount by which the carrying amount of an asset or a cash-generating unit exceeds its recoverable amount. The recoverable amount of an asset or a cash-generating unit is the higher of its fair value less costs of disposal ('net fair value') and its value in use.

BC3   Paragraph Aus32.1 to AASB 136, required not-for-profit (NFP) entities to determine the value in use of an asset as its depreciated replacement cost (DRC) when the future economic benefits of the asset are not primarily dependent on the asset's ability to generate net cash inflows and where the entity would, if deprived of the asset, replace its remaining future economic benefits. Paragraph Aus6.2 to AASB 136 defined DRC as "the current replacement cost of an asset less, where applicable, accumulated depreciation calculated on the basis of such cost to reflect the already consumed or expired future economic benefits of the asset". Paragraph Aus32.2 explained that "The current replacement cost of an asset is its cost measured by reference to the lowest cost at which the gross future economic benefits of that asset could currently be obtained in the normal course of business".

BC4   The AASB previously concluded that the Aus paragraphs were needed in AASB 136 to help ensure impairments are not recognised for non-cash-generating assets held by NFP entities when they still embody future economic benefits of a value equal to, or greater than, their carrying amounts. This was based on the view that entities might inappropriately recognise impairment due to the focus of IAS 36 *Impairment of Assets*, which is incorporated into AASB 136, on cash-generating assets. The value in use of a non-cash-generating asset based on cash flows would be zero or close to zero and the net fair value of the asset could be regarded as relating to a scrap value for a specialised asset.

The need to issue AASB 2016-4

BC5   Clarifications were sought by some constituents about the interaction between the notion of DRC for determining the value in use of assets held by NFP entities in the circumstances described in paragraph BC3 and the notion of current replacement cost (CRC) as a measure of the fair value of an asset under the cost approach in AASB 13 *Fair Value Measurement*. AASB 13 (paragraphs B8 and B9) identifies the cost approach as a valuation technique for measuring fair value. Under AASB 13, the cost approach reflects the amount that would be required currently to replace the service capacity of an asset.

BC6   Some commentators argued that, consistent with the role of CRC as a measure of fair value under AASB 13 (reflecting the assumptions that market participants would use when pricing the asset), DRC should not be an entity-specific measure of recoverable amount under AASB 136. These commentators supported the objective of the existing requirements of AASB 136 of not basing the recoverable amount of primarily non-cash-generating assets held by NFP entities on discounted cash flows. They also noted that when DRC was included in AASB 116 *Property, Plant and Equipment* (July 2004), there was ambiguity as to whether it was a measure of fair value or a measure of value in use and that with the publication of AASB 13 and its exposition of the cost approach, it became clear that DRC under the AASB 116 is a measure of fair value as is CRC under AASB 13. Accordingly, for such assets, they argued that DRC should be used to determine fair value as a measure of recoverable amount and noted that its designation as a measure of value in use under AASB 136 might be a source of confusion.

BC7   Other commentators argued that DRC is identified as a measure of fair value in paragraph 33 to AASB 116 (July 2004), in cases where there is no market-based evidence of fair value because of the specialised nature of the asset and the item is rarely sold, except as part of a continuing business. They noted that, with the publication of AASB 13, the cost approach plays a similar role as a measure of fair value when the market and income approaches to valuation are not applicable due to the specialised nature of the asset.

BC8   Further comments on the interaction between DRC under AASB 136 and CRC under AASB 13 were sought in AASB outreach with key stakeholders, such as preparers and auditors, and valuers of NFP entities' assets, particularly in regard to assets held by public sector entities.

BC9   Comments from some preparers in the public sector who participated in the outreach indicated that separate evaluations of CRC as a measure of fair value under AASB 13 and DRC as a measure of value in use under AASB 136 are not usually performed. These commentators noted that, although CRC as a measure of fair value under AASB 13 and DRC as a measure of value in use under AASB 136 are different in concept, for specialised assets where the market is typically inactive, the highest and best use is generally their current use. Accordingly, in their view the CRC of such assets under AASB 13 and their DRC under AASB 136 are, in practice, interchangeable. Some noted one reason for this outcome is that highest and best use requires consideration of reasonably possible uses, not every possible use.

BC10   Some valuers participating in staff outreach noted:

(a)   in the case of a NFP entity where the fair value of a specialised asset is based on the cost approach, the entity acts as the 'buyer' and is competing with other market participants in order to acquire the asset. They argue that this means CRC under AASB 13 should not be different from DRC under AASB 136;

(b)   CRC under AASB 13 and DRC under AASB 136 are regarded as similar measures of fair value and the existing use or alternative uses are considered and assessed on a case-by-case basis; and

(c)   the highest and best use of an asset determines its fair value, but restrictions (such as legal restrictions) on the use of an asset often mean that the highest and best use of an asset is its current use.

The AASB's initial deliberations

BC11   The AASB noted that DRC is identified as a measure of fair value in paragraph 33 to AASB 116 (July 2004) in cases where there is no market-based evidence of fair value because of the specialised nature of the asset and the item is rarely sold, except as part of a continuing business. The AASB also noted that, with the publication of AASB 13, CRC plays a similar role for assets that are specialised in nature and are rarely sold, such as many assets held by public sector entities. The AASB further noted that the cost of disposal of such assets is not expected to be material.

BC12   The AASB noted that fair value under AASB 13 is defined as an exit price. Therefore, CRC under AASB 13 is conceptually different from DRC as a measure of value in use under AASB 136, being an entry price. The AASB noted, however, that:

(a)   the description of the cost approach in AASB 13 indicates that CRC incorporates obsolescence as does the definition of DRC under AASB 136, where accumulated depreciation encompasses obsolescence;

(b)   valuers use similar approaches in determining DRC and CRC. Factors such as physical obsolescence, functional obsolescence and economic obsolescence are all considered in determining each measure; and

    (c)   valuers' practice involves considering as a starting point whether the valuation is of a specialised asset in its current use or an alternative use and whether there are any restrictions on the use of the asset.

BC13 The AASB concluded that DRC as a measure of value in use of specialised assets that are rarely sold is unlikely to be materially different from DRC (or CRC) as a measure of fair value of such assets. This is because, for non-cash-generating specialised assets, the market is typically inactive and their highest and best uses would usually be their current uses rather than their sale, resulting in CRC of such assets being not materially different from their DRC, as the following example shows:

Example

An entity self-constructs a specialised facility. Because this is the entity's specific practice in its industry, it can construct the facility for $8.5 million, whereas the cost of construction of the facility to any other market participant would be $10 million. As the construction of the facility has just been completed, there is no obsolescence or depreciation.

The issues are: (a) whether the CRC of the facility should be measured at $10 million or $8.5m under AASB 13; and (b) whether the DRC of the facility should be measured at $10m or $8.5m under AASB 136.

Analysis

Paragraph B9 to AASB 13 states that "a market participant buyer would not pay more for an asset than the amount for which it could replace the service capacity of that asset". The implication of that statement depends on whether the market participant buyer includes, or has the attributes of, the vendor. Paragraph BC78 of the IASB's Basis for Conclusions on IFRS 13 *Fair Value Measurement* states that, in relation to a specialised non-financial asset, "In effect, the market participant buyer *steps into the shoes of the entity* that holds that specialised asset" (emphasis added). Based on that comment, it seems appropriate in the above example to regard the market participant buyer as being capable of self-constructing the asset for $8.5 million, in which case CRC should be measured at $8.5 million under AASB 13. Because value in use is an entity-specific measure, the DRC of the facility would also be measured at $8.5 million under AASB 136.

BC14 The AASB noted that, when the AASB 136 impairment model (as per IAS 36) is applied to non-cash-generating specialised assets that are rarely sold, the value in use of the asset is typically less than its net fair value because the asset is generally held for continuing use of its service capacity, not the generation of cash inflows. Further, because these assets are rarely sold, their cost of disposal is typically negligible. The AASB concluded that, in such circumstances, the recoverable amount of the asset would be materially the same as fair value determined under AASB 13.

BC15 The AASB noted that AASB 13 has addressed the concerns identified in paragraph BC4 above that the net fair value of an asset could be regarded as relating to a scrap value for a specialised asset leading to an inappropriate recognition of impairment. Paragraph BC78 of the IASB's Basis for Conclusions on IFRS 13 refers to the concerns that an exit price would be based on scrap value (particularly given the requirement to maximise the use of observable inputs, such as market prices) and not reflect the value that an entity expects to generate by using the asset in its operations. It notes that, in such circumstances, the scrap value for an individual asset would be irrelevant because an exit price reflects the sale of the asset to a market participant that has, or can obtain, the complementary assets and the associated liabilities needed to use the specialised asset in its own operations. In effect, the market participant buyer steps into the shoes of the entity that holds that specialised asset.

BC16 The AASB noted that, with the issuance of AASB 13, the fair value of non-financial assets is determined under that Standard. Accordingly, with the CRC measure being available under AASB 13, the notion of DRC included in AASB 116 (July 2004) would no longer be applicable in estimating the fair value of specialised non-financial assets.

ED 269 proposals

BC17 The AASB published ED 269 *Recoverable Amount of Non-cash-generating Specialised Assets of Not-for-Profit Entities* proposing that:

(a) references to DRC as a measure of value in use in AASB 136 be deleted from that Standard; and

(b) paragraph Aus5.1 be included in AASB 136 to clarify that, because primarily non-cash-generating specialised assets held for continuing use of their service capacity are rarely sold, their cost of disposal is typically negligible and, accordingly, the recoverable amount of such assets is expected to be materially the same as fair value, determined under AASB 13.

BC18 The Board noted with the removal of DRC as a measure of value in use from AASB 136, the recoverable amount of a primarily non-cash-generating specialised asset held by an NFP entity for continuing use of its service capacity is determined as the higher of value in use and net fair value. The recoverable amount would be fair value since the value in use of a primarily non-cash-generating asset would be small or close to zero.

BC19 The ED 269 proposals identified implications for assets held both under the revaluation model and under the cost model as outlined below:

Revaluation model

NFP entities that regularly revalue their primarily non-cash-generating specialised assets to fair value would find the application of the impairment model under AASB 136 redundant.

Cost model

If there are indicators of impairment, NFP entities applying the cost model to their primarily non-cash-generating specialised assets would need to determine their recoverable amounts at fair value to establish whether there is a need to recognise impairment.

Redeliberation of ED 269 proposals

BC20 The AASB considered comments on the ED 269 proposals received via submissions and further AASB targeted outreach. The AASB noted that commentators were generally supportive of ED 269 proposals and discussed concerns raised about some aspects of the proposals.

Clarifying CRC

BC21 Some valuation industry participants consulted in AASB outreach were of the view that some constituents continue to see CRC under AASB 13 as the gross replacement cost of a new asset rather than the CRC of the remaining service capacity of the asset. The AASB observed that:

(a) paragraph B8 to AASB 13 describes CRC as the amount that would be required currently to replace the service capacity of an asset. This is a reference to replacement cost of the service capacity of the asset and not a new asset; and

(b) paragraph B9 to AASB 13 further clarifies that the price that would be received for the asset is based on the cost to a market participant buyer to acquire or construct a substitute asset of comparable utility, adjusted for obsolescence and that obsolescence encompasses physical deterioration, functional (technological) obsolescence and economic (external) obsolescence.

BC22 The AASB concluded that the description of CRC in AASB 13 is clear that CRC is not a gross value reflecting the replacement cost of a new asset, rather it is replacement cost of the remaining service capacity of the asset.

BC23 The AASB also confirmed its view that DRC under AASB 136 is equivalent to CRC under AASB 13. It was noted that the description of the cost approach in AASB 13 indicates that CRC incorporates obsolescence as did the definition of DRC under AASB 136, where accumulated depreciation encompasses obsolescence. It also noted that valuation industry participants in AASB outreach generally were of the view that the description of CRC in AASB 13 is consistent with their current valuation practice for determining DRC under a cost approach in that the replacement cost or reproduction cost of a new equivalent asset is adjusted for all relevant types of obsolescence and the issue of overcapacity is also considered in arriving at an optimised value.

BC24 Some commentators noted that the capitalisation of borrowing costs assumed in the example in paragraph BC14 to ED 269 was not common for NFP public sector entities because the ABS GFS Manual prohibits capitalisation of borrowing costs. The AASB noted that capitalisation of borrowing costs would need to be addressed as part of another project.

Disposal costs associated with specialised assets

BC25 Some participants in AASB outreach noted the costs of disposal might not be negligible in some cases where non-cash-generating specialised assets are involved. Some had in mind a range of costs they considered potentially material that could be associated with making an asset saleable. As an example, they noted those costs might include material costs of rezoning land.

BC26 The AASB noted that IFRS 13, Illustrative Example 8, clarifies the type of costs that would need to be considered in determining the fair value of assets. In illustrating the determination of highest and best use, the example contrasts the value of land currently developed for industrial use with the land as a vacant site for residential use. In identifying the fair value of the land as a vacant site for residential use it considers the costs of demolishing the factory and other costs necessary to convert the land to a vacant site.

BC27 The AASB noted that disposal costs are costs incurred to sell the asset in its existing state (target asset). The AASB confirmed that, consistent with the example noted in paragraph BC26, costs incurred to enhance the use of an asset, change its nature, or make it marketable would be considered in fair valuing the enhanced asset. Such costs would not be disposal costs of the target asset for the purpose of calculating net fair value. Accordingly, land rezoned for residential or commercial use is a different asset from land with zoning as public land and costs such as decommissioning costs or rezoning costs that change the nature of the asset are not classified as disposal costs of the land in its public use.

BC28 The AASB also noted that disposal costs are 'normal' incremental costs directly attributable to disposal of an asset and are not intended to include excessive costs arising from the processes to sell particular assets.

Impairment of revalued assets

BC29 Some commentators expressed the view that it was not sufficiently clear whether the proposed paragraph Aus5.1 would apply only to NFP entities as it does not explicitly preclude application by for-profit entities. The AASB confirmed that paragraph Aus5.1 would apply only to primarily non-cash-generating specialised assets of NFP entities held for their service capacity and would not apply to assets of for-profit entities whether or not held for their service capacity.

BC30 Some participants in AASB outreach commented that ED 269 is not clear as to whether it would mean that consideration does not need to be had to whether revalued assets of NFP entities would still need to be tested for impairment if an impairment trigger were present.

BC31 The AASB noted that the objective of removing references to DRC from AASB 136 and determining recoverable amount as fair value is to reduce financial reporting costs to NFP entities holding specialised assets that are held for continuing use of their service capacity. The AASB considered that this is consistent with its *Process for Modifying IFRSs for NFPs* which notes that "In some cases, the context or increased or reduced prevalence of a transaction or event for PBE/NFP as compared with for-profit entities, may require modifications to the relevant IFRS to ensure that user needs are met while considering the balance between costs and benefits". The AASB noted that revaluation of non-financial assets in the Australian NFP public sector is more prevalent than in the for-profit sector. The AASB concluded that when non-cash-generating specialised assets of NFP entities that are held for the continuing use of their service capacity are revalued regularly to fair value under the revaluation model in AASB 116 and AASB 138 *Intangible Assets*, the entity no longer applies AASB 136 to such assets. This is because regular revaluation ensures such assets are carried at an amount that is not materially different from fair value and any impairment would be taken into account as part of revaluation. For such assets, the issue of determining recoverable amount of the asset and magnitude of disposal costs would not be relevant.

BC32 The AASB noted that an entity holding an asset with the intention of selling it would need to apply AASB 5 *Non-current Assets Held for Sale and Discontinued Operations* and AASB 136 would not apply.

BC33 The AASB decided to proceed with the ED 269 proposals with amendments based on the conclusion noted in paragraph BC31.

BC34 The AASB noted that AASB 101 *Presentation of Financial Statements* and AASB 108 *Accounting Policies, Changes in Accounting Estimates and Errors* would apply in implementing the amendments and in respect of comparative information. The AASB also noted that it would not expect the amendments to AASB 136 to change current practice materially.

AASB 137
Provisions, Contingent Liabilities and Contingent Assets

(Reissued August 2015)

This note is not part of Accounting Standard AASB 137.

The following unincorporated amendments are not included in this Standard.

- AASB 17 *Insurance Contracts* — Appendix D sets out the amendments to other Standards that are a consequence of the AASB issuing AASB 17 *Insurance Contracts*. This Standard is applicable from 1 January 2021. Earlier application is permitted, but entities must apply AASB 9 *Financial Instruments* and AASB 15 *Revenue from Contracts with Customers* first.

- AASB 16 *Leases* — Appendix D sets out the amendments to other Standards that are a consequence of the AASB issuing this Standard. It is applicable from 1 January 2019. Earlier application is permitted, but entities must apply AASB 15 *Revenue from Contracts with Customers* before applying this Standard.

- AASB 2016-7 *Amendments to Australian Accounting Standards — Deferral of AASB 15 for Not-for-Profit Entities*. This Standard defers the consequential amendments that were originally set out in AASB 2014-5 *Amendments to Australian Accounting Standards arising from AASB 15*, by restating the effective date of the amendments set out in AASB 2015-8 *Amendments to Australian Accounting Standards* for not-for-profit entities. This Standard defers the application of AASB 15 to 1 January 2019. Earlier application is permitted provided AASB 1058 is also applied to the same period.

Entities early-adopting any amendments with later application dates will need to refer to the amending Standards that have not yet been incorporated into compilations. The abovementioned unincorporated amendments may be located on the AASB website at www.aasb.gov.au or on the Federal Register of Legislation website at www.legislation.gov.au.

CONTENTS

APPENDIX

A. AUSTRALIAN REDUCED DISCLOSURE REQUIREMENTS

IMPLEMENTATION GUIDANCE

A. TABLES – PROVISIONS, CONTINGENT LIABILITIES, CONTINGENT ASSETS
AND REIMBURSEMENTS

B. DECISION TREE

C. EXAMPLES: RECOGNITION

D. EXAMPLES: DISCLOSURES

DELETED IAS 37 TEXT

Australian Accounting Standard AASB 137 *Provisions, Contingent Liabilities and Contingent Assets* is
set out in paragraphs 1 – 101 and Appendix A. All the paragraphs have equal authority. Paragraphs in
bold type state the main principles. AASB 137 is to be read in the context of other Australian Accounting
Standards, including AASB 1048 *Interpretation of Standards*, which identifies the Australian Accounting
Interpretations, and AASB 1057 *Application of Australian Accounting Standards*. In the absence of explicit
guidance, AASB 108 *Accounting Policies, Changes in Accounting Estimates and Errors* provides a basis
for selecting and applying accounting policies.

COMPARISON WITH IAS 37

AASB 137 *Provisions, Contingent Liabilities and Contingent Assets* incorporates IAS
37 *Provisions, Contingent Liabilities and Contingent Assets* issued by the International
Accounting Standards Board (IASB). Australian-specific paragraphs (which are not included
in IAS 37) are identified with the prefix "Aus". Paragraphs that apply only to not-for-profit
entities begin by identifying their limited applicability.

Tier 1

For-profit entities complying with AASB 137 also comply with IAS 37.

Not-for-profit entities' compliance with IAS 37 will depend on whether any "Aus" paragraphs that specifically apply to not-for-profit entities provide additional guidance or contain applicable requirements that are inconsistent with IAS 37.

Tier 2

Entities preparing general purpose financial statements under Australian Accounting Standards – Reduced Disclosure Requirements (Tier 2) will not be in compliance with IFRSs.

AASB 1053 *Application of Tiers of Australian Accounting Standards* explains the two tiers of reporting requirements.

ACCOUNTING STANDARD AASB 137

The Australian Accounting Standards Board makes Accounting Standard AASB 137 *Provisions, Contingent Liabilities and Contingent Assets* under section 334 of the *Corporations Act 2001*.

	Kris Peach
Dated 14 August 2015	Chair – AASB

ACCOUNTING STANDARD AASB 137
PROVISIONS, CONTINGENT LIABILITIES AND CONTINGENT ASSETS

Objective

The objective of this Standard is to ensure that appropriate recognition criteria and measurement bases are applied to provisions, contingent liabilities and contingent assets and that sufficient information is disclosed in the notes to enable users to understand their nature, timing and amount.

Scope

1   This Standard shall be applied by all entities in accounting for provisions, contingent liabilities and contingent assets, except:

   (a)   those resulting from executory contracts, except where the contract is onerous; and

   (b)   [deleted]

   (c)   those covered by another Standard.

2   This Standard does not apply to financial instruments (including guarantees) that are within the scope of AASB 9 *Financial Instruments*.

3   Executory contracts are contracts under which neither party has performed any of its obligations or both parties have partially performed their obligations to an equal extent. This Standard does not apply to executory contracts unless they are onerous.

4   [Deleted]

5   When another Standard deals with a specific type of provision, contingent liability or contingent asset, an entity applies that Standard instead of this Standard. For example, some types of provisions are addressed in Standards on:

   (a)   [deleted]

   (b)   income taxes (see AASB 112 *Income Taxes*);

(c)   leases (see AASB 117 *Leases*). However, as AASB 117 contains no specific requirements to deal with operating leases that have become onerous, this Standard applies to such cases;

(d)   employee benefits (see AASB 119 *Employee Benefits*);

(e)   insurance contracts (see AASB 4 *Insurance Contracts*, AASB 1023 *General Insurance Contracts*, and AASB 1038 *Life Insurance Contracts*). However, this Standard applies to provisions, contingent liabilities and contingent assets of an insurer, other than those arising from its contractual obligations and rights under insurance contracts within the scopes of AASB 4, AASB 1023 or AASB 1038;

(f)   contingent consideration of an acquirer in a business combination (see AASB 3 *Business Combinations*); and

(g)   revenue from contracts with customers (see AASB 15 *Revenue from Contracts with Customers*). However, as AASB 15 contains no specific requirements to address contracts with customers that are, or have become, onerous, this Standard applies to such cases.

6   [Deleted]

7   This Standard defines provisions as liabilities of uncertain timing or amount. In some countries the term 'provision' is also used in the context of items such as depreciation, impairment of assets and doubtful debts: these are adjustments to the carrying amounts of assets and are not addressed in this Standard.

8   Other Standards specify whether expenditures are treated as assets or as expenses. These issues are not addressed in this Standard. Accordingly, this Standard neither prohibits nor requires capitalisation of the costs recognised when a provision is made.

9   This Standard applies to provisions for restructurings (including discontinued operations). When a restructuring meets the definition of a discontinued operation, additional disclosures may be required by AASB 5 *Non-current Assets Held for Sale and Discontinued Operations*.

Definitions

10   **The following terms are used in this Standard with the meanings specified:**

       A *provision* **is a liability of uncertain timing or amount.**

       A *liability* **is a present obligation of the entity arising from past events, the settlement of which is expected to result in an outflow from the entity of resources embodying economic benefits.**

       An *obligating event* **is an event that creates a legal or constructive obligation that results in an entity having no realistic alternative to settling that obligation.**

       A *legal obligation* **is an obligation that derives from:**

       (a)   a contract (through its explicit or implicit terms);

       (b)   legislation; or

       (c)   other operation of law.

       A *constructive obligation* **is an obligation that derives from an entity's actions where:**

       (a)   by an established pattern of past practice, published policies or a sufficiently specific current statement, the entity has indicated to other parties that it will accept certain responsibilities; and

       (b)   as a result, the entity has created a valid expectation on the part of those other parties that it will discharge those responsibilities.

A *contingent liability* is:

(a)   a possible obligation that arises from past events and whose existence will be confirmed only by the occurrence or non-occurrence of one or more uncertain future events not wholly within the control of the entity; or

(b)   a present obligation that arises from past events but is not recognised because:

(i)   it is not probable that an outflow of resources embodying economic benefits will be required to settle the obligation; or

(ii)   the amount of the obligation cannot be measured with sufficient reliability.

A *contingent asset* is a possible asset that arises from past events and whose existence will be confirmed only by the occurrence or non-occurrence of one or more uncertain future events not wholly within the control of the entity.

An *onerous contract* is a contract in which the unavoidable costs of meeting the obligations under the contract exceed the economic benefits expected to be received under it.

A *restructuring* is a programme that is planned and controlled by management, and materially changes either:

(a)   the scope of a business undertaken by an entity; or

(b)   the manner in which that business is conducted.

Provisions and other liabilities

11   Provisions can be distinguished from other liabilities such as trade payables and accruals because there is uncertainty about the timing or amount of the future expenditure required in settlement. By contrast:

(a)   trade payables are liabilities to pay for goods or services that have been received or supplied and have been invoiced or formally agreed with the supplier; and

(b)   accruals are liabilities to pay for goods or services that have been received or supplied but have not been paid, invoiced or formally agreed with the supplier, including amounts due to employees (for example, amounts relating to accrued vacation pay). Although it is sometimes necessary to estimate the amount or timing of accruals, the uncertainty is generally much less than for provisions.

Accruals are often reported as part of trade and other payables, whereas provisions are reported separately.

Relationship between provisions and contingent liabilities

12   In a general sense, all provisions are contingent because they are uncertain in timing or amount. However, within this Standard the term 'contingent' is used for liabilities and assets that are not recognised because their existence will be confirmed only by the occurrence or non-occurrence of one or more uncertain future events not wholly within the control of the entity. In addition, the term 'contingent liability' is used for liabilities that do not meet the recognition criteria.

13   This Standard distinguishes between:

(a)   provisions – which are recognised as liabilities (assuming that a reliable estimate can be made) because they are present obligations and it is probable that an outflow of resources embodying economic benefits will be required to settle the obligations; and

(b)   contingent liabilities – which are not recognised as liabilities because they are either:

(i)   possible obligations, as it has yet to be confirmed whether the entity has a present obligation that could lead to an outflow of resources embodying economic benefits; or

(ii)   present obligations that do not meet the recognition criteria in this Standard (because either it is not probable that an outflow of resources embodying economic benefits will be required to settle the obligation, or a sufficiently reliable estimate of the amount of the obligation cannot be made).

Recognition

Provisions

14   A *provision* shall be recognised when:

(a)   an entity has a present obligation (legal or constructive) as a result of a past event;

(b)   it is probable that an outflow of resources embodying economic benefits will be required to settle the obligation; and

(c)   a reliable estimate can be made of the amount of the obligation.

If these conditions are not met, no provision shall be recognised.

Present obligation

15   In rare cases it is not clear whether there is a present obligation. In these cases, a past event is deemed to give rise to a present obligation if, taking account of all available evidence, it is more likely than not that a present obligation exists at the end of the reporting period.

16   In almost all cases it will be clear whether a past event has given rise to a present obligation. In rare cases, for example in a lawsuit, it may be disputed either whether certain events have occurred or whether those events result in a present obligation. In such a case, an entity determines whether a present obligation exists at the end of the reporting period by taking account of all available evidence, including, for example, the opinion of experts. The evidence considered includes any additional evidence provided by events after the reporting period. On the basis of such evidence:

(a)   where it is more likely than not that a present obligation exists at the end of the reporting period, the entity recognises a provision (if the recognition criteria are met); and

(b)   where it is more likely that no present obligation exists at the end of the reporting period, the entity discloses a contingent liability, unless the possibility of an outflow of resources embodying economic benefits is remote (see paragraph 86).

Past event

17   A past event that leads to a present obligation is called an obligating event. For an event to be an obligating event, it is necessary that the entity has no realistic alternative to settling the obligation created by the event. This is the case only:

(a)   where the settlement of the obligation can be enforced by law; or

(b)   in the case of a constructive obligation, where the event (which may be an action of the entity) creates valid expectations in other parties that the entity will discharge the obligation.

18   Financial statements deal with the financial position of an entity at the end of its reporting period and not its possible position in the future. Therefore, no provision is recognised for costs that need to be incurred to operate in the future. The only liabilities recognised in an entity's statement of financial position are those that exist at the end of the reporting period.

19   It is only those obligations arising from past events existing independently of an entity's future actions (ie the future conduct of its business) that are recognised as provisions. Examples of such obligations are penalties or clean-up costs for

unlawful environmental damage, both of which would lead to an outflow of resources embodying economic benefits in settlement regardless of the future actions of the entity. Similarly, an entity recognises a provision for the decommissioning costs of an oil installation or a nuclear power station to the extent that the entity is obliged to rectify damage already caused. In contrast, because of commercial pressures or legal requirements, an entity may intend or need to carry out expenditure to operate in a particular way in the future (for example, by fitting smoke filters in a certain type of factory). Because the entity can avoid the future expenditure by its future actions, for example by changing its method of operation, it has no present obligation for that future expenditure and no provision is recognised.

20   An obligation always involves another party to whom the obligation is owed. It is not necessary, however, to know the identity of the party to whom the obligation is owed—indeed the obligation may be to the public at large. Because an obligation always involves a commitment to another party, it follows that a management or board decision does not give rise to a constructive obligation at the end of the reporting period unless the decision has been communicated before the end of the reporting period to those affected by it in a sufficiently specific manner to raise a valid expectation in them that the entity will discharge its responsibilities.

21   An event that does not give rise to an obligation immediately may do so at a later date, because of changes in the law or because an act (for example, a sufficiently specific public statement) by the entity gives rise to a constructive obligation. For example, when environmental damage is caused there may be no obligation to remedy the consequences. However, the causing of the damage will become an obligating event when a new law requires the existing damage to be rectified or when the entity publicly accepts responsibility for rectification in a way that creates a constructive obligation.

22   Where details of a proposed new law have yet to be finalised, an obligation arises only when the legislation is virtually certain to be enacted as drafted. For the purpose of this Standard, such an obligation is treated as a legal obligation. Differences in circumstances surrounding enactment make it impossible to specify a single event that would make the enactment of a law virtually certain. In many cases it will be impossible to be virtually certain of the enactment of a law until it is enacted.

Probable outflow of resources embodying economic benefits

23   For a liability to qualify for recognition there must be not only a present obligation but also the probability of an outflow of resources embodying economic benefits to settle that obligation. For the purpose of this Standard,[1] an outflow of resources or other event is regarded as probable if the event is more likely than not to occur, ie the probability that the event will occur is greater than the probability that it will not. Where it is not probable that a present obligation exists, an entity discloses a contingent liability, unless the possibility of an outflow of resources embodying economic benefits is remote (see paragraph 86).

24   Where there are a number of similar obligations (eg product warranties or similar contracts) the probability that an outflow will be required in settlement is determined by considering the class of obligations as a whole. Although the likelihood of outflow for any one item may be small, it may well be probable that some outflow of resources will be needed to settle the class of obligations as a whole. If that is the case, a provision is recognised (if the other recognition criteria are met).

Reliable estimate of the obligation

25   The use of estimates is an essential part of the preparation of financial statements and does not undermine their reliability. This is especially true in the case of provisions, which by their nature are more uncertain than most other items in the statement of financial position. Except in extremely rare cases, an entity will be able to determine a

---

1   The interpretation of 'probable' in this Standard as 'more likely than not' does not necessarily apply in other Standards.

range of possible outcomes and can therefore make an estimate of the obligation that is sufficiently reliable to use in recognising a provision.

26   In the extremely rare case where no reliable estimate can be made, a liability exists that cannot be recognised. That liability is disclosed as a contingent liability (see paragraph 86).

Recognition of liabilities arising from local government and government existing public policies, budget policies, election promises or statements of intent

Aus26.1   This paragraph and paragraph Aus26.2 relate to the recognition by a local government, government department or government of a liability arising from a local government or government existing public policy, budget policy, election promise or statement of intent. The intention to make payments to other parties, whether advised in the form of a local government or government budget policy, election promise or statement of intent, does not of itself create a present obligation which is binding. A liability would be recognised only when the entity is committed in the sense that it has little or no discretion to avoid the sacrifice of future economic benefits. For example, a government does not have a present obligation to sacrifice future economic benefits for social welfare payments that might arise in future reporting periods. A present obligation for social welfare payments arises only when entitlement conditions are satisfied for payment during a particular payment period. Similarly, a government does not have a present obligation to sacrifice future economic benefits under multi-year public policy agreements until the grantee meets conditions such as grant eligibility criteria, or has provided the services or facilities required under the grant agreement. In such cases, only amounts outstanding in relation to current or previous periods satisfy the definition of liabilities.

Aus26.2   Some such transactions or events may give rise to legal, social, political or economic consequences which leave little, if any, discretion to avoid a sacrifice of future economic benefits. In such circumstances, the definition of a liability is satisfied. An example of such an event is the occurrence of a disaster, where a government has a clear and formal policy to provide financial aid to victims of such disasters. In this circumstance, the government has little discretion to avoid the sacrifice of future economic benefits. However, the liability is recognised only when the amount of financial aid to be provided can be measured reliably.

Contingent liabilities

27   **An entity shall not recognise a contingent liability.**

28   A contingent liability is disclosed, as required by paragraph 86, unless the possibility of an outflow of resources embodying economic benefits is remote.

29   Where an entity is jointly and severally liable for an obligation, the part of the obligation that is expected to be met by other parties is treated as a contingent liability. The entity recognises a provision for the part of the obligation for which an outflow of resources embodying economic benefits is probable, except in the extremely rare circumstances where no reliable estimate can be made.

30   Contingent liabilities may develop in a way not initially expected. Therefore, they are assessed continually to determine whether an outflow of resources embodying economic benefits has become probable. If it becomes probable that an outflow of future economic benefits will be required for an item previously dealt with as a contingent liability, a provision is recognised in the financial statements of the period in which the change in probability occurs (except in the extremely rare circumstances where no reliable estimate can be made).

Contingent assets

31   **An entity shall not recognise a contingent asset.**

32 Contingent assets usually arise from unplanned or other unexpected events that give rise to the possibility of an inflow of economic benefits to the entity. An example is a claim that an entity is pursuing through legal processes, where the outcome is uncertain.

33 Contingent assets are not recognised in financial statements since this may result in the recognition of income that may never be realised. However, when the realisation of income is virtually certain, then the related asset is not a contingent asset and its recognition is appropriate.

34 A contingent asset is disclosed, as required by paragraph 89, where an inflow of economic benefits is probable.

35 Contingent assets are assessed continually to ensure that developments are appropriately reflected in the financial statements. If it has become virtually certain that an inflow of economic benefits will arise, the asset and the related income are recognised in the financial statements of the period in which the change occurs. If an inflow of economic benefits has become probable, an entity discloses the contingent asset (see paragraph 89).

Measurement

Best estimate

36 **The amount recognised as a provision shall be the best estimate of the expenditure required to settle the present obligation at the end of the reporting period.**

37 The best estimate of the expenditure required to settle the present obligation is the amount that an entity would rationally pay to settle the obligation at the end of the reporting period or to transfer it to a third party at that time. It will often be impossible or prohibitively expensive to settle or transfer an obligation at the end of the reporting period. However, the estimate of the amount that an entity would rationally pay to settle or transfer the obligation gives the best estimate of the expenditure required to settle the present obligation at the end of the reporting period.

38 The estimates of outcome and financial effect are determined by the judgement of the management of the entity, supplemented by experience of similar transactions and, in some cases, reports from independent experts. The evidence considered includes any additional evidence provided by events after the reporting period.

39 Uncertainties surrounding the amount to be recognised as a provision are dealt with by various means according to the circumstances. Where the provision being measured involves a large population of items, the obligation is estimated by weighting all possible outcomes by their associated probabilities. The name for this statistical method of estimation is 'expected value'. The provision will therefore be different depending on whether the probability of a loss of a given amount is, for example, 60 per cent or 90 per cent. Where there is a continuous range of possible outcomes, and each point in that range is as likely as any other, the mid-point of the range is used.

Example

An entity sells goods with a warranty under which customers are covered for the cost of repairs of any manufacturing defects that become apparent within the first six months after purchase. If minor defects were detected in all products sold, repair costs of 1 million would result. If major defects were detected in all products sold, repair costs of 4 million would result. The entity's past experience and future expectations indicate that, for the coming year, 75 per cent of the goods sold will have no defects, 20 per cent of the goods sold will have minor defects and 5 per cent of the goods sold will have major defects. In accordance with paragraph 24, an entity assesses the probability of an outflow for the warranty obligations as a whole.

The expected value of the cost of repairs is:

(75% of nil) + (20% of 1m) + (5% of 4m) = 400,000

---

40 Where a single obligation is being measured, the individual most likely outcome may be the best estimate of the liability. However, even in such a case, the entity considers other possible outcomes. Where other possible outcomes are either mostly higher or mostly lower than the most likely outcome, the best estimate will be a higher or lower amount. For example, if an entity has to rectify a serious fault in a major plant that it has constructed for a customer, the individual most likely outcome may be for the repair to succeed at the first attempt at a cost of 1,000, but a provision for a larger amount is made if there is a significant chance that further attempts will be necessary.

41 The provision is measured before tax, as the tax consequences of the provision, and changes in it, are dealt with under AASB 112.

Risks and uncertainties

42 The risks and uncertainties that inevitably surround many events and circumstances shall be taken into account in reaching the best estimate of a provision.

43 Risk describes variability of outcome. A risk adjustment may increase the amount at which a liability is measured. Caution is needed in making judgements under conditions of uncertainty, so that income or assets are not overstated and expenses or liabilities are not understated. However, uncertainty does not justify the creation of excessive provisions or a deliberate overstatement of liabilities. For example, if the projected costs of a particularly adverse outcome are estimated on a prudent basis, that outcome is not then deliberately treated as more probable than is realistically the case. Care is needed to avoid duplicating adjustments for risk and uncertainty with consequent overstatement of a provision.

44 Disclosure of the uncertainties surrounding the amount of the expenditure is made under paragraph 85(b).

Present value

45 Where the effect of the time value of money is material, the amount of a provision shall be the present value of the expenditures expected to be required to settle the obligation.

46 Because of the time value of money, provisions relating to cash outflows that arise soon after the reporting period are more onerous than those where cash outflows of the same amount arise later. Provisions are therefore discounted, where the effect is material.

47 The discount rate (or rates) shall be a pre-tax rate (or rates) that reflect(s) current market assessments of the time value of money and the risks specific to the liability. The discount rate(s) shall not reflect risks for which future cash flow estimates have been adjusted.

Future events

48 Future events that may affect the amount required to settle an obligation shall be reflected in the amount of a provision where there is sufficient objective evidence that they will occur.

49 Expected future events may be particularly important in measuring provisions. For example, an entity may believe that the cost of cleaning up a site at the end of its life will be reduced by future changes in technology. The amount recognised reflects a reasonable expectation of technically qualified, objective observers, taking account of all available evidence as to the technology that will be available at the time of the clean-up. Thus it is appropriate to include, for example, expected cost reductions associated with increased experience in applying existing technology or the expected cost of applying existing technology to a larger or more complex clean-up operation than has previously been carried out. However, an entity does not anticipate the development of a completely new technology for cleaning up unless it is supported by sufficient objective evidence.

50   The effect of possible new legislation is taken into consideration in measuring an existing obligation when sufficient objective evidence exists that the legislation is virtually certain to be enacted. The variety of circumstances that arise in practice makes it impossible to specify a single event that will provide sufficient, objective evidence in every case. Evidence is required both of what legislation will demand and of whether it is virtually certain to be enacted and implemented in due course. In many cases sufficient objective evidence will not exist until the new legislation is enacted.

Expected disposal of assets

51   **Gains from the expected disposal of assets shall not be taken into account in measuring a provision.**

52   Gains on the expected disposal of assets are not taken into account in measuring a provision, even if the expected disposal is closely linked to the event giving rise to the provision. Instead, an entity recognises gains on expected disposals of assets at the time specified by the Standard dealing with the assets concerned.

Reimbursements

53   **Where some or all of the expenditure required to settle a provision is expected to be reimbursed by another party, the reimbursement shall be recognised when, and only when, it is virtually certain that reimbursement will be received if the entity settles the obligation. The reimbursement shall be treated as a separate asset. The amount recognised for the reimbursement shall not exceed the amount of the provision.**

54   **In the statement of comprehensive income, the expense relating to a provision may be presented net of the amount recognised for a reimbursement.**

55   Sometimes, an entity is able to look to another party to pay part or all of the expenditure required to settle a provision (for example, through insurance contracts, indemnity clauses or suppliers' warranties). The other party may either reimburse amounts paid by the entity or pay the amounts directly.

56   In most cases the entity will remain liable for the whole of the amount in question so that the entity would have to settle the full amount if the third party failed to pay for any reason. In this situation, a provision is recognised for the full amount of the liability, and a separate asset for the expected reimbursement is recognised when it is virtually certain that reimbursement will be received if the entity settles the liability.

57   In some cases, the entity will not be liable for the costs in question if the third party fails to pay. In such a case the entity has no liability for those costs and they are not included in the provision.

58   As noted in paragraph 29, an obligation for which an entity is jointly and severally liable is a contingent liability to the extent that it is expected that the obligation will be settled by the other parties.

Changes in provisions

59   **Provisions shall be reviewed at the end of each reporting period and adjusted to reflect the current best estimate. If it is no longer probable that an outflow of resources embodying economic benefits will be required to settle the obligation, the provision shall be reversed.**

60   Where discounting is used, the carrying amount of a provision increases in each period to reflect the passage of time. This increase is recognised as borrowing cost.

Use of provisions

61   **A provision shall be used only for expenditures for which the provision was originally recognised.**

AASB

62   Only expenditures that relate to the original provision are set against it. Setting expenditures against a provision that was originally recognised for another purpose would conceal the impact of two different events.

Application of the recognition and measurement rules

Future operating losses

63   **Provisions shall not be recognised for future operating losses.**

64   Future operating losses do not meet the definition of a liability in paragraph 10 and the general recognition criteria set out for provisions in paragraph 14.

65   An expectation of future operating losses is an indication that certain assets of the operation may be impaired. An entity tests these assets for impairment under AASB 136 *Impairment of Assets*.

Onerous contracts

66   **If an entity has a contract that is onerous, the present obligation under the contract shall be recognised and measured as a provision.**

67   Many contracts (for example, some routine purchase orders) can be cancelled without paying compensation to the other party, and therefore there is no obligation. Other contracts establish both rights and obligations for each of the contracting parties. Where events make such a contract onerous, the contract falls within the scope of this Standard and a liability exists which is recognised. Executory contracts that are not onerous fall outside the scope of this Standard.

68   This Standard defines an onerous contract as a contract in which the unavoidable costs of meeting the obligations under the contract exceed the economic benefits expected to be received under it. The unavoidable costs under a contract reflect the least net cost of exiting from the contract, which is the lower of the cost of fulfilling it and any compensation or penalties arising from failure to fulfil it.

69   Before a separate provision for an onerous contract is established, an entity recognises any impairment loss that has occurred on assets dedicated to that contract (see AASB 136).

Restructuring

70   The following are examples of events that may fall under the definition of restructuring:

   (a)   sale or termination of a line of business;

   (b)   the closure of business locations in a country or region or the relocation of business activities from one country or region to another;

   (c)   changes in management structure, for example, eliminating a layer of management; and

   (d)   fundamental reorganisations that have a material effect on the nature and focus of the entity's operations.

71   A provision for restructuring costs is recognised only when the general recognition criteria for provisions set out in paragraph 14 are met. Paragraphs 72–83 set out how the general recognition criteria apply to restructurings.

72   **A constructive obligation to restructure arises only when an entity:**

   (a)   has a detailed formal plan for the restructuring identifying at least:

      (i)   the business or part of a business concerned;

      (ii)   the principal locations affected;

      (iii)   the location, function, and approximate number of employees who will be compensated for terminating their services;

>   (iv)   **the expenditures that will be undertaken; and**
>
>   (v)   **when the plan will be implemented; and**
>
> (b)   **has raised a valid expectation in those affected that it will carry out the restructuring by starting to implement that plan or announcing its main features to those affected by it.**

73   Evidence that an entity has started to implement a restructuring plan would be provided, for example, by dismantling plant or selling assets or by the public announcement of the main features of the plan. A public announcement of a detailed plan to restructure constitutes a constructive obligation to restructure only if it is made in such a way and in sufficient detail (ie setting out the main features of the plan) that it gives rise to valid expectations in other parties such as customers, suppliers and employees (or their representatives) that the entity will carry out the restructuring.

74   For a plan to be sufficient to give rise to a constructive obligation when communicated to those affected by it, its implementation needs to be planned to begin as soon as possible and to be completed in a timeframe that makes significant changes to the plan unlikely. If it is expected that there will be a long delay before the restructuring begins or that the restructuring will take an unreasonably long time, it is unlikely that the plan will raise a valid expectation on the part of others that the entity is at present committed to restructuring, because the timeframe allows opportunities for the entity to change its plans.

75   A management or board decision to restructure taken before the end of the reporting period does not give rise to a constructive obligation at the end of the reporting period unless the entity has, before the end of the reporting period:

    (a)   started to implement the restructuring plan; or

    (b)   announced the main features of the restructuring plan to those affected by it in a sufficiently specific manner to raise a valid expectation in them that the entity will carry out the restructuring.

    If an entity starts to implement a restructuring plan, or announces its main features to those affected, only after the reporting period, disclosure is required under AASB 110 *Events after the Reporting Period*, if the restructuring is material and non-disclosure could influence the economic decisions that users make on the basis of the financial statements.

76   Although a constructive obligation is not created solely by a management decision, an obligation may result from other earlier events together with such a decision. For example, negotiations with employee representatives for termination payments, or with purchasers for the sale of an operation, may have been concluded subject only to board approval. Once that approval has been obtained and communicated to the other parties, the entity has a constructive obligation to restructure, if the conditions of paragraph 72 are met.

77   In some countries, the ultimate authority is vested in a board whose membership includes representatives of interests other than those of management (eg employees) or notification to such representatives may be necessary before the board decision is taken. Because a decision by such a board involves communication to these representatives, it may result in a constructive obligation to restructure.

78   **No obligation arises for the sale of an operation until the entity is committed to the sale, ie there is a binding sale agreement.**

79   Even when an entity has taken a decision to sell an operation and announced that decision publicly, it cannot be committed to the sale until a purchaser has been identified and there is a binding sale agreement. Until there is a binding sale agreement, the entity will be able to change its mind and indeed will have to take another course of action if a purchaser cannot be found on acceptable terms. When the sale of an operation is envisaged as part of a restructuring, the assets of the operation are reviewed for impairment, under AASB 136. When a sale is only part of a restructuring, a

AASB

constructive obligation can arise for the other parts of the restructuring before a binding sale agreement exists.

80   A restructuring provision shall include only the direct expenditures arising from the restructuring, which are those that are both:

    (a)   necessarily entailed by the restructuring; and

    (b)   not associated with the ongoing activities of the entity.

81   A restructuring provision does not include such costs as:

    (a)   retraining or relocating continuing staff;

    (b)   marketing; or

    (c)   investment in new systems and distribution networks.

These expenditures relate to the future conduct of the business and are not liabilities for restructuring at the end of the reporting period. Such expenditures are recognised on the same basis as if they arose independently of a restructuring.

82   Identifiable future operating losses up to the date of a restructuring are not included in a provision, unless they relate to an onerous contract as defined in paragraph 10.

83   As required by paragraph 51, gains on the expected disposal of assets are not taken into account in measuring a restructuring provision, even if the sale of assets is envisaged as part of the restructuring.

Disclosure

84   For each class of provision, an entity shall disclose:

    (a)   the carrying amount at the beginning and end of the period;

    (b)   additional provisions made in the period, including increases to existing provisions;

    (c)   amounts used (ie incurred and charged against the provision) during the period;

    (d)   unused amounts reversed during the period; and

    (e)   the increase during the period in the discounted amount arising from the passage of time and the effect of any change in the discount rate.

Comparative information is not required.

85   An entity shall disclose the following for each class of provision:

    (a)   a brief description of the nature of the obligation and the expected timing of any resulting outflows of economic benefits;

    (b)   an indication of the uncertainties about the amount or timing of those outflows. Where necessary to provide adequate information, an entity shall disclose the major assumptions made concerning future events, as addressed in paragraph 48; and

    (c)   the amount of any expected reimbursement, stating the amount of any asset that has been recognised for that expected reimbursement.

86   Unless the possibility of any outflow in settlement is remote, an entity shall disclose for each class of contingent liability at the end of the reporting period a brief description of the nature of the contingent liability and, where practicable:

    (a)   an estimate of its financial effect, measured under paragraphs 36–52;

    (b)   an indication of the uncertainties relating to the amount or timing of any outflow; and

    (c)   the possibility of any reimbursement.

87 In determining which provisions or contingent liabilities may be aggregated to form a class, it is necessary to consider whether the nature of the items is sufficiently similar for a single statement about them to fulfil the requirements of paragraphs 85(a) and (b) and 86(a) and (b). Thus, it may be appropriate to treat as a single class of provision amounts relating to warranties of different products, but it would not be appropriate to treat as a single class amounts relating to normal warranties and amounts that are subject to legal proceedings.

88 Where a provision and a contingent liability arise from the same set of circumstances, an entity makes the disclosures required by paragraphs 84–86 in a way that shows the link between the provision and the contingent liability.

89 Where an inflow of economic benefits is probable, an entity shall disclose a brief description of the nature of the contingent assets at the end of the reporting period, and, where practicable, an estimate of their financial effect, measured using the principles set out for provisions in paragraphs 36–52.

90 It is important that disclosures for contingent assets avoid giving misleading indications of the likelihood of income arising.

91 Where any of the information required by paragraphs 86 and 89 is not disclosed because it is not practicable to do so, that fact shall be stated.

92 In extremely rare cases, disclosure of some or all of the information required by paragraphs 84–89 can be expected to prejudice seriously the position of the entity in a dispute with other parties on the subject matter of the provision, contingent liability or contingent asset. In such cases, an entity need not disclose the information, but shall disclose the general nature of the dispute, together with the fact that, and reason why, the information has not been disclosed.

Transitional provisions

93 [Deleted by the AASB]

94 [Deleted]

Commencement of the legislative instrument

Aus94.1 For legal purposes, this legislative instrument commences on 31 December 2017.

Withdrawal of AASB pronouncements

Aus94.2 This Standard repeals AASB 137 *Provisions, Contingent Liabilities and Contingent Assets* issued in July 2004. Despite the repeal, after the time this Standard starts to apply under section 334 of the Corporations Act (either generally or in relation to an individual entity), the repealed Standard continues to apply in relation to any period ending before that time as if the repeal had not occurred.

[Note: When this Standard applies under section 334 of the Corporations Act (either generally or in relation to an individual entity), it supersedes the application of the repealed Standard.]

Effective date

95 This Standard becomes operative for annual financial statements covering periods beginning on or after 1 January 2018. Earlier application is encouraged for periods beginning after 24 July 2014 but before 1 January 2018. If an entity applies this Standard for periods beginning before 1 January 2018, it shall disclose that fact.

AASB

96   [Deleted]

97   [Deleted]

98   [Deleted]

99   AASB 2014-1 *Amendments to Australian Accounting Standards*, issued in June 2014, amended paragraph 5 in the previous version of this Standard as a consequential amendment derived from the amendment to AASB 3. An entity shall apply that amendment prospectively to business combinations to which the amendment to AASB 3 applies.

100 AASB 2014-5 *Amendments to Australian Accounting Standards arising from AASB 15*, issued in December 2014, amended the previous version of this Standard as follows: amended paragraph 5 and deleted paragraph 6. An entity shall apply those amendments when it applies AASB 15.

101 AASB 2010-7 *Amendments to Australian Accounting Standards arising from AASB 9 (December 2010)* (as amended) amended paragraph 2 in the previous version of this Standard. Paragraph 97, added by AASB 2010-7, was deleted by AASB 2014-1 *Amendments to Australian Accounting Standards*. Paragraph 98, added by AASB 2014-1, was deleted by AASB 2014-7 *Amendments to Australian Accounting Standards arising from AASB 9 (December 2014)*. An entity shall apply those amendments when it applies AASB 9.

APPENDIX A
AUSTRALIAN REDUCED DISCLOSURE REQUIREMENTS

This appendix is an integral part of the Standard.

AusA1   **The following do not apply to entities preparing general purpose financial statements under Australian Accounting Standards – Reduced Disclosure Requirements:**

    (a)   paragraphs 84(b), 84(e) and 85(c);

    (b)   in paragraph 75, the text "If an entity starts to ... of the financial statements."; and

    (c)   in paragraph 85(b), the text ". Where necessary ... paragraph 48".

    Entities applying Australian Accounting Standards – Reduced Disclosure Requirements may elect to comply with some or all of these excluded requirements.

AusA2   The requirements that do not apply to entities preparing general purpose financial statements under Australian Accounting Standards – Reduced Disclosure Requirements are also identified in this Standard by shading of the relevant text.

GUIDANCE ON IMPLEMENTING AASB 137

This guidance accompanies, but is not part of, AASB 137.

A. Tables – provisions, contingent liabilities, contingent assets and reimbursements

The purpose of these tables is to summarise the main requirements of the Standard.

Provisions and contingent liabilities

Where, as a result of past events, there may be an outflow of resources embodying future economic benefits in settlement of: (a) a present obligation; or (b) a possible obligation whose existence will be confirmed only by the occurrence or non-occurrence of one or more uncertain future events not wholly within the control of the entity.		
There is a present obligation that probably requires an outflow of resources.	There is a possible obligation or a present obligation that may, but probably will not, require an outflow of resources.	There is a possible obligation or a present obligation where the likelihood of an outflow of resources is remote.
A provision is recognised (paragraph 14).	No provision is recognised (paragraph 27).	No provision is recognised (paragraph 27).
Disclosures are required for the provision (paragraphs 84 and 85).	Disclosures are required for the contingent liability (paragraph 86).	No disclosure is required (paragraph 86).

A contingent liability also arises in the extremely rare case where there is a liability that cannot be recognised because it cannot be measured reliably. Disclosures are required for the contingent liability.

Contingent assets

Where, as a result of past events, there is a possible asset whose existence will be confirmed only by the occurrence or non-occurrence of one or more uncertain future events not wholly within the control of the entity.		
The inflow of economic benefits is virtually certain.	The inflow of economic benefits is probable, but not virtually certain.	The inflow is not probable.
The asset is not contingent (paragraph 33).	No asset is recognised (paragraph 31).	No asset is recognised (paragraph 31).
	Disclosures are required (paragraph 89).	No disclosure is required (paragraph 89).

Reimbursements

Some or all of the expenditure required to settle a provision is expected to be reimbursed by another party.		
The entity has no obligation for the part of the expenditure to be reimbursed by the other party.	The obligation for the amount expected to be reimbursed remains with the entity and it is virtually certain that reimbursement will be received if the entity settles the provision.	The obligation for the amount expected to be reimbursed remains with the entity and the reimbursement is not virtually certain if the entity settles the provision.

(Continued)

AASB

(Continued)

The entity has no liability for the amount to be reimbursed (paragraph 57).	The reimbursement is recognised as a separate asset in the statement of financial position and may be offset against the expense in the statement of comprehensive income. The amount recognised for the expected reimbursement does not exceed the liability (paragraphs 53 and 54).	The expected reimbursement is not recognised as an asset (paragraph 53).
No disclosure is required.	The reimbursement is disclosed together with the amount recognised for the reimbursement (paragraph 85(c)).	The expected reimbursement is disclosed (paragraph 85(c)).

B. Decision tree

The purpose of this diagram is to summarise the main recognition requirements of the Standard for provisions and contingent liabilities.

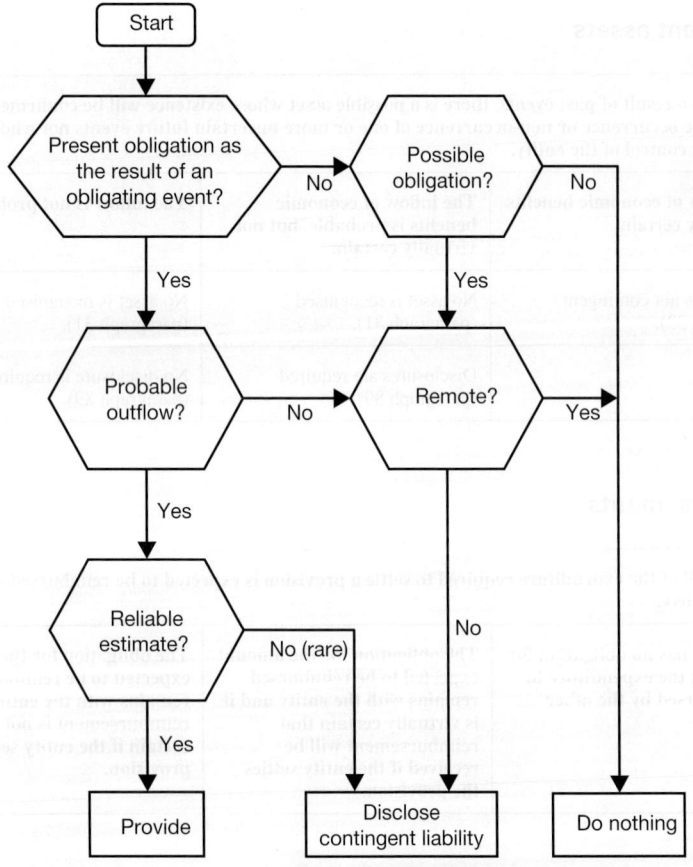

Note: In rare cases, it is not clear whether there is a present obligation. In these cases, a past event is deemed to give rise to a present obligation if, taking account of all available evidence, it is more likely than not that a present obligation exists at the end of the reporting period (paragraph 15 of the Standard).

C. Examples: Recognition

All the entities in the examples have 31 December year-ends. In all cases, it is assumed that a reliable estimate can be made of any outflows expected. In some examples the circumstances described may have resulted in impairment of the assets—this aspect is not dealt with in the examples.

The cross-references provided in the examples indicate paragraphs of the Standard that are particularly relevant.

References to 'best estimate' are to the present value amount, where the effect of the time value of money is material.

Example 1 Warranties

A manufacturer gives warranties at the time of sale to purchasers of its product. Under the terms of the contract for sale the manufacturer undertakes to make good, by repair or replacement, manufacturing defects that become apparent within three years from the date of sale. On past experience, it is probable (ie more likely than not) that there will be some claims under the warranties.

Present obligation as a result of a past obligating event – The obligating event is the sale of the product with a warranty, which gives rise to a legal obligation.

An outflow of resources embodying economic benefits in settlement – Probable for the warranties as a whole (see paragraph 24).

Conclusion – A provision is recognised for the best estimate of the costs of making good under the warranty products sold before the end of the reporting period (see paragraphs 14 and 24).

Example 2A Contaminated land – legislation virtually certain to be enacted

An entity in the oil industry causes contamination but cleans up only when required to do so under the laws of the particular country in which it operates. One country in which it operates has had no legislation requiring cleaning up, and the entity has been contaminating land in that country for several years. At 31 December 20X0 it is virtually certain that a draft law requiring a clean-up of land already contaminated will be enacted shortly after the year-end.

Present obligation as a result of a past obligating event – The obligating event is the contamination of the land because of the virtual certainty of legislation requiring cleaning up.

An outflow of resources embodying economic benefits in settlement – Probable.

Conclusion – A provision is recognised for the best estimate of the costs of the clean-up (see paragraphs 14 and 22).

Example 2B Contaminated land and constructive obligation

An entity in the oil industry causes contamination and operates in a country where there is no environmental legislation. However, the entity has a widely published environmental policy in which it undertakes to clean up all contamination that it causes. The entity has a record of honouring this published policy.

Present obligation as a result of a past obligating event – The obligating event is the contamination of the land, which gives rise to a constructive obligation because the conduct of the entity has created a valid expectation on the part of those affected by it that the entity will clean up contamination.

An outflow of resources embodying economic benefits in settlement – Probable.

Conclusion – A provision is recognised for the best estimate of the costs of clean-up (see paragraphs 10 (the definition of a constructive obligation), 14 and 17).

Example 3 Offshore oilfield

An entity operates an offshore oilfield where its licensing agreement requires it to remove the oil rig at the end of production and restore the seabed. Ninety per cent of the eventual costs relate to the removal of the oil rig and restoration of damage caused by building it, and 10 per cent arise through the extraction of oil. At the end of the reporting period, the rig has been constructed but no oil has been extracted.

Present obligation as a result of a past obligating event – The construction of the oil rig creates a legal obligation under the terms of the licence to remove the rig and restore the seabed and is thus an obligating event. At the end of the reporting period, however, there is no obligation to rectify the damage that will be caused by extraction of the oil.

An outflow of resources embodying economic benefits in settlement – Probable.

Conclusion – A provision is recognised for the best estimate of ninety per cent of the eventual costs that relate to the removal of the oil rig and restoration of damage caused by building it (see paragraph 14). These costs are included as part of the cost of the oil rig. The 10 per cent of costs that arise through the extraction of oil are recognised as a liability when the oil is extracted.

Example 4 Refunds policy

A retail store has a policy of refunding purchases by dissatisfied customers, even though it is under no legal obligation to do so. Its policy of making refunds is generally known.

Present obligation as a result of a past obligating event – The obligating event is the sale of the product, which gives rise to a constructive obligation because the conduct of the store has created a valid expectation on the part of its customers that the store will refund purchases.

An outflow of resources embodying economic benefits in settlement – Probable, a proportion of goods are returned for refund (see paragraph 24).

Conclusion – A provision is recognised for the best estimate of the costs of refunds (see paragraphs 10 (the definition of a constructive obligation), 14, 17 and 24).

Example 5A Closure of a division – no implementation before end of the reporting period

On 12 December 20X0 the board of an entity decided to close down a division. Before the end of the reporting period (31 December 20X0) the decision was not communicated to any of those affected and no other steps were taken to implement the decision.

Present obligation as a result of a past obligating event – There has been no obligating event and so there is no obligation.

Conclusion – No provision is recognised (see paragraphs 14 and 72).

Example 5B Closure of a division – communication/implementation before end of the reporting period

On 12 December 20X0, the board of an entity decided to close down a division making a particular product. On 20 December 20X0 a detailed plan for closing down the division was agreed by the board; letters were sent to customers warning them to seek an alternative source of supply and redundancy notices were sent to the staff of the division.

Present obligation as a result of a past obligating event – The obligating event is the communication of the decision to the customers and employees, which gives rise to a constructive obligation from that date, because it creates a valid expectation that the division will be closed.

An outflow of resources embodying economic benefits in settlement – Probable.

Conclusion – A provision is recognised at 31 December 20X0 for the best estimate of the costs of closing the division (see paragraphs 14 and 72).

Example 6 Legal requirement to fit smoke filters

Under new legislation, an entity is required to fit smoke filters to its factories by 30 June 20X1. The entity has not fitted the smoke filters.

(a)   At 31 December 20X0, the end of the reporting period

Present obligation as a result of a past obligating event – There is no obligation because there is no obligating event either for the costs of fitting smoke filters or for fines under the legislation.

Conclusion – No provision is recognised for the cost of fitting the smoke filters (see paragraphs 14 and 17–19).

(b)   At 31 December 20X1, the end of the reporting period

Present obligation as a result of a past obligating event – There is still no obligation for the costs of fitting smoke filters because no obligating event has occurred (the fitting of the filters). However, an obligation might arise to pay fines or penalties under the legislation because the obligating event has occurred (the non-compliant operation of the factory).

An outflow of resources embodying economic benefits in settlement – Assessment of probability of incurring fines and penalties by non-compliant operation depends on the details of the legislation and the stringency of the enforcement regime.

Conclusion – No provision is recognised for the costs of fitting smoke filters. However, a provision is recognised for the best estimate of any fines and penalties that are more likely than not to be imposed (see paragraphs 14 and 17–19).

Example 7 Staff retraining as a result of changes in the income tax system

The government introduces a number of changes to the income tax system. As a result of these changes, an entity in the financial services sector will need to retrain a large proportion of its administrative and sales workforce in order to ensure continued compliance with financial services regulation. At the end of the reporting period, no retraining of staff has taken place.

Present obligation as a result of a past obligating event – There is no obligation because no obligating event (retraining) has taken place.

Conclusion – No provision is recognised (see paragraphs 14 and 17–19).

Example 8 An onerous contract

An entity operates profitably from a factory that it has leased under an operating lease. During December 20X0 the entity relocates its operations to a new factory. The lease on the old factory continues for the next four years, it cannot be cancelled and the factory cannot be re-let to another user.

Present obligation as a result of a past obligating event – The obligating event is the signing of the lease contract, which gives rise to a legal obligation.

An outflow of resources embodying economic benefits in settlement – When the lease becomes onerous, an outflow of resources embodying economic benefits is probable. (Until the lease becomes onerous, the entity accounts for the lease under AASB 117 *Leases*.)

Conclusion – A provision is recognised for the best estimate of the unavoidable lease payments (see paragraphs 5(c), 14 and 66).

Example 9 A single guarantee

[Deleted]

Example 10 A court case

After a wedding in 20X0, ten people died, possibly as a result of food poisoning from products sold by the entity. Legal proceedings are started seeking damages from the entity but it disputes liability. Up to the date of authorisation of the financial statements for the year to 31 December 20X0 for issue, the entity's lawyers advise that it is probable that the entity will not be found liable. However, when the entity prepares the financial statements for the year to 31 December 20X1, its lawyers advise that, owing to developments in the case, it is probable that the entity will be found liable.

(a)   At 31 December 20X0

Present obligation as a result of a past obligating event – On the basis of the evidence available when the financial statements were approved, there is no obligation as a result of past events.

Conclusion – No provision is recognised (see paragraphs 15 and 16). The matter is disclosed as a contingent liability unless the probability of any outflow is regarded as remote (paragraph 86).

(b)   At 31 December 20X1

Present obligation as a result of a past obligating event – On the basis of the evidence available, there is a present obligation.

An outflow of resources embodying economic benefits in settlement – Probable.

Conclusion – A provision is recognised for the best estimate of the amount to settle the obligation (paragraphs 14–16).

Example 11 Repairs and maintenance

Some assets require, in addition to routine maintenance, substantial expenditure every few years for major refits or refurbishment and the replacement of major components. AASB 116 *Property, Plant and Equipment* gives guidance on allocating expenditure on an asset to its component parts where these components have different useful lives or provide benefits in a different pattern.

Example 11A Refurbishment costs – no legislative requirement

A furnace has a lining that needs to be replaced every five years for technical reasons. At the end of the reporting period, the lining has been in use for three years.

Present obligation as a result of a past obligating event – There is no present obligation.

Conclusion – No provision is recognised (see paragraphs 14 and 17–19).

The cost of replacing the lining is not recognised because, at the end of the reporting period, no obligation to replace the lining exists independently of the company's future actions—even the intention to incur the expenditure depends on the company deciding to continue operating the furnace or to replace the lining. Instead of a provision being recognised, the depreciation of the lining takes account of its consumption, ie it is depreciated over five years. The re-lining costs then incurred are capitalised with the consumption of each new lining shown by depreciation over the subsequent five years.

Example 11B Refurbishment costs – legislative requirement

An airline is required by law to overhaul its aircraft once every three years.

Present obligation as a result of a past obligating event – There is no present obligation.

Conclusion – No provision is recognised (see paragraphs 14 and 17–19).

The costs of overhauling aircraft are not recognised as a provision for the same reasons as the cost of replacing the lining is not recognised as a provision in example 11A. Even a legal requirement to overhaul does not make the costs of overhaul a liability, because no obligation exists to overhaul the aircraft independently of the entity's future actions—the entity could avoid the future expenditure by its future actions, for example by selling the aircraft. Instead of a provision being recognised, the depreciation of the aircraft takes account of the future incidence of maintenance costs, ie an amount equivalent to the expected maintenance costs is depreciated over three years.

D. Examples: disclosures

Two examples of the disclosures required by paragraph 85 are provided below.

Example 1 Warranties

A manufacturer gives warranties at the time of sale to purchasers of its three product lines. Under the terms of the warranty, the manufacturer undertakes to repair or replace items that fail to perform satisfactorily for two years from the date of sale. At the end of the reporting period, a provision of 60,000 has been recognised. The provision has not been discounted as the effect of discounting is not material. The following information is disclosed:

A provision of 60,000 has been recognised for expected warranty claims on products sold during the last three financial years. It is expected that the majority of this expenditure will be incurred in the next financial year, and all will be incurred within two years after the reporting period.

Example 2 Decommissioning costs

In 2000, an entity involved in nuclear activities recognises a provision for decommissioning costs of 300 million. The provision is estimated using the assumption that decommissioning will take place in 60–70 years' time. However, there is a possibility that it will not take place until 100–110 years' time, in which case the present value of the costs will be significantly reduced. The following information is disclosed:

A provision of 300 million has been recognised for decommissioning costs. These costs are expected to be incurred between 2060 and 2070; however, there is a possibility that decommissioning will not take place until 2100–2110. If the costs were measured based upon the expectation that they would not be incurred until 2100–2110 the provision would be reduced to 136 million. The provision has been estimated using existing technology, at current prices, and discounted using a real discount rate of 2 per cent.

An example is given below of the disclosures required by paragraph 92 where some of the information required is not given because it can be expected to prejudice seriously the position of the entity.

Example 3 Disclosure exemption

An entity is involved in a dispute with a competitor, who is alleging that the entity has infringed patents and is seeking damages of 100 million. The entity recognises a provision for its best estimate of the obligation, but discloses none of the information required by paragraphs 84 and 85 of the Standard. The following information is disclosed:

Litigation is in process against the company relating to a dispute with a competitor who alleges that the company has infringed patents and is seeking damages of 100 million. The information usually required by AASB 137 Provisions, Contingent Liabilities and Contingent Assets *is not disclosed on the grounds that it can be expected to prejudice seriously the outcome of the litigation. The directors are of the opinion that the claim can be successfully resisted by the company.*

DELETED IAS 37 TEXT

Deleted IAS 37 text is not part of AASB 137.

93   The effect of adopting this Standard on its effective date (or earlier) shall be reported as an adjustment to the opening balance of retained earnings for the period in which the Standard is first adopted. Entities are encouraged, but not required, to adjust the opening balance of retained earnings for the earliest period presented and to restate comparative information. If comparative information is not restated, this fact shall be disclosed.

AASB 138
Intangible Assets

(Compiled October 2015)

This compiled Standard applies to annual periods beginning on or after 1 January 2018 but before 1 January 2019. Earlier application is permitted for annual periods beginning on or after 1 January 2014 but before 1 January 2018. It incorporates relevant amendments made up to and including 22 October 2015.

Prepared on 20 March 2017 by the staff of the Australian Accounting Standards Board.

Compilation no. 1

Compilation date: 31 December 2016

This note is not part of Accounting Standard AASB 138.

The following unincorporated amendments are not included in this compiled Standard.

- AASB 17 *Insurance Contracts* — Appendix D sets out the amendments to other Standards that are a consequence of the AASB issuing AASB 17 *Insurance Contracts*. This Standard is applicable from 1 January 2021. Earlier application is permitted, but entities must apply AASB 9 *Financial Instruments* and AASB 15 *Revenue from Contracts with Customers* first.

- AASB 1058 *Income of Not-for-Profit Entities* — Appendix D sets out the amendments to other Australian Accounting Standards that are a consequence of the AASB issuing this Standard. It is applicable from 1 January 2019. Earlier application is permitted, but amendments to AASB 117 apply before 1 January 2019 only if AASB 1058 is also applied to an earlier period. In addition, AASB 1 and AASB 16 amendments are applied to an earlier period only if AASB 16 is also applied to that period.

- AASB 16 *Leases* — Appendix D sets out the amendments to other Standards that are a consequence of the AASB issuing this Standard. It is applicable from 1 January 2019. Earlier application is permitted, but entities must apply AASB 15 *Revenue from Contracts with Customers* before applying this Standard.

- AASB 2016-7 *Amendments to Australian Accounting Standards — Deferral of AASB 15 for Not-for-Profit Entities.* This Standard defers the consequential amendments that were originally set out in AASB 2014-5 *Amendments to Australian Accounting Standards arising from AASB 15,* by restating the effective date of the amendments set out in AASB 2015-8 *Amendments to Australian Accounting Standards* for not-for-profit entities. This Standard defers the application of AASB 15 to 1 January 2019. Earlier application is permitted provided AASB 1058 is also applied to the same period.

Entities early-adopting any amendments with later application dates will need to refer to the amending Standards that have not yet been incorporated into compilations. The abovementioned unincorporated amendments may be located on the AASB website at www.aasb.gov.au or on the Federal Register of Legislation website at www.legislation.gov.au.

CONTENTS

AASB

APPENDIX
A. AUSTRALIAN REDUCED DISCLOSURE REQUIREMENTS

ILLUSTRATIVE EXAMPLES
COMPILATION DETAILS
DELETED IAS 38 TEXT

BASIS FOR CONCLUSIONS ON IAS 38 (available on the website)

Australian Accounting Standard AASB 138 *Intangible Assets* (as amended) is set out in paragraphs 1 –
Aus133.2 and Appendix A. All the paragraphs have equal authority. Paragraphs in **bold type** state the main
principles. AASB 138 is to be read in the context of other Australian Accounting Standards, including
AASB 1048 *Interpretation of Standards*, which identifies the Australian Accounting Interpretations, and
AASB 1057 *Application of Australian Accounting Standards*. In the absence of explicit guidance, AASB
108 *Accounting Policies, Changes in Accounting Estimates and Errors* provides a basis for selecting and
applying accounting policies.

COMPARISON WITH IAS 38

AASB 138 *Intangible Assets* as amended incorporates IAS 38 *Intangible Assets* as issued
and amended by the International Accounting Standards Board (IASB). Australian-specific
paragraphs (which are not included in IAS 38) are identified with the prefix "Aus" or
"RDR". Paragraphs that apply only to not-for-profit entities begin by identifying their limited
applicability.

Tier 1

For-profit entities complying with AASB 138 also comply with IAS 38.

Not-for-profit entities' compliance with IAS 38 will depend on whether any "Aus" paragraphs
that specifically apply to not-for-profit entities provide additional guidance or contain
applicable requirements that are inconsistent with IAS 38.

Tier 2

Entities preparing general purpose financial statements under Australian Accounting
Standards – Reduced Disclosure Requirements (Tier 2) will not be in compliance with IFRSs.

AASB 1053 *Application of Tiers of Australian Accounting Standards* explains the two tiers
of reporting requirements.

ACCOUNTING STANDARD AASB 138

The Australian Accounting Standards Board made Accounting Standard AASB 138
Intangible Assets under section 334 of the *Corporations Act 2001* on 14 August 2015.

This compiled version of AASB 138 applies to annual periods beginning on or after 1
January 2018 but before 1 January 2019. It incorporates relevant amendments contained
in other AASB Standards made by the AASB up to and including 22 October 2015 (see
Compilation Details).

ACCOUNTING STANDARD AASB 138
INTANGIBLE ASSETS

Objective

1   The objective of this Standard is to prescribe the accounting treatment for intangible
assets that are not dealt with specifically in another Standard. This Standard requires

an entity to recognise an intangible asset if, and only if, specified criteria are met. The Standard also specifies how to measure the carrying amount of intangible assets and requires specified disclosures about intangible assets.

Scope

2 **This Standard shall be applied in accounting for intangible assets, except:**

(a) **intangible assets that are within the scope of another Standard;**

(b) **financial assets, as defined in AASB 132** *Financial Instruments: Presentation*;

(c) **the recognition and measurement of exploration and evaluation assets (see AASB 6** *Exploration for and Evaluation of Mineral Resources*); and

(d) **expenditure on the development and extraction of minerals, oil, natural gas and similar non-regenerative resources.**

3 If another Standard prescribes the accounting for a specific type of intangible asset, an entity applies that Standard instead of this Standard. For example, this Standard does not apply to:

(a) intangible assets held by an entity for sale in the ordinary course of business (see AASB 102 *Inventories*).

(b) deferred tax assets (see AASB 112 *Income Taxes*).

(c) leases that are within the scope of AASB 117 *Leases*.

(d) assets arising from employee benefits (see AASB 119 *Employee Benefits*).

(e) financial assets as defined in AASB 132. The recognition and measurement of some financial assets are covered by AASB 10 *Consolidated Financial Statements*, AASB 127 *Separate Financial Statements* and AASB 128 *Investments in Associates and Joint Ventures*.

(f) goodwill acquired in a business combination (see AASB 3 *Business Combinations*).

(g) deferred acquisition costs, and intangible assets, arising from an insurer's contractual rights under insurance contracts within the scope of AASB 4 *Insurance Contracts*. AASB 4 sets out specific disclosure requirements for those deferred acquisition costs but not for those intangible assets. Therefore, the disclosure requirements in this Standard apply to those intangible assets.

(h) non-current intangible assets classified as held for sale (or included in a disposal group that is classified as held for sale) in accordance with AASB 5 *Non-current Assets Held for Sale and Discontinued Operations*.

(i) assets arising from contracts with customers that are recognised in accordance with AASB 15 *Revenue from Contracts with Customers*.

4 Some intangible assets may be contained in or on a physical substance such as a compact disc (in the case of computer software), legal documentation (in the case of a licence or patent) or film. In determining whether an asset that incorporates both intangible and tangible elements should be treated under AASB 116 *Property, Plant and Equipment* or as an intangible asset under this Standard, an entity uses judgement to assess which element is more significant. For example, computer software for a computer-controlled machine tool that cannot operate without that specific software is an integral part of the related hardware and it is treated as property, plant and equipment. The same applies to the operating system of a computer. When the software is not an integral part of the related hardware, computer software is treated as an intangible asset.

5 This Standard applies to, among other things, expenditure on advertising, training, start-up, research and development activities. Research and development activities are directed to the development of knowledge. Therefore, although these activities may

result in an asset with physical substance (eg a prototype), the physical element of the asset is secondary to its intangible component, ie the knowledge embodied in it.

6   In the case of a finance lease, the underlying asset may be either tangible or intangible. After initial recognition, a lessee accounts for an intangible asset held under a finance lease in accordance with this Standard. Rights under licensing agreements for items such as motion picture films, video recordings, plays, manuscripts, patents and copyrights are excluded from the scope of AASB 117 and are within the scope of this Standard.

7   Exclusions from the scope of a Standard may occur if activities or transactions are so specialised that they give rise to accounting issues that may need to be dealt with in a different way. Such issues arise in the accounting for expenditure on the exploration for, or development and extraction of, oil, gas and mineral deposits in extractive industries and in the case of insurance contracts. Therefore, this Standard does not apply to expenditure on such activities and contracts. However, this Standard applies to other intangible assets used (such as computer software), and other expenditure incurred (such as start-up costs), in extractive industries or by insurers.

Definitions

8   **The following terms are used in this Standard with the meanings specified:**

Amortisation **is the systematic allocation of the depreciable amount of an intangible asset over its useful life.**

An *asset* **is a resource:**

(a)   controlled by an entity as a result of past events; and

(b)   from which future economic benefits are expected to flow to the entity.

Carrying amount **is the amount at which an asset is recognised in the statement of financial position after deducting any accumulated amortisation and accumulated impairment losses thereon.**

Cost **is the amount of cash or cash equivalents paid or the fair value of other consideration given to acquire an asset at the time of its acquisition or construction, or, when applicable, the amount attributed to that asset when initially recognised in accordance with the specific requirements of other Australian Accounting Standards, eg AASB 2** *Share-based Payment.*

Depreciable amount **is the cost of an asset, or other amount substituted for cost, less its residual value.**

Development **is the application of research findings or other knowledge to a plan or design for the production of new or substantially improved materials, devices, products, processes, systems or services before the start of commercial production or use.**

Entity-specific value **is the present value of the cash flows an entity expects to arise from the continuing use of an asset and from its disposal at the end of its useful life or expects to incur when settling a liability.**

Fair value **is the price that would be received to sell an asset or paid to transfer a liability in an orderly transaction between market participants at the measurement date. (See AASB 13** *Fair Value Measurement.*)

An *impairment loss* **is the amount by which the carrying amount of an asset exceeds its recoverable amount.**

An *intangible asset* **is an identifiable non-monetary asset without physical substance.**

Monetary assets **are money held and assets to be received in fixed or determinable amounts of money.**

Research is original and planned investigation undertaken with the prospect of gaining new scientific or technical knowledge and understanding.

The *residual value* of an intangible asset is the estimated amount that an entity would currently obtain from disposal of the asset, after deducting the estimated costs of disposal, if the asset were already of the age and in the condition expected at the end of its useful life.

Useful life is:

(a)   the period over which an asset is expected to be available for use by an entity; or

(b)   the number of production or similar units expected to be obtained from the asset by an entity.

Intangible assets

9   Entities frequently expend resources, or incur liabilities, on the acquisition, development, maintenance or enhancement of intangible resources such as scientific or technical knowledge, design and implementation of new processes or systems, licences, intellectual property, market knowledge and trademarks (including brand names and publishing titles). Common examples of items encompassed by these broad headings are computer software, patents, copyrights, motion picture films, customer lists, mortgage servicing rights, fishing licences, import quotas, franchises, customer or supplier relationships, customer loyalty, market share and marketing rights.

10   Not all the items described in paragraph 9 meet the definition of an intangible asset, ie identifiability, control over a resource and existence of future economic benefits. If an item within the scope of this Standard does not meet the definition of an intangible asset, expenditure to acquire it or generate it internally is recognised as an expense when it is incurred. However, if the item is acquired in a business combination, it forms part of the goodwill recognised at the acquisition date (see paragraph 68).

Identifiability

11   The definition of an intangible asset requires an intangible asset to be identifiable to distinguish it from goodwill. Goodwill recognised in a business combination is an asset representing the future economic benefits arising from other assets acquired in a business combination that are not individually identified and separately recognised. The future economic benefits may result from synergy between the identifiable assets acquired or from assets that, individually, do not qualify for recognition in the financial statements.

12   An asset is identifiable if it either:

(a)   is separable, ie is capable of being separated or divided from the entity and sold, transferred, licensed, rented or exchanged, either individually or together with a related contract, identifiable asset or liability, regardless of whether the entity intends to do so; or

(b)   arises from contractual or other legal rights, regardless of whether those rights are transferable or separable from the entity or from other rights and obligations.

Control

13   An entity controls an asset if the entity has the power to obtain the future economic benefits flowing from the underlying resource and to restrict the access of others to those benefits. The capacity of an entity to control the future economic benefits from an intangible asset would normally stem from legal rights that are enforceable in a court of law. In the absence of legal rights, it is more difficult to demonstrate control. However, legal enforceability of a right is not a necessary condition for control because an entity may be able to control the future economic benefits in some other way.

14   Market and technical knowledge may give rise to future economic benefits. An entity controls those benefits if, for example, the knowledge is protected by legal rights such as copyrights, a restraint of trade agreement (where permitted) or by a legal duty on employees to maintain confidentiality.

15   An entity may have a team of skilled staff and may be able to identify incremental staff skills leading to future economic benefits from training. The entity may also expect that the staff will continue to make their skills available to the entity. However, an entity usually has insufficient control over the expected future economic benefits arising from a team of skilled staff and from training for these items to meet the definition of an intangible asset. For a similar reason, specific management or technical talent is unlikely to meet the definition of an intangible asset, unless it is protected by legal rights to use it and to obtain the future economic benefits expected from it, and it also meets the other parts of the definition.

16   An entity may have a portfolio of customers or a market share and expect that, because of its efforts in building customer relationships and loyalty, the customers will continue to trade with the entity. However, in the absence of legal rights to protect, or other ways to control, the relationships with customers or the loyalty of the customers to the entity, the entity usually has insufficient control over the expected economic benefits from customer relationships and loyalty for such items (eg portfolio of customers, market shares, customer relationships and customer loyalty) to meet the definition of intangible assets. In the absence of legal rights to protect customer relationships, exchange transactions for the same or similar non-contractual customer relationships (other than as part of a business combination) provide evidence that the entity is nonetheless able to control the expected future economic benefits flowing from the customer relationships. Because such exchange transactions also provide evidence that the customer relationships are separable, those customer relationships meet the definition of an intangible asset.

Future economic benefits

17   The future economic benefits flowing from an intangible asset may include revenue from the sale of products or services, cost savings, or other benefits resulting from the use of the asset by the entity. For example, the use of intellectual property in a production process may reduce future production costs rather than increase future revenues.

Recognition and measurement

18   The recognition of an item as an intangible asset requires an entity to demonstrate that the item meets:

     (a)   the definition of an intangible asset (see paragraphs 8–17); and

     (b)   the recognition criteria (see paragraphs 21–23).

     This requirement applies to costs incurred initially to acquire or internally generate an intangible asset and those incurred subsequently to add to, replace part of, or service it.

19   Paragraphs 25–32 deal with the application of the recognition criteria to separately acquired intangible assets, and paragraphs 33–43 deal with their application to intangible assets acquired in a business combination. Paragraph 44 deals with the initial measurement of intangible assets acquired by way of a government grant, paragraphs 45–47 with exchanges of intangible assets, and paragraphs 48–50 with the treatment of internally generated goodwill. Paragraphs 51–67 deal with the initial recognition and measurement of internally generated intangible assets.

20   The nature of intangible assets is such that, in many cases, there are no additions to such an asset or replacements of part of it. Accordingly, most subsequent expenditures are likely to maintain the expected future economic benefits embodied in an existing intangible asset rather than meet the definition of an intangible asset and the

recognition criteria in this Standard. In addition, it is often difficult to attribute subsequent expenditure directly to a particular intangible asset rather than to the business as a whole. Therefore, only rarely will subsequent expenditure—expenditure incurred after the initial recognition of an acquired intangible asset or after completion of an internally generated intangible asset—be recognised in the carrying amount of an asset. Consistently with paragraph 63, subsequent expenditure on brands, mastheads, publishing titles, customer lists and items similar in substance (whether externally acquired or internally generated) is always recognised in profit or loss as incurred. This is because such expenditure cannot be distinguished from expenditure to develop the business as a whole.

21   **An intangible asset shall be recognised if, and only if:**

    (a)   **it is probable that the expected future economic benefits that are attributable to the asset will flow to the entity; and**

    (b)   **the cost of the asset can be measured reliably.**

22   **An entity shall assess the probability of expected future economic benefits using reasonable and supportable assumptions that represent management's best estimate of the set of economic conditions that will exist over the useful life of the asset.**

23   An entity uses judgement to assess the degree of certainty attached to the flow of future economic benefits that are attributable to the use of the asset on the basis of the evidence available at the time of initial recognition, giving greater weight to external evidence.

24   **An intangible asset shall be measured initially at cost.**

Aus24.1   **Notwithstanding paragraph 24, in respect of not-for-profit entities, where an asset is acquired at no cost, or for a nominal cost, the cost is its *fair value* as at the date of acquisition.**

Separate acquisition

25   Normally, the price an entity pays to acquire separately an intangible asset will reflect expectations about the probability that the expected future economic benefits embodied in the asset will flow to the entity. In other words, the entity expects there to be an inflow of economic benefits, even if there is uncertainty about the timing or the amount of the inflow. Therefore, the probability recognition criterion in paragraph 21(a) is always considered to be satisfied for separately acquired intangible assets.

26   In addition, the cost of a separately acquired intangible asset can usually be measured reliably. This is particularly so when the purchase consideration is in the form of cash or other monetary assets.

27   The cost of a separately acquired intangible asset comprises:

    (a)   its purchase price, including import duties and non-refundable purchase taxes, after deducting trade discounts and rebates; and

    (b)   any directly attributable cost of preparing the asset for its intended use.

28   Examples of directly attributable costs are:

    (a)   costs of employee benefits (as defined in AASB 119) arising directly from bringing the asset to its working condition;

    (b)   professional fees arising directly from bringing the asset to its working condition; and

    (c)   costs of testing whether the asset is functioning properly.

29   Examples of expenditures that are not part of the cost of an intangible asset are:

    (a)   costs of introducing a new product or service (including costs of advertising and promotional activities);

    (b)   costs of conducting business in a new location or with a new class of customer (including costs of staff training); and

    (c)   administration and other general overhead costs.

30   Recognition of costs in the carrying amount of an intangible asset ceases when the asset is in the condition necessary for it to be capable of operating in the manner intended by management. Therefore, costs incurred in using or redeploying an intangible asset are not included in the carrying amount of that asset. For example, the following costs are not included in the carrying amount of an intangible asset:

(a)   costs incurred while an asset capable of operating in the manner intended by management has yet to be brought into use; and

(b)   initial operating losses, such as those incurred while demand for the asset's output builds up.

31   Some operations occur in connection with the development of an intangible asset, but are not necessary to bring the asset to the condition necessary for it to be capable of operating in the manner intended by management. These incidental operations may occur before or during the development activities. Because incidental operations are not necessary to bring an asset to the condition necessary for it to be capable of operating in the manner intended by management, the income and related expenses of incidental operations are recognised immediately in profit or loss, and included in their respective classifications of income and expense.

32   If payment for an intangible asset is deferred beyond normal credit terms, its cost is the cash price equivalent. The difference between this amount and the total payments is recognised as interest expense over the period of credit unless it is capitalised in accordance with AASB 123 *Borrowing Costs*.

Acquisition as part of a business combination

33   In accordance with AASB 3 *Business Combinations*, if an intangible asset is acquired in a business combination, the cost of that intangible asset is its fair value at the acquisition date. The fair value of an intangible asset will reflect market participants' expectations at the acquisition date about the probability that the expected future economic benefits embodied in the asset will flow to the entity. In other words, the entity expects there to be an inflow of economic benefits, even if there is uncertainty about the timing or the amount of the inflow. Therefore, the probability recognition criterion in paragraph 21(a) is always considered to be satisfied for intangible assets acquired in business combinations. If an asset acquired in a business combination is separable or arises from contractual or other legal rights, sufficient information exists to measure reliably the fair value of the asset. Thus, the reliable measurement criterion in paragraph 21(b) is always considered to be satisfied for intangible assets acquired in business combinations.

34   In accordance with this Standard and AASB 3, an acquirer recognises at the acquisition date, separately from goodwill, an intangible asset of the acquiree, irrespective of whether the asset had been recognised by the acquiree before the business combination. This means that the acquirer recognises as an asset separately from goodwill an in-process research and development project of the acquiree if the project meets the definition of an intangible asset. An acquiree's in-process research and development project meets the definition of an intangible asset when it:

(a)   meets the definition of an asset; and

(b)   is identifiable, ie is separable or arises from contractual or other legal rights.

Intangible asset acquired in a business combination

35   If an intangible asset acquired in a business combination is separable or arises from contractual or other legal rights, sufficient information exists to measure reliably the fair value of the asset. When, for the estimates used to measure an intangible asset's fair value, there is a range of possible outcomes with different probabilities, that uncertainty enters into the measurement of the asset's fair value.

36 An intangible asset acquired in a business combination might be separable, but only together with a related contract, identifiable asset or liability. In such cases, the acquirer recognises the intangible asset separately from goodwill, but together with the related item.

37 The acquirer may recognise a group of complementary intangible assets as a single asset provided the individual assets have similar useful lives. For example, the terms 'brand' and 'brand name' are often used as synonyms for trademarks and other marks. However, the former are general marketing terms that are typically used to refer to a group of complementary assets such as a trademark (or service mark) and its related trade name, formulas, recipes and technological expertise.

38–41 [Deleted]

Subsequent expenditure on an acquired in-process research and development project

42 Research or development expenditure that:

    (a) **relates to an in-process research or development project acquired separately or in a business combination and recognised as an intangible asset; and**

    (b) **is incurred after the acquisition of that project**

shall be accounted for in accordance with paragraphs 54–62.

43 Applying the requirements in paragraphs 54–62 means that subsequent expenditure on an in-process research or development project acquired separately or in a business combination and recognised as an intangible asset is:

    (a) recognised as an expense when incurred if it is research expenditure;

    (b) recognised as an expense when incurred if it is development expenditure that does not satisfy the criteria for recognition as an intangible asset in paragraph 57; and

    (c) added to the carrying amount of the acquired in-process research or development project if it is development expenditure that satisfies the recognition criteria in paragraph 57.

Acquisition by way of a government grant

44 In some cases, an intangible asset may be acquired free of charge, or for nominal consideration, by way of a government grant. This may happen when a government transfers or allocates to an entity intangible assets such as airport landing rights, licences to operate radio or television stations, import licences or quotas or rights to access other restricted resources. In accordance with AASB 120 *Accounting for Government Grants and Disclosure of Government Assistance*, an entity may choose to recognise both the intangible asset and the grant initially at fair value.[1] If an entity chooses not to recognise the asset initially at fair value, the entity recognises the asset initially at a nominal amount (the other treatment permitted by AASB 120) plus any expenditure that is directly attributable to preparing the asset for its intended use.

Exchanges of assets

45 One or more intangible assets may be acquired in exchange for a non-monetary asset or assets, or a combination of monetary and non-monetary assets. The following discussion refers simply to an exchange of one non-monetary asset for another, but it also applies to all exchanges described in the preceding sentence. The cost of such an intangible asset is measured at fair value unless (a) the exchange transaction lacks commercial substance or (b) the fair value of neither the asset received nor the asset

---

1 [Aus] AASB 120 applies only to for-profit entities. Not-for-profit entities are required to recognise the intangible asset and the grant initially at fair value in accordance with AASB 1004 *Contributions*.

given up is reliably measurable. The acquired asset is measured in this way even if an entity cannot immediately derecognise the asset given up. If the acquired asset is not measured at fair value, its cost is measured at the carrying amount of the asset given up.

46   An entity determines whether an exchange transaction has commercial substance by considering the extent to which its future cash flows are expected to change as a result of the transaction. An exchange transaction has commercial substance if:

(a)   the configuration (ie risk, timing and amount) of the cash flows of the asset received differs from the configuration of the cash flows of the asset transferred; or

(b)   the entity-specific value of the portion of the entity's operations affected by the transaction changes as a result of the exchange; and

(c)   the difference in (a) or (b) is significant relative to the fair value of the assets exchanged.

For the purpose of determining whether an exchange transaction has commercial substance, the entity-specific value of the portion of the entity's operations affected by the transaction shall reflect post-tax cash flows. The result of these analyses may be clear without an entity having to perform detailed calculations.

47   Paragraph 21(b) specifies that a condition for the recognition of an intangible asset is that the cost of the asset can be measured reliably. The fair value of an intangible asset is reliably measurable if (a) the variability in the range of reasonable fair value measurements is not significant for that asset or (b) the probabilities of the various estimates within the range can be reasonably assessed and used when measuring fair value. If an entity is able to measure reliably the fair value of either the asset received or the asset given up, then the fair value of the asset given up is used to measure cost unless the fair value of the asset received is more clearly evident.

Internally generated goodwill

48   **Internally generated goodwill shall not be recognised as an asset.**

49   In some cases, expenditure is incurred to generate future economic benefits, but it does not result in the creation of an intangible asset that meets the recognition criteria in this Standard. Such expenditure is often described as contributing to internally generated goodwill. Internally generated goodwill is not recognised as an asset because it is not an identifiable resource (ie it is not separable nor does it arise from contractual or other legal rights) controlled by the entity that can be measured reliably at cost.

50   Differences between the fair value of an entity and the carrying amount of its identifiable net assets at any time may capture a range of factors that affect the fair value of the entity. However, such differences do not represent the cost of intangible assets controlled by the entity.

Internally generated intangible assets

51   It is sometimes difficult to assess whether an internally generated intangible asset qualifies for recognition because of problems in:

(a)   identifying whether and when there is an identifiable asset that will generate expected future economic benefits; and

(b)   determining the cost of the asset reliably. In some cases, the cost of generating an intangible asset internally cannot be distinguished from the cost of maintaining or enhancing the entity's internally generated goodwill or of running day-to-day operations.

Therefore, in addition to complying with the general requirements for the recognition and initial measurement of an intangible asset, an entity applies the requirements and guidance in paragraphs 52–67 to all internally generated intangible assets.

52   To assess whether an internally generated intangible asset meets the criteria for recognition, an entity classifies the generation of the asset into:

(a)   a research phase; and

(b)   a development phase.

Although the terms 'research' and 'development' are defined, the terms 'research phase' and 'development phase' have a broader meaning for the purpose of this Standard.

53   If an entity cannot distinguish the research phase from the development phase of an internal project to create an intangible asset, the entity treats the expenditure on that project as if it were incurred in the research phase only.

Research phase

54   No intangible asset arising from research (or from the research phase of an internal project) shall be recognised. Expenditure on research (or on the research phase of an internal project) shall be recognised as an expense when it is incurred.

55   In the research phase of an internal project, an entity cannot demonstrate that an intangible asset exists that will generate probable future economic benefits. Therefore, this expenditure is recognised as an expense when it is incurred.

56   Examples of research activities are:

(a)   activities aimed at obtaining new knowledge;

(b)   the search for, evaluation and final selection of, applications of research findings or other knowledge;

(c)   the search for alternatives for materials, devices, products, processes, systems or services; and

(d)   the formulation, design, evaluation and final selection of possible alternatives for new or improved materials, devices, products, processes, systems or services.

Development phase

57   An intangible asset arising from development (or from the development phase of an internal project) shall be recognised if, and only if, an entity can demonstrate all of the following:

(a)   the technical feasibility of completing the intangible asset so that it will be available for use or sale.

(b)   its intention to complete the intangible asset and use or sell it.

(c)   its ability to use or sell the intangible asset.

(d)   how the intangible asset will generate probable future economic benefits. Among other things, the entity can demonstrate the existence of a market for the output of the intangible asset or the intangible asset itself or, if it is to be used internally, the usefulness of the intangible asset.

(e)   the availability of adequate technical, financial and other resources to complete the development and to use or sell the intangible asset.

(f)   its ability to measure reliably the expenditure attributable to the intangible asset during its development.

58   In the development phase of an internal project, an entity can, in some instances, identify an intangible asset and demonstrate that the asset will generate probable future economic benefits. This is because the development phase of a project is further advanced than the research phase.

59   Examples of development activities are:

    (a)   the design, construction and testing of pre-production or pre-use prototypes and models;

    (b)   the design of tools, jigs, moulds and dies involving new technology;

    (c)   the design, construction and operation of a pilot plant that is not of a scale economically feasible for commercial production; and

    (d)   the design, construction and testing of a chosen alternative for new or improved materials, devices, products, processes, systems or services.

60   To demonstrate how an intangible asset will generate probable future economic benefits, an entity assesses the future economic benefits to be received from the asset using the principles in AASB 136 *Impairment of Assets*. If the asset will generate economic benefits only in combination with other assets, the entity applies the concept of cash-generating units in AASB 136.

61   Availability of resources to complete, use and obtain the benefits from an intangible asset can be demonstrated by, for example, a business plan showing the technical, financial and other resources needed and the entity's ability to secure those resources. In some cases, an entity demonstrates the availability of external finance by obtaining a lender's indication of its willingness to fund the plan.

62   An entity's costing systems can often measure reliably the cost of generating an intangible asset internally, such as salary and other expenditure incurred in securing copyrights or licences or developing computer software.

63   Internally generated brands, mastheads, publishing titles, customer lists and items similar in substance shall not be recognised as intangible assets.

64   Expenditure on internally generated brands, mastheads, publishing titles, customer lists and items similar in substance cannot be distinguished from the cost of developing the business as a whole. Therefore, such items are not recognised as intangible assets.

Cost of an internally generated intangible asset

65   The cost of an internally generated intangible asset for the purpose of paragraph 24 is the sum of expenditure incurred from the date when the intangible asset first meets the recognition criteria in paragraphs 21, 22 and 57. Paragraph 71 prohibits reinstatement of expenditure previously recognised as an expense.

66   The cost of an internally generated intangible asset comprises all directly attributable costs necessary to create, produce, and prepare the asset to be capable of operating in the manner intended by management. Examples of directly attributable costs are:

    (a)   costs of materials and services used or consumed in generating the intangible asset;

    (b)   costs of employee benefits (as defined in AASB 119) arising from the generation of the intangible asset;

    (c)   fees to register a legal right; and

    (d)   amortisation of patents and licences that are used to generate the intangible asset.

AASB 123 specifies criteria for the recognition of interest as an element of the cost of an internally generated intangible asset.

67   The following are not components of the cost of an internally generated intangible asset:

    (a)   selling, administrative and other general overhead expenditure unless this expenditure can be directly attributed to preparing the asset for use;

    (b)   identified inefficiencies and initial operating losses incurred before the asset achieves planned performance; and

    (c)   expenditure on training staff to operate the asset.

Example illustrating paragraph 65

An entity is developing a new production process. During 20X5, expenditure incurred was CU1,000,[a] of which CU900 was incurred before 1 December 20X5 and CU100 was incurred between 1 December 20X5 and 31 December 20X5. The entity is able to demonstrate that, at 1 December 20X5, the production process met the criteria for recognition as an intangible asset. The recoverable amount of the know-how embodied in the process (including future cash outflows to complete the process before it is available for use) is estimated to be CU500.

At the end of 20X5, the production process is recognised as an intangible asset at a cost of CU100 (expenditure incurred since the date when the recognition criteria were met, ie 1 December 20X5). The CU900 expenditure incurred before 1 December 20X5 is recognised as an expense because the recognition criteria were not met until 1 December 20X5. This expenditure does not form part of the cost of the production process recognised in the statement of financial position.

During 20X6, expenditure incurred is CU2,000. At the end of 20X6, the recoverable amount of the know-how embodied in the process (including future cash outflows to complete the process before it is available for use) is estimated to be CU1,900.

At the end of 20X6, the cost of the production process is CU2,100 (CU100 expenditure recognised at the end of 20X5 plus CU2,000 expenditure recognised in 20X6). The entity recognises an impairment loss of CU200 to adjust the carrying amount of the process before impairment loss (CU2,100) to its recoverable amount (CU1,900). This impairment loss will be reversed in a subsequent period if the requirements for the reversal of an impairment loss in AASB 136 are met.

(a)   In this Standard, monetary amounts are denominated in 'currency units (CU)'.

Recognition of an expense

68   **Expenditure on an intangible item shall be recognised as an expense when it is incurred unless:**

    (a)   it forms part of the cost of an intangible asset that meets the recognition criteria (see paragraphs 18–67); or

    (b)   the item is acquired in a business combination and cannot be recognised as an intangible asset. If this is the case, it forms part of the amount recognised as goodwill at the acquisition date (see AASB 3).

69   In some cases, expenditure is incurred to provide future economic benefits to an entity, but no intangible asset or other asset is acquired or created that can be recognised. In the case of the supply of goods, the entity recognises such expenditure as an expense when it has a right to access those goods. In the case of the supply of services, the entity recognises the expenditure as an expense when it receives the services. For example, expenditure on research is recognised as an expense when it is incurred (see paragraph 54), except when it is acquired as part of a business combination. Other examples of expenditure that is recognised as an expense when it is incurred include:

    (a)   expenditure on start-up activities (ie start-up costs), unless this expenditure is included in the cost of an item of property, plant and equipment in accordance with AASB 116. Start-up costs may consist of establishment costs such as legal and secretarial costs incurred in establishing a legal entity, expenditure to open a new facility or business (ie pre-opening costs) or expenditures for starting new operations or launching new products or processes (ie pre-operating costs).

    (b)   expenditure on training activities.

    (c)   expenditure on advertising and promotional activities (including mail order catalogues).

    (d)   expenditure on relocating or reorganising part or all of an entity.

69A   An entity has a right to access goods when it owns them. Similarly, it has a right to access goods when they have been constructed by a supplier in accordance with the terms of a supply contract and the entity could demand delivery of them in return for payment. Services are received when they are performed by a supplier in accordance with a contract to deliver them to the entity and not when the entity uses them to deliver another service, for example, to deliver an advertisement to customers.

70   Paragraph 68 does not preclude an entity from recognising a prepayment as an asset when payment for goods has been made in advance of the entity obtaining a right to access those goods. Similarly, paragraph 68 does not preclude an entity from recognising a prepayment as an asset when payment for services has been made in advance of the entity receiving those services.

Past expenses not to be recognised as an asset

71   **Expenditure on an intangible item that was initially recognised as an expense shall not be recognised as part of the cost of an intangible asset at a later date.**

Measurement after recognition

72   **An entity shall choose either the cost model in paragraph 74 or the revaluation model in paragraph 75 as its accounting policy. If an intangible asset is accounted for using the revaluation model, all the other assets in its class shall also be accounted for using the same model, unless there is no active market for those assets.**

73   A class of intangible assets is a grouping of assets of a similar nature and use in an entity's operations. The items within a class of intangible assets are revalued simultaneously to avoid selective revaluation of assets and the reporting of amounts in the financial statements representing a mixture of costs and values as at different dates.

Cost model

74   **After initial recognition, an intangible asset shall be carried at its cost less any accumulated amortisation and any accumulated impairment losses.**

Revaluation model

75   **After initial recognition, an intangible asset shall be carried at a revalued amount, being its fair value at the date of the revaluation less any subsequent accumulated amortisation and any subsequent accumulated impairment losses. For the purpose of revaluations under this Standard, fair value shall be measured by reference to an active market. Revaluations shall be made with such regularity that at the end of the reporting period the carrying amount of the asset does not differ materially from its fair value.**

76   The revaluation model does not allow:

   (a)   the revaluation of intangible assets that have not previously been recognised as assets; or

   (b)   the initial recognition of intangible assets at amounts other than cost.

77   The revaluation model is applied after an asset has been initially recognised at cost. However, if only part of the cost of an intangible asset is recognised as an asset because the asset did not meet the criteria for recognition until part of the way through the process (see paragraph 65), the revaluation model may be applied to the whole of that asset. Also, the revaluation model may be applied to an intangible asset that was received by way of a government grant and recognised at a nominal amount (see paragraph 44).

78   It is uncommon for an active market to exist for an intangible asset, although this may happen. For example, in some jurisdictions, an active market may exist for freely transferable taxi licences, fishing licences or production quotas. However, an active market cannot exist for brands, newspaper mastheads, music and film publishing rights, patents or trademarks, because each such asset is unique. Also, although intangible

assets are bought and sold, contracts are negotiated between individual buyers and sellers, and transactions are relatively infrequent. For these reasons, the price paid for one asset may not provide sufficient evidence of the fair value of another. Moreover, prices are often not available to the public.

79 The frequency of revaluations depends on the volatility of the fair values of the intangible assets being revalued. If the fair value of a revalued asset differs materially from its carrying amount, a further revaluation is necessary. Some intangible assets may experience significant and volatile movements in fair value, thus necessitating annual revaluation. Such frequent revaluations are unnecessary for intangible assets with only insignificant movements in fair value.

80 When an intangible asset is revalued, the carrying amount of that asset is adjusted to the revalued amount. At the date of the revaluation, the asset is treated in one of the following ways:

    (a) the gross carrying amount is adjusted in a manner that is consistent with the revaluation of the carrying amount of the asset. For example, the gross carrying amount may be restated by reference to observable market data or it may be restated proportionately to the change in the carrying amount. The accumulated amortisation at the date of the revaluation is adjusted to equal the difference between the gross carrying amount and the carrying amount of the asset after taking into account accumulated impairment losses; or

    (b) the accumulated amortisation is eliminated against the gross carrying amount of the asset.

The amount of the adjustment of accumulated amortisation forms part of the increase or decrease in the carrying amount that is accounted for in accordance with paragraphs 85 and 86.

81 **If an intangible asset in a class of revalued intangible assets cannot be revalued because there is no active market for this asset, the asset shall be carried at its cost less any accumulated amortisation and impairment losses.**

82 **If the fair value of a revalued intangible asset can no longer be measured by reference to an active market, the carrying amount of the asset shall be its revalued amount at the date of the last revaluation by reference to the active market less any subsequent accumulated amortisation and any subsequent accumulated impairment losses.**

83 The fact that an active market no longer exists for a revalued intangible asset may indicate that the asset may be impaired and that it needs to be tested in accordance with AASB 136.

84 If the fair value of the asset can be measured by reference to an active market at a subsequent measurement date, the revaluation model is applied from that date.

85 **If an intangible asset's carrying amount is increased as a result of a revaluation, the increase shall be recognised in other comprehensive income and accumulated in equity under the heading of revaluation surplus. However, the increase shall be recognised in profit or loss to the extent that it reverses a revaluation decrease of the same asset previously recognised in profit or loss.**

Aus85.1 **Notwithstanding paragraph 85, in respect of not-for-profit entities, if the carrying amount of a class of assets is increased as a result of a revaluation, the net revaluation increase shall be recognised in other comprehensive income and accumulated in equity under the heading of revaluation surplus. However, the net revaluation increase shall be recognised in profit or loss to the extent that it reverses a net revaluation decrease of the same class of assets previously recognised in profit or loss.**

86 **If an intangible asset's carrying amount is decreased as a result of a revaluation, the decrease shall be recognised in profit or loss. However, the decrease shall be recognised in other comprehensive income to the extent of any credit balance in the revaluation surplus in respect of that asset. The decrease recognised in**

other comprehensive income reduces the amount accumulated in equity under the heading of revaluation surplus.

Aus86.1   Notwithstanding paragraph 86, in respect of not-for-profit entities, if the carrying amount of a class of assets decreased as a result of a revaluation, the net revaluation decrease shall be recognised in profit or loss. However, the net revaluation decrease shall be recognised in other comprehensive income to the extent of any credit balance existing in any revaluation surplus in respect of that same class of assets. The net revaluation decrease recognised in other comprehensive income reduces the amount accumulated in equity under the heading of revaluation surplus.

Aus86.2   In respect of not-for-profit entities, revaluation increases and revaluation decreases relating to individual assets within a class of intangible assets shall be offset against one another within that class but shall not be offset in respect of assets in different classes.

87   The cumulative revaluation surplus included in equity may be transferred directly to retained earnings when the surplus is realised. The whole surplus may be realised on the retirement or disposal of the asset. However, some of the surplus may be realised as the asset is used by the entity; in such a case, the amount of the surplus realised is the difference between amortisation based on the revalued carrying amount of the asset and amortisation that would have been recognised based on the asset's historical cost. The transfer from revaluation surplus to retained earnings is not made through profit or loss.

Useful life

88   **An entity shall assess whether the useful life of an intangible asset is finite or indefinite and, if finite, the length of, or number of production or similar units constituting, that useful life. An intangible asset shall be regarded by the entity as having an indefinite useful life when, based on an analysis of all of the relevant factors, there is no foreseeable limit to the period over which the asset is expected to generate net cash inflows for the entity.**

89   The accounting for an intangible asset is based on its useful life. An intangible asset with a finite useful life is amortised (see paragraphs 97–106), and an intangible asset with an indefinite useful life is not (see paragraphs 107–110). The Illustrative Examples accompanying this Standard illustrate the determination of useful life for different intangible assets, and the subsequent accounting for those assets based on the useful life determinations.

90   Many factors are considered in determining the useful life of an intangible asset, including:

(a)   the expected usage of the asset by the entity and whether the asset could be managed efficiently by another management team;

(b)   typical product life cycles for the asset and public information on estimates of useful lives of similar assets that are used in a similar way;

(c)   technical, technological, commercial or other types of obsolescence;

(d)   the stability of the industry in which the asset operates and changes in the market demand for the products or services output from the asset;

(e)   expected actions by competitors or potential competitors;

(f)   the level of maintenance expenditure required to obtain the expected future economic benefits from the asset and the entity's ability and intention to reach such a level;

(g)   the period of control over the asset and legal or similar limits on the use of the asset, such as the expiry dates of related leases; and

(h) whether the useful life of the asset is dependent on the useful life of other assets of the entity.

91 The term 'indefinite' does not mean 'infinite'. The useful life of an intangible asset reflects only that level of future maintenance expenditure required to maintain the asset at its standard of performance assessed at the time of estimating the asset's useful life, and the entity's ability and intention to reach such a level. A conclusion that the useful life of an intangible asset is indefinite should not depend on planned future expenditure in excess of that required to maintain the asset at that standard of performance.

92 Given the history of rapid changes in technology, computer software and many other intangible assets are susceptible to technological obsolescence. Therefore, it will often be the case that their useful life is short. Expected future reductions in the selling price of an item that was produced using an intangible asset could indicate the expectation of technological or commercial obsolescence of the asset, which, in turn, might reflect a reduction of the future economic benefits embodied in the asset.

93 The useful life of an intangible asset may be very long or even indefinite. Uncertainty justifies estimating the useful life of an intangible asset on a prudent basis, but it does not justify choosing a life that is unrealistically short.

94 **The useful life of an intangible asset that arises from contractual or other legal rights shall not exceed the period of the contractual or other legal rights, but may be shorter depending on the period over which the entity expects to use the asset. If the contractual or other legal rights are conveyed for a limited term that can be renewed, the useful life of the intangible asset shall include the renewal period(s) only if there is evidence to support renewal by the entity without significant cost. The useful life of a reacquired right recognised as an intangible asset in a business combination is the remaining contractual period of the contract in which the right was granted and shall not include renewal periods.**

95 There may be both economic and legal factors influencing the useful life of an intangible asset. Economic factors determine the period over which future economic benefits will be received by the entity. Legal factors may restrict the period over which the entity controls access to these benefits. The useful life is the shorter of the periods determined by these factors.

96 Existence of the following factors, among others, indicates that an entity would be able to renew the contractual or other legal rights without significant cost:

(a) there is evidence, possibly based on experience, that the contractual or other legal rights will be renewed. If renewal is contingent upon the consent of a third party, this includes evidence that the third party will give its consent;

(b) there is evidence that any conditions necessary to obtain renewal will be satisfied; and

(c) the cost to the entity of renewal is not significant when compared with the future economic benefits expected to flow to the entity from renewal.

If the cost of renewal is significant when compared with the future economic benefits expected to flow to the entity from renewal, the 'renewal' cost represents, in substance, the cost to acquire a new intangible asset at the renewal date.

Intangible assets with finite useful lives

Amortisation period and amortisation method

97 **The depreciable amount of an intangible asset with a finite useful life shall be allocated on a systematic basis over its useful life. Amortisation shall begin when the asset is available for use, ie when it is in the location and condition necessary for it to be capable of operating in the manner intended by management. Amortisation shall cease at the earlier of the date that the asset is classified as held for sale (or included in a disposal group that is classified as held for**

sale) in accordance with AASB 5 and the date that the asset is derecognised. The amortisation method used shall reflect the pattern in which the asset's future economic benefits are expected to be consumed by the entity. If that pattern cannot be determined reliably, the straight-line method shall be used. The amortisation charge for each period shall be recognised in profit or loss unless this or another Standard permits or requires it to be included in the carrying amount of another asset.

98   A variety of amortisation methods can be used to allocate the depreciable amount of an asset on a systematic basis over its useful life. These methods include the straight-line method, the diminishing balance method and the units of production method. The method used is selected on the basis of the expected pattern of consumption of the expected future economic benefits embodied in the asset and is applied consistently from period to period, unless there is a change in the expected pattern of consumption of those future economic benefits.

98A   There is a rebuttable presumption that an amortisation method that is based on the revenue generated by an activity that includes the use of an intangible asset is inappropriate. The revenue generated by an activity that includes the use of an intangible asset typically reflects factors that are not directly linked to the consumption of the economic benefits embodied in the intangible asset. For example, revenue is affected by other inputs and processes, selling activities and changes in sales volumes and prices. The price component of revenue may be affected by inflation, which has no bearing upon the way in which an asset is consumed. This presumption can be overcome only in the limited circumstances:

   (a)   in which the intangible asset is expressed as a measure of revenue, as described in paragraph 98C; or

   (b)   when it can be demonstrated that revenue and the consumption of the economic benefits of the intangible asset are highly correlated.

98B   In choosing an appropriate amortisation method in accordance with paragraph 98, an entity could determine the predominant limiting factor that is inherent in the intangible asset. For example, the contract that sets out the entity's rights over its use of an intangible asset might specify the entity's use of the intangible asset as a predetermined number of years (ie time), as a number of units produced or as a fixed total amount of revenue to be generated. Identification of such a predominant limiting factor could serve as the starting point for the identification of the appropriate basis of amortisation, but another basis may be applied if it more closely reflects the expected pattern of consumption of economic benefits.

98C   In the circumstance in which the predominant limiting factor that is inherent in an intangible asset is the achievement of a revenue threshold, the revenue to be generated can be an appropriate basis for amortisation. For example, an entity could acquire a concession to explore and extract gold from a gold mine. The expiry of the contract might be based on a fixed amount of total revenue to be generated from the extraction (for example, a contract may allow the extraction of gold from the mine until total cumulative revenue from the sale of gold reaches CU2 billion) and not be based on time or on the amount of gold extracted. In another example, the right to operate a toll road could be based on a fixed total amount of revenue to be generated from cumulative tolls charged (for example, a contract could allow operation of the toll road until the cumulative amount of tolls generated from operating the road reaches CU100 million). In the case in which revenue has been established as the predominant limiting factor in the contract for the use of the intangible asset, the revenue that is to be generated might be an appropriate basis for amortising the intangible asset, provided that the contract specifies a fixed total amount of revenue to be generated on which amortisation is to be determined.

99   Amortisation is usually recognised in profit or loss. However, sometimes the future economic benefits embodied in an asset are absorbed in producing other assets. In this case, the amortisation charge constitutes part of the cost of the other asset and

is included in its carrying amount. For example, the amortisation of intangible assets used in a production process is included in the carrying amount of inventories (see AASB 102 *Inventories*).

Residual value

100 **The residual value of an intangible asset with a finite useful life shall be assumed to be zero unless:**

  (a) **there is a commitment by a third party to purchase the asset at the end of its useful life; or**

  (b) **there is an active market (as defined in AASB 13) for the asset and:**

   (i) **residual value can be determined by reference to that market; and**

   (ii) **it is probable that such a market will exist at the end of the asset's useful life.**

101 The depreciable amount of an asset with a finite useful life is determined after deducting its residual value. A residual value other than zero implies that an entity expects to dispose of the intangible asset before the end of its economic life.

102 An estimate of an asset's residual value is based on the amount recoverable from disposal using prices prevailing at the date of the estimate for the sale of a similar asset that has reached the end of its useful life and has operated under conditions similar to those in which the asset will be used. The residual value is reviewed at least at each financial year-end. A change in the asset's residual value is accounted for as a change in an accounting estimate in accordance with AASB 108 *Accounting Policies, Changes in Accounting Estimates and Errors*.

103 The residual value of an intangible asset may increase to an amount equal to or greater than the asset's carrying amount. If it does, the asset's amortisation charge is zero unless and until its residual value subsequently decreases to an amount below the asset's carrying amount.

Review of amortisation period and amortisation method

104 **The amortisation period and the amortisation method for an intangible asset with a finite useful life shall be reviewed at least at each financial year-end. If the expected useful life of the asset is different from previous estimates, the amortisation period shall be changed accordingly. If there has been a change in the expected pattern of consumption of the future economic benefits embodied in the asset, the amortisation method shall be changed to reflect the changed pattern. Such changes shall be accounted for as changes in accounting estimates in accordance with AASB 108.**

105 During the life of an intangible asset, it may become apparent that the estimate of its useful life is inappropriate. For example, the recognition of an impairment loss may indicate that the amortisation period needs to be changed.

106 Over time, the pattern of future economic benefits expected to flow to an entity from an intangible asset may change. For example, it may become apparent that a diminishing balance method of amortisation is appropriate rather than a straight-line method. Another example is if use of the rights represented by a licence is deferred pending action on other components of the business plan. In this case, economic benefits that flow from the asset may not be received until later periods.

Intangible assets with indefinite useful lives

107 **An intangible asset with an indefinite useful life shall not be amortised.**

108   In accordance with AASB 136, an entity is required to test an intangible asset with an indefinite useful life for impairment by comparing its recoverable amount with its carrying amount

    (a)   annually, and

    (b)   whenever there is an indication that the intangible asset may be impaired.

Review of useful life assessment

109   **The useful life of an intangible asset that is not being amortised shall be reviewed each period to determine whether events and circumstances continue to support an indefinite useful life assessment for that asset. If they do not, the change in the useful life assessment from indefinite to finite shall be accounted for as a change in an accounting estimate in accordance with AASB 108.**

110   In accordance with AASB 136, reassessing the useful life of an intangible asset as finite rather than indefinite is an indicator that the asset may be impaired. As a result, the entity tests the asset for impairment by comparing its recoverable amount, determined in accordance with AASB 136, with its carrying amount, and recognising any excess of the carrying amount over the recoverable amount as an impairment loss.

Recoverability of the carrying amount—impairment losses

111   To determine whether an intangible asset is impaired, an entity applies AASB 136. That Standard explains when and how an entity reviews the carrying amount of its assets, how it determines the recoverable amount of an asset and when it recognises or reverses an impairment loss.

Retirements and disposals

112   **An intangible asset shall be derecognised:**

    (a)   **on disposal; or**

    (b)   **when no future economic benefits are expected from its use or disposal.**

113   **The gain or loss arising from the derecognition of an intangible asset shall be determined as the difference between the net disposal proceeds, if any, and the carrying amount of the asset. It shall be recognised in profit or loss when the asset is derecognised (unless AASB 117 requires otherwise on a sale and leaseback.) Gains shall not be classified as revenue.**

114   The disposal of an intangible asset may occur in a variety of ways (eg by sale, by entering into a finance lease, or by donation). The date of disposal of an intangible asset is the date that the recipient obtains control of that asset in accordance with the requirements for determining when a performance obligation is satisfied in AASB 15. AASB 117 applies to disposal by a sale and leaseback.

115   If in accordance with the recognition principle in paragraph 21 an entity recognises in the carrying amount of an asset the cost of a replacement for part of an intangible asset, then it derecognises the carrying amount of the replaced part. If it is not practicable for an entity to determine the carrying amount of the replaced part, it may use the cost of the replacement as an indication of what the cost of the replaced part was at the time it was acquired or internally generated.

115A In the case of a reacquired right in a business combination, if the right is subsequently reissued (sold) to a third party, the related carrying amount, if any, shall be used in determining the gain or loss on reissue.

116   The amount of consideration to be included in the gain or loss arising from the derecognition of an intangible asset is determined in accordance with the requirements for determining the transaction price in paragraphs 47–72 of AASB 15. Subsequent changes to the estimated amount of the consideration included in the gain or loss shall

be accounted for in accordance with the requirements for changes in the transaction price in AASB 15.

117   Amortisation of an intangible asset with a finite useful life does not cease when the intangible asset is no longer used, unless the asset has been fully depreciated or is classified as held for sale (or included in a disposal group that is classified as held for sale) in accordance with AASB 5.

Disclosure

General

118   **An entity shall disclose the following for each class of intangible assets, distinguishing between internally generated intangible assets and other intangible assets:**

(a)   **whether the useful lives are indefinite or finite and, if finite, the useful lives or the amortisation rates used;**

(b)   **the amortisation methods used for intangible assets with finite useful lives;**

(c)   **the gross carrying amount and any accumulated amortisation (aggregated with accumulated impairment losses) at the beginning and end of the period;**

(d)   **the line item(s) of the statement of comprehensive income in which any amortisation of intangible assets is included;**

(e)   **a reconciliation of the carrying amount at the beginning and end of the period showing:**

(i)   **additions, indicating separately those from internal development, those acquired separately, and those acquired through business combinations;**

(ii)   **assets classified as held for sale or included in a disposal group classified as held for sale in accordance with AASB 5 and other disposals;**

(iii)   **increases or decreases during the period resulting from revaluations under paragraphs 75, 85 and 86 and from impairment losses recognised or reversed in other comprehensive income in accordance with AASB 136 (if any);**

(iv)   **impairment losses recognised in profit or loss during the period in accordance with AASB 136 (if any);**

(v)   **impairment losses reversed in profit or loss during the period in accordance with AASB 136 (if any);**

(vi)   **any amortisation recognised during the period;**

(vii)   **net exchange differences arising on the translation of the financial statements into the presentation currency, and on the translation of a foreign operation into the presentation currency of the entity; and**

(viii)   **other changes in the carrying amount during the period.**

119   A class of intangible assets is a grouping of assets of a similar nature and use in an entity's operations. Examples of separate classes may include:

(a)   brand names;

(b)   mastheads and publishing titles;

(c)   computer software;

(d)   licences and franchises;

(e) copyrights, patents and other industrial property rights, service and operating rights;

(f) recipes, formulae, models, designs and prototypes; and

(g) intangible assets under development.

The classes mentioned above are disaggregated (aggregated) into smaller (larger) classes if this results in more relevant information for the users of the financial statements.

120   An entity discloses information on impaired intangible assets in accordance with AASB 136 in addition to the information required by paragraph 118(e)(iii)–(v).

121   AASB 108 requires an entity to disclose the nature and amount of a change in an accounting estimate that has a material effect in the current period or is expected to have a material effect in subsequent periods. Such disclosure may arise from changes in:

(a) the assessment of an intangible asset's useful life;

(b) the amortisation method; or

(c) residual values.

122   An entity shall also disclose:

(a) for an intangible asset assessed as having an indefinite useful life, the carrying amount of that asset and the reasons supporting the assessment of an indefinite useful life. In giving these reasons, the entity shall describe the factor(s) that played a significant role in determining that the asset has an indefinite useful life.

(b) a description, the carrying amount and remaining amortisation period of any individual intangible asset that is material to the entity's financial statements.

(c) for intangible assets acquired by way of a government grant and initially recognised at fair value (see paragraph 44):

(i)   the fair value initially recognised for these assets;

(ii) their carrying amount; and

(iii) whether they are measured after recognition under the cost model or the revaluation model.

(d) the existence and carrying amounts of intangible assets whose title is restricted and the carrying amounts of intangible assets pledged as security for liabilities.

(e) the amount of contractual commitments for the acquisition of intangible assets.

123   When an entity describes the factor(s) that played a significant role in determining that the useful life of an intangible asset is indefinite, the entity considers the list of factors in paragraph 90.

Intangible assets measured after recognition using the revaluation model

124   If intangible assets are accounted for at revalued amounts, an entity shall disclose the following:

(a) by class of intangible assets:

(i)   the effective date of the revaluation;

(ii) the carrying amount of revalued intangible assets; and

      (iii)   the carrying amount that would have been recognised had the revalued class of intangible assets been measured after recognition using the cost model in paragraph 74; and

  (b)   the amount of the revaluation surplus that relates to intangible assets at the beginning and end of the period, indicating the changes during the period and any restrictions on the distribution of the balance to shareholders.

  (c)   [deleted]

Aus124.1   Notwithstanding paragraph 124(a)(iii), in respect of not-for-profit entities, for each revalued class of intangible assets, the requirement to disclose the carrying amount that would have been recognised had the assets been carried under the cost model does not apply.

125   It may be necessary to aggregate the classes of revalued assets into larger classes for disclosure purposes. However, classes are not aggregated if this would result in the combination of a class of intangible assets that includes amounts measured under both the cost and revaluation models.

Research and development expenditure

126   **An entity shall disclose the aggregate amount of research and development expenditure recognised as an expense during the period.**

127   Research and development expenditure comprises all expenditure that is directly attributable to research or development activities (see paragraphs 66 and 67 for guidance on the type of expenditure to be included for the purpose of the disclosure requirement in paragraph 126).

Other information

128   An entity is encouraged, but not required, to disclose the following information:

  (a)   a description of any fully amortised intangible asset that is still in use; and

  (b)   a brief description of significant intangible assets controlled by the entity but not recognised as assets because they did not meet the recognition criteria in this Standard.

Transitional provisions and effective date

129   [Deleted]

130   [Deleted by the AASB]

Aus130.1   An entity shall apply this Standard for annual periods beginning on or after 1 January 2018. Earlier application is encouraged for periods beginning on or after 1 January 2014 but before 1 January 2018. If an entity applies the Standard for a period beginning before 1 January 2018, it shall disclose that fact.

130A–130B [Deleted by the AASB]

130C AASB 2008-3 *Amendments to Australian Accounting Standards Arising from AASB 3 and AASB 127* amended the previous version of this Standard as follows: amended paragraphs 12, 33–35, 68, 69, 94 and 130, deleted paragraphs 38 and 129 and added paragraph 115A. AASB 2009-4 *Amendments to Australian Accounting Standards arising from the Annual Improvements Project*, issued in May 2009, amended paragraphs 36 and 37 in the previous version of this Standard. An entity shall apply those amendments prospectively for annual periods beginning on or after 1 July 2009. Therefore, amounts recognised for intangible assets and goodwill in prior business combinations shall not be adjusted. If an entity applies AASB 3 (revised 2008) for an earlier period, it shall apply the amendments for that earlier period and disclose that fact.

130D [Deleted by the AASB]

130E   [Deleted]

130F–130G [Deleted by the AASB]

130H   AASB 2014-1 *Amendments to Australian Accounting Standards*, issued in June 2014, amended paragraph 80 in the previous version of this Standard. An entity shall apply that amendment for annual periods beginning on or after 1 July 2014. Earlier application is permitted. If an entity applies that amendment for an earlier period it shall disclose that fact.

130I   An entity shall apply the amendment made by AASB 2014-1 to all revaluations recognised in annual periods beginning on or after the date of initial application of that amendment and in the immediately preceding annual period. An entity may also present adjusted comparative information for any earlier periods presented, but it is not required to do so. If an entity presents unadjusted comparative information for any earlier periods, it shall clearly identify the information that has not been adjusted, state that it has been presented on a different basis and explain that basis.

130J   AASB 2014-4 *Amendments to Australian Accounting Standards – Clarification of Acceptable Methods of Depreciation and Amortisation*, issued in August 2014, amended the previous version of this Standard as follows: amended paragraphs 92 and 98 and added paragraphs 98A–98C. An entity shall apply those amendments prospectively for annual periods beginning on or after 1 January 2016. Earlier application is permitted. If an entity applies those amendments for an earlier period it shall disclose that fact.

130K   AASB 2014-5 *Amendments to Australian Accounting Standards arising from AASB 15*, issued in December 2014, amended paragraphs 3, 114 and 116 in the previous version of this Standard. An entity shall apply those amendments when it applies AASB 15.

Exchanges of similar assets

131   [Deleted by the AASB]

Early application

132   [Deleted by the AASB]

Withdrawal of IAS 38 (issued 1998)

133   [Deleted by the AASB]

Commencement of the legislative instrument

Aus133.1   For legal purposes, this legislative instrument commences on 31 December 2016.

Withdrawal of AASB pronouncements

Aus133.2   This Standard repeals AASB 138 *Intangible Assets* issued in July 2004. Despite the repeal, after the time this Standard starts to apply under section 334 of the Corporations Act (either generally or in relation to an individual entity), the repealed Standard continues to apply in relation to any period ending before that time as if the repeal had not occurred.

[Note: When this Standard applies under section 334 of the Corporations Act (either generally or in relation to an individual entity), it supersedes the application of the repealed Standard.]

APPENDIX A
AUSTRALIAN REDUCED DISCLOSURE
REQUIREMENTS

This appendix is an integral part of the Standard.

AusA1   **Paragraphs 118(e)(vii), 120, 124(a)(iii), Aus124.1 and 128 of this Standard do not apply to entities preparing general purpose financial statements under Australian Accounting Standards – Reduced Disclosure Requirements. Entities applying Australian Accounting Standards – Reduced Disclosure Requirements may elect to comply with some or all of these excluded requirements.**

AusA2   The requirements that do not apply to entities preparing general purpose financial statements under Australian Accounting Standards – Reduced Disclosure Requirements are also identified in this Standard by shading of the relevant text, except for comparative disclosures subject to RDR paragraphs.

AusA3   **The RDR paragraph in this Standard applies only to entities preparing general purpose financial statements under Australian Accounting Standards – Reduced Disclosure Requirements.**

RDR118.1   **An entity applying Australian Accounting Standards – Reduced Disclosure Requirements is not required to disclose the reconciliations specified in paragraph 118(e) for prior periods.**

ILLUSTRATIVE EXAMPLES

These examples accompany, but are not part of, AASB 138.

Assessing the useful lives of intangible assets

The following guidance provides examples on determining the useful life of an intangible asset in accordance with AASB 138.

Each of the following examples describes an acquired intangible asset, the facts and circumstances surrounding the determination of its useful life, and the subsequent accounting based on that determination.

Example 1 An acquired customer list

A direct-mail marketing company acquires a customer list and expects that it will be able to derive benefit from the information on the list for at least one year, but no more than three years.

The customer list would be amortised over management's best estimate of its useful life, say 18 months. Although the direct-mail marketing company may intend to add customer names and other information to the list in the future, the expected benefits of the acquired customer list relate only to the customers on that list at the date it was acquired. The customer list also would be reviewed for impairment in accordance with AASB 136 *Impairment of Assets* by assessing at the end of each reporting period whether there is any indication that the customer list may be impaired.

Example 2 An acquired patent that expires in 15 years

The product protected by the patented technology is expected to be a source of net cash inflows for at least 15 years. The entity has a commitment from a third party to purchase that patent in five years for 60 per cent of the fair value of the patent at the date it was acquired, and the entity intends to sell the patent in five years.

The patent would be amortised over its five-year useful life to the entity, with a residual value equal to the present value of 60 per cent of the patent's fair value at the date it was acquired. The patent would also be reviewed for impairment in accordance with AASB 136 by assessing at the end of each reporting period whether there is any indication that it may be impaired.

Example 3 An acquired copyright that has a remaining legal life of 50 years

An analysis of consumer habits and market trends provides evidence that the copyrighted material will generate net cash inflows for only 30 more years.

The copyright would be amortised over its 30-year estimated useful life. The copyright also would be reviewed for impairment in accordance with AASB 136 by assessing at the end of each reporting period whether there is any indication that it may be impaired.

Example 4 An acquired broadcasting licence that expires in five years

The broadcasting licence is renewable every 10 years if the entity provides at least an average level of service to its customers and complies with the relevant legislative requirements. The licence may be renewed indefinitely at little cost and has been renewed twice before the most recent acquisition. The acquiring entity intends to renew the licence indefinitely and evidence supports its ability to do so. Historically, there has been no compelling challenge to the licence renewal. The technology used in broadcasting is not expected to be replaced by another technology at any time in the foreseeable future. Therefore, the licence is expected to contribute to the entity's net cash inflows indefinitely.

The broadcasting licence would be treated as having an indefinite useful life because it is expected to contribute to the entity's net cash inflows indefinitely. Therefore, the licence would not be amortised until its useful life is determined to be finite. The licence would be tested for impairment in accordance with AASB 136 annually and whenever there is an indication that it may be impaired.

Example 5 The broadcasting licence in Example 4

The licensing authority subsequently decides that it will no longer renew broadcasting licences, but rather will auction the licences. At the time the licensing authority's decision is made, the entity's broadcasting licence has three years until it expires. The entity expects that the licence will continue to contribute to net cash inflows until the licence expires.

Because the broadcasting licence can no longer be renewed, its useful life is no longer indefinite. Thus, the acquired licence would be amortised over its remaining three-year useful life and immediately tested for impairment in accordance with AASB 136.

Example 6 An acquired airline route authority between two European cities that expires in three years

The route authority may be renewed every five years, and the acquiring entity intends to comply with the applicable rules and regulations surrounding renewal. Route authority renewals are routinely granted at a minimal cost and historically have been renewed when the airline has complied with the applicable rules and regulations. The acquiring entity expects to provide service indefinitely between the two cities from its hub airports and expects that the related supporting infrastructure (airport gates, slots, and terminal facility leases) will remain in place at those airports for as long as it has the route authority. An analysis of demand and cash flows supports those assumptions.

Because the facts and circumstances support the acquiring entity's ability to continue providing air service indefinitely between the two cities, the intangible asset related to the route authority is treated as having an indefinite useful life. Therefore, the route authority would not be amortised until its useful life is determined to be finite. It would be tested for impairment in accordance with AASB 136 annually and whenever there is an indication that it may be impaired.

Example 7 An acquired trademark used to identify and distinguish a leading consumer product that has been a market-share leader for the past eight years

The trademark has a remaining legal life of five years but is renewable every 10 years at little cost. The acquiring entity intends to renew the trademark continuously and evidence supports its ability to do so. An analysis of (1) product life cycle studies, (2) market, competitive and environmental trends, and (3) brand extension opportunities provides evidence that the trademarked product will generate net cash inflows for the acquiring entity for an indefinite period.

The trademark would be treated as having an indefinite useful life because it is expected to contribute to net cash inflows indefinitely. Therefore, the trademark would not be amortised until its useful life is determined to be finite. It would be tested for impairment in accordance with AASB 136 annually and whenever there is an indication that it may be impaired.

Example 8 A trademark acquired 10 years ago that distinguishes a leading consumer product

The trademark was regarded as having an indefinite useful life when it was acquired because the trademarked product was expected to generate net cash inflows indefinitely. However, unexpected competition has recently entered the market and will reduce future sales of the product. Management estimates that net cash inflows generated by the product will be 20 per cent less for the foreseeable future. However, management expects that the product will continue to generate net cash inflows indefinitely at those reduced amounts.

As a result of the projected decrease in future net cash inflows, the entity determines that the estimated recoverable amount of the trademark is less than its carrying amount, and an impairment loss is recognised. Because it is still regarded as having an indefinite useful life, the trademark would continue not to be amortised but would be tested for impairment in accordance with AASB 136 annually and whenever there is an indication that it may be impaired.

Example 9 A trademark for a line of products that was acquired several years ago in a business combination

At the time of the business combination the acquiree had been producing the line of products for 35 years with many new models developed under the trademark. At the acquisition date the acquirer expected to continue producing the line, and an analysis of various economic factors indicated there was no limit to the period the trademark would contribute to net cash inflows. Consequently, the trademark was not amortised by the acquirer. However, management has recently decided that production of the product line will be discontinued over the next four years.

Because the useful life of the acquired trademark is no longer regarded as indefinite, the carrying amount of the trademark would be tested for impairment in accordance with AASB 136 and amortised over its remaining four-year useful life.

COMPILATION DETAILS

Accounting Standard AASB 138 *Intangible Assets* as amended

Compilation details are not part of AASB 138.

This compiled Standard applies to annual periods beginning on or after 1 January 2018 but before 1 January 2019. It takes into account amendments up to and including 22 October 2015 and was prepared on 20 March 2017 by the staff of the Australian Accounting Standards Board (AASB).

This compilation is not a separate Accounting Standard made by the AASB. Instead, it is a representation of AASB 138 (August 2015) as amended by other Accounting Standards, which are listed in the Table below.

Table of Standards

Standard	Date made	FRLI identifier	Commencement date	Effective date *(annual periods ... on or after ...)*	Application, saving or transitional provisions
AASB 138	14 Aug 2015	F2015L01558	31 Dec 2016	*(beginning)* 1 Jan 2018	see (a) below
AASB 2015-8	22 Oct 2015	F2015L01840	31 Dec 2016	*(beginning)* 1 Jan 2017	see (b) below
AASB 16	23 Feb 2016	F2016L00233	31 Dec 2018	*(beginning)* 1 Jan 2019	not compiled*
AASB 1058	9 Dec 2016	F2017L00042	31 Dec 2018	*(beginning)* 1 Jan 2019	not compiled*

* The amendments made by this Standard are not included in this compilation, which presents the principal Standard as applicable to annual reporting periods beginning on or after 1 January 2018 but before 1 January 2019.

(a) AASB 138 applies to annual periods beginning on or after 1 January 2018 (instead of 1 January 2017) as a result of amendments made by AASB 2015-8 *Amendments to Australian Accounting Standards – Effective Date of AASB 15*.

(b) Entities may elect to apply this Standard to annual periods beginning before 1 January 2017, provided that AASB 15 *Revenue from Contracts with Customers* is also applied.

Table of amendments

Paragraph affected	How affected	By ... [paragraph]
Aus130.1	amended	AASB 2015-8 [13]

DELETED IAS 38 TEXT

Deleted IAS 38 text is not part of AASB 138.

130 An entity shall apply this Standard:

    (a) to the accounting for intangible assets acquired in business combinations for which the agreement date is on or after 31 March 2004; and

    (b) to the accounting for all other intangible assets prospectively from the beginning of the first annual period beginning on or after 31 March 2004. Thus, the entity shall not adjust the carrying amount of intangible assets recognised at that date. However, the entity shall, at that date, apply this Standard to reassess the useful lives of such intangible assets. If, as a result of that reassessment, the entity changes its assessment of the useful life of an asset, that change shall be accounted for as a change in an accounting estimate in accordance with IAS 8.

130A An entity shall apply the amendments in paragraph 2 for annual periods beginning on or after 1 January 2006. If an entity applies IFRS 6 for an earlier period, those amendments shall be applied for that earlier period.

130B IAS 1 *Presentation of Financial Statements* (as revised in 2007) amended the terminology used throughout IFRSs. In addition it amended paragraphs 85, 86 and 118(e)(iii). An entity shall apply those amendments for annual periods beginning on or after 1 January 2009. If an entity applies IAS 1 (revised 2007) for an earlier period, the amendments shall be applied for that earlier period.

130D Paragraphs 69, 70 and 98 were amended and paragraph 69A was added by *Improvements to IFRSs* issued in May 2008. An entity shall apply those amendments for annual periods beginning on or after 1 January 2009. Earlier application is permitted. If an entity applies the amendments for an earlier period it shall disclose that fact.

130F IFRS 10 and IFRS 11 *Joint Arrangements*, issued in May 2011, amended paragraph 3(e). An entity shall apply that amendment when it applies IFRS 10 and IFRS 11.

130G IFRS 13, issued in May 2011, amended paragraphs 8, 33, 47, 50, 75, 78, 82, 84, 100 and 124 and deleted paragraphs 39–41 and 130E. An entity shall apply those amendments when it applies IFRS 13.

131 The requirement in paragraphs 129 and 130(b) to apply this Standard prospectively means that if an exchange of assets was measured before the effective date of this Standard on the basis of the carrying amount of the asset given up, the entity does not restate the carrying amount of the asset acquired to reflect its fair value at the acquisition date.

132 Entities to which paragraph 130 applies are encouraged to apply the requirements of this Standard before the effective dates specified in paragraph 130. However, if an entity applies this Standard before those effective dates, it also shall apply IFRS 3 and IAS 36 (as revised in 2004) at the same time.

133 This Standard supersedes IAS 38 *Intangible Assets* (issued in 1998).

AASB

AASB 140
Investment Property

(Compiled February 2017)

For-profit (FP) entities

This compiled Standard applies to annual periods beginning on or after 1 January 2018 but before 1 January 2019. Earlier application is permitted for annual periods beginning on or after 1 January 2014 but before 1 January 2018. It incorporates relevant amendments made up to and including 13 February 2017.

Not-for-profit (NFP) entities – early application only

This compiled Standard does not apply mandatorily to NFP entities. However, earlier application is permitted for annual reporting periods beginning on or after 1 January 2014 but before 1 January 2019.

Prepared on 20 March 2018 by the staff of the Australian Accounting Standards Board.

Compilation no. 2

Compilation date: 31 December 2017

This note is not part of Accounting Standard AASB 140.

The following unincorporated amendments are not included in this compiled Standard.

- AASB 17 *Insurance Contracts* — Appendix D sets out the amendments to other Standards that are a consequence of the AASB issuing AASB 17 *Insurance Contracts*. This Standard is applicable from 1 January 2021. Earlier application is permitted, but entities must apply AASB 9 *Financial Instruments* and AASB 15 *Revenue from Contracts with Customers* first.

- AASB 1058 *Income of Not-for-Profit Entities* — Appendix D sets out the amendments to other Australian Accounting Standards that are a consequence of the AASB issuing this Standard. It is applicable from 1 January 2019. Earlier application is permitted, but amendments to AASB 117 apply before 1 January 2019 only if AASB 1058 is also applied to an earlier period. In addition, AASB 1 and AASB 16 amendments are applied to an earlier period only if AASB 16 is also applied to that period.

- AASB 16 *Leases* — Appendix D sets out the amendments to other Standards that are a consequence of the AASB issuing this Standard. It is applicable from 1 January 2019. Earlier application is permitted, but entities must apply AASB 15 *Revenue from Contracts with Customers* before applying this Standard.

- AASB 2016-7 *Amendments to Australian Accounting Standards — Deferral of AASB 15 for Not-for-Profit Entities*. This Standard defers the consequential amendments that were originally set out in AASB 2014-5 *Amendments to Australian Accounting Standards arising from AASB 15*, by restating the effective date of the amendments set out in AASB 2015-8 *Amendments to Australian Accounting Standards* for not-for-profit entities. This Standard defers the application of AASB 15 to 1 January 2019. Earlier application is permitted provided AASB 1058 is also applied to the same period.

Entities early-adopting any amendments with later application dates will need to refer to the amending Standards that have not yet been incorporated into compilations. The abovementioned unincorporated amendments may be located on the AASB website at www.aasb.gov.au or on the Federal Register of Legislation website at www.legislation.gov.au.

CONTENTS

AASB

Australian Accounting Standard AASB 140 *Investment Property* (as amended) is set out in paragraphs 1 – Aus86.2 and Appendix A. All the paragraphs have equal authority. Paragraphs in **bold type** state the main principles. AASB 140 is to be read in the context of other Australian Accounting Standards, including AASB 1048 *Interpretation of Standards*, which identifies the Australian Accounting Interpretations, and AASB 1057 *Application of Australian Accounting Standards*. In the absence of explicit guidance, AASB 108 *Accounting Policies, Changes in Accounting Estimates and Errors* provides a basis for selecting and applying accounting policies.

COMPARISON WITH IAS 40

AASB 140 *Investment Property* as amended incorporates IAS 40 *Investment Property* as issued and amended by the International Accounting Standards Board (IASB). Australian-specific paragraphs (which are not included in IAS 40) are identified with the prefix "Aus" or

"RDR". Paragraphs that apply only to not-for-profit entities begin by identifying their limited applicability.

Tier 1

For-profit entities complying with AASB 140 also comply with IAS 40.

Not-for-profit entities' compliance with IAS 40 will depend on whether any "Aus" paragraphs that specifically apply to not-for-profit entities provide additional guidance or contain applicable requirements that are inconsistent with IAS 40.

Tier 2

Entities preparing general purpose financial statements under Australian Accounting Standards – Reduced Disclosure Requirements (Tier 2) will not be in compliance with IFRSs.

AASB 1053 *Application of Tiers of Australian Accounting Standards* explains the two tiers of reporting requirements.

ACCOUNTING STANDARD AASB 140

The Australian Accounting Standards Board made Accounting Standard AASB 140 *Investment Property* under section 334 of the *Corporations Act 2001* on 14 August 2015.

This compiled version of AASB 140 applies to annual periods beginning on or after 1 January 2018 but before 1 January 2019 for for-profit entities. It incorporates relevant amendments contained in other AASB Standards made by the AASB up to and including 13 February 2017 (see Compilation Details).

ACCOUNTING STANDARD AASB 140
INVESTMENT PROPERTY

Objective

1   The objective of this Standard is to prescribe the accounting treatment for investment property and related disclosure requirements.

Scope

2   **This Standard shall be applied in the recognition, measurement and disclosure of investment property.**

3   Among other things, this Standard applies to the measurement in a lessee's financial statements of investment property interests held under a lease accounted for as a finance lease and to the measurement in a lessor's financial statements of investment property provided to a lessee under an operating lease. This Standard does not deal with matters covered in AASB 117 *Leases*, including:

   (a)   classification of leases as finance leases or operating leases;

   (b)   recognition of lease income from investment property (see also AASB 15 *Revenue from Contracts with Customers*);

   (c)   measurement in a lessee's financial statements of property interests held under a lease accounted for as an operating lease;

   (d)   measurement in a lessor's financial statements of its net investment in a finance lease;

   (e)   accounting for sale and leaseback transactions; and

   (f)   disclosure about finance leases and operating leases.

4   This Standard does not apply to:

    (a)   biological assets related to agricultural activity (see AASB 141 *Agriculture* and AASB 116 *Property, Plant and Equipment*); and

    (b)   mineral rights and mineral reserves such as oil, natural gas and similar non-regenerative resources.

Definitions

5   **The following terms are used in this Standard with the meanings specified:**

Carrying amount **is the amount at which an asset is recognised in the statement of financial position.**

Cost **is the amount of cash or cash equivalents paid or the fair value of other consideration given to acquire an asset at the time of its acquisition or construction or, where applicable, the amount attributed to that asset when initially recognised in accordance with the specific requirements of other Standards, eg AASB 2** *Share-based Payment.*

Fair value **is the price that would be received to sell an asset or paid to transfer a liability in an orderly transaction between market participants at the measurement date. (See AASB 13** *Fair Value Measurement*).

Investment property **is property (land or a building—or part of a building—or both) held (by the owner or by the lessee under a finance lease) to earn rentals or for capital appreciation or both, rather than for:**

    (a)   use in the production or supply of goods or services or for administrative purposes; or

    (b)   sale in the ordinary course of business.

Owner-occupied property **is property held (by the owner or by the lessee under a finance lease) for use in the production or supply of goods or services or for administrative purposes.**

Classification of property as investment property or owner-occupied property

6   A *property interest* that is held by a lessee under an operating lease may be classified and accounted for as investment property if, and only if, the property would otherwise meet the definition of an investment property and the lessee uses the fair value model set out in paragraphs 33–55 for the asset recognised. This classification alternative is available on a property-by-property basis. However, once this classification alternative is selected for one such property interest held under an operating lease, all property classified as investment property shall be accounted for using the fair value model. When this classification alternative is selected, any interest so classified is included in the disclosures required by paragraphs 74–78.

7   Investment property is held to earn rentals or for capital appreciation or both. Therefore, an investment property generates cash flows largely independently of the other assets held by an entity. This distinguishes investment property from owner-occupied property. The production or supply of goods or services (or the use of property for administrative purposes) generates cash flows that are attributable not only to property, but also to other assets used in the production or supply process. AASB 116 applies to owner-occupied property.

8   The following are examples of investment property:

    (a)   land held for long-term capital appreciation rather than for short-term sale in the ordinary course of business.

    (b)   land held for a currently undetermined future use. (If an entity has not determined that it will use the land as owner-occupied property or for short-term sale in the ordinary course of business, the land is regarded as held for capital appreciation.)

(c)   a building owned by the entity (or held by the entity under a finance lease) and leased out under one or more operating leases.

(d)   a building that is vacant but is held to be leased out under one or more operating leases.

(e)   property that is being constructed or developed for future use as investment property.

9   The following are examples of items that are not investment property and are therefore outside the scope of this Standard:

(a)   property intended for sale in the ordinary course of business or in the process of construction or development for such sale (see AASB 102 *Inventories*), for example, property acquired exclusively with a view to subsequent disposal in the near future or for development and resale.

(b)   [deleted]

(c)   owner-occupied property (see AASB 116), including (among other things) property held for future use as owner-occupied property, property held for future development and subsequent use as owner-occupied property, property occupied by employees (whether or not the employees pay rent at market rates) and owner-occupied property awaiting disposal.

(d)   [deleted]

(e)   property that is leased to another entity under a finance lease.

Aus9.1   In respect of not-for-profit entities, property may be held to meet service delivery objectives rather than to earn rental or for capital appreciation. In such situations the property will not meet the definition of investment property and will be accounted for under AASB 116, for example:

(a)   property held for strategic purposes; and

(b)   property held to provide a social service, including those which generate cash inflows where the rental revenue is incidental to the purpose for holding the property.

10   Some properties comprise a portion that is held to earn rentals or for capital appreciation and another portion that is held for use in the production or supply of goods or services or for administrative purposes. If these portions could be sold separately (or leased out separately under a finance lease), an entity accounts for the portions separately. If the portions could not be sold separately, the property is investment property only if an insignificant portion is held for use in the production or supply of goods or services or for administrative purposes.

11   In some cases, an entity provides ancillary services to the occupants of a property it holds. An entity treats such a property as investment property if the services are insignificant to the arrangement as a whole. An example is when the owner of an office building provides security and maintenance services to the lessees who occupy the building.

12   In other cases, the services provided are significant. For example, if an entity owns and manages a hotel, services provided to guests are significant to the arrangement as a whole. Therefore, an owner-managed hotel is owner-occupied property, rather than investment property.

13   It may be difficult to determine whether ancillary services are so significant that a property does not qualify as investment property. For example, the owner of a hotel sometimes transfers some responsibilities to third parties under a management contract. The terms of such contracts vary widely. At one end of the spectrum, the owner's position may, in substance, be that of a passive investor. At the other end of the spectrum, the owner may simply have outsourced day-to-day functions while retaining significant exposure to variation in the cash flows generated by the operations of the hotel.

14 Judgement is needed to determine whether a property qualifies as investment property. An entity develops criteria so that it can exercise that judgement consistently in accordance with the definition of investment property and with the related guidance in paragraphs 7–13. Paragraph 75(c) requires an entity to disclose these criteria when classification is difficult.

14A Judgement is also needed to determine whether the acquisition of investment property is the acquisition of an asset or a group of assets or a business combination within the scope of AASB 3 *Business Combinations*. Reference should be made to AASB 3 to determine whether it is a business combination. The discussion in paragraphs 7–14 of this Standard relates to whether or not property is owner-occupied property or investment property and not to determining whether or not the acquisition of property is a business combination as defined in AASB 3. Determining whether a specific transaction meets the definition of a business combination as defined in AASB 3 and includes an investment property as defined in this Standard requires the separate application of both Standards.

15 In some cases, an entity owns property that is leased to, and occupied by, its parent or another subsidiary. The property does not qualify as investment property in the consolidated financial statements, because the property is owner-occupied from the perspective of the group. However, from the perspective of the entity that owns it, the property is investment property if it meets the definition in paragraph 5. Therefore, the lessor treats the property as investment property in its individual financial statements.

Recognition

16 **Investment property shall be recognised as an asset when, and only when:**

(a) **it is probable that the future economic benefits that are associated with the investment property will flow to the entity; and**

(b) **the cost of the investment property can be measured reliably.**

17 An entity evaluates under this recognition principle all its investment property costs at the time they are incurred. These costs include costs incurred initially to acquire an investment property and costs incurred subsequently to add to, replace part of, or service a property.

18 Under the recognition principle in paragraph 16, an entity does not recognise in the carrying amount of an investment property the costs of the day-to-day servicing of such a property. Rather, these costs are recognised in profit or loss as incurred. Costs of day-to-day servicing are primarily the cost of labour and consumables, and may include the cost of minor parts. The purpose of these expenditures is often described as for the 'repairs and maintenance' of the property.

19 Parts of investment properties may have been acquired through replacement. For example, the interior walls may be replacements of original walls. Under the recognition principle, an entity recognises in the carrying amount of an investment property the cost of replacing part of an existing investment property at the time that cost is incurred if the recognition criteria are met. The carrying amount of those parts that are replaced is derecognised in accordance with the derecognition provisions of this Standard.

Measurement at recognition

20 **An investment property shall be measured initially at its cost. Transaction costs shall be included in the initial measurement.**

Aus20.1 **Notwithstanding paragraph 20, in respect of not-for-profit entities, where an investment property is acquired at no cost or for nominal cost, its cost shall be deemed to be its fair value as at the date of acquisition.**

21   The cost of a purchased investment property comprises its purchase price and any directly attributable expenditure. Directly attributable expenditure includes, for example, professional fees for legal services, property transfer taxes and other transaction costs.

22   [Deleted]

23   The cost of an investment property is not increased by:

       (a)   start-up costs (unless they are necessary to bring the property to the condition necessary for it to be capable of operating in the manner intended by management),

       (b)   operating losses incurred before the investment property achieves the planned level of occupancy, or

       (c)   abnormal amounts of wasted material, labour or other resources incurred in constructing or developing the property.

24   If payment for an investment property is deferred, its cost is the cash price equivalent. The difference between this amount and the total payments is recognised as interest expense over the period of credit.

25   **The initial cost of a property interest held under a lease and classified as an investment property shall be as prescribed for a finance lease by paragraph 20 of AASB 117, ie the asset shall be recognised at the lower of the fair value of the property and the present value of the minimum lease payments. An equivalent amount shall be recognised as a liability in accordance with that same paragraph.**

26   Any premium paid for a lease is treated as part of the minimum lease payments for this purpose, and is therefore included in the cost of the asset, but is excluded from the liability. If a property interest held under a lease is classified as investment property, the item accounted for at fair value is that interest and not the underlying property. Guidance on measuring the fair value of a property interest is set out for the fair value model in paragraphs 33–35, 40, 41, 48, 50 and 52 and in AASB 13. That guidance is also relevant to the measurement of fair value when that value is used as cost for initial recognition purposes.

27   One or more investment properties may be acquired in exchange for a non-monetary asset or assets, or a combination of monetary and non-monetary assets. The following discussion refers to an exchange of one non-monetary asset for another, but it also applies to all exchanges described in the preceding sentence. The cost of such an investment property is measured at fair value unless (a) the exchange transaction lacks commercial substance or (b) the fair value of neither the asset received nor the asset given up is reliably measurable. The acquired asset is measured in this way even if an entity cannot immediately derecognise the asset given up. If the acquired asset is not measured at fair value, its cost is measured at the carrying amount of the asset given up.

28   An entity determines whether an exchange transaction has commercial substance by considering the extent to which its future cash flows are expected to change as a result of the transaction. An exchange transaction has commercial substance if:

       (a)   the configuration (risk, timing and amount) of the cash flows of the asset received differs from the configuration of the cash flows of the asset transferred, or

       (b)   the entity-specific value of the portion of the entity's operations affected by the transaction changes as a result of the exchange, and

       (c)   the difference in (a) or (b) is significant relative to the fair value of the assets exchanged.

For the purpose of determining whether an exchange transaction has commercial substance, the entity-specific value of the portion of the entity's operations affected by the transaction shall reflect post-tax cash flows. The result of these analyses may be clear without an entity having to perform detailed calculations.

29 The fair value of an asset is reliably measurable if (a) the variability in the range of reasonable fair value measurements is not significant for that asset or (b) the probabilities of the various estimates within the range can be reasonably assessed and used when measuring fair value. If the entity is able to measure reliably the fair value of either the asset received or the asset given up, then the fair value of the asset given up is used to measure cost unless the fair value of the asset received is more clearly evident.

Measurement after recognition

Accounting policy

30 **With the exceptions noted in paragraphs 32A and 34, an entity shall choose as its accounting policy either the fair value model in paragraphs 33–55 or the cost model in paragraph 56 and shall apply that policy to all of its investment property.**

31 AASB 108 *Accounting Policies, Changes in Accounting Estimates and Errors* states that a voluntary change in accounting policy shall be made only if the change results in the financial statements providing reliable and more relevant information about the effects of transactions, other events or conditions on the entity's financial position, financial performance or cash flows. It is highly unlikely that a change from the fair value model to the cost model will result in a more relevant presentation.

32 This Standard requires all entities to measure the fair value of investment property, for the purpose of either measurement (if the entity uses the fair value model) or disclosure (if it uses the cost model). An entity is encouraged, but not required, to measure the fair value of investment property on the basis of a valuation by an independent valuer who holds a recognised and relevant professional qualification and has recent experience in the location and category of the investment property being valued.

32A **An entity may:**

    (a) **choose either the fair value model or the cost model for all investment property backing liabilities that pay a return linked directly to the fair value of, or returns from, specified assets including that investment property; and**

    (b) **choose either the fair value model or the cost model for all other investment property, regardless of the choice made in (a).**

32B Some insurers and other entities operate an internal property fund that issues notional units, with some units held by investors in linked contracts and others held by the entity. Paragraph 32A does not permit an entity to measure the property held by the fund partly at cost and partly at fair value.

32C If an entity chooses different models for the two categories described in paragraph 32A, sales of investment property between pools of assets measured using different models shall be recognised at fair value and the cumulative change in fair value shall be recognised in profit or loss. Accordingly, if an investment property is sold from a pool in which the fair value model is used into a pool in which the cost model is used, the property's fair value at the date of the sale becomes its deemed cost.

Fair value model

33 **After initial recognition, an entity that chooses the fair value model shall measure all of its investment property at fair value, except in the cases described in paragraph 53.**

34 **When a property interest held by a lessee under an operating lease is classified as an investment property under paragraph 6, paragraph 30 is not elective; the fair value model shall be applied.**

35 **A gain or loss arising from a change in the fair value of investment property shall be recognised in profit or loss for the period in which it arises.**

36–39 [Deleted]

40   When measuring the fair value of investment property in accordance with AASB 13, an entity shall ensure that the fair value reflects, among other things, rental income from current leases and other assumptions that market participants would use when pricing investment property under current market conditions.

41   Paragraph 25 specifies the basis for initial recognition of the cost of an interest in a leased property. Paragraph 33 requires the interest in the leased property to be remeasured, if necessary, to fair value. In a lease negotiated at market rates, the fair value of an interest in a leased property at acquisition, net of all expected lease payments (including those relating to recognised liabilities), should be zero. This fair value does not change regardless of whether, for accounting purposes, a leased asset and liability are recognised at fair value or at the present value of minimum lease payments, in accordance with paragraph 20 of AASB 117. Thus, remeasuring a leased asset from cost in accordance with paragraph 25 to fair value in accordance with paragraph 33 should not give rise to any initial gain or loss, unless fair value is measured at different times. This could occur when an election to apply the fair value model is made after initial recognition.

42–47 [Deleted]

48   In exceptional cases, there is clear evidence when an entity first acquires an investment property (or when an existing property first becomes investment property after a change in use) that the variability in the range of reasonable fair value measurements will be so great, and the probabilities of the various outcomes so difficult to assess, that the usefulness of a single measure of fair value is negated. This may indicate that the fair value of the property will not be reliably measurable on a continuing basis (see paragraph 53).

49   [Deleted]

50   In determining the carrying amount of investment property under the fair value model, an entity does not double-count assets or liabilities that are recognised as separate assets or liabilities. For example:

      (a)   equipment such as lifts or air-conditioning is often an integral part of a building and is generally included in the fair value of the investment property, rather than recognised separately as property, plant and equipment.

      (b)   if an office is leased on a furnished basis, the fair value of the office generally includes the fair value of the furniture, because the rental income relates to the furnished office. When furniture is included in the fair value of investment property, an entity does not recognise that furniture as a separate asset.

      (c)   the fair value of investment property excludes prepaid or accrued operating lease income, because the entity recognises it as a separate liability or asset.

      (d)   the fair value of investment property held under a lease reflects expected cash flows (including contingent rent that is expected to become payable). Accordingly, if a valuation obtained for a property is net of all payments expected to be made, it will be necessary to add back any recognised lease liability, to arrive at the carrying amount of the investment property using the fair value model.

51   [Deleted]

52   In some cases, an entity expects that the present value of its payments relating to an investment property (other than payments relating to recognised liabilities) will exceed the present value of the related cash receipts. An entity applies AASB 137 *Provisions, Contingent Liabilities and Contingent Assets* to determine whether to recognise a liability and, if so, how to measure it.

Inability to measure fair value reliably

53   **There is a rebuttable presumption that an entity can reliably measure the fair value of an investment property on a continuing basis. However, in exceptional cases, there is clear evidence when an entity first acquires an investment property**

(or when an existing property first becomes investment property after a change in use) that the fair value of the investment property is not reliably measurable on a continuing basis. This arises when, and only when, the market for comparable properties is inactive (eg there are few recent transactions, price quotations are not current or observed transaction prices indicate that the seller was forced to sell) and alternative reliable measurements of fair value (for example, based on discounted cash flow projections) are not available. If an entity determines that the fair value of an investment property under construction is not reliably measurable but expects the fair value of the property to be reliably measurable when construction is complete, it shall measure that investment property under construction at cost until either its fair value becomes reliably measurable or construction is completed (whichever is earlier). If an entity determines that the fair value of an investment property (other than an investment property under construction) is not reliably measurable on a continuing basis, the entity shall measure that investment property using the cost model in AASB 116. The residual value of the investment property shall be assumed to be zero. The entity shall apply AASB 116 until disposal of the investment property.

53A   Once an entity becomes able to measure reliably the fair value of an investment property under construction that has previously been measured at cost, it shall measure that property at its fair value. Once construction of that property is complete, it is presumed that fair value can be measured reliably. If this is not the case, in accordance with paragraph 53, the property shall be accounted for using the cost model in accordance with AASB 116.

53B   The presumption that the fair value of investment property under construction can be measured reliably can be rebutted only on initial recognition. An entity that has measured an item of investment property under construction at fair value may not conclude that the fair value of the completed investment property cannot be measured reliably.

54   In the exceptional cases when an entity is compelled, for the reason given in paragraph 53, to measure an investment property using the cost model in accordance with AASB 116, it measures at fair value all its other investment property, including investment property under construction. In these cases, although an entity may use the cost model for one investment property, the entity shall continue to account for each of the remaining properties using the fair value model.

55   If an entity has previously measured an investment property at fair value, it shall continue to measure the property at fair value until disposal (or until the property becomes owner-occupied property or the entity begins to develop the property for subsequent sale in the ordinary course of business) even if comparable market transactions become less frequent or market prices become less readily available.

Cost model

56   After initial recognition, an entity that chooses the cost model shall measure all of its investment properties in accordance with AASB 116's requirements for that model, other than those that meet the criteria to be classified as held for sale (or are included in a disposal group that is classified as held for sale) in accordance with AASB 5 *Non-current Assets Held for Sale and Discontinued Operations*. Investment properties that meet the criteria to be classified as held for sale (or are included in a disposal group that is classified as held for sale) shall be measured in accordance with AASB 5.

Transfers

57   An entity shall transfer a property to, or from, investment property when, and only when, there is a change in use. A change in use occurs when the property meets, or ceases to meet, the definition of investment property and there is evidence of the change in use. In isolation, a change in management's intentions

for the use of a property does not provide evidence of a change in use. Examples of evidence of a change in use include:

(a)   commencement of owner-occupation, or of development with a view to owner-occupation, for a transfer from investment property to owner-occupied property;

(b)   commencement of development with a view to sale, for a transfer from investment property to inventories;

(c)   end of owner-occupation, for a transfer from owner-occupied property to investment property; ~~or~~ and

(d)   inception of an operating lease to another party, for a transfer from inventories to investment property.

(e)   [deleted]

58   When an entity decides to dispose of an investment property without development, it continues to treat the property as an investment property until it is derecognised (eliminated from the statement of financial position) and does not reclassify it as inventory. Similarly, if an entity begins to redevelop an existing investment property for continued future use as investment property, the property remains an investment property and is not reclassified as owner-occupied property during the redevelopment.

59   Paragraphs 60–65 apply to recognition and measurement issues that arise when an entity uses the fair value model for investment property. When an entity uses the cost model, transfers between investment property, owner-occupied property and inventories do not change the carrying amount of the property transferred and they do not change the cost of that property for measurement or disclosure purposes.

60   For a transfer from investment property carried at fair value to owner-occupied property or inventories, the property's deemed cost for subsequent accounting in accordance with AASB 116 or AASB 102 shall be its fair value at the date of change in use.

61   If an owner-occupied property becomes an investment property that will be carried at fair value, an entity shall apply AASB 116 up to the date of change in use. The entity shall treat any difference at that date between the carrying amount of the property in accordance with AASB 116 and its fair value in the same way as a revaluation in accordance with AASB 116.

62   Up to the date when an owner-occupied property becomes an investment property carried at fair value, an entity depreciates the property and recognises any impairment losses that have occurred. The entity treats any difference at that date between the carrying amount of the property in accordance with AASB 116 and its fair value in the same way as a revaluation in accordance with AASB 116. In other words:

(a)   any resulting decrease in the carrying amount of the property is recognised in profit or loss. However, to the extent that an amount is included in revaluation surplus for that property, the decrease is recognised in other comprehensive income and reduces the revaluation surplus within equity.

(b)   any resulting increase in the carrying amount is treated as follows:

(i)   to the extent that the increase reverses a previous impairment loss for that property, the increase is recognised in profit or loss. The amount recognised in profit or loss does not exceed the amount needed to restore the carrying amount to the carrying amount that would have been determined (net of depreciation) had no impairment loss been recognised.

(ii)   any remaining part of the increase is recognised in other comprehensive income and increases the revaluation surplus within equity. On subsequent disposal of the investment property, the revaluation surplus included in equity may be transferred to retained earnings. The transfer from revaluation surplus to retained earnings is not made through profit or loss.

63 **For a transfer from inventories to investment property that will be carried at fair value, any difference between the fair value of the property at that date and its previous carrying amount shall be recognised in profit or loss.**

64 The treatment of transfers from inventories to investment property that will be carried at fair value is consistent with the treatment of sales of inventories.

65 **When an entity completes the construction or development of a self-constructed investment property that will be carried at fair value, any difference between the fair value of the property at that date and its previous carrying amount shall be recognised in profit or loss.**

Disposals

66 **An investment property shall be derecognised (eliminated from the statement of financial position) on disposal or when the investment property is permanently withdrawn from use and no future economic benefits are expected from its disposal.**

67 The disposal of an investment property may be achieved by sale or by entering into a finance lease. The date of disposal for investment property is the date the recipient obtains control of the investment property in accordance with the requirements for determining when a performance obligation is satisfied in AASB 15. AASB 117 applies to a disposal effected by entering into a finance lease and to a sale and leaseback.

68 If, in accordance with the recognition principle in paragraph 16, an entity recognises in the carrying amount of an asset the cost of a replacement for part of an investment property, it derecognises the carrying amount of the replaced part. For investment property accounted for using the cost model, a replaced part may not be a part that was depreciated separately. If it is not practicable for an entity to determine the carrying amount of the replaced part, it may use the cost of the replacement as an indication of what the cost of the replaced part was at the time it was acquired or constructed. Under the fair value model, the fair value of the investment property may already reflect that the part to be replaced has lost its value. In other cases it may be difficult to discern how much fair value should be reduced for the part being replaced. An alternative to reducing fair value for the replaced part, when it is not practical to do so, is to include the cost of the replacement in the carrying amount of the asset and then to reassess the fair value, as would be required for additions not involving replacement.

69 **Gains or losses arising from the retirement or disposal of investment property shall be determined as the difference between the net disposal proceeds and the carrying amount of the asset and shall be recognised in profit or loss (unless AASB 117 requires otherwise on a sale and leaseback) in the period of the retirement or disposal.**

70 The amount of consideration to be included in the gain or loss arising from the derecognition of an investment property is determined in accordance with the requirements for determining the transaction price in paragraphs 47–72 of AASB 15. Subsequent changes to the estimated amount of the consideration included in the gain or loss shall be accounted for in accordance with the requirements for changes in the transaction price in AASB 15.

71 An entity applies AASB 137 or other Standards, as appropriate, to any liabilities that it retains after disposal of an investment property.

72 **Compensation from third parties for investment property that was impaired, lost or given up shall be recognised in profit or loss when the compensation becomes receivable.**

73 Impairments or losses of investment property, related claims for or payments of compensation from third parties and any subsequent purchase or construction of replacement assets are separate economic events and are accounted for separately as follows:

(a)   impairments of investment property are recognised in accordance with AASB 136;

(b)   retirements or disposals of investment property are recognised in accordance with paragraphs 66–71 of this Standard;

(c)   compensation from third parties for investment property that was impaired, lost or given up is recognised in profit or loss when it becomes receivable; and

(d)   the cost of assets restored, purchased or constructed as replacements is determined in accordance with paragraphs 20–29 of this Standard.

Disclosure

Fair value model and cost model

74   The disclosures below apply in addition to those in AASB 117. In accordance with AASB 117, the owner of an investment property provides lessors' disclosures about leases into which it has entered. An entity that holds an investment property under a finance or operating lease provides lessees' disclosures for finance leases and lessors' disclosures for any operating leases into which it has entered.

75   **An entity shall disclose:**

(a)   **whether it applies the fair value model or the cost model.**

(b)   **if it applies the fair value model, whether, and in what circumstances, property interests held under operating leases are classified and accounted for as investment property.**

(c)   **when classification is difficult (see paragraph 14), the criteria it uses to distinguish investment property from owner-occupied property and from property held for sale in the ordinary course of business.**

(d)   [deleted]

(e)   **the extent to which the fair value of investment property (as measured or disclosed in the financial statements) is based on a valuation by an independent valuer who holds a recognised and relevant professional qualification and has recent experience in the location and category of the investment property being valued. If there has been no such valuation, that fact shall be disclosed.**

(f)   **the amounts recognised in profit or loss for:**

    (i)   **rental income from investment property;**

    (ii)   **direct operating expenses (including repairs and maintenance) arising from investment property that generated rental income during the period;**

    (iii) **direct operating expenses (including repairs and maintenance) arising from investment property that did not generate rental income during the period; and**

    (iv)   **the cumulative change in fair value recognised in profit or loss on a sale of investment property from a pool of assets in which the cost model is used into a pool in which the fair value model is used (see paragraph 32C).**

(g)   **the existence and amounts of restrictions on the realisability of investment property or the remittance of income and proceeds of disposal.**

(h)   **contractual obligations to purchase, construct or develop investment property or for repairs, maintenance or enhancements.**

Fair value model

76   **In addition to the disclosures required by paragraph 75, an entity that applies the fair value model in paragraphs 33–55 shall disclose a reconciliation between the**

carrying amounts of investment property at the beginning and end of the period, showing the following:

(a)   additions, disclosing separately those additions resulting from acquisitions and those resulting from subsequent expenditure recognised in the carrying amount of an asset;

(b)   additions resulting from acquisitions through business combinations;

(c)   assets classified as held for sale or included in a disposal group classified as held for sale in accordance with AASB 5 and other disposals;

(d)   net gains or losses from fair value adjustments;

(e)   the net exchange differences arising on the translation of the financial statements into a different presentation currency, and on translation of a foreign operation into the presentation currency of the reporting entity;

(f)   transfers to and from inventories and owner-occupied property; and

(g)   other changes.

77   When a valuation obtained for investment property is adjusted significantly for the purpose of the financial statements, for example to avoid double-counting of assets or liabilities that are recognised as separate assets and liabilities as described in paragraph 50, the entity shall disclose a reconciliation between the valuation obtained and the adjusted valuation included in the financial statements, showing separately the aggregate amount of any recognised lease obligations that have been added back, and any other significant adjustments.

78   In the exceptional cases referred to in paragraph 53, when an entity measures investment property using the cost model in AASB 116, the reconciliation required by paragraph 76 shall disclose amounts relating to that investment property separately from amounts relating to other investment property. In addition, an entity shall disclose:

(a)   a description of the investment property;

(b)   an explanation of why fair value cannot be measured reliably;

(c)   if possible, the range of estimates within which fair value is highly likely to lie; and

(d)   on disposal of investment property not carried at fair value:

(i)   the fact that the entity has disposed of investment property not carried at fair value;

(ii)   the carrying amount of that investment property at the time of sale; and

(iii)   the amount of gain or loss recognised.

Cost model

79   In addition to the disclosures required by paragraph 75, an entity that applies the cost model in paragraph 56 shall disclose:

(a)   the depreciation methods used;

(b)   the useful lives or the depreciation rates used;

(c)   the gross carrying amount and the accumulated depreciation (aggregated with accumulated impairment losses) at the beginning and end of the period;

(d)   a reconciliation of the carrying amount of investment property at the beginning and end of the period, showing the following:

AASB

(i) additions, disclosing separately those additions resulting from acquisitions and those resulting from subsequent expenditure recognised as an asset;

(ii) additions resulting from acquisitions through business combinations;

(iii) assets classified as held for sale or included in a disposal group classified as held for sale in accordance with AASB 5 and other disposals;

(iv) depreciation;

(v) the amount of impairment losses recognised, and the amount of impairment losses reversed, during the period in accordance with AASB 136;

(vi) the net exchange differences arising on the translation of the financial statements into a different presentation currency, and on translation of a foreign operation into the presentation currency of the reporting entity;

(vii) transfers to and from inventories and owner-occupied property; and

(viii) other changes.

(e) the fair value of investment property. In the exceptional cases described in paragraph 53, when an entity cannot measure the fair value of the investment property reliably, it shall disclose:

(i) a description of the investment property;

(ii) an explanation of why fair value cannot be measured reliably; and

(iii) if possible, the range of estimates within which fair value is highly likely to lie.

Transitional provisions

80–84 [Deleted by the AASB]

Business combinations

84A AASB 2014-1 *Amendments to Australian Accounting Standards*, issued in June 2014, amended the previous version of this Standard as follows: added paragraph 14A and a heading before paragraph 6. An entity shall apply that amendment prospectively for acquisitions of investment property from the beginning of the first period for which it adopts that amendment. Consequently, accounting for acquisitions of investment property in prior periods shall not be adjusted. However, an entity may choose to apply the amendment to individual acquisitions of investment property that occurred prior to the beginning of the first annual period occurring on or after the effective date if, and only if, information needed to apply the amendment to those earlier transactions is available to the entity.

Transfers of investment property

84C AASB 2017-1 *Amendments to Australian Accounting Standards – Transfers of Investment Property, Annual Improvements 2014–2016 Cycle and Other Amendments*, issued in February 2017, amended paragraphs 57–58. An entity shall apply those amendments to changes in use that occur on or after the beginning of the annual reporting period in which the entity first applies the amendments (the date of initial application). At the date of initial application, an entity shall reassess the classification of property held at that date and, if applicable, reclassify property applying paragraphs 7–14 to reflect the conditions that exist at that date.

84D   Notwithstanding the requirements in paragraph 84C, an entity is permitted to apply the amendments to paragraphs 57–58 retrospectively in accordance with AASB 108 if, and only if, that is possible without the use of hindsight.

84E   If, in accordance with paragraph 84C, an entity reclassifies property at the date of initial application, the entity shall:

(a)   account for the reclassification applying the requirements in paragraphs 59–64. In applying paragraphs 59–64, an entity shall:

(i)   read any reference to the date of change in use as the date of initial application; and

(ii)   recognise any amount that, in accordance with paragraphs 59–64, would have been recognised in profit or loss as an adjustment to the opening balance of retained earnings at the date of initial application.

(b)   disclose the amounts reclassified to, or from, investment property in accordance with paragraph 84C. The entity shall disclose those amounts reclassified as part of the reconciliation of the carrying amount of investment property at the beginning and end of the period as required by paragraphs 76 and 79.

Effective date

85   An entity shall apply this Standard for annual periods beginning on or after 1 January 2018. Earlier application is encouraged for periods beginning on or after 1 January 2014 but before 1 January 2018. If an entity applies this Standard for a period beginning before 1 January 2018, it shall disclose that fact.

85A   [Deleted by the AASB]

85B   In the previous version of this Standard, paragraphs 8, 9, 48, 53, 54 and 57 were amended, paragraph 22 was deleted and paragraphs 53A and 53B were added by AASB 2008-5 *Amendments to Australian Accounting Standards arising from the Annual Improvements Project* issued in July 2008. An entity shall apply those amendments prospectively for annual periods beginning on or after 1 January 2009. An entity is permitted to apply the amendments to investment property under construction from any date before 1 January 2009 provided that the fair values of investment properties under construction were measured at those dates. Earlier application is permitted. If an entity applies the amendments for an earlier period it shall disclose that fact and at the same time apply the amendments to paragraphs 5 and 81E of IAS 16 *Property, Plant and Equipment*.

85C   [Deleted by the AASB]

85D   AASB 2014-1 *Amendments to Australian Accounting Standards*, issued in June 2014, amended the previous version of this Standard as follows: added headings before paragraph 6 and after paragraph 84 and added paragraphs 14A and 84A. An entity shall apply those amendments for annual periods beginning on or after 1 July 2014. Earlier application is permitted. If an entity applies those amendments for an earlier period it shall disclose that fact.

85E   AASB 2014-5 *Amendments to Australian Accounting Standards arising from AASB 15*, issued in December 2014, amended paragraphs 3(b), 9, 67 and 70 in the previous version of this Standard. An entity shall apply those amendments when it applies AASB 15.

85G   AASB 2017-1 *Amendments to Australian Accounting Standards – Transfers of Investment Property, Annual Improvements 2014–2016 Cycle and Other Amendments*, issued in February 2017, amended paragraphs 57–58 and added paragraphs 84C–84E. A for-profit entity shall apply those amendments for annual periods beginning on or after 1 January 2018. A not-for-profit entity shall apply those amendments for annual periods beginning on or after 1 January 2019. Earlier application is permitted. If an entity applies those amendments for an earlier period, it shall disclose that fact.

Withdrawal of IAS 40 (2000)

86 [Deleted by the AASB]

Commencement of the legislative instrument

Aus86.1 For legal purposes, this legislative instrument commences on 31 December 2016.

Withdrawal of AASB pronouncements

Aus86.2 This Standard repeals AASB 140 *Investment Property* issued in July 2004. Despite the repeal, after the time this Standard starts to apply under section 334 of the Corporations Act (either generally or in relation to an individual entity), the repealed Standard continues to apply in relation to any period ending before that time as if the repeal had not occurred.

[Note: When this Standard applies under section 334 of the Corporations Act (either generally or in relation to an individual entity), it supersedes the application of the repealed Standard.]

APPENDIX A
AUSTRALIAN REDUCED DISCLOSURE REQUIREMENTS

This appendix is an integral part of the Standard.

AusA1 **The following do not apply to entities preparing general purpose financial statements under Australian Accounting Standards – Reduced Disclosure Requirements:**

(a) **paragraphs 75(b), 75(c), 75(f), 76(e), 77, 79(d)(vi), 79(d)(vii) and 79(e);**

(b) **in paragraph 76(a), the text ", disclosing separately ... an asset"; and**

(c) **in paragraph 79(d)(i), the text ", disclosing separately ... an asset".**

Entities applying Australian Accounting Standards – Reduced Disclosure Requirements may elect to comply with some or all of these excluded requirements.

AusA2 The requirements that do not apply to entities preparing general purpose financial statements under Australian Accounting Standards – Reduced Disclosure Requirements are also identified in this Standard by shading of the relevant text, except for comparative disclosures subject to RDR paragraphs.

AusA3 **The RDR paragraph in this Standard applies only to entities preparing general purpose financial statements under Australian Accounting Standards – Reduced Disclosure Requirements.**

RDR76.1 **An entity applying Australian Accounting Standards – Reduced Disclosure Requirements is not required to disclose the reconciliation specified in paragraph 76 for prior periods.**

COMPILATION DETAILS

Accounting Standard AASB 140 *Investment Property* as amended

Compilation details are not part of AASB 140.

This compiled Standard applies to annual periods beginning on or after 1 January 2018 but before 1 January 2019 for for-profit entities. It takes into account amendments up to and including 13 February 2017 and was prepared on 20 March 2018 by the staff of the Australian Accounting Standards Board (AASB).

This compilation is not a separate Accounting Standard made by the AASB. Instead, it is a representation of AASB 140 (August 2015) as amended by other Accounting Standards, which are listed in the Table below.

Table of Standards

Standard	Date made	FRL identifier	Commence-ment date	Effective date *(annual periods ... on or after ...)*	Application, saving or transitional provisions
AASB 140	14 Aug 2015	F2015L01611	31 Dec 2016	*(beginning)* 1 Jan 2018	see (a) below
AASB 2015-8	22 Oct 2015	F2015L01840	31 Dec 2016	*(beginning)* 1 Jan 2017	see (b) below
AASB 16	23 Feb 2016	F2016L00233	31 Dec 2018	*(beginning)* 1 Jan 2019	not compiled*
AASB 1058	9 Dec 2016	F2017L00042	31 Dec 2018	*(beginning)* 1 Jan 2019	not compiled*
AASB 2016-7	9 Dec 2016	F2017L00043	31 Dec 2016	*(beginning)* 1 Jan 2017	see (c) below
AASB 2017-1	13 Feb 2017	F2017L00193	31 Dec 2017	FP *(beginning)* 1 Jan 2018 NFP *(beginning)* 1 Jan 2019	see (d) below
AASB 17	19 Jul 2017	F2017L01184	31 Dec 2020	*(beginning)* 1 Jan 2021	not compiled*

* The amendments made by this Standard are not included in this compilation, which presents the principal Standard as applicable to annual reporting periods beginning on or after 1 January 2018 but before 1 January 2019 for for-profit entities.

(a) AASB 140 applies to annual periods beginning on or after 1 January 2018 (instead of 1 January 2017) as a result of amendments made by AASB 2015-8 *Amendments to Australian Accounting Standards – Effective Date of AASB 15* Earlier application is permitted for periods beginning on or after 1 January 2014

(b) Entities may elect to apply this Standard to annual periods beginning before 1 January 2017, provided that AASB 15 *Revenue from Contracts with Customers* is also applied

(c) As a result of AASB 2016-7 deferring the effective date of AASB 15 *Revenue from Contracts with Customers* (and its consequential amendments in AASB 2014-5) for not-for-profit entities from 1 January 2018 to 1 January 2019, AASB 140 (2015) applies to not-for-profit entities only to annual reporting periods beginning on or after 1 January 2019, instead of 1 January 2018. However, earlier application is permitted, provided that AASB 15 is also applied.

(d) For-profit (FP) entities and not-for-profit (NFP) entities may elect to apply the amendments made to AASB 140 by this Standard early, in advance of their particular mandatory effective dates.

Table of amendments

Paragraph affected	How affected	By ... [paragraph/page]
57-58	amended	AASB 2017-1 [page 8]
84C-84E	added	AASB 2017-1 [page 9]
85	amended	AASB 2015-8 [13]
85G	added	AASB 2017-1 [page 9]

DELETED IAS 40 TEXT

Deleted IAS 40 text is not part of AASB 140.

80   **An entity that has previously applied IAS 40 (2000) and elects for the first time to classify and account for some or all eligible property interests held under operating leases as investment property shall recognise the effect of that election as an adjustment to the opening balance of retained earnings for the period in which the election is first made. In addition:**

    (a)   **if the entity has previously disclosed publicly (in financial statements or otherwise) the fair value of those property interests in earlier periods (measured on a basis that satisfies the definition of fair value in IFRS 13), the entity is encouraged, but not required:**

        (i)   **to adjust the opening balance of retained earnings for the earliest period presented for which such fair value was disclosed publicly; and**

        (ii)   **to restate comparative information for those periods; and**

    (b)   **if the entity has not previously disclosed publicly the information described in (a), it shall not restate comparative information and shall disclose that fact.**

81   This Standard requires a treatment different from that required by IAS 8. IAS 8 requires comparative information to be restated unless such restatement is impracticable.

82   When an entity first applies this Standard, the adjustment to the opening balance of retained earnings includes the reclassification of any amount held in revaluation surplus for investment property.

83   IAS 8 applies to any change in accounting policies that is made when an entity first applies this Standard and chooses to use the cost model. The effect of the change in accounting policies includes the reclassification of any amount held in revaluation surplus for investment property.

84   **The requirements of paragraphs 27–29 regarding the initial measurement of an investment property acquired in an exchange of assets transaction shall be applied prospectively only to future transactions.**

85A   IAS 1 *Presentation of Financial Statements* (as revised in 2007) amended the terminology used throughout IFRSs. In addition it amended paragraph 62. An entity shall apply those amendments for annual periods beginning on or after 1 January 2009. If an entity applies IAS 1 (revised 2007) for an earlier period, the amendments shall be applied for that earlier period.

85C   IFRS 13, issued in May 2011, amended the definition of fair value in paragraph 5, amended paragraphs 26, 29, 32, 40, 48, 53, 53B, 78–80 and 85B and deleted paragraphs 36–39, 42–47, 49, 51 and 75(d). An entity shall apply those amendments when it applies IFRS 13.

86   This Standard supersedes IAS 40 *Investment Property* (issued in 2000).

AASB 141

Agriculture

(Reissued August 2015)

This note is not part of Accounting Standard AASB 141.

The following unincorporated amendments are not included in this Standard.

- AASB 1058 *Income of Not-for-Profit Entities* — Appendix D sets out the amendments to other Australian Accounting Standards that are a consequence of the AASB issuing this Standard. It is applicable from 1 January 2019. Earlier application is permitted, but amendments to AASB 117 apply before 1 January 2019 only if AASB 1058 is also applied to an earlier period. In addition, AASB 1 and AASB 16 amendments are applied to an earlier period only if AASB 16 is also applied to that period.

- AASB 16 *Leases* — Appendix D sets out the amendments to other Standards that are a consequence of the AASB issuing this Standard. It is applicable from 1 January 2019. Earlier application is permitted, but entities must apply AASB 15 *Revenue from Contracts with Customers* before applying this Standard.

Entities early-adopting any amendments with later application dates will need to refer to the amending Standards that have not yet been incorporated into compilations. The abovementioned unincorporated amendments may be located on the AASB website at www.aasb.gov.au or on the Federal Register of Legislation website at www.legislation.gov.au.

CONTENTS

APPENDIX

A. AUSTRALIAN REDUCED DISCLOSURE REQUIREMENTS

DELETED IAS 41 TEXT

ILLUSTRATIVE EXAMPLES (available on the AASB website)

BASIS FOR CONCLUSIONS ON IAS 41 (available on the AASB website)

Accounting Standard AASB 141 *Agriculture* is set out in paragraphs 1 – 63 and Appendix A. All the paragraphs have equal authority. Paragraphs in **bold type** state the main principles. AASB 141 is to be read in the context of other Australian Accounting Standards, including AASB 1048 *Interpretation of Standards*, which identifies the Australian Accounting Interpretations, and AASB 1057 *Application of Australian Accounting Standards*. In the absence of explicit guidance, AASB 108 *Accounting Policies, Changes in Accounting Estimates and Errors* provides a basis for selecting and applying accounting policies.

COMPARISON WITH IAS 41

AASB 141 *Agriculture* incorporates IAS 41 *Agriculture* issued by the International Accounting Standards Board (IASB). Australian-specific paragraphs (which are not included in IAS 41) are identified with the prefix "Aus" or "RDR". Paragraphs that apply only to not-for-profit entities begin by identifying their limited applicability.

Tier 1

For-profit entities complying with AASB 141 also comply with IAS 41.

Not-for-profit entities' compliance with IAS 41 will depend on whether any "Aus" paragraphs that specifically apply to not-for-profit entities provide additional guidance or contain applicable requirements that are inconsistent with IAS 41.

Tier 2

Entities preparing general purpose financial statements under Australian Accounting Standards – Reduced Disclosure Requirements (Tier 2) will not be in compliance with IFRSs.

AASB 1053 *Application of Tiers of Australian Accounting Standards* explains the two tiers of reporting requirements.

ACCOUNTING STANGDARD AASB 141

The Australian Accounting Standards Board makes Accounting Standard AASB 141 *Agriculture* under section 334 of the *Corporations Act 2001*.

Kris Peach

Dated 14 August 2015   Chair – AASB

ACCOUNTING STANDARD AASB 141
AGRICULTURE

Objective

The objective of this Standard is to prescribe the accounting treatment and disclosures related to agricultural activity.

Scope

1 **This Standard shall be applied to account for the following when they relate to agricultural activity:**

   (a) **biological assets, except for bearer plants;**

   (b) **agricultural produce at the point of harvest; and**

   (c) **government grants covered by paragraphs 34 and 35.**

2 This Standard does not apply to:

   (a) land related to agricultural activity (see AASB 116 *Property, Plant and Equipment* and AASB 140 *Investment Property*).

   (b) bearer plants related to agricultural activity (see AASB 116). However, this Standard applies to the produce on those bearer plants.

   (c) government grants related to bearer plants (see AASB 120 *Accounting for Government Grants and Disclosure of Government Assistance*).

   (d) intangible assets related to agricultural activity (see AASB 138 *Intangible Assets*).

3 This Standard is applied to agricultural produce, which is the harvested produce of the entity's biological assets, at the point of harvest. Thereafter, AASB 102 *Inventories* or another applicable Standard is applied. Accordingly, this Standard does not deal with the processing of agricultural produce after harvest; for example, the processing of grapes into wine by a vintner who has grown the grapes. While such processing may be a logical and natural extension of agricultural activity, and the events taking place may bear some similarity to biological transformation, such processing is not included within the definition of agricultural activity in this Standard.

4 The table below provides examples of biological assets, agricultural produce, and products that are the result of processing after harvest:

Biological assets	Agricultural produce	Products that are the result of processing after harvest
Sheep	Wool	Yarn, carpet
Trees in a timber plantation	Felled trees	Logs, lumber
Dairy cattle	Milk	Cheese
Pigs	Carcass	Sausages, cured hams
Cotton plants	Harvested cotton	Thread, clothing
Sugarcane	Harvested cane	Sugar
Tobacco plants	Picked leaves	Cured tobacco
Tea bushes	Picked leaves	Tea
Grape vines	Picked grapes	Wine
Fruit trees	Picked fruit	Processed fruit

(Continued)

(Continued)

Biological assets	Agricultural produce	Products that are the result of processing after harvest
Oil palms	Picked fruit	Palm oil
Rubber trees	Harvested latex	Rubber products

Some plants, for example, tea bushes, grape vines, oil palms and rubber trees, usually meet the definition of a bearer plant and are within the scope of AASB 116. However, the produce growing on bearer plants, for example, tea leaves, grapes, oil palm fruit and latex, is within the scope of AASB 141.

Definitions

Agriculture-related definitions

5   The following terms are used in this Standard with the meanings specified:

Agricultural activity is the management by an entity of the biological transformation and harvest of biological assets for sale or for conversion into agricultural produce or into additional biological assets.

Agricultural produce is the harvested produce of the entity's biological assets.

A *bearer plant* is a living plant that:

(a)   is used in the production or supply of agricultural produce;

(b)   is expected to bear produce for more than one period; and

(c)   has a remote likelihood of being sold as agricultural produce, except for incidental scrap sales.

A *biological asset* is a living animal or plant.

Biological transformation comprises the processes of growth, degeneration, production, and procreation that cause qualitative or quantitative changes in a biological asset.

Costs to sell are the incremental costs directly attributable to the disposal of an asset, excluding finance costs and income taxes.

A *group of biological assets* is an aggregation of similar living animals or plants.

Harvest is the detachment of produce from a biological asset or the cessation of a biological asset's life processes.

5A   The following are not bearer plants:

(a)   plants cultivated to be harvested as agricultural produce (for example, trees grown for use as lumber);

(b)   plants cultivated to produce agricultural produce when there is more than a remote likelihood that the entity will also harvest and sell the plant as agricultural produce, other than as incidental scrap sales (for example, trees that are cultivated both for their fruit and their lumber); and

(c)   annual crops (for example, maize and wheat).

5B   When bearer plants are no longer used to bear produce they might be cut down and sold as scrap, for example, for use as firewood. Such incidental scrap sales would not prevent the plant from satisfying the definition of a bearer plant.

5C   Produce growing on bearer plants is a biological asset.

6   Agricultural activity covers a diverse range of activities; for example, raising livestock, forestry, annual or perennial cropping, cultivating orchards and plantations, floriculture and aquaculture (including fish farming). Certain common features exist within this diversity:

(a)   *Capability to change.* Living animals and plants are capable of biological transformation;

(b) *Management of change*. Management facilitates biological transformation by enhancing, or at least stabilising, conditions necessary for the process to take place (for example, nutrient levels, moisture, temperature, fertility, and light). Such management distinguishes agricultural activity from other activities. For example, harvesting from unmanaged sources (such as ocean fishing and deforestation) is not agricultural activity; and

(c) *Measurement of change*. The change in quality (for example, genetic merit, density, ripeness, fat cover, protein content, and fibre strength) or quantity (for example, progeny, weight, cubic metres, fibre length or diameter, and number of buds) brought about by biological transformation or harvest is measured and monitored as a routine management function.

7 Biological transformation results in the following types of outcomes:

(a) asset changes through (i) growth (an increase in quantity or improvement in quality of an animal or plant), (ii) degeneration (a decrease in the quantity or deterioration in quality of an animal or plant), or (iii) procreation (creation of additional living animals or plants); or

(b) production of agricultural produce such as latex, tea leaf, wool, and milk.

General definitions

8 The following terms are used in this Standard with the meanings specified:

Carrying amount is the amount at which an asset is recognised in the statement of financial position.

Fair value is the price that would be received to sell an asset or paid to transfer a liability in an orderly transaction between market participants at the measurement date. (See AASB 13 *Fair Value Measurement*.)

Government grants are as defined in AASB 120.

9 [Deleted]

Recognition and measurement

10 An entity shall recognise a biological asset or agricultural produce when, and only when:

(a) the entity controls the asset as a result of past events;

(b) it is probable that future economic benefits associated with the asset will flow to the entity; and

(c) the fair value or cost of the asset can be measured reliably.

11 In agricultural activity, control may be evidenced by, for example, legal ownership of cattle and the branding or otherwise marking of the cattle on acquisition, birth, or weaning. The future benefits are normally assessed by measuring the significant physical attributes.

12 A biological asset shall be measured on initial recognition and at the end of each reporting period at its fair value less costs to sell, except for the case described in paragraph 30 where the fair value cannot be measured reliably.

13 Agricultural produce harvested from an entity's biological assets shall be measured at its fair value less costs to sell at the point of harvest. Such measurement is the cost at that date when applying AASB 102 *Inventories* or another applicable Standard.

14 [Deleted]

15 The fair value measurement of a biological asset or agricultural produce may be facilitated by grouping biological assets or agricultural produce according to significant attributes; for example, by age or quality. An entity selects the attributes corresponding to the attributes used in the market as a basis for pricing.

16   Entities often enter into contracts to sell their biological assets or agricultural produce at a future date. Contract prices are not necessarily relevant in measuring fair value, because fair value reflects the current market conditions in which market participant buyers and sellers would enter into a transaction. As a result, the fair value of a biological asset or agricultural produce is not adjusted because of the existence of a contract. In some cases, a contract for the sale of a biological asset or agricultural produce may be an onerous contract, as defined in AASB 137 *Provisions, Contingent Liabilities and Contingent Assets*. AASB 137 applies to onerous contracts.

17–21   [Deleted]

22   An entity does not include any cash flows for financing the assets, taxation, or re-establishing biological assets after harvest (for example, the cost of replanting trees in a plantation forest after harvest).

23   [Deleted]

24   Cost may sometimes approximate fair value, particularly when:

     (a)   little biological transformation has taken place since initial cost incurrence (for example, for seedlings planted immediately prior to the end of a reporting period or newly acquired livestock); or

     (b)   the impact of the biological transformation on price is not expected to be material (for example, for the initial growth in a 30-year pine plantation production cycle).

25   Biological assets are often physically attached to land (for example, trees in a plantation forest). There may be no separate market for biological assets that are attached to the land but an active market may exist for the combined assets, that is, the biological assets, raw land, and land improvements, as a package. An entity may use information regarding the combined assets to measure the fair value of the biological assets. For example, the fair value of raw land and land improvements may be deducted from the fair value of the combined assets to arrive at the fair value of biological assets.

Gains and losses

26   **A gain or loss arising on initial recognition of a biological asset at fair value less costs to sell and from a change in fair value less costs to sell of a biological asset shall be included in profit or loss for the period in which it arises.**

27   A loss may arise on initial recognition of a biological asset, because costs to sell are deducted in determining fair value less costs to sell of a biological asset. A gain may arise on initial recognition of a biological asset, such as when a calf is born.

28   **A gain or loss arising on initial recognition of agricultural produce at fair value less costs to sell shall be included in profit or loss for the period in which it arises.**

29   A gain or loss may arise on initial recognition of agricultural produce as a result of harvesting.

Inability to measure fair value reliably

30   **There is a presumption that fair value can be measured reliably for a biological asset. However, that presumption can be rebutted only on initial recognition for a biological asset for which quoted market prices are not available and for which alternative fair value measurements are determined to be clearly unreliable. In such a case, that biological asset shall be measured at its cost less any accumulated depreciation and any accumulated impairment losses. Once the fair value of such a biological asset becomes reliably measurable, an entity shall measure it at its fair value less costs to sell. Once a non-current biological asset meets the criteria to be classified as held for sale (or is included in a disposal group that is classified as held for sale) in accordance with AASB 5 *Non-current Assets Held for Sale and Discontinued Operations*, it is presumed that fair value can be measured reliably.**

31   The presumption in paragraph 30 can be rebutted only on initial recognition. An entity that has previously measured a biological asset at its fair value less costs to sell continues to measure the biological asset at its fair value less costs to sell until disposal.

32   In all cases, an entity measures agricultural produce at the point of harvest at its fair value less costs to sell. This Standard reflects the view that the fair value of agricultural produce at the point of harvest can always be measured reliably.

33   In determining cost, accumulated depreciation and accumulated impairment losses, an entity considers AASB 102, AASB 116 and AASB 136 *Impairment of Assets*.

Government grants

34   An unconditional government grant related to a biological asset measured at its fair value less costs to sell shall be recognised in profit or loss when, and only when, the government grant becomes receivable.

35   If a government grant related to a biological asset measured at its fair value less costs to sell is conditional, including when a government grant requires an entity not to engage in specified agricultural activity, an entity shall recognise the government grant in profit or loss when, and only when, the conditions attaching to the government grant are met.

36   Terms and conditions of government grants vary. For example, a grant may require an entity to farm in a particular location for five years and require the entity to return all of the grant if it farms for a period shorter than five years. In this case, the grant is not recognised in profit or loss until the five years have passed. However, if the terms of the grant allow part of it to be retained according to the time that has elapsed, the entity recognises that part in profit or loss as time passes.

37   If a government grant relates to a biological asset measured at its cost less any accumulated depreciation and any accumulated impairment losses (see paragraph 30), AASB 120 is applied.

38   This Standard requires a different treatment from AASB 120, if a government grant relates to a biological asset measured at its fair value less costs to sell or a government grant requires an entity not to engage in specified agricultural activity. AASB 120 is applied only to a government grant related to a biological asset measured at its cost less any accumulated depreciation and any accumulated impairment losses.

Aus38.1   Notwithstanding paragraphs 34–38, not-for-profit entities recognise government grants related to a biological asset in accordance with AASB 1004 *Contributions*.

Disclosure

39   [Deleted]

General

40   An entity shall disclose the aggregate gain or loss arising during the current period on initial recognition of biological assets and agricultural produce and from the change in fair value less costs to sell of biological assets.

41   An entity shall provide a description of each group of biological assets.

42   The disclosure required by paragraph 41 may take the form of a narrative or quantified description.

43   An entity is encouraged to provide a quantified description of each group of biological assets, distinguishing between consumable and bearer biological assets or between mature and immature biological assets, as appropriate. For example, an entity may disclose the carrying amounts of consumable biological assets and bearer biological assets by group. An entity may further divide those carrying amounts between mature

and immature assets. These distinctions provide information that may be helpful in assessing the timing of future cash flows. An entity discloses the basis for making any such distinctions.

44   Consumable biological assets are those that are to be harvested as agricultural produce or sold as biological assets. Examples of consumable biological assets are livestock intended for the production of meat, livestock held for sale, fish in farms, crops such as maize and wheat, produce on a bearer plant and trees being grown for lumber. Bearer biological assets are those other than consumable biological assets; for example, livestock from which milk is produced and fruit trees from which fruit is harvested. Bearer biological assets are not agricultural produce but, rather, are held to bear produce.

45   Biological assets may be classified either as mature biological assets or immature biological assets. Mature biological assets are those that have attained harvestable specifications (for consumable biological assets) or are able to sustain regular harvests (for bearer biological assets).

46   If not disclosed elsewhere in information published with the financial statements, an entity shall describe:

    (a)   the nature of its activities involving each group of biological assets; and

    (b)   non-financial measures or estimates of the physical quantities of:

        (i)   each group of the entity's biological assets at the end of the period; and

        (ii)   output of agricultural produce during the period.

47–48 [Deleted]

49   An entity shall disclose:

    (a)   the existence and carrying amounts of biological assets whose title is restricted, and the carrying amounts of biological assets pledged as security for liabilities;

    (b)   the amount of commitments for the development or acquisition of biological assets; and

    (c)   financial risk management strategies related to agricultural activity.

50   An entity shall present a reconciliation of changes in the carrying amount of biological assets between the beginning and the end of the current period. The reconciliation shall include:

    (a)   the gain or loss arising from changes in fair value less costs to sell;

    (b)   increases due to purchases;

    (c)   decreases attributable to sales and biological assets classified as held for sale (or included in a disposal group that is classified as held for sale) in accordance with AASB 5;

    (d)   decreases due to harvest;

    (e)   increases resulting from business combinations;

    (f)   net exchange differences arising on the translation of financial statements into a different presentation currency, and on the translation of a foreign operation into the presentation currency of the reporting entity; and

    (g)   other changes.

51   The fair value less costs to sell of a biological asset can change due to both physical changes and price changes in the market. Separate disclosure of physical and price changes is useful in appraising current period performance and future prospects, particularly when there is a production cycle of more than one year. In such cases, an entity is encouraged to disclose, by group or otherwise, the amount of change in fair value less costs to sell included in profit or loss due to physical changes and due to price changes. This information is generally less useful when the production cycle is less than one year (for example, when raising chickens or growing cereal crops).

52   Biological transformation results in a number of types of physical change—
        growth, degeneration, production, and procreation, each of which is observable
        and measurable. Each of those physical changes has a direct relationship to future
        economic benefits. A change in fair value of a biological asset due to harvesting is
        also a physical change.

53   Agricultural activity is often exposed to climatic, disease and other natural risks. If
        an event occurs that gives rise to a material item of income or expense, the nature
        and amount of that item are disclosed in accordance with AASB 101 *Presentation of
        Financial Statements*. Examples of such an event include an outbreak of a virulent
        disease, a flood, a severe drought or frost, and a plague of insects.

Additional disclosures for biological assets where fair value cannot be measured reliably

54   If an entity measures biological assets at their cost less any accumulated
        depreciation and any accumulated impairment losses (see paragraph 30) at the
        end of the period, the entity shall disclose for such biological assets:

        (a)   a description of the biological assets;

        (b)   an explanation of why fair value cannot be measured reliably;

        (c)   if possible, the range of estimates within which fair value is highly likely to
                lie;

        (d)   the depreciation method used;

        (e)   the useful lives or the depreciation rates used; and

        (f)   the gross carrying amount and the accumulated depreciation (aggregated
                with accumulated impairment losses) at the beginning and end of the
                period.

55   If, during the current period, an entity measures biological assets at their cost
        less any accumulated depreciation and any accumulated impairment losses (see
        paragraph 30), an entity shall disclose any gain or loss recognised on disposal
        of such biological assets and the reconciliation required by paragraph 50 shall
        disclose amounts related to such biological assets separately. In addition, the
        reconciliation shall include the following amounts included in profit or loss related
        to those biological assets:

        (a)   impairment losses;

        (b)   reversals of impairment losses; and

        (c)   depreciation.

56   If the fair value of biological assets previously measured at their cost less
        any accumulated depreciation and any accumulated impairment losses becomes
        reliably measurable during the current period, an entity shall disclose for those
        biological assets:

        (a)   a description of the biological assets;

        (b)   an explanation of why fair value has become reliably measurable; and

        (c)   the effect of the change.

Government grants

57   An entity shall disclose the following related to agricultural activity covered by
        this Standard:

        (a)   the nature and extent of government grants recognised in the financial
                statements;

        (b)   unfulfilled conditions and other contingencies attaching to government
                grants; and

        (c)   significant decreases expected in the level of government grants.

Commencement of the legislative instrument

Aus57.1   For legal purposes, this legislative instrument commences on 31 December 2015.

Withdrawal of AASB pronouncements

Aus57.2   This Standard repeals AASB 141 *Agriculture* issued in July 2004. Despite the repeal, after the time this Standard starts to apply under section 334 of the Corporations Act (either generally or in relation to an individual entity), the repealed Standard continues to apply in relation to any period ending before that time as if the repeal had not occurred.

         [Note: When this Standard applies under section 334 of the Corporations Act (either generally or in relation to an individual entity), it supersedes the application of the repealed Standard.]

Effective date and transition

58   This Standard becomes operative for annual financial statements covering periods beginning on or after 1 January 2016. Earlier application is encouraged for periods beginning on or after 1 January 2014 but before 1 January 2016. If an entity applies this Standard for periods beginning before 1 January 2016, it shall disclose that fact.

59   This Standard does not establish any specific transitional provisions. The adoption of this Standard is accounted for in accordance with AASB 108 *Accounting Policies, Changes in Accounting Estimates and Errors*.

60   In the previous version of this Standard, paragraphs 5, 6, 17, 20 and 21 were amended and paragraph 14 deleted by AASB 2008-5 *Amendments to Australian Accounting Standards arising from the Annual Improvements Project* issued in July 2008. An entity shall apply those amendments prospectively for annual periods beginning on or after 1 January 2009. Earlier application is permitted. If an entity applies the amendments for an earlier period it shall disclose that fact.

61   [Deleted by the AASB]

62   AASB 2014-6 *Amendments to Australian Accounting Standards – Agriculture: Bearer Plants*, issued in December 2014, amended the previous version of this Standard as follows: amended paragraphs 1–5, 8, 24 and 44 and added paragraphs 5A–5C and 63. An entity shall apply those amendments for annual periods beginning on or after 1 January 2016. Earlier application is permitted. If an entity applies those amendments for an earlier period, it shall disclose that fact. An entity shall apply those amendments retrospectively in accordance with AASB 108.

63   In the reporting period when AASB 2014-6 is first applied an entity need not disclose the quantitative information required by paragraph 28(f) of AASB 108 for the current period. However, an entity shall present the quantitative information required by paragraph 28(f) of AASB 108 for each prior period presented.

APPENDIX A

AUSTRALIAN REDUCED DISCLOSURE REQUIREMENTS

This appendix is an integral part of the Standard.

AusA1   **Paragraphs 40, 43-46, 49, 51-53, 54(c), 55, 56 and 57(c) of this Standard do not apply to entities preparing general purpose financial statements under Australian Accounting Standards – Reduced Disclosure Requirements. Entities applying Australian Accounting Standards – Reduced Disclosure**

Requirements may elect to comply with some or all of these excluded requirements.

AusA2   The requirements that do not apply to entities preparing general purpose financial statements under Australian Accounting Standards – Reduced Disclosure Requirements are also identified in this Standard by shading of the relevant text.

AusA3   **The RDR paragraph in this Standard applies only to entities preparing general purpose financial statements under Australian Accounting Standards – Reduced Disclosure Requirements.**

RDR50.1   **An entity applying Australian Accounting Standards – Reduced Disclosure Requirements is not required to disclose the reconciliation specified in paragraph 50 for prior periods.**

DELETED IAS 41 TEXT

Deleted IAS 41 text is not part of AASB 141.

61   IFRS 13, issued in May 2011, amended paragraphs 8, 15, 16, 25 and 30 and deleted paragraphs 9, 17–21, 23, 47 and 48. An entity shall apply those amendments when it applies IFRS 13.

AASB 1004
Contributions

(Compiled January 2015)

This compiled Standard applies to annual reporting periods beginning on or after 1 July 2015. Early application is permitted for annual reporting periods beginning on or after 1 January 2014 but before 1 July 2015. It incorporates relevant amendments made up to and including 28 January 2015.

Prepared on 2 April 2015 by the staff of the Australian Accounting Standards Board.

This note is not part of Accounting Standard AASB 1004.

The following unincorporated amendments are not included in this compiled Standard.

- AASB 1058 *Income of Not-for-Profit Entities* — Appendix D sets out the amendments to other Australian Accounting Standards that are a consequence of the AASB issuing this Standard. It is applicable from 1 January 2019. Earlier application is permitted, but amendments to AASB 117 apply before 1 January 2019 only if AASB 1058 is also applied to an earlier period. In addition, AASB 1 and AASB 16 amendments are applied to an earlier period only if AASB 16 is also applied to that period.

Entities early-adopting any amendments with later application dates will need to refer to the amending Standards that have not yet been incorporated into compilations. The abovementioned unincorporated amendments may be located on the AASB website at www.aasb.gov.au or on the Federal Register of Legislation website at www.legislation.gov.au.

CONTENTS

Australian Accounting Standard AASB 1004 *Contributions* (as amended) is set out in paragraphs 1 – 68 and Appendix A. All the paragraphs have equal authority. Paragraphs in **bold type** state the main principles. AASB 1004 is to be read in the context of other Australian Accounting Standards, including AASB 1048 *Interpretation of Standards*, which identifies the Australian Accounting Interpretations. In the absence of explicit guidance, AASB 108 *Accounting Policies, Changes in Accounting Estimates and Errors* provides a basis for selecting and applying accounting policies.

COMPILATION DETAILS

Accounting Standard AASB 1004 *Contributions* as amended

This compiled Standard applies to annual reporting periods beginning on or after 1 July 2015. It takes into account amendments up to and including 28 January 2015 and was prepared on 2 April 2015 by the staff of the Australian Accounting Standards Board (AASB).

This compilation is not a separate Accounting Standard made by the AASB. Instead, it is a representation of AASB 1004 (December 2007) as amended by other Accounting Standards, which are listed in the Table below.

Table of Standards

Standard	Date made	Application date (*annual reporting periods ... on or after ...*)	Application, saving or transitional provisions
AASB 1004	13 Dec 2007	(*beginning*) 1 Jul 2008	see (a) below
AASB 2011-8	2 Sep 2011	(*beginning*) 1 Jan 2013	see (b) below
AASB 2015-3	28 Jan 2015	(*beginning*) 1 Jul 2015	see (c) below

(a) Entities may elect to apply this Standard to annual reporting periods beginning on or after 1 January 2005 but before 1 July 2008, provided that a number of updated, public-sector-related Standards are also applied to such periods, as set out in the Standard.

(b) AASB 2011-8 has been amended by AASB 2011-10 (made 5 September 2011) and AASB 2012-6 (made 10 September 2012).
Entities may elect to apply this Standard to annual reporting periods beginning on or after 1 January 2005 but before 1 January 2013, provided that AASB 13 Fair Value Measurement is also applied to such periods.

(c) Entities may elect to apply this Standard to annual reporting periods beginning on or after 1 January 2014 but before 1 July 2015.

Table of amendments

Paragraph affected	How affected	By … [paragraph]
9	deleted	AASB 2015-3 [13, 14]
11	amended	AASB 2011-8 [101]
44	amended	AASB 2011-8 [102]

COMPARISON WITH INTERNATIONAL PRONOUNCEMENTS

This Standard retains the requirements in AASB 1004 *Contributions* (as issued in July 2004) and incorporates relevant paragraphs from AAS 27 *Financial Reporting by Local Governments*, AAS 29 *Financial Reporting by Government Departments* and AAS 31 *Financial Reporting by Governments* in substantially unamended form (with some exceptions, as noted in Appendix B). Accordingly, the development of this Standard did not involve consideration of International Public Sector Accounting Standards (IPSASs) issued by the International Public Sector Accounting Standards Board or International Financial Reporting Standards (IFRSs) issued by the International Accounting Standards Board.

A review by the AASB of accounting for non-exchange income (which will incorporate a review of contributions) is in progress at the time of issue of this Standard. That review will involve consideration of international pronouncements.

AASB 1004 and IPSASs

Not-for-profit entities that comply with the requirements of AASB 1004 may not simultaneously be in compliance with the requirements of IPSAS 23 *Revenue from Non-Exchange Transactions (Taxes and Transfers)*. This is because the requirements in AASB 1004 are different from those in IPSAS 23. The more significant differences include:

(a) IPSAS 23 applies to all public sector entities other than government business enterprises, whereas the various requirements in AASB 1004 apply as detailed in the table at paragraph 6;

(b) IPSAS 23 requires an inflow of resources from a non-exchange transaction (such as a contribution) recognised as an asset to be recognised as revenue, except to the extent that a liability is recognised in respect of the same inflow. Conditions on a transferred asset give rise to a present obligation on initial recognition that is to be recognised as a liability provided it meets the liability recognition criteria. AASB 1004, on the other hand, requires contributions, other than contributions by owners, to be recognised as income when the transferee local government, government department, General Government Sector (GGS) or whole of government obtains control over them, irrespective of whether restrictions or conditions are imposed on the use of the contributions;

(c) under IPSAS 23 an entity may, but is not required to, recognise services in-kind as revenue and as an asset. Under AASB 1004, contributions of services to local governments, government departments, GGSs and whole of governments are recognised as income when, and only when, the fair value of those services can be reliably determined, and the services would have been purchased if they had not been donated; and

(d) AASB 1004 includes a number of disclosure requirements that are not included in IPSAS 23, such as the requirement for government departments to disclose information relating to compliance with parliamentary appropriations and other externally imposed requirements.

AASB 1004 and IFRSs

Not-for-profit entities that comply with the requirements of AASB 1004 may not simultaneously be in compliance with the requirements of IAS 20 *Accounting for Government Grants and Disclosure of Government Assistance*. This is because the recognition criteria in AASB 1004 are different from those in IAS 20.

AASB 1004 requires contributions received or receivable to be recognised immediately as revenue when:

(a)   the entity obtains control of the contribution or the right to receive the contribution;

(b)   it is probable that the economic benefits comprising the contribution will flow to the entity; and

(c)   the amount of the contribution can be measured reliably.

In contrast, IAS 20 requires government grants to be recognised as income on a systematic basis over the periods necessary to match them with the related costs which they are intended to compensate or by deducting the grant in arriving at the carrying amount of the asset when there is reasonable assurance that:

(a)   the entity will comply with the conditions attaching to them; and

(b)   the grants will be received.

ACCOUNTING STANDARD AASB 1004

The Australian Accounting Standards Board made Accounting Standard AASB 1004 *Contributions* under section 334 of the *Corporations Act 2001* on 13 December 2007.

This compiled version of AASB 1004 applies to annual reporting periods beginning on or after 1 July 2015. It incorporates relevant amendments contained in other AASB Standards made by the AASB up to and including 28 January 2015 (see Compilation Details).

ACCOUNTING STANDARD AASB 1004
CONTRIBUTIONS

Application

1   **Subject to paragraphs 2 to 5, this Standard applies to:**

    (a)   each not-for-profit entity that is required to prepare financial reports in accordance with Part 2M.3 of the Corporations Act and that is a reporting entity;

    (b)   general purpose financial statements of each other not-for-profit entity that is a reporting entity;

    (c)   financial statements of not-for-profit entities that are, or are held out to be, general purpose financial statements; and

    (d)   financial statements of General Government Sectors (GGSs) prepared in accordance with AASB 1049 *Whole of Government and General Government Sector Financial Reporting*.

2   **Paragraphs 31 to 43 and 63 to 68 only apply to government departments that are reporting entities.**

3   **Paragraphs 19 to 30, 44 to 47 and 60 to 62 only apply to local governments, government departments that are reporting entities, GGSs and whole of governments.**

(c)   **AASB 1051** *Land Under Roads*;

(d)   **AASB 1052** *Disaggregated Disclosures*;

(e)   **AASB 2007-9** *Amendments to Australian Accounting Standards arising from the Review of AASs 27, 29 and 31*; and

(f)   **AASB Interpretation 1038** *Contributions by Owners Made to Wholly-Owned Public Sector Entities.*

9   [Deleted by the AASB]

10   **When applicable, this Standard, together with the Standards referred to in paragraph 8, supersede:**

(a)   **AASB 1004** *Contributions* **as notified in the** *Commonwealth of Australia Gazette* **No S 294, 22 July 2004;**

(b)   **AAS 27** *Financial Reporting by Local Governments*, **as amended;**

(c)   **AAS 29** *Financial Reporting by Government Departments*, **as amended; and**

(d)   **AAS 31** *Financial Reporting by Governments*, **as amended.**

Measurement of contributions

11   **Income shall be measured at the fair value (see AASB 13** *Fair Value Measurement*) **of the** *contributions* **received or receivable.**

Recognition of contributions of assets

12   **Income arising from the contribution of an asset to the entity shall be recognised when, and only when, all the following conditions have been satisfied:**

(a)   **the entity obtains control of the contribution or the right to receive the contribution;**

(b)   **it is probable that the economic benefits comprising the contribution will flow to the entity; and**

(c)   **the amount of the contribution can be measured reliably.**

13   A contribution occurs when an entity receives an asset, including the right to receive cash or other forms of asset without directly giving approximately equal value to the other party or parties to the transfer; that is, when there is a *non-reciprocal transfer*. Contributions would, for example, include donated assets. Contributions that are income exclude *contributions by owners*.

14   In some cases it may be difficult to determine whether the entity has control of a contribution or the right to receive a contribution. One such case could be economic benefits expected to be received under a multi-year public policy agreement. The entity does not obtain control of a contribution under such an agreement until it has met conditions or provided services or facilities that make it eligible to receive a contribution. On this basis, under multi-year public policy agreements, income would be recognised only in relation to contributions received or receivable under policy agreements. Another example is where a donor pledges a donation to an entity. If the pledge is not enforceable against the donor, the entity does not control the contribution.

15   In some cases it may be difficult to determine whether the entity is giving approximately equal value to the other parties to a transfer. This is particularly the case where, for example, fees are charged by a not-for-profit entity for the potential use of a general pool of facilities. In circumstances where clubs and professional associations charge fees in return for contributors being able to enjoy the use of facilities, receive publications or practice in a particular vocation for a defined period, an exchange transaction can be presumed and the fees would not be treated as contributions. The

recipient of the fees would have a contractual or constructive obligation to refund some or all fees if it were unable to provide the facilities or services. In circumstances where the benefits to contributors are only nominal, such as acknowledgment letters, general information about the entity's activities and satisfaction of contributors' altruistic goals, the fees are in the nature of contributions.

Liabilities forgiven

16   The gross amount of a liability forgiven by a credit provider shall be recognised by the borrower as income.

17   Where equity is substituted for a liability, this is not treated as a forgiveness.

Disclosures

18   The following information shall be disclosed:

    (a)   contributions of assets, including cash and non-monetary assets; and

    (b)   the forgiveness of liabilities.

Recognition of contributions, other than contributions by owners, by local governments, government departments, GGSs or whole of governments

Paragraphs 19 to 30 of this Standard apply only to local governments, government departments, GGSs and whole of governments.

Contributions

19   Contributions, other than contributions by owners, to a local government, government department, GGS or whole of government are received in the form of involuntary transfers, such as rates, taxes and fines, and voluntary transfers, such as grants and donations. In the case of government departments, parliamentary appropriations, other than those that give rise to a liability or that are in the nature of a contribution by owners, may also be a type of contribution.

20   This Standard requires contributions, other than contributions by owners, to be recognised as income when the transferee local government, government department, GGS or whole of government obtains control over them, irrespective of whether restrictions or conditions are imposed on the use of the contributions. The transferee does not have a present obligation to sacrifice future economic benefits to the transferor, even though the transferee has a fiduciary responsibility to use the assets effectively and efficiently in pursuing its objectives. This fiduciary responsibility pertains to all assets and does not, of itself, create a present obligation to make sacrifices of future economic benefits to external parties. Accordingly, the receipt of contributions does not give rise to a liability.

21   For transfers to a local government, government department, GGS or whole of government to create a present obligation on that entity to make future sacrifices of economic benefits to external parties, the transfers must be reciprocal. Where assets are provided on the condition that the local government, government department, GGS or whole of government is to make a reciprocal transfer of economic benefits, and that transfer has not occurred prior to the reporting date, a liability is recognised as at the reporting date in respect of such amounts.

22   Reciprocal transfers are transfers in which the transferor and transferee directly receive and sacrifice approximately equal value. Examples of reciprocal transfers are sales of goods and services, the provision of loan funds, and the provision of employee services. A reciprocal transfer also occurs where, for example, assets are provided to

a government department on the condition that the government department renders particular services to the transferor of the assets and, if the services are not rendered, those assets are required to be remitted directly to the transferor. Another example of a reciprocal transfer is where a user charge is provided to a local government in advance for repairs to a private road, where the charge would be repayable directly to the provider or providers if the works were not performed.

23   For a transaction to be reciprocal, the transferor must have a right to receive the benefits directly. It is not sufficient that the transferor receives benefits indirectly as a result of the transfer. For example, when a government provides a grant to a local government, it does not receive value directly in exchange, although it (or those it represents) would indirectly receive a benefit as a result of the local government deploying the grant in providing goods or services to beneficiaries that the grantor government represents.

24   While involuntary transfers to local governments, government departments, GGSs and whole of governments may result in the provision of some goods or services to the transferor, they do not give the transferor a claim to receive directly benefits of approximately equal value. The receipt and sacrifice of approximately equal value may occur, but only by coincidence. For example, governments are not obliged to provide commensurate benefits, in the form of goods or services, to particular taxpayers in return for their taxes. For this reason, involuntary transfers are non-reciprocal transfers.

25   There could be instances where a transfer of economic benefits comprises a reciprocal component and a non-reciprocal component. For example, where another entity transfers a building to a local government, government department, GGS or whole of government at a price that intentionally is significantly lower than its fair value, the transfer is in part reciprocal (to the extent that approximately equal value is received directly in exchange) and in part non-reciprocal. In this circumstance, because a reciprocal transaction is involved, any unsatisfied obligation to provide consideration in return for the building is a liability of the local government, government department, GGS or whole of government.

26   If a local government, government department, GGS or whole of government failed to meet the specific conditions attaching to a contribution of assets and part or all of the contribution is required to be repaid, a liability and an expense would need to be recognised for the amount payable. In this circumstance, the transferee has a present obligation to the transferor that has arisen as a result of a past event: the failure of the transferee to meet the conditions for retention of the contribution.

Control over assets

27   Control of amounts in the nature of voluntary transfers arises when the transferee can benefit from funds transferred to it and deny or regulate the access of others to those benefits. Therefore, control arises when, for example, government departments can use funds granted or transferred to purchase goods and services or retain those funds for future purchases.

28   The timing of gaining control over assets acquired from voluntary non-reciprocal transfers, such as grants and donations, depends upon the arrangements between the transferor and the transferee. For example, where a State Government receives a single-year grant from the Commonwealth Government to provide services in the following reporting period, the State Government obtains control over the grant when the grant eligibility criteria have been satisfied or the services or facilities under the grant agreement (if any) have been provided, which may coincide with the date of its receipt. This is because when the State Government satisfies grant eligibility criteria or provides services or facilities under any grant agreement, it has the capacity to benefit from the grant and can deny or regulate the access of others to it. Correspondingly, in this circumstance, the Commonwealth Government would recognise an expense at the same time.

29   In the case of multi-year grant agreements from a government to another level of government or a government department, the transferee government or government

department does not control the contributed assets, and therefore should not recognise revenues, until the transferor government has a present obligation that is binding. For example, the transferee government or government department does not gain control of assets under a multi-year public policy grant agreement until it has met conditions such as grant eligibility criteria or provided the services or facilities that make it eligible to receive a contribution. On this basis, under multi-year public policy agreements, income would be recognised only in relation to grants received or receivable under any grant agreement.

30   Control over assets acquired from involuntary non-reciprocal transfers, such as rates, taxes and fines, is obtained when the underlying transaction or other event giving rise to control of the future economic benefits occurs. For example, taxes are recognised when the underlying transaction or event that gives rise to the GGS's or whole of government's right to collect the tax occurs and can be measured reliably. In some cases an inability to reliably measure taxes when the underlying transactions or events occur means that they may need to be recognised at a later time. In most cases, taxes will be recognised in the reporting period in which the tax assessments are due to be issued or during which the tax collections are received. For this reason, the disclosure of policies adopted for recognising taxes will enhance the understandability and comparability of information relating to them. Where the transfers arise from a periodical charge, such as a land tax, a government obtains control over the assets on the day on which the government becomes entitled to levy the land tax. Control over assets acquired from local government rates would be obtained at the commencement of the rating period or, where earlier, upon receipt.

Taxes collected by government departments and parliamentary appropriations to government departments

Paragraphs 31 to 38 of this Standard apply only to government departments.

Taxes collected by government departments

31   It is unlikely that taxes, for example, income tax, will qualify as income of the agency responsible for their collection. This is because the agency responsible for collecting taxes does not normally control the future economic benefits embodied in tax collections (see AASB 1050). Taxes are recognised when the definition of, and recognition criteria for, income is met. Accordingly, taxes which are controlled by the tax collection agency and which satisfy the recognition criteria for income specified in paragraph 12 of this Standard qualify for recognition as income in the reporting period during which control is obtained. This means that taxes are treated in the same manner as described in paragraph 30.

Parliamentary appropriations to government departments

32   **Parliamentary appropriations over which a government department gains control during the reporting period shall be recognised as:**

   (a)   **income of that reporting period where the appropriation:**

      (i)   **satisfies the definition of income in the *Framework for the Preparation and Presentation of Financial Statements* (the *Framework*); and**

      (ii)   **satisfies the recognition criteria for income;**

   (b)   **a direct adjustment to equity where the appropriation satisfies the definition of a contribution by owners; or**

   (c)   **a liability of the government department where the appropriation:**

      (i)   **satisfies the definition of liabilities in the *Framework*; and**

      (ii)   **satisfies the recognition criteria for liabilities in the *Framework*.**

AASB

33 Parliamentary appropriations may be designated as recurrent appropriations, capital or works and services appropriations or other appropriations. Irrespective of the designation given to a parliamentary appropriation, its recognition as income, a contribution by owners or a liability requires an evaluation of the characteristics of the parliamentary appropriation by reference to the definitions of income, contributions by owners and liabilities. This ensures that the substance, rather than the form, of the parliamentary appropriation is reported.

Parliamentary appropriations as income

34 The parliamentary appropriation process currently adopted in some jurisdictions in Australia is such that government departments do not gain control of funds appropriated for their use until obligations are incurred or expenditures are made by the government department. In these jurisdictions, appropriations recognised as income are in the nature of a recovery of costs incurred for the acquisition of goods and services or for amounts otherwise expended. As such, a government department usually only controls amounts appropriated by parliament for its use during the reporting period where those amounts have been expended or are required to meet obligations incurred during that reporting period.

35 However, the nature of parliamentary appropriations, and the circumstances that give rise to a government department's control of such appropriations, can vary across different jurisdictions in Australia, and may vary for different types of appropriations within a particular jurisdiction. In addition, a government department's authority and ability to maintain separate bank accounts and to retain funds that have been appropriated for its use but that have not been expended during a reporting period can change over time. Similarly, the nature and content of appropriation legislation, the manner in which government departments' activities are funded, and the mechanisms by which parliament and the government ensure that the government departments' use of public funds is appropriate and consistent with government priorities as sanctioned by parliament, can change over time. These changes can affect a government department's ability to control amounts appropriated for its use. Accordingly, the extent to which amounts appropriated for a government department's use are recognised as income of a particular reporting period is determined by reference to the characteristics of the appropriation process and the circumstances in which the government department obtains control of appropriated amounts.

36 Where the nature of parliamentary appropriations is such that a government department's control over appropriations is not dependent on expenditure or the incurrence of obligations or the completion of agreed outputs, services or facilities, the government department's control of the appropriated amounts occurs at the earliest of:

(a)   the commencement of the period to which the appropriation applies;

(b)   the receipt of the appropriated funds; and

(c)   the date on which the government department's authority to expend appropriated funds becomes effective.

37 Where a government department controls amounts appropriated to it for transfer to other parties, those amounts give rise to assets and income when the government department gains control of those appropriations. Where a government department controls the appropriations and the conditions for transfer to beneficiaries are satisfied during the reporting period but the amounts have not been transferred as at the reporting date, the government department recognises a liability in respect of such amounts. Where amounts are to be transferred in future reporting periods and the conditions for transfer are also to be satisfied in future reporting periods, the government department does not recognise a liability as at the reporting date in respect of such amounts.

38 Parliamentary appropriations made to enable a tax collection agency to perform its services are income of that agency. This is because the agency has the authority to deploy the appropriated funds for the achievement of its objectives and, consequently, controls the assets arising from the appropriation.

Liabilities of government departments assumed by other entities

Paragraphs 39 to 43 of this Standard apply only to government departments.

39   A liability of a government department that is assumed by the government or other entity shall be accounted for as follows:

    (a)   on initial incurrence of the liability by the government department, the government department shall recognise a liability and an expense;

    (b)   on assumption of the liability by the government or other entity, the government department shall extinguish the liability and:

        (i)   when the assumption is not in the nature of a contribution by owners, the government department shall recognise income of an amount equivalent to the liability assumed; or

        (ii)   when the assumption of the liability is in the nature of a contribution by owners, the government department shall make a direct adjustment to equity of an amount equivalent to the liability assumed.

40   The obligation to make payments to employees in respect of long-service leave and other employee benefits may rest with the government, a central agency or other entity. However, the costs of long-service leave and other employee benefits are part of the cost of the goods and services provided by the government department for which those employees work. Employment contracts or employment arrangements may be such that a government or other entity, rather than the government department, directly incurs the obligation to settle liabilities that arise in respect of benefits of the government department's employees. Alternatively, it may be that the government department initially incurs the obligation to settle such liabilities, and the government or other entity then assumes that obligation.

41   A government or other entity may initially incur, and then settle, obligations in respect of the wages, salaries and other costs of the employees of a government department during the reporting period. Similarly, other expenses of operating the government department during the reporting period, such as building occupancy expenses, may be incurred and settled by the government or other entity. In such cases, the government department does not recognise a liability when the expenses are initially incurred. Rather, the government department recognises income equivalent to the fair value of the employee services or other assets it receives, and recognises expenses of the same amount to reflect that the economic benefits represented by those employee services or other benefits have been consumed by the government department. For employee services, this normally occurs when the services are provided, but in some instances the costs of these services forms part of the cost of acquiring an asset.

42   When an employee transfers from one government department to another government department, the liability in respect of employee benefits accrued up to the transfer date is usually transferred to the transferee government department. In such cases, the transferor government department may make a payment to the transferee government department for the employee's accrued benefits. When an employee transfers from one government department to another government department:

    (a)   the transferor government department extinguishes any liability for employee benefits recognised in respect of the employee, and recognises income equivalent to the liability extinguished. When a payment is made or is to be made by the transferor government department in consideration for the assumption of the liability by the transferee government department, the transferor government department extinguishes the liability and recognises a decrease in assets (cash) or an increase in liabilities (cash payable). When the payment is less than the total amount of the liability, the transferor government department recognises income equal to the amount of that shortfall; and

(b)   the transferee government department recognises an expense and a liability in respect of any present obligations to pay accrued employee benefits in the future that are assumed as a consequence of the transfer. When a payment is made or is to be made to the transferee government department in consideration for the assumption of the liability, the transferee government department recognises the liability assumed and an increase in assets (cash or cash receivable). When the payment is less than the total amount of the liability for employee entitlements assumed, the transferee government department recognises an expense equal to the amount of that shortfall.

43   As noted in paragraphs 39 to 41, a government may initially incur or subsequently assume all obligations to make payments to employees of a government department in respect of long-service leave and other employee benefits. In such cases, the transfer of employees between government departments will not give rise to the need for the transferee government department to recognise expenses and liabilities or for the transferor government department to extinguish liabilities and recognise income as outlined in paragraph 42.

Contributions of services

Paragraphs 44 to 47 of this Standard apply only to local governments, government departments, GGSs and whole of governments.

44   Contributions of services to local governments, government departments, GGSs and whole of governments shall be recognised as income when and only when:

(a)   the fair value of those services can be reliably measured; and

(b)   the services would have been purchased if they had not been donated.

45   Local governments, government departments, GGSs and whole of governments may receive contributions of goods or services free of charge or for nominal consideration by way of gift or donation. The assets and income recognised by the recipient in respect of such contributions, subject to the requirements of paragraph 12 of this Standard, are measured at the fair value of the goods or services received. This ensures that the operating statement reports the change in resources controlled by the recipient as a result of the operations for the reporting period, and that the statement of financial position reports the assets and liabilities of the recipient as at the reporting date.

46   Some donated services, while useful, may not be central to the delivery of the outputs of the local government, government department, GGS or whole of government. In these cases, it is unlikely that the recipient would purchase the services if they were not donated. Recognition of the fair value of those services as income and expenses is not relevant to assessments of the cost of services provided by, or the financial performance of, the recipient. Accordingly, this Standard requires that contributed services only be recognised when the services would be purchased if not donated and when their fair value can be measured reliably.

47   In some cases, the gaining of control over the assets that result from contributions and the consumption of the future economic benefits embodied in those assets will be simultaneous. For example, donated services give rise to income and an asset of the recipient and, simultaneously, an expense as the future economic benefits embodied in the asset are consumed. Therefore, the net effect of the contribution of services is the recognition of income and an expense. Such recognition is important if the operating statement is to reflect fully the cost of services provided during the reporting period and the sources and amounts of the entity's income. Such information is useful in assessing the cost efficiency of an entity's performance and the amounts and sources of likely future resource requirements.

Contributions by owners and distributions to owners of local governments, government departments and whole of governments

Paragraphs 48 to 53 of this Standard apply only to local governments, government departments and whole of governments.

48   **Contributions by owners shall be recognised as a direct adjustment to equity when the contributed assets qualify for recognition.**

49   **Distributions to owners shall be recognised as a direct adjustment to equity when the associated reduction in assets, rendering of services or increase in liabilities qualifies for recognition.**

50   It is important to distinguish contributions by owners from other contributions. It may be argued that contributions that are provided on the condition that they be expended on assets that increase the capacity of the entity to provide particular services should be classified as contributions of equity. However, such contributions would be contributions by owners, as defined in Appendix A to this Standard, only when the contributor establishes by way of the contribution a financial interest in the net assets of the entity that:

(a)   conveys entitlement both to a financial return on the contribution and to distributions of any excess of assets over liabilities in the event of the entity being wound up; and/or

(b)   can be sold, transferred or redeemed.

51   Contributions by owners are examples of non-reciprocal transfers. Examples of contributions by owners (and distributions to owners) are non-reciprocal transfers between a government department and the controlling government acting in its capacity as owner. Transactions with owners in their capacity as owners are not common in a local government context. A local government may on occasions receive contributions by owners, as defined in Appendix A to this Standard, such as investments in the capital of companies controlled by the governing body of the local government. Such contributions would need to be recognised as contributions of equity.

52   Contributions by owners can occur upon establishment of the entity or at a subsequent stage of the entity's existence. Contributions by owners can be in the form of cash, nonmonetary assets such as property, plant and equipment, or the provision of services. In some instances, the contribution may result from the conversion of the entity's liabilities into equity.

53   Reductions in equity as a result of distributions to owners (either dividends or returns of capital) can be in the form of a transfer of assets, a rendering of services or an increase in liabilities. Distributions from government departments to governments are made at the discretion of the government.

Restructure of administrative arrangements

Paragraphs 54 to 59 of this Standard apply only to government controlled not-for-profit entities and for-profit government departments.

54   **In relation to a *restructure of administrative arrangements*, a government controlled not-for-profit transferor entity or a for-profit government department transferor entity shall recognise distributions to owners and a government controlled not-for-profit transferee entity or a for-profit government department transferee entity shall recognise contributions by owners in respect of assets transferred.**

55   **In relation to a restructure of administrative arrangements, a government controlled not-for-profit transferor entity or a for-profit government department transferor entity shall recognise contributions by owners and a government controlled not-for-profit transferee entity or a for-profit government**

department transferee entity shall recognise distributions to owners in respect of liabilities transferred.

56 When both assets and liabilities are transferred as a consequence of a restructure of administrative arrangements, a government controlled not-for-profit transferor entity or a for-profit government department transferor entity and a government controlled not-for-profit transferee entity or a for-profit government department transferee entity shall recognise a net contribution by owners or distribution to owners, as applicable.

57 When activities are transferred as a consequence of a restructure of administrative arrangements, a government controlled not-for-profit transferee entity or a for-profit government department transferee entity shall disclose the expenses and income attributable to the transferred activities for the reporting period, showing separately those expenses and items of income recognised by the transferor during the reporting period. If disclosure of this information would be impracticable, that fact shall be disclosed, together with an explanation of why this is the case.

58 For each material transfer, the assets and liabilities transferred as a consequence of a restructure of administrative arrangements during the reporting period shall be disclosed by class, and the counterparty transferor/transferee entity shall be identified. With respect to transfers that are individually immaterial, the assets and liabilities transferred shall be disclosed on an aggregate basis.

59 The disclosures required by paragraph 58 will assist users to identify the assets and liabilities recognised or derecognised as a result of a restructure of administrative arrangements separately from other assets and liabilities and to identify the transferor/transferee entity.

Disclosure of contributions

Paragraphs 60 to 62 of this Standard apply only to local governments, government departments, GGSs and whole of governments.

60 The complete set of financial statements shall disclose, separately by way of note, the amounts and nature of:

(a) contributions recognised as income during the reporting period in respect of which expenditure in a manner specified by a transferor contributor had yet to be made as at the reporting date, details of those contributions and the conditions attaching to them;

(b) contributions recognised as income during the reporting period that were provided specifically for the provision of goods or services over a future period;

(c) contributions recognised as income during the reporting period that were obtained in respect of a future rating or taxing period identified by the local government, GGS or whole of government for the purpose of establishing a rate or tax;

(d) the nature of the amounts referred to in (a), (b) and (c) above and, in respect of (b) and (c) above, the periods to which they relate; and

(e) contributions recognised as income in a previous reporting period that were obtained in respect of the current reporting period.

61 Where a local government, government department, GGS or whole of government receives contributions on the condition that the related assets shall be expended in a particular manner or used over a particular period, and those conditions are undischarged in part or in full as at the reporting date, the entity will have a strong fiduciary responsibility in relation to the deployment of those contributed assets. As noted in paragraph 20, this fiduciary responsibility does not constitute a liability. However, information about the contributions, including the conditions, is relevant to

users of the complete set of financial statements, particularly in assessing performance and the discharge of accountability obligations. Accordingly, this Standard requires disclosure of those conditions where they are yet to be discharged, in part or in full, as at the reporting date. In addition, disclosure of contributions recognised as income in a previous reporting period that were provided specifically in respect of the current reporting period will provide information relevant to users' assessments of the entity's recovery of the cost of goods and services it has provided during the current reporting period.

62   The complete set of financial statements shall disclose separately the fair value of goods and services received free of charge, or for nominal consideration, that are recognised during the reporting period.

Additional government department disclosures

Paragraph 63 of this Standard applies only to government departments.

63   The complete set of financial statements of a government department shall disclose separately:

   (a)   appropriations, by class; and

   (b)   liabilities that were assumed during the reporting period by the government or other entity.

Compliance with parliamentary appropriations and other externally-imposed requirements

Paragraphs 64 to 68 of this Standard apply only to government departments.

64   The complete set of financial statements of a government department shall disclose separately:

   (a)   a summary of the recurrent, capital or other major categories of appropriations, disclosing separately:

   (i)   the original amounts appropriated for the reporting period; and

   (ii)   the total amounts appropriated for the reporting period;

   (b)   amounts authorised other than by way of appropriation and advanced separately by the Treasurer, other minister or other legislative authority for the reporting period;

   (c)   the expenditures for the reporting period in respect of each of the items disclosed in (a) and (b) above;

   (d)   the reasons for any material variances between the amounts appropriated or otherwise authorised and the associated expenditures for the reporting period; and

   (e)   the nature and probable financial effect of any non-compliance by the government department with externally-imposed requirements for the reporting period, not already disclosed by virtue of (d) above, and that are relevant to assessments of the government department's performance, financial position or financing and investing activities.

65   The information disclosed about compliance with externally-imposed requirements shall be in a form that is relevant to users of that information, and that reflects the following:

   (a)   the operating characteristics of the government department;

   (b)   the structure of the appropriations;

   (c)   any other requirements that are imposed externally on the government department; and

   (d)   the general purpose nature of the complete set of financial statements.

66   For the purposes of economic decision making, including assessments of accountability, this Standard requires that users of the complete set of financial statements be provided with information about the amounts appropriated or otherwise authorised for a government department's use, and whether the government department's expenditures were as authorised. When spending limits imposed by parliamentary appropriation or other authorisation have not been complied with, information regarding the amount of, and reasons for, the non-compliance is relevant for assessing the performance of management, the likely consequences of non-compliance, and the ability of the government department to continue to provide services at a similar or different level in the future.

67   Broad summaries of the major categories of appropriations and associated expenditures, rather than detailed reporting of appropriations line-item by line-item for each activity, is sufficient for most users of a government department's complete set of financial statements. Determining the level of detail and the structure of the summarised information is a matter of judgement. The detailed information about compliance with spending mandates required by certain users should be provided in special purpose financial statements.

68   In addition to requirements to comply with expenditure limits imposed by parliamentary appropriations, government departments are subject to a range of legislative, regulatory and other externally-imposed requirements governing their operations. Knowledge of non-compliance with such requirements is relevant for accountability purposes and may affect users' assessments of the government department's performance and likely future operations. It may also influence decisions about resources to be allocated to that government department in the future.

APPENDIX A
DEFINED TERMS

This Appendix is an integral part of AASB 1004.

Contributions	Non-reciprocal transfers to the entity.
Contributions by owners	Future economic benefits that have been contributed to the entity by parties external to the entity, other than those which result in liabilities of the entity, that give rise to a financial interest in the net assets of the entity which:
	(a) conveys entitlement both to distributions of future economic benefits by the entity during its life, such distributions being at the discretion of the ownership group or its representatives, and to distributions of any excess of assets over liabilities in the event of the entity being wound up; and/or
	(b) can be sold, transferred or redeemed.
Non-reciprocal transfer	A transfer in which the entity receives assets or services or has liabilities extinguished without directly giving approximately equal value in exchange to the other party or parties to the transfer.
Restructure of administrative arrangements	The reallocation or reorganisation of assets, liabilities, activities and responsibilities amongst the entities that the government controls that occurs as a consequence of a rearrangement in the way in which activities and responsibilities as prescribed under legislation or other authority are allocated between the government's controlled entities.
	The scope of the requirements relating to restructures of administrative arrangements is limited to the transfer of a business (as defined in AASB 3 *Business Combinations*). The requirements do not apply to, for example, a transfer of an individual asset or a group of assets that is not a business.

APPENDIX B
COMPARISON OF AASB 1004 WITH AAS 27, AAS 29 AND AAS 31

This Appendix accompanies, but is not part of, AASB 1004.

Paragraphs 19 to 68 of this Standard broadly reproduce the requirements relating to contributions contained in AAS 27 *Financial Reporting by Local Governments*, AAS 29 *Financial Reporting by Government Departments* and AAS 31 *Financial Reporting by Governments*, with some exceptions. The more significant exceptions include:

(a)   requirements in this Standard relating to recognition of contributions other than contributions by owners (paragraphs 19 to 30), contributions of services (paragraphs 44 to 47) and disclosure of contributions (paragraphs 60 to 62) have been extended to apply to General Government Sectors (GGSs);

(b)   requirements in this Standard relating to recognition of non-reciprocal transfers (paragraph 30), including material from AAS 31 (paragraph 15.2.1) have been extended beyond whole of governments to local governments, government departments and GGSs;

(c)   requirements in this Standard relating to recognition and disclosure of contributions of services (paragraphs 44 to 47, and 62) have been extended beyond government departments to local governments, government departments, GGSs and whole of governments;

(d)   requirements in this Standard relating to the disclosure of contributions (paragraph 60) are more detailed than those that applied to government departments under AAS 29 and governments under AAS 31;

(e)   guidance in this Standard relating to contributions by owners and distributions to owners of local governments, government departments and whole of governments (paragraphs 48 to 53) has been amended to make it consistent with Interpretation 1038 *Contributions by Owners Made to Wholly-Owned Public Sector Entities*; and

(f)   requirements in this Standard relating to restructures of administrative arrangements (paragraphs 54 to 59) require that transfers of resources resulting from such restructures are to be treated as movements in owner's equity by government controlled not-for-profit entities and for-profit government departments that are transferees or transferors. This contrasts with the treatment under superseded AAS 29 and Interpretation 1038 that would have required treatment of the resource transfers as revenues or expenses in some circumstances. This Standard also includes a definition of 'restructure of administrative arrangements" (Appendix A).

The following table provides source references to paragraphs 19 – 68 of this Standard, most of which were derived from AASs 27, 29 and 31. It is provided to facilitate an understanding of, and assist in the application of, the requirements in this Standard.

Paragraphs in AASB 1004	Relevant source paragraphs in AASs 27, 29 and 31
19, 20, first sentence 21	60, 64-65 of AAS 27, 10.12.1 – 10.12.3 of AAS 29 and 14.1.1 – 14.1.3 of AAS 31
Second sentence of 21	67 of AAS 27 and 10.12.4 of AAS 29
22 – 23	61 of AAS 27, 10.12.2 and 10.12.4 of AAS 29 and 14.1.8 and 14.1.9 of AAS 31
24	62 of AAS 27 and 14.1.10 of AAS 31
25	14.1.11 of AAS 31
26	69 of AAS 27, 10.12.7 of AAS 29 and 14.1.4 of AAS 31
27	10.5.5 of AAS 29

(Continued)

(Continued)

Paragraphs in AASB 1004	Relevant source paragraphs in AASs 27, 29 and 31
28 – 29	10.12.5 of AAS 29 and 14.1.6 and 14.1.7 of AAS 31
30	68 of AAS 27, 10.5.10 of AAS 29 and 14.1.5 and 15.2.1 of AAS 31
31	10.5.9 of AAS 29
32	10.5 of AAS 29
33	10.5.1 of AAS 29
34 – 36	10.5.6 and 10.5.7 of AAS 29
37	10.5.17 of AAS 29
38	10.5.10 of AAS 29
39 – 43	8.2, 8.2.1 and 8.2.3 – 8.2.5 of AAS 29
44	10.12 of AAS 29
45	10.12.6 of AAS 29
46	10.12.9 of AAS 29
47	10.12.8 of AAS 29
48 – 53	63 and 70 of AAS 27, 11.1 – 11.2.4 of AAS 29 and 14.1.12 and 14.1.13 of AAS 31
54 – 59	7.4, 7.4.2 and 10.6 – 10.9.3 of AAS 29
60 – 61	92 and 93 of AAS 27 and 12.4 and 12.4.1 of AAS 29
62	12.2(d) of AAS 29
63	12.2(b) and (c) of AAS 29
64	12.6 of AAS 29
65	12.6.3 of AAS 29
66	12.6.2 of AAS 29
67	12.6.3 of AAS 29
68	12.6.4 of AAS 29

BASIS FOR CONCLUSIONS

This Basis for Conclusions accompanies, but is not part of, AASB 1004.

Introduction

BC1   This Basis for Conclusions summarises the Board's considerations in revising AASB 1004 *Contributions* in the context of the Board's short-term review of the requirements in AAS 27 *Financial Reporting by Local Governments*, AAS 29 *Financial Reporting by Government Departments* and AAS 31 *Financial Reporting by Governments*.

Background

BC2   The Board considered it timely to review the requirements in AASs 27, 29 and 31, in particular to:

(a)   review the extent to which local governments, government departments and governments should continue to be subject to requirements that differ from requirements applicable to other not-for-profit entities and for-profit entities contained in Australian Accounting Standards. The Board concluded that differences should be removed, where appropriate and timely, to improve the overall quality of financial reporting;

(b) bring requirements applicable to local governments, government departments and governments up-to-date with contemporary accounting thought;

(c) consider the implications of the outcomes of its project on the harmonisation of Generally Accepted Accounting Principles (GAAP) and Government Finance Statistics (GFS), in particular, on the requirements in AAS 31;

(d) decide whether the encouragements in AASs 27, 29 and 31 should be made mandatory or removed; and

(e) remove uncertainty in the application of cross-references to other Australian Accounting Standards and the override provisions in AASs 27, 29 and 31 that made the requirements in AASs 27, 29 and 31 take precedence over other requirements.

BC3 The Board considered the following alternative mechanisms for implementing the approach of updating and improving the requirements for local governments, government departments and governments:

(a) review the requirements in AASs 27, 29 and 31 and, where appropriate:

(i) amend other Australian Accounting Standards to pick up any issues that are addressed in AASs 27, 29 and 31 that are not adequately addressed in the latest Australian Accounting Standards and have them apply to local governments, government departments and governments; or

(ii) create public sector specific topic-based Standards;

and consequently withdraw AASs 27, 29 and 31; or

(b) review AASs 27, 29 and 31 and re-issue them in light of the latest Australian Accounting Standards, retaining/amending where necessary any issues that are addressed in AASs 27, 29 and 31 that are not adequately addressed in the latest Australian Accounting Standards.

BC4 The Board chose alternative (a) given the improvements in the quality of financial reporting by local governments, government departments and governments since AASs 27, 29 and 31 were first issued.

BC5 Where the Board identified that the material in AASs 27, 29 and 31 could be improved within time and resource constraints, improvements have been made. Much of the material in AASs 27, 29 and 31 has been retained substantively unamended. Improvements will be progressed in due course in line with the AASB's Public Sector Policy Paper *Australian Accounting Standards and Public Sector Entities*.

BC6 The first stage of the short-term review of the requirements in AASs 27, 29 and 31 was the preparation of a paragraph-by-paragraph analysis of each of AASs 27, 29 and 31, listing each paragraph of each Standard alongside corresponding Standards or other pronouncements that would apply to local governments, government departments or governments in the absence of AASs 27, 29 and 31. The Board's conclusions and rationale for the treatment of each paragraph in the context of the review were also provided in the analysis. The Board's primary focus was on dealing with the requirements from the three Standards in such a way as to not leave a vacuum.

BC7 Each paragraph from AASs 27, 29 and 31 was classified as being:

(a) no longer needed or adequately dealt with in other Standards;

(b) more appropriately dealt with in other Standards; or

(c) not adequately and/or appropriately dealt with in other Standards and therefore should be retained or improved and incorporated into other Standards.

The paragraph-by-paragraph analyses considered by the AASB in developing the Exposure Draft ED 156 *Proposals Arising from the Short-term Review of the*

Requirements in AAS 27, AAS 29 and AAS 31 that gave rise to this Standard are available on the AASB website. They support, but do not form part of, this Basis for Conclusions.

BC8   In reviewing the paragraphs, the Board noted that some material in AASs 27, 29 and 31 would, under the current style of writing Standards, be located in a separate Basis for Conclusions. Given the short-term nature of the review of AASs 27, 29 and 31, the Board concluded that explanations of technical issues that both originated in and are being relocated from AASs 27, 29 and 31 should, when appropriate, be located in the body of the Standard to which they are relocated.

BC9   The Board decided not to retain the illustrative general purpose financial reports provided in AASs 27, 29 and 31, because their purpose, which was to provide an educational tool in the initial stages of accrual reporting by local governments, government departments and governments is no longer needed.

BC10 The remainder of this Basis for Conclusions focuses on issues specific to contributions.

Contributions

General approach

BC11 The Board decided to broadly retain the material on contributions from AASs 27, 29 and 31 and locate it in separate sections within AASB 1004 because it was not adequately covered in existing Australian Accounting Standards.

BC12 The Board concluded that, in the short term, minimal changes should be made to the content of the material. The Board considered that it is appropriate to review the requirements and guidance for contributions as part of a longer-term project as outlined in the AASB's Public Sector Policy Paper. A review by the Board of non-exchange income, which will incorporate a review of contributions, is in progress at the time of revision of this Standard.

BC13 The Board considered two options for relocating the requirements on contributions into AASB 1004:

(a)   merging the AASs 27, 29 and 31 paragraphs into the then existing AASB 1004 requirements; or

(b)   adding the AASs 27, 29 and 31 paragraphs into the existing AASB 1004 as separate sections.

The paragraphs in AASs 27, 29 and 31 containing guidance about contributions were very detailed and contained a large amount of commentary whereas the then existing guidance in AASB 1004 was significantly less detailed. The Board concluded that merging the requirements in AASs 27, 29 and 31 with the AASB 1004 requirements would, in effect, require the redrafting of the entire Standard, which is beyond the scope of this project. The integration approach was also considered more likely to raise controversial revenue recognition issues for all not-for-profit entities that, as noted in paragraph BC12, the Board will deal with as a separate longer-term project applicable to a broader range of entities.

BC14 The Board also considered whether the guidance from AASs 27, 29 and 31 should be merged into a single set of generic requirements or expressed separately for local governments, government departments or governments. The Board concluded that the three sets of guidance from AASs 27, 29 and 31 were sufficiently similar to be merged to form one set of requirements – noting that such an approach results in some changes for some entities. One area where this occurs is the disclosure of contributions, where government departments and governments are now required to make disclosures not previously required, because AAS 27 was more onerous than AASs 29 and 31.

BC15 The Board decided to include specific references to the application of this Standard to General Government Sectors (GGSs) to support/clarify the AASB 1049 *Financial Reporting of General Government Sectors by Governments* requirement for GGSs to adopt other Australian Accounting Standards, including this Standard. As this

Standard has many parts, applicable to different groups of entities, the Board considered it would aid users to explicitly refer to GGSs in paragraph 1(d) and throughout this Standard.

BC16 In addition, the Board decided to extend the application of the requirements relating to 'contributions of services' to apply beyond government departments to local governments, GGSs and whole of governments, for consistency across these types of entities.

BC17 Because the guidance from AASs 27, 29 and 31 partly overlapped with the guidance in the superseded AASB 1004, the Board amended the requirements to reduce duplication.

BC18 The Board considered whether the paragraphs of AAS 29 that address the accounting for parliamentary appropriations, which are only applicable to government departments, should be incorporated into this Standard as a separate section. The Board noted the view that the requirements are no longer needed given the nature of current arrangements between governments and government departments for parliamentary appropriations compared with past arrangements and government departments' familiarity with accrual accounting. However, the Board concluded that the paragraphs should be retained, in keeping with Board's short-term intention of retaining the guidance from AASs 27, 29 and 31 where there are no comparable requirements in existing Australian Accounting Standards and thereby avoid creating a vacuum.

BC19 Paragraph 15.2.1 of AAS 31 dealt with the disclosure of policies adopted for recognising tax revenues. Given the nature of the commentary, the Board concluded that it would be most logical to locate the contents of this paragraph in paragraph 30 of this Standard within the area that relates to recognition of 'contributions, other than contributions by owners, by local governments, government departments, GGSs or whole of governments' and within the section 'control over assets' in a paragraph that discusses control over assets acquired from involuntary non-reciprocal transfers, such as rates, taxes and fines. In doing this, the Board decided to extend the requirements beyond whole of governments to local governments, government departments and GGSs.

Liabilities assumed by other entities

BC20 The Board decided to substantially retain the guidance in AAS 29 relating to the treatment of liabilities assumed by other entities in the financial statements of a government department. The Board concluded that, although the superseded AASB 1004 specified requirements for liabilities that are forgiven, it did not explicitly deal with liabilities that are assumed by other entities.

BC21 The Board considered whether to align the requirements in paragraphs 8.2, 8.2.1 and 8.2.3-8.2.5 of AAS 29 for derecognition of liabilities with the corresponding requirements in AASB 139 *Financial Instruments: Recognition and Measurement*. The Board noted that the AAS 29 requirements, which reflected a symmetrical accounting approach, may not be consistent with the criteria for derecognition of a liability in AASB 139, which does not necessarily result in symmetry and refers to liabilities arising from contracts. Given the relationship between an entity assuming a government department's liability (such as the controlling government) and the government department, the Board concluded that the symmetrical accounting adopted in AAS 29 is appropriate for derecognition of liabilities.

Government department disclosures relating to revenue

BC22 The Board decided that it would be most logical to incorporate the requirements from paragraphs 12.2(b)-(d) of AAS 29 relating to disclosure requirements for certain revenue items (that is, appropriations by class; liabilities that were assumed during the reporting period by the government or other entity; and the fair value of goods and services received free of charge, or for nominal consideration, and recognised during the reporting period) into this Standard. This is because they are disclosures of items of revenue that, for the purpose of the short-term review, are considered to be sufficiently related to the scope of the superseded AASB 1004.

BC23 The Board decided to limit the requirements in paragraphs 12.2(b) and (c) of AAS 29 to government departments, in keeping with its approach of retaining AASs 27, 29 and 31 requirements in the short term. In keeping with the Board's decision to extend the application of the section on 'contribution of services' to apply beyond government departments to local governments, GGSs and whole of governments (see paragraph BC16), the Board concluded that the disclosure requirements in paragraph 12.2(d) of AAS 29 relating to revenue disclosures about contributions of services should also be extended to apply to local governments, GGSs and whole of governments. Furthermore, the Board concluded that the paragraph in question should be amended to refer to recognised contributions of services to be consistent with the requirements under which not all contributions received would be required to be recognised.

Restructures of administrative arrangements

BC24 The Board considered it timely to amend the requirements in paragraphs 7.4, 7.4.2 and 10.6-10.9.3 of AAS 29 for restructures of administrative arrangements as part of the short-term review of AAS 29 and in light of the existing definition of contributions by owners that is contained in this Standard. The Board decided to define restructures of administrative arrangements and to specify that they are in the nature of transactions with owners in their capacity as owners to be recognised on a net basis. In particular, the Board concluded that a transfer of net assets arising as a consequence of a restructure of administrative arrangements is faithfully represented as a distribution to owners by the transferor and a contribution by owners by the transferee. The Board also noted that this would result in greater consistency in accounting for restructures of administrative arrangements. The Board concluded that this approach is preferable to the superseded approach whereby transfers need to be designated as contributions by owners at the time of the transfer to be treated as such. The Board noted that this would result in a significant change in the current AAS 29 requirements as the possibility of treating a transfer as a revenue/expense item would no longer be available, and would give rise to amendments to Interpretation 1038 *Contributions by Owners Made to Wholly-Owned Public Sector Entities* to make it consistent with this Standard. Consistent with the short-term nature of the review of AASs 27, 29 and 31, the Board intends making amendments to Interpretation 1038 to make it consistent with this Standard. In the longer term, the Board intends to undertake a fundamental review of Interpretation 1038.

BC25 The Board concluded that the effect of the requirements should be expanded beyond government departments to include all government controlled not-for-profit public sector entities and for-profit government departments, noting that this would increase the consistency with the scope of Interpretation 1038 which applies to all wholly-owned public sector entities that prepare general purpose financial statements, not just government departments. This will assist in harmonising requirements and guidance in relation to contributions by owners. It is not intended that the amended requirements for restructures of administrative arrangements necessarily apply in analogous circumstances. For example, it is not intended that the amended requirements apply in the accounting for restructures of commonly-controlled private sector entities.

BC26 Although assets and/or liabilities assumed by another entity as a consequence of a restructure of administrative arrangements were not explicitly dealt with in the superseded AASB 1004, the Board concluded that this Standard is an appropriate location for this material as it is the Standard that is best suited to dealing with contributions, including contributions by owners, to not-for-profit reporting entities and for-profit government departments.

BC27 In addition, in accordance with its decision to issue AASB 2005-6 *Amendments to Australian Accounting Standards [AASB 3]*, the Board concluded that AASB 3 *Business Combinations* is not an appropriate Standard in which to locate specific requirements relating to restructures of administrative arrangements because business combinations involving entities or businesses under common control are now excluded from the scope of AASB 3. However, a cross-reference from AASB 3 to AASB 1004 is provided to assist in understanding the relationship between the two Standards.

BC28 The Board also concluded that it is not necessary at this time to explicitly address the measurement basis to be adopted for transferred assets and liabilities due to a restructure of administrative arrangements. An asset acquired by a government controlled not-for-profit entity or a for-profit government department as a consequence of a restructure of administrative arrangements is considered to be a contribution by owners. Not specifying the measurement basis is consistent with Interpretation 1038, which also does not specify the measurement basis to be adopted with respect to contributions by owners or distributions to owners. In addition, AASB 3 does not address the measurement issue for a restructure of entities under common control. The Board also noted that measurement requirements in AASB 116 *Property, Plant and Equipment* (including paragraph Aus15.1) do not apply to assets transferred under a restructure of administrative arrangements because they are acquired by the transferee as part of a business. The Board acknowledges that, as the proposed amendments do not specify the measurement basis to be adopted, assets and liabilities transferred in the course of a restructure of administrative arrangements could be measured at fair value or book value.

BC29 The Board noted that the scope of the requirements relating to restructures of administrative arrangements is limited to the transfer of a business (as defined in AASB 3). The Board does not intend the requirements to apply where, for example, an individual asset or a group of assets that are not a business are transferred, noting that transfers of an individual asset and a group of assets are scoped out by the definition of a business in AASB 3.

Compliance with parliamentary appropriations and other externally-imposed requirements by government departments

BC30 The Board noted that issues relating to compliance with parliamentary appropriations and other externally-imposed requirements are important for government accountability. Accordingly, the Board concluded that the requirements in paragraphs 12.6 and 12.6.2-12.6.4 of AAS 29 for disclosure of compliance with parliamentary appropriations and other externally imposed requirements should be retained.

BC31 The Board concluded that the requirements for the disclosure by government departments of compliance with parliamentary appropriations and other externally-imposed requirements are sufficiently related to the topic of contributions to be incorporated into this Standard.

BC32 Consistent with the short-term nature of the project, the requirements are to be limited to government departments rather than applying them more broadly to not-for-profit public sector entities. In due course, the Board will consider extending the application of the requirements.

BC33 The Board concluded that it is appropriate to not retain paragraph 12.6.1 of AAS 29, which explains the meaning of parliamentary appropriations, as it is no longer necessary.

AASB 1023
General Insurance Contracts

(Compiled December 2017)

For-profit (FP) entities

This compiled Standard applies to annual reporting periods beginning on or after 1 January 2018 but before 1 January 2019. Earlier application is permitted for annual reporting periods beginning after 24 July 2014 but before 1 January 2018. It incorporates relevant amendments made up to and including 12 December 2017.

Not-for-profit (NFP) entities – early application only

This compiled Standard does not apply mandatorily to NFP entities. However, early application is permitted for annual reporting periods beginning after 24 July 2014 but before 1 January 2019.

Prepared on 20 May 2018 by the staff of the Australian Accounting Standards Board.

Compilation no. 14

Compilation date: 31 December 2017

This note is not part of Accounting Standard AASB 1023.

The following unincorporated amendments are not included in this compiled Standard.

- AASB 17 *Insurance Contracts* — Appendix D sets out the amendments to other Standards that are a consequence of the AASB issuing AASB 17 *Insurance Contracts*. This Standard is applicable from 1 January 2021. Earlier application is permitted, but entities must apply AASB 9 *Financial Instruments* and AASB 15 *Revenue from Contracts with Customers* first.

- AASB 16 *Leases* — Appendix D sets out the amendments to other Standards that are a consequence of the AASB issuing this Standard. It is applicable from 1 January 2019. Earlier application is permitted, but entities must apply AASB 15 *Revenue from Contracts with Customers* before applying this Standard.

- AASB 2016-7 *Amendments to Australian Accounting Standards — Deferral of AASB 15 for Not-for-Profit Entities*. This Standard defers the consequential amendments that were originally set out in AASB 2014-5 *Amendments to Australian Accounting Standards arising from AASB 15,* by restating the effective date of the amendments set out in AASB 2015-8 *Amendments to Australian Accounting Standards* for not-for-profit entities. This Standard defers the application of AASB 15 to 1 January 2019. Earlier application is permitted provided AASB 1058 is also applied to the same period.

Entities early-adopting any amendments with later application dates will need to refer to the amending Standards that have not yet been incorporated into compilations. The above mentioned unincorporated amendments may be located on the AASB website at www.aasb.gov.au or on the Federal Register of Legislation website at www.legislation.gov.au.

CONTENTS

AASB 1023 *GENERAL INSURANCE CONTRACTS*

Australian Accounting Standard AASB 1023 *General Insurance Contracts* (as amended) is set out in paragraphs 1.1 – 19.2 and the Appendix. All the paragraphs have equal authority. Paragraphs in **bold type** state the main principles. Terms defined in this Standard are in *italics* the first time they appear in the Standard. AASB 1023 is to be read in the context of other Australian Accounting Standards including AASB 1048 *Interpretation of Standards*, which identifies the Australian Accounting Interpretations. In the absence of explicit guidance, AASB 108 *Accounting Policies, Changes in Accounting Estimates and Errors* provides a basis for selecting and applying accounting policies.

COMPARISON WITH IFRS 4

AASB 1023 and IFRS 4

AASB 1023 *General Insurance Contracts* as amended incorporates the limited improvements to accounting for insurance contracts required by IFRS 4 *Insurance Contracts*.

General insurers applying this Standard and Australian equivalents to IFRSs will be compliant with IFRSs.

IFRS 4 is being implemented in Australia using three Accounting Standards:

(a)   AASB 4 *Insurance Contracts* (the Australian equivalent to IFRS 4), which applies to fixed-fee service contracts that meet the definition of an insurance contract;

(b)   AASB 1023, which applies to general insurance contracts; and

(c)   AASB 1038 *Life Insurance Contracts*, which applies to life insurance contracts.

IFRS 4 applies to all insurance contracts and financial instruments with discretionary participation features, whereas AASB 1023 only applies to general insurance contracts as well as certain aspects of accounting for assets that back general insurance liabilities. Whereas IFRS 4 only includes limited improvements to accounting for insurance contracts and disclosure requirements, AASB 1023 addresses all aspects of the recognition, measurement and disclosure of general insurance contracts.

IFRS 4 allows insurers to use a practice described as "shadow accounting". The revised AASB 1023 does not allow shadow accounting.

ACCOUNTING STANDARD AASB 1023

The Australian Accounting Standards Board made Accounting Standard AASB 1023 *General Insurance Contracts* under section 334 of the *Corporations Act 2001* on 15 July 2004.

This compiled version of AASB 1023 applies to annual reporting periods beginning on or after 1 January 2018 but before 1 January 2019 for for-profit entities. It incorporates relevant amendments contained in other AASB Standards made by the AASB and other decisions of the AASB up to and including 12 December 2017 (see Compilation Details).

ACCOUNTING STANDARD AASB 1023
GENERAL INSURANCE CONTRACTS

Application

1.1   This Standard applies to:

  (a)   each entity that is required to prepare financial reports in accordance with Part 2M.3 of the Corporations Act and that is a reporting entity;

  (b)   general purpose financial statements of each other reporting entity; and

  (c)   financial statements that are, or are held out to be, general purpose financial statements.

1.2   This Standard applies to annual reporting periods beginning on or after 1 January 2005.

[Note: For application dates of paragraphs changed or added by an amending Standard, see Compilation Details.]

1.3   This Standard shall not be applied to annual reporting periods beginning before 1 January 2005.

1.4   [Deleted by the AASB]

1.4.1   [Deleted by the AASB]

1.4.2   For the purposes of AASB 134 *Interim Financial Reporting*, the determination of the *outstanding claims liability* does not necessarily require a full actuarial valuation. In accordance with AASB 134, the outstanding claims liability would need to be determined on a reliable basis, would be based on reasonable estimates, would include a full review of all assumptions, and would not be materially different from the outstanding claims liability determined by a full actuarial valuation.

1.5   When applicable, this Standard supersedes:

   (a)   **Accounting Standard AASB 1023** *Financial Reporting of General Insurance Activities* **as approved by notice published in the** *Commonwealth of Australia Gazette* **No S 415, 6 November 1996; and**

   (b)   **AAS 26** *Financial Reporting of General Insurance Activities* **issued in November 1996.**

1.6   Both AASB 1023 (issued in November 1996) and AAS 26 remain applicable until superseded by this Standard.

1.7   Notice of this Standard was published in the *Commonwealth of Australia Gazette* No S 294, 22 July 2004.

Scope

General insurance contracts

2.1   **This Standard applies to:**

   (a)   **general insurance contracts (including** *general reinsurance contracts*) **that a general insurer issues and to general reinsurance contracts that it holds;**

   (b)   **certain assets backing general insurance liabilities;**

   (c)   *financial liabilities* **and** *financial assets* **that arise under** *non-insurance contracts*; **and**

   (d)   **certain assets backing financial liabilities that arise under non-insurance contracts.**

2.1.1   There are various types of *insurance contract*. This Standard deals with general insurance contracts (including general reinsurance contracts). General insurance contracts are defined as insurance contracts that are not *life insurance contracts*.

2.1.2   This Standard applies to general insurance contracts issued by Registered Health Benefits Organisations (RHBOs) registered under the *National Health Act 1953*. RHBOs apply this Standard to contracts that meet the definition of a general insurance contract and to certain assets backing general insurance liabilities.

2.1.3   For ease of reference, this Standard describes any entity that issues an insurance contract as an *insurer*, whether or not the issuer is regarded as an insurer for legal, regulatory or supervisory purposes.

2.1.4   A *reinsurance contract* is a type of insurance contract. Accordingly, all references in this Standard to insurance contracts also apply to reinsurance contracts.

2.1.5   *Weather derivatives* that meet the definition of a general insurance contract under this Standard are treated under this Standard. A contract that requires payment based on climatic, geological or other physical variables only where there is an adverse effect on the contract holder is a weather derivative that is an insurance contract. To meet the definition of a general insurance contract, the physical variable specified in the contract will be specific to a party to the contract.

Transactions outside the scope of this Standard

2.2   This Standard does not apply to:

(a)   life insurance contracts (see AASB 1038 *Life Insurance Contracts*);

(b)   product warranties issued directly by a manufacturer, dealer or retailer (see AASB 15 *Revenue from Contracts with Customers* and AASB 137 *Provisions, Contingent Liabilities and Contingent Assets*);

(c)   employers' assets and liabilities under employee benefit plans (see AASB 119 *Employee Benefits* and AASB 2 *Share-based Payment*) and retirement benefit obligations reported by defined benefit retirement plans (see AASB 1056 *Superannuation Entities*);

(d)   contingent consideration payable or receivable in a business combination (see AASB 3 *Business Combinations*);

(e)   contractual rights or contractual obligations that are contingent on the future use of, or right to use, a non-financial item (for example, some license fees, royalties, contingent lease payments and similar items), as well as a lessee's residual value guarantee embedded in a finance lease (see AASB 15, AASB 117 *Leases* and AASB 138 *Intangible Assets*);

(f)   *financial guarantee contracts* unless the issuer has previously asserted explicitly that it regards such contracts as insurance contracts and has used accounting applicable to insurance contracts, in which case the issuer may elect to apply either AASB 9 *Financial Instruments*, AASB 132 *Financial Instruments: Presentation* and AASB 7 *Financial Instruments: Disclosures* or this Standard to such financial guarantee contracts. The issuer may make that election contract by contract, but the election for each contract is irrevocable;

(g)   *direct insurance contracts* that the entity holds (that is direct insurance contracts in which the entity is a *policyholder*). However, a *cedant* shall apply this Standard to reinsurance contracts that it holds; and

(h)   fixed-fee service contracts, that meet the definition of an insurance contract, if the level of service depends on an uncertain event, for example maintenance contracts or roadside assistance contracts (see AASB 4 *Insurance Contracts*).

Embedded derivatives

2.3.1   AASB 9 *Financial Instruments* requires hybrid contracts that contain financial asset hosts to be classified and measured in their entirety in accordance with the requirements in paragraphs 4.1.1-4.1.5 of that Standard. However, AASB 9 requires an entity to separate some embedded derivatives from their financial liability hosts, measure them at *fair value* and include changes in their fair value in the statement of comprehensive income. AASB 9 applies to derivatives embedded in a general insurance contract unless the embedded derivative is itself a general insurance contract.

2.3.2   As an exception to the requirement in AASB 9, an insurer need not separate, and measure at fair value, a policyholder's option to surrender an insurance contract for a fixed amount (or for an amount based on a fixed amount and an interest rate) even if the exercise price differs from the carrying amount of the host *insurance liability*. However, the requirement in AASB 9 applies to a put option or cash surrender option embedded in an insurance contract if the surrender value varies in response to the change in a financial variable (such as an equity or commodity price or index), or a non-financial variable that is not specific to a party to the contract. Furthermore, that requirement also applies if the holder's ability to exercise a put option or cash surrender option is triggered by a change in such a variable (for example, a put option that can be exercised if a stock market index reaches a specified level).

Deposit components

2.4.1 Some general insurance contracts contain both an insurance component and a *deposit component*. In some cases, an insurer is required or permitted to *unbundle* those components.

    (a)   Unbundling is required if both the following conditions are met:

        (i)   the insurer can measure the deposit component (including any embedded surrender options) separately (that is, without considering the insurance component); and

        (ii)   the insurer's accounting policies do not otherwise require it to recognise all obligations and rights arising from the deposit component.

    (b)   Unbundling is permitted, but not required, if the insurer can measure the deposit component separately as in paragraph 2.4.1(a)(i) but its accounting policies require it to recognise all obligations and rights arising from the deposit component, regardless of the basis used to measure those rights and obligations.

    (c)   Unbundling is prohibited if an insurer cannot measure the deposit component separately as in paragraph 2.4.1(a)(i).

2.4.2 The following is an example of a case when an insurer's accounting policies do not require it to recognise all obligations arising from a deposit component. A cedant receives compensation for losses from a *reinsurer*, but the contract obliges the cedant to repay the compensation in future years. That obligation arises from a deposit component. If the cedant's accounting policies would otherwise permit it to recognise the compensation as income without recognising the resulting obligation, unbundling is required.

2.4.3 A general insurer, in considering the need to unbundle the deposit component of the general insurance contract, would consider all expected cash flows over the period of the contract and would consider the substance of the contract. For example, while some financial reinsurance contracts may require annual renewal, in substance they may be expected to be renewed for a number of years.

2.4.4 To unbundle a general insurance contract, an insurer shall:

    (a)   apply this Standard to the insurance component; and

    (b)   apply AASB 9 to the deposit component. When applying AASB 9, an insurer shall designate the deposit component as "at fair value through profit or loss", on first application of this Standard or on initial recognition of the deposit component.

Purpose of Standard

3.1   **The purpose of this Standard is to:**

    (a)   **specify the manner of accounting for general insurance contracts consistent with AASB 4;**

    (b)   **specify certain aspects of accounting for assets backing general insurance liabilities;**

    (c)   **specify certain aspects of accounting for non-insurance contracts; and**

    (d)   **require disclosure of information relating to general insurance contracts.**

Premium revenue

Classification

4.1.1 *Premium* revenue comprises:

    (a)   premiums from direct business, that is, premiums paid by a policyholder (that is neither an insurer nor reinsurer) to a general insurer; and

(b)   premiums from reinsurance business, that is, premiums received by a reinsurer from an insurer or from another reinsurer.

4.1.2   Premiums from direct business arise from contracts when a policyholder transfers significant *insurance risk* to an insurer.

4.1.3   Premiums from reinsurance business arise from contracts when an insurer or reinsurer transfers significant insurance risk to another reinsurer.

Recognition

4.2   Premium revenue shall be recognised from the *attachment date* as soon as there is a basis on which it can be reliably estimated.

4.2.1   The amount of premium is determined by a general insurer or reinsurer so as to cover anticipated *claims*, reinsurance premiums, administrative, acquisition and other costs, and a profit component (having regard to expected income from the investment of premiums). The amounts collected in respect of these components are income of an insurer on the basis that they are collected in consideration for the insurer rendering services by indemnifying those insured against specified losses.

4.2.2   For certain classes of general insurance business, government authorities may require the payment of levies and charges. For example, workers' compensation insurance levies, annual licence fees and fire brigade charges may apply. Such levies and charges are expenses of the insurer, rather than government charges directly upon those insured. The insurer is not acting simply as a collector of these levies and charges. Although not compelled to collect these amounts from those insured, the insurer is entitled to include in premiums an amount to cover the estimated amount of the levies and charges. The insurer is usually responsible for paying the levies and charges at a later date. The amount paid by the insurer does not depend on the amounts collected from those insured in relation to the levies and charges. Therefore, the amounts collected to meet levies and charges are income of the insurer. The insurer accrues for all levies and charges expected under the general insurance contracts written in the period.

4.2.3   In most States, stamp duty is charged on individual general insurance contracts and is separately identified by insurers on policy documents. The insurer is normally required to collect and pass on to the government an equivalent amount. Because such stamp duty is a tax collected on behalf of a third party and there is no choice on the part of the insurer but to collect the duty from the insured, it is not income of the insurer. Similarly, Goods and Services Tax (GST) is not income of the insurer.

4.2.4   Premium revenue needs to be recognised from the date of the attachment of risk in relation to each general insurance contract because insurers earn premium revenue by assuming insurance risks from that date on behalf of those insured. However, for reasons of practicality, many general insurers use bases of recognition that attempt to approximate this date. Such bases are acceptable provided that they do not result in the recognition of a materially different amount of premium revenue in a particular reporting period than would be the case if recognition occurred from the date of attachment of risk for each general insurance contract.

4.2.5   In recognising premium from the attachment date, an insurer may recognise premiums relating to general insurance contracts when the contract period commences after the reporting period, commonly referred to as premiums in advance. The attachment date is the date from which an insurer accepts risk. An insurer may accept risk prior to the date a contract commences: for example, it is not unusual for insurers to issue renewals, and for renewals to be paid for by policyholders, prior to the commencement date of an insurance contract. For commercial lines insurance, where the policyholder may be using the services of an insurance broker, the renewal terms could be agreed by both the insurer and policyholder prior to the commencement date and before the policyholder has paid the premium. In this situation, there may also have been a transfer of risk. As premiums in advance relate entirely to insurance cover to be provided in a future period, premiums in advance are recognised as part of the unearned premium liability. Premiums in advance are considered as part of the *liability adequacy test* required by section 9.

Reinsurance premiums

4.2.6 From the perspective of the reinsurer, reinsurance premiums accepted are akin to premiums accepted by a direct insurer. The reinsurer recognises *inwards reinsurance* premiums ceded to it as revenue in the same way as a direct insurer treats the acceptance of direct premiums as revenue.

4.2.7 Premiums accepted by the reinsurer are recognised from the attachment date, that is, the date from which the reinsurer bears its proportion of the relevant risks underwritten by the cedant. Reinsurers usually use bases of recognition that approximate the dates of bearing the risks. For example, the reinsurer may assume that its acceptance of risks occurs from the middle of the period for which the aggregate ceded premiums are advised by the cedant. This approach is acceptable provided that the premiums received or receivable in respect of the reporting period are recognised in that period, whether or not the periodic advice from the cedant has been received.

Measurement

4.3   Premium revenue shall be recognised in the statement of comprehensive income from the attachment date:

   (a)   over the period of the general insurance contract for direct business; or

   (b)   over the period of indemnity for reinsurance business;

   in accordance with the pattern of the incidence of risk expected under the general insurance contract.

4.4   In the case of business where the premium is subject to later adjustment, the adjusted premium shall be used, where possible, as the basis for recognising premium revenue. Where this is not possible, the *deposit premium*, adjusted for any other relevant information, shall be recognised as the premium revenue, provided that it is expected that this amount will not be materially different from the actual amount of premium.

4.4.1 Premium revenue is recognised in the statement of comprehensive income when it has been earned. An insurance contract involves the transfer of significant insurance risk. The insurer estimates the pattern of the incidence of risk over the period of the contract for direct business, or over the period of indemnity for reinsurance business, and the premium revenue is recognised in accordance with this pattern. This results in the allocation of the premium revenue and the *claims incurred* expense and hence the gross underwriting result over the period of the contract for direct business, or over the period of indemnity for reinsurance business, in accordance with the pattern of the incidence of risk.

4.4.2 Measuring premium revenue involves the following steps:

   (a)   estimating the total amount of premium revenue expected under the contract;

   (b)   estimating the total amount of *claims expenses* expected under the contract and estimating when the claims are expected to arise;

   (c)   estimating the pattern of the incidence of risk from the result of (b); and

   (d)   recognising the premium revenue under the contract identified in (a) when it will be earned, that is, in accordance with the pattern of the incidence of risk determined in (c).

4.4.3 For some general insurance contracts, especially complex multi-year reinsurance contracts, these estimations involve the use of significant judgement. The estimates are reassessed at the end of each reporting period. This prospective estimate of all of the income and expenses expected under the contract is also necessary for the purposes of the liability adequacy test. Refer to section 9.

Direct business

4.4.4 For most direct general insurance contracts the specified period of the contract is one year. For many direct insurance contracts the pattern of the incidence of risk will be

AASB

linear, that is, the risk of events occurring that will give rise to claims is evenly spread throughout the contract period. For these contracts the premium revenue will be earned evenly over the period of the contract. However, for some direct insurance contracts the risk of events occurring that will give rise to claims is not evenly spread throughout the contract. For example, with motor insurance contracts, the risk of events occurring that will give rise to claims may be subject to seasonal factors.

4.4.5   Insurers estimate the pattern of the incidence of risk expected under the general insurance contracts from the attachment date. An insurer may be able to reliably estimate the pattern for a particular type of insurance business based upon past experience. However, when there have been changes in the nature of the cover provided, or, when there has been a change in loss experience, the insurer reflects this in the estimations.

Reinsurance business

4.4.6   Reinsurers recognise reinsurance premiums over the period of indemnity provided by the reinsurance contract in accordance with the pattern of the incidence of risk. For a typical twelve-month proportional treaty, such as a quota share treaty, written on a "risks attaching basis", the period of indemnity will be twenty-four months, as the proportional treaty will indemnify the direct insurer (or, for retrocession, the reinsurer) for losses arising under direct policies written during the twelve-month contract period. Hence, an underlying annual direct contract written on the last day of the reinsurance contract has twelve months of insurance cover beyond the last day of the reinsurance contract. The reinsurer estimates the pattern of the incidence of risk over the twenty-four-month indemnity period.

4.4.7   The reinsurer may be able to reliably estimate the pattern for a particular type of reinsurance business based upon past experience. The reinsurer is likely to seek information from the cedant to estimate the pattern of the incidence of loss expected. When there have been changes in the nature of the cover provided or when there has been a change in loss experience the insurer will need to reflect this in the estimations.

4.4.8   To determine the pattern of the incidence of risk, reinsurers first determine the total reinsurance premiums expected under the contract. The premiums receivable under reinsurance treaties often depend on the volume of business written by the cedant after the reporting period but before the treaty expiry date. This is always true of proportional (quota share and surplus) treaties that span the end of the reporting period, and is often true of non-proportional treaties. For such treaties, to estimate the total premium revenue expected under the reinsurance contract, the reinsurer estimates the inwards reinsurance premium it will receive under the contract by estimating the gross premium revenue that the cedant is likely to receive. The reinsurer is likely to estimate this by communicating with the cedant, and by reviewing past experience.

4.4.9   For a typical non-proportional treaty, such as an excess of loss treaty, the period of indemnity is usually the same as the contract period. For example, an excess of loss treaty could indemnify a cedant for all claims incurred above the excess (either individual claims or in aggregate) during the contract period, or for all claims made during the contract period. For some of these contracts the pattern of the incidence of risk is likely to be linear and hence for these contracts the premium revenue expected under the contract is earned evenly over the contract period.

4.4.10   With a non-proportional treaty the reinsurer estimates the total liabilities that are likely to arise under the underlying insurance contracts to enable an estimation of the total inwards reinsurance premium revenue expected under the contract. Where relevant, the reinsurer estimates whether the cedant is likely to want to reinstate the contract, in which case the reinsurer considers the additional reinstatement premiums it is expected to receive and the extent that they may have been earned at the end of the reporting period. A reinsurer liaises closely with the cedant, reviews any market information on significant losses or events that may have arisen, for example a hailstorm or earthquake, and reviews past experience.

4.4.11   Some reinsurance contracts might involve an experience account. Whilst such contracts may require annual renewal, in substance the contract period is likely to be greater than one year. In estimating the total inwards reinsurance premium expected under the contract and in estimating the total reinsurance claims, to determine the pattern of the incidence of risk, the reinsurer considers the probability-weighted expected cash flows over the expected period of the contract, and discounts these cash flows to reflect the time value of money. Section 6 discusses the determination of discount rates. In determining the expected cash flows, the reinsurer considers any cash flows such as profit commissions and commission rebates.

Adjusted premiums

4.4.12   For some classes of insurance it is usual for the premium to be adjusted as a result of events and information that only become known during or after the insurance contract period. For example, marine cargo insurance is a type of "adjustable" business for which a deposit premium is paid at the beginning of the contract period and subsequently adjusted on the basis of a cargo declaration.

Unclosed business

4.5   Premium revenue relating to unclosed business shall be recognised in accordance with paragraphs 4.2, 4.3 and 4.4.

4.5.1   Frequently, there is insufficient information available at the end of a reporting period to enable a general insurer to accurately identify the business written close to the end of the reporting period for which the date of attachment of risk is prior to the end of the reporting period. This is often referred to as unclosed business. Consistent with the principle stated in paragraph 4.2, that premium revenue is to be recognised from the attachment date, all unclosed business is estimated and the premium relating to unclosed business included in premium revenue.

4.5.2   Estimates of the amount of unclosed business can be made using information from prior periods adjusted for the impact of recent trends and events. In addition, information about unclosed business may become available after the reporting period and before the financial statements are authorised for issue and may enable more reliable estimates to be made.

Outstanding claims liability

Recognition and measurement

5.1   An outstanding claims liability shall be recognised in respect of direct business and reinsurance business and shall be measured as the central estimate of the present value of the expected future payments for claims incurred with an additional risk margin to allow for the inherent uncertainty in the central estimate.

5.1.1   The recognition and measurement approach requires estimation of the probability-weighted expected cost (discounted to a present value) of settling claims incurred, and the addition of a risk margin to reflect inherent uncertainty in the central estimate.

5.1.2   The longer the expected period from the end of the reporting period to settlement, the more likely it is that the ultimate cost of settlement will be affected by inflationary factors likely to occur during the period to settlement. These factors include changes in specific price levels, for example, trends in average periods of incapacity and in the amounts of court awards for successful claims. For claims expected to be settled within one year of the end of the reporting period, the impact of inflationary factors might not be material.

5.1.3   For claims expected to be settled within one year of the end of the reporting period, where the amount of the expected future payments does not differ materially from the present value of those payments, insurers would not need to discount the expected future payments.

Central estimate

5.1.4   In estimating the outstanding claims liability, a central estimate is adopted. If all the possible values of the outstanding claims liability are expressed as a statistical distribution, the central estimate is the mean of that distribution.

5.1.5   In estimating the outstanding claims liability, an insurer may make use of case estimates of individual reported claims that remain unsettled at the end of the reporting period. An insurer may base case estimates on the most likely claim costs. Where the range in potential outcomes is small, the likely cost may be close to the mean cost. However, where the potential range in outcomes is large and where the probability distribution may be highly skewed, the most likely cost, or the mode, could be below the mean and hence below the central estimate. In this situation, the insurer would need to increase the case estimates accordingly to ensure that they represent the central estimate.

Risk margin

5.1.6   The outstanding claims liability includes, in addition to the central estimate of the present value of the expected future payments, a risk margin that relates to the inherent uncertainty in the central estimate of the present value of the expected future payments.

5.1.7   Risk margins are determined on a basis that reflects the insurer's business. Regard is had to the robustness of the valuation models, the reliability and volume of available data, past experience of the insurer and the industry and the characteristics of the classes of business written.

5.1.8   The risk margin is applied to the net outstanding claims for the entity as a whole. The overall net uncertainty has regard to:

(a)   the uncertainty in the gross outstanding claims liability;

(b)   the effect of reinsurance on (a); and

(c)   the uncertainty in reinsurance and other recoveries due.

5.1.9   In practice, however, outstanding claims liabilities are often estimated on a class-by-class basis, including an assessment of the uncertainty in each class and the determination of a risk margin by class of business. When these estimates are combined for all classes, the central estimates are combined, however the risk margin for all classes when aggregated may be determined by some insurers to be less than the sum of the individual risk margins. The extent of the difference that some insurers may decide to recognise is likely to depend upon the degree of diversification between the different classes and the degree of correlation between the experiences of these classes.

5.1.10   For the purposes of the liability adequacy test, required by section 9, the risk margin for the entity as a whole is apportioned across portfolios of contracts that are subject to broadly similar risks and are managed together as a single portfolio.

5.1.11   Risk margins adopted for regulatory purposes may be appropriate risk margins for the purposes of this Standard, or they may be an appropriate starting point in determining such risk margins.

Expected future payments

5.2   The expected future payments shall include:

(a)   amounts in relation to unpaid reported claims;

(b)   claims incurred but not reported (IBNR);

(c)   claims incurred but not enough reported (IBNER); and

(d)   costs, including claims handling costs, which the insurer expects to incur in settling these incurred claims.

5.2.1 It is important to identify the components of the ultimate cost to an insurer of settling incurred claims, for the purposes of determining the claims expense for the reporting period and determining the outstanding claims liability as at the end of the reporting period. These components comprise the policy benefit amounts required to be paid to or on behalf of those insured, and claims handling costs, that is, costs associated with achieving settlements with those insured. Claims handling costs include costs that can be associated directly with individual claims, such as legal and other professional fees, and costs that can only be indirectly associated with individual claims, such as claims administration costs.

5.2.2 Policy benefit amounts and direct claims handling costs are expenses of an insurer, representing the consumption or loss of economic benefits. The outstanding claims liability includes unpaid policy benefits and direct claims handling costs relating to claims arising during current and prior reporting periods, as they are outgoings that an insurer is presently obliged to meet as a result of past events.

5.2.3 Indirect claims handling costs incurred during the reporting period are also expenses of an insurer, and include a portion of the indirect claims handling costs to be paid in the future, being that portion which relates to handling claims incurred during the reporting period. The outstanding claims liability includes these unpaid indirect claims handling costs.

5.2.4 It is important to ensure that claims are recognised as expenses and liabilities for the correct reporting period. For contracts written on a claims incurred basis, claims arise from *insured events* that occur during the insurance contract period. Some events will occur and give rise to claims that are reported to the insurer and settled within the same reporting period. Other reported claims may be unsettled at the end of a particular reporting period. In addition, there may be events that give rise to claims that, at the end of a reporting period, have yet to be reported to the insurer. The latter are termed claims incurred but not reported (IBNR claims). The insurer also considers the need to recognise a liability for claims that may be re-opened after the reporting period.

5.2.5 For contracts written on a claims made basis, claims arise in respect of claims reported during the insurance contract period. The insured event that gave rise to the claim could have occurred in a previous period. While claims made insurance contracts should theoretically only give rise to outstanding claims liabilities and IBNER claims (see paragraph 5.2.10), as claims cannot be incurred but not reported under such a contract, this may not be the case for reinsurers. A reinsurer may have reinsured a claims made contract on a claims incurred basis. In this case whilst a loss or other event would be reported to the direct insurer during the period of insurance to generate a valid claim, the reinsurer may not have received information about the claim but would have an IBNR liability. Similarly, a reinsurer may have issued a claims made reinsurance contract but may need to consider that not all notices of claims may have been reported by the direct insurer. Insurers and reinsurers should also consider court rulings that may impact on the way claims made contracts are interpreted.

5.2.6 Claims arising from events that occur during a reporting period and which are settled during that same period are expenses of that period. In addition, a liability and corresponding expense is recognised for reported claims arising from events of the reporting period that have yet to be settled. This involves a process of estimation that includes assessment of individual claims and past claims experience.

5.2.7 When, based on knowledge of the business, IBNR claims are expected to exist, an estimate is made of the amount of the claims that will arise therefrom. This involves recognition of a liability and corresponding expense for the reporting period. As in the case of reported but unsettled claims, an estimate of the amount of the current claims incurred but not reported is based on past experience and takes into account any changes in circumstances, such as recent catastrophic events that may have occurred during the reporting period and changes in the volume or mix of insurance contracts underwritten, that may affect the pattern of unreported claims.

5.2.8 Some insurers use estimations or formulae, related to the amount of outstanding claims and based on the past experience of the insurer and the industry, to arrive at an estimate of direct and indirect claims handling costs.

5.2.9   Claims expense and the outstanding claims liability are adjusted on the basis of information, including re-opened claims, that becomes available after the initial recognition of claims, to enable the insurer to make a more accurate estimate of the ultimate cost of settlement. This is often referred to as claims development. As is the case with other liabilities, the effect of the adjustments to the liability for outstanding claims and to claims expense is recognised in the statement of comprehensive income when the information becomes available.

5.2.10   Where further information becomes available about reported claims and reveals that the ultimate cost of settling claims has been under-estimated, the upwards adjustment to claims expense and to the liability for outstanding claims is often referred to as claims incurred but not enough reported (IBNER claims). Where further information reveals that the ultimate cost of settling claims has been over-estimated, the adjustment is sometimes referred to as negative IBNER claims.

5.2.11   Appropriate allowance is made for *future claim* cost escalation when determining the central estimate of the present value of the expected future payments. Future claims payments may increase over current levels as a result of wage or price inflation, and as a result of superimposed inflation (cost increases) due to court awards, environmental factors or economic or other causes.

5.2.12   With inwards reinsurance claims the reinsurer will receive periodic advices from each cedant. These may include aggregate information relating to the claims liability. The reinsurer measures its outstanding claims liability on the basis of this information and its past experience of the claims payments made under reinsurance arrangements. The reinsurer also considers market knowledge of losses and other events such as hailstorms or earthquakes.

Discount rates

6.1   The outstanding claims liability shall be discounted for the time value of money using risk-free discount rates that are based on current observable, objective rates that relate to the nature, structure and term of the future obligations.

6.1.1   The discount rates adopted are not intended to reflect risks inherent in the liability cash flows, which might be allowed for by a reduction in the discount rate in a fair value measurement, nor are they intended to reflect the insurance and other non-financial risks and uncertainties reflected in the outstanding claims liability. The discount rates are not intended to include allowance for the cost of any options or guarantees that are separately measured within the outstanding claims liability.

6.1.2   Typically, government bond rates may be appropriate discount rates for the purposes of this Standard, or they may be an appropriate starting point in determining such discount rates.

6.1.3   The portion of the increase in the liability for outstanding claims from the end of the previous reporting period to the end of the current reporting period which is due to discounted claims not yet settled being one period closer to settlement, ought, conceptually, to be recognised as interest expense of the current reporting period. However, it is considered that the costs of distinguishing this component of the increase in the outstanding claims liability exceed the benefits that may be gained from its disclosure. Thus, such increase is included in claims expense for the current reporting period.

Unearned premium liability

7.1   Premium that has not been recognised in the statement of comprehensive income is premium that is unearned and shall be recognised in the statement of financial position as an unearned premium liability.

7.1.1   The unearned premium liability is to meet the costs, including the claims handling costs, of future claims that will arise under current general insurance contracts and the deferred acquisition costs that will be recognised as an expense in the statement of comprehensive income in future reporting periods.

Acquisition costs

8.1 **Acquisition costs incurred in obtaining and recording general insurance contracts shall be deferred and recognised as assets where they can be reliably measured and where it is probable that they will give rise to premium revenue that will be recognised in the statement of comprehensive income in subsequent reporting periods. Deferred acquisition costs shall be amortised systematically in accordance with the expected pattern of the incidence of risk under the related general insurance contracts.**

8.1.1 Acquisition costs are incurred in obtaining and recording general insurance contracts. They include commission or brokerage paid to agents or brokers for obtaining business for the insurer, selling and underwriting costs such as advertising and risk assessment, the administrative costs of recording policy information and premium collection costs.

8.1.2 Because such costs are usually incurred at acquisition whilst the pattern of earnings occurs throughout the contract periods, which may extend beyond the end of the reporting period, those acquisition costs which lead to obtaining future benefits for the insurer are recognised as assets.

8.1.3 For an asset to be recognised, it will be probable that the future economic benefits will eventuate, and that it possesses a cost or other value that can be measured reliably. Direct acquisition costs such as commission or brokerage are readily measurable. However, it may be difficult to reliably measure indirect costs that give rise to premium revenue, such as administration costs, because it is difficult to associate them with particular insurance contracts.

Liability adequacy test

9.1 **The adequacy of the unearned premium liability shall be assessed by considering current estimates of the present value of the expected future cash flows relating to future claims arising from the rights and obligations under current general insurance contracts. If the present value of the expected future cash flows relating to future claims arising from the rights and obligations under current general insurance contracts, plus an additional risk margin to reflect the inherent uncertainty in the central estimate, exceed the unearned premium liability less related intangible assets and related deferred acquisition costs, then the unearned premium liability is deficient. The entire deficiency shall be recognised in the statement of comprehensive income. In recognising the deficiency in the statement of comprehensive income the insurer shall first write-down any related intangible assets and then the related deferred acquisition costs. If an additional liability is required this shall be recognised in the statement of financial position as an unexpired risk liability. The liability adequacy test for the unearned premium liability shall be performed at the level of a portfolio of contracts that are subject to broadly similar risks and are managed together as a single portfolio.**

9.1.1 In determining the present value of the expected future cash flows relating to future claims arising from the rights and obligations under current general insurance contracts, the insurer applies sections 5 and 6 and includes an appropriate risk margin to reflect inherent uncertainty in the central estimate, as set out in paragraphs 5.1.6 to 5.1.11.

9.1.2 Whilst the probability of adequacy adopted in performing the liability adequacy test may be the same or similar to the probability of adequacy adopted in determining the outstanding claims liability, this Standard does not require the same or similar probabilities of adequacy. However, the users of financial statements need to be presented with information explaining any differences in probabilities of adequacy adopted, and insurers are required to disclose the reasons for any differences in accordance with paragraph 17.8(e).

9.1.3 The unearned premium liability may include premiums in advance as described in paragraph 4.2.5. Insurers also consider whether there are any additional general insurance contracts, where the premium revenue is not recognised in the unearned premium liability, under which the insurer has a constructive obligation to settle future claims that may arise. That is, there may be general insurance contracts where there has not been a transfer of risk, as described in paragraph 4.2.5, but where a constructive obligation has arisen. The cash flows expected under these contracts are considered as part of the liability adequacy test.

9.1.4 In reviewing expected future cash flows, the insurer takes into account both future cash flows under insurance contracts it has issued and the related reinsurance.

9.1.5 The related intangible assets referred to in paragraph 9.1 are those that arise under paragraph 13.3.1(b). As the liability adequacy test for the unearned premium liability is performed at the level of portfolios of contracts that are subject to broadly similar risks and are managed together as a single portfolio, the intangible asset is allocated on a reasonable basis across these portfolios.

9.1.6 As the liability adequacy test applies to deferred acquisition costs and to intangible assets, these assets are excluded from the scope of AASB 136 *Impairment of Assets*.

Outwards reinsurance expense

10.1 Premium ceded to reinsurers shall be recognised by the cedant as outwards reinsurance expense in the statement of comprehensive income from the attachment date over the period of indemnity of the reinsurance contract in accordance with the expected pattern of the incidence of risk.

10.1.1 It is common for general insurers or reinsurers to reinsure a portion of the risks that they accept. To secure reinsurance cover, the cedant passes on a portion of the premiums received to a reinsurer. This is known as outwards reinsurance expense.

10.1.2 The cedant accounts for direct insurance and reinsurance transactions on a gross basis, so that the extent and effectiveness of the reinsurance arrangements are apparent to the users of the financial statements, and an indication of the insurer's risk management performance is provided to users. The gross amount of premiums earned by the cedant during the reporting period is recognised as income because it undertakes to indemnify the full amount of the specified losses of those it has insured, regardless of the reinsurance arrangements. Correspondingly, the cedant recognises the gross amount of claims expense in the reporting period because it is obliged to meet the full cost of successful claims by those it has insured.

10.1.3 Accordingly, premium ceded to reinsurers is recognised in the statement of comprehensive income as an expense of the cedant on the basis that it is an outgoing incurred in undertaking the business of direct insurance underwriting, and is not to be netted off against premium revenue.

10.1.4 Outwards reinsurance expense is recognised in the statement of comprehensive income consistently with the recognition of reinsurance recoveries under the reinsurance contract. For proportional reinsurance the estimate of outwards reinsurance expense is based upon the gross premium of the underlying direct insurance contract. For non-proportional reinsurance the cedant estimates the total claims that are likely to be made under the contract and hence whether it needs to recognise additional outwards reinsurance expense under a minimum and deposit arrangement or whether it needs to recognise reinstatement premiums expense.

10.1.5 Some reinsurance contracts purchased by a cedant might involve an experience account. Whilst these contracts may require annual renewal, in substance, the contract period is likely to be greater than one year. In estimating the outwards reinsurance expense and reinsurance recoveries to be recognised in the reporting period the cedant considers the probability-weighted expected cash flows over the expected period of indemnity and discounts the cash flows to reflect the time value of money. In determining the discount rates to be adopted, an insurer applies the same principles that are used to determine the discount rates for outstanding claims liabilities outlined in section 6. In considering all expected cash flows the reinsurer considers any profit commissions and commission rebates.

Reinsurance recoveries and non-reinsurance recoveries

11.1 Reinsurance recoveries received or receivable in relation to the outstanding claims liability and non-reinsurance recoveries received or receivable shall be recognised as income of the cedant and shall not be netted off against the claims expense or outwards reinsurance expense in the statement of comprehensive income, or the outstanding claims liability or unearned premium liability in the statement of financial position.

11.1.1   The reinsurance recoveries receivable in the statement of financial position may not be received for some time. The reinsurance recoveries receivable are discounted on a basis consistent with the discounting of the outstanding claims liabilities outlined in section 6.

11.1.2   An insurer may also be entitled to non-reinsurance recoveries under the insurance contract such as salvage, subrogation and sharing arrangements with other insurers. Non-reinsurance recoveries are not offset against gross claims, but are recognised as income or assets, in the same way as, but separately from, reinsurance recoveries. The non-reinsurance recoveries receivable in the statement of financial position may not be received for some time. The non-reinsurance recoveries receivable are discounted on a basis consistent with the discounting of the outstanding claims liabilities outlined in section 6.

11.1.3   Amounts that reduce the liability to the policyholder, such as excesses or allowances for contributory negligence, are not non-reinsurance recoveries and are offset against the gross claims.

Impairment of reinsurance assets

12.1.1   If a cedant's *reinsurance asset* is impaired, the cedant shall reduce its carrying amount accordingly and recognise that impairment in the statement of comprehensive income. A reinsurance asset is impaired if, and only if:

(a)   there is objective evidence, as a result of an event that occurred after initial recognition of the reinsurance asset, that the cedant may not receive amounts due to it under the terms of the contract; and

(b)   that event has a reliably measurable impact on the amounts that the cedant will receive from the reinsurer.

Portfolio transfers and business combinations

13.1 Where the responsibility in relation to claims on transferred insurance business remains with the transferring insurer, the transfer shall be treated by the transferring insurer and the accepting insurer as reinsurance business.

13.1.1   Portfolio transfer is a term used to describe the process by which premiums and claims are transferred from one insurer to another. Transfers may be completed in a number of ways in relation to claims arising from events that occurred before the transfer. The receiving insurer may take responsibility in relation to all claims under the agreement or treaty that have not yet been paid, or it may take responsibility only in relation to those claims arising from events that occur after the date of transfer.

13.1.2 In relation to the transfer of insurance business, while the acquiring insurer agrees to meet the claims of those insured from a particular time, the contractual responsibility of the original insurer to meet those claims normally remains.

13.1.3 In relation to the withdrawal of a reinsurer from a reinsurance treaty arrangement, the contractual responsibility of the reinsurer to the direct insurer in relation to outstanding claims may be passed back to the direct insurer with a return of any premium relating to unexpired risk, or may be retained by the withdrawing reinsurer. In the former case, the direct insurer may choose to reinsure the outstanding claims with another reinsurer. This assuming reinsurer would be ceded premium for bearing liability in relation to existing outstanding claims.

13.1.4 Where the responsibility in relation to claims on transferred insurance business remains with the transferring insurer:

(a) the transferring insurer recognises the transferred premium revenue and the relevant outstanding claims in the same way as other outwards reinsurance business; and

(b) the accepting insurer recognises the premium revenue ceded to it and the relevant outstanding claims in the same way as other inwards reinsurance business.

13.2 Where the responsibility in relation to claims on transferred insurance business passes from the transferring insurer to the accepting insurer, the transfer shall be accounted for as a portfolio withdrawal by the transferring insurer and as a portfolio assumption by the accepting insurer.

13.3 A portfolio withdrawal shall be accounted for by the transferring insurer by eliminating the liabilities and assets connected with the risks transferred. A portfolio assumption shall be accounted for by the accepting insurer by recognising the relevant amount of unexpired premium revenue and the outstanding claims for which the transferring insurer is no longer responsible.

13.3.1 To comply with AASB 3, an insurer shall, at the acquisition date, measure at fair value the insurance liabilities assumed and *insurance assets* acquired in a business combination. However, an insurer is permitted, but not required, to use an expanded presentation that splits the fair value of acquired insurance contracts into two components:

(a) a liability measured in accordance with the insurer's accounting policies for general insurance contracts that it issues; and

(b) an intangible asset, representing the difference between:

(i) the fair value of the contractual insurance rights acquired and insurance obligations assumed; and

(ii) the amount described in paragraph 13.3.1(a).

The subsequent measurement of this asset shall be consistent with the measurement of the related insurance liability.

13.3.2 An insurer acquiring a portfolio of general insurance contracts may use an expanded presentation described in paragraph 13.3.1.

13.3.3 The intangible assets described in paragraphs 13.3.1 and 13.3.2 are excluded from the scope of AASB 136 and from the scope of AASB 138 in respect of recognition and measurement. AASB 136 and AASB 138 apply to customer lists and customer relationships reflecting the expectation of future contracts that are not part of the contractual insurance rights and contractual insurance obligations that existed at the date of a business combination or portfolio transfer.

13.3.4 AASB 138 includes specific disclosure requirements in relation to this intangible asset.

Underwriting pools and coinsurance

14.1 **Insurance business allocated through underwriting pools and coinsurance arrangements, by an entity acting as agent, shall be accounted for by the accepting insurer as direct insurance business.**

14.1.1 Direct insurers or reinsurers may form underwriting pools or enter coinsurance arrangements as vehicles for jointly insuring particular risks or types of risks. Premiums, claims and other expenses are usually shared in agreed ratios by insurers involved in these arrangements.

14.1.2 Many underwriting pools and coinsurance arrangements involve the acceptance of risks by an entity acting as an agent for pool members or coinsurers. The entity receives premiums and pays claims and expenses, and allocates shares of the business to each pool member or coinsurer in agreed ratios. As the entity acting as agent is not an insurer, the business allocated to pool members and coinsurers is not reinsurance business. Pool members and coinsurers treat such business allocated to them as direct insurance business.

14.2 **Business directly underwritten by a member of an underwriting pool or coinsurance arrangement shall be treated as direct insurance business and the portion of the risk reinsured by other pool members or coinsurers, determined by reference to the extent of the shares in the pool or arrangement of other pool members or coinsurers, shall be treated as outwards reinsurance. The pool member's or coinsurer's share of insurance business that other insurers place in the pool or arrangement shall be treated as inwards reinsurance.**

Assets backing general insurance liabilities

Fair value approach

15.1.1 Paragraphs 15.2 to 15.5 address the measurement of certain assets backing general insurance liabilities or financial liabilities that arise under non-insurance contracts. The fair value approach to the measurement of assets backing general insurance liabilities or financial liabilities that arise under non-insurance contracts is consistent with the present value measurement approach for general insurance liabilities, and the fair value measurement for financial liabilities that arise under non-insurance contracts, required by this Standard. Where assets are not backing general insurance liabilities or financial liabilities that arise under non-insurance contracts, general insurers apply the applicable accounting standards making use of any measurement choices available.

Measurement

15.2 **Financial assets that:**

(a) **are within the scope of AASB 9;**

(b) **back general insurance liabilities; and**

(c) **are permitted to be designated as "at fair value through profit or loss" under AASB 9;**

shall be designated as "at fair value through profit or loss" under AASB 9 on first application of this Standard, or on initial recognition.

15.2.1 An insurer applies AASB 9 to its financial assets. Under AASB 9 a financial asset is classified and measured at fair value through profit or loss when:

(a) it does not meet the criteria specified in paragraph 4.1.2 of AASB 9 to be classified at amortised cost; or

(b) it does not meet the criteria specified in paragraph 4.1.2A of AASB 9 to be classified at fair value through other comprehensive income; or

(c) it is designated as "at fair value through profit or loss" upon initial recognition in accordance with paragraph 4.1.5 of AASB 9.

AASB 1 *First-time Adoption of Australian Accounting Standards* permits entities to designate financial assets as "at fair value through profit or loss" on first application of the Standard.

15.2.2   The view adopted in this Standard is that financial assets, within the scope of AASB 9 that back general insurance liabilities, are permitted to be measured at fair value through profit or loss under AASB 9. This is because the measurement of general insurance liabilities under this Standard incorporates current information and measuring the financial assets backing these general insurance liabilities at fair value, eliminates or significantly reduces a potential measurement or recognition inconsistency which would arise if the assets were classified and measured at amortised cost or fair value through other comprehensive income (refer to AASB 9 paragraph B4.1.30(a)).

15.3   Investment property within the scope of AASB 140 *Investment Property* and that backs general insurance liabilities shall be measured using the fair value model under AASB 140 and AASB 13 *Fair Value Measurement*.

15.4   Property, plant and equipment that is within the scope of AASB 116 *Property, Plant and Equipment* and that backs general insurance liabilities, shall be measured using the revaluation model under AASB 116.

15.4.1-15.4.2 [Deleted by the IASB]

15.5   When preparing *separate financial statements*, those investments in subsidiaries, joint ventures and associates that:

(a)   are defined by AASB 10 *Consolidated Financial Statements*, AASB 11 *Joint Arrangements* and AASB 128 *Investments in Associates and Joint Ventures*;

(b)   back general insurance liabilities; and

(c)   are permitted to be designated as "at fair value through profit or loss" under AASB 9;

shall be designated as "at fair value through profit or loss" under AASB 9, on first application of this Standard or on initial recognition.

15.5.1   An insurer applies AASB 127 to its investments in subsidiaries, joint ventures and associates when preparing separate financial statements. Under AASB 127, in the parent's own financial statements, the investments in subsidiaries, joint ventures and associates can either be accounted for at cost or in accordance with AASB 9.

15.5.2   In the parent's separate financial statements, investments in subsidiaries, joint ventures and associates that are within the scope of AASB 127, that the insurer considers back general insurance liabilities, and that are permitted to be designated as "at fair value through profit or loss" under AASB 9, are designated as "at fair value through profit or loss" under AASB 9, on first application of this Standard or on initial recognition.

Non-insurance contracts regulated under the *Insurance Act 1973*

16.1   Non-insurance contracts regulated under the *Insurance Act 1973* shall be treated under AASB 9 to the extent that they give rise to financial assets or financial liabilities respectively. However, the financial assets and the financial liabilities that arise under these contracts shall be designated as "at fair value through profit or loss", on first application of this Standard, or on initial recognition of the financial assets or financial liabilities, where this is permitted under AASB 9.

16.1.1   In relation to non-insurance contracts regulated under the Insurance Act, an insurer applies AASB 9 to its financial assets and financial liabilities.

16.1.2   Under AASB 9 a financial asset is classified and measured at fair value through profit or loss when:

(a)   it does not meet the criteria specified in paragraph 4.1.2 of AASB 9 to be classified at amortised cost; or

(b)   it does not meet the criteria specified in paragraph 4.1.2A of AASB 9 to be classified at fair value through other comprehensive income; or

(c)   it is designated as "at fair value through profit or loss" upon initial recognition in accordance with paragraph 4.1.5 of AASB 9.

AASB 1 *First-time Adoption of Australian Accounting Standards* permits entities to designate financial assets as "at fair value through profit or loss" on first application of the Standard.

16.1.3   Under AASB 9 a financial liability at fair value through profit or loss is a financial liability that meets either of the following conditions:

(a)   it meets the definition of held for trading; or

(b)   it is designated as "at fair value through profit or loss" upon initial recognition in accordance with paragraph 4.2.2, because either:

      (i)   it eliminates or significantly reduces a measurement or recognition inconsistency (sometimes referred to as 'an accounting mismatch') that would otherwise arise from measuring assets or liabilities or recognising the gains and losses on them on different bases; or

      (ii)   a group of financial liabilities or financial assets and financial liabilities is managed and its performance is evaluated on a fair value basis, in accordance with a documented risk management or investment strategy, and information about the group is provided internally on that basis to the entity's key management personnel (as defined in AASB 124 *Related Party Disclosures*), for example the entity's board of directors and chief executive officer.

An entity may also use this designation when it is a contract with an embedded derivative and paragraph 4.3.3 of AASB 9 allows the entity to measure the hybrid contract as "at fair value through profit or loss".

AASB 1 *First-time Adoption of Australian Accounting Standards* permits entities to designate financial liabilities as "at fair value through profit or loss" on first application of the Standard.

16.2   Paragraphs 15.2, 15.3, 15.4 and 15.5 shall also be applied to the measurement of assets that back financial liabilities that arise under non-insurance contracts.

Disclosures

Statement of comprehensive income

17.1   In relation to the statement of comprehensive income, the financial statements shall disclose:

(a)   **the underwriting result for the reporting period, determined as the amount obtained by deducting the sum of claims expense, outwards reinsurance premium expense and underwriting expenses from the sum of direct and inwards reinsurance premium revenues and recoveries revenue;**

(b)   ***net claims incurred* shall be disclosed, showing separately:**

      (i)   **the amount relating to risks borne in the current reporting period; and**

      (ii)   **the amount relating to a reassessment of risks borne in all previous reporting periods.**

An explanation shall be provided where net claims incurred relating to a reassessment of risks borne in previous reporting periods are material; and

     (c)   in respect of **17.1(b)(i)** and **17.1(b)(ii)**, the following components shall be separately disclosed:

          (i)   gross claims incurred – undiscounted;

          (ii)   reinsurance and other recoveries – undiscounted; and

          (iii) discount movements shown separately for (i) and (ii).

17.1.1   This Standard requires the underwriting result for the reporting period to be disclosed. This disclosure gives an indication of an insurer's underwriting performance, including the extent to which underwriting activities rely on investment income for the payment of claims.

17.1.2   Based on the total movement in net claims incurred, it may appear that there has not been a material reassessment of risks borne in previous periods, however, there may be material movements at a business segment level, that mitigate each other. For example, the insurer may have seen a material deterioration in its motor portfolio, which has been mitigated by material savings in the professional indemnity portfolio, such that when both portfolios are aggregated there appears to have been little change in the reporting period. In such circumstances, the insurer provides an explanation of the reassessments that took place in the net claims incurred for previous periods during the reporting period at the business segment level.

Statement of financial position

17.2   The financial statements shall disclose in relation to the outstanding claims liability:

     (a)   the central estimate of the expected present value of future payments for claims incurred;

     (b)   the component related to the risk margin;

     (c)   the percentage risk margin adopted in determining the outstanding claims liability (determined from (a) and (b) above);

     (d)   the probability of adequacy intended to be achieved through adoption of the risk margin; and

     (e)   the process used to determine the risk margin, including the way in which diversification of risks has been allowed for.

17.3   An insurer shall disclose the process used to determine which assets back general insurance liabilities and which assets back financial liabilities arising under non-insurance contracts.

Non-insurance contracts

17.4   Where a general insurer has issued a non-insurance contract or holds a non-insurance contract as a cedant, and that non-insurance contract has a material financial impact on the statement of comprehensive income, statement of financial position or cash flows, the general insurer shall disclose:

     (a)   the nature of the non-insurance contract;

     (b)   the recognised assets, liabilities, income, expense and cash flows arising from the non-insurance contract; and

     (c)   information that helps users to understand the amount, timing and uncertainty of future cash flows from the non-insurance contract.

17.4.1   In applying paragraph 17.4 a non-insurance contract shall be considered together with any related contracts or side letters, when determining the need for disclosure, and in making the disclosures required.

17.5   [Deleted by the AASB]

17.5.1   [Deleted by the AASB]

Insurance contracts – explanation of recognised amounts

17.6 **An insurer shall disclose information that identifies and explains the amounts in its financial statements arising from insurance contracts.**

17.6.1   To comply with paragraph 17.6, an insurer shall disclose:

(a)   its accounting policies for insurance contracts and related assets, liabilities, income and expense;

(b)   the recognised assets, liabilities, income, expense and cash flows arising from insurance contracts. Furthermore, if the insurer is a cedant, it shall disclose:

(i)   gains and losses recognised in the statement of comprehensive income on buying reinsurance; and

(ii)   if the cedant defers and amortises gains and losses arising on buying reinsurance, the amortisation for the period and the amounts remaining unamortised at the beginning and end of the period;

(c)   the process used to determine the assumptions that have the greatest effect on the measurement of the recognised amounts described in (b). When practicable, an insurer shall also give quantified disclosure of those assumptions;

(d)   the effect of changes in assumptions used to measure insurance assets and insurance liabilities, showing separately the effect of each change that has a material effect on the financial statements; and

(e)   reconciliations of changes in insurance liabilities, reinsurance assets and, if any, related deferred acquisition costs.

17.6.2   In applying paragraph 17.6.1(b), the recognised assets and liabilities arising from insurance contracts would normally include:

(a)   gross outstanding claims liability;

(b)   reinsurance recoveries receivable arising from the outstanding claims liability;

(c)   gross unearned premium liability;

(d)   reinsurance recoveries receivable arising from the unearned premium liability;

(e)   unexpired risk liability;

(f)   other reinsurance recoveries receivable;

(g)   other recoveries receivable;

(h)   outwards reinsurance expense asset or liability;

(i)   direct premium revenue receivable;

(j)   inwards reinsurance premium revenue receivable;

(k)   deferred acquisition cost asset; and

(l)   intangible assets relating to acquired insurance contracts.

17.6.3   In applying paragraph 17.6.1(b), the recognised income and expenses arising from insurance contracts would normally include:

(a)   direct premium revenue;

(b)   inwards reinsurance premium revenue (including retrocessions);

(c)   reinsurance and other recoveries revenue;

(d)   direct claims expense;

(e)   reinsurance claims expense;

(f)   outwards reinsurance premium expense (including retrocessions);

(g)   acquisition costs expense; and

(h)   other underwriting expenses, including claims handling expenses.

17.6.4   When an insurer is presenting the disclosures required by paragraphs 17.6.1(c) and 17.6.1(d) the insurer determines the level and extent of disclosure that is appropriate having regard to its circumstances and the qualitative characteristics of financial statements under the *Framework for the Preparation and Presentation of Financial Statements* (as identified in AASB 1048 *Interpretation of Standards*).

17.6.5   For an insurer that is involved in a large number of insurance classes, across different jurisdictions, disclosure by class of business is likely to be voluminous and may not be understandable to the user of the financial statements. Furthermore, for such an insurer, disclosure for the entity as a whole is also likely to be at too high a level of aggregation to be relevant or comparable. It is expected that for most insurers disclosure at the major business segment level would normally be most appropriate. The insurer may believe that disclosure of a range of values would be relevant to the users of the financial statements.

17.6.6   Some of the assumptions that would normally have the greatest effect on the measurement of the recognised amounts described in paragraph 17.6.1(b), are discount rates, inflation rates, average weighted term to settlement from the claims reporting date, average claim frequency, average claim size and expense rates. The insurer determines whether these assumptions shall be disclosed given the requirements of paragraphs 17.6 and 17.6.1.

Nature and extent of risks arising from insurance contracts

17.7   An insurer shall disclose information that enables users of its financial statements to evaluate the nature and extent of risks arising from insurance contracts.

17.7.1   To comply with paragraph 17.7, an insurer shall disclose:

(a)   its objectives, policies and processes for managing risks arising from insurance contracts and the methods used to manage those risks;

(b)   information about insurance risk (both before and after risk mitigation by reinsurance), including information about:

(i)   sensitivity to insurance risk (see paragraph 17.7.5);

(ii)   concentrations of insurance risk, including a description of how management determines concentrations and a description of the shared characteristic that identifies each concentration (e.g. type of insured event, geographical area, or currency); and

(iii)   actual claims compared with previous estimates (i.e. claims development). The disclosure about claims development shall go back to the period when the earliest material claim arose for which there is still uncertainty about the amount and timing of the claims payments, but need not go back more than ten years. An insurer need not disclose this information for claims for which uncertainty about the amount and timing of claims payments is typically resolved within one year;

(c)   information about credit risk, liquidity risk and market risk that paragraphs 31-42 of AASB 7 *Financial Instruments: Disclosures* would require if the insurance contracts were within the scope of AASB 7. However:

(i)   an insurer need not provide the maturity analyses required by paragraphs 39(a) and (b) of AASB 7 if it discloses information about the estimated timing of the net cash outflows resulting from recognised insurance liabilities instead. This may take the form of an analysis, by estimated timing, of the amounts recognised in the statement of financial position; and

(ii) if an insurer uses an alternative method to manage sensitivity to market conditions, such as an embedded value analysis, it may use that sensitivity analysis to meet the requirement in paragraph 40(a) of AASB 7. Such an insurer shall also provide the disclosures required by paragraph 41 of AASB 7; and

(d) information about exposures to market risk arising from embedded derivatives contained in a host insurance contract if the insurer is not required to, and does not, measure the embedded derivatives at fair value.

17.7.2   For an insurer that is involved in a large number of insurance classes, across different jurisdictions, disclosure by class of business is likely to be voluminous and may not be understandable to the user of the financial statements. Furthermore, for such an insurer disclosure for the entity as a whole would normally be at too high a level of aggregation to be relevant or comparable. It is expected that for most insurers disclosure at the major business segment level would normally be most appropriate.

17.7.3   The claims development disclosure required by paragraph 17.7.1(b)(iii) only applies to classes of business where claims are not typically resolved within one year. The insurer, in disclosing claims development, ensures it is clear to the reader of the financial statements, which classes of business, or which segments of the business, are covered by the disclosures and which classes of business, or which segments of the business, are not covered by the disclosures.

17.7.4   IG Example 5 in the *Guidance on Implementing IFRS 4* Insurance Contracts, provides one possible format to meet the claims development disclosure requirements of this Standard. Such a format may be particularly appropriate for longer tail classes of business where the long tail nature of the claims is a significant aspect in the development of the claims, as this format illustrates the development of claims over a number of years. If this format is adopted, disclosure by accident year, gross and net of reinsurance, of undiscounted claims would normally be most relevant to the users of financial statements. The insurer explains the information presented. This includes whether the claims are discounted or undiscounted, gross or net of reinsurance and by accident year or underwriting year.

17.7.5   To comply with paragraph 17.7.1(b)(i), an insurer shall disclose either (a) or (b) as follows:

(a) a sensitivity analysis that shows how profit or loss and equity would have been affected had changes in the relevant risk variable that were reasonably possible at the end of the reporting period occurred; the methods and assumptions used in preparing the sensitivity analysis; and any changes from the previous period in the methods and assumptions used. However, if an insurer uses an alternative method to manage sensitivity to market conditions, such as an embedded value analysis, it may meet this requirement by disclosing that alternative sensitivity analysis and the disclosures required by paragraph 41 of AASB 7; and

(b) qualitative information about sensitivity, and information about those terms and conditions of insurance contracts that have a material effect on the amount, timing and uncertainty of the insurer's future cash flows.

Liability adequacy test

17.8 **In relation to the liability adequacy test in** section 9, **the financial statements shall disclose:**

(a) **where a deficiency has been identified, the amounts underlying the calculation performed, that is:**

(i) **unearned premium liability;**

(ii) **related reinsurance asset;**

      (iii)   deferred acquisition costs;

      (iv)   intangible assets;

      (v)   present value of expected future cash flows for future claims, showing expected reinsurance recoveries separately; and

      (vi)   deficiency;

  (b)   any write-down of deferred acquisition costs under the liability adequacy test;

  (c)   any write-down of intangible assets under the liability adequacy test;

  (d)   in relation to the present value of expected future cash flows for future claims:

      (i)   the central estimate of the present value of expected future cash flows;

      (ii)   the component of present value of expected future cash flows related to the risk margin;

      (iii)   the percentage risk margin adopted in determining the present value of expected future cash flows (determined from (i) and (ii) above);

      (iv)   the probability of adequacy intended to be achieved through adoption of the risk margin; and

      (v)   the process used to determine the risk margin, including the way in which diversification of risks has been allowed for;

  (e)   where the probability of adequacy disclosed in paragraph 17.2(d) is not the same or similar to the probability of adequacy disclosed in paragraph 17.8(d)(iv), the reasons for the difference; and

  (f)   where a surplus has been identified, the fact that the liability adequacy test identified a surplus.

Other disclosures

17.9.1   This Standard addresses disclosure requirements in relation to general insurance contracts. Other Australian Accounting Standards may be relevant to a general insurer's financial statements. In particular, the disclosure requirements in AASB 7 would normally be relevant to general insurers.

Transitional provisions

18.1   An entity need not apply the disclosure requirements in this Standard to comparative information that relates to annual periods beginning before 1 January 2005, except for the disclosures required by paragraphs 17.6.1(a) and 17.6.1(b) about accounting policies, and recognised assets, liabilities, income and expense and cash flows.

18.2   Where an entity applies the disclosure requirements in this Standard to comparative information that relates to annual periods beginning before 1 January 2005, if it is impracticable to apply a particular requirement of this Standard to comparative information that relates to annual periods beginning before 1 January 2005, an entity shall disclose that fact. AASB 108 *Accounting Policies, Changes in Accounting Estimates and Errors* explains the term "impracticable".

18.3   In applying paragraph 17.7.1(b)(iii), an entity need not disclose information about claims development that occurred earlier than five years before the end of the first annual reporting period in which it applies this Standard. Furthermore, if it is impracticable, when an entity first applies this Standard, to prepare information about claims development that occurred before the beginning of the earliest period for which an entity presents full comparative information that complies with this Standard, the entity shall disclose that fact.

18.3.1   There are also references to transitional measurement requirements in paragraphs 15.2.1, 15.2.2, 15.5, 15.5.2, 16.1 and 16.1.1.

18.4   [Deleted by the AASB]

18.5   [Deleted by the AASB]

Definitions

19.1   In this Standard:

attachment date means, for a direct insurer, the date as from which the insurer accepts risk from the insured under an insurance contract or endorsement or, for a reinsurer, the date from which the reinsurer accepts risk from the direct insurer or another reinsurer under a reinsurance arrangement

cedant means the policyholder under a reinsurance contract

claim means a demand by any party external to the entity for payment by the insurer on account of an alleged loss resulting from an insured event or events, that have occurred, alleged to be covered by an insurance contract

claims expense means the charge to the statement of comprehensive income for the reporting period and represents the sum of claims settled and claims management expenses relating to claims incurred in the period and the movement in the gross outstanding claims liability in the period

claims incurred means claims that have occurred prior to the end of the reporting period, whether reported or unreported at the end of the reporting period

deposit component means a contractual component that is not accounted for as a derivative under AASB 9 *Financial Instruments* and would be within the scope of AASB 9 if it were a separate instrument

deposit premium means the premium charged by the insurer at the inception of a contract under which the final premium depends on conditions prevailing over the contract period and so is not determined until the expiry of that period

direct insurance contract means an insurance contract that is not a reinsurance contract

fair value is the price that would be received to sell an asset or paid to transfer a liability in an orderly transaction between market participants at the measurement date. (See AASB 13.)

financial risk means the risk of a possible future change in one or more of a specified interest rate, financial instrument price, commodity price, foreign exchange rate, index of prices or rates, a credit rating or credit index or other variable, provided in the case of a non-financial variable that the variable is not specific to a party to the contract

future claims means claims in respect of insured events that are expected to occur in future reporting periods under policies where the attachment date is prior to the end of the reporting period

general insurance contract means an insurance contract that is not a life insurance contract

general insurer means an insurer that writes general insurance contracts

general reinsurance contract means a reinsurance contract that is not a *life reinsurance contract*

insurance asset means an insurer's net contractual rights under an insurance contract

insurance contract means a contract under which one party (the insurer) accepts significant insurance risk from another party (the policyholder) by agreeing to compensate the policyholder if a specified uncertain future event (the insured event) adversely affects the policyholder

(Refer to Appendix for additional guidance in applying this definition.)

insurance liability **means an insurer's net contractual obligations under an insurance contract**

insurance risk **means risk, other than financial risk, transferred from the holder of a contract to the issuer**

insured event **means an uncertain future event covered by an insurance contract and creates insurance risk**

insurer **means the party that has an obligation under an insurance contract to compensate a policyholder if an insured event occurs**

inwards reinsurance **means reinsurance contracts written by reinsurers**

liability adequacy test **means an assessment of whether the carrying amount of an insurance liability needs to be increased (or the carrying amount of the related deferred acquisition costs or related intangible assets decreased) based on a review of future cash flows**

life insurance contract **means an insurance contract, or a financial instrument with a discretionary participation feature, regulated under the** *Life Insurance Act 1995*, **and similar contracts issued by entities operating outside Australia**

life reinsurance contract **means a life insurance contract issued by one insurer (the reinsurer) to compensate another insurer (the cedant) for losses on one or more contracts issued by the cedant**

net claims incurred **means direct claims costs net of reinsurance and other recoveries, and indirect claims handling costs, determined on a discounted basis**

non-insurance contract **means a contract regulated under the** *Insurance Act 1973*, **and similar contracts issued by entities operating outside Australia, which fails to meet the definition of an insurance contract under this Standard**

(An example of a non-insurance contract might be a type of complex financial reinsurance contract.)

outstanding claims liability **means all unpaid claims and related claims handling expenses relating to claims incurred prior to the end of the reporting period**

policyholder **means a party that has a right to compensation under an insurance contract if an insured event occurs**

premium **means the amount charged in relation to accepting risk from the insured, but does not include amounts collected on behalf of third parties**

reinsurance assets **means a cedant's net contractual rights under a reinsurance contract**

reinsurance contract **means an insurance contract issued by one insurer (the reinsurer) to compensate another insurer (the cedant) for losses on one or more contracts issued by the cedant**

reinsurer **means the party that has an obligation under a reinsurance contract to compensate a cedant if an insured event occurs**

separate financial statements **are those presented by a parent, an investor in an associate or a venturer in a jointly controlled entity, in which the investments are accounted for on the basis of the direct equity interest rather than on the basis of the reported results and net assets of the investees**

unbundle **means to treat the components of a contract as if they were separate contracts**

weather derivative **means a contract that requires payment based on climatic, geological or other physical variables**

19.2   The following terms are defined in AASB 9 or AASB 132 and are used in this Standard with the meaning specified in those Standards:

    (a)   financial asset;

(b)   financial guarantee contract;

(c)   financial instrument; and

(d)   financial liability.

APPENDIX
DEFINITION OF AN INSURANCE CONTRACT

This Appendix is an integral part of AASB 1023.

1   This Appendix gives guidance on the definition of an insurance contract in section 19 of the Standard. It addresses the following issues:

(a)   the term 'uncertain future event' (paragraphs 2-4);

(b)   payments in kind (paragraphs 5-6);

(c)   insurance risk and other risks (paragraphs 7-16);

(d)   examples of insurance contracts (paragraphs 17-20);

(e)   significant insurance risk (paragraphs 21-26); and

(f)   changes in the level of insurance risk (paragraphs 27 and 28).

Uncertain future event

2   Uncertainty (or risk) is the essence of an insurance contract. Accordingly, at least one of the following is uncertain at the inception of an insurance contract:

(a)   whether an insured event will occur;

(b)   when it will occur; or

(c)   how much the insurer will need to pay if it occurs.

3   In some insurance contracts, the insured event is the discovery of a loss during the term of the contract, even if the loss arises from an event that occurred before the inception of the contract. In other insurance contracts, the insured event is an event that occurs during the term of the contract, even if the resulting loss is discovered after the end of the contract term.

4   Some insurance contracts cover events that have already occurred, but whose financial effect is still uncertain. An example is a reinsurance contract that covers the direct insurer against adverse development of claims already reported by policyholders. In such contracts, the insured event is the discovery of the ultimate cost of those claims.

Payments in kind

5   Some insurance contracts require or permit payments to be made in kind. An example is when the insurer replaces a stolen article directly, instead of reimbursing the policyholder. Another example is when an insurer uses its own hospitals and medical staff to provide medical services covered by the contracts.

6   Some fixed-fee service contracts in which the level of service depends on an uncertain event meet the definition of an insurance contract in this Standard but are not regulated as insurance contracts in some countries. One example is a maintenance contract in which the service provider agrees to repair specified equipment after a malfunction. The fixed service fee is based on the expected number of malfunctions, but it is uncertain whether a particular machine will break down. The malfunction of the equipment adversely affects its owner and the contract compensates the owner (in kind, rather than cash). Another example is a contract for car breakdown services in which the provider agrees, for a fixed annual fee, to provide roadside assistance or tow the car to a nearby garage. The latter contract could meet the definition of an insurance contract even if the provider does not agree to carry out repairs or replace parts.

Distinction between insurance risk and other risks

7   The definition of an insurance contract refers to insurance risk, which this Standard defines as risk, other than *financial risk*, transferred from the holder of a contract to the issuer. A contract that exposes the issuer to financial risk without significant insurance risk is not an insurance contract.

8   The definition of financial risk in section 19 of the Standard includes a list of financial and non-financial variables. That list includes non-financial variables that are not specific to a party to the contract, such as an index of earthquake losses in a particular region or an index of temperatures in a particular city. It excludes non-financial variables that are specific to a party to the contract, such as the occurrence or non-occurrence of a fire that damages or destroys an asset of that party. Furthermore, the risk of changes in the fair value of a non-financial asset is not a financial risk if the fair value reflects not only changes in market prices for such assets (a financial variable) but also the condition of a specific non-financial asset held by a party to a contract (a non-financial variable). For example, if a guarantee of the residual value of a specific car exposes the guarantor to the risk of changes in the car's physical condition, that risk is insurance risk, not financial risk.

9   Some contracts expose the issuer to financial risk, in addition to significant insurance risk. For example, many life insurance contracts both guarantee a minimum rate of return to policyholders (creating financial risk) and promise death benefits that at some times significantly exceed the policyholder's account balance (creating insurance risk in the form of mortality risk). Such contracts are insurance contracts.

10   Under some contracts, an insured event triggers the payment of an amount linked to a price index. Such contracts are insurance contracts, provided the payment that is contingent on the insured event can be significant. The link to the price index is an embedded derivative, but it also transfers insurance risk. If the resulting transfer of insurance risk is significant, the embedded derivative meets the definition of an insurance contract, in which case it need not be separated and measured at fair value (see paragraph 2.3.1 of this Standard).

11   The definition of insurance risk refers to risk that the insurer accepts from the policyholder. In other words, insurance risk is a pre-existing risk transferred from the policyholder to the insurer. Thus, a new risk created by the contract is not insurance risk.

12   The definition of an insurance contract refers to an adverse effect on the policyholder. The definition does not limit the payment by the insurer to an amount equal to the financial impact of the adverse event. For example, the definition does not exclude 'new-for-old' coverage that pays the policyholder sufficient to permit replacement of a damaged old asset by a new asset.

13   Some contracts require a payment if a specified uncertain event occurs, but do not require an adverse effect on the policyholder as a precondition for payment. Such a contract is not an insurance contract even if the holder uses the contract to mitigate an underlying risk exposure. For example, if the holder uses a derivative to hedge an underlying non financial variable that is correlated with cash flows from an asset of the entity, the derivative is not an insurance contract because payment is not conditional on whether the holder is adversely affected by a reduction in the cash flows from the asset. Conversely, the definition of an insurance contract refers to an uncertain event for which an adverse effect on the policyholder is a contractual precondition for payment. This contractual precondition does not require the insurer to investigate whether the event actually caused an adverse effect, but permits the insurer to deny payment if it is not satisfied that the event caused an adverse effect.

14   Lapse or persistency risk (i.e. the risk that the counterparty will cancel the contract earlier or later than the issuer had expected in pricing the contract) is not insurance risk because the payment to the counterparty is not contingent on an uncertain future event that adversely affects the counterparty. Similarly, expense risk (i.e. the risk of unexpected increases in the administrative costs associated with the servicing of a

contract, rather than in costs associated with insured events) is not insurance risk because an unexpected increase in expenses does not adversely affect the counterparty.

15 Therefore, a contract that exposes the issuer to lapse risk, persistency risk or expense risk is not an insurance contract unless it also exposes the issuer to insurance risk. However, if the issuer of that contract mitigates that risk by using a second contract to transfer part of that risk to another party, the second contract exposes that other party to insurance risk.

16 An insurer can accept significant insurance risk from the policyholder only if the insurer is an entity separate from the policyholder. In the case of a mutual insurer, the mutual accepts risk from each policyholder and pools that risk. Although policyholders bear that pooled risk collectively in their capacity as owners, the mutual has still accepted the risk that is the essence of an insurance contract.

Examples of general insurance contracts

17 The following are examples of contracts that are general insurance contracts, if the transfer of insurance risk is significant:

(a) insurance against theft or damage to property;

(b) insurance against product liability, professional liability, civil liability or legal expenses;

(c) medical cover;

(d) surety bonds, fidelity bonds, performance bonds and bid bonds (i.e. contracts that provide compensation if another party fails to perform a contractual obligation, for example an obligation to construct a building);

(e) credit insurance that provides for specified payments to be made to reimburse the holder for a loss it incurs because a specified debtor fails to make payment when due under the original or modified terms of a debt instrument. These contracts could have various legal forms, such as that of a guarantee, some types of letter of credit, a credit derivative default contract or an insurance contract. However, although these contracts meet the definition of an insurance contract, they also meet the definition of a financial guarantee contract in AASB 9 and are within the scope of AASB 7 and AASB 9, not this Standard (see paragraph 2.2(f)). Nevertheless, if an issuer of financial guarantee contracts has previously asserted explicitly that it regards such contracts as insurance contracts and has used accounting applicable to insurance contracts, the issuer may elect to apply either AASB 9 and AASB 7 or this Standard to such financial guarantee contracts;

(f) product warranties. Product warranties issued by another party for goods sold by a manufacturer, dealer or retailer are within the scope of this Standard. However, product warranties issued directly by a manufacturer, dealer or retailer are outside its scope, because they are within the scope of AASB 15 *Revenue from Contracts with Customers* and AASB 137 *Provisions, Contingent Liabilities and Contingent Assets*;

(g) title insurance (i.e. insurance against the discovery of defects in title to land that were not apparent when the insurance contract was written). In this case, the insured event is the discovery of a defect in the title, not the defect itself;

(h) travel assistance (i.e. compensation in cash or in kind to policyholders for losses suffered while they are travelling). Paragraphs 5 and 6 of this Appendix discuss some contracts of this kind;

(i) catastrophe bonds that provide for reduced payments of principal, interest or both if a specified event adversely affects the issuer of the bond (unless the specified event does not create significant insurance risk, for example if the event is a change in an interest rate or foreign exchange rate);

AASB

(j)   insurance swaps and other contracts that require a payment based on changes in climatic, geological or other physical variables that are specific to a party to the contract; and

(k)   reinsurance contracts.

18   The following are examples of items that are not general insurance contracts:

(a)   contracts that have the legal form of insurance, but pass all significant insurance risk back to the policyholder through non-cancellable and enforceable mechanisms that adjust future payments by the policyholder as a direct result of insured losses, for example some financial reinsurance contracts or some group contracts (such contracts are normally non-insurance *financial instruments* or service contracts, see paragraphs 19 and 20 of this Appendix);

(b)   self-insurance, in other words retaining a risk that could have been covered by insurance (there is no insurance contract because there is no agreement with another party);

(c)   contracts (such as gambling contracts) that require a payment if a specified uncertain future event occurs, but do not require, as a contractual precondition for payment, that the event adversely affects the policyholder. However, this does not preclude the specification of a predetermined payout to quantify the loss caused by a specified event such as an accident;

(d)   derivatives that expose one party to financial risk but not insurance risk, because they require that party to make payment based solely on changes in one or more of a specified interest rate, financial instrument price, commodity price, foreign exchange rate, index of prices or rates, credit rating or credit index or other variable, provided in the case of a non-financial variable that the variable is not specific to a party to the contract (see AASB 9 for derivative assets and AASB 9 for derivative liabilities);

(e)   a credit-related guarantee (or letter of credit, credit derivative default contract or credit insurance contract) that requires payments even if the holder has not incurred a loss on the failure of the debtor to make payments when due (see AASB 9);

(f)   contracts that require a payment based on a climatic, geological or other physical variable that is not specific to a party to the contract (commonly described as weather derivatives);

(g)   catastrophe bonds that provide for reduced payments of principal, interest or both, based on a climatic, geological or other physical variable that is not specific to a party to the contract; and

(h)   life insurance contracts.

19   If the contracts described in paragraph 18 of this Appendix create financial assets or financial liabilities, they are within the scope of AASB 9. Among other things, this means that the parties to the contract use what is sometimes called deposit accounting, which involves the following:

(a)   one party recognises the consideration received as a financial liability, rather than as revenue; and

(b)   the other party recognises the consideration paid as a financial asset, rather than as an expense.

20   If the contracts described in paragraph 18 of this Appendix do not create financial assets or financial liabilities, AASB 15 applies. Under AASB 15, revenue is recognised when (or as) an entity satisfies a performance obligation by transferring a promised good or service to a customer in an amount that reflects the consideration to which the entity expects to be entitled.

Significant insurance risk

21 A contract is an insurance contract only if it transfers significant insurance risk. Paragraphs 7 to 20 of this Appendix discuss insurance risk. The following paragraphs discuss the assessment of whether insurance risk is significant.

22 Insurance risk is significant if, and only if, an insured event could cause an insurer to pay significant additional benefits in any scenario, excluding scenarios that lack commercial substance (i.e. have no discernible effect on the economics of the transaction). If significant additional benefits would be payable in scenarios that have commercial substance, the condition in the previous sentence may be met even if the insured event is extremely unlikely or even if the expected (i.e. probability-weighted) present value of contingent cash flows is a small proportion of the expected present value of all the remaining contractual cash flows.

23 The additional benefits described in paragraph 22 of this Appendix refer to amounts that exceed those that would be payable if no insured event occurred (excluding scenarios that lack commercial substance). Those additional amounts include claims handling and claims assessment costs, but exclude:

(a) the loss of the ability to charge the policyholder for future services;

(b) a payment conditional on an event that does not cause a significant loss to the holder of the contract. For example, consider a contract that requires the issuer to pay one million currency units if an asset suffers physical damage causing an insignificant economic loss of one currency unit to the holder. In this contract, the holder transfers to the insurer the insignificant risk of losing one currency unit. At the same time, the contract creates non-insurance risk that the issuer will need to pay 999,999 currency units if the specified event occurs. Because the issuer does not accept significant insurance risk from the holder, this contract is not an insurance contract; and

(c) possible reinsurance recoveries. The insurer accounts for these separately.

24 An insurer shall assess the significance of insurance risk contract by contract, rather than by reference to materiality to the financial statements[1]. Thus, insurance risk may be significant even if there is a minimal probability of material losses for a whole book of contracts. This contract-by-contract assessment makes it easier to classify a contract as an insurance contract. However, if a relatively homogeneous book of small contracts is known to consist of contracts that all transfer insurance risk, an insurer need not examine each contract within that book to identify a few non-derivative contracts that transfer insignificant insurance risk.

25 Paragraph 22 of this Appendix refers to additional benefits. These additional benefits could include a requirement to pay benefits earlier if the insured event occurs earlier and the payment is not adjusted for the time value of money.

26 If an insurance contract is unbundled into a deposit component and an insurance component, the significance of insurance risk transfer is assessed by reference to the insurance component. The significance of insurance risk transferred by an embedded derivative is assessed by reference to the embedded derivative.

Changes in the level of insurance risk

27 Some contracts do not transfer any insurance risk to the issuer at inception, although they do transfer insurance risk at a later time.

28 A contract that qualifies as an insurance contract remains an insurance contract until all rights and obligations are extinguished or expire.

---

1 For this purpose, contracts entered into simultaneously with a single counterparty (or contracts that are otherwise interdependent) form a single contract.

COMPILATION DETAILS

Accounting Standard AASB 1023 *General Insurance Contracts* as amended

This compiled Standard applies to annual reporting periods beginning on or after 1 January 2018 but before 1 January 2019 for for-profit entities. It takes into account amendments up to and including 12 December 2017 and was prepared on 20 May 2018 by the staff of the Australian Accounting Standards Board (AASB).

This compilation is not a separate Accounting Standard made by the AASB. Instead, it is a representation of AASB 1023 (July 2004) as amended by other Accounting Standards, which are listed in the Table below.

Table of Standards

Standard	Date made	FRL identifier	Commencement date	Effective date *(annual reporting periods ... on or after ...)*	Application, saving or transitional provisions
AASB 1023	15 Jul 2004	F2005B01401	24 May 2005	*(beginning)* 1 Jan 2005	–
AASB 2005-2	3 Jun 2005	F2005L01699	30 Jun 2005	*(beginning)* 1 Jan 2005	–
AASB 2005-4	9 Jun 2005	F2005L01708	30 Jun 2005	*(beginning)* 1 Jan 2006	see (a) below
AASB 2005-9	6 Sep 2005	F2005L03009	7 Oct 2005	*(beginning)* 1 Jan 2006	see (a) below
AASB 2005-10	5 Sep 2005	F2005L02840	27 Sep 2005	*(beginning)* 1 Jan 2007	see (b) below
AASB 2005-12	8 Dec 2005	F2005L04207	24 Dec 2005	*(ending)* 31 Dec 2005	see (c) below
AASB 2007-3	26 Feb 2007	F2007L00551	8 Mar 2007	*(beginning)* 1 Jan 2009	see (d) below
AASB 2007-4	30 Apr 2007	F2007L01669	16 Jun 2007	*(beginning)* 1 Jul 2007	see (e) below
AASB 2007-8	24 Sep 2007	F2007L04130	26 Oct 2007	*(beginning)* 1 Jan 2009	see (f) below
AASB 2007-10	13 Dec 2007	F2008L04269	29 Oct 2008	*(beginning)* 1 Jan 2009	see (f) below
AASB 2008-5	24 Jul 2008	F2008L03030	16 Aug 2008	*(beginning)* 1 Jan 2009	see (g) below
AASB 2009-2	22 Apr 2009	F2009L01638	9 May 2009	*(beginning)* 1 Jan 2009 and *(ending)* 30 Apr 2009	see (h) below
AASB 2009-6	25 Jun 2009	F2009L02729	17 Jul 2009	*(beginning)* 1 Jan 2009 and *(ending)* 30 Jun 2009	see (i) below
Erratum	5 Oct 2009			*(beginning)* 1 Jan 2009 and *(ending)* 30 Jun 2009	see (j) below

Standard	Date made	FRL identifier	Commence-ment date	Effective date (*annual reporting periods ... on or after ...*)	Application, saving or transitional provisions
AASB 2009-11	7 Dec 2009	F2009L04690	23 Dec 2009	(*beginning*) 1 Jan 2018	see (k) below
AASB 2009-12	15 Dec 2009	F2009L04669	23 Dec 2009	(*beginning*) 1 Jan 2011	see (l) below
AASB 2010-5	27 Oct 2010	F2010L03081	25 Nov 2010	(*beginning*) 1 Jan 2011	see (l) below
AASB 2010-7	6 Dec 2010	F2011L00315	1 Mar 2011	(*beginning*) 1 Jan 2018	see (m) below
AASB 2011-7	29 Aug 2011	F2011L02017	5 Oct 2011	(*beginning*) 1 Jan 2013	see (n) below
AASB 2011-8	2 Sep 2011	F2011L02038	8 Oct 2011	(*beginning*) 1 Jan 2013	see (o) below
AASB 2012-10	18 Dec 2012	F2013L00080	23 Jan 2013	(*beginning*) 1 Jan 2013	see (p) below
AASB 2013-9	20 Dec 2013	F2014L00370	1 Apr 2014	Pt A (*ending*) 20 Dec 2013 Pt B (*beginning*) 1 Jan 2014	see (q) below see (r) below
AASB 2014-5	12 Dec 2014	F2015L00107	12 Dec 2014	(*beginning*) 1 Jan 2018	see (s) below
AASB 2014-7	17 Dec 2014	F2015L00135	17 Dec 2014	(*beginning*) 1 Jan 2018	see (t) below
AASB 2015-8	22 Oct 2015	F2015L01840	31 Dec 2016	(*beginning*) 1 Jan 2017	see (u) below
AASB 16	23 Feb 2016	F2016L00233	31 Dec 2018	(*beginning*) 1 Jan 2019	not compiled*
AASB 2016-7	9 Dec 2016	F2017L00043	31 Dec 2016	(*beginning*) 1 Jan 2017	see (v) below
AASB 17	19 Jul 2017	F2017L01184	31 Dec 2020	(*beginning*) 1 Jan 2021	not compiled*
AASB 2017-5	12 Dec 2017	F2018L00067	31 Dec 2017	(*beginning*) 1 Jan 2018	see (w) below

* The amendments made by this Standard are not included in this compilation, which presents the principal Standard as applicable to annual reporting periods beginning on or after 1 January 2018 but before 1 January 2019 for for-profit entities.

(a) Entities may elect to apply this Standard to annual reporting periods beginning on or after 1 January 2005 but before 1 January 2006.

(b) Entities may elect to apply this Standard to annual reporting periods beginning on or after 1 January 2005 but before 1 January 2007.

(c) Entities may elect to apply this Standard to annual reporting periods beginning on or after 1 January 2005 that end before 31 December 2005.

(d) Entities may elect to apply this Standard to annual reporting periods beginning on or after 1 January 2005 but before 1 January 2009, provided that AASB 8 *Operating Segments* is also applied to such periods.

(e) Entities may elect to apply this Standard to annual reporting periods beginning on or after 1 January 2005 but before 1 July 2007.

(f) Entities may elect to apply this Standard to annual reporting periods beginning on or after 1 January 2005 but before 1 January 2009, provided that AASB 101 *Presentation of Financial Statements* (September 2007) is also applied to such periods.

(Continued)

(Continued)

(g) Entities may elect to apply this Standard, or its amendments to individual Standards, to annual reporting periods beginning on or after 1 January 2005 but before 1 January 2009.

(h) Entities may elect to apply this Standard to annual reporting periods beginning on or after 1 January 2005 but before 1 January 2009 and to annual reporting periods beginning on or after 1 January 2009 that end before 30 April 2009.

(i) Entities may elect to apply this Standard to annual reporting periods beginning on or after 1 January 2005 but before 1 January 2009, provided that AASB 101 *Presentation of Financial Statements* (September 2007) is also applied to such periods, and to annual reporting periods beginning on or after 1 January 2009 that end before 30 June 2009.

(j) Entities may elect to apply this Erratum to annual reporting periods beginning on or after 1 January 2005, provided that AASB 2009-6 *Amendments to Australian Accounting Standards* is also applied to such periods.

(k) AASB 2009-11 has been amended by AASB 2010-10 (made 31 December 2010) and AASB 2012-6 (made 10 September 2012). AASB 2014-1 deferred the amendments set out in AASB 2009-11 to annual reporting periods beginning on or after 1 January 2018.

Entities may elect to apply this Standard to annual reporting periods ending on or after 31 December 2009 that begin before 1 January 2018, provided that AASB 9 (2009) *Financial Instruments* is also applied to such periods.

(l) Entities may elect to apply this Standard to annual reporting periods beginning on or after 1 January 2005 but before 1 January 2011.

(m) AASB 2010-7 has been amended by AASB 2010-10 (made 31 December 2010) and AASB 2012-6 (made 10 September 2012). AASB 2014-1 deferred the amendments set out in AASB 2010-7 to annual reporting periods beginning on or after 1 January 2018.

Entities may elect to apply this Standard as set out in paragraph 6 of AASB 2010-7.

(n) AASB 2011-7 has been amended by AASB 2012-6 (made 10 September 2012) and AASB 2012-10 (made 18 December 2012).

For-profit entities may elect to apply this Standard to annual reporting periods beginning on or after 1 January 2005 but before 1 January 2013. The Standard applies for not-for-profit entities to annual reporting periods beginning on or after 1 January 2014. Not-for-profit entities may elect to apply this Standard to annual reporting periods beginning on or after 1 January 2013 but before 1 January 2014. If an entity elects to apply this Standard to such annual reporting periods, it shall also apply AASB 10 *Consolidated Financial Statements* and associated Standards to such periods.

(o) AASB 2011-8 has been amended by AASB 2011-10 (made 5 September 2011) and AASB 2012-6 (made 10 September 2012).

Entities may elect to apply this Standard to annual reporting periods beginning on or after 1 January 2005 but before 1 January 2013, provided that AASB 13 *Fair Value Measurement* is also applied to such periods.

(p) Entities may elect to apply this Standard to annual reporting periods beginning on or after 1 January 2005 but before 1 January 2013.

(q) Entities may elect to apply Part A of this Standard to annual reporting periods beginning on or after 1 January 2005 that end before 20 December 2013, provided that AASB CF 2013-1 *Amendments to the Australian Conceptual Framework* and AASB 1048 *Interpretation of Standards* (December 2013) are also applied to the such periods.

(r) Early application of Part B of this Standard is not permitted.

(s) Entities may elect to apply this Standard to annual reporting periods beginning on or after 1 January 2005 but before 1 January 2018, provided that AASB 15 *Revenue from Contracts with Customers* is also applied to such periods. AASB 2015-8 updated the application date of the amendments in this Standard (and of AASB 15) to 1 January 2018.

(t) Entities may elect to apply this Standard to annual reporting periods beginning after 24 July 2014 but before 1 January 2018, provided that AASB 9 *Financial Instruments* (2014) is also applied to such periods.

(u) The amendments made by AASB 2014-5 are no longer required to apply to annual reporting periods beginning on or after 1 January 2017 but before 1 January 2018, as a consequence of AASB 2015-8 deferring the effective date of AASB 15 (and its consequential amendments in AASB 2014-5) from 1 January 2017 to 1 January 2018.

(v) As a result of AASB 2016-7 deferring the effective date of AASB 15 (and its consequential amendments in AASB 2014-5) for not-for-profit entities from 1 January 2018 to 1 January 2019, the amendments made by AASB 2014-5 apply to not-for-profit entities only to annual reporting periods beginning on or after 1 January 2019, instead of 1 January 2018. However, earlier application is permitted, provided that AASB 15 is also applied.

(w) Entities may elect to apply this Standard to annual periods beginning before 1 January 2018.

Table of amendments

Paragraph affected	How affected	By ... [paragraph]
1.4	deleted	AASB 2013-9B [37, 38]
1.4.1	deleted	AASB 2013-9B [40]
2.2	amended amended amended amended amended	AASB 2005-9 [12, 25] AASB 2007-4 [104] AASB 2010-7 [57] AASB 2014-5 [41] AASB 2017-5 [27]
2.3.1	amended amended	AASB 2009-11 [54] AASB 2010-7 [7, 57]
2.3.2	amended	AASB 2010-7 [56]
2.4.4	amended	AASB 2010-7 [56]
4.2.5	amended	AASB 2009-12 [19]
4.4.8	amended	AASB 2009-12 [19]
4.5.2	amended amended	AASB 2007-10 [95] AASB 2009-12 [19]
5.1.10	amended	AASB 2005-2 [7]
5.2.4	amended	AASB 2009-12 [19]
6.1.3	amended	Erratum, Oct 2009 [6]
9.1	amended	AASB 2005-2 [8]
9.1.1	deleted	AASB 2005-2 [9]
9.1.2	renumbered as 9.1.1 added	AASB 2005-2 [10] AASB 2005-2 [11]
9.1.5	amended	AASB 2005-2 [12]
13.3.1	amended	AASB 2007-4 [104]
15.2	amended amended amended	AASB 2005-4 [21] AASB 2009-11 [53] AASB 2010-7 [7, 56]
15.2.1	amended amended amended amended	AASB 2005-4 [21] AASB 2009-11 [54] AASB 2010-7 [7, 57] AASB 2014-7 [55]
15.2.2	amended amended amended amended	AASB 2005-4 [22] AASB 2009-11 [54] AASB 2010-7 [7, 57] AASB 2014-7 [55]
15.3	amended	AASB 2011-8 [103]
15.4.1-15.4.2	deleted	AASB 2012-10 [66]
15.5	amended amended amended amended amended amended amended	AASB 2005-4 [23] AASB 2005-12 [14] AASB 2007-4 [104] AASB 2008-5 [79] AASB 2009-11 [53] AASB 2010-7 [7, 56] AASB 2011-7 [53, A13]
15.5.1	amended amended amended	AASB 2009-11 [53] AASB 2010-7 [7, 56] AASB 2011-7 [54, A14]

(Continued)

(*Continued*)

Paragraph affected	How affected	By ... [paragraph]
15.5.2	amended amended amended amended amended	AASB 2005-4 [24] AASB 2008-5 [79] AASB 2009-11 [53] AASB 2010-7 [7, 56] AASB 2011-7 [54, A14]
15.5.3	deleted	AASB 2005-12 [15]
16.1	amended amended amended	AASB 2005-4 [25] AASB 2009-11 [54] AASB 2010-7 [7, 56]
16.1.1	amended amended amended	AASB 2005-4 [25] AASB 2009-11 [54] AASB 2010-7 [7, 57]
16.1.2	added added amended	AASB 2009-11 [54] AASB 2010-7 [7, 57] AASB 2014-7 [55]
16.1.3	added added	AASB 2009-11 [54] AASB 2010-7 [7, 57]
17.1(a), (b) & (c)	deleted	AASB 2005-2 [13]
17.1(d)	renumbered as 17.1(a)	AASB 2005-2 [14]
17.1(e)	renumbered as 17.1(b)	AASB 2005-2 [15]
17.1(f)	amended renumbered as 17.1(c)	AASB 2005-2 [16]
17.2	amended amended	AASB 2005-2 [17] AASB 2007-4 [104]
17.5 (and preceding heading)	deleted	AASB 2007-3 [17]
17.5.1	deleted	AASB 2007-3 [17]
17.6.4	amended	AASB 2013-9A [30]
17.7 (and preceding heading)	amended	AASB 2005-10 [41]
17.7.1	amended amended	AASB 2005-10 [41] AASB 2009-2 [13]
17.7.3	amended	AASB 2005-10 [42]
17.7.4	amended	AASB 2009-6 [100]
17.7.5	added	AASB 2005-10 [43]
17.8 (and preceding heading)	added amended	AASB 2005-2 [18] AASB 2007-4 [104]
17.8.1	renumbered as 17.9.1	AASB 2005-2 [19]
17.9.1	amended	AASB 2005-10 [44]
18.3	amended	AASB 2005-10 [45]
18.4	added deleted	AASB 2009-11 [54] AASB 2010-7 [7, 57]
18.5	added deleted	AASB 2010-7 [57] AASB 2014-7 [55]
19.1	amended amended amended amended	AASB 2007-4 [103,104] AASB 2010-5 [61] AASB 2010-7 [57] AASB 2011-8 [12]

Paragraph affected	How affected	By ... [paragraph]
19.2	added amended	AASB 2010-5 [62] AASB 2014-7 [55]
Appendix, 1	amended	AASB 2010-5 [63]
Appendix, 8	amended	AASB 2010-5 [63]
Appendix, 17	amended amended amended	AASB 2005-9 [13, 25] AASB 2010-7 [56] AASB 2014-5 [42]
Appendix, 18	amended amended amended	AASB 2005-9 [14] AASB 2009-11 [55] AASB 2010-7 [7, 56]
Appendix, 19	amended amended	AASB 2009-11 [55] AASB 2010-7 [7, 56]
Appendix, 20	amended	AASB 2014-5 [42]

General terminology amendments

The following amendments are not shown in the above Table of Amendments:

References to 'financial report(s)' were amended to 'financial statements' by AASB 2007-8 and AASB 2007-10, except in relation to specific Corporations Act references and interim financial reports.

References to 'income statement' and 'balance sheet' were amended to 'statement of comprehensive income' and 'statement of financial position' respectively by AASB 2007-8.

References to 'reporting date' and 'each reporting date' were amended to 'end of the reporting period' and 'the end of each reporting period' respectively by AASB 2007-8.

AASB

AASB 1038
Life Insurance Contracts
(Compiled December 2015)

This compiled Standard applies to annual reporting periods beginning on or after 1 January 2018. Early application is permitted for annual reporting periods beginning on or after 24 July 2014 but before 1 January 2018. It incorporates relevant amendments made up to and including 17 December 2015.

Prepared on 12 March 2015 by the staff of the Australian Accounting Standards Board.

This note is not part of Accounting Standard AASB 1038.

The following unincorporated amendments are not included in this compiled Standard.

- AASB 17 *Insurance Contracts* — Appendix D sets out the amendments to other Standards that are a consequence of the AASB issuing AASB 17 *Insurance Contracts*. This Standard is applicable from 1 January 2021. Earlier application is permitted, but entities must apply AASB 9 *Financial Instruments* and AASB 15 *Revenue from Contracts with Customers* first.

- AASB 2016-7 *Amendments to Australian Accounting Standards — Deferral of AASB 15 for Not-for-Profit Entities.* This Standard defers the consequential amendments that were originally set out in AASB 2014-5 *Amendments to Australian Accounting Standards arising from AASB 15,* by restating the effective date of the amendments set out in AASB 2015-8 *Amendments to Australian Accounting Standards* for not-for-profit entities. This Standard defers the application of AASB 15 to 1 January 2019. Earlier application is permitted provided AASB 1058 is also applied to the same period.

Entities early-adopting any amendments with later application dates will need to refer to the amending Standards that have not yet been incorporated into compilations. The abovementioned unincorporated amendments may be located on the AASB website at www.aasb.gov.au or on the Federal Register of Legislation website at www.legislation.gov.au.

CONTENTS

COMPILATION DETAILS
COMPARISON WITH IFRS 4
ACCOUNTING STANDARD
AASB 1038 *LIFE INSURANCE CONTRACTS*

    Chartered Accountants Australia and New Zealand

AASB

Australian Accounting Standard AASB 1038 *Life Insurance Contracts* (as amended) is set out in paragraphs 1.1 – 20.2 and the Appendix. All the paragraphs have equal authority. Paragraphs in **bold type** state the main principles. Terms defined in this Standard are in *italics* the first time they appear in the Standard. AASB 1038 is to be read in the context of other Australian Accounting Standards including AASB 1048 *Interpretation of Standards*, which identifies the Australian Accounting Interpretations. In the absence of explicit guidance, AASB 108 *Accounting Policies, Changes in Accounting Estimates and Errors* provides a basis for selecting and applying accounting policies.

COMPILATION DETAILS

Accounting Standard AASB 1038 *Life Insurance Contracts* as amended

This compiled Standard applies to annual reporting periods beginning on or after 1 January 2018. It takes into account amendments up to and including 17 December 2014 and was prepared on 12 March 2015 by the staff of the Australian Accounting Standards Board (AASB).

This compilation is not a separate Accounting Standard made by the AASB. Instead, it is a representation of AASB 1038 (July 2004) as amended by other Accounting Standards, which are listed in the Table below.

Table of Standards

Standard	Date made	Application date *(annual reporting periods ... on or after ...)*	Application, saving or transitional provisions
AASB 1038	15 Jul 2004	*(beginning)* 1 Jan 2005	
AASB 2005-4	9 Jun 2005	*(beginning)* 1 Jan 2006	see (a) below
AASB 2005-10	5 Sep 2005	*(beginning)* 1 Jan 2007	see (b) below
AASB 2005-12	8 Dec 2005	*(ending)* 31 Dec 2005	see (c) below
AASB 2007-3	26 Feb 2007	*(beginning)* 1 Jan 2009	see (d) below
AASB 2007-4	30 Apr 2007	*(beginning)* 1 Jul 2007	see (e) below
AASB 2007-8	24 Sep 2007	*(beginning)* 1 Jan 2009	see (f) below
AASB 2007-10	13 Dec 2007	*(beginning)* 1 Jan 2009	see (f) below
AASB 2008-5	24 Jul 2008	*(beginning)* 1 Jan 2009	see (g) below
AASB 2009-2	22 Apr 2009	*(beginning)* 1 Jan 2009 and *(ending)* 30 Apr 2009	see (h) below
AASB 2009-6	25 Jun 2009	*(beginning)* 1 Jan 2009 and *(ending)* 30 Jun 2009	see (i) below
Erratum	5 Oct 2009	*(beginning)* 1 Jan 2009 and *(ending)* 30 Jun 2009	see (j) below
AASB 2009-11	7 Dec 2009	*(beginning)* 1 Jan 2015	see (k) below
AASB 2010-5	27 Oct 2010	*(beginning)* 1 Jan 2011	see (l) below
AASB 2010-7	6 Dec 2010	*(beginning)* 1 Jan 2015	see (m) below
AASB 2011-7	29 Aug 2011	*(beginning)* 1 Jan 2013	see (n) below
AASB 2011-8	2 Sep 2011	*(beginning)* 1 Jan 2013	see (o) below
AASB 2012-10	18 Dec 2012	*(beginning)* 1 Jan 2013	see (p) below
AASB 2013-2	13 Mar 2013	*(ending)* 31 Mar 2013	see (q) below
AASB 2013-7	14 Oct 2013	*(beginning)* 1 Jan 2014	see (r) below
AASB 2013-9	20 Dec 2013	Pt A *(ending)* 20 Dec 2013 Pt B *(ending)* 1 Jan 2014	see (s) below see (t) below
AASB 2014-5	12 Dec 2014	*(beginning)* 1 Jan 2017	see (u) below
AASB 2014-7	17 Dec 2014	*(beginning)* 1 Jan 2018	see (v) below

(a) Entities may elect to apply this Standard to annual reporting periods beginning on or after 1 January 2005 but before 1 January 2006.

(b) Entities may elect to apply this Standard to annual reporting periods beginning on or after 1 January 2005 but before 1 January 2007.

(c) Entities may elect to apply this Standard to annual reporting periods beginning on or after 1 January 2005 that end before 31 December 2005.

(d) Entities may elect to apply this Standard to annual reporting periods beginning on or after 1 January 2005 but before 1 January 2009, provided that AASB 8 *Operating Segments* is also applied to such periods.

(e) Entities may elect to apply this Standard to annual reporting periods beginning on or after 1 January 2005 but before 1 July 2007.

(f) Entities may elect to apply this Standard to annual reporting periods beginning on or after 1 January 2005 but before 1 January 2009, provided that AASB 101 *Presentation of Financial Statements* (September 2007) is also applied to such periods.

(g) Entities may elect to apply this Standard, or its amendments to individual Standards, to annual reporting periods beginning on or after 1 January 2005 but before 1 January 2009.

(h) Entities may elect to apply this Standard to annual reporting periods beginning on or after 1 January 2005 but before 1 January 2009 and to annual reporting periods beginning on or after 1 January 2009 that end before 30 April 2009.

(i) Entities may elect to apply this Standard to annual reporting periods beginning on or after 1 January 2005 but before 1 January 2009, provided that AASB 101 *Presentation of Financial Statements* (September 2007) is also applied to such periods, and to annual reporting periods beginning on or after 1 January 2009 that end before 30 June 2009.

(j) Entities may elect to apply this Erratum to annual reporting periods beginning on or after 1 January 2005, provided that AASB 2009-6 *Amendments to Australian Accounting Standards* is also applied to such periods.

(k) AASB 2009-11 has been amended by AASB 2010-10 (made 31 December 2010) and AASB 2012-6 (made 10 September 2012).

Entities may elect to apply this Standard to annual reporting periods ending on or after 31 December 2009 that begin before 1 January 2015, provided that AASB 9 (2009) *Financial Instruments* is also applied to such periods.

(l) Entities may elect to apply this Standard to annual reporting periods beginning on or after 1 January 2005 but before 1 January 2011.

(m) AASB 2010-7 has been amended by AASB 2010-10 (made 31 December 2010) and AASB 2012-6 (made 10 September 2012).

Entities may elect to apply this Standard as set out in paragraph 6 of AASB 2010-7.

(n) AASB 2011-7 has been amended by AASB 2012-6 (made 10 September 2012) and AASB 2012-10 (made 18 December 2012).

For-profit entities may elect to apply this Standard to annual reporting periods beginning on or after 1 January 2005 but before 1 January 2013. The Standard applies for not-for-profit entities to annual reporting periods beginning on or after 1 January 2014. Not-for-profit entities may elect to apply this Standard to annual reporting periods beginning on or after 1 January 2013 but before 1 January 2014. If an entity elects to apply this Standard to such annual reporting periods, it shall apply AASB 10 *Consolidated Financial Statements* and associated Standards to such periods.

(o) AASB 2011-8 has been amended by AASB 2011-10 (made 5 September 2011) and AASB 2012-6 (made 10 September 2012).

Entities may elect to apply this Standard to annual reporting periods beginning on or after 1 January 2005 but before 1 January 2013, provided that AASB 13 *Fair Value Measurement* is also applied to such periods.

(p) Entities may elect to apply this Standard to annual reporting periods beginning on or after 1 January 2005 but before 1 January 2013.

(q) Entities may elect to apply this Standard to annual reporting periods ending on or after 1 January 2013 but before 31 March 2013.

(r) Entities may elect to apply this Standard to annual reporting periods ending on or after 1 January 2005 but before 1 January 2014, provided that AASB 10 *Consolidated Financial Statements* is also applied to such periods.

(s) Entities may elect to apply this Standard to annual reporting periods beginning on or after 1 January 2005 that end before 20 December 2013, provided that AASB CF 2013-1 *Amendments to the Australian Conceptual Framework* and AASB 1048 *Interpretation of Standards* (December 2013) are also applied to the such periods.

(t) Early application of Part B of this Standard is not permitted.

(u) Entities may elect to apply this Standard to annual reporting periods beginning on or after 1 January 2005 but before 1 January 2017, provided that AASB 15 *Revenue from Contracts with Customers* is also applied to such periods.

(v) Entities may elect to apply this Standard to annual reporting periods beginning on or after 24 July 2014 but before 1 January 2018, provided that AASB 9 *Financial Instruments* (2014) is also applied to such periods.

Table of amendments

Paragraph affected	How affected	By ... [paragraph]
1.1	amended amended	AASB 2007-4 [105] AASB 2007-10 [99]
1.1.1	deleted	AASB 2013-7 [7]
1.4	deleted	AASB 2013-9B [37, 38]
1.4.1	deleted	AASB 2013-9B [41]
2.1.6	amended	AASB 2005-10 [46]
2.2.1	amended amended	AASB 2009-11 [57] AASB 2010-7 [7, 59]
2.2.2	amended	AASB 2010-7 [58]
4 (section heading)	amended	AASB 2013-7 [6]
4.1 (and preceding heading)	deleted	AASB 2013-7 [6, 7]
4.1.1	deleted	AASB 2013-7 [7]
4.1.2	amended	AASB 2005-12 [5]
4.2 (and preceding heading)	deleted	AASB 2013-7 [8]
4.2.1- 4.2.2	deleted	AASB 2013-7 [8]
5.2.4	deleted	Erratum, Oct 2009 [7]
8.4.2	amended	Erratum, Oct 2009 [8]
9.2.2	amended	AASB 2005-12 [6]
10.1.1	amended	AASB 2009-6 [101]
10.2	amended amended amended amended	AASB 2005-4 [26] AASB 2007-4 [109] AASB 2009-11 [56] AASB 2010-7 [7, 58]
10.2.1	amended amended amended amended	AASB 2005-4 [26] AASB 2009-11 [57] AASB 2010-7 [7, 59] AASB 2014-7 [56]
10.2.2	amended amended amended amended	AASB 2005-4 [27] AASB 2009-11 [57] AASB 2010-7 [7, 59] AASB 2014-7 [56]
10.3	amended amended	AASB 2007-4 [109] AASB 2011-8 [104]
10.4.1-10.4.2	deleted	AASB 2012-10 [67]
10.5	amended amended amended amended amended	AASB 2005-4 [28] AASB 2005-12 [7] AASB 2009-11 [56] AASB 2010-7 [7, 58] AASB 2011-7 [55, A15]
10.5.1	amended amended amended	AASB 2009-11 [56] AASB 2010-7 [7, 58] AASB 2011-7 [55, A15]
10.6	amended amended amended amended amended	AASB 2005-4 [29] AASB 2005-12 [8] AASB 2009-11 [56] AASB 2010-7 [7, 58] AASB 2011-7 [55, A15]

Paragraph affected	How affected	By ... [paragraph]
10.6.1	amended amended amended	AASB 2009-11 [56] AASB 2010-7 [7, 58] AASB 2011-7 [55, A15]
10.7	amended amended amended amended amended	AASB 2005-4 [30] AASB 2008-5 [80] AASB 2009-11 [56] AASB 2010-7 [7, 58] AASB 2011-7 [55, A15]
10.7.1	amended amended amended	AASB 2009-11 [56] AASB 2010-7 [7, 58] AASB 2011-7 [56, A16]
10.7.2	amended amended amended amended amended	AASB 2005-4 [31] AASB 2008-5 [80] AASB 2009-11 [56] AASB 2010-7 [7, 58] AASB 2011-7 [56, A16]
10.7.3	deleted	AASB 2005-12 [9]
12.1	amended amended	AASB 2005-4 [32] AASB 2010-7 [58]
12.1.1	renumbered as 12.1.2 added amended	AASB 2005-4 [33] AASB 2010-7 [58]
12.1.2	amended amended amended amended	AASB 2007-4 [109] AASB 2010-5 [64] AASB 2010-7 [58] AASB 2014-5 [43]
14.1.4	amended	AASB 2007-4 [109]
14.1.5	amended	AASB 2007-4 [109]
14.1.7	amended	AASB 2013-9A [31]
15.1 (and preceding heading)	amended amended	AASB 2005-10 [47] AASB 2007-4 [109]
15.1.1	amended amended amended	AASB 2005-10 [47] AASB 2007-4 [109] AASB 2009-2 [14]
15.1.2	amended	AASB 2005-10 [49]
15.1.3 (and preceding heading)	added amended	AASB 2005-10 [48] AASB 2007-4 [109]
17.5.2	amended	AASB 2005-12 [10]
17.5.3	amended	AASB 2005-12 [11]
17.5.4	amended amended	AASB 2005-12 [12] AASB 2010-7 [58]
17.5.5	amended amended amended amended	AASB 2005-10 [50, 51] AASB 2005-12 [13] AASB 2007-4 [106, 107, 109] AASB 2010-7 [58]
17.8 (and preceding heading)	amended	AASB 2013-2 [6]
17.8.1	deleted	AASB 2013-2 [6]
17.10	amended	AASB 2013-2 [6]
17.13.1	amended	AASB 2005-10 [52]
18.2.1	amended	AASB 2007-4 [109]

(Continued)

(Continued)

Paragraph affected	How affected	By ... [paragraph]
18.2.2 (and preceding heading)	deleted	AASB 2007-3 [18]
19.3	amended	AASB 2005-10 [53]
19.4	added deleted	AASB 2009-11 [57] AASB 2010-7 [7, 59]
19.5	added deleted	AASB 2010-7 [59] AASB 2014-7 [56]
20.1	amended amended amended amended	AASB 2007-4 [108] AASB 2010-5 [65] AASB 2010-7 [59] AASB 2011-8 [12]
20.2	added	AASB 2010-5 [66]
Appendix, 16	amended amended	AASB 2007-4 [109] AASB 2010-7 [58]
Appendix, 17	amended	AASB 2010-7 [58]
Appendix, 18	amended	AASB 2014-5 [44]

General terminology amendments

The following amendments are not shown in the above Table of Amendments:

References to 'financial report(s)' were amended to 'financial statements' by AASB 2007-8 and AASB 2007-10, except in relation to specific Corporations Act references and interim financial reports.

References to 'income statement' and 'balance sheet' were amended to 'statement of comprehensive income' and 'statement of financial position' respectively by AASB 2007-8.

References to 'reporting date' and 'each reporting date' were amended to 'end of the reporting period' and 'the end of each reporting period' respectively by AASB 2007-8.

COMPARISON WITH IFRS 4

AASB 1038 and IFRS 4

AASB 1038 *Life Insurance Contracts* as amended incorporates the limited improvements to accounting for insurance contracts required by IFRS 4 *Insurance Contracts*.

Life insurers applying this Standard and Australian equivalents to other IFRSs will therefore be compliant with IFRSs.

IFRS 4 is being implemented in Australia using three Accounting Standards:

(a) AASB 4 *Insurance Contracts* (the Australian equivalent to IFRS 4), which applies to fixed-fee service contracts that meet the definition of an insurance contract;

(b) AASB 1023 *General Insurance Contracts*, which applies to general insurance contracts; and

(c) AASB 1038, which applies to life insurance contracts.

IFRS 4 applies to all insurance contracts and financial instruments with discretionary participation features, whereas AASB 1038 applies to life insurance contracts and financial instruments with discretionary participation features, certain aspects of accounting for life investment contracts as well as certain aspects of accounting for assets that back life insurance liabilities or life investment contract liabilities.

Whereas IFRS 4 only includes limited improvements to accounting for insurance contracts and disclosure requirements, AASB 1038 addresses all aspects of the recognition, measurement and disclosure of life insurance contracts.

IFRS 4 allows insurers to use a practice described as "shadow accounting". The revised AASB 1038 does not allow shadow accounting.

ACCOUNTING STANDARD AASB 1038

The Australian Accounting Standards Board made Accounting Standard AASB 1038 *Life Insurance Contracts* under section 334 of the *Corporations Act 2001* on 15 July 2004.

This compiled version of AASB 1038 applies to annual reporting periods beginning on or after 1 January 2018. It incorporates relevant amendments contained in other AASB Standards made by the AASB and other decisions of the AASB up to and including 17 December 2014 (see Compilation Details).

ACCOUNTING STANDARD AASB 1038
LIFE INSURANCE CONTRACTS

Application

1.1 This Standard applies to each entity that is:

    (a) a *life insurer*; or

    (b) the parent in a group that includes a life insurer;

    when the entity:

    (c) is a reporting entity that is required to prepare financial reports in accordance with Part 2M.3 of the Corporations Act;

    (d) is an other reporting entity and prepares general purpose financial statements; or

    (e) prepares financial statements that are, or are held out to be, general purpose financial statements.

1.2 This Standard applies to annual reporting periods beginning on or after 1 January 2005.

    [Note: For application dates of paragraphs changed or added by an amending Standard, see Compilation Details.]

1.3 This Standard shall not be applied to annual reporting periods beginning before 1 January 2005.

1.4 [Deleted by the AASB]

1.4.1 [Deleted by the AASB]

1.4.2 For the purposes of AASB 134 *Interim Financial Reporting*, the determination of *policy liabilities* does not necessarily require a full actuarial valuation. In accordance with AASB 134, policy liabilities would need to be determined on a reliable basis, would be based on reasonable estimates, would include a full review of all assumptions, and would not be materially different from the policy liabilities determined by a full actuarial valuation.

1.5 When operative, this Standard supersedes AASB 1038 *Life Insurance Business* as approved by public notice in the *Commonwealth of Australia Gazette* No 546, 19 November 1998.

1.6 AASB 1038 (issued in November 1998) remains applicable until superseded by this Standard.

1.7 Notice of this Standard was published in the *Commonwealth of Australia Gazette* No S 294, 22 July 2004.

Scope

Life insurance contracts

2.1   This Standard applies to:

   (a)   life insurance contracts (including *life reinsurance contracts*) that a life insurer issues and to life reinsurance contracts that it holds;

   (b)   certain aspects of accounting for *life investment contracts* that a life insurer issues, or, in the case of a life investment contract that is reinsured, that it holds; and

   (c)   certain assets backing *life insurance liabilities* or *life investment contract liabilities*.

2.1.1   A life insurance contract is:

   (a)   an *insurance contract*, as defined by this Standard, regulated under the *Life Insurance Act 1995*, or similar contracts issued by entities operating outside Australia; or

   (b)   a *financial instrument* with a *discretionary participation feature*, which is regulated under the Life Insurance Act, or similar contracts issued by entities operating outside Australia.

2.1.2   All other insurance contracts are *general insurance contracts* and are treated under AASB 1023 *General Insurance Contracts* or AASB 4 *Insurance Contracts*.

2.1.3   A life insurer is defined as an *insurer* or *reinsurer*, registered under the Life Insurance Act, who issues life insurance contracts or life investment contracts, or a similar entity operating outside Australia.

2.1.4   This Standard applies to life insurance contracts issued by friendly societies registered under the Life Insurance Act. Private health insurance contracts that are issued under the *National Health Act 1953* by friendly societies registered under the Life Insurance Act are excluded from the scope of this Standard. Private health insurance contracts issued under the National Health Act are treated under AASB 1023.

2.1.5   Life insurers often sell contracts that do not meet the definition of a life insurance contract in this Standard. These contracts are referred to as life investment contracts for the purposes of this Standard. Section 12 addresses the requirements in relation to life investment contracts.

2.1.6   A financial instrument with a discretionary participation feature, issued by a life insurer, is defined as a life insurance contract for the purposes of this Standard and in measuring the life insurance liability, issuers of such instruments would apply paragraph 8.9. AASB 7 *Financial Instruments: Disclosures* addresses additional disclosure in relation to these financial instruments.

Embedded derivatives

2.2.1   AASB 9 *Financial Instruments* requires hybrid contracts that contain financial asset hosts to be classified and measured in their entirety in accordance with the requirements in paragraphs 4.1.1-4.1.5 of that Standard. However, AASB 9 requires an entity to separate some embedded derivatives from their financial liability hosts, measure them at *fair value* and include changes in their fair value in the statement of comprehensive income. AASB 9 applies to derivatives embedded in a life insurance contract unless the embedded derivative is itself a life insurance contract.

2.2.2   As an exception to the requirement in AASB 9, an insurer need not separate, and measure at fair value, a *policyholder's* option to surrender an insurance contract for a fixed amount (or for an amount based on a fixed amount and an interest rate) even if the exercise price differs from the carrying amount of the host *insurance liability*. However, the requirement in AASB 9 applies to a put option or cash surrender option embedded in an insurance contract if the surrender value varies in response to the change in a financial variable (such as an equity or commodity price or index), or a non-financial variable that is not specific to a party to the contract. Furthermore, that requirement also applies if the holder's ability to exercise a put option or cash surrender option is triggered by a change in such a variable (for example, a put option that can be exercised if a stock market index reaches a specified level).

2.2.3 Paragraph 2.2.2 applies equally to options to surrender a financial instrument containing a discretionary participation feature.

Deposit components

2.3.1 Some life insurance contracts contain both an insurance component and a *deposit component*. In some cases, an insurer is permitted to *unbundle* those components.

2.3.2 Unbundling is permitted if the insurer can measure the deposit component separately.

2.3.3 If a life insurer cannot measure the deposit component separately, an insurer shall not unbundle the deposit component.

2.3.4 To unbundle a life insurance contract, a life insurer:

(a) treats the life insurance component as a life insurance contract in accordance with this Standard;

(b) subject to (c), treats the deposit component as a life investment contract in accordance with this Standard; and

(c) where the deposit component includes a discretionary participation feature, treats this component as a separate life insurance contract in accordance with this Standard.

Purpose of Standard

3.1 The purpose of this Standard is to:

(a) prescribe the accounting methods to be used for reporting on life insurance contracts consistent with AASB 4 *Insurance Contracts*, and the accounting methods to be used for certain aspects of life investment contracts;

(b) prescribe the accounting methods to be used in accounting for assets backing life insurance liabilities or life investment contract liabilities; and

(c) require disclosures about life insurance contracts and disclosures about certain aspects of life investment contracts.

Equity in a shareholder-owned life insurer

4.1.2 Equity in a shareholder-owned life insurer will generally comprise only shareholder equity. Although participants in the industry commonly refer to "policyholder retained profits", in relation to Australian business such amounts are unvested policyholder benefits liabilities. Under Australian legislation, "policyholder retained profits" relating to Australian life insurance business are paid to policyholders, although the timing of the payment is at the discretion of the life insurer. A life insurer may have unallocated surplus that is in the nature of "policyholder equity" if it is a friendly society or has foreign life insurance operations in a jurisdiction that permits retained profits to remain unallocated between policyholders and shareholders, and the policyholders' component has yet to be determined. A key factor in evaluating the classification as liability or equity of retained profits in a friendly society is the benefit fund rules of each particular benefit fund. If the rules of a benefit fund were such that all retained profits by default are for the benefit of policyholders, such retained profits would be classed as policyholder benefit liabilities.

Premiums and claims

5.1   Subject to paragraph 5.2, insurance components of life insurance contract premiums are income and insurance components of life insurance contract claims are expenses and shall be recognised separately in the statement of comprehensive income. Deposit components of life insurance contract premiums are not income and deposit components of life insurance contract claims are not expenses and shall be recognised as changes in life insurance liabilities.

5.2   For life insurance contracts where unbundling of the deposit component is prohibited under paragraph 2.3.3, premiums shall be recognised as income and claims shall be recognised as expenses.

5.2.1   A wide variety of products are offered by life insurers – risk or insurance products, investment products and numerous hybrids of these two products. There will be hybrid products that fall within the scope of this Standard that have both deposit and insurance components.

5.2.2   Premiums may comprise amounts that give rise to:

(a)   income that is earned by providing services, including the bearing of risks; and

(b)   amounts that are akin to deposits and which qualify for recognition as liabilities.

5.2.3   Similarly, claims may comprise amounts that give rise to:

(a)   expenses that are incurred in providing services, including the bearing of risks; and

(b)   amounts that are akin to withdrawals from deposits and which qualify for recognition as reductions in liabilities.

Reinsurance

Reporting by cedants

6.1   A *cedant* shall recognise:

(a)   premiums ceded to reinsurers as reinsurance expenses;

(b)   claim recoveries and commissions from reinsurers as income; and

(c)   claim recoveries and other inflows not yet received from a reinsurer as an asset.

6.1.1   Life insurers may reinsure some of their business. The cedant remains responsible for the total amount of successful claims of policyholders and, through reinsurance arrangements, may be entitled to recover amounts relating to some of those claims.

6.1.2   *Reinsurance contracts* are considered to be separate transactions from the original life insurance contracts and therefore give rise to separately recognisable amounts. The cedant recognises the gross amount of premiums received in accordance with paragraphs 5.1 and 5.2 and, where portions of the policies are reinsured, the ceded premiums are recognised as expenses (except where they would otherwise be recognised as deposits, if not reinsured). Any recoveries from reinsurers are recognised as income by the cedant (except for any amounts representing the return of deposits). Consistent with this approach, the gross amount of life insurance liabilities is recognised as a liability and claim recoveries not yet received from a reinsurer are recognised as a receivable by the cedant.

Reporting by reinsurers

6.2   Inwards reinsurance premiums and outwards reinsurance claims shall be recognised by the accepting reinsurer as for premiums and claims in accordance with paragraphs 5.1 and 5.2. Life insurance liabilities assumed shall be recognised as a liability by the accepting reinsurer in accordance with section 8.

6.2.1 From the perspective of the reinsurer, reinsurance premiums accepted are recognised in the same way as the cedant treats the acceptance of premiums under a *direct insurance contract*. Correspondingly, claims paid and payable to direct insurers are recognised as expenses by the reinsurer. Consistent with these treatments, life insurance liabilities assumed are recognised as a liability by the accepting reinsurer.

Impairment of reinsurance assets

7.1.1 If a cedant's *reinsurance asset* is impaired, the cedant shall reduce its carrying amount accordingly and recognise that impairment in the statement of comprehensive income. A reinsurance asset is impaired if, and only if:

(a) there is objective evidence, as a result of an event that occurred after initial recognition of the reinsurance asset, that the cedant may not receive amounts due to it under the terms of the contract; and

(b) that event has a reliably measurable impact on the amounts that the cedant will receive from the reinsurer.

Life insurance liabilities

Present value and best estimates

8.1 Obligations arising from life insurance contracts (life insurance liabilities) shall be recognised as liabilities and shall be measured at the end of each reporting period as:

(a) **the net present value of future receipts from and payments to policyholders, including participating benefits, allowing for the possibility of discontinuance before the end of insurance contract periods, plus planned margins of revenues over expenses relating to services yet to be provided to policyholders, on the basis of assumptions that are best estimates and using a discount rate determined in accordance with paragraphs 8.7 or 8.8; or**

(b) **the accumulated benefits to policyholders after allowing for the portion of *acquisition costs* expected to be recouped where the result would not be materially different from the application of paragraph 8.1(a).**

8.1.1 The participating benefits component of life insurance liabilities includes previously vested benefits and future supportable bonuses. In addition to life insurance liabilities, there may be other liabilities that relate to participating policyholders. Insurance contract benefits attributable to participating policyholders that are not yet vested with specific policyholders are recognised as liabilities. These are further discussed in section 9.

8.1.2 Premiums are generally received in advance of the provision of services to policyholders, including the payment of claims. In return for premiums, life insurers provide services sometimes over long periods. Entering into a life insurance contract is considered to be the event that gives rise to future benefits and present obligations under a policy.

8.1.3 Where there are a number of variables relating to future uncertainties, a net present value approach to measuring life insurance liabilities is likely to provide the most appropriate measurement basis. The obligations under these more complex contracts are generally measured as the present value of the expected inflows, such as premiums and fees, and outflows, such as claims and other expenses, based on assumptions relating to whole populations of policyholders, and taking into account applicable taxation.

8.1.4 An accumulation approach involves accruing the entitlements in policyholders' records at the end of the reporting period. If the fees expected to be charged by the life insurer to the policyholder in each future reporting period are expected to equal or exceed any expenses incurred by the life insurer, the life insurance liability calculated under the accumulation approach would not be materially different from that obtained using the approach in paragraph 8.1(a).

8.1.5 The ultimate cost of meeting claims under many life insurance contracts depends on the frequency of occurrence of particular future events such as death and surrender and in some cases may depend upon other factors such as the future levels of investment returns. Assumptions need to be made about these future events. In order to ensure that life insurance liabilities are measured reliably, such assumptions need to be "best estimates".

8.1.6 Best estimate assumptions used in determining the present value of life insurance liabilities, such as the best estimate of the bonus rate, are made on the basis of the assets available to the life insurer at the end of the reporting period and do not include any allowance for future contributions by owners and other funds which may be provided in the future to support the business.

Acquisition costs

8.1.7 Life insurance contracts written in one reporting period often give rise to benefits to the life insurer in subsequent reporting periods, such as future management fees and surrender penalties. Therefore, there are future benefits associated with the costs of acquiring life insurance contracts, and such costs are often substantial.

8.1.8 In the life insurance industry, acquisition costs are usually recognised as expenses in the reporting period in which they are incurred. This is generally offset by identifying a portion of the planned margins included in life insurance liabilities as relating to the recovery of acquisition costs. The most useful and reliable information available about the acquisition costs that will give rise to future economic benefits is the amount of future charges for acquisition costs identified as part of the process of determining life insurance liabilities.

Recognition of planned margins as revenues

8.2 Planned margins of revenues over expenses for life insurance contracts shall be recognised in the statement of comprehensive income over the reporting periods during which the services, to which those margins relate, are provided to policyholders, and the revenues, relating to those services, are received.

8.2.1 In setting premium rates, life insurers will include planned margins of revenues over expenses. As noted in paragraph 8.1.2, premiums are generally received in advance of the provision of services to policyholders.

8.2.2 In this Standard, planned margins are recognised in the statement of comprehensive income when, and only when, the life insurer has performed the services necessary to establish a valid claim to those margins and has received the revenues relating to those services. To ensure that planned margins are recognised during the reporting period in which the relevant services are provided, life insurance liabilities include a component relating to those margins. These margins are then "released" based on one or more factors or "profit carriers" which correspond to the performance of services and the earning of the margins. In relation to many products, the profit carrier might be premiums or claims.

Differences between actual and assumed experience

8.3 Except in relation to investment earnings rate assumptions for participating business, the effect of changes in life insurance liabilities resulting from a difference between actual and assumed experience determined during the reporting period shall be recognised in the statement of comprehensive income as income or expenses in the reporting period in which the changes occur.

8.3.1 The assumed patterns and frequencies of events used in determining life insurance liabilities are compared with actual events in each reporting period to assess their accuracy. The effects of differences between actual and assumed experience represents decreases or increases in the expected payments to policyholders and are income or expenses of the reporting period in which the differences occur. For example, where the assumed costs of death claims under a renewable term life product line are greater than the actual costs for a reporting period, income equal to the difference is recognised in the statement of comprehensive income for the current reporting period.

8.3.2 The recognition of the net amount of changes in life insurance liabilities resulting from a difference between actual and assumed experience identified during the reporting period as income or an expense is consistent with the use of assumptions that are best estimates as at the end of each reporting period.

Changes to underlying assumptions

8.4   Assumptions used for measuring life insurance liabilities shall be reviewed for each reporting period. Where the review leads to changes in assumptions, with the exception of new business, the changes shall be deemed to occur at the end of the reporting period.

8.4.1 Assumptions used for measuring new business may be deemed to have occurred at the beginning of the reporting period, or at the date of commencement of the new business or at the end of the reporting period.

8.4.2 In preparing interim financial reports, the end of the reporting period is the end of the interim reporting period. Accordingly, changes in assumptions are deemed to occur at the end of the interim reporting period.

8.5   The financial effects of changes to the assumptions underlying the measurement of life insurance liabilities made during the reporting period shall be recognised in the statement of comprehensive income over the future reporting periods during which services are provided to policyholders, except that:

(a)   any estimated excess of the present value of future expenses over the present value of future revenues for a group of related products arising during the reporting period shall be recognised as an expense of the reporting period;

(b)   the reversal of an expense previously recognised in accordance with paragraph 8.5(a) shall be recognised as income of the reporting period in which the reversal of the loss is recognised;

(c)   the effects of a change to adopted discount rates and related economic assumptions caused by changes in investment market and general economic conditions shall be recognised as income or expense of the reporting period in which the change occurs; and

(d)   material calculation errors and similar errors shall be treated in accordance with AASB 108 *Accounting Policies, Changes in Accounting Estimates and Errors.*

8.5.1 The assumptions underlying the measurement of life insurance liabilities are reviewed at the end of each reporting period. Based on past experience and revised expectations about the future, it may become apparent that particular assumptions are not consistent with likely future experience and need to be changed. Such changes are effectively a reassessment of the likely patterns and frequencies of future events. The normal revision of assumptions is not considered to be an error.

8.5.2 Apart from the circumstances identified in paragraph 8.5, changes to underlying assumptions are effectively recognised over future reporting periods by adjusting the planned margins included in life insurance liabilities. If the effect of a changed assumption is a decrease in the present value of present obligations to policyholders, the planned margin is increased. If the effect is an increase in the present value of obligations to policyholders, the planned margin is reduced. The overall amount of life insurance liabilities is not affected by these changes to underlying assumptions, as long as the planned margin of revenues over expenses is not eliminated.

8.5.3   Material calculation errors and similar errors are treated in accordance with AASB 108. Under AASB 108, except to the extent that it is impracticable to determine either the period-specific effects or the cumulative effect of the error, an entity corrects material prior period errors retrospectively in the first financial statements authorised for issue after their discovery by:

    (a)   restating the comparative amounts for the prior period(s) presented in which the error occurred; or

    (b)   if the error occurred before the earliest prior period presented, restating the opening balances of assets, liabilities and equity for the earliest prior period presented.

Changes to discount rates and related economic assumptions

8.5.4   As with other assumptions, the discount rates and related economic assumptions used in determining life insurance liabilities are reviewed at the end of each reporting period. The effects of a change to adopted discount rates and related economic assumptions caused by changes in investment market and economic conditions are recognised in the reporting period in which the change is made. For a life insurer with a typical spread of investments, if market yields fall, investment values generally rise and the resulting increases in investment values are recognised as income in the reporting period in which they occur. Where the discount rates are adjusted in line with such falls in market rates, life insurance liabilities for such contracts will increase and an expense will be recognised, having an offsetting (but not usually matching) effect on the increased investment values.

8.5.5   In relation to participating business (which is discussed in section 9), the effect of a change to the assumptions about discount rates, explained in paragraph 8.5.4, is a result of adjusting the best estimate of life insurance liabilities, including future participating benefits. For example, if market rates of return rise, investment values generally fall and the resulting decreases in investment values are recognised as an expense in the reporting period in which they occur. The fall in investment values will clearly impact on the ability of the life insurer to support future participating benefits. These are likely to be reduced, with an offsetting effect on the reduced investment values.

Liability adequacy test

8.6   Life insurers shall perform a *liability adequacy test*.

8.6.1   Situations may arise where the present value of the planned margin of revenues over expenses for a group of related products will be adjusted as a result of changing underlying assumptions to the extent that the planned margin is eliminated and becomes a planned loss. That is, a review of expected future cash flows indicates that the present value of estimated future expenses for a group of related products exceeds the present value of estimated future revenues. In such circumstances, the excess of the present value of expenses over revenues arising during the reporting period is recognised in the statement of comprehensive income in the reporting period in which the assessment is made. The loss reflects a higher present obligation due to adverse future experience, which is now expected in future years. Whilst the future cash flows giving rise to the loss are yet to occur, this treatment is justified on the basis that entering into life insurance contracts is an event that gives rise to a present obligation to meet the expected future claims.

8.6.2   A group of related products, for the purpose of the calculating the planned margin, performing the liability adequacy test and for disclosure, would be products that have substantially the same contractual terms and were priced on the basis of substantially the same assumptions.

8.6.3   In reviewing expected future cash flows, the insurer takes into account both future cash flows under insurance contracts it has issued and the related reinsurance contracts.

8.6.4   Where an intangible asset has arisen under paragraph 13.1.1(b), a loss arises when the present value of planned margins of revenues over expenses is less than the related intangible asset. This test is to be performed for groups of related products and the intangible asset is allocated, on a reasonable basis, across these groups. Any loss is recognised as an expense in the statement of comprehensive income. In recognising the loss in the statement of comprehensive income, the life insurer first writes down the related intangible asset and then reflects any additional liability in the life insurance liabilities.

Discount rates

8.7   To the extent that the benefits under life insurance contracts are not contractually linked to the performance of the assets held, the life insurance liabilities shall be discounted for the time value of money using risk-free discount rates based on current observable, objective rates that relate to the nature, structure and term of the future obligations.

8.8   To the extent that the benefits under life insurance contracts are contractually linked to the performance of the assets held, the life insurance liabilities shall be discounted using discount rates based on the market returns on assets backing life insurance liabilities.

8.8.1   In applying paragraph 8.7, the discount rates adopted are not intended to reflect risks inherent in the liability cash flows, which might be allowed for by a reduction in the discount rate in a fair value measurement, nor are they intended to reflect the insurance and other non-financial risks and uncertainties reflected in the life insurance liabilities. The discount rates are not intended to include allowance for the cost of any options or guarantees that are separately measured as part of the life insurance liabilities.

8.8.2   In applying paragraph 8.7, typically, government bond rates may be appropriate discount rates for the purposes of this Standard, or they may be an appropriate starting point in determining such discount rates.

Financial instruments with discretionary participation features

8.9   Financial instruments with discretionary participation features are life insurance contracts for the purposes of this Standard and shall be treated in accordance with paragraphs 8.1 to 8.8 and section 9.

Participating benefits

9.1   Except for transfers from unvested policyholder benefits liabilities, participating benefits vested in policyholders in relation to the reporting period shall be recognised in the statement of comprehensive income as expenses for the reporting period. Such benefits which remain payable as at the end of the reporting period shall be recognised as a component of life insurance liabilities.

9.2   Participating benefits that have been allocated in relation to the reporting period to participating policyholders generally, but that have not yet vested in specific policyholders, shall be recognised as expenses for the reporting period. Amounts that have been allocated to participating policyholders generally, but that have not vested in specific policyholders as at the end of the reporting period, shall be recognised as unvested policyholder benefits liabilities.

9.2.1   Some life insurers sell participating business. Participating policyholders are generally eligible to receive the same types of benefits as other policyholders and, in addition, are entitled to participate in the profits relating to participating business. For example, a participating policyholder may receive a low contractually determined rate of return on savings together with term life cover and, in addition, receive benefits that depend on the investment performance of the pool of assets associated with participating policies and on the risk experience of participating policyholders. These additional benefits are often called bonuses and are at the discretion of the life insurer. In some reporting periods the life insurer may withhold a portion of the "profits" from the pool of participating business and recognise these "profits" as unvested policyholder benefits liabilities. In other reporting periods the life insurer may "top up" the vested benefits to participating policyholders. Such vesting of benefits is often done to provide a reasonably level vesting of benefits over time, despite volatility in periodic profits from participating business.

9.2.2   It is sometimes argued that the discretionary nature of participating benefits means that they should be treated as appropriations of profit in the same way as dividends to shareholders. Because life insurance liabilities relating to all types of policyholders are recognised as liabilities under the Life Insurance Act (excluding some contracts issued by friendly societies), it is appropriate for the participating benefits vested in relation to the reporting period, other than transfers from unvested policyholder benefits liabilities, to be recognised as expenses of the reporting period.

9.2.3   Mutual life insurers are effectively owned by their policyholder members. Nevertheless, the mutual life insurer also has obligations to its policyholders. These obligations are classified as policy liabilities. Benefits vested in a mutual life insurer's policyholders, other than transfers from unvested policyholder benefits liabilities, are also to be recognised as expenses in the reporting period in which they are vested.

9.2.4   For financial reporting purposes, participating benefits vested in policyholders in a reporting period but not yet paid are included in life insurance liabilities and are measured at net present values. In the case of investment account participating business this may be approximately the same as the amount actually allocated to policyholder accounts. In the case of traditional participating business, there may be a significant difference between the net present value and the face value of the amount vested in policyholders. The net present value is relevant for financial reporting purposes because it is the best estimate of the net present value of the amount that the life insurer expects to pay out in the future using information based on experience up to the end of the reporting period.

9.2.5   Where a life insurer "tops up" the vested benefits from previously recognised unvested policyholder benefits liabilities, a transfer between liabilities is recognised. If a life insurer tops up the vested benefits for participating policyholders other than from unvested policyholder benefits liabilities, the amount of the "top up" is recognised as an expense of the reporting period in which the additional benefits are vested.

Assets backing life insurance liabilities or life investment contract liabilities

Fair value approach

10.1.1   Paragraphs 10.2 to 10.7.2 address the measurement of certain assets backing life insurance liabilities or life investment contract liabilities. The fair value approach to the measurement of assets backing life insurance liabilities or life investment contract liabilities is consistent with the present value measurement approach for life insurance liabilities required by this Standard and the fair value measurement approach for life investment contract liabilities required by this Standard. Where assets are not backing life insurance liabilities or life investment contract liabilities life insurers apply the applicable accounting standards making use of any measurement choices available.

Measurement

10.2   *Financial assets* **that:**

(a)   **are within the scope of AASB 9;**

(b)   **back life insurance liabilities or life investment contract liabilities; and**

(c)   **are permitted to be designated as "at fair value through profit or loss" under AASB 9;**

shall be designated as "at fair value through profit or loss" under AASB 9 on first application of this Standard, or on initial recognition.

10.2.1 An insurer applies AASB 9 to its financial assets. Under AASB 9 a financial asset is classified and measured at fair value through profit or loss when:

(a) it does not meet the criteria specified in paragraph 4.1.2 of AASB 9 to be classified at amortised cost; or

(b) it does not meet the criteria specified in paragraph 4.1.2A of AASB 9 to be classified at fair value through other comprehensive income, or

(c) it is designated as "at fair value through profit or loss" upon initial recognition in accordance with paragraph 4.1.5 of AASB 9.

AASB 1 *First-time Adoption of Australian Accounting Standards* permits entities to designate financial assets as "at fair value through profit or loss" on first application of the Standard.

10.2.2 The view adopted in this Standard is that, in all but rare cases, financial assets within the scope of AASB 9 that back life insurance liabilities or life investment contract liabilities are permitted to be measured at fair value through profit or loss under AASB 9. This is because the measurement of life insurance liabilities under this Standard incorporates current information and measuring the financial assets backing these life insurance liabilities at fair value eliminates or significantly reduces a potential measurement or recognition inconsistency which would arise if the assets were classified and measured at amortised cost or fair value through other comprehensive income (refer to AASB 9 paragraph B4.1.30(a)).

10.3 **Investment property that is within the scope of AASB 140 *Investment Property* and that backs life insurance liabilities or life investment contract liabilities shall be measured at fair value using the fair value model under AASB 140 and AASB 13 *Fair Value Measurement*.**

10.4 **Property, plant and equipment that is within the scope of AASB 116 *Property, Plant and Equipment* and that backs life insurance liabilities or life investment contract liabilities shall be measured using the revaluation model under AASB 116.**

10.4.1–10.4.2 [Deleted by the IASB]

10.5 **Investments in associates that:**

(a) **are defined by AASB 128 *Investments in Associates and Joint Ventures*;**

(b) **back either life insurance liabilities or life investment contract liabilities;**

(c) **are held by mutual funds, unit trusts and similar entities including *investment-linked* insurance funds; and**

(d) **are permitted to be designated as "at fair value through profit or loss" under AASB 9;**

shall be designated as "at fair value through profit or loss" under AASB 9 on first application of this Standard, or on initial recognition.

10.5.1 An insurer applies AASB 128 to its investments in associates. AASB 128 requires investments in associates to be accounted for using the equity method. When investments in associates are held by mutual funds, unit trusts and similar entities including investment-linked insurance funds, AASB 128 permits the investments in those associates to be measured at fair value through profit or loss in accordance with AASB 9.

10.6 **Venturers' interests in joint ventures that:**

(a) **are defined by AASB 11 *Joint Arrangements*;**

(b) **back either life insurance liabilities or life investment contract liabilities;**

(c) **are held by mutual funds, unit trusts and similar entities including investment-linked insurance funds; and**

(d) **are permitted to be designated as "at fair value through profit or loss" under AASB 9;**

AASB

shall be designated as "at fair value through profit or loss" under AASB 9, on first application of this Standard, or on initial recognition.

10.6.1 AASB 11 requires a joint venturer to recognise its interest in a joint venture as an investment and to account for that investment using the equity method in accordance with AASB 128 unless exempted from applying that method. AASB 128 permits mutual funds, unit trusts and similar entities including investment-linked insurance funds to measure investments in joint ventures at fair value through profit or loss in accordance with AASB 9.

Separate financial statements

10.7   When preparing *separate financial statements*, those investments in subsidiaries, joint ventures and associates that:

(a)   are within the scope of AASB 127 *Separate Financial Statements*;

(b)   back life insurance liabilities or life investment contract liabilities; and

(c)   are permitted to be designated as "at fair value through profit or loss" under AASB 9;

shall be designated as "at fair value through profit or loss" under AASB 9, on first application of this Standard or on initial recognition.

10.7.1 An insurer applies AASB 127 to its investments in subsidiaries, joint ventures and associates when preparing separate financial statements. Under AASB 127, in the parent's separate financial statements, the investments in subsidiaries, joint ventures and associates can either be accounted for at cost or in accordance with AASB 9.

10.7.2 In the parent's separate financial statements, investments in subsidiaries, joint ventures and associates, that are within the scope of AASB 127, that the insurer considers back life insurance liabilities or life investment contract liabilities, and that are permitted to be designated as "at fair value through profit or loss" under AASB 9, are designated as "at fair value through profit or loss" under AASB 9, on first application of this Standard or on initial recognition.

Imputed inflows and outflows

11.1   Subject to paragraph 18.3, a life insurer shall recognise imputed inflows and outflows as income and expenses when, and only when, such imputed flows relate to transactions with external entities.

11.1.1 Life insurers often impute inflows and outflows to different classes of policyholders in order to help ensure that they are treated equitably. For example, a life insurer may own the buildings that it occupies. The funds of a particular group of policyholders are used to acquire and operate such buildings whilst a wider group of policyholders and shareholders may benefit from the use of the buildings. In the owner-occupied building example, the life insurer imputes an inflow of rent income to the policyholders whose funds are used to acquire and operate the buildings and imputes an outflow of rent cost to the other policyholders and to shareholders.

11.1.2 In cases where there are no transactions with external entities, such as with owner-occupied buildings, the life insurer is dealing with itself. There is no transaction or other past event that gives rise to income or an expense. Any inflows and outflows imputed for internal management purposes would be eliminated in preparing external financial statements except in relation to the disaggregated disclosures required by paragraphs 18.1 and 18.2.

11.1.3 In some cases, life insurers impute inflows and outflows where external entities are involved. For example, life insurers often lend funds to their employees at concessional rates of interest with the funds being provided by a particular group of policyholders, whilst other policyholders and any shareholders benefit from the services provided by those employees. Because external parties are involved, such imputed inflows and outflows are recognised as income and expenses when they can be reliably measured.

Life investment contracts

12.1 **Life investment contract liabilities, that are permitted to be designated as "at fair value through profit or loss" under AASB 9, shall be designated as "at fair value through profit or loss" under AASB 9 on first application of this Standard, or on initial recognition.**

12.1.1 The view adopted in this Standard is that, in all but rare cases, life investment contract liabilities within the scope of AASB 9 are permitted to be measured at fair value through profit or loss under AASB 9. This is because, when a life investment contract liability is backed by a financial asset measured at fair value through profit or loss, designating the life investment contract liability at fair value through profit or loss eliminates or significantly reduces a potential measurement inconsistency which would arise if the life investment contract liability were measured at amortised cost. In addition, in the vast majority of cases, life investment contract liabilities would be managed and their performance would be evaluated on a fair value basis, in accordance with a documented risk management or investment strategy.

12.1.2 Some life investment contracts involve both the origination of one or more financial instruments and the provision of management services. Life investment contract liabilities arise under the financial instrument element and are treated under AASB 139. The management services element, including associated ~~acquisition~~ incremental costs of obtaining a contract, is treated under AASB 15 *Revenue from Contracts with Customers*; this element may also give rise to assets and liabilities.

Life insurance contracts acquired in a business combination or portfolio transfer

13.1.1 To comply with AASB 3 *Business Combinations*, an insurer shall, at the acquisition date, measure at fair value the insurance liabilities assumed and *insurance assets* acquired in a business combination. However, an insurer is permitted, but not required, to use an expanded presentation that splits the fair value of acquired insurance contracts into two components:

    (a)   a liability measured in accordance with the insurer's accounting policies for life insurance contracts that it issues; and

    (b)   an intangible asset, representing the difference between:

        (i)   the fair value of the contractual insurance rights acquired and insurance obligations assumed; and

        (ii)   the amount described in paragraph 13.1.1(a).

        The subsequent measurement of this asset shall be consistent with the measurement of the related life insurance liability.

13.1.2 An insurer acquiring a portfolio of life insurance contracts may use an expanded presentation described in paragraph 13.1.1.

13.1.3 The intangible assets described in paragraphs 13.1.1 and 13.1.2 are excluded from the scope of AASB 136 *Impairment of Assets* and from the scope of AASB 138 *Intangible Assets* in respect of recognition and measurement. AASB 136 and AASB 138 apply to customer lists and customer relationships reflecting the expectation of future contracts that are not part of the contractual insurance rights and contractual insurance obligations that existed at the date of a business combination or portfolio transfer.

13.1.4 AASB 138 includes disclosure requirements in relation to this intangible asset.

13.1.5 Where a life insurer recognises an intangible asset under paragraph 13.1.1(b), this intangible asset is considered when performing the liability adequacy test referred to in paragraph 8.6.

Life insurance contracts disclosure – explanation of recognised amounts

14.1   A life insurer shall disclose information that identifies and explains the amounts in its financial statements arising from life insurance contracts.

14.1.1 To comply with paragraph 14.1, a life insurer shall disclose:

(a)   its accounting policies for life insurance contracts and related assets, liabilities, income and expense;

(b)   the recognised assets, liabilities, income, expense and cash flows arising from life insurance contracts. Furthermore, if the life insurer is a cedant, it shall disclose:

(i)   gains and losses recognised in profit or loss at the time of buying reinsurance; and

(ii)   if the cedant defers and amortises gains and losses arising at the time of buying reinsurance, the amortisation for the period and the amounts remaining unamortised at the beginning and end of the period;

(c)   the process used to determine the assumptions that have the greatest effect on the measurement of the recognised amounts described in (b). When practicable, a life insurer shall also give quantified disclosure of those assumptions;

(d)   the effect of changes in assumptions used to measure life insurance assets and life insurance liabilities, showing separately the effect of each change that has a material effect on the financial statements; and

(e)   reconciliations of changes in life insurance liabilities and reinsurance assets.

14.1.2 When applying paragraph 14.1.1(b) and disclosing recognised income arising from life insurance contracts, life insurers would normally disclose income from direct and reinsurance business. In accordance with the principles embodied in this Standard, with the exception of premium revenue recognised in accordance with paragraph 5.1, all revenues are recognised and disclosed before the effects of any transfers to or from life insurance liabilities. Disclosure of the effects of transfers to and from life insurance liabilities is required by paragraph 14.1.1(e).

14.1.3 In accordance with the principles embodied in this Standard, with the exception of claims expense recognised in accordance with paragraph 5.1, all expenses are recognised and disclosed before the effects of any transfers to or from life insurance liabilities. Disclosure of the effects of transfers to and from life insurance liabilities is required by paragraph 14.1.1(e).

14.1.4 To disclose and explain the expenses arising from life insurance contracts, life insurers would normally disclose:

(a)   outwards reinsurance expense;

(b)   operating expenses:

(i)   claims expense;

(ii)   policy acquisition expenses, separated into material components including commission;

(iii) policy maintenance expenses; and

(iv)   investment management expenses; and

    (c)   the basis for the apportionment of operating expenses between:

        (i)   life insurance contract acquisition;

        (ii)   life insurance contract maintenance;

        (iii)   investment management expenses;

        (iv)   life investment contract acquisition;

        (v)   life investment contract maintenance; and

        (vi)   other expenses.

14.1.5 When applying paragraphs 14.1.1(c) and 14.1.1(d) and disclosing the process used to determine assumptions, quantified disclosure of assumptions and the effect of changes in assumptions, the life insurer would normally show the impact of changes in assumptions on future profit margins and life insurance liabilities. The assumptions that would normally have the greatest effect on the measurement of recognised amounts described in paragraph 14.1.1(b) are:

    (a)   discount rates and inflation rates;

    (b)   profit carriers used for each major product group;

    (c)   future maintenance and investment management expenses, the rate of inflation applicable to them and any automatic indexation of benefits and premiums;

    (d)   rates of taxation;

    (e)   mortality and morbidity, by reference to the identity of the tables;

    (f)   rates of discontinuance;

    (g)   surrender values;

    (h)   rates of growth of unit prices in respect of unit-linked benefits;

    (i)   rates of future supportable participating benefits; and

    (j)   the crediting policy adopted in determining future supportable participating benefits.

14.1.6 When applying paragraph 14.1.1(b) and disclosing the recognised liabilities arising from life insurance contracts, life insurers would normally disclose the following components of life insurance liabilities:

    (a)   future policy benefits, including participating benefits;

    (b)   balance of future expenses;

    (c)   planned margins of revenues over expenses;

    (d)   future charges for acquisition costs; and

    (e)   balance of future revenues.

14.1.7 When a life insurer is presenting the disclosures required by paragraphs 14.1.1(c) and 14.1.1(d) the insurer determines the level and extent of disclosure that is appropriate having regard to its circumstances and the qualitative characteristics of financial statements under the *Framework for the Preparation and Presentation of Financial Statements* (as identified in AASB 1048 *Interpretation of Standards*).

Nature and extent of risks arising from life insurance contracts

15.1   **A life insurer shall disclose information that enables users of its financial statements to evaluate the nature and extent of risks arising from life insurance contracts.**

15.1.1 To comply with paragraph 15.1, a life insurer shall disclose:

    (a)   its objectives, policies and processes for managing risks arising from life insurance contracts and the methods used to manage those risks;

(b)   information about *insurance risk* (both before and after risk mitigation by reinsurance), including information about:

   (i)   sensitivity to insurance risk (see paragraph 15.1.3);

   (ii)   concentrations of insurance risk, including a description of how management determines concentrations and a description of the shared characteristic that identifies each concentration (e. g. type of *insured event*, geographical area, or currency); and

   (iii)   actual claims compared with previous estimates (i. e. claims development). The disclosure about claims development shall go back to the period when the earliest material claim arose for which there is still uncertainty about the amount and timing of the claims payments, but need not go back more than ten years. A life insurer need not disclose this information for claims for which uncertainty about the amount and timing of claims payments is typically resolved within one year;

(c)   information about credit risk, liquidity risk and market risk that paragraphs 31-42 of AASB 7 would require if the life insurance contracts were within the scope of AASB 7. However:

   (i)   a life insurer need not provide the maturity analyses required by paragraphs 39(a) and (b) of AASB 7 if it discloses information about the estimated timing of the net cash outflows resulting from recognised insurance liabilities instead. This may take the form of an analysis, by estimated timing, of the amounts recognised in the statement of financial position; and

   (ii)   if a life insurer uses an alternative method to manage sensitivity to market conditions, such as an embedded value analysis, it may use that sensitivity analysis to meet the requirement in paragraph 40(a) of AASB 7. Such a life insurer shall also provide the disclosures required by paragraph 41 of AASB 7; and

(d)   information about exposures to market risk arising from embedded derivatives contained in a host insurance contract if the life insurer is not required to, and does not, measure the embedded derivatives at fair value.

15.1.2   The claims development disclosure required by paragraph 15.1.1(b)(iii) only applies to classes of business where claims are not typically resolved within one year. For many life insurance products this disclosure would not normally be required. Furthermore, claims development disclosure would not normally be needed for annuity contracts, for example, because each periodic payment arises, in effect, from a separate claim about which there is no uncertainty.

15.1.3   To comply with paragraph 15.1.1(b)(i), a life insurer shall disclose either (a) or (b) as follows:

(a)   a sensitivity analysis that shows how profit or loss and equity would have been affected had changes in the relevant risk variable that were reasonably possible at the end of the reporting period occurred; the methods and assumptions used in preparing the sensitivity analysis; and any changes from the previous period in the methods and assumptions used. However, if a life insurer uses an alternative method to manage sensitivity to market conditions, such as an embedded value analysis, it may meet this requirement by disclosing that alternative sensitivity analysis and the disclosures required by paragraph 41 of AASB 7; and

(b)   qualitative information about sensitivity, and information about those terms and conditions of life insurance contracts that have a material effect on the amount, timing and uncertainty of the life insurer's future cash flows.

Other disclosures relating to life insurance contracts

16.1 Where any premiums and any claims are separated into their revenue, expense and change in life insurance liability components in accordance with paragraph 5.1, total premiums and total claims shall be disclosed.

16.1.1 The mix of products written by a life insurer will vary between life insurers. Comparability between life insurers is enhanced by the disclosure of total premiums and total claims.

Disclosures relating to life insurance contracts and life investment contracts

Financial performance

17.1 The following components of profit or loss shall be shown, separated between policyholder and shareholder interests:

    (a)   profit related to movement in life insurance liabilities;

    (b)   profit related to movement in life investment contract liabilities and movement in assets or liabilities arising in respect of the management services element of life investment contracts;

    (c)   investment earnings on assets in excess of policy liabilities; and

    (d)   other items, separated into material components.

17.2 The following components of profit related to movements in life insurance liabilities, life investment contract liabilities and assets or liabilities arising in respect of the management services element of life investment contracts shall be shown:

    (a)   planned margins of revenues over expenses;

    (b)   the difference between actual and assumed experience;

    (c)   the effects of changes to underlying assumptions;

    (d)   loss recognition on groups of related products or reversal of previously recognised losses required by paragraph 8.6; and

    (e)   other movements, separated into material components.

Restrictions on assets

17.3 Restrictions attaching to assets held for the benefit of policyholders shall be disclosed.

17.3.1 There are a number of restrictions on the use of assets invested for policyholders in *statutory funds*. It is important that these restrictions be disclosed so that users of the financial statements can assess their impact.

Guaranteed or assured returns of funds invested

17.4 A life insurer shall separately disclose:

    (a)   in respect of contracts with discretionary participation features, the amount of policy liabilities that relates to the *guaranteed element*;

    (b)   in respect of investment-linked contracts, the amount of policy liabilities subject to investment performance guarantees; and

    (c)   in respect of any other contracts not addressed in (a) or (b) with a fixed or guaranteed termination value, the amount of the current termination values.

17.4.1 Many life insurers issue contracts that provide some form of guarantee or assurance about the return of funds invested. It is useful for users of life insurers' financial statements to have information about the extent of such guarantees or assurances, since they involve the life insurer bearing investment risks on behalf of policyholders.

Equity

17.5   The following components of equity shall be disclosed:

   (a)   retained earnings wholly attributable to shareholders; and

   (b)   retained earnings where the allocation between participating policyholders and shareholders has yet to be determined.

17.5.1   Information about the different components of retained earnings is useful in meeting the accountability obligations of the life insurer for the whole business and in showing the relative positions of the major stakeholders.

17.5.2   A life insurer that has issued participating business may have "retained profits" generated from that business. In relation to Australian participating policyholders, these "retained profits" are liabilities in accordance with the Life Insurance Act. However, in friendly societies or foreign life insurance operations, "retained profits" may exist which have yet to be allocated between policyholders and shareholders. Such "retained profits" are separately disclosed. It is relevant to note that "retained profits" directly attributable to shareholders may reside in both statutory funds and a shareholder fund.

17.5.3   Where, in friendly societies or foreign life operations, "retained profits" exist, which have yet to be allocated and which are treated as equity then the insurer applies paragraphs 17.5.4 and 17.5.5 to this participating business.

17.5.4   Where a life insurance contract with a discretionary participation feature is issued by a friendly society or foreign life operation, the issuer of such a contract:

   (a)   may, but need not, recognise the guaranteed element separately from the discretionary participation feature. If the issuer does not recognise them separately, it classifies the whole contract as a liability. If the issuer classifies them separately, it classifies the guaranteed element as a liability;

   (b)   shall, if it recognises the discretionary participation feature separately from the guaranteed element, classify that feature as either a liability or a separate component of equity. This Standard does not specify how the issuer determines whether that feature is a liability or equity. The issuer may split that feature into liability and equity components and shall use a consistent accounting policy for that split. The issuer shall not classify that feature as an intermediate category that is neither liability nor equity;

   (c)   may recognise all premiums received as revenue without separating any portion that relates to the equity component. The resulting changes in the guaranteed element and in the portion of the discretionary participation feature classified as a liability shall be recognised in profit or loss. If part of the entire discretionary participation feature is classified in equity, a portion of profit or loss may be attributable to that feature (in the same way that a portion may be attributable to minority interests). The issuer shall recognise the portion of profit or loss attributable to any equity component of a discretionary participation feature as an allocation of profit or loss, not as expense or income (see AASB 101 *Presentation of Financial Statements*);

   (d)   shall, if the contract contains an embedded derivative within the scope of AASB 9, apply AASB 9 to that embedded derivative; and

   (e)   shall, in all respects not described in paragraphs 14-20 of AASB 4 and paragraphs 34(a)-(d) of AASB 4, continue its existing accounting policies for such contracts, unless it changes those accounting policies in a way that complies with paragraphs 21-30 of AASB 4.

17.5.5   The requirements in paragraph 17.5.4 also apply to a life investment contract issued by a friendly society or foreign life insurer that contains a discretionary participation feature. In addition:

(a) if the issuer classifies the entire discretionary participation feature as a liability, it shall apply the liability adequacy test in paragraph 8.6 to the whole contract (i.e. both the guaranteed element and the discretionary participation feature). The issuer need not determine the amount that would result from applying AASB 9 to the guaranteed element;

(b) if the issuer classifies part or all of the discretionary participation feature as a separate component of equity, the liability recognised for the whole contract shall not be less than the amount that would result from applying AASB 9 to the guaranteed element. That amount shall include the intrinsic value of an option to surrender the contract, but need not include its time value if paragraph 2.2.2 exempts that option from measurement at fair value. The issuer need not disclose the amount that would result from applying AASB 9 to the guaranteed element, nor need it present that amount separately. Furthermore, the issuer need not determine that amount if the total liability recognised is clearly higher;

(c) although these contracts are financial instruments, the issuer may continue to recognise the premiums for those contracts as revenue and recognise as an expense the resulting increase in the carrying amount of the liability, subject to the requirements of paragraphs 5.1 and 5.2; and

(d) although these contracts are financial instruments, an issuer applying paragraph 20(b) of AASB 7 to contracts with a discretionary participation feature shall disclose the total interest expense recognised in profit or loss, but need not calculate such interest expense using the effective interest method.

Regulatory capital information

17.8 **A life insurer shall disclose the regulatory capital position of each statutory fund. In consolidated financial statements a group shall disclose the regulatory capital position of each life insurer in the group.**

Managed funds and other fiduciary activities

17.9 **The nature and amount of the life insurer's activities relating to managed funds and trust activities, and whether arrangements exist to ensure that such activities are managed independently from its other activities, shall be disclosed.**

Actuarial information

17.10 **The following shall be disclosed in notes:**

(a) **if other than the end of the reporting period, the effective date of the actuarial report on policy liabilities and regulatory capital reserves;**

(b) **the name and qualifications of the actuary;**

(c) **whether the amount of policy liabilities has been determined in accordance with the requirements of the Life Insurance Act; and**

(d) **whether the actuary is satisfied as to the accuracy of the data from which the amount of policy liabilities has been determined.**

Assets backing life insurance liabilities or life investment contract liabilities

17.11 **An insurer shall disclose the process used to determine which assets back life insurance liabilities or life investment contract liabilities.**

Other disclosures

17.12.1 Australian Accounting Standards and the Life Insurance Act differ in their requirements. Accordingly, life insurers are encouraged to disclose a reconciliation between:

AASB

      (a)   the profit for the reporting period reported under Australian Accounting Standards and the profit for the reporting period reported under the Life Insurance Act; and

      (b)   the retained earnings at the end of the reporting period in accordance with Australian Accounting Standards and the retained earnings at the end of the reporting period in accordance with the Life Insurance Act.

17.13.1 This Standard addresses disclosure requirements in relation to life insurance contracts and certain disclosure requirements in relation to life investment contracts. Other Australian Accounting Standards may be relevant to a life insurer's financial statements. In particular, the disclosure requirements in AASB 7 would normally be relevant to life insurers.

Disaggregated information

Statutory funds and the shareholder fund

18.1   **For each statutory fund and for the shareholder fund the following shall be disclosed:**

    (a)   **investment assets;**

    (b)   **other assets;**

    (c)   **life insurance liabilities;**

    (d)   **life investment contract liabilities and assets or liabilities arising in respect of the management services element of life investment contracts;**

    (e)   **liabilities other than life insurance liabilities or life investment contract liabilities;**

    (f)   **retained earnings, showing the amount directly attributable to shareholders and other retained earnings;**

    (g)   **premium revenue split between life insurance contracts and life investment contracts;**

    (h)   **investment income;**

    (i)   **claims expense split between life insurance contracts and life investment contracts;**

    (j)   **other operating expenses;**

    (k)   **investment income paid or allocated to policyholders;**

    (l)   **profit or loss before tax;**

    (m) **profit or loss after tax; and**

    (n)   **transfers to or from other funds.**

18.1.1 Disaggregated information for each life fund and the shareholder fund is useful because, under Australian legislation, each life insurer may have more than one fund and, in general, the assets of each life fund are only available to meet the liabilities and expenses of that life fund.

Investment-linked and non-investment-linked business

18.2   **A life insurer shall disclose the information required by paragraphs 18.1(a) to 18.1(m) disaggregated between those amounts relating to investment-linked business and those relating to *non-investment-linked business*.**

18.2.1 The risks and potential rewards for a life insurer differ substantially as between investment-linked business and non-investment-linked business. Accordingly, disaggregated information about these is considered to be useful in assessing the financial performance and financial position of a life insurer. The information required by paragraph 18.2 is for the entity's life insurance business as a whole; it is not required for each life fund.

18.2.2 [Deleted by the AASB]

Imputed inflows and outflows

18.3 **Disclosures required by paragraphs 18.1 and 18.2 shall include all imputed inflows and outflows as income and expenses where they can be reliably measured.**

18.3.1 As discussed in paragraph 11.1.1, life insurers often impute inflows and outflows to different classes of policyholders and shareholders to help ensure that they are treated equitably. Whereas, in relation to the statement of comprehensive income and the statement of financial position, paragraph 11.1 only permits the recognition of imputed inflows and outflows relating to transactions with external parties, paragraph 18.3 requires all imputed inflows and outflows to be included in the disaggregated information to reflect the performance of each segment of the life insurer.

Transitional provisions

19.1 **An entity need not apply the disclosure requirements in this Standard to comparative information that relates to annual periods beginning before 1 January 2005, except for the disclosures required by paragraphs 14.1.1(a) and 14.1.1(b) about accounting policies, and recognised assets, liabilities, income and expense and cash flows.**

19.2 **When an entity applies the disclosure requirements in this Standard to comparative information that relates to annual periods beginning before 1 January 2005, if it is impracticable to apply a particular requirement of this Standard to comparative information that relates to annual periods beginning before 1 January 2005, an entity shall disclose that fact. AASB 108 explains the term "impracticable".**

19.3 **In applying paragraph 15.1.1(b)(iii), an entity need not disclose information about claims development that occurred earlier than five years before the end of the first annual reporting period in which it applies this Standard. Furthermore, if it is impracticable, when an entity first applies this Standard, to prepare information about claims development that occurred before the beginning of the earliest period for which an entity presents full comparative information that complies with this Standard, the entity shall disclose that fact.**

19.3.1 There are also references to transitional measurement requirements in paragraphs 10.2-10.2.2, 10.5, 10.6, 10.7, 10.7.2 and 12.1.

19.4 [Deleted by the AASB]

19.5 [Deleted by the AASB]

Definitions

20.1 **In this Standard:**

acquisition costs **means the fixed and variable costs of acquiring new business, including commissions and similar distribution costs, and costs of accepting, issuing and initially recording policies**

(Acquisition costs relate to the costs incurred in acquiring specific life insurance contracts during the reporting period. They do not include the general growth and development costs incurred by a life insurer.)

cedant **means the policyholder under a life reinsurance contract**

deposit component **means a contractual component that is not accounted for as a derivative under AASB 9** *Financial Instruments* **and would be within the scope of AASB 9** *Financial Instruments* **if it were a separate instrument**

direct insurance contract means an insurance contract that is not a reinsurance contract

discretionary participation feature means a contractual right to receive, as a supplement to *guaranteed benefits*, additional benefits:

(a)   that are likely to be a significant portion of the total contractual benefits;

(b)   whose amount or timing is contractually at the discretion of the issuer; and

(c)   that are contractually based on:

    (i)   the performance of a specified pool of contracts or a specified type of contract;

    (ii)   realised and/or unrealised investment returns on a specified pool of assets held by the issuer; or

    (iii)   the profit or loss of the company, fund or other entity that issues the contract

fair value is the price that would be received to sell an asset or paid to transfer a liability in an orderly transaction between market participants at the measurement date. (See AASB 13.)

financial risk means the risk of a possible future change in one or more of a specified interest rate, financial instrument price, commodity price, foreign exchange rate, index of prices or rates, a credit rating or credit index or other variable, provided in the case of a non-financial variable that the variable is not specific to a party to the contract

general insurance contract means an insurance contract that is not a life insurance contract

guaranteed benefits means payments or other benefits to which a particular policyholder or investor has an unconditional right that is not subject to the contractual discretion of the issuer

guaranteed element means an obligation to pay guaranteed benefits included in a contract that contains a discretionary participation feature

insurance asset means an insurer's net contractual rights under an insurance contract

insurance contract means a contract under which one party (the insurer) accepts significant insurance risk from another party (the policyholder) by agreeing to compensate the policyholder if a specified uncertain future event (the insured event) adversely affects the policyholder

(Refer to Appendix for additional guidance in applying this definition.)

insurance liability means an insurer's net contractual obligations under an insurance contract

insurance risk means risk, other than financial risk, transferred from the holder of a contract to the issuer

insured event means an uncertain future event covered by an insurance contract and creates insurance risk

insurer means the party that has an obligation under an insurance contract to compensate a policyholder if an insured event occurs

investment-linked means where the benefit amount under a life insurance contract or life investment contract is directly linked to the market value of the investments held in the particular investment-linked fund

liability adequacy test means an assessment of whether the carrying amount of an insurance liability needs to be increased (or the carrying amount of the related deferred acquisition costs or related intangible assets decreased) based on a review of future cash flows

life insurance business means all life insurance contract and life investment contract business conducted by a life insurer

life insurance contract means an insurance contract, or a financial instrument with a discretionary participation feature, regulated under the Life Insurance Act, and similar contracts issued by entities operating outside Australia

(Private health insurance contracts issued under the *National Health Act 1953* but written by friendly societies registered under the Life Insurance Act, are not life insurance contracts but are general insurance contracts.)

life insurance liability means a life insurer's net contractual obligations under a life insurance contract

life insurer means an entity registered under the *Life Insurance Act 1995*, that issues life insurance contracts or life investment contracts, and similar entities operating outside Australia

life investment contract means a contract which is regulated under the *Life Insurance Act 1995* but which does not meet the definition of a life insurance contract in this Standard, and similar contracts issued by entities operating outside Australia

life investment contract liability means a life insurer's net contractual obligations under a life investment contract which arise under the financial instrument component of a life investment contract

life reinsurance contract means a life insurance contract issued by one insurer (the reinsurer) to compensate another insurer (the cedant) for losses on one or more contracts issued by the cedant

non-investment-linked business means life insurance business other than investment-linked business

policyholder means a party that has a right to compensation under an insurance contract if an insured event occurs

policy liability means a liability that arises under a life insurance contract or a life investment contract including any asset or liability arising in respect of the management services element of a life investment contract

reinsurance assets means a cedant's net contractual rights under a reinsurance contract

reinsurance contract means an insurance contract issued by one insurer (the reinsurer) to compensate another insurer (the cedant) for losses on one or more contracts issued by the cedant

reinsurer means the party that has an obligation under a reinsurance contract to compensate a cedant if an insured event occurs

separate financial statements are those presented by a parent, an investor in an associate or a venturer in a jointly controlled entity, in which the investments are accounted for on the basis of the direct equity interest rather than on the basis of the reported results and net assets of the investees

statutory fund means a statutory fund under the *Life Insurance Act 1995*

unbundle means to account for the components of a contract as if they were separate contracts

20.2   The following terms are defined in AASB 132 *Financial Instruments: Presentation* and are used in this Standard with the meaning specified in AASB 132:

    (a)   financial asset;

    (b)   financial instrument; and

    (c)   financial liability.

APPENDIX
DEFINITION OF AN INSURANCE CONTRACT

This appendix is an integral part of AASB 1038.

1   This Appendix gives guidance on the definition of an insurance contract in section 20 of this Standard. It addresses the following issues:

(a)   the term 'uncertain future event' (paragraphs 2-4);

(b)   insurance risk and other risks (paragraphs 5-14);

(c)   examples of life insurance contracts (paragraphs 15-18);

(d)   significant insurance risk (paragraphs 19-25); and

(e)   changes in the level of insurance risk (paragraphs 26 and 27).

Uncertain future event

2   Uncertainty (or risk) is the essence of an insurance contract. Accordingly, at least one of the following is uncertain at the inception of an insurance contract:

(a)   whether an insured event will occur;

(b)   when it will occur; or

(c)   how much the insurer will need to pay if it occurs.

3   In some insurance contracts, the insured event is the discovery of a loss during the term of the contract, even if the loss arises from an event that occurred before the inception of the contract. In other insurance contracts, the insured event is an event that occurs during the term of the contract, even if the resulting loss is discovered after the end of the contract term.

4   Some insurance contracts cover events that have already occurred, but whose financial effect is still uncertain. An example is a reinsurance contract that covers the direct insurer against adverse development of claims already reported by policyholders. In such contracts, the insured event is the discovery of the ultimate cost of those claims.

Distinction between insurance risk and other risks

5   The definition of an insurance contract refers to insurance risk, which this Standard defines as risk, other than *financial risk*, transferred from the holder of a contract to the issuer. A contract that exposes the issuer to financial risk without significant insurance risk is not an insurance contract.

6   The definition of financial risk in section 20 of this Standard includes a list of financial and non-financial variables. That list includes non-financial variables that are not specific to a party to the contract, such as an index of earthquake losses in a particular region or an index of temperatures in a particular city. It excludes non-financial variables that are specific to a party to the contract.

7   Some contracts expose the issuer to financial risk, in addition to significant insurance risk. For example, many life insurance contracts both guarantee a minimum rate of return to policyholders (creating financial risk) and promise death benefits that at some times significantly exceed the policyholder's account balance (creating insurance risk in the form of mortality risk). Such contracts are insurance contracts.

8   Under some contracts, an insured event triggers the payment of an amount linked to a price index. Such contracts are insurance contracts, provided the payment that is contingent on the insured event can be significant. For example, a life-contingent annuity linked to a cost-of-living index transfers insurance risk because payment is triggered by an uncertain event – the survival of the annuitant. The link to the price index is an embedded derivative, but it also transfers insurance risk. If the resulting transfer of insurance risk is significant, the embedded derivative meets the definition

of an insurance contract, in which case it need not be separated and measured at fair value (see paragraph 2.2.1 of this Standard).

9   The definition of insurance risk refers to risk that the insurer accepts from the policyholder. In other words, insurance risk is a pre-existing risk transferred from the policyholder to the insurer. Thus, a new risk created by the contract is not insurance risk.

10   The definition of an insurance contract refers to an adverse effect on the policyholder. The definition does not limit the payment by the insurer to an amount equal to the financial impact of the adverse event. For example, the definition does not limit payment under a term life insurance contract to the financial loss suffered by the deceased's dependants, nor does it preclude the payment of predetermined amounts to quantify the loss caused by death or an accident.

11   Some contracts require a payment if a specified uncertain event occurs, but do not require an adverse effect on the policyholder as a precondition for payment. Such a contract is not an insurance contract even if the holder uses the contract to mitigate an underlying risk exposure. For example, if the holder uses a derivative to hedge an underlying non-financial variable that is correlated with cash flows from an asset of the entity, the derivative is not an insurance contract because payment is not conditional on whether the holder is adversely affected by a reduction in the cash flows from the asset. Conversely, the definition of an insurance contract refers to an uncertain event for which an adverse effect on the policyholder is a contractual precondition for payment. This contractual precondition does not require the insurer to investigate whether the event actually caused an adverse effect, but permits the insurer to deny payment if it is not satisfied that the event caused an adverse effect.

12   Lapse or persistency risk (i. e. the risk that the counterparty will cancel the contract earlier or later than the issuer had expected in pricing the contract) is not insurance risk because the payment to the counterparty is not contingent on an uncertain future event that adversely affects the counterparty. Similarly, expense risk (i. e. the risk of unexpected increases in the administrative costs associated with the servicing of a contract, rather than in costs associated with insured events) is not insurance risk because an unexpected increase in expenses does not adversely affect the counterparty.

13   Therefore, a contract that exposes the issuer to lapse risk, persistency risk or expense risk is not an insurance contract unless it also exposes the issuer to insurance risk. However, if the issuer of that contract mitigates that risk by using a second contract to transfer part of that risk to another party, the second contract exposes that other party to insurance risk.

14   An insurer can accept significant insurance risk from the policyholder only if the insurer is an entity separate from the policyholder. In the case of a mutual insurer, the mutual accepts risk from each policyholder and pools that risk. Although policyholders bear that pooled risk collectively in their capacity as owners, the mutual has still accepted the risk that is the essence of an insurance contract.

Examples of life insurance contracts

15   The following are examples of contracts that are life insurance contracts, if the transfer of insurance risk is significant:

     (a)   life insurance contracts (although death is certain, it is uncertain when death will occur or, for some types of life insurance, whether death will occur within the period covered by the insurance);

     (b)   life-contingent annuities and pensions (i. e. contracts that provide compensation for the uncertain future event – the survival of the annuitant or pensioner – to assist the annuitant or pensioner in maintaining a given standard of living, which would otherwise be adversely affected by his or her survival); and

     (c)   life reinsurance contracts.

16   The following are examples of items that are not life insurance contracts:

(a)   investment contracts that are governed under the *Life Insurance Act 1995* but do not expose the insurer to significant insurance risk, for example life insurance contracts in which the insurer bears no significant mortality risk (such contracts are non-insurance financial instruments or service contracts: see paragraphs 17 and 18 of this Appendix);

(b)   contracts that have the legal form of insurance, but pass all significant insurance risk back to the policyholder through non-cancellable and enforceable mechanisms that adjust future payments by the policyholder as a direct result of insured losses, for example some financial reinsurance contracts or some group contracts (such contracts are normally non-insurance financial instruments or service contracts: see paragraphs 17 and 18 of this Appendix);

(c)   self-insurance, in other words retaining a risk that could have been covered by insurance (there is no insurance contract because there is no agreement with another party);

(d)   contracts (such as gambling contracts) that require a payment if a specified uncertain future event occurs, but do not require, as a contractual precondition for payment, that the event adversely affects the policyholder. However, this does not preclude the specification of a predetermined payout to quantify the loss caused by a specified event such as death or an accident;

(e)   derivatives that expose one party to financial risk but not insurance risk, because they require that party to make payment based solely on changes in one or more of a specified interest rate, financial instrument price, commodity price, foreign exchange rate, index of prices or rates, credit rating or credit index or other variable, provided in the case of a non-financial variable that the variable is not specific to a party to the contract (see AASB 9); and

(f)   general insurance contracts.

17   If the contracts described in paragraph 16 of this Appendix create financial assets or financial liabilities, they are within the scope of AASB 9. Among other things, this means that the parties to the contract use what is sometimes called deposit accounting, which involves the following:

(a)   one party recognises the consideration received as a financial liability, rather than as revenue; and

(b)   the other party recognises the consideration paid as a financial asset, rather than as an expense.

18   If the contracts described in paragraph 16 of this Appendix do not create financial assets or financial liabilities, AASB 15 applies. Under AASB 15, revenue is recognised when (or as) an entity satisfies a performance obligation by transferring a promised good or service to a customer in an amount that reflects the consideration to which the entity expects to be entitled.

Significant insurance risk

19   A contract is an insurance contract only if it transfers significant insurance risk. Paragraphs 5 to 14 of this Appendix discuss insurance risk. The following paragraphs discuss the assessment of whether insurance risk is significant.

20   Insurance risk is significant if, and only if, an insured event could cause an insurer to pay significant additional benefits in any scenario, excluding scenarios that lack commercial substance (i. e. have no discernible effect on the economics of the transaction). If significant additional benefits would be payable in scenarios that have commercial substance, the condition in the previous sentence may be met even if the insured event is extremely unlikely or even if the expected (i. e. probability-weighted) present value of contingent cash flows is a small proportion of the expected present value of all the remaining contractual cash flows.

21   The additional benefits described in paragraph 20 of this Appendix refer to amounts that exceed those that would be payable if no insured event occurred (excluding scenarios that lack commercial substance). Those additional amounts include claims handling and claims assessment costs, but exclude:

(a)   the loss of the ability to charge the policyholder for future services. For example, in an investment-linked life insurance contract, the death of the policyholder means that the insurer can no longer perform investment management services and collect a fee for doing so. However, this economic loss for the insurer does not reflect insurance risk, just as a mutual fund manager does not take on insurance risk in relation to the possible death of the client. Therefore, the potential loss of future investment management fees is not relevant in assessing how much insurance risk is transferred by a contract;

(b)   waiver on death of charges that would be made on cancellation or surrender. Because the contract brought those charges into existence, the waiver of these charges does not compensate the policyholder for a pre-existing risk. Hence, they are not relevant in assessing how much insurance risk is transferred by a contract;

(c)   a payment conditional on an event that does not cause a significant loss to the holder of the contract. For example, consider a contract that requires the issuer to pay one million currency units if an asset suffers physical damage causing an insignificant economic loss of one currency unit to the holder. In this contract, the holder transfers to the insurer the insignificant risk of losing one currency unit. At the same time, the contract creates non-insurance risk that the issuer will need to pay 999,999 currency units if the specified event occurs. Because the issuer does not accept significant insurance risk from the holder, this contract is not an insurance contract; and

(d)   possible reinsurance recoveries. The insurer accounts for these separately.

22   An insurer shall assess the significance of insurance risk contract by contract, rather than by reference to materiality to the financial statements[1]. Thus, insurance risk may be significant even if there is a minimal probability of material losses for a whole book of contracts. This contract-by-contract assessment makes it easier to classify a contract as an insurance contract. However, if a relatively homogeneous book of small contracts is known to consist of contracts that all transfer insurance risk, an insurer need not examine each contract within that book to identify a few non-derivative contracts that transfer insignificant insurance risk.

23   It follows from paragraphs 20 to 22 of this Appendix that if a contract pays a death benefit exceeding the amount payable on survival, the contract is an insurance contract unless the additional death benefit is insignificant (judged by reference to the contract rather than to an entire book of contracts). As noted in paragraph 21(b) of this Appendix, the waiver on death of cancellation or surrender charges is not included in this assessment if this waiver does not compensate the policyholder for a pre-existing risk. Similarly, an annuity contract that pays out regular sums for the rest of a policyholder's life is an insurance contract, unless the aggregate life contingent payments are insignificant.

24   Paragraph 20 of this Appendix refers to additional benefits. These additional benefits could include a requirement to pay benefits earlier if the insured event occurs earlier and the payment is not adjusted for the time value of money. An example is whole life insurance for a fixed amount (in other words, insurance that provides a fixed death benefit whenever the policyholder dies, with no expiry date for the cover). It is certain that the policyholder will die, but the date of death is uncertain. The insurer will suffer a loss on those individual contracts for which policyholders die early, even if there is no overall loss on the whole book of contracts.

---

1   For this purpose, contracts entered into simultaneously with a single counterparty (or contracts that are otherwise interdependent) form a single contract.

25   If an insurance contract is unbundled into a deposit component and an insurance
      component, the significance of insurance risk transfer is assessed by reference to the
      insurance component. The significance of insurance risk transferred by an embedded
      derivative is assessed by reference to the embedded derivative.

Changes in the level of insurance risk

26   Some contracts do not transfer any insurance risk to the issuer at inception, although
      they do transfer insurance risk at a later time. For example, consider a contract that
      provides a specified investment return and includes an option for the policyholder
      to use the proceeds of the investment on maturity to buy a life-contingent annuity
      at the current annuity rates charged by the insurer to other new annuitants when the
      policyholder exercises the option. The contract transfers no insurance risk to the issuer
      until the option is exercised, because the insurer remains free to price the annuity on
      a basis that reflects the insurance risk transferred to the insurer at that time. However,
      if the contract specifies the annuity rates (or a basis for setting the annuity rates), the
      contract transfers insurance risk to the issuer at inception.

27   A contract that qualifies as an insurance contract remains an insurance contract until
      all rights and obligations are extinguished or expire.

AASB 1039
Concise Financial Reports
(Compiled January 2015)

This compiled Standard applies to annual reporting periods beginning on or after 1 January 2017. Early application is permitted for annual reporting periods beginning on or after 1 January 2014 but before 1 January 2017. It incorporates relevant amendments made up to and including 28 January 2015.

Prepared on 2 April 2015 by the staff of the Australian Accounting Standards Board.

This note is not part of Accounting Standard AASB 1039.

The following unincorporated amendments are not included in this compiled Standard.

- AASB 2016-7 *Amendments to Australian Accounting Standards — Deferral of AASB 15 for Not-for-Profit Entities.* This Standard defers the consequential amendments that were originally set out in AASB 2014-5 *Amendments to Australian Accounting Standards arising from AASB 15,* by restating the effective date of the amendments set out in AASB 2015-8 *Amendments to Australian Accounting Standards* for not-for-profit entities. This Standard defers the application of AASB 15 to 1 January 2019. Earlier application is permitted provided AASB 1058 is also applied to the same period.

Entities early-adopting any amendments with later application dates will need to refer to the amending Standards that have not yet been incorporated into compilations. The abovementioned unincorporated amendments may be located on the AASB website at www.aasb.gov.au or on the Federal Register of Legislation website at www.legislation.gov.au.

AASB

CONTENTS

COMPILATION DETAILS
ACCOUNTING STANDARD
AASB 1039 *CONCISE FINANCIAL REPORTS*

Australian Accounting Standard AASB 1039 *Concise Financial Reports* (as amended) is set out in paragraphs 1 – 37. All the paragraphs have equal authority. Paragraphs in **bold type** state the main principles. AASB 1039 is to be read in the context of other Australian Accounting Standards, including AASB 1048 *Interpretation of Standards*, which identifies the Australian Accounting Interpretations. In the absence of explicit guidance, AASB 108 *Accounting Policies, Changes in Accounting Estimates and Errors* provides a basis for selecting and applying accounting policies.

COMPILATION DETAILS
ACCOUNTING STANDARD AASB 1039 *CONCISE FINANCIAL REPORTS* AS AMENDED

This compiled Standard applies to annual reporting periods beginning on or after 1 January 2017. It takes into account amendments up to and including 28 January 2015 and was prepared on 2 April 2015 by the staff of the Australian Accounting Standards Board (AASB).

This compilation is not a separate Accounting Standard made by the AASB. Instead, it is a representation of AASB 1039 (August 2008) as amended by other Accounting Standards, which are listed in the Table below.

Table of Standards

Standard	Date made	Application date *(annual reporting periods ... on or after ...)*	Application, saving or transitional provisions
AASB 1039	27 Aug 2008	*(beginning)* 1 Jan 2009	see (a) below
AASB 2009-6	25 Jun 2009	*(beginning)* 1 Jan 2009 and *(ending)* 30 Jun 2009	see (b) below
AASB 2011-9	5 Sep 2011	*(beginning)* 1 Jul 2012	see (c) below
AASB 2012-10	18 Dec 2012	*(beginning)* 1 Jan 2013	see (d) below
AASB 2014-5	12 Dec 2014	*(beginning)* 1 Jan 2017	see (e) below
AASB 2015-3	28 Jan 2015	*(beginning)* 1 Jul 2015	see (f) below

(a) Entities may elect to apply this Standard to annual reporting periods beginning on or after 1 January 2005 but before 1 January 2009, provided that AASB 101 *Presentation of Financial Statements* (September 2007) and AASB 8 *Operating Segments* are also applied to such periods.

(b) Entities may elect to apply this Standard to annual reporting periods beginning on or after 1 January 2005 but before 1 January 2009, provided that AASB 101 *Presentation of Financial Statements* (September 2007) is also applied to such periods, and to annual reporting periods beginning on or after 1 January 2009 that end before 30 June 2009.

(c) Entities may elect to apply this Standard to annual reporting periods beginning on or after 1 January 2005 but before 1 July 2012.

(d) Entities may elect to apply this Standard to annual reporting periods beginning on or after 1 January 2005 but before 1 January 2013.

(e) Entities may elect to apply this Standard to annual reporting periods beginning on or after 1 January 2005 but before 1 January 2017, provided that AASB 15 *Revenue from Contracts with Customers* is also applied to such periods.

(f) Entities may elect to apply this Standard to annual reporting periods beginning on or after 1 January 2014 but before 1 July 2015.

Table of amendments

Paragraph affected	How affected	By ... [paragraph]
5	deleted	AASB 2015-3 [13, 14]
18-19	amended	AASB 2011-9 [24]
27	amended	AASB 2011-9 [24]
30	amended	AASB 2012-10 [68]
	amended	AASB 2014-5 [45]
	amended	AASB 2015-3 [15]
31	amended	AASB 2009-6 [102]

ACCOUNTING STANDARD AASB 1039

The Australian Accounting Standards Board made Accounting Standard AASB 1039 *Concise Financial Reports* under section 334 of the *Corporations Act 2001* on 27 August 2008.

This compiled version of AASB 1039 applies to annual reporting periods beginning on or after 1 January 2017. It incorporates relevant amendments contained in other AASB Standards made by the AASB up to and including 28 January 2015 (see Compilation Details).

ACCOUNTING STANDARD AASB 1039

CONCISE FINANCIAL REPORTS

Application

1 **This Standard applies to a concise financial report prepared by an entity in accordance with paragraph 314(2)(a) in Part 2M.3 of the Corporations Act.**

2 Under the Corporations Act a company, registered scheme or disclosing entity can elect to send to its members for a financial year a concise report, which includes a concise financial report, instead of the financial report.

3 **Where an entity is the parent of a group, this Standard applies to the consolidated financial statements of the entity and the notes to those statements, and does not require that parent financial information be provided.**

4 If the entity provides parent financial information in addition to consolidated financial information, the parent financial information is also subject to the requirements of this Standard.

5 [Deleted by the AASB]

Operative date

6 **This Standard applies to annual reporting periods beginning on or after 1 January 2009.** [Note: For application dates of paragraphs changed or added by an amending Standard, see Compilation Details.]

7 **This Standard may be applied to annual reporting periods beginning on or after 1 January 2005 but before 1 January 2009 provided that AASB 101** *Presentation of Financial Statements* **(September 2007) and AASB 8** *Operating Segments* **are also applied to the period. If an entity adopts this Standard for an earlier period, it shall disclose that fact.**

8 **When applied or operative, this Standard supersedes AASB 1039** *Concise Financial Reports* **made on 14 April 2005.**

Purpose of Standard

9 **The purpose of this Standard is to specify the minimum content of a concise financial report.**

10 The requirements of the Corporations Act relating to concise financial reports are based on the view that a concise financial report can provide members with information relevant to evaluating the business, without giving them fully detailed accounting disclosures. For some members, the provision of less detailed information is expected to be sufficient to meet their needs for an understanding of the financial performance, financial position and financing and investing activities of the company, registered scheme or disclosing entity.

11   The minimum content required by this Standard is intended also to provide sufficient information to permit members to identify if and when they consider it would be useful to obtain more comprehensive and detailed information by requesting a copy of the financial report.

Preparation and presentation

12   The financial statements and specific disclosures (identified in paragraphs 28 to 32 of this Standard) required in a concise financial report shall be derived from the financial report of the entity. Any other information included in a concise financial report shall be consistent with the financial report of the entity.

13   In order to achieve consistency and comparability with information included in the financial report, this Standard requires the accounting policies relating to recognition and measurement applied in the preparation of a concise financial report to be the same as those adopted in the preparation of the financial report.

14   This Standard prescribes the minimum information to be disclosed in a concise financial report but does not prescribe the format in which that information is presented. The format for the presentation of information in a concise financial report is developed having regard to the particular circumstances of the entity and the presentation of relevant, reliable, understandable and comparable information about the entity's financial performance, financial position and financing and investing activities. Entities are encouraged to develop a format that best meets the information needs of their members.

15   The consistency required by paragraph 12 means that information voluntarily included in the concise financial report is determined in accordance with the treatment adopted in the financial report. When the information in the financial report was determined in accordance with an Accounting Standard, the same treatment is adopted in the concise financial report.

16   The nature and estimated magnitude of particular items are disclosed if it is likely that the concise financial report would be misleading without such disclosures.

17   The content of a concise financial report specified in this Standard constitutes the minimum level of disclosure. Where there are particular features of the operations and activities of the entity that are significant, the entity may need to provide additional information in the concise financial report in order to comply with paragraph 16. Similarly, members benefit from industry-specific disclosures, for example, disclosure of additional information by mining companies in relation to exploration and evaluation expenditure and decommissioning costs, and by banks and other financial institutions in relation to doubtful debts.

Financial statements

18   A concise financial report shall include the following financial statements:

   (a)   a statement of profit or loss and other comprehensive income for the annual reporting period;

   (b)   a statement of financial position as at the end of the annual reporting period;

   (c)   a statement of cash flows for the annual reporting period; and

   (d)   a statement of changes in equity for the annual reporting period.

19   In accordance with paragraph 10A of AASB 101 *Presentation of Financial Statements*, an entity may present all items of income and expense recognised in a period in a single statement of profit or loss and other comprehensive income or present the profit or loss section in a separate statement of profit or loss.

20   **Each financial statement shall be presented as it is in the financial report, in accordance with other Accounting Standards, except for the omission of cross-references to notes to the financial statements in the financial report.**

21   All the notes to the financial statements required by other Accounting Standards are not required in the concise financial report. For example, this Standard does not require an entity that uses the direct method in the statement of cash flows to provide a reconciliation of cash flows arising from operating activities to profit or loss. However, information required in some notes by other Accounting Standards is required when specified in this Standard.

22   It is recommended that the financial statements in the concise financial report be cross-referenced, where appropriate, to disclosures included in the concise financial report.

23   When the entity is a parent and only the consolidated financial statements are presented, the lack of financial statements for the parent would not be regarded as contravening paragraph 21.

24   **The financial statements of entities other than listed companies shall be accompanied by discussion and analysis to assist the understanding of members.**

25   Listed companies are not required by this Standard to provide discussion and analysis in the concise financial report because, unlike other entities, they are required by section 299A of the Corporations Act to provide an operational and financial report in the Directors' Report that is part of the concise report. Paragraph 24 only exempts listed companies from the statutory obligation to provide discussion and analysis of the financial statements. It does not prohibit a listed company from providing any discussion and analysis that it considers would assist a reader to understand the financial statements in the concise financial report.

26   The information reported in the financial statements will be enhanced by a discussion and analysis of the principal factors affecting the financial performance, financial position and financing and investing activities of the entity. The extent of the discussion and analysis provided will vary from entity to entity, and from year to year, as is necessary in the circumstances to help compensate for the brevity of the concise financial report compared with the financial report.

27   In most situations, the content of the discussion and analysis would cover at least the following areas:

    (a)   in relation to the statement of profit or loss and other comprehensive income:

         (i)   trends in revenues;

         (ii)   the effects of significant economic or other events on the operations of the entity;

         (iii)   the main influences on costs of operations; and

         (iv)   measures of financial performance such as return on sales, return on assets and return on equity;

    (b)   in relation to the statement of financial position:

         (i)   changes in the composition of assets;

         (ii)   the relationship between debt and equity; and

         (iii)   significant movements in assets, liabilities and equity items;

    (c)   in relation to the statement of cash flows:

         (i)   changes in cash flows from operations;

         (ii)   financing of capital expenditure programs; and

         (iii)   servicing and repayment of borrowings; and

AASB

    (d)   in relation to the statement of changes in equity:

           (i)   changes in the composition of the components of equity; and

           (ii)   causes of significant changes in subscribed capital, such as rights issues, share buy-backs or capital reductions.

Specific disclosures

28   When the entity has prepared its financial report on the basis that the entity is not a going concern, or where the going concern basis has become inappropriate after the reporting date, this fact shall be disclosed.

29   The following information shall be disclosed for each reportable segment identified in the financial report in accordance with AASB 8 *Operating Segments*:

    (a)   revenues from sales to external customers and revenues from transactions with other operating segments of the same entity if the specified amounts are included in the measure of segment profit or loss reviewed by the chief operating decision maker or are otherwise regularly provided to the chief operating decision maker, even if not included in that measure of segment profit or loss;

    (b)   a measure of profit or loss;

    (c)   a measure of total assets; and

    (d)   a measure of liabilities if such amount is regularly provided to the chief operating decision maker.

30   The following items for the period shall be disclosed even if the amounts are zero:

    (a)   the amount of revenue recognised in accordance with AASB 15 *Revenue from Contracts with Customers*;

    (b)   the amount of dividends, in aggregate and per share, in respect of each class of shares included in equity, identifying:

           (i)   dividends paid during the period and date of payment; and

           (ii)   dividends proposed or declared before the financial report was authorised for issue, and the expected date of payment, separately identifying, where relevant, those recognised from those not recognised as a distribution to equity holders during the period; and

    (c)   where the entity is required to comply with AASB 133 *Earnings per Share*, the amount of basic earnings per share and diluted earnings per share.

31   The following items shall be disclosed:

    (a)   the presentation currency used;

    (b)   in respect of each event occurring after the reporting date that does not relate to conditions existing at the reporting date, the information required by paragraph 21 of AASB 110 *Events after the Reporting Period*; and

    (c)   where there is a change in accounting policy or estimates from those used in the preceding reporting period, or a correction of a prior period error, which has a material effect in the current reporting period or is expected to have a material effect in a subsequent reporting period, the information required about such a change or correction by the relevant Accounting Standards that are applicable to the current reporting period.

32   The concise financial report for the period when an entity first adopts Australian equivalents to IFRSs shall provide directions as to the location in the financial report of the reconciliations and other disclosures required by paragraphs 39 and 40 of AASB 1 *First-time Adoption of Australian Accounting Standards*. A summary of this information shall be included in the concise financial report.

Relationship to financial report

33   The first page of the concise financial report shall prominently display advice to the effect that:

(a)   the concise financial report is an extract from the financial report;

(b)   the financial statements and specific disclosures included in the concise financial report have been derived from the financial report;

(c)   the concise financial report cannot be expected to provide as full an understanding of the financial performance, financial position and financing and investing activities of the entity as the financial report; and

(d)   further financial information can be obtained from the financial report and that the financial report is available, free of charge, on request to the entity.

Comparative information

34   Any requirements relating to comparative information in other Accounting Standards that have been adopted in the preparation of the financial report are applicable in this Standard.

35   When disclosure is not required with respect to the current reporting period for an item in paragraphs 28 to 32 of this Standard but was required in the preceding reporting period, it is still necessary to disclose the comparative information.

Definitions

36   In this Standard, technical terms have the same meaning as in the relevant Accounting Standards applied in the preparation of the financial report for the current reporting period.

37   The terms 'concise report', 'concise financial report', 'financial report', 'listed company' and 'members' have the meanings as given or used in Chapter 2M of the Corporations Act.

AASB 1048

Interpretation of Standards

(Reissued December 2017)

CONTENTS

PREFACE
COMPARISON WITH INTERNATIONAL PRONOUNCEMENTS
ACCOUNTING STANDARD
AASB 1048 *INTERPRETATION OF STANDARDS*

Australian Accounting Standard AASB 1048 *Interpretation of Standards* is set out in paragraphs 1 – 13. All the paragraphs have equal authority. Paragraphs in **bold type** state the main principles. AASB 1048 is to be read in the context of other Australian Accounting Standards, including AASB 1057 *Application of Australian Accounting Standards*. In the absence of explicit guidance, AASB 108 *Accounting Policies, Changes in Accounting Estimates and Errors* provides a basis for selecting and applying accounting policies.

PREFACE

Introduction

The Australian Accounting Standards Board (AASB) is an Australian Government entity under the *Australian Securities and Investments Commission Act 2001*. The AASB develops, issues and maintains Australian Accounting Standards, including Interpretations. These are to be applied by:

(a)   entities required by the *Corporations Act 2001* to prepare financial reports;

(b)   governments in preparing financial statements for the whole of government and the General Government Sector (GGS); and/or

(c)   entities in the private or public for-profit or not-for-profit sectors that are reporting entities or that prepare general purpose financial statements.

AASB 1053 *Application of Tiers of Australian Accounting Standards* establishes a differential reporting framework consisting of two tiers of reporting requirements for preparing general purpose financial statements:

(a)   Tier 1: Australian Accounting Standards; and

(b)   Tier 2: Australian Accounting Standards – Reduced Disclosure Requirements.

What does this Standard require?

This Standard identifies the Australian Interpretations and classifies them into two groups: those that correspond to an International Accounting Standards Board (IASB) Interpretation and those that do not. Entities are required to apply each relevant Australian Interpretation in preparing financial statements that are within the scope of the Standard.

In respect of the first group (Table 1), it is necessary for those Australian Interpretations, where relevant, to be applied in order for an entity to be able to make an explicit and unreserved statement of compliance with International Financial Reporting Standards (IFRS Standards). The IASB defines IFRS Standards to include both IFRIC and SIC Interpretations.

In the second group (Table 2), this Standard lists the other Australian Interpretations, which do not correspond to the IASB Interpretations, to assist financial statement preparers and users to identify the other authoritative pronouncements necessary for compliance in the Australian context.

This Standard (see Table 3) also updates references to the *Framework for the Preparation and Presentation of Financial Statements* in other Standards to refer to an amended version of the *Framework*, as identified in this Standard.

The Standard will be reissued when necessary to keep the Tables up to date.

When does it apply?

This Standard is applicable to annual reporting periods ending on or after 31 December 2017 (see paragraph 2). Earlier application is permitted as specified in paragraph 3, subject to paragraphs 7, 9 and 11 of this Standard.

What are the changes?

This Standard (issued in December 2017) supersedes the previous version of AASB 1048, issued in August 2015.

The main differences between the previous version and this version include:

(a)   the removal from Tables 1 and 2 of versions of Interpretations that do not apply to any of the reporting periods to which this Standard mandatorily applies (see paragraph 2);

(b)   the addition of two Australian Interpretations incorporating an IFRIC Interpretation to Table 1, as set out in the following table:

Principal additions to Table 1

Interpretation *Issue Date*	Title	Application Date (annual reporting periods)	IFRIC or SIC Interp'n
22 *February* 2017	Foreign Currency Transactions and Advance Consideration	(beginning) 1 January 2018	IFRIC 22
23 *July 2017*	Uncertainty over Income Tax Treatments	(beginning) 1 January 2019	IFRIC 23

(c)   the addition of amended versions of Interpretations in Tables 1 and 2, where applicable to any reporting period to which this Standard mandatorily applies. This reflects amended versions of Interpretations arising as a result of the deferral of AASB 15 *Revenue from Contracts with Customers* and its consequential amendments, and consequential amendments arising from the issuance of AASB 16 *Leases*, AASB 17 *Insurance Contracts*, AASB 1058 *Income of Not-for-Profit Entities* and AASB 1059 *Service Concession Arrangements: Grantors*.

Why have we issued this Standard?

This Standard clarifies that all Australian Interpretations have the same authoritative status. Those that incorporate the IASB Interpretations must be applied to achieve compliance with IFRS Standards. Australian Interpretations issued by the AASB comprise both AASB and

UIG Interpretations. UIG Interpretations were developed by the Urgent Issues Group, a former committee of the AASB.

This Standard also updates references in other Standards to the *Framework for the Preparation and Presentation of Financial Statements* to subsequent versions.

Need for a service Standard

Australian Interpretations

In the Australian context, Australian Interpretations do not have the same legal status as Standards (delegated legislation) and are treated as 'external documents' by the *Acts Interpretation Act 1901* and the *Legislation Act 2003*. Although references in one Standard to a second Standard are ambulatory (automatically moving forward to refer to the most recently-issued version of the second Standard), references in a Standard to external documents are stationary (being fixed in time to refer to the contents of the external document when the Standard was issued). A simple reference to an Australian Interpretation in a Standard can refer only to the Interpretation that existed when the Standard was issued. It cannot refer to any revised version of the Interpretation that may exist at a later reporting date. However, a Standard can refer to a second Standard and, when the first Standard is applied at a later reporting date, the reference will be to the then-current version of the second Standard, even if it has been reissued since the first Standard was issued.

The service Standard approach, as applied to Australian Interpretations, involves issuing this Standard to list the Australian Interpretations, and referring to this Standard in every other Standard where necessary to refer to an Interpretation. This enables references to the Interpretations in all other Standards to be updated by reissuing the service Standard.

This approach preserves the status of Australian Interpretations as 'external documents' referred to in a Standard. It does not treat the Interpretations as delegated legislation or confer ambulatory status on the reference. In each Standard where there is a need to refer to an Australian Interpretation, the reference will be to this Standard, phrased as "Interpretation [number] [title] as identified in AASB 1048" (or similar). This reference, being to another Standard, is ambulatory and will refer to the version of this Standard that is in force from time to time. AASB 1048 itself will contain the direct references to the external documents and will be reissued periodically.

This approach to clarifying the status of Australian Interpretations ensures there is no difference between the status in the hierarchy accorded to Interpretations in IAS 8 *Accounting Policies, Changes in Accounting Estimates and Errors* compared with AASB 108 *Accounting Policies, Changes in Accounting Estimates and Errors*.

Australian conceptual framework

In the Australian context, an Australian conceptual framework pronouncement, such as the *Framework for the Preparation and Presentation of Financial Statements* (*Framework*), also does not have the same legal status as a Standard (delegated legislation) and, like Interpretations, is treated as an 'external document' by the *Acts Interpretation Act 1901* and the *Legislation Act 2003*.

The service Standard approach, as applied to the Australian conceptual framework, involves issuing this Standard to update references to the *Framework* in other Standards. This approach preserves the status of the *Framework* as an 'external document' referred to in a Standard. It does not treat the *Framework* as delegated legislation or confer ambulatory status on the reference.

COMPARISON WITH INTERNATIONAL PRONOUNCEMENTS

There is no International Accounting Standards Board (IASB) Standard that directly corresponds to AASB 1048. However, Table 1 in AASB 1048 (see paragraph 6) contains a list of Australian Interpretations identifying the corresponding IASB Interpretations.

Tier 1

For-profit entities complying with the Australian Interpretations designated in this Standard as corresponding to the IASB Interpretations also comply with the Interpretations referred to by the IASB in its definition of International Financial Reporting Standards (IFRS Standards).

Not-for-profit entities' compliance with IASB Interpretations will depend on whether any "Aus" paragraphs or Interpretations that specifically apply to not-for-profit entities provide additional guidance or contain applicable requirements that are inconsistent with IASB Interpretations.

Tier 2

Entities preparing general purpose financial statements under Australian Accounting Standards – Reduced Disclosure Requirements (Tier 2) will not be in compliance with all IASB Interpretations.

AASB 1053 *Application of Tiers of Australian Accounting Standards* explains the two tiers of reporting requirements.

Conceptual framework

In relation to references to the *Framework for the Preparation and Presentation of Financial Statements* in other Standards, the approach taken in this Standard to clarifying the applicable framework pronouncement ensures there is no difference between the version of the conceptual framework referred to in IAS 8 *Accounting Policies, Changes in Accounting Estimates and Errors* and AASB 108 *Accounting Policies, Changes in Accounting Estimates and Errors*, and in other Standards.

ACCOUNTING STANDARD AASB 1048

The Australian Accounting Standards Board makes Accounting Standard AASB 1048 *Interpretation of Standards* (December 2017) under section 334 of the *Corporations Act 2001*.

Dated 12 December 2017

Kris Peach

Chair – AASB

ACCOUNTING STANDARD AASB 1048
INTERPRETATION OF STANDARDS

Objective

1   The objective of this Standard is to provide an up-to-date listing of Australian Interpretations and to ensure the effectiveness of references in Australian Accounting Standards to Australian Interpretations and to the *Framework for the Preparation and Presentation of Financial Statements* (*Framework*). AASB and UIG Interpretations are referred to collectively in this Standard as Australian Interpretations.

Application

2   **This Standard applies to annual reporting periods ending on or after 31 December 2017.**

3   **This Standard may be applied to annual reporting periods that end before 31 December 2017.**

Interpretations

4   This Standard refers to all Australian Interpretations currently approved by the AASB and applicable to any period[1] specified in paragraph 2 (by either mandatory or early application), classified according to whether they correspond to Interpretations adopted by the International Accounting Standards Board (IASB).

5   For ease of presentation, the Australian Interpretations are set out in two separate tables: in paragraph 6, Table 1 lists those corresponding to IASB Interpretations and, in paragraph 8, Table 2 lists the other Interpretations. Each reference to an Interpretation in a row in each of the Tables 1 and 2 is to be treated as a separate provision of this Standard.

Australian Interpretations corresponding to IASB Interpretations

6   **An entity shall apply each relevant Australian Interpretation listed in Table 1 below.**

Table 1   Australian Interpretations corresponding to IASB Interpretations

Interpretation *Issue Date*	Title	Application Date (annual reporting periods)	IFRIC or SIC Interp'n
1 *February 2016* [as amended to]	Changes in Existing Decommissioning, Restoration and Similar Liabilities	(beginning) 1 January 2019	IFRIC 1
1 *July 2015*	Changes in Existing Decommissioning, Restoration and Similar Liabilities	(beginning) 1 January 2016	IFRIC 1
2 *July 2015*	Members' Shares in Co-operative Entities and Similar Instruments	(beginning) 1 January 2018	IFRIC 2
2 *December 2014* [as amended to]	Members' Shares in Co-operative Entities and Similar Instruments	(beginning) 1 January 2018	IFRIC 2
2 *June 2014* [as amended to]	Members' Shares in Co-operative Entities and Similar Instruments	(beginning) 1 January 2018	IFRIC 2
2 *December 2013* [as amended to]	Members' Shares in Co-operative Entities and Similar Instruments	(beginning) 1 January 2014	IFRIC 2
4 *August 2015*	Determining whether an Arrangement contains a Lease	(beginning) 1 January 2016	IFRIC 4
5 *August 2015*	Rights to Interests arising from Decommissioning, Restoration and Environmental Rehabilitation Funds	(beginning) 1 January 2018	IFRIC 5
5 *December 2014* [as amended to]	Rights to Interests arising from Decommissioning, Restoration and Environmental Rehabilitation Funds	(beginning) 1 January 2018	IFRIC 5
5 *June 2014* [as amended to]	Rights to Interests arising from Decommissioning, Restoration and Environmental Rehabilitation Funds	(beginning) 1 January 2018	IFRIC 5
5 *December 2013* [as amended to]	Rights to Interests arising from Decommissioning, Restoration and Environmental Rehabilitation Funds	(beginning) 1 January 2014	IFRIC 5

(Continued)

---

1   Periods no longer than 18 months.

Interpretation *Issue Date*	Title	Application Date (annual reporting periods)	IFRIC or SIC Interp'n
6 *August 2015*	Liabilities arising from Participating in a Specific Market – Waste Electrical and Electronic Equipment	(beginning) 1 January 2016	IFRIC 6
7 *August 2015*	Applying the Restatement Approach under AASB 129 *Financial Reporting in Hyperinflationary Economies*	(beginning) 1 January 2016	IFRIC 7
9 *December 2013* [as amended to]	Reassessment of Embedded Derivatives	(beginning) 1 January 2014	IFRIC 9
10 *August 2015*	Interim Financial Reporting and Impairment	(beginning) 1 January 2018	IFRIC 10
10 *December 2014* [as amended to]	Interim Financial Reporting and Impairment	(beginning) 1 January 2018	IFRIC 10
10 *June 2014* [as amended to]	Interim Financial Reporting and Impairment	(beginning) 1 January 2018	IFRIC 10
10 *December 2013* [as amended to]	Interim Financial Reporting and Impairment	(beginning) 1 January 2014	IFRIC 10
12 *December 2017* [as amended to]	Service Concession Arrangements	(beginning) 1 January 2019	IFRIC 12
12 *February 2016* [as amended to]	Service Concession Arrangements	(beginning) 1 January 2019	IFRIC 12
12 *December 2017* [as amended to]	Service Concession Arrangements	(beginning) 1 January 2018	IFRIC 12
12 *February 2016* [as amended to]	Service Concession Arrangements	(beginning) 1 January 2019	IFRIC 12
12 *December 2016* [as amended to]	Service Concession Arrangements	(beginning) 1 January 2018	IFRIC 12
12 *October 2015* [as amended to]	Service Concession Arrangements	(beginning) 1 January 2018	IFRIC 12
12 *August 2015*	Service Concession Arrangements	(beginning) 1 January 2018	IFRIC 12
12 *December 2014* [as amended to]	Service Concession Arrangements	(beginning) 1 January 2018	IFRIC 12
12 *June 2014* [as amended to]	Service Concession Arrangements	(beginning) 1 January 2018	IFRIC 12
12 *December 2013* [as amended to]	Service Concession Arrangements	(beginning) 1 January 2014	IFRIC 12

(Continued)

(Continued)

Interpretation Issue Date	Title	Application Date (annual reporting periods)	IFRIC or SIC Interp'n
13 December 2013 [as amended to]	Customer Loyalty Programmes	(beginning) 1 January 2014	IFRIC 13
14 August 2015	AASB 119 – The Limit on a Defined Benefit Asset, Minimum Funding Requirements and their Interaction	(beginning) 1 January 2016	IFRIC 14
15 December 2013 [as amended to]	Agreements for the Construction of Real Estate	(beginning) 1 January 2014	IFRIC 15
16 August 2015	Hedges of a Net Investment in a Foreign Operation	(beginning) 1 January 2018	IFRIC 16
16 December 2014 [as amended to]	Hedges of a Net Investment in a Foreign Operation	(beginning) 1 January 2018	IFRIC 16
16 June 2014 [as amended to]	Hedges of a Net Investment in a Foreign Operation	(beginning) 1 January 2018	IFRIC 16
16 December 2013 [as amended to]	Hedges of a Net Investment in a Foreign Operation	(beginning) 1 January 2014	IFRIC 16
17 August 2015	Distributions of Non-cash Assets to Owners	(beginning) 1 January 2016	IFRIC 17
18 December 2013 [as amended to]	Transfers of Assets from Customers	(beginning) 1 January 2014	IFRIC 18
19 August 2015	Extinguishing Financial Liabilities with Equity Instruments	(beginning) 1 January 2018	IFRIC 19
19 December 2014 [as amended to]	Extinguishing Financial Liabilities with Equity Instruments	(beginning) 1 January 2018	IFRIC 19
19 June 2014 [as amended to]	Extinguishing Financial Liabilities with Equity Instruments	(beginning) 1 January 2018	IFRIC 19
19 December 2013 [as amended to]	Extinguishing Financial Liabilities with Equity Instruments	(beginning) 1 January 2014	IFRIC 19
20 August 2015	Stripping Costs in the Production Phase of a Surface Mine	(beginning) 1 January 2016	IFRIC 20
21 August 2015	Levies	(beginning) 1 January 2016	IFRIC 21
22 February 2017	Foreign Currency Transactions and Advance Consideration	(beginning) 1 January 2018	IFRIC 22
23 July 2017	Uncertainty over Income Tax Treatments	(beginning) 1 January 2019	IFRIC 23
107 August 2015	Introduction of the Euro	(beginning) 1 January 2018	SIC-7
107 June 2014 [as amended to]	Introduction of the Euro	(beginning) 1 January 2018	SIC-7

Interpretation _Issue Date_	Title	Application Date (annual reporting periods)	IFRIC or SIC Interp'n
107 _December 2013_ [as amended to]	Introduction of the Euro	(beginning) 1 January 2014	SIC-7
110 _August 2015_	Government Assistance – No Specific Relation to Operating Activities	(beginning) 1 January 2016	SIC-10
115 _August 2015_	Operating Leases – Incentives	(beginning) 1 January 2016	SIC-15
125 _August 2015_	Income Taxes – Changes in the Tax Status of an Entity or its Shareholders	(beginning) 1 January 2016	SIC-25
127 _July 2017_ [as amended to]	Evaluating the Substance of Transactions Involving the Legal Form of a Lease	(beginning) 1 January 2021	SIC-27
127 _December 2016_ [as amended to]	Evaluating the Substance of Transactions Involving the Legal Form of a Lease	(beginning) 1 January 2018	SIC-27
127 _October 2015_ [as amended to]	Evaluating the Substance of Transactions Involving the Legal Form of a Lease	(beginning) 1 January 2018	SIC-27
127 _August 2015_	Evaluating the Substance of Transactions Involving the Legal Form of a Lease	(beginning) 1 January 2018	SIC-27
127 _December 2014_ [as amended to]	Evaluating the Substance of Transactions Involving the Legal Form of a Lease	(beginning) 1 January 2018	SIC-27
127 _December 2013_ [as amended to]	Evaluating the Substance of Transactions Involving the Legal Form of a Lease	(beginning) 1 January 2014	SIC-27
129 _July 2017_ [as amended to]	Service Concession Arrangements: Disclosures	(beginning) 1 January 2019	SIC-29
129 _February 2016_ [as amended to]	Service Concession Arrangements: Disclosures	(beginning) 1 January 2019	SIC-29
129 _August 2015_	Service Concession Arrangements: Disclosures	(beginning) 1 January 2016	SIC-29
131 _December 2013_ [as amended to]	Revenue – Barter Transactions Involving Advertising Services	(beginning) 1 January 2014	SIC-31
132 _February 2016_ [as amended to]	Intangible Assets – Web Site Costs	(beginning) 1 January 2019	SIC-32
132 _December 2016_ [as amended to]	Intangible Assets – Web Site Costs	(beginning) 1 January 2018	SIC-32
132 _October 2015_ [as amended to]	Intangible Assets – Web Site Costs	(beginning) 1 January 2018	SIC-32
132 _December 2013_ [as amended to]	Intangible Assets – Web Site Costs	(beginning) 1 January 2014	SIC-32

AASB

7   The principal application date listed in Table 1 for each Interpretation is a reference to annual reporting periods beginning or ending (as indicated) on or after the date specified. An entity may elect to apply an individual Interpretation to annual reporting periods in advance of that stated for the Interpretation in Table 1, subject to the early application requirements of the Interpretation.

Other Australian Interpretations

8   **An entity shall apply each relevant Australian Interpretation listed in Table 2 below.**

Table 2   Other Australian Interpretations

Interpretation *Issue Date*	Title	Application Date (annual reporting periods)
1003 *December 2013* [as amended to]	Australian Petroleum Resource Rent Tax	(beginning) 1 January 2014
1019 *December 2013* [as amended to]	The Superannuation Contributions Surcharge	(beginning) 1 January 2014
1030 *December 2013* [as amended to]	Depreciation of Long-Lived Physical Assets: Condition-Based Depreciation and Related Methods	(beginning) 1 January 2014
1031 *December 2016* [as amended to]	Accounting for the Goods and Services Tax (GST)	(beginning) 1 January 2018
1031 *October 2015* [as amended to]	Accounting for the Goods and Services Tax (GST)	(beginning) 1 January 2018
1031 *December 2013* [as amended to]	Accounting for the Goods and Services Tax (GST)	(beginning) 1 January 2014
1038 *December 2016* [as amended to]	Contributions by Owners Made to Wholly-Owned Public Sector Entities	(beginning) 1 January 2019
1038 *December 2016* [as amended to]	Contributions by Owners Made to Wholly-Owned Public Sector Entities	(beginning) 1 January 2018
1038 *October 2015* [as amended to]	Contributions by Owners Made to Wholly-Owned Public Sector Entities	(beginning) 1 January 2018
1038 *December 2013* [as amended to]	Contributions by Owners Made to Wholly-Owned Public Sector Entities	(beginning) 1 January 2014
1042 *December 2013* [as amended to]	Subscriber Acquisition Costs in the Telecommunications Industry	(beginning) 1 January 2014
1047 *July 2017* [as amended to]	Professional Indemnity Claims Liabilities in Medical Defence Organisations	(beginning) 1 January 2021
1047 *December 2013* [as amended to]	Professional Indemnity Claims Liabilities in Medical Defence Organisations	(beginning) 1 January 2014
1052 *December 2016* [as amended to]	Tax Consolidation Accounting	(beginning) 1 January 2018
1052 *October 2015* [as amended to]	Tax Consolidation Accounting	(beginning) 1 January 2018
1052 *December 2013* [as amended to]	Tax Consolidation Accounting	(beginning) 1 January 2014
1055 *December 2013* [as amended to]	Accounting for Road Earthworks	(beginning) 1 January 2014

9   The principal application date listed in Table 2 for each Interpretation is a reference to annual reporting periods beginning or ending (as indicated) on or after the date specified. An entity may elect to apply an individual Interpretation to annual reporting periods in advance of that stated for the Interpretation in Table 2, subject to the early application requirements of the Interpretation.

Conceptual framework

10   Each reference to the *Framework for the Preparation and Presentation of Financial Statements* (or *Framework*) in other Australian Accounting Standards (including Interpretations) is taken to be a reference to the relevant pronouncement listed in Table 3 below. Each row in Table 3 is to be treated as a separate provision of this Standard.

Table 3   Australian conceptual framework pronouncements

Issue Date	Title	Application Date (annual reporting periods)
June 2014 [as amended to]	Framework for the Preparation and Presentation of Financial Statements (or Framework)	(beginning) 1 July 2014

11   This Standard updates references to the *Framework* in Australian Accounting Standards (including Interpretations) to the relevant amended version of the *Framework*. The principal application date listed in each row of Table 3 is a reference to annual reporting periods beginning or ending (as indicated) on or after the date specified. An entity may elect to apply an amended version of the pronouncement to annual reporting periods in advance of that stated in Table 3, subject to any early application paragraphs.

Commencement of the legislative instrument

12   For legal purposes, this legislative instrument commences on 30 December 2017.

Withdrawal of AASB pronouncements

13   This Standard repeals AASB 1048 *Interpretation of Standards* issued in August 2015. Despite the repeal, after the time this Standard starts to apply under section 334 of the Corporations Act (either generally or in relation to an individual entity), the repealed Standard continues to apply in relation to any period ending before that time as if the repeal had not occurred.

[Note: When this Standard applies under section 334 of the Corporations Act (either generally or in relation to an individual entity), it supersedes the application of the repealed Standard.]

Note: The name of this instrument was amended on registration as the instrument as lodged did not have a unique name (see subsection 10(2), *Legislation Rule 2016*).

AASB 1049

Whole of Government and General Government Sector Financial Reporting

(Compiled March 2015)

This compiled Standard applies to annual reporting periods beginning on or after 1 July 2016 but before 1 January 2018. Early application is permitted. It incorporates relevant amendments made up to and including 31 March 2015.

Prepared on 6 June 2016 by the staff of the Australian Accounting Standards Board.

This note is not part of Accounting Standard AASB 1049.

Even though the Standard specifies applicable for periods prior to 1 January 2018, this compiled Standard remains in force for the 2018–19 reporting year.

The following unincorporated amendments are not included in this compiled Standard.

- AASB 2016-7 *Amendments to Australian Accounting Standards — Deferral of AASB 15 for Not-for-Profit Entities.* This Standard defers the consequential amendments that were originally set out in AASB 2014-5 *Amendments to Australian Accounting Standards arising from AASB 15,* by restating the effective date of the amendments set out in AASB 2015-8 *Amendments to Australian Accounting Standards* for not-for-profit entities. This Standard defers the application of AASB 15 to 1 January 2019. Earlier application is permitted provided AASB 1058 is also applied to the same period.

Entities early-adopting any amendments with later application dates will need to refer to the amending Standards that have not yet been incorporated into compilations. The abovementioned unincorporated amendments may be located on the AASB website at www.aasb.gov.au or on the Federal Register of Legislation website at www.legislation.gov.au.

CONTENTS

     Chartered Accountants Australia and New Zealand

Australian Accounting Standard AASB 1049 *Whole of Government and General Government Sector Financial Reporting* (as amended) is set out in paragraphs 1 – 58 and Appendix A. All the paragraphs have equal authority. Paragraphs in **bold type** state the main principles. Terms defined in this Standard are in *italics* the first time they appear in the Standard. AASB 1049 is to be read in the context of other Australian Accounting Standards, including AASB 1048 *Interpretation of Standards*, which identifies the Australian Accounting Interpretations. In the absence of explicit guidance, AASB 108 *Accounting Policies, Changes in Accounting Estimates and Errors* provides a basis for selecting and applying accounting policies.

COMPILATION DETAILS

Accounting Standard AASB 1049 *Whole of Government and General Government Sector Financial Reporting* as amended

This compiled Standard applies to annual reporting periods beginning on or after 1 July 2016 but before 1 January 2018. It takes into account amendments up to and including 31 March 2015 and was prepared on 6 June 2016 by the staff of the Australian Accounting Standards Board (AASB).

This compilation is not a separate Accounting Standard made by the AASB. Instead, it is a representation of AASB 1049 (October 2007) as amended by other Accounting Standards, which are listed in the Table below.

Table of Standards

Standard	Date made	Application date (*annual reporting periods ... on or after ...*)	Application, saving or transitional provisions
AASB 1049	30 Oct 2007	(*beginning*) 1 Jul 2008	see (a) below
AASB 2008-9	24 Sep 2008	(*beginning*) 1 Jan 2009	see (b) below
AASB 2011-3	20 May 2011	(*beginning*) 1 Jul 2012	see (c) below
AASB 2011-9	5 Sep 2011	(*beginning*) 1 Jul 2012	see (d) below
AASB 2011-10	5 Sep 2011	(*beginning*) 1 Jan 2013	see (e) below
AASB 2011-13	14 Dec 2011	(*beginning*) 1 Jul 2012	see (f) below
AASB 2012-8	17 Dec 2012	(*beginning*) 1 Jul 2012	–
AASB 2012-10	18 Dec 2012	(*beginning*) 1 Jan 2013	see (g) below
AASB 2013-1	5 Mar 2013	(*beginning*) 1 Jul 2014	see (h) below
AASB 2013-8	31 Oct 2013	(*beginning*) 1 Jan 2014	see (i) below
AASB 2013-9	20 Dec 2013	Pt B (*beginning*) 1 Jan 2014	see (j) below
AASB 2014-5	12 Dec 2014	(*beginning*) 1 Jan 2017	not compiled*
AASB 2014-7	17 Dec 2014	(*beginning*) 1 Jan 2018	not compiled*
AASB 2015-2	28 Jan 2015	(*beginning*) 1 Jan 2016	see (k) below
AASB 2015-6	31 Mar 2015	(*beginning*) 1 Jul 2016	see (l) below
AASB 2015-8	22 Oct 2015	(*beginning*) 1 Jan 2017	not compiled*

*   The amendments made by this Standard are not included in this compilation, which presents the principal Standard as applicable to annual reporting periods beginning on or after 1 July 2016 but before 1 January 2018. AASB 2015-8 has the effect of reversing the amendments originally set out in AASB 2014-5.

(a) Entities may elect to apply this Standard to annual reporting periods beginning before 1 July 2008.

(b) Entities may elect to apply this Standard to annual reporting periods beginning on or after 1 January 2005 but before 1 January 2009, provided that AASB 101 *Presentation of Financial Statements* (September 2007) is also applied to such periods.

(c) Entities may elect to apply this Standard to annual reporting periods beginning on or after 1 January 2009 but before 1 July 2012.

(d) Entities may elect to apply this Standard to annual reporting periods beginning on or after 1 January 2005 but before 1 July 2012.

(e) Entities may elect to apply this Standard to annual reporting periods beginning on or after 1 January 2005 but before 1 January 2013, provided that AASB 119 *Employee Benefits* (September 2011) is also applied to such periods.

(f) Entities may elect to apply this Standard to annual reporting periods beginning on or after 1 January 2009 but before 1 July 2012, provided that AASB 2011-3 *Amendments to Australian Accounting Standards – Orderly Adoption of Changes to the ABS GFS Manual and Related Amendments* is also applied to such periods.

(g) Entities may elect to apply this Standard to annual reporting periods beginning on or after 1 January 2005 but before 1 January 2013.

(h) Entities may elect to apply this Standard to annual reporting periods beginning on or after 1 January 2009 but before 1 July 2014, provided that AASB 1055 *Budgetary Reporting* is also applied to the same period.

(i) Entities may elect to apply this Standard to annual reporting periods beginning on or after 1 January 2013 but before 1 January 2014, provided that AASB 10 *Consolidated Financial Statements* and AASB 12 *Disclosure of Interests in Other Entities* are also applied to such periods.

(j) Early application of Part B of this Standard is not permitted.

(k) Entities may elect to apply this Standard to annual reporting periods beginning on or after 1 January 2005 but before 1 January 2016.

(l) Entities may elect to apply this Standard to annual reporting periods beginning on or after 1 January 2005 but before 1 July 2016. The amendments shall be applied prospectively as of the beginning of the annual reporting period in which the Standard is initially applied.

Table of amendments to Standard

Paragraph affected	How affected	By ... [paragraph]
1	amended	AASB 2008-9 [5]
3-4	amended	AASB 2008-9 [6]
5	amended deleted	AASB 2008-9 [6] AASB 2013-9B [37, 38]
6	amended amended	AASB 2008-9 [6] AASB 2012-10 [69]
7	amended amended	AASB 2008-9 [7] AASB 2011-13 [8]
8	amended	AASB 2011-13 [9]
9 (preceding heading)	amended	AASB 2011-13 [10]
10	amended amended	AASB 2008-9 [8] AASB 2013-8 [12]
11	amended	AASB 2015-6 [12]
12	amended amended	AASB 2008-9 [9] AASB 2013-8 [13]
13	amended	AASB 2011-13 [11]
13A	added	AASB 2011-13 [11]
13B	added amended	AASB 2011-3 [7] AASB 2012-8 [5]
13C	added	AASB 2012-8 [5]
14	amended amended amended	AASB 2008-9 [10] AASB 2011-10 [18] AASB 2013-9B [57]
15	amended amended	AASB 2008-9 [5, 11] AASB 2015-2 [15]
16-17	amended	AASB 2008-9 [12]
18	amended	AASB 2011-13 [12]
18A-18D	added	AASB 2011-13 [12]
19	amended amended	AASB 2008-9 [13] AASB 2013-8 [14]
20	amended	AASB 2008-9 [14]
23	amended amended	AASB 2008-9 [15] AASB 2011-13 [13]
25 (and preceding heading)	deleted	AASB 2008-9 [16]
26	deleted	AASB 2008-9 [16]
27 (and preceding heading)	amended	AASB 2008-9 [5, 17]
29 (and preceding heading)	amended	AASB 2008-9 [18]
30	amended	AASB 2011-13 [14]
30A	added	AASB 2011-13 [14]
31	amended amended	AASB 2011-10 [18] AASB 2011-13 [14]
33	amended amended	AASB 2008-9 [19] AASB 2011-9 [25]

(Continued)

AASB

(Continued)

Paragraph affected	How affected	By ... [paragraph]
34	amended deleted	AASB 2008-9 [20] AASB 2011-10 [19]
34A (and preceding heading)	added	AASB 2008-9 [21]
34B	added amended	AASB 2008-9 [21] AASB 2011-13 [15]
35 (and preceding heading)	amended	AASB 2008-9 [5, 22]
37	amended	AASB 2008-9 [5]
38	amended	AASB 2008-9 [23]
39	amended amended amended amended	AASB 2008-9 [24] AASB 2011-3 [8] AASB 2011-13 [16] AASB 2012-8 [6]
39A	added	AASB 2011-3 [8]
40	amended	AASB 2008-9 [24]
41	amended amended	AASB 2008-9 [25] AASB 2011-13 [17]
42	amended amended	AASB 2011-13 [18] AASB 2013-8 [14]
43	amended	AASB 2008-9 [26]
44	amended amended amended	AASB 2008-9 [27] AASB 2011-13 [19] AASB 2013-9B [58]
45	amended deleted	AASB 2008-9 [28] AASB 2013-8 [15]
47	amended	AASB 2008-9 [29]
48	amended amended	AASB 2008-9 [30] AASB 2011-13 [20]
50	amended	AASB 2011-13 [20]
51	amended	AASB 2008-9 [31]
52	amended amended	AASB 2008-9 [32] AASB 2011-13 [21]
53	amended	AASB 2008-9 [32]
54	amended	AASB 2008-9 [33]
55	amended	AASB 2011-13 [22]
58	amended	AASB 2008-9 [34]
59 (preceding heading)	deleted	AASB 2013-1 [6]
59	amended amended deleted	AASB 2008-9 [35] AASB 2011-13 [23] AASB 2013-1 [6]
60-62	deleted	AASB 2013-1 [6]
63	amended amended deleted	AASB 2011-13 [23] AASB 2012-10 [70] AASB 2013-1 [6]

Paragraph affected	How affected	By ... [paragraph]
64	amended amended deleted	AASB 2008-9 [36] AASB 2011-13 [23] AASB 2013-1 [6]
65	amended deleted	AASB 2008-9 [37] AASB 2013-1 [6]
65A	added deleted	AASB 2008-9 [38] AASB 2011-13 [24]
66-70	deleted	AASB 2011-13 [24]
Appendix A	amended amended amended	AASB 2008-9 [39] AASB 2011-3 [9] AASB 2013-8 [12]

Table of amendments to illustrative examples

Paragraph affected	How affected	By ... [paragraph]
Illustrative Examples	amended amended amended amended amended amended amended amended	AASB 2008-9 [40] AASB 2011-3 [10-12] AASB 2011-9 [26, 27] AASB 2011-13 [25-32] AASB 2011-10 [20, 21] AASB 2012-10 [71-73] AASB 2013-1 [7] AASB 2013-8 [12]

General terminology amendments

The following amendments made by AASB 2008-9 are not shown in the above Tables of Amendments:

> References to 'financial report(s)' were amended to 'financial statements', except in relation to specific Corporations Act references.

> References to 'balance sheet(s)' and 'cash flow statement(s)' were amended to 'statement(s) of financial position' and 'statement(s) of cash flows' respectively, except in relation to ABS GFS Manual references.

> References to 'operating statement(s)' were amended to 'statement(s) of comprehensive income'.

> The phrases 'on the face(s) of', 'movements in equity' and 'transactions with owners as owners' were amended to 'in', 'changes in equity' and 'transactions with owners in their capacity as owners' respectively.

The following amendments made by AASB 2011-13 are not shown in the above Tables of Amendments:

> References to 'other non-owner changes in equity' and 'other changes in equity' were amended to 'other comprehensive income'.

COMPARISON WITH IASB PRONOUNCEMENTS

AASB 1049 and International Financial Reporting Standards

There is no specific Standard issued by the International Accounting Standards Board dealing with whole of government financial statements and GGS financial statements.

Many of the issues addressed in this Standard are addressed in International Financial Reporting Standards (IFRSs). To the extent this Standard incorporates by cross-reference other Australian Accounting Standards, those Standards provide a comparison of this Standard with IFRSs. In addition, in some significant respects, this Standard amends the requirements of other Australian Accounting Standards for the purposes of whole of government financial statements and GGS financial statements, and thereby differs from the requirements in IFRSs. In relation to whole of government financial statements and GGS financial statements, differences relate to the presentation of the financial statements, especially the statement of comprehensive income, and notes. In relation to GGS financial statements, a difference relates to the specification of the entities to be consolidated and the consequential accounting for investments in controlled entities in other sectors that are not consolidated.

ACCOUNTING STANDARD AASB 1049

The Australian Accounting Standards Board made Accounting Standard AASB 1049 *Whole of Government and General Government Sector Financial Reporting* on 30 October 2007.

This compiled version of AASB 1049 applies to annual reporting periods beginning on or after 1 July 2016 but before 1 January 2018. It incorporates relevant amendments contained in other AASB Standards made by the AASB up to and including 31 March 2015 (see Compilation Details).

ACCOUNTING STANDARD AASB 1049
WHOLE OF GOVERNMENT AND GENERAL GOVERNMENT SECTOR FINANCIAL REPORTING

Objective

1   The objective of this Standard is to specify requirements for *whole of government general purpose financial statements* and *General Government Sector (GGS)* financial statements of each *government*. This Standard requires compliance with other applicable Australian Accounting Standards except as specified in this Standard. It also requires disclosure of additional information such as reconciliations to *key fiscal aggregates* determined in accordance with the *ABS GFS Manual* and, for the whole of government, sector information (GGS, *Public Non-Financial Corporations (PNFC) sector* and *Public Financial Corporations (PFC) sector*). Whole of government financial statements and GGS financial statements prepared in accordance with this Standard provide users with:

(a)   information about the stewardship by each government and accountability for the resources entrusted to it;

(b)   information about the financial position, performance and cash flows of each government and its sectors; and

(c)   information that facilitates assessments of the macro-economic impact of each government and its sectors.

Application

2   **This Standard applies to each government's whole of government general purpose financial statements and GGS financial statements.**

3   **This Standard applies to annual reporting periods beginning on or after 1 January 2009.**

[Note: For application dates of paragraphs changed or added by an amending Standard, see Compilation Details.]

4   This Standard may be applied to annual reporting periods beginning before 1 January 2009, provided there is early adoption for the same annual reporting period of AASB 101 *Presentation of Financial Statements* (September 2007).

5   [Deleted by the AASB]

6   When applicable, this Standard supersedes AASB 1049 *Financial Reporting of General Government Sectors by Governments* (September 2006) and AAS 31 *Financial Reporting by Governments* (November 1996), as amended.

Financial statements to be prepared

7   A government shall prepare both whole of government financial statements and GGS financial statements, whether presented together or separately in accordance with the requirements of this Standard.

8   A government shall, at all times, make its GGS financial statements available at the same time that its whole of government financial statements are made available.

Compliance with Australian Accounting Standards and the ABS GFS Manual

9   Unless otherwise specified in this Standard, the whole of government financial statements and the GGS financial statements shall adopt the same accounting policies and be prepared in a manner consistent with other applicable Australian Accounting Standards.

10   With limited significant exceptions, this Standard requires the definition, recognition, measurement, classification, consolidation, presentation and disclosure requirements specified in other applicable Australian Accounting Standards to be adopted. This Standard only requires a different treatment from another applicable Australian Accounting Standard when the requirements of this Standard directly conflict with the requirements of that other Standard. In particular, in relation to the GGS, in conflict with AASB 10 *Consolidated Financial Statements*, paragraph 19 prohibits the consolidation of controlled entities in other sectors.

11   Where an Australian Accounting Standard:

(a)   explicitly excludes from its scope not-for-profit entities, such as AASB 8 *Operating Segments*; or

(b)   [deleted by the AASB]

(c)   only applies to certain entities, such as listed companies, that are required to prepare financial reports in accordance with Part 2M.3 of the *Corporations Act 2001*, such as AASB 133 *Earnings per Share*;

the whole of government financial statements and the GGS financial statements are not required to adopt the requirements of that Standard.

12   Paragraph 9 of AASB 1054 *Australian Additional Disclosures* applies to the whole of government. It does not apply to the GGS. Accordingly, the GGS is not required to disclose whether its financial statements are general purpose financial statements or special purpose financial statements.

13   **In satisfying paragraph 9 of this Standard, subject to paragraph 13A, where compliance with the ABS GFS Manual would not conflict with Australian Accounting Standards, the principles and rules in the ABS GFS Manual shall be applied. In particular, certain Australian Accounting Standards allow optional treatments within their scope. Those optional treatments in Australian Accounting Standards aligned with the principles or rules in the ABS GFS Manual shall be applied.**

13A   A government is not required to early adopt Australian Accounting Standards.

13B   Subject to paragraph 13C, for the purpose of this Standard, a government shall apply the version of the ABS GFS Manual effective at the beginning of the previous annual reporting period or any version effective at a later date, as the basis for GFS information included in the financial statements under this Standard. The date on which amendments to the ABS GFS Manual become effective is, for the purpose of this Standard, the publication date if no effective date is specified by the ABS.

13C   A government may elect not to apply Chapter 2 *Amendments to Defence Weapons Platforms* of the ABS publication *Amendments to Australian System of Government Finance Statistics, 2005* (ABS Catalogue No. 5514.0) – published on the ABS website on 5 April 2011 – in the financial statements prepared in accordance with this Standard for reporting periods ending before 30 June 2015.

14   Examples of particular optional treatments in Australian Accounting Standards that paragraph 13 of this Standard has the effect of limiting, include:

   (a)   assets within the scope of AASB 116 *Property, Plant and Equipment*, AASB 138 *Intangible Assets* or AASB 140 *Investment Property* that may be measured at cost or at fair value. Those assets that are assets under the ABS GFS Manual that are within the scope of those Standards are required to be measured at fair value because the ABS GFS Manual requires those assets to be measured at market value.

   However, the fair value options allowed under AASB 116, AASB 138 and AASB 140 are not amended by paragraph 13 of this Standard. If the fair value of an asset cannot be reliably measured in accordance with an Australian Accounting Standard that allows a choice between fair value and cost, then that asset is to be measured at cost. Where historical cost is adopted because fair value cannot be measured reliably, historical cost is not characterised as fair value. Also, for example, the requirement for the fair value of an intangible asset to be determined by reference to an active market under AASB 138 continues to apply;

   (b)   certain financial instruments that may be measured at fair value or on another basis under AASB 139 *Financial Instruments: Recognition and Measurement*. Where financial instruments meet the criteria for measurement at fair value under AASB 139, they are required to be measured at fair value where the ABS GFS Manual requires market value as the measurement basis.

   Although fair value measurement in the statement of financial position may be mandated through paragraph 13 of this Standard, the accounting for changes in fair value in the statement of comprehensive income is not mandated by paragraph 13. Rather, changes in fair value are classified in the statement of comprehensive income in accordance with AASB 139. AASB 139 anticipates certain financial assets being classified as either:

      (i)   'fair value through profit or loss', with changes in fair value included in operating result; or

      (ii) 'available-for-sale', with changes in fair value included in the other comprehensive income section of the statement of comprehensive income;

   (c)   [deleted]

   (d)   [deleted]

   (e)   cash flows from operating activities that may be reported using either the direct method or the indirect method in the statement of cash flows under AASB 107 *Statement of Cash Flows*. Because the direct method is consistent with the format of the cash flow statement under the ABS GFS Manual, paragraph 13 of this Standard has the effect of requiring the direct method to be adopted;

    (f)   dividends paid by entities within the PNFC sector and PFC sector that may be classified by those sectors as a financing cash flow or as a component of cash flows from operating activities under AASB 107. Because classification as a financing cash flow is consistent with the format of the cash flow statement under the ABS GFS Manual, paragraph 13 of this Standard has the effect of requiring classification of dividends paid as a financing cash flow; and

    (g)   government grants accounted for by entities within the PNFC sector and PFC sector in accordance with AASB 120 *Accounting for Government Grants and Disclosure of Government Assistance*. In accordance with paragraphs 52(b)(i) and 53 of this Standard, information about the PNFC sector and PFC sector disclosed for the whole of government is prepared in a manner consistent with the accounting policies adopted in the whole of government statement of financial position, statement of comprehensive income, statement of changes in equity and statement of cash flows. Therefore, the options in AASB 120 are not adopted and instead the principles in AASB 1004 *Contributions* are applied.

15   Certain Australian Accounting Standards do not prescribe specific treatments for all items and issues within their scope. An example is AASB 101, which requires additional line items, headings and subtotals to be presented when such presentation is relevant to an understanding of the entity's financial position. The ABS GFS Manual specifies principles and rules for the presentation of a balance sheet prepared for GFS purposes. Those ABS GFS Manual principles and rules are required to be applied in the presentation of the whole of government statement of financial position and the GGS statement of financial position to the extent that they do not conflict with AASB 101.

16   Subject to paragraphs 41(a)(i)(A) and 52(b)(ii)(A) of this Standard, key fiscal aggregates that are disclosed for the whole of government or the GGS, either because they are required by this Standard or a government elects to provide additional information, shall be measured in a manner that is consistent with amounts recognised in the corresponding statement of financial position, statement of comprehensive income, statement of changes in equity and statement of cash flows.

17   This Standard requires certain information that is relevant to an assessment of the macro-economic impact of:

    (a)   a whole of government and GGS to be included in the statements of financial position, statements of comprehensive income and statements of cash flows (see paragraphs 28, 32 and 37); and

    (b)   a government's sectors to be included in the sector statements of financial position, statements of comprehensive income and statements of cash flows required to be disclosed for the whole of government by paragraph 52(b)(i).

This Standard requires the information to be determined in a manner consistent with other amounts recognised in the statement of financial position, statement of comprehensive income, statement of changes in equity and statement of cash flows. Corresponding amounts, determined in accordance with the ABS GFS Manual, are required to be disclosed in the notes where they differ from the amounts presented in the statement of financial position, statement of comprehensive income and statement of cash flows (see paragraphs 41(a)(i)(A) and 52(b)(ii)(A)).

18   A government may elect to disclose key fiscal aggregates (as defined) or other information additional to the requirements of this Standard. If a government elects to make additional disclosures, they are made in a way that does not detract from the information prescribed in this Standard.

18A   Examples of additional disclosures that may be made voluntarily include the classification of *other economic flows* consistent with Table 7.4 of the ABS publication *Australian System of Government Finance Statistics: Concepts, Sources and Methods, 2005* (ABS Catalogue No. 5514.0) and additional key fiscal aggregates, such as change in *net worth* due to revaluations and change in net worth due to other changes in the volume of assets.

18B   Consistent with the requirements in paragraph 16 of this Standard, additional key fiscal aggregates are measured in a manner consistent with recognised amounts. Consistent with paragraphs 41(a)(i) and 52(b)(ii) of this Standard, where they differ, corresponding key fiscal aggregates measured in accordance with the ABS GFS Manual are disclosed, together with a reconciliation of the two measures of each key fiscal aggregate.

18C   Fiscal aggregates that are not measured in a manner consistent with recognised amounts or the ABS GFS Manual may be disclosed, but are not presented as key fiscal aggregates.

18D   If a government elects to disclose aggregates that are not key fiscal aggregates, they are made in a way that clearly differentiates them from key fiscal aggregates.

Presentation and scope of GGS financial statements

19   **A government shall present GGS financial statements in which it consolidates only entities that are within the GGS, using the consolidation procedures specified in AASB 10.**

GGS investment in PNFC sector and PFC sector entities

20   **A GGS equity investment in a government controlled entity that is within the PNFC sector or PFC sector shall be recognised as an asset in the GGS statement of financial position. It shall be measured:**

   (a)   **at fair value, where fair value is reliably measurable; or**

   (b)   **at the government's proportional share of the carrying amount of net assets of the PNFC sector or PFC sector entity before consolidation eliminations, where fair value is not reliably measurable and the carrying amount of net assets before consolidation eliminations is not less than zero; or**

   (c)   **at zero, where fair value is not reliably measurable and the carrying amount of net assets of the PNFC sector or PFC sector entity before consolidation eliminations is less than zero.**

   Any change in the carrying amount of the investment from period to period shall be accounted for as if the change in carrying amount is a change in fair value and accounted for in a manner consistent with the requirements in AASB 139.

21   If the carrying amount of net assets of a PNFC sector or PFC sector entity is less than zero, a liability may need to be recognised by the GGS to the extent a present obligation exists.

22   Income from GGS investments in controlled entities in the PNFC sector and PFC sector is accounted for in accordance with AASB 118 *Revenue* and AASB 139. Dividends are classified as revenue consistent with AASB 118. A change in the carrying amount of the investment over the reporting period that does not arise from the government acquiring or disposing of an interest or undistributed dividends is classified as a gain or loss. The gain or loss is included in the operating result or other comprehensive income, depending on whether the investment is classified in the same manner as 'fair value through profit or loss' investments or in the same manner as 'available- for-sale' investments consistent with the principles in AASB 139.

23   For the purposes of determining the carrying amount of net assets of entities within the PNFC sector and PFC sector recognised and measured in accordance with paragraph 20(b):

   (a)   each PNFC sector and PFC sector entity's accounting policies are adjusted to align with the accounting policies adopted for the whole of government for the same period;

(b)   intersector balances between the GGS and entities within the PNFC sector and PFC sector are not eliminated; and

(c)   individual amounts for each PNFC sector and PFC sector entity are presented in aggregate.

GGS investment in jointly controlled entities and associates

24   **Investments in jointly controlled entities and associates shall be measured using the equity method of accounting, unless the investment is classified as held for sale in accordance with AASB 5** *Non-current Assets Held for Sale and Discontinued Operations,* **in which case AASB 5 is applied.**

25   [Deleted]

26   [Deleted]

Whole of government and GGS statements of financial position

27   **The whole of government statement of financial position and the GGS statement of financial position, and notes thereto, shall be presented in a manner consistent with the requirements in AASB 101.**

28   **Net worth shall be presented in the whole of government statement of financial position and GGS statement of financial position, measured in a manner consistent with other amounts recognised in the respective statements of financial position.**

Whole of government and GGS statements of comprehensive income

29   **The whole of government statement of comprehensive income and GGS statement of comprehensive income, and notes thereto, shall be presented in a manner consistent with the requirements for a single statement of comprehensive income in AASB 101.**

30   **For the purpose of presentation, all amounts relating to an item included in the determination of comprehensive result (total change in net worth [before transactions with owners in their capacity as owners]) shall be classified as** *transactions* **or other economic flows in a manner that is consistent with applying the principles in the ABS GFS Manual from the GAAP perspective.**

30A   In accordance with paragraph 30:

(a)   where GAAP and GFS both recognise the item in the reporting period, amounts relating to that item shall be classified in accordance with the ABS GFS Manual; and

(b)   where GAAP recognises an item that GFS does not recognise in the reporting period, subject to paragraph 55(b), amounts relating to that item shall be classified by applying GFS principles to the underlying event giving rise to the amounts, as if the amounts were recognised under GFS, using an analogous GFS item.

31   The following examples illustrate how the approach in paragraphs 30 and 30A applies to particular items:

(a)   in both a whole of government and GGS financial reporting context, where GAAP and GFS both recognise the item in the reporting period:

(i)   net profit/(loss) from associates potentially comprises two components under GFS classification – dividends from associates and the remainder.

AASB

Accordingly, dividends are classified as transactions and the remainder is classified as other economic flows. Such dividends are not included in the line item that includes dividends from entities other than associates;

(ii) changes in the fair value of financial instruments measured at fair value, that do not arise from undistributed interest or dividends, are classified as other economic flows, irrespective of whether the instruments are classified as 'fair value through profit or loss' or 'available-for-sale';

(iii) remeasurements of the defined benefit liability (asset) relating to defined benefit superannuation plans are classified as other economic flows;

(iv) changes in the fair value of investment property potentially comprise two components under GFS classification – consumption of capital and price changes. Accordingly, the expense arising from consumption of capital is classified as transactions and the gains and losses arising from price changes are classified as other economic flows. Although the consumption of capital may be considered to be similar in nature to depreciation, it is not included in the line item that includes depreciation; and

(v) bad debts expense is classified as transactions to the extent it is mutually agreed, otherwise it is classified as other economic flows; and

(b) in both a whole of government and GGS financial reporting context, where GAAP recognises an item that GFS does not recognise in the reporting period:

(i) income that arises from the amortisation of a prepayment received for a licence involving the licensee having rights over a specified period of time (that GFS treated in a previous period as a sale of intangible asset) is classified as transactions, by analogy with the GFS classification of the amortisation of a prepayment received for a service to be rendered;

(ii) doubtful debts expense that arises from the impairment of loans and receivables is classified as other economic flows, by analogy with the GFS classification of revaluation of financial assets;

(iii) an expense that arises from the initial recognition of the difference between the fair value of a concessionary loan and the transaction price (the loan proceeds) is classified as transactions, by analogy with the GFS classification of subsidies; and

(iv) an expense that arises from the initial recognition of a provision for decommissioning costs for which there is no counterparty that recognises a related financial asset is classified as transactions, by analogy with the GFS classification of an expense arising from the initial recognition of a liability. Subsequent changes in the measurement of such provisions arising from changes in estimates of the expenditure required to settle the present obligation are classified as other economic flows, by analogy with the GFS classification of revaluation of liabilities; and

(c) in a GGS financial reporting context, dividends from PNFC sector and PFC sector entities are classified as transactions to the extent the ABS GFS Manual accounts for them as dividends and otherwise as other economic flows.

In some cases the approach in paragraphs 30 and 30A facilitates the reduction of differences between GAAP and GFS, particularly at the key fiscal aggregate level. Illustrative Examples A and B illustrate the classification between transactions and other economic flows for some of the items listed above and other possible circumstances where items recognised in the whole of government statement of comprehensive income and the GGS statement of comprehensive income do not have GFS equivalents.

32   **The following shall be presented in the whole of government statement of comprehensive income and the GGS statement of comprehensive income:**

(a) *net operating balance*;

(b) total change in net worth (before transactions with owners in their capacity as owners, where they exist); and

(c) *net lending/(borrowing)* and its derivation from net operating balance;

measured in a manner consistent with other amounts recognised in the respective statements of comprehensive income.

33 Under AASB 101, an entity may present a single statement of profit or loss and other comprehensive income, with profit or loss and other comprehensive income presented in two sections. The sections shall be presented together, with the profit or loss section presented first followed directly by the other comprehensive income section. An entity may present the profit or loss section in a separate statement of profit or loss. If so, the separate statement of profit or loss shall immediately precede the statement presenting comprehensive income. This Standard requires a single statement of profit or loss and other comprehensive income option to be adopted, and therefore requires all recognised income and expenses to be included in a single statement that presents the comprehensive result (total change in net worth [before transactions with owners in their capacity as owners, where they exist]).

34 [Deleted]

Whole of government and GGS statements of changes in equity

34A The whole of government statement of changes in equity and the GGS statement of changes in equity, and notes thereto, shall be presented in a manner consistent with the requirements in AASB 101.

34B Generally, transactions with owners in their capacity as owners do not arise in a GGS context because there is no ownership group identified for the GGS. They may arise in a whole of government context in relation to partly-owned subsidiaries. They may also arise between PNFC sector and PFC sector entities and their owner, the GGS.

Whole of government and GGS statements of cash flows

35 The whole of government statement of cash flows and the GGS statement of cash flows, and notes thereto, shall be presented in a manner consistent with the requirements in AASB 107.

36 Cash flows relating to investing in financial assets for policy purposes and for liquidity management purposes shall be presented separately, determined in a manner consistent with the ABS GFS Manual, in the whole of government statement of cash flows and the GGS statement of cash flows.

37 The whole of government statement of cash flows and the GGS statement of cash flows shall also include *cash surplus/(deficit)* and its derivation, measured in a manner consistent with other amounts recognised in the respective statements of cash flows, without the deduction of the value of assets acquired under finance leases and similar arrangements.

Illustrative examples

38 An example of an acceptable whole of government statement of financial position, statement of comprehensive income, statement of changes in equity and statement of cash flows format and GGS statement of financial position, statement of comprehensive income, statement of changes in equity and statement of cash flows format that are in accordance with this Standard is provided in Illustrative Examples A and B respectively.

Notes

Summary of significant accounting policies

39   In addition to the disclosures required by other Australian Accounting Standards in the note containing the summary of significant accounting policies, the following disclosures shall be made prominently in that note:

    (a)   for the whole of government and the GGS:

        (i)   a statement that the financial statements are prepared in accordance with this Standard;

        (ii)   a reference to the version of the ABS GFS Manual used as the basis for GFS information included in the financial statements, and when an entity has not applied the most recent version of the ABS GFS Manual (including when an entity has elected to adopt the relief available in paragraph 13C):

            (A)   this fact; and

            (B)   known or reasonably estimable information relevant to assessing the possible impact that application of the latest version of the ABS GFS Manual will have on the financial statements in the period of initial application; and

        (iii)   where the GGS financial statements and whole of government financial statements are presented separately from each other, a cross-reference to each other; and

    (b)   for the GGS only:

        (i)   a statement of the purpose for which the GGS financial statements are prepared;

        (ii)   a description of the GGS; and

        (iii)   a description of how the GGS financial statements differ from the whole of government financial statements in terms of the treatment of the government's investments in PNFC sector and PFC sector entities.

39A   In complying with paragraph 39(a)(ii), an entity considers disclosing:

    (a)   the version of the latest ABS GFS Manual;

    (b)   the nature of the impending change or changes in the ABS GFS Manual;

    (c)   the date by which application of the latest version of the ABS GFS Manual is required;

    (d)   the date as at which it plans to apply the latest version of the ABS GFS Manual initially; and

    (e)   either:

        (i)   a discussion of the impact that initial application of the latest version of the ABS GFS Manual is expected to have on the entity's financial statements; or

        (ii)   if that impact is not known or reasonably estimable, a statement to that effect.

40   An example of the information to be included in the summary of significant accounting policies disclosed for the GGS in accordance with paragraph 39 is provided in Illustrative Example C.

Other explanatory notes

41   In addition to the disclosures required to be made in other explanatory notes in accordance with other applicable Australian Accounting Standards, the following disclosures shall be made:

     (a)   for the whole of government and the GGS:

         (i)   where the key fiscal aggregates measured in accordance with the ABS GFS Manual differ from the key fiscal aggregates provided pursuant to paragraph 16 of this Standard:

             (A)   the key fiscal aggregates measured in accordance with the ABS GFS Manual; and

             (B)   a reconciliation of the two measures of key fiscal aggregates and an explanation of the differences; and

         (ii)   where the key fiscal aggregates measured in accordance with the ABS GFS Manual do not differ from the key fiscal aggregates provided pursuant to paragraph 16, a statement of that fact; and

         (iii)   explanations of key technical terms used; and

     (b)   for the GGS:

         (i)   a list of entities within the GGS, and any changes to that list that have occurred since the previous reporting date and the reasons for those changes;

         (ii)   a list of significant investments in PNFC sector and PFC sector entities, including:

             (A)   the name;

             (B)   proportion of ownership interest and, if different, proportion of voting power held; and

             (C)   the measurement basis adopted for the amount recognised in accordance with paragraph 20; and

         (iii)   the aggregate amount of dividends and other distributions to owners in their capacity as owners from PNFC sector and PFC sector entities to the GGS and the aggregate amount of the comprehensive result attributable to the GGS of the PNFC sector and PFC sector entities disclosed in the whole of government statement of comprehensive income by sector for the reporting period.

42   In relation to the requirements in paragraph 41(a)(i), differences in the key fiscal aggregates determined under the ABS GFS Manual and pursuant to paragraph 16 of this Standard arise from differences in definition, recognition, measurement and certain classification requirements. Each difference gives rise to the need for disclosure of a reconciliation and an explanation of the difference. Examples of such differences include:

     (a)   in a whole of government and GGS context:

         (i)   doubtful debts – although the ABS GFS Manual recognises bad debts written off, it does not recognise write-downs of accounts receivable in relation to doubtful debts;

         (ii)   provisions recognised as liabilities – in the absence of a counter-party recognising a related financial asset, the ABS GFS Manual does not recognise a liability arising from a constructive obligation;

         (iii)   inventories – under the ABS GFS Manual, inventories are measured at current prices, whereas under AASB 102 *Inventories* (as amended by AASB 2007-5 *Amendments to Australian Accounting Standard – Inventories Held for Distribution by Not-for-Profit Entities*), depending on their nature, inventories are measured at the lower of cost and net realisable value or at cost adjusted when applicable for any loss of service potential; and

(iv)   investments in associates – under the ABS GFS Manual, those assets are measured at current prices where current prices exist, whereas under AASB 128 *Investments in Associates* the equity method of accounting generally applies; and

(b)   in a whole of government context only:

(i)   non-controlling interest in controlled entities – under the ABS GFS Manual, minority interest is classified as a liability and measured at current prices, whereas under AASB 10 non-controlling interest that is classified as equity is not remeasured; and

(ii)   outgoing dividends – under the ABS GFS Manual, outgoing dividends are classified as an expense, whereas under AASB 101 a dividend is treated as a distribution to owners.

Illustrative Examples A and B illustrate some of these and other possible circumstances where differences arise and the manner in which they are reflected in reconciliation notes.

43   In relation to the whole of government, for the purpose of paragraph 41(a)(i)(A), the ABS GFS Manual key fiscal aggregate that corresponds to the requirement in paragraph 32(b) to present 'total change in net worth before transactions with owners in their capacity as owners' is 'total change in net worth' (after transactions with owners in their capacity as owners). Accordingly, the reconciliation required to be disclosed for the whole of government by paragraph 41(a)(i)(B) is from 'total change in net worth before transactions with owners in their capacity as owners' as presented in accordance with paragraph 32(b) to 'total change in net worth' measured in accordance with the ABS GFS Manual. As noted in paragraph 34B, transactions with owners in their capacity as owners do not arise in a GGS context.

44   Some differences between GAAP and GFS requirements relate to differences in classification or differences in consolidation eliminations that do not cause a difference in measurements of key fiscal aggregates and therefore do not need to be included in the reconciliation notes. However, they do give rise to the need for explanations of the differences to be disclosed. Examples of such differences include:

(a)   for both the whole of government and the GGS:

(i)   AASB 132 *Financial Instruments: Presentation* classifies certain prepaid expenses as non-financial assets, whereas the ABS GFS Manual classifies them as financial assets;

(ii)   AASB 137 *Provisions, Contingent Liabilities and Contingent Assets* may classify an amount within provisions, whereas the ABS GFS Manual classifies them as accounts payable; and

(iii)   paragraph 31(a)(iv) of this Standard notes that consumption of capital of investment property is classified separately from depreciation, whereas the ABS GFS Manual classifies it as depreciation; and

(b)   for the whole of government, consolidation eliminations. Under the ABS GFS Manual, certain transactions between the GGS and entities within the PNFC sector and PFC sector are not eliminated on whole of government consolidation, whereas under AASB 10 intragroup transactions that are not, in substance, transactions with external parties are eliminated in full. The GFS treatment has the effect of 'grossing up' both GFS revenue and GFS expenses by equal amounts and though the key fiscal aggregates remain the same, the differences in GAAP and GFS revenues and expenses should be disclosed. For example, a GGS may compensate a PNFC sector entity for a community service obligation, imposed by the GGS, that requires the PNFC sector entity to provide free services to a cohort of private individuals. The compensation provided by the GGS to the PNFC sector entity is not eliminated for whole of government reporting under the ABS GFS Manual (instead it is 'rerouted' through the household sector of the economy and therefore treated as an expense of the GGS to the household sector, and an expense of the household sector to the PNFC sector entity, and therefore revenue of the PNFC sector entity).

45   The GGS is not subject to the disclosures required by AASB 12 *Disclosure of Interests in Other Entities*. The requirements in AASB 12 are either addressed elsewhere in this Standard or are not significant for GGS financial reporting.

46   In relation to the requirement in paragraph 41(a)(iii) to disclose explanations of key technical terms, key technical terms include:

(a)   transactions;

(b)   other economic flows;

(c)   net operating balance;

(d)   net lending/(borrowing);

(e)   financial assets;

(f)   non-financial assets;

(g)   net worth;

(h)   cash surplus/(deficit);

(i)   operating result;

(j)   comprehensive result (total change in net worth [before transactions with owners in their capacity as owners]);

(k)   total change in net worth; and

(l)   net debt.

An example of the disclosures required by paragraph 41(a)(iii) is provided in Illustrative Example D.

47   Paragraph 112 of AASB 101 requires additional information to be provided in notes that is not presented in the statement of financial position, statement of comprehensive income, statement of changes in equity and statement of cash flows but is relevant to an understanding of them. Consistent with this, the components of aggregate numbers presented in those statements, including key fiscal aggregates, are disclosed in the notes where relevant.

Functional information

48   **In respect of each broad function identified in** Table 2.6 "Government Purpose Classification: Major Groups" **of the ABS publication** *Australian System of Government Finance Statistics: Concepts, Sources and Methods, 2005* **(ABS Catalogue No. 5514.0), the whole of government and the GGS shall disclose by way of note:**

(a)   **a description of that function;**

(b)   **the carrying amount of assets recognised in the respective statements of financial position that are reliably attributable to that function; and**

(c)   **expenses, excluding losses, included in operating result in the respective statements of comprehensive income for the reporting period that are reliably attributable to that function.**

49   **The information provided by way of note in accordance with paragraph 48 shall be aggregated. A reconciliation of the aggregate amount of expenses, excluding losses, included in operating result to the aggregate of expenses from transactions recognised in the statement of comprehensive income shall be disclosed.**

50   Paragraph 48 requires disclosure of information about the recognised expenses, excluding losses, included in operating result and assets that are reliably attributable

to broad functions determined to at least the ABS GFS Manual two-digit level of classification shown in Table 2.6 of the ABS publication *Australian System of Government Finance Statistics: Concepts, Sources and Methods, 2005* (ABS Catalogue No. 5514.0). Disclosure of this information assists users in identifying the resources committed to particular functions and the costs of service delivery that are reliably attributable to those functions. Functional classification of financial information, where it can be determined reliably, will also assist users in assessing the significance of financial or non-financial performance indicators reported by the government.

51   AASB 114 (AASB 8) does not apply to the whole of government or the GGS. The bases used in the ABS GFS Manual for identifying functions do not necessarily accord with the criteria for identifying segments contained in AASB 114 (AASB 8). However, AASB 114 (AASB 8) may be useful in identifying the expenses, excluding losses, included in operating result and assets that are reliably attributable to each function. An example of the disclosures required by paragraphs 48(b) and 48(c) in respect of each function of the whole of government and the GGS is provided in Illustrative Examples A and B respectively.

Whole of government sector information

52   **The whole of government shall disclose by way of note, in respect of the GGS, PNFC sector and PFC sector as defined in the ABS GFS Manual:**

(a)   **a description of each sector;**

(b)   **for each sector:**

(i)   **a statement of financial position, statement of comprehensive income, statement of changes in equity and statement of cash flows that are consistent with the whole of government's corresponding financial statements prepared in accordance with this Standard;**

(ii)   **where the key fiscal aggregates measured in accordance with the ABS GFS Manual differ from the key fiscal aggregates determined in a manner consistent with paragraph 16 of this Standard:**

(A)   **the key fiscal aggregates measured in accordance with the ABS GFS Manual; and**

(B)   **a reconciliation of the two measures of key fiscal aggregates and an explanation of the differences; and**

(iii)   **where the key fiscal aggregates measured in accordance with the ABS GFS Manual do not differ from the key fiscal aggregates determined in a manner consistent with paragraph 16, a statement of that fact; and**

(c)   **a reconciliation between the information disclosed for the sectors in total and the corresponding information in the whole of government's statement of financial position, statement of comprehensive income, statement of changes in equity and statement of cash flows (see, for example, Illustrative Example A).**

53   Sector information prepared in accordance with paragraph 52(b) is determined before consolidation eliminations. Accordingly, GGS investments in PNFC sector and PFC sector entities are included in the GGS information that is disclosed for the whole of government. They are measured at the carrying amount of net assets disclosed by the whole of government for the PNFC sector and PFC sector.

54   Notes to the sector statements of financial position, statements of comprehensive income, statements of changes in equity and statements of cash flows, other than those required by paragraph 52, are not required to be disclosed.

55   In relation to the requirements in paragraph 52(b)(ii), differences in the key fiscal aggregates determined under the ABS GFS Manual and consistent with paragraph 16 of this Standard arise from differences in definition, recognition, measurement and

certain classification requirements. Each difference gives rise to the need for disclosure of a reconciliation and an explanation of the difference. Examples of such differences for the PNFC sector and the PFC sector include those identified in paragraph 42 of this Standard, as well as:

(a) ownership interest in PNFC sector and PFC sector entities – in contrast to Australian Accounting Standards, under the ABS GFS Manual, the carrying amount of ownership interest in PNFC sector and PFC sector entities is deducted in the determination of net worth of those sectors. In particular:

    (i) where the market value of ownership interest in PNFC sector and PFC sector entities is reliably measurable, GFS deducts it in determining net worth of those sectors. Accordingly, negative GFS net worth arises if the market value exceeds the recognised carrying amount of net assets. Under Australian Accounting Standards, the market value of ownership interest is not recognised; and

    (ii) where ownership interest in PNFC sector and PFC sector entities is measured by GFS at the carrying amount of net assets, GFS net worth is nil. Under Australian Accounting Standards, the carrying amount of net assets is not deducted in determining net worth; and

(b) deferred tax assets and deferred tax liabilities of PNFC sector and PFC sector entities – the ABS GFS Manual does not recognise deferred tax assets and deferred tax liabilities that are recognised by PNFC sector and PFC sector entities in accordance with AASB 112 *Income Taxes*. Like the approach in paragraph 61A of AASB 112, a deferred tax revenue or expense recognised in accordance with AASB 112 is classified in the statement of comprehensive income as a transaction or an other economic flow consistent with the underlying event giving rise to the related deferred tax asset or liability. For example, when a deferred tax liability arises from the revaluation of an asset, the related deferred tax expense is classified as an other economic flow because the asset revaluation itself is recognised as an other economic flow.

56 For the purpose of paragraph 52(b)(ii)(A), the ABS GFS Manual key fiscal aggregate that corresponds to the requirement implicit in paragraph 52(b)(i) to present 'total change in net worth before transactions with owners in their capacity as owners' for the PNFC sector and PFC sector is 'total change in net worth' (after transactions with owners in their capacity as owners). Accordingly, the reconciliation required to be disclosed by paragraph 52(b)(ii)(B) is from 'total change in net worth before transactions with owners in their capacity as owners' as presented in accordance with paragraph 52(b)(i) to 'total change in net worth' measured in accordance with the ABS GFS Manual.

57 A government may choose to disclose sectors in addition to the GGS, PNFC sector and PFC sector. For example, a government may disclose information about the total non-financial public sector, comprising the GGS and PNFC sector. Where that is the case, the additional sectors are disclosed on a comparable basis to the information disclosed for the GGS, PNFC sector and PFC sector.

58 The sector statements of financial position, statements of comprehensive income, statements of changes in equity and statements of cash flows could be presented in a single schedule that includes an adjustments column or row to facilitate reconciliation to the corresponding whole of government statements in accordance with paragraph 52(c). Alternatively, those sector financial statements may be presented in columns, with or without an adjustments column, in the whole of government statement of financial position, statement of comprehensive income, statement of changes in equity and statement of cash flows. Where an adjustments column is not provided in those whole of government financial statements, the reconciliation required by paragraph 52(c) is provided in the notes. Disclosure of the individual eliminations between the sectors is not required.

APPENDIX A
DEFINED TERMS

This appendix is an integral part of AASB 1049.

ABS GFS Manual	Australian Bureau of Statistics (ABS) publications *Australian System of Government Finance Statistics: Concepts, Sources and Methods, 2005* (ABS Catalogue No. 5514.0) and *Amendments to Australian System of Government Finance Statistics, 2005* (ABS Catalogue No. 5514.0) published on the ABS website.
cash surplus/(deficit)	Net cash flows from operating activities plus net cash flows from acquisition and disposal of non- financial assets less distributions paid less value of assets acquired under finance leases and similar arrangements. Defined in the ABS GFS Manual (paragraph 2.124).
General Government Sector (GGS)	Institutional sector comprising all *government units* and *non-profit institutions* controlled and mainly financed by government. Defined in the ABS GFS Manual (Glossary, page 256).
government	The Australian Government, the Government of the Australian Capital Territory, New South Wales, the Northern Territory, Queensland, South Australia, Tasmania, Victoria or Western Australia.
government units	Unique kinds of legal entities established by political processes which have legislative, judicial or executive authority over other *institutional units* within a given area and which: (i) provide goods and services to the community and/or individuals free of charge or at prices that are not economically significant; and (ii) redistribute income and wealth by means of taxes and other compulsory transfers. Defined in the ABS GFS Manual (Glossary, page 257).
institutional unit	An economic entity that is capable, in its own right, of owning assets, incurring liabilities and engaging in economic activities and in transactions with other entities. Defined in the ABS GFS Manual (Glossary, page 257).
key fiscal aggregates	Referred to as analytical balances in the ABS GFS Manual, are data identified in the ABS GFS Manual as useful for macro-economic analysis purposes, including assessing the impact of a government and its sectors on the economy. They are: opening net worth, net operating balance, net lending/(borrowing), change in net worth due to revaluations, change in net worth due to other changes in the volume of assets, total change in net worth, closing net worth and cash surplus/(deficit).
net lending/ (borrowing)	The financing requirement of government, calculated as the net operating balance less the net acquisition of non-financial assets. A positive result reflects a net lending position and a negative result reflects a net borrowing position. Based on the definition in the ABS GFS Manual (Glossary, page 259).
net operating balance	This is calculated as income from transactions minus expenses from transactions. Based on the definition in the ABS GFS Manual (Glossary, page 259).
net worth	Assets less liabilities and shares/contributed capital. For the GGS, net worth is assets less liabilities since shares and contributed capital is zero. It is an economic measure of wealth and reflects the contribution of governments to the wealth of Australia. Defined in the ABS GFS Manual (Glossary, page 259).

(Continued)

(Continued)

non-profit institution	A legal or social entity that is created for the purpose of producing or distributing goods and services but is not permitted to be a source of income, profit or other financial gain for the units that establish, control or finance it. Defined in the ABS GFS Manual (Glossary, page 260).
other economic flows	Changes in the volume or value of an asset or liability that do not result from transactions (i.e. revaluations and other changes in the volume of assets). Defined in the ABS GFS Manual (Glossary, page 260).
Public Financial Corporations (PFC) sector	Institutional sector comprising resident government controlled corporations and *quasi- corporations* mainly engaged in financial intermediation or provision of auxiliary financial services. Based on the definition in the ABS GFS Manual (Glossary, page 261).
Public Non-Financial Corporations (PNFC) sector	Institutional sector comprising resident government controlled corporations and quasi- corporations mainly engaged in the production of market goods and/or non-financial services. Based on the definition in the ABS GFS Manual (Glossary, page 261).
quasi-corporation	An unincorporated enterprise that functions as if it were a corporation, has the same relationship with its owner as a corporation, and keeps a separate set of accounts. Defined in the ABS GFS Manual (Glossary, page 261).
transactions	Interactions between two institutional units by mutual agreement or actions within a unit that it is analytically useful to treat as transactions. Defined in the ABS GFS Manual (Glossary, page 263).
whole of government general purpose financial statements (also referred to as 'whole of government financial statements' in this Standard)	General purpose financial statements prepared by a government that are prepared in accordance with Australian Accounting Standards, including AASB 10 *Consolidated Financial Statements*, and thereby separately recognise assets, liabilities, income, expenses and cash flows of all entities under the control of the government on a line-by- line basis.

BASIS FOR CONCLUSIONS ON AASB 1049
WHOLE OF GOVERNMENT AND GENERAL GOVERNMENT SECTOR FINANCIAL REPORTING

This Basis for Conclusions accompanies, but is not part of, AASB 1049.

Introduction

BC1   The Preface to this Standard outlines the broad strategic direction issued to the Australian Accounting Standards Board (AASB) by the Financial Reporting Council (FRC) that gave rise to AASB 1049 *Whole of Government and General Government Sector Financial Reporting*. This Basis for Conclusions summarises the Board's considerations in developing the Standard. It focuses on the issues that the Board considers to be of greatest significance.

BC2   In developing the Standard, the Board first considered GAAP/GFS harmonisation issues from a General Government Sector (GGS) perspective. This resulted in the issue of AASB 1049 *Financial Reporting of General Government Sectors by Governments* in September 2006. It included a requirement that a government not make its GGS financial report available prior to its whole of government financial report being made available. The Board became aware that no jurisdiction intended to early adopt AASB 1049 (September 2006) because of this requirement, combined with concern that the whole of government accounting basis (then specified in AAS 31 *Financial Reporting by Governments*) was, at the time, different from the GGS accounting basis (specified in AASB 1049).

BC3 In addressing this concern, the Board considered the extent to which the principles in AASB 1049 (September 2006) should apply to whole of government financial reporting. The Board concluded that the requirements for GAAP/GFS harmonised whole of government financial reports, incorporating requirements for information about the GGS, the Public Non-Financial Corporations (PNFC) sector and the Public Financial Corporations (PFC) sector, should be based on the principles in AASB 1049 (September 2006). This reflects the relationship between the GGS of a government, the other sectors of a government and the whole of government and is a response to an assessment of user needs. Given the relationship between the GGS and whole of government, an alternative approach that would result in fundamentally different accounting bases for GGS financial reports and whole of government financial reports has the potential to confuse some users.

BC4 The Board developed a separate Exposure Draft (ED 155 *Financial Reporting by Whole of Governments*) for the purpose of exposing its proposals for GAAP/GFS harmonisation requirements for whole of government financial reporting, rather than present the proposals integrated with the requirements in AASB 1049 (September 2006). However, the Board indicated its intention in ED 155 that the Standard to be developed would be an amended AASB 1049 that specifies, in an integrated way, the GAAP/GFS harmonised requirements for GGS financial reports and whole of government financial reports. The Board concluded that a single integrated Standard is justified on the basis that:

(a) it more effectively acknowledges the strong relationship between whole of government financial reports and GGS financial reports. An integrated Standard is consistent with the requirement that GGS financial reports not be made available prior to the release of whole of government financial reports (see paragraphs BC18-BC20);

(b) it is more consistent with a topic-based approach to setting Standards; and

(c) it imposes a greater discipline on the Board to ensure that the requirements are expressed in the same way for GGS and whole of government, and only differ where intended.

GGS financial reports

Preparation of GGS financial reports [paragraphs 2 and 7]

The nature of a GGS financial report

BC5 Due to the unique circumstances related to the GGS, its relationship to the whole of government (see paragraphs BC18-BC20) and its macro-economic significance, the Board concluded that a Standard should require the preparation of financial reports of a federal, state or territory government's GGS. The Board also supported the GGS presenting a financial report on the basis that whole of government financial reports are to be available at the same time as the GGS financial report (see paragraph BC18).

BC6 The Board concluded that it is not necessary to specify whether the GGS is a reporting entity and whether the GGS financial report prepared in accordance with the Standard is a general purpose financial report (GPFR) because the Standard itself prescribes the particular requirements for the scope of the GGS and the form and content of the GGS financial report.

GGS financial report prepared on a partial consolidation basis

BC7 It is inherent in the definition of a GGS that government controlled entities within the PNFC sector and PFC sector are not consolidated in the GGS financial report (see paragraphs BC11-BC13). Only government controlled entities that fall within the boundary of a GGS are consolidated. Accordingly, the Board concluded that a government should produce a GGS financial report on a partial consolidation basis (see paragraph 19).

BC8 This focus on the GGS and consequently the partial consolidation approach is consistent with, to some extent, the 'through the eyes of management' approach adopted in AASB 8 *Operating Segments*. The information used to manage a government includes GGS information prepared on a partial consolidated basis because, essentially, the GGS equates to the budget sector of Australian governments, and reporting of budget outcomes is a major focus.

BC9 The Board's decisions reflect that:

(a) the GGS is a significant sector of a government that warrants prominence in financial reporting;

(b) GGS financial information is relevant to users and is widely distributed;

(c) GGS financial information should be made available to the public in a manner that meets the key characteristics of comparability, understandability, relevance, reliability and timeliness set out in AASB *Framework for the Preparation and Presentation of Financial Statements*; and

(d) GGS financial information is necessary to provide a link to GGS budgets, which are a means by which governments outline their taxing policies and resource allocation decisions (see paragraphs BC57-BC62).

BC10 An alternative view considered by the Board is that, because a GGS is a sector of the whole of government, GGS financial information prepared on a partial consolidation basis should only be included in the whole of government GPFR (see also paragraph BC20). When that GGS financial information is presented in a financial report that is separate from the whole of government GPFR, it should be characterised as a special purpose financial report. However, as explained in paragraph BC6, the Board decided that, because the Standard prescribes the form and content of the GGS financial report, it is not necessary to take such an approach.

Accounting for GGS investments in PNFC sector and PFC sector entities in GGS financial reports [paragraphs 19 and 20]

BC11 The issue of the accounting for GGS investments in PNFC sector and PFC sector entities in the GGS financial report is closely related to the basis on which the GGS financial report is prepared and to the issue of partial consolidation (see paragraphs BC7-BC10).

BC12 The Board decided that, consistent with GFS principles and rules, entities that are controlled by a government, but are not part of the GGS of the government, should be recognised in the GGS financial report as investments.

BC13 Furthermore, the Board concluded that GGS controlling investments in PNFC sector and PFC sector entities should be measured at, depending on circumstances, fair value, the government's proportional share of the carrying amount of net assets (as a surrogate for fair value) or zero. Measurement at fair value, or at the government's proportional share of the carrying amount of net assets where fair value is not reliably measurable, is consistent with GFS. Not allowing investments to be measured below zero is consistent with the principles elsewhere in GAAP (for example, AASB 128 *Investments in Associates* does not allow negative investment values when using the equity method).

BC14 When a GGS's controlling investment in a PNFC sector or PFC sector entity is measured at the government's proportional share of the carrying amount of net assets, for consistency with GFS principles, it should be accounted for as a financial asset consistent with AASB 139 *Financial Instruments: Recognition and Measurement*, rather than as if it were an investment in an associate accounted for using the equity method of accounting.

Accounting for GGS investments in jointly controlled entities and associates in GGS financial reports [paragraph 24]

BC15 The Board concluded that investments in jointly controlled entities and associates should be measured using the equity method of accounting, except when the investment is classified as held for sale in accordance with AASB 5 *Non-current Assets Held for Sale and Discontinued Operations*. This is on the basis that, consistent with paragraph 19 of this Standard that prescribes the use of the consolidation procedures in AASB 127 *Consolidated and Separate Financial Statements*, the GGS financial report is treated as if it is a consolidated financial report rather than as 'separate financial statements', as defined in AASB 127.

Disclosures about the GGS in the summary of significant accounting policies note [paragraph 39(b)]

BC16 The Board concluded that additional disclosures relating to the nature of the GGS and its relationship to the whole of government financial report should be made as part of the note in the GGS financial report containing the summary of significant accounting policies. These disclosures are intended to help overcome concerns that users might perceive the GGS financial report as being a substitute for the whole of government financial report. Furthermore, the disclosures are intended to help users understand the nature of the GGS and its financial reports to provide a greater link to the budget outcome reports, to the extent they focus solely on the GGS.

Other disclosures specific to the GGS [paragraph 41(b)]

BC17 Given this Standard encompasses GFS concepts and definitions for the GGS, the Board considered it appropriate to require additional disclosures to be included in the GGS financial report. The additional disclosures include:

(a) a list of entities within the GGS and any changes to that list since the previous reporting date and reasons for the changes (paragraph 41(b)(i)). This disclosure informs users of the controlled entities that have been consolidated into the GGS financial report and, for the purposes of year to year comparisons, the changes to the list of entities. The reasons for changes should be capable of being traced back to the ABS GFS Manual definition of the GGS and should reflect a fundamental change to the nature of an entity's functions and purpose;

(b) a list of significant investments in PNFC sector and PFC sector entities (paragraph 41(b)(ii)). This disclosure informs users of the controlled entities that have not been consolidated into the GGS financial report and the effect of GGS management decisions to retain or divest these investments and their effect on the balance sheet of the GGS; and

(c) the aggregate amount of dividends and other distributions to owners as owners from PNFC sector and PFC sector entities to the GGS and the aggregate amount of the comprehensive result of the PNFC sector and PFC sector entities that is attributable to the GGS for the reporting period (paragraph 41(b)(iii)). This disclosure provides further information about the relationship between the GGS and PNFC sector and PFC sector entities.

Relationship between GGS financial reports and whole of government financial reports [paragraphs 8 and 39(b)(iv)]

BC18 As noted in paragraph BC2, the Board concluded that, because of the relationship between the GGS (partially consolidated) financial report and the whole of government (fully consolidated) financial report, the GGS financial report should not be made available prior to the whole of government financial report being made available. Furthermore, the GGS financial report should include a cross-reference to the whole of government financial report (see paragraph 39(b)(iv)). This approach ensures that GGS financial reports are given due prominence within an appropriate context. That context is the whole of government financial reports that provide information about all the resources controlled by the government.

BC19 Board consultations indicated that most jurisdictions would be able to meet the requirement for the whole of government financial report to be available at the time the GGS financial report is prepared in the short term. One jurisdiction faced a number of impediments, including legislative provisions, to achieving completion of the whole of government financial report at the same time as a GGS financial report could be prepared. The Board therefore decided to specify a mandatory operative date for the Standard of the year beginning 1 July 2008, and to allow early adoption (see paragraphs 3 and 4). The Board's decision not to permit the preparation and presentation of GGS financial reports at an earlier date than for the whole of government financial report is consistent, by analogy, with the requirements in AASB 127 that parent entity financial reports cannot be prepared and presented unless consolidated financial statements are available.

BC20 Prior to this Standard, Australian Accounting Standards only anticipated that sectors of a whole of government (including the GGS) might be disclosed in the whole of government financial report in the form of disaggregated information. That is, separate financial reporting of a GGS was not contemplated. The Board considered whether, consistent with this disaggregated information approach, the proposals in International Public Sector Accounting Standards Board (IPSASB) Exposure Draft ED 28 *Disclosure of Financial Information about the General Government Sector*, since reflected in IPSAS 22 *Disclosure of Financial Information About the General Government Sector*, should be adopted in Australia. When a government elects to disclose information about its GGS in its whole of government financial reports, IPSAS 22 requires the information to conform with the accounting policies of the whole of government financial report (which are not GAAP/GFS harmonised) except for consolidation requirements and the accounting for investments in controlled PNFC sector and PFC sector entities. The Board concluded that such an approach would not adequately facilitate the presentation of GGS information and GFS information with appropriate prominence.

Whole of government financial reports

Specification of requirements for whole of government financial reports

BC21 AAS 31 was first issued in 1996 and specified requirements for general purpose financial reporting by governments. Since then, AAS 31 had only been subject to limited reviews, the most recent in June 1998.[1] The Board considered it timely to undertake a comprehensive review of the requirements in AAS 31 through two concurrent and interrelated AASB projects:

(a) the GAAP/GFS Harmonisation project; and

(b) the Short-term Review of the Requirements in AAS 27 *Financial Reporting by Local Governments*, AAS 29 *Financial Reporting by Government Departments* and AAS 31 *Financial Reporting by Governments*.

BC22 This Standard, which is a result of the GAAP/GFS Harmonisation project, together with the new, amending and revised Standards being developed from the Short-term Review of the Requirements in AASs 27, 29 & 31, supersede AAS 31.

BC23 This Standard requires governments to prepare GPFRs that adopt applicable Australian Accounting Standards, except when otherwise specified (see paragraph 9). The Short-term Review of the Requirements in AASs 27, 29 & 31 retains or amends the AAS 31 requirements by amending, where appropriate, the Australian Accounting Standards that this Standard requires to be adopted by governments. The Bases for Conclusions accompanying Exposure Draft ED 156 *Proposals Arising from the Short-term Review of the Requirements in AAS 27, AAS 29 and AAS 31* and to accompany the resulting new, amending or revised Standards, contain the Board's rationale for its treatment of

---

1 Although AAS 31A *Amendments to the Transitional Provisions in AAS 31* was issued in December 1999 and AASB 1045 *Land Under Roads: Amendments to AAS 27A, AAS 29 & AAS 31* was issued in October 2002, they only had the effect of extending the transitional provisions for land under roads.

the requirements in AAS 31. This Basis for Conclusions provides the Board's rationale for adopting GAAP/GFS harmonisation principles for whole of governments.

BC24 The Board concluded that adopting the GAAP/GFS harmonisation principles in this Standard would help ensure that the multiple needs of users for both GAAP and GFS based information prepared under a harmonised framework at a whole of government level (incorporating sector information) are satisfied.

Preparation of whole of government financial reports [paragraphs 2 and 7]

BC25 Due to the nature of governments, the Board concluded that a Standard should continue to specify requirements for the preparation of whole of government GPFRs of the federal and each state and territory government.

Consolidation of non-resident entities

BC26 Generally, the controlled entities that are not consolidated within the GGS would be consolidated under both GAAP and GFS in whole of government financial reports, and therefore one of the more controversial aspects dealt with in the context of GGS financial reporting (see paragraphs BC5-BC13) does not arise in the context of whole of government. However, a different kind of non- consolidation issue conceivably arises. Under GAAP, irrespective of residency, all controlled entities are consolidated. Under GFS, controlled non-residents are not consolidated. For example, an off- shore subsidiary of a PNFC sector entity or PFC sector entity is not consolidated under GFS because it is not part of the Australian economic territory. Instead GFS records the parent PNFC sector or PFC sector entity as having an equity investment in the non-resident subsidiary and deriving dividend income from it. The non-resident subsidiary is an institutional unit in the economic territory of the other economy that would be part of that other economy's private sector.

BC27 The Board concluded that, consistent with AASB 127, all controlled entities should be consolidated on a line-by-line basis in whole of government financial reports. If material, the GFS non-consolidation of non-resident subsidiaries would be shown as a reconciling difference (see paragraphs BC40(c) and BC52). The Board noted that Australian jurisdictions either do not have non-resident subsidiaries or have immaterial non-resident subsidiaries. Given that the issue is not significant in practice, the Board concluded that it is not necessary for the Standard to explicitly refer to the issue.

Consolidation of PNFC sector and PFC sector entities

BC28 The Board noted that under AASB 1049 (September 2006), and carried over with some clarification into this Standard, the GGS recognises its investment in PNFC sector and PFC sector entities at, depending on circumstances, fair value, proportional share of the carrying amount of net assets (as a surrogate for fair value) or zero (see paragraph BC13).

BC29 The Board considered the whole of government consolidation implications of GGS investments in PNFC sector and PFC sector entities potentially being measured at fair value in GGS financial reports. The Board noted that if the whole of government financial report were to consolidate PNFC sector and PFC sector entities at fair value, this would result in the recognition of, among other things, internally generated goodwill. The Board concluded that it is not appropriate for a government to recognise internally generated goodwill, noting that internally generated goodwill is also not recognised under GFS. Accordingly, the Board concluded that PNFC sector and PFC sector entities should be consolidated at the carrying amount of their net assets on a line-by-line basis, determined in a manner consistent with GAAP/GFS harmonisation principles.

BC30 The Board noted that no PNFC sector and PFC sector entities in any Australian jurisdiction currently have traded shares and therefore the principle in this Standard would be expected to result in the investments being measured at the carrying amount of net assets, which is consistent with GFS in these circumstances. Therefore, the question of consolidating PNFC sector and PFC sector entities at fair value is not expected to arise frequently in practice.

Disclosure of whole of government sector information [paragraph 52]

PNFC sector and PFC sector information as note disclosure in whole of government financial reports

BC31 The Board concluded that financial statements for the GGS, PNFC sector and PFC sector and reconciliations between GFS and GAAP measures of key fiscal aggregates for each sector should be disclosed in the whole of government financial report. The Board concluded that such information, together with related information, is sufficient to satisfy user needs in a general purpose financial reporting context and therefore it is not necessary to require the preparation of separate PNFC sector and PFC sector financial reports. To facilitate a presentation format that provides sufficient prominence to the various sectors relative to each other and the whole of government, the Board concluded that the sector financial statements could be presented:

(a) as a table in the notes to the whole of government financial statements comprising all sectors, an adjustments column and the whole of government; or

(b) on the face of the government's financial statements.

BC32 The Board considered whether to make the sector information disclosure requirements less onerous by only requiring disclosure of sector financial statements prepared on a GFS basis. The Board noted that this would in some respects broadly align with the 'through the eyes of management' approach adopted in AASB 8. However, the Board concluded that this approach should not be adopted because:

(a) sectors are different in nature from operating segments;

(b) such an approach would not be consistent with the approach to GAAP/GFS harmonisation adopted for the GGS financial report; and

(c) there would be a potential for user confusion if GGS financial reports adopt an accounting basis fundamentally different from that used for the GGS financial information presented in the whole of government financial report.

BC33 The Board also considered whether to not require disclosure of reconciliations of GAAP and GFS measures of key fiscal aggregates for the PNFC sector and PFC sector (see paragraph BC52), noting a view expressed by some that having to provide such information is onerous for preparers. The Board concluded that such information is useful for a significant group of users and therefore should be included in the whole of government financial report.

BC34 The Board noted that a government may choose to present information about additional sectors, such as the total non-financial public sector (comprising the GGS and PNFC sector). The Board concluded that it is not necessary to prescribe the disclosure of additional sectors, because the GGS, PNFC sector and PFC sector comprise a comprehensive disaggregation of the whole of government. However, where a government elects to disclose information about additional sectors, this should be made on a comparable basis. This ensures that information contained in the financial report is consistent.

GGS investment in PNFC sector and PFC sector entities

BC35 The Board addressed the question of whether the GGS information disclosed in the whole of government financial report should be consistent with the GGS financial report or the whole of government consolidated amounts. It therefore considered whether GGS investments in PNFC sector and PFC sector entities should be disclosed, and how they should be measured (fair value, carrying amount of net assets or zero). The Board noted that if a GGS investment in PNFC sector and PFC sector entities were to be measured at fair value in the whole of government financial report's sector information disclosures, there would be a disconnect between that amount and the carrying amount of net assets disclosed for the PNFC sector and PFC sector.

BC36 The Board concluded that GGS investments in PNFC sector and PFC sector entities should be included in the sector information disclosures, and be measured at the carrying amount of net assets disclosed for the PNFC sector and PFC sector in the whole of government financial report. The Board notes that it is conceivable, although unlikely in practice, that information about the GGS investment in PNFC and PFC sectors in the GGS financial report might differ from the GGS financial information disclosed in the whole of government financial report. This is appropriate given the different contexts in which the two sets of GGS information are presented. GGS financial reports treat the GGS as akin to a separate reporting entity whereas the GGS information disclosed in whole of government financial reports treats the GGS as a sector of a reporting entity.

Issues common to whole of government financial reports and GGS financial reports

GAAP or GFS [paragraph 9]

BC37 The Board considered whether GAAP or GFS principles should prevail for financial reporting purposes. The Board concluded that GAAP definition, recognition and measurement principles should be applied in accordance with other Australian Accounting Standards, unless otherwise specified, to accommodate GFS principles. In particular, in the interests of GAAP/GFS harmonisation, the Board concluded that GAAP presentation principles should be modified to accommodate GFS principles. Although this issue was considered in a GGS context, the Board concluded that there is no reason to adopt a different approach in a whole of government context.

BC38 An alternative approach to adopting GAAP with limited exceptions would have been to decide, for the purposes of preparing financial reports, that the GFS framework should apply. Making that declaration in a Standard would mean that GFS would become part of GAAP. However, the Board formed the view that its objective of promulgating an Australian Accounting Standard that provides useful information in a financial reporting context could be achieved without overriding entirely the GAAP framework. Accordingly, the Board's starting point was the principles and framework of GAAP, and the Board concluded that to simply adopt GFS in the Standard would be an inappropriate approach. To have adopted the GFS framework and principles as the starting point for the development of a Standard within the GAAP context, would have required the Board to become closely involved with all elements of the GFS framework. This would include any ongoing changes to the GFS framework, over which the Board has no control.

BC39 The Board's decision to adopt GAAP with limited exceptions was made on the basis that the accounting prescribed under Australian Accounting Standards is appropriate for events that occur within the not-for-profit sector, including the government. The Board noted that, in developing those Australian Accounting Standards, where the International Financial Reporting Standards (IFRSs) upon which the Standards are based do not sufficiently deal with not-for-profit circumstances, Aus paragraphs have been or will be inserted by the Board or separate Standards have been or will be issued to deal with those circumstances.

BC40 The Board's conclusion facilitates GAAP/GFS harmonisation for whole of government financial reports and GGS financial reports by:

(a) amending presentation requirements to encompass a comprehensive operating statement (paragraphs 29 and 52(b)(i)) that retains the GAAP classification system but overlays it with a transactions/other economic flows classification system based on GFS (paragraphs 30 and 52(b)(i));

(b) expanding disclosure requirements to accommodate, on the face of the statements, key fiscal aggregates under GFS (paragraphs 28, 32, 37 and 52(b)(i)) and the distinction between cash flows relating to investing in financial assets for policy purposes and for liquidity management purposes adopted by GFS (paragraphs 36 and 52(b)(i)); and

(c)   specifying supplementary disclosure requirements, including GFS measures of key fiscal aggregates, reconciliations between GAAP and GFS measures of key fiscal aggregates and explanations of differences between GAAP and GFS (paragraphs 41 and 52) – (see paragraphs BC48-BC53).

BC41 The Board decided to utilise the GFS principles related to the distinction between transactions and other economic flows for presentation purposes in the operating statement as it facilitates GAAP/GFS harmonisation in a number of areas – especially at the key fiscal aggregates level. The Board formed the view that applying the GFS principles in this way is possible without breaching the principles of GAAP because the GAAP classification system has been retained but overlayed with the GFS classification system. Furthermore, GAAP disclosure requirements have been retained.

BC42 In a whole of government context, including the disclosure of information about the PNFC sector and PFC sector, the Board considered the manner in which transactions with owners as owners should be treated. It concluded that, because they are different in nature from amounts recognised on the face of the operating statement, such transactions should be disclosed in the notes or a separate statement. However, consistent with AASB 1049 (September 2006) and paragraph 97(b) and (c) of AASB 101 *Presentation of Financial Statements*, and subject to paragraph 93B of AASB 119 *Employee Benefits*, movements in reserves should be disclosed in notes, on the face of the operating statement or in a separate statement.

Limitation of GAAP options [paragraph 13]

BC43 The Board concluded that, where other Australian Accounting Standards allow optional treatments, only those treatments that align with GFS should be applied. The Board concluded that this is appropriate because it results in the selection of the accounting policies that advance the objective of GAAP/GFS harmonisation. The Board noted that this would in turn improve consistency and comparability between jurisdictions. Although this issue was considered in a GGS context, the Board concluded that there is no reason to adopt a different approach in a whole of government context.

BC44 This approach, which results in mandating a particular accounting policy or limiting an otherwise broader choice of policies, is a crucial element of GAAP/GFS harmonisation as it facilitates the adoption of GFS treatments within the GAAP framework.

BC45 A contrary view considered by the Board is that all Australian Accounting Standards should apply, without exception, including the full range of optional treatments in those Standards. Under this view, any optional treatments available under GAAP would be available even where they do not align with GFS. It was also suggested that mandating particular optional treatments undermines the transaction neutrality principle. The Board rejected this view as not supporting the objective of GAAP/GFS harmonisation.

Adoption of ABS GFS Manual [paragraph 13]

BC46 The Board concluded that this Standard should cross-reference to the GFS Manual published by the ABS as amended from time to time, rather than the International Monetary Fund's *Government Finance Statistics Manual 2001* (IMF GFSM 2001). It did so, notwithstanding the context of international harmonisation, on the basis that:

(a)   the ABS has a similar role to the role that the Board plays for GAAP. That is, the ABS GFS Manual refines the generic requirements of IMF GFSM 2001 into more specific and relevant requirements for the Australian context, and the Board refines the requirements of IFRSs in issuing Australian Accounting Standards in relation to not-for-profit entities. [Chapter 7 of the ABS GFS Manual includes a section on the relationship of the ABS GFS Manual to IMF GFSM 2001];

(b)   there is no compelling reason for preferring IMF GFSM 2001 over the ABS GFS Manual. Both the IMF and the ABS are independent authorities; and

(c)   Australia remains ahead of international developments in the field of GAAP/GFS harmonisation.

Although this issue was considered in a GGS context, the Board concluded that there is no reason to adopt a different approach in a whole of government context.

BC47 The reference to the ABS GFS Manual is an ambulatory reference, rather than a static one. This means that the ABS GFS Manual referred to is that which may be amended from time to time. In the absence of an ambulatory reference, it may be necessary for the Board to revise its Standard more frequently than would otherwise be the case.

Presentation of key fiscal aggregates [paragraphs 16, 28, 32, 37, 41(a)(i) and 52(b)(ii)]

BC48 The Board concluded that, as well as requiring presentation of the usual GAAP aggregates, the Standard should require or allow certain GFS named key fiscal aggregates to be presented on the face of the financial statements. Although this issue was considered in a GGS context, the Board concluded that there is no reason to adopt a different approach in a whole of government context. These aggregates reflect some of the reporting features of the GFS system by including indicators of the macro-economic impact of a particular government's policy decisions on the economy as a whole, and its overall financing impact on capital markets. These GFS aggregates are important to an understanding of a GGS and a whole of government (including its sectors) and therefore they should be displayed with an appropriate level of prominence in the financial reports.

BC49 The Board concluded that the key fiscal aggregates should be measured in a manner consistent with other amounts recognised on the face of the financial statements. The Board was mindful of the potential distortion of what might be regarded by some as 'pure GFS' measures of key fiscal aggregates. Nevertheless, the Board considered that the approach adopted increases understanding as to the manner in which the key fiscal aggregates are derived and interconnected with the existing GAAP concepts.

BC50 Depending on the jurisdiction concerned, it is possible that the measurement differences will not be of great significance, and the Board expects that, over time, several of the measurement differences will be resolved. In any event, measurement differences are included in the reconciliations and explanations required by paragraphs 41(a)(i)(B) and 52(b)(ii)(B) (see paragraph BC52).

BC51 The Board also noted some concerns about the GFS nomenclature being used to describe the key fiscal aggregates. Despite these concerns, the same GFS nomenclature has been retained on the basis that to do otherwise would require the introduction of further definitions and terminology that could cause confusion for users. This approach is consistent with the Board's expectation that, over time, several of the differences will be resolved. The Board further noted that GAAP and GFS already share other terminology, such as assets and depreciation, despite being subject to different definition, recognition and measurement requirements.

BC52 Following the Board's decision to require the presentation of the key fiscal aggregates on the face of the financial statements, the Board also concluded that it is appropriate to stipulate certain disclosure requirements. Where the key fiscal aggregates presented on the face of the financial statements differ from those measured in accordance with the ABS GFS Manual, a reconciliation of the two measures and/or an explanation of the differences is required to be disclosed so that users are informed about the relationship between GAAP and GFS.

BC53 The level of prominence of these disclosures is not prescribed in the Standard.

Disclosure of functional information [paragraphs 48 and 49]

BC54 The Board concluded that disaggregated/functional information disclosure requirements should be limited to expenses (excluding losses) recognised in operating result and assets. It noted that this disaggregation provides information that is useful in understanding the disbursement of the overall resources of a government. Although this issue was considered in a GGS context, the Board concluded that there is no reason to adopt a different approach in a whole of government context.

BC55 In drawing this conclusion, the Board took into account that AASB 114 *Segment Reporting* (and AASB 8) does not apply to not- for-profit entities. The Board is monitoring the implementation of the International Accounting Standards Board (IASB) and the IPSASB Standards on segment reporting, and this may lead to an amendment to the requirements for not-for-profit entities more generally.

BC56 The Board noted that governments are already providing comparable disaggregated information of GFS expenses and net acquisitions of GFS non-financial assets as part of their GFS reporting requirements and it does not appear to be unduly onerous. The Standard makes it clear that disaggregation should only occur where it can be reliably attributable to a function.

Budgetary information [paragraph 59]

BC57 The FRC's broad strategic direction makes specific mention of budgetary information. The direction is, among other things, to achieve an Australian Accounting Standard " ... in which the outcome statements are directly comparable with the relevant budget statements".

BC58 The Board concluded that the Standard should require disclosure of certain budgetary information where budgetary information is presented to parliament, including the original budgeted financial statements. The Board also concluded that explanations of major variances between the actual amounts presented on the face of the financial statements and corresponding budget amounts should be disclosed. Although this issue was considered in a GGS context, the Board concluded that there is no reason to adopt a different approach in a whole of government context. In doing so, the Board noted that Australian Accounting Standards, including this Standard, do not prescribe the preparation of a budget. The Board also noted that governments typically budget on a GGS basis rather than on a whole of government basis.

BC59 The Board concluded that the 'presented' budget is more relevant to users than the 'adopted' budget. The presented budget is the one most widely publicised and, accordingly, is the primary reference point for any assessment of the reliability of budgeting, identification of major variances and assessment of the quality of stewardship in relation to the period. Therefore, this Standard mandates inclusion of the first budget presented to parliament. This Standard also allows for revised budgeted financial statements to be disclosed, acknowledging that revised budgets may occur late in the financial period and their disclosure can play a role in demonstrating an aspect of stewardship.

BC60 The Board concluded that the requirement for disclosure of explanations of major variances should be a key feature within the Standard. It did so on the basis that the information is useful and relevant to users and that merely recording the amount of the variance is not sufficient to meet accountability needs. An explanation of major variances is critical if users are to find comparisons between actual and budget valuable input to their analysis of the performance of government. A similar requirement exists within the New Zealand Accounting Standard NZ IAS 1 *Presentation of Financial Statements* (paragraphs NZ41.1 and NZ41.2) – see also paragraph 70 of NZ FRS-42 *Prospective Financial Statements*.

BC61 This is not an area in which the IASB has developed an IFRS. The Board considered IPSAS 24 *Presentation of Budget Information in Financial Statements* and concluded that it does not provide an appropriate basis for budgetary reporting in the Australian environment, particularly because it gives primacy to the budget basis over the accounting basis and contemplates explanations of variances being disclosed outside the financial report.

BC62 The Board also noted that, as part of the Uniform Presentation Framework, typically Australian jurisdictions publish GGS budget information together with budget information relating to the PNFC sector (and the Non-Financial Public Sector, comprising the GGS and PNFC sector) but not the PFC sector. The Board considered whether sector-based budgetary information should be required to be disclosed in the whole of government financial report. The Board concluded that because the PNFC sector and PFC sector are not required by Australian Accounting Standards to prepare separate financial reports, a requirement to disclose budget information for the PNFC sector and PFC sector in whole of government financial reports would be onerous and of limited use to users even if that budget information is presented to parliament. The Board also noted that GGS budgetary information is required to be disclosed in GGS financial reports in accordance with this Standard. Accordingly, the Board concluded that sector-based budgetary information should not be required to be disclosed in whole of government financial reports.

Performance indicators

BC63 The proposals in Exposure Draft ED 142 *Financial Reporting of General Government Sectors by Governments* (issued July 2005) relating to performance indicators were modelled on the requirements that were contained within AAS 27, AAS 29 and AAS 31 at that time. Most respondents to ED 142 supported the principles but seemed to interpret the proposals as potentially mandating disclosure of performance indicators in the GGS financial reports. Many claimed it would be premature to mandate disclosure of performance indicators.

BC64 The Board decided to not retain the proposed requirements and guidance for either whole of government financial reports or GGS financial reports. It intends to consider issues relating to performance indicators more comprehensively in a separate project in due course.

Transitional requirements [paragraphs 66-68]

BC65 Consistent with the general approach adopted in this Standard, the Board decided that the requirements relating to changes in accounting policies in AASB 108 *Accounting Policies, Changes in Accounting Estimates and Errors* should apply to the first financial report prepared in accordance with this Standard and that it is not necessary to specify such a requirement in this Standard.

BC66 The Board noted that jurisdictions adopted Australian equivalents to IFRSs for their whole of government financial reports for annual reporting periods ending on 30 June 2006 (under AAS 31 and AASB 1 *First-time Adoption of Australian Equivalents to International Financial Reporting Standards*) and AASB 1049 requires the date of transition of the GGS to be the date of transition used in the whole of government financial reports. The Board also noted that all jurisdictions intended deferring adopting AASB 1049 (September 2006) until a whole of government harmonised Standard is in place (see paragraph BC2). Accordingly, the Board concluded that it is only necessary to provide specific transitional requirements in a whole of government GAAP/GFS harmonised Standard to the extent necessary to facilitate consistency between GGS and whole of government financial reporting and between GAAP and GFS.

BC67 The Board concluded that AASB 1 should be applied by GGSs in their first financial report prepared in accordance with this Standard, with certain exceptions.

BC68 As noted in paragraph BC66, the Board concluded that, in relation to the GGS, the date of transition should be the date of transition used in the whole of government financial report and that the whole of government elections under AASB 1 that align with GFS should be adopted by the GGS. This is on the basis that the GGS is part of the whole of government. The Board noted that to do otherwise would inappropriately give rise to potential differences between the amounts in the GGS financial report and the whole of government financial report.

BC69 The Board concluded that GGSs should be relieved from the disclosure requirements on transition, including the reconciliation from previous GAAP to Australian equivalents to IFRSs, in paragraphs 38 to 46 of AASB 1. The Board considers that the disclosures would not be relevant given that the date of transition of the GGS is the same as the date of transition used in the whole of government financial report, which is likely to be two or three years earlier than the first time the GGS applies this Standard.

BC70 The Board also concluded that GGSs and whole of governments should be subject to the other aspects of AASB 1 to enable governments to avail themselves of the various forms of optional relief provided under AASB 1 to facilitate GAAP/GFS harmonisation. The extent to which that relief is available is limited to some extent by the operation of paragraphs 13, 66 and 68(c) of this Standard.

BASIS FOR CONCLUSIONS ON AASB 2008-9

This Basis for Conclusions accompanies, but is not part of, AASB 1049. The Basis for Conclusions was originally published with AASB 2008-9 Amendments to AASB 1049 for Consistency with AASB 101 (September 2008).

Background

BC1 This Basis for Conclusions summarises the Australian Accounting Standards Board's considerations in reaching the conclusions in this Standard. Individual Board members gave greater weight to some factors than to others.

Significant issues

BC2 AASB 101 *Presentation of Financial Statements* (as issued in October 2006) required the presentation of an income statement that included items of income and expense recognised in profit or loss. It required items of income and expense not recognised in profit or loss to be presented in the statement of changes in equity, potentially together with owner changes in equity. Revised AASB 101 (issued September 2007) includes requirements for income and expenses to be presented in one statement (a statement of comprehensive income) or in two statements (a separate income statement and a statement of comprehensive income), separately from owner changes in equity. As a result of these changes, revised AASB 101 more closely aligned with the principles in AASB 1049 (issued October 2007), and it became possible for AASB 1049 to rely more heavily on the principles in AASB 101 by cross-reference rather than express requirements directly in AASB 1049. The changes help reinforce the approach taken in AASB 1049 of relying on other Standards rather than re-expressing the principles in those Standards directly in AASB 1049.

BC3 The Board noted that a consequence of relying on the revised AASB 101 is a requirement to present a statement of changes in equity. Previously, AASB 1049 contemplated information pertinent to a statement of changes in equity being presented in a note or a separate statement to the extent the information is not included in the statement of comprehensive income. This is because of the way in which superseded AASB 101 treated such items. For example, superseded AASB 101 required changes in reserves to be presented in what was then a statement of changes in equity (which included components of comprehensive income) or in the notes. It also contemplated transactions with owners in their capacity as owners being presented in the statement of changes in equity or in the notes. Revised AASB 101 requires changes in reserves and transactions with owners in their capacity as owners to be presented in the statement of changes in equity. Therefore, this Standard amends AASB 1049 to require the presentation of a statement of changes in equity.

BC4 With minor exceptions, the Board decided to align the terminology used in AASB 1049 with the terminology in revised AASB 101 to ensure greater consistency across the suite of Australian Accounting Standards. The reference to 'comprehensive result' and 'operating result' is retained, despite revised AASB 101's use of the terms 'total comprehensive income' and 'profit or loss'. The Board concluded that, for the purpose of the Standard, the terms 'comprehensive result' and 'operating result' are more appropriate in a not-for-profit public sector context.

BC5 Consistent with revised AASB 101, the financial statement titles 'balance sheet', 'operating statement' and 'cash flow statement' have been replaced by 'statement of financial position', 'statement of comprehensive income' and 'statement of cash flows' respectively. However, the Board notes that, consistent with the flexibility on statement titles allowed for in revised AASB 101, whole of governments and GGSs would not be restricted by AASB 1049 to using the titles used in AASB 1049.

BC6 The Board decided that the transitional requirements in the revised AASB 1049 should not be available to governments that have previously applied AASB 1049 as issued in October 2007. This is because the transitional requirements should only be available once, on the initial transition to GAAP/GFS harmonisation.

BC7 Following feedback on AASB 1049 from constituents the Board decided to clarify that:

(a) the whole of government statement of comprehensive income disclosures referred to in paragraph 41(b)(iii) of AASB 1049 relate to the sector statements of comprehensive income that are disclosed for the whole of government; and

(b) the budget information disclosure requirements in paragraph 59 of AASB 1049 only relate to the budgeted financial statement(s) that were initially presented to parliament.

BC8 To assist in implementing the changes to AASB 1049 the Board decided to incorporate the changes into the Illustrative Examples in the Standard, including the addition of illustrations of the statement of changes in equity.

BC9 Following feedback from constituents on ED 163 the Board decided:

(a) to require that, where the revised AASB 1049 is applied to annual reporting periods beginning before 1 January 2009, there is early adoption for the same annual reporting period of AASB 101 (September 2007). This will help to ensure consistency in application of the two Standards; and

(b) to illustrate the statement of changes in equity for the whole of government by sector in a down-the-page, rather than an across-the-page, format in an attempt to make it more understandable.

BASIS FOR CONCLUSIONS ON AASB 2011-3

This Basis for Conclusions accompanies, but is not part of, AASB 1049. The Basis for Conclusions was originally published with AASB 2011-3 Amendments to Australian Accounting Standards – Orderly Adoption of Changes to the ABS GFS Manual and Related Amendments *(May 2011).*

Background

BC1 This Basis for Conclusions summarises the Australian Accounting Standards Board (AASB) considerations in reaching the conclusions in this Standard. Individual Board members gave greater weight to some factors than to others.

BC2 Given the substantial change to financial reporting brought about by AASB 1049 *Whole of Government and General Government Sector Financial Reporting* (October 2007), the Board decided to undertake a post-implementation review of that Standard. The objective was to identify any material issues at an operational level with a view to improving financial reporting. The post-implementation review included consideration of the consistency of application of AASB 1049 across jurisdictions.

BC3 Various methods were used to identify the AASB 1049 implementation issues, some of which are the subject of this Standard. These methods included consulting with personnel with AASB 1049 implementation experience from each jurisdiction's Department of Treasury and Finance and Auditor-General's Office.

BC4 After reviewing the implementation issues identified, the Board proposed amendments to AASB 1049 in Exposure Draft ED 211 *Proposed Amendments to AASB 1049* (Issued in March 2011). The Exposure Draft was structured to focus on two sets of proposals:

(a) Part 1, open for a 30-day comment period, relates to the definition of the ABS GFS Manual, relief from adopting the latest version of the ABS GFS Manual, and related disclosures; and

(b) Part 2, open for a 90-day comment period, relates to other proposals.

Part 1 had a 30-day comment period because of the Board's aim to provide relief as early as possible from the requirement to adopt the latest version of the ABS GFS Manual, so that the relief would be available for the reporting period ending on 30 June 2011. Therefore, this Standard arises from the Part 1 proposals in ED 211. The second set of proposals will be considered in due course.

Issues giving rise to amendments to AASB 1049

Orderly adoption of changes to the ABS GFS Manual [paragraphs 13B, 39(a)(ii) & 39A]

BC5 The Board considered how best to draft requirements into AASB 1049 that would help facilitate the orderly adoption of future amendments to the ABS GFS Manual for the purposes of GAAP/GFS harmonised financial reporting. The Board noted that there are potentially two broad aspects to this issue:

(a) the manner in which a change to the ABS GFS Manual should be initially adopted in the GAAP/GFS harmonised financial statements for the purposes of determining GFS information included in those statements; and

(b) the time lag to allow between the change being issued and it becoming mandatory for the GAAP/GFS harmonised financial statements.

BC6 In relation to the manner in which a change in the ABS GFS Manual should be initially adopted, the Board noted that if AASB 1049 were to override, or even merely clarify, GFS transitional arrangements, it would arguably go beyond the Board's role, and potentially result in the Board interpreting or effectively modifying the ABS GFS Manual. To avoid this, consistent with the approach in AASB 1049, the Board decided that AASB 1049 should adopt the ABS GFS Manual as it is. The Board noted that to do otherwise would create the potential for there to be a permanent difference between the amounts presented as GFS in the financial statements and amounts published by the ABS. However, the Board noted this decision only pertains to GFS information, and therefore GAAP requirements (including those relating to retrospectivity in AASB 108 *Accounting Policies, Changes in Accounting Estimates and Errors*) apply, unamended, to the manner in which a change in accounting policy is initially adopted.

BC7 In relation to time lag, the Board noted that providing relief through a 'time lag' has the potential to give rise to temporary differences between the amounts presented as GFS in the financial statements and amounts published by the ABS. After considering alternative approaches on how to give an effective time lag between the issue of an amendment to the ABS GFS Manual and when it becomes mandatory for GAAP/GFS harmonised financial reporting purposes, the Board decided AASB 1049 should specify that references to the ABS GFS Manual are to the version of the Manual effective at the beginning of the previous annual reporting period or any version effective at a later date. The Board decided to allow jurisdictions to adopt a version of the ABS GFS Manual for AASB 1049 financial reporting purposes, even if that version was not effective until after the beginning of the reporting period, consistent with the Board's usual policy of allowing early adoption of Australian Accounting Standards.

BC8 The Board noted that this approach is broadly aligned with the Board's normal approach to specifying transitional requirements for changes to GAAP because it:

(a) specifies, albeit in an ambulatory two year lagged way, a mandatory operative date for changes to the ABS GFS Manual;

(b) provides a reasonable time for entities to implement changes to the ABS GFS Manual that could affect comparative information; and

(c) allows, but does not require, entities to adopt changes to the ABS GFS Manual prior to mandatory operative dates.

BC9 The Board also noted that this approach would warrant an amendment to paragraph 39 of AASB 1049, to help ensure users are informed about the version of the ABS GFS Manual adopted as the basis for GFS information included in financial statements. Consequently, amendments are made to Illustrative Example C 'Extract from the Note Containing the Summary of Significant Accounting Policies of a General Government Sector', which provides an illustration of disclosures required by paragraph 39. Also, consistent with paragraph 30 of AASB 108 relating to new but not yet effective Standards, the Board decided that AASB 1049 should require the disclosure of information about the latest version of the ABS GFS Manual that has not yet had an impact on the financial statements.

BC10 To address concerns about uncertainties that arise from the ABS potentially not specifying effective dates for amendments to the ABS GFS Manual, the Board decided to clarify that the date on which amendments to the ABS GFS Manual become effective is, for the purpose of AASB 1049, the publication date if no effective date is specified by the ABS.

Definition of the ABS GFS Manual [appendix A]

BC11 The Board decided that the ABS GFS Manual continues to be the appropriate authoritative source for GFS matters that are pertinent to general purpose financial reporting. After consulting with the ABS, which had clarified the boundaries of the ABS GFS Manual on its website since ED 211 was issued, the Board also decided the ABS GFS Manual should be defined as "Australian Bureau of Statistics publications *Australian System of Government Finance Statistics: Concepts, Sources and Methods, 2005* (ABS Catalogue No. 5514.0) and *Amendments to Australian System of Government Finance Statistics, 2005* (ABS Catalogue No. 5514.0) published on the ABS website". Consequently, amendments are made to the illustrated explanation of the key technical term 'Government Finance Statistics (GFS)' provided in Illustrative Example D 'Key Technical Terms Used in the Complete Sets of Financial Statements' to make it consistent with the revised definition of the ABS GFS Manual.

BASIS FOR CONCLUSIONS ON AASB 2011-13

This Basis for Conclusions accompanies, but is not part of, AASB 1049. The Basis for Conclusions was originally published with AASB 2011-13 Amendments to Australian Accounting Standard – Improvements to AASB 1049 *(December 2011).*

Background

BC1 This Basis for Conclusions summarises the Australian Accounting Standards Board (AASB) considerations in reaching the conclusions in this Standard. Individual Board members gave greater weight to some factors than to others.

BC2 Given the substantial change to financial reporting brought about by AASB 1049 *Whole of Government and General Government Sector Financial Reporting* (October 2007, as amended), the Board decided to undertake a post-implementation review of that Standard. The objective was to identify any material issues at an operational level with a view to improving financial reporting. The post- implementation review included consideration of the consistency of application of AASB 1049 across jurisdictions.

BC3   Various methods were used to identify the AASB 1049 implementation issues that gave rise to the amendments in this Standard. These methods included consulting with personnel with AASB 1049 implementation experience from each jurisdiction's Department of Treasury and Finance and Auditor-General's Office.

BC4   The Board noted that the post-implementation review work to date has not identified any major flaws in the Standard. However, the Board identified a number of aspects of AASB 1049 where improvements could be made. After reviewing the implementation issues identified, the Board issued Exposure Draft ED 211 *Proposed Amendments to AASB 1049* containing proposals to amend AASB 1049 to clarify some of its requirements.

BC5   The Board issued AASB 2011-3 *Amendments to Australian Accounting Standards – Orderly Adoption of Changes to the ABS GFS Manual and Related Amendments* [AASB 1049] in May 2011. The amendments in AASB 2011-3 arise from the proposals in ED 211 relating to the definition of the ABS GFS Manual, and related disclosures. AASB 2011-3 was issued early so that the relief would be available for the reporting period ending on 30 June 2011.

BC6   The amendments in this Standard arise from the remaining proposals in ED 211, with the bases for amendments outlined in paragraphs BC7-BC22. In addition, the Board decided that some issues raised in the post-implementation review did not warrant amendments to AASB 1049, on the bases outlined in paragraphs BC23-BC40.

Issues giving rise to amendments to AASB 1049

Alignment to terminology used in AASB 101

BC7   Consistent with the terminology used in AASB 101 *Presentation of Financial Statements*, wherever the term 'other non-owner changes in equity' or 'other changes in equity' is used in AASB 1049 to refer to the other comprehensive income section in the statement of comprehensive income, the Board decided to amend the term to 'other comprehensive income'.

Preparation of GGS and whole of government financial statements [paragraph 7][1]

BC8   Consistent with the original intention of paragraph 7 of AASB 1049 (see for example paragraphs BC5 and BC25 of AASB 1049) the Board decided to clarify within the body of the Standard that both whole of government and GGS financial statements are required to be prepared. The amendment addresses the concern that some could conceivably interpret AASB 1049 as merely specifying requirements for financial statements if they are prepared.

Relative timing and cross-referencing of GGS and whole of government financial statements [paragraphs 8, 39(a) and 39(b)]

BC9   AASB 1049 previously allowed GGS financial statements to be made available later than whole of government financial statements being made available. Where the GGS financial statements were presented separately from the whole of government financial statements, a cross-reference from the GGS financial statements to the whole of government financial statements was required to be made. The Board decided that AASB 1049 should be amended to require, at all times, GGS and whole of government financial statements to be made available at the same time and cross-referenced to each other. This is on the basis that:

---

1   References to paragraphs in the headings of this Basis for Conclusions are to paragraphs in AASB 1049.

(a)   GGS financial statements provide useful information (e.g. budgetary information) for users, and users should receive such information on a timely basis;

(b)   GGS financial statements provide a bridge between a government's budget and its whole of government financial statements; and

(c)   given that GGS is a sector of whole of government, whole of government financial statements provide a context to the GGS financial statements.

Adoption of options in GAAP that align with GFS [paragraphs 13-15]

Early adoption of new or revised standards

BC10   The Board noted that paragraph 13 of AASB 1049 could be interpreted as requiring early adoption of a new or revised Standard if its adoption is more in line with GFS than the requirements of the Standard being superseded. The Board decided that such an interpretation is not the intention of paragraph 13 as it would potentially undermine the Board's intention of facilitating the orderly adoption of new or revised requirements. Accordingly, the Board decided to amend AASB 1049 to clarify that AASB 1049, in mandating a particular accounting policy or limiting an otherwise broader choice of policies for the objective of GAAP/GFS harmonisation, does not require that a new or revised Standard must be adopted early, even if early adoption would more quickly allow alignment with GFS.

Disclosure of key fiscal aggregates

Presentation of additional fiscal aggregates [paragraphs 16 & 18]

BC11   The Board noted that AASB 1049 allows jurisdictions to disclose fiscal aggregates that are additional to the key fiscal aggregates required by AASB 1049. However, the Board noted the concern that, in practice, these other fiscal aggregates are not necessarily clearly distinguished from those key fiscal aggregates in the financial statements. To address this concern, the Board decided that AASB 1049 should be amended to require a clear differentiation between key fiscal aggregates and other fiscal aggregates, to help avoid potential confusion for users.

Disclosure of other measures of key fiscal aggregates [paragraphs 16, 18, 41(a)(i) & 52(b)(ii)]

BC12   AASB 1049 previously only allowed key fiscal aggregates measured in a manner consistent with recognised amounts or the ABS GFS Manual to be disclosed. Other measures of key fiscal aggregates were not allowed to be disclosed. The Board decided that AASB 1049 should be amended to allow disclosure of other measures of key fiscal aggregates (i.e. not measured in a manner consistent with recognised amounts or the ABS GFS Manual) on the basis that preparers should not be prevented from disclosing information they believe is useful to users, as long as it does not detract from the information required by the Standard. Accordingly, paragraphs 41(a)(i) and 52(b)(ii) have been amended by removing the requirement that prohibits the disclosure of other measures of key fiscal aggregates. Furthermore, the amendments to paragraph 18 in AASB 1049 clarify that other measures of key fiscal aggregates should not be presented as key fiscal aggregates, to help avoid potential confusion for users.

Determination of the amount to be recognised for GGS investments in PNFC and PFC sector entities [paragraphs 20(c), 21 & 23(c)]

BC13   Paragraph 20 of AASB 1049 requires GGS controlling investments in PNFC sector and PFC sector entities to be measured at, depending on circumstances, fair value, or the government's proportional share of the carrying amount of net assets, or zero. Therefore, an investment is not recognised at an amount below zero. As noted in paragraph BC13 of AASB 1049 measurement at fair value, or at the government's proportional share of the carrying amount of net assets where fair value is not reliably measurable, is consistent with GFS. That paragraph also notes that not allowing investments to be measured below zero is consistent with the principles elsewhere in GAAP (for example, AASB 128 *Investments in Associates* does not allow negative investment values when using the equity method).

BC14 With that background, in relation to paragraph 20 of AASB 1049, the Board noted the view of some practitioners that paragraph 23(c) of AASB 1049 is inconsistent with paragraph 20(c) because paragraph 23(c), which refers to 'net basis', implies individual amounts may be less than zero whereas paragraph 20(c) requires individual amounts to be not less than zero for the purposes of measuring a GGS equity investment in a PNFC sector or PFC sector entity. Consistent with the rationale in paragraph BC13 of AASB 1049, the Board decided the last sentence of paragraph 23(c) should be amended to be consistent with paragraph 20(c).

Classification of items between transactions and other economic flows [paragraphs 30, 31 & 55(b)]

BC15 The Board acknowledged the view that paragraph 30 should be amended to provide further guidance for the classification of items between transactions and other economic flows to help facilitate greater consistency in its application by jurisdictions, particularly for circumstances where items arising under GAAP are not recognised under GFS in the reporting period. The Board noted that for circumstances where items arising under GAAP are also recognised under GFS in the reporting period, the principle for classification between transactions and other economic flows are already in AASB 1049. The Board decided to amend AASB 1049 to clarify the principle for classification between transactions and other economic flows in circumstances where items arising under GAAP are not recognised under GFS in the reporting period. In addition, to assist in applying the clarified principle, the Board decided to provide additional examples of how the clarified principles would apply in particular circumstances.

BC16 Related to this issue, the Board considered whether classification of GAAP items that are also recognised under GFS in the reporting period should be grouped together, and presented separately in the statement of comprehensive income from classification of GAAP items that are not recognised under GFS in the reporting period. However, the Board decided against imposing such a requirement, on the basis that it was not identified as an issue in the post-implementation review of AASB 1049.

Defence weapons platforms [paragraphs 31(a)(v) and 44(a)(iv) of AASB 1049, and the illustrative examples A and B accompanying AASB 1049]

BC17 Consistent with the ABS GFS Manual, which now recognises and measures defence weapons platforms in the same way as other non-financial assets, the relevant paragraphs in AASB 1049 and the relevant sections of the Illustrative Examples accompanying AASB 1049 are amended. There would now be no convergence difference between GAAP and GFS in relation to defence weapons platforms.

Transactions with owners as owners in a GGS context [paragraph 34B]

BC18 The Board noted that, although not common, transactions with owners in their capacity as owners that are not eliminated on consolidation could arise because of non-controlling interest attributable to entities outside the GGS. Therefore, the Board decided that paragraph 34B should be amended to acknowledge that this could occur.

Interpretation of 'presented on a basis that is consistent with' in the context of budgetary information [paragraphs 59(e), 63 & 64]

BC19 Paragraph 59(e) of AASB 1049 required disclosure of the original budgeted financial statements, presented on a basis that is consistent with the basis prescribed for the financial statements by AASB 1049. The Board noted that some practitioners questioned the meaning of 'presented on a basis that is consistent with'. In particular, it was questioned whether the budget would be required to be recast solely for presentation and classification or whether the requirement extends to recognition and measurement. The Board noted the practical difficulties of recasting for recognition and measurement differences – e.g. retrospectively determining 'budgeted' fair values when hindsight is likely to influence such a determination. Therefore, the Board decided that paragraph 59(e) of AASB 1049 should be amended to clarify that the budget should be recast solely for presentation and classification matters, not for recognition and measurement matters. This amendment gave rise to consequential amendments to paragraphs 63 and 64 to focus them on presentation and classification.

BC20 In relation to the requirement in paragraph 59(f) to disclose explanations of major variances between actual and budget amounts, the Board noted that variances might arise from recognition and measurement principles adopted in the budget being different from the recognition and measurement principles adopted in the financial statements.

Transitional requirements [paragraphs 65A, 66, 67, 68, 69 & 70]

BC21 The Board noted it is no longer necessary to specify transitional requirements because all jurisdictions have previously first-time adopted AASB 1049 for their whole of government and GGS financial statements.

Tax-effect accounting by GGS [explanatory note r(ii) to the illustrative examples accompanying AASB 1049]

BC22 The Board noted that of those jurisdictions that recognise deferred tax liabilities at the PNFC/PFC level, only some reflect corresponding amounts in the GGS statement of financial position as deferred tax assets. The Board also noted:

(a) the view that, from a GAAP perspective, such 'mirror' accounting can be justified given the amount is known in a 'closed system' (i.e. the taxpayer and taxing authority are within the government); and

(b) the question of whether the amounts are in the nature of a tax or distribution to owners as owners.

After considering these issues, the Board considered whether to remove the text in square brackets in Explanatory Note r(ii) on the basis that the subject matter of that text is beyond the scope of the GAAP/GFS Harmonisation project. However, the Board noted that the tax regime assumed is in the context of an illustrative example and thus is non-prescriptive. The Board decided to retain the text, on the basis that it provides a useful explanation of why there is no convergence difference for GGS in relation to deferred tax balances as illustrated in Example A, with some editorial amendments to the text to clarify that the tax regime assumed is for the purpose of an illustrative example.

Significant issues that did not give rise to amendments to AASB 1049

Purpose of the GGS financial report [paragraphs 12 & BC6]

BC23 The Board noted that paragraph 12 does not require disclosure of whether GGS financial statements are general purpose financial statements or special purpose financial statements and considered whether the absence of such a requirement gives rise to implementation issues. The Board decided AASB 1049 should not be amended in relation to this issue at this time because the AASB 1049 approach to the issue has not created insurmountable practical problems for jurisdictions, particularly because, in practice, GGS financial statements are not presented separately from the general purpose financial statements of the whole of government. The Board notes that, in due course, it may be appropriate to revisit the way AASB 1049 deals with the issue, depending on the outcome of future work to be undertaken on the Board's Differential Reporting project.

Adoption of options in GAAP that align with GFS [paragraphs 13 & 14]

Examples of particular optional treatments in GAAP

BC24 The Board noted the view that the Board should fully analyse optional treatments in GAAP and specify directly in AASB 1049 those treatments to be adopted, to avoid the need for preparers to refer directly to the ABS GFS Manual. The Board decided that the relatively principles-based approach in AASB 1049 should be retained, rather than including an exhaustive list of GAAP options that align with GFS, on the basis that it is not the Board's role to interpret GFS. Also, the Board decided to monitor the development of any further guidance by other interested parties on this issue and expressed a willingness to collaborate with Treasuries and the ABS in developing such guidance if Treasuries decide to develop separate guidance.

BC25 The Board noted that some practitioners questioned the application of paragraph 12 of AASB 108 *Accounting Policies, Changes in Accounting Estimates and Errors* in the context of aligning optional treatments in GAAP with GFS and whether the wording in that paragraph of 'most recent pronouncements of other standard setting bodies' included the ABS GFS Manual.

Paragraph 12 of AASB 108 states:

"In making the judgement described in paragraph 10, management may also consider the most recent pronouncements of other standard setting bodies that use a similar conceptual framework to develop accounting standards, other accounting literature and accepted industry practices, to the extent that these do not conflict with the sources in paragraph 11."

The Board decided that the ABS GFS Manual should not be included in the AASB 108 hierarchy, on the basis that GFS, per se, is not a part of GAAP.

Presentation of the whole of government/GGS statements of financial position [paragraph 15]

BC26 The Board noted that the Illustrative Examples accompanying AASB 1049 subclassify non-financial assets between 'produced' and 'non-produced' categories even though the ABS GFS Manual does not explicitly require such a subclassification. The Board decided it is not necessary to amend AASB 1049 to remove the subclassification because the Illustrative Examples are not prescriptive.

BC27 The Board also noted the view that AASB 1049 should be amended to clarify requirements relating to the presentation of statements of financial position based on liquidity. However, the Board decided it is not necessary to amend AASB 1049 in relation to this issue because the principles in AASB 1049 are sufficiently clear and the Illustrative Examples are not prescriptive.

Presentation of operating result on the face [paragraph 29]

BC28 The Board noted the view that AASB 1049 should be amended to allow the operating result (a GAAP subtotal) not to be presented on the face of the single statement of comprehensive income on the basis that its presentation on the face clutters the statement. This is consistent with a view that users are most interested in the 'net result from transactions – net operating balance', and that including the 'operating result' on the face has the potential to confuse users. However, the Board decided that paragraph 29 should continue to require jurisdictions to present the operating result on the face of the single statement of comprehensive income because, consistent with the fundamental basis upon which AASB 1049 was developed, such a presentation is required by AASB 101.

Treatment of non-cash items in relation to cash flow statements [paragraphs 18 & 37]

BC29 The Board noted that some jurisdictions present the value of assets acquired under finance leases and similar arrangements on the face of the cash flow statements. The

Board also noted the concern expressed by some about such non-cash flows being included in cash flow statements. However, the Board decided it is not necessary to amend AASB 1049 for this issue because it is already obvious in GAAP (including AASB 1049) that an entity should clearly distinguish between information that is and is not cash flow information.

GAAP/GFS reconciliation requirements [paragraphs 41(a)(i)(B) & 52(b)(ii)(B)]

BC30 The Board noted that AASB 1049 requires disclosure of reconciliations of GAAP and GFS measures of certain key fiscal aggregates, and an explanation of the differences. The Board also noted the view that such disclosures are unnecessary and therefore that the reconciliation requirement should be removed. However, the Board decided paragraphs 41(a)(i)(B) and 52(b)(ii)(B) should continue to require the reconciliations and explanations because they provide useful information for users in the context of GAAP/GFS harmonisation and the reconciliation schedule is a critical part of AASB 1049.

BC31 On a related issue, the Board considered whether it is necessary to amend AASB 1049 to explicitly address the circumstances where GFS amounts determined by the ABS differ from and are published after amounts disclosed as GFS amounts in the financial statements. The question arises as to which GFS amounts should be reconciled to in the comparative information disclosed in the following year's financial statements. The Board decided that it is not necessary to explicitly address this issue in AASB 1049, noting that the GFS amounts previously reported in the financial statements would be the relevant amounts.

Disclosure of the aggregates of dividends and other distributions to owners as owners [paragraph 41(b)(iii)]

BC32 The Board noted that paragraph 41(b)(iii) requires the GGS financial statements to disclose the aggregate amount of dividends and other distributions to owners as owners from PNFC sector and PFC sector entities to the GGS. The Board also noted the suggestion that the wording in paragraph 41(b)(iii) should be amended because it is unclear as to what is meant by 'other distributions'. The Board decided paragraph 41(b)(iii) should not be amended in relation to this issue on the basis that there is apparently no significant issue in complying with the requirement in paragraph 41(b)(iii). The Board particularly noted it is a matter of professional judgement based on circumstances whether income tax equivalent income is in the nature of a distribution to owners as owners.

BC33 The Board noted the view that paragraph 41(b)(iii) should be amended to require the disclosure of contributions from the GGS in its capacity as owner to PNFC sector and PFC sector entities to enable derivation of 'net distributions'. However, the Board noted that typically such information is already disclosed and therefore it is not necessary for AASB 1049 to mandate it.

Carrying amounts of assets attributable to functions [paragraphs 48(b), 50 & 51]

BC34 The Board noted that AASB 1049 requires disclosure of the carrying amount of recognised assets that are reliably attributable to each function (paragraph 48(b)). The Board also noted that the relevance of such a disclosure when it is not based on an ABS GFS Manual concept was questioned by some. The Board decided paragraph 48(b) should continue to require the disclosure on the basis that the disclosure would assist users in identifying resources committed to particular functions relative to the costs of service delivery that are reliably attributable to those functions, which facilitates comparisons between jurisdictions. The Board also noted that, in due course, its Disaggregated Disclosures project will address, amongst other things, issues raised in the post-implementation review of AASB 1049. The Board noted that retaining the requirement would avoid the risk of otherwise removing the requirement and then potentially reinstating it as a result of the Disaggregated Disclosures project.

'Expenses, excluding losses, included in operating result' by function [paragraphs 48(c), 50 & 51]

BC35 Consistent with the decision to retain the requirement in AASB 1049 to disclose carrying amount of recognised assets that are reliably attributable to each function (see paragraph BC34), the Board decided to retain the requirement to disclose 'expenses, excluding losses, included in operating result' (paragraph 48(c)).

BC36 The Board noted that 'expenses excluding losses' is not explicitly described in AASB 1049. Furthermore, the Board noted the view that inclusion of this term in the functional information could confuse users (and preparers) as there is no clear definition of what is intended to be included in the calculation and that the phrase should be replaced with the phrase 'expenses from transactions', which would avoid the reconciliation required by paragraph 49. However, the Board decided paragraph 48(c) should not be amended for the following reasons:

(a) if the reference to 'excluding losses' were omitted, it would seem to be anomalous to include losses, but not gains, given that gains and losses relating to an item might be netted off; and

(b) 'expenses excluding losses' more closely aligns with GAAP than 'expenses from transactions', because 'expenses from transactions' does not include GAAP expenses classified as other economic flows.

Explanations of variances from budget [paragraphs 59(f) & 65]

BC37 The Board noted that the AASB 1049 requirement to include explanations of variances between budgeted and actual financial information was questioned by some practitioners for two primary reasons:

(a) the requirement to explain variances is unnecessary as the variance explanations are not relevant to users because variance explanations are more relevant at entity level and the reasons for changes in budgetary assumptions are explained every time the budgets are updated; and

(b) the inclusion of unaudited budgetary information within the audited financial statements results in audit report comments in relation to budget information within the statements. In particular, whilst audit of variances between budgeted and actual data is possible at the higher levels, at a lower level there is insufficient evidence available to make assessments.

BC38 The Board decided not to amend paragraph 59(f) in relation to this issue on the basis that disclosure of variance information provides useful information for users and facilitates the discharge of accountability by governments. Paragraph BC60 of AASB 1049 contains the Board's rationale for the requirement for disclosure of explanations of major variances between the actual amounts presented on the face of the financial statements and corresponding budget amounts.

Capital management disclosures

BC39 The Board considered whether the exemption provided by paragraph Aus1.7 of AASB 101 for whole of governments and GGSs from presenting certain capital management disclosures required by paragraphs 134-136 of AASB 101 should be retained or removed.

BC40 The Board decided it would be inappropriate to reconsider the exemption as part of the post-implementation review of AASB 1049, on the basis that the issue should be considered in the context of a broader range of not-for-profit entities than whole of governments and GGSs.

BASIS FOR CONCLUSIONS ON AASB 2012-8

This Basis for Conclusions accompanies, but is not part of, AASB 1049. The Basis for Conclusions was originally published with AASB 2012-8 Amendments to AASB 1049 – Extension of Transitional Relief for the Adoption of Amendments to the ABS GFS Manual relating to Defence Weapons Platforms *(December 2012).*

Background

BC1 This Basis for Conclusions summarises the Australian Accounting Standards Board's considerations in reaching the conclusions in the Standard, following consideration of comments received in response to Exposure Draft ED 227 *Proposed Amendments to AASB 1049 – Extension of Transitional Relief for the Adoption of Amendments to the ABS GFS Manual relating to Defence Weapons Platforms*, issued in October 2012. Individual Board members gave greater weight to some factors than to others.

BC2 On 5 April 2011, the ABS published on its website, Chapter 2 *Amendments to Defence Weapons Platforms* of the ABS publication *Amendments to Australian Government Finance Statistics, 2005* (ABS Catalogue No. 5514.0). Due to the interrelationship between the ABS GFS Manual and AASB 1049 *Whole of Government and General Government Sector Financial Reporting*, the effect of the ABS Chapter 2 Amendments would be to require assets that are the subject of Chapter 2 to be measured at fair value, where reliably measurable, in the financial statements prepared in accordance with AASB 1049 for reporting periods beginning on or after 1 July 2012.

Considerations in extending the transitional relief

BC3 Prior to issuing ED 227, the Board considered a submission arguing that more time was needed to measure assets classified as defence weapons platforms at fair value, for the purposes of financial reporting under AASB 1049, due to the magnitude and complexity of the valuation exercise for such assets. Constituents familiar with the nature and quantity of the assets involved advised the Board that an extension of transitional relief for two years would be required to comply. The Board agreed that the extension is warranted, and considered that such an extension should be sufficient and therefore would not expect to provide further relief for such assets in the future.

BC4 The Board also considered the existing disclosure requirements in paragraphs 39(a)(ii) and 39A of AASB 1049 and decided that, in principle, they would be adequate during the extended period in which the ABS Chapter 2 Amendments are not applied in financial statements prepared in accordance with AASB 1049. However, to address concern that there might be potential confusion as to whether the disclosure requirements of paragraphs 39(a)(ii) and 39A would apply to an entity that elects to adopt the extended transitional relief, the Board decided to clarify in paragraph 39(a)(ii) that such an entity is regarded as not having applied the latest version of the ABS GFS Manual.

BC5 One Board member, Ian McPhee, abstained from voting on the issue of this Standard, which has the potential to significantly affect only the Australian Government, due to his role as the Auditor-General of that Government.

ILLUSTRATIVE EXAMPLES

The following examples accompany, but are not part of, AASB 1049.

Illustrative Examples A and B provide examples of acceptable formats for whole of government and GGS financial statements respectively, that are consistent with the requirements of this Standard and the assumptions made for the purpose of the illustrations. They also illustrate an acceptable style and format for reconciliation notes and functional information. Furthermore, sector information is illustrated for the whole of government in Illustrative Example A.

The styles and formats illustrated are not mandatory. Other styles and formats may be equally appropriate if they meet the requirements of this Standard.

To assist an understanding of the illustrations, particularly in relation to differences between GAAP and GFS, explanatory notes are provided at the end of Illustrative Example B and relate to both Illustrative Examples A and B. They do not form part of the illustrative financial statements or notes.

Illustrative Examples A and B do not purport to identify all possible differences between GAAP and GFS, nor to present in the financial statements all the line items as might be required by a different set of assumptions. Additionally, they do not illustrate the disclosure of comparative period information or the notes required by paragraphs 39[1], 41 (except the relevant reconciliation notes)[2], 52(a) and the explanation of differences required by 52(b)(ii)(B). They also do not illustrate all the disclosures required by other Australian Accounting Standards, such as the disclosure of budgetary information required by AASB 1055 *Budgetary Reporting*.

The amounts used are based on assumptions made for illustrative purposes only.

---

1   Illustrative Example C provides an example of the information to be included in the summary of significant accounting policies of the GGS in accordance with paragraph 39(b).

2   Illustrative Example D provides an example of the information to be included in the other explanatory notes of the whole of government and GGS regarding explanations of key technical terms in accordance with paragraph 41(a)(iii).

ILLUSTRATIVE EXAMPLE A

Whole of government statement of comprehensive income, statement of financial position, statement of changes in equity, statement of cash flows and selected notes

Statement of comprehensive income for the whole of government of the ABC Government for the year ended 30 June 20XX

	Notes	$m
Revenue from Transactions		
Taxation revenue		209,178
Other revenue		
Interest, other than swap interest		3,298
Dividends from associates (part of share of net profit/(loss) from associates)		3
Sales of goods and services		12,862
Other current revenues		2,792
		228,133
Expenses from Transactions		
Employee benefits expense		
Wages, salaries and supplements		(20,866)
Superannuation		(2,477)
Use of goods and services		(40,710)
Depreciation		(3,823)
Interest, other than swap interest and superannuation interest expenses		(4,841)
Subsidy expenses		(5,253)
Grants		(69,494)
Social benefits		(71,730)
Superannuation net interest expenses		(4,902)
Loss on write-off of financial assets at fair value through operating result		(380)
		(224,476)
NET RESULT FROM TRANSACTIONS – NET OPERATING BALANCE		**3,657**
Other Economic Flows – Included in Operating Result		
Other revenue		
Net swap interest revenue		577
Net foreign exchange gains		2,120
Net gain on sale of non-financial assets		343
Net gain on financial assets or liabilities at fair value through operating result		265
Amortisation of non-produced assets		(119)
Doubtful debts		(604)
Share of net profit/(loss) from associates, excluding dividends		(26)
		2,556
OPERATING RESULT		**6,213**
Other Economic Flows – Other Comprehensive Income		
Items that will not be reclassified to operating result		
Revaluations		1,589
Remeasurements of the defined benefit liability		866

AASB 1049   **Chartered Accountants Australia and New Zealand**

	Notes	$m
Items that may be reclassified subsequently to operating result		
Net gain on financial assets measured at fair value		2,946
		5,401
COMPREHENSIVE RESULT – TOTAL CHANGE IN NET WORTH BEFORE TRANSACTIONS WITH OWNERS IN THEIR CAPACITY AS OWNERS		**11,614**
KEY FISCAL AGGREGATES		
NET LENDING/(BORROWING)	S2	**5,100**
plus Net acquisition/(disposal) of non-financial assets from transactions		(1,443)
NET OPERATING BALANCE	S1	**3,657**
plus Net other economic flows		7,957
TOTAL CHANGE IN NET WORTH BEFORE TRANSACTIONS WITH OWNERS IN THEIR CAPACITY AS OWNERS	S3	**11,614**

Statement of financial position for the whole of government of the ABC Government as at 30 June 20XX

	Notes	$m
Assets		
Financial Assets		
Cash and deposits		14,070
Accounts receivable		18,080
Securities other than shares		78,438
Loans		9,956
Advances		7,758
Shares and other equity		
Investments accounted for using equity method		695
Investments in other entities		1,142
		130,139
Non-Financial Assets		
Produced assets		
Inventories		5,346
Machinery and equipment		67,014
Buildings and structures		16,654
Intangibles		1,380
Valuables		6,867
Non-produced assets		
Land		9,876
Intangibles		1,193
		108,330
TOTAL ASSETS		**238,469**

AASB

	Notes	$m
Liabilities		
Deposits held		81,311
Accounts payable		5,080
Securities other than shares		21,520
Borrowing		9,346
Superannuation		89,858
Provisions		30,298
TOTAL LIABILITIES		**237,413**
NET ASSETS/(LIABILITIES)		**1,056**
Accumulated surplus/(deficit)		(33,041)
Other reserves		34,097
NET WORTH	T	**1,056**

Statement of changes in equity for the whole of government of the ABC Government for the year ended 30 June 20XX

	Accumulated surplus/(deficit)	Asset revaluation reserve	Accumulated net gain on financial assets	Total equity
	$m	$m	$m	$m
Equity at 1 July 20XX-1	(40,120)	16,887	12,675	(10,558)
Total comprehensive result	7,079	1,589	2,946	11,614
EQUITY AT 30 JUNE 20XX	**(33,041)**	**18,476**	**15,621**	**1,056**

Statement of cash flows for the whole of government of the ABC Government for the year ended 30 June 20XX

	Notes	$m
Cash Flows from Operating Activities		
Cash received		
Taxes received		206,343
Sales of goods and services		10,624
Interest, excluding swap interest		3,298
Dividends from associates		3
Other receipts		3,161
		223,429
Cash paid		
Payments to and on behalf of employees		(19,996)
Purchases of goods and services		(41,019)
Interest, excluding swap interest		(4,841)
Subsidies		(5,253)

	Notes	$m
Grants		(69,494)
Social benefits		(70,597)
Other payments		(4,123)
		(215,323)
NET CASH FLOWS FROM OPERATING ACTIVITES		**8,106**

Cash Flows from Investing Activities
Non-Financial Assets

Sales of non-financial assets		3,036
Purchases of new non-financial assets		(5,238)
Net cash flows from investments in non-financial assets		(2,202)

Financial Assets (Policy Purposes)

Purchases of investments		(1,641)
Net cash flows from investments in financial assets (policy purposes)		(1,641)

Financial Assets (Liquidity Management Purposes)

Sales of investments		1,778
Purchases of investments		(9,084)
Net cash flows from investments in financial assets (liquidity management purposes)		(7,306)
NET CASH FLOWS FROM INVESTING ACTIVITIES		**(11,149)**

Cash Flows from Financing Activities
Cash received

Borrowing		9,692
Deposits received		6,947
Swap interest		3,617
Other financing		2,857
		23,113

Cash paid

Borrowing		(15,325)
Deposits paid		(1,841)
Swap interest		(3,040)
Other financing		(1,870)
		(22,076)
NET CASH FLOWS FROM FINANCING ACTIVITIES		**1,037**

NET INCREASE IN CASH AND CASH EQUIVALENTS		**(2,006)**
Cash and cash equivalents at beginning of year		16,076
CASH AND CASH EQUIVALENTS AT END OF YEAR		**14,070**

KEY FISCAL AGGREGATE

Net cash flows from operating activities		8,106
Net cash flows from investments in non-financial assets		(2,202)
CASH SURPLUS/(DEFICIT)	U	**5,904**

AASB

R1 Statement of comprehensive income for the whole of government by sector of the ABC Government for the year ended 30 June 20XX

	Notes	GGS $m	PNFC sector $m	PFC sector $m	Eliminations $m	Whole of Government $m
Revenue from Transactions						
Taxation revenue		209,178	-	-	-	209,178
Other revenue						
Interest, other than swap interest		1,304	113	3,969	(2,088)	3,298
Dividends and income tax from other sector entities		1,399			(1,399)	
Dividends from associates (part of share of net profit/(loss) from associates)		1	2			3
Sales of goods and services		4,314	6,079	3,677	(1,208)	12,862
Other current revenues		2,684	130	176	(198)	2,792
		218,880	6,324	7,822	(4,893)	228,133
Expenses from Transactions						
Employee benefits expense						
Wages, salaries and supplements		(14,178)	(6,302)	(386)		(20,866)
Superannuation		(2,069)	(395)	(13)		(2,477)
Use of goods and services		(37,898)	(2,855)	(550)	593	(40,710)
Depreciation		(3,672)	(125)	(26)		(3,823)
Interest, other than swap interest and superannuation interest expenses		(4,201)	(513)	(2,215)	2,088	(4,841)
Subsidy expenses		(5,742)			489	(5,253)
Grants		(69,692)			198	(69,494)
Social benefits		(71,856)			126	(71,730)
Income tax expenses			(200)	(151)	351	
Superannuation net interest expenses		(4,898)	(3)	(1)		(4,902)
Loss on write-off of financial assets at fair value through operating result		(380)				(380)
		(214,586)	(10,393)	(3,342)	3,845	(224,476)
NET RESULT FROM TRANSACTIONS – NET OPERATING BALANCE		**4,294**	**(4,069)**	**4,480**	**(1,048)**	**3,657**
Other Economic Flows – Included in Operating Result						
Other revenue						
Net swap interest revenue		340	69	168		577
Dividends from other sector entities		300		(300)		-

	Notes	GGS $m	PNFC sector $m	PFC sector $m	Eliminations $m	Whole of Government $m
Net foreign exchange gains/(losses)		599	(3)	1,524	-	2,120
Net gain on sale of non-financial assets		200	145	(2)	-	343
Net gain on financial assets or liabilities at fair value through operating result		220	-	45	-	265
Amortisation of non-produced assets		(75)	(43)	(1)	-	(119)
Doubtful debts		(500)	(63)	(41)	-	(604)
Share of net profit/(loss) from associates, excluding dividends		(51)	25	-	-	(26)
		1,033	130	1,693	(300)	2,556
OPERATING RESULT		**5,327**	**(3,939)**	**6,173**	**(1,348)**	**6,213**
Other Economic Flows – Other Comprehensive Income						
Items that will not be reclassified to operating result						
Revaluations		1,552	20	17	-	1,589
Remeasurements of the defined benefit liability		840	21	5	-	866
Items that may be reclassified subsequently to operating result						
Net gain on equity investments in other sector entities measured at proportional share of the carrying amount of net assets/(liabilities)		1,072	-	-	(1,072)	-
Net gain on financial assets measured at fair value		1,000	15	1,931	-	2,946
		4,464	56	1,953	(1,072)	5,401
COMPREHENSIVE RESULT – TOTAL CHANGE IN NET WORTH BEFORE TRANSACTIONS WITH OWNERS IN THEIR CAPACITY AS OWNERS		**9,791**	**(3,883)**	**8,126**	**(2,420)**	**11,614**
KEY FISCAL AGGREGATES						
NET LENDING/(BORROWING)	S2	**4,967**	**(3,347)**	**4,528**	**(1,048)**	**5,100**
plus Net acquisition/(disposal) of non-financial assets from transactions		(673)	(722)	(48)	-	(1,443)
NET OPERATING BALANCE	S1	**4,294**	**(4,069)**	**4,480**	**(1,048)**	**3,657**
plus Net other economic flows		5,497	186	3,646	(1,372)	7,957
TOTAL CHANGE IN NET WORTH BEFORE TRANSACTIONS WITH OWNERS IN THEIR CAPACITY AS OWNERS	S3	**9,791**	**(3,883)**	**8,126**	**(2,420)**	**11,614**

AASB

R3 Statement of changes in equity for the whole of government by sector of the ABC Government for the year ended 30 June 20XX

	Equity at 1 July 20XX-1 $m	Total comprehensive result $m	Dividends $m	Equity at 30 June 20XX $m
GGS				
Accumulated surplus/(deficit)	(26,491)	6,167	-	(20,324)
Asset revaluation reserve	12,161	1,552	-	13,713
Accumulated net gain on equity investments in other sector entities measured at proportional share of the carrying amount of net assets/(liabilities)	500	1,072	-	1,572
Accumulated net gain on financial assets measured at fair value	4,589	1,000	-	5,589
	(9,241)	9,791	-	550
PNFC sector				
Contributed equity	6,900	-	-	6,900
Accumulated surplus/(deficit)	15,334	(3,918)	(559)	10,857
Asset revaluation reserve	2,030	20	-	2,050
Accumulated net gain on financial assets measured at fair value	185	15	-	200
	24,449	(3,883)	(559)	20,007
PFC sector				
Contributed equity	350	-	-	350
Accumulated surplus/(deficit)	(4,526)	6,178	(789)	863
Asset revaluation reserve	1,690	17	-	1,707
Accumulated net gain on financial assets measured at fair value	7,901	1,931	-	9,832
	5,415	8,126	(789)	12,752
Eliminations	(31,181)	(2,420)	1,348	(32,253)
Total Whole of Government	**(10,558)**	**11,614**	**-**	**1,056**

Explanatory Note: Shares and contributed equity do not exist in a GGS context.

R4 Statement of cash flows for the whole of government by sector of the ABC Government for the year ended 30 June 20XX

	Notes	GGS $m	PNFC sector $m	PFC sector $m	Eliminations $m	Whole of Government $m
Cash Flows from Operating Activities						
Cash received						
Taxes received		206,343	-	-	-	206,343
Sales of goods and services		4,314	5,615	1,899	(1,204)	10,624
Interest, excluding swap interest		1,304	113	3,969	(2,088)	3,298
Dividends and income tax receipts		1,399	-	-	(1,399)	-
Dividends from associates		1	2	-	-	3
Other receipts		2,935	275	159	(208)	3,161
		216,296	6,005	6,027	(4,899)	223,429
Cash paid						
Income tax paid		-	(200)	(151)	351	-
Payments to and on behalf of employees		(16,247)	(3,397)	(352)	-	(19,996)
Purchases of goods and services		(37,898)	(3,151)	(559)	589	(41,019)
Interest, excluding swap interest		(4,201)	(513)	(2,215)	2,088	(4,841)
Subsidies		(5,742)	-	-	489	(5,253)
Grants		(69,692)	-	-	198	(69,494)
Social benefits		(70,723)	-	-	126	(70,597)
Other payments		(2,134)	(1,157)	(842)	10	(4,123)
		(206,637)	(8,418)	(4,119)	3,851	(215,323)
NET CASH FLOWS FROM OPERATING ACTIVITES		**9,659**	**(2,413)**	**1,908**	**(1,048)**	**8,106**
Cash Flows from Investing Activities						
Non-Financial Assets						
Sales of non-financial assets		1,734	1,234	68	-	3,036
Purchases of new non-financial assets		(4,504)	(689)	(45)	-	(5,238)
Net cash flows from investments in non-financial assets		(2,770)	545	23	-	(2,202)

(Continued)

AASB

(Continued)

	Notes	GGS $m	PNFC sector $m	PFC sector $m	Eliminations $m	Whole of Government $m
Financial Assets (Policy Purposes)						
Dividends received out of proceeds from sale of PNFC sector assets		300	-	-	(300)	-
Purchases of investments		(1,641)			-	(1,641)
Net cash flows from investments in financial assets (policy purposes)		(1,341)	-	-	(300)	(1,641)
Financial Assets (Liquidity Management Purposes)						
Sales of investments		500	45	1,977	(744)	1,778
Purchases of investments		(3,500)	(5)	(9,934)	4,355	(9,084)
Net cash flows from investments in financial assets (liquidity management purposes)		(3,000)	40	(7,957)	3,611	(7,306)
NET CASH FLOWS FROM INVESTING ACTIVITIES		**(7,111)**	**585**	**(7,934)**	**3,311**	**(11,149)**
Cash Flows from Financing Activities						
Cash received						
Borrowing		13,597	450	-	(4,355)	9,692
Deposits received		899	20	6,028	-	6,947
Swap interest		1,912	110	1,595	-	3,617
Other financing		233	169	2,455	-	2,857
		16,641	749	10,078	(4,355)	23,113
Cash paid						
Borrowing		(15,032)	(677)	(360)	744	(15,325)
Deposits paid		(213)	(7)	(1,621)	-	(1,841)
Swap interest		(1,572)	(41)	(1,427)	-	(3,040)
Dividends paid out of proceeds from sale of assets		-	(300)	-	300	-
Other dividends paid		-	(259)	(789)	1,048	-
Other financing		(765)	(990)	(115)	-	(1,870)
		(17,582)	(2,274)	(4,312)	2,092	(22,076)
NET CASH FLOWS FROM FINANCING ACTIVITIES		**(941)**	**(1,525)**	**5,766**	**(2,263)**	**1,037**
NET INCREASE IN CASH AND CASH EQUIVALENTS		**1,607**	**(3,353)**	**(260)**	**-**	**(2,006)**

	Notes	GGS $m	PNFC sector $m	PFC sector $m	Eliminations $m	Whole of Government $m	Explanatory Notes
Cash and cash equivalents at beginning of year		8,984	4,292	2,800	-	16,076	
CASH AND CASH EQUIVALENTS AT END OF YEAR		10,591	939	2,540	-	14,070	
KEY FISCAL AGGREGATE							
Net cash flows from operating activities		9,659	(2,413)	1,908	(1,048)	8,106	
Net cash flows from investments in non-financial assets		(2,770)	545	23	-	(2,202)	
Dividends paid out of proceeds from sale of assets		-	(300)	-	300	-	
Other dividends paid		-	(259)	(789)	1,048	-	
CASH SURPLUS/(DEFICIT)	U	6,889	(2,427)	1,142	300	5,904	
Note S1 – Reconciliation to GFS Net Operating Balance*							
Net result from transactions – net operating balance		4,294	(4,069)	4,480	(1,048)	3,657	
Convergence differences							
Use of goods and services – development costs		(45)	(41)	-	-	(86)	a
Depreciation – development costs		6	5	-	-	11	b
Social benefits		94	-	-	-	94	c
Dividends to GGS from other sector entities		-	(259)	(789)	1,048	-	d
Total convergence differences		55	(295)	(789)	1,048	19	
GFS NET OPERATING BALANCE		4,349	(4,364)	3,691	-	3,676	e
Note S2 – Reconciliation to GFS Net Lending/(Borrowing)*							
Net lending/(borrowing)	S1	4,967	(3,347)	4,528	(1,048)	5,100	
Convergence differences							
Relating to net operating balance		55	(295)	(789)	1,048	19	
Relating to net acquisition/(disposal) of non-financial assets from transactions		(100)	(7)	(1)	-	(108)	f
Total convergence differences		(45)	(302)	(790)	1,048	(89)	
GFS NET LENDING/(BORROWING)		4,922	(3,649)	3,738	-	5,011	

(Continued)

AASB

(*Continued*)

Note S3 – Reconciliation to GFS Total Change in Net Worth*

	Notes	GGS $m	PNFC sector $m	PFC sector $m	Eliminations $m	Whole of Government $m	Explanatory Notes
Comprehensive result – total change in net worth before transactions with owners in their capacity as owners		9,791	(3,883)	8,126	(2,420)	11,614	
Convergence differences							
Relating to net operating balance	S1	55	(295)	(789)	1,048	19	
Relating to other economic flows							
Dividends to GGS out of proceeds from sale of PNFC sector assets		(300)			300	-	g
Doubtful debts		500	63	41	-	604	h
Net gain on equity investments in other sector entities measured at proportional share of the carrying amount of net assets/(liabilities)		390			(390)	-	i
Share of net profit/(loss) from associates (excluding dividends)		51				51	j
Revaluations – market value of investments		(55)				(55)	k(i)
Revaluations – intangible assets		130	12			142	k(ii)
Revaluations – property			10		(10)	-	k(iii)
Remeasurement of shares and other contributed capital		-	4,093	(7,378)	3,285	-	l
Total convergence differences		771	3,883	(8,126)	4,233	761	
GFS TOTAL CHANGE IN NET WORTH		**10,562**	-	-	**1,813**	**12,375**	

* Determined in accordance with the ABS GFS Manual.

	Notes	GGS $m	PNFC sector $m	PFC sector $m	Eliminations $m	Whole of Government $m	Explanatory Notes
Note T – Reconciliation to GFS Net Worth*							
Net worth		550	20,007	12,752	(32,253)	1,056	
Convergence differences							
Assets							
Accounts receivable		1,800	165	298	-	2,263	m
Shares and other equity							
Investments accounted for using equity method		36	-	-	-	36	n
Investments in other sector entities		900	-	-	(900)	-	o
Non-financial assets							
Machinery and equipment		(30,745)	-	-	-	(30,745)	p(i)
Intangible assets – research and development		(400)	(69)	-	-	(469)	p(ii)
Intangible assets – no active market		150	-	-	-	150	
Liabilities							
Provisions		94	-	-	-	94	q(i)
Deferred tax liability		-	506	-	(506)	-	q(ii)
Shares and other contributed capital		-	(20,609)	(13,050)	33,659	-	r
Total convergence differences		(28,165)	(20,007)	(12,752)	32,253	(28,671)	
GFS NET WORTH		**(27,615)**	**-**	**-**	**-**	**(27,615)**	s
Note U – Reconciliation to GFS Cash Surplus/(Deficit)*							
Cash surplus/(deficit)		6,889	(2,427)	1,142	300	5,904	
Convergence difference							t
Adjustments to cash flows from investments in non-financial assets		-	-	-	-	-	
Finance leases and similar arrangements		(4)	-	-	-	(4)	u
GFS CASH SURPLUS/(DEFICIT)		**6,885**	**(2,427)**	**1,142**	**300**	**5,900**	

* Determined in accordance with the ABS GFS Manual.

Disaggregated information

Z Functional classification for whole of government

	Expenses, excluding losses, included in operating result 20XX $m	Assets 20XX $m
General public services	(52,194)	10,009
Defence	(13,018)	55,759
Public order and safety	(2,521)	5,587
Education	(14,156)	8,645
Health	(32,569)	2,002
Social security and welfare	(70,139)	4,045
Housing and community amenities	(1,727)	5,533
Recreation and culture	(2,291)	3,003
Fuel and energy	(1,546)	990
Agriculture, forestry, fishing and hunting	(3,711)	2,572
Mining and mineral resources, other than fuels; manufacturing; and construction	(3,756)	2,515
Transport and communications	(9,509)	37,051
Other economic affairs	(1,502)	1,046
Other purposes[b]	(15,576)	99,712
TOTAL	**(224,215)**	**238,469**

b   Explanatory note: For the purpose of this illustration, financial assets that are not allocated to other functions are included in the 'Other purposes' function.

Reconciliation of 'expenses, excluding losses, included in the operating result' to 'expenses from transactions' in the statement of comprehensive income

	20XX $m
Expenses from transactions	224,476
Less: loss on write-off of financial assets at fair value through operating result	(380)
	224,096
Plus: amortisation of non-produced assets	119
Expenses, excluding losses, included in operating result	**224,215**

ILLUSTRATIVE EXAMPLE B

General government sector statement of comprehensive income, statement of financial position, statement of changes in equity, statement of cash flows and selected notes

Statement of comprehensive income for the general government sector of the ABC Government for the year ended 30 June 20XX

	Notes	$m
Revenue from Transactions		
Taxation revenue		209,178
Other revenue		
Interest, other than swap interest		1,304
Dividends and income tax from other sector entities		1,399
Dividends from associates (part of share of net profit/(loss) from associates)		1
Sales of goods and services		4,314
Other current revenues		2,684
		218,880
Expenses from Transactions		
Employee benefits expense		
Wages, salaries and supplements		(14,178)
Superannuation		(2,069)
Use of goods and services		(37,898)
Depreciation		(3,672)
Interest, other than swap interest and superannuation interest expenses		(4,201)
Subsidy expenses		(5,742)
Grants		(69,692)
Social benefits		(71,856)
Superannuation net interest expenses		(4,898)
Loss on write-off of financial assets at fair value through operating result		(380)
		(214,586)
NET RESULT FROM TRANSACTIONS – NET OPERATING BALANCE		**4,294**
Other Economic Flows – Included in Operating Result		
Other revenue		
Net swap interest revenue		340
Dividends from other sector entities		300
Net foreign exchange gains		599
Net gain on sale of non-financial assets		200
Net gain on financial assets or liabilities at fair value through operating result		220
Amortisation of non-produced assets		(75)
Doubtful debts		(500)
Share of net profit/(loss) from associates, excluding dividends		(51)
		1,033
OPERATING RESULT		**5,327**

(Continued)

(Continued)

	Notes	$m
Other Economic Flows – Other Comprehensive Income		
Items that will not be reclassified to operating result		
Revaluations		1,552
Remeasurements of the defined benefit liability		840
Items that may be reclassified subsequently to operating result		
Net gain on equity investments in other sector entities measured at proportional share of carrying amount of net assets/(liabilities)		1,072
Net gain on financial assets measured at fair value		1,000
		4,464
COMPREHENSIVE RESULT – TOTAL CHANGE IN NET WORTH		**9,791**
KEY FISCAL AGGREGATES		
NET LENDING/(BORROWING)	S2	**4,967**
plus Net acquisition/(disposal) of non-financial assets from transactions		(673)
NET OPERATING BALANCE	S1	**4,294**
plus Net other economic flows		5,497
TOTAL CHANGE IN NET WORTH	S3	**9,791**

Statement of financial position for the general government sector of the ABC Government as at 30 June 20XX

	Notes	$m
Assets		
Financial Assets		
Cash and deposits		10,591
Accounts receivable		16,748
Securities other than shares		24,188
Loans		10,302
Advances		7,758
Shares and other equity		
Investments accounted for using equity method		365
Investments in other sector entities		32,759
		102,711
Non-Financial Assets		
Produced assets		
Inventories		4,832
Machinery and equipment		54,367
Buildings and structures		14,152
Intangibles		1,250
Valuables		6,442
Non-produced assets		
Land		5,196
Intangibles		747
		86,986
TOTAL ASSETS		**189,697**

	Notes	$m
Liabilities		
Deposits held		364
Accounts payable		5,253
Securities other than shares		60,650
Borrowing		6,246
Superannuation		88,540
Provisions		28,094
TOTAL LIABILITIES		**189,147**
NET ASSETS/(LIABILITIES)		**550**
Accumulated surplus/(deficit)		(20,324)
Other reserves		20,874
NET WORTH	T	**550**

Statement of changes in equity for the general government sector of the ABC Government for the year ended 30 June 20XX

	Accumulated surplus/(deficit)	Asset revaluation reserve	Accumulated net gain on equity investments in other sector entities	Accumulated net gain on other financial assets	Total equity
	$m	$m	$m	$m	$m
Equity at 1 July 20XX-1	(26,491)	12,161	500	4,589	(9,241)
Total comprehensive result	6,167	1,552	1,072	1,000	9,791
EQUITY AT 30 JUNE 20XX	**(20,324)**	**13,713**	**1,572**	**5,589**	**550**

Statement of cash flows for the general government sector of the ABC Government for the year ended 30 June 20XX

	Notes	$m
Cash Flows from Operating Activities		
Cash received		
Taxes received		206,343
Sales of goods and services		4,314
Interest, excluding swap interest		1,304
Dividends and income tax receipts		1,399
Dividends from associates		1
Other receipts		2,935
		216,296
		(Continued)

(Continued)

	Notes	$m
Cash paid		
Payments to and on behalf of employees		(16,247)
Purchases of goods and services		(37,898)
Interest, excluding swap interest		(4,201)
Subsidies		(5,742)
Grants		(69,692)
Social benefits		(70,723)
Other payments		(2,134)
		(206,637)
NET CASH FLOWS FROM OPERATING ACTIVITES		**9,659**
Cash Flows from Investing Activities		
Non-Financial Assets		
Sales of non-financial assets		1,734
Purchases of new non-financial assets		(4,504)
Net cash flows from investments in non-financial assets		(2,770)
Financial Assets (Policy Purposes)		
Dividends received out of proceeds from sale of PNFC sector assets		300
Purchases of investments		(1,641)
Net cash flows from investments in financial assets (policy purposes)		(1,341)
Financial Assets (Liquidity Management Purposes)		
Sales of investments		500
Purchases of investments		(3,500)
Net cash flows from investments in financial assets (liquidity management purposes)		(3,000)
NET CASH FLOWS FROM INVESTING ACTIVITIES		**(7,111)**
Cash Flows from Financing Activities		
Cash received		
Borrowing		13,597
Deposits received		899
Swap interest		1,912
Other financing		233
		16,641
Cash paid		
Borrowing		(15,032)
Deposits paid		(213)
Swap interest		(1,572)
Other financing		(765)
		(17,582)
NET CASH FLOWS FROM FINANCING ACTIVITIES		**(941)**
NET INCREASE IN CASH AND CASH EQUIVALENTS		**1,607**
Cash and cash equivalents at beginning of year		8,984
CASH AND CASH EQUIVALENTS AT END OF YEAR		**10,591**
KEY FISCAL AGGREGATE		
Net cash flows from operating activities		9,659
Net cash flows from investments in non-financial assets		(2,770)
CASH SURPLUS/(DEFICIT)	U	**6,889**

	Notes	$m	Explanatory Notes
Note S1 – Reconciliation to GFS Net Operating Balance*			
Net result from transactions – net operating balance		4,294	
Convergence differences			
Use of goods and services – development costs		(45)	a
Depreciation – development costs		6	b
Social benefits		94	c
Total convergence differences		55	
GFS NET OPERATING BALANCE		**4,349**	e
Note S2 – Reconciliation to GFS Net Lending/(Borrowing)*			
Net lending/(borrowing)		4,967	
Convergence differences			
Relating to net operating balance	S1	55	
Relating to net acquisition/(disposal) of non-financial assets from transactions		(100)	f
Total convergence differences		(45)	
GFS NET LENDING/(BORROWING)		**4,922**	
Note S3 – Reconciliation to GFS Total Change in Net Worth*			
Comprehensive result – total change in net worth		9,791	
Convergence differences			
Relating to net operating balance	S1	55	
Relating to other economic flows			
Dividends to GGS out of proceeds from sale of PNFC sector assets		(300)	g
Doubtful debts		500	h
Net gain on equity investments in other sector entities measured at proportional share of the carrying amount of net assets/(liabilities)		390	i
Share of net profit/(loss) from associates (excluding dividends)		51	j
Revaluations – market value of investments		(55)	k(i)
Revaluations – intangible assets		130	k(ii)
Total convergence differences		771	
GFS TOTAL CHANGE IN NET WORTH		**10,562**	

* Determined in accordance with the ABS GFS Manual.

(*Continued*)

(Continued)

	Notes	$m	Explanatory Notes
Note T – Reconciliation to GFS Net Worth*			
Net worth		550	
Convergence differences			
Assets			
Accounts receivable		1,800	m
Shares and other equity			
Investments accounted for using equity method		36	n
Investments in other sector entities		900	o
Non-financial assets			
Machinery and equipment		(30,745)	
Intangible assets – research and development		(400)	p(i)
Intangible assets – no active market		150	p(ii)
Liabilities			
Provisions		94	q(i)
Total convergence differences		(28,165)	
GFS NET WORTH		**(27,615)**	s
Note U – Reconciliation to GFS Cash Surplus/(Deficit)*			
Cash surplus/(deficit)		6,889	
Convergence differences			
Adjustments to cash flows from investments in non-financial assets			
Finance leases and similar arrangements		(4)	t
GFS CASH SURPLUS/(DEFICIT)		**6,885**	u

* Determined in accordance with the ABS GFS Manual.

Disaggregated information

Z Functional classification for general government sector

	Expenses, excluding losses, included in operating result 20XX $m	Assets 20XX $m
General public services	(50,661)	7,149
Defence	(13,018)	55,759
Public order and safety	(2,401)	3,991
Education	(13,482)	6,175
Health	(31,971)	1,430
Social security and welfare	(69,036)	2,899
Housing and community amenities	(1,645)	3,952

(Continued)

(Continued)

	Expenses, excluding losses, included in operating result 20XX $m	Assets 20XX $m
Recreation and culture	(2,182)	2,145
Fuel and energy	(1,473)	707
Agriculture, forestry, fishing and hunting	(3,535)	1,837
Mining and mineral resources, other than fuels; manufacturing; and construction	(3,578)	1,797
Transport and communications	(4,295)	13,418
Other economic affairs	(1,431)	747
Other purposes[b]	(15,573)	87,691
TOTAL	**(214,281)**	**189,697**

b   Explanatory note: For the purpose of this illustration, financial assets that are not allocated to other functions are included in the 'Other purposes' function.

Reconciliation of 'expenses, excluding losses, included in operating result' to 'expenses from transactions' in the statement of comprehensive income

	20XX $m
Expenses from transactions	214,586
Less: loss on write-off of financial assets at fair value through operating result	(380)
	214,206
Plus: amortisation of non-produced assets	75
Expenses, excluding losses, included in operating result	**214,281**

Explanatory notes supporting illustrative examples A and B

The following notes are for explanatory purposes only, and do not form part of the financial statements or accompanying notes illustrated in Illustrative Examples A or B.

The notes provide explanations of the convergence differences between the key fiscal aggregates presented in each of the financial statements and GFS measures of the key fiscal aggregates for the whole of government (including the sectors) and GGS.

Convergence differences relating to the statements of comprehensive income
Net operating balance
a   **Expenses from Transactions – Use of Goods and Services**

The convergence difference of ($45m) in the GGS and ($41m) in the PNFC sector arises because GFS expenses certain development costs and classifies them as expenses from transactions. However, the development costs are not recognised as expenses from transactions in the statement of comprehensive income because they are recognised as intangible assets upon acquisition. GFS treats goods and services used for research and development as use of goods and services expenses from transactions, rather than as acquisitions of intangible assets, even though some development activities are expected to bring benefits for more than one year (refer also to Note (b)).

The total difference of ($86m) flows through to the whole of government amounts.

b   **Expenses from Transactions – Depreciation**

The convergence difference of $6m in the GGS and $5m in the PNFC sector arises because GFS recognises a smaller amortisation of produced intangibles than is recognised as an expense from transactions in the statement of comprehensive income. GFS treats goods and services used for research and development as use of goods and services expense from transactions, rather than as acquisitions of intangible assets, even though some development activities may bring benefits for more than one year (refer also to Note (a)).

The total difference of $11m flows through to the whole of government amounts.

c   **Expenses from Transactions – Social Benefits**

The convergence difference of $94m in the GGS arises because GFS does not recognise a liability relating to the potential beneficiaries of a social benefit scheme who had not registered for benefits as at the reporting date. Therefore, GFS does not recognise the associated expense from transactions, whereas such an amount is recognised in the statement of comprehensive income and classified as expenses from transactions.

This difference flows through to the whole of government amounts.

d   **Dividends to GGS from Other Sector Entities**

The convergence difference comprises ($259m) in the PNFC sector and ($789m) in the PFC sector because GFS treats dividends to owners as an expense, whereas such an amount is not recognised as an expense in the statement of comprehensive income because it is treated as a distribution to owners and therefore a direct debit to equity.

The total difference of ($1,048m) does not flow through to the whole of government amounts as it arises from intersector transactions.

e   **Other Differences Included in the GFS Net Operating Balance**

A classification difference arises in the whole of government and the GGS, because GFS classifies the debt security written off by mutual agreement of $380m as a capital grant expense from transactions, whereas, although it is recognised as an expense from transactions in the statement of comprehensive income, it is classified as loss on write-off of financial assets at fair value through operating result. [For the purpose of Illustrative Examples A and B, the debt security is assumed to have satisfied the criteria in AASB 139 *Financial Instruments: Recognition and Measurement* for classification as a 'fair value through profit or loss' financial asset.] The write-off arose from the Government agreeing to forgive the outstanding debt of a Country. The classification difference has no impact on the amount of the GFS Net Operating Balance.

A GGS/PNFC elimination difference arises in respect of the treatment of $25m of the social benefits. Under GFS, certain transactions between the GGS and entities within the PNFC and PFC sectors are not eliminated on consolidation, whereas under AASB 10 *Consolidated Financial Statements* intragroup transactions that are not in substance transactions with external parties are eliminated in full. The GFS treatment has the effect of 'grossing up' both GFS 'revenue from transactions – other current revenues' and GFS 'expenses from transactions – grants' of the whole of government by equal amounts even though the key fiscal aggregates remain the same. [For the purpose of this illustration, it is assumed the GGS has compensated a PNFC entity for $25m of community service obligations, imposed by the GGS, that requires the PNFC entity to provide free services to a cohort of private individuals.] The compensation provided by the GGS to the PNFC entity is not eliminated under GFS (instead it is 'rerouted' through the household sector of the economy and therefore treated as an expense of the GGS to the household sector, and an expense of the household sector to the PNFC entity and therefore revenue of the PNFC entity). This convergence difference has no impact on the amount of the whole of government's GFS Net Operating Balance. This difference does not affect the GGS or the PNFC and PFC sectors but impacts the total of revenues and expenses in the whole of government statement of comprehensive income.

Net lending/(borrowing)

f   Net Acquisition/(Disposal) of Non-Financial Assets from Transactions

The convergence differences are explained as follows:

	Statement of Comprehensive Income $m	GFS $m	Convergence Difference $m	For explanations see notes
GGS				
Gross fixed capital formation	3,932	1,847	2,085	(a)
Depreciation	(3,747)	(1,562)	(2,185)	(b) #
Change in inventory	300	300	-	
Other transactions in non-financial assets	(1,158)	(1,158)	-	
Net acquisition/(disposal) of non-financial assets from transactions	(673)	(573)	(100)	
PNFC Sector				
Gross fixed capital formation	342	301	41	(a)
Depreciation	(168)	(120)	(48)	(b) #
Change in inventory	(9)	(9)	-	
Other transactions in non-financial assets	(887)	(887)	-	
Net acquisition/(disposal) of non-financial assets from transactions	(722)	(715)	(7)	
PFC Sector				
Gross fixed capital formation	18	18	-	
Depreciation	(27)	(26)	(1)	#
Change in inventory	2	2	-	
Other transactions in non-financial assets	(41)	(41)	-	
Net acquisition/(disposal) of non-financial assets from transactions	(48)	(47)	(1)	
Whole of Government				
Gross fixed capital formation	4,292	2,166	2,126	(a)
Depreciation	(3,942)	(1,708)	(2,234)	(b) #
Change in inventory	293	293	-	
Other transactions in non-financial assets	(2,086)	(2,086)	-	
Net acquisition/(disposal) of non-financial assets from transactions	(1,443)	(1,335)	(108)	

\#   Depreciation shown in the statement of comprehensive income column includes both depreciation and amortisation from non-produced assets. Note (b) explains the convergence difference so far as it relates to the item described as depreciation in the statement of comprehensive income. The convergence differences shown in this note also include the amounts for 'amortisation of non-produced assets' presented in the statement of comprehensive income of $75m for the GGS, $43m for the PNFC sector and $1m for the PFC sector.

AASB

Net other economic flows

g   **Other Economic Flows – Included in Operating Result – Other Revenue – Dividends to GGS from the sale of PNFC sector assets**

The convergence difference of ($300m) arises in the GGS because GFS classifies $300m of the distributions from other sector entities as a transaction in financial assets (that is, as a withdrawal of equity because it is funded from proceeds from sale of assets), whereas the statement of comprehensive income recognises it as dividend revenue and classifies it as other economic flows (refer also to Note i).

This difference does not flow through to the whole of government amounts as it arises from intersector transactions.

h   **Other Economic Flows – Included in Operating Result – Doubtful Debts**

The convergence differences of $500m in the GGS, $63m in the PNFC sector and $41m in the PFC sector arise because GFS does not recognise doubtful debts, whereas the statement of comprehensive income recognises doubtful debts and classifies it as other economic flows. In this example, no bad debts were written off from doubtful debts. GFS recognises amounts written off when there is mutual agreement with debtors as capital grants expenses in the period of the write-off, and recognises those written off unilaterally by the government as other economic flows also in the period of the write-off.

The total difference of $604m flows through to the whole of government amounts.

i   **Other Economic Flows – Other Comprehensive Income – Net Gain on Equity Investments in Other Sector Entities Measured at Proportional Share of the Carrying Amount of Net Assets/(Liabilities)**

The convergence differences comprise:

$90m in the GGS: The carrying amount of net assets (and therefore the change in carrying amount of net assets) of other sector entities determined under GFS principles and rules differs from the carrying amount of net assets (and therefore the change in carrying amount of net assets) of the subsidiaries recognised in the statement of financial position (being the carrying amount of net assets determined before elimination of intersector balances).

The difference is therefore equivalent to the total of those convergence differences affecting the total change in net worth impacting either through the net operating balance (itemised in Note S1 of Illustrative Example A) or other economic flows (other than transactions with owners in their capacity as owners in the form of dividends paid – itemised in Note S3 of Illustrative Example A). The components are:

	$m
Use of goods and services – development costs [PNFC]	(41)
Depreciation – development costs [PNFC]	5
Doubtful debts [PNFC]	63
Doubtful debts [PFC]	41
Revaluations – intangible assets [PNFC]	12
Revaluations – property [PNFC]	10
TOTAL	90

$300m in the GGS: GFS treats this amount as a distribution from other sector entities classified as a transaction in financial assets (that is, as a withdrawal of equity because it is funded from proceeds from sale of assets), whereas the statement of comprehensive income recognises it as dividend revenue and classifies it as other economic flows (refer also to Note g). Under GFS, the holding gain on other sector entities is determined after taking into account additions to and withdrawals from equity that have occurred.

The total difference of $390m does not flow through to the whole of government amounts as it arises from intersector items.

j   Other Economic Flows – Included in Operating Result – Share of Net Profit/(Loss) from Associates (Excluding Dividends)

The convergence difference of $51m arises in the GGS because GFS does not recognise the share of the associate's loss (excluding dividends), whereas consistent with the equity method of accounting, it is recognised as an expense of $51m and classified as an other economic flow and dividends are recognised as a revenue of $1m and classified as a transaction in the statement of comprehensive income. GFS recognises the decrease in the market value of investments in associates of $55m as an other economic flow (refer to Note k(ii)), and the dividends on such investments of $1m as dividend revenue from transactions.

This difference flows through to the whole of government amounts.

k   Other Economic Flows – Other Comprehensive Income – Revaluations

The convergence differences comprise:

k(i)   ($55m) in the GGS because GFS recognises the decrease in the market value of investments in associates of $55m as an other economic flow, whereas it is not recognised in the statement of comprehensive income. Consistent with the equity method of accounting, the statement of comprehensive income recognises the share of the associate's loss of $50m as a loss of $51m classified as other economic flows and revenue (from dividends) of $1m (refer also to Note j).

This difference flows through to the whole of government amounts.

k(ii) $130m in the GGS and $12m in the PNFC sector because GFS recognises the net increase in the revalued intangible assets as an other economic flow, whereas it is not recognised in the statement of comprehensive income. In accordance with paragraph 81 of AASB 138 *Intangible Assets*, the intangible assets in this example are not revalued because there is no active market for them.

The total difference of $142m flows through to the whole of government amounts.

k(iii) $10m in the PNFC sector because while GFS recognises the gross increase in the revalued asset (in Illustrative Example A, assumed to have arisen from an upward asset revaluation of properties), it does not recognise as an offset part of the increase in the revalued asset as being due to a corresponding increase in the deferred tax liability. (Refer also to Note q(ii))

This difference does not flow through to the whole of government amounts as the whole of government does not have a deferred tax liability.

l   Remeasurement of Shares and Other Contributed Capital

The convergence differences of $4,093m in the PNFC sector and ($7,378m) in the PFC sector arise because GFS measures net worth as assets less liabilities less share capital/contributed capital (remeasured). Because in Illustrative Example A PNFC and PFC sectors are 100 per cent owned by the GGS, the GFS net worth, and therefore the GFS change in net worth, of these sectors is zero. In effect, all of the convergence differences that impact on the comprehensive result are netted off for the PNFC and PFC sectors against the GFS remeasurement of shares and other contributed capital.

The total difference of ($3,285m) does not flow through to the whole of government amounts as they relate to the GGS ownership interest in PNFC/PFC sectors.

Convergence differences relating to the statements of financial position
Net worth

m   Assets – Financial Assets – Accounts Receivable

The convergence differences of $1,800m in the GGS, $165m in the PNFC sector and $298m in the PFC sector arise because GFS does not recognise doubtful debts, whereas a provision for doubtful debts is recognised in the statement of financial position.

This total difference of $2,263m flows through to the whole of government amounts.

n   **Assets – Financial Assets – Shares and Other Equity – Investments Accounted for Using Equity Method**

The convergence difference of $36m arises in the GGS because GFS recognises the net decrease in the market value of investments in associates, whereas the equity method of accounting is applied in the calculation of the carrying amount recognised in the statement of financial position.

This difference flows through to the whole of government amounts.

o   **Assets – Financial Assets – Shares and Other Equity – GGS Investments in Other Sector Entities**

The convergence difference of $900m arises in the GGS in relation to the measurement of equity investments in other sector entities measured at proportional share of the carrying amount of net assets/(liabilities), due to different definition, recognition and measurement principles and rules for certain assets and liabilities under GFS.

The difference is therefore equivalent to the total of those convergence differences affecting Net Worth (as itemised in Note T). The components are:

	$m
Amounts receivable [PNFC]	165
Amounts receivable [PFC]	298
Intangible assets – research and development [PNFC]	(69)
Deferred tax liability [PNFC]	506
TOTAL	900

This difference does not flow through to the whole of government amounts as it arises from an intersector item.

p   **Assets – Non-Financial Assets – Produced Assets – Intangibles**

The convergence differences comprise:

p(i)   ($400m) in the GGS and ($69m) in the PNFC sector because GFS treats research and development costs as use of goods and services expenses from transactions, whereas some are treated as acquisitions of intangible assets for the statement of financial position because some development activities are expected to bring benefits for more than one year.

This total difference of ($469m) flows through to the whole of government amounts.

p(ii) $150m in the GGS because GFS recognises the revaluation of certain intangible assets, whereas those intangible assets have not been revalued in the statement of financial position because there is no active market (in accordance with paragraph 81 of AASB 138).

This difference flows through to the whole of government amounts.

q   **Liabilities – Provisions**

The convergence differences comprise:

q(i) $94m in the GGS because GFS does not recognise certain provisions that are recognised in the statement of financial position as liabilities (for example, to the extent that they arise from constructive obligations for which there is no counterparty recognising a related financial asset).

This difference flows through to the whole of government amounts.

q(ii) $506m in the PNFC sector because GFS does not recognise the deferred tax liability.

This difference does not flow through to the whole of government amounts as it arises from a PNFC sector liability that is not a whole of government liability.

[Note: Depending on the arrangements operating in a particular jurisdiction, a GGS, as an income tax collector, may not be able to recognise a related revenue unless it meets the criteria in AASB 1004 *Contributions*. Under the tax regime assumed for the purpose of this example, the GGS, as the tax collector, does not recognise deferred tax balances because the tax events associated with the PNFC sector's deferred tax balances have not occurred, even though from the PNFC sector's viewpoint, the event is the recognition of the underlying assets and/or liabilities in accordance with AASB 112 *Income Taxes*. This treatment in the GGS accords with GFS, which does not recognise deferred tax assets. Therefore, no convergence difference arises.]

r   **Shares and Other Contributed Capital**

The convergence differences of ($20,609m) in the PNFC sector and ($13,050m) in the PFC sector arise because GFS measures net worth as assets less liabilities less shares/contributed capital, whereas shares/contributed capital are not deducted in the determination of GAAP net worth. Because in this example GFS measures shares/contributed capital of the PNFC and PFC sectors at the carrying amount of net assets of those sectors, PNFC and PFC sector GFS net worth is nil.

The total difference of ($33,659m) does not flow through to the whole of government amounts as they relate to the GGS ownership interest in the PNFC and PFC sectors.

s   **Classification Difference Included in the GFS Net Worth**

A classification difference arises in the GGS because GFS classifies $28,000m of the $28,094m of provisions as other accounts payable. The classification difference has no impact on the amount of the GFS Net Worth.

This difference flows through to whole of government amounts.

Convergence differences relating to the statements of cash flows
Cash surplus/(deficit)

t   **Cash Flows from Investments in Non-Financial Assets**

The convergence difference of ($4m) in the GGS arises because GFS recognises a notional cash outflow relating to new finance leases and similar arrangements in calculating cash surplus/(deficit), whereas the statement of cash flows does not recognise notional cash flows.

This difference flows through to the whole of government amounts.

u   **Classification Differences Included in the GFS Cash Surplus/(Deficit)**

For the whole of government and GGS, amounts of $41,019m and $37,898m respectively have been recognised as payments for purchases of goods and services from operating activities in the statement of cash flows.

Under GFS, the corresponding amounts are $41,105m and $37,943m respectively.

The convergence difference of $45m in the GGS is due to capitalised development costs that are classified as purchases of non-financial assets – which are investing activities in the statement of cash flows.

For the PNFC sector, an amount of $3,151m has been recognised as payments for purchases of goods and services from operating activities in the statement of cash flows. Under GFS, the corresponding amount is $3,192m.

The convergence difference of $41m comprises capitalised development costs that are classified as purchases of non-financial assets – which are classified as investing activities in the statement of cash flows.

The total convergence difference of $86m flows through to whole of government.

These classification differences have no impact on the amount of the GFS Cash Surplus/(Deficit).

ILLUSTRATIVE EXAMPLE C

Extract from the note containing the summary of significant accounting policies of a general government sector

> The following is an example of an extract from Note 1 of the financial statements for a year subsequent to the first year of adoption of this Standard, consistent with the requirements of paragraph 39. This example assumes that the GGS financial statements are presented separately from the whole of government financial statements, and that the most recent version of the ABS GFS Manual has been applied.

The financial statements of the General Government Sector (GGS) of *[name of the Government]* have been prepared in accordance with AASB 1049 *Whole of Government and General Government Sector Financial Reporting*, which requires compliance with all Australian Accounting Standards except those identified below. The purpose of the financial statements is to provide users with information about the stewardship by the Government in relation to its GGS and accountability for the resources entrusted to it; information about the financial position, changes in net assets/(liabilities), performance and cash flows of the Government's GGS; and information that facilitates assessments of the macro-economic impact of the Government's GGS.

The GGS of *[name of the Government]* is a component of the Whole of Government of *[name of the Government]*. The GGS is determined in accordance with the principles and rules contained in the Australian Bureau of Statistics publications:

(a)   *Australian System of Government Finance Statistics: Concepts, Sources and Methods, 2005* (ABS Catalogue No. 5514.0); and

(b)   *Amendments to Australian System of Government Finance Statistics, 2005* (ABS Catalogue No. 5514.0)

published on the ABS website on *[publication date, or refer to effective date if specified by the ABS]* (ABS GFS Manual). The GGS consists of all government units and non-profit institutions controlled and mainly financed by government. Government units are legal entities established by political processes that have legislative, judicial, or executive authority over other units and which provide goods and services to the community or to individuals on a non-market basis; and make transfer payments to redistribute income and wealth. Non-profit institutions are created for the purpose of producing or distributing goods and services but are not a source of income, profit or other financial gain for the government.

The Standard under which the GGS financial statements are prepared does not require full application of AASB 10 *Consolidated Financial Statements* and AASB 139 *Financial Instruments: Recognition and Measurement*. Assets, liabilities, income, expenses and cash flows of government controlled entities that are in the Public Non-Financial Corporations sector and the Public Financial Corporations sector are not separately recognised in the GGS of *[name of the Government's]* financial statements. Instead, the GGS financial statements recognise an asset, being the controlling equity investment in those entities, and recognise a gain or loss relating to changes in the carrying amount of that asset, measured in accordance with AASB 1049. Readers are referred to the Whole of Government general purpose financial statements of *[name of the Government]* for the year ended 30 June 20XX for financial information that separately recognises assets, liabilities, income, expenses and cash flows of all entities under the control of the *[name of the Government]*.

The ABS GFS Manual also provides the basis upon which Government Finance Statistics (GFS) information that is contained in the financial statements is prepared. In particular, notes disclosing key fiscal aggregates of net worth, net operating balance, total change in net worth, net lending/(borrowing) and cash surplus/(deficit) determined using the principles and rules in the ABS GFS Manual are included in the financial statements, together with a reconciliation of those key fiscal aggregates to the corresponding key fiscal aggregates recognised in the financial statements.

ILLUSTRATIVE EXAMPLE D

Key technical terms used in the complete sets of financial statements

> This illustration provides an example of the presentation of explanations of selected key technical terms used in the Whole of Government and GGS Financial Statements and Selected Notes (Illustrative Examples A and B), as required by paragraph 41(a)(iii) of this Standard.
>
> This illustration presents generic explanations, suitable in both a whole of government and GGS context, except where indicated. In instances where the generic definition is not necessarily appropriate, further guidance has been provided.

Cash surplus/(deficit) is net cash flows from operating activities plus net cash flows from acquisition and disposal of non-financial assets and less distributions paid. GFS cash surplus/(deficit) also deducts the value of assets acquired under finance leases and similar arrangements.

Comprehensive result (total change in net worth before transactions with owners in their capacity as owners)[5] is the net result of all items of income and expense recognised for the period. It is the aggregate of operating result and other comprehensive income, other than transactions with owners in their capacity as owners.

Convergence difference is the difference between the amounts recognised in the financial statements compared with the amounts determined for GFS purposes as a result of differences in definition, recognition, measurement, classification and consolidation principles and rules.

Financial asset is any asset that is:

(a)   cash;

(b)   an equity instrument of another entity;

(c)   a contractual right:

    (i)   to receive cash or another financial asset from another entity; or

    (ii)   to exchange financial assets or financial liabilities with another entity under conditions that are potentially favourable to the entity; or

(d)   a contract that will or may be settled in the entity's own equity instruments and is:

    (i)   a non-derivative for which the entity is or may be obliged to receive a variable number of the entity's own equity instruments; or

    (ii)   a derivative that will or may be settled other than by the exchange of a fixed amount of cash or another financial asset for a fixed number of the entity's own equity instruments. For this purpose the entity's own equity instruments do not include instruments that are themselves contracts for the future receipt or delivery of the entity's own equity instruments.

General Government Sector (GGS) is the institutional sector comprising all government units and non-profit institutions controlled and mainly financed by government.

Government Finance Statistics (GFS) enable policymakers and analysts to study developments in the financial operations, financial position and liquidity situation of the government. More details about the GFS can be found in the Australian Bureau of Statistics (ABS) publications *Australian System of Government Finance Statistics: Concepts, Sources and Methods, 2005* (ABS Catalogue No. 5514.0) and *Amendments to Australian System of*

---

5   Explanatory note: The term 'transactions with owners in their capacity as owners' is most pertinent in a whole of government context. Such transactions may occur between the GGS, as owner, and the PNFC/PFC sectors and are therefore required to be disclosed in the sector information included in the whole of government financial statements. In addition, transactions with owners in their capacity as owners may occur in a whole of government context in relation to partly-owned subsidiaries. Accordingly, the GGS financial statements could use the alternative term 'Comprehensive result (total change in net worth)' defined as the net result of all items of income and expense recognised for the period. It is the aggregate of operating result and other changes in equity.

Government Finance Statistics, 2005 (ABS Catalogue No. 5514.0) published on the ABS website.

Gross fixed capital formation is the value of acquisition less disposals of new and existing produced assets that can be used in production, other than inventories.

Mutually agreed bad debts are financial assets written off where there was prior knowledge and consent by the counterparties.

Net acquisition/(disposal) of non-financial assets from transactions is gross fixed capital formation less depreciation plus changes in inventories plus other transactions in non-financial assets.

Net actuarial gains includes actuarial gains and losses on defined benefit superannuation plans.

Net cash flows from investments in financial assets (liquidity management purposes) is cash receipts from liquidation or repayment of investments in financial assets for liquidity management purposes less cash payments for such investments. Investment for liquidity management purposes means making funds available to others with no policy intent and with the aim of earning a commercial rate of return.

Net cash flows from investments in financial assets (policy purposes) is cash receipts from the repayment and liquidation of investments in financial assets for policy purposes less cash payments for acquiring financial assets for policy purposes. Acquisition of financial assets for policy purposes is distinguished from investments in financial assets (liquidity management purposes) by the underlying government motivation for acquiring the assets. Acquisition of financial assets for policy purposes is motivated by government policies such as encouraging the development of certain industries or assisting citizens affected by natural disaster.

Net gain on equity investments in other sector entities measured at proportional share of the carrying amount of net assets/(liabilities) comprises the net gains relating to the equity held by the GGS in other sector entities. It arises from a change in the carrying amount of net assets of the subsidiaries. The net gains are measured based on the proportional share of the subsidiary's carrying amount of net assets/(liabilities) before elimination of intersector balances.

Net lending/(borrowing) is net operating balance minus the net acquisition/(disposal) of non-financial assets. It is also equal to transactions in the net acquisition/(disposal) of financial assets minus the net incurrence of liabilities. It indicates the extent to which financial resources are placed at the disposal of the rest of the economy or the utilisation of financial resources generated by the rest of the economy. It is an indicator of the financial impact on the rest of the economy.

Net other economic flows is the net change in the volume or value of assets and liabilities that does not result from transactions.

Net result from transactions – net operating balance is revenue from transactions minus expenses from transactions. It is a summary measure of the ongoing sustainability of operations. It excludes gains and losses resulting from changes in price levels and other changes in the volume of assets. It is the component of the change in net worth that is due to transactions and can be attributed directly to government policies.

Net worth is assets less liabilities and shares/contributed capital. For the GGS, net worth is assets less liabilities, since shares and contributed capital do not exist in a GGS context[6]. It is an economic measure of wealth and reflects the contribution to the wealth of Australia. The change in net worth is the preferred measure for assessing the sustainability of fiscal activities.

Non-financial assets are all assets that are not 'financial assets'.

Non-produced assets are assets needed for production that have not themselves been produced. They include land, subsoil assets, and certain intangible assets.

---

6   Explanatory note: The reference to shares/contributed capital is most pertinent in a whole of government context. As an alternative, the GGS financial statements could define 'net worth' as 'assets less liabilities' because shares and contributed capital do not exist in a GGS context.

Non-produced intangibles are intangible assets needed for production that have not themselves been produced. They include constructs of society such as patents.

Operating result is a measure of financial performance of the operations for the period. It is the net result of items of revenue, gains and expenses (including losses) recognised for the period, excluding those that are classified as 'other comprehensive income'.

Other current revenues refers to current revenue other than current revenue from taxes, sales of goods and services, and property income. It includes revenue from fines other than penalties imposed by tax authorities.

Other economic flows – see definition of 'net other economic flows' above.

Other sector entities are government controlled entities that are not part of the GGS.

Public Financial Corporations (PFC) sector is the institutional sector comprising resident government controlled corporations and quasi- corporations mainly engaged in financial intermediation or provision of auxiliary financial services.

Public Non-Financial Corporations (PNFC) sector is the institutional sector comprising resident government controlled corporations and quasi- corporations mainly engaged in the production of market goods and/or non- financial services.

Quasi-corporation is an unincorporated enterprise that functions as if it were a corporation, has the same relationship with its owner as a corporation, and keeps a separate set of accounts.

Securities other than shares are negotiable financial instruments serving as evidence of the obligations to settle by means of providing cash, a financial instrument, or some other item of economic value. The security normally specifies a schedule for interest payments and principal repayments. Some examples are: bills, bonds and debentures, commercial paper, and securitised mortgage loans.

Social benefits are transfers in cash or in kind to relieve households of the burden of a defined set of social risks. Social risks are events or circumstances that may adversely affect the welfare of households either by imposing additional demands on their resources or by reducing their incomes.

Transactions are interactions between two units by mutual agreement or an action within a unit that is analytically useful to treat as a transaction.

Unilaterally determined bad debts are financial assets written off without an agreement with the debtor in cases such as bankruptcy of the debtor.

Use of goods and services is the total value of goods and services used in production, and use of goods acquired for resale. Goods and services acquired for use as direct in-kind transfers to households or as grants are excluded.

Valuables are produced goods of considerable value that are acquired and held primarily as stores of value over time and are not used primarily for purposes of production or consumption. They include works of art not used primarily in museums to produce services for the public.

Wages, salaries and supplements consist of all uncapitalised compensation of employees except for superannuation. It includes pay in cash or in-kind.

Whole of government financial statements are financial statements that are prepared in accordance with Australian Accounting Standards, including AASB 10 *Consolidated Financial Statements*, and thereby separately recognise assets, liabilities, income, expenses, and cash flows of all entities under the control of the government on a line-by-line basis.

AASB 1050

Administered Items

(Compiled December 2013)

This compiled Standard applies to annual reporting periods beginning on or after 1 January 2014. Early application is not permitted. It incorporates relevant amendments made up to and including 20 December 2013.

Prepared on 1 July 2014 by the staff of the Australian Accounting Standards Board.

CONTENTS

COMPILATION DETAILS
COMPARISON WITH INTERNATIONAL PRONOUNCEMENTS
ACCOUNTING STANDARD
AASB 1050 *ADMINISTERED ITEMS*

Australian Accounting Standard AASB 1050 *Administered Items* (as amended) is set out in paragraphs 1 – 25. All the paragraphs have equal authority. Paragraphs in **bold type** state the main principles. AASB 1050 is to be read in the context of other Australian Accounting Standards, including AASB 1048 *Interpretation of Standards*, which identifies the Australian Accounting Interpretations. In the absence of explicit guidance, AASB 108 *Accounting Policies, Changes in Accounting Estimates and Errors* provides a basis for selecting and applying accounting policies.

COMPILATION DETAILS

Accounting Standard AASB 1050 *Administered Items* as amended

This compiled Standard applies to annual reporting periods beginning on or after 1 January 2014. It takes into account amendments up to and including 20 December 2013 and was prepared on 1 July 2014 by the staff of the Australian Accounting Standards Board (AASB).

This compilation is not a separate Accounting Standard made by the AASB. Instead, it is a representation of AASB 1050 (December 2007) as amended by other Accounting Standards, which are listed in the Table below.

Table of Standards

Standard	Date made	Application date *(annual reporting periods ... on or after ...)*	Application, saving or transitional provisions
AASB 1050	13 Dec 2007	*(beginning)* 1 Jul 2008	see (a) below
AASB 2010-2	30 Jun 2010	*(beginning)* 1 Jul 2013	see (b) below
AASB 2013-9	20 Dec 2013	Pt B *(beginning)* 1 Jan 2014	see (c) below

(a) Entities may elect to apply this Standard to annual reporting periods beginning on or after 1 January 2005 but before 1 July 2008, provided that the Standards listed in paragraph 4 are also applied to such periods.

(b) Entities may elect to apply this Standard to annual reporting periods beginning on or after 1 July 2009 but before 1 July 2013, provided that AASB 1053 *Application of Tiers of Australian Accounting Standards* is also applied to such periods.

(c) Early application of Part B of this Standard is not permitted.

Table of amendments

Paragraph affected	How affected	By ... [paragraph]
5	deleted	AASB 2013-9B [37, 38]
6A-6B (and preceding heading)	added	AASB 2010-2 [47]

COMPARISON WITH INTERNATIONAL PRONOUNCEMENTS

This Standard contains relevant requirements for the disclosure of administered items by government departments that have been relocated from AAS 29 *Financial Reporting by Government Departments* in substantially unamended form (with some exceptions, as noted in Appendix A). Accordingly, the development of this Standard did not involve consideration of International Public Sector Accounting Standards (IPSASs) issued by the International Public Sector Accounting Standards Board (IPSASB) or International Financial Reporting Standards (IFRSs) issued by the International Accounting Standards Board (IASB).

The longer-term review of accounting for administered items will involve consideration of international pronouncements.

AASB 1050 and IPSASs

At the date of issue, this Standard has no corresponding IPSAS dealing specifically with administered items. Consistent with this Standard, paragraph 12 of IPSAS 9 *Revenue from Exchange Transactions* notes that amounts collected on behalf of third parties in a custodial or agency relationship are excluded from revenue.

The IPSASB is undertaking a project to develop a public sector conceptual framework. Administered items is a topic that will be addressed as part of that project.

AASB 1050 and IFRSs

At the date of issue, this Standard has no corresponding IFRS dealing specifically with administered items. Consistent with this Standard, paragraph 8 of IAS 18 *Revenue* notes that amounts collected on behalf of third parties in an agency relationship are not revenue. In addition, where a bank is engaged in significant trust activities (which excludes safe custody functions), paragraph 55 of IAS 30 *Disclosures in the Financial Statements of Banks and Similar Financial Institutions* (superseded by IFRS 7 *Financial Instruments: Disclosures* from 1 January 2007) requires the disclosure of that fact and an indication of the extent of those activities.

ACCOUNTING STANDARD AASB 1050

The Australian Accounting Standards Board made Accounting Standard AASB 1050 *Administered Items* on 13 December 2007.

This compiled version of AASB 1050 applies to annual reporting periods beginning on or after 1 January 2014. It incorporates relevant amendments contained in other AASB Standards made by the AASB up to and including 20 December 2013 (see Compilation Details).

ACCOUNTING STANDARD AASB 1050
ADMINISTERED ITEMS

Objective

1   The objective of this Standard is to specify requirements for government departments relating to administered items. Disclosures made in accordance with this Standard provide users with information relevant to assessing the performance of a government department, including accountability for resources entrusted to it.

Application

2   **This Standard applies to general purpose financial statements of government departments.**

3   **This Standard applies to annual reporting periods beginning on or after 1 July 2008.**
       [Note: For application dates of paragraphs changed or added by an amending Standard, see Compilation Details.]

4   **This Standard may be applied to annual reporting periods beginning on or after 1 January 2005 but before 1 July 2008, provided there is early adoption for the same annual reporting period of the following pronouncements being issued at about the same time, as applicable:**

       (a)   **AASB 1004 *Contributions*;**

       (b)   **AASB 1049 *Whole of Government and General Government Sector Financial Reporting*;**

       (c)   **AASB 1051 *Land Under Roads*;**

       (d)   **AASB 1052 *Disaggregated Disclosures*;**

       (e)   **AASB 2007-9 *Amendments to Australian Accounting Standards arising from the Review of AASs 27, 29 and 31*; and**

       (f)   **AASB Interpretation 1038 *Contributions by Owners Made to Wholly-Owned Public Sector Entities*.**

5   [Deleted by the AASB]

6　When applicable, this Standard, together with the Standards referred to in paragraph 4, supersede AAS 29 *Financial Reporting by Government Departments* as issued in June 1998, as amended.

Reduced disclosure requirements

6A　The following do not apply to entities preparing general purpose financial statements under Australian Accounting Standards – Reduced Disclosure Requirements:

(a)　paragraphs 7(a)(ii), 7(b)(ii) and 8; and

(b)　in paragraph 14, the words "and by activity" in the third sentence.

Entities applying Australian Accounting Standards – Reduced Disclosure Requirements may elect to comply with some or all of these excluded requirements.

6B　The requirements that do not apply to entities preparing general purpose financial statements under Australian Accounting Standards – Reduced Disclosure Requirements are identified in this Standard by shading of the relevant text.

Disclosure of administered income, expenses, assets and liabilities

7　A government department shall disclose the following in its complete set of financial statements in relation to activities administered by the government department:

(a)　administered income, showing separately:

　(i)　each major class of income; and

　(ii)　in respect of each major class of income, the amounts reliably attributable to each of the government department's activities and the amounts not attributable to activities;

(b)　administered expenses, showing separately:

　(i)　each major class of expense; and

　(ii)　in respect of each major class of expense, the amounts reliably attributable to each of the government department's activities and the amounts not attributable to activities;

(c)　administered assets, showing separately each major class of asset; and

(d)　administered liabilities, showing separately each major class of liability.

8　AASB 1052 specifies requirements for the disclosure of income and expenses attributable to a government department's activities. The principles in that Standard are applied in disclosing administered income and expenses reliably attributable to activities in accordance with paragraphs 7(a)(ii) and 7(b)(ii) of this Standard.

9　A government department's operating statement only recognises income and expenses of the government department. Similarly, a government department's statement of financial position only recognises assets that the government department controls and liabilities that involve a future sacrifice of the government department's assets.

10　Items recognised in the statement of financial position include the assets and liabilities of the trusts that the government department controls and from whose activities the government department obtains benefits.

11　The responsibilities of a government department may encompass the levying or collection of taxes, fines and fees, the provision of goods and services at a charge to recipients, and the transfer of funds to eligible beneficiaries. These activities may give rise to income and expenses that are not attributable to the government department.

This occurs, for example, where the government department is unable to use for its own purposes the proceeds of user charges, taxes, fines and fees it collects without further authorisation, or where the transfer of funds to eligible beneficiaries does not involve a reduction in the assets recognised in the government department's statement of financial position. In addition, the government department may manage government assets in the capacity of an agent and may incur liabilities that, for example, while involving a future disbursement from the Consolidated Revenue Fund or other Fund will not involve a sacrifice of the assets that the government department controls as at the end of the reporting period. This administered income and these administered expenses, assets and liabilities are not recognised in the government department's operating statement or statement of financial position.

12   A government department's ability to control all, or a portion of, the proceeds of the user charges, fines and fees it levies may be subject to complex arrangements. Consistent with those arrangements, where a government department does not control any of the proceeds of the user charges, fines and fees that it levies, it does not recognise any of the proceeds of those user charges, fines and fees as income. Similarly, where, as a result of automatic appropriations or other authority, a government department controls some but not all of the proceeds of user charges, fines and fees, the department recognises as income only those amounts that it controls.

13   If taxes, fines, fees and other amounts that are not controlled by a government department were to be recognised as assets or income by the collecting government department, users could incorrectly assume that these amounts were available for the government department's use.

14   The tax revenues, user charges, fines and fees administered by a government department and the amount of funds transferred to eligible beneficiaries are an important indicator of the government department's performance in achieving its objectives. Therefore, paragraph 7 requires disclosure of income and expenses administered by a government department that are not recognised in the government department's operating statement. Disclosure of this information by major class and by activity facilitates an assessment of activity costs and cost recoveries, and is therefore relevant to parliamentary decision making and enhances the discharge of accountability obligations. Even though a government department does not control such items, the effective and efficient administration of these items is an important role of the government department.

Taxes

15   It is unlikely that taxes, for example, income tax, will qualify as income of the agency responsible for their collection, for example, the Australian Taxation Office, or the central agency responsible for management of the Consolidated Revenue Fund, Trust Fund or other Fund, for example, Treasury. This is because the agency responsible for collecting taxes does not normally control the future economic benefits embodied in tax collections. Similarly, Treasury may be responsible for bank accounts into which tax collections are deposited, but until parliament has 'appropriated funds' for Treasury use or authorised the Treasury to make payments, the Treasury will not control those tax revenues.

16   Parliamentary appropriations made to enable the tax collection agency to perform its services are income of that agency. This is because the agency has the authority to deploy the appropriated funds for the achievement of its objectives and, consequently, controls the assets arising from the appropriation.

Transfer payments

17   A government department does not recognise as income and expenses those amounts that the government department is responsible for transferring to eligible beneficiaries, consistent with legislation or other authority, but that the government department does not control. If these amounts were recognised as income on receipt by the

government department and as expenses on payment by the government department, users could incorrectly assume that the government department controlled these amounts. Nevertheless, this Standard requires such amounts to be disclosed in the complete set of financial statements because that information may be relevant for understanding the government department's financial performance, including assessments of accountability. Even though a government department does not control such items, their effective and efficient administration is an important role of the government department.

18   Consistent with a government department's objectives and with legislation or other authority, amounts appropriated to government departments may include amounts to be transferred to third parties or recoupment of such amounts previously transferred by the government department. Such transfers may encompass payments for unemployment benefits, family allowances, age and invalid pensions, disaster relief, and grants and subsidies made to other governments or to other government or private sector entities.

19   Whether a government department recognises the amounts appropriated for transfer during the reporting period as income, and the amounts transferred during that reporting period as expenses, depends on whether the government department controls the assets to be transferred, and whether the amounts subsequently transferred constitute a reduction in the net assets of the government department.

20   Where amounts are transferred to eligible beneficiaries and the identity of the beneficiaries and the amounts to be transferred to them are determined by reference to legislation or other authority, it is unlikely that the government department controls the funds to be transferred. The government department is merely the agent responsible for the administration of the transfer process. As such, the government department does not benefit from the assets held for transfer, nor does it have the capacity to deny or regulate the access of eligible beneficiaries to the assets. Accordingly, the government department does not recognise assets and income in respect of amounts appropriated for transfer, nor expenses in respect of the amounts subsequently transferred.

21   Although transfers not controlled by a government department do not qualify for recognition in the financial statements, information about their nature and amount is relevant for understanding the government department's financial performance.

22   Details of the broad categories of recipients and the amounts transferred to those recipients shall be disclosed in the government department's complete set of financial statements.

23   In some cases it may not be clear whether the government department controls amounts to be transferred to eligible beneficiaries. For example, amounts may be appropriated to a government department for subsequent transfer, but the government department can exercise significant discretion in determining the amount or timing of payment, the identity of beneficiaries and the conditions under which the payments are to be made. In such cases, preparers and auditors use their judgement in deciding whether the government department controls the amounts to be transferred.

Accounting basis

24   To facilitate the assessment of the costs incurred and the cost recoveries generated as a result of the government department's activities, administered income, expenses, assets and liabilities are reported on the same basis adopted for the recognition of the elements of the financial statements.

Display of information about administered items

25   The manner in which administered transactions are displayed in the financial statements of a government department will depend on the administrative arrangements adopted by the controlling government, and may therefore vary from jurisdiction to jurisdiction. For example, in some jurisdictions it may be appropriate for administered transactions to be displayed as a separate schedule

to the operating statement and/or the statement of financial position. In other jurisdictions, a government department's accountability for administered transactions may mean that it is appropriate for administered transactions to be displayed with, but clearly distinguishable from, the government department's operating statement and/or statement of financial position.

APPENDIX A

COMPARISON OF AASB 1050 WITH AAS 29

This Appendix accompanies, but is not part of, AASB 1050.

This Standard reproduces the requirements relating to administered items contained in AAS 29, except that:

(a) paragraph 5.2.5 of AAS 29 encouraged disclosure of items collected or distributed on behalf of another entity or held in legal custody that are neither administered nor controlled. This Standard does not contain such an encouragement;

(b) in relation to transfer payments, paragraph 10.5.15 of AAS 29 noted that transfer payments not controlled by a government department do not qualify for recognition. However, the paragraph contemplated disclosure of the broad categories of recipients and the amounts transferred to those recipients. Paragraph 22 of this Standard requires such disclosures;

(c) paragraph 12.9.4 of AAS 29 encouraged the disclosure of information about administered assets and administered liabilities on an activity basis. This Standard does not contain such an encouragement; and

(d) paragraph 8 of this Standard requires the principles in AASB 1052 *Disaggregated Disclosures* to be applied in disclosing administered income and expenses reliably attributable to activities. AAS 29 did not include such a specific requirement.

The following table provides source references to paragraphs 7–25 of this Standard, most of which were derived from AAS 29. It is provided to facilitate an understanding of, and assist in the application of, the requirements in this Standard.

Paragraph in AASB 1050	Relevant source paragraph/s in AAS 29
7	12.9
8	New paragraph
9	12.9.1
10	5.2.5
11	12.9.2
12	10.4.2
13	6.3.11
14	12.9.3 and last sentence of 6.3.11
15	10.5.9
16	First two sentences of paragraph 10.5.10
17	6.3.12
18	10.5.11
19	10.5.12
20	10.5.13
21–22	10.5.15

Paragraph in AASB 1050	Relevant source paragraph/s in AAS 29
23	10.5.16
24	12.9.6
25	12.9.5

BASIS FOR CONCLUSIONS

This Basis for Conclusions accompanies, but is not part of, AASB 1050.

Introduction

BC1 This Basis for Conclusions summarises the Board's considerations in developing this Standard in the context of the Board's short-term review of the requirements in AAS 27 *Financial Reporting by Local Governments*, AAS 29 *Financial Reporting by Government Departments* and AAS 31 *Financial Reporting by Governments*.

Background

BC2 The Board considered it timely to review the requirements in AASs 27, 29 and 31, in particular to:

    (a) review the extent to which local governments, government departments and governments should continue to be subject to requirements that differ from requirements applicable to other not-for-profit entities and for-profit entities contained in Australian Accounting Standards. The Board concluded that differences should be removed, where appropriate and timely, to improve the overall quality of financial reporting;

    (b) bring requirements applicable to local governments, government departments and governments up-to-date with contemporary accounting thought;

    (c) consider the implications of the outcomes of its project on the harmonisation of Generally Accepted Accounting Principles (GAAP) and Government Finance Statistics (GFS), in particular on the requirements in AAS 31;

    (d) decide whether the encouragements in AASs 27, 29 and 31 should be made mandatory or removed; and

    (e) remove uncertainty in the application of cross-references to other Australian Accounting Standards and the override provisions in AASs 27, 29 and 31 that made the requirements in AASs 27, 29 and 31 take precedence over other requirements.

BC3 The Board considered the following alternative mechanisms for implementing the approach of updating and improving the requirements for local governments, government departments and governments:

    (a) review the requirements in AASs 27, 29 and 31 and where appropriate:

        (i) amend other Australian Accounting Standards to pick up any issues that are addressed in AASs 27, 29 and 31 that are not adequately addressed in the latest Australian Accounting Standards and have them apply to local governments, government departments and governments; or

        (ii) create public sector specific topic-based Standards; and consequently withdraw AASs 27, 29 and 31; or

    (b) review AASs 27, 29 and 31 and re-issue them in light of the latest Australian Accounting Standards, retaining/amending where necessary any issues that are addressed in AASs 27, 29 and 31 that are not adequately addressed in the latest Australian Accounting Standards.

BC4   The Board chose alternative (a), given the improvements in the quality of financial reporting by local governments, government departments and governments since AASs 27, 29 and 31 were first issued.

BC5   Where the Board identified that the material in AASs 27, 29 and 31 could be improved within time and resource constraints, improvements have been made. Much of the material in AASs 27, 29 and 31 has been retained substantively unamended. Improvements will be progressed in due course in line with the AASB's Public Sector Policy Paper *Australian Accounting Standards and Public Sector Entities*.

BC6   The first stage of the short-term review of the requirements in AASs 27, 29 and 31 was the preparation of a paragraph-by-paragraph analysis of each of AASs 27, 29 and 31, listing each paragraph of each Standard alongside corresponding Standards or other pronouncements that would apply to local governments, government departments or governments in the absence of AASs 27, 29 and 31. The Board's conclusions and rationale for the treatment of each paragraph in the context of the review were also provided in the analysis. The Board's primary focus was on dealing with the requirements from the three Standards in such a way as to not leave a vacuum.

BC7   Each paragraph from AASs 27, 29 and 31 was classified as being:

(a)   no longer needed or adequately dealt with in other Standards;

(b)   more appropriately dealt with in other Standards; or

(c)   not adequately and/or appropriately dealt with in other Standards and therefore should be retained or improved and incorporated into other Standards.

The paragraph-by-paragraph analyses considered by the AASB in developing the Exposure Draft ED 156 *Proposals Arising from the Short-term Review of the Requirements in AAS 27, AAS 29 and AAS 31* that gave rise to this Standard are available on the AASB website. They support, but do not form part of, this Basis for Conclusions.

BC8   In reviewing the paragraphs, the Board noted that some material in AASs 27, 29 and 31 would, under the current style of writing Standards, be located in a separate Basis for Conclusions. For example, paragraph 6.3.12 of AAS 29 provides a rationale for the disclosure of information about administered items. Given the short-term nature of the review of AASs 27, 29 and 31, the Board concluded that explanations of technical issues that both originated in and are being relocated from AASs 27, 29 and 31 should, when appropriate, be located in the body of the Standard to which the relevant requirements are being relocated.

BC9   The Board decided not to retain the illustrative general purpose financial reports provided in AASs 27, 29 and 31, because their purpose, which was to provide an educational tool in the initial stages of accrual reporting by local governments, government departments and governments, is no longer needed.

BC10   The remainder of this Basis for Conclusions focuses on issues specific to administered items.

Administered items

Location of requirements

BC11   Consistent with paragraphs BC3(a)(ii) and BC7(c), the Board decided to retain the existing requirements and guidance relating to administered items from AAS 29 and include them, substantively unchanged (although see paragraphs BC15–BC17 below).

BC12   As an alternative, the Board considered locating the material in an existing Standard such as AASB 101 *Presentation of Financial Statements*. However, the Board concluded that:

(a)   the material is sufficiently dissimilar from the other requirements of AASB 101 to warrant a separate Standard; and

(b) a new Standard on administered items would make the requirements easily identifiable by those financial report preparers and auditors most affected by the requirements.

Short-term retention of acknowledged inadequacies

BC13 The Board noted that some of the acknowledged inadequacies in AAS 29 are retained, including the lack of extensive guidance for identifying administered items and the potential inadequate prominence given to administered items in a complete set of financial statements. The Board decided that this is justified on the basis that this Standard is a short-term measure until such time as the Board undertakes a longer-term project on administered items as part of a broader review.

Application limited to government departments

BC14 The Board concluded that it is appropriate for government departments, including for-profit government departments, to be subject to this Standard, consistent with the range of entities that were subject to AAS 29. The Board also concluded that it is appropriate to limit the application of this Standard to government departments because extending the application of the requirements as part of the short-term review would delay the short-term project and impinge on the issues to be addressed in the longer term. The Board noted that, as a part of the Board's fundamental longer-term review of the requirements in AAS 29, consideration will be given to the different treatments available that would result in administered items being given more prominence and disclosed in more detail in the general purpose financial statements of government departments and other entities.

Treatment of encouragements in AAS 29

BC15 In line with paragraph BC2(d), the Board considered whether the encouragement in paragraph 5.2.5 of AAS 29 should be removed or amended to require items collected or distributed on behalf of another entity or held in legal custody that are neither administered nor controlled to be disclosed. The Board concluded that the encouragement should be removed. This is in acknowledgement of the implementation difficulties related to the lack of clarity in the short term about the definition of 'items that a government department collects or distributes on behalf of another entity that are neither controlled nor administered items'. The Board noted that this issue will be addressed as part of the planned longer-term more fundamental review of requirements relating to administered items.

BC16 Also consistent with paragraph BC2(d), the Board decided that, although transfers not controlled by a government department (such as, in general, pensions paid to beneficiaries) do not qualify for recognition, details of the broad categories of recipients and the amounts transferred to those recipients should be required to be disclosed in a complete set of financial statements (see paragraph 22 of this Standard). This is because the resulting information is relevant for understanding the government department's financial performance.

BC17 Paragraph 12.9.4 of AAS 29 encouraged the disclosure of information about administered assets and administered liabilities on an activity basis. Again, consistent with paragraph BC2(d), the Board concluded that the encouragement should be removed, noting that its removal does not create a vacuum.

Other changes to requirements in AAS 29

BC18 The Board decided to delete the following sentence in paragraph 12.9.6 of AAS 29: "In some jurisdictions, this may mean that the basis adopted by a government department for reporting administered items may differ from the basis adopted by the government itself". The Board considers this sentence to be redundant, given that government departments are typically directed to adopt particular policies by their controlling government.

AASB 1051

Land Under Roads

(Compiled December 2013)

This compiled Standard applies to annual reporting periods beginning on or after 1 January 2014. Early application is not permitted. It incorporates relevant amendments made up to and including 20 December 2013.

Prepared on 1 July 2014 by the staff of the Australian Accounting Standards Board.

CONTENTS

COMPILATION DETAILS
COMPARISON WITH INTERNATIONAL PRONOUNCEMENTS
ACCOUNTING STANDARD
AASB 1051 *LAND UNDER ROADS*

Australian Accounting Standard AASB 1051 *Land Under Roads* (as amended) is set out in paragraphs 1 – 15 and Appendix A. All the paragraphs have equal authority. Paragraphs in **bold type** state the main principles. Terms defined in this Standard are in *italics* the first time they appear in the Standard. AASB 1051 is to be read in the context of other Australian Accounting Standards, including AASB 1048 *Interpretation of Standards*, which identifies the Australian Accounting Interpretations. In the absence of explicit guidance, AASB 108 *Accounting Policies, Changes in Accounting Estimates and Errors* provides a basis for selecting and applying accounting policies.

COMPILATION DETAILS

Accounting Standard AASB 1051 *Land Under Roads* as amended

This compiled Standard applies to annual reporting periods beginning on or after 1 January 2014. It takes into account amendments up to and including 20 December 2013 and was prepared on 1 July 2014 by the staff of the Australian Accounting Standards Board (AASB).

This compilation is not a separate Accounting Standard made by the AASB. Instead, it is a representation of AASB 1051 (December 2007) as amended by other Accounting Standards, which are listed in the Table below.

Table of Standards

Standard	Date made	Application date *(annual reporting periods ... on or after ...)*	Application, saving or transitional provisions
AASB 1051	13 Dec 2007	*(beginning)* 1 Jul 2008	see (a) below
AASB 2013-9	20 Dec 2013	Pt B *(beginning)* 1 Jan 2014	see (b) below

(a) Entities may elect to apply this Standard to annual reporting periods beginning on or after 1 January 2005 but before 1 July 2008, provided that the Standards and Interpretation listed in paragraph 4 of this Standard are also applied to such periods.

(b) Early application of Part B of this Standard is not permitted.

Table of amendments

Paragraph affected	How affected	By ... [paragraph]
5	deleted	AASB 2013-9B [37, 38]

COMPARISON WITH INTERNATIONAL PRONOUNCEMENTS

AASB 1051 and International Public Sector Accounting Standards

International Public Sector Accounting Standards (IPSASs) are issued by the International Public Sector Accounting Standards Board (IPSASB).

Land under roads falls within the scope of IPSAS 17 *Property, Plant and Equipment* (issued December 2001, amended February 2007).

IPSAS 17 does not require recognition of land under roads (and other property, plant and equipment) for reporting periods beginning on a date within five years following the date of first adoption of accrual accounting in accordance with IPSASs. However, at the expiry of the transitional period, holdings of land under roads must be recognised where they satisfy the recognition criteria. The effect of the initial recognition of land under roads is accounted for as an adjustment to the opening balance of accumulated surpluses or deficits. When an entity elects to not recognise land under roads within the transitional period, certain disclosures must be made.

This Standard does not require the recognition of land under roads acquired before the end of the first reporting period ending on or after 31 December 2007. If an entity decides to recognise such land then, under this Standard, the entity may elect, in certain circumstances, to apply the fair value or a previous revaluation under the "fair value or revaluation as deemed cost" exemptions in AASB 1 *First-time Adoption of Australian Accounting Standards*. In contrast, IPSAS 17 requires an entity that adopts accrual accounting for the first time in accordance with IPSASs to initially recognise land under roads at cost or fair value. For items acquired at no cost, or for a nominal cost, cost is the item's fair value as at the date of acquisition.

Land under roads acquired after the end of the first reporting period ending on or after 31 December 2007 is accounted for under AASB 116 *Property, Plant and Equipment*. AASB 116 contains a comparison with the corresponding IPSAS 17.

AASB 1051 and International Financial Reporting Standards

Land under roads falls within the scope of IAS 16 *Property, Plant and Equipment*, which does not contain requirements or choices equivalent to this Standard for land under roads acquired before the end of the first reporting period ending on or after 31 December 2007.

Land under roads acquired after the end of the first reporting period ending on or after 31 December 2007 is accounted for under AASB 116. AASB 116 contains a comparison with the corresponding IAS 16.

This Standard allows an entity to elect, in certain circumstances, to apply the fair value or a previous revaluation under the "fair value or revaluation as deemed cost exemptions" in AASB 1. AASB 1 contains a comparison with the corresponding IFRS 1 *First-time Adoption of International Financial Reporting Standards.*

ACCOUNTING STANDARD AASB 1051

The Australian Accounting Standards Board made Accounting Standard AASB 1051 *Land Under Roads* on 13 December 2007.

This compiled version of AASB 1051 applies to annual reporting periods beginning on or after 1 January 2014. It incorporates relevant amendments contained in other AASB Standards made by the AASB up to and including 20 December 2013 (see Compilation Details).

ACCOUNTING STANDARD AASB 1051
LAND UNDER ROADS

Objective

1   The objective of this Standard is to specify the requirements for financial reporting of *land under roads* by local governments, government departments, General Government Sectors (GGSs) and whole of governments.

Application

2   **This Standard applies to general purpose financial statements of local governments, government departments and whole of governments, and financial statements of GGSs.**

3   **This Standard applies to annual reporting periods beginning on or after 1 July 2008.**

[Note: For application dates of paragraphs changed or added by an amending Standard, see Compilation Details.]

4   **This Standard may be applied to annual reporting periods beginning on or after 1 January 2005 but before 1 July 2008, provided there is early adoption for the same annual reporting period of the following pronouncements being issued at about the same time, as applicable:**

     (a)   **AASB 1004** *Contributions*;

     (b)   **AASB 1049** *Whole of Government and General Government Sector Financial Reporting*;

     (c)   **AASB 1050** *Administered Items*;

     (d)   **AASB 1052** *Disaggregated Disclosures*;

     (e)   **AASB 2007-9** *Amendments to Australian Accounting Standards arising from the Review of AASs 27, 29 and 31*; **and**

     (f)   **AASB Interpretation 1038** *Contributions by Owners Made to Wholly-Owned Public Sector Entities.*

5   [Deleted by the AASB]

6   **When applicable, this Standard, together with the Standards referred to in paragraph 4, supersede:**

(a) AAS 27 *Financial Reporting by Local Governments* as issued in June 1996, as amended;

(b) AAS 29 *Financial Reporting by Government Departments* as issued in June 1998, as amended; and

(c) AAS 31 *Financial Reporting by Governments* as issued in June 1998, as amended.

Land under roads

7 **Other Australian Accounting Standards (including AASB 116 *Property, Plant and Equipment*) apply to land under roads, except to the extent that this Standard requires or permits otherwise.**

8 **An entity may elect to recognise (including continue to recognise or to recognise for the first time), subject to satisfaction of the asset recognition criteria, or not to recognise (including continue not to recognise or to derecognise) as an asset, land under roads acquired before the end of the first reporting period ending on or after 31 December 2007.**

9 **An entity shall make a final election under paragraph 8 effective as at the first day of the next reporting period following the end of the first reporting period ending on or after 31 December 2007. Any adjustments that arise from a final election that is made effective as at that first day shall be made against the opening balance of accumulated surplus (deficiency) of that next reporting period.**

10 Adjustments arising under paragraph 9 include those relating to a revision of recognised amounts of previously recognised land under roads acquired before the end of the first reporting period ending on or after 31 December 2007, made to reflect a reassessment of the factors used to determine those recognised amounts. Any adjustments that arise from an election that is made effective:

(a) before the first day of the next reporting period following the end of the first reporting period ending on or after 31 December 2007, is made against accumulated surplus (deficiency) of the earliest prior period presented, and therefore comparative data is adjusted; and

(b) on the first day of the next reporting period following the end of the first reporting period ending on or after 31 December 2007, is made against the opening balance of accumulated surplus (deficiency) of that next reporting period, and therefore comparative data is not adjusted.

11 **An entity shall disclose its accounting policy for land under roads acquired before the end of the first reporting period ending on or after 31 December 2007, in each reporting period to which this Standard is applied.**

12 **The nature and net amount of each adjustment made in accordance with paragraph 9 shall be disclosed.**

13 **Where an entity recognises land under roads in accordance with paragraphs 8 and 9, but after the entity's first-time adoption of Australian equivalents to International Financial Reporting Standards (IFRSs), the entity may, in relation to land under roads, elect to adopt the fair value (as at the date of that election) or a previous revaluation under the "fair value or revaluation as deemed cost" exemptions contained in AASB 1 *First-time Adoption of Australian Equivalents to International Financial Reporting Standards*, as if it were adopting Australian equivalents to IFRSs for the first time.**

14 Paragraph 13 enables an entity that recognises land under roads acquired before the end of the first reporting period ending on or after 31 December 2007, after its first-time adoption of Australian equivalents to IFRSs and under paragraphs 8 and 9, to elect to:

AASB

(a)   measure the fair value of land under roads as at the date of the election made under paragraph 13 and use that fair value as the deemed cost;

(b)   use an earlier revaluation of land under roads as its deemed cost; or

(c)   use an earlier deemed cost of land under roads established from an event-driven fair value measurement as its deemed cost.

15   Land under roads acquired after the end of the first reporting period ending on or after 31 December 2007 is accounted for in accordance with AASB 116.

APPENDIX A
DEFINED TERMS

This Appendix is an integral part of AASB 1051.

land under roads	Land under roadways, and road reserves, including land under footpaths, nature strips and median strips.

APPENDIX B
COMPARISON OF AASB 1051 WITH AASs 27, 29 AND 31

This Appendix accompanies, but is not part of, AASB 1051.

The requirements of this Standard differ from the requirements contained in AASs 27 *Financial Reporting by Local Governments*, AAS 29 *Financial Reporting by Government Departments* and AAS 31 *Financial Reporting by Governments* (as amended), and expresses the requirements generically. The main differences between AASB 1051 and AASs 27, 29 and 31 (as amended) are:

(a)   this Standard extends indefinitely the relief from the requirement to recognise land under roads acquired before the end of the first reporting period ending on or after 31 December 2007. AASs 27, 29 and 31 provided recognition relief only for a transitional period;

(b)   AASs 27, 29 and 31 encouraged entities to recognise land under roads as an asset wherever it can be measured reliably. Consistent with the AASB's policy of not including encouragements within Standards, this encouragement has not been included in this Standard;

(c)   this Standard notes that AASB 116 *Property, Plant and Equipment* applies to land under roads acquired after the end of the first reporting period ending on or after 31 December 2007. AASs 27, 29 and 31 would have required that AASB 116 be retrospectively applied to land under roads after the end of the transitional period;

(d)   in certain circumstances this Standard allows an entity, in relation to land under roads acquired before the end of the first reporting period ending on or after 31 December 2007, to elect to adopt the fair value (as at the date of that election) or a previous revaluation under the "fair value or revaluation as deemed cost" exemptions contained in AASB 1 *First-time Adoption of Australian Equivalents to International Financial Reporting Standards*, as if it were adopting Australian equivalents to IFRSs for the first time. AASs 27, 29 and 31 did not contain this relief;

(e)   AASs 29 and 31 did not explicitly require that, if the recognised amounts of land under roads acquired before the end of the first reporting period ending on or after 31 December 2007 are revised, up until the first day of the next reporting period, to reflect a reassessment of the factors used to determine those recognised amounts, the net amount of the resultant adjustments be made against accumulated surplus (deficiency) in the reporting periods in which the recognised amounts are revised; and

(f) this Standard extends the requirements to General Government Sectors.

APPENDIX C
IMPLEMENTATION GUIDANCE

This Appendix accompanies, but is not part of, AASB 1051.

The following diagram illustrates the effect of the requirements in this Standard for land under roads acquired before 1 July 2008, assuming an entity with a 1 July 2008 to 30 June 2009 reporting period makes a final election under paragraphs 8 and 9 as at 1 July 2008. (Note that land under roads acquired after 30 June 2008 is accounted for in accordance with AASB 116.)

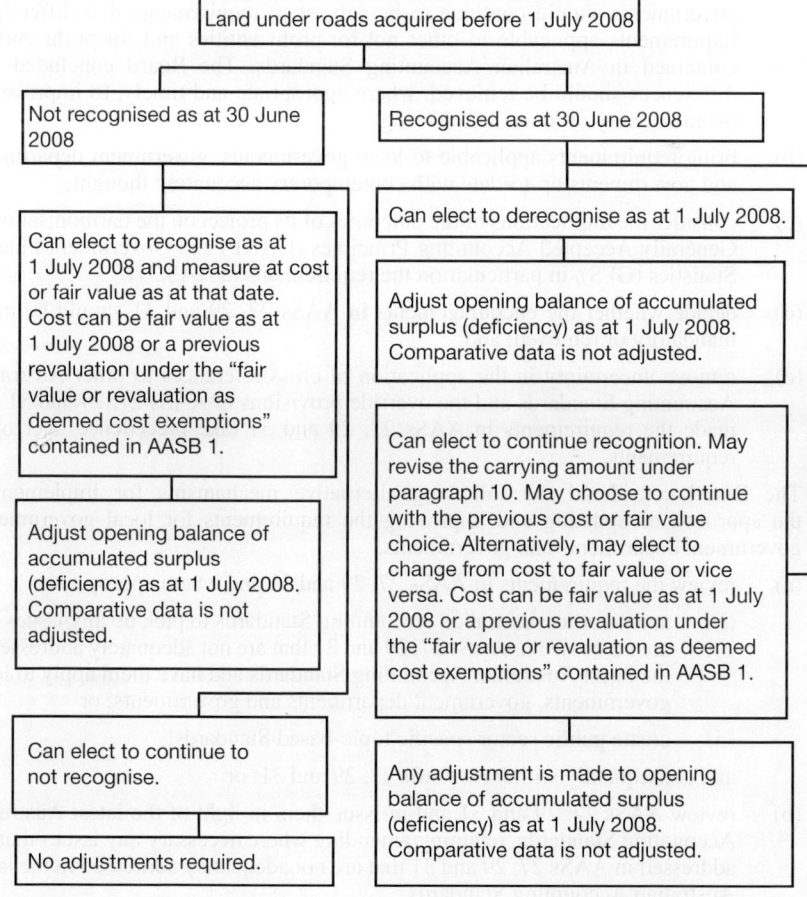

BASIS FOR CONCLUSIONS

This Basis for Conclusions accompanies, but is not part of, AASB 1051.

Introduction

BC1   This Basis for Conclusions summarises the Board's considerations in developing this Standard in the context of the Board's short-term review of the requirements in AAS 27 *Financial Reporting by Local Governments*, AAS 29 *Financial Reporting by Government Departments* and AAS 31 *Financial Reporting by Governments*.

Background

BC2   The Board considered it timely to review the requirements in AASs 27, 29 and 31, in particular to:

(a)   review the extent to which local governments, government departments and governments should continue to be subject to requirements that differ from requirements applicable to other not-for-profit entities and for-profit entities contained in Australian Accounting Standards. The Board concluded that differences should be removed, where appropriate and timely, to improve the overall quality of financial reporting;

(b)   bring requirements applicable to local governments, government departments and governments up-to-date with contemporary accounting thought;

(c)   consider the implications of the outcomes of its project on the harmonisation of Generally Accepted Accounting Principles (GAAP) and Government Finance Statistics (GFS), in particular on the requirements in AAS 31;

(d)   decide whether the encouragements in AASs 27, 29 and 31 should be made mandatory or removed; and

(e)   remove uncertainty in the application of cross-references to other Australian Accounting Standards and the override provisions in AASs 27, 29 and 31 that made the requirements in AASs 27, 29 and 31 take precedence over other requirements.

BC3   The Board considered the following alternative mechanisms for implementing the approach of updating and improving the requirements for local governments, government departments and governments:

(a)   review the requirements in AASs 27, 29 and 31 and where appropriate:

(i)   amend other Australian Accounting Standards to pick up any issues that are addressed in AASs 27, 29 and 31 that are not adequately addressed in the latest Australian Accounting Standards and have them apply to local governments, government departments and governments; or

(ii)   create public sector specific topic-based Standards;

and consequently withdraw AASs 27, 29 and 31; or

(b)   review AASs 27, 29 and 31 and re-issue them in light of the latest Australian Accounting Standards, retaining/amending where necessary any issues that are addressed in AASs 27, 29 and 31 that are not adequately addressed in the latest Australian Accounting Standards.

BC4   The Board chose alternative (a) given the improvements in the quality of financial reporting by local governments, government departments and governments since AASs 27, 29 and 31 were first issued.

BC5   Where the Board identified that the material in AASs 27, 29 and 31 could be improved within time and resource constraints, improvements have been made. Much of the material in AASs 27, 29 and 31 has been retained substantively unamended.

Improvements will be progressed in due course in line with the AASB's Public Sector Policy Paper *Australian Accounting Standards and Public Sector Entities*.

BC6 The first stage of the short-term review of the requirements in AASs 27, 29 and 31 was the preparation of a paragraph-by-paragraph analysis of each of AASs 27, 29 and 31, listing each paragraph of each Standard alongside corresponding Standards or other pronouncements that would apply to local governments, government departments or governments in the absence of AASs 27, 29 and 31. The Board's conclusions and rationale for the treatment of each paragraph in the context of the review were also provided in the analysis. The Board's primary focus was on dealing with the requirements from the three Standards in such a way as to not leave a vacuum.

BC7 Each paragraph from AASs 27, 29 and 31 was classified as being:

(a) no longer needed or adequately dealt with in other Standards;

(b) more appropriately dealt with in other Standards; or

(c) not adequately and/or appropriately dealt with in other Standards and therefore should be retained or improved and incorporated into other Standards.

The paragraph-by-paragraph analyses considered by the AASB in developing the Exposure Draft ED 156 *Proposals Arising from the Short-term Review of the Requirements in AAS 27, AAS 29 and AAS 31* that gave rise to this Standard are available on the AASB website. They support, but do not form part of, this Basis for Conclusions.

BC8 In reviewing the paragraphs, the Board noted that some material in AASs 27, 29 and 31 would, under the current style of writing Standards, be located in a separate Basis for Conclusions. Given the short-term nature of the review of AASs 27, 29 and 31, the Board concluded that explanations of technical issues that both originated in and are being relocated from AASs 27, 29 and 31 should, when appropriate, be located in the body of the Standard to which the relevant requirements are being relocated.

BC9 The Board decided not to retain the illustrative general purpose financial reports provided in AASs 27, 29 and 31, because their purpose, which was to provide an educational tool in the initial stages of accrual reporting by local governments, government departments and governments, is no longer needed.

BC10 The remainder of this Basis for Conclusions focuses on issues specific to land under roads.

Land under roads

BC11 The Board decided to issue this Standard as part of the short-term review of the requirements in AASs 27, 29 and 31 and to amend the previous transitional relief for land under roads, to allow entities to elect whether to recognise land under roads acquired before the end of the first reporting period ending on or after 31 December 2007. This decision is in acknowledgement of the potentially onerous demands on entities if they were to be required to retrospectively identify, assess the recognition criteria, recognise and measure land under roads previously acquired.

BC12 The Board decided that a final election relating to the recognition of land under roads acquired before the end of the first reporting period ending on or after 31 December 2007 should be made effective as at the first day of the next reporting period. The final election can be made at any time prior to the completion of the financial statements for that next reporting period, but will be effective as at the first day of that period. The Board also decided that, to facilitate the transition to the new requirements, any adjustments arising from an election be made against accumulated surplus (deficiency); and that there would be no requirement to adjust comparative data for earlier periods when the election is made effective as at that first day. The Board noted that the extent to which an entity could change its recognition policy after that date would be constrained by the requirements of AASB 108 *Accounting Policies, Changes in Accounting Estimates and Errors* relating to voluntary change in accounting policy. Accordingly, subsequent changes to the accounting policy relating to the recognition of land under roads acquired before the end of the first reporting period ending on or after 31 December 2007 could only be made to recognise land under roads that it previously elected to not recognise (or, conceivably, vice versa) if that change could be justified based on paragraph 14 of AASB 108.

BC13 Consistent with the entities that were subject to AASs 27, 29 and 31, this Standard applies to local governments, government departments (including for-profit government departments), and whole of governments. In addition, the application of this Standard extends to General Government Sectors (GGSs), which facilitates consistency in financial reporting by GGSs and whole of governments.

BC14 In relation to GGSs and whole of governments, the Board considered the relationship between this Standard and the principle in AASB 1049 *Whole of Government and General Government Sector Financial Reporting* that GGSs and whole of governments should adopt optional treatments in Australian Accounting Standards that align with the principles or rules in the Australian Bureau of Statistics (ABS) Government Finance Statistics (GFS) Manual. The Board noted that the recognition relief provided in this Standard for land under roads is potentially inconsistent with GFS principles. However, the Board also noted that land under roads is not recognised under GFS in practice in certain circumstances, depending on the availability of information pertinent to measurement. Accordingly, the Board concluded that the impact of AASB 1049 relative to this Standard on the recognition of land under roads would be expected to be limited.

BC15 Accordingly, the Board decided that the broad principle adopted in AASB 1049 that a GAAP option should be adopted where it aligns with GFS should be retained without an exception for land under roads. In making this decision, the Board also noted that any difference between GFS principles and practice is beyond the control of the AASB, and that land under roads does not create unique issues in a GAAP/GFS harmonisation context.

BC16 The Board concluded that, in principle, land under roads is property and therefore falls within the scope of AASB 116. Accordingly, it is appropriate that land under roads acquired after the end of the first reporting period ending on or after 31 December 2007 is accounted for in accordance with AASB 116. In making this decision, the Board noted that AASB 116, including paragraph Aus15.1, requires:

(a) assets acquired at no cost, or for a nominal cost, to be initially measured at fair value as at the date of acquisition where fair value can be measured reliably; and

(b) requires assets acquired at a cost to be initially measured at cost, but does not require adoption of the revaluation model. The Board also noted that issues relating to reliable measurement of fair value are not unique to land under roads and therefore could be dealt with in the same manner in which issues for other classes of assets are dealt with under AASB 116.

BC17 The Board also concluded that further requirements should replicate, in certain circumstances, the fair value or a previous revaluation (in accordance with, for example, AASB 1041 *Revaluation of Non-Current Assets* or AASB 116 *Property, Plant and Equipment*) under the "fair value or revaluation as deemed cost" exemptions in AASB 1 *First-time Adoption of Australian Equivalents to International Financial Reporting Standards* on the basis that this would facilitate the initial recognition of land under roads under AASB 116. The requirements would be used when a local government, government department, GGS or whole of government elects to recognise and measure land under roads acquired before the end of the first reporting period ending on or after 31 December 2007 under paragraphs 8 and 9 of this Standard, after its first-time adoption of Australian equivalents to International Financial Reporting Standards.

AASB 1052
Disaggregated Disclosures

(Compiled June 2014)

This compiled Standard applies to annual reporting periods beginning on or after 1 July 2014. Early application is permitted for annual reporting periods beginning on or after 1 January 2014 but before 1 July 2014. It incorporates relevant amendments made up to and including 4 June 2014.

Prepared on 1 September 2014 by the staff of the Australian Accounting Standards Board.

CONTENTS

Australian Accounting Standard AASB 1052 *Disaggregated Disclosures* (as amended) is set out in paragraphs 1 – 21. All the paragraphs have equal authority. Paragraphs in **bold type** state the main principles. AASB 1052 is to be read in the context of other Australian Accounting Standards, including AASB 1048 *Interpretation Standards*, which identifies the Australian Accounting Interpretations. In the absence of explicit guidance, AASB 108 *Accounting Policies, Changes in Accounting Estimates and Errors* provides a basis for selecting and applying accounting policies.

COMPILATION DETAILS

Accounting Standard AASB 1052 *Disaggregated Disclosures* as amended

This compiled Standard applies to annual reporting periods beginning on or after 1 July 2014. It takes into account amendments up to and including 4 June 2014 and was prepared on 1 September 2014 by the staff of the Australian Accounting Standards Board (AASB).

This compilation is not a separate Accounting Standard made by the AASB. Instead, it is a representation of AASB 1052 (December 2007) as amended by other Accounting Standards, which are listed in the Table below.

Table of Standards

Standard	Date made	Application date *(annual reporting periods ... on or after ...)*	Application, saving or transitional provisions
AASB 1052	13 Dec 2007	*(beginning)* 1 Jul 2008	see (a) below
AASB 2010-2	30 Jun 2010	*(beginning)* 1 Jul 2013	see (b) below
AASB 2013-9	20 Dec 2013	Pt B *(beginning)* 1 Jan 2014	see (c) below
AASB 2014-1	4 Jun 2014	Pt A *(beginning)* 1 Jul 2014	see (d) below

(a) Entities may elect to apply this Standard to annual reporting periods beginning on or after 1 January 2005 but before 1 July 2008, provided that the Standards listed in paragraph 7 are also applied to such periods.

(b) Entities may elect to apply this Standard to annual reporting periods beginning on or after 1 July 2009 but before 1 July 2013, provided that AASB 1053 *Application of Tiers of Australian Accounting Standards* is also applied to such periods.

(c) Early application of Part B of this Standard is not permitted.

(d) Entities may elect to apply Part A of this Standard to annual reporting periods beginning on or after 1 January 2005 but before 1 July 2014.

Table of amendments

Paragraph affected	How affected	By ... [paragraph]
9	deleted	AASB 2013-9B [37, 38]
10A-10B (and preceding heading)	added	AASB 2010-2 [48]
14	amended	AASB 2014-1A [40]
20	amended	AASB 2013-9B [42]

COMPARISON WITH INTERNATIONAL PRONOUNCEMENTS

This Standard contains relevant requirements relating to reporting of disaggregated information by local governments and government departments that have been relocated from AAS 27 *Financial Reporting by Local Governments* and AAS 29 *Financial Reporting by Government Departments* in substantially unamended form (with some exceptions, as noted in Appendix A). Accordingly, the development of this Standard did not involve consideration of International Public Sector Accounting Standards (IPSASs) issued by the International Public Sector Accounting Standards Board or International Financial Reporting Standards (IFRSs) issued by the International Accounting Standards Board.

The longer-term review of disaggregated disclosures for local governments and government departments will involve consideration of International pronouncements.

AASB 1052 and IPSASs

IPSAS 18 *Segment Reporting* addresses segment reporting issues and specifies requirements for all public sector entities other than government business enterprises. It contains more detailed requirements and guidance than this Standard. For example, IPSAS 18:

(a)   defines a segment as a distinguishable activity or group of activities of an entity for which it is appropriate to separately report financial information for the purpose of evaluating the entity's past performance in achieving its objectives and for making decisions about the future allocation of resources;

(b)   provides detailed guidance on determining segments;

(c)   requires specific disclosures about segments, including segment revenue, expenses, assets, liabilities and capital expenditure; and

(d)   requires specific disclosures for assets that are jointly used by two or more segments.

AASB 1052 and IFRSs

IFRS 8 *Operating Segments* does not apply to the general purpose financial statements of local governments and government departments. IFRS 8 specifies requirements that differ substantially from the requirements in this Standard.

ACCOUNTING STANDARD AASB 1052

The Australian Accounting Standards Board made Accounting Standard AASB 1052 *Disaggregated Disclosures* on 13 December 2007.

This compiled version of AASB 1052 applies to annual reporting periods beginning on or after 1 July 2014. It incorporates relevant amendments contained in other AASB Standards made by the AASB up to and including 4 June 2014 (see Compilation Details).

ACCOUNTING STANDARD AASB 1052
DISAGGREGATED DISCLOSURES

Objective

1   The objective of this Standard is to specify principles for reporting:

(a)   financial information by function or activity by local governments; and

(b)   financial information about service costs and achievements by government departments.

2   Disclosures made in accordance with this Standard provide users with information relevant to assessing the performance of a local government or government department, including accountability for resources entrusted to it.

Application

3   **Subject to paragraphs 4 and 5, this Standard applies to general purpose financial statements of local governments and government departments.**

4   **Paragraphs 11 to 14 only apply to general purpose financial statements of local governments.**

5   **Paragraphs 15 to 21 only apply to general purpose financial statements of government departments.**

6   **This Standard applies to annual reporting periods beginning on or after 1 July 2008.**

[Note: For application dates of paragraphs changed or added by an amending Standard, see Compilation Details.]

7   **This Standard may be applied to annual reporting periods beginning on or after 1 January 2005 but before 1 July 2008, provided there is early adoption for the same annual reporting period of the following pronouncements being issued at about the same time, as applicable:**

(a)   **AASB 1004 *Contributions*;**

    (b)   **AASB 1049** *Whole of Government and General Government Sector Financial Reporting*;

    (c)   **AASB 1050** *Administered Items*;

    (d)   **AASB 1051** *Land Under Roads*;

    (e)   **AASB 2007-9** *Amendments to Australian Accounting Standards arising from the Review of AASs 27, 29 and 31*; and

    (f)   **AASB Interpretation 1038** *Contributions by Owners Made to Wholly-Owned Public Sector Entities*.

8   This Standard does not specify disaggregated disclosure requirements for whole of governments or General Government Sectors (GGSs). The requirements for disaggregated disclosures for whole of governments and GGSs are contained in AASB 1049.

9   [Deleted by the AASB]

10   **When applicable, this Standard, together with the Standards referred to in paragraph 7, supersede:**

    (a)   **AAS 27** *Financial Reporting by Local Governments* **as issued in June 1996, as amended; and**

    (b)   **AAS 29** *Financial Reporting by Government Departments* **as issued in June 1998, as amended.**

Reduced disclosure requirements

10A   **Paragraphs 11–21 of this Standard do not apply to entities preparing general purpose financial statements under Australian Accounting Standards – Reduced Disclosure Requirements. Entities applying Australian Accounting Standards – Reduced Disclosure Requirements may elect to comply with some or all of these excluded requirements.**

10B   The requirements that do not apply to entities preparing general purpose financial statements under Australian Accounting Standards – Reduced Disclosure Requirements are identified in this Standard by shading of the relevant text.

Classification according to function or activity by local governments

Paragraphs 11 to 14 only apply to local governments.

11   **The complete set of financial statements of a local government shall disclose in respect of each broad function or activity:**

    (a)   **by way of note:**

        (i)   **the nature and objectives of that function/activity; and**

        (ii)   **the carrying amount of assets that are reliably attributable to that function/activity; and**

    (b)   **by way of note or otherwise:**

        (i)   **income for the reporting period that is reliably attributable to that function/activity, with component revenues from related grants disclosed separately as a component thereof; and**

        (ii)   **expenses for the reporting period that are reliably attributable to that function/activity.**

12   **The information provided by way of note in accordance with paragraph 11 shall be aggregated and reconciled to agree with the related information in the financial statements of the local government.**

13   This Standard requires disclosure of information about the assets, income and expenses of the local government according to the broad functions or activities of the local government, whether they be related to service delivery or undertaken for commercial objectives. Disclosure of this information assists users in identifying the resources committed to particular functions/activities of the local government, the costs of service delivery that are reliably attributable to those functions/activities, and the extent to which the local government has recovered those costs from income that is reliably attributable to those functions/activities. Function/activity classification of financial information will also assist users in assessing the significance of any financial or non-financial performance indicators reported by the local government.

14   AASB 8 *Operating Segments* is not applicable to local governments. The bases considered appropriate for identifying broad functions or activities of local governments would not necessarily accord with the criteria for identification of segments contained in that Standard. However, preparers of the complete set of financial statements may find that the guidance contained in that Standard is useful in identifying the income, expenses and assets that are reliably attributable to the broad functions or activities of the local government.

Disclosure of service costs and achievements by government departments

Paragraphs 15 to 21 only apply to government departments.

15   The complete set of financial statements of a government department shall disclose:

(a)   in summarised form, the identity and purpose of each major activity undertaken by the government department during the reporting period;

(b)   if not otherwise disclosed in, or in conjunction with, the government department's complete set of financial statements, a summary of the government department's objectives;

(c)   expenses reliably attributable to each of the activities identified in (a) above, showing separately each major class of expenses; and

(d)   income reliably attributable to each of the activities identified in (a) above, showing separately user charges, income from government and other income by major class of income.

16   The complete set of financial statements of a government department shall also disclose the assets deployed and liabilities incurred that are reliably attributable to each of the activities identified in paragraph 15(a).

17   Government departments are required to achieve service delivery as well as financial objectives. Accordingly, a government department's performance is assessed by reference to the effectiveness, economy and efficiency with which the government department achieves its service delivery and financial objectives. Financial information is therefore only a subset of the information necessary to enable an adequate assessment of a government department's performance. Accordingly, the complete set of financial statements is presented as part of an annual report that discloses information about such matters as the government department's objectives and service delivery achievements during the reporting period. To enhance the quality of information available for assessing performance, paragraph 15 requires that a summary of the government department's objectives be disclosed in the complete set of financial statements where the government department's annual report does not include this disclosure.

18   Paragraphs 15 and 16 require disclosure of information about the expenses, income, assets and liabilities attributable to the major activities of a government department for the reporting period. This information is relevant in assessing the effectiveness, efficiency and economy of operations and of resource allocation decisions. It is

AASB

also necessary for reviewing existing expenditure commitments and service delivery arrangements, and for considering the long-term funding implications of new initiatives.

19   However, in some instances it may not be possible to reliably attribute all expenses, income, assets and liabilities to each of the major activities of a government department. Paragraphs 15 and 16 require that the complete set of financial statements of a government department only disclose, on an activity by activity basis, information about the expenses, income, assets and liabilities that can be reliably attributed to major activities.

Identifying major activities of government departments

20   Judgement is required to identify those activities of a government department that warrant separate disclosure in the complete set of financial statements. Exercising this judgement involves a consideration of the following:

(a)   the objectives of the government department;

(b)   the likely users of the general purpose financial statements;

(c)   the activity level that may be relevant to users' assessments of the performance of the government department; and

(d)   the concept of materiality. AASB 101 *Presentation of Financial Statements* and AASB 108 *Accounting Policies, Changes in Accounting Estimates and Errors* define an item as material if its omission or misstatement could influence the economic decisions of users of the financial statements.

21   AASB 1050 also contains requirements relating to the disclosure of administered income and expenses attributable to a government department's activities. The principles in this Standard are used in satisfying the requirements in AASB 1050.

APPENDIX A
COMPARISON OF AASB 1052 WITH AASs 27 AND 29

This Appendix accompanies, but is not part of, AASB 1052.

This Standard reproduces the material relating to disaggregated disclosures contained in AAS 27 and AAS 29, except that:

(a)   Appendix 1 to AAS 27 contained an illustrative example of the disclosures required in respect of the broad functions/activities of a local government. This Standard does not provide an illustration;

(b)   AAS 29 (paragraph 12.7.2) encouraged a government department to disclose the assets deployed and liabilities incurred that are reliably attributable to each of its activities. This Standard (paragraph 16) requires such disclosure; and

(c)   this Standard (paragraph 21) notes that its principles are used in satisfying the requirement in AASB 1050 *Administered Items* to disclose administered income and expenses attributable to a government department's activities. AASs 27 and 29 contained no such reference.

The following table provides source references to paragraphs 11–21 of this Standard, most of which were derived from AASs 27 and 29. It is provided to facilitate an understanding of, and assist in the application of, the requirements in this Standard.

Paragraphs in AASB 1052	Relevant source paragraphs in AASs 27 & 29
11–14	86–89 of AAS 27
15–20	12.7–12.7.4 of AAS 29
21	New paragraph

BASIS FOR CONCLUSIONS

This Basis for Conclusions accompanies, but is not part of, AASB 1052.

Introduction

BC1 This Basis for Conclusions summarises the Board's considerations in developing this Standard in the context of the Board's short-term review of the requirements in AAS 27 *Financial Reporting by Local Governments*, AAS 29 *Financial Reporting by Government Departments* and AAS 31 *Financial Reporting by Governments*.

Background

BC2 The Board considered it timely to review the requirements in AASs 27, 29 and 31, in particular to:

(a) review the extent to which local governments, government departments and governments should continue to be subject to requirements that differ from requirements applicable to other not-for-profit entities and for-profit entities contained in Australian Accounting Standards. The Board concluded that differences should be removed, where appropriate and timely, to improve the overall quality of financial reporting;

(b) bring requirements applicable to local governments, government departments and governments up-to-date with contemporary accounting thought;

(c) consider the implications of the outcomes of its project on the harmonisation of Generally Accepted Accounting Principles (GAAP) and Government Finance Statistics (GFS), in particular on the requirements in AAS 31;

(d) decide whether the encouragements in AASs 27, 29 and 31 should be made mandatory or removed; and

(e) remove uncertainty in the application of cross-references to other Australian Accounting Standards and the override provisions in AASs 27, 29 and 31 that made the requirements in AASs 27, 29 and 31 take precedence over other requirements.

BC3 The Board considered the following alternative mechanisms for implementing the approach of updating and improving the requirements for local governments, government departments and governments:

(a) review the requirements in AASs 27, 29 and 31 and where appropriate:

(i) amend other Australian Accounting Standards to pick up any issues that are addressed in AASs 27, 29 and 31 that are not adequately addressed in the latest Australian Accounting Standards and have them apply to local governments, government departments and governments; or

(ii) create public sector specific topic-based Standards;

and consequently withdraw AASs 27, 29 and 31; or

(b) review AASs 27, 29 and 31 and re-issue them in light of the latest Australian Accounting Standards, retaining/amending where necessary any issues that are addressed in AASs 27, 29 and 31 that are not adequately addressed in the latest Australian Accounting Standards.

BC4 The Board chose alternative (a) given the improvements in the quality of financial reporting by local governments, government departments and governments since AASs 27, 29 and 31 were first issued.

BC5 Where the Board identified that the material in AASs 27, 29 and 31 could be improved within time and resource constraints, improvements have been made. Much of the material in AASs 27, 29 and 31 has been retained substantively unamended.

Improvements will be progressed in due course in line with the AASB's Public Sector Policy Paper *Australian Accounting Standards and Public Sector Entities*.

BC6 The first stage of the short-term review of the requirements in AASs 27, 29 and 31 was the preparation of a paragraph-by-paragraph analysis of each of AASs 27, 29 and 31, listing each paragraph of each Standard alongside corresponding Standards or other pronouncements that would apply to local governments, government departments or governments in the absence of AASs 27, 29 and 31. The Board's conclusions and rationale for the treatment of each paragraph in the context of the review were also provided in the analysis. The Board's primary focus was on dealing with the requirements from the three Standards in such a way as to not leave a vacuum.

BC7 Each paragraph from AASs 27, 29 and 31 was classified as being:

(a) no longer needed or adequately dealt with in other Standards;

(b) more appropriately dealt with in other Standards; or

(c) not adequately and/or appropriately dealt with in other Standards and therefore should be retained or improved and incorporated into other Standards.

The paragraph-by-paragraph analyses considered by the AASB in developing the Exposure Draft ED 156 *Proposals Arising from the Short-term Review of the Requirements in AAS 27, AAS 29 and AAS 31* that gave rise to this Standard are available on the AASB website. They support, but do not form part of, this Basis for Conclusions.

BC8 In reviewing the paragraphs, the Board noted that some material in AASs 27, 29 and 31 would, under the current style of writing Standards, be located in a separate Basis for Conclusions. Given the short-term nature of the review of AASs 27, 29 and 31, the Board concluded that explanations of technical issues that both originated in and are being relocated from AASs 27, 29 and 31 should, when appropriate, be located in the body of the Standard to which they are relocated.

BC9 The Board decided not to retain the illustrative general purpose financial reports provided in AASs 27, 29 and 31, because their purpose, which was to provide an educational tool in the initial stages of accrual reporting by local governments, government departments and governments, is no longer needed.

BC10 The remainder of this Basis for Conclusions focuses on issues specific to disaggregated disclosures.

Disaggregated disclosures

BC11 The Board decided to retain, substantially unchanged, the requirements relating to segment-like reporting from paragraphs 86 to 89 of AAS 27 and paragraphs 12.7 to12.7.4 of AAS 29 and relocate them into a separate new topic-based Standard. Because of the differing requirements, the Board concluded that they should be expressed separately for local governments and government departments. A longer-term separate project on disaggregated disclosures for local governments and government departments will be progressed in due course.

BC12 The Board considered relocating the material into AASB 114 *Segment Reporting* (and subsequently AASB 8 *Operating Segments*), but rejected this option consistent with its intention to retain requirements substantively unchanged in the short term. The guidance in AASB 114 (and AASB 8), which is not applicable to not-for-profit entities or for-profit government departments, comprehensively addresses segment reporting issues and specifies requirements that differ substantially from those required under AASs 27, 29 and 31.

BC13 The Board considered whether for-profit government departments should be subject to AASB 114 (and AASB 8) rather than this Standard. The Board noted that for-profit government departments typically do not exist in practice. Consistent with the general approach to the short-term review of AASs 27, 29 and 31, and because

AAS 29 applied to government departments, including for-profit government departments, the Board decided that for-profit government departments should continue to adopt policies that are consistent with not-for-profit government departments to the extent previously required by AAS 29. This approach will be reviewed as part of the Board's longer-term consideration of the definition of government departments in the context of the reporting entity concept.

BC14 Paragraph 12.7.2 of AAS 29 encouraged the disclosure of information about assets deployed and liabilities incurred in relation to each major activity undertaken by a government department. Consistent with paragraph BC2(d), the Board decided that, in relation to disaggregated information, assets deployed and liabilities incurred in relation to and reliably attributable to each major activity undertaken by a government department should be required to be disclosed (see paragraph 16). The information is relevant in assessing the effectiveness, efficiency and economy of operations and of resource allocation decisions.

BC15 The Board decided not to retain the requirements relating to segment-like reporting from paragraphs 15.12 to 15.12.2 of AAS 31. It is not necessary for this Standard to specify disaggregated disclosure requirements for governments, as AASB 1049 *Whole of Government and General Government Sector Financial Reporting* addresses disaggregated disclosure requirements for governments.

AASB

AASB 1053

Application of Tiers of Australian Accounting Standards

(Compiled January 2015)

This compiled Standard applies to annual reporting periods beginning on or after 1 January 2017. Early application is permitted for annual reporting periods beginning on or after 1 January 2014 but before 1 January 2017. It incorporates relevant amendments made up to and including 28 January 2015.

Prepared on 2 April 2015 by the staff of the Australian Accounting Standards Board.

This note is not part of Accounting Standard AASB 1053.

The following unincorporated amendments are not included in this compiled Standard.

- AASB 2016-7 *Amendments to Australian Accounting Standards — Deferral of AASB 15 for Not-for-Profit Entities*. This Standard defers the consequential amendments that were originally set out in AASB 2014-5 *Amendments to Australian Accounting Standards arising from AASB 15*, by restating the effective date of the amendments set out in AASB 2015-8 *Amendments to Australian Accounting Standards* for not-for-profit entities. This Standard defers the application of AASB 15 to 1 January 2019. Earlier application is permitted provided AASB 1058 is also applied to the same period.

Entities early-adopting any amendments with later application dates will need to refer to the amending Standards that have not yet been incorporated into compilations. The abovementioned unincorporated amendments may be located on the AASB website at www.aasb.gov.au or on the Federal Register of Legislation website at www.legislation.gov.au.

CONTENTS

Australian Accounting Standard AASB 1053 *Application of Tiers of Australian Accounting Standards* (as amended) is set out in paragraphs 1 – 24 and Appendices A and B. All the paragraphs have equal authority. Paragraphs in **bold type** state the main principles. AASB 1053 is to be read in the context of other Australian Accounting Standards, including AASB 1048 *Interpretation of Standards*, which identifies the Australian Accounting Interpretations. In the absence of explicit guidance, AASB 108 *Accounting Policies, Changes in Accounting Estimates and Errors* provides a basis for selecting and applying accounting policies.

COMPILATION DETAILS

Accounting Standard AASB 1053 *Application of Tiers of Australian Accounting Standards* as amended

This compiled Standard applies to annual reporting periods beginning on or after 1 January 2017. It takes into account amendments up to and including 28 January 2015 and was prepared on 2 April 2015 by the staff of the Australian Accounting Standards Board (AASB).

This compilation is not a separate Accounting Standard made by the AASB. Instead, it is a representation of AASB 1053 (June 2010) as amended by other Accounting Standards, which are listed in the Table below.

Table of Standards

Standard	Date made	Application date (*annual reporting periods ... on or after ...*)	Application, saving or transitional provisions
AASB 1053	30 Jun 2010	(*beginning*) 1 Jul 2013	see (a) below
AASB 2014-2	23 Jun 2014	(*beginning*) 1 Jul 2014	see (b) below
AASB 2014-5	12 Dec 2014	(*beginning*) 1 Jan 2017	see (c) below
AASB 2015-3	28 Jan 2015	(*beginning*) 1 Jul 2015	see (d) below

(a) Entities may elect to apply this Standard to annual reporting periods beginning on or after 1 July 2009 but before 1 July 2013.
(b) Entities may elect to apply this Standard to annual reporting periods beginning on or after 1 July 2009 but before 1 July 2014.
(c) Entities may elect to apply this Standard to annual reporting periods beginning on or after 1 January 2005 but before 1 January 2017, provided that AASB 15 *Revenue from Contracts with Customers* is also applied to such periods.
(d) Entities may elect to apply this Standard to annual reporting periods beginning on or after 1 January 2014 but before 1 July 2015.

Table of amendments to Standard

Paragraph affected	How affected	By ... [paragraph]
6	deleted	AASB 2015-3 [13, 14]
13	amended	AASB 2014-2 [7]
15	amended	AASB 2014-2 [8]
17 (preceding heading)	replaced	AASB 2014-2 [9]
17	amended	AASB 2014-2 [10]
18 (and preceding heading)	replaced	AASB 2014-2 [11]
18A-18B	added	AASB 2014-2 [12]
19 (preceding heading)	added	AASB 2014-2 [13]
19	replaced	AASB 2014-2 [14]
19A-19B	added	AASB 2014-2 [14]
20	replaced	AASB 2014-2 [15]
21-22	amended	AASB 2014-2 [16]
24 (preceding heading)	added	AASB 2014-2 [17]
24	added	AASB 2014-2 [18]

Table of amendments to guidance

Paragraph affected	How affected	By ... [paragraph]
Appendix C (rubric)	amended	AASB 2014-2 [19]
Appendix C, Chart 1-2	replaced	AASB 2014-2 [20]
Appendix C, Chart 3-4	added	AASB 2014-2 [20]
Appendix D	added	AASB 2014-2 [21]

Basis for Conclusions paragraph BC81 has been amended by AASB 2014-5 *Amendments to Australian Accounting Standards arising from AASB 15*. This amendment is not shown in the above Tables of amendments.

COMPARISON WITH *IFRS FOR SMEs*

The disclosures required by Tier 2 and the disclosures required by the IASB's *International Financial Reporting Standard for Small and Medium-sized Entities (IFRS for SMEs)* are highly similar. However, Tier 2 requirements and the *IFRS for SMEs* are not directly comparable as a consequence of Tier 2 including recognition and measurement requirements corresponding to those in IFRSs, whereas the *IFRS for SMEs* includes limited modifications to those requirements.

In addition, the recognition, measurement and disclosure requirements that apply in accordance with Tier 2 are to be revised as Australian Accounting Standards are revised, whereas the *IFRS for SMEs* is expected to be revised only periodically for revisions of IFRSs.

ACCOUNTING STANDARD AASB 1053

The Australian Accounting Standards Board made Accounting Standard AASB 1053 *Application of Tiers of Australian Accounting Standards* under section 334 of the *Corporations Act 2001* on 30 June 2010.

This compiled version of AASB 1053 applies to annual reporting periods beginning on or after 1 January 2017. It incorporates relevant amendments contained in other AASB Standards made by the AASB up to and including 28 January 2015 (see Compilation Details).

ACCOUNTING STANDARD AASB 1053
APPLICATION OF TIERS OF AUSTRALIAN ACCOUNTING STANDARDS

Objective

1   The objective of this Standard is to set out the application of Tiers of Australian Accounting Standards to different categories of entities preparing *general purpose financial statements*.

Application

2   This Standard applies to[1]:

   (a)   each entity that is required to prepare financial reports in accordance with Part 2M.3 of the Corporations Act;

   (b)   general purpose financial statements of each *reporting entity*;

   (c)   financial statements that are, or are held out to be, general purpose financial statements; and

   (d)   financial statements of General Government Sectors (GGSs) prepared in accordance with AASB 1049 *Whole of Government and General Government Sector Financial Reporting*.

3   This Standard applies to annual reporting periods beginning on or after 1 July 2013.

   [Note: For application dates of paragraphs changed or added by an amending Standard, see Compilation Details.]

4   **This Standard may be applied to annual reporting periods beginning on or after 1 July 2009 but before 1 July 2013. When an entity applies this Standard to such an annual reporting period it shall disclose that fact.**

5   When an entity elects to early adopt this Standard for an annual reporting period beginning on or after 1 July 2009 but before 1 July 2013 and prepares Tier 2 general purpose financial statements, it shall also adopt the relevant Standards that specify Tier 2 reporting requirements.

6   [Deleted by the AASB]

Tiers of reporting requirements

7   Australian Accounting Standards consist of two Tiers of reporting requirements for preparing general purpose financial statements:

   (a)   Tier 1: Australian Accounting Standards; and

   (b)   Tier 2: Australian Accounting Standards – Reduced Disclosure Requirements.

8   Tier 1 incorporates International Financial Reporting Standards (IFRSs) issued by the International Accounting Standards Board (IASB) and include requirements that are specific to Australian entities.

---

1   This application paragraph does not amend the application paragraphs of other Standards that are restricted to reporting entities.

9   Tier 2 comprises the recognition and measurement requirements of Tier 1 but substantially reduced disclosure requirements. Except for the presentation of a third statement of financial position under Tier 1[2], the presentation requirements under Tier 1 and Tier 2 are the same.

10   Each Australian Accounting Standard specifies the entities to which it applies and, where necessary, sets out disclosure requirements from which Tier 2 entities are exempt.

Application of Australian Accounting Standards under the Differential Reporting Framework

Application of Tier 1 reporting requirements

11   Tier 1 reporting requirements shall apply to the general purpose financial statements of the following types of entities:

(a)   for-profit private sector entities that have *public accountability*; and

(b)   the Australian Government and State, Territory and Local Governments.

12   Subject to AASB 1049, GGSs of the Australian Government and State and Territory Governments shall apply Tier 1 reporting requirements.

Application of Tier 2 reporting requirements

13   Tier 2 reporting requirements shall, as a minimum, apply to the general purpose financial statements of the following types of entities:

(a)   for-profit private sector entities that do not have public accountability;

(b)   not-for-profit private sector entities; and

(c)   public sector entities, whether for-profit or not-for-profit, other than the Australian Government and State, Territory and Local Governments.

These types of entities may elect to apply Tier 1 reporting requirements in preparing general purpose financial statements.

14   Entities applying Tier 2 reporting requirements would not be able to state compliance with IFRSs.

15   Whilst Tier 2 reporting requirements are available under this Standard for general purpose financial statements of non-publicly accountable for-profit private sector entities, not-for-profit private sector entities and public sector entities (both for-profit or not-for-profit) other than those required to apply Tier 1 reporting requirements, regulators might exercise a power to require the application of Tier 1 reporting requirements.

16   Disclosures under Tier 2 reporting requirements are the minimum disclosures required to be included in general purpose financial statements. Entities may include additional disclosures using Tier 1 reporting requirements as a guide if, in their judgement, such additional disclosures are consistent with the objective of general purpose financial statements.

Application of AASB 1

17   Some of the disclosure requirements in AASB 1 *First-time Adoption of Australian Accounting Standards* have been excluded from Tier 2 reporting requirements.

---

2   Under AASB 101 *Presentation of Financial Statements*, a complete set of financial statements includes a statement of financial position as at the beginning of the earliest comparative period when an entity applies an accounting policy retrospectively or makes a retrospective restatement of items in its financial statements, or when it reclassifies items in its financial statements.

Accordingly, entities adopting Tier 2 reporting requirements for the first time that are required to apply AASB 1 shall comply with the reduced disclosure requirements in AASB 1, including for the purposes of paragraph 18A(a).

First-time adoption of Australian Accounting Standards

18   When applying Tier 1 reporting requirements for the first time, an entity that prepared its most recent previous financial statements in the form of special purpose financial statements shall apply all the relevant requirements of AASB 1.

18A   When applying Tier 2 reporting requirements for the first time, an entity that prepared its most recent previous financial statements in the form of special purpose financial statements:

(a)   without applying, or only selectively applying, applicable recognition and measurement requirements of Australian Accounting Standards shall apply either:

(i)   all the relevant requirements of AASB 1; or

(ii)   Tier 2 reporting requirements directly using the requirements in AASB 108; and

(b)   applying all applicable recognition and measurement requirements of Australian Accounting Standards shall not apply AASB 1.

18B   An entity applying paragraph 18A(b) continues applying the applicable recognition and measurement requirements of Australian Accounting Standards, whether it had previously initially applied recognition and measurement requirements consistent with AASB 1 or a predecessor to AASB 108, whichever was applicable at the time.

Reapplication of Australian Accounting Standards other than transitioning between Tiers

19   Subject to paragraphs 19A and 21, an entity that:

(a)   has applied Tier 1 reporting requirements or IFRSs in a previous reporting period; but

(b)   whose most recent previous annual financial statements did not contain an explicit and unreserved statement of compliance with Tier 1 reporting requirements[3] or IFRSs; and

(c)   is resuming or commencing the application of Tier 1 reporting requirements;

        shall apply all the relevant requirements of AASB 1, or the AASB 1 option for retrospective application of Australian Accounting Standards in accordance with AASB 108 as if the entity had never stopped applying Australian Accounting Standards or IFRSs.

19A   An entity that is to claim IFRS compliance on resuming Tier 1 reporting requirements under paragraph 19, shall not use the AASB 1 option for retrospective application of Australian Accounting Standards in accordance with AASB 108 if it was not previously IFRS compliant.

19B   Subject to paragraph 23, an entity that:

(a)   has applied Tier 2 reporting requirements in a previous reporting period; but

---

3   Compliance with Tier 1 reporting requirements is a reference to compliance with Australian Accounting Standards (Tier 1).

APPENDIX C
TRANSITION

This appendix accompanies, but is not part of, AASB 1053.

This Appendix is intended to facilitate the application of the requirements in paragraphs 17–23 of the Standard for the application of Tiers, and the transition between Tiers, of Australian Accounting Standards.

Chart 1: First-time Adoption of Tier 1 or Tier 2 Reporting Requirements (paragraphs 18–18B)

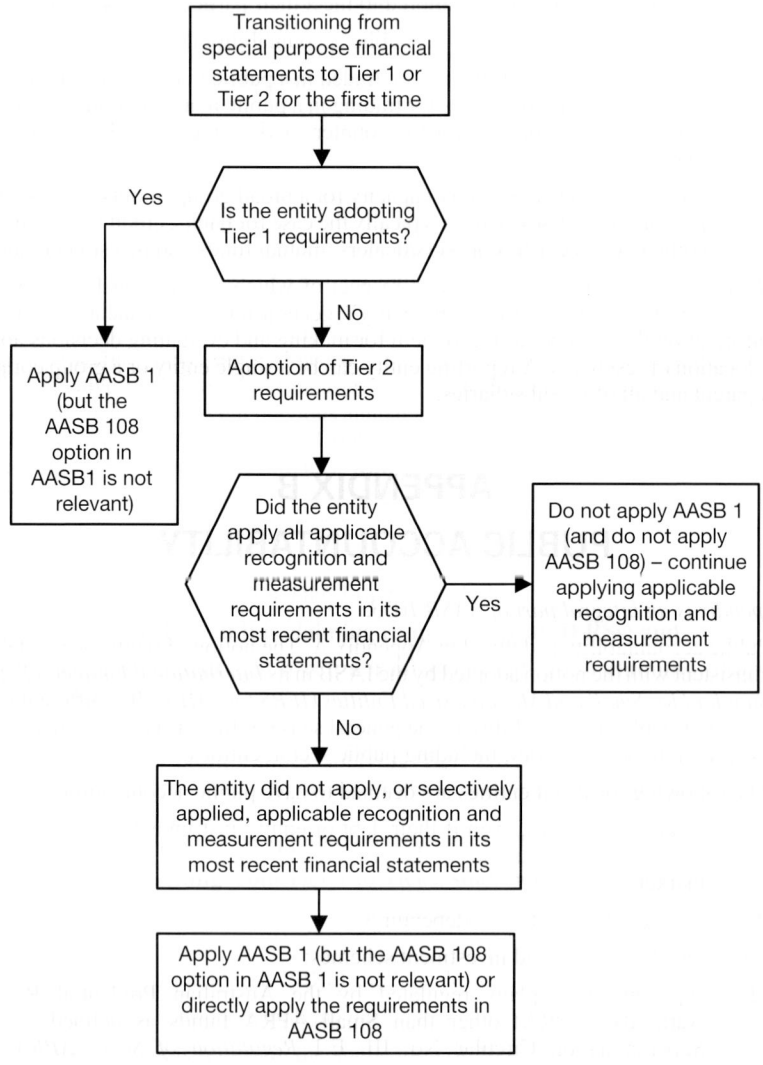

Chart 2: Re-application of Tier 1 Reporting Requirements (paragraphs 19 and 19A)

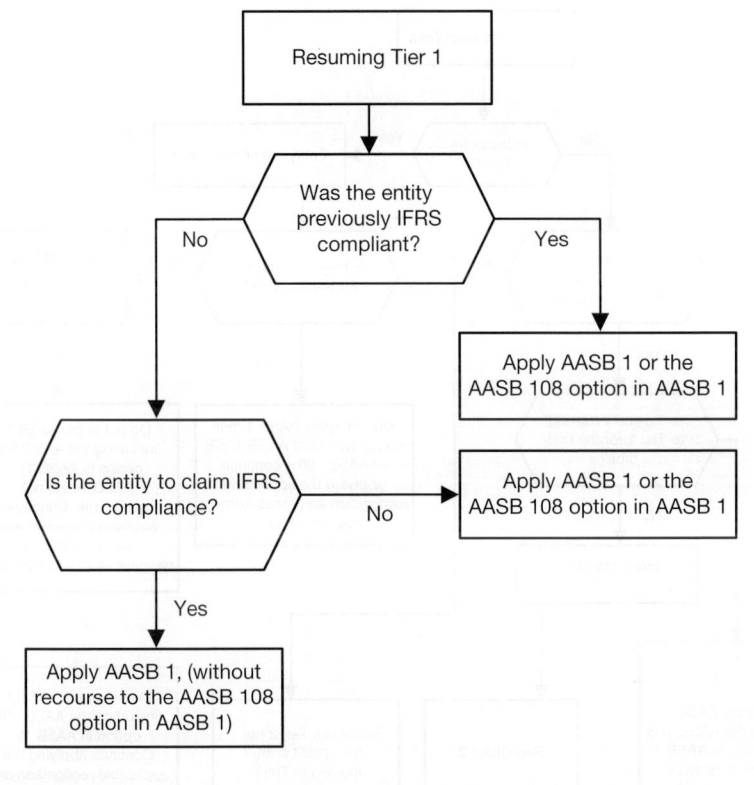

Chart 3: Re-application of Tier 2 Reporting Requirements (paragraph 19B)

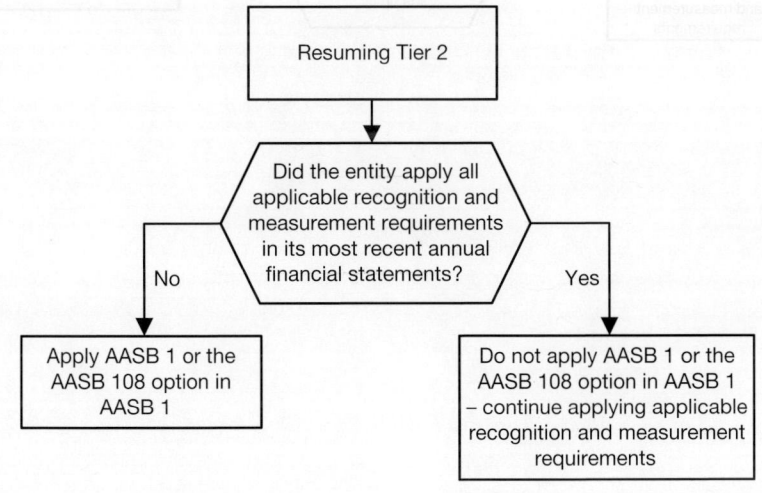

Chart 4: Moving between Tiers (paragraphs 21 and 23)

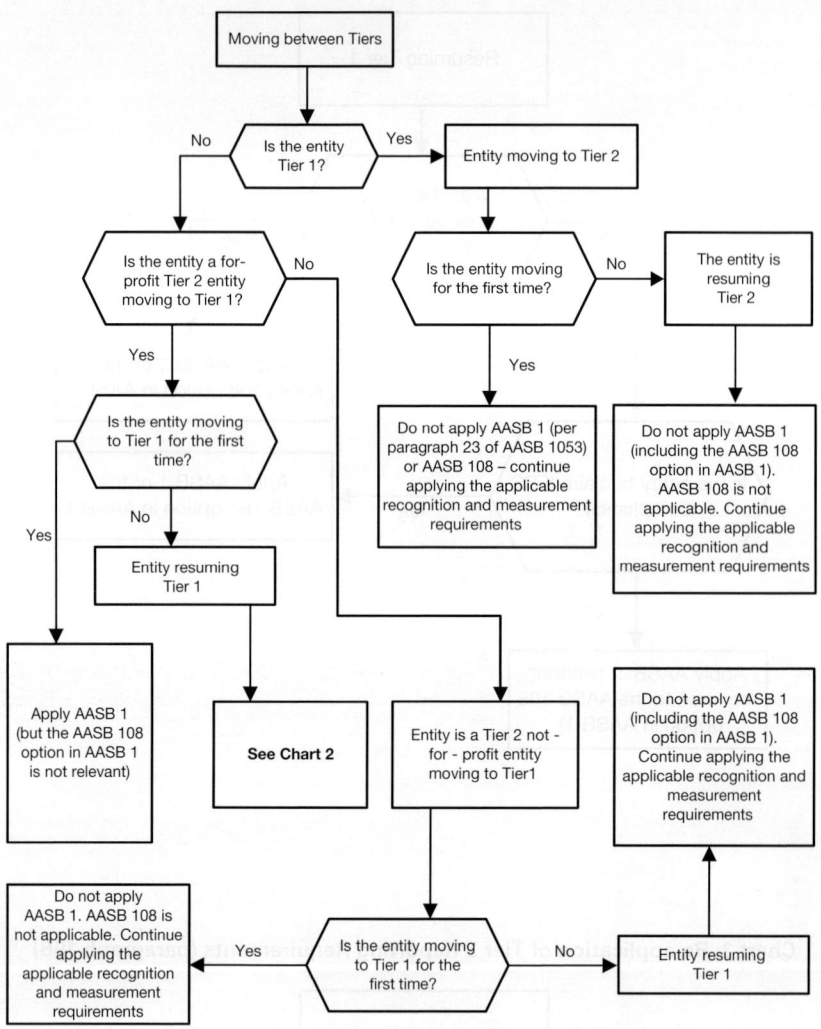

APPENDIX D
TRANSITION SCENARIOS[6]

This appendix accompanies, but is not part of AASB 1053. It is intended to summarise which paragraphs of AASB 1053 (as revised by AASB 2014–2 Amendments to AASB 1053 – Transition to and between Tiers, and related Tier 2 Disclosure Requirements) would apply in particular common scenarios, and their consequences.

A previous reporting period	The most recent previous reporting period	Current reporting period	Applicable paragraph of AASB 1053	Consequence	Rationale	Basis for Conclusions paragraph accompanying AASB 2014–2
		First time adopt T1				
SPFSs	SPFSs using R&M	T1 IFRS	18	AASB 1	IFRS adoption	BC17
SPFSs	SPFSs using R&M	T1 non-IFRS	18	AASB 1	Consistent with IFRS	BC17
SPFSs	SPFSs not using R&M	T1 IFRS	18	AASB 1	IFRS adoption	BC17
SPFSs	SPFSs not using R&M	T1 non-IFRS	18	AASB 1	Consistent with IFRS	BC17
SPFSs	T2	T1 IFRS	21(a)	AASB 1	IFRS adoption	BC22
SPFSs	T2	T1 non-IFRS	21(b)	Not AASB 1	Continue R&M, & BC93 of AASB 1053[7]	BC22
		First time adopt T2				
SPFSs	SPFSs using R&M	T2	18A(b)	Not AASB 1	Continue R&M, & BC93 of AASB 1053	BC18
SPFSs	SPFSs not using R&M	T2	18A(a)	AASB 1 or directly through AASB 108	Cost/benefit considerations	BC17&BC19
SPFSs	T1 IFRSs	T2	23	Not AASB 1	Continue R&M, & BC93 of AASB 1053	BC22
SPFSs	T1 non-IFRS	T2	23	Not AASB 1	Continue R&M, & BC93 of AASB 1053	BC22

6 Legend:
SPFSs: special purpose financial statements;
R&M: recognition and measurement in Australian Accounting Standards;
T1: Tier 1;
T2: Tier 2; and
BC: Basis for Conclusions.

7 AASB 1053 *Application of Tiers of Australian Accounting Standards* (June 2010).

A previous reporting period	The most recent previous reporting period	Current reporting period	Applicable paragraph of AASB 1053	Consequence	Rationale	Basis for Conclusions paragraph accompanying AASB 2014–2
		Resume T1				
T1 IFRS	SPFSs using R&M	T1 IFRS	19	AASB 1 or AASB 108 option in AASB 1	IFRS adoption	BC13
T1 IFRS	SPFSs using R&M	T1 non-IFRS	19	AASB 1 or AASB 108 option in AASB 1	Consistent with IFRS	BC13
T1 IFRS	SPFSs not using R&M	T1 IFRS	19	AASB 1 or AASB 108 option in AASB 1	IFRS adoption	BC13
T1 IFRS	SPFSs not using R&M	T1 non-IFRS	19	AASB 1 or AASB 108 option in AASB 1	Consistent with IFRS	BC13
T1 IFRS	T2	T1 IFRS	21(a)	AASB 1 or AASB 108 option in AASB 1	IFRS adoption	BC22
T1 IFRS	T2	T1 non-IFRS	21(b)	Not AASB 1	Continue R&M, & BC93 of AASB 1053	BC22
T1 non-IFRS	SPFSs using R&M	T1 IFRS	19A	AASB 1 (but not AASB 108 option in AASB 1)	IFRS adoption	BC12
T1 non-IFRS	SPFSs using R&M	T1 non-IFRS	19	AASB 1 or AASB 108 option in AASB 1	Consistent with IFRS	
T1 non-IFRS	SPFSs not using R&M	T1 IFRS	19A	AASB 1 (but not AASB 108 option in AASB 1)	IFRS adoption	BC12
T1 non-IFRS	SPFSs not using R&M	T1 non-IFRS	19	AASB 1 or AASB 108 option in AASB 1	Consistent with IFRS	
T1 non-IFRS	T2	T1 IFRS	19A&21(a)	AASB 1 (but not AASB 108 option in AASB 1)	IFRS adoption	BC12&BC22
T1 non-IFRS	T2	T1 non-IFRS	21(b)	Not AASB 1	Continue R&M, & BC93 of AASB 1053	BC22

A previous reporting period	The most recent previous reporting period	Current reporting period	Applicable paragraph of AASB 1053	Consequence	Rationale	Basis for Conclusions paragraph accompanying AASB 2014–2
		Resume T2				
T2	SPFSs using R&M	T2	19B(e)	Not AASB 1 or AASB 108 option in AASB 1	Continue R&M, & BC93 of AASB 1053	BC14
T2	SPFSs not using R&M	T2	19B(d)	AASB 1 or AASB 108 option in AASB 1	Consistent with IFRS	
T2	T1 IFRS	T2	23	Not AASB 1 or AASB 108 option in AASB 1	Continue R&M, & BC93 of AASB 1053	BC22
T2	T1 non-IFRS	T2	23	Not AASB 1 or AASB 108 option in AASB 1	Continue R&M, & BC93 of AASB 1053	BC22

BASIS FOR CONCLUSIONS

The Basis for Conclusions accompanies, but is not part of, AASB 1053.

BC1 This Basis for Conclusions summarises the Australian Accounting Standards Board's considerations in reaching the conclusions in AASB 1053 *Application of Tiers of Australian Accounting Standards*. It also provides a context for the Board's decisions about disclosures from which 'Tier 2' entities are exempt, which are reflected in AASB 2010-2 *Amendments to Australian Accounting Standards arising from Reduced Disclosure Requirements*. It focuses on the issues that the Board considers to be of greatest significance. Individual Board members gave greater weight to some factors than to others.

Background to Differential Reporting in Australia

BC2 A form of differential reporting has been incorporated in Accounting Standards in Australia since the early 1990s. The concept of 'reporting entity' is at the core of this differential reporting regime. Statement of Accounting Concepts SAC 1 *Definition of the Reporting Entity* deals with the reporting entity concept. The AASB *Glossary of Defined Terms* includes the definition of a reporting entity[1] as:

> An entity in respect of which it is reasonable to expect the existence of users who rely on the entity's general purpose financial statement for information that will be useful to them for making and evaluating decisions about the allocation of resources. A reporting entity can be a single entity or a group comprising a parent and all of its subsidiaries.

BC3 Most Australian Accounting Standards include the requirements of corresponding International Financial Reporting Standards (IFRSs) and have the following application paragraph:

> This Standard applies to:
>
> (a)   each entity that is required to prepare financial reports in accordance with Part 2M.3 of the Corporations Act and that is a reporting entity;

---

1   This definition is included in paragraph Aus7.2 of AASB 101 *Presentation of Financial Statements*.

(b)   general purpose financial statements of each other reporting entity; and

(c)   financial statements that are, or are held out to be, general purpose financial statements.

Prior to AASB 1053, for-profit and not-for-profit (NFP) entities falling within the scope of this application paragraph were subject to all the recognition, measurement, presentation and disclosure requirements of those Standards. These entities included entities incorporated under the *Corporations Act 2001* that are reporting entities.

BC4   Under the Corporations Act, disclosing entities, public companies (including companies limited by guarantee), large proprietary companies and registered schemes must prepare and lodge financial statements that comply with accounting standards. Large proprietary companies are those companies that meet at least two of the three size thresholds set out in the Corporations Act relating to:

(a)   the consolidated revenue for the financial year of the company and the entities it controls (if any);

(b)   the value of the consolidated gross assets at the end of the financial year of the company and the entities it controls (if any); and

(c)   the number of employees of the company and the entities it controls (if any) at the end of the financial year.

These Corporations Act size thresholds effectively remove the external reporting obligations for small proprietary companies.[2]

BC5   Accordingly, prior to AASB 1053, a reporting burden that is less than compliance with full Australian Accounting Standards was only available to non-reporting entities in the preparation of financial statements that are not general purpose financial statements. The financial statements of non-reporting entities are classified as special purpose financial statements and, like general purpose financial statements, are subject to true and fair view requirements of the Corporations Act where they fall within the scope of that Act.

BC6   Entities eligible for this reduced reporting burden included those incorporated under the Corporations Act that are not reporting entities but are required to prepare financial statements. Only AASB 101 *Presentation of Financial Statements*, AASB 107 *Statement of Cash Flows*, AASB 108 *Accounting Policies, Changes in Accounting Estimates and Errors*, AASB 1031 *Materiality* and AASB 1048 *Interpretation of Standards* apply to such entities, by virtue of the application paragraphs in those Standards.

BC7   The Australian Securities and Investment Commission (ASIC) has expressed the view[3] that non-reporting entities required to prepare financial statements in accordance with Chapter 2M of the Corporations Act should comply with the recognition and measurement requirements of all accounting standards. Under ASIC's view, the only 'relief' for these entities is not having to apply the disclosure requirements contained in Standards other than AASB 101, AASB 107 and AASB 108.

BC8   In addition to AASB pronouncements that incorporate IFRSs, there are Australian Accounting Standards (including Interpretations) that apply specifically to some or all NFP entities, including:

(a)   AASB 1004 *Contributions*;

(b)   AASB 1049 *Whole of Government and General Government Sector Financial Reporting*;

---

2   Under Sections 292(2), 293 and 294 of the Corporations Act, small proprietary companies must prepare and lodge financial reports in certain circumstances such as when the Australian Securities and Investments Commission (ASIC) directs them, or they are controlled by a foreign company, or 5% of shareholders vote to have a financial report.

3   ASIC Regulatory Guide 85 *Reporting requirements for non-reporting entities.*

(c)   AASB 1050 *Administered Items*;

(d)   AASB 1051 *Land Under Roads*;

(e)   AASB 1052 *Disaggregated Disclosures*; and

(f)   AASB Interpretation 1038 *Contributions by Owners Made to Wholly-owned Public Sector Entities*.

BC9   Prior to AASB 1053, entities not incorporated under the Corporations Act, (which include many NFP entities and most public sector entities), were required to apply, where applicable, the recognition, measurement, presentation and disclosure requirements of these and other Australian Accounting Standards if they were reporting entities or holding out financial statements to be general purpose financial statements.

The Need to Review the Differential Reporting Framework

BC10   The Board identified a number of concerns with the differential reporting framework that existed prior to AASB 1053. These concerns included that:

(a)   costs of preparing general purpose financial statements for some entities were greater than benefits for the users of those general purpose financial statements, because the framework resulted in requirements for general purpose financial statements that were overly burdensome for many entities; and

(b)   user needs were not being satisfied for other entities, because the framework was being applied in a way that some entities (which should prepare general purpose financial statements) were being treated as non-reporting entities and preparing only special purpose financial statements.

BC11   When it was initially considering these concerns, the Board noted that the International Accounting Standards Board (IASB) was developing an *IFRS for SMEs* that would result in general purpose financial statements that would not be compliant with IFRSs. Accordingly, the Board decided that, in revising its differential reporting framework, it was appropriate for the Board to also consider requirements for general purpose financial statements that differ from (full) Australian Accounting Standards. The Financial Reporting Council has been kept apprised of these developments.

BC12   The Board issued a number of consultative documents containing its proposals for addressing the concerns noted in paragraph BC10. These documents were, in sequence:

(a)   Invitation to Comment ITC 12 *Request for Comment on a Proposed Revised Differential Reporting Regime for Australia and IASB Exposure Draft of A Proposed IFRS for Small and Medium-sized Entities* – issued in May 2007;

(b)   Consultation Paper *Differential Financial Reporting – Reducing Disclosure Requirements (A Proposed Reduced Disclosure Regime for Non-publicly Accountable For-profit Private Sector Entities and Certain Entities in the Not-for-profit Private Sector and Public Sector)* – issued in February 2010; and

(c)   Exposure Draft ED 192 *Differential Reporting Framework* – also issued in February 2010.

BC13   These consultative documents contained proposals relating to both of the concerns (a) and (b) noted in paragraph BC10 above. The Board refined its ITC 12 proposals in the light of comments it received on the ITC, and reflected its revised proposals in the Consultation Paper and accompanying ED 192. After considering constituent comments on ED 192, the Board decided to issue AASB 1053 in response to concern (a), and to undertake further research prior to deciding how it would deal with concern (b).

BC14 In relation to concern (b), many constituents agreed with the manner in which the Board proposed to address the concern, which was to change the focus from reporting entity to general purpose financial statements and clarify the meaning of general purpose financial statements in an Australian context. This was on the grounds that:

(a)   the application of reporting entity involves a high degree of subjectivity and the term is open to differing interpretations; and

(b)   the use of reporting entity for differential reporting is not universally understood.

This group was of the view that the use of the reporting entity concept does not provide the intended result, and the uncertainty surrounding its application reduces its usefulness as a robust criterion for differential reporting purposes.

BC15 In contrast, other constituents expressed the view that the concept of reporting entity works well and should be retained as one aspect of differential reporting. They commented that they have not seen evidence of major problems with its application. This group, therefore, considered that those entities that currently claim to be non-reporting entities and prepare special purpose financial statements do not have dependent users and the evidence does not support a view that there is a systemic problem with reporting entities claiming a non-reporting entity status to evade their reporting responsibilities under Australian Accounting Standards.

BC16 The Board concluded that, in the light of these contrasting claims, further research should be carried out on the impact of the ED 192 proposals on those entities currently preparing special purpose financial statements. This is primarily with a view to ensuring that those entities currently appropriately preparing special purpose financial statements are not disadvantaged by the proposals. Consistent with this, the Board decided that, under the first stage of revisions to the differential reporting framework, concern (a) should be addressed. The Board's approach to dealing with concern (a) leaves the current differential reporting framework based on the reporting entity concept and general purpose financial statements intact, including the requirement for entities required to prepare financial reports in accordance with Part 2M.3 of the Corporations Act to apply AASB 101, AASB 107, AASB 108, AASB 1031 and AASB 1048, by virtue of the application paragraphs in those Standards.

BC17 The remainder of this Basis for Conclusions focuses on the basis for the Board's conclusions relating to concern (a).

Different Tiers of Requirements for General Purpose Financial Statements

BC18 The Board decided to retain full IFRSs as adopted in Australia as the first Tier (Tier 1) of reporting requirements, and make it mandatory for a relatively small number of entities in the private and public sectors in their preparation of general purpose financial statements. These entities are limited to publicly accountable entities in the for-profit private sector and Governments in the public sector (see paragraphs BC25 and BC52). Accordingly, AASB 1053 does not reduce the reporting burden of those entities. Retention of full IFRSs as adopted in Australia requirements for these entities is consistent with the approach adopted by the IASB to require certain entities to continue to comply with full IFRSs in order to claim IFRS compliance.

BC19 The Board decided to introduce a second Tier (Tier 2) of requirements to substantially reduce the burden of financial reporting for other entities in both the private and public sectors in their preparation of general purpose financial statements. Tier 2 retains the recognition, measurement and presentation requirements[4] of full IFRSs as adopted in Australia, but requires disclosures that are substantially reduced when compared with those required under full IFRSs as adopted in Australia.

---

4   Except for presentation of a third balance sheet required under Tier 1.

BC20 The Board regards AASB 1053 as a pragmatic and substantive response to the need to reduce the burden of disclosure requirements on Australian reporting entities. However, the Board does not regard it as a complete or final answer to that need. In addition to the further research referred to in paragraph BC16 above, the Board intends continuing its deliberations on revising the differential reporting framework with a view to ongoing improvements (including having regard to decisions made by the IASB in relation to its *IFRS for SMEs* – see paragraph BC98). The Board concluded that the reforms in AASB 1053 should not be delayed while consideration of other possible areas of reform continues. The Board notes that important reforms are also being considered to reduce the complexity of full IFRSs, including in the area of financial instruments, which would help reduce reporting complexities when adopted in Australia, including for entities that would be subject to Tier 1 requirements. The IASB is expected to move beyond financial instruments in its efforts to simplify requirements and the AASB will continue to encourage and support those efforts.

BC21 The new Tier 2 requirements do not change the current AASB policy of the same transactions and other events being subject to the same accounting requirements to the extent feasible (that is, transaction neutrality), for all entities preparing general purpose financial statements (whether for-profit or NFP).

BC22 The Board considered whether a third tier of reporting requirements for general purpose financial statements should be introduced to provide simpler financial reporting requirements for smaller NFP entities since those entities might find the adoption of Tier 2 requirements overly burdensome on cost-benefit grounds. The Board noted that many NFP entities in the private sector are established as companies limited by guarantee under the Corporations Act or as associations under relevant Incorporated Associations Acts in each State and Territory. Moreover, many non-trading cooperatives are regulated by State or Territory Acts. Having regard to this legislation, the Board noted that a reason for contemplating the need for a third tier was that there is generally no NFP equivalent to the outright exemption from reporting that exists for small proprietary companies (see paragraph BC4 above).

BC23 The Board noted that while there is some support from constituents for creating a third tier, there are different views about the requirements of such a tier and the way entities applying those requirements should be identified. The Board also considered the proposals for reporting relief in the Discussion Paper published by the Australian Government in June 2007 titled *Financial Reporting by Unlisted Public Companies* in relation to the creation of a third tier of reporting requirements for companies limited by guarantee[5].

BC24 The Board decided not to introduce a third tier of reporting requirements on the basis that:

(a) the Government intended to alleviate the reporting burden of small companies limited by guarantee through amendments to the Corporations Act; and

(b) Tier 2 requirements for preparing general purpose financial statements would help reduce the disclosure burden of NFP entities significantly.

Applicability of the Different Tiers to For-Profit Entities

Public Accountability

BC25 The Board concluded that for-profit entities that are publicly accountable (as defined in *International Financial Reporting Standard for Small and Medium-sized Entities* [*IFRS for SMEs*]) should be required to apply full IFRSs as adopted in Australia. This is on the basis of consistency with international reporting requirements in the for-profit private sector. The Board noted that, since Australia has adopted full IFRSs, it would be logical to use the public accountability notion used by the IASB in determining

---

5 The outcome of the proposals in the Discussion Paper are included in the *Corporations Amendment (Corporate Reporting Reform) Act 2010*.

which entities in the for-profit sector should apply Australian Accounting Standards in full.

BC26 The Board acknowledged constituents' comments about some aspects of the definition of public accountability that the application of the definition in some cases may involve interpretation or judgement. Some respondents to ED 192 noted it would be helpful for the Board to clarify certain terms used in the definition. These include the term 'public market' referred to in the first leg of the definition and the terms 'fiduciary', 'broad', 'outsiders' and 'primary business' referred to in the second leg of the definition. However, the Board noted it is not a policy of the Board to further interpret the IASB's terms and definitions. Accordingly, the Board decided that, instead of interpreting the terms in the definition, AASB 1053 should identify entities that the Board deems to be publicly accountable in the Australian context, to supplement the IASB's definition of public accountability (see Appendix B of AASB 1053).

BC27 In relation to identifying entities that should be deemed to be publicly accountable in the Australian context, some respondents to ED 192 questioned whether captive insurers should be classified as publicly accountable since, in their view, there is unlikely to be a broad group of outsiders involved. The Board noted that the nature of captive insurers varies. Some only provide insurance to subsidiaries within their group while others also insure joint venture businesses. Some captive insurers, such as association captive insurers, can insure a wide range of members. Those that provide insurance to subsidiaries within groups may also deal with outsiders. For example, they may offer products that have public beneficiaries (such as public or product liability, or professional indemnity).

BC28 The Board concluded that, whilst it expects that most insurance companies will be publicly accountable, there may be certain general insurers, such as some captive insurers, that may not be publicly accountable. Accordingly, the Board did not deem all regulated insurance entities as publicly accountable.

BC29 Some respondents to ED 192 also questioned whether Small Australian Prudential Regulation Authority (APRA) Funds (SAFs) should be deemed to be publicly accountable, given the small number of members and the limited users of their financial statements.

BC30 The Board noted that SAFs are usually similar in size to self-managed super funds (SMSFs) but, unlike SMSFs (which are regulated by the Australian Taxation Office [ATO]), are regulated by APRA because they do not meet all conditions to be a SMSF. The Board noted there may be users (such as regulators and trustees) of the financial statements of SAFs who can command information they need and the outsiders for whom the SAF holds assets in a fiduciary capacity. Accordingly, those users do not seem to constitute a broad group and the Board decided not to deem SAFs as publicly accountable.

BC31 Furthermore, some respondents questioned whether all entities holding an Australian Financial Services Licence (AFSL) would meet the definition of publicly accountable.

BC32 The Board noted that AFSL holders undertake a range of activities and are a diverse group of entities. The Board concluded that whether an AFSL holder is publicly accountable depends on the circumstances, including the nature of the services they provide. Therefore, it would not be appropriate for the Board to deem AFSL holders as publicly accountable or not publicly accountable.

Size Thresholds

BC33 The Board proposed in ITC 12 that for-profit entities that do not satisfy the definition of a publicly accountable entity, nevertheless may be viewed as being 'important' from a public interest perspective because of their large size, and should be subject to Tier 1 requirements. The size thresholds proposed were:

- Consolidated revenue for the financial year of the entity and the entities it controls (if any) of $500m.

- Consolidated assets at financial year end of the entity and the entities it controls (if any) of $250m.

BC34 The Board considered constituents' comments on the issue and decided not to require entities that are 'important' because of their large size to adopt Tier 1 requirements on the grounds that:

(a) size thresholds are arbitrary;

(b) using public accountability (as defined by the IASB) for the for-profit sector in Australia would be consistent with international requirements;

(c) large non-publicly accountable entities would still be required to prepare high-quality general purpose financial statements under the requirements of Tier 2; and

(d) keeping size thresholds that identify 'important' entities up-to-date would entail additional maintenance and monitoring costs.

For-Profit Entities in the Public Sector

BC35 The Board noted that the definition of public accountability it has adopted has a for-profit private sector orientation as it is based on the definition included in the *IFRS for SMEs*. The Board noted that the nature of for-profit entities in the public sector may differ from that in the private sector in that many Government Business Enterprises (GBEs) also undertake social policy obligations. Moreover, the ownership group in many for-profit public sector entities is not a broad group. The Board noted that, although these entities are typically seen as publicly accountable in the general sense of the term, they do not typically fall under the definition of public accountability used for the private sector.

BC36 Some respondents to ED 192 expressed the view that GBEs should be included in Tier 1 because of their commercial significance and their participation in markets in competition with private sector for-profit entities. Others noted that, while it is acknowledged there is a relatively high level of public interest in relation to GBEs, it is also important that those public sector entities that compete with private sector entities in Tier 2 are not disadvantaged through the application of more onerous financial reporting requirements.

BC37 Some respondents supported an approach where GBEs would by default be classified as Tier 2 entities, with the caveat that the public sector entity that 'regulates' the respective entities would determine whether individual entities should apply the disclosure requirements of Tier 1. This approach, it was noted, could result in GBEs achieving the same level of financial reporting as for-profit private sector entities of similar nature and size.

BC38 The Board concluded that, consistent with the role of other regulators under the revised differential reporting framework (see paragraphs BC40-BC41), the determination of the Tiers of reporting requirements under which for-profit public sector entities should report would best be left to relevant public sector regulators in each jurisdiction.

Entities Eligible for Tier 2 Requirements can Elect to Adopt Tier 1 Requirements

BC39 The Board concluded that an entity that is eligible to adopt Tier 2 requirements should be permitted to adopt Tier 1 requirements. This is on the basis that:

(a) a relevant regulator may decide that in certain circumstances it is more beneficial to the users of financial statements, including the public at large, to include more comprehensive information in the general purpose financial statements;

(b) a subsidiary may be required to apply Tier 1 requirements by its parent; and

(c)   some entities may find it more convenient or beneficial to continue to apply Tier 1 requirements in their circumstances. Examples include entities:

(i)   contemplating future listing on the stock exchange;

(ii)   planning to engage in activities as their primary business that would classify them as holders of assets in a fiduciary capacity for a broad group of outsiders; and

(iii) preferring to state compliance with full IFRSs because they are primarily engaged in international business.

The Role of Other Regulators

BC40 The Board noted that other regulators, legislators and stakeholders play an important role in the application of Standards, including providing exemptions in certain circumstances. For example, as noted in paragraph BC4, small proprietary companies are exempted from financial reporting under the Corporations Act.

BC41 The Board noted that some respondents to ITC 12 expressed concern about possible inconsistencies in practice that may arise if the Board were to specify rules rather than principles for determining which Tier of reporting is applicable to which entities. This is due to complexities involved in determining the application of different Tiers of reporting requirements to entities of different sizes and with varying levels of economic, social and political significance across different economic sectors. To help avoid these inconsistencies and to facilitate the application of different Tiers of reporting requirements in an effective and efficient manner, the Board decided that other regulators, legislators or stakeholders should have a role in determining the application of Standards under the revised framework. Accordingly, the Board decided that, except for the cases where a clear-cut and timeless application criterion can be used by the Board or a clear-cut judgement can be made based on relevant factors, the application issue would best be dealt with by other regulators, legislators and stakeholders (see, for example, paragraphs BC39(a) and (b)).

Applicability of the Different Tiers to NFP Entities

Public Accountability

BC42 The Board considered whether the notion of public accountability as defined by the IASB could usefully be applied to the NFP sector. It noted that, although there are some who argue that the IASB definition of public accountability may cover some NFP entities on the grounds that they hold funds in a fiduciary capacity for a broad group of outsiders, the IASB definition has a for-profit context that makes it unsuitable for the NFP sector.

BC43 The Board also considered using a modified definition of public accountability in the NFP sector context. The Board noted the disparate views among constituents about whether such a notion can effectively be modified and used to identify entities falling under different reporting Tiers in the NFP sector.

BC44 The Board noted that some constituents believe that the level of public accountability, for example, for each charity, depends on a number of entity-specific factors, which reduce the usefulness of 'public accountability' as a stand-alone criterion for differential reporting purposes in the NFP sector. Some constituents argued that the degree of public accountability of a charity has a direct relationship to the following.

(a)   *Sources of funds*: for example, if the sources of funds are public donations (particularly those that are tax deductible by the donor) or government grants, then a high degree of public accountability is expected. Voluntary labour may be regarded as a form of donation and, therefore, a high degree of public accountability might be expected when significant voluntary labour is involved. Generally the level of public accountability is high where public funds are involved, such as when community or social activities are carried out on behalf of government. However, when the source of funds is an individual or a corporation, a much lower degree of public accountability is expected on the basis that the individual or corporation involved can probably access the financial information they need. A moderate level of public accountability may be envisaged when the sources of funds are grants from foundations or sponsors.

(b) *Number of stakeholders in the entity*: the wider the spectrum of stakeholders, the higher the expected level of public accountability.

(c) *Scale of operations and geographical coverage*: generally charities active at the national or international level are seen as being publicly accountable at a high level.

BC45 The Board concluded that a modified definition of public accountability in the NFP private sector context would not provide a robust basis for identifying entities falling under different reporting Tiers since NFP private sector entities, (with the likely exception of smaller member-based entities), are typically seen as having differing degrees of public accountability in the general sense of the term.

BC46 The Board reached a similar conclusion about whether a definition of public accountability could provide a robust basis for identifying NFP public sector entities falling under different reporting Tiers. This is on the basis that these entities are regarded as publicly accountable in the general sense of the term.

Size Thresholds

BC47 The Board proposed in ITC 12 that NFP entities that prepare general purpose financial statements that exceed nominated size thresholds should be required to apply Tier 1 requirements. The size thresholds proposed were:

- Consolidated revenue for the financial year of the entity and the entities it controls (if any) of $25m.

- Consolidated assets at the end of the financial year of the entity and the entities it controls (if any) of $12.5m.

BC48 Some respondents to ITC 12 preferred the use of size thresholds in comparison to the use of a modified notion of public accountability as the basis for identifying reporting Tiers on the grounds that it is relatively objective and would provide consistency in identifying entities that fall under different Tiers. However, other respondents were concerned about using size thresholds, citing the following reasons:

(a) size thresholds are arbitrary;

(b) size thresholds will become outdated over time; and

(c) particularly in the public sector, unless jurisdiction-specific thresholds are prescribed, it would lead to similar entities applying different requirements across different State and Territory jurisdictions.

BC49 There were also differences of view between respondents as to the amounts of the appropriate thresholds. Some thought the thresholds noted in paragraph BC47 are too low and should be raised to be comparable to 'important' entity thresholds contemplated for the for-profit sector noted in paragraph BC33. Others thought the thresholds being contemplated are too high, which would mean that too few NFP entities would apply full IFRSs as adopted in Australia. Yet others thought that the ratio of thresholds (revenue twice the assets) is not appropriate for many asset-rich entities in the NFP sector.

BC50 Respondents' comments on the comparability of thresholds between private and public sector NFP entities and their difference from those contemplated for 'important' entities in the for-profit sector did not reflect any convergence of views. Some respondents thought that public sector NFP entities are inherently of greater public interest than private sector NFP entities. Others thought that the thresholds should take account of the fact that the resources at the disposal of public sector NFP entities are generally significantly greater than those at the disposal of private sector NFP entities.

Some expressed the view that public interest would not differ between the for-profit and NFP sectors. Others expressed the view that entities within the public sector are all of public interest and expressed concern that size thresholds would give a misleading perception of an increase in public interest proportional to an increase in an entity's size.

BC51 Consistent with the Board's conclusions in relation to size thresholds for for-profit entities, the Board concluded that size thresholds do not provide a robust basis for differential reporting purposes in a NFP context because of the complexities involved and that the disadvantages of using size thresholds would exceed any advantages that may arise from their use. The Board also noted that keeping size thresholds up-to-date would entail additional maintenance and monitoring costs.

Governments

BC52 The Board concluded that the Australian Government and State, Territory and Local Governments should be subject to Tier 1 requirements. This is on the basis that these entities clearly satisfy the criteria cited in paragraph BC63 as a whole, including in particular their coercive power to tax, rate or levy. Consistent with this conclusion, the Board also decided that General Government Sectors of the Australian Government and State and Territory Governments should continue to apply AASB 1049 *Whole of Government and General Government Sector Financial Reporting*, without the reduction in disclosures provided by Tier 2.

Public Sector NFP Universities

BC53 ED 192 proposed that universities in the public sector should be subject to Tier 1 requirements. Some respondents concurred with the proposal on the grounds that universities in the public sector are government funded. However, others had reservations, which included the following:

(a)   since universities are statutory bodies (in some jurisdictions), then they should be subject to the same reporting requirements that apply to other statutory bodies in the relevant jurisdiction – that is, the decision as to whether universities should be subject to Tier 1 or Tier 2 requirements should be left to the local regulator;

(b)   while it is acknowledged they are large entities, there would appear to be no conceptual reason mandating the classification of universities under Tier 1 – for example, they have no coercive power to tax, rate or levy;

(c)   funding by government or receipt of voluntary donations, by itself, does not suffice to classify universities as Tier 1 entities since many other public sector entities fall in the same category; and

(d)   the proposal would not be consistent with transaction-neutrality principles, because it would result in public sector NFP universities being treated differently from private sector universities.

BC54 The Board noted that because universities differ from jurisdiction to jurisdiction, it may not enable regulators in those jurisdictions to apply criteria that they regard as appropriate in their circumstances, if the Board were to make a universal decision on the reporting Tier under which they fall. Accordingly the Board decided that universities should be allowed to apply Tier 2 requirements in preparing their general purpose financial statements unless a relevant public sector regulator requires the application of Tier 1 requirements.

Private Sector NFP Entities

BC55 The Board considered the issue of possible subclassifications of different types of NFP entities within the NFP sector for differential reporting purposes. The Board noted commentators' views on ITC 14 *Proposed Definition and Guidance for Not-for-Profit*

Entities that NFP entities can generally be identified as being in one of three categories based on the nature of their operations and sources of funding:

(a) charities;

(b) member-based entities; and

(c) public sector entities;

and that there may be a need for a fourth 'other' category to cater for entities such as schools and religious organisations. The Board noted the significant disparities in the size of entities within each of the above categories.

BC56 Some constituents argued that the disclosures required by full IFRSs (or the *IFRS for SMEs*) would not satisfy the information needs of users of financial statements of, for example, charities. These Standards, it was noted, have a for-profit focus while the nature of charities' activities is such that not all disclosures in these Standards are pertinent to the needs of users of the financial statements of charities. Moreover, there are disclosures that relate to the nature of operations of charities and specific issues of public interest that are not required by these Standards and that may be within the scope of financial reporting. It was argued that the stakeholders of a charity are interested in the accountability of the entity in achieving objectives stated in the entity's mission statement using funds provided by those stakeholders. They noted that donors, grantors and other contributors who provide resources in the form of money or voluntary services and the public at large (which includes the beneficiaries of charitable activity) are all interested in the accountability of charities.

BC57 The Board noted that a similar view exists in regard to all NFP entities. This view links accountability to the objective of each NFP entity and advocates disclosure of particular performance-related information to help inform a wide range of stakeholders about the way a NFP entity is utilising its resources in achieving its purpose.

BC58 The Board decided that there should not be subclassifications of different types of entities in the NFP sector other than between private and public sector entities, for differential reporting purposes. In arriving at this decision, the Board noted that:

(a) in a transaction-neutral reporting environment, subclassifications should not make a reporting difference as far as the recognition and measurement of transactions are concerned; and

(b) a choice between Tier 1 and Tier 2 requirements would provide different levels of disclosures appropriate for entities with different levels of activities.

BC59 The Board noted that its conclusion on this matter does not rule out specific projects directed at particular types of NFP entities and decided that its separate project on Disclosures by Private Sector Not-for-Profit Entities should be the vehicle through which it determines whether disclosures in addition to those required by full IFRSs as adopted in Australia should be required of Tier 1 or Tier 2 NFP entities. The Board also noted that much of the information relating to the extent to which a NFP entity has achieved its purpose set out in its mission statement may not be of a financial nature.

Entities Eligible for Tier 2 Requirements can Elect to Adopt Tier 1 Requirements

BC60 The Board concluded that a NFP entity that is eligible to adopt Tier 2 requirements should be permitted to adopt Tier 1 requirements. This is on the basis that, as noted in relation to the for-profit sector in paragraph BC39, in some jurisdictions, a relevant regulator may decide that in certain circumstances it is more beneficial to the users of financial statements, including the public at large, to include more comprehensive information in the general purpose financial statements. A NFP entity may also find it beneficial to choose to apply Tier 1 requirements in order to claim compliance with full IFRSs as adopted in Australia with a view to enhancing its credibility internationally, in particular in relation to major users of financial statements such as donors and governments.

The Role of Other Regulators

BC61 The Board acknowledges that, although AASB 1053 allows the vast majority of entities in the NFP sector to adopt Tier 2 requirements, other regulators may decide that some of those entities should adopt Tier 1 requirements.

BC62 Some respondents to ED 192 particularly commented that, while they welcome the choice that the Board has provided to public sector regulators in determining which of the Tiers should be followed by entities other than those required by the Board to apply Tier 1 requirements, the Board should develop non-mandatory guidance, in the form of qualitative criteria, to help public sector regulators consistently identify entities falling under each of the two Tiers of reporting requirements.

BC63 The Board explored the possibility of providing guidance, noting there are a range of qualitative factors that could be considered, including the following:

(a) *the entity's coercive power to obtain public funds*: the Board noted this notion of coercive power is a narrow criterion and on its own would be helpful only in a limited number of cases for jurisdictions in identifying entities falling under each Tier;

(b) *level of public funds used by the entity*: entities in the public sector vary in the degree to which they are publicly funded, the discretion over the distribution or expenditure of public funds, and the nature of that spending (for example, operational compared with income redistribution);

(c) *risk profile*: generally, risk in the public sector is a reference to uncertainty in achieving an organisation's objectives and more comprehensive disclosures may be warranted where an entity is seen as having a high risk profile;

(d) *level of complexity*: the level of complexity of public sector entities varies with the nature, diversity and range of their activities, which may also point to the existence of a wide range of stakeholders; and

(e) *financial profile*: the financial profile of a public sector entity may point to its economic significance and ability in providing services, which would in turn have an impact on the level of public interest.

BC64 The Board noted that, while each of the above factors may be a useful indicator to help regulators in identifying entities that should disclose more comprehensive information in their general purpose financial statements, no single criterion, by itself, would be likely to provide a conclusive basis for a jurisdiction to distinguish between Tier 1 and Tier 2 entities in the public sector.

BC65 The Board noted these factors as a whole were taken into account in its decision to classify the Australian Government and State, Territory and Local Governments as Tier 1 entities (see paragraph BC52). Accordingly, the Board concluded that these factors as a whole would be likely to benefit regulators across public sector jurisdictions in identifying the population of entities that could be of greater interest to users of general purpose financial statements, including the public at large. The Board noted regulators may develop their own size thresholds to identify those entities about which there would be sufficient interest to justify applying Tier 1 requirements. To arrive at consistent results, the Board noted it might be appropriate to use a number of different size indicators such as total assets, revenue, and number of employees as the basis for thresholds.

Tier 2 Requirements

BC66 The Board decided to adopt the Reduced Disclosure Requirements (RDR) reflected in AASB 1053, rather than the *IFRS for SMEs*, as Tier 2 requirements. The Board noted that the two approaches are fundamentally different because the RDR involve applying the same recognition and measurement requirements as Tier 1, whereas the *IFRS for SMEs* modifies the recognition and measurement requirements of full IFRSs. In deciding between the RDR and the *IFRS for SMEs*, the Board also considered whether entities subject to Tier 2 requirements should be provided with an option of adopting the RDR or the *IFRS for SMEs*.

Reasons for Not Adopting *IFRS for SMEs*

BC67 Constituents' comments on the *IFRS for SMEs* were mixed. While many supported its reduction in disclosure requirements, they expressed concern about introducing recognition and measurement requirements that are different from those included in full IFRSs.

BC68 There was also concern expressed about the differences in the hierarchies for determining accounting policies under the *IFRS for SMEs* and full IFRSs in the absence of a specific requirement. It was noted that the hierarchy adopted in the *IFRS for SMEs* would lead to disparities in the choice of accounting policies by different entities as it gives precedence to the Conceptual Framework over full IFRSs as the source of guidance for determining accounting policies in the absence of a specific requirement.

BC69 Other respondents noted the additional initial and ongoing costs of training and education for two sets of standards both for the profession and at the tertiary level.

BC70 In its submission to the IASB on the proposed *IFRS for SMEs*, the AASB noted that the *IFRS for SMEs* in its proposed form would not be a stand-alone document and that to meet its stand-alone objective more topics and more treatment options would need to be included from full IFRSs.

BC71 Based on comments received from constituents, the AASB commented in its submission to the IASB that:

> Some subsidiaries of publicly accountable entities would find it burdensome to apply the proposed *IFRS for SMEs* in preparing their general purpose financial statements. They would need to prepare financial information based on the recognition and measurement requirements of full IFRSs for the purposes of the parent entity consolidation. If such subsidiaries are not themselves publicly accountable but apply full IFRSs (as they are already applying full IFRS recognition and measurement for consolidation purposes), they are required to disclose information that is onerous to prepare and is often of no benefit to users. If they were to adopt the *IFRS for SMEs* as proposed, they could choose to refer to a full IFRS for an option that is not included in the *IFRS for SMEs*. However, they are then required to follow the disclosure requirements of that full IFRS. A stand-alone *IFRS for SMEs* that includes only the absolute minimum necessary disclosures, more topics and more of the treatment options from full IFRSs may alleviate the problem. However, it seems likely that subsidiaries within large groups would be involved in a wider range of activities and transactions than an equivalent SME that is not part of a group. Accordingly, it may be necessary for the IASB to consider permitting subsidiaries of publicly accountable entities to prepare general purpose financial statements by applying all the recognition and measurement requirements of full IFRSs, but permitting reduced disclosures similar to those required by the *IFRS for SMEs*.

BC72 However, the *IFRS for SMEs*, published in July 2009, did not address many of the Australian constituents' concerns. The *IFRS for SMEs* changes some of the full IFRS recognition and measurement accounting policy options by mandating or eliminating a particular option or introducing 'new' options. That means some of the full IFRS recognition and measurement accounting policy options are not available to SMEs and there are some that differ from comparable full IFRS recognition and measurement requirements.

BC73 The AASB discussed the *IFRS for SMEs* with a view to assessing its suitability as Tier 2 requirements. The AASB noted that there are concerns about adopting the *IFRS for SMEs* in Australia for the following reasons:

(a) some of the accounting policy options that have been removed would be the favoured accounting policies for many Australian entities;

(b)   changes to full IFRS recognition and measurement requirements under the *IFRS for SMEs* and the absence of some accounting policy options from the *IFRS for SMEs* would force subsidiaries to adjust accounting policies for consolidation purposes when parents apply full IFRSs;

(c)   entities applying the *IFRS for SMEs* would be deprived of improvements and simplifications as they become available at the full IFRS level because the IASB has stated that it will only update the *IFRS for SMEs* once there have been two years of broad adoption and, thereafter, every three years;

(d)   possible benefits that might result from comparability with overseas entities applying the *IFRS for SMEs* would:

     (i)   depend on how widely adopted it becomes;

     (ii)   be limited because entities seeking to access international capital markets would generally apply full IFRSs; and

     (iii)   be mitigated due to a loss of comparability across all types of entities' general purpose financial statements within Australia;

(e)   having different streams of recognition and measurement requirements involves different streams of knowledge, such that education and training at the tertiary level and within the accounting profession would become more costly;

(f)   there would be start up costs because entities preparing general purpose financial statements have already made the effort to apply full IFRSs;

(g)   adoption of the *IFRS for SMEs* may be seen as a retrograde step in a country that has already adopted full IFRS recognition and measurement accounting policy options;

(h)   the actual changes in recognition and measurement requirements in the *IFRS for SMEs* would not produce any real economies for Australian SMEs; and

(i)   in the event that an entity moves to, or from, full IFRSs, there would be costs involved in migrating from the recognition and measurement requirements of one Tier of reporting to another.

BC74   The Board concluded that the *IFRS for SMEs* is not presently a suitable set of requirements for Tier 2 in Australia. However, the Board decided it will continue to monitor and contribute to further changes in the *IFRS for SMEs* and that it is open to the possibility of adopting the *IFRS for SMEs* in future should the changes in that Standard make it practicable in an integrated for-profit/NFP sector reporting environment.

BC75   The Board noted that the introduction of the RDR as Tier 2 is supported by a majority of respondents to ED 192 who have also provided reasons for not supporting the adoption of the *IFRS for SMEs* as Tier 2 in place of the RDR or as an alternative alongside it.

Approach to Determining Disclosure Requirements under the RDR

BC76   In determining the RDR, the Board sought to balance the need to reduce disclosures with the need to satisfy the objective of general purpose financial statements. From amongst a number of possible approaches to determining disclosure requirements under the RDR, the Board decided to adopt an approach that:

(a)   draws on the *IFRS for SMEs* to identify disclosures in cases where the recognition and measurement accounting policy options available or requirements under the RDR align with those under the *IFRS for SMEs*; and

(b)   applies 'user need' and 'cost-benefit' principles (that is, the same basic principles used by the IASB in determining disclosures under the *IFRS for SMEs*) to arrive at reduced disclosure requirements in cases where the recognition and measurement accounting policy options or requirements under the RDR differ from those under the *IFRS for SMEs*.

In applying this approach, the Board concluded that satisfying the objective of general purpose financial statements should be the overriding basis for determining the disclosures under the RDR whether or not the recognition and measurement accounting policy options available or required under that regime align with those provided under the *IFRS for SMEs*. The Board applied this approach to each disclosure requirement in each Australian Accounting Standard. The results are reflected in AASB 2010-2.

BC77 The Board noted that its approach would help minimise the cost of determining and maintaining disclosures under the RDR.

BC78 Consistent with the IASB's approach in the *IFRS for SMEs*, the AASB concluded that users of general purpose financial statements of non-publicly accountable for-profit entities are particularly interested in information about:

(a) short-term cash flows and about obligations, commitments or contingencies, whether or not recognised as liabilities;

(b) liquidity and solvency;

(c) measurement uncertainties;

(d) the entity's accounting policy choices;

(e) disaggregations of amounts presented in the financial statements; and

(f) transactions and other events and conditions encountered by such entities.

BC79 The Board also concluded that, in addition to the particular information needs of users of non-publicly accountable for-profit entities noted in paragraph BC78, the information needs of the users of general purpose financial statements of NFP entities in both the private and public sectors would be satisfied by adopting a similar approach, having regard to the specific needs of users of NFP, including public sector, entity financial statements. The AASB uses its *Process for Modifying IFRSs for PBE/NFP* in assessing the need for specific requirements relating to NFP entities.

BC80 The Board noted that, although the *IFRS for SMEs* has been developed to apply to for-profit private sector entities, broadly it is considered reasonable to rely on the judgements made in developing the *IFRS for SMEs* in respect of both for-profit and NFP (including public sector) entities in Australia given that IFRSs are generally applied to all types of Australian entities.

Application of Standards

BC81 AASB 2010-2 specifies the disclosures in each Australian Accounting Standard from which Tier 2 entities are exempted. However, some Standards are equally applicable to both Tier 1 and Tier 2 entities. Accordingly, such Standards do not provide reduced disclosures for Tier 2 entities. Examples are AASB 4 *Insurance Contracts* and AASB 1004 *Contributions*.

BC82 Some Standards apply only to Tier 1 entities, but Tier 2 entities may elect to use them. Examples are AASB 8 *Operating Segments* and AASB 133 *Earnings per Share*, which generally apply only to entities that access public capital markets, as stated in their application paragraphs.

BC83 AASB 134 *Interim Financial Reporting* applies to disclosing entities' half-year financial statements. Consistent with the Board's approach to other Standards in respect of annual general purpose financial statements, other Tier 1 entities and Tier 2 entities that elect to prepare interim general purpose financial statements would be required to apply AASB 134 (which specifies reduced disclosure requirements under Tier 2), by virtue of the application paragraph in that Standard.

BC84 Entities applying AASB 134 may prepare condensed interim financial statements or present a complete set of financial statements as interim financial statements. Tier 2 entities are exempted from some disclosures when preparing condensed financial statements and would apply Tier 2 requirements in AASB 101 when preparing a complete set of financial statements as their interim financial statements.

BC85 There are also Standards that are only applicable to Tier 1 entities, and Tier 2 entities cannot elect to apply them in preparing financial statements. These Standards are identified by virtue of their application paragraphs. Currently the only example is AASB 1049 *Whole of Government and General Government Sector Financial Reporting*.

BC86 In considering possible reductions in disclosure requirements of:

(a)   AASB 4 *Insurance Contracts*, AASB 1023 *General Insurance Contracts* and AASB 1038 *Life Insurance Contracts* for insurers that might not be publicly accountable, such as potentially some captive insurers (see paragraphs BC27-BC28); and

(b)   AAS 25 *Financial Reporting by Superannuation Plans* for superannuation plans that might not be publicly accountable, such as SAFs (see paragraphs BC29-BC30);

the Board noted that such decisions should be made after applying further due process, including public exposure of proposed reductions. This is because ED 192 did not include proposed reduced disclosures for AASB 4, AASB 1023, AASB 1038 and AAS 25. In particular, the Board considered it would need to consult widely about whether some life insurers could be given relief from disclosures under AASB 1038 because the Board's initial view is that life insurance is of high public interest and comprehensive information on life insurance is needed by users of general purpose financial statements.

BC87 The Board noted that, until the above due process is completed, all insurers and superannuation plans preparing general purpose financial statements would continue to apply these Standards in full. Accordingly, if there are any Tier 2 insurers or superannuation plans preparing general purpose financial statements, the only benefits of reduced disclosure requirements available to them would be through the reduced disclosures in other Standards.

Transition

BC88 The Board considered the transitional requirements for entities adopting Tier 2 requirements for the first time and moving between Tiers. The Board identified three main scenarios for transition that should be dealt with in AASB 1053:

(a)   transition by an entity that prepared its most recent previous financial statements in the form of special purpose financial statements to Tier 1 or Tier 2;

(b)   transition by an entity applying Tier 1 to Tier 2; and

(c)   transition by an entity applying Tier 2 to Tier 1.

BC89 The Board noted that, for transitioning from special purpose financial statements to general purpose financial statements, an assessment of whether the preparer has applied recognition and measurement requirements in its most recent previous financial statements is of paramount importance. Accordingly, an entity that has applied recognition and measurement requirements of Australian Accounting Standards selectively or not at all in its special purpose financial statements should be treated differently from one that has applied the recognition and measurement requirements of applicable Australian Accounting Standards, including those of AASB 1 *First-time Adoption of Australian Accounting Standards*.

BC90 AASB 1 includes disclosure requirements. Entities transitioning from special purpose financial statements to Tier 2 are exempted from some of the disclosure requirements in that Standard, using the principles applied in determining disclosures under Tier 2 (see paragraph BC78).

BC91 Entities transitioning from Tier 1 to Tier 2 would not apply AASB 1. However, entities transitioning from Tier 2 to Tier 1 would need to apply AASB 1 in full to claim compliance with IFRSs, as under Tier 2 they would only have applied some of the disclosure requirements of AASB 1. This is consistent with the Board's policy that for-profit entities complying with Australian Accounting Standards simultaneously comply with IFRSs.

BC92 Entities that transition to Tier 1 need to apply AASB 1 in full in order to be able to claim compliance with IFRSs, in accordance with AASB 101, including making an unreserved statement of compliance as required by AASB 101.

BC93 The Board considered whether entities transitioning between Tiers for which compliance with IFRSs is not pertinent, in particular NFP entities that are subject to Aus paragraphs, should be subject to AASB 1 on transition. The Board concluded that AASB 1 is not applicable in those circumstances because, at the time of transition between Tiers, Australian Accounting Standards or Australian Accounting Standards – Reduced Disclosure Requirements, which have common recognition and measurement requirements, have previously been complied with. Accordingly, it would not be appropriate to imply, through application of AASB 1, that the basis of accounting has changed.

Operative Date

BC94 The Board concluded that mandatory application of Tier 2 requirements should be annual reporting periods beginning on or after 1 July 2013. The Board noted a long transitional period is particularly required to allow entities that prepare special purpose financial statements to make necessary preparations for transitioning to Tier 2 requirements should they choose to prepare general purpose financial statements under Tier 2. The Board considered it would be beneficial to have a relatively long transition period to allow these entities to prepare their internal reporting systems for transition.

BC95 However, the Board decided to allow early adoption of Tier 2 requirements for those entities that want to avail themselves of the reduced disclosure requirements under that Tier before the mandatory application date of 1 July 2013. Early adoption is permitted for annual reporting periods that begin on or after 1 July 2009 but before 1 July 2013. The Board decided not to permit early adoption for annual reporting periods that begin before 1 July 2009 due to the difficulty of identifying relevant Standards applying to those earlier periods and making consistent judgments as to which disclosures in those Standards would be applicable under Tier 2.

BC96 The Board also noted that a long transition period would potentially enable any outcome of the second stage of the project to be made operative from the same date as the first stage, to facilitate minimal disruption on transition. The Board will not decide whether the second stage should be progressed until the results of the research project it has commissioned are known.

BC97 The transition period is also consistent with the Board's normal policy regarding transition periods for its Standards. The Board concluded that making Tier 2 requirements mandatory from the date of issue of relevant Standards may inappropriately require entities that currently apply Tier 1 to select that Tier and make disclosures related to that selection rather than continue their current accounting disclosures that comply with current GAAP.

Maintenance of Tier 2 Requirements

BC98 The Board decided that Tier 2 requirements should be maintained on a continuous basis, rather than waiting for the IASB to update its *IFRS for SMEs*, which the IASB plans to undertake only every few years, by which time there would be an accumulation of possible changes. The AASB intends that each future Exposure Draft or Invitation to Comment involving changes to Tier 1 that includes disclosure proposals would seek comment about which disclosures should be included in Tier 2, and may include the AASB's proposed reduced disclosures.

Post-implementation Review

BC99 The Board decided that Tier 2 requirements should be subject to review and revision taking account of implementation experience and international developments.

BC100 The Board plans to monitor implementation experience with Tier 2 requirements and use it as a basis for providing feedback to the IASB to assist with its further deliberations on differential reporting matters and to help shape future amendments to the *IFRS for SMEs*.

Trans-Tasman Convergence

BC101 AASB 1053 was developed in the context of the Prime Ministers of Australia and New Zealand having signed on 20 August 2009 a Joint Statement of Intent that agreed on a framework of Outcome Proposals for developing cross-border economic initiatives. A range of shared Outcome Proposals have been identified across a wide range of business law areas, including in relation to financial reporting. The outcomes are expected to accelerate and deepen trans-Tasman regulatory integration as part of a broader single economic market initiative. Outcome Proposals relating to financial reporting include:

For-profit entities

(a) "Profit entities are able to use a single set of accounting standards and prepare only one set of financial statements (timeframe: short term – within two years)"

(b) "Trans-Tasman companies have to prepare only one set of financial statements to one set of standards (timeframe: short term – within two years)"

Not-for-profit entities

"Not-for-profit entities are able to use a single set of accounting standards and prepare only one set of financial statements (timeframe: medium term – within five years)".

BC102 These Outcome Proposals are intended to reduce compliance costs for entities operating across the Tasman and support trans-Tasman investment through the consistency of financial statements. The use of full IFRSs as the foundation standards in both countries provides a sound basis for achieving the above Outcome Proposals. However, further harmonisation in regard to financial reporting by entities other than those that are required to apply full IFRSs as adopted in Australia would be necessary to achieve the Outcome Proposals. This would be achieved by convergence of the differential reporting frameworks in the two countries.

BC103 New Zealand already adopts a differential reporting regime (that is different from the regime in Australia both before and after AASB 1053), which is expected to undergo restructuring in the light of the New Zealand Ministry of Economic Development review of standard setting arrangements. Close monitoring of these developments by the two countries would help identify an appropriate approach to converge the differential reporting frameworks in the two countries in due course.

BC104 The convergence of differential reporting frameworks is likely to be conducted in stages, with the first stage relating to for-profit private sector entities. New Zealand is expected to employ a notion of public accountability that is close to the IASB's definition to distinguish between for-profit entities that apply NZ IFRSs and those that can avail themselves of concessions under the differential reporting framework. The AASB noted that the use of the IASB's notion of public accountability under Tier 2 requirements in Australia provides common ground to discuss the harmonisation of the two countries' differential reporting frameworks in regard to for-profit private sector entities.

AASB 1054

Australian Additional Disclosures

(Compiled January 2015)

This compiled Standard applies to annual reporting periods beginning on or after 1 July 2015. Early application is permitted for annual reporting periods beginning on or after 1 January 2014 but before 1 July 2015. It incorporates relevant amendments made up to and including 28 January 2015.

Prepared on 2 April 2015 by the staff of the Australian Accounting Standards Board.

CONTENTS

COMPILATION DETAILS
COMPARISON WITH IFRSs
ACCOUNTING STANDARD
AASB 1054 *AUSTRALIAN ADDITIONAL DISCLOSURES*

Australian Accounting Standard AASB 1054 *Australian Additional Disclosures* (as amended) is set out in paragraphs 1 – 16. All the paragraphs have equal authority. Paragraphs in **bold type** state the main principles. AASB 1054 is to be read in the context of other Australian Accounting Standards, including AASB 1048 *Interpretation of Standards*, which identifies the Australian Accounting Interpretations. In the absence of explicit guidance, AASB 108 *Accounting Policies, Changes in Accounting Estimates and Errors* provides a basis for selecting and applying accounting policies.

COMPILATION DETAILS

Accounting Standard AASB 1054 *Australian Additional Disclosures* as amended

This compiled Standard applies to annual reporting periods beginning on or after 1 July 2015. It takes into account amendments up to and including 28 January 2015 and was prepared on 2 April 2015 by the staff of the Australian Accounting Standards Board (AASB).

This compilation is not a separate Accounting Standard made by the AASB. Instead, it is a representation of AASB 1054 (May 2011) as amended by other Accounting Standards, which are listed in the Table below.

Table of Standards

Standard	Date made	Application date (annual reporting periods ... on or after ...)	Application, saving or transitional provisions
AASB 1054	11 May 2011	(beginning) 1 Jul 2011	see (a) below
AASB 2011-2	11 May 2011	(beginning) 1 Jul 2013	see (b) below
AASB 2015-3	28 Jan 2015	(beginning) 1 Jul 2015	see (c) below

(a) Entities may elect to apply this Standard, or individual disclosure requirements, to annual reporting periods beginning on or after 1 January 2005 but before 1 July 2011, provided that AASB 2011-1 *Amendments to Australian Accounting Standards arising from the Trans-Tasman Convergence Project*, or the relevant individual amendments, is also applied to such periods.

(b) Entities may elect to apply this Standard to annual reporting periods beginning on or after 1 July 2009 but before 1 July 2013, provided that AASB 1053 *Application of Tiers of Australian Accounting Standards*, AASB 1054 *Australian Additional Disclosures* and AASB 2011-1 *Amendments to Australian Accounting Standards arising from the Trans-Tasman Convergence Project* are also applied to such periods.

(c) Entities may elect to apply this Standard to annual reporting periods beginning on or after 1 January 2014 but before 1 July 2015.

Table of amendments

Paragraph affected	How affected	By ... [paragraph]
5	deleted	AASB 2015-3 [13, 14]
5A-5C (and preceding heading)	added	AASB 2011-2 [8]
RDR7.1	added	AASB 2011-2 [8]

COMPARISON WITH IFRSs

AASB 1054 *Australian Additional Disclosures* includes disclosure requirements and definitions which are additional to International Financial Reporting Standards issued by the International Accounting Standards Board (IASB).

Compliance with AASB 1054 is not needed for IFRS compliance.

ACCOUNTING STANDARD AASB 1054

The Australian Accounting Standards Board made Accounting Standard AASB 1054 *Australian Additional Disclosures* under section 334 of the *Corporations Act 2001* on 11 May 2011.

This compiled version of AASB 1054 applies to annual reporting periods beginning on or after 1 July 2015. It incorporates relevant amendments contained in other AASB Standards made by the AASB up to and including 28 January 2015 (see Compilation Details).

ACCOUNTING STANDARD AASB 1054
AUSTRALIAN ADDITIONAL DISCLOSURES

Objective

1   The objective of this Standard is to set out Australian-specific disclosure requirements that are in addition to disclosure requirements in International Financial Reporting Standards.

Application

2   This Standard applies to:

(a)   each entity that is required to prepare financial reports in accordance with Part 2M.3 of the Corporations Act;

(b)   general purpose financial statements of each reporting entity; and

(c)   financial statements that are, or are held out to be, general purpose financial statements.

3   This Standard applies to *annual reporting periods* beginning on or after 1 July 2011. [Note: For application dates of paragraphs changed or added by an amending Standard, see Compilation Details.]

4   This Standard, or individual disclosure requirements, may be applied to annual reporting periods beginning on or after 1 January 2005 but before 1 July 2011, provided that AASB 2011-1 *Amendments to Australian Accounting Standards arising from the Trans-Tasman Convergence Project*, or its relevant individual amendments, is also adopted early for the same period. When an entity applies this Standard, or individual disclosure requirements, to such an annual reporting period, it shall disclose that fact.

5   [Deleted by the AASB]

Reduced disclosure requirements

5A   Paragraphs 10-16 of this Standard do not apply to entities preparing general purpose financial statements under Australian Accounting Standards – Reduced Disclosure Requirements. Entities applying Australian Accounting Standards – Reduced Disclosure Requirements may elect to comply with some or all of these excluded requirements.

5B   The requirements that do not apply to entities preparing general purpose financial statements under Australian Accounting Standards – Reduced Disclosure Requirements are identified in this Standard by shading of the relevant text.

5C   RDR paragraphs in this Standard apply only to entities preparing general purpose financial statements under Australian Accounting Standards – Reduced Disclosure Requirements.

Definitions

6   The following terms are used in this Standard with the meanings specified.

Annual reporting period means the financial year or similar period to which annual financial statements relate.

Special purpose financial statements are financial statements other than general purpose financial statements.

Compliance with Australian Accounting Standards

7   An entity whose financial statements comply with Australian Accounting Standards shall make an explicit and unreserved statement of such compliance in the notes. An entity shall not describe financial statements as complying with Australian Accounting Standards unless they comply with all the requirements of Australian Accounting Standards.

RDR7.1   An entity whose financial statements comply with Australian Accounting Standards – Reduced Disclosure Requirements shall make an explicit and unreserved statement of such compliance in the notes. An entity shall not describe financial statements as complying with Australian Accounting Standards – Reduced Disclosure Requirements unless they comply with all the requirements of Australian Accounting Standards – Reduced Disclosure Requirements.

Reporting framework

8   An entity shall disclose in the notes:

(a)   the statutory basis or other reporting framework, if any, under which the financial statements are prepared; and

(b)   whether, for the purposes of preparing the financial statements, it is a for-profit or not-for-profit entity.

General purpose or special purpose financial statements

9   An entity shall disclose in the notes whether the financial statements are general purpose financial statements or *special purpose financial statements*.

Audit fees

10   An entity shall disclose fees to each auditor or reviewer, including any network firm, separately for:

(a)   the audit or review of the financial statements; and

(b)   all other services performed during the reporting period.

11   For paragraph 10(b) above, an entity shall describe the nature of other services.

Imputation credits

12   The term 'imputation credits' is used in paragraphs 13-15 to also mean 'franking credits'. The disclosures required by paragraphs 13 and 15 shall be made separately in respect of any New Zealand imputation credits and any Australian imputation credits.

13   An entity shall disclose the amount of imputation credits available for use in subsequent reporting periods.

14   For the purposes of determining the amount required to be disclosed in accordance with paragraph 13, entities may have:

(a)   imputation credits that will arise from the payment of the amount of the provision for income tax;

(b)   imputation debits that will arise from the payment of dividends recognised as a liability at the reporting date; and

(c)   imputation credits that will arise from the receipt of dividends recognised as receivables at the reporting date.

15   Where there are different classes of investors with different entitlements to imputation credits, disclosures shall be made about the nature of those entitlements for each class where this is relevant to an understanding of them.

Reconciliation of net operating cash flow to profit (loss)

16   When an entity uses the direct method to present its statement of cash flows, the financial statements shall provide a reconciliation of the net cash flow from operating activities to profit (loss).

BASIS FOR CONCLUSIONS

This Basis for Conclusions accompanies, but is not part of, AASB 1054.

Background

BC1   This Basis for Conclusions summarises the considerations of the Australian Accounting Standards Board and the Financial Reporting Standards Board (FRSB) of the New Zealand Institute of Chartered Accountants (NZICA) in reaching the conclusions in AASB 1054. It also provides a context for the Boards' decisions about harmonising the disclosure requirements. It focuses on the issues that the Boards consider to be of greatest significance. Individual Board members gave greater weight to some factors than to others.

Location of additional disclosures

BC2   The Boards discussed the merits of locating the additional domestic disclosure requirements in a separate disclosure standard compared with locating them within topic-based standards, which is the current practice. Some members supported a separate disclosure standard largely on the basis that it would facilitate the topic-based standards being identical to International Financial Reporting Standards (IFRSs). Other members expressed a preference for locating additional disclosures within topic-based standards for ease of use. On balance, with the benefit of constituent responses to AASB ED 200B / FRSB ED 122 *Proposed Separate Disclosure Standards*, the Boards decided to locate the additional disclosures in separate disclosure standards on the basis that they view bringing the wording of Australian and New Zealand Standards closer to IFRSs as one of the greatest benefits of the Trans-Tasman Convergence project.

Definitions

BC3   The definition of 'annual reporting period' has been retained on the basis that it is used in application paragraphs of AASB Standards, consistent with terminology in the Australian *Corporations Act 2001*.

BC4   The definition of 'special purpose financial statements' has been retained on the basis that it is used in a disclosure requirement related to the AASB's differential reporting framework.

Audit fees

BC5   The AASB and the FRSB have relocated and amended the audit fee disclosure requirements contained in AASB 101 *Presentation of Financial Statements* and NZ IAS 1 *Presentation of Financial Statements* to their respective separate disclosure Standards and harmonised the disclosure requirements across both jurisdictions.

BC6   The AASB and the FRSB consider that the disclosure of audit fees is a matter of accountability and, given that the accountability environment is similar in both jurisdictions, they should have the same audit fee disclosure requirements. The Boards also took the opportunity to simplify the disclosure requirements on the basis that in recent times both preparers and users have indicated that disclosures in financial statements have become overly complex.

BC7   The AASB and FRSB noted the usefulness of the notion of 'related practice' in audit fee disclosures in AASB 101 and decided to incorporate a similar notion that is common to both jurisdictions in the harmonised disclosures. Accordingly, the Boards decided to include the notion of 'network firm' from APES 110 *Code of Ethics for Professional Accountants* issued by Accounting and Professional Ethical Standards Board (APESB) (February 2008) and *Code of Ethics: Independence in Assurance Engagements* issued by the NZICA (September 2008). The Boards also decided not to define or provide explanatory material for 'network firm' on the basis that the notion is generally understood and preparers and auditors could refer to the relevant APESB and NZICA pronouncements.

BC8   The AASB and FRSB note that disclosures are made in the context of the scope of the entity reporting. Accordingly, in the case of a group, disclosures made in accordance with paragraph 10 would include fees paid by the parent and its subsidiaries for each of the parent and its subsidiaries.

Imputation credits

BC9   The AASB and the FRSB have relocated the imputation credit disclosure requirements contained in AASB 101 and NZ IAS 12 *Income Taxes* to their respective separate disclosure Standards and to harmonise the disclosure requirements across both jurisdictions.

BC10   The AASB and the FRSB noted that Australia and New Zealand are among a limited number of jurisdictions that have an imputation tax regime and acknowledge the decision usefulness of information about imputation credits to users of financial information. Accordingly, the AASB and the FRSB decided that these disclosure requirements should be retained.

BC11   Given that both jurisdictions have disclosure requirements about imputation credits, and that the imputation regimes in each jurisdiction are highly similar, the Boards have harmonised the wording across both jurisdictions. The Boards also took the opportunity to simplify the disclosure requirements on the basis that in recent times both preparers and users have indicated that disclosures in financial statements have become overly complex.

Reconciliation of net operating cash flow to profit (loss)

BC12   The AASB and the FRSB have relocated the requirement to disclose a reconciliation of net operating cash flow to profit or loss when an entity uses the direct method to present its statement of cash flows [that were contained in AASB 107 *Statement of Cash Flows* and NZ IAS 7 *Statement of Cash Flows*] to their respective separate disclosure standards and to harmonise the disclosure requirements across both jurisdictions.

BC13   The Boards, in forming the view to retain the requirement for a reconciliation of net operating cash flow to profit or loss, acknowledged the weight of comments received on AASB ED 200B / FRSB ED 122 from constituents who opposed the proposal to remove this requirement.

BC14   The Boards noted that the IASB has recently considered requiring a reconciliation of net operating cash flow to profit or loss in the context of its Financial Statement Presentation project.

AASB 1055
Budgetary Reporting

(Compiled December 2013)

This compiled Standard applies to annual reporting periods beginning on or after 1 July 2014. Early application is permitted for annual reporting periods beginning on or after 1 January 2014 but before 1 July 2014. It incorporates relevant amendments made up to and including 20 December 2013.

Prepared on 2 July 2014 by the staff of the Australian Accounting Standards Board.

CONTENTS

COMPILATION DETAILS

COMPARISON WITH IASB PRONOUNCEMENTS

ACCOUNTING STANDARD

AASB 1055 *BUDGETARY REPORTING*

Australian Accounting Standard AASB 1055 *Budgetary Reporting* (as amended) is set out in paragraphs 1 – 15 and Appendix A. All the paragraphs have equal authority. Paragraphs in **bold type** state the main principles. Terms defined in Appendix A are in *italics* the first time they appear in the Standard. AASB 1055 is to be read in the context of other Australian Accounting Standards, including AASB 1048 *Interpretation of Standards*, which identifies the Australian Accounting Interpretations. In the absence of explicit guidance, AASB 108 *Accounting Policies, Changes in Accounting Estimates and Errors* provides a basis for selecting and applying accounting policies.

COMPILATION DETAILS

Accounting Standard AASB 1055 *Budgetary Reporting* as amended

This compiled Standard applies to annual reporting periods beginning on or after 1 July 2014. It takes into account amendments up to and including 20 December 2013 and was prepared on 2 July 2014 by the staff of the Australian Accounting Standards Board (AASB).

This compilation is not a separate Accounting Standard made by the AASB. Instead, it is a representation of AASB 1055 (March 2013) as amended by other Accounting Standards, which are listed in the Table below.

Table of Standards

Standard	Date made	Application date (*annual reporting periods ... on or after ...*)	Application, saving or transitional provisions
AASB 1055	5 Mar 2013	*(beginning)* 1 Jul 2014	see (a) below
AASB 2013-9	20 Dec 2013	Pt B *(beginning)* 1 Jan 2014	see (b) below

(a) Entities may elect to apply this Standard to annual reporting periods beginning on or after 1 January 2009 but before 1 July 2014, provided that AASB 2013-1 *Amendments to AASB 1049 – Relocation of Budgetary Reporting Requirements* is also applied to such periods.
(b) Early application of Part B of this Standard is not permitted.

Table of amendments

Paragraph affected	How affected	By ... [paragraph]
5	deleted	AASB 2013-9B [37, 38]

COMPARISON WITH IASB PRONOUNCEMENTS

AASB 1055 and International Financial Reporting Standards

There is no specific Standard issued by the International Accounting Standards Board dealing with budgetary information to be included in:

(a)   the financial statements of the GGS;

(b)   whole of government general purpose financial statements; or

(c)   the general purpose financial statements of not-for-profit entities within the GGS;

of the Australian Government and State and Territory Governments.

ACCOUNTING STANDARD AASB 1055

The Australian Accounting Standards Board made Accounting Standard AASB 1055 *Budgetary Reporting* on 5 March 2013.

This compiled version of AASB 1055 applies to annual reporting periods beginning on or after 1 July 2014. It incorporates relevant amendments contained in other AASB Standards made by the AASB up to and including 20 December 2013 (see Compilation Details).

ACCOUNTING STANDARD AASB 1055
BUDGETARY REPORTING

Objective

1   The objective of this Standard is to specify budgetary disclosure requirements for the whole of government, *General Government Sector* (GGS) and not-for-profit *entities within the GGS* of each *government*. Disclosures made in accordance with this Standard provide users with information relevant to assessing performance of an entity, including accountability for resources entrusted to it.

Application and scope

2   This Standard applies to:

(a)   **whole of government general purpose financial statements of each government;**

    (b)   financial statements of each government's GGS;

    (c)   general purpose financial statements of each not-for-profit reporting entity within the GGS; and

    (d)   financial statements of each not-for-profit entity within the GGS that are, or are held out to be, general purpose financial statements.

3   **This Standard applies to annual reporting periods beginning on or after 1 July 2014.**
[Note: For application dates of paragraphs changed or added by an amending Standard, see Compilation Details.]

4   **This Standard may be applied to annual reporting periods beginning before 1 July 2014, provided that AASB 2013-1** *Amendments to AASB 1049 – Relocation of Budgetary Reporting Requirements* **is also applied to the same period.**

5   [Deleted by the AASB]

Budgetary information

6   **Where an entity's budgeted:**

    (a)   **statement of financial position;**

    (b)   **statement of profit or loss and other comprehensive income;**

    (c)   **statement of changes in equity; or**

    (d)   **statement of cash flows;**

    reflecting controlled items is presented to parliament and is separately identified as relating to that entity, the entity shall disclose for the reporting period:

    (e)   **that original budgeted financial statement presented to parliament, presented and classified on a basis that is consistent with the presentation and classification adopted in the corresponding financial statement prepared in accordance with Australian Accounting Standards; and**

    (f)   **explanations of major variances between the actual amounts presented in the financial statements and the corresponding original budget amounts.**

7   **Where an entity within the GGS's budgeted financial information reflecting major classes of administered income and expenses, or major classes of administered assets and liabilities, is presented to parliament and is separately identified as relating to that entity, the entity shall disclose for the reporting period:**

    (a)   **that original budgeted financial information presented to parliament, presented and classified on a basis that is consistent with the presentation and classification adopted for the corresponding information about administered items disclosed in accordance with AASB 1050** *Administered Items***; and**

    (b)   **explanations of major variances between the actual amounts disclosed in the financial statements in accordance with AASB 1050 and the corresponding original budget amounts.**

8   **Comparative budgetary information in respect of the previous period need not be disclosed.**

9   The original budget is the first budget presented to parliament in respect of the reporting period.

10   Under AASB 101 *Presentation of Financial Statements* an entity may present a statement of profit or loss and other comprehensive income as:

(a)   a single statement of profit or loss and other comprehensive income, with profit or loss and other comprehensive income presented in two sections; or

(b)   the profit or loss section in a separate statement of profit or loss, and a separate statement presenting comprehensive income that begins with profit or loss.

AASB 1049 *Whole of Government and General Government Sector Financial Reporting* limits the presentation of the statement of profit or loss and other comprehensive income of a GGS and a whole of government to the format described in (a) above. Accordingly, if a GGS or whole of government budget presented to parliament is in the format described in (b), in accordance with paragraph 6(e) of this Standard, that budgeted information would need to be restated for disclosure purposes to align with the format described in (a).

11   Any revised budget that is presented to parliament during the reporting period may be disclosed in the financial statements in addition to the original budget and might need to be referred to in explanations of major variances as noted in paragraph 15.

12   Information provided in accordance with paragraph 6 or 7 facilitates users of financial statements (including taxpayers) making and evaluating decisions about the allocation of scarce resources and for assessing the discharge of an entity's accountability. The budget information is disclosed on the same presentation and classification bases adopted for the corresponding actual information in the financial statements, to facilitate a comparison of actual outcomes against the budget. Accordingly:

(a)   in relation to controlled items, to the extent the presentation and classification bases adopted in the budget presented to parliament are not consistent with the corresponding financial statements, the budget presented to parliament is restated for disclosure purposes to align with the presentation and classification bases adopted in the corresponding financial statements. As such, the budget information may be presented in the corresponding financial statements; and

(b)   in relation to administered items of entities within the GGS, to the extent the presentation and classification bases adopted in the budget presented to parliament are not consistent with the corresponding information about administered items disclosed in accordance with AASB 1050, the budget presented to parliament is restated for disclosure purposes to align with the presentation and classification bases adopted for the corresponding information about administered items disclosed in accordance with AASB 1050. As such, the budget information may be disclosed with the corresponding information about administered items, including where the corresponding information about administered items is disclosed with the financial statements.

13   Budgeted financial information reflecting administered income and expenses, or assets and liabilities, presented to parliament that is subject to the requirements of paragraph 7 would, consistent with AASB 1050, at a minimum, contain information about major classes of administered income and expenses, or major classes of administered assets and liabilities. Accordingly, if the budgeted information of an entity within a GGS is presented to parliament only at a more highly summarised level, for example, budgeted aggregate of administered income and expenses, that entity would not be required to report the budgetary information specified in paragraph 7. Similarly, the requirements in paragraph 6 do not apply where parliament only receives information about an entity's budgeted controlled items at a more highly summarised level than the level of information required by Australian Accounting Standards to be presented in the financial statements.

14   The budgetary reporting requirements in this Standard only apply to an entity within the GGS where budgeted information about controlled or administered items is separately identified as relating to that entity within the budgetary information presented to parliament. Accordingly, for example, where:

(a) a consolidated GGS budget presented to parliament incorporates a budget of an entity within the GGS in a way that the individual entity's budget is not separately identified as relating to that entity; and

(b) a separate individual budget is not presented to parliament for that entity;

that entity's budget is not regarded as having been presented to parliament and therefore the entity is not required to report the budgetary information specified in this Standard.

15 The explanations of major variances required to be disclosed by paragraph 6(f) or 7(b) are those relevant to an assessment of the discharge of accountability and to an analysis of performance of an entity, not merely focusing on the numerical differences between original budget and actual amounts. They include high-level explanations of the causes of major variances rather than merely the nature of the variances. Furthermore, if revised budgets are presented to parliament, even when there are no major numerical differences between the original budget and actual amounts, an entity might need to have regard to those revised budgets and include explanations for major numerical differences between them and actual amounts. Such explanations are made when they are relevant for the assessment of the discharge of accountability and to an analysis of the performance of an entity.

APPENDIX A
DEFINED TERMS

This appendix is an integral part of AASB 1055.

ABS GFS Manual	Australian Bureau of Statistics (ABS) publications *Australian System of Government Finance Statistics: Concepts, Sources and Methods, 2005* (ABS Catalogue no. 5514.0) and *Amendments to Australian System of Government Finance Statistics, 2005* (ABS Catalogue No. 5514.0) published on the ABS website.
entity within the GGS	Any legal, administrative, or fiduciary arrangement, organisational structure or other party (including a person) within the GGS having the capacity to deploy scarce resources in order to achieve objectives.
General Government Sector (GGS)	Institutional sector comprising all *government units* and *non-profit institutions* controlled and mainly financed by government. Defined in the ABS GFS Manual (Glossary, page 256).
government	The Australian Government, the Government of the Australian Capital Territory, New South Wales, the Northern Territory, Queensland, South Australia, Tasmania, Victoria or Western Australia.
government units	Unique kinds of legal entities established by political processes which have legislative, judicial or executive authority over other *institutional units* within a given area and which: (i) provide goods and services to the community and/or individuals free of charge or at prices that are not economically significant; and (ii) redistribute income and wealth by means of taxes and other compulsory transfers. Defined in the ABS GFS Manual (Glossary, page 257).
institutional unit	An economic entity that is capable, in its own right, of owning assets, incurring liabilities and engaging in economic activities and in transactions with other entities. Defined in the ABS GFS Manual (Glossary, page 257).
non-profit institution	A legal or social entity that is created for the purpose of producing or distributing goods and services but is not permitted to be a source of income, profit or other financial gain for the units that establish, control or finance it. Defined in the ABS GFS Manual (Glossary, page 260).

BASIS FOR CONCLUSIONS

This Basis for Conclusions accompanies, but is not part of, AASB 1055.

Background

BC1   AASB 1055 *Budgetary Reporting* arises from the Australian Accounting Standards Board's deliberations of the proposals in Exposure Draft ED 212 *Not-for-Profit Entities within the General Government Sector* (issued in June 2011) relating to budgetary reporting.

BC2   This is not an area in which the International Accounting Standards Board (IASB) has developed an International Financial Reporting Standard (IFRS). The Board considered the International Public Sector Accounting Standards Board's IPSAS 24 *Presentation of Budget Information in Financial Statements* and concluded that it does not provide an appropriate basis for budgetary reporting in the Australian environment, particularly because it gives primacy to the budget basis of presentation and classification over the accounting basis of presentation and classification and contemplates explanations of variances being disclosed outside the financial report.

BC3   Consistent with its general approach of issuing topic-based rather than industry-based standards, the Board decided to locate budgetary reporting requirements for not-for-profit entities within the GGS in a separate topic-based Standard. Accordingly, the Board also decided to relocate the budgetary reporting requirements from paragraphs 59-65 of AASB 1049 *Whole of Government and General Government Sector Financial Reporting*[1] (without substantive amendment) into AASB 1055. Hence, the Board issued, at the same time as AASB 1055, AASB 2013-1 *Amendments to AASB 1049 – Relocation of Budgetary Reporting Requirements* to remove the budgetary reporting requirements for each government's whole of government and GGS from AASB 1049.

BC4   As explained in paragraphs BC7 and BC12 below, the Board decided that the principles underpinning the budgetary reporting requirements in AASB 1049 should apply to not-for-profit entities within the GGS. Accordingly, in AASB 1055, the budgetary reporting requirements that were in AASB 1049 are integrated with the budgetary reporting requirements for not-for-profit entities within the GGS.

BC5   In relation to not-for-profit entities within the GGS, AASB 1055 provides guidance on how the budgetary reporting principles previously in AASB 1049 apply in the context of an entity within the GGS, including guidance relating to administered items, for circumstances where:

(a)   an entity's budgetary information is incorporated into a consolidated budget of its parent; or

(b)   only summarised budgetary information is presented to parliament.

BC6   This Basis for Conclusions summarises the Board's main considerations in reaching the conclusions in developing AASB 1055. It comprises the Board's main considerations relating to budgetary reporting requirements previously included in the Basis for Conclusions of AASB 1049 and AASB 2011-13 *Amendments to Australian Accounting Standard – Improvements to AASB 1049*, as well as the Board's subsequent deliberations relating to the relevant proposals in ED 212. Individual Board members gave greater weight to some factors than to others.

---

1   As noted in the Basis for Conclusions accompanying AASB 1049, AASB 1049 was issued in response to the Financial Reporting Council's direction. The direction was, among other things, to achieve an Australian Accounting Standard "... in which the outcome statements are directly comparable with the relevant budget statements". The budgetary reporting requirements previously included in AASB 1049 were consistent with this aspect of the FRC's direction.

Entities subject to the requirements

BC7   The Board decided to extend the application of the principles underpinning the budgetary reporting requirements in AASB 1049 to not-for-profit entities within the GGS, which include government departments and statutory authorities. This was on the basis that adoption of those principles has the potential to improve the financial reporting by those entities in the relatively short term. Furthermore, such entities are a significant group for which there is a convention or formal requirement that budgets are published. Accordingly, the current conventions or requirements for governments to present budgets to parliament provide a context for specifying the budgetary reporting requirements for not-for-profit entities within the GGS.

BC8   In limiting the types of entities that are included within the scope of AASB 1055, the Board noted that governments typically budget on a GGS basis rather than on a whole of government basis, and might present budgets for individual not-for-profit entities within the GGS to parliament.

Entities not subject to the requirements

BC9   The Board considered expanding the scope of the budgetary reporting requirements to a broader range of public sector entities, for example, local governments or not-for-profit entities controlled by government outside the GGS. However, for the reasons given in paragraph BC7, the Board decided to limit the scope of AASB 1055 to each government's whole of government and GGS and not-for-profit entities within the GGS. The Board noted it could in the future, as a separate project, address budgetary reporting requirements of a broader range of public sector entities.

BC10 The Board decided not to consider budgetary reporting requirements for private sector entities (whether for-profit or not-for-profit) on the basis that, in contrast to the public sector, it is not typical for there to be a convention or formal requirement to make a private sector entity's budgets public.

BC11 In developing the budgetary reporting requirements that were previously in AASB 1049, the Board noted that, as part of the Uniform Presentation Framework, typically Australian jurisdictions publish GGS budget information together with budget information relating to the Public Non-Financial Corporation (PNFC) sector (and the Non-Financial Public Sector, comprising the GGS and PNFC sector) but not the Public Financial Corporation (PFC) sector. The Board considered whether sector-based budgetary information should be required to be disclosed in the whole of government financial report. The Board concluded that because the PNFC sector and PFC sector are not required by Australian Accounting Standards to prepare separate financial reports, a requirement to disclose budget information for the PNFC sector and PFC sector in whole of government financial reports would be onerous and of limited use to users even if that budget information is presented to parliament. The Board also noted that GGS budgetary information is required to be disclosed in GGS financial statements in accordance with AASB 1055. Accordingly, the Board concluded that sector-based budgetary information should not be required to be disclosed in whole of government financial statements.

Budgetary reporting requirements

BC12 In issuing AASB 1055, the Board noted that Australian Accounting Standards, including AASB 1055, do not prescribe the preparation of a budget. Within that context, as noted in paragraph BC7, the Board decided that budgetary reporting requirements for not-for-profit entities within the GGS should be consistent with the budgetary reporting requirements previously included in AASB 1049. This was on the basis that the requirements are working satisfactorily in practice, as evidenced by the post-implementation review of that Standard conducted in March 2010, and there is no conceptual reason to not subject such entities to similar budgetary reporting requirements under similar circumstances.

BC13 The Board decided to extend the application of the budgetary reporting principles in AASB 1049 to not-for-profit entities within the GGS after considering the implications of that decision from the perspective of its role as a standard setter, the scope of financial reporting and its transaction neutral policy. Overall, the Board was persuaded by the importance of budgetary reporting for accountability purposes of those entities. The Board particularly noted that, for those entities, comparisons of current period actuals to the previous period actuals would provide an incomplete picture without the comparisons from budgets to actuals. This was because, for example, in relation to not-for-profit entities within the GGS, machinery of government changes in one period can often cause period to period comparisons to be less informative without the budget against actual comparisons.

BC14 Accordingly, consistent with the principles underpinning the budgetary reporting requirements previously in AASB 1049, the Board concluded that AASB 1055 should require disclosure of certain budgetary information where budgetary information is presented to parliament, including the original budgeted financial statements, reflecting controlled items. Similarly, where an entity within the GGS's budgeted information reflecting administered items is presented to parliament, the Board concluded that AASB 1055 should require disclosure of original budgeted information reflecting administered items. In addition, the Board concluded that AASB 1055 should require explanations of major variances between actual amounts and the corresponding budget amounts to be disclosed. Specific aspects of these decisions are explained in paragraphs BC15-BC28 below.

BC15 In relation to extending the budgetary reporting requirements to administered items of not-for-profit entities within the GGS (a government's whole of government and GGS do not have administered items), the Board noted its decision not to proceed with the proposal in ED 212 to require disclosure of information for administered items 'coupled' with controlled items, on the basis that administered items would be the subject of a more fundamental review under the Board's Control in the Not-for-Profit Sector project. However, the Board considered the proposal relating to budgetary information about administered items to be a separate issue. On that basis, consistent with the budgetary reporting requirements for controlled items, the Board decided that if original budgeted information about administered items is presented to parliament it should be required to be disclosed in the financial report, restated if necessary to align with the presentation and classification adopted in the financial report for the information about administered items disclosed in accordance with AASB 1050.

BC16 The Board noted that AASB 1055 cannot explicitly cover all of the circumstances in which reporting against original budgets will need to be considered under the Standard. Judgement will need to be exercised to meet the objective of the Standard. Furthermore, there is a variety of circumstances that could occur that would make difficult the application of the principle that budgeted and actual numbers should be reported and variances explained. For example, after an original budget is presented to parliament, entities might be divided or combined (i.e. restructured) in ways that mean actual numbers do not directly relate meaningfully to original budget numbers. However, the Board noted that the principles in AASB 1055 could still be applicable in such circumstances. For example, in some of these circumstances, the original budgets presented to parliament can sensibly be divided or combined in a way that aligns with a post-budget restructure and thereby facilitate explanations of individual variances. However, the Board also noted that in other circumstances it might be necessary to explain a restructuring descriptively because any allocation of the original budget presented to parliament would be quite arbitrary and may not have been replaced for the new entities involved by other budgets presented to parliament in the period of the restructuring.

Budget presented to parliament [paragraphs 6, 7 and 14]

BC17 The Board concluded that the budget first 'presented' to parliament is more relevant to users than the budget that is first 'adopted' by parliament. This is because the presented budget is the one most widely publicised and, accordingly, is the primary reference point for any assessment of the reliability of budgeting, identification of major variances and assessment of an entity's performance in relation to the period.

BC18 As noted in paragraph BC5, the Board identified the need to provide additional guidance to facilitate the application of the principles previously in AASB 1049 to an individual entity within the GGS relating to budgets incorporated into a parent's consolidated budget or where only summarised budget information is presented to parliament. Accordingly, the Board decided to clarify the meaning of the phrase 'budget ... presented to parliament' for not-for-profit entities within the GGS in paragraph 14 of AASB 1055.

Original versus revised budget [paragraphs 6(e), 7(a), 9 and 11]

BC19 For the same reason outlined in paragraph BC17 relating to the presented versus the adopted budget, the Board concluded that the original budget, rather than a subsequently revised budget, is a primary reference point for assessing accountability. This is because a revised budget, possibly revised late in a period, would limit the ability of users to assess how well an entity performed over the whole period against its objectives reflected in the original budget. Accordingly, the Board decided that the budgetary disclosures required by AASB 1055 should be based on the original budget, with a discretion to disclose any additional revised budgets, acknowledging that disclosure of revised budgets may occur late in the financial period and their disclosure can provide useful input to assessments of an entity's performance and inform users of budget updates.

Restating the presentation and classification of budgetary information [paragraphs 6(e), 7(a), and 12]

BC20 The Board decided that the budgetary information required by AASB 1055 should be restated, if necessary, to align with the presentation and classification adopted in the financial statements for controlled items and the information about administered items disclosed in accordance with AASB 1050.

BC21 The Board considered whether the budget should also be required to be recast to align with recognition and measurement principles adopted for actual amounts. The Board noted the practical difficulties of recasting amounts for recognition and measurement differences – e.g. retrospectively determining 'budgeted' fair values when hindsight is likely to influence such a determination. Accordingly, the requirements in paragraphs 6(e), 7(a) and 12 of AASB 1055 are expressed in a way that the budget should be restated solely for presentation and classification matters, not for recognition and measurement matters.

BC22 The Board noted that as a result of this conclusion variances might arise from recognition and measurement principles adopted in the budget being different from the recognition and measurement principles adopted in the financial statements. Accordingly, AASB 1055 requires disclosure of explanations of major variances between actual and budget amounts that might include variances arising from recognition and measurement differences.

Explanation of major variances [paragraphs 6(f), 7(b) and 15]

BC23 The Board noted that the requirement to include explanations of major variances between budgeted and actual financial information is questioned by some practitioners for two primary reasons:

    (a)   in relation to whole of government and GGS financial statements, the requirement to explain variances is unnecessary as the variance explanations are not relevant to users because variance explanations are more relevant at entity level and the reasons for changes in budgetary assumptions are explained every time the budgets are updated; and

(b)   the inclusion of unaudited budgetary information within the audited financial statements results in references in an audit report in relation to budget information within the statements.

BC24 However, the Board concluded that the requirement for disclosure of explanations of major variances should be a key feature within the Standard. It did so on the basis that the information is relevant to users and that merely recording the amount of the variance is not sufficient to meet accountability needs. An explanation of major variances is critical if users are to find comparisons between actual and budget valuable input to their analysis of the performance of an entity. A similar requirement exists within the New Zealand Accounting Standards.

BC25 Although the budgetary disclosures in AASB 1055 are to be based on the original budget, the Board noted that the requirement to disclose explanations of major variances between an original budget and actual amounts might need to include references to revisions during a period, particularly if an entity's structure or objectives are changed during the period, or government policy changes during the period have affected the original budget. For example, where there are major numerical differences between the actual and revised budget amounts, the explanations of major variances might need to include causes that led to such differences, even if there were no major numerical differences between original budget and actual amounts. This would be particularly when omission of such explanations would result in misleading users' analysis of an entity's performance for a period or assessment of accountability.

BC26 The Board also noted that some question the suitability of referring to 'major' variances, given the role materiality plays in standards. The Board decided to retain the reference, given it was used in AASB 1049 without insurmountable practice issues being identified. However, the Board decided that it would reconsider the matter in due course as part of a broader consideration of terminology associated with 'materiality' used in a range of standards.

Auditability of budgetary information

BC27 The Board noted the concerns expressed by some about the auditability of the budgetary information (including explanations of major variances) that would be required to be disclosed. The Board noted that the auditors would need to understand the budget and the budget processes in order to plan the audit approach to meet the objectives of the audit. However, the auditor does not provide an opinion on the budget. Furthermore, such concerns appear to have been resolved in practice (as evident from the post-implementation review of AASB 1049). In any event, the Board noted that if any audit related issues arise, they would be matters more suited for consideration by the Auditing and Assurance Standards Board (AUASB) rather than the AASB.

The relationship of budgetary requirements in AASB 1055 and disclosure requirements about appropriations in AASB 1004

BC28 The Board considered the relationship of AASB 1055 to paragraph 64 of AASB 1004 *Contributions*, which requires government departments to provide disclosures of appropriations and other amounts authorised other than by way of appropriations, expenditures against those appropriations or other amounts and material variances between expenditures and appropriations or other amounts. The Board decided that paragraph 64 of AASB 1004 contains fundamentally different requirements from AASB 1055 and should be retained, as it is focused on information concerning the acquittal of appropriations and other advances rather than the more broadly-based requirements in AASB 1055 for actual to budget variance analysis.

Reduced disclosure requirements for entities applying Tier 2 reporting requirements

BC29 The Board noted that, under AASB 1053 *Application of Tiers of Australian Accounting Standards*, all not-for-profit entities within the GGS are Tier 2 entities (albeit that they might elect or be directed by a regulator to adopt Tier 1 requirements). Accordingly, the Board considered whether all the disclosure requirements of AASB 1055 should be applied to all not-for-profit entities within the GGS, or only those applying Tier 1 requirements. In making this assessment, the Board applied the principles it adopted in determining the disclosures in other standards of which Tier 2 entities should be relieved. Accordingly, having regard to user needs and cost/benefit considerations, the Board decided that not-for-profit entities within the GGS applying Tier 2 requirements should be subject to all the disclosure requirements of AASB 1055.

Transitional requirements

BC30 The Board noted that comparative budgetary information in respect of the previous period is not required to be disclosed by AASB 1055. Accordingly, the Board concluded that the requirements in AASB 1055 do not warrant specific transitional relief.

Operative date

BC31 The Board considered the date from which AASB 1055 should become mandatory. Given the nature of the requirements, which affects only presentation and classification, and no comparative budgetary information required to be disclosed, AASB 1055 is unlikely to cause insurmountable difficulty in its implementation. Thus, the Board decided that a period of about two years from the issue of AASB 1055 before it becomes mandatory would be sufficient. The Board also decided to allow early adoption of AASB 1055.

AASB 1056

Superannuation Entities

(Issued June 2014)

This note is not part of Accounting Standard AASB 1056.

The following unincorporated amendments are not included in this Standard.

- AASB 2014-5 *Amendments to Australian Accounting Standards arising from AASB 15 Revenue from Contracts with Customers*. This Standard makes amendments to AASB 1056 *Superannuation Entities* to reporting periods beginning 1 January 2017.

- AASB 2015-8 *Amendments to AAS — Deferral of AASB 15 Revenue from Contracts with Customers*. This Standard amends the mandatory effective date of AASB 15 to reporting periods beginning on or after 1 January 2018 instead of 1 January 2017. Therefore, this Standard also defers the consequential amendments to AASB 1056 set out in AASB 2014-5.

- AASB 2016-7 *Amendments to Australian Accounting Standards — Deferral of AASB 15 for Not-for-Profit Entities*. This Standard defers the consequential amendments that were originally set out in AASB 2014-5 *Amendments to Australian Accounting Standards arising from AASB 15*, by restating the effective date of the amendments set out in AASB 2015-8 *Amendments to Australian Accounting Standards* for not-for-profit entities. This Standard defers the application of AASB 15 to 1 January 2019. Earlier application is permitted provided AASB 1058 is also applied to the same period.

Entities early-adopting any amendments with later application dates will need to refer to the amending Standards that have not yet been incorporated into compilations. The abovementioned unincorporated amendments may be located on the AASB website at www.aasb.gov.au or on the Federal Register of Legislation website at www.legislation.gov.au.

CONTENTS

PREFACE

COMPARISON WITH IAS 26

ACCOUNTING STANDARD

AASB 1056 *SUPERANNUATION ENTITIES*

Paragraphs

Australian Accounting Standard AASB 1056 *Superannuation Entities* is set out in paragraphs 1 – 37 and Appendices A and B. All the paragraphs have equal authority. Paragraphs in **bold type** state the main principles. Terms defined in Appendix A are in *italics* the first time they appear in the Standard. AASB 1056 is to be read in the context of other Australian Accounting Standards, including AASB 1048 *Interpretation of Standards*, which identifies the Australian Accounting Interpretations. In the absence of explicit guidance, AASB 108 *Accounting Policies, Changes in Accounting Estimates and Errors* provides a basis for selecting and applying accounting policies.

AASB (side tab)

PREFACE

Introduction

The Australian Accounting Standards Board (AASB) makes Australian Accounting Standards, including Interpretations, to be applied by:

(a)   entities required by the *Corporations Act 2001* to prepare financial reports;

(b)   governments in preparing financial statements for the whole of government and the General Government Sector (GGS); and

(c)   entities in the private or public for-profit or not-for-profit sectors that are reporting entities or that prepare general purpose financial statements.

AASB 1053 *Application of Tiers of Australian Accounting Standards* establishes a differential reporting framework consisting of two tiers of reporting requirements for preparing general purpose financial statements:

(a)   Tier 1: Australian Accounting Standards; and

(b)   Tier 2: Australian Accounting Standards – Reduced Disclosure Requirements.

Tier 1 requirements incorporate International Financial Reporting Standards (IFRS), including Interpretations, issued by the International Accounting Standards Board (IASB), with the addition of paragraphs on the applicability of each Standard in the Australian environment.

Publicly accountable for-profit private sector entities are required to adopt Tier 1 requirements, and therefore are required to comply with IFRS. Furthermore, other for-profit private sector entities complying with Tier 1 requirements will simultaneously comply with IFRS. Some other entities complying with Tier 1 requirements will also simultaneously comply with IFRS.

Tier 2 requirements comprise the recognition and measurement requirements of Tier 1 but substantially reduced disclosure requirements in comparison with Tier 1.

AASB 1053 specifically deems superannuation plans regulated by the Australian Prudential Regulation Authority (APRA), other than Small APRA Funds,[1] to be entities that have public accountability. Accordingly, those APRA-regulated superannuation plans that are classified as 'large' prepare Tier 1 general purpose financial statements.

AASB 1056 *Superannuation Entities* does not permit Tier 2 general purpose financial statements for superannuation entities.

AASB 1056 is among a number of Australian Accounting Standards that are specific to Australian entities.

Some other Australian Accounting Standards, which incorporate IFRS, also include requirements that are specific to Australian entities. In most instances, these requirements are either restricted to the not-for-profit or public sectors or include additional disclosures that address domestic, regulatory or other issues.

In developing requirements for public sector entities, the AASB considers the requirements of International Public Sector Accounting Standards (IPSASs), as issued by the International Public Sector Accounting Standards Board (IPSASB) of the International Federation of Accountants.

Purpose of developing AASB 1056

AASB 1056 replaces AAS 25 *Financial Reporting by Superannuation Plans*, which was issued in 1993. AASB 1056 has been developed in light of significant changes in recent years, including developments in the superannuation industry and Australia's adoption of IFRS. AASB 1056 also addresses deficiencies in AAS 25 and makes the requirements for superannuation entities more consistent with current requirements in Australian Accounting Standards.

Paragraphs BC3 to BC6 provide more background on the purpose of developing AASB 1056.

COMPARISON WITH IAS 26

AASB 1056 *Superannuation Entities* has been developed by the Australian Accounting Standards Board (AASB) to replace AAS 25 *Financial Reporting by Superannuation Plans*.

IAS 26 *Accounting and Reporting by Retirement Benefit Plans* was originally issued by the International Accounting Standards Committee in January 1987 and adopted by the International Accounting Standards Board in April 2001. When Australia first adopted International Financial Reporting Standards, AAS 25 was considered to be more appropriate for Australian superannuation entities than IAS 26. The AASB considers that the AASB's reasons for not adopting IAS 26 remain valid in respect of AASB 1056. Those reasons are outlined in paragraphs BC7 to BC11 of the Basis for Conclusions.

The main differences between AASB 1056 and IAS 26 include the following.

(a)   AASB 1056 requires the presentation of a comprehensive set of financial statements for superannuation entities, whether they constitute one or more superannuation plans and whether they have defined contribution members or defined benefit members, or both. In contrast IAS 26 requires a defined contribution plan to present a statement of net assets available for benefits, and permits a defined benefit plan to present either:

---

1   As defined by APRA Superannuation Circular No. III.E.1 *Regulation of Small APRA Funds,* December 2000.

(i) a statement showing net assets available for benefits, an actuarial present value of promised retirement benefits, and a resulting excess or deficit; or

(ii) a statement of net assets available for benefits including either a note disclosing an actuarial present value of promised retirement benefits, or a reference to this information in an accompanying actuarial report.

(b) AASB 1056 requires most assets to be measured at fair value; whereas IAS 26 permits investment assets to be measured at an amount other than fair value when "an estimate of fair value is not possible".

(c) AASB 1056 requires measurement of defined benefit member liabilities to involve assumptions that would include projected salary levels; whereas IAS 26 permits the "actuarial present value of promised retirement benefits" to be based on either current or projected salary levels.

ACCOUNTING STANDARD AASB 1056

The Australian Accounting Standards Board makes Accounting Standard AASB 1056 *Superannuation Entities*.

Kevin M. Stevenson
Chair – AASB

Dated 5 June 2014

ACCOUNTING STANDARD AASB 1056
SUPERANNUATION ENTITIES

Objective

1   The objective of this Standard is to specify requirements for the general purpose financial statements of *superannuation entities* with a view to providing users with information useful for decision making in a superannuation entity context.

Application

2   **This Standard applies to:**

(a) **general purpose financial statements of each superannuation entity that is a reporting entity; and**

(b) **financial statements of a superannuation entity that are held out to be general purpose financial statements.**

3   **This Standard applies to annual reporting periods beginning on or after 1 July 2016.**

4   **This Standard may be applied to annual reporting periods beginning before 1 July 2016. When an entity applies this Standard to such an annual reporting period, it shall disclose that fact.**

5   When applied or operative, this Standard supersedes AAS 25 *Financial Reporting by Superannuation Plans* as issued in March 1993 and amended to December 2013.

Compliance with Australian Accounting Standards

6   **Unless otherwise specified in this Standard, the financial statements of a superannuation entity shall be prepared in accordance with other applicable Australian Accounting Standards.**

7   Except in specified circumstances, this Standard requires a superannuation entity to apply other applicable Australian Accounting Standards. One of the main exceptions is to require most assets to be measured at fair value.

Presentation of financial statements

8   A superannuation entity shall present:

      (a)   a statement of financial position as at the end of the reporting period;

      (b)   an income statement for the period;

      (c)   a statement of changes in equity/reserves for the period;

      (d)   a statement of cash flows for the period;

      (e)   a statement of changes in member benefits for the period; and

      (f)   notes to the financial statements.

Income statement

9   The income statement shall include line items that present, when applicable, the following amounts for the period:

      (a)   income, in aggregate or subclassified, subject to paragraph 10;

      (b)   expenses, in aggregate or subclassified, subject to paragraph 10;

      (c)   net benefits allocated to *defined contribution member* accounts;

      (d)   the net change in *defined benefit member* liabilities;

      (e)   net result, subject to paragraph 10; and

      (f)   income tax expense or benefit attributable to net result.

10   When a superannuation entity acts in the capacity of an insurer in respect of defined contribution members, the income statement or notes to the financial statements shall separately present insurance premiums, claim expenses, reinsurance expenses, reinsurance recoveries, and the net result from insurance activities.

Statement of changes in member benefits

11   A statement of changes in member benefits shall present opening and closing balances for member liabilities and, when applicable, include the following line items for the period:

      (a)   employer contributions;

      (b)   member contributions;

      (c)   taxes on contributions;

      (d)   benefits transferred into the entity from other superannuation entities;

      (e)   benefits to members or their beneficiaries;

      (f)   insurance premiums charged to defined contribution member accounts;

      (g)   net benefits allocated to defined contribution member accounts;

      (h)   net changes to defined benefit member *accrued benefits*; and

      (i)   amounts allocated to members from reserves.

12   Current tax and deferred tax shall be charged or credited directly to member liabilities and presented in the statement of changes in member benefits when the tax relates to items that are credited or charged, in the same or a different period, directly to member liabilities.

Assets and liabilities measured at fair value

13   **All recognised assets and liabilities except member liabilities, tax assets and liabilities, acquired goodwill, insurance assets and liabilities, and employer-sponsor receivables shall be measured at fair value at each reporting date.**

Member liabilities

Recognition

14 Obligations relating to member entitlements shall be recognised as member liabilities.

Measurement

15 Member liabilities shall be measured as the accrued benefits of members as set out in paragraphs 16 and 17.

16 Defined contribution member liabilities shall be measured as the amount of member account balances as at the reporting date.

17 Defined benefit member liabilities shall be measured as the amount of a portfolio of investments that would be needed as at the reporting date to yield future net cash inflows that would be sufficient to meet accrued benefits as at that date when they are expected to fall due.

Employer-sponsor receivables

Recognition

18 An asset relating to an employer-sponsor receivable shall be recognised to the extent there is a difference between a defined benefit member liability and the fair value of assets available to meet that liability that meets the definition and recognition criteria for an asset in the *Framework for the Preparation and Presentation of Financial Statements*.

Measurement

19 An asset recognised in accordance with paragraph 18 shall be measured consistently with the measurement of defined benefit member liabilities less the relevant amount of the other recognised assets held to meet those liabilities.

Disclosure

20 Paragraph AG5 of Appendix B includes guidance on the approach to disclosure principles and requirements in other Australian Accounting Standards that a superannuation entity applies when relevant.

Nature of member benefits

21 A superannuation entity shall disclose information that provides users with a basis for understanding the benefits the entity provides to members. These disclosures shall include the types of benefits the superannuation entity provides and, when applicable, whether the superannuation entity can accept new defined benefit members.

Nature of income and expense items

22 A superannuation entity shall disclose information that provides users with a basis for understanding the nature and amounts of income and expenses.

Member liabilities

23 A superannuation entity shall disclose information that provides users with a basis for understanding member liabilities.

24   In relation to defined contribution member liabilities, to meet the objective in paragraph 23, when applicable, an entity:

   (a)   applies the disclosure requirements of AASB 7 *Financial Instruments: Disclosures* in respect of credit risk, market risk and liquidity risk, as if defined contribution member liabilities were financial liabilities; and

   (b)   discloses the amount of any net assets attributable to defined contribution members but not allocated to those members as at the end of the period.

25   In relation to defined benefit member liabilities, to meet the objective in paragraph 23, the disclosures would include:

   (a)   information in relation to the key assumptions used in measuring defined benefit member liabilities, including:

      (i)   the basis for the key assumptions, including the manner in which they have been determined;

      (ii)   the key assumptions used, as percentages or in other quantitative terms or in qualitative form; and

      (iii)   the sensitivity of the liabilities to reasonably possible changes in the key assumptions;

   (b)   the amount of *vested benefits* at the end of the period;

   (c)   whether the actual level of contributions is consistent with the actuary's recommendations;

   (d)   information about the manner in which the entity manages liquidity risk; and

   (e)   where the entity's actual investment portfolio differs from the portfolio used in measuring defined benefit member liabilities in accordance with paragraph 17, an explanation of why that is the case.

Employer-sponsor receivables

26   **When an employer-sponsor receivable is recognised in accordance with paragraph 18, the main features of the specific contractual or statutory arrangement in place between the superannuation entity and the relevant employer-sponsor(s) shall be disclosed.**

27   To meet the objective in paragraph 26, the disclosures would include:

   (a)   whether the arrangement is contractual or statutory and, in the latter case, the name of the statute;

   (b)   the identity of the employer-sponsor(s); and

   (c)   the manner in which the receivable is expected to be realised by the entity.

Net assets attributable to defined benefit members

28   **Where the amount of net assets attributable to defined benefit members differs from defined benefit member liabilities determined in accordance with this Standard, the entity shall disclose information that provides users with a basis for understanding the nature, causes of and any strategies for addressing the difference between the two amounts.**

29   To meet the objective in paragraph 28, the disclosures would include:

   (a)   whether the difference has arisen, in whole or in part, as a consequence of applying different assumptions for the purposes of determining funding levels and measuring defined benefit member liabilities and, if so, the nature of the differences between the assumptions; and

   (b)   in the case of a difference not wholly explained by (a):

      (i)   the entity's strategy for addressing the difference and the anticipated timeframe over which the difference is expected to be eliminated; and

      (ii)   any plans or processes in place for employer-sponsors to seek to be paid some or all of a surplus or to reduce the level of their contributions in the future.

Explaining changes in defined benefit member liabilities

30   **A superannuation entity shall disclose information that provides users with a basis for understanding the overall change in defined benefit member liabilities.**

31   To meet the objective in paragraph 30, the disclosures would include quantitative or qualitative information about changes to key assumptions.

Disaggregated financial information

32   **A superannuation entity shall disclose disaggregated information when it is necessary to explain the risks and benefit arrangements relating to different categories of members.**

Insurance arrangements

33   **A superannuation entity acting in the capacity of an insurer shall:**

    (a)   recognise liabilities and assets arising from its insurance and reinsurance arrangements;

    (b)   measure liabilities and assets arising from insurance and reinsurance arrangements using the approach to measuring defined benefit member liabilities; and

    (c)   if reinsurance assets are impaired, reduce the carrying amount of those assets and recognise the impairment in the income statement.

34   A reinsurance asset is impaired if, and only if:

    (a)   there is objective evidence, as a result of an event that occurred after initial recognition of the reinsurance asset, that the entity may not receive amounts due to it under the terms of the contract; and

    (b)   that event has a reliably measurable impact on the amounts that the entity will receive from the reinsurer.

35   **A superannuation entity acting in the capacity of an insurer in respect of defined contribution members that recognises insurance liabilities and assets shall disclose information that provides a basis for understanding the amount, timing and uncertainty of future cash flows relating to those liabilities and assets.**

36   To meet the objective in paragraph 35, the disclosures would include quantitative or qualitative information in relation to:

    (a)   key assumptions used in measuring liabilities arising from insurance arrangements the superannuation entity provides to its members;

    (b)   any uncertainties surrounding those key assumptions; and

    (c)   any uncertainties surrounding reinsurance assets.

Transition on initial application

37   **On initial application of this Standard, superannuation entities need not present a statement of financial position as at the beginning of the earliest comparative period.**

AASB

APPENDIX A
DEFINED TERMS

This appendix is an integral part of AASB 1056.

accrued benefits	Benefits the superannuation entity is presently obliged to transfer to members or their beneficiaries in the future as a result of membership up to the end of the reporting period.
approved deposit fund	An entity that is an approved deposit fund within the meaning of section 10 of the *Superannuation Industry (Supervision) Act 1993*.
defined benefit member	A member whose benefits are specified, or are determined, at least in part, by reference to a formula based on their years of membership and/or salary level.
	Members identified as defined benefit members based on the definition in this Standard are not expected to be different from members identified as defined benefit members under prudential regulation.
defined contribution member	A member whose benefits are determined by reference to accumulated contributions made on their behalf and/or by them, together with investment earnings thereon.
	If an individual member's benefit entitlements have characteristics of both defined benefit and defined contribution entitlements, the member is regarded as a defined benefit member for the purpose of this Standard.
superannuation entity	An entity that constitutes one or more *superannuation plan(s)* or an *approved deposit fund*.
superannuation plan	An entity that is:
	(a) regulated under the *Superannuation Industry (Supervision) Act 1993*, or similar legislative requirements in the case of an exempt public sector superannuation plan; and
	(b) established and maintained:
	(i) in order to receive superannuation contributions; and
	(ii) for the primary purpose of providing benefits to members upon their retirement, death, disablement or other event that qualifies as a condition of release for member benefits.
	Superannuation plans may be constituted as separate entities or as a number of separate entities established to administer aspects of the plan (such as when one entity administers contributions and another administers benefit payments).
vested benefits	The value of benefits to which members or their beneficiaries would be entitled on voluntary withdrawal from the superannuation entity or on becoming entitled to a pension or deferred benefit as at the end of the reporting period.
	In the context of a defined benefit member's vested benefits, withdrawal means withdrawal by a member from either the defined benefit section of their superannuation plan or withdrawal from the plan itself.

APPENDIX B
APPLICATION GUIDANCE

CONTENTS

Paragraphs

APPENDIX B
APPLICATION GUIDANCE

This appendix is an integral part of AASB 1056.

Definition of superannuation entity

AG1   This Standard applies to the general purpose financial statements of superannuation entities, as defined in Appendix A. The definition of 'superannuation entity' includes regulated superannuation funds under the *Superannuation Industry (Supervision) Act 1993* (SIS Act). It also includes various public sector superannuation arrangements, but does not include pooled superannuation trusts. Accordingly the term has a different meaning in this Standard from its meaning in the SIS Act.

AG2   In some cases, entities administering superannuation arrangements, particularly in the public sector, would need to consider the nature of their activities and the boundaries of their arrangements to determine whether they are superannuation entities that would apply this Standard. They may instead be only custodial arrangements under which member liabilities rest directly and solely with employer-sponsors.

Compliance with principles and requirements in other Australian Accounting Standards (paragraphs 6 and 7)

AG3   When the recognition, measurement and disclosure principles and requirements in this Standard address the same items or events as the recognition, measurement and disclosure principles and requirements in other Australian Accounting Standards, a superannuation entity need not apply those other Standards. For example, a superannuation entity applying this Standard would:

    (a)   measure financial assets at fair value and recognise fair value changes in the income statement and not apply AASB 9 *Financial Instruments*; which might otherwise require some financial assets to be measured at amortised cost or fair value through other comprehensive income; and

(b)   disclose information about expenses in accordance with paragraphs 9 and 22 and need not disclose information in accordance with paragraphs 99-105 of AASB 101 *Presentation of Financial Statements* regarding an analysis of expenses.

AG4   Additionally, when the measurement principles in this Standard are different from the measurement principles in other Australian Accounting Standards, the disclosure requirements related to the measurement requirements in those other Australian Accounting Standards do not apply. For example, a superannuation entity that holds plant and equipment is not required to disclose the carrying amounts that would have been recognised had the assets been measured under the cost model in accordance with paragraph 77(e) of AASB 116 *Property, Plant and Equipment*.

AG5   When a superannuation entity applies the recognition and measurement principles and requirements in other Australian Accounting Standards, the entity would also apply any relevant disclosure principles and requirements contained in those other Standards unless they are specifically modified by this Standard. Australian Accounting Standards that contain disclosure principles and requirements, some or all of which a superannuation entity would apply, when relevant, include but are not limited to the following:

(a)   AASB 7 *Financial Instruments: Disclosures*;[2]

(b)   AASB 12 *Disclosure of Interests in Other Entities*;

(c)   AASB 101 *Presentation of Financial Statements*;

(d)   AASB 107 *Statement of Cash Flows*;

(e)   AASB 108 *Accounting Policies, Changes in Accounting Estimates and Errors*;

(f)   AASB 110 *Events after the Reporting Period*;

(g)   AASB 112 *Income Taxes*;

(h)   AASB 118 *Revenue*; and

(i)   AASB 124 *Related Party Disclosures*.

AG6   When a superannuation entity applies other Australian Accounting Standards, the entity also applies relevant Australian Interpretations listed in AASB 1048 *Interpretation of Standards*.

Presentation of financial statements (paragraphs 8 to 12)

AG7   Consistent with AASB 101, alternative titles can be used for the financial statements to suit the circumstances. For example, the statement of changes in equity might be better described as a statement of changes in reserves in some circumstances.

Statement of financial position

AG8   Where a superannuation entity's total assets differs from its total liabilities (including defined contribution member liabilities, defined benefit member liabilities and any obligations to employer-sponsors), the difference is classified as equity and presented in accordance with applicable Australian Accounting Standards. In these circumstances, consistent with paragraph 55 of AASB 101, the entity may need to present additional line items, headings and subtotals in the statement of financial position when such presentation is relevant to an understanding of the entity's financial position.

AG9   Differences between the total assets and total liabilities of a superannuation entity commonly arise in relation to matters such as operational risk reserves and, in respect

---

2   Although, refer to paragraph AG36 in respect of the fair value disclosure requirements of AASB 7.

of defined benefit members, due to factors such as differences between actual and assumed experience.

AG10 A superannuation entity that has both defined contribution and defined benefit members would present separately its obligations for the two types of benefits in accordance with paragraph 32.

AG11 Superannuation entities would be expected to present the various classes of their investments in a meaningful way, consistent with the requirements of AASB 101.

AG12 Judgement needs to be exercised in the context of a superannuation entity about how to describe investments presented in its statement of financial position so as to explain the nature of investments to users. For example, an investment in a unit trust might need to be described so as to reflect the nature of the assets underlying the unit trust.

Income statement

AG13 Revenues and expenses are presented in relevant subclassifications in the income statement or notes to the financial statements.

AG14 Gains and losses arising from the remeasurement of assets and liabilities measured at fair value are included in the income statement. An example of a liability measured at fair value is a derivative financial instrument that is a liability.

AG15 The income tax expense or benefit attributable to profit or loss does not include the taxes levied on concessional contributions, which is included in the statement of changes in member benefits and impacts on the amount of net benefits allocated to members.

AG16 The net change in defined benefit member liabilities for a period is the difference between the opening and closing balances of the defined benefit member liabilities for the period, after adjusting for inwards and outwards movements, including:

    (a)   contributions;

    (b)   tax on contributions;

    (c)   benefits to members; and

    (d)   transfers between reserves and accrued benefits.

AG17 A superannuation entity that presents an income statement in accordance with this Standard does not present a single statement of comprehensive income, or separate income statement and statement of comprehensive income, in accordance with AASB 101.

Statement of changes in member benefits

AG18 In the context of the line items that might appear in a statement of changes in member benefits in accordance with paragraph 11:

    (a)   employer contributions include both routine contributions and any 'top-up' contributions made to fund defined benefit member liabilities;

    (b)   net benefits allocated to defined contribution members include the investment returns and fair value movements allocated to these members – the line item might be positive or negative; and

    (c)   net changes to defined benefit members may include a number of components because the service element for a period might be different from actual contributions for that period and because of the interest cost associated with the liability – the line item might be positive or negative.

AG19 When a surplus in a defined benefit plan is being used to fund employer contributions to defined contribution members within the one superannuation entity, the entity determines the most relevant presentation in the statement of changes in member benefits in the circumstances. That might include presenting a transfer from defined benefit member benefits to defined contribution member benefits as separate line items in relation to sources of contributions.

AG20 In relation to the net amount allocated to defined contribution member accounts, when appropriate, there shall be separate disclosure of net investment income and the administration costs charged to member accounts in the statement of changes in member benefits or in the notes to the financial statements.

Statement of changes in equity/reserves

AG21 Under this Standard, the interests of members of superannuation entities are liabilities and are not regarded as meeting the definition of an 'equity instrument' in paragraph 11 of AASB 132 *Financial Instruments: Presentation*, which is "any contract that evidences a residual interest in the assets of an entity after deducting all of its liabilities". Superannuation entities would not disclose 'equity' information equivalent to that required by paragraphs 79(a) and 80 of AASB 101, in relation to member liabilities.

AG22 Paragraph 6 of AASB 101 notes: entities that do not have equity as defined in AASB 132 may need to adapt the financial statement presentation of members' interests. Consistent with this notion, superannuation entities need to exercise judgement in preparing the statement of changes in equity/reserves, including the title and content of that statement.

Assets and liabilities measured at fair value (paragraph 13)

AG23 This Standard requires assets and liabilities, other than member liabilities, tax assets and liabilities, acquired goodwill and insurance assets and liabilities, to be measured at fair value with fair value changes recognised through the income statement. This would include:

(a)   financial assets and liabilities, including derivatives;

(b)   investment property; and

(c)   property, plant and equipment.

AG24 In determining the fair value measurements and accounting for any transaction costs, a superannuation entity applies the relevant principles and requirements in other applicable Australian Accounting Standards, including in particular AASB 13 *Fair Value Measurement*. Superannuation entities shall not apply AASB 5 *Non-current Assets Held for Sale and Discontinued Operations*.

Measurement of defined benefit member liabilities (paragraph 17)

AG25 The amount of defined benefit member liabilities measured in accordance with paragraph 17 is a present value based on a portfolio of investments estimated to yield future net cash inflows that would be sufficient to meet accrued benefit payments when they are expected to fall due. In this context:

(a)   the amount relates to members' service up to the reporting date;

(b)   it is assumed the accrued benefits will be fulfilled and, accordingly, there is no adjustment for the superannuation entity's own credit risk;

(c)   the expected cash outflows relevant to measuring the liability take into account the timing and probabilities attaching to various factors that reflect the characteristics of the members/beneficiaries and the features of entitlements (including expected rates of: member turnover; mortality and disability; salary adjustment; early retirement; and member choice of available options, such as lump sum and pension options). The relevant portfolio of investments would not necessarily be a portfolio of instruments that is expected to yield contractual net cash inflows that match the timing of the expected net cash outflows relating to the liability. It might be a portfolio that is expected to yield either contractual or non-contractual net cash inflows that match the timing of expected net cash outflows relating to the liability;

(d)   the investment returns relevant to measuring the liability are those expected on a portfolio of investments that reflects the opportunities available in investment markets and not necessarily the actual investments held by the superannuation entity to meet accrued defined benefit member liabilities. Accordingly, the measurement is not dependent on whether the benefits are fully funded, under/over funded or completely unfunded. However, in many cases there would be a strong relationship between the portfolio of investments used for measurement purposes and, where relevant, the superannuation entity's actual portfolio of investments, consistent with its investment strategy in respect of meeting defined benefit member liabilities;

(e)   the accrued benefit amount might be more or less than the value of vested benefits; and

(f)   the discount rate would exclude risks incorporated in the expected cash flows (to avoid 'double-counting' of the impacts of risks).

AG26   In applying the defined benefit member liability measurement requirements of this Standard, superannuation entities may use estimates, averages and computational shortcuts provided that application of those shortcut techniques yield a reasonable approximation of the defined benefit member liabilities.

Employer-sponsor receivables (paragraphs 18 and 19)

AG27   A specific contractual or statutory arrangement in place between the superannuation entity and the relevant employer-sponsor(s) in relation to funding defined benefit member liabilities might give rise to an asset recognised in accordance with paragraph 18.

AG28   A receivable meeting the definition and recognition criteria for an asset in the *Framework for the Preparation and Presentation of Financial Statements* would be measured at its intrinsic value. That is, the difference between the defined benefit member liabilities and the amount of the other recognised assets held to meet those liabilities, unless the amount of the receivable is capped in some manner.

Disclosures (paragraphs 20 to 32)

Nature of income and expense items

AG29   To meet the objectives in paragraph 22, when relevant, the superannuation entity discloses:

(a)   income by class, such as interest, dividends and rentals;

(b)   net gain or loss arising from the remeasurement of assets and liabilities measured at fair value;

(c)   net gain or loss attributable to liabilities and assets arising from insurance arrangements the superannuation entity provides to its members;

(d)   administration expenses;

(e)   investment expenses, such as investment manager fees, investment consultant fees and custodian fees;

(f)   actuarial fees;

(g)   audit fees;

(h)   commissions paid directly by the superannuation entity;

(i)   trustee fees and reimbursements; and

(j)   sponsorship and advertising expenses.

Member liabilities

AG30 Paragraph 23 requires a superannuation entity to disclose information that provides users with a basis for understanding member liabilities. Paragraph 24(a) requires a superannuation entity to treat its defined contribution member liabilities as being within the scope of AASB 7 for the purposes of disclosing information about credit risk, market risk and liquidity risk. The fair value disclosure requirements of AASB 7 need not be applied in respect of member liabilities.

AG31 In applying the relevant principles and requirements of AASB 7 in respect of credit risk, market risk and liquidity risk, an entity would give consideration to the characteristics of member benefits in determining the information it would provide. For example, the entity would consider disclosing:

(a) the mechanism by which market risk is passed on to members, such as through frequent crediting of member accounts; and

(b) how it manages the liquidity risk associated with meeting withdrawals and, when relevant, pension payments.

AG32 Paragraph 25(a)(iii) identifies disclosure of the sensitivity of defined benefit member liabilities to changes in key assumptions used in their measurement as being required to meet the objective of paragraph 23. The subject of the disclosures is reasonably possible changes in the key assumptions. When there is more than one key assumption for which a change is judged to be reasonably possible, the analysis can be performed on a univariate basis or on a multivariate basis.

Disaggregated information

AG33 When a superannuation entity has multiple defined benefit plans, judgement needs to be applied to determine the most relevant levels of aggregation at which to disclose information, particularly where the information differs from plan to plan. Depending on the circumstances, the requirements might be able to be satisfied through aggregate disclosures about multiple plans or they might need to involve plan-by-plan disclosure.

AG34 In meeting the requirement in paragraph 32 to present disaggregated information, a superannuation entity that has material member liabilities relating to different types of members, such as defined contribution members and defined benefit members, would need to consider separately presenting:

(a) line items in the statement of financial position for each of the different membership types in respect of member liabilities; and

(b) either a single statement of changes in member benefits with columns or notes showing the amounts relating to different membership types or separate statements of changes in member benefits for each different type of members.

This would be in addition to presenting the aggregated information.

AG35 Depending on the circumstances of the superannuation entity, other disaggregated information might also be necessary to explain the risks to which different categories of members are exposed.

Financial instruments

AG36 For the purpose of applying the disclosure principles and requirements in AASB 7, an entity would consider financial assets and any financial liabilities to be measured at fair value through profit or loss and, accordingly, the fair value disclosure requirements of AASB 7 need not be applied to these assets and liabilities.

AG37 For the purpose of applying the disclosure principles and requirements in AASB 7, an entity would read references in AASB 7 to 'statement of comprehensive income' to mean 'income statement'.

Comparative information

AG38 In complying with the comparative information requirements of AASB 101 a superannuation entity discloses:

(a) key assumptions used in measuring defined benefit member liabilities at the end of the last annual reporting period; and

(b) how, if at all, those assumptions differ from the corresponding key assumptions used in measuring defined benefit member liabilities at the end of the current period.

Related parties

AG39 A trustee of a superannuation entity is a related party of the entity for the purpose of applying AASB 124.

Insurance arrangements (paragraphs 33 to 36)

AG40 Superannuation entities often have insurance arrangements in place for their members and the extent to which they affect the financial statements varies depending on the nature of those arrangements. Some superannuation entities act only as agents for external insurers. Other superannuation entities act in the capacity of insurers and, therefore, take on insurance risks.

AG41 Factors that might be considered in determining whether a superannuation entity is acting as an agent in respect of the insurance arrangements provided to members include:

(a) members (or their beneficiaries) will only receive insurance benefits if the external insurer/reinsurer pays claims;

(b) insurance premiums are only paid through the superannuation entity for administrative reasons; and

(c) insurance premiums are effectively set directly by reference to premiums set by an external insurer.

AG42 It is not necessarily indicative of a superannuation entity taking on the role of an insurer simply because:

(a) (group) insurance cover is taken out in the name of the superannuation entity trustee;

(b) claim benefits are paid to members (or their beneficiaries) via the superannuation entity; and

(c) ex gratia payments have occasionally been made by the trustees in respect of death and disability benefits.

Superannuation entities acting only as agents

AG43 When a superannuation entity is acting only as an agent for an external insurer, premiums are not revenues or expenses of the superannuation entity and do not give rise to insurance contract liabilities or reinsurance assets. However, the impacts on the financial statements could include:

(a) premium cash inflows collected from members and premium cash outflows paid to insurers in the statement of cash flows; and

(b) premiums charged to member accounts and insurance benefits paid to members via the superannuation entity in the statement of changes in member benefits.

Superannuation entities as insurers

AG44 When a superannuation entity is taking on the role of an insurer, the impacts on the financial statements could include:

(a)   insurance contract revenue, incurred claims expense, reinsurance expense and reinsurance recoveries recognised in the income statement;

(b)   insurance contract liabilities and reinsurance contract assets recognised in the statement of financial position; and

(c)   insurance contract cash inflows, reinsurance contract cash outflows, claims cash outflows and reinsurance recoveries cash inflows recognised in the statement of cash flows.

AG45   Depending on the conditions set out in the relevant trust deed, defined benefit members or beneficiaries might be promised, for example, a lump sum benefit on retirement or resignation, a lump sum benefit on death or disablement, a pension on retirement for their remaining lifetime and/or a pension for the remaining lifetime of a spouse, and the pension may or may not be indexed in some way. The defined benefit member liability is effectively the sum of the expected values associated with the various ways in which members might be paid their benefits. It is relevant to consider the defined benefit member liability as a single item made up of inter-related components, rather than to seek to identify particular components for presentation purposes, such as an insurance component. Accordingly, liabilities and assets arising from insurance arrangements a superannuation entity provides to defined benefit members need not be presented as a separate liability in the statement of financial position. Furthermore, unless there are explicit direct premiums, claims, reinsurance premiums or claim recoveries relating to insurance risks, revenues and/or expenses relating to insurance arrangements a superannuation entity provides to defined benefit members need not be presented separately in the income statement or statement of changes in member benefits.

AG46   Liabilities arising from insurance arrangements a superannuation entity provides to defined contribution members shall be presented separately from the entity's liabilities for such members' benefits in the statement of financial position.

AG47   Assets arising from the reinsurance arrangements of a superannuation entity related to defined contribution members shall be presented separately.

AG48   Insurance contract liabilities and reinsurance contract assets are recognised and measured in accordance with the approach to measuring defined benefit member liabilities, whether they relate to defined contribution or defined benefit members. Shortcut techniques could be applied to measure insurance contract liabilities, for example, deferring and matching premiums over the period, provided the amount is not materially different from the amount that would be determined using the approach to measuring defined benefit member liabilities.

AG49   If a reinsurance asset is impaired, its carrying amount shall be reduced accordingly and an impairment expense recognised in the income statement. A reinsurance asset is impaired if, and only if:

(a)   there is objective evidence, as a result of an event that occurred after initial recognition of the reinsurance asset, that the amounts due from the reinsurer may not be received under the terms of the contract; and

(b)   that event has a reliably measurable impact on the amounts receivable from the reinsurer.

Preparation and presentation of consolidated financial statements

AG50   AASB 10 *Consolidated Financial Statements*, as amended by AASB 2013-5 *Amendments to Australian Accounting Standards – Investment Entities*, is applicable to periods beginning on or after 1 January 2014, and can be applied early.

AG51   AASB 10 is relevant for determining when consolidated financial statements must be presented. The AASB 2013-5 amendments provide an exception from consolidated financial statements for 'investment entities', which could include superannuation entities. The exception applies to all subsidiaries of investment entities, other than subsidiaries that provide services relating to the investment entity's investment activities. A parent must account for its subsidiaries that are subject to the exception at fair value through profit or loss.

AG52 It is possible that now or in the future there may be superannuation entities that have subsidiaries and do not qualify to be treated as investment entities; or, that there are superannuation entities that qualify to be treated as investment entities and have subsidiaries that provide services relating to their investment activities. Such superannuation entities would:

(a) present consolidated financial statements in accordance with the requirements of AASB 10; and

(b) initially measure any non-controlling interests applying the fair value approach in accordance with AASB 3 *Business Combinations* at the subsidiary's acquisition date and in accordance with AASB 10 at the end of each subsequent period.

MAIN DIFFERENCES BETWEEN AASB 1056 AND AAS 25

This summary accompanies, but is not part of, AASB 1056.

This summary highlights the main differences between AASB 1056 *Superannuation Entities* and its predecessor, AAS 25 *Financial Reporting by Superannuation Plans*.

Application of Australian Accounting Standards

AAS 25 required superannuation entities to apply, where appropriate, Australian Accounting Standards, but with some significant exceptions. AASB 1056 takes a similar approach, but is far more integrated with other Australian Accounting Standards (and therefore with International Financial Reporting Standards).

Under AAS 25, superannuation plans whose only assets (other than temporary deposits at call with a bank) are endowment, whole of life or other long-term insurance policies that match and fully guarantee the benefits to be paid to individual members were not required to comply with a number of the recognition, measurement and disclosure requirements of AAS 25 [paragraph 66]. The general purpose financial report of such plans needed only to report a limited amount of information.

No equivalent exemption is provided in AASB 1056.

Superannuation entity definition

AASB 1056 defines a 'superannuation entity' as an entity that constitutes one or more superannuation plan(s) or an approved deposit fund. A 'superannuation plan' is an entity that is:

(a) regulated under the *Superannuation Industry (Supervision) Act 1993* or similar legislative requirements in the case of an exempt public sector superannuation plan; and

(b) established and maintained: (i) in order to receive superannuation contributions; and (ii) for the primary purpose of providing benefits to members upon their retirement, death, disablement or other event that qualifies as a condition of release for member benefits.

AAS 25 had a different definition; namely: an arrangement whereby it is agreed, between trustees and employers, employees or self-employed persons, that benefits be provided upon retirement of plan members or upon their resignation, death, disablement or other specified event(s).

However, the entities identified as having to apply AASB 1056 are not necessarily expected to differ from those identified as having to apply AAS 25.

Presentation of financial statements

AASB 1056 requires that superannuation entities present:

(a) a statement of financial position;

(b) an income statement;

(c) a statement of changes in equity/reserves;

(d) a statement of cash flows; and

(e) a statement of changes in member benefits.

AAS 25 required a defined contribution plan, and permitted a defined benefit plan, to present a statement of financial position, operating statement, and statement of cash flows. Alternatively, defined benefit plans could present a statement of net assets and a statement of changes in net assets.

Income statement

Items AASB 1056 requires to be presented in the income statement include:

(a) income in aggregate or subclassified;

(b) expenses in aggregate or subclassified;

(c) net benefits allocated to defined contribution member accounts;

(d) net change in defined benefit member liabilities;

(e) net result; and

(f) income tax expense or benefit attributable to net result.

AASB 1056 treats contributions from employers and members and benefits to members as affecting member liabilities, not as income and expenses.

AAS 25 required changes in the net market value of assets and financial liabilities to be included as a component of income. Contributions from employers and members and benefits to members were accounted for as income and expenses.

Statement of changes in equity/reserves

AASB 1056 envisages that a difference may exist between total assets and liabilities (including member liabilities and any obligations to employer-sponsors) in the nature of equity/reserves that would be presented in the statement of financial position, with changes from period to period presented in a statement of changes in equity/reserves.

AAS 25 did not explicitly address this topic.

Statement of changes in member benefits

AASB 1056 requires a statement of changes in member benefits to be presented and that it includes:

(a) contributions, separately for employers and members;

(b) taxes on contributions;

(c) benefits to members;

(d) net benefits allocated to defined contribution members; and

(e) net changes to defined benefit member accrued benefits.

AAS 25 did not require presentation of a statement of changes in member benefits.

Assets and liabilities measured at fair value

AASB 1056 requires assets and liabilities to be measured at 'fair value through profit or loss' with specific exceptions. The exceptions include member liabilities and tax balances.

AAS 25 required assets and financial liabilities to be measured at 'net market values' with similar exceptions to those applying under AASB 1056.

Member liabilities

AASB 1056 requires both defined contribution and defined benefit member liabilities to be recognised and measured as the amount of accrued benefits. The measurement principle in AASB 1056 for a defined benefit member liability is the amount of a portfolio of investments that would be needed as at the reporting date to yield future net cash inflows that would be sufficient to meet accrued benefits as at that date when they are expected to fall due.

AASB 1056 requires defined benefit member liabilities to be measured at each reporting date. However, AASB 1056 does not identify any particular methodologies that might be employed in measuring defined benefit member liabilities, for example, when an actuary is not engaged to conduct a full actuarial valuation, but notes that superannuation entities may use estimates, averages and computational shortcuts provided that any shortcut techniques used yield a reliable approximation of the defined benefit member liabilities.

AAS 25 required defined contribution member liabilities to be determined as the difference between assets and 'other' liabilities. It required defined benefit member liabilities to be determined as the present value of expected future payments (remeasured at least once each three years).

Employer-sponsor receivables

AASB 1056 requires an asset to be recognised when there is a receivable from an employer-sponsor in respect of a difference between a defined benefit member liability and the fair value of assets available to meet that liability that meets the definition and recognition criteria for an asset. The asset is required to be measured at its 'intrinsic value' (the amount of the difference, unless capped). The requirement is expected to give rise to the recognition of an asset in only a limited number of cases.

AAS 25 did not address employer-sponsor receivables.

Disclosure

AASB 1056 has of a number of disclosure 'principles', including requiring the following disclosures:

(a) information that provides users with a basis for understanding the nature of the entity, the benefits provided to members and the expenses it incurs;

(b) information about changes in key components of defined benefit member liabilities that provides users with a basis for understanding the overall change;

(c) deeming defined contribution member liabilities to be within the scope of AASB 7 *Financial Instruments: Disclosure* in respect of credit risk, market risk and liquidity risk (but not the fair value disclosures);

(d) in relation to accrued defined benefit member liabilities, the basis for the assumptions used in measurement, including the manner in which they are determined, the impact of changes to demographic assumptions compared with changes in financial assumptions, and the sensitivity of the liabilities to reasonably possible changes in key assumptions;

(e)   when net assets attributable to defined benefit members differs from defined benefit member liabilities, information explaining the policies for managing the difference; and

(f)   disaggregated financial information where that would help to explain the risks to which different categories of members are exposed.

AAS 25 required some relatively specific disclosures regarding classes of assets, liabilities, investment revenue and expenses. Many of these related to member liabilities and would be captured in the statement of changes in member benefits required by AASB 1056.

Insurance arrangements

Whether a superannuation entity has an obligation under insurance arrangements, or is only acting as an agent will depend on the nature of the arrangements. AASB 1056 requires that, when a superannuation entity is acting in the capacity of an insurer and has an obligation under insurance arrangements provided to members (whether defined contribution or defined benefit), any insurance contract liabilities and assets are measured in a manner consistent with the way in which defined benefit member liabilities are measured. In respect of defined contribution members, any insurance liabilities, assets, insurance premiums, claim expenses, reinsurance expenses and reinsurance recoveries would be shown separately in the statement of financial position, income statement, or notes to the financial statements. However, liabilities and assets arising from insurance arrangements a superannuation entity provides to defined benefit members need not be presented separately from the entity's liabilities for such members' benefits. Furthermore, unless there are explicit direct premiums, claims, reinsurance premiums or claim recoveries relating to insurance risks, revenues and/or expenses relating to insurance arrangements a superannuation entity provides to defined benefit members need not be presented separately.

AAS 25 did not address insurance arrangements provided to members other than in the context of providing an exemption from some of the requirements of AAS 25 for a plan that purchases insurance policies that match and guarantee benefits to members.

Consolidated financial statements

Consolidated financial statements are not explicitly addressed in AASB 1056. The requirements of AASB 10 *Consolidated Financial Statements*, as amended by AASB 2013-5 *Amendments to Australian Accounting Standards – Investment Entities*, would apply.

Consolidated financial statements were also not explicitly addressed in AAS 25 and the requirements in AASB 127 *Consolidated and Separate Financial Statements* and AASB 10 applied.[3]

AASB 10 is relevant for determining when a consolidation takes place. The AASB 2013-5 amendments provide an exception from consolidation for investment entities, which could include superannuation entities. The exception applies to all subsidiaries of investment entities except subsidiaries that provide services relating to the investment entity's investment activities.

ILLUSTRATIVE EXAMPLES

These illustrative examples accompany, but are not part of, AASB 1056.

---

3   Depending on the reporting period concerned and the choices made by the entity, either AASB 127 *Consolidated and Separate Financial Statements* (which preceded AASB 127 *Separate Financial Statements*) or AASB 10 *Consolidated Financial Statements* would have applied.

CONTENTS

Illustrative Examples I and II provide examples of acceptable styles and formats for a superannuation entity that are consistent with the requirements of AASB 1056 *Superannuation Entities*. They are not comprehensive.

The styles and formats illustrated are not mandatory. Other styles and formats may be equally appropriate if they meet the requirements of AASB 1056 and other applicable Australian Accounting Standards.

For illustrative convenience, particular notes have been located next to the financial statements to which they most closely relate. Some of the information illustrated as appearing on the face of the financial statements could be disclosed in the notes, and some of the information illustrated as appearing in the notes could be shown on the face of the financial statements.

For simplicity of presentation, comparative information is not shown.

For the purposes of the examples, the following insurance arrangements are assumed.

-   The superannuation entity with only defined contribution members has insurance arrangements that involve taking on insurance risk and the entity fully reinsures those risks, giving rise to both insurance liabilities and assets of the entity.

-   The hybrid superannuation entity is acting as an agent in respect of the insurance arrangements it has in place for defined contribution members. These insurance arrangements do not give rise to insurance liabilities and assets of the entity. Some components of the benefits for defined benefit members are in the nature of insurance, but separate amounts are not presented in respect of those components.

Illustrative example I

As at 30 June 20XX, Defined Contribution Superannuation Plan (the Plan) has 425,301 members and is a public offer fund open to new members. The Plan is a defined contribution style plan and, as such, members' accounts are credited or debited each year with contributions and a proportionate share of net investment income and expenses (including income tax expense) of the Plan.

**Statement of Financial Position for Defined Contribution
Superannuation Plan as at 30 June 20XX**

	Note	$000
Assets		
Cash		240,510
Receivables		324,909
Units in unlisted cash management trusts		4,921,700
Listed Australian shares held directly		7,490,663
Units in international share trusts		3,944,033
Units in unlisted property trusts		1,269,828
Australian fixed interest securities held directly		4,212,948
Overseas fixed interest securities held directly		879,034

(Continued)

(*Continued*)

	Note	$000
Property held directly		436,978
Reinsurance assets		6,458
Deferred tax assets		52,358
Total assets		**23,779,419**
Liabilities		
Payables		(236,641)
Income tax payable		(148,561)
Deferred tax liabilities		(364,903)
Insurance liabilities	A	(6,519)
Total liabilities excluding member benefits		**(756,624)**
Net assets available for member benefits		**23,022,795**
Member benefits		**(22,965,083)**
Total net assets		**57,712**
Equity		
Investment reserve	B	(1,655)
Operational risk reserve	C	(56,057)
Total equity		**(57,712)**

Note A – Insurance contract liabilities

Members can elect to take out term life cover with the Plan up to a maximum of $500,000 per member. The Plan uses the services of an actuary to determine its insurance contract liabilities who bases the calculations on relevant industry-focused mortality tables and the entity's own claims experience. The entity has reinsured all of its direct insurance risks with EFG Reinsurance (Australia).

Note B – Investment reserve

The investment reserve comprises the difference between the cumulative amount of investment income (net of investment expenses) allocated to members' accounts compared to the cumulative investment income (net of investment expenses) earned.

Note C – Operational risk reserve

An operational risk reserve is required under Australian Prudential Regulation Authority Standards to maintain adequate financial resources to address potential losses arising from operational risks. The Trustee has assessed a reserve of approximately 0.25% of funds under management as being appropriate for the Plan.

**Income Statement for Defined Contribution
Superannuation Plan for the year ended 30 June 20XX**

	Note	$000
Superannuation activities		
Interest revenue – direct cash deposits		8,152
Distributions from cash management trusts		211,534

	Note	$000
Interest from Australian securities held directly		282,045
Interest from overseas securities held directly		66,283
Dividend revenue – listed Australian shares held directly		286,794
Distributions from wholesale international share trusts		99,325
Net rentals from directly held property		28,068
Distributions from unlisted property trusts		82,407
Net remeasurement changes in assets measured at fair value		1,903,074
Total superannuation activities revenue		**2,967,682**
Investment expenses		(55,972)
Administration expenses		(41,662)
Other operating expenses	E	(1,642)
Total expenses		**(99,276)**
Net income from superannuation activities		**2,868,406**
Net loss from insurance activities	F	**(36)**
Profit from operating activities		**2,868,370**
Less: Net benefits allocated to members' accounts		(2,635,776)
Profit before income tax		**232,594**
Income tax expense		(235,553)
Loss after income tax		**(2,959)**

Note D – Total revenue	$000
Superannuation activities revenue	2,967,682
Insurance contract revenue	77,810
	3,045,492

Note E – Other operating expenses	$000
Trustee fees	(298)
Commissions paid directly	(323)
Audit fees	(309)
Advertising and sponsorship	(712)
Other operating expenses	**(1,642)**

Note F – Insurance activities	$000
Insurance contract revenue	77,810
Less: Outwards reinsurance premiums	(77,806)
Net premium revenue	4
Reinsurance recoveries revenues	23,219
Insurance contract claims expenses	(22,833)

(Continued)

(Continued)

Note F – Insurance activities	$000
Movement in insurance liabilities	(1,059)
Movement in reinsurance assets	633
Net loss from insurance activities	**(36)**

Statement of Changes in Member Benefits for Defined Contribution Superannuation Plan for the year ended 30 June 20XX

	$000
Opening balance of member benefits	**18,014,382**
Contributions:	
Employer	2,622,940
Member	241,812
Transfers from other superannuation plans	704,162
Government co-contributions	27,746
Income tax on contributions (refer Note G)	(416,373)
Net after tax contributions	3,180,287
Benefits to members	(811,432)
Insurance premiums charged to members' accounts	(77,810)
Death and disability benefits credited to members' accounts	23,880
Benefits allocated to members' accounts, comprising:	
Net investment income	2,677,097
Administration fees	(41,321)
	2,635,776
Closing balance of member benefits	**22,965,083**

Note G – Income tax on contributions	$000
Contributions tax	(415,616)
Contributions surcharge	(757)
	(416,373)

Statement of Changes in Reserves for Defined Contribution Superannuation Plan for the year ended 30 June 20XX

	Unallocated surplus/ (deficiency)	Investment reserve	Operational risk	Total equity
	$000	$000	$000	$000
Opening balance	–	3,330	57,341	60,671
Profit/(Loss) for period	(2,959)	–	–	(2,959)
Net transfers to/from reserves	2,959	(1,675)	(1,284)	–
Closing balance	–	1,655	56,057	57,712

Statement of Cash Flows for Defined Contribution Superannuation Plan
for the year ended 30 June 20XX

Cash flows from operating activities	$000
Interest from cash deposits and cash management trusts	189,667
Interest on Australian fixed interest securities held directly	310,760
Interest on overseas fixed interest securities held directly	27,819
Dividends from listed Australian shares held directly	267,104
Net rentals from property held directly	25,982
Unlisted property trust distributions	83,691
Insurance premiums (inwards)	77,810
Reinsurance recoveries	22,016
Other income	3,785
Administration expenses	(42,846)
Investment expenses	(55,094)
Reinsurance premiums (outward)	(77,270)
Other expenses	(693)
Income tax paid	(134,470)
Net cash inflows from operating activities	**698,261**
Cash flows from investing activities	
Proceeds from sales of units in unlisted cash management trusts	680,654
Proceeds from sales of shares in Australian listed corporations	803,730
Proceeds from sales of units in wholesale international share trusts	845,218
Proceeds from sales of overseas fixed interest securities	444,826
Proceeds from sales of units in unlisted property trusts	259,428
Purchases of units in unlisted cash management trusts	(1,285,930)
Purchases of Australian fixed interest securities	(498,898)
Purchases of shares in Australian listed corporations	(944,767)
Purchases of units in wholesale international share trusts	(2,684,406)
Purchases of units in unlisted property trusts	(517,326)
Purchases of other assets	(201)
Net cash outflows from investing activities	**(2,897,672)**
Cash flows from financing activities	
Employer contributions	2,554,872
Member contributions	235,548
Transfers from other superannuation plans received	704,162
Government co-contributions received	27,746
Benefits paid to members	(807,070)
Income tax paid on contributions received	(407,417)
Contributions surcharge tax paid	(674)
Net cash inflows from financing activities	**2,307,167**
Net increase in cash	**107,756**
Cash at the beginning of the financial period	**132,754**
Cash at the end of the financial period	**240,510**

Illustrative example II

As at 30 June 20XX, Hybrid Superannuation Plan (the Plan) has 51,109 defined contribution members and 23,918 defined benefit members. The defined contribution part of the Plan is open to new members. All four of the defined benefit plans in the Plan are closed to new members. The defined contribution members have accounts that are credited or debited each year with contributions and a proportionate share of net investment income and expenses (including income tax expense) of the Plan. The defined benefit members have promised benefits that are determined on the basis of various formulae based on members' salaries in the final years before they retire.

Statement of Financial Position for Hybrid Superannuation Plan as at 30 June 20XX

	Note	$000
Assets		
Cash		467,803
Receivables		210,980
Shares in Australian listed corporations held directly		2,788,084
Units in international shares trusts		621,631
Fixed interest securities held directly		3,214,391
Investment-linked insurance contracts		289,148
Unlisted property trusts		1,918,116
Derivatives		32,328
Deferred tax assets		38,333
Other assets		5,345
Total assets		**9,586,159**
Liabilities		
Benefits payable		(148,058)
Other payables		(42,347)
Income tax payable		(202,812)
Deferred tax liabilities		(797)
Total liabilities excluding member benefits		**(394,014)**
Net assets available for member benefits		**9,192,145**
Defined contribution member liabilities	A	(2,258,229)
Defined benefit member liabilities	B	(6,954,622)
Total net liabilities		**(20,706)**
Equity		
Operational Risk Reserve	C	(25,895)
Investment reserve	D	(2,980)
Defined benefits that are (over) or under funded	E	49,581
Total equity		**20,706**

Note A – Defined contribution member liabilities

Defined contribution members bear the investment risk relating to the underlying assets and unit prices used to measure defined contribution member liabilities. Unit prices are updated each day for movements in investment markets.

Hybrid Superannuation Plan manages market risks, including foreign exchange rate risk, interest rate risk, commodity price risk and equity price risk by obtaining exposure to major asset classes through investment managers with highly-diversified portfolios.

The credit risk on investments in bonds and similar interest-bearing instruments is managed by selecting relevant fund managers that have well-established frameworks and supporting policies for managing credit risk across their portfolios. Those policies include managing concentration of credit risks and managing the balance between secured and unsecured debt.

The Plan closely monitors the inflows of contributions and the withdrawals from its various superannuation plans with a view to maintaining an adequate balance of liquid assets at all times to facilitate paying benefits to any exiting members within the statutory timelines.

Note B – Defined benefit member liabilities

In aggregate for the Plan's four defined benefit superannuation plans, there were no unexpected events that changed defined benefit member liabilities materially. In line with general market expectations, discount rates are slightly higher at the current reporting date compared with the previous reporting date across all four plans, which had the effect of reducing defined benefit member liabilities. The Plan has no information that would lead it to adjust the assumptions around salary adjustment rates, pension index rates, resignations and mortality, which are all unchanged from the previous reporting period.

The Plan engages qualified actuaries on an annual basis to measure the defined benefit member liabilities in each of its four defined benefit plans. The Plan uses sensitivity analysis to monitor the potential impact of changes to key variables about which assumptions need to be made. The Plan has identified two assumptions (discount rate and rate of salary adjustment) for which changes are reasonably possible that would have a material impact on the amount of the liabilities.

The assumed discount rate for the four plans has been determined by reference to the investment returns expected on the investment portfolio that reflects the opportunities reasonably available to the Plan in investment markets, which also reflects the Plan's actual investments and investment strategy in respect of defined benefit member liabilities. The assumed discount rate is the same for each of the four defined benefit plans.

Defined member benefits in each of the Plan's four plans are based on an average of each member's salary at specified anniversary dates in each of the last three years of their expected membership of their plan. The assumed annual salary adjustments for each of the entity's four plans has been determined by reference to the Wage Price Index produced by the Australian Bureau of Statistics and in consultation with the employer-sponsors. The rate is the same for each of the ABC, OPQ and RST defined benefit plans. XYZ members are in an industry that is expected to experience generally higher than average salary adjustments.

The other variables about which assumptions have been made in measuring defined benefit member liabilities and for which changes are not considered reasonably possible, or for which reasonably possible changes would not be expected to have a material effect, include: pension index rates, mortality rates and resignations.

The following are sensitivity calculations on a univariate basis for the discount rate and rate of salary adjustment assumptions for the XYZ defined benefit plan and for the ABC, OPQ and RST defined benefit plans in aggregate.

Assumption for XYZ plan	Assumed at reporting date	Reasonably possible change	Amount of (increase) decrease in member benefit liability – $000
Discount rate	5.0%	+0.5% –0.5%	2,280 (2,549)
Salary adjustment rate	4.0%	+1.0% –1.0%	(3,001) 3,350

Assumption for ABC, OPQ and RST plans	Assumed at reporting date	Reasonably possible change	Amount of (increase) decrease in member benefit liability – $000
Discount rate	5.0%	+0.5% –0.5%	4,378 (4,809)
Salary adjustment rate	3.0%	+1.0% –1.0%	(5,762) 6,143

Note C – Operational risk reserve

The Trustee has assessed an operational risk reserve of approximately 0.25% of funds under management as appropriate for the Plan in respect of both defined contribution member interests and defined benefit member interests.

Operational risk reserve	$000
Defined contribution membership	5,657
Defined benefit membership	20,238
	25,895

Note D – Investment reserve

The Investment reserve comprises the difference between the cumulative amount of investment income (net of investment expenses) allocated to members' accounts compared with the cumulative investment income (net of investment expenses) earned.

Note E – Defined benefit plans that are (over) or under funded

	Note	$000
ABC	F	2,316
OPQ	G	(2,589)
RST	H	42,897
XYZ	H	6,957
		49,581

Note F – plan ABC

Based on the existing contribution rate of the employer-sponsor of plan ABC, member benefits are projected, based on current assumptions, to be fully funded within the next two financial years.

Note G – plan OPQ

The employer-sponsor of plan OPQ intends to reduce contributions to the minimum amount required to meet its superannuation guarantee obligations, which is projected, based on current assumptions, to eliminate the surplus to zero within three years.

Note H – plans RST and XYZ

The employer-sponsors of plans RST and XYZ intend to increase their contributions for a period of three financial years to a level that is projected, based on current assumptions, to result in member liabilities being fully funded by the end of those three years.

Note I – Net assets attributable to defined benefit members

In respect of all four defined benefit plans, the entity has worked with the relevant employer-sponsors to develop a contributions strategy to fund the deficits that exist in three of the plans (ABC, RST and XYZ) and use up the surplus in one of the plans (OPQ). At the current rate of contributions from those employer-sponsors, each plan that currently has a deficit of liabilities over assets is scheduled to be fully funded within three years, and the plan that currently has a surplus is scheduled to be in balance within two years.

Income Statement for Hybrid Superannuation Plan
for the year ended 30 June 20XX

	Note	$000
Superannuation activities		
Interest revenue		190,696
Dividend revenue – listed Australian shares held directly		91,338
Distributions from wholesale international share trusts		12,881
Unlisted property trust distributions		261,878
Other income		1,496
Net remeasurement changes in assets measured at fair value		170,804
Total revenue		**729,093**
Investment expenses		(27,404)
Administration expenses		(12,042)
Other operating expenses	J	(998)
Total expenses		**(40,444)**
Operating result		**688,649**
Net benefits allocated to defined contribution member accounts		(142,293)
Net change in defined benefit member benefits		(580,138)
Operating result before income tax expense		**(33,782)**
Income tax expense		(38,470)
Operating result after income tax		**(72,252)**

Note J – Other operating expenses	$000
Trustee fees	(198)
Actuarial fees	(272)
Audit fees	(216)
Commissions paid directly	(123)
Advertising and sponsorship	(189)
Other operating expenses	**(998)**

Statement of Changes in Member Benefits for Hybrid Superannuation
Plan for the year ended 30 June 20XX

	DC member benefits $000	DB member benefits $000	Totals $000
Opening balance	2,185,275	6,555,825	8,741,100
Employer contributions	127,355	349,814	477,169
Member contributions	17,717	93,153	110,870
Transfers from other super entities	29,987	–	29,987
Transfers to other super entities	(40,737)	–	(40,737)
Income tax on contributions	(20,148)	(66,445)	(86,593)
Net after tax contributions	114,174	376,522	490,696

(Continued)

(*Continued*)

	DC member benefits $000	DB member benefits $000	Totals $000
Benefits to members	(187,093)	(561,278)	(748,371)
Insurance premiums charged to members	(105)	(312)	(417)
Death/disability benefits credited	1,233	3,699	4,932
Reserve transfers to (from) members:			
Investment reserves	1,239	–	1,239
Operational risk reserves	1,213	28	1,241
Net benefits allocated, comprising:			
Net investment income	145,701		
Net administration fees	(3,408) 142,293	–	142,293
Net change in DB member benefits	–	580,138	580,138
Closing balance	**2,258,229**	**6,954,622**	**9,212,851**

Statement of Changes in Reserves for Hybrid Superannuation Plan for the year ended 30 June 20XX

	Investment Note E	Operational risk Note C	Unallocated surplus/ (deficiency)	Total equity
	$000	**$000**	**$000**	**$000**
Opening balance	4,219	27,136	22,671	54,026
Transfers to DC member accounts	(1,239)	(1,213)	–	(2,452)
Transfers to DB member accounts	–	(28)	–	(28)
Operating result	–	–	(72,252)	(72,252)
Closing balance	**2,980**	**25,895**	**(49,581)**	**(20,706)**

Statement of Cash Flows for Hybrid Superannuation Plan for the year ended 30 June 20XX

	$000
Cash flows from operating activities	
Interest on cash deposits and debt securities	128,368
Dividends from Australian listed corporations	210,250
Distributions from international share trusts	12,981
Insurance premiums	4,558
Other income	1,295
Administration expenses	(11,289)
Investment expenses	(26,560)
Other expenses	(714)
Income tax	(98,299)
Net cash inflows (outflows) from operating activities	**220,590**
Cash flows from investing activities	
Sales of shares in Australian listed corporations	601,110
Sales of fixed interest securities	128,908
Sales of derivatives	4,219
Sales of investment-linked insurance contracts	530,886
Purchases of shares in Australian listed corporations	(842,316)

Cash flows from operating activities	$000
Purchases of fixed interest securities	(179,108)
Net cash inflows (outflows) from investing activities	**243,699**
Cash flows from financing activities	
Employer contributions	487,185
Member contributions	110,870
Transfers from other superannuation entities	29,428
Transfers to other superannuation entities	(41,436)
Benefit payments to members	(769,353)
Tax paid on contributions	(89,224)
Net cash inflows from financing activities	**(272,530)**
Net increase in cash	**191,759**
Cash at the beginning of the financial period	**276,044**
Cash at the end of the financial period	**467,803**

BASIS FOR CONCLUSIONS ON
AASB 1056 *SUPERANNUATION ENTITIES*

This Basis for Conclusions accompanies, but is not part of, AASB 1056.

Introduction

BC1 This Basis for Conclusions summarises the Australian Accounting Standards Board's (AASB's) reasons for reaching the conclusions in AASB 1056 *Superannuation Entities*, which is the replacement Standard for AAS 25 *Financial Reporting by Superannuation Plans*. This includes the development of the proposals made in two Exposure Drafts (ED 179 *Superannuation Plans and Approved Deposit Funds* and ED 223 *Superannuation Entities*) and the AASB's re-deliberations of those proposals. Individual Board members gave greater weight to some factors than to others.

BC2 In the process of developing AASB 1056, the AASB also identified a number of topics that are beyond the scope of AASB 1056 or are linked to issues that would have an impact on a wide range of entities. These topics include issues around the measurement of liabilities using discounted cash flow techniques and the nature of the reporting entity in a superannuation context, which are likely to form the basis of future research by the AASB Research Centre. The outcomes of this research might impact on issues the AASB raises with the International Accounting Standards Board (IASB) or impact on the application of Australian Accounting Standards.

Background

Comprehensive review of general purpose financial reporting requirements for superannuation entities

BC3 When originally drafted, AAS 25 was intended to provide the main recognition, measurement and disclosure requirements applicable to superannuation plans. Accordingly, the Standard was intended to apply in the place of other Australian Accounting Standards on financial reporting issues that were considered most significant to superannuation plans. AAS 25 was also intended to address the financial reporting issues that superannuation plans were specifically dealing with at the time (the early 1990s).

BC4   However, in recent years, developments in the superannuation industry and the adoption of International Financial Reporting Standards (IFRS) mean there has been the need for a comprehensive review of the general purpose financial reporting requirements applicable to superannuation entities, particularly the requirements in AAS 25. For example, the increasing significance of superannuation entities that have both defined contribution members and defined benefit members (hybrid superannuation entities) highlights deficiencies in AAS 25, which had requirements that lead defined contribution and defined benefit superannuation plans to prepare their financial statements on different bases.

BC5   There were also deficiencies in AAS 25 when compared to the requirements in Australian Accounting Standards applied by other entities. These include AAS 25 permitting entities not to recognise member liabilities in respect of defined benefit members.

BC6   Only limited improvements were made to AAS 25 since its issue in 1993.[4]

The AASB's policy on IFRS

BC7   In 2004, when the AASB was implementing the decision to adopt IFRS, it considered the merits of IAS 26 *Accounting and Reporting by Retirement Benefit Plans*, which was originally issued in 1987 and has changed little since that time. The AASB concluded that IAS 26 should not be adopted in Australia because its application by Australian superannuation entities would be unlikely to result in financial statements that meet users' information needs and would potentially reduce the quality of financial reporting by superannuation entities.

BC8   In particular, the AASB considered that IAS 26 would not result in useful information on the capacity of a superannuation entity to meet its member liabilities. For example, IAS 26:

(a)   contemplates that a plan would invest in assets for which it is impossible to estimate fair value, and permits those assets to be measured at an amount other than fair value; and

(b)   permits the actuarial present value of 'promised retirement benefits' to be based on either current or projected salary levels.

BC9   In contrast to IAS 26, AAS 25 required all assets held by a superannuation plan to be measured at a current value (consistent with Australian prudential measurement requirements). The AASB also considered other relevant IFRS being adopted in Australia and noted that the requirements of IAS 26 are highly dissimilar from the requirements of most other IFRS. For example, in contrast to IAS 26, IAS 19 *Employee Benefits* (AASB 119 *Employee Benefits*) requires plan assets attributable to defined benefit obligations to be measured at fair value in determining an employer-sponsor's net defined benefit obligations.

BC10   The AASB considers that the reasons identified for not adopting IAS 26 (and retaining AAS 25) remain valid in respect of AASB 1056.

BC11   The AASB also considered the implications of withdrawing AAS 25 and requiring superannuation entities to apply, where appropriate, Australian Accounting Standards. The AASB concluded that, while the financial reporting requirements for superannuation entities can, in many respects, be enhanced by being more closely aligned with corresponding requirements of other Standards, there remains a need for

---

4   In late 2005, as a result of a process involving the issue of Invitation to Comment ITC 9 *Superannuation Plans – Financial Liabilities*, the AASB made two amendments to AAS 25 through AASB 2005-13 *Amendments to Australian Accounting Standards*. One amendment was to require a hedging instrument or derivative to be recognised at net market value, whether it has a debit or credit balance, with any changes recognised in profit or loss for the period. A second amendment confirmed that a superannuation plan holding a controlling interest in another entity would apply AASB 3 *Business Combinations* and AASB 127 *Consolidated and Separate Financial Statements*. AAS 25 was also amended in 2013 to remove references to the materiality Standard through AASB 2013-9 *Amendments to Australian Accounting Standards – Conceptual Framework, Materiality and Financial Instruments*.

a specific Standard to help ensure the general purpose financial statements (GPFSs) of superannuation entities cater for the needs of users.

Users of the general purpose financial statements of superannuation entities

BC12 The AASB concluded that the following are most prominent among the users of GPFSs of superannuation entities:

(a) current and potential members and beneficiaries;

(b) parties that act on behalf of members and beneficiaries, such as financial analysts, advisors and unions; and

(c) employer-sponsors.

BC13 This is because the primary responsibility of superannuation entities is to provide retirement benefits to their members, and both employees and employers contribute to those entities.

BC14 Financial analysts and advisors are generally servicing a wide variety of existing and potential superannuation entity members and may use superannuation entity financial statements in the course of their work.

BC15 The *Superannuation Guarantee (Administration) Act 2002* provides most superannuation members the right to choose the superannuation entity managing their entitlements, thereby reducing the incentives for employers to provide corporate superannuation arrangements. An employer without a plan of its own is required to identify an appropriate default plan for employees. Consequently, employers seeking a superannuation entity to meet their employees' superannuation needs might use the financial statements of an entity to gain assurances regarding its financial position and performance.

BC16 Employers that provide defined benefit entitlements, particularly through master trusts and other similar arrangements, are interested in a superannuation entity's financial statements in order to evaluate whether the arrangement is cost-beneficial and the capacity of the assets to fund entitlements as and when they fall due.

BC17 The AASB concluded that, for some items, the reporting requirements that would otherwise apply under Australian Accounting Standards would not necessarily give rise to relevant financial information for users of superannuation entity financial statements. This is particularly the case in relation to measuring assets, recognising member liabilities, measuring defined benefit member liabilities and disclosing information about the amount of, and the entity's capacity to meet, member liabilities. As a consequence, the AASB concluded there is a need to:

(a) require superannuation entities to depart from Australian Accounting Standards on some topics;

(b) limit the accounting treatments available to superannuation entities in other Australian Accounting Standards; and

(c) require superannuation entities to provide information about items and events specific to them.

A replacement Standard for AAS 25

BC18 In May 2009, the AASB published ED 179 containing proposals for a replacement Standard for AAS 25. The AASB received 20 comment letters on ED 179 from a range of constituents, including superannuation plans, superannuation industry representative bodies, accounting firms, professional accounting and actuarial bodies and service providers to the superannuation industry. The AASB also held roundtable discussions on ED 179 with a range of constituents with an interest in the superannuation industry to enable them to discuss the proposals directly with AASB members.

BC19 Based on the responses to ED 179 and the AASB's redeliberations, in December 2011, the AASB published ED 223 containing revised proposals for a replacement Standard for AAS 25. The AASB received 17 comment letters on ED 223 from a range of constituents and also held roundtable discussions on ED 223. The feedback from both ED 179 and ED 223 and other forms of outreach that the AASB has performed between 2012 and 2014 have shaped AASB 1056.

BC20 The majority of respondents to both ED 179 and ED 223 expressed broad support for developing a replacement Standard that:

(a) provides greater transparency and consistency in reporting by superannuation entities; and

(b) substantially aligns the reporting practices of superannuation entities with other entities applying Australian Accounting Standards, thereby facilitating greater comparability.

BC21 Each of the respondents expressed concerns with one or more of the proposals in ED 179, particularly on cost-benefit grounds, which the AASB considered in developing ED 223. Further revisions have been made in developing AASB 1056 in response to issues raised by constituents on the revised proposals in ED 223. The revisions arising from the consultative process include matters relating to:

(a) presenting financial statements, including a statement of changes in member benefits;

(b) recognising defined benefit member liabilities;

(c) measuring both defined contribution member and defined benefit member liabilities;

(d) measuring assets;

(e) accounting for liabilities and assets that might arise from insurance arrangements provided to members;

(f) disclosing information about the nature, extent and management of credit, liquidity and market risks; and

(g) disclosing disaggregated information.

BC22 In the process of finalising AASB 1056, the AASB approved a Draft AASB 1056 for fatal flaw review that was published in December 2013 for a 60-day comment period. The comments received during that process helped the AASB to refine its requirements before making AASB 1056.

Application of the replacement Standard

The reporting entity concept and superannuation entities

BC23 AAS 25 applies to the financial statements of each private or public sector superannuation plan that is a reporting entity or is not a reporting entity and prepares financial statements which purport to be GPFSs.

BC24 The AASB considered the advantages and disadvantages of the replacement Standard for AAS 25 applying to different types of superannuation entities, including superannuation plans, approved deposit funds, eligible rollover funds, pooled superannuation trusts, Small Australian Prudential Regulation Authority (APRA) Funds (SAFs) and self-managed superannuation funds (SMSFs).

BC25 The AASB proposed in ED 179 and ED 223 that the replacement Standard for AAS 25 should retain the reporting entity concept, particularly in view of the AASB's current research on the concept. Accordingly, the replacement Standard would apply to each reporting entity that is a defined contribution plan, defined benefit plan, 'hybrid' plan (comprising both defined contribution and defined benefit members), private sector plan, public sector plan, eligible rollover fund or approved deposit fund.

BC26 Whilst a number of respondents to ED 179 and ED 223 argued that some SMSFs would often be reporting entities, the AASB concluded that an entity such as a SMSF would not normally be a reporting entity because:

(a) each member is required to be a trustee (or a director of a corporate trustee) and to have access to the entity's financial information; and

(b) the primary external user is the Australian Taxation Office, which requires specific information for compliance and regulatory purposes.

BC27 During its deliberations, the AASB gave particular consideration to whether the replacement Standard for AAS 25 should apply to pooled superannuation trusts. The AASB noted pooled superannuation trusts and superannuation plans, particularly defined contribution superannuation plans, share a number of characteristics. For example, they are both required to comply with many of the same prudential requirements, are taxed at the same concessional tax rate and accept monies from other superannuation entities.

BC28 However, the AASB concluded pooled superannuation trusts are more in the nature of investment trusts, such as managed investment schemes, because they have unitholders rather than members, and there are no member-based restrictions over when they can distribute funds to a unitholder. Accordingly, to facilitate comparable financial reporting among investment-type trusts, the AASB concluded pooled superannuation trusts should apply Australian Accounting Standards in the same manner as managed investment schemes.

BC29 Respondents to ED 179 and ED 223 expressed general agreement with the proposed scope and the AASB concluded that the replacement Standard for AAS 25 should reflect those application proposals.

Tiers of Australian Accounting Standards

BC30 Subsequent to issuing ED 179, the AASB promulgated AASB 1053 *Application of Tiers of Australian Accounting Standards*, which establishes a differential reporting framework consisting of two tiers of reporting requirements for preparing GPFSs:

(a) Tier 1: Australian Accounting Standards; and

(b) Tier 2: Australian Accounting Standards – Reduced Disclosure Requirements (RDR).

BC31 In the process of developing AASB 1053, the AASB issued ED 192 *Differential Reporting Framework* (February 2010), which noted that:

"AAS 25 *Financial Reporting by Superannuation Plans* has been excluded from the RDR on the grounds that entities applying AAS 25 would be superannuation plans registered with the Australian Prudential Regulation Authority, which are regarded as publicly accountable in this Exposure Draft. Superannuation entities that apply AAS 25 and prepare general purpose financial statements are required, under the *Superannuation Industry (Supervision) Act 1993*, to hold assets in a fiduciary capacity for their members. In addition, most superannuation entities, particularly public offer superannuation plans and approved deposit funds, have a broad range of members who have no involvement in the day-to-day operations of the entity."

BC32 Some respondents to ED 192 questioned whether all APRA-regulated entities, particularly SAFs, should be considered to have 'public accountability'. They noted that, while SAFs lodge financial statements with APRA, they are not made publicly available, APRA does not mandate that SAFs prepare GPFSs and most, if not all, SAFs are similar in nature and size to SMSFs.

BC33 During its redeliberations on ED 179, the AASB noted SAFs are defined by APRA as superannuation plans with less than five members and have an Extended Public Offer Entity licence. As such, members of a SAF appoint a trustee with a Public Offer Entity licence to manage the plan on their behalf. While SAFs must lodge APRA returns that include information reported in their financial statements, this information is not publicly available for individual SAFs. In addition, the AASB noted SAFs would not be considered publicly accountable or reporting entities because they are small, have few members who have a close relationship with the trustee and SAFs normally prepare special purpose financial statements.

BC34 ED 223 included a question asking constituents whether there are any superannuation entities that would meet the criteria in AASB 1053 for applying Tier 2 disclosure requirements and the AASB also conducted targeted outreach on the issue, including in respect of so-called 'paragraph 66 plans'. Paragraph 66 of AAS 25 permits superannuation plans whose only assets (other than temporary deposits at call with a bank) are endowment, whole of life or other long-term insurance policies which match and fully guarantee the benefits to be paid to individual members to apply only a sub-set of its recognition, measurement and disclosure requirements, provided they report items such as: whether those policies have been fully maintained as directed by the insurer(s), the identity of the insurer(s), and amounts contributed by employers and members during the reporting period, and the expenses of the plan incurred by the trustees during the reporting period.

BC35 The AASB concluded superannuation entities are currently divided between Tier 1 entities (including industry plans, public sector plans, retail plans, eligible rollover funds, corporate plans and approved deposit funds) and non-reporting entities (including SAFs and SMSFs). Accordingly, in the context of AASB 1056, there are entities that prepare GPFSs by applying all the relevant Australian Accounting Standards and those that need not prepare GPFSs. Consistent with AASB 1053, there is no applicable second Tier of general purpose financial reporting requirements for superannuation entities.

Definitions

Superannuation entity

BC36 AAS 25 defines a superannuation plan as "an arrangement whereby it is agreed, between trustees, employers or self-employed persons, that benefits be provided upon retirement of plan members or upon their resignation, death, disablement or other specific event(s)." It also includes commentary that notes a superannuation plan may be constituted as either a separate entity or a number of separate entities established to administer aspects of the plan, such as when one entity manages contributions and another administers benefit payments. AAS 25 applies regardless of whether a separate pool of assets from which benefits are paid is created.

BC37 In recognition of the significant legislative and other changes that have occurred in a superannuation context, ED 179 and ED 223 proposed:

(a)   a definition of 'superannuation entity'; and

(b)   definitions for the terms 'superannuation plan' and 'approved deposit fund' (to form the basis for the 'superannuation entity' definition) that are consistent with the equivalent definitions in the *Superannuation Industry (Supervision) Act 1993* and accompanying Regulations.

BC38 The AASB noted that, given the extent of regulation about the forms superannuation arrangements can take, particularly in the private sector, the proposed definitions received general support from those responding to ED 179 and ED 223. However, the AASB also noted that some of the superannuation arrangements in the public sector are not as straight-forward.

BC39 The AASB concluded that the proposed definitions are appropriate for AASB 1056. However, the AASB also noted that entities, particularly in the public sector, would need to consider the nature of their activities and the boundaries of the entity to determine if they are superannuation entities or only custodial arrangements. For example, there may be cases in the public sector where an entity administers information about members and their benefits, but is not liable for paying benefits to members.

Defined contribution member and defined benefit member

BC40 Due to the increasing significance of superannuation entities that have both defined contribution members and defined benefit members, AASB 1056 does not have definitions of 'defined benefit plan' and 'defined contribution plan' (as in AAS 25). The AASB instead developed definitions of 'defined benefit member' and 'defined contribution member'. These are based on the AASB 'plan' definitions and the relevant definitions in AASB 119. These definitions were generally supported in the comments received on ED 179 and ED 223.

BC41 In the context of the Draft AASB 1056 for fatal flaw review, some constituents commented that the AASB should consider using the definition of 'defined benefit member' in the prudential regulation. However, the AASB concluded that the regulatory definition might change in ways that would not necessarily suit the aims of AASB 1056. Nevertheless, in terms of the current definitions, the AASB does not expect there to be any difference between those members identified as being either defined benefit members or defined contribution members based on definitions in AASB 1056 and those members identified as being either defined benefit members or defined contribution members based on the defined benefit member definition under prudential regulation.

Applying recognition and measurement requirements in Australian Accounting Standards

BC42 Under AAS 25, a superannuation plan applied other relevant Australian Accounting Standards with the key exceptions of some aspects of: financial statement presentation (defined benefit plans can present a statement of net assets and a statement of changes in net assets), asset measurement (net market value is required), and defined benefit member liability measurement (actuarial valuations performed on at least a triennial basis).

BC43 The AASB decided there are no compelling reasons for retaining this approach and concluded that a superannuation entity should apply the presentation, recognition and measurement requirements in other relevant Australian Accounting Standards, except in relation to:

(a) measuring most assets at fair value through profit or loss;[5]

(b) presenting a statement of changes in member benefits;

(c) measuring defined benefit member liabilities; and

(d) measuring liabilities and assets arising from insurance arrangements it might provide to its members.

Measurement of assets at fair value

BC44 AAS 25 required a superannuation plan to measure its assets at market value less costs that would be expected to be incurred in realising the proceeds from their disposal. The AASB considered a number of alternative approaches, including measuring assets:

(a) in a manner consistent with the approach under AAS 25;

(b) in accordance with the various requirements of relevant Australian Accounting Standards; and

(c) in a manner consistent with AASB 1023 *General Insurance Contracts* and AASB 1038 *Life Insurance Contracts*, under which assets are required to be measured at fair value through profit or loss where that is required or permitted in other Australian Accounting Standards.

---

5   This exception includes fair valuing acquired intangible assets each period, but would apply only when a superannuation entity is required to prepare consolidated financial statements in accordance with AASB 10, as amended by AASB 2013-5 *Amendments to Australian Accounting Standards – Investment Entities.*

BC45 With respect to approaches (b) and (c), the AASB noted some Australian Accounting Standards currently provide a choice between alternative measurement methods, particularly cost and fair value through profit or loss, and some require cost or fair value through other comprehensive income, for particular types of assets. However, the AASB regards measurement of superannuation entity assets at cost or at fair value through other comprehensive income to be inconsistent with the needs of users in the investment performance of superannuation entities, and inconsistent with the prudential measurement requirements.

BC46 The AASB concluded the AAS 25 approach is an appropriate starting point, and that there are a number of compelling arguments in favour of requiring a superannuation entity to use fair value through profit or loss rather than net market value.

BC47 Both net market value measurements and fair value measurements provide useful information for users of the financial statements of a superannuation entity about:

(a) the capacity of a superannuation entity with defined contribution members to pay benefits as the information reflects the interests of members; and

(b) the financial position (solvency) of a superannuation entity with defined benefit members as the information reflects the capacity of the entity to meet member liabilities.

However, the approach for measuring assets under AAS 25 is inconsistent with the approach for measuring equivalent assets under other Australian Accounting Standards. In addition, fair value measurement is more comprehensively dealt with in the accounting literature, in particular, AASB 13 *Fair Value Measurement*. Accordingly, the AASB considers requiring fair value measurement would enhance the comparability of the financial statements of superannuation entities with other entities.

BC48 Both ED 179 and ED 223 proposed that superannuation entities measure their assets at fair value through profit or loss, with the exception of tax assets, and any assets arising from insurance arrangements the entity provides to its members.

BC49 Most of the respondents that specifically commented on the ED 179 and ED 223 asset measurement proposals expressed general agreement with them. One respondent expressed concern that assets be measured at 'bid' prices and liabilities be measured at 'ask' prices. However, the AASB noted that entities reporting under AAS 25 should, in principle, measure their assets at bid prices and liabilities other than member liabilities at ask prices because AAS 25 is based on an exit value model. The AASB also noted that, while some superannuation entities may be currently measuring assets at their 'mid' prices, this is presumably because any differences between the assets' bid and mid prices are not material.

BC50 In the interests of providing useful information on investment performance and in light of respondents' comments, the AASB concluded the replacement Standard for AAS 25 should require fair value through profit or loss measurement for most assets.

BC51 In coming to this conclusion, the AASB noted:

(a) a superannuation entity would apply AASB 13, which takes a principles-based approach to determining fair value measurement; and

(b) any implementation issues a superannuation entity might encounter in applying AASB 13 are unlikely to be unique and would potentially arise in the context of other investment-type entities, such as managed investment schemes.

Accordingly, the AASB concluded it is not necessary to include additional fair value measurement guidance in the replacement Standard for AAS 25.

Transaction costs

BC52 Under AAS 25, a superannuation plan is required to measure its assets net of anticipated disposal costs. In developing ED 179, the AASB considered a number of different treatments for transaction costs, including:

(a) separate recognition as an expense when incurred; and

(b)   as a reduction of the carrying amounts of assets.

BC53 The AASB concluded ED 179 should propose transaction costs be treated as a reduction in the carrying amounts of assets because:

(a)   members and beneficiaries would regard information about assets net of transaction costs as useful as it might have a direct bearing on assessing a superannuation entity's capacity to pay benefits;

(b)   it would facilitate alignment between financial reporting requirements and member reporting practices; and

(c)   it is consistent with the treatment of assets under some Australian Accounting Standards, such as AASB 5 *Non-current Assets Held for Sale and Discontinued Operations* in respect of assets held for immediate sale.

BC54 Several respondents to ED 179 expressed disagreement with the proposal to adjust fair value amounts for transaction costs because:

(a)   the treatment is inconsistent with the approach required under most Australian Accounting Standards, including AASB 139 *Financial Instruments: Recognition and Measurement*;[6] and

(b)   transaction costs are generally an immaterial amount relative to a superannuation entity's net assets.

BC55 During its redeliberations on ED 179, the AASB also noted:

(a)   AASB 13 requires that, while transaction costs be considered when determining the most advantageous market, the price used to measure the fair value of an asset (or liability) should, in principle, not be adjusted for such costs. As noted in paragraph 25 of AASB 13:

"... Transaction costs are not a characteristic of an asset or a liability; rather, they are specific to a transaction and will differ depending on how an entity enters into a transaction for the asset or liability ... "; and

(b)   defined contribution members and beneficiaries would regard information about assets net of transaction costs as useful because it may help clarify whether all members and beneficiaries are being treated equitably, including different generations of members.[7] However, the AASB rejected the intergenerational equity argument, noting that it would be better facilitated by a superannuation entity determining crediting rates for defined contribution members on a basis that reflects anticipated transaction costs. The AASB also noted that these types of intergenerational equity issues are not as relevant in a defined benefit context because benefits are determined on the basis of a member's salary.

BC56 In light of respondents' comments, ED 223 proposed not permitting the carrying amounts of assets measured at fair value to be adjusted for transaction costs. The AASB also proposed that, to facilitate consistency across superannuation entities in relation to transaction costs, the application of AASB 5 should be prohibited.

BC57 There was general support from constituents commenting on the asset measurement proposals in ED 223 and the AASB concluded fair values should not be adjusted for transaction costs.

---

6   AASB 9 *Financial Instruments* had not yet been issued.

7   Intergenerational inequities can arise when exiting members do not 'pay' a share of the transaction costs because the superannuation entity has the capacity to pay departing member benefits out of cash on hand or else out of ongoing contributions and income. In such circumstances, members who remain in the entity may eventually incur transaction costs that would otherwise have been shared equally amongst all members if they had all exited the entity at the same time. In addition, members with relatively large account balances may be charged transaction costs as a consequence of their superannuation plan selling some of its assets whereas other members with relatively smaller balances may not be charged transaction costs if their entitlements are paid out of funds from other sources.

Measurement of liabilities other than tax liabilities, member liabilities and liabilities arising from insurance arrangements provided to members

BC58 AAS 25 required a superannuation plan to measure its financial liabilities at net market value.

BC59 During its deliberations on the proposals in ED 179 and ED 223, the AASB considered the different ways in which a liability can be measured under Australian Accounting Standards, in particular:

(a)   at fair value; and

(b)   at amortised cost.

BC60 The AASB decided amortised cost is not an appropriate basis in a superannuation context because it would not result in useful information to users. Accordingly, the AASB proposed that a superannuation entity should measure its liabilities at fair value, with the exception of member liabilities, tax liabilities, and liabilities arising from insurance arrangements the entity might provide to its members. In addition, consistent with its decision in relation to the treatment of transaction costs in respect of assets, the AASB proposed in ED 223 that a superannuation entity should treat transaction costs attributable to each liability measured at fair value as an increase in its carrying amount.

BC61 Consistent with constituent comments on measuring assets, the majority of respondents agreed with the ED 223 measurement proposals for liabilities. The AASB concluded it should require fair value measurement for liabilities other than member liabilities, tax liabilities and liabilities arising from insurance arrangements. Consistent with its conclusions on transaction costs in relation to assets, the AASB also concluded it should require that:

(a)   the carrying amount of liabilities measured at fair value not be adjusted for transaction costs; and

(b)   costs attributable to issuing a liability be treated in accordance with the relevant Australian Accounting Standards.

Presentation of financial statements

BC62 AAS 25 required a defined contribution plan, and permits a defined benefit plan, to present a statement of financial position, operating statement, and statement of cash flows. Alternatively, defined benefit plans can present a statement of net assets and a statement of changes in net assets.

BC63 In relation to ED 179 and ED 223, the AASB decided to propose that the existing AAS 25 approach should not be retained because financial statements may not be comparable between superannuation entities and the approach does not cater for (hybrid) entities that have both defined contribution members and defined benefit members.

BC64 The AASB considered the implications of superannuation entities applying AASB 101 *Presentation of Financial Statements* and decided to propose that they present:

(a)   a statement of financial position, a statement of cash flows and, where relevant, a statement of changes in equity, in accordance with applicable Australian Accounting Standards;

(b)   an income statement instead of a single statement of comprehensive income or a separate income statement and a statement of comprehensive income;

(c)   a statement of changes in member benefits; and

(d)   notes in accordance with other relevant Australian Accounting Standards except where the disclosure principles and requirements in other Australian Accounting Standards are not consistent with the measurement requirements or the disclosure principles for superannuation entities.

Statement of financial position

BC65 The AASB noted a superannuation entity would recognise a difference between total assets and total liabilities (including members' accrued benefits and any obligations to employer-sponsors) in a number of circumstances, including when:

(a)   it has an operational risk reserve; and

(b)   the amount of net assets attributable to defined benefit members is greater or less than such members' accrued benefits.

BC66 The AASB noted the net assets attributable to defined benefit members would not exceed such members' accrued benefits if:

(a)   the relevant trust deed terms or legislation required any surplus be applied for the benefit of members, in which case the entity would be presently obliged to such members;

(b)   an employer-sponsor agreed to apply surplus assets to enhance defined benefit members' benefits in the past, and it is reasonable to assume that this practice would continue, in which case the employer-sponsor would arguably have a constructive obligation to meet the enhanced benefits; or

(c)   the trustee agreed to pay surplus assets to an employer-sponsor and this meets the relevant prudential requirements, in which case the entity would be presently obliged to the employer-sponsor.

BC67 The AASB also noted that, where trust deeds or the relevant legislation is silent with respect to surplus assets, and there is no established practice, the entity would present a residual interest in the net assets as equity because the entity has no present obligation with respect to surplus assets.

BC68 Where net assets attributable to defined benefit members is less than defined benefit members' accrued benefits, the AASB noted in the Bases for Conclusions to ED 179 and ED 223, that unless there is a specific contractual arrangement between the entity and employer-sponsor, the deficit would not in itself give rise to a receivable controlled by the entity. (However, also see paragraphs BC138 to BC141.) This is because, in the absence of a contract, the payment of any future contributions by the employer-sponsor to address the deficit:

(a)   would not meet the definition of a financial instrument under AASB 132 *Financial Instruments: Presentation*; and

(b)   would not be virtually certain to be received, as required to recognise a 'reimbursement' under AASB 137 *Provisions, Contingent Liabilities and Contingent Assets*.

BC69 In relation to ED 179 and ED 223, the AASB decided, where the amount of a superannuation entity's total assets does not equal its total liabilities (including defined contribution members' vested benefits, defined benefit members' accrued benefits and any obligations to employer-sponsors), the residual is in the nature of equity in the context of Australian Accounting Standards. Accordingly, to ensure consistency with other entities, a superannuation entity should present any residual interest as equity in accordance with applicable Standards.

Statement of changes in equity

BC70 Under AAS 25, a superannuation entity is not required to present a statement of changes in equity.

BC71 The AASB noted that, while superannuation entities have no equityholders as such, they often have equity, particularly in the form of reserves. The AASB also noted that an entity's reserving policy could have implications for the amounts credited to defined contribution members' accounts. Accordingly, ED 179 and ED 223 proposed that, when appropriate, a superannuation entity should present a statement of changes in equity in accordance with AASB 101.

Responses to ED 179 and ED 223 proposals on statement of financial position and statement of changes in equity

BC72 Some respondents expressed concerns with presenting a difference between total assets and total liabilities in the statement of financial position. They suggested such presentation might be misleading to users where, for example:

(a)   an entity has several groups of defined benefit members and the difference is attributable to only one or some of these groups;

(b)   there is no specific contractual arrangement between the entity and relevant employer-sponsor(s) but it is probable the employer-sponsor(s) will make sufficient future contributions to eliminate any deficit; or

(c)   there is an expectation any surplus (reserves) of the entity will be used for the future benefit of members.

BC73 The AASB noted these concerns, but concluded they are not sufficient to justify an entity not presenting a difference between assets and liabilities in its financial statements because:

(a)   the extent of any surplus or deficit of net assets is useful information regarding the entity's capacity to pay defined contribution members' benefits and/or financial position (solvency) with respect to defined benefit members' entitlements;

(b)   if an entity considers users of its financial statements might misunderstand the implications of any surplus or deficit, consistent with paragraph 55 of AASB 101, the entity would present additional line items by way of explanation, and/or make further note disclosures; and

(c)   unless there is a present obligation at reporting date to pay reserves to a member and/or employer-sponsor, the reserve is equity in accordance with Australian Accounting Standards.

BC74 Several respondents were also concerned an entity might be permitted or required to present its liabilities for defined contribution and defined benefit members' benefits as a single line item under the ED 179 proposals. The AASB noted, because defined contribution member liabilities are different in nature and would be measured on a different basis from defined benefit member liabilities; consistent with the approach in paragraph 59 of AASB 101 and, when appropriate, the entity would present separately its liabilities for the two types of benefits.

BC75 Several respondents suggested that a statement of changes in equity would not provide sufficient useful information to users in a superannuation context to justify the cost of preparation and audit. They suggested the information that would otherwise be presented in a statement of changes in equity be included in:

(a)   the statement of changes in member benefits because equity in a superannuation context is normally small (if not immaterial) and in most cases would comprise reserves that will ultimately be used for the benefit of members; or

(b)   a note to the financial statements.

BC76 The AASB concluded it should require the recognition of the difference between total assets and total liabilities in the statement of financial position and require a statement of changes in equity. However, the AASB noted that there may be situations when a statement of changes in equity may not be material.

BC77 The AASB also concluded that, consistent with the sentiments in paragraphs 5 and 6 of AASB 101, superannuation entities should employ terminology that best suits their circumstances. Accordingly, superannuation entities might use a term such as 'reserve' rather than 'equity' in referring to line items or in naming statements.

Income statement

BC78 The AASB considered whether superannuation entities should present a single statement of profit or loss and comprehensive income or a single statement of comprehensive income in accordance with AASB 101 and concluded neither would be appropriate in a superannuation context because:

(a) all remeasurement changes in assets and liabilities, other than tax items credited or charged directly to member benefits, should be recognised in an income statement in the period they occur; and

(b) 'comprehensive income' encompasses items that would not be recognised in equity in a superannuation context and, accordingly, requiring a statement of comprehensive income may be misleading.

Income and expense items

BC79 Under AAS 25, superannuation entities recognise all income and expense items, including remeasurements of assets at net market value, in profit or loss when they occur.

BC80 The AASB considered the merits of retaining this approach and noted that defined contribution members may choose between superannuation entities based on investment returns. In addition, some employer-sponsors of entities with defined benefit members would rely on investment returns to minimise the likelihood of being required to make additional future contributions.

BC81 The AASB also noted that some Australian Accounting Standards require remeasurements of some types of assets to be debited or credited to comprehensive income. However, the AASB concluded all remeasurements, other than tax items, that are credited or charged directly to member benefits should be presented in the income statement when they occur to facilitate a clear presentation of a superannuation entity's financial performance. The AASB also noted this treatment is generally consistent with prudential reporting and to require otherwise may increase reporting costs.

Presentation of contributions, rollovers, transfers and benefit payments

BC82 Under AAS 25, contributions, rollovers and other inwards transfers are treated as revenues, and benefits to members are treated as expenses.

BC83 The AASB decided this treatment should not be retained because:

(a) for defined contribution members, member contributions, transfers and rollovers and employer contributions fully vest in members and are payable to, or on behalf of, members upon demand (if they rollover their benefits to another superannuation entity or meet a condition of release) and therefore give rise to liabilities; and

(b) employer contributions on behalf of defined benefit members assist in funding the obligations to such members.

BC84 Accordingly, the AASB concluded these flows increase the liabilities of superannuation entities and benefit payments reduce those liabilities, and they are not in the nature of revenues and expenses.

Net benefits allocated to defined contribution members' accounts

BC85 Under AAS 25, the difference between a defined contribution superannuation entity's revenues and expenses is presented in the operating statement as benefits accrued for members and their beneficiaries during the period.

BC86 The AASB noted this could be interpreted by some users to mean all revenues and expenses attributable to defined contribution members are allocated to their accounts and vest with them. However, this might not be the case where, for example, a trustee creates a reserve of unallocated assets. The AASB also noted:

(a) other Australian Accounting Standards that permit or require liabilities to be remeasured generally require recognition of remeasurement changes in profit or loss when they occur;[8] and

(b) it had concluded that most of a superannuation entity's assets and other liabilities should be measured at fair value, with remeasurement changes recognised in the income statement when they occur.

BC87 The AASB concluded that a superannuation entity should present the net benefits allocated to defined contribution members' accounts for a period as an allocation of operating profit or loss in the income statement for that period. This is in the interests of having information that provides users with an understanding of net benefits allocated to defined contribution members' accounts.

Net changes in defined benefit member liabilities

BC88 Under AAS 25, a defined benefit superannuation plan that measures members' accrued benefits at the end of each period is permitted (but not required) to recognise the remeasurement change for the period as an expense in the operating statement. In contrast, an entity that does not measure those benefits at the end of each period would disclose in the notes the amounts of members' accrued benefits at the most recent measurement date and at the previous measurement date.

BC89 The AASB noted that:

(a) the AAS 25 requirements do not facilitate the provision of comparable information useful for users in a superannuation context because defined benefit superannuation entities that are similar in all significant respects could prepare their financial statements on different bases;

(b) it has concluded, in the interests of providing users with useful information on a timely basis, and consistent with the treatment of similar types of liabilities, such as insurance contract liabilities, a superannuation plan should recognise defined benefit members' accrued benefits as a liability and measure them as at the end of each period;

(c) other Australian Accounting Standards that permit or require liabilities to be remeasured generally require remeasurement changes to be recognised in profit or loss in the period they occur; and

(d) it has concluded most of a superannuation entity's assets and other liabilities should be measured at fair value, with remeasurement changes recognised in profit or loss in the period they occur.

BC90 However, the AASB also noted, unlike many other types of liabilities, defined benefit member liabilities are funded, at least in part, by contributions from members' employers and the members themselves. Consequently, the 'cost' to a superannuation entity of providing defined benefit entitlements for a reporting period is the net rather than gross change in the entity's obligations for defined benefit member liabilities for the period. The net change is the difference between the opening and closing balances of defined benefit member liabilities for the period, after adjusting for movements of member benefits into and out of the defined benefit plan, including net after tax contributions, benefits, transfers between reserves and accrued benefits, and any gains and losses on non-routine settlements, curtailments and plan amendments. Accordingly, the AASB concluded a superannuation entity should recognise and present the net change in defined benefit member liabilities for a reporting period as a gain or loss in the income statement.

Statement of changes in member benefits

BC91 The AASB noted that paragraph 80 of AASB 101 requires an entity without share capital to disclose information in relation to owners' interests equivalent to that

---

8 For example, under AASB 137, changes in provisions are recognised as gains or losses in profit or loss in the period they occur.

required by paragraph 79(a) of AASB 101. However, the AASB concluded the presentation of member benefits in accordance with paragraph 79(a) of AASB 101 may not facilitate useful information to users in a superannuation context. For example, much of the information described in paragraph 79(a) of AASB 101 does not readily relate to a superannuation context.

BC92 Although some respondents to ED 179 and ED 223 raised concerns about the number of financial statements superannuation entities might have to prepare, given the significance of member benefits, the AASB concluded the financial statements of a superannuation entity should clearly present information that provides users with a basis for understanding changes in member liabilities. Accordingly, the AASB concluded that a statement of changes in member benefits is necessary to ensure that contributions, rollovers, transfers and benefits to members are clearly presented in a manner that enables users to evaluate their significance in relation to the entity's financial position.

Presentation of taxation amounts

BC93 Tax is levied on superannuation entities in respect of concessional contributions received and taxable earnings.[9]

BC94 Under AAS 25, tax attributable to concessional contributions is recognised as a part of income tax expense in the period contributions are received, consistent with the treatment of contributions under AAS 25. However, consistent with contributions not being treated as revenues, ED 179 and ED 223 proposed that tax levied on concessional contributions be presented separately in the statement of changes in member benefits.

BC95 Some respondents to ED 179 and ED 223 considered that it would be more useful to present all tax amounts in one statement and, preferably, the income statement. However, other respondents acknowledged the distinction between the tax on investment income and tax on concessional contributions and the relevance of presenting them in different statements.

BC96 The AASB concluded that tax levied on concessional contributions should be presented separately in the statement of changes in member benefits because:

(a) information about tax on contributions is important for decision making by users;

(b) tax on concessional contributions is effectively paid by a superannuation entity on behalf of members and should be associated with member benefits; and

(c) recognising tax on contributions as a part of income tax expense attributable to earnings would understate the entity's operating and investment performance.

BC97 The AASB also noted that, under Interpretation 1019 *The Superannuation Contributions Surcharge*, an obligation for the surcharge gives rise to a liability and an expense of a superannuation entity. The AASB also noted that, while the surcharge specifically dealt with in Interpretation 1019 no longer applies to deductible contributions, it will continue to be paid by defined benefit members who have made surchargeable contributions or who had surchargeable contributions made on their behalf between 1996 and 2005 and the surcharge has not yet been paid. Accordingly, under Interpretation 1019, accrued interest on a surcharge amount payable is treated as an expense by the entity. In addition, a new surcharge on superannuation contributions for high income earners has recently been implemented.

BC98 The AASB considered the nature of the surcharge dealt with under Interpretation 1019 and concluded the superannuation entity is essentially acting as an agent for its members because the surcharge was determined on the basis of members' personal taxable income. The AASB also considered contribution surcharge amounts are unlikely to be material in the context of member liabilities.

---

9   In relation to approved deposit funds, tax is normally only levied on earnings because these entities are not permitted to receive concessional contributions.

BC99 The AASB concluded it will reconsider the status of Interpretation 1019 and whether it might need to address the surcharge on superannuation contributions for high income earners introduced in 2013, once the impact of the implementation of that surcharge is clear.[10]

Member liabilities

Recognition

BC100 Under AAS 25, a defined contribution superannuation plan must recognise its members' accrued benefits as a liability whereas a defined benefit superannuation plan can choose to either disclose its members' accrued benefits in a note or recognise them as a liability.

BC101 During its deliberations on ED 179 and ED 223, the AASB considered the merits of retaining these reporting requirements, particularly the requirements for defined benefit superannuation plans, and noted:

(a)   the disclosure of liabilities that would otherwise be recognised in the statement of financial position is inconsistent with other Australian Accounting Standards; and

(b)   liabilities could be legal (including contractual) obligations or be constructive in nature.

BC102 The AASB considered the respective legal/contractual and constructive obligations of superannuation entities and employer-sponsors and concluded that member liabilities should be recognised as liabilities of superannuation entities because:

(a)   the obligation to fund a member's defined contribution entitlements falls on the member's superannuation entity and the obligation is legally enforceable; and

(b)   the obligation to fund a member's defined benefit entitlements, as specified in the relevant trust deed, falls primarily on the member's plan and the obligation is contractual and/or constructive in nature.

BC103 The AASB also considered the main characteristics of superannuation members' vested and accrued benefits and noted:

(a)   member contributions and benefit transfers into a superannuation entity fully vest in the member upon receipt by the entity;

(b)   employer contributions on behalf of a defined contribution member fully vest with the member upon their receipt by the superannuation entity whereas employer contributions on behalf of a defined benefit member may only vest with the member progressively in line with the relevant benefit formula. Accordingly, for the vast majority of defined contribution members, the difference between defined contribution members' vested and accrued benefits is immaterial. However, for some defined benefit members, the amount of defined benefit members' vested benefits may be materially different from the amount of such members' accrued benefits; and

(c)   most defined contribution members are entitled to transfer their vested benefits to another regulated superannuation entity under the Superannuation Guarantee (Administration) Act, whereas most defined benefit members are prohibited from transferring their defined benefit entitlements by the same legislation.

BC104 Accordingly, the AASB proposed in ED 179 and ED 223 that:

(a)   consistent with the treatment of a financial liability with a demand feature under AASB 139, defined contribution members' vested benefits should be recognised as liabilities of superannuation entities; and

---

10   The surcharge was introduced in the *Superannuation (Sustaining the Superannuation Contribution Concession) Imposition Act 2013*.

(b)   consistent with the recognition of net defined benefit member liabilities of employers under AASB 119, superannuation entities should recognise defined benefit member liabilities.

BC105   Most respondents to ED 179 and ED 223 agreed with the proposal to recognise member liabilities. However, many of them disagreed with the measurement proposals (refer to paragraphs BC120 to BC123 and BC127).

Puttable financial instruments and obligations arising on liquidation

BC106   The AASB considered the implications of applying to superannuation entities the exception to the definition of 'financial liability' in AASB 132 to classify as equity instruments certain puttable financial instruments and certain instruments that impose on an entity an obligation to deliver to another party a pro rata share of the net assets of the entity only on liquidation of the entity.[11]

BC107   The AASB noted that applying the puttable instruments exception could give rise to inconsistent reporting outcomes – for example:

(a)   defined contribution members' entitlements held by an entity with only defined contribution members might meet the criteria necessary to be classified as equity; and

(b)   defined contribution members' entitlements held by a hybrid plan and defined benefit members' entitlements would not generally meet the criteria necessary to be classified as equity.

BC108   The AASB considered that having different reporting outcomes depending upon the impact of the puttable instruments requirements would be inconsistent with principles-based standard-setting and would diminish the comparability and usefulness of the financial statements of superannuation entities. Both ED 179 and ED 223 identified the issue with puttable instruments in a superannuation entity context. The consensus from those commenting on the matter is that it would not be useful to show some or all member benefits as equity of a superannuation entity. Accordingly, the AASB concluded that the puttable instruments exception should not apply to superannuation entities.

Measurement

Defined contribution members' vested benefits

BC109   In both ED 179 and ED 223, the AASB identified defined contribution members' vested benefits as representing the amount that would be payable on demand:

(a)   upon the member's retirement, death, disablement or other event that qualifies as a condition for releasing their superannuation benefits; or

(b)   to another regulated superannuation entity under the Superannuation Guarantee (Administration) Act.

BC110   The AASB noted the net assets attributable to defined contribution members would include items that it proposes be measured at amounts other than their fair values, such as tax liabilities and tax assets. However, the AASB concluded that, as most assets and liabilities attributable to defined contribution members would be measured at their fair values, the difference between defined contribution members' vested benefits measured entirely at fair value or in accordance with AASB 119 would in most cases not be expected to be material.

BC111   Some respondents to ED 179 and ED 223 commented that the expression 'amount payable on demand' is inappropriate because it might imply that members could

---

11   AASB 2008-2 *Amendments to Australian Accounting Standards – Puttable Financial Instruments and Obligations arising on Liquidation* amended AASB 132 in February 2008.

immediately access their benefits without meeting a condition of release. Some respondents also queried why 'vested benefits' should be specified for defined contribution member liabilities, yet 'accrued benefits' is specified for defined benefit member liabilities.

BC112 The AASB concluded that it could achieve its intended outcome with modified wording and decided to refer to defined contribution member liabilities being measured at the amount of account balances at the reporting date. The AASB also concluded that it should specify the measurement of 'accrued benefits' of defined contribution members to be consistent with the requirements in other Australian Accounting Standards and to be internally consistent in respect of both defined contribution member liabilities and defined benefit member liabilities.

Defined benefit members' accrued benefits

BC113 In developing ED 179 and ED 223, the AASB considered a number of bases for measuring defined benefit member liabilities, including:

(a) at fair value consistent with the IASB Discussion Paper proposals that have now led to AASB 13;

(b) at current exit value consistent with a model in the IASB's Discussion Paper *Preliminary Views on Insurance Contracts*;[12]

(c) at present value of the expected future benefit payments consistent with the requirements of AAS 25; and

(d) at present value of the expected future benefit payments consistent with AASB 119 for defined benefit member liabilities.

BC114 With respect to paragraphs BC113(a) and BC113(b), the AASB noted:

(a) a fair value or current exit value could potentially:

(i) provide useful information to users, particularly in relation to the amount, timing and uncertainty of future benefit payments; and

(ii) facilitate consistency of reporting (with most assets being measured at fair value);

(b) defined benefit member liabilities are not traded as stand-alone items and are generally extinguished in the normal course of business. While the absence of an active market for defined benefit member liabilities does not preclude such fair value measurement, the issues that would need to be addressed to achieve consistency across superannuation entities would be potentially insurmountable. The issues include estimating risk margins, service margins and costs of capital, and putting a price on the 'moral hazard' implications of one or more (third party) employer-sponsors deciding on employees' salary adjustments; and

(c) fair value or current exit value would be inconsistent with:

(i) achieving closer alignment between the treatment of defined benefit member liabilities recognised by employer-sponsors and superannuation entities;

(ii) thinking included in the IASB Exposure Draft of proposed amendments to IAS 37 *Provisions, Contingent Liabilities and Contingent Assets* and IAS 19 *Employee Benefits*,[13] that the amount an entity would rationally pay to extinguish a liability is the lower of its settlement or transfer amounts; and

---

12 Issued in May 2007.

13 Issued in June 2005

(iii) the reasoning behind the proposals to apply a 'fulfilment approach' in the AASB's ED 244 *Insurance Contracts*, which incorporates the IASB's ED/2013/7 *Insurance Contracts*.[14]

BC115 Due to the relative weight of argument, the AASB concluded against proposing that defined benefit members' accrued benefits be measured at fair value or current exit value.

BC116 In relation to paragraph BC113(c), the AASB noted that, while the requirements in AAS 25 for measuring defined benefit members' accrued benefits are conceptually consistent with the requirements in AASB 119 for measuring defined benefit member liabilities, AAS 25 is arguably more permissive. For example, AAS 25:

(a) does not specify the actuarial valuation method required to measure defined benefit members' accrued benefits;

(b) provides little or no guidance in relation to assumptions used in measuring defined benefit member liabilities; and

(c) requires a superannuation plan to measure its defined benefit members' accrued benefits as frequently as required for statutory purposes, which might not be annually.

BC117 The AASB also noted AAS 25 required a superannuation plan to discount defined benefit members' accrued benefits at the rate of return the plan anticipates it could achieve if, at the measurement date, sufficient funds were available to meet members' accrued benefits as they fall due. The AASB considered the merits of this approach and rejected it because the discount rate might be affected by the actual types of assets held by a plan and AAS 25 does not establish a sufficient link between that rate and the nature or amounts of the plan's liabilities. The AASB was particularly concerned that, under AAS 25, a plan could potentially recognise a smaller amount for its defined benefit member liabilities than it would otherwise by holding riskier assets with potentially higher expected rates of return.

BC118 In relation to paragraph BC113(d), the AASB decided that, to achieve greater consistency across superannuation entities, and to facilitate consistency with the measurement of defined benefit and other liabilities by other entities, the approach in AASB 119 should be proposed in ED 179, on the following basis:

(a) use actuarial techniques and assumptions to make a reliable estimate of expected future cash flows;

(b) determine the present value of liabilities using the projected unit credit method;

(c) be permitted to apply estimates, averages and computational shortcuts for determining its liabilities; and

(d) measure liabilities at the end of each reporting period to help ensure users have useful information on a timely basis.

BC119 However, the AASB also decided some of the AASB 119 measurement requirements in respect of defined benefit member liabilities may need to be modified for application in a superannuation entity context. In particular, the AASB decided ED 179 should propose that:

(a) expected administration costs not be included because, although they may be regarded as a component of the ultimate cost of an employer in meeting defined benefit member liabilities, they do not constitute a part of members' accrued benefits;

(b) if a superannuation plan's benefit formula prescribes that members accrue materially higher levels of benefits as they near retirement age, rather than attribute benefits to reporting periods on a straight-line basis, the

---

14   Issued in June 2013

superannuation entity would attribute member benefits to reporting periods on a basis appropriate to its circumstances;[15]

(c)   consistent with the *Framework*, a superannuation entity would consider its assumptions to be unbiased if they are not imprudent or conservative (AASB 119 states actuarial assumptions are unbiased if they are neither imprudent nor excessively conservative); and

(d)   expected future benefit payments be discounted for the time value of money using a risk-free discount rate based on current observable, objective rates that relate to the nature, structure and terms of the obligations for future benefit payments. The AASB decided the AASB 119 requirement to determine discount rates by reference to market yields on high quality corporate bonds, or by applying yields on government bonds, is not relevant in a superannuation entity context.

BC120   Many respondents to ED 179 disagreed with the measurement proposals for defined benefit members' accrued benefits. The reasons they cited include the following.

(a)   Superannuation plans must currently calculate at least two, and potentially three, different liability measures:

(i)   vested benefits on a quarterly basis for prudential reporting, and sometimes more frequently for trustee monitoring and reporting to employer-sponsors;

(ii)   accrued benefits (discounted at the entity's estimated earnings rate) at least every three years for funding purposes and to meet prudential and legislative requirements; and

(iii) accrued benefits are potentially required to be calculated every year for the purpose of financial reporting by employer-sponsors under AASB 119.

Accordingly, requiring another liability measure would not be justified on cost-benefit grounds.

(b)   The amount of defined benefit members' accrued benefits measured under ED 179 would be likely to differ from the amount for the same members measured under AASB 119, which could give rise to confusion among users.

(c)   The amount of defined benefit members' accrued benefits measured under ED 179 would be likely to be greater than the amount for the same members measured for the actuarial review because the entity's estimated earnings rate will generally be used to discount future benefits for the purpose of the actuarial review and will generally be greater than a risk-free rate. Accordingly, deficits would be more likely to be reported under ED 179. As employer-sponsors are generally disinclined to make contributions above those needed for funding purposes, members may incorrectly conclude their entitlements are at risk.

BC121   Some respondents to ED 179 preferred that defined benefit member liabilities be measured at the amount of vested benefits for a number of reasons, including:

(a)   the amount of vested benefits is easier and less costly to calculate than accrued benefits;

(b)   users, particularly members, are more familiar with the concept of vested benefits (as it is reported in individual benefit statements). Also, users arguably

---

15   When a benefit formula prescribes that members accrue materially higher levels of benefits as they near retirement age, the allocation of service cost to reporting periods in accordance with the benefit formula would not provide a reliable measure of the employer's periodic cost of providing such benefits to employees, particularly in the earlier years of service. Accordingly, in such circumstances, AASB 119 requires employers to attribute defined benefits to reporting periods on a straight-line basis to more closely reflect the periodic cost of providing such benefits to employees. Unlike employers, superannuation entities do not receive services from members in exchange for entitlements and it would be more relevant for a plan to attribute member benefits to reporting periods on a basis appropriate to the plan's particular circumstances, taking into account the formal terms of the plan and any constructive obligations that go beyond the formal terms of the plan.

have relatively less understanding of accrued benefits and what they mean in the context of a superannuation entity's financial position;

(c) the amount of accrued benefits is relevant to an employer-sponsor that promises a future benefit, but arguably less relevant if a plan limits its legal obligation to members to the amount of its assets net of any obligations other than member liabilities;

(d) vested benefits can be a reasonable proxy for accrued benefits, particularly when members are close to expected retirement age; and

(e) measuring defined benefit member liabilities as vested benefits would be consistent with the proposed measurement of defined contribution member liabilities.

BC122 Other respondents to ED 179 expressed a preference for defined benefit member liabilities being measured in accordance with the approach in AASB 119 for defined benefit member liabilities, noting that such an approach:

(a) would facilitate greater consistency between employer-sponsor and superannuation entity financial statements;

(b) would not impose significant additional preparation and audit costs on superannuation entities; and

(c) would be likely to yield a figure that is similar to the amount that would be calculated under ED 179 because:

(i) expected administration costs are generally not material and not normally included in calculating defined benefit member liabilities under AASB 119;

(ii) Superannuation Guarantee minimum benefits have meant few entities provide defined benefit entitlements that accrue materially higher levels of benefits as members approach retirement age; and

(iii) most defined benefit member liabilities for employers are discounted using a rate determined on the basis of government bond yields, which would generally be consistent with a risk-free rate.

BC123 However, the AASB noted the following drawbacks of requiring superannuation entities to measure defined benefit member liabilities as vested benefits or in accordance with the approach in AASB 119.

(a) A vested benefits approach is inconsistent with the going concern concept because it is somewhat akin to a liquidation value and therefore not consistent with the long-term nature of defined benefit member liabilities and the approaches required under Australian Accounting Standards for measuring similar liabilities, such as insurance contract liabilities.

(b) A superannuation plan with an employer-sponsor that applies AASB 119 may still incur additional preparation and audit costs in applying the approach in AASB 119 for defined benefit member liabilities where:

(i) the employer-sponsor's reporting date is different from the superannuation entity's reporting date; or

(ii) there is a multi-employer plan and the criteria in AASB 119 are met that enable the employer-sponsor to account for the plan as if it were a defined contribution plan.

BC124 The AASB also considered that measuring defined benefit member liabilities in accordance with the approach in AASB 119 for defined benefit member liabilities within the APRA reporting timeframe (within four months of period end) may pose challenges for some superannuation entities. However, the AASB decided not to provide special guidance on materiality in respect of measuring defined benefit member liabilities to facilitate plans meeting reporting deadlines because it would arguably need to be rules-based, which is contrary to the AASB's general approach.

BC125 The AASB noted AASB 119 permits the use of particular estimates, averages or computational shortcuts in measuring defined benefit member liabilities in some cases. Accordingly, an entity would be permitted to use those shortcuts that it considers appropriate (including, but not limited to, the shortcut techniques used by employer-sponsors of defined benefit members under AASB 119), provided that the amount calculated using the shortcut techniques is not materially different from the amount that would otherwise have been determined using the comprehensive approach.

BC126 In light of the comments and recommendations of respondents, the AASB decided that, on cost-benefit grounds, ED 223 should propose that a superannuation plan be required to measure its defined benefit member liabilities in accordance with the approach in AASB 119 (without modification) for defined benefit member liabilities.

BC127 In relation to ED 223, respondents reiterated many of the points made above in relation to the ED 179 proposals. In particular, many regard the requirements in AASB 119 in respect of defined benefit member liabilities to be flawed and could identify costs of applying the AASB 119 model in a superannuation entity context and few benefits. In response, the AASB conducted further targeted outreach on the cost and timeliness of implementing a principle similar to the requirements in AAS 25, but with more direction on its implementation designed to overcome the short-comings of the AAS 25 requirement.

BC128 After noting that there is not a consistent approach across the various Australian Accounting Standards to measuring different types of liabilities and having regard to the nature of defined benefit member liabilities and the regulatory environment in which superannuation entities operate, the AASB concluded it should identify a measurement principle for defined benefit member liabilities. That principle is to measure defined benefit member liabilities as the amount of a portfolio of investments that would be needed as at the reporting date to yield future net cash inflows that would be sufficient to meet accrued benefits at that date when they are expected to fall due.

BC129 The AASB noted this principle is consistent with the notion that the superannuation entity needs to fund the liability, taking into account the timing and probabilities attaching to various factors that reflect the characteristics of the members/beneficiaries. Those characteristics include: expected mortality; rates of member turnover, disability, and early retirement; salaries and rates of salary adjustment; member choices of available options, such as lump sum or pension options; and any other risks specific to the liability. The AASB further concluded that it would require:

(a) expected cash flows to be discounted by a rate that reflects the expected notional returns, including fair value changes, on a portfolio of investments that is judged by the trustees to be the optimal way to generate the net cash inflows needed to meet benefit payments, based on a realistic assessment of the relative risks and returns on those assets;

(b) the relevant portfolio of investments might not be the same as the existing portfolio of investments, for example, because the existing investments are currently in different asset classes, or the defined benefit member liability is under-funded/unfunded; and

(c) to the extent the relevant portfolio of investments is not the same as the existing portfolio of investments, it would need to be based on investment opportunities that are realistically available to the entity.

BC130 The AASB acknowledged that, in applying the above measurement principle and the concept of materiality, there would often be approaches to measuring defined benefit member liabilities that could be employed which do not involve undertaking a comprehensive actuarial assessment. For example, the AASB noted that vested benefit calculations, including an assessment of the relationship between vested benefits and accrued benefits and the stability of that relationship, are the basis for some of the approaches that might be used in practice to measure defined benefit member liabilities for financial reporting purposes. However, the AASB noted that, because of the varied circumstances facing different plans, it would be inappropriate to identify particular approaches as being those that would apply in any particular cases.

BC131 The AASB discussed an alternative view that a risk-free rate representing only the time value of money should be applied to present value expected cash outflows. The AASB noted that, although arguably facilitating comparability among entities, this would tend to result in overstated defined benefit member liabilities and give rise to up-front deficits that would later reverse.

'Higher of' benefit options

BC132 During its deliberations on measuring member liabilities, the AASB noted the issues regarding a 'higher of' benefit that arises in a case where members are entitled to the higher of a defined benefit entitlement and a contributions-based amount.

BC133 In its Discussion Paper *Preliminary Views on Amendments to IAS 19 Employee Benefits*, the IASB proposed that an employer-sponsor account for a higher of benefit option in a manner consistent with an embedded option under IAS 39 *Financial Instruments: Recognition and Measurement* such that an employer-sponsor would:

(a) recognise and account for the host defined benefit promise in the same way as a defined benefit member liability under IAS 19; and

(b) account for the higher of benefit option separately, measured at its fair value assuming the terms of the benefit promise will not change.

BC134 The AASB concluded ED 179 should seek input from constituents on accounting for a higher of benefit option separately from member liabilities, and how the benefit option might be measured (prior to making any proposals on the matter), since the IASB's proposals were at an early stage of development and had been specifically developed for application by employer-sponsors.

BC135 Respondents to ED 179 confirmed that higher of benefit options are presently measured at their 'intrinsic values' as:

(a) the difference between the defined benefit members' accrued benefits and their account balances when account balances are greater than accrued benefits; and

(b) at nil when account balances are less than accrued benefits.

BC136 In addition, most of the respondents to ED 179 disagreed with the IASB's proposed approach because:

(a) there are no compelling reasons to depart from current practice under AAS 25 and AASB 119, which ensures accrued benefits are measured on the basis of future benefit payments that members are likely to receive;

(b) in the Australian context, some higher of benefit options can change depending upon various factors, including investment returns, salary increases, and members' ages and service periods, and a reliable measurement is not feasible; and

(c) using an option valuation technique is not justified on cost-benefit grounds, particularly since the separate recognition of a higher of benefit option could potentially confuse some users.

BC137 Based on the feedback received on ED 179 and the lack of progress at the IASB on its post-employment benefits work, the AASB concluded that neither ED 223 nor AASB 1056 should address higher of benefit options.

Employer-sponsor receivables

BC138 Neither ED 179 nor ED 223 included explicit recognition or measurement proposals about receivables from an employer-sponsor where there is a net difference between the assets and liabilities of a defined benefit plan. Both exposure drafts proposed disclosure of the main features of any specific contractual arrangement in place between the trustee and the relevant employer-sponsor in relation to funding a 'deficit'. Both also mentioned in their Bases for Conclusions that, unless there is a specific contractual arrangement between the entity and employer-sponsor, the deficit would not in itself give rise to a receivable controlled by the entity.

BC139   Respondents to ED 179 and ED 223 confirmed the AASB's thinking that specific contractual arrangements between the entity and employer-sponsor are rarely, if ever, encountered. However, the AASB's targeted outreach with public sector superannuation entities revealed that legislative guarantees of funding are relatively common in that sector. In addition, some respondents sought guidance on the circumstances in which a plan would recognise contributions receivable in respect of defined benefit members for which there is a deficit of net assets.

BC140   The AASB concluded that AASB 1056 should include a requirement to recognise a receivable from an employer-sponsor to the extent that it meets the definition and recognition criteria for an asset in the *Framework*.

BC141   The AASB considered the various approaches that could be taken to measuring such a receivable and concluded that it should be measured on a basis consistent with the measurement principle for the underlying defined benefit member liability less the fair value of any assets held by the entity to meet that liability, which is effectively the 'intrinsic value' of the asset. The AASB concluded that any other measurement principle for an employer-sponsor receivable in respect of defined benefit member liabilities would be likely to involve taking into account employer-sponsor credit risk, which would not be appropriate for the reasons identified in paragraph BC194(d) in relation to risk disclosure proposals.

BC142   A number of constituents commenting on the Draft AASB 105X for fatal flaw review sought to know why there would be no requirements in relation to whether entities should accrue for contributions receivable from employers for payroll of the reporting period. The AASB noted that this type of accrual is the subject of other Australian Accounting Standards and the general conventions underpinning accounting, and should not be specifically addressed in AASB 1056.

Tax liabilities and tax assets

BC143   Under AAS 25, the recognition and measurement requirements of AASB 112 apply in determining income tax expense.

BC144   The AASB considered the merits of requiring superannuation entities to measure tax liabilities and tax assets at fair value, which would imply a need for discounting in some circumstances, thereby requiring such entities to depart from AASB 112. The AASB noted:

(a)   AASB 112 prohibits discounting deferred tax assets and liabilities to their present values on the basis that the detailed scheduling necessary to undertake that discounting is usually impracticable or highly complex;

(b)   a significant proportion of many superannuation entity tax balances are attributable to unrealised gains and losses on assets held to fund member benefits and measuring those assets at fair value helps ensure that any associated tax balances determined under AASB 112 would be recognised at amounts approximating fair value;[16] and

(c)   most of the 'transaction costs' associated with tax balances relate to measuring the assets held to fund member benefits and maintaining adequate records for tax purposes, and the transaction costs directly attributable to extinguishing or settling a tax liability or tax asset are immaterial.

---

16   For example, if a superannuation entity sold an asset for its carrying amount at the end of the period, and that amount is above its tax base, the tax liability measured in accordance with AASB 112 would generally be materially the same as the present value of tax the entity would have to pay in relation to the asset.

BC145 ED 179 and ED 223 proposed that superannuation entities should measure tax balances in accordance with AASB 112 because:

(a) users' needs do not appear to justify a departure from AASB 112 as the difference between a tax balance measured at fair value or in accordance with AASB 112 would, in most cases, be immaterial; and

(b) the benefits to users from fair valuing deferred tax assets and liabilities are unlikely to be outweighed by the costs incurred in determining their fair values.

BC146 The majority of the respondents to ED 179 and ED 223 that specifically commented on the recognition and measurement proposals for tax liabilities and tax assets generally agreed with the proposals. Accordingly, the AASB concluded that superannuation entities should be required to measure tax balances in accordance with AASB 112.

Liabilities and assets arising from insurance contracts

BC147 During its deliberations on the proposals in ED 179, the AASB noted many superannuation entities offer life and disability insurance cover to their members and some also offer income protection insurance, and that AAS 25 is silent about how to account for such arrangements. The AASB also noted the forms of these insurance arrangements differ across entities, including those where cover is:

(a) offered to members, with the entity only acting as agent;

(b) offered to members with the entity accepting insurance risk; and

(c) provided to defined benefit members in relation to their projected retirement benefit.

BC148 The AASB noted that, in the case of (a), a superannuation entity is unlikely to be exposed to significant insurance risk as members or their beneficiaries would not generally have recourse to the assets of the plan, even in the event the insurer fails. In other circumstances the entity may have significant insurance risk, even if it reinsures 100% of the risk with a third-party (re)insurer. The AASB noted that, under the insurance standards, reinsurance does not nullify the direct contract with the policyholder.

BC149 The AASB considered a number of approaches to accounting for insurance arrangements that involve a superannuation entity having significant insurance risk, including applying AASB 137, AASB 4 *Insurance Contracts*, AASB 1023 and AASB 1038.

BC150 The AASB considered that many of the insurance contracts entered into by superannuation entities would meet the 'insurance contract' definition. The AASB decided ED 179 should propose that superannuation entities account for any liabilities and assets arising from the insurance arrangements they provide to their members by applying the recognition, measurement and disclosure requirements of AASB 1038 on the basis that:

(a) insurance arrangements provided to superannuation members generally have the same characteristics as life insurance contracts and would meet the 'life insurance contract' definition were it not for the fact that it is confined to contracts regulated under the *Life Insurance Act 1995*;

(b) AASB 1038 has comprehensive requirements;

(c) AASB 4 does not include initial liability recognition requirements or comprehensive measurement requirements;

(d) the liability recognition and measurement requirements of AASB 1023 are based on a premium deferral model, which would not suit the circumstances of superannuation entities that would generally not receive significant premiums in advance that could be deferred; and

(e) AASB 137 applies only to liability recognition and measurement.

BC151 The AASB noted that applying AASB 1038 would potentially change the way in which many superannuation entities account for insurance arrangements and, where the insurance arrangements give rise to obligations, entities would be required to recognise:

(a) insurance contract premiums and claim recoveries as income;

(b) insurance contract claims and premiums ceded to reinsurers as expenses;

(c) claim recoveries and other inflows not yet received from reinsurers as assets; and

(d) insurance contract liabilities.

BC152 In response to ED 179, a number of respondents acknowledged that a superannuation entity that:

(a) 'self-insures' members' benefits (that is, does not reinsure all of the members' insurance benefits with a third-party insurer);

(b) pays discretionary insurance benefits in addition to the benefits provided by a third-party insurer; or

(c) is liable for insurance claims under its trust deeds that are not met by a third-party insurer;

is potentially exposed to insurance risk and therefore should arguably provide information regarding these risks.

BC153 However, nearly all of those commenting on the proposed application of AASB 1038 expressed concerns, including:

(a) applying the recognition and measurement principles and requirements in AASB 1038 would be difficult because:

(i) contributions in respect of self-insured defined benefit members do not include explicit insurance premium components and, while a plan's actuary would normally estimate that component for tax purposes, that may not meet the relevant requirements;

(ii) for some plans, a member's resignation benefits and death and/or disability benefits are linked and would be included as part of the defined benefit member liability, with the death and/or disability component not being separately calculated; and

(iii) the amount of any self-insured defined death and/or disability benefit may not be readily identifiable where the benefit is not defined in terms of an accrued (retirement) amount plus an insured component;

(b) the proposals are not justified on cost-benefit grounds, because:

(i) applying AASB 1038 would impose significant additional costs, including the cost of systems for capturing the necessary information; and

(ii) insurance risks are generally not significant in the context of a superannuation entity's operations as a whole because few superannuation entities are self-insured; the provision of insurance arrangements is only an ancillary benefit offered to members; and most plans reinsure all of the relevant risks with third party (re)insurers; and

(c) the potential implications of the changes to AASB 1038 that would result from the IASB's comprehensive insurance contracts project in the next few years.

BC154 Respondents to ED 179 also identified a number of alternative approaches the AASB could adopt, including:

(a) only addressing accounting for insurance arrangements in a superannuation context once the IASB's comprehensive insurance contracts project is completed;

(b) a disclosure-only approach, for example, requiring disclosure of the insurance arrangements provided, the risk exposures and any reserves established in respect of such exposures; or

(c) requiring any liabilities or assets arising from insurance arrangements to be accounted for in a manner consistent with the basis adopted for measuring member liabilities.

BC155 In redeliberating the proposals in ED 179, the AASB noted that, in many cases, superannuation entities act only as agents in respect of the insurance arrangements they have for members and would not be affected by requirements to account for insurance contracts. However, whilst insurance risks may not be significant for many superannuation entities, the AASB noted that some may be exposed to significant insurance risk. For example, (re)insuring member liabilities with a third-party (re)insurer may not mitigate the insurance risks to which a plan is exposed because:

(a) the superannuation entity remains exposed to credit and other performance risk of the (re)insurer, including the possibility a reinsurer declines a claim but the entity remains obliged to meet the benefit;

(b) the excesses and/or deductibles under a group policy might leave the entity exposed to some or all members' insurance claims; and/or

(c) the (re)insurer is in 'run off' and unwilling or unable to pay claims.

BC156 The AASB also noted that self-insured arrangements may expose an entity to non-performance risk and/or economic dependency risk in relation to the employer-sponsor, particularly when there exists a deficit in a defined benefit plan.

BC157 The AASB concluded that it should reconsider the accounting for the insurance arrangements once the IASB's comprehensive insurance contracts project is completed, but that this should not be a barrier to addressing the matter now. In its response to the IASB's ED/2010/8 *Insurance Contracts*, the AASB recommended that the IASB consider the implications of the findings on insurance contracts as a part of its proposed comprehensive review of the accounting for post-employment benefits.

BC158 The AASB concluded a 'disclosure only' approach is not adequate because it would mean assets and liabilities would remain unrecognised.

BC159 The AASB considers the main risks to which most superannuation entities are exposed in relation to insured benefits are credit and operational risks of the (re)insurer, and risks associated with the plan administering policies (such as the risk of higher than expected claims administration expenses).

BC160 The AASB also noted that:

(a) insurance contract liabilities in respect of defined benefit members are measured as part of members' accrued benefits under AAS 25;

(b) for the purpose of recognising a net defined benefit member liability under AASB 119, the level of aggregation (unit of account) is the cohort of employees with defined benefit entitlements and any insurance contract liabilities are calculated as a part of the 'best estimate' cash flows, which contrasts with AASB 1038, which is designed to cater for life insurers and incorporates the notions of experience adjustments as well as adjusting planned margins for the impacts of changes to assumptions;

(c) insurance contract liabilities in respect of defined benefit members are likely to be measured at a similar amount under the accumulation approach in AASB 1038 as they would be under the approach in AASB 119 for defined benefit member liabilities;

(d) under AASB 119, no distinction is made between retirement benefits and insurance benefits in respect of the measurement or presentation of defined benefit member liabilities; and

(e) an entity could use estimates, averages or computational shortcuts permitted in AASB 119 in measuring its defined benefit member liabilities, such as a cash premiums basis to measure the insurance component of its liability to defined benefit members, or its liabilities arising from insurance arrangements provided to defined contribution members, if the outcomes are not materially different from those that would otherwise be achieved using an expected present value basis.

BC161 Accordingly, the AASB decided ED 223 should propose that insurance obligations to members be:

(a) recognised (and derecognised) using the AASB 119 approach for defined benefit member liabilities;

(b) for defined benefit members, measured as part of accrued benefits using the measurement approach in AASB 119 for defined benefit member liabilities;

(c) for defined contribution members, measured using the approach in AASB 119 for defined benefit member liabilities, to facilitate consistency with the requirements for defined benefit member liabilities;

(d) presented separately from any liabilities for defined contribution members' vested benefits (when material) – separate presentation should not be required in relation to defined benefit members' accrued benefits, consistent with the approach in AASB 119; and

(e) any reinsurance assets should be recognised in accordance with AASB 1038.

BC162 The AASB also decided ED 223 should propose that information should be disclosed that explains and provides users with a basis for understanding the amount, timing and uncertainty of future cash flows arising from insurance obligations to members.

BC163 In response to ED 223, a number of respondents made the following points:

(a) it is clear those superannuation entities that 'self-insure' should be accounting for any insurance assets and liabilities, and that AASB 119 is a reasonable basis for recognising and measuring the liabilities – it was noted that such self-insurance is becoming less prevalent;

(b) some superannuation entities clearly state that members will only receive insurance benefits if the insurer/reinsurer pays. Accordingly, although superannuation entities may control cash and accrue receivables and payables arising from their insurance arrangements, they are not taking on insurance risk;

(c) those superannuation entities offering group insurance cover that members can elect to have would reinsure those risks with a registered insurer. In many of these arrangements it may not be entirely clear whether the superannuation entities are taking on insurance risk that should cause them to account for insurance assets and liabilities;

(d) in most cases, the insurance offered to defined contribution members can be re-priced at short notice. That is, the premiums charged to member accounts can be adjusted as the insurance costs faced by the superannuation entities change (for example, as the reinsurance premiums change). Accordingly, in such cases, any insurance contracts that might exist between the superannuation entities and their members are short in duration and the associated insurance assets and liabilities might be immaterial;

(e) superannuation entities occasionally make ex gratia payments in respect of death and disability claims where the trustees judge that a benefit should be paid even though it is not covered by reinsurance, but they would not be material;

(f) referring to both AASB 119 and AASB 1038 in relation to insurance is potentially confusing, particularly to those who are not familiar with accounting for insurance contract liabilities; and

(g) further guidance should be provided on when superannuation entities would be considered to be acting as agents.

BC164 The AASB concluded it should include the requirements relating to reinsurance assets from AASB 1038 in the replacement standard, rather than referencing to AASB 1038; particularly in view of the fact that AASB 1038 will be replaced at some stage.

BC165 The AASB also concluded it should proceed with the other recognition and measurement requirements consistent with the proposals in ED 223, but noted that it had concluded on an approach to measuring defined benefit member liabilities, and therefore insurance liabilities, that is different from ED 223. The AASB also concluded that further guidance should be provided on:

(a) factors that are indicative of a superannuation entity acting as an agent in respect of the insurance cover provided to members (or their beneficiaries); and

(b) factors that are indicative of a superannuation entity acting as an insurer.

BC166 The AASB noted that, in the case of superannuation entities acting as agents in relation to insurance arrangements provided to members, whilst these arrangements do not give rise to revenues and expenses of the entity, amounts from members account balances are typically applied to pay insurance premiums and some claims may be received via member accounts. (Many claims would be received directly by members/beneficiaries and would not appear in a superannuation entity's financial statements.) The AASB concluded that, in respect of the premium amounts and any claim amounts that flow through the superannuation entity, it provides useful information about insurance arrangements a superannuation entity provides as an agent for the statement of cash flows and statement of changes in member benefits to reflect those amounts.

BC167 In arriving at the above conclusions, the AASB was aware of the relatively new regulation designed to phase out so-called 'self-insurance' through prudential regulation. Nevertheless, the AASB concluded that the requirements relating to recognising assets, liabilities, revenues and expenses in relation to insurance arrangements might still apply. This is because a superannuation entity that has insurance policies with registered insurers that 'fully support' insurance cover provided to members may still leave the superannuation entity acting in the capacity of an insurer (albeit one with reinsurance cover).

Consolidated and separate financial statements

Consolidated financial statements

BC168 At the time of preparing both ED 179 and ED 223, the AASB noted there is an expectation that under AASB 127 *Consolidated and Separate Financial Statements* and AASB 10 *Consolidated Financial Statements*,[17] superannuation entities would generally be required to prepare consolidated financial statements. Following the developments explained below, the IASB (and ultimately the AASB) changed the landscape for consolidation when it decided to apply a different approach to 'investment entities' that, generally, would not require consolidation.

BC169 The AASB deliberated at length on the manner in which superannuation entities should prepare consolidated financial statements. Those deliberations were conducted prior to the issue of AASB 2013-5 *Amendments to Australian Accounting Standards – Investment Entities*. They included considering feedback on an AASB Consultation Paper *Consolidation of Subsidiaries by Superannuation Entities* (September 2007) and the consolidation proposals in ED 179 and ED 223. During that process, the AASB considered a number of different ways in which a parent superannuation entity could treat a subsidiary in its consolidated financial statements, including:

---

17 AASB 10 superseded AASB 127 for periods beginning on or after 1 January 2013.

(a)　on a full fair value basis that involves all assets and liabilities, whether recognised or unrecognised in the separate financial statements of the parent or a subsidiary, being measured at fair values;

(b)　on a basis that involves all assets and liabilities recognised by a subsidiary being measured at fair values when fair value is required or permitted under the relevant Australian Accounting Standards;[18]

(c)　as per (b) above with the addition, when applicable, of a balancing item in relation to subsidiaries.[19] That balancing item would comprise:

  (i)　acquired goodwill remaining at period end;

  (ii)　changes in internally generated goodwill associated with subsidiaries subsequent to their acquisition; and

  (iii)　measurement differences resulting from subsidiaries' assets and liabilities being recognised in consolidated financial statements at amounts other than their fair values adjusted for transaction costs;

(d)　in accordance with AASB 3 and AASB 127,[20] under which a subsidiary's identifiable assets and liabilities are recognised in the consolidated financial statements at their fair values at the subsidiary's date of acquisition, and subsequent to acquisition, a subsidiary's assets and liabilities are recognised in accordance with relevant Australian Accounting Standards, which treat the fair values of assets or liabilities acquired in business combinations as 'cost' for the purposes of subsequent accounting;

(e)　a proportionate consolidation model that ensures the net asset amounts reported in the parent's separate and consolidated financial statements are the same; and

(f)　recognition of net investments in subsidiaries as a single line item with detailed note disclosure.

BC170　In relation to ED 179, the AASB decided that a parent superannuation entity would be best served by recognising in its consolidated statement of financial position all assets and liabilities of a subsidiary, whether recognised or unrecognised in the statement of financial position of the subsidiary.

BC171　In light of the comments received on ED 179 from respondents the AASB decided, consistent with ED 179, that ED 223 should propose that a parent superannuation entity present consolidated financial statements. However, in contrast to ED 179, the consolidated financial statements would be prepared in accordance with AASB 3 and AASB 10, including in relation to accounting for acquired goodwill. Superannuation entities would also be required to apply the fair value option to measuring non-controlling interests at inception, without subsequent remeasurement, in accordance with AASB 3.

BC172　Consistent with ED 179, under ED 223 it was proposed to require remeasuring acquired intangible assets at fair value at each reporting date in the consolidated financial statements; whether or not they had been acquired in a business combination. The AASB noted that this would be a departure from AASB 3 and AASB 138 *Intangible Assets* when there are not active markets for the intangible assets concerned.

BC173　At the time of preparing ED 223, the AASB also noted the proposals in IASB ED/2011/4 *Investment Entities*[21] to account for most subsidiaries at fair value through profit or loss might address some of the concerns raised by constituents. However, the AASB decided that it would be premature for the AASB to propose in ED 223

18　Consistent with the approach currently applied under AASB 1023 and AASB 1038.

19　Similar to the approach in the now superseded AASB 1038 *Life Insurance Business* (1998).

20　AASB 10 had not yet been issued.

21　ED/2011/4 *Investment Entities* (August 2011) was open for comment by 5 January 2012. ED/2011/4 was incorporated in AASB ED 220 *Investment Entities* for comment by 30 November 2011.

permitting or requiring parent superannuation entities to apply investment entity accounting before there is an outcome from the IASB's project.

Responses to the ED 179 and ED 223 consolidation proposals

BC174 Overall, respondents expressed mixed views on the proposals in ED 179 and ED 223 that a parent superannuation entity present consolidated financial statements. Many of them identified practical difficulties, including:

(a) identifying entities controlled and the times when control arises or is lost;

(b) monitoring changes in holdings in collective investment entities, particularly when there is a high turnover of ownership interests in the investee;

(c) obtaining relevant, reliable and timely information to prepare consolidated financial statements, particularly in relation to 'fund of fund' investment vehicles; and

(d) consolidating for only part of a period because the investment in the subsidiary fluctuates either side of a controlling level (say around 50%) in its outstanding ownership interests.

BC175 Based on these practical difficulties, some constituents recommended the AASB would need to provide application guidance on how the concept of control should be interpreted and applied in a superannuation context. To this end, some suggested a 'substance over form' approach be taken whereby entities that a parent 'actively' controls are consolidated and entities in which there is a 'passive' investment be accounted for as investments.

BC176 Other respondents suggested that, due to the nature of superannuation arrangements in Australia, in some circumstances the parent may be incapable of controlling an investee that would otherwise meet the definition of a subsidiary in a manner consistent with the notions of control in AASB 127 and AASB 10 because:

(a) members exercise investment choice and might collectively acquire a controlling interest in another entity, and the superannuation entity may not be considered to have the power to govern the investee so as to obtain benefits from its activities because the superannuation entity is subject to the independent investment choice decisions of its members; and

(b) the 'sole purpose test' in the Superannuation Industry (Supervision) Act is generally considered to prohibit trustees from being involved in day-to-day operations of the businesses in which their superannuation entities invest.

BC177 The AASB considered the concerns expressed in a superannuation context and noted that most, if not all, the practical difficulties identified are not unique to superannuation entities and are encountered by many other entities, including investment-type entities reporting under Australian Accounting Standards.

BC178 A number of the respondents opposed parent superannuation entities being required to present consolidated financial statements on the grounds that users, particularly members, are unlikely to consider consolidated information useful. They noted that, unlike shareholders in a company, members of a superannuation entity do not necessarily have a notional interest in all the net assets. In particular, some members may have no exposure to a subsidiary held by their superannuation entity because that investment is not part of some members' chosen investment options.

BC179 Some respondents to ED 223 noted their support for the proposals in IASB ED/2011/4 to account for most subsidiaries at fair value through profit or loss.

Separate financial statements

BC180 The AASB considered whether there is any information that a user of the GPFSs of a superannuation parent might need that is not available in consolidated financial statements and concluded that consolidated financial statements would normally provide such users with the information they need in a superannuation context.

However, if a parent superannuation entity prepares separate financial statements for general purpose users, the AASB reasoned the entity presumably considers this information necessary for an understanding of the reported results of the group. Accordingly, for the purposes of both ED 179 and ED 223, the AASB decided to propose that a parent superannuation entity that prepares separate financial statements for general purpose users should present them together with its consolidated financial statements.

Responses to the ED 179 and ED 223 separate financial statements proposals

BC181 Some respondents to ED 179 and ED 223 expressed concerns about the apparent inconsistency between the proposals about separate financial statements and the prudential reporting requirements in respect of separate financial statements that apply to APRA-regulated superannuation entities. The AASB acknowledged the concerns but concluded its proposals would not prevent an APRA-regulated superannuation entity from preparing separate financial statements for the specific purpose of fulfilling its prudential reporting obligations.

AASB conclusions on consolidated and separate financial statements

BC182 Given the amendments made through AASB 2013-5, the AASB concluded that there should not be special requirements on consolidated or separate financial statements for superannuation entities. Accordingly, they would be required to account for their subsidiaries under AASB 10. If a superannuation entity qualifies as an 'investment entity' it would be required to account at fair value through profit or loss for its subsidiaries, except for any subsidiary that provides services relating to its investment activities, which would still need to be consolidated.

BC183 The AASB acknowledged this may mean that parent superannuation entities would generally account for their subsidiaries at fair value through profit or loss and not prepare consolidated financial statements. However, the AASB also concluded that superannuation entities that qualify as investment entities might have subsidiaries that provide services that relate to its investment activities[22] and/or it is conceivable that, now or in the future, there may be a superannuation entity that has subsidiaries and does not qualify to be treated as an 'investment entity'. In both these cases, when material, superannuation entities would still need to prepare consolidated financial statements under AASB 10.

Disclosures

BC184 As outlined in the *Framework*, financial statement disclosures provide information about the risks and uncertainties affecting an entity. In many circumstances, the disclosure requirements of Australian Accounting Standards would provide users of the financial statements of a superannuation entity with useful information for their decision making. However, some disclosure principles and requirements of those Standards may not facilitate the provision of useful information in a superannuation context. For example, AASB 116 *Property, Plant and Equipment* requires entities applying the revaluation model to disclose the carrying amount of each revalued class of property, plant and equipment as it would have been measured under the cost model. However, there are very few circumstances in which users of superannuation entity financial statements might require historical cost information.

BC185 The AASB decided that ED 179 and ED 223 should propose the use of the disclosure requirements in many of the existing Australian Accounting Standards, but should also propose some disclosure principles that particularly suit the superannuation environment, in place of the requirements of some of those other Standards.

---

22   Refer to paragraph 32 of AASB 10 as amended by AASB 2013-5.

BC186 Accordingly, ED 179 and ED 223 proposed that:

    (a)   a superannuation entity apply the disclosure principles and requirements in other applicable Australian Accounting Standards unless they:

        (i)   are not consistent with the measurement requirements for superannuation entities; or

        (ii)   address the same items or events as the principles or requirements in the replacement Standard;

    (b)   superannuation-specific guidance in relation to the disclosure principles and requirements in other Australian Accounting Standards be provided only where it is necessary to facilitate their reliable and consistent application; and

    (c)   a superannuation entity disclose information that provides users, particularly members and beneficiaries, with a basis for understanding transactions and events specific to superannuation entities that are relevant to the users' decision making needs.

Expense items

BC187 Most defined contribution members can choose the superannuation entity that manages their retirement benefits. However, to make informed decisions, members need to be able to compare plans, particularly with respect to expenses. Defined contribution members bear the costs associated with the management of their retirement benefits and the level of a plan's expenses can help provide a basis for understanding the level of fees that might be charged to members' accounts.

BC188 Employers would also be interested in information about the nature and amount of expenses, for example, in attempting to identify a default defined contribution plan for employees or because they sponsor defined benefit arrangements for their employees (and generally bear the costs of providing such arrangements).

BC189 In line with other Australian Accounting Standards, ED 179 and ED 223 proposed a superannuation entity disclose information about the nature and amount of expenses.

BC190 ED 179 and ED 223 also proposed that expense items of particular relevance, such as administration costs and trustees' fees, should be separately disclosed. Most respondents to both exposure drafts who commented on the proposals supported requiring these disclosures.

Management expense ratio

BC191 The AASB considered whether a superannuation entity should be required to disclose a management expense ratio (MER) for the entity as a whole. The AASB concluded that a better focus of Australian Accounting Standards is to facilitate the provision of information from which users can calculate their own ratios for their particular needs. The AASB also noted MERs of superannuation entities are publicly available from other sources; and other investment-type entities are not required to disclose MERs under Australian Accounting Standards.

Nature, extent and management of risks

BC192 Having considered the types of risks to which a superannuation entity could be exposed, the AASB decided ED 179 should propose that:

    (a)   the disclosure requirements in paragraphs 6 to 30 of AASB 7 should not apply; and

    (b)   disclosure principles based on paragraphs 31 to 42 of AASB 7 and tailored for a superannuation context would facilitate the disclosure of useful information about significant risks to which an entity is exposed.

BC193 The AASB concluded that paragraphs 6 to 30 of AASB 7 are generally not relevant in a superannuation context. For example:

(a) superannuation entities are not permitted to issue compound financial instruments with multiple embedded derivatives;

(b) paragraphs 9 to 11 of AASB 7 are intended to help explain an entity's choice to designate financial instruments at fair value through profit or loss,[23] whereas applying that measurement basis is the subject of specific requirements;

(c) paragraphs 25 to 30 of AASB 7 do not seem relevant because financial assets and any financial liabilities are measured at fair value through profit or loss; and for assets and liabilities relating to member benefits, there are the challenges noted in paragraph BC114(b) about obtaining fair values; and

(d) superannuation entities generally do not have loans and are prohibited from holding a borrowing directly, and therefore accounting mismatches of related loans and liabilities are generally not relevant.

BC194 In light of constituent feedback on ED 179, the AASB redeliberated the risk disclosure proposals and noted:

(a) the support for not requiring the application of paragraphs 6 to 30 of AASB 7 for the reasons in paragraph BC193;

(b) there may be less need for specific principles for superannuation entities regarding disclosures about the nature and extent of risks than assumed for the purposes of ED 179;

(c) although AASB 7 scopes out obligations arising from employee benefit plans to which AASB 119 applies, a member liability meets the financial liability definition. This is because meeting members' benefits can be considered a contractual obligation of the superannuation entity (in the sense that defined contribution entitlements must be met and defined benefit entitlements are specified in trust deeds), and members' benefits are normally paid in cash;

(d) information in relation to the risk an employer-sponsor of defined benefit members will not be able to make contributions at a level that would be expected to permit the superannuation entity to meet members' accrued benefits is of critical importance in understanding a superannuation entity's overall financial position (solvency), irrespective of whether there is a surplus or deficit, and such risk is more in the nature of non-performance or economic dependency risk than credit risk; and

(e) additional liquidity risk disclosure about any non-financial liabilities other than tax liabilities of a superannuation entity can be justified on the basis that trustees are required to have an investment strategy that has regard to the entity's overall circumstances, including the liquidity of its investments and its expected cash flow requirements. Accordingly, entities with non-financial liabilities other than tax liabilities (such as provisions) would be expected to have considered the relevant liquidity risks and how they will be managed for prudential purposes. In this regard, the AASB noted that many superannuation entities would not have material non-financial liabilities other than those related to tax.

BC195 Based on its deliberations on the comments on ED 179, the AASB decided ED 223 should propose:

(a) a superannuation entity apply the principles and requirements in AASB 7, as appropriate, and should only include guidance considered necessary to facilitate their application in a superannuation entity context;

(b) a superannuation entity make disclosures consistent with the types of information disclosed under AASB 7 in relation to the liquidity risks arising from any non-financial liabilities other than tax liabilities; and

---

23 The Bases for Conclusions to IAS 32, IAS 39 and IFRS 7 suggest that paragraphs 9 to 11 of IFRS 7 are intended to address concerns about how entities exercise their choice to designate financial instruments at fair value through profit or loss.

(c) a superannuation entity with defined benefit members provide qualitative disclosures about non-performance risk and/or economic dependency risk relating to the employer-sponsor(s).

BC196 Respondents to ED 223 expressed concerns that a requirement to disclose qualitative information about non-performance risk and/or economic dependency risk to which the plan is exposed in relation to employer-sponsors would give rise to 'boilerplate' disclosure. This is because, in some cases, the trustees would have no more information about a superannuation entity's reliance on employer-sponsors than is already publicly available and, in other cases, such a requirement might put the trustees in a position where they have to make judgements about the overall viability of an employer that may already be the subject of speculation in the business community.

BC197 Some respondents suggested the disclosure should instead focus on the process superannuation entities use to assess risks associated with employer-sponsors, or provide information focusing on the funding plans of a superannuation entity in relation to defined benefits.

BC198 In relation to defined contribution member liabilities, the AASB concluded the disclosure principles in AASB 7 would be relevant. However, in relation to defined benefit member liabilities, the AASB considers most of the disclosure principles in AASB 7 are not readily applicable, and concluded AASB 1056 should set out disclosure principles and related guidance on explaining the quantitative and/or qualitative information that would be useful, including:

(a) how any funding deficit is expected to be met – in terms of the nature, causes of, and any strategies for, addressing the deficit;

(b) the basis for assumptions and manner in which they are determined; and

(c) the sensitivity of the liabilities to changes in key assumptions.

BC199 The AASB concluded that, consistent with the principles in AASB 7, the subject of the sensitivity disclosures should be reasonably possible changes in the key assumptions, and when there is more than one key assumption for which a change is judged to be reasonably possible, the analysis can be performed on a univariate basis or on a multivariate basis.

BC200 Given the obligations of trustees to have an investment strategy that has regard to the entity's overall circumstances, including the liquidity of its investments and its expected cash flow requirements, the AASB also concluded that, where the entity's actual investment portfolio differs from the portfolio used in measuring defined benefit member liabilities, an explanation should be required of why that is the case.

Disaggregated financial information

BC201 Information about the way a superannuation entity arranges and manages assets attributable to different groups of members, and the related member liabilities, can help provide users with a basis for understanding the financial performance, financial position and risk exposures of the entity as a whole.

BC202 In framing its ED 179 proposals, the AASB decided the 'through the eyes of management' approach applied to operating segments under AASB 8 *Operating Segments* would be an appropriate approach for superannuation entities to apply in respect of disclosing information about assets attributable to different groups of members and the related member liabilities because:

(a) whilst they generally do not have identifiable operating segments, some superannuation entities segregate their assets into different member groups to facilitate meeting liabilities to those different groups. Users would arguably benefit from these entities disclosing information about such asset groups and the related member liabilities that corresponds to information provided in management reports;

(b) the approach is sufficiently generic to be applied in disclosing information about assets attributable to different member groups;

(c) the approach should be generally less costly to apply than alternative approaches because it uses information already generated for management's use; and

(d) the approach is consistent with that proposed for other disclosures, such as disclosures about risks and risk management arrangements.

BC203 Some respondents to ED 179 agreed with the principle of having segment disclosures, particularly if they result in improved disclosures about risks attaching to different member groups. However, many other constituents expressed concerns about requiring segment-type disclosures because such requirements would:

(a) make some entities' note disclosures excessively long and complex, thereby diminishing their overall usefulness; and

(b) not assist users in understanding the overall financial position and performance of an entity that has member groups with different entitlements but 'pools' all its assets for investment purposes.

BC204 Of significance to many constituents were the potential practical implications of applying a segment-type approach in a superannuation context, including identifying segregated groups of assets. While trustees generally manage member liabilities on a segregated basis, most pool assets to achieve efficiencies. Some respondents expressed concern that some relatively common situations that arise with pooled assets may nevertheless satisfy the criteria for managing assets on a segregated basis. For example, they were concerned entities that provide investment choices to members may be required to treat each investment choice as a segregated asset group because entities' trustees might often:

(a) adjust actual allocations between asset classes within a particular investment option to match target allocations following movements in investment markets; and

(b) adjust actual allocations of assets between investment options to match member liabilities.

BC205 Others were concerned about applying the proposals to master trusts and multi-employer-sponsored plans, some of which have in excess of 100 sub-plans, which comprise members with the same or related employer-sponsors. While trustees generally monitor the financial position of sub-plans in relation to defined benefit members on a regular basis, they do not monitor the financial performance of each sub-plan because a significant proportion of the plan's expenses are not capable of being reliably attributed to individual sub-plans. Accordingly, given the likely cost of determining, presenting and understanding this information, it is unlikely the ED 179 segment disclosure proposals would give rise to sufficient benefits in the context of master trusts and multi-employer-sponsored plans.

BC206 Others are keen to avoid duplication of effort, by aligning any segment-type disclosures with prudential reporting requirements.

BC207 Based on responses to ED 179, the AASB:

(a) noted that a significant number of superannuation entities are managed by their trustees on a segmented basis, although segmentation will often not be clear from the way the entity's assets are managed;

(b) decided that disaggregated financial disclosures would provide useful information for users, particularly for hybrid entities because they are exposed to different types and levels of risks; and

(c) decided that there is a need to mitigate the practical issues identified by constituents.

BC208 The AASB noted that requiring superannuation entities to provide disaggregated disclosures on the basis of member groups would facilitate a hybrid superannuation entity providing risk-based disclosures in respect of its liabilities to the different classes of members and it would potentially address some concerns of constituents around investment options and sub-plans being the subject of disaggregated disclosure. However, disaggregated disclosures may, for example, not be useful for showing how a hybrid plan with a small number of defined benefit members arranges and manages activities.

BC209 The AASB also noted that requiring the use of the principles and requirements in AASB 8, as appropriate, might have drawbacks, including:

(a) some of the terms used in AASB 8 may be ambiguous or irrelevant in a superannuation context. For example, a characteristic of an operating segment is that its operating results are regularly reviewed by the entity's chief operating decision maker to make decisions about resource allocations. However, some could interpret this to mean that investment options are not operating segments because members generally decide how the assets of the plan are allocated; and

(b) some entities may provide only limited segment information under the principles and requirements in AASB 8, even when they have both defined contribution and defined benefit members because the operating results regularly reviewed by the trustees do not distinguish between the two groups of members or their related assets.

BC210 Based on these considerations, the AASB decided ED 223 should propose that a superannuation entity provide disaggregated disclosures in accordance with the principles and requirements in AASB 8, except where it is appropriate to modify the requirements for application in a superannuation context. This was intended to provide trustees with more flexibility and enable them to provide disaggregated information that reflects the manner in which they arrange and manage the assets and liabilities of their entity.

BC211 In coming to these proposals, the AASB noted paragraph 19 of AASB 8 comments that there may be a practical limit to the number of reportable segments an entity separately discloses beyond which segment information may become too detailed.

BC212 Respondents to ED 223 raised many of the same concerns with the proposals as were expressed in relation to the ED 179 proposals.

BC213 In redeliberating its approach, the AASB noted that the role of a trustee in a superannuation entity differs from the role of a chief operating decision maker in the context of AASB 8, and the main focus in a superannuation entity context should be on information about different categories of members. Accordingly, the AASB concluded there should be no specific disaggregated information disclosure requirements, but there should be a general requirement to disclose disaggregated information when that would help to explain the risks to which different categories of members are exposed.

Expected rates of return

BC214 The AASB considered whether a superannuation entity should be required to disclose its expected rates of return. The AASB noted other Australian Accounting Standards do not typically require 'forecast-type' information and that requiring disclosure of expected rates of return in the context of member investment choice would arguably not be helpful. Accordingly, the AASB concluded that AASB 1056 should not require expected rates of return disclosure.

Member liabilities

BC215 The nature of a defined contribution member liability differs from the nature of a defined benefit member liability. As these differences are likely to affect a user's understanding of a superannuation entity's member liabilities, the AASB concluded a superannuation entity should disclose information that provides users with a basis for understanding the entity's member liabilities.

BC216   AAS 25 required disclosure of defined benefit members' vested benefits at the end of the period. The AASB considered the merits of continuing to require this information and concluded that it is useful information to users because:

    (a)   items that may be regarded as analogous to vested benefits are reported by other entities. For example, 'demand deposits' are reported by banks; and

    (b)   vested benefits may be regarded as akin to the current portion of defined benefit member liabilities, and AASB 101 includes classification requirements for separate presentation of current and non-current liabilities.

AASB 119 requirements

BC217   The AASB considered whether the disclosures required in AASB 119 about member benefits should be required of superannuation entities. This included considering proposals in AASB ED 195, which incorporated the IASB's ED/2010/3 *Defined Benefit Plans – Proposed amendments to IAS 19* (May 2010) as a part of a project to improve accounting for employee benefits. Consistent with ED 195, ED 179 and ED 223 proposed a superannuation entity disclose the main components of any remeasurement changes in defined benefit liabilities, including benefit cost, interest cost and actuarial gains and losses.

BC218   However, ED 179 and ED 223 did not incorporate some other ED 195 disclosure proposals, including disclosure of defined benefit member liabilities adjusted to exclude the effect of projected growth in salaries ('accumulated benefit obligation'), because it is inconsistent with the presumption employers will meet their defined benefit member liabilities in full.

BC219   The AASB considered whether ED 223 should propose that a superannuation entity disclose information required by AASB 119 (as amended in 2011) and decided those requirements are generally not relevant in a superannuation entity context. This was mainly because AASB 119 has an employer perspective, which differs from the member perspective of superannuation entities.

BC220   Instead, the AASB concluded that more relevant information would result by requiring disclosures that satisfy principles regarding providing users with an understanding of the nature of member benefits and the risks associated with them.

Net assets attributable to defined benefit members

BC221   At any particular time, the amount of net assets attributable to defined benefit members may differ from the amount of such members' accrued benefits. However, the existence of a surplus or deficit does not necessarily mean the superannuation entity will or will not be able to pay these benefits when due. Other factors can influence the capacity to pay defined benefit members, including the expected earnings rate on the net assets attributable to such members and the expected level of future contributions by defined benefit members and/or their employer-sponsors. Nevertheless, knowledge of the relationship between the net assets attributable to defined benefit members and such members' accrued benefits is important for an understanding of a plan's financial position, including its solvency. The AASB concluded that information about the size, nature, causes of, and any strategies for addressing a surplus or deficit should be disclosed.

Remeasurement changes in defined benefit members' accrued benefits

BC222   During its deliberations on the proposals in ED 179, the AASB considered whether separate disclosures of the components of remeasurement changes in defined benefit members' accrued benefits, particularly benefit cost, interest cost and actuarial gains and losses, would be useful information. The AASB noted some users might consider the amount of benefit cost for a period to be useful in providing an indication of the recurring cost to the superannuation entity of providing defined benefit entitlements. The AASB also noted some users might consider the amount of any actuarial gains and losses for a period to be useful information as it provides an indication of how accurately the superannuation plan has estimated the key determinants of defined benefit members' accrued benefits. However, the AASB also noted information about the components of remeasurement changes in defined benefit member liabilities might be regarded as relatively more useful in an employer-sponsor context. Accordingly, the AASB decided ED 179 should ask constituents whether the separate disclosure of the components of remeasurement changes would provide useful information for users in a superannuation context and, if so, how it should be presented.

BC223 The majority of respondents to ED 179 expressed a view that the disclosures should be required. Other respondents:

(a) did not agree with the proposal that defined benefit member liabilities be measured at the amount of such members' accrued benefits; and/or

(b) did not consider such disclosures would be justified on cost-benefit grounds because the number of defined benefit members is declining.

BC224 The AASB included similar proposals in ED 223. A number of respondents to ED 223 noted that, in the general course of measuring defined benefit member liabilities, an actuarial report would not usually provide quantitative information on components of the change from one period to the next and nor would any of the potential shortcut methods of achieving materially the same measure as would be provided by a full actuarial assessment. They also noted that such information might only be relevant in an employer context where the employer is recognising the net difference between the liabilities and the assets supporting the liabilities.

BC225 Based on the responses received on ED 223, and in view of the likely costs involved in determining quantitative information on components of the change from one period to the next, the AASB concluded disclosure of explanations in either quantitative or qualitative terms about changes in defined benefit member liabilities should be required.

Related parties

BC226 The AASB noted that, while the disclosure principles and requirements of AASB 124 *Related Party Disclosures* would apply to most of the related party relationships and transactions that a superannuation entity would be involved in, they may not facilitate consistent disclosures across all superannuation entities.

BC227 At the time the AASB deliberated on the proposals in ED 179, the definition of related party in AASB 124 focused predominantly upon relationships premised on control, joint control or significant influence. Nevertheless, the AASB concluded that trustees and employer-sponsors are, in essence, related parties of superannuation entities because they can affect those entities' financing and operating policies. ED 179 proposed disclosure about the entity's relationships with its trustee(s) and employer-sponsor(s), any transactions with trustees or employer-sponsors during the reporting period, and any outstanding balances with trustees and employer-sponsors at the end of the reporting period, if the nature of these relationships, transactions or balances were not considered 'normal' in a superannuation context.

BC228 Some ED 179 respondents expressed concerns with the proposed manner in which related party disclosures would be dealt with and suggested that:

(a) the proposals do not appear to include the materiality threshold that applies in relation to AASB 124; and

(b) the term 'normal' may be difficult to apply in some circumstances to determine whether a transaction and/or balance between a plan, its trustee or an employer-sponsor should be disclosed.

BC229 AASB 124 was reissued in 2009 and related parties of post-employment benefit plans now explicitly include their sponsoring employer(s).

BC230 The AASB decided ED 223 should propose that a superannuation entity apply, when appropriate, the principles and requirements in AASB 124. The AASB also decided it should propose that a trustee be specifically identified as a related party of its superannuation entity, primarily because trustees have the ability to affect the financing and operating policies. Based on the responses received on ED 223, the AASB concluded that a trustee of a superannuation entity is a related party of the entity for the purpose of applying AASB 124.

BC231 The AASB also noted that an employer of members of a superannuation entity (that the employer does not sponsor) may, in some cases, be a related party of the entity. However, the AASB concluded that this would need to be decided on the basis of the facts in each case and that there is no need to specifically identify employers as related parties.

Insurance contracts

BC232 The AASB included proposed disclosure requirements in ED 179 and ED 223 to complement the proposed recognition and measurement requirements relating to insurance arrangements a superannuation entity provides to its members. Constituents' comments on the ED 179 and ED 223 proposals tended to focus on the recognition and measurement issues, however, the constituents comment on the Draft AASB 1056 for fatal flaw review included feedback on the disclosure issues.

BC233 Based on the feedback received, the AASB concluded that a superannuation entity taking on the role of an insurer in relation to its defined contribution members should separately disclose in their financial statements items such as:

(a)   insurance contract revenue, incurred claims expense, reinsurance expense and reinsurance recoveries recognised in the income statement;

(b)   insurance contract liabilities and reinsurance contract assets recognised in the statement of financial position; and

(c)   insurance contract cash inflows, reinsurance contract cash outflows, claims cash outflows and reinsurance recoveries cash inflows recognised in the statement of cash flows.

BC234 In relation to defined benefit members, the AASB noted that, depending on the conditions set out in the relevant trust deed, those members (or their beneficiaries) might be promised, for example, a lump sum benefit on retirement or resignation, a lump sum benefit on death or disablement, a pension on retirement for their remaining lifetime and/or a pension for the remaining lifetime of a spouse, and the pension may or may not be indexed in some way. The AASB noted that the defined benefit member liability is effectively the sum of the expected values associated with the various ways in which members might be paid their benefits, and can be regarded as a single item made up of inter-related components. Accordingly, the AASB concluded that liabilities and assets arising from insurance arrangements a superannuation entity provides to defined benefit members need not be presented separately from the entity's liabilities for such members' benefits in the statement of financial position. Furthermore, unless there are explicit direct premiums, claims, reinsurance premiums or claim recoveries relating to insurance risks, the AASB concluded that amounts relating to insurance arrangements a superannuation entity provides to defined benefit members need not be presented separately in the income statement, statement of changes in member benefits or statement of cash flows.

Definitions

BC235 AAS 25 defines a number of terms and phrases relevant to a superannuation context. However, some of these terms are no longer consistent with the definitions of the same or equivalent terms in Australian Accounting Standards. In addition, the AASB decided that some of the terms and phrases defined in AAS 25 are no longer necessary.

BC236 Consistent with its current policies, the AASB decided:

(a) there is no need to define terms in AASB 1056 that are defined elsewhere or are similar to terms defined elsewhere in Australian Accounting Standards, such as 'general purpose financial report' and 'reporting date'; and

(b) to include in AASB 1056 definitions of specific relevance in a superannuation entity context, such as 'defined contribution member' and 'defined benefit member' based on the AAS 25 definitions for 'defined contribution plan' or 'defined benefit plan' (which themselves are not included in AASB 1056 because that entity-based dichotomy is no longer relevant).

Other issues raised on definitions

BC237 In ED 179, the AASB proposed that:

(a) the definition of the term 'vested benefits' should be based on the definition of the same term in AASB 119, but amended to reflect the nature of such benefits in a superannuation context; and

(b) the term 'accrued benefits' should be defined broadly to cover both defined contribution and defined benefit arrangements.

BC238 Several respondents to ED 179 raised concerns with the applicability of the definition of vested benefits in the context of defined benefit members. The AASB noted, for a superannuation entity with only defined contribution members, the amount of its member liabilities may not change as a consequence of the timing or circumstances of a member's departure (for example, resignation, retrenchment or retirement). However, depending on the relevant trust deed, different timing or circumstances may give rise to different entitlements for defined benefit members. Accordingly, in ED 223 the AASB proposed the definition of vested benefits be amended to clarify that:

(a) vested benefits are the benefits a member would be entitled to on voluntary withdrawal from their superannuation entity at the end of the period; and

(b) in the context of defined benefit members' vested benefits, the term 'withdrawal' could be interpreted to mean voluntary withdrawal by the member from either the defined benefit section of the entity or from the entity itself.

BC239 One respondent to ED 179 noted the proposed 'defined benefit member' definition did not identify the employer-sponsor's responsibility for investment risk as a distinguishing feature, and is not adequately distinguished from defined contribution members. However, the AASB was not persuaded by this view because investment risk is not a defining characteristic of such arrangements, for example, for employer-sponsors of unfunded defined benefit public sector schemes.

Effective date and transition on initial application

BC240 The AASB noted that, given the extent of the changes, unless comparative information is prepared on the same basis as the current period information in the year of transition, the comparative information would not be useful. Accordingly, the AASB concluded the AASB 1056 requirements should be applied retrospectively in accordance with paragraphs 19 to 27 of AASB 108 *Accounting Policies, Changes in Accounting Estimates and Errors* and, therefore, the comparative information on transition should be prepared on the basis of the AASB 1056 requirements.

BC241 The AASB considered the time that superannuation entities would need to adjust their financial reporting systems in order to transition from applying the requirements of AAS 25 to applying the requirements of AASB 1056. In particular, the AASB noted the changes that might need to be made by superannuation entities with defined

AASB

benefit members liabilities and entities that are so-called 'paragraph 66 plans' (also see paragraph BC34).

BC242 In light of the expected financial reporting impacts on superannuation entities of replacing AAS 25 with AASB 1056 and the need to present comparative information in accordance with AASB 1056, the AASB considered that there should be a period of at least two years between the making of AASB 1056 and its mandatory application date. In particular, the AASB noted that, for superannuation entities that undertake a comprehensive valuation of some or all of their defined benefit member liabilities on a triennial basis, it might be most practicable for there to be at least three year-ends (including the comparative year-end) between the making of AASB 1056 and the year-end relating to the mandatory application date.

BC243 The AASB also noted that paragraph 10(f) of AASB 101 would generally require a statement of financial position to be presented for the beginning of the earliest comparative period, which based on the thinking in paragraph BC242 would mean a mandatory application date of 1 July 2017. The AASB considers this to be an excessively long time to elapse before the mandatory application date and concluded that:

(a) the mandatory application date should be annual reporting periods beginning on or after 1 July 2016; and

(b) superannuation entities should be specifically exempted from presenting a statement of financial position as at the beginning of the earliest comparative period for which information is included in its financial statements when they transition to AASB 1056.

Implications of the review of the governance, structure and operation of Australia's superannuation system

BC244 On 30 June 2010, the report on the *Review of the Governance, Efficiency, Structure and Operation of Australia's Superannuation System* (the Review) was presented to the Federal Minister for Financial Services, Superannuation and Corporate Law. As a part of its terms of reference, the Review considered issues in relation to the fees, costs and investment returns of superannuation entities, and improving transparency around these items through reporting to advisers, researchers, analysts, regulators and members.

BC245 The Review Panel concluded that the Australian superannuation system currently lacks transparency, comparability and accountability in relation to costs, fees and investment returns. It also concluded that, while the proposals in ED 179 would improve financial reporting by superannuation plans, they would not materially improve the information required by individual users, particularly individual members.

BC246 The Review Panel considered the superannuation industry and members are more concerned about the performance of the investment options in which they are invested than the whole-of-fund information required by AAS 25. It also noted a perceived disconnect between the information provided by superannuation entities in GPFSs and the information needs of users, particularly members, which would be unlikely to be rectified under the proposals in ED 179. However, there was an acknowledgement by the Review Panel that a plan member can be affected by factors impacting on their plan as a whole.[24]

BC247 The AASB considered the Panel's findings and noted, even though the GPFSs of superannuation entities are not targeted at each member's particular interest, the

---

24 As noted in the Review Panel's Final Report (page 173) " ... during the GFC, previously liquid assets held by some superannuation funds became illiquid due to capital freezes in mortgage, cash management and property trusts. In order to meet portability, switching and capital drawdown requests, some trustees were forced to sell equities into a depressed market, while trustees who were unable to meet these requests applied to APRA for a variation or suspension of portability requirements."

whole-of-fund financial information is useful to members and other users for their decision making.

BC248 In addition, the AASB concluded financial statements play an important role within the current regulatory arrangements by providing a basis for information reported in trustees' annual reports to members and members' individual benefit statements, even though these would not include the same level of disclosure or necessarily have been audited. Consequently, under the current arrangements financial statements are a key medium through which trustees discharge their accountability responsibilities.

BC249 The Stronger Super reforms implemented from 1 July 2013 are the government response to the Review recommendations and the AASB has monitored those reforms and, where relevant, considered them in developing AASB 1056.

Certain other matters raised by respondents to ED 179 and ED 223 that the AASB decided not to pursue

BC250 Some respondents to ED 179 and ED 223 sought specific guidance in relation to superannuation entities on the following:

    (a) the preparation and presentation of consolidated financial statements under AASB 3 and AASB 10;

    (b) presentation of statements of cash flows and disclosures in relation to non-cash transactions under AASB 107 *Statement of Cash Flows*. In doing so, the AASB noted AASB 107 requires entities to:

        (i) disclose a reconciliation of cash flows arising from operating activities to profit or loss;

        (ii) report cash flows from operating, investing and financing activities on a gross basis; and

        (iii) disclose non-cash investing and financing transactions in a way that provides relevant information about such transactions;

    (c) risk-based disclosures in relation to asset concentrations and sensitivity analyses;

    (d) disclosures in relation to business, non-financial and emerging risks;

    (e) disclosures in relation to information about reserves;

    (f) how a superannuation entity's tax liability for a period might be allocated between the income statement and the statement of changes in member benefits, particularly since the *Income Tax Assessment Act 1997* does not generally distinguish between income tax on investment earnings and tax on contributions The AASB noted that superannuation entities would currently need to distinguish between tax on earnings and tax attributable to contributions in order to determine member benefits and that non-superannuation entities are required to perform similar calculations under other Australian Accounting Standards;

    (g) facilitating separate presentation of realised and unrealised gains and losses. The AASB noted that superannuation entities would not be prevented from presenting or disclosing such additional information if it provides useful information to users of its financial statements;

    (h) presentation of 'netted off' revenue and expense items, particularly in relation to entities conducting their investment arrangements through investment managers and/or custodians;

    (i) circumstances in which contributions in respect of defined contribution members should be recognised on an accrual basis or a cash basis; and

(j)   circumstances in which benefits payable would be disclosed as a current liability. The AASB noted that AASB 101 has relevant criteria for distinguishing between current and non-current liabilities.

BC251   The AASB concluded that the issues underlying some of those concerns:

(a)   are outside the scope of general purpose financial reporting;

(b)   are dealt with in other Australian Accounting Standards; and/or

(c)   arise under other Australian Accounting Standards and are dealt with by non-superannuation entities without additional guidance.

The AASB also noted that providing superannuation-specific guidance on the application of the principles and requirements in other Australian Accounting Standards would run the risk of interpreting IFRS principles and requirements in a way that is not consistent with the way they are interpreted in other contexts.

BC252   Some respondents raised issues about better identifying the 'reporting entity' in a superannuation industry context. They noted that, in the private sector, Registrable Superannuation Entities (RSE) would typically be the entities that apply AAS 25 and would apply AASB 1056, but that this may not be the appropriate entity level at which general purpose financial reporting should take place. At this stage, the AASB concluded that this topic would need to be the subject of future research (refer to paragraph BC2).

AASB 1057

Application of Australian Accounting Standards

(Compiled November 2015)

This compiled Standard applies to annual periods beginning on or after 1 January 2016. Earlier application is permitted for annual periods beginning before 1 January 2016. It incorporates relevant amendments made up to and including 11 November 2015.

Prepared on 7 December 2015 by the staff of the Australian Accounting Standards Board.

This note is not part of Accounting Standard AASB 1057.

The following unincorporated amendments are not included in this compiled Standard.

- AASB 17 *Insurance Contracts* — Appendix D sets out the amendments to other Standards that are a consequence of the AASB issuing AASB 17 *Insurance Contracts*. This Standard is applicable from 1 January 2021. Earlier application is permitted, but entities must apply AASB 9 *Financial Instruments* and AASB 15 *Revenue from Contracts with Customers* first.

- AASB 1058 *Income of Not-for-Profit Entities* — Appendix D sets out the amendments to other Australian Accounting Standards that are a consequence of the AASB issuing this Standard. It is applicable from 1 January 2019. Earlier application is permitted, but amendments to AASB 117 apply before 1 January 2019 only if AASB 1058 is also applied to an earlier period. In addition, AASB 1 and AASB 16 amendments are applied to an earlier period only if AASB 16 is also applied to that period.

Entities early-adopting any amendments with later application dates will need to refer to the amending Standards that have not yet been incorporated into compilations. The abovementioned unincorporated amendments may be located on the AASB website at www.aasb.gov.au or on the Federal Register of Legislation website at www.legislation.gov.au.

CONTENTS

ACCOUNTING STANDARD
AASB 1057 *APPLICATION OF AUSTRALIAN ACCOUNTING STANDARDS*

Australian Accounting Standard AASB 1057 *Application of Australian Accounting Standards* (as amended) is set out in paragraphs 1 – 27 and the Appendix. All the paragraphs have equal authority. Paragraphs in **bold type** state the main principles. Terms defined in the Appendix are in *italics* the first time they appear in the Standard. AASB 1057 is to be read in the context of other Australian Accounting Standards, including AASB 1048 *Interpretation of Standards*, which identifies the Australian Accounting Interpretations. In the absence of explicit guidance, AASB 108 *Accounting Policies, Changes in Accounting Estimates and Errors* provides a basis for selecting and applying accounting policies.

ACCOUNTING STANDARD AASB 1057

The Australian Accounting Standards Board made Accounting Standard AASB 1057 *Application of Australian Accounting Standards* under section 334 of the *Corporations Act 2001* on 24 July 2015.

This compiled version of AASB 1057 applies to annual periods beginning on or after 1 January 2016. It incorporates relevant amendments contained in other AASB Standards made by the AASB up to and including 11 November 2015 (see Compilation Details).

ACCOUNTING STANDARD AASB 1057
APPLICATION OF AUSTRALIAN ACCOUNTING STANDARDS

Objective

1   The objective of this Standard is to specify the types of entities and financial statements to which Australian Accounting Standards (including Interpretations) apply. Each reference to an Interpretation refers to that Interpretation as identified in AASB 1048 *Interpretation of Standards*.

Application of this Standard

2   This Standard applies to:

(a)   **each entity that is required to prepare financial reports in accordance with Part 2M.3 of the Corporations Act;**

(b)   *general purpose financial statements* of each *reporting entity*;

(c)   **financial statements that are, or are held out to be, general purpose financial statements; and**

(d)   **financial statements of General Government Sectors (GGSs) prepared in accordance with AASB 1049** *Whole of Government and General Government Sector Financial Reporting***.**

3   This Standard applies to annual periods beginning on or after 1 January 2016.

4   This Standard may be applied to annual periods beginning before 1 January 2016.

Application of Australian Accounting Standards

5   **Unless specified otherwise in paragraphs 6–21, Australian Accounting Standards apply to:**

(a)   **each entity that is required to prepare financial reports in accordance with Part 2M.3 of the Corporations Act and that is a reporting entity;**

(b)   **general purpose financial statements of each other reporting entity; and**

(c)   **financial statements that are, or are held out to be, general purpose financial statements.**

6   AASB 8 *Operating Segments* applies to:

    (a)   each for-profit entity that is required to prepare financial reports in accordance with Part 2M.3 of the Corporations Act and that is a reporting entity;

    (b)   general purpose financial statements of each other for-profit reporting entity other than for-profit government departments; and

    (c)   financial statements of a for-profit entity other than for-profit government departments that are, or are held out to be, general purpose financial statements.

7   AASB 101 *Presentation of Financial Statements*, AASB 107 *Statement of Cash Flows*, AASB 108 *Accounting Policies, Changes in Accounting Estimates and Errors*, AASB 1048 *Interpretation of Standards* and AASB 1054 *Australian Additional Disclosures* apply to:

    (a)   each entity that is required to prepare financial reports in accordance with Part 2M.3 of the Corporations Act;

    (b)   general purpose financial statements of each reporting entity; and

    (c)   financial statements that are, or are held out to be, general purpose financial statements.

8   AASB 120 *Accounting for Government Grants and Disclosure of Government Assistance* applies to:

    (a)   each for-profit entity that is required to prepare financial reports in accordance with Part 2M.3 of the Corporations Act and that is a reporting entity;

    (b)   general purpose financial statements of each other for-profit reporting entity; and

    (c)   financial statements of a for-profit entity that are, or are held out to be, general purpose financial statements.

9   AASB 133 *Earnings per Share* applies to each entity that is required to prepare financial reports in accordance with Part 2M.3 of the Corporations Act and that is a reporting entity or discloses earnings per share.

10   AASB 134 *Interim Financial Reporting* applies to:

    (a)   each disclosing entity required to prepare half-year financial reports in accordance with Part 2M.3 of the Corporations Act;

    (b)   interim financial reports that are general purpose financial statements of each other reporting entity; and

    (c)   interim financial reports that are, or are held out to be, general purpose financial statements.

11   AASB 1004 *Contributions* applies to:

    (a)   each not-for-profit entity that is required to prepare financial reports in accordance with Part 2M.3 of the Corporations Act and that is a reporting entity;

    (b)   general purpose financial statements of each other not-for-profit entity that is a reporting entity;

    (c)   financial statements of not-for-profit entities that are, or are held out to be, general purpose financial statements; and

    (d)   financial statements of GGSs prepared in accordance with AASB 1049.

AASB

12   AASB 1038 *Life Insurance Contracts* applies to:

(a)   a life insurer; or

(b)   the parent in a group that includes a life insurer;

when the entity:

(c)   is a reporting entity that is required to prepare financial reports in accordance with Part 2M.3 of the Corporations Act;

(d)   is an other reporting entity and prepares general purpose financial statements; or

(e)   prepares financial statements that are, or are held out to be, general purpose financial statements.

13   AASB 1039 *Concise Financial Reports* applies to a concise financial report prepared by an entity in accordance with paragraph 314(2)(a) in Part 2M.3 of the Corporations Act.

14   AASB 1049 applies to each government's whole of government general purpose financial statements and GGS financial statements.

15   AASB 1050 *Administered Items* applies to general purpose financial statements of government departments.

16   AASB 1051 *Land Under Roads* applies to general purpose financial statements of local governments, government departments and whole of governments, and financial statements of GGSs.

17   AASB 1052 *Disaggregated Disclosures* applies to general purpose financial statements of local governments and government departments.

18   AASB 1053 *Application of Tiers of Australian Accounting Standards* applies to:

(a)   each entity that is required to prepare financial reports in accordance with Part 2M.3 of the Corporations Act;

(b)   general purpose financial statements of each reporting entity;

(c)   financial statements that are, or are held out to be, general purpose financial statements; and

(d)   financial statements of GGSs prepared in accordance with AASB 1049.

19   AASB 1055 *Budgetary Reporting* applies to:

(a)   whole of government general purpose financial statements of each government;

(b)   financial statements of each government's GGS;

(c)   general purpose financial statements of each not-for-profit reporting entity within the GGS; and

(d)   financial statements of each not-for-profit entity within the GGS that are, or are held out to be, general purpose financial statements.

20   AASB 1056 *Superannuation Entities* applies to:

(a)   general purpose financial statements of each superannuation entity that is a reporting entity; and

(b)   financial statements of a superannuation entity that are held out to be general purpose financial statements.

21   AAS 25 *Financial Reporting by Superannuation Plans* applies to general purpose financial reports of each superannuation plan in the private or public sector that is a reporting entity.

Application of Australian Interpretations

22   Unless specified otherwise in paragraphs 23–26, Interpretations apply to:

(a)   each entity that is required to prepare financial reports in accordance with Part 2M.3 of the Corporations Act and that is a reporting entity;

(b)   general purpose financial statements of each other reporting entity; and

(c)   financial statements that are, or are held out to be, general purpose financial statements.

23   Interpretation 110 *Government Assistance – No Specific Relation to Operating Activities* applies to:

(a)   each for-profit entity that is required to prepare financial reports in accordance with Part 2M.3 of the Corporations Act and that is a reporting entity;

(b)   general purpose financial statements of each other for-profit reporting entity; and

(c)   financial statements of a for-profit entity that are, or are held out to be, general purpose financial statements.

24   Interpretation 1019 *The Superannuation Contributions Surcharge* applies to:

(a)   each superannuation plan that is required to prepare financial reports in accordance with Part 2M.3 of the Corporations Act and that is a reporting entity;

(b)   general purpose financial statements of each other superannuation plan that is a reporting entity; and

(c)   financial statements of a superannuation plan that are, or are held out to be, general purpose financial statements.

25   Interpretation 1038 *Contributions by Owners Made to Wholly-Owned Public Sector Entities* applies to public sector entities as follows:

(a)   each entity that is required to prepare financial reports in accordance with Part 2M.3 of the Corporations Act and that is a reporting entity;

(b)   general purpose financial statements of each other reporting entity; and

(c)   financial statements that are, or are held out to be, general purpose financial statements.

26   Interpretation 1047 *Professional Indemnity Claims Liabilities in Medical Defence Organisations* applies to entities that are or include medical defence organisations as follows:

(a)   each entity that is required to prepare financial reports in accordance with Part 2M.3 of the Corporations Act and that is a reporting entity;

(b)   general purpose financial statements of each other reporting entity; and

(c)   financial statements that are, or are held out to be, general purpose financial statements.

Commencement of the legislative instrument

27   For legal purposes, this legislative instrument commences on 31 December 2015.

APPENDIX
DEFINED TERMS

This appendix is an integral part of AASB 1057.

general purpose financial statements	Financial statements that are intended to meet the needs of users who are not in a position to require an entity to prepare reports tailored to their particular information needs.
reporting entity	An entity in respect of which it is reasonable to expect the existence of users who rely on the entity's general purpose financial statements for information that will be useful to them for making and evaluating decisions about the allocation of resources. A reporting entity can be a single entity or a group comprising a parent and all of its subsidiaries.

COMPILATION DETAILS

Accounting Standard AASB 1057 *Application of Australian Accounting Standards* as amended

Compilation details are not part of AASB 1057.

This compiled Standard applies to annual periods beginning on or after 1 January 2016. It takes into account amendments up to and including 11 November 2015 and was prepared on 7 December 2015 by the staff of the Australian Accounting Standards Board (AASB).

This compilation is not a separate Accounting Standard made by the AASB. Instead, it is a representation of AASB 1057 (July 2015) as amended by other Accounting Standards, which are listed in the Table below.

Table of Standards

Standard	Date made	FRLI identifier	Commence-ment date	Application date (*annual periods ... on or after ...*)	Application, saving or transitional provisions
AASB 1057	24 Jul 2015	F2015L01620	31 Dec 2015	(*beginning*) 1 Jan 2016	see (a) below
AASB 2015-9	11 Nov 2015	F2015L01832	31 Dec 2015	(*beginning*) 1 Jan 2016	see (a) below

(a)   Entities may elect to apply this Standard to annual periods beginning before 1 January 2016.

Table of amendments

Paragraph affected	How affected	By ... [paragraph]
6	amended	AASB 2015-9 [11]
9	amended	AASB 2015-9 [11]

BASIS FOR CONCLUSIONS

This Basis for Conclusions accompanies, but is not part of, AASB 1057.

BC1   This Basis for Conclusions summarises the Australian Accounting Standards Board's considerations in reaching the conclusions in AASB 1057 *Application of Australian Accounting Standards*. Individual Board members gave greater weight to some factors than to others.

BC2   In 2005 when Australia transitioned to adopting International Financial Reporting Standards (IFRSs), Australian Accounting Standards (including Interpretations) were issued using IFRSs as a base. Australian-specific paragraphs (labelled as 'Aus' paragraphs), including application paragraphs, were added to the IFRS text. These application paragraphs identified, in each Standard, the entities and financial reports to which the Standard applied. For example, most Standards apply explicitly to reporting entities and to general purpose financial statements. Other minor amendments were also made to the IFRS text (eg Australian terminology and punctuation).

BC3   At its May 2015 meeting, the Board decided to revise Australian Accounting Standards that incorporate IFRSs to minimise Australian-specific wording even further. Therefore, because IFRSs do not contain such application paragraphs, the application paragraphs that were previously in each Australian Accounting Standard were moved to this Standard. In doing so, the application requirements have not been amended. These application paragraphs also do not affect requirements in other Standards that specify that certain paragraphs apply only to certain types of entities.

BC4   For consistency, the application paragraphs of Australian-specific Standards have also been included in this Standard, without amendment. When those Standards are amended for other reasons, their application paragraphs are expected to be removed.

AASB 1058
Income of Not-for-Profit Entities
(Issued December 2016)

This note is not part of Accounting Standard AASB 1058.

The following unincorporated amendments are not included in this Standard.

- AASB 2018-3 *Amendments to Australian Accounting Standards — Reduced Disclosure Requirements*. This Standard makes amendments to AASB 16 *Leases* and AASB 1058 *Income of Not-for-Profit Entities*. These amendments establish Reduced Disclosure Requirements for entities preparing general purpose financial statements under *Australian Accounting Standards — Reduced Disclosure Requirements*. It applies to annual periods beginning on or after 1 January 2019, but earlier application is permitted.

- AASB 17 *Insurance Contracts* — Appendix D sets out the amendments to other Standards that are a consequence of the AASB issuing AASB 17 *Insurance Contracts*. This Standard is applicable from 1 January 2021. Earlier application is permitted, but entities must apply AASB 9 *Financial Instruments* and AASB 15 *Revenue from Contracts with Customers* first.

Entities early-adopting any amendments with later application dates will need to refer to the amending Standards that have not yet been incorporated into compilations. The abovementioned unincorporated amendments may be located on the AASB website at www.aasb.gov.au or on the Federal Register of Legislation website at www.legislation.gov.au.

CONTENTS

PREFACE

ACCOUNTING STANDARD

AASB 1058 *INCOME OF NOT-FOR-PROFIT ENTITIES*

APPENDICES

A. DEFINED TERMS

B. APPLICATION GUIDANCE

C. EFFECTIVE DATE AND TRANSITION

D. AMENDMENTS TO OTHER STANDARDS

ILLUSTRATIVE EXAMPLES

BASIS FOR CONCLUSIONS

> Australian Accounting Standard AASB 1058 *Income of Not-for-Profit Entities* is set out in paragraphs 1 –
> 42 and Appendices A – D. All the paragraphs have equal authority. Paragraphs in **bold type** state the main
> principles. Terms defined in Appendix A are in *italics* the first time they appear in the Standard. AASB 1058
> is to be read in the context of other Australian Accounting Standards, including AASB 1048 *Interpretation
> of Standards*, which identifies the Australian Accounting Interpretations, and AASB 1057 *Application of
> Australian Accounting Standards*. In the absence of explicit guidance, AASB 108 *Accounting Policies,
> Changes in Accounting Estimates and Errors* provides a basis for selecting and applying accounting policies.

PREFACE

Introduction

The Australian Accounting Standards Board (AASB) develops, issues and maintains
Australian Accounting Standards, including Interpretations. The AASB is a Commonwealth
entity under the *Australian Securities and Investments Commission Act 2001*.

AASB 1057 *Application of Australian Accounting Standards* identifies the application of
Standards to entities and financial statements. AASB 1053 *Application of Tiers of Australian
Accounting Standards* establishes a differential reporting framework consisting of two tiers
of reporting requirements for preparing general purpose financial statements.

What this Standard requires

This Standard clarifies and simplifies the income recognition requirements that apply to
not-for-profit (NFP) entities, in conjunction with AASB 15 *Revenue from Contracts with
Customers*. These Standards supersede all the income recognition requirements relating to
private sector NFP entities, and the majority of income recognition requirements relating to
public sector NFP entities, previously in AASB 1004 *Contributions*. The requirements of
this Standard more closely reflect the economic reality of NFP entity transactions that are
not contracts with customers. The timing of income recognition depends on whether such a
transaction gives rise to a liability or other performance obligation (a promise to transfer a
good or service), or a contribution by owners, related to an asset (such as cash or another
asset) received by an entity.

This Standard applies when a NFP entity receives volunteer services or enters into other
transactions where the consideration to acquire an asset is significantly less than the fair value
of the asset principally to enable the entity to further its objectives. In the latter case, the entity
recognises and measures the asset at fair value in accordance with the applicable Australian
Accounting Standard (eg AASB 116 *Property, Plant and Equipment*).

Upon initial recognition of the asset, this Standard requires the entity to consider whether any
other financial statement elements (called 'related amounts') should be recognised, such as:

(a)   contributions by owners;

(b)   revenue, or a contract liability arising from a contract with a customer;

(c)   a lease liability;

(d)   a financial instrument; or

(e)   a provision.

These related amounts are accounted for in accordance with the applicable Australian Accounting Standard.

If the transaction is a transfer of a financial asset to enable an entity to acquire or construct a recognisable non-financial asset to be controlled by the entity (ie an in-substance acquisition of a non-financial asset), the entity recognises a liability for the excess of the fair value of the transfer over any related amounts recognised. The entity recognises income as it satisfies its obligations under the transfer similarly to income recognition in relation to performance obligations under AASB 15.

If the transaction does not enable an entity to acquire or construct a recognisable non-financial asset to be controlled by the entity, then any excess of the initial carrying amount of the recognised asset over the related amounts is recognised as income.

When an entity receives volunteer services and can reliably measure the fair value of those services, the entity may elect to recognise the services as an asset (provided the relevant asset recognition criteria are met) or an expense. Local governments, government departments, general government sectors (GGSs) and whole of governments are required to recognise volunteer services if they would have been purchased if not provided voluntarily and the fair value of those services can be measured reliably.

Application date

This Standard applies to annual reporting periods beginning on or after 1 January 2019. Earlier application is permitted, provided entities also apply AASB 15 *Revenue from Contracts with Customers* to the same period.

ACCOUNTING STANDARD AASB 1058

The Australian Accounting Standards Board makes Accounting Standard AASB 1058 *Income of Not-for-Profit Entities* under section 334 of the *Corporations Act 2001*.

Kris Peach

Dated 9 December 2016   Chair – AASB

ACCOUNTING STANDARD AASB 1058
INCOME OF NOT-FOR-PROFIT ENTITIES

Objective

1   **This Standard establishes principles for not-for-profit entities that apply to:**

    (a)   transactions where the consideration to acquire an asset is significantly less than fair value principally to enable a not-for-profit entity to further its objectives; and

    (b)   the receipt of volunteer services.

2   If the consideration provided to acquire an asset, including cash, is significantly less than the fair value of that asset, or if no consideration was provided, and the difference is principally to enable the entity to further its objectives, such a transaction is within the scope of this Standard. For example, an entity that receives a cash grant to be used to further its objectives might not have provided any consideration in exchange for that cash. As another example, governments are entitled to non-contractual receivables arising from statutory requirements such as *taxes* and rates without providing consideration to the other party – those receivables provide income to the government to further its objectives. This Standard addresses the accounting for the income arising from such transactions.

Meeting the objective

3   To meet the objective in paragraph 1(a), an entity shall initially recognise:

(a)   an asset in accordance with the applicable Australian Accounting Standard;

(b)   any related *contributions by owners*, contract liabilities, financial liabilities, lease liabilities and other liabilities and revenue, measured in accordance with the applicable Australian Accounting Standard;

(c)   any liabilities for obligations arising from transfers to enable the entity to acquire or construct non-financial assets to be controlled by the entity; and

(d)   related income, representing the residual amount of resources received.

4   To meet the objective in paragraph 1(b), certain types of public sector entities shall recognise assets or expenses for volunteer services received if the fair value of those services can be measured reliably and the entity would have purchased those services if they had not been donated. Any not-for-profit entity may elect to recognise volunteer services received if their fair value can be measured reliably irrespective of whether that entity would have purchased those services if not donated.

5   AASB 15 *Revenue from Contracts with Customers* defines income as increases in economic benefits during the accounting period in the form of inflows or enhancements of assets or decreases of liabilities that result in increases in equity, other than those relating to contributions by equity participants (that is, owners). This Standard addresses income arising from the acquisition of assets for consideration that is significantly less than the fair value of the asset when that difference is principally to enable the not-for-profit entity to further its objectives. This Standard applies to those differences that result in increases in equity, other than those relating to contributions by owners or those accounted for under another Standard (eg AASB 15). Other Australian Accounting Standards (eg AASB 1004 *Contributions*) address income arising from decreases of liabilities and the accounting for contributions by owners.

6   An entity shall apply the requirements of this Standard to each transaction based on the substance of the transaction, rather than its legal form or the description given to it (eg grants or donations), so as to provide a faithful representation of the economic substance of the transaction.

Scope (paragraphs B2–B11)

7   An entity shall apply this Standard to transactions where the consideration to acquire an asset is significantly less than fair value principally to enable the entity to further its objectives, and the receipt of volunteer services, except for:

(a)   share-based payment transactions within the scope of AASB 2 *Share-based Payment*;

(b)   business combinations within the scope of AASB 3 *Business Combinations*;

(c)   insurance contracts within the scope of AASB 4 *Insurance Contracts*, AASB 1023 *General Insurance Contracts* or AASB 1038 *Life Insurance Contracts*;

(d)   licences outside the scope of AASB 15;

(e)   income taxes within the scope of AASB 112 *Income Taxes*; and

(f)   restructures of administrative arrangements within the scope of AASB 1004.

Recognition and measurement

Recognition and measurement of an asset

8   Except as set out in paragraphs 18–22, an entity shall apply the requirements of other Australian Accounting Standards (as relevant) to an asset arising from a transaction within the scope of this Standard. Examples include:

    (a)   AASB 9 *Financial Instruments* (eg cash received);

    (b)   AASB 16 *Leases*;

    (c)   AASB 116 *Property, Plant and Equipment*; and

    (d)   AASB 138 *Intangible Assets*.

Recognition and measurement of income and related amounts (paragraphs B12–B31)

9   On initial recognition of an asset, an entity shall recognise any related contributions by owners, increases in liabilities, decreases in assets, and revenue ('related amounts') in accordance with other Australian Accounting Standards. For example, related amounts may take the form of:

    (a)   *contributions by owners*, in accordance with AASB 1004;

    (b)   revenue or a contract liability arising from a contract with a customer, in accordance with AASB 15;

    (c)   a lease liability in accordance with AASB 16;

    (d)   a financial instrument, in accordance with AASB 9; or

    (e)   a provision, in accordance with AASB 137 *Provisions, Contingent Liabilities and Contingent Assets*.

10   Except as set out in paragraphs 15–17, an entity shall recognise income immediately in profit or loss for the excess of the initial carrying amount of an asset over the related amounts recognised in accordance with paragraph 9.

11   Appendix F *Australian Implementation Guidance for Not-for-Profit Entities* of AASB 15 provides guidance on the identification of a contract with a customer in a not-for-profit entity context. The Appendix also clarifies the measurement of revenue and contract liabilities where the transaction price includes an amount that would otherwise be separately recognised and accounted for as income immediately in accordance with this Standard.

12   For the purposes of this Standard, income is determined as the difference between the consideration for an asset and the asset's fair value, after recognising any other related amounts. An entity applies judgement in determining the extent to which the acquisition of an asset gives rise to income as specified by this Standard or to revenue, a liability or a contribution by owners recognised in accordance with another Australian Accounting Standard.

13   An entity might acquire an asset and also recognise related amounts that in total exceed the initial measurement of the asset. In such cases, the entity shall reassess whether it has appropriately identified and measured all the related amounts. If an excess remains after restating any related amounts, the entity shall recognise an expense immediately in profit or loss for the excess of the related amounts over the carrying amount of the asset acquired. An entity does not adjust the excess against the recognised related amounts.

14   An entity shall subsequently apply the requirements of other Australian Accounting Standards applicable to the related amounts referred to in paragraph 9.

Transfers to enable an entity to acquire or construct a recognisable non-financial asset to be controlled by the entity

15   A transfer of a financial asset to enable an entity to acquire or construct a recognisable non-financial asset that is to be controlled by the entity is one that:

    (a)   requires the entity to use that financial asset to acquire or construct a recognisable non-financial asset to identified specifications;

    (b)   does not require the entity to transfer the non-financial asset to the transferor or other parties; and

    (c)   occurs under an enforceable agreement.

16   An entity shall recognise a liability for the excess of the initial carrying amount of a financial asset received in a transfer to enable the entity to acquire or construct a recognisable non-financial asset that is to be controlled by the entity over any related amounts recognised in accordance with paragraph 9. The entity shall recognise income in profit or loss when (or as) the entity satisfies its obligations under the transfer.

17   In such circumstances, the transferor has in substance transferred a recognisable non-financial asset to the entity. The entity recognises the financial asset received in accordance with AASB 9 and subsequently recognises the acquired or constructed non-financial asset in accordance with the applicable Australian Accounting Standard (eg AASB 116 for property, plant and equipment). This Standard requires the entity to initially recognise a liability representing the entity's obligation to acquire or construct the non-financial asset and, if applicable, other performance obligations under AASB 15, which involve the transfer of goods or services to other parties. The liability in relation to acquiring or constructing the non-financial asset is initially measured at the carrying amount of the financial asset received from the transferor that is not attributable to related amounts for performance obligations under AASB 15, contributions by owners, etc. The liability is recognised until such time when (or as) the entity satisfies its obligations under the transfer.

Volunteer services

18   Local governments, government departments, general government sectors (GGSs) and whole of governments shall recognise an inflow of resources in the form of volunteer services as an asset (or an expense, when the definition of an asset is not met) if:

(a)   the fair value of those services can be measured reliably; and

(b)   the services would have been purchased if they had not been donated.

19   Any not-for-profit entity (including those listed in the preceding paragraph) may, as an accounting policy choice, elect to recognise volunteer services, or a class of volunteer services, if the fair value of those services can be measured reliably, whether or not the services would have been purchased if they had not been donated.

20   Some volunteer services, such as professional services, might have readily observable market prices. In such circumstances, obtaining a reliable measure of fair value would be relatively straightforward. An entity is not required to perform an exhaustive search for volunteer services that might meet the recognition criteria in this Standard. Volunteer services that would have been purchased if they were not donated should be readily identifiable from the entity's operational requirements.

21   Recognised volunteer services shall be measured at fair value.

22   On the initial recognition of volunteer services as an asset or an expense, an entity shall recognise any related amounts in accordance with paragraph 9 (such as contributions by owners or revenue) and the applicable Australian Accounting Standards. The entity shall recognise the excess of the fair value of the volunteer services over the recognised related amounts as income immediately in profit or loss.

Disclosure

23   The objective of the disclosure requirements is for an entity to disclose sufficient information to enable users of financial statements to understand the effects of volunteer services and other transactions where an entity acquires an asset for consideration that is significantly less than fair value principally to enable the entity to further its objectives on the financial position, financial performance and cash flows of the entity. Paragraphs 24–41 specify requirements relating to this objective.

24   An entity shall consider the level of detail necessary to satisfy the disclosure objective and how much emphasis to place on each of the various requirements. An entity shall aggregate or disaggregate disclosures so that useful information is not obscured by either the inclusion of a large amount of insignificant detail or the aggregation of items that have substantially different characteristics.

25   An entity need not disclose information in accordance with this Standard if it has provided the information in accordance with another Standard.

26   An entity shall disclose income recognised during the period, disaggregated into categories that reflect how the nature and amount of income (and the resultant cash flows) are affected by economic factors. An entity considers disclosing separately the following categories of income:

    (a)   grants, bequests and donations of cash, other financial assets and goods;

    (b)   recognised volunteer services; and

    (c)   for government departments and other public sector entities, appropriation amounts recognised as income, by class of appropriation.

27   To assist users to make informed judgements about the contribution of volunteer services and inventories to the achievement of the entity's objectives during the reporting period, and the entity's dependence on such contributions for the achievement of its objectives in the future, an entity is encouraged to disclose qualitative information, by major class of transaction, about the nature of the entity's dependence arising from:

    (a)   volunteer services it receives, including those not recognised; and

    (b)   inventories held but not recognised as assets during the period.

Non-contractual income arising from statutory requirements

28   An entity shall disclose income arising from statutory requirements (such as taxes, rates and *fines*) recognised during the period, disaggregated into categories that reflect how the nature and amount of income (and the resultant cash flows) are affected by economic factors.

29   To meet the objective in paragraph 23, an entity shall consider disclosing information about assets and liabilities recognised at the reporting date in accordance with this Standard, including the amounts of:

    (a)   receivables that are not a financial asset as defined in AASB 132 *Financial Instruments: Presentation* (eg income tax receivable from a taxpayer), and:

        (i)   interest income recognised in relation to such receivables during the period; and

        (ii)   impairment losses recognised in relation to such receivables during the period; and

    (b)   financial liabilities relating to prepaid taxes or rates for which the *taxable event* has yet to occur, and the future period(s) to which those taxes or rates relate.

30   Other information that may be appropriate for an entity to disclose includes, for each class of taxation income that the entity cannot measure reliably during the period in which the taxable event occurs (see paragraphs B28–B31):

    (a)   information about the nature of the tax;

    (b)   the reason(s) why that income cannot be measured reliably; and

    (c)   when that uncertainty might be resolved.

Transfers to enable an entity to acquire or construct a recognisable non-financial asset to be controlled by the entity

31   An entity shall disclose the opening and closing balances of financial assets arising from transfers to enable an entity to acquire or construct recognisable non-financial

assets to be controlled by the entity and the associated liabilities arising from such transfers, if not otherwise separately presented or disclosed. An entity shall also disclose income recognised in the reporting period arising from the reduction of an associated liability.

32 An entity shall disclose information about its obligations under such transfers, including a description of when the entity typically satisfies its obligations (for example, as the asset is constructed, upon completion of construction or when the asset is acquired).

33 An entity shall disclose an explanation of when it expects to recognise as income any liability for unsatisfied obligations as at the end of the reporting period. An entity may disclose this information in either of the following ways:

(a) on a quantitative basis using the time bands that would be most appropriate for the duration of the remaining obligations; or

(b) through qualitative information.

34 An entity shall disclose the judgements, and changes in the judgements, made in applying this Standard that significantly affect the determination of the amount and timing of income arising from transfers to enable an entity to acquire or construct a recognisable non-financial asset to be controlled by the entity. In particular, an entity shall explain the judgements, and changes in the judgements, made in determining the timing of satisfaction of obligations (see paragraphs 35 and 36).

35 For obligations that an entity satisfies over time, an entity shall disclose both of the following:

(a) the methods used to recognise income (for example, a description of the output methods or input methods used and how those methods are applied); and

(b) an explanation of why the methods used provide a faithful depiction of the entity's progress toward satisfying its obligations.

36 For obligations satisfied at a point in time, an entity shall disclose the significant judgements made in evaluating when it has satisfied its obligations.

Restrictions

37 An entity is encouraged to disclose information about externally imposed restrictions that limit or direct the purpose for which resources controlled by the entity may be used. For example, an entity may elect to disclose an explanation of the judgements used in determining whether funds are restricted and any of, or any combination of, the following:

(a) assets to be used for specified purposes;

(b) components of equity divided into restricted and unrestricted amounts; and

(c) total comprehensive income divided into restricted and unrestricted amounts – either on the face of the statement of profit or loss and other comprehensive income or in the notes.

Compliance with parliamentary appropriations and other related authorities for expenditure

38 **Paragraphs 39–41 apply only to government departments and other public sector entities that obtain part or all of their spending authority for the period from a parliamentary appropriation. The amounts disclosed in accordance with paragraphs 39–41 include any amounts appropriated in respect of which the entity recognises revenue or other income in accordance with another Australian Accounting Standard.**

39 **An entity shall disclose:**

(a) **a summary of the recurrent, capital or other major categories of amounts authorised for expenditure (including parliamentary appropriations), disclosing separately:**

      (i)   the original amounts appropriated; and

      (ii)   the total of any supplementary amounts appropriated and amounts authorised other than by way of appropriation (eg by the Treasurer, other Minister or other legislative authority);

  (b)   the expenditures in respect of each of the items disclosed in (a) above; and

  (c)   the reasons for any material variances between the amounts appropriated or otherwise authorised and the resulting associated expenditures, and any financial consequences for the entity of unauthorised expenditure.

40   For the purposes of resource allocation decisions, including assessments of accountability, this Standard requires that users of financial statements of government departments and other public sector entities that obtain part or all of their spending authority for the period from a parliamentary appropriation be provided with information about the amounts appropriated or otherwise authorised for the entity's use, and whether the entity's expenditures were as authorised. This information may be based on acquittal processes applied by an entity. When spending limits imposed by parliamentary appropriation or other authorisation have not been complied with, information regarding the amount of, and reasons for, the non-compliance is relevant for assessing the performance of management, the likely consequences of non-compliance, and the ability of the entity to continue to provide services at a similar or different level in the future.

41   Broad summaries of the major categories of appropriations and associated expenditures, rather than detailed reporting of appropriations for each activity or output, is sufficient for most users of such an entity's financial statements. Determining the level of detail and the structure of the summarised information is a matter of judgement. To develop effective disclosures, entities also subject to AASB 1055 *Budgetary Reporting* might consider the variance disclosure requirements in that Standard at the same time.

Commencement of the legislative instrument

42   For legal purposes, this legislative instrument commences on 31 December 2018.

APPENDIX A
DEFINED TERMS

This appendix is an integral part of the Standard.

contributions by owners	Future economic benefits that have been contributed to the entity by parties external to the entity, other than those which result in liabilities of the entity, that give rise to a financial interest in the net assets of the entity which:
	(a) conveys entitlement both to distributions of future economic benefits by the entity during its life, such distributions being at the discretion of the ownership group or its representatives, and to distributions of any excess of assets over liabilities in the event of the entity being wound up; and/or
	(b) can be sold, transferred or redeemed.
fines	Economic benefits received or receivable by an entity, as determined by a court or other law enforcement body, as a consequence of a breach of a law or regulation.
payable tax credits	Tax credits that are not limited to the amount of a taxpayer's tax liability for the period, because they are available to beneficiaries regardless of whether they pay taxes.
tax relief	Preferential provisions of the tax law that provide particular taxpayers with concessions that are not available to others. Tax relief excludes **payable tax credits**.

taxable event	The event that the government, legislature or other authority has determined will be subject to taxation.
taxes	Economic benefits compulsorily paid or payable to public sector entities in accordance with laws and/or regulations established to provide income to the government. Taxes exclude **fines**.

APPENDIX B

APPLICATION GUIDANCE

This appendix is an integral part of the Standard. It describes the application of paragraphs 1–41.

Application of this Standard

B1   The following flowcharts summarise the main requirements of this Standard to assist in its application.

Chart 1 – Transactions other than Volunteer Services

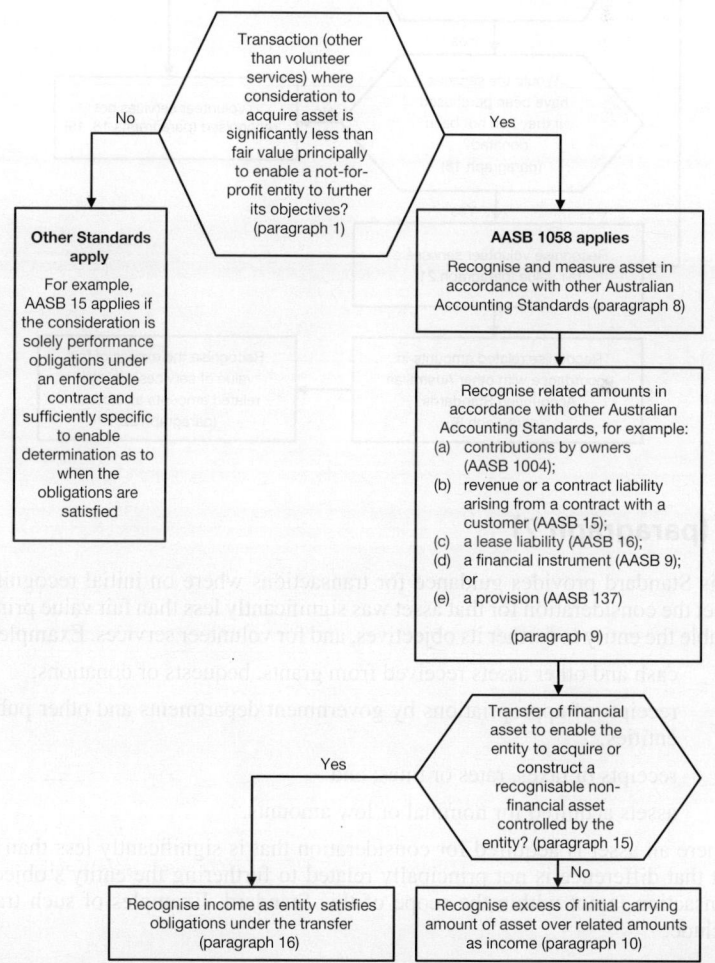

Chart 2 – Volunteer Services

```
        ┌─────────────────────┐
        │ Can the fair        │
        │ value of            │
        │ volunteer           │              No
        │ services be         │ ─────────────────────────────┐
        │ measured            │                              │
        │ reliably?           │                              │
        │ (paragraphs 18, 19) │                              │
        └─────────────────────┘                              │
                  │ Yes                                       │
                  ▼                                           │
  Yes   ┌─────────────────────────────────┐                  │
 ┌──────│ Does the entity elect to        │                  │
 │      │ recognise volunteer services?   │                  │
 │      │ (paragraph 19)                  │                  │
 │      └─────────────────────────────────┘                  │
 │                │ No                                        │
 │                ▼                                           │
 │      ┌─────────────────────┐                              │
 │      │ Is the entity a     │                              │
 │      │ local government,   │              No              │
 │      │ government          │ ────────────────────────┐    │
 │      │ department, GGS or  │                         │    │
 │      │ whole of            │                         │    │
 │      │ government?         │                         │    │
 │      │ (paragraph 18)      │                         │    │
 │      └─────────────────────┘                         │    │
 │                │ Yes                                  │    │
 │                ▼                                      ▼    ▼
 │      ┌─────────────────────┐           ┌──────────────────────────┐
 │      │ Would the services  │    No     │ Volunteer services not   │
 │      │ have been purchased │ ────────► │ recognised               │
 │      │ if they had not been│           │ (paragraphs 18, 19)      │
 │      │ donated?            │           └──────────────────────────┘
 │      │ (paragraph 18)      │
 │      └─────────────────────┘
 │                │ Yes
 │                ▼
 │      ┌─────────────────────────────┐
 └─────►│ Recognise volunteer services│
        │ at fair value (paragraph 21)│
        └─────────────────────────────┘
                  │
                  ▼
   ┌─────────────────────────────┐        ┌──────────────────────────┐
   │ Recognise related amounts in│        │ Recognise the excess of  │
   │ accordance with other       │ ─────► │ fair value of services   │
   │ Australian Accounting       │        │ over the related amounts │
   │ Standards (paragraph 9)     │        │ as income (paragraph 22) │
   └─────────────────────────────┘        └──────────────────────────┘
```

Scope (paragraph 7)

B2   This Standard provides guidance for transactions where on initial recognition of an asset the consideration for that asset was significantly less than fair value principally to enable the entity to further its objectives, and for volunteer services. Examples include:

(a)   cash and other assets received from grants, bequests or donations;

(b)   receipts of appropriations by government departments and other public sector entities;

(c)   receipts of taxes, rates or fines; and

(d)   assets acquired for nominal or low amounts.

B3   Where an asset is acquired for consideration that is significantly less than fair value but that difference is not principally related to furthering the entity's objectives, the transaction is not within the scope of this Standard. Examples of such transactions include:

(a)   distress sales; and

(b)   trade discounts.

B4   When assessing whether the consideration for an asset is less than fair value principally to enable the entity to further its objectives, the entity may consider whether another entity could have obtained the asset under the same terms and conditions. If those terms and conditions are generally not available to other entities of the same class/nature, it is more likely that the difference between the consideration for the asset and the fair value of the asset acquired is principally for enabling the entity to further its objectives. For example, trade discounts available to all not-for-profit entities, but not to for-profit entities, are not considered principally to further the specific not-for-profit entity's objectives.

B5   Where the consideration provided under a transaction solely involves performance obligations recognised in accordance with AASB 15, the asset is not acquired for consideration that is significantly less than fair value. Therefore, the transaction is not within the scope of this Standard.

B6   Transfers with consideration significantly less than fair value primarily to enable a not-for-profit entity to further its objectives may be called grants, bequests, donations or appropriations and are usually made voluntarily. Such transfers could be in the form of cash or another financial asset, goods, or volunteer services, and may or may not be made with restrictions or conditions on their use. Transactions may include elements with consideration that is significantly less than fair value primarily to enable the not-for-profit entity to further its objectives and other elements with consideration at fair value. For example, a donation by a customer may be present in a contract in which a customer promises consideration in exchange for goods or services (eg a fundraising dinner).

B7   Volunteer services are services transferred by individuals or other entities without charge or for consideration significantly less than the fair value of those services. Whether such services (when recognised in accordance with paragraphs 18 and 19) are recognised as an asset or an expense depends on the entity's determination whether it is probable that economic benefits will flow to the entity beyond the current accounting period. In many instances, the economic benefits of volunteer services will be consumed as the services are acquired. In some cases, the volunteer services will contribute to the development of an asset and be included in the carrying amount of that asset.

B8   Entities may be recipients of volunteer services under voluntary or compulsory schemes operated in the public interest, for example:

(a)   technical assistance from other governments or international organisations;

(b)   persons convicted of offences who are required to perform community service for the entity;

(c)   hospitals receiving the services of volunteers;

(d)   schools receiving voluntary services from parents as teachers' aides or as board members; and

(e)   local governments receiving the services of volunteer firefighters.

B9   Entities may also be recipients of volunteer professional services that support their broader activities. For example, charities and religious organisations may receive free professional accounting or legal services.

B10   Government appropriations, which establish the authority to spend money for particular purposes, are a form of a transfer made voluntarily as the government is not compelled to make particular payments of amounts appropriated.

B11   Taxes, rates and fines are forms of transfers made compulsorily.

Recognition and measurement of income and related amounts (paragraphs 9–17)

B12   An entity recognises related contributions by owners, liabilities and revenue ('related amounts') on initial recognition of an asset in accordance with another Australian Accounting Standard where the consideration for that asset is significantly less than fair value principally to further the entity's objectives.

B13   Any income recognised in accordance with paragraph 10 is strictly the residual of the difference between the fair value of the asset recognised and the consideration for that asset, after deducting any other related amounts described in paragraph 9. However, income is not recognised under paragraph 10 where another Standard addresses the accounting for the difference, such as the "day one gain/loss" requirements in AASB 9.

Refund obligations

B14   An entity typically has the ability, through its own actions, to avoid the circumstances that would give rise to a breach of conditions or requirements in an agreement necessitating a return of funds received. In such cases, liabilities recognised in accordance with other Standards do not include refund obligations that apply in the event of a breach, unless the breach has occurred or is expected to occur. For example, a grant agreement may require the funds provided to an entity to be spent only in a particular period, failing which repayment to the grantor will be required. As the entity has the discretion whether to spend funds received in advance of the specified period, a refund liability is not recognised unless the entity breaches the condition or a breach is expected.

Transfers to enable an entity to acquire or construct a recognisable non-financial asset to be controlled by the entity

B15   An entity that receives a financial asset, such as cash, in a transfer to enable the entity to acquire or construct a recognisable non-financial asset to be controlled by the entity shall apply the requirements of AASB 9 to that financial asset. The acquisition or construction of the non-financial asset is accounted for separately to the transfer of the financial asset, in accordance with other Standards. If the non-financial asset is not permitted to be recognised by another Standard (eg knowledge or intellectual property developed through research, which cannot be recognised as an asset in accordance with AASB 138), paragraphs 15–17 do not apply. The key criterion is that the recognisable non-financial asset will be under the control of the entity (ie for its own use) – it will not be transferred to the transferor or other parties. Therefore, the transfer of the financial asset (or the relevant part) to the entity does not occur under a contract with a customer and is not subject to AASB 15. However, the recognisable non-financial asset could increase the entity's ability or capacity to provide goods or services to other parties pursuant to other transactions, which are separate to the transfer that enabled the entity to acquire or construct the non-financial asset for its own use.

B16   On initial recognition of the financial asset, the entity recognises the requirement to acquire or construct the recognisable non-financial asset as an obligation and considers whether there are other conditions that give rise to performance obligations that require the entity to transfer goods or services to other entities (which are accounted for under AASB 15). The obligation to acquire or construct the non-financial asset is accounted for similarly to a performance obligation under AASB 15. For each obligation, the entity shall determine whether the obligation would be satisfied over time or at a point in time. If an entity does not satisfy an obligation over time, the obligation would be satisfied at a point in time.

B17   An entity shall apply a single method of measuring progress for each obligation satisfied over time and the entity shall apply that method consistently to similar obligations and in similar circumstances. At the end of each reporting period, an entity shall remeasure its progress towards complete satisfaction of each obligation that is satisfied over time, and shall recognise income over time on that basis.

Endowments

B18   An endowment is a transfer of an asset to an entity for the ongoing support of the entity's objectives, and may (but not necessarily) be made as part of a bequest. An endowment may be made for the perpetual benefit of the entity in that the transfer is made with a requirement for the principal to be preserved, and only income earned on investment activity to be available for use in furthering the entity's objectives.

B19   An endowment may include conditions pertaining to investment of the principal and the purpose to which investment income must be applied. For example, an endowment made to a university may be made on condition that the principal is invested and the investment income used for annual scholarships. An entity shall consider whether the conditions of the transfer give rise to any related contribution by owners, liabilities or revenue that is recognised at the same time as the entity recognises an asset. For example, an entity may determine the conditions give rise to a financial liability within the scope of AASB 9 for the obligation to provide a financial asset into the future, or a contract liability within the scope of AASB 15 for unperformed performance obligations relating to the transfer of goods or services under the terms of the endowment.

Bequests

B20   A bequest is a transfer made according to the provisions of a deceased person's will. Whether the initial recognition of bequeathed items as assets in accordance with another Standard simultaneously gives rise to the recognition of income will depend on whether the entity recognises a liability, or other related amounts, as a result of the bequest. For example, the terms of a bequest may establish a contract between an entity and the estate that is within the scope of AASB 15 and give rise to a contract liability.

Provisions

Constructive obligations

B21   When an entity recognises an asset in accordance with another Australian Accounting Standard for consideration that is significantly less than fair value principally to enable the entity to further its objectives, the entity applies paragraph 9 to recognise any related amounts. When applying that paragraph, an entity considers whether a provision should be recognised in accordance with AASB 137 for a constructive obligation.

B22   Critical to recognising a provision for a constructive obligation, an entity must demonstrate that its published policies, past practices or current statements are sufficiently specific to raise a valid expectation on the part of other parties that the entity will discharge its responsibilities under those policies, practices or statements. Determining whether an entity's policies, practices or statements are sufficiently specific to create such an expectation among other parties is a matter of judgement. However, it is unlikely that an entity's charter or stated objectives would satisfy the definition of a constructive obligation.

B23   An established pattern of past practices might also create a valid expectation among other parties that the entity will continue to adhere to those practices in the future. While entities might establish a general pattern for utilising assets received, they often do not adhere to those patterns to such a degree as to create a valid expectation among other parties.

Legal obligations

B24   Contractual terms (implicit or explicit), legislation or another operation of the law might create a legal non-financial obligation for an entity. In these circumstances an entity applies AASB 137 to recognise a provision, if any, arising from those legal obligations.

B25   Provisions might arise from terms included in a lease, such as an obligation to return
       or restore the leased asset in its original condition. Paragraphs 24 and 25 of AASB
       16 provide guidance on accounting for an obligation to maintain, or restore, assets to
       conditions specified in a lease. Where such an obligation exists, the obligation is also
       accounted for in accordance with AASB 137.

Parliamentary appropriations as income

B26   The nature of parliamentary appropriations, and the circumstances that give rise
       to a government department's recognition of such appropriations, can vary across
       different jurisdictions in Australia, and may vary for different types of appropriations
       within a particular jurisdiction. Similarly, the nature and content of appropriation
       legislation, the manner in which government departments' activities are funded,
       and the mechanisms by which parliament and the government ensure that the
       government departments' use of public funds is appropriate and consistent with
       government priorities as sanctioned by parliament, can change over time. Accordingly,
       the extent to which amounts appropriated for a government department's use are
       recognised as income of a particular reporting period is determined by reference to
       the characteristics of the appropriation process and the circumstances in which the
       government department recognises appropriated amounts.

B27   For example, the parliamentary appropriation process currently adopted in some
       jurisdictions in Australia is such that the government departments do not gain control
       of funds appropriated for their use until obligations are incurred or expenditures are
       made by the government department. In these jurisdictions, appropriations recognised
       as income are in the nature of a recovery of costs incurred for the acquisition of goods
       and services or for amounts otherwise expended.

Non-contractual income arising from statutory requirements

B28   Taxes, rates and fines do not give rise to a contract liability or revenue recognised in
       accordance with AASB 15, even when they are raised in respect of specific goods or
       services. This is because the entity does not promise to provide goods or services in an
       agreement that creates obligations enforceable against the entity by legal or equivalent
       means.

B29   Taxes, rates and fines are not contributions by owners acting in their capacity as owners.

Payable tax credits and other tax relief

B30   Amounts of *tax relief* that enter directly into the calculation of a taxpayer's tax liability
       (including tax allowances, exemptions and deductions, and 'non-payable tax credits')
       are treated as reductions in income (ie foregone income), rather than expenses. A
       'non-payable tax credit' is a tax credit limited to the amount of the taxpayer's tax
       liability for the period. An example of tax relief that enters directly into the calculation
       of a taxpayer's tax liability is where taxpayers are permitted tax deductions for self-
       education expenses. These types of concessions are available only to taxpayers. If an
       entity (including a natural person) does not pay tax, it cannot access the concession.

B31   In contrast, a *payable tax credit* is a tax credit that is not limited to the amount of the
       taxpayer's tax liability for the period; that is, any excess of the tax credit over the tax
       liability for the period would be payable to the taxpayer. Such tax credits might be
       payable to taxpayers as part of a programme in which the same amount of benefit
       is paid to taxpayers and non-taxpayers alike (the latter being payable exclusively
       in the form of a cash benefit). For example, a government may use the tax system
       as a convenient method of paying benefits to taxpayers, which would otherwise be
       paid using another payment method, such as writing a cheque, directly depositing
       the amount in a taxpayer's bank account, or settling another account on behalf of
       the taxpayer. For example, a government may pay part of an individual's health
       insurance premiums, to encourage the uptake of such insurance, either by reducing
       the individual's tax liability (by providing payable tax credits), making a payment by
       cheque or by paying an amount directly to the insurer. In these cases, the amount is

payable irrespective of whether the individual pays taxes. Consequently, this amount is an expense of the government and is recognised separately from its tax income. Tax income is measured gross of any expenses incurred by granting payable tax credits.

Volunteer services (paragraphs 18–22)

B32   A not-for-profit entity that makes an accounting policy choice to recognise volunteer services under paragraph 19 shall only change its accounting policy if the change meets the criteria in AASB 108 *Accounting Policies, Changes in Accounting Estimates and Errors* (paragraph 14). That is, an entity can change an accounting policy only if the change:

(a)   is required by an Australian Accounting Standard; or

(b)   results in the financial statements providing reliable and more relevant information about the effects of transactions, other events or conditions on the entity's financial position, financial performance or cash flows.

APPENDIX C

EFFECTIVE DATE AND TRANSITION

This appendix is an integral part of the Standard.

Effective date

C1   An entity shall apply this Standard for annual reporting periods beginning on or after 1 January 2019. Earlier application is permitted provided that entities apply AASB 15 *Revenue from Contracts with Customers* to the same period. If an entity applies this Standard earlier, it shall disclose that fact.

Transition

C2   For the purposes of the transition requirements in paragraphs C3–C12:

(a)   the date of initial application is the beginning of the annual reporting period in which an entity first applies this Standard; and

(b)   a completed contract is a contract or transaction for which the entity has recognised all of the income in accordance with AASB 1004 *Contributions*.

C3   An entity shall apply this Standard either:

(a)   retrospectively to each prior reporting period presented in accordance with AASB 108 *Accounting Policies, Changes in Accounting Estimates and Errors*; or

(b)   retrospectively with the cumulative effect of initially applying this Standard recognised at the date of initial application in accordance with paragraphs C6–C11.

C4   Notwithstanding the requirements of paragraph 28 of AASB 108, when this Standard is first applied, an entity need only present the quantitative information required by paragraph 28(f) of AASB 108 for the annual reporting period immediately preceding the first annual reporting period for which this Standard is applied (the 'immediately preceding period') and only if the entity applies this Standard retrospectively in accordance with paragraph C3(a). An entity may also present this information for the current period or for earlier comparative periods, but is not required to do so.

C5   When applying this Standard retrospectively in accordance with paragraph C3(a), as a practical expedient an entity need not restate completed contracts or transactions that:

(a)   begin and end within the same annual reporting period; or

(b)   are completed contracts or transactions at the beginning of the earliest period presented.

If an entity applies this expedient, it shall do so consistently to all completed contracts or transactions within all reporting periods presented and shall disclose the use of this expedient.

C6   If an entity elects to apply this Standard retrospectively in accordance with paragraph C3(b), the entity shall not restate comparative information. Instead, the entity shall recognise the cumulative effect of initially applying this Standard as an adjustment to the opening balance of retained earnings (or other component of equity, as appropriate) at the date of initial application. Under this transition method, an entity may elect to apply this Standard retrospectively only to contracts and transactions that are not completed contracts at the date of initial application.

C7   For the reporting period that includes the date of initial application, an entity shall provide both of the following additional disclosures if this Standard is applied retrospectively in accordance with paragraph C3(b):

(a)   the amount by which each financial statement line item is affected in the current reporting period by the application of this Standard as compared to AASB 1004 *Contributions* before the change; and

(b)   an explanation of the reasons for significant changes identified in paragraph C7(a).

Assets acquired for significantly less than fair value

C8   Assets acquired for consideration that was significantly less than fair value principally to enable the entity to further its objectives may have been measured on initial recognition under other Australian Accounting Standards at a cost that was significantly less than fair value. As a practical expedient, such assets are not required to be remeasured at fair value, whether the entity elects to apply this Standard retrospectively in accordance with paragraph C3(a) or C3(b).

Leases with significantly below-market terms and conditions

Leases classified as operating leases

C9   If an entity applies this Standard before applying AASB 16 *Leases*, and notwithstanding the requirements in paragraph C3, for leases that (1) at inception had significantly below-market terms and conditions principally to enable the entity to further its objectives and (2) were classified as operating leases in accordance with AASB 117 *Leases*, the entity shall not apply the requirements of this Standard to recognise any asset or income. Instead, the entity shall continue to apply its accounting policy under AASB 117 to those operating leases. On transition to AASB 16 *Leases*, the entity shall apply the transition requirements of that Standard to leases classified as operating leases in accordance with AASB 117.

Leases classified as finance leases

C10   If an entity applies this Standard before applying AASB 16, for leases that (1) at inception had significantly below-market terms and conditions principally to enable the entity to further its objectives and (2) were classified as finance leases in accordance with AASB 117, and if an entity elects to apply this Standard in accordance with:

(a)   paragraph C3(a) – the entity shall:

(i)   measure the leased asset at fair value at the beginning of the earliest period presented;

      (ii)   measure the lease liability in accordance with AASB 117;

      (iii)   recognise any related items in accordance with paragraph 9; and

      (iv)   recognise any income arising as an adjustment to the opening balance of retained earnings (or other component of equity, as appropriate) at the beginning of the earliest period presented; or

(b)   paragraph C3(b) – the entity shall:

      (i)   measure the leased asset at fair value at the date of initial application of this Standard;

      (ii)   measure the lease liability in accordance with AASB 117;

      (iii)   recognise any related items in accordance with paragraph 9; and

      (iv)   recognise any income arising as an adjustment to the opening balance of retained earnings (or other component of equity, as appropriate) at the date of initial application of this Standard.

C11   An entity may, as a practical expedient, apply paragraph C10 to a portfolio of leases with similar characteristics if the entity reasonably expects that the effects on the financial statements of this approach would not differ materially from applying paragraph C10 to the individual leases within that portfolio. If accounting for a portfolio, an entity shall use estimates and assumptions that reflect the size and composition of the portfolio.

References to AASB 9

C12   If an entity applies this Standard but does not yet apply AASB 9 *Financial Instruments*, any reference in this Standard to AASB 9 shall be read as a reference to AASB 139 *Financial Instruments: Recognition and Measurement*.

APPENDIX D
AMENDMENTS TO OTHER STANDARDS

This appendix sets out the amendments to other Australian Accounting Standards that are a consequence of the AASB issuing this Standard.

The amendments set out in this appendix apply to entities and financial statements in accordance with the application of the Standards and Interpretations set out in AASB 1057 *Application of Australian Accounting Standards* (as amended).

The amendments apply to annual reporting periods beginning on or after 1 January 2019, except that the amendment to AASB 117 applies to periods beginning before 1 January 2019 if AASB 1058 is applied to an earlier period.

If an entity applies this Standard to an earlier period, it shall also apply these amendments to that earlier period. However, the AASB 1 and AASB 16 amendments are applied to an earlier period only if AASB 16 is also applied to that period.

Amendments are made to the latest principal version of a Standard (or an Interpretation), unless otherwise indicated. The amendments also apply, as far as possible, to earlier principal versions of the amended Standards and Interpretations when this Standard is applied for earlier periods, as necessary.

This appendix uses underlining, striking out and other typographical material to identify some of the amendments to a Standard or an Interpretation, in order to make the amendments more understandable. However, the amendments made by this appendix do not include that underlining, striking out or other typographical material. Amended paragraphs are shown with deleted text struck through and new text underlined. Ellipses (...) are used to help provide the context within which amendments are made and also to indicate text that is not amended.

AASB 1 *First-time Adoption of Australian Accounting Standards* (July 2015)

In Appendix D, paragraphs AusD7.1, AusD9D.1 and AusD9D.2 are added. Paragraphs D5–D7, D9 and D9B–D9D have not been amended, but are included for ease of reference.

Deemed cost

D5   An entity may elect to measure an item of property, plant and equipment at the date of transition to Australian Accounting Standards at its fair value and use that fair value as its deemed cost at that date.

D6   A first-time adopter may elect to use a previous GAAP revaluation of an item of property, plant and equipment at, or before, the date of transition to Australian Accounting Standards as deemed cost at the date of the revaluation, if the revaluation was, at the date of the revaluation, broadly comparable to:

(a)   fair value; or

(b)   cost or depreciated cost in accordance with Australian Accounting Standards, adjusted to reflect, for example, changes in a general or specific price index.

D7   The elections in paragraphs D5 and D6 are also available for:

(a)   ...

(aa)   right-of-use assets (AASB 16 *Leases*); and

(b)   ...

AusD7.1   Notwithstanding paragraphs D5–D7, where a lessee is a not-for-profit entity and the lease had at inception significantly below-market terms and conditions principally to enable the entity to further its objectives, the entity shall measure the right-of-use asset at fair value at the beginning of the current period presented in the entity's first Australian-Accounting-Standards financial statements or at the previous GAAP valuation if that valuation broadly reflects that fair value.

...

Leases

D9   A first-time adopter may assess whether a contract existing at the date of transition to Australian Accounting Standards contains a lease by applying paragraphs 9–11 of AASB 16 to those contracts on the basis of facts and circumstances existing at that date.

D9B   When a first-time adopter that is a lessee recognises lease liabilities and right-of-use assets, it may apply the following approach to all of its leases (subject to the practical expedients described in paragraph D9D):

(a)   measure a lease liability at the date of transition to Australian Accounting Standards. A lessee following this approach shall measure that liability at the present value of the remaining lease payments (see paragraph D9E), discounted using the lessee's incremental borrowing rate (see paragraph D9E) at the date of transition to Australian Accounting Standards.

(b)   measure a right-of-use asset at the date of transition to Australian Accounting Standards. The lessee shall choose, on a lease-by-lease basis, to measure that right-of-use asset at either:

(i)   its carrying amount as if AASB 16 had been applied since the commencement date of the lease (see paragraph D9E), but discounted using the lessee's incremental borrowing rate at the date of transition to Australian Accounting Standards; or

      (ii)   an amount equal to the lease liability, adjusted by the amount of any prepaid or accrued lease payments relating to that lease recognised in the statement of financial position immediately before the date of transition to Australian Accounting Standards.

  (c)   apply AASB 136 to right-of-use assets at the date of transition to Australian Accounting Standards.

D9C   Notwithstanding the requirements in paragraph D9B, a first-time adopter that is a lessee shall measure the right-of-use asset at fair value at the date of transition to Australian Accounting Standards for leases that meet the definition of investment property in AASB 140 and are measured using the fair value model in AASB 140 from the date of transition to Australian Accounting Standards.

D9D   A first-time adopter that is a lessee may do one or more of the following at the date of transition to Australian Accounting Standards, applied on a lease-by-lease basis:

  (a)   ...

AusD9D.1   Notwithstanding paragraphs D9B–D9D, where a lessee is a not-for-profit entity and the lease had at inception significantly below-market terms and conditions principally to enable the entity to further its objectives, all references in those paragraphs to the date of transition to Australian Accounting Standards shall be read as referring to the beginning of the current period presented in the entity's first Australian-Accounting-Standards financial statements. Consequently, the entity shall measure the lease liability and the right-of-use asset at that date. The right-of-use asset shall be measured in accordance with paragraph AusD7.1.

AusD9D.2   Where a lessee is a not-for-profit entity and the lease had at inception significantly below-market terms and conditions principally to enable the entity to further its objectives, the entity shall also recognise any related items in accordance with paragraph 9 of AASB 1058 *Income of Not-for-Profit Entities*. Any income arising shall be recognised as an adjustment to the opening balance of retained earnings (or another component of equity, as appropriate) at the beginning of the current period presented in the entity's first Australian-Accounting-Standards financial statements.

AASB 15 *Revenue from Contracts with Customers* (December 2014)

> In Appendix C, paragraph AusC2.1 is added.

AusC2.1   In respect of not-for-profit entities, the reference in paragraph C2(b) to a completed contract also includes contracts for which the entity has recognised all of the revenue in accordance with AASB 1004 *Contributions*, or revenue in combination with a provision in accordance with AASB 137 *Provisions, Contingent Liabilities and Contingent Assets*.

AASB 16 *Leases* (February 2016)

> Paragraph Aus25.1 and, in Appendix C, paragraphs AusC5.1, AusC5.2, AusC8.1 and AusC11.1 are added.

Aus25.1   **Notwithstanding paragraphs 23–25, where the lessee is a not-for-profit entity and the lease has significantly below-market terms and conditions principally to enable the entity to further its objectives, the right-of-use asset shall initially be measured at fair value in accordance with AASB 13 *Fair Value Measurement*. AASB 1058 *Income of Not-for-Profit Entities* addresses the recognition of related amounts.**

AusC5.1   Not-for-profit entities applying this Standard retrospectively in accordance with paragraph C5(a) to leases that at inception had significantly below-market terms and conditions principally to enable the entity to further its objectives shall:

(a)   measure the right-of-use asset at fair value;

(b)   measure the lease liability in accordance with this Standard; and

(c)   recognise any related items in accordance with paragraph 9 of AASB 1058 *Income of Not-for-Profit Entities.*

Any income arising shall be recognised as an adjustment to the opening balance of retained earnings (or other component of equity, as appropriate) at the beginning of the earliest prior period presented.

AusC5.2   Notwithstanding paragraph AusC5.1, not-for-profit entities that adopted AASB 1058 in an earlier reporting period are not required to remeasure the fair value of the right-of-use asset arising from leases that (1) at inception had significantly below-market terms and conditions principally to enable the entity to further its objectives and (2) were previously classified as finance leases applying AASB 117. Instead, the entity shall transition those leases in accordance with paragraph C11, regardless of which transition option in paragraph C5 is applied.

AusC8.1   Not-for-profit entities applying this Standard retrospectively in accordance with paragraph C5(b) to leases that (1) at inception had significantly below-market terms and conditions principally to enable the entity to further its objectives and (2) were previously classified as operating leases applying AASB 117 shall:

(a)   notwithstanding paragraph C8(b), measure the right-of-use asset at fair value at the date of initial application of this Standard;

(b)   measure the lease liability in accordance with paragraph C8(a); and

(c)   recognise any related items in accordance with paragraph 9 of AASB 1058.

Any income arising shall be recognised as an adjustment to the opening balance of retained earnings (or other component of equity, as appropriate) at the date of initial application of this Standard.

AusC11.1   Subject to paragraph AusC5.2 and notwithstanding paragraph C11, not-for-profit entities applying this Standard retrospectively in accordance with paragraph C5(b) to leases that (1) at inception had significantly below-market terms and conditions principally to enable the entity to further its objectives and (2) were previously classified as finance leases applying AASB 117 shall:

(a)   measure the right-of-use asset at fair value at the date of initial application of this Standard;

(b)   measure the lease liability in accordance with this Standard; and

(c)   recognise any related items in accordance with paragraph 9 of AASB 1058.

Any income arising shall be recognised as an adjustment to the opening balance of retained earnings (or other component of equity, as appropriate) at the date of initial application of this Standard.

AASB 101 *Presentation of Financial Statements* (July 2015)

Paragraph Aus16.2 is deleted.

Aus16.2   [Deleted by the AASB]

AASB 102 *Inventories* (July 2015)

> Paragraph Aus10.1 is amended and paragraph Aus10.2 is added.

Aus10.1   Notwithstanding paragraph 10 and subject to paragraph Aus10.2, in respect of not-for-profit entities shall initially measure the cost of inventories at current replacement cost where the consideration for those inventories is significantly less than fair value principally to enable the entity to further its objectives, where inventories are acquired at no cost, or for nominal consideration, the cost shall be the current replacement cost as at the date of acquisition. AASB 1058 *Income of Not-for-Profit Entities* addresses the recognition of related amounts.

Aus10.2   As a practical expedient, where a not-for-profit entity acquires inventory for consideration that is significantly less than fair value principally to enable the entity to further its objectives, the entity may elect to recognise an item of inventory based on an assessment of the materiality either of the individual item or of inventories at an aggregate or portfolio level.

AASB 112 *Income Taxes* (August 2015)

> Paragraphs 4 and Aus33.1 are amended. Paragraph Aus4.1 is added.

4   This Standard does not deal with the methods of accounting for government grants (see AASB 120 *Accounting for Government Grants and Disclosure of Government Assistance* or, for not-for-profit entities, AASB 1004 *Contributions*) or investment tax credits. However, this Standard does deal with the accounting for temporary differences that may arise from such grants or investment tax credits.

Aus4.1   In respect of not-for-profit entities, AASB 1058 *Income of Not-for-Profit Entities* and AASB 15 *Revenue from Contracts with Customers* address the accounting for government grants.

...

Aus33.1   In respect of not-for-profit entities, a deferred tax asset will not arise on a non-taxable government grant relating to an asset. For example, Under AASB 1004 *Contributions* under AASB 1058 *Income of Not-for-Profit Entities*, where a not-for-profit entity accounts for the receipt of non-taxable government grants as income rather than as deferred income when those grants are controlled by the entity. As such, a temporary difference does not arise.

AASB 116 *Property, Plant and Equipment* (August 2015)

> Paragraph Aus15.2 is deleted, and paragraphs Aus15.1 and Aus15.3 are amended.

Aus15.1   Notwithstanding paragraph 15, in respect of not-for-profit entities,shall initially measure the cost of an item of property, plant and equipment at fair value in accordance with AASB 13 *Fair Value Measurement* where the consideration for the asset is significantly less than fair value principally to enable the entity to further its objectives where an asset is acquired at no cost, or for a nominal cost, the cost is its *fair value* as at the date of acquisition. AASB 1058 *Income of Not-for-Profit Entities* addresses the recognition of related amounts.

Aus15.3   In respect of not-for-profit entities, for the purposes of this Standard, the initial recognition and measurement at fair value of an item of property, plant and equipment, ~~acquired at no or nominal cost, consistent with the requirements of paragraph Aus15.1~~ in accordance with paragraph Aus15.1, does not constitute a revaluation. Accordingly, the revaluation requirements in paragraph 31, and the supporting commentary in paragraphs ~~32 to~~ 34 and 35, only apply where an entity elects to revalue an item of property, plant and equipment ~~in subsequent reporting periods~~ after its recognition.

Paragraph Aus6.2 in Appendix A *Australian defined terms* is amended.

Aus6.2   Examples of property, plant and equipment held by not-for-profit public sector entities ~~and for-profit government departments~~ include, but are not limited to, infrastructure, cultural, community and heritage assets.

The scoping guidance to the Australian implementation guidance accompanying AASB 116 is amended.

Australian implementation guidance

This guidance accompanies, but is not part of, AASB 116. This guidance is pertinent to not-for-profit public sector entities ~~and for-profit government departments~~ that hold heritage or cultural assets.

AASB 117 *Leases* (August 2015)

The amendment to AASB 117 applies to periods beginning before 1 January 2019. This means that the amendment applies only if AASB 1058 is applied to an earlier period.

Paragraph Aus20.1 is added.

Aus20.1   **Notwithstanding paragraph 20, the leased asset shall initially be measured at fair value in accordance with AASB 13 *Fair Value Measurement* where:**

                (a)   at inception the lease has significantly below-market terms and conditions principally to enable the lessee to further its objectives; and

                (b)   the lessee applies AASB 1058 *Income of Not-for-Profit Entities* to the period.

                AASB 1058 addresses the recognition of related amounts.

AASB 128 *Investments in Associates and Joint Ventures* (August 2015)

Paragraph Aus10.1 is added.

Aus10.1   Notwithstanding paragraph 10, not-for-profit entities shall initially measure the cost of an investment in an associate or joint venture at fair value in accordance with AASB 13 *Fair Value Measurement* where the consideration for the investment is significantly less than fair value principally to enable the entity to further its objectives. AASB 1058 *Income of Not-for-Profit Entities* addresses the recognition of related amounts.

AASB 138 *Intangible Assets* (August 2015)

> Paragraph Aus24.1 is amended.

Aus24.1   Notwithstanding paragraph 24, ~~in respect of~~ not-for-profit entities, ~~where an asset is acquired at no cost, or for a nominal cost,~~ shall initially measure the cost of the asset at ~~is its~~ *fair value* ~~as at the date of acquisition~~ where the consideration for the asset is significantly less than fair value principally to enable the entity to further its objectives. AASB 1058 *Income of Not-for-Profit Entities* addresses the recognition of related amounts.

> The footnote to paragraph 44 is amended.

AASB 120 only applies to for-profit entities. Not-for-profit entities shall initially measure the intangible asset at fair value where the consideration for the asset is significantly less than the fair value of the asset principally to enable the entity to further its objectives ~~are required to recognise the intangible asset and the grant initially at fair value in accordance with AASB 1004 *Contributions*~~.

AASB 140 *Investment Property* (August 2015)

> Paragraph Aus20.1 is amended.

Aus20.1   Notwithstanding paragraph 20, ~~in respect of~~ not-for-profit entities, shall initially measure the cost of the asset at fair value in accordance with AASB 13 *Fair Value Measurement* where the consideration for the asset is significantly less than fair value principally to enable the entity to further its objectives ~~where an investment property is acquired at no cost or for nominal cost, its cost shall be deemed to be its fair value as at the date of acquisition~~. AASB 1058 *Income of Not-for-Profit Entities* addresses the recognition of related amounts.

AASB 141 *Agriculture* (August 2015)

> Paragraph Aus38.1 is amended.

Aus38.1   Notwithstanding paragraphs 34-38, not-for-profit entities ~~recognises~~shall account for government grants related to a biological asset in accordance with ~~AASB 1004 *Contributions*~~ AASB 1058 *Income of Not-for-Profit Entities*.

AASB 1004 *Contributions* (December 2007)

> Paragraphs 1–5 are deleted and paragraph 6 is replaced.

6   The following table identifies which paragraphs are applicable to each type of entity to which this Standard applies:

Type of entity to which the paragraph is applicable	Content of paragraphs	Para No.
Government departments	Parliamentary appropriations	32
	Liabilities of government departments assumed by other entities	39 – 43A
	Contributions by owners and distributions to owners	48 – 53
	Restructure of administrative arrangements	54 – 59
Other government controlled not-for-profit entities	Restructure of administrative arrangements	54 – 59
Local governments and whole of governments	Contributions by owners and distributions to owners	48 – 53

Paragraphs 11–31, 33–38, 44–47 and 60–68 and the related headings and scoping guidance are deleted. Paragraph 32 is amended and scoping guidance added. The scoping guidance before paragraph 39 is amended. Paragraph 43A is added. Appendix B *Comparison of AASB 1004 with AAS 27, AAS 29 and AAS 31* accompanying AASB 1004 is deleted.

Parliamentary appropriations to government departments

Paragraph 32 of this Standard applies only to government departments.

32   Parliamentary appropriations over which a government department gains control during the reporting period shall be recognised as:

(a)   income of that reporting period where the appropriation:

(i)   satisfies the definition of income in the Framework for the Preparation and Presentation of Financial Statements (the Framework); and

(ii)   satisfies the recognition criteria for income;

(b)   a direct adjustment to equity where the appropriation satisfies the definition of a contribution by owners; or

(c)   a liability of the government department where the appropriation:

(i)   satisfies the definition of liabilities in the *Framework*; and

(ii)   satisfies the recognition criteria for liabilities in the *Framework*.

...

Liabilities of government departments assumed by other entities

Paragraphs 39 to 43 43A of this Standard apply only to government departments.

...

43A   A government department shall disclose liabilities that were assumed during the reporting period by the government or other entity.

Paragraphs 54–57 and the related scoping guidance are amended.

Restructure of administrative arrangements

Paragraphs 54 to 59 of this Standard apply only to government departments and other government controlled not-for-profit entities and for-profit government departments.

54   In relation to a *restructure of administrative arrangements*, a government controlled not-for-profit transferor entity or a for-profit government department

~~transferor entity~~ shall recognise distributions to owners and a government controlled not-for-profit transferee entity ~~or a for-profit government department transferee entity~~ shall recognise contributions by owners in respect of assets transferred.

55   In relation to a restructure of administrative arrangements, a government controlled not-for-profit transferor entity ~~or a for-profit government department transferor entity~~ shall recognise contributions by owners and a government controlled not-for-profit transferee entity ~~or a for-profit government department transferee entity~~ shall recognise distributions to owners in respect of liabilities transferred.

56   When both assets and liabilities are transferred as a consequence of a restructure of administrative arrangements, a government controlled not-for-profit transferor entity ~~or a for-profit government department transferor entity~~ and a government controlled not-for-profit transferee entity ~~or a for-profit government department transferee entity~~ shall recognise a net contribution by owners or distribution to owners, as applicable.

57   When activities are transferred as a consequence of a restructure of administrative arrangements, a government controlled not-for-profit transferee entity ~~or a for-profit government department transferee entity~~ shall disclose the expenses and income attributable to the transferred activities for the reporting period, showing separately those expenses and items of income recognised by the transferor during the reporting period. If disclosure of this information would be impracticable, that fact shall be disclosed, together with an explanation of why this is the case.

AASB 1049 *Whole of Government and General Government Sector Financial Reporting* (October 2007)

> In the Illustrative Examples accompanying AASB 1049, the explanatory notes supporting illustrative examples A and B are amended.

Explanatory notes supporting illustrative examples A and B

...

q   **Liabilities – Provisions**

    ...

q(ii) ...

    [Note: Depending on the arrangements operating in a particular jurisdiction, a GGS, as an income tax collector, may not be able to recognise revenue unless it meets the criteria in ~~AASB 1004 *Contributions*~~ AASB 1058 *Income of Not-for-Profit Entities*.

    ...

AASB 1057 *Application of Australian Accounting Standards*

> Paragraphs 6 and 11 are amended. Paragraph 20A is added.

6   **AASB 8 *Operating Segments* applies to:**

    (a)   **each for-profit entity that is required to prepare financial reports in accordance with Part 2M.3 of the Corporations Act and that is a reporting entity;**

    (b)   **general purpose financial statements of each for-profit reporting entity ~~other than for-profit government departments~~; and**

ILLUSTRATIVE EXAMPLES

These illustrative examples accompany, but are not part of, AASB 1058. They illustrate aspects of AASB 1058, but are not intended to provide interpretative guidance.

IE1   The following examples portray hypothetical situations. They are intended to illustrate how a not-for-profit entity might apply some of the requirements of AASB 1058 *Income of Not-for-Profit Entities* to particular types of transactions, on the basis of the limited facts presented. Although some aspects of the examples might be present in actual fact patterns, all relevant facts and circumstances of a particular fact pattern need to be evaluated when applying AASB 1058.

Recognition and measurement of income and related amounts (paragraphs 9–22)

IE2   Examples 1–8 illustrate the requirements in AASB 1058 for identifying related amounts and income to be recognised in accordance with paragraphs 9 and 10 on the initial recognition of an asset. The following requirements are illustrated in the examples in identifying related amounts in the form of:

(a)   contributions by owners, in accordance with AASB 1004;

(b)   a financial instrument, in accordance with AASB 9;

(c)   a lease liability arising in a lease contract, in accordance with AASB 16; and

(d)   revenue or a contract liability arising from a contract with a customer, in accordance with AASB 15.

Contributions by owners

Example 1 – Contributions by owners – transfer of cash appropriation

A Government department transfers cash appropriations of $730,000 to its controlled entity and designates the transfer before it occurs as an equity contribution in accordance with paragraph 8(c) of AASB Interpretation 1038 *Contributions by Owners Made to Wholly-Owned Public Sector Entities*, as identified in AASB 1048 *Interpretation of Standards*.

Scope and asset recognition

The controlled entity determines:

•   the cash appropriation is an asset acquired by the controlled entity for no consideration to further the objectives of the controlled entity. Accordingly, the appropriation is within the scope of AASB 1058; and

•   it controls a financial asset within the scope of AASB 9.

Accounting treatment

In accordance with paragraph 9, the related amount for the cash asset is a contribution by owners, which is recognised in equity, as it meets the requirements of AASB Interpretation 1038 and AASB 1004.

The journal entry on initial recognition by the controlled entity is:

	Debit	Credit
Cash	730,000	
Equity – contributed capital		730,000

Example 2 — Contributions by owners to a private sector not-for-profit entity

Charity P makes a contribution of $500,000 to establish Company S, which operates child care centres. There are no repayment terms to the contribution and there are no goods or services to be provided to Charity P in return for the contribution. Company S is a company limited by guarantee with required member contributions of $10. Charity P controls the voting rights and in accordance with AASB 10 *Consolidated Financial Statements* consolidates Company S.

Scope and asset recognition

Company S determines:

- the cash from the contribution is an asset acquired by Company S for no consideration to further the objectives of Company S. Accordingly, the cash injection is within the scope of AASB 1058; and

- it controls a financial asset within the scope of AASB 9.

Accounting treatment

In accordance with paragraph 9, the related amount for the cash asset is accounted for as a contribution by owners. Charity P is a member (owner) of Company S, and the transfer is from an owner acting in their capacity as an owner. No services are required of Company S as a result of the contribution, nor is there an obligation to repay the funds.

The journal entry on initial recognition by Company S is:

	Debit	Credit
Cash	500,000	
Equity – contributed capital		500,000

Financial instruments, bequests and endowments

IE3   Examples 3 and 4 illustrate the requirements of paragraphs 9 and 10 in AASB 1058 for the accounting treatment for financial instruments, bequests and endowments. Examples 3A and 4 illustrate the identification of related amounts in the form of a financial instrument, in accordance with AASB 9. Receiving a bequest or endowment in the form of cash, or paying out the principal and/or interest in the form of cash, requires the application of the financial instrument accounting requirements in AASB 9.

Example 3 — Endowment made to a university

An alumnus transferred $2 million cash to University A as an endowment. Under the terms of the endowment:

- the $2 million cash can be invested at the university's discretion;

- subject to preserving the real value of the principal, all income generated from investing the principal is required to be applied towards cash scholarships of $20,000 per student for the student to use at their discretion; and

- if the university breaches the terms of the endowment, the university is required to return the real value of the principal to the alumnus.

Scope and asset recognition

University A determines:

- it has an enforceable agreement with the alumnus, as the university can be required to return the endowment in the event it breaches the terms under which it was given;

- the $2 million endowment is an asset the university acquired for no consideration to further the objectives of the university. Accordingly, the endowment is within the scope of AASB 1058; and

- it controls a financial asset ($2 million) within the scope of AASB 9.

Example 3A – Financial instrument (cash scholarships, not goods or services)

Based on the facts and circumstances outlined above, as the income generated from the principal amount (excluding the income required to preserve the real value of the principal) must be applied towards funding cash scholarships at some time in the future (at its discretion), the university considers whether it has incurred a financial liability under AASB 9 as a related amount. The university also considers whether derecognition of the financial asset is appropriate under Chapter 3 'Recognition and derecognition' of AASB 9, instead of the recognition of a financial liability.

In this example, no transfer of specific goods or services is required under the terms of the endowment. The scholarship is paid in cash rather than through the provision of goods or services. Accordingly, the university determines that it does not have a contract with a customer (the alumnus) that would be accounted for in accordance with AASB 1058.

Similarly, the endowment does not give rise to the following types of related amounts:

- a contribution by owners, as the alumnus does not control or have an ownership interest in the university;

- a lease liability as defined in AASB 16, as the endowment does not provide a right to use a specified asset; and

- a provision within the scope of AASB 137, as the agreement provides legal obligations and there are no other constructive obligations that are sufficiently specific to consider.

Accounting treatment

In accordance with paragraph 9, University A accounts for the endowment under AASB 9. In accordance with paragraph B13, any difference between the $2 million financial asset recognised and a related financial liability recognised would be accounted for under AASB 9. Paragraph 10 of AASB 1058 does not apply in this case.

Example 3B – Income (provision of services, no sufficiently specific performance obligation)

In this example, the facts of Example 3 apply, except that:

- University A is required to provide free student accommodation each year for one student for one year, for as long as University A continues to operate as a university and subject to the real value of the principal of $2 million being preserved;

- income generated from investment of the principal may be applied to provide the student accommodation; and

- any excess income generated from the investment of the principal is permitted to be spent on other university activities.

Based on these facts and circumstances, on gaining control of the endowment of $2 million, University A determines that there are no related amounts for the $2 million as the endowment does not give rise to:

- a contribution by owners, as the alumnus does not control or have an ownership interest in University A;

- a contract with a customer within the scope of AASB 15. Although the promise to provide student accommodation is a promise to transfer goods or services, it is not a sufficiently specific performance obligation relating to the controlled asset. While the promise to provide student accommodation is distinct and the university can identify at the end of each year whether or not it has delivered the accommodation for one student, it cannot identify when its obligation is fully satisfied and cannot allocate the transaction price as the promise is continuous as long as University A continues to operate as a university. University A must be able to identify when the performance obligation is satisfied for the promise to be identified as sufficiently specific (paragraph F20 of AASB 15);

- a lease liability as defined in AASB 16, as the endowment agreement does not provide a right to use a specified asset (the accommodation provided can vary from year to year);

- a financial liability within the scope of AASB 9 as there is no obligation to provide cash or other financial assets to other parties, only accommodation; or

- a provision within the scope of AASB 137, as the agreement provides legal obligations and there are no other constructive obligations that are sufficiently specific to consider.

Accounting treatment

In accordance with paragraph 10, the endowment of $2 million is accounted for by University A as income immediately in profit or loss on recognition of the financial asset in accordance with AASB 9.

The journal entry on initial recognition is:

	Debit	Credit
Cash	2,000,000	
Income		2,000,000

Example 3C – Contract liability under AASB 15

In this example, the facts of Example 3B apply, except that University A is required to provide the annual scholarship for one student's accommodation for a defined period of 30 years.

University A determines:

- it controls a financial asset ($2 million) within the scope of AASB 9; and

- on gaining control of the endowment, the university does not have related amounts in the form of contributions by owners, a lease liability, a financial liability or a provision.

However, the promise to provide student accommodation is a sufficiently specific performance obligation related to the asset that AASB 15 applies, as the obligation to provide student accommodation for one student each year is distinct, and the university is able to identify that its obligation under the agreement will be satisfied by the end of 30 years (paragraph F20 of AASB 15). The endowment is also an enforceable agreement. Accordingly, as the consideration provided for the endowment is solely a performance obligation within the scope of AASB 15, AASB 1058 does not apply.

Accounting treatment

On recognition of the endowment financial asset in accordance with AASB 9, University A also recognises a contract liability in a contract with a customer in accordance with AASB 15 for its performance obligation to transfer an annual scholarship for 30 years. University A recognises income immediately in profit or loss for any excess of the fair value of the cash transferred ($2 million) over the contract liability recognised in accordance with paragraph 106 of AASB 15.

The journal entry on initial recognition is:

	Debit	Credit
Cash	2,000,000	
Contract liability		1,850,000
Income		150,000

Example 4—Refundable prepaid local government rates

Local Council A calculates the rates it charges local residents on an annual basis approximately two months prior to the annual period to which the rates relate. Residents and other ratepayers are able to pay their rates in advance on a quarterly or annual basis. Rate payments received before the annual rateable period begins are fully refundable up to the beginning of the rateable period for which the payment is made. For example, if the Council receives a payment in May 20X6 for the rateable period from 1 July 20X6 to 30 June 20X7, the receipt is refundable in May and June 20X6.

The following transactions have occurred during May and June 20X6, in aggregate:

- ratepayers prepaid 20X6/X7 rates of $120,000; and
- refunds of prepaid rates totalling $7,000 were paid to ratepayers.

On receipt of prepaid rates, the Council determines that it has acquired cash (a financial asset) for no consideration to further the objectives of the Council. Accordingly, the transaction is within the scope of AASB 1058, and the Council seeks to identify any related amounts for recognition.

As the taxable event for the rates has not yet occurred (see AASB 9, Appendix C), the prepaid rates are refundable at the request of the ratepayer. Until the taxable event occurs, the prepaid rates do not have the character of non-contractual amounts arising from statutory requirements. Therefore, during the refundable period, the rates received in advance give rise to a financial liability that is within the scope of AASB 9. This is the related amount to be recognised in accordance with paragraph 9.

Accounting treatment

On recognition of the prepaid-rates financial asset, in accordance with paragraph 9 the Council also recognises the related amount of the financial liability in accordance with AASB 9, and no income is recognised by the Council. Following the occurrence of the taxable event on 1 July 20X6, the financial liability is extinguished and the Council recognises income for the prepaid rates that have not been refunded.

The journal entries for the accounting (aggregating the journal entries in May and June 20X6 for individual transactions) are:

	Debit	Credit
Receipt of prepaid rates (aggregate)		
Cash	120,000	
Financial liability		120,000
Refunds of prepaid rates (aggregate)		
Financial liability	7,000	
Cash		7,000
Taxable event occurs **1 July 20X6**		
Financial liability	113,000	
Income		113,000

Leases

IE4   Example 5 illustrates the requirements in AASB 1058 regarding the recognition of a lease liability in accordance with AASB 16.

Example 5—Lease with significantly below-market minimum lease payments

Charity A (lessee) enters a 30 year lease with a local government (the lessor) for the use of a facility. The lease contract specifies lease payments of $100 per annum. At the inception of the lease, the entity assesses the terms and conditions of the lease, including restrictions, and determines the fair value of the right to use the facility for 30 years is $360,000. The leased premises must be used to provide services to the homeless, or else Charity A will no longer be able to use the facility.

There are no other conditions specified in the lease contract.

Scope and asset recognition

Charity A determines:

* the $360,000 right-of-use asset is an asset the charity acquired for consideration significantly below fair value to further the objectives of the charity. Accordingly, the asset is within the scope of AASB 1058; and

* it controls a leased asset ($360,000) within the scope of AASB 16.

On recognition of the right-of-use asset, Charity A determines the lease does not give rise to related amounts of the following types:

* a contribution by owners, as the local government does not have an ownership interest in Charity A;

* a contract with a customer in accordance with AASB 15, because the lease liability arises from a lease contract within the scope of AASB 16 and there are no other sufficiently specific performance obligations requiring transfers of goods or services to the local government or others associated with the lease contracts. Use of the facility to provide services to the homeless is not sufficiently specific to identify when the services have been provided. Accordingly, AASB 15 does not apply;

* a provision within the scope of AASB 137, as the agreement provides legal obligations and there are no other constructive obligations that are sufficiently specific to consider; and

* a financial instrument, because lease contracts within the scope of AASB 16 are scoped out of AASB 9.

Accounting treatment

In accordance with AASB 16, Charity A recognises a right-of-use asset of $360,000 and a lease liability of $1,537, being the present value of the future lease payments discounted at Charity A's incremental borrowing rate of 5% per annum (as the interest rate implicit in the lease is not readily determinable). Charity A also recognises the difference of $358,463 between the fair value of leased asset and the lease liability as income at inception of the lease in accordance with paragraph 10 of AASB 1058.

The journal entry on initial recognition is:

	Debit	Credit
Right-of-use asset	360,000	
Lease liability		1,537
Income		358,463

Contract with a customer – revenue and income

IE5   Examples 6–8 illustrate the requirements in AASB 1058 regarding recognition of revenue and a contract liability in accordance with AASB 15. To be in the scope of AASB 15, the contract must:

(a)   be enforceable;

(b)   contain performance obligations to transfers goods or services to another party that are sufficiently specific to enable determination of when the obligation has been satisfied; and

(c)   not result in the goods or services specified being retained by the entity, ie the goods or services will be transferred to the customer or to other parties on behalf of the customer.

Example 6—Enforceable agreement, performance obligations and restrictions on timing of expenditure

Charity B receives a government grant of $2.4 million on 31 May 20X6, which is refundable if the money is not spent in the period 1 July 20X6 to 30 June 20X7.

Scope and asset recognition

Charity B determines:

- the $2.4 million grant is an asset the charity acquired to further the objectives of the charity; and

- it controls a financial asset ($2.4 million cash) within the scope of AASB 9.

The above fact pattern and analysis applies to Examples 6A and 6B, described below. Each example is considered in isolation.

Example 6A – Enforceable agreement, no specific performance obligations but restrictions on timing of expenditure

This example contains the additional fact that Charity B's agreement with the grantor specifies that the grant must be used in accordance with the charity's overall objectives. The agreement does not specify the services that the grant must be used for.

Charity B analyses the terms of the grant agreement and notes:

- the agreement is enforceable as the grantor can enforce its rights in the contract to require Charity B to return the cash of $2.4 million if Charity B does not spend the amount in the year ending 30 June 20X7;

- the required use of the funds to further the entity's objectives is not sufficiently specific to know when goods or services have been transferred and the obligation satisfied; and

- the time restriction on use of the funds is not sufficiently specific of itself to create a performance obligation to transfer goods or services to the grantor or a third party so that it can be identified when the obligation is satisfied. When funds have been commingled with other funds, such as general purpose funds, used to fund administrative services as well as those related to the objectives of the entity, it is not possible to reliably determine what transfer of goods or services may have occurred using the specific funds. The time restriction is also not sufficiently specific of itself to create a constructive obligation.

Consequently, Charity B concludes that the transaction is not a contract with a customer as defined under AASB 15. Because the $2.4 million grant is an asset the charity acquired for no consideration to further its objectives, the grant is within the scope of AASB 1058.

Accounting treatment

Charity B determines that there are no related amounts to recognise in accordance with paragraph 9. Therefore, Charity B recognises income of $2.4 million in accordance with paragraph 10 of AASB 1058 on 31 May 20X6 on recognition of the financial asset in accordance with AASB 9.

Furthermore, on 31 May 20X6, Charity B does not have a liability under AASB 9 for the potential breach of contract, as it has the discretion not to spend the grant money before 1 July 20X6. If Charity B breaches the contract by spending the money before 1 July 20X6 or failing to spend the grant in full by 30 June 20X7, the breach is the obligating event giving rise to a liability (in this instance, a penalty). For this reason, Charity B recognises the grant of $2.4 million as income as at 31 May 20X6. If Charity B breaches the contract, it recognises a liability and equivalent expense for the amount due for repayment when the breach occurs.

The journal entry for the accounting treatment is:

31 May 20X6	Debit	Credit
Cash	2,400,000	
Income		2,400,000

Example 6B – Enforceable agreement, sufficiently specific performance obligations and restrictions on timing of expenditure

This example contains the following additional facts relating to Charity B:

- Charity B's charter states its purpose is to provide counselling to victims of violence and emergency accommodation to the homeless; and

- Charity B has an agreement with the grantor that specifies the grant must be spent providing crisis counselling services for a given number of hours per week for the entire year ending 30 June 20X7. Charity B expects to fulfil its promise to provide the counselling services.

Based on the facts and circumstances outlined above, on gaining control of the grant of $2.4 million, Charity B determines that the grant agreement does not give rise to related amounts of the following types:

- a contribution by owners, as the government does not have an ownership interest in Charity B;

- a lease liability as defined in AASB 16, as the grant agreement is not a lease and does not contain a lease;

- a financial liability within the scope of AASB 9, as there is no unconditional obligation to repay the grant and the conditions requiring repayment of the grant are under the control of Charity B; and

- a provision within the scope of AASB 137, as the agreement provides legal obligations and there are no other sufficiently specific constructive obligations to consider.

Charity B concludes its agreement with the grantor is a contract with a customer as defined in AASB 15. This is on the basis that:

- the agreement is enforceable (refer to paragraphs F11–F19 of AASB 15), as the grantor can enforce its rights in the contract to require Charity B to return the funds if Charity B does not fulfil the specific performance obligations under the contract (ie by providing the counselling services for the specified number of hours per week for the entire year); and

- Charity B's obligation to provide the specific services (identified counselling services for a specific number of hours per week in 20X6/X7 to victims of violence) in return for the consideration from the grantor is sufficiently specific to determine when the obligation is satisfied, as it will be clear at the end of each week whether the specified hours of counselling have been provided (refer to paragraph F20 of AASB 15). The services are also provided to third parties and not consumed by Charity B.

Accounting treatment

In accordance with paragraph 9, the related amount for the $2.4 million is accounted for by Charity B as a contract liability in accordance with AASB 15 on recognition of the financial asset in accordance with AASB 9.

The journal entry for the initial recognition is:

31 May 20X6	Debit	Credit
Cash	2,400,000	
Contract liability		2,400,000

Example 7—Donations, management intent and discretionary use

Charity C's publicly stated objective is to build water wells to provide clean drinking water in developing countries.

Charity C received 200 donations of $800 each. The donors indicated the donations are to be used for the purpose of building water wells.

The above fact pattern applies to Examples 7A–7D, described below. Each example is considered in isolation.

Example 7A – Pledges

In this example, the facts in Example 7 apply, except the 200 donations of $800 each are pledged by donors to Charity C in a telethon, and no cash has yet been received by Charity C.

Charity C determines it does not control the future economic benefits associated with pledged amounts before receipt of the cash, as it does not have an enforceable right to require the donors to meet their pledge. Accordingly, the charity does not recognise an asset until the requirements of AASB 9 are satisfied. No journal entry is required.

Example 7B – Management intent, no legal or constructive obligations

In this example, the facts in Example 7 apply, except the Board of Charity C determined at a board meeting that funds raised from the public appeal from which the donated funds arose are to be used only for building water wells in Kenya. The Board has not publicly communicated this intention and its public statements are limited to those that appear in the Example 7 fact pattern above.

Scope and asset recognition

Charity C determines:

- the $160,000 in donations is an asset the charity acquired for no consideration to further the objectives of the charity. Accordingly, the donation is within the scope of AASB 1058; and

- it controls a financial asset ($160,000) within the scope of AASB 9.

Based on the facts and circumstances, on gaining control of the donations, Charity C determines that the donations do not give rise to related amounts of the following types:

- a contribution by owners, as the donors do not have an ownership interest in Charity C, or if they are owners, the donations were not made in their capacity as owners;

- a lease liability as defined in AASB 16, as the agreement Charity C enters into with the donors with respect to the donations is not a lease, and does not contain a lease;

- a financial liability within the scope of AASB 9, as there is no obligation to provide cash or another financial asset to other parties; and

- a provision within the scope of AASB 137, as the agreement provides legal obligations and there are no other constructive obligations to consider – there is no constructive obligation as past practice indicates water wells have been built in a number of different developing countries and the possible obligation to build water wells is not sufficiently specific to know when those funds received have been spent on water wells, or whether they have been spent on other purposes.

Charity C assesses whether it has any related amounts in the form of revenue from a contract with a customer in accordance with AASB 15. Charity C determines its arrangement with donors is not an enforceable agreement in accordance with paragraph 10 of AASB 15 as there is no return obligation, and although management intends to spend the monies to build wells in a particular country, there is no public statement that would establish an enforceable contractual arrangement. The Board noting that the donation is to be spent on water wells is not sufficiently specific to enable enforcement of the contract, and there is no return obligation if not spent on water wells.

Accounting treatment

Accordingly, Charity C recognises the donations as income when it gains control of the donated cash, in accordance with AASB 1058.

The journal entry for the initial recognition (in aggregate) is:

	Debit	Credit
Cash	160,000	
Income		160,000

Voluntary disclosure of restrictions

Although not an enforceable performance obligation, Charity C determines the donor expectations that the donations are intended to be used for the purpose of building water wells represents a restriction that is externally imposed on the donations. Consequently, Charity C elects to disclose the following information regarding the externally imposed restrictions on the donations by dividing total comprehensive income into restricted and unrestricted amounts in the statement of profit or loss and other comprehensive income in accordance with paragraph 37 of AASB 1058.

Summary of Statement of Profit and Loss and Other Comprehensive Income of Charity C

	$
Donation income – restricted	160,000
Donation income – unrestricted	230,000
Other revenue	10,000
Total revenue	**400,000**
Total expenses	220,000
Total comprehensive income	**180,000**
Total comprehensive income – restricted	160,000
Total comprehensive income – unrestricted	20,000

Charity C also elects to disclose restricted funds in the statement of financial position by presenting restricted and unrestricted components of retained profits.

Example 7C – Not enforceable and for discretionary use

In this example, the facts in Example 7 apply, except Charity C collected the donations as part of a campaign to raise funds for building water wells in Kenya. However, Charity C indicated that any funds not required would be spent on other purposes in Kenya.

Subsequently, Charity C suspended the construction of the water wells due to a disease outbreak in Kenya and redirected some of the donations received for the construction of the water wells to emergency food and medical supplies for the affected people in that country.

Consistent with Example 7B, Charity C determines it controls a financial asset within the scope of AASB 9 and does not have a related contribution by owners, lease liability, financial liability or provision, as specified in another Australian Accounting Standard.

Consistent with Example 7B, Charity C assesses whether it has any related amounts in the form of revenue from a contract with a customer in accordance with AASB 15. Charity C's promise to transfer goods or services related to the donations is not an enforceable arrangement with the donors. Charity B has the discretion to direct the use of the donated money, provided the use is consistent with the overall objectives of the charity, and the donors would not have recourse against Charity B for redirecting the donations. Consequently, Charity B does not have a contract with a customer as defined under AASB 15.

Accounting treatment

Accordingly, Charity B recognises the donations as income when it gains control of the donated cash, in accordance with AASB 1058.

The journal entry for the initial recognition (in aggregate) is:

	Debit	Credit
Cash	160,000	
Income		160,000

Example 7D – Enforceable and sufficiently specific performance obligation

At the public launch of Charity B's appeal for donations, Charity B:

- reaffirmed its 20-year history of building water wells in Kenya, with the funds raised for building water wells having been used only for that purpose and in that country. This has been the established practice despite its disclaimer that donated money may be used for other aid activities in response to changing circumstances;

- publicly reinforced its commitment that the funds raised through this appeal are to be used only in respect of building wells in the identified country;

- pledged to return the donated funds if Charity B is unable or not required to spend the funds to build wells in Kenya. This is despite the disclaimer that Charity B can redirect the funds to other aid activities in response to changing circumstances; and

- publicly stated that each donation of $800 will construct two water wells. (The cost of well construction can vary from that, depending on any problems faced and efficiencies achieved.)

Consistent with Examples 7B and 7C, Charity C determines it controls a financial asset within the scope of AASB 9 and does not have a related contribution by owners, lease liability, financial liability or provision, as specified in another Australian Accounting Standard.

In contrast to Examples 7B and 7C, Charity C determines that the donations arise under contracts with customers, as defined under AASB 15. This is because:

- the expectations raised through the commitment to refund unspent funds makes the agreements enforceable; and

- the public statements it has made and its long-standing practices, which create a valid expectation that the funds will be spent on the task of building wells in the identified country, are sufficiently specific as Charity B has committed that each donation of $800 will construct two water wells.

Accounting treatment

Charity B recognises each donation as a contract liability in accordance with AASB 15, when it gains control of the donated cash. Income is not recognised in respect of a donation until the specified two water wells have been built.

The journal entries for the accounting (aggregating the journal entries for individual donations) are:

	Debit	Credit
Initial recognition (aggregate)		
Cash	160,000	
Contract liability		160,000
Wells built (aggregate)		
Contract liability	160,000	
Income		160,000
Expenses – construction of 400 wells	153,000	
Cash		153,000

Example 8—Multi-year cash grant

The Local Government enters into an agreement with the State Government in the form of a Memorandum of Understanding (MOU) to receive a multi-year cash grant of $90,000 from the State Government, which is received in full on 24 June 20X0. The grant is to fund education programs over three years commencing 1 July 20X0, with the objective of increasing the literacy of students of a specific rural area.

The fact pattern and analysis applies to Examples 8A–8C, described below. Each example is considered in isolation.

Example 8A – Enforceable, no sufficiently specific performance obligation

This example contains the following additional facts:

- the MOU does not specify the activities the grant must be used for, other than an education program to increase literacy in a particular area; and

- the State Government can enforce the repayment of the grant if the entity does not apply the funds to relevant education programs.

Scope and asset recognition

The Local Government determines:

- the $90,000 grant is an asset the Local Government acquired to further the objectives of the Local Government; and

- it controls a financial asset ($90,000) within the scope of AASB 9.

Based on the facts and circumstances, on gaining control of the grant, the Local Government determines that there are no related amounts under paragraph 9 of AASB 1058 as the grant does not give rise to:

- a contribution by owners, as the State Government does not control the Local Government;

- a contract with a customer within the scope of AASB 15. The agreement is enforceable as the grantor can enforce its rights in the contract to require the Local Government to return the funds if the Local Government does not undertake relevant programs. However, the Local Government's performance obligation to provide relevant education programs is not sufficiently specific to be able to determine when the obligation is satisfied.

- a lease liability as defined in AASB 16, as the grant agreement is not a lease and does not contain a lease;

- a financial liability within the scope of AASB 9, as there is no obligation to provide cash or another financial asset to other parties; or

- a provision within the scope of AASB 137, as the agreement does not set out specific constructive obligations.

The Local Government concludes that the grant is an asset acquired for consideration that is significantly less than the fair value of the grant principally to further its objectives, and so the grant is within the scope of AASB 1058.

Accounting treatment

The Local Government determines that there are no related amounts to recognise under the MOU and so recognises the grant as income in accordance with paragraph 10 of AASB 1058 on 24 June 20X0.

The journal entry for the accounting is:

24 June 20X0	Debit	Credit
Cash	90,000	
Income		90,000

Example 8B – Enforceable and sufficiently specific performance obligation

This example contains the following additional facts:

- the MOU outlines the agreed activities of education programs that are tailored to the literacy needs of the students. The Local Government is required to provide to the State Government an annual report on the activities undertaken and the progress of the program. The Local Government is able to identify when its specific performance obligations are satisfied and expects to fulfil its promise to provide the agreed activities; and

- the State Government can enforce the repayment of the grant if the specified activities are not undertaken by requiring direct repayment or otherwise deducting unspent monies from future funding.

Scope and asset recognition

The Local Government determines:

- the $90,000 grant is an asset the Local Government acquired to further the objectives of the Local Government; and
- it controls a financial asset ($90,000) within the scope of AASB 9.

Based on the facts and circumstances, on gaining control of the grant, the Local Government determines that the grant agreement (the MOU) does not give rise to related amounts of the following types:

- a contribution by owners, as the State Government does not control the Local Government;
- a lease liability as defined in AASB 16, as the grant agreement is not a lease and does not contain a lease;
- a financial liability within the scope of AASB 9, as there is no obligation to provide cash or another financial asset to other parties; and
- a provision within the scope of AASB 137, as the agreement specifies legal obligations and there are no other sufficiently specific constructive obligations to consider.

The Local Government analyses the terms and conditions of the grant, and notes:

- the agreement is enforceable (refer to paragraphs F10–F18 of AASB 15), as the grantor can enforce its rights in the contract to require the Local Government to return the funds if the Local Government does not fulfil its specific performance obligations under the agreement (i.e. by providing literacy programs tailored to the needs of the students and annual reports to the State Government); and
- the Local Government's obligation to transfer the specific services in return for the consideration from the State Government is sufficiently specific so as to be able to determine when the obligation is satisfied.

Consequently, the Local Government concludes that the grant is a contract with a customer as defined under AASB 15. The cost to be incurred by the Local Government in providing the literacy programs can vary from the amount of the grant received.

Accounting treatment

In accordance with AASB 15, the Local Government:

- identifies each performance obligation relating to the grant;
- recognises a contract liability for its obligations under the agreement; and
- recognises revenue as it satisfies its performance obligations.

The journal entries for the accounting treatment (to the end of the first year) are:

Initial recognition	Debit	Credit
24 June 20X0		
Cash	90,000	
Contract liability		90,000
Year 1		
30 June 20X1		
Contract liability	30,000	
Revenue		30,000
Expenses – literacy program	32,000	
Cash		32,000

Example 8C – Multi-year conditional grant

This example contains the following additional facts:

- the Local Government receives $30,000 in the first year; and

- in the following years, the grant is paid in two equal portions, with each payment conditional on the Local Government's adequate progress toward advancing literacy in the previous year.

In this case, the Local Government recognises a receivable for the first year's grant. However, the Local Government has no control over the cash flows that are conditional on its future performance. Accordingly, the Local Government will only recognise those future cash flows once the Local Government becomes unconditionally entitled to them.

The journal entries for the accounting treatment for the first year's grant are:

Initial recognition	Debit	Credit
24 June 20X0		
Cash	30,000	
Contract liability		30,000
Year 1		
30 June 20X1		
Contract liability	30,000	
Revenue		30,000
Expenses – literacy program	32,000	
Cash		32,000

Transfers to enable an entity to acquire or construct a recognisable non-financial asset to be controlled by the entity (paragraphs 15–17)

IE6   Examples 9 and 10 illustrate the requirements in AASB 1058 regarding a transfer of a financial asset to enable an entity to acquire or construct a recognisable non-financial asset to be controlled by the entity, and when revenue is recognised. Example 11 illustrates a transfer to enable an entity to develop a non-financial asset that cannot be recognised under Australian Accounting Standards, and hence does not meet the criteria for the accounting for transfers of financial assets set out in paragraphs 15–17.

Example 9—Cash grant for the construction of a recognisable asset – income recognised over time

On 1 July 20X1, a private sector not-for-profit school, School A, receives a cash grant of $2 million from the State Government to build an early learning centre (ELC) on the school's land to the standard specified by government department regulations applicable to early learning (EL) programs for children.

The terms of the agreement require School A to:

- construct the ELC to include two rooms for the delivery of the EL programs and retain control of the ELC;

- return all unspent, uncommitted funding after building the ELC; and

- reimburse the State Government the whole or a portion of the grant amount (calculated on a pro-rata basis) if the ELC ceases to be used for the provision of EL programs within ten years of the date on which the funds have been fully paid.

At the end of the School's financial year (30 June 20X2), a survey of work completed indicated that the construction of the ELC was 60 percent complete and $1.2 million of the funding had been spent. The ELC was completed on 30 June 20X3 and the $2 million was fully spent.

Scope and asset recognition

School A determines:

- the $2 million grant is an asset the school acquired for consideration that is significantly less than the fair value of the grant to further the objectives of the school. Accordingly, the grant is within the scope of AASB 1058; and

- it controls a financial asset ($2 million) within the scope of AASB 9.

School A determines its agreement with the State Government is a transfer of a financial asset to enable it to construct a recognisable non-financial asset to be controlled by the school that meets the criteria in paragraph 15 of AASB 1058. That is, the agreement:

- requires the transfer of a financial asset to enable the school to acquire or construct a non-financial asset, the ELC, to the identified specification;

- relates to a non-financial asset (the ELC) that the school will be able to recognise as an asset under another Standard (AASB 116);

- does not involve a transfer of the non-financial asset to or on behalf of the State Government; and

- is enforceable, as it requires the school to refund the grant received to the State Government if the money is not used as specified in the agreement (eg non-construction of the ELC, unspent funds or EL programs cease to be provided within ten years).

School A applies paragraph 16 and determines that it does not need to recognise related amounts of the following types:

- a contribution by owners, as the grantor does not control or have an ownership interest in School A;

- a contract with a customer within the scope of AASB 15. The grant to construct an asset to be controlled by School A does not require a sufficiently specific transfer of goods or services to the grantor or another party (see paragraph F20 of AASB 15) and the requirement to continue using the school for EL programs is not sufficiently specific to know when the service has been provided. This is because it is not possible to know at the time an EL program is delivered whether it is a program that satisfies requirements of the grant;

- a lease liability as defined in AASB 16, as the agreement does not provide a right to use a specified asset;

- a financial liability within the scope of AASB 9, as there is no obligation to provide cash or another financial asset to other parties; and

- a provision within the scope of AASB 137, as the agreement specifies legal obligations and there are no other sufficiently specific constructive obligations to consider.

Accounting treatment

In accordance with paragraph 16 of AASB 1058, School A:

- identifies each obligation relating to the receipt of the cash grant and allocates the entire grant ($2 million) to those obligations – the work to be undertaken to construct the ELC;

- recognises a liability for its obligation under the agreement; and

- recognises income as it satisfies its obligation to construct the school.

In accordance with paragraph 16 of AASB 1058, income is recognised over time as the building is constructed.

The journal entries for the accounting treatment are:

Initial recognition	Debit	Credit
1 July 20X1		
Cash	2,000,000	
Obligation		2,000,000
Year 1		
30 June 20X2		
Obligation	1,200,000	
Income		1,200,000
Building – work in progress	1,200,000	
Cash		1,200,000
Year 2		
30 June 20X3		
Obligation	800,000	
Income		800,000
Building – work in progress	800,000	
Cash		800,000

The entries shown as 30 June 20X2 and 20X3 represent an aggregation of the entries occurring during each financial year. For example, income recognition might occur during a financial year according to specific target points in the construction agreement, such as the completion of foundations, framing, roofing, lock-up, and so on.

Example 10—Cash grant for the construction of a recognisable asset – income recognised at a point in time

The State Government makes a cash grant of $100,000 to Hospital X to acquire 16 intensive care hospital beds that are to be controlled by the entity and used in its operations. Six beds are acquired by the hospital in its first purchase, and the remaining ten beds in a second purchase.

Scope and asset recognition

Hospital X determines:

- the $100,000 grant is an asset Hospital X acquired for consideration that is significantly less than the fair value of the grant to further the objectives of the hospital. Accordingly, the grant is within the scope of AASB 1058; and

- it controls a financial asset ($100,000) within the scope of AASB 9.

Hospital X determines its agreement with the State Government is a transfer of a financial asset to enable it to acquire a recognisable non-financial asset to be controlled by the hospital that meets the criteria in paragraph 15 of AASB 1058. That is, the agreement:

- requires the transfer of a financial asset to enable Hospital X to acquire non-financial assets (the hospital beds) that conform to identified technical specifications;

- relates to non-financial assets that the hospital will be able to recognise as assets under another Standard (AASB 116);

- does not involve a transfer of a non-financial asset to or on behalf of the State Government; and

- is enforceable, as the Government may sue for specific performance or transfer of the ownership of any assets acquired with the funds if the money is not used to acquire the non-financial assets.

Hospital X applies paragraph 16 and determines that it does not need to recognise related amounts of the following types:

- a contribution by owners, as the grantor does not control or have an ownership interest in Hospital X;
- a contract with a customer within the scope of AASB 15. The grant to acquire the hospital beds for Hospital X does not require a sufficiently specific transfer of goods or services to the grantor or another party (see paragraph F20 of AASB 15);
- a lease liability as defined in AASB 16, as the agreement does not provide a right to use a specified asset;
- a financial liability within the scope of AASB 9, as there is no obligation to provide cash or another financial asset to other parties; and
- a provision within the scope of AASB 137, as the agreement specifies legal obligations and there are no other constructive obligations to consider.

Accounting treatment

In accordance with paragraph 16 of AASB 1058, Hospital X recognises the grant initially as a liability at the point in time when it obtains control of the funds. Hospital X recognises income as it acquires and controls the hospital beds.

The journal entries for the accounting treatment are:

	Debit	Credit
Initial recognition		
Cash	100,000	
Obligation		100,000
First purchase		
Obligation	37,500	
Income		37,500
Equipment – ICU	37,500	
Cash		37,500
Second purchase		
Obligation	62,500	
Income		62,500
Equipment – ICU	62,500	
Cash		62,500

Example 11 — Cash grant for the development of an unrecognisable asset – immediate income

The State Government makes a cash grant of $170,000 to Research Institute N to research improvements to long-range rainfall prediction models for agricultural areas in the west of the State. This will develop the intellectual property of the institute.

The terms of the agreement require Institute N to:

- develop its existing prediction models with the aim of improving the accuracy of six-month and twelve-month forecasts;
- provide semi-annual budget reports that detail how the funds have been spent; and
- return any funds that remain unspent after eighteen months.

Scope and asset recognition

Research Institute N determines:

- the agreement is enforceable as grant funds are refundable if the research is not undertaken or the funds are not fully expended under the project;

- the agreement is not a contract with a customer as defined in AASB 15 since no transfer of goods or services to the Government or other parties is required;

- the $170,000 grant is an asset acquired by Institute N for consideration that is significantly less than the fair value of the grant to further the objectives of the institute. Accordingly, the grant is within the scope of AASB 1058; and

- it controls a financial asset ($170,000) within the scope of AASB 9.

Institute N determines its agreement with the State Government is a transfer of a financial asset to enable it to acquire a non-financial asset (intellectual property) to be controlled by the institute. However, the institute concludes that the agreement does not meet the criteria in paragraph 15 of AASB 1058, since the non-financial asset cannot be recognised under other Standards: AASB 138 does not permit the recognition of research as an asset. Accordingly, the institute is not able to apply paragraph 16 to recognise a liability in relation to the obligation under the agreement to develop the non-financial asset.

Institute N therefore applies paragraph 9 and determines that it does not need to recognise related amounts of the following types:

- a contribution by owners, as the grantor does not control or have an ownership interest in Institute N;

- a contract with a customer within the scope of AASB 15 (as noted above);

- a lease liability as defined in AASB 16, as the agreement does not provide a right to use a specified asset;

- a financial liability within the scope of AASB 9, as there is no obligation to provide cash or another financial asset to other parties; and

- a provision within the scope of AASB 137, as the agreement does not set out any constructive obligations – the refund obligation is recognised only in the event of a breach of the agreement or when a breach is expected.

Accounting treatment

In accordance with paragraph 10 of AASB 1058, Institute N recognises the grant as income when it obtains control of the funds.

The journal entry for the initial recognition is:

	Debit	Credit
Cash	170,000	
Income		170,000

Volunteer services (paragraphs 18–22)

IE7   Example 12 illustrates the requirements in AASB 1058 for recognising the receipt of volunteer services as income and as an asset or an expense.

Example 12 — Volunteer services

A Local Government operates 35 preschools and employs 105 qualified educators to provide a quality education program for children. The program operates five days per week for 40 weeks a year. Preschools are subject to an externally imposed staff-to-children ratio. To satisfy the required ratio while employed staff take lunch breaks across a two-hour period, the Local Government obtains the services of volunteer qualified educators for the 35 preschools to relieve the employed staff for the two-hour period each day of the program.

The Local Government assesses whether it meets the criteria in paragraph 18 (or 19) to require (or permit) the recognition of these volunteer services as income:

- the fair value of the volunteer services received can be measured reliably by reference to the casual pay rates applicable to qualified educators. The Local Government estimates the fair value of the volunteer services at $30 per hour and measures the fair value of the volunteer services received for the financial year as $420,000. This is based on the calculation of $30 × 35 (relieving educators) × 2 (hours) × 5 (days) × 40 (weeks); and

- the services would have been purchased if they had not been donated, in order to meet the staff-to-children ratio at all times.

Accounting treatment

As the Local Government meets the criteria in paragraph 18, it is required to recognise volunteer services income of $420,000. The services of the volunteers do not result in the acquisition of an asset, and so an equivalent expense is also recognised.

The journal entry to recognise the volunteer services for the year is:

	Debit	Credit
Expenses – Preschools – Volunteers	420,000	
Income		420,000

Disclosure

Restrictions (paragraph 37)

IE8   Example 13 illustrates disclosures about externally imposed restrictions that limit or direct the purpose for which resources controlled by an entity may be used. Such disclosures are encouraged by this Standard but not required. This example extends Example 6A to illustrate possible disclosures about time restrictions on the expenditure of grant monies received. This example illustrates voluntary disclosures about restricted and unrestricted donation income in the Statement of Profit and Loss and Other Comprehensive Income, as well as disclosures relating to restricted net assets. Example 7B also illustrates voluntary disclosures of restrictions.

Example 13 — Voluntary disclosure regarding restrictions on timing of expenditure

As per Example 6A, Charity B receives a government grant of $2.4 million on 31 May 20X6, which is refundable if the money is not spent in the period 1 July 20X6 to 30 June 20X7. The grantor specifies that the grant must be used in accordance with the charity's overall objectives. The agreement does not specify the services that the grant must be used for.

Charity B concludes that the transaction is not a contract with a customer as defined under AASB 15. The charity determines that there are no related amounts to recognise in accordance with paragraph 9 of AASB 1058. Charity B does not have a liability under AASB 9 for a potential breach of contract, as it has the discretion not to spend the grant money before 1 July 20X6. Therefore, Charity B recognises income of $2.4 million in accordance with paragraph 10 on 31 May 20X6, on recognition of the financial asset in accordance with AASB 9.

Voluntary disclosure

Charity B elects to make the following disclosures in its financial statements for the year ended 30 June 20X6 to identify donations that are subject to some form of restriction in how the charity can use them, such as time restrictions imposed by donors.

Summary of Statement of Profit and Loss and Other Comprehensive Income of Charity B

	20X6	20X5
	$	$
Donation income – unrestricted	800,000	700,000
Donation income – restricted	2,400,000	3,000,000
Other revenue	850,000	820,000
Total revenue	**4,050,000**	**4,520,000**
Total expenses	1,700,000	1,300,000
Total comprehensive income	**2,350,000**	**3,220,000**
Total comprehensive income – unrestricted	(50,000)	220,000
Total comprehensive income – restricted	2,400,000	3,000,000

Notes to the Financial Statements

Note X – Changes in Restricted Net Assets	20X6	20X5
	$	$
Opening balance	3,000,000	900,000
Grant income received – time restrictions	2,400,000	3,000,000
Grant funds – time restrictions expired during the year	(1,000,000)	(900,000)
Closing balance	**4,400,000**	**3,000,000**

During the year, Charity B received a grant of $2.4 million from the government. This grant is to be spent in accordance with our charter in the 20X6/X7 year. Accordingly, the full amount of the grant received is treated as restricted net assets at the current reporting date.

The grant of $3 million received in June 20X5 was restricted by the donor (Outback Health Services Trust) to the provision of health services over a three-year period from 1 July 20X5. Therefore, $2 million of this grant continues to be identified as restricted net assets at the current reporting date.

Transition (paragraphs C2–C7)

IE9   Example 14 illustrates the modified retrospective initial application of this Standard to peppercorn leases.

Example 14—Peppercorn leases and modified retrospective initial application

School A, a not-for-profit school, was built on land leased to it by Church B. Church B (the lessor) leases the land to School A (the lessee) for a payment of $10 per year for 99 years (ie a peppercorn lease). On the date of transition to this Standard, the present value of the remaining lease payments is $100.

School A has a reporting period ending 30 June and recognises a right to use land under AASB 16 for the first time for its reporting period ending 30 June 2020. The fair value of the right of use of the land is $2 million at 1 July 2019. Prior to applying AASB 1058, School A had not previously recognised a right-of-use asset for land or a lease liability.

AASB 1058 (effective date 1 January 2019) also applies to School A for the first time for its reporting period ending 30 June 2020. As there is a significantly below-market lease at inception of the lease, School A identifies that the transaction is within the scope of AASB 1058 and elects to apply the modified retrospective approach permitted on transition to AASB 1058.

School A accounts for the peppercorn lease in accordance with the transition requirements of AASB 1058 by:

- recognising the right-of-use asset for the land as at 1 July 2019 at the fair value of $2 million;

- recognising the lease liability under AASB 16 of $100 (this accounting treatment is unaffected by AASB 1058); and

- recognising the difference between the fair value of the right-of-use asset and the lease liability as an adjustment to the opening balance of School A's retained earnings as at 1 July 2019.

Accounting treatment

The journal entry for the accounting is:

1 July 2019	Debit	Credit
Right-of-use asset – land	2,000,000	
Lease liability		100
Opening retained earnings		1,999,900

BASIS FOR CONCLUSIONS

This Basis for Conclusions accompanies, but is not part of, AASB 1058.

Introduction

BC1   This Basis for Conclusions summarises the Australian Accounting Standards Board's considerations in reaching the conclusions in AASB 1058. It sets out the reasons why the AASB developed the Standard, the approach taken to developing the Standard and the key decisions made. In making decisions, individual Board members gave greater weight to some factors than to others.

The need for change

BC2   Prior to the issue of this Standard and AASB 15 *Revenue from Contracts with Customers*, the recognition and measurement requirements for transactions giving rise to income depended on whether the transaction was reciprocal or non-reciprocal in nature. The accounting for income arising from reciprocal transactions was predominantly addressed in AASB 118 *Revenue* and AASB 111 *Construction Contracts*. The accounting for income arising from non-reciprocal transactions was addressed in AASB 1004 *Contributions*.

BC3   The Board observed determining whether a transaction was reciprocal or non-reciprocal in practice was not always straightforward. Entities found it challenging to determine whether approximately equal value had been provided in exchange to the other party or parties to the transfer, and contended that in many instances the immediate recognition of income in a non-reciprocal transaction did not faithfully represent the underlying financial performance of the entity. Diverse interpretations existed, with some entities recognising transactions with return obligations and specified performance outcomes as reciprocal transactions and some not.

BC4   Constituents were particularly concerned about the income recognition requirements as applied to grants, appropriations and other transfers of assets made on the condition that the not-for-profit entity deliver goods or services to nominated third parties. The Board heard that constituents who are preparers find it difficult to discuss financial information with grantors and donors, and challenging to explain why a not-for-profit entity needed additional resources when the financial statements indicated no such need. Users noted they did not think the financial statements were reflective of the economic reality of a not-for-profit entity's financial circumstances. Having regard to the feedback from constituents, the Board decided to undertake a project to conduct a fundamental review of the income recognition requirements applying to not-for-profit entities.

BC5 The Board observed that the International Accounting Standards Board had completed developments in the accounting for revenue with the issue of IFRS 15 *Revenue from Contracts with Customers* in May 2014. The Board noted it still needed to determine what, if any, amendments and guidance would be required to enable not-for-profit entities to apply the equivalent Australian Accounting Standard, AASB 15. In addition, the Board noted that the application of the performance obligation approach to revenue recognition adopted in AASB 15, using a broader concept of customer, had the potential to resolve some of the issues noted with AASB 1004. Consequently, the Board considered that this was an appropriate time to undertake a project to review the income recognition requirements applying to not-for-profit entities.

BC6 As part of its current project, the Board noted there is currently divergence in practice in the accounting for leases with significantly below-market terms and conditions, such as 'peppercorn' leases where a nominal amount is made as payment to the lessor. Some entities consider AASB 117 *Leases* takes precedence over AASB 1004 and accordingly, currently recognise such leases at nominal values; others consider the reverse applies and recognise such leases at fair value, together with a related contribution. The Board decided its project should also clarify the accounting for such leases.

BC7 The Board also observed that various Australian Accounting Standards required a not-for-profit entity to recognise assets received at fair value (or current replacement cost, in relation to inventories) only where the asset had been acquired for no or nominal consideration (for example, AASB 116 *Property, Plant and Equipment* and AASB 138 *Intangible Assets*). The Board perceived there to be a gap in the accounting for those transactions where an asset has been acquired for consideration that is below market but is more than nominal. The Board noted that under existing recognition and measurement rules at that time, an entity would likely not have recognised any income on the transaction, but measured the asset acquired at the amount of the consideration transferred. The Board considered that, in many instances, such transactions were unlikely to be conceptually different to those for which no consideration was transferred, and consequently decided to also consider the accounting for such transactions as part of this project.

Previous stages of this project

BC8 In previous stages of this project, the Board had previously exposed proposals on income recognition requirements for similar transactions as part of the following Exposure Drafts:

    (a)   ED 125 *Financial Reporting by Local Governments* (October 2003). This ED also addressed other issues;

    (b)   ED 144 *Proposed Guidance to accompany AASB 1004* Contributions (November 2005);

    (c)   ED 147 *Revenue from Non-Exchange Transactions (Including Taxes and Transfers)* (February 2006); and

    (d)   ED 180 *Income from Non-exchange Transactions (Including Taxes and Transfers)* (June 2009).

BC9 However, having regard to constituent feedback and developments in accounting internationally subsequent to the issue of each such Exposure Draft, the Board had decided not to finalise those previous Exposure Drafts. The last such Exposure Draft, ED 180, was closely based on IPSAS 23 *Income from Non-exchange Transactions (Taxes and Transfers)*. At that time, the Board decided, having regard to feedback received on the ED and the progress the IASB was making on a project to replace

IAS 18 *Revenue*, not to finalise the proposals set out in ED 180, but instead to refocus its project following issue of IFRS 15 *Revenue from Contracts with Customers*.

Alternative approaches considered

BC10 In developing this Standard, the Board considered whether to base the income recognition and measurement principles for a not-for-profit entity on those set out in:

(a)   AASB 1004 *Contributions*;

(b)   IPSAS, including IPSAS 23;

(c)   AASB 120 *Accounting for Government Grants and Disclosure of Government Assistance*; or

(d)   AASB 15 *Revenue from Contracts with Customers*.

BC11 The Board decided not to develop proposals based on the accounting specified by AASB 1004 (as in force at that time), having regard to constituent feedback leading to the Board undertaking the project. In addition, the Board observed that the approach in AASB 1004 does not acknowledge that a non-reciprocal transfer may be made on terms and conditions representative of a liability as defined in the *Framework for the Preparation and Presentation of Financial Statements*.

Using the IPSAS 23 exchange/ non-exchange approach

BC12 Unlike the income recognition requirements in AASB 1004, IPSAS 23 requires liabilities to be recognised in relation to non-exchange transactions when transferred assets are received on the condition that the recipient entity must:

(a)   consume the future economic benefits embodied in the transferred assets as specified; or if not,

(b)   return the future economic benefits to the transferor.

BC13 The Board observed that it had previously considered adopting an approach similar to that used in IPSAS, and exposed this for comment as part of ED 180. However, the Board had received constituent feedback that the:

(a)   definition of a 'non-exchange transaction' in IPSAS (a transaction in which "an entity either receives value from another entity without directly giving approximately equal value in exchange, or gives value to another entity without directly receiving equal value in exchange") was similar to the non-reciprocal definition and therefore would still be ambiguous and difficult to apply in practice; and

(b)   the notion of a liability in ED 180 was too narrow.

BC14 Having regard to the above, the Board decided not to develop proposals based on IPSAS in this project for the following reasons (see also paragraphs BC177–BC179):

(a)   IPSAS employs an exchange/non-exchange distinction to determine the accounting for income; with non-exchange being defined similarly to non-reciprocal in Australian Accounting Standards. The Board observed that part of the reason for undertaking this project was in response to constituent feedback of challenges in identifying a transaction as a reciprocal/non-reciprocal transaction, and concerns that the consequential accounting did not reflect the true underlying financial performance of the entity. Accordingly, the Board considered that basing its project proposals on existing IPSAS would not meet its objective in undertaking this project; and

(b)   the IPSASB is currently developing new standards-level requirements and guidance on revenue to amend or supersede that currently in IPSAS. As part of that project, the IPSASB is expected to have regard to the requirements set out in IFRS 15. The IPSASB is not expected to complete its project before 2019. Having regard to the effective date of AASB 15, the Board considered that it is necessary for it to develop guidance at this time to assist not-for-profit entities in implementing AASB 15 in advance of the IPSASB project.

Extending the scope of AASB 120

BC15 As part of its deliberations about an appropriate approach, the Board observed that extending the scope of AASB 120 to not-for-profit entities would allow government grants to be accounted for under a strict transaction-neutral approach. However, the Board was reluctant to do so, given the:

(a) limited scope of transfers addressed by AASB 120 compared to the varied transfers received by a not-for-profit entity; and

(b) application of the recognition and presentation requirements in that Standard could result in an entity's assets being materially understated. For example:

     (i) government grants of non-monetary assets may be measured at a nominal amount;

     (ii) government grants relating to assets may be deducted in determining the carrying amount of the assets; and

     (iii) grants are not to be recognised by an entity until there is reasonable assurance that the entity will comply with the conditions attaching to the grants and the grants will be received (however, conditions attaching to grants are relevant to whether liabilities exist, not to whether assets have been received).

BC16 The Board observed that extending the application of requirements in AASB 120 to all transfers of a not-for-profit entity would require a not-for-profit entity to defer income recognition for every form of transfer until there is reasonable assurance that the entity will comply with any conditions attached to the transfer. AASB 120 does not define 'conditions', and consequently, the Board was concerned there would be inconsistency in application of the requirements. For example, whether conditions include only performance conditions (as used in the IFRS for SMEs), akin to performance obligations of the form specified by AASB 15, or whether conditions include other conditions. The Board also considered it unclear whether the 'conditions' of some transfers, for example, an endowment that must be used to provide an annual scholarship, could ever be said to be met. Accordingly, the Board was not convinced that developing proposals based on AASB 120 would achieve its objectives in undertaking this project.

BC17 In addition, the Board discussed recent international developments for the recognition of income, and noted AASB 120 was less consistent with current conceptual thinking (compared to AASB 15) as it does not articulate the nature of obligations giving rise to a liability rather than income, or when these obligations can be said to have been satisfied. The Board observed that the principles in IAS 20 *Accounting for Government Grants and Disclosure of Government Assistance* had not been reconsidered fully at the time of issue of IFRS 15. However, the IASB considered the approach in IAS 20 when developing the *IFRS for SMEs* Standard. The IASB ultimately decided to adopt an approach that refers to the recognition of income when performance conditions are satisfied. This approach may be considered to be similar to the IFRS 15 performance obligation approach. Further, the Board observed that the IASB has no current plans to review IAS 20. Having regard to the significance of grants, taxes, donations and similar transfers to the income of a not-for-profit entity, the Board decided to confirm again its 2004 decision not to extend AASB 120 to apply also to not-for-profit entities.

Based on AASB 15

BC18 The Board issued AASB 15 in December 2014, incorporating IFRS 15 *Revenue from Contracts with Customers*, and superseding AASB 118 and AASB 111 (among other pronouncements). The AASB 15 revenue recognition model replaced the risk and rewards approach of AASB 118, introducing a performance obligation approach to the recognition of revenue. The five-step model in AASB 15 focuses on:

(a) identifying the contract;

(b) identifying performance obligations;

(c)   determining the transaction price;

(d)   allocating the transaction price; and

(e)   recognising revenue.

BC19   In the process of issuing AASB 15, the AASB decided that, consistent with AASB 118, AASB 15 should apply to not-for-profit entities as well as for-profit entities. In this project, the AASB considered whether income from non-reciprocal transfers should continue to be treated differently from revenue from reciprocal transfers. The Board concluded that, for any entity, a performance obligation (that is, a promise to transfer a good or a service to a customer in a contract) gives rise to a contract liability when the customer pays consideration for the good or service. Consequently, the Board decided that the principles in AASB 15 on performance obligations should apply to any entity, whether for-profit or not-for-profit, in the private sector or public sector.

BC20   Overall, the Board considered the financial reporting of not-for-profit entities would be best improved by, as a starting point, aligning the applicable recognition and measurement principles with the principles of AASB 15, and drawing on the guidance available in IPSAS where not inconsistent with Australian Accounting Standards. This is in keeping with the Board's policy on transaction neutrality.

Issue of ED 260

BC21   The Board's proposals with respect to the accounting for income of not-for-profit entities finalised in this Standard were exposed for public comment in April 2015 as part of ED 260 *Income of Not-for-Profit Entities*. In developing ED 260, the Board considered both the feedback received on ED 180 and the requirements of AASB 15. ED 260 proposed both revisions to the income recognition principles in AASB 1004, and development of guidance and illustrative examples to assist not-for-profit entities in implementing AASB 15.

BC22   Part B of ED 260 proposed the issue of a draft Standard establishing the principles that a not-for-profit entity shall apply to report useful information to users of financial statements about the nature and amount of assets, liabilities, income and cash flows arising from inflows (or net inflows) of resources from donations, grants, taxes, and similar transactions and events. The ED proposed that income is immediately recognised for the excess of an asset acquired over any related liabilities or contributions by owners. Related liabilities include contract liabilities arising in a contract with a customer within the scope of AASB 15.

BC23   In June 2015, the Board held roundtables in Melbourne, Canberra, Brisbane and Sydney to seek feedback on its proposals set out in ED 260. The ED proposals were also presented at various forums, workshops and discussion groups. In addition, the Board conducted targeted meetings to help ensure the Board understood the implications of its proposals to entities with different not-for-profit objectives (for example, charities and local governments).

BC24   The Board received feedback on its proposals through receipt of 34 formal comment letters on ED 260. The Board also obtained feedback via means such as email, meetings with constituents, presentations to various bodies and social media. About half the respondents to the Exposure Draft explicitly considered that overall, the proposals would result in financial statements that would be useful to users. Many respondents to ED 260 expressed support for no longer basing income recognition requirements on a reciprocal/non-reciprocal transfer distinction as previously specified by AASB 1004, but on requirements based on satisfying a performance obligation.

BC25   Many respondents to ED 260 qualified their support that a resulting Standard would result in financial statements that would be useful to users. The main concerns raised about the proposals were:

(a)   the proposals would not fully resolve the current dissatisfaction with existing income recognition requirements as entities would not be able to fully defer income recognition to such time as related expenses are recognised. The

Board noted that responding fully to such concerns would result in liabilities being recognised inconsistent with the *Framework for the Preparation and Presentation of Financial Statements* and that with no conceptual basis it would be difficult to distinguish which receipts should be deferred and which should not. In response, the Board decided to add disclosure encouraging entities to disclose information in the financial statements (including on the face of the financial statements) of externally imposed restrictions on an entity. The Board considered this would go some way to addressing constituent concerns that financial performance is misrepresented to users as it allows preparers to better explain their financial performance to others;

(b)   the proposals were presented in an overly complicated manner, and consequently the interaction with other Australian Accounting Standards was not necessarily clear. In response, the Board decided to redraft the pronouncements to clarify the specified requirements when finalising this Standard (and AASB 2016-8), and to add further illustrative examples to illustrate the operation of the Standard, including its interaction with AASB 15 and other Australian Accounting Standards. As part of this, the Board decided that this Standard should not address the recognition of assets that are already the subject of existing Australian Accounting Standards (see paragraphs BC58–BC59).

BC26 Given the significance of this project to not-for-profit entities, the Board decided to establish a Project Advisory Panel consisting of preparers and advisors. The Panel provided valuable insights to the AASB during the Board's redeliberations of the ED, enabling the Board to make better informed decisions about whether, and how, to finalise the proposals in ED 260.

BC27 In addition, the Board decided to invite public comment on draft pronouncements incorporating the Board's decisions following completion of its redeliberations. Draft Standards were issued in September 2016 for public comment primarily seeking feedback on matters constituents considered to be a 'fatal flaw' with the pronouncements. The Board received seven formal submissions, and also obtained feedback via various presentations and meetings held with other constituents and with Panel members.

Finalisation of ED 260

BC28 Following the consultation period, and after considering constituent comments received, the Board decided to proceed with issuing revised principles for the recognition and measurement of income of not-for-profit entities largely as exposed. The Board considered the identified benefits of the revised requirements to exceed the costs of the revised requirements.

BC29 The Board observed some of the costs of the new requirements to be:

(a)   costs of changing systems and processes to reflect the revised requirements;

(b)   costs of reviewing the terms of existing contracts, funding agreements and similar to determine the impact on transition. The Board observed that it expects the operation of the transitional provisions to largely negate these costs;

(c)   increased costs associated with the requirement to measure more assets at fair value (or current replacement cost, in relation to inventories) at initial recognition. The Board observed that while the consequential amendments made by this Standard will require more assets to be recognised and measured at fair value, these requirements better reflect the value transferred to the entity. The Board noted this Standard does not require assets (including assets obtained in a 'peppercorn' lease where a nominal amount is made as payment to the lessor) to be measured at fair value on an ongoing basis, but only on initial recognition (or in some instances, on transition to this Standard). Further, the Standard does not require the valuations to be conducted by a professional valuation expert. In addition, the Board noted the Standard does not require assets in the form of donated inventory to be recognised and measured at current replacement cost where the item donated is not material;

(d)   increased costs associated with the requirement to separately identify components not related to a transfer of goods or services. In response, the Board has limited the instances in which an entity is required to separately account for such components in a contract with a customer, and only requires the accounting to be applied where the component is material;

(e)   increased costs associated with identifying whether transactions are contracts with customers within the scope of AASB 15, or to be accounted for in accordance with this Standard. The Board noted it had added further guidance on enforceability and further illustrative examples to the Standard to assist entities in understanding whether the accounting for income arising from an arrangement was likely to be addressed by AASB 15 or by this Standard; and

(f)   costs of educating users of the financial statements of the new approach.

BC30 The Board considered some of the benefits of the revised requirements to be:

(a)   the approach adopted in AASB 1058 and AASB 15 (as amended by AASB 2016-8) best responds to constituent concerns about the operation of the income recognition requirements formerly set out in AASB 1004, compared to the alternatives considered (see paragraphs BC10–BC17 above);

(b)   the Board's policy of transaction neutrality means that the application of AASB 15 to not-for-profit entities needed to be addressed at this time; however the concept of performance obligations in AASB 15 has enabled a fundamental change to income recognition for not-for-profit entities. The performance obligation approach is more comprehensible than the reciprocal approach of AASB 1004;

(c)   AASB 1058 and AASB 15 (as amended by AASB 2016-8) provide a better reflection of the underlying substance of transfers made to a not-for-profit entity recipient – under the revised principles, in general, income is deferred where an entity has a contractual obligation to deliver specified goods or services;

(d)   there will be greater transparency of an entity's assets and liabilities which results in better accountability and stewardship. Assets will be measured at fair value (or current replacement cost, in relation to inventories) at initial recognition where the asset has been acquired for consideration that is significantly less than its fair value, or if no consideration was provided, and the difference is principally to enable the entity to further its objectives. This helps address the current ambiguity in accounting by a not-for-profit lessee for leases with significantly below-market lease payments and for other assets where the consideration is more than nil or nominal amount but significantly less than the asset's fair value;

(e)   while the principles in this Standard do not completely address constituent concerns about potential misrepresentation of the not-for-profit entity's financial position and financial performance to users, the Board has managed this through encouraging entities to disclose information distinguishing for users amounts that are restricted in their use (but which may have been recognised as income immediately in accordance with this Standard). The Board considered that, as there is no contractual liability, the entity has the ability to use the assets acquired in alternative ways if that best reflects the needs of the entity, although the entity may currently have every intention of continuing to use the assets acquired in a designated way;

(f)   the revised principles are more conceptually consistent with the *Framework for the Preparation and Presentation of Financial Statements* as they require the recognition of a liability (a contract liability in accordance with AASB 15 or obligation to construct an asset in accordance with this Standard) where an obligation exists.

BC31 The Board noted that while neither the underlying approach exposed nor the scope of the transactions the project was intended to address has changed between ED 260 and the final pronouncements, in response to the feedback received, it had amended or clarified various proposals in ED 260, and finalised them in a form different to that exposed. More significant changes from the ED include:

(a) asset recognition requirements to be specified only by other Australian Accounting Standards. However, the Board observed this Standard makes consequential amendments to other Standards to extend the requirement to measure recognised assets at fair value (or current replacement cost, in relation to inventories) on initial recognition to a broader range of assets;

(b) AASB 1058 to specify requirements for an in-substance transfer of a non-financial asset to the entity for its own use;

(c) additional disclosures;

(d) additional transitional provisions;

(e) additional guidance and illustrative examples; and

(f) deferral of the effective date.

BC32 The Board considered that, overall, its decisions on this project have not significantly departed from those exposed in a manner that adversely affects entities applying the Standard. The Board decided to finalise its proposals exposed in ED 260 by:

(a) issuing AASB 1058 to address the accounting for income of not-for-profit entities. The Standard establishes principles for not-for-profit entities that apply to transactions where the consideration to acquire an asset is significantly less than fair value principally to enable a not-for-profit entity to further its objectives, and to the receipt of volunteer services;

(b) issuing AASB 2016-8 *Amendments to Australian Accounting Standards – Australian Implementation Guidance for Not-for-Profit Entities* to add implementation guidance and illustrative examples to AASB 15 to assist not-for-profit entities in applying the Standard. In addition, AASB 2016-8 adds implementation guidance to AASB 9 on the initial measurement and recognition of non-contractual receivables arising from statutory requirements;

(c) retaining AASB 1004 *Contributions*, amended to exclude transactions now addressed by AASB 1058; and

(d) issuing AASB 2016-7 *Amendments to Australian Accounting Standards – Deferral of AASB 15 for Not-for-Profit Entities* to defer the effective date of AASB 15 for application by not-for-profit entities.

BC33 The remainder of this Basis for Conclusions primarily focuses on issues pertaining to transfers of resources to a not-for-profit entity that are not contracts with customers within the scope of AASB 15, and the Board's decisions with respect to contributions by owners. The Board's considerations in reaching the conclusions in AASB 2016-8 are set out in the Basis for Conclusions to AASB 2016-8.

Objective

BC34 The Board noted that it had proposed a resulting Standard to address the accounting for inflows of resources arising from donations, grants, taxes, and similar transactions and events. In finalising this Standard, the Board decided to express the objective of this Standard in:

(a) a broader manner, to avoid inadvertently excluding some transactions from the scope of the Standard; and

(b) 'plainer' language, so that users can clearly understand the purpose of the Standard.

Scope

Income, including revenue, of not-for-profit entities

BC35 The Board considered whether to define the scope of AASB 1058 based on revenue of not-for-profit entities (except revenue within the scope of AASB 15 or another Australian Accounting Standard) or on income of not-for-profit entities arising from inflows of resources. The Board noted:

(a) revenue is defined in AASB 15 as income arising the course of an entity's ordinary activities; and

(b) some types of income of not-for-profit entities (such as bequests and other donations, which historically fell within the scope of AASB 1004) can arise from transactions and other events outside the course of an entity's ordinary activities. Limiting the scope of AASB 1058 to revenue could therefore omit requirements and guidance on potentially significant types of income of not-for-profit entities and only partially meet the objective of this project.

BC36 Accordingly, the Board based its proposals in ED 260 on the concept of income of an not-for-profit entity arising from inflows of resources because, in its view, revenue of not-for-profit entities did not capture all transactions that the Board intended AASB 1058 to provide requirements for. The Board observed that this does not mean that income recognised in accordance with this Standard is not also revenue of a not-for-profit entity; the extent to which amounts recognised in accordance with this Standard meets the definition of revenue to the entity (that is, income arising the course of an entity's ordinary activities) is a matter of facts and circumstances.

Assets acquired for more than no or nominal cost, but significantly less than fair value

BC37 In ED 260, the Board proposed that, if:

(a) a vendor in a transaction in which a not-for-profit entity acquires an asset, or

(b) a lessor, in a finance lease entered into by a not-for-profit entity;

makes a donation in the sale or lease contract, the not-for-profit entity should measure the cost of the asset at fair value. Accordingly, a broader range of assets may need to be measured at fair value on initial recognition than currently required, and a corresponding amount may be recognised as income to the extent no related liabilities or equity contributions arise on the transaction.

BC38 The Board decided to finalise its proposals in this regard, largely as proposed, by way of consequential amendments to various other Australian Accounting Standards. The Board's considerations in forming this decision are set out in paragraphs BC60–BC68 below.

Significantly less than fair value principally to enable the entity to further its objectives

BC39 Having regard to feedback received, in its redeliberations the Board decided to finalise these proposals, but to shift the focus of AASB 1058 away from emphasising the identification of donations, grants and similar transfers towards requiring an entity to identify whether an asset (other than volunteer services) was acquired for consideration that was significantly less than fair value principally to enable the entity to further its objectives. The Board considered this does not change the scope exposed in ED 260, but:

(a) avoids inadvertently limiting the extent of transactions that might give rise to income on initial recognition of an asset; and

(b) gives entities a clear indication of the transactions that are captured within the scope of AASB 1058;

(c) has the benefit of not requiring the entity to make an assessment of the transferor's intent; and

(d)   continues to exclude acquisitions of assets at discounts attributable to auction, distress sale and trade discount pricings.

BC40 In developing its articulation of a revised scope for the Standard, the Board was conscious it did not intend for this Standard to apply to transactions such as trade discounts and distress sales, for which the consideration paid for an asset may be significantly below the asset's fair value. The Board's view is that such discounts, where made available to all market participants (or a particular market segment) regardless of the participants' objectives, are not specific to the not-for-profit sector: other Australian Accounting Standards specify the accounting for such transactions.

BC41 The Board observed that 'significant' is a term used in other Standards, and considered its meaning therefore would be readily understandable by users of this Standard. The Board also noted that expressing the scope of AASB 1058 by reference to transactions "significantly less than fair value ... " means that transactions where the consideration is only marginally less than fair value are not expressly covered. Therefore, such transactions may be accounted for consistently with the requirements of AASB 1058 or with the accounting applicable to for-profit entities. Although this could mean less consistency in the accounting by not-for-profit entities for all asset transactions with consideration less than fair value, the Board regarded this approach as an appropriate balancing of the costs and benefits in accounting for transactions with consideration that is less than fair value, but not significantly less than fair value.

BC42 Some respondents to ED 260 were concerned that the Standard would require the not-for-profit recipient to make an assessment of the transferor's intentions in undertaking a transaction with the entity. For this reason, in developing its articulation of a revised scope for AASB 1058, the Board wanted to avoid using language that implied a need to assess the vendor's intentions. Accordingly, the Board decided to articulate in the scope that its interest is in transactions occurring principally to enable the entity to further its objectives. The Board considered the term 'principally':

(a)   provides a link between the significantly reduced purchase price (compared to fair value) and the purpose of that reduction being to enable a not-for-profit entity to further its objectives;

(b)   is more likely to be better understood as it is also currently used in Commonwealth grant applications and in taxation law (for example, in relation to principal place of business); and

(c)   is useful as there may be more than one reason for setting the terms and conditions of the transactions.

BC43 The Board considered using the term 'specifically' or 'particularly' in place of 'principally'. However, the Board decided not to finalise the Standard using this language due to:

(a)   the similarity of the term 'specifically' to 'sufficiently specific' (as used in AASB 15); and

(b)   concern that the term 'particularly' is too broad, and could give rise to differences in practice as to whether certain transactions are within the scope of this Standard.

BC44 This Standard makes consequential amendments to AASB 16 *Leases* to require a not-for-profit lessee to measure the right-to-use asset in a lease at its fair value where the lease has been undertaken on significantly below-market terms and conditions principally to enable the entity to further its objectives. AASB 117 is similarly amended in respect of the leased asset recognised in a finance lease. The Board observed that the lease payments (the consideration) to acquire the asset in such transactions will be significantly less than the asset's fair value. Consequently, leases undertaken on significantly below-market terms and conditions principally to enable the entity to further its objectives are within the scope of AASB 1058.

Scope exclusions

BC45 While not wanting to limit the extent of transactions that might give rise to income on initial recognition of an asset, the Board acknowledged that in some cases other Standards provide more detailed income recognition requirements. Accordingly, the Board decided to exclude transactions within the scope of the following Standards from AASB 1058:

(a)   AASB 3 *Business Combinations*;

(b)   AASB 4 *Insurance Contracts*, AASB 1023 *General Insurance Contracts* and AASB 1038 *Life Insurance Contracts*; and

(c)   AASB 112 *Income Taxes*.

BC46 The Board expects it would be rare for a not-for-profit entity to acquire an asset for consideration in the form of share-based payment valued significantly below the asset's fair value, on terms made principally in order to further the entity's objectives. However, the Board decided to exclude AASB 2 *Share-based Payment* from this Standard for avoidance of doubt.

BC47 The Board also decided to exclude, from the scope of AASB 1058:

(a)   licences outside the scope of AASB 15 (see paragraph BC48 below); and

(b)   restructures of administrative arrangements within the scope of AASB 1004 *Contributions* (see paragraph BC49).

BC48 In its redeliberations on the ED, the Board discussed a concern that AASB 1058 would apply to a transfer of a licence to a not-for-profit entity, where that transaction is not within the scope of AASB 15. The Board heard that the accounting for licences in the public sector is a significant issue, and observed that the Board had not before considered whether public sector licences should be accounted for in accordance with AASB 1058, or whether the licences are more appropriately accounted for by analogy to AASB 15. The Board signalled its intention to undertake a separate project on the accounting for public sector licences, and as it did not want to presuppose the accounting outcomes of that project, decided to exclude licences that are outside the scope of AASB 15 from this Standard. The Board noted that not-for-profit entities with such licences should develop an accounting policy in accordance with AASB 108, and that this policy could extend to applying the accounting set out in AASB 1058 by analogy.

BC49 The Board noted that the requirements of AASB 1058 could be interpreted to apply to restructures of administrative arrangements, which are addressed in AASB 1004 (see paragraph BC173 below). To avoid confusion as to which Standard applies to these transactions, the Board decided to exclude them from the scope of AASB 1058.

Terminology

BC50 NFP entities might acquire, or obtain, an asset in a number of circumstances. Various terms are commonly used to describe acquisitions of assets under terms and conditions that also provide a significant benefit to an entity, including 'grant', 'donation', 'bequest', 'assistance' and 'endowment'. These terms are not necessarily synonymous but are at times used interchangeably. Therefore, while these terms might be familiar to not-for-profit entities the Board decided not to develop accounting requirements based upon them.

BC51 When considering the underlying transactions associated with the above terms the Board observed the term used for a particular transaction is not important; rather, it is the characteristics or substance of the transaction that should determine the appropriate accounting. Accordingly, the Board decided to express the principles in AASB 1058 as far as possible without reference to such commonly used terminology.

BC52 However, the Board noted in order for AASB 1058 to remain accessible to preparers and other users, it could not completely avoid the use of such terms, especially in guidance material accompanying the Standard. Accordingly, the Board decided to clarify in AASB 1058 that an entity considers the substance, rather than the form, of transfers of resources to a not-for-profit entity for consideration significantly less than fair value principally to enable the entity to achieve its objectives in identifying the applicable requirements of AASB 1058.

Extending the scope to not-for-profit transferors and for-profit entities

BC53 The Board considered whether the scope of its project should be extended to address the accounting by not-for-profit transferors in arrangements giving rise to inflows of resources to a not-for-profit entity. The Board decided not to address this issue as part of the current project for the following reasons:

(a) the Board aims to address not-for-profit specific requirements for a topic as promptly as possible after an IFRS Standard for a similar topic is issued; and

(b) to ensure timely issue of these requirements. The Board was concerned broadening the scope of this project to address transferor accounting would raise issues not addressed in IFRS 15, and therefore delay the finalisation of pronouncements under this project.

BC54 The Board also considered whether the principles in this Standard should be extended to similar transactions of for-profit entities. The Board noted its policy on IFRS compliance for such entities, and decided not to extend the application of this Standard to these entities. The Board confirmed its decision as part of its redeliberations on this project, not having received significant contrary feedback in this regard. Accordingly, the accounting for certain transfers (eg government grants) may differ between that of a for-profit applying AASB 120 *Accounting for Government Grants and Disclosure of Government Assistance* and a not-for-profit public sector entity applying this Standard.

Recognition and measurement

Approach taken in this Standard

BC55 The Board considered that AASB 1058 should operate on a 'residual' basis, meaning that entities first apply other applicable Australian Accounting Standards to a transaction before recognising income in accordance with AASB 1058. This approach was exposed in ED 260 and generally accepted.

BC56 To assist readers of AASB 1058 the Board decided to insert common examples of 'related amounts' that could be recognised on the acquisition of an asset. These include:

(a) contributions of equity;

(b) revenue or a contract liability arising from a contract with a customer;

(c) a lease liability;

(d) a financial instrument; or

(e) a provision.

BC57 Many respondents to ED 260 expressed support for the inclusion of examples illustrating the interaction of other Australian Accounting Standards with AASB 1058. The Board considered constituent feedback seeking further specific examples, and improved articulation of how each example illustrates the principles of the Standard. The Board was conscious that illustrative examples cannot consider all situations, and that the particular circumstances of each transaction must be considered to determine the appropriate accounting treatment. However, in response to the feedback received, the Board decided to add several further examples to assist users of the Standard to understand the intended operation of the Standard, and to simplify examples proposed in ED 260.

Recognition of assets

BC58 Consistent with the approach taken in AASB 1004, in ED 260 the Board proposed asset recognition requirements for AASB 1058 that arguably overrode the recognition criteria of other Australian Accounting Standards. Under those proposals, entities would have recognised an asset and measured it at fair value in accordance with the proposed requirements and then subsequently measured that asset in accordance with its applicable Standard. In its redeliberations on ED 260, the Board noted it was not their intent to override the recognition criteria for an asset in other Standards when proposing asset recognition criteria be included in this Standard.

BC59 Having regard to the above, the Board decided not to proceed with the asset recognition requirements it proposed in ED 260 (other than for volunteer services). Accordingly, this Standard does not specify asset recognition criteria or the guidance on control that had been proposed in ED 260. Instead, the Board decided to clarify consequential amendments to other Standards that specify the initial measurement requirements for transactions within the scope of AASB 1058 and to direct that this Standard applies to assets recognised in accordance with other Australian Accounting Standards, where that asset had been acquired for consideration that is significantly less than fair value principally to enable the entity to further its objectives.

Measurement of assets

BC60 As noted in paragraph BC7, various Australian Accounting Standards presently require a not-for-profit entity to recognise assets received at fair value (or current replacement cost, in relation to inventories) where the asset had been acquired for no or nominal consideration. Part of the Board's reason for undertaking this project was to address the perceived gap in the accounting for transactions where an asset has been acquired for reduced consideration that is more than a nominal amount; the reduced consideration representing a donation (or other transfer) to the entity to further its objectives.

BC61 The Board considered that, generally, assets and liabilities of not-for-profit entities arising from transactions within the scope of a pronouncement resulting from this project should initially be measured in accordance with the measurement requirements of any other Standard applying to that class of assets or liabilities (for example, AASB 9, AASB 15 or AASB 116), because there is not a not-for-profit-entity-specific reason to depart from those measurement requirements. However, the Board considered that, if a vendor, in a transaction in which a not-for-profit entity acquires an asset, or a lessor, in a finance lease entered by a not-for-profit entity, makes a donation in the sale or lease contract, the not-for-profit entity should measure the cost of the asset at fair value with a corresponding amount recognised as income (assuming there are no related amounts to recognise on the transaction in accordance with paragraph 9 of the Standard). The Board noted that this view is consistent with the requirement in paragraph 66 of AASB 15 for an entity to measure any non-cash consideration at fair value to determine the transaction price in respect of a contract in which a customer promises consideration in a form other than cash.

BC62 The Board exposed this view as part of ED 260. The Board observed that this proposal was not limited to acquisitions of assets at no cost or for nominal consideration. Consequently, in ED 260 the Board proposed:

(a)   extending the scope of the corresponding requirements in AASB 102, AASB 116, AASB 138, AASB 140 and AASB 141 that specify that the cost of an asset is measured at its fair value (or current replacement cost, in relation to inventories) as at the date of acquisition if the asset was acquired at no cost or for nominal consideration;

(b)   some finance lease assets of lessees would consequently be initially measured at fair value, rather than at the lower of the fair value of the leased property and the present value of the minimum lease payments (see AASB 117). The Board observed its proposed modification of the leasing requirements in this regard would achieve consistency with the Standards referred to in paragraph BC62(a); and

(c)   other assets recognised in accordance with Part B of ED 260 would also be required to be initially recognised at fair value.

BC63 The Board considered that the previous limitation on the use of fair value (or current replacement cost, in relation to inventories) to measure cost (ie when assets are acquired at no cost or for nominal consideration) was too narrow, for the following reasons:

(a)   significant donations made by vendors are not recognised when the consideration paid by the entity is greater than nominal;

(b)   as a consequence of (a), donations are treated inconsistently (for example, because a cash donation is recognised but a donation in the form of a discount on an asset purchase is not); and

(c)   the different treatment of donated assets, according to whether consideration is greater than 'nominal', means that it is important to identify when consideration is 'nominal'; however, that term is undefined and its application may require subjective assessments.

BC64 Accordingly, the Board considered further modification of the asset measurement requirements set out in Australian Accounting Standards may be warranted. The Board proposed this modification in ED 260 as it considered the benefits of further modifying IFRS requirements in this regard to outweigh any additional costs to a not-for-profit entity, having regard to the scale of such transactions in the not-for-profit sector and noting that the modification would improve comparability by requiring consistent accounting for transactions of the same nature. In its redeliberations, the Board confirmed its view in this regard and decided to finalise its proposals largely as exposed, amended to reflect its revised articulation of the scope of this Standard. However, in response to feedback about the undue complexity of a resulting pronouncement and to facilitate understanding of the interaction between AASB 1058 and other Standards, the Board decided not to specify measurement requirements in respect of an asset (other than for volunteer services) in AASB 1058, but to reflect these within the specific other Australian Accounting Standards. Accordingly, this Standard makes consequential amendments to AASB 16, AASB 102, AASB 116, AASB 117, AASB 128, AASB 138, AASB 140 and AASB 141 to extend the requirement to measure assets at fair value (or current replacement cost, in relation to inventories) to include all assets acquired where the consideration for the asset is significantly less than fair value principally to enable the entity to further its objectives. The Board observed that income may arise on the initial recognition of a broader set of assets under the revised requirements set out in this Standard (including Appendix D) compared to the previous requirements.

BC65 The Board observed that under the revised requirements, a not-for-profit entity may be required to account for certain transactions made on significantly below-market terms and conditions differently to a for-profit entity. For example, a for-profit entity that negotiates a favourable price to acquire a property will initially measure that asset at the amount of consideration transferred. In contrast, a not-for-profit entity that negotiates a similar favourable price to acquire property will initially measure that asset at the asset's fair value for transactions where that price was provided to the entity in support of the not-for-profit entity's objectives, and the price is significantly different to the asset's fair value. The Board noted that this is not in keeping with a strict transaction neutrality policy. However, the Board considered its revised requirements appropriately reflect the substance of the transaction between a vendor and a not-for-profit entity and that the scale of such transactions in the not-for-profit sector is sufficiently greater than that in the for-profit sector to warrant the adoption of requirements for not-for-profit entities that differ from those for for-profit entities based on IFRS Standards.

BC66 In keeping with its decision not to specify measurement requirements in respect of an asset that is already the subject of an existing Australian Accounting Standard, the Board decided not to finalise proposed guidance on the measurement of taxation income (and other non-contractual receivables arising from statutory requirements) in AASB 1058, but as an amendment to AASB 9, made via AASB 2016-8.

AASB

Inventory

BC67 In its redeliberations, the Board noted that it had proposed in ED 260 for inventories acquired in a transaction that includes a donation by the vendor to measure the cost of those inventories at their fair value. The Board observed that, before issue of this Standard, a not-for-profit entity is required to measure all inventory acquired at nil or nominal cost at current replacement cost (defined in paragraph Aus6.1 of AASB 102 *Inventories* as 'the cost the entity would incur to acquire the asset at the end of the reporting period'). The subsequent measurement requirements for inventories held for distribution refer to current replacement cost as one possible basis for identifying a loss in service potential.

BC68 The Board discussed a concern that it may be inappropriate to require all inventories acquired for consideration significantly less than fair value principally to enable the entity to further its objectives to be initially measured at fair value. The Board observed that a day-one loss might arise in instances where current replacement cost (subsequent measurement requirements) as defined in AASB 102 was determined to be less than the fair value on initial recognition of inventories held for distribution. Consequently, in finalising this Standard, the Board decided to instead require inventories acquired for consideration significantly less than fair value principally to enable the entity to further its objectives to be measured, on initial recognition, at their current replacement cost, rather than at fair value as proposed. The Board considered this avoids inadvertently potentially creating new inventory measurement issues. The Board decided to consider fair value measurement as part of a future project.

Bequests and endowments

BC69 In its redeliberations on ED 260, the Board observed differing treatments in practice as to when control of an item bequeathed to a not-for-profit entity is obtained, as some argue that control of a bequeathed item is obtained upon the death of the deceased person who made the Will, on the basis that the entity has a privileged position of being named as a beneficiary in that Will. The Board considered that until no other party holds a right to challenge the Will, the entity does not have an enforceable right to receive the bequeathed items, and that it is likely that a not-for-profit entity does not gain control of the asset until such time. Consistent with its decision to exclude asset recognition criteria from this Standard, the Board decided not to include guidance on when an entity may gain control of a bequest.

BC70 In commenting on the Exposure Draft, respondents also expressed concerns about the accounting for endowments made for the perpetual benefit of the entity. Respondents sought clarification of the accounting for such endowments, including:

(a)   the form, if any, of the asset controlled; and

(b)   whether the endowment is a contract with customer within the scope of AASB 15, or is recognised as income immediately on obtaining control.

BC71 The Board decided there was no need to develop any new principles in relation to endowments. Also, consistent with its decision to exclude asset recognition criteria from this Standard, the Board decided not to include guidance on when an entity may gain control of an endowment. However, having regard to the concerns raised by constituents, the Board decided to include illustrative examples to assist an entity in understanding whether a contract liability may need to be recognised on gaining control of an endowment.

Transactions including a contract with a customer

BC72 A customer may enter into a contract with a not-for-profit entity with a dual purpose of obtaining goods or services and to help the not-for-profit entity achieve its objectives. The Board considered that such a contract should be separated into component parts to faithfully represent the impact of the transaction on the entity's financial performance.

BC73 The Board initially explored using a measurement-driven 'residual' approach to identify donation components of contracts with customers. Under this approach,

(a) performance obligations of a not-for-profit entity arising from a particular contract would be measured at the stand-alone selling price for the unit of account for the usual sale of the promised goods or services; and

(b) the residual after deducting the measure of the performance obligations in (a) above from the total contract consideration (ie transaction price) would be recognised immediately as donation income.

BC74 The Board decided not to proceed with this approach having regard to:

(a) the risk of mistakenly identifying donation components in contracts with customers, because of measurement error; and

(b) the time and cost of estimating the aggregate of the stand-alone selling prices of the promised goods or services separately from the transaction price would often exceed the benefits to users.

BC75 Consequently, in ED 260 the Board proposed that a not-for-profit entity be required to account for a separately identifiable donation component of a contract with a customer separately from the revenue that is recognised when the entity transfers a good or service to the customer, where that donation component is material. That is, the contract would be partly accounted for in accordance with this Standard (in respect of the donation component), and partly in accordance with AASB 15 (in respect of any performance obligations).

BC76 The Board proposed that the identification of whether a contract with a customer includes a donation component to be accounted for separately requires a qualitative assessment of whether:

(a) the customer intended to make a donation to the entity; and, if so,

(b) the donation is separately identifiable from the goods or services promised in the contract. A donation is separately identifiable from the goods or services promised in the contract if:

(i) there is evidence that part of the consideration paid or payable by the customer is not part of the consideration to which the entity expects to be entitled in exchange for the promised good or service;

(ii) the entity's entitlement to retain the donation is not conditional on that entity transferring a good or service to the customer (donor); and

(iii) the amount of the donation component can be measured reliably.

BC77 Some respondents to ED 260 considered that accounting separately for donation components does not provide information sufficiently useful to justify the cost. However, the majority of respondents to ED 260 agreed that any donation component included in a contract with a customer should be separated from the contract and accounted for in accordance with AASB 1058. Some of these respondents did not support the proposed qualitative assessment of whether a donation component is separately identifiable (based, in part, on whether the customer intended to make a donation). These constituents argued that it is unnecessary and unworkable to impose a 'customer intention' test for separately identifying a donation component.

BC78 In addition, the Board received feedback from its Project Advisory Panel that while understanding customer relationships was fundamental to the operation of AASB 15, the proposed approach to accounting for transactions involving both a contract with a customer and a donation component was not intuitive. The Board discussed feedback that the approach proposed in ED 260 overcomplicates the accounting, implies that the not-for-profit entity needs to 'stand in the shoes' of the transferor, and prioritises non-refundability as a distinguishing factor.

BC79 In its redeliberations, having regard to the feedback received, the Board confirmed its decision that the underlying principle that applies is for each component of a transaction to be accounted for separately, where material. However, acknowledging the constituent concerns described above, the Board decided not to require income to be recognised in accordance with this Standard in every such situation.

AASB

BC80 Instead, the Board decided to develop a rebuttable presumption (set out in Appendix F to AASB 15) that the transaction price in a contract with a customer is treated as wholly related to the transfer of promised goods or services. The Board decided that this presumption should be rebutted where the transaction price is partially refundable in the event the entity does not deliver the promised goods or services. That is, for transactions including a contract with a customer, only where these criteria are met may an entity have to possibly recognise an amount as income in accordance with paragraph 10 of this Standard. The Board considered whether the rebuttable presumption needed to also refer to separate identifiability of the element that is not related to the transfer of promised goods or services. The Board decided that this was not necessary, as this element – and any associated amount ascribed to it – represents the residual remaining after allocating the transaction price to the performance obligations in that contract. The Board's considerations in forming this decision are set out in its Basis for Conclusions to AASB 2016-8.

BC81 The rebuttable presumption is set out in Appendix F to AASB 15 (inserted via AASB 2016-8). However, the Board considered it important to highlight to users, as part of this Standard, that the requirements with respect to the accounting for contracts with customers where the transaction price includes an amount that would otherwise be separately recognised and accounted for as income immediately in accordance with this Standard is specified by AASB 15.

Leases with significantly below-market terms and conditions

BC82 In ED 260 the Board proposed a consequential amendment to AASB 117 *Leases* that would require entities to measure the lease asset and lease liability arising from a finance lease at the fair value of the leased asset. Constituents questioned the application of the requirements, observing in particular:

(a) applying the amendment would result in equal measurement of the asset and the liability associated with the finance lease. A residual amount would never arise and therefore no income would be recognised in accordance with AASB 1058;

(b) the lease asset in a finance lease represents the right to use that asset for the lease term and therefore measuring it with respect to the leased property would not accurately reflect the economic benefits arising from the lease; and

(c) the lease liability would not reflect an entity's ongoing obligations in respect of the lease if measured with reference to the fair value of the leased property.

BC83 The Board agreed with constituent concerns, noting that it intended for the amendment to reflect the objective of AASB 1058. Consequently, the Board revised the amendment to require:

(a) the lease asset be measured with reference to the right to use the underlying asset in accordance with the terms and conditions of the lease;

(b) the lease liability be measured in accordance with the applicable Standard; and

(c) any residual amount be accounted for in accordance with AASB 1058.

BC84 The Board observed that AASB 16 *Leases* would require amendment in addition to AASB 117. In this respect the Board noted that AASB 16 measures the right-of-use asset with reference to the lease liability. The Board noted that where an entity enters into a lease with below-market terms and conditions it is unlikely that the lease liability would reflect an appropriate starting point to measure the right-of-use asset and accurately reflect the substance of the lease transaction. Consequently, the Board decided to specify that the right-of-use asset be initially measured at the fair value of the right to use the underlying asset in accordance with the terms and conditions of the lease. This Standard does not require that right-of-use asset to be subsequently measured at fair value – the subsequent measurement requirements that apply are specified by other Australian Accounting Standards.

BC85 The Board noted that leases with below-market terms and conditions were of particular interest for constituents and therefore decided to specifically identify them in the examples of related financial statement elements that could arise from a transaction within the scope of AASB 1058.

Transactions involving financial instruments

BC86 The Board observed a transfer of a financial instrument (or a net transfer of financial instruments) to a not-for-profit entity may include an element of assisting the not-for-profit entity to achieve its objectives, for example in the form of a below-market interest rate on the financial instrument. When developing the proposals for ED 260 the Board noted:

    (a)   paragraph 5.1.1 of AASB 9 requires a financial instrument to be initially measured at its fair value; and

    (b)   paragraphs B5.1.1–B5.1.2A of AASB 9 specify the accounting requirements in respect of any difference between the transaction price and the fair value of the instrument(s) transferred, including when any deferred difference is recognised as a gain or loss.

BC87 The Board discussed whether to require an element arising on transfer of a financial instrument (net transfer of financial instruments) on terms significantly below fair value primarily to enable a not-for-profit entity to achieve its objectives to be accounted for in accordance with AASB 1058, or in accordance with paragraphs B5.1.1–B5.1.2A of AASB 9. The Board weighed the benefits of treating the beneficial element similarly to other forms of transfers to the entity against that of treating a below-market loan differently to a negotiated loan (which may also be provided on better terms to 'market'). The Board noted that overall, paragraphs B5.1.1–B5.1.2A specify that the difference between the transaction price and the fair value of the instrument could qualify for recognition as part of another asset, or otherwise be accounted for in accordance with paragraph B5.1.2A.

BC88 The Board concluded to propose no amendment to AASB 9 in this regard and to finalise its proposals largely as exposed, on consideration of the costs involved in requiring an entity to separately account for these transactions compared to the benefits of more accurately reflecting the substance of part of the transaction. That is, when applying paragraph 9 of AASB 1058, an entity measures any financial instruments identified as a 'related amount' in accordance with AASB 9, and does not account for the difference between the transaction price and the fair value of the instrument in accordance with this Standard.

Provisions

BC89 ED 260 specifically mentioned provisions as a related liability that could be recognised in relation to an inflow of a resource. When developing the proposals in ED 260, the Board noted that not-for-profit entities could enter into arrangements that satisfy the criteria to recognise a provision. However, ED 260 did not contain any further guidance on this point.

BC90 The Board observed that not-for-profit entities often provide specific reasons for their fundraising activities, and that at times the purpose for fundraising could be very specific but not legally binding. The Board discussed when a not-for-profit entity may have a constructive obligation, in the absence of a legal obligation, on acquiring an asset in a transaction where consideration is significantly below fair value principally to further the entity's objectives, such that a related provision is recognised on initial recognition of the asset.

BC91 In its discussion, the Board had regard to paragraph 20 of AASB 137 *Provisions, Contingent Liabilities and Contingent Assets*, which states:

    "... Because an obligation always involves a commitment to another party, it follows that a management or board decisions does not give rise to a constructive obligation at the end of the reporting period unless the decisions has been communicated before the end of the reporting period to those affected by it in a sufficiently specific manner to raise a valid expectation in them that the entity will discharge its responsibilities."

Hence, the Board considered that it would be unlikely, for example, for a not-for-profit entity's charter or stated objectives to be a sufficiently specific statement creating a valid expectation on the part of other parties such that a provision should be recognised in accordance with AASB 137.

BC92 The Board decided it would be useful to set out its views in this regard in Appendix B of the Standard and also as part of the Illustrative Examples accompanying AASB 1058.

Onerous contracts

BC93 Some not-for-profit entities enter into enforceable agreements where both a grantor and a service recipient both compensate the not-for-profit entity for the delivery of a specified good or service. The grantor may transfer an amount over to the not-for-profit entity in advance of the services being provided, but require a certain sum to be repaid where the service is not delivered.

BC94 The Board discussed a concern that a not-for-profit entity will be required to recognise an onerous contract for the costs of delivering future services when entering into such arrangements. The Board observed that each arrangement will need to be assessed based on its specific terms and conditions, and that judgement is involved in identifying whether an onerous contract which is part of the same economic event as the transfer from the grantor exists. The Board decided not to address the accounting for onerous contracts in AASB 1058 (or in AASB 15) as:

(a) the accounting for onerous contracts is specified by AASB 137 and is outside the scope of its current project; and

(b) agreements in which different parties pay collectively for a specified good or service are not limited to not-for-profit entities.

Transfers for the purpose of enabling an entity to acquire or construct a recognisable non-financial asset to be controlled by the entity

BC95 Some respondents to ED 260 sought clarification on whether a transfer made for the purposes of enabling an entity to acquire or construct a recognisable non-financial asset for its own use would be recognised as income immediately, or whether a contract liability determined in accordance with AASB 15 arises. The Board noted that these concerns specifically related to whether a transfer of financial assets to enable an entity to acquire or construct a non-financial asset would result in a transfer of goods or services to the transferor or another party. If such a transfer does not result in the transfer of goods or services to the transferor or another party it will be outside the scope of AASB 15 and no contract liability is recognisable; and consequently, under the proposals, the transfer recognised as income on receipt.

BC96 The Board heard feedback from constituents from the university sector that universities presently recognise a cash grant received to build an educational facility at the time of receiving the grant (that is, on gaining control). Some constituents hold the view that this accounting treatment does not appropriately reflect the relationship of the grant and its related expenditure as the related expenditure is recognised over a number of reporting periods as the educational facility is built.

BC97 The Board discussed whether such transfers were within the scope of AASB 15, as had been suggested by ED 260. The Board considered that in the absence of guidance, diverse practice may arise in this regard, for example, some may consider that:

(a) the construction or acquisition of a recognisable non-financial asset on behalf of the grantor is an activity representing services being transferred to the grantor, similar to research activities undertaken on behalf of the grantor but benefiting the community at large. Under this view, an entity would conclude there had been a transfer of goods or services to the transferor or another party;

(b) the construction or acquisition of the recognisable non-financial asset is not an activity representing services being transferred to the grantor as the asset remains with the not-for-profit entity. Under this view, an entity would conclude that the transfer is not a contract with a customer within the scope of AASB 15; and

(c) AASB 15 applies, but does not require any originally transferred cash and an associated contract liability to be recognised. Instead, the underlying recognisable non-financial asset and income is recognised as the asset is constructed, akin to treating the transaction as an in-substance transfer of the underlying asset as consideration for the construction or acquisition service.

BC98 For avoidance of doubt, the Board decided to identify the accounting that applies to such transfers. In its redeliberations, the Board observed that in such arrangements, in substance, the transferor had intended to transfer a recognisable non-financial asset to the not-for-profit entity. The Board considered that an in-substance transfer of a good for use by the entity itself should not result in income until the recipient has satisfied its obligation to construct or acquire the asset. That is, the timing of income recognition should reflect the entity receiving the asset directly, rather than the cash to construct or acquire the asset. Accordingly, the Board decided that the accounting for such transactions should reflect that of the approach in AASB 15. However, given the diverse views as to whether AASB 15 applies, the Board decided to specify instead requirements in AASB 1058 to mirror, to the extent appropriate, the accounting that would be achieved had the transaction been accounted for had it been incontestably a contract with a customer within the scope of AASB 15.

BC99 The Board sought feedback on its proposals in this regard as part of the public 'fatal flaw' review of the draft Standard. Respondents to the draft Standard were generally supportive of the proposal to include specific requirements for such arrangements.

BC100 The Board discussed the following concerns about the proposal:

(a) what is meant by 'own use';

(b) whether the specified accounting could apply also in instances where the non-financial asset acquired is a resource controlled that meets the definition of an asset but that is not permitted to be recognised by an Accounting Standard; and

(c) whether the specified accounting should be extended to apply also in instances where a non-financial asset (for example, construction materials) are made available to the entity, instead of cash or another financial asset.

BC101 The Board discussed feedback seeking clarification whether the specified accounting could apply to instances where an asset is constructed as directed but used by others as part of furthering the not-for-profit entity's objectives. For example, a not-for-profit entity whose mission is to provide housing services may receive a grant to construct public housing, however, the not-for-profit entity would not itself occupy the building when constructed. The Board observed its intention was for the scope of the accounting specified to include such transfers. In finalising AASB 1058, the Board decided to refer instead to "a recognisable non-financial asset to be controlled by the entity" and to add guidance to clarify the types of arrangements that could be within scope.

BC102 The Board also discussed whether the specified accounting could apply also in instances where the non-financial asset acquired is a resource controlled that meets the definition of an asset but that is not permitted to be recognised by an Accounting Standard. For example, a not-for-profit entity may be provided a grant to conduct research services with any detailed research data collected and rights to any commercial use of the data retained by the not-for-profit entity. AASB 138 *Intangible Assets* does not permit research activity to be recognised as an asset.

BC103 The Board considered whether to:

(a) limit the application of paragraphs 15–17 of the Standard to only grants (and other transfers) to develop a non-financial asset that qualifies for recognition under another Australian Accounting Standard; or

(b)   clearly articulate that the application of paragraphs 15–17 of the Standard includes grants (and other transfers) to develop a non-financial asset for which recognition is prohibited by another Australian Accounting Standard.

BC104   The Board discussed the scope of these paragraphs having regard to grants received to conduct specified research activity; the related intellectual property of which may or may not be controlled by the not-for-profit entity recipient. The Board observed that extending the application of paragraphs 15-17 of the Standard to include grants (and other transfers) to develop a non-financial asset for which recognition is prohibited by another Australian Accounting Standard would be consistent with the underlying principle being that the grantor intended to transfer a good (rather than a financial asset) to the not-for-profit recipient. However, the Board was concerned that extending the paragraphs in this manner would:

(a)   create ambiguity in the distinction between a service and a good, and lack of clarity as to whether an implicit good component in a contract needs to be separately identified from the service. The Board observed that many service contracts in both the not-for-profit and for-profit sector arguably give rise to (unrecognised) knowledge or expertise to the service renderer;

(b)   result in a lack of comparability, as some constituents may contend that all the value in such a contract is attributable to the unrecognised good acquired; while others contend that the value remains with the service rendered (ie the good is an incidental product that the customer does not value in entering the contract). Yet others may contend that some apportionment is appropriate;

(c)   be seen as being inconsistent with the Board's decision not to extend the accounting specified by AASB 15 to all transactions of not-for-profit entities, regardless of whether a contract with a customer exists. The Board could not see a clear distinction why the accounting should differ between transactions that through the conduct of an activity result in incidentally gaining control of intellectual property assets, and an arrangement to deliver services for which income may be recognised immediately in accordance with this Standard; and

(d)   create confusion as to whether this Standard would allow certain intangible assets to be recognised, where their recognition is otherwise prohibited.

Consequently, the Board decided that the accounting set out in paragraphs 15–17 of the Standard should be limited to transactions that will result in a recognisable non-financial asset controlled by the entity.

BC105   The Board observed that universities (and other not-for-profit recipients of grants to perform research) would need to determine whether the accounting for a grant to perform research is specified by AASB 15 or AASB 1058. The Board considered its decision to limit the scope of paragraphs 15–17 of the Standard will not result in significant additional costs to affected entities, as the entity would already be required to assess a funding arrangement within the scope of AASB 15 for whether revenue is recognised over time, or at a point in time.

BC106   However, given the significance of grants to conduct research to universities and other not-for-profit recipients, the Board decided to develop several implementation examples to AASB 15 to set out the accounting in this regard. The examples illustrate scenarios where income would be recognised immediately on gaining control of the financial asset in accordance with this Standard, or recognised over time, or at the end of the agreement, in accordance with AASB 15. The Board's considerations in this regard are set out in its Basis for Conclusions to AASB 2016-8.

Volunteer services

BC107   AASB 1004 (December 2007) required local governments, government departments, General Government Sectors (GGSs) and whole of government reporting entities to recognise services received free of charge or for nominal consideration, provided the fair value of those services could be measured reliably, and the services would have been purchased if they had not been donated. The Board decided to carry forward these aspects into AASB 1058 as it was concerned that a wide-ranging review of the recognition requirements for volunteer services could take significant time and potentially delay the completion of this project.

BC108 AASB 1004 does not specifically indicate the circumstances in which not-for-profit entities other than those specifically identified can recognise volunteer services. Consequently, not-for-profit entities may elect to recognise volunteer services based on an accounting policy developed in accordance with AASB 108. ED 260 proposed clarifying that not-for-profit entities may elect to recognise volunteer services if the fair value of those services can be measured reliably, without necessarily needing to have been purchased had the services not been donated. In forming the proposal, the Board observed the purchase pre-requisite in AASB 1004 was primarily focused on limiting the scope of volunteer services for which recognition by particular public sector not-for-profit entities is required. The Board considered not-for-profit entities should be able to elect to recognise volunteer services with a fair value that can be measured reliably even if those services would not have been purchased if they had not been donated.

BC109 The Board noted that carrying forward the treatment of volunteer services from AASB 1004 almost unchanged retains an inconsistency between private sector and public sector not-for-profit entities regarding the scope of the recognition requirements for volunteer services. The Board acknowledged the inconsistency reflects the transfer of recognition requirements for volunteer services to AASB 1004 upon the withdrawal of Australian Accounting Standards for specific types of public sector entity (namely, AAS 27 *Financial Reporting by Local Governments*, AAS 29 *Financial Reporting by Government Departments* and AAS 31 *Financial Reporting by Governments*) in 2007, rather than a difference in information needs of users of financial statements of not-for-profit entities in the private and public sectors.

BC110 Many respondents to ED 260 were of the view that the requirements with respect to the recognition of volunteer services should be the same for all not-for-profit entities. However, many opined that the recognition of volunteer services should be optional, primarily for cost–benefit reasons. Some encouraged the Board to expedite consideration of whether there was differentiation between entities in the sector to justify different accounting requirements. Others suggested that the treatment and location of information about volunteer services be reconsidered by the Board.

BC111 The Board considered how to progress its consideration of the accounting for volunteer services, having regard to the feedback received. The Board noted further consideration and due process would be required before it could finalise any broad changes to the current accounting requirements in this regard. Accordingly, the Board decided, as a short-term solution, to finalise the recognition and measurement proposals largely unamended from those exposed. (See also paragraphs BC123–BC124 below.)

BC112 The Board expects to consider the accounting requirements for volunteer services as part of a separate future project.

Receipts of inventory

BC113 ED 260 proposed that an assessment of whether a transfer of inventory for no consideration is material for recognition should be made at a transaction level, and need not be reassessed at another unit of account, such as at a portfolio of similar transactions. The Board considered such a treatment would be likely to achieve a better balance of costs and benefits having regard to the extent of transfers of goods for no consideration to charities.

BC114 The Board sought specific feedback from constituents as to its proposed approach to the recognition and measurement of inventories donated other than as part of a contract with a customer. Most expressed support for the proposal to assess materiality of a donation of inventory at the transaction level rather than at a portfolio level.

BC115 In its redeliberations, the Board observed that it had presented its discussion on materiality in ED 260 both within the general principles for recognition and within specific requirements pertaining to donated inventory. The Board confirmed it had not intended to propose that materiality should only be assessed at a transaction level for all transactions (for example, volunteer services or small grants of non-financial assets), as evidenced by its specific question pertaining to inventory and requirements of volunteer services.

BC116 The Board considered whether further due process is necessary if the final pronouncement limited the proposal that materiality need only be assessed at the transaction level, rather than also at a portfolio level, only to donations of inventory, rather than all inflows of assets. The Board decided that no further due process is necessary, as not finalising its proposals in that regard would, in the main, maintain the current status quo. In addition, the Board decided to express the relief in this regard as a practical expedient, rather than a requirement.

BC117 AASB 101 defines materiality as "omissions or misstatements of items are material if they could, individually or collectively, influence the economic decisions that users make on the basis of the financial statements". The Board observed that materiality is commonly understood as applying to the whole financial statements as well as at an individual transaction level. The Board concluded it was not providing guidance on interpreting materiality, but providing relief from the normal manner in which materiality would otherwise apply to the entity in respect of inventories. That is, in the absence of the practical expedient, an entity would be required to recognise receipts of inventories for which the consideration paid was significantly less than fair value (including transfers for no or nominal consideration) where the inventory overall could materially affect the entity's financial position and financial performance.

Grant income

BC118 The Board noted that constituents in local government were particularly concerned about the implications of the revised recognition requirements to certain periodic grant funding received by these entities. The Board considered the application of the underlying principles in this Standard to such grants, and decided there was no conceptual basis for supporting an exception to the general requirements in the Standard.

Rates received in advance of the rating period

BC119 The Board observed that under the former income recognition requirements, rates received by local governments were generally recognised as income on receipt by the local government. The Board heard that some constituents considered income to be prematurely recognised where amounts were received in advance of the rating period, as the local government is obliged to refund the amount prepaid until the start of the rating period. The Board expects that it may be possible for the timing of income recognition to be later under this Standard compared to the previous requirements. In acknowledgement of the significance of rates to a local government's financial performance, the Board decided to confirm its decision in ED 260 for the final Standard to include an example on rates received in advance, to explain the accounting that applies under this Standard (and its interaction with other Australian Accounting Standards).

Disclosure

BC120 The Board decided that, consistent with other recent Australian Accounting Standards, AASB 1058 should specify a disclosure objective. The Board observed that specifying an overall disclosure objective avoids the need for detailed and prescriptive disclosure requirements to accommodate the varied types of transactions within the scope of AASB 1058.

BC121 The Board decided to include disclosure requirements to help an entity meet the disclosure objective. The Board observed that those disclosures should not be viewed as a checklist of minimum disclosures, because some disclosures may be relevant for some entities but may be irrelevant for others. The Board also observed that it is important for an entity to consider the adequacy of its disclosures having regard to the disclosure objective, and materiality.

BC122 In its redeliberations, the Board considered the adequacy of the disclosures proposed in ED 260, having regard to its other decisions on the project (for example, to require a liability to be recognised in respect of certain transfers to enable an entity to construct a non-financial asset for its own use), and in response to constituent feedback on the proposed disclosures. The Board decided to finalise some disclosures in a form different to that proposed, and include certain specified additional disclosures, as well as encouraging other disclosures.

Volunteer services and donated inventory

BC123 In its redeliberations on ED 260, the Board observed that the operations of many not-for-profit entities rely heavily upon volunteer services and/or donated inventories. The Board considered that users of a not-for-profit entity's financial statements would find it useful to understand the contribution made by such donations to the achievement of the entity's objectives during the reporting period and the entity's dependency on donated inventories and volunteer services for the future achievement of its objectives.

BC124 The Board observed that it had not proposed a disclosure of this nature as part of ED 260 nor received much feedback seeking such disclosure. In addition, the Board considered whether requiring disclosure of an entity's dependency on volunteer services as part of this project may be seen as pre-empting the outcomes of the Board's project on Reporting Service Performance Information and a possible future project relating to volunteer services (see paragraph BC112 above). Accordingly, the Board decided to encourage entities to disclose qualitative information about the entity's dependence on volunteer services (recognised and unrecognised) and donated inventory held but not recognised as assets.

Transfers to enable an entity to acquire or construct a recognisable non-financial asset to be controlled by the entity

BC125 Consistent with the Board's decision to include requirements in AASB 1058 that substantially mirror those in AASB 15 for transfers to enable an entity to acquire or construct a non-financial asset to be controlled by the entity, the Board decided to replicate various AASB 15 disclosure requirements in AASB 1058. The Board noted that these disclosures provide useful information to users of a not-for-profit entity's financial statements and that similar disclosures would have been required had the agreement been determined to be within the scope of AASB 15.

Restrictions on the use of an asset

BC126 In its redeliberations, the Board discussed feedback querying whether AASB 1058 should require the disclosure of restrictions on the use and purpose of amounts recognised as income, including restrictions on an entity's ability to liquidate a related asset or to use it as security. These constituents considered that the disclosure of restrictions is necessary to enable users of financial statements to understand the effects of inflows of resources on the financial position, financial performance and cash flows of the entity. The Board agreed that it would be useful to a user of the financial statements of a not-for-profit entity, for example, to understand the nature and extent of externally imposed restrictions on resources controlled. The Board noted these disclosures will go some way to addressing respondent concerns that the proposals in ED 260 do not permit the deferral of income to match expenses in all scenarios where a not-for-profit entity considers funds to have been fully committed to a specific purpose.

BC127 The Board observed that international standard-setters have specified varying disclosures in this regard. The Board considered whether it would be appropriate to specify a particular disclosure in this Standard (for example, disclosure of components of equity divided into restricted and unrestricted amounts), but decided that the form of the disclosure should be determined by the not-for-profit entity. This allows an entity to adopt an approach that best aligns with the manner in which it manages and presents its financial statements. For the same reason, the Board decided not to define "externally imposed restrictions".

BC128   To assist users of the Standard, the Board decided to include examples of various forms the disclosure could take. The Board acknowledged a concern some preparers have with the proposed Standard is that they consider the primary financial statements will continue to misrepresent to users the resources available to the entity (as the timing of income recognition may be in advance of the expenses the income received is meant to compensate). In response to this feedback, the Board decided to specify in particular, that a not-for-profit entity may separately identify on the face of the statement of profit or loss and other comprehensive income, the amount of total comprehensive income that is:

(a)   subject to externally imposed restrictions; and

(b)   is not subject to any externally imposed restrictions (the 'unrestricted' amount).

Disclosing information about its externally imposed restrictions in this form allows entities to distinguish between 'committed' and 'uncommitted' amounts recognised immediately as income in instances where there is no obligation on the not-for-entity recipient to return assets received in the event the social expectation is not met. The Board expects this disclosure to alleviate, through communication, the concern that users of a not-for-profit entity's financial statements do not appreciate the "true" financial position and financial performance of the entity, while maintaining the Board's policy on transaction neutrality. Further, the Board noted by identifying in the Standard that the disclosure may be made on the face of the financial statements (for example, as a subtotal) will avoid ambiguity of whether this is a permissible manner of satisfying the encouraged disclosure.

BC129   The Board discussed whether disclosure about externally imposed restrictions should be required, or merely encouraged. The Board noted that it had not exposed a proposal in this regard, and accordingly, decided to encourage the disclosure of information in this regard as opposed to requiring entities to make that disclosure.

BC130   In addition, the Board observed that:

(a)   AASB 107 *Statement of Cash Flows* requires disclosure of the amount of significant cash and cash equivalent balances held by an entity that are not available for use by its group, together with commentary about these balances;

(b)   AASB 116 *Property, Plant and Equipment* and AASB 138 *Intangible Assets* require disclosure of the existence and carrying amounts of assets whose title is restricted; and

(c)   AASB 7 *Financial Instruments: Disclosures* requires disclosure of information that enables users of its financial statements to evaluate the significance of financial instruments for its financial position and performance, and the nature and extent of risks arising from financial instruments to which the entity is exposed at the end of the reporting period.

The Board noted there may be some overlap between the disclosures set out in paragraph 37 of this Standard, and these other Australian Accounting Standards.

Disclosure of parliamentary appropriations and other related authorities for expenditure

BC131   When developing AASB 1004 (December 2007), the Board decided to defer consideration of whether disclosures of parliamentary appropriations should apply to not-for-profit public sector entities other than government departments, given the short-term nature of its project at that time. The Board noted that in due course, it would consider extending the application of the requirements.

BC132 As part of this project, the Board reviewed the specified disclosures of compliance with parliamentary appropriations and other externally-imposed requirements required of government departments which had been included in AASB 1004 (now deleted from that Standard). The Board decided, in light of changes in public sector financial management arrangements since originally developing these requirements, to propose extending the scope of disclosures in this regard to include other public sector entities that obtain part or all of their spending authority from parliamentary appropriations.

BC133 In reviewing the disclosures, the Board acknowledged constituent concerns that the interaction between two of the specified disclosures was unclear, as the scope of paragraph 64(e) of AASB 1004 was broader than the scope of paragraph 64(d). The Board decided to clarify its requirements in this regard by proposing in ED 260:

(a) not to carry forward the text of paragraph 64(e) into AASB 1058; and

(b) to require disclosure of the financial consequences of an unauthorised expenditure.

BC134 Respondents to the ED were generally supportive of the Board's proposals in this regard. In its redeliberations, the Board noted a concern raised that by extending the application of these disclosure requirements beyond government departments some might interpret the disclosure requirements as applying to for-profit entities in the public sector. The Board observed that the scope of AASB 1058 is limited to not-for-profit entities and therefore for-profit public sector entities would not be subject to these disclosures.

BC135 The Board discussed a concern whether the proposed disclosure requirements duplicate existing disclosures in AASB 1055 *Budgetary Reporting*. The Board reaffirmed its view that these disclosures contain fundamentally different requirements from AASB 1055 and should be retained, as the disclosures are focused on information concerning how appropriations and other advances received have been expended, rather than the more broadly based requirements in AASB 1055 for actual to budget variance analysis (see paragraph BC28 in AASB 1055).

BC136 In addition, as part of its deliberations, the Board discussed whether to relocate disclosures about a government department's compliance with parliamentary appropriations and other externally-imposed requirements from AASB 1004 to AASB 1054 *Australian Additional Disclosures*, rather than this Standard. The Board concluded it would be more user-friendly to include these disclosure requirements in AASB 1058 given the nexus between the income of government departments and appropriated amounts.

BC137 Having regard to the feedback received, the Board decided to finalise the disclosure in this regard largely as exposed in ED 260.

Reduced disclosure requirements (Tier 2)

BC138 The Board decided, in light of its current project to review the principles underlying Tier 2 reporting requirements, not to specify any reduction in applicable disclosures in making AASB 1058. Through a separate due process, the AASB will consider whether relief from certain specified disclosure requirements should be provided to entities that adopt Tier 2 Reduced Disclosure Requirements.

Transition

BC139 The Board considered whether it should provide transitional relief to entities on adopting AASB 1058 and decided that, consistent with the IASB's decisions on IFRS 15, some form of transition relief would be appropriate.

BC140 In developing ED 260, the Board observed there did not appear to be any not-for-profit specific reason for AASB 1058 to depart from the general features of the transitional provisions in AASB 15 as arrangements giving rise to income are not specific to not-for-profit entities. Accordingly, the Board proposed transitional relief on initial application of AASB 1058 be limited to permitting entities the option of recognising the cumulative effect of initially applying AASB 1058 in opening retained earnings (or another component of equity, as appropriate) at the date of initial application of AASB 1058, to be consistent with AASB 15.

BC141 Many respondents were not supportive of the Board's limited proposals in this regard. In its redeliberations, the Board noted concerns about the absence of any specific transitional provisions:

(a) for existing research, donation and grant funded projects;

(b) for assets acquired for no cost or a nominal consideration (including "peppercorn" leases where a nominal amount is made as payment to the lessor); and

(c) in acknowledgement of the short lead time between issue and implementation of AASB 1058.

BC142 Having regard to the feedback received, the Board decided to confirm its proposal to allow entities an option between fully retrospectively applying the Standard, or recognising the cumulative effect of initially applying the Standard at the date of initial application (that is, not to restate comparative information). The Board decided entities should be encouraged, but not required, to restate comparative information on adoption of AASB 1058. In addition, the Board redeliberated whether further transitional relief was necessary.

BC143 The Board observed that not-for-profit entities commonly receive assets through donations, taxes and other similar transfers. The Board acknowledged constituent concerns about the transition requirements for inflows of resources previously accounted for in AASB 1004 but now within the scope of this Standard or AASB 15. The Board noted that in the absence of any transitional provisions in AASB 1058 or amendment to AASB 15, not-for-profit entities would be required to retrospectively apply the requirements of AASB 1058 or AASB 15 (where the transaction is within the scope) to contracts for which the associated inflow of resources had already been fully recognised in accordance with AASB 1004.

BC144 The Board was concerned that this imposed a greater implementation burden on not-for-profit entities compared to for-profit entities. Consequently, the Board decided to extend the transitional relief in AASB 1058 to permit relief from retrospective application for contracts for which the entity has recognised all of the income in accordance with AASB 1004, to be consistent with the relief available in IFRS 15 for completed contracts. The Board also additionally amended the definition of a completed contract in AASB 15 to include contracts for which the entity has recognised all of the revenue in accordance with AASB 1004, or revenue in combination with a provision in accordance with AASB 137. The extent of the relief is dependent on the entity's elections on retrospective application.

BC145 In ED 260, the Board proposed requiring an asset that has been acquired for consideration that is below market but that is more than nominal to be measured at fair value. The Board decided to finalise the proposal in issuing this Standard (other than with respect to inventory). However, the Board observed that an entity would not have previously applied AASB 1004 to these transactions, nor recognised any income on the transaction as the asset acquired will generally have been measured at the amount of the consideration transferred. Accordingly, in the absence of any transitional provisions, a not-for-profit entity will be required to apply the requirements of AASB 1058 retrospectively to such transactions, including determining the fair value (or, in respect of inventory, current replacement cost) of the asset on acquisition.

BC146 In its redeliberations, the Board considered that the costs of applying AASB 1058 retrospectively to all such assets would exceed the benefits of doing so, having regard to the need for an entity to identify and value such assets still existing at reporting date. Accordingly, the Board determined some form of transitional relief to be appropriate. The Board decided to consider transitional provisions for leases made on significantly below-market terms and conditions separately from any transitional provisions for other assets. The Board's considerations with respect to transitional provisions for leases made on significantly below-market terms and conditions is set out in paragraphs BC150–BC153 below.

BC147   With respect to assets other than lease assets, the Board decided not to require a not-for-profit entity to revisit the accounting that previously applied on initial recognition of these assets. The Board made this decision having regard to costs involved in identifying and measuring the various assets held on adoption of this Standard that may have been acquired at an amount that was more than nil or nominal, but significantly less than fair value, and the associated discount to fair value. The Board considered these costs to outweigh the benefits of retrospective application of the Standard, as these assets are already recognised (generally at cost on initial recognition) in the statement of financial position, and noting that there is unlikely to be any deferred income to recognise in future periods in accordance with this Standard.

BC148   The Board observed that, consequently, the statement of financial position will reflect a mixed measurement position for assets acquired for consideration that is significantly less than fair value but more than nominal. Those acquired for more than a nominal amount prior to the application of AASB 1058 would continue to be reflected at cost on initial recognition. Assets acquired under similar circumstances after adoption of AASB 1058 will generally be initially measured at fair value (or current replacement cost, in relation to inventories).

BC149   The Board decided that the transitional relief for other assets need not be aligned with transitional relief for leases. In making this decision, the Board considered:

    (a)   the quantum of transactions involving a lease. The Board observed it expects an entity to have undertaken fewer transactions involving leases, and that the terms and conditions of these transactions to be clearly identifiable, compared to acquisitions of other assets at a discount to fair value; and

    (b)   that a lessee may not necessarily have recognised an amount in its statement of financial position in respect of the right-to-use asset in an operating lease.

Leases with significantly below-market terms and conditions

BC150   The Board decided to consider transitional relief for leases on significantly below-market terms and conditions separately from transitional relief for other assets. The Board made this decision having regard to:

    (a)   the diversity in accounting for such leases under previous requirements (see paragraph BC6 above);

    (b)   the potential significance of leases made on such terms to the financial position of a not-for-profit entity; and

    (c)   the prevalence of below-market leases in the not-for-profit sector.

BC151   The Board considered whether to:

    (a)   require retrospective application of this Standard, without any relief on initial application;

    (b)   permit a not-for-profit lessee to continue its existing accounting for such leases, in a similar manner to the relief specified for other transactions; or

    (c)   permit a not-for-profit lessee access to a similar level of relief on initial application of this Standard as is available to a for-profit entity on adoption of AASB 16.

BC152   The Board decided that it should, at a minimum, permit a not-for-profit lessee access to a similar level of relief on initial application of this Standard as is available to a for-profit entity on adoption of AASB 16. However, having regard to its decisions on the measurement of assets acquired in a lease (see paragraph BC84 above), the Board concluded it would be appropriate to modify the transitional provisions set out in AASB 16 to require the lease asset, on initial adoption of this Standard, to be measured at its fair value rather than by reference to the lease liability.

BC153 In its discussion, the Board decided not to permit a not-for-profit lessee to continue its existing accounting for such leases, in a similar manner to the relief specified for other transactions. The Board made this decision having regard to its concern the financial position of a not-for-profit entity may be misrepresented, and the lack of comparability between entities if such leases were entered into before and after adoption of this Standard.

Early adoption of AASB 1058 before AASB 16

BC154 The Board did not want to unintentionally require a lessee to fair value a right-of-use asset twice, once on transition to AASB 1058, if early adopted, and again on transition to AASB 16. Having regard to this and the feedback received about the adequacy of the transitional provisions in ED 260, the Board decided to add early adoption transition requirements to AASB 1058.

BC155 The scope of AASB 1058 extends to leases provided to a not-for-profit entity on significantly below-market terms and conditions at inception principally to enable an entity to further its objectives. Not-for-profit entities can apply AASB 1058 early before the mandatory application date of AASB 16, thereby applying AASB 1058 alongside AASB 117. Under AASB 117, leases classified as operating leases do not give rise to a recognised asset of the lessee. The Board considered whether a not-for-profit lessee should be required to recognise right-of-use assets arising from operating leases at fair value when applying AASB 1058 before adopting AASB 16, noting this approach would be consistent with the objective of this Standard. However, the Board was conscious that it were to do so, it would place an additional burden on not-for-profit lessees, and would not be in keeping with its policy on transaction neutrality. Consequently, and having regard to the short lead time before AASB 16 becomes effective, the Board decided to require entities to continue applying the requirements of AASB 117 in respect of operating leases until transition to AASB 16.

BC156 With respect to finance leases within the scope of AASB 117, the Board noted that a lessee may not have previously measured a finance lease asset, in a lease made on significantly below-market terms and conditions at inception principally to enable an entity to further its objectives, at fair value on initial recognition. The Board considered the costs to a lessee of having to fully retrospectively apply AASB 1058 to such leases were likely to outweigh the benefits to users of doing so. Consequently, the Board decided to require a lessee to measure the fair value of a finance leased asset at the date of initial application of AASB 1058 (if paragraph C3(b) applies) or at the beginning of the earliest period presented (if paragraph C3(a) applies). The Board decided it was not necessary to require the entity to remeasure the leased asset to fair value again on adoption of AASB 16.

First-time adoption of Australian Accounting Standards

BC157 The Board considered whether any amendment is necessary to AASB 1 *First-time Adoption of Australian Accounting Standards* to assist not-for-profit entities on first-time adoption of Australian Accounting Standards. In making its decision, the Board had regard to the extent of amendment to AASB 1 as a consequence of the issue of AASB 15 and AASB 16.

BC158 The Board noted that a not-for-profit entity applying AASB 1 would be able to access the relief specified in AASB 15 in respect of contracts for which the entity has previously fully recognised income in accordance with AASB 1004 (refer paragraphs D34-D35 of AASB 1). Consequently, the Board decided no further amendment was required in this regard.

BC159 The Board observed that AASB 1 specifies the accounting on first-time adoption of Australian Accounting Standards for lease assets and lease liabilities, including practical expedients that may be adopted. The Board noted, in the absence of developing Australian specific amendments to AASB 1, it is unclear how a lease within the scope of AASB 1058 should be treated in the financial statements of a first-time adopter of Australian Accounting Standards.

BC160 The Board considered whether the general features of the exemptions available for lease assets and lease liabilities in AASB 1 should apply also to leases with significantly below-market terms and conditions at inception. The Board noted if it did so, assets acquired through such leases could remain understated in a first-time adopter's financial statements. The Board considered this reduced comparability between a not-for-profit first-time adopter and a not-for-profit entity that is already applying Australian Accounting Standards. Accordingly, the Board decided not to extend this exemption to leases for which the initial recognition and measurement is specified by AASB 1058. However, the Board considered that some measure of transitional relief is necessary, and decided a first-time adopter should have access to similar relief in this regard as an entity already applying Australian Accounting Standards.

Effective date

BC161 The Board considered feedback it received from several constituents requesting the Board defer the effective date of AASB 1058 (and related pronouncements) beyond 1 January 2018. The Board discussed the effective date of AASB 1058 (and AASB 2016-8, also issued as part of this project), noting its intention had been to align the effective date of any pronouncements resulting from this project with the effective date of AASB 15. The Board was concerned that an effective date of 1 January 2018 could disadvantage not-for-profit entities compared to for-profit entities applying AASB 15, as not-for-profit entities would have significantly less lead time before implementation of AASB 1058. The Board considered that the transitional provisions may not provide sufficient relief to entities in this regard.

BC162 In addition, the Board considered whether to similarly defer the application date of AASB 15 for not-for-profit entities. The Board discussed the interaction between AASB 15, AASB 1004 and AASB 1058 should the application date of AASB 15 differ from that of AASB 1058, including:

(a) whether the scope of AASB 1004 should take precedence over AASB 15 for affected entities. (that is, transaction types subject to AASB 1004 would continue to be subject to that Standard, until such time as AASB 1058 became effective); and

(b) the effect on comparability for transactions that may be accounted for in accordance with AASB 1004 by not-for-profit entities but in accordance with AASB 15 by for-profit entities.

BC163 The Board considered that it would be preferable for the effective date of AASB 1058, AASB 2016-8 and AASB 15 to be aligned for application by not-for-profit entities, rather than adopt a stepped approach to adopting the revised income recognition requirements. Having regard to the timing of finalisation of this project, the Board decided, for not-for-profit entities, to defer the application date of AASB 1058, AASB 2016-8 and AASB 15 to 1 January 2019. The amendment to defer the application date of AASB 15 to 1 January 2019 for not-for-profit entities is made by AASB 2016-7.

BC164 The Board decided to permit entities to early adopt AASB 1058, provided AASB 15 and AASB 2016-8 are applied at the same time. The ability to early adopt means that a not-for-profit entity wishing to adopt the revised requirements at the same time as a for-profit entity is not prevented from doing so.

Other

Forthcoming amendments to the Australian Conceptual Framework

BC165 The Board observed that an active project on its work program is the development of a revised Australian Conceptual Framework. The Board expects that there will be amendments to the definitions of various elements of the financial statements resulting from that project, at least for for-profit entities.

BC166 The Board considered whether AASB 1058 should be developed having regard to the proposals exposed in ED 264 *Conceptual Framework for Financial Reporting* (incorporating IASB ED/2015/3 of the same name) and any subsequent decisions of the IASB to date on its project. The Board concluded it would be inappropriate to base its decisions in AASB 1058 on expected forthcoming amendments, noting that it had not yet deliberated the extent of any amendment that may be necessary to the IASB Conceptual Framework for application by Australian not-for-profit entities.

BC167 The Board noted it may, at a future time, consider undertaking a project to review the requirements of AASB 1058 against a revised Australian Conceptual Framework.

Contributions by owners

BC168 In developing ED 260, the Board noted the concerns of some constituents with the existing definition of "contributions by owners" (see Appendix A of AASB 1058) and Interpretation 1038 that includes for-profit public sector entities within its scope. The Board observed:

(a) the IASB has not defined a similar term employed within the definition of 'income' in IFRS Standards; and

(b) the IPSASB's Public Sector Conceptual Framework includes a broader definition of 'ownership contributions' than that in Australian Accounting Standards.

BC169 Acknowledging constituent concerns about application of the term, the Board decided to invite comment on the defined term "contributions by owners" as part of this project. The Board did not make a specific proposal regarding the definition of "contributions by owners". Instead, ED 260 illustrated what a replacement Standard for AASB 1004 would look like without that definition and particular related guidance, and posed related questions including whether a definition of 'contributions by owners' is still necessary, or appropriate.

BC170 In responding to the ED, constituents noted the definition in AASB 1004 can be problematic, identified a need for a definition of contributions by owners and expressed their support for applying the IPSASB definition or using the IPSASB definition as the basis for an Australian definition. Many respondents considered a definition was necessary to minimise diversity in practice.

BC171 In addition, the majority of respondents to ED 260 responding on this topic supported the withdrawal of Interpretation 1038.

BC172 Having regard to the feedback received, the Board considered whether to:

(a) withdraw and not replace the current definition in AASB 1004 and Interpretation 1038;

(b) replace the current definition in AASB 1004 with the definition of ownership contributions adopted by the IPSASB, and separately consider whether to retain an amended Interpretation 1038; or

(c) address the accounting for contributions by owners as part of a separate project.

BC173 The Board was conscious of the need to finalise its proposals on other aspects of its current project in a timely manner. The Board considered that developing any amendment to the definition, including ensuring adequate due process, would delay finalisation of its current project. Accordingly, the Board decided to progress consideration of 'contributions by owners' and the related requirements as part of a separate project. Consequently, the Board decided to retain, for the interim:

(a) the terms 'contributions' and 'contributions by owners' as presently defined in Australian Accounting Standards;

(b) the requirements specified in AASB 1004 and AASB Interpretation 1038 *Contributions by Owners Made to Wholly-Owned Public Sector Entities* with respect to contributions by owners and distributions to owners; and

(c)   the requirements specified in AASB 1004 with respect to contributions by owners and distributions to owners, including those arising in relation to restructures of administrative arrangements.

GAAP/GFS convergence

BC174 The Board discussed implications of its decisions on GAAP/GFS harmonisation. The Board noted that differences between Generally Accepted Accounting Principles (GAAP) and Government Finance Statistics (GFS) may arise in relation to the following:

(a)   timing of recognition of income tax revenue – income tax revenue is recognised under GFS in advance of AASB 1058 (see Appendix C of AASB 9);

(b)   timing of recognition of property tax revenue – property tax revenue is recognised under GFS later than AASB 1058 (see Appendix C of AASB 9). The Board considered constituent feedback that GFS requires income to be recognised progressively over the period of the levy;

(c)   timing of revenue recognition on transfer of goods – GFS generally recognises revenue on legal change in title, while AASB 1058, with limited exception, requires income to be recognised on recognition of the asset. Under Australian Accounting Standards, an entity must control the asset for recognition to occur, which could be at a point in time earlier than on legal change in title;

(d)   recognised income for certain volunteer services received – GFS does not recognise any income representing the fair value of volunteer services received; and

(e)   recognition of provisions in accordance with AASB 137 Provisions, Contingent Liabilities and Contingent Assets – the amount of income recognised under GAAP and GFS will differ where a provision relating to the transaction or event is recognised in accordance with Australian Accounting Standards but not under GFS.

BC175 The Board weighed its policy on GAAP/GFS harmonisation against its policy of transaction neutrality. The Board observed that some areas of potential difference were known when developing AASB 1049. Others were more likely to give rise to differences only in interim reporting periods, or are driven by a difference in the underlying principles. Further, some differences could only be addressed by making changes to the underlying principles in AASB 1058 and AASB 15.

BC176 On balance, the Board considered that it was not necessary to amend its decisions reflected in AASB 1058 in order to achieve GAAP/GFS harmonisation. The Board noted that AASB 1049 Whole of Government and General Government Sector Financial Reporting will require entities to identify and explain any differences arising from different requirements in GAAP as compared to GFS.

Comparison with International Public Sector Accounting Standards

BC177 As part of its deliberations, the Board considered the accounting for income of not-for-profit entities specified by the International Public Sector Accounting Standards Board (IPSASB). The Board noted the following International Public Sector Accounting Standards (IPSAS) specified the accounting in this regard:

(a)   IPSAS 9 *Revenue from Exchange Transactions;*

(b)   IPSAS 11 *Construction Contracts;*

(c)   IPSAS 23 *Revenue from Non-exchange Transactions (Taxes and Transfers).*

BC178 The Board observed IPSAS 9 and IPSAS 11 are based on the principles of superseded IAS 18 *Revenue* (incorporated into AASB 118 *Revenue*) and IAS 11 *Construction Contracts* (incorporated into AASB 111 *Construction Contracts*), rather than those of IFRS 15 *Revenue from Contracts with Customers* (incorporated into AASB 15). In addition, it noted that IPSAS 23 was issued prior to the issue of IFRS 15. The requirements of IPSAS 23 were therefore not necessarily developed with reference to similar principles of IFRS 15. The Board concluded these IPSASB Standards do not provide an appropriate basis for financial reporting in the Australian environment, particularly because they require different income recognition depending on whether the transaction is an exchange transaction or a non-exchange transaction, and IPSAS 9 and IPSAS 11 adopt a 'risks and rewards' approach that is not consistent with the performance obligation approach in IFRS 15.

BC179 The Board further noted the IPSASB is currently developing proposals for the accounting of non-exchange expenses. The IPSASB is also developing a related project on revenue, which uses IFRS 15 as a starting point and looks at the type of modifications that would be required for IFRS 15 to be suitable for application to a wide range of revenue transactions in the public sector. This may result in revisions to, or a replacement of, the existing revenue recognition requirements. The Board noted that the issues to be considered under the IPSASB revenue project could result in outcomes that are similar to what the Board had achieved in finalising AASB 1058. The IPSASB expects to complete these projects in 2019. The Board noted that it would consider undertaking a project to review the accounting specified by AASB 1058 following the completion of these projects.

BC180 The Board noted the following differences between AASB 1058 and IPSAS 9, IPSAS 11 and IPSAS 23 arise as a result of its decisions in finalising AASB 1058:

(a) recognition criteria – the Board decided not to specify asset recognition criteria in AASB 1058, but to require an entity to recognise assets as specified by other Australian Accounting Standards (other than in respect of volunteer services). In contrast, IPSAS 23 specifies that an asset is recognised where it is probable that future economic benefits or service potential will flow to the entity and its fair value can be measured reliably;

(b) fair value of an asset – the consequential amendments arising from AASB 1058 require various assets acquired for consideration that is significantly less than the fair value of the asset principally to enable the entity to further its objectives, to be initially measured at fair value in accordance with AASB 13. AASB 1058 also requires any related amounts to the asset to be recognised and measured in accordance with other Australian Accounting Standards. The IPSASB does not have a fair value measurement standard similar to AASB 13 and therefore IPSAS 9, IPSAS 11 and IPSAS 23 do not include such a reference;

(c) exchange and non-exchange transactions – IPSAS 9 and IPSAS 23 require income recognition based on whether it is an exchange or non-exchange transaction (a transaction in which the entity receives value from another entity without giving approximately equal value in exchange) respectively. IPSAS 23 requires a non-exchange transfer to be recognised as an asset and corresponding revenue when the entity does not have a liability in respect of the same asset. Where a liability is initially recognised, an entity recognises revenue and reduces the liability when it satisfies the present obligations associated with the asset. Except in certain specified instances, AASB 1058 requires an entity to recognise as income immediately in profit or loss the excess of the initial carrying amount of an asset over the related amounts recognised in accordance with other Australian Accounting Standards in the form of contributions by owners, liabilities and revenue;

(d) volunteer services – IPSAS 23 permits an entity to elect whether to recognise services in-kind (ie volunteer services) as revenue and an asset. AASB 1058 requires local government, government departments, general government sectors and whole of government to recognise volunteer services as income (or where appropriate, a contribution by owner) if the fair value of the services can be measured reliably and if the services would have been purchased if they had not been donated. All other entities may elect to recognise volunteer services if those services can be measured reliably; and

(e) disclosure – AASB 1058 includes a number of disclosure requirements that are not included in IPSAS 9, IPSAS 11 and IPSAS 23, such as the requirement for government departments to disclose information relating to compliance with parliamentary appropriations and other externally imposed requirements. IPSAS 9 and IPSAS 23 require some disclosures that are not included in AASB 1058, such as the disclosure of the methods adopted to determine the stage of completion of transactions involving the rendering of services. Additionally, IPSAS 23 encourages, but does not require, the disclosure about the nature and type of all volunteer services received, whether they are recognised or not. This contrasts with AASB 1058, which requires the disclosure of volunteer services that are recognised during the period, and encourages disclosure about the nature of the entity's dependence on volunteer services, including those not recognised.

AASB 1059
Service Concession Arrangements: Grantors

(Issued July 2017)

This note is not part of Accounting Standard AASB 1059.

The following unincorporated amendments are not included in this Standard.

- AASB 2018-5 *Amendments to Australian Accounting Standards — Deferral of AASB 1059.* This Standard makes amendments to AASB 1059 *Service Concession Arrangements: Grantors.* This Standard amends the mandatory effective date of AASB 1059 to reporting periods beginning on or after 1 January 2020 instead of 1 January 2019. Therefore, this Standard also defers the consequential amendments to other pronouncements set out in AASB 1059.

Entities early-adopting any amendments with later application dates will need to refer to the amending Standards that have not yet been incorporated into compilations. The abovementioned unincorporated amendments may be located on the AASB website at www.aasb.gov.au or on the Federal Register of Legislation website at www.legislation.gov.au.

CONTENTS

PREFACE

COMPARISON WITH INTERNATIONAL PRONOUNCEMENTS

ACCOUNTING STANDARD

AASB 1059 *SERVICE CONCESSION ARRANGEMENTS: GRANTORS*

APPENDICES

A. DEFINED TERMS

B. APPLICATION GUIDANCE

C. EFFECTIVE DATE AND TRANSITION

D. AMENDMENTS TO OTHER STANDARDS

IMPLEMENTATION GUIDANCE
ILLUSTRATIVE EXAMPLES
BASIS FOR CONCLUSIONS

> Australian Accounting Standard AASB 1059 *Service Concession Arrangements: Grantors* is set out in paragraphs 1 –30 and Appendices A – D. All the paragraphs have equal authority. Paragraphs in **bold type** state the main principles. Terms defined in Appendix A are in *italics* the first time they appear in the Standard. AASB 1059 is to be read in the context of other Australian Accounting Standards, including AASB 1048 *Interpretation of Standards*, which identifies the Australian Accounting Interpretations, and AASB 1057 *Application of Australian Accounting Standards*. In the absence of explicit guidance, AASB 108 *Accounting Policies, Changes in Accounting Estimates and Errors* provides a basis for selecting and applying accounting policies.

PREFACE

Introduction

The Australian Accounting Standards Board (AASB) develops, issues and maintains Australian Accounting Standards, including Interpretations. The AASB is a Commonwealth entity under the *Australian Securities and Investments Commission Act 2001*.

AASB 1057 *Application of Australian Accounting Standards* identifies the application of Standards to entities and financial statements. AASB 1053 *Application of Tiers of Australian Accounting Standards* establishes a differential reporting framework consisting of two tiers of reporting requirements for preparing general purpose financial statements.

What this Standard requires

This Standard addresses the accounting for a service concession arrangement by a grantor that is a public sector entity by prescribing the accounting for the arrangement from the grantor's perspective. The Standard is based on International Public Sector Accounting Standard IPSAS 32 *Service Concession Arrangements: Grantor* and is informed by AASB Interpretation 12 *Service Concession Arrangements*, which sets out the accounting for the operator in a public-to-private service concession arrangement. For example, the principles for recognition of a service concession asset are broadly consistent with AASB Interpretation 12.

The Standard applies to arrangements that involve an operator providing public services related to a service concession asset on behalf of a public sector grantor for a specified period of time and managing at least some of those services. An arrangement within the scope of this Standard typically involves an operator constructing the assets used to provide the public service or upgrading the assets (for example, by increasing their capacity) and operating and maintaining the assets for a specified period of time. Such arrangements are often described as build-operate-transfer or rehabilitate-operate-transfer service concession arrangements or public-private partnerships (PPPs).

The Standard requires the grantor to:

(a) recognise a service concession asset constructed, developed or acquired from a third party by the operator, including an upgrade to an existing asset of the grantor, when the grantor controls the asset. The grantor controls the asset if the grantor controls or regulates the services the operator must provide with the asset, to whom it must provide them and at what price, and if the grantor controls any significant residual interest in the asset at the end of the term of the arrangement;

(b) reclassify an existing asset (including recognising previously unrecognised identifiable intangible assets and land under roads) as a service concession asset when it meets the criteria for recognition as a service concession asset;

(c) initially measure a service concession asset constructed, developed or acquired by the operator or reclassified by the grantor at current replacement cost in accordance with the cost approach to fair value in AASB 13 *Fair Value Measurement*. Subsequent to the initial recognition or reclassification of the asset, the service concession asset is accounted for in accordance with AASB 116 *Property, Plant and Equipment* or AASB 138 *Intangible Assets*, as appropriate, except as specified in this Standard;

(d) recognise a corresponding liability measured initially at the fair value (current replacement cost) of the service concession asset, adjusted for any other consideration between the grantor and the operator. The liability is recognised using either or both of the following models:

    (i) the financial liability model – this model applies where the grantor has an obligation to deliver cash or another financial asset to the operator for the delivery of the service concession asset. This model requires the grantor to allocate the payments to the operator under the contract and account for them according to their substance as payments relating to the liability recognised or charges for services provided by the operator; and

    (ii) the grant of a right to the operator model – this model applies where the grantor grants the operator the right to earn revenue from third-party users of the service concession asset. This model requires the grantor to recognise a liability reflecting the unearned portion of the revenue arising from the exchange of the assets between the grantor and the operator. The grantor recognises revenue over the period of the service concession arrangement according to the substance of the arrangement and reduces the liability as the revenue is recognised; and

(e) disclose sufficient information to enable users of financial statements to understand the nature, amount, timing and uncertainty of assets, liabilities, revenue and cash flows arising from service concession arrangements, by considering the disclosure of information such as the following:

    (i) a description of the arrangements;

    (ii) significant terms of the arrangements that may affect the amount, timing and uncertainty of future cash flows;

    (iii) the nature and extent of the grantor's rights and obligations (such as rights to receive specified services and assets from the operator, and obligations to provide the operator with access to service concession assets or other revenue-generating assets) and renewal and termination options; and

    (iv) changes in arrangements during the reporting period.

Application date

This Standard applies to annual reporting periods beginning on or after 1 January 2019. Earlier application is permitted for periods beginning before 1 January 2019.

COMPARISON WITH INTERNATIONAL PRONOUNCEMENTS

AASB 1059 *Service Concession Arrangements: Grantors* applies to all public sector entities irrespective of whether they are for-profit or not-for-profit entities.

AASB 1059 and IPSASs

AASB 1059 is based on IPSAS 32 *Service Concession Arrangements: Grantor*. However, public sector entities that comply with AASB 1059 may not be in compliance with IPSAS 32 because of differences between the Standards. The more significant differences include the following:

(a) AASB 1059 applies to public sector entities in both the for-profit and not-for-profit sectors, whereas IPSAS 32 applies only to not-for-profit public sector entities;

(b)   AASB 1059 requires the grantor to initially measure a service concession asset provided by the operator at current replacement cost in accordance with the cost approach to fair value in AASB 13 *Fair Value Measurement*. IPSAS 32 specifies measurement at fair value generally;

(c)   an existing asset of the grantor, including a previously unrecognised identifiable intangible asset or land under roads, that is reclassified as a service concession asset is measured at fair value (current replacement cost) at the date of reclassification under AASB 1059. IPSAS 32 does not permit such remeasurement or the recognition of previously unrecognised identifiable intangible assets or land under roads;

(d)   AASB 1059 requires the grantor to recognise a financial liability where the grantor has a contractual obligation to pay cash to the operator for third-party usage of a service concession asset, with or without guaranteeing a minimum amount to the operator. IPSAS 32 refers to such an arrangement as a 'shadow toll' arrangement and requires the grantor to account for the payments as an expense when paid instead of recognising a financial liability at the commencement of the arrangement;

(e)   AASB 1059 provides more guidance on the term 'public service' than IPSAS 32; and

(f)   IPSAS 32 includes additional application guidance for other revenues. Other revenues relate to compensation by the operator to the grantor for access to the service concession asset by providing the grantor with a series of predetermined inflows of resources such as an upfront payment or a stream of payments (eg rent payments) and revenue-sharing provisions.

AASB 1059 and IFRS Standards

Public sector entities, including for-profit entities, that comply with AASB 1059 may not be in compliance with International Financial Reporting Standards issued by the International Accounting Standards Board (IASB). The IASB has issued an IFRIC Interpretation addressing the accounting by private sector operators of service concession arrangements but has not issued a pronouncement regarding the accounting by grantors.

AASB 1059 requires a grantor to initially measure a service concession asset at current replacement cost in accordance with the cost approach to fair value in AASB 13. However, AASB 13 and the corresponding IFRS 13 *Fair Value Measurement* do not specify which valuation technique to use. Instead IFRS 13 requires the use of valuation techniques that are appropriate in the circumstances and for which sufficient data are available to measure fair value, maximising the use of relevant observable inputs and minimising the use of unobservable inputs. Three widely used valuation techniques set out in IFRS 13 are the market approach, the cost approach and the income approach. The requirement of AASB 1059 to initially measure a service concession asset at current replacement cost in accordance with the cost approach may not be compliant with IFRS 13.

AASB 1059 requires a grantor to recognise an identifiable intangible asset as a service concession asset where the grantor controls the asset as set out in paragraph 5 or 6, even if the asset does not qualify for recognition under AASB 138/IAS 38 *Intangible Assets*. This Standard also permits revaluation of the asset in the absence of an active market.

AASB 15 *Revenue from Contracts with Customers* requires a licensor of intellectual property to recognise revenue from granting the licence using either the right-to-use or right-to-access methods, depending on the specific facts and circumstances. The general requirement in AASB 1059 to recognise revenue from granting a right to the operator over the term of the service concession arrangement on an appropriate basis may not be compliant with IFRS 15 *Revenue from Contracts with Customers*.

Consequently, a public sector grantor that is a for-profit entity may not be able to state that its financial statements comply with IFRS Standards.

ACCOUNTING STANDARD AASB 1059

The Australian Accounting Standards Board makes Accounting Standard AASB 1059 *Service Concession Arrangements: Grantors* under section 334 of the *Corporations Act 2001*.

Kris Peach

Dated 14 July 2017   Chair – AASB

ACCOUNTING STANDARD AASB 1059
SERVICE CONCESSION ARRANGEMENTS: GRANTORS

Objective

1   The objective of this Standard is to prescribe the accounting for a *service concession arrangement* by a *grantor* that is a public sector entity.

Scope (paragraphs B1–B3)

2   **This Standard shall be applied to service concession arrangements, which involve an *operator*:**

   (a)   providing public services related to a *service concession asset* on behalf of a grantor; and

   (b)   managing at least some of those services under its own discretion, rather than at the direction of the grantor.

3   Arrangements outside the scope of this Standard include those that do not involve the delivery of a public service, those where the operator manages the public services merely as an agent of the grantor, and those that involve service and management components where the asset is not controlled by the grantor as described in paragraph 5, or paragraph 6 for a whole-of-life asset.

4   This Standard does not specify the accounting by operators. Guidance on accounting for service concession arrangements by private sector operators can be found in AASB Interpretation 12 *Service Concession Arrangements*.

Recognition and measurement of service concession assets (paragraphs B14–B59)

5   **The grantor shall recognise an asset provided by the operator and an upgrade to or a major component replacement for an existing asset of the grantor as a service concession asset if the grantor controls the asset. The grantor controls the asset if, and only if:**

   (a)   the grantor controls or regulates what services the operator must provide with the asset, to whom it must provide them, and at what price; and

   (b)   the grantor controls – through ownership, beneficial entitlement or otherwise – any significant residual interest in the asset at the end of the term of the arrangement.

6   **The grantor shall recognise an asset that will be used in a service concession arrangement for its entire economic life (a 'whole-of-life' asset) if the conditions in paragraph 5(a) are met. In this case, the condition in paragraph 5(b) is not relevant and therefore the grantor controls the whole-of-life asset if the conditions in paragraph 5(a) are met.**

7   The grantor shall initially measure the service concession asset recognised in accordance with paragraph 5 (or paragraph 6 for a whole-of-life asset) at current replacement cost in accordance with the cost approach to fair value in AASB 13 *Fair Value Measurement*.

8   Where an existing asset of the grantor meets the conditions specified in paragraph 5 (or paragraph 6 for a whole-of-life asset), the grantor shall reclassify the existing asset as a service concession asset and shall measure the asset at current replacement cost in accordance with the cost approach to fair value in AASB 13 as at the date of reclassification. The grantor shall recognise any difference at that date between the carrying amount of the asset and its fair value (current replacement cost) as if it is a revaluation of the asset. This approach does not mean that the grantor has adopted the revaluation model.

9   After initial recognition or reclassification, the grantor shall account for a service concession asset during the term of the service concession arrangement as follows:

(a)   depreciate or amortise the depreciable amount of the asset over the useful life in accordance with AASB 116 *Property, Plant and Equipment* or AASB 138 *Intangible Assets*, as appropriate, with any impairment recognised in accordance with AASB 136 *Impairment of Assets*; and

(b)   references to fair value in other Standards shall be read as references to current replacement cost for service concession assets. For example, this means that current replacement cost is the basis for fair value measurement of service concession assets under a revaluation model. Furthermore, the active market requirements in AASB 138 for the revaluation of an intangible asset shall not apply.

10   The grantor shall account for a service concession asset after the end of the term of the service concession arrangement in accordance with other Accounting Standards and as specified below. In particular:

(a)   the grantor reclassifies the asset based on its nature or function;

(b)   references to fair value in other Standards shall no longer be read as references to current replacement cost. For example, any of the approaches in AASB 13 to fair value measurement may be applied to the asset under a revaluation model, as appropriate. Furthermore, the active market requirements in AASB 138 for the revaluation of an intangible asset shall apply; and

(c)   the grantor derecognises the asset in accordance with AASB 116 or AASB 138, as appropriate, only when the grantor loses control of the asset. For example, internally generated intangible assets that were recognised as service concession assets (including those that do not qualify for recognition under AASB 138) are not derecognised at the end of the term of the service concession arrangement, unless the grantor loses control of the asset at that time.

Recognition and measurement of liabilities (paragraphs B60–B74)

11   Where the grantor recognises a service concession asset in accordance with paragraph 5 (or paragraph 6 for a whole-of-life asset), the grantor shall also recognise a liability. The grantor shall not recognise a liability when an existing asset of the grantor is reclassified as a service concession asset in accordance with paragraph 8, except in circumstances where additional consideration is provided by the operator, as noted in paragraph 12.

12   The liability recognised in accordance with paragraph 11 shall be initially measured at the same amount as the service concession asset, adjusted by the

amount of any other consideration (eg the transfer of an existing asset) from the grantor to the operator, or from the operator to the grantor.

13 The nature of the liability recognised is based on the nature of the consideration exchanged between the grantor and the operator. The nature of the consideration given by the grantor to the operator is determined by reference to the terms of the *contract*.

14 In exchange for the service concession asset, the grantor might compensate the operator for the service concession asset by any combination of:

(a) making payments to the operator (the 'financial liability' model); and

(b) compensating the operator by other means (the 'grant of a right to the operator' model), such as granting the operator:

(i) the right to earn revenue from third-party users of the service concession asset; or

(ii) access to another revenue-generating asset for the operator's use (eg a private wing of a hospital where the remainder of the hospital is used by the grantor to treat public patients or a private parking facility adjacent to a public facility).

Financial liability model

15 **Where the grantor has a contractual obligation to deliver cash or another financial asset to the operator for the construction, development, acquisition or upgrade of a service concession asset, the grantor shall account for the liability recognised in accordance with paragraph 11 as a financial liability.**

16 The grantor has a contractual obligation to pay cash if it has agreed to pay the operator specified or determinable amounts, such as payments relating to the following:

(a) third-party usage of a service concession asset, with or without guaranteeing a minimum amount to the operator; or

(b) the shortfall, if any, between amounts received by the operator from users of the service concession asset and any other specified or determinable amounts payable by the grantor, even if the payment is contingent on the operator ensuring that the service concession asset meets specified quality or efficiency requirements.

17 AASB 9 *Financial Instruments*, AASB 132 *Financial Instruments: Presentation* and AASB 7 *Financial Instruments: Disclosures* apply to the financial liability recognised under paragraph 11, except where this Standard specifies otherwise.

18 **The grantor shall allocate the payments to the operator under the contract and account for them according to their substance as payments relating to the liability recognised in accordance with paragraph 11 or charges for services provided by or to be provided by the operator (including the future replacement of components of the service concession asset).**

19 **Charges for services provided by the operator (other than replacement components) in a service concession arrangement determined in accordance with paragraph 18 shall be accounted for in accordance with other relevant Standards.**

20 **Where the asset and service components of a service concession arrangement are separately identifiable, the service component of payments from the grantor to the operator shall be allocated accordingly (see paragraph B53). Where the asset and service components are not separately identifiable, the service component of payments from the grantor to the operator shall be determined using estimation techniques (see paragraph B54).**

Grant of a right to the operator model

21 **Where the grantor does not have a contractual obligation to pay cash or another financial asset to the operator for the construction, development, acquisition, or**

upgrade of a service concession asset, and instead grants the operator the right to earn revenue from third-party users or access to another revenue-generating asset, the grantor shall account for the liability recognised in accordance with paragraph 11 as the unearned portion of the revenue arising from the exchange of assets between the grantor and the operator.

22   **The grantor shall recognise revenue, and accordingly reduce the liability noted in paragraph 21, according to the economic substance of the service concession arrangement (see paragraph B71).**

23   Where the grantor compensates the operator for the service concession asset and the provision of services by granting the operator the right to earn revenue from third-party users of the service concession asset or access to another revenue-generating asset, the exchange is regarded as a transaction that will generate revenue for the grantor. As the right granted to the operator to access the grantor's underlying service concession asset is effective for the period of the service concession arrangement, the grantor does not recognise revenue from the exchange immediately. Instead, a liability is recognised for revenue that is not yet earned. The revenue is then recognised according to the economic substance of the service concession arrangement, and the liability is reduced as revenue is recognised.

Dividing the arrangement

24   **If the grantor compensates the operator for the provision of a service concession asset partly by incurring a financial liability and partly by the grant of a right to the operator, it is necessary to account separately for each part of the total liability recognised in accordance with paragraph 11. The amount initially recognised for the total liability shall be the same amount as that specified in paragraph 12.**

25   The grantor shall account for each part of the liability referred to in paragraph 24 in accordance with paragraphs 15–23. The financial liability part shall be measured first, and the remainder of the total liability allocated to the part related to the grant of the right to the operator (see paragraphs B73 and B74).

Other liabilities, commitments, contingent liabilities and contingent assets (paragraphs B75–B78)

26   **The grantor shall account for other liabilities, commitments, contingent liabilities and contingent assets arising from a service concession arrangement in accordance with AASB 9, AASB 137 *Provisions, Contingent Liabilities and Contingent Assets*, and any other relevant Standards.**

Other revenues

27   **The grantor shall account for revenues arising from a service concession arrangement, other than those specified in paragraphs 21–23, in accordance with AASB 15 *Revenue from Contracts with Customers* or AASB 1058 *Income of Not-for-Profit Entities*, as appropriate.**

Presentation and disclosure (paragraphs B79–B80)

28   **The objective of the disclosure requirements is for an entity to disclose sufficient information to enable users of financial statements to understand the nature, amount, timing and uncertainty of assets, liabilities, revenue and cash flows arising from service concession arrangements. To achieve this, an entity shall consider disclosing qualitative and quantitative information about its service concession arrangements, including the following:**

      (a)   a description of the arrangements;

      (b)   significant terms of the arrangements that may affect the amount, timing and uncertainty of future cash flows (eg the period of the arrangement, re-pricing dates and the basis upon which re-pricing or renegotiation is determined);

      (c)   the nature and extent (eg quantity, time period, or amount, as appropriate) of:

           (i)   rights to receive specified services from the operator;

           (ii)   the carrying amount of service concession assets as at the end of the reporting period, including separate disclosure for existing assets of the grantor reclassified as service concession assets during the reporting period;

           (iii)   rights to receive specified assets at the end of an arrangement;

           (iv)   renewal and termination options;

           (v)   other rights and obligations (eg major overhaul of service concession assets); and

           (vi)   obligations to provide the operator with access to service concession assets or other revenue-generating assets; and

      (d)   changes in arrangements occurring during the reporting period.

29   The disclosures provided by an entity in accordance with paragraph 28 are provided individually for each material service concession arrangement or in aggregate for service concession arrangements involving services of a similar nature, in addition to disclosures required by AASB 116 and AASB 138. Service concession assets of a similar nature may form a subset of a class of assets disclosed in accordance with AASB 116 or AASB 138 or may be included in more than one class of assets disclosed in accordance with AASB 116 or AASB 138. For example, for the purposes of AASB 116, a toll bridge may be included in the same class as other bridges, and for the purposes of paragraph 28 may be included with service concession assets reported in aggregate as toll roads.

Commencement of the legislative instrument

30   For legal purposes, this legislative instrument commences on 31 December 2018.

APPENDIX A
DEFINED TERMS (paragraphs B4–B13)

This appendix is an integral part of the Standard.

contract	An agreement between two or more parties that creates enforceable rights and obligations.
grantor	The entity that grants the right to access the **service concession asset** to the **operator**.
operator	The entity that has a right of access to the **service concession asset** to provide public services.

service concession arrangement	A **contract** effective during the reporting period between a **grantor** and an **operator** in which:
	(a) the **operator** has the right of access to the **service concession asset** (or assets) to provide public services on behalf of the **grantor** for a specified period of time;
	(b) the **operator** is responsible for at least some of the management of the public services provided through the asset and does not act merely as an agent on behalf of the grantor; and
	(c) the **operator** is compensated for its services over the period of the **service concession arrangement**.
service concession asset	An asset (other than goodwill) to which the **operator** has the right of access to provide public services on behalf of the **grantor** in a **service concession arrangement** that:
	(a) the **operator** constructs, develops, upgrades or replaces major components, or acquires from a third party or is an existing asset of the **operator**; or
	(b) is an existing asset of the **grantor**, including a previously unrecognised identifiable intangible asset and land under roads, or an upgrade to or replacement of a major component of an existing asset of the **grantor**.

APPENDIX B
APPLICATION GUIDANCE

This appendix is an integral part of the Standard.

Scope (paragraphs 2–4)

B1   This Standard is informed by AASB Interpretation 12, which sets out the accounting requirements for the private sector operator in a service concession arrangement. For example, the principles for recognition of a service concession asset are broadly consistent with AASB Interpretation 12. However, because this Standard deals with the accounting by the public sector grantor, this Standard addresses the issues identified in AASB Interpretation 12 from the grantor's point of view, as follows:

(a)   the grantor recognises a financial liability when it is obliged to make a payment or series of payments to the operator for provision of a service concession asset (ie constructed, developed, acquired or upgraded). Under paragraphs 12, 14 and 20 of AASB Interpretation 12, the operator recognises revenue for the construction, development, acquisition, upgrade and operation services it provides. Under paragraph 16 of AASB Interpretation 12, the operator recognises a financial asset;

(b)   the grantor recognises a liability when it grants the operator the right to earn revenue from third-party users of the service concession asset or another revenue-generating asset. Under paragraph 17 of AASB Interpretation 12, the operator recognises an intangible asset; and

(c)   the grantor derecognises an asset it grants to the operator and over which it no longer has control and reduces the liability recognised under paragraph 11 of this Standard. Under paragraph 27 of AASB Interpretation 12, the operator accounts for the asset as part of the transaction price if the asset forms part of the consideration payable by the grantor for the services.

B2   Paragraph 2 of this Standard specifies that an arrangement within the scope of this Standard involves an operator providing a public service related to a service concession asset on behalf of a grantor. In many jurisdictions, governments have introduced contractual service arrangements to attract private sector participation in the development, financing, operation and maintenance of infrastructure and other assets used to provide public services. The assets may already exist, or may be constructed or upgraded during the period of the service arrangement. An arrangement within the scope of this Standard typically involves an operator constructing the assets used to provide the public services or upgrading the assets (for example, by increasing their capacity) and operating and maintaining the assets for a specified period of time. Such arrangements are often described as build-operate-transfer or rehabilitate-operate-transfer service concession arrangements or public-private partnerships (PPPs).

B3   Paragraph 3 of the Standard illustrates the types of arrangements that are outside the scope of this Standard, such as arrangements that do not deliver a public service (for example, assets used for commercial purposes), arrangements where the operator does not provide and manage at least some of the public services under its own discretion (for example, outsourcing service agreements where the public sector entity has control of the asset) and arrangements that involve service and management components where the asset is not controlled by the grantor (for example, privatised assets that are subject to price regulation).

Definitions (Appendix A)

Public service

B4   Appendix A defines a service concession arrangement. A feature of a service concession arrangement is the public service nature of the obligation to be undertaken by the operator in a commercial transaction. The public service nature of the services to be provided using the service concession asset is assessed irrespective of the identity of the party that operates the services. A service concession arrangement contractually obliges the operator to provide some, if not all, of the services to the public on behalf of the public sector entity. Other common features of a service concession arrangement within the scope of this Standard are:

(a)   the grantor is a public sector entity;

(b)   the operator is responsible for at least some of the management of the service concession asset and related services and does not merely act as an agent on behalf of the grantor;

(c)   the arrangement sets or limits the initial prices to be levied by the operator and regulates price revisions over the period of the service concession arrangement;

(d)   the operator is obliged to hand over the service concession asset to the grantor in a specified condition at the end of the period of the arrangement, for little or no incremental consideration, irrespective of which party initially financed it; and

(e)   the arrangement is governed by a contract that sets out performance standards, mechanisms for adjusting prices, and arrangements for arbitrating disputes.

B5   Appendix A defines a service concession asset. Examples of service concession assets include roads (and land under roads), bridges, tunnels, prisons, hospitals, airports, water distribution facilities, energy supply and telecommunication networks, permanent installations for military and other operations, registries and databases, and other tangible or intangible assets that are expected to be used during more than one reporting period in delivering public services.

Asset provides public services

B6   Assessing whether an asset provides public services requires judgement, taking into account the nature and relative significance of each component and the services provided. For example, a courthouse building provides multiple services, such as courts, administrative offices and associated services. However, the primary purpose of the building is to provide court services, which are considered to be public services. The court services are necessary or essential to the general public and are generally expected to be provided by a public sector entity in accordance with government policy or regulation. The court services are accessible to the public, even if it is a subset of the community that uses the services. The services provided by the administrative offices may be unrelated to the court services and therefore considered ancillary if they are insignificant to the arrangement as a whole, and in that case would not affect the assessment that the building provides public services. However, if the unrelated administrative services were significant to the arrangement as a whole, the courthouse building might be assessed as not providing public services.

B7   If an arrangement provides public services principally through a primary asset, and a secondary asset is used or is mainly used to complement the primary asset, such as student accommodation for a public university, the secondary asset would be regarded as providing public services as well. As another example, a hospital car park constructed by an operator as part of the arrangement to construct a hospital that largely provides public services would be considered part of the hospital service concession arrangement. The car park may provide limited ancillary services without affecting the assessment that the car park is used to provide public services. However, if the car park was not constructed as part of the hospital service concession arrangement (eg subsequent to the construction of the hospital or with a different party) and is largely of a commercial nature (eg car parking is available to the general public, including hospital patrons), the car park would be regarded as an asset that does not provide public services, and therefore outside the scope of this Standard.

B8   Where the services provided by an asset are used wholly internally by a public sector entity for the purpose of assisting the public sector entity to deliver public services, but managed by an external party, the arrangement is likely to be an outsourcing arrangement or a lease, rather than a service concession arrangement. For example, the provision of information technology services to a government department providing emergency services to the public is likely to be an outsourcing contract, which may contain a lease of the information technology hardware. The accompanying Implementation Guidance also illustrates common types of arrangements.

B9   For an asset to provide public services, it is not necessary for the public to have physical access to the asset. For example, a military base provides public services (defence activities) even though the public is unlikely to have physical access to the military base.

Operator manages at least some of the public services

B10   For an arrangement to be within the scope of this Standard, the operator must be responsible for providing public services through the service concession asset and for managing at least some of the public services and related services, and not act merely as an agent on behalf of the grantor through an outsourcing arrangement. For example, an operator in an arrangement to construct and operate a hospital in accordance with the grantor's directions would need to provide services more managerial in nature than cleaning, building maintenance and security services for the hospital after its construction in order for the arrangement to be considered a service concession arrangement. Cleaning, building maintenance and security services would generally be regarded as relatively insignificant to the public services provided by the hospital. Therefore, if the operator is responsible only for constructing the hospital and then providing all or any of those services, the operator is unlikely to be considered to be responsible for some of the management of the public services provided by the hospital. However, if after constructing the hospital the operator also provides scheduling of staff and resources (even if provided by the grantor), the operator is likely to be responsible for some of the management of the hospital public services, and not acting like an agent of the grantor. In contrast, if the maintenance contributes significantly to the public services provided by the asset, then the operator would be responsible for at least some of the management of the public services provided by the asset. For example, this would be the case for an arrangement where an operator constructs and maintains (at its discretion) a toll road on behalf of the grantor, because maintenance services are a significant component of the public services provided by the toll road.

Changes in an arrangement

B11   A grantor assesses at the commencement of an arrangement whether an asset provides public services and whether the operator is responsible for providing and managing at least some of the public services provided through the asset and does not act merely as an agent on behalf of the grantor. The initial assessment applies for the duration of the service concession arrangement. Where there is a significant modification to the terms and conditions of the arrangement, the arrangement should be reassessed to determine whether the asset still provides public services, and whether the operator is responsible for providing and managing at least some of the public services provided through the asset under its own discretion – and therefore whether the arrangement is still within the scope of this Standard. If service concession accounting is no longer appropriate, the grantor determines whether the service concession asset and liabilities continue to be recognised and accounted for under other Accounting Standards or else derecognised.

Contracts

B12   Appendix A also defines a contract. The term 'agreement' in the definition of a 'contract' encompasses an arrangement entered into under the direction of another party (eg when assets are transferred to an entity with a directive that they be deployed to provide specified services).

B13   Contracts can be written, oral or implied by an entity's customary practices in performing or conducting its activities. For not-for-profit entities, Appendix F to AASB 15 includes guidance regarding when an agreement creates enforceable rights and obligations.

Recognition and initial measurement of service concession assets (paragraphs 5–10)

Recognition of service concession assets

B14   A service concession arrangement typically includes many assets, rather than one asset. References in this Standard to a service concession asset apply to all of the assets encompassed by the arrangement. If a service concession arrangement encompasses a business as defined in AASB 3 *Business Combinations*, the grantor shall recognise the assets (including any identifiable intangible assets) and liabilities of the business when the conditions in paragraph 5 or 6 are satisfied. Goodwill shall not be recognised by the grantor.

Control

B15   Paragraph 5 of this Standard specifies the conditions under which an asset, other than a whole-of-life asset, is recognised by the grantor. Paragraph 6 of the Standard specifies the condition under which a whole-of-life asset is recognised by the grantor. The assessment of whether a service concession asset should be recognised in accordance with paragraph 5 (or paragraph 6 for a whole-of-life asset) is made on the basis of all of the facts and circumstances of the arrangement.

B16   The fundamental principle reflected in paragraphs 5 and 6 is determining whether the grantor controls the underlying asset or assets of a service concession arrangement. The ability to exclude or regulate the access of others to the benefits of an asset is an essential element of control that distinguishes an entity's assets from public goods that all entities can access and benefit from. If the service concession arrangement provides for the grantor to control the price (for example, the contract may set the initial prices to be levied by the operator and regulate price revisions over the period of the service concession arrangement), the services to be provided and to whom the services must be provided, then the grantor controls the service concession asset regardless of whether there is any regulation by a third-party regulator.

B17 Control should be distinguished from management. If the grantor has both the degree of control described in paragraph 5(a) and any significant residual interest in the asset (as noted in paragraph 5(b)), the operator is only managing the asset on the grantor's behalf – even though, in many cases, it may have wide managerial discretion.

B18 The control or regulation referred to in paragraph 5(a) could be by contract, or otherwise. If the contract specifies that the grantor controls or regulates the price, the services to be provided and to whom the operator must provide the services, the conditions specified in paragraph 5(a) are met.

Regulation

B19 If a service concession contract by itself does not result in the grantor having explicit control over the services and/or pricing of the services, the grantor might still have control of the service concession asset as a result of regulation by a third party. Regulation of what services the operator must provide, to whom it must provide them, and at what price, in the manner specified in paragraph 5(a), is a means by which a grantor can demonstrate control of the substantive benefits of the service concession asset. Grantor control of a service concession asset through regulation does not require the contract to refer to the regulation or the grantor to control or be related to the regulator. The third-party regulator might, for example, regulate other entities that operate in the same industry or sector as the grantor. This includes circumstances in which the grantor buys all of the services as well as those in which some or all of the services are bought by other users.

Regulation of pricing

B20 Control or regulation of the pricing of the services is one of the three factors set out in paragraph 5(a) to be considered in determining whether the grantor controls an asset and should recognise it as a service concession asset. For example, a regulated price includes a specified price, which may be zero, that the operator can charge for the services of the asset. The grantor would also have to control the services to be provided and the recipients of the services in order to recognise a service concession asset. This approach is consistent with the fundamental principle in paragraph B16 of an entity controlling an asset if it has the ability to exclude or regulate the access of others to the benefits of the asset. For example, for the purpose of paragraph 5(a), the grantor does not need to have complete control of the price: it is sufficient for the price to be regulated by the grantor, or by a third-party regulator (eg by a capping mechanism). Prices are regarded as controlled by the grantor in a regulated environment when a third-party regulator regulates the pricing of the services provided with a service concession asset. The regulation removes the ability of the operator to determine the price and, for the purpose of paragraph 5(a), the pricing of the services is considered to be set implicitly by the grantor as the contract between the grantor and the operator effectively incorporates the price regulation. In some cases, the grantor could have specified an alternative pricing regime but has chosen not to do so, effectively asserting 'passive' control of the pricing. If the contract specifies the grantor controls the services and the recipients of the services, the third-party regulation of the pricing of the services means that the operator does not control the pricing or the other criteria specified in paragraph 5(a), and accordingly the grantor controls the asset. If the operator is able to determine to whom the services are provided, but is subject to grantor control over what services may be provided and the pricing, the grantor does not control the asset. The accompanying Implementation Guidance illustrates common types of arrangements where the grantor or the operator might control the various factors.

B21 Where a third-party regulator regulates the pricing or the services that the asset must provide (as specified in paragraph 5(a)), it is not essential for the grantor to control or direct the activities of the third-party regulator for the grantor to have control of the service concession asset. For example, a State grantor in a service concession arrangement might meet the regulated pricing condition specified in paragraph 5(a) even though the relevant regulation is carried out by an independent Commonwealth regulator. Furthermore, it is not necessary for the grantor to refer to the regulator in the contract. The grantor might rely on the regulator exercising its powers within the parameters applicable to the regulator at the inception of the contract.

B22 Governments often have the power to regulate the behaviour of entities operating in certain sectors of the economy, either directly or through specifically created agencies. For the purpose of paragraph 5(a), such broad regulatory powers do not constitute control. In this Standard, the term 'regulate' is intended to be applied only in the context of the terms and conditions of the service concession arrangement. For example, a regulator of rail services may determine rates that apply to the rail industry as a whole. Depending on the legal framework in a jurisdiction, such rates may be implicit in the contract governing a service concession arrangement involving the provision of railway transportation, or they may be specifically referred to therein. However, in both cases, the control of the pricing of the service concession asset is derived from either the contract or the specific regulation applicable to rail services, without considering whether the grantor is related to the regulator of rail services.

B23 Where a service concession arrangement does not clearly fall within an existing regulatory framework (eg where there is more than one possible source of regulation), the contract will need to incorporate the specific regulatory framework that stipulates the services, the users and/or the pricing to be charged for the services in order for the requirements of paragraph 5(a) to be met.

B24 For a grantor to control any of the factors listed in paragraph 5(a) through third-party regulation, the regulation must be substantive. Non-substantive features, such as a cap that will apply only in remote circumstances, shall be ignored. Conversely, if, for example, an arrangement purports to give the operator freedom to set prices but any excess profit is returned to the grantor, the operator's return is capped and the price element of the control test is met.

Partly regulated asset

B25 Sometimes the use of a service concession asset is partly regulated in the manner described in paragraph 5(a) and partly unregulated. These arrangements may take a variety of forms, such as:

(a)   any asset that is physically separable and capable of being operated independently and meets the definition of a cash-generating unit as defined in AASB 136 is analysed separately to determine whether the conditions set out in paragraph 5(a) are met if it is used wholly for unregulated purposes (eg this might apply to a private wing of a hospital, where the remainder of the hospital is used to treat public patients); and

(b)   when purely ancillary activities (such as a hospital shop) are unregulated, the control tests shall be applied as if those services did not exist, because in cases in which the grantor controls the services in the manner described in paragraph 5(a), the existence of ancillary activities does not detract from the grantor's control of the service concession asset.

B26 There may be arrangements that include unregulated services that are neither purely ancillary nor delivered by using a physically separable portion of the total asset. For example, a grantor may control prices charged to children and seniors at a sports facility but the amounts charged to adults are not controlled. The same facilities are being used by all, regardless of the amount they pay. Alternatively, prices could be regulated by the grantor for services provided at certain times of the day rather than for different classes of users. In such cases, it will be a matter of judgement whether enough of the service is regulated in order to demonstrate that the grantor has control of the asset.

B27 The operator may have a right to use the separable asset described in paragraph B25(a), or the facilities used to provide ancillary unregulated services described in paragraph

B25(b). In either case, there may in substance be a lease from the grantor to the operator; if so, it shall be accounted for in accordance with AASB 16 *Leases*.

Control concept in other Australian Accounting Standards

B28   If an asset meets the conditions in paragraph 5 (or paragraph 6), the grantor controls the use of the asset and therefore recognises the asset in accordance with this Standard. An asset that does not meet the control criteria of this Standard is assessed to determine whether it is recognised under another Accounting Standard, such as AASB 16, AASB 116 or AASB 138. The Implementation Guidance accompanying this Standard contains a table that highlights the continuum of typical arrangements and relevant accounting requirements.

Long-term leases, outsourcing or privatisation

B29   Assessment of whether long-term leasing, outsourcing, service and privatisation arrangements are within the scope of this Standard addresses whether the 'grantor' entity controls the underlying asset(s) of the arrangement in accordance with the control criteria of paragraph 5 (or paragraph 6). For example:

(a)   if the grantor does not retain control of an existing asset under such an arrangement, the grantor considers whether to derecognise the asset as a sale or privatisation; or

(b)   if the grantor retains control of an existing asset and gives the 'operator' the right to use the asset, or the operator controls an asset and gives the grantor the right to use the asset, the grantor considers whether to recognise a lease in relation to the asset as lessor or lessee respectively. This contrasts with a service concession arrangement, where the grantor provides the operator with the right to access the service concession asset, rather than a right to use the asset.

Changes in control

B30   The grantor's control of the service concession asset may change during the term of the service concession arrangement. The change in the grantor's control of the asset may arise from changes in the terms of the service concession contract, or changes in third-party regulation of the price and/or services.

B31   Where there is a change in facts or circumstances that indicate the grantor's control of the asset may have changed, the grantor assesses whether the asset is still within the scope of this Standard or should be reclassified within the scope of another Standard. Where the grantor no longer has control of the asset in accordance with this Standard, the grantor determines whether the asset continues to be recognised and accounted for under other Accounting Standards or else derecognised, except internally generated identifiable intangible assets initially recognised by the grantor under a service concession arrangement continue to be recognised by the grantor while control is retained, rather than derecognised under AASB 138.

Residual interest

B32   The grantor must also control through ownership, beneficial entitlement or otherwise any significant residual interest in the asset at the end of the term of the arrangement (paragraph 5(b)).

B33   For the purpose of paragraph 5(b), the grantor's control over any significant residual interest would both restrict the operator's practical ability to sell or pledge the asset (by acknowledging the grantor's residual interest in the asset) and effectively give the grantor control of the asset throughout the period of the service concession arrangement. Consequently, where the grantor has substantive, rather than merely protective, rights to prevent the operator selling or pledging the asset during the service concession arrangement (eg the grantor must formally approve the transferee, rather than being able to refuse merely on the grounds that the transferee is not fit and proper), then the grantor is likely to have control of any significant residual interest in the asset.

B34   The residual interest in the asset is the estimated fair value (current replacement cost) of the asset, determined at the inception of the arrangement, as if it were already of the age and in the condition expected at the end of the service concession arrangement.

B35   Paragraph 5 identifies whether the asset, including any replacements required, is controlled by the grantor for the whole of its economic life, beyond the term of the service concession arrangement. For example, if the operator has to replace part of an asset during the period of the arrangement (eg the top layer of a road or the roof of a building), the asset shall be considered as a whole. Thus the condition in paragraph 5(b) is met for the whole of the asset, including the part that is replaced, if the grantor controls any significant residual interest in the final replacement of that part. However, replacements of major components are treated as a separate service concession asset (see paragraphs B38 and B48).

Whole-of-life assets

B36   For the purpose of paragraph 6, a whole-of-life asset is an asset that will be used in a service concession arrangement for either its entire economic life or the major part of its economic life. In both cases, there is no significant residual interest in the asset at the end of the arrangement, so that the condition in paragraph 5(b) is not relevant.

Existing assets of the grantor

B37   The arrangement may involve an existing asset (tangible or intangible) of the grantor:

   (a)   to which the grantor gives the operator access for the purpose of the service concession arrangement; or

   (b)   to which the grantor gives the operator access for the purpose of the operator generating revenues as compensation for the service concession asset.

B38   Existing assets of the grantor used in the service concession arrangement shall be classified under this Standard (paragraph 8) as service concession assets. This includes identifiable intangible assets and land under roads of the grantor that have not been recognised previously by the grantor. The grantor shall recognise the upgrade of an existing asset of the grantor (eg an increase in capacity) or the replacement of a major component of an asset as a service concession asset in accordance with paragraph 5 (or paragraph 6 for a whole-of-life asset). The grantor also recognises a corresponding liability, when the upgrade or replacement occurs.

Intangible assets and land under roads

B39   In applying paragraphs 8–10 and B38 to an identifiable intangible asset or land under roads that has not been recognised previously by the grantor, the grantor shall:

   (a)   initially recognise the asset as a service concession asset, measured at current replacement cost in accordance with the cost approach to fair value in AASB 13. In accordance with paragraphs 8 and 11, the grantor shall account for the recognition of the asset at fair value (current replacement cost) as if it is a revaluation of the asset (ie as a revaluation surplus) and shall recognise a liability only to the extent of additional consideration provided by the operator;

   (b)   after initial recognition of the asset and while controlled by the grantor, account for the asset in accordance with AASB 116 or AASB 138, as appropriate, subject to paragraph 9, as follows:

      (i)   depreciate or amortise the depreciable amount of the asset over its useful life; and

      (ii)   if applying the revaluation model to the asset, current replacement cost continues to be used as the basis for fair value measurement without applying, in the case of an intangible asset, the active market requirements in AASB 138; and

   (c)   after the end of the service concession arrangement, account for the asset in accordance with other Accounting Standards. This requires the grantor to reclassify the asset, continue to recognise the intangible asset while controlled by the grantor, and account for depreciation or amortisation over its useful life and revaluation in accordance with the other Standards and derecognise the asset in accordance with AASB 116 or AASB 138 only when control is lost. For example, this means that an internally generated intangible asset is not derecognised under AASB 138 until control is lost, even if the asset would not have satisfied the initial recognition criteria in AASB 138.

Impairment and loss of control

B40   In applying the impairment tests to service concession assets accounted for under the cost model in AASB 116 or AASB 138, as appropriate, the grantor does not necessarily consider the granting of the service concession to the operator as a circumstance that causes impairment, unless there has been a change in use of the asset that affects its future economic benefits or service potential. The grantor shall refer to AASB 136 to determine whether any of the indicators of impairment have been triggered under such circumstances. AASB 136 does not apply to primarily non-cash-generating specialised assets of not-for-profit entities that are regularly revalued to fair value (current replacement cost) under the revaluation model in AASB 116 or AASB 138.

B41   Subject to paragraph B39(c), if the asset no longer meets the conditions for recognition in paragraph 5 (or paragraph 6 for a whole-of-life asset), the grantor shall follow the principles in AASB 116 or AASB 138, as appropriate. For example, if control of the asset is transferred to the operator on a permanent basis, it shall be derecognised. Alternatively, the grantor may be required to derecognise the asset when it or a third-party regulator no longer regulates the pricing, but rather allows the operator to freely set prices for the services provided through the service concession asset.

B42   If control of the asset is transferred on a temporary basis, the grantor considers the substance of this term of the service concession arrangement in determining whether the asset should be derecognised. In such cases, the grantor shall also consider whether the arrangement is a lease transaction or a sale and leaseback transaction that should be accounted for in accordance with AASB 16.

Existing assets of the operator

B43   The operator may provide an asset for use in the service concession arrangement that it has not constructed, developed, or acquired for the purpose of the arrangement. If the arrangement involves an existing asset of the operator that the operator uses for the purpose of the service concession arrangement, the grantor shall determine whether the asset meets the conditions in paragraph 5 (or paragraph 6 for a whole-of-life asset). If the conditions for recognition are met, the grantor shall recognise the asset as a service concession asset and account for it in accordance with this Standard.

Constructed or developed assets

B44   When a constructed or developed asset meets the conditions in paragraph 5 (or paragraph 6 for a whole-of-life asset), the grantor shall recognise and measure the asset in accordance with this Standard. This recognition also depends on the asset meeting the recognition criteria in AASB 116 or AASB 138:

(a)   AASB 116 requires that the cost of an item of property, plant and equipment shall be recognised as an asset if, and only if:

    (i)   it is probable that future economic benefits associated with the asset will flow to the entity; and

    (ii)   the cost of the item can be measured reliably;

(b)   AASB 138 requires that an intangible asset shall be recognised if, and only if:

    (i)   it is probable that the expected future economic benefits that are attributable to the asset will flow to the entity; and

    (ii)   the cost of the asset can be measured reliably.

B45   Those criteria, together with the terms and conditions of the contract, need to be considered by the grantor in determining whether to recognise the service concession asset during the period in which the asset is constructed or developed. For property, plant and equipment and intangible assets, if the recognition criteria are met during the construction or development period, the grantor recognises the service concession asset to the appropriate extent during that period.

B46   The first recognition criterion requires the flow of economic benefits to the grantor. According to the *Framework for the Preparation and Presentation of Financial Statements*, as identified in AASB 1048 *Interpretation of Standards*, for not-for-profit entities, future economic benefits are synonymous with the notion of service potential. From the grantor's point of view, the primary purpose of a service concession asset is to provide service potential on behalf of the public sector grantor. Similar to an asset the grantor constructs or develops for its own use, the grantor would assess, at the time the costs of construction or development are incurred, the terms of the contract to determine whether, in addition to retaining control of the land on which the service concession asset is being developed, economic benefits embodied in the service concession asset are controlled by the grantor at that time.

B47   The second recognition criterion requires that the cost of the asset can be measured reliably. Accordingly, to meet the recognition criteria in AASB 116 or AASB 138, as appropriate, the grantor must have reliable information about the cost of the asset during its construction or development. For example, if the service concession arrangement requires the operator to provide the grantor with progress reports during the asset's construction or development, the costs incurred may be measurable, and would therefore meet the recognition criteria in AASB 116 for constructed assets or in AASB 138 for developed intangible assets. Also, where the grantor has little ability to avoid accepting an asset constructed or developed to meet the specifications of the service concession arrangement, the costs shall be recognised as progress is made towards completion of the asset. Thus, the grantor shall recognise a service concession asset and an associated liability.

Upgrades or replacement of major components

B48   The grantor shall recognise an upgrade, or the replacement of a major component, of (1) an existing asset of the grantor, or (2) an asset constructed, developed, acquired or otherwise provided by the operator, as a separate service concession asset in accordance with paragraph 5 (or paragraph 6 for a whole-of-life asset). The grantor shall also recognise the related liability in accordance with paragraph 11 when the upgrade or replacement occurs.

Measurement of service concession assets

B49   Paragraph 7 requires service concession assets recognised in accordance with paragraph 5 (or paragraph 6 for a whole-of-life asset) to be measured initially at current replacement cost. This is in accordance with the cost approach to fair value in AASB 13. In particular, the cost approach is used to determine the cost of a constructed or developed service concession asset or the cost of any upgrades to existing assets, on initial recognition. The requirement to measure the asset at current replacement cost also applies to existing assets, both tangible and intangible, of the grantor that are reclassified as service concession assets, in accordance with paragraph 8 of this Standard. The use of fair value (current replacement cost) on initial recognition or reclassification of a service concession asset does not constitute a revaluation under AASB 116 or AASB 138. Therefore, future revaluations of the asset are not required unless the entity adopts the revaluation model under the relevant Standard.

Types of compensation

B50   Service concession arrangements are rarely, if ever, the same: technical requirements vary by sector and by jurisdiction. Furthermore, the terms of the arrangement may also depend on the specific features of the overall legal framework, including contract law, of the particular jurisdiction.

B51 Depending on the terms of the service concession arrangement, the grantor may compensate the operator for the service concession asset and service provision by any combination of the following:

(a) making payments (eg cash) to the operator; and

(b) compensating the operator by other means, such as:

(i) granting the operator the right to earn revenue from third-party users of the service concession asset; or

(ii) granting the operator access to another revenue-generating asset for its use.

B52 When the grantor compensates the operator for the service concession asset by making payments to the operator, the asset and service components of the payments may be separately identifiable (eg the contract specifies the amount of the predetermined payment or series of payments to be allocated to the service concession asset). The asset and service components of the service concession arrangement are accounted for separately, in accordance with paragraph 20.

Separately identifiable payments

B53 A service concession arrangement may have separately identifiable asset and service components of the payments in a variety of circumstances, including, but not limited to, the following:

(a) part of a payment stream that varies according to the availability of the service concession asset itself and another part that varies according to usage or performance of certain services can be identified;

(b) different components of the service concession arrangement run for different periods or can be terminated separately. For example, an individual service component can be terminated without affecting the continuation of the rest of the arrangement; or

(c) different components of the service concession arrangement can be renegotiated separately. For example, the upgrade or replacement of major components of a service concession asset are addressed separately, or a service component is market tested and some or all of the cost increases or reductions are passed on to the grantor in such a way that the part of the payment by the grantor that relates specifically to that service can be identified.

Payments not separately identifiable

B54 For the purpose of applying the requirements of this Standard, payments and other consideration required by the arrangement are allocated at the inception of the arrangement or upon a reassessment of the arrangement into those for the service concession asset and those for other components of the service concession arrangement (eg maintenance and operation services) on the basis of their relative fair values. The fair value (current replacement cost) of the service concession asset represents amounts related to the asset and excludes other components of the service concession arrangement. In some cases, identifying payments for the asset and payments for other components of the service concession arrangement will require the grantor to use an estimation technique. For example, a grantor may estimate the payments related to the asset by reference to the fair value of a comparable asset in an agreement that contains no other components, or by estimating the payments for the other components in the service concession arrangement by reference to comparable arrangements and then deducting these payments from the total payments under the arrangement.

Operator receives other forms of compensation

B55 The types of compensation transactions referred to in paragraph 14(b) are non-monetary exchange transactions. Paragraph 24 of AASB 116 and paragraph 45 of AASB 138, as appropriate, provide guidance on these circumstances.

B56   When the operator is granted the right to earn revenue from third-party users of the service concession asset, or from another revenue-generating asset, or receives non-cash compensation from the grantor, the grantor does not incur a cost directly for acquiring the service concession asset. These forms of consideration to the operator may be intended to compensate the operator both for the cost of the service concession asset and for operating it during the term of the service concession arrangement. The grantor therefore needs to initially measure the asset component in a manner consistent with paragraph 7.

Fair value measurement

B57   A service concession asset is an asset that is obtained through construction, development, upgrade, major component replacement or acquisition, an existing asset or upgrade or major component replacement of an existing asset, to provide public services in a service concession arrangement. The capacity or service potential of the asset is used to achieve public service objectives irrespective of whether the cost of the asset will be recovered by the expected cash flows that the asset may generate. The asset is initially measured at fair value, which is the current replacement cost under the cost approach. The current replacement cost reflects the amount that would be required at the time to replace the service capacity of an asset. The asset is measured at current replacement cost whether the related liability is measured under the financial liability model, the grant of the right to the operator model, or both.

Subsequent measurement

B58   For consistency with the approach to the initial measurement of service concession assets recognised in accordance with this Standard, references to fair value in other Standards shall be read as references to current replacement cost for service concession assets, during the term of the service concession arrangement. If the grantor retains control of the asset after the end of the service concession arrangement, any fair value measurement of the asset is no longer restricted to the cost approach in AASB 13.

B59   After initial recognition, a grantor applies AASB 116 or AASB 138 to the subsequent measurement and derecognition of a service concession asset and to subsequent costs incurred. For the purposes of applying AASB 116 or AASB 138, service concession assets of a similar nature may form a subset of a class, or classes, of assets. Subsequent costs include lifecycle costs incurred to maintain the asset during the operating and maintenance phase of the service concession arrangement. However, upgrades or replacements of major components of service concession assets would be recognised as service concession assets in accordance with paragraph B48. AASB 136 is also applied in considering whether there is any indication that a service concession asset is impaired. The reference to fair value in AASB 136 for such assets refers to the current replacement cost of the asset.

Recognition and measurement of liabilities (paragraphs 11–25)

B60   The grantor recognises a liability in accordance with paragraph 11 when a service concession asset is recognised in accordance with paragraph 5 (or paragraph 6 for a whole-of-life asset). The nature of the liability recognised in accordance with paragraph 11 differs in the circumstances described in paragraphs B51(a) and B51(b) according to their substance. However, in each case, the liability recognised in accordance with paragraph 11 shall be initially measured at the same amount as the service concession asset, being the fair value (current replacement cost) of the asset in accordance with AASB 13.

B61   The grantor also recognises a liability in accordance with paragraph 11 when an existing asset of the grantor is reclassified as a service concession asset and the operator provides additional consideration to the grantor. The grantor first recognises the reclassification of its existing asset as a service concession asset in accordance with paragraph 8, treating any difference between the carrying amount of the asset and its fair value (current replacement cost) as if it is a revaluation of the asset. The second step for the grantor is to recognise the additional consideration provided by the operator (cash or other assets), and a financial liability or a liability under the grant of a right to the operator model or both, depending on the nature of the service concession arrangement.

B62 Payments made by an operator to a grantor that are separate from the service concession arrangement are accounted for based on the nature of the payments. If the payments are:

(a) for a right to goods or services, the grantor accounts for the payments as other revenues in accordance with AASB 15 or AASB 1058, as appropriate; or

(b) for the right to use an asset, the grantor assesses whether the arrangement contains a lease. If the arrangement contains a lease, the grantor accounts for the payments in accordance with AASB 16 (paragraph B29(b)).

Financial liability model

B63 When the grantor has a contractual obligation to make a predetermined series of payments to the operator, the liability is a financial liability as defined in AASB 9. The grantor has a contractual obligation if it has little, if any, discretion to avoid the obligation, which is usually the case because a contract with an operator normally is enforceable by law. For example, when an arrangement involves the grantor making payments to the operator for third-party usage of the service concession asset, the grantor accounts for the liability in the arrangement as a financial liability, regardless of whether the grantor has contractually agreed to provide a minimum guaranteed amount to the operator.

Initial measurement

B64 When the grantor provides compensation to the operator for the cost of the service concession asset and service provision in the form of a predetermined payment or series of payments, an amount reflecting the fair value (current replacement cost) of the service concession asset is recognised as a liability in accordance with paragraph 11. The grantor shall use the contractually specified interest rate in the arrangement to initially measure the financial liability component of a hybrid arrangement in accordance with AASB 9. If it is not practicable to determine the contractually specified interest rate, the grantor shall determine an appropriate rate using the prevailing market rate(s) of interest for a similar instrument with a similar credit rating. Examples of rates for a similar instrument include the operator's cost of capital specific to the service concession asset, the grantor's incremental borrowing rate, or another rate appropriate to the terms and conditions of the arrangement.

Subsequent measurement

B65 After initial recognition, the grantor applies AASB 9 to the subsequent measurement of a financial liability. For example, when the financial liability is measured at amortised cost and there is a difference between the expected payments and the actual payments by the grantor to the operator based on third-party usage of the service concession asset, the amortised cost is recalculated based on revised estimated cash flows discounted at the original effective interest rate. The adjustment is recognised in profit or loss as income or expense.

B66 When the grantor makes any payments to the operator in advance of the service concession asset being recognised, the grantor accounts for those payments as prepayments.

B67 When the financial liability is subsequently measured at amortised cost in accordance with AASB 9, the finance charge is determined based on the effective interest method. When the financial liability is subsequently measured at fair value through profit or loss, AASB 9 requires the fair value movements in the financial liability to be recognised as a gain or loss in profit or loss.

B68   The finance charge (if any) related to the liability in a service concession arrangement is presented consistently with other finance charges in accordance with AASB 101 *Presentation of Financial Statements*, AASB 123 *Borrowing Costs* and AASB 7 *Financial Instruments: Disclosures*.

B69   The financial liability does not include the grantor's payments to the operator for service components identified in paragraph 18. The service component of payments is normally recognised as expenses (and as liabilities prior to payment) as the services are provided.

Grant of a right to the operator model

B70   Under the grant of a right to the operator model, the grantor compensates the operator for the service concession asset and service provision by granting the operator the right to earn revenue from third-party users of the service concession asset.

B71   Revenue is not recognised immediately by the grantor at the inception of the service concession arrangement. Instead, a liability is recognised (as noted in paragraph 21) and subsequently reduced as revenue is recognised in accordance with paragraph 22 based on the economic substance of the service concession arrangement. Revenue is usually recognised as access to the service concession asset is provided to the operator over the term of the service concession arrangement. Paragraph B51 states that the grantor may compensate the operator by a combination of payments and granting a right to earn revenue directly from third-party users. In cases where the operator's right to earn third-party revenues significantly reduces or eliminates the grantor's predetermined series of payments to the operator, the liability related to the grant of the right to the operator usually would still be reduced (and revenue recognised) over the term of the arrangement as access is provided to the operator.

B72   When the grantor compensates the operator for the service concession asset and services by the provision of a revenue-generating asset, other than the service concession asset, the liability related to the grant of the right to the operator is reduced and revenue relating to the remaining liability is recognised in a manner similar to that described in the previous paragraph. In such cases, the grantor also considers the derecognition requirements in AASB 116 or AASB 138, as appropriate. If the grantor derecognises the revenue-generating asset, the grantor recognises a gain or loss for the difference between the carrying amount of the asset and its fair value (current replacement cost), and reduces the service concession liability accordingly.

Dividing the arrangement

B73   If the operator is compensated for the service concession asset partly by a predetermined payment or series of payments and partly by receiving the right to earn revenue from third-party use of either the service concession asset or another revenue-generating asset, it is necessary to account separately for each portion of the total liability related to the grantor's consideration. In these circumstances, the consideration to the operator is divided into a financial liability portion for the payments and a liability portion for the right granted to the operator to earn revenue from third-party use of the service concession asset or another revenue-generating asset.

B74   Arrangements described in paragraph B73 are commonly referred to as hybrid arrangements. Consistent with paragraph 12, the total liability recognised for a hybrid arrangement is initially measured at the same amount as the fair value (current replacement cost) of the service concession asset. The financial liability portion of the liability under the hybrid arrangement is measured first, with the remainder of the fair value (current replacement cost) of the service concession asset allocated to the portion of the liability relating to the grant of the right to the operator model. The financial liability portion is measured initially in accordance with paragraph B64.

Other liabilities, commitments, contingent liabilities and contingent assets (paragraph 26)

B75 Service concession arrangements may include various forms of financial guarantees (eg a guarantee, security, or indemnity related to the debt incurred by the operator to finance construction, development, acquisition or upgrade of a service concession asset) or performance guarantees (eg a guarantee of minimum revenue streams, including compensation for shortfalls).

B76 The grantor determines whether guarantees provided by the grantor as part of a service concession arrangement meet the definition of a financial guarantee contract. If so, the grantor applies AASB 7, AASB 9 and AASB 132 in accounting for the guarantee. Where the guarantee is regarded as an insurance contract, the grantor can elect to apply AASB 4 *Insurance Contracts* or AASB 1023 *General Insurance Contracts* instead if it has previously used accounting applicable to insurance contracts for such guarantees.

B77 Guarantees and commitments that do not meet the requirements in AASB 9 and AASB 132 relating to financial guarantee contracts and are not accounted for as insurance contracts are accounted for in accordance with AASB 137.

B78 Contingent assets or liabilities may arise from disputes over the terms of the service concession arrangement. Such contingencies are accounted for in accordance with AASB 137.

Presentation and disclosure (paragraphs 28–29)

B79 Disclosures relating to various aspects of service concession arrangements may be addressed in other Standards. This Standard addresses only the additional disclosures relating to service concession arrangements. Where the accounting for a particular aspect of a service concession arrangement is addressed in another Standard, the grantor follows the relevant disclosure requirements of that Standard in addition to those set out in paragraphs 28 and 29. The grantor also applies the relevant presentation and disclosure requirements in other Standards as they pertain to assets, liabilities, revenues, and expenses recognised under this Standard.

B80 AASB 101 requires finance costs (if any) to be presented separately in the statement of profit and loss and other comprehensive income. Finance charges (if any) determined in accordance with paragraph B67 that are expensed are included in this item.

APPENDIX C
EFFECTIVE DATE AND TRANSITION

This appendix is an integral part of the Standard.

Effective date

C1 An entity shall apply this Standard for annual reporting periods beginning on or after 1 January 2019. Earlier application is permitted for periods beginning before 1 January 2019. If an entity applies this Standard for an earlier period, it shall disclose that fact.

Transition

C2 For the purposes of the transition requirements, the date of initial application is the beginning of the earliest reporting period for which comparative information is presented in the financial statements.

C3 A grantor shall apply this Standard either:

(a) retrospectively to each prior period presented in accordance with AASB 108 *Accounting Policies, Changes in Accounting Estimates and Errors*; or

(b)   retrospectively by recognising and measuring service concession assets and related liabilities at the date of initial application.

C4   If a grantor elects to apply this Standard retrospectively in accordance with paragraph C3(b), the grantor shall:

(a)   measure the deemed cost of a service concession asset (including an existing asset of the grantor reclassified as a service concession asset) at fair value (current replacement cost) at the date of initial application;

(b)   measure a financial liability arising under a service concession arrangement in accordance with this Standard at the date of initial application;

(c)   measure a liability representing the unearned portion of any revenue arising from the receipt of a service concession asset under the grant of a right to the operator model at the fair value (current replacement cost) of the related service concession asset at the date of initial application, adjusted to reflect the remaining period of the service concession arrangement relative to the remaining economic life of the asset, less any related financial liabilities measured in accordance with paragraph (b);

(d)   recognise any net adjustments to the amounts of assets and liabilities as an adjustment to the opening balance of accumulated surplus (deficiency) at the date of initial application; and

(e)   disclose that it has applied this transition approach and information relating to the measurement of the assets and liabilities in support of the disclosure objective in paragraph 28.

C5   Retrospective application of this Standard in accordance with either paragraph C3(a) or C3(b) may require the derecognition or adjustment of any service concession assets and liabilities recognised under previous accounting policies or the initial recognition of service concession assets and liabilities. Any net adjustment on initial application of this Standard is recognised as an adjustment to the opening balance of accumulated surplus (deficiency). If the grantor applies the revaluation model in AASB 116 or AASB 138 as its accounting policy, the net adjustment is included in accumulated surplus (deficiency) and not revaluation surplus.

C6   The initial measurement of service concession assets at fair value (current replacement cost) does not mean that the assets are measured under the revaluation model. Subsequent revaluations are not required unless the grantor applies the revaluation model as its accounting policy.

C7   If a grantor applies this Standard retrospectively in accordance with paragraph C3(b), the measurement of liabilities arising under the financial liability model at the date of initial application is addressed in paragraph C4(b). Paragraph C4(c) addresses liability measurement under both the grant of a right to the operator model and hybrid arrangements, as it requires the measurement of the liability relating to the grant of a right to the operator to exclude any related financial liabilities.

References to superseded Standards

C8   If an entity applies this Standard but does not yet apply AASB 9, any reference in this Standard to AASB 9 shall be read as a reference to AASB 139 *Financial Instruments: Recognition and Measurement*.

C9   If an entity applies this Standard but does not yet apply AASB 15 or AASB 1058, any reference in this Standard to those Standards shall be read as a reference to AASB 118 *Revenue* or AASB 1004 *Contributions*, as appropriate.

C10   If an entity applies this Standard but does not yet apply AASB 16, any reference in this Standard to AASB 16 shall be read as a reference to AASB 117 *Leases*.

APPENDIX D
AMENDMENTS TO OTHER STANDARDS

This appendix sets out the amendments to other Australian Accounting Standards that are a consequence of the AASB issuing this Standard.

The amendments set out in this appendix apply to entities and financial statements in accordance with the application of the Standards and Interpretations set out in AASB 1057 *Application of Australian Accounting Standards* (as amended).

The amendments apply to annual reporting periods beginning on or after 1 January 2019.

If an entity applies this Standard to an earlier period, it shall also apply these amendments to that earlier period.

Amendments are made to the latest principal version of a Standard (or an Interpretation), unless otherwise indicated. The amendments also apply, as far as possible, to earlier principal versions of the amended Standards and Interpretations when this Standard is applied for earlier periods, as necessary.

This appendix uses underlining, striking out and other typographical material to identify some of the amendments to a Standard or an Interpretation, in order to make the amendments more understandable. However, the amendments made by this appendix do not include that underlining, striking out or other typographical material. Amended paragraphs are shown with deleted text struck through and new text underlined. Ellipses (...) are used to help provide the context within which amendments are made and also to indicate text that is not amended.

AASB 16 *Leases* (February 2016)

Paragraph Aus3.1 is added.

Aus3.1   This Standard does not apply to service concession assets recognised in accordance with AASB 1059 *Service Concession Arrangements: Grantors*.

AASB 138 *Intangible Assets* (August 2015)

Paragraph Aus3.1 is added.

Aus3.1   This Standard does not apply to intangible assets recognised as service concession assets in accordance with AASB 1059 *Service Concession Arrangements: Grantors*, except as set out in that Standard.

AASB 1051 *Land Under Roads* (December 2007)

Paragraph 7 is amended.

7   Other Australian Accounting Standards (including AASB 116 *Property, Plant and Equipment*) apply to land under roads, except to the extent that this Standard requires or permits otherwise. **This Standard does not apply to land under roads that are service concession assets in accordance with AASB 1059 *Service Concession Arrangements: Grantors*.**

Interpretation 129 *Service Concession Arrangements: Disclosures* (August 2015)

Paragraph 4 and 6 are amended.

4   The issue is what information should be disclosed in the notes in financial statements
        of an operator ~~and a grantor~~.

5   All aspects of a service concession arrangement shall be considered in determining
        the appropriate disclosures in the notes. An operator ~~and a grantor~~ shall disclose the
        following in each period:

        (a)   ...

IMPLEMENTATION GUIDANCE

This implementation guidance accompanies, but is not part of, AASB 1059.

IG1   The purpose of this Implementation Guidance is to illustrate certain aspects of the
        requirements of AASB 1059. Except in respect of arrangements that are concluded to
        be service concession arrangements, the implementation guidance identifies the parties
        to an arrangement as the grantor and the operator for convenience, without reference
        to the definitions in Appendix A.

Accounting framework for service concession arrangements

IG2   The diagram below summarises some of the key decisions in determining whether an
        arrangement is a service concession arrangement within the scope of AASB 1059.
        It does not address the period of time or operator compensation requirements of the
        definition of a service concession arrangement.

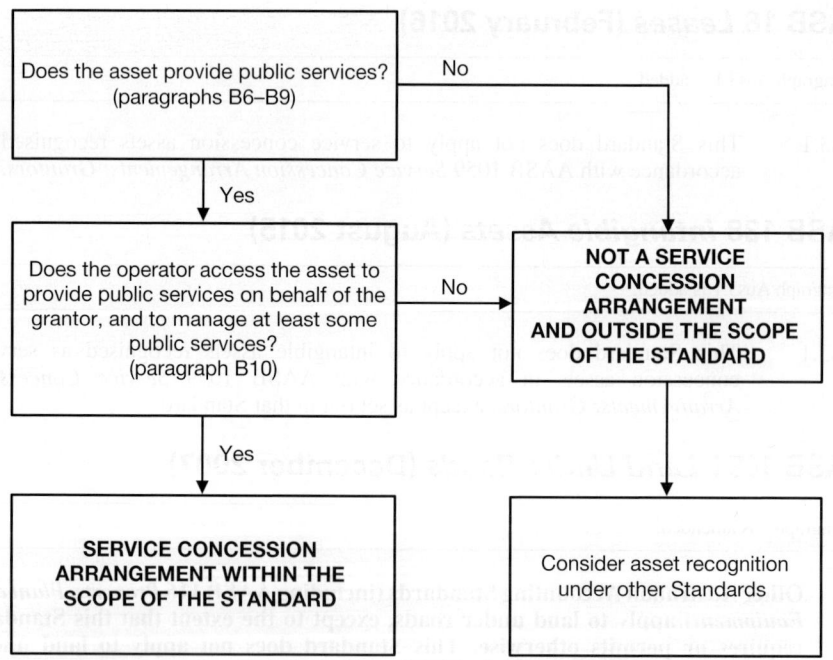

Guidance examples

IG3   The guidance examples below illustrate the key decisions outlined in the diagram
        in paragraph IG2 for assessing whether an arrangement is a service concession
        arrangement – and therefore within the scope of AASB 1059, assuming that the
        period of time and operator compensation requirements are met – in the following
        circumstances:

    (a)   the operator provides limited services for the asset; and

    (b)   the operator has management responsibilities for some services.

Example 1: Limited operator services

IG4   In this example, the relevant terms of the arrangement for assessing whether it is within the scope of AASB 1059 are:

    (a)   a grantor enters into an arrangement that involves the operator constructing a school;

    (b)   the school provides public services as the basic purpose of the school is to provide education services that are necessary or essential to the general public. The education services provided by the school are accessible to the public, even if it is a subset of the community that uses the services. The assessment of the public service nature of the school is consistent with paragraph B6;

    (c)   the grantor is responsible for the services relating to the delivery of education and operational services such as the recruitment of teachers and administration staff, and the maintenance of the school facilities; and

    (d)   the operator is responsible for cleaning and security services for the school.

IG5   Based on these facts and circumstances, the grantor concludes the operator does not access the school to provide public services as its provision of cleaning and security services does not constitute management of at least some of the public services provided by the school (refer paragraph B10). Accordingly, the arrangement is not a service concession arrangement and is outside the scope of AASB 1059 (paragraph 2). The cleaning and security services represent an outsourced service to the grantor to enable it to provide the public services through the school.

Example 2(a): Facility maintenance at discretion of operator

IG6   In this example, the facts in Example 1 apply, except that the operator is also responsible for maintenance of the school facilities by maintaining the school to a specified condition. The operator has discretion as to when and how it conducts maintenance of the school facilities.

IG7   Based on the facts and circumstances, whilst the operator provides maintenance of the school facilities, facility maintenance does not represent a significant component of the public services provided by the school. Therefore, the operator's responsibility for maintenance does not involve the operator in managing the school services (refer paragraph B10). Accordingly, the arrangement is not a service concession arrangement and is outside the scope of AASB 1059 (paragraph 2). The maintenance services represent an outsourced service to the grantor to enable it to provide the public services through the school.

Example 2(b): Operator has management responsibilities

IG8   In this example, the facts in Example 1 apply, except that the operator is also responsible for certain operational services, in determining how many staff are required and organising classes, teachers and administrative staff, and for maintenance of the school facilities by providing upgrades and maintaining the school to a specified condition. The operator has discretion as to when and how it carries out these responsibilities.

IG9   Based on these facts and circumstances, the grantor concludes the operator accesses the school to provide public services and is responsible for at least some of the management of the school services. The operator fulfils this management responsibility through its significant operational and maintenance responsibilities, even though the staff are provided by the grantor (refer paragraph B10). Accordingly, the arrangement is a service concession arrangement within the scope of AASB 1059.

IG10   The diagram below summarises the accounting for service concession arrangements in accordance with AASB 1059.

AASB

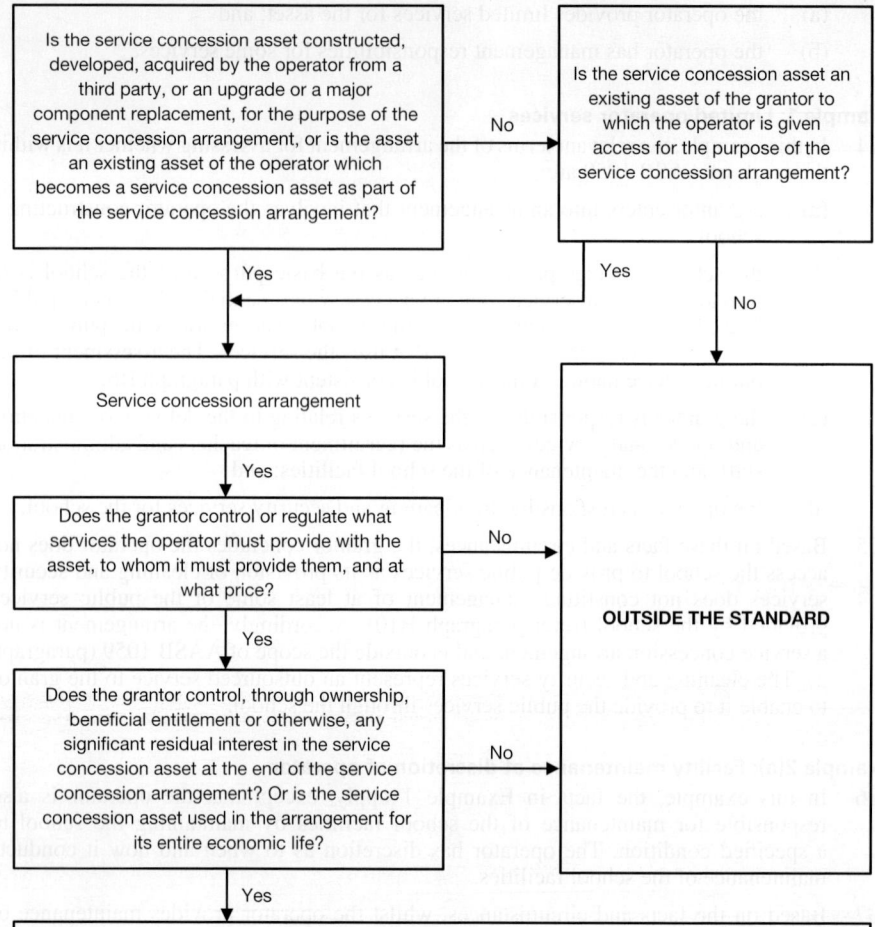

Is the service concession asset constructed, developed, acquired by the operator from a third party, or an upgrade or a major component replacement, for the purpose of the service concession arrangement, or is the asset an existing asset of the operator which becomes a service concession asset as part of the service concession arrangement?

No →

Is the service concession asset an existing asset of the grantor to which the operator is given access for the purpose of the service concession arrangement?

Yes

Yes

No

Service concession arrangement

Yes

Does the grantor control or regulate what services the operator must provide with the asset, to whom it must provide them, and at what price?

No →

Yes

OUTSIDE THE STANDARD

Does the grantor control, through ownership, beneficial entitlement or otherwise, any significant residual interest in the service concession asset at the end of the service concession arrangement? Or is the service concession asset used in the arrangement for its entire economic life?

No →

Yes

ACCOUNTING UNDER THE STANDARD

- Grantor initially recognises a service concession asset, or reclassifies an existing asset as a service concession asset, measured at current replacement cost in accordance with the cost approach to fair value in AASB 13
- After the initial recognition or reclassification, the grantor depreciates/amortises the service concession asset as property, plant and equipment or an identifiable intangible asset in accordance with AASB 116 or AASB 138, as appropriate
- After the initial recognition or reclassification of an identifiable intangible asset, the grantor accounts for the asset in accordance with AASB 138, except for the active market requirement for the revaluation of an intangible service concession asset – current replacement cost continues to be used as the basis for fair value measurement
- Grantor follows impairment testing as set out in AASB 136 for a service concession asset that is accounted for under the cost model or (in some cases) the revaluation model
- Grantor initially recognises a related liability equal to the initial amount of the SCA asset (AASB 9, AASB 132 and AASB 7)
- Grantor recognises revenues and expenses related to the service concession arrangement (AASB 15 or AASB 1058)
- After the end of the term of the arrangement, the grantor accounts for depreciation or amortisation of the asset in accordance with AASB 116 or AASB 138 , and continues to recognise the asset until control is lost.

References to Australian Accounting Standards that apply to typical types of arrangements involving an asset combined with provision of a service

IG11 The table below sets out the typical types of arrangements for private sector participation in the provision of public sector services and provides references to Accounting Standards that may apply to those arrangements. The list of arrangement types is not exhaustive. The purpose of the table is to highlight the continuum of arrangements. It is not the AASB's intention to convey the impression that bright lines exist between the accounting requirements for various types of arrangements.

IG12 The shaded text shows arrangements within the scope of AASB 1059.

Category	Lease	Service provision			Sale	
Typical arrangement types	Lease (e.g. operator leases asset from grantor)	Service outsourcing contract (specific tasks eg debt collection)	Rehabilitate-operate-transfer	Build-operate-transfer	Build-own-operate	100% Divestment/ Privatisation/ Corporation
Asset ownership	Grantor				Operator	
Capital investment	Grantor			Operator		
Demand risk	Shared	Grantor	Grantor and/or Operator		Operator	
Typical duration	8–20 years	1–5 years	25-30 years		Indefinite (or may be limited by contract or licence)	
Significant residual interest	Grantor				Operator	
Relevant Accounting Standards	AASB 16	AASB 101	This Standard/ AASB 116/ AASB 138		AASB 116/ AASB 138 (derecognition)	

IG13 The table below compares the key features of various common types of arrangements for private sector participation in the provision of public services. This table presents simple arrangements, however the classification of an arrangement as a construction contract with a service outsourcing contract, lease, service concession arrangement, or sale or privatisation will depend on the specific terms and conditions of the arrangement.

Features	Construction contract with service outsourcing contract[1]	Lease[2] (grantor is lessor)	Service concession arrangement[3]	Sale/Privatisation[4]
Determining whether arrangement is within the scope of AASB 1059 (paragraphs 2, IG2)	*Conclusion* (based on analysis below) – **Outside** the scope of AASB 1059 and grantor controls the asset.	*Conclusion* (based on analysis below) – **Depending** on terms of arrangement, can be outside or within the scope of AASB 1059.	*Conclusion* (based on analysis below) – **Within** the scope of AASB 1059 and grantor controls the asset.	*Conclusion* (based on analysis below) – **Outside** the scope of AASB 1059 and grantor does not control the asset.

(Continued)

(Continued)

Features	Construction contract with service outsourcing contract[1]	Lease[2] (grantor is lessor)	Service concession arrangement[3]	Sale/Privatisation[4]
Operator provides public services related to the asset on behalf of the grantor and is responsible for at least some of the management of the asset (paragraph B10)?	Operator provides construction services, **not public services**. Operator provides management of asset and related services as **predetermined by the grantor**.	Operator involvement in the management of the asset and related services **varies**, depending on the lease terms (ie operator may have **full involvement or be limited** to facility management pre-determined by the grantor).	Operator involved in management of service concession asset that is **not predetermined by grantor** (ie operator has discretion how the asset is managed).	Operator **does not** provide public services **on behalf of the grantor**, despite any protective rights of the grantor.
Determining whether grantor controls the asset for recognition as service concession asset (paragraph 5(a))	**Grantor** controls or regulates all three aspects.	**Operator** typically controls all three aspects in a lease, but **grantor might** control or regulate some.	**Grantor** controls or regulates all three aspects.	**Grantor might** control or regulate any of these aspects (especially pricing) but not all three aspects.
Grantor controls or regulates services provided by operator with the asset?	**Grantor** controls or regulates services.	**Operator** typically controls services.	**Grantor** controls or regulates services.	**Operator** typically controls services.
Grantor controls or regulates recipients of services?	**Grantor** controls recipients of services.	**Operator** typically controls recipients of services.	**Grantor** controls recipients of services.	**Operator** typically controls recipients of services.
Grantor controls or regulates pricing of services?	**Grantor** controls pricing of services.	**Operator** typically controls pricing of services.	**Grantor** controls pricing of services.	**Operator** might not control pricing of services.
Grantor controls underlying use of the asset?	**Grantor** controls the asset and the right to use the asset.	**Operating lease**: Grantor (lessor) retains control of the asset and operator (lessee) has right-of-use asset. **Finance lease**: Grantor (lessor) relinquishes control of asset to operator (lessee): • lessor derecognises asset and recognises receivable • lessee recognises right-of-use asset.	**Grantor retains** control of asset and the right to use the asset. **Operator** only has a right to access the asset.	**Operator** controls the asset and the right to use the asset.

Features	Construction contract with service outsourcing contract[1]	Lease[2] (grantor is lessor)	Service concession arrangement[3]	Sale/Privatisation[4]
Determining whether grantor controls any significant residual interest in the asset at the end of the arrangement (paragraph 5(b))	**Grantor** controls any significant residual interest at end of arrangement.	**Depending** on terms of arrangement, grantor or operator might control residual interest in the asset.	**Grantor** controls any significant residual interest at end of arrangement.	**Depending** on terms of arrangement, grantor or operator might control residual interest in the asset.
Grantor controls any <u>significant residual interest</u> at end of arrangement?	**Grantor** controls any significant residual interest at end of arrangement.	**Operating lease**: <u>Grantor</u> (lessor) controls significant residual interest. **Finance lease**: <u>No significant residual interest</u> expected.	**Grantor** controls any significant residual interest at end of arrangement.	**Sale**: <u>No significant residual interest</u> expected. **Privatisation**: Grantor may control any significant residual interest.
Grantor's interest <u>restricts operator's practical ability</u> to sell or pledge asset (paragraph B33)?	Operator has no ability to sell or pledge the asset.	**Operating lease**: Grantor's (lessor's) interest **restricts operator's (lessee's) practical ability** to sell or pledge asset. **Finance lease**: Protective rights of the grantor (lessor) typically define the scope of the operator's (lessee's) right of use.	Grantor's interest **restricts operator's practical ability** to sell or pledge asset.	**Sale**: Not applicable. **Privatisation**: Grantor's interest **restricts operator's practical ability** to sell or pledge asset.
Relevant Accounting Standards	AASB 116 AASB 101	AASB 16	AASB 1059	AASB 116 / AASB 138

NOTES:

1 A construction contract with a service outsourcing contract is a contract for the construction of an asset or a combination of assets with provision of services over a specified period.

2 A lease is a contract that conveys the right to use a specified asset for a period of time in exchange for consideration (as defined in AASB 16).

3 A service concession arrangement is a contract between a grantor and an operator in which the operator has the right to access the service concession asset to provide public services on behalf of the grantor, the operator is responsible for at least some of the management of the public services, and the operator is compensated for the services over the period of the service concession arrangement (as defined in AASB 1059).

4 A sale or privatisation is an arrangement that transfers the asset and its related services from public to private ownership/ control.

AASB

Guidance examples

IG14   The guidance examples below illustrate the features of the types of arrangements for private sector participation in the provision of public services that are outlined in the table in paragraph IG13:

(a)   an arrangement that is a construction contract with a service contract;

(b)   an arrangement that contains a lease;

(c)   an arrangement that contains a service concession arrangement that is partly regulated and partly unregulated; and

(d)   an arrangement that is a sale or privatisation.

Example 3: Construction contract with limited operator services

IG15   This example illustrates an arrangement that involves the operator agreeing to construct an asset or group of assets (a school) for the grantor with a contract for the provision of cleaning and security services over a specified period of time. The example is based on the facts and circumstances in Example 1 (paragraphs IG4–IG5). The grantor:

(a)   in accordance with paragraph 2 – determines the arrangement for the construction of the school and the provision of the services is outside the scope of AASB 1059, consistent with paragraphs IG4–IG5; and

(b)   assesses whether it controls the school or has a right to use the school for recognition under another Accounting Standard. In making this assessment, the grantor considers that:

•   the services the operator provides with the school would be based on the service contract agreed by the grantor and the operator; and

•   the control of or right to use the asset would depend on the service contract, including who has title to the land on which the school is built, the terms of the arrangement and the disposition of any residual interest.

Example 4: Lease and service concession arrangement – regulated and unregulated

IG16   Example 4 illustrates an arrangement that involves the operator agreeing to construct an asset or group of assets for the grantor with a contract for the provision of services or maintenance (including facilities maintenance) of the asset(s) over a specified period of time. The arrangement is partly regulated and unregulated by the grantor. The relevant terms of the arrangement are:

(a)   a grantor enters into an arrangement that involves the operator constructing a hospital and then maintaining the hospital buildings. The grantor determines the hospital is capable of being operated with separately identifiable public and private wings;

(b)   the public wing of the hospital is expected to provide health services to the general public for no cost to the patients. The grantor is responsible for the services relating to the delivery of medical services and operational services, including setting key performance requirements, but the operator is responsible for the employment of the doctors, nurses and administration staff and scheduling the various services;

(c)   the private wing of the hospital is expected to provide health services to private patients of the hospital. The operator is responsible for the services relating to the delivery of medical services and operational services, including the employment of doctors, nurses and administration staff. The operator also determines the pricing of the services charged to patients;

(d)   the hospital is considered to provide public services, as the basic purpose of the hospital is to provide health services that are necessary or essential to the general public. The health services provided by the hospital are accessible to the public, even if it is a subset of the community that uses the services and notwithstanding that the private wing of the hospital is to be used by private patients. The assessment of the public service nature of the hospital is consistent with paragraph B6;

(e)   the operator is responsible for the cleaning and security services and facility maintenance of both the public wing and the private wing of the hospital. The operator has discretion as to when and how it conducts the facility maintenance of providing upgrades and maintenance of the hospital to a specified condition;

(f)   the grantor is entitled to the residual interest in both the public wing and the private wing of the hospital at the end of the term of the arrangement, as both wings will transfer to the grantor. During the term of the arrangement, the grantor's residual interest and the requirement for the grantor to specifically approve any transferee restricts the operator from selling or pledging the hospital; and

(g)   both the public and private wings are built on government land, leased to the operator for a nominal fee.

IG17 The grantor assesses separately (consistent with paragraphs B6–B7) whether the public wing and the private wing are within the scope of AASB 1059.

Hospital – Public wing (regulated)

Scope

IG18 Based on the facts and circumstances, the grantor determines:

(a)   the operator accesses the public wing of the hospital to provide public services and is responsible for at least some of the management of the hospital services. The operator fulfils this management responsibility by employing the staff and scheduling services; and

(b)   the public wing of the hospital is a service concession arrangement that is within the scope of AASB 1059, in accordance with paragraph 2.

Grantor's control of asset for recognition under paragraph 5

IG19 Based on the facts and circumstances, the grantor determines it controls the underlying asset (the public wing of the hospital) in the service concession arrangement, as the arrangement entered into by the grantor and the operator specifies:

(a)   the grantor controls or regulates (as required by paragraph 5(a)):

- the services provided by the public wing of the hospital – the grantor is responsible for the delivery and standard of performance of the medical and operational services;

- the recipients of the services – the public wing of the hospital is expected to provide health services to the general public; and

- the pricing of the services – the public wing of the hospital is to provide health services at no cost to the patients; and

(b)   the grantor controls the significant residual interest in the asset (the public wing of the hospital) at the end of the arrangement in accordance with paragraph 5(b), as the grantor is entitled to this residual interest. Additionally, during the term of the arrangement, the operator is restricted from selling or pledging the public wing of the hospital (refer paragraphs B32–B33).

Recognition of arrangement

IG20 Given the public wing of the hospital is within the scope of AASB 1059 (paragraph 2) and the grantor controls the asset in accordance with paragraphs 5(a) and (b), the grantor recognises the public wing of the hospital provided by the operator as a service concession asset.

Hospital – Private wing (unregulated)
Scope

IG21 Based on the facts and circumstances, the grantor determines:

(a) the operator uses the private wing of the hospital to provide services to private patients of the hospital. The operator is also responsible for the management of the private wing by providing the medical and operational services and staff; and

(b) the private wing of the hospital is not a service concession arrangement, in accordance with paragraph 2, because the services in the private wing are not being provided to the public on behalf of a public sector entity.

Recognition of arrangement

IG22 Notwithstanding the grantor cannot recognise the private wing of the hospital as a service concession asset, the grantor assesses whether it controls the asset (the private wing of the hospital) under another Accounting Standard, such as AASB 16. In this example, as the grantor controls the land on which the private wing is located, which provides legal control of the private wing, and the operator is prevented from selling or pledging its interest in the private wing, the grantor controls the private wing. However, the arrangement provides the operator with the right to use the private wing, because the private wing is a separately identifiable asset and the operator controls the services provided, which patients will be admitted, and the prices to be charged during the specified arrangement term. Accordingly:

(a) where the grantor retains substantially all the risks and rewards incidental to ownership, the grantor is the lessor in an operating lease; or

(b) where the operator has substantially all the risks and rewards incidental to ownership, the grantor derecognises the asset and recognises a receivable in accordance with the accounting for a finance lease.

IG23 In this example, the wings of the hospital are capable of being separated into a public wing (regulated portion) and a private wing (unregulated portion). However, some service concession arrangements may involve a hospital that is partly regulated and partly unregulated based on the number of patients that are admitted as a public patient or a private patient, instead of being physically separate as per paragraph IG16(a). In such circumstances, judgement will be required as to the relative significance of the regulated versus unregulated activities in order to determine whether the grantor has control of the asset and/or has granted a right of use to the operator. For example, if the hospital admissions are expected to comprise substantially public patients, then the admission of private patients would be considered as ancillary (unregulated) activities of the hospital and the hospital considered to be used wholly for regulated purposes in addressing the accounting for the service concession asset. In addition, a lease from the grantor to the operator requires a specifically identifiable asset with a right of use granted for a specified time, so in these circumstances it is unlikely a lease could be identified.

Example 5(a): Sale

IG24 This example illustrates an arrangement that involves a public sector entity (a State Government – the grantor) selling an asset (electricity distribution business) to a private sector entity (the operator). The relevant terms of the arrangement are:

(a) in exchange for the sale of the electricity distribution business, the grantor receives cash relating to the sale of its interest in the net assets of the business, and settlement by the operator of the liabilities of the business;

(b) the operator is able to operate the electricity distribution business subject to regulation by a third-party regulator of electricity distributors. Additionally, although the operator has discretion to set the prices of the electricity services, the operator must seek the third-party regulator's approval for changes in pricing; and

(c)   the operator controls:

-    the operating activities of the electricity distribution business, including decisions to expand or modify the distribution network or to continue providing electricity services, subject to protective rights of the grantor to ensure electricity supply in certain circumstances. If the operator decides to discontinue providing electricity services, the grantor has an option to buy back the business from the operator at fair value; and

-    the recipients of the services – the operator can expand the distribution network beyond the network existing at the time of entering the contract without requiring the grantor's approval.

Scope

IG25   Based on the facts and circumstances, the grantor concludes the arrangement for the electricity distribution business is outside the scope of AASB 1059 (paragraph 2) – although electricity distribution would be regarded as public services, the operator does not provide the services on behalf of the grantor and the arrangement is not for a specific period of time. The grantor's protective rights do not mean that the operator provides the services on behalf of the grantor. The protective rights would have the same impact as for an operator that had developed its own electricity network rather than purchasing it from a grantor – the rights do not give the grantor control of the distribution network.

Grantor's control of asset for recognition

IG26   The grantor would also be unable to recognise a service concession asset in these circumstances, because the grantor is able to control or regulate only some of the aspects addressed in paragraph 5(a), as follows:

(a)   the grantor controls the pricing of the services provided by the operator, as the requirement for the operator to seek approval from the third-party regulator removes the operator's ability to regulate the pricing and, for the purpose of paragraph 5(a), the pricing of the services is therefore considered to be set implicitly by the grantor (refer paragraph B20);

(b)   the operator controls the services to be provided by the business. The grantor's protective rights and option to buy back the business from the operator, in the event the operator decides to discontinue the provision of electricity services, do not prevent the operator determining the services to be provided; and

(c)   the operator controls the recipients of the services as outlined in paragraph IG24(c).

IG27   There is no residual interest in the arrangement, as the sale is not limited to a specified period, and so the grantor would also not satisfy the requirements of paragraph 5(b). Furthermore, the grantor's buy-back option is exercisable only at fair value and so does not give the grantor any significant residual interest. As the asset need not be used for the provision of public services for its entire remaining economic life (the operator has discretion as to how to use the asset) and the criteria in paragraph 5(a) are not met, the conditions in paragraph 6 for a whole-of-life asset are not met.

IG28   Although the grantor cannot recognise a service concession asset, the grantor assesses whether it controls the electricity distribution network, has the right to use the network, or controls any other rights requiring recognition under another Accounting Standard. In making this assessment, the grantor takes into account the factors noted in the previous paragraphs.

Recognition of arrangement

IG29　Based on the assessment in paragraphs IG26–IG27, the grantor determines that it does not control the asset or have a right to use the asset subsequent to the sale of the electricity distribution business. The grantor therefore derecognises the asset under another Accounting Standard, such as AASB 116.

Example 5(b): Privatisation

IG30　In this example, the facts in Example 5(a) apply, except that:

(a)　the State Government (the grantor) enters into an arrangement with a private sector entity (the operator) to operate the electricity distribution business for 100 years, instead of the operator purchasing the business from the grantor; and

(b)　at the end of the arrangement (ie in 100 years' time), the distribution network reverts to the grantor. The operator must maintain the electricity distribution network to the specified age and condition at the end of the arrangement.

IG31　Based on the facts and circumstances, the grantor determines:

(a)　the arrangement for the operator to operate the electricity distribution network is outside the scope of AASB 1059, as the grantor's protective rights to ensure electricity supply in certain circumstances do not mean that the operator provides the services on behalf of the grantor;

(b)　even if the arrangement was a service concession arrangement, it does not control the asset for recognition under paragraph 5(a), for the reasons outlined in paragraphs IG26(a)–(c); and

(c)　it controls the significant residual interest at the end of the arrangement, as the electricity distribution network reverts to the grantor at the end of the arrangement. Accordingly, the arrangement is a privatisation and not a sale.

IG32　Based on the assessment in the previous paragraph, the grantor determines that it does not control the asset (the electricity distribution network) or have a right to use the asset under the arrangement. The grantor's protective rights do not give the grantor any more significant interest in the distribution network than it would have with those same rights in relation to an operator that had developed its own network. The grantor therefore derecognises the asset under another Accounting Standard, such as AASB 116, and determines whether it controls any other rights requiring recognition under another Accounting Standard.

ILLUSTRATIVE EXAMPLES

These illustrative examples accompany, but are not part of, AASB 1059.

IE1　These examples consider only three of many possible types of service concession arrangements. Their purpose is to illustrate the accounting treatment for some features that are commonly found in practice. To make the illustrations as clear as possible:

(a)　It is assumed in Examples 6–7 that the term of the service concession arrangement is only ten years and that the operator's annual receipts are constant over that period. In practice, terms may be much longer and annual revenues may increase over time;

(b)　Examples 6 and 7 do not illustrate the accounting by the grantor for existing assets of the grantor used in the service concession arrangement, such as land under roads; and

(c)　Example 8 presents only relevant terms of the arrangement that illustrate the requirements for dividing the liability under a hybrid service concession arrangement into the financial liability and the grant of the right to the operator liability.

IE2　In these examples, monetary amounts are denominated in 'currency units' (CU) – rounded to the nearest unit.

Arrangement terms and assumptions (common to Examples 6–7)

IE3　These terms are common to the two examples that follow.

IE4　The terms of the arrangement require an operator to construct a road on land owned by the grantor – completing construction within two years – and maintain and operate the road to a specified standard for eight years (ie years 3–10). The arrangement is within the scope of this Standard and the road meets the conditions for recognition of a service concession asset in paragraph 5.

IE5　The terms of the arrangement also require the operator to resurface the road when the original surface has deteriorated below a specified condition. The operator estimates that it will have to undertake the resurfacing at the end of year 8 at a fair value (current replacement cost) of CU110. The compensation to the operator for this service is included in the predetermined series of payments and/or the revenue the operator has the right to earn from the service concession asset or another revenue-generating asset granted to the operator by the grantor. The compensation to the operator also covers the annual operating costs of CU12.

IE6　It is assumed that the original road surface is a separate component of the service concession asset and meets the criteria for recognition specified in AASB 116 when the service concession asset is initially recognised. The road surface is therefore recognised as a separate component of the initial fair value (current replacement cost) of the service concession asset and depreciated over years 3–8. This depreciation period is shorter than that for the road base, and takes into account that resurfacing would ordinarily occur every six years, compared with replacing the road base in 25 years. During the construction phase, it is assumed that only the road base is constructed in year 1, and that the road only becomes ready to use at the end of year 2.

IE7　The replacement of a major component of the road as a separate component of the service concession asset occurs in year 8, and is recognised as a new service concession asset when the resurfacing work is performed. This also results in an increase in the liability recognised by the grantor, in accordance with paragraph B48. Where the liability relates to the grant of a right to the operator model, additional revenue in respect of this increase is recognised evenly over the remaining term of the arrangement. However, if the expenditure represented an improvement in service potential such as a new traffic lane rather than restoration to original service capability then it would be appropriate to instead recognise revenue relevant to that improvement only once it has occurred.

IE8　At the beginning of year 3, the total fair value (current replacement cost) of the road is CU1,082, comprised of CU972 related to the base layers (including implied funding costs due to the extended construction period) and CU110 related to the surface layers. The fair value of the surface layers is used to estimate the fair value of the resurfacing (which is treated as a replacement component in accordance with AASB 116). The estimated life of surface layers (ie six years) is also used to estimate the depreciation of the replacement component in years 9 and 10.

IE9　The road base has an economic life of 25 years. Annual depreciation is recognised by the grantor on a straight-line basis. It is therefore CU39 (CU972/25) for the base layers. The surface layers are depreciated over 6 years (years 3–8 for the original component, and starting in year 9 for the replacement component). Annual depreciation related to the original surface layers and the replacement surface layers is CU18 (CU110/6).

IE10　The effective interest rate in the service concession arrangement is 6.18 per cent per year.

IE11　It is assumed that all cash flows take place at the end of the year.

IE12　It is assumed that the time value of money is not significant.

IE13　At the end of year 10, the arrangement will end and the operator will transfer the operation of the road to the grantor.

IE14   The total compensation to the operator under each of the two examples is inclusive of each of the components of the service concession arrangement and reflects the fair values (current replacement cost) for each of the assets and services, which are set out in Table 6.

IE15   The grantor's accounting policies include:

(a)   service concession assets (property, plant, and equipment) – measured initially at fair value (current replacement cost) and subsequently in accordance with the cost model. Impairment is recognised when the carrying amount exceeds the current replacement cost;

(b)   financial liabilities – subsequently measured at amortised cost using the effective interest method; and

(c)   borrowing costs – expensed in the period incurred regardless of how the borrowings are applied.

Table 6   Fair values of the components of the arrangement (currency units)

Contract component	Fair value
Road – base layers	972
Road – original surface layers	110
Total fair value of road	1,082
Annual service component	12
Effective interest rate	6.18%

Example 6: The grantor makes a predetermined series of payments to the operator (paragraphs 15–20)

Additional arrangement terms

IE16   The terms of the arrangement require the grantor to pay the operator CU200 per year in years 3–10 for making the road available to the public. The total consideration (payment of CU200 in each of years 3–10) reflects the fair values (current replacement cost) for each of the assets and services indicated in Table 6. These payments are intended to cover the cost of constructing the road, annual operating costs of CU12 and reimbursement to the operator for the cost of resurfacing the road in year 8 of CU110.

Financial statement impact

IE17   The grantor initially recognises the service concession asset as property, plant, and equipment at its fair value, measured at current replacement cost (total CU1,082, determined as CU940 related to construction of the base layers, CU110 related to construction of the original surface layers and CU32 for funding costs related to the costs incurred in year 1 for base layers). The asset is recognised as it is constructed (CU525 in year 1 and CU557 in year 2). Depreciation is recognised annually (CU57, comprised of CU39 (CU972/25) for the base layers and CU18 (CU110/6) for the surface layers), starting from year 3.

IE18   The grantor initially recognises a financial liability equal to the fair value (current replacement cost) of the service concession asset under construction at the end of year 1 (CU525). The liability is increased at the end of year 2 to reflect both the fair value of the additional construction (CU525) and the finance charge (CU32) on the outstanding financial liability. Because the amount of the predetermined payment related to the service component of the service concession arrangement is known, the grantor is able to determine the amount of the annual payment that reduces the liability each period.

A finance charge at the effective interest rate of 6.18 per cent is recognised annually. The liability is subsequently measured at amortised cost, that is, the amount initially recognised plus the finance charge on that amount calculated using the effective interest method, minus repayments. The initial liability excludes the annual operating costs of CU12 and the compensation for the road resurfacing, as these components of the arrangement represent equally proportionately unperformed contracts.

IE19   The compensation for the road resurfacing is included in the predetermined series of payments. There is no additional direct cash flow impact related to the road resurfacing beyond the predetermined payments; however, the grantor recognises the resurfacing as an asset when the work is undertaken and recognises depreciation expense of CU110/6 = CU18, beginning in year 9. When the resurfacing occurs, the grantor also recognises the related liability.

IE20   The compensation for maintenance and operating the road (CU12) is also included in the predetermined series of payments. There is no additional cash flow impact related to this service expense beyond those payments; however, the grantor recognises an expense annually.

Overview of cash flows, statement of profit and loss and other comprehensive income, and statement of financial position

IE21   The grantor's cash flows, statement of profit and loss and other comprehensive income, and statement of financial position over the duration of the arrangement will be as illustrated in Tables 6.1 to 6.3. In addition, Table 6.4 shows the changes in the financial liability.

Table 6.1 Cash flows (currency units)

Year	1	2	3	4	5	6	7	8	9	10	Total
Predetermined series of payments	–	–	(200)	(200)	(200)	(200)	(200)	(200)	(200)	(200)	(1,600)
Net inflow/(outflow)	–	–	(200)	(200)	(200)	(200)	(200)	(200)	(200)	(200)	(1,600)

Table 6.2 Statement of profit and loss and other comprehensive income (currency units)

Year	1	2	3	4	5	6	7	8	9	10	Total
Service expense	–	–	(12)	(12)	(12)	(12)	(12)	(12)	(12)	(12)	(96)
Finance charge*	–	(32)	(67)	(59)	(51)	(43)	(34)	(25)	(22)	(11)	(344)
Depreciation – base layers	–	–	(39)	(39)	(39)	(39)	(39)	(39)	(39)	(39)	(312)
Depreciation – original surface layers	–	–	(18)	(19)	(18)	(18)	(19)	(18)	–	–	(110)
Depreciation – replacement surface layers	–	–	–	–	–	–	–	–	(18)	(19)	(37)
Total depreciation	–	–	(57)	(58)	(57)	(57)	(58)	(57)	(57)	(58)	(459)
Annual surplus/(deficit)	–	(32)	(136)	(129)	(120)	(112)	(104)	(94)	(91)	(81)	(899)
Revaluation surplus †	–	32	–	–	–	–	–	–	–	–	32

(Continued)

(Continued)

NOTES:

1. Depreciation in years 3–8 reflects the depreciation on the original road. The road surface is fully depreciated over that period. Depreciation in years 9–10 reflects the depreciation on the new service concession asset component (the replacement surface) recognised in year 8. The depreciation calculations are set out in paragraph IE9.
2. Although these Illustrative Examples use a straight-line depreciation method, it is not intended that this method be used in all cases. Paragraph 60 of AASB 116 requires that, "The depreciation method used shall reflect the pattern in which the asset's future economic benefits are expected to be consumed by the entity." Likewise, for intangible assets, paragraph 97 of AASB 138 requires that, "The depreciable amount of an intangible asset with a finite useful life shall be allocated on a systematic basis over its useful life."

* Financial liability at start of year (Table 6.4) x 6.18%.

† Adjustment of current replacement cost to include funding cost in measuring the service concession asset in year 2, since the grantor's accounting policy is to expense borrowing costs.

Table 6.3   Statement of financial position (currency units)

Year	1	2	3	4	5	6	7	8	9	10
Service concession asset – base layers *	525	972	933	894	855	816	777	738	699	660
Service concession asset – original surface layers *	–	110	92	73	55	37	18	–	–	–
Service concession asset – replacement surface layers	–	–	–	–	–	–	–	110	92	73
Total service concession asset	525	1,082	1,025	967	910	853	795	848	791	733
Cash (Table 6.1)	–	–	(200)	(400)	(600)	(800)	(1,000)	(1,200)	(1,400)	(1,600)
Financial liability (Table 6.4)	(525)	(1,082)	(961)	(832)	(695)	(550)	(396)	(343)	(177)	–
Cumulative surplus/(deficit)	–	(32)	(168)	(297)	(417)	(529)	(633)	(727)	(818)	(899)
Revaluation surplus (Table 6.2)	–	32	32	32	32	32	32	32	32	32

NOTES:

1. In this example, the resurfacing occurs as expected in year 8, when the original road surface is fully depreciated. If the resurfacing occurred earlier, the original road surface would not be fully depreciated, and would need to be derecognised in accordance with AASB 116 before the new component of the service concession asset related to the resurfacing is recognised.
2. The new component of the service concession asset related to the resurfacing is recognised in year 8. Years 9–10 reflect depreciation on this additional component (Table 6.2).
3. The financial liability is increased in year 8 for the recognition of the new component of the service concession asset.

* From year 3, opening balance less depreciation for the year (Table 6.2).

Table 6.4   Changes in the financial liability (currency units)

Year	1	2	3	4	5	6	7	8	9	10
Balance brought forward	–	525	1,082	961	832	695	550	396	343	177
Liability recognised along with initial service concession asset*	525	525	–	–	–	–	–	–	–	–
Finance charge added to liability prior to payments being made*	–	32	–	–	–	–	–	–	–	–
Portion of predetermined series of payments that reduces the liability†	–	–	(121)	(129)	(137)	(145)	(154)	(163)	(166)	(177)
Liability recognised along with replacement surface layers	–	–	–	–	–	–	–	110	–	–
Balance carried forward	525	1,082	961	832	695	550	396	343	177	–

NOTES:

* See paragraph IE18.
† Annual payment (Table 6.1) less service payment and finance charge payment (Table 6.2).

Example 7: The grantor grants the operator the right to charge users a toll for use of the road (paragraphs 21–23)

Additional arrangement terms

IE22   The terms of the arrangement allow the operator to collect tolls from drivers using the road. The operator forecasts that vehicle numbers will remain constant over the duration of the arrangement and that it will receive tolls of CU200 in each of years 3–10. The total consideration (tolls of CU200 in each of years 3–10) reflects the fair values (current replacement cost) for each of the assets and services indicated in Table 6, and is intended to cover the cost of constructing the road, annual operating costs of CU12 and reimbursement to the operator for the cost of resurfacing the road in year 8 of CU110.

Financial statement impact

IE23   The grantor initially recognises the service concession asset as property, plant, and equipment at its fair value (current replacement cost) (total CU1,082, determined as CU940 related to construction of the base layers, CU110 related to construction of the original surface layers and CU32 for implied funding costs related to the costs incurred in year 1 for base layers). The asset is recognised as it is constructed (CU525 in year 1 and CU557 in year 2). Depreciation is recognised annually (CU57, comprised of CU39 (CU972/25) for the base layers and CU18 (CU110/6) for the surface layers), starting from year 3.

IE24   As consideration for the service concession asset, the grantor recognises a liability under the grant of a right to the operator model for granting the operator the right to collect tolls of CU200 in years 3–10. The liability is recognised as the asset is recognised. The liability is measured initially at the same amount as the asset, which includes an implied funding cost in the measurement of the current replacement cost.

IE25   The liability is reduced over years 3–10, and the grantor recognises revenue on that basis because access to the service concession asset is expected to be provided evenly over the term of the service concession arrangement from the point at which the asset is capable of providing economic benefits.

IE26   The compensation for the road resurfacing is included in the tolls the operator expects to earn over the term of the service concession arrangement. There is no additional cash flow impact related to the road resurfacing; however, the grantor recognises the resurfacing (the replacement of a major component of the road) as a service concession asset when the work is undertaken and recognises depreciation expense of CU110/6 = CU18, beginning in year 9. When the resurfacing occurs, the grantor also recognises the related liability.

IE27   The compensation for maintenance and operating the road (CU12) is also included in the tolls the operator expects to earn over the term of the service concession arrangement. There is no financial statement impact related to this service expense. It does not affect cash flow because the grantor has no cash inflow or outflow. It is not recognised as an operating expense because the fair value (current replacement cost) of the asset and liability initially recognised do not include any service costs the operator may incur.

Overview of cash flows, statement of profit or loss and other comprehensive income, and statement of financial position

IE28   The grantor's cash flows, statement of profit and loss and other comprehensive income, and statement of financial position over the duration of the arrangement will be as illustrated in Tables 7.1 to 7.2. In addition, Table 7.3 shows the changes in the liability.

IE29   Because no payments are made by the grantor to the operator, there are no cash flow impacts for this example.

Table 7.1   Statement of profit and loss and other comprehensive income (currency units)

Year	1	2	3	4	5	6	7	8	9	10	Total
Revenue (reduction of liability) (Table 7.3)	–	–	135	135	135	136	135	135	190	191	1,192
Depreciation – base layers	–	–	(39)	(39)	(39)	(39)	(39)	(39)	(39)	(39)	(312)
Depreciation – original surface layers	–	–	(18)	(19)	(18)	(18)	(19)	(18)	–	–	(110)
Depreciation – replacement surface layers	–	–	–	–	–	–	–	–	(18)	(19)	(37)
Total depreciation	–	–	(57)	(58)	(57)	(57)	(58)	(57)	(57)	(58)	(459)
Annual surplus/(deficit)	–	–	78	77	78	79	77	78	133	133	733

NOTES:

1. Depreciation in years 3–8 reflects the depreciation on the original road. The road surface is fully depreciated over that period. The depreciation calculations are set out in paragraph IE23.

(Continued)

(Continued)

2. Depreciation in years 9–10 reflects the depreciation on the new service concession asset component (surface) recognised in year 8, as set out in paragraph IE26.
3. The revenue (reduction of the liability) includes revenue from the additional liability (Table 7.3).
4. All revenue is recognised evenly over the remaining term of the arrangement, once the liability has been recognised and the service concession asset is operating.

Table 7.2   Statement of financial position (currency units)

Year	1	2	3	4	5	6	7	8	9	10
Service concession asset – base layers *	525	972	933	894	855	816	777	738	699	660
Service concession asset – original surface layers *	–	110	92	73	55	37	18	–	–	–
Service concession asset – replacement surface layers	–	–	–	–	–	–	–	110	92	73
Total service concession asset	525	1,082	1,025	967	910	853	795	848	791	733
Cash	–	–	–	–	–	–	–	–	–	–
Liability (Table 7.3)	(525)	(1,082)	(947)	(812)	(677)	(541)	(406)	(381)	(191)	–
Cumulative surplus/(deficit)	–	–	78	155	233	312	389	467	600	733

NOTES:

1. In this example, the resurfacing occurs as expected in year 8, when the original road surface is fully depreciated. If the resurfacing occurred earlier, the original road surface would not be fully depreciated, and would need to be derecognised in accordance with AASB 116 before the new component of the service concession asset related to the resurfacing is recognised.
2. The new component of the service concession asset related to the resurfacing is recognised in year 8. Years 9–10 reflect depreciation on this additional component (Table 7.1).
3. The liability is increased in year 8 for the recognition of the new component of the service concession asset.
* From year 3, opening balance less depreciation for the year (Table 7.1).

Table 7.3   Changes in the liability (currency units)

Year	1	2	3	4	5	6	7	8	9	10
Balance brought forward	–	525	1,082	947	812	677	541	406	381	191
Liability recognised along with initial service concession asset *	525	525	–	–	–	–	–	–	–	–
Implied funding cost included in current replacement cost of asset *	–	32	–	–	–	–	–	–	–	–

Year	1	2	3	4	5	6	7	8	9	10
Revenue (reduction of liability) †	–	–	(135)	(135)	(135)	(136)	(135)	(135)	(190)	(191)
Liability recognised along with replacement surface layers	–	–	–	–	–	–	–	110	–	–
Balance carried forward	525	1,082	947	812	677	541	406	381	191	–

NOTES:

* See paragraph IE24.
† Revenue related to the initial liability of CU135 (CU1,082/8) in years 3–10, plus revenue related to the resurfacing liability of CU55 (CU110/2) in years 9–10.

Example 8: Allocation of liabilities in a hybrid arrangement

IE30   Example 8 illustrates the requirements in paragraphs 24–25 and B73–B74 for dividing a hybrid service concession arrangement by measuring the financial liability part first and then allocating the remainder of the total liability to the part related to the grant of the right to the operator.

Arrangement terms

IE31   The relevant terms of the arrangement in the example are:

    (a)   the operator is required to construct a road on land owned by the grantor – completing construction within two years – and maintain and operate the road to a specified standard for eighteen years (ie years 3–20);

    (b)   the grantor is required to pay the operator CU100 each year for eight years (ie years 3–10) for making the road available to the public. These payments are intended to partially cover the cost of constructing the road. It is assumed all cash flows take place at the end of the year. The contractually specified interest rate in the arrangement is 4% per annum. The present value of the payments is CU673. However, unlike a typical loan, the grantor incurs the liability two years before cash payments commence from year 3. Consequently, the effective interest rate for the financial liability is 3.2% per annum, reflecting this timing difference. The grantor's accounting policy for the financial liability is to subsequently measure the financial liability at amortised cost using the effective interest method;

    (c)   the operator is permitted to collect tolls from drivers using the road for eighteen years (ie years 3–20);

    (d)   the initial fair value (current replacement cost) of the construction cost of the service concession asset is CU1,800, once construction is complete at the end of the second year; and

    (e)   at the end of year 20, the arrangement will end, and the operator will transfer the operation of the road to the grantor.

IE32   The arrangement is within the scope of this Standard and the road meets the conditions for recognition as a service concession asset in paragraph 5 (or paragraph 6 for a whole-of-life asset).

Financial statement impact

IE33 It is necessary to divide the grantor's consideration to the operator into two parts – the financial liability for the predetermined payments and the liability related to the grant of the right to the operator to charge tolls.

IE34 The grantor recognises:

(a) the service concession asset as property, plant and equipment at current replacement cost in accordance with the cost approach to fair value (current replacement cost) in AASB 13 totalling CU1,822 at the end of year 2, related to construction of the road (CU900 in both year 1 and year 2) and funding costs related to the financial liability recognised in year 1 (CU22 in year 2);

(b) the total liability equal to the same amount as the current replacement cost of the service concession asset (total CU1,822). The total liability is allocated:

(i) in year 1 – first to the financial liability measured at present value under AASB 9. In this example, the present value of the grantor's payments to the operator is CU673. Second, the remainder of the CU900 is allocated to the liability under the grant of the right to the operator model for the right to collect tolls (CU227);

(ii) in year 2 – to the liability under the grant of the right to the operator model for the right to collect tolls (CU900) as the remainder of the liability related to the construction costs; and

(iii) in year 2 – the borrowing costs of CU22 are allocated to the financial liability;

(c) a finance charge expense (CU22) in year 2 relating to the financial liability in year 1, in accordance with the grantor's accounting policy; and

(d) a revaluation surplus of CU22 to reflect the inclusion of funding costs relating to the construction period in the current replacement cost of the service concession asset.

IE35 The journal entries for the accounting treatment set out in paragraph IE34 are:

	Debit	Credit
End of year 1	CU	CU
Service concession asset – PPE	900	
Financial liability		673
Liability		227
End of year 2		
Service concession asset – PPE	922	
Liability		900
Revaluation surplus		22
Finance charge	22	
Financial liability		22

Example 9: Initial recognition of intangible assets in a business

IE36 Example 9 illustrates the requirements in paragraphs B14 and B39(a) for the initial recognition of the assets of a business that is subject to a service concession arrangement, including identifiable intangible assets.

Arrangement terms

IE37   The relevant terms of the arrangement in the example are:

    (a)   a grantor enters into an arrangement that involves an operator providing public services related to a business, on behalf of the grantor. The business is a business as defined in AASB 3 *Business Combinations*, with customer lists and property, plant and equipment. The customer lists are intangible assets as they would meet the separability criterion in AASB 3. They were developed and are owned by the grantor;

    (b)   the initial fair value (current replacement cost) of the business and the identifiable assets of the business are set out in Table 9;

    (c)   the operator has the right to collect revenue in relation to updating the customer lists; and

    (d)   at the commencement of the arrangement, the operator provides the grantor with cash consideration of CU300.

Table 9   Fair values of the components of the arrangement (currency units)

Contract component	Carrying amount	Fair value
Business	n/a	300
Property, plant and equipment	60	100
Customer lists	–	150

IE38   The arrangement is within the scope of this Standard and, as existing assets of the grantor, the property, plant and equipment and customer lists meet the conditions for a service concession asset in paragraph 5 (or paragraph 6 for a whole-of-life asset).

Financial statement impact

IE39   The grantor has not previously recognised the customer lists as an intangible asset as they are precluded from recognition as an intangible asset under AASB 138. As a result of entering into the service concession arrangement, the grantor recognises the assets of the business, excluding any internally generated goodwill, as service concession assets. Therefore the grantor initially:

    (a)   reclassifies the property, plant and equipment as a service concession asset and recognises the asset at fair value (current replacement cost) (CU100), representing a revaluation surplus of CU40 over the carrying amount of CU60;

    (b)   reclassifies the customer lists as an intangible service concession asset and recognises the asset at fair value (current replacement cost) (CU150) and a corresponding amount as revaluation surplus; and

    (c)   recognises a liability under the grant of a right to the operator model for the additional consideration (CU300) provided by the operator.

IE40   The journal entries for the accounting treatment set out in paragraph IE39 are:

	Debit	Credit
Year 1	CU	CU
Service concession asset – PPE	60	
Property, plant and equipment		60
Service concession asset – PPE	40	

	Debit	Credit
Year 1	CU	CU
Service concession asset – Customer lists	150	
Revaluation surplus		190
Cash	300	
Liability		300

Example 10: Transition – measuring the liability under the grant of a right to the operator model at the date of initial application

IE41   In accordance with the transition requirements set out in Appendix C of the Standard, a grantor may elect to apply the Standard retrospectively by recognising and measuring service concession assets and related liabilities at the date of initial application (paragraph C3(b)). The date of initial application is the beginning of the earliest reporting period for which comparative information is presented in the financial statements.

IE42   This example illustrates the approach set out in paragraph C4(c) to measuring a liability under the grant of a right to the operator model at the date of initial application. The liability related to the grant of a right to the operator is required to be measured at the fair value (current replacement cost) of the related service concession asset at the date of initial application, adjusted to reflect the remaining period of the service concession arrangement relative to the remaining economic life of the asset, less any related financial liabilities.

IE43   Assuming that the service concession arrangement in this example does not also give rise to a financial liability for the grantor, the information needed for measuring the liability is illustrated in the following table:

Table 10   Estimates at the date of initial application

Parameter	Amount or period
Fair value (current replacement cost) of the service concession asset	CU1,200
Remaining economic life of the asset	20 years
Remaining service concession period	10 years
Apportionment for the liability re grant of rights to the operator	CU1,200 X 10/20 = CU600

IE44   If the service concession arrangement is a hybrid arrangement, then the financial liability would be measured separately under the financial liability model at the date of initial application. The amount of the financial liability would then be deducted from the apportioned amount for the liability re the grant of rights to the operator as per the table in order to derive the amount to be recognised for the liability.

IE45   The measurement approach illustrated in this example is a simplified transition method, as it does not require the service concession asset or the liability to be measured at the inception of the service concession arrangement, as would be required under the full retrospective transition method in accordance with AASB 108 *Accounting Policies, Changes in Accounting Estimates and Errors.*

BASIS FOR CONCLUSIONS

This Basis for Conclusions accompanies, but is not part of, AASB 1059.

Introduction

BC1   This Basis for Conclusions summarises the Australian Accounting Standards Board's considerations in reaching the conclusions in AASB 1059. In making decisions, individual Board members gave greater weight to some factors than to others.

Background

Reasons for issuing this Standard

BC2   In Australia, public sector entities enter into service concession arrangements (also called public-private partnerships (PPPs), build-own-operate-transfer (BOOT) arrangements and other similar names) as a means of developing and delivering infrastructure and other assets for public services such as roads, bridges, tunnels, prisons, hospitals, airports, water distribution facilities, energy supply and telecommunication networks, permanent installations for military and other operations, registries and databases, and other tangible or intangible assets that are expected to be used during more than one reporting period in delivering public services. The public sector entity (the grantor) typically engages another entity (the operator) to construct or otherwise provide the underlying infrastructure and other assets through which the operator will provide public services on behalf of the grantor. In exchange for the asset (or assets) and services, the grantor makes payments to the operator or grants the operator a right to charge users of the service concession asset (or assets).

BC3   Prior to the issue of this Standard, there was no specific Australian Accounting Standard that prescribed the accounting for service concession arrangements from the grantor's perspective.

BC4   In determining an accounting policy for service concession arrangements in accordance with AASB 108 *Accounting Policies, Changes in Accounting Estimates and Errors*, in the absence of AASB 1059, an Australian public sector entity might consider existing accounting requirements for service concession arrangements, including:

(a)   AASB Interpretation 12 *Service Concession Arrangements* – AASB Interpretation 12 (which incorporates IFRIC 12 *Service Concession Arrangements*) provides the accounting requirements for service concession arrangements by the operator of a service concession arrangement. AASB Interpretation 12 does not apply to a grantor;

(b)   AASB 16 *Leases* – AASB 16 provides guidance where the grantor makes payments to the operator, but does not provide guidance where the grantor grants the operator a right to charge users of the service concession asset;

(c)   AASB Interpretation 4 *Determining whether an Arrangement contains a Lease* – AASB Interpretation 4 provides guidance for the application of AASB 16; and

(d)   IPSAS 32 *Service Concession Arrangements: Grantor* – the International Public Sector Accounting Standards Board (IPSASB) published IPSAS 32 in October 2011. IPSAS 32 prescribes the accounting for service concession assets, liabilities, revenues and expenses by grantors. IPSAS 32 mirrors IFRIC 12 in most aspects.

Australian public sector entities had also considered previous requirements in the United Kingdom set out in Financial Reporting Standard FRS 5 *Reporting the Substance of Transactions*, issued by the UK Accounting Standard Board. FRS 5 required an entity to recognise an asset and a liability where the entity had substantially all or the majority of risks and rewards incident to the ownership of a service concession asset.

BC5   The lack of a specific Australian Accounting Standard that prescribed the accounting for a service concession arrangement from the grantor's perspective resulted in divergence in the accounting for such arrangements. For example, some grantors recognised service concession assets and liabilities in their statement of financial position while others did not. Given the significance of service concession arrangements to the Australian economy, it is important that the AASB issue an Accounting Standard to address the lack of explicit requirements for accounting for such arrangements. Recognition of service concession assets and related liabilities is important in assisting users of financial statements to understand the resources and obligations of a grantor involved in the provision of public services.

BC6   The Board considered a range of alternatives for the accounting for service concession arrangements by a grantor. This included consideration of:

(a)   whether under the hierarchy for selecting accounting policies set out in AASB 108, the grantor could apply AASB Interpretation 12 by analogy. The Board (in December 2007) noted that, in accordance with AASB 108, the management of an entity must use its judgement in developing and applying an accounting policy that results in information that is both relevant and reliable to the economic decision-making needs of users, including that the financial statements reflect the economic substance of the transaction or event. In making this judgement, management must refer to, and consider the applicability of, the requirements and guidance in Australian Accounting Standards (including Interpretations) dealing with similar and related issues, and the definitions, recognition criteria and measurement concepts in the *Framework for the Preparation and Presentation of Financial Statements*. The Board concluded public sector grantors are required to consider Interpretation 12 in developing their accounting policy for service concession arrangements, and could choose to follow the Interpretation, although it does not apply mandatorily;

(b)   the IPSASB's project on grantor accounting for service concession arrangements, which the Board followed closely by issuing the IPSASB's consultation documents in Australia as Invitation to Comment ITC 16 *Request for Comment on IPSASB Consultation Paper* Accounting and Financial Reporting for Service Concession Arrangements (April 2008) and Exposure Draft ED 194 *Request for Comment on IPSASB Exposure Draft* Service Concession Arrangements: Grantor (April 2010). The Board considered the feedback from constituents in preparing its submissions on the IPSASB proposals; and

(c)   other approaches to the accounting for service concession arrangements, which are identified further in this Basis for Conclusions.

Issue of ED 261 and additional public versions

BC7   After considering the alternatives, the Board decided to develop an Australian Accounting Standard on grantor accounting for service concession arrangements, based on IPSAS 32, to address the lack of guidance. The Board issued Exposure Draft ED 261 *Service Concession Arrangements: Grantor* in May 2015. The Board took into account its policy of making Australian Accounting Standards with a view to requiring like transactions and events to be accounted for in a like manner by all types of entities, referred to as 'transaction neutrality', in restricting the scope of ED 261 to a grantor that is a public sector entity. The Board noted that it is highly unlikely that a service concession arrangement would involve a grantor that is a private sector entity. Consequently, only in rare instances would a private sector grantor require specific guidance on the accounting for a service concession arrangement.

BC8   The Board conducted extensive outreach on the proposals in ED 261, including roundtable discussions in Melbourne, Brisbane and Sydney, field tests in a number of Australian jurisdictions and other targeted outreach.

BC9   The Board received ten comment letters in response to ED 261. The key responses to ED 261 were:

      (a)   all respondents were supportive of the proposals set out in ED 261 on the basis that the proposals would provide a consistent approach to the accounting for service concession arrangements from a public sector grantor perspective;

      (b)   some respondents commented that the proposals were more rule-based than principle-based. These respondents recommended that a principle-based Standard be developed so that the Standard could address emerging innovative service concession arrangements that perhaps a rule-based Standard would not be able to adequately address; and

      (c)   overall, respondents requested additional guidance and examples on the concept of control, fair value measurement of service concession assets and liabilities, and accounting for the arrangements when transitioning to the Standard.

BC10   As the Board considered a broad range of issues in developing this Standard following the ED 261 exposure process, numerous issues papers and draft wording for paragraphs of the Standard were published as Board agenda papers. This gave constituents the opportunity to follow the debate and to provide comments on the issues and drafting contemporaneously.

BC11   In February 2017, the Board also issued a Fatal-Flaw Review version of the Standard for public comment. Submissions were received from seven constituents. The majority of the respondents were supportive of the Board's approach in the Fatal-Flaw Review version. However, some respondents had concerns particularly over the proposed requirement for a grantor to recognise as a service concession asset an intangible asset that the grantor had not been previously recognised and the proposed guidance on public services. Single respondents also objected strongly to (1) the approach to determining the grantor's control or regulation of the pricing of the services of a service concession asset and (2) the proposed requirement to recognise a service concession arrangement that involves the grant of a right to the operator.

BC12   The Board considered these issues and the comments received at its March and May 2017 meetings. In particular, the Board added additional implementation guidance to illustrate the differences between service concession arrangements and other types of arrangements (construction and service contracts, leases, and sale and privatisation arrangements). The Board also clarified the treatment of previously unrecognised intangible service concession assets and the application guidance regarding public services, for example.

BC13   The proposed requirements were then finalised in June 2017 in the form of a Pre-Ballot Draft of the Standard. This version, which typically is distributed only to Board members, was also circulated to the respondents to the Fatal-Flaw Review version that had provided substantive comments. Further comments were received from those respondents and were considered by the Board in finalising the Standard. As a result of those comments, for example, the definition of 'service concession arrangement' was extended to refer to the operator being responsible for at least some of the management of the public services provided through the service concession asset, which had featured in the application guidance and in some of the implementation guidance examples. References to land under roads as service concession assets were also added, and the accounting for upgrades and the replacement of major components of service concession assets clarified.

Scope

BC14   The Board considered various types of arrangements involving public and private sector entities and deliberated whether the Standard should be consistent with IPSAS 32 by applying only to not-for-profit public sector entities.

BC15 The Board decided that ED 261 should propose application to all public sector entities, rather than being limited to not-for-profit public sector entities, consistent with the Board's policy of transaction neutrality, as applied to public sector grantors of service concession arrangements. The Board noted that this scope would be wider than that of IPSAS 32 as International Public Sector Accounting Standards do not apply to for-profit entities.

BC16 The Board considered the constituents' feedback on ED 261 and additional outreach, in particular some constituents' concerns that a for-profit grantor applying this Standard may not be able to state that its financial statements comply with International Financial Reporting Standards (IFRS Standards) issued by the International Accounting Standards Board (IASB) (see paragraphs BC124–BC127 for a comparison with IFRS Standards). The Board also noted the constituents' feedback that although they prefer a for-profit entity to be able to state compliance with IFRS Standards when applying this Standard, transaction neutrality across the entire public sector is more important in this instance. The Board therefore reaffirmed its view that the Standard should apply to all public sector entities, whether for-profit or not-for-profit. The Board concluded that this was an appropriate, limited exception to its general policy that compliance with Australian Accounting Standards by for-profit entities would result in compliance with IFRS Standards. The Board noted this approach would reduce or eliminate any incentive for structuring service concession arrangements through for-profit public sector grantors.

Terminology

BC17 IPSAS 32 is expressed in jurisdiction-neutral language. The Board considered that some of the terminology in IPSAS 32 does not readily translate to the Australian environment and decided that different terms and phrases would be appropriate for entities applying Australian Accounting Standards. For example, consistent with the terminology used in other Australian Accounting Standards, the Standard adopts the term 'contract' rather than the term 'binding arrangement', and the Standard refers to operator 'access' rather than 'use' as in the definitions of a 'grantor' and an 'operator' in IPSAS 32.

BC18 ED 261 proposed defining the term 'public service' as "A service that is provided by government or one of its controlled entities, as part of the usual government function, to the community, either directly (through the public sector) or by financing the provision of services". Constituents in their feedback on ED 261 stated that although they supported the inclusion of a 'public service' definition, the proposed definition was unclear. The Board concluded that any definition of 'public service' would result in similar interpretative issues as those raised by constituents in relation to the definition proposed in ED 261. The Board therefore decided, instead of providing a definition, the Standard should include guidance on 'public service' for assessing whether an arrangement is within the scope of the Standard. The Board also noted this approach is consistent with IPSAS 32 and AASB Interpretation 12, which do not contain a definition of 'public service'. The Board decided that the guidance should be in the form of examples and features to be considered, such as:

(a) an operator must be responsible for at least some of the management of the service concession asset and related services, and not act merely as an agent of the grantor; and

(b) services that are insignificant to the arrangement as a whole may be ancillary services.

BC19 The Board also decided to amend the 'service concession asset' definition (as proposed in ED 261) so that it refers to an asset accessed by the operator to provide public services on behalf of the grantor, for consistency with the public service guidance.

Recognition of service concession assets

Control

BC20 The Board considered a number of alternative approaches in developing the proposed guidance for assessing whether a grantor controls the service concession asset, including:

(a)   the risks and rewards approach;

(b)   the rights and obligations approach;

(c)   the control or regulation approach (the IPSAS 32 concept of control); and

(d)   an approach analogous to the principles of control specified in AASB 10 *Consolidated Financial Statements*.

BC21 The Board decided to adopt the IPSAS 32 concept of control (the control or regulation approach) for the following reasons.

BC22 In considering the merits of the risks and rewards and the control-based approach to assess whether the grantor should recognise the asset, the Board noted that the risks and rewards approach focuses on the economic aspects of the terms and conditions in the arrangement. The Board did not consider this focus to be appropriate for service concession arrangements in the Australian public sector. This is because the primary purpose of a service concession asset, from the grantor's point of view, is to provide specified public services on behalf of the grantor and not to provide economic benefits such as revenue generated by such assets (eg from user fees). A control-based approach focuses on control over the service potential of the service concession asset.

BC23 Service concession arrangements are often entered into to share the risks between the grantor and the operator. The Board questioned whether objective criteria could be established as the basis for consistent assessments of the risks and rewards. In addition, the weighting of various risks and rewards was seen to be problematic. The Board also noted the IASB has progressively been moving away from the risks and rewards approach to focus on the concept of control when determining what assets should be recognised (eg AASB 10 and AASB 16 have a primary focus on control, with risks and rewards a secondary consideration). The Board also considered its transaction neutrality approach and noted the risks and rewards approach would be inconsistent with the principles in AASB Interpretation 12. The Board concluded that the risks and rewards approach was not appropriate for an Australian Accounting Standard addressing grantor accounting for service concession arrangements.

BC24 In considering the rights and obligations approach, the Board noted that although this could have conceptual merit, it would represent a significant change in the accounting for and financial reporting of assets and liabilities for public sector entities that could have implications beyond service concession arrangements. The Board concluded that the rights and obligations approach was not appropriate at this time for an Australian Accounting Standard addressing grantor accounting for service concession arrangements.

BC25 The Board discussed application of the concept of control in AASB 10 by analogous interpretation, and decided that the principles for assessing control of an entity may not necessarily be appropriate for assessing control of an individual asset.

BC26 The Board concluded that the IPSAS 32 approach (the control or regulation approach) was the most appropriate approach as it is consistent with AASB Interpretation 12. Accordingly, this approach would lead to greater consistency in the accounting requirements for the operator and the grantor. The Board noted that this approach would require both the operator and the grantor under a service concession arrangement to apply the same principles in determining which party should recognise the asset in the arrangement. The Board considered that this approach would reduce the possibility of an asset being recognised by both parties, or by neither party to the arrangement.

BC27 The Board noted that the IPSASB confirmed the control approach in IPSAS 32 in the Basis for Conclusions to *The Conceptual Framework for General Purpose Financial Reporting by Public Sector Entities* (October 2014), where the IPSASB concluded that consideration of "the risks and rewards associated with particular transactions and events, and which party to any transaction or event bears the majority of those risks and rewards, may be relevant and useful in identifying the nature of the asset controlled by parties to the transaction or event. It may also be useful in determining how to quantify and associate the economic rights and obligations with particular parties. However, it is not of itself an indicator of the party that controls an asset. The IPSASB therefore decided not to include the risks and rewards of ownership as an indicator of control" (paragraph BC5.14).

BC28 In considering the concept of control for the recognition of service concession assets, the Board decided that the grantor recognises an asset provided by the operator and an upgrade to or major component replacement of an existing asset of the grantor provided by the operator as a service concession asset if the grantor controls the asset. The grantor essentially controls the asset if the grantor satisfies the specific control criteria in paragraphs 5(a) and (b): the grantor "controls or regulates what services the operator must provide with the asset, to whom it must provide them, and at what price" and controls the residual value (if significant), thus controlling the asset for the majority of its economic life. This mirrors the control concept in AASB Interpretation 12. The Board noted that a broader concept of control currently applies in other Accounting Standards and that an asset that does not meet the control definition of this Standard may still need to be recognised under other Accounting Standards. The Board decided to include application guidance to make explicit the requirement to apply the broader concept of control.

Regulation

BC29 In developing the Application Guidance for the control concept, the Board formed the view that there are three main circumstances in which a grantor controls or regulates the price, the services and/or to whom the services must be provided in accordance with paragraph 5(a). The three main circumstances are where the service concession contract:

(a) *specifies that the grantor controls or regulates* the price, the services and/or to whom the services must be provided;

(b) *specifies that a third-party regulator regulates* the price, the services and/or to whom the services must be provided – under this circumstance, the regulation by the third-party regulator removes the ability of the operator to set or regulate the price, the services and/or to whom the services must be provided and the regulation is considered to be set implicitly by the grantor. Additionally, it is not essential for the grantor to direct the activities of the third-party regulator for the grantor to have control over the service concession arrangements (paragraph B20); and

(c) *does not specify that a third-party regulator regulates* the price, the services and/or to whom the services must be provided – under these circumstances, many governments have the power to regulate the behaviour of entities operating in certain sectors of the economy, either directly or through specifically created agencies. For the purpose of paragraph 5(a), such broad regulatory powers do not constitute control without a specific arrangement or contract (paragraph B21). Instead the grantor, operating under such a regulatory framework, derives control of the service concession asset either from the contract or the specific regulation applicable to the industry or service. However, where a service concession arrangement does not clearly fall within an existing regulatory framework (eg where there is more than one possible source of regulation), the arrangement will need to incorporate the specific regulatory framework that stipulates the services, the users and/or the pricing to be charged for the services in order for the grantor to have control of the service concession asset (paragraph B22).

BC30 The Board decided that the circumstances noted in the preceding paragraph should form part of the application guidance to assist entities in assessing whether the service concession asset is controlled by the grantor.

BC31 The Board deliberated whether long-term arrangements, privatisation and outsourcing arrangements should be scoped out of the requirements of the Standard, or whether they should be assessed to determine whether they meet the control criteria of paragraphs 5 or 6 of the Standard. The Board decided that where the arrangements meet the criteria of paragraphs 5 or 6, the arrangements should be accounted for as service concession arrangements. This approach would ensure the substance of an arrangement determines whether the arrangement is subject to this Standard.

Changes in control

BC32 The Board considered whether the Application Guidance should require that where there is a change in facts and circumstances indicating the grantor's control of the asset may have changed, the arrangement should be reassessed to determine whether it is still within the scope of the Standard. The Board concluded that the Standard should include such Application Guidance, similar to existing requirements in AASB 16 and AASB Interpretation 4. The Application Guidance should also require that where the grantor no longer controls the asset, as specified in the Standard, the grantor assesses whether the asset should be recognised under another Accounting Standard.

Residual interest and whole-of-life assets

BC33 The Board considered whether the Application Guidance should provide guidance on what constitutes a 'significant residual interest', including the determination of 'fair value' and its relationship with a 'whole-of-life' asset, in addressing whether the grantor controls a significant residual interest as set out in paragraph 5(b).

BC34 The Board decided that:

(a) what constitutes 'significant' varies from one entity to another and is a matter of judgement for the individual entity and not a decision for the Board. The judgement should be based on substance rather than form: for example, any residual interest is not necessarily a significant residual interest; and

(b) the term 'significant' is used in numerous Standards without specific guidance as to what would constitute 'significant'. The Board did not consider specific guidance on the term would be appropriate in this Standard. If the Board were to provide guidance on the term, the Board may need to refer the matter to the IASB for consideration with reference to maintaining compliance with IFRS Standards. Consideration by the IASB on this issue would most likely have implications beyond service concession arrangements.

BC35 This Standard requires the residual interest in the asset to be measured as the estimated fair value (current replacement cost) of the asset as if it were already of the age and in the condition expected at the end of the service concession arrangement. The Board considered whether guidance should be provided in determining 'fair value' and its relationship to the asset's residual interest, and concluded it was not necessary to provide additional guidance (see paragraph BC69).

BC36 The Board also considered the relationship between 'significant residual interest' and a 'whole-of-life' asset in determining whether the grantor has control of an asset. The Board decided that if the term of the service concession arrangement:

(a) is not the economic life of the asset, then paragraph 5 of the Standard applies; or

(b) is the economic life of the asset, then paragraph 6 of the Standard applies.

The Board noted this is consistent with the general observation that the amount of residual interest at the end of an arrangement is inversely related to the term of the service concession arrangement relative to the economic life of the asset. That is, the residual interest at the end of the arrangement is likely to be significant if the term of the arrangement is not at least the majority portion of the economic life of the asset. Consequently, such an arrangement would be subject to paragraphs 5(a) and (b). Alternatively, where the residual interest is insignificant, the arrangement would be subject either to paragraph 5(a) or, for a whole-of-life asset, paragraph 6.

BC37 Paragraph 6 of this Standard requires the grantor to recognise an asset that will be used in a service concession arrangement for its economic life (a whole-of-life asset) if the conditions in paragraph 5(a) are met. The Board decided to use the term 'economic life' instead of 'useful life' as proposed in ED 261 (paragraph 9). The economic life of an asset is the period over which future economic benefits are expected from all possible users of the asset, and may be the entire physical life of the asset. Consequently, an asset used in a service concession arrangement for its economic life will not have a significant residual interest at the end of the arrangement, and the condition in paragraph 5(b) will not be relevant. This contrasts with the term 'useful life', which is defined in AASB 116 *Property, Plant and Equipment* as the period over which an asset is expected to be available for use by an entity. An asset used in a service concession arrangement for its useful life (to the grantor) could have a significant residual interest at the end of the arrangement if the arrangement is not for all or the major part of its economic life. In this case, the condition in paragraph 5(b) would be relevant, and paragraph 6 is not applicable.

Upgrades or replacement of major components

BC38 The Board extended the definition of 'service concession asset' to refer explicitly to upgrades and to replacements of major components of assets, whether of assets provided by the operator or existing assets of the grantor. The Board clarified that upgrades and major component replacements of service concession assets would be recognised by the grantor when the upgrade or replacement occurs, provided that the control criteria in paragraphs 5 or 6 were satisfied. The Board concluded that such upgrades and major component replacements are treated as service concession assets in their own right, and consequently the grantor also recognises a related liability in accordance with paragraph 11.

Intangible assets

BC39 The Board considered whether the requirement in paragraph 8 that the grantor reclassify and measure an existing asset that is used in a service concession arrangement should apply to an identifiable intangible asset that has not been recognised previously by the grantor. The intangible asset would not have been recognised previously if the asset did not meet the criteria of AASB 138 *Intangible Assets* for recognition as an intangible asset. The Board decided that AASB 1059 should override AASB 138 and require a grantor to recognise and measure an existing but unrecognised identifiable intangible asset when the conditions in paragraph 5 or 6 for recognition as a service concession asset are met. This would apply even to intangible assets that are specifically precluded from recognition under paragraph 63 of AASB 138: internally generated brands, mastheads, publishing titles, customer lists and items similar in substance. The accounting for intangible assets of the grantor that are part of a service concession arrangement is set out in paragraphs B38–B39.

BC40 The Board took the view that a service concession arrangement represents a transaction with an external party that identifies and values all identifiable assets involved in the arrangement. Therefore, with the exception of goodwill (see paragraph BC42), the accounting should be similar to that for business combinations under AASB 3 *Business Combinations*, in which all assets and liabilities acquired are recognised, including those not previously recognised by the acquiree. This approach means that intangible assets encompassed by a service concession arrangement should be recognised by the grantor as intangible service concession assets (when the conditions in paragraph 5 or

6 are met), regardless of whether the assets were already recognised by the grantor as intangible assets.

BC41 The Board considered whether the recognition of previously unrecognised intangible assets as service concession assets should result in revenue for the grantor. The Board decided that the recognition of revenue would not be appropriate since the grantor is not obtaining control of such assets for the first time, but continues to control such assets. Instead, the Board concluded that the recognition is like a remeasurement of the assets, with a corresponding adjustment to revaluation surplus. This aligns with the grantor recognising a liability in respect of service concession assets provided by the operator, since the grantor obtains control of those assets only through the service concession arrangement. Those liabilities are reduced as revenue is recognised in accordance with the substance of the arrangement.

BC42 The Board noted that a service concession arrangement might encompass a business of the grantor, as defined in AASB 3. This raised the issue of whether the grantor should recognise internally generated goodwill as an asset of the business. The Board considered whether to follow the approach in AASB 3 and require goodwill to be recognised by the grantor. Under this approach, the grantor would measure the business at fair value (current replacement cost) and allocate this amount to the identifiable assets (such as property, plant and equipment and identifiable intangible assets) in the business, measured at their fair value (current replacement cost), with the remaining amount allocated to internally generated goodwill after recognising any liabilities of the business.

BC43 The Board acknowledged the conceptual merit in applying the AASB 3 approach to identify the assets for recognition in a service concession arrangement, in that the grantor has provided the operator with the right to access the whole business (including any goodwill) for the purpose of providing public services. However, the Board noted that this approach would give rise to difficulties in subsequently assessing goodwill annually for impairment under AASB 136 *Impairment of Assets*, since the revenue to be recognised by the grantor under the service concession arrangement would be limited to the related liabilities recognised, rather than reflecting cash flows of the service concession assets. The Board concluded that the approach in AASB 3 would be difficult to apply in practice, with the costs likely to outweigh the benefits. Consequently, the Board decided not to apply the approach in AASB 3. Instead, the grantor is required by AASB 1059 to recognise only the tangible assets and intangible assets in the business, measured at fair value (current replacement cost) and liabilities of the business. Goodwill is not permitted to be recognised.

BC44 The Board considered that at the end of a service concession arrangement an intangible service concession asset should continue to be recognised as an intangible asset and accounted for in accordance with AASB 138, excluding the recognition criteria of AASB 138. The Board decided that AASB 1059 would override the recognition criteria of AASB 138, so that an intangible asset would not be derecognised at the end of the service concession arrangement merely because it could not satisfy the recognition requirements of AASB 138. However, the derecognition criteria in AASB 138 would apply, so that the grantor would be required to derecognise the intangible asset if the grantor loses control of the asset.

Land under roads

BC45 The Board noted that a service concession arrangement might involve land under roads. AASB 1051 *Land Under Roads* requires land under roads to be recognised as an asset only by local governments, government departments, General Government Sectors and whole of governments, and only in respect of land under roads acquired after the end of the first reporting period that ended on or after 31 December 2007. AASB 1051 notes that AASB 116 applies to land under roads when recognised. The Board concluded that, to be consistent with the requirement in this Standard for a grantor to recognise previously unrecognised identifiable intangible assets that are controlled by the grantor as service concession assets, grantors would also be required to recognise land under roads as service concession assets when the control criteria in paragraphs 5 or 6 were satisfied. The Board decided that this requirement would apply to all grantors, not just grantors that were subject to AASB 1051.

Measurement of service concession assets

BC46 The Standard addresses subsequent measurement of service concession assets by reference to AASB 116 and AASB 138, on the grounds that service concession arrangements relating to other types of assets are unlikely. That does not prevent application of this Standard to other types of assets included within a service concession arrangement.

BC47 The Board considered the measurement of a service concession asset at fair value in accordance with AASB 13 in relation to the characteristics of the asset and valuation techniques for measuring the fair value of the asset.

Characteristics of the asset

BC48 In considering the characteristics of the asset when measuring fair value, the Board noted AASB 13 requires the grantor to consider the characteristics of the service concession asset that market participants would take into account when pricing the asset at the measurement date. Characteristics include the condition and location of the asset as well as any restrictions on the sale, transfer or use of the asset. The effect of restrictions on the sale, transfer or use of the service concession asset depends on whether the restriction is deemed to be a characteristic of the asset or a characteristic of the grantor that controls the asset. Where a restriction would transfer with the asset in an assumed sale or transfer, the restriction would generally be regarded as a characteristic of the asset and likely to be considered by a market participant in pricing the asset. On the other hand, a restriction that is specific to the grantor and that would not transfer with the asset in an assumed sale would not be considered in measuring the fair value of the asset. Whether a restriction is a characteristic of the service concession asset or specific to the grantor requires judgement based on the specific facts and circumstances of the arrangement.

BC49 A market participant may consider that the right of access provided by the grantor to the operator does not represent a restriction on the grantor's use of the asset. In a service concession arrangement, control of the asset and therefore the right to use the asset is retained by the grantor (and transferred to the market participant in a hypothetical transaction). Under this view, the right of access provided to the operator would not represent a restriction on the use of the asset.

BC50 The assessment of restrictions is important for service concession arrangements involving the grant of a right to the operator (GORTO) model, where the grantor provides the operator with a right to charge the users of the service concession asset. To the extent that a market participant (acting in its economic best interest) would take into account in measuring the fair value of the asset the fact that a third-party operator has been granted a right to charge users, this could result in a different fair value compared to that for an equivalent asset without such a characteristic, such as the service concession asset under an arrangement that involves only the financial liability model. In the latter case, any obligation to pay the operator under the financial liability model that would be transferred to the market participant would be separately recognised, not netted against the asset.

BC51 The Board discussed the unit of account in AASB 13, which defines it as the level at which an asset or a liability is aggregated or disaggregated in a Standard for recognition purposes. The Board noted there are three possible bases for identifying a service concession asset: the service concession period, the economic life after the end of the arrangement (the residual), or both the concession period and any remaining economic life.

BC52 The Board noted some may view the grant of a right to the operator to earn revenue from third-party users of the asset means that the grantor's service concession asset is only the residual interest in the asset after the service concession period. Under this view, the grantor's interest in the service concession period component of the asset is effectively derecognised, consistent with a rights and obligations approach.

BC53 In the development of IFRIC 12, the IFRIC decided that when the operator in a service concession arrangement does not have the right to control the underlying use of the asset, the operator instead has access to operate the asset to provide a service on behalf of the grantor. In essence, the operator acts as a service provider (IFRIC 12, paragraphs BC24–BC25). Accordingly, it is the grantor that has control of the underlying use of the asset during both the service concession period and any residual period thereafter. The Board therefore concluded the unit of account is the entire service concession asset, not just the residual interest after the service concession arrangement ends.

Valuation techniques for measuring fair value

BC54 AASB 13 outlines three 'widely used' valuation techniques for measuring fair value (paragraph 62): the market approach, the income approach and the cost approach. AASB 13 does not specify which valuation technique is more appropriate. Instead, AASB 13 states that:

(a)   an entity uses the valuation techniques that are appropriate in the circumstances and for which sufficient data are available to measure fair value, maximising the use of relevant observable inputs and minimising the use of unobservable inputs;

(b)   the inputs selected should be consistent with the characteristics of the asset or liability that market participants would take into account in a transaction for the asset or liability; and

(c)   the fair value hierarchy (Level 1, 2 and 3 inputs) prioritises the inputs to the valuation techniques, not the valuation techniques used to measure fair value.

Market approach

BC55 The Board noted service concession assets are subject to terms and conditions determined on a project by project basis and are rarely exchanged between willing sellers and buyers. Accordingly, it is highly unlikely that the market approach would be applicable to measuring service concession assets, although this would depend on the facts and circumstances.

Income approach

BC56 The income approach converts future amounts (eg cash flows or income and expenses) to a single current (ie discounted) amount. When the income approach is used, the fair value measurement reflects current market expectations about those future amounts (AASB 13, paragraph B10).

BC57 Service concession assets are used to provide goods or services to achieve public service objectives and consequently the prices that might be charged for those goods or services may be regulated. Price regulation would have the effect of restricting the future cash flows that could be obtained from the assets. The fees the operator can charge users may be at a significant discount and hence this would not reflect the fair value of the asset based on what a market participant may choose to charge under commercial terms. Service potential (ie capacity to provide future services) rather than future economic benefits (ie future cash flows) is likely to drive decisions regarding service concession assets.

BC58 The Board considered whether the grantor's contractual obligation to make a predetermined payment or series of payments to the operator under the financial liability model could be a measure of the fair value of the asset. Where the grantor's payments to the operator represent the price that the operator expects for the construction, development, acquisition or upgrade of a service concession asset based on the expectations of the cash flows which could be generated by the asset, this method may be appropriate for determining fair value at initial recognition as a surrogate for the income approach. However, the cash payments promised to the operator under the financial liability model might have no direct relationship to the cash flows expected to be generated from the asset (for example, the grantor may choose not to charge users) and the income approach would not be appropriate.

BC59 The Board noted some may view the grant of a right to the operator to earn revenue from third-party users of the asset as a restriction that a market participant would recognise when using the income approach (see also paragraph BC50). Under this view, the asset should be measured only in relation to the service potential of the asset after the service concession period has expired, ie at the fair value of the residual interest in the asset (see also paragraphs BC52–BC53). This is on the basis that the market participant buyer will not have the right to all the cash flows that could be generated by the asset as the right to the cash flows for the service concession period has been granted to the operator (effectively the service concession period component of the asset would be derecognised). Under this view, the service concession asset's fair value relates only to the cash flows that can be directly generated for the grantor by the asset. Consequently, the fair value of the asset would be measured at the asset's residual value.

BC60 However, the Board noted a public sector entity uses a service concession asset's capacity or service potential to provide goods or services to achieve public service objectives, replacing the asset irrespective of whether the replacement cost will be recovered by the expected cash flows that the asset may generate. The Board also noted the view that the service potential of a service concession asset (such as a road) under a service concession arrangement involving the financial liability model and the service potential of an identical asset (such as a toll road) under a service concession arrangement involving the GORTO model is the same from the grantor's perspective as both assets will provide the same utility to the public. Under this view, the fair value of these assets should therefore be measured consistently. The Board concluded that the fair value of the asset would be understated if it was measured at the fair value of the residual interest in the asset.

BC61 The Board also noted its decision to recognise, under the GORTO model, a contract liability that is initially recognised and then reduced as revenue is recognised (see paragraphs B71–B72 and BC80). The Board considered whether the amortisation profile of the contract liability should be determined so that the net balance of the service concession asset and the contract liability approximates the fair value of the residual interest in the asset. Whilst this would effectively mean a more consistent outcome with the financial liability model, the Board considered this approach would be practically difficult, with the costs likely to outweigh the benefits. The Board also expected that in many instances there would not be a material difference between this net approach and amortisation of the liability on a time basis. The Board therefore concluded that this approach was not appropriate.

Cost approach

BC62 The cost approach "reflects the amount that would be required currently to replace the service capacity of an asset (often referred to as current replacement cost)" (AASB 13, paragraph B8). This approach uses Level 2 and/or Level 3 inputs, which are observable or unobservable inputs. Current replacement cost is the "cost to a market participant buyer to acquire or construct a substitute asset of comparable utility, adjusted for obsolescence" (AASB 13, paragraph B9). The Board noted that current replacement cost is often used to measure the fair value of assets that are used in combination with other assets or with other assets and liabilities. This is particularly relevant if the service concession asset is part of an integrated network of assets, such as the provision of a transport network.

BC63 The Board noted (in paragraph BC60) a public sector entity uses a service concession asset's capacity or service potential to provide goods or services to achieve public service objectives, replacing the asset irrespective of whether the replacement cost will be recovered by the expected cash flows that the asset may generate. This view would be consistent with measuring the asset using current replacement cost under the cost approach in AASB 13.

BC64 Additionally the Board's view (in paragraph BC60) is that the service potential of a service concession asset under a service concession arrangement involving the financial liability model and the service potential of an identical asset involving the GORTO model is the same from the grantor's perspective, as both assets will provide the same utility to the public. The fair value of these assets should therefore be measured consistently.

BC65 Unlike the other valuation methodologies, current replacement cost would result in the same value under both the financial liability model and the GORTO model. Current replacement cost would not include the restriction on the asset (see paragraph BC49) of the grantor having granted the operator the right to charge users as the restriction relates to future cash flows from the asset rather than the costs to replace the asset to provide its current service potential. The Board's considerations of whether the granting of the right to future cash flows should be recognised as a separate liability are set out in paragraphs BC79–BC80.

BC66 The Board concluded a service concession asset is an asset that is obtained through construction, development, acquisition, upgrade or replacement of a major component of an asset. The asset's capacity or service potential is used to achieve public service objectives irrespective of whether the cost of the asset will be recovered by the expected cash flows that the asset may generate. The Board therefore concluded that it is appropriate to initially measure service concession assets at fair value using only current replacement cost under the cost approach to fair value. The Board noted that this approach applies to for-profit public sector grantors as well as to not-for-profit public sector grantors, given the objective of the Standard. The Board preferred the same measurement basis for all public sector grantors, even though it is possible that a for-profit grantor might hold service concession assets for both their service potential and their future cash flows.

Measuring reclassified assets at fair value

BC67 The Board deliberated whether an existing asset of a grantor that is reclassified as a service concession asset should be measured at current replacement cost in accordance with the cost approach to fair value in AASB 13. The Board concluded the reclassification of the grantor's existing asset represents a change in the nature of the asset (even an intangible asset) to a service concession asset and should therefore be measured on the same basis as a service concession asset acquired through the operator.

BC68 The Board acknowledged the requirement for a grantor to initially measure a service concession asset at fair value (current replacement cost) in accordance with the cost approach in AASB 13 may result in a for-profit grantor not being able to state that its financial statements comply with IFRS Standards. This is because AASB 13 (and the corresponding IFRS 13 *Fair Value Measurement*) permits other valuation techniques (see paragraphs BC124–BC125).

BC69 The Board decided not to provide additional guidance on the measurement of a service concession asset on the grounds that this would best be developed in the future through a separate project on the measurement of public sector assets. The Board also considered whether the Standard should include additional guidance in the following areas and decided there is sufficient guidance in the Standard and/or other Standards:

    (a)   determination of the fair value of a partly constructed asset – the Board noted there is a broad range of techniques in AASB 15 *Revenue from Contracts with Customers* that, depending on the nature of the contract, could be used to establish the fair value of a partly constructed asset;

(b) the valuation approach for intangible service concession assets – the Board decided intangible service concession assets should not be treated differently from tangible service concession assets on initial recognition. In both cases, the asset's capacity or service potential is used to achieve public service objectives irrespective of whether the cost of the asset will be recovered by the expected cash flows that the asset may generate. Consequently, the measurement of the asset at initial recognition should not be affected by whether the service concession asset is a tangible or intangible asset; and

(c) accounting for economic obsolescence in determining the fair value of the asset – as noted in paragraph BC66, the Board concluded that the fair value of a service concession asset should be measured using the cost approach. The cost approach (the current replacement cost) reflects the amount required currently to replace the service capacity of an asset. Current replacement cost takes obsolescence into consideration. AASB 13 provides examples of obsolescence, such as physical deterioration, functional (technological) obsolescence and economic (external) obsolescence, and notes that it is broader than depreciation.

Intangible assets

BC70 The Board decided that after the initial recognition of an intangible service concession asset, it should be accounted for in accordance with AASB 138, subject to the provisos in paragraph 9 of this Standard. The depreciable amount of the intangible asset would be amortised over its useful life. However, if the grantor elected (or was required) to measure the asset under the revaluation model, current replacement cost would continue to be used as the basis for fair value measurement, overriding the active market requirements in AASB 138 for the revaluation of intangible assets. The Board noted this approach is consistent with its decision to measure an asset at fair value (current replacement cost) on the basis of the asset's service potential, rather than on the basis of whether there is an active market for the fair value of the asset.

Recognition and measurement of a liability

Financial liability model

BC71 The Board considered issues relating to the recognition of a financial liability and, consistent with the key principles of IPSAS 32, decided that a financial liability should be recognised when the grantor has a contractual obligation to deliver cash or another financial asset to the operator.

BC72 A financial liability arises when the grantor is obligated to make a determinable payment or series of payments to the operator. The Board agreed with the IPSASB conclusion that when there is a determinable payment or series of payments of cash or cash equivalents, the payments should be allocated as a reduction of the liability, an imputed finance charge (if any), and charges for services provided by the operator under the service concession arrangement. The Board determined that wherever possible the existing guidance in AASB 9 *Financial Instruments* should apply.

BC73 The Board considered whether a financial liability arises when an arrangement requires the grantor to make payments to the operator based on third-party usage of the service concession asset without guaranteeing a minimum amount to the operator. The Board considered the application of the financial liability model to this case by assessing the notion that the grantor may not have a contractual obligation to pay the operator specified or determinable amounts at the inception of the arrangement as specified in paragraph 15. As noted in paragraph B63, the grantor has a financial liability if it does not have an unconditional ability to avoid the obligation to make the payments to the operator. The grantor is not able to avoid the payments as it cannot control the usage of the service concession asset by third parties, and any attempt to restrict usage may result in penalties under the arrangement. The amounts payable by the grantor to the operator are contingent upon the level of third-party usage of the service concession asset. Paragraph 25 of AASB 132 *Financial Instruments: Presentation* affirms this view that a grantor may have a contractual obligation in the form of a financial liability when the amounts are not specified or determinable at inception but are contingent on the occurrence or non-occurrence of uncertain future events. The Board also decided that AASB 9 should be applied to the accounting for the financial liability subsequent to its initial recognition. Accordingly, the Board decided that, for the arrangement under consideration, the financial liability model should be applied (as set out in paragraph 16(a)), with the financial liability initially recognised at the same amount as the fair value of the service concession asset, and the grantor applying AASB 9 subsequently to the accounting for the financial liability. The Board noted this view is consistent with its decision to not include in ED 261 or AASB 1059 the guidance in paragraph AG49 of IPSAS 32 relating to treating shadow tolls payable by the grantor as payments for the usage and not the acquisition of the service concession asset.

BC74 The Board noted that the approach described in paragraph BC73 may result in asymmetry in accounting for the same arrangement by the operator. This is due to AASB Interpretation 12 (paragraph 16) permitting the operator to recognise a financial asset only to the extent that it has an unconditional present right to receive cash from or at the direction of the grantor. The operator has an unconditional contractual right to receive cash if the grantor contractually guarantees the operator's cash flows. In the absence of a guarantee from the grantor, the operator's contractual right is conditional on third-party usage of the service concession asset, and the operator recognises an intangible asset rather than a financial asset. The Board concluded the principles appropriate to this Standard are more important than achieving symmetry in accounting by the parties to the service concession arrangement.

BC75 Consistent with AASB Interpretation 12, this Standard requires the application of the financial instrument Standards to the financial liability recognised under paragraph 11, except where this Standard requires otherwise. In deliberating the application of the financial instrument Standards to the recognition of a financial liability, the Board considered the following:

(a)   whether the financial liability should be measured in accordance with AASB 9 rather than measured initially at the same amount as the service concession asset (current replacement cost). The Board noted that consistent with AASB 9 there is no day-one gain or loss to be recognised, and concluded that the costs of separately measuring the fair value of the financial liability would outweigh the benefits of doing so;

(b)   whether to retain, in paragraph 18, the requirement proposed in ED 261 that the grantor allocates the payments to the operator under the contract and accounts separately for the finance charge. The Board noted this proposed requirement would apply if the financial liability is subsequently measured at amortised cost in accordance with AASB 9. However, AASB 9 permits other methods in the subsequent measurement of a financial liability, such as fair value through profit or loss. The subsequent measurement of a financial liability at fair value through profit or loss would not require separate accounting for a finance charge. The Board decided, given AASB 9 addresses the separate accounting for a finance charge, it is sufficient for AASB 1059 to refer to the financial instrument Standards in this respect without providing additional guidance;

(c)   whether to retain the guidance proposed in ED 261 relating to the appropriate interest rate for determining the finance charge (if any). The Board decided to replace the reference in ED 261 to determining the finance charge using the rate implicit in the arrangement. The Standard (paragraph B67) instead refers to determining the finance charge using the effective interest method when the financial liability is subsequently measured at amortised cost in accordance with AASB 9; and

(d)   whether to include guidance relating to the appropriate interest rate for initially measuring the financial liability component in a hybrid arrangement, since the financial liability component is measured first, and an interest rate is needed in order to discount the expected future cash flows to a present value. The Board decided to include application guidance (see paragraph B64) that the grantor shall, in the first instance, use the contractually specified interest rate in the arrangement to initially measure the financial liability component of a hybrid arrangement in accordance with AASB 9. If it is not practicable to determine the contractually specified interest rate, the grantor would determine the appropriate rate using the prevailing market rate(s) of interest for a similar instrument with a similar credit rating, following the requirements of AASB 9. Examples of rates for a similar instrument include the operator's cost of capital specific to the service concession asset, the grantor's incremental borrowing rate, or another rate appropriate to the terms and conditions of the arrangement.

Grant of a right to the operator (GORTO) model

BC76 The GORTO model applies when the grantor grants the operator the right to earn revenue from third-party users of the service concession asset. Under the GORTO model, the grantor transfers to the operator an intangible asset (being a right to charge users of the service concession asset) in exchange for the construction, development, acquisition or upgrade of a service concession asset and the provision of related future services. The Board considered whether the grantor should initially recognise revenue or a liability when it obtains control of the service concession asset arising from a service concession arrangement. The Board noted that IPSAS 32 requires a grantor to initially recognise a liability when the grantor recognises the service concession asset. Given its policy of transaction neutrality, the Board considered whether the requirements of Australian Accounting Standards, specifically the application of AASB 15 either directly or by analogy, would support:

(a)   the recognition of a liability (consistent with IPSAS 32); or

(b)   the recognition of revenue on the basis that the grantor has no remaining obligations to the operator once it has transferred to the operator the right to charge users.

BC77 The Board concluded that, from a grantor's perspective, the application of AASB 15 without further guidance may lead to divergence in accounting for a service concession arrangement, as significant judgement would be required to determine whether a service concession arrangement in which the grantor transfers an intangible asset to the operator is within the scope of AASB 15. The Board noted differing views on whether a service concession arrangement involves a contract with a customer (ie whether the right to charge users is considered a licence, whether the operator is considered a customer, or whether the ordinary activities of government include undertaking service concession arrangements as a grantor), and depending on the specific facts and circumstances some service concession arrangements might be a right-of-use licence and others a right of access. The Board preferred the view that the substance of the transaction appears more akin to financing the construction of the service concession asset, rather than a contract with a customer.

BC78 The Board also noted, in a service concession arrangement, the grantor makes promises, either explicitly or implicitly, to undertake activities in relation to the service concession asset that will benefit the operator. This reflects the fact that a service concession asset is controlled and managed by the grantor to provide public services. The Board acknowledged that the grantor's promise, or the operator's expectation, that the grantor will undertake activities that benefit the operator may in some instances be comparable to promises made by a licensor or expectations of a licensee that the licensor will undertake activities in relation to intellectual property that will benefit the licensee. AASB 15 identifies such licences as licences that provide the licensee with a right to access the underlying intellectual property. AASB 15 specifies that the promise of a right to access intellectual property is a performance obligation that is satisfied over time and the licensor would recognise a contract liability for its remaining performance obligation to provide access.

BC79 The Board decided that facts and circumstances would need to be assessed for each arrangement to determine whether the arrangement represented a right-of-access licence or a right-of-use licence. The Board preferred all service concession arrangements to be treated the same way, as it did not see the substance of service concession arrangements being different in respect to commitments under the arrangements. The Board also noted that recognising revenue immediately on a service concession asset that would otherwise be considered loss making from a cashflow perspective would not reflect the economic substance of the arrangement and would overstate current year financial performance. The Board further noted that immediate recognition of revenue (rather than a liability) would result in overstatement of the financial position as the requirement to use current replacement cost as fair value recognises the asset in full, even though the right to charge users of the asset has been transferred to the operator.

BC80 Consequently, the Board concluded the grantor's promises to undertake activities in relation to the service concession asset that will benefit the operator should also be accounted similarly to a contract liability. The grantor would subsequently recognise revenue as the 'access' is provided to the operator over the service concession period.

BC81 In some service concession arrangements, the right to charge users is described as a licence. The Board noted that accounting for licences other than those relating to service concession arrangements should be subject to further research to inform the Board as to whether a separate project would be required. Determining whether a particular licence granted by a government is within the scope of AASB 15 would depend on the facts and circumstances.

BC82 Given the importance of service concession arrangements to governments and the lack of accounting guidance for such arrangements in the absence of AASB 1059, the Board decided that service concession arrangements should be treated separately from other licences granted by governments.

BC83 The Board considered whether the Standard should include additional guidance on the principle-based approach to recognising revenue under the GORTO model. The Standard (paragraph 22) specifies that the grantor recognises revenue and reduces the GORTO liability according to the economic substance of the arrangement. The Board assessed the following options of whether to:

(a) require revenue to be recognised on a systematic and rational basis using the straight-line method. This option would eliminate divergent approaches to recognising revenue but would not be consistent with the objective of the Board to develop a principle-based accounting standard; or

(b) not provide additional guidance in the final Standard on the basis there is sufficient guidance in the Standard. Paragraph B71 requires revenue to be recognised and the liability reduced based on the economic substance of the arrangement, usually as access to the service concession asset is provided to the operator over the term of the service concession arrangement.

BC84 The Board decided not to add additional guidance. Revenue recognition should be based on the economic substance of the specific arrangement as assessed by the grantor and should not be prescribed by the Board.

Other liability recognition and measurement models

BC85 The Board considered the following alternative recognition and measurement models to the GORTO model:

(a) applying the financial liability model to all service concession arrangements;

(b) accounting for the assets of the arrangement and not the right to charge users for the use of the service concession asset that has been granted by the grantor to the operator; and

(c) application of AASB 140 *Investment Property* by analogy.

BC86 In analysing whether the financial liability model could be applied to all service concession arrangements, the Board considered:

(a) whether the nature of the party (the grantor or the users of the service concession asset) that makes the payment to the operator determines the accounting model for the grantor to recognise a service concession liability. Consistent with AASB Interpretation 12, the Board concluded the party that has the responsibility to make payments to the operator is important in determining the accounting model for the grantor's recognition of the liability. This view takes into account who bears the demand risk (ie the ability and willingness of the users to use and pay for the services). This view is consistent with the models in this Standard and mirrors the requirements of AASB Interpretation 12. That is, under the financial liability model, the grantor is the party with the primary responsibility to make payments to the operator for the services. This contrasts with the GORTO model, where the operator is the party that bears the demand risks. Accordingly, the use of different models (ie the financial liability model and the GORTO model) to account for the liability is more appropriate; and

(b) whether the grantor has a financial liability when the operator has been granted the right to charge third-party users for the use of the asset. The Board concluded that the grantor does not have a financial liability under GORTO arrangements. That is, the grantor does not have a contractual obligation to deliver cash or another financial asset to the operator nor exchange financial assets or financial liabilities with the operator under potentially unfavourable conditions.

BC87 The Board considered whether the more appropriate approach under the GORTO model is to recognise only the cash flows that the service concession asset can generate directly (the residual cash flows to the grantor). The implication is that the fair value of the asset could be measured at the asset's residual value (which could be zero), excluding the cash flows generated by the asset that have been granted to the operator. However, the Board concluded that the fair value of the asset should be measured using the current replacement cost under the cost approach irrespective of whether the cost of replacing the asset will be recovered by the expected cash flows that the asset may generate (see paragraphs BC63–BC66). In addition, the grantor would recognise a GORTO contract liability (see paragraphs BC79–BC80).

BC88 The Board also considered the application of AASB 140 by analogy to address the implication of measuring the asset's fair value based on only the cash flows that are directly generated by the service concession asset for the grantor. Although this approach might be appropriate under AASB 13, the resulting fair value of the service concession asset would be understated in relation to the service concession arrangement. The application of AASB 140 by analogy attempts to overcome this.

BC89 Under AASB 140, the fair value of investment property reflects expected future cash flows, including any future rental receipts. AASB 140 (paragraph 50) makes clear that in determining the carrying amount of investment property under the fair value model, it is necessary to avoid double-counting assets or liabilities that are recognised separately, such as prepaid or accrued rental income and lease incentives. In such cases, the fair value (carrying amount) of the investment property is adjusted so that in total the combination of all related amounts gives the fair value of the investment property.

BC90 The Board considered that to apply the AASB 140 approach to the GORTO model, the fair value of the service concession asset would first be determined on a gross basis (ie current replacement cost for the full service potential of the asset). Then a GORTO contract liability would be recognised, so that in total the combination of the service concession asset and the liability would give on a net basis the appropriate measure of the service concession asset, reflecting the cash flows expected to be generated for the grantor. This approach would avoid measuring the service concession asset at a net amount, such as the residual value of the asset.

BC91 However, the Board decided that the investment property model should not be applied by analogy. The Board concluded (see paragraph BC66) that service concession assets should be measured at fair value (current replacement cost) in relation to the service potential of the asset, rather than reflecting only the expected future cash flows for the grantor.

Dividing an arrangement

BC92 In response to constituents' comments, the Board decided to revise the approach to dividing a hybrid arrangement that had been proposed in ED 261. Instead of noting that each component of the service concession liability should be measured at fair value, the Standard requires that:

(a) the liability recognised under a hybrid arrangement is initially measured at the same amount as the fair value (current replacement cost) of the service concession asset; and

(b) the method for dividing the liability under a hybrid arrangement is to determine the financial liability part of the liability first, with the remainder of the fair value (current replacement cost) of the service concession asset allocated to the part related to the grant of the right to the operator.

BC93 The Board, in making the decision in paragraph BC92(b), considered whether the amounts allocated to the financial liability and the GORTO liability should depend on the entity's ability to determine the fair value of the service concession asset to be accounted for in relation to each liability model in the hybrid arrangement. For example, if the fair value of the service concession asset related to the grant of the right to the operator could be reliably determined, a method of dividing the hybrid arrangement might be to allocate this amount to the GORTO liability, with the remainder of the total liability to be allocated to the financial liability. However, the Board took the view that it would be difficult to determine fair values for the portions of a service concession asset related to each of the two liabilities, if it were possible. Similarly, it would be difficult to determine fair values for both liabilities directly, to allow the fair value (current replacement cost) of the service concession asset to be allocated to each liability based on their relative fair values, following the approach in AASB 15 to allocating the transaction price to performance obligations. Furthermore, since the liability is not measured directly at fair value under the financial liability model (see paragraph BC75), it would be inappropriate to require such measurement in relation to recognising a hybrid arrangement.

BC94 The Board concluded the appropriate approach would be to measure the financial liability part of the total liability first, with the remainder of the total liability allocated to the GORTO part of the liability. This approach avoids understating the financial liability, which might occur if the GORTO liability is measured first. Overstatement of the GORTO liability would mean overstatement of the revenues recognised by the grantor under the service concession arrangement. The financial liability is measured and recognised first, even where the service concession asset is under construction. This is illustrated in Example 8 of the Illustrative Examples accompanying this Standard.

Accounting issues addressed in other Australian Accounting Standards

BC95 Due to the complexity of many service concession arrangements, there may be additional accounting issues related to certain terms in the contract (for example, revenues, expenses, guarantees and contingencies). The Board decided that it was not necessary to repeat in this Standard guidance that appears in other Standards. Accordingly, when another Australian Accounting Standard specifies the accounting and reporting for a component of a service concession arrangement, this Standard references the specific Standard without necessarily providing additional guidance. However, the Board noted some cases (for example, revenue recognition) when the application of another Standard might be difficult, given certain unique features in service concession arrangements. To facilitate consistent implementation of this Standard, the Board decided to provide additional guidance on applying the principles in other Standards when appropriate.

Other revenues

BC96 The Board considered whether to include in this Standard the Application Guidance paragraphs AG55–AG64 of IPSAS 32 for other revenues. Other revenues relate to compensation by the operator to the grantor for access to the service concession asset by providing the grantor with a series of predetermined inflows of resources, including the following:

(a) an upfront payment or a stream of payments;

(b) revenue-sharing provisions;

(c) a reduction in a predetermined series of payments the grantor is required to make to the operator; and

(d) rent payments for providing the operator access to a revenue-generating asset.

BC97 The Board decided this guidance was not necessary in the Australian context as the existing revenue recognition guidance in Australian Accounting Standards was sufficient.

BC98 In setting the requirement in paragraph 12, the Board noted deliberations by the IFRS Interpretations Committee on IFRIC 12 with respect to payments by the operator to the grantor. The Board concluded no additional guidance was necessary in relation to the requirement that the grantor recognise the liability initially at the same amount as the service concession asset, adjusted by the amount of any other consideration from the grantor to the operator, or from the operator to the grantor.

BC99 The Board observed that adjusting the liability for additional consideration from the operator to the grantor differed from the approach set out in an IFRIC agenda decision (July 2016). The IFRIC agenda decision noted that where the operator recognised a financial asset under a service concession arrangement, the operator would account for the payments to the grantor as a reduction of the transaction price, reducing the operator's revenue. Under this Standard, the payments from the operator would increase the grantor's liability, rather than reduce the carrying amount of the service concession asset. The asset is measured at fair value (current replacement cost) as a fundamental principle of this Standard, in order to reflect the service potential of the asset rather than future cash flows. The adjustment to the liability affects the grantor's revenue based on the pattern of revenue recognition during the period of the service concession arrangement.

Disclosures

BC100 The Board proposed in ED 261 only minor changes to the disclosure requirements in IPSAS 32. In finalising the Standard, the Board added the objective of the disclosure requirements to paragraph 28, and clarified in paragraph 29 the flexibility for a grantor to classify service concession assets across more than one class of assets for the purposes of AASB 116 or AASB 138, as appropriate, and for the disclosures required by this Standard.

Transition

BC101 This Standard requires an entity to apply the Standard retrospectively either in accordance with AASB 108 or under a simplified approach from the beginning of the earliest period for which comparative information is presented in the financial statements (the date of initial application). The modified retrospective approach requires a grantor to recognise and measure service concession assets and related liabilities at the date of initial application, rather than at an earlier date.

BC102 The general requirement in AASB 108 is that accounting policy changes should be accounted for retrospectively, except to the extent that retrospective application would be impracticable. The Board noted that there are two aspects to retrospective application: reclassification and measurement. The Board took a similar view to the IPSASB that it will usually be practicable to determine retrospectively the appropriate classification of all amounts previously included in a grantor's statement of financial position, but that retrospective measurement of service concession assets might not always be practicable, particularly if an entity has not previously recognised service concession assets and related liabilities, revenues and expenses.

BC103 As proposed in ED 261, the Board decided that the modified retrospective approach should be available to grantors that have previously recognised service concession assets and related liabilities, as well as to grantors that have not done so. This contrasts with IPSAS 32, which limits this option to grantors that have not previously recognised service concession assets and liabilities. The Board concluded that since the retrospective restatement of service concession assets might not always be practicable, the modified approach would be made available to all grantors.

BC104 Under the modified retrospective approach (see paragraph C4 of the Standard), the deemed cost of service concession assets is measured at fair value (current replacement cost) at the date of initial application. The Board decided this measurement basis should also apply to assets of the grantor that are reclassified as service concession assets on initial application of the Standard, thus requiring the remeasurement of such assets. The Board noted that this would be consistent with the requirement in paragraph 8 for grantors to measure existing assets that are reclassified as service concession assets at current replacement cost in accordance with the cost approach to fair value at the date of reclassification. ED 261 had not proposed any remeasurement for reclassified assets.

BC105 The Board considered the approach to the initial recognition by a grantor of previously unrecognised identifiable intangible assets and land under roads as service concession assets on transition, and concluded that no additional transition relief was required. A grantor may elect to apply the modified retrospective approach, requiring measurement of service concession assets at the date of initial application of the Standard, to simplify the measurement of such assets.

BC106 The Board decided to clarify in the Standard the approach to measuring a liability under the GORTO model when the grantor adopts the modified retrospective transition approach. The starting point is to measure the fair value (current replacement cost) of the service concession asset at the date of initial application, and then adjust that measure to reflect that part of the term of the service concession arrangement has passed. There were different views as to how to make that adjustment. The Board concluded that the adjustment should reflect the remaining service concession period relative to the remaining economic life of the service concession asset, on the grounds that the current measurement of the asset represented the future benefits inherent in the asset. The Board decided to include an example to illustrate the adjustment required.

BC107 The Standard requires that any net adjustment to the carrying amounts of assets and liabilities is recognised as an adjustment to the opening balance of accumulated surplus (deficiency) at the date of initial application. Accordingly, the Standard requires that if the grantor elects as its accounting policy the revaluation model in AASB 116 or AASB 138 (or is required to adopt that policy), any relevant adjustment is included in accumulated surplus (deficiency) and not revaluation surplus. The Board noted that the amount of such an adjustment could not be used to offset future changes in the values of an asset or liability. This is consistent with the treatment in

AASB 108 for a change in accounting policy. However, this differs from the approach permitted by IPSAS 32, where such an adjustment would be included in revaluation surplus.

Effective date

BC108 The Board noted that ED 261 had proposed an effective date of annual reporting periods beginning on or after 1 January 2017, which was no longer feasible. The Board decided the effective date of the Standard should be annual reporting periods beginning on or after 1 January 2019, on the basis that that date would:

(a) effectively provide two years, from the issue date, for implementing the Standard for entities that have a 30 June reporting date. This aligns with constituents' comments that this Standard will need a significant amount of time to implement; and

(b) align with the effective date of AASB 15 and AASB 1058 *Income of Not-for-Profit Entities*, which this Standard cross-references (see paragraph 27). Although the effective date of this Standard need not align with those Standards, the Board considered having the same effective date would assist grantors in the overall implementation of the Standards.

GAAP/GFS convergence

BC109 The Board discussed implications of its decisions on GAAP/GFS harmonisation. The Board noted that key differences between Generally Accepted Accounting Principles (GAAP) and Government Finance Statistics (GFS) may arise in relation to the following:

(a) service concession arrangement terminology – GFS refers to such arrangements as 'Public Private Partnerships' (PPP);

(b) assessment of whether the grantor recognises a service concession asset – assessment is based on the risks and rewards approach under GFS rather than the control and regulation approach in this Standard;

(c) accounting for a service concession arrangement – the arrangement is accounted for as a finance lease under GFS, but with some differences to AASB 16. The difference in accounting will likely result in differences between GAAP and GFS in the amounts of the assets and liabilities recognised both initially and during the term of the arrangement;

(d) revaluation of service concession assets – GFS requires the asset to be measured using the revaluation model. This Standard references AASB 116 and AASB 138, which permit the cost and revaluation models. AASB 1049 *Whole of Government and General Government Sector Financial Reporting* requires fair value measurement and the revaluation of assets consistent with the market value measurement requirements of GFS; and

(e) the liability recognised under the GORTO model – GFS acknowledges the GORTO model but does not provide specific accounting requirements. Instead, GFS notes most PPPs are unique and the accounting is to be considered on a case by case basis.

BC110 The Board weighed its policy on GAAP/GFS harmonisation against its policy of transaction neutrality. The Board observed that some areas of potential difference were known when developing AASB 1049. Others are driven by a difference in the underlying principles. Further, some differences could only be addressed by making changes to the underlying principles in AASB 1059.

BC111 On balance, the Board considered that it was not necessary to amend its decisions reflected in AASB 1059 in order to better achieve GAAP/GFS harmonisation. The

Board noted that AASB 1049 will require entities to identify and explain any material differences arising from different requirements in GAAP as compared with GFS.

Comparison with IPSAS 32

BC112 This Standard incorporates the key requirements of IPSAS 32, with the main differences detailed in the paragraphs below.

Scope

BC113 This Standard applies to all public sector entities in both the for-profit and not-for-profit sectors. This is wider than the scope of IPSAS 32, which applies to public sector not-for-profit entities.

Recognition and measurement of service concession assets

BC114 This Standard includes Application Guidance on the following matters, which is additional to that in IPSAS 32:

(a)   the fundamental principle of control of a service concession asset, including guidance on:

   (i)   when the grantor would control the service concession asset in an environment where the services provided and/or the service pricing is regulated by a third-party regulator;

   (ii)   the need to assess whether long-term leases, outsourcing or privatisation arrangements are within the scope of this Standard; and

   (iii)   changes in the grantor's control of the service concession asset; and

(b)   the relationship between the residual interest of the asset at the end of the service concession arrangement and a whole-of-life asset.

BC115 This Standard requires the grantor to initially measure the service concession asset at current replacement cost in accordance with the cost approach to fair value in AASB 13. IPSAS 32 instead specifies measurement of fair value generally – there is no IPSAS corresponding to AASB 13.

BC116 This Standard requires an existing asset of the grantor, including a previously unrecognised identifiable intangible asset or land under roads, that is reclassified as a service concession asset to be measured at fair value (current replacement cost) at the date of reclassification. IPSAS 32 does not permit such measurement or the recognition of previously unrecognised identifiable intangible assets or land under roads.

Recognition and measurement of liabilities

BC117 This Standard requires the grantor to recognise a financial liability when the grantor has a contractual obligation to pay cash to the operator for third-party usage of a service concession asset, with or without guaranteeing a minimum amount to the operator. IPSAS 32 refers to such an arrangement as a 'shadow toll' arrangement and requires the grantor to account for the payments as an expense when paid instead of recognising a financial liability at the commencement of the service concession arrangement.

BC118 This Standard references the application of the financial instrument Standards to a financial liability, while IPSAS 32 explicitly requires the grantor to allocate the payments to the operator under the contract as a reduction in the liability recognised, a finance charge and charges for services. Additionally, IPSAS 32 provides guidance that the finance charge is determined based on the operator's cost of capital specific to the service concession asset, if this is practicable to determine. If this is not practicable, the rate implicit in the arrangement, the grantor's incremental borrowing rate, or another rate appropriate to the terms and conditions of the arrangement is used. In contrast, this Standard provides guidance that the grantor uses the contractually specified interest rate in the arrangement to initially measure the financial liability component for the purpose of dividing a hybrid arrangement. Where this is not practicable, prevailing market rate(s) of interest for a similar instrument with similar credit ratings are applied, as required by the financial instrument Standards.

BC119 This Standard requires the grantor in a hybrid arrangement to measure the financial liability first, with the remainder of the total liability allocated to the liability related to the grant of the right to the operator. IPSAS 32 requires the grantor to account for the liability in a hybrid arrangement in accordance with the liability recognition requirements in IPSAS 32 generally.

Other revenues

BC120 IPSAS 32 includes additional application guidance for other revenues, which is not included in this Standard. Other revenues relate to compensation by the operator to the grantor for access to the service concession asset by providing the grantor with a series of predetermined inflows of resources such as an upfront payment or a stream of payments (eg rent payments) and revenue-sharing provisions. This Standard instead references AASB 15 and AASB 1058 for application.

Definitions

BC121 This Standard modifies the defined terms of IPSAS 32. This Standard:

(a) replaces the IPSAS 32 term 'binding arrangement', which "describes contracts and other arrangements that confer similar rights and obligations on the parties to it as if they were in the form of a contract", with the term 'contract', which is defined as an "agreement between two or more parties that creates enforceable rights and obligations". This Standard also provides Application Guidance on the term 'contract';

(b) modifies the IPSAS 32 definition of a 'grantor' to refer to the grantor granting a 'right to access' the service concession asset to the operator, rather than a 'right to use' the asset;

(c) modifies the IPSAS 32 definition of an 'operator' from an entity that "uses the service concession asset" to an entity that has a "right of access to the service concession asset";

(d) modifies the IPSAS 32 definition of 'service concession arrangement' to require the operator to be responsible for at least some of the management of the public services provided through the service concession asset and not act merely as an agent on behalf of the grantor. IPSAS 32 identifies this only as a common feature of a service concession arrangement;

(e) modifies the IPSAS 32 definition of 'service concession asset' to expressly include major component replacements and previously unrecognised identifiable intangible assets and land under roads, and to exclude goodwill; and

(f) provides guidance on the term 'public service' that is not in IPSAS 32.

Transition

BC122 This Standard modifies the transition approach of IPSAS 32 to require any net adjustment on transition to be included as an adjustment to the opening balance of accumulated surplus (deficiency) at the date of initial application. IPSAS 32 requires a relevant adjustment to be included in revaluation surplus when the revaluation model is applied. Unlike IPSAS 32, this Standard also permits a grantor that has previously recognised service concession assets and related liabilities to apply the Standard retrospectively in accordance with the modified retrospective approach.

Illustrative examples

BC123　This Standard includes some differences in the illustrative examples based on those in IPSAS 32, such as:

(a)　the examples of the financial liability model (Example 6) and the grant of a right to the operator model (Example 7) both include a funding cost in the measurement of the service concession asset at fair value (current replacement cost), whereas the corresponding IPSAS 32 examples do not. Consequently, Examples 6 and 7 in this Standard both show the service concession asset and the liability measured initially at the same amount, which is not the case for the financial liability example (Example 1) in IPSAS 32; and

(b)　in Example 7, no revenue is recognised by the grantor in relation to the replacement of a major component of the service concession asset until the replacement occurs. The corresponding IPSAS 32 example (Example 2) allocates all revenue evenly over the term of the service concession arrangement.

The Standard also includes additional implementation guidance examples to illustrate the differences between service concession arrangements and other types of arrangements.

Comparison with IFRS Standards

BC124　Entities that comply with this Standard may not be in compliance with IFRS Standards issued by the IASB. The IASB has issued IFRIC Interpretation 12 addressing the accounting by operators of public-to-private service concession arrangements but has not issued a pronouncement regarding the accounting by grantors. The following paragraphs set out requirements in this Standard for the accounting by grantors that may not be compliant with IFRS Standards. A grantor that is a for-profit entity would not be able to state that its financial statements comply with IFRS Standards if it applies requirements that are not compliant with IFRS Standards.

BC125　This Standard requires a grantor to initially measure a service concession asset at current replacement cost in accordance with the cost approach to fair value in AASB 13. However, AASB 13 and the corresponding IFRS 13 do not specify which valuation technique to use. Instead IFRS 13 requires the use of valuation techniques that are appropriate in the circumstances and for which sufficient data are available to measure fair value, maximising the use of relevant observable inputs and minimising the use of unobservable inputs. Three widely used valuation techniques set out in IFRS 13 are the market approach, the cost approach and the income approach. The requirement of this Standard to initially measure a service concession asset at current replacement cost in accordance with the cost approach may not be compliant with IFRS 13.

BC126　This Standard requires a grantor to recognise an identifiable intangible asset as a service concession asset where the grantor controls the asset as set out in paragraph 5 or 6, even if the asset does not qualify for recognition under AASB 138/IAS 38 *Intangible Assets*. This approach is explained in paragraph BC39.

BC127　Under this Standard, a grantor recognises revenue from granting a right to the operator over the term of the service concession arrangement on an appropriate basis. This may not be compliant with the permitted approaches to revenue recognition for licences of intellectual property, if IFRS 15 *Revenue from Contracts with Customers* applied in the absence of grantor accounting requirements. In developing this Standard, the Board decided not to apply the licence revenue requirements of AASB 15 by analogy.

Comparison with AASB Interpretation 12

BC128 This Standard addresses the key requirements of AASB Interpretation 12 from a grantor's perspective, in particular the criteria for the recognition of a service concession asset in paragraphs 5 and 6. The main differences between this Standard and AASB Interpretation 12 are detailed in the paragraphs below.

BC129 The scope of this Standard does not explicitly state whether the operator should be a public or private sector entity. This contrasts with AASB Interpretation 12, which states that the Interpretation gives guidance on the accounting by operators for public-to-private service concession arrangements (paragraph 4).

BC130 This Standard applies to arrangements involving a 'service concession asset', including intangible assets and land under roads. This is broader than AASB Interpretation 12, which is applicable to infrastructure but does not refer explicitly to such assets.

BC131 This Standard requires the grantor to recognise a financial liability when the grantor has a contractual obligation to pay cash to the operator for third-party usage of a service concession asset, with or without guaranteeing a minimum amount to the operator. This contrasts with AASB Interpretation 12, which links the recognition of a financial asset by an operator to a guarantee of the cash flows by the grantor. Under Interpretation 12, the operator's cash flows are conditional on usage when it has no such guarantee.

AASB